W. E. VINE'S

NEW TESTAMENT WORD PICTURES

MATTHEW TO ACTS

Every Verse Explained

W. E. VINE'S

NEW TESTAMENT WORD PICTURES

MATTHEW TO ACTS

EVERY VERSE EXPLAINED

W. E. VINE WITH **F. F. BRUCE**

EDITED BY MARTIN H. MANSER
ASSISTANT EDITOR: NICOLA L. BULL

THOMAS NELSON
Since 1798

NASHVILLE MEXICO CITY RIO DE JANEIRO

Published in Nashville, Tennessee by Thomas Nelson. Thomas Nelson is a trademark of HarperCollins Christian Publishing, Inc.

Design and layout by Kevin Wade, kwgraphicdesign

Thomas Nelson titles may be purchased in bulk for educational, business, fund-raising, or sales promotional use. For information, please e-mail SpecialMarkets@ThomasNelson.com.

ISBN: 978-0-7180-3689-8

Contents

MATTHEW TO ACTS

Introduction

Welcome to *W. E. Vine's New Testament Word Pictures*.

It's Saturday evening and you have to finish preparing your talk for tomorrow from Matthew's Gospel. You may have used *Vine's Expository Dictionary of New Testament Words* before, but you cannot face the daunting task of looking up every word in each verse of your passage to see if there's a nugget that will set your congregation, class or group alight. Relax – we've done the hard work for you!

We've taken every key word that's in Vine's and re-sorted each one out of its original alphabetical sequence into a handy verse-by-verse order, covering every verse of the New Testament. To make it even more helpful to use, we've also:

- given the text of the KJV to provide the context for the key words
- included the Strong's numbers for the key words
- selected the relevant paragraphs of the entries
- kept W. E. Vine's original comments on alternative readings from the Revised Version
- provided you with inspirational quotations to give your talk that fresh edge.

The text before you is an edited version of the *Expository Dictionary of New Testament Words* by W. E. Vine, originally published in 1940, which has helped countless Bible preachers and teachers to explain the text of the New Testament.

W. E. Vine's original text used the scholarship of Bishop Westcott, W. F. Moulton, A. T. Robertson and James Hastings; forewords were written by the eminent scholars W. Graham Scroggie and F. F. Bruce.

This new reference work makes Vine's material even more accessible, because the edited text has been re-arranged in Bible book order and then by chapter and verse. So this means that if you are preparing to give a talk on Matthew chapter 4, you can look up that chapter here and all the words discussed with reference to that chapter in *Vine's Expository Dictionary of New Testament Words* are presented here in a convenient verse-by-verse order. Of course you can still explore the entire riches of the complete *Vine's Expository Dictionary of New Testament Words*.

We are pleased to have worked with Thomas Nelson in producing this text, and you can of course still buy *Vine's Expository Dictionary of New Testament Words* and *Vine's Complete Expository Dictionary of Old and New Testament Words with Topical Index* as books, online, or as Bible software. See www.logos.com.

This unique text contains elements of a Dictionary, Concordance and Commentary, not merely listing the key words of the Bible text, but also explaining the meaning behind them. And because it is keyed to Strong's numbers, you can use it with any version of the Bible.

We trust that this companion will help you explore God's word to discover fresh inspiration you can communicate to others, directing them to God's Word to all humanity, Jesus Christ himself.

Martin Manser
Editor

Thank you, Professor F. F. Bruce

"Give honor to whom honor is due."

Not long after I took on the stewardship of the works of the late W. E. Vine, I was privileged to come to know three of his then-surviving daughters and Mr. Vine's personal Secretary, John Williamson.

Through our conversations, I began to realize the major contribution of Professor F. F. Bruce to the unique book created by Mr. Vine – his *Expository Dictionary of New Testament Words*. Originally published in four volumes, it is now available as a single volume, which is the basis of this book.

Mr. Vine and Prof. Bruce had many things in common academically. They both gained their qualifications by studying the Greek classics, and both were familiar with the many ancient manuscripts that stand behind the Greek New Testament. They were also students of the Greek manuscripts of the Old Testament that were in existence before the first century and which were frequently quoted in the New Testament. In addition to their academic similarity, they both belonged to Brethren assemblies, a group known in the United States as Plymouth Brethren.

Mr. Williamson and Mr. Vine's daughters told me that when Mr. Vine began work on his *Dictionary*, he sent it, section by section, to Prof. Bruce. Interestingly, Mr. Vine's daughter Jeannette manually typed the text. Prof. Bruce then checked the draft script against all reliable sources, making additions and corrections as well as offering suggestions – and these were returned to Mr. Vine.

Mr. Vine incorporated the recommendations into a second draft, which was then sent back to Prof. Bruce. Jeannette informed me that Mr. Vine seldom saw anything in Prof. Bruce's work on which he raised a query.

Prof. Bruce then prepared the text for typesetting, which in those days was a major task. Unusually, Mr. Vine paid for the typesetting himself, rather than having the publisher pay for it, as is more common. The typesetting was then sent to the printer who created a "proof." Prof. Bruce again checked everything on the proof before giving his approval to publish the book.

Martin Manser, who undertook the editorial work for this edition of the *Dictionary*, has told me that there were very few mistakes in the original. This is clear evidence of the professionalism of both Mr. Vine and Prof. Bruce.

While Mr. Vine will always be acknowledged as the originating author of this work, the level of scholarship and assistance that Prof. Bruce contributed means that in today's world he would have been acknowledged alongside Mr. Vine as co-author – as we have done in this edition. Prof. Bruce made significant changes to Mr. Vine's text, effectively rewriting much of the material, bringing his own scholarship to the work. Mr. Vine trusted Prof. Bruce's judgment, allowing Bruce to make changes as necessary without questioning. So, a belated "Thank you" to Professor F. F. Bruce for bringing his significant academic skills to the work of W. E. Vine.

Robert F. Hicks
Publisher

Matthew

Chapter 1

1:1 The book of the generation of Jesus Christ, the son of David, the son of Abraham.

Book *biblos* (976), (Eng. "Bible") was the inner part, or rather the cellular substance, of the stem of the papyrus (Eng. "paper"). It came to denote the paper made from this bark in Egypt, and then a written "book," roll, or volume. It is used in referring to "books" of Scripture, the "book," or scroll, of Matthew's Gospel, **Matt. 1:1**; the Pentateuch, as the "book" of Moses, Mark 12:26; Isaiah, as "the book of the words of Isaiah," Luke 3:4; the Psalms, Luke 20:42 and Acts 1:20; "the prophets," Acts 7:42; to "the Book of Life," Phil. 4:3; Rev. 3:5; 20:15. Once only it is used of secular writings, Acts 19:19.

Generation *genesis* (1078), denotes "an origin, a lineage, or birth," translated "generation" in **Matt. 1:1**.

Jesus *iesous* (2424), is a transliteration of the Heb. "Joshua," meaning "Jehovah is salvation," i.e., "is the Savior," "a common name among the Jews, e.g., Ex. 17:9; Luke 3:29 (RV); Col. 4:11. It was given to the Son of God in Incarnation as His personal name, in obedience to the command of an angel to Joseph, the husband of His Mother, Mary, shortly before He was born, **Matt. 1:21**. By it He is spoken of throughout the Gospel narratives generally, but not without exception, as in Mark 16:19, 20; Luke 7:13, and a dozen other places in that Gospel, and a few in John.

"'Jesus Christ' occurs only in **Matt. 1:1, 18; 16:21**, marg.; Mark 1:1; John 1:17; 17:3. In Acts the name 'Jesus' is found frequently. 'Lord Jesus' is the normal usage, as in Acts 8:16; 19:5, 17; see also the reports of the words of Stephen, 7:59, of Ananias, 9:17, and of Paul, 16:31; though both Peter, 10:36, and Paul, 16:18, also used 'Jesus Christ.' In the Epistles of James, Peter, John and Jude, the personal name is not once found alone, but in Rev. eight times (RV), 1:9; 12:17; 14:12; 17:6; 19:10 (twice); 20:4; 22:16. In the Epistles of Paul 'Jesus' appears alone just thirteen times, and in the Hebrews eight times; in the latter the title 'Lord' is added once only, at 13:20. In the Epistles of James, Peter, John, and Jude, men who had companied with the Lord in the days of His flesh, 'Jesus Christ' is the invariable order (in the RV) of the Name and Title, for this was the order of their experience; as 'Jesus' they knew Him first, that He was Messiah they learnt finally in His resurrection. But Paul came to know Him first in the glory of heaven, Acts 9:1-6, and his experience being thus the reverse of theirs, the reverse order, 'Christ Jesus,' is of frequent occurrence in his letters, but, with the exception of Acts 24:24, does not occur elsewhere in the RV. In Paul's letters the order is always in harmony with the context. Thus 'Christ Jesus' describes the Exalted One who emptied Himself, Phil. 2:5, and testifies to His pre-existence; 'Jesus Christ' describes the despised and rejected One Who was afterwards glorified, Phil. 2:11, and testifies to His resurrection. 'Christ Jesus' suggests His grace, 'Jesus Christ' suggests His glory."

1:2 Abraham begat Isaac; and Isaac begat Jacob; and Jacob begat Judas and his brethren;

Begat *gennao* (1080), "to beget," in the passive voice, "to be born," is chiefly used of men "begetting" children, **Matt. 1:2-16**; more rarely of women "begetting" children, Luke 1:13, 57, "brought forth"; 23:29; John 16:21, "is delivered of," and of the child, "is born." In Gal. 4:24, it is used allegorically, to contrast Jews under bondage to the Law, and spiritual Israel, KJV, "gendereth," RV, "bearing children," to contrast the natural birth of Ishmael and the supernatural birth of Isaac. In

Matt. 1:20 it is used of conception, "that which is conceived in her."

Brethren Male children of the same parents, **Matt. 1:2; 14:3**.

1:3-6 And Judas begat Phares and Zara of Thamar; and Phares begat Esrom; and Esrom begat Aram;

And Aram begat Aminadab; and Aminadab begat Naasson; and Naasson begat Salmon;

And Salmon begat Booz of Rachab; and Booz begat Obed of Ruth; and Obed begat Jesse;

And Jesse begat David the king; and David the king begat Solomon of her *that had been the wife* of Urias;

King *basileus* (935), "a king" (cf. Eng., "Basil"), e.g., **Matt. 1:6**, is used of the Roman emperor in 1 Pet. 2:13, 17 (a command of general application); this reference to the emperor is illustrated frequently in the *Koine*; of Herod the Tetrarch (used by courtesy), **Matt. 14:9**; of Christ, as the "King" of the Jews, e.g., **Matt. 2:2**; **27:11**, **29**, **37**; as the "King" of Israel, Mark 15:32; John 1:49; 12:13; as "King of kings," Rev. 17:14; 19:16; as "the King" in judging nations and men at the establishment of the millennial kingdom, **Matt. 25:34**, **40**; of God, "the great King," **Matt. 5:35**; "the King eternal, incorruptible, invisible," 1 Tim. 1:17; "King of kings," 1 Tim. 6:15; "King of the ages," Rev. 15:3, RV (KJV, "saints"). Christ's "kingship" was predicted in the OT, e.g., Ps. 2:6, and in the NT, e.g., Luke 1:32, 33; He came as such, e.g., **Matt. 2:2**; John 18:37; was rejected and died as such, Luke 19:14; **Matt. 27:37**; is now a "King" Priest, after the order of Melchizedek, Heb. 5:6; 7:1, 17; and will reign for ever and ever, Rev. 11:15.

Wife In John 19:25 the article stands idiomatically for "the *wife* (of)"; in **Matt. 1:6**, the article is rendered "her *that had been the wife* (of)."

1:7-11 And Solomon begat Roboam; and Roboam begat Abia; and Abia begat Asa;

And Asa begat Josaphat; and Josaphat begat Joram; and Joram begat Ozias;

And Ozias begat Joatham; and Joatham begat Achaz; and Achaz begat Ezekias;

And Ezekias begat Manasses; and Manasses begat Amon; and Amon begat Josias;

And Josias begat Jechonias and his brethren, about the time they were carried away to Babylon:

Carried away *metoikesia* (3350), "a change of abode, or a carrying away by force" (*meta*, implying "change," *oikia*, "a dwelling"), is used only of the carrying away to Babylon, **Matt. 1:11-12, 17**.

1:12 And after they were brought to Babylon, Jechonias begat Salathiel; and Salathiel begat Zorobabel;

Brought *see* Carried away at *Matthew 1:11*.

1:13-16 And Zorobabel begat Abiud; and Abiud begat Eliakim; and Eliakim begat Azor;

And Azor begat Sadoc; and Sadoc begat Achim; and Achim begat Eliud;

And Eliud begat Eleazar; and Eleazar begat Matthan; and Matthan begat Jacob;

And Jacob begat Joseph the husband of Mary, of whom was born Jesus, who is called Christ.

Husband *aner* (435), denotes, in general, "a man, an adult male" (in contrast to *anthropos*, which generically denotes "a human being, male or female"); it is used of man in various relations, the context deciding the meaning; it signifies "a husband," e.g., **Matt. 1:16**, **19**; Mark 10:12; Luke 2:36; 16:18; John 4:16, 17, 18; Rom. 7:23.

Called *lego* (3004), "to speak," is used of all kinds of oral communication, e.g., "to call, to call by name," to surname, **Matt. 1:16**; **26:36**; John 4:5; 11:54; 15:15; Rev. 2:2, RV, "call themselves," etc.

1:17 So all the generations from Abraham to David *are* fourteen generations; and from David until the carrying away into Babylon *are* fourteen generations; and from the carrying away into Babylon unto Christ *are* fourteen generations.

Carrying away *see* Carried away at *Matthew 1:11*.

Christ *christos* (5547), "anointed," translates, in the Sept., the word "Messiah," a term applied to the priests who were anointed with the holy oil, particularly the high priest, e.g., Lev. 4:3, 5, 16. The prophets are called *hoi christoi Theou*, "the anointed of God," Ps. 105:15. A king of Israel was described upon occasion as *christos tou Kuriou*, "the anointed of the Lord," 1 Sam. 2:10, 35; 2 Sam. 1:14; Ps. 2:2; 18:50; Hab. 3:13; the term is used even of Cyrus, Isa. 45:1. The title *ho Christos*, "the Christ," is not used of Christ in the Sept. version of the inspired books of the OT. In the NT the word is frequently used with the article, of the Lord Jesus, as an appellative rather than a title, e.g., **Matt. 2:4**; Acts 2:31; without the article, Luke 2:11; 23:2; John 1:41. Three times the title was expressly accepted by the Lord Himself, **Matt. 16:17**; Mark 14:61-62;

John 4:26. It is added as an appellative to the proper name "Jesus," e.g., John 17:3, the only time when the Lord so spoke of Himself; Acts 9:34; 1 Cor. 3:11; 1 John 5:6. It is distinctly a proper name in many passages, whether with the article, e.g., **Matt. 1:17; 11:2**; Rom. 7:4, 9:5; 15:19; 1 Cor. 1:6, or without the article, Mark 9:41; Rom. 6:4; 8:9, 17; 1 Cor. 1:12; Gal. 2:16. The single title Christos is sometimes used without the article to signify the One who by His Holy Spirit and power indwells believers and molds their character in conformity to His likeness, Rom. 8:10; Gal. 2:20; 4:19; Eph. 3:17. As to the use or absence of the article, the title with the article specifies the Lord Jesus as "the Christ"; the title without the article stresses His character and His relationship with believers. Again, speaking generally, when the title is the subject of a sentence it has the article; when it forms part of the predicate the article is absent.

Fourteen *tessares* (5064), "four," is not found in the NT outside the Gospels, the Acts and Revelation; in the last it is very frequent. *Tetartos*, "fourth," is found in **Matt. 14:25**; Mark 6:48 and seven times in Revelation; also in Acts 10:30, "four days ago," lit., "from a fourth day." *Dekatessares*, "fourteen" (lit., "ten-four"), is found in **Matt. 1:17**; 2 Cor. 12:2; Gal. 2:1; *tessareskaidekatos*, "fourteenth" (lit., "four-and-tenth"), Acts 27:27, 33; *tetrakosia*, "four hundred," Acts 5:36; 7:6; 13:20; Gal. 3:17. In Acts 7:6 the 400 years refers to Abraham's descendants and to the sojourning and the bondage. This agrees with Gen. 15:13. In Exod. 12:40 the 430 years dates from the call of Abraham himself. Likewise the giving of the Law was 430 years from the promise in Gen. 12:3, which agrees with Gal. 3:17. In John 11:39 *tetartaios*, lit., "a fourth day (one)," is rendered "four days."

Generations *genea* (1074), connected with *ginomai*, "to become," primarily signifies "a begetting, or birth"; hence, that which has been begotten, a family; or successive members of a genealogy, **Matt. 1:17**, or of a race of people, possessed of similar characteristics, pursuits, etc., (of a bad character) **Matt. 17:17**; Mark 9:19; Luke 9:41; 16:8; Acts 2:40; or of the whole multitude of men living at the same time, **Matt. 24:34**; Mark 13:30; Luke 1:48; 21:32; Phil. 2:15, and especially of those of the Jewish race living at the same period, **Matt. 11:16**, etc. Transferred from people to the time in which they lived, the word came to mean "an age," i.e., a period ordinarily occupied by each successive generation, say, of thirty or forty years, Acts 14:16; 15:21; Eph. 3:5; Col. 1:26; see also, e.g., Gen. 15:16. In Eph. 3:21 *genea* is combined with *aion* in a remarkable phrase in a doxology: "Unto Him be the glory in the church and in Christ Jesus, unto all generations for ever and ever (wrongly in KJV 'all ages, world without end')." The word *genea* is to be distinguished from *aion*, as not denoting a period of unlimited duration.

1:18 Now the birth of Jesus Christ was on this wise: When as his mother Mary was espoused to Joseph, before they came together, she was found with child of the Holy Ghost.

Birth *gennesis* (1083), "a birth, begetting, producing" (related to *gennao*, "to beget"), is used in **Matt. 1:18** and Luke 1:14. Some mss. have *genesis*, "lineage, birth" (from *ginomai*, "to become").

Jesus *see Matthew 1:1.*

On this wise *houtos* or *houto* (3779), "in this way, so, thus," is used (a) with reference to what precedes, e.g., Luke 1:25; 2:48; (b) with reference to what follows, e.g., Luke 19:31, rendered "on this wise," in **Matt. 1:18**; John 21:1, and before quotations, Acts 7:6; 13:34; Rom. 10:6, KJV (RV, "thus"); Heb. 4:4; (c) marking intensity, rendered "so," e.g., Gal. 1:6; Heb. 12:21; Rev. 16:18; (d) in comparisons, rendered "so," e.g., Luke 11:30; Rom. 5:15.

Mother *meter* (3384), is used (a) of the natural relationship, e.g., **Matt. 1:18**; 2 Tim. 1:5; (b) figuratively, (1) of "one who takes the place of a mother," **Matt. 12:49, 50**; Mark 3:34, 35; John 19:27; Rom. 16:13; 1 Tim. 5:2; (2) of "the heavenly and spiritual Jerusalem," Gal. 4:26, which is "free" (not bound by law imposed externally, as under the Law of Moses), "which is our mother" (RV), i.e., of Christians, the metropolis, mother-city, used allegorically, just as the capital of a country is "the seat of its government, the center of its activities, and the place where the national characteristics are most fully expressed"; (3) symbolically, of "Babylon," Rev. 17:5, as the source from which has proceeded the religious harlotry of mingling pagan rites and doctrines with the Christian faith.

Espoused *mnesteuo* (3423), "to woo and win, to espouse or promise in marriage," is used in the passive voice in **Matt. 1:18**; Luke 1:27; 2:5, all with reference to the Virgin Mary, RV, "betrothed," for KJV, "espoused," in each case.

Before *prin* (4250), "before, formerly" (etymologically akin to *pro*, "before"), has the force of a conjunction, e.g., **Matt. 1:18; 26:34, 75**; John 14:29; Acts 7:2.

Was When not part of another verb, or phrase, these translate *eimi*, "to be," e.g., **Matt. 1:18**, or the following: (a) *ginomai*, "to become," e.g., **Matt. 8:26**; (b) *huparcho*, "to exist," especially when referring to an already existing condition, e.g., Luke 8:41; Acts 5:4 (2nd part); 16:3; 27:12; Rom. 4:19, KJV, "when he was" (RV, "he being"); (c) *echo*, "to have," e.g., Acts 12:15; (d) *apecho*, "to be away, to be distant," e.g., Luke 7:6; 24:13; (e) *mello*, "to be about to," e.g., Luke 19:4; Acts 21:27, 37, KJV (RV, "was about to"); (f) *sumbaino*, "to come to pass, happen," e.g., Acts 21:35; (g) in Gal. 4:28, the preposition *kata*, "according to," is rendered "was," in the phrase "as Isaac was," lit., "like Isaac"; as Isaac's birth came by divine interposition, so does the spiritual birth of every believer.

Holy *hagios* (40), from the same root as *hagnos* (found in *hazo*, "to venerate"), fundamentally signifies "separated" (among the Greeks, dedicated to the gods), and hence, in Scripture in its moral and spiritual significance, separated from sin and therefore consecrated to God, sacred.

(a) It is predicated of God (as the absolutely "Holy" One, in His purity, majesty and glory): of the Father, e.g., Luke 1:49; John 17:11; 1 Pet. 1:15, 16; Rev. 4:8; 6:10; of the Son, e.g., Luke 1:35; Acts 3:14; 4:27, 30; 1 John 2:20; of the Spirit, e.g., **Matt. 1:18** and frequently in all the Gospels, Acts, Romans, 1 and 2 Cor., Eph., 1 Thess.; also in 2 Tim. 1:14; Titus 3:5; 1 Pet. 1:12; 2 Pet. 1:21; Jude 20.

(b) It is used of men and things in so far as they are devoted to God. Indeed the quality, as attributed to God, is often presented in a way which involves divine demands upon the conduct of believers. These are called *hagioi*, "saints," i.e., "sanctified" or "holy" ones.

Holy Ghost The "Holy Spirit" is spoken of under various titles in the NT ("Spirit" and "Ghost" are renderings of the same word, *pneuma;* the advantage of the rendering "Spirit" is that it can always be used, whereas "Ghost" always requires the word "Holy" prefixed.) In the following list the omission of the definite article marks its omission in the original (concerning this see below): "Spirit, **Matt. 22:43**; Eternal Spirit, Heb. 9:14; the Spirit, **Matt. 4:1**; Holy Spirit, **Matt. 1:18**; the Holy Spirit, **Matt. 28:19**; the Spirit, the Holy, **Matt. 12:32**; the Spirit of promise, the Holy, Eph. 1:13; Spirit of God, Rom. 8:9; Spirit of (the) living God, 2 Cor. 3:3; the Spirit of God, 1 Cor. 2:11; the Spirit of our God, 1 Cor. 6:11; the Spirit of God, the Holy, Eph. 4:30; the Spirit of glory and of God, 1 Pet. 4:14; the Spirit of Him that raised up Jesus from the dead (i.e., God), Rom. 8:11; the Spirit of your Father, **Matt. 10:20**; the Spirit of His Son, Gal. 4:6; Spirit of (the) Lord, Acts 8:39; the Spirit of (the) Lord, Acts 5:9; (the) Lord, (the) Spirit, 2 Cor. 3:18; the Spirit of Jesus, Acts 16:7; Spirit of Christ, Rom. 8:9; the Spirit of Jesus Christ, Phil. 1:19; Spirit of adoption, Rom. 8:15; the Spirit of truth, John 14:17; the Spirit of life, Rom. 8:2; the Spirit of grace, Heb. 10:29."

The use or absence of the article in the original where the "Holy Spirit" is spoken of cannot always be decided by grammatical rules, nor can the presence or absence of the article alone determine whether the reference is to the "Holy Spirit." Examples where the Person is meant when the article is absent are **Matt. 22:43** (the article is used in Mark 12:36); Acts 4:25, RV (absent in some texts); 19:2, 6; Rom. 14:17; 1 Cor. 2:4; Gal. 5:25 (twice); 1 Pet. 1:2. Sometimes the absence is to be accounted for by the fact that *Pneuma* (like *Theos*) is substantially a proper name, e.g., in John 7:39. As a general rule the article is present where the subject of the teaching is the Personality of the Holy Spirit, e.g., John 14:26, where He is spoken of in distinction from the Father and the Son. See also 15:26 and cf. Luke 3:22. In Gal. 3:3, in the phrase "having begun in the Spirit," it is difficult to say whether the reference is to the "Holy Spirit" or to the quickened spirit of the believer; that it possibly refers to the latter is not to be determined by the absence of the article, but by the contrast with "the flesh"; on the other hand, the contrast may be between the "Holy Spirit" who in the believer sets His seal on the perfect work of Christ, and the flesh which seeks to better itself by works of its own. There is no preposition before either noun, and if the reference is to the quickened spirit it cannot be dissociated from the operation of the "Holy Spirit." In Gal. 4:29 the phrase "after the Spirit" signifies "by supernatural power," in contrast to "after the flesh," i.e., "by natural power," and the reference must be to the "Holy Spirit"; so in 5:17. The full title with the article before both *pneuma* and *hagios* (the "resumptive" use of the article), lit., "the Spirit the Holy," stresses the character of the Person, e.g., **Matt. 12:32**; Mark 3:29; 12:36; 13:11; Luke 2:26; 10:21 (RV); John 14:26; Acts 1:16; 5:3; 7:51; 10:44, 47; 13:2; 15:28; 19:6; 20:23, 28; 21:11; 28:25; Eph. 4:30; Heb. 3:7; 9:8; 10:15. The Personality of the Spirit is emphasized at the expense of strict grammatical procedure in John 14:26; 15:26; 16:8, 13, 14, where the emphatic pronoun *ekeinos*, "He," is used of Him in the masculine, whereas the noun *pneuma* is neuter in Greek, while the corresponding word in Aramaic, the language in which our Lord probably spoke, is feminine (*rucha*, cf. Heb. *ruach*). The rendering "itself" in Rom. 8:16, 26, due to the Greek gender, is corrected to "Himself" in the RV. The subject of the "Holy Spirit" in the NT may be considered as to His divine attributes; His distinct Personality in the Godhead; His operation in connection with the Lord Jesus in His birth, His life, His baptism, His death; His operations in the world; in the church; His having been sent at Pentecost by the Father and by Christ; His operations in the individual believer; in local churches; His operations in the production of Holy Scripture; His work in the world, etc.

1:19 Then Joseph her husband, being a just *man*, and not willing to make her a publick example, was minded to put her away privily.

Husband *see Matthew 1:16*.

Just *dikaios* (1342), was first used of persons observant of *dike*, "custom, rule, right," especially in the fulfillment of duties towards gods and men, and of things that were in accordance with right. The Eng. word "righteous" was formerly spelt "rightwise," i.e., (in a) straight way. In the NT it denotes "righteous," a state of being right, or right conduct, judged whether by the divine standard, or according to human standards, of what is right. Said of God, it designates the perfect agreement between His nature and His acts (in which He is the standard for all men). It is used (1) in the broad sense, of persons: (a) of God, e.g., John 17:25; Rom. 3:26; 1 John 1:9; 2:29; 3:7; (b) of Christ, e.g., Acts 3:14; 7:52; 22:14; 2 Tim. 4:8; 1 Pet. 3:18; 1 John 2:1; (c) of men, **Matt. 1:19**; Luke 1:6; Rom. 1:17; 2:13; 5:7. (2) of things; blood (metaphorical), **Matt. 23:35**; Christ's judgment, John 5:30; any circumstance, fact or deed, **Matt. 20:4** (v. 7, in some mss.); Luke 12:57; Acts 4:19; Eph. 6:1; Phil. 1:7; 4:8; Col. 4:1; 2 Thess. 1:6; "the commandment" (the Law), Rom. 7:12; works, 1 John 3:12; the ways of God, Rev. 15:3. In the following the RV substitutes "righteous" for the KJV "just"; **Matt. 1:19**; **13:49**; **27:19**, **24**; Mark 6:20; Luke 2:25; 15:7; 20:20; 23:50; John 5:30; Acts 3:14; 7:52; 10:22; 22:14; Rom. 1:17; 7:12; Gal. 3:11; Heb. 10:38; Jas. 5:6; 1 Pet. 3:18; 2 Pet. 2:7; 1 John 1:9; Rev. 15:3.

Example *deigmatizo* (1165), "to make a show of, to expose," is translated "to make a public example," in **Matt. 1:19** (some mss. have the strengthened form *paradeigmatizo* here; "put ... to an open shame," Heb. 6:6); in Col. 2:15, "made a show of."

Minded *boulomai* (1014), "to wish, will, desire, purpose" (akin to *boule*, "counsel, purpose"), is translated "was minded" in **Matt. 1:19**; Acts 15:37, RV (KJV, "determined"); 18:27, RV (KJV, "was disposed"); 19:30, RV (KJV, "would have"); 5:33, RV, "were minded" (KJV, "took counsel"); 18:15, RV, "I am (not) minded (to be)," KJV, "I will (be no)"; Heb. 6:17, "being minded," RV (KJV, "willing"), said of God.

Put *apoluo* (630), "to set free, let go," is rendered "to put away" in reference to one who is betrothed, **Matt. 1:19**; a wife, **5:31**, **32** (twice; in 2nd part, RV; KJV, "is divorced"); **19:3**, **7**, **8**, **9** (twice); Mark 10:2, 4, 11, 12; Luke 16:18 (twice).

Privily *lathra* (2977), "secretly, covertly" (from a root *lath-* indicating "unnoticed, unknown," seen in *lanthano*, "to escape notice," *lethe*, "forgetfulness"), is translated "privily" in **Matt. 1:19**; **2:7**; Acts 16:37; "secretly" in John 11:28 (in some mss., Mark 5:33).

1:20 But while he thought on these things, behold, the angel of the Lord appeared unto him in a dream, saying, Joseph, thou son of David, fear not to take unto thee Mary thy wife: for that which is conceived in her is of the Holy Ghost.

Thought *enthumeomai* (1760), "to reflect on, ponder," is used in **Matt. 1:20**; **9:4**. Cf. *enthumesis*, "consideration".

Behold *idou* (2400), e.g., **Matt. 1:20**, **23**; very frequent in the Synoptists and Acts and Revelation.

Appeared *phaino* (5316), signifies, in the active voice, "to shine"; in the passive, "to be brought forth into light, to become evident, to appear." In Rom. 7:13, concerning sin, the RV has "might be shewn to be," for KJV, "appear." It is used of the "appearance" of Christ to the disciples, Mark 16:9; of His future "appearing" in glory as the Son of Man, spoken of as a sign to the world, **Matt. 24:30**; there the genitive is subjective, the sign being the "appearing" of Christ Himself; of Christ as the light, John 1:5; of John the Baptist, 5:35; of the "appearing" of an angel of the Lord, either visibly, **Matt. 1:20**, or in a dream, **2:13**; of a star, **2:7**; of men who make an outward show, **Matt. 6:5**; **6:18** (see the RV); **23:27-28**; 2 Cor. 13:7; of tares, **Matt. 13:26**; of a vapor, Jas. 4:14; of things physical in general, Heb. 11:3; used impersonally in **Matt. 9:33**, "it was never so seen"; also of what appears to the mind, and so in the sense of to think, Mark 14:64, or to seem, Luke 24:11 (RV, "appeared").

Dream *onar* (3677), is "a vision in sleep," in distinction from a waking vision, **Matt. 1:20**; **2:12-13**, **19**, **22**; **27:19**.

Take *paralambano* (3880), besides its meaning "to receive," denotes "to take to (or with) oneself," of "taking" a wife, e.g., **Matt. 1:20**, **24**; of "taking" a person or persons with one, e.g., **Matt. 2:13**, **14**, **20**, **21**; **4:5**, **8**; of demons, **12:45**; of Christ and His disciples, **17:1**; **20:17**; Mark 9:2; 10:32; 14:33; of witnesses, **Matt. 18:16**; of the removal of persons from the earth in judgment, when "the Son of Man is revealed," **Matt. 24:40**, **41**; Luke 17:34, 35 (cf. the means of the removal of corruption, in v. 37); of the "taking" of Christ by the soldiers for scourging, **Matt. 27:27**, RV, and to crucifixion, John 19:16; see also Acts 15:39; 16:33; 21:24, 26, 32; 23:18.

Thy One of the oblique cases of *su*, "thou"; *sou*, "of thee," e.g., **Matt. 1:20**; **7:3** (2nd part), "thine own"; *soi*, "to thee," e.g., Mark 5:9; with *meno*, "to remain," Acts 5:4 (1st part), "thine own," lit., "remain to thee"; in **Matt. 26:18**, *pros se*, "at thy house," lit., "with thee".

Wife *gune* (1135), denotes (1) "a woman, married or unmarried"; (2) "a wife," e.g., **Matt. 1:20**; 1 Cor. 7:3, 4; in 1 Tim. 3:11, RV, "women," the reference may be to the "wives" of deacons, as the KJV takes it.

Conceived *see* Begat at *Matthew 1:2.*

1:21 And she shall bring forth a son, and thou shalt call his name JESUS: for he shall save his people from their sins.

Bring *tikto* (5088), "to beget, bring forth," **Matt. 1:21**, **23**, **25**; Jas. 1:15 (first part of verse, according to the best mss.); Rev. 12:5 (RV, "was delivered of").

Jesus *see Matthew 1:1.*

He *autos* (846), "he himself and no other," emphatic, e.g., **Matt. 1:21**, where the RV brings out the emphasis by the rendering "it is He"; **3:11** (last clause), where the repeated "He" brings out the emphasis; in some cases it can be marked only by a circumlocution which would not constitute a translation, e.g., **8:24**; this use is very frequent, especially in the Gospels, the epistles of John and Revelation; see also, e.g., Eph. 2:14; 4:11; 5:23, 27.

Save *sozo* (4982), "to save," is used (as with the noun *soteria*, "salvation") (a) of material and temporal deliverance from danger, suffering, etc., e.g., **Matt. 8:25**; Mark 13:20; Luke 23:35; John 12:27; 1 Tim. 2:15; 2 Tim. 4:18 (KJV, "preserve"); Jude 5; from sickness, **Matt. 9:22**, "made ... whole" (RV, marg., "saved"); so Mark 5:34; Luke 8:48; Jas. 5:15; (b) of the spiritual and eternal salvation granted immediately by God to those who believe on the Lord Jesus Christ, e.g., Acts 2:47, RV "(those that) were being saved"; 16:31; Rom. 8:24, RV, "were we saved"; Eph. 2:5, 8; 1 Tim. 2:4; 2 Tim. 1:9; Titus 3:5; of human agency in this, Rom. 11:14; 1 Cor. 7:16; 9:22; (c) of the present experiences of God's power to deliver from the bondage of sin, e.g., **Matt. 1:21**; Rom. 5:10; 1 Cor. 15:2; Heb. 7:25; Jas. 1:21; 1 Pet. 3:21; of human agency in this, 1 Tim. 4:16; (d) of the future deliverance of believers at the second coming of Christ for His saints, being deliverance from the wrath of God to be executed upon the ungodly at the close of this age and from eternal doom, e.g., Rom. 5:9; (e) of the deliverance of the nation of Israel at the second advent of Christ, e.g., Rom. 11:26; (f) inclusively for all the blessings bestowed by God on men in Christ, e.g., Luke 19:10; John 10:9; 1 Cor. 10:33; 1 Tim. 1:15; (g) of those who endure to the end of the time of the Great Tribulation, **Matt. 10:22**; Mark 13:13; (h) of the individual believer, who, though losing his reward at the judgment seat of Christ hereafter, will not lose his salvation, 1 Cor. 3:15; 5:5; (i) of the deliverance of the nations at the Millennium, Rev. 21:24 (in some mss.).

1:22 Now all this was done, that it might be fulfilled which was spoken of the Lord by the prophet, saying,

Fulfilled *pleroo* (4137), signifies (1) "to fill"; (2) "to fulfill, complete," (a) of time, e.g., Mark 1:15; Luke 21:24; John 7:8 (KJV, "full come"); Acts 7:23, RV, "he was wellnigh forty years old" (KJV, "was full" etc.), lit., "the time of forty years was fulfilled to him"; v. 30, KJV, "were expired"; 9:23; 24:27 (KJV, "after two years"; RV, "when two years were fulfilled"); (b) of number, Rev. 6:11; (c) of good pleasure, 2 Thess. 1:11; (d) of joy, Phil. 2:2; in the passive voice, "to be fulfilled," John 3:29 and 17:13; in the following the verb is rendered "fulfilled" in the RV, for the KJV, "full," John 15:11; 16:24; 1 John 1:4; 2 John 12; (e) of obedience, 2 Cor. 10:6; (f) of works, Rev. 3:2; (g) of the future Passover, Luke 22:16; (h) of sayings, prophecies, etc., e.g., **Matt. 1:22** (twelve more times in Matt., **2:15**, **17**, **23**; **4:14**; **8:17**; **12:17**; **13:35**; **21:4**; **26:54**, **56**; **27:9**, **35**; two in Mark, four in Luke, eight in John, two in Acts); Jas. 2:23; in Col. 1:25 the word signifies to preach "fully," to complete the ministry of the Gospel appointed.

Spoken *eiro* (3004), has a 1st aorist, passive participle *rhethen*, "spoken" or "spoken of," used in **Matt. 1:22**;

2:15, 17, 23; **3:3**; **4:14**; **8:17**; **12:17**; **13:35**; **21:4**; **22:31**; **24:15**; **27:9** (in some texts in **27:35** and Mark 13:14).

Of For *hupo*, "by," see the RV of **Matt. 1:22**; **2:16**; **11:27**; Luke 9:7; Acts 15:4; 1 Cor. 14:24; 2 Cor. 8:19; Phil. 3:12.

Lord *kurios* (2962), properly an adjective, signifying "having power" (*kuros*) or "authority," is used as a noun, variously translated in the NT, "'Lord,' 'master,' 'Master,' 'owner,' 'Sir,' a title of wide significance, occurring in each book of the NT save Titus and the Epistles of John. It is used (a) of an owner, as in Luke 19:33, cf. **Matt. 20:8**; Acts 16:16; Gal. 4:1; or of one who has the disposal of anything, as the Sabbath, **Matt. 12:8**; (b) of a master, i.e., one to whom service is due on any ground, **Matt. 6:24**; **24:50**; Eph. 6:5; (c) of an Emperor or King, Acts 25:26; Rev. 17:14; (d) of idols, ironically, 1 Cor. 8:5, cf. Isa. 26:13; (e) as a title of respect addressed to a father, **Matt. 21:30**, a husband, 1 Pet. 3:6, a master, **Matt. 13:27**; Luke 13:8, a ruler, **Matt. 27:63**, an angel, Acts 10:4; Rev. 7:14; (f) as a title of courtesy addressed to a stranger, John 12:21; 20:15; Acts 16:30; from the outset of His ministry this was a common form of address to the Lord Jesus, alike by the people, **Matt. 8:2**; John 4:11, and by His disciples, **Matt. 8:25**; Luke 5:8; John 6:68; (g) *kurios* is the Sept. and NT representative of Heb. Jehovah ('LORD' in Eng. versions), see **Matt. 4:7**; Jas. 5:11, e.g., of *adon*, Lord, **Matt. 22:44**, and of *Adonay*, Lord, **1:22**; it also occurs for *Elohim*, God, 1 Pet. 1:25.

"Thus the usage of the word in the NT follows two main lines: *one-a-f*, customary and general, the other, *g*, peculiar to the Jews, and drawn from the Greek translation of the OT. Christ Himself assumed the title, **Matt. 7:21**, **22**; **9:38**; **22:41-45**; Mark 5:19 (cf. Ps. 66:16; the parallel passage, Luke 8:39, has 'God'); Luke 19:31; John 13:13, apparently intending it in the higher senses of its current use, and at the same time suggesting its OT associations. His purpose did not become clear to the disciples until after His resurrection, and the revelation of His Deity consequent thereon. Thomas, when he realized the significance of the presence of a mortal wound in the body of a living man, immediately joined with it the absolute title of Deity, saying, 'My Lord and my God,' John 20:28. Thereafter, except in Acts 10:4 and Rev. 7:14, there is no record that *kurios* was ever again used by believers in addressing any save God and the Lord Jesus; cf. Acts 2:47 with 4:29, 30. How soon and how completely the lower meaning had been superseded is seen in Peter's declaration in his first sermon after the resurrection, 'God hath made Him—Lord,' Acts 2:36, and that in the house of Cornelius, 'He is Lord of all,' 10:36, cf. Deut. 10:14; **Matt. 11:25**; Acts 17:24. In his writings the implications of his early teaching are confirmed and developed. Thus Ps. 34:8, 'O taste and see that Jehovah is good,' is applied to the Lord Jesus, 1 Pet. 2:3, and 'Jehovah of Hosts, Him shall ye sanctify,' Isa. 8:13, becomes 'sanctify in your hearts Christ as Lord,' 3:15. So also James who uses *kurios* alike of God, 1:7 (cf. v. 5); 3:9; 4:15; 5:4, 10, 11, and of the Lord Jesus, 1:1 (where the possibility that *kai* is intended epexegetically, i.e. = even, cf. 1 Thess. 3:11, should not be overlooked); 2:1 (lit., 'our Lord Jesus Christ of glory,' cf. Ps. 24:7; 29:3; Acts 7:2; 1 Cor. 2:8); 5:7, 8, while the language of 4:10; 5:15, is equally applicable to either. Jude, v. 4, speaks of 'our only—Lord, Jesus Christ,' and immediately, v. 5, uses 'Lord' of God (see the remarkable marg. here), as he does later, vv. 9, 14."

1:23 Behold, a virgin shall be with child, and shall bring forth a son, and they shall call his name Emmanuel, which being interpreted is, God with us.

Behold *see Matthew 1:20.*

Virgin *parthenos* (3933), is used (a) of "the Virgin Mary," **Matt. 1:23**; Luke 1:27; (b) of the ten "virgins" in the parable, **Matt. 25:1**, **7**, **11**; (c) of the "daughters" of Philip the evangelist, Acts 21:9; (d) those concerning whom the apostle Paul gives instructions regarding marriage, 1 Cor. 7:25, 28, 34; in vv. 36, 37, 38, the subject passes to that of "virgin *daughters*" (RV), which almost certainly formed one of the subjects upon which the church at Corinth sent for instructions from the apostle; one difficulty was relative to the discredit which might be brought upon a father (or guardian), if he allowed his daughter or ward to grow old unmarried. The interpretation that this passage refers to a man and woman already in some kind of relation by way of a spiritual marriage and living together in a vow of virginity and celibacy, is untenable if only in view of the phraseology of the passage; (e) figuratively, of "a local church" in its relation to Christ, 2 Cor. 11:2; (f) metaphorically of "chaste persons," Rev. 14:4.

Bring *see Matthew 1:21.*

Interpreted *methermeneuo* (3177), "to change or translate from one language to another (*meto*, implying change), to interpret," is always used in the passive voice in the NT, "being interpreted," of interpreting the names, Immanuel, **Matt. 1:23**; Golgotha, Mark 15:22; Barnabas, Acts 4:36; in Acts 13:8, of Elymas, the verb is rendered "is ... by interpretation," lit., "is interpreted"; it is used of interpreting or translating sentences in Mark 5:41; 15:34; in the best mss., John 1:38 (Rabbi, interpreted as "Master"); v. 41 (Messiah, interpreted as "Christ").

1:24 Then Joseph being raised from sleep did as the angel of the Lord had bidden him, and took unto him his wife:

Raised *anistemi* (450), is translated "to raise or raise up," (a) of the resurrection of the dead by Christ, John 6:39, 40, 44, 54; (b) of the resurrection of Christ from the dead, Acts 2:24 (for v. 30 see RV, *kathizo*, "to set," as in the best texts); 2:32; 13:34, see (c) below; Acts 17:31; (c) of "raising" up a person to occupy a place in the midst of a nation, said of Christ, Acts 3:26; 7:37; 13:33, RV, "raised up Jesus," not here by resurrection from the dead, as the superfluous "again" of the KJV would suggest; this is confirmed by the latter part of the verse, which explains the "raising" up as being by way of His incarnation, and by the contrast in v. 34, where stress is laid upon His being "raised" from the dead, the same verb being used: (d) of "raising" up seed, **Matt. 22:24**; (e) of being "raised" from natural sleep, **Matt. 1:24**, KJV, "being raised" (RV, "arose"); here some mss. have *diegeiro*, "to arouse completely".

Bidden *prostasso* (4367), denotes "to arrange or set in order towards" (*pros*, "towards," *tasso*, "to arrange"); hence "to prescribe, give command," **Matt. 1:24**; **8:4**; Mark 1:44; Luke 5:14; Acts 10:33, 48.

Took *see* Take at *Matthew 1:20*.

1:25 And knew her not till she had brought forth her firstborn son: and he called his name JESUS.

Knew *ginosko* (1097), signifies "to be taking in knowledge, to come to know, recognize, understand," or "to understand completely," e.g., Mark 13:28, 29; John 13:12; 15:18; 21:17; 2 Cor. 8:9; Heb. 10:34; 1 John 2:5; 4:2, 6 (twice), 7, 13; 5:2, 20; in its past tenses it frequently means "to know in the sense of realizing," the aorist or point tense usually indicating definiteness, **Matt. 13:11**; Mark 7:24; John 7:26; in 10:38 "that ye may know (aorist tense) and understand, (present tense)"; 19:4; Acts 1:7; 17:19; Rom. 1:21; 1 Cor. 2:11 (2nd part), 14; 2 Cor. 2:4; Eph. 3:19; 6:22; Phil. 2:19; 3:10; 1 Thess. 3:5; 2 Tim. 2:19; Jas. 2:20; 1 John 2:13 (twice), 14; 3:6; 4:8; 2 John 1; Rev. 2:24; 3:3, 9. In the passive voice, it often signifies "to become known," e.g., **Matt. 10:26**; Phil. 4:5. In the sense of complete and absolute understanding on God's part, it is used, e.g., in Luke 16:15; John 10:15 (of the Son as well as the Father); 1 Cor. 3:20. In Luke 12:46, KJV, it is rendered "he is ... aware." In the NT *ginosko* frequently indicates a relation between the person "knowing" and the object known; in this respect, what is "known" is of value or importance to the one who knows, and hence the establishment of the relationship, e.g., especially of God's "knowledge," 1 Cor. 8:3, "if any man love God, the same is known of Him"; Gal. 4:9, "to be known of God"; here the "knowing" suggests approval and bears the meaning "to be approved"; so in 2 Tim. 2:19; cf. John 10:14, 27; Gen. 18:19; Nah. 1:7; the relationship implied may involve remedial chastisement, Amos 3:2. The same idea of appreciation as well as "knowledge" underlies several statements concerning the "knowledge" of God and His truth on the part of believers, e.g., John 8:32; 14:20, 31; 17:3; Gal. 4:9 (1st part); 1 John 2:3-13, 14; 4:6, 8, 16; 5:20; such "knowledge" is obtained, not by mere intellectual activity, but by operation of the Holy Spirit consequent upon acceptance of Christ. Nor is such "knowledge" marked by finality; see e.g., 2 Pet. 3:18; Hos. 6:3, RV. The verb is also used to convey the thought of connection or union, as between man and woman, **Matt. 1:25**; Luke 1:34.

Brought *see* Bring at *Matthew 1:21*.

Chapter 2

2:1 Now when Jesus was born in Bethlehem of Judaea in the days of Herod the king, behold, there came wise men from the east to Jerusalem,

Judea *ioudaios* (2453), is used (a) adjectivally, with the lit. meaning, "Jewish," sometimes with the addition of *aner*, "a man," Acts 10:28; 22:3; in 21:39 with *anthropos*, in some mss. (a man in the generic sense); the best mss. omit the phrase here; in 13:6, lit., "a Jewish false-prophet"; in John 3:22, with the word *chora*, "land" or "country," signifying "Judean," lit., "Judean country"; used by metonymy for the people of the country; (b) as a noun, "a Jew, Jews," e.g., **Matt. 2:2**; Mark 7:3. It also denotes Judea, e.g., **Matt. 2:1**; Luke 1:5; John 4:3, the word "country" being understood [cf. (a) above]. In Luke 23:5 and John 7:1, where the KJV has "Jewry," the RV translates it as usual, "Judea."

Came *paraginomai* (3854), *para*, "near or by," denotes to "arrive, to be present," e.g., **Matt. 2:1**.

Wise men *magos* (3097), denotes "a Magian," one of a sacred caste, originally Median, who apparently conformed to the Persian religion while retaining their old beliefs; it is used in the plural, **Matt. 2:1, 7, 16** (twice), "wise men."

East *anatole* (395), primarily "a rising," as of the sun and stars, corresponds to *anatello*, "to make to rise," or, intransitively, "to arise," which is also used of the sunlight, as well as of other objects in nature. In Luke 1:78 it is used metaphorically of Christ as "the Dayspring," the One through whom light came into the world, shining immediately into Israel, to dispel the darkness which was upon all nations. Cf. Mal. 4:2. Elsewhere it denotes the "east," as the quarter of the sun's rising, **Matt. 2:1-2, 9; 8:11; 24:27**; Luke 13:29; Rev. 7:2; 16:12; 21:13. The "east" in general stands for that side of things upon which the rising of the sun gives light. In the heavenly city itself, Rev. 21:13, the reference to the "east" gate points to the outgoing of the influence of the city "eastward."

2:2 Saying, Where is he that is born King of the Jews? for we have seen his star in the east, and are come to worship him.

Born *tikto* (5088), "to bring forth," Luke 1:57; John 16:21; Heb. 11:11; Rev. 12:2, 4, or, "to be born," said of the Child, **Matt. 2:2**; Luke 2:11, is used metaphorically in Jas. 1:15, of lust as bringing forth sin.

King *see Matthew 1:6.*

Jews *see* Judea at *Matthew 2:1.*

Star *aster* (792), "a star," **Matt. 2:2–10; 24:29**; Mark 13:25; 1 Cor. 15:41; Rev. 6:13; 8:10-12; 9:1; 12:1, 4, is used metaphorically, (a) of Christ, as "the morning star," figurative of the approach of the day when He will appear as the "sun of righteousness," to govern the earth in peace, an event to be preceded by the rapture of the Church, Rev. 2:28; 22:16, the promise of the former to the overcomer being suggestive of some special personal interest in Himself and His authority; (b) of the angels of the seven churches, Rev. 1:16, 20; 2:1; 3:1; (c) of certain false teachers, described as "wandering stars," Jude 13, as if the "stars," intended for light and guidance, became the means of deceit by irregular movements.

Worship *proskuneo* (4352), "to make obeisance, do reverence to" (from *pros*, "towards," and *kuneo*, "to kiss"), is the most frequent word rendered "to worship." It is used of an act of homage or reverence (a) to God, e.g., **Matt. 4:10**; John 4:21-24; 1 Cor. 14:25; Rev. 4:10; 5:14; 7:11; 11:16; 19:10 (2nd part) and 22:9; (b) to Christ, e.g., **Matt. 2:2, 8, 11; 8:2; 9:18; 14:33; 15:25; 20:20; 28:9, 17**; John 9:38; Heb. 1:6, in a quotation from the Sept. of Deut. 32:43, referring to Christ's second advent; (c) to a man, **Matt. 18:26**; (d) to the Dragon, by men, Rev. 13:4; (e) to the Beast, his human instrument, Rev. 13:4, 8, 12; 14:9, 11; (f) the image of the Beast, 13:15; 14:11; 16:2; (g) to demons, Rev. 9:20; (h) to idols, Acts 7:43.

2:3 When Herod the king had heard *these things*, he was troubled, and all Jerusalem with him.

Troubled *tarosso* (5015), is used (1) in a physical sense, John 5:7 (in some mss. v. 4), (2) metaphorically, (a) of the soul and spirit of the Lord, John 11:33, where the true rendering is "He troubled Himself"; (b) of the hearts of disciples, 14:1, 27; (c) of the minds of those in

"The coming of Jesus into the world is the most stupendous event in human history."

MALCOLM MUGGERIDGE

fear or perplexity, **Matt. 2:3; 14:26**; Mark 6:50; Luke 1:12; 24:38; 1 Pet. 3:14; (d) of subverting the souls of believers, by evil doctrine, Acts 15:24; Gal. 1:7; 5:10; (e) of stirring up a crowd, Acts 17:8; v. 13 in the best texts, "troubling (the multitudes)," RV.

All *pas* (3956), radically means "all." Used without the article it means "every," every kind or variety. So the RV marg. in Eph. 2:21, "every building," and the text in 3:15, "every family," and the RV marg. of Acts 2:36, "every house"; or it may signify "the highest degree," the maximum of what is referred to, as, "with all boldness" Acts 4:29. Before proper names of countries, cities and nations, and before collective terms, like "Israel," it signifies either "all" or "the whole," e.g., **Matt. 2:3**; Acts 2:36. Used with the article, it means the whole of one object. In the plural it signifies "the totality of the persons or things referred to." Used without a noun it virtually becomes a pronoun, meaning "everyone" or "anyone." In the plural with a noun it means "all." The neuter singular denotes "everything" or "anything whatsoever." One form of the neuter plural (*panta*) signifies "wholly, together, in all ways, in all things," Acts 20:35; 1 Cor. 9:25. The neuter plural without the article signifies "all things severally," e.g., John 1:3; 1 Cor. 2:10; preceded by the article it denotes "all things," as constituting a whole, e.g., Rom. 11:36; 1 Cor. 8:6; Eph. 3:9.

2:4 And when he had gathered all the chief priests and scribes of the people together, he demanded of them where Christ should be born.

Gathered *sunago* (4863), "to gather or bring together," is said of (a) persons, e.g., **Matt. 2:4**; (b) things, e.g., **Matt. 13:30**; in Luke 15:13 the idea is that of "gathering" his goods together for sale, i.e., "having sold off all."

Chief *archiereus* (749), "a chief priest, high priest" (*arche*, "first," *hiereus*, "a priest"), is frequent in the Gospels, Acts and Hebrews, but there only in the NT. It is used of Christ, e.g., in Heb. 2:17; 3:1; of "chief" priests, including ex-high-priests and members of their families, e.g., **Matt. 2:4**; Mark 8:31.

Priests *archiereus* (749), designates (a) "the high priests" of the Levitical order, frequently called "chief priests" in the NT, and including "ex-high priests" and members of "high priestly" families, e.g., **Matt. 2:4**; **16:21**; **20:18**; **21:15**; in the singular, a "high priest," e.g., Abiathar, Mark 2:26; Annas and Caiaphas, Luke 3:2, where the RV rightly has "in the high priesthood of A. and C." (cf. Acts 4:6). As to the combination of the two in this respect, Annas was the "high priest" from AD 7-14, and, by the time referred to, had been deposed for some years; his son-in-law, Caiaphas, the fourth "high priest" since his deposition, was appointed about AD 24. That Annas was still called the "high priest" is explained by the facts (1) that by the Mosaic law the high priesthood was held for life, Num. 35:25; his deposition was the capricious act of the Roman procurator, but he would still be regarded legally and religiously as "high priest" by the Jews; (2) that he probably still held the office of deputy-president of the Sanhedrin (cf. 2 Kings 25:18); (3) that he was a man whose age, wealth and family connections gave him a preponderant influence, by which he held the real sacerdotal power; indeed at this time the high priesthood was in the hands of a clique of some half dozen families; the language of the writers of the Gospels is in accordance with this, in attributing the high priesthood rather to a caste than a person; (4) the "high priests" were at that period mere puppets of Roman authorities who deposed them at will, with the result that the title was used more loosely than in former days.

Scribes *grammateus* (1122), from *gramma*, "a writing," denotes "a scribe, a man of letters, a teacher of the law"; the "scribes" are mentioned frequently in the Synoptists, especially in connection with the Pharisees, with whom they virtually formed one party (see Luke 5:21), sometimes with the chief priests, e.g., **Matt. 2:4**; Mark 8:31; 10:33; 11:18, 27; Luke 9:22. They are mentioned only once in John's Gospel, 8:3, three times in the Acts, 4:5; 6:12; 23:9; elsewhere only in 1 Cor. 1:20, in the singular. They were considered naturally qualified to teach in the synagogues, Mark 1:22. They were ambitious of honor, e.g., **Matt. 23:5–11**, which they demanded especially from their pupils, and which was readily granted them, as well as by the people generally. Like Ezra (Ezra 7:12), the "scribes" were found originally among the priests and Levites. The priests being the official interpreters of the Law, the "scribes" ere long became an independent company; though they never held political power, they became leaders of the people. Their functions regarding the Law were to teach it, develop it, and use it in connection with the Sanhedrin and various local courts. They also occupied themselves with the sacred writings both historical and didactic. They attached the utmost importance to ascetic elements, by which the nation was especially separated from the Gentiles. In their regime piety was reduced to external formalism. Only that was of value which was governed by external precept. Life under them became a burden; they themselves sought to evade certain of their own precepts, **Matt. 23:13**ff.; Luke 11:46; by their traditions the Law, instead of being a help in moral and spiritual life, became an instrument for preventing true access to God, Luke 11:52. Hence the Lord's stern denunciations of them and the Pharisees.

Demanded *punthanomai* (4441), "to inquire," is translated "inquired" in **Matt. 2:4**, and Acts 21:33, RV (KJV, "demanded"); in Luke 15:26; 18:36 and Acts 4:7 (KJV, "asked"); "inquired" (KJV, "inquired") in John 4:52; "inquire" (KJV, "inquire") in Acts 23:20; in Acts 23:34 it denotes "to learn by inquiry," KJV, and RV, "when (he) understood"; elsewhere it is rendered by the verb "to ask," Acts 10:18, 29; 23:19.

Christ *see Matthew 1:17.*

2:5-6 And they said unto him, In Bethlehem of Judaea: for thus it is written by the prophet,
And thou Bethlehem, in the land of Juda, art not the least

among the princes of Juda: for out of thee shall come a Governor, that shall rule my people Israel.

Thou Frequently this forms part of the translation of a verb in the 2nd person, singular. Otherwise it translates (a) the pronoun *su*, used for emphasis or contrast, e.g., John 1:19, 21 (twice), 25, 42 (twice); 8:5, 13, 25, 33, 48, 52, 53; Acts 9:5; in addressing a person or place, e.g., **Matt. 2:6**; Luke 1:76; John 17:5; perhaps also in the phrase *su eipas*, "thou hast said," e.g., **Matt. 26:64** (sometimes without emphasis, e.g., Acts 13:33); (b) in the oblique cases, e.g., the dative *soi*, lit., "to thee," e.g., **Matt. 17:25**, "what thinkest thou?" (lit., "what does it seem to thee?"); (c) *autos*, "self," e.g., Luke 6:42; Acts 21:24, "thou thyself"; (d) the reflexive pronoun, *seauton*, Rom. 2:19, "thou thyself."

Least *elachistos* (1646), "least," is a superlative degree formed from the word *elachus*, "little," the place of which was taken by *mikros* (the comparative degree being *elasson*, "less"); it is used of (a) size, Jas. 3:4; (b) amount; of the management of affairs, Luke 16:10 (twice), 19:17, "very little"; (c) importance, 1 Cor. 6:2, "smallest (matters)"; (d) authority: of commandments, **Matt. 5:19**; (e) estimation, as to persons, **Matt. 5:19** (2nd part); **25:40, 45**; 1 Cor. 15:9; as to a town, **Matt. 2:6**; as to activities or operations, Luke 12:26; 1 Cor. 4:3, "a very small thing."

Come *exerchomai* (1831), "to come out, or go out or forth" (*ek*, "out"), e.g., **Matt. 2:6**.

Governor *hegemon* (2232), is a term used (a) for "rulers" generally, Mark 13:9; 1 Pet. 2:14; translated "princes" (i.e., leaders) in **Matt. 2:6**; (b) for the Roman procurators, referring, in the Gospels to Pontius Pilate, e.g., **Matt. 27:2**; Luke 20:20 (so designated by Tacitus, *Annals*, xv. 44); to Felix, Acts 23:26. Technically the procurator was a financial official under a proconsul or propretor, for collecting the imperial revenues, but entrusted also with magisterial powers for decisions of questions relative to the revenues. In certain provinces, of which Judea was one (the procurator of which was dependent on the legate of Syria), he was the general administrator and supreme judge, with sole power of life and death. Such a governor was a person of high social standing. Felix, however, was an ex-slave, a freedman, and his appointment to Judea could not but be regarded by the Jews as an insult to the nation. The headquarters of the governor of Judea was Caesarea, which was made a garrison town. For *anthupatos*, "a proconsul."

Rule *poimaino* (4165), "to act as a shepherd, tend flocks," is translated "to rule" in Rev. 2:27; 12:5; 19:15, all indicating that the governing power exercised by the Shepherd is to be of a firm character; in **Matt. 2:6**, KJV, "shall rule" (RV, "shall be shepherd of").

People *laos* (2992), is used of (a) "the people at large," especially of people assembled, e.g., **Matt. 27:25**; Luke 1:21; 3:15; Acts 4:27; (b) "a people of the same race and language," e.g., Rev. 5:9; in the plural, e.g., Luke 2:31; Rom. 15:11; Rev. 7:9; 11:9; especially of Israel, e.g., **Matt. 2:6; 4:23**; John 11:50; Acts 4:8; Heb. 2:17; in distinction from their rulers and priests, e.g., **Matt. 26:5**; Luke 20:19; Heb. 5:3; in distinction from Gentiles, e.g., Acts 26:17, 23; Rom. 15:10; (c) of Christians as the people of God, e.g., Acts 15:14; Titus 2:14; Heb. 4:9; 1 Pet. 2:9.

2:7 Then Herod, when he had privily called the wise men, enquired of them diligently what time the star appeared.

Then *tote* (5119), a demonstrative adverb of time, denoting "at that time," is used (a) of concurrent events, e.g., **Matt. 2:17**; Gal. 4:8, "at that time"; v. 29, "then"; 2 Pet. 3:6, "(the world) that then was," lit., "(the) then (world)"; (b) of consequent events, "then, thereupon," e.g., **Matt. 2:7**; Luke 11:26; 16:16, "[from (KJV, "since")] that time"; John 11:14; Acts 17:14; (c) of things future, e.g., **Matt. 7:23**; **24:30** (twice), **40**; eight times in ch. **25**; 1 Cor. 4:5; Gal. 6:4; 1 Thess. 5:3; 2 Thess. 2:8. It occurs 90 times in Matthew, more than in all the rest of the NT together.

Privily *see Matthew 1:19.*

Wise men *see Matthew 2:1.*

Enquired ... diligently *akriboo* (198), "to learn carefully," is so translated in **Matt. 2:7, 16**, RV (KJV, "diligently enquired").

Time *chronos* (5550), whence Eng. words beginning with "chron"–, denotes "a space of time," whether long or short: (a) it implies duration, whether longer, e.g., Acts 1:21, "(all the) time"; Acts 13:18; 20:18, RV, "(all the) time" (KJV, "at all seasons"); or shorter, e.g., Luke 4:5; (b) it sometimes refers to the date of an occurrence, whether past, e.g., **Matt. 2:7**, or future, e.g., Acts 3:21; 7:17. Broadly speaking, *chronos* expresses the duration of a period, *kairos* stresses it as marked by certain features; thus in Acts 1:7, "the Father has set within His own authority" both the times (*chronos*), the lengths of the periods, and the "seasons" (*kairos*), epochs characterized by certain events; in 1 Thess. 5:1, "times" refers to the length of the interval before the Parousia takes place (the presence of Christ with the saints when He comes to receive them to Himself at the Rapture), and to the length of time the Parousia will occupy; "seasons" refers to the special features of the period before, during, and after the Parousia. In Rev. 10:6 *chronos* has the meaning "delay" (RV, marg.), an important rendering for the understanding of the passage (the word being akin to *chronizo*, "to take time, to linger, delay," **Matt. 24:48**; Luke 12:45).

Appeared *see Matthew 1:20.*

2:8 And he sent them to Bethlehem, and said, Go and search diligently for the young child; and when ye have found *him*, bring me word again, that I may come and worship him also.

Search *exetazo* (1833), "to search out" (*ek*, "out," intensive, *etazo*, "to examine"), is translated "ask," in John 21:12, KJV (RV, "inquire"); in **Matt. 2:8**, KJV, "search"; RV, "search out," expressing the intensive force of the verb, so **Matt. 10:11** (KJV, "inquire").

Diligently *akribos* (199), means "accurately, exactly." The KJV translates it "diligently" in **Matt. 2:8** and Acts 18:25; "perfectly" in 1 Thess. 5:2 (cf. Luke 1:3).

Child *paidion* (3813), a diminutive of *pais*, signifies "a little or young child"; it is used of an infant just born, John 16:21, of a male child recently born, e.g., **Matt. 2:8**; Heb. 11:23; of a more advanced child, Mark 9:24; of a son, John 4:49; of a girl, Mark 5:39, 40, 41; in the plural, of "children," e.g., **Matt. 14:21**. It is used metaphorically of believers who are deficient in spiritual understanding, 1 Cor. 14:20, and in affectionate and familiar address by the Lord to His disciples, almost like the Eng., "lads," John 21:5; by the apostle John to the youngest believers in the family of God, 1 John 2:13, 18; there it is to be distinguished from *teknia*, which term he uses in addressing all his readers (vv. 1, 12, 28).

Bring *apangello* (518), "to announce," is translated "bring word" in **Matt. 2:8**, RV (the KJV unnecessarily adds "again"); **28:8**.

Worship *see Matthew 2:2.*

2:9 When they had heard the king, they departed; and, lo, the star, which they saw in the east, went before them, till it came and stood over where the young child was.

Departed *poreuo* (4198), akin to *poros*, "a passage," in the middle voice signifies "to go on one's way, to depart from one place to another." In some places, where the KJV has the verb "to depart," the RV translates by "to go one's way," e.g., **Matt. 2:9**, "went their way"; **11:7**; **24:1**, "was going on His way." In the following the RV has the verb "to go," for the KJV "depart," Luke 4:42 (latter part of verse); 13:31; John 16:7; 2 Tim. 4:10. In Luke 21:8, "go (after)," is said of disciples or partisans. In some places both KJV and RV translate by the verb "to depart," e.g., **Matt. 19:15**; **25:41**; Acts 5:41; Acts 22:21. This verb is to be distinguished from others signifying "to go." It is best rendered, as often as possible, "to go on one's way."

East *see Matthew 2:1.*

Went *proago* (4254), "to lead forth," used intransitively signifies "to go before," usually of locality, e.g., **Matt. 2:9**; figuratively, in 1 Tim. 1:18, "went before" (RV, marg., "led the way to"), of the exercise of the gifts of prophecy which pointed to Timothy as one chosen by God for the service to be committed to him; in 5:24, of sins "going before unto judgment." In 2 John 9, where the best mss. have this verb (instead of *parabaino*, "to transgress," KJV), the RV renders it "goeth onward" (marg., "taketh the lead"), of not abiding in the doctrine of Christ. Cf. Mal. 4:4.

Stood *histemi* (2476), (a) transitively, denotes "to cause to stand, to set"; in the passive voice, "to be made to stand," e.g., **Matt. 2:9**, lit., "was made to stand"; so Luke 11:18; 19:8 (Col. 4:12 in some mss.); in Rev. 13:1 the RV follows the best texts, "he stood" (not as KJV, "I stood"); the reference is to the Dragon. In the middle voice, "to take one's stand, place oneself," e.g., Rev. 18:15; (b) intransitively, in the 2nd aorist and perfect active, "to stand, stand by, stand still," e.g., **Matt. 6:5**; **20:32**, "stood still"; in Luke 6:8, "stand forth" and "stood forth"; metaphorically, "to stand firm," John 8:44 (negatively), in the truth; Rom. 5:2, in grace; 1 Cor. 15:1, in the gospel; Rom. 11:20, "by thy faith," RV; 2 Cor. 1:24, "by faith" (marg., "by your faith"); of steadfastness, 1 Cor. 7:37; Eph. 6:11, 13, 14; Col. 4:12.

2:10 When they saw the star, they rejoiced with exceeding great joy.

Exceeding *sphodra* (4970), properly the neuter plural of *sphodros*, "excessive, violent" (from a root indicating restlessness), signifies "very, very much, exceedingly," **Matt. 2:10**; **17:6**, "sore"; **17:23**; **18:31**, RV, "exceeding," for KJV, "very"; **19:25**; **26:22**; **27:54**, RV, "exceedingly" for KJV, "greatly"; Mark 16:4, "very"; Luke 18:23 (ditto); Acts 6:7, RV, "exceedingly," for KJV, greatly; Rev. 16:21.

2:11 And when they were come into the house, they saw the young child with Mary his mother, and fell down, and worshipped him: and when they had opened their treasures, they presented unto him gifts; gold, and frankincense, and myrrh.

House *oikia* (3614), in Attic law *oikos* denoted the whole estate, *oikia* stood for the dwelling only; this distinction was largely lost in later Greek. In the NT it denotes (a) "a house, a dwelling," e.g., **Matt. 2:11; 5:15; 7:24-27**; 2 Tim. 2:20; 2 John 10; it is not used of the Tabernacle or the Temple; (b) metaphorically, the heavenly abode, spoken of by the Lord as "My Father's house," John 14:2, the eternal dwelling place of believers; the body as the dwelling place of the soul, 2 Cor. 5:1; similarly the resurrection body of believers (*id.*); property, e.g., Mark 12:40; by metonymy, the inhabitants of a house, a household, e.g., **Matt. 12:25**; John 4:53; 1 Cor. 16:15.

Fell *pipto* (4098), "to fall," is used (a) of descent, to "fall" down from, e.g., **Matt. 10:29; 13:4**; (b) of a lot, Acts 1:26; (c) of "falling" under judgment, Jas. 5:12 (cf. Rev. 18:2, RV); (d) of persons in the act of prostration, to prostrate oneself, e.g., **Matt. 17:6**; John 18:6; Rev. 1:17; in homage and worship, e.g., **Matt. 2:11**; Mark 5:22; Rev. 5:14; 19:4; (e) of things, "falling" into ruin, or failing, e.g., **Matt. 7:25**; Luke 16:17, RV, "fall," for KJV, "fail"; Heb. 11:30; (f), of "falling" in judgment upon persons, as of the sun's heat, Rev. 7:16, RV, "strike," KJV, "light"; of a mist and darkness, Acts 13:11 (some mss. have *epipipto*); (g) of persons, in "falling" morally or spiritually, Rom. 14:4; 1 Cor. 10:8, 12; Rev. 2:5.

Worshipped *see* **Worship** at *Matthew 2:2*.

Opened *anoigo* (455), is used (1) transitively, (a) literally, of "a door or gate," e.g., Acts 5:19; graves, **Matt. 27:52**; a sepulchre, Rom. 3:13; a book, e.g., Luke 4:17; Rev. 5:2-5; 10:8; the seals of a roll, e.g., Rev. 5:9; 6:1; the eyes, Acts 9:40; the mouth of a fish, **Matt. 17:27**; "the pit of the abyss," Rev. 9:2, RV; heaven and the heavens, **Matt. 3:16**; Luke 3:21; Acts 10:11; Rev. 19:11; "the temple of the tabernacle of the testimony in heaven," Rev. 15:5; by metonymy, for that which contained treasures, **Matt. 2:11**; (b) metaphorically, e.g., **Matt. 7:7-8; 25:11**; Rev. 3:7; Hebraistically, "to open the mouth," of beginning to speak, e.g., **Matt. 5:2; 13:35**; Acts 8:32, 35; 10:34; 18:14; Rev. 13:6 (cf., e.g., Num. 22:28; Job. 3:1; Isa. 50:5); and of recovering speech, Luke 1:64; of the earth "opening," Rev. 12:16; of the "opening" of the eyes, Acts 26:18; the ears, Mark 7:35 (in the best mss.); (2) intransitively (perfect tense, active, in the Greek), (a) literally, of "the heaven," John 1:51, RV, "opened;" (b) metaphorically, of "speaking freely," 2 Cor. 6:11.

Treasures *thesauros* (2344), denotes (1) "a place of safe keeping" (possibly akin to *tithemi*, "to put"), (a) "a casket," **Matt. 2:11**; (b) "a storehouse," **Matt. 13:52**; used metaphorically of the heart, **Matt. 12:35**, twice (RV, "out of his treasure"); Luke 6:45; (2) "a treasure," **Matt. 6:19, 20, 21; 13:44**; Luke 12:33, 34; Heb. 11:26; "treasure" (in heaven or the heavens), **Matt. 19:21**; Mark 10:21; Luke 18:22; in these expressions (which are virtually equivalent to that in **Matt. 6:1**, "with your Father which is in Heaven") the promise does not simply refer to the present life, but looks likewise to the hereafter; in 2 Cor. 4:7 it is used of "the light of the knowledge of the glory of God in the face of Jesus Christ," descriptive of the gospel, as deposited in the earthen vessels of the persons who proclaim it (cf. v. 4); in Col. 2:3, of the wisdom and knowledge hidden in Christ.

Presented *prosphero* (4374), primarily, "to bring to" (*pros*, "to," *phero*, "to bring"), also denotes "to offer," (a) of the sacrifice of Christ Himself, Heb. 8:3; of Christ in virtue of his High Priesthood (RV, "this *high priest*"; KJV, "this man"); 9:14, 25 (negative), 28; 10:12; (b) of offerings under, or according to, the Law, e.g., **Matt. 8:4**; Mark 1:44; Acts 7:42; 21:26; Heb. 5:1, 3; 8:3; 9:7, 9; 10:1-2, 8, 11; (c) of "offerings" previous to the Law, Heb. 11:4, 17 (of Isaac by Abraham); (d) of gifts "offered" to Christ, **Matt. 2:11**, RV, "offered" (KJV, "presented unto"); (e) of prayers "offered" by Christ, Heb. 5:7; (f) of the vinegar "offered" to Him in mockery by the soldiers at the cross, Luke 23:36; (g) of the slaughter of disciples by persecutors, who think they are "offering" service to God, John 16:2, RV (KJV, "doeth"); (h) of money "offered" by Simon the sorcerer, Acts 8:18.

Gifts *doron* (1435), akin to *didomi*, "to give," is used (a) of "gifts" presented as an expression of honor, **Matt. 2:11**; (b) of "gifts" for the support of the temple and the needs of the poor, **Matt. 15:5**; Mark 7:11; Luke 21:1, 4; (c) of "gifts" offered to God, **Matt. 5:23, 24; 8:4; 23:18, 19**; Heb. 5:1; 8:3, 4; 9:9; 11:4; (d) of salvation by grace as the "gift" of God, Eph. 2:8; (e) of "presents" for mutual celebration of an occasion, Rev. 11:10.

Gold *chrusos* (5557), is used (a) of "coin," **Matt. 10:9**; Jas. 5:3; (b) of "ornaments," **Matt. 23:16, 17**; Jas. 5:3 (perhaps both coin and ornaments); Rev. 18:12; some mss. have it in 1 Cor. 3:12; (c) of "images," Acts 17:29; (d) of "the metal in general," **Matt. 2:11**; Rev. 9:7 (some mss. have it in Rev. 18:16).

Frankincense *libanos* (2030), from a Semitic verb signifying "to be white," is a vegetable resin, bitter and glittering, obtained by incisions in the bark of the *arbor thuris*, "the incense tree," and especially imported through Arabia; it was used for fumigation at sacrifices, Exod. 30:7, etc., or for perfume, Song of Sol. 3:6. The Indian variety is called *looban*. It was among the offerings brought by the wise men, **Matt. 2:11**. In Rev. 18:13 it is listed among the commodities of Babylon. The "incense" of Rev. 8:3 should be "frankincense."

Myrrh *smurna* (4666), whence the name "Smyrna," a word of Semitic origin, Heb., *mor*, from a root meaning "bitter," is a gum resin from a shrubby tree, which grows in Yemen and neighboring regions of Africa; the fruit is smooth and somewhat larger than a pea. The color of myrrh varies from pale reddish-yellow to reddish-brown or red. The taste is bitter, and the substance astringent, acting as an antiseptic and a stimulant. It was used as a perfume, Ps. 45:8, where the language is symbolic of the graces of the Messiah; Prov. 7:17; Song of Sol. 1:13; 5:5; it was one of the ingredients of the "holy anointing oil" for the priests, Ex. 30:23 (RV, "flowing myrrh"); it was used also for the purification of women, Esth. 2:12; for embalming, John 19:39; as an anodyne), it was one of the gifts of the Magi, **Matt. 2:11**.

2:12 And being warned of God in a dream that they should not return to Herod, they departed into their own country another way.

Warned *chrematizo* (5537), is translated "to warn" in **Matt. 2:12, 22**; Acts 10:22; Heb. 8:5, RV (KJV, "admonished"); 11:7; 12:25, RV (KJV, "spake").

Dream *see Matthew 1:20.*

Return *anakampto* (344), "to turn or bend back," occurs in **Matt. 2:12**; Luke 10:6 (i.e., as if it was unsaid); Acts 18:21; Heb. 11:15.

Departed *anachoreo* (402), "to go back, recede, retire" (*ana*, "back or up," *choreo*, "to make room for, betake oneself," *choros*, "a place"), is translated "departed" in **Matt. 2:12–14; 4:12** (RV, "withdrew"); so in **14:13** and **15:21**, but "departed" in **27:5**; "withdrew" in John 6:15. In **Matt. 2:22** the RV has "withdrew," which is preferable to the KJV, "turned aside." The most suitable translation wherever possible, is by the verb "to withdraw."

Their *auton*, the genitive plur. of *autos*, "he," e.g., **Matt. 2:12**.

Country *chora* (5561), properly denotes "the space lying between two limits or places"; accordingly it has a variety of meanings: "country," **Matt. 2:12; 8:28**; Mark 1:5, RV (KJV, "land"); 5:1, 10; Luke 2:8; 8:26; 15:13-14, RV (KJV, "land"), 15; 19:12; 21:21; Acts 10:39, RV (KJV, "land"); 12:20; 26:20, RV (KJV, "coasts"); 27:27; in Mark 6:55 (in the best mss.) and Acts 18:23, RV, region.

2:13 And when they were departed, behold, the angel of the Lord appeareth to Joseph in a dream, saying, Arise, and take the young child and his mother, and flee into Egypt, and be thou there until I bring thee word: for Herod will seek the young child to destroy him.

Appeareth *see* Appeared at *Matthew 1:20.*

Take *see Matthew 1:20.*

There *ekei* (1563), signifies (a) "there," e.g., **Matt. 2:13**, frequently in the Gospels; (b) "thither," e.g., Luke 17:37; in Rom. 15:24, "thitherward."

Bring ... word *lego* (3004), and the 2nd aorist form *eipon*, used to supply this tense in *lego*, are frequently translated "to tell," e.g., **Matt. 2:13**, RV, "I tell," KJV, "I bring (thee) word"; **10:27**.

Will *mello* (3195), "to be about to," is translated "will" in **Matt. 2:13** and John 7:35 (twice); "wilt," John 14:22; "will," Acts 17:31; "wouldest," 23:20; "will," 27:10 and Rev. 3:16.

Destroy *apollumi* (622), a strengthened form of *ollumi*, signifies "to destroy utterly"; in middle voice, "to perish." The idea is not extinction but ruin, loss, not of being, but of well-being. This is clear from its use, as, e.g., of the marring of wine skins, Luke 5:37; of lost sheep, i.e., lost to the shepherd, metaphorical of spiritual destitution, Luke 15:4, 6, etc.; the lost son, 15:24; of the perishing of food, John 6:27; of gold, 1 Pet. 1:7. So of persons, **Matt. 2:13**, "destroy"; **8:25**, "perish"; **22:7; 27:20**; of the loss of well-being in the case of the unsaved hereafter, **Matt. 10:28**; Luke 13:3, 5; John 3:16 (v. 15 in some mss.); 10:28; 17:12; Rom. 2:12; 1 Cor. 15:18; 2 Cor. 2:15, "are perishing"; 4:3; 2 Thess. 2:10; Jas. 4:12; 2 Pet. 3:9.

2:14 When he arose, he took the young child and his mother by night, and departed into Egypt:

Arose *egeiro* (1453), is frequently used in the NT in the sense of "raising" (active voice), or "rising" (middle and passive voices): (a) from sitting, lying, sickness, e.g., **Matt. 2:14; 9:5, 7, 19**; Jas. 5:15; Rev. 11:1; (b) of causing to appear, or, in the passive, appearing, or raising up so as to occupy a place in the midst of people, **Matt. 3:9**; **11:11**; Mark 13:22; Acts 13:22. It is thus said of Christ in Acts 13:23; (c) of rousing, stirring up, or "rising" against, **Matt. 24:7**; Mark 13:8; (d) of "raising buildings," John 2:19-20; (e) of "raising or rising" from the dead; (1) of Christ, **Matt. 16:21**; and frequently elsewhere (but not in Phil., 2 Thess., 1 Tim., Titus, Jas., 2 Pet., 1, 2, 3 John, and Jude); (2) of Christ's "raising" the dead, **Matt. 11:5**; Mark 5:41; Luke 7:14; John 12:1, 9, 17; (3) of the act of the disciples, **Matt. 10:8**; (4) of the resurrection of believers, **Matt. 27:52**; John 5:21; 1 Cor. 15:15-16, 29, 32, 35, 42-44, 52; 2 Cor. 1:9; 4:14; of unbelievers, **Matt. 12:42** (cf. v. **41**). *Egeiro* stands in contrast to *anistemi* (when used with reference to resurrection) in this respect, that *egeiro* is frequently used both in the transitive sense of "raising up" and the intransitive of "rising," whereas *anistemi* is comparatively infrequent in the transitive use.

Took *see* **Take** at *Matthew 1:20.*

Night *nux* (3571), is used (I) literally, (a) of "the alternating natural period to that of the day," e.g., **Matt. 4:2**; **12:40**; 2 Tim. 1:3; Rev. 4:8; (b) of "the period of the absence of light," the time in which something takes place, e.g., **Matt. 2:14** (**27:64**), in some mss.); Luke 2:8; John 3:2 (7:50, in some mss.); Acts 5:19; 9:25; (c) of "point of time," e.g., **Matt. 14:27** (in some mss.), **30**; Luke 12:20; Acts 27:23; (d) of "duration of time," e.g., Luke 2:37; 5:5; Acts 20:31; 26:7 (note the difference in the phrase in Mark 4:27); (II) metaphorically, (a) of "the period of man's alienation from God," Rom. 13:12; 1 Thess. 5:5, lit., "not of night," where "of" means 'belonging to;' cf. "of the Way," Acts 9:2; "of shrinking back" and "of faith," Heb. 10:39, marg.; (b) of "death," as the time when work ceases, John 9:4.

2:15 And was there until the death of Herod: that it might be fulfilled which was spoken of the Lord by the prophet, saying, Out of Egypt have I called my son.

Death *teleute* (5054), "an end, limit" (cf. *telos*), hence, "the end of life, death," is used of the "death" of Herod, **Matt. 2:15**.

Fulfilled *see Matthew 1:22.*

Spoken *see Matthew 1:22.*

2:16 Then Herod, when he saw that he was mocked of the wise men, was exceeding wroth, and sent forth, and slew all the children that were in Bethlehem, and in all the coasts thereof, from two years old and under, according to the time which he had diligently enquired of the wise men.

Mocked *empaizo* (1702), a compound of *paizo*, "to play like a child" (*pais*), "to sport, jest," prefixed by *en*, "in" or "at," is used only in the Synoptists, and, in every instance, of the "mockery" of Christ, except in **Matt. 2:16** (there in the sense of deluding, or deceiving, of Herod by the wise men) and in Luke 14:29, of ridicule cast upon the one who after laying a foundation of a tower is unable to finish it. The word is used (a) prophetically by the Lord, of His impending sufferings, **Matt. 20:19**; Mark 10:34; Luke 18:32; (b) of the actual insults inflicted upon Him by the men who had taken Him from Gethsemane, Luke 22:63; by Herod and his soldiers, Luke 23:11; by the soldiers of the governor, **Matt. 27:29, 31**; Mark 15:20; Luke 23:36; by the chief priests, **Matt. 27:41**; Mark 15:31.

Of *see Matthew 1:22.*

Wise men *see Matthew 2:1.*

Exceeding *lian* (3029), "very, exceedingly," is translated "exceeding" in **Matt. 2:16**; **4:8**; **8:28**; Mark 9:3; Luke 23:8.

Wroth *thumoo* (2373), signifies "to be very angry" (from *thumos*, "wrath, hot anger"), "to be stirred into passion," **Matt. 2:16**, of Herod (passive voice).

Slew *anaireo* (337), "to take away, destroy, kill," is rendered "to slay" in **Matt. 2:16**; Acts 2:23; 5:33, 36; 9:29, KJV (RV, "to kill"); 10:39; 13:28; 22:20; 23:15, RV; in 2 Thess. 2:8 the best texts have this verb (for *analisko*, "to consume," KJV and RV marg.); hence the RV, "shall slay," of the destruction of the man of sin.

Children *pais* (3816), signifies (a) "a child in relation to descent," (b) "a boy or girl in relation to age," (c) "a servant, attendant, maid, in relation to condition." As an instance of (a) see **Matt. 21:15**, "children," and Acts 20:12 (RV, "lad"). In regard to (b) the RV has "boy" in **Matt. 17:18** and Luke 9:42. In Luke 2:43 it is used of the Lord Jesus. In regard to (c), see **Matt. 8:6, 8, 13**, etc. As to (a) note **Matt. 2:16**, RV, male children.

Coasts *horion* (3725), "the border of a country or district" (cf. Eng., "horizon"), is always used in the plural. The KJV has "coasts," but "borders" in **Matt. 4:13**; the RV always "borders," **Matt. 2:16**; **4:13**; **8:34**; **15:22, 39**; **19:1**; Mark 5:17; 7:31 (twice); 10:1; Acts 13:50. In some of these it signifies territory.

Years *dietes* (1332), denotes "lasting two years, two years old," **Matt. 2:16**.

Under *katotero* (2736), the comparative degree of *kato*, "below, beneath," occurs in **Matt. 2:16**, "under." *Kato* signifies (a) "down, downwards," **Matt. 4:6**; Luke 4:9; John 8:6, 8; Acts 20:9; (b) "below, beneath," of place, Mark 14:66; the realms that lie below in contrast to heaven, John 8:23; the earth, as contrasted with the heavens, Acts 2:19; with *heos*, "unto," **Matt. 27:51**; Mark 15:38.

Diligently enquired *see* Enquired ... diligently at *Matthew 2:7*.

2:17 Then was fulfilled that which was spoken by Jeremy the prophet, saying,

Then *see Matthew 2:7*.

Fulfilled *see Matthew 1:22*.

Spoken *see Matthew 1:22*.

2:18 In Rama was there a voice heard, lamentation, and weeping, and great mourning, Rachel weeping *for* her children, and would not be comforted, because they are not.

Voice *phone* (5456), "a sound," is used of the voice (a) of God, **Matt. 3:17**; John 5:37; 12:28, 30; Acts 7:31; 10:13, 15; 11:7, 9; Heb. 3:7, 15; 4:7; 12:19, 26; 2 Pet. 1:17, 18; Rev. 18:4; 21:3; (b) of Christ, (1) in the days of His flesh, **Matt. 12:19** (negatively); John 3:29; 5:25; 10:3, 4, 16, 27; 11:43; 18:37; (2) on the cross, **Matt. 27:46**, and parallel passages; (3) from heaven, Acts 9:4, 7; 22:7, 9, 14; 26:14; Rev. 1:10, 12 (here, by metonymy, of the speaker), 15; 3:20; (4) at the resurrection "to life," John 5:28; 1 Thess. 4:16, where "the voice of the archangel" is, lit., "a voice of an archangel," and probably refers to the Lord's voice as being of an archangelic character; (5) at the resurrection to judgment, John 5:28 [not the same event as (4)]; (c) of human beings on earth, e.g., **Matt. 2:18**; **3:3**; Luke 1:42, in some texts, KJV, "voice", and frequently in the Synoptists; (d) of angels, Rev. 5:11, and frequently in Revelation; (e) of the redeemed in heaven, e.g., Rev. 6:10; 18:22; 19:1, 5; (f) of a pagan god, Acts 12:22; (g) of things, e.g., wind, John 3:8, RV, "voice" (KJV, "sound").

Lamentation *threneo*, "to sing a dirge, to lament," is rendered "wail" in **Matt. 11:17**, RV; "mourned" in Luke 7:32; "to lament" in Luke 23:27 and John 16:20. *Threnos*, "lamentation," occurs in **Matt. 2:18**.

Weeping *klauthmos* (2805), denotes "weeping, crying," **Matt. 2:18**; **8:12**; **13:42**, **50**, RV (KJV, "wailing"); **22:13**; **24:51**; **25:30**; Luke 13:28; Acts 20:37.

Mourning *odurmos* (3602), "lamentation, mourning," is translated "mourning" in **Matt. 2:18** and 2 Cor. 7:7.

Comforted *parakaleo* (3870), has a variety of meanings, e.g., **Matt. 2:18**; 1 Thess. 3:2, 7; 4:18. In 2 Cor. 13:11, it signifies "to be comforted" (so the RV).

2:19 But when Herod was dead, behold, an angel of the Lord appeareth in a dream to Joseph in Egypt,

Dead *teleutao* (5053), "to end" (from *telos*, "an end"), hence, "to end one's life," is used (a) of the "death" of the body, **Matt. 2:19**; **9:18**; **15:4**, where "die the death" means "surely die," RV, marg., lit., "let him end by death"; Mark 7:10; **Matt. 22:25**, "deceased"; Luke 7:2; John 11:39; Acts 2:29; 7:15; Heb. 11:22 (RV, "his end was nigh"); (b) of the gnawings of conscience in self reproach, under the symbol of a worm, Mark 9:48 (vv. 44 and 46, KJV).

Dream *see Matthew 1:20*.

2:20 Saying, Arise, and take the young child and his mother, and go into the land of Israel: for they are dead which sought the young child's life.

Take *see Matthew 1:20*.

Land *ge* (1093), in one of its usages, denotes (a) "land" as distinct from sea or other water, e.g., Mark 4:1; 6:47; Luke 5:3; John 6:21; (b) "land" as subject to cultivation, e.g., Luke 14:35; (c) "land" as describing a country or region, e.g., **Matt. 2:20**, **21**; **4:15**; Luke 4:25; in 23:44, RV, "(the whole) land," KJV, "(all the) earth"; Acts 7:29; Heb. 11:9, RV, "a land (not his own)," KJV, "a (strange) country;" Jude 5. In Acts 7:11 the KJV follows a reading of the noun with the definite article which necessitates the insertion of "land."

Sought *zeteo* (2212), signifies (a) "to seek, to seek for," e.g., **Matt. 7:7**, **8**; **13:45**; Luke 24:5; John 6:24; of plotting against a person's life, **Matt. 2:20**; Acts 21:31; Rom. 11:3; metaphorically, to "seek" by thinking, to "seek" how to do something, or what to obtain, e.g., Mark 11:18; Luke 12:29; to "seek" to ascertain a meaning, John 16:19, "do ye inquire"; to "seek" God, Acts 17:27, RV; Rom. 10:20; (b) "to seek or strive after, endeavor, to desire," e.g., **Matt. 12:46**, **47**, RV, "seeking" (KJV, "desiring"); Luke 9:9, RV, "sought" (KJV, "desired"); John 7:19, RV, "seek ye" (KJV, "go ye about"); so v. 20; Rom. 10:3, RV, "seeking" (KJV, "going about"); of "seeking" the kingdom of God and His righteousness, in the sense of coveting earnestly, striving after, **Matt. 6:33**; "the things that are above," Col. 3:1; peace, 1 Pet. 3:11; (c) "to require or demand," e.g., Mark 8:12; Luke 11:29; 1 Cor. 4:2, "it is required"; 2 Cor. 13:3, "ye seek."

Life *psuche* (5590), denotes "the breath, the breath of life," then "the soul," in its various meanings. The NT uses "may be analyzed approximately as follows:

(a) the natural life of the body, **Matt. 2:20**; Luke 12:22; Acts 20:10; Rev. 8:9; 12:11; cf. Lev. 17:11; 2 Sam. 14:7; Esth. 8:11; (b) the immaterial, invisible part of man, **Matt. 10:28**; Acts 2:27; cf. 1 Kings 17:21; (c) the disembodied (or "unclothed" or "naked," 2 Cor. 5:3, 4) man, Rev. 6:9; (d) the seat of personality, Luke 9:24, explained as = "own self," v. 25; Heb. 6:19; 10:39; cf. Isa. 53:10 with 1 Tim. 2:6; (e) the seat of the sentient element in man, that by which he perceives, reflects, feels, desires, **Matt. 11:29**; Luke 1:46; 2:35; Acts 14:2, 22; cf. Ps. 84:2; 139:14; Isa. 26:9; (f) the seat of will and purpose, **Matt. 22:37**; Acts 4:32; Eph. 6:6; Phil. 1:27; Heb. 12:3; cf. Num. 21:4; Deut. 11:13; (g) the seat of appetite, Rev. 18:14; cf. Ps. 107:9; Prov. 6:30; Isa. 5:14 ("desire"); 29:8; (h) persons, individuals, Acts 2:41, 43; Rom. 2:9; Jas. 5:20; 1 Pet. 3:20; 2 Pet. 2:14; cf. Gen. 12:5; 14:21 ("persons"); Lev. 4:2 ("any one"); Ezek. 27:13; of dead bodies, Num. 6:6, lit., "dead soul"; and of animals, Lev. 24:18, lit., "soul for soul"; (i) the equivalent of the personal pronoun, used for emphasis and effect:—1st person, John 10:24 ("us"); Heb. 10:38; cf. Gen. 12:13; Num. 23:10; Jud. 16:30; Ps. 120:2 ("me"); 2nd person, 2 Cor. 12:15; Heb. 13:17; Jas. 1:21; 1 Pet. 1:9; 2:25; cf. Lev. 17:11; 26:15; 1 Sam. 1:26; 3rd person, 1 Pet. 4:19; 2 Pet. 2:8; cf. Exod. 30:12; Job 32:2, Heb. "soul," Sept. "self"; (j) an animate creature, human or other, 1 Cor. 15:45; Rev. 16:3; cf. Gen. 1:24; 2:7, 19; (k) "the inward man," the seat of the new life, Luke 21:19 (cf. **Matt. 10:39**); 1 Pet. 2:11; 3 John 2.

"Body and soul are the constituents of the man according to **Matt. 6:25**; **10:28**; Luke 12:20; Acts 20:10; body and spirit according to Luke 8:55; 1 Cor. 5:3; 7:34; Jas. 2:26. In **Matt. 26:38** the emotions are associated with the soul, in John 13:21 with the spirit; cf. also Ps. 42:11 with 1 Kings 21:5. In Ps. 35:9 the soul rejoices in God, in Luke 1:47 the spirit."

2:21 And he arose, and took the young child and his mother, and came into the land of Israel.

Took *see* Take at *Matthew 1:20.*

Land *see Matthew 2:20.*

2:22 But when he heard that Archelaus did reign in Judaea in the room of his father Herod, he was afraid to go thither: notwithstanding, being warned of God in a dream, he turned aside into the parts of Galilee:

Reign *basileuo* (936), "to reign," is used (I) literally, (a) of God, Rev. 11:17; 19:6, in each of which the aorist tense (in the latter, translated "reigneth") is "ingressive," stressing the point of entrance; (b) of Christ, Luke 1:33; 1 Cor. 15:25; Rev. 11:15; as rejected by the Jews, Luke 19.14, 27; (c) of the saints, hereafter, 1 Cor. 4:8 (2nd part), where the apostle, casting a reflection upon the untimely exercise of authority on the part of the church at Corinth, anticipates the due time for it in the future; Rev. 5:10; 20:4, where the aorist tense is not simply of a "point" character, but "constative," that is, regarding a whole action as having occurred, without distinguishing any steps in its progress (in this instance the aspect is future); v. 6; 22:5; (d) of earthly potentates, **Matt. 2:22**; 1 Tim. 6:15, where "kings" is, lit., "them that reign"; (II), metaphorically, (a) of believers, Rom. 5:17, where "shall reign in life" indicates the activity of life in fellowship with Christ in His sovereign power, reaching its fullness hereafter; 1 Cor. 4:8 (1st part), of the carnal pride that laid claim to a power not to be exercised until hereafter; (b) of divine grace, Rom. 5:21; (c) of sin, Rom. 5:21; 6:12; (d) of death, Rom. 5:14, 17.

Room *anti* (473), "in place of, instead of," is translated "in the room of" in **Matt. 2:22**.

Father *pater* (3962), from a root signifying "a nourisher, protector, upholder" (Lat., *pater*, Eng., "father," are akin), is used (a) of the nearest ancestor, e.g., **Matt. 2:22**; (b) of a more remote ancestor, the progenitor of the people, a "forefather," e.g., **Matt. 3:9**; **23:30**; 1 Cor. 10:1; the patriarchs, 2 Pet. 3:4; (c) one advanced in the knowledge of Christ, 1 John 2:13; (d) metaphorically, of the originator of a family or company of persons animated by the same spirit as himself, as of Abraham, Rom. 4:11, 12, 16, 17, 18, or of Satan, John 8:38, 41, 44; (e) of one who, as a preacher of the gospel and a teacher, stands in a "father's" place, caring for his spiritual children, 1 Cor. 4:15 (not the same as a mere title of honor, which the Lord prohibited, **Matt. 23:9**); (f) of the members of the Sanhedrin, as of those who exercised religious authority over others, Acts 7:2; 22:1; (g) of God in relation to those who have been born anew (John 1:12, 13), and so are believers, Eph. 2:18; 4:6 (cf. 2 Cor. 6:18), and imitators of their "Father," **Matt. 5:45**, **48**; **6:1**, **4**, **6**, **8**, **9**, etc. Christ never associated Himself with them by using the personal pronoun "our"; He always used the singular, "My Father," His relationship being unoriginated and essential, whereas theirs is by grace and regeneration, e.g., **Matt.**

11:27; **25:34**; John 20:17; Rev. 2:27; 3:5, 21; so the apostles spoke of God as the "Father" of the Lord Jesus Christ, e.g., Rom. 15:6; 2 Cor. 1:3; 11:31; Eph. 1:3; Heb. 1:5; 1 Pet. 1:3; Rev. 1:6; (h) of God, as the "Father" of lights, i.e., the Source or Giver of whatsoever provides illumination, physical and spiritual, Jas. 1:17; of mercies, 2 Cor. 1:3; of glory, Eph. 1:17; (i) of God, as Creator, Heb. 12:9 (cf. Zech. 12:1).

Warned *see Matthew 2:12.*

Dream *see Matthew 1:20.*

Turned aside *anachoreo* (402), is translated "to withdraw" in the RV of **Matt. 2:22** and John 6:15; RV and KJV in **Matt. 12:15** and Mark 3:7. See also **Departed** at *Matthew 2:12.*

Parts *meros* (3313), denotes (a) "a part, portion," of the whole, e.g., John 13:8; Rev. 20:6; 22:19; hence, "a lot" or "destiny," e.g., Rev. 21:8; in **Matt. 24:51** and Luke 12:46, "portion"; (b) "a part" as opposite to the whole, e.g., Luke 11:36; John 19:23; 21:6, "side"; Acts 5:2; 23:6; Eph. 4:16; Rev. 16:19; a party, Acts 23:9; the divisions of a province, e.g., **Matt. 2:22**; Acts 2:10; the regions belonging to a city, e.g., **Matt. 15:21**, RV, "parts" (KJV, "coasts"); **16:13** (ditto); Mark 8:10, KJV and RV, "parts"; "the lower parts of the earth," Eph. 4:9; this phrase means the regions beneath the earth; (c) "a class," or "category" (with *en*, in, "in respect of"), Col. 2:16; "in this respect," 2 Cor. 3:10; 9:3, RV (KJV, "in this behalf").

2:23 And he came and dwelt in a city called Nazareth: that it might be fulfilled which was spoken by the prophets, He shall be called a Nazarene.

Fulfilled *see Matthew 1:22.*

Spoken *see Matthew 1:22.*

Chapter 3

3:1 In those days came John the Baptist, preaching in the wilderness of Judaea,

Came *paraginomai* (3854), lit., "to become near," hence, "to come on the scene," **Matt. 3:1**, of John the Baptist, is translated, "arrive" in the RV of 1 Cor. 16:3, for KJV, "come."

Preaching *kerusso* (2784), signifies (a) "to be a herald," or, in general, "to proclaim," e.g., **Matt. 3:1**; Mark 1:45, "publish"; in Luke 4:18, RV, "to proclaim," KJV, "to preach"; so verse 19; Luke 12:3; Acts 10:37; Rom. 2:21; Rev. 5:2. In 1 Pet. 3:19 the probable reference is, not to glad tidings (which there is no real evidence that Noah preached, nor is there evidence that the spirits of antediluvian people are actually "in prison"), but to the act of Christ after His resurrection in proclaiming His victory to fallen angelic spirits; (b) "to preach the gospel as a herald," e.g., **Matt. 24:14**; Mark 13:10, RV, "be preached" (KJV, "be published"); 14:9; 16:15, 20; Luke 8:1; 9:2; 24:47; Acts 8:5; 19:13; 28:31; Rom. 10:14, present participle, lit., "(one) preaching," "a preacher"; 10:15 (1st part); 1 Cor. 1:23; 15:11, 12; 2 Cor. 1:19; 4:5; 11:4; Gal. 2:2; Phil. 1:15; Col. 1:23; 1 Thess. 2:9; 1 Tim. 3:16; (c) "to preach the word," 2 Tim. 4:2 (of the ministry of the Scriptures, with special reference to the gospel).

3:2 And saying, Repent ye: for the kingdom of heaven is at hand.

At hand *engizo* (1448), "to draw near, to approach," from *engus*, "near," is used (a) of place and position, literally and physically, **Matt. 21:1**; Mark 11:1; Luke 12:33; 15:25; figuratively, of drawing near to God, **Matt. 15:8**; Heb. 7:19; Jas. 4:8; (b) of time, with reference to things that are imminent, as the kingdom of heaven, **Matt. 3:2**; **4:17**; **10:7**; the kingdom of God, Mark 1:15; Luke 10:9, 11; the time of fruit, **Matt. 21:34**; the desolation of Jerusalem, Luke 21:8; redemption, 21:28; the fulfillment of a promise, Acts 7:17; the Day of Christ in contrast to the present night of the world's spiritual darkness, Rom. 13:12; Heb. 10:25; the coming of the Lord, Jas. 5:8; the end of all things, 1 Pet. 4:7. It is also said of one who was drawing near to death, Phil. 2:30.

3:3 For this is he that was spoken of by the prophet Esaias, saying, The voice of one crying in the wilderness, Prepare ye the way of the Lord, make his paths straight.

Spoken *see Matthew 1:22.*

Voice *see Matthew 2:18.*

Crying *boao* (994), signifies (a) "to raise a cry," whether of joy, Gal. 4:27, or vexation, Acts 8:7; (b) "to speak with a strong voice," **Matt. 3:3**; Mark 1:3; 15:34; Luke 3:4; 9:38 (some mss. have *anaboao* here); John 1:23; Acts 17:6; 25:24 (some mss. have *epiboao* here); (c) "to cry out for help," Luke 18:7, 38.

Prepare *hetoimazo* (2090), "to prepare, make ready," is used (I) absolutely, e.g., Mark 14:15; Luke 9:52; (II) with an object, e.g., (a) of those things which are ordained (1) by God, such as future positions of authority, **Matt. 20:23**; the coming Kingdom, **25:34**; salvation personified in Christ, Luke 2:31; future blessings, 1 Cor. 2:9; a city, Heb. 11:16; a place of refuge for the Jewish remnant, Rev. 12:6; Divine judgments on the world, Rev. 8:6; 9:7, 15; 16:12; eternal fire, for the Devil and his angels, **Matt. 25:41**; (2) by Christ: a place in Heaven for

His followers, John 14:2, 3; (b) of human "preparation" for the Lord, e.g., **Matt. 3:3**; **26:17, 19**; Luke 1:17 ("make ready"), 76; 3:4, KJV (RV, "make ye ready"); 9:52 ("to make ready"); 23:56; Rev. 19:7; 21:2; in 2 Tim. 2:21, of "preparation" of oneself for "every good work"; (c) of human "preparations" for human objects, e.g., Luke 12:20, RV, "thou hast prepared" (KJV, "provided"); Acts 23:23; Philem. 22.

Paths *tribos* (5147), "a beaten track" (akin to *tribo*, "to rub, wear down"), "a path," is used in **Matt. 3:3**; Mark 1:3; Luke 3:4.

Straight *euthus* (2117), "direct, straight, right," is translated "straight," figuratively, of the paths of the Lord, **Matt. 3:3**; Mark 1:3; Luke 3:4; in v. 5 of the rectification of the crooked, with reference to moral transformation; in Acts 9:11, the name of a street in Damascus, still one of the principal thoroughfares.

3:4 And the same John had his raiment of camel's hair, and a leathern girdle about his loins; and his meat was locusts and wild honey.

Had *echo* (2192), the usual verb for "to have," is used with the following meanings: (a) "to hold, in the hand," etc., e.g., Rev. 1:16; 5:8; (b) "to hold fast, keep," Luke 19:20; metaphorically, of the mind and conduct, e.g., Mark 16:8; John 14:21; Rom. 1:28; 1 Tim. 3:9; 2 Tim. 1:13; (c) "to hold on, cling to, be next to," e.g., of accompaniment, Heb. 6:9, "things that accompany (salvation)," lit., "the things holding themselves of salvation" (RV, marg., "are near to"); of place, Mark 1:38, "next (towns)," lit., "towns holding nigh"; of time, e.g., Luke 13:33, "(the day) following," lit., "the holding (day)"; Acts 13:44; 20:15; 21:26; (d) "to hold, to count, consider, regard," e.g., **Matt. 14:5**; **21:46**; Mark 11:32; Luke 14:18; Philem. 17; (e) "to involve," Heb. 10:35; Jas. 1:4; 1 John 4:18; (f) "to wear," of clothing, arms, etc., e.g., **Matt. 3:4**; **22:12**; John 18:10; (g) "to be with child," of a woman, Mark 13:17; Rom. 9:10 (lit., "having conception"); (h) "to possess," the most frequent use, e.g., **Matt. 8:20**; **19:22**; Acts 9:14; 1 Thess. 3:6; (i) of complaints, disputes, **Matt. 5:23**; Mark 11:25; Acts 24:19; Rev. 2:4, 20; (j) of ability, power, e.g., Luke 12:4; Acts 4:14 (lit., "had nothing to say"); (k) of necessity, e.g., Luke 12:50; Acts 23:17-19; (l) "to be in a certain condition," as of readiness, Acts 21:12 (lit., "I have readily"); of illness, **Matt. 4:24**, "all that were sick" (lit., "that had themselves sickly"); Mark 5:23, "lieth (lit., "hath herself") at the point of death"; Mark 16:18 "they shall recover" (lit., "shall have themselves well"), John 4:52, "he began to amend" (lit., "he had himself better"); of evil works, 1 Tim. 5:25, "they that are otherwise," (lit., "the things having otherwise"); to be so, e.g., Acts 7:1, "are these things so?" (lit., "have these things thus?"), of time, Acts 24:25, "for this time" (lit., "the thing having now").

Raiment *enduma* (1742), akin to *enduo*, denotes "anything put on, a garment of any kind." It was used of the clothing of ancient prophets, in token of their contempt of earthly splendor, 1 Kings 19:13; 2 Kings 1:8, RV; Zech. 13:4. In the NT it is similarly used of John the Baptist's raiment, **Matt. 3:4**: of raiment in general, **Matt. 6:25, 28**; Luke 12:23; metaphorically, of sheep's clothing, **Matt. 7:15**; of a wedding garment, **22:11-12**; of the raiment of the angel at the tomb of the Lord after His resurrection, **28:3**.

Hair *thrix* (2359), denotes the "hair," whether of beast, as of the camel's "hair" which formed the raiment of John the Baptist, **Matt. 3:4**; Mark 1:6; or of man. Regarding the latter (a) it is used to signify the minutest detail, as that which illustrates the exceeding care and protection bestowed by God upon His children, **Matt. 10:30**; Luke 12:7; 21:18; Acts 27:34; (b) as the Jews swore by the "hair," the Lord used the natural inability to make one "hair" white or black, as one of the reasons for abstinence from oaths, **Matt. 5:36**; (c) while long "hair" is a glory to a woman, and to wear it loose or dishevelled is a dishonor, yet the woman who wiped Christ's feet with her "hair" (in place of the towel which Simon the Pharisee omitted to provide), despised the shame in her penitent devotion to the Lord (slaves were accustomed to wipe their masters' feet), Luke 7:38, 44 (RV, "hair"); see also John 11:2; 12:3; (d) the dazzling whiteness of the head and "hair" of the Son of Man in the vision of Rev. 1 (v. 14) is suggestive of the holiness and wisdom of "the Ancient of Days"; (e) the long "hair" of the spirit-beings described as locusts in Rev. 9:8 is perhaps indicative of their subjection to their satanic master (cf. 1 Cor. 11:10, RV); (f) Christian women are exhorted to refrain from adorning their "hair" for outward show, 1 Pet. 3:3.

Leathern *dermatinos* (1193), denotes "of skin, leather" (from *derma*, "skin, hide of beasts," akin to *dero*, "to flay"; whence Eng., "derm," "dermal," "dermatology"); it is translated "leather" in **Matt. 3:4**, of John the Baptist's girdle; in Mark 1:6, RV (KJV, "of a skin").

Girdle *zone* (2223), Eng., "zone," denotes "a belt or girdle," **Matt. 3:4**; Mark 1:6; Acts 21:11; Rev. 1:13;

15:6; it was often hollow, and hence served as a purse, **Matt. 10:9**; Mark 6:8.

Loins *osphus* (3751), is used (a) in the natural sense in **Matt. 3:4**; Mark 1:6; (b) as "the seat of generative power," Heb. 7:5, 10; metaphorically in Acts 2:30; (c) metaphorically, (1) of girding the "loins" in readiness for active service for the Lord, Luke 12:35; (2) the same, with truth, Eph. 6:14, i.e., bracing up oneself so as to maintain perfect sincerity and reality as the counteractive in Christian character against hypocrisy and falsehood; (3) of girding the "loins" of the mind, 1 Pet. 1:13, RV, "girding," suggestive of the alertness necessary for sobriety and for setting one's hope perfectly on "the grace to be brought ... at the revelation of Jesus Christ" (the present participle, "girding," is introductory to the rest of the verse).

Meat *trophe* (5160), denotes "nourishment, food" (akin to *trepho*, "to rear, nourish, feed"); it is used literally, in the Gospels, Acts and Jas. 2:15; metaphorically, in Heb. 5:12, 14, RV, "(solid) food," KJV, "(strong) meat," i.e., deeper subjects of the faith than that of elementary instruction. The word is always rendered "food" in the RV, where the KJV has "meat"; e.g., **Matt. 3:4**; **6:25**; **10:10**; **24:45**; Luke 12:23; John 4:8; Acts 2:46, "did take their food," RV (KJV, "did eat their meat"); 9:19, "took food"; 27:33, 34, 36. The KJV also has "food" in Acts 14:17 and Jas. 2:15.

Locusts *akris* (200), occurs in **Matt. 3:4** and Mark 1:6, of the animals themselves, as forming part of the diet of John the Baptist; they are used as food; the Arabs stew them with butter, after removing the head, legs and wings. In Rev. 9:3, 7, they appear as monsters representing satanic agencies, let loose by divine judgments inflicted upon men for five months, the time of the natural life of the "locust." For the character of the judgment see the whole passage.

Wild *agrios* (66), denotes (a) "of or in fields" (*agros*, "a field"), hence, "not domestic," said of honey, **Matt. 3:4**; Mark 1:6; (b) "savage, fierce," Jude 13, RV, metaphorically, "wild (waves)," KJV, "raging." It is used in the papyri of a malignant wound.

Honey *meli* (3192), occurs with the adjective *agrios*, "wild," in **Matt. 3:4**; Mark 1:6; in Rev. 10:9, 10, as an example of sweetness. As "honey" is liable to ferment, it was precluded from offerings to God, Lev. 2:11. The liquid "honey" mentioned in Ps. 19:10 and Prov. 16:24 is regarded as the best; a cruse of it was part of the present brought to Ahijah by Jeroboam's wife, 1 Kings 14:3.

3:5 Then went out to him Jerusalem, and all Judaea, and all the region round about Jordan,

Region *perichoros* (4066), "a country or region round about" *peri*), is translated "region round about" in **Matt. 3:5**; **14:35**, RV; Mark 1:28 (in some mss. Mark 6:55); Luke 3:3, RV; 4:14; 4:37, RV; 7:17; Acts 14:6.

3:6 And were baptized of him in Jordan, confessing their sins.

Confessing *exomologeo* (1843), "to confess forth," i.e., "freely, openly," is used (a) "of a public acknowledgment or confession of sins," **Matt. 3:6**; Mark 1:5; Acts 19:18; Jas. 5:16; (b) "to profess or acknowledge openly," **Matt. 11:25** (translated "thank," but indicating the fuller idea); Phil. 2:11 (some mss. have it in Rev. 3:5); (c) "to confess by way of celebrating, giving praise," Rom. 14:11; 15:9. In Luke 10:21, it is translated "I thank," the true meaning being "I gladly acknowledge." In Luke 22:6 it signifies to consent (RV), for KJV, "promised."

3:7 But when he saw many of the Pharisees and Sadducees come to his baptism, he said unto them, O generation of vipers, who hath warned you to flee from the wrath to come?

Many *polus* (4183), "much, many great," is used especially of number when its significance is "many," e.g., **Matt. 8:30**; **9:10**; **13:17**; so the RV of **Matt. 12:15**, where some mss. follow the word by *ochloi*, "multitudes"; 1 Cor. 12:12; Rev. 1:15; it is more frequently used as a noun, "many (persons)," e.g., **Matt. 3:7**; **7:22**; **22:14**; with the article, "the many," e.g., **Matt. 24:12**, RV; Mark 9:26, RV, "the more part" (KJV "many"); Rom. 5:15, 19 (twice), RV; 12:5; 1 Cor. 10:17; v. 33, RV; so 2 Cor. 2:17; in 1 Cor. 11:30, RV, "not a few." In Luke 12:47 it is translated "many stripes," the noun being understood.

Come *mello* (3195), "to be about (to do something)," often implying the necessity and therefore the certainty of what is to take place, is frequently rendered "to come," e.g., **Matt. 3:7**; **11:14**; Eph. 1:21; 1 Tim. 4:8; 6:19; Heb. 2:5.

Generation *gennema* (1081), akin to *gennao*, "to beget," denotes "the offspring of men and animals," **Matt. 3:7**; **12:34**; **23:33**; Luke 3:7, RV, "offspring" (KJV, "generation").

Vipers *echidna* (2191), is probably a generic term for "poisonous snakes." It is rendered "viper" in the NT, (a) of the actual creature, Acts 28:3; (b) metaphorically in **Matt. 3:7**; **12:34**; **23:33**; Luke 3:7.

Warned *hupodeiknumi* (5263), primarily, "to show secretly" (*hupo*, "under," *deiknumi*, "to show"), hence, generally, "to teach, make known," is translated "to warn" in **Matt. 3:7**; Luke 3:7; 12:5, RV (KJV, "forewarn").

Wrath *orge* (3709), originally any "natural impulse, or desire, or disposition," came to signify "anger," as the strongest of all passions. It is used of the wrath of man, Eph. 4:31; Col. 3:8; 1 Tim. 2:8; Jas. 1:19-20; the displeasure of human governments, Rom. 13:4-5; the sufferings of the Jews at the hands of the Gentiles, Luke 21:23; the terrors of the Law, Rom. 4:15; "the anger" of the Lord Jesus, Mark 3:5; God's "anger" with Israel in the wilderness, in a quotation from the OT, Heb. 3:11; 4:3; God's present "anger" with the Jews nationally, Rom. 9:22; 1 Thess. 2:16; His present "anger" with those who disobey the Lord Jesus in His gospel, John 3:36; God's purposes in judgment, **Matt. 3:7**; Luke 3:7; Rom. 1:18; 2:5, 8; 3:5; 5:9; 12:19; Eph. 2:3; 5:6; Col. 3:6; 1 Thess. 1:10; 5:9.

3:8 Bring forth therefore fruits meet for repentance:

Bring *poieo* (4160), "to make, to do," used of the bringing forth of fruit, **Matt. 3:8, 10; 7:17, 18**.

Meet *axios* (514), has the meaning of being of "weight, value, worth"; also "befitting, becoming, right on the ground of fitness," e.g., **Matt. 3:8**, KJV, "meet" (RV, "worthy"); so Acts 26:20; Luke 3:8 ("worthy"); 23:41 ("due reward").

Repentance *metanoia* (3341), "afterthought, change of mind, repentance," is used of "repentance" from sin or evil, except in Heb. 12:17, where the word "repentance" seems to mean, not simply a change of Isaac's mind, but such a change as would reverse the effects of his own previous state of mind. Esau's birthright-bargain could not be recalled; it involved an irretrievable loss. As regards "repentance" from sin, (a) the requirement by God on man's part is set forth, e.g., in **Matt. 3:8**; Luke 3:8; Acts 20:21; 26:20; (b) the mercy of God in giving "repentance" or leading men to it is set forth, e.g., in Acts 5:31; 11:18; Rom. 2:4; 2 Tim. 2:25. The most authentic mss. omit the word in **Matt. 9:13** and Mark 2:17, as in the RV.

3:9 And think not to say within yourselves, We have Abraham to *our* father: for I say unto you, that God is able of these stones to raise up children unto Abraham.

Think *dokeo* (1380), "to suppose, to think, to form an opinion," which may be either right or wrong, is sometimes rendered "to think," e.g., **Matt. 3:9; 6:7**.

Say *lego* (3004), primarily "to pick out, gather," chiefly denotes "to say, speak, affirm," whether of actual speech, e.g., **Matt. 11:17**, or of unspoken thought, e.g., **Matt. 3:9**, or of a message in writing, e.g., 2 Cor. 8:8. The 2nd aorist form *eipon* is used to supply that tense, which is lacking in *lego*. Concerning the phrase "he answered and said," it is a well known peculiarity of Hebrew narrative style that a speech is introduced, not simply by "and he said," but by prefixing "and he answered" (*apokrinomai*, with *eipon*). In **Matt. 14:27**, "saying," and Mark 6:50, "and saith," emphasis is perhaps laid on the fact that the Lord, hitherto silent as He moved over the lake, then addressed His disciples. That the phrase sometimes occurs where no explicit question has preceded (e.g., **Matt. 11:25; 17:4; 28:5**; Mark 11:14; 12:35; Luke 13:15; 14:3; John 5:17, 19), illustrates the use of the Hebrew idiom.

Yourselves The reflexive pronoun "yourselves" represents the various plural forms of the reflexive pronoun *heautou* (frequently governed by some preposition), e.g., **Matt. 3:9; 16:8; 23:31; 25:9**; Mark 9:50; Luke 3:8; 12:33, 57; 16:9; 21:30, "of your own selves"; 21:34; Acts 5:35; in Rom. 11:25, "in your own (conceits)," lit., "in (*en;* some texts have *para,* 'among') yourselves"; so 12:16 (with *para*); 1 Pet. 4:8; Jude 20, 21; in Eph. 5:19, RV, "one to another" (KJV, and RV marg., "to yourselves").

Father *see Matthew 2:22*.

Able *dunamai* (1410), "to be able, to have power," whether by virtue of one's own ability and resources, e.g., Rom. 15:14; or through a state of mind, or through favorable circumstances, e.g., 1 Thess. 2:6; or by permission of law or custom, e.g., Acts 24:8, 11; or simply "to be able, powerful," **Matt. 3:9**; 2 Tim. 3:15, etc.

These In Acts 17:32 the RV rightly omits "*matter*"; in Heb. 4:5 "*place*" is italicized; it is frequently rendered "this man," e.g., **Matt. 9:3**; John 6:52; "of this sort," 2 Tim. 3:6, KJV (RV, "of these"); (b) as an adjective with a noun, either with the article and before it, e.g., **Matt. 12:32**, or after the noun (which is preceded by the article), e.g., **Matt. 3:9** and **4:3**, "these stones"; or without the article often forming a predicate, e.g., John 2:11; 2 Cor. 13:1.

Raise *see* Arose at *Matthew 2:14*.

3:10 And now also the axe is laid unto the root of the trees: therefore every tree which bringeth not forth good fruit is hewn down, and cast into the fire.

Now *ede* (2235), denotes "already, now already," "the subjective present, with a suggested reference to some other time, or to some expectation" (Thayer), e.g., **Matt. 3:10**; **14:24**; Luke 11:7; John 6:17; Rom. 1:10; 4:19; 13:11; Phil. 4:10.

Axe *axine* (513), "an axe," akin to *agnumi*, "to break," is found in **Matt. 3:10** and Luke 3:9.

Laid *keimai* (2749), "to be laid, to lie," is used as the passive voice of *tithemi*, "to put," and is translated by some part of the verb "to be laid" in **Matt. 3:10** and Luke 3:9, of an axe; Luke 12:19, of goods; John 21:9, where the verb has been omitted from the translation, after the words "a fire of coals"; 1 Cor. 3:11, of Christ, as a foundation.

Root *rhiza* (4491), is used (a) in the natural sense, **Matt. 3:10**; **13:6**, **21**; Mark 4:6, 17, 11:20; Luke 3:9; 8:13; (b) metaphorically (1) of "cause, origin, source," said of persons, ancestors, Rom. 11:16, 17, 18 (twice); of things, evils, 1 Tim. 6:10, RV, of the love of money as a "root" of all "kinds of evil" (marg., "evils", KJV, "evil"); bitterness, Heb. 12:15; (2) of that which springs from a "root," a shoot, said of offspring, Rom. 15:12; Rev. 5:5; 22:16.

Every *pas* (3956), signifies (1) with nouns without the article, (a) "every one" of the class denoted by the noun connected with *pas*, e.g., **Matt. 3:10**, "every tree"; Mark 9:49, "every sacrifice"; see also John 2:10; Acts 2:43; Rom. 2:9; Eph. 1:21; 3:15; 2 Thess. 2:4; 2 Tim. 3:16, RV; (b) "any and every, of every kind, all manner of," e.g., **Matt. 4:23**; "especially with nouns denoting virtues or vices, emotions, condition, indicating every mode in which a quality manifests itself; or any object to which the idea conveyed by the noun belongs" (GrimmThayer). This is often translated "all," e.g., Acts 27:20; Rom. 15:14; 2 Cor. 10:6; Eph. 4:19, 31; Col. 4:12, "all the will of God," i.e., everything God wills; (2) without a noun, "every one, everything, every man" (i.e., person), e.g., Luke 16:16; or with a negative, "not everyone," e.g., Mark 9:49; with a participle and the article, equivalent to a relative clause, everyone who, e.g., 1 Cor. 9:25; Gal. 3:10, 13; 1 John 2:29; 3:3-4, 6, 10, 15, rendered "whosoever." So in the neuter, 1 John 2:16; 5:4, often rendered "whatsoever"; governed by the preposition *en*, "in," without a noun following, it signifies "in every matter, or condition," Phil. 4:6; 1 Thess. 5:18; "in every way or particular," 2 Cor. 4:8, translated "on every side"; so 2 Cor. 7:5; "in everything," Eph. 5:24; Phil. 4:12, lit., "in everything and (perhaps "even") in all things."

Bringeth *see* **Bring** at **Matthew** *3:8*.

Good *kalos* (2570), denotes that which is intrinsically "good," and so, "goodly, fair, beautiful," as (a) of that which is well adapted to its circumstances or ends, e.g., fruit, **Matt. 3:10**; a tree, **12:33**; ground, **13:8**, **23**; fish, **13:48**; the Law, Rom. 7:16; 1 Tim. 1:8; every creature of God, 1 Tim. 4:4; a faithful minister of Christ and the doctrine he teaches, 4:6; (b) of that which is ethically good, right, noble, honorable e.g., Gal. 4:18; 1 Tim. 5:10, 25; 6:18; Titus 2:7, 14; 3:8, 14. The word does not occur in Revelation, nor indeed after 1 Peter. Christians are to "take thought for things honorable" (*kalos*), 2 Cor. 8:21, RV; to do that which is honorable, 13:7; not to be weary in well doing, Gal. 6:9; to hold fast "that which is good," 1 Thess. 5:21; to be zealous of good works, Titus 2:14; to maintain them, 3:8; to provoke to them, Heb. 10:24; to bear testimony by them, 1 Pet. 2:12.

Hewn *ekkopto* (1581), lit., "to cut or strike out," "to cut down," is used (a) literally, **Matt. 5:30** (in **3:10** and **7:19** and Luke 3:9, "hewn down"); **18:8**; Luke 13:7, 9; (b) metaphorically, of "cutting off" from spiritual blessing, Rom. 11:22, 24; of depriving persons of an occasion for something, 2 Cor. 11:12.

3:11 I indeed baptize you with water unto repentance: but he that cometh after me is mightier than I, whose shoes I am not worthy to bear: he shall baptize you with the Holy Ghost, and *with* fire:

Indeed *men* (3303), a conjunctive particle (originally a form of *men*, "verily, truly," found in Heb. 6:14.), usually related to an adversative conjunction or particle, like *de*, in the following clause, which is placed in opposition to it. Frequently it is untranslatable; sometimes it is rendered "indeed," e.g., **Matt. 3:11**; **13:32**; **17:11**, RV (KJV, "truly"); **20:23**; **26:41**; (some mss. have it in Mark 1:8); Mark 9:12, RV (KJV, "verily").

Baptize *baptizo* (907), "to baptize," primarily a frequentative form of *bapto*, "to dip," was used among the Greeks to signify the dyeing of a garment, or the drawing of water by dipping a vessel into another, etc. Plutarchus uses it of the drawing of wine by dipping the cup into the bowl (*Alexis*, 67) and Plato, metaphorically, of being overwhelmed with questions (*Euthydemus*, 277 D). It is used in the NT in Luke 11:38 of washing oneself (as in 2 Kings 5:14, "dipped himself," Sept.); see also Isa. 21:4, lit., "lawlessness overwhelms me." In the early chapters of the four Gospels and in Acts 1:5; 11:16; 19:4, it is used of the rite performed by John the Baptist who called upon the people to repent that they might receive remission of sins. Those who obeyed came "confessing their sins," thus acknowledging their unfitness to be in the Messiah's coming kingdom. Distinct from this is the "baptism" enjoined by Christ, **Matt. 28:19**, a "baptism" to be undergone by believers, thus witnessing to their identification with Him in death, burial and resurrection, e.g., Acts 19:5; Rom. 6:3-4; 1 Cor. 1:13-17; 12:13; Gal. 3:27; Col. 2:12. The phrase in **Matt. 28:19**, "baptizing them into the Name" (RV; cf. Acts 8:16, RV), would indicate that the "baptized" person was closely bound to, or became the property of, the one into whose name he was "baptized." In Acts 22:16 it is used in the middle voice, in the command given to Saul of Tarsus, "arise and be baptized," the significance of the middle voice form being "get thyself baptized." The experience of those who were in the ark at the time of the Flood was a figure or type of the facts of spiritual death, burial, and resurrection, Christian "baptism" being an *antitupon*, "a corresponding type," a "like figure," 1 Pet. 3:21. Likewise the nation of Israel was figuratively baptized when made to pass through the Red Sea under the cloud, 1 Cor. 10:2. The verb is used metaphorically also in two distinct senses: firstly, of "baptism" by the Holy Spirit, which took place on the Day of Pentecost; secondly, of the calamity which would come upon the nation of the Jews, a "baptism" of the fire of divine judgment for rejection of the will and word of God, **Matt. 3:11**; Luke 3:16.

He *see Matthew 1:21.*

Mightier *ischuroteros* (2478), "stronger, mightier," is translated "mightier" in **Matt. 3:11**; Mark 1:7; Luke 3:16; "stronger" in Luke 11:22; 1 Cor. 1:25; 10:22.

Shoes *hupodemo* (5266), denotes "a sole bound under the foot" (*hupo*, "under," *deo*, "to bind"; cf. *hupodeo*, "to bind under"), "a sandal," always translated "shoes," e.g., **Matt. 3:11**; **10:10**; Mark 1:7.

Worthy *hikanos* (2425), "sufficient," is translated "worthy" in this sense in **Matt. 3:11** (marg., "sufficient"); so **8:8**; Mark 1:7; Luke 3:16; 7:6.

Bear *bastazo* (941), signifies "to support as a burden." It is used with the meaning (a) "to take up," as in picking up anything stones, John 10:31; (b) "to carry" something, **Matt. 3:11**; Mark 14:13; Luke 7:14; 22:10; Acts 3:2; 21:35; Rev. 17:7; "to carry" on one's person, Luke 10:4; Gal. 6:17; in one's body, Luke 11:27; "to bear" a name in testimony, Acts 9:15; metaphorically, of a root "bearing" branches, Rom. 11:18; (c) "to bear" a burden, whether physically, as of the cross, John 19:17, or metaphorically in respect of sufferings endured in the cause of Christ, Luke 14:27; Rev. 2:3; it is said of physical endurance, **Matt. 20:12**; of sufferings "borne" on behalf of others, **Matt. 8:17**; Rom. 15:1; Gal. 6:2; of spiritual truths not able to be "borne," John 16:12; of the refusal to endure evil men, Rev. 2:2; of religious regulations imposed on others, Acts 15:10; of the burden of the sentence of God to be executed in due time, Gal. 5:10; of the effect at the judgment seat of Christ, to be "borne" by the believer for failure in the matter of discharging the obligations of discipleship, Gal. 6:5; (d) to "bear" by way of carrying off, John 12:6; 20:15.

Fire *pur* (4442), (akin to which are *pura*, and *puretos*, "a fever," Eng., "fire," etc.) is used (besides its ordinary natural significance): (a) of the holiness of God, which consumes all that is inconsistent therewith, Heb. 10:27; 12:29; cf. Rev. 1:14; 2:18; 10:1; 15:2; 19:12; similarly of the holy angels as His ministers, Heb. 1:7; in Rev. 3:18 it is symbolic of that which tries the faith of saints, producing what will glorify the Lord. (b) of the divine judgment, testing the deeds of believers, at the judgment seat of Christ, 1 Cor. 3:13 and 15. (c) of the fire of divine judgment upon the rejectors of Christ, **Matt. 3:11** (where a distinction is to be made between the baptism of the Holy Spirit at Pentecost and the "fire" of divine retribution; Acts 2:3 could not refer to baptism): Luke 3:16. (d) of the judgments of God at the close of the present age previous to the establishment of the kingdom of Christ in the world, 2 Thess. 1:8; Rev. 18:8. (e) of the "fire" of Hell, to be endured by the ungodly hereafter, **Matt. 5:22**; **13:42**, **50**; **18:8**, **9**; **25:41**; Mark 9:43, 48; Luke 3:17. (f) of human hostility both to the Jews and to Christ's followers, Luke 12:49. (g) as illustrative of retributive judgment upon the luxurious and tyrannical rich, Jas. 5:3. (h) of the future overthrow of the Babylonish religious system at the hands of the Beast and the nations under him, Rev. 17:16. (i) of turning the heart of an enemy to repentance by repaying his unkindness by kindness, Rom. 12:20. (j) of the tongue, as governed by a "fiery" disposition and as exercising a destructive influence over others, Jas. 3:6. (k) as symbolic of the danger of destruction, Jude 23.

3:12 Whose fan *is* in his hand, and he will throughly purge his floor, and gather his wheat into the garner; but he will burn up the chaff with unquenchable fire.

Fan *ptuon* (4425), denotes "a winnowing shovel or fan," with which grain is thrown up against the wind, in order to separate the chaff, **Matt. 3:12**; Luke 3:17.

Purge *diakatharizo* (1245), "to cleanse thoroughly," is translated "will throughly purge" in **Matt. 3:12**, KJV.

Floor *halon* (257), "a threshing floor," is so translated in **Matt. 3:12**, and Luke 3:17, RV (KJV, "floor"), perhaps by metonymy for the grain.

Wheat *sitos* (4621), "wheat, corn"; in the plural, "grain," is translated "corn" in Mark 4:28; "wheat," **Matt. 3:12**; **13:25, 29-30**; Luke 3:17; 12:18 (some mss. have *genemata*, "fruits," here); 16:7; 22:31; John 12:24; Acts 27:38; 1 Cor. 15:37; Rev. 6:6; 18:13.

Garner *apotheke* (596), lit., "a place where anything is stored" (Eng., "apothecary"), hence denoted a garner, granary, barn, **Matt. 3:12**; **6:26**; **13:30**; Luke 3:17; 12:18, 24.

Burn *katakaio* (2618), signifies "to burn up, burn utterly," as of chaff, **Matt. 3:12**; Luke 3:17; tares, **Matt. 13:30**, **40**; the earth and its works, 2 Pet. 3:10; trees and grass, Rev. 8:7. This form should be noted in Acts 19:19; 1 Cor. 3:15; Heb. 13:11, Rev. 17:16. In each place the full rendering "burn utterly" might be used, as in Rev. 18:8.

Chaff *achuron* (892), "chaff, the stalk of the grain from which the kernels have been beaten out, or the straw broken up by a threshing machine," is found in **Matt. 3:12** and Luke 3:17.

Unquenchable *asbestos* (762), "not quenched," is used of the doom of persons described figuratively as "chaff," **Matt. 3:12** and Luke 3:17, "unquenchable"; of the fire of Gehenna, Mark 9:43, RV, "unquenchable fire" (in some mss. v. 45). In the Sept., Job 20:26.

3:13-14 Then cometh Jesus from Galilee to Jordan unto John, to be baptized of him.

But John forbad him, saying, I have need to be baptized of thee, and comest thou to me?

Forbad *diakoluo* (1254), a strengthened form, "to hinder thoroughly," is used in **Matt. 3:14**, of John the Baptist's endeavor to "hinder" Christ from being baptized, KJV, "forbad," RV, "would have hindered," lit., "was hindering."

Need *chreia* (5532), denotes "a need," in such expressions as "there is a need"; or "to have need of" something, e.g., **Matt. 3:14**; **6:8**; **9:12**, RV, "(have no) need," KJV, "need (not)," the RV adheres to the noun form; so in **14:16**; Mark 14:63; Luke 5:31; 22:71; Eph. 4:28; 1 Thess. 4:9; in the following, however, both RV and KJV use the verb form, "to need" (whereas the original has the verb *echo*, "to have," with the noun *chreia* as the object, as in the instances just mentioned): Luke 15:7; John 2:25; 13:10; 16:30; 1 Thess. 1:8; 1 John 2:27; Rev. 22:5; in all these the verb "to have" could well have been expressed in the translation. In Luke 10:42 it is translated "needful," where the "one thing" is surely not one dish, or one person, but is to be explained according to **Matt. 6:33** and **16:26**. In Eph. 4:29, for the KJV, "(to) the use (of edifying)," the RV more accurately has "(for edifying) as the need may be," marg., "the building up of the need," i.e., "to supply that which needed in each case"; so Westcott, who adds "The need represents a gap in the life which the wise word 'builds up,' fills up solidly and surely." In Phil. 4:19 the RV has "every need of yours" (KJV, "all your need"); in 1 Thess. 4:12, RV, "need" (KJV, "lack"); in Acts 28:10, RV, "(such things) as we needed" (KJV, "as were necessary"), lit., "the things for the needs (plural)."

And *kai* In some passages *kai* has the meaning "and yet," e.g., **Matt. 3:14**, "and yet comest Thou to me?"; **6:26**, "and yet (RV 'and,' KJV, 'yet') your Heavenly Father feedeth them"; Luke 18:7, "and yet He is longsuffering"; John 3:19, "and yet men loved the darkness"; 4:20, "and yet we say"; 6:49, "and yet they died"; 1 Cor. 5:2, "and yet ye are puffed up"; 1 John 2:9, "and yet hateth his brother." The same is probably the case in John 7:30, "and yet no man laid hands on Him", some rule this and similar cases out because of the negative in the sentence following the *kai*, but that seems hardly tenable.

3:15 And Jesus answering said unto him, Suffer *it to be so* now: for thus it becometh us to fulfil all righteousness. Then he suffered him.

Suffer, Suffered *aphiemi* (863), "to send away," signifies "to permit, suffer," in **Matt. 3:15** (twice); **Matt. 19:14**; **23:13**; Mark 1:34; 5:19, 37; 10:14; 11:16; Luke 8:51; 12:39, KJV (RV, "left"); 18:16; John 12:7, RV, KJV and RV marg., "let (her) alone"; Rev. 11:9.

Now *arti* (737), expressing "coincidence," and denoting "strictly present time," signifies "just now, this moment," in contrast (a) to the past, e.g., **Matt. 11:12**; John 2:10; 9:19, 25; 13:33; Gal. 1:9-10; (b) to the future, e.g., John 13:37; 16:12, 31; 1 Cor. 13:12; 2 Thess. 2:7; 1 Pet. 1:6, 8; (c) sometimes without necessary reference to either, e.g., **Matt. 3:15**; **9:18**; **26:53**; Gal. 4:20; Rev. 12:10.

Becometh *prepo* (4241), means "to be conspicuous among a number, to be eminent, distinguished by a thing," hence, "to be becoming, seemly, fit." The adornment of good works "becometh women professing godliness," 1 Tim. 2:10. Those who minister the truth are to speak "the things which befit the sound doctrine," Titus 2:1. Christ, as a High Priest "became us," Heb. 7:26. In the impersonal sense, it signifies "it is fitting, it becometh," **Matt. 3:15**; 1 Cor. 11:13; Eph. 5:3; Heb. 2:10.

Righteousness *dikaiosune* (1343), is "the character or quality of being right or just"; it was formerly spelled "rightwiseness," which clearly expresses the meaning. It is used to denote an attribute of God, e.g., Rom. 3:5, the context of which shows that "the righteousness of God" means essentially the same as His faithfulness, or truthfulness, that which is consistent with His own nature and promises; Rom. 3:25, 26 speaks of His "righteousness" as exhibited in the death of Christ, which is sufficient to show men that God is neither indifferent to sin nor regards it lightly. On the contrary, it demonstrates that quality of holiness in Him which must find expression in His condemnation of sin. "*Dikaiosune* is found in the sayings of the Lord Jesus, (a) of whatever is right or just in itself, whatever conforms to the revealed will of God, **Matt. 5:6, 10, 20**; John 16:8, 10; (b) whatever has been appointed by God to be acknowledged and obeyed by man, **Matt. 3:15**; **21:32**; (c) the sum total of the requirements of God, **Matt. 6:33**; (d) religious duties, **Matt. 6:1** (distinguished as almsgiving, man's duty to his neighbor, vv. **2-4**, prayer, his duty to God, vv. **5-15**, fasting, the duty of self-control, vv. **16-18**)."

3:16 And Jesus, when he was baptized, went up straightway out of the water: and, lo, the heavens were opened unto him, and he saw the Spirit of God descending like a dove, and lighting upon him:

Opened *see Matthew 2:11.*

Dove *peristera* (4058), denotes "a dove or pigeon," **Matt. 3:16**; **10:16** (indicating its proverbial harmlessness); **21:12**; Mark 1:10; 11:15; Luke 2:24 (pigeons"); 3:22; John 1:32; 2:14, 16.

Lighting In **Matt. 3:16**, KJV, *erchomai*, "to come," is translated "lighting"; RV, "coming."

3:17 And lo a voice from heaven, saying, This is my beloved Son, in whom I am well pleased.

Voice *see Matthew 2:18.*

This *houtos*, which is used (a) as a noun, "this one," followed by no noun, e.g., **Matt. 3:17**; translated in Luke 2:34, "this *child*"; in 1 Cor. 5:3, RV, "this thing" (KJV, "this deed").

Beloved *agapetos* (27), from *agapao*, "to love," is used of Christ as loved by God, e.g., **Matt. 3:17**; of believers (ditto), e.g., Rom. 1:7; of believers, one of another, 1 Cor. 4:14; often, as a form of address, e.g., 1 Cor. 10:14. Whenever the KJV has "dearly beloved," the RV has "beloved"; so, "well beloved" in 3 John 1; in 1 John 2:7, KJV, "brethren" (*adelphos*), the RV has "beloved," according to the mss. which have *agapetos*.

Son *The Son of God* In this title the word "Son" is used sometimes (a) of relationship, sometimes (b) of the expression of character. "Thus, e.g., when the disciples so addressed Him, **Matt. 14:33**; **16:16**; John 1:49, when the centurion so spoke of Him, **Matt. 27:54**, they probably meant that (b) He was a manifestation of God in human form. But in such passages as Luke 1:32, 35; Acts 13:33, which refer to the humanity of the Lord Jesus, ... the word is used in sense (a).

"The Lord Jesus Himself used the full title on occasion, John 5:25; 9:35 [some mss. have 'the Son of Man'; see RV marg.]; 11:4, and on the more frequent occasions on which He spoke of Himself as 'the Son,' the words are to be understood as an abbreviation of 'the Son

> *"The cross of Jesus Christ and his baptism express the same thing. Our Lord was not a martyr; he was not merely a good man; he was God Incarnate. He came down to the lowest reach of creation in order to bring back the whole human race to God, and in order to do this he must take upon him, as representative man, the whole massed sin of the race."*
>
> OSWALD CHAMBERS

of God,' not of 'The Son of Man'; this latter He always expressed in full; see Luke 10:22; John 5:19, etc.

"John uses both the longer and shorter forms of the title in his Gospel, see 3:16-18; 20:31, e.g., and in his Epistles; cf. Rev. 2:18. So does the writer of Hebrews, 1:2; 4:14; 6:6, etc. An eternal relation subsisting between the Son and the Father in the Godhead is to be understood. That is to say, the Son of God, in His eternal relationship with the Father, is not so entitled because He at any time began to derive His being from the Father (in which case He could not be co-eternal with the Father), but because He is and ever has been the expression of what the Father is; cf. John 14:9, 'he that hath seen Me hath seen the Father.' The words of Heb. 1:3, 'Who being the effulgence of His (God's) glory, and the very image of His (God's) substance' are a definition of what is meant by 'Son of God.' Thus absolute Godhead, not Godhead in a secondary or derived sense, is intended in the title."

Other titles of Christ as the "Son of God" are: "His Son," 1 Thess. 1:10 (in Acts 13:13, 26, RV, *pais* is rendered "servant"); "His own Son," Rom. 8:32; "My beloved Son," **Matt. 3:17**; "His Only Begotten Son," John 3:16; "the Son of His love," Col. 1:13.

"The Son is the eternal object of the Father's love, John 17:24, and the sole Revealer of the Father's character, John 1:14; Heb. 1:3. The words, 'Father' and 'Son,' are never in the NT so used as to suggest that the Father existed before the Son; the Prologue to the Gospel according to John distinctly asserts that the Word existed 'in the beginning,' and that this Word is the Son, Who 'became flesh and dwelt among us.'"

In addressing the Father in His prayer in John 17 He says, "Thou lovedst Me before the foundation of the world." Accordingly in the timeless past the Father and the "Son" existed in that relationship, a relationship of love, as well as of absolute Deity. In this passage the "Son" gives evidence that there was no more powerful plea in the Father's estimation than that coeternal love existing between the Father and Himself.

Son of Man In the NT this is a designation of Christ, almost entirely confined to the Gospels. Elsewhere it is found in Acts 7:56, the only occasion where a disciple applied it to the Lord and in Rev. 1:13; 14:14. "Son of Man" is the title Christ used of Himself; John 12:34 is not an exception, for the quotation by the multitude was from His own statement. The title is found especially in the Synoptic Gospels. The occurrences in John's Gospel, 1:51; 3:13, 14; 5:27; 6:27, 53, 62; 8:28 (9:35 in some texts); 12:23, 34 (twice); 13:31, are not parallel to those in the Synoptic Gospels. In the latter the use of the title falls into two groups, (a) those in which it refers to Christ's humanity, His earthly work, sufferings and death, e.g., **Matt. 8:20**; **11:19**; **12:40**; **26:2, 24**; (b) those which refer to His glory in resurrection and to that of His future advent, e.g., **Matt. 10:23**; **13:41**; **16:27, 28**; **17:9**; **24:27, 30** (twice), **37, 39, 44**.

Pleased *eudokeo* (2106), signifies (a) "to be well pleased, to think it good," not merely an understanding of what is right and good as in *dokeo*, but stressing the willingness and freedom of an intention or resolve regarding what is good, e.g., Luke 12:32, "it is (your Father's) good pleasure"; so Rom. 15:26, 27, RV; 1 Cor. 1:21; Gal. 1:15; Col. 1:19; 1 Thess. 2:8, RV, "we were well pleased" (KJV, "we were willing"); this meaning is frequently found in the papyri in legal documents; (b) "to be well pleased with," or "take pleasure in," e.g., **Matt. 3:17**; **12:18**; **17:5**; 1 Cor. 10:5; 2 Cor. 12:10; 2 Thess. 2:12; Heb. 10:6, 8, 38; 2 Pet. 1:17.

Chapter 4

4:1 Then was Jesus led up of the Spirit into the wilderness to be tempted of the devil.

Led *anago* (321), "to lead up" (*ana*, "up"), is used of Christ in being "led" up by the Spirit into the wilderness, **Matt. 4:1**; Luke 4:5 (KJV, "taking up"); by the elders of the people into their council, Luke 22:66, "led away."

Spirit *pneuma* (4151), primarily denotes "the wind" (akin to *pneo*, "to breathe, blow"); also "breath"; then, especially "the spirit," which, like the wind, is invisible, immaterial and powerful. The NT uses of the word may be analyzed approximately as follows:

"(a) the wind, John 3:8 (where marg. is, perhaps, to be preferred); Heb. 1:7; cf. Amos 4:13, Sept.; (b) the breath, 2 Thess. 2:8; Rev. 11:11; 13:15; cf. Job 12:10, Sept.; (c) the immaterial, invisible part of man, Luke 8:55; Acts 7:59; 1 Cor. 5:5; Jas. 2:26; cf. Eccl. 12:7, Sept.; (d) the disembodied (or 'unclothed,' or 'naked,' 2 Cor. 5:3, 4) man, Luke 24:37, 39; Heb. 12:23; 1 Pet. 4:6; (e) the resurrection body, 1 Cor. 15:45; 1 Tim. 3:16; 1 Pet. 3:18; (f) the sentient element in man, that by which he perceives, reflects, feels, desires, **Matt. 5:3**; **26:41**; Mark 2:8; Luke 1:47, 80; Acts 17:16; 20:22; 1 Cor. 2:11; 5:3, 4; 14:4, 15; 2 Cor. 7:1; cf. Gen. 26:35; Isa. 26:9; Ezek. 13:3; Dan. 7:15; (g) purpose, aim, 2 Cor. 12:18; Phil. 1:27; Eph.

4:23; Rev. 19:10; cf. Ezra 1:5; Ps. 78:8; Dan. 5:12; (h) the equivalent of the personal pronoun, used for emphasis and effect: 1st person, 1 Cor. 16:18; cf. Gen. 6:3; 2nd person, 2 Tim. 4:22; Philem. 25; cf. Ps. 139:7; 3rd person, 2 Cor. 7:13; cf. Isa. 40:13; (i) character, Luke 1:17; Rom. 1:4; cf. Num. 14:24; (j) moral qualities and activities: bad, as of bondage, as of a slave, Rom. 8:15; cf. Isa. 61:3; stupor, Rom. 11:8; cf. Isa. 29:10; timidity, 2 Tim. 1:7; cf. Josh. 5:1; good, as of adoption, i.e., liberty as of a son, Rom. 8:15; cf. Ps. 51:12; meekness, 1 Cor. 4:21; cf. Prov. 16:19; faith, 2 Cor. 4:13; quietness, 1 Pet. 3:4; cf. Prov. 14:29; (k) the Holy Spirit, e.g., **Matt. 4:1**; Luke 4:18; (l) 'the inward man' (an expression used only of the believer, Rom. 7:22; 2 Cor. 4:16; Eph. 3:16); the new life, Rom. 8:4-6, 10, 16; Heb. 12:9; cf. Ps. 51:10; (m) unclean spirits, demons, **Matt. 8:16**; Luke 4:33; 1 Pet. 3:19; cf. 1 Sam. 18:10; (n) angels, Heb. 1:14; cf. Acts 12:15; (o) divine gift for service, 1 Cor. 14:12, 32; (p) by metonymy, those who claim to be depositories of these gifts, 2 Thess. 2:2; 1 John 4:1-3; (q) the significance, as contrasted with the form, of words, or of a rite, John 6:63; Rom. 2:29; 7:6; 2 Cor. 3:6; (r) a vision, Rev. 1:10; 4:2; 17:3; 21:10." *See also* **Holy** at ***Matthew 1:18.***

Tempted *peirazo* (3985), signifies (1) "to try, attempt, assay"; (2) "to test, try, prove," in a good sense, said of Christ and of believers, Heb. 2:18, where the context shows that the temptation was the cause of suffering to Him, and only suffering, not a drawing away to sin, so that believers have the sympathy of Christ as their High Priest in the suffering which sin occasions to those who are in the enjoyment of communion with God; so in the similar passage in 4:15; in all the temptations which Christ endured, there was nothing within Him that answered to sin. There was no sinful infirmity in Him. While He was truly man, and His divine nature was not in any way inconsistent with His Manhood, there was nothing in Him such as is produced in us by the sinful nature which belongs to us; in Heb. 11:37, of the testing of OT saints; in 1 Cor. 10:13, where the meaning has a wide scope, the verb is used of "testing" as permitted by God, and of the believer as one who should be in the realization of his own helplessness and his dependence upon God; in a bad sense, "to tempt" (a) of attempts to ensnare Christ in His speech, e.g., **Matt. 16:1**; **19:3**; **22:18**, **35**, and parallel passages; John 8:6; (b) of temptations to sin, e.g., Gal. 6:1, where one who would restore an erring brother is not to act as his judge, but as being one with him in liability to sin, with the possibility of finding himself in similar circumstances, Jas. 1:13, 14; of temptations mentioned as coming from the Devil, **Matt. 4:1**; and parallel passages; 1 Cor. 7:5; 1 Thess. 3:5; (c) of trying or challenging God, Acts 15:10; 1 Cor. 10:9 (2nd part); Heb. 3:9; the Holy Spirit, Acts 5:9.

4:2 And when he had fasted forty days and forty nights, he was afterward an hungred.

Fasted *nesteuo* (3522), "to fast, to abstain from eating", is used of voluntary "fasting," **Matt. 4:2**; **6:16**, **17**, **18**; **9:14**, **15**; Mark 2:18, 19, 20; Luke 5:33, 34, 35; 18:12; Acts 13:2, 3. Some of these passages show that teachers to whom scholars or disciples were attached gave them special instructions as to "fasting." Christ taught the need of purity and simplicity of motive. The answers of Christ to the questions of the disciples of John and of the Pharisees reveal His whole purpose and method. No doubt He and His followers observed such a fast as that on the Day of Atonement, but He imposed no frequent "fasts" in addition. What He taught was suitable to the change of character and purpose which He designed for His disciples. His claim to be the Bridegroom, **Matt. 9:15**, and the reference there to the absence of "fasting," virtually involved a claim to be the Messiah (cf. Zech. 8:19). Some mss. have the verb in Acts 10:30.

Forty *tessarakonta* (5062), is used in circumstances in Scripture which indicate the number as suggesting probation, separation or judgment, e.g., **Matt. 4:2**; Acts 1:3; Heb. 3:9, 17.

Nights *see* **Night** at *Matthew 2:14.*

Afterward *husteron* (5305), "afterwards," with the suggestion of at length, is found in **Matt. 4:2**; **21:29**, **32**, **37** (KJV, "last of all"); **22:27**; **25:11**; **26:60** (KJV, "at the last"), Mark 16:14; Luke 4:2; 20:32 (KJV, "last"), John 13:36; Heb. 12:11.

Hungred *peinao* (3983), "to hunger, be hungry, hungered," is used (a) literally, e.g., **Matt. 4:2**; **12:1**; **21:18**; Rom. 12:20; 1 Cor. 11:21, 34; Phil. 4:12; Rev. 7:16; Christ identifies Himself with His saints in speaking of Himself as suffering in their sufferings in this and other respects, **Matt. 25:35**, **42**; (b) metaphorically, **Matt. 5:6**; Luke 6:21, 25; John 6:35.

4:3 And when the tempter came to him, he said, If thou be the Son of God, command that these stones be made bread.

Tempter The present participle of *peirazo*, "to tempt," preceded by the article, lit., "the (one) tempting," is used as a noun, describing the Devil in this character, **Matt. 4:3**; 1 Thess. 3:5.

Came *proserchomai* (4334), denotes "to come or go near to" (*pros*, "near to"), e.g., **Matt. 4:3**; Heb. 10:1, KJV, "comers," RV, them that draw nigh.

Command *epo* (2036), denotes "to speak" (connected with *eipon*, "to say"); hence, among various renderings, "to bid, command," **Matt. 4:3**; Mark 5:43; 8:7; Luke 4:3; 19:15.

These *see Matthew 3:9*.

Stones *lithos* (3037), is used (I) literally, of (a) the "stones" of the ground, e.g., **Matt. 4:3, 6; 7:9**; (b) "tombstones," e.g., **Matt. 27:60, 66**; (c) "building stones," e.g., **Matt. 21:42**; (d) "a millstone," Luke 17:2; cf. Rev. 18:21; (e) the "tables (or tablets)" of the Law, 2 Cor. 3:7; (f) "idol images," Acts 17:29; (g) the "treasures" of commercial Babylon, Rev. 18:12, 16; (II), metaphorically, of (a) Christ, Rom. 9:33; 1 Pet. 2:4, 6, 8; (b) believers, 1 Pet. 2:5; (c) spiritual edification by scriptural teaching, 1 Cor. 3:12; (d) the adornment of the foundations of the wall of the spiritual and heavenly Jerusalem, Rev. 21:19; (e) the adornment of the seven angels in Rev. 15:6, RV (so the best texts; some have *linon*, "linen," KJV); (f) the adornment of religious Babylon, Rev. 17:4; (III) figuratively, of Christ, Rev. 4:3; 21:11, where "light" stands for "Light-giver" (*phoster*).

4:4 But he answered and said, It is written, Man shall not live by bread alone, but by every word that proceedeth out of the mouth of God.

Man *anthropos* (444), is used (a) generally, of "a human being, male or female," without reference to sex or nationality, e.g., **Matt. 4:4; 12:35**; John 2:25; (b) in distinction from God, e.g., **Matt. 19:6**; John 10:33; Gal. 1:11; Col. 3:23; (c) in distinction from animals, etc., e.g., Luke 5:10; (d) sometimes, in the plural, of "men and women," people, e.g., **Matt. 5:13, 16**; in Mark 11:2 and 1 Tim. 6:16, lit., "no one of men"; (e) in some instances with a suggestion of human frailty and imperfection e.g., 1 Cor. 2:5; Acts 14:15 (2nd part) ... (i) often joined with another noun, e.g., **Matt. 11:19**, lit., "a man, a glutton"; **13:52**, lit., "a man, a householder"; **18:23**, "a certain king," lit., "a man, a king;" (j) as equivalent simply to "a person," or "one," whether "man" or woman, e.g., Acts 19:16; Rom. 3:28; Gal. 2:16; Jas. 1:19; 2:24; 3:8 (like the pronoun *tis*, "someone"; *tis* is rendered "man" in **Matt. 8:28**); or, again (as *tis* sometimes signifies), "a man," e.g., **Matt. 17:14**; Luke 13:19; (k) definitely, with the article, of some particular person, **Matt. 12:13**; Mark 3:3, 5; or with the demonstrative pronoun and the article, e.g., **Matt. 12:45**; Luke 14:30.

Live *zao* (2198), "to live, be alive," is used in the NT of "(a) God, **Matt. 16:16**; John 6:57; Rom. 14:11; (b) the Son in Incarnation, John 6:57; (c) the Son in Resurrection, John 14:19; Acts 1:3; Rom. 6:10; 2 Cor. 13:4; Heb. 7:8; (d) spiritual life, John 6:57; Rom. 1:17; 8:13b; Gal. 2:19, 20; Heb. 12:9; (e) the present state of departed saints, Luke 20:38; 1 Pet. 4:6; (f) the hope of resurrection, 1 Pet. 1:3; (g) the resurrection of believers, 1 Thess. 5:10; John 5:25; Rev. 20:4, and of unbelievers, v. 5, cf. v. 13; (h) the way of access to God through the Lord Jesus Christ, Heb. 10:20; (i) the manifestation of divine power in support of divine authority, 2 Cor. 13:4b; cf. 12:10, and 1 Cor. 5:5; (j) bread, figurative of the Lord Jesus, John 6:51; (k) a stone, figurative of the Lord Jesus, 1 Pet. 2:4; (l) water, figurative of the Holy Spirit, John 4:10; 7:38; (m) a sacrifice, figurative of the believer, Rom. 12:1; (n) stones, figurative of the believer, 1 Pet. 2:5; (o) the oracles, *logion*, Acts 7:38, and word, *logos*, Heb. 4:12; 1 Pet. 1:23, of God; (p) the physical life of men, 1 Thess. 4:15; **Matt. 27:63**; Acts 25:24; Rom. 14:9; Phil. 1:21 (in the infinitive mood used as a noun with the article, 'living'), 22; 1 Pet. 4:5; (q) the maintenance of physical life, **Matt. 4:4**; 1 Cor. 9:14; (r) the duration of physical life, Heb. 2:15; (s) the enjoyment of physical life, 1 Thess. 3:8; (t) the recovery of physical life from the power of disease, Mark 5:23; John 4:50; (u) the recovery of physical life from the power of death, **Matt. 9:18**; Acts 9:41; Rev. 20:5; (v) the course, conduct, and character of men, (1) good, Acts 26:5; 2 Tim. 3:12; Titus 2:12; (2) evil, Luke 15:13; Rom. 6:2; 8:13a; 2 Cor. 5:15b; Col. 3:7; (3) undefined, Rom. 7:9; 14:7; Gal. 2:14; (w) restoration after alienation, Luke 15:32."

Alone *monos* (3441), denotes "single, alone, solitary," **Matt. 4:4**, etc.

Proceedeth *ekporeuomai* (1607), "to go forth," is translated "to proceed out of" in **Matt. 4:4; 15:11**, RV; **15:18**; Mark 7:15, RV; 7:20, RV; 7:21; 7:23, RV; Luke 4:22; John 15:26; Eph. 4:29; Rev. 1:16, RV; 4:5; 9:17, 18, RV (KJV, "issued"); 11:5; 19:15, RV; 19:21, KJV (RV, "came forth"); 22:1.

4:5 Then the devil taketh him up into the holy city, and setteth him on a pinnacle of the temple,

Taketh *see Matthew 1:20*.

Setteth *histemi* (2476), "to cause to stand," is translated "to set" in **Matt. 4:5** (aorist tense in the best texts; some have the present, as in KJV);

18:2; **25:33**; Mark 9:36; Luke 4:9; 9:47; John 8:3; Acts 4:7; 5:27; 6:6; v. 13, "set up"; 22:30; in Jude 24, RV, "to set" (KJV, "to present").

Pinnacle *pterugion* (4419), denotes (a) "a little wing" (diminutive of *pterux*, "a wing"); (b) "anything like a wing, a turret, battlement," of the temple in Jerusalem, **Matt. 4:5** and Luke 4:9 (of the *hieron*, "the entire precincts," or parts of the main building, as distinct from the *naos*, "the sanctuary"). This "wing" has been regarded (1) as the apex of the sanctuary, (2) the top of Solomon's porch, (3) the top of the Royal Portico, which Josephus describes as of tremendous height (*Antig.* xv. 11.5). It is used in the Sept. of the fins of fishes, e.g. Lev. 11:9-12; of the part of a dress, hanging down in the form of a wing, Ruth 3:9; 1 Sam. 24:5.

4:6 And saith unto him, If thou be the Son of God, cast thyself down: for it is written, He shall give his angels charge concerning thee: and in *their* hands they shall bear thee up, lest at any time thou dash thy foot against a stone.

Thyself *seauton*, "(as) thyself," Rom. 13:9; *seautou*, "of thyself," e.g., **Matt. 4:6**; *seauto*, "to thyself," Acts 16:28.

Charge *entellomai* (1781), to order, command, enjoin (from *en*, in, used intensively, and *teleo*, to fulfil), is translated by the verb to give charge, **Matt. 4:6**; **17:9** (AV); Luke 4:10.

Lest *me pote* (3379), lit., "lest ever," "lest haply," e.g., Luke 14:29, of laying a foundation, with the possibility of being unable to finish the building; Acts 5:39, of the possibility of being found fighting against God; Heb. 3:2, RV, "lest haply," of the possibility of having an evil heart of unbelief. The RV usually has "lest haply" (KJV "lest at any time"), e.g., **Matt. 4:6**; **5:25**; **13:15**; Mark 4:12; Luke 4:11; 21:34; Heb. 2:1; in **Matt. 25:9**, the RV has "peradventure"; in 2 Tim. 2:25, KJV and RV, have "if peradventure"; in John 7:26 the RV has "Can it be that," for the word "Do" in the KJV.

Dash *proskopto* (4350), denotes "to beat upon or against, to strike against, dash against" (*pros*, "to or against," *kopto*, "to strike, beat"); hence, of the foot, to stumble, "dash" (KJV and RV), **Matt. 4:6**; Luke 4:11.

Stone *see* Stones at *Matthew 4:3*.

4:7 Jesus said unto him, It is written again, Thou shalt not tempt the Lord thy God.

Tempt *ekpeirazo* (1598), an intensive form, is used in much the same way as in Christ's quotation from Deut. 6:16, in reply to the Devil, **Matt. 4:7**; Luke 4:12; so in 1 Cor. 10:9, RV, "the Lord" (KJV, "Christ"); of the lawyer who "tempted" Christ, Luke 10:25. In the Sept., Deut. 6:16; 8:2, 16; Ps. 78:15. Cf. *dokimazo*.

Lord *see Matthew 1:22*.

4:8 Again, the devil taketh him up into an exceeding high mountain, and sheweth him all the kingdoms of the world, and the glory of them;

Taketh *see Matthew 1:20*.

Exceeding *see Matthew 2:16*.

High *hupselos* (5308), "high, lofty," is used (a) naturally, of mountains, **Matt. 4:8**; **17:1**; Mark 9:2; Rev. 21:10; of a wall, Rev. 21:12; (b) figuratively, of the arm of God, Acts 13:17; of heaven, "on high," plural, lit., "in high (places)," Heb. 1:3; (c) metaphorically, Luke 16:15, RV, "exalted" (KJV, "highly esteemed"); Rom. 11:20, in the best texts, "high-minded" [lit., "mind (not) high things"]; 12:16.

Sheweth *deiknumi, or deiknuo*, (1166), denotes (a) "to show, exhibit," e.g., **Matt. 4:8**; **8:4**; John 5:20; 20:20; 1 Tim. 6:15; (b) "to show by making known," **Matt. 16:21**; Luke 24:40; John 14:8, 9; Acts 10:28; 1 Cor. 12:31; Rev. 1:1; 4:1; 22:6; (c) "to show by way of proving," Jas. 2:18; 3:13.

Kingdoms *basileia* (932), is primarily an abstract noun, denoting "sovereignty, royal power, dominion," e.g., Rev. 17:18, translated "(which) reigneth," lit., "hath a kingdom" (RV marg.); then, by metonymy, a concrete noun, denoting the territory or people over whom a king rules, e.g., **Matt. 4:8**; Mark 3:24. It is used especially of the "kingdom" of God and of Christ.

"The Kingdom of God is (a) the sphere of God's rule, Ps. 22:28; 145:13; Dan. 4:25; Luke 1:52; Rom. 13:1, 2. Since, however, this earth is the scene of universal rebellion against God, e.g., Luke 4:5, 6; 1 John 5:19; Rev. 11:15-18, the "kingdom" of God is (b) the sphere in which, at any given time, His rule is acknowledged. God has not relinquished His sovereignty in the face of rebellion, demoniac and human, but has declared His purpose to establish it, Dan. 2:44; 7:14; 1 Cor. 15:24, 25. Meantime, seeking willing obedience, He gave His law to a nation and appointed kings to administer His "kingdom" over it, 1 Chron. 28:5. Israel, however, though declaring still a nominal allegiance shared in the common rebellion, Isa. 1:2-4, and, after they had rejected the Son of God, John 1:11 (cf. **Matt. 21:33-43**), were "cast away," Rom. 11:15, 20, 25. Henceforth God calls upon men everywhere, without distinction of race or nationality, to submit voluntarily to His rule. Thus the "kingdom" is said to be "in mystery" now, Mark 4:11, that is, it does not come within the range of the natural powers of observation, Luke 17:20, but is spiritually discerned, John 3:3 (cf. 1 Cor. 2:14). When, hereafter, God asserts His rule universally, then the "kingdom" will be in glory, that is, it will be manifest to all; cf. **Matt. 25:31-34**; Phil. 2:9-11; 2 Tim. 4:1, 18. Thus, speaking generally, references to the Kingdom fall into two classes, the first, in which it is viewed as present and involving suffering for those who enter it, 2 Thess. 1:5; the second, in which it is viewed as future and is associated with reward, **Matt. 25:34**, and glory, **13:43**. See also Acts 14:22. The fundamental principle of the Kingdom is declared in the words of the Lord spoken in the midst of a company of Pharisees, "the Kingdom of God is in the midst of you," Luke 17:21, marg., that is, where the King is, there is the Kingdom. Thus at the present time and so far as this earth is concerned, where the King is and where His rule is acknowledged, is, first, in the heart of the individual believer, Acts 4:19; Eph. 3:17; 1 Pet. 3:15; and then in the churches of God, 1 Cor. 12:3, 5, 11; 14:37; cf. Col. 1:27, where for "in" read "among." Now, the King and His rule being refused, those who enter the Kingdom of God are brought into conflict with all who disown its allegiance, as well as with the desire for ease, and the dislike of suffering and unpopularity, natural to all. On the other hand, subjects of the Kingdom are the objects of the care of God, **Matt. 6:33**, and of the rejected King, Heb. 13:5. Entrance into the Kingdom of God is by the new birth, **Matt. 18:3**; John 3:5, for nothing that a man may be by nature, or can attain to by any form of self-culture, avails in the spiritual realm. And as the new nature, received in the new birth, is made evident by obedience, it is further said that only such as do the will of God shall enter into His Kingdom, **Matt. 7:21**, where, however, the context shows that the reference is to the future, as in 2 Pet. 1:10, 11. Cf. also 1 Cor. 6:9, 10; Gal. 5:21; Eph. 5:5. The expression 'Kingdom of God' occurs four times in Matthew, 'Kingdom of the Heavens' usually taking its place. The latter (cf. Dan. 4:26) does not occur elsewhere in NT, but see 2 Tim. 4:18, "His heavenly Kingdom." ... This Kingdom is identical with the Kingdom of the Father (cf. **Matt. 26:29** with Mark 14:25), and with the Kingdom of the Son (cf. Luke 22:30). Thus there is but one Kingdom, variously described: of the Son of Man, **Matt. 13:41**; of Jesus, Rev. 1:9; of Christ Jesus, 2 Tim. 4:1; "of Christ and God," Eph. 5:5; "of our Lord, and of His Christ," Rev. 11:15; "of our God, and the authority of His Christ," 12:10; "of the Son of His love," Col. 1:13. Concerning the future, the Lord taught His disciples to pray, "Thy Kingdom come," **Matt. 6:10**, where the verb is in the point tense, precluding the notion of gradual progress and development, and implying a sudden catastrophe as declared in 2 Thess. 2:8."

4:9-10 And saith unto him, All these things will I give thee, if thou wilt fall down and worship me.

Then saith Jesus unto him, Get thee hence, Satan: for it is written, Thou shalt worship the Lord thy God, and him only shalt thou serve.

Get *hupago* (5217), "to go away, withdraw," is rendered "get," "get ... hence," in **Matt. 4:10**; **16:23**; Mark 8:33; some mss. have it in Luke 4:8.

Satan *satanas* (4567), a Greek form derived from the Aramaic (Heb., *Satan*), "an adversary," is used (a) of an angel of Jehovah in Num. 22:22 (the first occurrence of the Word in the OT); (b) of men, e.g., 1 Sam. 29:4; Ps. 38:20; 71:13; four in Ps. 109; (c) of "Satan," the Devil, some seventeen or eighteen times in the OT; in Zech. 3:1, where the name receives its interpretation, "to be (his) adversary," RV (see marg.; KJV, "to resist him"). In the NT the word is always used of "Satan," the adversary (a) of God and Christ, e.g., **Matt. 4:10**; **12:26**; Mark 1:13; 3:23, 26; 4:15; Luke 4:8 (in some mss.); 11:18; 22:3; John 13:27; (b) of His people, e.g., Luke 22:31; Acts 5:3; Rom. 16:20; 1 Cor. 5:5; 7:5; 2 Cor. 2:11; 11:14; 12:7; 1 Thess. 2:18; 1 Tim. 1:20; 5:15; Rev. 2:9, 13 (twice), 24; 3:9; (c) of mankind, Luke 13:16; Acts 26:18; 2 Thess. 2:9; Rev. 12:9; 20:7.

His doom, sealed at the Cross, is foretold in its stages in Luke 10:18; Rev. 20:2, 10. Believers are assured of victory over him, Rom. 16:20. The appellation was given by the Lord to Peter, as a "Satan-like" man, on the occasion when he endeavored to dissuade Him from death, **Matt. 16:23**; Mark 8:33.

Worship *see Matthew 2:2*.

Only *monos* (3441), "alone, solitary," is translated "only," e.g., in **Matt. 4:10**; **12:4**; **17:8**; 1 Cor. 9:6; 14:36; Phil. 4:15; Col. 4:11; 2 John 1; it is used as an attribute of God in John 5:44; 17:3; Rom. 16:27; 1 Tim. 1:17; 1 Tim. 6:15-16; Jude 4, 25; Rev. 15:4.

Serve *latreuo* (3000), primarily "to work for hire" (akin to *latris*, "a hired servant"), signifies (1) to worship, (2) to "serve"; in the latter sense it is used of service (a) to God, **Matt. 4:10**; Luke 1:74 ("without fear");

4:8; Acts 7:7; 24:14, RV, "serve" (KJV, "worship"); 26:7; 27:23; Rom. 1:9 ("with my spirit"); 2 Tim. 1:3; Heb. 9:14; 12:28, KJV, "we may serve," RV, "we may offer service"; Rev. 7:15; (b) to God and Christ ("the Lamb"), Rev. 22:3; (c) in the tabernacle, Heb. 8:5, RV; 13:10; (d) to "the host of heaven," Acts 7:42, RV, "to serve" (KJV, "to worship"); (e) to "the creature," instead of the Creator, Rom. 1:25, of idolatry.

4:11 Then the devil leaveth him, and, behold, angels came and ministered unto him.

Leaveth *aphiemi* (863), *apo*, "from," and *hiemi*, "to send," has three chief meanings, (a) "to send forth, let go, forgive"; (b) "to let, suffer, permit"; (c) "to leave, leave alone, forsake, neglect." It is translated by the verb "to leave" (c), in **Matt. 4:11**; **4:20**, **22**, and parallel passages; **5:24**; **8:15**, and parallel passages; **8:22**, RV, "leave (the dead)," KJV, "let," and the parallel passage; **13:36**, RV, "left (the multitude)," KJV, "sent ... away"; **18:12**; **19:27**, and parallel passages, RV, "we have left" (KJV, "we have forsaken"), so v. **29**; **22:22**, **25**; **23:23**, RV, "have left undone" (KJV, "have omitted," in the 1st part, "leave undone" in the second); **23:38**, and the parallel passage; **24:2**, **40**, **41**, and parallel passages; **26:56**, RV, "left"; Mark 1:18, "left"; 1:31; 7:8, RV, "ye leave"; 8:13; 10:28, 29; 12:12, 19-22; 13:34; Luke 10:30; 11:42 (in some mss.); Luke 12:39, RV "have left," KJV "have suffered"; John 4:3, 28, 52; 8:29; 10:12; 14:18, 27; 16:28, 32; Rom. 1:27; 1 Cor. 7:11, RV, "leave" (KJV "put away"); 7:13 (KJV and RV); Heb. 2:8; 6:1; Rev. 2:4.

Ministered *diakoneo* (1247), signifies "to be a servant, attendant, to serve, wait upon, minister." In the following it is translated "to minister," except where "to serve" is mentioned: it is used (a) with a general significance, e.g., **Matt. 4:11**; **20:28**; Mark 1:13; 10:45; John 12:26 ("serve," twice); Acts 19:22; Philem. 13; (b) of waiting at table, "ministering" to the guests, **Matt. 8:15**; Luke 4:39; 8:3; 12:37; 17:8, "serve"; 22:26, "serve," v. 27, "serveth," twice; the 2nd instance, concerning the Lord, may come under (a); so of women preparing food, etc., Mark 1:31; Luke 10:40, "serve"; John 12:2, "served"; (c) of relieving one's necessities, supplying the necessaries of life, **Matt. 25:44**; **27:55**; Mark 15:41; Acts 6:2, "serve"; Rom. 15:25; Heb. 6:10; more definitely in connection with such service in a local church, 1 Tim. 3:10, 13 [there is nothing in the original representing the word "office"; RV, "let them serve as deacons," "they that have served (well) as deacons"]; (d) of attending, in a more general way, to anything that may serve another's interests, as of the work of an amanuensis, 2 Cor. 3:3 (metaphorical): of the conveyance of material gifts for assisting the needy, 2 Cor. 8:19, 20, RV, "is ministered" (KJV, "is administered"); of a variety of forms of service, 2 Tim. 1:18; of the testimony of the OT prophets, 1 Pet. 1:12; of the ministry of believers one to another in various ways, 1 Pet. 4:10, 11 (not here of discharging ecclesiastical functions).

4:12 Now when Jesus had heard that John was cast into prison, he departed into Galilee;

Cast *paradidomi* (3860), "to betray" (*para*, "up," *didomi*, "to give"), lit., "to give over," is used either (a) in the sense of delivering a person or thing to be kept by another, to commend, e.g., Acts 28:16; (b) to deliver to prison or judgment, e.g., **Matt. 4:12**; 1 Tim. 1:20; (c) to deliver over treacherously by way of "betrayal," **Matt. 17:22** (RV, "delivered"); **26:16**; John 6:64, etc.; (d) to hand on, deliver, e.g., 1 Cor. 11:23; (e) to allow of something being done, said of the ripening of fruit, Mark 4:29, RV, "is ripe" (marg., "alloweth").

Prison In **Matt. 4:12**, KJV, *paradidomi*, "to betray, deliver up," is translated "was cast into prison" (RV, "was delivered up"). In Mark 1:14, KJV, "was put in prison," RV, as in **Matt. 4:12**.

Departed *see Matthew 2:12*.

4:13 And leaving Nazareth, he came and dwelt in Capernaum, which is upon the sea coast, in the borders of Zabulon and Nephthalim:

Leaving *kataleipo* (2641), a strengthened form of *leipo*, "to leave," signifies (a) "to leave, to leave behind," e.g., **Matt. 4:13**; (b) "to leave remaining, reserve," e.g., Luke 10:40; (c) "to forsake," in the sense of abandoning, translated "to forsake" in the RV of Luke 5:28 and Acts 6:2; in Heb. 11:27 and 2 Pet. 2:15, KJV and RV. In this sense it is translated "to leave," in Mark 10:7; 14:52; Luke 15:4; Eph. 5:31.

Sea *parathalassios* (3864), "by the sea," **Matt. 4:13**, the phrase "upon the sea coast," **Matt. 4:13**, KJV, translates *parathalassios* (*para*, "by," *thalassa*, "the sea"), RV, "by the sea."

Borders *horion* (3725), "a bound, boundary, limit, frontier" (akin to *horizo*, "to bound, limit"), is rendered "coasts" ten times in the KJV, but "borders" in **Matt. 4:13**, and is always translated "borders" in the RV. *See also* Coasts at *Matthew 2:16*.

4:14 That it might be fulfilled which was spoken by Esaias the prophet, saying,

Fulfilled *see Matthew 1:22*.

Spoken *see Matthew 1:22*.

4:15 The land of Zabulon, and the land of Nephthalim, *by* the way of the sea, beyond Jordan, Galilee of the Gentiles;

Land *see Matthew 2:20.*

Gentiles *ethnos* (1484), whence Eng., "heathen," denotes, (a) "a nation," e.g., **Matt. 24:7**; Acts 10:35; "the Jewish people," e.g., Luke 7:5; Acts 10:22; 28:19; (b) in the plural, "the rest of mankind" in distinction from Israel or the Jews, e.g., **Matt. 4:15**; Acts 28:28; (c) "the people of a city," Acts 8:9; (d) gentile Christians, e.g., Rom. 10:19; 11:13; 15:27; Gal. 2:14.

4:16 The people which sat in darkness saw great light; and to them which sat in the region and shadow of death light is sprung up.

Sat *kathemai* (2521), is used (a) of the natural posture, e.g., **Matt. 9:9**, most frequently in Revelation, some 32 times; frequently in the Gospels and Acts; elsewhere only in 1 Cor. 14:30; Jas. 2:3 (twice); and of Christ's position of authority on the throne of God, Col. 3:1, KJV, "sitteth" (RV, "is, seated"); Heb. 1:13 (cf. **Matt. 22:44**; **26:64** and parallel passages in Mark and Luke, and Acts 2:34); often as antecedent or successive to, or accompanying, another act (in no case a superfluous expression), e.g., **Matt. 15:29**; **27:36**; Mark 2:14; 4:1; (b) metaphorically in **Matt. 4:16** (twice); Luke 1:79; of inhabiting a place (translated "dwell"), Luke 21:35; Rev. 14:6, RV marg., "sit" (in the best texts: some have *katoikeo*, "to dwell").

Darkness *skotia* (4653), is used (a) of physical darkness, "dark," John 6:17, lit., "darkness had come on," and 20:1, lit., "darkness still being"; (b) of secrecy, in general, whether what is done therein is good or evil, **Matt. 10:27**; Luke 12:3; (c) of spiritual or moral "darkness," emblematic of sin, as a condition of moral or spiritual depravity, **Matt. 4:16**; John 1:5; 8:12; 12:35, 46; 1 John 1:5; 2:8-9, 11.

Region *chora* (5561), "a space lying between two limits, a country, land," is translated "region" in **Matt. 4:16**; Luke 3:1; Acts 8:1; 13:49; 16:6; 18:23, RV. In the last three passages it has the technical sense of a subdivision of a Roman province.

Shadow *skia* (4639), is used (a) of "a shadow," caused by the interception of light, Mark 4:32; Acts 5:15; metaphorically of the darkness and spiritual death of ignorance, **Matt. 4:16**; Luke 1:79; (b) of "the image" or "outline" cast by an object, Col. 2:17, of ceremonies under the Law; of the tabernacle and its appurtenances and offerings, Heb. 8:5; of these as appointed under the Law, Heb. 10:1.

Sprung *anatello* (393), "to arise," is used especially of things in the natural creation, e.g., "the rising" of the sun, moon and stars; metaphorically, of light, in **Matt. 4:16**, "did spring up"; of the sun, **Matt. 5:45**; **13:6** (RV); Mark 4:6; Jas. 1:11; in Mark 16:2 the RV has "when the sun was risen," keeping to the verb form, for the KJV, "at the rising of"; of a cloud, Luke 12:54; of the day-star, 2 Pet. 1:19; in Heb. 7:14 metaphorically, of the Incarnation of Christ: "Our Lord hath sprung out of Judah," more lit., "Our Lord hath arisen out of Judah," as of the rising of the light of the sun.

4:17 From that time Jesus began to preach, and to say, Repent: for the kingdom of heaven is at hand.

Repent In the NT the subject chiefly has reference to "repentance" from sin, and this change of mind involves both a turning from sin and a turning to God. The parable of the Prodigal Son is an outstanding illustration of this. Christ began His ministry with a call to "repentance," **Matt. 4:17**, but the call is addressed, not as in the OT to the nation, but to the individual. In the Gospel of John, as distinct from the Synoptic Gospels, referred to above, "repentance" is not mentioned, even in connection with John the Baptist's preaching; in John's Gospel and 1st epistle the effects are stressed, e.g., in the new birth, and, generally, in the active turning from sin to God by the exercise of faith (John 3:3; 9:38; 1 John 1:9), as in the NT in general.

At hand *see Matthew 3:2.*

4:18 And Jesus, walking by the sea of Galilee, saw two brethren, Simon called Peter, and Andrew his brother, casting a net into the sea: for they were fishers.

Net *amphiblestron* (293), lit., "something thrown around" (*amphi*, "around," *ballo*, "to throw"), denotes "a casting net," a somewhat small "net," cast over the shoulder, spreading out in a circle and made to sink by weights, **Matt. 4:18** (in some mss. in Mark 1:16: the best have the verb *amphiballo* alone).

Sea *thalassa* (2281), is used (a) chiefly literally, e.g., "the Red Sea," Acts 7:36; 1 Cor. 10:1; Heb. 11:29; the "sea" of Galilee or Tiberias, **Matt. 4:18**; **15:29**; Mark 6:48, 49, where the acts of Christ testified to His deity; John 6:1; 21:1; in general, e.g., Luke 17:2; Acts 4:24; Rom. 9:27; Rev. 16:3; 18:17; 20:8, 13; 21:1; in combination with *pelagos*, **Matt. 18:6**; (b) metaphorically, of "the ungodly men" described in Jude 13 (cf. Isa. 57:20); (c) symbolically, in the apocalyptic vision of "a glassy sea like unto crystal," Rev. 4:6, emblematic of the fixed purity and holiness of all that appertains to the authority and judicial dealings of God; in 15:2, the same, "mingled with fire," and, standing by it (RV) or on it (KJV and RV marg.), those who had "come victorious from the beast" (ch. 13); of the wild and restless condition of nations, Rev. 13:1 (see 17:1, 15), where "he stood" (RV) refers to the dragon, not John (KJV); from the midst of this state arises the beast, symbolic of the final gentile power dominating the federated nations of the Roman world (see Dan., chs. 2, 7, etc.).

Fishers *halieus* (231), "a fisherman, fisher" (from *hals*, "the sea"), occurs in **Matt. 4:18, 19**; Mark 1:16, 17; Luke 5:2.

4:19 And he saith unto them, Follow me, and I will make you fishers of men.

Follow In **Matt. 4:19**, *deute*, "come hither," with *opiso*, "after," is translated "come ye after," RV (KJV, "follow").

Make *poieo* (4160), "to do, to make," is used in the latter sense (a) of constructing or producing anything, of the creative acts of God, e.g., **Matt. 19:4** (2nd part); Acts 17:24; of the acts of human beings, e.g., **Matt. 17:4**; Acts 9:39; (b) with nouns denoting a state or condition, to be the author of, to cause, e.g., peace, Eph. 2:15; Jas. 3:18; stumbling blocks, Rom. 16:17; (c) with nouns involving the idea of action (or of something accomplished by action), so as to express the idea of the verb more forcibly (the middle voice is commonly used in this respect, suggesting the action as being of special interest to the doer); for the active voice see, e.g., Mark 2:23, of "making" one's way, where the idea is not that the disciples "made" a path through the standing corn, but simply that they went, the phrase being equivalent to going, "(they began) as they went (to pluck the ears)"; other instances of the active are Rev. 13:13, 14; 16:14; 19:20; for the middle voice (the dynamic or subjective middle), see, e.g., John 14:23, "will make Our abode"; in Acts 20:24, "none of these things move me," lit., "I make account of none of these things"; 25:17, "I made no delay" RV, Rom. 15:26; Eph. 4:16; Heb. 1:2; 2 Pet. 1:10; (d) to "make" ready or prepare, e.g., a dinner, Luke 14:12; a supper, John 12:2; (e) to acquire, provide a thing for oneself, **Matt. 25:16**; Luke 19:18; (f) to render or "make" one or oneself anything, or cause a person or thing to become something, e.g., **Matt. 4:19**; **12:16**, "make (Him known)"; John 5:11, 15, to "make" whole; 16:2, lit., "they shall make (you put out of the synagogue)"; Eph. 2:14; Heb. 1:7; to change one thing into another, **Matt. 21:13**; John 2:16; 4:46; 1 Cor. 6:15; (g) to constitute one anything, e.g., Acts 2:36, (h) to declare one or oneself anything, John 5:18, "making (Himself equal with God)"; 8:53; 10:33; 19:7, 12; 1 John 1:10; 5:10; (i) to "make" one do a thing, e.g., Luke 5:34; John 6:10; Rev. 3:9.

Fishers *see Matthew 4:18.*

4:20 And they straightway left *their* nets, and followed him.

Left *see* Leaveth at *Matthew 4:11.*

Nets *diktuon* (1350), a general term for a "net" (from an old verb *diko*, "to cast": akin to *diskos*, "a quoit"), occurs in **Matt. 4:20-21**; Mark 1:18-19; Luke 5:2, 4-6; John 21:6, 8, 11 (twice). In the Sept. it was used for a "net" for catching birds, Prov. 1:17, in other ways, e.g., figuratively of a snare, Job 18:8; Prov. 29:5.

4:21 And going on from thence, he saw other two brethren, James *the son* of Zebedee, and John his brother, in a ship with Zebedee their father, mending their nets; and he called them.

Going on *probaino* (4260), "to go on, forwards, advance," is used of locality, **Matt. 4:21**; Mark 1:19; for the metaphorical use with reference to age, Luke 1:7, 18; 2:36.

Thence *ekeithen* (1564), is used (a) of place, e.g., **Matt. 4:21**, "from thence"; **5:26**; in Acts 20:13, "there"; often preceded by *kai*, written *kakeithen*, e.g., Mark 9:30 and Luke 11:53 (in the best texts); Acts 7:4; 14:26; (b) of time, Acts 13:21, "and afterward."

Mending *katartizo* (2675), from *kata*, "down," intensive and *artios*, "fit," has three meanings, (a) "to mend, repair," **Matt. 4:21**; Mark 1:19, of nets; (b) "to complete, furnish completely, equip, prepare," Luke 6:40; Rom. 9:22; Heb, 11:3 and in the middle voice, **Matt. 21:16**; Heb. 10:5; (c) "ethically, to prepare, perfect," Gal. 6:1; 1 Thess. 3:10; 1 Pet. 5:10; Heb. 13:21; and in the passive voice, 1 Cor. 1:10; 2 Cor. 13:11.

4:22 And they immediately left the ship and their father, and followed him.

Left *see* Leaveth at *Matthew 4:11.*

4:23 And Jesus went about all Galilee, teaching in their synagogues, and preaching the gospel of the kingdom, and healing all manner of sickness and all manner of disease among the people.

Went about *periago* (4013), "to lead about," as in 1 Cor. 9:5, is used intransitively with the meaning "to go about"; "went about," **Matt. 4:23, 9:35**; Mark 6:6; Acts 13:11; in **Matt. 23:15**, "ye compass."

Teaching *didasko* (1321), is used (a) absolutely, "to give instruction," e.g., **Matt. 4:23**; **9:35**; Rom. 12:7; 1 Cor. 4:17; 1 Tim. 2:12; 4:11; (b) transitively, with an object, whether persons, e.g., **Matt. 5:2**; **7:29**, and frequently in the Gospels and Acts, or things "taught," e.g., **Matt. 15:9**; **22:16**; Acts 15:35; 18:11; both persons and things, e.g., John 14:26; Rev. 2:14, 20.

Gospel *euangelion* (2098), originally denoted a reward for good tidings; later, the idea of reward dropped, and the word stood for "the good news" itself. The Eng. word "gospel," i.e. "good message," is the equivalent of *euangelion* (Eng., "evangel"). In the NT it denotes the "good tidings" of the kingdom of God and of salvation through Christ, to be received by faith, on the basis of His expiatory death, His burial, resurrection, and ascension, e.g., Acts 15:7; 20:24; 1 Pet. 4:17. Apart from those references and those in the Gospels of Matthew and Mark, and Rev. 14:6, the noun is confined to Paul's epistles. The apostle uses it of two associated yet distinct things, (a) of the basic facts of the death, burial and resurrection of Christ, e.g., 1 Cor. 15:1-3; (b) of the interpretation of these facts, e.g., Rom. 2:16; Gal. 1:7, 11; 2:2; in (a) the "gospel" is viewed historically, in (b) doctrinally, with reference to the interpretation of the facts, as is sometimes indicated by the context. The following phrases describe the subjects or nature or purport of the message; it is the "gospel" of God, Mark 1:14; Rom. 1:1; 15:16; 2 Cor. 11:7; 1 Thess. 2:2, 9; 1 Pet. 4:17; God, concerning His Son, Rom. 1:1-3; His Son, Rom. 1:9; Jesus Christ, the Son of God, Mark 1:1; our Lord Jesus, 2 Thess. 1:8; Christ, Rom. 15:19, etc.; the glory of Christ, 2 Cor. 4:4; the grace of God, Acts 20:24; the glory of the blessed God, 1 Tim. 1:11; your salvation, Eph. 1:13; peace, Eph. 6:15. Cf. also "the gospel of the Kingdom," **Matt. 4:23**; **9:35**; **24:14**; "an eternal gospel," Rev. 14:6.

The following expressions are used in connection with the "gospel": (a) with regard to its testimony; (1) *kerusso*, "to preach it as a herald," e.g., **Matt. 4:23**; Gal. 2:2; (2) *laleo*, "to speak," 1 Thess. 2:2; (3) *diamarturomai*, "to testify (thoroughly)," Acts 20:24; (4) *euangelizo*, "to preach," e.g., 1 Cor. 15:1; 2 Cor. 11:7; Gal. 1:11; (5) *katangello*, "to proclaim," 1 Cor. 9:14; (6) *douleuo eis*, "to serve unto" ("in furtherance of"), Phil. 2:22; (7) *sunathleo en*, "to labor with in," Phil. 4:3; (8) *hierourgeo*, "to minister," Rom. 15:16; (8) *pleroo*, "to preach fully," Rom. 15:19; (10) *sunkakopatheo*, "to suffer hardship with," 2 Tim. 1:8; (b) with regard to its reception or otherwise: (1) *dechomai*, "to receive," 2 Cor. 11:4; *hupakouo*, "to hearken to, or obey," Rom. 10:16; 2 Thess. 1:8; *pisteuo en*, "to believe in," Mark 1:15; *metastrepho*, "to pervert," Gal. 1:7.

All *holos* (3650), "the whole, all," is most frequently used with the article followed by a noun, e.g., **Matt. 4:23**. It is used with the article alone, in John 7:23, "every whit"; Acts 11:26; 21:31; 28:30; Titus 1:11; Luke 5:5, in the best texts. *See also* **Every** at ***Matthew 3:10***.

Sickness *nosos* (3554), akin to Lat. *nocere*, "to injure" (Eng., "nosology"), is the regular word for "disease, sickness," **Matt. 4:23**; **8:17**; **9:35**; **10:1**, RV, "disease," KJV, "sickness"; in **Matt. 4:24**; Mark 1:34; Luke 4:40; 6:17; 9:1; Acts 19:12, KJV and RV render it "diseases." In Luke 7:21, KJV has "infirmities." The most authentic mss. omit the word in Mark 3:15.

Disease *malakia* (3119), primarily denotes "softness" (cf. *malakos*, "soft," **Matt. 11:8**, etc.); hence, "debility, disease." It is found in Matthew only, **4:23**; **9:35**; **10:1**. It is frequent in the Sept., e.g., Gen. 42:4; 44:29; Deut. 7:15; 28:61; Isa. 38:9; 53:3.

People *see* ***Matthew 2:6***.

4:24 And his fame went throughout all Syria: and they brought unto him all sick people that were taken with divers diseases and torments, and those which were possessed with devils, and those which were lunatick, and those that had the palsy; and he healed them.

Fame *akoe* (189), denotes (a) "the sense of hearing," 1 Cor. 12:17; 2 Pet. 2:8; a combination of verb and noun is used in phrases which have been termed Hebraic as they express somewhat literally an OT phraseology, e.g., "By hearing ye shall hear," **Matt. 13:14**; Acts 28:26, RV, a mode of expression conveying emphasis; (b) "the organ of hearing," Mark 7:35, "ears"; Luke 7:1, RV, "ears," for KJV, "audience"; Acts 17:20; 2 Tim. 4:3, 4; Heb. 5:11, "dull of hearing," lit., "dull as to ears"; (c) "a thing heard, a message or teaching," John 12:38, "report"; Rom. 10:16; 1 Thess. 2:13, "the word of the message," lit. "the word of hearing" (KJV, "which ye heard"); Heb. 4:2, "the word of hearing," RV, for KJV, "the word preached"; in a somewhat similar sense, "a rumor, report," **Matt. 4:24**; **14:1**; Mark 1:28, KJV, "fame," RV, "report"; **Matt. 24:6**; Mark

13:7, "rumors (of wars)"; (d) "the receiving of a message," Rom. 10:17, something more than the mere sense of "hearing" [see (a)]; so with the phrase "the hearing of faith," Gal. 3:2, 5, which it seems better to understand so than under (c).

Sick *kakos* (2560), "badly, evilly," is used in the physical sense, "to be sick," e.g., **Matt. 4:24**; Mark 1:32, 34; Luke 5:31. In **Matt. 21:41** this adverb is used with the adjective, "He will miserably destroy those miserable men," more lit., "He will evilly destroy those men (evil as they are)," with stress on the adjective; in the moral sense, "to speak evilly," John 18:23; Acts 23:5; to ask evilly, Jas. 4:3.

Taken with *sunecho* (4912), "to hold in, hold fast," is used, in the passive voice, of "being seized or afflicted by ills," Acts 28:8, "sick" (of the father of Publius, cf. **Matt. 4:24**; Luke 4:38, taken with).

Divers *poikilos* (4164), denotes "particolored, variegated" (*poikillo* means "to make gay": the root of the first syllable is *pik–*, found in Eng., "picture"), hence "divers," **Matt. 4:24**; Mark 1:34; Luke 4:40; 2 Tim. 3:6; Titus 3:3; Heb. 2:4 (RV, "manifold"), 13:9; Jas. 1:2 (RV, "manifold"); in 1 Pet. 1:6 and 4:10, "manifold," both KJV and RV.

Diseases *see* **Disease** at *Matthew 4:23*.

Torments *basanos* (931), primarily "a touchstone," employed in testing metals, hence, "torment," is used (a) of physical diseases, **Matt. 4:24**; (b) of a condition of retribution in Hades, Luke 16:23, 28.

Possessed with devils *daimonizomai* (1139), signifies "to be possessed of a demon, to act under the control of a demon." Those who were thus afflicted expressed the mind and consciousness of the "demon" or "demons" indwelling them, e.g., Luke 8:28. The verb is found chiefly in Matt. and Mark; **Matt. 4:24; 8:16, 28, 33; 9:32; 12:22; 15:22**; Mark 1:32; 5:15-16, 18; elsewhere in Luke 8:36 and John 10:21, "him that hath a devil (demon)."

Lunatick *seleniazo* (4583), lit., "to be moon struck" (from *selene*, "the moon"), is used in the passive voice with active significance, RV, "epileptic," for KJV, "lunatick," **Matt. 4:24; 17:15**; the corresponding English word is "lunatic." Epilepsy was supposed to be influenced by the moon.

Had *see Matthew 3:4*.

Palsy *paralutikos* (3885), "paralytic, sick of the palsy," is found in **Matt. 4:24** (RV, "palsied"); **8:6; 9:2** (twice), **6**; Mark 2:3, 4, 5, 9, 10; in some mss. Luke 5:24.

4:25 And there followed him great multitudes of people from Galilee, and *from* Decapolis, and *from* Jerusalem, and *from* Judaea, and *from* beyond Jordan.

Followed *akoloutheo* (190), to be an *akolouthos*, "a follower," or "companion" (from the prefix *a*, here expressing "union, likeness," and *keleuthos*, "a way"; hence, "one going in the same way"), is used (a) frequently in the literal sense, e.g., **Matt. 4:25**; (b) metaphorically, of "discipleship," e.g., Mark 8:34; 9:38; 10:21. It is used 77 times in the Gospels, of "following" Christ, and only once otherwise, Mark 14:13.

Multitudes *ochlos* (3793), is used frequently in the four Gospels and the Acts; elsewhere only in Rev. 7:9; 17:15; 19:1, 6; it denotes (a) "a crowd or multitude of persons, a throng," e.g., **Matt. 14:14, 15; 15:33**; often in the plural, e.g., **Matt. 4:25; 5:1**; with *polus*, "much" or "great," it signifies "a great multitude," e.g., **Matt. 20:29**, or "the common people," Mark 12:37, perhaps preferably "the mass of the people." The mass of the people was attracted to Him (for the statement "heard Him gladly" cf. what is said in Mark 6:20 of Herod Antipas concerning John the Baptist); in John 12:9, "the common people," RV, stands in contrast with their leaders (v. 10); Acts 24:12, RV, "crowd"; (b) "the populace, an unorganized multitude," in contrast to *demos*, "the people as a body politic," e.g., **Matt. 14:5; 21:26**; John 7:12 (2nd part); (c) in a more general sense, "a multitude or company," e.g., Luke 6:17, RV, "a (great) multitude (of His disciples)," KJV, "the company"; Acts 1:15, "a multitude (of persons)," RV, KJV, "the number (of names)"; Acts 24:18, RV, "crowd" (KJV, "multitude").

Chapter 5

5:1 And seeing the multitudes, he went up into a mountain: and when he was set, his disciples came unto him:

Multitudes *see Matthew 4:25*.

Mountain *oros* (3735), is used (a) without specification, e.g., Luke 3:5 (distinct from *bounos*, "a hill"); John 4:20; (b) of "the Mount of Transfiguration," **Matt. 17:1, 9**; Mark 9:2, 9; Luke 9:28, 37 (KJV, "hill"); 2 Pet. 1:18; (c) of "Zion," Heb. 12:22; Rev. 14:1; (d) of "Sinai," Acts 7:30, 38; Gal. 4:24, 25; Heb. 8:5; 12:20; (e) of "the Mount of Olives," **Matt. 21:1; 24:3**; Mark 11:1; 13:3; Luke 19:29, 37; 22:39; John 8:1; Acts 1:12; (f) of "the hill districts as distinct from the lowlands," especially of the hills above the Sea of Galilee, e.g., **Matt. 5:1; 8:1; 18:12**; Mark 5:5; (g) of "the

"'Poor in spirit' refers, not precisely to humility, but to an attitude of dependence on God and detachment from earthly supports."

RONALD ARBUTHNOTT KNOX

mountains on the east of Jordan" and "those in the land of Ammon" and "the region of Petra," etc., **Matt. 24:16**; Mark 13:14; Luke 21:21; (h) proverbially, "of overcoming difficulties, or accomplishing great things," 1 Cor. 13:2; cf. **Matt. 17:20**; **21:21**; Mark 11:23; (i) symbolically, of "a series of the imperial potentates of the Roman dominion, past and future," Rev. 17:9.

Set *kathizo* (2523), is used (a) transitively, "to make sit down," Acts 2:30; (b) intransitively, "to sit down," e.g., **Matt. 5:1**, RV, "when (He) had sat down" (KJV, "was set"); **19:28**; **20:21**, **23**; **23:2**; **25:31**; **26:36**; Mark 11:2, 7; 12:41; Luke 14:28, 31; 16:6; John 19:13; Acts 2:3 (of the tongues of fire); 8:31; 1 Cor. 10:7; 2 Thess. 2:4, "he sitteth," aorist tense, i.e., "he takes his seat" (as, e.g., in Mark 16:19); Rev. 3:21 (twice), RV, "to sit down" and "sat down"; 20:4.

5:2 And he opened his mouth, and taught them, saying,

Opened *see Matthew 2:11.*

Taught *see* Teaching at *Matthew 4:23.*

5:3 Blessed *are* the poor in spirit: for theirs is the kingdom of heaven.

Blessed *makarios* (3107), is used in the beatitudes in **Matt. 5** and Luke 6, is especially frequent in the Gospel of Luke, and is found seven times in Revelation, 1:3; 14:13; 16:15; 19:9; 20:6; 22:7, 14. It is said of God twice, 1 Tim. 1:11; 6:15. In the beatitudes the Lord indicates not only the characters that are "blessed," but the nature of that which is the highest good.

Poor *ptochos* (4434), has the broad sense of "poor," (a) literally, e.g., **Matt. 11:5**; **26:9, 11**; Luke 21:3 (with stress on the word, "a conspicuously poor widow"); John 12:5, 6, 8; 13:29; Jas. 2:2, 3, 6; the "poor" are constantly the subjects of injunctions to assist them, **Matt. 19:21**; Mark 10:21; Luke 14:13, 21; 18:22; Rom. 15:26; Gal. 2:10; (b) metaphorically, **Matt. 5:3**; Luke 6:20; Rev. 3:17.

Spirit *see Matthew 4:1.*

5:4 Blessed *are* they that mourn: for they shall be comforted.

Mourn *pentheo* (3996), "to mourn for, lament," is used (a) of mourning in general, **Matt. 5:4**; **9:15**; Luke 6:25; (b) of sorrow for the death of a loved one, Mark 16:10; (c) of "mourning" for the overthrow of Babylon and the Babylonish system, Rev. 18:11, 15, RV, "mourning" (KJV, "wailing"); v. 19 (ditto); (d) of sorrow for sin or for condoning it, Jas. 4:9; 1 Cor. 5:2; (e) of grief for those in a local church who show no repentance for evil committed, 2 Cor. 12:21, RV, "mourn" (KJV, "bewail").

5:5 Blessed *are* the meek: for they shall inherit the earth.

Meek *praus* or *praos* (4239), denotes "gentle, mild, meek"; Christ uses it of His own disposition, **Matt. 11:29**; He gives it in the third of His Beatitudes, **5:5**; it is said of Him as the King Messiah, **21:5**, from Zech. 9:9; it is an adornment of the Christian profession, 1 Pet. 3:4. Cf. *epios*, "gentle, of a soothing disposition," 1 Thess. 2:7; 2 Tim. 2:24.

Inherit *kleronomeo* (2816), strictly means "to receive by lot" (*kleros*, "a lot," *nemomai*, "to possess"); then, in a more general sense, "to possess oneself of, to receive as one's own, to obtain." The following list shows how in the NT the idea of inheriting broadens out to include all spiritual good provided through and in Christ, and particularly all that is contained in the hope grounded on the promises of God. The verb is used of the following objects: "(a) birthright, that into the possession of which one enters in virtue of sonship, not because of a price paid or of a task accomplished, Gal. 4:30; Heb. 1:4; 12:17; (b) that which is received as a gift, in contrast with that which is received as the reward of law-keeping, Heb. 1:14; 6:12 ("through," i.e., "through experiences that called for the exercise of faith and patience,' but not 'on the ground of the exercise of faith and patience.'); (c) that which is received on condition of obedience to certain precepts, 1 Pet. 3:9, and of faithfulness to God amidst opposition, Rev. 21:7; (d) the reward of that condition of soul which forbears retaliation and self-vindication, and expresses itself in gentleness of behavior.... **Matt. 5:5**. The phrase "inherit the earth," or "land," occur several times in OT. See especially Ps. 37:11, 22; (e) the reward (in the coming age, Mark 10:30) of the acknowledgment of the paramountcy of the claims of Christ, **Matt. 19:29**. In the three accounts given of this incident, see Mark 10:17-31; Luke 18:18-30, the words of the question put to the Lord are, in Matthew, "that I may have," in Mark and Luke, "that I may inherit." In the report of the Lord's word to Peter in reply to his subsequent question, Matthew has "inherit eternal life," while Mark and Luke have "receive eternal life." It seems to follow that the meaning of the word "inherit" is here ruled by the words "receive" and "have," with which it is interchanged in each of the three Gospels, i.e., the less common word "inherit" is to be regarded as equivalent to the more common words "receive" and "have." Cf. Luke 10:25; (f) the reward of those who have shown kindness to the "brethren" of the Lord in their distress, **Matt. 25:34;** (g) the kingdom of God, which the morally corrupt cannot "inherit," 1 Cor. 6:9, 10, the "inheritance" of which is likewise impossible to the present physical constitution of man, 1 Cor. 15:50; (h) incorruption, impossible of "inheritance" by corruption, 1 Cor. 15:50."

5:6 Blessed *are* they which do hunger and thirst after righteousness: for they shall be filled.

Hunger *see* Hungred at *Matthew 4:2.*

Thirst *dipsao* (1372), is used (a) in the natural sense, e.g., **Matt. 25:35, 37, 42**; in v. **44**, "athirst" (lit., "thirsting"); John 4:13, 15; 19:28; Rom. 12:20; 1 Cor. 4:11; Rev. 7:16; (b) figuratively, of spiritual "thirst," **Matt. 5:6**; John 4:14; 6:35; 7:37; in Rev. 21:6 and 22:17, "that is athirst."

Righteousness *see Matthew 3:15.*

Filled *chortazo* (5526), "to fill or satisfy with food," e.g., **Matt. 15:33**; Phil. 4:12, is used metaphorically in **Matt. 5:6**; Luke 6:21.

5:7 Blessed *are* the merciful: for they shall obtain mercy.

Merciful *eleemon* (1655), "merciful," not simply possessed of pity but actively compassionate, is used of Christ as a High Priest, Heb. 2:17, and of those who are like God, **Matt. 5:7** (cf. Luke 6:35, 36, where the RV, "sons" is to be read, as representing characteristics resembling those of their Father).

Obtain For the phrase "to obtain mercy," the passive voice of *eleeo* in **Matt. 5:7**; Rom. 11:30-31; 1 Cor. 7:25; 2 Cor. 4:1 (RV); 1 Tim. 1:13, 16; 1 Pet. 2:10 (twice).

Mercy *eleeo* (1653), signifies, in general, "to feel sympathy with the misery of another," and especially sympathy manifested in act, (a) in the active voice, "to have pity or mercy on, to show mercy" to, e.g., **Matt. 9:27; 15:22; 17:15; 18:33; 20:30, 31** (three times in Mark, four in Luke); Rom. 9:15, 16, 18; 11:32; 12:8; Phil. 2:27; Jude 22, 23; (b) in the passive voice, "to have pity or mercy shown one, to obtain mercy," **Matt. 5:7**; Rom. 11:30, 31; 1 Cor. 7:25; 2 Cor. 4:1; 1 Tim. 1:13, 16; 1 Pet. 2:10.

5:8 Blessed *are* the pure in heart: for they shall see God.

Pure *katharos* (2513), "free from impure admixture, without blemish, spotless," is used (a) physically, e.g., **Matt. 23:26; 27:59**; John 13:10 (where the Lord, speaking figuratively, teaches that one who has been entirely "cleansed," needs not radical renewal, but only to be "cleansed" from every sin into which he may fall); 15:3; Heb. 10:22; Rev. 15:6; 19:8, 14; 21:18, 21; (b) in a Levitical sense, Rom. 14:20; Titus 1:15, "pure"; (c) ethically, with the significance free from corrupt desire, from guilt, **Matt. 5:8**; John 13:10-11; Acts 20:26; 1 Tim. 1:5; 3:9; 2 Tim. 1:3; 2:22; Titus 1:15; Jas. 1:27; blameless, innocent (a rare meaning for this word), Acts 18:6; (d) in a combined Levitical and ethical sense ceremonially, Luke 11:41, "all things are clean unto you."

5:9 Blessed *are* the peacemakers: for they shall be called the children of God.

Peacemakers *eirenopoios* (1518), an adjective signifying peace making (*eirene*, and *poieo*, "to make"), is used in **Matt. 5:9**, "peacemakers."

Children *huios* (5207), primarily signifies the relation of offspring to parent (see John 9:18-20; Gal. 4:30). It is often used metaphorically of prominent moral characteristics. "It is used in the NT of (a) male offspring, Gal. 4:30; (b) legitimate, as opposed to illegitimate offspring, Heb. 12:8; (c) descendants, without reference to sex, Rom. 9:27; (d) friends attending a wedding, **Matt. 9:15**; (e) those who enjoy certain privileges, Acts 3:25; (f) those who act in a certain way, whether evil, **Matt. 23:31**, or good, Gal. 3:7; (g) those who manifest a certain character, whether evil, Acts 13:10; Eph. 2:2, or good, Luke 6:35; Acts 4:36; Rom. 8:14; (h) the destiny that corresponds with the character, whether evil, **Matt. 23:15**; John 17:12; 2 Thess. 2:3, or good, Luke 20:36; (i) the dignity of the relationship with God whereinto men are brought by the Holy Spirit when they believe on the Lord Jesus Christ, Rom. 8:19; Gal. 3:26....

"The Apostle John does not use *huios*, 'son,' of the believer, he reserves that title for the Lord; but he does use *teknon*, 'child,' as in his Gospel, 1:12; 1 John 3:1, 2; Rev. 21:7 (*huios*) is a quotation from 2 Sam. 7:14.

"The Lord Jesus used *huios* in a very significant way, as in **Matt. 5:9**,

'Blessed are the peacemakers, for they shall be called the sons of God,' and vv. **44, 45**, 'Love your enemies, and pray for them that persecute you; that ye may be (become) sons of your Father which is in heaven.' The disciples were to do these things, not in order that they might become children of God, but that, being children (note 'your Father' throughout), they might make the fact manifest in their character, might 'become sons.' See also 2 Cor. 6:17, 18.

"As to moral characteristics, the following phrases are used: (a) sons of God, **Matt. 5:9, 45**; Luke 6:35; (b) sons of the light, Luke 16:8; John 12:36; (c) sons of the day, 1 Thess. 5:5; (d) sons of peace, Luke 10:6; (e) sons of this world, Luke 16:8; (f) sons of disobedience, Eph. 2:2; (g) sons of the evil one, **Matt. 13:38**, cf. 'of the Devil,' Acts 13:10; (h) son of perdition, John 17:12; 2 Thess. 2:3. It is also used to describe characteristics other than moral, as: (i) sons of the resurrection, Luke 20:36; (j) sons of the Kingdom, **Matt. 8:12**; **13:38**; (k) sons of the bridechamber, Mark 2:19; (l) sons of exhortation, Acts 4:36; (m) sons of thunder, Boanerges, Mark 3:17."

5:10 Blessed *are* they which are persecuted for righteousness' sake: for theirs is the kingdom of heaven.

Persecuted *dioko* (1377), has the meanings (a) "to put to flight, drive away," (b) "to pursue," whence the meaning "to persecute," **Matt. 5:10-12, 44**; **10:23**; **23:34**; Luke 11:49; 21:12; John 5:16; 15:20 (twice); Acts 7:52; 9:4, 5, and similar passages; Rom. 12:14; 1 Cor. 4:12; 15:9; 2 Cor. 4:9, KJV (RV, "pursued"); Gal. 1:13, 23; 4:29; Gal. 5:11, RV, "am ... persecuted" (KJV, "suffer persecution"); so 6:12; Phil. 3:6; 2 Tim. 3:12, "shall suffer persecution"; Rev. 12:13.

Righteousness *see Matthew 3:15.*

5:11 Blessed are ye, when *men* shall revile you, and persecute *you*, and shall say all manner of evil against you falsely, for my sake.

Revile *oneidizo* (3679), signifies (a), in the active voice, "to reproach, upbraid," **Matt. 5:11**, RV, "shall reproach" (KJV, "shall revile"); **11:20**, "to upbraid"; **27:44**, RV, "cast ... reproach" [KJV, "cast ... in (His) teeth"]; Mark 15:32 RV, "reproached" (KJV, "reviled"); 16:14 "upbraided"; Luke 6:22 "shall reproach", Rom. 15:3; Jas. 1:5, "upbraideth"; (b) in the passive voice, "to suffer reproach, be reproached," 1 Tim. 4:10 (in some mss. in the 2nd part); 1 Pet. 4:14.

Evil *kakos* (2556), stands for "whatever is evil in character, base," in distinction (wherever the distinction is observable) from *poneros*, which indicates "what is evil in influence and effect, malignant." *Kakos* is the wider term and often covers the meaning of *poneros*. *Kakos* is antithetic to *kalos*, "fair, advisable, good in character," and to *agathos*, "beneficial, useful, good in act"; hence it denotes what is useless, incapable, bad; *poneros* is essentially antithetic to *chrestos*, "kind, gracious, serviceable"; hence it denotes what is destructive, injurious, evil. As evidence that *poneros* and *kakos* have much in common, though still not interchangeable, each is used of thoughts, cf. **Matt. 15:19** with Mark 7:21; of speech, **Matt. 5:11** with 1 Pet. 3:10; of actions, 2 Tim. 4:18 with 1 Thess. 5:15; of man, **Matt. 18:32** with **24:48**. The use of *kakos* may be broadly divided as follows: (a) of what is morally or ethically "evil," whether of persons, e.g., **Matt. 21:41**; **24:48**; Phil. 3:2; Rev. 2:2, or qualities, emotions, passions, deeds, e.g., Mark 7:21; John 18:23, 30; Rom. 1:30; 3:8; 7:19, 21; 13:4; 14:20; 16:19; 1 Cor. 13:5; 2 Cor. 13:7; 1 Thess. 5:15; 1 Tim. 6:10; 2 Tim. 4:14; 1 Pet. 3:9, 12; (b) of what is injurious, destructive, baneful, pernicious, e.g., Luke 16:25; Acts 16:28; 28:5; Titus 1:12; Jas. 3:8; Rev. 16:2, where *kakos* and *poneros* come in that order, "noisome and grievous."

poneros (4190), akin to *ponos*, "labor, toil," denotes "evil that causes labor, pain, sorrow, malignant evil"; it is used (a) with the meaning bad, worthless, in the physical sense, **Matt. 7:17-18**; in the moral or ethical sense, "evil," wicked; of persons, e.g., **Matt. 7:11**; Luke 6:45; Acts 17:5; 2 Thess. 3:2; 2 Tim. 3:13; of "evil" spirits, e.g., **Matt. 12:45**; Luke 7:21; Acts 19:12-13, 15-16; of a generation, **Matt. 12:39, 45**; **16:4**; Luke 11:29; of things, e.g., **Matt. 5:11**; **6:23**; **20:15**; Mark 7:22; Luke 11:34; John 3:19; 7:7; Acts 18:14; Gal. 1:4; Col. 1:21; 1 Tim. 6:4; 2 Tim. 4:18; Heb. 3:12; 10:22; Jas. 2:4; 4:16; 1 John 3:12; 2 John 11; 3 John 10; (b) with the meaning toilsome, painful, Eph. 5:16; 6:13; Rev. 16:2. Cf. *poneria*, "iniquity, wickedness." It is used, e.g., of thoughts, **Matt. 15:19** (cf. *kakos*, in Mark 7:21); of speech, **Matt. 5:11** (cf. *kakos*, in 1 Pet. 3:10); of acts, 2 Tim. 4:18. Where *kakos* and *poneros* are put together, *kakos* is always put first and signifies "bad in character, base," *poneros*, "bad in effect, malignant": see 1 Cor. 5:8, and Rev. 16:2. *Kakos* has a wider meaning, *poneros* a stronger meaning. *Poneros* alone is used of Satan and might well be translated "the malignant one," e.g., **Matt. 5:37** and five times in 1 John (2:13-14; 3:12; 5:18-19, RV); of demons, e.g., Luke 7:21. Once it is translated bad, **Matt. 22:10**.

See also ***Matthew 5:37***.

Falsely *pseudo* (5574), "to deceive by lies," is used in the middle voice, translated "to say ... falsely," in **Matt. 5:11**; it is elsewhere rendered "to lie," Acts 5:3-4; Rom. 9:1; 2 Cor. 11:31; Gal. 1:20; Col. 3:9; 1 Tim. 2:7.

5:12 Rejoice, and be exceeding glad: for great *is* your reward in heaven: for so persecuted they the prophets which were before you.

Rejoice *chairo* (5463), "to rejoice," is most frequently so translated. As to this verb, the following are grounds and occasions for "rejoicing," on the part of believers: in the Lord, Phil. 3:1; 4:4; His incarnation, Luke 1:14; His power, Luke 13:17; His presence with the Father, John 14:28; His presence with them, John 16:22; 20:20; His ultimate triumph, 8:56; hearing the gospel, Acts 13:48; their salvation, Acts 8:39; receiving the Lord, Luke 19:6; their enrollment in Heaven, Luke 10:20; their liberty in Christ, Acts 15:31; their hope, Rom. 12:12 (cf. Rom. 5:2; Rev. 19:7); their prospect of reward, **Matt. 5:12**; the obedience and godly conduct of fellow believers, Rom. 16:19, RV, "I rejoice" (KJV, "I am glad"); 2 Cor. 7:7, 9; 13:9; Col. 2:5; 1 Thess. 3:9; 2 John 4; 3 John 3; the proclamation of Christ, Phil. 1:18; the gospel harvest, John 4:36; suffering with Christ, Acts 5:41; 1 Pet. 4:13; suffering in the cause of the gospel, 2 Cor. 13:9 (1st part); Phil. 2:17 (1st part); Col. 1:24; in persecutions, trials and afflictions, **Matt. 5:12**; Luke 6:23; 2 Cor. 6:10; the manifestation of grace, Acts 11:23; meeting with fellow believers, 1 Cor. 16:17, RV, "I rejoice"; Phil. 2:28; receiving tokens of love and fellowship, Phil. 4:10; the "rejoicing" of others, Rom. 12:15; 2 Cor. 7:13; learning of the well-being of others, 2 Cor. 7:16.

Glad *agalliao* (21), "to exult, rejoice greatly," is chiefly used in the middle voice (active in Luke 1:47; some mss. have the passive in John 5:35, "to be made glad"). In the OT, it is found abundantly in the Psalms, from 2:11 onward to 149:2, 5 (Sept.). It conveys the idea of jubilant exultation, spiritual "gladness," **Matt. 5:12**, "be exceeding glad," the Lord's command to His disciples; Luke 1:47, in Mary's song; 10:21, of Christ's exultation ("rejoiced"); cf Acts 2:26, "(My tongue) was glad," KJV (RV, "rejoiced"); John 8:56, of Abraham; Acts 16:34, RV, "rejoiced greatly" (of the Philippian jailor); 1 Pet. 1:6, 8; 4:13 ("with exceeding joy"), of believers in general; in Rev. 19:7, RV, "be exceeding glad" (KJV, "rejoice").

Reward *misthos* (3408), primarily "wages, hire," and then, generally, "reward," (a) received in this life, **Matt. 5:46**; **6:2**, **5**, **16**; Rom. 4:4; 1 Cor. 9:17, 18; of evil "rewards," Acts 1:18; (b) to be received hereafter, **Matt. 5:12**; **10:41** (twice), 42; Mark 9:41; Luke 6:23, 35; 1 Cor. 3:8, 14; 2 John 8; Rev. 11:18; 22:12.

Prophets *prophetes* (4396), "one who speaks forth or openly", "a proclaimer of a divine message," denoted among the Greeks an interpreter of the oracles of the gods. In the Sept. it is the translation of the word *roeh*, "a seer"; 1 Sam. 9:9, indicating that the "prophet" was one who had immediate intercourse with God. It also translates the word *nabhi*, meaning "either one in whom the message from God springs forth" or "one to whom anything is secretly communicated." Hence, in general, "the prophet" was one upon whom the Spirit of God rested, Num. 11:17-29, one, to whom and through whom God speaks, Num. 12:2; Amos 3:7, 8. In the case of the OT prophets their messages were very largely the proclamation of the divine purposes of salvation and glory to be accomplished in the future; the "prophesying" of the NT "prophets" was both a preaching of the divine counsels of grace already accomplished and the foretelling of the purposes of God in the future. In the NT the word is used (a) of "the OT prophets," e.g., **Matt. 5:12**; Mark 6:15; Luke 4:27; John 8:52; Rom. 11:3; (b) of "prophets in general," e.g., **Matt. 10:41**; **21:46**; Mark 6:4; (c) of "John the Baptist," **Matt. 21:26**; Luke 1:76; (d) of "prophets in the churches," e.g., Acts 13:1; 15:32; 21:10; 1 Cor. 12:28, 29; 14:29, 32, 37; Eph. 2:20; 3:5; 4:11; (e) of "Christ, as the aforepromised Prophet," e.g., John 1:21; 6:14; 7:40; Acts 3:22; 7:37, or, without the article, and, without reference to the Old Testament, Mark 6:15; Luke 7:16; in Luke 24:19 it is used with *aner*, "a man"; John 4:19; 9:17; (f) of "two witnesses" yet to be raised up for special purposes, Rev. 11:10, 18; (g) of "the Cretan poet Epimenides," Titus 1:12; (h) by metonymy, of "the writings of prophets," e.g., Luke 24:27; Acts 8:28.

"The character which we find in the Beatitudes is, beyond all question, nothing less than our Lord's own character, put into words. It is the description set side by side with an example."

BILLY GRAHAM

5:13 Ye are the salt of the earth: but if the salt have lost his savour, wherewith shall it be salted? it is thenceforth good for nothing, but to be cast out, and to be trodden under foot of men.

Ye These are most frequently the translations of various inflections of a verb; sometimes of the article before a nominative used as a vocative, e.g., Rev. 18:20, "ye saints, and ye apostles, and ye prophets" (lit., "the saints, etc."). When the 2nd person plural pronouns are used separately from a verb, they are usually one or other of the forms of *humeis*, the plural of *su*, "thou," and are frequently emphatic, especially when they are subjects of the verb, an emphasis always to be noticed, e.g., **Matt. 5:13**, **14**, **48**; **6:9**, **19**, **20**; Mark 6:31, 37; John 15:27a; Rom. 1:6; 1 Cor. 3:17, 23; Gal. 3:28, 29a; Eph. 1:13a; 2:8; 2:11, 13; Phil. 2:18; Col. 3:4, 7a; 4:1; 1 Thess. 1:6; 2:10, 19, 20; 3:8; 2 Thess. 3:13; Jas. 5:8; 1 Pet. 2:9a; 1 John 2:20, 24 (1st and 3rd occurrences), 27a; 4:4; Jude 17, 20.

Salt *halas* (251), a late form of *hals* (found in some mss. in Mark 9:49), is used (a) literally in **Matt. 5:13** (2nd part); Mark 9:50 (1st part, twice); Luke 14:34 (twice); (b) metaphorically, of "believers," **Matt. 5:13** (1st part); of their "character and condition," Mark 9:50 (2nd part); of "wisdom" exhibited in their speech, Col.4:6. Being possessed of purifying, perpetuating and antiseptic qualities, "salt" became emblematic of fidelity and friendship among eastern nations. To eat of a person's "salt" and so to share his hospitality is still regarded thus among the Arabs. So in Scripture, it is an emblem of the covenant between God and His people, Num. 18:19; 2 Chron. 13:5; so again when the Lord says "Have salt in yourselves, and be at peace one with another" (Mark 9:50). In the Lord's teaching it is also symbolic of that spiritual health and vigor essential to Christian virtue and counteractive of the corruption that is in the world, e.g., **Matt. 5:13**, see (b) above. Food is seasoned with "salt"; every meal offering was to contain it, and it was to be offered with all offerings presented by Israelites, as emblematic of the holiness of Christ, and as betokening the reconciliation provided for man by God on the ground of the death of Christ, Lev. 2:13. To refuse God's provision in Christ and the efficacy of His expiatory sacrifice is to expose oneself to the doom of being "salted with fire," Mark 9:49. While "salt" is used to fertilize soil, excess of it on the ground produces sterility (e.g., Deut. 29:23; Judg. 9:45; Jer. 17:6; Zeph. 2:9).

Savour *moraino* (3471), primarily, "to be foolish," is used of salt that has lost its "savor," **Matt. 5:13**; Luke 14:34.

Salted *halizo* (233), signifies "to sprinkle" or "to season with salt," **Matt. 5:13**; Mark 9:49.

Thenceforth *eti* (2089), "yet, still, further," is rendered "thenceforth" in **Matt. 5:13**.

Good for nothing *ischuo* (2480), signifies (a) "to be strong in body, to be robust, in sound health," **Matt. 9:12**; Mark 2:17; (b) "to have power," as of the gospel, Acts 19:20; to prevail against, said of spiritual enemies, Rev. 12:8; of an evil spirit against exorcists, Acts 19:16; (c) "to be of force, to be effective, capable of producing results," **Matt. 5:13** ("it is good for nothing"; lit., "it availeth nothing"); Gal. 5:6; in Heb. 9:17 it apparently has the meaning "to be valid" (RV, "for doth it ever avail ...?", for KJV, "it is of no strength"). It is translated "avail" with reference to prayer, in Jas. 5:16; cf. the strengthened form *exischuo* in Eph. 3:18.

Nothing *ouden* (3762), the neuter of *oudeis*, "no one," occurs, e.g., in **Matt. 5:13**; **10:26**; **23:16**; adverbially, e.g., in **Matt. 27:24**; 2 Cor. 12:11 (1st part), "in nothing"; 1 Tim. 4:4; in the dative case, after *en*, "in," Phil. 1:20. Westcott and Hort adopt the spelling *outhen* in Luke 22:35; 23:14; Acts 15:9; 19:27; 26:26; 1 Cor. 13:2.

Trodden *katapateo* (2662), "to tread down, trample under foot," is used (a) literally, **Matt. 5:13**; **7:6**; Luke 8:5; 12:1; (b) metaphorically, of "treading under foot" the Son of God, Heb. 10:29, i.e., turning away from Him, to indulge in willful sin.

Men *see* Man at *Matthew 4:4.*

5:14 Ye are the light of the world. A city that is set on an hill cannot be hid.

Ye *see Matthew 5:13.*

Light *phos* (5457), akin to *phao*, "to give light" (from roots *pha*– and *phan*–, expressing "light as seen by the eye," and, metaphorically, as "reaching the mind," whence *phaino*, "to make to appear," *phaneros*, "evident," etc.); cf. Eng., "phosphorus" (lit., "light-bearing"). "Primarily light is a luminous emanation, probably of force, from certain bodies, which enables the eye to discern form and color. Light requires an organ adapted for its reception (**Matt. 6:22**). Where the eye is absent, or where it has become impaired from any cause, light is useless. Man, naturally, is incapable of receiving spiritual light inasmuch as he lacks the capacity for spiritual things, 1 Cor. 2:14. Hence believers are called 'sons of light,' Luke 16:8, not merely because they have received a revelation from God, but because in the New Birth they have received the spiritual capacity for it.

"Apart from natural phenomena, light is used in Scripture of (a) the glory of God's dwelling-place, 1 Tim. 6:16; (b) the nature of God, 1 John 1:5; (c) the impartiality of God, Jas. 1:17; (d) the favor of God, Ps. 4:6; of the King, Prov. 16:15; of an influential man, Job 29:24; (e) God, as the illuminator of His people, Isa. 60:19, 20; (f) the Lord Jesus as the illuminator of men, John 1:4, 5, 9; 3:19; 8:12; 9:5; 12:35, 36, 46; Acts 13:47; (g) the illuminating power of the Scriptures, Ps. 119:105; and of the judgments and commandments of God, Isa. 51:4; Prov. 6:23, cf. Ps. 43:3; (h) the guidance of God, Job 29:3; Ps. 112:4; Isa. 58:10; and, ironically, of the guidance of man, Rom. 2:19; (i) salvation, 1 Pet. 2:9; (j) righteousness, Rom. 13:12; 2 Cor. 11:14, 15; 1 John 2:9, 10; (k) witness for God, **Matt. 5:14, 16**; John 5:35; (l) prosperity and general well-being, Esth. 8:16; Job 18:18; Isa. 58:8-10."

World *kosmos* (2889), primarily "order, arrangement, ornament, adornment" (1 Pet. 3:3), is used to denote (a) the "earth," e.g., **Matt. 13:35**; John 21:25; Acts 17:24; Rom. 1:20 (probably here the universe: it had this meaning among the Greeks, owing to the order observable in it); 1 Tim. 6:7; Heb. 4:3; 9:26; (b) the "earth" in contrast with Heaven, 1 John 3:17 (perhaps also Rom. 4:13); (c) by metonymy, the "human race, mankind," e.g., **Matt. 5:14**; John 1:9 [here "that cometh (RV, 'coming') into the world" is said of Christ, not of "every man"; by His coming into the world He was the light for all men]; v. 10; 3:16, 17 (thrice), 19; 4:42, and frequently in Rom., 1 Cor. and 1 John; (d) "Gentiles" as distinguished from Jews, e.g., Rom. 11:12, 15, where the meaning is that all who will may be reconciled (cf. 2 Cor. 5:19); (e) the "present condition of human affairs," in alienation from and opposition to God, e.g., John 7:7; 8:23; 14:30; 1 Cor. 2:12; Gal. 4:3; 6:14; Col. 2:8; Jas. 1:27; 1 John 4:5 (thrice); 5:19; (f) the "sum of temporal possessions," **Matt. 16:26**; 1 Cor. 7:31 (1st part); (g) metaphorically, of the "tongue" as "a world (of iniquity)," Jas. 3:6, expressive of magnitude and variety.

Set *keimai* (2749), "to lie, to be laid" (used as the passive voice of *tithemi*), is translated "to be set," e.g., in **Matt. 5:14** (of a city); Luke 2:34 (of Christ); John 2:6 (of waterpots); 19:29 (of a vessel of vinegar); Phil. 1:16, RV (v. 17, KJV) (of the apostle Paul); Rev. 4:2 (of the throne in heaven).

Hill *oros* (3735), "a hill or mountain," is translated "hill" in **Matt. 5:14**; Luke 4:29; "mountain" in Luke 9:37, RV, KJV, "hill" (of the mount of transfiguration) as in v. 28.

Hid *krupto* (2928), "to cover, conceal, keep secret" (Eng., "crypt," "cryptic," etc.), is used (a) in its physical significance, e.g., **Matt. 5:14**; **13:44**; **25:18**; (b) metaphorically, e.g., **Matt. 11:25**; **13:35**, RV, "(things) hidden"; KJV, "(things) which have been kept secret"; Luke 18:34; 19:42; John 19:38, "secretly."

5:15 Neither do men light a candle, and put it under a bushel, but on a candlestick; and it giveth light unto all that are in the house.

Light *kaio* (2545), "to set fire to, to light"; in the passive voice, "to be lighted, to burn," **Matt. 5:15**; John 15:6; Heb. 12:18; Rev. 4:5; 8:8, 10; 19:20; 21:8; 1 Cor. 13:3, is used metaphorically of the heart, Luke 24:32; of spiritual light, Luke 12:35; John 5:35.

Candle *luchnos* (3088), frequently mistranslated "candle," is a portable "lamp" usually set on a stand; the word is used literally, **Matt. 5:15**; Mark 4:21; Luke 8:16; 11:33, 36; 15:8; Rev. 18:23; 22:5; (b) metaphorically, of Christ as the Lamb, Rev. 21:23, RV, "lamp" (KJV, "light"); of John the Baptist, John 5:35, RV, "the lamp" (KJV, "a ... light"); of the eye, **Matt. 6:22**, and Luke 11:34, RV, "lamp"; of spiritual readiness, Luke 12:35, RV, "lamps"; of "the word of prophecy," 2 Pet. 1:19, RV, "lamp."

Put *tithemi* (5087), "to place, lay, set, put," is translated "to put" in **Matt. 5:15**; **12:18**; in **Matt. 22:44**, RV, "put (underneath Thy feet)"; Mark 4:21 (1st part), in the 2nd part, RV, "put"; 10:16, KJV (RV, "laying"); Luke 8:16 (1st part); 2nd part, RV (KJV, "setteth"); 11:33; John 19:19; Acts 1:7, KJV (RV, "set"), 4:3, 5:18, 25; 12:4; Rom. 14:13; 1 Cor. 15:25; 2 Cor. 3:13; 1 Tim. 1:12, KJV (RV, "appointing"); Rev. 11:9, KJV (RV, "laid").

Bushel *modios* (3426), was a dry measure containing about a peck, **Matt. 5:15**; Mark 4:21; Luke 11:33.

Candlestick *luchnia* (3087), is mistranslated "candlestick" in every occurrence in the KJV and in certain places in the RV; the RV has "stand" in **Matt. 5:15**; Mark 4:21; Luke 8:16; 11:33; "candlestick" in Heb. 9:2; Rev. 1:12, 13, 20 (twice); 2:1, 5; 11:4, the RV marg., gives "lampstands" in the passages in Rev., but not in Heb. 9:2.

And *kai* Sometimes it has the consecutive meaning of "and so": e.g., **Matt. 5:15**, "and so it shineth"; Phil. 4:7, "and so the peace ..."; Heb. 3:19, "and so we see."

Light *lampo* (2989), "to shine as a torch," occurs in **Matt. 5:15, 16**; **17:2**; Luke 17:24; Acts 12:7; 2 Cor. 4:6 (twice).

House *see Matthew 2:11.*

5:16 Let your light so shine before men, that they may see your good works, and glorify your Father which is in heaven.

Light *see Matthew 5:14.*

"We have too many men of science, too few men of God. We have grasped the mystery of the atom, and rejected the Sermon on the Mount. The world has achieved brilliance without wisdom, power without conscience."

OMAR NELSON BRADLEY

Shine *see* **Light** at *Matthew 5:15.*

Before *emprocthen* (1715), is used of place or position only; adverbially, signifying "in front," Luke 19:28; Phil. 3:13; Rev. 4:6; as a preposition, e.g., **Matt. 5:24**; John 10:4; with the meaning "in the sight of a person," e.g., **Matt. 5:16**; **6:1**; **17:2**; Luke 19:27; John 12:37; 1 Thess. 2:19, RV, "before"; KJV, "in the presence of"; Rev. 19:10, RV, "before," especially in phrases signifying in the sight of God, as God wills, **Matt. 11:26**; **18:14** (lit., "a thing willed before your Father," RV, marg.); Luke 10:21; in the sense of "priority of rank or position or dignity," John 1:15, 30 (in some texts, v. 27); in an antagonistic sense, "against," **Matt. 23:13** (RV, marg., "before").

Men *see* **Man** at *Matthew 4:4.*

Works *ergon* (2041), denotes (I) "work, employment, task," e.g., Mark 13:34; John 4:34; 17:4; Acts 13:2; Phil. 2:30; 1 Thess. 5:13; in Acts 5:38 with the idea of enterprise; (II) "a deed, act," (a) of God, e.g., John 6:28, 29; 9:3; 10:37; 14:10; Acts 13:41; Rom. 14:20; Heb. 1:10; 2:7; 3:9; 4:3, 4, 10; Rev. 15:3; (b) of Christ, e.g., **Matt. 11:2**; especially in John, 5:36; 7:3, 21; 10:25, 32, 33, 38; 14:11, 12; 15:24; Rev. 2:26; (c) of believers, e.g., **Matt. 5:16**; Mark 14:6; Acts 9:36; Rom. 13:3; Col. 1:10; 1 Thess. 1:3, "work of faith," here the initial act of faith at conversion (turning to God, v. 9); in 2 Thess. 1:11, "*every* work of faith," RV, denotes every activity undertaken for Christ's sake; 2:17; 1 Tim. 2:10; 5:10; 6:18; 2 Tim. 2:21; 3:17; Titus 2:7, 14; 3:1, 8, 14; Heb. 10:24; 13:21; frequent in James, as the effect of faith [in 1:25, KJV, "(a doer) of the work," RV, "(a doer) that worketh"]; 1 Pet. 2:12; Rev. 2:2 and in several other places in chs. 2 and 3; 14:13; (d) of unbelievers, e.g., **Matt. 23:3**, **5**; John 7:7; Acts 7:41 (for idols); Rom. 13:12; Eph. 5:11; Col. 1:21; Titus 1:16 (1st part); 1 John 3:12; Jude 15, RV; Rev. 2:6, RV; of those who seek justification by works, e.g., Rom. 9:32; Gal. 3:10; Eph. 2:9; described as the works of the law, e.g., Gal. 2:16; 3:2, 5; dead works, Heb. 6:1; 9:14; (e) of Babylon, Rev. 18:6; (f) of the Devil, John 8:41; 1 John 3:8.

Glorify *doxazo* (1392), primarily denotes "to suppose" (from *doxa*, "an opinion"); in the NT (a) "to magnify, extol, praise" (see *doxa* below), especially of "glorifying"; God, i.e., ascribing honor to Him, acknowledging Him as to His being, attributes and acts, i.e., His glory, e.g., **Matt. 5:16**; **9:8**; **15:31**; Rom. 15:6, 9; Gal. 1:24; 1 Pet. 4:16; the Word of the Lord, Acts 13:48; the Name of the Lord, Rev. 15:4; also of "glorifying" oneself, John 8:54; Rev. 18:7; (b) "to do honor to, to make glorious," e.g., Rom. 8:30; 2 Cor. 3:10; 1 Pet. 1:8, "full of glory," passive voice (lit., "glorified"); said of Christ, e.g., John 7:39; 8:54, RV, "glorifieth," for KJV, "honor" and "honoreth" (which would translate *timao*, "to honor"); of the Father, e.g., John 13:31, 32; 21:19; 1 Pet. 4:11; of "glorifying" one's ministry, Rom. 11:13, RV, "glorify" (KJV, "magnify"); of a member of the body, 1 Cor. 12:26, "be honored" (RV marg., "be glorified").

Heaven *ouranos* (3772), probably akin to *ornumi*, "to lift, to heave," is used in the NT (a) of "the aerial heavens," e.g., **Matt. 6:26**; **8:20**; Acts 10:12; 11:6 (RV, "heaven," in each place, KJV, "air"); Jas. 5:18; (b) "the sidereal," e.g., **Matt. 24:29**, **35**; Mark 13:25, 31; Heb. 11:12, RV, "heaven," KJV, "sky"; Rev. 6:14; 20:11; they, (a) and (b), were created by the Son of God, Heb. 1:10, as also by God the Father, Rev. 10:6; (c) "the eternal dwelling place of God," **Matt. 5:16**; **12:50**; Rev. 3:12; 11:13; 16:11; 20:9. From thence the Son of God descended to become incarnate, John 3:13, 31; 6:38, 42. In His ascension Christ "passed through the heavens," Heb. 4:14, RV; He "ascended far above all the heavens," Eph. 4:10, and was "made higher than the heavens," Heb. 7:26; He "sat down on the right hand of the throne of the Majesty in the heavens," Heb. 8:1; He is "on the right hand of God," having gone into heaven, 1 Pet. 3:22. Since His ascension it is the scene of His present life and activity, e.g., Rom. 8:34; Heb. 9:24. From thence the Holy Spirit descended at Pentecost, 1 Pet. 1:12. It is the abode of the angels, e.g., **Matt. 18:10**; **22:30**; cf. Rev. 3:5. Thither Paul was "caught up," whether in the body or out of the body, he knew not, 2 Cor. 12:2. It is to be the eternal dwelling place of the saints in resurrection glory, 2 Cor. 5:1. From thence Christ will descend to the air to receive His saints at the Rapture, 1 Thess. 4:16; Phil. 3:20, 21, and will subsequently come with His saints and with His holy angels at His second advent, **Matt. 24:30**; 2 Thess. 1:7. In the present life "heaven" is the region of the spiritual citizenship of believers, Phil. 3:20. The present "heavens," with the earth, are to pass away, 2 Pet. 3:10, "being on fire," v. 12 (see v. 7); Rev. 20:11, and new "heavens" and earth are to be created, 2 Pet. 3:13; Rev. 21:1, with Isa. 65:17, e.g.

5:17 Think not that I am come to destroy the law, or the prophets: I am not come to destroy, but to fulfil.

Think *nomizo* (3543), "to consider, suppose, think," is rendered "to suppose" in **Matt. 20:10**; Luke 2:34; 3:23; Acts 7:25; 14:19; 16:27; 21:29; 1 Tim. 6:5; in 1 Cor. 7:26, KJV (RV, "I think"); in Acts 16:13, the RV adheres to the meaning "to suppose," "(where) we supposed (there was a place of prayer)"; this word also signifies "to practice a custom" (*nomos*) and is commonly so used by Greek writers. Hence the KJV, "was wont (to be made)"; it is rendered "to think" in **Matt. 5:17**; **10:34**; Acts 8:20; 17:29; 1 Cor. 7:36.

Destroy *kataluo* (2647), "to destroy utterly, to overthrow completely," is rendered "destroy," in **Matt. 5:17**, twice, of the Law; **Matt. 24:2**; **26:61**; **27:40**; Mark 13:2; 14:58; 15:29; Luke 21:6, of the Temple; in Acts 6:14, of Jerusalem; in Gal. 2:18, of the Law as a means of justification; in Rom. 14:20 (KJV, "destroy," RV, "overthrow"), of the marring of a person's spiritual well-being (in v. 15 *apollumi*, is used in the same sense); in Acts 5:38 and 39 (RV, "overthrow") of the failure of purposes; in 2 Cor. 5:1, of the death of the body ("dissolved").

Law *nomos* (3551), akin to *nemo*, "to divide out, distribute," primarily meant "that which is assigned"; hence, "usage, custom," and then, "law, law as prescribed by custom, or by statute"; the word *ethos*, "custom," was retained for unwritten "law," while *nomos* became the established name for "law" as decreed by a state and set up as the standard for the administration of justice. In the NT it is used:

(a) of "law" in general, e.g., Rom. 2:12, 13, "a law" (RV), expressing a general principle relating to "law"; v. 14, last part; 3:27, "By what manner of law?" i.e., "by what sort of principle (has the glorying been excluded)?"; 4:15 (last part); 5:13, referring to the period between Adam's trespass and the giving of the Law; 7:1 (1st part, RV marg., "law"); against those graces which constitute the fruit of the Spirit "there is no law," Gal. 5:23 ...

(c) of the Mosaic Law, the "law" of Sinai, (1) with the definite article, e.g., **Matt. 5:18**; John 1:17; Rom. 2:15, 18, 20, 26, 27; 3:19; 4:15; 7:4, 7, 14, 16, 22; 8:3, 4, 7; Gal. 3:10, 12, 19, 21, 24; 5:3; Eph. 2:15; Phil. 3:6; 1 Tim. 1:8; Heb. 7:19; Jas. 2:9; (2) without the article, thus stressing the Mosaic Law in its quality as "law," e.g., Rom. 2:14 (1st part); 5:20; 7:9, where the stress in the quality lies in this, that "the commandment which was unto (i.e., which he thought would be a means of) life," he found to be "unto (i.e., to have the effect of revealing his actual state of) death"; 10:4; 1 Cor. 9:20; Gal. 2:16, 19, 21; 3:2, 5, 10 (1st part), 11, 18, 23; 4:4, 5, 21 (1st part); 5:4, 18; 6:13; Phil. 3:5, 9; Heb. 7:16; 9:19; Jas. 2:11; 4:11; (in regard to the statement in Gal. 2:16, that "a man is not justified by the works of the Law," the absence of the article before *nomos* indicates the assertion of a principle, "by obedience to law," but evidently the Mosaic Law is in view. Here the apostle is maintaining that submission to circumcision entails the obligation to do the whole "Law." Circumcision belongs to the ceremonial part of the "Law," but, while the Mosaic Law is actually divisible into the ceremonial and the moral, no such distinction is made or even assumed in Scripture. The statement maintains the freedom of the believer from the "law" of Moses in its totality as a means of justification);

(d) by metonymy, of the books which contain the "law," (1) of the Pentateuch, e.g., **Matt. 5:17**; **12:5**; Luke 16:16; 24:44; John 1:45; Rom. 3:21; Gal. 3:10; (2) of the Psalms, John 10:34; 15:25; of the Psalms, Isaiah, Ezekiel and Daniel, 12:34, the Psalms and Isaiah, Rom. 3:19 (with vv. 10-18); Isaiah, 1 Cor. 14:21; from all this it may be inferred that "the law" in the most comprehensive sense was an alternative title to "The Scriptures."

The following phrases specify "laws" of various kinds; (a) "the law of Christ," Gal. 6:2, i.e., either given by Him (as in the Sermon on the Mount and in John 13:14, 15; 15:4), or the "law" or principle by which Christ Himself lived (**Matt. 20:28**; John 13:1); these are not actual alternatives, for the "law" imposed by Christ was always that by which He Himself lived in the "days of His flesh." He confirmed the "Law" as being of divine authority (cf. **Matt. 5:18**); yet He presented a higher standard of life than perfunctory obedience to the current legal rendering of the "Law," a standard which, without annulling the "Law," He embodied in His own character and life (see, e.g., **Matt. 5:21-48**; this breach with legalism is especially seen in regard to the ritual or ceremonial part of the "Law" in its wide scope); He showed Himself superior to all human interpretations of it; (b) "a law of faith," Rom. 3:27, i.e., a principle which demands only faith on man's part; (c) "the law of my mind," Rom. 7:23, that principle which governs the new nature in virtue of the new birth; (d) "the law of sin," Rom. 7:23, the principle by which sin exerts its influence and power despite the desire to do what is right; "of sin and death," 8:2, death being the effect; (e) "the law of liberty," Jas. 1:25; 2:12, a term comprehensive of all the Scriptures, not a "law" of compulsion enforced from without, but meeting with ready obedience through the desire and delight of the renewed being who is subject to it; into it he looks, and in its teaching he delights; he is "under law (*ennomos*, "in law," implying union and subjection) to Christ," 1 Cor. 9:21; cf, e.g., Ps. 119:32, 45, 97; 2 Cor. 3:17; (f) "the royal law," Jas. 2:8, i.e., the "law" of love, royal in the majesty of its power, the "law" upon which all others hang, **Matt. 22:34-40**; Rom. 13:8; Gal. 5:14.

5:18 For verily I say unto you, Till heaven and earth pass, one jot or one tittle shall in no wise pass from the law, till all be fulfilled.

Earth *ge* (1093), denotes (a) "earth as arable land," e.g., **Matt. 13:5, 8, 23**; in 1 Cor. 15:47 it is said of the "earthly" material of which "the first man" was made, suggestive of frailty; (b) "the earth as a whole, the world," in contrast, whether to the heavens, e.g., **Matt. 5:18, 35**, or to heaven, the abode of God, e.g., **Matt. 6:19**, where the context suggests the "earth" as a place characterized by mutability and weakness; in Col. 3:2 the same contrast is presented by the word "above"; in John 3:31 (RV, "of the earth," for KJV, "earthly") it describes one whose origin and nature are "earthly" and whose speech is characterized thereby, in contrast with Christ as the One from heaven; in Col. 3:5 the physical members are said to be "upon the earth," as a sphere where, as potential instruments of moral evils, they are, by metonymy, spoken of as the evils themselves; (c) "the inhabited earth," e.g., Luke 21:35; Acts 1:8; 8:33; 10:12; 11:6; 17:26; 22:22; Heb. 11:13; Rev. 13:8. In the following the phrase "on the earth" signifies "among men," Luke 12:49; 18:8; John 17:4, (d) "a country, territory," e.g., Luke 4:25; John 3:22; (e) "the ground," e.g., **Matt. 10:29**; Mark 4:26, RV, "(upon the) earth," for KJV, "(into the) ground"; (f) "land," e.g., Mark 4:1; John 21:8-9, 11. Cf. Eng. words beginning with *ge*–, e.g., "geodetic," "geodesy," "geology," "geometry," "geography."

Pass *parerchomai* (3928), from *para*, "by," *erchomai*, "to come" or "go," denotes (I), literally, "to pass, pass by," (a) of persons, **Matt. 8:28**; Mark 6:48; Luke 18:37; Acts 16:8; (b) of things, **Matt. 26:39, 42**; of time, **Matt. 14:15**; Mark 14:35; Acts 27:9, KJV, "past" (RV, "gone by"); 1 Pet. 4:3; (II), metaphorically, (a) "to pass away, to perish," **Matt. 5:18; 24:34, 35**; Mark 13:30, 31; Luke 16:17; 21:32, 33; 2 Cor. 5:17; Jas. 1:10; 2 Pet. 3:10; (b) "to pass by, disregard, neglect, pass over," Luke 11:42; 15:29, "transgressed." For the meaning "to come forth or come," see Luke 12:37; 17:7, RV (Acts 24:7 in some mss.).

Jot *iota* (2503), from the Heb. *uod*, the smallest Hebrew letter, is mentioned by the Lord in **Matt. 5:18** (together with *keraia*, "a little horn, a tittle, the point or extremity" which distinguishes certain Hebrew letters from others), to express the fact that not a single item of the Law will pass away or remain unfulfilled.

Tittle *keraia* or *kerea* (2762), "a little horn" (*keras*, "a horn"), was used to denote the small stroke distinguishing one Hebrew letter from another. The rabbis attached great importance to these; hence the significance of the Lord's statements in **Matt. 5:18** and Luke 16:17, charging the Pharisees with hypocrisy, because, while professing the most scrupulous reverence to the Law, they violated its spirit. Grammarians used the word to denote the accents in Greek words.

Law *see Matthew 5:17.*

Fulfilled *ginomai*, "to become, to take place," is rendered "fulfilled" in the KJV of **Matt. 5:18; 24:34**; Luke 21:32, RV, "accomplished," in each place.

5:19 Whosoever therefore shall break one of these least commandments, and shall teach men so, he shall be called the least in the kingdom of heaven: but whosoever shall do and teach *them*, the same shall be called great in the kingdom of heaven.

Break *luo* (3089), "to loosen," especially by way of deliverance, sometimes has the meaning of "breaking, destructively," e.g., of "breaking" commandments, not only infringing them, but loosing the force of them, rendering them not binding, **Matt. 5:19**; John 5:18; of "breaking" the Law of Moses, John 7:23; Scripture, John 10:35; of the "breaking up" of a ship, Acts

27:41; of the "breaking down" of the middle wall of partition, Eph. 2:14; of the marriage tie, 1 Cor. 7:27.

Commandments *entole* (1785), denotes, in general, "an injunction, charge, precept, commandment." It is the most frequent term, and is used of moral and religious precepts, e.g., **Matt. 5:19**; it is frequent in the Gospels, especially that of John, and in his Epistles. See also, e.g., Acts 17:15; Rom. 7:8-13; 13:9; 1 Cor. 7:19; Eph. 2:15; Col. 4:10.

He *houtos* (3778), "this, this person here," is always emphatic; it is used with this meaning, sometimes to refer to what precedes, e.g., **Matt. 5:19**, "he (shall be called great)"; John 6:46, "he (hath seen)"; often rendered "this," e.g., Rom. 9:9, or "this man," e.g., **Matt. 27:58**, RV; Jas. 1:25; "the same," e.g., Luke 9:48.

Least *see Matthew 2:6.*

5:20 For I say unto you, That except your righteousness shall exceed *the righteousness* of the scribes and Pharisees, ye shall in no case enter into the kingdom of heaven.

Righteousness *see Matthew 3:15.*

Exceed *perisseuo* (4052), is used intransitively (a) "of exceeding a certain number, or measure, to be over, to remain," of the fragments after feeding the multitude (cf. *perisseuma*), Luke 9:17; John 6:12-13; "to exist in abundance"; as of wealth, Luke 12:15; 21:4; of food, 15:17 ...

(c) "to be abundantly furnished, to abound in a thing," as of material benefits, Luke 12:15; Phil. 4:18 of spiritual gifts; 1 Cor. 14:12, or "to be pre-eminent, to excel, to be morally better off," as regards partaking of certain meats; 1 Cor. 8:8, "are we the better", "to abound" in hope, Rom. 15:13; the work of the Lord, 1 Cor. 15:58; faith and grace, 2 Cor. 8:7; thanksgiving, Col. 2:7; walking so as to please God, Phil. 1:9; 1 Thess. 4:1, 10; of righteousness, **Matt. 5:20**; of the Gospel, as the ministration of righteousness, 2 Cor. 3:9, "exceed."

It is used transitively, in the sense of "to make to abound," e.g., to provide a person richly so that he has "abundance," as of spiritual truth, **Matt. 13:12**; the right use of what God has entrusted to us, **25:29**; the power of God in conferring grace, 2 Cor. 9:8; Eph. 1:8; to "make abundant" or to cause to excel, as of the effect of grace in regard to thanksgiving, 2 Cor. 4:15; His power to make us "to abound" in love, 1 Thess. 3:12.

pleion (4119), the comparative of *polus*, is used (a) as an adjective, "greater, more," e.g., Acts 15:28; (b) as a noun, e.g., **Matt. 12:41**, "a greater (than Jonah)"; v. **42**, "a greater (than Solomon)" or with a noun understood, e.g., **Matt. 20:10**; Mark 12:43; Acts 19:32 and 27:12, "the more part"; 1 Cor. 9:19; in these instances the neuter *pleion*, "something greater," is "a fixed or stereotyped form" of the word; in 1 Cor. 15:6, "the greater part" (masculine plural); (c) as an adverb, e.g., **Matt. 5:20**, lit., "(except your righteousness abound) more greatly (than of scribes and Pharisees)"; so **26:53**, "more"; Luke 9:13.

Case In **Matt. 5:20** the strong double negative *ou me* is translated "in no case" (KJV): RV, "in no wise."

5:21 Ye have heard that it was said by them of old time, Thou shalt not kill; and whosoever shall kill shall be in danger of the judgment:

Old *archaios* (744), "original, ancient" (from *arche*, "a beginning": Eng., "archaic," "archaeology," etc.), is used (a) of persons belonging to a former age, "(to) them of old time," **Matt. 5:21, 33**, RV; in some mss. v. **27**; the RV rendering is right; not ancient teachers are in view; what was said to them of old time was "to be both recognized in its significance and estimated in its temporary limitations, Christ intending His words to be regarded not as an abrogation, but a deepening and fulfilling" (Cremer); of prophets, Luke 9:8, 19; (b) of time long gone by, Acts 15:21; (c) of days gone by in a person's experience, Acts 15:7, "a good while ago," lit., "from old (days)," i.e., from the first days onward in the sense of originality, not age; (d) of Mnason, "an early disciple," Acts 21:16, RV, not referring to age, but to his being one of the first who had accepted the gospel from the beginning of its proclamation; (e) of things which are "old" in relation to the new, earlier things in contrast to things present, 2 Cor. 5:17, i.e., of what characterized and conditioned the time previous to conversion in a believer's experience, RV, "they are become new," i.e., they have taken on a new complexion and are viewed in an entirely different way; (f) of the world (i.e., the inhabitants of the world) just previous to the Flood, 2 Pet. 2:5; (g) of the Devil, as "that old serpent," Rev. 12:9; 20:2, "old," not in age, but as characterized for a long period by the evils indicated.

Kill *phoneuo* (5407), "to murder," akin to *phoneus*, "a murderer," is always rendered by the verb "to kill" (except in **Matt. 19:18**, KJV, "do ... murder," and in **Matt. 23:35**, KJV and RV, "ye slew"); **Matt. 5:21** (twice); **23:31**; Mark 10:19; Luke 18:20; Rom. 13:9; Jas. 2:11 (twice); 4:2; 5:6.

Danger *enochos* (1777), lit., "held in, contained in" (*en*, "in," *echo*, "to have, hold"), hence, "bound under obligation to, liable to, subject to," is used in the sense of being in "danger" of the penal effect of a misdeed, i.e., in a forensic sense, signifying the connection of a person with (a) his crime, "guilty of an eternal sin," Mark 3:29, RV; (b) the trial or tribunal, as a result of which sentence is passed, **Matt. 5:21-22**, "the judgment," "the council"; *enochos* here has the obsolete sense of control (J. Hastings); (c) the penalty itself, **5:22**, "the hell of fire," and, with the translation "worthy" (KJV, "guilty"), of the punishment determined to be inflicted on Christ, **Matt. 26:66** and Mark 14:64, "death"; (d) the person or thing against whom or which the offense is committed, 1 Cor. 11:27, "guilty," the crime being against "the body and blood of the Lord"; Jas. 2:10, "guilty" of an offense against all the Law, because of a breach of one commandment.

Judgment *krisis* (2920), (a) denotes "the process of investigation, the act of distinguishing and separating"; hence "a judging, a passing of judgment upon a person or thing"; it has a variety of meanings, such as judicial authority, John 5:22, 27; justice, Acts 8:33; Jas. 2:13; a tribunal, **Matt. 5:21-22**; a trial, John 5:24; 2 Pet. 2:4; a judgment, 2 Pet. 2:11; Jude 9; by metonymy, the standard of judgment, just dealing, **Matt. 12:18**, **20**; **23:23**; Luke 11:42; divine judgment executed, 2 Thess. 1:5; Rev. 16:7; (b) sometimes it has the meaning "condemnation," and is virtually equivalent to *krima* (a); see **Matt. 23:33**; John 3:19; Jas. 5:12, *hupo krisin*, "under judgment." *See also* **Law** at ***Matthew 5:17.***

5:22 But I say unto you, That whosoever is angry with his brother without a cause shall be in danger of the judgment: and whosoever shall say to his brother, Raca, shall be in danger of the council: but whosoever shall say, Thou fool, shall be in danger of hell fire.

Angry *orgizo* (3710), "to provoke, to arouse to anger," is used in the middle voice in the eight places where it is found, and signifies "to be angry, wroth." It is said of individuals, in **Matt. 5:22**; **18:34**; **22:7**; Luke 14:21; 15:28, and Eph. 4:26 (where a possible meaning is "be ye angry with yourselves"); of nations, Rev. 11:18; of Satan as the Dragon, 12:17

Brother Any man, a neighbor, Luke 10:29; **Matt. 5:22**; **7:3**.

Cause *eike*, "in vain," "without a cause," **Matt. 5:22** (KJV), is absent from the most authentic mss.

Danger *see* ***Matthew 5:21.***

Raca *raka* (4469), is an Aramaic word akin to the Heb. *req*, "empty," the first *a* being due to a Galilean change. In the KJV of 1611 it was spelled *racha*; in the edition of 1638, *raca*. It was a word of utter contempt, signifying "empty," intellectually rather than morally, "empty-headed," like Abimelech's hirelings, Judg. 9:4, and the "vain" man of Jas. 2:20. As condemned by Christ, **Matt. 5:22**, it was worse than being angry, inasmuch as an outrageous utterance is worse than a feeling unexpressed or somewhat controlled in expression; it does not indicate such a loss of self-control as the word rendered "fool," a godless, moral reprobate.

Fool *moros* (3474), primarily denotes "dull, sluggish" (from a root *muh*, "to be silly"); hence, "stupid, foolish"; it is used (a) of persons, **Matt. 5:22**, "Thou fool"; here the word means morally worthless, a scoundrel, a more serious reproach than "Raca"; the latter scorns a man's mind and calls him stupid; *moros* scorns his heart and character; hence the Lord's more severe condemnation; in **7:26**, "a foolish man"; **23:17**, **19**, "fools"; **25:2**, **3**, **8**, "foolish"; in 1 Cor. 3:18, "a fool"; the apostle Paul uses it of himself and his fellow workers, in 4:10, "fools" (i.e., in the eyes of opponents); (b) of things, 2 Tim. 2:23, "foolish and ignorant questionings"; so Titus 3:9; in 1 Cor. 1:25, "the foolishness of God," not *moria*, "foolishness" as a personal quality, but adjectivally, that which is considered by the ignorant as a "foolish" policy or mode of dealing, lit., "the foolish (thing)"; so in v. 27, "the foolish (things) of the world."

Hell *geenna* (1067), represents the Hebrew Ge-Hinnom (the valley of Tophet) and a corresponding Aramaic word; it is found twelve times in the NT, eleven of which are in the Synoptists, in every instance as uttered by the Lord Himself. He who says to his brother, Thou fool, will be in danger of "the hell of fire," **Matt. 5:22**; it is better to pluck out (a metaphorical description of irrevocable law) an eye that causes its possessor to stumble, than that his "whole body be cast into hell," v. **29**; similarly with the hand, v. **30**; in **Matt. 18:8**, **9**, the admonitions are repeated, with an additional mention of the foot; here, too, the warning concerns the person himself (for which obviously the "body" stands in chapt. **5**); in v. **8**, "the eternal fire" is mentioned as the doom, the character of the region standing for the region itself, the two being combined in the phrase "the hell of fire," v. **9**. To the passage in **Matt. 18**, that in Mark 9:43-47, is parallel; here to the word "hell" are applied the extended descriptions "the unquenchable fire" and "where their worm dieth not and the fire is not quenched." That God, "after He hath killed, hath power to cast into hell," is assigned as a reason why He should be feared with the fear that keeps from evil doing, Luke 12:5; the parallel passage to this in **Matt. 10:28** declares, not the casting in, but the doom which follows, namely, the destruction (not the loss of being, but of well-being) of "both soul and body." In **Matt. 23** the Lord denounces the scribes and Pharisees, who in proselytizing a person "make him two-fold more a son of hell" than themselves (v. **15**), the phrase here being expressive of moral characteristics, and declares the impossibility of their escaping "the judgment of hell," v. **33**. In Jas. 3:6 "hell" is described as the source of the evil done by misuse of the tongue; here the word stands for the powers of darkness, whose characteristics and destiny are those of "hell." For terms descriptive of "hell," see, e.g., **Matt. 13:42; 25:46**; Phil. 3:19; 2 Thess. 1:9; Heb. 10:39; 2 Pet. 2:17; Jude 13; Rev. 2:11; 19:20; 20:6, 10, 14; 21:8.

Fire *see Matthew 3:11.*

5:23 Therefore if thou bring thy gift to the altar, and there rememberest that thy brother hath ought against thee;

Bring *prosphero* (4374), means (a) "to bring (in addition)," **Matt. 25:20**; "to bring unto," **Matt. 5:23** (RV, "art offering"); Mark 10:13; (b) to offer, **Matt. 5:24**.

Gift *see* Gifts at *Matthew 2:11.*

Altar *thuciasterion* (2379), probably the neuter of the adjective *thuciaterioc*, is derived from *thuciazo*, "to sacrifice." Accordingly it denotes an "altar" for the sacrifice of victims, though it was also used for the "altar" of incense, e.g., Luke 1:11. In the NT this word is reserved for the "altar" of the true God, **Matt. 5:23-24; 23:18-20, 35**; Luke 11:51; 1 Cor. 9:13; 10:18, in contrast to *bomos*. In the Sept. *thuciasterion* is mostly, but not entirely, used for the divinely appointed altar; it is used for idol "altars," e.g., in Judg. 2:2; 6:25; 2 Kings 16:10.

Hath *see* Had at *Matthew 3:4.*

5:24 Leave there thy gift before the altar, and go thy way; first be reconciled to thy brother, and then come and offer thy gift.

Leave *see* Leaveth at *Matthew 4:11.*

Gift *see* Gifts at *Matthew 2:11.*

Before *see Matthew 5:16.*

Reconciled *katallasso* (2644), properly denotes "to change, exchange" (especially of money); hence, of persons, "to change from enmity to friendship, to reconcile." With regard to the relationship between God and man, the use of this and connected words shows that primarily "reconciliation" is what God accomplishes, exercising His grace towards sinful man on the ground of the death of Christ in propitiatory sacrifice under the judgment due to sin, 2 Cor. 5:19, where both the verb and the noun are used. By reason of this men in their sinful condition and alienation from God are invited to be "reconciled" to Him; that is to say, to change their attitude, and accept the provision God has made, whereby their sins can be remitted and they themselves be justified in His sight in Christ...

When the writers of the NT speak upon the subject of the wrath of God, "the hostility is represented not as on the part of God, but of man. And this is the reason why the apostle never uses *diallasso* [a word used only in **Matt. 5:24**, in the NT] in this connection, but always *katallasso*, because the former word denotes mutual concession after mutual hostility [frequently exemplified in the Sept.], an idea absent from *katallasso*" (Lightfoot, *Notes on the Epistles of Paul*, p. 288).

Offer *see* Bring at *Matthew 5:23.*

5:25 Agree with thine adversary quickly, whiles thou art in the way with him; lest at any time the adversary deliver thee to the judge, and the judge deliver thee to the officer, and thou be cast into prison.

Agree *eunoeo* (2132), lit., "to be well-minded, well-disposed" (*eu*, "well," *nous*, "the mind"), is found in **Matt. 5:25**, "agree with."

Adversary *antidikos* (476), firstly, "an opponent in a lawsuit," **Matt. 5:25** (twice); Luke 12:58; 18:3, is also used to denote "an adversary or an enemy," without reference to legal affairs, and this is perhaps its meaning in 1 Pet. 5:8, where it is used of the Devil. Some would regard the word as there used in a legal sense, since the Devil accuses men before God.

Quickly *tachu* (5035), the neuter of *tachus*, "swift, quick," signifies "quickly," **Matt. 5:25; 28:7, 8**; Mark 9:39, RV (KJV, "lightly"); Luke 15:22; John 11:29; Rev. 2:16 (v. 5 in some mss.); 3:11; 11:14; 22:7, 12, 20.

Whiles The conjunction *heos*, "until," etc., has the meaning "while" in **Matt. 14:22**; Mark 6:45; 14:32; in some texts, John 9:4; 12:35, 36; with *hotou*, "whatever" (an oblique case, neuter, of *hostis*, "whoever"), "whiles," **Matt. 5:25**.

Lest *see Matthew 4:6.*

Judge *krites* (2923), "a judge" (from *krino*), is used (a) of God, Heb. 12:23, where the order in the original is "to a Judge who is God of all"; this is really the significance; it suggests that He who is the Judge of His people is at the same time their God; that is the order in 10:30; the word is also used of God in Jas. 4:12, RV; (b) of Christ, Acts 10:42; 2 Tim. 4:8; Jas. 5:9; (c) of a ruler in Israel in the times of the Judges, Acts 13:20; (d) of a Roman procurator, Acts 24:10; (e) of those whose conduct provides a standard of "judging," **Matt. 12:27**; Luke 11:19; (f) in the forensic sense, of one who tries and decides a case, **Matt. 5:25** (twice); Luke 12:14; 12:58 (twice); 18:2; 18:6 (lit., "the judge of unnghteousness," expressing subjectively his character); Acts 18:15; (g) of one who passes, or arrogates to himself, judgment on anything, Jas. 2:4 (see the RV); 4:11.

Officer *huperetes* (5257), is translated "officer," with the following applications, (a) to a magistrate's attendant, **Matt. 5:25**; (b) to officers of the synagogue, or officers or bailiffs of the Sanhedrin, **Matt. 26:58**; Mark 14:54, 65; John 7:32, 45-46; 18:3, 12, 18, 22; 19:6; Acts 5:22, 26.

5:26 Verily I say unto thee, Thou shalt by no means come out thence, till thou hast paid the uttermost farthing.

Means The double negative *ou me*, i.e., "no not," "not at all," is translated "by no means," **Matt. 5:26**; in Luke 10:19, "by any means," KJV (RV, "in any wise"); Luke 12:59, RV, "by no means" (KJV, "not").

Thence *see Matthew 4:21.*

Paid *apodidomi* (591), signifies "to give up or back, to restore, return, render what is due, to pay, give an account," e.g., of an account. **Matt. 5:26**; **12:36**; Luke 16:2; Acts. 19:40; Heb. 13:17; 1 Pet. 4:5; of wages, etc., e.g., **Matt. 18:25-34**; **20:8**; of conjugal duty, 1 Cor. 7:3; of a witness, Acts 4:33; frequently of recompensing or rewarding, 1 Tim. 5:4; 2 Tim. 4:8, 14; 1 Pet. 3:9; Rev. 18:6; 22:12. In the middle voice it is used of "giving" up what is one's own; hence, "to sell," Acts 5:8; 7:9; Heb. 12:16.

Uttermost *eschatos* (2078), "last, utmost, extreme," is used (a) of place, e.g., Luke 14:9, 10, "lowest;" Acts 1:8 and 13:47, "uttermost part;" (b) of rank, e.g., Mark 9:35; (c) of time, relating either to persons or things, e.g., **Matt. 5:26**, "the last (farthing)," RV (KJV, "uttermost"); **Matt. 20:8**, **12**, **14**; Mark 12:6, 22; 1 Cor. 4:9, of apostles as "last" in the program of a spectacular display; 1 Cor. 15:45, "the last Adam"; Rev. 2:19; of the "last" state of persons, **Matt. 12:45**, neuter plural, lit., "the last (things)"; so Luke 11:26; 2 Pet. 2:20, RV, "the last state" (KJV, "the latter end"); of Christ as the Eternal One, Rev. 1:17 (in some mss. v. 11); 2:8; 22:13; in eschatological phrases as follows: (a) "the last day," a comprehensive term including both the time of the resurrection of the redeemed, John 6:39, 40, 44, 54 and 11:24, and the ulterior time of the judgment of the unregenerate, at the Great White Throne, John 12:48; (b) "the last days," Acts 2:17, a period relative to the supernatural manifestation of the Holy Spirit at Pentecost and the resumption of the divine interpositions in the affairs of the world at the end of the present age, before "the great and notable Day of the Lord," which will usher in the messianic kingdom; (c) in 2 Tim. 3:1, "the last days" refers to the close of the present age of world conditions; (d) in Jas. 5:3, the phrase "in the last days" (RV) refers both to the period preceding the Roman overthrow of the city and the land in AD 70, and to the closing part of the age in consummating acts of gentile persecution including "the time of Jacob's trouble" (cf. verses 7, 8); (e) in 1 Pet. 1:5, "the last time" refers to the time of the Lord's second advent; (f) in 1 John 2:18, "the last hour" (RV) and, in Jude 18, "the last time" signify the present age previous to the Second Advent.

Farthing *kodrantes* (2835), was the Latin *quadrans*, "the fourth part of an as", about two thirds of a farthing, **Matt. 5:26**; Mark 12:42.

5:27 Ye have heard that it was said by them of old time, Thou shalt not commit adultery:

Old *see Matthew 5:21.*

Adultery *moicheuo* (3431), is used in **Matt. 5:27-28**, **32**; **19:18**; Mark 10:19; Luke 16:18; 18:20; John 8:4; Rom. 2:22; 13:9; Jas. 2:11; in Rev. 2:22, metaphorically, of those who are by a Jezebel's solicitations drawn away to idolatry.

5:28 But I say unto you, That whosoever looketh on a woman to lust after her hath committed adultery with her already in his heart.

Whosoever In Mark 7:14, KJV, the plural of *pas*, "all" (so RV), is translated "every one"; in **Matt. 5:28**, KJV, *pas*, with the article, is translated "whosoever" (RV, "every one who").

Lust *epithumeo* (1937), has the same twofold meaning as the noun, namely (a) "to desire," used of the Holy Spirit against the flesh, Gal. 5:17; of the Lord Jesus, Luke 22:15, "I have desired;" of the holy angels, 1 Pet. 1:12; of good men, for good things, **Matt. 13:17**; 1 Tim. 3:1; Heb. 6:11; of men, for things without moral quality, Luke 15:16; 16:21;

17:22; Rev. 9:6; (b) of "evil desires," in respect of which it is translated "to lust" in **Matt. 5:28**; 1 Cor. 10:6; Gal. 5:17; Jas. 4:2; to covet, Acts 20:23; Rom. 7:7; 13:9.

Heart *kardia* (2588), "the heart" (Eng., "cardiac," etc.), the chief organ of physical life ("for the life of the flesh is in the blood," Lev. 17:11), occupies the most important place in the human system. By an easy transition the word came to stand for man's entire mental and moral activity, both the rational and the emotional elements. In other words, the heart is used figuratively for the hidden springs of the personal life. "The Bible describes human depravity as in the 'heart,' because sin is a principle which has its seat in the center of man's inward life, and then 'defiles' the whole circuit of his action, **Matt. 15:19, 20.** On the other hand, Scripture regards the heart as the sphere of Divine influence, Rom. 2:15; Acts 15:9.... The heart, as lying deep within, contains 'the hidden man,' 1 Pet. 3:4, the real man. It represents the true character but conceals it" (J. Laidlaw, in *Hastings' Bible Dic.*). As to its usage in the NT it denotes (a) the seat of physical life, Acts 14:17; Jas. 5:5; (b) the seat of moral nature and spiritual life, the seat of grief, John 14:1; Rom. 9:2; 2 Cor. 2:4; joy, John 16:22; Eph. 5:19; the desires, **Matt. 5:28**; 2 Pet. 2:14; the affections, Luke 24:32; Acts 21:13; the perceptions, John 12:40; Eph. 4:18; the thoughts, **Matt. 9:4**; Heb. 4:12; the understanding, **Matt. 13:15**; Rom. 1:21; the reasoning powers, Mark 2:6; Luke 24:38; the imagination, Luke 1:51; conscience, Acts 2:37; 1 John 3:20; the intentions, Heb. 4:12, cf. 1 Pet. 4:1; purpose, Acts 11:23; 2 Cor. 9:7; the will, Rom. 6:17; Col. 3:15; faith, Mark 11:23; Rom. 10:10; Heb. 3:12.

5:29 And if thy right eye offend thee, pluck it out, and cast *it* from thee: for it is profitable for thee that one of thy members should perish, and not *that* thy whole body should be cast into hell.

Right *dexios* (1188), an adjective, used (a) of "the right" as opposite to the left, e.g., **Matt. 5:29, 30**; Rev. 10:5, RV, "right hand"; in connection with armor (figuratively), 2 Cor. 6:7; with *en*, followed by the dative plural, Mark 16:5; with *ek*, and the genitive plural, e.g., **Matt. 25:33, 34**; Luke 1:11; (b) of giving the "right hand" of fellowship, Gal. 2:9, betokening the public expression of approval by leaders at Jerusalem of the course pursued by Paul and Barnabas among the Gentiles; the act was often the sign of a pledge, e.g., 2 Kings 10:15; 1 Chron. 29:24, marg.; Ezra 10:19; Ezek. 17:18; figuratively, Lam. 5:6; it is often so used in the papyri; (c) metaphorically of "power" or "authority," Acts 2:33; with *ek*, signifying "on," followed by the genitive plural, **Matt. 26:64**; Mark 14:62; Heb. 1:13; (d) similarly of "a place of honor in the messianic kingdom," **Matt. 20:21**; Mark 10:37.

Offend *see* **Offended** at *Matthew 13:57.*

Pluck *exaireo* (1807), "to take out" (*ex* for *ek*, "out," haireo, "to take"), is translated "pluck out," of the eye as the occasion of sin, in **Matt. 5:29; 18:9**, indicating that, with determination and promptitude, we are to strike at the root of unholy inclinations, ridding ourselves of whatever would stimulate them.

Profitable *sumphero* (4851), signifies (a), transitively, lit., "to bring together," (*sun*, "with," *phero*, "to bring"), Acts 19:19; (b) intransitively, "to be an advantage, profitable, expedient" (not merely 'convenient'); it is used mostly impersonally, "it is (it was) expedient"; so in **Matt. 19:10**, RV (negatively), KJV, "it is (not) good"; John 11:50; 16:7; 18:14; 1 Cor. 6:12; 10:23; 2 Cor. 8:10; 12:1; "it is profitable," **Matt. 5:29-30; 18:6**, RV; "was profitable," Acts 20:20; "to profit withal," 1 Cor. 12:7; in Heb. 12:10, used in the neuter of the present participle with the article as a noun, "for (our) profit." Cf. the adjective *sumphoros* (or *sumpheron*), "profitable," used with the article as a noun, 1 Cor. 7:35; 10:33.

Members *melos* (3196), "a limb of the body," is used (a) literally, **Matt. 5:29-30**; Rom. 6:13 (twice), 19 (twice); 7:5, 23 (twice); 12:4 (twice); 1 Cor. 12:12 (twice), 14, 18-20, 22, 25-26 (twice); Jas. 3:5, 6; 4:1; in Col. 3:5, "mortify therefore your members which are upon the earth"; since our bodies and their "members" belong to the earth, and are the instruments of sin, they are referred to as such (cf. **Matt. 5:29-30**; Rom. 7:5, 23, mentioned above); the putting to death is not physical, but ethical; as the physical "members" have distinct individualities, so those evils, of which the physical "members" are agents, are by analogy regarded as examples of the way in which the "members" work if not put to death; this is not precisely the same as "the old man," v. 9, i.e., the old nature, though there is a connection; (b) metaphorically, "of believers as members of Christ," 1 Cor. 6:15 (1st part); of one another, Rom. 12:5 (as with the natural illustration, so with the spiritual analogy, there is not only vital unity, and harmony in operation, but diversity, all being essential to effectivity; the unity is not due to external organization but to common and vital union in Christ); there is stress in v. 5 upon "many" and "in Christ" and "members;" 1 Cor. 12:27 (of the "members" of a local church as a body); Eph. 4:25 (of the "members" of the whole Church as the mystical body of Christ); in 1 Cor. 6:15 (2nd part), of one who practices fornication.

Perish *apollumi* (622), "to destroy," signifies, in the middle voice, "to perish," and is thus used (a) of things, e.g., **Matt. 5:29, 30**; Luke 5:37; Acts 27:34, RV, "perish" (in some texts *pipto*, "to fall," as KJV); Heb. 1:11; 2 Pet. 3:6; Rev. 18:14 (2nd part), RV, "perished" (in some texts *aperchomai*, "to depart," as KJV); (b) of persons, e.g., **Matt. 8:25**; John 3:15), 16; 10:28; 17:12, RV, "perished" (KJV, "is lost"); Rom. 2:12; 1 Cor. 1:18, lit., "the perishing," where the perfective force of the verb implies the completion of the process of destruction (Moulton, *Proleg.*, p. 114); 8:11; 15:18; 2 Pet. 3:9; Jude 11.

Whole *holos* (3650), signifies "whole," (a) with a noun, e.g., **Matt. 5:29, 30**; Mark 8:36; 15:1, 16, 33; Luke 11:36 (1st part), though *holon* may here be used adverbially with *photeinon*, "wholly light" [as in the 2nd part, RV, "wholly (full of light)"]; John 11:50; 1 Cor. 12:17 (1st part); 1 John 2:2; 5:19; (b) absolutely, as a noun, e.g., **Matt. 13:33**; 1 Cor. 12:17 (2nd part).

Body *soma* (4983), is "the body as a whole, the instrument of life," whether of man living, e.g., **Matt. 6:22**, or dead, **Matt. 27:52**; or in resurrection, 1 Cor. 15:44; or of beasts, Heb. 13:11; of grain, 1 Cor. 15:37-38; of the heavenly hosts, 1 Cor. 15:40. In Rev. 18:13 it is translated "slaves." In its figurative uses the essential idea is preserved. Sometimes the word stands, by *synecdoche*, for "the complete man," **Matt. 5:29**; **6:22**; Rom. 12:1; Jas. 3:6; Rev. 18:13. Sometimes the person is identified with his or her "body," Acts 9:37; 13:36, and this is so even of the Lord Jesus, John 19:40 with 42. The "body" is not the man, for he himself can exist apart from his "body," 2 Cor. 12:2-3. The "body" is an essential part of the man and therefore the redeemed are not perfected till the resurrection, Heb. 11:40; no man in his final state will be without his "body," John 5:28-29; Rev. 20:13.

Hell *see Matthew 5:22.*

5:30 And if thy right hand offend thee, cut it off, and cast *it* from thee: for it is profitable for thee that one of thy members should perish, and not *that* thy whole body should be cast into hell.

Right *see Matthew 5:29.*

Offend *see* **Offended** at *Matthew 13:57.*

Cut *see* **Hewn** at *Matthew 3:10.*

Cast *ballo* (906), "to throw, hurl, in contrast to striking," is frequent in the four Gospels and Revelation; elsewhere it is used only in Acts. In **Matt. 5:30** some mss. have this verb (KJV, "should be cast"); the most authentic have *aperchomai* "to go away," RV, "go."

Profitable *see Matthew 5:29.*

Perish *see Matthew 5:29.*

Whole *see Matthew 5:29.*

Hell *see Matthew 5:22.*

5:31 It hath been said, Whosoever shall put away his wife, let him give her a writing of divorcement:

Put *see Matthew 1:19.*

Divorcement *apostasion* (647), primarily, "a defection," lit., "a standing off" (*apo*, "from," *stasis*, "a standing"; cf. *aphistemi*, "to cause to withdraw"), denotes, in the NT, "a writing or bill of divorcement," **Matt. 5:31**; **19:7**; Mark 10:4. In Sept., Deut. 24:3; Isa. 50:1; Jer. 3:8.

5:32 But I say unto you, That whosoever shall put away his wife, saving for the cause of fornication, causeth her to commit adultery: and whosoever shall marry her that is divorced committeth adultery.

Put *see Matthew 1:19.*

Saving *parektos* (3924), is used (a) as an adverb, signifying "without," 2 Cor. 11:28; lit., "the things without," i.e., the things happening without; (b) as a preposition signifying "except"; in **Matt. 5:32**, "saving"; in Acts 26:29, except; **Matt. 5:32** (in some mss., **19:9**).

Cause *logos* (3056), "a word spoken for any purpose," denotes, in one place, a cause or reason assigned, **Matt. 5:32.**

Fornication *porneia* (4202), is used (a) of "illicit sexual intercourse," in John 8:41; Acts 15:20, 29; 21:25; 1 Cor. 5:1; 6:13, 18; 2 Cor. 12:21; Gal. 5:19; Eph. 5:3; Col. 3:5; 1 Thess. 4:3; Rev. 2:21; 9:21; in the plural in 1 Cor. 7:2; in **Matt. 5:32** and **19:9** it stands for, or includes, adultery; it is distinguished from it in **15:19** and Mark 7:21; (b) metaphorically, of "the association of pagan idolatry with doctrines of, and professed adherence to, the Christian faith," Rev. 14:8; 17:2, 4; 18:3; 19:2; some suggest this as the sense in 2:21.

Causeth In **Matt. 5:32** the RV translates *poieo* "maketh (her an adulteress)": in Rev. 13:12, RV, "maketh," for KJV, "causeth."

Adultery *see Matthew 5:27.*

Marry *gameo* (1060), "to marry," is used (a) of "the man," **Matt. 5:32; 19:9, 10; 22:25** (RV; KJV, "married a wife"); v. **30; 24:38;** Mark 6:17; 10:11; 12:25; Luke 14:20; 16:18; 17:27, RV, "married" (KJV, "married wives"); 20:34, 35; 1 Cor. 7:28 (1st part); v. 33; (b) of "the woman," in the active voice, Mark 10:12; 1 Cor. 7:28 (last part); ver. 34; 1 Tim. 5:11, 14; in the passive voice, 1 Cor. 7:39; (c) of "both sexes," 1 Cor. 7:9, 10, 36; 1 Tim. 4:3.

Divorced *see* Put at *Matthew 1:19.*

Adultery *moichao* (3429), used in the middle voice in the NT, is said of men in **Matt. 5:32; 19:9;** Mark 10:11; of women in Mark 10:12.

5:33 Again, ye have heard that it hath been said by them of old time, Thou shalt not forswear thyself, but shalt perform unto the Lord thine oaths:

Again *palin* (3825), the regular word for "again," is used chiefly in two senses, (a) with reference to repeated action; (b) rhetorically, in the sense of "moreover" or "further," indicating a statement to be added in the course of an argument, e.g., **Matt. 5:33;** or with the meaning "on the other hand, in turn," Luke 6:43; 1 Cor. 12:21; 2 Cor. 10:7; 1 John 2:8. In the first chapter of Hebrews, v. 5, *palin* simply introduces an additional quotation; in v. 6 this is not so. There the RV rightly puts the word "again" in connection with "He bringeth in the firstborn into the world," "When He again bringeth, etc." That is to say, *palin* is here set in contrast to the time when God *first* brought His Son into the world. This statement, then, refers to the future second advent of Christ. The word is used far more frequently in the Gospel of John than in any other book in the New Testament.

Old *see Matthew 5:21.*

Forswear *epiorkeo* (1964), signifies "to swear falsely, to undo one's swearing, forswear oneself" (*epi*, "against," *orkos*, "an oath"), **Matt. 5:33.** Cf. *epiorkos*, "a perjured person, a perjurer," 1 Tim. 1:10, "false swearers."

Perform *apodidomi* (591), "to give back, or in full," is translated "thou ... shalt perform" in **Matt. 5:33.**

Oaths *horkos* (3727), is primarily equivalent to *herkos*, "a fence, an enclosure, that which restrains a person"; hence, "an oath." The Lord's command in **Matt. 5:33** was a condemnation of the minute and arbitrary restrictions imposed by the scribes and Pharisees in the matter of adjurations, by which God's Name was profaned. The injunction is repeated in Jas. 5:12. The language of the apostle Paul, e.g., in Gal. 1:20 and 1 Thess. 5:27 was not inconsistent with Christ's prohibition, read in the light of its context. Contrast the "oaths" mentioned in **Matt. 14:7, 9; 26:72;** Mark 6:26. Heb. 6:16 refers to the confirmation of a compact among men, guaranteeing the discharge of liabilities; in their disputes "the oath is final for confirmation." This is referred to in order to illustrate the greater subject of God's "oath" to Abraham, confirming His promise; cf. Luke 1:73; Acts 2:30.

5:34 But I say unto you, Swear not at all; neither by heaven; for it is God's throne:

Swear *omnumi* or *omnuo* (3660), is used of "affirming or denying by an oath," e.g., **Matt. 26:74;** Mark 6:23; Luke 1:73; Heb. 3:11, 18; 4:3; 7:21; accompanied by that by which one swears, e.g., **Matt. 5:34, 36; 23:16;** Heb. 6:13, 16; Jas. 5:12; Rev. 10:6.

All *holos* (3654), signifies "at all," **Matt. 5:34;** 1 Cor. 15:29; "actually," 1 Cor. 5:1, RV (KJV, wrongly, "commonly"); "altogether," 1 Cor. 6:7 (KJV, "utterly").

Throne *thronos* (2362), "a throne, a seat of authority," is used of the "throne" (a) of God, e.g., Heb. 4:16, "the throne of grace," i.e., from which grace proceeds; 8:1; 12:2; Rev. 1:4; 3:21 (2nd part); 4:2 (twice); 5:1; frequently in Rev.; in 20:12, in the best texts, "the throne" (some have *Theos*, "God," KJV); cf. 21:3; **Matt. 5:34; 23:22;** Acts 7:49; (b) of Christ, e.g., Heb. 1:8; Rev. 3:21 (1st part); 22:3; His seat of authority in the Millennium, **Matt. 19:28** (1st part); (c) by metonymy for angelic powers, Col. 1:16; (d) of the Apostles in millennial authority, **Matt. 19:28** (2nd part); Luke 22:30; (e) of the elders in the heavenly vision, Rev. 4:4 (2nd and 3rd parts), RV, "thrones" (KJV, "seats"); so 11:16; (f) of David, Luke 1:32; Acts 2:30; (g) of Satan, Rev. 2:13, RV, "throne" (KJV, "seat"); (h) of "the beast," the final and federal head of the revived Roman Empire, Rev. 13:2; 16:10.

5:35 Nor by the earth; for it is his footstool: neither by Jerusalem; for it is the city of the great King.

Earth *see Matthew 5:18.*

Footstool *hupopodion* (5286), from *hupo*, "under," and *pous*, "a foot," is used (a) literally in Jas. 2:3, (b) metaphorically, of the earth as God's "footstool," **Matt. 5:35;** of the foes of the Lord, **Matt. 22:44** (in some mss.); Mark 12:36, "underneath" (in some mss.), Luke 20:43; Acts 2:35; 7:49; Heb. 1:13; 10:13. The RV, adhering to the literal rendering, translates the phrase "the footstool of My (Thy, His) feet," for the KJV, "My (etc.) footstool," but in **Matt. 22:44**, "(till I put Thine enemies) underneath thy feet."

King *see Matthew 1:6.*

5:36 Neither shalt thou swear by thy head, because thou canst not make one hair white or black.

Swear *see Matthew 5:34.*

Hair *see Matthew 3:4.*

White *leukos* (3022), is used of (a) clothing (sometimes in the sense of "bright"), **Matt. 17:2; 28:3**; Mark 9:3; 16:5; Luke 9:29; John 20:12; Acts 1:10; symbolically, Rev. 3:4, 5, 18; 4:4; 6:11; 7:9, 13; 19:14 (2nd part); (b) hair, **Matt. 5:36**; Christ's head and hair (in a vision; cf. Dan. 7:9), Rev. 1:14 (twice); ripened grain, John 4:35; a stone, Rev. 2:17, an expression of the Lord's special delight in the overcomer, the new name on it being indicative of a secret communication of love and joy; a horse (in a vision), 6:2; 19:11-14 (1st part); a cloud, 14:14; the throne of God, 20:11.

Black *melas* (3189), "black," **Matt. 5:36**; Rev. 6:5, 12, is derived from a root *mal*–, meaning "to be dirty"; hence Latin, *malus*, bad.

5:37 But let your communication be, Yea, yea; Nay, nay: for whatsoever is more than these cometh of evil.

Communication *logos* (3056), "a word, that which is spoken" (*lego*, "to speak"), is used in the plural with reference to a conversation; "communication," Luke 24:17. Elsewhere with this significance the RV renders it "speech," **Matt. 5:37**; Eph. 4:29.

Yea *nai* (3483), a particle of affirmation, is used (a) in answer to a question, **Matt. 9:28; 11:9; 13:51; 17:25; 21:16**; Luke 7:26; John 11:27; 21:15, 16; Acts 5:8; 22:27; Rom. 3:29; (b) in assent to an assertion, **Matt. 15:27**, RV (KJV, "truth"); Mark 7:28; Rev. 14:13; 16:7, RV (KJV, "even so"); (c) in confirmation of an assertion, **Matt. 11:26** and Luke 10:21, RV (KJV, "even so"); Luke 11:51, RV (KJV, "verily"); 12:5; Phil. 4:3 (in the best texts); Philem. 20; (d) in solemn asseveration, Rev. 1:7 (KJV and RV, "even so"); 22:20, RV (KJV, "surely"); (e) in repetition for emphasis, **Matt. 5:37**; 2 Cor. 1:17; Jas. 5:12; (f) singly in contrast to *ou*, "nay," 2 Cor. 1:18, 19 (twice), 20, "(the) yea," RV.

Nay *ou* (3756), "no, not," expressing a negation absolutely, is rendered "nay," e.g., in **Matt. 5:37; 13:29**; John 7:12, KJV (RV, "not so"); Acts 16:37; 2 Cor. 1:17-19; Jas. 5:12.

More *perissos* (4053), "more than sufficient, over and above, abundant," is translated "more," e.g., in **Matt. 5:37-47**. In John 10:10 the neuter form is rendered "more abundantly," KJV, RV, "abundantly" (marg., "abundance").

Evil *poneros* (4190), the adjective, is used as a noun, (a) of Satan as the "evil" one, **Matt. 5:37; 6:13; 13:19, 38**; Luke 11:4 (in some texts); John 17:15; Eph. 6:16; 2 Thess. 3:3; 1 John 2:13-14; 3:12; 5:18-19; (b) of human beings, **Matt. 5:45**; (probably v. **39**); **13:49; 22:10**; Luke 6:35; 1 Cor. 5:13; (c) neuter, "evil (things)," **Matt. 9:4; 12:35**; Mark 7:23; Luke 3:19; "that which is evil," Luke 6:45; Rom. 12:9; Acts 28:21, "harm." *See also* ***Matthew 5:11.***

5:38 Ye have heard that it hath been said, An eye for an eye, and a tooth for a tooth:

Eye *ophthalmos* (3788), akin to *opsis*, "sight," probably from a root signifying "penetration, sharpness" (Curtius, Gk. Etym.) (cf. Eng., "ophthalmia," etc.) is used (a) of the physical organ, e.g., **Matt. 5:38**; of restoring sight, e.g., **Matt. 20:33**; of God's power of vision, Heb. 4:13; 1 Pet. 3:12; of Christ in vision, Rev. 1:14; 2:18; 19:12; of the Holy Spirit in the unity of Godhood with Christ, Rev. 5:6; (b) metaphorically, of ethical qualities, evil, **Matt. 6:23**; Mark 7:22 (by metonymy, for envy); singleness of motive, **Matt. 6:22**; Luke 11:34; as the instrument of evil desire, "the principal avenue of temptation," 1 John 2:16; of adultery, 2 Pet. 2:14; (c) metaphorically, of mental vision, **Matt. 13:15**; John 12:40; Rom. 11:8; Gal. 3:1, where the metaphor of the "evil eye" is altered to a different sense from that of bewitching (the posting up or placarding of an "eye" was used as a charm, to prevent mischief); by gospel-preaching Christ had been, so to speak, placarded before their "eyes"; the question may be paraphrased, "What evil teachers have been malignly fascinating you?"; Eph. 1:18, of the "eyes of the heart," as a means of knowledge.

Tooth *odous* (3599), is used in the sing. in **Matt. 5:38** (twice); elsewhere in the plural, of "the gnashing of teeth," the gnashing being expressive of anguish and indignation, **Matt. 8:12; 13:42, 50; 22:13; 24:51; 25:30**; Mark 9:18; Luke 13:28; Acts 7:54; in Rev. 9:8, of the beings seen in a vision and described as locusts.

5:39 But I say unto you, That ye resist not evil: but whosoever shall smite thee on thy right cheek, turn to him the other also.

Resist *anthistemi* (436), "to set against" (*anti*, "against," *histemi*, "to cause to stand"), used in the middle (or passive) voice and in the intransitive 2nd aorist and perfect active, signifying "to withstand, oppose, resist," is translated "to resist" in **Matt. 5:39**; Acts 6:10, KJV (RV, withstand); Rom. 9:19, KJV (RV, "withstandeth"); 13:2 (2nd and 3rd parts), KJV (RV, "withstandeth" and "withstand"); Gal. 2:11, RV (KJV, "withstood"); 2 Tim. 3:8 (2nd part), KJV (RV, "withstand"); Jas. 4:7; 1 Pet. 5:9, KJV (RV, "withstand"); "to withstand" in Acts 13:8; Eph. 6:13; 2 Tim. 3:8 (1st part); 4:15.

Evil *see Matthew 5:37.*

Smite *rhapizo* (4474), primarily "to strike with a rod" (*rhapis*, "a rod"), then, "to strike the face with the palm of the hand or the clenched fist," is used in **Matt. 5:39**; **26:67**, where the marg. of KJV and RV has "with rods."

Cheek *siagon* (4600), primarily denotes "the jaw, the jaw-bone"; hence "cheek," **Matt. 5:39**; Luke 6:29.

Turn *strepho* (4762), denotes (1) in the active voice, (a) "to turn" (something), **Matt. 5:39**; (b) "to bring back," **Matt. 27:3** (in the best texts); (c) reflexively, "to turn oneself, to turn the back to people," said of God, Acts 7:42; (d) "to turn one thing into another," Rev. 11:6 (the only place where this word occurs after the Acts); (2) in the passive voice, (a) used reflexively, "to turn oneself," e.g. **Matt. 7:6**; John 20:14, 16; (b) metaphorically, **Matt. 18:3**, RV, "(except) ye turn" (KJV, "... be converted"); John 12:40 (in the best texts).

Other *allos* (243), indicates numeral distinction of objects of similar character, and is used (a) absolutely, e.g., **Matt. 20:3** (plural); (b) attached to a noun, e.g., **Matt. 21:36**; (c) with the article, e.g., **Matt. 5:39**; 1 Cor. 14:29 (plural, RV); in **Matt. 13:5**; Luke 9:19; John 9:9, e.g., RV, "others" (KJV, "some"); in **Matt. 25:20**, RV, "other" (KJV, "beside them ... more").

Also *kai* The particle *kai*, "and," chiefly used for connecting words, clauses and sentences (the copulative or connective use), not infrequently signifies "also." This is the *adjunctive*, or *amplificatory*, use, and it is to be distinguished from the purely copulative significance "and." A good illustration is provided in **Matt. 8:9**, in the words of the centurion, "I also am a man under authority." Other instances are **Matt. 5:39**, **40**; **8:9**; **10:18**; **18:33**; **20:4**; Luke 11:49; 12:41, 54, 57; 20:3; John 5:26, "the Son also," RV; 7:3; 12:10; 14:1, 3, 7, 19; 15:9, 27; 17:24; Acts 11:17; Rom. 1:13; 6:11; 1 Cor. 7:3; 11:25; 15:30; Gal. 6:1; Phil. 4:12, "I know also," RV, 1 Thess. 3:12. In 1 Cor. 2:13 the *kai* phrase signifies "which are the very things we speak, with the like power of the Holy Spirit." This use includes the meanings "so," or "just so," by way of comparison, as in **Matt. 6:10**, and "so also," e.g., John 13:33; cf. Rom. 11:16. In Heb. 7:26 the most authentic mss. have *kai* in the first sentence, which may be rendered "for such a High Priest also became us." Here it virtually has the meaning "precisely."

5:40 And if any man will sue thee at the law, and take away thy coat, let him have *thy* cloke also.

Law *krino* (2919), primarily denotes "to separate, select, choose"; hence, "to determine," and so "to judge, pronounce judgment." "The uses of this verb in the NT may be analyzed as follows: (a) to assume the office of a judge, **Matt. 7:1**; John 3:17; (b) to undergo process of trial, John 3:18; 16:11; 18:31; Jas. 2:12; (c) to give sentence, Acts 15:19; 16:4; 21:25; (d) to condemn, John 12:48; Acts 13:27; Rom. 2:27; (e) to execute judgment upon, 2 Thess. 2:12; Acts 7:7; (f) to be involved in a lawsuit, whether as plaintiff, **Matt. 5:40**; 1 Cor. 6:1; or as defendant, Acts 23:6; (g) to administer affairs, to govern, **Matt. 19:28**; cf. Judg. 3:10; (h) to form an opinion, Luke 7:43; John 7:24; Acts 4:19; Rom. 14:5; (i) to make a resolve, Acts 3:13; 20:161 Cor. 2:2."

Take *lambano* (2983), "to take, lay hold of," besides its literal sense, e.g., **Matt. 5:40**; **26:26**, **27**, is used metaphorically, of fear, in "taking" hold of people, Luke 7:16, RV (KJV, "came ... on"); of sin in "finding (occasion)," RV (KJV, "taking"), Rom. 7:8, 11, where sin is viewed as the corrupt source of action, an inward element using the commandment to produce evil effects; of the power of temptation, 1 Cor. 10:13; of "taking" an example, Jas. 5:10; of "taking" peace from the earth, Rev. 6:4; of Christ in "taking" the form of a servant, Phil. 2:7; of "taking" rightful power (by the Lord, hereafter), Rev. 11:17.

Let *aphiemi* (863), frequently denotes "to let, suffer, permit," e.g., **Matt. 5:40** (translated "let ... have"); **7:4**; **13:30**; **15:14**; **27:49** and Mark 15:36, RV, "let be," probably short for "let us see" (Moulton and Milligan, *Vocab.*); Mark 7:27; 11:6 ("let ... go"); 14:6 ("let ... alone"); so Luke 13:8; John 11:48; in Acts 5:38 (where some mss. have *eao*, "to permit, let, suffer"); in John 11:44 and 18:8 ("let"); 1 Cor. 7:11, 12, RV, "let ... leave," KJV, "let ... put away"; 7:13 ("let ... leave").

Cloke *chiton* (5509), denotes "the inner vest or undergarment," and is to be distinguished, as such, from the *himation*. The distinction is made, for instance, in the Lord's command in **Matt. 5:40**: "If any man would go to law with thee, and take away thy coat (*chiton*), (*himation*) also." The order is reversed in Luke 6:29, and the difference lies in this, that in **Matt. 5:40** the Lord is referring to a legal process, so the claimant is supposed to claim the inner garment, the less costly. The defendant is to be willing to let him have the more valuable one too. In the passage in Luke an act of violence is in view, and there is no mention of going to law. So the outer garment is the first one which would be seized.

Also *see Matthew 5:39.*

5:41 And whosoever shall compel thee to go a mile, go with him twain.

Compel *angareuo* (29), "to dispatch as an *angaros*" (a Persian courier kept at regular stages with power of impressing men into service), and hence, in general, "to impress into service," is used of "compelling" a person to go a mile, **Matt. 5:41**; of the impressing of Simon to bear Christ's cross, **Matt. 27:32**; Mark 15:21.

Mile *milion* (3400), "a Roman mile," a word of Latin origin (1680 yards), is used in **Matt. 5:41**.

Twain *duo* (1417), is rendered "twain" in **Matt. 5:41**; **19:5**, **6**; **21:31**; **27:21**, **51**; Mark 10:8 (twice); 15:38; in 1 Cor. 6:16 and Eph. 5:31, RV (KJV, "two"); Eph. 2:15; in Rev. 19:20, RV (KJV, "both").

5:42 Give to him that asketh thee, and from him that would borrow of thee turn not thou away.

Borrow *daneizo* (1155), in the active voice signifies "to lend money," as in Luke 6:34-35, in the middle voice, "to have money lent to oneself, to borrow," **Matt. 5:42**. Cf. *dan(e)ion*, "a debt," **Matt. 18:27**, and *dan(e)istes*, "a creditor," Luke 7:41.

Turn *apostrepho* (654), denotes (a) "to cause to turn away (*apo*), to remove," Rom. 11:26; 2 Tim. 4:4 (1st clause); metaphorically, "to turn away from allegiance, pervert," Luke 23:14; (b) "to make to return, put back," **Matt. 26:52**, (c) in the passive voice, used reflexively, "to turn oneself away from," **Matt. 5:42**; 2 Tim. 1:15; Titus 1:14; Heb. 12:25; in the active voice, Acts 3:26.

5:43 Ye have heard that it hath been said, Thou shalt love thy neighbour, and hate thine enemy.

Neighbour *plesion* (4139), the neuter of the adjective *plesios* (from *pelas*, "near"), is used as an adverb accompanied by the article, lit., "the (one) near"; hence, one's "neighbor." This has a wider range of meaning than that of the Eng. word "neighbor." There were no farmhouses scattered over the agricultural areas of Palestine; the populations, gathered in villages, went to and fro to their toil. Hence domestic life was touched at every point by a wide circle of neighborhood. The terms for neighbor were therefore of a very comprehensive scope. This may be seen from the chief characteristics of the privileges and duties of neighborhood as set forth in Scripture, (a) its helpfulness, e.g., Prov. 27:10; Luke 10:36; (b) its intimacy, e.g., Luke 15:6, 9; Heb. 8:11; (c) its sincerity and sanctity, e.g., Ex. 22:7, 10; Prov. 3:29; 14:21; Rom. 13:10; 15:2; Eph. 4:25; Jas. 4:12. The NT quotes and expands the command in Lev. 19:18, "to love one's neighbor as oneself"; see, e.g., **Matt. 5:43**; **19:19**; **22:39**; Mark 12:31, 33; Luke 10:27; Gal. 5:14; Jas. 2:8. See also Acts 7:27.

Enemy *echthros* (2190), an adjective, primarily denoting "hated" or "hateful" (akin to *echthos*, "hate"; perhaps associated with *ekos*, "outside"), hence, in the active sense, denotes "hating, hostile"; it is used as a noun signifying an "enemy," adversary, and is said (a) of the Devil, **Matt. 13:39**; Luke 10:19; (b) of death, 1 Cor. 15:26; (c) of the professing believer who would be a friend of the world, thus making himself an enemy of God, Jas. 4:4; (d) of men who are opposed to Christ, **Matt. 13:25**, **28**; **22:44**; Mark 12:36; Luke 19:27; 20:43; Acts 2:35; Rom. 11:28; Phil. 3:18; Heb. 1:13; 10:13; or to His servants, Rev. 11:5, 12; to the nation of Israel, Luke 1:71, 74; 19:43; (e) of one who is opposed to righteousness, Acts 13:10; (f) of Israel in its alienation from God, Rom. 11:28; (g) of the unregenerate in their attitude toward God, Rom. 5:10; Col. 1:21; (h) of believers in their former state, 2 Thess. 3:15; (i) of foes, **Matt. 5:43-44**; **10:36**; Luke 6:27, 35; Rom. 12:20; 1 Cor. 15:25; of the apostle Paul because he told converts "the truth," Gal. 4:16. Cf. *echthra*, "enmity".

5:44 But I say unto you, Love your enemies, bless them that curse you, do good to them that hate you, and pray for them which despitefully use you, and persecute you;

Curse *kataraomai* (2672), primarily signifies "to pray against, to wish evil against a person or thing"; hence "to curse," **Matt. 25:41**; Mark 11:21; Luke 6:28; Rom. 12:14; Jas. 3:9. Some mss. have it in **Matt. 5:44**.

Good *kalos* (2573), "well, finely," is used in some mss. in **Matt. 5:44**, with *poieo*, "to do," and translated "do good." In Jas. 2:3 it is rendered "in a good place" (KJV marg., "well" or "seemly").

Despitefully *epereazo* (1908), is found in some mss. in **Matt. 5:44**, and translated "despitefully use," KJV (the RV follows the mss. which omit the sentence). In the corresponding passage in Luke 6:28, the KJV and RV have "despitefully use"; in 1 Pet. 3:16, KJV, "falsely accuse," RV, "revile."

Persecute *see* Persecuted at *Matthew 5:10.*

5:45 That ye may be the children of your Father which is in heaven: for he maketh his sun to rise on the evil and on the good, and sendeth rain on the just and on the unjust.

Children *see Matthew 5:9.*

Father *see Matthew 2:22.*

Sun *helios* (2246), whence Eng. prefix "helio-," is used (a) as a means of the natural benefits of light and heat, e.g., **Matt. 5:45**, and power, Rev. 1:16; (b) of its qualities of brightness and glory, e.g., **Matt. 13:43**; **17:2**; Acts 26:13; 1 Cor. 15:41; Rev. 10:1; 12:1; (c) as a means of destruction, e.g., **Matt. 13:6**; Jas. 1:11; of physical misery, Rev. 7:16; (d) as a means of judgment, e.g., **Matt. 24:29**; Mark 13:24; Luke 21:25; 23:45; Acts 2:20; Rev. 6:12; 8:12; 9:2; 16:8.

Rise *see* Sprung at *Matthew 4:16.*

Evil *see Matthew 5:37.*

Good *agathos* (18), describes that which, being "good" in its character or constitution, is beneficial in its effect; it is used (a) of things physical, e.g., a tree, **Matt. 7:17**; ground, Luke 8:8; (b) in a moral sense, frequently of persons and things. God is essentially, absolutely and consummately "good," **Matt. 19:17**; Mark 10:18; Luke 18:19. To certain persons the word is applied in **Matt. 20:15**; **25:21**, **23**; Luke 19:17; 23:50; John 7:12; Acts 11:24; Titus 2:5; in a general application, **Matt. 5:45**; **12:35**; Luke 6:45; Rom. 5:7; 1 Pet. 2:18. The neuter of the adjective with the definite article signifies that which is "good," lit., "the good," as being morally honorable, pleasing to God, and therefore beneficial. Christians are to prove it, Rom. 12:2; to cleave to it, 12:9; to do it, 13:3; Gal. 6:10; 1 Pet. 3:11 (here, and here only, the article is absent); John 5:29 (here, the neuter plural is used, "the good things"); to work it, Rom. 2:10; Eph. 4:28; 6:8; to follow after it, 1 Thess. 5:15; to be zealous of it, 1 Pet. 3:13; to imitate it, 3 John 11; to overcome evil with it, Rom. 12:21. Governmental authorities are ministers of "good," i.e., that which is salutary, suited to the course of human affairs, Rom. 13:4. In Philem. 14, "thy goodness," RV (lit., "thy good"), means "thy benefit." As to **Matt. 19:17**, "why askest thou Me concerning that which is good?" the RV follows the most ancient mss.

Rain *brecho* (1026), signifies (a) "to wet," Luke 7:38, 44, RV (KJV, to wash); (b) "to send rain," **Matt. 5:45**; to rain, Luke 17:29 (of fire and brimstone); Jas. 5:17, used impersonally (twice); Rev. 11:6, where *huetos* is used as the subject, lit., "(that) rain rain (not)."

Unjust *adikos* (94), "not in conformity with dike, 'right,'" is rendered "unjust" in the KJV and RV in **Matt. 5:45**; Luke 18:11; Acts 24:15; elsewhere for the KJV "unjust" the RV has "unrighteous.

5:46 For if ye love them which love you, what reward have ye? do not even the publicans the same?

Reward *see Matthew 5:12.*

Even *kai* (2532), a conjunction, is usually a mere connective, meaning "and"; it frequently, however, has an ascensive or climactic use, signifying "even," the thing that is added being out of the ordinary, and producing a climax. The determination of this meaning depends on the context. Examples are **Matt. 5:46-47**; Mark 1:27; Luke 6:33 (RV); 10:17; John 12:42; Gal. 2:13, 17, where "also" should be "even"; Eph. 5:12. Examples where the RV corrects the KJV "and" or "also," by substituting "even," are Luke 7:49; Acts 17:28; Heb. 11:11; in 1 John 4:3 the RV rightly omits "even." When followed by "if" or "though," *kai* often signifies "even," e.g., **Matt. 26:35**; John 8:14. So sometimes when preceded by "if," e.g., 1 Cor. 7:11, where "but and if" should be "but even if." The epexegetic or explanatory use of *kai* followed by a noun in apposition, and meaning "namely," or "even" is comparatively rare. Winer's cautionary word needs heeding, that "this meaning has been introduced into too many passages" (Gram. of the NT, p. 546.). Some think it has this sense in John 3:5, "water, even the Spirit," and Gal. 6:16, "even the Israel of God."

"You never so touch the ocean of God's love as when you forgive and love your enemies."

CORRIE TEN BOOM

Publicans *telones* (5057), primarily denoted "a farmer of the tax" (from *telos*, "toll, custom, tax"), then, as in the NT, a subsequent subordinate of such, who collected taxes in some district, "a tax gatherer"; such were naturally hated intensely by the people; they are classed with "sinners," **Matt. 9:10, 11; 11:19**; Mark 2:15, 16; Luke 5:30; 7:34; 15:1; with harlots, **Matt. 21:31, 32**; with "the Gentile," **Matt. 18:17**; some mss. have it in **Matt. 5:47**, the best have *ethnikoi*, "Gentiles." See also **Matt. 5:46; 6:7; 10:3**; Luke 3:12; 5:27, 29; 7:29; 18:10, 11, 13.

Same *autos* (846), denotes "the same" when preceded by the article, and either with a noun following, e.g., Mark 14:39; Phil. 1:30; 1 Cor. 12:4, or without, e.g., **Matt. 5:46, 47**; Rom. 2:1; Phil. 2:2; 3:1; Heb. 1:12; 13:8. It is thus to be distinguished from uses as a personal and a reflexive pronoun.

5:47 And if ye salute your brethren only, what do ye more *than others*? do not even the publicans so?

Brethren Persons united by a common interest, **Matt. 5:47**.

Only *monon* (3441), "only, exclusively," is translated "only," e.g., in **Matt. 5:47; 8:8**; John 5:18; 11:52; 12:9; 13:9; frequently in Acts, Romans and Galatians.

Even *see Matthew 5:46.*

Publicans *see Matthew 5:46.*

So *see* Same at *Matthew 5:46.*

5:48 Be ye therefore perfect, even as your Father which is in heaven is perfect.

Ye *see Matthew 5:13.*

Perfect *teleios* (5049), signifies "having reached its end" (*telos*), "finished, complete perfect." It is used (I) of persons, (a) primarily of physical development, then, with ethical import, "fully grown, mature," 1 Cor. 2:6; 14:20 ("men"; marg., "of full age"); Eph. 4:13; Phil. 3:15; Col. 1:28; 4:12; in Heb. 5:14, RV, "full-grown" (marg., "perfect"), KJV, "of full age" (marg., "perfect"); (b) "complete," conveying the idea of goodness without necessary reference to maturity or what is expressed under (a) **Matt. 5:48; 19:21**; Jas. 1:4 (2nd part); 3:2. It is used thus of God in **Matt. 5:48**; (II), of "things, complete, perfect," Rom. 12:2; 1 Cor. 13:10 (referring to the complete revelation of God's will and ways, whether in the completed Scriptures or in the hereafter); Jas. 1:4 (of the work of patience); v. 25; 1 John 4:18.

Father *see Matthew 2:22.*

Chapter 6

6:1 Take heed that ye do not your alms before men, to be seen of them: otherwise ye have no reward of your Father which is in heaven.

Heed *prosecho* (4337), lit., "to hold to," signifies "to turn to, turn one's attention to"; hence, "to give heed"; it is rendered "take heed" in **Matt. 6:1**; Luke 17:3; 21:34; Acts 5:35; 20:28; 2 Pet. 1:19; to give heed to, in Acts 8:6, 10; in v. 11 (KJV, "had regard to"); 16:14 (KJV, "attended unto"); 1 Tim. 1:4; 4:1, 13 (KJV, "give attendance to"); Titus 1:14; Heb. 2:1, lit., "to give heed more earnestly."

Alms *eleemosune* (1654), connected with *eleemon*, "merciful," signifies (a) "mercy, pity, particularly in giving alms," **Matt. 6:1, 2-4**; Acts 10:2; 24:17; (b) the benefaction itself, the "alms" (the effect for the cause), Luke 11:41; 12:33; Acts 3:2-3, 10; 9:36, "alms-deeds"; 10:2, 4, 31. In **Matt. 6:1**, the RV, translating *dikaiosune*, according to the most authentic texts, has "righteousness," for KJV, "alms." *See also* **Righteousness** at *Matthew 3:15.*

Before *see Matthew 5:16.*

Seen *theaomai* (2300), "to view attentively, to see with admiration, desire, or regard," stresses more especially the action of the person beholding; it is used in **Matt. 11:7** (RV, "to behold"), while *idein*, the infinitive of *eidon*, is used in the questions in the next two verses; in verse **7** the interest in the onlooker is stressed, in vv. **8, 9**, the attention is especially directed to the object "seen." The verb is translated "to see" in the KJV and RV of **Matt. 6:1**; Mark 16:11, 14; John 6:5; Acts 8:18 (in some mss.); 21:27; Rom. 15:24; elsewhere, for the KJV, "to see," the RV uses the verb "to behold," bringing out its force more suitably.

Otherwise The phrase *ei*, "if," de, "but," *mege*, "not indeed," i.e., "but if not indeed," is translated "otherwise" in the KJV of **Matt. 6:1**; Luke 5:36 (RV, "else," in each place); in 2 Cor. 11:16, KJV, "if otherwise" (RV, "but if *ye do*").

Have *apecho* (568), denotes (a) transitively, "to have in full, to have received"; so the RV in **Matt. 6:2, 5, 16** (for KJV, "they have"); Luke 6:24, KJV, and RV; in all these instances the present tense (to which the KJV incorrectly adheres in the **Matt. 6** verses) has a perfective force, consequent upon the combination with the prefix *apo* ("from"), not that it stands for the perfect tense, but that it views the action in its accomplished result; so in Phil. 4:18, where the KJV and RV translate it "I have"; in Philem. 15, "(that) thou shouldest have (him for ever)," KJV, "shouldest receive"; (b) intransitively, "to be away, distant," used with *porro*, "far," **Matt. 15:8**; Mark 7:6; with *makran*, "far off, afar," Luke 7:6; 15:20; without an accompanying adverb, Luke 24:13, "which was from."

Reward *see* Treasures at *Matthew 2:11.*

Father *see Matthew 2:22.*

6:2 Therefore when thou doest *thine* alms, do not sound a trumpet before thee, as the hypocrites do in the synagogues and in the streets, that they may have glory of men. Verily I say unto you, They have their reward.

Alms *see Matthew 6:1. See also* Righteousness at *Matthew 3:15.*

Sound a trumpet *salpizo* (4537), "to sound a trumpet" (*salpinx*), occurs in **Matt. 6:2**; 1 Cor. 15:52, "the trumpet shall sound"; Rev. 8:6-8, 10, 12, 13; 9:1, 13; 10:7; 11:15.

Hypocrites *pharisaios* (5330), from an Aramaic word *peras* (found in Dan. 5:28), signifying "to separate," owing to a different manner of life from that of the general public. The "Pharisees" and Sadducees appear as distinct parties in the latter half of the 2nd cent. BC, though they represent tendencies traceable much earlier in Jewish history, tendencies which became pronounced after the return from Babylon (537 B.C.). The immediate progenitors of the two parties were, respectively, the Hasidaeans and the Hellenizers; the latter, the antecedents of the Sadducees, aimed at removing Judaism from its narrowness and sharing in the advantages of Greek life and culture. The Hasidaeans, a transcription of the Hebrew *chasidim*, i.e., "pious ones," were a society of men zealous for religion, who acted under the guidance of the scribes, in opposition to the godless Hellenizing party; they scrupled to oppose the legitimate high priest even when he was on the Greek side. Thus the Hellenizers were a political sect, while the Hasidaeans, whose fundamental principle was complete separation from non-Jewish elements, were the strictly legal party among the Jews, and were ultimately the more popular and influential party. In their zeal for the Law they almost deified it and their attitude became merely external, formal, and mechanical. They laid stress, not upon the righteousness of an action, but upon its formal correctness. Consequently their opposition to Christ was inevitable; His manner of life and teaching was essentially a condemnation of theirs; hence His denunciation of them, e.g., **Matt. 6:2, 5, 16; 15:7** and chapter **23**.

Synagogues *sunagoge* (4864), properly "a bringing together" (*sun*, "together," *ago*, "to bring"), denoted (a) "a gathering of things, a collection," then, of "persons, an assembling, of Jewish religious gatherings," e.g., Acts 9:2; an assembly of Christian Jews, Jas. 2:2, RV, "synagogue" (KJV, marg.; text, "assembly"); a company dominated by the power and activity of Satan, Rev. 2:9; 3:9; (b) by metonymy, "the building" in which the gathering is held, e.g. **Matt. 6:2**, Mark 1:21. The origin of the Jewish "synagogue" is probably to be assigned to the time of the Babylonian exile. Having no temple, the Jews assembled on the Sabbath to hear the Law read, and the practice continued in various buildings after the return. Cf. Ps. 74:8.

Streets *rhume* (4505), in earlier Greek meant "the force or rush or swing of a moving body" in later times, "a narrow road lane or street", it is translated "lanes" in Luke 14:21; "streets" in **Matt. 6:2**; "street" in Acts 9:11; 12:10. In the Sept., Isa. 15:3.

Have *see Matthew 6:1.*

Reward *see Matthew 5:12.*

6:3 But when thou doest alms, let not thy left hand know what thy right hand doeth:

Left *aristeros* (710), is used (a) of the "left" hand, in **Matt. 6:3**, the word "hand" being understood; in connection with the armor of righteousness, in 2 Cor. 6:7, "(on the right hand and) on the left," lit., "(of the weapons ... the right and) the left"; (b) in the phrase "on the left," formed by *ex* (for *ek*), "from," and the genitive plural of this adjective, Mark 10:37; Luke 23:33.

6:4 That thine alms may be in secret: and thy Father which seeth in secret himself shall reward thee openly.

Secret *kruptos* (2927), "secret, hidden" (akin to *krupto*, "to hide"), Eng., "crypt," "cryptic," etc., is used as an adjective and rendered "secret" in Luke 8:17, KJV (RV, "hid"); in the neuter, with *en*, "in," as an adverbial phrase, "in secret," with the article, **Matt. 6:4, 6** (twice in each v.), without the article, John 7:4, 10; 18:20; in the neuter plural, with the article, "the secrets (of men)," Rom. 2:16; of the heart, 1 Cor. 14:25; in Luke 11:33, KJV, "a secret place" (RV, "cellar").

Father *see Matthew 2:22.*

Seeth *blepo* (991), "to have sight," is used of bodily vision, e.g., **Matt. 11:4**; and mental, e.g. **Matt. 13:13, 14**; it is said of God the Father in **Matt. 6:4, 6, 18**; of Christ as "seeing" what the Father doeth, John 5:19. It especially stresses the thought of the person who "sees."

Reward *apodidomi* (591), "to give back," is nowhere translated "to reward" in the RV; KJV, **Matt. 6:4, 6, 18; 16:27**; 2 Tim. 4:14; Rev. 18:6.

Openly In some mss. in **Matt. 6:4, 6, 18**, the phrase *en to phanero*, lit., "in the manifest," is found (KJV, "openly"); see the RV.

6:5 And when thou prayest, thou shalt not be as the hypocrites *are*: for they love to pray standing in the synagogues and in the corners of the streets, that they may be seen of men. Verily I say unto you, They have their reward.

Hypocrites *see Matthew 6:2.*

Standing *see* Stood at *Matthew 2:9.*

Corners *gonia* (1137), "an angle" (Eng., "coign"), signifies (a) "an external angle," as of the "corner" of a street, **Matt. 6:5**; or of a building, **21:42**; Mark 12:10; Luke 20:17; Acts 4:11; 1 Pet. 2:7, "the corner stone or head-stone of the corner"; or the four extreme limits of the earth, Rev. 7:1; 20:8; (b) "an internal corner," a secret place, Acts 26:26.

Streets *plateia* (4113), grammatically the feminine of *platus*, "broad," is used as a noun (*hodos*, "a way," being understood, i.e., "a broad way"), "a street," **Matt. 6:5**; **12:19** (in some texts, Mark 6:56); Luke 10:10; 13:26; 14:21; Acts 5:15; Rev. 11:8; 21:21; 22:2.

Seen *phaino* (5316), "to cause to appear," and in the passive voice, "to appear, be manifest," is rendered "(that) they may be seen" in **Matt. 6:5**; "it was (never so) seen," **9:33**. *See also* Appeared at *Matthew 1:20.*

Have *see Matthew 6:1.*

Reward *see Matthew 5:12.*

6:6 But thou, when thou prayest, enter into thy closet, and when thou hast shut thy door, pray to thy Father which is in secret; and thy Father which seeth in secret shall reward thee openly.

Prayest, Pray "Prayer is properly addressed to God the Father, **Matt. 6:6**; John 16:23; Eph. 1:17; 3:14, and the Son, Acts 7:59; 2 Cor. 12:8; but in no instance in the NT is prayer addressed to the Holy Spirit distinctively, for whereas the Father is in Heaven, **Matt. 6:9**, and the Son is at His right hand, Rom. 8:34, the Holy Spirit is in and with the believers, John 14:16, 17.

"Prayer is to be offered in the Name of the Lord Jesus, John 14:13, that is, the prayer must accord with His character, and must be presented in the same spirit of dependence and submission that marked Him, **Matt. 11:26**; Luke 22:42. The Holy Spirit, being the sole interpreter of the needs of the human heart, makes His intercession therein; and inasmuch as prayer is impossible to man apart from His help, Rom. 8:26, believers are exhorted to pray at all seasons in the Spirit, Eph. 6:18; cf. Jude 20, and Jas. 5:16, the last clause of which should probably be read 'the inwrought [i.e., by the Holy Spirit] supplication of righteous man availeth much' (or 'greatly prevails' *ischuo*, as in Acts 19:16, 20). None the less on this account is the understanding to be engaged in prayer, 1 Cor. 14:15, and the will, Col. 4:12; Acts 12:5 (where 'earnestly' is, lit., 'stretched out') and so in Luke 22:44. Faith is essential to prayer, **Matt. 21:22**; Mark 11:24; Jas. 1:5-8, for faith is the recognition of, and the committal of ourselves and our matters to, the faithfulness of God."

Closet *tameion* (5009), denotes, firstly, "a store-chamber," then, "any private room, secret chamber," **Matt. 6:6**; RV, "inner chamber" (KJV, "closet"); **24:26**, "inner (KJV, secret) chambers"; Luke 12:3, RV, ditto, for KJV, "closets"; it is used in Luke 12:24 ("store-chamber") of birds.

Shut *kleio* (2808), is used (a) of things material, **Matt. 6:6**; **25:10**; Luke 11:7; John 20:19, 26; Acts 5:23; 21:30; Rev. 20:3; figuratively, 21:25; (b) metaphorically, of the kingdom of heaven, **Matt. 23:13**; of heaven, with consequences of famine, Luke 4:25; Rev. 11:6; of compassion, 1 John 3:17, RV (KJV, "bowels *of compassion*"); of the blessings accruing from the promises of God regarding David, Rev. 3:7; of a door for testimony, 3:8.

Door *thura* (2374), "a door, gate" (Eng., "door" is connected), is used (a) literally, e.g., **Matt. 6:6**; **27:60**; (b) metaphorically, of Christ, John 10:7, 9; of faith, by acceptance of the gospel, Acts 14:27; of "openings" for preaching and teaching the Word of God, 1 Cor. 16:9; 2 Cor. 2:12; Col. 4:3; Rev. 3:8; of "entrance" into the Kingdom of God, **Matt. 25:10**; Luke 13:24-25; of Christ's "entrance" into a repentant believer's heart, Rev. 3:20; of the nearness of Christ's second advent, **Matt. 24:33**; Mark 13:29; cf. Jas. 5:9; of "access" to behold visions relative to the purposes of God, Rev. 4:1.

Father *see Matthew 2:22.*

Secret *see Matthew 6:4.*

Seeth *see Matthew 6:4.*

Reward *see Matthew 6:4.*

Openly *see Matthew 6:4.*

6:7 But when ye pray, use not vain repetitions, as the heathen *do*: for they think that they shall be heard for their much speaking.

Repetitions *battalogeo* or *battologeo* (945), "to repeat idly," is used in **Matt. 6:7**, "use (not) vain repetitions"; the meaning "to stammer" is scarcely to be associated with this word. The word is probably from an

Aramaic phrase and onomatopoeic in character. The rendering of the Sinaitic Syriac is "Do not be saying *battalatha*, idle things," i.e., meaningless and mechanically repeated phrases, the reference being to pagan (not Jewish) modes of prayer. *Battalos*, "the Gabbler," was a nickname for Demosthenes, the great orator, assigned to him by his rivals.

Heathen *see* Publicans at *Matthew 5:47*.

Think *see Matthew 3:9*.

Heard *eisakouo* (1522), "to listen to," has two meanings, (a) "to hear and to obey," 1 Cor. 14:21, "they will not hear"; (b) "to hear so as to answer," of God's answer to prayer, **Matt. 6:7**; Luke 1:13; Acts 10:31; Heb. 5:7.

Speaking *polulogia* (4180), "loquacity," "much speaking" (*polus*, "much," *logos*, "speech"), is used in **Matt. 6:7**. In the Sept., Prov. 10:19.

6:8 Be not ye therefore like unto them: for your Father knoweth what things ye have need of, before ye ask him.

Like unto *homoioo* (3666), "to make like," is used (a) especially in the parables, with the significance of comparing, "likening," or, in the passive voice, "being likened," **Matt. 7:24, 26; 11:16; 13:24; 18:23; 22:2** (RV, "likened"); **25:1**; Mark 4:30; Luke 7:31; 13:18, RV, "liken" (KJV, "resemble"); v. 20; in several of these instances the point of resemblance is not a specific detail, but the whole circumstances of the parable; (b) of making "like," or, in the passive voice, of being made or becoming "like," **Matt. 6:8**; Acts 14:11, "in the likeness of (men)," lit., "being made like" (aorist participle, passive); Rom. 9:29; Heb. 2:17, of Christ in being "made like" unto His brethren, i.e., in partaking of human nature, apart from sin (cf. v. 14).

Father *see Matthew 2:22*.

Knoweth *oida* (1492), from the same root as *eidon*, "to see," is a perfect tense with a present meaning, signifying, primarily, "to have seen or perceived"; hence, "to know, to have knowledge of," whether absolutely, as in divine knowledge, e.g., **Matt. 6:8, 32**; John 6:6, 64; 8:14; 11:42; 13:11; 18:4; 2 Cor. 11:31; 2 Pet. 2:9; Rev. 2:2, 9, 13, 19; 3:1, 8, 15; or in the case of human "knowledge," to know from observation, e.g., 1 Thess. 1:4, 5; 2:1; 2 Thess. 3:7. The differences between *ginosko* and *oida* demand consideration: (a) *ginosko*, frequently suggests inception or progress in "knowledge," while *oida* suggests fullness of "knowledge," e.g., John 8:55, "ye have not known Him" (*ginosko*), i.e., begun to "know," "but I know Him" (*oida*), i.e., "know Him perfectly"; 13:7, "What I do thou knowest not now," i.e. Peter did not yet perceive (*oida*) its significance, "but thou shalt understand," i.e., "get to know (*ginosko*), hereafter"; 14:7, "If ye had known Me" (*ginosko*), i.e., "had definitely come to know Me," "ye would have known My Father also" (*oida*), i.e., "would have had perception of": "from henceforth ye know Him" (*ginosko*), i.e., having unconsciously been coming to the Father, as the One who was in Him, they would now consciously be in the constant and progressive experience of "knowing" Him; in Mark 4:13, "Know ye not (*oida*) this parable? and how shall ye know (*ginosko*) all the parables?" (RV), i.e., "Do ye not understand this parable? How shall ye come to perceive all ..." the intimation being that the first parable is a leading and testing one; (b) while *ginosko* frequently implies an active relation between the one who "knows" and the person or thing "known," *oida* expresses the fact that the object has simply come within the scope of the "knower's" perception; thus in **Matt. 7:23** "I never knew you" (*ginosko*) suggests "I have never been in approving connection with you," whereas in **25:12**, "I know you not" (*oida*) suggests "you stand in no relation to Me."

Need *see Matthew 3:14*.

6:9 After this manner therefore pray ye: Our Father which art in heaven, Hallowed be thy name.

Manner *houtos* or *houto* (3779), "thus, in this way," is rendered "after this manner" in **Matt. 6:9**; 1 Pet. 3:5; Rev. 11:5.

Pray *see* Prayest, Pray at *Matthew 6:6*.

Ye *see Matthew 5:13*.

Our This usually translates *hemon*, the genitive of *hemeis*, "we," lit., "of us," e.g., **Matt. 6:9, 11-12**. It is translated "ours," e.g., in Mark 12:7; Luke 20:14; 1 Cor. 1:2; 2 Cor. 1:14.

Father *see Matthew 2:22*.

Hallowed *hagiazo* (37), "to make holy" (from *hagios*, "holy"), signifies to set apart for God, to sanctify, to make a person or thing the opposite of *koinos*, "common"; it is translated "Hallowed," with reference to the name of God the Father in the Lord's Prayer, **Matt. 6:9**; Luke 11:2.

Name *onoma* (3686), is used (I) in general of the "name" by which a person or thing is called, e.g., Mark 3:16, 17, "(He) surnamed," lit., "(He added) the name"; 14:32, lit., "(of which) the name (was)"; Luke 1:63; John 18:10, sometimes translated "named," e.g., Luke 8:5, "named (Zacharias)," lit., "by name"; in the same verse, "named (Elizabeth)," lit., "the name of her," an elliptical phrase, with "was" understood; Acts 8:9, RV, "by name," 10:1; the "name" is put for the reality in Rev.

3:1; in Phil. 2:9, the "Name" represents "the title and dignity" of the Lord, as in Eph. 1:21 and Heb. 1:4;

(II) for all that a "name" implies, of authority, character, rank, majesty, power, excellence, etc., of everything that the "name" covers: (a) of the "Name" of God as expressing His attributes, etc., e.g., **Matt. 6:9**; Luke 1:49; John 12:28; 17:6, 26; Rom. 15:9; 1 Tim. 6:1; Heb. 13:15; Rev. 13:6; (b) of the "Name" of Christ, e.g., **Matt. 10:22**; **19:29**; John 1:12; 2:23; 3:18; Acts 26:9; Rom. 1:5; Jas. 2:7; 1 John 3:23; 3 John 7; Rev. 2:13; 3:8; also the phrases rendered "in the name"; these may be analyzed as follows: (1) representing the authority of Christ, e.g., **Matt. 18:5** (with *epi*, "on the ground of My authority"); so **Matt. 24:5** (falsely) and parallel passages; as substantiated by the Father, John 14:26; 16:23 (last clause), RV; (2) in the power of (with *en*, "in"), e.g., Mark 16:17; Luke 10:17; Acts 3:6; 4:10; 16:18; Jas. 5:14; (3) in acknowledgement or confession of, e.g., Acts 4:12; 8:16; 9:27, 28; (4) in recognition of the authority of (sometimes combined with the thought of relying or resting on), **Matt. 18:20**; cf. **28:19**; Acts 8:16; 9:2 (*eis*, "into"); John 14:13; 15:16; Eph. 5:20; Col. 3:17; (5) owing to the fact that one is called by Christ's "Name" or is identified with Him, e.g. 1 Pet. 4:14 (with *en*, "in"); with *heneken*, "for the sake of," e.g., **Matt. 19:29**; with *dia*, "on account of," **Matt. 10:22**; **24:9**; Mark 13:13; Luke 21:17; John 15:21; 1 John 2:12; Rev. 2:3.

6:10 Thy kingdom come. Thy will be done in earth, as *it is* in heaven.

Kingdom *see* Kingdoms at *Matthew 4:8*.

As *see* Also at *Matthew 5:39*.

6:11 Give us this day our daily bread.

Our *see Matthew 6:9*.

Daily *epiousios* (1967), is found in **Matt. 6:11** and Luke 11:3. Some would derive the word from *epi*, "upon," and *eimi*, "to be," as if to signify "(bread) present," i.e., sufficient bread, but this formation is questionable. The same objection applies to the conjecture, that it is derived from *epi*, and *ousia*, and signifies "(bread) for sustenance." The more probable derivation is from *epi*, and *eimi*, "to go," (bread) for going on, i.e., for the morrow and after, or (bread) coming (for us). See the RV marg. This suits the added *semeron*, "to-day," i.e., the prayer is to be for bread that suffices for this day and next, so that the mind may conform to Christ's warning against anxiety for the morrow. Confirmation of this derivation is also to be found in the word *epious*, in the phrase "the next day," Acts 7:26; 16:11.

Bread *artos* (740), "bread" (perhaps derived from *aro*, "to fit together," or from a root *ar*–, "the earth"), signifies (a) "a small loaf or cake," composed of flour and water, and baked, in shape either oblong or round, and about as thick as the thumb; these were not cut, but broken and were consecrated to the Lord every Sabbath and called the "shewbread" (loaves of presentation), **Matt. 12:4**; when the "shewbread" was reinstituted by Nehemiah (Neh. 10:32) a poll-tax of 1/3 shekel was laid on the Jews, **Matt. 17:24**; (b) "the loaf at the Lord's Supper," e.g., **Matt. 26:26** ("Jesus took a loaf," RV, marg.); the breaking of "bread" became the name for this institution, Acts 2:42; 20:7; 1 Cor. 10:16; 11:23; (c) "bread of any kind," **Matt. 16:11**; (d) metaphorically, "of Christ as the Bread of God, and of Life," John 6:33, 35; (e) "food in general," the necessities for the sustenance of life, **Matt. 6:11**; 2 Cor. 9:10, etc.

> *"If you do not wish for His kingdom, don't pray for it. But if you do, you must do more than pray for it; you must work for it."*
>
> JOHN RUSKIN

6:12 And forgive us our debts, as we forgive our debtors.

Forgive *aphiemi* (863), primarily, "to send forth, send away" (*apo*, "from," *hiemi*, "to send"), denotes, besides its other meanings, "to remit or forgive" (a) debts, **Matt. 6:12**; **18:27**, **32**, these being completely cancelled; (b) sins, e.g., **Matt. 9:2**, **5**, **6**; **12:31**, **32**; Acts 8:22 ("the thought of thine heart"); Rom. 4:7; Jas. 5:15; 1 John 1:9; 2:12. In this latter respect the verb, like its corresponding noun (below), firstly signifies the remission of the punishment due to sinful conduct, the deliverance of the sinner from the penalty divinely, and therefore righteously, imposed; secondly, it involves the complete removal of the cause of offense; such remission is based upon the vicarious and propitiatory sacrifice of Christ. In the OT atoning sacrifice and "forgiveness" are often associated, e.g., Lev. 4:20, 26. The verb is used in the NT with reference to trespasses (*paraptoma*), e.g., **Matt. 6:14**, **15**; sins (*hamartia*), e.g., Luke 5:20; debts (*opheilema*), **Matt. 6:12**; (*opheile*), **18:32**; (*daneion*), **18:27**; the thought (*dianoia*) of the heart, Acts 8:22. Cf. *kalupto*, "to cover," 1 Pet. 4:8; Jas. 5:20; and *epikalupto*, "to cover over," Rom. 4:7, representing the Hebrew words for "atonement." Human "forgiveness" is to be strictly analogous to divine "forgiveness," e.g., **Matt. 6:12**. If certain conditions are fulfilled, there is no limitation to Christ's law of "forgiveness," **Matt. 18:21**, **22**. The conditions are repentance and confession, **Matt. 18:15-17**; Luke 17:3. As to limits to the possibility of divine "forgiveness," see **Matt. 12:32**, 2nd part and 1 John 5:16.

Debts *sopheilema* (3783), expressing a "debt," is used (a) literally, of that which is legally due, Rom. 4:4; (b) metaphorically, of sin as a "debt," because it demands expiation, and thus payment by way of punishment, **Matt. 6:12**.

Debtors *opheiletes* (3781), "one who owes anything to another," primarily in regard to money; in **Matt. 18:24**, "who owed" (lit., "one was brought, a debtor to him of ten thousand talents"). The slave could own property, and so become a "debtor" to his master, who might seize him for payment. It is used metaphorically, (a) of a person who is under an obligation, Rom. 1:14, of Paul, in the matter of preaching the gospel; in Rom. 8:12, of believers, to mortify the deeds of the body; in Rom. 15:27, of gentile believers, to assist afflicted Jewish believers; in Gal. 5:3, of those who would be justified by circumcision, to do the whole Law: (b) of those who have not yet made amends to those whom they have injured, **Matt. 6:12**, "our debtors"; of some whose disaster was liable to be regarded as a due punishment, Luke 13:4 (RV, "offenders"; KJV, "sinners"; marg, "debtors").

6:13 And lead us not into temptation, but deliver us from evil: For thine is the kingdom, and the power, and the glory, for ever. Amen.

Lead *eisphero* (1533), "to bring in, or into," is translated "lead (us not) into," in **Matt. 6:13** and Luke 11:4 (RV, "bring ... into"), of temptation.

Temptation *peirasmos* (3986), is used of (1) "trials" with a beneficial purpose and effect, (a) of "trials" or "temptations," divinely permitted or sent, Luke 22:28; Acts 20:19; Jas. 1:2; 1 Pet. 1:6; 4:12, RV, "to prove," KJV, "to try"; 2 Pet. 2:9 (singular); Rev. 3:10, RV, "trial" (KJV, "temptation"); in Jas. 1:12, "temptation" apparently has meanings (1) and (2) combined, and is used in the widest sense; (b) with a good or neutral significance, Gal. 4:14, of Paul's physical infirmity, "a temptation" to the Galatian converts, of such a kind as to arouse feelings of natural repugnance; (c) of "trials" of a varied character, **Matt. 6:13** and Luke 11:4, where believers are commanded to pray not to be led into such by forces beyond their own control; **Matt. 26:41**; Mark 14:38; Luke 22:40, 46, where they are commanded to watch and pray against entering into "temptations" by their own carelessness or disobedience; in all such cases God provides "the way of escape," 1 Cor. 10:13 (where *peirasmos* occurs twice). (2) Of "trial" definitely designed to lead to wrong doing, "temptation," Luke 4:13; 8:13; 1 Tim. 6:9; (3) of "trying" or challenging God, by men, Heb. 3:8.

Deliver *rhuomai* (4506), "to rescue from, to preserve from," and so, "to deliver," the word by which it is regularly translated, is largely synonymous with *sozo*, "to save," though the idea of "rescue from" is predominant in *rhuomai* (see **Matt. 27:43**), that of "preservation from," in *sozo*. In Rom. 11:26 the present participle is used with the article, as a noun, "the Deliverer." This is the construction in 1 Thess. 1:10, where Christ is similarly spoken of. Here the KJV wrongly has "which delivered" (the tense is not past); RV, "which delivereth"; the translation might well be (as in Rom. 11:26), "our Deliverer," that is, from the retributive calamities with which God will visit men at the end of the present age. From that wrath believers are to be "delivered." The verb is used with *apo*, "away from," in **Matt. 6:13**; Luke 11:4 (in some mss.); so also in 11:4; Rom. 15:31; 2 Thess. 3:2; 2 Tim. 4:18; and with *ek*, "from, out of," in Luke 1:74; Rom. 7:24; 2 Cor. 1:10; Col. 1:13, from bondage; in 2 Pet. 2:9, from temptation, in 2 Tim. 3:11, from persecution; but *ek* is used of ills impending, in 2 Cor. 1:10; in 2 Tim. 4:17, *ek* indicates that the danger was more imminent than in v. 18, where *apo* is used. Accordingly the meaning "out of the midst of" cannot be pressed in 1 Thess. 1:10.

Evil *see Matthew 5:37.*

6:14 For if ye forgive men their trespasses, your heavenly Father will also forgive you:

Forgive *see Matthew 6:12.*

Trespasses *paraptoma* (3900), primarily "a false step, a blunder" (akin to *parapipto*, "to fall away," Heb. 6:6), lit., "a fall beside," used ethically, denotes "a trespass," a deviation, from uprightness and truth, **Matt. 6:14**, **15** (twice); **18:35**, in some mss.; Mark 11:25,

"The Lord's Prayer may be committed to memory quickly, but it is slowly learnt by heart."

JOHN FREDERICK DENISON MAURICE

26; in Romans the RV substitutes "trespass" and "trespasses" for KJV, "offense" and "offenses," 4:25, "for (i.e., because of) our trespasses"; 5:15 (twice), where the trespass is that of Adam (in contrast to the free gift of righteousness, v. 17, a contrast in the nature and the effects); 5:16, where "of many trespasses" expresses a contrast of quantity; the condemnation resulted from one "trespass," the free gift is "of (*ek*, expressing the origin, and throwing stress upon God's justifying grace in Christ) many trespasses"; v. 17, introducing a contrast between legal effects and those of divine grace; v. 18, where the RV, "through one trespass," is contrasted with "one act of righteousness"; this is important, the difference is not between one man's "trespass" and Christ's righteousness (as KJV), but between two acts, that of Adam's "trespass" and the vicarious death of Christ; v. 20; in 2 Cor. 5:19, KJV and RV, "trespasses"; in Eph. 1:7, RV, "trespasses" (KJV, "sins"); in 2:1, RV, "(dead through your) trespasses," KJV, "(dead in) trespasses"; 2:5, RV, "(dead through our) trespasses," KJV, "(dead in) sins"; so Col. 2:13 (1st part); in the 2nd part, KJV and RV, "trespasses." In Gal. 6:1, RV, "(in any) trespass" (KJV, "fault"), the reference is to "the works of the flesh" (5:19), and the thought is that of the believer's being found off his guard, the "trespass" taking advantage of him; in Jas. 5:16, KJV, "faults" (RV, "sins" translates the word *hamartias*, which is found in the best texts), auricular confession to a priest is not in view here or anywhere else in Scripture; the command is comprehensive, and speaks either of the acknowledgment of sin where one has wronged another, or of the unburdening of a troubled conscience to a godly brother whose prayers will be efficacious, or of open confession before the church. In Rom. 11:11, 12, the word is used of Israel's "fall," i.e., their deviation from obedience to God and from the fulfillment of His will (to be distinguished from the verb *ptaio*, "fall," in the 1st part of v. 11, which indicates the impossibility of recovery).

Heavenly *ouranios* (3770), signifying "of heaven, heavenly," is used (a) as an appellation of God the Father, **Matt. 6:14**, **26**, **32**, "your heavenly Father"; **15:13**, "My heavenly Father"; (b) as descriptive of the holy angels, Luke 2:13; (c) of the vision seen by Paul, Acts 26:19.

6:15 But if ye forgive not men their trespasses, neither will your Father forgive your trespasses.

Forgive *see Matthew 6:12.*

Trespasses *see Matthew 6:14.*

6:16 Moreover when ye fast, be not, as the hypocrites, of a sad countenance: for they disfigure their faces, that they may appear unto men to fast. Verily I say unto you, They have their reward.

Fast *see* Fasted at *Matthew 4:2.*

Hypocrites *see Matthew 6:2.*

Countenance *skuthropos*, "of a sad countenance" (*skuthros*, "gloomy, sad," *ops*, "an eye"), is used in **Matt. 6:16** and Luke 24:17, "sad."

Disfigure *aphanizo* (853), primarily means "to cause to disappear," hence (a) "to make unsightly, to disfigure," as of the face, **Matt. 6:16**; (b) "to cause to vanish away, consume," **Matt. 6:19**, **20**; (c) in the passive voice, "to perish," Acts 13:41, or "to vanish away," Jas. 4:14.

Faces *prosopon* (4383), denotes "the countenance," lit., "the part towards the eyes" (from *pros*, "towards," *ops*, "the eye"), and is used (a) of the "face," **Matt. 6:16-17**; 2 Cor. 3:7, 2nd part (KJV, "countenance"); in 2 Cor. 10:7, in the RV, "things that are before your face" (KJV, "outward appearance"), the phrase is figurative of superficial judgment; (b) of the look, i.e., the "face," which by its various movements affords an index of inward thoughts and feelings, e g., Luke 9:51, 53; 1 Pet. 3:12; (c) the presence of a person, the "face" being the noblest part, e.g., Acts 3:13, RV, "before the face of," KJV, "in the presence of"; 5:41, "presence"; 2 Cor. 2:10, "person"; 1 Thess. 2:17 (first part), "presence"; 2 Thess. 1:9, RV, "face," KJV, "presence"; Rev. 12:14, "face"; (d) the person himself, e.g., Gal. 1:22; 1 Thess. 2:17 (second part); (e) the appearance one presents by his wealth or poverty, his position or state, **Matt. 22:16**; Mark 12:14; Gal. 2:6; Jude 16; (f) the outward appearance of inanimate things, **Matt. 16:3**; Luke 12:56; 21:35; Acts 17:26. "To spit in a person's face" was an expression of the utmost scorn and aversion, e.g., **Matt. 26:67** (cf. **27:30**; Mark 10:34; Luke 18:32).

Have *see Matthew 6:2.*

Reward *see Matthew 5:12.*

6:17 But thou, when thou fastest, anoint thine head, and wash thy face;

Fastest *see* Fasted at *Matthew 4:2*.

Anoint *aleipho* (218), is a general term used for "an anointing" of any kind, whether of physical refreshment after washing, e.g., in the Sept. of Ruth 3:3; 2 Sam. 12:20; Dan. 10:3; Micah 6:15; in the NT, **Matt. 6:17**; Luke 7:38, 46; John 11:2; 12:3; or of the sick, Mark 6:13; Jas. 5:14; or a dead body, Mark 16:1. The material used was either oil, or ointment, as in Luke 7:38, 46. In the Sept. it is also used of "anointing" a pillar, Gen. 31:13, or captives, 2 Chron. 28:15, or of daubing a wall with mortar, Ezek. 13:10-12, 14-15; and, in the sacred sense, of "anointing" priests, in Exod. 40:15 (twice), and Num. 3:3.

Wash *nipto* (3538), is chiefly used of "washing part of the body," John 13:5-6, 8 (twice, figuratively in 2nd clause), 12, 14 (twice); in 1 Tim. 5:10, including the figurative sense; in the middle voice, to wash oneself, **Matt. 6:17**; **15:2**; Mark 7:3; John 9:7, 11, 15; 13:10. For the corresponding noun.

6:18 That thou appear not unto men to fast, but unto thy Father which is in secret: and thy Father, which seeth in secret, shall reward thee openly.

Appear *see* Appeared at *Matthew 1:20*.

Fast *see* Fasted at *Matthew 4:2*.

Secret *kruphaios* (2928), occurs in the best mss. in **Matt. 6:18** (twice).

Seeth *see Matthew 6:4*.

Reward *see Matthew 6:4*.

Openly *see Matthew 6:4*.

6:19 Lay not up for yourselves treasures upon earth, where moth and rust doth corrupt, and where thieves break through and steal:

Lay *thesaurizo* (2343), "to lay up, store up" (akin to *thesauros*, "a treasury, a storehouse, a treasure"), is used of "laying" up treasures, on earth, **Matt. 6:19**; in Heaven, v. **20**; in the last days, Jas. 5:3, RV, "ye have laid up your treasure" (KJV, "ye have heaped treasure together"); in Luke 12:21, "that layeth up treasure (for himself)"; in 1 Cor. 16:2, of money for needy ones (here the present participle is translated "in store," lit., "treasuring" or "storing," the "laying by" translating the preceding verb *tithemi*); in 2 Cor. 12:14, negatively, of children for parents; metaphorically, of "laying" up wrath, Rom. 2:5, "treasurest up." In 2 Pet. 3:7 the passive voice is used of the heavens and earth as "stored up" for fire, RV (marg., "stored" with fire), KJV, "kept in store."

Yourselves *see* Ye at *Matthew 5:13*.

Treasures *see Matthew 2:11*.

Earth *see Matthew 5:18*.

Moth *ses* (4597), denotes "a clothes moth," **Matt. 6:19**, **20**; Luke 12:33. In Job 4:19 "crushed before the moth" alludes apparently to the fact that woolen materials, riddled by the larvae of "moths," become so fragile that a touch demolishes them. In Job 27:18 "He buildeth his house as a "moth" alludes to the frail covering which a larval "moth" constructs out of the material which it consumes. The rendering "spider" (marg.) seems an attempt to explain a difficulty.

Rust *brosis* (1035), "an eating" (akin to *bibrosko*, "to eat"), is used metaphorically to denote "rust" in **Matt. 6:19, 20**.

Corrupt *aphanizo* (853), lit., "to cause to disappear, put out of sight," came to mean "to do away with" (*a*, negative, *phaino*, "to cause to appear"), said of the destructive work of moth and rust, **Matt. 6:19-20** (RV, "consume," KJV, "corrupt"). *See also* Disfigure at *Matthew 6:16*.

Thieves *kleptes* (2812), is used (a) literally, **Matt. 6:19**, **20**; **24:43**; Luke 12:33, 39; John 10:1, 10; 12:6; 1 Cor. 6:10; 1 Pet. 4:15; (b) metaphorically of "false teachers," John 10:8; (c) figuratively, (1) of the personal coming of Christ, in a warning to a local church, with most of its members possessed of mere outward profession and defiled by the world, Rev. 3:3; in retributive intervention to overthrow the foes of God, 16:15; (2) of the Day of the Lord, in divine judgment upon the world, 2 Pet. 3:10 and 1 Thess. 5:2, 4; in v. 2, according to the order in the original "the word 'night' is not to be read with 'the day of the Lord,' but with 'thief,' i.e., there is no reference to the time of the coming, only to the manner of it. To avoid ambiguity the phrase may be paraphrased, 'so comes as a thief in the night comes.' The use of the present tense instead of the future emphasizes the certainty of the coming.... The unexpectedness of the coming of the thief, and the unpreparedness of those to whom he comes, are the essential elements in the figure; cf. the entirely different figure used in **Matt. 25:1-13**."

Break *diorusso* (1358), lit., "to dig through" (*dia*, "through," *orusso*, "to dig"), is used of the act of thieves in "breaking" into a house, **Matt. 6:19**, **20**; **24:43**; Luke 12:39.

Steal *klepto* (2813), "to steal," akin to *kleptes*, "a thief" (cf. Eng., "kleptomania"), occurs in **Matt. 6:19**, **20**; **19:18**; **27:64**; **28:13**; Mark 10:19;

Luke 18:20; John 10:10; Rom. 2:21 (twice); 13:9; Eph. 4:28 (twice).

6:20 But lay up for yourselves treasures in heaven, where neither moth nor rust doth corrupt, and where thieves do not break through nor steal:

Lay *see Matthew 6:19.*

Yourselves *see* Ye at *Matthew 5:13.*

Treasures *see Matthew 2:11.*

Moth *see Matthew 6:19.*

Rust *see Matthew 6:19.*

Corrupt *see* Disfigure at *Matthew 6:16.*

Thieves *see Matthew 6:19.*

Break *see Matthew 6:19.*

Steal *see Matthew 6:19.*

6:21 For where your treasure is, there will your heart be also.

Treasure *see* Treasures at *Matthew 2:11.*

6:22 The light of the body is the eye: if therefore thine eye be single, thy whole body shall be full of light.

"Money is emphasized in Scripture simply because our temptation to love it is inexplicably powerful."

ERWIN W. LUTZER

Light *photeinos* (5460), from *phos,* "bright," is rendered "full of light" in **Matt. 6:22**; Luke 11:34, 36 (twice), figuratively, of the single-mindedness of the eye, which acts as the lamp of the body; in **Matt. 17:5**, "bright," of a cloud. *See also Matthew 5:14. See also* **Candle** at *Matthew 5:15.*

Body *see Matthew 5:29.*

Eye *see Matthew 5:38.*

Single *haplous* (573), "simple, single," is used in a moral sense in **Matt. 6:22** and Luke 11:34, said of the eye; "singleness" of purpose keeps us from the snare of having a double treasure and consequently a divided heart. The papyri provide instances of its use in other than the moral sense, e.g., of a marriage dowry, to be repaid pure and simple by a husband (Moulton and Milligan). In the Sept., Prov. 11:25.

6:23 But if thine eye be evil, thy whole body shall be full of darkness. If therefore the light that is in thee be darkness, how great is that darkness!

Eye *see Matthew 5:38.*

Evil *see Matthew 5:11.*

Darkness *skoteinos* (4652), "full of darkness, or covered with darkness," is translated "dark" in Luke 11:36; "full of darkness," in **Matt. 6:23**; *skotos* (4655), a neuter noun frequent in the Sept., is used in the NT, (a) of "physical darkness," **Matt. 27:45**; 2 Cor. 4:6; (b) of "intellectual darkness," Rom. 2:19; (c) of "blindness," Acts 13:11; (d) by metonymy, of the "place of punishment," e.g., **Matt. 8:12**; 2 Pet. 2:17; Jude 13; (e) metaphorically, of "moral and spiritual darkness," e.g., **Matt. 6:23**; Luke 1:79; 11:35; John 3:19; Acts 26:18; 2 Cor. 6:14; Eph. 6:12; Col. 1:13; 1 Thess. 5:4-5; 1 Pet. 2:9; 1 John 1:6; (f) by metonymy, of "those who are in moral or spiritual darkness," Eph. 5:8; (g) of "evil works," Rom. 13:12; Eph. 5:11; (h) of the "evil powers that dominate the world," Luke 22:53; (i) "of secrecy." While *skotos* is used more than twice as many times as *skotia* in the NT, the apostle John uses *skotos* only once, 1 John 1:6, but *skotia* 15 times out of the 18.

Great *posos* (4214), an adjective of number, magnitude, degree, etc., is rendered "how great" in **Matt. 6:23**.

6:24 No man can serve two masters: for either he will hate the one, and love the other; or else he will hold to the one, and despise the other. Ye cannot serve God and mammon.

Serve *douleuo* (1398), "to serve as a *doulos,*" is used (a) of serving God (and the impossibility of serving mammon also), **Matt. 6:24** and Luke 16:13; Rom. 7:6; in the gospel, Phil. 2:22; (b) Christ, Acts 20:19; Rom. 12:11; 14:18; 16:18; Eph. 6:7; Col. 3:24; (c) the law of God, Rom. 7:25; (d) one another, Gal. 5:13, RV, "be servants to" (KJV, "serve"); (e) a father, Luke 15:29 (with a suggestion of acting as a slave); (f) earthly masters, **Matt. 6:24**; Luke 16:13; 1 Tim. 6:2, RV, "serve"; (g) the younger by the elder, Rom. 9:12; (h) of being in bondage to a nation, Acts 7:7; Gal. 4:25, to the Romans, actually, though also spiritually to Judaizers; (i) to idols, Gal. 4:8, RV, "were in bondage" (KJV, "did service"); (j) to "the weak and beggarly rudiments," v. 9 (RV), "to be in bondage" (aorist tense in the best texts, suggesting "to enter into bondage"), i.e., to the religion of the Gentiles ("rudiments" being used in v. 3 of the religion of the Jews); (k) sin, Rom. 6:6, RV, "be in bondage" (KJV, "serve"); (l) "divers lusts and pleasures," Titus 3:3; (m) negatively, to any man – a proud and thoughtless denial by the Jews, John 8:33.

Masters *kurios* (2962), "a lord, one who exercises power," is translated "masters" in **Matt. 6:24; 15:27**; Mark 13:35; Luke 16:13; Acts 16:16, 19; Rom. 14:4, KJV (RV, "lord"); Eph. 6:5, 9 (twice), the 2nd time of Christ; so in Col. 3:22; 4:1. *See also* **Lord** at *Matthew 1:22*.

Either *e* (2228), is a disjunctive particle. One of its uses is to distinguish things which exclude each other, or one of which can take the place of another. It is translated "either" in **Matt. 6:24; 12:33**; Luke 16:13; Acts 17:21; 1 Cor. 14:6. The RV rightly omits it in Luke 6:42, and translates it by "or" in Luke 15:8; Phil. 3:12 and Jas. 3:12.

Hate *miseo* (3404), "to hate," is used especially (a) of malicious and unjustifiable feelings towards others, whether towards the innocent or by mutual animosity, e.g., **Matt. 10:22; 24:10**; Luke 6:22, 27; 19:14; John 3:20, of "hating" the light (metaphorically); 7:7; 15:18, 19, 23-25; Titus 3:3; 1 John 2:9, 11; 3:13, 15; 4:20; Rev. 18:2, where "hateful" translates the perfect participle passive voice of the verb, lit., "hated," or "having been hated"; (b) of a right feeling of aversion from what is evil; said of wrongdoing, Rom. 7:15; iniquity, Heb. 1:9; "the garment (figurative) spotted by the flesh," Jude 23; "the works of the Nicolaitans," Rev. 2:6 (and v. 15, in some mss.; see the KJV); (c) of relative preference for one thing over another, by way of expressing either aversion from, or disregard for, the claims of one person or thing relatively to those of another, **Matt. 6:24**, and Luke 16:13, as to the impossibility of serving two masters; Luke 14:26, as to the claims of parents relatively to those of Christ; John 12:25, of disregard for one's life relatively to the claims of Christ; Eph. 5:29, negatively, of one's flesh, i.e. of one's own, and therefore a man's wife as one with him.

One *heis* (1520), the first cardinal numeral, masculine (feminine and neuter nominative forms are *mia* and *hen*, respectively), is used to signify (1) (a) "one" in contrast to many, e.g., **Matt. 25:15**; Rom. 5:18, RV, "(through) one (trespass)," i.e., Adam's transgression, in contrast to the "one act of righteousness," i.e., the death of Christ (not as KJV, "the offense of one," and "the righteousness of one"); (b) metaphorically, "union" and "concord," e.g., John 10:30; 11:52; 17:11, 21-22; Rom. 12:4-5; Phil. 1:27; (2) emphatically, (a) a single ("one"), to the exclusion of others, e.g., **Matt. 21:24**; Rom. 3:10; 1 Cor. 9:24; 1 Tim. 2:5 (twice); (b) "one, alone," e.g., Mark 2:7, RV (KJV, "only"); 10:18; Luke 18:19; (c) "one and the same," e.g., Rom. 3:30, RV, "God is one," i.e., there is not "one" God for the Jew and one for the Gentile; cf. Gal. 3:20, which means that in a promise there is no other party; 1 Cor. 3:8; 11:5; 12.11, 1 John 5:8 (lit., "and the three are into one," i.e., united in "one" and the same witness); (3) a certain "one," in the same sense as the indefinite pronoun *tis*, e.g., **Matt. 8:19**, RV, "a (scribe)," marg., "one (scribe)," KJV, "a certain (scribe)"; **19:16**, "one;" in Rev. 8:13, RV marg., "one (eagle)"; *heis tis* are used together in Luke 22:50; John 11:49; this occurs frequently in the papyri (Moulton, *Prol.*, p. 96); (4) distributively, with *hekastos*, "each," i.e., "every one," e.g., Luke 4:40; Acts 2:6, "every man" (lit., "every one"); in the sense of "one ... and one," e.g., John 20:12; or "one" ... followed by *allos* or *heteros*, "the other," e.g., **Matt. 6:24**; or by a second *heis*, e.g., **Matt. 24:40**, RV, "one"; John 20:12; in Rom. 12:5 *heis* is preceded by *kata* (*kath'*) in the sense of "severally (members) one (of another)," RV (KJV, "every one ... one"); cf. Mark 14:19; in 1 Thess. 5:11 the phrase in the 2nd part, "each other," RV (KJV, "one another"), is, lit., "one the one"; (5) as an ordinal number, equivalent to *protos*, "first," in the phrase "the first day of the week," lit. and idiomatically, "one of sabbaths," signifying "the first day after the sabbath," e.g., **Matt. 28:1**; Mark 16:2; Acts 20:7; 1 Cor. 16:2. Moulton remarks on the tendency for certain cardinal numerals to replace ordinals (*Prol.*, p. 96).

Hold *antecho* (472), signifies in the middle voice, (a) "to hold firmly to, cleave to," of "holding" or cleaving to a person, **Matt. 6:24**; Luke 16:13; of "holding" to the faithful word, Titus 1:9, RV, KJV, "holding fast"; (b) "to support," 1 Thess. 5:14 (the weak).

Despise *kataphroneo* (2706), lit., "to think down upon or against anyone" (*kata*, "down," *phren*, "the mind"), hence signifies "to think slightly of, to despise," **Matt. 6:24; 18:10**; Luke 16:13; Rom. 2:4; 1 Cor. 11:22; 1 Tim. 4:12; 6:2; Heb. 12:2; 2 Pet. 2:10.

Mammon *mamonas* (3126), a common Aramaic word for "riches," akin to a Hebrew word signifying "to be firm, steadfast" (whence "Amen"), hence, "that which is to be trusted"; Gesenius regards it as derived from a Heb. word signifying "treasure" (Gen. 43:23); it is personified in **Matt. 6:24**; Luke 16:9, 11, 13.

6:25 Therefore I say unto you, Take no thought for your life, what ye shall eat, or what ye

shall drink; nor yet for your body, what ye shall put on. Is not the life more than meat, and the body than raiment?

Thought *merimnao* (3309), denotes "to be anxious, careful." For the KJV, "to take thought," the RV substitutes "to be anxious" in **Matt. 6:25, 27, 28, 31, 34; 10:19**; Luke 12:11, 22, 25, 26.

Life *see Matthew 2:20.*

Put *enduo* (1746), used in the middle voice, of "putting" on oneself, or on another, is translated "to put on" (a) literally, **Matt. 6:25; 27:31**; Mark 6:9; 15:20; Luke 12:22; 15:22; (b) metaphorically, of "putting" on the armor of light, Rom. 13:12; the Lord Jesus Christ, 13:14; Christ, Gal. 3:27; incorruption and immortality (said of the body of the believer), 1 Cor. 15:53, 54; the new man, Eph. 4:24; Col. 3:10; the whole armor of God, Eph. 6:11; the breastplate of righteousness, 6:14, RV; the breastplate of faith and love, 1 Thess. 5:8; various Christian qualities, Col. 3:12.

More *pleion* (4119), "more, greater," the comparative degree of *polus*, "much," is translated "more excellent" in Heb. 11:4, of Abel's sacrifice; *pleion* is used sometimes of that which is superior by reason of inward worth, cf. 3:3, "more (honor)"; in **Matt. 6:25**, of the life in comparison with meat.

Meat *see Matthew 3:4.*

Raiment *see Matthew 3:4.*

6:26 Behold the fowls of the air: for they sow not, neither do they reap, nor gather into barns; yet your heavenly Father feedeth them. Are ye not much better than they?

Behold *emblepo* (1689), expresses "earnest looking," e.g., in the Lord's command to "behold" the birds of the heaven, with the object of learning lessons of faith from them, **Matt. 6:26**. See also **19:26**; Mark 8:25; 10:21, 27; 14:67; Luke 20:17; 22:61; John 1:36; of the Lord's looking upon Peter, John 1:42; Acts 1:11; 22:11.

"Anxiety is the natural result when our hopes are centered in anything short of God and his will for us."

BILLY GRAHAM

Fowls *peteinon* (4071), signifies "that which is able to fly, winged." It is connected with *ptenon* signifying "feathered, winged," which is used in 1 Cor. 15:39. Cf. *petomai* and *petaomai*, "to fly." In the Gospels the RV always translates it "birds," e.g., **Matt. 6:26**; but "fowls" in Acts 10:12; 11:6. The KJV unsuitably has "fowls," in the Gospels, except **Matt. 8:20; 13:32**; Luke 9:58.

Reap *therizo* (2325), "to reap" (akin to *theros*, "summer, harvest"), is used (a) literally, **Matt. 6:26; 25:24, 26**; Luke 12:24; 19:21, 22; Jas. 5:4 (2nd part), KJV, "have reaped"; (b) figuratively or in proverbial expressions, John 4:36 (twice), 37, 38, with immediate reference to bringing Samaritans into the kingdom of God, in regard to which the disciples would enjoy the fruits of what Christ Himself had been doing in Samaria; the Lord's words are, however, of a general application in respect of such service; in 1 Cor. 9:11, with reference to the right of the apostle and his fellow missionaries to receive material assistance from the church, a right which he forbore to exercise; in 2 Cor. 9:6 (twice), with reference to rendering material help to the needy, either "sparingly" or "bountifully," the "reaping" being proportionate to the sowing; in Gal. 6:7, 8 (twice), of "reaping" corruption, with special reference, according to the context, to that which is naturally shortlived transient (though the statement applies to every form of sowing to the flesh), and of "reaping" eternal life (characteristics and moral qualities being in view), as a result of sowing "to the Spirit," the reference probably being to the new nature of the believer, which is, however, under the controlling power of the Holy Spirit, v. 9, the "reaping" (the effect of well doing) being accomplished, to a limited extent, in this life, but in complete fulfillment at and beyond the judgment seat of Christ; diligence or laxity here will then produce proportionate results; in Rev. 14:15 (twice), 16; figurative of the discriminating judgment divinely to be fulfilled at the close of this age, when the wheat will be separated from the tares (see **Matt. 13:30**).

Barns *see* Garner at *Matthew 3:12.*

Yet *see* And at *Matthew 3:14.*

Heavenly *see* Heaven at *Matthew 5:16.*

Feedeth *trepho* (5142), signifies (a) "to make to grow, bring up, rear," Luke 4:16, "brought up"; (b) "to nourish, feed," **Matt. 6:26; 25:37**; Luke 12:24; Acts 12:20; Rev. 12:6, 14; of a mother, "to give suck," Luke 23:29 (some mss. here have *thelazo*, "to suckle"); "to fatten," as of fattening animals, Jas. 5:5, "ye have nourished (your hearts)."

Better *diaphero* (1308), used (a) transitively, means "to carry through" or "about" (*dia*, "through," *phero*, "to carry"), Mark 11:16 ("carry ... through"); Acts 13:49; 27:27 ("driven to and fro"); (b) intransitively, (1) "to differ," Rom. 2:18; Gal. 2:6; Phil. 1:10; (2) "to excel, be better," e.g., **Matt. 6:26**; **10:31** ("of more value"); **12:12**; Luke 12:7, 24; 1 Cor. 15:41; Gal. 4:1; some would put Rom. 2:18 and Phil. 1:10 here (see marg.).

6:27 Which of you by taking thought can add one cubit unto his stature?

Which This is the translation of (a) the article with nouns, adjectives, numerals, participles, etc., e.g., "that which," etc.; (b) the relative pronoun *hos*, "who," in one of its forms (a frequent use); (c) *hostis*, "whoever," differing from *hos* by referring to a subject in general, as one of a class, e.g., Rom. 2:15; Gal. 4:24 (twice); 5:19; Rev. 2:24; 20:4; (d) the interrogative pronoun *tis*, "who? which?," e.g., **Matt. 6:27**; John 8:46; (e) *hoios*, "of what kind," e.g., Phil. 1:30; (f) *poios*, the interrogative of (e), e.g., John 10:32; (g) *hosos*, "whatsoever," etc.; plural, how many, translated "which" in Acts 9:39.

Thought *see Matthew 6:25.*

Cubit *pechus* (4083), denotes the forearm, i.e., the part between the hand and the elbow-joint; hence, "a measure of length," not from the wrist to the elbow, but from the tip of the middle finger to the elbow joint, i.e., about a foot and a half, or a little less than two feet, **Matt. 6:27**; Luke 12:25; John 21:8; Rev. 21:17.

Stature *helikia* (2244), primarily "an age," as a certain length of life, came to mean (a) "a particular time of life," as when a person is said to be "of age," John 9:21, 23, or beyond a certain stage of life, Heb. 11:11; (b) elsewhere only "of stature," e.g., **Matt. 6:27**; Luke 2:52; 12:25; 19:3; Eph. 4:13. Some regard **Matt. 6:27** and Luke 12:25 as coming under (a). It is to be distinguished from *aion* and *genea*, since it has to do simply with matters relating to an individual, either his time of life or his height.

6:28 And why take ye thought for raiment? Consider the lilies of the field, how they grow; they toil not, neither do they spin:

Thought *see Matthew 6:25.*

Raiment *see Matthew 3:4.*

Consider *katamanthano* (2648), lit., "to learn thoroughly" (*kata*, "down," intensive, *manthano*, "to learn"), hence, "to note accurately, consider well," is used in the Lord's exhortation to "consider" the lilies. **Matt. 6:28.**

Lilies *krinon* (2918), occurs in **Matt. 6:28** and Luke 12:27; in the former the Lord speaks of "the lilies of the field"; the "lily" referred to was a flower of rich color, probably including the gladiolus and iris species. The former "grow among the grain, often overtopping it and illuminating the broad fields with their various shades of pinkish purple to deep violet purple and blue.... Anyone who has stood among the wheat fields of Galilee ... will see at once the appropriateness of our Savior's allusion. They all have a reedy stem, which, when dry, would make such fuel as is used in the ovens. The beautiful irises ... have gorgeous flowers, and would suit our Savior's comparison even better than the above. But they are plants of pasture grounds and swamps, and seldom found in grain fields. If, however, we understand by 'lilies of the field' simply wild lilies, these would also be included in the expression. Our Savior's comparison would then be like a 'composite photograph,' a reference to all the splendid colors and beautiful shapes of the numerous wild plants comprehended under the name 'lily'" (G. E. Post, in *Hastings' Bib. Dic.*).

Field *agros* (68), denotes (a) "a field" (cf. Eng., "agriculture"), e.g., **Matt. 6:28**; (b) "the country," e.g., Mark 15:21, or, in the plural, "country places, farms," Mark 5:14; 6:36, 56; Luke 8:34; 9:12; (c) "a piece of ground," e.g., Mark 10:29; Acts 4:37; "a farm," **Matt. 22:5**.

Grow *auxano* (837), "to grow or increase," of the growth of that which lives, naturally or spiritually, is used (a) transitively, signifying to make to increase, said of giving the increase, 1 Cor. 3:6, 7; 2 Cor. 9:10, the effect of the work of God, according to the analogy of His operations in nature; "to grow, become greater," e.g., of plants and fruit, **Matt. 6:28**; used in the passive voice in **13:32** and Mark 4:8, "increase"; in the active in Luke 12:27; 13:19; of the body, Luke 1:80; 2:40; of Christ, John 3:30, "increase"; of the work of the gospel of God, Acts 6:7, "increased"; 12:24; 19:20; of people, Acts 7:17; of faith, 2 Cor. 10:15 (passive voice), RV, "groweth" (KJV, "is increased"); of believers individually, Eph. 4:15; Col. 1:6, RV, 10 (passive voice), "increasing"; 1 Pet. 2:2; 2 Pet. 3:18; of the church, Col. 2:19; of churches, Eph. 2:21.

Toil *kopiao* (2872), "to be weary, to labor," is rendered "to toil" in **Matt. 6:28**; Luke 5:5 (12:27), in some mss.); in 1 Cor. 4:12, RV (KJV, "we labor").

Spin *netho* (3514), "to spin," is found in **Matt. 6:28** and Luke 12:27, of the lilies of the field.

6:29 And yet I say unto you, That even Solomon in all his glory was not arrayed like one of these.

Like *hos* (5613), used as a relative adverb of manner, means "as, like as," etc., and is translated "like," e.g., in **Matt. 6:29**; Mark 4:31; Luke 12:27; in Acts 3:22 and 7:37 (see RV, marg.); in 8:32 (2nd part), RV, "as" (KJV, "like"); Rev. 2:18, RV (the rendering should have been "as" here); 18:21, RV, "as it were" (KJV, "like"); 21:11, 2nd part (ditto).

6:30 Wherefore, if God so clothe the grass of the field, which to day is, and to morrow is cast into the oven, *shall he* not much more *clothe* you, O ye of little faith?

Clothe *amphiennumi* (294), "to put clothes round" (*amphi*, "around," *hennumi*, "to clothe"), "to invest," signifies, in the middle voice, to put clothing on oneself, e.g., **Matt. 6:30**; **11:8**; Luke 7:25; 12:28.

Grass *chortos* (5528), primarily denoted "a feeding enclosure" (whence Latin *hortus*, "a garden"; Eng., "yard," and "garden"); then, "food," especially grass for feeding cattle; it is translated "grass" in **Matt. 6:30**; **14:19**; Mark 6:39 (where "the green grass" is the first evidence of early spring); Luke 12:28; John 6:10; Jas. 1:10, 11; 1 Pet. 1:24; Rev. 8:7; 9:4; "blade" in **Matt. 13:26**; Mark 4:28; "hay" in 1 Cor. 3:12, used figuratively. In Palestine or Syria there are 90 genera and 243 species of grass.

Morrow *aurion* (839), an adverb denoting "tomorrow," is used (a) with this meaning in **Matt. 6:30**; Luke 12:28; 13:32, 33; Acts 23:15 (in some mss.), 20; 25:22; 1 Cor. 15:32; Jas. 4:13; (b) with the word *hemera*, "day," understood (occurring thus in the papyri), translated as a noun, "(the) morrow," **Matt. 6:34** (twice); Luke 10:35; Acts 4:3 (KJV, "next day"); 4:5; Jas. 4:14.

Oven *klibanos* (2823), is mentioned in **Matt. 6:30** and Luke 12:28. The form of "oven" commonly in use in the east indicates the kind in use as mentioned in Scripture. A hole is sunk in the ground about 3 feet deep and somewhat less in diameter. The walls are plastered with cement. A fire is kindled inside, the fuel being grass, or dry twigs, which heat the oven rapidly and blacken it with smoke and soot (see Lam. 5:10). When sufficiently heated the surface is wiped, and the dough is molded into broad thin loaves, placed one at a time on the wall of the "oven" to fit its concave inner circle. The baking takes a few seconds. Such ovens are usually outside the home, and often the same "oven" serves for several families (Lev. 26:26). An "oven" of this sort is doubtless referred to in Ex. 8:3 (see *Hastings' Bib. Dic.*).

Faith *oligopistos* (3640), lit., "little of faith" (*oligos*, "little," *pistis*, "faith"), is used only by the Lord, and as a tender rebuke, for anxiety, **Matt. 6:30** and Luke 12:28; for fear, **Matt. 8:26**; **14:31**; **16:8**.

6:31 Therefore take no thought, saying, What shall we eat? or, What shall we drink? or, Wherewithal shall we be clothed?

Thought *see Matthew 6:25.*

6:32 (For after all these things do the Gentiles seek:) for your heavenly Father knoweth that ye have need of all these things.

Seek *epizeteo* (1934), "to seek after" (directive, *epi*, "towards") is always rendered in the RV, by some form of the verb "to seek," Acts 13:7, "sought" (KJV, "desired"); 19:39, "seek" (KJV, "inquire"); Phil. 4:17, "seek for" (KJV, "desire"), twice; elsewhere, **Matt. 6:32**; **12:39**; **16:4**; Mark 8:12 (in some texts); Luke 12:30; Acts 12:19; Rom. 11:7; Heb. 11:14; 13:14.

Heavenly *see Matthew 6:14.*

Knoweth *see Matthew 6:8.*

Need *chrezo* (5535), "to need, to have need of" (akin to *chre*, "it is necessary, fitting"), is used in **Matt. 6:32**; Luke 11:8; 12:30; Rom. 16:2, RV, "may have need" (KJV, "hath need"); 2 Cor. 3:1.

6:33 But seek ye first the kingdom of God, and his righteousness; and all these things shall be added unto you.

Seek *see* Sought at Matthew *2:20.*

Kingdom *see* Kingdoms at Matthew *4:8.*

Righteousness *see Matthew 3:15.*

6:34 Take therefore no thought for the morrow: for the morrow shall take thought for the things of itself. Sufficient unto the day *is* the evil thereof.

Thought *see Matthew 6:25.*

Morrow *see Matthew 6:30.*

Sufficient *arketos* (713), "sufficient," akin to *arkeo*, is rendered "enough" in **Matt. 10:25**; "sufficient" in **Matt. 6:34**; "suffice" in 1 Pet. 4:3, lit., "(is) sufficient."

Evil *kakia* (2549), primarily, "badness" in quality, denotes (a) "wickedness, depravity, malignity," e.g., Acts 8:22, "wickedness"; Rom. 1:29, "maliciousness"; in Jas. 1:21, KJV, "naughtiness"; (b) "the evil of trouble, affliction," **Matt. 6:34**, only, and here alone translated "evil."

Chapter 7

7:1 Judge not, that ye be not judged.

Judge, Judged *see* Law at *Matthew 5:40.*

7:2 For with what judgment ye judge, ye shall be judged: and with what measure ye mete, it shall be measured to you again.

Judgment *krima* (2917), denotes the result of the action signified by the verb *krino,* "to judge"; it is used (a) of a decision passed on the faults of others, **Matt. 7:2**; (b) of "judgment" by man upon Christ, Luke 24:20; (c) of God's "judgment" upon men, e.g., Rom. 2:2, 3; 3:8; 5:16; 11:33; 13:2; 1 Cor. 11:29; Gal. 5:10; Heb. 6:2; Jas. 3:1; through Christ, e.g., John 9:39; (d) of the right of "judgment," Rev. 20:4; (e) of a lawsuit, 1 Cor. 6:7.

Measure *metron* (3358), denotes (I) "that which is used for measuring, a measure," (a) of "a vessel," figuratively, **Matt. 23:32**; Luke 6:38 (twice); in John 3:34, with the preposition *ek*, "(He giveth not the Spirit) by measure," RV (which is a necessary correction; the italicized words "*unto him*," KJV, detract from the meaning). Not only had Christ the Holy Spirit without "measure," but God so gives the Spirit through Him to others. It is the ascended Christ who gives the Spirit to those who receive His testimony and set their seal to this, that God is true. The Holy Spirit is imparted neither by degrees, nor in portions, as if He were merely an influence, He is bestowed personally upon each believer, at the time of the New Birth; (b) of "a graduated rod or rule for measuring," figuratively, **Matt. 7:2**; Mark 4:24; literally, Rev. 21:15 (in the best mss.; see the RV); v. 17; (II) "that which is measured, a determined extent, a portion measured off," Rom. 12:3; 2 Cor. 10:13 (twice); Eph. 4:7, "(according to the) measure (of the gift of Christ)"; the gift of grace is "measured" and given according to the will of Christ; whatever the endowment, His is the bestowment and the adjustment; v. 13, "the measure (of the stature of the fullness of Christ)," the standard of spiritual stature being the fullness which is essentially Christ's; v. 16, "(according to the working in due) measure (of each several part)," i.e., according to the effectual working of the ministration rendered in due "measure" by every part.

Mete *metreo* (3354), "to measure," is used (a) of space, number, value, etc., Rev. 11:1, 2; 21:15, 16, 17; metaphorically, 2 Cor. 10:12; (b) in the sense of "measuring" out, giving by "measure," **Matt. 7:2**, "ye mete"; Mark 4:24; in some mss. in Luke 6:38.

Measured *antimetreo* (488), "to measure in return," is used in the passive voice, and found in some mss. in **Matt. 7:2**; in Luke 6:38 the most authentic have this verb. It is not found in the Sept.

7:3 And why beholdest thou the mote that is in thy brother's eye, but considerest not the beam that is in thine own eye?

Mote *karphos* (2595), "a small, dry stalk, a twig, a bit of dried stick" (from *karpho*, "to dry up"), or "a tiny straw or bit of wool," such as might fly into the eye, is used metaphorically of a minor fault, **Matt. 7:3, 4, 5**; Luke 6:41, 42 (twice), in contrast with *dokos*, "a beam supporting the roof of a building". In the Sept., Gen. 8:11.

Thy The possessive pronoun *sos*, and its inflections, e.g., **Matt. 7:3** (1st part); it is used as a noun with the article, in the phrases *to son*, "that which is thine," **Matt. 20:14; 25:25**, "thine own"; *hoi soi*, "thy friends," Mark 5:19; *ta sa*, "thy goods," Luke 6:30, lit., "the thine."

> *"Do not think of the faults of others but of what is good in them and faulty in yourself."*
>
> ST. TERESA OF AVILA

Brother *see Matthew 5:22.*

Considerest *katanoeo* (2657), "to perceive clearly" (*kata*, intensive, and *noeo*), "to understand fully, consider closely," is used of not "considering" thoroughly the beam in one's own eye, **Matt. 7:3** and Luke 6:41 (KJV, "perceivest"); of carefully "considering" the ravens, Luke 12:24; the lilies, v. 27; of Peter's full "consideration" of his vision, Acts 11:6; of Abraham's careful "consideration" of his own body, and Sarah's womb, as dead, and yet accepting by faith God's promise, Rom. 4:19 (RV); of "considering" fully the Apostle and High Priest of our confession, Heb. 3:1; of thoughtfully "considering" one another to provoke unto love and good works, Heb. 10:24. It is translated by the verbs "behold," Acts 7:31-32; Jas. 1:23-24; "perceive," Luke 20:23; "discover," Acts 27:39.

Beam *dokos* (1385), "a beam," is perhaps etymologically connected with the root *dek–*, seen in the word *dechomai*, "to receive," "beams" being received at their ends into walls or pieces of timber. The Lord used it metaphorically, in contrast to a mote, "of a great fault, or vice," **Matt. 7:3-5**; Luke 6:41-42.

Thine *see* **Thy** at *Matthew 1:20.*

7:4 Or how wilt thou say to thy brother, Let me pull out the mote out of thine eye; and, behold, a beam *is* in thine own eye?

Say *eiro* (3004), an obsolete verb, has the future tense *ereo*, used, e.g., in **Matt. 7:4**; Luke 4:23 (2nd part); 13:25 (last part); Rom. 3:5; 4:1; 6:1; 7:7 (1st part); 8:31; 9:14, 19, 20, 30; 11:19; 1 Cor. 15:35; 2 Cor. 12:6; Jas. 2:18. The perfect is used, e.g., in John 12:50. The 1st aorist passive, "it was said," is used in Rom. 9:12, 26; Rev. 6:11.

Let *see Matthew 5:40.*

Pull *ekballo*, "to cast out," is translated "to pull out" in **Matt. 7:4** and Luke 6:42 (twice), KJV (RV, "cast out").

Mote *see Matthew 7:3.*

7:5 Thou hypocrite, first cast out the beam out of thine own eye; and then shalt thou see clearly to cast out the mote out of thy brother's eye.

See clearly *diablepo* (1227), "to see clearly," is used in **Matt. 7:5**; Luke 6:42; in Mark 8:25, RV, "he looked steadfastly."

Mote *see Matthew 7:3.*

7:6 Give not that which is holy unto the dogs, neither cast ye your pearls before swine, lest they trample them under their feet, and turn again and rend you.

Dogs *kuon* (2965), is used in two senses, (a) natural, **Matt. 7:6**; Luke 16:21; 2 Pet. 2:22; (b) metaphorical, Phil. 3:2; Rev. 22:15, of those whose moral impurity will exclude them from the New Jerusalem. The Jews used the term of Gentiles, under the idea of ceremonial impurity. Among the Greeks it was an epithet of impudence. Lat., *canis*, and Eng., "hound" are etymologically akin to it.

Pearls *margarites* (3135), "a pearl" (Eng., Margaret), occurs in **Matt. 7:6** (proverbially and figuratively); **13:45, 46**; 1 Tim. 2:9; Rev. 17:4; 18:12, 16; 21:21 (twice).

Swine *choiros* (5519), "a swine," is used in the plural, in the Synoptic Gospels only, **Matt. 7:6**; **8:30, 31, 32**; Mark 5:11, 13, 16; Luke 8:32, 33; Luke 15:15, 16. It does not occur in the OT.

Lest *see Matthew 4:6.*

Trample *katapateo* (2662), "to tread down, trample under foot," is rendered "trample" in **Matt. 7:6**. See also **Trodden** at *Matthew 5:13.*

Under The preposition *en*, "in," is rendered "under" in **Matt. 7:6**; Rom. 3:19 (1st part).

Turn *see Matthew 5:39.*

Rend *rhegnumi* (4486), "to tear, rend," is translated "to rend" in **Matt. 7:6**, of swine.

7:7 Ask, and it shall be given you; seek, and ye shall find; knock, and it shall be opened unto you:

Ask *aiteo* (154), "to ask," frequently suggests the attitude of a suppliant, the petition of one who is lesser in position than he to whom the petition is made; e.g., in the case of men in asking something from God, **Matt. 7:7**; a child from a parent, **Matt. 7:9-10**; a subject from a king, Acts 12:20; priests and people from Pilate, Luke 23:23 (RV, "asking" for KJV, "requiring"); a beggar from a passer by, Acts 3:2. With reference to petitioning God, this verb is found in Paul's epistles in Eph. 3:20 and Col. 1:9; in James four times, 1:5-6; 4:2-3; in 1 John, five times, 3:22; 5:14, 15 (twice), 16.

Seek *see* **Sought** at *Matthew 2:20.*

Find *heurisko* (2147), denotes (a) "to find," either with previous search, e.g., **Matt. 7:7, 8**, or without, e.g., **Matt. 27:32**; in the passive voice, of Enoch's disappearance, Heb. 11:5; of mountains, Rev. 16:20; of Babylon and its occupants, 18:21, 22; (b) metaphorically, "to find out by enquiry," or "to learn, discover," e.g., Luke 19:48; John 18:38; 19:4, 6; Acts 4:21; 13:28; Rom. 7:10; Gal. 2:17, which indicates "the surprise of the Jew" who learned for the first time that before God he had no moral superiority over the Gentiles whom he superciliously dubbed "sinners," while he esteemed himself to be "righteous"; 1 Pet. 1:7; Rev. 5:4; (c) in the middle voice, "to find for oneself, gain, procure, obtain," e.g. **Matt. 10:39; 11:29**, "ye shall find (rest)"; Luke 1:30; Acts 7:46; 2 Tim. 1:18.

Knock *krouo* (2925), "to strike, knock," is used in the NT of "knocking" at a door, (a) literally, Luke 12:36; Acts 12:13, 16; (b) figuratively, **Matt. 7:7, 8**; Luke 11:9, 10 (of importunity in dealing with God); 13:25; Rev. 3:20.

Opened *see Matthew 2:11.*

7:8 For every one that asketh receiveth; and he that seeketh findeth; and to him that knocketh it shall be opened.

Receiveth *lambano* (2983), denotes either "to take" or "to receive," (I) literally, (a) without an object, in contrast to asking, e.g., **Matt. 7:8**; Mark 11:24, RV, "have received" (the original has no object); (b) in contrast to giving, e.g., **Matt.**

10:8; Acts 20:35; (c) with objects, whether things, e.g., Mark 10:30; Luke 18:30, in the best mss.; John 13:30; Acts 9:19, RV, "took" (KJV, "received"); 1 Cor. 9:25, RV, "receive" (KJV, "obtain"); or persons, e.g., John 6:21; 13:20; 16:14, RV, "take"; 2 John 10; in Mark 14:65, RV, "received (Him with blows of their hands)"; this has been styled a vulgarism; (II) metaphorically, of the word of God, **Matt. 13:20**; Mark 4:16; the sayings of Christ, John 12:48; the witness of Christ, John 3:11; a hundredfold in this life, and eternal life in the world to come, Mark 10:30; mercy, Heb. 4:16, RV, "may receive" (KJV, "may obtain"); a person (*prosopon*), Luke 20:21, "acceptest," and Gal. 2:6, "accepteth," an expression used in the OT either in the sense of being gracious or kind to a person, e.g., Gen. 19:21; 32:20, or (negatively) in the sense of being impartial, e.g., Lev. 19:15; Deut. 10:17; this latter is the meaning in the two NT passages just mentioned.

Seeketh *see* Sought at *Matthew 2:20.*

Findeth *see* Find at *Matthew 7:7.*

Knocketh *see* Knock at *Matthew 7:7.*

7:9 Or what man is there of you, whom if his son ask bread, will he give him a stone?

Ask *see Matthew 7:7.*

Give *epididomi* (1929), signifies (a) "to give by handing, to hand" (*epi*, "over"), e.g., **Matt. 7:9**, **10**; Luke 4:17; 24:30, here of the Lord's act in "handing" the broken loaf to the two at Emmaus, an act which was the means of the revelation of Himself as the crucified and risen Lord; the simple verb, *didomi*, is used of His "handing" the bread at the institution of the Lord's Supper, **Matt. 26:26**; Mark 14:22; Luke 22:19; this meaning of the verb *epididomi* is found also in Acts 15:30, "they delivered"; (b) "to give in, give way," Acts 27:15, RV, "we gave way to it."

Stone *see* Stones at *Matthew 4:3.*

7:10 Or if he ask a fish, will he give him a serpent?

Fish *ichthus* (2486), denotes "a fish," **Matt. 7:10**; Mark 6:38, etc.; apart from the Gospels, only in 1 Cor. 15:39.

Give *see Matthew 7:9.*

Serpent *ophis* (3789), the characteristics of the "serpent" as alluded to in Scripture are mostly evil (though **Matt. 10:16** refers to its caution in avoiding danger); its treachery, Gen. 49:17; 2 Cor. 11:3; its venom, Ps. 58:4; 1 Cor. 10:9; Rev. 9:19; its skulking, Job 26:13; its murderous proclivities, e.g., Ps. 58:4; Prov. 23:32; Eccl. 10:8, 11; Amos 5:19; Mark 16:18; Luke 10:19; the Lord used the word metaphorically of the scribes and Pharisees, **Matt. 23:33** (cf. *echidna*, "viper," in **Matt. 3:7**; **12:34**). The general aspects of its evil character are intimated in the Lord's rhetorical question in **Matt. 7:10** and Luke 11:11. Its characteristics are concentrated in the archadversary of God and man, the Devil, metaphorically described as the serpent, 2 Cor. 11:3; Rev. 12:9, 14, 15; 20:2. The brazen "serpent" lifted up by Moses was symbolical of the means of salvation provided by God, in Christ and His vicarious death under the divine judgment upon sin, John 3:14. While the living "serpent" symbolizes sin in its origin, hatefulness, and deadly effect, the brazen "serpent" symbolized the bearing away of the curse and the judgment of sin; the metal was itself figurative of the righteousness of God's judgment.

7:11 If ye then, being evil, know how to give good gifts unto your children, how much more shall your Father which is in heaven give good things to them that ask him?

Evil *see Matthew 5:11.*

Gifts *doma* (1390), lends greater stress to the concrete character of the "gift," than to its beneficent nature, **Matt. 7:11**; Luke 11:13; Eph. 4:8; Phil. 4:17.

7:12-13 Therefore all things whatsoever ye would that men should do to you, do ye even so to them: for this is the law and the prophets.

Enter ye in at the strait gate: for wide *is* the gate, and broad *is* the way, that leadeth to destruction, and many there be which go in thereat:

Enter *eiserchomai* (1525), "to come into" (*eis*, "in," *erchomai*, "to come"), is frequently rendered "entered" in the RV for KJV, "went into," e.g., **Matt. 9:25**; **21:12**; or "go in," e.g., **Matt. 7:13**; Luke 8:51; "go," Luke 18:25; "was coming in," Acts 10:25.

Strait *stenos* (4728), from a root *sten-*, seen in *stenazo*, "to groan," *stenagmos*, "groaning" (Eng., "stenography," lit., "narrow writing"), is used figuratively in **Matt. 7:13**, **14**, of the gate which provides the entrance to eternal life, "narrow" because it runs counter to natural inclinations, and "the way" is similarly characterized; so in Luke 13:24 (where the more intensive word *agonizomai*, "strive," is used); RV, "narrow" (KJV, "strait") in each place. Cf. *stenochoreo*, "to be straitened," and *stenochoria*, "narrowness, anguish, distress."

Gate *pule* (4439), is used (a) literally, for a larger sort of "gate," in the wall either of a city or palace or temple, Luke 7:12, of Nain (burying places were outside the "gates" of cities); Acts 3:10; 9:24; 12:10; Heb. 13:12; (b) metaphorically, of the "gates" at the entrances of the ways leading to life and to destruction, **Matt. 7:13, 14**; some mss. have *pule*, for *thura*, "a door," in Luke 13:24 (see the RV); of the "gates" of Hades, **Matt. 16:18**, than which nothing was regarded as stronger. The importance and strength of "gates" made them viewed as synonymous with power. By metonymy, the "gates" stood for those who held government and administered justice there.

Broad *euruchoros* (2149), from *eurus*, "broad," and *chora*, "a place," signifies, lit., "(with) a broad place," i.e., "broad, spacious," **Matt. 7:13**.

Way *hodos* (3598), denotes (a) "a natural path, road, way," frequent in the Synoptic Gospels; elsewhere, e.g., Acts 8:26; 1 Thess. 3:11; Jas. 2:25; Rev. 16:12; (b) "a traveler's way"; (c) metaphorically, of "a course of conduct," or "way of thinking," e.g., of righteousness, **Matt. 21:32**; 2 Pet. 2:21; of God, **Matt. 22:16**, and parallels, i.e., the "way" instructed and approved by God; so Acts 18:26 and Heb. 3:10, "My ways" (cf. Rev. 15:3); of the Lord, Acts 18:25; "that leadeth to destruction," **Matt. 7:13**; "... unto life," **7:14**; of peace, Luke 1:79; Rom. 3:17; of Paul's "ways" in Christ, 1 Cor. 4:17 (plural); "more excellent" (of love), 1 Cor. 12:31; of truth, 2 Pet. 2:2; of the right "way," 2:15; of Balaam (*id.*), of Cain, Jude 11; of a "way" consisting in what is from God, e.g., of life, Acts 2:28 (plural); of salvation, Acts 16:17; personified, of Christ as the means of access to the Father, John 14:6; of the course followed and characterized by the followers of Christ, Acts 9:2; 19:9, 23; 24:22.

Leadeth *apago* (520), "to lead away" (*apo*, "away"), is used of a way "leading" to destruction, **Matt. 7:13**, to life, v. **14**; of those who "led" Christ away from Gethsemane, Mark 14:44; in some mss., John 18:13, to Annas; to Caiaphas, **Matt. 26:57**; Mark 14:53; to Pilate, **Matt. 27:2**; to the Praetorium, Mark 15:16; to crucifixion, **Matt. 27:31**; Luke 23:26; in some mss. John 19:16; of "leading" an animal away to watering, Luke 13:15; of being "led" away to idolatry, 1 Cor. 12:2, RV, "led away" (KJV, "carried away"). Some mss. have it in Acts 24:7 (KJV, "took away"). It is translated "bring" in 23:17. In 12:19 it signifies "to put to death."

Destruction *apoleia* (684), indicating "loss of well-being, not of being," is used (a) of things, signifying their waste, or ruin; of ointment, **Matt. 26:8**; Mark 14:4; of money, Acts 8:20 ("perish"); (b) of persons, signifying their spiritual and eternal perdition, **Matt. 7:13**; John 17:12; 2 Thess. 2:3, where "son of perdition" signifies the proper destiny of the person mentioned; metaphorically of men persistent in evil, Rom. 9:22, where "fitted" is in the middle voice, indicating that the vessels of wrath fitted themselves for "destruction", of the adversaries of the Lord's people, Phil. 1:28 ("perdition"); of professing Christians, really enemies of the cross of Christ, Phil. 3:19 (RV, "perdition"); of those who are subjects of foolish and hurtful lusts, 1 Tim. 6:9; of professing Hebrew adherents who shrink back into unbelief, Heb. 10:39; of false teachers, 2 Pet. 2:1, 3; of ungodly men, 3:7; of those who wrest the Scriptures, 3:16; of the Beast, the final head of the revived Roman Empire, Rev. 17:8, 11; (c) of impersonal subjects, as heresies, 2 Pet. 2:1, where "destructive heresies" (RV; KJV, "damnable") is, lit., "heresies of destruction" (marg., "sects of perdition"); in v. 2 the most authentic mss. have *aselgeiais*, "lascivious," instead of *apoleiais*.

Thereat The phrase *di'autes*, lit., "by (*dia*) it," is rendered "thereat" in **Matt. 7:13**, KJV (RV, "thereby").

7:14 Because strait *is* the gate, and narrow *is* the way, which leadeth unto life, and few there be that find it.

Strait *see Matthew 7:13.*

Gate *see Matthew 7:13.*

Narrow *thlibo* (2346), "to press," is translated "narrow" in **Matt. 7:14**, KJV, lit., "narrowed" (RV, "straitened"; the verb is in the perfect participle, passive voice), i.e., hemmed in, like a mountain gorge; the way is rendered "narrow" by the divine conditions, which make it impossible for any to enter who think the entrance depends upon self-merit, or who still incline towards sin, or desire to continue in evil.

Way *see Matthew 7:13.*

Leadeth *see Matthew 7:13.*

Few *oligos* (3641), used of number quantity, and size, denotes "few, little, small, slight," e.g., **Matt. 7:14**; **9:37**; **15:34**; **20:16**; neuter plural, "a few things," **Matt. 25:21, 23**; Rev. 2:14 (20 in some mss.); in Eph. 3:3, the phrase *en oligo*, in brief, is translated "in a few words."

7:15 Beware of false prophets, which come to you in sheep's clothing, but inwardly they are ravening wolves.

Beware *prosecho* (4337), lit., "to hold to" (*pros*, "to," *echo*, "to have, to hold"), hence, "to turn one's mind or attention to a thing by being on one's guard against it," is translated "beware" in **Matt. 7:15**; **10:17**; **16:6, 11-12**; Luke 12:1; 20:46.

Prophets *pseudoprophetes* (5578), "a false prophet," is used of such (a) in OT times, Luke 6:26; 2 Pet. 2:1; (b) in the present period since Pentecost, **Matt. 7:15**; **24:11**, **24**; Mark 13:22; Acts 13:6; 1 John 4:1; (c) with reference to a false "prophet" destined to arise as the supporter of the "Beast" at the close of this age, Rev. 16:13; 19:20; 20:10 (himself described as "another beast," 13:11).

Sheep *probaton* (4263), from *probaino*, "to go forward," i.e., of the movement of quadrupeds, was used among the Greeks of small cattle, sheep and goats; in the NT, of "sheep" only (a) naturally, e.g., **Matt. 12:11**, **12**; (b) metaphorically, of those who belong to the Lord, the lost ones of the house of Israel, **Matt. 10:6**; of those who are under the care of the Good Shepherd, e.g., **Matt. 26:31**; John 10:1, lit., "the fold of the sheep," and vv. 2-27; 21:16, 17 in some texts; Heb. 13:20; of those who in a future day, at the introduction of the millennial kingdom, have shown kindness to His persecuted earthly people in their great tribulation, **Matt. 25:33**; of the clothing of false shepherds, **Matt. 7:15**; (c) figuratively, by way of simile, of Christ, Acts 8:32; of the disciples, e.g., **Matt. 10:16**; of true followers of Christ in general, Rom. 8:36; of the former wayward condition of those who had come under His Shepherd care, 1 Pet. 2:25; of the multitudes who sought the help of Christ in the days of His flesh, **Matt. 9:36**; Mark 6:34.

Clothing *see* Raiment at *Matthew 3:4.*

Inwardly *esothen* (2081), is used in Luke 11:39, as a noun with the article, "part" being understood, "(your) inward part"; in **Matt. 7:15** it has its normal use as an adverb, "inwardly."

Ravening *harpax* (727), an adjective signifying "rapacious," is translated "ravening" (of wolves) in **Matt. 7:15**.

Wolves *lukos* (3074), occurs in **Matt. 10:16**; Luke 10:3; John 10:12 (twice); metaphorically, **Matt. 7:15**; Acts 20:29.

7:16 Ye shall know them by their fruits. Do men gather grapes of thorns, or figs of thistles?

Fruits *karpos* (2590), "fruit," is used (I) of the fruit of trees, fields, the earth, that which is produced by the inherent energy of a living organism, e.g., **Matt. 7:17**; Jas. 5:7, 18; plural, e.g., in Luke 12:17 and 2 Tim. 2:6; of the human body, Luke 1:42; Acts 2:30; (II) metaphorically, (a) of works or deeds, "fruit" being the visible expression of power working inwardly and invisibly, the character of the "fruit" being evidence of the character of the power producing it, **Matt. 7:16**. As the visible expressions of hidden lusts are the works of the flesh, so the invisible power of the Holy Spirit in those who are brought into living union with Christ (John 15:2-8, 16) produces "the fruit of the Spirit," Gal. 5:22, the singular form suggesting the unity of the character of the Lord as reproduced in them, namely, "love, joy, peace, longsuffering, kindness, goodness, faithfulness, meekness, temperance," all in contrast with the confused and often mutually antagonistic "works of the flesh." So in Phil. 1:11, marg., "fruit of righteousness." In Heb. 12:11, "the fruit of righteousness" is described as "peaceable fruit," the outward effect of divine chastening; "the fruit of righteousness is sown in peace," Jas. 3:18, i.e., the seed contains the fruit; those who make peace, produce a harvest of righteousness; in Eph. 5:9, "the fruit of the light" (RV, and see context) is seen in "goodness and righteousness and truth," as the expression of the union of the Christian with God (Father, Son and Holy Spirit); for God is good, Mark 10:18, the Son is "the righteous One," Acts 7:52, the Spirit is "the Spirit of truth," John 16:13; (b) of advantage, profit, consisting (1) of converts as the result of evangelistic ministry, John 4:36; Rom. 1:13; Phil. 1:22; (2) of sanctification, through deliverance from a life of sin and through service to God, Rom. 6:22, in contrast to (3) the absence of anything regarded as advantageous as the result of former sins, v. 21; (4) of the reward for ministration to servants of God, Phil. 4:17; (5) of the effect of making confession to God's Name by the sacrifice of praise, Heb. 13:15.

Gather *sullego* (4816), "to collect, gather up or out" (*sun*, "with" *lego*, "to pick out"), is said of "gathering" grapes and figs, **Matt. 7:16**; Luke 6:44; tares, **Matt. 13:28**, **29**, **30**, **40**; good fish, **13:48**; "all things that cause stumbling, and them that do iniquity," **13:41**

Grapes *staphule* (4718), denotes "a bunch of grapes, or a grape," **Matt. 7:16**; Luke 6:44; Rev. 14:18. It is to be distinguished from *omphax*, "an unripe grape" (not in NT), e.g., in the Sept. of Job 15:33, and from *botrus*, "a cluster," used together with *staphule* in Rev. 14:18.

Thorns *akantha* (173), "a brier, a thorn" (from *ake*, "a point"), is always used in the plural in the NT, **Matt. 7:16** and parallel passage in Luke 6:44; **Matt. 13:7** (twice), **22** and parallels in Mark and Luke; in **Matt. 27:29** and John 19:2, of the crown of "thorns" placed on Christ's head in mock imitation of the garlands worn by emperors. They were the effects of the divine curse on the ground (Gen. 3:18; contrast Isa. 55:13). The "thorns" of the crown plaited by the soldiers, are usually identified with those of the *Zizyphus spina Christi*, some 20 feet high or more, fringing the Jordan and abundant in Palestine; its twigs are flexible. Another species, however, the Arabian *qundaul*, crowns of which are plaited and sold in Jerusalem as representatives of Christ's crown, seems likely to be the one referred to. The branches are easily woven and adapted to the torture intended. The word *akantha* occurs also in Heb. 6:8.

Figs *sukon* (4810), denotes "the ripe fruit of a *suke*, a fig-tree," **Matt. 7:16**; Mark 11:13; Luke 6:44; Jas. 3:12.

Thistles *tribolos* (5146), occurs in **Matt. 7:16** and Heb. 6:8 (KJV, "briers"). In the Sept., Gen. 3:18; 2 Sam. 12:31; Prov. 22:5; Hos. 10:8.

7:17 Even so every good tree bringeth forth good fruit; but a corrupt tree bringeth forth evil fruit.

Even so *houtos* (3778), or *houto*, "so, thus," is frequently rendered "even so," e.g., **Matt. 7:17**; **12:45**; **18:14**; **23:28**; "so" in 1 Cor. 11:12 and 1 Thess. 2:4, RV.

Good *see Matthew 5:45.*

Tree *dendron* (1186), "a living, growing tree" (cf. Eng., "rhododendron," lit., "rose tree"), known by the fruit it produces, **Matt. 12:33**; Luke 6:44; certain qualities are mentioned in the NT; "a good tree," **Matt. 7:17, 18; 12:33**; Luke 6:43; "a corrupt tree" (ditto); in Jude 12, metaphorically, of evil teachers, "autumn trees (KJV, 'trees whose fruit withereth') without fruit, twice dead, plucked up by the roots," RV; in Luke 13:19 in some texts, "a great tree," KJV (RV, "a tree"); and **Matt. 13:32**; in Luke 21:29 "the fig tree" is illustrative of Israel, "all the trees" indicating gentile nations.

Bringeth *see* Bring at *Matthew 3:8.*

Fruit *see* Fruits at *Matthew 7:16.*

Corrupt *sapros* (4550), "corrupt, rotten" (akin to *sepo*, "to rot"), primarily, of vegetable and animal substances, expresses what is of poor quality, unfit for use, putrid. It is said of a tree and its fruit, **Matt. 7:17-18**; **12:33**; Luke 6:43; of certain fish, **Matt. 13:48** (here translated "bad"); of defiling speech, Eph. 4:29.

Evil *see Matthew 5:11.*

7:18 A good tree cannot bring forth evil fruit, neither *can* a corrupt tree bring forth good fruit.

Tree *see Matthew 7:17.*

Bring *see Matthew 3:8.*

7:19 Every tree that bringeth not forth good fruit is hewn down, and cast into the fire.

Hewn *see Matthew 3:10.*

7:20 Wherefore by their fruits ye shall know them.

Wherefore *ara*, "so," 2 Cor. 7:12, KJV (RV, "so"); with *ge*, "at least," **Matt. 7:20**, KJV (RV, "therefore").

7:21 Not every one that saith unto me, Lord, Lord, shall enter into the kingdom of heaven; but he that doeth the will of my Father which is in heaven.

Lord *see Matthew 1:22.*

Kingdom *see* Kingdoms at *Matthew 4:8.*

7:22 Many will say to me in that day, Lord, Lord, have we not prophesied in thy name? and in thy name have cast out devils? and in thy name done many wonderful works?

Many *see Matthew 3:7.*

Lord *see Matthew 1:22.*

Prophesied *propheteuo* (4395), "to be a prophet, to prophesy," is used (a) with the primary meaning of telling forth the divine counsels, e.g., **Matt. 7:22**; **26:68**; 1 Cor. 11:4, 5; 13:9; 14:1, 3-5, 24, 31, 39; Rev. 11:3; (b) of foretelling the future, e.g., **Matt. 15:7**; John 11:51; 1 Pet. 1:10; Jude 14.

Wonderful *dunamis* (1411), "power," (a) used relatively, denotes "inherent ability, capability, ability to perform anything," e.g., **Matt. 25:15**, "ability"; Acts 3:12, "power"; 2 Thess. 1:7, RV, "(angels) of His power" (KJV, "mighty"); Heb. 11:11, RV, "power" (KJV, "strength"); (b) used absolutely, denotes (1) "power to work, to carry something into effect," e.g., Luke 24:49; (2) "power in action," e.g., Rom. 1:16; 1 Cor. 1:18; it is translated "might" in the KJV of Eph. 1:21 (RV, "power"); so 3:16; Col. 1:11 (1st clause); 2 Pet. 2:11; in Rom. 15:19, KJV, this noun is rendered "mighty"; RV, "(in the) power of signs." The RV consistently avoids the rendering "might" for *dunamis;* the usual rendering is "power." Under this heading comes the rendering "mighty works," e.g., **Matt. 7:22**, RV (KJV, "wonderful works"); **11:20-23**; singular number in Mark 6:5; in **Matt. 14:2** and Mark 6:14 the RV has "powers"; in 2 Cor. 12:12, RV, "mighty works" (KJV, "mighty deeds").

7:23 And then will I profess unto them, I never knew you: depart from me, ye that work iniquity.

Then *see Matthew 2:7.*

Profess *homologeo* (3670), lit., "to speak the same thing" (*homos*, "same," *lego*, "to speak"), "to assent, accord, agree with," denotes, (a) "to confess, declare, admit," John 1:20; e.g., Acts 24:14; Heb. 11:13; (b) "to confess by way of admitting oneself guilty of what one is accused of, the result of inward conviction," 1 John 1:9; (c) "to declare openly by way of speaking out freely, such confession being the effect of deep conviction of facts," **Matt. 7:23**; **10:32** (twice) and Luke 12:8 (see next par.); John 9:22; 12:42; Acts 23:8; Rom. 10:9-10 ("confession is made"); 1 Tim. 6:12 (RV); Titus 1:16; 1 John 2:23; 4:2, 15; 2 John 7 (in John's epistle it is the necessary antithesis to Gnostic doceticism); Rev. 3:5, in the best mss.; (d) "to confess by way of celebrating with praise," Heb. 13:15; (e) "to promise," **Matt. 14:7**. In **Matt. 10:32** and Luke 12:8 the construction of this verb with *en*, "in," followed by the dative case of the personal pronoun, has a special significance, namely, to "confess" in a person's name, the nature of the "confession" being determined by the context, the suggestion being to make a public "confession." Thus the statement, "every one … who shall confess Me (lit. "in Me," i.e., in My case) before men, him (lit., "in him," i.e., in his case) will I also confess before My Father … ," conveys the thought of "confessing" allegiance to Christ as one's Master and Lord, and, on the other hand, of acknowledgment, on His part, of the faithful one as being His worshipper and servant, His loyal follower; this is appropriate to the original idea in *homologeo* of being identified in thought or language.

Never *oudepote* (3763), from *oude*, "not even," and *pote*, "at any time," is used in definite negative statements, e.g., **Matt. 7:23**; 1 Cor. 13:8; Heb. 10:1, 11, or questions, e.g., **Matt. 21:16**, **42**; in Luke 15:29 (1st part), RV, "never" (KJV, "neither … at any time"); KJV and RV, "never" (2nd part).

Knew *see* Knoweth at *Matthew 6:8*.

Depart *apochoreo* (672), "to depart from" (*apo*), is so translated in **Matt. 7:23**; Luke 9:39; Acts 13:13 (both KJV and RV). Some mss. have it in Luke 20:20.

Iniquity *anomia* (458), lit., "lawlessness" (*a*, negative, *nomos*, "law"), is used in a way which indicates the meaning as being lawlessness or wickedness. Its usual rendering in the NT is "iniquity," which lit. means unrighteousness. It occurs very frequently in the Sept., especially in the Psalms, where it is found about 70 times. It is used (a) of iniquity in general, **Matt. 7:23**; **13:41**; **23:28**; **24:12**; Rom. 6:19 (twice); 2 Cor. 6:14, RV, "iniquity" (KJV, "unrighteousness"); 2 Thess. 2:3, in some mss.; the KJV and RV follow those which have *hamartia*, "(man of) sin"; 2:7, RV, "lawlessness" (KJV, "iniquity"); Titus 2:14; Heb. 1:9; 1 John 3:4 (twice), RV, "(doeth) … lawlessness" and "lawlessness" (KJV, "transgresseth the law" and "transgression of the law"); (b) in the plural, of acts or manifestations of lawlessness, Rom. 4:7; Heb. 10:17 (some inferior mss. have it in 8:12, for the word *hamartia*).

7:24 Therefore whosoever heareth these sayings of mine, and doeth them, I will liken him unto a wise man, which built his house upon a rock:

Liken *see* Like unto at *Matthew 6:8*.

Wise *phronimos* (5429), "prudent, sensible, practically wise," **Matt. 7:24**; **10:16**; **24:45**; **25:2**, **4**, **8**, **9**; Luke 12:42; 16:8 (comparative degree, *phronimoteros*); 1 Cor. 10:15; in an evil sense, "wise (in your own conceits)," lit., "wise (in yourselves)," i.e., "judged by the standard of your self-complacency," Rom. 11:25; 12:16; ironically, 1 Cor. 4:10; 2 Cor. 11:19.

Built … house *oikodomeo* (3618), lit., "to build a house" (*oikos*, "a house," *domeo*, "to build"), hence, to build anything, e.g., **Matt. 7:24**; Luke 4:29; 6:48, RV, "well builded" (last clause of verse); John 2:20; is frequently used figuratively, e.g., Acts 20:32; Gal. 2:18; especially of edifying, Acts 9:31; Rom. 15:20; 1 Cor. 10:23; 14:4; 1 Thess. 5:11 (RV). In 1 Cor. 8:10 it is translated "emboldened" (marg., "builded up"). The participle with the article (equivalent to a noun) is rendered "builder," **Matt. 21:42**; Acts 4:11; 1 Pet. 2:7. *See also* House at *Matthew 2:11*.

Rock *petra* (4073), denotes "a mass of rock," as distinct from *petros*, "a detached stone or boulder," or a stone that might be thrown or easily moved. For the nature of *petra*, see **Matt. 7:24**, **25**; **27:51**, **60**; Mark 15:46; Luke 6:48 (twice), a type of a sure foundation (here the true reading is as in the RV, "because it had been well builded"); Rev. 6:15, 16 (cf. Isa. 2:19ff.; Hos. 10:8); Luke 8:6, 13, used illustratively; 1 Cor. 10:4 (twice), figuratively, of Christ; in Rom. 9:33 and 1 Pet. 2:8, metaphorically, of Christ; in **Matt. 16:18**, metaphorically, of Christ and the testimony concerning Him.

7:25 And the rain descended, and the floods came, and the winds blew, and beat upon that house; and it fell not: for it was founded upon a rock.

Rain *broche* (1028), lit., "a wetting," hence, "rain," is used in **Matt. 7:25**,

27. In the Sept., Ps. 68:9; 105:32. It is found in the papyri in connection with irrigation in Egypt (Deissmann, *Light from the Ancient East*).

Floods *potamos* (4215), denotes (a) "a stream," Luke 6:48, 49; (b) "a flood or floods," **Matt. 7:25, 27**; (c) "a river," natural, **Matt. 3:6**, RV; Mark 1:5; Acts 16:13; 2 Cor. 11:26, RV (KJV, "waters"); Rev. 8:10; 9:14; 16:4, 12; symbolical, Rev. 12:15 (1st part), RV, "river" (KJV, "flood"); so v. 16; 22:1, 2 (cf. Gen. 2:10; Ezek. 47); figuratively, John 7:38, "the effects of the operation of the Holy Spirit in and through the believer."

Blew *pneo* (4154), signifies (a) "to blow," e.g., **Matt. 7:25**; John 3:8; in Acts 27:40 the present participle is used as a noun, lit., "to the blowing" (i.e., to the wind); (b) "to breathe."

Beat *prospipto* (4363), "to fall upon" (*pros*, "to," *pipto*, "to fall"), is translated "beat" in **Matt. 7:25**; elsewhere, "to fall down at or before."

Fell *see Matthew 2:11.*

Founded *themelioo* (2311), "to lay a foundation, to found," is used (a) literally, **Matt. 7:25**; Luke 6:48; Heb. 1:10; (b) metaphorically, Eph. 3:17, "grounded (in love)"; Col. 1:23 (ditto, "in the faith"); 1 Pet. 5:10, KJV, "settle."

Rock *see Matthew 7:24.*

7:26 And every one that heareth these sayings of mine, and doeth them not, shall be likened unto a foolish man, which built his house upon the sand:

Likened *see* Like unto at *Matthew 6:8.*

Foolish *see* Fool at *Matthew 5:22.*

Sand *ammos* (285), "sand" or "sandy ground," describes (a) an insecure foundation, **Matt. 7:26**; (b) numberlessness, vastness, Rom. 9:27; Heb. 11:12; Rev. 20:8; (c) symbolically in Rev. 13:1, RV, the position taken up by the Dragon (not, as in the KJV, by John), in view of the rising of the Beast out of the sea (emblematic of the restless condition of nations).

"Everything Jesus Christ taught was contrary to common sense. Not one thing in the Sermon on the Mount is common sense. The basis of Christianity is neither common sense nor rationalism."

OSWALD CHAMBERS

7:27 And the rain descended, and the floods came, and the winds blew, and beat upon that house; and it fell: and great was the fall of it.

Rain *see Matthew 7:25.*

Floods *see Matthew 7:25.*

Beat *proskopto* (4350), "to stumble, to strike against" (*pros*, "to or against," *kopto*, "to strike"), is once used of a storm "beating" upon a house, **Matt. 7:27**.

Fall *ptosis* (4431), "a fall," is used (a) literally, of the "overthrow of a building," **Matt. 7:27**; (b) metaphorically, Luke 2:34, of the spiritual "fall" of those in Israel who would reject Christ; the word "again" in the KJV of the next clause is misleading; the "rising up" (RV) refers to those who would acknowledge and receive Him, a distinct class from those to whom the "fall" applies. The "fall" would be irretrievable, cf. (a); such a lapse as Peter's is not in view.

7:28 And it came to pass, when Jesus had ended these sayings, the people were astonished at his doctrine:

Ended *sunteleo* (4931), "to end together, bring quite to an end" (*sun*, "together," intensive, *telos*, "an end"), is said (a) of the "completion" of a period of days, Luke 4:2; Acts 21:27; (b) of "completing" something; some mss. have it in **Matt. 7:28**, of the Lord, in ending His discourse (the best mss. have *teleo*, "to finish"); of God, in finishing a work, Rom. 9:28, in making a new covenant, Heb. 8:8, marg., "accomplish"; of the fulfillment of things foretold, Mark 13:4; of the Devil's temptation of the Lord, Luke 4:13.

Doctrine *didache* (1322), denotes "teaching," either (a) that which is taught, e.g., **Matt. 7:28**, KJV, "doctrine," RV, "teaching"; Titus 1:9, RV; Rev. 2:14-15, 24, or (b) the act of teaching, instruction, e.g., Mark 4:2, KJV, "doctrine," RV, "teaching" the RV has "the doctrine" in Rom. 16:17.

7:29 For he taught them as *one* having authority, and not as the scribes.

Taught *see* Teaching at *Matthew 4:23.*

Chapter 8

8:1 When he was come down from the mountain, great multitudes followed him.

Come *katabaino* (2597), signifies "to come down," e.g., **Matt. 8:1**.

Mountain *see Matthew 5:1*.

8:2 And, behold, there came a leper and worshipped him, saying, Lord, if thou wilt, thou canst make me clean.

Leper *lepros* (3015), an adjective, primarily used of "psoriasis," characterized by an eruption of rough scaly patches; later, "leprous," but chiefly used as a noun, "a leper," **Matt. 8:2**; **10:8**; **11:5**; Mark 1:40; Luke 4:27; 7:22; 17:12; especially of Simon, mentioned in **Matt. 26:6**; Mark 14:3.

Worshipped *see* Worship at *Matthew 2:2*.

Lord *see Matthew 1:22*.

Clean *katharizo* (2511), signifies (1) "to make clean, to cleanse" (a) from physical stains and dirt, as in the case of utensils, **Matt. 23:25** (figuratively in verse **26**); from disease, as of leprosy, **Matt. 8:2**; (b) in a moral sense, from the defilement of sin, Acts 15:9; 2 Cor. 7:1; Heb. 9:14; Jas. 4:8, "cleanse" from the guilt of sin, Eph. 5:26; 1 John 1:7; (2) "to pronounce clean in a Levitical sense," Mark 7:19, RV; Acts 10:15; 11:9; "to consecrate by cleansings," Heb. 9:22, 23; 10:2.

8:3 And Jesus put forth *his* hand, and touched him, saying, I will; be thou clean. And immediately his leprosy was cleansed.

Put forth *ekteino* (1614), "to stretch out or forth," is so rendered in **Matt. 12:13** (twice), **49**; **14:31**; **26:51**; Mark 3:5 (twice), Luke 6:10; in **Matt. 8:3**; Mark 1:41 and Luke 5:13, RV (KJV, "put forth"); Luke 22:53; John 21:18; Acts 4:30; 26:1. For Acts 27:30.

Touched *hapto* (681), primarily, "to fasten to," hence, of fire, "to kindle," denotes, in the middle voice (a) "to touch," e.g., **Matt. 8:3**, **15**; **9:20**, **21**, **29**; (b) "to cling to, lay hold of," John 20:17; here the Lord's prohibition as to clinging to Him was indicative of the fact that communion with Him would, after His ascension, be by faith, through the Spirit; (c) "to have carnal intercourse with a woman," 1 Cor. 7:1; (d) "to have fellowship and association with unbelievers," 2 Cor. 6:17; (e) (negatively) "to adhere to certain Levitical and ceremonial ordinances," in order to avoid contracting external defilement, or to practice rigorous asceticism, all such abstentions being of "no value against the indulgence of the flesh," Col. 2:21, KJV (RV, "handle"); (f) "to assault," in order to sever the vital union between Christ and the believer, said of the attack of the Evil One, 1 John 5.18.

Leprosy *lepra* (3014), akin to *lepros*, is mentioned in **Matt. 8:3**; Mark 1:42; Luke 5:12, 13. In the removal of other maladies the verb "to heal" (*iaomai*) is used, but in the removal of "leprosy," the verb "to cleanse" (*katharizo*), save in the statement concerning the Samaritan, Luke 17:15, "when he saw that he was healed." **Matt. 10:8** and Luke 4:27 indicate that the disease was common in the nation. Only twelve cases are recorded in the NT, but these are especially selected.

8:4 And Jesus saith unto him, See thou tell no man; but go thy way, shew thyself to the priest, and offer the gift that Moses commanded, for a testimony unto them.

See *horao* (3708), with the form *eidon*, serving for its aorist tense, and *opsomai*, for its future tense (middle voice), denotes "to see," of bodily vision, e.g., John 6:36; and mental, e.g., **Matt. 8:4**; it is said of Christ as "seeing" the Father, John 6:46, and of what He had "seen" with the Father, 8:38. It especially indicates the direction of the thought to the object "seen."

Shew *see* Sheweth at *Matthew 4:8*.

Priest *hiereus* (2409), "one who offers sacrifice and has the charge of things pertaining thereto," is used (a) of a "priest" of the pagan god Zeus, Acts 14:13; (b) of Jewish "priests," e.g., **Matt. 8:4**; **12:4**, **5**; Luke 1:5, where allusion is made to the 24 courses of "priests" appointed for service in the Temple (cf. 1 Chron. 24:4ff.); John 1:19; Heb. 8:4; (c) of believers, Rev. 1:6; 5:10; 20:6. Israel was primarily designed as a nation to be a kingdom of "priests," offering service to God, e.g., Ex. 19:6, the Israelites having renounced their obligations, Ex. 20:19, the Aaronic priesthood was selected for the purpose, till Christ came to fulfil His ministry in offering up Himself; since then the Jewish priesthood has been abrogated, to be resumed nationally, on behalf of Gentiles, in the millennial kingdom, Is. 61:6; 66:21. Meanwhile all believers, from Jews and Gentiles, are constituted "a kingdom of priests," Rev. 1:6, "a holy priesthood," 1 Pet. 2:5, and "royal," v. 9. The NT knows nothing of a sacerdotal class in contrast to the laity; all believers are commanded to offer the sacrifices mentioned in Rom. 12:1; Phil. 2:17; 4:18; Heb. 13:15, 16; 1 Pet. 2:5; (d) of Christ,

Heb. 5:6; 7:11, 15, 17, 21; 8:4 (negatively); (e) of Melchizedek, as the foreshadower of Christ, Heb. 7:1, 3.

Offer *see* Presented at *Matthew 2:11.*

Gift *see* Gifts at *Matthew 2:11.*

Commanded *see* Bidden at *Matthew 1:24.*

8:5 And when Jesus was entered into Capernaum, there came unto him a centurion, beseeching him,

Centurion *hekatontarchos* (1543), "a centurion," denotes a military officer commanding from 50 to 100 men, according to the size of the legion of which it was a part (*hekaton*, "a hundred," *archo*, "to rule"), e.g., **Matt. 8:5, 8.**

8:6 And saying, Lord, my servant lieth at home sick of the palsy, grievously tormented.

Servant *pais* (3816), also denotes "an attendant"; it is translated "servant" (a) of natural conditions, in **Matt. 8:6, 8, 13; 14:2**; Luke 7:7 ("menservants" in 12:45); 15:26; (b) of spiritual relation to God, (1) of Israel, Luke 1:54; (2) of David, Luke 1:69; Acts 4:25; (3) of Christ, so declared by God the Father, **Matt. 12:18**; spoken of in prayer, Acts 4:27, 30, RV (KJV, "child"); the argument advanced by Dalman for the rendering "Child" in these passages, is not sufficiently valid as against the RV, "Servant" in Acts 4, and the KJV and RV in **Matt. 12** (cf, e.g., the use of *pais* in the Sept. of Gen. 41:38; Jer. 36:24). The **Matt. 12** passage by direct quotation, and the Acts 4 passages by implication, refer to the ideal "Servant of Jehovah" (Sept., *pais Kuriou*), of Isa. 42:1 and following passages, thus identifying the Servant with the Lord Jesus; for the same identification, cf. Acts 8:35. *See also* Children at *Matthew 2:16.*

Lieth *ballo* (906), "to throw, cast," is used in the passive voice, with reference to the sick, with the meaning "to be laid, to lie," in **Matt. 8:6**, "(my servant) lieth (in the house)," lit., "is laid"; **8:14**, "lying," RV, (KJV, "laid"); **9:2**, "lying (on a bed)."

At home In John 16:32, this phrase is rendered "to his own" (of the predicted scattering of the disciples), KJV marg., "his own home"; cf. John 1:11, "His own things," RV, marg. (i.e., "His possessions"). For *oikia* in **Matt. 8:6**, KJV, "at home."

Palsy *see Matthew 4:24.*

Grievously *deinos* (1171), akin to *deos*, "fear," signifies (a) "terribly," **Matt. 8:6**, "grievously (tormented)"; (b) "vehemently," Luke 11:53.

Tormented *basanizo* (928), is translated "to torment," (a) of sickness, **Matt. 8:6**; (b) of the doom of evil spirits, Mark 5:7; Luke 8:28; (c) of retributive judgments upon impenitent mankind at the close of this age, Rev. 9:5; 11:10; (d) upon those who worship the Beast and his image and receive the mark of his name, 14:10; (e) of the doom of Satan and his agents, 20:10.

8:7-8 And Jesus saith unto him, I will come and heal him.

The centurion answered and said, Lord, I am not worthy that thou shouldest come under my roof: but speak the word only, and my servant shall be healed.

Centurion *see Matthew 8:5.*

Worthy *see Matthew 3:11.*

Roof *stege* (4721), "a covering" (*stego*, "to cover"), denotes "a roof," Mark 2:4; said of entering a house, **Matt. 8:8**; Luke 7:6.

Only *see Matthew 5:47.*

Servant *see Matthew 8:6.*

8:9 For I am a man under authority, having soldiers under me: and I say to this *man*, Go, and he goeth; and to another, Come, and he cometh; and to my servant, Do this, and he doeth *it*.

Soldiers *stratiotes* (4757), "a soldier," is used (a) in the natural sense, e.g., **Matt. 8:9; 27:27; 28:12**; Mark 15:16; Luke 7:8; 23:36; six times in John; thirteen times in Acts; not again in the NT; (b) metaphorically of one who endures hardship in the cause of Christ, 2 Tim. 2:3.

Me *emautou* (1683), a reflexive pronoun, of the first person, lit., "of myself," is used (a) frequently after various prepositions, e.g., *hupo*, "under," **Matt. 8:9**; Luke 7:8; RV, "under myself"; *peri*, "concerning," John 5:31; 8:14, 18; Acts 24:10; *apo*, "from," John 5:30; 7:17, RV, "from" (KJV, "of," which is ambiguous); so v. 28; 8:28, 42; 10:18; 14:10 (RV, "from"); *pros*, "unto," John 12:32, RV, "unto Myself"; 14:3; Philem. 13, "with me"; *eis*, "to," 1 Cor. 4:6; *huper*, "on behalf of," 2 Cor. 12:5; *ek* (*ex*), "out of," or "from," John 12:49, RV, "from Myself"; (b) as the direct object of a verb, Luke 7:7; John 8:54; 14:21; 17:19; Acts 26:2; 1 Cor. 4:3; 9:19; 2 Cor. 11:7, 9; Gal. 2:18; Phil. 3:13; (c) in other oblique cases of the pronoun, without a preposition, e.g., Acts 20:24, "unto" (or to); 26:9, "with" (or "to"); Rom. 11:4, RV, "for" (KJV, "to"); 1 Cor. 4:4, RV, "against myself" (KJV, inaccurately, "by"); in all these instances the pronoun is in the dative case; in 1 Cor. 10:33, "mine own" (the genitive case); in 1 Cor. 7:7, "I myself" (the accusative case).

Servant *doulos* (1401), from *deo*, "to bind," "a slave," originally the lowest term in the scale of servitude, came also to mean "one who gives himself up to the will of another," e.g., 1 Cor. 7:23; Rom. 6:17, 20, and became the most common and general word for "servant," as in **Matt. 8:9**, without any idea of bondage. In calling himself, however, a "bondslave of Jesus Christ," e.g., Rom. 1:1, the apostle Paul intimates (1) that he had been formerly a "bondslave" of Satan, and (2) that, having been bought by Christ, he was now a willing slave, bound to his new Master. The feminine, *doule*, signifies "a handmaid," Luke 1:38, 48; Acts 2:18.

8:10 When Jesus heard *it*, he marvelled, and said to them that followed, Verily I say unto you, I have not found so great faith, no, not in Israel.

Great *tosoutos* (5118), "so great, so many, so much," of quantity, size, etc., is rendered "so great," in **Matt. 8:10**, and Luke 7:9, of faith; **Matt. 15:33**, of a multitude; Heb. 12:1, of a cloud of witnesses; Rev. 18:17, of riches.

8:11 And I say unto you, That many shall come from the east and west, and shall sit down with Abraham, and Isaac, and Jacob, in the kingdom of heaven.

East *see Matthew 2:1.*

West *dusme* (1424), "the quarter of the sun-setting" (*dusis*, "a sinking, setting"; *duno*, "to sink"), hence, "the west," occurs in **Matt. 8:11**; **24:27**; Luke 12:54 (some regard this as the sunset); 13:29; Rev. 21:13.

Sit *anaklino* (347), "to cause to recline, make to sit down," is used in the active voice, in Luke 12:37 (also in 2:7, of "laying" the infant Christ in the manger); in the passive, **Matt. 8:11**; **14:19**; Mark 6:39 (in the best texts); in some texts, Luke 7:36 and 9:15; 13:29.

8:12 But the children of the kingdom shall be cast out into outer darkness: there shall be weeping and gnashing of teeth.

Children *see Matthew 5:9.*

Outer *exoteros* (1857), the comparative degree of *exo*, "without," is used of the "outer" darkness, **Matt. 8:12**; **22:13**; **25:30**.

Darkness *see Matthew 6:23.*

Weeping *see Matthew 2:18.*

Gnashing *brugmos* (1030), denotes "gnashing" ("of teeth" being added), **Matt. 8:12**; **13:42**, **50**; **22:13**; **24:51**; **25:30**; Luke 13:28.

Teeth *see* Tooth at *Matthew 5:38.*

8:13 And Jesus said unto the centurion, Go thy way; and as thou hast believed, *so* be it done unto thee. And his servant was healed in the selfsame hour.

Servant *see Matthew 8:6.*

Selfsame In **Matt. 8:13**, KJV, *ekeinos*, with the article, "that," RV, is rendered "that selfsame."

Hour *hora* (5610), whence Lat., *hora*, Eng., "hour," primarily denoted any time or period, especially a season. In the NT it is used to denote (a) "a part of the day," especially a twelfth part of day or night, an "hour," e.g., **Matt. 8:13**; Acts 10:3, 9; 23:23; Rev. 9:15; in 1 Cor. 15:30, "every hour" stands for "all the time"; in some passages it expresses duration, e.g., **Matt. 20:12**; **26:40**; Luke 22:59; inexactly, in such phrases as "for a season," John 5:35; 2 Cor. 7:8; "for an hour," Gal. 2:5; "for a short season," 1 Thess. 2:17, RV (KJV, "for a short time," lit., "for the time of an hour"); (b) "a period more or less extended," e.g., 1 John 2:18, "it is the last hour," RV; (c) "a definite point of time," e.g., **Matt. 26:45**, "the hour is at hand"; Luke 1:10; 10:21; 14:17, lit., "at the hour of supper"; Acts 16:18; 22:13; Rev. 3:3; 11:13; 14:7; a point of time when an appointed action is to begin, Rev. 14:15; in Rom. 13:11, "it is high time," lit., "it is already an hour," indicating that a point of time has come later than would have been the case had responsibility been realized. In 1 Cor. 4:11, it indicates a point of time previous to which certain circumstances have existed.

8:14 And when Jesus was come into Peter's house, he saw his wife's mother laid, and sick of a fever.

Wife's mother *penthera* (3994), denotes "a mother-in-law," **Matt. 8:14**; **10:35**; Mark 1:30; Luke 4:38; 12:53 (twice).

Laid *ballo* (906), "to cast, throw, place, put," is used in the passive voice signifying "to be laid," e.g., Mark 7:30; Luke 16:20; for **Matt. 8:14**, RV, "lying" (KJV, "laid") and **9:2**. *See also* Lieth at *Matthew 8:6.*

Fever *puresso* (4445), signifies "to be ill of a fever," **Matt. 8:14**; Mark 1:30.

8:15 And he touched her hand, and the fever left her: and she arose, and ministered unto them.

Touched *see Matthew 8:3.*

Fever *puretos* (4446), "feverish heat" (from *pur*, "fire"), hence, "a fever," occurs in **Matt. 8:15**; Mark 1:31; John 4:52; Acts 28:8; in Luke 4:38, with *megas*, "great, a high fever"; v. 39. Luke, as a physician, uses the medical distinction by which the ancients classified fevers into great and little. In the Sept., Deut. 28:22.

"Jesus came to save persons, not just souls. He came to help the suffering in whatever way they were suffering. Sickness of the body was part of the kingdom of Satan he had come to destroy."

FRANCIS MACNUTT

Left *see* Leaveth at Matthew *4:11*.

Ministered *see Matthew 4:11*.

8:16 When the even was come, they brought unto him many that were possessed with devils: and he cast out the spirits with *his* word, and healed all that were sick:

Devils *see Matthew 4:24*.

Spirits *see* Spirit at *Matthew 4:1*.

Sick *see Matthew 4:24*.

8:17 That it might be fulfilled which was spoken by Esaias the prophet, saying, Himself took our infirmities, and bare *our* sicknesses.

Fulfilled *see Matthew 1:22*.

Spoken *see Matthew 1:22*.

Bare *see* Bear at *Matthew 3:11*. [cf. Spirits at 8:16]

Sicknesses *astheneia* (769), lit., "lacking strength" (*a*, negative, *sthenos*, "strength"), "weakness, infirmity," is translated "diseases" in **Matt. 8:17**, RV, for KJV, "sicknesses," and in Acts 28:9. Its usual rendering is "infirmity" or "infirmities"; "sickness," in John 11:4. *See also* Sickness at *Matthew 4:23*.

8:18 Now when Jesus saw great multitudes about him, he gave commandment to depart unto the other side.

Depart *aperchomai* (565), lit., "to come or go away" (*apo*), hence, "to set off, depart," e.g., **Matt. 8:18**, is frequent in the Gospels and Acts; Rev. 18:14, RV, "are gone."

Side *peran* (4008), an adverb, signifying "beyond, on the other side," is used (a) as a preposition and translated "on the other side of," e.g., in Mark 5:1; Luke 8:22; John 6:1, RV; 6:22, 25; (b) as a noun with the article, e.g., **Matt. 8:18, 28; 14:22; 16:5**.

8:19 And a certain scribe came, and said unto him, Master, I will follow thee whithersoever thou goest.

Certain *see* One at *Matthew 6:24*.

Master *didaskalos* (1320), "a teacher" (from *didasko*, "to teach"), is frequently rendered "Master" in the four Gospels, as a title of address to Christ, e.g., **Matt. 8:19**; Mark 4:38 (there are more instances in Luke than in the other Gospels); John 1:38, where it interprets "Rabbi"; 20:16, where it interprets "Rabboni." It is used by Christ of Himself in **Matt. 23:8** and John 13:13-14; by others concerning Him, **Matt. 17:24; 26:18**; Mark 5:35; 14:14; Luke 8:49; 22:11; John 11:28. In John 3:10, the Lord uses it in addressing Nicodemus, RV, "the teacher" (KJV, "a master"), where the article does not specify a particular "teacher," but designates the member of a class; for the class see Luke 2:46, "the doctors" (RV, marg., "teachers"). It is used of the relation of a disciple to his "master," in **Matt. 10:24, 25**; Luke 6:40. It is not translated "masters" in the rest of the NT, save in the KJV of Jas. 3:1 "(be not many) masters," where obviously the RV "teachers" is the meaning.

8:20 And Jesus saith unto him, The foxes have holes, and the birds of the air *have* nests; but the Son of man hath not where to lay *his* head.

Foxes *alopex* (258), is found in **Matt. 8:20**; Luke 9:58; metaphorically, of Herod, in Luke 13:32.

Have *see* Had at *Matthew 3:4*.

Holes *pholeos* (5454), "a lair, burrow, den or hole," is used of foxes in **Matt. 8:20** and Luke 9:58.

Birds *see* Fowls at *Matthew 6:26*.

Air *ouranos* (3772), denotes "the heaven." The RV always renders it "heaven." The KJV translates it "air" in **Matt. 8:20**. In the phrase "the fowls (or birds) of the heaven" the KJV always has "air"; "sky" in **Matt. 16:2-3**; Luke 12:56; in all other instances "heaven." The word is probably derived from a root meaning to cover or encompass. *See also* Heaven at *Matthew 5:16*.

Nests *kataskenosis* (2682), properly "an encamping, taking up one's quarters," then, "a lodging, abode" (*kata*, "down over," *skene*, "a tent"), is used of birds' "nests" in **Matt. 8:20** and Luke 9:58. In the Sept., 1 Chron. 28:2, "the building"; Ezek. 37:27, "(My) tabernacle." The word *nossia*, signifying "a brood," Luke 13:34, used in the Sept. to denote a "nest," e.g., in Deut. 22:6; 32:11, signifies the actual receptacle built by birds in which to lay their eggs (having special reference to the prospective brood); but the word *kataskenosis*, used by the Lord, denotes "a resting or roosting place." This lends force to His comparison. Not only was He without a home, He had not even a lodging place (cf. *kataskenoo*, "to lodge," e.g., **Matt. 13:32**; Acts 2:26, RV marg., "shall tabernacle".

Son *see Matthew 3:17*.

Lay *klino* (2827), "to make to bend, to bow," or "to make to lean, to rest," is used in **Matt. 8:20** and Luke 9:58, in the Lord's statement, "the Son of man hath not where to lay His head"; it is significant that this verb is used in John 19:30 of the Lord's act at the moment of His death in placing His head into a position of rest, not a helpless drooping of the head as in all other cases of crucifixion. He reversed the natural order, by first reclining His head (indicative of His submission to His Father's will), and then "giving up His spirit." The rest He found not on earth in contrast to His creatures the foxes and birds, He found in this consummating act on the cross.

8:21 And another of his disciples said unto him, Lord, suffer me first to go and bury my father.

Suffer *epitrepo* (2010) "to permit," is rendered "to suffer" in KJV and RV in **Matt. 8:21**; Mark 10:4; Luke 9:59; Acts 28:16; RV only, Luke 9:61 (KJV, "let"); KJV only, Acts 21:39; in some texts, **Matt. 8:31**, KJV only.

First *proton* (4412), the neuter of the adjective *protos*, is used as an adverb, signifying "first, firstly," e.g., of time, **Matt. 8:21**; of order, Rom. 3:2 (KJV, "chiefly"); in John 7:51, RV, "except it first hear from himself" (the KJV "before it hear him").

Bury *thapto* (2290), occurs in **Matt. 8:21-22**, and parallels in Luke; **Matt. 14:12**; Luke 16:22; Acts 2:29; 5:6, 9-10; of Christ's "burial," 1 Cor. 15:4.

8:22 But Jesus said unto him, Follow me; and let the dead bury their dead.

Let *see* Leaveth at *Matthew 4:11*.

Dead *nekros* (3498), is used of (a) the death of the body, cf. Jas. 2:26, its most frequent sense: (b) the actual spiritual condition of unsaved men, **Matt. 8:22**; John 5:25; Eph. 2:1, 5; 5:14; Phil. 3:11; Col. 2:13; cf. Luke 15:24: (c) the ideal spiritual condition of believers in regard to sin, Rom. 6:11: (d) a church in declension, inasmuch as in that state it is inactive and barren, Rev. 3:1: (e) sin, which apart from law cannot produce a sense of guilt, Rom. 7:8: (f) the body of the believer in contrast to his spirit, Rom. 8:10: (g) the works of the Law, inasmuch as, however good in themselves, Rom. 7:13, they cannot produce life, Heb. 6:1; 9:14: (h) the faith that does not produce works, Jas. 2:17, 26; cf. v. 20.

Their *heauton*, "of themselves," the genitive plur. of *heautou*, "of himself," e.g., **Matt. 8:22**; Rom. 16:4, 18, "their own"; or the accusative plur. *heautous*, e.g., 2 Cor. 8:5, "their own selves."

8:23 And when he was entered into a ship, his disciples followed him.

Entered *embaino* (1684), "to go in" (*en*, "in"), is used only in the Gospels, of "entering" a boat, **Matt. 8:23**; **9:1**; **13:2**; **14:22**, **32**; **15:39**; Mark 4:1; 5:18; 6:45; 8:10, 13; Luke 5:3; 8:22, 37; John 6:17, (in some mss., in v. 22), 24, RV, "got into the boats," for KJV, "took shipping"; 21:3; Acts 21:6 (in the best mss.); of stepping into water, John 5:4 (RV omits the verb).

8:24 And, behold, there arose a great tempest in the sea, insomuch that the ship was covered with the waves: but he was asleep.

Arose *ginomai* (1096), "to become, to take place," is sometimes suitably translated "arise"; e.g., **Matt. 8:24**; Mark 4:37, "there arose a great tempest." So of the arising of persecution, **Matt. 13:21**; Mark 4:17; this might be translated "taketh place"; of a tumult, **Matt. 27:24**, RV, "arising," for KJV, "made"; of a flood, Luke 6:48; a famine, 15:14; a questioning, John 3:25; a murmuring, Acts 6:1; a tribulation, 11:19 (RV); a stir in the city, 19:23; a dissension, 23:7; a great clamor, v. 9.

Tempest *seismos* (4578), "a shaking, a shock," from *seio*, "to move to and fro, to shake," chiefly with the idea of concussion (Eng., "seismic," "seismology," "seismometry"), is used (a) of a "tempest" in the sea, **Matt. 8:24**; (b) of "earthquakes," **Matt. 24:7**; **27:54**; **28:2**; Mark 13:8; Luke 21:11; Acts 16:26; Rev. 6:12; 8:5; 11:13 (twice), 19; 16:18 (twice).

Insomuch that *hoste* (5620), a consecutive particle, is used with the meaning "insomuch that," or "so that," or "that," to express the effect or result of anything, e.g., **Matt. 8:24**; **13:54**; **15:31**; **27:14**; Acts 1:19 (KJV, "insomuch as"); 5:15; 19:12 (KJV, "so that"); 2 Cor. 1:8; Gal. 2:13.

Covered *kalupto* (2572), signifies "to cover," **Matt. 8:24**; **10:26**; Luke 8:16; 23:30; Jas. 5:20 (RV); 1 Pet. 4:8; to veil, in 2 Cor. 4:3 (RV; KJV, "hid).

Waves *kuma* (2949), from *kuo*, "to be pregnant, to swell," is used (a) literally in the plural, **Matt. 8:24**; **14:24**; Mark 4:37 (Acts 27:41, in some mss.); (b) figuratively, Jude 13.

He *see Matthew 1:21*.

8:25 And his disciples came to *him*, and awoke him, saying, Lord, save us: we perish.

Awoke *egeiro* (1453), is used, (a) in the active voice, of "arousing a person from sleep" in **Matt. 8:25** of the act of the disciples in awaking the Lord; in Acts 12:7, of the awaking of Peter, RV, "awake him"; (b) in the passive voice, with a middle significance, of the virgins, in "arousing themselves" from their slumber, **Matt. 25:7**; in Rom. 13:11, and Eph. 5:14, metaphorically, "of awaking from a state of moral sloth.

Lord *see Matthew 1:22.*

Save *see Matthew 1:21.*

Perish *apollumi* (622), signifies (I) In the active voice, (a) "to destroy, destroy utterly, kill," e.g., **Matt. 10:28**; Mark 1:24; 9:22; (b) "to lose utterly," e.g., **Matt. 10:42**, of "losing" a reward; Luke 15:4 (1st part), of "losing" a sheep; Luke 9:25, of "losing" oneself (of the "loss" of well-being hereafter); metaphorically, John 6:39, of failing to save; 18:9, of Christ's not "losing" His own; (II) in the middle voice (a) "to perish," of things, e.g., John 6:12 "(that nothing) be lost"; of persons, e.g., **Matt. 8:25**, "we perish;" of the "loss" of eternal life, usually (always in the RV) translated to perish, John 3:16; 17:12, KJV, "is lost," RV, "perished"; 2 Cor. 4:3, "are perishing," KJV, "are lost"; (b) "to be lost," e.g., Luke 15:4 (2nd part), "which is lost"; metaphorically, from the relation between shepherd and flock, of spiritual destitution and alienation from God, **Matt. 10:6**, "(the) lost (sheep)" of the house of Israel; Luke 19:10 (the perfect tense translated "lost" is here intransitive). *See also* ***Matthew 5:29.*** *See also* **Destroy** at ***Matthew 2:13.***

8:26 And he saith unto them, Why are ye fearful, O ye of little faith? Then he arose, and rebuked the winds and the sea; and there was a great calm.

Fearful *deilos* (1169), "cowardly," "timid," is used in **Matt. 8:26**; Mark 4:40; Rev. 21:8 (here "the fearful" are first in the list of the transgressors).

Faith *see Matthew 6:30.*

Rebuked *epitimao* (2008), primarily, "to put honor upon," then, "to adjudge," hence signifies "to rebuke." Except for 2 Tim. 4:2 and Jude 9, it is confined in the NT to the Synoptic Gospels, where it is frequently used of the Lord's rebukes to (a) evil spirits, e.g., **Matt. 17:18**; Mark 1:25; 9:25; Luke 4:35, 41; 9:42; (b) winds, **Matt. 8:26**; Mark 4:39; Luke 8:24; (c) fever, Luke 4:39; (d) disciples, Mark 8:33; Luke 9:55; contrast Luke 19:39. For rebukes by others see **Matt. 16:22**; **19:13**; **20:31**; Mark 8:32; 10:13; 10:48, RV, "rebuked" (KJV, "charged"); Luke 17:3; 18:15, 39; 23:40.

Was *see Matthew 1:18.*

Calm *galene* (1055), primarily signifies "calmness, cheerfulness" (from a root *gal-*, from which *gelao*, "to smile," is also derived, hence the "calm" of the sea, the smiling ocean being a favorite metaphor of the poets), **Matt. 8:26**; Mark 4:39; Luke 8:24.

8:27 But the men marvelled, saying, What manner of man is this, that even the winds and the sea obey him!

Manner *potapos* (4217), primarily, "from what country," then, "of what sort," is rendered "what manner of man." **Matt. 8:27**: so 2 Pet. 3:11; Mark 13:1 (twice); Luke 1:29; 7:39; 1 John 3:1.

Obey *hupakouo* (5219), "to listen, attend" (as in Acts 12:13), and so, "to submit, to obey," is used of "obedience" (a) to God, Heb. 5:9; 11:8; (b) to Christ, by natural elements, **Matt. 8:27**; Mark 1:27; 4:41; Luke 8:25; (c) to disciples of Christ, Luke 17:6; (d) to the faith, Acts 6:7; the gospel, Rom. 10:16; 2 Thess. 1:8; Christian doctrine, Rom. 6:17 (as to a form or mold of teaching); (e) to apostolic injunctions, Phil. 2:12; 2 Thess. 3:14; (f) to Abraham by Sarah, 1 Pet. 3:6; (g) to parents by children, Eph. 6:1; Col. 3:20; (h) to masters by servants, Eph. 6:5; Col. 3:22; (i) to sin, Rom. 6:12; (j) in general, Rom. 6:16.

8:28 And when he was come to the other side into the country of the Gergesenes, there met him two possessed with devils, coming out of the tombs, exceeding fierce, so that no man might pass by that way.

Side *see Matthew 8:18.*

Country *see Matthew 2:12.*

Met *hupantao* (5221), "to go to meet, to meet," is used in **Matt. 8:28**; Luke 8:27; John 11:20, 30, and, in the most authentic mss., in **Matt. 28:9**; Mark 5:2; Luke 14:31 (of meeting in battle); John 4:51; 12:18 and Acts 16:16.

Devils *see Matthew 4:24.*

Tombs *mnemeion* (3419), is almost invariably rendered "tomb" or "tombs" in the RV, never "grave," sometimes "sepulchre"; in the KJV, "tomb" in **Matt. 8:28**; **27:60**; Mark 5:2; 6:29.

Exceeding *see Matthew 2:16.*

Fierce *chalepos* (5467), "hard," (a) "hard to do or deal with, difficult, fierce," is said of the Gadarene demoniacs, **Matt. 8:28**; (b) "hard to bear, painful, grievous," said of the last times, 2 Tim. 3:1, RV, "grievous," for KJV, "perilous."

No man In some mss. the negative *me* and the indefinite pronoun *tis*, "some one, anyone," appear as one word, *metis* (always separated in the best mss.), e.g., **Matt. 8:28**, "no man"; so in 1 Cor. 16:11; 2 Cor. 11:16; 2 Thess. 2:3. The words are separated also in **Matt. 24:4**; 2 Cor. 8:20 (RV, "any man," after "avoiding"); Rev. 13:17. These instances represent either impossibility or prohibition; contrast *ouch* (i.e., *ou*) ... *tis* in Heb. 5:4, "no man (taketh)," where a direct negative statement is made.

Man *see Matthew 4:4.*

Might In **Matt. 8:28**, KJV, *ischuo*, "to have strength, be strong, be well able," is translated "might" (RV, "could").

Pass *see Matthew 5:18.*

8:29 And, behold, they cried out, saying, What have we to do with thee, Jesus, thou Son of God? art thou come hither to torment us before the time?

Have In **Matt. 27:19**, "Have thou nothing to do with that righteous man" translates what is lit. "nothing to thee and that righteous man," the verb being omitted. Similarly with the phrase, "What have I to do with thee?" lit., "what (is) to me and thee?" Mark 5:7; Luke 8:28; John 2:4, where Westcott translates it "What is there to Me and to thee?"; Ellicott, "What is that to Me and to thee," i.e., "What is My concern and thine in the matter?" There is certainly nothing disparaging in the question. On the contrary, it answers what must have been the thought in Mary's heart, and suggests that while there is no obligation either on Him or her, yet the need is a case for rendering help. For the construction with the plural pronoun see **Matt. 8:29**; Mark 1:24; Luke 4:34.

Hither *hode* (5602), primarily an adverb of manner then, of place, (a) of "motion" or "direction towards a place," e.g., **Matt. 8:29**; Mark 11:3; Luke 9:41; John 6:25; (b) of "position."

Time *kairos* (2540), primarily, "due measure, fitness, proportion," is used in the NT to signify "a season, a time, a period" possessed of certain characteristics, frequently rendered "time" or "times"; in the following the RV substitutes "season" for the KJV "time," thus distinguishing the meaning from *chronos*: **Matt. 11:25**; **12:1**; **14:1**; **21:34**; Mark 11:13; Acts 3:19; 7:20; 17:26; Rom. 3:26; 5:6; 9:9; 13:11; 1 Cor. 7:5; Gal. 4:10; 1 Thess. 2:17, lit., "for a season (of an hour)"; 2 Thess. 2:6; in Eph. 6:18, "at all seasons" (KJV, "always"); in Titus 1:3, "His own seasons" (marg., "its"; KJV, "in due times"); in the preceding clause *chronos* is used. The characteristics of a period are exemplified in the use of the term with regard, e.g. to harvest, **Matt. 13:30**; reaping, Gal. 6:9; punishment, **Matt. 8:29**; discharging duties, Luke 12:42; opportunity for doing anything, whether good, e.g., **Matt. 26:18**; Gal. 6:10 ("opportunity"); Eph. 5:16; or evil, e.g., Rev. 12:12; the fulfillment of prophecy, Luke 1:20; Acts 3:19; 1 Pet. 1:11; a time suitable for a purpose, Luke 4:13, lit., "until a season"; 2 Cor. 6:2.

8:30 And there was a good way off from them an herd of many swine feeding.

Way off *makran* (3112), properly a feminine form of the adjective above, denotes "a long way, far," (a) literally, **Matt. 8:30**, RV, "afar off." Luke 7:6; 15:20, RV, "afar off"; John 21:8; Acts 17:27; 22:21; (b) metaphorically, "far (from the kingdom of God)," Mark 12:34; in spiritual darkness, Acts 2:39; Eph. 2:13, 17.

Herd *agele* (34), from *ago*, "to lead," is used, in the NT, only of swine, **Matt. 8:30**, **31**, **32**; Mark 5:11, 13; Luke 8:32, 33.

Many *see Matthew 3:7.*

Swine *see Matthew 7:6.*

Feeding *bosko* (1006), "to feed," is primarily used of a herdsman (from *boo*, "to nourish," the special function being to provide food; the root is *bo*, found in *boter*, "a herdsman or herd," and *botane*, "fodder, pasture"), its uses are (a) literal, **Matt. 8:30**; in v. **33**, the RV corrects the KJV, "they that kept," to "they that fed," as in Mark. 5:14 (KJV and RV) and Luke 8:34; in Mark 5:11 and Luke 8:32, "feeding"; Luke 15:15; (b) metaphorical, of spiritual ministry, John 21:15, 17.

8:31 So the devils besought him, saying, If thou cast us out, suffer us to go away into the herd of swine.

Devils *daimon* (1142), "a demon," signified, among pagan Greeks, an inferior deity, whether good or bad. In the NT it denotes "an evil spirit." It is used in **Matt. 8:31**, mistranslated "devils." Some would derive the word from a root *da*–, meaning "to distribute." More probably it is from a similar root *da*–, meaning "to know," and hence means "a knowing one."

Suffer *see Matthew 8:21.*

Herd *see Matthew 8:30.*

Swine *see Matthew 7:6.*

8:32 And he said unto them, Go. And when they were come out, they went into the herd of swine: and, behold, the whole herd of swine ran violently down a steep place into the sea, and perished in the waters.

Herd *see Matthew 8:30.*

Swine *see Matthew 7:6.*

Whole *pas* (3956), is sometimes translated "the whole" when used with the article, e.g., **Matt. 8:32, 34;** Rom. 8:22.

Ran violently *hormao,* "to set in motion, urge on," but intransitively, "to hasten on, rush," is always translated "to rush" in the RV; KJV, "ran violently," **Matt. 8:32;** Mark 5:13; Luke 8:33; "ran," Acts 7:57; "rushed", 19:29.

Steep *kremnos* (2911), "a steep bank" (akin to *kremannumi,* "to hang"), occurs in **Matt. 8:32;** Mark 5:13; Luke 8:33, RV, "the steep" (KJV, "a steep place"). In the Sept., 2 Chron. 25:12.

Perished *apothnesko* (599), lit., "to die off or out," is used (a) of the separation of the soul from the body, i.e., the natural "death" of human beings, e.g., **Matt. 9:24;** Rom. 7:2; by reason of descent from Adam, 1 Cor. 15:22; or of violent "death," whether of men or animals; with regard to the latter it is once translated "perished," **Matt. 8:32;** of vegetation, Jude 12; of seeds, John 12:24; 1 Cor. 15:36; it is used of "death" as a punishment in Israel under the Law, in Heb. 10:28; (b) of the separation of man from God, all who are descended from Adam not only "die" physically, owing to sin, see (a) above, but are naturally in the state of separation from God, 2 Cor. 5:14. From this believers are freed both now and eternally, John 6:50; 11:26, through the "death" of Christ, Rom. 5:8, e.g.; unbelievers, who "die" physically as such, remain in eternal separation from God, John 8:24. Believers have spiritually "died" to the Law as a means of life, Gal. 2:19; Col. 2:20; to sin, Rom. 6:2, and in general to all spiritual association with the world and with that which pertained to their unregenerate state, Col. 3:3, because of their identification with the "death" of Christ, Rom. 6:8. As life never means mere existence, so "death," the opposite of life, never means nonexistence.

8:33 And they that kept them fled, and went their ways into the city, and told every thing, and what was befallen to the possessed of the devils.

Kept In **Matt. 8:33,** *bosko,* "to feed" (swine, etc.), is translated "(they that) fed," RV for KJV "(they that) kept." *See also* **Feeding** at *Matthew 8:30.*

Told *apangello* (518), "to announce, declare, report" (usually as a messenger), is frequently rendered "to tell," e.g., **Matt. 8:33; 14:12.**

What In **Matt. 8:33** "what" is, lit., "the things" (neuter plural of the article).

Befallen The phrase in **Matt. 8:33,** "what was befallen to them that were possessed with demons," is, lit., "the things of the demonized."

Devils *see Matthew 4:24.*

8:34 And, behold, the whole city came out to meet Jesus: and when they saw him, they besought *him* that he would depart out of their coasts.

Whole *see Matthew 8:32.*

City *polis* (4172), primarily "a town enclosed with a wall" (perhaps from a root *ple*—, signifying "fullness," whence also the Latin *pleo,* "to fill," Eng., "polite, polish, politic, etc."), is used also of the heavenly Jerusalem, the abode and community of the redeemed, Heb. 11:10, 16; 12:22; 13:14. In Revelation it signifies the visible capital of the heavenly kingdom, as destined to descend to earth in a coming age, e.g., Rev. 3:12; 21:2, 14, 19. By metonymy the word stands for the inhabitants, as in the English use, e.g., **Matt. 8:34; 12:25; 21:10;** Mark 1:33; Acts 13:44.

Meet *hupantesis* (5222), "a going to meet," preceded by the preposition *eis,* "unto," lit., "unto a meeting," translated "to meet," is found in John 12:13, and in the most authentic mss. in **Matt. 8:34** and **25:1.** *Sunantesis* (4877), "a coming to meet with," is found in some mss. in **Matt. 8:34,** of the coming out of all the people of a city to meet the Lord.

Depart *metabaino* (3327), is rendered "to depart" in **Matt. 8:34; 11:1; 12:9; 15:29;** John 7:3; 13:1; Acts 18:7.

Coasts *see Matthew 2:16.*

Chapter 9

9:1 And he entered into a ship, and passed over, and came into his own city.

Entered *see Matthew 8:23.*

Passed *diaperao* (1276), "to pass over, to cross over" (*dia,* "through," *perao,* "to pass": akin to this are *peran,* "across," *peras,* "a boundary," Latin, *porta,* "a gate," Eng., "portal, port," etc.), is translated by the verb "to cross" in the RV, but differently in the KJV; in **Matt. 9:1;** Mark 5:21; 6:53 (KJV, "passed"); **Matt. 14:34** (KJV, "were gone"); Luke 16:26 (KJV, "neither can they pass"); Acts 21:2 (KJV, "sailing"). In the Sept., Deut. 30:13; Isa. 23:2.

9:2 And, behold, they brought to him a man sick of the palsy,

lying on a bed: and Jesus seeing their faith said unto the sick of the palsy; Son, be of good cheer; thy sins be forgiven thee.

Palsy *see Matthew 4:24.*

Lying *see* Laid at *Matthew 8:14. See also* Lieth at *Matthew 8:6.*

Bed *kline* (2825), akin to *klino*, "to lean" (Eng., "recline, incline," etc.), "a bed," e.g., Mark 7:30, also denotes a "couch" for reclining at meals, Mark 4:21, or a "couch" for carrying the sick, **Matt. 9:2, 6**. The metaphorical phrase "to cast into a bed," Rev. 2:22, signifies to afflict with disease (or possibly, to lay on a bier). In Mark 7:4 the KJV curiously translates the word "tables" (marg., "beds"), RV, marg. only, "couches."

Cheer *tharseo* (2293), "to be of good courage, of good cheer" (*tharsos*, "courage, confidence"), is used only in the imperative mood, in the NT; "be of good cheer," **Matt. 9:2, 22; 14:27**; Mark 6:50; 10:49; Luke 8:48; John 16:33; Acts 23:11.

Forgiven *see* Forgive at *Matthew 6:12.*

9:3 And, behold, certain of the scribes said within themselves, This man blasphemeth.

Scribes *nomikos* (3544), an adjective, "learned in the law," is used as a noun, "a lawyer," **Matt. 22:35**; Luke 7:30; 10:25; 11:45, 46, 52 (v. 53 in some mss.); 14:3; Titus 3:13, where Zenas is so named. As there is no evidence that he was one skilled in Roman jurisprudence, the term may be regarded in the usual NT sense as applying to one skilled in the Mosaic Law. The usual name for a scribe is *grammateus*, a man of letters; for a doctor of the law, *nomodidaskalos*, "A comparison of Luke 5:17 with v. 21 and Mark 2:6 and **Matt. 9:3** shows that the three terms were used synonymously, and did not denote three distinct classes. The scribes were originally simply men of letters, students of Scripture, and the name first given to them contains in itself no reference to the law; in course of time, however, they devoted themselves mainly, though by no means exclusively, to the study of the law. They became jurists rather than theologians, and received names which of themselves called attention to that fact. Some would doubtless devote themselves more to one branch of activity than to another; but a 'lawyer' might also be a 'doctor,' and the case of Gamaliel shows that a 'doctor' might also be a member of the Sanhedrin, Acts 5:34" (Eaton, in *Hastings' Bib. Dic.*).

This *see* These at *Matthew 3:9.*

Blasphemeth *blasphemeo* (987), "to blaspheme, rail at or revile," is used (a) in a general way, of any contumelious speech, reviling, calumniating, railing at, etc., as of those who railed at Christ, e.g., **Matt. 27:39**; Mark 15:29; Luke 22:65 (RV, "reviling"); 23:39; (b) of those who speak contemptuously of God or of sacred things, e.g., **Matt. 9:3**; Mark 3:28; Rom. 2:24; 1 Tim. 1:20; 6:1; Rev. 13:6; 16:9, 11, 21; "hath spoken blasphemy," **Matt. 26:65**; "rail at," 2 Pet. 2:10; Jude 8, 10; "railing," 2 Pet. 2:12; "slanderously reported," Rom. 3:8; "be evil spoken of," Rom. 14:16; 1 Cor. 10:30; 2 Pet. 2:2; "speak evil of," Titus 3:2; 1 Pet. 4:4; "being defamed," 1 Cor. 4:13. The verb (in the present participial form) is translated "blasphemers" in Acts 19:37; in Mark 2:7, "blasphemeth," RV, for KJV, "speaketh blasphemies." There is no noun in the original representing the English "blasphemer." This is expressed either by the verb, or by the adjective *blasphemos*.

9:4 And Jesus knowing their thoughts said, Wherefore think ye evil in your hearts?

Thoughts *enthumesis* (1761), is translated "thoughts" in **Matt. 9:4; 12:25**; Heb. 4:12.

Wherefore *hina*, "in order that," with *ti*, "what," **Matt. 9:4**.

Think *see* Thought at *Matthew 1:20.*

Evil *see Matthew 5:37.*

Hearts *see* Heart at *Matthew 5:28.*

9:5 For whether is easier, to say, *Thy* sins be forgiven thee; or to say, Arise, and walk?

Easier *eukopoteros* (2123), the comparative degree of *eukopos*, "easy, with easy labor" (*eu*, "well," *kopos*, "labor"), hence, of that which is "easier to do," is found in the Synoptics only, **Matt. 9:5; 19:24**; Mark 2:9; 10:25; Luke 5:23; 16:17; 18:25.

Forgiven *see* Forgive at *Matthew 6:12.*

Arise *see* Arose at *Matthew 2:14.*

9:6 But that ye may know that the Son of man hath power on earth to forgive sins, (then saith he to the sick of the palsy,) Arise, take up thy bed, and go unto thine house.

Power *exousia* (1849), denotes "authority" (from the impersonal verb *exesti*, "it is lawful"). From the meaning of "leave or permission," or liberty of doing as one pleases, it passed to that of "the ability or strength with which one is endued," then to that of the "power of authority," the right to exercise power, e.g., **Matt. 9:6; 21:23**; 2 Cor. 10:8; or "the power of rule or government," the power of one whose will and commands must be obeyed by others, e.g., **Matt. 28:18**; John 17:2; Jude 25; Rev. 12:10; 17:13; more specifically of apostolic "authority," 2 Cor. 10:8; 13:10; the "power" of judicial decision, John 19:10; of "managing domestic affairs," Mark 13:34. By metonymy, or name-change (the substitution of a suggestive word for the name of the thing meant), it stands for "that which is subject to authority or rule," Luke 4:6 (RV, "authority," for the KJV "power"); or, as with the English "authority," "one who possesses authority, a ruler, magistrate," Rom. 13:1-3; Luke 12:11; Titus 3:1; or "a spiritual potentate," e.g., Eph. 3:10; 6:12; Col. 1:16; 2:10, 15; 1 Pet. 3:22. The RV usually translates it "authority." In 1 Cor. 11:10 it is used of the veil with which a woman is required to cover herself in an assembly or church, as a sign of the Lord's "authority" over the church.

Forgive *see Matthew 6:12.*

Palsy *see Matthew 4:24.*

Bed *see Matthew 9:2.*

House *oikos* (3624), denotes (a) "a house, a dwelling," e.g., **Matt. 9:6, 7; 11:8**; it is used of the Tabernacle, as the House of God, **Matt. 12:4**, and the Temple similarly, e.g., **Matt. 21:13**; Luke 11:51, KJV, "temple," RV, "sanctuary"; John 2:16, 17; called by the Lord "your house" in **Matt. 23:38** and Luke 13:35 (some take this as the city of Jerusalem); metaphorically of Israel as God's house, Heb. 3:2, 5, where "his house" is not Moses', but God's; of believers, similarly, v. 6, where Christ is spoken of as "over God's House" (the word "own" is rightly omitted in the RV); Heb. 10:21; 1 Pet. 2:5; 4:17; of the body, **Matt. 12:44**; Luke 11:24; (b) by metonymy, of the members of a household or family, e.g., Luke 10:5; Acts 7:10; 11:14; 1 Tim. 3:4, 5, 12; 2 Tim. 1:16; 4:19, RV (KJV, "household"); Titus 1:11 (plural); of a local church, 1 Tim. 3:15; of the descendants of Jacob (Israel) and David, e.g., **Matt. 10:6**; Luke 1:27, 33; Acts 2:36; 7:42.

9:7 And he arose, and departed to his house.

Arose *see Matthew 2:14.*

House *see Matthew 9:6.*

9:8 But when the multitudes saw *it*, they marvelled, and glorified God, which had given such power unto men.

Marvelled In **Matt. 9:8**, KJV translates this verb; RV, *phobeo*, "were afraid."

Glorified *see* Glorify at Matthew *5:16.*

9:9 And as Jesus passed forth from thence, he saw a man, named Matthew, sitting at the receipt of custom: and he saith unto him, Follow me. And he arose, and followed him.

Passed *parago* (3855), "to pass by, pass away," in **Matt. 9:9**, RV, "passed by" (KJV, "forth"), is used in the middle voice in 1 John 2:8, RV, "is passing away" (KJV, "is past"), of the "passing" of spiritual darkness through the light of the gospel, and in v. 17 of the world.

Named In **Matt. 9:9** and Mark 15:7, KJV, the verb *lego*, "to speak, to call by name," is rendered "named" (RV, "called").

Sitting *see* Sat at *Matthew 4:16.*

Custom *telonion* (5058), denotes "a custom-house," for the collection of the taxes, **Matt. 9:9**; Mark 2:14; Luke 5:27 (RV, "place of toll").

9:10 And it came to pass, as Jesus sat at meat in the house, behold, many publicans and sinners came and sat down with him and his disciples.

Sat *anakeimai* (345), "to recline at table" (*ana*, "up" *keimai*, "to lie"), is rendered "to sit at meat" in **Matt. 9:10** (RV, marg., "reclined"); **26:7; 26:20**, RV, "He was sitting at meat" (KJV, "He sat down"); Mark 16:14; in some mss. Luke 7:37; 22:27 (twice); in Mark 14:18, "sat"; in John 6:11, "were set down"; John 12:2 in the best texts.

Many *see Matthew 3:7.*

Publicans *see Matthew 5:46.*

Sat *sunanakeimai* (4873), "to recline at table with or together," "to sit at meat or at table with," occurs in **Matt. 9:10**, "sat down"; **14:9**; Mark 2:15, RV, "sat down with" (KJV, "sat ... together with"); 6:22; Luke 7:49; 14:10, 15; John 12:2 (in some texts).

9:11 And when the Pharisees saw *it*, they said unto his disciples, Why eateth your Master with publicans and sinners?

Publicans *see Matthew 5:46.*

9:12 But when Jesus heard *that*, he said unto them, They that be whole need not a physician, but they that are sick.

Whole *ischuo* (2480), "to be strong," is rendered "they that are whole" in **Matt. 9:12** and Mark 2:17.

Need *see Matthew 3:14.*

Physician *iatros* (2395), akin to *iaomai*, "to heal," "a physician," occurs in **Matt. 9:12**; Mark 2:17; 5:26; Luke 4:23; 5:31 (in some mss., 8:43); Col. 4:14.

Sick *see Matthew 4:24.*

9:13 But go ye and learn what *that* meaneth, I will have mercy, and not sacrifice: for I am not come to call the righteous, but sinners to repentance.

Learn *manthano* (3129), denotes (a) "to learn" (akin to *mathetes*, "a disciple"), "to increase one's knowledge," or "be increased in knowledge," frequently "to learn by inquiry, or observation," e.g., **Matt. 9:13; 11:29; 24:32**; Mark 13:28; John 7:15; Rom. 16:17; 1 Cor. 4:6; 14:35; Phil. 4:9; 2 Tim. 3:14; Rev. 14:3; said of "learning" Christ, Eph. 4:20, not simply the doctrine of Christ, but Christ Himself, a process not merely of getting to know the person but of so applying the knowledge as to walk differently from the rest of the Gentiles; (b) "to ascertain," Acts 23:27, RV, "learned" (KJV, "understood"); Gal. 3:2, "This only would I learn from you," perhaps with a tinge of irony in the enquiry, the answer to which would settle the question of the validity of the new Judaistic gospel they were receiving; (c) "to learn by use and practice, to acquire the habit of, be accustomed to," e.g., Phil. 4:11; 1 Tim. 5:4, 13; Titus 3:14; Heb. 5:8.

Meaneth *eimi* (1510), "to be," in certain of its forms, has an explicative force, signifying "to denote, to import," e.g., **Matt. 9:13; 12:7**, "(what this) meaneth," lit. "(what this) is"; Luke 18:36, "meant" (lit., "might be"); Acts 10:17, "might mean," RV (lit., "might be"); in Luke 15:26 the RV keeps to the verb "to be," "(what these things) might be" (KJV, "meant"). In Acts 2:12 the verb "to be" is preceded by *thelo*, "to will," and the phrase is translated "(what) meaneth (this)," lit., "(what) does (this) will to be?" in 17:20, lit., "(what do these things) will to be."

Will *thelo* (2309), "to will, to wish," implying volition and purpose, frequently a determination, is most usually rendered "to will." It is translated "to desire" in the RV of the following: **Matt. 9:13; 12:7**; Mark 6:19; Luke 10:29; 14:28; 23:20; Acts 24:27; 25:9; Gal. 4:17; 1 Tim. 5:11; Heb. 12:17; 13:18.

Mercy *eleos* (1656), "is the outward manifestation of pity; it assumes need on the part of him who receives it, and resources adequate to meet the need on the part of him who shows it. It is used (a) of God, who is rich in mercy, Eph. 2:4, and who has provided salvation for all men, Titus 3:5, for Jews, Luke 1:72, and Gentiles, Rom. 15:9. He is merciful to those who fear him, Luke 1:50, for they also are compassed with infirmity, and He alone can succor them. Hence they are to pray boldly for mercy, Heb. 4:16, and if for themselves, it is seemly that they should ask for mercy for one another, Gal. 6:16; 1 Tim. 1:2. When God brings His salvation to its issue at the Coming of Christ, His people will obtain His mercy, 2 Tim. 1:16; Jude 21; (b) of men; for since God is merciful to them, He would have them show mercy to one another, **Matt. 9:13; 12:7; 23:23**; Luke 10:37; Jas. 2:13. Wherever the words mercy and peace are found together they occur in that order, except in Gal. 6:16. Mercy is the act of God, peace is the resulting experience in the heart of man. Grace describes God's attitude toward the lawbreaker and the rebel; mercy is His attitude toward those who are in distress."

Sacrifice *thusia* (2378), primarily denotes "the act of offering"; then, objectively, "that which is offered" (a) of idolatrous "sacrifice," Acts 7:41; (b) of animal or other "sacrifices," as offered under the Law, **Matt. 9:13; 12:7**; Mark 9:49; 12:33; Luke 2:24; 13:1; Acts 7:42; 1 Cor. 10:18; Heb. 5:1; 7:27 (RV, plural); 8:3; 9:9; 10:1, 5, 8 (RV, plural), 11; 11:4; (c) of Christ, in His "sacrifice" on the cross, Eph. 5:2; Heb. 9:23, where the plural antitypically comprehends the various forms of Levitical "sacrifices" in their typical character; 9:26; 10:12, 26; (d) metaphorically, (1) of the body of the believer, presented to God as a living "sacrifice," Rom. 12:1; (2) of faith, Phil. 2:17; (3) of material assistance rendered to servants of God, Phil. 4:18; (4) of praise, Heb, 13:15; (5) of doing good to others and communicating with their needs, Heb. 13:16; (6) of spiritual "sacrifices" in general, offered by believers as a holy priesthood, 1 Pet. 2:5.

Repentance *see Matthew 3:8.*

9:14 Then came to him the disciples of John, saying, Why do we and the Pharisees fast oft, but thy disciples fast not?

Disciples *mathetes* (3101), lit., "a learner" (from *manthano*, "to learn," from a root *math–*, indicating thought accompanied by endeavor), in contrast to *didaskalos*, "a teacher"; hence it denotes "one who follows one's teaching," as the "disciples" of John, **Matt. 9:14**; of the Pharisees, **Matt. 22:16**; of Moses, John 9:28; it is used of the "disciples" of Jesus (a) in a wide sense, of Jews who became His adherents, John 6:66; Luke 6:17, some being secretly so, John 19:38; (b) especially of the twelve apostles, **Matt. 10:1**; Luke 22:11, e.g.; (c) of all who manifest that they are His "disciples" by abiding in His Word, John 8:31, cf. 13:35; 15:8; (d) in the Acts, of those who believed upon Him and confessed Him, 6:1-2, 7; 14:20, 22, 28; 15:10; 19:1, etc. A "disciple" was not only a pupil, but an adherent; hence they are spoken of as imitators of their teacher; cf. John 8:31; 15:8.

Fast *see* **Fasted** at *Matthew 4:2.*

Oft *polla* (4183), the neuter plural of *polus*, is translated "oft" in **Matt. 9:14**; some ancient authorities omit it here (see RV marg.); in Rom. 15:22, with the article, RV, "these many times" (KJV, "much").

9:15 And Jesus said unto them, Can the children of the bridechamber mourn, as long as the bridegroom is with them? but the days will come, when the bridegroom shall be taken from them, and then shall they fast.

Children *see Matthew 5:9.*

Bridechamber *numphon* (3567), signifies (a) "the room or dining hall in which the marriage ceremonies were held," **Matt. 22:10**; some mss. have *gamos*, "a wedding," here; (b) "the chamber containing the bridal bed," "the sons of the bridechamber" being the friends of the bridegroom, who had the charge of providing what was necessary for the nuptials, **Matt. 9:15**; Mark 2:19; Luke 5:34.

Mourn *see Matthew 5:4.*

Taken *apairo* (522), "to lift off," is used, in the passive voice, of Christ, metaphorically as the Bridegroom of His followers, **Matt. 9:15**; Mark 2:20; Luke 5:35.

Fast *see* Fasted at *Matthew 4:2.*

9:16 No man putteth a piece of new cloth unto an old garment, for that which is put in to fill it up taketh from the garment, and the rent is made worse.

Putteth *epiballo* (1911), "to put to or unto," is so translated in **Matt. 9:16**; Luke 5:36; 9:62; in Acts 12:1, RV, "put forth (his hands)," KJV, "stretched forth."

Piece *epiblema* (1915), primarily denotes "that which is thrown over, a cover" (*epi*, "over," *ballo*, "to throw"); then, "that which is put on, or sewed on, to cover a rent, a patch," **Matt. 9:16**; Mark 2:21; in the next sentence, RV, "that which should fill" (KJV, "the new piece that filled"), there is no word representing "piece" (lit., "the filling," *pleroma*).

New *agnaphos* (46), "uncarded" (*a*, negative, *knapto*, "to card wool"), is rendered "undressed," of cloth, in **Matt. 9:16** and Mark 2:21, RV (KJV, "new").

Cloth *rhakos* (4470), denotes "a ragged garment, or a piece of cloth torn off, a rag"; hence, a piece of undressed "cloth," **Matt. 9:16**; Mark 2:21.

Old *palaios* (3820), (Eng., "paleontology," etc.), "of what is of long duration, old in years," etc., a garment, wine (in contrast to *neos*), **Matt. 9:16–17**; Mark 2:21-22 (twice); Luke 5:36-37, 39 (twice); of the treasures of divine truth, **Matt. 13:52** (compared with *kainos*); of what belongs to the past, e.g., the believer's former self before his conversion, his "old man," "old" because it has been superseded by that which is new, Rom. 6:6; Eph. 4:22 (in contrast to *kainos*); Col. 3:9 (in contrast to *neos*); of the covenant in connection with the Law, 2 Cor. 3:14; of leaven, metaphorical of moral evil, 1 Cor. 5:7, 8 (in contrast to *neos*); of that which was given long ago and remains in force, an "old" commandment, 1 John 2:7 (twice), that which was familiar and well known in contrast to that which is fresh (*kainos*).

Put In **Matt. 9:16**, KJV, *pleroma*, "the fullness or filling," is rendered "(that) which is put in to fill it up," RV, "(that) which should fill it up."

Fill *pleroma* (4138), fullness, has two meanings, (a) in the active sense, "that which fills up," a piece of undressed cloth on an old garment, **Matt. 9:16**; Mark 2:21, lit., "the filling" (RV, "that which should fill it up"), i.e., "the patch," which is probably the significance; (b) "that which has been completed, the fullness," e.g., Mark 8:20.

Rent *schisma* (4978), "a rent, division," signifies a "rent" in wineskins in **Matt. 9:16**; Mark 2:21.

Made *ginomai* (1096), "to become," is sometimes translated by the passive voice of the verb to make, e.g., **Matt. 9:16**; John 1:3 (three times), 10; 8:33; Rom. 11:9; 1 Cor. 1:30; 3:13; 4:9, 13; Eph. 2:13; 3:7; Phil. 2:7 (but RV marg., "becoming"); Col. 1:23, 25; Heb. 5:5; 6:4; 7:12, 16, 21, 26; 11:3; Jas. 3:9; 1 Pet. 2:7. In many places the RV translates otherwise, and chiefly by the verb to become, e.g., **Matt. 25:6**, "there is"; **27:24**, "was arising"; John 1:14, "became"; John 2:9, "become"; Rom. 1:3, "born"; 2:25, "is become"; 10:20, "became"; Gal. 3:13, "having become"; 4:4, "born" (twice); Heb. 3:14, "are become", 7:22, "hath … become."

Worse *cheiron* (5501), used as the comparative degree of *kakos*, "evil," describes (a) the condition of certain men, **Matt. 12:45**; Luke 11:26; 2 Pet. 2:20; (b) evil men themselves and seducers, 2 Tim. 3:13; (c) indolent men who refuse to provide for their own households, and are worse than unbelievers, 1 Tim. 5:8, RV; (d) a rent in a garment, **Matt. 9:16**; Mark 2:21; (e) an error, **Matt. 27:64**; (f) a person suffering from a malady, Mark 5:26; (g) a possible physical affliction, John 5:14; (h) a punishment, Heb. 10:29, "sorer."

9:17 Neither do men put new wine into old bottles: else the bottles break, and the wine runneth out, and the bottles

perish: but they put new wine into new bottles, and both are preserved.

Put *ballo* (906), "to throw, cast, put," is translated "to put," in **Matt. 9:17** (twice); **25:27**; **27:6**; Mark 2:22; 7:33; Luke 5:37; John 5:7; 12:6; 13:2 (of "putting" into the heart by the Devil); 18:11 (of "putting" up a sword); 20:25 (RV twice, KJV, "put" and "thrust"); v. 27, RV; Jas, 3:3; Rev. 2:24 (RV, "cast").

New *neos* (3501), signifies "new" in respect of time, that which is recent; it is used of the young, and so translated, especially the comparative degree "younger"; accordingly what is *neos* may be a reproduction of the old in quality or character. *Neos* and *kainos* are sometimes used of the same thing, but there is a difference, as already indicated. Thus the "new man" in Eph. 2:15 (*kainos*) is "new" in differing in character; so in 4:24; but the "new man" in Col. 3:10 (*neos*) stresses the fact of the believer's "new" experience, recently begun, and still proceeding. "The old man in him ... dates as far back as Adam; a new man has been born, who therefore is fitly so called" [i.e., *neos*], Trench, *Syn.* §lx. The "New" Covenant in Heb. 12:24 is "new" (*neos*) compared with the Mosaic, nearly fifteen hundred years before; it is "new" (*kainos*) compared with the Mosaic, which is old in character, ineffective, 8:8, 13; 9:15. The "new" wine of **Matt. 9:17**; Mark 2:22; Luke 5:37-39, is *neos*, as being of recent production; the "new" wine of the kingdom, **Matt. 26:29**; Mark 14:25, is *kainos*, since it will be of a different character from that of this world. The rendering "new" (*neos*) is elsewhere used metaphorically in 1 Cor. 5:7, "a new lump."

Wine *oinos* (3631), is the general word for "wine." The mention of the bursting of the wineskins, **Matt. 9:17**; Mark 2:22; Luke 5:37, implies fermentation. See also Eph. 5:18 (cf. John 2:10; 1 Tim. 3:8; Titus 2:3). In **Matt. 27:34**, the RV has "wine" (KJV, "vinegar," translating the inferior reading *oxos*). The drinking of "wine" could be a stumbling block and the apostle enjoins abstinence in this respect, as in others, so as to avoid giving an occasion of stumbling to a brother, Rom. 14:21. Contrast 1 Tim. 5:23, which has an entirely different connection. The word is used metaphorically (a) of the evils ministered to the nations by religious Babylon, 14:8; 17:2; 18:3; (b) of the contents of the cup of divine wrath upon the nations and Babylon, Rev. 14:10; 16:19; 19:15.

Bottles *askos* (779), "a leather bottle, wineskin," occurs in **Matt. 9:17** (four times); Mark 2:22 (four times); Luke 5:37 (three times), 38; in each place, RV, "wineskins" or "skins," for KJV, "bottles." A whole goatskin, for example, would be used with the apertures bound up, and when filled, tied at the neck. They were tanned with acacia bark and left hairy on the outside. New wines, by fermenting, would rend old skins (cf. Josh. 9:13; Job 32:19). Hung in the smoke to dry, the skin-bottles become shriveled (see Ps. 119:83).

Break *rhegnumi* (4486), "to tear, rend, as of garments, etc.," is translated "break" in the KJV, of **Matt. 9:17**, of wine-skins (RV, "burst"); as in Mark 2:22 and Luke 5:37; "break forth" in Gal. 4:27.

Runneth In **Matt. 9:17**, KJV, *ekcheo*, "to pour out," used in the passive voice (RV, "is spilled"), is translated "runneth out."

Preserved *suntereo* (4933), denotes "to preserve, keep safe, keep close," in Luke 2:19, as in v. 51, of the mother of Jesus in regard to the words of the shepherds; in Mark 6:20 it is used of Herod's preservation of John the Baptist from Herodias, RV, "kept (him) safe," KJV, "observed (him)" (marg., "kept"); in **Matt. 9:17** (in some mss., Luke 5:38), of the preservation of wineskins.

9:18 While he spake these things unto them, behold, there came a certain ruler, and worshipped him, saying, My daughter is even now dead: but come and lay thy hand upon her, and she shall live.

Ruler *archon* (758), the present participle of the verb *archo*, "to rule"; denotes "a ruler, a prince." It is used as follows ("p" denoting "prince," or "princes"; "r," "ruler" or "rulers"): (a) of Christ, as "the Ruler (KJV, Prince) of the kings of the earth," Rev. 1:5; (b) of rulers of nations, **Matt. 20:25**, RV, "r," KJV, "p"; Acts 4:26, "r"; 7:27, "r"; 7:35, "r" (twice); (c) of judges and magistrates, Acts 16:19, "r"; Rom. 13:3, "r"; (d) of members of the Sanhedrin, Luke 14:1, RV, "r" (KJV, "chief"); 23:13, 35, "r"; so 24:20, John 3:1; 7:26, 48; 12:42, RV, "r" (KJV, "chief r."); "r" in Acts 3:17; 4:5, 8; 13:27; 14:5; (e) of rulers of synagogues, **Matt. 9:18**, **23**, "r"; so Luke 8:41; 18:18; (f) of the Devil, as "prince" of this world, John 12:31; 14:30; 16:11; of the power of the air, Eph. 2:2, "the air" being that sphere in which the inhabitants of the world live and which, through the rebellious and godless condition of humanity, constitutes the seat of his authority; (g) of Beelzebub, the "prince" of the demons, **Matt. 9:24**; **12:24**; Mark 3:22; Luke 11:15.

Worshipped *see* Worship at *Matthew 2:2*.

Now *see Matthew 3:15.*

Dead *see Matthew 2:19.*

Lay *epitithemi* (2007), "to add to, lay upon," etc., is used of "laying" hands on the sick, for healing, **Matt. 9:18; 19:13**, RV, "lay" (KJV, "put"); **19:15**; Mark 5:23; 6:5; 7:32; 8:23, RV, "laid" (KJV, "put"); so in v. 25; 16:18; Luke 4:40; 13:13; Acts 6:6; 8:17, 19; 9:12 and 17, RV, "laying" (KJV, "putting"); 13:3; 19:6; 28:8; in some mss. in Rev. 1:17; of "laying" hands on a person by way of public recognition, 1 Tim. 5:22; of a shepherd's "laying" a sheep on his shoulders, Luke 15:5; of "laying" the cross on Christ's shoulders, Luke 23:26; of "laying" on stripes, Acts 16:23; wood on a fire, 28:3; metaphorically, of "laying" burden's on men's shoulders, **Matt. 23:4**; similarly of "giving" injunctions, Acts 15:28 (cf. "put ... upon" in v. 10).

Live *see Matthew 4:4.*

9:19 And Jesus arose, and followed him, and *so did* his disciples.

Arose *see Matthew 2:14.*

9:20 And, behold, a woman, which was diseased with an issue of blood twelve years, came behind *him*, and touched the hem of his garment:

Blood *haimorrhoeo* (131), from *haima*, "blood," *rheo*, "to flow" (Eng., "hemorrhage"), signifies "to suffer from a flow of blood," **Matt. 9:20**.

Years *etos* (2094), is used (a) to mark a point of time at or from which events take place, e.g., Luke 3:1 (dates were frequently reckoned from the time when a monarch began to reign); in Gal. 3:17 the time of the giving of the Law is stated as 430 "years" after the covenant of promise given to Abraham; there is no real discrepancy between this and Ex. 12:40; the apostle is not concerned with the exact duration of the interval, it certainly was not less than 430 "years"; the point of the argument is that the period was very considerable; Gal. 1:18 and 2:1 mark events in Paul's life; as to the former the point is that three "years" elapsed before he saw any of the apostles; in 2:1 the 14 "years" may date either from his conversion or from his visit to Peter mentioned in 1:18; the latter seems the more natural (for a full discussion of the subject see *Notes on Galatians* by Hogg and Vine, pp. 55ff.); (b) to mark a space of time, e.g., **Matt. 9:20**; Luke 12:19; 13:11; John 2:20; Acts 7:6, where the 400 "years" mark not merely the time that Israel was in bondage in Egypt, but the time that they sojourned or were strangers there (the RV puts a comma after the word "evil"); the Genevan Version renders Gen. 15:13 "thy posterity shall inhabit a strange land for 400 years"; Heb. 3:17; Rev. 20:2-7; (c) to date an event from one's birth, e.g., Mark 5:42; Luke 2:42; 3:23; John 8:57; Acts 4:22; 1 Tim. 5:9; (d) to mark recurring events, Luke 2:41 (with *kata*, used distributively); 13:7; (e) of an unlimited number, Heb. 1:12.

Behind *opisthen* (3693), "behind," is used only of place, e.g., **Matt. 9:20**; Mark 5:27; Luke 8:44; Rev. 4:6; as a preposition, **Matt. 15:23** ("after"), and Luke 23:26; in Rev. 5:1, RV, "on the back"; KJV, "backside."

Touched *see Matthew 8:3.*

Hem *kraspedon* (2899), was primarily "the extremity or prominent part of a thing, an edge"; hence "the fringe of a garment, or a little fringe," hanging down from the edge of the mantle or cloak. The Jews had these attached to their mantles to remind them of the Law, according to Num. 15:38-39; Deut. 22:12; Zech. 8:23. This is the meaning in **Matt. 23:5**. In **Matt. 9:20; 14:36**; Mark 6:56; Luke 8:44, it is used of the border of Christ's garment (KJV "hem," in the first two places).

9:21 For she said within herself, If I may but touch his garment, I shall be whole.

Touch *see* Touched at *Matthew 8:3.*

Whole *sozo* (4982), "to save," is sometimes rendered "to make whole," and, in the passive voice, "to be made whole," or "to be whole," e.g., **Matt. 9:21, 22** (twice), and parallel passages; Acts 4:9.

9:22 But Jesus turned him about, and when he saw her, he said, Daughter, be of good comfort; thy faith hath made thee whole. And the woman was made whole from that hour.

Comfort *see* Cheer at *Matthew 9:2.*

Whole *see Matthew 9:21. See also* Save at *Matthew 1:21.*

9:23 And when Jesus came into the ruler's house, and saw the minstrels and the people making a noise,

Ruler *see Matthew 9:18.*

Minstrels *auletes* (834), "a flute-player" (from *auleo*, "to play the flute"), occurs in **Matt. 9:23** (KJV, "minstrel"), and Rev. 18:22 (KJV "pipers"). In the papyri writings of the time the word is chiefly associated with religious matters (Moulton and Milligan, *Vocab.*).

People *ochlos* (3793), "a confused throng," is usually translated "multitude." The RV translates it "crowd" (KJV, "press" in some) in **Matt. 9:23, 25**; Mark 2:4; 3:9; 5:27, 30; Luke 8:19; 19:3; Acts 21:34-35; 24:12, 18.

Noise *thorubeo* (2350), "to make an uproar, to throw into confusion, or to wail tumultuously," is rendered "make ... ado," in Mark 5:39; elsewhere in **Matt. 9:23**; Acts 17:5; 20:10.

9:24 He said unto them, Give place: for the maid is not dead, but sleepeth. And they laughed him to scorn.

Place *anachoreo* (402), "to withdraw" (*ana*, "back," *choreo*, "to make room, retire"), is translated "give place" in **Matt. 9:24**.

Maid *korasion* (2877), a diminutive of *kore*, "a girl," denotes "a little girl" (properly a colloquial word, often used disparagingly, but not so in later writers); in the NT it is used only in familiar conversation, **Matt. 9:24-25** (KJV, "maid"); **14:11**; Mark 5:41-42; 6:22, 28.

Dead *see* Perished at *Matthew 8:32*.

Sleepeth *katheudo* (2518), "to go to sleep," is chiefly used of natural "sleep," and is found most frequently in the Gospels, especially Matthew and Luke. With reference to death it is found in the Lord's remark concerning Jairus' daughter, **Matt. 9:24**; Mark 5:39; Luke 8:52. In the epistles of Paul it is used as follows: (a) of natural "sleep," e.g., 1 Thess. 5:7; (b) of carnal indifference to spiritual things on the part of believers, Eph. 5:14; 1 Thess. 5:6, 10 (as in Mark 13:36), a condition of insensibility to divine things involving conformity to the world (cf. *hupnos*).

Laughed *katagelao* (2606), denotes "to laugh scornfully at," signifies derisive laughter, **Matt. 9:24**; Mark 5:40; Luke 8:53. Cf. *ekmukterizo*, "to deride."

9:25 But when the people were put forth, he went in, and took her by the hand, and the maid arose.

People *see Matthew 9:23*.

Put *ekballo* (1544), "to cast out," is translated "to put forth or out" in **Matt. 9:25**; Mark 5:40 (Luke 8:54 in some mss.); John 10:4; Acts 9:40.

Went *see* Enter at *Matthew 7:13*.

Took *krateo* (2902), "to take hold of, get possession of," is translated "to take" in **Matt. 9:25**; **22:6**; **26:4**; Mark 1:31; 5:41; 9:27; 14:1, 44, 46, 49; Luke 8:54; Acts 24:6.

Maid *see Matthew 9:24*.

9:26 And the fame hereof went abroad into all that land.

Fame *pheme* (5345), originally denoted "a divine voice, an oracle"; hence, "a saying or report" (akin to *phemi*, "to say," from a root meaning "to shine, to be clear"; hence, Lat., *fama*, Eng., "fame"), is rendered "fame" in **Matt. 9:26** and Luke 4:14.

Hereof This translates the word *haute*, "this," the feminine of *houtos*, "this," in **Matt. 9:26**, lit., "this (fame)," KJV, and RV marg.

9:27 And when Jesus departed thence, two blind men followed him, crying, and saying, *Thou* Son of David, have mercy on us.

Departed *parago* (3855), used intransitively, means "to pass by" (*para*, "by, beside"), and is so translated everywhere in the Gospels, except in the KJV of **Matt. 9:27**, "departed"; RV, "passed by." Outside the Gospels it is used in its other meaning, "to pass away," 1 Cor. 7:31; 1 John 2:8 (RV), 17.

Mercy *see Matthew 5:7*.

9:28 And when he was come into the house, the blind men came to him: and Jesus saith unto them, Believe ye that I am able to do this? They said unto him, Yea, Lord.

Yea *see Matthew 5:37*.

9:29 Then touched he their eyes, saying, According to your faith be it unto you.

Touched *see Matthew 8:3*.

9:30 And their eyes were opened; and Jesus straitly charged them, saying, See *that* no man know *it*.

Straitly For *embrimaomai*, KJV, "charge straitly" (RV, "strictly") in **Matt. 9:30**; Mark 1:43.

Charged *embrimaomai* (1690), from *en*, "in," intensive, and *brime*, "strength," primarily signifies "to snort with anger, as of horses." Used of men it signifies "to fret, to be painfully moved"; then, "to express indignation against"; hence, "to rebuke sternly, to charge strictly," **Matt. 9:30**; Mark 1:43, it is rendered "murmured against" in Mark 14:5; "groaned" in John 11:33; "groaning" in v. 38.

9:31 But they, when they were departed, spread abroad his fame in all that country.

Departed *exerchomai* (1831), denotes "to come out, or go out of, to go forth." It is frequently translated by the verb "to depart," e.g., **Matt. 9:31**; in Luke 4:42, for the KJV, "He departed and went," the RV has "He came out and went"; in 9:6 the KJV and RV agree.

Spread abroad *diaphemizo* (1310), "to spread broad" (*dia*, "throughout," *phemizo*, "to speak"), is so translated in the RV in **Matt. 9:31**; **28:15** (KJV, "commonly reported"); Mark 1:45 (KJV, "blaze abroad").

Fame *diaphemizo* (1310), signifies "to spread abroad a matter," **Matt. 28:15**, RV; Mark 1:45, RV (from *dia*, "throughout," and *phemi*, "to say"); hence, "to spread abroad one's fame," **Matt. 9:31**. All the passages under this heading relate to the testimony concerning Christ in the days of His flesh.

Country *ge*, "earth, land," is translated "country" in the KJV of **Matt. 9:31** and Acts 7:3; RV, "land."

9:32 As they went out, behold, they brought to him a dumb man possessed with a devil.

Dumb *kophos* (2974), akin to *kopto*, "to beat," and *kopiao*, "to be tired" (from a root *kop*–, "to cut"), signifies "blunted, dull," as of a weapon; hence, "blunted in tongue, dumb," **Matt. 9:32**, etc.; "in hearing, deaf," **Matt. 11:5**; Mark 7:32, 37; 9:25; Luke 7:22.

Devil *see* Devils at *Matthew 4:24*.

9:33 And when the devil was cast out, the dumb spake: and the multitudes marvelled, saying, It was never so seen in Israel.

Seen *see Matthew 6:5. See also* Appeared at *Matthew 1:20*.

9:34-35 But the Pharisees said, He casteth out devils through the prince of the devils.

And Jesus went about all the cities and villages, teaching in their synagogues, and preaching the gospel of the kingdom, and healing every sickness and every disease among the people.

Went about *see Matthew 4:23*.

Teaching *see Matthew 4:23*.

Gospel *see Matthew 4:23*.

Disease *see Matthew 4:23*.

9:36 But when he saw the multitudes, he was moved with compassion on them, because they fainted, and were scattered abroad, as sheep having no shepherd.

Compassion *splanchnizomai* (4697), "to be moved as to one's inwards (*splanchna*), to be moved with compassion, to yearn with compassion," is frequently recorded of Christ towards the multitude and towards individual sufferers, **Matt. 9:36**; **14:14**; **15:32**; **18:27**; **20:34**; Mark 1:41; 6:34; 8:2; 9:22 (of the appeal of a father for a demon-possessed son); Luke 7:13; 10:33; of the father in the parable of the Prodigal Son, 15:20. (Moulton and Milligan consider the verb to have been coined in the Jewish dispersion).

Fainted *ekluo* (1590), denotes (a) "to loose, release" (*ek*, "out," *luo*, "to loose"); (b) "to unloose," as a bowstring, "to relax," and so, "to enfeeble," and is used in the passive voice with the significance "to be faint, grow weary," (1) of the body, **Matt. 15:32**; (some mss. have it in **9:36**); Mark 8:3; (2) of the soul, Gal. 6:9 (last clause), in discharging responsibilities in obedience to the Lord; in Heb. 12:3, of becoming weary in the strife against sin; in v. 5, under the chastening hand of God. It expresses the opposite of *anazonnumi*, "to gird up," 1 Pet. 1:13.

Scattered *rhipto* (4496), denotes "to throw with a sudden motion, to jerk, cast forth"; "cast down," **Matt. 15:30** and **27:5**; "thrown down," Luke 4:35; "thrown," 17:2 (KJV, "cast"); [*rhipteo* in Acts 22:23 (KJV, "cast off"), of the "casting" off of clothes (in the next sentence *ballo* is used of "casting" dust into the air)]; in 27:19 "cast out," of the tackling of a ship, in v. 29 "let go" (KJV, "cast"), of anchors; in **Matt. 9:36**, "scattered," said of sheep.

Sheep *see Matthew 7:15*.

Shepherd *poimen* (4166), is used (a) in its natural significance, **Matt. 9:36**; **25:32**; Mark 6:34; Luke 2:8, 15, 18, 20; John 10:2, 12; (b) metaphorically of Christ, **Matt. 26:31**; Mark 14:27; John 10:11, 14, 16; Heb. 13:20; 1 Pet. 2:25; (c) metaphorically of those who act as pastors in the churches, Eph. 4:11.

9:37 Then saith he unto his disciples, The harvest truly *is* plenteous, but the labourers *are* few;

Harvest *therismos* (2326), akin to *therizo*, "to reap," is used (a) of "the act of harvesting," John 4:35; (b) "the time of harvest," figuratively, **Matt. 13:30**, **39**; Mark 4:29; (c) "the crop," figuratively, **Matt. 9:37**, **38**; Luke 10:2; Rev. 14:15. The beginning of "harvest" varied according to natural conditions, but took place on the average about the middle of April in the eastern lowlands of Palestine, in the latter part of the month in the coast plains and a little later in high districts. Barley "harvest" usually came first and then wheat. "Harvesting" lasted about seven weeks, and was the occasion of festivities.

Plenteous *polus* (4183), "much, many, great," is used of number, e.g., Luke 5:6; Acts 11:21; degree, e.g., of harvest, **Matt. 9:37**; mercy, 1 Pet. 1:3, RV "great" (KJV, "abundant"); glory, **Matt. 24:30**; joy, Philem. 7, RV, "much" (KJV, "great"); peace, Acts 24:2. The best mss. have it in Acts 8:8 (RV, "much"), of joy.

Labourers *ergates* (2040), akin to *ergazomai*, "to work," and *ergon*, "work," denotes (a) "a field laborer, a husbandman," **Matt. 9:37**, **38**; **20:1**, **2**, **8**; Luke 10:2 (twice); Jas. 5:4; (b) "a workman, laborer," in a general sense, **Matt. 10:10**; Luke 10:7; Acts 19:25; 1 Tim. 5:18; it is used (c) of false apostles and evil teachers, 2 Cor. 11:13; Phil. 3:2, (d) of a servant of Christ, 2 Tim. 2:15; (e) of evildoers, Luke 13:27.

Few *see Matthew 7:14.*

9:38 Pray ye therefore the Lord of the harvest, that he will send forth labourers into his harvest.

Pray *deomai* (1189), "to desire, to long for," usually representing the word "need," is sometimes translated "beseech," e.g., Luke 5:12; Acts 21:39; 2 Cor. 10:2; Gal. 4:12. It is used of prayer to God, in **Matt. 9:38**; Luke 10:2; 21:36; 22:32; Acts 4:31; 8:22, 24; 10:2; Rom. 1:10; 1 Thess. 3:10.

Lord *see Matthew 1:22.*

Harvest *see Matthew 9:37.*

Labourers *see Matthew 9:37.*

Chapter 10

10:1 And when he had called unto *him* his twelve disciples, he gave them power *against* unclean spirits, to cast them out, and to heal all manner of sickness and all manner of disease.

Called *proskaleo* (4341), signifies (a) "to call to oneself, to bid to come"; it is used only in the middle voice, e.g., **Matt. 10:1**; Acts 5:40; Jas. 5:14; (b) "God's call to Gentiles through the gospel," Acts 2:39; (c) the divine call in entrusting men with the preaching of the gospel," Acts 13:2; 16:10.

Disciples *see Matthew 9:14.*

Spirits *daimonion* (1140), the neuter of the adjective *daimonios*, pertaining to a demon, is also mistranslated "devil," "devils." In Acts 17:18, it denotes an inferior pagan deity. "Demons" are the spiritual agents acting in all idolatry. The idol itself is nothing, but every idol has a "demon" associated with it who induces idolatry, with its worship and sacrifices, 1 Cor. 10:20-21; Rev. 9:20; cf. Deut. 32:17; Isa. 13:21; 34:14; 65:3, 11. They disseminate errors among men, and seek to seduce believers, 1 Tim. 4:1. As seducing spirits they deceive men into the supposition that through mediums (those who have "familiar spirits," Lev. 20:6, 27, e.g.) they can converse with deceased human beings. Hence the destructive deception of spiritism, forbidden in Scripture, Lev. 19:31; Deut. 18:11; Isa. 8:19. "Demons" tremble before God, Jas. 2:19; they recognized Christ as Lord and as their future Judge, **Matt. 8:29**; Luke 4:41. Christ cast them out of human beings by His own power. His disciples did so in His name, and by exercising faith, e.g., **Matt. 17:20**. Acting under Satan (cf. Rev. 16:13-14), "demons" are permitted to afflict with bodily disease, Luke 13:16. Being unclean they tempt human beings with unclean thoughts, **Matt. 10:1**; Mark 5:2; 7:25; Luke 8:27-29; Rev. 16:13; 18:2, e.g. They differ in degrees of wickedness, **Matt. 12:45**. They will instigate the rulers of the nations at the end of this age to make war against God and His Christ, Rev. 16:14.

Disease *see Matthew 4:23.*

10:2-3 Now the names of the twelve apostles are these; The first, Simon, who is called Peter, and Andrew his brother; James *the son* of Zebedee, and John his brother;

Philip, and Bartholomew; Thomas, and Matthew the publican; James *the son* of Alphaeus, and Lebbaeus, whose surname was Thaddaeus;

Publican *see* Publicans at *Matthew 5:46.*

Surname *epikaleo* (1941), "to put a name upon" (*epi*, "upon," *kaleo*, "to call"), "to surname," is used in this sense in the passive voice, in some texts in **Matt. 10:3** (it is absent in the best); in Luke 22:3, in some texts (the best have *kaleo*, "to call"); Acts 1:23; 4:36; 10:5, 18, 32; 11:13; 12:12, 25; in some texts, 15:22 (the best have *kaleo*).

10:4-6 Simon the Canaanite, and Judas Iscariot, who also betrayed him.

These twelve Jesus sent forth, and commanded them, saying, Go not into the way of the Gentiles, and into *any* city of the Samaritans enter ye not:

But go rather to the lost sheep of the house of Israel.

Rather *mallon* (3123), the comparative degree of *mala*, "very, very much," is frequently translated "rather," e.g., **Matt. 10:6, 28**; 1 Cor. 14:1, 5; sometimes followed by "than," with a connecting particle, e.g., **Matt. 18:13** ("more than"); or without, e.g., John 3:19; Acts 4:19, RV (KJV, "more"); in 1 Cor. 9:12, KJV, "rather" (RV, "yet more"); 12:22, RV, "rather" (KJV, "more"); 2 Cor. 3:9 (ditto); Philem. 16 (ditto); in 2 Pet. 1:10, KJV, "the rather" (RV, "the more").

Lost *see* Perish at *Matthew 8:25.*

Sheep *see Matthew 7:15.*

House *see Matthew 9:6.*

10:7-8 And as ye go, preach, saying, The kingdom of heaven is at hand.

Heal the sick, cleanse the lepers, raise the dead, cast out devils: freely ye have received, freely give.

Sick *astheneo* (770), lit., "to be weak, feeble" (*a*, negative, *sthenos*, "strength"), is translated "to be sick," e.g., in **Matt. 10:8**, "(the) sick"; **25:36**; v. **39** in the best texts; Mark 6:56; Luke 4:40; 7:10 (RV omits the word); 9:2; John 4:46; 5:3, RV (KJV, "impotent folk"); v. 7; 6:2, RV (KJV, "were diseased"); 11:1-3, 6; Acts 9:37; 19:12, Phil. 2:26, 27; 2 Tim. 4:20; Jas. 5:14.

Lepers *see* Leper at *Matthew 8:2*.

Raise *egeiro* (1453), is used (a) of "raising" the dead, active and passive voices, e.g., of the resurrection of Christ, **Matt. 16:21**; **17:23**; **20:19**, RV; **26:32**, RV, "(after) I am raised up" (KJV, "... risen again"); Luke 9:22; 20:37; John 2:19; Acts 3:15; 4:10 [not 5:30, see (c) below]; 10:40 [not 13:23 in the best texts, see (c) below]; 13:30, 37; Rom. 4:24, 25; 6:4, 9; 7:4; 8:11 (twice); 8:34, RV; 10:9; 1 Cor. 6:14 (1st part); 15:13, 14, RV; 15:15 (twice), 16, 17; 15:20, RV; 2 Cor. 4:14; Gal. 1:1; Eph. 1:20; Col. 2:12; 1 Thess. 1:10; 1 Pet. 1:21; in 2 Tim. 2:8, RV, "risen"; (b) of the resurrection of human beings, **Matt. 10:8**; **11:5**; **Matt. 27:52**., RV (KJV, "arose"); Mark 12:26, RV; Luke 7:22; John 5:21; 12:1, 9, 17; Acts 26:8; 1 Cor. 15:29 and 32, RV; 15:35, 42, 43 (twice), 44, 52; 2 Cor. 1:9; 4:14; Heb. 11:19; (c) of "raising" up a person to occupy a place in the midst of a people, said of Christ, Acts 5:30; in 13:23, KJV only (the best texts have *ago*, to bring, RV, "hath ... brought"); of David, Acts 13:22; (d) metaphorically, of a horn of salvation, Luke 1:69; (e) of children, from stones, by creative power, Luke 3:8; (f) of the Temple, as the Jews thought, John 2:20, RV, "wilt Thou raise (it) Up" (KJV, "rear"); (g) of "lifting" up a person, from physical infirmity, Mark 1:31, RV, "raised ... up" (KJV, "lifted"); so 9:27; Acts 3:7; 10:26, RV (KJV, "took"); Jas. 5:15, "shall raise ... up"; (h) metaphorically, of "raising" up affliction, Phil. 1:17, RV (in the best texts; the KJV, v. 16, following those which have *epiphero*, has "to add"). *See also* Arose at *Matthew 2:14*.

Received *see* Receiveth at *Matthew 7:8*.

Freely *dorean* (1432), from *dorea*, "a gift" is used as an adverb in the sense "freely," in **Matt. 10:8**; Rom. 3:24; 2 Cor. 11:7 (RV, "for nought"); Rev. 21:6; 22:17. Here the prominent thought is the grace of the Giver.

10:9 Provide neither gold, nor silver, nor brass in your purses,

Provide *ktaomai* (2932), "to acquire, procure for oneself, gain," is rendered "get" in the RV of **Matt. 10:9** and KJV marg. (KJV, text, "provide"); in Luke 18:12 (for KJV, "possess").

Gold *see Matthew 2:11*.

Silver *arguros* (696), akin to *argos*, "shining," denotes "silver." In each occurrence in the NT it follows the mention of gold, **Matt. 10:9**; Acts 17:29; Jas. 5:3; Rev. 18:12. For *drachme*, Luke 15:8.

Brass *chalkos* (5475), primarily, "copper," became used for metals in general, later was applied to bronze, a mixture of copper and tin, then, by metonymy, to any article made of these metals, e.g., money, **Matt. 10:9**; Mark 6:8; 12:41, or a sounding instrument, 1 Cor. 13:1, figurative of a person destitute of love. See Rev. 18:12.

Purses *zone*, "a girdle or belt," also served as "a purse for money," **Matt. 10:9**; Mark 6:8. *See also* Girdle at *Matthew 3:4*.

10:10 Nor scrip for *your* journey, neither two coats, neither shoes, nor yet staves: for the workman is worthy of his meat.

Scrip *pera* (4082), "a traveler's leather bag or pouch for holding provisions," is translated "wallet" in the RV (KJV, "scrip"), **Matt. 10:10**; Mark 6:8; Luke 9:3; 10:4; 22:35, 36. Deissmann (*Light from the Ancient East*) regards it as an alms-bag.

Shoes *see Matthew 3:11*.

Staves *rhabdos* (4464), "a staff, rod, scepter," is used (a) of Aaron's "rod," Heb. 9:4; (b) a staff used on a journey, **Matt. 10:10**, RV, "staff" (KJV, "staves"); so Luke 9:3; Mark 6:8, "staff"; Heb. 11:21, "staff"; (c) a ruler's staff, a "scepter," Heb. 1:8 (twice); elsewhere a "rod," Rev. 2:27; 12:5; 19:15; (d) a "rod" for chastisement (figuratively), 1 Cor. 4:21; (e) a measuring rod, Rev. 11:1.

Workman *ergates* (2040), is translated "workers" in Luke 13:27 ("of iniquity"); 2 Cor. 11:13 ("deceitful"); Phil. 3:2 ("evil"); "workman," **Matt. 10:10**, KJV (RV, "laborer"); "workman," 2 Tim. 2:15; "workmen," Acts 19:25. *See also* **Labourers** at *Matthew 9:37*.

Worthy *axios* (514), "of weight, worth, worthy," is said of persons and their deeds: (a) in a good sense, e.g., **Matt. 10:10**, **11**, **13** (twice), 37 (twice), 38; **22:8**; Luke 7:4; 10:7; 15:19, 21; John 1:27; Acts 13:25; 1 Tim. 5:18; 6:1; Heb. 11:38; Rev. 3:4; 4:11; 5:2, 4, 9, 12; (b) in a bad sense, Luke 12:48; 23:15; Acts 23:29; 25:11, 25; 26:31; Rom. 1:32; Rev. 16:6.

Meat *see Matthew 3:4*.

10:11 And into whatsoever city or town ye shall enter, enquire who in it is worthy; and there abide till ye go thence.

Whatsoever Frequently by the addition of the particle *an*, or the conjunction *ean*, "if," the phrase has the more general idea of "whatsoever," e.g., with *hos*, **Matt. 10:11**; with *hosos*, **Matt. 17:12**; with *hostis*, neuter form, Luke 10:35.

Town *kome* (2968), "a village," or "country town without walls." The RV always renders this "village" or "villages," KJV, "town" or "towns," **Matt. 10:11**; Mark 8:23, 26 (twice), 27; Luke 5:17; 9:6, 12; John 7:42; 11:1, 30.

Enquire *see* **Search** at *Matthew 2:8*.

Worthy *see Matthew 10:10*.

Abide *meno* (3306), used (a) of place, e.g., **Matt. 10:11**, metaphorically 1 John 2:19, is said of God, 1 John 4:15; Christ, John 6:56; 15:4, etc.; the Holy Spirit, John 1:32-33; 14:17; believers, John 6:56; 15:4; 1 John 4:15, etc.; the Word of God, 1 John 2:14; the truth, 2 John 2, etc.; (b) of time; it is said of believers, John 21:22-23; Phil. 1:25; 1 John 2:17; Christ, John 12:34; Heb. 7:24; the Word of God, 1 Pet. 1:23; sin, John 9:41; cities, **Matt. 11:23**; Heb. 13:14; bonds and afflictions, Acts 20:23; (c) of qualities; faith, hope, love, 1 Cor. 13:13; Christ's love, John 15:10; afflictions, Acts 20:23; brotherly love, Heb. 13:1; the love of God, 1 John 3:17; the truth, 2 John 2. The RV usually translates it by "abide," but "continue" in 1 Tim. 2:15; in the following, the RV substitutes "to abide" for the KJV, "to continue," John 2:12; 8:31; 15:9; 2 Tim. 3:14; Heb. 7:24; 13:14; 1 John 2:24.

10:12-13 And when ye come into an house, salute it.

And if the house be worthy, let your peace come upon it: but if it be not worthy, let your peace return to you.

Worthy *see Matthew 10:10*.

Peace *eirene* (1515), "occurs in each of the books of the NT, save 1 John and save in Acts 7:26 ['(at) one again'] it is translated "peace" in the RV. It describes (a) harmonious relationships between men, **Matt. 10:34**; Rom. 14:19; (b) between nations, Luke 14:32; Acts 12:20; Rev. 6:4; (c) friendliness, Acts 15:33; 1 Cor. 16:11; Heb. 11:31; (d) freedom from molestation, Luke 11:21; 19:42; Acts 9:31 (RV, 'peace,' KJV, 'rest'); 16:36; (e) order, in the State, Acts 24:2 (RV, 'peace,' KJV, 'quietness'); in the churches, 1 Cor. 14:33; (f) the harmonized relationships between God and man, accomplished through the gospel, Acts 10:36; Eph. 2:17; (g) the sense of rest and contentment consequent thereon, **Matt. 10:13**; Mark 5:34; Luke 1:79; 2:29; John 14:27; Rom. 1:7; 3:17; 8:6; in certain passages this idea is not distinguishable from the last, Rom. 5:1."

10:14 And whosoever shall not receive you, nor hear your words, when ye depart out of that house or city, shake off the dust of your feet.

Receive *dechomai* (1209), "to receive by deliberate and ready reception of what is offered," is used of (a) taking with the hand, taking hold, taking hold of or up, e.g., Luke 2:28, RV, "he received (Him)," KJV, "took he (Him) up"; 16:6, 7; 22:17; Eph. 6:17; (b) "receiving," said of a place "receiving" a person, of Christ into the Heavens, Acts 3:21; or of persons in giving access to someone as a visitor, e.g., John 4:45; 2 Cor. 7:15; Gal. 4:14; Col. 4:10; by way of giving hospitality, etc., e.g., **Matt. 10:14, 40** (four times), **41** (twice); **18:5**; Mark 6:11; 9:37; Luke 9:5, 48, 53; 10:8, 10; 16:4; v. 9, of reception, "into the eternal tabernacles," said of followers of Christ who have used "the mammon of unrighteousness" to render assistance to ("make ... friends of") others; of Rahab's reception of the spies, Heb. 11:31; of the reception, by the Lord, of the spirit of a departing believer, Acts 7:59; of "receiving" a gift, 2 Cor. 8:4 (in some mss.; RV follows those which omit it); of the favorable reception of testimony and teaching, etc., Luke 8:13; Acts 8:14; 11:1; 17:11; 1 Cor. 2:14; 2 Cor. 8:17; 1 Thess. 1:6; 2:13, where *paralambano* is used in the 1st part, "ye received," *dechomai* in the 2nd part, "ye accepted," RV (KJV, "received"), the former refers to the ear, the latter, adding the idea of appropriation, to the heart; Jas. 1:21; in 2 Thess. 2:10, "the love of the truth:" i.e., love for the truth; cf. **Matt. 11:14**, "if ye are willing to receive it," an elliptical construction frequent in Greek writings; of "receiving," by way of bearing with, enduring, 2 Cor. 11:16; of "receiving" by way of getting, Acts 22:5; 28:21, of becoming partaker of benefits, Mark 10:15; Luke 18:17; Acts 7:38; 2 Cor. 6:1; 11:4 (last clause "did accept": cf. *lambano* in previous clauses); Phil. 4:18.

Shake *ektinasso* (1621), "to shake out," is used of "shaking off" the dust from the feet, **Matt. 10:14**; Mark 6:11; Acts 13:51; of "shaking out" one's raiment, Acts 18:6.

Dust *koniortos* (2868), "raised or flying dust" (*konia*, "dust," *ornumi*, "to stir up"), is found in **Matt. 10:14**; Luke 9:5; 10:11; Acts 13:51; 22:23.

Feet *pous* (4228), besides its literal meaning, is used, by metonymy, of "a person in motion," Luke 1:79; Acts 5:9; Rom. 3:15; 10:15; Heb. 12:13. It is used in phrases expressing subjection, 1 Cor. 15:27, RV; of the humility and receptivity of discipleship, Luke 10:39; Acts 22:3; of obeisance and worship, e.g., **Matt. 28:9**; of scornful rejection,

Matt. 10:14; Acts 13:51. Washing the "feet" of another betokened the humility of the service and the comfort of the guest, and was a feature of hospitality, Luke 7:38; John 13:5; 1 Tim. 5:10 (here figuratively).

10:15 Verily I say unto you, It shall be more tolerable for the land of Sodom and Gomorrha in the day of judgment, than for that city.

Tolerable *anektos* (414), (akin to *anecho*, in the middle voice, "to endure") is used in its comparative form, *anektoteros*, in **Matt. 10:15; 11:22, 24**; Luke 10:12, 14; some texts have it in Mark 6:11.

10:16 Behold, I send you forth as sheep in the midst of wolves: be ye therefore wise as serpents, and harmless as doves.

I *ego* (1473), is the nominative case of the first personal pronoun. The pronoun, "I," however, generally forms a part of the verb itself in Greek; thus *luo* itself means "I loose," the pronoun being incorporated in the verb form. Where the pronoun *ego* is added to the verb, it is almost invariably, if not entirely, emphatic. The emphasis may not be so apparent in some instances, as e.g., **Matt. 10:16**, but even here it may be taken that something more of stress is present than if the pronoun were omitted. By far the greater number of instances are found in the Gospel of John, and there in the utterances of the Lord concerning Himself, e.g., 4:14, 26, 32, 38; 5:34, 36, 43, 45; 6:35, 40, 41, 48, 51 (twice), 63, 70 instances in the Epistles are Rom. 7:9, 14, 17, 20 (twice), 24, 25; there are more in that chapter than in any other outside the Gospel of John. In other cases of the pronoun than the nominative, the pronoun is usually more necessary to the meaning, apart from any stress.

Send *apostello* (649), lit., "to send forth" (*apo*, "from"), akin to *apostolos*, "an apostle," denotes (a) "to send on service, or with a commission." (1) of persons; Christ, sent by the Father, **Matt. 10:40; 15:24; 21:37**; Mark 9:37; 12:6; Luke 4:18, 43; 9:48; 10:16; John 3:17; 5:36, 38; 6:29, 57; 7:29; 8:42; 10:36; 11:42; 17:3, 8, 18 (1st part), 21, 23, 25; 20:21; Acts 3:20 (future); 3:26; 1 John 4:9, 10, 14; the Holy Spirit, Luke 24:49; 1 Pet. 1:12; Rev. 5:6; Moses, Acts 7:35; John the Baptist, John 1:6; 3:28; disciples and apostles, e.g., **Matt. 10:16**; Mark 11:1; Luke 22:8; John 4:38; 17:18 (2nd part); Acts 26:17; servants, e.g., **Matt. 21:34**; Luke 20:10; officers and officials, Mark 6:27; John 7:32; Acts 16:35; messengers, e.g., Acts 10:8, 17, 20; 15:27; evangelists, Rom. 10:15; angels, e.g., **Matt. 24:31**; Mark 13:27; Luke 1:19, 26; Heb. 1:14; Rev. 1:1; 22:6; demons, Mark 5:10; (2) of things, e.g., **Matt. 21:3**; Mark 4:29, RV, marg., "sendeth forth," text, "putteth forth" (KJV, "... in"); Acts 10:36; 11:30; 28:28; (b) "to send away, dismiss," e.g., Mark 8:26; 12:3; Luke 4:18, "to set (at liberty)."

Sheep *see Matthew 7:15.*

Wolves *see Matthew 7:15.*

Wise *see Matthew 7:24.*

Serpents *see* **Serpent** at *Matthew 7:10.*

Harmless *akeraios* (185), lit., "unmixed, with absence of foreign mixture" (from *a*, negative, and *kerannumi*, "to mix"), "pure," is used metaphorically in the NT of what is guileless, sincere, **Matt. 10:16**, "harmless" (marg., "simple"), i.e., with the simplicity of a single eye, discerning what is evil, and choosing only what glorifies God; Rom. 16:19, "simple (unto that which is evil)," KJV marg., "harmless"; Phil. 2:15, "harmless," KJV marg., "sincere." The Greeks used it of wine unmixed with water, of unalloyed metal; in the papyri writings it is used of a loan the interest of which is guaranteed (Moulton and Milligan, *Vocab.*). Trench compares it and synonymous words as follows: "as the *akakos* has no harmfulness in him, and the *adolos* no guile, so the *akeraios* no foreign mixture, and the *haplous* no folds" (*Syn.* Sec.lvi).

Doves *see* **Dove** at *Matthew 3:16.*

10:17 But beware of men: for they will deliver you up to the councils, and they will scourge you in their synagogues;

Beware *see Matthew 7:15.*

Councils *sunedrion* (4892), properly, "a settling together" (*sun*, "together," *hedra*, "a seat"), hence, (a) "any assembly or session of persons deliberating or adjusting," as in the Sept. of Ps. 26:4 (lit., "with a council of vanity"); Prov. 22:10; Jer. 15:17, etc.; in the NT, e.g., **Matt. 10:17**; Mark 13:9; John 11:47, in particular, it denoted (b) "the Sanhedrin," the Great Council at Jerusalem, consisting of 71 members, namely, prominent members of the families of the high priest, elders and scribes. The Jews trace the origin of this to Num. 11:16. The more important causes came up before this tribunal. The Roman rulers of Judea permitted the Sanhedrin to try such cases, and even to pronounce sentence of death, with the condition that such a sentence should be valid only if confirmed by the Roman procurator. In John 11:47, it is used of a meeting of the Sanhedrin; in Acts 4:15, of the place of meeting.

Scourge *mastigoo* (3146), akin to *mastix*, is used of Jewish "scourgings," **Matt. 10:17** and **23:34**; and metaphorically, in Heb. 12:6, of the "chastening" by the Lord administered in love to His spiritual sons.

Synagogues *sunagoge* (4864), is, lit., "a place where people assemble." In Acts 13:43 the RV suitably has "synagogue," for the KJV "congregation," the building standing by metonymy for the people therein (cf. **Matt. 10:17**, etc.). In Jas. 2:2 (KJV, "assembly") the word is "synagogue" (RV).

10:18 And ye shall be brought before governors and kings for my sake, for a testimony against them and the Gentiles.

And *see* Also at *Matthew 5:39.*

10:19 But when they deliver you up, take no thought how or what ye shall speak: for it shall be given you in that same hour what ye shall speak.

Thought *see Matthew 6:25.*

10:20 For it is not ye that speak, but the Spirit of your Father which speaketh in you.

Spirit *see* Holy Ghost at *Matthew 1:18.*

10:21 And the brother shall deliver up the brother to death, and the father the child: and the children shall rise up against *their* parents, and cause them to be put to death.

Rise *epanistamai*, "to rise up against," occurs in **Matt. 10:21**; Mark 13:12.

Parents *goneus* (1118), "a begetter, a father" (akin to *ginomai*, "to come into being, become"), is used in the plural in the NT, **Matt. 10:21**; Mark 13:12; six times in Luke (in Luke 2:43, RV, "His parents," KJV, "Joseph and His mother"); six in John; elsewhere, Rom. 1:30; 2 Cor. 12:14 (twice); Eph. 6:1; Col. 3:20; 2 Tim. 3:2.

Death *thanatoo* (2289), "to put to death," in **Matt. 10:21**; Mark 13:12; Luke 21:16, is translated "shall ... cause (them) to be put to death," lit., "shall put (them) to death" (RV marg.). It is used of the death of Christ in **Matt. 26:59**; **27:1**; Mark 14:55 and 1 Pet. 3:18. In Rom. 7:4 (passive voice) it is translated "ye ... were made dead," RV (for KJV, "are become"), with reference to the change from bondage to the Law to union with Christ; in 8:13, "mortify" (marg., "make to die"), of the act of the believer in regard to the deeds of the body; in 8:36, "are killed"; so in 2 Cor. 6:9.

10:22 And ye shall be hated of all *men* for my name's sake: but he that endureth to the end shall be saved.

Hated *see* Hate at *Matthew 6:24.*

Name *see Matthew 6:9.*

Endureth *hupomeno* (5278), denotes "to abide under, to bear up courageously" (under suffering), **Matt. 10:22**; **24:13**; Mark 13:13; Rom. 12:12, translated "patient"; 1 Cor. 13:7; 2 Tim. 2:10, 12 (KJV, "suffer"); Heb. 10:32; 12:2-3, 7; Jas. 1:12; 5:11; 1 Pet. 2:20, "ye shall take it patiently." It has its other significance, "to tarry, wait for, await," in Luke 2:43; Acts 17:14 (in some mss., Rom. 8:24). Cf. *makrothumeo*, to be longsuffering".

End The following phrases contain *telos* (the word itself coming under one or other of the above): *eis telos*, "unto the end," e.g., **Matt. 10:22**; **24:13**; Luke 18:5, "continual"; John 13:1; 2 Cor. 3:13, "on the end" (RV); *heos telous*, "unto the end," 1 Cor. 1:8; 2 Cor. 1:13; *achri telous*, "even to the end" (a stronger expression than the preceding); Heb. 6:11; Rev. 2:26 (where "even" might well have been added); *mechri telous*, with much the same meaning as *achri telous*, Heb. 3:6, 14.

Saved *see* Save at *Matthew 1:21.*

10:23 But when they persecute you in this city, flee ye into another: for verily I say unto you, Ye shall not have gone over the cities of Israel, till the Son of man be come.

Persecute *see* Persecuted at *Matthew 5:10.*

Gone *teleo* (5055), "to finish," is rendered "to go through or over" in **Matt. 10:23**, of "going through" the cities of Israel (KJV, marg., "end," or "finish").

Son *see Matthew 3:17.*

10:24 The disciple is not above *his* master, nor the servant above his lord.

Master *see Matthew 8:19.*

10:25 It is enough for the disciple that he be as his master, and the servant as his lord. If they have called the master of the house Beelzebub, how much more *shall they call* them of his household?

Enough *see* Sufficient at *Matthew 6:34.*

Master *see Matthew 8:19.*

Called, Call *epikaleo* (1941), denotes (a) "to surname"; (b) "to be called by a person's name"; hence it is used of being declared to be dedicated to a person, as to the Lord, Acts 15:17 (from Amos 9:12); Jas. 2:7; (c) "to call a person by a name by charging him with an offense," as the Pharisees charged Christ with doing His works by the help of Beelzebub, **Matt. 10:25** (the most authentic reading has *epikaleo*, for *kaleo*); (d) "to call upon, invoke"; in the middle voice, "to call upon for oneself" (i.e., on one's behalf), Acts 7:59, or "to call upon a person as a witness," 2 Cor. 1:23, or to appeal to an authority, Acts 25:11, etc.; (e) "to call upon by way of adoration, making use of the Name of the Lord," Acts 2:21; Rom. 10:12-14; 2 Tim. 2:22.

Master of the house *oikodespotes* (3617), "a master of a house" (*oikos*, "a house," *despotes*, "a master"), is rendered "master of the house" in **Matt. 10:25**; Luke 13:25, and 14:21, where the context shows that the authority of the "householder" is stressed; in **Matt. 24:43** and Luke 12:39, the RV "master of the house" (KJV, "goodman of the house," does not give the exact meaning); "householder" is the rendering in both versions in **Matt. 13:27, 52; 20:1; 21:33**; so the RV in **20:11** (for KJV, "goodman of the house"); both have "goodman of the house" in Mark 14:14; in Luke 22:11, "goodman."

Household *oikiakos* (3615), denotes "belonging to one's household, one's own"; it is used in **Matt. 10:25, 36**.

10:26 Fear them not therefore: for there is nothing covered, that shall not be revealed; and hid, that shall not be known.

Nothing *see Matthew 5:13.*

Covered *see Matthew 8:24.*

Revealed *apokalupto* (601), signifies "to uncover, unveil" (*apo*, "from," *kalupto*, "to cover"); both verbs are used in **Matt. 10:26**; in Luke 12:2, *apokalupto* is set in contrast to *sunkalupto*, "to cover up, cover completely." "The NT occurrences of this word fall under two heads, subjective and objective. The subjective use is that in which something is presented to the mind directly, as, (a) the meaning of the acts of God, **Matt. 11:25**; Luke 10:21; (b) the secret of the Person of the Lord Jesus, **Matt. 16:17**; John 12:38; (c) the character of God as Father, **Matt. 11:27**; Luke 10:22; (d) the will of God for the conduct of His children, Phil. 3:15; (e) the mind of God to the prophets of Israel, 1 Pet. 1:12, and of the Church, 1 Cor. 14:30; Eph. 3:5."

Hid *kruptos* (2927), "hidden, secret," is translated "hid" in **Matt. 10:26**; Mark 4:22; Luke 8:17, RV, for KJV, "secret"; 12:2 (last part); in 1 Cor. 4:5, "hidden (things of darkness)"; 2 Cor. 4:2, "hidden (things of shame)"; 1 Pet. 3:4, "hidden (man of the heart)."

Known *see* Knew at *Matthew 1:25.*

10:27 What I tell you in darkness, *that* speak ye in light: and what ye hear in the ear, *that* preach ye upon the housetops.

Tell *see* **Bring ... word** at *Matthew 2:13.*

Darkness *see Matthew 4:16.*

Ear *ous* (3775), Latin *auris*, is used (a) of the physical organ, e.g., Luke 4:21; Acts 7:57; in Acts 11:22, in the plural with *akouo*, "to hear," lit., "was heard into the ears of someone," i.e., came to the knowledge of, similarly, in the singular, **Matt. 10:27**, in familiar private conversation; in Jas. 5:4 the phrase is used with *eiserchomai*, "to enter into"; in Luke 1:44, with *ginomai*, "to become, to come"; in Luke 12:3, with *lalein*, "to speak" and *pros*, "to", (b) metaphorically, of the faculty of perceiving with the mind, understanding and knowing, **Matt. 13:16**; frequently with *akouo*, "to hear," e.g., **Matt. 11:15; 13:9, 43**; Rev. 2 and 3, at the close of each of the messages to the churches, in **Matt. 13:15** and Acts 28:27, with *bareos*, "heavily," of being slow to understand and obey; with a negative in Mark 8:18; Rom. 11:8; in Luke 9:44 the lit. meaning is "put those words into your ears," i.e., take them into your mind and keep them there, in Acts 7:51 it is used with *aperitmetos*, "uncircumcised." As seeing is metaphorically associated with conviction, so hearing is with obedience (*hupakoe*, lit., "hearing under"; the Eng., "obedience" is etymologically "hearing over against," i.e., with response in the hearer).

Preach *kerusso* (2784), is translated "to proclaim" in the RV, for KJV, "to preach," in **Matt. 10:27**; Luke 4:19; Acts 8:5; 9:20.

Housetops *doma* (1430), akin to *demo*, "to build," denotes a housetop. The housetop was flat, and guarded by a low parapet wall (see Deut. 22:8). It was much frequented and used for various purposes, e.g., for proclamations, **Matt. 10:27**; Luke 12:3; for prayer, Acts 10:9. The house was often built round a court, across the top of which cords were fixed from the parapet walls for supporting a covering from the heat. The housetop could be reached by stairs outside the building; the paralytic in Luke 5:19 could be let down into the court or area by rolling back the covering. External flight from the housetop in time or danger is enjoined in **Matt. 24:17**; Mark 13:15; Luke 17:31.

10:28 And fear not them which kill the body, but are not able to kill the soul: but rather fear him which is able to destroy both soul and body in hell.

Fear *phobos* (5401), first had the meaning of "flight," that which is caused by being scared; then, "that which may cause flight," (a) "fear, dread, terror," always with this significance in the four Gospels; also, e.g., in Acts 2:43; 19:17; 1 Cor. 2:3; 1 Tim. 5:20 (lit., "may have fear"); Heb. 2:15; 1 John 4:18; Rev. 11:11; 18:10, 15; by metonymy, that which causes "fear," Rom. 13:3; 1 Pet. 3:14, RV, "(their) fear," KJV "(their) terror," an adaptation of the Sept. of Isa. 8:12, "fear not their fear"; hence some take it to mean, as there, "what they fear," but in view of **Matt. 10:28**, e.g., it seems best to understand it as that which is caused by the intimidation of adversaries; (b) "reverential fear," (1) of God, as a controlling motive of the life, in matters spiritual and moral, not a mere "fear" of His power and righteous retribution, but a wholesome dread of displeasing Him, a "fear" which banishes the terror that shrinks from His presence, Rom. 8:15, and which influences the disposition and attitude of one whose circumstances are guided by trust in God, through the indwelling Spirit of God, Acts 9:31; Rom. 3:18; 2 Cor. 7:1; Eph. 5:21 (RV, "the fear of Christ"); Phil. 2:12; 1 Pet. 1:17 (a comprehensive phrase: the reverential "fear" of God will inspire a constant carefulness in dealing with others in His "fear"); 3:2, 15; the association of "fear and trembling," as, e.g., in Phil. 2:12, has in the Sept. a much sterner import, e.g., Gen. 9:2; Exod. 15:16; Deut. 2:25; 11:25; Ps. 55:5; Isa. 19:16; (2) of superiors, e.g., Rom. 13:7; 1 Pet. 2:18.

Kill *apokteino* (615), "to kill," is used (a) physically, e.g., **Matt. 10:28; 14:5**, "put ... to death," similarly rendered in John 18:31; often of Christ's death; in Rev. 2:13, RV "was killed" (KJV, "was slain"); 9:15, RV, "kill" (KJV, "slay"); 11:13, RV, "were killed" (KJV, "were slain"); so in 19:21; (b) metaphorically, Rom. 7:11, of the power of sin, which is personified, as "finding occasion, through the commandment," and inflicting deception and spiritual death, i.e., separation from God, realized through the presentation of the commandment to conscience, breaking in upon the fancied state of freedom; the argument shows the power of the Law, not to deliver from sin, but to enhance its sinfulness; in 2 Cor. 3:6, "the letter killeth," signifies not the literal meaning of Scripture as contrasted with the spiritual, but the power of the Law to bring home the knowledge of guilt and its punishment; in Eph. 2:16 "having slain the enmity" describes the work of Christ through His death in annulling the enmity, "the Law" (v. 15), between Jew and Gentile, reconciling regenerate Jew and Gentile to God in spiritual unity "in one body."

Soul *see* Life at *Matthew 2:20*.

Rather *see Matthew 10:6*.

Destroy *see Matthew 2:13*. *See also* Perish at *Matthew 8:25*.

Hell *see Matthew 5:22*.

10:29 Are not two sparrows sold for a farthing? and one of them shall not fall on the ground without your Father.

Sparrows *strouthion* (4765), a diminutive of *strouthos*, "a sparrow," occurs in **Matt. 10:29, 31**; Luke 12: 6, 7.

Farthing *assarion* (787), a diminutive of the Latin *as*, was one-tenth of a drachma, or one-sixteenth of a Roman *denarius*, i.e., about three farthings, **Matt. 10:29**; Luke 12:6.

Fall *see* Fell at *Matthew 2:11*.

Ground *ge* (1093), "the earth, land," etc., often denotes "the ground," e.g., **Matt. 10:29**; Mark 8:6. *See also* Earth at *Matthew 5:18*.

Without The opposite of *choris* is *sun*, "with." A synonymous preposition, *aneu*, denotes "without," **Matt. 10:29**; 1 Pet. 3:1 and 4:9.

Father *theos* (2316), (I) in the polytheism of the Greeks, denoted "a god or deity," e.g., Acts 14:11; 19:26; 28:6; 1 Cor. 8:5; Gal. 4:8.

(II) (a) Hence the word was appropriated by Jews and retained by Christians to denote "the one true God." In the Sept. *theos* translates (with few exceptions) the Hebrew words *Elohim* and *Jehovah*, the former indicating His power and preeminence, the latter His unoriginated, immutable, eternal and self-sustained existence. In the NT, these and all the other divine attributes are predicated of Him. To Him are ascribed, e.g., His unity, or monism, e.g., Mark 12:29; 1 Tim. 2:5; self-existence, John 5:26; immutability, Jas. 1:17; eternity, Rom. 1:20; universality, **Matt. 10:29**; Acts 17:26-28; almighty power, **Matt. 19:26**; infinite knowledge, Acts 2:23; 15:18; Rom. 11:33, creative power, Rom. 11:36; 1 Cor. 8:6; Eph. 3:9; Rev. 4:11; 10:6; absolute holiness, 1 Pet. 1:15; 1 John 1:5; righteousness, John 17:25; faithfulness, 1 Cor. 1:9; 10:13; 1 Thess. 5:24; 2 Thess. 3:3; 1 John 1:9; love, 1 John 4:8, 16; mercy, Rom. 9:15, 18; truthfulness, Titus 1:2; Heb. 6:18.

(b) The divine attributes are likewise indicated or definitely predicated of Christ, e.g., **Matt. 20:18-19**; John 1:1-3; 1:18, RV, marg.; 5:22-29; 8:58; 14:6; 17:22-24; 20:28; Rom. 1:4; 9:5; Phil. 3:21; Col. 1:15; 2:3; Titus 2:13, RV; Heb. 1:3; 13:8; 1 John 5:20; Rev. 22:12, 13.

(c) Also of the Holy Spirit, e.g., **Matt. 28:19**; Luke 1:35; John 14:16; 15:26; 16:7-14; Rom. 8:9, 26; 1 Cor. 12:11; 2 Cor. 13:14.

(d) *Theos* is used (1) with the definite article, (2) without (i.e., as an anarthrous noun). "The English may or may not have need of the article in translation. But that point cuts no figure in the Greek idiom. Thus in Acts 27:23 ('the God whose I am,' RV) the article points out the special God whose Paul is, and is to be preserved in English. In the very next verse (*ho theos*) we in English do not need the article" (A. T. Robertson, *Gram. of Greek, NT*, p. 758).

In the following titles God is described by certain of His attributes; the God of glory, Acts 7:2; of peace, Rom. 15:33; 16:20; Phil. 4:9; 1 Thess. 5:23; Heb. 13:20; of love and peace, 2 Cor. 13:11; of patience and comfort, Rom. 15:5; of all comfort, 2 Cor. 1:3; of hope, Rom. 15:13; of all grace, 1 Pet. 5:10. These describe Him, not as in distinction from other persons, but as the source of all these blessings; hence the employment of the definite article. In such phrases as "the God of a person," e.g., **Matt. 22:32**, the expression marks the relationship in which the person stands to God and God to him ...

(f) The phrase "the things of God" (translated literally or otherwise) stands for (1) His interests, **Matt. 16:23**; Mark 8:33; (2) His counsels, 1 Cor. 2:11; (3) things which are due to Him, **Matt. 22:21**; Mark 12:17; Luke 20:25. The phrase "things pertaining to God," Rom. 15:17; Heb. 2:17; 5:1, describes, in the Heb. passages, the sacrificial service of the priest; in the Rom. passage the gospel ministry as an offering to God.

10:30 But the very hairs of your head are all numbered.

Very Sometimes it translates the conjunction *kai*, in the sense of "even," e.g., **Matt. 10:30**; in **24:24**, KJV, "very" (RV, "even"); Luke 12:59.

Hairs *see* Hair at *Matthew 3:4*.

Numbered *arithmeo* (705), is found in **Matt. 10:30**; Luke 12:7; Rev. 7:9.

10:31 Fear ye not therefore, ye are of more value than many sparrows.

More value *see* Better at *Matthew 6:26*.

Sparrows *see Matthew 10:29*.

10:32 Whosoever therefore shall confess me before men, him will I confess also before my Father which is in heaven.

Confess *see* Profess at *Matthew 7:23*.

10:33 But whosoever shall deny me before men, him will I also deny before my Father which is in heaven.

Deny *arneomai* (720), signifies (a) "to say ... not, to contradict," e.g., Mark 14:70; John 1:20; 18:25, 27; 1 John 2:22; (b) "to deny" by way of disowning a person, as, e.g., the Lord Jesus as master, e.g., **Matt. 10:33**; Luke 12:9; John 13:38 (in the best mss.); 2 Tim. 2:12; or, on the other hand, of Christ Himself, "denying" that a person is His follower, **Matt. 10:33**; 2 Tim. 2:12; or to "deny" the Father and the Son, by apostatizing and by disseminating pernicious teachings, to "deny" Jesus Christ as master and Lord by immorality under a cloak of religion, 2 Pet. 2:1; Jude 4; (c) "to deny oneself," either in a good sense, by disregarding one's own interests, Luke 9:23, or in a bad sense, to prove false to oneself, to act quite unlike oneself, 2 Tim. 2:13; (d) to "abrogate, forsake, or renounce a thing," whether evil, Titus 2:12, or good, 1 Tim. 5:8; 2 Tim. 3:5; Rev. 2:13; 3:8; (e) "not to accept, to reject" something offered, Acts 3:14; 7:35, "refused"; Heb. 11:24 "refused."

10:34 Think not that I am come to send peace on earth: I came not to send peace, but a sword.

Think *see Matthew 5:17*.

Peace *see Matthew 10:13*.

Send *ballo* (906), "to cast, throw," is translated "to send (peace)" in **Matt. 10:34** (twice), (RV, marg., "cast").

Sword *machaira* (3162), "a short sword or dagger," e.g., **Matt. 26:47, 51, 52** and parallel passages; Luke 21:24; 22:38, possibly "a knife" (Field, *Notes on the Translation of the NT*); Heb. 4:12; metaphorically and by metonymy, (a) for ordinary violence, or dissensions, that destroy peace, **Matt. 10:34**; (b) as the instrument of a magistrate or judge, e.g., Rom. 13:4; (c) of the Word of God, "the sword of the Spirit," probing the conscience, subduing the impulses to sin, Eph. 6:17.

10:35 For I am come to set a man at variance against his father, and the daughter against her mother, and the daughter in law against her mother in law.

Variance *dichazo* (1369), "to cut apart, divide in two," is used metaphorically in **Matt. 10:35**, "to set at variance."

Daughter, Daughter in law *numphe* (3565), (Eng., "nymph"), denotes "a bride," John 3:29; also "a daughter-in-law," **Matt. 10:35**; Luke 12:53.

Mother in law *see* Wife's mother at *Matthew 8:14*.

10:36 And a man's foes *shall be* they of his own household.

Foes *echthros* (2190), an adjective signifying "hated, hateful, or hostile," is used also as a noun denoting "an enemy," translated "foes" in **Matt. 10:36** and the KJV of Acts 2:35. *See also* Enemy at *Matthew 5:43*.

Household *see Matthew 10:25*.

10:37 He that loveth father or mother more than me is not worthy of me: and he that loveth son or daughter more than me is not worthy of me.

More Various uses of the word "more" occur in connection with other words, especially in the comparative degree. The phrase "more than" translates certain prepositions and particles: in Rom. 1:25, KJV, *para*, "beside, compared with," is translated "more than" (RV, "rather than"): cf. Rom. 12:3 *huper*, "over, above," "more than," in **Matt. 10:37** (twice); in Philem. 21, KJV, "more than" (RV, "beyond"). In Mark 14:5, KJV, *epano*, "above," is translated "more than" (RV, "above"). In Luke 15:7 the particle *e*, "than," is necessarily rendered "more than"; cf. Luke 17:2 and 1 Cor. 14:19, "rather than." In Mark 8:14, the conjunction *ei*, "if," with the negative *me*, lit., "if not," signifying "except," is translated "more than (one loaf)."

10:38 And he that taketh not his cross, and followeth after me, is not worthy of me.

He that *hos* (3739), the relative pronoun "who," is sometimes rendered "he that," e.g., **Matt. 10:38**; with the particle *an*, expressing possibility, uncertainty or a condition, signifying "whosoever," Mark 3:29, KJV (RV, "whosoever"); 4:25 and 9:40 (with *an*, in the best mss.).

Cross *stauros* (4716), denotes, primarily, "an upright pale or stake." On such malefactors were nailed for execution. Both the noun and the verb *stauroo*, "to fasten to a stake or pale," are originally to be distinguished from the ecclesiastical form of a two beamed "cross." The shape of the latter had its origin in ancient Chaldea, and was used as the symbol of the god Tammuz (being in the shape of the mystic Tau, the initial of his name) in that country and in adjacent lands, including Egypt. By the middle of the 3rd cent. AD the churches had either departed from, or had travestied, certain doctrines of the Christian faith. In order to increase the prestige of the apostate ecclesiastical system pagans were received into the churches apart from regeneration by faith, and were permitted largely to retain their pagan signs and symbols. Hence the Tau or T, in its most frequent form, with the cross-piece lowered, was adopted to stand for the "cross" of Christ. The method of execution was borrowed by the Greeks and Romans from the Phoenicians. The *stauros* denotes (a) "the cross, or stake itself," e.g., **Matt. 27:32**; (b) "the crucifixion suffered," e.g., 1 Cor. 1:17-18, where "the word of the cross," RV, stands for the gospel; Gal. 5:11, where crucifixion is metaphorically used of the renunciation of the world, that characterizes the true Christian life; 6:12, 14; Eph. 2:16; Phil. 3:18. The judicial custom by which the condemned person carried his stake to the place of execution, was applied by the Lord to those sufferings by which His faithful followers were to express their fellowship with Him, e.g., **Matt. 10:38**.

10:39 He that findeth his life shall lose it: and he that loseth his life for my sake shall find it.

> *"The service that counts is the service that costs."*
>
> HOWARD G. HENDRICKS

Findeth *see* Find at *Matthew 7:7*.

Life *see Matthew 2:20*.

10:40 He that receiveth you receiveth me, and he that receiveth me receiveth him that sent me.

Receiveth *see* Receive at *Matthew 10:14*.

Sent *see* Send at *Matthew 10:16*.

10:41 He that receiveth a prophet in the name of a prophet shall receive a prophet's reward; and he that receiveth a righteous man in the name of a righteous man shall receive a righteous man's reward.

Receiveth, Receive *see* Receive at *Matthew 10:14*.

Prophet *see* Prophets at *Matthew 5:12*.

Reward *see Matthew 5:12*.

10:42 And whosoever shall give to drink unto one of these little ones a cup of cold *water* only in the name of a disciple, verily I say unto you, he shall in no wise lose his reward.

Drink *potizo* (4222), "to give to drink, to make to drink," is used (a) in the material sense, in **Matt. 10:42, 25:35, 37, 42** (here of "ministering" to those who belong to Christ and thus doing so virtually to Him); **27:48**; Mark 9:41; 15:36; Luke 13:15 ("to watering"); Rom. 12:20; 1 Cor. 3:7-8; (b) figuratively, with reference to "teaching" of an elementary character, 1 Cor. 3:2, "I fed (you with milk)"; of "spiritual watering by teaching" the Word of God, 3:6; of being "provided" and "satisfied" by the power and blessing of the Spirit of God, 1 Cor. 12:13; of the effect upon the nations of "partaking" of the abominable mixture, provided by Babylon, of paganism with details of the Christian faith, Rev. 14:8.

Little *mikros* (3398), "little, small" (the opposite of *megos*, "great"), is used (a) of persons, with regard to (1) station, or age, in the singular, Mark 15:40, of James "the less" (RV marg., "little"), possibly referring to age; Luke 19:3; in the plural, "little" ones, **Matt. 18:6**, **10**, **14**; Mark 9:42; (2) rank or influence, e.g., **Matt. 10:42** (see context); Acts 8:10; 26:22, "small," as in Rev. 11:18; 13:16; 19:5, 18; 20:12; (b) of things, with regard to (1) size, e.g., Jas. 3:5; (2) quantity, Luke 12:32; 1 Cor. 5:6; Gal. 5:9; Rev. 3:8; (3) time, John 7:33; 12:35; Rev. 6:11; 20:3.

Cup *poterion* (4221), a diminutive of *poter*, denotes, primarily, a "drinking vessel"; hence, "a cup" (a) literal, as, e.g., in **Matt. 10:42**. The "cup" of blessing, 1 Cor. 10:16, is so named from the third (the fourth according to Edersheim) "cup" in the Jewish Passover feast, over which thanks and praise were given to God. This connection is not to be rejected on the ground that the church at Corinth was unfamiliar with Jewish customs. That the contrary was the case, see 5:7; (b) figurative, of one's lot or experience, joyous or sorrowful (frequent in the Psalms; cf. Ps. 116:18, "cup of salvation"); in the NT it is used most frequently of the sufferings of Christ, **Matt. 20:22-23**; **26:39**; Mark 10:38-39; 14:36; Luke 22:42; John 18:11; also of the evil deeds of Babylon, Rev. 17:4; 18:6; of divine punishments to be inflicted, Rev. 14:10; 16:19. Cf. Ps. 11:6; 75:8; Isa. 51:17; Jer. 25:15; Ezek. 23:32-34; Zech. 12:2.

Cold *psuchros* (5593), "cool, fresh, cold, chilly" (fuller in expression than *psuchos*), is used in the natural sense in **Matt. 10:42**, "cold water"; metaphorically in Rev. 3:15-16.

Lose *see* **Perish** at *Matthew 8:25*.

Chapter 11

11:1 And it came to pass, when Jesus had made an end of commanding his twelve disciples, he departed thence to teach and to preach in their cities.

End *teleo* (5055), "to complete, finish, bring to an end," is translated "had made an end," in **Matt. 11:1**.

Commanding *diatasso* (1299), signifies "to set in order, appoint, command," **Matt. 11:1**; Luke 8:55; 17:9-10; Acts 18:2; 23:31; "gave order," 1 Cor. 16:1, RV. So in Acts 24:23, where it is in the middle voice.

Departed *see* **Depart** at *Matthew 8:34*.

11:2 Now when John had heard in the prison the works of Christ, he sent two of his disciples,

Prison *desmoterion* (1201), "a place of bonds" (from *desmos*, "a bond," *deo*, "to bind"), "a prison," occurs in **Matt. 11:2**, in Acts 5:21, 23 and 16:26, RV, "prison house" (KJV, "prison").

Works *see Matthew 5:16*.

Christ *see Matthew 1:17*.

Sent *pempo* (3992), "to send," is used (a) of persons: Christ, by the Father, Luke 20:13; John 4:34; 5:23, 24, 30, 37; 6:38, 39, (40), 44; 7:16, 18, 28, 33; 8:16, 18, 26, 29; 9:4; 12:44, 45, 49; 13:20 (2nd part); 14:24; 15:21; 16:5; Rom. 8:3; the Holy Spirit, John 14:26; 15:26; 16:7; Elijah, Luke 4:26; John the Baptist, John 1:33; disciples and apostles, e.g., **Matt. 11:2**; John 20:21; servants, e.g., Luke 20:11, 12; officials, **Matt. 14:10**; messengers, e.g., Acts 10:5, 32, 33; 15:22, 25; 2 Cor. 9:3, Eph. 6:22; Phil. 2:19, 23, 25; 1 Thess. 3:2, 5; Titus 3:12; a prisoner, Acts 25:25, 27; potentates, by God, 1 Pet. 2:14; an angel, Rev. 22:16, demons, Mark 5:12; (b) of things, Acts 11:29; Phil. 4:16; 2 Thess. 2:11; Rev. 1:11; 11:10; 14:15, 18, RV, "send forth" (KJV, "thrust in").

11:3 And said unto him, Art thou he that should come, or do we look for another?

Look for *prosdokao* (4328), "to await, expect" (*pros*, "to" or "towards," *dokeo*, "to think, be of opinion"), is translated "to look for," e.g., in **Matt. 11:3**; 2 Pet. 3:12, 13, 14; the RV renders it by the verb "to expect, to be in expectation," in some instances, as does the KJV in Luke 3:15; Acts 3:5.

Another *allos* (243), and *heteros* (2087) have a difference in meaning, which despite a tendency to be lost, is to be observed in numerous passages. *Allos* expresses a numerical difference and denotes "another of the same sort"; *heteros* expresses a qualitative difference and denotes "another of a different sort." Christ promised to send "another Comforter" (*allos*, "another like Himself," not *heteros*), John 14:16. Paul says "I see a different (KJV, "another") law," *heteros*, a law different from that of the spirit of life (not *allos*, "a law of the same sort"), Rom. 7:23. After Joseph's death "another king arose," *heteros*, one of quite a different character, Acts 7:18. Paul speaks of "a different gospel (*heteros*), which is not another" (*allos*, another like the one he preached), Gal. 1:6-7. See *heteros* (not *allos*) in **Matt. 11:3**, and Acts 27:1; in Luke 23:32 *heteroi* is used of the two malefactors crucified with Christ. The two words are only apparently interchanged in 1 Cor. 1:16 and 6:1; 12:8-10; 14:17 and 19, e.g., the difference being present, though not so readily discernible.

11:4 Jesus answered and said unto them, Go and shew John again those things which ye do hear and see:

Shew *anangello* ("to declare"), **Matt. 11:4**, "tell"; John 16:13-15, "declare"; 16:25, "shall tell"; Acts 19:18 and 20:20, "declaring". Also, *apangello* ("to announce"), **Matt. 11:4**, "tell"; 12:18, "declare"; **28:11**, "told"; Luke 14:21, "told"; Acts 26:20, "declared"; 28:21, "report"; 1 Thess. 1:9, "report"; 1 John 1:2, "declare".

See *see* Seeth at *Matthew 6:4*.

11:5 The blind receive their sight, and the lame walk, the lepers are cleansed, and the deaf hear, the dead are raised up, and the poor have the gospel preached to them.

Sight *anablepo* (308), denotes (a) "to look up," e.g., **Matt. 14:19**; Mark 8:24 (in some mss. v. 25); (b) "to recover sight," e.g., **Matt. 11:5**; **20:34**, RV, "received their sight"; John 9:11. Cf. *anablepsis*, "recovering of sight," Luke 4:18.

Lame *cholos* (5560), "lame," is translated "halt" in **Matt. 18:8**; Mark 9:45; John 5:3, in Acts 14:8, "cripple"; in Luke 14:21, KJV, "halt," RV, "lame"; elsewhere, "lame," **Matt. 11:5**; **15:30**, **31**; **21:14**: Luke 7:22; 14:13; Acts 3:2; 8:7; Heb. 12:13; some mss. have it in Acts 3:11 (KJV, "the lame man"), RV, "he," translating *autou*, as in the best texts.

Lepers *see* Leper at *Matthew 8:2*.

Deaf *see* Dumb at Matthew *9:32*.

Raised *see* Raise at *Matthew 10:8*. *See also* Arose at *Matthew 2:14*.

Poor *see Matthew 5:3*.

Gospel *euangelizo* (2097), "to bring or announce glad tidings" (Eng., "evangelize"), is used (a) in the active voice in Rev. 10:7 ("declared") and 14:6 ("to proclaim," RV, KJV, "to preach"); (b) in the passive voice, of matters to be proclaimed as "glad tidings," Luke 16:16; Gal. 1:11; 1 Pet. 1:25; of persons to whom the proclamation is made, **Matt. 11:5**; Luke 7:22; Heb. 4:2, 6; 1 Pet. 4:6; (c) in the middle voice, especially of the message of salvation, with a personal object, either of the person preached, e.g., Acts 5:42; 11:20; Gal. 1:16, or, with a preposition, of the persons evangelized, e.g., Acts 13:32, "declare glad tidings"; Rom. 1:15; Gal. 1:8; with an impersonal object, e.g., "the word," Acts 8:4; "good tidings," 8:12; "the word of the Lord," 15:35; "the gospel," 1 Cor. 15:1; 2 Cor. 11:7; "the faith," Gal. 1:23; "peace," Eph. 2:17; "the unsearchable riches of Christ, 3:8.

11:6 And blessed is *he*, whosoever shall not be offended in me.

Offended *see Matthew 13:57*.

11:7 And as they departed, Jesus began to say unto the multitudes concerning John, What went ye out into the wilderness to see? A reed shaken with the wind?

Departed *see Matthew 2:9*.

See *see* Seen at *Matthew 6:1*.

Reed *kalamos* (2563), denotes (a) "the reed" mentioned in **Matt. 11:7**; **12:20**; Luke 7:24, the same as the Heb., *qaneh* (among the various reeds in the OT), e.g., Isa. 42:3, from which **Matt. 12:20** is quoted (cf. Job 40:21; Ezek. 29:6, "a reed with jointed, hollow stalk"); (b) "a reed staff, staff," **Matt. 27:29**, **30**, **48**; Mark 15:19, 36 (cf. *rhabdos*, "a rod"; in 2 Kings 18:21, *rhabdos kalamine*); (c) "a measuring reed or rod," Rev. 11:1; 21:15, 16; (d) "a writing reed, a pen," 3 John 13.

Shaken *saleuo* (4531), "to agitate, shake," primarily of the action of stormy winds, waves, etc., is used (a) literally, of a reed, **Matt. 11:7**; Luke 7:24; a vessel, "shaken" in filling, Luke 6:38; a building, Luke 6:48; Acts 4:31; 16:26; the natural forces of the heavens and heavenly bodies, **Matt. 24:29**; Mark 13:25; Luke 21:26; the earth, Heb. 12:26, "shook"; (b) metaphorically, (1) of "shaking" so as to make insecure, Heb. 12:27 (twice); (2) of casting down from a sense of security, Acts 2:25, "I should (not) be moved"; (3) to stir up (a crowd), Acts 17:13; (4) to unsettle, 2 Thess. 2:2, "(to the end that) ye be not (quickly) shaken (from your mind)," i.e., from their settled conviction and the purpose of heart begotten by it, as to the return of Christ before the Day of the Lord begins; the metaphor may be taken from the loosening of a ship from its moorings by a storm.

11:8 But what went ye out for to see? A man clothed in soft raiment? behold, they that wear soft *clothing* are in kings' houses.

See *see* Seen at *Matthew 6:1*.

Clothed *see* Clothe at *Matthew 6:30*.

Soft *malakos* (3120), "soft, soft to the touch" (Lat., *mollis*, Eng., "mollify," "emollient," etc.), is used (a) of raiment, **Matt. 11:8** (twice); Luke 7:25; (b) metaphorically, in a bad sense, 1 Cor. 6:9, "effeminate," not simply of a male who practices forms of lewdness, but persons in general, who are guilty of addiction to sins of the flesh, voluptuous. *See also* Disease at *Matthew 4:23*.

Wear *phoreo* (5409), a frequentative form of *phero*, "to bear," and denoting "repeated or habitual action," is chiefly used of clothing, weapons, etc., of soft raiment, **Matt. 11:8**; fine clothing, Jas. 2:3; the crown of thorns, John 19:5.

Houses *see* House at *Matthew 9:6*.

11:9 But what went ye out for to see? A prophet? yea, I say unto you, and more than a prophet.

See *see* Seen at *Matthew 6:1*.

Yea *see Matthew 5:37*.

More *perissoteros* (4055), is translated as follows: in **Matt. 11:9**, and Luke 7:26, RV, "much more" (KJV, "more"); in Mark 12:40, "greater"; in Luke 12:4, 48, "more"; in 1 Cor. 12:23-24, "more abundant"; in 2 Cor. 2:7, "overmuch"; in 2 Cor. 10:8, RV, "abundantly"; KJV, "more."

11:10 For this is *he*, of whom it is written, Behold, I send my messenger before thy face, which shall prepare thy way before thee.

Messenger *angelos* (32), "a messenger, an angel, one sent," is translated "messenger," of John the Baptist, **Matt. 11:10**; Mark 1:2; Luke 7:27; in the plural, of John's "messengers," 7:24; of those whom Christ sent before Him when on His journey to Jerusalem, 9:52; of Paul's "thorn in the flesh," "a messenger of Satan," 2 Cor. 12:7; of the spies as received by Rahab, Jas. 2:25.

Prepare *kataskeuazo* (2680), "to prepare, make ready" (*kata*, used intensively, *skeue*, "equipment"), is so translated in **Matt. 11:10**; Mark 1:2; Luke 1:17; 7:27; Heb. 9:2, RV (KJV, "made"); 9:6, RV (KJV, "were ... ordained"); 11:7; 1 Pet. 3:20.

11:11 Verily I say unto you, Among them that are born of women there hath not risen a greater than John the Baptist: notwithstanding he that is least in the kingdom of heaven is greater than he.

Born *gennetos* (1084), "born" (related to *gennao*), is used in **Matt. 11:11** and Luke 7:28 in the phrase "born of women," a periphrasis for "men," and suggestive of frailty.

Woman *gune* (1135), is used of a "woman" unmarried or married, e.g., **Matt. 11:11**; **14:21**; Luke 4:26, of a "widow"; Rom. 7:2; in the vocative case, used in addressing a "woman," it is a term not of reproof or severity, but of endearment or respect, **Matt. 15:28**; John 2:4, where the Lord's words to His mother at the wedding in Cana, are neither rebuff nor rebuke. The question is, lit., "What to Me and to thee?" and the word "woman," the term of endearment, follows this. The meaning is "There is no obligation on Me or you, but love will supply the need." She confides in Him, He responds to her faith. There was lovingkindness in both hearts. His next words about "His hour" suit this; they were not unfamiliar to her. Cana is in the path to Calvary; Calvary was not yet, but it made the beginning of signs possible. See also 4:21; 19:26.

Risen *see* Arose at *Matthew 2:14*.

Greater *meizon* (3187), is the comparative degree of *megas*, e.g., **Matt. 11:11**; in **Matt. 13:32**, the RV rightly has "greater than" (KJV, "the greatest among"); **23:17**; in Luke 22:26, RV, "the greater (among you)" (KJV, "greatest"); in Jas. 3:1, RV, "the heavier (marg., greater) judgment" (KJV, "the greater condemnation"); it is used in the neuter plural in John 1:50, "greater things"; in 14:12, "greater works" (lit., "greater things"); in 1 Cor. 12:31, RV, "the greater," KJV, "the best".

Least *mikroteros* (3398), is used of (a) size, **Matt. 13:32**, KJV, "the least," RV, "less;" Mark 4:31; (b) estimation, **Matt. 11:11** and Luke 7:28, KJV, "least," RV, "but little," marg., "lesser" (in the kingdom of heaven), those in the kingdom itself being less than John the Baptist; Luke 9:48.

11:12 And from the days of John the Baptist until now the kingdom of heaven suffereth violence, and the violent take it by force.

Now *see Matthew 3:15*.

Violence *biazo* (971), in the passive voice, is rendered "suffereth violence" in **Matt. 11:12**. Some, e.g., Cremer (*Lexicon*) and Dalman (*Words of Jesus*, pp. 139ff.), hold that the reference is to the antagonism of the enemies of the kingdom, but Luke 16:16 (middle voice: RV, "entereth violently") indicates the meaning as referring to those who make an effort to enter the kingdom in spite of violent opposition.

Violent *biastes* (973), "a forceful or violent man," is used in **Matt. 11:12**.

Take ... by force *harpazo* (726), "to snatch or catch away," is said of the act of the Spirit of the Lord in regard to Philip in Acts 8:39; of Paul in being "caught" up to paradise, 2 Cor. 12:2, 4; of the rapture of the saints at the return of the Lord, 1 Thess. 4:17; of the rapture of the man child in the vision of Rev. 12:5. This verb conveys the idea of force suddenly exercised, as in **Matt. 11:12**, "take (it) by force"; **12:29**, "spoil" (some mss. have *diarpazo* here), in **13:19**, RV, "snatcheth"; for forceful seizure, see also John 6:15; 10:12 28-29; Acts 23:10; in Jude 23, RV, "snatching."

11:13-14 For all the prophets and the law prophesied until John.

And if ye will receive *it*, this is Elias, which was for to come.

Receive *see Matthew 10:14.*

This *autos*; "he," rendered "this" in **Matt. 11:14**, lit., "he"; in John 12:7, KJV (RV, "it"); in the feminine, Luke 13:16.

Come *see Matthew 3:7.*

1:15 He that hath ears to hear, let him hear.

Ears *see* Ear at *Matthew 10:27.*

Hear *akouo* (191), the usual word denoting "to hear," is used (a) intransitively, e.g., **Matt. 11:15**; Mark 4:23; (b) transitively when the object is expressed, sometimes in the accusative case, sometimes in the genitive. Thus in Acts 9:7, "hearing the voice," the noun "voice" is in the partitive genitive case [i.e., hearing (something) of], whereas in 22:9, "they heard not the voice," the construction is with the accusative. This removes the idea of any contradiction. The former indicates a "hearing" of the sound, the latter indicates the meaning or message of the voice (this they did not hear). "The former denotes the sensational perception, the latter (the accusative case) the thing perceived" (Cremer). In John 5:25, 28, the genitive case is used, indicating a "sensational perception" that the Lord's voice is sounding; in 3:8, of "hearing" the wind, the accusative is used, stressing "the thing perceived."

11:16 But whereunto shall I liken this generation? It is like unto children sitting in the markets, and calling unto their fellows,

Liken *homoios* (3664), "like, resembling, such as, the same as," is used (a) of appearance or form John 9:9; Rev. 1:13, 15; 2:18; 4:3 (twice), 6, 7; 9:7 (twice), 10, 19; 11:1; 13:2, 11; 14:14; (b) of ability, condition, nature, **Matt. 22:39**; Acts 17:29; Gal. 5:21, "such like," lit., "and the (things) similar to these"; 1 John 3:2; Rev. 13:4; 18:18; 21:11, 18; (c) of comparison in parables, **Matt. 13:31, 33, 44, 45, 47; 20:1**; Luke 13:18, 19, 21; (d) of action, thought, etc. **Matt. 11:16; 13:52**; Luke 6:47, 48, 49; 7:31, 32; 12:36; John 8:55; Jude 7.

Generation *see* Generations at *Matthew 1:17.*

Like unto *see Matthew 6:8.*

Children *paidarion* (3808), another diminutive of *pais*, is used of "boys and girls," in **Matt. 11:16** (the best texts have *paidiois* here), and a "lad," John 6:9; the tendency in colloquial Greek was to lose the diminutive character of the word.

Markets *agora* (58), primarily "an assembly," or, in general, "an open space in a town" (akin to *ageiro*, "to bring together"), became applied, according to papyri evidences, to a variety of things, e.g., "a judicial assembly," "a market," or even "supplies, provisions" (Moulton and Milligan, *Vocab.*). In the NT it denotes "a place of assembly, a public place or forum, a marketplace." A variety of circumstances, connected with it as a public gathering place, is mentioned, e.g., business dealings such as the hiring of laborers, **Matt. 20:3**; the buying and selling of goods, Mark 7:4 (involving risk of pollution); the games of children, **Matt. 11:16**; Luke 7:32; exchange of greetings, **Matt. 23:7**; Mark 12:38; Luke 11:43; 20:46; the holding of trials, Acts 16:19; public discussions, Acts 17:17. Mark 6:56 records the bringing of the sick there. The word always carries with it the idea of publicity, in contrast to private circumstances. The RV always translates it "marketplace" or in the plural. The KJV sometimes changes the rendering to "markets" and translates it "streets" in Mark 6:56.

Calling *prosphoneo* (4377), "to address, call to," is rendered "spake unto" (or "to") in Luke 23:20; Acts 21:40; 22:2; "to call unto" (or "to") in **Matt. 11:16**; Luke 6:13; 7:32; 13:12.

Fellows *hetairos* (2083), "a companion, comrade," is translated "fellows" in **Matt. 11:16** [where, however, the most authentic mss. have *heterois*, "(the) others"]. The word is used only by Matthew and is translated "friend" in **20:13; 22:12; 26:50**.

11:17 And saying, We have piped unto you, and ye have not danced; we have mourned unto you, and ye have not lamented.

Saying *see* Say at *Matthew 3:9.*

Piped *auleo* (832), "to play on an *aulos*," is used in **Matt. 11:17**; Luke 7:32; 1 Cor. 14:7 (2nd part).

Danced *orcheo* (3738), (cf. Eng., "orchestra"), probably originally signified "to lift up," as of the feet; hence, "to leap with regularity of motion." It is always used in the middle voice, **Matt. 11:17**; **14:6**; Mark 6:22; Luke 7:32. The performance by the daughter of Herodias is the only clear instance of artistic dancing, a form introduced from Greek customs.

Mourned *threneo* (2354), "to lament, wail" (akin to *threnos*, "a lamentation, a dirge"), is used (a) in a general sense, of the disciples during the absence of the Lord, John 16:20, "lament"; (b) of those who sorrowed for the sufferings and the impending crucifixion of the Lord, Luke 23:27, "lamented"; the preceding word is *kopto*; (c) of "mourning" as for the dead, **Matt. 11:17**, RV, "wailed" (KJV, "have mourned"); Luke 7:32 (ditto).

Lamented *kopto* (2875), primarily, "to beat, smite"; then, "to cut off," **Matt. 21:8**; Mark 11:8, is used in the middle voice, of beating oneself, beating the breast, as a token of grief; hence, "to bewail," **Matt. 11:17** (RV, "mourn," for KJV, "lament"); **24:30**, "mourn"; Rev. 1:7 (RV, "mourn"; KJV, "wail"); in Luke 8:52; 23:27 "bewail"; in Rev. 18:9, "wail" (for KJV, "lament"). Cf. *kopetos*, "lamentation," Acts 8:2. *See also* Lamentation at *Matthew 2:18*.

11:18-19 For John came neither eating nor drinking, and they say, He hath a devil.

The Son of man came eating and drinking, and they say, Behold a man gluttonous, and a winebibber, a friend of publicans and sinners. But wisdom is justified of her children.

Son *see Matthew 3:17*.

Man *see Matthew 4:4*.

"The greatest blessing we ever get from God is to know that we are destitute spiritually."

OSWALD CHAMBERS

Gluttonous *phagos* (5314), akin to *phago*, "to eat," a form used for the aorist or past tense of *esthio*, denotes "a glutton," **Matt. 11:19**; Luke 7:34.

Winebibber *oinopotes* (3630), "a wine drinker" (*oinos*, and *potes*, "a drinker"), is used in **Matt. 11:19**; Luke 7:34. In the Sept., Prov. 23:20.

Friend *philos* (5384), primarily an adjective, denoting "loved, dear, or friendly," became used as a noun, (a) masculine, **Matt. 11:19**; fourteen times in Luke (once feminine, 15:9); six in John; three in Acts; two in James, 2:23, "the friend of God"; 4:4, "a friend of the world"; 3 John 14 (twice); (b) feminine, Luke 15:9, "her friends."

Publicans *see Matthew 5:46*.

Wisdom *sophia* (4678), is used with reference to (a) God, Rom. 11:33; 1 Cor. 1:21, 24; 2:7; Eph. 3:10; Rev. 7:12; (b) Christ, **Matt. 13:54**; Mark 6:2; Luke 2:40, 52; 1 Cor. 1:30; Col. 2:3; Rev. 5:12; (c) "wisdom" personified, **Matt. 11:19**; Luke 7:35; 11:49; (d) human "wisdom" (1) in spiritual things, Luke 21:15; Acts 6:3, 10; 7:10; 1 Cor. 2:6 (1st part); 12:8; Eph. 1:8, 17; Col. 1:9, RV, "(spiritual) wisdom," 28; 3:16; 4:5; Jas. 1:5; 3:13, 17; 2 Pet. 3:15; Rev. 13:18; 17:9; (2) in the natural sphere, **Matt. 12:42**; Luke 11:31; Acts 7:22; 1 Cor. 1:17, 19, 20, 21 (twice), 22; 2:1, 4, 5, 6 (2nd part), 13; 3:19; 2 Cor. 1:12; Col. 2:23; (3) in its most debased form, Jas. 3:15, "earthly, sensual, devilish" (marg., "demoniacal").

Justified *dikaioo* (1344), primarily "to deem to be right," signifies, in the NT, (a) "to show to be right or righteous"; in the passive voice, to be justified, **Matt. 11:19**; Luke 7:35; Rom. 3:4; 1 Tim. 3:16; (b) "to declare to be righteous, to pronounce righteous," (1) by man, concerning God, Luke 7:29 (see Rom. 3:4, above); concerning himself, Luke 10:29; 16:15; (2) by God concerning men, who are declared to be righteous before Him on certain conditions laid down by Him.

11:20 Then began he to upbraid the cities wherein most of his mighty works were done, because they repented not:

Upbraid *see* Revile at *Matthew 5:11*.

Most *pleistos* (4118), the superlative degree of *polus*, is used (a) as an adjective in **Matt. 11:20**; **21:8**, RV, "(the) most part of" (KJV, "a very great"); (b) in the neuter, with the article, adverbially, "at the most," 1 Cor. 14:27; (c) as an elative (i.e., intensively) in Mark 4:1 (in the best mss.; some have *polus*), "a very great (multitude)."

Mighty *see* Wonderful at *Matthew 7:22*.

11:21 Woe unto thee, Chorazin! woe unto thee, Bethsaida! for if the mighty works, which were done in you, had been done in Tyre and Sidon, they would have repented long ago in sackcloth and ashes.

Woe *ouai* (3759), an interjection, is used (a) in denunciation, **Matt. 11:21**; **18:7** (twice); eight times in ch. **23** (verses **13**, **14**, **15**, **16**, **23**, **25**, **27**, **29**); **24:19**; **26:24**; Mark 13:17; 14:21; Luke 6:24, 25 (twice), 26; 10:13; six times in ch. 11; 17:1; 21:23; 22:22; 1 Cor. 9:16; Jude 11; Rev. 8:13 (thrice); 12:12; as a noun, Rev. 9:12 (twice); 11:14 (twice); (b) in grief, "alas," Rev. 18:10, 16, 19 (twice in each).

Sackcloth *sakkos* (4526), "a warm material woven from goat's or camel's hair," and hence of a dark color, Rev. 6:12; Jerome renders it *saccus cilicinus* (being made from the hair of the black goat of Cilicia; the Romans called it *cilicium*); cf. Isa. 50:3; it was also used for saddlecloths, Josh. 9:4; also for making sacks, e.g., Gen. 42:25, and for garments worn as expressing mourning or penitence, **Matt. 11:21**; Luke 10:13, or for purposes of prophetic testimony, Rev. 11:3.

Ashes *spodos* (4700), "ashes", is found three times, twice in association with sackcloth, **Matt. 11:21** and Luke 10:13, as tokens of grief (cf. Esth. 4:1, 3; Isa. 58:5; 61:3; Jer. 6:26; Jonah 3:6); of the ashes resulting from animal sacrifices, Heb. 9:13; in the OT, metaphorically, of one who describes himself as dust and "ashes," Gen. 18:27, etc.

11:22 But I say unto you, It shall be more tolerable for Tyre and Sidon at the day of judgment, than for you.

Tolerable *see Matthew 10:15.*

11:23 And thou, Capernaum, which art exalted unto heaven, shalt be brought down to hell: for if the mighty works, which have been done in thee, had been done in Sodom, it would have remained until this day.

Exalted *hupsoo* (5312), "to lift up" (akin to *hupsos*, "height"), is used (a) literally of the "lifting" up of Christ in His crucifixion, John 3:14; 8:28; 12:32, 34; illustratively, of the serpent of brass, John 3:14; (b) figuratively, of spiritual privileges bestowed on a city, **Matt. 11:23**; Luke 10:15; of "raising" to dignity and happiness, Luke 1:52; Acts 13:17; of haughty self-exaltation, and, contrastingly, of being "raised" to honor, as a result of self-humbling, **Matt. 23:12**; Luke 14:11; 18:14; of spiritual "uplifting" and revival, Jas. 4:10; 1 Pet. 5:6; of bringing into the blessings of salvation through the gospel, 2 Cor. 11:7; (c) with a combination of the literal and metaphorical, of the "exaltation" of Christ by God the Father, Acts 2:33; 5:31.

Brought *katabibazo* (2601), in the active voice, "to cause to go down," is used in the passive in the sense of "being brought down," Luke 10:15 (KJV, "thrust down"); "go down" in **Matt. 11:23** (marg., "be brought down"). In **Matt. 11:23** and Luke 10:15 the best texts have *katabaino*, "to go down" (RV), instead of *katabibazo*, in the passive voice, "to be thrust down or brought down" (KJV).

Hell *hades* (86), "the region of departed spirits of the lost" (but including the blessed dead in periods preceding the ascension of Christ). It has been thought by some that the word etymologically meant "the unseen" (from *a*, negative, and *eido*, "to see"), but this derivation is questionable; a more probable derivation is from *hado*, signifying "all-receiving." It corresponds to "Sheol" in the OT. In the KJV of the OT and NT; it has been unhappily rendered "hell," e.g., Ps. 16:10; or "the grave," e.g., Gen. 37:35; or "the pit," Num. 16:30, 33; in the NT the revisers have always used the rendering "hades"; in the OT, they have not been uniform in the translation, e.g., in Isa. 14:15 "hell" (marg., "Sheol"); usually they have "Sheol" in the text and "the grave" in the margin. It never denotes the grave, nor is it the permanent region of the lost; in point of time it is, for such, intermediate between decease and the doom of Gehenna. For the condition, see Luke 16:23-31. The word is used four times in the Gospels, and always by the Lord, **Matt. 11:23**; **16:18**; Luke 10:15; 16:23; it is used with reference to the soul of Christ, Acts 2:27, 31; Christ declares that He has the keys of it, Rev. 1:18; in Rev. 6:8 it is personified, with the signification of the temporary destiny of the doomed; it is to give up those who are therein, 20:13, and is to be cast into the lake of fire, v. 14.

Remained *meno* (3306), "to stay, abide," is frequently rendered "to remain," e.g., **Matt. 11:23**; Luke 10:7; John 1:33, KJV (RV, "abiding"); 9:41 (in 15:11, the best texts have the verb to be, see RV); 15:16, KJV (RV, "abide"); 19:31; Acts 5:4 (twice), RV, "whiles it remained, did it (not) remain (thine own)?"; 27:41; 1 Cor 7:11; 15:6; 2 Cor. 3:11, 14; 9:9, KJV (RV, "abideth"); Heb. 12:27; 1 John 3:9. *See also* **Abide** at *Matthew 10:11.*

11:24 But I say unto you, That it shall be more tolerable for the land of Sodom in the day of judgment, than for thee.

Tolerable *see Matthew 10:15.*

11:25 At that time Jesus answered and said, I thank thee, O Father, Lord of heaven and earth, because thou hast hid these things from the wise and prudent, and hast revealed them unto babes.

Time *see Matthew 8:29.*

Answered *apokrinomai* (611), signifies either "to give an answer to a question" (its more frequent use) or "to begin to speak," but always where something has preceded, either statement or act to which the remarks refer, e.g., **Matt. 11:25**; Luke 14:3; John 2:18. The RV translates by "answered," e.g., **Matt. 28:5**; Mark 12:35; Luke 3:16, where some have suggested "began to say" or "uttered solemnly," whereas the speaker is replying to the unuttered thought or feeling of those addressed by him. See also **Confessing** at *Matthew 3:6.*

Said *see* **Say** at *Matthew 3:9.*

Thank *exomologeo* (1843), in the middle voice, signifies "to make acknowledgment," whether of sins (to confess), or in the honor of a person, as in Rom. 14:11; 15:9 (in some mss. in Rev. 3:5); this is the significance in the Lord's address to the Father, "I thank (Thee)," in **Matt. 11:25** and Luke 10:21, the meaning being "I make thankful confession" or "I make acknowledgment with praise."

Lord *see Matthew 1:22.*

Hid *see Matthew 5:14.*

Wise *sophos* (4680), is used of (a) God, Rom. 16:27; in 1 Tim. 1:17 and Jude 25 *sophos* is absent, in the best mss. (see the RV), the comparative degree, *sophoteros*, occurs in 1 Cor. 1:25, where "foolishness" is simply in the human estimate; (b) spiritual teachers in Israel, **Matt. 23:34**; (c) believers endowed with spiritual and practical wisdom, Rom. 16:19; 1 Cor. 3:10; 6:5; Eph. 5:15; Jas. 3:13; (d) Jewish teachers in the time of Christ, **Matt. 11:25**; Luke 10:21; (e) the naturally learned, Rom. 1:14, 22; 1 Cor. 1:19, 20, 26, 27; 3:15-20.

Prudent *sunetos* (4908), signifies "intelligent, sagacious, understanding" (akin to *suniemi*, "to perceive"), translated "prudent" in **Matt. 11:25**, KJV (RV, "understanding"); Luke 10:21 (ditto); Acts 13:7, RV, "(a man) of understanding"; in 1 Cor. 1:19, "prudent," RV and KJV. Cf. *asunetos*, "without understanding."

Revealed *see Matthew 10:26.*

Babes *nepios* (3516), lit., "without the power of speech," denotes "a little child," the literal meaning having been lost in the general use of the word. It is used (a) of "infants," **Matt. 21:16**; (b) metaphorically, of the unsophisticated in mind and trustful in disposition, **Matt. 11:25** and Luke 10:21, where it stands in contrast to the wise; of those who are possessed merely of natural knowledge, Rom. 2:20; of those who are carnal, and have not grown, as they should have done, in spiritual understanding and power, the spiritually immature, 1 Cor. 3:1, those who are so to speak partakers of milk, and "without experience of the word of righteousness," Heb. 5:13; of the Jews, who, while the Law was in force, were in a state corresponding to that of childhood, or minority, just as the word "infant" is used of a minor, in English law, Gal. 4:3, "children"; of believers in an immature condition, impressionable and liable to be imposed upon instead of being in a state of spiritual maturity, Eph. 4:14, "children." "Immaturity" is always associated with this word.

11:26 Even so, Father: for so it seemed good in thy sight.

Even so *nai* (3483), a particle of strong affirmation, "yea, verily, even so," is rendered "even so" in the KJV, "yea" in the RV, in **Matt. 11:26**; Luke 10:21; Rev. 16:7; both KJV and RV have it in Rev. 1:7; the most authentic mss. omit it in 22:20. *See also* **Yea** at *Matthew 5:37.*

Good *eudokia* (2107), lit., "good pleasure" (*eu*, "well," *dokeo*, "to seem"), implies a gracious purpose, a good object being in view, with the idea of a resolve, showing the willingness with which the resolve is made. It is often translated "good pleasure," e.g., Eph. 1:5, 9; Phil. 2:13; in Phil. 1:15, "good will"; in Rom. 10:1, "desire," (marg., "good pleasure"); in 2 Thess. 1:11, RV, "desire," KJV and RV, marg., "good pleasure." It is used of God in **Matt. 11:26** ("well pleasing," RV, for KJV, "seemed good"); Luke 2:14, RV, "men in whom He is well pleased," lit., "men of good pleasure" (the construction is objective); 10:21; Eph. 1:5, 9; Phil. 2:13.

Sight *emprosthen* (1715), is translated "in the sight of" in **Matt. 11:26**; Luke 10:21; 1 Thess. 1:3, KJV. *See also* **Before** at *Matthew 5:16.*

11:27 All things are delivered unto me of my Father: and no man knoweth the Son, but the Father; neither knoweth any man the Father, save the Son, and *he* to whomsoever the Son will reveal *him*.

Of *see Matthew 1:22.*

Father *see Matthew 2:22.* Whereas the everlasting power and divinity of God are manifest in creation, His "Fatherhood" in spiritual relationship through faith is the subject of NT revelation, and waited for the presence on earth of the Son, **Matt. 11:27**; John 17:25. The spiritual relationship is not universal, John 8:42, 44 (cf. John 8:12 and Gal. 3:26).

Will *boulomai* (1014), usually expresses the deliberate exercise of volition more strongly than *thelo*, and is rendered as follows in the RV, where the KJV has "will": **Matt. 11:27** and Luke 10:22, "willeth"; Jas. 4:4, "would"; in Jas. 3:4, RV, "willeth" (KJV, "listeth"). In Jas. 1:18 the perfect participle is translated "of His own will," lit., "having willed."

Reveal *see* **Revealed** at *Matthew 10:26*.

11:28 Come unto me, all *ye* that labour and are heavy laden, and I will give you rest.

Labour *kopiao* (2872), has the two different meanings (a) "growing weary," (b) "toiling"; it is sometimes translated "to bestow labor". It is translated by the verb "to labor" in **Matt. 11:28**; John 4:38 (2nd part); Acts 20:35; Rom. 16:12 (twice); 1 Cor. 15:10; 16:16; Eph. 4:28; Phil. 2:16; Col. 1:29; 1 Thess. 5:12; 1 Tim. 4:10; 5:17; 2 Tim. 2:6; Rev. 2:3; 1 Cor. 4:12, RV, "toil" (KJV, "labor").

Laden *phortizo* (5412), "to load" (akin to *phero*, "to bear"), is used in the active voice in Luke 11:46, "ye lade"; in the passive voice, metaphorically, in **Matt. 11:28**, "heavy laden." In the Sept., Ezek. 16:33.

Rest *anapauo* (373), signifies "to give intermission from labor, to give rest, to refresh," **Matt. 11:28**; 1 Cor. 16:18, "have refreshed"; Philem. 20, "refresh"; passive voice, "to be rested, refreshed," 2 Cor. 7:13, "was refreshed", Philem. 7, "are refreshed"; in the middle voice, "to take or enjoy rest," **Matt. 26:45**; Mark 6:31; 14:41; Luke 12:19, "take thine ease"; 1 Pet. 4:14; Rev. 6:11; 14:13. In the papyri it is found as an agricultural term, e.g., of giving land "rest" by sowing light crops upon it. In inscriptions it is found on gravestones of Christians, followed by the date of death (Moulton and Milligan).

11:29 Take my yoke upon you, and learn of me; for I am meek and lowly in heart: and ye shall find rest unto your souls.

Yoke *zugos* (2218), "a yoke," serving to couple two things together, is used (1) metaphorically, (a) of submission to authority, **Matt. 11:29, 30**, of Christ's "yoke," not simply imparted by Him but shared with Him; (b) of bondage, Acts 15:10 and Gal. 5:1, of bondage to the Law as a supposed means of salvation; (c) of bond service to masters, 1 Tim. 6:1; (2) to denote "a balance," Rev. 6:5.

Learn *see Matthew 9:13*.

Meek *see Matthew 5:5*.

Lowly *tapeinos* (5011), primarily signifies "low-lying." It is used always in a good sense in the NT, metaphorically, to denote (a) "of low degree, brought low," Luke 1:52; Rom. 12:16, KJV, "(men) of low estate," RV, "(things that are) lowly" (i.e., of low degree); 2 Cor. 7:6, KJV, "cast down," RV, "lowly"; the preceding context shows that this occurrence belongs to (a); Jas. 1:9, "of low degree"; (b) humble in spirit, **Matt. 11:29**; 2 Cor. 10:1, RV, "lowly," KJV "base"; Jas. 4:6; 1 Pet. 5:5.

Find *see Matthew 7:7*.

Rest *anapausis* (372), "cessation, refreshment, rest" (*ana*, "up," *pauo*, "to make to cease"), the constant word in the Sept. for the Sabbath "rest," is used in **Matt. 11:29**; here the contrast seems to be to the burdens imposed by the Pharisees. Christ's "rest" is not a "rest" from work, but in work, "not the rest of inactivity but of the harmonious working of all the faculties and affections – of will, heart, imagination, conscience – because each has found in God the ideal sphere for its satisfaction and development" (J. Patrick, in *Hastings' Bib. Dic.*); it occurs also in **Matt. 12:43**; Luke 11:24; Rev. 4:8, RV, "(they have no) rest" [KJV, "(they) rest (not)"], where the noun is the object of the verb *echo*, "to have"; so in 14:11.

> *"Meekness is not weakness. It is power under control."*
>
> WARREN W. WIERSBE

Soul *see* **Life** at *Matthew 2:20*.

11:30 For my yoke is easy, and my burden is light.

Yoke *see Matthew 11:29*.

Easy *chrestos* (5543), primarily signifies "fit for use, able to be used" (akin to *chraomai*, "to use"), hence, "good, virtuous, mild, pleasant" (in contrast to what is hard, harsh, sharp, bitter). It is said (a) of the character of God as "kind, gracious," Luke 6:35; 1 Pet. 2:3; "good," Rom. 2:4, where the neuter of the adjective is used as a noun, "the goodness" (cf. the corresponding noun *chrestotes*, "goodness," in the same verse); of the yoke of Christ, **Matt. 11:30**, "easy" (a suitable rendering would be "kindly"); (c) of believers, Eph. 4:32; (d) of things, as wine, Luke 5:39, RV, "good," for KJV, "better" (cf. Jer. 24:3, 5, of figs); (e) ethically, of manners, 1 Cor. 15:33.

Burden *phortion* (5413), lit., "something carried" (from *phero*, "to bear"), is always used metaphorically (except in Acts 27:10, of the lading of a ship); of that which, though "light," is involved in discipleship of Christ, **Matt. 11:30**; of tasks imposed by the scribes, Pharisees and lawyers, **Matt. 23:4**; Luke 11:46; of that which will be the result, at the judgment-seat of Christ, of each believer's work, Gal. 6:5.

Light *elaphros* (1645), "light in weight, easy to bear," is used of the burden imparted by Christ, **Matt. 11:30**; of affliction, 2 Cor. 4:17.

Chapter 12

12:1 At that time Jesus went on the sabbath day through the corn; and his disciples were an hungred, and began to pluck the ears of corn, and to eat.

Time *see Matthew 8:29.*

Sabbath *sabbaton* (4521), or *sabbata:* the latter, the plural form, was transliterated from the Aramaic word, which was mistaken for a plural; hence the singular, *sabbaton,* was formed from it. The root means "to cease, desist" (Heb., *shabath*; cf. Arab., *sabata,* "to intercept, interrupt"); the doubled *b* has an intensive force, implying a complete cessation or a making to cease, probably the former. The idea is not that of relaxation or refreshment, but cessation from activity. The observation of the seventh day of the week, enjoined upon Israel, was a sign between God and His earthly people, based upon the fact that after the six days of creative operations He rested, Exod. 31:16, 17, with 20:8-11. The OT regulations were developed and systematized to such an extent that they became a burden upon the people (who otherwise rejoiced in the rest provided) and a byword for absurd extravagance. Two treatises of the Mishna (the *Shabbath* and *Erubin*) are entirely occupied with regulations for the observance; so with the discussions in the Gemara, on rabbinical opinions. The effect upon current opinion explains the antagonism roused by the Lord's cures wrought on the "Sabbath," e.g., **Matt. 12:9-13**; John 5:5-16, and explains the fact that on a "Sabbath" the sick were brought to be healed after sunset, e.g., Mark 1:32. According to rabbinical ideas, the disciples, by plucking ears of corn (**Matt. 12:1**; Mark 2:23), and rubbing them (Luke 6:1), broke the "sabbath" in two respects; for to pluck was to reap, and to rub was to thresh. The Lord's attitude towards the "sabbath" was by way of freeing it from these vexatious traditional accretions by which it was made an end in itself, instead of a means to an end (Mark 2:27). In **Matt. 12:1** and **11**, where the plural is used, the KJV (as the RV) rightly has the singular, "the sabbath day"; in v. **5** the KJV has the plural. Where the singular is used the RV omits the word "day," v. **2**; **24:20**; Mark 6:2; Luke 6:1 ("on a sabbath"); 14:3; John 9:14 ("it was the sabbath on the day when ..."). As to the use or omission of the article the omission does not always require the rendering "a sabbath"; it is absent, e.g., in **Matt. 12:2**.

Corn *sporimos* (4702), lit., "sown, or fit for sowing" (*speiro* "to sow, scatter seed"), denotes, in the plural, "sown fields, fields of grain, cornfields," **Matt. 12:1**, RV; Mark 2:23; Luke 6:1 (cf. *spora,* 1 Pet. 1:23, and *sporos,* "seed").

Disciples *see* **Servant** at *Matthew 8:6.*

Hungred *see Matthew 4:2.*

Pluck *tillo* (5089), is used of "plucking off ears of corn," **Matt. 12:1**; Mark 2:23; Luke 6:1. In the Sept., Isa. 18:7.

Ears of corn *stachus* (4719), means "an ear of grain," **Matt. 12:1**; Mark 2:23; 4:28; Luke 6:1. Cf. the name *Stachys* in Rom. 16:9.

12:2 But when the Pharisees saw *it*, they said unto him, Behold, thy disciples do that which is not lawful to do upon the sabbath day.

Sabbath *see Matthew 12:1.*

12:3 But he said unto them, Have ye not read what David did, when he was an hungred, and they that were with him;

Read *anaginosko* (314), primarily, "to know certainly, to know again, recognize" (*ana,* "again," *ginosko,* "to know"), is used of "reading" written characters, e.g., **Matt. 12:3**, **5**; **21:16**; **24:15**; of the private "reading" of Scripture, Acts 8:28, 30, 32; of the public "reading" of Scripture, Luke 4:16; Acts 13:27; 15:21; 2 Cor. 3:15; Col. 4:16 (thrice); 1 Thess. 5:27; Rev. 1:3. In 2 Cor. 1:13 there is a purposive play upon words; firstly, "we write none other things unto you, than what ye read (*anaginosko*)" signifies that there is no hidden or mysterious meaning in his epistles; whatever doubts may have arisen and been expressed in this respect, he means what he says; then follows the similar verb *epiginosko,* "to acknowledge," "or even acknowledge, and I hope ye will acknowledge unto the end." The *paronomasia* can hardly be reproduced in English. Similarly, in 3:2 the verb *ginosko,* "to know," and *anaginosko,* "to read," are put in that order, and metaphorically applied to the church at Corinth as being an epistle, a message to the world, written by the apostle and his fellow missionaries, through their ministry of the gospel and the consequent change in the lives of the converts, an epistle "known and read of all men."

12:4 How he entered into the house of God, and did eat the

shewbread, which was not lawful for him to eat, neither for them which were with him, but only for the priests?

House *see Matthew 9:6.*

Shewbread The phrase rendered "the shewbread" is formed by the combination of the nouns *prothesis*, "a setting forth" (*pro*, "before," *tithemi*, "to place") and *artos*, "a loaf" (in the plural), each with the article, **Matt. 12:4**; Mark 2:26 and Luke 6:4, lit., "the loaves of the setting forth"; in Heb. 9:2, lit., "the setting forth of the loaves." The corresponding OT phrases are lit., "bread of the face," Exod. 25:30, i.e., the presence, referring to the Presence of God (cf. Isa. 63:9 with Exod. 33:14, 15); "the bread of ordering," 1 Chron. 9:32, marg. In Num. 4:7 it is called "the continual bread"; in 1 Sam. 21:4, 6, "holy bread" (KJV, "hallowed"). In the Sept. of 1 Kings 7:48, it is called "the bread of the offering" (*prosphora*, "a bearing towards"). The twelve loaves, representing the tribes of Israel, were set in order every Sabbath day before the Lord, "on the behalf of the children," Lev. 24:8, RV (marg., and KJV, "from"), "an everlasting covenant." The loaves symbolized the fact that on the basis of the sacrificial atonement of the Cross, believers are accepted before God, and nourished by Him in the person of Christ. The showbread was partaken of by the priests, as representatives of the nation. Priesthood now being coextensive with all who belong to Christ, 1 Pet. 2:5, 9, He, the Living Bread, is the nourishment of all, and where He is, there, representatively, they are. *See also* Bread at *Matthew 6:11.*

Only *see Matthew 4:10.*

Priests *see* Priest at *Matthew 8:4.*

12:5 Or have ye not read in the law, how that on the sabbath days the priests in the temple profane the sabbath, and are blameless?

Read *see Matthew 12:3.*

Law *see Matthew 5:17.*

Sabbath *see Matthew 12:1.*

Priests *see* Priest at *Matthew 8:4.*

Profane *bebeloo* (953), primarily, "to cross the threshold," hence, "to profane, pollute," occurs in **Matt. 12:5** and Acts 24:6 (the latter as in 21:28, 29).

Blameless *anaitios* (338), "guiltless" (*a*, negative, *n*, euphonic, and *aitia*, "a charge"), is translated, "blameless" in the KJV of **Matt. 12:5**, "guiltless" in **12:7**. The RV has "guiltless" in both places. In the Sept., in Deut. 19:10, 13, and 21:8-9.

12:6 But I say unto you, That in this place is *one* greater than the temple.

This place *hode* (5602), an adverb signifying (a) "here" (of place), e.g., **Matt. 12:6**; Mark 9:1; used with the neuter plural of the article, Col. 4:9, "(all) things (that are done) here," lit., "(all) the (things) here"; in **Matt. 24:23**, *hode* is used in both parts, hence the RV, "Lo, here (is the Christ, or) Here"; in Mark 13:21 *hode* is followed by *ekei*, "there." The word is used metaphorically in the sense of "in this circumstance," or connection, in 1 Cor. 4:2; Rev. 13:10, 18; 14:12; 17:9.

12:7 But if ye had known what *this* meaneth, I will have mercy, and not sacrifice, ye would not have condemned the guiltless.

Meaneth *see Matthew 9:13.*

Will *see Matthew 9:13.*

Mercy *see Matthew 9:13.*

Sacrifice *see Matthew 9:13.*

Condemned *katadikazo* (2613), signifies "to exercise right or law against anyone"; hence, "to pronounce judgment, to condemn" (*kata*, "down, or against," *dike*, "justice"), **Matt. 12:7, 37**; Luke 6:37; Jas. 5:6.

Guiltless *see* Blameless at *Matthew 12:5.*

12:8 For the Son of man is Lord even of the sabbath day.

Lord *see Matthew 1:22.*

12:9 And when he was departed thence, he went into their synagogue:

Departed *see* Depart at *Matthew 8:34.*

12:10 And, behold, there was a man which had *his* hand withered. And they asked him, saying, Is it lawful to heal on the sabbath days? that they might accuse him.

Withered *xeros* (3584), is used (a) naturally, of "dry" land, Heb. 11:29; or of land in general, **Matt. 23:15**, "land"; or of physical infirmity, "withered," **Matt. 12:10**; Mark 3:3; Luke 6:6, 8; John 5:3; (b) figuratively, in Luke 23:31, with reference to the spiritual "barrenness" of the Jews, in contrast to the character of the Lord. Cf. Ps. 1:3; Isa. 56:3; Ezek. 17:24; 20:47.

Accuse *kategoreo* (2723), "to speak against, accuse," is used (a) in a general way, "to accuse," e.g., Luke 6:7, RV, "how to accuse"; Rom. 2:15; Rev. 12:10; (b) before a judge, e.g., **Matt. 12:10**; Mark 15:4 (RV, "witness against"); Acts 22:30; 25:16. In Acts 24:19, RV renders it "make accusation," for the KJV, "object."

12:11 And he said unto them, What man shall there be among you, that shall have one sheep, and if it fall into a pit on the sabbath day, will he not lay hold on it, and lift *it* out?

Sheep *see Matthew 7:15.*

Fall *empipto* (1706), "to fall into, or among," is used (a) literally, **Matt. 12:11**; Luke 6:39; 10:36; some mss. have it in 14:5; (b) metaphorically, into condemnation, 1 Tim. 3:6; reproach, 3:7; temptation and snare, 6:9; the hands of God in judgment, Heb. 10:13.

Pit *bothunos* (999), any kind of "deep hole or pit" (probably connected with *bathos*, "deep"), is translated "ditch" in the KJV of **Matt. 15:14** and Luke 6:39, RV, "pit" in each place, as in both versions of **Matt. 12:11**.

Sabbath *see Matthew 12:1.*

Hold *krateo* (2902), "to be strong, mighty, to prevail," (1) is most frequently rendered "to lay or take hold on" (a) literally, e.g., **Matt. 12:11**; **14:3**; **18:28** and **21:46**, RV (KJV, "laid hands on"); **22:6**, RV (KJV, "took"); **26:55**, KJV (RV, "took"); **28:9**, RV, "took hold of" (KJV, "held by"); Mark 3:21; 6:17; 12:12; 14:51; Act 24:6, RV (KJV, "took"); Rev. 20:2; (b) metaphorically, of "laying hold of the hope of the Lord's return," Heb. 6:18; (2) also signifies "to hold" or "hold fast," i.e., firmly, (a), literally, **Matt. 26:48**, KJV (RV, "take"); Acts 3:11; Rev. 2:1; (b) metaphorically, of "holding fast a tradition or teaching," in an evil sense, Mark 7:3, 4, 8; Rev. 2:14, 15; in a good sense, 2 Thess. 2:15; Rev. 2:25; 3:11; of "holding" Christ, i.e., practically apprehending Him, as the head of His church, Col. 2:19; a confession, Heb. 4:14; the name of Christ, i.e., abiding by all that His name implies, Rev. 2:13; of restraint, Luke 24:16, "(their eyes) were holden"; of the winds, Rev. 7:1; of the impossibility of Christ's being "holden" of death, Acts 2:24.

Lift *egeiro* (1453), "to awaken, raise up," is used in **Matt. 12:11**, of "lifting" a sheep out of a pit. In the following the RV has "raised" for KJV, "lifted": Mark 1:31; 9:27; Acts 3:7.

12:12 How much then is a man better than a sheep? Wherefore it is lawful to do well on the sabbath days.

Better *see Matthew 6:26.*

Sheep *see Matthew 7:15.*

12:13 Then saith he to the man, Stretch forth thine hand. And he stretched *it* forth; and it was restored whole, like as the other.

Man *see Matthew 4:4.*

Stretch forth *see* Put forth at *Matthew 8:3.*

Restored *apokathistemi* or the alternative form *apokathistano* (600), is used (a) of "restoration" to a former condition of health, **Matt. 12:13**; Mark 3:5; 8:25; Luke 6:10; (b) of the divine "restoration" of Israel and conditions affected by it, including the renewal of the covenant broken by them, **Matt. 17:11**; Mark 9:12; Acts 1:6; (c) of "giving" or "bringing" a person back, Heb. 13:19. In the papyri it is used of financial restitution, of making good the breaking of a stone by a workman by his substituting another, of the reclamation of land, etc. (Moulton and Milligan).

Whole *hugies* (5199), (cf. Eng., "hygiene") is used especially in the Gospels of making sick folk "whole," **Matt. 12:13**; **15:31**; Mark 3:5; 5:34; Luke 6:10; John 5:4, 6, 9, 11, 14, 15; 7:23; also Acts 4:10; of "sound (speech)," Titus 2:8.

12:14 Then the Pharisees went out, and held a council against him, how they might destroy him.

Held In **Matt. 12:14**, RV, *lambano*, "to take," is translated "took (counsel)," KJV, "held (a council)."

Council *sumboulion* (4824), "a uniting in counsel" (*sun*, "together," *boule*, "counsel, advice"), denotes (a) "counsel" which is given, taken and acted upon, e.g., **Matt. 12:14**, RV, "took counsel," for KJV, "held a council"; **22:15**; hence (b) "a council," an assembly of counsellors or persons in consultation, Acts 25:12, of the "council" with which Festus conferred concerning Paul. The governors and procurators of provinces had a board of advisers or assessors, with whom they took "counsel," before pronouncing judgment.

12:15 But when Jesus knew *it*, he withdrew himself from thence: and great multitudes followed him, and he healed them all;

Knew *ginosko* (1097), "to know by experience and observation," is translated "to perceive" in **Matt. 12:15**, RV (KJV, "knew"); **16:8**; **21:45**; **22:18**; **26:10**, RV, (KJV, "understood"); Mark 8:17; 12:12 and 15:10, RV (KJV, "knew"); so Luke 9:11; 18:34; in Luke 7:39, RV (KJV, "known"); 20:19; John 6:15; 8:27, RV (KJV, "understood"); 16:19, RV (KJV, "knew"); Acts 23:6; Gal. 2:9; in 1 John 3:16, KJV, "perceive" (RV, "know," perfect tense, lit., "we have perceived," and therefore "know").

Withdrew *see* Turned aside at *Matthew 2:22.*

Multitudes *see* Many at *Matthew 3:7.*

12:16 And charged them that they should not make him known:

Charged *epitimao* (2008), signifies (a) to put honor upon (*epi*, upon, *time*, honor); (b) to adjudge, to find fault with, rebuke; hence to charge, or rather, to charge strictly (*epi*, intensive), e.g., **Matt. 12:16**; Mark 3:12, "charged much"; Mark 8:30; in 10:48, RV, "rebuked."

Make *see Matthew 4:19.*

Known *phaneros* (5318), "visible, manifest," is translated "known" in **Matt. 12:16** and Mark 3:12.

12:17 That it might be fulfilled which was spoken by Esaias the prophet, saying,

Fulfilled *see Matthew 1:22.*

Spoken *see Matthew 1:22.*

12:18 Behold my servant, whom I have chosen; my beloved, in whom my soul is well pleased: I will put my spirit upon him, and he shall shew judgment to the Gentiles.

Servant *see Matthew 8:6.*

Chosen *hairetizo* (140), akin to the verbal adjective *hairetos*, "that which may be taken", signifies "to take," with the implication that what is taken is eligible or suitable; hence, "to choose," by reason of this suitability, **Matt. 12:18**, of God's delight in Christ as His "chosen." It is frequent in the Sept., e.g., Gen. 30:20; Num. 14:8; Ps. 25:12; 119:30, 173; 132:13-14; Hos. 4:18; Hag. 2:23 ("he hath chosen the Canaanites"), Zech. 1:17; 2:12; Mal. 3:17.

Pleased *see Matthew 3:17.*

Put *see Matthew 5:15.*

Judgment *see Matthew 5:21.*

12:19 He shall not strive, nor cry; neither shall any man hear his voice in the streets.

Strive *erizo* (2051), "to wrangle, strive" (*eris*, "strife"), is used in **Matt. 12:19**.

Cry *kraugazo* (2905), a stronger form of "to make a clamor or outcry," is used in **Matt. 12:19**, in a prophecy from Isaiah of Christ; in Luke 4:41 (in the best mss., instead of *krazo*); John 11:43; 12:13 (in the best mss.); 18:40; 19:6, 12:15; Acts 22:23.

Voice *see Matthew 2:18.*

Streets *see Matthew 6:5.*

12:20 A bruised reed shall he not break, and smoking flax shall he not quench, till he send forth judgment unto victory.

Bruised *suntribo* (4937), lit., "to rub together," and so "to shatter, shiver, break in pieces by crushing," is said of the bruising of a reed, **Matt. 12:20**; the "breaking" of fetters in pieces, Mark 5:4; the "breaking" of an alabaster cruse, Mark 14:3; an earthenware vessel, Rev. 2:27; of the physical bruising of a person possessed by a demon, Luke 9:39; concerning Christ, "a bone of Him shall not be broken," John 19:36; metaphorically of the crushed condition of a "broken-hearted" person, Luke 4:18 (KJV only); of the eventual crushing of Satan, Rom. 16:20. This verb is frequent in the Sept. in the passive voice, e.g., Ps. 51:17; Isa. 57:15, of a contrite heart, perhaps a figure of stones made smooth by being rubbed together in streams. Cf. *suntrimma*, "destruction."

Reed *see Matthew 11:7.*

Break *katagnumi* (2608), is used of the "breaking" of a bruised reed, **Matt. 12:20**, and of the "breaking" of the legs of those who were crucified, John 19:31, 32, 33.

Smoking *tupho* (5188), "to raise a smoke" [akin to *tuphos*, "smoke" (not in the NT), and *tuphoo*, "to puff up with pride], is used in the passive voice in **Matt. 12:20**, "smoking (flax)," lit., "caused to smoke," of the wick of a lamp which has ceased to burn clearly, figurative of mere nominal religiousness without the Spirit's power. The Sept. uses the verb *kapnizo*.

Flax *linon* (3043), primarily denotes "flax" (Eng., "linen"); then, that which is made of it, "a wick of a lamp," **Matt. 12:20**; several ancient mss. have the word in Rev. 15:6 (KJV only, "linen").

Quench *sbennumi* (4570), is used (a) of "quenching" fire or things on fire, **Matt. 12:20**, quoted from Isa. 42:3, figurative of the condition of the feeble; Heb. 11:34; in the passive voice, **Matt. 25:8**, of torches, RV, "are going out," lit., "are being quenched"; of the retributive doom hereafter of sin unrepented of and unremitted in this life, Mark 9:48 (in some mss. in vv. 44, 46); (b) metaphorically, of "quenching" the fire-tipped darts of the evil one, Eph. 6:16; of "quenching" the Spirit, by hindering His operations in oral testimony in the church gatherings of believers, 1 Thess. 5:19. "The peace, order, and edification of the saints were evidence of the ministry of the Spirit among them, 1 Cor. 14:26, 32, 33, 40, but if, through ignorance of His ways, or through failure to recognize, or refusal to submit to, them, or through impatience with the ignorance or self-will of others, the Spirit were quenched, these happy results would be absent. For there was always the danger that the impulses of the flesh might usurp the place of the energy of the Spirit in the assembly, and the endeavor to restrain this evil by natural means would have the effect of hindering His ministry also. Apparently then, this injunction was intended to warn believers against the substitution of a mechanical order for the restraints of the Spirit." Cf. Song of Sol. 8:7.

Judgment *see Matthew 5:21.*

Victory *nikos* (3534), is used in **Matt. 12:20**; 1 Cor. 15:54, 55, 57.

12:21 And in his name shall the Gentiles trust.

Trust *elpizo* (1679), "to hope," is not infrequently translated in the KJV, by the verb "to trust"; the RV adheres to some form of the verb "to hope," e.g., John 5:45, "Moses, on whom ye have set your hope"; 2 Cor. 1:10, "on whom we have set our hope"; so in 1 Tim. 4:10; 5:5; 6:17; see also, e.g., **Matt. 12:21**; Luke 24:21; Rom. 15:12, 24.

12:22 Then was brought unto him one possessed with a devil, blind, and dumb: and he healed him, insomuch that the blind and dumb both spake and saw.

Devil *see* Devils at *Matthew 4:24.*

12:23 And all the people were amazed, and said, Is not this the son of David?

Amazed *existemi* (1839), primarily and lit. means "to put out of position, displace": hence, (a) "to amaze," Luke 24:22 (for KJV, "make ... astonished"); Acts 8:9, 11 (KJV, "bewitched"); or "to be amazed, astounded," **Matt. 12:23**; Mark 6:51; (b) "to be out of one's mind, to be beside oneself," Mark 3:21; 2 Cor. 5:13, in the latter of which it is contrasted with *sophroneo*, "to be of a sound mind, sober."

12:24 But when the Pharisees heard *it*, they said, This *fellow* doth not cast out devils, but by Beelzebub the prince of the devils.

Prince *see* Ruler at Matthew *9:18.*

12:25 And Jesus knew their thoughts, and said unto them, Every kingdom divided against itself is brought to desolation; and every city or house divided against itself shall not stand:

Thoughts *see Matthew 9:4.*

Divided *merizo* (3307), akin to *meros*, "a part, to part, divide into," in the middle voice means "to divide anything with another, to share with." The usual meaning is "to divide," **Matt. 12:25, 26**; Mark 3:24-26; 6:41; Luke 12:13 (middle voice); Rom. 12:3, "hath dealt"; 1 Cor. 1:13; Heb. 7:2, RV (KJV, "gave a part"). Elsewhere with other meanings, 1 Cor. 7:17, 34; 2 Cor. 10:13.

Desolation *eremoo* (2049), signifies "to make desolate, lay waste." From the primary sense of "making quiet" comes that of "making lonely." It is used only in the passive voice in the NT; in Rev. 17:16, "shall make desolate" is, lit., "shall make her desolated"; in 18:17, 19, "is made desolate"; in **Matt. 12:25** and Luke 11:17, "is brought to desolation."

City *see Matthew 8:34.*

House *see Matthew 2:11.*

12:26 And if Satan cast out Satan, he is divided against himself; how shall then his kingdom stand?

Satan *see Matthew 4:10.*

Divided *see Matthew 12:25.*

12:27 And if I by Beelzebub cast out devils, by whom do your children cast *them* out? therefore they shall be your judges.

Judges *see* Judge at *Matthew 5:25.*

12:28 But if I cast out devils by the Spirit of God, then the kingdom of God is come unto you.

Come *phthano* (5348), denotes "to anticipate, to come sooner than expected," 1 Thess. 2:16, "is come upon," of divine wrath; cf. Rom. 9:31, "did not arrive at"; or to "come" in a different manner from what was expected, **Matt. 12:28**, "come upon"; Luke 11:20, of the kingdom of God; so of coming to a place, 2 Cor. 10:14.

12:29 Or else how can one enter into a strong man's house, and spoil his goods, except he first bind the strong man? and then he will spoil his house.

Strong *ischuros* (2478), "strong, mighty," is used of (a) persons: (1) God, Rev. 18:8; (2) angels, Rev. 5:2; 10:1; 18:21; (3) men, **Matt. 12:29** (twice) and parallel passages; Heb. 11:34, KJV, "valiant" (RV, "mighty"); Rev. 6:15; 19:18, "mighty"; metaphorically, (4) the church at Corinth, 1 Cor. 4:10, where the apostle reproaches them ironically with their unspiritual and self-complacent condition; (5) of young men in Christ spiritually strong, through the Word of God, to overcome the evil one, 1 John 2:14; of (b) things: (1) wind, **Matt. 14:30** (in some mss.), "boisterous"; (2) famine, Luke 15:14; (3) things in the mere human estimate, 1 Cor. 1:27; (4) Paul's letters, 2 Cor. 10 :10; (5) the Lord's crying and tears, Heb. 5:7; (6) consolation, 6:18; (7) the voice of an angel, Rev. 18:2 (in the best texts; some have *megas*, "great");

(8) Babylon, Rev. 18:10; (9) thunderings, Rev. 19:6.

Spoil *harpazo* (726), "to seize, snatch away," is rendered "spoil" in **Matt. 12:29a**. *See also* **Take ... by force** at *Matthew 11:12*.

Goods *skeuos* (4632), "a vessel," denotes "goods" in **Matt. 12:29**; Mark 3:27; Luke 17:31, RV (KJV, "stuff").

Spoil *diarpazo* (1283), "to plunder," is found in **Matt. 12:29**, 2nd part (the 1st has *harpazo*, in the best texts), lit., "(then) he will completely (*dia*, intensive) spoil (his house)"; Mark 3:27 (twice).

12:30 He that is not with me is against me; and he that gathereth not with me scattereth abroad.

Scattereth *skorpizo* (4650), "to scatter" (probably from a root, *skarp-*, signifying "to cut asunder," akin to *skorpios*, "a scorpion"), is used in **Matt. 12:30**; Luke 11:23; John 10:12; 16:32; in the RV of 2 Cor. 9:9, "scattered abroad" (KJV, "he hath dispersed abroad"), of one who liberally dispenses benefits.

12:31 Wherefore I say unto you, All manner of sin and blasphemy shall be forgiven unto men: but the blasphemy *against* the *Holy* Ghost shall not be forgiven unto men.

Wherefore Some phrases introduced by the preposition *dia*, "on account of," *dia touto*, "on account of this," e.g., **Matt. 12:31**; Rom. 5:12; Eph. 1:15; 3 John 10; *dia hen* (the accusative feminine of *hos*, "who"), "on account of which" (*aitia*, "a cause," being understood), e.g., Acts 10:21 (with *aitia*, expressed, Titus 1:13; Heb. 2:11); *dia ti* "on account of what?" (sometimes as one word, *diati*) e.g., Luke 19:23; Rom. 9:32; 2 Cor. 11:11; Rev. 17:7.

Manner In **Matt. 12:31**; Luke 11:42; Rev. 18:12, KJV, *pas*, "every" (so RV), is translated "all manner."

Sin *hamartia* (266), is, lit., "a missing of the mark," but this etymological meaning is largely lost sight of in the NT. It is the most comprehensive term for moral obliquity. It is used of "sin" as (a) a principle or source of action, or an inward element producing acts, e.g., Rom. 3:9; 5:12, 13, 20; 6:1, 2; 7:7 (abstract for concrete); 7:8 (twice), 9, 11, 13, "sin, that it might be shown to be sin," i.e., "sin became death to me, that it might be exposed in its heinous character": in the last clause, "sin might become exceeding sinful," i.e., through the holiness of the Law, the true nature of sin was designed to be manifested to the conscience.

(b) a governing principle or power, e.g., Rom. 6:6, "(the body) of sin," here "sin" is spoken of as an organized power, acting through the members of the body, though the seat of "sin" is in the will (the body is the organic instrument); in the next clause, and in other passages, as follows, this governing principle is personified, e.g., Rom. 5:21; 6:12, 14, 17; 7:11, 14, 17, 20, 23, 25; 8:2; 1 Cor. 15:56; Heb. 3:13; 11:25; 12:4; Jas. 1:15 (2nd part).

(c) a generic term (distinct from specific terms such as *hamartema* yet sometimes inclusive of concrete wrong doing, e.g., John 8:21, 34, 46; 9:41; 15:22, 24; 19:11); in Rom. 8:3, "God, sending His own Son in the likeness of sinful flesh," lit., "flesh of sin," the flesh stands for the body, the instrument of indwelling "sin" [Christ, preexistently the Son of God, assumed human flesh, "of the substance of the Virgin Mary"; the reality of incarnation was His, without taint of sin], and *as an offering* for sin," i.e., "a sin offering" (so the Sept., e.g., in Lev. 4:32; 5:6, 7, 8, 9), "condemned sin in the flesh," i.e., Christ, having taken human nature, "sin" apart (Heb. 4:15), and having lived a sinless life, died under the condemnation and judgment due to our "sin"; for the generic sense see further, e.g., Heb. 9:26; 10:6, 8, 18; 13:11; 1 John 1:7, 8; 3:4 (1st part; in the 2nd part, "sin" is defined as "lawlessness," RV), 8, 9; in these verses the KJV use of the verb to commit is misleading; not the committal of an act is in view, but a continuous course of "sin," as indicated by the RV, "doeth." The apostle's use of the present tense of *poieo*, "to do," virtually expresses the meaning of *prasso*, "to practice," which John does not use (it is not infrequent in this sense in Paul's Epp., e.g., Rom. 1:32, RV; 2:1; Gal. 5:21; Phil. 4:9);1 Pet. 4:1 (singular in the best texts), lit., "has been made to cease from sin," i.e., as a result of suffering in the flesh, the mortifying of our members, and of obedience to a Savior who suffered in flesh. Such no longer lives in the flesh, "to the lusts of men, but to the will of God"; sometimes the word is used as virtually equivalent to a condition of "sin," e.g., John 1:29, "the sin (not sins) of the world": 1 Cor. 15:17; or a course of "sin," characterized by continuous acts, e.g., 1 Thess. 2:16; in 1 John 5:16 (2nd part) the RV marg., is probably to be preferred, "there is sin unto death," not a special act of "sin," but the state or condition producing acts; in v. 17, "all unrighteousness is sin" is not a definition of "sin" (as in 3:4), it gives a specification of the term in its generic sense.

(d) a sinful deed, an act of "sin," e.g., **Matt. 12:31**; Acts 7:60; Jas. 1:15 (1st part); 2:9; 4:17; 5:15, 20; 1 John 5:16 (1st part).

Forgiven *see* **Forgive** at *Matthew 6:12*.

12:32 And whosoever speaketh a word against the Son of man,

it shall be forgiven him: but whosoever speaketh against the Holy Ghost, it shall not be forgiven him, neither in this world, neither in the *world* to come.

Forgiven *see* Forgive at *Matthew 6:12*.

Holy Ghost *see Matthew 1:18*.

This *see* These at *Matthew 3:9*.

12:33 Either make the tree good, and his fruit good; or else make the tree corrupt, and his fruit corrupt: for the tree is known by *his* fruit.

Either *see Matthew 6:24*.

Tree *see Matthew 7:17*.

Good *see Matthew 3:10*.

Corrupt *see Matthew 7:17*.

12:34 O generation of vipers, how can ye, being evil, speak good things? for out of the abundance of the heart the mouth speaketh.

Generation *see Matthew 3:7*.

Vipers *see Matthew 3:7*.

Abundance *perisseuma* (4051), denotes "abundance" in a slightly more concrete form, 2 Cor. 8:13-14, where it stands for the gifts in kind supplied by the saints. In **Matt. 12:34** and Luke 6:45 it is used of the "abundance" of the heart; in Mark 8:8, of the broken pieces left after feeding the multitude "that remained over" (KJV "that was left"). In the Sept., Eccl. 2:15.

Mouth *stoma* (4750), akin to *stomachos* (which originally meant "a throat, gullet"), is used (a) of "the mouth" of man, e.g., **Matt. 15:11**; of animals, e.g., **Matt. 17:27**; 2 Tim. 4:17 (figurative); Heb. 11:33; Jas. 3:3; Rev. 13:2 (2nd occurrence); (b) figuratively of "inanimate things," of the "edge" of a sword, Luke 21:24; Heb. 11:34; of the earth, Rev. 12:16; (c) figuratively, of the "mouth," as the organ of speech, (1) of Christ's words, e.g., **Matt. 13:35**; Luke 11:54; Acts 8:32; 22:14; 1 Pet. 2:22; (2) of human, e.g., **Matt. 18:16**; **21:16**; Luke 1:64; Rev. 14:5; as emanating from the heart, **Matt. 12:34**; Rom. 10:8, 9; of prophetic ministry through the Holy Spirit, Luke 1:70; Acts 1:16; 3:18; 4:25; of the destructive policy of two world potentates at the end of this age, Rev. 13:2, 5, 6; 16:13 (twice); of shameful speaking, Eph. 4:29 and Col. 3:8; (3) of the Devil speaking as a dragon or serpent, Rev. 12:15, 16; 16:13; (d) figuratively, in the phrase "face to face" (lit., "mouth to mouth"), 2 John 12; 3 John 14; (e) metaphorically, of "the utterances of the Lord, in judgment," 2 Thess. 2:8; Rev. 1:16; 2:16; 19:15, 21; of His judgment upon a local church for its lukewarmness, Rev. 3:16; (f) by metonymy, for "speech," **Matt. 18:16**; Luke 19:22; 21:15; 2 Cor. 13:1.

12:35 A good man out of the good treasure of the heart bringeth forth good things: and an evil man out of the evil treasure bringeth forth evil things.

Good *see Matthew 5:45*.

Man *see Matthew 4:4*.

Treasure *see* Treasures at *Matthew 2:11*.

Bringeth *ekballo* (1544), "to cast out," used of bringing forth good and evil things from the heart, **Matt. 12:35**.

Evil *see Matthew 5:37*.

12:36 But I say unto you, That every idle word that men shall speak, they shall give account thereof in the day of judgment.

Idle *argos* (692), denotes "inactive, idle, unfruitful, barren" (*a*, negative, and *ergon*, "work"; cf. the verb *katargeo*, "to reduce to inactivity"); it is used (a) literally, **Matt. 20:3**, **6**; 1 Tim. 5:13 (twice); Titus 1:12, RV, "idle (gluttons)"; 2 Pet. 1:8, RV, "idle," KJV, "barren"; (b) metaphorically in the sense of "ineffective, worthless," as of a word, **Matt. 12:36**; of faith unaccompanied by works, Jas. 2:20 (some mss. have *nekra*, "dead").

Word *rhema* (4487), denotes "that which is spoken, what is uttered in speech or writing"; in the singular, "a word," e.g., **Matt. 12:36**; **27:14**; 2 Cor. 12:4; 13:1; Heb. 12:19; in the plural, speech, discourse, e.g., John 3:34; 8:20; Acts 2:14; 6:11, 13; 11:14; 13:42; 26:25; Rom. 10:18; 2 Pet. 3:2; Jude 17; it is used of the gospel in Rom. 10:8 (twice), 17, RV, "the word of Christ" (i.e., the "word" which preaches Christ); 10:18; 1 Pet. 1:25 (twice); of a statement, command, instruction, e.g., **Matt. 26:75**; Luke 1:37, RV, "(no) word (from God shall be void of power)", v. 38; Acts 11:16; Heb. 11:3. The significance of *rhema* (as distinct from *logos*) is exemplified in the injunction to take "the sword of the Spirit, which is the word of God," Eph. 6:17; here the reference is not to the whole Bible as such, but to the individual scripture which the Spirit brings to our remembrance for use in time of need, a prerequisite being the regular storing of the mind with Scripture.

Give *see* Paid at *Matthew 5:26*.

Account *logos* (3056), "a word or saying," also means "an account which one gives by word of mouth," **Matt. 12:36**; **Matt. 18:23**, RV, "reckoning"; **16:2**; Acts 19:40; 20:24 (KJV, "count"); Rom. 14:12; Phil. 4:17; Heb. 13:17; 1 Pet. 4:5.

12:37 For by thy words thou shalt be justified, and by thy words thou shalt be condemned.

Condemned *see Matthew 12:7.*

12:38 Then certain of the scribes and of the Pharisees answered, saying, Master, we would see a sign from thee.

Sign *semeion* (4592), "a sign, mark, indication, token," is used (a) of that which distinguished a person or thing from others, e.g., **Matt. 26:48**; Luke 2:12; Rom. 4:11; 2 Cor. 12:12 (1st part); 2 Thess. 3:17, "token," i.e., his autograph attesting the authenticity of his letters; (b) of a "sign" as a warning or admonition, e.g., **Matt. 12:39**, "the sign of (i.e., consisting of) the prophet Jonas"; **16:4**; Luke 2:34; 11:29, 30; (c) of miraculous acts (1) as tokens of divine authority and power, e.g., **Matt. 12:38, 39** (1st part); John 2:11, RV, "signs"; 3:2 (ditto); 4:54, "(the second) sign," RV; 10:41 (ditto); 20:30; in 1 Cor. 1:22, "the Jews ask for signs," RV, indicates that the Apostles were met with the same demand from Jews as Christ had been: "signs were vouchsafed in plenty, signs of God's power and love, but these were not the signs which they sought.... They wanted signs of an outward Messianic Kingdom, of temporal triumph, of material greatness for the chosen people.... With such cravings the Gospel of a 'crucified Messiah' was to them a stumbling-block indeed" (Lightfoot); 1 Cor. 14:22; (2) by demons, Rev. 16:14; (3) by false teachers or prophets, indications of assumed authority, e.g., **Matt. 24:24**; Mark 13:22; (4) by Satan through his special agents, 2 Thess. 2:9; Rev. 13:13, 14; 19:20; (d) of tokens portending future events, e. g., **Matt. 24:3**, where "the sign of the Son of Man" signifies, subjectively, that the Son of Man is Himself the "sign" of what He is about to do; Mark 13:4; Luke 21:7, 11, 25; Acts 2:19; Rev. 12:1, RV; 12:3, RV; 15:1.

12:39 But he answered and said unto them, An evil and adulterous generation seeketh after a sign; and there shall no sign be given to it, but the sign of the prophet Jonas:

Evil *see Matthew 5:11.*

Adulterous *moichalis* (3428), "an adulteress," is used (a) in the natural sense, 2 Pet. 2:14; Rom. 7:3; (b) in the spiritual sense, Jas. 4:4; here the RV rightly omits the word "adulterers." It was added by a copyist. As in Israel the breach of their relationship with God through their idolatry, was described as "adultery" or "harlotry" (e.g., Ezek. 16:15, etc.; 23:43), so believers who cultivate friendship with the world, thus breaking their spiritual union with Christ, are spiritual "adulteresses," having been spiritually united to Him as wife to husband, Rom. 7:4. It is used adjectivally to describe the Jewish people in transferring their affections from God, **Matt. 12:39**; **16:4**; Mark 8:38. In 2 Pet. 2:14, the lit. translation is "full of an adulteress" (RV, marg.).

Seeketh *see* Seek at *Matthew 6:32.*

Sign *see Matthew 12:38.*

12:40 For as Jonas was three days and three nights in the whale's belly; so shall the Son of man be three days and three nights in the heart of the earth.

Nights *see* Night at *Matthew 2:14.*

Whale *ketos* (2785), denotes "a huge fish, a sea monster," **Matt. 12:40**. In the Sept., Gen. 1:21; Job 3:8; 9:13; 26:12; Jonah 1:17 (twice); 2:1, 10.

Son *see Matthew 3:17.*

12:41 The men of Nineveh shall rise in judgment with this generation, and shall condemn it: because they repented at the preaching of Jonas; and, behold, a greater than Jonas *is* here.

Rise *anistemi* (450), "to stand up or to make to stand up," according as its use is intransitive or transitive (*ana*, "up," *histemi*, "to stand"), is used (a) of a physical change of position, e.g., of "rising" from sleep, Mark 1:35; from a meeting in a synagogue, Luke 4:29; of the illegal "rising" of the high priest in the tribunal in **Matt. 26:62**; of an invalid "rising" from his couch, Luke 5:25; the "rising" up of a disciple from his vocation to follow Christ, Luke 5:28; cf. John 11:31; "rising" up from prayer, Luke 22:45; of a whole company, Acts 26:30; 1 Cor. 10:7; (b) metaphorically, of "rising" up antagonistically against persons, e.g., of officials against people, Acts 5:17; of a seditious leader, 5:36, of the "rising" up of Satan, Mark 3:26; of false teachers, Acts 20:30; (c) of "rising" to a position of preeminence or power; e.g., of Christ as a prophet, Acts 3:22; 7:37; as God's servant in the midst of the nation of Israel, Acts 3:26; as the Son of God in the midst of the nation, 13:33 (not here of resurrection, but with reference to the Incarnation: the KJV "again" has nothing corresponding to it in the original, it was added as a misinterpretation: the mention of His resurrection is in the next verse, in which it is stressed by way of contrast and by the addition, "from the dead"); as a priest, Heb. 7:11, 15; as king over the nations, Rom. 15:12; (d) of a spiritual awakening from lethargy, Eph. 5:14; (e) of resurrection from the dead: (1) of the resurrection of Christ, **Matt. 17:9; 20:19**; Mark 8:31; 9:9-10, 31; 10:34; Luke 18:33; 24:7, 46; John 20:9; Acts 2:24, 32; 10:41; 13:34; 17:3, 31; 1 Thess. 4:14; (2) of believers, John 6:39-40, 44, 54; 11:24; 1 Thess. 4:16; of unbelievers, **Matt. 12:41**. *See also* Arose at *Matthew 2:14.*

Condemn *katakrino* (2632), signifies "to give judgment against, pass sentence upon"; hence, "to condemn," implying (a) the fact of a crime, e.g., Rom. 2:1; 14:23; 2 Pet. 2:6; some mss. have it in Jas. 5:9; (b) the imputation of a crime, as in the "condemnation" of Christ by the Jews, **Matt. 20:18**; Mark 14:64. It is used metaphorically of "condemning" by a good example, **Matt. 12:41-42**; Luke 11:31-32; Heb. 11:7.

Preaching *kerugma* (2782), "a proclamation by a herald," denotes "a message, a preaching" (the substance of what is "preached" as distinct from the act of "preaching"), **Matt. 12:41**; Luke 11:32; Rom. 16:25; 1 Cor. 1:21; 2:4; 15:14; in 2 Tim. 4:17 and Titus 1:3, RV, "message," marg., "proclamation," KJV, "preaching." In the Sept., 2 Chron. 30:5; Prov. 9:3; Jonah 3:2.

Greater *see* Exceed at *Matthew 5:20.*

12:42 The queen of the south shall rise up in the judgment with this generation, and shall condemn it: for she came from the uttermost parts of the earth to hear the wisdom of Solomon; and, behold, a greater than Solomon *is* here.

Queen *basilissa* (938), the feminine of *basileus,* "a king," is used (a) of the "Queen of Sheba," **Matt. 12:42**; Luke 11:31; of "Candace," Acts 8:27; (b) metaphorically, of "Babylon," Rev. 18:7.

South *notos* (3558), denotes (a) "the south wind," Luke 12:55; Acts 27:13; 28:13; (b) "south," as a direction, Luke 13:29; Rev. 21:13; (c) "the South," as a region, **Matt. 12:42**; Luke 11:31.

Rise *see* Arose at *Matthew 2:14.*

Uttermost *peras* (4009), "a limit, boundary" (from *pera,* "beyond"), is used (a) of space, chiefly in the plural, **Matt. 12:42**, RV, "ends," for KJV, "uttermost parts"; so Luke 11:31 (KJV, "utmost"); Rom. 10:18 (KJV and RV, "ends"); (b) of the termination of something occurring in a period, Heb. 6:16, RV, "final," for KJV, "an end," said of strife.

Parts *peras* (4009), "an end, boundary," is translated "utmost parts" in the KJV of **Matt. 12:42** and Luke 11:31.

Wisdom *see Matthew 11:19.*

Greater *see* Exceed at *Matthew 5:20.*

12:43 When the unclean spirit is gone out of a man, he walketh through dry places, seeking rest, and findeth none.

Walketh through *dierchomai* (1330), denotes "to pass through or over," (a) of persons, e.g., **Matt. 12:43**, RV, "passeth (KJV, walketh) through"; Mark 4:35, KJV, "pass (RV, go) over"; Luke 19:1, 4; Heb. 4:14, RV, "passed through" (KJV "into"); Christ "passed through" the created heavens to the throne of God; (b) of things, e.g., **Matt. 19:24**, "to go through"; Luke 2:35, "shall pierce through" (metaphorically of a sword).

Dry *anudros* (504), "waterless" (*a,* negative, *n,* euphonic, *hudor,* "water"), is rendered "dry" in **Matt. 12:43**, KJV, and Luke 11:24 (RV, "waterless"); "without water" in 2 Pet. 2:17 and Jude 12.

Rest *see Matthew 11:29.*

12:44 Then he saith, I will return into my house from whence I came out; and when he is come, he findeth *it* empty, swept, and garnished.

Return *epistrepho* (1994), "to turn about," or "towards," is translated "to return" in **Matt. 12:44; 24:18**; Mark 13:16, RV (KJV, "turn back again"); Luke 2:39; 8:55, RV (KJV, "came again"); 17:31; Acts 15:36, RV (KJV, "go again").

House *see Matthew 9:6.*

Whence *hothen* (which denotes "whence," when used of direction or source, e.g., **Matt. 12:44**), used of cause and denoting "wherefore" in Heb. 2:17; 3:1; 7:25; 8:3.

Empty *scholazo* (4980), from *schole,* "leisure," that for which leisure is employed, such as "a lecture" (hence, "the place where lectures are given"; Eng., "school"), is used of persons, to have time for anything and so to be occupied in, 1 Cor. 7:5; of things, to be unoccupied, empty, **Matt. 12:44** (some mss. have it in Luke 11:25).

Swept *saroo* (4563), occurs in **Matt. 12:44**; Luke 11:25; 15:8.

Garnished *kosmeo* (2885), primarily "to arrange, to put in order" (Eng., "cosmetic"), is used of furnishing a room, **Matt. 12:44**; Luke 11:25, and of trimming lamps, **Matt. 25:7**. Hence, "to adorn, to ornament," as of garnishing tombs, **Matt. 23:29**; buildings, Luke 21:5; Rev. 21:19; one's person, 1 Tim. 2:9; 1 Pet. 3:5; Rev. 21:2; metaphorically, of "adorning a doctrine, Titus 2:10.

12:45 Then goeth he, and taketh with himself seven other spirits more wicked than himself, and they enter in and dwell there: and the last *state* of that man is worse than the first. Even so shall it be also unto this wicked generation.

Taketh *see* Take at *Matthew 1:20.*

Spirits *see* Devils at *Matthew 8:28.*

Wicked *poneros* (4190), is translated "wicked" in the KJV and RV in **Matt. 13:49**; **18:32**; **25:26**; Luke 19:22; Acts 18:14; 1 Cor. 5:13; in the following the RV substitutes "evil" for KJV, "wicked": **Matt. 12:45** (twice); **13:19**; **16:4**; Luke 11:26; Col. 1:21; 2 Thess. 3:2; and in the following, where Satan is mentioned as "the (or that) evil one": **Matt. 13:38**; Eph. 6:16; 1 John 2:13, 14; 3:12 (1st part); 5:18; in v. 19 for KJV, "wickedness"; he is so called also in KJV and RV in John 17:15; 2 Thess. 3:3; KJV only in Luke 11:4; in 3 John 10, KJV, the word is translated "malicious," RV, "wicked." *See also* Evil at *Matthew 5:11.*

Last state *eschatos* (2078), "last, utmost, extreme," is used as a noun (a) of time, rendered "end" in Heb. 1:2, RV, "at the "end" of these days," i.e., at the "end" of the period under the Law, for KJV, "in these last days"; so in 1 Pet. 1:20, "at the end of the times." In 2 Pet. 2:20, the plural, *ta eschata*, lit., "the last things," is rendered "the latter end," KJV, (RV, "the last state"); the same phrase is used in **Matt. 12:45**; Luke 11:26; (b) of place, Acts 13:47, KJV, "ends (of the earth)," RV, "uttermost part." *See also* Uttermost at *Matthew 5:26.*

Man *see Matthew 4:4.*

Worse *see Matthew 9:16.*

First *protos* (4413), the superlative degree of *pro*, "before," is used (I) "of time or place," (a) as a noun, e.g., Luke 14:18; Rev. 1:17; opposite to "the last," in the neuter plural, **Matt. 12:45**; Luke 11:26; 2 Pet. 2:20; in the neuter singular, opposite to "the second," Heb. 10:9; in 1 Cor. 15:3, *en protois*, lit., "in the first (things, or matters)" denotes "first of all"; (b) as an adjective, e.g., Mark 16:9, used with "day" understood, lit., "the first (day) of (i.e., after) the Sabbath," in which phrase the "of" is objective, not including the Sabbath, but following it; in John 20:4, 8; Rom. 10:19, e.g., equivalent to an English adverb; in John 1:15, lit., "first of me," i.e., "before me" (of superiority); (II) "of rank or dignity."

Even so *see Matthew 7:17.*

12:46 While he yet talked to the people, behold, *his* mother and his brethren stood without, desiring to speak with him.

Yet *eti* (2089), "yet, still, further," is used (a) of time, most usually translated "yet," e.g., **Matt. 12:46**; or negatively, "any more," "no more," e.g., Heb. 8:12; (b) of degree, translated "further," or "any further," **Matt. 26:65**; Mark 5:35; 14:63; Luke 22:71; Heb. 7:11 in Acts 21:28, RV, "moreover" (KJV, "further").

Talked *laleo* (2980), "to speak, say," is always translated "to speak" in the RV, where the KJV renders it by "to talk," **Matt. 12:46**; Mark 6:50; Luke 24:32; John 4:27 (twice); 9:37; 14:30; Acts 26:31; Rev. 4:1; 17:1; 21:9, 15. The RV rendering is preferable; the idea of "chat" or "chatter" is entirely foreign to the NT, and should never be regarded as the meaning in 1 Cor. 14:34, 35.

Without This is a translation of *exo*, "outside," e.g., Matt. 12:46, 47; "(them that are) without," 1 Cor. 5:12, 13; Col. 4:5; 1 Thess. 4:12 (the unregenerate); Heb. 13:11-13.

Desiring *zeteo*, "to seek"; in **Matt. 12:46–47**, RV, "seeking"; in Luke 9:9, RV, "sought." *See also* Sought at *Matthew 2:20.*

12:47 Then one said unto him, Behold, thy mother and thy brethren stand without, desiring to speak with thee.

Without *see Matthew 12:47.*

Desiring *see* Sought at *Matthew 2:20.*

12:48-49 But he answered and said unto him that told him, Who is my mother? and who are my brethren?

And he stretched forth his hand toward his disciples, and said, Behold my mother and my brethren!

Stretched *see* Put forth at *Matthew 8:3.*

Mother *see Matthew 1:18.*

12:50 For whosoever shall do the will of my Father which is in heaven, the same is my brother, and sister, and mother.

Heaven *see Matthew 5:16.*

Sister *adelphe* (79), is used (a) of natural relationship, e.g., **Matt. 19:29**; of the "sisters" of Christ, the children of Joseph and Mary after the virgin birth of Christ, e.g., **Matt. 13:56**; (b) of "spiritual kinship" with Christ, an affinity marked by the fulfillment of the will of the Father, **Matt. 12:50**; Mark 3:35; of spiritual relationship based upon faith in Christ, Rom. 16:1; 1 Cor. 7:15; 9:5, KJV and RV marg.; Jas. 2:15; Philem. 2, RV.

Mother *see Matthew 1:18.*

Chapter 13

13:1-2 The same day went Jesus out of the house, and sat by the sea side.

And great multitudes were gathered together unto him, so that he went into a ship, and sat; and the whole multitude stood on the shore.

Went into *see* Entered at *Matthew 8:23.*

Shore *aigialos* (123), translated "shore" in the KJV in each place where it is used, **Matt. 13:2, 48**; John 21:4; Acts 21:5; 27:39-40, is always in the RV translated "beach." It is derived from a root signifying "to press, drive"; *aigis* denotes "a wind-storm."

13:3 And he spake many things unto them in parables, saying, Behold, a sower went forth to sow;

Parables *parabole* (3850), lit. denotes "a placing beside" (akin to *paraballo*, "to throw" or "lay beside, to compare"). It signifies "a placing of one thing beside another" with a view to comparison (some consider that the thought of comparison is not necessarily contained in the word). In the NT it is found outside the Gospels, only in Heb. 9:9 and 11:19. It is generally used of a somewhat lengthy utterance or narrative drawn from nature or human circumstances, the object of which is to set forth a spiritual lesson, e.g., those in **Matt. 13** and Synoptic parallels; sometimes it is used of a short saying or proverb, e.g., **Matt. 15:15**; Mark 3:23; 7:17; Luke 4:23; 5:36; 6:39. It is the lesson that is of value; the hearer must catch the analogy if he is to be instructed (this is true also of a proverb). Such a narrative or saying, dealing with earthly things with a spiritual meaning, is distinct from a fable, which attributes to things what does not belong to them in nature. Christ's "parables" most frequently convey truths connected with the subject of the kingdom of God. His withholding the meaning from His hearers as He did from the multitudes, **Matt. 13:34**, was a divine judgment upon the unworthy. Two dangers are to be avoided in seeking to interpret the "parables" in Scripture, that of ignoring the important features, and that of trying to make all the details mean something.

Sower, Sow *speiro* (4687), "to sow seed," is used (1) literally, especially in the Synoptic Gospels; elsewhere, 1 Cor. 15:36, 37; 2 Cor. 9:10, "the sower", (2) metaphorically, (a) in proverbial sayings, e.g., **Matt. 13:3, 4**; Luke 19:21, 22; John 4:37; 2 Cor. 9:6; (b) in the interpretation of parables, e.g., **Matt. 13:19-23** (in these vv., RV, "was sown," for KJV, "received seed"); (c) otherwise as follows: of "sowing" spiritual things in preaching and teaching, 1 Cor. 9:11; of the interment of the bodies of deceased believers, 1 Cor. 15:42-44; of ministering to the necessities of others in things temporal (the harvest being proportionate to the "sowing"), 2 Cor. 9:6, 10; of "sowing" to the flesh, Gal. 6:7, 8 ("that" in v. 7 is emphatic, "that and that only," what was actually "sown"); in v. 8, *eis*, "unto," signifies "in the interests of"; of the "fruit of righteousness" by peacemakers, Jas. 3:18.

13:4 And when he sowed, some *seeds* fell by the way side, and the fowls came and devoured them up:

Fell *see Matthew 2:11.*

Sowed *see* Sower, Sow at *Matthew 13:3.*

Devoured *katesthio* and *kataphago* (2719), signifies (a) "to consume by eating, to devour," said of birds, **Matt. 13:4**; Mark 4:4; Luke 8:5; of the Dragon, Rev. 12:4; of a prophet, "eating" up a book, suggestive of spiritually "eating" and digesting its contents, Rev. 10:9 (cf. Ezek. 2:8; 3:1-3; Jer. 15:16); (b) metaphorically, "to squander, to waste," Luke 15:30; "to consume" one's physical powers by emotion, John 2:17; "to devour" by forcible appropriation, as of widows' property, **Matt. 23:14** (KJV only); Mark 12:40; "to demand maintenance," as false apostles did to the church at Corinth, 2 Cor. 11:20; "to exploit or prey on one another," Gal. 5:15, where "bite ... devour ... consume" form a climax, the first two describing a process, the last the act of swallowing down; to "destroy" by fire, Rev. 11:5; 20:9.

13:5 Some fell upon stony places, where they had not much earth: and forthwith they sprung up, because they had no deepness of earth:

Some In the following *alloi*, "others" ("some" in the KJV), is translated "others" in the RV, **Matt. 13:5, 7**; Mark 4:7 ("other"); 8:28; Luke 9:19; John 9:9. Followed by a correlative expression it denotes "some," e.g., Acts 19:32; 21:34. *See also* Other at *Matthew 5:39.*

Stony *petrodes* (4075), "rock-like" (*petra*, "a rock," *eidos*, "a form, appearance"), is used of "rock" underlying shallow soil, **Matt. 13:5, 20**, RV, "the rocky places" (KJV, "stony places"); Mark 4:5, RV, "the rocky ground" (KJV, "stony ground"); v. 16, RV, "rocky places" (KJV, "stony ground").

Much *polus* (4183), is used (a) as an adjective of degree, e.g., **Matt. 13:5**, "much (earth)"; Acts 26:24, "much (learning)"; in v. 29, in the answer to Agrippa's "with but little persuasion," some texts have *pollo* (some *megalo*, "with great"), RV, "(whether with little or) with much"; of number, e.g., Mark 5:24, RV, "a great (multitude)," KJV, "much (people)"; so Luke 7:11; John 12:12; Rev. 19:1, etc.; (b) in the neuter singular form (*polu*), as a noun, e.g., Luke 16:10 (twice); in the plural (*polla*), e.g., Rom. 16:6, 12, "(labored) much," lit., "many things"; (c) adverbially, in the neuter singular, e.g., Acts 18:27; James 5:16; **Matt. 26:9** (a genitive of price); in the plural, e.g., Mark 5:43, RV, "much" (KJV, "straitly"); Mark 9:26, RV, "much" (KJV, "sore"); John 14:30; and with the article, Acts 26:24; Rom. 15:22; 1 Cor. 16:19; Rev. 5:4.

Earth *see Matthew 5:18.*

Forthwith *eutheos* (2112), "at once, straightway" (from the adjective, *euthus*, "straight"), is translated "forthwith," in the KJV of **Matt. 13:5**; **26:49**; (it occurs in some mss. in Mark 5:13; the RV omits it); Acts 12:10; 21:30 (RV, "straightway," in each place).

Sprung *exanatello* (1816), is used of the "springing" up of seeds, **Matt. 13:5**; Mark 4:5.

Deepness *bathos* (899), is used (a) naturally, in **Matt. 13:5**, "deepness"; Mark 4:5, KJV, "depth," RV, "deepness"; Luke 5:4, of "deep" water; Rom. 8:39 (contrasted with *hupsoma*, "height"); (b) metaphorically, in Rom. 11:33, of God's wisdom and knowledge; in 1 Cor. 2:10, of God's counsels; in Eph. 3:18, of the dimensions of the sphere of the activities of God's counsels, and of the love of Christ which occupies that sphere; in 2 Cor. 8:2, of "deep" poverty; some mss. have it in Rev. 2:24.

13:6 And when the sun was up, they were scorched; and because they had no root, they withered away.

Sun *see Matthew 5:45.*

Up In **Matt. 13:6** and Mark 4:6, KJV, *anatello*, "to rise" (of the sun), is rendered "was up." *See also* **Sprung** at *Matthew 4:16.*

Scorched *kaumatizo* (2739), "to scorch" (from *kauma*, "heat"), is used (a) of seed that had not much earth, **Matt. 13:6**; Mark 4:6; (b) of men, stricken retributively by the sun's heat, Rev. 16:8, 9.

Root *see Matthew 3:10.*

Withered *xeraino* (3583), "to dry up, parch, wither," is translated "to wither," (a) of plants, **Matt. 13:6**; **21:19**, **20**; Mark 4:6; 11:20, RV (KJV, "dried up"), 21; Luke 8:6; John 15:6; Jas. 1:11; 1 Pet. 1:24; (b) of members of the body, Mark 3:1, and, in some texts, 3.

13:7 And some fell among thorns; and the thorns sprung up, and choked them:

Some *see Matthew 13:5.*

Thorns *see Matthew 7:16.*

Sprung *anabaino* (305), "to go up," is rendered "sprang up" in **Matt. 13:7**, KJV, of thorns, and Mark 4:8, of seed (RV, "grew up").

Choked *apopnigo* (638), is used metaphorically, of "thorns crowding out seed sown and preventing its growth," **Matt. 13:7**; Luke 8:7. It is Luke's word for "suffocation by drowning," Luke 8:33 (cf. Mark 5:13, above).

13:8 But other fell into good ground, and brought forth fruit, some an hundredfold, some sixtyfold, some thirtyfold.

Good *see Matthew 3:10.*

Ground *see* **Earth** at *Matthew 5:18.*

Brought forth *didomi* (1325), "to give," is translated "to yield," i.e., "to produce," in **Matt. 13:8**, RV (KJV, "brought forth"); Mark 4:7, 8.

Hundredfold *hekaton* (1540), an indeclinable numeral, denotes "a hundred," e.g., **Matt. 18:12**, **28**; it also signifies "a hundredfold," **Matt. 13:8**, **23**, and the RV in the corresponding passage, Mark 4:8, 20 (for KJV, "hundred"), signifying the complete productiveness of sown seed. In the passage in Mark the phrase is, lit., "in thirty and in sixty and in a hundred." In Mark 6:40 it is used with the preposition *kata*, in the phrase "by hundreds." It is followed by other numerals in John 21:11; Acts 1:15; Rev. 7:4; 14:1, 3; 21:17.

Sixtyfold *hexekonta* (1835), occurs in **Matt. 13:8**, RV (KJV, "sixty-fold"); **13:23**; Mark 4:8, where the RV and KJV reverse the translation, as in **Matt. 13:8**, while in Mark 4:20 the RV has "sixtyfold," KJV, "sixty"; in Rev. 13:18, RV, "sixty" (KJV, "threescore"). It is rendered "threescore" in Luke 24:13; 1 Tim. 5:9; Rev. 11:3; 12:6.

Thirtyfold *triakonta* (5144), is usually rendered "thirty," e.g., **Matt. 13:23**; "thirtyfold," in **Matt. 13:8**, KJV only; in Mark 4:8, RV only; in Mark 4:20, KJV and RV.

13:9 Who hath ears to hear, let him hear.

Ears *see* **Ear** at *Matthew 10:27.*

13:10-11 And the disciples came, and said unto him, Why speakest thou unto them in parables?

He answered and said unto them, Because it is given unto

you to know the mysteries of the kingdom of heaven, but to them it is not given.

Know *see* Knew at *Matthew 1:25*.

Mysteries *musterion* (3466), primarily that which is known to the *mustes*, "the initiated" (from *mueo*, "to initiate into the mysteries"; cf. Phil. 4:12, *mueomai*, "I have learned the secret," RV). In the NT it denotes, not the mysterious (as with the Eng. word), but that which, being outside the range of unassisted natural apprehension, can be made known only by divine revelation, and is made known in a manner and at a time appointed by God, and to those only who are illumined by His Spirit. In the ordinary sense a "mystery" implies knowledge withheld; its Scriptural significance is truth revealed. Hence the terms especially associated with the subject are "made known," "manifested," "revealed," "preached," "understand," "dispensation." The definition given above may be best illustrated by the following passage: "the mystery which hath been hid from all ages and generations: but now hath it been manifested to His saints" (Col. 1:26, RV). "It is used of: "(a) spiritual truth generally, as revealed in the gospel, 1 Cor. 13:2; 14:2. Among the ancient Greeks 'the mysteries' were religious rites and ceremonies practiced by secret societies into which any one who so desired might be received. Those who were initiated into these 'mysteries' became possessors of certain knowledge, which was not imparted to the uninitiated, and were called 'the perfected,' cf. 1 Cor. 2:6-16 where the Apostle has these 'mysteries' in mind and presents the gospel in contrast thereto; here 'the perfected' are, of course the believers, who alone can perceive the things revealed; (b) Christ, who is God Himself revealed under the conditions of human life, Col. 2:2; 4:3, and submitting even to death, 1 Cor. 2:1 [in some mss., for *marturion*, testimony], 7, but raised from among the dead, 1 Tim. 3:16, that the will of God to coordinate the universe in Him, and subject it to Him, might in due time be accomplished, Eph. 1:9 (cf. Rev. 10:7), as is declared in the gospel, Rom. 16:25; Eph. 6:19; (c) the Church, which is Christ's Body, i.e., the union of redeemed men with God in Christ, Eph. 5:32; (d) the rapture into the presence of Christ of those members of the Church which is His Body who shall be alive on the earth at His Parousia, 1 Cor. 15:51; (e) the operation of those hidden forces that either retard or accelerate the Kingdom of Heaven (i.e., of God), **Matt. 13:11**; Mark 4:11; (f) the cause of the present condition of Israel, Rom. 11:25; (g) the spirit of disobedience to God, 2 Thess. 2:7; Rev. 17:5, 7, cf. Eph. 2:2." To these may be added (h) the seven local churches, and their angels, seen in symbolism, Rev. 1:20; (i) the ways of God in grace, Eph. 3:9. The word is used in a comprehensive way in 1 Cor. 4:1.

Them E.g., **Matt. 13:11**. Regarding *allelon*, "of one another," and its other forms, the RV substitutes "one another" for the KJV "themselves" in Mark 8:16; 9:34; Luke 4:36; John 6:52; 11:56; 16:17; 19:24; Acts 26:31; 28:4; Rom. 2:15, but adheres to the rendering "themselves" in Mark 15:31; Acts 4:15; 28:25.

13:12 For whosoever hath, to him shall be given, and he shall have more abundance: but whosoever hath not, from him shall be taken away even that he hath.

Abundance *see* Exceed at *Matthew 5:20*.

13:13 Therefore speak I to them in parables: because they seeing see not; and hearing they hear not, neither do they understand.

Seeing *see* Seeth at *Matthew 6:4*.

See *blepo* (991), is also used of (a) bodily and (b) mental vision, (a) "to perceive," e.g., **Matt. 13:13**; (b) "to take heed," e.g., Mark 13:23, 33; it indicates greater vividness than *horao*, expressing a more intent, earnest contemplation; in Luke 6:41, of "beholding" the mote in a brother's eye; Luke 24:12, of "beholding" the linen clothes in the empty tomb; Acts 1:9, of the gaze of the disciples when the Lord ascended. The greater earnestness is sometimes brought out by the rendering "regardest," **Matt. 22:16**.

Understand *suniemi* (4920), primarily, "to bring or set together," is used metaphorically of "perceiving, understanding, uniting" (*sun*), so to speak, the perception with what is perceived, e.g., **Matt. 13:13-15, 19, 23, 51; 15:10; 16:12; 17:13**, and similar passages in Mark and Luke; Acts 7:25 (twice); 28:26, 27; in Rom. 3:11, the present participle, with the article, is used as a noun, lit., "there is not the understanding (one)," in a moral and spiritual sense; Rom. 15:21; 2 Cor. 10:12, RV, "are (without) understanding," KJV, "are (not) wise"; Eph. 5:17, RV, "understand."

13:14 And in them is fulfilled the prophecy of Esaias, which saith, By hearing ye shall hear, and shall not understand; and seeing ye shall see, and shall not perceive:

Fulfilled *anapleroo* (378), "to fill up, fill completely," is used (a) of Isaiah's prophecy of Israel's rejection of God, fulfilled in the rejection

"Wherever God rules over the human heart as King, there is the kingdom of God established."

PAUL W. HARRISON

of His Son, **Matt. 13:14**; (b) of the status of a person in a church, RV, "filleth the place," for KJV, "occupieth the room," 1 Cor. 14:16; (c) of an adequate supply of service, 1 Cor. 16:17, "supplied"; Phil. 2:30, "to supply"; (d) of sins, 1 Thess. 2:16; (e) of the law of Christ; Gal. 6:2.

Prophecy *propheteia* (4394), signifies "the speaking forth of the mind and counsel of God" (*pro*, "forth," *phemi*, "to speak"); in the NT it is used (a) of the gift, e.g., Rom. 12:6; 1 Cor. 12:10; 13:2; (b) either of the exercise of the gift or of that which is "prophesied," e.g., **Matt. 13:14**; 1 Cor. 13:8; 14:6, 22 and 1 Thess. 5:20, "prophesying (s)"; 1 Tim. 1.18; 4:14; 2 Pet. 1:20, 21; Rev. 1:3; 11:6; 19:10; 22:7, 10, 18, 19. "Though much of OT prophecy was purely predictive, see Micah 5:2, e.g., and cf. John 11:51, prophecy is not necessarily, nor even primarily, fore-telling. It is the declaration of that which cannot be known by natural means, **Matt. 26:68**, it is the forth-telling of the will of God, whether with reference to the past, the present, or the future, see Gen. 20:7; Deut. 18:18; Rev. 10:11; 11:3."

Hearing, Hear *see* Fame at *Matthew 4:24*.

Seeing, See *see* Seeth at *Matthew 6:4*.

Perceive *eidon* (3708), (akin to *oida*, "to know"), an aorist form used to supply that tense of *horao*, "to see," is translated "to perceive" in **Matt. 13:14**; Mark 4:12; Acts 28:26; in Luke 9:47, KJV (RV, "saw"); in Acts 14:9, KJV, "perceiving" (RV, "seeing").

13:15 For this people's heart is waxed gross, and *their* ears are dull of hearing, and their eyes they have closed; lest at any time they should see with *their* eyes, and hear with *their* ears, and should understand with *their* heart, and should be converted, and I should heal them.

Heart *see Matthew 5:28*.

Gross *pachuno* (3975), from *pachus*, "thick," signifies "to thicken, fatten"; in the passive voice, "to grow fat"; metaphorically said of the heart, to wax gross or dull, **Matt. 13:15**; Acts 28:27.

Ears *see* Ear at *Matthew 10:27*.

Dull of hearing *bareos* (917), "heavily, with difficulty" (*barus*, "heavy"), is used with *akouo*, "to hear," in **Matt. 13:15**, and Acts 28:27 (from Isa. 6:10), lit., "to hear heavily, to be dull of hearing." In the Sept., Gen. 31:35 (lit., "bear it not heavily"); Isa. 6:10.

Eyes *see* Eye at *Matthew 5:38*.

Closed *kammuo* (2576), derived by syncope (i.e., shortening and assimilation of *t* to *m*) from *katamuo*, i.e., *kata*, "down," and *muo*, from a root *mu-*, pronounced by closing the lips, denotes "to close down"; hence, "to shut the eyes," **Matt. 13:15** and Acts 28:27, in each place of the obstinacy of Jews in their opposition to the gospel.

Lest *see Matthew 4:6*.

Converted *epistrepho* (1994), "to turn about, turn towards," is used transitively, and so rendered "convert" (of causing a person to turn) in Jas. 5:19-20. Elsewhere, where the KJV translates this verb, either in the middle voice and intransitive use, or the passive, the RV adheres to the middle voice significance, and translates by "turn again," **Matt. 13:15**; Mark 4:12; Luke 22:32; Acts 3:19; 28:27.

Heal *iaomai* (4390), "to heal," is used (a) of physical treatment 22 times; in Mark 5:28, KJV, "made whole," RV, "healed"; so in Acts 9:34; (b) figuratively, of spiritual "healing," **Matt. 13:15**; John 12:40; Acts 28:27; Heb. 12:13; 1 Pet. 2:24; possibly, Jas. 5:16 includes both (a) and (b); some mss. have the word, with sense (b), in Luke 4:18. Apart from this last, Luke, the physician, uses the word fifteen times.

13:16 But blessed *are* your eyes, for they see: and your ears, for they hear.

Ears *see* Ear at *Matthew 10:27*.

13:17 For verily I say unto you, That many prophets and righteous *men* have desired to see *those things* which ye see, and have not seen *them*; and to hear *those things* which ye hear, and have not heard *them*.

Many *see Matthew 3:7*.

Desired *see* Lust at *Matthew 5:28*.

13:18-19 Hear ye therefore the parable of the sower.

When any one heareth the word of the kingdom, and understandeth *it* not, then cometh the wicked *one*, and catcheth away that which was sown in his heart. This is he which received seed by the way side.

Understandeth *see* Understand at *Matthew 13:13*.

Wicked *see Matthew 12:45. See also* Evil at *Matthew 5:37.*

Catcheth *harpazo* (726), "to snatch," is translated "to snatch" in the RV only, in **Matt. 13:19**, KJV, "catcheth away"; John 10:12, KJV, "catcheth"; 10:28, 29, KJV, "pluck"; Jude 23, KJV, "pulling." *See also* **Take ... by force** at *Matthew 11:12.*

Sown *see* **Sower, Sow** at *Matthew 13:3.*

Received In the KJV of **Matt. 13:19, 20, 22, 23**, *speiro*, "to sow seed," is translated "received seed".

Seed *sperma* (4690), akin to *speiro*, "to sow" (Eng., "sperm," "spermatic," etc.), has the following usages, (a) agricultural and botanical, e.g., **Matt. 13:24, 27, 32** (for the KJV of vv. **19, 20, 22, 23**); 1 Cor. 15:38; 2 Cor. 9:10; (b) physiological, Heb. 11:11; (c) metaphorical and by metonymy for "offspring, posterity," (1) of natural offspring, e.g., **Matt. 22:24, 25**, RV, "seed" (KJV, "issue"); John 7:42; 8:33, 37; Acts 3:25; Rom. 1:3; 4:13, 16, 18; 9:7 (twice), 8, 29; 11:1; 2 Cor. 11:22; Heb. 2:16; 11:18; Rev. 12:17; Gal. 3:16, 19, 29; in the 16th v., "He saith not, And to seeds, as of many; but as of one, And to thy seed, which is Christ," quoted from the Sept. of Gen. 13:15 and 17:7, 8, there is especial stress on the word "seed," as referring to an individual (here, Christ) in fulfillment of the promises to Abraham – a unique use of the singular.

13:20 But he that received the seed into stony places, the same is he that heareth the word, and anon with joy receiveth it;

Received, Receiveth *see* Receiveth at Matthew *7:8.*

Seed *see Matthew 13:19.*

Stony *see Matthew 13:5.*

Word *logos* (3056), denotes (I) "the expression of thought" – not the mere name of an object – (a) as embodying a conception or idea, e.g., Luke 7:7; 1 Cor. 14:9, 19; (b) a saying or statement, (1) by God, e.g., John 15:25; Rom. 9:9; 9:28, RV, "word" (KJV, "work"); Gal. 5:14; Heb. 4:12; (2) by Christ, e.g., **Matt. 24:35** (plur.); John 2:22; 4:41; 14:23 (plur.); 15:20. In connection with (1) and (2) the phrase "the word of the Lord," i.e., the revealed will of God (very frequent in the OT), is used of a direct revelation given by Christ, 1 Thess. 4:15; of the gospel, Acts 8:25; 13:49; 15:35, 36; 16:32; 19:10; 1 Thess. 1:8; 2 Thess. 3:1; in this respect it is the message from the Lord, delivered with His authority and made effective by His power (cf. Acts 10:36); for other instances relating to the gospel see Acts 13:26; 14:3; 15:7; 1 Cor. 1:18, RV; 2 Cor. 2:17; 4:2; 5:19; 6:7; Gal. 6:6; Eph. 1:13; Phil. 2:16; Col. 1:5; Heb. 5:13; sometimes it is used as the sum of God's utterances, e.g., Mark 7:13; John 10:35; Rev. 1:2, 9; (c) discourse, speech, of instruction, etc., e.g., Acts 2:40; 1 Cor. 2:13; 12:8; 2 Cor. 1:18; 1 Thess. 1:5; 2 Thess. 2:15; Heb. 6:1, RV, marg.; doctrine, e.g., **Matt. 13:20**; Col. 3:16; 1 Tim. 4:6; 2 Tim. 1:13; Titus 1:9; 1 John 2:7; (II) "The Personal Word," a title of the Son of God.

Anon This is the KJV rendering of *euthus*, in **Matt. 13:20** and Mark 1:30, RV, "straightway."

13:21 Yet hath he not root in himself, but dureth for a while: for when tribulation or persecution ariseth because of the word, by and by he is offended.

Root *see Matthew 3:10.*

While In **Matt. 13:21**, *proskairos estin*, lit., "is for a season," is rendered "dureth (RV, endureth) for a while."

Tribulation *thlipsis* (2347), primarily means "a pressing, pressure," anything which burdens the spirit. In two passages in Paul's Epistles it is used of future retribution, in the way of "affliction," Rom. 2:9; 2 Thess. 1:6. In **Matt. 24:9**, the KJV renders it as a verb, "to be afflicted," (RV, "unto tribulation"). It is coupled with *stenochoria*, "anguish," in Rom. 2:9; 8:35; with *ananke*, "distress," 1 Thess. 3:7; with *diogmos*, "persecution," **Matt. 13:21**; Mark 4:17; 2 Thess. 1:4. It is used of the calamities of war, **Matt. 24:21, 29**; Mark 13:19, 24; of want, 2 Cor. 8:13, lit., "distress for you"; Phil. 4:14 (cf. 1:16); Jas. 1:27; of the distress of woman in childbirth, John 16:21; of persecution, Acts 11:19; 14:22; 20:23; 1 Thess. 3:3, 7; Heb. 10:33; Rev. 2:10; 7:14; of the "afflictions" of Christ, from which (His vicarious sufferings apart) his followers must not shrink, whether sufferings of body or mind, Col. 1:24; of sufferings in general, 1 Cor. 7:28; 1 Thess. 1:6, etc.

Persecution *diogmos* (1375), occurs in **Matt. 13:21**; Mark 4:17; 10:30; Acts 8:1; 13:50; Rom. 8:35; 2 Cor. 12:10; 2 Thess. 1:4; 2 Tim. 3:11, twice. In the Sept., Prov. 11:19; Lam. 3:19.

Ariseth *see* **Arose** at *Matthew 8:24.*

By The phrase "by and by" in the KJV is in several places misleading. The three words *exautes*, Mark 6:25, *euthus*, **Matt. 13:21**, and *eutheos*, Luke 17:7; 21:9, mean "straightway," "immediately."

Offended *see Matthew 13:57.*

13:22 He also that received seed among the thorns is he that heareth the word; and the care of this world, and the deceitfulness of riches, choke the word, and he becometh unfruitful.

Received *see Matthew 13:19.*

Seed *see Matthew 13:19.*

Thorns *see Matthew 7:16.*

Care *merimna* (3308), probably connected with *merizo,* "to draw in different directions, distract," hence signifies "that which causes this, a care, especially an anxious care," **Matt. 13:22**; Mark 4:19; Luke 8:14; 21:34; 2 Cor. 11:28 (RV, "anxiety for"), 1 Pet. 5:7 (RV, "anxiety").

World *aion* (165), "an age, a period of time," marked in the NT usage by spiritual or moral characteristics, is sometimes translated "world"; the RV marg. always has "age." The following are details concerning the world in this respect; its cares, **Matt. 13:22**; its sons, Luke 16:8; 20:34; its rulers, 1 Cor. 2:6, 8; its wisdom, 1 Cor. 1:20; 2:6; 3:18; its fashion, Rom. 12:2; its character, Gal. 1:4; its god, 2 Cor. 4:4. The phrase "the end of the world" should be rendered "the end of the age," in most places; in 1 Cor. 10:11, KJV, "the ends (*tele*) of the world," RV, "the ends of the ages," probably signifies the fulfillment of the divine purposes concerning the ages in regard to the church. In Heb. 11:3 [lit., "the ages (have been prepared)"] the word indicates all that the successive periods contain; cf. 1:2. *Aion* is always to be distinguished from *kosmos,* even where the two seem to express the same idea, e.g., 1 Cor. 3.18, *aion,* v. 19, *kosmos;* the two are used together in Eph. 2:2, lit., "the age of this world."

Deceitfulness *apate* (539), "deceit or deceitfulness" (akin to *apatao,* "to cheat, deceive, beguile"), that which gives a false impression, whether by appearance, statement or influence, is said of riches, **Matt. 13:22**; Mark 4:19; of sin, Heb. 3:13. The phrase in Eph. 4:22, "deceitful lusts," KJV, "lusts of deceit," RV, signifies lusts excited by "deceit," of which "deceit" is the source of strength, not lusts "deceitful" in themselves. In 2 Thess. 2:10, "all deceit of unrighteousness," RV, signifies all manner of unscrupulous words and deeds designed to "deceive" (see Rev. 13:13-15). In Col. 2:8, "vain deceit" suggests that "deceit" is void of anything profitable.

Riches *ploutos* (4149), is used in the singular (I) of material "riches," used evilly, **Matt. 13:22**: Mark 4:19; Luke 8:14; 1 Tim. 6:17; Jas. 5:2; Rev. 18:17; (II) of spiritual and moral "riches," (a) possessed by God and exercised towards men, Rom. 2:4, "of His goodness and forbearance and longsuffering"; 9:23 and Eph. 3:16, "of His glory" (i.e., of its manifestation in grace towards believers); Rom. 11:33, of His wisdom and knowledge; Eph. 1:7 and 2:7, "of His grace"; 1:18, "of the glory of His inheritance in the saints"; 3:8, "of Christ"; Phil. 4:19, "in glory in Christ Jesus," RV; Col. 1:27, "of the glory of this mystery ... Christ in you, the hope of glory"; (b) to be ascribed to Christ, Rev. 5:12; (c) of the effects of the gospel upon the Gentiles, Rom. 11:12 (twice); (d) of the full assurance of understanding in regard to the mystery of God, even Christ, Col. 2:2, RV; (e) of the liberality of the churches of Macedonia, 2 Cor. 8:2 (where "the riches" stands for the spiritual and moral value of their liberality); (f) of "the reproach of Christ" in contrast to this world's treasures, Heb. 11:26.

Choke *sumpnigo* (4846), gives the suggestion of "choking together" (*sun,* "with"), i.e., by crowding, **Matt. 13:22**; Mark 4:7, 19; Luke 8:14. It is used in Luke 8:42, of the crowd that thronged the Lord, almost, so to speak, to suffocation.

Unfruitful *akarpos* (175), "unfruitful," is used figuratively (a) of "the word of the Kingdom," rendered "unfruitful" in the case of those influenced by the cares of the world and the deceitfulness of riches, **Matt. 13:22**; Mark 4:19; (b) of the understanding of one praying with a "tongue," which effected no profit to the church without an interpretation of it, 1 Cor. 14:14; (c) of the works of darkness, Eph. 5:11; (d) of believers who fail "to maintain good works," indicating the earning of one's living so as to do good works to others, Titus 3:14; of the effects of failing to supply in one's faith the qualities of virtue, knowledge, temperance, patience, godliness, love of the brethren, and love, 2 Pet. 1:8. In Jude 12 it is rendered "without fruit," of ungodly men, who oppose the gospel while pretending to uphold it, depicted as "autumn trees." In the Sept., Jer. 2:6.

13:23 But he that received seed into the good ground is he that heareth the word, and understandeth *it;* which also beareth fruit, and bringeth forth, some an hundredfold, some sixty, some thirty.

Received *see Matthew 13:19.*

Seed *see Matthew 13:19.*

Good *see Matthew 3:10.*

Ground *see* Earth at *Matthew 5:18.*

Understandeth *see* Understand at *Matthew 13:13.*

Fruit *karpophoreo* (2592), "to bear or bring forth fruit," is used (a) in the natural sense, of the "fruit of the earth," Mark 4:28; (b) metaphorically, of conduct, or that which takes effect in conduct, **Matt. 13:23**;

Mark 4:20; Luke 8:15; Rom. 7:4, 5 (the latter, of evil "fruit," borne "unto death," of activities resulting from a state of alienation from God); Col. 1:6 in the middle voice; Col. 1:10.

Hundredfold *see Matthew 13:8.*

Sixty *see* Sixtyfold at *Matthew 13:8.*

Thirty *see* Thirtyfold at *Matthew 13:8.*

13:24 Another parable put he forth unto them, saying, The kingdom of heaven is likened unto a man which sowed good seed in his field:

Put *paratithemi* (3908), "to set before" (*para*, "beside" or "before"), is rendered "to put forth" (of a parable) in **Matt. 13:24, 31**, KJV (RV, "set before").

Likened unto *see* Like unto at *Matthew 6:8.*

Seed *see Matthew 13:19.*

13:25 But while men slept, his enemy came and sowed tares among the wheat, and went his way.

While In Acts 27:33 and Heb. 3:13 *achri* (or *achris*) followed by *hou*, the genitive case of the relative pronoun *hos*, lit., "until which," is rendered "while"; cf. *en ho*, in Mark 2:19; Luke 5:34; John 5:7; *en to*, in Luke 1:21, RV, "while"; in Heb. 3:15, "while it is said," is, lit., "in the being said" (*en*, with the article and the pres. infin., passive of *lego*); so, e.g., in **Matt. 13:25**.

Enemy *see Matthew 5:43.*

Tares *zizanion* (2215), is a kind of darnel, the commonest of the four species, being the bearded, growing in the grain fields, as tall as wheat and barley, and resembling wheat in appearance. It was credited among the Jews with being degenerate wheat. The rabbis called it "bastard." The seeds are poisonous to man and herbivorous animals, producing sleepiness, nausea, convulsions and even death (they are harmless to poultry). The plants can be separated out, but the custom, as in the parable, is to leave the cleaning out till near the time of harvest, **Matt. 13:25-27, 29, 30, 36, 38, 40**. The Lord describes the tares as "the sons of the evil *one*"; false teachings are indissociable from their propagandists. For the Lord's reference to the Kingdom.

Among *mesos* (3319), an adjective denoting "middle, in the middle or midst," is used in the following, in which the English requires a phrase, and the adjectival rendering must be avoided: Luke 22:55, "Peter sat in the midst of them," lit., "a middle one of (them)"; Luke 23:45, of the rending of the veil "in the midst"; here the adjective idiomatically belongs to the verb "was rent," and is not to be taken literally, as if it meant "the middle veil"; John 1:26, "in the midst of you (standeth One)," RV (lit., "a middle One"); Acts 1:18, where the necessity of avoiding the lit. rendering is obvious. Cf. the phrases "at midday," "at midnight." *Mesos* is used adverbially, in prepositional phrases, (a) *ana m.*, e.g., 1 Cor. 6:5, "between"; **Matt. 13:25**, "among"; Rev. 7:17, "in the midst"; (b) *dia m.*, e.g., Luke 4:30; 17:11, "through the midst"; (c) *en m.*, Luke 10:3, RV, "in the midst," KJV, "among"; so 22:27; 1 Thess. 2:7; with the article after *en*, e.g., **Matt. 14:6**, RV, "in the midst," KJV, "before"; (d) *eis m.*, Mark 14:60, "in the midst"; with the article, e.g., Mark 3:3, "forth" (lit., "into the midst"); (e) *ek m.*, "out of the way," lit., "out of the midst," Col. 2:14; 2 Thess. 2:7, where, however, removal is not necessarily in view; there is no accompanying verb signifying removal, as in each of the other occurrences of the phrase; with the article, e.g., 1 Cor. 5:2; 2 Cor. 6:17; (f) *kata m.*, Acts 27:27, "about mid(night)."

Wheat *see Matthew 3:12.*

Way *aperchomai*, "to go away," is rendered "to go one's way," e.g., **Matt. 13:25; 20:4**; Mark 11:4; 12:12; Luke 19:32; John 11:46; Acts 9:17; Jas. 1:24.

13:26 But when the blade was sprung up, and brought forth fruit, then appeared the tares also.

Blade *see* Grass at *Matthew 6:30.*

Sprung *blastano* (985), "to sprout," is rendered "to spring up" in **Matt. 13:26**, of tare blades, and Mark 4:27, of seed.

Appeared *see Matthew 1:20.*

13:27 So the servants of the householder came and said unto him, Sir, didst not thou sow good seed in thy field? from whence then hath it tares?

Householder *see* Master of the house at *Matthew 10:25.*

Sir *see* Lord at *Matthew 1:22.*

Seed *see Matthew 13:19.*

13:28 He said unto them, An enemy hath done this. The servants said unto him, Wilt thou then that we go and gather them up?

Enemy *see Matthew 5:43.*

Gather *see Matthew 7:16.*

13:29 But he said, Nay; lest while ye gather up the tares,

ye root up also the wheat with them.

Said *phemi* (5346), "to declare, say," (a) is frequently used in quoting the words of another, e.g., **Matt. 13:29; 26:61**; (b) is interjected into the recorded words, e.g., Acts 23:35; (c) is used impersonally, 2 Cor. 10:10.

Nay *see Matthew 5:37.*

Gather *see Matthew 7:16.*

Tares *see Matthew 13:25.*

Root *ekrizoo* (1610), "to pluck up by the roots" (*ek*, "out," *rhiza*, "a root"), is so translated in Jude 12 (figuratively), and in the KJV in Luke 17:6, RV, "rooted up"; "root up," **Matt. 13:29**; "shall be rooted up," **15:13**.

Wheat *see Matthew 3:12.*

13:30 Let both grow together until the harvest: and in the time of harvest I will say to the reapers, Gather ye together first the tares, and bind them in bundles to burn them: but gather the wheat into my barn.

Let *see Matthew 5:40.*

Grow *sunauxano* (4885), "to grow together," is in **Matt. 13:30**.

Harvest *see Matthew 9:37.*

Time *see Matthew 8:29.*

Reapers *theristes* (2327), "a reaper" (akin to *therizo*), is used of angels in **Matt. 13:30, 39**. *See also* Reap at *Matthew 6:26.*

Gather *see* Gathered at *Matthew 2:4.*

Tares *see Matthew 13:25.*

Bundles *desme* (1197), from *deo*, "to bind" (similarly, Eng. "bundle" is akin to "bind"), is used in **Matt. 13:30**.

Burn *see Matthew 3:12.*

Barn *see* Garner at *Matthew 3:12.*

13:31 Another parable put he forth unto them, saying, The kingdom of heaven is like to a grain of mustard seed, which a man took, and sowed in his field:

Put *see Matthew 13:24.*

Like to *see* Like unto at *Matthew 11:16.*

Grain *kokkos* (2848), denotes "a grain," **Matt. 13:31; 17:20**; Mark 4:31; Luke 13:19; 17:6; John 12:24 (KJV, "corn"); 1 Cor. 15:37 (where the RV has "a ... grain," to distinguish it from "grain" in general).

Mustard *sinapi* (4615), a word of Egyptian origin, is translated "mustard seed" in the NT. "The conditions to be fulfilled by the mustard are that it should be a familiar plant, with a very small seed, **Matt. 17:20**; Luke 17:6, sown in the earth, growing larger than garden herbs, **Matt. 13:31**, having large branches, Mark 4:31, ... attractive to birds, Luke 13:19 [RV, '(became) a tree']. The cultivated mustard is *sinapis nigra*. The seed is well known for its minuteness. The mustards are annuals, reproduced with extraordinary rapidity ... In fat soil they often attain a height of 10 or 12 feet, and have branches which attract passing birds" (A. E. Post, in *Hastings' Bib. Dic.*).

13:32 Which indeed is the least of all seeds: but when it is grown, it is the greatest among herbs, and becometh a tree, so that the birds of the air come and lodge in the branches thereof.

Indeed *see Matthew 3:11.*

Least *see Matthew 11:11.*

Seeds *see* Seed at *Matthew 13:19.*

Grown *see* Grow at *Matthew 6:28.*

Greatest *meizon* (3187), is sometimes translated "greatest," where the RV corrects the KJV, "greatest" to "greater" (**Matt. 13:32** and Luke 22:26), the RV itself has "greatest" for this comparative in the following, and relegates "greater" to the margin, **Matt. 18:1, 4; 23:11**; Mark 9:34; Luke 9:46; 22:24. *See also* Greater at *Matthew 11:11.*

Herbs *lachanon* (3001), denotes "a garden herb, a vegetable" (from *lachaino*, "to dig"), in contrast to wild plants, **Matt. 13:32**; Mark 4:32; Luke 11:42; Rom. 14:2.

Tree *see Matthew 7:17.*

Birds *see* Fowls at *Matthew 6:26.*

Nest *see* Nests at *Matthew 8:20.*

Lodge *kataskenoo* (2681), "to pitch one's tent" (*kata*, "down," *skene*, "a tent"), is rendered "to lodge," of birds, in **Matt. 13:32**; Mark 4:32; Luke 13:19. In Acts 2:26, it is used of the body of the Lord in the tomb, as dwelling in hope, RV, "shall dwell" (marg., "tabernacle"), KJV, "shall rest." Cf. *katoskenosis*, "a roosting place."

Branches *klados* (2798), from *klao*, "to break" (cf. *klasma*, "a broken piece"), properly a young tender shoot, "broken off" for grafting, is used for any kind of branch, **Matt. 13:32; 21:8; 24:32**; Mark 4:32; 13:28; Luke 13:19; the descendants of Israel, Rom. 11:16-19, 21.

13:33 Another parable spake he unto them; The kingdom of heaven is like unto leaven, which a woman took, and hid in three measures of meal, till the whole was leavened.

Like unto *see Matthew 11:16.*

Leaven *zume* (2219), "leaven, sour dough, in a high state of fermentation," was used in general in making bread. It required time to fulfill the process. Hence, when food was required at short notice, unleavened cakes were used, e.g., Gen. 18:6; 19:3; Exod. 12:8. The Israelites were forbidden to use "leaven" for seven days at the time of Passover, that they might be reminded that the Lord brought them out of Egypt "in haste," Deut. 16:3, with Exod. 12:11; the unleavened bread, insipid in taste, reminding them, too, of their afflictions, and of the need of self-judgment, is called "the bread of affliction." "Leaven" was forbidden in all offerings to the Lord by fire, Lev. 2:11; 6:17. Being bred of corruption and spreading through the mass of that in which it is mixed, and therefore symbolizing the pervasive character of evil, "leaven" was utterly inconsistent in offerings which typified the propitiatory sacrifice of Christ. In the OT "leaven" is not used in a metaphorical sense. In the NT it is used (a) metaphorically (1) of corrupt doctrine, **Matt. 13:33** and Luke 13:21, of error as mixed with the truth (there is no valid reason for regarding the symbol here differently from its application elsewhere in the NT); **Matt. 16:6, 11**; Mark 8:15 (1st part); Luke 12:1; that the kingdom of heaven is likened to "leaven," does not mean that the kingdom is "leaven." The same statement, as made in other parables, shows that it is the whole parable which constitutes the similitude of the kingdom; the history of Christendom confirms the fact that the pure meal of the doctrine of Christ has been adulterated with error; (2) of corrupt practices, Mark 8:15 (2nd part), the reference to the Herodians being especially applied to their irreligion; 1 Cor. 5:7, 8; (b) literally in **Matt. 16:12**, and in the general statements in 1 Cor. 5:6 and Gal. 5:9, where the implied applications are to corrupt practice and corrupt doctrine respectively.

Hid *enkrupto* (1470), "to hide in anything," is used in **Matt. 13:33**, of leaven "hidden" in meal.

Measures *saton* (4568), is a Hebrew dry measure (Heb., *seah*), about a peck and a half, **Matt. 13:33**; Luke 13:21; "three measures" would be the quantity for a baking (cf. Gen. 18:6; Judg. 6:19; 1 Sam. 1:24; the "ephah" of the last two passages was equal to three *sata*).

Meal *aleuron* (224), "meal" (akin to *aleuo*, "to grind," and therefore, lit., "what is ground"), occurs in **Matt. 13:33**; Luke 13:21.

Whole *holos* (3650), "whole," is rendered "altogether" in John 9:34. It is sometimes subjoined to an adjective or a verb, as in this case, to show that the idea conveyed by the adjective or verb belongs to the whole person or thing referred to. So here, lit., "thou wast altogether (i.e., completely) born in sins." Cf. **Matt. 13:33**, RV; Luke 11:36; 13:21; John 13:10, RV (rendered "every whit"). *See also Matthew 5:29.*

Leavened *zumoo* (2220), signifies "to leaven, to act as leaven," passive voice in **Matt. 13:33** and Luke 13:21; active voice in 1 Cor. 5:6 and Gal. 5:9.

13:34 All these things spake Jesus unto the multitude in parables; and without a parable spake he not unto them:

Parables *see Matthew 13:3.*

13:35 That it might be fulfilled which was spoken by the prophet, saying, I will open my mouth in parables; I will utter things which have been kept secret from the foundation of the world.

Fulfilled *see Matthew 1:22.*

Spoken *see Matthew 1:22.*

Open *see* **Opened** at *Matthew 2:11.*

Mouth *see Matthew 12:34.*

Utter *ereugomai* (2044), primarily, "to spit or spue out," or, of oxen, "to bellow, roar," hence, "to speak aloud, utter," occurs in **Matt. 13:35**. This affords an example of the tendency for certain words to become softened in force in late Greek.

Secret *krupto* (2928), "to hide," is translated "secretly" in John 19:38 [perfect participle, passive voice, lit., "(but) having been hidden"], referring to Nicodemus as having been a "secret" disciple of Christ; in **Matt. 13:35**, KJV, it is translated "kept secret" (RV, "hidden"). *See also* **Hid** at *Matthew 5:14.*

Foundation *katabole* (2602), lit., "a casting down," is used (a) of "conceiving seed," Heb. 11:11; (b) of "a foundation," as that which is laid down, or in the sense of founding; metaphorically, of "the foundation of the world"; in this respect two phrases are used, (1) "from the foundation of the world," **Matt. 25:34** (in the most authentic mss. in **13:35** there is no phrase representing "of the world"); Luke 11:50; Heb. 4:3; 9:26; Rev. 13:8; 17:8; (2) "before the foundation of the world," John 17:24; Eph. 1:4; 1 Pet. 1:20. The latter phrase looks back to the past eternity.

World *see Matthew 5:14.*

13:36 Then Jesus sent the multitude away, and went into the house: and his disciples came unto him, saying, Declare unto us the parable of the tares of the field.

Sent In **Matt. 13:36**, KJV, *aphiemi*, "to leave," is translated "He sent

... away" (RV, "He left"); so in Mark 4:36, KJV, "they had sent away," RV, "leaving." *See also* **Leaveth** at *Matthew 4:11.*

Declare *phrazo* (5419), "to declare," occurs in **Matt. 15:15** and (in some texts) in **13:36** (as KJV).

Tares *see Matthew 13:25.*

13:37-38 He answered and said unto them, He that soweth the good seed is the Son of man;
The field is the world; the good seed are the children of the kingdom; but the tares are the children of the wicked *one*;

Children *see Matthew 5:9.*

Tares *see Matthew 13:25.*

Wicked *see Matthew 12:45. See also* Evil at *Matthew 5:37.*

13:39 The enemy that sowed them is the devil; the harvest is the end of the world; and the reapers are the angels.

Enemy *see Matthew 5:43.*

Harvest *see Matthew 9:37.*

End *sunteleia* (4930), signifies "a bringing to completion together" (*sun* "with," *teleo*, "to complete," akin to *telos*), marking the "completion" or consummation of the various parts of a scheme. In **Matt. 13:39-40, 49; 24:3; 28:20**, the rendering "the end of the world" (KJV and RV, text) is misleading; the RV marg., "the consummation of the age," is correct. The word does not denote a termination, but the heading up of events to the appointed climax. *Aion* is not the world, but a period or epoch or era in which events take place. In Heb. 9:26, the word translated "world" (KJV) is in the plural, and the phrase is "the consummation of the ages." It was at the heading up of all the various epochs appointed by divine counsels that Christ was manifested (i.e., in His Incarnation) "to put away sin by the sacrifice of Himself."

Reapers *see Matthew 13:30.*

13:40 As therefore the tares are gathered and burned in the fire; so shall it be in the end of this world.

Tares *see Matthew 13:25.*

Gathered *see* Gather at *Matthew 7:16.*

Burned *see* Burn at *Matthew 3:12.*

13:41 The Son of man shall send forth his angels, and they shall gather out of his kingdom all things that offend, and them which do iniquity;

Son *see Matthew 3:17.*

Gather *see Matthew 7:16.*

Kingdom *see* Kingdoms at *Matthew 4:8.*

Things that offend *skandalon* (4625), originally was "the name of the part of a trap to which the bait is attached, hence, the trap or snare itself, as in Rom. 11:9, RV, 'stumblingblock,' quoted from Psa. 69:22, and in Rev. 2:14, for Balaam's device was rather a trap for Israel than a stumblingblock to them, and in **Matt. 16:23**, for in Peter's words the Lord perceived a snare laid for Him by Satan. "In NT *skandalon* is always used metaphorically, and ordinarily of anything that arouses prejudice, or becomes a hindrance to others, or causes them to fall by the way. Sometimes the hindrance is in itself good, and those stumbled by it are the wicked." Thus it is used (a) of Christ in Rom. 9:33, "(a rock) of offense"; so 1 Pet. 2:8; 1 Cor. 1:23 (KJV and RV, "stumblingblock"), and of His cross, Gal. 5:11 (RV, ditto); of the "table" provided by God for Israel, Rom. 11:9; (b) of that which is evil, e.g., **Matt. 13:41**, RV, "things that cause stumbling" (KJV, "things that offend"), lit., "all stumblingblocks"; **18:7**, RV, "occasions of stumbling" and "occasion"; Luke 17:1 (ditto); Rom. 14:13, RV, "an occasion of falling" (KJV, "an occasion to fall"), said of such a use of Christian liberty as proves a hindrance to another; 16:17, RV, "occasions of stumbling," said of the teaching of things contrary to sound doctrine; 1 John 2:10, "occasion of stumbling," of the absence of this in the case of one who loves his brother and thereby abides in the light. Love, then, is the best safeguard against the woes pronounced by the Lord upon those who cause others to stumble.

Iniquity *see Matthew 7:23.*

13:42 And shall cast them into a furnace of fire: there shall be wailing and gnashing of teeth.

Furnace *kaminos* (2575), "an oven, furnace, kiln" (whence Lat. *caminus*, Eng., chimney), used for smelting, or for burning earthenware, occurs in **Matt. 13:42, 50**; Rev. 1:15; 9:2.

Fire *see Matthew 3:11. See also* **Hell** at *Matthew 5:22.*

Wailing For *klauthmos*, rendered "wailing" in **Matt. 13:42, 50**, KJV. See also **Weeping** at *Matthew 2:18.*

Gnashing *see Matthew 8:12.*

Teeth *see* Tooth at *Matthew 5:38.*

13:43 Then shall the righteous shine forth as the sun in the kingdom of their Father. Who hath ears to hear, let him hear.

Shine *eklampo* (1584), "to shine forth," is used in **Matt. 13:43**, of the future shining "forth" of the righteous "in the Kingdom of their Father."

Sun *see Matthew 5:45.*

Kingdom *see* Kingdoms at *Matthew 4:8.*

Ears *see* Ear at *Matthew 10:27.*

13:44 Again, the kingdom of heaven is like unto treasure hid in a field; the which when a man hath found, he hideth, and for joy thereof goeth and selleth all that he hath, and buyeth that field.

Like unto *see Matthew 11:16.*

Treasure *see* Treasures at *Matthew 2:11.*

Hid *see Matthew 5:14.*

13:45 Again, the kingdom of heaven is like unto a merchant man, seeking goodly pearls:

Like unto *see Matthew 11:16.*

Merchant *emporos* (1713), denotes "a person on a journey" (*poros*, "a journey"), "a passenger on shipboard"; then, "a merchant," **Matt. 13:45**; Rev. 18:3, 11, 15, 23.

Seeking *see* Sought at *Matthew 2:20.*

Pearls *see Matthew 7:6.*

13:46 Who, when he had found one pearl of great price, went and sold all that he had, and bought it.

Pearl *see* Pearls at *Matthew 7:6.*

Price *polutimos* (4186), lit., "of great value," is used of a pearl, **Matt. 13:46**; of spikenard, John 12:3 (RV, "very precious," KJV "very costly"). The comparative *polutimo (v.l.io) teros*, "much more precious," is used in 1 Pet. 1:7.

Sold *piprasko* (4097), from an earlier form, *perao*, "to carry across the sea for the purpose of selling or to export," is used (a) literally, **Matt. 13:46**; **18:25**; **26:9**; Mark 14:5; John 12:5; Acts 2:45; 4:34; 5:4; (b) metaphorically, Rom. 7:14, "sold under sin," i.e., as fully under the domination of sin as a slave is under his master; the statement evinces an utter dissatisfaction with such a condition; it expresses, not the condemnation of the unregenerate state, but the evil of bondage to a corrupt nature, involving the futility of making use of the Law as a means of deliverance.

13:47 Again, the kingdom of heaven is like unto a net, that was cast into the sea, and gathered of every kind:

Like unto *see Matthew 11:16.*

Net *sagene* (4522), denotes "a dragnet, a seine"; two modes were employed with this, either by its being let down into the water and drawn together in a narrowing circle, and then into the boat, or as a semicircle drawn to the shore, **Matt. 13:47**. The Greek historian Herodotus uses the corresponding verb *sageneuo* of a device by which the Persians are said to have cleared a conquered island of its inhabitants.

Kind *genos* (1085), akin to *ginomai*, "to become," denotes (a) "a family," Acts 4:6, "kindred;" 7:13, RV, "race" (KJV, "kindred"); 13:26, "stock"; (b) "an offspring," Acts 17:28; Rev. 22:16; (c) "a nation, a race," Mark 7:26, RV, "race" (KJV, "nation"); Acts 4:36, RV "(a man of Cyprus) by race," KJV, "of the country (of Cyprus);" *genos* does not mean "a country;" the word here signifies "parentage" (Jews had settled in Cyprus from, or even before, the reign of Alexander the Great); 7:19, RV, "race" (KJV, "kindred"); 18:2, 24, RV, "by race" (KJV, "born"); 2 Cor. 11:26, "countrymen"; Gal. 1:14, RV, "countrymen" (KJV, "nation"); Phil. 3:5, "stock"; 1 Pet. 2:9, RV, "race" (KJV, "generation"); (d) "a kind, sort, class," **Matt. 13:47**, "kind"; in some mss. in **17:21**, KJV, "kind;" Mark 9:29, "kind"; 1 Cor. 12:10, 28, "kinds" (KJV, "diversities"); 14:10 (ditto).

13:48 Which, when it was full, they drew to shore, and sat down, and gathered the good into vessels, but cast the bad away.

Full *pleroo* (4137), denotes (I) "to make full, to fill to the full"; in the passive voice, "to be filled, made full"; it is used (1) of things: a net, **Matt. 13:48**; a building, John 12:3; Acts 2:2; a city, Acts 5:28; needs, Phil. 4:19, KJV "supply," RV, "fulfill"; metaphorically, of valleys, Luke 3:5; figuratively, of a measure of iniquity, **Matt. 23:32**; (2) of persons: (a) of the members of the church, the body of Christ, as filled by Him, Eph. 1:23 ("all things in all the members"); 4:10; in 3:19, of their being filled "into" (*eis*), RV, "unto," KJV, "with" (all the fullness of God); of their being "made full" in Him, Col. 2:10 (RV, for KJV, "complete"); (b) of Christ Himself: with wisdom, in the days of His flesh, Luke 2:40; with joy, in His return to the Father, Acts 2:28; (c) of believers: with the Spirit, Eph. 5:18; with joy, Acts 13:52; 2 Tim. 1:4; with joy and peace, Rom. 15:13; with knowledge, Rom. 15:14; with comfort, 2 Cor. 7:4; with the fruits of righteousness, Phil. 1:11 (Gk. "fruit"); with the knowledge of God's will, Col. 1:9; with abundance through material supplies by fellow believers, Phil. 4:18; (d) of the hearts of believers as the seat of emotion and volition, John 16:6 (sorrow); Acts 5:3 (deceitfulness); (e) of the unregenerate who refuse recognition of God, Rom. 1:29; (II) "to accomplish, complete, fulfill.

Drew *anabibazo* (307), a causal form of *anabaino*, "to go up," denotes, lit., "to make go up, cause to ascend" (*ana*, "up," *bibazo*, "to cause to mount"), hence, "to draw a boat up on land," **Matt. 13:48**.

Shore *see Matthew 13:2.*

Gathered *see* Gather at *Matthew 7:16.*

Good *see Matthew 3:10.*

Vessels *angos* (30), denotes "a jar" or "pail," **Matt. 13:48**, in the best texts. It is used, in an inscription, of a cinerary urn.

Bad *see* Corrupt at *Matthew 7:17.*

13:49 So shall it be at the end of the world: the angels shall come forth, and sever the wicked from among the just,

End *see Matthew 13:39.*

Sever *aphorizo* (873), "to mark off by bounds" (*apo*, "from," *horizo*, "to determine"; *horos*, "a limit"), "to separate," is used of "(a) the Divine action in setting men apart for the work of the gospel, Rom. 1:1; Gal. 1:15; (b) the Divine judgment upon men, **Matt. 13:49**; **25:32**; (c) the separation of Christians from unbelievers, Acts 19:9; 2 Cor. 6:17; (d) the separation of believers by unbelievers, Luke 6:22; (e) the withdrawal of Christians from their brethren, Gal. 2:12. In (c) is described what the Christian must do, in (d) what he must be prepared to suffer, and in (e) what he must avoid."

Wicked *see Matthew 12:45. See also* Evil at *Matthew 5:37.*

Just *see Matthew 1:19.*

13:50 And shall cast them into the furnace of fire: there shall be wailing and gnashing of teeth.

Furnace *see Matthew 13:42.*

Fire *see Matthew 3:11.*

Wailing *see Matthew 13:42. See also* Weeping at *Matthew 2:18.*

Gnashing *see Matthew 8:12.*

Teeth *see* Tooth at *Matthew 5:38.*

13:51 Jesus saith unto them, Have ye understood all these things? They say unto him, Yea, Lord.

Understood *see* Understand at *Matthew 13:13.*

Yea *see Matthew 5:37.*

13:52 Then said he unto them, Therefore every scribe *which is* instructed unto the kingdom of heaven is like unto a man *that is* an householder, which bringeth forth out of his treasure *things* new and old.

Instructed *matheteuo* (3100), is used in the active voice, intransitively, in some mss., in **Matt. 27:57**, in the sense of being the "disciple" of a person; here, however, the best mss. have the passive voice, lit., "had been made a disciple," as in **Matt. 13:52**, RV, "who hath been made a disciple." It is used in this transitive sense in the active voice in **28:19** and Acts 14:21.

Like unto *see Matthew 6:8.*

Man *see Matthew 4:4.*

Householder *see* Master of the house at *Matthew 10:25.*

Treasure *see* Treasures at *Matthew 2:11.*

Old *see Matthew 9:16.*

13:53 And it came to pass, *that* when Jesus had finished these parables, he departed thence.

Finished *teleo* (5055), "to bring to an end" (*telos*, "an end"), in the passive voice, "to be finished," is translated by the verb "to finish" in **Matt. 13:53**; **19:1**; **26:1**; John 19:28, where the RV "are ... finished" brings out the force of the perfect tense (the same word as in v. 30, "It is finished"), which is missed in the KJV; as Stier says, "the word was in His heart before He uttered it", 2 Tim. 4:7; Rev. 10:7; 11:7; 20:3, RV, "should be finished" (KJV, "fulfilled"), 5, 7, RV, "finished" (KJV, "expired"). In Rev. 15:1 the verb is rightly translated "is finished," RV. In 15:8 the RV, "should be finished" corrects the KJV, "were fulfilled."

Departed *metairo* (3332), "to make a distinction, to remove, to lift away" (in its transitive sense), is used intransitively in the NT, signifying "to depart," and is said of Christ, in **Matt. 13:53**; **19:1**. It could be well translated "removed."

13:54 And when he was come into his own country, he taught them in their synagogue, insomuch that they were astonished, and said, Whence hath this *man* this wisdom, and *these* mighty works?

Country *patris* (3968), primarily signifies "one's fatherland, native country, of one's own town," **Matt. 13:54**, **57**; Mark 6:1, 4; Luke 4: 23-24; John 4:44; Heb. 11:14.

Insomuch that *see Matthew 8:24.*

Wisdom *see Matthew 11:19.*

13:55 Is not this the carpenter's son? is not his mother called Mary? and his brethren, James, and Joses, and Simon, and Judas?

Carpenter *tekton* (5405), denotes any craftsman, but especially a worker in wood, a carpenter, **Matt. 13:55**; Mark 6:3.

Brethren Male children of the same mother, **Matt. 13:55**; 1 Cor. 9:5; Gal. 1:19.

13:56 And his sisters, are they not all with us? Whence then hath this *man* all these things?

Sisters *see* Sister at *Matthew 12:50* Sister.

13:57 And they were offended in him. But Jesus said unto them, A prophet is not without honour, save in his own country, and in his own house.

Offended *skandalizo* (4624), from *skandalon* (offense), signifies "to put a snare or stumblingblock in the way," always metaphorically in the NT, in the same ways as the noun, which see. It is used 14 times in Matthew, 8 in Mark, twice in Luke, twice in John; elsewhere in 1 Cor. 8:13 (twice) and 2 Cor. 11:29. It is absent in the most authentic mss. in Rom. 14:21. The RV renders it by the verb "to stumble," or "cause to stumble," in every place save the following, where it uses the verb "to offend," **Matt. 13:57**; **15:12**; **26:31, 33**; Mark 6:3; 14:27, 29.

Without honour *atimos* (820), without honor (*a*, negative, or privative, *time*, "honor"), "despised," is translated "without honor" in **Matt. 13:57**; Mark 6:4; "dishonor" in 1 Cor. 4:10, RV (KJV, "despised"). The comparative degree *atimoteros* is used in the best mss. in 1 Cor. 12:23, "less honorable."

Country *see Matthew 13:54.*

13:58 And he did not many mighty works there because of their unbelief.

Unbelief The negative noun *apistia*, "unbelief," is used twice in Matthew (**13:58**; **17:20**), three times in Mark (6:6; 9:24; 16:14), four times in Romans (3:3; 4:20; 11:20, 23); elsewhere in 1 Tim. 1:13 and Heb. 3:12, 19.

Chapter 14

14:1 At that time Herod the tetrarch heard of the fame of Jesus,

Time *see Matthew 8:29.*

Tetrarch *tetraarches or tetrarches* (5076), denotes "one of four rulers" (*tetra*, "four," *arche*, "rule"), properly, "the governor of the fourth part of a region"; hence, "a dependent princeling," or "any petty ruler" subordinate to kings or ethnarchs; in the NT, Herod Antipas, **Matt. 14:1**; Luke 3:19; 9:7; Acts 13:1.

Fame *see Matthew 4:24.*

14:2 And said unto his servants, This is John the Baptist; he is risen from the dead; and therefore mighty works do shew forth themselves in him.

Servants *see* Servant at *Matthew 8:6*.

Mighty *see* Wonderful at *Matthew 7:22*.

Works In **Matt. 14:2** and Mark 6:14, KJV, *dunameis*, "powers," RV, is translated "mighty works"; in Acts 2:22, RV, "mighty works," KJV, "miracles."

14:3 For Herod had laid hold on John, and bound him, and put *him* in prison for Herodias' sake, his brother Philip's wife.

Hold *see Matthew 12:11.*

Brother *see* Brethren at *Matthew 1:2*.

14:4-5 For John said unto him, It is not lawful for thee to have her.

And when he would have put him to death, he feared the multitude, because they counted him as a prophet.

Have *see* Had at *Matthew 3:4*.

Put … to death *see* Kill at *Matthew 10:28*.

Multitude *see* Multitudes at *Matthew 4:25*.

Counted *echo* (2192), "to have, to hold"; then, "to hold in the mind, to regard, to count," has this significance in **Matt. 14:5**, "they counted Him as a prophet"; Philem. 17, "If then thou countest me a partner"; Mark 11:32, KJV, (RV, "hold"); Acts 20:24, KJV.

14:6 But when Herod's birthday was kept, the daughter of Herodias danced before them, and pleased Herod.

Birthday *genesia* (1077), a neuter plural (akin to *genesis*, "lineage," from *ginomai*), primarily denoted "the festivities of a birthday, a birthday feast," though among the Greeks it was also used of a festival in commemoration of a deceased friend. It is found in **Matt. 14:6** and Mark 6:21. Some have regarded it as the day of the king's accession, but this meaning is not confirmed in Greek writings.

Kept In **Matt. 14:6** some mss. have the verb *ago*, "to lead, hold" (of a feast), of "keeping" Herod's birthday; the most authentic have *ginomai*, "to become, take place"; hence the RV, "when Herod's birthday came." The verb *ago* is used in Acts 19:38 of "keeping" certain occasions, as of the holding of law courts, RV "(the courts) are open," KJV marg., "court days are kept"; Moulton and Milligan illustrate from the papyri the use of the adjective *agoraios*, in the plural with *hemerai*, "days," understood, in regard to certain market days; certain court days are what are indicated here. The conjecture that the meaning is "courts are now being held" (*sunodoi* being understood as meetings of the court instead of "days") is scarcely so appropriate to the circumstances.

Danced *see Matthew 11:17.*

Before *see* Among at *Matthew 13:25.*

Pleased *aresko* (700), signifies (a) "to be pleasing to, be acceptable to," **Matt. 14:6**; Mark 6:22; Acts 6:5; Rom. 8:8; 15:2; 1 Cor. 7:32-34; Gal. 1:10; 1 Thess. 2:15; 4:1 (where the preceding *kai*, "and," is epexegetical, "even," explaining the "walking," i.e., Christian manner of life as "pleasing" God; in Gen. 5:22, where the Hebrew has "Enoch walked with God," the Sept. has "Enoch pleased God"; cf. Mic. 6:8; Heb. 11:5); 2 Tim. 2:4; (b) "to endeavor to please," and so, "to render service," doing so evilly in one's own interests, Rom. 15:1, which Christ did not, v. 3; or unselfishly, 1 Cor. 10:33; 1 Thess. 2:4. This sense of the word is illustrated by Moulton and Milligan (*Vocab.*) from numerous inscriptions, especially describing "those who have proved themselves of use to the commonwealth."

14:7 Whereupon he promised with an oath to give her whatsoever she would ask.

Promised *homologeo* (3670), "to agree, confess," signifies "to promise" in **Matt. 14:7**. *See also* Profess at *Matthew 7:23.*

Oath *see* Oaths at *Matthew 5:33.*

14:8 And she, being before instructed of her mother, said, Give me here John Baptist's head in a charger.

Instructed *probibazo* (4264), "to lead forward, lead on" (the causal of *probaino*, "to go forward"; *pro*, "forward," *bibazo*, "to lift up"), is used in the passive voice. In **Matt. 14:8**, and translated, KJV, "being before instructed," RV, "being put forward." Some mss. have it in Acts 19:33.

Charger *pinax* (4094), primarily "a board or plank," came to denote various articles of wood; hence, "a wooden trencher, charger," **Matt. 14:8, 11**; Mark 6:25, 28; Luke 11:39.

14:9 And the king was sorry: nevertheless for the oath's sake, and them which sat with him at meat, he commanded *it* to be given *her*.

King *see Matthew 1:6.*

Sorry *lupeo* (3076), is rendered "to be sorry" (passive voice) in **Matt. 14:9**, KJV (RV, "grieved"); **17:23**; **18:31**; 2 Cor. 2:2 [1st part, active voice, "make sorry" (as in 7:8, twice); 2nd part, passive]; 2:4, RV, "made sorry"; 9:9 and 11, RV, "ye were made sorry."

Oath *see* Oaths at *Matthew 5:33.*

Sat *see Matthew 9:10.*

Commanded *keleuo* (2753), "to urge, incite, order," suggests a strong injunction, **Matt. 14:9**, **19**; **15:35**; **18:25**; **27:58**, **64**; Luke 18:40; Acts 4:15 (frequently in Acts, not subsequently in the NT).

14:10 And he sent, and beheaded John in the prison.

Sent *see Matthew 11:2.*

Beheaded *apokephalizo* (607), *apo*, "from, off," *kephale*, "a head," is found in **Matt. 14:10**; Mark 6:16, 27; Luke 9:9.

Prison *phulake* (5438), denotes a "prison," e.g., **Matt. 14:10**; Mark 6:17; Acts 5:19; 2 Cor. 11:23; in 2 Cor. 6:5 and Heb. 11:36 it stands for the condition of imprisonment; in Rev. 2:10; 18:2, "hold" (twice, RV, marg., "prison"; in the 2nd case, KJV, "cage"); 20:7.

14:11 And his head was brought in a charger, and given to the damsel: and she brought *it* to her mother.

Charger *see Matthew 14:8.*

Damsel *see* Maid at *Matthew 9:24.*

14:12 And his disciples came, and took up the body, and buried it, and went and told Jesus.

Body *ptoma* (4430), denotes, lit., "a fall" (akin to *pipto*, "to fall"); hence, "that which is fallen, a corpse," **Matt. 14:12**; **24:28**, "carcase"; Mark 6:29; 15:45, "corpse"; Rev. 11:8-9, "dead bodies" (Gk., "carcase," but plural in the 2nd part of v. 9).

Buried *see* Bury at *Matthew 8:21.*

Told *see Matthew 8:33.*

14:13 When Jesus heard *of it*, he departed thence by ship into a desert place apart: and when the people had heard *thereof*, they followed him on foot out of the cities.

Departed *see Matthew 2:12.*

Desert *eremos* (2048), used as a noun, has the same meaning as *eremia*, in Luke 5:16 and 8:29, RV, "deserts," for KJV, "wilderness"; in **Matt. 24:26** and John 6:31, RV, "wilderness," for KJV, "desert." As an adjective, it denotes (a), with reference to persons, "deserted," desolate, deprived of the friends and kindred, e.g., of a woman deserted by a husband, Gal 4:21; (b) so of a city, as Jerusalem, **Matt. 23:38**; or uninhabited places, "desert," e.g., **Matt. 14:13**, **15**; Acts 8:26; in Mark 1:35, RV, "desert," for KJV, "solitary."

Foot *poderes* (4158), signifies "reaching to the feet," from *pous*, and *aro*, "to fit," and is said of a garment, Rev. 1:13. In the Sept. it is used of the high priest's garment, e.g., Ex. 28:4. 2. *pezos* (3978), an adjective, "on foot," is used in one of its forms as an adverb in **Matt. 14:13**, and Mark 6:33, in each place signifying "by land," in contrast to by sea. Cf. *pezeuo*, "to go on foot," Acts 20:3, RV, "to go by land" (marg., "on foot").

14:14 And Jesus went forth, and saw a great multitude, and was moved with compassion toward them, and he healed their sick.

Multitude *see* Multitudes at *Matthew 4:25.*

Compassion *see Matthew 9:36.*

Sick *arrhostos* (732), "feeble, sickly" (*a*, negative, *rhonnumi*, "to be strong"), is translated "sick" in **Matt. 14:14**; Mark 16:18; "sick folk" in Mark 6:5; "that were sick" in 6:13; "sickly" in 1 Cor. 11:30, here also of the physical state. In the Sept., 1 Kings 14:5; Mal. 1:8.

14:15 And when it was evening, his disciples came to him, saying, This is a desert place, and the time is now past; send the multitude away, that they may go into the villages, and buy themselves victuals.

Desert *see Matthew 14:13.*

Time *hora* (5610), primarily, "any time or period fixed by nature," is translated "time" in **Matt. 14:15**; Luke 14:17; Rom. 13:11, "high time"; in the following the RV renders it "hour," for KJV, "time," **Matt. 18:1**; Luke 1:10; John 16:2, 4, 25; 1 John 2:18 (twice); Rev. 14:15; in Mark 6:35, RV, "day"; in 1 Thess. 2:17, RV, "a short (season)," lit., "(the season, KJV, 'time') of an hour."

Past *see* Pass at *Matthew 5:18.*

Send *apoluo* (630), denotes (a) "to set free, release," translated "loosed" in Luke 13:12, of deliverance from an infirmity; in **Matt. 18:27**, KJV, "loosed" (RV, "released"), of a debtor; (b) "to let go, dismiss," e.g., **Matt. 14:15, 22**.

Multitude *see* Multitudes at Matthew *4:25.*

Buy *agorazo* (59), primarily, "to frequent the market-place," the *agora*, hence "to do business there, to buy or sell," is used lit., e.g., in **Matt. 14:15**. Figuratively Christ is spoken of as having bought His redeemed, making them His property at the price of His blood (i.e., His death through the shedding of His blood in expiation for their sins), 1 Cor. 6:20; 7:23; 2 Pet. 2:1; see also Rev. 5:9; 14:3-4 (not as KJV, "redeemed"). *Agorazo* does not mean "to redeem."

Victuals *broma* (1033), "food" (akin to *bibrosko*, "to eat," John 6:13), solid food in contrast to milk, is translated "food" in **Matt. 14:15**, RV (KJV, "victuals"); "meats," Mark 7:19; 1 Cor. 6:13 (twice); 1 Tim. 4:3; Heb. 9:10; 13:9; "meat," John 4:34; Rom. 14:15 (twice), 20; 1 Cor. 3:2; 8:8, 13; 10:3; "food," RV, for KJV, "meat," Luke 3:11; 9:13.

14:16 But Jesus said unto them, They need not depart; give ye them to eat.

Need *see Matthew 3:14.*

14:17-19 And they say unto him, We have here but five loaves, and two fishes.

He said, Bring them hither to me.

And he commanded the multitude to sit down on the grass, and took the five loaves, and the two fishes, and looking up to heaven, he blessed, and brake, and gave the loaves to *his* disciples, and the disciples to the multitude.

Commanded *see Matthew 14:9.*

Sit *see Matthew 8:11.*

Grass *see Matthew 6:30.*

Looking *see* Sight at *Matthew 11:5.*

Brake *klao* or *klazo* (2806), "to break, to break off pieces," is used of "breaking bread," (a) of the Lord's act in providing for people, **Matt. 14:19**; **15:36**; Mark 8:6, 19; (b) of the "breaking of bread" in the Lord's Supper, **Matt. 26:26**; Mark 14:22; Luke 22:19; Acts 20:7; 1 Cor. 10:16; 11:24; (c) of an ordinary meal, Acts 2:46; 20:11; 27:35; (d) of the Lord's act in giving evidence of His resurrection, Luke 24:30.

14:20 And they did all eat, and were filled: and they took up of the fragments that remained twelve baskets full.

Filled *pleres* (4134), denotes "full," (a) in the sense of "being filled," materially, **Matt. 14:20**; **15:37**; Mark 8:19 (said of baskets "full" of bread crumbs); of leprosy, Luke 5:12; spiritually, of the Holy Spirit, Luke 4:1; Acts 6:3; 7:55; 11:24; grace and truth, John 1:14; faith, Acts 6:5; grace and power, 6:8; of the effects of spiritual life and qualities, seen in good works, Acts 9:36; in an evil sense, of guile and villany, Acts 13:10; wrath, 19:28; (b) in the sense of "being complete," "full corn in the ear," Mark 4:28; of a reward hereafter, 2 John 8.

Fragments *klasma* (2801), "a broken piece, fragment," is always used of remnants of food, **Matt. 14:20**; **15:37** and corresponding passages.

Remained *perisseuo* (4052), "to be over and above" (the number), hence, "to be or remain over," is translated "was left," in **Matt. 15:37**, KJV (RV, "remained over," as in **14:20**; Luke 9:17; John 6:12 and v. 13, where the KJV adds "and above"), of the broken fragments after the feeding of the multitudes.

Baskets *kophinos* (2894), was "a wicker basket," originally containing a certain measure of capacity, **Matt. 14:20**; **16:9**; Mark 6:43 (RV, "basketfuls"); 8:19; Luke 9:17; 13:8 in some mss.; John 6:13.

14:21 And they that had eaten were about five thousand men, beside women and children.

About *hosei* (5616), "as if," before numerals, denotes "about, nearly, something like," with perhaps an indication of greater indefiniteness, e.g., **Matt. 14:21**; Luke 3:23; 9:14, 28; Acts 2:41; with a measure of space, Luke 22:41, "about a stone's cast."

Five *pente* (4002), is derived by some from words suggesting the fingers of a hand, or a fist. The word is frequent in the Gospels. *Pentakis*, "five times," is found in 2 Cor. 11:24; *pentakosioi*, "five hundred," in Luke 7:41; 1 Cor. 15:6; *pentakischilioi*, "five thousand" (*chilios*, "a thousand"), in **Matt. 14:21**; **16:9** and corresponding passages.

Thousand The following compounds represent different multiples of a thousand: *dischilioi*, 2,000, Mark 5:13; *trischilioi*, 3,000, Acts 2:41; *tetrakischilioi*, 4,000, **Matt. 15:38**; **16:10**; Mark 8:9, 20; Acts 21:35; *pentakischilioi*, 5,000, **Matt. 14:21**; **16:9**; Mark 6:44; 8:9; Luke 9:14; John 6:10; *heplakischilioi*, 7,000, Rom. 11:4.

Beside *choris* (5565), "separately, apart from, besides," is translated "beside" in **Matt. 14:21**; **15:38**; 2 Cor. 11:28.

Women *see Matthew 11:11.*

Children *see* Child at *Matthew 2:8.*

14:22 And straightway Jesus constrained his disciples to get into a ship, and to go before him unto the other side, while he sent the multitudes away.

Constrained *anankazo* (315), denotes "to put constraint upon (from *ananke*, 'necessity'), to constrain, whether by threat, entreaty, force or persuasion"; Christ "constrained" the disciples to get into a boat, **Matt. 14:22**; Mark 6:45; the servants of the man who made a great supper were to constrain people to come in, Luke 14:23 (RV, "constrain"); Saul of Tarsus "strove" to make saints blaspheme, Acts 26:11, RV (KJV, "compelled"); Titus, though a Greek, was not "compelled" to be circumcised, Gal. 2:3, as Galatian converts were, 6:12, RV; Peter was "compelling" Gentiles to live as Jews, Gal. 2:14; Paul was "constrained" to appeal to Caesar, Acts 28:19, and was "compelled" by the church at Corinth to become foolish in speaking of himself, 2 Cor. 12:11.

Get into *see* Entered at *Matthew 8:23.*

Side *see Matthew 8:18.*

While *see* Whiles at *Matthew 5:25.*

Sent *see* Send at *Matthew 14:15.*

14:23 And when he had sent the multitudes away, he went up into a mountain apart to pray: and when the evening was come, he was there alone.

Sent *see* Send at *Matthew 14:15.*

14:24 But the ship was now in the midst of the sea, tossed with waves: for the wind was contrary.

Now *see Matthew 3:10.*

Midst The neuter, *meson*, is used adverbially in **Matt. 14:24**, in some mss., "in the midst (of the waves)"; in Phil. 2:15 in the best mss. (where some mss. have *en m....*).

Tossed *basanizo* (928), properly signifies "to test by rubbing on the touchstone" (*basanos*, "a touchstone"), then, "to question by applying torture"; hence "to vex, torment"; in the passive voice, "to be harassed, distressed"; it is said of men struggling in a boat against wind and waves, **Matt. 14:24**, RV, "distressed" (KJV, "tossed"); Mark 6:48, RV, "distressed" (KJV, "toiling").

Waves *see Matthew 8:24.*

Contrary *enantios* (1727), "over against" (*en*, "in," *antios*, "against"), is used primarily of place, Mark 15:39; of an opposing wind, **Matt. 14:24**; Mark 6:48; Acts 27:4; metaphorically, opposed as an adversary, antagonistic, Acts 26:9; 1 Thess. 2:15; Titus 2:8; Acts 28:17, "against."

14:25 And in the fourth watch of the night Jesus went unto them, walking on the sea.

Fourth *see* Fourteen at *Matthew 1:17.*

Watch *phulake* (5438), is used (a) with the meaning "a watch," actively, "a guarding," Luke 2:8, lit., "(keeping, *phulasso*) watches"; (b) of "the time during which guard was kept by night, a watch of the night," **Matt. 14:25**; **24:43**; Mark 6:48; Luke 12:38.

14:26 And when the disciples saw him walking on the sea, they were troubled, saying, It is a spirit; and they cried out for fear.

Troubled *see Matthew 2:3.*

Spirit *phantasma* (5326), "a phantasm or phantom" (from *phaino*, "to appear"), is translated "apparition" in the RV of **Matt. 14:26** and Mark 6:49 (KJV, "spirit"). In the Sept., Job 20:8; Isa. 28:7.

14:27 But straightway Jesus spake unto them, saying, Be of good cheer; it is I; be not afraid.

Cheer *see Matthew 9:2.*

Saying *see* Say at *Matthew 3:9.*

14:28 And Peter answered him and said, Lord, if it be thou, bid me come unto thee on the water.

Bid *keleuo* (2753), "to command," is translated "bid" in **Matt. 14:28**, only.

14:29-30 And he said, Come. And when Peter was come down out of the ship, he walked on the water, to go to Jesus.
But when he saw the wind boisterous, he was afraid; and beginning to sink, he cried, saying, Lord, save me.

Boisterous The KJV "boisterous" in **Matt. 14:30** is a rendering of the word *ischuros*, "strong" (see margin); it is not in the most authentic mss. *See* **Strong** at *Matthew 12:29.*

Sink *katapontizo* (2670), "to throw into the sea" (*kata*, "down," *pontos*, "the open sea"), in the passive voice, "to be sunk in, to be drowned," is translated "were drowned," in **Matt. 18:6**, KJV (RV, "should be sunk"); elsewhere in **14:30**, "(beginning) to sink."

14:31 And immediately Jesus stretched forth *his* hand, and caught him, and said unto him, O thou of little faith, wherefore didst thou doubt?

Stretched *see* Put forth at *Matthew 8:3.*

Faith *see Matthew 6:30.*

Wherefore *eis*, "unto," with *ti*, "what," **Matt. 14:31**; with *ho*, "which" (the accusative neuter of *hos*), 2 Thess. 1:11, KJV (RV, "to which end").

Doubt *distazo* (1365), "to stand in two ways" (*dis*, "double," *stasis*, "a standing"), implying "uncertainty which way to take," is used in **Matt. 14:31** and **28:17**; said of believers whose faith is small.

14:32 And when they were come into the ship, the wind ceased.

Come into *see* Entered at *Matthew 8:23.*

Ceased *kopazo* (2869), "to cease through being spent with toil, to cease raging" (from *kopos*, "labor, toil," *kopiao*, "to labor"), is said of the wind only, **Matt. 14:32**; Mark 4:39; 6:51.

14:33 Then they that were in the ship came and worshipped him, saying, Of a truth thou art the Son of God.

Worshipped *see* Worship at *Matthew 2:2.*

Of a truth *alethos* (230), "truly, surely," is rendered "of a truth" in **Matt. 14:33**; **26:73** and Mark 14:70, RV, (KJV, "surely"); Luke 9:27; 12:44; 21:3; John 6:14; 7:40; 17:8, RV, "of a truth (KJV, "surely"); Acts 12:11, RV (KJV, "of a surety"); "in truth," 1 Thess. 2:13; "truly," **Matt. 27:54**; Mark 15:39.

Son *see Matthew 3:17.*

14:34 And when they were gone over, they came into the land of Gennesaret.

Gone *see* Passed at *Matthew 9:1.*

14:35 And when the men of that place had knowledge of him, they sent out into all that country round about, and brought unto him all that were diseased;

Country *see* Region at *Matthew 3:5.*

Diseased *see* Sick at *Matthew 4:24.*

14:36 And besought him that they might only touch the hem of his garment: and as many as touched were made perfectly whole.

Hem *see Matthew 9:20.*

Many *hosos* (3745), "how much, how many, how great, as much as, as many as," is translated "as many as," e.g., in **Matt. 14:36**; Mark 3:10; Luke 9:5, RV (KJV, "whosoever"); Acts 2:39; in 9:16, RV, "how many things" (KJV, "how great things"); in Rom. 6:3 the RV renders it by "all we who" (KJV, "so many of us as"), a necessary alteration, not singling out some believers from others, as if some were not baptized, but implying what was recognized as true of all (see Acts 18:8); in 2 Cor. 1:20, RV, "how many soever be" (KJV, "all").

Whole *diosozo* (1295), "to save thoroughly" (dia), is used in the passive voice and rendered "were made whole" in **Matt. 14:36**, RV (KJV, "were made perfectly whole").

Chapter 15

15:1-2 Then came to Jesus scribes and Pharisees, which were of Jerusalem, saying,
Why do thy disciples transgress the tradition of the elders? for they wash not their hands when they eat bread.

Transgress *parabaino* (3845), lit., "to go aside" (*para*), hence "to go beyond," is chiefly used metaphorically of "transgressing" the tradition of the elders, **Matt. 15:2**; the commandment of God, **15:3**; in Acts 1:25, of Judas, KJV, "by transgression fell" (RV, "fell away"); in 2 John 9 some texts have this verb (KJV, "transgresseth"), the best have *proago*.

Tradition *paradosis* (3862), "a handing down or on" (akin to *paradidomi*, "to hand over, deliver"), denotes "a tradition," and hence, by metonymy, (a) "the teachings of the rabbis," interpretations of the Law, which was thereby made void in practice, **Matt. 15:2, 3, 6**; Mark 7:3, 5, 8, 9, 13; Gal. 1:14; Col. 2:8; (b) of "apostolic teaching," 1 Cor. 11:2, RV, "traditions" (KJV, "ordinances"), of instructions concerning the gatherings of believers (instructions of wider scope than ordinances in the limited sense); in 2 Thess. 2:15, of Christian doctrine in general, where the apostle's use of the word constitutes a denial that what he preached originated with himself, and a claim for its divine authority (cf. *paralambano*, "to receive," 1 Cor. 11:23; 15:3); in 2 Thess. 3:6, it is used of instructions concerning everyday conduct.

Elders *presbuteros* (4245), an adjective, the comparative degree of *presbus*, "an old man, an elder," is used (a) of age, whether of the "elder" of two persons, Luke 15:25, or more, John 8:9, "the eldest", or of a person advanced in life, a senior, Acts 2:17; in Heb. 11:2, the "elders" are the forefathers in Israel so in **Matt. 15:2**; Mark 7:3, 5 the feminine of the adjective is used of "elder" women in the churches, 1 Tim. 5:2, not in respect of position but in seniority of age; (b) of rank or positions of responsibility, (1) among Gentiles, as in the Sept. of Gen. 50:7; Num. 22:7, (2) in the Jewish nation, firstly, those who were the heads or leaders of the tribes and families, as of the seventy who assisted Moses, Num. 11:16; Deut. 27:1, and those assembled by Solomon; secondly, members of the Sanhedrin, consisting of the chief priests, "elders" and scribes, learned in Jewish law, e.g., **Matt. 16:21**; **26:47**; thirdly, those who managed public affairs in the various cities, Luke 7:3; (3) in the Christian churches those who, being raised up and qualified by the work of the Holy Spirit, were appointed to have the spiritual care of, and to exercise oversight over, the churches. To these the term "bishops," *episkopoi*, or "overseers," is applied (see Acts 20, v. 17 with v. 28, and Titus 1:5 and 7), the latter term indicating the nature of their work *presbuteroi* their maturity of spiritual experience. The divine arrangement seen throughout the NT was for a plurality of these to be appointed in each church, Acts 14:23; 20:17; Phil. 1:1; 1 Tim. 5:17; Titus 1:5. The duty of "elders" is described by the verb *episkopeo*. They were appointed according as they had given evidence of fulfilling the divine qualifications, Titus 1:6 to 9; cf. 1 Tim. 3:1-7 and 1 Pet. 5:2; (4) the twenty-four "elders" enthroned in heaven around the throne of God, Rev. 4:4, 10; 5:5-14; 7:11, 13; 11:16; 14:3; 19:4. The number twenty-four is representative of earthly conditions.

Wash *see Matthew 6:17.*

15:3 But he answered and said unto them, Why do ye also transgress the commandment of God by your tradition?

Transgress *see Matthew 15:2.*

Tradition *see Matthew 15:2.*

15:4 For God commanded, saying, Honour thy father and mother: and, He that curseth father or mother, let him die the death.

Honour *timao* (5091), "to honor," is used of (a) valuing Christ at a price, **Matt. 27:9**; (b) "honoring" a person: (1) the "honor" done by Christ to the Father, John 8:49; (2) "honor" bestowed by the Father upon him who serves Christ, John 12:26; (3) the duty of all to "honor" the Son equally with the Father, 5:23; (4) the duty of children to "honor" their parents, **Matt. 15:4**; **19:19**; Mark 7:10; 10:19; Luke 18:20; Eph. 6:2; (5) the duty of Christians to "honor" the king, and all men, 1 Pet. 2:17; (6) the respect and material assistance to be given to widows "that are widows indeed," 1 Tim. 5:3; (7) the "honor" done to Paul and his companions by the inhabitants of Melita, Acts 28:10; (8) mere lip profession of "honor" to God, **Matt. 15:8**; Mark 7:6.

Curseth *kakologeo* (2551), "to speak evil" (*kakos*, "evil," *lego*, "to speak"), is translated by the verb "to curse" in **Matt. 15:4**, and Mark 7:10, "to speak evil of father and mother," not necessarily "to curse," is what the Lord intended (RV). KJV and RV have the verb "to speak evil" in Mark 9:39 and Acts 19:9.

Die *see* Dead at *Matthew 2:19.*

15:5 But ye say, Whosoever shall say to *his* father or *his* mother, *It is* a gift, by whatsoever thou mightest be profited by me;

Gift *see* Gifts at *Matthew 2:11.*

Profited *opheleo* (5623), is translated "to profit" in **Matt. 15:5**; **16:26**; Mark 7:11; 8:36; Luke 9:25, RV; John 6:63; Rom. 2:25; 1 Cor. 13:3; 14:6; Gal. 5:2; Heb. 4:2; 13:9.

"Put everything you have into the care of your heart, for it determines what your life amounts to."

DALLAS WILLARD

15:6 And honour not his father or his mother, *he shall be free*. Thus have ye made the commandment of God of none effect by your tradition.

Free In **Matt. 15:6** and Mark 7:11, the words "he shall be free," KJV, have nothing to represent them in the Greek.

Of none effect *akuroo* (208), signifies "to render void, deprive of force and authority" (from *a*, negative, and *kuros*, "might, authority"; *kurios*, "a lord," is from the same root), the opposite to *kuroo*, "to confirm". It is used of making "void" the Word of God, **Matt. 15:6**; Mark 7:13 (KJV, "making of none effect"), and of the promise of God to Abraham as not being deprived of authority by the Law 430 years after, Gal. 3:17, "disannul."

Tradition *see Matthew 15:2.*

15:7 *Ye* hypocrites, well did Esaias prophesy of you, saying,

Hypocrites *see Matthew 6:2.*

Prophesy *see* Prophesied at *Matthew 7:22.*

15:8 This people draweth nigh unto me with their mouth, and honoureth me with *their* lips; but their heart is far from me.

Draweth nigh *see* At hand at *Matthew 3:2.*

Honoureth *see* Honour at *Matthew 15:4.*

Lips *cheilos* (5491), is used (a) of the organ of speech, **Matt. 15:8** and Mark 7:6, where "honoring with the lips," besides meaning empty words, may have reference to a Jewish custom of putting to the mouth the tassel of the tallith (the woollen scarf wound round the head and neck during prayer), as a sign of acceptance of the Law from the heart; Rom. 3:13; 1 Cor. 14:21 (from Isa. 28:11, 12, speaking of the Assyrian foe as God's message to disobedient Israel); Heb. 13:15; 1 Pet. 3:10; (b) metaphorically, of "the brink or edge of things," as of the sea shore, Heb. 11:12, lit., "the shore (of the sea)."

Far *porro* (4206), is used (a) literally, Luke 14:32, "a great way off"; the comparative degree *porroteron*, "further," is used in 24:28; (b) metaphorically, of the heart in separation from God, **Matt. 15:8**; Mark 7:6. Cf. *porrothen*, "afar off." *See also* Have at *Matthew 6:1.*

15:9 But in vain they do worship me, teaching *for* doctrines the commandments of men.

Vain *maten* (3155), properly the accusative case of *mate*, "a fault, a folly," signifies "in vain, to no purpose," **Matt. 15:9**; Mark 7:7.

Worship *sebomai* (4576), "to revere," stressing the feeling of awe or devotion, is used of "worship" (a) to God, **Matt. 15:9**; Mark 7:7; Acts 16:14; 18:7, 13; (b) to a goddess, Acts 19:27.

Teaching *see Matthew 4:23.*

Doctrines *didaskalia* (1319), denotes (a) "that which is taught, doctrine," **Matt. 15:9**; Mark 7:7; Eph. 4:14; Col. 2:22; 1 Tim. 1:10; 4:1, 6; 6:1, 3; 2 Tim. 4:3; Titus 1:9 ("doctrine," in last part of verse); 2:1, 10; (b) "teaching, instruction," Rom. 12:7, "teaching"; 15:4, "learning", 1 Tim. 4:13, KJV, "doctrine," RV, "teaching"; v. 16, KJV, "the doctrine," RV, (correctly) "thy teaching;" 5:17, KJV, "doctrine," RV "teaching"; 2 Tim. 3:10, 16 (ditto); Titus 2:7, "thy doctrine."

Commandments *entalma* (1778), marks "the thing commanded, a commission"; in **Matt. 15:9**; Mark 7:7; Col. 2:22, RV, "precepts," KJV, "commandments."

15:10 And he called the multitude, and said unto them, Hear, and understand:

Understand *see Matthew 13:13.*

15:11 Not that which goeth into the mouth defileth a man; but that which cometh out of the mouth, this defileth a man.

Mouth *see Matthew 12:34.*

Defileth *koinoo* (2840), denotes (a) "to make common"; hence, in a ceremonial sense, "to render unholy, unclean, to defile," **Matt. 15:11, 18, 20**; Mark 7:15, 18, 20, 23; Acts 21:28 (RV, "defiled"; KJV, "polluted"); Heb. 9:13 (RV, "them that have been defiled," KJV, "the unclean"); (b) "to count unclean," Acts 10:15; 11:9. In Rev. 21:27, some mss. have this verb, "defileth"; the most authentic have the adjective, *koinos*, "unclean."

Cometh *see* Proceedeth at *Matthew 4:4.*

15:12 Then came his disciples, and said unto him, Knowest thou that the Pharisees were offended, after they heard this saying?

Offended *see Matthew 13:57.*

15:13 But he answered and said, Every plant, which my heavenly Father hath not planted, shall be rooted up.

Plant *phuteia* (5451), firstly, "a planting," then "that which is planted, a plant" (from *phuo*, "to bring forth, spring up, grow," *phuton*, "a plant"), occurs in **Matt. 15:13**. In the Sept., 2 Kings 19:29; Ezek. 17:7; Mic. 1:6.

Heavenly *see Matthew 6:14.*

Planted *phuteuo* (5452), "to plant," is used (a) literally, **Matt. 21:33**; Mark 12:1; Luke 13:6; 17:6, 28; 20:9; 1 Cor. 9:7; (b) metaphorically, **Matt. 15:13**; 1 Cor. 3:6, 7, 8.

Rooted *see* Root at *Matthew 13:29.*

15:14 Let them alone: they be blind leaders of the blind. And if the blind lead the blind, both shall fall into the ditch.

Let *see Matthew 5:40.*

Alone *aphiemi* (863), signifies "to send away, set free"; also "to let alone," **Matt. 15:14**; Mark 14:6; Luke 13:8; John 11:48; 12:7 (RV, "suffer her"); in Acts 5:38 some texts have *easate* from *eao*, "to permit."

Leaders *hodegos* (3595), "a leader on the way" (*hodos*, "a way," *hegeomai*, "to lead"), "a guide," is used (a) literally, in Acts 1:16; (b) figuratively, **Matt. 15:14**, RV, "guides" (KJV, "leaders"); **Matt. 23:16, 24**, "guides"; Rom. 2:19, "a guide."

Lead *hodegeo* (3594), "to lead the way," is used (a) literally, RV, "guide" (KJV, "lead"), of "guiding" the blind, in **Matt. 15:14**; Luke 6:39; of "guiding" unto fountains of waters of life, Rev. 7:17; (b) figuratively, in John 16:13, of "guidance" into the truth by the Holy Spirit; in Acts 8:31, of the interpretation of Scripture.

Ditch *see* Pit at *Matthew 12:11.*

15:15 Then answered Peter and said unto him, Declare unto us this parable.

Declare *see Matthew 13:36.*

Parable *see* Parables at *Matthew 13:3.*

15:16 And Jesus said, Are ye also yet without understanding?

Yet *akmen*, "even to this point of time" (the accusative case of *akme*, "a point"), **Matt. 15:16**.

Understanding *asunetos* (801), "without understanding or discernment" (*a*, negative, *sunetos*, "intelligent, understanding"), is translated "without understanding" in **Matt. 15:16**; Mark 7:18; Rom. 1:31; 10:19, RV, "void of understanding" (KJV, "foolish"); in Rom. 1:21, RV, "senseless" (KJV, "foolish").

15:17 Do not ye yet understand, that whatsoever entereth in at the mouth goeth into the belly, and is cast out into the draught?

Understand *noeo* (3539), "to perceive with the mind," as distinct from perception by feeling, is so used in **Matt. 15:17**, KJV, "understand," RV, "perceive"; **16:9, 11; 24:15** (here rather perhaps in the sense of considering) and parallels in Mark (not in Luke); John 12:40; Rom. 1:20; 1 Tim. 1:7; Heb. 11:3; in Eph. 3:4, KJV, "may understand" (RV, "can perceive"); 3:20, "think"; 2 Tim. 2:7, "consider."

Entereth *eisporeuomai* (1531), "to go into," found only in the Synoptists and Acts, is translated "to enter," in the RV of Mark 1:21; 6:56; 11:2; Luke 8:16; 11:33 (KJV, "come in"); 19:30 (KJV, "at your entering"); 22:10; in the following the RV has the verb "to go," for the KJV, "to enter," **Matt. 15:17**; Mark 5:40; 7:15, 18-19; in Acts 28:30, "went," KJV, "came"; in 9:28, RV, "going," KJV, "coming"; in the following both KJV and RV have the verb "to enter," Mark 4:19; Luke 18:24 (in the best mss.); Acts 3:2; 8:3.

> *"There's none so blind as those who will not see."*
>
> MATTHEW HENRY

Goeth *choreo* (5562), signifies (a), lit., "to give space, make room" (*chora*, "a place"); hence, transitively, "to have space or room for a thing, to contain," said of the waterpots as "containing" a certain quantity, John 2:6; of a space large enough to hold a number of people, Mark 2:2; of the world as not possible of "containing" certain books, John 21:25; (b) "to go," **Matt. 15:17**; "to have place," John 8:37; "to come," 2 Pet. 3:9; (c) metaphorically, "of receiving with the mind," **Matt. 19:11, 12**; or "into the heart," 2 Cor. 7:2.

Draught *aphedron* (856), "a latrine, a sink, drain," is found in **Matt. 15:17** and Mark 7:19.

15:18 But those things which proceed out of the mouth come forth from the heart; and they defile the man.

Proceed *see* Proceedeth at *Matthew 4:4.*

Defile *see* Defileth at *Matthew 15:11.*

15:19 For out of the heart proceed evil thoughts, murders, adulteries, fornications, thefts, false witness, blasphemies:

Heart *see Matthew 5:28.*

Proceed *exerchomai* (1831), is translated "proceed" in **Matt. 15:19**, KJV

(RV, "come forth"); John 8:42, RV, "came forth"; Jas. 3:10. The verb "to proceed" is not so suitable.

Evil *see Matthew 5:11.*

Thoughts *dialogismos* (1261), "reasoning," is translated "thoughts" in **Matt. 15:19**; Mark 7:21; Luke 2:35; 6:8; in 5:22, KJV, RV, "reasonings"; in 9:47, KJV, RV, "reasoning," and 24:38, KJV, RV, "reasonings"; so 1 Cor. 3:20; in Luke 9:46, KJV and RV, "reasoning"; "thoughts" in Jas. 2:4, KJV and RV.

Murders *phonos* (5408), is used (a) of a special act, Mark 15:7; Luke 23:19, 25; (b) in the plural, of "murders" in general, **Matt. 15:19**; Mark 7:21 (Gal. 5:21, in some inferior mss.); Rev. 9:21; in the singular, Rom. 1:29; (c) in the sense of "slaughter," Heb. 11:37, "they were slain with the sword," lit., "(they died by) slaughter (of the sword)"; in Acts 9:1, "slaughter."

Adulteries *moicheia* (3430), "adultery," is found in **Matt. 15:19**; Mark 7:21; John 8:3 (KJV only).

Fornications *see* Fornication at *Matthew 5:32.*

Thefts *klope* (2829), akin to *klepto*, "to steal," is used in the plural in **Matt. 15:19**; Mark 7:22.

Witness *pseudomarturia* (5577), "false witness," occurs in **Matt. 15:19**; **26:59**.

Blasphemies *blasphemia* (988), either from *blax*, "sluggish, stupid," or, probably, from *blapto*, "to injure," and *pheme*, "speech," (Eng. "blasphemy") is so translated thirteen times in the RV, but "railing" in **Matt. 15:19**; Mark 7:22; Eph. 4:31; Col. 3:8; 1 Tim. 6:4; Jude 9. The word "blasphemy" is practically confined to speech defamatory of the Divine Majesty.

15:20 These are *the things* which defile a man: but to eat with unwashen hands defileth not a man.

Defile, Defileth *see* Defileth at *Matthew 15:11.*

Unwashen *aniptos* (449), "unwashed" (*a*, negative, *nipto*, "to wash"), occurs in **Matt. 15:20**; Mark 7:2 (v. 5 in some mss.).

15:21 Then Jesus went thence, and departed into the coasts of Tyre and Sidon.

Departed *see Matthew 2:12.*

Coasts *meros*, "a part," is translated "coasts" in **Matt. 15:21**; **16:13**, KJV (RV, "parts,"); "country," RV, in Acts 19:1, KJV "coasts"; this refers to the high land in the interior of Asia Minor. *See also* Parts at *Matthew 2:22.*

15:22 And, behold, a woman of Canaan came out of the same coasts, and cried unto him, saying, Have mercy on me, O Lord, *thou* Son of David; my daughter is grievously vexed with a devil.

Coasts *see Matthew 2:16.*

Cried *krazo* (2896), "to cry out," an onomatopoeic word, used especially of the "cry" of the raven; then, of any inarticulate cries, from fear, pain, etc.; of the "cry" of a Canaanitish woman, **Matt. 15:22** (so the best mss., instead of *kraugazo*); of the shouts of the children in the Temple, **Matt. 21:15**; of the people who shouted for Christ to be crucified, **27:23**; Mark 15:13-14; of the "cry" of Christ on the Cross at the close of His sufferings, **Matt. 27:50**; Mark 15:39. In John's Gospel it is used three times, out of the six, of Christ's utterances, 7:28, 37; 12:44. In the Acts it is not used of "cries" of distress, but chiefly of the shouts of opponents; in Revelation, chiefly of the utterances of heavenly beings concerning earthly matters; in Rom. 8:15 and Gal. 4:6, of the appeal of believers to God the Father; in Rom. 9:27, of a prophecy concerning Israel; in Jas. 5:4, metaphorically, of hire kept back by fraud.

Mercy *see Matthew 5:7.*

Grievously *kakos* (2560), "badly, ill," is translated "grievously (vexed)," in **Matt. 15:22**.

Devil *see* Devils at *Matthew 4:24.*

15:23 But he answered her not a word. And his disciples came and besought him, saying, Send her away; for she crieth after us.

After *see* Behind at *Matthew 9:20.*

15:24 But he answered and said, I am not sent but unto the lost sheep of the house of Israel.

Sent *see* Send at *Matthew 10:16.*

15:25 Then came she and worshipped him, saying, Lord, help me.

Worshipped *see* Worship at *Matthew 2:2.*

Help *boetheo* (997), "to come to the aid of anyone, to succor," is used in **Matt. 15:25**; Mark 9:22, 24; Acts 16:9; 21:28; 2 Cor. 6:2, "did I succour"; Heb. 2:18, "to succour"; Rev. 12:16.

15:26 But he answered and said, It is not meet to take the children's bread, and to cast *it* to dogs.

Meet *kalos* (2570), "good," is translated "meet" in **Matt. 15:26** and Mark 7:27.

Dogs *kunarion* (2952), a diminutive, "a little dog, a puppy," is used in **Matt. 15:26-27**; Mark 7:27, 28.

15:27 And she said, Truth, Lord: yet the dogs eat of the crumbs which fall from their masters' table.

Truth *see* Yea at *Matthew 5:37.*

Crumbs *psichion* (5589), "a small morsel," a diminutive of *psix*, "a bit, or crumb", of bread or meat, it is used in **Matt. 15:27** and Mark 7:28; some mss. have it in Luke 16:21.

Masters *see Matthew 6:24.*

Table *trapeza* (5132), primarily "a table," denotes (a) an eating-table, e.g., **Matt. 15:27**; (b) food, etc. placed on "a table," Acts 6:2; 16:34; (c) "a feast, a banquet," 1 Cor. 10:21; (d) "the table or stand" of a moneychanger, where he exchanged money for a fee, or dealt with loans and deposits, **Matt. 21:12**; Mark 11:15; Luke 19:23; John 2:15.

15:28 Then Jesus answered and said unto her, O woman, great *is* thy faith: be it unto thee even as thou wilt. And her daughter was made whole from that very hour.

Woman *see* Women at *Matthew 11:11.*

Even *hos* (5613), "as," in comparative sentences, is sometimes translated "even as," **Matt. 15:28**; Mark 4:36; Eph. 5:33; 1 Pet. 3:6 (KJV only); Jude 7.

Whole *iaomai* (2390), "to heal," is rendered "to make whole," **Matt. 15:28**; Acts 9:34, KJV (RV, "healeth").

15:29 And Jesus departed from thence, and came nigh unto the sea of Galilee; and went up into a mountain, and sat down there.

Departed *see* Depart at *Matthew 8:34.*

Nigh *para* (3844), "beside, alongside of," is translated "nigh unto" in **Matt. 15:29**; in Mark 5:21, RV, "by" (KJV, "nigh unto").

Sea *see Matthew 4:18.*

Sat *see Matthew 4:16.*

15:30 And great multitudes came unto him, having with them *those that were* lame, blind, dumb, maimed, and many others, and cast them down at Jesus' feet; and he healed them:

Lame *see Matthew 11:5.*

Maimed *kullos* (2948), denotes "crooked crippled" (akin to *kulio*, "to roll"); in **Matt. 15:30, 31**, translated "maimed"; so in **18:8**, KJV (RV, "halt") and Mark 9:43 (KJV and RV).

Cast *see* Scattered at *Matthew 9:36.*

15:31 Insomuch that the multitude wondered, when they saw the dumb to speak, the maimed to be whole, the lame to walk, and the blind to see: and they glorified the God of Israel.

Insomuch *see Matthew 8:24.*

Maimed *see Matthew 15:30.*

Whole *see Matthew 12:13.*

Lame *see Matthew 11:5.*

Glorified *see* Glorify at *Matthew 5:16.*

15:32 Then Jesus called his disciples *unto him*, and said, I have compassion on the multitude, because they continue with me now three days, and have nothing to eat: and I will not send them away fasting, lest they faint in the way.

Compassion *see Matthew 9:36.*

Continue *prosmeno* (4357), "to remain with," "to continue with a person," is said of the people with Christ, **Matt. 15:32**; Mark 8:2 (KJV, "been with"); of "continuing" in supplications and prayers, 1 Tim. 5:5.

Fasting *nestis* (3523), "not eating", "fasting," is used of lack of food, **Matt. 15:32**; Mark 8:3.

Faint *see* Fainted at *Matthew 9:36.*

15:33 And his disciples say unto him, Whence should we have so much bread in the wilderness, as to fill so great a multitude?

Much The adjective *tosoutos*, "so great, so much," is translated "so much (bread)," in **Matt. 15:33**, plural, RV, "so many (loaves)"; in the genitive case, of price, in Acts 5:8, "for so much"; in the dative case, of degree, in Heb. 1:4, RV, "by so much" (KJV, "so much"); so in Heb. 10:25; in Heb. 7:22 "by so much" translates the phrase *kata tosouto;* in Rev. 18:7, "so much."

Wilderness *eremia* (2047), "an uninhabited place," is translated "wilderness" in the KJV of **Matt. 15:33** and Mark 8:4 (RV, "a desert place"); RV and KJV, "wilderness" in 2 Cor. 11:26.

Fill *see* Filled at *Matthew 5:6.*

Great *see Matthew 8:10.*

Multitude *see* Multitudes at *Matthew 4:25.*

15:34 And Jesus saith unto them, How many loaves have ye? And they said, Seven, and a few little fishes.

Many *posos* (4214), "how much, how great, how many," has the last meaning in **Matt. 15:34; 16:9, 10; 27:13** ("how many things"); Mark 6:38; 8:5, 19, 20; 15:4 ("how many things); Luke 15:17; Acts 21:20.

Few *see Matthew 7:14.*

Fishes *ichthudion* (2485), "a little fish," **Matt. 15:34**; Mark 8:7.

15:35 And he commanded the multitude to sit down on the ground.

Commanded *see Matthew 14:9.*

Sit *anapipto* (377), "to fall back" (*ana*, "back," *pipto*, "to fall"), denotes, in the NT, "to recline for a repast," **Matt. 15:35**; Mark 6:40; 8:6; Luke 11:37; 14:10; 17:7; 22:14; John 6:10 (twice); 13:12; in John 13:25 and 21:20 it is used of leaning on the bosom of Christ. In the Sept., Gen. 49:9.

15:36 And he took the seven loaves and the fishes, and gave thanks, and brake *them*, and gave to his disciples, and the disciples to the multitude.

Thanks *eucharisteo* (2168), "to give thanks," (a) is said of Christ, **Matt. 15:36**; **26:27**; Mark 8:6; 14:23; Luke 22:17, 19; John 6:11, 23; 11:41; 1 Cor. 11:24; (b) of the Pharisee in Luke 18:11 in his selfcomplacent prayer; (c) is used by Paul at the beginning of all his epistles, except 2 Cor. (see, however, *eulogetos* in 1:3), Gal., 1 Tim., 2 Tim. (see, however, *charin echo*, 1:3), and Titus, (1) for his readers, Rom. 1:8; Eph. 1:16; Col. 1:3; 1 Thess. 1:2; 2 Thess. 1:3 (cf. 2:13); virtually so in Philem. 4; (2) for fellowship shown, Phil. 1:3; (3) for God's gifts to them, 1 Cor. 1:4; (d) is recorded (1) of Paul elsewhere, Acts 27:35; 28:15; Rom. 7:25; 1 Cor. 1:14; 14:18; (2) of Paul and others, Rom. 16:4; 1 Thess. 2:13; of himself, representatively, as a practice, 1 Cor. 10:30; (3) of others, Luke 17:16; Rom. 14:6 (twice); 1 Cor. 14:17; Rev. 11:17; (e) is used in admonitions to the saints, the Name of the Lord Jesus suggesting His character and example, Eph. 5:20; Col. 1:12; 3:17; 1 Thess. 5:18; (f) as the expression of a purpose, 2 Cor. 1:11, RV; (g) negatively of the ungodly, Rom. 1:21. "Thanksgiving" is the expression of joy Godward, and is therefore the fruit of the Spirit (Gal. 5:22); believers are encouraged to abound in it (e.g., Col. 2:7).

Brake *see Matthew 14:19.*

15:37 And they did all eat, and were filled: and they took up of the broken *meat* that was left seven baskets full.

Filled *see Matthew 14:20.*

Broken *see* Fragments at *Matthew 14:20.*

Meat In **Matt. 15:37** and Mark 8:8, the KJV translates the plural of *klasma*, "a broken piece" (from *klao*, "to break"), "broken meat" (RV, "broken pieces").

Left *see* Remained at *Matthew 14:20.*

Baskets *spuris* (4711), or *sphuris*, signifies "something round, twisted or folded together" (connected with *speira*, "anything rolled into a circle"; Eng., "sphere"); hence a reed basket, plaited, a capacious kind of hamper, sometimes large enough to hold a man, **Matt. 15:37**; **16:10**; Mark 8:8, 20 (RV, "basketfuls"); Acts 9:25.

15:38 And they that did eat were four thousand men, beside women and children.

Thousand *see Matthew 14:21.*

Beside *see Matthew 14:21.*

15:39 And he sent away the multitude, and took ship, and came into the coasts of Magdala.

Came *see* Entered at *Matthew 8:23.*

Coasts *see Matthew 2:16.*

Chapter 16

16:1 The Pharisees also with the Sadducees came, and tempting desired him that he would shew them a sign from heaven.

Tempting *see* Tempted at *Matthew 4:1.*

Desired *eperotao* (1905), is frequently used in the Synoptic Gospels, but only twice in the Gospel of John, 18:7, 21. In Rom. 10:20 it is rendered "asked of" (KJV, "asked after"). The more intensive character of the "asking" may be observed in Luke 2:46; 3:14; 6:9; 17:20; 20:21, 27, 40; 22:64, 23:3, 6, 9. In **Matt. 16:1**, it virtually signifies to demand (its meaning in later Greek).

Shew *epideiknumi* (1925), signifies (a) "to exhibit, display," **Matt. 16:1**; **22:19**; **24:1**; Luke 17:14 (in some mss. 24:40); in the middle voice, "to display," with a special interest in one's own action, Acts 9:39; (b) "to point out, prove, demonstrate," Acts 18:28; Heb. 6:17.

16:2 He answered and said unto them, When it is evening, ye say, *It will be* fair weather: for the sky is red.

Say *see* Account at *Matthew 12:36.*

Fair *eudia* (2105), denotes "fair weather," **Matt. 16:2**, from *eudios*, "calm"; from *eu*, "good," and *dios*, "divine," among the pagan Greeks, akin to the name for the god Zeus, or Jupiter. Some would derive *Dios* and the Latin *deus* (god) and *dies* (day) from a root meaning "bright." Cf. the Latin *sub divo*, "under a bright, open sky."

Weather *eudia* (2105), akin to *eudios*, "calm," denotes "fair weather," **Matt. 16:2**.

Sky *see* Air at *Matthew 8:20.*

Red *purrhazo* (4449), "to be fiery red," is used of the sky, **Matt. 16:2**, **3**. In the Sept., *purrhizo*, Lev. 13:19, 42, 43, 49; 14:37.

16:3 And in the morning, *It will be* foul weather to day: for the sky is red and lowring. O *ye* hypocrites, ye can discern the face of the sky; but can ye not *discern* the signs of the times?

Morning *proi* (4404), "early," is translated "in the morning" in **Matt. 16:3**; **20:1** (with *hama*, "early"); **21:18**; Mark 1:35; 11:20; 13:35; 15:1; "early" in Mark 16:2 (with *lian*, "very"; KJV, "early in the morning"); 16:9; **Matt. 21:18** and John 18:28; 20:1; Acts 28:23 (with *apo*, "from").

Weather *cheimon* (5494), "winter," also "a winter storm," is translated "foul weather" in **Matt. 16:3**.

Red *see Matthew 16:2*.

Lowring *stugnazo* (4768), "to have a gloomy, somber appearance" (akin to *stugnos*, "somber, gloomy," from a root *stug*–, "to hate"; cf. *stugetos*, "hateful," Titus 3:3), is said of the human countenance, Mark 10:22, RV, "his countenance fell" (KJV, "he was sad"); of the sky, **Matt. 16:3**, "lowring."

Can *ginosko* (1097), "to know," is so rendered in the RV of **Matt. 16:3**, "ye know how to," for KJV, "ye can" (*dunamai* is used in the next sentence). This verb represents knowledge as the effect of experience. In Acts 21:37, for "canst thou speak Greek?" the RV has dost ...

Discern *diakrino* (1252), signifies "to separate, discriminate"; then, "to learn by discriminating, to determine, decide." It is translated "discern" in **Matt. 16:3**, of discriminating between the varying conditions of the sky, and in 1 Cor. 11:29, with reference to partaking of the bread and the cup of the Lord's Supper unworthily, by not "discerning" or discriminating what they represent; in v. 31, the RV has "discerned," for the KJV, "would judge," of trying oneself, "discerning" one's condition, and so judging any evil before the Lord; in 14:29, regarding oral testimony in a gathering of believers, it is used of "discerning" what is of the Holy Spirit, RV, "discern" (KJV, "judge").

Face *see* Faces at *Matthew 6:16*.

16:4 A wicked and adulterous generation seeketh after a sign; and there shall no sign be given unto it, but the sign of the prophet Jonas. And he left them, and departed.

Wicked *see Matthew 12:45. See also* Evil at *Matthew 5:11*.

Adulterous *see Matthew 12:39*.

Seeketh *see* Seek at *Matthew 6:32*.

Sign *see Matthew 12:38*.

16:5 And when his disciples were come to the other side, they had forgotten to take bread.

Side *see Matthew 8:18*.

Forgotten *epilanthanomai* (1950), "to forget, or neglect," is said (a) negatively of God, indicating His remembrance of sparrows, Luke 12:6, and of the work and labor of love of His saints, Heb. 6:10; (b) of the disciples regarding taking bread, **Matt. 16:5**: Mark 8:14; (c) of Paul regarding "the things which are behind," Phil. 3:13; (d) of believers, as to showing love to strangers, Heb. 13:2, RV, and as to doing good and communicating, v. 16; (e) of a person who after looking at himself in a mirror, forgets what kind of person he is, Jas. 1:24.

16:6 Then Jesus said unto them, Take heed and beware of the leaven of the Pharisees and of the Sadducees.

Heed *horao* (3708), "to see," usually expressing the sense of vision, is rendered "take heed" in **Matt. 16:6**; **18:10**, KJV (RV, "see"); Mark 8:15; Luke 12:15; Acts 22:26 (KJV only).

Beware *see Matthew 7:15*.

Leaven *see Matthew 13:33*

16:7 And they reasoned among themselves, saying, *It is* because we have taken no bread.

Reasoned *dialogizomai* (1260), "to bring together different reasons and reckon them up, to reason," is used in the NT (a) chiefly of thoughts and considerations which are more or less objectionable, e.g., of the disciples who "reasoned" together, through a mistaken view of Christ's teaching regarding leaven, **Matt. 16:7**, **8** and Mark 8:16, 17; of their "reasoning" as to who was the greatest among them, Mark 9:33, RV, "were ye reasoning," KJV, "ye disputed"; of the scribes and Pharisees in criticizing Christ's claim to forgive sins, Mark 2:6, 8 (twice) and Luke 5:21, 22; of the chief priests and elders in considering how to answer Christ's question regarding John's baptism, **Matt. 21:25**; Mark 11:31 (some mss. have *logizomai*, here, which is nowhere else rendered "to reason"); of the wicked husbandmen, and their purpose to murder the heir and seize his inheritance, Luke 20:14; of the rich man who "reasoned" within himself, RV (KJV, "thought"), as to where to bestow his fruits, Luke 12:17 (some mss. have it in John 11:50, the best have *logizomai*); (b) of considerations not objectionable, Luke 1:29, "cast in (her) mind"; 3:15, RV and KJV, marg., "reasoned" (KJV, "mused").

16:8 *Which* when Jesus perceived, he said unto them, O ye of little faith, why reason ye among yourselves, because ye have brought no bread?

Perceived *see* Knew at *Matthew 12:15.*

Faith *see Matthew 6:30.*

Reason *see* Reasoned at *Matthew 16:7.*

Ye, Yourselves *see* Yourselves at *Matthew 3:9.*

Brought In **Matt. 16:8** some mss. have *lambano* (KJV, "ye have brought").

16:9 Do ye not yet understand, neither remember the five loaves of the five thousand, and how many baskets ye took up?

Understand *see Matthew 15:17.*

Remember *mnemoneuo* (3421), signifies "to call to mind, remember"; it is used absolutely in Mark 8:18; everywhere else it has an object, (a) persons, Luke 17:32; Gal. 2:10; 2 Tim. 2:8, where the RV rightly has "remember Jesus Christ, risen from the dead"; Paul was not reminding Timothy (nor did he need to) that Christ was raised from the dead (KJV), what was needful for him was to "remember" (to keep in mind) the One who rose, the Source and Supplier of all his requirements; (b) things, e.g., **Matt. 16:9**; John 15:20; 16:21; Acts 20:35; Col. 4:18; 1 Thess. 1:3; 2:9; Heb. 11:15, "had been mindful of"; 13:7; Rev. 18:5; (c) a clause, representing a circumstance, etc., John 16:4; Acts 20:31; Eph. 2:11; 2 Thess. 2:5; Rev. 2:5; 3:3; in Heb. 11:22 it signifies "to make mention of."

Five *see Matthew 14:21.*

Thousand *see Matthew 14:21.*

Many *see Matthew 15:34.*

Baskets *see Matthew 14:20.*

16:10 Neither the seven loaves of the four thousand, and how many baskets ye took up?

Thousand *see Matthew 14:21.*

Many *see Matthew 15:34.*

Baskets *see Matthew 14:20.*

16:11 How is it that ye do not understand that I spake *it* not to you concerning bread, that ye should beware of the leaven of the Pharisees and of the Sadducees?

Understand *see Matthew 15:17.*

Bread *see Matthew 6:11.*

Beware *see Matthew 7:15.*

Leaven *see Matthew 13:33.*

16:12 Then understood they how that he bade *them* not beware of the leaven of bread, but of the doctrine of the Pharisees and of the Sadducees.

Understood *see* Understand at *Matthew 13:13.*

Bade *eipon* (3004), used as the aorist tense of *lego*, "to speak, to say," sometimes has the meaning of "commanding, or bidding," and is translated "bid," or "bade," e.g., in **Matt. 16:12; 23:3**; Luke 10:40; 9:54, KJV, "command," RV, "bid"; Acts 11:12; "bidding," Acts 22:24, RV.

Leaven *see Matthew 13:33.*

16:13 When Jesus came into the coasts of Caesarea Philippi, he asked his disciples, saying, Whom do men say that I the Son of man am?

Coasts *see Matthew 15:21. See also* Parts at *Matthew 2:22.*

16:14-16 And they said, Some *say that thou art* John the Baptist: some, Elias; and others, Jeremias, or one of the prophets.
He saith unto them, But whom say ye that I am?
And Simon Peter answered and said, Thou art the Christ, the Son of the living God.

Son *see Matthew 3:17.*

Living *see* Live at *Matthew 4:4.*

16:17 And Jesus answered and said unto him, Blessed art thou, Simon Barjona: for flesh and blood hath not revealed *it* unto thee, but my Father which is in heaven.

Jesus *see* Christ at *Matthew 1:17.*

Blood *haima* (129), (hence Eng., prefix *haem*-, besides its natural meaning, stands, (a) in conjunction with *sarx*, "flesh," "flesh and blood," **Matt. 16:17**; 1 Cor. 15:50; Gal. 1:16; the original has the opposite order, blood and flesh, in Eph. 6:12 and Heb. 2:14; this phrase signifies, by *synecdoche*, "man, human beings." It stresses the limitations of humanity; the two are essential elements in man's physical being; "the life of the flesh is in the blood," Lev. 17:11; (b) for human generation, John 1:13; (c) for "blood" shed by violence, e.g., **Matt. 23:35**; Rev. 17:6; (d) for the "blood" of sacrificial victims, e.g., Heb. 9:7; of the "blood" of Christ, which betokens His death by the shedding of His "blood" in expiatory sacrifice; to drink His "blood" is to appropriate the saving effects of His expiatory death, John 6:53. As "the life of the flesh is in the blood," Lev. 17:11, and was forfeited by sin, life eternal can be imparted only by the expiation made, in the giving up of the life by the sinless Savior.

Revealed *see Matthew 10:26.*

16:18 And I say also unto thee, That thou art Peter, and upon this rock I will build my church; and the gates of hell shall not prevail against it.

Rock *see Matthew 7:24.*

Church *ekklesia* (1577), from *ek*, "out of," and *klesis*, "a calling" (*kaleo*, "to call"), was used among the Greeks of a body of citizens "gathered" to discuss the affairs of state, Acts 19:39. In the Sept. it is used to designate the "gathering" of Israel, summoned for any definite purpose, or a "gathering" regarded as representative of the whole nation. In Acts 7:38 it is used of Israel; in 19:32, 41, of a riotous mob. It has two applications to companies of Christians, (a) to the whole company of the redeemed throughout the present era, the company of which Christ said, "I will build My Church," **Matt. 16:18**, and which is further described as "the Church which is His Body," Eph. 1:22; 5:23; (b) in the singular number (e.g., **Matt. 18:17**, RV marg., "congregation"), to a company consisting of professed believers, e.g., Acts 20:28; 1 Cor. 1:2; Gal. 1:13; 1 Thess. 1:1; 2 Thess. 1:1; 1 Tim. 3:5, and in the plural, with reference to churches in a district. There is an apparent exception in the RV of Acts 9:31, where, while the KJV has "churches," the singular seems to point to a district; but the reference is clearly to the church as it was in Jerusalem, from which it had just been scattered, 8:1. Again, in Rom. 16:23, that Gaius was the host of "the whole church," simply suggests that the "assembly" in Corinth had been accustomed to meet in his house, where also Paul was entertained.

Gates *see* Gate at *Matthew 7:13.*

Hell *see Matthew 11:23.*

Prevail *katischuo* (2729), "to be strong against," is used in **Matt. 16:18**, negatively of the gates of hades; in Luke 21:36 (in the most authentic mss., some have *kataxioo*, "to count worthy"; see KJV), of "prevailing" to escape judgments at the close of this age; in Luke 23:23, of the voices of the chief priests, rulers and people against Pilate regarding the crucifixion of Christ.

16:19 And I will give unto thee the keys of the kingdom of heaven: and whatsoever thou shalt bind on earth shall be bound in heaven: and whatsoever thou shalt loose on earth shall be loosed in heaven.

Keys *kleis* (2807), "a key," is used metaphorically (a) of "the keys of the kingdom of heaven," which the Lord committed to Peter, **Matt. 16:19**, by which he would open the door of faith, as he did to Jews at Pentecost, and to Gentiles in the person of Cornelius, acting as one commissioned by Christ, through the power of the Holy Spirit; he had precedence over his fellow disciples, not in authority, but in the matter of time, on the ground of his confession of Christ (v. **16**); equal authority was committed to them (**18:18**); (b) of "the key of knowledge," Luke 11:52, i.e., knowledge of the revealed will of God, by which men entered into the life that pleases God; this the religious leaders of the Jews had presumptuously "taken away," so that they neither entered in themselves, nor permitted their hearers to do so; (c) of "the keys of death and of Hades," Rev. 1:18, RV, indicative of the authority of the Lord over the bodies and souls of men; (d) of "the key of David," Rev. 3:7, a reference to Isa. 22:22, speaking of the deposition of Shebna and the investiture of Eliakim, in terms evidently messianic, the metaphor being that of the right of entrance upon administrative authority; the mention of David is symbolic of complete sovereignty; (e) of "the key of the pit of the abyss," Rev. 9:1; here the symbolism is that of competent authority; the pit represents a shaft or deep entrance into the region, from whence issued smoke, symbolic of blinding delusion; (f) of "the key of the abyss," Rev. 20:1; this is to be distinguished from (e): the symbolism is that of the complete supremacy of God over the region of the lost, in which, by angelic agency, Satan is destined to be confined for a thousand years.

Bind *deo* (1210), "to bind," is used (a) literally, of any sort of "binding," e.g., Acts 22:5; 24:27, (b) figuratively, of the Word of God, as not being "bound," 2 Tim. 2:9, i.e., its ministry, course and efficacy were not hindered by the bonds and imprisonment suffered by the apostle. A woman who was bent together, had been "bound" by Satan through the work of a demon, Luke 13:16. Paul speaks of himself, in Acts 20:22, as being "bound in the spirit," i.e. compelled by his convictions, under the constraining power of the Spirit of God, to go to Jerusalem. A wife is said to be "bound" to her husband, Rom. 7:2; 1 Cor. 7:39; and the husband to the wife, 1 Cor. 7:27. The Lord's words to the apostle Peter in **Matt. 16:19**, as to "binding," and to all the disciples in **18:18**, signify, in the former case, that the apostle, by his ministry of the Word of Life, would keep unbelievers outside the kingdom of God, and admit those who believed. So with regard to **18:18**, including the exercise of disciplinary measures in the sphere of the local church; the application of the rabbinical sense of forbidding is questionable.

16:20 Then charged he his disciples that they should tell no man that he was Jesus the Christ.

Charged *diastellomai* (1291), lit., "to draw asunder" (*dia*, "asunder," *stello*, "to draw"), signifies "to admonish, order, charge," **Matt. 16:20**; Mark 5:43; 7:36 (twice); 8:15; 9:9. In Acts 15:24 it is translated "gave commandment"; in Heb. 12:20, KJV, "commanded," RV, "enjoined."

16:21 From that time forth began Jesus to shew unto his disciples, how that he must go unto Jerusalem, and suffer many things of the elders and chief priests and scribes, and be killed, and be raised again the third day.

Jesus *see Matthew 1:1*.

Shew *see* Sheweth at *Matthew 4:8*.

Suffer *pascho* (3958), "to suffer," is used (I) of the "sufferings" of Christ (a) at the hands of men, e.g., **Matt. 16:21**; **17:12**; 1 Pet. 2:23; (b) in His expiatory and vicarious sacrifice for sin, Heb. 9:26; 13:12; 1 Pet. 2:21; 3:18; 4:1; (c) including both (a) and (b), Luke 22:15; 24:26, 46; Acts 1:3, "passion"; 3:18; 17:3; Heb. 5:8; (d) by the antagonism of the evil one, Heb. 2:18; (II) of human "suffering" (a) of followers of Christ, Acts 9:16; 2 Cor. 1:6; Gal. 3:4; Phil. 1:29; 1 Thess. 2:14; 2 Thess. 1:5; 2 Tim. 1:12; 1 Pet. 3:14, 17; 5:10; Rev. 2:10; in identification with Christ in His crucifixion, as the spiritual ideal to be realized, 1 Pet. 4:1; in a wrong way, 4:15; (b) of others, physically, as the result of demoniacal power, **Matt. 17:15**, RV, "suffereth (grievously)," KJV, "is (sore) vexed"; cf. Mark 5:26; in a dream, **Matt. 27:19**; through maltreatment, Luke 13:2; 1 Pet. 2:19, 20; by a serpent (negatively), Acts 28:5, RV, "took" (KJV, "felt"); (c) of the effect upon the whole body through the "suffering" of one member, 1 Cor. 12:26, with application to a church.

Elders *see Matthew 15:2*.

Priests *see Matthew 2:4*.

Raised *see* **Raise** at *Matthew 10:8*. *See also* **Arose** at *Matthew 2:14*.

Third *tritos* (5154), is used (a) as a noun, e.g., Luke 20:12, 31; in Rev. 8:7-12 and 9:15, 18, "the third part," lit., "the third"; (b) as an adverb, with the article, "the third time," e.g., Mark 14:41; John 21:17 (twice); without the article, lit., "a third time," e.g., John 21:14; 2 Cor. 12:14; 13:1; in enumerations, in **Matt. 26:44**, with *ek*, "from," lit., "from the third time" (the *ek* indicates the point of departure, especially in a succession of events, cf. John 9:24; 2 Pet. 2:8); absolutely, in the accusative neuter, in 1 Cor. 12:28, "thirdly"; (c) as an adjective (its primary use), e.g., in the phrase the third heaven, 2 Cor. 12:2; in the phrase "the third hour," **Matt. 20:3**; Mark 15:25; Acts 2:15 ("... of the day"); 23:23 ("... of the night"); in a phrase with *hemera*, "a day," "on the third day" (i.e., "the next day but one"), e.g., **Matt. 16:21**; Luke 24:46; Acts 10:40; in this connection the idiom "three days and three nights," **Matt. 12:40**, is explained by ref. to 1 Sam. 30:12, 13, and Esth. 4:16 with 5:1; in Mark 9:31 and 10:34, the RV, "after three days," follows the texts which have this phrase, the KJV, "the third day," those which have the same phrase as in **Matt. 16:21**, etc.

16:22 Then Peter took him, and began to rebuke him, saying, Be it far from thee, Lord: this shall not be unto thee.

Took *proslambano* (4355), "to take to oneself" (*pros*), is used of food, Acts 27:33-36; of persons, of Peter's act toward Christ, **Matt. 16:22**; Mark 8:32; for evil purposes, Acts 17:5; for good purposes, 18:26.

Rebuke *see* **Rebuked** at *Matthew 8:26*.

Far In **Matt. 16:22**, Peter's word to the Lord "be it far from Thee" translates the phrase *hileos soi*, lit., "(God be) propitious to Thee," RV, marg., "God have mercy on Thee." Some would translate it "God avert this from Thee!" Others render it "God forbid!" Luther's translation is "spare Thyself." Lightfoot suggests "Nay, verily!" or "Away with the thought!" It was the vehement and impulsive utterance of Peter's horrified state of mind. *Hileos* signifies "propitious, merciful," Heb. 8:12.

16:23 But he turned, and said unto Peter, Get thee behind me, Satan: thou art an offence unto me: for thou savourest not the things that be of God, but those that be of men.

Get *see Matthew 4:10*.

Satan *see Matthew 4:10*.

Offence *see* **Things that offend** at *Matthew 13:41*.

Savourest In the KJV of **Matt. 16:23** and Mark 8:33, *phroneo*, "to think, to mind," is translated "thou savorest" (RV, "thou mindest").

God *see* Father at *Matthew 10:29*.

16:24 Then said Jesus unto his disciples, If any *man* will come after me, let him deny himself, and take up his cross, and follow me.

Will *thelo* (2309), usually expresses "desire" or "design"; it is most frequently translated by "will" or "would"; see especially Rom. 7:15, 16, 18-21. In 1 Tim. 2:4, RV, "willeth" signifies the gracious "desire" of

God for all men to be saved; not all are "willing" to accept His condition, depriving themselves either by the self-established criterion of their perverted reason, or because of their self-indulgent preference for sin. In John 6:21, the KJV renders the verb "willingly" (RV, "they were willing"); in 2 Pet. 3:5, KJV, the present participle is translated "willingly" (RV, "wilfully"). The following are RV renderings for the KJV, "will": **Matt. 16:24, 25**, "would"; "wouldest," **19:21** and **20:21**; "would," **20:26, 27**; Mark 8:34, 35; 10:43, 44; "would fain," Luke 13:31; "would," John 6:67; "willeth," 7:17; in 8:44, "it is your will (to do)"; "wouldest," Rom. 13:3; "would," 1 Cor. 14:35 and 1 Pet. 3:10.

Deny *aparneomai* (533), means (a) "to deny utterly," to abjure, to affirm that one has no connection with a person, as in Peter's denial of Christ, **Matt. 26:34-35, 75**; Mark 14:30-31, 72; Luke 22:34, 61 (some mss. have it in John 13:38). This stronger form is used in the Lord's statements foretelling Peter's "denial," and in Peter's assurance of fidelity; the simple verb (*arneomai*) is used in all the records of his actual denial. The strengthened form is the verb used in the Lord's warning as to being "denied" in the presence of the angels, Luke 12:9; in the preceding clause, "he that denieth Me," the simple verb *arneomai* is used; the rendering therefore should be "he that denieth Me in the presence of men, shall be utterly denied in the presence of the angels of God"; (b) "to deny oneself" as a follower of Christ, **Matt. 16:24**; Mark 8:34; Luke 9:23.

16:25 For whosoever will save his life shall lose it: and whosoever will lose his life for my sake shall find it.

Will *see Matthew 16:24.*

Save *zoogoneo* (2225), denotes "to preserve alive" (from *zoos*, "alive," and *ginomai*, "to come to be, become, be made"); in Luke 17:33, "shall preserve (it)," i.e., his life, RV marg., "save (it) alive"; cf. the parallels *sozo*, "to save," in **Matt. 16:25**, and *phulaso*, "to keep," in John 12:25; in Acts 7:19, "live," negatively of the efforts of Pharaoh to destroy the babes in Israel; in 1 Tim. 6:13, according to the best mss. (some have *zoopoieo*, "to cause to live"), "quickeneth" (RV, marg., "preserveth ... alive," the preferable rendering).

16:26 For what is a man profited, if he shall gain the whole world, and lose his own soul? or what shall a man give in exchange for his soul?

Profited *see Matthew 15:5.*

Gain *kerdaino* (2770), signifies (I) literally, (a) "to gain something," **Matt. 16:26; 25:16** (in the best mss.), **17, 20, 22**; Mark 8:36; Luke 9:25; (b) "to get gain, make a profit," Jas. 4:13; (II), metaphorically, (a) "to win persons," said (1) of "gaining" an offending brother who by being told privately of his offense, and by accepting the representations, is won from alienation and from the consequences of his fault, **Matt. 18:15**; (2) of winning souls into the kingdom of God by the gospel, 1 Cor. 9:19, 20 (twice), 21, 22, or by godly conduct, 1 Pet. 3:1 (RV, "gained"); (3) of so practically appropriating Christ to oneself that He becomes the dominating power in and over one's whole being and circumstances, Phil. 3:8 (RV, "gain"); (b) "to gain things," said of getting injury and loss, Acts 27:21, RV, "gotten."

World *see Matthew 5:14.*

"To take up the cross of Christ is no great action done once for all; it consists in the continual practice of small duties which are distasteful to us."

JOHN HENRY NEWMAN

Lose *zemioo* (2210), "to damage" (akin to *zemia*, "damage," e.g., Acts 27:10, 21), is used in the NT, in the passive voice, signifying "to suffer loss, forfeit, lose," **Matt. 16:26**; Mark 8:36, of losing one's soul or life; Luke 9:25, RV, "forfeit (his own self)," KJV, "be cast away"; 1 Cor. 3:15, "he shall suffer loss," i.e., at the Judgment-Seat of Christ (see v. 13 with 2 Cor. 5:10); 2 Cor. 7:9, "(that) ye might suffer loss," RV (KJV, "might receive damage"); though the apostle did regret the necessity of making them sorry by his letter, he rejoiced that they were made sorry after a godly sort, and that they thus suffered no spiritual loss, which they would have done had their sorrow been otherwise than after a godly manner; in Phil. 3:8, "I suffered the loss (of all things)," RV, i.e., of all things which he formerly counted gain (especially those in verses 5 and 6, to which the article before "all things" points).

Exchange *antallagma* (465), "the price received as an equivalent of, or in exchange for, an article, an exchange" (*anti*, "instead of," *allasso*, "to change," akin to *allos*, "another"), hence denotes the price at which the "exchange" is effected, **Matt. 16:26**; Mark 8:37. Connected with this is the conception of atonement, as in the word *lutron*, "a ransom." Cf *allagma* in the Sept., e.g., in Isa. 43:3.

16:27 For the Son of man shall come in the glory of his Father with his angels; and then he shall reward every man according to his works.

Son *see Matthew 3:17.*

Shall *mello* (3195), "to be about (to be or do)," is used of purpose, certainty, compulsion or necessity. It is rendered simply by "shall" or "should" (which frequently represent elsewhere part of the future tense of the verb) in the following (the RV sometimes translates differently, as noted): **Matt. 16:27** (1st part), lit., "is about to come"; **17:12, 22; 20:22**, RV, "am about"; **24:6**; Mark 13:4 (2nd part), RV, "are about"; Luke 9:44; 21:7 (2nd part), RV, "are about"; v. 36; Acts 23:3; 24:15; 26:2, RV, "I am (to)"; Rom. 4:24; 8:13 (1st part), RV, "must"; v. 18; 2 Tim. 4:1; Heb. 1:14; 10:27; Jas. 2:12, RV "are to"; 1 Pet. 5:1; Rev. 1:19; 2:10 (1st and 2nd parts), RV, "art about," "is about"; 3:10, RV, "is (to)"; 17:8 (1st part), RV, "is about."

Reward *apodidomi* (591), to give up or back," is translated "to render," (a) of righteous acts, (1) human, **Matt. 21:41; 22:21**; Mark 12:17; Luke 16:2, RV (KJV, "give"); Luke 20:25; Rom. 13:7, 1 Cor. 7:3; (2) divine, **Matt. 16:27**, RV, "shall render" (KJV, "shall reward"), an important RV change; Rom. 2:6; 2 Tim. 4:14, RV (KJV, "reward"); Rev. 18:6 (ditto); 22:12, RV (KJV, "give"); (b) of unrighteous acts. Rom. 12:17, RV (KJV, "recompense"); 1 Thess. 5:15; 1 Pet. 3:9. *See also* ***Matthew 6:4.***

Works *praxis* (4234), denotes "a doing, transaction, a deed the action of which is looked upon as incomplete and in progress" (cf. *prasso*, "to practice"); in **Matt. 16:27**, RV, "deeds," for KJV, "works"; in Luke 23:51, "deed"; in v. 41, the verb is used; Acts 19:18; Rom. 8:13; Col. 3:9. In Rom. 12:4 it denotes an "action," business, or function, translated "office."

16:28 Verily I say unto you, There be some standing here, which shall not taste of death, till they see the Son of man coming in his kingdom.

Son *see Matthew 3:17.*

Verily *amen* (281), is transliterated from Hebrew into both Greek and English. "Its meanings may be seen in such passages as Deut. 7:9, 'the faithful (the Amen) God,' Isa. 49:7, 'Jehovah that is faithful.' 65:16, 'the God of truth,' marg., 'the God of Amen.' And if God is faithful His testimonies and precepts are "sure (*amen*)," Ps. 19:7; 111:7, as are also His warnings, Hos. 5:9, and promises, Isa. 33:16; 55:3. 'Amen' is used of men also, e.g., Prov. 25:13.

"Once in the NT 'Amen' is a title of Christ, Rev. 3:14, because through Him the purposes of God are established, 2 Cor. 1:20. The early Christian churches followed the example of Israel in associating themselves audibly with the prayers and thanksgivings offered on their behalf, 1 Cor. 14:16, where the article 'the' points to a common practice. Moreover this custom conforms to the pattern of things in the Heavens, see Rev. 5:14, etc. The individual also said 'Amen' to express his 'let it be so' in response to the Divine 'thus it shall be,' Rev. 22:20. Frequently the speaker adds 'Amen' to his own prayers and doxologies, as is the case at Eph. 3:21, e.g. The Lord Jesus often used 'Amen,' translated 'verily,' to introduce new revelations of the mind of God. In John's Gospel it is always repeated, 'Amen, Amen,' but not elsewhere. Luke does not use it at all, but where Matthew, **16:28**, and Mark, 9:1, have 'Amen,' Luke has 'of a truth'; thus by varying the translation of what the Lord said, Luke throws light on His meaning."

Taste *geuo* (1089), "to make to taste," is used in the middle voice, signifying "to taste" (a) naturally, **Matt. 27:34**; Luke 14:24; John 2:9; Col. 2:21; (b) metaphorically, of Christ's "tasting" death, implying His personal experience in voluntarily undergoing death, Heb. 2:9; of believers (negatively) as to "tasting" of death, **Matt. 16:28**; Mark 9:1; Luke 9:27; John 8:52; of "tasting" the heavenly gift (different from receiving it), Heb. 6:4; "the good word of God, and the powers of the age to come," 6:5; "that the Lord is gracious," 1 Pet. 2:3.

Chapter 17

17:1 And after six days Jesus taketh Peter, James, and John his brother, and bringeth them up into an high mountain apart,

Six *hex* (1803), whence Eng. prefix, "hex"-, is used separately from other numerals in **Matt. 17:1**; Mark 9:2; Luke 4:25; 13:14; John 2:6; 12:1; Acts 11:12; 18:11; Jas. 5:17; Rev. 4:8. It sometimes suggests incompleteness, in comparison with the perfect number seven.

Taketh *see* **Take** at ***Matthew 1:20.***

Bringeth *anaphero* (399), denotes "to bring up," **Matt. 17:1**.

High *see Matthew 4:8.*

Mountain *see Matthew 5:1.*

17:2 And was transfigured before them: and his face did shine as the sun, and his raiment was white as the light.

Transfigured *metamorphoo* (3339), "to change into another form" (*meta*, implying change, and *morphe*, "form"), is used in the passive voice (a) of Christ's "transfiguration," **Matt. 17:2**; Mark 9:2; Luke (in 9:29) avoids this term, which might have suggested to gentile readers the metamorphoses of heathen gods, and uses the phrase *egeneto heteron*, "was altered", lit., "became (*ginomai*) different (*heteros*)"; (b) of believers, Rom. 12:2, "be ye transformed," the obligation being to undergo a complete change which, under the power of God, will find expression in character and conduct; *morphe* lays stress on the inward change, *schema* (see the preceding verb in that verse, *suschematizo*) lays stress on the outward; the present continuous tenses indicate a process; 2 Cor. 3:18 describes believers as being "transformed (RV) into the same image" (i.e., of Christ in all His moral excellencies), the change being effected by the Holy Spirit.

Before *see Matthew 5:16.*

Shine *see* Light at *Matthew 5:15.*

Sun *see Matthew 5:45.*

Raiment *himation* (2440), "an outer garment, a mantle, thrown over the *chiton*." In the plural, "clothes" (the "cloke" and the tunic), e.g., **Matt. 17:2; 26:65; 27:31, 35.**

White *see Matthew 5:36.*

17:3 And, behold, there appeared unto them Moses and Elias talking with him.

Talking *sullaleo* (4814), "to speak together with" (*sun*, "with," *laleo*, "to speak"), is translated "to talk with," **Matt. 17:3**; Mark 9:4; Luke 9:30.

17:4 Then answered Peter, and said unto Jesus, Lord, it is good for us to be here: if thou wilt, let us make here three tabernacles; one for thee, and one for Moses, and one for Elias.

Said *see* Say at *Matthew 3:9.*

Lord *rabbei* (4461), was an Aramaic word signifying "my master," a title of respectful address to Jewish teachers. "The Aramaic word *rabbei*, transliterated into Greek, is explicitly recognized as the common form of address to Christ, **Matt. 26:25** (cf., however, v. **22**, *kurios*); **26:49**; Mark 9:5, but **Matt. 17:4**, *kurios*" (Dalman, *The Words of Jesus*). In the following the RV has "Rabbi" for KJV "Master"; **Matt. 26:25, 49**; Mark 9:5; 11:21; 14:45; John 4:31; 9:2; 11:8. In other passages the KJV has "Rabbi," **Matt 23:7-8**; John 1:38, 49; 3:2, 26; 6:25.

Make *poieo* (4160), signifies (a) "to make," (b) "to do," i.e., to adopt a way of expressing by act the thoughts and feelings. It stands for a number of such acts, chiefly "to make, produce, create, cause," e.g., **Matt. 17:4.** *See also Matthew 4:19.*

Tabernacles *skene* (4633), "a tent, booth, tabernacle," is used of (a) tents as dwellings, **Matt. 17:4**; Mark 9:5; Luke 9:33; Heb. 11:9, KJV, "tabernacles" (RV, "tents"); (b) the Mosaic tabernacle, Acts 7:44; Heb. 8:5; 9:1 (in some mss.); 9:8, 21, termed "the tent of meeting," RV (i.e., where the people were called to meet God), a preferable description to "the tabernacle of the congregation," as in the KJV in the OT; the outer part, 9:2, 6; the inner sanctuary, 9:3; (c) the heavenly prototype, Heb. 8:2; 9:11; Rev. 13:6; 15:5; 21:3 (of its future descent); (d) the eternal abodes of the saints, Luke 16:9, RV, "tabernacles" (KJV, "habitations"); (e) the Temple in Jerusalem, as continuing the service of the tabernacle, Heb. 13:10; (f) the house of David, i.e., metaphorically of his people, Acts 15:16; (g) the portable shrine of the god Moloch, Acts 7:43.

17:5 While he yet spake, behold, a bright cloud overshadowed them: and behold a voice out of the cloud, which said, This is my beloved Son, in whom I am well pleased; hear ye him.

Bright *see* Light at *Matthew 6:22.*

Cloud *nephele* (3507), "a definitely shaped cloud, or masses of clouds possessing definite form," is used, besides the physical element, (a) of the "cloud" on the mount of transfiguration, **Matt. 17:5**; (b) of the "cloud" which covered Israel in the Red Sea, 1 Cor. 10:1-2; (c) of "clouds" seen in the Apocalyptic visions, Rev. 1:7; 10:1; 11:12; 14:14-16; (d) metaphorically in 2 Pet. 2:17, of the evil workers there mentioned; but RV, "and mists" (*homichle*), according to the most authentic mss. In 1 Thess. 4:17, the "clouds" referred to in connection with the rapture of the saints are probably the natural ones, as also in the case of those in connection with Christ's second advent to the earth. See **Matt. 24:30; 26:64**, and parallel passages. So at the Ascension, Acts 1:9.

Overshadowed *episkiazo* (1982), "to throw a shadow upon" (*epi*, "over," *skia*, "a shadow"), "to overshadow," is used (a) of the bright cloud at the Transfiguration, **Matt. 17:5**; Mark 9:7; Luke 9:34; (b) metaphorically of the power of "the Most High" upon the Virgin Mary, Luke 1:35; (c) of the apostle Peter's shadow upon the sick, Acts 5:15.

Pleased *see Matthew 3:17.*

17:6 And when the disciples heard *it*, they fell on their face, and were sore afraid.

Fell *see Matthew 2:11.*

Sore *sphodra* (4970), "very, very much," is translated "sore" in **Matt. 17:6** (of fear). *See also* **Exceeding** at *Matthew 2:10.*

17:7-8 And Jesus came and touched them, and said, Arise, and be not afraid.

And when they had lifted up their eyes, they saw no man, save Jesus only.

Lifted *epairo* (1869), "to lift up, raise," is used of "lifting" up the eyes, **Matt. 17:8**; Luke 6:20; 16:23, 18:13; John 4:35; 6:5; 17:1; the head, Luke 21:28; the hands, Luke 24:50; 1 Tim. 2:8; the voice, Luke 11:27; Acts 2:14; 14:11; 22:22; a foresail, Acts 27:40 ("hoisting," RV); metaphorically, of the heel, John 13:18, as of one "lifting" up the foot before kicking; the expression indicates contempt and violence; in the passive voice, Acts 1:9, of Christ's ascension, "was taken up"; 2 Cor. 10:5, "is exalted" (with pride); 11:20, "exalteth himself."

No man The RV often substitutes "one" for "man," e.g., **Matt. 17:8** (*oudeis*, "no one"); 1 Cor. 3:21 (i.e., "no person"); 1 Cor. 15:35; 1 Thess. 5:15; 2 Tim. 4:16; 1 John 2:27; 3:3.

Only *see Matthew 4:10.*

17:9 And as they came down from the mountain, Jesus charged them, saying, Tell the vision to no man, until the Son of man be risen again from the dead.

From The preposition *ek* (or *ex*), which frequently signifies "out of" or "from the midst of," has a variety of meanings, among which is "from," as virtually equivalent to *apo*, "away from," e.g., 2 Cor. 1:10, "who delivered us out of so great a death, and will deliver"; since death was not actually experienced, but was impending, *ek* here does not signify "out of the midst of." In Acts 12:7 it is used in the statement "his chains fell off from his hands." In **Matt. 17:9** it is used of descending from a mountain, not "out of"; "we are not to suppose that they had been in a cave" (Dr. A. T. Robertson, *Gram. of the Greek NT*). In 1 Thess. 1:10, "even Jesus, which delivereth us from the wrath to come," RV, the question whether *ek* here means "out of the midst of" or "away from," is to be determined by some statement of Scripture where the subject is specifically mentioned; this is provided, e.g., in 5:9, the context of which makes clear that believers are to be delivered from (not "out of") the divine wrath to be executed on the nations at the end of the present age.

Mountain *see Matthew 5:1.*

Charged *see* **Charge** at *Matthew 4:6.*

Vision *horama* (3705), "that which is seen" (*horao*), denotes (a) "a spectacle, sight," **Matt. 17:9**; Acts 7:31 ("sight"); (b) "an appearance, vision," Acts 9:10 (v. 12 in some mss.): 10:3, 17, 19; 11:5; 12:9; 16:9, 10; 18:9.

Son *see Matthew 3:17.*

Risen *see* **Rise** at *Matthew 12:41.*

17:10 And his disciples asked him, saying, Why then say the scribes that Elias must first come?

Must *dei* (1163), an impersonal verb, signifying "it is necessary" or "one must," "one ought," is found most frequently in the Gospels, Acts and Revelation, and is used (a) of a necessity lying in the nature of the case e.g., John 3:30; 2 Tim. 2:6; (b) of necessity brought about by circumstances, e.g., **Matt. 26:35**, RV, "must," KJV, "should"; John 4:4; Acts 27:21, "should"; 2 Cor. 11:30; in the case of Christ, by reason of the Father's will, e.g., Luke 2:49; 19:5; (c) of necessity as to what is required that something may be brought about, e.g., Luke 12:12, "ought"; John 3:7; Acts 9:6; 1 Cor. 11:19; Heb. 9:26; (d) of a necessity of law, duty, equity, e.g., **Matt. 18:33**, "shouldest"; **23:23**, "ought"; Luke 15:32, "it was meet"; Acts 15:5, "it is needful" (RV); Rom. 1:27, RV, "was due," KJV, "was meet" (of a recompense due by the law of God); frequently requiring the rendering "ought," e.g., Rom. 8:26; 12:3; 1 Cor. 8:2; (e) of necessity arising from the determinate will and counsel of God, e.g., **Matt. 17:10**; **24:6**; **26:54**; 1 Cor. 15:53, especially regarding the salvation of men through the death, resurrection and ascension of Christ, e.g., John 3:14; Acts 3:21; 4:12.

17:11 And Jesus answered and said unto them, Elias truly shall first come, and restore all things.

Truly *see* **Indeed** at *Matthew 3:11.*

Restore *see* **Restored** at *Matthew 12:13.*

17:12 But I say unto you, That Elias is come already, and they knew him not, but have done unto him whatsoever they listed. Likewise shall also the Son of man suffer of them.

Whatsoever *see Matthew 10:11.*

Listed *thelo* (2309), "to will, wish," is translated by the verb "to list" in **Matt. 17:12**; Mark 9:13; John 3:8.

Likewise In **Matt. 17:12** and Rom. 6:11, KJV, the adverb *houtos*, "thus, so," is translated "likewise" (RV, "so"); in Luke 15:7 and 10, KJV, "likewise," RV, "even so", in Luke 14:33, KJV, followed by *oun*, "therefore," it is rendered "so likewise" (RV, "so therefore").

Shall *see Matthew 16:27.*

Suffer *see Matthew 16:21.*

17:13 Then the disciples understood that he spake unto them of John the Baptist.

Understood *see* **Understand** at *Matthew 13:13.*

17:14 And when they were come to the multitude, there came to him a *certain* man, kneeling down to him, and saying,

Man *see Matthew 4:4.*

Kneeling *gonupeteo* (1120), denotes "to bow the knees, kneel," from *gonu* and *pipto*, "to fall prostrate," the act of one imploring aid, **Matt. 17:14**; Mark 1:40; of one expressing reverence and honor, Mark 10:17; in mockery, **Matt. 27:29**.

17:15 Lord, have mercy on my son: for he is lunatick, and sore vexed: for ofttimes he falleth into the fire, and oft into the water.

Mercy *see Matthew 5:7.*

Lunatick *see Matthew 4:24.*

Sore vexed *echo* (2192) *poneros* (4190), idiomatic phrase (lit., "hath badly"), is rendered "suffereth grievously," RV (KJV, "is ... sore vexed"). *See also* **Suffer** at *Matthew 16:21.*

Ofttimes *pollakis* (4178), akin to *polus*, "much, many," is variously translated, e.g., "ofttimes," **Matt. 17:15** (KJV, "oft," 2nd part); "many times," 2 Cor. 8:22, RV (KJV, "oftentimes"); "oft," 2 Cor. 11:23; "often" (v. 26).

17:16 And I brought him to thy disciples, and they could not cure him.

Cure *therapeuo* (2323), (Eng., "therapeutics," etc.), denotes (a) primarily, "to serve" (cf. *therapeia* and *therapon*), Acts 17:25 (KJV, "worshiped"); then, (b) "to heal, restore to health, to cure"; it is usually translated "to heal," but "cure" in **Matt. 17:16, 18**; Luke 7:21; 9:1; John 5:10; Acts 28:9, RV.

17:17 Then Jesus answered and said, O faithless and perverse generation, how long shall I be with you? how long shall I suffer you? bring him hither to me.

Faithless *apistos* (571), (a) "untrustworthy," not worthy of confidence or belief, is said of things "incredible," Acts 26:8 (b) "unbelieving, distrustful," used as a noun, "unbeliever," Luke 12:46; 1 Tim. 5:8 (RV, for KJV, "infidel"); in Titus 1:15 and Rev. 21:8, "unbelieving"; "faithless" in **Matt. 17:17**; Mark 9:19; Luke 9:41; John 20:27. The word is most frequent in 1 and 2 Corinthians. (In the Sept., Prov. 17:6; 28:25; Isa. 17:10.).

Perverse *diastrepho* (1294), "to distort, twist" (*dia*, "through," and *strepho*), is translated "to pervert" in Luke 23:2; Acts 13:10 [in v. 8, "to turn aside" (KJV, "away")]; in the perfect participle, passive voice, it is translated "perverse," lit., "turned aside, corrupted," in **Matt. 17:17**; Luke 9:41; Acts 20:30; Phil. 2:15.

Generation *see* **Generations** at *Matthew 1:17.*

Suffer *anecho* (430), in the middle voice, "to bear with," is rendered "to suffer" in **Matt. 17:17** and parallel passages; KJV only, 1 Cor. 4:12 (RV, "endure"); 2 Cor. 11:19, 20 and Heb. 13:22 (RV, "bear with").

17:18 And Jesus rebuked the devil; and he departed out of him: and the child was cured from that very hour.

Rebuked *see Matthew 8:26.*

Child *pais* (3816), denotes "a boy" (in contrast to *paidion*, a diminutive of *pais*, and to *teknon*, "a child"). With reference to Christ, instead of the KJV "child," the RV suitably translates otherwise as follows: Luke 2:43, "the boy Jesus"; Acts 4:27, 30, "Thy Holy Servant, Jesus." So in the case of others, **Matt. 17:18** and Luke 9:42 ("boy"). *See also* **Children** at *Matthew 2:16.*

Cured *see* **Cure** at *Matthew 17:16.*

17:19-20 Then came the disciples to Jesus apart, and said, Why could not we cast him out?

And Jesus said unto them, Because of your unbelief: for verily I say unto you, If ye have faith as a grain of mustard seed, ye shall say unto this mountain, Remove hence to yonder place; and it shall remove; and nothing shall be impossible unto you.

Unbelief *see Matthew 13:58.*

Grain *see Matthew 13:31.*

Mustard *see Matthew 13:31.*

Mountain *see Matthew 5:1.*

Remove *metabaino* (3327), "to pass over from one place to another" (*meta*, implying "change," and *baino*, "to go"), is translated "to remove" in **Matt. 17:20** (twice).

Hence *enthen* (1782), is found in the best mss. in **Matt. 17:20**; Luke 16:26.

Yonder *ekei* (1563), "there," is rendered "yonder" in **Matt. 26:36**; "to yonder place," **17:20**.

Impossible *adunateo* (101), signifies "to be impossible," "unable"; in the NT it is used only of things, **Matt. 17:20**, "(nothing) shall be impossible (unto you)"; Luke 1:37. KJV "(with God nothing) shall be impossible"; RV, "(no word from God—a different construction in the best mss.) shall be void of power"; *rhema* may mean either "word" or "thing" (i.e., fact). In the Sept. the verb is always used of things and signifies either to be "impossible" or to be impotent, e.g., Gen. 18:14; Lev. 25:35, "he fail"; Deut. 17:8; Job 4:4, "feeble"; 42:2; Dan. 4:6; Zech. 8:6.

17:21 Howbeit this kind goeth not out but by prayer and fasting.

Kind *see Matthew 13:47.*

Fasting *nesteia* (3521), "a fasting, fast" (from *ne*, a negative prefix, and *esthio*, "to eat"), is used (a) of voluntary abstinence from food, Luke 2:37; Acts 14:23 (some mss. have it in **Matt. 17:21** and Mark 9:29); "fasting" had become a common practice among Jews, and was continued among Christians; in Acts 27:9, "the Fast" refers to the Day of Atonement, Lev. 16:29; that time of the year would be one of dangerous sailing; (b) of involuntary abstinence (perhaps voluntary is included), consequent upon trying circumstances, 2 Cor. 6:5; 11:27.

17:22 And while they abode in Galilee, Jesus said unto them, The Son of man shall be betrayed into the hands of men:

Abode *anastrepho* (390), used once in the sense of "abiding," **Matt. 17:22**, frequently denotes "to behave oneself, to live a certain manner of life"; here the most reliable mss. have *sustrephomai*, "to travel about."

Shall *see Matthew 16:27.*

Betrayed *see* Prison at *Matthew 4:12.*

Hands *cheir* (5495), "the hand" (cf. Eng., "chiropody"), is used, besides its ordinary significance, (a) in the idiomatic phrases, "by the hand of," "at the hand of," etc., to signify "by the agency of," Acts 5:12; 7:35; 17:25; 14:3; Gal. 3:19 (cf. Lev. 26:46); Rev. 19:2; (b) metaphorically, for the power of God, e.g., Luke 1:66; 23:46; John 10:28, 29; Acts 11:21; 13:11; Heb. 1:10; 2:7; 10:31; (c) by metonymy, for power, e.g., **Matt. 17:22**; Luke 24:7; John 10:39; Acts 12:11.

17:23 And they shall kill him, and the third day he shall be raised again. And they were exceeding sorry.

Third *treis* (5143), is regarded by many as a number sometimes symbolically indicating fullness of testimony or manifestation, as in the three persons in the Godhead, cf. 1 Tim. 5:19; Heb. 10:28; the mention in 1 John 5:7 is in a verse which forms no part of the original; no Greek ms. earlier than the 14th century contained it; no version earlier than the 5th cent. in any other language contains it, nor is it quoted by any of the Greek or Latin "Fathers" in their writings on the Trinity. That there are those who bear witness in Heaven is not borne out by any other Scripture. It must be regarded as the interpolation of a copyist. In Mark 9:31 and 10:34 the best texts have *meta treis hemeras*, "after three days," which idiomatically expresses the same thing as *te tritehemera*, "on the third day," which some texts have here, as, e.g., the phrase "the third day" in **Matt. 17:23**; **20:19**; Luke 9:22; 18:33, where the repetition of the article lends stress to the number, lit., "the day the third"; 24:7, 46; Acts 10:40.

Raised *see* Raise at *Matthew 10:8.*

Exceeding *see Matthew 2:10.*

Sorry *see Matthew 14:9.*

17:24 And when they were come to Capernaum, they that received tribute *money* came to Peter, and said, Doth not your master pay tribute?

Master *see Matthew 8:19.*

Pay *teleo* (5055), "to bring to an end, complete, fulfill," has the meaning "to pay" in **Matt. 17:24** and Rom. 13:6.

Tribute *didrachmon* (1323), "a half-shekel" (i.e., *dis*, "twice," *drachme*, "a drachma," the coin mentioned in Luke 15:8, 9), was the amount of the tribute in the 1st cent., AD, due from every adult Jew for the maintenance of the Temple services, **Matt. 17:24** (twice). This was based on Exod. 30:13, 24 (see also 38:24-26; Lev. 5:15; 27:3, 25; Num. 3:47, 50; 7:13ff.; 18:16).

17:25 He saith, Yes. And when he was come into the house, Jesus prevented him, saying, What thinkest thou, Simon? of whom do the kings of the earth take custom or tribute? of their own children, or of strangers?

Yes *see* Yea at *Matthew 5:37.*

Come *katantao* (2658), "to come to, arrive at", is used (a) literally, of locality, Acts 16:1, "came to"; so 18:19, 24; 20:15 ("came"); 21:7; 25:13; 27:12 (KJV, "attain to," RV, "reach"); 28:13; (b) metaphorically, of attainment, Acts 26:7, "attain"; so Eph. 4:13; Phil. 3:11. In 1 Cor. 10:11 ("upon whom the ends of the ages are come," RV), the metaphor is apparently that of an inheritance as coming down or descending to an heir, the "ends" (*tele* being the spiritual revenues (cf. **Matt. 17:25**, revenues derived from taxes, and Rom. 13:7, where the singular, *telos*, "custom," is used); the inheritance metaphor is again seen in 1 Cor. 14:36, of the coming (or descending) of the Word of God to the Corinthians.

Prevented *prophthano* (4399), "to anticipate" (an extension, by *pro*, "before," of *phthano*, which has the same meaning), is rendered "spake first" in **Matt. 17:25**, RV (KJV, "prevented").

Thou *see Matthew 2:6.*

Custom *telos* (5056), "an end, termination," whether of time or purpose, denotes, in its secondary significance, "what is paid for public ends, a toll, tax, custom," **Matt. 17:25** (RV, "toll"); Rom. 13:7 (RV and KJV, "custom"). In Palestine the Herods of Galilee and Perea received the "custom"; in Judea it was paid to the procurator for the Roman government.

Tribute *kensos* (2778), Lat. and Eng., "census," denotes "a poll tax," **Matt. 17:25; 22:17, 19**; Mark 12:14.

Strangers *allotrios* (245), "strangers," **Matt. 17:25, 26**; John 10:5 (twice).

17:26 Peter saith unto him, Of strangers. Jesus saith unto him, Then are the children free.

Strangers *see Matthew 17:25.*

Free *eleutheros* (1658), primarily of "freedom to go wherever one likes," is used (a) of "freedom from restraint and obligation" in general, **Matt. 17:26**; Rom. 7:3; 1 Cor. 7:39, RV, "free," of the second marriage of a woman; 9:1, 19; 1 Pet. 2:16; from the Law, Gal. 4:26; from sin, John 8:36; with regard to righteousness, Rom. 6:20 (i.e., righteousness laid no sort of bond upon them, they had no relation to it); (b) in a civil sense, "free" from bondage or slavery, John 8:33; 1 Cor. 7:21, 22, 2nd part; 12:13; Gal. 3:28; Eph. 6:8; Rev. 13:16; 19:18; as a noun, "freeman," Col. 3:11, RV; Rev. 6:15; "freewoman," Gal. 4:22, 23, 30, and v. 31.

17:27 Notwithstanding, lest we should offend them, go thou to the sea, and cast an hook, and take up the fish that first cometh up; and when thou hast opened his mouth, thou shalt find a piece of money: that take, and give unto them for me and thee.

Offend *see Matthew 13:57.*

Hook *ankistron* (44), "a fish-hook" (from *ankos*, "a bend"; Lat. *angulus*; Eng., "anchor" and "angle" are akin), is used in **Matt. 17:27**. In the Sept., 2 Kings 19:28; Job 40:20; Isa. 19:8; Ezek. 32:3; Hab. 1:15.

Opened *see Matthew 2:11.*

Mouth *see Matthew 12:34.*

Piece of money In **Matt. 17:27**, KJV, *stater* ("a coin," estimated at a little over three shillings, equivalent to four *drachmae*, the temple-tax for two persons), is translated "piece of money" (RV, "shekel").

Chapter 18

18:1 At the same time came the disciples unto Jesus, saying, Who is the greatest in the kingdom of heaven?

Time *see Matthew 14:15.*

Greatest *see Matthew 13:32.*

18:2 And Jesus called a little child unto him, and set him in the midst of them,

Set *see* Setteth at *Matthew 4:5.*

18:3 And said, Verily I say unto you, Except ye be converted, and become as little children, ye shall not enter into the kingdom of heaven.

Converted *strepho* (4762), "to turn," is translated "be converted" in **Matt. 18:3**, KJV. *See also* Turn at *Matthew 5:39.*

Kingdom *see* Kingdoms at *Matthew 4:8.*

18:4 Whosoever therefore shall humble himself as this little child, the same is greatest in the kingdom of heaven.

Humble *tapeinoo* (5013), signifies "to make low," (a) literally, "of mountains and hills," Luke 3:5 (passive voice); (b) metaphorically, in the active voice, **Matt. 18:4; 23:12** (2nd part); Luke 14:11 (2nd part); 18:14 (2nd part); 2 Cor. 11:7 ("abasing"); 12:21; Phil. 2:8; in the passive voice, **Matt. 23:12** (1st part), RV, "shall be humbled," KJV, "shall be abased"; Luke 14:11 (ditto); 18:14 (ditto); Phil. 4:12, "to be abased"; in the passive, with middle voice sense, Jas. 4:10, "humble yourselves"; 1 Pet. 5:6 (ditto).

Greatest *see Matthew 13:32.*

18:5 And whoso shall receive one such little child in my name receiveth me.

Receive, Receiveth *see* Receive at *Matthew 10:14.*

Name *see Matthew 6:9.*

18:6 But whoso shall offend one of these little ones which believe in me, it were better for him that a millstone were hanged about his neck, and *that* he were drowned in the depth of the sea.

Offend *see Matthew 13:57.*

Little *see Matthew 10:42.*

Better *see* Profitable at *Matthew 5:29.*

Millstone *mulos* (3458), denotes "a handmill," consisting of two circular stones, one above the other, the lower being fixed. From the center of the lower a wooden pin passes through a hole in the upper, into which the grain is thrown, escaping as flour between the stones and falling on a prepared material below them. The handle is inserted into the upper stone near the circumference. Small stones could be turned by one woman (millgrinding was a work deemed fit only for women and slaves; cf. Judg. 16:21); larger ones were turned by two (cf. **Matt. 24:41**), or more. Still larger ones were turned by an ass (*onikos*), **Matt. 18:6**, RV, "a great millstone" (marg., "a millstone turned by an ass"), indicating the immediate and overwhelming drowning of one who causes one young believer to stumble; Mark 9:42 (where some mss. have *lithos mulikos*, "a stone of a mill," as in Luke 17:2); Rev. 18:22 (some mss. have it in v. 21).

Hanged *kremannumi* (2910), is used (a) transitively in Acts 5:30; 10:39; in the passive voice, in **Matt. 18:6**, of a millstone about a neck, and in Luke 23:39, of the malefactors; (b) intransitively, in the middle voice, in **Matt. 22:40**, of the dependence of "the Law and the prophets" (i.e., that which they enjoin) upon the one great principle of love to God and one's neighbor (as a door "hangs" on a hinge, or as articles "hang" on a nail); in Acts 28:4, of the serpent "hanging" from Paul's hand; in Gal. 3:13 the word is used in a quotation from the Sept. of Deut. 21:23.

Neck *trachelos* (5137), is used (a) literally, **Matt. 18:6**; Mark 9:42; Luke 17:2; of "embracing," Luke 15:20; Acts 20:37; (b) metaphorically, in Acts 15:10, of "putting a yoke upon": Rom. 16:4, singular in the original, "(laid down their) neck," indicating the figurative use of the term rather than the literal. Prisca and Aquila in some way had risked their lives for the apostle (the phrase is found with this significance in the papyri).

Drowned *see* Sink at *Matthew 14:30.*

Depth *pelagos* (3989), "the sea," Acts 27:5, denotes also "the depth" (of the sea), **Matt. 18:6**. The word is most probably connected with a form of *plesso*, "to strike," and *plege*, "a blow," suggestive of the tossing of the waves. Some would connect it with *plax*, "a level board," but this is improbable, and less applicable to the general usage of the word, which commonly denotes the sea in its restless character.

Sea *see Matthew 4:18.*

18:7 Woe unto the world because of offences! for it must needs be that offences come; but woe to that man by whom the offence cometh!

Woe *see Matthew 11:21.*

Offences *see* Things that offend at *Matthew 13:41.*

Needs *ananke* (318), "a necessity, need," is translated "it must needs be" in **Matt. 18:7**, with the verb "to be" understood (according to the best mss.); in Luke 14:18, "I must needs" translates the verb *echo*, "to have," with this noun as the object, lit., "I have need"; in Rom. 13:5 "(ye) must needs," lit., "(it is) necessary (to be subject)."

18:8 Wherefore if thy hand or thy foot offend thee, cut them off, and cast *them* from thee: it is better for thee to enter into life halt or maimed, rather than having two hands or two feet to be cast into everlasting fire.

Offend *see Matthew 13:57.*

Halt *see* Lame at *Matthew 11:5.*

Maimed *see Matthew 15:30.*

Everlasting *aionios* (166), "describes duration, either undefined but not endless, as in Rom. 16:25; 2 Tim. 1:9; Titus 1:2; or undefined because endless as in Rom. 16:26, and the other sixty-six places in the NT. "The predominant meaning of *aionios*, that in which it is used everywhere in the NT, save the places noted above, may be seen in 2 Cor. 4:18, where it is set in contrast with *proskairos*, lit., 'for a season,' and in Philem. 15, where only in the NT it is used without a noun. Moreover it is used of persons and things which are in their nature endless, as, e.g., of God, Rom. 16:26; of His power, 1 Tim. 6:16, and of His glory, 1 Pet. 5:10; of the Holy Spirit, Heb. 9:14; of the redemption effected by Christ, Heb. 9:12, and of the consequent salvation of men, 5:9, as well as of His future rule, 2 Pet. 1:11, which is elsewhere declared to be without end, Luke

1:33; of the life received by those who believe in Christ, John 3:16, concerning whom He said, 'they shall never perish,' 10:28, and of the resurrection body, 2 Cor. 5:1, elsewhere said to be 'immortal,' 1 Cor. 15:53, in which that life will be finally realized, **Matt. 25:46**; Titus 1:2. *Aionios* is also used of the sin that 'hath never forgiveness,' Mark 3:29, and of the judgment of God, from which there is no appeal, Heb. 6:2, and of the fire, which is one of its instruments, **Matt. 18:8; 25:41**; Jude 7, and which is elsewhere said to be 'unquenchable,' Mark 9:43."

Fire *see Matthew 3:11. See also* **Hell** at *Matthew 5:22.*

18:9 And if thine eye offend thee, pluck it out, and cast *it* from thee: it is better for thee to enter into life with one eye, rather than having two eyes to be cast into hell fire.

Offend *see Matthew 13:57.*

Pluck *see Matthew 5:29.*

With one eye *monophthalmos* (3442), "oneeyed, deprived of one eye," is used in the Lord's warning in **Matt. 18:9**; Mark 9:47.

Hell *see Matthew 5:22.*

Fire *see Matthew 3:11.*

18:10 Take heed that ye despise not one of these little ones; for I say unto you, That in heaven their angels do always behold the face of my Father which is in heaven.

Heed *see Matthew 16:6.*

Despise *see Matthew 6:24.*

Little *see Matthew 10:42.*

Heaven *see Matthew 5:16.*

Angels *angelos* (32), "a messenger" (from *angello*, "to deliver a message"), sent whether by God or by man or by Satan, "is also used of a guardian or representative in Rev. 1:20, cf. **Matt. 18:10**; Acts 12:15 (where it is better understood as 'ghost'), but most frequently of an order of created beings, superior to man, Heb. 2:7; Ps. 8:5, belonging to Heaven, **Matt. 24:36**; Mark 12:25, and to God, Luke 12:8, and engaged in His service, Ps. 103:20. "Angels" are spirits, Heb. 1:14, i.e., they have not material bodies as men have; they are either human in form, or can assume the human form when necessary, cf. Luke 24:4, with v. 23, Acts 10:3 with v. 30. "They are called 'holy' in Mark 8:38, and 'elect,' 1 Tim. 5:21, in contrast with some of their original number, **Matt. 25:41**, who 'sinned,' 2 Pet. 2:4, 'left their proper habitation,' Jude 6, *oiketerion*, a word which occurs again, in the NT, only in 2 Cor. 5:2. Angels are always spoken of in the masculine gender, the feminine form of the word does not occur."

18:11-12 For the Son of man is come to save that which was lost.

How think ye? if a man have an hundred sheep, and one of them be gone astray, doth he not leave the ninety and nine, and goeth into the mountains, and seeketh that which is gone astray?

Have *ginomai* (1096), "to begin to be, come to pass, happen," is rendered "have" in **Matt. 18:12**; "had" in Acts 15:2; "shall have" in 1 Cor. 4:5, lit., "praise shall be," or come to pass.

Hundred *see* **Hundredfold** at *Matthew 13:8.*

Gone astray *planao* (4105), (Eng., "planet"), in the passive form sometimes means "to go astray, wander," **Matt. 18:12**; 1 Pet. 2:25; Heb. 11:38; frequently active, "to deceive, by leading into error, to seduce," e.g., **Matt. 24:4, 5, 11, 24**; John 7:12, "leadeth astray," RV (cf. 1 John 3:7). In Rev. 12:9 the present participle is used with the definite article, as a title of the Devil, "the Deceiver," lit., "the deceiving one." Often it has the sense of "deceiving oneself," e.g., 1 Cor. 6:9; 15:33; Gal. 6:7; Jas. 1:16, "be not deceived," RV, "do not err," KJV.

Leave *see* **Leaveth** at *Matthew 4:11.*

Ninety *enenekonta*, or *ennen-* (1767), is found in **Matt. 18:12-13**; Luke 15:4, 7.

Mountains *see* **Mountain** at *Matthew 5:1.*

18:13 And if so be that he find it, verily I say unto you, he rejoiceth more of that *sheep*, than of the ninety and nine which went not astray.

Than *see* **Rather** at *Matthew 10:6.*

Of *epi*, "over," is so translated in **Matt. 18:13**, RV; "concerning" in Acts 4:9.

18:14 Even so it is not the will of your Father which is in heaven, that one of these little ones should perish.

Even so *see Matthew 7:17.*

Will *thelema* (2307), signifies (a) objectively, "that which is willed, of the will of God," e.g., **Matt. 18:14**; Mark 3:35, the fulfilling being a sign of spiritual relationship to the Lord, John 4:34; 5:30; 6:39, 40; Acts 13:22, plural, "my desires"; Rom. 2:18; 12:2, lit., "the will of God, the good and perfect and acceptable"; here the repeated article is probably resumptive, the adjectives describing the will, as in the Eng. versions; Gal. 1:4; Eph. 1:9; 5:17, "of the Lord"; Col. 1:9; 4:12; 1 Thess. 4:3; 5:18, where it means "the gracious design," rather than "the determined resolve"; 2 Tim. 2:26, which should read "which have been taken captive by him" [(*autou*), i.e., by the Devil; the RV, "by the Lord's servant" is an interpretation; it does not correspond to the Greek] unto His (*ekeinou*) will" (i.e., "God's will"; the different pronoun refers back to the subject of the sentence, viz., God); Heb. 10:10; Rev. 4:11, RV, "because of Thy will"; of human will, e.g., 1 Cor. 7:37; (b) subjectively, the "will" being spoken of as the emotion of being desirous, rather than as the thing "willed"; of the "will" of God, e.g., Rom. 1:10; 1 Cor. 1:1; 2 Cor. 1:1; 8:5; Eph. 1:1, 5, 11; Col. 1:1; 2 Tim. 1:1; Heb. 10:7, 9, 36; 1 John 2:17; 5:14; of human "will," e.g., John 1:13; Eph. 2:3, "the desires of the flesh"; 1 Pet. 4:3 (in some texts); 2 Pet. 1:21. *See also* Before at *Matthew 5:16*.

Little *see Matthew 10:42*.

18:15 Moreover if thy brother shall trespass against thee, go and tell him his fault between thee and him alone: if he shall hear thee, thou hast gained thy brother.

Moreover *de* (1161), a particle signifying "and" or "but," is translated "moreover" in **Matt. 18:15**, KJV (RV, "and"); Acts 11:12 (RV, "and"); Rom. 5:20, KJV (RV, "but"); 8:30 ("and"); 1 Cor. 15:1 (RV, "now"); 2 Cor. 1:23 (RV, "but"); 2 Pet. 1:15 (RV, "yea").

Trespass *hamartano* (264), lit., "to miss the mark," is used in the NT (a) of "sinning" against God, (1) by angels, 2 Pet. 2:4; (2) by man, **Matt. 27:4**; Luke 15:18, 21 (heaven standing, by metonymy, for God); John 5:14; 8:11; 9:2, 3; Rom. 2:12 (twice); 3:23; 5:12, 14, 16; 6:15; 1 Cor. 7:28 (twice), 36; 15:34; Eph. 4:26; 1 Tim. 5:20; Titus 3:11; Heb. 3:17; 10:26; 1 John 1:10; in 2:1 (twice), the aorist tense in each place, referring to an act of "sin"; on the contrary, in 3:6 (twice), 8, 9, the present tense indicates, not the committal of an act, but the continuous practice of "sin"; in 5:16 (twice) the present tense indicates the condition resulting from an act, "unto death" signifying "tending towards death"; (b) against Christ, 1 Cor. 8:12; (c) against man, (1) a brother, **Matt. 18:15**, RV, "sin" (KJV, "trespass"); v. **21**; Luke 17:3, 4, RV, "sin" (KJV, "trespass"); 1 Cor. 8:12; (2) in Luke 15:18, 21, against the father by the Prodigal Son, "in thy sight" being suggestive of befitting reverence; (d) against Jewish law, the Temple, and Caesar, Acts 25:8, RV, "sinned" (KJV, "offended"); (e) against one's own body, by fornication, 1 Cor. 6:18; (f) against earthly masters by servants, 1 Pet. 2:20, RV, "(when) ye sin (and are buffeted for it)," KJV, "(when ye be buffeted) for your faults," lit., "having sinned."

Fault *elencho* (1651), "to convict, reprove, rebuke," is translated "shew (him) his fault" in **Matt. 18:15**.

Between *metaxu* (3342), "in the midst, or between" (from *meta*, and *xun*, i.e., *sun*, "with"), is used as a preposition, (a) of mutual relation, **Matt. 18:15**; Acts 15:9; Rom. 2:15, RV, "one with another," lit., "between one another," for KJV, "the meanwhile"; (b) of place, **Matt. 23:35**; Luke 11:51; 16:26; Acts 12:6; (c) of time, "meanwhile," John 4:31. In Acts 13:42, the KJV marg. has "in the week between," the literal rendering

Gained *see* Gain at *Matthew 16:26*.

18:16 But if he will not hear *thee, then* take with thee one or two more, that in the mouth of two or three witnesses every word may be established.

Take *see Matthew 1:20*.

More *eti* (2089), "yet, as yet, still," used of degree is translated "more" in **Matt. 18:16**, "(one or two) more"; Heb. 8:12 and 10:17, "(will I remember no) more"; 10:2, "(no) more (conscience)"; 11:32, "(what shall I) more (say)?" Rev. 3:12, "(he shall go out thence no) more"; 7:16, "(no) more" and "any more;" 9:12, KJV "more" (RV, "hereafter"); 18:21-23, "(no) more," "any more" (5 times); 20:3, "(no) more"; 21:1, 4 (twice); 22:3.

Mouth *see Matthew 12:34*.

Witnesses *martus* or *martur* (3144), (whence Eng., "martyr," one who bears "witness" by his death) denotes "one who can or does aver what he has seen or heard or knows"; it is used (a) of God, Rom. 1:9; 2 Cor. 1:23; Phil. 1:8; 1 Thess. 2:5, 10 (2nd part); (b) of Christ, Rev. 1:5; 3:14; (c) of those who "witness" for Christ by their death, Acts 22:20; Rev. 2:13; Rev. 17:6; (d) of the interpreters of God's counsels, yet to "witness" in Jerusalem in the times of the Antichrist, Rev. 11:3; (e) in a forensic sense, **Matt. 18:16**; **26:65**; Mark 14:63; Acts 6:13; 7:58; 2 Cor. 13:1; 1 Tim. 5:19; Heb. 10:28; (f) in a historical sense, Luke 11:48; 24:48; Acts 1:8, 22; 2:32; 3:15; 5:32; 10:39, 41; 13:31; 22:15; 26:16; 1 Thess. 2:10 (1st part); 1 Tim. 6:12; 2 Tim. 2:2; Heb. 12:1, "(a cloud) of witnesses," here of those mentioned in ch. 11, those whose lives and actions testified to the worth and effect of faith, and whose faith received "witness" in Scripture; 1 Pet. 5:1.

18:17 And if he shall neglect to hear them, tell *it* unto the church: but if he neglect to hear the church, let him be unto thee as an heathen man and a publican.

Neglect For *parakouo*, "to refuse to hear," RV in **Matt. 18:17** (twice).

Hear *parakouo* (3878), primarily signifies "to overhear, hear amiss or imperfectly"; then (in the NT) "to hear without taking heed, to neglect to hear," **Matt. 18:17** (twice); in Mark 5:36 the best mss. have this verb, which the RV renders "not heeding" (marg., "overhearing"); some mss. have "hearing." It seems obvious that the Lord paid no attention to those from the ruler's house and their message that his daughter was dead. Cf. the noun *parakoe*, "disobedience."

Church *see Matthew 16:18.*

Publican *see* **Publicans** at *Matthew 5:46.*

18:18 Verily I say unto you, Whatsoever ye shall bind on earth shall be bound in heaven: and whatsoever ye shall loose on earth shall be loosed in heaven.

Bind *see Matthew 16:19.*

18:19 Again I say unto you, That if two of you shall agree on earth as touching any thing that they shall ask, it shall be done for them of my Father which is in heaven.

Agree *sumphoneo* (4856), lit., "to sound together" (*sun*, "together," *phone*, "a sound"), i.e., "to be in accord, primarily of musical instruments," is used in the NT of the "agreement" (a) of persons concerning a matter, **Matt. 18:19**; **20:2, 13**; Acts 5:9; (b) of the writers of Scripture, Acts 15:15; (c) of things that are said to be congruous in their nature, Luke 5:36.

Thing *pragma* (4229), is translated "thing" in **Matt. 18:19**, as part of the word "anything," lit., "every thing"; Luke 1:1, KJV only; Acts 5:4; in Heb. 6:18; 10:1, and 11:1, "things."

18:20 For where two or three are gathered together in my name, there am I in the midst of them.

Name *see Matthew 6:9.*

18:21 Then came Peter to him, and said, Lord, how oft shall my brother sin against me, and I forgive him? till seven times?

Oft *posakis* (4212), an interrogative numeral adverb, "how many times, how oft (or often)?" occurs in **Matt. 18:21**; **23:37**; Luke 13:34.

Sin *see* Trespass at Matthew *18:15.*

Forgive *see Matthew 6:12.*

Seven times *heptakis* (2034), occurs in **Matt. 18:21, 22**; Luke 17:4 (twice).

18:22 Jesus saith unto him, I say not unto thee, Until seven times: but, Until seventy times seven.

Seven times *see Matthew 18:21.*

Seventy times *hebdomekontakis* (1441), occurs in **Matt. 18:22**, where it is followed by *hepta*, "seven," "seventy times seven"; RV marg. has "seventy times and seven," which many have regarded as the meaning; cf. Gen. 4:24. The Lord's reply "until seventy times seven" was indicative of completeness, the absence of any limit, and was designed to turn away Peter's mind from a merely numerical standard. God's forgiveness is limitless; so should man's be.

18:23 Therefore is the kingdom of heaven likened unto a certain king, which would take account of his servants.

Likened *see* Like unto at *Matthew 6:8.*

Man *see Matthew 4:4.*

Take account *sunairo* (4868), "to take up together" (*sun*, "with," *airo*, "to take"), is used with the noun *logos*, "an account," signifying "to settle accounts," **Matt. 18:23**, RV, "make a reckoning" (KJV, "take account"); v. **24**, KJV and RV, "to reckon" (*logos* being understood); **25:19**, RV, "maketh a reckoning" (KJV, "reckoneth"). This phrase occurs not infrequently in the papyri in the sense of settling accounts (see Deissmann, *Light from the Ancient East*, 118). In the Sept. the verb occurs in its literal sense in Exod. 23:5, "thou shalt help to raise" (lit., "raise with"). *See also* **Account** at *Matthew 12:36.*

18:24 And when he had begun to reckon, one was brought unto him, which owed him ten thousand talents.

Reckon *see* Take account at *Matthew 18:23.*

Owed *opheiletes* (3781), "a debtor," is translated "which owed" in **Matt. 18:24**, lit., "a debtor (of ten thousand talents)." *See also* **Debtors** at *Matthew 6:12.*

Ten thousand *murias* (3461), denotes either "ten thousand," or, "indefinitely, a myriad, a numberless host," in the plural, Acts 19:19; lit. "five ten-thousands," Rev. 5:11; 9:16; in the following, used of vast numbers, Luke 12:1, KJV, "an innumerable multitude," RV, "the many thousands" (RV marg., "the myriads"); Acts 21:20, "thousands"; Heb. 12:22, "innumerable hosts"; Jude 14, "ten thousands" (RV, marg., in each place, "myriads"). Cf. the adjective *murios*, "ten thousand," **Matt. 18:24**; 1 Cor. 4:15; 14:19.

18:25 But forasmuch as he had not to pay, his lord commanded him to be sold, and his wife,

and children, and all that he had, and payment to be made.

Pay *see* Paid at *Matthew 5:26.*

Commanded *see Matthew 14:9.*

Sold *see Matthew 13:46.*

18:26 The servant therefore fell down, and worshipped him, saying, Lord, have patience with me, and I will pay thee all.

Worshipped *see* Worship at *Matthew 2:2.*

Patience *makrothumeo* (3114), "to be long-tempered," is translated "to have patience," or "to be patient," in **Matt. 18:26, 29**; 1 Thess. 5:14, KJV (RV, "be longsuffering"); Jas. 5:7 (1st part, "be patient"; 2nd part, RV, "being patient," KJV, "hath long patience"); in Heb. 6:15, RV, "having (KJV, after he had) patiently endured."

Pay *see* Paid at *Matthew 5:26.*

18:27 Then the lord of that servant was moved with compassion, and loosed him, and forgave him the debt.

Compassion *see Matthew 9:36.*

Forgave *see* Forgive at *Matthew 6:12.*

Loosed *apoluo* (630), "to loose from," is translated "to release" in **Matt. 18:27**, RV (KJV, "loosed"); **27:15, 17, 21, 26**; Mark 15:6, 9, 11, 15; Luke 6:37 (twice), RV (KJV, "forgive" and "ye shall be forgiven"); 23:16 (v. 17, in some mss.), 18, 20, 25; 23:22, RV (KJV, "let ... go"); John 18:39 (twice); 19:10; in 19:12, in the 1st part, KJV and RV; in the 2nd part, RV, "release" (KJV, "let ... go"); so in Acts 3:13. *See also* Send at *Matthew 14:15.*

Debt *daneion* (1156), "a loan" (akin to *danos*, "a gift"), is translated "debt" in **Matt. 18:27** (RV, marg., "loan"), of the ten thousand talents debtor. Cf. *daneizo*, "to lend," and *daneistes*, "a money-lender, a creditor." *See also* Borrow at *Matthew 5:42.*

18:28 But the same servant went out, and found one of his fellowservants, which owed him an hundred pence: and he laid hands on him, and took *him* by the throat, saying, Pay me that thou owest.

Fellowservants *sundoulos* (4889), "a fellow servant," is used (a) of natural conditions, **Matt. 18:28, 29, 31, 33; 24:49**; (b) of "servants" of the same divine Lord, Col. 1:7; 4:7; Rev. 6:11; of angels, Rev. 19:10; 22:9.

Owed, Owest *opheilo* (3784), "to owe, to be a debtor" (in the passive voice, "to be owed, to be due"), is translated by the verb "to owe" in **Matt. 18:28** (twice); Luke 7:41; 16:5, 7; Rom. 13:8; in 15:27, RV, "they (gentile converts) owe it" (KJV, "it is their duty"); Philem. 18.

Hundred *see* Hundredfold at *Matthew 13:8.*

Pence *denarion* (1220), a Roman coin, a *denarius*, a little less than the value of the Greek *drachme*, now estimated as amounting to about 9 ½d. in the time of our Lord, occurs in the singular, e.g., **Matt. 20:2; 22:19**; Mark 12:15; Rev. 6:6; in the plural, e.g., **Matt. 18:28**; Mark 14:5; Luke 7:41; 10:35; John 12:5; "pennyworth" in Mark 6:37 and John 6:7, lit., "(loaves of two hundred) pence." Considering the actual value, "shilling" would have been a more accurate translation, as proposed by the American translators, retaining "penny" for the *as*, and "farthing" for the *quadrans*.

Laid hands on *see* Hold at *Matthew 12:11.*

Throat *pnigo* (4155), "to choke," is rendered "took ... by the throat" in **Matt. 18:28.**

Pay *see* Paid at *Matthew 5:26.*

18:29 And his fellowservant fell down at his feet, and besought him, saying, Have patience with me, and I will pay thee all.

Fellowservant *see* Fellowservants at *Matthew 18:28.*

Patience *see Matthew 18:26.*

Pay *see* Paid at *Matthew 5:26.*

18:30 And he would not: but went and cast him into prison, till he should pay the debt.

Pay *see* Paid at *Matthew 5:26.*

Debt *opheilo* (3784), signifies "to owe, to be indebted," especially financially, **Matt. 18:30**, RV, "that which was due"; **18:34**, "all that was due," translated "debt" in the KJV.

18:31 So when his fellowservants saw what was done, they were very sorry, and came and told unto their lord all that was done.

Fellowservants *see Matthew 18:28.*

Very *see* Exceeding at *Matthew 2:10.*

Sorry *see Matthew 14:9.*

Told *diasapheo* (1285), "to make clear" (*dia*, "throughout," *saphes*, "clear"), explain fully, is translated "told" in **Matt. 18:31.** *See also* Declare at *Matthew 13:36.*

18:32 Then his lord, after that he had called him, said unto him, O thou wicked servant, I forgave thee all that debt, because thou desiredst me:

Wicked *see Matthew 12:45. See also* Evil at *Matthew 5:11.*

Forgave *see* Forgive at *Matthew 6:12.*

Debt *opheile* (3782), "that which is owed," is translated "debt" in **Matt. 18:32**; in the plural, "dues," Rom. 13:7; "(her) due," 1 Cor. 7:3, of conjugal duty: some texts here have *opheilomenen* (*eunoian*) "due (benevolence)," KJV; the context confirms the RV.

18:33 Shouldest not thou also have had compassion on thy fellowservant, even as I had pity on thee?

Shouldest *mello* (3195), "to be about to," e.g., Mark 10:32, RV, "were to"; Luke 19:11, RV, "was to"; "should" in 22:23; 24:21; John 6:71; 7:39, RV, "were to"; 11:51; 12:4, 33; 18:32; Acts 11:28; 23:27, RV, "was about (to be slain)"; 1 Thess. 3:4, RV, "are to"; Rev. 6:11. *See also* Must at *Matthew 17:10.*

Also *see Matthew 5:39.*

Compassion *eleeo* (1653), "to have mercy (*eleos*, "mercy"), to show kindness, by beneficence, or assistance," is translated "have compassion" in **Matt. 18:33** (KJV); Mark 5:19 and Jude 22.

Fellowservant *see* Fellowservants at *Matthew 18:28.*

Pity *see* Mercy at *Matthew 5:7.*

18:34 And his lord was wroth, and delivered him to the tormentors, till he should pay all that was due unto him.

Wroth *orgizo* (3710), always in the middle or passive voice in the NT, is rendered "was (were) wroth" in **Matt. 18:34**; **22:7**; Rev. 11:18, RV, (KJV, "were angry"); 12:17, RV, "waxed wroth." *See also* Angry at *Matthew 5:22.*

Tormentors *basanistes* (930), properly, "a torturer" (akin to *basanizo*), "one who elicits information by torture," is used of jailors, **Matt. 18:34.**

Pay *see* Paid at *Matthew 5:26.*

Due *see* Debt at *Matthew 18:30.*

18:35 So likewise shall my heavenly Father do also unto you, if ye from your hearts forgive not every one his brother their trespasses.

Likewise *kai* (2532), "and, even," is translated "likewise" in the KJV and RV of **Matt. 20:10** (last *kai* in the verse), more lit., "even they"; elsewhere the RV has "also," for the KJV, "likewise," **Matt. 18:35**; **24:33**; Luke 3:14; 17:10; 19:19; 21:31; Acts 3:24; 1 Cor. 14:9; Col. 4:16; 1 Pet. 4:1; in **Matt. 21:24**, the KJV has "in like wise" (RV, "likewise").

Heavenly *epouranios* (2032), "heavenly," what pertains to, or is in, heaven (*epi*, in the sense of "pertaining to," not here, "above"). It is used (a) of God the Father, **Matt. 18:35**; (b) of the place where Christ "sitteth at the right hand of God" (i.e., in a position of divine authority), Eph. 1:20; and of the present position of believers in relationship to Christ, Eph 2:6; where they possess "every spiritual blessing," 1:3; (c) of Christ as "the Second Man," and all those who are related to Him spiritually, 1 Cor. 15:48; (d) of those whose sphere of activity or existence is above, or in contrast to that of earth, of "principalities and powers," Eph. 3:10; of "spiritual hosts of wickedness," 6:12, RV, "in heavenly places," for KJV, "in high places"; (e) of the Holy Spirit, Heb. 6:4; (f) of "heavenly things," as the subjects of the teaching of Christ, John 3:12, and as consisting of the spiritual and "heavenly" sanctuary and "true tabernacle" and all that appertains thereto in relation to Christ and His sacrifice as antitypical of the earthly tabernacle and sacrifices under the Law, Heb. 8:5; 9:23; (g) of the "calling" of believers, Heb. 3:1; (h) of heaven as the abode of the saints, "a better country" than that of earth, Heb. 11:16, and of the spiritual Jerusalem, 12:22; (i) of the kingdom of Christ in its future manifestation, 2 Tim. 4:18; (j) of all beings and things, animate and inanimate, that are "above the earth," Phil. 2:10; (k) of the resurrection and glorified bodies of believers, 1 Cor. 15:49; (l) of the "heavenly orbs," 1 Cor. 15:40 ("celestial," twice, and so rendered here only).

Trespasses *see Matthew 6:14.*

Chapter 19

19:1 And it came to pass, *that* when Jesus had finished these sayings, he departed from Galilee, and came into the coasts of Judaea beyond Jordan;

Finished *see Matthew 13:53.*

Departed *see Matthew 13:53.*

Coasts *see Matthew 2:16.*

19:2-3 And great multitudes followed him; and he healed them there.

The Pharisees also came unto him, tempting him, and saying unto him, Is it lawful for a man to put away his wife for every cause?

Tempting *see* Tempted at *Matthew 4:1.*

Put *see Matthew 1:19.*

19:4 And he answered and said unto them, Have ye not read, that he which made *them* at the beginning made them male and female,

Made *see* Make at *Matthew 4:19.*

Male *arsen* or *arren* (730), is translated "men" in Rom. 1:27 (three times); "man child" in Rev. 12:5 (v. 13 in some mss.); "male" in **Matt. 19:4**; Mark 10:6; Luke 2:23; Gal. 3:28, "(there can be no) male (and female)," RV, i.e. sex distinction does not obtain in Christ; sex is no barrier either to salvation or the development of Christian graces.

Female *thelus* (2338), an adjective (from *thele*, "a breast"), is used in the form *thelu* (grammatically neuter) as a noun, "female," in **Matt. 19:4**; Mark 10:6; Gal. 3:28; in the feminine form *theleia*, in Rom. 1:26, "women"; v. 27 "woman."

19:5 And said, For this cause shall a man leave father and mother, and shall cleave to his wife: and they twain shall be one flesh?

Cleave *kollao* (2853), "to join fast together, to glue, cement," is primarily said of metals and other materials (from *kolla*, "glue"). In the NT it is used only in the passive voice, with reflexive force, in the sense of "cleaving unto," as of cleaving to one's wife, **Matt. 19:5**; some mss. have the intensive verb *proskollao* (4347) here; 1 Cor. 6:16-17, "joined." In the corresponding passage in Mark 10:7, the most authentic mss. omit the sentence. In Luke 10:11 it is used of the "cleaving" of dust to the feet; in Acts 5:13; 8:29; 9:26; 10:28; 17:34, in the sense of becoming associated with a person so as to company with him, or be on his side, said, in the last passage, of those in Athens who believed: in Rom. 12:9, ethically, of "cleaving" to that which is good.

Twain *see Matthew 5:41.*

Flesh *sarx* (4561), has a wider range of meaning in the NT than in the OT. Its uses in the NT may be analyzed as follows: "(a) "the substance of the body," whether of beasts or of men, 1 Cor. 15:39; (b) "the human body," 2 Cor. 10:3a; Gal. 2:20; Phil. 1:22; (c) by synecdoche, of "mankind," in the totality of all that is essential to manhood, i.e., spirit, soul, and body, **Matt. 24:22**; John 1:13; Rom. 3:20; (d) by synecdoche, of "the holy humanity" of the Lord Jesus, in the totality of all that is essential to manhood, i.e., spirit, soul, and body, John 1:14; 1 Tim. 3:16; 1 John 4:2; 2 John 7, in Heb. 5:7, "the days of His flesh," i.e., His past life on earth in distinction from His present life in resurrection; (e) by synecdoche, for "the complete person," John 6:51-57; 2 Cor. 7:5; Jas. 5:3; (f) "the weaker element in human nature," **Matt. 26:41**; Rom. 6:19; 8:3a; (g) "the unregenerate state of men," Rom. 7:5; 8:8, 9; (h) "the seat of sin in man" (but this is not the same thing as in the body), 2 Pet. 2:18; 1 John 2:16; (i) "the lower and temporary element in the Christian," Gal. 3:3; 6:8, and in religious ordinances, Heb. 9:10; (j) "the natural attainments of men," 1 Cor. 1:26; 2 Cor. 10:2, 3b; (k) "circumstances," 1 Cor. 7:28; the externals of life, 2 Cor. 7:1; Eph. 6:5; Heb. 9:13; (l) by metonymy, "the outward and seeming," as contrasted with the spirit, the inward and real, John 6:63; 2 Cor. 5:16; (m) "natural relationship, consanguine," 1 Cor. 10:18; Gal. 4:23, or marital, **Matt. 19:5**." In **Matt. 26:41**; Rom. 8:4, 13; 1 Cor. 5:5; Gal. 6:8 (not the Holy Spirit, here), "flesh" is contrasted with spirit, in Rom. 2:28, 29, with heart and spirit; in Rom. 7:25, with the mind; cf. Col. 2:1, 5. It is coupled with the mind in Eph. 2:3, and with the spirit in 2 Cor. 7:1.

19:6 Wherefore they are no more twain, but one flesh. What therefore God hath joined together, let not man put asunder.

No more *ouketi* (3765), a negative adverb of time, signifies "no longer, no more" (*ou*, "not," *k*, euphonic, *eti* "longer"), denying absolutely and directly, e.g., **Matt. 19:6**; John 4:42, "now ... not"; 6:66; Acts 20:25, 38; 2 Cor. 1:23, KJV, "not as yet"; Eph. 2:19; with another negative, to strengthen the negation, e.g., **Matt. 22:46**; Mark 14:25; 15:5, RV, "no more (anything)," KJV, "yet ... no (thing)"; Acts 8:39; Rev. 18:11, 14.

Twain *see Matthew 5:41.*

Joined *su(n)zeugnumi* (4801), "to yoke together" (*sun*, "with," *zugos*, "a yoke"), is used metaphorically of union in wedlock, in **Matt. 19:6**; Mark 10:9.

Man *see Matthew 4:4.*

Put *chorizo* (5563), "to separate, divide" (cf. *choris*, "apart, separate from"), is translated "to put asunder" in **Matt. 19:6**; Mark 10:9, of "putting" away a wife.

19:7 They say unto him, Why did Moses then command to give a writing of divorcement, and to put her away?

Command *entello* (1781), signifies "to enjoin upon, to charge with"; it is used in the Middle Voice in the sense of commanding, **Matt. 19:7**; **28:20**; Mark 10:3; 13:34; John 8:5; 15:14, 17; Acts 13:47; Heb. 9:20; 11:22, "gave commandment."

Writing *biblion* (975), had in Hellenistic Greek almost lost its diminutive force and was ousting *biblos* in ordinary use; it denotes "a scroll or a small book." It is used in Luke 4:17, 20, of the "book" of Isaiah; in John 20:30, of the Gospel of John; in Gal. 3:10 and Heb. 10:7, of the whole of the OT; in Heb. 9:19, of the "book" of Exodus; in Rev. 1:11; 22:7, 9-10, 18 (twice), 19, of Revelation; in John 21:25 and 2 Tim. 4:13, of "books" in general; in Rev. 13:8; 17:8; 20:12; 21:27, of the "Book" of Life; in Rev. 20:12, of other "books" to be opened in the Day of Judgment, containing, it would seem, the record of human deeds. In Rev. 5:1-9 the "Book" represents the revelation of God's purposes and counsels concerning the world. So with the "little book" in Rev. 10:8. In 6:14 it is used of a scroll, the rolling up of which illustrates the removal of the heaven. In **Matt. 19:7** and Mark 10:4 the word is used of a bill of divorcement.

Put *see Matthew 1:19.*

19:8 He saith unto them, Moses because of the hardness of your hearts suffered you to put away your wives: but from the beginning it was not so.

Hardness of … hearts *sklerokardia* (4641), "hardness of heart" (*skleros*, "hard," and *kardia*), is used in **Matt. 19:8**; Mark 10:5; 16:14. In the Sept., Deut. 10:16; Jer. 4:4.

Put *see Matthew 1:19.*

19:9 And I say unto you, Whosoever shall put away his wife, except *it be* for fornication, and shall marry another, committeth adultery: and whoso marrieth her which is put away doth commit adultery.

Put *see Matthew 1:19.*

Except *In* **Matt. 19:9**, the KJV and RV, translating the mss. which have the negative *me*, followed by *epi*, render it "except for." The authorities mentioned in the RV marg. have *parektos*, followed by *logou*, i.e., "saving for the cause of." *See also* Saving at *Matthew 5:32.*

Fornication *see Matthew 5:32.*

Marry, Marrieth *see* Marry at *Matthew 5:32.*

Adultery *see Matthew 5:32.*

19:10 His disciples say unto him, If the case of the man be so with *his* wife, it is not good to marry.

Good *In* **Matt. 19:10**, KJV, *sumphero*, "to be profitable, expedient" (*sun*, "together," *phero*, "to bring"); is rendered with a negative "it is not good" (RV, "it is not expedient"). *See also* Profitable at *Matthew 5:29.*

Marry *see Matthew 5:32.*

19:11 But he said unto them, All *men* cannot receive this saying, save *they* to whom it is given.

Receive *choreo* (5562), "to give space, make room for" (*chora*, "a place"), is used metaphorically, of "receiving" with the mind, **Matt. 19:11, 12**; into the heart, 2 Cor. 7:2, RV, "open your hearts," marg., "make room" (KJV, receive). *See also* Goeth at *Matthew 15:17.*

19:12 For there are some eunuchs, which were so born from *their* mother's womb: and there are some eunuchs, which were made eunuchs of men: and there be eunuchs, which have made themselves eunuchs for the kingdom of heaven's sake. He that is able to receive *it*, let him receive *it*.

Eunuchs *eunouchizo* (2134), "to make a eunuch," is used in **Matt. 19:12**; and in the passive voice, "were made eunuchs," probably an allusion by the Lord to the fact that there were eunuchs in the courts of the Herods, as would be well known to His hearers.

Womb *koilia* (2836), denotes "the womb," **Matt. 19:12**; Luke 1:15, 41, 42, 44; 2:21; 11:27; 23:29; John 3:4; Acts 3:2; 14:8; Gal. 1:15.

Eunuchs *eunouchos* (2135), denotes (a) "an emasculated man, a eunuch," **Matt. 19:12**; (b) in the 3rd instance in that verse, "one naturally incapacitated for, or voluntarily abstaining from, wedlock"; (c) one such, in a position of high authority in a court, "a chamberlain," Acts 8:27-39.

Receive *see Matthew 19:11. See also* Goeth at *Matthew 15:17.*

19:13 Then were there brought unto him little children, that he should put *his* hands on them, and pray: and the disciples rebuked them.

Put *epitithemi* (2007), "to put on, upon," is so rendered in **Matt. 19:13**, KJV (RV, "lay"); so Mark 7:32; 8:25 (some mss. have *tithemi* here); **Matt. 21:7; 27:29**; John 9:15; 19:2 (1st part); Acts 9:12 (RV, "laying … on"); 15:10. *See also* Lay at *Matthew 9:18.*

Rebuked *see Matthew 8:26.*

19:14 But Jesus said, Suffer little children, and forbid them not, to come unto me: for of such is the kingdom of heaven.

Suffer *see Matthew 3:15.*

19:15 And he laid *his* hands on them, and departed thence.

Laid *see* Lay at *Matthew 9:18*.

Departed *see Matthew 2:9*.

19:16 And, behold, one came and said unto him, Good Master, what good thing shall I do, that I may have eternal life?

One *see Matthew 6:24*.

19:17 And he said unto him, Why callest thou me good? *there* is none good but one, *that is*, God: but if thou wilt enter into life, keep the commandments.

Callest *In* **Matt. 19:17**, the RV, following the most authentic mss., has "Why askest (*erotao*) thou Me concerning that which is good."

Good *see Matthew 5:45*.

Keep *tereo* (5083), denotes (a) "to watch over, preserve, keep, watch," e.g., Acts 12:5, 6; 16:23; in 25:21, RV (1st part), "kept" (KJV, "reserved"); the present participle is translated "keepers" in **Matt. 28:4**, lit. "the keeping (ones)"; it is used of the "keeping" power of God the Father and Christ, exercised over His people, John 17:11, 12, 15; 1 Thess. 5:23, "preserved"; 1 John 5:18, where "He that was begotten of God," RV, is said of Christ as the Keeper ("keepeth him," RV, for KJV, "keepeth himself"); Jude 1, RV, "kept for Jesus Christ" (KJV, "preserved in Jesus Christ"), Rev. 3:10; of their inheritance, 1 Pet. 1:4 ("reserved"); of judicial reservation by God in view of future doom, 2 Pet. 2:4, 9, 17; 3:7; Jude 6, 13; of "keeping" the faith, 2 Tim. 4:7; the unity of the Spirit, Eph. 4:3; oneself, 2 Cor. 11:9; 1 Tim. 5:22; Jas. 1:27; figuratively, one's garments, Rev. 16:15; (b) "to observe, to give heed to," as of keeping commandments, etc., e.g., **Matt. 19:17**; John 14:15; 15:10; 17:6; Jas. 2:10; 1 John 2:3, 4, 5; 3:22, 24; 5:2 (in some mss.), 3; Rev. 1:3; 2:26; 3:8, 10; 12:17; 14:12; 22:7, 9.

19:18 He saith unto him, Which? Jesus said, Thou shalt do no murder, Thou shalt not commit adultery, Thou shalt not steal, Thou shalt not bear false witness,

Murder *In* **Matt. 19:18**, KJV, *phoneuo*, "to kill" (akin to *phoneus*), is translated "thou shalt do (no) murder" (RV, "thou shalt (not) kill"). *See also* Kill at *Matthew 5:21*.

Adultery *see Matthew 5:27*.

Steal *see Matthew 6:19*.

Witness *pseudomartureo* (5576), "to bear false witness" (*pseudes*, "false"), occurs in **Matt. 19:18**; Mark 10:19; 14:56, 57; Luke 18:20; in some texts, Rom. 13:9.

19:19 Honour thy father and *thy* mother: and, Thou shalt love thy neighbour as thyself.

Honour *see Matthew 15:4*.

Neighbour *see Matthew 5:43*.

19:20 The young man saith unto him, All these things have I kept from my youth up: what lack I yet?

Young *neaniskos* (3495), "a youth, a young man," occurs in **Matt. 19:20, 22**; Mark 14:51 (1st part; RV omits in 2nd part); 16:5; Luke 7:14; Acts 2:17; 5:10 (i.e., attendants); 23:18 (in the best texts), 22; 1 John 2:13, 14, of the second branch of the spiritual family.

Kept *phulasso* (5442), denotes (a) "to guard, watch, keep watch," e.g., Luke 2:8; in the passive voice, 8:29; (b) "to keep by way of protection," e.g., Luke 11:21; John 12:25; 17:12 (2nd part); (c) metaphorically, "to keep a law precept," etc., e.g., **Matt. 19:20** and Luke 18:21, "have observed"; Luke 11:28; John 12:47 (in the best mss.); Acts 7:53; 16:4; 21:24; Rom. 2:26; Gal. 6:13; 1 Tim. 5:21 ("observe"); in the middle voice, Mark 10:20 ("have observed"); (d) in the middle voice, "to keep oneself from," Acts 21:25; elsewhere translated by the verb "to beware."

Youth *neotes* (3503), from *neos*, "new," occurs in Mark 10:20; Luke 18:21; Acts 26:4; 1 Tim. 4:12 (in some mss., **Matt. 19:20**).

Lack *hustereo* (5302), "to come or be behind," is used in the sense of "lacking" certain things, **Matt. 19:20**; Mark 10:21 ("one thing"; cf. *leipo* in Luke 18:22); Luke 22:35; in the sense of being inferior, 1 Cor. 12:24 (middle voice). Elsewhere it is translated in various ways.

19:21 Jesus said unto him, If thou wilt be perfect, go *and* sell that thou hast, and give to the poor, and thou shalt have treasure in heaven: and come *and* follow me.

Wilt *see* Will at *Matthew 16:24*.

Perfect *see Matthew 5:48*.

Hast *huparcho* (5225), "to be in existence, to be ready, at hand," is translated by the verb "to have" in Acts 3:6, lit., "silver and gold is not to me" (in the next clause, "such as I have," *echo* is used); 4:37, "having (land)," lit., "(land) being (to him)"; **Matt. 19:21**, "that (thou) hast," lit., "(things that) are (thine)," i.e., "thy belongings"; similarly Luke 12:33; 44; 14:33.

Poor *see Matthew 5:3*.

Treasure *see* Treasures at Matthew *2:11*.

Come *deuro,* "hither, here," is used (sometimes with verbs of motion) in the singular number, in calling a person to come, **Matt. 19:21**; Mark 10:21; Luke 18:22; John 11:43; Acts 7:3, 34; Rev. 17:1; 21:9. It has a plural, *deute,* frequent in the Gospels; elsewhere in Rev. 19:17.

19:22 But when the young man heard that saying, he went away sorrowful: for he had great possessions.

Young *see Matthew 19:20.*

Had *see Matthew 3:4.*

Possessions *ktema* (2933), denotes "a possession, property," **Matt. 19:22**; Mark 10:22; Acts 2:45; 5:1.

19:23 Then said Jesus unto his disciples, Verily I say unto you, That a rich man shall hardly enter into the kingdom of heaven.

Rich *plousios* (4145), "rich, wealthy," is used (I) literally, (a) adjectivally (with a noun expressed separately) in **Matt. 27:57**; Luke 12:16; 14:12; 16:1, 19; (without a noun), 18:23; 19:2; (b) as a noun, singular, a "rich" man (the noun not being expressed), **Matt. 19:23, 24**; Mark 10:25; 12:41; Luke 16:21, 22; 18:25; Jas. 1:10, 11, "the rich," "the rich (man)"; plural, Mark 12:41, lit., "rich (ones)"; Luke 6:24 (ditto); 21:1; 1 Tim. 6:17, "(them that are) rich," lit., "(the) rich"; Jas. 2:6, RV, "the rich"; 5:1, RV, "ye rich"; Rev. 6:15 and 13:16, RV, "the rich"; (II) metaphorically, of God, Eph. 2:4 ("in mercy"); of Christ, 2 Cor. 8:9; of believers, Jas. 2:5, RV, "(*to be*) rich (in faith)"; Rev. 2:9, of spiritual "enrichment" generally; 3:17, of a false sense of "enrichment."

Hardly *duskolos* (1423), is used in **Matt. 19:23**; Mark 10:23; Luke 18:24 of the danger of riches.

19:24 And again I say unto you, It is easier for a camel to go through the eye of a needle, than for a rich man to enter into the kingdom of God.

Easier *see Matthew 9:5.*

Camel *kamelos* (2574), from a Hebrew word signifying "a bearer, carrier," is used in proverbs to indicate (a) "something almost or altogether impossible," **Matt. 19:24**, and parallel passages; (b) "the acts of a person who is careful not to sin in trivial details, but pays no heed to more important matters," **Matt. 23:24**.

Go through *see* **Walketh through** at *Matthew 12:43.*

Eye *trumalia* (5168), is used of the "eye" of a needle, Mark 10:25 (from *trume,* "a hole," *truo,* "to wear away"). Cf. *trema,* "a hole, perforation," **Matt. 19:24** (some texts have *trupema,* "a hole," from *trupao,* "to bore a hole") and Luke 18:25, as in the most authentic mss. (some texts have *trumalia* here).

Needle *rhaphis* (4476), from *rhapto,* "to sew," occurs in **Matt. 19:24**; Mark 10.25.

Rich *see Matthew 19:23.*

19:25 When his disciples heard *it*, they were exceedingly amazed, saying, Who then can be saved?

Exceedingly *see* **Exceeding** at *Matthew 2:10.*

Amazed *ekplesso* (1605), from *ek,* "out of," *plesso,* "to strike," lit., "to strike out," signifies "to be exceedingly struck in mind, to be astonished" (*ek,* intensive). The English "astonish" should be used for this verb, and "amaze" for *existemi,* as in the RV; see **Matt. 19:25**; Luke 2:48; 9:43.

19:26 But Jesus beheld *them*, and said unto them, With men this is impossible; but with God all things are possible.

Beheld *see* **Behold** at *Matthew 6:26.*

Impossible *adunatos* (102), from *a,* negative, and *dunatos,* "able, strong," is used (a) of persons, Acts 14:8, "impotent"; figuratively, Rom. 15:1, "weak"; (b) of things, "impossible," **Matt. 19:26**; Mark 10:27; Luke 18:27; Heb. 6:4, 18; 10:4; 11:6; in Rom. 8:3, "for what the Law could not do," is, more lit., "the inability of the law"; the meaning may be either "the weakness of the Law," or "that which was impossible for the Law"; the latter is perhaps preferable; literalism is ruled out here, but the sense is that the Law could neither justify nor impart life.

God *see* **Father** at *Matthew 10:29.*

Possible *dunatos* (1415), "strong, mighty, powerful, able (to do)," in its neuter form signifies "possible," **Matt. 19:26; 24:24; 26:39**; Mark 9:23; 10:27; 13:22; 14:35, 36; Luke 18:27; Acts 2:24; 20:16 (27:39, in some mss; *dunamai,* "to be able," in the most authentic, RV, "they could"); Rom. 12:18; Gal. 4:15.

19:27 Then answered Peter and said unto him, Behold, we have forsaken all, and followed thee; what shall we have therefore?

Forsaken *see* **Leaveth** at *Matthew 4:11.*

Have *eimi* (1510), "to be," is often used in its various forms with some case of the personal pronoun, to signify "to be to," or "of, a person," e.g., **Matt. 19:27**, "(what then) shall we have," lit., "what then shall be to us?"; Acts 21:23, "we have four men," lit., "there are to us, etc."

19:28 And Jesus said unto them, Verily I say unto you, That ye which have followed me, in the regeneration when the Son of man shall sit in the throne of his glory, ye also shall sit upon twelve thrones, judging the twelve tribes of Israel.

Regeneration *palingenesia* (3824), "new birth" (*palin*, "again," *genesis*, "birth"), is used of "spiritual regeneration," Titus 3:5, involving the communication of a new life, the two operating powers to produce which are "the word of truth," Jas. 1:18; 1 Pet. 1:23, and the Holy Spirit, John 3:5, 6; the *loutron*, "the laver, the washing," is explained in Eph. 5:26, "having cleansed it by the washing (*loutron*) of water with the word." The new birth and "regeneration" do not represent successive stages in spiritual experience; they refer to the same event but view it in different aspects. The new birth stresses the communication of spiritual life in contrast to antecedent spiritual death; "regeneration" stresses the inception of a new state of things in contrast with the old; hence the connection of the use of the word with its application to Israel, in **Matt. 19:28**. Some regard the *kai* in Titus 3:5 as epexegetic, "even"; but, as Scripture marks two distinct yet associated operating powers, there is not sufficient ground for this interpretation. In **Matt. 19:28** the word is used, in the Lord's discourse, in the wider sense, of the "restoration of all things" (Acts 3:21, RV), when, as a result of the second advent of Christ, Jehovah "sets His King upon His holy hill of Zion" (Ps. 2:6), and Israel, now in apostasy, is restored to its destined status, in the recognition and under the benign sovereignty of its Messiah. Thereby will be accomplished the deliverance of the world from the power and deception of Satan and from the despotic and antichristian rulers of the nations. This restitution will not in the coming millennial age be universally a return to the pristine condition of Edenic innocence previous to the Fall, but it will fulfill the establishment of God's covenant with Abraham concerning his descendants, a veritable rebirth of the nation, involving the peace and prosperity of the Gentiles. That the worldwide subjection to the authority of Christ will not mean the entire banishment of evil, is clear from Rev. 20:7, 8. Only in the new heavens and earth, "wherein dwelleth righteousness," will sin and evil be entirely absent.

Sit *see* Set at *Matthew 5:1.*

Twelve *dodeka* (1427), is used frequently in the Gospels for the twelve apostles, and in Acts 6:2; 1 Cor. 15:5; Rev. 21:14b; of the tribes of Israel, **Matt. 19:28**; Luke 22:30; Jas. 1:1; Rev. 21:12c (cf. 7:5-8; 12:1); in various details relating to the heavenly Jerusalem, Rev. 21:12-21; 22:2. The number in general is regarded as suggestive of divine administration.

Thrones *see* Throne at *Matthew 5:34.*

Judging *see* Law at *Matthew 5:40.*

Tribes *phule* (5443), "a company of people united by kinship or habitation, a clan, tribe," is used (a) of the peoples of the earth, **Matt. 24:30**; in the following the RV has "tribe(-s)," for KJV, "kindred(-s)," Rev. 1:7; 5:9; 7:9; 11:9; 13:7; 14:6; (b) of the "tribes" of Israel, **Matt. 19:28**; Luke 2:36; 22:30; Acts 13:21; Rom. 11:1; Phil. 3:5; Heb. 7:13, 14; Jas. 1:1; Rev. 5:5; 7:4-8; 21:12.

19:29-30 And every one that hath forsaken houses, or brethren, or sisters, or father, or mother, or wife, or children, or lands, for my name's sake, shall receive an hundredfold, and shall inherit everlasting life.

But many *that are* first shall be last; and the last *shall be* first.

Forsaken *see* Leaveth at *Matthew 4:11.*

Sisters *see* Sister at *Matthew 12:50.*

Lands *agros* (68), "a field," or "piece of ground," or "the country" as distinct from the town, is translated "lands" in **Matt. 19:29**; Mark 10:29, 30; Acts 4:37.

Name *see Matthew 6:9.*

Hundredfold *hekatontaplasion* (1542), an adjective, denotes "a hundredfold," Mark 10:30; Luke 8:8; the best mss. have it in **Matt. 19:29** for *pollaplasion* (4179), "many times more." See the RV margin.

Inherit *see Matthew 5:5.*

Chapter 20

20:1 For the kingdom of heaven is like unto a man *that is* an householder, which went out early in the morning to hire labourers into his vineyard.

Like unto *see* Liken at *Matthew 11:16.*

Householder *oikodespotes* (3617), denotes "the master of a house" (*oikos*, "a house," *despotes*, "a master"), "a householder." It occurs only in the Synoptists, and there 12 times. It is rendered "goodman" in Luke 22:11, where "of the house" is put separately; in **Matt. 20:11**, where the KJV has "the goodman of the house" for the one word, the RV renders it by "householder," as in v. **1**; in **24:43**, "master"; so in Luke 12:39; in Mark 14:14, both have "the goodman of the house.

See also Master of the house at *Matthew 10:25.*

Early In **Matt. 20:1**, *hama*, "at once," is rendered "early."

Morning *see Matthew 16:3.*

Hire *misthoo* (3409), "to let out for hire," is used in the middle voice, signifying "to hire, to engage the services of anyone by contract," **Matt. 20:1, 7.**

Labourers *see Matthew 9:37.*

20:2 And when he had agreed with the labourers for a penny a day, he sent them into his vineyard.

Agreed *see* Agree at *Matthew 18:19.*

Labourers *see Matthew 9:37.*

Penny *see* Pence at *Matthew 18:28.*

20:3 And he went out about the third hour, and saw others standing idle in the marketplace,

Third *see* Three at *Matthew 12:40.*

Others *see* Other at *Matthew 5:39.*

Idle *see Matthew 12:36.*

Marketplace *see* Markets at *Matthew 11:16.*

20:4 And said unto them; Go ye also into the vineyard, and whatsoever is right I will give you. And they went their way.

Also *see Matthew 5:39.*

Right *dikaios* (1342), "just, righteous, that which is in accordance with," *dike*, "rule, right, justice," is translated "right" in **Matt. 20:4**; v. 7, KJV only (RV omits, according to the most authentic mss., the clause having been inserted from v. **4**, to the detriment of the narrative); Luke 12:57; Acts 4:19; Eph. 6:1; Phil. 1:7, RV (KJV, "meet"); 2 Pet. 1:13 (KJV, "meet"). *See also* Just at *Matthew 1:19.*

Way *see Matthew 13:25.*

20:5 Again he went out about the sixth and ninth hour, and did likewise.

Sixth *hektos* (1623), is used (a) of a month, Luke 1:26, 36; (b) an hour, **Matt. 20:5; 27:45** and parallel passages; John 4:6; (c) an angel, Rev. 9:13, 14; 16:12; (d) a seal of a roll, in vision, Rev. 6:12; (e) of the "sixth" precious stone, the sardius, in the foundations of the wall of the heavenly Jerusalem, Rev. 21:20.

Ninth *enatos*, or *enn-* (1766), is found in reference (a) to "the ninth hour" (3 o'clock, p.m.) in **Matt. 20:5; 27:45-46**; Mark 15:33-34; Luke 23:44; Acts 3:1; 10:3, 30; (b) to "the topaz" as the "ninth" foundation of the city wall in the symbolic vision in Rev. 21 (v. 20).

Likewise *hosautos* (5615), a strengthened form of *hos*, "as," denotes "in like manner, just so, likewise"; it is sometimes translated "likewise," e.g., **Matt. 20:5; 21:30.**

20:6 And about the eleventh hour he went out, and found others standing idle, and saith unto them, Why stand ye here all the day idle?

Eleventh *hendekatos* (1734), an adjective derived from the above, is found in **Matt. 20:6, 9**; Rev. 21:20.

Idle *see Matthew 12:36.*

20:7 They say unto him, Because no man hath hired us. He saith unto them, Go ye also into the vineyard; and whatsoever is right, *that* shall ye receive.

Hired *see* Hire at *Matthew 20:1.*

Right *see Matthew 20:4. See also* Just at *Matthew 1:19.*

20:8 So when even was come, the lord of the vineyard saith unto his steward, Call the labourers, and give them *their* hire, beginning from the last unto the first.

Lord *see Matthew 1:22.*

Steward *epitropos* (2012), is rendered "steward" in **Matt. 20:8**; Luke 8:3.

Call *kaleo* (2564), derived from the root *kal-*, whence Eng. "call" and "clamor," is used (a) with a personal object, "to call anyone, invite, summon," e.g., **Matt. 20:8; 25:14**; it is used particularly of the divine call to partake of the blessings of redemption, e.g., Rom. 8:30; 1 Cor. 1:9; 1 Thess. 2:12; Heb. 9:15; (b) of nomenclature or vocation, "to call by a name, to name"; in the passive voice, "to be called by a name, to bear a name." Thus it suggests either vocation or destination; the context determines which, e.g., Rom. 9:25-26; "surname," in Acts 15:37, KJV, is incorrect (RV, "was called").

Labourers *see Matthew 9:37.*

Give *see* Paid at *Matthew 5:26.*

Hire *misthos* (3408), denotes (a) "wages, hire," **Matt. 20:8**; Luke 10:7; Jas. 5:4; in 1 Tim. 5:18; 2 Pet. 2:13; Jude 11, RV, "hire" (KJV, "reward"); in 2 Pet. 2:15, RV, "hire" (KJV, "wages").

Last *see* Uttermost at *Matthew 5:26.*

20:9 And when they came that *were hired* about the eleventh hour, they received every man a penny.

Hired In v. **9** there is no word for "hired" in the original.

Eleventh *see Matthew 20:6.*

Every man *ana* (303), in **Matt. 20:9-10**, the preposition *ana*, "upward" (used distributively), governing the noun *denarion*, is translated "every man (a penny)." There is no word for "every man," and an appropriate rendering would be "a penny apiece"; cf. Luke 9:14, "fifty each," RV; 10:1, "two and two"; John 2:6, "two or three ... apiece"; Rev. 4:8, "each ... six wings."

20:10 But when the first came, they supposed that they should have received more; and they likewise received every man a penny.

Supposed *see* Think at *Matthew 5:17*.

More *see* Exceed *pleion* (4119) at *Matthew 5:20*.

Likewise *see Matthew 18:35*.

20:11 And when they had received *it*, they murmured against the goodman of the house,

Murmured *gonguzo* (1111), "to mutter, murmur, grumble, say anything in a low tone" (Eng., "gong"), an onomatopoeic word, representing the significance by the sound of the word, as in the word "murmur" itself, is used of the laborers in the parable of the householder, **Matt. 20:11**; of the scribes and Pharisees, against Christ, Luke 5:30; of the Jews, John 6:41, 43, of the disciples, 6:61; of the people, 7:32 (of debating secretly); of the Israelites, 1 Cor. 10:10 (twice), where it is also used in a warning to believers. In the papyri it is used of the "murmuring" of a gang of workmen, also in a remark interposed, while the Emperor (late 2nd cent. AD) was interviewing a rebel, that the Romans were then "murmuring" (Moulton and Milligan, *Vocab.*).

Goodman *see* Householder at *Matthew 20:1*. *See also* Master of the house at *Matthew 10:25*.

20:12 Saying, These last have wrought *but* one hour, and thou hast made them equal unto us, which have borne the burden and heat of the day.

Last *see* Uttermost at *Matthew 5:26*.

Wrought *poieo* (4160), "to do," is rendered "to work" in **Matt. 20:12**, KJV (RV, "spent"); Acts 15:12, "had wrought"; 19:11; 21:19; Heb. 13:21; Rev. 16:14; 19:20; 21:27, KJV (RV, "maketh"; marg., "doeth").

Hour *see Matthew 8:13*.

Borne *see* Bear at *Matthew 3:11*.

Burden *baros* (922), denotes "a weight, anything pressing on one physically," **Matt. 20:12**, or "that makes a demand on one's resources," whether material, 1 Thess. 2:6 (to be burdensome), or spiritual, Gal. 6:2; Rev. 2:24, or religious, Acts 15:28. In one place it metaphorically describes the future state of believers as "an eternal weight of glory," 2 Cor. 4:17.

Heat *kauson* (2742), denotes "a burning heat" (from *kaio*, "to burn"; cf. Eng., "caustic," "cauterize"), **Matt. 20:12**; Luke 12:55 (KJV, "heat"), RV, in each place, "scorching heat" (marg. "hot wind"); in Jas. 1:11, "a burning heat," KJV, RV, "the scorching wind" like the sirocco. Cf. Amos 4:9, where the Sept. has *purosis*, "burning" (*pur*, "fire").

20:13 But he answered one of them, and said, Friend, I do thee no wrong: didst not thou agree with me for a penny?

Friend *see* Fellows at *Matthew 11:16*.

Wrong *adikeo* (91), "to do wrong," is used (a) intransitively, to act unrighteously, Acts 25:11, RV, "I am a wrongdoer" (KJV, "... an offender"); 1 Cor. 6:8; 2 Cor. 7:12 (1st part); Col. 3:25 (1st part); cf. Rev. 22:11; (b) transitively, "to wrong," **Matt. 20:13**; Acts 7:24 (passive voice), 26, 27; 25:10; 2 Cor. 7:2, v. 12 (2nd part; passive voice); Gal. 4:12, "ye did (me no) wrong," anticipating a possible suggestion that his vigorous language was due to some personal grievance; the occasion referred to was that of his first visit; Col. 3:25 (2nd part), lit., "what he did wrong," which brings consequences both in this life and at the judgment seat of Christ; Philem. 18; 2 Pet. 2:13 (1st part); in the middle or passive voice, "to take or suffer wrong, to suffer (oneself) to be wronged," 1 Cor. 6:7.

Agree *see Matthew 18:19*.

20:14 Take *that* thine *is*, and go thy way: I will give unto this last, even as unto thee.

Thine, Thy *see* Thy at *Matthew 7:3*.

Last *see* Uttermost at Matthew *5:26*.

20:15 Is it not lawful for me to do what I will with mine own? Is thine eye evil, because I am good?

Mine *emos* (1699), a possessive adjective of the first person, often used as a possessive pronoun with greater emphasis than the oblique forms of *ego*, a measure of stress which should always be observed; it denotes (I) subjectively, (a) "what I possess," e.g., John 4:34; 7:16 (1st part); 13:35; 1 Cor. 16:21; Gal. 6:11; Col. 4:18 (1st clause); as a pronoun, absolutely (i.e., not as an adjective), e.g., **Matt. 20:15**; **25:27**; Luke 15:31, RV, "(all that is) mine," KJV, "(all that) I have"; John 16:14, 15; 17:10; (b) "proceeding from me," e.g. Mark 8:38; John 7:16 (2nd part); 8:37 (here the repetition of the article with the pronoun, after the article with the noun, lends special stress to the pronoun; more lit., "the word, that which is mine"); so in John 15:12. Such instances are to be distinguished from the less emphatic order where the pronoun comes between the article and the noun, as in John 7:16, already mentioned; (c) in the phrase "it is mine" (i.e., "it rests with me"), e.g., **Matt. 20:23**; Mark 10:40; (II) objectively, "pertaining or relating to me": (a) "appointed for me," e.g., John 7:6, "My time" (with the repeated article and special stress just referred to); (b) equivalent to an objective genitive ("of me") e.g., Luke 22:19, "(in remembrance) of Me" (lit., "in My remembrance"); so 1 Cor. 11:24.

Evil *see Matthew 5:11.*

Good *see Matthew 5:45.*

20:16 So the last shall be first, and the first last: for many be called, but few chosen.

Called *kletos* (2822), "called, invited," is used, (a) "of the call of the gospel," **Matt. 20:16**; **22:14**, not there "an effectual call," as in the Epistles, Rom. 1:1, 6-7; 8:28; 1 Cor. 1:2, 24; Jude 1; Rev. 17:14; in Rom. 1:7 and 1 Cor. 1:2 the meaning is "saints by calling"; (b) of "an appointment to apostleship," Rom. 1:1; 1 Cor. 1:1.

Few *see Matthew 7:14.*

Chosen *eklektos* (1588), lit. signifies "picked out, chosen" (*ek*, "from," *lego*, "to gather, pick out"), and is used of (a) Christ, the "chosen" of God, as the Messiah, Luke 23:35, and metaphorically as a "living Stone," "a chief corner Stone," 1 Pet. 2:4, 6; some mss. have it in John 1:34, instead of *huios*, "Son"; (b) angels, 1 Tim. 5:21, as "chosen" to be of especially high rank in administrative association with God, or as His messengers to human beings, doubtless in contrast to fallen angels (see 2 Pet. 2:4 and Jude 6); (c) believers (Jews or Gentiles), **Matt. 24:22, 24, 31**; Mark 13:20, 22, 27; Luke 18:7; Rom. 8:33; Col. 3:12; 2 Tim. 2:10; Titus 1:1; 1 Pet. 1:1; 2:9 (as a spiritual race); **Matt. 20:16**; **22:14** and Rev. 17:14, "chosen"; individual believers are so mentioned in Rom. 16:13; 2 John 1, 13.

20:17 And Jesus going up to Jerusalem took the twelve disciples apart in the way, and said unto them,

Took *see* Take at *Matthew 1:20.*

20:18 Behold, we go up to Jerusalem; and the Son of man shall be betrayed unto the chief priests and unto the scribes, and they shall condemn him to death,

Son *see* Father at *Matthew 10:29.*

Priests *see Matthew 2:4.*

Condemn *see Matthew 12:41.*

20:19 And shall deliver him to the Gentiles to mock, and to scourge, and to crucify *him*: and the third day he shall rise again.

Mock *see* Mocked at *Matthew 2:16.*

Scourge *mastigoo* (3146), in John 19:1 the "scourging" of Christ is thus described, as also in His prophecy of His sufferings, **Matt. 20:19**; Mark 10:34; Luke 18:33. In Acts 22:25 the similar punishment about to be administered to Paul is described by *mastizo* (the "scourging" of Roman citizens was prohibited by the Porcian law of 197 BC).

Crucify *stauroo* (4717), signifies (a) "the act of crucifixion," e.g., **Matt. 20:19**; (b) metaphorically, "the putting off of the flesh with its passions and lusts," a condition fulfilled in the case of those who are "of Christ Jesus," Gal. 5:24, RV; so of the relationship between the believer and the world, 6:14.

Third *see Matthew 17:23.*

Rise *see Matthew 12:41. See also* Raise at *Matthew 10:8.*

20:20 Then came to him the mother of Zebedee's children with her sons, worshipping *him*, and desiring a certain thing of him.

Worshipping *see* Worship at *Matthew 2:2.*

Desiring *aiteo* (154), "to ask," is rendered "to desire" in KJV, e.g., in **Matt. 20:20**; Luke 23:25 [RV, always "to ask (for)"].

Certain The indefinite pronoun *tis* signifies "anyone, some one, a certain one"; the neuter, *ti*, "a certain thing," e.g., **Matt. 20:20**; Mark 14:51.

20:21 And he said unto her, What wilt thou? She saith unto him, Grant that these my two sons may sit, the one on thy right hand, and the other on the left, in thy kingdom.

Wilt *see* Will at *Matthew 16:24.*

Sit *see* Set at *Matthew 5:1.*

Right *see Matthew 5:29.*

Left *euonumos* (2176), lit., "of good name," or "omen" (*eu*, "well," *onoma*, "a name"), a word adopted to avoid the ill-omen attaching to the "left" (omens from the "left" being unlucky, but a good name being desired for them, cf. *aristeros*, lit., "better of two," euphemistic for the ill-omened *laios* and *skaios*; cf, too, the Eng., "sinister," from the Latin word meaning "left"), is used euphemistically, either (a) simply as an adjective in Rev. 10:2, of the "left" foot; in Acts 21:3, "on the left" (lit., "left"); or (b) with the preposition *ex* (for *ek*), signifying "on the left hand," **Matt. 20:21, 23; 25:33, 41; 27:38**; Mark 10:40 (for v. 37, in some mss.); 15:27.

20:22 But Jesus answered and said, Ye know not what ye ask. Are ye able to drink of the cup that I shall drink of, and to be baptized with the baptism that I am baptized with? They say unto him, We are able.

Drink *pino* (4095), "to drink," is used chiefly in the Gospels and in 1 Cor., whether literally (most frequently), or figuratively, (a) of "drinking" of the blood of Christ, in the sense of receiving eternal life, through His death, John 6:53-54, 56; (b) of "receiving" spiritually that which refreshes, strengthens and nourishes the soul, John 7:37; (c) of "deriving" spiritual life from Christ, John 4:14, as Israel did typically, 1 Cor. 10:4; (d) of "sharing" in the sufferings of Christ humanly inflicted, **Matt. 20:22-23**; Mark 10:38-39; (e) of "participating" in the abominations imparted by the corrupt religious and commercial systems emanating from Babylon, Rev. 18:3; (f) of "receiving" divine judgment, through partaking unworthily of the Lord's Supper, 1 Cor. 11:29; (g) of "experiencing" the wrath of God, Rev. 14:10; 16:6; (h) of the earth's "receiving" the benefits of rain, Heb. 6:7.

Cup *see Matthew 10:42.*

Shall *see Matthew 16:27.*

Baptized, Baptism *baptisma* (908), "baptism," consisting of the processes of immersion, submersion and emergence (from *bapto*, "to dip"), is used (a) of John's "baptism," (b) of Christian "baptism"; (c) of the overwhelming afflictions and judgments to which the Lord voluntarily submitted on the cross, e.g., Luke 12:50; (d) of the sufferings His followers would experience, not of a vicarious character, but in fellowship with the sufferings of their Master. Some mss. have the word in **Matt. 20:22-23**; it is used in Mark 10:38-39, with this meaning.

20:23 And he saith unto them, Ye shall drink indeed of my cup, and be baptized with the baptism that I am baptized with: but to sit on my right hand, and on my left, is not mine to give, but *it shall be given to them* for whom it is prepared of my Father.

Indeed *see Matthew 3:11.*

My *see* Mine at *Matthew 20:15.*

Sit *see* Set at *Matthew 5:1.*

Left *see Matthew 20:21.*

Prepared *see* Prepare at *Matthew 3:3.*

20:24 And when the ten heard *it*, they were moved with indignation against the two brethren.

Indignation *aganakteo* (23), "to be indignant, to be moved with indignation" (from *agan*, "much," *achomai*, "to grieve"), is translated "were moved with indignation" of the ten disciples against James and John, **Matt. 20:24**; in Mark 10:41, RV (KJV, "they began to be much displeased"); in **Matt. 21:15**, of the chief priests and scribes, against Christ and the children, RV, "they were moved with indignation" (KJV, "they were sore displeased"); in **26:8**, of the disciples against the woman who anointed Christ's feet, "they had indignation"; so Mark 14:4; in Mark 10:14, of Christ, against the disciples, for rebuking the children, "He was moved with indignation," RV (KJV, "he was much displeased"); in Luke 13:14, of the ruler of the synagogue against Christ for healing on the Sabbath, "being moved with indignation," RV, KJV, "(answered) with indignation."

20:25 But Jesus called them *unto him*, and said, Ye know that the princes of the Gentiles exercise dominion over them, and they that are great exercise authority upon them.

Princes *see* Ruler at *Matthew 9:18.*

Exercise The following verbs contain in translation the word "exercise" but belong to other headings: *exousiazo*, "to exercise authority over," Luke 22:25 (*exousia*, "authority"); in the first part of this verse, the verb *kurieuo*, "to be lord," is translated "exercise lordship," KJV (RV, "have lordship"); *katexousiazo*, a strengthened form of the preceding (*kata*, "down," intensive), **Matt. 20:25**; Mark 10:42, "exercise authority" (in the first part of these verses the synonymous verb *katakurieuo* is rendered "lord it," RV, for KJV, "exercise dominion," and "exercise lordship," respectively); *episkopeo*, "to look over or upon" (*epi*, "over," *skopeo*, "to look"), "to care for," 1 Pet. 5:2 (absent in some mss.), RV, "exercising the oversight," for KJV "taking, etc."

Dominion *katakurieuo* (2634), "to exercise, or gain, dominion over, to lord it over," is used of (a) the "lordship" of gentile rulers, **Matt. 20:25**, KJV, "exercise dominion," RV, "lord it", Mark 10:42, KJV, "exercise lordship," RV, "lord it"; (b) the power of demons over men, Acts 19:16, KJV, "overcame," RV, "mastered"; (c) of the evil of elders in "lording" it over the saints under their spiritual care, 1 Pet. 5:3.

Great *megas* (3173), is used (a) of external form, size, measure, e.g., of a stone, **Matt. 27:60**; fish, John 21:11; (b) of degree and intensity, e.g., of fear, Mark 4:41; wind, John 6:18; Rev. 6:13, RV, "great" (KJV, "mighty"); of a circumstance, 1 Cor. 9:11; 2 Cor. 11:15; in Rev. 5:2, 12, the RV has "great" (KJV, "loud"), of a voice; (c) of rank, whether of persons, e.g., God, Titus 2:13; Christ as a "great Priest," Heb. 10:21, RV; Diana, Acts 19:27, Simon Magus, Acts 8:9 "(some) great one"; in the plural "great ones," **Matt. 20:25**; Mark 10:42, those who hold positions of authority in gentile nations; or of things, e.g., a mystery, Eph. 5:32. Some mss. have it in Acts 8:8, of joy.

Authority *katexousiazo* (2175), "to exercise authority upon," is used in **Matt. 20:25**, and Mark 10:42.

20:26 But it shall not be so among you: but whosoever will be great among you, let him be your minister;

Will *see Matthew 16:24.*

Minister *diakonos* (1249), (Eng., "deacon"), primarily denotes a "servant," whether as doing servile work, or as an attendant rendering free service, without particular reference to its character. The word is probably connected with the verb *dioko*, "to hasten after, pursue" (perhaps originally said of a runner). "It occurs in the NT of domestic servants, John 2:5, 9; the civil ruler, Rom. 13:4; Christ, Rom. 15:8; Gal. 2:17; the followers of Christ in relation to their Lord, John 12:26; Eph. 6:21; Col. 1:7; 4:7; the followers of Christ in relation to one another, **Matt. 20:26**; **23:11**; Mark 9:35; 10:43; the servants of Christ in the work of preaching and teaching, 1 Cor. 3:5; 2 Cor. 3:6; 6:4; 11:23; Eph. 3:7; Col. 1:23, 25; 1 Thess. 3:2; 1 Tim. 4:6; those who serve in the churches, Rom. 16:1 (used of a woman here only in NT); Phil. 1:1; 1 Tim. 3:8, 12; false apostles, servants of Satan, 2 Cor. 11:15. Once *diakonos* is used where, apparently, angels are intended, **Matt. 22:13**; in v. **3**, where men are intended, *doulos* is used." *Diakonos* is, generally speaking, to be distinguished from *doulos*, "a bondservant, slave"; *diakonos* views a servant in relationship to his work, *doulos* views him in relationship to his master. See, e.g., **Matt. 22:2-14**; those who bring in the guests (vv. **3-4**, **6**, **8**, **10**) are *douloi* those who carry out the king's sentence (v. **13**) are *diakonoi*.

"Self-chosen authority is an impertinence. Jesus said that the great ones in this world exercise authority but that in his kingdom it is not so; no one exercises authority over another because in his kingdom the king is servant of all. If a saint tries to exercise authority, it is a proof he is not rightly related to Jesus Christ."

OSWALD CHAMBERS

20:27 And whosoever will be chief among you, let him be your servant:

Will *see Matthew 16:24.*

Chief *protos* (4413), denotes "the first," whether in time or place. It is translated "chief" in Mark 6:21, RV, of men of Galilee; in Acts 13:50, of men in a city; in 28:7, of the "chief" man in the island of Melita; in 17:4, of "chief" women in a city; in 28:17, of Jews; in 1 Tim. 1:15-16, of a sinner. In the following, where the KJV has "chief," or "chiefest," the RV renderings are different: **Matt. 20:27** and Mark 10:44, "first"; Luke 19:47 and Acts 25:2, "principal men"; Acts 16:12, said of Philippi, "the first (city) of the district," RV, for incorrect KJV, "the chief city of that part of Macedonia." Amphipolis was the "chief" city of that part. *Protos* here must mean the first in the direction in which the apostle came.

20:28 Even as the Son of man came not to be ministered unto, but to minister, and to give his life a ransom for many.

Even as *hosper* (5618), is translated "even as" in **Matt. 20:28**.

Ministered, Minister *see* **Ministered** at *Matthew 4:11. See also* **Law** at *Matthew 5:17.*

Ransom *lutron* (3383), lit., "a means of loosing" (from *luo*, "to loose"), occurs frequently in the Sept., where it is always used to signify "equivalence." Thus it is used of the "ransom" for a life, e.g., Exod. 21:30, of the redemption price of a slave, e.g., Lev. 19:20, of land, 25:24, of the price of a captive, Isa. 45:13. In the NT it occurs in **Matt. 20:28** and Mark

10:45, where it is used of Christ's gift of Himself as "a ransom for many." Some interpreters have regarded the "ransom" price as being paid to Satan; others, to an impersonal power such as death, or evil, or "that ultimate necessity which has made the whole course of things what it has been." Such ideas are largely conjectural, the result of an attempt to press the details of certain Old Testament illustrations beyond the actual statements of New Testament doctrines. That Christ gave up His life in expiatory sacrifice under God's judgment upon sin and thus provided a "ransom" whereby those who receive Him on this ground obtain deliverance from the penalty due to sin, is what Scripture teaches. What the Lord states in the two passages mentioned involves this essential character of His death. In these passages the preposition is *anti*, which has a vicarious significance, indicating that the "ransom" holds good for those who, accepting it as such, no longer remain in death since Christ suffered death in their stead. The change of preposition in 1 Tim. 2:6, where the word *antilutron*, a substitutionary "ransom," is used, is significant. There the preposition is *huper*, "on behalf of," and the statement is made that He "gave Himself a ransom for all," indicating that the "ransom" was provisionally universal, while being of a vicarious character. Thus the three passages consistently show that while the provision was universal, for Christ died for all men, yet it is actual for those only who accept God's conditions, and who are described in the Gospel statements as "the many." The giving of His life was the giving of His entire person, and while His death under divine judgment was alone expiatory, it cannot be dissociated from the character of His life which, being sinless, gave virtue to His death and was a testimony to the fact that His death must be of a vicarious nature.

20:29 And as they departed from Jericho, a great multitude followed him.

Departed *ekporeuo* (1607), *ek*, "from," in the middle and passive, "to proceed from or forth," more expressive of a definite course than simply "to go forth," is translated "go forth," in Mark 6:11; "went out" in **Matt. 20:29**, RV (KJV, "departed"); both have "depart" in Acts 25:4. It is frequently translated by the verb "to proceed," and is often best so rendered, e.g., in Rev. 9:17-18, RV, for KJV, "issued."

Multitude *see* Multitudes at *Matthew 4:25.*

20:30 And, behold, two blind men sitting by the way side, when they heard that Jesus passed by, cried out, saying, Have mercy on us, O Lord, *thou* Son of David.

Mercy *see Matthew 5:7.*

20:31 And the multitude rebuked them, because they should hold their peace: but they cried the more, saying, Have mercy on us, O Lord, *thou* Son of David.

Rebuked *see Matthew 8:26.*

Peace *siopao* (4623), "to be silent or still, to keep silence" (from *siope*, "silence"), is translated "to hold one's peace," in **Matt. 20:31**; **26:63**; Mark 3:4; 9:34; 10:48; 14:61; Luke 19:40; Acts 18:9; in the Lord's command to the sea, in Mark 4:39, it is translated "peace"; in Luke 1:20, RV, "thou shalt be silent" (KJV, "dumb").

More *meizon* (3187), the neuter of *meizon*, "greater," the comparative degree of *megas*, "great," is used as an adverb, and translated "the more" in **Matt. 20:31**.

Mercy *see Matthew 5:7.*

20:32 And Jesus stood still, and called them, and said, What will ye that I shall do unto you?

Stood *see Matthew 2:9.*

Called *phoneo* (5455), "to sound" (Eng., "phone"), is used of the crowing of a cock, e.g., **Matt. 26:34**; John 13:38; of "calling" out with a clear or loud voice, to cry out, e.g. Mark 1:26 (some mss. have *krazo* here); Acts 16:28; of "calling" to come to oneself, e.g., **Matt. 20:32**; Luke 19:15; of "calling" forth, as of Christ's call to Lazarus to come forth from the tomb, John 12:17; of inviting, e.g., Luke 14:12; of "calling" by name, with the implication of the pleasure taken in the possession of those "called," e.g., John 10:3; 13:13.

20:33 They say unto him, Lord, that our eyes may be opened.

Eyes *omma* (3659), "sight," is used in the plural in **Matt. 20:34** (*opthalmos* is used in v. **33**); Mark 8:23. The word is more poetical in usage than *ophthalmos*, and the writers may have changed the word with a view to distinguishing the simple desire of the blind man from the tender act of the Lord Himself. *See also* Eye at *Matthew 5:38.*

20:34 So Jesus had compassion *on them*, and touched their eyes: and immediately their eyes received sight, and they followed him.

Compassion *see Matthew 9:36.*

Eyes *see Matthew 20:33.*

Sight *see Matthew 11:5.*

Chapter 21

21:1 And when they drew nigh unto Jerusalem, and were come to Bethphage, unto the mount of Olives, then sent Jesus two disciples,

Drew nigh *see* At hand at *Matthew 3:2.*

Mount *see* Mountain at *Matthew 5:1.*

Olives *elaia* (1636), denotes (a) "an olive tree," Rom. 11:17, 24; Rev. 11:4 (plural); the Mount of Olives was so called from the numerous olive trees there, and indicates the importance attached to such; the Mount is mentioned in the NT in connection only with the Lord's life on earth, **Matt. 21:1**; **24:3**; **26:30**; Mark 11:1; 13:3; 14:26; Luke 19:37; 22:39; John 8:1; (b) "an olive," Jas. 3:12, RV (KJV, "olive berries").

21:2 Saying unto them, Go into the village over against you, and straightway ye shall find an ass tied, and a colt with her: loose *them*, and bring *them* unto me.

Over against The most authentic mss. have *katenanti*, "over against," in **Matt. 21:2**.

Tied *deo* (1210), "to bind," is rendered "to tie" in **Matt. 21:2**; Mark 11:2, 4; Luke 19:30.

Colt *polos* (4454), "a foal," whether "colt or filly," had the general significance of "a young creature"; in **Matt. 21:2**, and parallel passages, "an ass's colt."

Loose *luo* (3089), denotes (a) "to loose, unbind, release," (1) of things, e.g., in Acts 7:33, RV, "loose (the shoes)," KJV, "put off"; Mark 1:7; (2) of animals, e.g., **Matt. 21:2**; (3) of persons, e.g., John 11:44; Acts 22:30; (4) of Satan, Rev. 20:3, 7, and angels, Rev. 9:14, 15; (5) metaphorically, of one diseased, Luke 13:16; of the marriage tie, 1 Cor. 7:27; of release from sins, Rev. 1:5 (in the most authentic mss.); (b) "to loosen, break up, dismiss, dissolve, destroy"; in this sense it is translated "to loose" in Acts 2:24, of the pains of death; in Rev. 5:2, of the seals of a roll.

21:3 And if any *man* say ought unto you, ye shall say, The Lord hath need of them; and straightway he will send them.

Send *see Matthew 10:16.*

21:4 All this was done, that it might be fulfilled which was spoken by the prophet, saying,

Fulfilled *see Matthew 1:22.*

Spoken *see Matthew 1:22.*

21:5 Tell ye the daughter of Sion, Behold, thy King cometh unto thee, meek, and sitting upon an ass, and a colt the foal of an ass.

Daughter *thugater* (2364), "a daughter," (etymologically, Eng., "daughter" is connected), is used of (a) the natural relationship (frequent in the Gospels); (b) spiritual relationship to God, 2 Cor. 6:18, in the sense of the practical realization of acceptance with, and the approval of, God (cf. Isa. 43:6), the only place in the NT where it applies to spiritual relationship; (c) the inhabitants of a city or region, **Matt. 21:5**; John 12:15 ("of Zion"); cf. Isa. 37:22; Zeph. 3:14 (Sept.); (d) the women who followed Christ to Calvary, Luke 23:28; (e) women of Aaron's posterity, Luke 1:5; (f) a female descendant of Abraham, Luke 13:16.

Meek *see Matthew 5:5.*

And *kai* The *epexegetic* or *explanatory* use. This may be represented by the expressions "namely," "again," "and indeed," "that is to say"; it is usually translated by "and." In such cases not merely an addition is in view. In **Matt. 21:5**, "and upon a colt" means "that is to say, upon a colt." In John 1:16 the clause "and grace for grace" is explanatory of the "fullness." In John 12:48, "and receiveth not My sayings," is not simply an addition to "that rejecteth Me," it explains what the rejection involves, as the preceding verse shows. In Mark 14:1, "and the unleavened bread" is perhaps an instance, since the Passover feast is so defined in Luke 22:1. In Acts 23:6 the meaning is "the hope, namely, the resurrection of the dead." In Rom. 1:5 "grace and apostleship" may signify "grace expressed in apostleship." In Eph. 1:1 "and the faithful" does not mark a distinct class of believers, it defines "the saints"; but in this case it goes a little further than what is merely epexegetical, it adds a more distinctive epithet than the preceding and may be taken as meaning "yes indeed."

Sitting upon *epibaino* (1910), "to go upon" (*epi*, "upon," *baino*, "to go"), is used of Christ's "riding" into Jerusalem, **Matt. 21:5**, RV, "riding" (KJV, "sitting").

Ass *hupozugion* (5268), lit., "under a yoke" (*hupo*, "under," *zugos*, "a yoke"), is used as an alternative description of the same animal, in **Matt. 21:5**, where both words are found together, "Behold, thy king cometh unto thee, meek and riding upon an ass (*onos*), and upon a colt the foal of an ass (*hupozugion*)." It was upon the colt that the Lord sat, John 12:14. In 2 Pet. 2:16, it is used of Balaam's "ass."

Foal *huios* (5207), "a son," is always so translated in the RV, except in the phrase "children of Israel," e.g., **Matt. 27:9**; and with reference to a foal, **Matt. 21:5**.

21:6 And the disciples went, and did as Jesus commanded them,

Commanded In **Matt. 21:6**, the RV, translating *suntasso*, as in the best mss., has "appointed," KJV, "commanded." *See also* **Bidden** at *Matthew 1:24*.

21:7 And brought the ass, and the colt, and put on them their clothes, and they set *him* thereon.

Put *see Matthew 19:13*.

Set In Heb. 8:1, *kathizo* is used intransitively, RV, "sat down" (KJV, "is set"); so in 12:2, RV, "hath sat down" (KJV, "is set down"); Rev. 3:21, RV, "I ... sat down" (KJV, "am set down"). So *epikathizo* in **Matt. 21:7** (last part), RV, "He sat" [some mss. have the plural in a transitive sense, KJV, "they set (Him)]."

21:8 And a very great multitude spread their garments in the way; others cut down branches from the trees, and strawed *them* in the way.

Great In **Matt. 21:8**, *pleistos*, the superlative of *polus*, said of a multitude, is rendered "very great" in the KJV (RV, "the most part"). *See also* **Most** at *Matthew 11:20*.

Spread, Strawed *stronnuo* or *stronnumi* (4766), "to spread," is used of "furnishing a room," Mark 14:15; Luke 22:12; of "making a bed," Acts 9:34; in **Matt. 21:8**; Mark 11:8, "spread" (KJV, "strawed," twice).

Cut *kopto* (2875), denotes "to cut by a blow," e.g., branches, **Matt. 21:8**; Mark 11:8. *See also* **Lamented** at *Matthew 11:17*.

Branches *see Matthew 13:32*.

21:9 And the multitudes that went before, and that followed, cried, saying, Hosanna to the Son of David: Blessed *is* he that cometh in the name of the Lord; Hosanna in the highest.

Blessed *eulogeo* (2127), lit., "to speak well of" (*eu*, "well," *logos*, "a word"), signifies, (a) "to praise, to celebrate with praises," of that which is addressed to God, acknowledging His goodness, with desire for His glory, Luke 1:64; 2:28; 24:51, 53; Jas. 3:9; (b) "to invoke blessings upon a person," e.g., Luke 6:28; Rom. 12:14. The present participle passive, "blessed, praised," is especially used of Christ in **Matt. 21:9; 23:39**, and the parallel passages; also in John 12:13; (c) "to consecrate a thing with solemn prayers, to ask God's blessing on a thing," e.g., Luke 9:16; 1 Cor. 10:16; (d) "to cause to prosper, to make happy, to bestow blessings on," said of God, e.g., in Acts 3:26; Gal. 3:9; Eph. 1:3. Cf. the synonym *aineo*, "to praise."

Hosanna *hosanna* (5614), in the Hebrew, means "save, we pray." The word seems to have become an utterance of praise rather than of prayer, though originally, probably, a cry for help. The people's cry at the Lord's triumphal entry into Jerusalem (**Matt. 21:9, 15**; Mark 11:9, 10; John 12:13) was taken from Ps. 118, which was recited at the Feast of Tabernacles in the great Hallel (Psalms 113 to 118) in responses with the priest, accompanied by the waving of palm and willow branches. "The last day of the feast" was called "the great Hosanna"; the boughs also were called "hosannas."

Highest *hupsistos* (5310), is used in the plural in the phrase "in the highest," i.e., in the "highest" regions, the abode of God, **Matt. 21:9**; Mark 11:10; Luke omits the article, Luke 2:14; 19:38; for its use as a title of God.

21:10 And when he was come into Jerusalem, all the city was moved, saying, Who is this?

City *see Matthew 8:34*.

Moved *seio* (4579), "to shake, move to and fro," usually of violent concussion (Eng., "seismic," "seismograph," "seismology"), is said (a) of the earth as destined to be shaken by God, Heb. 12:26; (b) of a local convulsion of the earth, at the death of Christ, **Matt. 27:51**, "did quake"; (c) of a fig tree, Rev. 6:13; (d) metaphorically, to stir up with fear or some other emotion, **Matt. 21:10**, of the people of a city; **28:4**, of the keepers or watchers, at the Lord's tomb, RV, "did quake" (KJV, "did shake").

21:11-12 And the multitude said, This is Jesus the prophet of Nazareth of Galilee.

And Jesus went into the temple of God, and cast out all them that sold and bought in the temple, and overthrew the tables of the moneychangers, and the seats of them that sold doves,

Went into *see* **Enter** at *Matthew 7:13*.

Overthrew *katastrepho* (2690), lit. and primarily, "to turn down" or "turn over," as, e.g., the soil, denotes to "overturn, overthrow," **Matt. 21:12**; Mark 11:15; in Acts 15:16, passive voice, "ruins," lit., "the overthrown (things) of it" (some mss. have *kataskapto*, "to dig down").

Tables *see* **Table** at *Matthew 15:27*.

Moneychangers *kollubistes* (2855), from *kollubos* (lit., "clipped"), "a small coin or rate of change" (*koloboo* signifies "to cut off, to clip, shorten," **Matt. 24:22**), denotes "a money-changer," lit., money-clipper, **Matt. 21:12**; Mark 11:15; John 2:15.

Seats *kathedra* (2515), from *kata*, "down," and *hedra*, "a seat," denotes "a seat" (Eng., "cathedral"), "a chair," **Matt. 21:12**; Mark 11:15; of teachers, **Matt. 23:2**.

Doves *see* Dove at *Matthew 3:16*.

21:13 And said unto them, It is written, My house shall be called the house of prayer; but ye have made it a den of thieves.

House *see Matthew 9:6*.

Made *see* Make at *Matthew 4:19*.

Den *spelaion* (4693), "a grotto, cavern, den" (Lat., *spelunca*), "cave," John 11:38, is said of the grave of Lazarus; in the RV in Heb. 11:38 and Rev. 6:15 (KJV, "dens"); in the Lord's rebuke concerning the defilement of the Temple, **Matt. 21:13**; Mark 11:17; Luke 19:46, "den" is used.

Thieves *lestes* (3027), "a robber, brigand" (akin to *leia*, "booty"), "one who plunders openly and by violence" (in contrast to *kleptes*, "a thief,"), is always translated "robber" or "robbers" in the RV, as the KJV in John 10:1, 8, 18:40; 2 Cor. 11:26; the KJV has "thief" or "thieves" in **Matt. 21:13**, and parallel passages; **26:55**, and parallel passages; **27:38, 44** and Mark 15:27; Luke 10:30, 36; but "thief" is the meaning of *kleptes*.

21:14 And the blind and the lame came to him in the temple; and he healed them.

Lame *see Matthew 11:5*.

21:15 And when the chief priests and scribes saw the wonderful things that he did, and the children crying in the temple, and saying, Hosanna to the Son of David; they were sore displeased,

Priests *see Matthew 2:4*.

Wonderful In **Matt. 21:15**, the neuter plural of the adjective *thaumasios*, "wonderful," is used as a noun, "wonderful things," lit., "wonders."

Children *see Matthew 2:16*.

Crying *see* Cried at *Matthew 15:22*.

Hosanna *see Matthew 21:9*.

Sore In **Matt. 21:15**, *aganakteo*, "to be moved with indignation" (RV), is translated "they were sore displeased."

Displeased *see* Indignation at *Matthew 20:24*.

21:16 And said unto him, Hearest thou what these say? And Jesus saith unto them, Yea; have ye never read, Out of the mouth of babes and sucklings thou hast perfected praise?

Yea *see Matthew 5:37*.

Never *see Matthew 7:23*.

Read *see Matthew 12:3*.

Mouth *see Matthew 12:34*.

Babes *see Matthew 11:25*.

Sucklings *thelazo* (2337), from *thele*, "a breast," is used (a) of the mother, "to suckle," **Matt. 24:19**; Mark 13:17; Luke 21:23; in some texts in 23:29 (the best have *trepho*); (b) of the young, "to suck," **Matt. 21:16**, "sucklings," Luke 11:27.

Perfected *see* Mending at *Matthew 4:21*.

Praise *ainos* (136), primarily "a tale, narration," came to denote "praise"; in the NT only of praise to God, **Matt. 21:16**; Luke 18:43.

21:17 And he left them, and went out of the city into Bethany; and he lodged there.

Lodged *aulizomai* (835), properly, "to lodge in a courtyard" (*aule*, "court"), then, "to lodge in the open," denotes, in the NT, "to pass the night, to lodge anywhere," **Matt. 21:17**; Luke 21:37, RV, "lodged" (KJV, "abode"). See the metaphorical use in the Sept. and the Heb. of Ps. 30:5, "(weeping) may come in to lodge (at even)," i.e., as a passing stranger.

21:18 Now in the morning as he returned into the city, he hungered.

Morning *proios* (4405), "early, at early morn" (from *pro*, "before"), is used as a noun in the feminine form *proia*, "morning" in **Matt. 27:1** and John 21:4 (in some mss. in **Matt. 21:18** and John 18:28). Its adjectival force is retained by regarding it as qualifying the noun *hora*, "an hour," i.e., "at an early hour." *See also Matthew 16:3*.

Returned *epanago* (1877), "to bring up or back" (primarily a nautical term for "putting to sea"), is used intransitively, in **Matt. 21:18**, "He returned."

Hungered *see* Hungred at *Matthew 4:2*.

21:19 And when he saw a fig tree in the way, he came to it, and found nothing thereon, but leaves only, and said unto it, Let no fruit grow on thee henceforward for ever. And presently the fig tree withered away.

Fig tree *suke* or *sukea* (4808), "a fig tree," is found in **Matt. 21:19, 20, 21; 24:32**; Mark 11:13, 20, 21; 13:28; Luke 13:6, 7; 21:29; John 1:48, 50, Jas. 3:12; Rev. 6:13.

Leaves *phullon* (5444), "a leaf" (originally *phulion*, Lat., *folium*, Eng., "folio," "foliaceous," "foliage," "foliate," "folious," etc.), is found in **Matt. 21:19**; **24:32**; Mark 11:13 (twice); 13:28; Rev. 22:2.

No *meketi* (3371), generally expressing a prohibition, e.g., **Matt. 21:19**; John 5:14; Rom. 14:13; Eph. 4:28; 1 Tim. 5:23; 1 Pet. 4:2; indicating some condition expressed or implied, e.g., 1 Thess. 3:5; or nonexistence, when the existence might have been possible under certain conditions, e.g., Mark 1:45; 2:2, RV, "no longer" (KJV, "no").

Grow In **Matt. 21:19**, for KJV, "let (no fruit) grow," the RV, more strictly, has "let there be (no fruit)."

Henceforward Negatively, "henceforth ... not" (or "no more") translates one or other of the negative adverbs *ouketi* and *meketi*, "no longer," e.g., Acts 4:17, KJV, and RV, "henceforth (to no man)"; in the following the RV has "no longer" for the KJV, "henceforth" (with a negative), John 15:15; Rom. 6:6; 2 Cor. 5:15; Eph. 4:17; in 2 Cor. 5:16 (last part), RV, "no more"; in **Matt. 21:19** and Mark 11:14, "no (fruit ...) henceforward"; KJV in the latter, "hereafter."

Presently *parachrema* (3916), lit., "with the matter (or business) itself" (*para*, "with," *chrema*, "a business," or "event"), and so, "immediately," **Matt. 21:19** (KJV, "presently"), **20**; Luke 1:64; 4:39; 5:25; 8:44, 47, 55; 13:13; 18:43; 19:11; 22:60; Acts 3:7; 5:10; 12:23; 13:11; 16:26, 33; it is thus used by Luke only, save for the two instances in Matthew. It is also rendered "presently," "soon," "straightway."

Withered *see Matthew 13:6.*

21:20 And when the disciples saw *it*, they marvelled, saying, How soon is the fig tree withered away!

Soon *see* **Presently** at *Matthew 21:19.*

Fig tree *see Matthew 21:19.*

Withered *see Matthew 13:6.*

21:21 Jesus answered and said unto them, Verily I say unto you, If ye have faith, and doubt not, ye shall not only do this *which is done* to the fig tree, but also if ye shall say unto this mountain, Be thou removed, and be thou cast into the sea; it shall be done.

Doubt *diakrino* (1252), lit., "to separate throughout, to make a distinction," Acts 15:9, RV, is translated "to make to differ," in 1 Cor. 4:7. In Jude 22, where the middle voice is used, the KJV has "making a difference"; the RV, adopting the alternative reading, the accusative case, has "who are in doubt," a meaning found in **Matt. 21:21**; Mark 11:23; Acts 10:20; Rom. 14:23; Jas. 1:6; 2:4.

This The article *ho*, **Matt. 21:21** (*to*, the neuter), KJV (RV, "what"); in Rom. 13:9 (1st part); Gal. 5:14; Heb. 12:27, the article *to* is virtually equivalent to "the following."

Fig tree *see Matthew 21:19.*

Mountain *see Matthew 5:1.*

Removed In **Matt. 21:21** and Mark 11:23, *airo*, "to lift, take up," is translated "be thou removed" (RV, "be thou taken up").

21:22 And all things, whatsoever ye shall ask in prayer, believing, ye shall receive.

Prayer *proseuche* (4335), denotes (a) "prayer" (to God), the most frequent term, e.g., **Matt. 21:22**; Luke 6:12, where the phrase is not to be taken literally as if it meant, "the prayer of God" (subjective genitive), but objectively, "prayer to God." In Jas. 5:17, "He prayed fervently," RV, is, lit., "he prayed with prayer" (a Hebraistic form). *See also* **Prayest, Pray** at *Matthew 6:6.*

21:23 And when he was come into the temple, the chief priests and the elders of the people came unto him as he was teaching, and said, By what authority doest thou these things? and who gave thee this authority?

What Other words are (a) *hoios*, "of what kind," e.g., 2 Cor. 10:11, RV (KJV, "such as"); 1 Thess. 1:5, "what manner of men"; 2 Tim. 3:11 (twice), lit., "what sorts of things," "what sorts of persecutions"; (b) *poios*, "what sort of," e.g., **Matt. 21:23**, **24**, **27**; **24:42**, **43**; Luke 5:19; 6:32-34; 20:2, 8; 24:19; John 12:33, "what manner of"; so in 18:32; 21:19; Rom. 3:27; 1 Cor. 15:35; in Jas. 4:14, "what"; 1 Pet. 2:20 and Rev. 3:3 (ditto); 1 Pet. 1:11, "what manner of"; (c) *hopoios*, "what sort of," 1 Cor. 3:13; "what manner of," 1 Thess. 1:9; (d) *hosos*, "how great," Mark 6:30 (twice), RV, "whatsoever"; Acts 15:12; Rom. 3:19, "what things soever"; Jude 10 (1st part), "what soever things," RV; (2nd part) "what"; (e) *posos*, "how great, how much," 2 Cor. 7:11, "what (earnest care)," RV (*posos* here stands for the repeated words in the Eng. versions, the adjective not being repeated in the original); (f) *hostis*, "what (things)," Phil. 3:7; (g) in **Matt. 26:40**, *houtos*, "thus, so," is used as an exclamatory expression, translated "What" (in a word immediately addressed by the Lord to Peter), lit., "So"; (h) for *potapos*, rendered "what" in Mark 13:1 (2nd part), KJV; (i) in 1 Cor. 6:16, 19, KJV, the particle *e*, "or" (RV), is rendered "What?"; in 1 Cor. 14:36, KJV and RV, "what?" (j) in 1 Cor. 11:22, *gar*, "in truth, indeed," has its exclamatory use "What."

Authority *see* Power at *Matthew 9:6*.

21:24 And Jesus answered and said unto them, I also will ask you one thing, which if ye tell me, I in like wise will tell you by what authority I do these things.

One *see Matthew 6:24*.

Thing *logos* (3056), "a word, an account," etc., is translated "thing" in **Matt. 21:24**, KJV (1st part), and Luke 20:3, KJV, RV, "question" (in **Matt. 21:24**, 2nd part, "these things" translates *tauta*, the neut. plur. of *houtos*, "this"); Luke 1:4; Acts 5:24, KJV (RV, "words").

Tell *eiro* (3004), is rendered "to tell" in **Matt. 21:24**; Mark 11:29; John 14:29; Rev. 17:7.

Like wise *see* Likewise at *Matthew 18:35*.

What *see Matthew 21:23*.

21:25 The baptism of John, whence was it? from heaven, or of men? And they reasoned with themselves, saying, If we shall say, From heaven; he will say unto us, Why did ye not then believe him?

Of The following are instances in which "of" translates *ek*, or *ex*, "out of, from," **Matt. 21:25** (RV, "from"); 1 Cor. 1:30; 15:6; 2 Cor. 5:1 (RV, "from"); Jas. 4:1.

Reasoned *see Matthew 16:7*.

21:26 But if we shall say, Of men; we fear the people; for all hold John as a prophet.

People *see* Multitudes at *Matthew 4:25*.

Hold *echo* (2192), "to have or hold," is used of mental conception, "to consider, account," e.g., **Matt. 21:26**; of "steadfast adherence to faith, or the faith," e.g., 1 Tim. 1:19; 3:9; 2 Tim. 1:13.

Prophet *see* Prophets at Matthew *5:12*.

21:27 And they answered Jesus, and said, We cannot tell. And he said unto them, Neither tell I you by what authority I do these things.

Cannot *oida* (1492), "to know by perception," is the word in Pilate's remark "make it as sure as ye can" (marg. "sure, as ye know"), **Matt. 27:65**. The phrases "cannot tell," "canst not tell," etc., are in the RV rendered "know not," etc., **Matt. 21:27**; Mark 11:33; Luke 20:7; John 3:8; 8:14; 16:18; 2 Cor. 12:2-3.

Tell In the following, *oida*, "to know," is translated "tell" in the KJV (RV, "know"), **Matt. 21:27**; Mark 11:33; Luke 20:7; John 3:8; 8:14; 16:18; 2 Cor. 12:2.

What *see Matthew 21:23*.

21:28 But what think ye? A *certain* man had two sons; and he came to the first, and said, Son, go work to day in my vineyard.

Work *ergazomai* (2038), is used (I) intransitively, e.g., **Matt. 21:28**; John 5:17; 9:4 (2nd part); Rom. 4:4, 5; 1 Cor. 4:12; 9:6; 1 Thess. 2:9; 4:11; 2 Thess. 3:8, 10-12; (II) transitively, (a) "to work something, produce, perform," e.g., **Matt. 26:10**, "she hath wrought"; John 6:28, 30; 9:4 (1st part); Acts 10:35; 13:41; Rom. 2:10; 13:10; 1 Cor. 16:10; 2 Cor. 7:10a; Gal. 6:10, RV, "let us work"; Eph. 4:28; Heb. 11:33; 2 John 8; (b) "to earn by working, work for," John 6:27, RV, "work" (KJV, "labor").

21:29 He answered and said, I will not: but afterward he repented, and went.

Afterward *see Matthew 4:2*.

Repented *metamelomai* (3338), is used in the passive voice with middle voice sense, signifying "to regret, to repent oneself," **Matt. 21:29**, RV, "repented himself"; v. **32**, RV, "ye did (not) repent yourselves" (KJV, "ye repented not"); **27:3**, "repented himself"; 2 Cor. 7:8 (twice), RV, "regret" in each case; Heb. 7:21, where alone in the NT it is said (negatively) of God.

21:30 And he came to the second, and said likewise. And he answered and said, I *go*, sir: and went not.

Likewise *see Matthew 20:5*.

Sir *see* Lord at *Matthew 1:22*.

21:31 Whether of them twain did the will of *his* father? They say unto him, The first. Jesus saith unto them, Verily I say unto you, That the publicans and the harlots go into the kingdom of God before you.

Twain *see Matthew 5:41*.

First *husteros* (5306), denotes "later" or "latter" and is used in 1 Tim. 4:1, RV, "in later (times)," KJV, "in (the) latter (times)." Several mss. have it in **Matt. 21:31**, "the former," for *protos*, "the first."

Publicans *see Matthew 5:46*.

Harlots *porne* (4204), "a prostitute, harlot" (from *pernemi*, "to sell"), is used (a) literally, in **Matt. 21:31, 32**, of those who were the objects of the mercy shown by Christ; in Luke 15:30, of the life of the Prodigal; in 1 Cor. 6:15, 16, in a warning to the Corinthian church against the prevailing licentiousness which had made Corinth a byword; in Heb. 11:31 and Jas. 2:25, of Rahab; (b) metaphorically, of mystic Babylon, Rev. 17:1, 5 (KJV, "harlots"), 15, 16; 19:2, RV, for KJV, "whore."

21:32 For John came unto you in the way of righteousness, and ye believed him not: but the publicans and the harlots believed him: and ye, when ye had seen *it*, repented not afterward, that ye might believe him.

Way *see Matthew 7:13.*

Righteousness *see Matthew 3:15.*

Publicans *see Matthew 5:46.*

Harlots *see Matthew 21:31.*

Repented *see Matthew 21:29.*

Afterward *see Matthew 4:2.*

21:33 Hear another parable: There was a certain householder, which planted a vineyard, and hedged it round about, and digged a winepress in it, and built a tower, and let it out to husbandmen, and went into a far country:

Householder *see* Master of the house at *Matthew 10:25.*

Planted *see Matthew 15:13.*

Hedged *phragmos* (5418), denotes any sort of fence, hedge, palings or wall (akin to *phrasso*, "to fence in, stop"). It is used (a) in its literal sense, in **Matt. 21:33**, lit. "(he put) a hedge (around)"; Mark 12:1; Luke 14:23; (b) metaphorically, of the "partition" which separated Gentile from Jew, which was broken down by Christ through the efficacy of His expiatory sacrifice, Eph. 2:14.

Digged *orusso* (3736), "to dig, dig up soil, dig a pit," is said of a place for a winepress, **Matt. 21:33**; Mark 12:1; of "digging" a pit for hiding something, **Matt. 25:15**.

Winepress *lenos* (3025), denotes "a trough or vat," used especially for the treading of grapes, **Matt. 21:33**. Not infrequently they were dug out in the soil or excavated in a rock, as in the rock vats in Palestine today. In Rev. 14:19, 20 (twice) and 19:15 (where *oinos* is added, lit.. "the winepress of the wine") the word is used metaphorically with reference to the execution of divine judgment upon the gathered foes of the Jews at the close of this age preliminary to the establishment of the millennial kingdom.

Tower *purgos* (4444), is used of "a watchtower in a vineyard," **Matt. 21:33**; Mark 12:1; probably, too, in Luke 14:28 (cf. Isa. 5:2); in Luke 13:4, of the "tower in Siloam," the modern Silwan, which is built on a steep escarpment of rock.

Let ... out *ekdidomi* (1554), primarily, "to give out, give up, surrender" (*ek*, "out, from," *didomi*, "to give"), denotes "to let out for hire"; in the NT it is used, in the middle voice, with the meaning "to let out to one's advantage," in the parable of the husbandman and his vineyard, **Matt. 21:33, 41**; Mark 12:1; Luke 20:9, KJV, "let ... forth"; RV, "let out."

Husbandmen *georgos* (1092), from *ge*, "land, ground," and *ergo* (or *erdo*), "to do" (Eng., "George"), denotes (a) "a husbandman," a tiller of the ground, 2 Tim. 2:6; Jas. 5:7; (b) "a vinedresser," **Matt. 21:33-35, 38, 40, 41**; Mark 12:1, 2, 7, 9; Luke 20:9, 10, 14, 16; John 15:1, where Christ speaks of the Father as the "Husbandman," Himself as the Vine, His disciples as the branches, the object being to bear much fruit, life in Christ producing the fruit of the Spirit, i.e., character and ways in conformity to Christ.

Far country *apodemeo* (589), signifies "to go or travel into a far country," lit., "to be away from one's people" (*apo*, "from," *demos*, "a people"), **Matt. 21:33; 25:14**; in v. **15** the verb is translated in the RV, "went on his journey" (KJV, "took his journey"); Mark 12:1; Luke 20:9, "went into another country," RV. In Luke 15:13 both versions translate by "took his journey" ("into a far country" being separately expressed). Cf. *apodemos*, lit., "away from one's own people, gone abroad," Mark 13:34. *See also* **Kingdoms** at *Matthew 4:8.*

21:34 And when the time of the fruit drew near, he sent his servants to the husbandmen, that they might receive the fruits of it.

Time *see Matthew 8:29.*

Drew near *engizo* (1448), transitively, "to bring near" (not in NT; in the Sept., e.g., Gen. 48:10; Isa. 5:8); intransitively, "to draw near," e.g., **Matt. 21:34**; Luke 18:40; 19:41, RV, "draw nigh." *See also* **At hand** at *Matthew 3:2.*

Sent The "sending" of the Son by the Father was from the glory which He had with the Father into the world, by way of the Incarnation, not a "sending" out into the world after His birth, as if denoting His mission among and His manifestation to the people. "Hofmann, in support of his view that Jesus is called the Son of God only in virtue of His being born of man, vainly urges that the simple accusative after *apostello* also denotes what the Person is or becomes by being sent. What he states is true but only when the name of the object spoken of is chosen to correspond with the purposed mission, as, e.g., in Mark 1:2; Luke 14:32; 19:14. We can no more say, 'God sent Jesus that He should be His Son' than we can render 'he sent his servants,' **Matt. 21:34**, in this manner. That the Sonship of Christ is anterior to His mission to the world ... is clear from John 16:28; cf. especially also the double accusative in 1 John

4:14, 'the Father sent the Son the Savior of the world.' The expression that Jesus is sent by God denotes the mission which He has to fulfill and the authority which backs Him" (Cremer, *Lexicon of NT Greek*). *See also* Send at *Matthew 10:16.*

21:35 And the husbandmen took his servants, and beat one, and killed another, and stoned another.

Beat *dero* (1194), from a root *der-*, "skin" (*derma,* "a skin," cf. Eng., "dermatology"), primarily "to flay," then "to beat, thrash or smite," is used of the treatment of the servants of the owner of the vineyard by the husbandmen, in the parable in **Matt. 21:35**; Mark 12:3, 5; Luke 20:10-11; of the treatment of Christ, Luke 22:63, RV, "beat," for KJV, "smote"; John 18:23; of the followers of Christ, in the synagogues, Mark 13:9; Acts 22:19; of the punishment of unfaithful servants, Luke 12:47-48; of the "beating" of apostles by the High Priest and the Council of the Sanhedrin, Acts 5:40; by magistrates, 16:37. The significance of flogging does not always attach to the word; it is used of the infliction of a single blow, John 18:23; 2 Cor. 11:20, and of "beating" the air, 1 Cor. 9:26. The usual meaning is that of "thrashing or cudgelling," and when used of a blow it indicates one of great violence.

Stoned *lithoboleo* (3036), "to pelt with stones," "to stone to death," occurs in **Matt. 21:35**; **23:37**; Luke 13:34 (John 8:5 in some mss.); Acts 7:58, 59; 14:5; Heb. 12:20.

21:36 Again, he sent other servants more than the first: and they did unto them likewise.

Other *see Matthew 5:39.*

21:37 But last of all he sent unto them his son, saying, They will reverence my son.

Last of all *see* Afterward at *Matthew 4:2.*

Sent *see* Send at *Matthew 10:16.*

Reverence *entrepo* (1788), lit., "to turn in" (i.e., upon oneself), "to put to shame," denotes, when used in the passive voice, "to feel respect for, to show deference to, to reverence," **Matt. 21:37**; Mark 12:6; Luke 20:13; Heb. 12:9.

21:38 But when the husbandmen saw the son, they said among themselves, This is the heir; come, let us kill him, and let us seize on his inheritance.

Husbandmen *see Matthew 21:33.*

Heir *kleronomos* (2818), lit. denotes "one who obtains a lot or portion (*kleros,* "a lot," *nemomai,* "to possess"), especially of an inheritance. The NT usage may be analyzed as under: "(a) the person to whom property is to pass on the death of the owner, **Matt. 21:38**; Mark 12:7; Luke 20:14; Gal. 4:1; (b) one to whom something has been assigned by God, on possession of which, however, he has not yet entered, as Abraham, Rom. 4:13, 14; Heb. 6:17; Christ, Heb. 1:2; the poor saints, Jas. 2:5; (c) believers, inasmuch as they share in the new order of things to be ushered in at the return of Christ, Rom. 8:17; Gal. 3:29; 4:7; Titus 3:7; (d) one who receives something other than by merit, as Noah, Heb. 11:7." In the Sept., Judg. 18:7; 2 Sam. 14:7; Jer. 8:10; Mic. 1:15.

Seize In **Matt. 21:38**, the best texts have *echo,* "to have" ("to take," RV); some have *katecho,* "to lay hold of" (KJV, "seize on").

Inheritance *kleronomia* (2817), "a lot," properly "an inherited property, an inheritance." "It is always rendered inheritance in NT, but only in a few cases in the Gospels has it the meaning ordinarily attached to that word in English, i.e., that into possession of which the heir enters only on the death of an ancestor. The NT usage may be set out as follows: (a) that property in real estate which in ordinary course passes from father to son on the death of the former, **Matt. 21:38**; Mark 12:7; Luke 12:13; 20:14; (b) a portion of an estate made the substance of a gift, Acts 7:5; Gal. 3:18, which also is to be included under (c); (c) the prospective condition and possessions of the believer in the new order of things to be ushered in at the return of Christ, Acts 20:32; Eph. 1:14; 5:5; Col. 3:24; Heb. 9:15; 1 Pet. 1:4; (d) what the believer will be to God in that age, Eph. 1:18."

21:39 And they caught him, and cast *him* out of the vineyard, and slew *him*.

Caught *lambano* (2983), "to receive," is once used of "catching" by fraud, circumventing, 2 Cor. 12:16. In **Matt. 21:39** and Mark 12:3, RV "took," for KJV "caught."

21:40 When the lord therefore of the vineyard cometh, what will he do unto those husbandmen?

Husbandmen *see Matthew 21:33.*

21:41 They say unto him, He will miserably destroy those wicked men, and will let out *his* vineyard unto other husbandmen, which shall render him the fruits in their seasons.

Miserably *kakos* (2560), "badly, ill," is translated "miserably" in **Matt.**

21:41. Adhering to the meaning "evil," and giving the designed stress, the sentence may be rendered, "evil (as they are) he will evilly destroy them."

Wicked *see* Evil at *Matthew 5:11*.

Let out *see* Let ... out at *Matthew 21:33*.

Husbandmen *see Matthew 21:33*.

Render *see* Reward at *Matthew 16:27*.

21:42 Jesus saith unto them, Did ye never read in the scriptures, The stone which the builders rejected, the same is become the head of the corner: this is the Lord's doing, and it is marvellous in our eyes?

Never *see Matthew 7:23*.

Scriptures *graphe* (1124), akin to *grapho*, "to write" (Eng., "graph," "graphic," etc.), primarily denotes "a drawing, painting"; then "a writing," (a) of the OT Scriptures, (1) in the plural, the whole, e.g., **Matt. 21:42**; **22:29**; John 5:39; Acts 17:11; 18:24; Rom. 1:2, where "the prophets" comprises the OT writers in general; 15:4; 16:26, lit., "prophetic writings," expressing the character of all the Scriptures; (2) in the singular in reference to a particular passage, e.g., Mark 12:10; Luke 4:21; John 2:22; 10:35 (though applicable to all); 19:24, 28, 36, 37; 20:9; Acts 1:16; 8:32, 35; Rom. 4:3; 9:17; 10:11; 11:2; Gal. 3:8, 22; 4:30; 1 Tim. 5:18, where the 2nd quotation is from Luke 10:7, from which it may be inferred that the apostle included Luke's Gospel as "Scripture" alike with Deuteronomy, from which the first quotation is taken; in reference to the whole, e.g. Jas. 4:5 (see RV, a separate rhetorical question from the one which follows); in 2 Pet. 1:20, "no prophecy of Scripture," a description of all, with special application to the OT in the next verse; (b) of the OT Scriptures (those accepted by the Jews as canonical) and all those of the NT which were to be accepted by Christians as authoritative, 2 Tim. 3:16.

Stone *see* Stones at *Matthew 4:3*.

Builders *oikodomeo* (3618), lit., "to build a house," usually signifies "to build," whether literally, or figuratively; the present participle, lit., "the (ones) building," is used as a noun, "the builders," in **Matt. 21:42**; Mark 12:10; Luke 20:17; Acts 4:11 (in some mss.; the most authentic have the noun *oikodomos;*) 1 Pet. 2:7. *See also* **Built ... house** at *Matthew 7:24*.

Rejected *apodokimazo* (593), "to reject" as the result of examination and disapproval (*apo*, "away from," *dokimazo*, "to approve"), is used (a) of the "rejection" of Christ by the elders and chief priests of the Jews, **Matt. 21:42**; Mark 8:31; 12:10; Luke 9:22; 20:17; 1 Pet. 2:4, 7 (KJV, "disallowed"); by the Jewish people, Luke 17:25; (b) of the "rejection" of Esau from inheriting "the blessing," Heb. 12:17. Cf. and contrast *exoutheneo*, Acts 4:11.

Head *kephale* (2776), besides its natural significance, is used (a) figuratively in Rom. 12:20, of heaping coals of fire on a "head"; in Acts 18:6, "Your blood be upon your own heads," i.e., "your blood-guiltiness rest upon your own persons," a mode of expression frequent in the OT, and perhaps here directly connected with Ezek. 3:18, 20; 33:6, 8; see also Lev. 20:16; 2 Sam. 1:16; 1 Kings 2:37; (b) metaphorically, of the authority or direction of God in relation to Christ, of Christ in relation to believing men, of the husband in relation to the wife, 1 Cor. 11:3; of Christ in relation to the Church, Eph. 1:22; 4:15; 5:23; Col. 1:18; 2:19; of Christ in relation to principalities and powers, Col. 2:10. As to 1 Cor. 11:10, taken in connection with the context, the word "authority" probably stands, by metonymy, for a sign of authority (RV), the angels being witnesses of the preeminent relationship as established by God in the creation of man as just mentioned, with the spiritual significance regarding the position of Christ in relation to the Church; cf. Eph. 3:10; it is used of Christ as the foundation of the spiritual building set forth by the Temple, with its "corner stone," **Matt. 21:42**; symbolically also of the imperial rulers of the Roman power, as seen in the apocalyptic visions, Rev. 13:1, 3; 17:3, 7, 9.

Corner *see* Corners at *Matthew 6:5*.

Doing *ginomai* (1096), "to become," is sometimes translated "do" or "done," e.g., Luke 4:23, "done (at Capernaum)," followed by *poieo* in the next clause. In **Matt. 21:42** and Mark 12:11, this verb is translated, in the KJV, "(the Lord's) doing"; RV, "this was from the Lord."

Marvellous *thaumastos* (2298), "marvellous," is said (a) of the Lord's doing in making the rejected Stone the Head of the corner, **Matt. 21:42**; Mark 12:11; (b) of the erstwhile blind man's astonishment that the Pharisees knew not from whence Christ had come, and yet He had given him sight, John 9:30, RV, "the marvel," KJV, "a marvellous thing"; (c) of the spiritual light into which believers are brought, 1 Pet. 2:9; (d) of the vision of the seven angels having the seven last plagues, Rev. 15:1; (e) of the works of God, 15:3.

21:43 Therefore say I unto you, The kingdom of God shall be taken from you, and given to a nation bringing forth the fruits thereof.

Nation *ethnos* (1484), originally "a multitude," denotes (a) "a nation" or "people," e.g., **Matt. 24:7**; Acts 10:35; the Jewish people, e.g., Luke 7:5; 23:2; John 11:48, 50-52; Acts 10:22; 24:2, 10, 17; in **Matt. 21:43**, the reference is to Israel in its restored condition, (b) in the plural "the nations" as distinct from Israel.

21:44 And whosoever shall fall on this stone shall be broken: but on whomsoever it shall fall, it will grind him to powder.

Broken *sunthlao* (4917), *sun*, "together" (intensive), and *thlao*, "to break or crush, to break in pieces, to shatter," is used in **Matt. 21:44** and Luke 20:18 of the physical effect of falling on a stone.

Grind In **Matt. 21:44** and Luke 20:18, *likmao*, "to winnow," as of grain, by throwing it up against the wind, to scatter the chaff and straw, hence has the meaning "to scatter," as chaff or dust, and is translated "will scatter ... as dust," RV (KJV, "will grind ... to powder"). In the Sept. it is used of being scattered by the wind or of sifting (cf. Amos 9:9). The use of the verb in the papyri writings suggests the meaning, "to ruin, destroy" (Deissmann).

21:45 And when the chief priests and Pharisees had heard his parables, they perceived that he spake of them.

Perceived *see* Knew at *Matthew 12:15.*

21:46 But when they sought to lay hands on him, they feared the multitude, because they took him for a prophet.

Lay hands *see* Hold at *Matthew 12:11.*

Took *echo* (2192), "to have, to hold," is used in **Matt. 21:46** in the sense of regarding a person as something, "they took (Him) for (a prophet)." *See also* Had at *Matthew 3:4.*

Prophet *see* Prophets at *Matthew 5:12.*

Chapter 22

22:1-2 And Jesus answered and spake unto them again by parables, and said,

The kingdom of heaven is like unto a certain king, which made a marriage for his son,

Like unto *see Matthew 6:8.*

Marriage *gamos* (1062), "a marriage, wedding," or "wedding feast," is used to denote (a) the ceremony and its proceedings, including the "marriage feast," John 2:1, 2; of the "marriage ceremony" only, figuratively, Rev. 19:7, as distinct from the "marriage feast" (v. 9); (b) "the marriage feast," RV in **Matt. 22:2-4, 9**; in v. **8, 10**, "wedding;" in **25:10**, RV "marriage feast;" so Luke 12:36; 14:8; in **Matt. 22:11, 12**, the "wedding garment" is, lit., "a garment of a wedding." In Rev. 19, where, under the figure of a "marriage," the union of Christ, as the Lamb of God, with His heavenly bride is so described, the marriage itself takes place in heaven during the Parousia, v. 7 (the aorist or point tense indicating an accomplished fact; the bride is called "His wife"); the "marriage feast" or supper is to take place on earth, after the Second Advent, v. 9. That Christ is spoken of as the Lamb points to His atoning sacrifice as the ground upon which the spiritual union takes place. The background of the phraseology lies in the OT description of the relation of God to Israel, e.g., Isa. 54:4ff.; Ezek. 16:7ff.; Hos. 2:19; (c) "marriage" in general, including the "married" state, which is to be "had in honor," Heb. 13:4, RV.

22:3 And sent forth his servants to call them that were bidden to the wedding: and they would not come.

Servants *see* Minister at *Matthew 20:26.*

Bidden *kaleo* (2564), "to call," often means "to bid," in the sense of "invite," e.g., **Matt. 22:3-4, 8, 9**; Luke 14:7-10, 13, RV; Rev. 19:9, RV.

Wedding *see* Marriage at *Matthew 22:2.*

22:4 Again, he sent forth other servants, saying, Tell them which are bidden, Behold, I have prepared my dinner: my oxen and *my* fatlings *are* killed, and all things *are* ready: come unto the marriage.

Dinner *ariston* (712), primarily, "the first food," taken early in the morning before work; the meal in the Pharisee's house, in Luke 11:37, was a breakfast or early meal (see RV, marg.); the dinner was called *deipnon*. Later the breakfast was called *akratisma* (not in NT), and dinner, *ariston*, as in **Matt. 22:4**; Luke 11:38; 14:12.

Oxen *tauros* (5022), Latin *taurus*, is translated "oxen" in **Matt. 22:4** and Acts 14:13; "bulls" in Heb. 9:13 and 10:4.

Fatlings *sitistos* (4619), "fattened," lit., "fed with grain" (fiom *siteuo*, "to feed, to fatten"), is used as a neuter plural noun, "fatlings," in **Matt. 22:4**.

Killed *thuo* (2380), primarily denotes "to offer firstfruits to a god"; then (a) "to sacrifice by slaying a victim,"

Acts 14:13, 18, to do sacrifice; 1 Cor. 10:20, to sacrifice; 1 Cor. 5:7, "hath been sacrificed," of the death of Christ as our Passover; (b) "to slay, kill," **Matt. 22:4**; Mark 14:12; Luke 15:23, 27, 30; 22:7; John 10:10; Acts 10:13; 11:7.

Ready *hetoimos* (2092), "prepared, ready" (akin to *hetoimasia*, "preparation"), is used (a) of persons, **Matt. 24:44**; **25:10**; Luke 12:40; 22:33; Acts 23:15, 21 (for 2 Cor. 10:6); Titus 3:1; 1 Pet. 3:15; (b) of things, **Matt. 22:4** (2nd part), **8**; Mark 14:15, RV, "ready" (KJV, "prepared"); Luke 14:17; John 7:6; 2 Cor. 9:5; 10:16, RV, "things ready" (KJV, "things made ready"); 1 Pet. 1:5.

Marriage *see Matthew 22:2.*

22:5 But they made light of *it*, and went their ways, one to his farm, another to his merchandise:

Made light of *ameleo* (272), denotes "to be careless, not to care" (*a*, negative, and *melei*, an impersonal verb, signifying "it is a care") **Matt. 22:5**, "they made light of (it)," lit. "making light of (it)," aorist participle, indicating the definiteness of their decision.

His These translate (a) forms of pronouns under he (a frequent use: in 1 Pet. 2:24, "His own self"); the form *autou*, "his," becomes emphatic when placed between the article and the noun, e.g., 1 Thess. 2:19; Titus 3:5; Heb. 2:4; also in which "his" is emphasized, e.g., John 5:47; 9:28; 1 Cor. 10:28; 2 Cor. 8:9; 2 Tim. 2:26; Titus 3:7; 2 Pet. 1:16; (b) *heautou*, "of himself, his own"; the RV rightly puts "his own," for the KJV, "his," in Luke 11:21; 14:26; Rom. 4:19; 5:8, "His own (love)"; 1 Cor. 7:37; Gal. 6:8; Eph. 5:28, 33; 1 Thess. 2:11, 12; 4:4; in Rev. 10:7 the change has not been made; it should read "his own servants"; (c) *idios*, "one's own," "his own," in the RV, in **Matt. 22:5**; John 5:18; 2 Pet. 2:16; in **Matt. 25:15**, it is rendered "his several"; in John 19:27, "his own home," lit., "his own things"; in 1 Tim. 6:15, RV, "its own (times)," referring to the future appearing of Christ; in Heb. 4:10 (end of verse), both KJV and RV have "his," where it should be "his own"; so in Acts 24:23, for KJV and RV, "his"; in 1 Cor. 7:7, RV, "his own," KJV, "his proper"; (d) in Acts 17:28, the genitive case of the definite article, "His (offspring)," lit., "of the" (i.e., the one referred to, namely, God).

Farm *see* **Field** at *Matthew 6:28.*

Merchandise *emporia* (1711), denotes "commerce, business, trade" [akin to *emporos*, "one on a journey" (*en*, "in," *poros*, "a journey"), "a merchant"], occurs in **Matt. 22:5**.

22:6 And the remnant took his servants, and entreated *them* spitefully, and slew *them*.

Remnant *loipos* (3062), an adjective (akin to *leipo*, "to leave") signifying "remaining," is used as a noun and translated "the rest" in the RV, where the KJV has "the remnant," **Matt. 22:6**; Rev. 11:13; 12:17; 19:21.

Took *see Matthew 9:25. See also* **Hold** at *Matthew 12:11.*

Servants *see* **Minister** at *Matthew 20:26.*

Entreated ... spitefully *hubrizo* (5195), used transitively, denotes "to outrage, treat insolently"; "to entreat shamefully" in **Matt. 22:6**, RV (KJV, "spitefully"); so in Luke 18:32, RV; in Acts 14:5 (KJV, "use despitefully"); in 1 Thess. 2:2, KJV and RV; in Luke 11:45, "reproachest."

22:7 But when the king heard *thereof*, he was wroth: and he sent forth his armies, and destroyed those murderers, and burned up their city.

Wroth *see Matthew 18:34. See also* **Angry** at *Matthew 5:22.*

Armies *strateuma* (4753), denotes (a) "an army" of any size, large or small, **Matt. 22:7**; Rev. 9:16; 19:14, 19 (twice); (b) "a company of soldiers," such as Herod's bodyguard, Luke 23:11 (RV, "soldiers"), or the soldiers of a garrison, Acts 23:10, 27 (RV, "the soldiers," for KJV, "an army").

Destroyed *see* **Destroy** at *Matthew 2:13.*

Murderers *phoneus* (5406), akin to *phoneuo* and *phonos*, is used (a) in a general sense, in the singular, 1 Pet. 4:15; in the plural, Rev. 21:8; 22:15; (b) of those guilty of particular acts, **Matt. 22:7**; Acts 3:14, lit. "a man (*aner*), a murderer"; 7:52; 28:4.

22:8 Then saith he to his servants, The wedding is ready, but they which were bidden were not worthy.

Servants *see* **Minister** at *Matthew 20:26.*

Wedding *see* **Marriage** at *Matthew 22:2.*

Ready *see Matthew 22:4.*

Bidden *see Matthew 22:3.*

Worthy *see Matthew 10:10.*

22:9 Go ye therefore into the highways, and as many as ye shall find, bid to the marriage.

Highways *hodos* (3598), "a way, path, road," is rendered "highways" in **Matt. 22:10**; Luke 14:23; in Mark 10:46, RV, "way side," KJV, "highway side"; in **Matt. 22:9**, the word is used with *diexodoi* ("ways out through"), and the phrase is rightly rendered in the RV, "the partings of the highways" (i.e., the crossroads), KJV, "the highways."

Bid *see* Bidden at *Matthew 22:3.*

Marriage *see Matthew 22:2.*

22:10 So those servants went out into the highways, and gathered together all as many as they found, both bad and good: and the wedding was furnished with guests.

Servants *see* Minister at *Matthew 20:26.*

Highways *see Matthew 22:9.*

Bad *see* Evil at *Matthew 5:11. See also* Evil at *Matthew 5:37.*

Wedding *see* Marriage at *Matthew 22:2. See also* Bridechamber at *Matthew 9:15.*

Furnished *pimplemi* (4130), and *pletho* (4130), lengthened forms of *pleo*, "to fill" (*pletho* supplies certain tenses of *pimplemi*), is used (1) of things; boats, with fish, Luke 5:7; a sponge, with vinegar, **Matt. 27:48** (some mss. have this verb in John 19:29); a city, with confusion, Acts 19:29; a wedding, with guests, **Matt. 22:10**; (2) of persons (only in Luke's writings): (a) with the Holy Spirit, Luke 1:15, 41, 67; Acts 2:4; 4:8, 31; 9:17; 13:9; (b) with emotions: wrath, Luke 4:28; fear, 5:26; madness, 6:11; wonder, amazement, Acts 3:10; jealousy, 5:17, RV, for KJV, "indignation," and 13:45 (KJV, "envy"). For its other significance, "to complete."

Guests *anakeimai* (345), "to recline at table," frequently rendered "to sit at meat," is used in its present participial form (lit., "reclining ones") as a noun denoting "guests," in **Matt. 22:10, 11.**

22:11 And when the king came in to see the guests, he saw there a man which had not on a wedding garment:

Guests *see Matthew 22:10.*

Wedding *see Matthew 22:2.*

Garment The fact of the wedding garment, *enduma* in **Matt. 22**, vv. **11, 12**, indicates that persons of high rank showed their magnificence by providing the guests with festal garments. For *himation*, the usual word for "garment," also *esthesis* (translated "garments" in the KJV of Luke 24:4, RV, "apparel"), *enduma, chiton*, and *stole* (RV, "robe" in Mark 16:5). *See also* Raiment at *Matthew 3:4.*

22:12 And he saith unto him, Friend, how camest thou in hither not having a wedding garment? And he was speechless.

Friend *see* Fellows at *Matthew 11:16.*

Having *see* Had at *Matthew 3:4.*

Wedding *see Matthew 22:2.*

Garment *see Matthew 22:11.*

Speechless *phimoo* (5392), "to close the mouth with a muzzle" (*phimos*), is used (a) of "muzzling" the ox when it treads out the corn, 1 Cor. 9:9, KJV, "muzzle the mouth of," RV, "muzzle," and 1 Tim. 5:18, with the lesson that those upon whom spiritual labor is bestowed should not refrain from ministering to the material needs of those who labor on their behalf; (b) metaphorically, of putting to silence, or subduing to stillness, **Matt. 22:12, 34**; Mark 1:25; 4:39; Luke 4:35; 1 Pet. 2:15.

22:13 Then said the king to the servants, Bind him hand and foot, and take him away, and cast *him* into outer darkness; there shall be weeping and gnashing of teeth.

Servants *diakonos* (1249), is translated "servant" or "servants" in **Matt. 22:13** (RV marg., "ministers"); **23:11** (RV marg., ditto); Mark 9:35, KJV (RV, "minister"); John 2:5, 9; 12:26; Rom. 16:1. *See also* Minister at *Matthew 20:26.*

Outer *see Matthew 8:12.*

Weeping *see Matthew 2:18.*

Gnashing *see Matthew 8:12.*

Teeth *see* Tooth at *Matthew 5:38.*

22:14 For many are called, but few *are* chosen.

Many *see Matthew 3:7.*

Called *see Matthew 20:16.*

Chosen *eklektos* (1588), signifies "chosen out, select," e.g., **Matt. 22:14**; Luke 23:35; Rom. 16:13 (perhaps in the sense of "eminent"), Rev. 17:14. In 1 Pet. 2:4, 9, the RV translates it "elect." *See also Matthew 20:16.*

22:15 Then went the Pharisees, and took counsel how they might entangle him in *his* talk.

Counsel *see* Council at *Matthew 12:14.*

Entangle *pagideuo* (3802), "to entrap, lay snares for" (from *pagis*, "anything which fixes or grips," hence, "a snare"), is used in **Matt. 22:15**, of the efforts of the Pharisees to "entrap" the Lord in His speech, KJV, "entangle."

Talk *logos* (3056), a word, is translated "talk" in **Matt. 22:15**; Mark 12:13.

22:16 And they sent out unto him their disciples with the Herodians, saying, Master, we know that thou art true, and

teachest the way of God in truth, neither carest thou for any *man*: for thou regardest not the person of men.

Disciples *see Matthew 9:14.*

True, Truth *alethes* (227), primarily, "unconcealed, manifest" (*a*, negative, *letho*, "to forget," = *lanthano*, "to escape notice"), hence, actual, "true to fact," is used (a) of persons, "truthful," **Matt. 22:16**; Mark 12:14; John 3:33; 7:18; 8:26; Rom. 3:4; 2 Cor. 6:8; (b) of things, "true," conforming to reality, John 4:18, "truly," lit., "true"; 5:31, 32; in the best texts, 6:55 (twice), "indeed"; 8:13, 14 (v. 16 in some texts), 17; 10:41; 19:35; 21:24; Acts 12:9; Phil. 4:8; Titus 1:13; 1 Pet. 5:12; 2 Pet. 2:22; 1 John 2:8, 27; 3 John 1:2.

Way *see Matthew 7:13.*

Teachest *see* Teaching at *Matthew 4:23.*

Carest *melei* (3199), the third person sing. of *melo*, used impersonally, signifies that "something is an object of care," especially the care of forethought and interest, rather than anxiety, **Matt. 22:16**; Mark 4:38; 12:14; Luke 10:40; John 10:13; 12:6; Acts 18:17; 1 Cor. 9:9 (RV, "Is it for the oxen that God careth?" The KJV seriously misses the point. God does "care" for oxen, but there was a divinely designed significance in the OT passage, relating to the service of preachers of the gospel); 7:21; 1 Pet. 5:7.

Regardest *blepo* (991), "to behold, look, perceive, see," has the sense of "regarding" by way of partiality, in **Matt. 22:16** and Mark 12:14. *See also* See at *Matthew 13:13.*

Person *prosopon* (4383), is translated "person" or "persons" in **Matt. 22:16**; Mark 12:14; Luke 20:21; 2 Cor. 1:11; 2 Cor. 2:10; Gal. 2:6; Jude 16, lit., "(admiring, or showing respect of, RV) persons." *See also* Faces at *Matthew 6:16.*

22:17 Tell us therefore, What thinkest thou? Is it lawful to give tribute unto Caesar, or not?

Tribute *see Matthew 17:25.*

22:18 But Jesus perceived their wickedness, and said, Why tempt ye me, *ye* hypocrites?

Perceived *see* Knew at *Matthew 12:15.*

Wickedness *poneria* (4189), akin to *poneo*, "to toil" (cf. *poneros*, "bad, worthless"), denotes "wickedness," and is so translated in **Matt. 22:18**; Mark 7:22 (plural); Luke 11:39; Rom. 1:29; 1 Cor. 5:8; Eph. 6:12; in Acts 3:26, "iniquities." Cf. *kakia*, "evil."

Tempt *see* Tempted at *Matthew 4:1.*

22:19 Shew me the tribute money. And they brought unto him a penny.

Shew *see Matthew 16:1.*

Tribute *see Matthew 17:25.*

Money *nomisma* (3546), primarily "that which is established by custom" (*nomos*, "a custom, law"), hence, "the current coin of a state, currency," is found in **Matt. 22:19**, "(tribute) money." In the Sept., Neh. 7:71.

Penny *see* Pence at *Matthew 18:28.*

22:20 And he saith unto them, Whose *is* this image and superscription?

Image *eikon* (1504), denotes "an image"; the word involves the two ideas of representation and manifestation. "The idea of perfection does not lie in the word itself, but must be sought from the context" (Lightfoot); the following instances clearly show any distinction between the imperfect and the perfect likeness. The word is used ... of an "image" or a coin (not a mere likeness), **Matt. 22:20**; Mark 12:16; Luke 20:24; so of a statue or similar representation (more than a resemblance), Rom. 1:23; Rev. 13:14, 15 (thrice); 14:9, 11; 15:2; 16:2; 19:20; 20:4; of the descendants of Adam as bearing his image, 1 Cor. 15:49, each a representation derived from the prototype.

Superscription *epigraphe* (1923), lit., "an overwriting" (*epi*, "over," *grapho*, "to write") (the meaning of the anglicized Latin word "superscription"), denotes "an inscription, a title." On Roman coins the emperor's name was inscribed, **Matt. 22:20**; Mark 12:16; Luke 20:24. In the Roman Empire, in the case of a criminal on his way to execution, a board on which was inscribed the cause of his condemnation, was carried before him or hung round his neck; the inscription was termed a "title" (*titlos*). The four Evangelists state that at the crucifixion of Christ the title was affixed to the cross, Mark (15:26), and Luke (23:38), call it a "superscription"; Mark says it was "written over" (*epigrapho*, the corresponding verb). Matthew calls it "His accusation"; John calls it "a title" (a technical term). The wording varies: the essential words are the same, and the variation serves to authenticate the narratives, showing that there was no consultation leading to an agreement as to the details.

22:21 They say unto him, Caesar's. Then saith he unto them, Render therefore unto Caesar the things which are Caesar's; and unto God the things that are God's.

Render *see* Reward at *Matthew 16:27*.

God *see* Father at *Matthew 10:29*.

22:22 When they had heard *these words*, they marvelled, and left him, and went their way.

Left *see* Leaveth at *Matthew 4:11*.

22:23 The same day came to him the Sadducees, which say that there is no resurrection, and asked him,

Resurrection *anastasis* (386), denotes (I) "a raising up," or "rising" (*ana*, "up," and *histemi*, "to cause to stand"), Luke 2:34, "the rising up"; the KJV "again" obscures the meaning; the Child would be like a stone against which many in Israel would stumble while many others would find in its strength and firmness a means of their salvation and spiritual life; (II) of "resurrection" from the dead, (a) of Christ, Acts 1:22; 2:31; 4:33; Rom. 1:4; 6:5; Phil. 3:10; 1 Pet. 1:3; 3:21; by metonymy, of Christ as the Author of "resurrection," John 11:25; (b) of those who are Christ's at His Parousia, Luke 14:14, "the resurrection of the just"; Luke 20:33, 35, 36; John 5:29 (1st part), "the resurrection of life"; 11:24; Acts 23:6; 24:15 (1st part); 1 Cor. 15:21, 42; 2 Tim. 2:18; Heb. 11:35 (2nd part); Rev. 20:5, "the first resurrection"; hence the insertion of "is" stands for the completion of this "resurrection," of which Christ was "the firstfruits"; 20:6; (c) of "the rest of the dead," after the Millennium (cf. Rev. 20:5); John 5:29 (2nd part), "the resurrection of judgment"; Acts 24:15 (2nd part), "of the unjust"; (d) of those who were raised in more immediate connection with Christ's "resurrection," and thus had part already in the first "resurrection," Acts 26:23 and Rom. 1:4 (in each of which "dead" is plural; see **Matt. 27:52**); (e) of the "resurrection" spoken of in general terms, **Matt. 22:23**; Mark 12:18; Luke 20:27; Acts 4:2; 17:18; 23:8; 24:21; 1 Cor. 15:12, 13; Heb. 6:2; (f) of those who were raised in OT times, to die again, Heb. 11:35 (1st part), lit., "out of resurrection."

22:24 Saying, Master, Moses said, If a man die, having no children, his brother shall marry his wife, and raise up seed unto his brother.

Man *tis* (5100), "some one, a certain one," is rendered "a man," "a certain man," e.g., in **Matt. 22:24**; Mark 8:4, KJV (RV, "one"); 12:19; John 3:3, 5; 6:50; 14:23; 15:6, 13; Acts 13:41, KJV (RV, "one"); 1 Cor. 4:2; 1 Tim. 1:8; 2 Tim. 2:5, 21; Jas. 2:14, 18; 1 Pet. 2:19; 1 John 4:20.

Marry *epigambreuo* (1918), "to take to wife after" (*epi*, "upon," *gambros*, "a connection by marriage"), signifies "to marry" (of a deceased husband's next of kin, **Matt. 22:24**). Cf. Gen. 38:8.

Raise *see* Raised at *Matthew 1:24*.

Seed *see Matthew 13:19*.

22:25 Now there were with us seven brethren: and the first, when he had married a wife, deceased, and, having no issue, left his wife unto his brother:

Married *see* Marry at *Matthew 5:32*.

Deceased *teleutao* (5053), lit., "to end," is used intransitively and translated "deceased" in **Matt. 22:25**. *See also* Dead at *Matthew 2:19*.

Issue In **Matt. 22:25**, KJV, *sperma*, "seed," is translated "issue" (RV, "seed"). *See also* Seed at *Matthew 13:19*.

Left *see* Leaveth at *Matthew 4:11*.

22:26 Likewise the second also, and the third, unto the seventh.

Likewise *homoios* (3668), "in like manner" (from the adjective *homoios*), is rendered "likewise" in the KJV of **Matt. 22:26; 27:41**, Luke 10:32; 16:25; John 5:19; Jas. 2:25; 1 Pet. 3:1, 7; Jude 8; Rev. 8:12 (in all these the RV has "in like manner"); in the following, KJV and RV have "likewise"; **Matt. 26:35**; Luke 5:33; 6:31; 10:37; 17:28, 31; 22:36; John 6:11; 21:13; Rom. 1:27; 1 Pet. 5:5.

Second *deuteros* (1208), denotes "second in order" with or without the idea of time, e.g., **Matt. 22:26, 39**; 2 Cor. 1:15; Rev. 2:11; in Rev. 14:8, RV only ("a second angel"); it is used in the neuter, *deuteron*, adverbially, signifying a "second" time, e.g., John 3:4; 21:16; Acts 7:13; Rev. 19:3, RV (KJV, "again"); Jude 5, "afterward" (RV, marg., "the second time"); used with *ek* ("of") idiomatically, the preposition signifying "for (the second time)," Mark 14:72; John 9:24 and Acts 11:9, RV (KJV, "again"); Heb. 9:28; in 1 Cor. 12:28, KJV, "secondarily," RV, "secondly."

Seventh *hepta* (2033), whence Eng. words beginning with "hept" ,corresponds to the Heb. *sheba'* (which is akin to *saba'*, signifying "to be full, abundant"), sometimes used as an expression of fullness, e.g., Ruth 4:15: it generally expresses completeness, and is used most frequently in Revelation; it is not found in the Gospel of John, nor between the Acts and Revelation, except in Heb. 11:30 (in Rom. 11:4 the numeral is *heptakischilioi*, "seven thousand"); in **Matt. 22:26** it is translated "seventh" (marg., "seven").

22:27 And last of all the woman died also.

Last of all *see* Afterward at *Matthew 4:2*.

22:28-29 Therefore in the resurrection whose wife shall she be of the seven? for they all had her.

Jesus answered and said unto them, Ye do err, not knowing the scriptures, nor the power of God.

Err *planao* (4105), in the active voice, signifies "to cause to wander, lead astray, deceive" (*plane*, "a wandering"; cf. Eng., "planet"); in the passive voice, "to be led astray, to err." It is translated "err," in **Matt. 22:29**; Mark 12:24, 27; Heb. 3:10; Jas. 1:16 (KJV, "do not err," RV, "be not deceived"); 5:19.

Scriptures *see Matthew 21:42.*

22:30 For in the resurrection they neither marry, nor are given in marriage, but are as the angels of God in heaven.

Marry *see Matthew 5:32.*

Marriage *gamizo* (1061), "to give in marriage," is used in the passive voice in **Matt. 22:30** (2nd clause), some mss. have *ekgamizo* here; Mark 12:25 (*gamisko* in some mss.); Luke 17:27 (*ekgamizo* in some mss.); 20:35 (last word), passive (*gamisko* and *ekgamisko* in some mss.); in the active voice **Matt. 24:38** (*gamisko* and *ekgamizo* in some mss.); further, of giving a daughter in "marriage," 1 Cor. 7:38 (twice), RV (*ekgamizo* in some mss.), which, on the whole, may be taken as the meaning. In this part of the Epistle, the apostle was answering a number of questions on matters about which the church at Corinth had written to him, and in this particular matter the formal transition from "marriage" in general to the subject of giving a daughter in "marriage," is simple. Eastern customs naturally would involve the inclusion of the latter in the inquiry and the reply.

Heaven *see Matthew 5:16.*

22:31 But as touching the resurrection of the dead, have ye not read that which was spoken unto you by God, saying,

Spoken *see Matthew 1:22.*

22:32 I am the God of Abraham, and the God of Isaac, and the God of Jacob? God is not the God of the dead, but of the living.

God *see* Father at *Matthew 10:29.*

22:33-34 And when the multitude heard *this*, they were astonished at his doctrine.

But when the Pharisees had heard that he had put the Sadducees to silence, they were gathered together.

Silence *phimoo* (5392), "to muzzle," is rendered "to put to silence" in **Matt. 22:34**; 1 Pet. 2:15. *See also* Speechless at *Matthew 22:12.*

Together In the following, "together" translates the phrase *epi to auto*, lit., "to (upon, or for) the same," **Matt. 22:34**; Luke 17:35; Acts 1:15; 2:44 (3:1, in some texts); 4:26; 1 Cor. 7:5; 14:23, RV.

22:35 Then one of them, *which was* a lawyer, asked *him a question*, tempting him, and saying,

Lawyer *see* Scribes at *Matthew 9:3.*

Question *eperotao* (1905), "to ask," is translated "asked ... a question," in **Matt. 22:35, 41**; in Luke 2:46, "asking ... questions"; "questioned" in Luke 23:9.

Tempting *see* Tempted at *Matthew 4:1.*

22:36 Master, which *is* the great commandment in the law?

Law *see Matthew 5:17.*

22:37 Jesus said unto him, Thou shalt love the Lord thy God with all thy heart, and with all thy soul, and with all thy mind.

Love *phileo* (5368), is to be distinguished from *agapao* in this, that *phileo* more nearly represents "tender affection." The two words are used for the "love" of the Father for the Son, John 3:35 (*agapao*), and 5:20 (*phileo*); for the believer, 14:21 (*agapao*) and 16:27 (*phileo*); both, of Christ's "love" for a certain disciple, 13:23 (*agapao*), and 20:2 (*phileo*). Yet the distinction between the two verbs remains, and they are never used indiscriminately in the same passage; if each is used with reference to the same objects, as just mentioned, each word retains its distinctive and essential character.

Phileo is never used in a command to men to "love" God; it is, however, used as a warning in 1 Cor. 16:22; *agapao* is used instead, e.g., **Matt. 22:37**; Luke 10:27; Rom. 8:28; 1 Cor. 8:3; 1 Pet. 1:8; 1 John 4:21. The distinction between the two verbs finds a conspicuous instance in the narrative of John 21:15-17. The context itself indicates that *agapao* in the first two questions suggests the "love" that values and esteems (cf. Rev. 12:11). It is an unselfish "love," ready to serve. The use of *phileo* in Peter's answers and the Lord's third question, conveys the thought of cherishing the Object above all else, of manifesting an affection characterized by constancy, from the motive of the highest veneration.

Again, to "love" (*phileo*) life, from an undue desire to preserve it, forgetful of the real object of living, meets with the Lord's reproof, John 12:25. On the contrary, to "love" life (*agapao*) as used in 1 Pet. 3:10, is to consult the true interests of living. Here the word *phileo* would be quite inappropriate.

Soul *see* Life at *Matthew 2:20.*

Mind *dianoia* (1271), lit. "a thinking through, or over, a meditation, reflecting," signifies (a) "the faculty of knowing, understanding, or moral reflection," (1) with an evil significance, a consciousness characterized by a perverted moral impulse, Eph. 2:3 (plural); 4:18; (2) with a good significance, the faculty renewed by the Holy Spirit, **Matt. 22:37**; Mark 12:30; Luke 10:27; Heb. 8:10; 10:16; 1 Pet. 1:13; 1 John 5:20; (b) "sentiment, disposition" (not as a function but as a product); (1) in an evil sense, Luke 1:51, "imagination"; Col. 1:21; (2) in a good sense, 2 Pet. 3:1.

22:38-39 This is the first and great commandment.
And the second *is* like unto it, Thou shalt love thy neighbour as thyself.

Second *see Matthew 22:26.*

Like unto *see Matthew 11:16.*

Neighbour *see Matthew 5:43.*

22:40 On these two commandments hang all the law and the prophets.

Hang *see* Hanged at *Matthew 18:6.*

22:41 While the Pharisees were gathered together, Jesus asked them,

Jesus *see* Lord at *Matthew 1:22.*

Asked In **Matt. 22:41**, there is no word in the original for "question." *See also* Question at *Matthew 22:35.*

22:42-43 Saying, What think ye of Christ? whose son is he? They say unto him, *The Son* of David.
He saith unto them, How then doth David in spirit call him Lord, saying,

Then *oun* (3767), a particle expressing sequence or consequence, is rendered "then," e.g., **Matt. 22:43**; 27:22; Luke 11:13.

Spirit *see* Holy Ghost at *Matthew 1:18.*

22:44 The LORD said unto my Lord, Sit thou on my right hand, till I make thine enemies thy footstool?

Lord *see Matthew 1:22.*

Sit *see* Sat at *Matthew 4:16.*

Make *tithemi* (5087), "to put," is used in **Matt. 22:44**, Mark 12:36; Luke 20:43; Acts 2:35; 1 Cor. 9:18 (of making the gospel without charge); Heb. 1:13; 10:13; 2 Pet. 2:6.

Enemies *see* Enemy at *Matthew 5:43.*

Footstool *see Matthew 5:35.*

22:45-46 If David then call him Lord, how is he his son?
And no man was able to answer him a word, neither durst any *man* from that day forth ask him any more *questions*.

Durst *tolmao* (5111), signifies "to dare," (a) in the sense of not dreading or shunning through fear, **Matt. 22:46**; Mark 12:34; Mark 15:43, "boldly," lit., "having dared, went in"; Luke 20:40; John 21:12; Acts 5:13; 7:32; Rom. 15:18; 2 Cor. 10:2, RV, "show courage," (KJV, "be bold"); 10:12, RV, "are (not) bold", 11:21; Phil. 1:14, "are bold"; Jude 9; (b) in the sense of bearing, enduring, bringing oneself to do a thing, Rom. 5:7; 1 Cor. 6:1. Cf. *apotolmao*, "to be very bold," Rom. 10:20.

Forth In **Matt. 26:16**, the RV omits "forth," as the similar *apo tote*, "from then," simply means "from that time"; in the similar phrase "from that day forth," **Matt. 22:46**; John 11:53, there is no word in the original representing "forth."

More *see* No more at *Matthew 19:6.*

Chapter 23

23:1-2 Then spake Jesus to the multitude, and to his disciples,
Saying, The scribes and the Pharisees sit in Moses' seat:

Sit *see* Set at *Matthew 5:1.*

Seat *see* Seats at *Matthew 21:12.*

23:3 All therefore whatsoever they bid you observe, *that* observe and do; but do not ye after their works: for they say, and do not.

Bid *see* Bade at *Matthew 16:12.*

Works *ergon* (2041), denotes "a work" (Eng., "work" is etymologically akin), "deed, act." When used in the sense of a "deed or act," the idea of "working" is stressed, e.g., Rom. 15:18; it frequently occurs in an ethical sense of human actions, good or bad, e.g., **Matt. 23:3**; **26:10**; John 3:20-21; Rom. 2:7, 15; 1 Thess. 1:3; 2 Thess. 1:11, etc.; sometimes in a less concrete sense, e.g., Titus 1:16; Jas. 1:25 (RV, "that worketh," lit., "of work"). *See also* **Matthew 5:16.**

23:4 For they bind heavy burdens and grievous to be borne, and lay *them* on men's shoulders; but they *themselves* will not move them with one of their fingers.

Bind *desmeuo* or *desmeo* (1195), signifies "to put in fetters or any kind of bond," Luke 8:29; Acts 22:4, or "to bind a burden upon a person," **Matt. 23:4.**

Heavy *barus* (926), denotes "heavy, burdensome"; it is always used metaphorically in the NT, and is translated "heavy" in **Matt. 23:4**, of Pharisaical ordinances; in the comparative degree "weightier," **23:23**, of details of the law of God; "grievous," metaphorically of wolves, in

Acts 20:29; of charges, 25:7; negatively of God's commandments, 1 John 5:3 (causing a burden on him who fulfills them); in 2 Cor. 10:10, "weighty," of Paul's letters.

Burdens *see* Burden at *Matthew 11:30.*

Grievous *dusbastaktos* (1419), "hard to be borne" (from *dus*, an inseparable prefix, like Eng. "mis-," and "un-," indicating "difficulty, injuriousness, opposition," etc., and *bastazo*, "to bear"), is used in Luke 11:46 and, in some mss., in **Matt. 23:4**, "grievous to be borne"; in the latter the RV marg. has "many ancient authorities omit."

"God is not deceived by externals."

C. S. LEWIS

Lay *see Matthew 9:18.*

Shoulders *omos* (5606), occurs in **Matt. 23:4** and Luke 15:5, and is suggestive (as in the latter passage) of strength and safety.

Move *kineo* (2795), "to set in motion, move" (hence, e.g., Eng. "kinematics," "kinetics," "cinema"), is used (a) of wagging the head, **Matt. 27:39**; Mark 15:29; (b) of the general activity of the human being, Acts 17:28; (c) of the "moving" of mountains, Rev. 6:14, in the sense of removing, as in Rev. 2:5, of removing a lampstand (there figuratively of causing a local church to be discontinued); (d) figuratively, of exciting, stirring up feelings and passions, Acts 21:30 (passive voice); 24:5, "a mover"; (e) of "moving burdens," **Matt. 23:4**. Cf. *sunkineo*, "to stir up," Acts 6:12.

Fingers *daktulos* (1147), **Matt. 23:4**; Mark 7:33; Luke 11:46; 16:24; John 8:6; 20:25, 27, is used metaphorically in Luke 11:20, for the power of God, the effects of which are made visible to men.

23:5 But all their works they do for to be seen of men: they make broad their phylacteries, and enlarge the borders of their garments,

Works *see Matthew 5:16.*

Make broad *platuno* (4115), connected with *plak*, "a flat, broad surface," signifies "to make broad"; said of phylacteries, **Matt. 23:5**; used figuratively in 2 Cor. 6:11, 13, "to be enlarged," in the ethical sense, of the heart.

Phylacteries *phulakterion* (5440), primarily "an outpost," or "fortification" (*phulax*, "a guard"), then, "any kind of safeguard," became used especially to denote "an amulet." In the NT it denotes a prayer fillet, "a phylactery," a small strip of parchment, with portions of the Law written on it; it was fastened by a leather strap either to the forehead or to the left arm over against the heart, to remind the wearer of the duty of keeping the commandments of God in the head and in the heart; cf. Ex. 13:16; Deut. 6:8; 11:18. It was supposed to have potency as a charm against evils and demons. The Pharisees broadened their "phylacteries" to render conspicuous their superior eagerness to be mindful of God's Law, **Matt. 23:5**.

Enlarge *megaluno* (3170), denotes "to make great" (from *megas*, "great"), **Matt. 23:5**, "enlarge"; 2 Cor. 10:15, KJV, "enlarged," RV, "magnified"; elsewhere in the KJV it is rendered by the verb "to magnify," except in Luke 1:58, KJV, "had showed great (mercy)," RV, "had magnified (His mercy); see Luke 1:46; Acts 5:13; 10:46; 19:17; Phil. 1:20.

Borders *see* Hem at *Matthew 9:20.*

23:6 And love the uppermost rooms at feasts, and the chief seats in the synagogues,

Uppermost rooms *protoklisia* (4411), "the chief reclining place at table," is rendered "uppermost rooms," in **Matt. 23:6**, KJV (RV, "chief place"); in Mark 12:39, "uppermost rooms," KJV (RV, "chief places"); in Luke 14:7, "chief rooms," KJV (RV, "chief seats"); in v. 8, KJV, "highest room" (RV, "chief seat"); in 20:46, KJV, "highest seats" (RV, "chief seats").

Feasts *deipnon* (1173), denotes (a) "the chief meal of the day," dinner or supper, taken at or towards evening; in the plural "feasts," **Matt. 23:6**; Mark 6:21; 12:39; Luke 20:46; otherwise translated "supper," Luke 14:12, 16, 17, 24; John 12:2; 13:2, 4; 21:20; 1 Cor. 11:21 (of a social meal); (b) "the Lord's Supper," 1 Cor. 11:20; (c) "the supper or feast" which will celebrate the marriage of Christ with His spiritual Bride, at the inauguration of His Kingdom, Rev. 19:9; (d) figuratively, of that to which the birds of prey will be summoned after the overthrow of the enemies of the Lord at the termination of the war of Armageddon, 19:17 (cf. Ezek. 39:4, 17-20).

Chief seats *protokathedria* (4410), "a sitting in the first or chief seat" (*protos*, "first," *kathedra*, "a seat"), is found in **Matt. 23:6**; Mark 12:39; Luke 11:43; 20:46.

23:7 And greetings in the markets, and to be called of men, Rabbi, Rabbi.

Greetings *aspamos* (783), a salutation, is always so rendered in the RV; KJV, "greetings" in **Matt. 23:7**;

Luke 11:43; 20:46, it is used (a) orally in those instances and in Mark 12:38; Luke 1:29, 41, 44; (b) in written salutations, 1 Cor. 16:21; Col. 4:18; 2 Thess. 3:17.

Markets *see Matthew 11:16.*

Rabbi *rabbei* or *rabbi* (4461), from a word *rab*, primarily denoting "master" in contrast to a slave; this with the added pronominal suffix signified "my master" and was a title of respect by which teachers were addressed. The suffix soon lost its specific force, and in the NT the word is used as courteous title of address. It is applied to Christ in **Matt. 26:25**, **49**; Mark 9:5; 11:21; 14:45; John 1:38 (where it is interpreted as *didaskalos*, "master," marg., "teacher" (see also "Rabboni" in John 20:16); v. 49; 3:2; 4:31; 6:25; 9:2; 11:8; to John the Baptist in John 3:26. In **Matt. 23:7**, **8**, Christ forbids his disciples to covet or use it. In the latter verse it is again explained as *didaskalos*, "master" (some mss. have *kathegetes*, "a guide"). *See also* Lord at *Matthew 17:4.*

23:8 But be not ye called Rabbi: for one is your Master, *even* Christ; and all ye are brethren.

Rabbi *see Matthew 23:7.*

Master *kathegetes* (2519), properly "a guide" (akin to *kathegeomai*, "to go before, guide"; *kata*, "down," *hegeomai*, "to guide"), denotes "a master, a teacher," **Matt. 23:10** (twice); some mss. have it in v. **8**, where the most authentic have *didaskalos* (1320); this is rendered "teacher" or "teachers" in **Matt. 23:8**, by Christ, of Himself; in John 3:2 of Christ; of Nicodemus in Israel, 3:10, RV; of "teachers" of the truth in the churches, Acts 13:1; 1 Cor. 12:28, 29; Eph. 4:11; Heb. 5:12; Jas. 3:1, RV; by Paul of his work among the churches, 1 Tim. 2:7; 2 Tim. 1:11; of "teachers," wrongfully chosen by those who have "itching ears," 2 Tim. 4:3. *See also Matthew 8:19.*

Brethren Believers, apart from sex, **Matt. 23:8**; Acts 1:15; Rom. 1:13; 1 Thess. 1:4; Rev. 19:10 (the word "sisters" is used of believers, only in 1 Tim. 5:2).

23:9 And call no *man* your father upon the earth: for one is your Father, which is in heaven.

Father *see Matthew 2:22.*

23:10 Neither be ye called masters: for one is your Master, *even* Christ.

Master *see Matthew 23:8.*

23:11 But he that is greatest among you shall be your servant.

Greatest *see Matthew 13:32.*

Servant *see* Servants at *Matthew 22:13. See also* Minister at *Matthew 20:26.*

23:12 And whosoever shall exalt himself shall be abased; and he that shall humble himself shall be exalted.

Exalt, Exalted *see* Exalted at *Matthew 11:23.*

Abased *see* Humble at *Matthew 18:4.*

He that In **Matt. 23:12**, *hostis*, combined with the indefinite pronoun *tis*, is properly rendered "whosoever," RV, for KJV, "he that."

Humble *see Matthew 18:4.*

23:13 But woe unto you, scribes and Pharisees, hypocrites! for ye shut up the kingdom of heaven against men: for ye neither go in *yourselves*, neither suffer ye them that are entering to go in.

Woe *see Matthew 11:21.*

Scribes *see Matthew 2:4.*

Shut *see Matthew 6:6.*

Suffer *see Matthew 3:15.*

23:14 Woe unto you, scribes and Pharisees, hypocrites! for ye devour widows' houses, and for a pretence make long prayer: therefore ye shall receive the greater damnation.

Woe *see Matthew 11:21.*

Scribes *see Matthew 2:4.*

Devour *see* Devoured at *Matthew 13:4.*

Pretence *prophasis* (4392), either from *pro*, "before," and *phaino*, "to cause to appear, shine," or, more probably, from *pro*, and *phemi*, "to say," is rendered "cloke" (of covetousness) in 1 Thess. 2:5; "excuse" in John 15:22 (KJV, "cloke"); "pretense" in **Matt. 23:14**; Mark 12:40; Luke 20:47 (KJV, "show"); Phil. 1:18; "color" in Acts 27:30. It signifies the assuming of something so as to disguise one's real motives.

Long *makros* (3117), is used of "long prayers" (**Matt. 23:14**, in some mss.), Mark 12:40; Luke 20:47. It denotes "far" in Luke 15:13; 19:12.

23:15 Woe unto you, scribes and Pharisees, hypocrites! for ye compass sea and land to make one proselyte, and when he is made, ye make him twofold more the child of hell than yourselves.

Woe *see Matthew 11:21.*

Scribes *see Matthew 2:4.*

Compass *see* Went about at *Matthew 4:23.*

Land *xeros* (3584), "dry," "dry land," **Matt. 23:15** (*ge*, "land," being understood); Heb. 11:29. *See also* Withered at *Matthew 12:10*.

Proselyte *proselutos* (4339), akin to *proserchomai*, "to come to," primarily signifies "one who has arrived, a stranger"; in the NT it is used of converts to Judaism, or foreign converts to the Jewish religion, **Matt. 23:15**; Acts 2:10; 6:5; 13:43. There seems to be no connection necessarily with Palestine, for in Acts 2:10 and 13:43 it is used of those who lived abroad. Cf. the Sept., e.g., in Exod. 22:21; 23:9; Deut. 10:19, of the "stranger" living among the children of Israel.

Twofold *diplous* (1362), denotes "twofold, double," 1 Tim. 5:17; Rev. 18:6 (twice). The comparative degree *diploteron* (neuter) is used adverbially in **Matt. 23:15**, "twofold more."

Child *see* Children at *Matthew 5:9*.

Hell *see Matthew 5:22*.

23:16 Woe unto you, *ye* blind guides, which say, Whosoever shall swear by the temple, it is nothing; but whosoever shall swear by the gold of the temple, he is a debtor!

Woe *see Matthew 11:21*.

Guides *see* Leaders at *Matthew 15:14*.

Swear *see Matthew 5:34*.

Nothing *see Matthew 5:13*.

Gold *see Matthew 2:11*.

Debtor In **Matt. 23:16** *opheilo*, "to owe", is translated "he is a debtor." The RV marg., keeping the verbal form, has "bound by his oath" (KJV, marg., "bound"). In the 18th verse the KJV, "he is guilty," means that he is under obligation to make amends for his misdeeds.

23:17 *Ye* fools and blind: for whether is greater, the gold, or the temple that sanctifieth the gold?

Fools *see* Fool at *Matthew 5:22*.

Greater *see Matthew 11:11*.

Gold *see Matthew 2:11*.

Sanctifieth *hagiazo* (37), "to sanctify," "is used of (a) the gold adorning the Temple and of the gift laid on the altar, **Matt. 23:17, 19**; (b) food, 1 Tim. 4:5; (c) the unbelieving spouse of a believer, 1 Cor. 7:14; (d) the ceremonial cleansing of the Israelites, Heb. 9:13; (e) the Father's Name, Luke 11:2; (f) the consecration of the Son by the Father, John 10:36; (g) the Lord Jesus devoting Himself to the redemption of His people, John 17:19; (h) the setting apart of the believer for God, Acts 20:32; cf. Rom. 15:16; (i) the effect on the believer of the Death of Christ, Heb. 10:10, said of God, and 2:11; 13:12, said of the Lord Jesus; (j) the separation of the believer from the world in his behavior – by the Father through the Word, John 17:17, 19; (k) the believer who turns away from such things as dishonor God and His gospel, 2 Tim. 2:21; (l) the acknowledgment of the Lordship of Christ, 1 Pet. 3:15. "Since every believer is sanctified in Christ Jesus, 1 Cor. 1:2, cf. Heb. 10:10, a common NT designation of all believers is 'saints,' *hagioi*, i.e., 'sanctified' or 'holy ones.' Thus sainthood, or sanctification, is not an attainment, it is the state into which God, in grace, calls sinful men, and in which they begin their course as Christians, Col. 3:12; Heb. 3:1."

23:18 And, Whosoever shall swear by the altar, it is nothing; but whosoever sweareth by the gift that is upon it, he is guilty.

Altar *see Matthew 5:23*.

Gift *see* Gifts at *Matthew 2:11*.

Guilty In **Matt. 23:18**, *opheilo*, to owe, to be indebted, to fail in duty, be a delinquent," is misrendered "guilty" in the KJV; RV, "a debtor."

23:19 *Ye* fools and blind: for whether *is* greater, the gift, or the altar that sanctifieth the gift?

Fools *see* Fool at *Matthew 5:22*.

Gift *see* Gifts at *Matthew 2:11*.

Sanctifieth *see Matthew 23:17*.

23:20-22 Whoso therefore shall swear by the altar, sweareth by it, and by all things thereon.

And whoso shall swear by the temple, sweareth by it, and by him that dwelleth therein.

And he that shall swear by heaven, sweareth by the throne of God, and by him that sitteth thereon.

Throne *see Matthew 5:34*.

23:23 Woe unto you, scribes and Pharisees, hypocrites! for ye pay tithe of mint and anise and cummin, and have omitted the weightier *matters* of the law, judgment, mercy, and faith: these ought ye to have done, and not to leave the other undone.

Woe *see Matthew 11:21*.

Scribes *see Matthew 2:4*.

Pay In **Matt. 23:23**, KJV, *apodekatoo*, "to tithe," is translated "ye pay tithe" (RV, "ye tithe").

Tithe *apodekatoo* (586), denotes (a) "to tithe" (*apo*, "from," *dekatos*, "tenth"), **Matt. 23:23** (KJV, "pay tithe of"); Luke 11:42; in Luke 18:12 (where the best texts have the alternative form *apodekateuo*), "I give tithes"; (b) "to exact tithes" from Heb. 7:5.

Mint *heduosmon* (2238), an adjective denoting sweet-smelling (*hedus*, "sweet," *osme*, "a smell"), is used as a neuter noun signifying "mint," **Matt. 23:23**; Luke 11:42.

Anise *anethon* (432), "dill, anise," was used for food and for pickling, **Matt. 23:23**.

Cummin *kuminon* (2951), is an umbelliferous plant with aromatic seeds, used as a condiment, **Matt. 23:23**.

Weightier *barus* (926), "heavy," is rendered "weighty" in 2 Cor. 10:10, of Paul's letters. The comparative degree is used in the neuter plural in **Matt. 23:23**, "(the) weightier matters (of the Law)." *See also* Heavy at *Matthew 23:4*.

Judgment *see Matthew 5:21*.

Mercy *see Matthew 9:13*.

Faith *pistis* (4102), primarily, "firm persuasion," a conviction based upon hearing (akin to *peitho*, "to persuade"), is used in the NT always of "faith in God or Christ, or things spiritual."

The word is used of (a) trust, e.g., Rom. 3:25; 1 Cor. 2:5; 15:14, 17; 2 Cor. 1:24; Gal. 3:23; Phil. 1:25; 2:17; 1 Thess. 3:2; 2 Thess. 1:3; 3:2; (b) trust-worthiness, e.g., **Matt. 23:23**; Rom. 3:3, RV, "the faithfulness of God", Gal. 5:22 (RV, "faithfulness"), Titus 2:10, "fidelity"; (c) by metonymy, what is believed, the contents of belief, the "faith," Acts 6:7; 14:22; Gal. 1:23; 3:25 [contrast 3:23, under (a)]; 6:10; Phil. 1:27; 1 Thess. 3:10; Jude 3, 20 (and perhaps 2 Thess. 3:2); (d) a ground for "faith," an assurance, Acts 17:31 (not as in KJV, marg., "offered faith"); (e) a pledge of fidelity, plighted "faith," 1 Tim. 5:12.

Ought *see* Must at *Matthew 17:10*.

Leave *see* Leaveth at *Matthew 4:11*.

Other *ekeinos* (1565), signifying "that one," implying remoteness as compared with *houtos*, "this," is translated "the other," e.g., in **Matt. 23:23**; Luke 11:42; 18:14.

23:24 *Ye* blind guides, which strain at a gnat, and swallow a camel.

Guides *see* Leaders at *Matthew 15:14*.

Strain *diulizo* (1368), primarily denotes "to strain thoroughly" (*dia*, "through," intensive, *hulizo*, "to strain"), then, "to strain out," as through a sieve or strainer, as in the case of wine, so as to remove the unclean midge, **Matt. 23:24**, RV (KJV, "strain at"). In the Sept., Amos 6:6.

Gnat *konops* (2971), denotes "the winegnat or midge," which breeds in fermenting or evaporating wine, **Matt. 23:24**, where the KJV, "strain at" is corrected to "strain out," in the RV.

Swallow *katapino* (2666), "to drink down" (*kata*, and *pino*, "to drink"), "to swallow," is used with this meaning (a) physically, but figuratively, **Matt. 23:24**; Rev. 12:16; (b) metaphorically, in the passive voice, of death (by victory), 1 Cor. 15:54; of being overwhelmed by sorrow, 2 Cor. 2:7; of the mortal body (by life), 5:4.

Camel *see Matthew 19:24*.

23:25 Woe unto you, scribes and Pharisees, hypocrites! for ye make clean the outside of the cup and of the platter, but within they are full of extortion and excess.

Woe *see Matthew 11:21*.

Clean *see Matthew 8:2*.

Outside *exothen* (1855), an adverb formed from *exo*, "without," properly signifies "from without," Mark 7:18 (in v. 15 it is used as a preposition); with the article it is equivalent to a noun, "the outside," **Matt. 23:25** (for v. **27**, "outward"); Luke 11:39; in v. 40, RV, "the outside" (KJV, "that which is without").

Platter *paropsis* (3953), firstly, "a side dish of dainties" (*para*, "beside," *opson*, "cooked"); then, "the dish itself," **Matt. 23:25**; v. **26**, in some mss.

Within This is a translation of (a) *entos*; in Luke 17:21 the RV marg., "in the midst of," is to be preferred; the kingdom of God was not in the hearts of the Pharisees; (b) *en*, "of thinking or saying within oneself," e.g., Luke 7:39, 49 (marg., "among"); locally, e.g., Luke 19:44; (c) *esothen*, 2 Cor. 7:5; Rev. 4:8; 5:1; "from within," Mark 7:21, 23; Luke 11:7; "within," **Matt. 23:25**; Luke 11:40, RV, "inside"; in **Matt. 23:27, 28**, RV, "inwardly"; (d) *eso*, John 20:26; Acts 5:23; 1 Cor. 5:12 (i.e., "within" the church); (e) *pros*, to, or with, in Mark 14:4, KJV, "within" (RV, "among"); (f) *dia*, "through," rendered "within (three days)" in Mark 14:58, KJV (RV, "in," looking through the time to the event, and in keeping with the metaphor of building); (g) *esoteros*, Heb. 6:19, the comparative degree of *eso*, used with the article translated "that within," lit., "the inner (part of the veil)," i.e., "inside"; (h) in Luke 11:41, RV, *eneimi*, "to be in," is rendered "are within" (KJV, "ye have").

Full *gemo* (1073), "to be full, to be heavily laden with," was primarily used of a ship; it is chiefly used in the NT of evil contents, such as extortion and excess, **Matt. 23:25**; dead men's bones, v. **27**; extortion and wickedness, Luke 11:39;

cursing, Rom. 3:14; blasphemy, Rev. 17:3; abominations, v. 4; of divine judgments 15:7; 21:9; (RV, "laden," KJV, "full"); of good things, 4:6, 8; 5:8.

Extortion *harpage* (724), denotes "pillage, plundering, robbery, extortion" (akin to *harpazo*, "to seize, carry off by force," and *harpagmos*, "a thing seized, or the act of seizing"; from the root *arp*, seen in Eng., "rapacious"; an associated noun, with the same spelling, denoted a rake, or hook for drawing up a bucket); it is translated "extortion" in **Matt. 23:25**; Luke 11:39, RV, KJV, "ravening"; Heb. 10:34, "spoiling."

Excess *akrasia* (192), lit. denotes "want of strength" (*a*, negative, *kratos*, "strength"), hence, "want of self-control, incontinence," **Matt. 23:25**, "excess"; 1 Cor. 7:5, "incontinency." Cf. *akrates*, "powerless, incontinent," 2 Tim. 3:3, RV, "without self-control."

23:26 *Thou* blind Pharisee, cleanse first that *which is* within the cup and platter, that the outside of them may be clean also.

Cleanse, Clean *see* Clean at *Matthew 5:8.*

Within *entos* (1787), an adverb denoting "within," or "among," is once used with the article, as a noun, of "the inside (of the cup and of the platter)," **Matt. 23:26**, RV (KJV, "that which is within, etc."); elsewhere, Luke 17:21.

Platter *see Matthew 23:25.*

Outside *ektos* (1622), is once used with the article, "the outside," **Matt. 23:26**.

23:27 Woe unto you, scribes and Pharisees, hypocrites! for ye are like unto whited sepulchres, which indeed appear beautiful outward, but are within full of dead *men's* bones, and of all uncleanness.

Woe *see Matthew 11:21.*

Like unto *paromoiazo* (3945), "to be like" (from *para*, "by," and a verbal form from *homoios*), is used in **Matt. 23:27** (perhaps with intensive force), in the Lord's comparison of the scribes and Pharisees to whitened sepulchres.

Whited *koniao* (2867), from *konia*, "dust, lime," denotes "to whiten, whitewash," of tombs, **Matt. 23:27**; figuratively of a hypocrite, Acts 23:3. In the Sept., Deut. 27:2, 4; Prov. 21:9.

Sepulchres *taphos* (5028), akin to *thapto*, "to bury," originally "a burial," then, "a place for burial, a tomb," occurs in **Matt. 23:27**; v. 29, RV (KJV, "tombs"); 27:61, 64, 66; 28:1; metaphorically, Rom. 3:13.

Appear *see* Appeared at *Matthew 1:20.*

Beautiful *horaios* (5611), describes "that which is seasonable, produced at the right time," as of the prime of life, or the time when anything is at its loveliest and best (from *hora*, "a season," a period fixed by natural laws and revolutions, and so the best season of the year). It is used of the outward appearance of whited sepulchres in contrast to the corruption within **Matt. 23:27**; of the Jerusalem gate called "Beautiful," Acts 3:2, 10; of the feet of those that bring glad tidings, Rom. 10:15. In the Sept. it is very frequent, and especially in Genesis and the Song of Solomon. In Genesis it is said of all the trees in the garden of Eden, 2:9, especially of the tree of the knowledge of good and evil, 3:6; of the countenances of Rebekah, 26:7, Rachel, 29:17 and Joseph, 39:6. It is used five times in the Song of Solomon, 1:16; 2:14; 4:3 and 6:3, 5.

Outward *exothen* (1855), is translated "outward" in **Matt. 23:27** (RV, "outwardly"); it is used with the article, adjectivally, in 1 Pet. 3:3, of "outward" adorning. *See also* Outside at *Matthew 23:25.*

Within *see Matthew 23:25.*

Full *see Matthew 23:25.*

Bones *osteon* (3747), probably from a word signifying strength, or firmness, sometimes denotes "hard substances other than bones," e.g., the stone or kernel of fruit. In the NT it always denotes "bones," **Matt. 23:27**; Luke 24:39; John 19:36; Heb. 11:22.

Uncleanness *akatharsia* (167), denotes "uncleanness," (a) physical, **Matt. 23:27** (instances in the papyri speak of tenants keeping houses in good condition); (b) moral, Rom. 1:24; 6:19; 2 Cor. 12:21; Gal. 5:19; Eph. 4:19; 5:3; Col. 3:5; 1 Thess. 2:3 (suggestive of the fact that sensuality and evil doctrine are frequently associated); 4:7.

23:28 Even so ye also outwardly appear righteous unto men, but within ye are full of hypocrisy and iniquity.

Even so *see Matthew 7:17.*

Within *see Matthew 23:25.*

Full *mestos* (3324), probably akin to a root signifying "to measure," hence conveys the sense of "having full measure," (a) of material things, a vessel, John 19:29; a net, 21:11; (b) metaphorically, of thoughts and feelings, exercised (1) in evil things, hypocrisy, **Matt. 23:28**; envy, murder, strife, deceit, malignity, Rom. 1:29; the utterances of the tongue, Jas. 3:8; adultery, 2 Pet. 2:14; (2) in virtues, goodness, Rom. 15:14; mercy, etc., Jas. 3:17.

Hypocrisy *hupokrisis* (5272), primarily denotes "a reply, an answer" (akin to *hupokrinomai*, "to answer"); then, "play-acting," as the actors spoke in dialogue; hence, "pretence, hypocrisy"; it is translated "hypocrisy" in **Matt. 23:28**; Mark 12:15; Luke 12:1; 1 Tim. 4:2; the plural in 1 Pet. 2:1. For Gal. 2:13 and *anupokritos*, "without hypocrisy," in Jas. 3:17.

Iniquity *see Matthew 7:23.*

23:29 Woe unto you, scribes and Pharisees, hypocrites! because ye build the tombs of the prophets, and garnish the sepulchres of the righteous,

Woe *see Matthew 11:21.*

Tombs *taphos* (5028), akin to *thapto*, "to bury," is translated "tombs" in **Matt. 23:29**; elsewhere "sepulchre."

Garnish *see* Garnished at *Matthew 12:44.*

Sepulchres *mnemeion* (3419), primarily denotes "a memorial" (akin to *mnaomai*, "to remember"), then, "a monument" (the significance of the word rendered "tombs," KJV, "sepulchres," in Luke 11:47), anything done to preserve the memory of things and persons; it usually denotes a tomb, and is translated either "tomb" or "sepulchre" or "grave." Apart from the Gospels, it is found only in Acts 13:29. Among the Hebrews it was generally a cavern, closed by a door or stone, often decorated. Cf. **Matt. 23:29**.

23:30 And say, If we had been in the days of our fathers, we would not have been partakers with them in the blood of the prophets.

Fathers *see* Father at *Matthew 2:22.*

Partakers *koinonos* (2844), an adjective, signifying "having in common" (*koinos*, "common"), is used as a noun, denoting "a companion, partner, partaker," translated "partakers" in **Matt. 23:30**; 1 Cor. 10:18, KJV; 2 Cor. 1:7; Heb. 10:33, RV; 2 Pet. 1:4; "partaker" in 1 Pet. 5:1.

23:31 Wherefore ye be witnesses unto yourselves, that ye are the children of them which killed the prophets.

Witnesses *martureo* (3140), denotes (I) "to be a *martus*," or "to bear witness to," sometimes rendered "to testify"; it is used of the witness (a) of God the Father to Christ, John 5:32, 37; 8:18 (2nd part); 1 John 5:9, 10; to others, Acts 13:22; 15:8; Heb. 11:2, 4 (twice), 5, 39; (b) of Christ, John 3:11, 32; 4:44; 5:31; 7:7; 8:13, 14, 18 (1st part); 13:21; 18:37; Acts 14:3; 1 Tim. 6:13; Rev. 22:18, 20; of the Holy Spirit, to Christ, John 15:26; Heb. 10:15; 1 John 5:7, 8, RV, which rightly omits the latter part of v. 7 (it was a marginal gloss which crept into the original text); it finds no support in Scripture; (c) of the Scriptures, to Christ, John 5:39; Heb. 7:8, 17; (d) of the works of Christ, to Himself, and of the circumstances connected with His death, John 5:36; 10:25; 1 John 5:8; (e) of prophets and apostles, to the righteousness of God, Rom. 3:21; to Christ, John 1:7, 8, 15, 32, 34; 3:26; 5:33, RV; 15:27; 19:35; 21:24; Acts 10:43; 23:11; 1 Cor. 15:15; 1 John 1:2; 4:14; Rev. 1:2; to doctrine, Acts 26:22 (in some texts, so KJV); to the Word of God, Rev. 1:2; (f) of others, concerning Christ, Luke 4:22; John 4:39; 12:17; (g) of believers to one another, John 3:28; 2 Cor. 8:3; Gal. 4:15; Col. 4:13; 1 Thess. 2:11 (in some texts); 3 John 3, 6, 12 (2nd part); (h) of the apostle Paul concerning Israel, Rom. 10:2; (i) of an angel, to the churches, Rev. 22:16; (j) of unbelievers, concerning themselves, **Matt. 23:31**; concerning Christ, John 18:23; concerning others, John 2:25; Acts 22:5; 26:5; (II) "to give a good report, to approve of," Acts 6:3; 10:22; 16:2; 22:12; 1 Tim. 5:10; 3 John 12 (1st part); some would put Luke 4:22 here.

Yourselves *see Matthew 3:9.*

Children *see Matthew 5:9.*

Killed *see* Kill at *Matthew 5:21.*

23:32 Fill ye up then the measure of your fathers.

Fill *see* Full at *Matthew 13:48.*

Measure *see Matthew 7:2.*

23:33 *Ye* serpents, *ye* generation of vipers, how can ye escape the damnation of hell?

Serpents *see* Serpent at *Matthew 7:10.*

Generation *see Matthew 3:7.*

Vipers *see Matthew 3:7.*

Escape *pheugo* (5343), "to flee" (Lat., *fuga*, "flight," etc.; cf. Eng., "fugitive, subterfuge"), is rendered "escape" in **Matt. 23:33**; Heb. 11:34.

Damnation *see* Judgment at *Matthew 5:21.*

Hell *see Matthew 5:22.*

23:34 Wherefore, behold, I send unto you prophets, and wise men, and scribes: and *some* of them ye shall kill and crucify; and *some* of them shall ye scourge in your synagogues, and persecute *them* from city to city:

Wise *see Matthew 11:25.*

Scourge *see Matthew 10:17.*

Persecute *see* Persecuted at *Matthew 5:10.*

23:35 That upon you may come all the righteous blood shed upon the earth, from the blood of righteous Abel unto the blood of Zacharias son of Barachias, whom ye slew between the temple and the altar.

Righteous *see* Just at *Matthew 1:19*.

Blood *see Matthew 16:17*.

Shed *ekchuno*, or *ekchunno* (1632), is used of the voluntary giving up of His life by Christ through the "shedding" of His blood in crucifixion as an atoning sacrifice, **Matt. 26:28**; Mark 14:24; Luke 22:20, KJV, "is shed," RV, "is poured out"; these passages do not refer to the effect of the piercing of His side (which took place after His death); of the murder of servants of God, **Matt. 23:35**; Luke 11:50; Acts 22:20 (in the best texts); of the love of God in the hearts of believers through the Holy Spirit, Rom. 5:5.

Slew *phoneuo* (5407), "to kill, to murder," is rendered "ye slew" in **Matt. 23:35**. *See also* **Kill** at *Matthew 5:21*.

Between *see Matthew 18:15*.

Temple *naos* (3485), is used of the inner part of the Temple in Jerusalem, in **Matt. 23:35**, RV, "sanctuary."

Altar *see Matthew 5:23*.

23:36 Verily I say unto you, All these things shall come upon this generation.

Come *heko* (2240), means (a) "to come, to be present"; (b) "to come upon, of time and events," **Matt. 24:14**; John 2:4; 2 Pet. 3:10; Rev. 18:8; (c) metaphorically, "to come upon one, of calamitous times, and evils," **Matt. 23:36**; Luke 19:43.

23:37 O Jerusalem, Jerusalem, *thou* that killest the prophets, and stonest them which are sent unto thee, how often would I have gathered thy children together, even as a hen gathereth her chickens under *her* wings, and ye would not!

Stonest *see* Stoned at *Matthew 21:35*.

Often *see* Oft at *Matthew 18:21*.

Gathered, Gathereth *episunago* (1996), "to gather together," suggesting stress upon the place at which the "gathering" is made (*epi*, "to"), is said of a hen and her chickens, **Matt. 23:37**; and so of the Lord's would-be protecting care of the people of Jerusalem, *id*, and Luke 13:34; of the "gathering" together of the elect, **Matt. 24:31**; Mark 13:27; of the "gathering" together of a crowd, Mark 1:33; Luke 12:1.

Even as In **Matt. 23:37**, "even as" translates the phrase *hon tropon*, lit., "(in) what manner."

Hen *ornis* (3733), "a bird," is used, in the NT, only of a "hen," **Matt. 23:37**; Luke 13:34.

Chickens *nossos* or *neossos* (3502), "a young bird," is translated "young" in Luke 2:24. Cf. *nossia*, "a brood," Luke 13:34, and the noun *nossion*, used in the neuter plural, *nossia*, in **Matt. 23:37**, "chickens"; *nossion* is the diminutive of *nossos*.

Wings *pterux* (4420), is used of birds, **Matt. 23:37**; Luke 13:34; symbolically in Rev. 12:14, RV, "the two wings of the great eagle" (KJV, "two wings of a great eagle"), suggesting the definiteness of the action, the "wings" indicating rapidity and protection, an allusion, perhaps, to Exod. 19:4 and Deut. 32:11, 12; of the "living creatures" in a vision, Rev. 4:8; 9:9. Cf. *pterugion*, "a pinnacle."

23:38 Behold, your house is left unto you desolate.

House *see Matthew 9:6*.

Left *see* Leaveth at *Matthew 4:11*.

Desolate *eremos* (2048), is translated "desolate" in the Lord's words against Jerusalem, **Matt. 23:38**; some mss. have it in Luke 13:35; in reference to the habitation of Judas, Acts 1:20, and to Sarah, from whom, being barren, her husband had turned, Gal. 4:27. *See also* Desert at *Matthew 14:13*.

23:39 For I say unto you, Ye shall not see me henceforth, till ye shall say, Blessed *is* he that cometh in the name of the Lord.

Blessed *see Matthew 21:9*.

Chapter 24

24:1 And Jesus went out, and departed from the temple: and his disciples came to *him* for to shew him the buildings of the temple.

Departed In Luke 8:14, KJV, *poreuomai*, "to go on one's way" (RV), is rendered "go forth"; in 13:33, KJV, "walk" (RV, "go on my way"); in **Matt. 24:1**, KJV, it is rendered "departed" (RV, "was going on his way"). *See also* **Matthew 2:9**.

Shew *see Matthew 16:1*.

Buildings *oikodome* (3619), "a building, or edification," is used (a) literally, e.g., **Matt. 24:1**; Mark 13:1-2; (b) figuratively, e.g., Rom. 14:19 (lit., "the things of building up"); 15:2 of a local church as a spiritual building, 1 Cor. 3:9, or the whole church, the body of Christ, Eph. 2:21. It expresses the strengthening effect of teaching, 1 Cor. 14:3, 5, 12, 26; 2 Cor. 10:8; 12:19; 13:10, or other ministry, Eph. 4:12, 16, 29 (the idea conveyed is progress resulting from patient effort). It is also used of the believer's resurrection body, 2 Cor. 5:1.

24:2 And Jesus said unto them, See ye not all these things? verily I say unto you, There shall not be left here one stone upon another, that shall not be thrown down.

Left *see* Leaveth at *Matthew 4:11.*

One ... another In **Matt. 24:2**; Mark 13:2; Luke 19:44, and 21:6, "one (stone upon) another" is, lit., "stone upon stone."

Thrown *kataluo* (2647), lit., "to loosen down," is rendered "to throw down" (of the stones of the Temple) in **Matt. 24:2** and parallel passages. *See also* Destroy at *Matthew 5:17.*

24:3 And as he sat upon the mount of Olives, the disciples came unto him privately, saying, Tell us, when shall these things be? and what *shall be* the sign of thy coming, and of the end of the world?

Mount *see* Mountain at *Matthew 5:1.*

Olives *see Matthew 21:1.*

Sign *see Matthew 12:38.*

Coming *parousia* (3952), lit., "a presence," *para,* "with," and *ousia,* "being" (from *eimi,* "to be"), denotes both an "arrival" and a consequent "presence with." For instance, in a papyrus letter a lady speaks of the necessity of her parousia in a place in order to attend to matters relating to her property there. Paul speaks of his *parousia* in Philippi, Phil. 2:12 (in contrast to his *apousia,* "his absence"). Other words denote "the arrival" (see *eisodos* and *eleusis,* above). *Parousia* is used to describe the presence of Christ with His disciples on the Mount of Transfiguration, 2 Pet. 1:16. When used of the return of Christ, at the rapture of the church, it signifies, not merely His momentary "coming" for His saints, but His presence with them from that moment until His revelation and manifestation to the world. In some passages the word gives prominence to the beginning of that period, the course of the period being implied, 1 Cor. 15:23; 1 Thess. 4:15; 5:23; 2 Thess. 2:1; Jas. 5:7-8; 2 Pet. 3:4. In some, the course is prominent, **Matt. 24:3, 37**; 1 Thess. 3:13; 1 John 2:28; in others the conclusion of the period, **Matt. 24:27**; 2 Thess. 2:8. The word is also used of the Lawless One, the Man of Sin, his access to power and his doings in the world during his *parousia,* 2 Thess. 2:9. In addition to Phil. 2:12 (above), it is used in the same way of the apostle, or his companions, in 1 Cor. 16:17; 2 Cor. 7:6-7; 10:10; Phil. 1:26; of the Day of God, 2 Pet. 3:12.

End *see Matthew 13:39.*

24:4 And Jesus answered and said unto them, Take heed that no man deceive you.

Heed *blepo* (991), "to look," see, usually implying more especially an intent, earnest contemplation, is rendered "take heed" in **Matt. 24:4**; Mark 4:24; 13:5, 9, 23, 33; Luke 8:18; 21:8; 1 Cor. 3:10; 8:9; 10:12; Gal. 5:15; Col. 2:8 (KJV, "beware"); 4:17; Heb. 3:12.

No man *see Matthew 8:28.*

Deceive *see* Gone astray at *Matthew 18:12.*

24:5 For many shall come in my name, saying, I am Christ; and shall deceive many.

Name *see Matthew 6:9.*

Deceive *see* Gone astray at *Matthew 18:12.*

"He who loves the coming of the Lord is not he who affirms it is far off, nor is it he who says it is near. It is he who, whether it be far or near, awaits it with sincere faith, steadfast hope, and fervent love."

ST. AUGUSTINE OF HIPPO

24:6 And ye shall hear of wars and rumours of wars: see that ye be not troubled: for all *these things* must come to pass, but the end is not yet.

Shall *see Matthew 16:27.*

Hear *see* Fame at *Matthew 4:24.*

Wars *polemos* (4171), "war," is so translated in the RV, for KJV, "battle," 1 Cor. 14:8; Rev. 9:7, 9; 16:14; 20:8; for KJV, "fight," Heb. 11:34; KJV and RV in Jas. 4:1, hyperbolically of private "quarrels"; elsewhere, literally, e.g., **Matt. 24:6**; Rev. 11:7.

Rumours *akoe* (189), "a hearing," is translated "rumor" in **Matt. 24:6**; Mark 13:7.

Troubled *throeo* (2360), "to make an outcry" (*throos,* "a tumult"), is used in the passive voice, **Matt. 24:6**; Mark 13:7; Luke 24:37; 2 Thess. 2:2. In the Sept., Song of Sol. 5:4.

Must *see Matthew 17:10.*

24:7 For nation shall rise against nation, and kingdom against kingdom: and there shall be famines, and pestilences, and earthquakes, in divers places.

Nation *see Matthew 21:43.*

Rise *see* Arose at *Matthew 2:14.*

Kingdom *see* Land at *Matthew 4:15.*

Famines *limos* (3042), is translated "hunger" in Luke 15:17; 2 Cor. 11:27; elsewhere it signifies "a famine," and is so translated in each place in the RV; the KJV has the word "dearth" in Acts 7:11 and 11:28, and "hunger" in Rev. 6:8; the RV "famine" is preferable there; see **Matt. 24:7**; Mark 13:8; Luke 4:25; 15:14; 21:11; Rom. 8:35; Rev. 18:8.

Pestilences *loimos* (3061), "a pestilence, any deadly infectious malady," is used in the plural in Luke 21:11 (in some mss., **Matt. 24:7**); in Acts 24:5, metaphorically, "a pestilent fellow."

Earthquakes *see* Tempest at *Matthew 8:24.*

Divers places The phrase *kata topous,* lit., "throughout places" (*kata,* "down, or throughout," in a distributive sense, *topos,* "a place"), is translated "in divers places," in **Matt. 24:7**; Mark 13:8 and Luke 21:11.

24:8 All these *are* the beginning of sorrows.

Sorrows *odin* (5604), "a birth pang, travail pain," is rendered "travail," metaphorically, in **Matt. 24:8** and Mark 13:8, RV (KJV, "sorrows"); by way of comparison, in 1 Thess. 5:3; translated "pains (of death)," Acts 2:24 (RV, "pangs"). Cf. *odino,* "to travail in birth."

24:9 Then shall they deliver you up to be afflicted, and shall kill you: and ye shall be hated of all nations for my name's sake.

Afflicted *thlipsis* (2347), is translated "tribulation" in the RV (for KJV, "affliction") in Mark 4:17; 13:19; plural in 2 Thess. 1:4, KJV, "tribulations," RV, "afflictions"; in Acts 14:22 "many tribulations" (KJV, "much tribulation"); in **Matt. 24:9**, "unto tribulation" (KJV, "to be afflicted"); in 2 Cor. 1:4; 7:4; 2 Thess. 1:6, KJV, "tribulation," for RV, "affliction"; RV and KJV, "tribulation(-s)," e.g., in Rom. 2:9; 5:3 (twice); 8:35; 12:12; Eph. 3:13; Rev. 1:9; 2:9, 10, 22. In Rev. 7:14, "the great tribulation," RV, lit., "the tribulation, the great one" (not as KJV, without the article), is not that in which all saints share; it indicates a definite period spoken of by the Lord in **Matt. 24:21**, **29**; Mark 13:19, 24, where the time is mentioned as preceding His second advent, and as a period in which the Jewish nation, restored to Palestine in unbelief by gentile instrumentality, will suffer an unprecedented outburst of fury on the part of the antichristian powers confederate under the Man of Sin (2 Thess. 2:10-12; cf. Rev. 12:13-17); in this tribulation gentile witnesses for God will share (Rev. 7:9), but it will be distinctly "the time of Jacob's trouble" (Jer. 30:7); its beginning is signalized by the setting up of the "abomination of desolation" (**Matt. 24:15**; Mark 13:14, with Dan. 11:31; 12:11). *See also* Tribulation at *Matthew 13:21.*

Name *see Matthew 6:9.*

24:10 And then shall many be offended, and shall betray one another, and shall hate one another.

Offended *see Matthew 13:57.*

Hate *see Matthew 6:24.*

24:11 And many false prophets shall rise, and shall deceive many.

Prophets *see Matthew 7:15.*

Deceive *see* Gone astray at *Matthew 18:12.*

24:12 And because iniquity shall abound, the love of many shall wax cold.

Iniquity *see Matthew 7:23.*

Abound *plethuno* (4129), a lengthened form of *pletho,* "to fill," signifies "to increase, to multiply," and, in the passive voice, "to be multiplied," e.g., of iniquity, **Matt. 24:12**, RV.

Many *see Matthew 3:7.*

Cold *psucho* (5594), "to breathe, blow, cool by blowing," passive voice, "grow cool," is used metaphorically in **Matt. 24:12**, in the sense of waning zeal or love.

24:13 But he that shall endure unto the end, the same shall be saved.

Endure *see* Endureth at *Matthew 10:22.*

End *see Matthew 10:22.*

24:14 And this gospel of the kingdom shall be preached in all the world for a witness unto all nations; and then shall the end come.

Gospel *see Matthew 4:23.*

Preached *see* Preaching at *Matthew 3:1.*

World *oikoumene* (3625), "the inhabited earth", is used (a) of the whole inhabited world, **Matt. 24:14**; Luke 4:5; 21:26; Rom. 10:18; Heb. 1:6; Rev. 3:10; 16:14; by metonymy, of its inhabitants, Acts 17:31; Rev. 12:9; (b) of the Roman Empire, the world as viewed by the writer or speaker, Luke 2:1; Acts 11:28; 24:5; by metonymy, of its inhabitants, Acts 17:6; 19:27; (c) the inhabited world in a coming age, Heb. 2:5.

Witness *marturion* (3142), "testimony or witness as borne, a declaration of facts," is translated "witness" in **Matt. 24:14**, KJV; Acts 4:33; 7:44 (KJV); Jas. 5:3 (KJV).

Come *see Matthew 23:36.*

24:15 When ye therefore shall see the abomination of desolation, spoken of by Daniel the prophet, stand in the holy place, (whoso readeth, let him understand:)

Abomination *bdelugma* (946), denotes an "object of disgust, an abomination." This is said of the image to be set up by Antichrist, **Matt. 24:15**; Mark 13:14; of that which is highly esteemed amongst men, in contrast to its real character in the sight of God, Luke 16:15. The constant association with idolatry suggests that what is highly esteemed among men constitutes an idol in the human heart. In Rev. 21:27, entrance is forbidden into the Holy City on the part of the unclean, or one who "maketh an abomination and a lie." It is also used of the contents of the golden cup in the hand of the evil woman described in Rev. 17:4, and of the name ascribed to her in the following verse.

Desolation *eremosis* (2050), denotes "desolation," (a) in the sense of "making desolate," e.g., in the phrase "the abomination of desolation," **Matt. 24:15**; Mark 13:14; the genitive is objective, "the abomination that makes desolate"; (b) with stress upon the effect of the process, Luke 21:20, with reference to the "desolation" of Jerusalem. *See also* **Afflicted** at *Matthew 24:9.*

Spoken *see Matthew 1:22.*

Readeth *see* **Read** at *Matthew 12:3.*

Understand *see Matthew 15:17.*

24:16 Then let them which be in Judaea flee into the mountains:

Mountains *see* **Mountain** at *Matthew 5:1.*

24:17 Let him which is on the housetop not come down to take any thing out of his house:

Housetop *see* **Housetops** at *Matthew 10:27.*

24:18 Neither let him which is in the field return back to take his clothes.

Return *see Matthew 12:44.*

24:19 And woe unto them that are with child, and to them that give suck in those days!

Woe *see Matthew 11:21.*

Suck *see* **Sucklings** at *Matthew 21:16.*

24:20 But pray ye that your flight be not in the winter, neither on the sabbath day:

Flight *phuge* (5437), akin to *pheugo*, is found in **Matt. 24:20**. Some inferior mss. have it in Mark 13:18.

Winter *cheimon* (5494), denotes "winter," in **Matt. 24:20**; Mark 13:18; John 10:22; 2 Tim. 4:21.

Sabbath *see Matthew 12:1.*

24:21 For then shall be great tribulation, such as was not since the beginning of the world to this time, no, nor ever shall be.

Tribulation *see Matthew 13:21. See also* **Afflicted** at *Matthew 24:9.*

Such as "Such as" is a rendering of certain relative pronouns: *hoios*, "what sort of," e.g., **Matt. 24:21**; 2 Cor. 12:20 (twice); Rev. 16:18; *hostis*, "whoever," e.g., Mark 4:20; *hopoios*, "of what sort," preceded by *toioutos*, "of such a sort," Acts 26:29.

Time In 1 Cor. 16:12, KJV, nun, "now" (RV), is rendered "at this time"; in Acts 24:25, the phrase *to nun echon*, lit., "the now having," is rendered "at this time" (the verb is adjectival); the phrase is more expressive than the simple "now." Cf. *heos tou nun*, "until now," **Matt. 24:21** and Mark 13:19, RV, KJV, "unto (this time)."

24:22 And except those days should be shortened, there should no flesh be saved: but for the elect's sake those days shall be shortened.

Shortened *koloboo* (2856), denotes "to cut off, amputate" (*kolobos*, "docked"); hence, "to curtail, shorten," said of the "shortening" by God of the time of the great tribulation, **Matt. 24:22** (twice); Mark 13:20 (twice). In the Sept., 2 Sam. 4:12. *See also* **Moneychangers** at *Matthew 21:12.*

Flesh *see Matthew 19:5.*

Elect *see* **Chosen** at *Matthew 20:16.*

24:23 Then if any man shall say unto you, Lo, here *is* Christ, or there; believe *it* not.

Here *see* **This place** at *Matthew 12:6.*

There In **Matt. 24:23** (2nd part), KJV, *hode*, "here" (RV), is translated "there."

24:24 For there shall arise false Christs, and false prophets, and shall shew great signs and wonders; insomuch that, if *it were* possible, they shall deceive the very elect.

False Christs *pseudochristos* (5580), denotes "one who falsely lays claim to the name and office of the Messiah," **Matt. 24:24**; Mark 13:22.

Prophets *see Matthew 7:15.*

Shew *didomi* (1325), "to give," is rendered "to show" in **Matt. 24:24**.

Signs *see* Sign at *Matthew 12:38.*

Wonders *teras* (5059), "something strange," causing the beholder to marvel, is always used in the plural, always rendered "wonders," and generally follows *semeia,* "signs"; the opposite order occurs in Acts 2:22, 43; 6:8, RV; 7:36; in Acts 2:19 "wonders" occurs alone. A sign is intended to appeal to the understanding, a "wonder" appeals to the imagination, a power (*dunamis*) indicates its source as supernatural. "Wonders" are manifested as divine operations in thirteen occurrences (9 times in Acts); three times they are ascribed to the work of Satan through human agents, **Matt. 24:24**; Mark 13:22 and 2 Thess. 2:9.

Possible *see Matthew 19:26.*

Deceive *see* Gone astray at *Matthew 18:12.*

Very *see Matthew 10:30.*

Elect *see* Chosen at *Matthew 20:16.*

24:25 Behold, I have told you before.

Told *proeiro (prolego)* (4280), "to tell before," is so rendered in **Matt. 24:25**. *proeipon* (4302), and *proereo,* "to say before," used as aorist and future respectively of *prolego,* is used (a) of prophecy, e.g., Rom. 9:29; "to tell before," **Matt. 24:25**; Mark 13:23; "were spoken before," 2 Pet. 3:2; Jude 17; (b) of "saying" before, 2 Cor. 7:3; 13:2, RV (KJV, "to tell before" and "foretell"); Gal. 1:9; 5:21; in 1 Thess. 4:6, "we forewarned," RV.

24:26 Wherefore if they shall say unto you, Behold, *he is* in the desert; go not forth: behold, he is in the secret chambers; believe *it* not.

Wherefore *oun,* a particle expressing sequence or consequence, e.g., **Matt. 24:26**; Acts 6:3.

Desert *eremos* (2048), an adjective signifying "desolate, deserted, lonely," is used as a noun, and rendered "wilderness" 32 times in the KJV; in **Matt. 24:26** and John 6:31, RV, "wilderness" (KJV, "desert"). *See also Matthew 14:13.*

Secret *tameion,* translated "secret chambers" in **Matt. 24:26**.

Chambers *see* Closet at *Matthew 6:6.*

24:27 For as the lightning cometh out of the east, and shineth even unto the west; so shall also the coming of the Son of man be.

Lightning *astrape* (796), denotes (a) "lightning," **Matt. 24:27; 28:3**; Luke 10:18; 17:24; in the plural, Rev. 4:5; 8:5; 11:19; 16:18; (b) "bright shining," or "shining brightness," Luke 11:36.

East *see Matthew 2:1.*

Shineth *phaino* (5316), "to cause to appear," denotes, in the active voice, "to give light, shine," John 1:5; 5:35; in **Matt. 24:27**, passive voice; so Phil. 2:15, RV, "ye are seen" (for KJV, "ye shine"); 2 Pet. 1:19 (active); so 1 John 2:8, Rev. 1:16; in 8:12 and 18:23 (passive); 21:23 (active).

West *see Matthew 8:11.*

Coming *see Matthew 24:3.*

Son *see Matthew 3:17.*

24:28 For wheresoever the carcase is, there will the eagles be gathered together.

Carcase *see* Body at *Matthew 14:12.*

Eagles *aetos* (105), "an eagle" (also a vulture), is perhaps connected with *aemi,* "to blow," as of the wind, on account of its windlike flight. In **Matt. 24:28** and Luke 17:37 the vultures are probably intended. The meaning seems to be that, as these birds of prey gather where the carcass is, so the judgments of God will descend upon the corrupt state of humanity. The figure of the "eagle" is used in Ezek. 17 to represent the great powers of Egypt and Babylon, as being employed to punish corrupt and faithless Israel. Cf. Job 39:30; Prov. 30:17. The "eagle" is mentioned elsewhere in the NT in Rev. 4:7; 8:13 (RV); 12:14. There are eight species in Palestine.

24:29 Immediately after the tribulation of those days shall the sun be darkened, and the moon shall not give her light, and the stars shall fall from heaven, and the powers of the heavens shall be shaken:

Tribulation *see Matthew 13:21. See also* Afflicted at *Matthew 24:9.*

Sun *see Matthew 5:45.*

Darkened *skotizo* (4654), "to deprive of light, to make dark," is used in the NT in the passive voice only, (a) of the heavenly bodies **Matt. 24:29**; Mark 13:24; Rev. 8:12; (b) metaphorically, of the mind, Rom. 1:21; 11:10; (some mss. have it in Luke 23:45).

Moon *selene* (4582), from *selas,* "brightness" (the Heb. words are *yareach,* "wandering," and *lebanah,* "white"), occurs in **Matt. 24:29**; Mark 13:24; Luke 21:25; Acts 2:20; 1 Cor. 15:41; Rev. 6:12; 8:12; 12:1; 21:23. In Rev. 12:1, "the moon under her feet" is suggestive of derived authority, just as her being clothed with the sun is suggestive of supreme authority, everything in the symbolism of the passage centers in Israel. In 6:12 the similar symbolism of the sun and "moon" is suggestive of the supreme authority over the world, and of derived authority, at the time of the execution of divine judgments upon nations at the close of the present age.

Light *phengos* (5338), "brightness, luster," is used of the "light" of the moon, **Matt. 24:29**; Mark 13:24; of a lamp, Luke 11:33 (some mss. have *phos*, here).

Stars *see* Star at *Matthew 2:2*.

Heavens *see* Heaven at *Matthew 5:16*.

Shaken *see Matthew 11:7*.

24:30 And then shall appear the sign of the Son of man in heaven: and then shall all the tribes of the earth mourn, and they shall see the Son of man coming in the clouds of heaven with power and great glory.

Then *see Matthew 2:7*.

Appear *see* Appeared at *Matthew 1:20*.

Son *see Matthew 3:17*.

Heaven *see Matthew 5:16*.

Tribes *see Matthew 19:28*.

Mourn *kopto* (2875), to cut or beat, used in the middle voice of "beating the breast or head in mourning" (cf. Luke 23:27), is translated "shall mourn" in **Matt. 24:30**. *See also* Mourned at *Matthew 11:17*.

Clouds *see* Cloud at *Matthew 17:5*.

Great *see* Plenteous at *Matthew 9:37*.

24:31 And he shall send his angels with a great sound of a trumpet, and they shall gather together his elect from the four winds, from one end of heaven to the other.

Send *see Matthew 10:16*.

Sound *phone* (5456), most frequently "a voice," is translated "sound" in **Matt. 24:31** (KJV marg., "voice"); John 3:8, KJV (RV, "voice"); so 1 Cor. 14:7 (1st part), 8; Rev. 1:15; 18:22 (2nd part, RV, "voice"); KJV and RV in 9:9 (twice); in Acts 2:6, RV, "(this) sound (was heard)," KJV, "(this) was noised abroad."

Trumpet *salpinx* (4536), is used (1) of the natural instrument, 1 Cor. 14:8; (2) of the supernatural accompaniment of divine interpositions, (a) at Sinai, Heb. 12:19; (b) of the acts of angels at the second advent of Christ, **Matt. 24:31**; (c) of their acts in the period of divine judgments preceding this, Rev. 8:2, 6, 13; 9:14; (d) of a summons to John to the presence of God, Rev. 1:10; 4:1; (e) of the act of the Lord in raising from the dead the saints who have fallen asleep and changing the bodies of those who are living, at the Rapture of all to meet Him in the air, 1 Cor. 15:52, where "the last trump" is a military allusion, familiar to Greek readers, and has no connection with the series in Rev. 8:6 to 11:15; there is a possible allusion to Num. 10:2-6, with reference to the same event, 1 Thess. 4:16, "the (lit., a) trump of God" (the absence of the article suggests the meaning "a trumpet such as is used in God's service").

Gather *see* Gathered at *Matthew 23:37*.

Elect *see* Chosen at *Matthew 20:16*.

Winds *anemos* (417), besides its literal meaning, is used metaphorically in Eph. 4:14, of variable teaching. In **Matt. 24:31** and Mark 13:27 the four "winds" stand for the four cardinal points of the compass; so in Rev. 7:1, "the four winds of the earth" (cf. Jer. 49:36; Dan. 7:2); the contexts indicate that these are connected with the execution of divine judgments.

End In **Matt. 24:31**, the prepositions *apo*, "from," and *heos*, "unto," are used with the plural of *akros*, "highest, extreme," signifying "from one end ... to the other," lit., "from extremities ... to extremities."

24:32 Now learn a parable of the fig tree; When his branch is yet tender, and putteth forth leaves, ye know that summer *is* nigh:

Learn *see Matthew 9:13*.

Fig tree *see Matthew 21:19*.

Branch *see* Branches at *Matthew 13:32*.

Tender *hapalos* (527), "soft, tender," is used of the branch of a tree, **Matt. 24:32**; Mark 13:28.

Putteth *ekphuo* (1631), "to cause to grow out, put forth" (*ek*, "out," *phuo*, "to bring forth, produce, beget"), is used of the leaves of a tree, **Matt. 24:32**; Mark 13:28, "putteth forth."

Leaves *see Matthew 21:19*.

Summer *theros* (2330), akin to *thero*, "to heat," occurs in **Matt. 24:32**; Mark 13:28; Luke 21:30.

Nigh *engus* (1451), "nigh" or "near," is translated in both ways in **Matt. 24:32-33** and Mark 13:28-29, KJV (RV, "nigh" in both); in Acts 1:12, with *echon*, present participle neuter of *echo*, "to have," RV, "nigh unto ... off" (KJV, "from").

24:33 So likewise ye, when ye shall see all these things, know that it is near, *even* at the doors.

Likewise *see Matthew 18:35.*

Doors *see* Door at *Matthew 6:6.*

24:34 Verily I say unto you, This generation shall not pass, till all these things be fulfilled.

Generation *see* Generations at *Matthew 1:17.*

Pass *see Matthew 5:18.*

Fulfilled *see Matthew 5:18.*

24:35 Heaven and earth shall pass away, but my words shall not pass away.

Heaven *see Matthew 5:16.*

Pass *see Matthew 5:18.*

Words *see* Word at *Matthew 13:20.*

24:36 But of that day and hour knoweth no *man*, no, not the angels of heaven, but my Father only.

Angels *see Matthew 18:10.*

24:37 But as the days of Noe *were*, so shall also the coming of the Son of man be.

Coming *see Matthew 24:3.*

Son *see Matthew 3:17.*

24:38 For as in the days that were before the flood they were eating and drinking, marrying and giving in marriage, until the day that Noe entered into the ark,

Flood *kataklusmos* (2627), "a deluge" (Eng., "cataclysm"), akin to *katakluzo*, "to inundate," 2 Pet. 3:6, is used of the "flood" in Noah's time, **Matt. 24:38, 39**; Luke 17:27; 2 Pet. 2:5.

Eating *trogo* (5176), primarily, "to gnaw, to chew," stresses the slow process; it is used metaphorically of the habit of spiritually feeding upon Christ, John 6:54, 56-58 (the aorists here do not indicate a definite act, but view a series of acts seen in perspective); of the constant custom of "eating" in certain company, John 13:18; of a practice unduly engrossing the world, **Matt. 24:38.** In John 6, the change in the Lord's use from the verb *esthio (phago)* to the stronger verb *trogo*, is noticeable. The more persistent the unbelief of His hearers, the more difficult His language and statements became. In vv. 49 to53 the verb *phago* is used; in 54, 58, *trogo* (in v. 58 it is put into immediate contrast with *phago*). The use of *trogo* in **Matt. 24:38** and John 13:18 is a witness against pressing into the meaning of the word the sense of munching or gnawing; it had largely lost this sense in its common usage.

Marrying, Marriage *see* Marry at *Matthew 5:32.*

Ark *kibotos* (2787), "a wooden box, a chest," is used of (a) Noah's vessel, **Matt. 24:38**; Luke 17:27; Heb. 11:7; 1 Pet. 3:20; (b) the "ark" of the covenant in the tabernacle, Heb. 9:4; (c) the "ark" seen in vision in the heavenly temple, Rev. 11:19.

24:39 And knew not until the flood came, and took them all away; so shall also the coming of the Son of man be.

Flood *see Matthew 24:38.*

Son *see Matthew 3:17.*

24:40 Then shall two be in the field; the one shall be taken, and the other left.

Then *see Matthew 2:7.*

One *see Matthew 6:24.*

Taken *see* Take at *Matthew 1:20.*

Other *heis* (1520), "one," is sometimes translated "other" when expressing the second of a pair, e.g., **Matt. 24:40**, KJV (RV, "one").

Left *see* Leaveth at *Matthew 4:11.*

24:41 Two *women shall be* grinding at the mill; the one shall be taken, and the other left.

Grinding *aletho* (229), signifies "to grind at the mill," **Matt. 24:41**; Luke 17:35. The Sept. has both the earlier form *aleo*, Isa. 47:2,, and the later one *aletho*, used in the *Koine* period, Num. 11:8; Judg. 16:21; Eccl. 12:3, 4.

Mill *mulon* (3459), denotes "a mill house," where the millstone is, **Matt. 24:41**; some mss. have *mulos* (see next word). In the Sept., Jer. 52:11, "grinding house" (lit., "house of a mill"). *See also* **Millstone** at *Matthew 18:6.*

Taken *see* Take at *Matthew 1:20.*

Left *see* Leaveth at *Matthew 4:11.*

24:42 Watch therefore: for ye know not what hour your Lord doth come.

What *see Matthew 21:23.*

24:43 But know this, that if the goodman of the house had known in what watch the thief would come, he would have watched, and would not have suffered his house to be broken up.

This *ekeinos*, "that one," rendered "this" in **Matt. 24:43.**

Goodman *see* Householder at *Matthew 20:1. See also* Master of the house at *Matthew 10:25.*

What *see Matthew 21:23.*

Watch *phulake* (5438), from *phulasso*, "to guard," denotes (a) "a watching, keeping watch," Luke 2:8; (b) "persons keeping watch, a guard,"

Acts 12:10; (c) "a period during which watch is kept," e.g., **Matt. 24:43**; (d) "a prison, a hold." In Rev. 18:2, KJV, Babylon is described figuratively, first as a "hold" and then as a "cage" of every unclean and hateful bird (RV, "hold" in both clauses, marg., "prison"). The word is almost invariably translated prison. *See also Matthew 14:25.*

Thief *see* Thieves at *Matthew 6:19.*

Watched *gregoreo* (1127), "to watch," is used (a) of "keeping awake," e.g., **Matt. 24:43; 26:38, 40, 41**; (b) of "spiritual alertness," e.g., Acts 20:31; 1 Cor. 16:13; Col. 4:2; 1 Thess. 5:6, 10; 1 Pet. 5:8, RV, "be watchful" (KJV, "be vigilant"); Rev. 3:2, 3; 16:15.

Suffered *eao* (1439), "to let, permit," is translated "to suffer" in **Matt. 24:43**; Luke 4:41; 22:51; Acts 14:16; 16:7; 19:30; 28:4; 1 Cor. 10:13. *See also* Leaveth at *Matthew 4:11.*

Broken *see* Break at *Matthew 6:19.*

24:44 Therefore be ye also ready: for in such an hour as ye think not the Son of man cometh.

Ready *see Matthew 22:4.*

Son *see Matthew 3:17.*

24:45 Who then is a faithful and wise servant, whom his lord hath made ruler over his household, to give them meat in due season?

Faithful *pistos* (4103), a verbal adjective, akin to *peitho*, is used in two senses, (a) passive, "faithful, to be trusted, reliable," said of God, e.g., 1 Cor. 1:9; 10:13; 2 Cor. 1:18 (KJV, "true"); 2 Tim. 2:13; Heb. 10:23; 11:11; 1 Pet. 4:19; 1 John 1:9; of Christ, e.g., 2 Thess. 3:3; Heb. 2:17; 3:2; Rev. 1:5; 3:14; 19:11; of the words of God, e.g., Acts 13:34, "sure"; 1 Tim. 1:15; 3:1 (KJV, "true"); 4:9; 2 Tim. 2:11; Titus 1:9; 3:8; Rev. 21:5; 22:6; of servants of the Lord, **Matt. 24:45; 25:21, 23**; Acts 16:15; 1 Cor. 4:2, 17; 7:25; Eph. 6:21; Col. 1:7; 4:7, 9; 1 Tim. 1:12; 3:11; 2 Tim. 2:2; Heb. 3:5; 1 Pet. 5:12; 3 John 5; Rev. 2:13; 17:14; of believers, Eph. 1:1; Col. 1:2; (b) active, signifying "believing, trusting, relying," e.g., Acts 16:1 (feminine); 2 Cor. 6:15; Gal. 3:9 seems best taken in this respect, as the context lays stress upon Abraham's "faith" in God, rather than upon his "faithfulness." In John 20:27 the context requires the active sense, as the Lord is reproaching Thomas for his want of "faith." With regard to believers, they are spoken of sometimes in the active sense, sometimes in the passive, i.e., sometimes as believers, sometimes as "faithful." See Lightfoot on Galatians, p. 155.

Wise *see Matthew 7:24.*

Made *kathistemi* (2525), usually signifies "to appoint a person to a position." In this sense the verb is often translated "to make" or "to set," in appointing a person to a place of authority, e.g., a servant over a household, **Matt. 24:45, 47; 25:21, 23**; Luke 12:42, 44; a judge, Luke 12:14; Acts 7:27, 35; a governor, Acts 7:10; man by God over the work of His hands, Heb. 2:7. It is rendered "appoint," with reference to the so-called seven deacons in Acts 6:3. The RV translates it by "appoint" in Titus 1:5, instead of "ordain," of the elders whom Titus was to "appoint" in every city in Crete. Not a formal ecclesiastical ordination is in view, but the "appointment," for the recognition of the churches, of those who had already been raised up and qualified by the Holy Spirit, and had given evidence of this in their life and service. It is used of the priests of old, Heb. 5:1; 7:28; 8:3 (RV, "appointed").

Ruler In **Matt. 24:45**, KJV, *kathistemi*, "to appoint," is translated "hath made ruler" (RV, "hath set"); so in v. **47; 25:21, 23**; Luke 12:42, 44.

Household *oiketeia* (3610), denotes "a household of servants," **Matt. 24:45.**

Meat *see Matthew 3:4.*

Due In the phrases "in due season" in **Matt. 24:45**; Luke 12:42; Rom. 5:6 (lit., "according to time"), and "in due time," 1 Pet. 5:6, there is no word representing "due" in the original, and the phrases are, lit., "in season," "in time."

24:46-47 Blessed *is* that servant, whom his lord when he cometh shall find so doing.

Verily I say unto you, That he shall make him ruler over all his goods.

Make *see* Made at *Matthew 24:45.*

Ruler *see Matthew 24:45.*

Goods The neuter plural of the present participle of *huparcho*, is used as a noun denoting "goods," in **Matt. 24:47**, KJV "his goods," RV, "that he hath"; "goods" in **Matt. 25:14**; Luke 11:21; 16:1; 19:8; 1 Cor. 13:3; in Heb. 10:34 (1st part).

24:48 But and if that evil servant shall say in his heart, My lord delayeth his coming;

Evil *see Matthew 5:11.*

Delayeth *chronizo* (5549), from *chronos*, "time," lit. means "to while away time," i.e., by way of lingering, tarrying, "delaying"; "delayeth," **Matt. 24:48**; Luke 12:45, "tarried" **Matt. 25:5**; "tarried so long," Luke 1:21; "will (not) tarry," Heb. 10:37. *See also* Time at *Matthew 2:7.*

24:49 And shall begin to smite *his* fellowservants, and to eat and drink with the drunken;

Smite *tupto* (5180), "to strike, smite, beat," is rendered "to smite" in **Matt. 24:49**, KJV (RV, "beat"); **27:30**; Mark 15:19; Luke 6:29; 18:13; in some texts in 22:64 (1st part: RV omits); 23:48; Acts 23:2, 3 (twice).

Fellowservants *see Matthew 18:28.*

Eat *esthio* (2068), signifies "to eat" (as distinct from *pino,* "to drink"); it is a lengthened form from *edo* (Lat., *edo;* cf. Eng., "edible"); in Heb. 10:27, metaphorically, "devour"; it is said of the ordinary use of food and drink, 1 Cor. 9:7; 11:22; of partaking of food at table, e.g., Mark 2:16; of reveling, **Matt. 24:49**; Luke 12:45. Cf. the strengthened, form *katesthio,* and the verb *sunesthio,* below.

Drunken *methuo* (3184), signifies "to be drunk with wine" (from *methu,* "mulled wine"; hence Eng., "mead, honey-wine"); originally it denoted simply "a pleasant drink." The verb is used of "being intoxicated" in **Matt. 24:49**; Acts 2:15; 1 Cor. 11:21; 1 Thess. 5:7*b*; metaphorically, of the effect upon men of partaking of the abominations of the Babylonish system, Rev. 17:2; of being in a state of mental "intoxication," through the shedding of men's blood profusely, v. 6.

24:50 The lord of that servant shall come in a day when he looketh not for *him,* and in an hour that he is not aware of,

Lord *see Matthew 1:22.*

Day *hemera* (2250), "a day," is used of (a) the period of natural light, Gen. 1:5; Prov. 4:18; Mark 4:35; (b) the same, but figuratively, for a period of opportunity for service, John 9:4; Rom. 13:13; (c) one period of alternate light and darkness, Gen. 1:5; Mark 1:13; (d) a period of undefined length marked by certain characteristics, such as "the day of small things," Zech. 4:10; of perplexity and distress, Isa. 17:11; Obad. 12-14; of prosperity and of adversity, Ecc. 7:14; of trial or testing, Ps. 95:8; of salvation, Isa. 49:8; 2 Cor. 6:2; cf. Luke 19:42; of evil, Eph. 6:13; of wrath and revelation of the judgments of God, Rom. 2:5; (e) an appointed time, Ecc. 8:6; Eph. 4:30; (f) a notable defeat in battle, etc., Isa. 9:4; Psa. 137:7; Ezek. 30:9; Hos. 1:11; (g) by metonymy = "when," "at the time when"; (1), of the past, Gen. 2:4; Num. 3:13; Deut. 4:10, (2), of the future, Gen. 2:17; Ruth 4:5; **Matt. 24:50**; Luke 1:20; (h) a judgment or doom, Job 18:20. (i) of a time of life, Luke 1:17-18 ("years").

Looketh *prosdokao* (4328), "to watch toward, to look for, expect" (*pros,* "toward," *dokeo,* "to think": *dokao* "does not exist"), is translated "expecting" in **Matt. 24:50** and Luke 12:46, RV (KJV, "looketh for"); Luke 3:15, "were in expectation"; Acts 3:5, "expecting" (KJV and RV); 28:6 (twice), "expected that," RV (KJV, "looked when") and "when they were long in expectation" (KJV, "after they had looked a great while").

24:51 And shall cut him asunder, and appoint *him* his portion with the hypocrites: there shall be weeping and gnashing of teeth.

Cut *dichotomeo* (1371), lit., to cut into two parts" (*dicha,* "apart," *temno,* "to cut," *tome,* "a cutting"), **Matt. 24:51**, "to cut asunder," is used in Luke 12:46. Some take the reference to be to the mode of punishment by which criminals and captives were "cut" in two; others, on account of the fact that in these passages the delinquent is still surviving after the treatment, take the verb to denote "to cut up" by scourging, to scourge severely, the word being used figuratively. As to **Matt. 24:51**, it has been remarked that the "cutting asunder" was an appropriate punishment for one who had lived a double life. In both passages the latter part of the sentence applies to retribution beyond this life. In the Sept. the verb is used in Exod. 29:17 of the dividing of the ram as a whole burnt offering at the consecration of the priests. The corresponding noun is found in Gen. 15:11, 17; Ex. 29:17; Lev. 1:8; Ezek. 24:4.

Appoint *tithemi* (5087), "to put," is used of "appointment" to any form of service. Christ used it of His followers, John 15:16 (RV, "appointed" for KJV, "ordained"). "I set you" would be more in keeping with the metaphor of grafting. The verb is used by Paul of his service in the ministry of the gospel, 1 Tim. 1:12 (RV, "appointing" for "putting"); 2:7 (RV, "appointed" for "ordained"); and 2 Tim. 1:11 (RV, "appointing" for "putting"); of the overseers, or bishops, in the local church at Ephesus, as those "appointed" by the Holy Ghost, to tend the church of God, Acts 20:28 ("hath made"); of the Son of God, as appointed Heir of all things, Heb. 1:2. It is also used of "appointment" to punishment, as of the unfaithful servant, **Matt. 24:51**; Luke 12:46; of unbelieving Israel, 1 Pet. 2:8. Cf. 2 Pet. 2:6.

Portion *meros* (3313), "a part," is translated "portion" in **Matt. 24:51**; Luke 12:46; 15:12. *See also* **Parts** at *Matthew 2:22.*

Weeping *see Matthew 2:18.*

Gnashing *see Matthew 8:12.*

Teeth *see* **Tooth** at *Matthew 5:38.*

Chapter 25

25:1 Then shall the kingdom of heaven be likened unto ten virgins, which took their lamps, and went forth to meet the bridegroom.

Likened unto *see* Like unto at *Matthew 6:8.*

Virgins *see* Virgin at *Matthew 1:23.*

Lamps *lampas* (2985), denotes "a torch" (akin to *lampo*, "to shine"), frequently fed, like a "lamp," with oil from a little vessel used for the purpose (the *angeion* of **Matt. 25:4**); they held little oil and would frequently need replenishing. Rutherford (*The New Phrynichus*) points out that it became used as the equivalent of *luchnos*, as in the parable of the ten virgins, **Matt. 25:1, 3, 4, 7, 8**; John 18:3, "torches"; Acts 20:8, "lights"; Rev. 4:5; 8:10 (RV, "torch," KJV, "lamp"). Cf. *phanos*, "a torch," John 18:3 (translated "lanterns").

Meet *apantesis* (529), "a meeting," occurs in **Matt. 25:6** (in some mss. in v. **1**, and in **27:32**, in some mss.); Acts 28:15; 1 Thess. 4:17. It is used in the papyri of a newly arriving magistrate. "It seems that the special idea of the word was the official welcome of a newly arrived dignitary" (Moulton, *Greek Test. Gram.* Vol. 1, p. 14). *See also* **Matthew** *8:34.*

25:2 And five of them were wise, and five *were* foolish.

Wise *see Matthew 7:24.*

Foolish *see* Fool at *Matthew 5:22.*

25:3 They that *were* foolish took their lamps, and took no oil with them:

They In Acts 5:16, *hoitines*, the plural of *hostis*, "anyone who," is translated "they"; so in 23:14, translated "and they"; in 17:11, "in that they" (some texts have it in **Matt. 25:3**).

Foolish *see* Fool at *Matthew 5:22.*

Lamps *see Matthew 25:1.*

Oil *elaion* (1637), "olive oil," is mentioned over 200 times in the Bible. Different kinds were known in Palestine. The "pure," RV (KJV, beaten), mentioned in Exod. 27:20; 29:40; Lev. 24:2; Num. 28:5 (now known as virgin oil), extracted by pressure, without heat, is called "golden" in Zech. 4:12. There were also inferior kinds. In the NT the uses mentioned were (a) for lamps, in which the "oil" is a symbol of the Holy Spirit, **Matt. 25:3-4, 8**; (b) as a medicinal agent, for healing, Luke 10:34; (c) for anointing at feasts, Luke 7:46; (d) on festive occasions, Heb. 1:9, where the reference is probably to the consecration of kings; (e) as an accompaniment of miraculous power, Mark 6:13, or of the prayer of faith, Jas. 5:14. For its general use in commerce, see Luke 16:6; Rev. 6:6; 18:13.

25:4 But the wise took oil in their vessels with their lamps.

Wise *see Matthew 7:24.*

Vessels *angeion* (30), denotes "a small vessel," e.g., for carrying oil, **Matt. 25:4.**

Lamps *see Matthew 25:1.*

25:5 While the bridegroom tarried, they all slumbered and slept.

Tarried *chronizo* (5549), "to spend or while away time"; "to tarry," **Matt. 25:5**; Luke 1:21; Heb. 10:37. *See also* Delayeth at *Matthew 24:48.*

Slumbered *nustazo* (3573), denotes "to nod in sleep" (akin to *neuo*, "to nod"), "fall asleep," and is used (a) of natural slumber, **Matt. 25:5**; (b) metaphorically in 2 Pet. 2:3, negatively, of the destruction awaiting false teachers.

25:6 And at midnight there was a cry made, Behold, the bridegroom cometh; go ye out to meet him.

Midnight In **Matt. 25:6** "at midnight" translates the adjective *mesos*, and noun *nux*, "night," in the combined adverbial phrase. In Acts 27:27 "about midnight" translates an adverbial phrase consisting of *kata*, "towards," followed by *mesos*, "middle" and *nux*, "night," with the article, lit., "towards (the) middle of the night."

Cry *krauge* (2906), an onomatopoeic word, is used in **Matt. 25:6**; Luke 1:42 (some mss. have *phone*); Acts 23:9, RV, "clamor"; Eph. 4:31, "clamor"; Heb. 5:7; Rev. 21:4, "crying." Some mss. have it in Rev. 14:18 (the most authentic have *phone*).

Made *see Matthew 9:16.*

Meet *see Matthew 25:1.*

25:7 Then all those virgins arose, and trimmed their lamps.

Virgins *see* Virgin at *Matthew 1:23.*

Arose *see* Awoke at *Matthew 8:25.*

Trimmed *kosmeo* (2885), "to arrange, adorn," is used of "trimming" lamps, **Matt. 25:7**. *See also* Garnished at *Matthew 12:44.*

Lamps *see Matthew 25:1.*

25:8 And the foolish said unto the wise, Give us of your oil; for our lamps are gone out.

Foolish *see* Fool at *Matthew 5:22.*

Wise *see Matthew 7:24.*

Oil *see Matthew 25:3.*

Lamps *see Matthew 25:1.*

Gone out *sbennumi* (4570), "to quench," is used in the passive voice, of the going out of the light of a torch or lamp, **Matt. 25:8**, "are going out" (RV). *See also* **Quench** at *Matthew 12:20.*

25:9 But the wise answered, saying, *Not so*; lest there be not enough for us and you: but go ye rather to them that sell, and buy for yourselves.

Wise *see Matthew 7:24.*

Lest *mepote* (3379), often written as two words, usually signifies "lest ever, lest haply, haply"; in indirect questions, "if haply" or "whether haply," e.g., Luke 3:15, RV; in **Matt. 25:9**, RV, "peradventure" (KJV, "lest"); "if peradventure," in 2 Tim. 2:25. *See also Matthew 4:6.*

Enough *arkeo* (714), "to ward off"; hence, "to aid, assist"; then, "to be strong enough," i.e., "to suffice, to be enough," is translated "be enough" in **Matt. 25:9**.

Yourselves *see Matthew 3:9.*

25:10 And while they went to buy, the bridegroom came; and they that were ready went in with him to the marriage: and the door was shut.

Ready *see Matthew 22:4.*

Marriage *see Matthew 22:2.*

Door *see Matthew 6:6.*

Shut *see Matthew 6:6.*

25:11 Afterward came also the other virgins, saying, Lord, Lord, open to us.

Afterwards *see* **Afterward** at *Matthew 4:2.*

Other *loipos* (3062), signifies "remaining, the rest." It is translated "other," or "others," e.g., in **Matt. 25:11**: Mark 4:19; Luke 18:9; 24:10 (in v. 9, "the rest"); but in Luke 8:10; Acts 28:9; Rom. 1:13; 1 Cor. 9:5; Eph. 2:3; 1 Thess. 4:13; 5:6; 1 Tim. 5:20, e.g., the RV renders this word "the rest" (KJV, "other" or "others"); in Eph. 4:17, some mss. have *loipa*, neuter plural, KJV, "other (Gentiles)"; see the RV.

Virgins *see* **Virgin** at *Matthew 1:23.*

Open *see* **Opened** at *Matthew 2:11.*

25:12 But he answered and said, Verily I say unto you, I know you not.

Know *see* **Knoweth** at *Matthew 6:8.*

25:13-14 Watch therefore, for ye know neither the day nor the hour wherein the Son of man cometh.

For *the kingdom of heaven is* as a man travelling into a far country, *who* called his own servants, and delivered unto them his goods.

Travelling *apodemeo* (589), "to be abroad," is translated "going into another country," in **Matt. 25:14** (KJV, "traveling, etc.").

Far country *see Matthew 21:33.*

Called *see* **Call** at *Matthew 20:8.*

Goods *see Matthew 24:47.*

25:15 And unto one he gave five talents, to another two, and to another one; to every man according to his several ability; and straightway took his journey.

One *see Matthew 6:24.*

Talents That the "talent" denotes "something weighed" has provided the meaning of the Eng. word as "a gift or ability," especially under the influence of the parable of the talents (**Matt. 25:14-30**).

His *see Matthew 22:5.*

Several *idios* (2398), "one's own," is translated "several (ability)," in **Matt. 25:15**.

Ability *see* **Wonderful** at *Matthew 7:22.*

Journey *see* **Far country** at *Matthew 21:33.*

25:16 Then he that had received the five talents went and traded with the same, and made *them* other five talents.

Traded *ergazomai* (2038), "to work," is rendered "traded" in **Matt. 25:16**; in Rev. 18:17, KJV, "trade," RV, "gain their living." *See also* **Gain** at *Matthew 16:26.*

Made *see* **Make** at *Matthew 4:19.*

25:17 And likewise he that *had received* two, he also gained other two.

Gained *see* **Gain** at *Matthew 16:26.*

25:18 But he that had received one went and digged in the earth, and hid his lord's money.

Hid *see Matthew 5:14.*

Money *argurion* (694), properly, "a piece of silver," denotes (a) "silver," e.g., Acts 3:6; (b) a "silver coin," often in the plural, "pieces of silver," e.g., **Matt. 26:15**; so **28:12**, where the meaning is "many, (*hikanos*) pieces of silver"; (c) "money"; it has this meaning in **Matt. 25:18, 27; 28:15**; Mark 14:11; Luke 9:3; 19:15, 23; 22:5; Acts 8:20 (here the RV has "silver").

25:19 After a long time the lord of those servants cometh, and reckoneth with them.

Long *polus* (4183), "much," is used with *chronos*, "time," in **Matt. 25:19**; John 5:6; in Acts 27:21, with *asitia*, KJV, "long abstinence," RV, "long without food."

Reckoneth *see* Take account at *Matthew 18:23*.

25:20 And so he that had received five talents came and brought other five talents, saying, Lord, thou deliveredst unto me five talents: behold, I have gained beside them five talents more.

Brought *see* Bring at *Matthew 5:23*.

Other *see Matthew 5:39*.

Behold *ide* (2396), an aorist or point tense, marking a definite point of time, of the imperative mood of *eidon*, "to see" (taken as part of *horao*, "to see"), is used as an interjection, addressed either to one or many persons, e.g., **Matt. 25:20**, **22**, **25**; John 1:29, 36, 47; Gal. 5:2, the only occurrence outside Matthew, Mark and John.

Gained *see* Gain at *Matthew 16:26*.

More In **Matt. 25:20** (2nd part), KJV, *allos*, "other" (so the RV), is translated "more."

25:21 His lord said unto him, Well done, *thou* good and faithful servant: thou hast been faithful over a few things, I will make thee ruler over many things: enter thou into the joy of thy lord.

Well *eu* (2095), primarily the neuter of an old word, *eus*, "noble, good," is used (a) with verbs, e.g., Mark 14:7, "do (*poieo*) ... good"; Acts 15:29 (*prasso*); Eph. 6:3 (*ginomai*, "to be"); (b) in replies, "good," "well done," **Matt. 25:21**, **23**; in Luke 19:17, *eu ge* (in the best texts). The word is the opposite of *kakos*, "evilly."

Good *see Matthew 5:45*.

Faithful *see Matthew 24:45*.

Few *see Matthew 7:14*.

Make *see* Made at *Matthew 24:45*.

Ruler *see Matthew 24:45*.

Joy *chara* (5479), "joy, delight" (akin to *chairo*, "to rejoice"), is found frequently in Matthew and Luke, and especially in John, once in Mark (4:16, RV, "joy," KJV, "gladness"); it is absent from 1 Cor. (though the verb is used three times), but is frequent in 2 Cor., where the noun is used five times, and the verb eight times, suggestive of the apostle's relief in comparison with the circumstances of the 1st Epistle; in Col. 1:11, KJV, "joyfulness," RV, "joy." The word is sometimes used, by metonymy, of the occasion or cause of "joy," Luke 2:10 (lit., "I announce to you a great joy"); in 2 Cor. 1:15, in some mss., for *charis*, "benefit"; Phil. 4:1, where the readers are called the apostle's "joy"; so 1 Thess. 2:19, 20; Heb. 12:2, of the object of Christ's "joy"; Jas. 1:2, where it is connected with falling into trials; perhaps also in **Matt. 25:21**, **23**, where some regard it as signifying, concretely, the circumstances attending cooperation in the authority of the Lord.

25:22 He also that had received two talents came and said, Lord, thou deliveredst unto me two talents: behold, I have gained two other talents beside them.

Behold *see Matthew 25:20*.

Gained *see* Gain at Matthew *16:26*.

25:23 His lord said unto him, Well done, good and faithful servant; thou hast been faithful over a few things, I will make thee ruler over many things: enter thou into the joy of thy lord.

> *"Faithfulness in little things is a big thing."*
>
> ST. JOHN CHRYSOSTOM

Well *see Matthew 25:21*.

Good *see Matthew 5:45*.

Faithful *see Matthew 24:45*.

Few *see Matthew 7:14*.

Make *see* Made at *Matthew 24:45*.

Ruler *see Matthew 24:45*

Joy *see Matthew 25:21*.

25:24 Then he which had received the one talent came and said, Lord, I knew thee that thou art an hard man, reaping where thou hast not sown, and gathering where thou hast not strawed:

Hard Synonymous with *austeros*, but to be distinguished from it, is *skleros* (from *skello*, "to be dry"). It was applied to that which lacks moisture, and so is rough and disageeable to the touch, and hence came to denotes "harsh, stern, hard." It is used by Matthew to describe the unprofitable servant's remark concerning his master, in the parable corresponding to that in Luke 19 (see *austeros*, above). *Austeros* is derived from a word having to do with the taste, *skleros*, "with the touch." *Austeros* is not necessarily a term of reproach, whereas *skleros* is always so, and indicates a harsh, even inhuman character. *Austeros* is "rather the exaggeration of a virtue pushed too far, than an absolute vice" (Trench, *Syn.* Sec. xiv). *Skleros* is used of the character of a man, **Matt. 25:24**; of a saying, John 6:60; of the difficulty and pain of kicking against the ox-goads, Acts 9:5; 26:14; of rough winds, Jas. 3:4 and of harsh speeches, Jude 15. Cf. *sklerotes,* "hardness," *skleruno,* "to harden," *sklerokardia,* "hardness of heart," and *sklerotrachelos,* "stiff-necked."

Reaping *see* Reap at *Matthew 6:26.*

Strawed *diaskorpizo* (1287), "to scatter abroad," is rendered "to scatter" in **Matt. 25:24, 26**, RV (KJV, "strawed"); **26:31**; Mark 14:27; Luke 1:51; John 11:52; Acts 5:37, RV.

25:25 And I was afraid, and went and hid thy talent in the earth: lo, *there* thou hast *that is* thine.

Thy *see Matthew 7:3.*

Lo *see* Behold at *Matthew 25:20.*

25:26 His lord answered and said unto him, *Thou* wicked and slothful servant, thou knewest that I reap where I sowed not, and gather where I have not strawed:

Wicked *see Matthew 12:45.*

Slothful *okneros* (3636), "shrinking, irksome," is translated "slothful" in **Matt. 25:26**, and Rom. 12:11, where "in diligence not slothful," RV, might be rendered "not flagging in zeal."

Reap *see Matthew 6:26.*

Strawed *see Matthew 25:24.*

25:27 Thou oughtest therefore to have put my money to the exchangers, and *then* at my coming I should have received mine own with usury.

Put *see Matthew 9:17.*

My *see* Mine at *Matthew 20:15.*

Money *see Matthew 25:18.*

Exchangers *trapezites* (5133), a "money-changer, broker, banker"; translated "bankers" in **Matt. 25:27**, RV (KJV, "exchangers").

Received *komizo* (2865), denotes "to bear, carry," e.g., Luke 7:37; in the middle voice, "to bear for oneself," hence (a) "to receive," Heb. 10:36; 11:13 (in the best texts; some have *lambano*), 39; 1 Pet. 1:9; 5:4; in some texts in 2 Pet. 2:13 (in the best mss. *adikeomai,* "suffering wrong," RV); (b) "to receive back, recover," **Matt. 25:27**; Heb. 11:19; metaphorically, of requital, 2 Cor. 5:10; Col. 3:25, of "receiving back again" by the believer at the judgment seat of Christ hereafter, for wrong done in this life; Eph. 6:8, of "receiving," on the same occasion, "whatsoever good thing each one doeth, RV.

Interest *tokos* (5110), primarily "a bringing forth, birth" (from *tikto,* "to beget"), then, "an offspring," is used metaphorically of the produce of money lent out, "interest," usury, **Matt. 25:27**; Luke 19:23.

25:28-29 Take therefore the talent from him, and give *it* unto him which hath ten talents.

For unto every one that hath shall be given, and he shall have abundance: but from him that hath not shall be taken away even that which he hath.

Abundance *see* Exceed at *Matthew 5:20.*

25:30 And cast ye the unprofitable servant into outer darkness: there shall be weeping and gnashing of teeth.

Unprofitable *achreios* (888), "useless" (*chreia,* "use"), "unprofitable," occurs in **Matt. 25:30** and Luke 17:10. In the Sept., 2 Sam. 6:22.

Outer *see Matthew 8:12.*

Weeping *see Matthew 2:18.*

Gnashing *see Matthew 8:12.*

Teeth *see* Tooth at *Matthew 5:38.*

25:31 When the Son of man shall come in his glory, and all the holy angels with him, then shall he sit upon the throne of his glory:

Sit *see* Set at *Matthew 5:1.*

25:32 And before him shall be gathered all nations: and he shall separate them one from another, as a shepherd divideth *his* sheep from the goats:

Separate *see* Sever at *Matthew 13:49.*

One another This translates a number of words and phrases, (a) *allelon,* a reciprocal pronoun in the genitive plural, signifying "of, or from, one another" (akin to *allos,* "another"), e.g., **Matt. 25:32**; John 13:22; Acts 15:39; 19:38; 1 Cor. 7:5; Gal. 5:17; the accusative *allelous* denotes "one another," e.g., Acts 7:26, lit., "why do ye wrong one another?"; 2 Thess. 1:3, RV; in Eph. 4:32 and Col. 3:13, e.g., RV, "each other"; in 1 Thess. 5:15, "one (toward) another," RV; the dative *allelois* denotes "one to another," e.g., Luke 7:32; (b) different forms of the plural of *heautou,* "of himself," used as a reciprocal pronoun, e.g., Eph. 5:19, RV, "one to another" (KJV, and RV marg., "to yourselves").

Shepherd *see Matthew 9:36.*

Divideth *aphorizo* (873), lit., "to mark off by boundaries or limits" (*apo,* "from," *horizo,* "to determine, mark out"), denotes "to separate"; "divideth," **Matt. 25:32**, KJV; RV, "separateth," as in the preceding part of the verse.

Goats *eriphos* (2056), denotes "a kid or goat," **Matt. 25:32** (RV, marg., "kids"); Luke 15:29, "a kid"; some mss. have *eriphion* here, indicating a sneer on the part of the elder son, that his father had never given him even a tiny kid.

25:33 And he shall set the sheep on his right hand, but the goats on the left.

Set *see* Setteth at *Matthew 4:5.*

Sheep *see Matthew 7:15.*

Right *see Matthew 5:29.*

Goats *eriphion* (2055), a diminutive, is used in **Matt. 25:33**. In v. **32** *eriphos* is purely figurative; in v. **33**, where the application is made, though metaphorically, the change to the diminutive is suggestive of the contempt which those so described bring upon themselves by their refusal to assist the needy.

Left *see Matthew 20:21.*

25:34 Then shall the King say unto them on his right hand, Come, ye blessed of my Father, inherit the kingdom prepared for you from the foundation of the world:

King *see Matthew 1:6.*

Right *see Matthew 5:29.*

Father *see Matthew 2:22.*

Inherit *see Matthew 5:5.*

Kingdom *see* Kingdoms at *Matthew 4:8.*

Prepared *see* Prepare at *Matthew 3:3.*

Foundation *see Matthew 13:35.*

25:35 For I was an hungred, and ye gave me meat: I was thirsty, and ye gave me drink: I was a stranger, and ye took me in:

Hungred *see Matthew 4:2.*

Meat *phago* (5315), "to eat," is used as a noun, in the infinitive mood, and translated "meat" in **Matt. 25:35, 42** (lit., "to eat"); in Luke 8:55 the RV translates it literally, "to eat" (KJV, "meat").

Thirsty *see* Thirst at *Matthew 5:6.*

Drink *see Matthew 10:42.*

Stranger *xenos* (3581), "strange", denotes "a stranger, foreigner," **Matt. 25:35, 38, 43, 44; 27:7**; Acts 17:21; Eph. 2:12, 19; Heb. 11:13; 3 John 5.

Took *sunago* (4863), "to bring together," is used of "taking" a person into one's house receiving hospitality, "took ... in," **Matt. 25:35, 38, 43**; so in Acts 11:26, RV, "were gathered together," KJV, "assembled"; perhaps the meaning is "they were entertained."

25:36 Naked, and ye clothed me: I was sick, and ye visited me: I was in prison, and ye came unto me.

Naked *gumnos* (1131), signifies (a) "unclothed," Mark 14:52; in v. 51 it is used as a noun ("*his*" and "*body*" being italicized); (b) "scantily or poorly clad," **Matt. 25:36, 38, 43, 44**; Acts 19:16 (with torn garments); Jas. 2:15; (c) "clad in the undergarment only" (the outer being laid aside), John 21:7; (d) metaphorically, (1) of "a bare seed," 1 Cor. 15:37; (2) of "the soul without the body," 2 Cor. 5:3; (3) of "things exposed to the allseeing eye of God," Heb. 4:13; (4) of "the carnal condition of a local church," Rev. 3:17; (5) of "the similar state of an individual," 16:15; (6) of "the desolation of religious Babylon," 17:16.

Clothed *periballo,* (4016), "to cast around or about, to put on, array," or, in the middle and passive voices, "to clothe oneself," e.g., **Matt. 25:36, 38, 43**, is most frequent in Revelation, where it is found some 12 times.

"Keep Jesus Christ in your hearts and you will recognize his face in every human being. You will want to help him out in all his needs; the needs of your brothers and sisters."

JOHN PAUL II

Sick *see Matthew 10:8.*

Visited *episkeptomai* (1980), primarily, "to inspect" (a late form of *episkopeo*, "to look upon, care for, exercise oversight"), signifies (a) "to visit" with help, of the act of God, Luke 1:68, 78; 7:16; Acts 15:14; Heb. 2:6; (b) "to visit" the sick and afflicted, **Matt. 25:36, 43**; Jas. 1:27; (c) "to go and see," "pay a visit to," Acts 7:23; 15:36; (d) "to look out" certain men for a purpose, Acts 6:3.

25:37 Then shall the righteous answer him, saying, Lord, when saw we thee an hungred, and fed *thee*? or thirsty, and gave *thee* drink?

Fed *see* Feedeth at *Matthew 6:26.*

Thirsty *see* Thirst at *Matthew 5:6.*

Drink *see Matthew 10:42.*

25:38 When saw we thee a stranger, and took *thee* in? or naked, and clothed *thee*?

Stranger *see Matthew 25:35.*

Took *see Matthew 25:35.*

Naked *see Matthew 25:36.*

Clothed *see Matthew 25:36.*

25:39 Or when saw we thee sick, or in prison, and came unto thee?

Sick *asthenes* (772), lit., "without strength," hence, "feeble, weak," is used of "bodily debility," **Matt. 25:43** (for v. **39**, *astheneo*), **44**; some texts have it in Luke 9:2 (the best omit it, the meaning being "to heal" in general); 10:9; Acts 5:15, 16; in 4:9 it is rendered "impotent. *See also Matthew 10:8.*

25:40 And the King shall answer and say unto them, Verily I say unto you, Inasmuch as ye have done *it* unto one of the least of these my brethren, ye have done *it* unto me.

King *see Matthew 1:6.*

Least *see Matthew 2:6.*

Brethren Mankind, **Matt. 25:40**; Heb. 2:17.

25:41 Then shall he say also unto them on the left hand, Depart from me, ye cursed, into everlasting fire, prepared for the devil and his angels:

Left *see Matthew 20:21.*

Depart *see* Departed at *Matthew 2:9.*

Cursed *see* Curse at *Matthew 5:44.*

Everlasting *see Matthew 18:8.*

Fire *see Matthew 3:11.*

Prepared *see* Prepare at *Matthew 3:3.*

Devil *diabolos* (1228), "an accuser, a slanderer" (from *diaballo*, "to accuse, to malign"), is one of the names of Satan. From it the English word "Devil" is derived, and should be applied only to Satan, as a proper name. *Daimon*, "a demon," is frequently, but wrongly, translated "devil"; it should always be translated "demon," as in the RV margin. There is one "Devil," there are many demons. Being the malignant enemy of God and man, he accuses man to God, Job 1:6-11; 2:1-5; Rev. 12:9, 10, and God to man, Gen. 3. He afflicts men with physical sufferings, Acts 10:38. Being himself sinful, 1 John 3:8, he instigated man to sin, Gen. 3, and tempts man to do evil, Eph. 4:27; 6:11, encouraging him thereto by deception, Eph. 2:2. Death having been brought into the world by sin, the "Devil" had the power of death, but Christ through His own death, has triumphed over him, and will bring him to nought, Heb. 2:14; his power over death is intimated in his struggle with Michael over the body of Moses, Jude 9. Judas, who gave himself over to the "Devil," was so identified with him, that the Lord described him as such, John 6:70 (see 13:2). As the "Devil" raised himself in pride against God and fell under condemnation, so believers are warned against similar sin, 1 Tim. 3:6; for them he lays snares, v. 7, seeking to devour them as a roaring lion, 1 Pet. 5:8; those who fall into his snare may be recovered therefrom unto the will of God, 2 Tim. 2:26, "having been taken captive by him (i.e., by the 'Devil')"; "by the Lord's servant" is an alternative, which some regard as confirmed by the use of *zogreo* ("to catch alive") in Luke 5:10; but the general use is that of taking captive in the usual way. If believers resist he will flee from them, Jas. 4:7. His fury and malignity will be especially exercised at the end of the present age, Rev. 12:12. His doom is the lake of fire, **Matt. 25:41**; Rev. 20:10. The noun is applied to slanderers, false accusers, 1 Tim. 3:11; 2 Tim. 3:3; Titus 2:3.

> *"God will never send anybody to hell. If man goes to hell, he goes by his own free choice. Hell was created for the devil and his angels, not for man. God never meant that man should go there."*
>
> BILLY GRAHAM

Angels *see Matthew 18:10.*

25:42 For I was an hungred, and ye gave me no meat: I was thirsty, and ye gave me no drink:

Hungred *see Matthew 4:2.*

Meat *see Matthew 25:35.*

Thirsty *see* Thirst at Matthew *5:6.*

Drink *see Matthew 10:42.*

25:43 I was a stranger, and ye took me not in: naked, and ye clothed me not: sick, and in prison, and ye visited me not.

Stranger *see Matthew 25:35.*

Took *see Matthew 25:35.*

Naked *see Matthew 25:36.*

Clothed *see Matthew 25:36.*

Sick *see Matthew 25:39.*

Visited *see Matthew 25:36.*

25:44 Then shall they also answer him, saying, Lord, when saw we thee an hungred, or athirst, or a stranger, or naked, or sick, or in prison, and did not minister unto thee?

Athirst *see* Thirst at *Matthew 5:6*.

Stranger *see Matthew 25:35*.

Naked *see Matthew 25:36*.

Sick *see Matthew 25:39*.

Minister *see* Ministered at *Matthew 4:11*.

25:45 Then shall he answer them, saying, Verily I say unto you, Inasmuch as ye did *it* not to one of the least of these, ye did *it* not to me.

Least *see Matthew 2:6*.

25:46 And these shall go away into everlasting punishment: but the righteous into life eternal.

Everlasting *see Matthew 18:8*.

Punishment *kolasis* (2851), akin to *kolazo*, "punishment," is used in **Matt. 25:46**, "(eternal) punishment," and 1 John 4:18, "(fear hath) punishment," RV (KJV, "torment"), which there describes a process, not merely an effect; this kind of fear is expelled by perfect love; where God's love is being perfected in us, it gives no room for the fear of meeting with His reprobation; the "punishment" referred to is the immediate consequence of the sense of sin, not a holy awe but a slavish fear, the negation of the enjoyment of love. *See also* Hell at *Matthew 5:22*.

Chapter 26

26:1 And it came to pass, when Jesus had finished all these sayings, he said unto his disciples,

Finished *see Matthew 13:53*.

26:2 Ye know that after two days is *the feast of* the passover, and the Son of man is betrayed to be crucified.

Passover *pascha* (3957), the Greek spelling of the Aramaic word for the Passover, from the Hebrew *pasach*, "to pass over, to spare," a feast instituted by God in commemoration of the deliverance of Israel from Egypt, and anticipatory of the expiatory sacrifice of Christ. The word signifies (I) "the Passover Feast," e.g., **Matt. 26:2**; John 2:13, 23; 6:4; 11:55; 12:1; 13:1; 18:39; 19:14; Acts 12:4; Heb. 11:28; (II) by metonymy, (a) "the Paschal Supper," **Matt. 26:18, 19**; Mark 14:16; Luke 22:8, 13; (b) "the Paschal lamb," e.g., Mark 14:12 (cf. Exod. 12:21); Luke 22:7; (c) "Christ Himself," 1 Cor. 5:7.

Son *see Matthew 3:17*.

26:3 Then assembled together the chief priests, and the scribes, and the elders of the people, unto the palace of the high priest, who was called Caiaphas,

Palace *aule* (833), primarily, "an uncovered space around a house, enclosed by a wall, where the stables were," hence was used to describe (a) "the courtyard of a house"; in the OT it is used of the "courts" of the tabernacle and Temple; in this sense it is found in the NT in Rev. 11:2; (b) "the courts in the dwellings of well-to-do folk," which usually had two, one exterior, between the door and the street (called the *proaulion*, or "porch," Mark 14:68.), the other, interior, surrounded by the buildings of the dwellings, as in **Matt. 26:69** (in contrast to the room where the judges were sitting); Mark 14:66; Luke 22:55; KJV, "hall"; RV "court" gives the proper significance, **Matt. 26:3, 58**; Mark 14:54; 15:16 (RV, "Praetorium"); Luke 11:21; John 18:15. It is here to be distinguished from the Praetorium, translated "palace." For the other meaning "sheepfold," John 10:1, 16.

26:4 And consulted that they might take Jesus by subtilty, and kill *him*.

Consulted *sumbouleuo* (4823), "to take counsel together," is translated "consulted together," in **Matt. 26:4**, KJV (RV, "took counsel.")

Take *see* Took at *Matthew 9:25*.

Subtilty *dolos* (1388), "a bait, snare, deceit," is rendered "guile" in John 1:47, negatively of Nathanael; Acts 13:10, RV, KJV, "subtlety" (of Bar-Jesus); 2 Cor. 12:16, in a charge made against Paul by his detractors, of catching the Corinthian converts by "guile" (the apostle is apparently quoting the language of his critics); 1 Thess. 2:3, negatively, of the teaching of the apostle and his fellow missionaries; 1 Pet. 2:1, of that from which Christians are to be free; 2:22, of the guileless speech of Christ; 3:10, of the necessity that the speech of Christians should be guileless. See also **Matt. 26:4**; Mark 7:22; 14:1.

26:5 But they said, Not on the feast *day*, lest there be an uproar among the people.

Uproar *thorubos* (2351), "a noise, uproar, tumult," is rendered "tumult" in **Matt. 27:24** and Mark 5:38; in **Matt. 26:5**, RV (KJV, "uproar"), so in Mark 14:2; in Acts 20:1, "uproar," KJV and RV; in 24:18, "tumult"; in 21:34, KJV, "tumult" (RV, "uproar").

People *see Matthew 2:6.*

26:6 Now when Jesus was in Bethany, in the house of Simon the leper,

Leper *see Matthew 8:2.*

26:7 There came unto him a woman having an alabaster box of very precious ointment, and poured it on his head, as he sat *at meat*.

Box *alabastron* (211), "an alabaster vessel," is translated in the KJV of **Matt. 26:7**; Mark 14:3; Luke 7:37, "box," RV, "cruse." The breaking refers to the seal, not to the box or cruse.

Very In **Matt. 26:7**, *barutimos* (*barus*, "weighty," *time* "value"), is rendered "exceeding precious," RV, for KJV, "very precious."

Precious *barutimos* (927), "of great value, exceeding precious" (*barus*, "weighty," *time*, value), is used in **Matt. 26:7**.

Ointment *muron* (3464), a word derived by the ancients from *muro*, "to flow," or from *murra*, "myrrh-oil" (it is probably of foreign origin). The "ointment" is mentioned in the NT in connection with the anointing of the Lord on the occasions recorded in **Matt. 26:7, 9, 12**; Mark 14:3-4; Luke 7:37-38, 46; John 11:2; 12:3 (twice), 5. The alabaster cruse mentioned in the passages in Matthew, Mark and Luke was the best of its kind, and the spikenard was one of the costliest of perfumes. "Ointments" were used in preparing a body for burial, Luke 23:56 ("ointments"). Of the act of the woman mentioned in **Matt. 26:6-13**, the Lord said, "she did it to prepare Me for burial"; her devotion led her to antedate the customary ritual after death, by showing both her affection and her understanding of what was impending. For the use of the various kinds of "ointments" as articles of commerce, see Rev. 18:13.

Sat *see Matthew 9:10.*

Poured *katacheo* (2708), "to pour down upon" (*kata*, "down," *cheo*, "to pour"), is used in **Matt. 26:7** and Mark 14:3, of ointment.

26:8 But when his disciples saw *it*, they had indignation, saying, To what purpose is this waste?

Indignation *see Matthew 20:24.*

Purpose The following phrases are translated with the word "purpose": (a) *eis auto touto*, "for this same (or very) purpose," lit., "unto this same (thing)," Rom. 9:17; Eph. 6:22; Col. 4:8; (b) *eis touto*, "for this purpose," Acts 26:16, KJV (RV, "to this end"), lit., "unto this"; so 1 John 3:8; (c) *eis ti*, "to what purpose," **Matt. 26:8**, lit., "unto what"; Mark 14:4, RV, "to what purpose" (KJV, "why").

Waste *see* **Destruction** at *Matthew 7:13.*

26:9 For this ointment might have been sold for much, and given to the poor.

Ointment *see Matthew 26:6.*

Might *dunamai* (1410), "to be able, have power," whether by personal ability, permission, or opportunity, is sometimes rendered "may" or "might," e.g., **Matt. 26:9**; Mark 14:5; Acts 17:19; 1 Thess. 2:6. In the following the RV substitutes "can," "canst," "couldst," for the KJV, e.g., **Matt. 26:42**; Mark 4:32; 14:7; Luke 16:2; Acts 24:11; 25:11; 27:12; 1 Cor. 7:21; 14:31 (here the alteration is especially important, as not permission for all to prophesy, but ability to do so, is the meaning); Eph. 3:4. In the following the RV substitutes the verb "to be able," Acts 19:40; 24:8; Rev. 13:17.

Sold *see Matthew 13:46.*

Much *see Matthew 13:5.*

Poor *see Matthew 5:3.*

26:10 When Jesus understood *it*, he said unto them, Why trouble ye the woman? for she hath wrought a good work upon me.

Understood *ginosko* (1097), "to know, to come to know," is translated "to understand" in the KJV in **Matt. 26:10** and John 8:27 (RV, "to perceive"); KJV and RV in John 8:43; 10:6; in 10:38, RV (in some texts *pisteuo*, KJV, "believe"); KJV and RV in 12:16; 13:7 RV, KJV, "know"; Acts 8:30; in Phil. 1:12, KJV, RV, "know" (in some texts, Acts 24:11, KJV). *See also* **Knew** at *Matthew 12:15.*

Trouble The noun *kopos*, "a striking, beating," then, "laborious toil, trouble," used with *parecho*, "to furnish, to supply," is rendered "to trouble" (lit., "to give trouble to"), in **Matt. 26:10**; Mark 14:6; Luke 11:7; 18:5; Gal. 6:17; the meaning is to embarrass a person by distracting his attention, or to give occasion for anxiety. In the last passage the apostle expresses his determination not to allow the Judaizing teachers to distract him any further.

Wrought *see* **Work** at *Matthew 21:28.*

Good In 3 John 5 the RV has "thou doest a faithful work," for KJV, "thou doest faithfully." The lit. rendering is "thou doest (*poieo*) a faithful thing, whatsoever thou workest (*ergazo*)." That would not do as a translation. To do a "faithful" work is to do what is worthy of a "faithful" man. The KJV gives a meaning but is not exact as a translation. Westcott suggests "thou makest sure (*piston*) whatsoever thou workest" (i.e., it will not lose its reward). The change between *poieo*, "to do," and *ergazo*, "to work," must be maintained. Cf. **Matt. 26:10** (*ergazo* and *ergon*).

Work *see* Works at *Matthew 23:3*.

26:11 For ye have the poor always with you; but me ye have not always.

Poor *see Matthew 5:3*.

26:12 For in that she hath poured this ointment on my body, she did *it* for my burial.

Poured *ballo* (906), "to throw," is used of "pouring" liquids, **Matt. 26:12**, RV, marg., "cast" (of ointment); John 13:5 (of water). *See also Matthew 26:7*.

Ointment *see Matthew 26:6*.

My In **Matt. 26:12**, "for My burial" translates a phrase consisting of the preposition *pros* ("towards") governing the article with the infinitive mood, aorist tense, of *entaphiazo*, "to bury," followed by the personal pronoun "Me," as the object, where the infinitive is virtually a noun, lit., "towards the burying (of) Me."

Burial *entaphiazo* (1779), "to prepare a body for burial," is used of any provision for this purpose, **Matt. 26:12**; John 19:40.

26:13 Verily I say unto you, Wheresoever this gospel shall be preached in the whole world, *there* shall also this, that this woman hath done, be told for a memorial of her.

Told *laleo* (2980), is usually rendered "to speak," in the RV (for KJV, "to tell"), e.g., **Matt. 26:13**; Luke 1:45; 2:17, 18, 20; Acts 11:14; 27:25; but RV and KJV, "to tell" in John 8:40; Acts 9:6; 22:10.

Memorial *mnemosunon* (3422), denotes "a memorial," that which keeps alive the memory of someone or something (from *mnemon*, "mindful"), **Matt. 26:13**; Mark 14:9; Acts 10:4.

26:14-15 Then one of the twelve, called Judas Iscariot, went unto the chief priests,
And said *unto them*, What will ye give me, and I will deliver him unto you? And they covenanted with him for thirty pieces of silver.

And *kai* Occasionally it has almost the sense of *hoti*, "that," e.g., **Matt. 26:15** (first part); Mark 14:40 (last part); Luke 5:12, 17, where, if the *kai* had been translated, the clause might be rendered "that, behold, a man ...," lit., "and behold ..."; so v. 17; see also 9:51, where *kai*, "that," comes before "He steadfastly set"; in 12:15, "take heed that ye keep." What is said under (d), regarding the influence of the Septuagint, is applicable also to this significance.

Covenanted In **Matt. 26:15** the KJV translates *histemi* (2476), "to place (in the balances)," i.e., to weigh, "they covenanted with"; RV, "they weighed unto."

Pieces *argurion* (694), which frequently denotes "money," also represents "a silver coin," of the value of a shekel or *tetradrachmon* (four times the *drachme*); it is used in the plural in **Matt. 26:15; 27:3-9**. In Acts 19:19, "fifty thousand pieces of silver," is, lit., "fifty thousand of silver" (probably drachmas).

> *"The poor come to all of us in many forms. Let us be sure that we never turn our backs on them, wherever we may find them. For when we turn our backs on the poor, we turn them on Jesus Christ."*
>
> MOTHER TERESA

Silver *see* Money at *Matthew 25:18*.

26:16 And from that time he sought opportunity to betray him.

From that time *see* Forth at *Matthew 22:46*.

Opportunity *eukairia* (2120), "a fitting time, opportunity," occurs in **Matt. 26:16** and Luke 22:6. Cf. *eukairos*, "seasonable".

Betray *see* Prison at *Matthew 4:12*.

26:17 Now the first *day* of the *feast of* unleavened bread the disciples came to Jesus, saying unto him, Where wilt thou that we prepare for thee to eat the passover?

Bread *azumos* (106), denotes "unleavened bread," i.e., without any process of fermentation; hence, metaphorically, "of a holy, spiritual condition," 1 Cor. 5:7, and of "sincerity and truth" (v. 8). With the article it signifies the feast of unleavened bread, **Matt. 26:17**; Mark 14:1, 12; Luke 22:1, 7; Acts 12:3; 20:6.

Prepare *see Matthew 3:3.*

26:18 And he said, Go into the city to such a man, and say unto him, The Master saith, My time is at hand; I will keep the passover at thy house with my disciples.

Such *deina,* **Matt. 26:18**, denotes "such a one" (whom one cannot, or will not, name).

Master *see Matthew 8:19.*

Time *see Matthew 8:29.*

At hand *engus* (1451), "near, nigh," frequently rendered "at hand," is used (a) of place, e.g., of the Lord's sepulchre, John 19:42, "nigh at hand"; (b) of time, e.g., **Matt. 26:18**; Luke 21:30, 31, RV, "nigh," KJV, "nigh at hand"; in Phil. 4:5, "the Lord is at hand," it is possible to regard the meaning as that either of (a) or (b); the following reasons may point to (b): (1) the subject of the preceding context has been the return of Christ, 3:20, 21; (2) the phrase is a translation of the Aramaic "Maranatha," 1 Cor. 16:22, a Christian watchword, and the use of the title "the Lord" is appropriate; (3) the similar use of the adverb in Rev. 1:3 and 22:10; (4) the similar use of the corresponding verb in Rom. 13:12; Heb. 10:25, "drawing nigh," RV; Jas. 5:8; cf. 1 Pet. 4:7.

Keep *poieo* (4160), "to do, make," signifies "to keep," in **Matt. 26:18**, in the Lord's statement, "I will keep the passover;" so in Acts 18:21, in some mss.; in John 7:19, where the KJV has "keepeth (the law)," the RV adheres to the usual meaning "doeth."

Passover *see Matthew 26:2.*

Thy *see Matthew 1:20.*

26:19 And the disciples did as Jesus had appointed them; and they made ready the passover.

Appointed *suntasso* (4929), lit., "to arrange together with", hence "to appoint, prescribe," is used twice, in **Matt. 26:19** of what the Lord "appointed" for His disciples, and in **27:10**, in a quotation concerning the price of the potter's field.

Made ready *see* Prepare at *Matthew 3:3.*

Passover *see Matthew 26:2.*

26:20 Now when the even was come, he sat down with the twelve.

Sat *see Matthew 9:10.*

26:21-22 And as they did eat, he said, Verily I say unto you, that one of you shall betray me.

And they were exceeding sorrowful, and began every one of them to say unto him, Lord, is it I?

Exceeding *see Matthew 2:10.*

Every *hekastos* (1538), "each" or "every," is used of any number separately, either (a) as an adjective qualifying a noun, e.g., Luke 6:44; John 19:23; Heb. 3:13, where "day by day," is, lit., "according to each day"; or, more emphatically with *heis,* "one," in **Matt. 26:22**; Luke 4:40; 16:5; Acts 2:3, 6, 20:31; 1 Cor. 12:18; Eph. 4:7, 16, RV, "each (several)," for KJV, "every"; Col. 4:6; 1 Thess. 2:11; 2 Thess. 1:3; (b) as a distributive pronoun, e.g., Acts 4:35; Rom. 2:6; Gal. 6:4; in Phil. 2:4, it is used in the plural; some mss. have it thus in Rev. 6:11. The repetition in Heb. 8:11 is noticeable "every man" (i.e., everyone). Prefixed by the preposition *ana,* "apiece" (a colloquialism), it is used, with stress on the individuality, in Rev. 21:21, of the gates of the heavenly city, "each one of the several," RV; in Eph. 5:33, preceded by *kath' hena,* "by one," it signifies "each (one) his own."

Lord *see Matthew 17:4.*

26:23 And he answered and said, He that dippeth *his* hand with me in the dish, the same shall betray me.

Dippeth *embapto* (1686), "to dip into," is used of the act of Judas in "dipping" his hand with that of Christ in the dish, **Matt. 26:23**; Mark 14:20.

Dish *trublion* (5165), denotes "a bowl," somewhat deep, **Matt. 26:23**; Mark 14:20; among the Greeks it was a measure in medical prescriptions.

26:24 The Son of man goeth as it is written of him: but woe unto that man by whom the Son of man is betrayed! it had been good for that man if he had not been born.

Son *see Matthew 3:17.*

Woe *see Matthew 11:21.*

26:25 Then Judas, which betrayed him, answered and said, Master, is it I? He said unto him, Thou hast said.

Master *see* Lord at *Matthew 17:4. See also* Rabbi at *Matthew 23:7.*

26:26 And as they were eating, Jesus took bread, and blessed *it*, and brake *it*, and gave *it* to the disciples, and said, Take, eat; this is my body.

Took *see* Take at *Matthew 5:40.*

Bread *see Matthew 6:11.*

Brake *see Matthew 14:19.*

Gave *see* Give at *Matthew 7:9.*

26:27 And he took the cup, and gave thanks, and gave *it* to them, saying, Drink ye all of it;

Took *see* Take at *Matthew 5:40.*

Thanks *see Matthew 15:36.*

26:28 For this is my blood of the new testament, which is shed for many for the remission of sins.

New *kainos* (2537), denotes "new," of that which is unaccustomed or unused, not "new" in time, recent, but "new" as to form or quality, of different nature from what is contrasted as old. " 'The new tongues,' kainos, of Mark 16:17 are the 'other tongues,' heteros, of Acts 2:4. These languages, however, were 'new' and 'different,' not in the sense that they had never been heard before, or that they were new to the hearers, for it is plain from v. 8 that this is not the case; they were new languages to the speakers, different from those in which they were accustomed to speak. "The new things that the Gospel brings for present obedience and realization are: a new covenant, **Matt. 26:28** in some texts; a new commandment, John 13:34; a new creative act, Gal. 6:15, a new creation, 2 Cor. 5:17; a new man, i.e., a new character of manhood, spiritual and moral, after the pattern of Christ, Eph. 4:24; a new man, i.e., 'the Church which is His (Christ's) body,' Eph. 2:15. The new things that are to be received and enjoyed hereafter are: a new name, the believer's, Rev. 2:17; a new name, the Lord's, Rev. 3:12; a new song, Rev. 5:9; a new Heaven and a new Earth, Rev. 21:1; the new Jerusalem, Rev. 3:12; 21:2; 'And He that sitteth on the Throne said, Behold, I make all things new,' Rev. 21:5."

Testament *diatheke* (1242), primarily signifies "a disposition of property by will or otherwise." In its use in the Sept., it is the rendering of a Hebrew word meaning a "covenant" or agreement (from a verb signifying "to cut or divide," in allusion to a sacrificial custom in connection with "covenant-making," e.g., Gen. 15:10, "divided" Jer. 34:18-19). In contradistinction to the English word "covenant" (lit., "a coming together"), which signifies a mutual undertaking between two parties or more, each binding himself to fulfill obligations, it does not in itself contain the idea of joint obligation, it mostly signifies an obligation undertaken by a single person. For instance, in Gal. 3:17 it is used as an alternative to a "promise" (vv. 16-18). God enjoined upon Abraham the rite of circumcision, but His promise to Abraham, here called a "covenant," was not conditional upon the observance of circumcision, though a penalty attached to its nonobservance.

"The NT uses of the word may be analyzed as follows: (a) a promise or undertaking, human or divine, Gal. 3:15; (b) a promise or undertaking on the part of God, Luke 1:72; Acts 3:25; Rom. 9:4; 11:27; Gal. 3:17; Eph. 2:12; Heb. 7:22; 8:6, 8, 10; 10:16; (c) an agreement, a mutual undertaking, between God and Israel, see Deut. 29-30 (described as a 'commandment,' Heb. 7:18, cf. v. 22); Heb. 8:9; 9:20; (d) by metonymy, the token of the covenant, or promise, made to Abraham, Acts 7:8, (e) by metonymy, the record of the covenant, 2 Cor. 3:14; Heb. 9:4; cf. Rev. 11:19; (f) the basis, established by the death of Christ, on which the salvation of men is secured, **Matt. 26:28**; Mark 14:24; Luke 22:20; 1 Cor. 11:25; 2 Cor. 3:6; Heb. 10:29; 12:24; 13:20.

"This covenant is called the 'new,' Heb. 9:15, the 'second,' 8:7, the 'better,' 7:22. In Heb. 9:16-17, the translation is much disputed. There does not seem to be any sufficient reason for departing in these verses from the word used everywhere else. The English word 'Testament' is taken from the titles prefixed to the Latin Versions."

Shed *see Matthew 23:35.*

Remission *aphesis* (859), "a dismissal, release" (from *aphiemi*), is used of the forgiveness of sins and translated "remission" in **Matt. 26:28**; Mark 1:4; Luke 1:77; 3:3; 24:47; Acts 2:38; 5:31 (KJV, "forgiveness"); 10:43; 13:38, RV (KJV, "forgiveness"); 26:18 (ditto); Heb. 9:22; 10:18.

26:29 But I say unto you, I will not drink henceforth of this fruit of the vine, until that day when I drink it new with you in my Father's kingdom.

Fruit *genema* (1096), from *ginomai*, "to come into being," denotes "fruit" (a) as the produce of the earth, e.g., the vine; in the following the best mss. have this noun, **Matt. 26:29**; Mark 14:25; Luke 22:18; [12:18 in some mss.,]; (b) metaphorically, as "the fruits of ... righteousness" (i.e., of material ministrations to the needy), 2 Cor. 9:10.

Vine *ampelos* (288), is used (a) lit., e.g., **Matt. 26:29** and parallel passages; Jas. 3:12; (b) figuratively, (1) of Christ, John 15:1, 4, 5; (2) of His enemies, Rev. 14:18, 19, "the vine of the earth" (RV, "vintage" in v. 19), probably figurative of the remaining mass of apostate Christendom.

New *see Matthew 9:17.*

Kingdom *see* Kingdoms at *Matthew 4:8.*

26:30 And when they had sung an hymn, they went out into the mount of Olives.

*"Here, O my Lord,
I see thee face
to face;
Here would I touch
and handle things
unseen,
Here grasp with
firmer hand
th'eternal grace,
And all my
weariness upon
thee lean."*

HORATIUS BONAR

Hymn *humneo* (5214), is used (a) transitively, **Matt. 26:30**; Mark 14:26, where the "hymn" was that part of the Hallel consisting of Psalms 113-118; (b) intransitively, where the verb itself is rendered "to sing praises" or "praise," Acts 16:25; Heb. 2:12. The Psalms are called, in general, "hymns," by Philo; Josephus calls them "songs and hymns."

Olives *see Matthew 21:1.*

26:31 Then saith Jesus unto them, All ye shall be offended because of me this night: for it is written, I will smite the shepherd, and the sheep of the flock shall be scattered abroad.

Offended *see Matthew 13:57.*

Smite *patasso* (3960), "to strike, smite," is used (I) literally, of giving a blow with the hand, or fist or a weapon, **Matt. 26:51**, RV, "smote" (KJV, "struck"); Luke 22:49, 50; Acts 7:24; 12:7; (II) metaphorically, (a) of judgment meted out to Christ, **Matt. 26:31**; Mark 14:27; (b) of the infliction of disease, by an angel, Acts 12:23; of plagues to be inflicted upon men by two divinely appointed witnesses, Rev. 11:6; (c) of judgment to be executed by Christ upon the nations, Rev. 19:15, the instrument being His Word, described as a sword.

Shepherd *see Matthew 9:36.*

Sheep *see Matthew 7:15.*

Flock *poimne* (4167), akin to *poimen*, "a shepherd," denotes "a flock" (properly, of sheep), **Matt. 26:31**; Luke 2:8; 1 Cor. 9:7; metaphorically, of Christ's followers, John 10:16, RV, for the erroneous KJV, "fold." What characterizes Christ's sheep is listening to His voice, and the "flock" must be one as He is one.

Scattered *see* Strawed at *Matthew 25:24.*

26:32 But after I am risen again, I will go before you into Galilee.

Risen *see* Raise at *Matthew 10:8.*

26:33 Peter answered and said unto him, Though all *men* shall be offended because of thee, *yet* will I never be offended.

Offended *see Matthew 13:57.*

26:34 Jesus said unto him, Verily I say unto thee, That this night, before the cock crow, thou shalt deny me thrice.

Before *see Matthew 1:18.*

Cock *alektor* (220), "a cock," perhaps connected with a Hebrew phrase for the oncoming of the light, is found in the passages concerning Peter's denial of the Lord, **Matt. 26:34, 74-75**; Mark 14:30, 68, 72; Luke 22:34, 60-61; John 13:38; 18:27.

Crow *phoneo* (5455), "to utter a loud sound or cry," whether of animals, e.g., **Matt. 26:34**; or persons, Luke 8:8; 16:24; this is the word which Luke uses to describe the "cry" of the Lord at the close of His sufferings on the cross, Luke 23:46 (see under *anaboao* and *krazo*, above); also, e.g., Acts 16:28; Rev. 14:18. *See also* **Called** at *Matthew 20:32.*

Deny *see Matthew 16:24.*

Thrice *tris* (5151), occurs in **Matt. 26:34, 75** and parallel passages; in Acts 10:16 and 11:10, preceded by *epi*, "up to"; 2 Cor. 11:25 (twice); 12:8.

26:35 Peter said unto him, Though I should die with thee, yet will I not deny thee. Likewise also said all the disciples.

Though *see* Even at *Matthew 5:46.*

Should *see* Must at *Matthew 17:10.*

Likewise *see Matthew 22:26.*

26:36 Then cometh Jesus with them unto a place called Gethsemane, and saith unto the disciples, Sit ye here, while I go and pray yonder.

Place *chorion* (5564), "a region" (a diminutive of *chora*, "a land, country"), is used of Gethsemane, **Matt. 26:36**; Mark 14:32.

Called *see Matthew 1:16.*

Sit *see* Set at *Matthew 5:1.*

Here *autou* (847), the genitive case of *autos*, "self," signifies "just here" in **Matt. 26:36**.

Yonder *see Matthew 17:20.*

26:37 And he took with him Peter and the two sons of Zebedee, and began to be sorrowful and very heavy.

Heavy *ademoneo* (85), "to be troubled, much distressed," is used of the Lord's sorrow in Gethsemane, **Matt. 26:37**; Mark 14:33, KJV, "to be very heavy," RV, "to be sore troubled"; of Epaphroditus, because the saints at Philippi had received news of his sickness, Phil. 2:26, KJV, "was full of heaviness," RV, "was sore troubled.

26:38 Then saith he unto them, My soul is exceeding sorrowful, even unto death: tarry ye here, and watch with me.

Soul *see* Life at *Matthew 2:20.*

Sorrowful *perilupos* (4036), "very sad, deeply grieved" (*peri*, intensive), is used in **Matt. 26:38** and Mark 14:34, "exceeding sorrowful"; Mark 6:26; Luke 18:23 (v. 24 in some mss.).

Tarry *meno* (3306), "to abide," is translated by the verb "to abide," in the RV, for KJV, "to tarry," in **Matt. 26:38**; Mark 14:34; Luke 24:29; John 4:40; Acts 9:43; 18:20; the RV retains the verb "to tarry" in John 21:22, 23; in Acts 20:5, KJV, "tarried" (RV, "were waiting"). Some mss. have it in Acts 20:15 (KJV, "tarried").

Watch *see* Watched at *Matthew 24:43.*

26:39 And he went a little further, and fell on his face, and prayed, saying, O my Father, if it be possible, let this cup pass from me: nevertheless not as I will, but as thou *wilt*.

Went *proerchomai* (4281), "to go before, precede, go forward or farther" (*pro*, "before"), is used of (a) place, e.g., **Matt. 26:39**; Acts 12:10, "passed on through"; (b) time, Luke 1:17; Acts 20:5, 13; 2 Cor. 9:5.

Little *mikron* (3397), is used adverbially (a) of distance, **Matt. 26:39**; Mark 14:35; (b) of quantity, 2 Cor. 11:1, 16; (c) of time, **Matt. 26:73**, "a while"; Mark 14:70; John 13:33, "a little while", 14:19; 16:16-9; Heb. 10:37, with the repeated *hoson*, "how very," lit., "a little while, how little, how little."

Possible *see Matthew 19:26.*

Cup *see Matthew 10:42.*

Pass *see Matthew 5:18.*

26:40 And he cometh unto the disciples, and findeth them asleep, and saith unto Peter, What, could ye not watch with me one hour?

What *see Matthew 21:23.*

Watch *see* Watched at *Matthew 24:43.*

Hour *see Matthew 8:13.*

26:41 Watch and pray, that ye enter not into temptation: the spirit indeed *is* willing, but the flesh *is* weak.

Watch *see* Watched at *Matthew 24:43.*

Temptation *see Matthew 6:13.*

Spirit *see Matthew 4:1.*

Indeed *see Matthew 3:11.*

Willing *prothumos* (4289), "predisposed, willing" (akin to *prothumia*), is translated "ready" in Rom. 1:15, expressive of willingness, eagerness: in Mark 14.38, RV, "willing" (KJV, "ready"); in **Matt. 26:41**. "willing."

Flesh *see Matthew 19:5.*

Weak *asthenes* (772), lit., "strengthless", is translated "weak," (a) of physical "weakness," **Matt. 26:41**; Mark 14:38; 1 Cor. 1:27; 4:10; 11:30 (a judgment upon spiritual laxity in a church); 2 Cor. 10:10; 1 Pet. 3:7 (comparative degree); (b) in the spiritual sense, said of the rudiments of Jewish religion, in their inability to justify anyone, Gal. 4:9; of the Law, Heb. 7:18; in Rom. 5:6, RV, "weak" (KJV, "without strength"), of the inability of man to accomplish his salvation; (c) morally or ethically, 1 Cor. 8:7, 10; 9:22; (d) rhetorically, of God's actions according to the human estimate, 1 Cor. 1:25, "weakness," lit., "the weak things of God."

26:42 He went away again the second time, and prayed, saying, O my Father, if this cup may not pass away from me, except I drink it, thy will be done.

May *see* Might at *Matthew 26:9.*

Pass *see Matthew 5:18.*

26:43 And he came and found them asleep again: for their eyes were heavy.

Heavy *bareo* (916), is used of the effect of drowsiness, "were heavy," **Matt. 26:43**; Mark 14:40; Luke 9:32; of the effects of gluttony, Luke 21:34 ("overcharged"); of the believer's present physical state in the body, 2 Cor. 5:4; of persecution, 2 Cor. 1:8; of a charge upon material resources, 1 Tim. 5:16 (RV).

26:44 And he left them, and went away again, and prayed the third time, saying the same words.

Third *see* Three at *Matthew 12:40.*

26:45 Then cometh he to his disciples, and saith unto them, Sleep on now, and take *your* rest: behold, the hour is at hand, and the Son of man is betrayed into the hands of sinners.

Rest *see Matthew 11:28.*

Hour *see Matthew 8:13.*

26:46 Rise, let us be going: behold, he is at hand that doth betray me.

Going *ago* (71), "to bring, lead," is used intransitively, signifying "let us go" (as if to say, "let us be leading on," with the point of departure especially in view), **Matt. 26:46**; Mark 1:38; 14:42; John 11:7, 15, 16; 14:31.

26:47 And while he yet spake, lo, Judas, one of the twelve, came, and with him a great multitude with swords and staves, from the chief priests and elders of the people.

Swords *see* Sword at *Matthew 10:34.*

Staves *xulon* (3586), "wood," then, "anything made of wood," e.g., "a cudgel" or "staff," is rendered "staves" in **Matt. 26:47, 55** and parallel passages.

Elders *see Matthew 15:2.*

26:48 Now he that betrayed him gave them a sign, saying, Whomsoever I shall kiss, that same is he: hold him fast.

Sign *see Matthew 12:38.*

Kiss *phileo* (5368), "to love," signifies "to kiss," in **Matt. 26:48**; Mark 14:44; Luke 22:47.

Hold *see Matthew 12:11.*

26:49 And forthwith he came to Jesus, and said, Hail, master; and kissed him.

Forthwith *see Matthew 13:5.*

Hail *chairo* (5463), "to rejoice," is used in the imperative mood, (a) as a salutation, only in the Gospels; in this respect it is rendered simply "hail," in mockery of Christ, **Matt. 26:49; 27:29**; Mark 15:18; John 19:3; (b) as a greeting, by the angel Gabriel to Mary, Luke 1:28, and, in the plural, by the Lord to the disciples after His resurrection, **Matt. 28:9**.

Master *see* Lord at *Matthew 17:4. See also* Rabbi at *Matthew 23:7.*

Kissed *kataphileo* (2705), denotes "to kiss fervently"; the stronger force of this verb has been called in question, but the change from *phileo* to *kataphileo* in **Matt. 26:49** and Mark 14:45 can scarcely be without significance, and the act of the traitor was almost certainly more demonstrative than the simple kiss of salutation. So with the kiss of genuine devotion, Luke 7:38, 45; 15:20; Acts 20:37, in each of which this verb is used.

26:50 And Jesus said unto him, Friend, wherefore art thou come? Then came they, and laid hands on Jesus, and took him.

Friend *see* Fellows at *Matthew 11:16.*

Wherefore In **Matt. 26:50**, *epi*, "unto," with *ho*, "which" (the accusative neuter of *hos*), 2 Thess. 1:11, KJV (RV, "to which end").

Come *pareimi* (3918), signifies (a) "to be by, at hand or present," of persons, e.g., Luke 13:1; Acts 10:33; 24:19; 1 Cor. 5:3; 2 Cor. 10:2, 11; Gal. 4:18, 20; of things, John 7:6, of a particular season in the Lord's life on earth, "is (not yet) come," or "is not yet at hand"; Heb. 12:11, of chastening "(for the) present" (the neuter of the present participle, used as a noun); in 13:5 "such things as ye have" is, lit., "the things that are present"; 2 Pet. 1:12, of the truth "(which) is with (you)" (not as KJV, "the present truth," as if of special doctrines applicable to a particular time); in v. 9 "he that lacketh" is lit., "to whom are not present"; (b) "to have arrived or come," **Matt. 26:50**, "thou art come," RV; John 11:28; Acts 10:21; Col. 1:6.

26:51 And, behold, one of them which were with Jesus stretched out *his* hand, and drew his sword, and struck a servant of the high priest's, and smote off his ear.

Stretched *see* Put forth at *Matthew 8:3.*

Drew *apospao* (645), "to draw away," lit., "to wrench away from," is used of a sword, **Matt. 26:51**, of "drawing" away disciples into error, Acts 20:30; of Christ's "withdrawal" from the disciples, in Gethsemane, Luke 22:41, KJV, "was withdrawn," RV, "was parted" (or "was reft away from them"); of "parting" from a company, Acts 21:1 (KJV, "were gotten," RV, "were parted").

Sword *see Matthew 10:34.*

Struck *see* Smite at *Matthew 26:31.*

Smote *aphaireo* (851), "to take away, remove," is translated "cut off" in Mark 14:47, KJV, and Luke 22:50, and "smote off" in **Matt. 26:51**; RV, "struck off" in each place.

Ear *otion* (5621), a diminutive, but without the diminutive force, it being a common tendency in everyday speech to apply a diminutive form to most parts of the body, is used in **Matt. 26:51**; Mark 14:47 (in some mss.); Luke 22:51; John 18:10 (in some mss.) and v. 26, all with reference to the "ear" of Malchus.

26:52 Then said Jesus unto him, Put up again thy sword into his place: for all they that take the sword shall perish with the sword.

Put *apostrepho* (654), "to turn away, remove, return," is used of "putting" up again a sword into its sheath, **Matt. 26:52**. *See also* Turn at *Matthew 5:42*.

Sword *see Matthew 10:34*.

Place *topos* (5117), (Eng., "topic," "topography," etc.) is used of "a region" or "locality," frequently in the Gospels and Acts, in Luke 2:7 and 14:22, "room"; of a place which a person or thing occupies, a couch at table, e.g., Luke 14:9, 10, RV, "place" (KJV, "room"); of the destiny of Judas Iscariot, Acts 1:25; of the condition of the "unlearned" or nongifted in a church gathering, 1 Cor. 14:16, RV, "place"; the sheath of a sword, **Matt. 26:52**; a place in a book, Luke 4:17; see also Rev. 2:5; 6:14; 12:8; metaphorically, of "condition, occasion, opportunity" Acts 25:16, RV, "opportunity" (KJV, "license"); Rom. 12:19; Eph. 4:27.

26:53 Thinkest thou that I cannot now pray to my Father, and he shall presently give me more than twelve legions of angels?

Now *see Matthew 3:15*.

Pray *parakaleo*, "to call to one's aid," is rendered by the verb "to pray" in the KJV in the following: **Matt. 26:53** (RV, "beseech"); so Mark 5:17, 18; Acts 16:9; in 24:4, RV, "intreat"; in 27:34, RV, "beseech."

Give For *paristemi*, "to place by," rendered "give" in **Matt. 26:53**, KJV (RV, "send").

More *see* Exceed at *Matthew 5:20*.

Legions *legion* (3003), otherwise spelled *legeon*, "a legion," occurs in **Matt. 26:53**, of angels; in Mark 5:9, 15, and Luke 8:30, of demons. Among the Romans a "legion" was primarily a chosen (*lego*, "to choose") body of soldiers divided into ten cohorts, and numbering from 4,200 to 6,000 men (Gk. *speira*). In the time of our Lord it formed a complete army of infantry and cavalry, of upwards of 5,000 men. The "legions" were not brought into Judea till the outbreak of the Jewish war (AD 66), as they were previously employed in the frontier provinces of the Empire. Accordingly in its NT use the word has its other and more general significance "of a large number."

26:54 But how then shall the scriptures be fulfilled, that thus it must be?

Fulfilled *see Matthew 1:22*.

Must *see Matthew 17:10*.

26:55 In that same hour said Jesus to the multitudes, Are ye come out as against a thief with swords and staves for to take me? I sat daily with you teaching in the temple, and ye laid no hold on me.

Thief *see* Thieves at *Matthew 21:13*.

Staves *see Matthew 26:47*.

Take *sullambano* (4815), "to seize, take," is rendered "to take" in **Matt. 26:55** and Mark 14:48, KJV (RV, "seize"); Luke 5:9; Acts 1:16; in 12:3 and 23:27, KJV (RV, "seize").

Sat *kathezomai* (2516), "to sit (down)," is used in **Matt. 26:55**; Luke 2:46; John 4:6; 11:20; 20:12; Acts 6:15.

Hold *see Matthew 12:11*.

26:56 But all this was done, that the scriptures of the prophets might be fulfilled. Then all the disciples forsook him, and fled.

Fulfilled *see Matthew 1:22*.

Forsook *see* Leaveth at *Matthew 4:11*.

26:57 And they that had laid hold on Jesus led *him* away to Caiaphas the high priest, where the scribes and the elders were assembled.

Led *see* Leadeth at *Matthew 7:13*.

26:58 But Peter followed him afar off unto the high priest's palace, and went in, and sat with the servants, to see the end.

Afar *makrothen* (3113), also from *makros*, signifies "afar off, from far," **Matt. 26:58**; **27:55**, etc. It is used with *apo*, "from," in Mark 5:6; 14:54; 15:40, etc.; outside the Synoptists, three times, Rev. 18:10, 15, 17.

Palace *see Matthew 26:3*.

Servants *huperetes* (5257), is translated "servants" in the KJV of **Matt. 26:58**; Mark 14:65 (RV, "officers"); in John 18:36, KJV and RV (RV, marg., "officers"). *See also* **Officer** at *Matthew 5:25*.

End *telos* (5056), signifies (a) "the limit," either at which a person or thing ceases to be what he or it was up to that point, or at which previous activities were ceased, 2 Cor. 3:13; 1 Pet. 4:7; (b) "the final issue or result" of a state or process, e.g., Luke 1:33; in Rom. 10:4, Christ is described as "the end of the Law unto righteousness to everyone that believeth"; this is best explained by Gal. 3:23-26; cf. Jas. 5:11; the following more especially point to the issue or fate of a thing, **Matt. 26:58**; Rom. 6:21; 2 Cor. 11:15; Phil. 3:19; Heb. 6:8; 1 Pet. 1:9; (c) "a fulfillment," Luke 22:37, KJV, "(have) an end"; (d) "the utmost degree" of an act, as of the love of Christ towards His disciples, John 13:1; (e) "the aim or purpose" of a thing, 1 Tim. 1:5; (f) "the last" in a succession or series Rev. 1:8 (KJV, only, "ending"); 21:6; 22:13.

26:59 Now the chief priests, and elders, and all the council, sought false witness against Jesus, to put him to death;

Witness *see Matthew 15:19.*

Death *see Matthew 10:21.*

26:60 But found none: yea, though many false witnesses came, *yet* found they none. At the last came two false witnesses,

At the last *see* Afterward at *Matthew 4:2.*

False witnesses *pseudomartus* or *-tur* (5571 and 3144) denotes "a false witness," **Matt. 26:60**; 1 Cor. 15:15.

26:61 And said, This *fellow* said, I am able to destroy the temple of God, and to build it in three days.

Said *see Matthew 13:29.*

Destroy *see Matthew 5:17.*

26:62 And the high priest arose, and said unto him, Answerest thou nothing? what *is it which* these witness against thee?

Arose *see* Rise at *Matthew 12:41.*

Witness *katamartureo* (2649), denotes "to witness against" (*kata*), **Matt. 26:62; 27:13**; Mark 14:60 (in some mss., 15:4, for *kategoreo*, "to accuse," RV).

26:63 But Jesus held his peace. And the high priest answered and said unto him, I adjure thee by the living God, that thou tell us whether thou be the Christ, the Son of God.

Peace *see Matthew 20:31.*

Adjure *exorkizo* (1844), an intensive form, signifies "to appeal by an oath, to adjure," **Matt. 26:63**. In the Sept., Gen. 24:3; Judg. 17:2; 1 Kings 22:16.

26:64 Jesus saith unto him, Thou hast said: nevertheless I say unto you, Hereafter shall ye see the Son of man sitting on the right hand of power, and coming in the clouds of heaven.

Thou *see Matthew 2:6.*

Hereafter Positively, "henceforth" stands for the following: (a) *ap' arti* (i.e., *apo arti*), lit., "from now," e.g., **Matt. 26:64**; Luke 22:69; John 13:19, RV, and KJV marg., "from henceforth"; Rev. 14:13 (where *aparti* is found as one word in the best mss.); (b) *to loipon*, lit., "(for) the remaining (time)," Heb. 10:13; *tou loipou*, Gal. 6:17; (c) *apo tou nun*, lit., "from the now," e.g., Luke 1:48; 5:10; 12:52; Acts 18:6; 2 Cor. 5:16 (1st part).

Sitting *see* Sat at *Matthew 4:16.*

Right *see Matthew 5:29.*

Power *dunamis* (1411), is sometimes used, by metonymy, of persons and things, e.g., (a) of God, **Matt. 26:64**; Mark 14:62; (b) of angels, e.g., perhaps in Eph. 1:21, RV, "power," KJV, "might" (cf. Rom. 8:38; 1 Pet. 3:22); (c) of that which manifests God's "power": Christ, 1 Cor. 1:24; the gospel, Rom. 1:16; (d) of mighty works (RV, marg., "power" or "powers"), e.g., Mark 6:5, "mighty work"; so 9:39, RV (KJV, "miracle"); Acts 2:22 (ditto); 8:13, "miracles"; 2 Cor. 12:12, RV, "mighty works" (KJV, "mighty deeds").

Clouds *see* Cloud at *Matthew 17:5.*

26:65 Then the high priest rent his clothes, saying, He hath spoken blasphemy; what further need have we of witnesses? behold, now ye have heard his blasphemy.

Rent *diarrhesso*, or *diaresso* (1284), a late form of *diarrhegnumi*, "to break asunder, rend", is used of "rending" one's garments, **Matt. 26:65**; Mark 14:63; Acts 14:14.

Clothes *see* Raiment at *Matthew 17:2.*

Blasphemy *see* Blasphemeth at *Matthew 9:3.*

Further *see* Yet at *Matthew 12:46.*

Witnesses *see Matthew 18:16.*

26:66 What think ye? They answered and said, He is guilty of death.

Guilty *enochos* (1777), "held in, bound by," is translated "worthy (of death)" in **Matt. 26:66** and Mark 14:64, RV (marg., "liable to"; KJV, "guilty").

Death *see* Danger at *Matthew 5:21.*

26:67 Then did they spit in his face, and buffeted him; and others smote *him* with the palms of their hands,

Spit *emptuo* (1716), "to spit upon," occurs in **Matt. 26:67; 27:30**; Mark 10:34; 14:65; 15:19; Luke 18:32. In the Sept., Num. 12:14, in some texts; Deut. 25:9.

Face *see* Faces at *Matthew 6:16.*

Buffeted *kolaphizo* (2852), signifies "to strike with clenched hands, to buffet with the fist" (*kolaphos*, "a fist"), **Matt. 26:67**; Mark 14:65; 1 Cor. 4:11; 2 Cor. 12:7; 1 Pet. 2:20.

Smote *see* Smite at *Matthew 5:39.*

26:68 Saying, Prophesy unto us, thou Christ, Who is he that smote thee?

Prophesy *see* Prophecy at *Matthew 13:14.*

Smote *paio* (3817), signifies "to strike or smite" (a) with the hand or fist,

Matt. 26:68; Luke 22:64; (b) with a sword, Mark 14:47; John 18:10, KJV (RV, "struck"); (c) with a sting, Rev. 9:5, "striketh."

26:69 Now Peter sat without in the palace: and a damsel came unto him, saying, Thou also wast with Jesus of Galilee.

Palace *see Matthew 26:3.*

Damsel *paidiske* (3814), a diminutive, is translated "maid," "maids," in the KJV and RV in Mark 14:66, 69; Luke 22:56, in the RV (KJV, "damsel"), in Matt. 26:69; John 18:17; Acts 12:13; 16:16; in Luke 12:45, "maidservants" (KJV "maidens"); in Gal. 4:22, 23, 30, 31, RV, "handmaid" (KJV, "bondmaid" or "bondwoman").

26:70-71 But he denied before *them* all, saying, I know not what thou sayest.

And when he was gone out into the porch, another *maid* saw him, and said unto them that were there, This *fellow* was also with Jesus of Nazareth.

Porch *pulon* (440), akin to *pule*, "a gate" (Eng., "pylon"), is used of "a doorway, porch or vestibule" of a house or palace, Matt. 26:71. In the parallel passage Mark 14:68, *proaulion* is used, and *pulon* doubtless stands in Matt. 26 for *proaulion.*

26:72 And again he denied with an oath, I do not know the man.

Oath *see* Oaths at *Matthew 5:33.*

26:73 And after a while came unto *him* they that stood by, and said to Peter, Surely thou also art *one* of them; for thy speech bewrayeth thee.

Little *see Matthew 26:39.*

Surely In the KJV of Matt. 26:73; Mark 14:70; John 17:8, *alethos*, "truly," is rendered "surely" (RV, "of a truth"); so *pantos*, "at all events, altogether," in Luke 4:23 (RV, "doubtless"), and *nai*, "yea," in Rev. 22:20 (RV, "yea"). *See also* Of a truth at *Matthew 14:33.*

Speech *lalia* (2981), akin to *laleo*, denotes "talk, speech," (a) of "a dialect," Matt. 26:73; Mark 14:70; (b) "utterances," John 4:42, RV, "speaking" (KJV, "saying"); 8:43.

Bewrayeth *delos* (1212), properly signifying "visible, clear to the mind, evident," is translated "evident" in Gal. 3:11 and 1 Cor. 15:27, RV (KJV, "manifest"); "bewrayeth," Matt. 26:73; "certain," 1 Tim. 6:7, KJV. The word "bewrayeth," Matt. 26:73, is a translation of *poieo*, "to make," with *delos*, "manifest, evident"; lit., "maketh thee manifest."

26:74 Then began he to curse and to swear, *saying*, I know not the man. And immediately the cock crew.

Curse *katanathematizo* (2653), a strengthened form, denotes "to utter curses against," Matt. 26:74; cf. Mark's word concerning the same occasion.

Swear *see Matthew 5:34.*

Cock *see Matthew 26:34.*

26:75 And Peter remembered the word of Jesus, which said unto him, Before the cock crow, thou shalt deny me thrice. And he went out, and wept bitterly.

Word *see Matthew 12:36.*

Before *see Matthew 1:18.*

Deny *see Matthew 16:24.*

Thrice *see Matthew 26:34.*

Bitterly *pikros* (4090), "bitterly," is used of the poignant grief of Peter's weeping for his denial of Christ, Matt. 26:75; Luke 22:62.

Chapter 27

27:1 When the morning was come, all the chief priests and elders of the people took counsel against Jesus to put him to death:

Morning *see Matthew 21:18.*

Death *see Matthew 10:21.*

27:2 And when they had bound him, they led *him* away, and delivered him to Pontius Pilate the governor.

Led *see* Leadeth at *Matthew 7:13.*

Governor *see Matthew 2:6.*

27:3 Then Judas, which had betrayed him, when he saw that he was condemned, repented himself, and brought again the thirty pieces of silver to the chief priests and elders,

Repented *see Matthew 21:29. See also* Turn at *Matthew 5:39.*

Brought *apostrepho* (654), "to turn, or put, back," is translated "brought back" in Matt. 27:3.

Pieces *see Matthew 26:15.*

27:4 Saying, I have sinned in that I have betrayed the innocent blood. And they said, What *is that* to us? see thou *to that*.

Sinned *see* Trespass at *Matthew 18:15.*

Innocent *athoos* (121), primarily denotes "unpunished" (*a*, negative, *thoe*, "a penalty"); then, "innocent," Matt. 27:4, "innocent blood," i.e., the blood of an "innocent" person, the word "blood" being used both by synecdoche (a part standing for the whole), and by metonymy (one thing standing for another), i.e., for death by execution (some mss. have *dikaion*, "righteous");

v. 24, where Pilate speaks of himself as "innocent."

See *horao* (3708), "to see", has the meaning of "seeing to" or "caring for a thing" in **Matt. 27:4**, "see (thou to it);" in Acts 18:15, "look to it (yourselves)"; the future (sing. *opsei*, plural, *opsesthe*), is used for the tense which is wanting in *horao*, and stands for the imperative.

27:5 And he cast down the pieces of silver in the temple, and departed, and went and hanged himself.

Cast *see* Scattered at *Matthew 9:36*.

Departed *see Matthew 2:12*.

Hanged *apancho* (519), signifies "to strangle"; in the middle voice, to "hang" oneself, **Matt. 27:5**. In the Sept., it is said of Ahithophel (2 Sam. 17:23).

27:6 And the chief priests took the silver pieces, and said, It is not lawful for to put them into the treasury, because it is the price of blood.

Put *see Matthew 9:17*.

Treasury *korbanas* (2878), signifying "the place of gifts," denoted the Temple "treasury," **Matt. 27:6**.

Price *time* (5092), denotes "a valuing," hence, objectively, (a) "price paid or received," **Matt. 27:6, 9**; Acts 4:34 (plural); 5:2, 3; 7:16, RV, "price (in silver)," KJV, "sum (of money)"; 19:19 (plural); 1 Cor. 6:20; 7:23; (b) "value, honor, preciousness."

27:7 And they took counsel, and bought with them the potter's field, to bury strangers in.

Potter *kerameus* (2763), "a potter" (from *kerannumi*, "to mix," akin to *keramos*, "potter's clay"), is used (a) in connection with the "potter's field," **Matt. 27:7, 10**; (b) illustratively of the "potter's" right over the clay, Rom. 9:21, where the introductory "or" suggests the alternatives that either there must be a recognition of the absolute discretion and power of God, or a denial that the "potter" has power over the clay. There is no suggestion of the creation of sinful beings, or of the creation of any simply in order to punish them. What the passage sets forth is God's right to deal with sinful beings according to His own counsel.

Bury *taphe* (5027), "a burial" (cf. Eng., "epitaph"), is found in **Matt. 27:7**, with *eis*, "unto," lit. "with a view to a buriai (place) for strangers."

Strangers *see* Stranger at *Matthew 25:35*.

27:8 Wherefore that field was called, The field of blood, unto this day.

Wherefore *dio* = *dia ho* (the neuter of the relative pronoun *hos*), "on account of which (thing)," e.g., **Matt. 27:8**; Acts 15:19; 20:31; 24:26; 25:26; 27:25, 34; Rom. 1:24; 15:7; 1 Cor. 12:3; 2 Cor. 2:8; 5:9; 6:17; Eph. 2:11; 3:13; 4:8, 25; 5:14; Phil. 2:9; 1 Thess. 5:11; Philem. 8; Heb. 3:7, 10; 10:5; 11:16; 12:12, 28; 13:12; Jas. 1:21; 4:6; 1 Pet. 1:13; 2 Pet. 1:10, 12; 3:14.

27:9 Then was fulfilled that which was spoken by Jeremy the prophet, saying, And they took the thirty pieces of silver, the price of him that was valued, whom they of the children of Israel did value;

Fulfilled *see Matthew 1:22*.

Spoken *see Matthew 1:22*.

Valued, Value *timao* (5091), "to fix the value, to price," is translated "was priced" and "did price" in the RV of **Matt. 27:9** (KJV, "was valued" and "did value"). *See also* Price at *Matthew 27:6*.

Children *see* Foal at *Matthew 21:5*.

27:10 And gave them for the potter's field, as the Lord appointed me.

Potter *see Matthew 27:7*.

Appointed *see Matthew 26:19*.

27:11 And Jesus stood before the governor: and the governor asked him, saying, Art thou the King of the Jews? And Jesus said unto him, Thou sayest.

King *see Matthew 1:6*.

27:12-13 And when he was accused of the chief priests and elders, he answered nothing.
Then said Pilate unto him, Hearest thou not how many things they witness against thee?

Many *see Matthew 15:34*.

Witness *see Matthew 26:62*.

27:14 And he answered him to never a word; insomuch that the governor marvelled greatly.

Word *see Matthew 12:36*.

Insomuch that *see Matthew 8:24*.

Greatly *lian* (3029), "very, exceedingly," is rendered "greatly" in **Matt. 27:14**, of wonder 2 Tim. 4:15, of opposition; 2 John 4 and 3 John 3, of joy.

27:15 Now at *that* feast the governor was wont to release unto the people a prisoner, whom they would.

Wont *etho* (1486), "to be accustomed," is used in the pluperfect tense (with imperfect meaning), *eiotha*, rendered "was wont" in **Matt. 27:15**; Mark 10:1.

Release *see* Loosed at *Matthew 18:27.*

Prisoner *desmios* (1198), an adjective, primarily denotes "binding, bound," then, as a noun, "the person bound, a captive, prisoner" (akin to *deo*, "to bind"), **Matt. 27:15, 16**; Mark 15:6; Acts 16:25, 27; 23:18; 25:14, RV (KJV, "in bonds"), 27; 28:16, 17; Eph. 3:1; 4:1; 2 Tim. 1:8; Philem. 1, 9; in Heb. 10:34 and 13:3, "in bonds."

27:16 And they had then a notable prisoner, called Barabbas.

Notable *episemos* (1978), primarily meant "bearing a mark," e.g., of money "stamped, coined," (from *epi*, "upon," and *sema*, "a mark, a sign"; cf. *semaino*, "to give a sign, signify, indicate," and *semeioo*, "to note"); it is used in the NT, metaphorically, (a) in a good sense, Rom. 16:7, "of note, illustrious," said of Andronicus and Junias; (b) in a bad sense, **Matt. 27:16**, "notable," of the prisoner Barabbas. In the Sept., Gen. 30:42; Esth. 5:4; 8:13, toward the end of the verse, "a distinct (day)."

Prisoner *see Matthew 27:15.*

27:17 Therefore when they were gathered together, Pilate said unto them, Whom will ye that I release unto you? Barabbas, or Jesus which is called Christ?

Release *see* Loosed at *Matthew 18:27.*

27:18 For he knew that for envy they had delivered him.

Envy *phthonos* (5355), "envy," is the feeling of displeasure produced by witnessing or hearing of the advantage or prosperity of others; this evil sense always attaches to this word, **Matt. 27:18**; Mark 15:10; Rom. 1:29; Gal. 5:21; Phil. 1:15; 1 Tim. 6:4; Titus 3:3; 1 Pet. 2:1; so in Jas. 4:5, where the question is rhetorical and strongly remonstrative, signifying that the Spirit (or spirit) which God made to dwell in us was certainly not so bestowed that we should be guilty of "envy."

27:19 When he was set down on the judgment seat, his wife sent unto him, saying, Have thou nothing to do with that just man: for I have suffered many things this day in a dream because of him.

Set In **Matt. 27:19**, KJV, *kathemai*, "to sit," is rendered "he was set down" (RV, "he was sitting").

Judgment seat *bema* (968), primarily, "a step, a pace" (akin to *baino*, "to go"), as in Acts 7:5, translated "to set (his foot) on," lit., "footroom," was used to denote a raised place or platform, reached by steps, originally that at Athens in the Pnyx Hill, where was the place of assembly; from the platform orations were made. The word became used for a tribune, two of which were provided in the law courts of Greece, one for the accuser and one for the defendant; it was applied to the tribunal of a Roman magistrate or ruler, **Matt. 27:19**; John 19:13; Acts 12:21, translated "throne"; 18:12, 16, 17; 25:6, 10, 17. In two passages the word is used of the divine tribunal before which all believers are hereafter to stand. In Rom. 14:10 it is called "The judgement seat of God," RV (KJV, "of Christ"), according to the most authentic mss. The same tribunal is called "the judgment seat of Christ," 2 Cor. 5:10, to whom the Father has given all judgment, John 5:22, 27. At this *bema* believers are to be made manifest, that each may "receive the things done in (or through) the body," according to what he has done, "whether it be good or bad." There they will receive rewards for their faithfulness to the Lord. For all that has been contrary in their lives to His will they will suffer loss, 1 Cor. 3:15. This judgment seat is to be distinguished from the premillennial, earthly throne of Christ, **Matt. 25:31**, and the postmillennial "Great White Throne," Rev. 20:11, at which only "the dead" will appear. The judgment seat of Christ will be a tribunal held "in His Parousia," i.e., His presence with His saints after His return to receive them to Himself.

Have *see Matthew 8:29.*

Nothing *meden* (3367), the neuter of *medeis*, "no one," is found, not in direct negative statements, but in warnings, prohibitions, etc., e.g., **Matt. 27:19**; Acts 19:36; in expressions conveying certain impossibilities, e.g., Acts 4:21; comparisons, e.g., 2 Cor. 6:10; intimating a supposition to the contrary, 1 Tim. 6:4; adverbially, e.g., 2 Cor. 11:5, "not a whit." Westcott and Hort adopt the spelling *methen* in Acts 27:33.

Just *see Matthew 1:19.*

Suffered *see* Suffer at *Matthew 16:21.*

Dream *see Matthew 1:20.*

27:20 But the chief priests and elders persuaded the multitude that they should ask Barabbas, and destroy Jesus.

Persuaded *peitho* (3982), in the active voice, signifies "to apply persuasion, to prevail upon or win over, to persuade," bringing about a change of mind by the influence of reason or moral considerations, e.g., in **Matt. 27:20**; **28:14**; Acts 13:43; 19:8; in the passive voice, "to be persuaded, believe," e.g., Luke 16:31; 20:6; Acts 17:4, RV (KJV, "believed"); 21:14; 26:26; Rom. 8:38; 14:14; 15:14; 2 Tim. 1:5, 12; Heb. 6:9; 11:13, in some mss.; 13:18, RV (KJV, "trust").

Destroy *see Matthew 2:13.*

27:21 The governor answered and said unto them, Whether of the twain will ye that I release unto you? They said, Barabbas.

Twain *see Matthew 5:41.*

Release *see* Loosed at *Matthew 18:27.*

27:22 Pilate saith unto them, What shall I do then with Jesus which is called Christ? *They* all say unto him, Let him be crucified.

Then *see Matthew 22:43.*

27:23 And the governor said, Why, what evil hath he done? But they cried out the more, saying, Let him be crucified.

Cried *see Matthew 15:22.*

More *perissos* (4057), is found in **Matt. 27:23**, RV, "exceedingly," KJV, "the more"; Mark 10:26, RV, "exceedingly," KJV, "out of measure"; 15:14; Acts 26:11, "exceedingly."

27:24 When Pilate saw that he could prevail nothing, but *that* rather a tumult was made, he took water, and washed *his* hands before the multitude, saying, I am innocent of the blood of this just person: see ye *to it*.

Prevail *opheleo* (5623), "to benefit, do good, profit," is translated "prevailed" in **Matt. 27:24**, RV (KJV, "could prevail"), of the conclusion formed by Pilate concerning the determination of the chief priests, elders and people. The meaning of the verb with the negative is better expressed by the phrase "he would do no good"; so in John 12:19, "ye prevail (nothing)," lit., "ye are doing no good."

Nothing *see Matthew 5:13.*

Tumult *see* Uproar at *Matthew 26:5.*

Made *see Matthew 9:16.*

Washed *aponipto* (633), "to wash off," is used in the middle voice, in **Matt. 27:24**.

Before *apenanti* (561), denotes (a) "opposite," **Matt. 27:61**; (b) "in the sight of, before," **Matt. 27:24**; Acts 3:16; Rom. 3:18; (c) "against," Acts 17:7.

Innocent *see Matthew 27:4.*

Just *see Matthew 1:19.*

Person In **Matt. 27:24**, RV, *toutou*, "of this ... (man)," is translated "of this ... person" (KJV).

See *see Matthew 27:4.*

27:25 Then answered all the people, and said, His blood *be* on us, and on our children.

People *see Matthew 2:6.*

27:26 Then released he Barabbas unto them: and when he had scourged Jesus, he delivered *him* to be crucified.

Released *see* **Loosed** at *Matthew 18:27.*

Scourged *phragelloo* (5417), (akin to Latin, *flagello;* Eng., "flagellate"), is the word used in **Matt. 27:26**, and Mark 15:15, of the "scourging" endured by Christ and administered by the order of Pilate. Under the Roman method of "scourging," the person was stripped and tied in a bending posture to a pillar, or stretched on a frame. The "scourge" was made of leather thongs, weighted with sharp pieces of bone or lead, which tore the flesh of both the back and the breast (cf. Ps. 22:17). Eusebius (*Chron.*) records his having witnessed the suffering of martyrs who died under this treatment.

27:27 Then the soldiers of the governor took Jesus into the common hall, and gathered unto him the whole band *of soldiers*.

Soldiers *see Matthew 8:9.*

Take *see* Take at *Matthew 1:20.*

Hall *praitorion* (4232), is translated "common hall" in **Matt. 27:27**, KJV (RV, "palace"); "Praetorium" in Mark 15:16; "hall of judgment" or "judgment hall" in John 18:28, 33; 19:9; Acts 23:35 (RV, "palace," in each place); "praetorian guard," Phil. 1:13 (KJV, "palace"). "In the Gospels the term denotes the official residence in Jerusalem of the Roman governor, and the various translations of it in our versions arose from a desire either to indicate the special purpose for which that residence was used on the occasion in question, or to explain what particular building was intended. But whatever building the governor occupied was the Praetorium. It is most probable that in Jerusalem he resided in the well-known palace of Herod.... Pilate's residence has been identified with the castle of Antonia, which was occupied by the regular garrison. The probability is that it was the same as Herod's palace. Herod's palace in Caesarea was used as the Praetorium there, and the expression in Acts 23:35, marg., 'Herod's praetorium,' is abbreviated from 'the praetorium of Herod's palace'" (*Hastings' Bib. Dic.*).

Band *speira* (4686), primarily "anything round," and so "whatever might be wrapped round a thing, a twisted rope," came to mean "a body of men at arms," and was the equivalent of the Roman *manipulus*. It was also used for a larger body of men, a cohort, about 600 infantry, commanded by a tribune. It is confined to its military sense. See, e.g., **Matt. 27:27**, and corresponding passages.

27:28 And they stripped him, and put on him a scarlet robe.

Stripped *ekduo* (1562), "to take off, strip off," is used especially of clothes, and rendered "to strip" in **Matt. 27:28** (some mss. have *enduo*, "to clothe"), and Luke 10:30, to take off, **Matt. 27:31**; Mark 15:20; figuratively, 2 Cor. 5:4, "unclothed" (middle voice), of putting off the body at death (the believer's state of being unclothed does not refer to the body in the grave but to the spirit, which awaits the "body of glory" at the resurrection).

Put *peritithemi* (4060), "to put around or on," is so used in **Matt. 27:28**; Mark 15:17, RV, "put on" (KJV, "... about"); 15:36; John 19:29.

Scarlet *kokkinos* (2847), is derived from *kokkos*, used of the "berries" (clusters of the eggs of an insect) collected from the *ilex coccifera;* the color, however, is obtained from the cochineal insect, which attaches itself to the leaves and twigs of the coccifera oak; another species is raised on the leaves of the *cactus ficus*. The Arabic name for this insect is *qirmiz*, whence the word "crimson." It is used (a) of "scarlet" wool, Heb. 9:19; cf. in connection with the cleansing of a leper, Lev. 14:4, 6, "scarlet"; with the offering of the red heifer, Num. 19:6; (b) of the robe put on Christ by the soldiers, **Matt. 27:28**; (c) of the "beast" seen in symbolic vision in Rev. 17:3, "scarlet-colored"; (d) of the clothing of the "woman" as seen sitting on the "beast," 17:4; (e) of part of the merchandise of Babylon, 18:12; (f) figuratively, of the glory of the city itself, 18:16; the neuter is used in the last three instances.

Robe *chlamus* (5511), "a cloak," is translated "robe" in **Matt. 27:28, 31**.

27:29 And when they had platted a crown of thorns, they put *it* upon his head, and a reed in his right hand: and they bowed the knee before him, and mocked him, saying, Hail, King of the Jews!

Platted *pleko* (4120), "to weave, twist, plait," is used of the crown of thorns inflicted on Christ, **Matt. 27:29**; Mark 15:17; John 19:2.

Crown *stephanos* (4735), primarily, "that which surrounds, as a wall or crowd" (from *stepho*, "to encircle"), denotes (a) "the victor's crown," the symbol of triumph in the games or some such contest; hence, by metonymy, a reward or prize; (b) "a token of public honor" for distinguished service, military prowess, etc., or of nuptial joy, or festal gladness, especially at the parousia of kings. It was woven as a garland of oak, ivy, parsley, myrtle, or olive, or in imitation of these in gold. In some passages the reference to the games is clear, 1 Cor. 9:25; 2 Tim. 4:8 ("crown of righteousness"); it may be so in 1 Pet. 5:4, where the fadeless character of "the crown of glory" is set in contrast to the garlands of earth. In other passages it stands as an emblem of life, joy, reward and glory, Phil. 4:1; 1 Thess. 2:19; Jas. 1:12 ("crown of life "); Rev. 2:10 (ditto); 3:11; 4:4, 10: of triumph, 6:2; 9:7; 12:1; 14:14. It is used of "the crown of thorns" which the soldiers plaited and put on Christ's head, **Matt. 27:29**; Mark 15:17; John 19:2, 5. At first sight this might be taken as an alternative for *diadema*, "a kingly crown," but considering the blasphemous character of that masquerade, and the materials used, obviously *diadema* would be quite unfitting and the only alternative was *stephanos* (see Trench *Syn.* Sec.xxxii).

Thorns *see Matthew 7:16.*

Put *see Matthew 19:13.*

Reed *see Matthew 11:7.*

Bowed the knee For *gonupeteo*, "to bow the knee," **Matt. 27:29**. *See also* **Kneeling** at *Matthew 17:14.*

Mocked *see Matthew 2:16.*

Hail *see Matthew 26:49.*

King *see Matthew 1:6.*

27:30 And they spit upon him, and took the reed, and smote him on the head.

Spit *see Matthew 26:67.*

Reed *see Matthew 11:7.*

Smote *tupto* (5180), from a root *tup-*, meaning "a blow," (*tupos*, "a figure or print:" (Eng., "type") denotes "to smite, strike, or beat," usually not with the idea of giving a thrashing as with *dero*. It frequently signifies a "blow" of violence, and, when used in a continuous tense, indicates a series of "blows." In **Matt. 27:30** the imperfect tense signifies that the soldiers kept on striking Christ on the head. So Mark 15:19. The most authentic mss. omit it in Luke 22:64. In that verse the word *paio*, "to smite," is used of the treatment given to Christ (*dero* in the preceding verse). The imperfect tense of the verb is again used in

Acts 18:17, of the beating given to Sosthenes. Cf. Acts 21:32, which has the present participle. It is used in the metaphorical sense of "wounding," in 1 Cor. 8:12. *See also* **Smite** at *Matthew 5:39; 24:49.*

Head *see* **Faces** at *Matthew 6:16.*

27:31 And after that they had mocked him, they took the robe off from him, and put his own raiment on him, and led him away to crucify *him*.

Mocked *see Matthew 2:16.*

Took ... off *ekduo* (1562), "to take off a garment from a person," is so rendered with reference to the soldiers' treatment of Christ, **Matt. 27:31**; Mark 15:20. *See also* **Stripped** at *Matthew 27:28.*

Robe *see Matthew 27:28.*

Put *see Matthew 6:25.*

Raiment *see Matthew 17:2.*

Led *see* **Leadeth** at *Matthew 7:13.*

27:32 And as they came out, they found a man of Cyrene, Simon by name: him they compelled to bear his cross.

Found *see* **Find** at *Matthew 7:7. See also* **Meet** at *Matthew 25:1.*

Compelled *see* **Compel** at *Matthew 5:41.*

Cross *see Matthew 10:38.*

27:33 And when they were come unto a place called Golgotha, that is to say, a place of a skull,

Skull *kranion* (2898), Lat., *cranium* (akin to *kara*, "the head"), is used of the scene of the Crucifixion, **Matt. 27:33**; Mark 15:22; John 19:17; in Luke 23:33, RV, "(the place which is called) The skull," KJV, "Calvary" (from Latin *calvaria*, "a skull": marg., "the place of a skull"). The locality has been identified by the traces of the resemblance of the hill to a "skull". In the Sept., Judg. 9:53; 2 Kings 9:35.

27:34 They gave him vinegar to drink mingled with gall: and when he had tasted *thereof*, he would not drink.

Vinegar *oxos* (3690), akin to *oxus*, "sharp," denotes "sour wine," the ordinary drink of laborers and common soldiers; it is used in the four Gospels of the "vinegar" offered to the Lord at His crucifixion. In **Matt. 27:34** the best texts have *oinos*, "wine" (RV). Some have *oxos* (KJV, "vinegar"), but Mark 15:23 (KJV and RV) confirms the RV in the passage in Matthew. This, which the soldiers offered before crucifying, was refused by Him, as it was designed to alleviate His sufferings; the "vinegar" is mentioned in Mark 15:36; so Luke 23:36, and John 19:29, 30. In the Sept., Num. 6:3; Ruth 2:14; Ps. 69:21; Prov. 25:20. *See also* **Wine** at *Matthew 9:17.*

Mingled *mignumi* (3396), "to mix, mingle" (from a root *mik*; Eng., "mix" is akin), is always in the NT translated "to mingle," **Matt. 27:34**; Luke 13:1; Rev. 8:7; 15:2.

Gall *chole* (5521), a word probably connected with *chloe*, "yellow," denotes "gall," (a) literal, **Matt. 27:34** (cf. Ps. 69:21); some regard the word here as referring to myrrh, on account of Mark 15:23; (b) metaphorical, Acts 8:23, where "gall of bitterness" stands for extreme wickedness, productive of evil fruit. In the OT it is used (a) of a plant characterized by bitterness (probably wormwood), Deut. 29:18; Hos. 10:4; Amos 6:12; (b) as the translation of the word *mererah*, "bitterness," Job. 13:26, e.g.; (c) as the translation of *rosh*, "venom"; in Deut. 32:32 "(grapes) of gall." In Job 20:25, the gall bladder is referred to (the receptacle of bile). The ancients supposed that the poison of serpents lay in the gall (see Job 20:14).

Tasted *see* **Taste** at *Matthew 16:28.*

27:35 And they crucified him, and parted his garments, casting lots: that it might be fulfilled which was spoken by the prophet, They parted my garments among them, and upon my vesture did they cast lots.

Parted *diamerizo* (1266), "to part among, to distribute," is translated by the verb "to part" (a) in the middle voice, with reference to the Lord's garments, **Matt. 27:35**, 1st part (in some mss., 2nd part); Mark 15:24; Luke 23:34; John 19:24; (b) in the active voice, of "the proceeds of the sale of possessions and goods," Acts 2:45; (c) in the passive voice in Acts 2:3, of the "parting asunder" (RV) of tongues like fire (KJV, "cloven").

Garments *himatismos* (2441), in form a collective word, denoting "vesture, garments," is used generally of "costly or stately raiment," the apparel of kings, of officials, etc. See Luke 7:25, where "gorgeously apparelled" is, lit., "in gorgeous vesture." See also Acts 20:33 and 1 Tim. 2:9, "costly raiment." This is the word used of the Lord's white and dazzling raiment on the Mount of Transfiguration, Luke 9:29. It is also used of His *chiton*, His undergarment, for which the soldiers cast lots, John 19:23-24, "vesture"; in **Matt. 27:35** it is also translated vesture. *See also* **Raiment** at *Matthew 17:2.*

Lots *kleros* (2819), denotes (a) an object used in casting or drawing lots, which consisted of bits, or small tablets, of wood or stone (the probable derivation is from *klao*, "to break"); these were sometimes inscribed with the names of persons, and were put into a receptacle or a garment ("a lap," Prov. 16:33), from which they were cast, after being shaken together; he whose "lot" first fell out was the one chosen. The method was employed in a variety of circumstances, e.g., of dividing or assigning property, **Matt. 27:35**; Mark 15:24; Luke 23:34; John 19:24 (cf., e.g., Num. 26:55); of appointing to office, Acts 1:26 (cf, e.g., 1 Sam. 10:20); for other occurrences in the OT, see, e.g., Josh. 7:14 (the earliest instance in Scripture), Lev.16:7-10; Esth. 3:7; 9:24; (b) "what is obtained by lot, an allotted portion," e.g., of the ministry allotted to the apostles, Acts 1:17, RV, "portion," marg., "lot" (KJV, "part"); in some mss. v. 25, KJV, "part" (the RV follows those which have *topos*, "place"); Acts 8:21; it is also used like *kleronomia*, "an inheritance," in Acts 26:18, of what God has in grace assigned to the sanctified; so Col. 1:12; in 1 Pet. 5:3 it is used of those the spiritual care of, and charge over, whom is assigned to elders, RV, "the charge allotted to you" (plural, lit., "the charges"), KJV, "(God's) heritage." From *kleros* the word "clergy" is derived (a transposition in the application of the term).

Fulfilled *see Matthew 1:22.*

Spoken *see Matthew 1:22.*

27:36 And sitting down they watched him there;

Sitting *see* Sat at *Matthew 4:16.*

Watched *tereo* (5083), "to keep," is rendered "to watch," of those who kept guard at the cross, **Matt. 27:36, 54; 28:4**, RV, "watchers" (KJV, "keepers"), lit., "the watching ones."

27:37 And set up over his head his accusation written, THIS IS JESUS THE KING OF THE JEWS.

Set *epitithemi* (2007), "to put, set or lay upon," is used of the placing over the head of Christ on the cross "His accusation," **Matt. 27:37**, "set up"; of attacking a person, Acts 18:10, "shall set on."

Accusation *aitia* (156), probably has the primary meaning of "a cause, especially an occasion of something evil, hence a charge, an accusation." It is used in a forensic sense, of (a) an accusation, Acts 25:18 (RV, "charge"), 27; (b) a crime, **Matt. 27:37**; Mark 15:26, John 18:38; 19:4, 6; Acts 13:28; 23:28; 28:18.

King *see Matthew 1:6.*

27:38 Then were there two thieves crucified with him, one on the right hand, and another on the left.

Thieves *see Matthew 21:13.*

Left *see Matthew 20:21.*

27:39 And they that passed by reviled him, wagging their heads,

Passed *paraporeuomai* (3899), primarily, "to go beside, accompany" (*para*, "beside," *poreuomai*, "to proceed"), denotes "to go past, pass by," **Matt. 27:39**; Mark 9:30, "passed through" (some mss. have *poreuomai*); 11:20; 15:29; in Mark 2:23, "going ... through."

Reviled *blasphemeo* (987), "to blaspheme, rail, revile," is translated "to rail at, or on," in **Matt. 27:39**, RV (KJV, "reviled"); Mark 15:29; Luke 23:39; 2 Pet. 2:10, RV (KJV, "to speak evil of"); 2:12, RV (KJV, "speak evil of"). Cf. *loidoreo*, "to revile." *See also* Blasphemeth at *Matthew 9:3.*

> *"If we would live aright it must be by the contemplation of Christ's death."*
>
> CHARLES HADDON SPURGEON

Wagging *kineo* (2795), "to move," is used of those who mocked the Lord at His crucifixion, nodding their heads in the direction of the cross as if sneering at this supposed ending of His career, **Matt. 27:39**; Mark 15:29. Cf. 2 Kings 19:21; Job 16:4; Ps. 22:7; 109:25; Isa. 37:22. *See also* Move at *Matthew 23:4.*

27:40 And saying, Thou that destroyest the temple, and buildest *it* in three days, save thyself. If thou be the Son of God, come down from the cross.

Destroyest *see* Destroy at *Matthew 5:17.*

27:41 Likewise also the chief priests mocking *him*, with the scribes and elders, said,

Likewise *homoios* (3668), akin to the adjective *homoios*, "like," signifies in "like manner, equally"; in the following the RV has "in like manner" for KJV, "likewise"; **Matt. 27:41**; Mark 4:16; Luke 10:32; 13:3; 16:25; John 5:19; (Heb. 9:21); Jas. 2:25; 1 Pet. 3:1, 7; Rev. 8:12; in Rev. 2:15 the KJV "which thing I hate" translates a variant reading (*ho miso*). *See also Matthew 22:26.*

Mocking *see* Mocked at *Matthew 2:16.*

27:42-43 He saved others; himself he cannot save. If he be the King of Israel, let him now come down from the cross, and we will believe him.

He trusted in God; let him deliver him now, if he will have him: for he said, I am the Son of God.

Trusted *peitho* (3982), intransitively, in the perfect and pluperfect active, "to have confidence, trust," is rendered "to trust" in **Matt. 27:43**; Mark 10:24; Luke 11:22; 18:9; 2 Cor. 1:9; 10:7; Phil. 2:24; 3:4, KJV (RV, "to have confidence"); Heb. 2:13; in the present middle, Heb. 13:18, KJV (RV, "are persuaded").

Deliver *see Matthew 6:13.*

27:44 The thieves also, which were crucified with him, cast the same in his teeth.

Thieves *see Matthew 21:13.*

Crucified *sustauroo* (4957), "to crucify with" (*su-*, "for," *sun*, "with"), is used (a) of actual "crucifixion" in company with another, **Matt. 27:44**; Mark 15:32; John 19:32; (b) metaphorically, of spiritual identification with Christ in His death, Rom. 6:6 and Gal. 2:20.

Cast For *oneidizo*, **Matt. 27:44** (KJV, "cast in one's teeth"). *See also* **Revile** at *Matthew 5:11.*

27:45 Now from the sixth hour there was darkness over all the land unto the ninth hour.

Sixth *see Matthew 20:5.*

Darkness *see Matthew 6:23.*

Ninth *see Matthew 20:5.*

27:46 And about the ninth hour Jesus cried with a loud voice, saying, Eli, Eli, lama sabachthani? that is to say, My God, my God, why hast thou forsaken me?

Cried *anaboao* (310), "to lift up the voice, cry out," is said of Christ at the moment of His death, a testimony to His supernatural power in giving up His life, **Matt. 27:46**; in some mss. in Mark 15:8, of the shouting of a multitude; in some mss. in Luke 9:38, of the "crying" out of a man in a company.

Loud *megas* (3173), "great," is used, besides other meanings, of intensity, as, e.g., of the force of a voice, e.g., **Matt. 27:46, 50**; in the following the RV has "great" for the KJV, "loud," Rev. 5:2, 12; 6:10; 7:2, 10; 8:13; 10:3; 12:10; 14:7, 9, 15, 18.

Voice *see Matthew 2:18.*

Lama *lama* (2982), is the Hebrew word for "Why?" (the variant *lema* is the Aramaic form), **Matt. 27:46**; Mark 15:34.

Sabachthani *sabachthanei* (4518), an Aramaic word signifying "Thou hast forsaken Me," is recorded as part of the utterance of Christ on the cross, **Matt. 27:46**; Mark 15:34, a quotation from Ps. 22:1. Recently proposed renderings which differ from those of the KJV and RV have not been sufficiently established to require acceptance.

Say The phrase *tout' esti* (i.e., *touto esti*), "that is," is so translated in **Matt. 27:46**, RV (KJV, "that is to say"); so Acts 1:19; in Heb. 9:11 and 10:20, KJV and RV, "that is to say"; in Mark 7:11 the phrase is *ho esti*, lit., "which is"; the phrase *ho legetai*, lit., "which is said," John 1:38 and 20:16, is rendered "which is to say."

Forsaken *enkataleipo* (1459), denotes (a) "to leave behind, among, leave surviving," Rom. 9:29; (b) "to forsake, abandon, leave in straits, or helpless," said by, or of, Christ, **Matt. 27:46**; Mark 15:34; Acts 2:27, 31; of men, 2 Cor. 4:9; 2 Tim. 4:10, 16; by God, Heb. 13:5; of things, by Christians (negatively), Heb. 10:25.

27:47-48 Some of them that stood there, when they heard *that*, said, This *man* calleth for Elias.

And straightway one of them ran, and took a spunge, and filled *it* with vinegar, and put *it* on a reed, and gave him to drink.

Ran *trecho* (5143), "to run," is used (a) literally, e.g., **Matt. 27:48** (*dramon*, an aorist participle, from an obsolete verb *dramo*, but supplying certain forms absent from *trecho*, lit., "having run, running," expressive of the decisiveness of the act); the same form in the indicative mood is used, e.g., in **Matt. 28:8**; in the Gospels the literal meaning alone is used; elsewhere in 1 Cor. 9:24 (twice in 1st part); Rev. 9:9, KJV, "running" (RV, "rushing"); (b) metaphorically, from the illustration of "runners" in a race, of either swiftness or effort to attain an end, Rom. 9:16, indicating that salvation is not due to human effort, but to God's sovereign right to exercise mercy; 1 Cor. 9:24 (2nd part), and v. 26, of persevering activity in the Christian course with a view to obtaining the reward; so Heb. 12:1; in Gal. 2:2 (1st part), RV, "(lest) I should be running," continuous present tense referring to the activity of the special service of his mission to Jerusalem; (2nd part) "had run," aorist tense, expressive of the continuous past, referring to the activity of his antagonism to the Judaizing teachers at Antioch, and his consent to submit the case to the judgment of the church in Jerusalem; in 5:7 of the erstwhile faithful course doctrinally of the Galatian believers; in Phil. 2:16, of the apostle's manner of life among the Philippian believers; in 2 Thess. 3:1, of the free and rapid progress of "the word of the Lord."

Spunge *spongos* (4699), was the medium by which vinegar was carried to the mouth of Christ on the cross, **Matt. 27:48**; Mark 15:36; John 19:29.

Filled *gemizo* (1072), "to fill or load full," is used of a boat, Mark 4:37 (RV, "was filling"); a sponge, Mark 15:36 (cf. **Matt. 27:48**) a house, Luke 14:23; the belly, Luke 15:16; waterpots, John 2:1; baskets, 6:13; bowls, with fire, Rev. 8:5; the temple, with smoke, 15:8. Cf. *gemo*, "to be full." *See also* **Furnished** at *Matthew 22:10*.

Reed *see Matthew 11:7*.

Drink *see Matthew 10:42*.

27:49 The rest said, Let be, let us see whether Elias will come to save him.

Let *see Matthew 5:40*.

27:50 Jesus, when he had cried again with a loud voice, yielded up the ghost.

Cried *see Matthew 15:22*.

Loud *see Matthew 27:46*.

Yielded *aphiemi* (863), "to send away," is translated "yielded up (His spirit)" in **Matt. 27:50** (cf. *paratithemi*, "I commend," Luke 23:46, and *paradidomi*, "He gave up," John 19:30).

Ghost *ekpneo* (1606), lit., "to breathe out" (*ek*, "out," *pneo*, "to breathe"), "to expire," is used in the NT, without an object, "soul" or "life" being understood, Mark 15:37, 39, and Luke 23:46, of the death of Christ. In **Matt. 27:50** and John 19:30, where different verbs are used, the act is expressed in a way which stresses it as of His own volition: in the former, "Jesus ... yielded up His spirit (*pneuma*)"; in the latter, "He gave up His spirit."

27:51 And, behold, the veil of the temple was rent in twain from the top to the bottom; and the earth did quake, and the rocks rent;

Veil *katapetasma* (2665), lit., "that which is spread out" (*petannumi*) "before" (*kata*), hence, "a veil," is used (a) of the inner "veil" of the tabernacle, Heb. 6:19; 9:3; (b) of the corresponding "veil" in the Temple, **Matt. 27:51**; Mark 15:38; Luke 23:45; (c) metaphorically of the "flesh" of Christ, Heb. 10:20, i.e., His body which He gave up to be crucified, thus by His expiatory death providing a means of the spiritual access of believers, the "new and living way," into the presence of God.

Rent *schizo* (4977), "to split, rend open," translated "to rend" in **Matt. 27:51** (twice); Mark 1:10, RV, "rent asunder" (KJV, "open"); 15:38; Luke 5:36, RV, "rendeth (from)"; the KJV follows the mss. which omit it in the 1st part of this verse; 23:45; John 19:24; 21:11, RV, "rent" (KJV, "broken"), of a net.

Twain In the following phrases the numeral is used distributively: (a) *ana duo*, "two apiece," John 2:6 (in some mss., Luke 9:3); in Luke 10.1, "two and two" ("by twos"); (b) *kata duo*, "by two," 1 Cor. 14:27; (c) *duo duo*, "by two and two," lit., "two (and) two," Mark 6:7 (not a Hebraism; the form of expression is used in the papyri); (d) *eis duo*, "into two," "in twain," **Matt. 27:51** and Mark 15:38. *See also* ***Matthew 5:41***.

Top *anothen* (509), "from above," is used of place, (a) with the meaning "from the top," **Matt. 27:51**; Mark 15:38, of the temple veil; in John 19:23, of the garment of Christ, lit., "from the upper parts" (plural); (b) of things which come from heaven, or from God in Heaven, John 3:31; 19:11; Jas. 1:17; 3:15, 17. It is also used in the sense of "again."

> *"Christ understands loneliness; he's been through it."*
>
> PAUL STROMBERG REES

Bottom *see* **Under** at *Matthew 2:16*.

Quake *seio* (4579), "did quake," **Matt. 27:51**, and **28:4**, RV (KJV, "did shake"). *See also* **Moved** at *Matthew 21:10*.

Rocks *see* **Rock** at *Matthew 7:24*.

27:52 And the graves were opened; and many bodies of the saints which slept arose,

Opened *see Matthew 2:11*.

Bodies *see* **Body** at *Matthew 5:29*.

Slept *koimaomai* (2837), is used of natural "sleep," **Matt. 28:13**; Luke 22:45; John 11:12; Acts 12:6; of the death of the body, but only of such as are Christ's; yet never of Christ Himself, though He is "the firstfruits of them that have fallen asleep," 1 Cor. 15:20, of saints who departed before Christ came, **Matt. 27:52**; Acts 13:36; of Lazarus, while Christ was yet upon the earth, John 11:11; of believers since the Ascension, 1 Thess. 4:13-15 and Acts 7:60; 1 Cor. 7:39; 11:30; 15:6, 18, 51; 2 Pet. 3:4.

Arose *see Matthew 2:14*. *See also* **Raise** at *Matthew 10:8;* **Resurrection** at *Matthew 22:23*.

27:53 And came out of the graves after his resurrection, and went into the holy city, and appeared unto many.

Resurrection *egersis* (1454), "a rousing" (akin to *egeiro*, "to arouse, to raise"), is used of the "resurrection" of Christ, in **Matt. 27:53**.

Appeared *emphanizo* (1718), from *en*, "in," intensive, and *phaino*, "to shine," is used, either of "physical manifestation," **Matt. 27:53**; Heb. 9:24; cf. John 14:22, or, metaphorically, of "the manifestation of Christ" by the Holy Spirit in the spiritual experience of believers who abide in His love, John 14:21. It has another, secondary meaning, "to make known, signify, inform." This is confined to the Acts, where it is used five times, 23:15, 22; 24:1; 25:2, 15. There is perhaps a combination of the two meanings in Heb. 11:14, i.e., to declare by oral testimony and to "manifest" by the witness of the life.

27:54 Now when the centurion, and they that were with him, watching Jesus, saw the earthquake, and those things that were done, they feared greatly, saying, Truly this was the Son of God.

Watching *see* Watched at *Matthew 27:36*.

Earthquake *see* Tempest at *Matthew 8:24*.

Greatly *see* Exceeding at *Matthew 2:10*.

Truly *see* Of a truth at *Matthew 14:33*.

Son *see Matthew 3:17*.

27:55 And many women were there beholding afar off, which followed Jesus from Galilee, ministering unto him:

Afar *see Matthew 26:58*.

Ministering *see* Ministered at *Matthew 4:11*.

27:56-57 Among which was Mary Magdalene, and Mary the mother of James and Joses, and the mother of Zebedee's children.

When the even was come, there came a rich man of Arimathaea, named Joseph, who also himself was Jesus' disciple:

Rich *see Matthew 19:23*.

Disciple *see* Instructed at *Matthew 13:52*.

27:58 He went to Pilate, and begged the body of Jesus. Then Pilate commanded the body to be delivered.

He *see Matthew 5:19*.

Begged "Begged" in **Matt. 27:58** and Luke 23:52, RV, "asked for," translates the verb *aiteo*.

Commanded *see Matthew 14:9*.

Delivered *apodidomi* (591), "to give away," hence, "to give back or up," is used in Pilate's command for the Lord's body to be "given up," **Matt. 27:58**; in the sense of "giving back," of the Lord's act in giving a healed boy back to his father, Luke 9:42.

27:59 And when Joseph had taken the body, he wrapped it in a clean linen cloth,

Wrapped *entulisso* (1794), "to wrap up, roll round or about," is translated "rolled up" in John 20:7, RV, of the cloth or "napkin" that had been wrapped around the head of the Lord before burial. Both the RV and the KJV, "wrapped together," might suggest that this cloth had been "rolled" or wrapped up and put in a certain part of the tomb at the Lord's resurrection, whereas, as with the body wrappings, the head cloth was lying as it had been "rolled" round His head, an evidence, to those who looked into the tomb, of the fact of His resurrection without any disturbance of the wrappings either by friend or foe or when the change took place. It is followed by *en*, "in," and translated "wrapped" in **Matt. 27:59**, a meaning and construction which Moulton and Milligan illustrate from the papyri; in Luke 23:53 it is followed by the dative of the noun *sindon*, "linen cloth," used instrumentally.

Clean *see* Pure at *Matthew 5:8*.

Linen *sindon* (4616), was "a fine linen cloth, an article of domestic manufacture" (Prov. 31:24) used (a) as a garment or wrap, the "linen cloth" of Mark 14:51, 52; (b) as shrouds or winding sheets, **Matt. 27:59**; Mark 15:46, RV, "linen cloth," for KJV, "linen"; Luke 23:53 (ditto). In the Sept., Judg. 14:2, "(thirty) sheets"; Prov. 31:24. The Mishna (the great collection of legal decisions by the ancient Rabbis) records that the material was sometimes used for curtains.

27:60 And laid it in his own new tomb, which he had hewn out in the rock: and he rolled a great stone to the door of the sepulchre, and departed.

Laid *tithemi* (5087), "to put, place, set," frequently signifies "to lay," and is used of (a) "laying" a corpse in a tomb, **Matt. 27:60**; Mark 6:29; 15:47; 16:6; Luke 23:53, 55; John 11:34; 19:41, 42; 20:2, 13, 15; Acts 7:16; 13:29; Rev. 11:9, RV, "to be laid" (KJV, "to be put"); in an upper chamber, Acts 9:37; (b) "laying" the sick in a place, Mark 6:56; Luke 5:18; Acts 3:2; 5:15; (c) "laying" money at the apostles' feet, Acts 4:35, 37; 5:2; (d) Christ's "laying" His hands upon children, Mark 10:16, RV, "laying" (KJV, "put"); upon John, Rev. 1:17 (in the best mss.); (e) "laying" down one's life, (1) of Christ, John 10:11, RV, "layeth down" (KJV, "giveth"); vv. 17, 18 (twice); 1 John 3:16; (2) of Peter for Christ's sake, John 13:37, 38; (3) of Christ's followers, on behalf of others, 1 John 3:16; (4) of anyone, for his friends, John 15:13; (f) "laying" up sayings in one's heart, Luke 1:66 (middle voice, in the sense of "for themselves"); in 9:44, of letting Christ's words "sink" (middle voice, in the sense of "for oneself"; KJV, "sink down") into the ears; (g) "laying" a foundation (1) literally, Luke 6:48; 14:29; (2) metaphorically, of Christ in relation to an assembly, 1 Cor. 3:10, 11; (h) in "laying" Christ as a "stone of stumbling" for Israel, Rom. 9:33; (i) Christ's "laying" aside His garments, John 13:4; (j) Christians, in "laying" money in store for the help of the needy, 1 Cor. 16:2 (lit., "let him put"); (k) "depositing" money, Luke 19:21, 22.

Tomb *see* Tombs at *Matthew 8:28*.

Hewn *latomeo* (2998), signifies "to hew out stones" (from *latomos*, "a stone-cutter"; *las*, "a stone," *temno*, "to cut"), and is used of the sepulchre which Joseph of Arimathaea had "hewn" out of a rock for himself, where the body of the Lord was buried, **Matt. 27:60**; Mark 15:46.

Rock *see Matthew 7:24*.

Rolled *proskulio* (4351), "to roll up or to" (*pros*), is used in **Matt. 27:60**; Mark 15:46, of the sepulchre stone.

Great *see Matthew 20:25*.

Stone *see* Stones at *Matthew 4:3*.

Door *see Matthew 6:6*.

27:61 And there was Mary Magdalene, and the other Mary, sitting over against the sepulchre.

Over against *see* Before at *Matthew 27:24*.

27:62 Now the next day, that followed the day of the preparation, the chief priests and Pharisees came together unto Pilate,

Next day *epaurion* (1887), the RV always translates it "on (the) morrow"; in the following the KJV has "(the) next day," **Matt. 27:62**; John 1:29, 35 ("the next day after"); 12:12; Acts 14:20; 21:8; 25:6; "(the) day following," John 1:43; 6:22; "the morrow after," Acts 10:24.

Preparation *paraskeue* (3904), denotes "preparation, equipment." The day on which Christ died is called "the Preparation" in Mark 15:42 and John 19:31; in John 19:42 "the Jews' Preparation," RV; in 19:14 it is described as "the Preparation of the Passover"; in Luke 23:54, RV, "the day of the Preparation (and the Sabbath drew on)." The same day is in view in **Matt. 27:62**, where the events recorded took place on "the day after the Preparation" (RV). The reference would be to the 6th day of the week. The title arose from the need of preparing food, etc., for the Sabbath. Apparently it was first applied only to the afternoon of the 6th day; later, to the whole day. In regard to the phraseology in John 19:14, many hold this to indicate the "preparation" for the paschal feast. It probably means "the Preparation day," and thus falls in line with the Synoptic Gospels. In modern Greek and ecclesiastical Latin, *Parasceve* = Friday.

Came *sunago*, "to gather together," is always so rendered in RV, e.g., **Matt. 27:62**; Mark 7:1; Luke 22:66; Acts 13:44; 15:6; 20:7.

27:63 Saying, Sir, we remember that that deceiver said, while he was yet alive, After three days I will rise again.

Sir *see* Lord at *Matthew 1:22*.

Deceiver *planos* (4108), is, properly, an adjective, signifying "wandering, or leading astray, seducing," 1 Tim. 4:1, "seducing (spirits)", used as a noun, it denotes an impostor of the vagabond type, and so any kind of "deceiver" or corrupter, **Matt. 27:63**; 2 Cor. 6:8; 2 John 7 (twice), in the last of which the accompanying definite article necessitates the translation "the deceiver," RV.

Alive *see* Live at *Matthew 4:4*.

27:64 Command therefore that the sepulchre be made sure until the third day, lest his disciples come by night, and steal him away, and say unto the people, He is risen from the dead: so the last error shall be worse than the first.

Command *see* Commanded at *Matthew 14:9*.

Sure *asphalizo* (805), "to make secure, safe, firm" (akin to *asphales*, "safe"), (*a*, negative, and *sphallo*, "to trip up"), is translated "make ... fast," in Acts 16:24, of prisoners' feet in the stocks. In **Matt. 27:64**, **65**, **66**, it is rendered "to make sure."

Lest *see Matthew 4:6*.

Night *see Matthew 2:14*.

Steal *see Matthew 6:19*.

Error *plane* (4106), akin to *planao*, "a wandering, a forsaking of the right path," see Jas. 5:20, whether in doctrine, 2 Pet. 3:17; 1 John 4:6, or in morals, Rom. 1:27; 2 Pet. 2:18;

Jude 11, though, in Scripture, doctrine and morals are never divided by any sharp line. See also **Matt. 27:64**, where it is equivalent to 'fraud.'" "Errors" in doctrine are not infrequently the effect of relaxed morality, and vice versa. In Eph. 4:14 the RV has "wiles of error," for KJV, "they lie in wait to deceive"; in 1 Thess. 2:3, RV, "error," for KJV, "deceit"; in 2 Thess. 2:11, RV, "a working of error," for KJV, "strong delusion." Cf. *planetes*, "a wandering," Jude 13, and the adjective *planos*, "leading astray, deceiving, a deceiver."

Worse *see Matthew 9:16.*

27:65 Pilate said unto them, Ye have a watch: go your way, make *it* as sure as ye can.

Watch *koustodia* (2892), from Lat., *custodia* (cf. Eng., "custody"), is rendered "watch" in **Matt. 27:65, 66** and **28:11**, KJV.

Sure *see Matthew 27:64.*

Can *see* **Cannot** at *Matthew 21:27.*

27:66 So they went, and made the sepulchre sure, sealing the stone, and setting a watch.

Sure *see Matthew 27:64.*

Sealing *sphragizo* (4972), "to seal," is used to indicate (a) security and permanency (attempted but impossible), **Matt. 27:66**; on the contrary, of the doom of Satan, fixed and certain, Rev. 20:3, RV, "sealed it over"; (b) in Rom. 15:28, "when ... I have ... sealed to them this fruit," the formal ratification of the ministry of the churches of the Gentiles in Greece and Galatia to needy saints in Judea, by Paul's faithful delivery of the gifts to them; this material help was the fruit of his spiritual ministry to the Gentiles, who on their part were bringing forth the fruit of their having shared with them in spiritual things; the metaphor stresses the sacred formalities of the transaction (Deissmann illustrates this from the papyri of Fayyum, in which the "sealing" of sacks guarantees the full complement of the contents); (c) secrecy and security and the postponement of disclosure, Rev. 10:4; in a negative command, 22:10; (d) ownership and security, together with destination, Rev. 7:3, 4, 5 (as with the noun in v. 2); the same three indications are conveyed in Eph. 1:13, in the metaphor of the "sealing" of believers by the gift of the Holy Spirit, upon believing (i.e., at the time of their regeneration, not after a lapse of time in their spiritual life, "having also believed" – not as KJV, "after that ye believed" – ;the aorist participle marks the definiteness and completeness of the act of faith); the idea of destination is stressed by the phrase "the Holy Spirit of promise" (see also v. 14); so 4:30, "ye were sealed unto the day of redemption"; so in 2 Cor. 1:22, where the middle voice intimates the special interest of the Sealer in His act; (e) authentication by the believer (by receiving the witness of the Son) of the fact that "God is true," John 3:33; authentication by God in sealing the Son as the Giver of eternal life (with perhaps a figurative allusion to the impress of a mark upon loaves), 6:27.

Stone *see* **Stones** at *Matthew 4:3.*

Setting In **Matt. 27:66** there is no word in the Greek representing the KJV "setting"; the RV has "the guard being with them," lit., "with (*meta*) the guard."

Watch *see Matthew 27:65.*

Chapter 28

28:1 In the end of the sabbath, as it began to dawn toward the first *day* of the week, came Mary Magdalene and the other Mary to see the sepulchre.

End *opse* (3796), "long after, late, late in the day, at evening" (in contrast to *proi*, "early," e.g., **Matt. 20:1**), is used practically as a noun in Mark 11:11, lit., "the hour being at eventide"; 11:19; 13:35; in **Matt. 28:1** it is rendered "late on," RV, for KJV, "in the end of." Here, however, the meaning seems to be "after," a sense in which the word was used by late Greek writers. In the Sept., Gen. 24:11; Exod. 30:8; Jer. 2:23; Isa. 5:11.

Dawn *epiphosko* (2020), "to grow light" (*epi*, "upon," *phos*, "light"), in the sense of shining upon, is used in **Matt. 28:1**; in Luke 23:54, "drew on" (of the Sabbath-day); RV, marg., "began to dawn."

First *see* **One** at *Matthew 6:24.*

Week *sabbaton* (4521), is used (a) in the plural in the phrase "the first day of the week," **Matt. 28:1**; Mark 16:2, 9; Luke 24:1; John 20:1, 19; Acts 20:7; 1 Cor. 16:2.; (b) in the singular, Luke 18:12, "twice in the week," lit., "twice of the sabbath," i.e., twice in the days after the sabbath.

See *theoreo* (2334), denotes "to be a spectator of," indicating the careful perusal of details in the object; it points especially, as in *blepo*, to the action of the person beholding, e.g., **Matt. 28:1**; the RV frequently renders it by "to behold," for the KJV, "to see," e.g., John 14:17, 19; 16:10, 16, 17, 19. The difference between this verb and *blepo* and *horao* is brought out in John 20:5, 6, 8; in v. 5 *blepo* is used of John's sight of the linen cloths in the tomb, without his entering in; he "saw" at a glance the Lord was not there; in v. 6 the closer contemplation by Peter is expressed in the verb *theoreo*. But in v. 8 the grasping by John of the significance of the undisturbed cloths is denoted by *eidon*.

28:2 And, behold, there was a great earthquake: for the angel of the Lord descended from heaven, and came and rolled back the stone from the door, and sat upon it.

Earthquake *see* Tempest at *Matthew 8:24*.

Rolled *apokulio* or *apokulizo* (617), "to roll away" (*apo*, "from," *kulio*, "to roll"; cf. Eng., "cylinder," etc.), is used of the sepulchre stone, **Matt. 28:2**; Mark 16:3 (v. 4 in some mss.); Luke 24:2. In the Sept., Gen. 29:3, 8, 10.

28:3 His countenance was like lightning, and his raiment white as snow:

Countenance *eidea* (5324), "an aspect, appearance," is used in **Matt. 28:3**, RV, "appearance"; KJV, "countenance."

Lightning *see Matthew 24:27*.

Raiment *see Matthew 3:4*.

White *see Matthew 5:36*.

Snow *chion* (5510), occurs in **Matt. 28:3**; Rev. 1:14. Some mss. have it in Mark 9:3 (KJV).

28:4 And for fear of him the keepers did shake, and became as dead *men*.

Keepers *see* Keep at *Matthew 19:17*. *See also* Watched at *Matthew 27:36*.

Shake *seio* (4579), "to shake to and fro," is rendered "to shake" in **Matt. 28:4**, KJV; Heb. 12:26, KJV; Rev. 6:13, KJV and RV. *See also* Moved at *Matthew 21:10;* Quake at *Matthew 27:51*.

28:5 And the angel answered and said unto the women, Fear not ye: for I know that ye seek Jesus, which was crucified.

Answered *see Matthew 11:25*.

Said *see* Say at *Matthew 3:9*.

28:6 He is not here: for he is risen, as he said. Come, see the place where the Lord lay.

Lay *keimai* (2749), "to be laid, to lie," used as the passive voice of *tithemi*, "to lay", is said (a) of the Child Jesus, Luke 2:12, 16; (b) of the dead body of the Lord, **Matt. 28:6**; John 20:12; in Luke 23:53, "had ... lain," RV, KJV, "was laid," in the tomb as hitherto empty; (c) of the linen cloths, John 20:5, 6, 7; (d) figuratively of a veil as "lying" upon the hearts of the Jews, 2 Cor. 3:15, RV, "lieth" (KJV, "is"); (e) metaphorically, of the world as "lying" in the evil one, 1 John 5:19, RV; (f) of the heavenly city, Rev. 21:16.

28:7 And go quickly, and tell his disciples that he is risen from the dead; and, behold, he goeth before you into Galilee; there shall ye see him: lo, I have told you.

Quickly *see Matthew 5:25*.

28:8 And they departed quickly from the sepulchre with fear and great joy; and did run to bring his disciples word.

Quickly *see Matthew 5:25*.

Run *see* Ran at *Matthew 27:48*.

Bring *see Matthew 2:8*.

28:9 And as they went to tell his disciples, behold, Jesus met them, saying, All hail. And they came and held him by the feet, and worshipped him.

"The resurrection is not a miracle like any other. It is a unique manifestation within this world of the transition God makes for us out of this way of being into another."

AUSTIN FARRER

Met *apantao* (528), "to go to meet, to meet" (*apo*, "from," *antao*, "to meet with, come face to face with"), is used in Mark 14:13 and Luke 17:12. Some mss. have this verb in **Matt. 28:9**; Mark 5:2; Luke 14:31; John 4:51; Acts 16:16. *See also Matthew 8:28*.

Hail *see Matthew 26:49*.

Held *see* Hold at *Matthew 12:11*.

Feet *see Matthew 10:14*.

Worshipped *see* Worship at *Matthew 2:2*.

28:10 Then said Jesus unto them, Be not afraid: go tell my brethren that they go into Galilee, and there shall they see me.

Brethren The disciples, and so, by implication, all believers, **Matt. 28:10**; John 20:17.

28:11 Now when they were going, behold, some of the watch came into the city, and shewed unto the chief priests all the things that were done.

Watch *see Matthew 27:65.*

Shewed *see* Shew at *Matthew 11:4.*

28:12 And when they were assembled with the elders, and had taken counsel, they gave large money unto the soldiers,

Large *hikanos* (2425), of persons, denotes "sufficient, competent, fit"; of things, "sufficient, enough, much, many (so of time)"; it is translated "large" in **Matt. 28:12**, of money.

Money *see Matthew 25:18.*

Soldiers *see Matthew 8:9.*

28:13 Saying, Say ye, His disciples came by night, and stole him *away* while we slept.

Stole *see* Steal at *Matthew 6:19.*

Slept *see Matthew 27:52.*

28:14 And if this come to the governor's ears, we will persuade him, and secure you.

Ears In **Matt. 28:14**, the verb *akouo* is used with the preposition *epi*, "upon or before" (or *hupo*, "by," in some mss.), lit., "if this come to a hearing before the governor."

Persuade *see* Persuaded at *Matthew 27:20.*

Secure In **Matt. 28:14**, KJV, *amerimnos*, "without anxiety," with *poieo*, "to make," is translated "we will ... secure (you)," RV, "we will ... rid (you) of care." The Eng. "secure" is derived from the Latin *se*, "free from," and *cura*, "care."

28:15 So they took the money, and did as they were taught: and this saying is commonly reported among the Jews until this day.

Money *see Matthew 25:18.*

Saying *muthos* (3454), primarily signifies "speech, conversation." The first syllable comes from a root *mu-*, signifying "to close, keep secret, be dumb"; whence, *muo*, "to close" (eyes, mouth) and *musterion*, "a secret, a mystery"; hence, "a story, narrative, fable, fiction" (Eng., "myth"). The word is used of gnostic errors and of Jewish and profane fables and genealogies, in 1 Tim. 1:4; 4:7; 2 Tim. 4:4; Titus 1:14; of fiction, in 2 Pet. 1:16. *Muthos* is to be contrasted with *aletheia*, "truth," and with *logos*, "a story, a narrative purporting to set forth facts," e.g., **Matt. 28:15**, a "saying" (i.e., an account, story, in which actually there is a falsification of facts); Luke 5:15, RV, "report."

Commonly reported In **Matt. 28:15**, *diaphemizo*, "to spread abroad" (as in the RV), is rendered in the KJV, "is commonly reported." *See also* Spread abroad at *Matthew 9:31;* Fame at *Matthew 9:31.*

28:16 Then the eleven disciples went away into Galilee, into a mountain where Jesus had appointed them.

Eleven *hendeka* (1733), lit., "one ten" (Lat., *undecim*), is used only of the eleven apostles remaining after the death of Judas Iscariot, **Matt. 28:16**; Mark 16:14; Luke 24:9, 33; Acts 1:26; 2:14.

Appointed *tasso* (5021), "to place in order, arrange," signifies "to appoint," e.g., of the place where Christ had "appointed" a meeting with His disciples after His resurrection, **Matt. 28:16**; of positions of military and civil authority over others, whether "appointed" by men, Luke 7:8, or by God, Rom. 13:1, "ordained." It is said of those who, having believed the gospel, "were ordained to eternal life," Acts 13:48. The house of Stephanas at Corinth had "set themselves" to the ministry of the saints (KJV, "addicted"), 1 Cor. 16:15. Other instances of the arranging of special details occur in Acts 15:2; 22:10; 28:23.

28:17 And when they saw him, they worshipped him: but some doubted.

Worshipped *see* Worship at *Matthew 2:2.*

Doubted *see* Doubt at *Matthew 14:31.*

28:18 And Jesus came and spake unto them, saying, All power is given unto me in heaven and in earth.

Power *see Matthew 9:6.*

28:19 Go ye therefore, and teach all nations, baptizing them in the name of the Father, and of the Son, and of the Holy Ghost:

Teach *see* Instructed at *Matthew 13:52.*

Baptizing *see* Baptize at *Matthew 3:11.*

Name *see Matthew 6:9.*

Father *see Matthew 10:29.*

Holy Ghost *see Matthew 1:18.*

28:20 Teaching them to observe all things whatsoever I have commanded you: and, lo, I am with you alway, *even* unto the end of the world. Amen.

Commanded *see* Command at *Matthew 19:7.*

Alway Two phrases, rendered "always" or "alway" in the KJV, are *en panti kairo* (lit., "in every season"), Luke 21:36, RV, "at every season," Eph. 6:18, RV, "at all seasons," and *pasas tas hemeras*, (lit., "all the days"), **Matt. 28:20**, KJV and RV, "alway."

End *see Matthew 13:39.*

Mark

Chapter 1

1:1 The beginning of the gospel of Jesus Christ, the Son of God;

Gospel *euangelion* (2098), originally denoted a reward for good tidings; later, the idea of reward dropped, and the word stood for "the good news" itself. The Eng. word "gospel," i.e. "good message," is the equivalent of *euangelion* (Eng., "evangel"). In the NT it denotes the "good tidings" of the kingdom of God and of salvation through Christ, to be received by faith, on the basis of His expiatory death, His burial, resurrection, and ascension, e.g., Acts 15:7; 20:24; 1 Pet. 4:17. Apart from those references and those in the Gospels of Matthew and Mark, and Rev. 14:6, the noun is confined to Paul's epistles. The following phrases describe the subjects or nature or purport of the message; it is the "gospel" of God, **Mark 1:14**; Rom. 1:1; 15:16; 2 Cor. 11:7; 1 Thess. 2:2, 9; 1 Pet. 4:17; God, concerning His Son, Rom. 1:1-3; His Son, Rom. 1:9; Jesus Christ, the Son of God, **Mark 1:1**; our Lord Jesus, 2 Thess. 1:8; Christ, Rom. 15:19, etc.; the glory of Christ, 2 Cor. 4:4; the grace of God, Acts 20:24; the glory of the blessed God, 1 Tim. 1:11; your salvation, Eph. 1:13; peace, Eph. 6:15. Cf. also "the gospel of the Kingdom," Matt. 4:23; 9:35; 24:14; "an eternal gospel," Rev. 14:6.

The following expressions are used in connection with the "gospel": (a) with regard to its testimony; (1) *kerusso*, "to preach it as a herald, e.g., Matt. 4:23; Gal. 2:2; (2) *laleo*, "to speak," 1 Thess. 2:2; (3) *diamarturomai*, "to testify (thoroughly)," Acts 20:24; (4) *euangelizo*, "to preach," e.g., 1 Cor. 15:1; 2 Cor. 11:7; Gal. 1:11); (5) *katangello*, "to proclaim," 1 Cor. 9:14; (6) *douleuo eis*, "to serve unto" ("in furtherance of"), Phil. 2:22; (7) *sunathleo en*, "to labor with in," Phil. 4:3; (8) *hierourgeo*, "to minister," Rom. 15:16; (9) *pleroo*, "to preach fully," Rom. 15:19; (10) *sunkakopatheo*, "to suffer hardship with," 2 Tim. 1:8; (b) with regard to its reception or otherwise: (1) *dechomai*, "to receive," 2 Cor. 11:4; *hupakouo*, "to hearken to, or obey," Rom. 10:16; 2 Thess. 1:8; *pisteuo en*, "to believe in," **Mark 1:15**; *metastrepho*, "to pervert," Gal. 1:7.

Jesus *iesous* (2424), is a transliteration of the Heb. "Joshua," meaning "Jehovah is salvation," i.e., "is the Savior," "a common name among the Jews, e.g., Ex. 17:9; Luke 3:29 (RV); Col. 4:11. It was given to the Son of God in Incarnation as His personal name, in obedience to the command of an angel to Joseph, the husband of His Mother, Mary, shortly before He was born, Matt. 1:21. By it He is spoken of throughout the Gospel narratives generally, but not without exception, as in **Mark 16:19, 20**; Luke 7:13, and a dozen other places in that Gospel, and a few in John.

"'Jesus Christ' occurs only in Matt. 1:1, 18; 16:21, marg.; **Mark 1:1**; John 1:17; 17:3. In Acts the name 'Jesus' is found frequently. 'Lord Jesus' is the normal usage, as in Acts 8:16; 19:5, 17; see also the reports of the words of Stephen, 7:59, of Ananias, 9:17, and of Paul, 16:31; though both Peter, 10:36, and Paul, 16:18, also used 'Jesus Christ.'" (From *Notes on Thessalonians*, by Hogg and Vine, pp. 16, 29.)

> *"The gospel was not good advice but good news."*
>
> WILLIAM RALPH INGE

1:2 As it is written in the prophets, Behold, I send my messenger before thy face, which shall prepare thy way before thee.

Written *grapho* (1125), is used of "writing directions or giving information," e.g., Rom. 10:5, "(Moses) writeth," RV (KJV, "describeth"); 15:15; 2 Cor. 7:12; and of "that which contained a record or message," e.g., **Mark 10:4, 5**; John 19:19; 21:25; Acts 23:25.

Send The "sending" of the Son by the Father was from the glory which He had with the Father into the world, by way of the Incarnation, not a "sending" out into the world after His birth, as if denoting His mission among and His manifestation to the people. "Hofmann, in support of his view that Jesus is called the Son of God only in virtue of His being born of man, vainly urges that the simple accusative after *apostello* also denotes what the Person is or becomes by being sent. What he states is true but only when the name of the object spoken of is chosen to correspond with the purposed mission, as, e.g., in **Mark 1:2**; Luke 14:32; 19:14. We can no more say, 'God sent Jesus that He should be His Son' than we can render 'he sent his servants,' Matt. 21:34, in this manner. That the Sonship of Christ is anterior to His mission to the world ... is clear from John 16:28; cf. especially also the double accusative in 1 John 4:14, 'the Father sent the Son the Savior of the world.' The expression that Jesus is sent by God denotes the mission which He has to fulfill and the authority which backs Him" (Cremer, *Lexicon of NT Greek*).

Messenger *angelos* (32), "a messenger, an angel, one sent," is translated "messenger," of John the Baptist, Matt. 11:10; **Mark 1:2**; Luke 7:27; in the plural, of John's "messengers," 7:24; of those whom Christ sent before Him when on His journey to Jerusalem, 9:52; of Paul's "thorn in the flesh," "a messenger of Satan," 2 Cor. 12:7; of the spies as received by Rahab, Jas. 2:25.

Prepare *kataskeuazo* (2680), "to prepare, make ready" (*kata*, used intensively, *skeue*, "equipment"), is so translated in Matt. 11:10; **Mark 1:2**; Luke 1:17; 7:27; Heb. 9:2, RV (KJV, "made"); 9:6, RV (KJV, "were ... ordained"); 11:7; 1 Pet. 3:20.

1:3 The voice of one crying in the wilderness, Prepare ye the way of the Lord, make his paths straight.

Crying *boao* (994), signifies (a) "to raise a cry," whether of joy, Gal. 4:27, or vexation, Acts 8:7; (b) "to speak with a strong voice," Matt. 3:3; **Mark 1:3**; **15:34**; Luke 3:4; 9:38 (some mss. have *anaboao* here); John 1:23; Acts 17:6; 25:24 (some mss. have *epiboao* here); (c) "to cry out for help," Luke 18:7, 38.

Paths *tribos* (5147), "a beaten track" (akin to *tribo*, "to rub, wear down"), "a path," is used in Matt. 3:3; **Mark 1:3**; Luke 3:4.

Straight *euthus* (2117), "direct, straight, right," is translated "straight," figuratively, of the paths of the Lord, Matt. 3:3; **Mark 1:3**; Luke 3:4; in v. 5 of the rectification of the crooked, with reference to moral transformation; in Acts 9:11, the name of a street in Damascus, still one of the principal thoroughfares.

1:4 John did baptize in the wilderness, and preach the baptism of repentance for the remission of sins.

Remission *aphesis* (859), "a dismissal, release" (from *aphiemi*), is used of the forgiveness of sins and translated "remission" in Matt. 26:28; **Mark 1:4**; Luke 1:77; 3:3; 24:47; Acts 2:38; 5:31 (KJV, "forgiveness"); 10:43; 13:38, RV (KJV, "forgiveness"); 26:18 (ditto); Heb. 9:22; 10:18.

1:5 And there went out unto him all the land of Judaea, and they of Jerusalem, and were all baptized of him in the river of Jordan, confessing their sins.

Land *chora* (5561), properly denotes "the space lying between two limits or places"; accordingly it has a variety of meanings: "country," Matt. 2:12; 8:28; **Mark 1:5**, RV (KJV, "land"); **5:1, 10**; Luke 2:8; 8:26; 15:13-14, RV (KJV, "land"), 15; 19:12; 21:21; Acts 10:39, RV (KJV, "land"); 12:20; 26:20, RV (KJV, "coasts"); 27:27; in **Mark 6:55** (in the best mss.) and Acts 18:23, RV, "region," as also in, e.g., Matt. 4:16; Luke 3:1; Acts 8:1; 13:49; 16:6; of property, Luke 12:16, "ground."

River *potamos* (4215), denotes (a) "a stream," Luke 6:48, 49; (b) "a flood or floods," Matt. 7:25, 27; (c) "a river," natural, Matt. 3:6, RV; **Mark 1:5**; Acts 16:13; 2 Cor. 11:26, RV (KJV, "waters"); Rev. 8:10; 9:14; 16:4, 12; symbolical, Rev. 12:15 (1st part), RV, "river" (KJV, "flood"); so v. 16; 22:1, 2 (cf. Gen. 2:10; Ezek. 47); figuratively, John 7:38, "the effects of the operation of the Holy Spirit in and through the believer."

Confessing *exomologeo* (1843), *ek*, "out," intensive, and *homologeo*, and accordingly stronger than *homologeo*, "to confess forth," i.e., "freely, openly," is used (a) "of a public acknowledgment or confession of sins," Matt. 3:6; **Mark 1:5**; Acts 19:18; Jas. 5:16; (b) "to profess or acknowledge openly," Matt. 11:25 (translated "thank," but indicating the fuller idea); Phil. 2:11 (some mss. have it in Rev. 3:5); (c) "to confess by way of celebrating, giving praise," Rom. 14:11; 15:9. In Luke 10:21, it is translated "I thank," the true meaning being "I gladly acknowledge." In Luke 22:6 it signifies to consent (RV), for KJV, "promised."

1:6 And John was clothed with camel's hair, and with a girdle of a skin about his loins; and he did eat locusts and wild honey;

Clothed *enduo* (1746), (Eng., "endue"), signifies "to enter into, get into," as into clothes, "to put on," e.g., **Mark 1:6**; Luke 8:27 (in the best mss.); 24:49 (KJV, "endued"); 2 Cor. 5:3; Rev. 1:13; 19:14.

Hair *thrix* (2359), denotes the "hair," whether of beast, as of the camel's "hair" which formed the raiment of John the Baptist, Matt. 3:4; **Mark 1:6**; or of man.

Girdle *zone* (2223), Eng., "zone," denotes "a belt or girdle," Matt. 3:4; **Mark 1:6**; Acts 21:11; Rev. 1:13; 15:6; it was often hollow, and hence served as a purse, Matt. 10:9; **Mark 6:8.**

Skin *dermatinos* (1193), denotes "of skin, leather" (from *derma*, "skin, hide of beasts," akin to *dero*, "to flay"; whence Eng., "derm," "dermal," "dermatology"); it is translated "leather" in Matt. 3:4, of John the Baptist's girdle; in **Mark 1:6**, RV (KJV, "of a skin").

Loins *osphus* (3751), is used (a) in the natural sense in Matt. 3:4; **Mark 1:6**; (b) as "the seat of generative power," Heb. 7:5, 10; metaphorically in Acts 2:30; (c) metaphorically, (1) of girding the "loins" in readiness for active service for the Lord, Luke 12:35; (2) the same, with truth, Eph. 6:14, i.e., bracing up oneself so as to maintain perfect sincerity and reality as the counteractive in Christian character against hypocrisy and falsehood; (3) of girding the "loins" of the mind, 1 Pet. 1:13, RV, "girding," suggestive of the alertness necessary for sobriety and for setting one's hope perfectly on "the grace to be brought ... at the revelation of Jesus Christ" (the present participle, "girding," is introductory to the rest of the verse).

Locusts *akris* (200), occurs in Matt. 3:4 and **Mark 1:6**, of the animals themselves, as forming part of the diet of John the Baptist; they are used as food; the Arabs stew them with butter, after removing the head, legs and wings. In Rev. 9:3, 7, they appear as monsters representing satanic agencies, let loose by divine judgments inflicted upon men for five months, the time of the natural life of the "locust." For the character of the judgment, see the whole passage.

Wild *agrios* (66), denotes (a) "of or in fields" (*agros*, "a field"), hence, "not domestic," said of honey, Matt. 3:4; **Mark 1:6**; (b) "savage, fierce," Jude 13, RV, metaphorically, "wild (waves)," KJV, "raging." It is used in the papyri of a malignant wound.

Honey *meli* (3192), occurs with the adjective *agrios*, "wild," in Matt. 3:4; **Mark 1:6**; in Rev. 10:9, 10, as an example of sweetness. As "honey" is liable to ferment, it was precluded from offerings to God, Lev. 2:11. The liquid "honey" mentioned in Ps. 19:10 and Prov. 16:24 is regarded as the best; a cruse of it was part of the present brought to Ahijah by Jeroboam's wife, 1 Kings 14:3.

1:7 And preached, saying, There cometh one mightier than I after me, the latchet of whose shoes I am not worthy to stoop down and unloose.

One In **Mark 1:7**, KJV, the article *ho*, "the," is rendered "one" (RV, "he that").

Mightier *ischuroteros* (2478), "stronger, mightier," the comparative degree, is translated "mightier" in Matt. 3:11; **Mark 1:7**; Luke 3:16; "stronger" in Luke 11:22; 1 Cor. 1:25; 10:22. It is used (a) of Christ, Matt. 3:11; **Mark 1:7**; Luke 3:16; (b) of "the weakness of God," as men without understanding regard it, 1 Cor. 1:25; (c) of a man of superior physical strength, Luke 11:22; (d) in 1 Cor. 10:22, in a rhetorical question, implying the impossibility of escaping the jealousy of God when it is kindled.

Latchet *himas* (2438), denotes "a thong, strap," whether for binding prisoners, Acts 22:25, "(the) thongs," or for fastening sandals, **Mark 1:7**; Luke 3:16; John 1:27. "Among the Orientals everything connected with the feet and shoes is defiled and debasing, and the stooping to unfasten the dusty latchet is the most insignificant in such service" (Mackie, in *Hastings' Bib. Dic.*).

Worthy *hikanos* (2425), "sufficient," is translated "worthy" in this sense in Matt. 3:11 (marg., "sufficient"); so 8:8; **Mark 1:7**; Luke 3:16; 7:6.

Stoop *kupto* (2955), "to bow the head, stoop down," occurs in **Mark 1:7**; John 8:6, 8.

Unloose *luo* (3089), denotes (a) "to loose, unbind, release," (1) of things, e.g., in Acts 7:33, RV, "loose (the shoes)," KJV, "put off"; **Mark 1:7**; (2) of animals, e.g., Matt. 21:2; (3) of persons, e.g., John 11:44; Acts 22:30; (4) of Satan, Rev. 20:3, 7, and angels, Rev. 9:14, 15; (5) metaphorically, of one diseased, Luke 13:16; of the marriage tie, 1 Cor. 7:27; of release from sins, Rev. 1:5 (in the most authentic mss.); (b) "to loosen, break up, dismiss, dissolve, destroy"; in this sense it is translated "to loose" in Acts 2:24, of the pains of death; in Rev. 5:2, of the seals of a roll. It is rendered "to unloose" in **Mark 1:7**; Luke 3:16; John 1:27; in Acts 13:25, RV.

Shoe *hupodemo* (5266), denotes "a sole bound under the foot" (*hupo*, "under," *deo*, "to bind"; cf. *hupodeo*, "to bind under"), "a sandal," always translated "shoes," e.g., Matt. 3:11; 10:10; **Mark 1:7**.

1:8 I indeed have baptized you with water: but he shall baptize you with the Holy Ghost.

Indeed *men* (3303), a conjunctive particle (originally a form of *men*, "verily, truly," found in Heb. 6:14.), usually related to an adversative conjunction or particle, like *de*, in the following clause, which is placed in opposition to it. Frequently it is untranslatable; sometimes it is rendered "indeed," e.g., Matt. 3:11; 13:32; 17:11, RV (KJV, "truly"); 20:23; 26:41; (some mss. have it in **Mark 1:8**); **Mark 9:12**, RV (KJV, "verily").

1:9-10 And it came to pass in those days, that Jesus came from Nazareth of Galilee, and was baptized of John in Jordan.

And straightway coming up out of the water, he saw the heavens opened, and the Spirit like a dove descending upon him:

Opened *schizo* (4977), "to split, to rend open," is said of the veil of the temple, Matt. 27:51; the rending of rocks, Matt. 27:51; the rending of the heavens, **Mark 1:10**; a garment, Luke 5:36; John 19:24; a net, John 21:11; in the passive voice, metaphorically, of being divided into factions, Acts 14:4; 23:7.

Like In the following the most authentic mss. have *hos*, "as," for *hosei*, "like," in the KJV; **Mark 1:10**; Luke 3:22; John 1:32; Rev. 1:14

Dove *peristera* (4058), denotes "a dove or pigeon," Matt. 3:16; 10:16 (indicating its proverbial harmlessness); 21:12; **Mark 1:10**; **11:15**; Luke 2:24 (pigeons"); 3:22; John 1:32; 2:14, 16.

"The cross of Jesus Christ and his baptism express the same thing. Our Lord was not a martyr; he was not merely a good man; he was God Incarnate. He came down to the lowest reach of creation in order to bring back the whole human race to God, and in order to do this he must take upon him, as representative man, the whole massed sin of the race."

OSWALD CHAMBERS

1:11-12 And there came a voice from heaven, *saying*, Thou art my beloved Son, in whom I am well pleased.

And immediately the Spirit driveth him into the wilderness.

Driveth *ekballo* (1544), denotes, lit., "to cast forth," with the suggestion of force (*ek*, "out," *ballo*, "to cast"); hence "to drive out or forth." It is translated "driveth" in **Mark 1:12**, RV, "driveth forth." In John 2:15 for the KJV, "drove," the RV has "cast," the more usual translation.

1:13 And he was there in the wilderness forty days, tempted of Satan; and was with the wild beasts; and the angels ministered unto him.

Days *hemera* (2250), "a day," is used of (a) the period of natural light, Gen. 1:5; Prov. 4:18; **Mark 4:35**; (b) the same, but figuratively, for a period of opportunity for service, John 9:4; Rom. 13:13; (c) one period of alternate light and darkness, Gen. 1:5; **Mark 1:13**.

Satan *satanas* (4567), a Greek form derived from the Aramaic (Heb., *Satan*), "an adversary," is used (a) of an angel of Jehovah in Num. 22:22 (the first occurrence of the Word in the OT); (b) of men, e.g., 1 Sam. 29:4; Ps. 38:20; 71:13; four in Ps. 109; (c) of "Satan," the Devil, some seventeen or eighteen times in the OT; in Zech. 3:1, where the name receives its interpretation, "to be (his) adversary," RV (see marg.; KJV, "to resist him").

In the NT the word is always used of "Satan," the adversary (a) of God and Christ, e.g., Matt. 4:10; 12:26; **Mark 1:13**; **3:23**, **26**; **4:15**; Luke 4:8 (in some mss.); 11:18; 22:3; John 13:27; (b) of His people, e.g., Luke 22:31; Acts 5:3; Rom. 16:20; 1 Cor. 5:5; 7:5; 2 Cor. 2:11; 11:14; 12:7; 1 Thess. 2:18; 1 Tim. 1:20; 5:15; Rev. 2:9, 13 (twice), 24; 3:9; (c) of mankind, Luke 13:16; Acts 26:18; 2 Thess. 2:9; Rev. 12:9; 20:7. His doom, sealed at the Cross, is foretold in its stages in Luke 10:18; Rev. 20:2, 10. Believers are assured of victory over him, Rom.

16:20. The appellation was given by the Lord to Peter, as a "Satan-like" man, on the occasion when he endeavored to dissuade Him from death, Matt. 16:23; **Mark 8:33**.

Ministered *diakoneo* (1247), signifies "to be a servant, attendant, to serve, wait upon, minister." In the following it is translated "to minister," except where "to serve" is mentioned: it is used (a) with a general significance, e.g., Matt. 4:11; 20:28; **Mark 1:13**; **10:45**; John 12:26 ("serve," twice); Acts 19:22; Philem. 13; (b) of waiting at table, "ministering" to the guests, Matt. 8:15; Luke 4:39; 8:3; 12:37; 17:8, "serve"; 22:26, "serve," v. 27, "serveth," twice; the 2nd instance, concerning the Lord, may come under (a); so of women preparing food, etc., **Mark 1:31**; Luke 10:40, "serve"; John 12:2, "served"; (c) of relieving one's necessities, supplying the necessaries of life, Matt. 25:44; 27:55; **Mark 15:41**; Acts 6:2, "serve"; Rom. 15:25; Heb. 6:10; 1 Tim. 3:10, 13.

1:14 Now after that John was put in prison, Jesus came into Galilee, preaching the gospel of the kingdom of God,

Put in *paradidomi* (3860), "to deliver over," in Rom. 6:17, RV, "that form of teaching whereunto ye were delivered," the figure being that of a mold which gives its shape to what is cast in it (not as the KJV). In Rom. 8:32 it is used of God in "delivering" His Son to expiatory death; so 4:25; see **Mark 9:31**; of Christ in "delivering" Himself up, Gal. 2:20; Eph. 5:2, 25. In **Mark 1:14**, RV, it is used of "delivering" John the Baptist to prison. In Matt. 4:12, KJV, *paradidomi*, "to betray, deliver up," is translated "was cast into prison" (RV, "was delivered up").

Gospel *see Mark 1:1.*

1:15 And saying, The time is fulfilled, and the kingdom of God is at hand: repent ye, and believe the gospel.

Fulfilled *pleroo* (4137), signifies (1) "to fill"; (2) "to fulfill, complete," (a) of time, e.g., **Mark 1:15**; Luke 21:24; John 7:8 (KJV, "full come"); Acts 7:23, RV, "he was wellnigh forty years old" (KJV, "was full," etc.), lit., "the time of forty years was fulfilled to him"; v. 30, KJV, "were expired"; 9:23; 24:27 (KJV, "after two years"; RV, "when two years were fulfilled"); (b) of number, Rev. 6:11; (c) of good pleasure, 2 Thess. 1:11; (d) of joy, Phil. 2:2; in the passive voice, "to be fulfilled," John 3:29 and 17:13; in the following the verb is rendered "fulfilled" in the RV, for the KJV, "full," John 15:11; 16:24; 1 John 1:4; 2 John 12; (e) of obedience, 2 Cor. 10:6; (f) of works, Rev. 3:2; (g) of the future Passover, Luke 22:16; (h) of sayings, prophecies, etc., e.g., Matt. 1:22 (twelve times in Matt., two in Mark, four in Luke, eight in John, two in Acts); Jas. 2:23; in Col. 1:25 the word signifies to preach "fully," to complete the ministry of the Gospel appointed.

At hand *engizo* (1448), "to draw near, to approach," from *engus*, "near," is used (a) of place and position, literally and physically, Matt. 21:1; **Mark 11:1**; Luke 12:33; 15:25; figuratively, of drawing near to God, Matt. 15:8; Heb. 7:19; Jas. 4:8; (b) of time, with reference to things that are imminent, as the kingdom of heaven, Matt. 3:2; 4:17; 10:7; the kingdom of God, **Mark 1:15**; Luke 10:9, 11; the time of fruit, Matt. 21:34; the desolation of Jerusalem, Luke 21:8; redemption, 21:28; the fulfillment of a promise, Acts 7:17; the Day of Christ in contrast to the present night of the world's spiritual darkness, Rom. 13:12; Heb. 10:25; the coming of the Lord, Jas. 5:8; the end of all things, 1 Pet. 4:7. It is also said of one who was drawing near to death, Phil. 2:30.

Gospel *see Mark 1:1.*

1:16 Now as he walked by the sea of Galilee, he saw Simon and Andrew his brother casting a net into the sea: for they were fishers.

Walked In **Mark 1:16**, KJV, *parago*, "to pass along" (RV, "passing along"), is translated "walked."

Casting *amphiballo* (97 and 906), "to cast around," occurs **Mark 1:16**.

Net *amphiblestron* (293), lit., "something thrown around" (*amphi*, "around," *ballo*, "to throw"), denotes "a casting net," a somewhat small "net," cast over the shoulder, spreading out in a circle and made to sink by weights, Matt. 4:18 (in some mss. in **Mark 1:16**: the best have the verb *amphiballo* alone).

Fishers *halieus* (231), "a fisherman, fisher" (from *hals*, "the sea"), occurs in Matt. 4:18, 19; **Mark 1:16**, **17**; Luke 5:2.

1:17 And Jesus said unto them, Come ye after me, and I will make you to become fishers of men.

Fishers *see Mark 1:16.*

1:18 And straightway they forsook their nets, and followed him.

Forsook *aphiemi* (863), sometimes has the significance of "forsaking," **Mark 1:18**; **14:50** (RV, "left"); so Luke 5:11. It has three chief meanings, (a) "to send forth, let go, forgive"; (b) "to let, suffer, permit"; (c) "to leave, leave alone, forsake, neglect." It is translated by the verb "to leave" (c), in Matt. 4:11; 4:20,

"We will never understand the full meaning of Jesus' richly varied ministry unless we see how the many things are rooted in the one thing: listening to the Father in the intimacy of perfect love."

HENRI J. M. NOUWEN

22, and parallel passages; 5:24; 8:15, and parallel passages; 8:22, RV, "leave (the dead)," KJV, "let," and the parallel passage; 13:36, RV, "left (the multitude)," KJV, "sent ... away"; 18:12; 19:27, and parallel passages, RV, "we have left" (KJV, "we have forsaken"), so v. 29; 22:22, 25; 23:23, RV, "have left undone" (KJV, "have omitted," in the 1st part, "leave undone" in the second); 23:38, and the parallel passage; 24:2, 40, 41, and parallel passages; 26:56, RV, "left"; **Mark 1:18**, "left"; **1:31**; **7:8**, RV, "ye leave"; **8:13**; **10:28, 29**; **12:12, 19-22**; **13:34**; Luke 10:30; 11:42 (in some mss.); Luke 12:39, RV "have left," KJV "have suffered"; John 4:3, 28, 52; 8:29; 10:12; 14:18, 27; 16:28, 32; Rom. 1:27; 1 Cor. 7:11, RV, "leave" (KJV "put away"); 7:13 (KJV and RV); Heb. 2:8; 6:1; Rev. 2:4.

Nets *diktuon* (1350), a general term for a "net" (from an old verb *diko*, "to cast": akin to *diskos*, "a quoit"), occurs in Matt. 4:20-21; **Mark 1:18-19**; Luke 5:2, 4-6; John 21:6, 8, 11 (twice). In the Sept. it was used for a "net" for catching birds, Prov. 1:17, in other ways, e.g., figuratively of a snare, Job 18:8; Prov. 29:5.

1:19 And when he had gone a little further thence, he saw James the *son* of Zebedee, and John his brother, who also were in the ship mending their nets.

Gone *probaino* (4260), "to go on, forwards, advance," is used of locality, Matt. 4:21; **Mark 1:19**; for the metaphorical use with reference to age, Luke 1:7, 18; 2:36.

Little *oligon* (3641), is used adverbially of (a) time, **Mark 6:31**, "a while;" 1 Pet. 1:6, RV, "a little while (KJV, "a season"); 5:10, RV, "a little while" (KJV, "a while"); Rev. 17:10, RV, "a little while" (KJV, "a short space"); (b) space, **Mark 1:19**; Luke 5:3; (c) extent, with the preposition *pros*, "for," in 1 Tim. 4:8, RV, "(for) a little" (KJV, and RV marg., "little"), where, while the phrase might refer to duration (as KJV marg.), yet the antithesis "for all things" clearly indicates extent, i.e., "physical training is profitable towards few objects in life."

Mending *katartizo* (2675), from *kata*, "down," intensive, and *artios*, "fit," has three meanings: (a) "to mend, repair," Matt. 4:21; **Mark 1:19**, of nets; (b) "to complete, furnish completely, equip, prepare," Luke 6:40; Rom. 9:22; Heb, 11:3 and in the middle voice, Matt. 21:16; Heb. 10:5; (c) "ethically, to prepare, perfect," Gal. 6:1; 1 Thess. 3:10; 1 Pet. 5:10; Heb. 13:21; and in the passive voice, 1 Cor. 1:10; 2 Cor. 13:11.

1:20 And straightway he called them: and they left their father Zebedee in the ship with the hired servants, and went after him.

Hired servants *misthotos* (3411), an adjective denoting "hired," is used as a noun, signifying "one who is hired," "hired servants," **Mark 1:20**; "hireling," John 10:12, 13; here, it expresses, not only one who has no real interest in his duty (that may or may not be present in its use in **Mark 1:20**), but one who is unfaithful in the discharge of it; that sense attaches always to the word rendered "hireling."

1:21 And they went into Capernaum; and straightway on the sabbath day he entered into the synagogue, and taught.

Entered *eisporeuomai* (1531), "to go into," found only in the Synoptists and Acts, is translated "to enter," in the RV of **Mark 1:21**; **6:56**; **11:2**; Luke 8:16; 11:33 (KJV, "come in"); 19:30 (KJV, "at your entering"); 22:10; in the following the RV has the verb "to go," for the KJV, "to enter," Matt. 15:17; **Mark 5:40**; **7:15, 18-19**; in Acts 28:30, "went," KJV, "came"; in 9:28, RV, "going," KJV, "coming"; in the following both KJV and RV have the verb "to enter," **Mark 4:19**; Luke 18:24 (in the best mss.); Acts 3:2; 8:3.

Synagogue *sunagoge* (4864), properly "a bringing together" (*sun*, "together," *ago*, "to bring"), denoted (a) "a gathering of things, a collection," then, of "persons, an assembling, of Jewish religious gatherings," e.g., Acts 9:2; an assembly of Christian Jews, Jas. 2:2, RV, "synagogue" (KJV, marg.; text, "assembly"); a company dominated by the power and activity of Satan, Rev. 2:9; 3:9; (b) by metonymy, "the building" in which the gathering is held, e.g., Matt. 6:2; **Mark 1:21**. The origin of the Jewish "synagogue" is probably to be assigned to the time of the Babylonian exile. Having no temple, the Jews assembled on the Sabbath to hear the Law read, and the practice continued in various buildings after the return. Cf. Ps. 74:8.

1:22 And they were astonished at his doctrine: for he taught them as one that had authority, and not as the scribes.

Scribes *grammateus* (1122), from *gramma*, "a writing," denotes "a scribe, a man of letters, a teacher of the law"; the "scribes" are mentioned frequently in the Synoptists, especially in connection with the Pharisees, with whom they virtually formed one party (see Luke 5:21), sometimes with the chief priests, e.g., Matt. 2:4; **Mark 8:31**; **10:33**; **11:18**, **27**; Luke 9:22. They are mentioned only once in John's Gospel, 8:3, three times in the Acts, 4:5; 6:12; 23:9; elsewhere only in 1 Cor. 1:20, in the singular. They were considered naturally qualified to teach in the synagogues, **Mark 1:22**. They were ambitious of honor, e.g., Matt. 23:5–11, which they demanded especially from their pupils, and which was readily granted them, as well as by the people generally. Like Ezra (Ezra 7:12), the "scribes" were found originally among the priests and Levites. The priests being the official interpreters of the Law, the "scribes" ere long became an independent company; though they never held political power, they became leaders of the people. Their functions regarding the Law were to teach it, develop it, and use it in connection with the Sanhedrin and various local courts. They also occupied themselves with the sacred writings both historical and didactic. They attached the utmost importance to ascetic elements, by which the nation was especially separated from the Gentiles. In their regime piety was reduced to external formalism. Only that was of value which was governed by external precept. Life under them became a burden; they themselves sought to evade certain of their own precepts, Matt. 23:16ff.; Luke 11:46; by their traditions the Law, instead of being a help in moral and spiritual life, became an instrument for preventing true access to God, Luke 11:52. Hence the Lord's stern denunciations of them and the Pharisees.

1:23 And there was in their synagogue a man with an unclean spirit; and he cried out,

Cried out *anakrazo* (349), *ana*, "up," intensive, and *krazo*, signifies "to cry out loudly," **Mark 1:23**; **6:49**; Luke 4:33; 8:28; 23:18.

1:24 Saying, Let *us* alone; what have we to do with thee, thou Jesus of Nazareth? art thou come to destroy us? I know thee who thou art, the Holy One of God.

Have ... to do In Matt. 27:19, "Have thou nothing to do with that righteous man" translates what is lit. "nothing to thee and that righteous man," the verb being omitted. Similarly with the phrase, "What have I to do with thee?" lit., "what (is) to me and thee?" **Mark 5:7**; Luke 8:28; John 2:4, where Westcott translates it "What is there to Me and to thee?"; Ellicott, "What is that to Me and to thee," i.e., "What is My concern and thine in the matter?" There is certainly nothing disparaging in the question. On the contrary, it answers what must have been the thought in Mary's heart, and suggests that while there is no obligation either on Him or her, yet the need is a case for rendering help. For the construction with the plural pronoun see Matt. 8:29; **Mark 1:24**; Luke 4:34.

Destroy *apollumi* (622), signifies (I) In the active voice, (a) "to destroy, destroy utterly, kill," e.g., Matt. 10:28; **Mark 1:24**; **9:22**; (b) "to lose utterly," e.g., Matt. 10:42, of "losing" a reward; Luke 15:4 (1st part), of "losing" a sheep; Luke 9:25, of "losing" oneself (of the "loss" of well-being hereafter); metaphorically, John 6:39, of failing to save; 18:9, of Christ's not "losing" His own; (II) in the middle voice (a) "to perish," of things, e.g., John 6:12 "(that nothing) be lost"; of persons, e.g., Matt. 8:25, "we perish;" of the "loss" of eternal life, usually (always in the RV) translated to perish, John 3:16; 17:12, KJV, "is lost," RV, "perished"; 2 Cor. 4:3, "are perishing," KJV, "are lost"; (b) "to be lost," e.g., Luke 15:4 (2nd part), "which is lost"; metaphorically, from the relation between shepherd and flock, of spiritual destitution and alienation from God, Matt. 10:6, "(the) lost (sheep)" of the house of Israel; Luke 19:10 (the perfect tense translated "lost" is here intransitive).

1:25 And Jesus rebuked him, saying, Hold thy peace, and come out of him.

Rebuke *epitimao* (2008), primarily, "to put honor upon," then, "to adjudge," hence signifies "to rebuke." Except for 2 Tim. 4:2 and Jude 9, it is confined in the NT to the Synoptic Gospels, where it is frequently used of the Lord's rebukes to (a) evil spirits, e.g., Matt. 17:18; **Mark 1:25**; **9:25**; Luke 4:35, 41; 9:42; (b) winds, Matt. 8:26; **Mark 4:39**; Luke 8:24; (c) fever, Luke 4:39; (d) disciples, **Mark 8:33**; Luke 9:55; contrast Luke 19:39. For rebukes by others, see Matt. 16:22; 19:13; 20:31; **Mark 8:32**; **10:13**; **10:48**, RV, "rebuked" (KJV, "charged"); Luke 17:3; 18:15, 39; 23:40.

Hold thy peace *phimoo* (5392), "to close the mouth with a muzzle" (*phimos*), is used (a) of "muzzling" the ox when it treads out the corn, 1 Cor. 9:9, KJV, "muzzle the mouth of," RV, "muzzle," and 1 Tim. 5:18, with the lesson that those upon whom spiritual labor is bestowed should not refrain from ministering to the material needs of those who labor on their behalf; (b) metaphorically, of putting to silence, or subduing to stillness, Matt. 22:12, 34; **Mark 1:25**; **4:39**; Luke 4:35; 1 Pet. 2:15.

1:26 And when the unclean spirit had torn him, and cried with a loud voice, he came out of him.

Torn *sparasso* (4682), denotes "to tear, rend, convulse," **Mark 1:26**; **9:20** (in some mss.), 26, RV, "having ... torn" (KJV, "rent"); Luke 9:39. In the Sept., 2 Sam. 22:8, of the foundations of heaven; Jer. 4:18, of the heart.

Cried *phoneo* (5455), "to sound" (Eng., "phone"), is used of the crowing of a cock, e.g., Matt. 26:34; John 13:38; of "calling" out with a clear or loud voice, to cry out, e.g., **Mark 1:26** (some mss. have *krazo* here), Acts 16:28; of "calling" to come to oneself, e.g., Matt. 20:32; Luke 19:15; of "calling" forth, as of Christ's call to Lazarus to come forth from the tomb, John 12:17; of inviting, e.g., Luke 14:12; of "calling" by name, with the implication of the pleasure taken in the possession of those "called," e.g., John 10:3; 13:13.

1:27 And they were all amazed, insomuch that they questioned among themselves, saying, What thing is this? what new doctrine *is* this? for with authority commandeth he even the unclean spirits, and they do obey him.

And *kai* (2532), a conjunction, is usually a mere connective, meaning "and"; it frequently, however, has an ascensive or climactic use, signifying "even," the thing that is added being out of the ordinary, and producing a climax. The determination of this meaning depends on the context. Examples are Matt. 5:46-47; **Mark 1:27**; Luke 6:33 (RV); 10:17; John 12:42; Gal. 2:13, 17, where "also" should be "even"; Eph. 5:12. Examples where the RV corrects the KJV "and" or "also," by substituting "even," are Luke 7:49; Acts 17:28; Heb. 11:11; in 1 John 4:3 the RV rightly omits "even."

Amazed *thambeo* (2284), is used in **Mark 1:27**; **10:24**, **32** (and Acts 9:6, KJV). The RV has "amazed" in each place; KJV "astonished," in Mark **10:24**.

Questioned *suzeteo* (4802), or *sunzeteo*, "to search together," "to discuss, dispute," is translated "to question" (or "question with or together") in **Mark 1:27**; **8:11**; **9:10**, **14**, **16**; **12:28**, RV (KJV, "reasoning together"); Luke 22:23, RV (KJV, "inquire"); 24:15, RV (KJV, "reasoned").

Commandeth *epitasso* (2004), signifies to appoint over, put in charge (*epi*, "over," *tasso*, "to appoint"); then, "to put upon one as a duty, to enjoin," **Mark 1:27**; **6:27**, **39**; **9:25**; Luke 4:36; 8:25, 31; 14:22; Acts 23:2; Philem. 8.

Obey *hupakouo* (5219), "to listen, attend" (as in Acts 12:13), and so, "to submit, to obey," is used of "obedience" (a) to God, Heb. 5:9; 11:8; (b) to Christ, by natural elements, Matt. 8:27; **Mark 1:27**; **4:41**; Luke 8:25; (c) to disciples of Christ, Luke 17:6; (d) to the faith, Acts 6:7; the gospel, Rom. 10:16; 2 Thess. 1:8; Christian doctrine, Rom. 6:17 (as to a form or mold of teaching); (e) to apostolic injunctions, Phil. 2:12; 2 Thess. 3:14; (f) to Abraham by Sarah, 1 Pet. 3:6; (g) to parents by children, Eph. 6:1; Col. 3:20; (h) to masters by servants, Eph. 6:5; Col. 3:22; (i) to sin, Rom. 6:12; (j) in general, Rom. 6:16.

1:28 And immediately his fame spread abroad throughout all the region round about Galilee.

Fame *akoe* (189), denotes (a) "the sense of hearing," 1 Cor. 12:17; 2 Pet. 2:8; a combination of verb and noun is used in phrases which have been termed Hebraic as they express somewhat literally an OT phraseology, e.g., "By hearing ye shall hear," Matt. 13:14; Acts 28:26, RV, a mode of expression conveying emphasis; (b) "the organ of hearing," **Mark 7:35**, "ears"; Luke 7:1, RV, "ears," for KJV, "audience"; Acts 17:20; 2 Tim. 4:3, 4; Heb. 5:11, "dull of hearing," lit., "dull as to ears"; (c) "a thing heard, a message or teaching," John 12:38, "report"; Rom. 10:16; 1 Thess. 2:13, "the word of the message," lit. "the word of hearing" (KJV, "which ye heard"); Heb. 4:2, "the word of hearing," RV, for KJV, "the word preached"; in a somewhat similar sense, "a rumor, report," Matt. 4:24; 14:1; **Mark 1:28**, KJV, "fame," RV, "report"; Matt. 24:6; **Mark 13:7**, "rumors (of wars)"; (d) "the receiving of a message," Rom. 10:17, something more than the mere sense of "hearing" [see (a)]; so with the phrase "the hearing of faith," Gal. 3:2, 5, which it seems better to understand so than under (c).

Spread In **Mark 1:28** and 1 Thess. 1:8, KJV, *exerchomai*, "to go out or forth" (RV), is rendered "to spread abroad."

Abroad *pantachou* (3837), is translated "everywhere" in **Mark 1:28**, RV, of the report throughout Galilee concerning Christ; in **Mark 16:20**, of preaching; Luke 9:6, of healing; Acts 17:30, of a divine command for repentance; 28:22, of disparagement of Christians; 1 Cor. 4:17, of apostolic teaching; in Acts 24:3, it is rendered "in all places." In the Sept., Isa. 42:22.

Region round about *perichoros* (4066), *peri*, "around," and *chora*, signifies "country round about," Luke 8:37; "country about," Luke 3:3, KJV (RV, "region round about"); in Matt. 14:35 and Luke 4:37, KJV, "country round about" (RV, "region round about"); Matt. 3:5; **Mark 1:28**; Luke 4:14; 7:17; Acts 14:6.

1:29 And forthwith, when they were come out of the synagogue, they entered into the house of Simon and Andrew, with James and John.

Forthwith *euthus* (2117), an alternative adverb, is translated "forthwith" in the KJV of **Mark 1:29**; **1:43** (in the best mss.), and John 19:34 (RV, "straightway").

Entered *erchomai*, "to come," is never translated "to enter," in the RV; in the KJV, **Mark 1:29**; Acts 18:7.

1:30 But Simon's wife's mother lay sick of a fever, and anon they tell him of her.

Wife's mother *penthera* (3994), the feminine of *pentheros* ("a father-in-law"), occurs in Matt. 8:14; 10:35; **Mark 1:30**; Luke 4:38; 12:53 (twice).

Lay *katakeimai* (2621), "to lie down" (*kata*, "down," and *keimai*), is used of the sick, **Mark 1:30**; **2:4**; Luke 5:25; John 5:3, 6; Acts 28:8; in Acts 9:33 it is rendered "had kept (his bed)," lit., "lying (on a bed)."

Sick of a fever *puresso* (4445), signifies "to be ill of a fever," Matt. 8:14; **Mark 1:30**.

Anon This is the KJV rendering of *euthus*, in Matt. 13:20 and **Mark 1:30**, RV, "straightway."

1:31 And he came and took her by the hand, and lifted her up; and immediately the fever left her, and she ministered unto them.

Took *krateo* (2902), "to take hold of, get possession of," is translated "to take" in Matt. 9:25; 22:6; 26:4; **Mark 1:31**; **5:41**; **9:27**; **14:1**, **44**, **46**, **49**; Luke 8:54; Acts 24:6.

Lifted *egeiro* (1453), is used (a) of "raising" the dead, active and passive voices, e.g., of the resurrection of Christ, Matt. 16:21; 17:23; 20:19, RV; 26:32, RV, "(after) I am raised up" (KJV, "... risen again"); Luke 9:22; 20:37; John 2:19; Acts 3:15; 4:10 [not 5:30, see (c) below]; 10:40 [not 13:23 in the best texts, see (c) below]; 13:30, 37; Rom. 4:24, 25; 6:4, 9; 7:4; 8:11 (twice); 8:34, RV; 10:9; 1 Cor. 6:14 (1st part); 15:13, 14, RV; 15:15 (twice), 16, 17; 15:20, RV; 2 Cor. 4:14; Gal. 1:1; Eph. 1:20; Col. 2:12; 1 Thess. 1:10; 1 Pet. 1:21; in 2 Tim. 2:8, RV, "risen"; (b) of the resurrection of human beings, Matt. 10:8; 11:5; Matt. 27:52, RV (KJV, "arose"); **Mark 12:26**, RV; Luke 7:22; John 5:21; 12:1, 9, 17; Acts 26:8; 1 Cor. 15:29 and 32, RV; 15:35, 42, 43 (twice), 44, 52; 2 Cor. 1:9; 4:14; Heb. 11:19; (c) of "raising" up a person to occupy a place in the midst of a people, said of Christ, Acts 5:30; in 13:23, KJV only (the best texts have *ago*, to bring, RV, "hath ... brought"); of David, Acts 13:22; (d) metaphorically, of a horn of salvation, Luke 1:69; (e) of children, from stones, by creative power, Luke 3:8; (f) of the Temple, as the Jews thought, John 2:20, RV, "wilt Thou raise (it) up" (KJV, "rear"); (g) of "lifting" up a person, from physical infirmity, **Mark 1:31**, RV, "raised ... up" (KJV, "lifted"); so **9:27**; Acts 3:7; 10:26, RV (KJV, "took"); Jas. 5:15, "shall raise ... up"; (h) metaphorically, of "raising" up affliction, Phil. 1:17, RV (in the best texts; the KJV, v. 16, following those which have *epiphero*, has "to add").

Fever *puretos* (4446), "feverish heat" (from *pur*, "fire"), hence, "a fever," occurs in Matt. 8:15; **Mark 1:31**; John 4:52; Acts 28:8; in Luke 4:38, with *megas*, "great, a high fever"; v. 39. Luke, as a physician, uses the medical distinction by which the ancients classified fevers into great and little. In the Sept., Deut. 28:22.

Left *see* **Forsook** at *Mark 1:18*.

Ministered *see Mark 1:13*.

1:32 And at even, when the sun did set, they brought unto him all that were diseased, and them that were possessed with devils.

Even *opsia* (3798), the feminine of the adjective *opsios*, "late," used as a noun, denoting "evening," with *hora*, "understood", is found seven times in Matthew, five in Mark, two in John, and in these places only in the NT (some mss. have it in **Mark 11:11**). The word really signifies the "late evening," the latter of the two "evenings" as reckoned by the Jews, the first from 3 p.m. to sunset, the latter after sunset; this is the usual meaning. It is used, however, of both, e.g., **Mark 1:32** (cf. *opsimos*, "latter," said of rain, Jas. 5:7).

Set *duno* (1416), "to sink into," is used of the "setting" of the sun, **Mark 1:32**, "did set"; Luke 4:40, "was setting." The sun, moon and stars were conceived of as sinking into the sea when they set.

Diseased *kakos* (2560), "badly, evilly," is used in the physical sense, "to be sick," e.g., Matt. 4:24; **Mark 1:32**, **34**; Luke 5:31. In Matt. 21:41 this adverb is used with the adjective, "He will miserably destroy those miserable men," more lit., "He will evilly destroy those men (evil as they are)," with stress on the adjective; in the moral sense, "to speak evilly," John 18:23; Acts 23:5; "to ask evilly," Jas. 4:3. The adverb *kakos*, "evilly ill," with *echo*, "to hold, to have," is rendered "to be sick," in Matt. 4:24, RV, "that were sick"; 8:16; 9:12; 14:35 and **Mark 1:32**, RV (KJV, "diseased"); **1:34**; **2:17**; **6:55**; Luke 5:31; 7:2.

Possessed with devils *daimonizomai* (1139), signifies "to be possessed of a demon, to act under the control of a demon." Those who were thus afflicted expressed the mind and consciousness of the "demon" or "demons" indwelling them, e.g., Luke 8:28. The verb is found chiefly in Matt. and Mark; Matt. 4:24; 8:16, 28, 33; 9:32; 12:22; 15:22; **Mark 1:32**; **5:15-16**, **18**; elsewhere in Luke 8:36 and John 10:21, "him that hath a devil (demon)."

1:33 And all the city was gathered together at the door.

City *polis* (4172), primarily "a town enclosed with a wall" (perhaps from a root *ple–*, signifying "fullness," whence also the Latin *pleo*, "to fill," Eng., "polite, polish, politic, etc."), is used also of the heavenly Jerusalem, the abode and community of the redeemed, Heb. 11:10, 16; 12:22; 13:14. In Revelation it signifies the visible capital of the heavenly kingdom, as destined to descend to earth in a coming age, e.g., Rev. 3:12; 21:2, 14, 19. By metonymy the word stands for the inhabitants, as in the English use, e.g., Matt. 8:34; 12:25; 21:10; **Mark 1:33**; Acts 13:44.

Gathered *episunago* (1996), "to gather together," suggesting stress upon the place at which the "gathering" is made (*epi*, "to"), is said of a hen and her chickens, Matt. 23:37; and so of the Lord's would-be protecting care of the people of Jerusalem, *id*, and Luke 13:34; of the "gathering" together of the elect, Matt. 24:31; **Mark 13:27**; of the "gathering" together of a crowd, **Mark 1:33**; Luke 12:1. It is found only in the Synoptic Gospels; twice of the "gathering" together of people, **Mark 1:33**; Luke 12:1; twice of the desire of the Lord to "gather" together the inhabitants of Jerusalem, Matt. 23:37; Luke 13:34; twice of His future act in "gathering" together His elect through the instrumentality of the angels, Matt. 24:31; **Mark 13:27**.

1:34 And he healed many that were sick of divers diseases, and cast out many devils; and suffered not the devils to speak, because they knew him.

Sick *see* **Diseased** at *Mark 1:32*.

Divers *poikilos* (4164), denotes "particolored, variegated" (*poikillo* means "to make gay": the root of the first syllable is *pik–*, found in Eng., "picture"), hence "divers," Matt. 4:24; **Mark 1:34**; Luke 4:40; 2 Tim. 3:6; Titus 3:3; Heb. 2:4 (RV, "manifold"), 13:9; Jas. 1:2 (RV, "manifold"); in 1 Pet. 1:6 and 4:10, "manifold," both KJV and RV.

Diseases *nosos* (3554), akin to Lat. *nocere*, "to injure" (Eng., "nosology"), is the regular word for "disease, sickness," Matt. 4:23; 8:17; 9:35; 10:1, RV, "disease," KJV, "sickness"; in Matt. 4:24; **Mark 1:34**; Luke 4:40; 6:17; 9:1; Acts 19:12, KJV and RV render it "diseases." In Luke 7:21, KJV has "infirmities." The most authentic mss. omit the word in **Mark 3:15**.

Devils *see* **Possessed with devils** at *Mark 1:32*.

Suffered *aphiemi* (863), "to send away," signifies "to permit, suffer," in Matt. 3:15 (twice); Matt. 19:14; 23:13; **Mark 1:34**; **5:19**, **37**; **10:14**; **11:16**; Luke 8:51; 12:39, KJV (RV, "left"); 18:16; John 12:7, RV, KJV and RV marg., "let (her) alone"; Rev. 11:9.

1:35 And in the morning, rising up a great while before day, he went out, and departed into a solitary place, and there prayed.

In the morning *proi* (4404), "early," is translated "in the morning" in Matt. 16:3; 20:1 (with *hama*, "early"); 21:18; **Mark 1:35**; **11:20**; **13:35**; **15:1**; "early" in **Mark 16:2** (with *lian*, "very"; KJV, "early in the morning"); **16:9**; Matt. 21:18 and John 18:28; 20:1; Acts 28:23 (with *apo*, "from").

Rising *anistemi* (450), "to stand up or to make to stand up," according as its use is intransitive or transitive (*ana*, "up," *histemi*, "to stand"), is used (a) of a physical change of position, e.g., of "rising" from sleep, **Mark 1:35**; from a meeting in a synagogue, Luke 4:29; of the illegal "rising" of the high priest in the tribunal in Matt. 26:62; of an invalid "rising" from his couch, Luke 5:25; the "rising" up of a disciple from his vocation to follow Christ, Luke 5:28; cf. John 11:31; "rising" up from prayer, Luke 22:45; of a whole company, Acts 26:30; 1 Cor. 10:7; (b) metaphorically, of "rising" up antagonistically against persons, e.g., of officials against people, Acts 5:17; of a seditious leader, 5:36, of the "rising" up of Satan, **Mark 3:26**; of false teachers, Acts 20:30; (c) of "rising" to a position of preeminence or power; e.g., of Christ as a prophet, Acts 3:22; 7:37; as God's servant in the midst of the nation of Israel, Acts 3:26; as the Son of God in the midst of the nation, 13:33 (not here of resurrection, but with reference to the Incarnation: the KJV "again" has nothing corresponding to it in the original, it was added as a misinterpretation: the mention of His resurrection is in the next verse, in which it is stressed by way of contrast and by the addition, "from the dead"); as a priest, Heb. 7:11, 15; as king over the nations, Rom. 15:12; (d) of a spiritual awakening from lethargy, Eph. 5:14; (e) of resurrection from the dead: (1) of the resurrection of Christ, Matt. 17:9; 20:19; **Mark 8:31; 9:9-10, 31; 10:34**; Luke 18:33; 24:7, 46; John 20:9; Acts 2:24, 32; 10:41; 13:34; 17:3, 31; 1 Thess. 4:14; (2) of believers, John 6:39-40, 44, 54; 11:24; 1 Thess. 4:16; of unbelievers, Matt. 12:41.

Great In **Mark 1:35**, the adverb *lian*, exceedingly, is rendered "a great while."

Day *ennucha* (1773), the neuter plural of *ennuchos*, used adverbially, lit., "in night" (*en*, "in," *nux*, "night," with *lian*, "very"), signifies "very early, yet in the night," "a great while before day," **Mark 1:35**.

Solitary place *eremos* (2048), used as a noun, has the same meaning as *eremia*, in Luke 5:16 and 8:29, RV, "deserts," for KJV, "wilderness", in Matt. 24:26 and John 6:31, RV, "wilderness," for KJV, "desert." As an adjective, it denotes (a), with reference to persons, "deserted," desolate, deprived of the friends and kindred, e.g., of a woman deserted by a husband, Gal 4:21; (b) so of a city, as Jerusalem, Matt. 23:38; or uninhabited places, "desert," e.g., Matt. 14:13, 15; Acts 8:26; in **Mark 1:35**, RV, "desert," for KJV, solitary.

1:36 And Simon and they that were with him followed after him.

Followed *katadioko* (2614), "to follow up or closely," with the determination to find (*kata*, "down," intensive, giving the idea of a hard, persistent search, and *dioko*), **Mark 1:36**, "followed after (Him)," is said of the disciples in going to find the Lord who had gone into a desert place to pray. The verb is found, e.g., in 1 Sam. 30:22; Ps. 23:6, and with hostile intent in Gen. 31:36.

1:37-38 And when they had found him, they said unto him, All *men* seek for thee.

And he said unto them, Let us go into the next towns, that I may preach there also: for therefore came I forth.

Go *ago* (71), "to bring, lead," is used intransitively, signifying "let us go" (as if to say, "let us be leading on," with the point of departure especially in view), Matt. 26:46; **Mark 1:38; 14:42**; John 11:7, 15, 16; 14:31.

Next *echo* (2192), the usual verb for "to have," is used with the following meanings: (a) "to hold, in the hand," etc., e.g., Rev. 1:16; 5:8; (b) "to hold fast, keep," Luke 19:20; metaphorically, of the mind and conduct, e.g., **Mark 16:8**; John 14:21; Rom. 1:28; 1 Tim. 3:9; 2 Tim. 1:13; (c) "to hold on, cling to, be next to," e.g., of accompaniment, Heb. 6:9, "things that accompany (salvation)," lit., "the things holding themselves of salvation" (RV, marg., "are near to"); of place, **Mark 1:38**, "next (towns)," lit., "towns holding nigh"; of time, e.g., Luke 13:33, "(the day) following," lit., "the holding (day)"; Acts 13:44; 20:15; 21:26; (d) "to hold, to count, consider, regard," e.g., Matt. 14:5; 21:46; **Mark 11:32**; Luke 14:18; Philem. 17; (e) "to involve," Heb. 10:35; Jas. 1:4; 1 John 4:18; (f) "to wear," of clothing, arms, etc., e.g., Matt. 3:4; 22:12; John 18:10; (g) "to be with child," of a woman, **Mark 13:17**; Rom. 9:10 (lit., "having conception"); (h) "to possess," the most frequent use, e.g., Matt. 8:20; 19:22; Acts 9:14; 1 Thess. 3:6; (i) of complaints, disputes, Matt. 5:23; **Mark 11:25**; Acts 24:19; Rev. 2:4, 20; (j) of ability, power, e.g., Luke 12:4; Acts 4:14 (lit., "had nothing to say"); (k) of necessity, e.g., Luke 12:50; Acts 23:17-19; (l) "to be in a certain condition," as of readiness, Acts 21:12 (lit., "I have readily"); of illness, Matt. 4:24, "all that were sick" (lit., "that had themselves sickly"); **Mark 5:23**, "lieth (lit., "hath herself") at the point of death"; **Mark 16:18** "they shall recover" (lit., "shall have themselves well"), John 4:52, "he began to amend" (lit., "he had himself better"); of evil works, 1 Tim. 5:25, "they that are otherwise," (lit., "the things having otherwise"); to be so, e.g., Acts 7:1, "are these things so?" (lit., "have these things thus?"), of time, Acts 24:25, "for this time" (lit., "the thing having now").

Towns *komopolis* (2969), denotes a country town," **Mark 1:38**, "a large village" usually without walls.

Therefore The phrase *eis touto*, lit., "unto this," signifies "to this end," John 18:37, RV (twice; KJV, "for this cause," in the second clause); so **Mark 1:38**; Acts 26:16; Rom. 14:9; 2 Cor. 2:9; 1 Tim. 4:10 (KJV, "therefore"); 1 Pet. 4:6; 1 John 3:8 (KJV, "for this purpose").

1:39-40 And he preached in their synagogues throughout all Galilee, and cast out devils.

And there came a leper to him, beseeching him, and kneeling down to him, and saying unto him, If thou wilt, thou canst make me clean.

Leper *lepros* (3015), an adjective, primarily used of "psoriasis," characterized by an eruption of rough scaly patches; later, "leprous," but chiefly used as a noun, "a leper,"

"Jesus Christ served others first; he spoke to those to whom no one spoke; he dined with the lowest members of society; he touched the untouchable. He had no throne, no crown, no bevy of servants or armored guards."

CHARLES W. COLSON

Matt. 8:2; 10:8; 11:5; **Mark 1:40**; Luke 4:27; 7:22; 17:12; especially of Simon, mentioned in Matt. 26:6; **Mark 14:3**.

Kneeling *gonupeteo* (1120), denotes "to bow the knees, kneel," from *gonu* and *pipto*, "to fall prostrate," the act of one imploring aid, Matt. 17:14; **Mark 1:40**; of one expressing reverence and honor, **Mark 10:17**; in mockery, Matt. 27:29.

1:41 And Jesus, moved with compassion, put forth *his* hand, and touched him, and saith unto him, I will; be thou clean.

Compassion *splanchnizomai* (4697), "to be moved as to one's inwards (*splanchna*), to be moved with compassion, to yearn with compassion," is frequently recorded of Christ towards the multitude and towards individual sufferers, Matt. 9:36; 14:14; 15:32; 18:27; 20:34; **Mark 1:41**; **6:34**; **8:2**; **9:22** (of the appeal of a father for a demon-possessed son); Luke 7:13; 10:33; of the father in the parable of the Prodigal Son, 15:20.

Put forth *ekteino* (1614), "to stretch out or forth," is so rendered in Matt. 12:13 (twice), 49; 14:31; 26:51; **Mark 3:5** (twice), Luke 6:10; in Matt. 8:3; **Mark 1:41** and Luke 5:13, RV (KJV, "put forth"); Luke 22:53; John 21:18; Acts 4:30; 26:1.

1:42 And as soon as he had spoken, immediately the leprosy departed from him, and he was cleansed.

Leprosy *lepra* (3014), akin to *lepros*, is mentioned in Matt. 8:3; **Mark 1:42**; Luke 5:12, 13. In the removal of other maladies the verb "to heal" (*iaomai*) is used, but in the removal of "leprosy," the verb "to cleanse" (*katharizo*), save in the statement concerning the Samaritan, Luke 17:15, "when he saw that he was healed." Matt. 10:8 and Luke 4:27 indicate that the disease was common in the nation. Only twelve cases are recorded in the NT, but these are especially selected.

1:43 And he straitly charged him, and forthwith sent him away;

Charged *embrimaomai* (1690), from *en*, "in," intensive, and *brime*, "strength," primarily signifies "to snort with anger, as of horses." Used of men it signifies "to fret, to be painfully moved"; then, "to express indignation against"; hence, "to rebuke sternly, to charge strictly," Matt. 9:30; **Mark 1:43**; it is rendered "murmured against" in **Mark 14:5**; "groaned" in John 11:33; "groaning" in v. 38.

Forthwith *see Mark 1:29*.

Sent *ekballo* (1544), "to cast out," or "send out," is translated "sent out" in **Mark 1:43**, RV (KJV, "sent away"), and in KJV and RV in Jas. 2:25.

1:44 And saith unto him, See thou say nothing to any man: but go thy way, shew thyself to the priest, and offer for thy cleansing those things which Moses commanded, for a testimony unto them.

Offer *prosphero* (4374), primarily, "to bring to" (*pros*, "to," *phero*, "to bring"), also denotes "to offer," (a) of the sacrifice of Christ Himself, Heb. 8:3; of Christ in virtue of his High Priesthood (RV, "this *high priest*"; KJV, "this man"); 9:14, 25 (negative), 28; 10:12; (b) of offerings under, or according to, the Law, e.g., Matt. 8:4; **Mark 1:44**; Acts 7:42; 21:26; Heb. 5:1, 3; 8:3; 9:7, 9; 10:1-2, 8, 11; (c) of "offerings" previous to the Law, Heb. 11:4, 17 (of Isaac by Abraham); (d) of gifts "offered" to Christ, Matt. 2:11, RV, "offered" (KJV, "presented unto"); (e) of prayers "offered" by Christ, Heb. 5:7; (f) of the vinegar "offered" to Him in mockery by the soldiers at the cross, Luke 23:36; (g) of the slaughter of disciples by persecutors, who think they are "offering" service to God, John 16:2, RV (KJV, "doeth"); (h) of money "offered" by Simon the sorcerer, Acts 8:18.

Cleansing *katharismos* (2512), denotes "cleansing," (a) both the action and its results, in the Levitical sense, **Mark 1:44**; Luke 2:22, "purification"; 5:14, "cleansing"; John 2:6; 3:25, "purifying"; (b) in the moral sense, from sins, Heb. 1:3; 2 Pet. 1:9, RV, "cleansing."

Commanded *prostasso* (4367), denotes "to arrange or set in order towards" (*pros*, "towards," *tasso*, "to arrange"); hence "to prescribe, give command," Matt. 1:24; 8:4; **Mark 1:44**; Luke 5:14; Acts 10:33, 48.

1:45 But he went out, and began to publish *it* much, and to blaze abroad the matter, insomuch that Jesus could no more openly enter into the city, but was without in desert places: and they came to him from every quarter.

Publish *kerusso* (2784), signifies (a) "to be a herald," or, in general, "to proclaim," e.g., Matt. 3:1; **Mark 1:45**, "publish"; in Luke 4:18, RV, "to proclaim," KJV, "to preach"; so verse 19; Luke 12:3; Acts 10:37; Rom. 2:21; Rev. 5:2. In 1 Pet. 3:19 the probable reference is, not to glad tidings (which there is no real evidence that Noah preached, nor is there evidence that the spirits of antediluvian people are actually "in prison"), but to the act of Christ after His resurrection in proclaiming His victory to fallen angelic spirits; (b) "to preach the gospel as a herald," e.g., Matt. 24:14; **Mark 13:10**, RV, "be preached" (KJV, "be published"); **14:9**; **16:15**, **20**; Luke 8:1; 9:2; 24:47; Acts 8:5; 19:13; 28:31; Rom. 10:14, present participle, lit., "(one) preaching," "a preacher"; 10:15 (1st part); 1 Cor. 1:23; 15:11, 12; 2 Cor. 1:19; 4:5; 11:4; Gal. 2:2; Phil. 1:15; Col. 1:23; 1 Thess. 2:9; 1 Tim. 3:16; (c) "to preach the word," 2 Tim. 4:2 (of the ministry of the Scriptures, with special reference to the gospel).

Much *polus* (4183), is used in the neuter singular (*polu*) or the plural (*polla*), as an adverb; in the sing., e.g., **Mark 12:27**; in the plural, e.g., **Mark 1:45**, "much"; **5:23**, "greatly" (RV, "much"); v. **38**, KJV and RV, "greatly"; 1 Cor. 16:12 (RV, much).

Blaze abroad *diaphemizo* (1310), "to spread broad" (*dia*, "throughout," *phemizo*, "to speak"), is so translated in the RV in Matt. 9:31; 28:15 (KJV, "commonly reported"); **Mark 1:45** (KJV, "blaze abroad").

Matter *logos* (3056), "a word, speech, discourse, account," hence also "that which is spoken of, a matter, affair, thing," is translated "matter" in **Mark 1:45**; Acts 8:21; 15:6; 19:38; RV of Phil. 4:15, "in the matter of" (KJV, "concerning").

No more *meketi* (3371), generally expressing a prohibition, e.g., Matt. 21:19; John 5:14; Rom. 14:13; Eph. 4:28; 1 Tim. 5:23; 1 Pet. 4:2; indicating some condition expressed or implied, e.g., 1 Thess. 3:5; or nonexistence, when the existence might have been possible under certain conditions, e.g., **Mark 1:45**; **2:2**, RV, "no longer" (KJV, "no").

Openly *phaneros* (5320), manifestly, is rendered "openly" in **Mark 1:45**; "publicly" in John 7:10, RV (opposite to "in secret"); in Acts 10:3, RV, "openly," for KJV, evidently.

Every quarter *pantothen* (3840), or *pantachothen*, "from all sides," is translated "from every quarter," **Mark 1:45**; in Luke 19:43, "on every side"; in Heb. 9:4, "round about."

Chapter 2

2:1 And again he entered into Capernaum after *some* days; and it was noised that he was in the house.

Noised *akouo* (191), "to hear," is translated "it was noised" in **Mark 2:1** (passive voice), of the rapid spread of the information that Christ was "in the house" in Capernaum.

2:2 And straightway many were gathered together, insomuch that there was no room to receive *them*, no, not so much as about the door: and he preached the word unto them.

No room *meketi* (3371), also means "no more, no longer," but generally suggests what is a matter of thought or supposition, rather than a matter of fact. It is rendered "any longer" in Acts 25:24; "no longer," in **Mark 2:2**, RV, "no longer (room)," KJV, "no (room);" 2 Cor. 5:15, RV (KJV, "not henceforth"); Eph. 4:14, RV (KJV, "no more"); 4:17, RV (KJV, "henceforth ... not"); 1 Thess. 3:1, 5; 1 Tim. 5:23; 1 Pet. 4:2. *See also* **No more** at ***Mark 1:45***.

Room to receive *choreo* (5562), signifies (a), lit., "to give space, make room" (*chora*, "a place"); hence, transitively, "to have space or room for a thing, to contain," said of the waterpots as "containing" a certain quantity, John 2:6; of a space large enough to hold a number of people, **Mark 2:2**; of the world as not possible of "containing" certain books, John 21:25; (b) "to go," Matt. 15:17; "to have place," John 8:37; "to come," 2 Pet. 3:9; (c) metaphorically, "of receiving with the mind," Matt. 19:11, 12; or "into the heart," 2 Cor. 7:2.

Much The negatives *oude* and *mede*, "not even" (RV) are translated "not so much as" in the KJV in **Mark 2:2**; Luke 6:3 and 1 Cor. 5:1; in the following the RV and KJV translate them "not so much as," **Mark 3:20** (some mss. have *mete*, with the same meaning); Acts 19:2; in **Mark 6:31** "no (leisure) so much as."

Preached *laleo*, "to speak," is translated "preached," **Mark 2:2**, KJV, "preached" (RV, "spake"); in Acts 8:25, 1st part, KJV (RV, "spoken"); so in 13:42 and 14:25; "preaching" in Acts 11:19, KJV, but what is indicated here is not a formal "preaching" by the believers scattered from Jerusalem, but a general testimony to all with whom they came into contact; in 16:6, RV, "to speak" (KJV, "to preach").

2:3 And they come unto him, bringing one sick of the palsy, which was borne of four.

Palsy (sick of) *paralutikos* (3885), "paralytic, sick of the palsy," is found in Matt. 4:24 (RV, "palsied"); 8:6; 9:2 (twice), 6; **Mark 2:3**, 4, 5, 9, 10; in some mss. Luke 5:24.

2:4 And when they could not come nigh unto him for the press, they uncovered the roof where he was: and when they had broken *it* up, they let down the bed wherein the sick of the palsy lay.

Come *prosengizo* (4331), denotes "to come near" (*pros*, "to," *engizo*, "to be near, to approach"), **Mark 2:4**, used of those who tried to bring a palsied man to Christ.

Press *ochlos* (3793), "a confused throng," is usually translated "multitude." The RV translates it "crowd" (KJV, "press" in some) in Matt. 9:23, 25; **Mark 2:4**; **3:9**; **5:27**, **30**; Luke 8:19; 19:3; Acts 21:34-35; 24:12, 18.

Uncovered *apostegazo* (648), signifies "to unroof" (*apo*, from, *stege*, "a roof"), **Mark 2:4**.

Roof *stege* (4721), "a covering" (*stego*, "to cover"), denotes "a roof," **Mark 2:4**; said of entering a house, Matt. 8:8; Luke 7:6.

Broken *exorusso* (1846), lit., "to dig out," is said of the "breaking up" of part of a roof, **Mark 2:4**, and, in a vivid expression, of plucking out the eyes, Gal. 4:15.

Let down *chalao* (5465), "to slacken, loosen, let loose," denotes in the NT, "to let down, to lower"; it is used with reference to (a) the paralytic, in **Mark 2:4**; (b) Saul of Tarsus, Acts 9:25, "lowering"; 2 Cor. 11:33, "was I let down" (passive voice); (c) nets, Luke 5:4, 5 (in the latter, RV, "nets"; KJV, "net"); (d) the gear of a ship, Acts 27:17, RV, "they lowered (the gear)," KJV, "they strake (sail)"; (e) a ship's boat, v. 30, RV, "lowered" (KJV, "let down").

Bed *krabbatos* (2895), a Macedonian word (Lat. *grabatus*), is "a somewhat mean bed, pallet, or mattress for the poor," **Mark 2:4**, **9**, **11-12**; **6:55**; John 5:8-11; Acts 5:15; 9:33.

Palsy (sick of) *see Mark 2:3.*

Lay *see Mark 1:30.*

2:5 When Jesus saw their faith, he said unto the sick of the palsy, Son, thy sins be forgiven thee.

Palsy (sick of) *see Mark 2:3.*

2:6 But there were certain of the scribes sitting there, and reasoning in their hearts,

Scribes *nomikos* (3544), an adjective, "learned in the law" (see Titus 3:9), is used as a noun, "a lawyer," Matt. 22:35; Luke 7:30; 10:25; 11:45, 46, 52 (v. 53 in some mss.); 14:3; Titus 3:13, where Zenas is so named. As there is no evidence that he was one skilled in Roman jurisprudence, the term may be regarded in the usual NT sense as applying to one skilled in the Mosaic Law. The usual name for a scribe is *grammateus*, a man of letters; for a doctor of the law, *nomodidaskalos*, "A comparison of Luke 5:17 with v. 21 and **Mark 2:6** and Matt. 9:3 shows that the three terms were used synonymously, and did not denote three distinct classes. The scribes were originally simply men of letters, students of Scripture, and the name first given to them contains in itself no reference to the law; in course of time, however, they devoted themselves mainly, though by no means exclusively, to the study of the law. They became jurists rather than theologians, and received names which of themselves called attention to that fact. Some would doubtless devote themselves more to one branch of activity than to another; but a 'lawyer' might also be a 'doctor,' and the case of Gamaliel shows that a 'doctor' might also be a member of the Sanhedrin, Acts 5:34" (Eaton, in *Hastings' Bib. Dic.*).

Reasoning *dialogizomai* (1260), "to bring together different reasons and reckon them up, to reason," is used in the NT (a) chiefly of thoughts and considerations which are more or less objectionable, e.g., of the disciples who "reasoned" together, through a mistaken view of Christ's teaching regarding leaven, Matt. 16:7, 8 and **Mark 8:16**, **17**; of their "reasoning" as to who was the greatest among them, **Mark 9:33**, RV, "were ye reasoning," KJV, "ye disputed"; of the scribes and Pharisees in criticizing Christ's claim to forgive sins, **Mark 2:6**, **8** (twice) and Luke 5:21, 22; of the chief priests and elders in considering how to answer Christ's question regarding John's baptism, Matt. 21:25; **Mark 11:31** (some mss. have *logizomai* here, which is nowhere else rendered "to reason"); of the wicked husbandmen, and their purpose to murder the heir and seize his inheritance, Luke 20:14; of the rich man who "reasoned" within himself, RV (KJV, "thought"), as to where to bestow his fruits, Luke 12:17 (some mss. have it in John 11:50, the best have *logizomai*); (b) of considerations not objectionable, Luke 1:29, "cast in (her) mind"; 3:15, RV, and KJV, marg., "reasoned" (KJV, "mused").

Hearts *kardia* (2588), "the heart" (Eng., "cardiac," etc.), the chief organ of physical life ("for the life of the flesh is in the blood," Lev. 17:11), occupies the most important place in the human system. By an easy transition the word came to stand for man's entire mental and moral activity, both the rational and the emotional elements. In other words, the heart is used figuratively for the hidden springs of the personal life. As to its usage in the NT it denotes (a) the seat of physical life, Acts 14:17; Jas. 5:5; (b) the seat of moral nature and spiritual life, the seat of grief, John 14:1; Rom. 9:2; 2 Cor. 2:4; joy, John 16:22; Eph. 5:19; the desires, Matt. 5:28; 2 Pet. 2:14; the affections, Luke 24:32; Acts 21:13; the perceptions, John 12:40; Eph. 4:18; the thoughts, Matt. 9:4; Heb. 4:12; the understanding, Matt. 13:15; Rom. 1:21; the reasoning powers, **Mark 2:6**; Luke 24:38; the imagination, Luke 1:51; conscience, Acts 2:37; 1 John 3:20; the intentions, Heb. 4:12, cf. 1 Pet. 4:1; purpose, Acts 11:23; 2 Cor. 9:7; the will, Rom. 6:17; Col. 3:15; faith, **Mark 11:23**; Rom. 10:10; Heb. 3:12.

2:7 Why doth this *man* thus speak blasphemies? who can forgive sins but God only?

This *houtos*, "this," is translated "this fellow" in the KJV of Luke 23:2 (RV, "this man"). So in John 9:29. Both versions have "this man," e.g., in **Mark 2:7**; John 6:52, in the same contemptuous sense.

Blasphemies *blasphemeo* (987), "to blaspheme, rail at or revile," is used (a) in a general way, of any contumelious speech, reviling, calumniating, railing at, etc., as of those who railed at Christ, e.g., Matt. 27:39; **Mark 15:29**; Luke 22:65 (RV, "reviling"); 23:39; (b) of those who speak contemptuously of God or of sacred things, e.g., Matt. 9:3; **Mark 3:28**; Rom. 2:24; 1 Tim. 1:20; 6:1; Rev. 13:6; 16:9, 11, 21; "hath spoken blasphemy," Matt. 26:65; "rail at," 2 Pet. 2:10; Jude 8, 10; "railing," 2 Pet. 2:12; "slanderously reported," Rom. 3:8; "be evil spoken of," Rom. 14:16; 1 Cor. 10:30; 2 Pet. 2:2; "speak evil of," Titus 3:2; 1 Pet. 4:4; "being defamed," 1 Cor. 4:13. The verb (in the present participial form) is translated "blasphemers" in Acts 19:37; in **Mark 2:7**, "blasphemeth," RV, for KJV, "speaketh blasphemies."

There is no noun in the original representing the English "blasphemer." This is expressed either by the verb, or by the adjective *blasphemos*.

Only *heis* (1520), the first cardinal numeral, masculine (feminine and neuter nominative forms are *mia* and *hen*, respectively), is used to signify (1) (a) "one" in contrast to many, e.g., Matt. 25:15; Rom. 5:18, RV, "(through) one (trespass)," i.e., Adam's transgression, in contrast to the "one act of righteousness," i.e., the death of Christ (not as KJV, "the offense of one," and "the righteousness of one"); (b) metaphorically, "union" and "concord," e.g., John 10:30; 11:52; 17:11, 21-22; Rom. 12:4-5; Phil. 1:27; (2) emphatically, (a) a single ("one"), to the exclusion of others, e.g., Matt. 21:24; Rom. 3:10; 1 Cor. 9:24; 1 Tim. 2:5 (twice); (b) "one, alone," e.g., **Mark 2:7**, RV (KJV, "only"); **10:18**; Luke 18:19; (c) "one and the same," e.g., Rom. 3:30, RV, "God is one," i.e., there is not "one" God for the Jew and one for the Gentile; cf. Gal. 3:20, which means that in a promise there is no other party; 1 Cor. 3:8; 11:5; 12:11; 1 John 5:8 (lit., "and the three are into one," i.e., united in "one" and the same witness); (3) a certain "one," in the same sense as the indefinite pronoun *tis*, e.g., Matt. 8:19, RV, "a (scribe)," marg., "one (scribe)," KJV, "a certain (scribe)"; 19:16, "one;" in Rev. 8:13, RV marg., "one (eagle)"; *heis tis* are used together in Luke 22:50; John 11:49; this occurs frequently in the papyri (Moulton, *Prol.*, p. 96); (4) distributively, with *hekastos*, "each," i.e., "every one," e.g., Luke 4:40; Acts 2:6, "every man" (lit., "every one"); in the sense of "one ... and one," e.g., John 20:12; or "one" ... followed by *allos* or *heteros*, "the other," e.g., Matt. 6:24; or by a second *heis*, e.g., Matt. 24:40, RV, "one"; John 20:12; in Rom. 12:5 *heis* is preceded by *kata* (*kath'* in the sense of "severally (members) one (of another)," RV (KJV, "every one ... one"); cf. **Mark 14:19**; in 1 Thess. 5:11 the phrase in the 2nd part, "each other," RV (KJV, "one another"), is, lit., "one the one"; (5) as an ordinal number, equivalent to *protos*, "first," in the phrase "the first day of the week," lit. and idiomatically, "one of sabbaths," signifying "the first day after the sabbath," e.g., Matt. 28:1; **Mark 16:2**; Acts 20:7; 1 Cor. 16:2. Moulton remarks on the tendency for certain cardinal numerals to replace ordinals (*Prol.*, p. 96).

2:8 And immediately when Jesus perceived in his spirit that they so reasoned within themselves, he said unto them, Why reason ye these things in your hearts?

Spirit *pneuma* (4151), primarily denotes "the wind" (akin to *pneo*, "to breathe, blow"); also "breath"; then, especially "the spirit," which, like the wind, is invisible, immaterial and powerful. The NT uses of the word include the sentient element in man, that by which he perceives, reflects, feels, desires, Matt. 5:3; 26:41; **Mark 2:8**; Luke 1:47, 80; Acts 17:16; 20:22; 1 Cor. 2:11; 5:3, 4; 14:4, 15; 2 Cor. 7:1; cf. Gen. 26:35; Isa. 26:9; Ezek. 13:3; Dan. 7:15.

Reasoned *see* Reasoning at *Mark 2:6*.

2:9 Whether is it easier to say to the sick of the palsy, *Thy* sins be forgiven thee; or to say, Arise, and take up thy bed, and walk?

Easier *eukopoteros* (2123), the comparative degree of *eukopos*, "easy, with easy labor" (*eu*, "well," *kopos*, "labor"), hence, of that which is "easier to do," is found in the Synoptics only, Matt. 9:5; 19:24; **Mark 2:9**; **10:25**; Luke 5:23; 16:17; 18:25.

Palsy (sick of) *see Mark 2:3.*

Bed *see Mark 2:4.*

2:10 But that ye may know that the Son of man hath power on earth to forgive sins, (he saith to the sick of the palsy,)

Palsy (sick of) *see Mark 2:3.*

2:11 I say unto thee, Arise, and take up thy bed, and go thy way into thine house.

Bed *see Mark 2:4.*

2:12 And immediately he arose, took up the bed, and went forth before them all; insomuch that they were all amazed, and glorified God, saying, We never saw it on this fashion.

Fashion *houtos* (3779), "thus, so, in this way," is rendered "on this fashion" in **Mark 2:12**.

2:13 And he went forth again by the sea side; and all the multitude resorted unto him, and he taught them.

Resorted *erchomai* (2064), "to come," is translated "resorted" in **Mark 2:13**; in John 10:41 (RV, "came").

2:14 And as he passed by, he saw Levi the *son* of Alphaeus sitting at the receipt of custom, and said unto him, Follow me. And he arose and followed him.

Sitting *kathemai* (2521), is used (a) of the natural posture, e.g., Matt. 9:9, most frequently in Revelation, some 32 times; frequently in the Gospels and Acts; elsewhere only in 1 Cor. 14:30; Jas. 2:3 (twice); and of Christ's position of authority on the throne of God, Col. 3:1, KJV, "sitteth" (RV, "is, seated"); Heb. 1:13 (cf. Matt. 22:44; 26:64 and parallel passages in Mark and Luke, and Acts 2:34); often as antecedent or successive to, or accompanying, another act (in no case a superfluous expression), e.g., Matt. 15:29; 27:36; **Mark 2:14**; **4:1**; (b) metaphorically in Matt. 4:16 (twice); Luke 1:79; of inhabiting a place (translated "dwell"), Luke 21:35; Rev. 14:6, RV marg., "sit" (in the best texts: some have *katoikeo*, "to dwell").

Custom *telonion* (5058), denotes "a custom-house," for the collection of the taxes, Matt. 9:9; **Mark 2:14**; Luke 5:27 (RV, "place of toll").

2:15 And it came to pass, that, as Jesus sat at meat in his house, many publicans and sinners sat also together with Jesus and his disciples: for there were many, and they followed him.

Sat *katakeimai* (2621), "to lie down" (*kata*, "down," and *keimai*), is used of "reclining at a meal," **Mark 2:15**; **14:3**; Luke 5:29, RV, "were sitting at meat" (KJV, "sat down"); 7:37 (in the best texts); 1 Cor. 8:10.

Publicans *telones* (5057), primarily denoted "a farmer of the tax" (from *telos*, "toll, custom, tax"), then, as in the NT, a subsequent subordinate of such, who collected taxes in some district, "a tax gatherer"; such were naturally hated intensely by the people; they are classed with "sinners," Matt. 9:10, 11; 11:9; **Mark 2:15**, **16**; Luke 5:30; 7:34; 15:1; with harlots, Matt. 21:31, 32; with "the Gentile," Matt. 18:17; some mss. have it in Matt. 5:47, the best have *ethnikoi*, "Gentiles." See also Matt. 5:46; 10:3; Luke 3:12; 5:27, 29; 7:29; 18:10, 11, 13.

Sat ... together with *sunanakeimai* (4873), "to recline at table with or together" (*sun*, and *anakeimai*), "to sit at meat or at table with," occurs in Matt. 9:10, "sat down"; 14:9; **Mark 2:15**, RV, "sat down with" (KJV, "sat ... together with"); **6:22**; Luke 7:49; 14:10, 15; John 12:2 (in some texts).

2:16 And when the scribes and Pharisees saw him eat with publicans and sinners, they said unto his disciples, How is it that he eateth and drinketh with publicans and sinners?

Eat with *esthio* (2068), signifies "to eat" (as distinct from *pino*, "to drink"); it is a lengthened form from *edo* (Lat., *edo;* cf. Eng., "edible"); in Heb. 10:27, metaphorically, "devour"; it is said of the ordinary use of food and drink, 1 Cor. 9:7; 11:22; of partaking of food at table, e.g., **Mark 2:16**; of reveling, Matt. 24:49; Luke 12:45.

Publicans *see Mark 2:15.*

2:17 When Jesus heard *it*, he saith unto them, They that are whole have no need of the physician, but they that are sick: I came not to call the righteous, but sinners to repentance.

Whole *ischuo* (2480), "to be strong," is rendered "they that are whole" in Matt. 9:12 and **Mark 2:17**.

Physician *iatros* (2395), akin to *iaomai*, "to heal," "a physician," occurs in Matt. 9:12; **Mark 2:17**; **5:26**; Luke 4:23; 5:31 (in some mss., 8:43); Col. 4:14.

Sick *see* **Diseased** at *Mark 1:32*.

Repentance *metanoia* (3341), "afterthought, change of mind, repentance," is used of "repentance" from sin or evil, except in Heb. 12:17, where the word "repentance" seems to mean, not simply a change of Isaac's mind, but such a change as would reverse the effects of his own previous state of mind. Esau's birthright-bargain could not be recalled; it involved an irretrievable loss. As regards "repentance" from sin, (a) the requirement by God on man's part is set forth, e.g., in Matt. 3:8; Luke 3:8; Acts 20:21; 26:20; (b) the mercy of God in giving "repentance" or leading men to it is set forth, e.g., in Acts 5:31; 11:18; Rom. 2:4; 2 Tim. 2:25. The most authentic mss. omit the word in Matt. 9:13 and **Mark 2:17**, as in the RV.

2:18 And the disciples of John and of the Pharisees used to fast: and they come and say unto him, Why do the disciples of John and of the Pharisees fast, but thy disciples fast not?

Fast *nesteuo* (3522), "to fast, to abstain from eating," is used of voluntary "fasting," Matt. 4:2; 6:16, 17, 18; 9:14, 15; **Mark 2:18, 19, 20**; Luke 5:33, 34, 35; 18:12; Acts 13:2, 3. Some of these passages show that teachers to whom scholars or disciples were attached gave them special instructions as to "fasting." Christ taught the need of purity and simplicity of motive.

The answers of Christ to the questions of the disciples of John and of the Pharisees reveal His whole purpose and method. No doubt He and His followers observed such a fast as that on the Day of Atonement, but He imposed no frequent "fasts" in addition. What He taught was suitable to the change of character and purpose which He designed for His disciples. His claim to be the Bridegroom, Matt. 9:15, and the reference there to the absence of "fasting," virtually involved a claim to be the Messiah (cf. Zech. 8:19). Some mss. have the verb in Acts 10:30.

2:19 And Jesus said unto them, Can the children of the bridechamber fast, while the bridegroom is with them? as long as they have the bridegroom with them, they cannot fast.

Children *huios* (5207), primarily signifies the relation of offspring to parent (see John 9:18-20; Gal. 4:30).

"As to moral characteristics, the following phrases are used: (a) sons of God, Matt. 5:9, 45; Luke 6:35; (b) sons of the light, Luke 16:8; John 12:36; (c) sons of the day, 1 Thess. 5:5; (d) sons of peace, Luke 10:6; (e) sons of this world, Luke 16:8; (f) sons of disobedience, Eph. 2:2; (g) sons of the evil one, Matt. 13:38, cf. 'of the Devil,' Acts 13:10; (h) son of perdition, John 17:12; 2 Thess. 2:3. It is also used to describe characteristics other than moral, as: (i) sons of the resurrection, Luke 20:36; (j) sons of the Kingdom, Matt. 8:12; 13:38; (k) sons of the bridechamber, **Mark 2:19**; (l) sons of exhortation, Acts 4:36; (m) sons of thunder, Boanerges, **Mark 3:17**."

Bridechamber *numphon* (3567), signifies (a) "the room or dining hall in which the marriage ceremonies were held," Matt. 22:10; some mss. have *gamos*, "a wedding," here; (b) "the chamber containing the bridal bed," "the sons of the bridechamber" being the friends of the bridegroom, who had the charge of providing what was necessary for the nuptials, Matt. 9:15; **Mark 2:19**; Luke 5:34.

Fast *see Mark 2:18*.

While In Acts 27:33 and Heb. 3:13 *achri* (or *achris*) followed by *hou*, the genitive case of the relative pronoun *hos*, lit., "until which," is rendered "while"; cf. *en ho*, in **Mark 2:19**; Luke 5:34; John 5:7; *en to*, in Luke 1:21, RV, "while"; in Heb. 3:15, "while it is said," is, lit., "in the being said" (*en*, with the article and the pres. infin., passive of *lego*); so, e.g., in Matt. 13:25.

2:20 But the days will come, when the bridegroom shall be taken away from them, and then shall they fast in those days.

Taken *apairo* (522), "to lift off" (*apo*, "from," *airo*), is used, in the passive voice, of Christ, metaphorically as the Bridegroom of His followers, Matt. 9:15; **Mark 2:20**; Luke 5:35.

Fast *see Mark 2:18*.

2:21 No man also seweth a piece of new cloth on an old garment: else the new piece that filled it up taketh away from the old, and the rent is made worse.

Seweth *epirapto* or *epirrhapto* (1976), (*epi*, "upon," *rhapto*, "to sew or stitch"), is used in **Mark 2:21**.

Piece *epiblema* (1915), primarily denotes "that which is thrown over, a cover" (*epi*, "over," *ballo*, "to throw"); then, "that which is put on, or sewed on, to cover a rent, a patch," Matt. 9:16; **Mark 2:21**; in the next sentence, RV, "that which should fill" (KJV, "the new piece that filled"), there is no word representing "piece" (lit., "the filling," *pleroma*).

New *agnaphos* (46), "uncarded" (*a*, negative, *knapto*, "to card wool"), is rendered "undressed," of cloth, in Matt. 9:16 and **Mark 2:21**, RV (KJV, "new").

Cloth *rhakos* (4470), denotes "a ragged garment, or a piece of cloth torn off, a rag"; hence, a piece of undressed "cloth," Matt. 9:16; **Mark 2:21**.

Old *palaios* (3820), (Eng., "paleontology," etc.), "of what is of long duration, old in years," etc., a garment, wine (in contrast to *neos*), Matt. 9:16-17; **Mark 2:21-22** (twice); Luke 5:36-37, 39 (twice); of the treasures of divine truth, Matt. 13:52 (compared with *kainos*); of what belongs to the past, e.g., the believer's former self before his conversion, his "old man," "old" because it has been superseded by that which is new, Rom. 6:6; Eph. 4:22 (in contrast to *kainos*); Col. 3:9 (in contrast to *neos*); of the covenant in connection with the Law, 2 Cor. 3:14; of leaven, metaphorical of moral evil, 1 Cor. 5:7, 8 (in contrast to *neos*); of that which was given long ago and remains in force, an "old" commandment, 1 John 2:7 (twice), that which was familiar and well known in contrast to that which is fresh (*kainos*).

Filled *pleroma* (4138), fullness, has two meanings, (a) in the active sense, "that which fills up," a piece of undressed cloth on an old garment, Matt. 9:16; **Mark 2:21**, lit., "the filling" (RV, "that which should fill it up"), i.e., "the patch," which is probably the significance; (b) "that which has been completed, the fullness," e.g., **Mark 8:20**.

Rent *schisma* (4978), (Eng., "schism"), denotes "a cleft, a rent," Matt. 9:16; **Mark 2:21**, then, metaphorically, "a division dissension," John 7:43; 9:16; 10:19; 1 Cor. 1:10; 11:18; in 1 Cor. 12:25 it is translated "schism" (marg., "division"). The root is *skid*– seen in the corresponding verb *schizo*, "to cleave" (Lat. *scindo*). Cf. *hairesis*, a sect.

Worse *cheiron* (5501), used as the comparative degree of *kakos*, "evil," describes (a) the condition of certain men, Matt. 12:45; Luke 11:26; 2 Pet. 2:20; (b) evil men themselves and seducers, 2 Tim. 3:13; (c) indolent men who refuse to provide for their own households, and are worse than unbelievers, 1 Tim. 5:8, RV; (d) a rent in a garment, Matt. 9:16; **Mark 2:21**; (e) an error, Matt. 27:64; (f) a person suffering from a malady, **Mark 5:26**; (g) a possible physical affliction, John 5:14; (h) a punishment, Heb. 10:29, "sorer."

2:22 And no man putteth new wine into old bottles: else the new wine doth burst the bottles, and the wine is spilled, and the bottles will be marred: but new wine must be put into new bottles.

Putteth, Put *ballo* (906), "to throw, cast, put," is translated "to put," in Matt. 9:17 (twice); 25:27; 27:6; **Mark 2:22**; **7:33**; Luke 5:37; John 5:7; 12:6; 13:2 (of "putting" into the heart by the Devil); 18:11 (of "putting" up a sword); 20:25 (RV twice, KJV, "put" and "thrust"); v. 27, RV; Jas, 3:3; Rev. 2:24 (RV, "cast"). *Bleteos* (992) (a gerundive form from *ballo*), meaning "(that which) one must put," is found in Luke 5:38, and, in some mss., **Mark 2:22**.

New *kainos* (2537), denotes "new," of that which is unaccustomed or unused, not "new" in time, recent, but "new" as to form or quality, of different nature from what is contrasted as old. "'The new tongues,' *kainos*, of **Mark 16:17** are the 'other tongues,' heteros, of Acts 2:4. These languages, however, were 'new' and 'different,' not in the sense that they had never been heard before, or that they were new to the hearers, for it is plain from v. 8 that this is not the case; they were new languages to the speakers, different from those in which they were accustomed to speak. *Kainos* is translated "fresh" in the RV of Matt. 9:17; **Mark 2:22** (in the best texts) and Luke 5:38, of wineskins. Cf. *kainotes*, "newness." The "new" wine of Matt. 9:17; **Mark 2:22**; Luke 5:37-39, is *neos*, as being of recent production; the "new" wine of the kingdom, Matt. 26:29; **Mark 14:25**, is *kainos*, since it will be of a different character from that of this world. The rendering "new" (*neos*) is elsewhere used metaphorically in 1 Cor. 5:7, "a new lump."

Wine *oinos* (3631), is the general word for "wine." The mention of the bursting of the wineskins, Matt. 9:17; **Mark 2:22**; Luke 5:37, implies fermentation. See also Eph. 5:18 (cf. John 2:10; 1 Tim. 3:8; Titus 2:3). In Matt. 27:34, the RV has "wine" (KJV, "vinegar," translating the inferior reading *oxos*).

Bottles *askos* (779), "a leather bottle, wineskin," occurs in Matt. 9:17 (four times); **Mark 2:22** (four times); Luke 5:37 (three times), 38; in each place, RV, "wineskins" or "skins," for KJV, "bottles." A whole goatskin, for example, would be used with the apertures bound up, and when filled, tied at the neck. They were tanned with acacia bark and left hairy on the outside. New wines, by fermenting, would rend old skins (cf. Josh. 9:13; Job 32:19). Hung in the smoke to dry, the skin-bottles become shriveled (see Ps. 119:83).

Burst *rhegnumi* (4486), "to tear, rend, as of garments, etc.," is translated "break" in the KJV, of Matt. 9:17, of wine-skins (RV, "burst"); as in **Mark 2:22** and Luke 5:37; "break forth" in Gal. 4:27.

Spilled Some texts have *ekcheo* in **Mark 2:22** (so KJV). The form in Luke 5:37 might also come from *ekcheo*.

Marred In **Mark 2:22**, *apollumi*, "to destroy, perish," is found in the most authentic mss. as applying both to the wine and the wine skins, RV, "perisheth"; the KJV follows the mss. which tell of the wine being "spilled" (*ekcheo*, "to pour out"), and the skins (KJV, "bottles") being "marred."

2:23 And it came to pass, that he went through the corn fields on the sabbath day; and his disciples began, as they went, to pluck the ears of corn.

Went *paraporeuomai* (3899), primarily, "to go beside, accompany" (*para*, "beside," *poreuomai*, "to proceed"), denotes "to go past, pass by," Matt. 27:39; **Mark 9:30**, "passed through" (some mss. have *poreuomai*); **11:20**; **15:29**; in **Mark 2:23**, "going ... through."

Sabbath *sabbaton* (4521), or *sabbata:* the latter, the plural form, was transliterated from the Aramaic word, which was mistaken for a plural; hence the singular, *sabbaton*, was formed from it. The root means "to cease, desist" (Heb., *shabath*; cf. Arab., *sabata*, "to intercept, interrupt"); the doubled *b* has an intensive force, implying a complete cessation or a making to cease, probably the former. The idea is not that of relaxation or refreshment, but cessation from activity.

The observation of the seventh day of the week, enjoined upon Israel, was a sign between God and His earthly people, based upon the fact that after the six days of creative operations He rested, Exod. 31:16, 17, with 20:8-11. The OT regulations were developed and systematized to such an extent that they became a burden upon the people (who otherwise rejoiced in the rest provided) and a byword for absurd extravagance. Two treatises of the Mishna (the *Shabbath* and *Erubin*) are entirely occupied with regulations for the observance; so with the discussions in the Gemara, on rabbinical opinions. The effect upon current opinion explains the antagonism roused by the Lord's cures wrought on the "Sabbath," e.g., Matt. 12:9-13; John 5:5-16, and explains the fact that on a "Sabbath" the sick were brought to be healed after sunset, e.g., **Mark 1:32**. According to rabbinical ideas, the disciples, by plucking ears of corn (Matt. 12:1; **Mark 2:23**), and rubbing them (Luke 6:1), broke the "sabbath" in two respects; for to pluck was to reap, and to rub was to thresh. The Lord's attitude towards the "sabbath" was by way of freeing it from these vexatious traditional accretions by which it was made an end in itself, instead of a means to an end (**Mark 2:27**).

Went *poieo* (4160), "to do, to make," is used in the latter sense (a) of constructing or producing anything, of the creative acts of God, e.g., Matt. 19:4 (2nd part); Acts 17:24; of the acts of human beings, e.g., Matt. 17:4; Acts 9:39; (b) with nouns denoting a state or condition, to be the author of, to cause, e.g., peace, Eph. 2:15; Jas. 3:18; stumbling blocks, Rom. 16:17; (c) with nouns involving the idea of action (or of something accomplished by action), so as to express the idea of the verb more forcibly (the middle voice is commonly used in this respect, suggesting the action as being of special interest to the doer); for the active voice see, e.g., **Mark 2:23**, of "making" one's way, where the idea is not that the disciples "made" a path through the standing corn, but simply that they went, the phrase being equivalent to going, "(they began) as they went (to pluck the ears)"; other instances of the active are Rev. 13:13, 14; 16:14; 19:20.

Corn fields *sporimos* (4702), signifies "fit for sowing" (from *speiro*, "to sow"), and denotes "a cornfield," Matt. 12:1; **Mark 2:23**; Luke 6:1. In the Sept., Gen. 1:29; Lev. 11:37.

Pluck *tillo* (5089), is used of "plucking off ears of corn," Matt. 12:1; **Mark 2:23**; Luke 6:1. In the Sept., Isa. 18:7.

Ears of corn *stachus* (4719), is found in Matt. 12:1; **Mark 2:23**; **4:28** ("ear," twice); Luke 6:1. The first part of the word is derived from the root *sta*— found in parts of the verb *histemi*, "to cause to stand." It is used as a proper name in Rom. 16:9.

2:24-26 And the Pharisees said unto him, Behold, why do they on the sabbath day that which is not lawful?

And he said unto them, Have ye never read what David did, when he had need, and was an hungred, he, and they that were with him?

How he went into the house of God in the days of Abiathar the high priest, and did eat the shewbread, which is not lawful to eat but for the priests, and gave also to them which were with him?

Days In **Mark 2:26**, KJV, "in the days of," there is no word for "days" in the original; RV (from best mss.), "when" in Acts 11:28, "in the days of."

Priest *archiereus* (749), designates (a) "the high priests" of the Levitical order, frequently called "chief priests" in the NT, and including "ex-high priests" and members of "high priestly" families, e.g., Matt. 2:4; 16:21; 20:18; 21:15; in the singular, a "high priest," e.g., Abiathar, **Mark 2:26**; Annas and Caiaphas, Luke 3:2.

Shewbread The phrase rendered "the shewbread" is formed by the combination of the nouns *prothesis*, "a setting forth" (*pro*, "before," *tithemi*, "to place") and *artos*, "a loaf" (in the plural), each with the article, Matt. 12:4; **Mark 2:26** and Luke 6:4, lit., "the loaves of the setting forth"; in Heb. 9:2, lit., "the setting forth of the loaves." The corresponding OT phrases are lit., "bread of the face," Exod. 25:30, i.e., the presence, referring to the Presence of God (cf. Isa. 63:9 with Exod. 33:14, 15); "the bread of ordering," 1 Chron. 9:32, marg. In Num. 4:7 it is called "the continual bread"; in 1 Sam. 21:4, 6, "holy bread" (KJV, "hallowed"). In the Sept. of 1 Kings 7:48, it is called "the bread of the offering" (*prosphora*, "a bearing towards"). The twelve loaves, representing the tribes of Israel, were set in order every Sabbath day before the Lord, "on the behalf of the children," Lev. 24:8, RV (marg., and KJV, "from"), "an everlasting covenant." The loaves symbolized the fact that on the basis of the sacrificial atonement of the Cross, believers are accepted before God, and nourished by Him in the person of Christ. The showbread was partaken of by the priests, as representatives of the nation. Priesthood now being coextensive with all who belong to Christ, 1 Pet. 2:5, 9, He, the Living Bread, is the nourishment of all, and where He is, there, representatively, they are.

2:27-28 And he said unto them, The sabbath was made for man, and not man for the sabbath:

Therefore the Son of man is Lord also of the sabbath.

Sabbath *see Mark 2:23.*

Chapter 3

3:1 And he entered again into the synagogue; and there was a man there which had a withered hand.

Withered *xeraino* (3583), "to dry up, parch, wither," is translated "to wither," (a) of plants, Matt. 13:6; 21:19, 20; **Mark 4:6; 11:20**, RV (KJV, "dried up"), 21; Luke 8:6; John 15:6; Jas. 1:11; 1 Pet. 1:24; (b) of members of the body, **Mark 3:1**.

3:2 And they watched him, whether he would heal him on the sabbath day; that they might accuse him.

Watched *paratereo* (3906), "to observe," especially with sinister intent, is rendered "to watch" in **Mark 3:2**; Luke 6:7; 14:1; 20:20; Acts 9:24.

3:3 And he saith unto the man which had the withered hand, Stand forth.

Man *anthropos* (444), is used (a) generally, of "a human being, male or female," without reference to sex or nationality, e.g., Matt. 4:4; 12:35; John 2:25; (b) in distinction from God, e.g., Matt. 19:6; John 10:33; Gal. 1:11; Col. 3:23; (c) in distinction from animals, etc., e.g., Luke 5:10; (d) sometimes, in the plural, of "men and women," people, e.g., Matt. 5:13, 16; in **Mark 11:2** and 1 Tim. 6:16, lit., "no one of men"; (e) in some instances with a suggestion of human frailty and imperfection, e.g., 1 Cor. 2:5; Acts 14:15 (2nd part); (f) in the phrase translated "after man," "after the manner of men," "as a man" (KJV), lit. "according to (*kata*) man," is used only by the apostle Paul, of "(1) the practices of fallen humanity 1 Cor. 3:3; (2) anything of human origin, Gal. 1:11; (3) the laws that govern the administration of justice among men, Rom. 3:5; (4) the standard generally accepted among men, Gal. 3:15; (5) an illustration not drawn from Scripture, 1 Cor. 9:8; (6) probably = 'to use a figurative expression' (see KJV, marg.), i.e., to speak evil of men with whom he had contended at Ephesus as 'beasts' (cf. 1 Cor. 4:6), 1 Cor. 15:32; Lightfoot prefers 'from worldly motives'; but the other interpretation, No. (4), seems to make better sense. See also Rom. 6:19, where, however, the Greek is slightly different, *anthropinos*, 'pertaining to mankind'." ... (k) definitely, with the article, of some particular person, Matt. 12:13; **Mark 3:3, 5**; or with the demonstrative pronoun and the article, e.g., Matt. 12:45; Luke 14:30.

Withered *xeros* (3584), is used (a) naturally, of "dry" land, Heb. 11:29; or of land in general, Matt. 23:15, "land"; or of physical infirmity, "withered," Matt. 12:10; **Mark 3:3**; Luke 6:6, 8; John 5:3; (b) figuratively, in Luke 23:31, with reference to the spiritual "barrenness" of the Jews, in contrast to the character of the Lord. Cf. Ps. 1:3; Isa. 56:3; Ezek. 17:24; 20:47.

Stand In **Mark 3:3**, *egeiro*, "to raise," followed by the phrase *eis to meson*, "into the midst," is translated "stand forth."

Forth *mesos* (3319), an adjective denoting "middle, in the middle or midst," is used in the following, in which the English requires a phrase, and the adjectival rendering must be avoided: Luke 22:55, "Peter sat in the midst of them," lit., "a middle one of (them)"; Luke 23:45, of the rending of the veil "in the midst"; here the adjective idiomatically belongs to the verb "was rent," and is not to be taken literally, as if it meant "the middle veil"; John 1:26, "in the midst of you (standeth One)," RV (lit., "a middle One"); Acts 1:18, where the necessity of avoiding the lit. rendering is obvious. Cf. the phrases "at midday," "at midnight." *Mesos* is used adverbially, in prepositional phrases, (a) *ana m.*, e.g., 1 Cor. 6:5, "between"; Matt. 13:25, "among"; Rev. 7:17, "in the midst"; (b) *dia m.*, e.g., Luke 4:30; 17:11, "through the midst"; (c) *en m.*, Luke 10:3, RV, "in the midst," KJV, "among"; so 22:27; 1 Thess. 2:7; with the article after *en*, e.g., Matt. 14:6, RV, "in the midst," KJV, "before"; (d) *eis m.*, **Mark 14:60**, "in the midst"; with the article, e.g., **Mark 3:3**, "forth" (lit., "into the midst").

3:4 And he saith unto them, Is it lawful to do good on the sabbath days, or to do evil? to save life, or to kill? But they held their peace.

To do good *agathopoieo* (15), "to do," is used (a) in a general way, "to do well," 1 Pet. 2:15, 20; 3:6, 17; 3 John 11; (b) with pointed reference "to the benefit of another," Luke 6:9, 33, 35; in **Mark 3:4** the parts of the word are separated in some mss. Some mss. have it in Acts 14:17. Cf. the noun *agathopoiia*, "well-doing," 1 Pet. 4:19, and the adjective *agathopoios*, "doing well," 1 Pet. 2:14.

To do evil *kakopoieo* (2554), signifies "to do evil," **Mark 3:4** is so rendered in the RV of **Mark 3:4** and Luke 6:9 (KJV, "to do evil"), with reference to the moral character of what is done; in 1 Pet. 3:17, "evil doing"; 3 John 11, "doeth evil."

Held their peace *siopao* (4623), "to be silent or still, to keep silence" (from *siope*, "silence"), is translated "to hold one's peace," in Matt. 20:31; 26:63; **Mark 3:4**; **9:34**; **10:48**; **14:61**; Luke 19:40; Acts 18:9; in the Lord's command to the sea, in **Mark 4:39**, it is translated "peace"; in Luke 1:20, RV, "thou shalt be silent" (KJV, "dumb").

3:5 And when he had looked round about on them with anger, being grieved for the hardness of their hearts, he saith unto the man, Stretch forth thine hand. And he stretched *it* out: and his hand was restored whole as the other.

Looked *periblepo* (4017), "to look about, or round about, on," is used in the middle voice, **Mark 3:5**, **34**, **5:32**; **9:8**; **10:23**; **11:11**; Luke 6:10.

Anger *orge* (3709), originally any "natural impulse, or desire, or disposition," came to signify "anger," as the strongest of all passions. It is used of the wrath of man, Eph. 4:31; Col. 3:8; 1 Tim. 2:8; Jas. 1:19-20; the displeasure of human governments, Rom. 13:4-5; the sufferings of the Jews at the hands of the Gentiles, Luke 21:23; the terrors of the Law, Rom. 4:15; "the anger" of the Lord Jesus, **Mark 3:5**; God's "anger" with Israel in the wilderness, in a quotation from the OT, Heb. 3:11; 4:3; God's present "anger" with the Jews nationally, Rom. 9:22; 1 Thess. 2:16; His present "anger" with those who disobey the Lord Jesus in His gospel, John 3:36; God's purposes in judgment, Matt. 3:7; Luke 3:7; Rom. 1:18; 2:5, 8; 3:5; 5:9; 12:19; Eph. 2:3; 5:6; Col. 3:6; 1 Thess. 1:10; 5:9.

Grieved *sunlupeo* (4818), or *sullupeo*, is used in the passive voice in **Mark 3:5**, "to be grieved" or afflicted together with a person, said of Christ's "grief" at the hardness of heart of those who criticized His healing on the Sabbath day; it here seems to suggest the sympathetic nature of His grief because of their self-injury. Some suggest that the *sun* indicates the mingling of "grief" with His anger.

Hardness *porosis* (4457), denotes "a hardening," a covering with a *poros*, a kind of stone, indicating "a process," and is used metaphorically of dulled spiritual perception, **Mark 3:5**, RV, "at the hardening of their hearts"; Rom. 11:25, RV, "a hardening" (KJV, "blindness"), said of the state of Israel; Eph. 4:8, RV, "hardening," of the heart of Gentiles.

Man *see Mark 3:3*.

Stretch *see* Put forth at *Mark 1:41*.

Restored *apokathistemi* or the alternative form *apokathistano* (600), is used (a) of "restoration" to a former condition of health, Matt. 12:13; **Mark 3:5**; **8:25**; Luke 6:10; (b) of the divine "restoration" of Israel and conditions affected by it, including the renewal of the covenant broken by them, Matt. 17:11; **Mark 9:12**; Acts 1:6; (c) of "giving" or "bringing" a person back, Heb. 13:19. In the papyri it is used of financial restitution, of making good the breaking of a stone by a workman by his substituting another, of the reclamation of land, etc. (Moulton and Milligan).

Whole *hugies* (5199), (cf. Eng., "hygiene") is used especially in the Gospels of making sick folk "whole," Matt. 12:13; 15:31; **Mark 3:5**; **5:34**; Luke 6:10; John 5:4, 6, 9, 11, 14, 15; 7:23; also Acts 4:10; of "sound (speech)," Titus 2:8.

3:6 And the Pharisees went forth, and straightway took counsel with the Herodians against him, how they might destroy him.

Took *didomi* (1325), "to give," found in the best texts in **Mark 3:6**, is rendered "took (counsel)"; some have *poieo*, "to make."

3:7 But Jesus withdrew himself with his disciples to the sea: and a great multitude from Galilee followed him, and from Judaea,

Withdrew *anachoreo* (402), is translated "to withdraw" in the RV of Matt. 2:22 and John 6:15; RV and KJV in Matt. 12:15 and **Mark 3:7**.

Multitude *plethos* (4128), lit., "a fullness," hence, "a large company, a multitude," is used (a) of things: of fish, Luke 5:6; John 21:6; of sticks ("bundle"), Acts 28:3; of stars and of sand, Heb. 11:12; of sins, Jas. 5:20; 1 Pet. 4:8; (b) of persons, (1) a "multitude": of people, e.g., **Mark 3:7, 8**; Luke 6:17; John 5:3; Acts 14:1; of angels, Luke 2:13; (2) with the article, the whole number, the "multitude," the populace, e.g., Luke 1:10; 8:37; Acts 5:16; 19:9; 23:7; a particular company, e.g., of disciples, Luke 19:37; Acts 4:32; 6:2, 5; 15:30; of elders, priests, and scribes, 23:7; of the apostles and the elders of the Church in Jerusalem, Acts 15:12.

3:8 And from Jerusalem, and from Idumaea, and *from* beyond Jordan; and they about Tyre and Sidon, a great multitude, when they had heard what great things he did, came unto him.

Multitude *see Mark 3:7.*

3:9 And he spake to his disciples, that a small ship should wait on him because of the multitude, lest they should throng him.

Ship *ploiarion* (4142), is translated "ship" in the KJV of **Mark 3:9; 4:36** and John 21:8; "(took) shipping" in John 6:24, KJV, RV "(got into the) boats."

Wait *proskartereo* (4342), lit., "to be strong towards" (*pros*, "towards," used intensively, and *kartereo*, "to be strong"), "to endure in, or persevere in, to be continually steadfast with a person or thing," is used of "continuing" in prayer with others, Acts 1:14; Rom. 12:12; Col. 4:2; in the apostles' teaching, Acts 2:42; in the Temple, 2:46 ("continuing steadfastly," RV), the adverb representing the intensive preposition; in prayer and the ministry, 6:4 (RV, "will continue steadfastly"); of Simon Magus with Philip, 8:13. In **Mark 3:9** and Acts 10:7, it signifies "to wait on"; in Rom. 13:6, to attend "continually" upon.

Multitude *see* Press at *Mark 2:4*.

Throng *thlibo* (2346), "to suffer affliction, to be troubled," has reference to sufferings due to the pressure of circumstances, or the antagonism of persons, 1 Thess. 3:4; 2 Thess. 1:6-7; "straitened," in Matt. 7:14 (RV); "throng," **Mark 3:9**; "afflicted," 2 Cor. 1:6; 7:5 (RV); 1 Tim. 5:10; Heb. 11:37; "pressed," 2 Cor. 4:8. Both the verb and the noun, when used of the present experience of believers, refer almost invariably to that which comes upon them from without.

3:10 For he had healed many; insomuch that they pressed upon him for to touch him, as many as had plagues.

Press *epipipto* (1968), "to fall upon," is used (a) literally, **Mark 3:10**, "pressed upon"; Acts 20:10, 37; (b) metaphorically, of fear, Luke 1:12; Acts 19:17; Rev. 11:11; reproaches, Rom. 15:3; of the Holy Spirit, Acts 8:16; 10:44; 11:15.

Many *hosos* (3745), "how much, how many, how great, as much as, as many as," is translated "as many as," e.g., in Matt. 14:36; **Mark 3:10**; Luke 9:5, RV (KJV, "whosoever"); Acts 2:39; in 9:16, RV, "how many things" (KJV, "how great things"); in Rom. 6:3 the RV renders it by "all we who" (KJV, "so many of us as"), a necessary alteration, not singling out some believers from others, as if some were not baptized, but implying what was recognized as true of all (see Acts 18:8); in 2 Cor. 1:20, RV, "how many soever be" (KJV, "all").

Plagues *mastix* (3148), "a whip, scourge," Acts 22:24, "by scourging"; Heb. 11:36, "scourgings," is used metaphorically of "disease" or "suffering," **Mark 3:10; 5:29, 34**; Luke 7:21.

3:11 And unclean spirits, when they saw him, fell down before him, and cried, saying, Thou art the Son of God.

Fell *prospipto* (4363), "to fall towards anything" (*pros*, "towards"), "to strike against," is said of "wind," Matt. 7:25; it also signifies to "fall" down at one's feet, "fall" prostrate before, **Mark 3:11; 5:33; 7:25**; Luke 5:8; 8:28, 47; Acts 16:29.

3:12 And he straitly charged them that they should not make him known.

Charged *epitimao* (2008), signifies (a) to put honor upon (*epi*, upon, *time*, honor); (b) to adjudge, to find fault with, rebuke; hence to charge, or rather, to charge strictly (*epi*, intensive), e.g., Matt. 12:16; **Mark 3:12**, "charged much"; **Mark 8:30**; in **10:48**, RV, "rebuked."

Known *phaneros* (5318), "visible, manifest," is translated "known" in Matt. 12:16 and **Mark 3:12**.

3:13 And he goeth up into a mountain, and calleth *unto him* whom he would: and they came unto him.

Came *aperchomai*, "to come away or from," is differently translated in the RV; see, e.g., **Mark 3:13** where it signifies that they went from the company or place where they were to Him; it usually denotes "to go away."

3:14 And he ordained twelve, that they should be with him, and that he might send them forth to preach,

Ordained In **Mark 3:14**, KJV, *poieo*, "to make," is translated "ordained" (RV, "appointed").

3:15 And to have power to heal sicknesses, and to cast out devils:

Sicknesses *see* Diseases at *Mark 1:34*.

3:16 And Simon he surnamed Peter;

Surnamed In **Mark 3:16, 17**, "He surnamed" is a translation of *epitithemi*, "to put upon, to add to," with *onoma*, "a name," as the object. *Onoma* (3686), is used (I) in general of the "name" by which a person or thing is called, e.g., **Mark 3:16, 17**, "(He) surnamed," lit., "(He added) the name"; **14:32**, lit., "(of which) the name (was)"; Luke 1:63; John 18:10, sometimes translated "named," e.g., Luke 8:5, "named (Zacharias)," lit., "by name"; in the same verse, "named (Elizabeth)," lit., "the name of her," an elliptical phrase, with "was" understood; Acts 8:9, RV, "by name," 10:1; the "name" is put for the reality in Rev. 3:1; in Phil. 2:9, the "Name" represents "the title and dignity" of the Lord, as in Eph. 1:21 and Heb. 1:4; (II) for all that a "name" implies, of authority, character, rank, majesty, power, excellence, etc., of everything that the "name" covers: (a) of the "Name" of God as expressing His attributes, etc., e.g., Matt. 6:9; Luke 1:49; John 12:28; 17:6, 26; Rom. 15:9; 1 Tim. 6:1; Heb. 13:15; Rev. 13:6; (b) of the "Name" of Christ, e.g., Matt. 10:22; 19:29; John 1:12; 2:23; 3:18; Acts 26:9; Rom. 1:5; Jas. 2:7; 1 John 3:23; 3 John 7; Rev. 2:13; 3:8; also the phrases rendered "in the name"; these may be analyzed as follows: (1) representing the authority of Christ, e.g., Matt. 18:5 (with *epi*, "on the ground of My authority"); so Matt. 24:5 (falsely) and parallel passages; as substantiated by the Father, John 14:26; 16:23 (last clause), RV; (2) in the power of (with *en*, "in"), e.g., **Mark 16:17**; Luke 10:17; Acts 3:6; 4:10; 16:18; Jas. 5:14; (3) in acknowledgement or confession of, e.g., Acts 4:12; 8:16; 9:27, 28; (4) in recognition of the authority of (sometimes combined with the thought of relying or resting on), Matt. 18:20; cf. 28:19; Acts 8:16; 9:2 (*eis*, "into"); John 14:13; 15:16; Eph. 5:20; Col. 3:17; (5) owing to the fact that one is called by Christ's "Name" or is identified with Him, e.g., 1 Pet. 4:14 (with *en*, "in"); with *heneken*, "for the sake of," e.g., Matt. 19:29; with *dia*, "on account of," Matt. 10:22; 24:9; **Mark 13:13**; Luke 21:17; John 15:21; 1 John 2:12; Rev. 2:3.

3:17 And James the *son* of Zebedee, and John the brother of James; and he surnamed them Boanerges, which is, The sons of thunder:

Son *see* Children at *Mark 2:19*.

Surnamed *see Mark 3:16*.

Thunder *bronte* (1027), in **Mark 3:17** "sons of thunder" is the interpretation of Boanerges, the name applied by the Lord to James and John; their fiery disposition is seen in **9:38** and Luke 9:54; perhaps in the case of James it led to his execution. The name and its interpretation have caused much difficulty; some suggest the meaning "the twins." It is however most probably the equivalent of the Aramaic *bene regesh*, "sons of tumult"; the latter of the two words was no doubt used of "thunder" in Palestinian Aramaic; hence the meaning "the sons of thunder"; the cognate Hebrew word *ragash*, "to rage," is used in Ps. 2:1 and there only. In John 12:29 *bronte* is used with *ginomai*, "to take place," and rendered "it had thundered"; lit., "there was thunder"; elsewhere, Rev. 4:5; 6:1; 8:5; 10:3, 4; 11:19; 14:2; 16:18; 19:6.

3:18-19 And Andrew, and Philip, and Bartholomew, and Matthew, and Thomas, and James the *son* of Alphaeus, and Thaddaeus, and Simon the Canaanite,

And Judas Iscariot, which also betrayed him: and they went into an house.

House In **Mark 3:19**, the KJV and RV marg., have "home," for the text "to a house"; the latter seems the more probable.

3:20 And the multitude cometh together again, so that they could not so much as eat bread.

Much *see Mark 2:2*.

3:21 And when his friends heard *of it*, they went out to lay hold on him: for they said, He is beside himself.

Friends The phrase *hoi para autou*, in **Mark 3:21**, "his friends," lit. means "the (ones) beside Him," i.e., those belonging to him.

Hold *krateo* (2902), "to be strong, mighty, to prevail," (1) is most frequently rendered "to lay or take hold on" (a) literally, e.g., Matt. 12:11; 14:3; 18:28 and 21:46, RV (KJV, "laid hands on"); 22:6, RV (KJV, "took"); 26:55, KJV (RV, "took"); 28:9, RV, "took hold of" (KJV, "held by"); **Mark 3:21**; **6:17**; **12:12**; **14:51**; Acts 24:6, RV (KJV, "took"); Rev. 20:2; (b) metaphorically, of "laying hold of the hope of the Lord's return," Heb. 6:18; (2) also signifies "to hold" or "hold fast," i.e., firmly, (a) literally, Matt. 26:48, KJV (RV, "take"); Acts 3:11; Rev. 2:1; (b) metaphorically, of "holding fast a tradition or teaching," in an evil sense, **Mark 7:3**, **4**, **8**; Rev. 2:14, 15; in a good sense, 2 Thess. 2:15; Rev. 2:25; 3:11; of "holding" Christ, i.e., practically apprehending Him, as the head of His church, Col. 2:19; a confession, Heb. 4:14; the name of Christ, i.e., abiding by all that His name implies, Rev. 2:13; of restraint, Luke 24:16, "(their eyes) were holden"; of the winds, Rev. 7:1; of the impossibility of Christ's being "holden" of death, Acts 2:24.

Beside himself *existemi* (1839), primarily and lit. means "to put out of position, displace": hence, (a) "to amaze," Luke 24:22 (for KJV, "make ... astonished"); Acts 8:9, 11 (KJV, "bewitched"); or "to be amazed, astounded," Matt. 12:23; **Mark 6:51**; (b) "to be out of one's mind, to be beside oneself," **Mark 3:21**; 2 Cor. 5:13, in the latter of which it is contrasted with *sophroneo*, "to be of a sound mind, sober."

3:22 And the scribes which came down from Jerusalem said, He hath Beelzebub, and by the prince of the devils casteth he out devils.

Prince *archon* (758), the present participle of the verb *archo*, "to rule"; denotes "a ruler, a prince." It is used as follows ("p" denoting "prince," or "princes"; "r," "ruler" or "rulers"): (a) of Christ, as "the Ruler (KJV, Prince) of the kings of the earth," Rev. 1:5; (b) of rulers of nations, Matt. 20:25, RV, "r," KJV, "p"; Acts 4:26, "r"; 7:27, "r"; 7:35, "r" (twice); (c) of judges and magistrates, Acts 16:19, "r"; Rom. 13:3, "r"; (d) of members of the Sanhedrin, Luke 14:1, RV, "r" (KJV, "chief"); 23:13, 35, "r"; so 24:20, John 3:1; 7:26, 48; 12:42, RV, "r" (KJV, "chief"); "r" in Acts 3:17; 4:5, 8; 13:27; 14:5; (e) of rulers of synagogues, Matt. 9:18, 23, "r"; so Luke 8:41; 18:18; (f) of the Devil, as "prince" of this world, John 12:31; 14:30; 16:11; of the power of the air, Eph. 2:2, "the air" being that sphere in which the inhabitants of the world live and which, through the rebellious and godless condition of humanity, constitutes the seat of his authority; (g) of Beelzebub, the "prince" of the demons, Matt. 9:24; 12:24; **Mark 3:22**; Luke 11:15.

3:23 And he called them *unto him*, and said unto them in parables, How can Satan cast out Satan?

Parables *parabole* (3850), lit. denotes "a placing beside" (akin to *paraballo*, "to throw" or "lay beside, to compare"). It signifies "a placing of one thing beside another" with a view to comparison (some consider that the thought of comparison is not necessarily contained in the word). In the NT it is found outside the Gospels, only in Heb. 9:9 and 11:19. It is generally used of a somewhat lengthy utterance or narrative drawn from nature or human circumstances, the object of which is to set forth a spiritual lesson, e.g., those in Matt. 13 and Synoptic parallels; sometimes it is used of a short saying or proverb, e.g., Matt. 15:15; **Mark 3:23**; **7:17**; Luke 4:23; 5:36; 6:39. It is the lesson that is of value; the hearer must catch the analogy if he is to be instructed (this is true also of a proverb). Such a narrative or saying, dealing with earthly things with a spiritual meaning, is distinct from a fable, which attributes to things what does not belong to them in nature. Christ's "parables" most frequently convey truths connected with the subject of the kingdom of God. His withholding the meaning from His hearers as He did from the multitudes, Matt. 13:34, was a divine judgment upon the unworthy. Two dangers are to be avoided in seeking to interpret the "parables" in Scripture, that of ignoring the important features, and that of trying to make all the details mean something.

Satan *see Mark 1:13.*

3:24 And if a kingdom be divided against itself, that kingdom cannot stand.

Kingdom *basileia* (932), is primarily an abstract noun, denoting "sovereignty, royal power, dominion," e.g., Rev. 17:18, translated "(which) reigneth," lit., "hath a kingdom" (RV marg.); then, by metonymy, a concrete noun, denoting the territory or people over whom a king rules, e.g., Matt. 4:8; **Mark 3:24**. It is used especially of the "kingdom" of God and of Christ.

Divided *merizo* (3307), akin to *meros*, "a part, to part, divide into," in the middle voice means "to divide anything with another, to share with." The usual meaning is "to divide," Matt. 12:25, 26; **Mark 3:24-26**; **6:41**; Luke 12:13 (middle voice); Rom. 12:3, "hath dealt"; 1 Cor. 1:13; Heb. 7:2, RV (KJV, "gave a part"). Elsewhere with other meanings, 1 Cor. 7:17, 34; 2 Cor. 10:13.

3:25-26 And if a house be divided against itself, that house cannot stand.

And if Satan rise up against himself, and be divided, he cannot stand, but hath an end.

Rise *see* Rising at *Mark 1:35.*

Satan *see Mark 1:13.*

3:27 No man can enter into a strong man's house, and spoil his goods, except he will first bind the strong man; and then he will spoil his house.

Spoil *diarpazo* (1283), "to plunder," is found in Matt. 12:29, 2nd part (the 1st has *harpazo,* in the best texts), lit., "(then) he will completely (*dia,* intensive) spoil (his house)"; **Mark 3:27** (twice).

Goods *skeuos* (4632), is used (a) of "a vessel or implement" of various kinds, **Mark 11:16**; Luke 8:16; John 19:29; Acts 10:11, 16; 11:5; 27:17 (a sail); Rom. 9:21; 2 Tim. 2:20; Heb. 9:21; Rev. 2:27; 18:12; (b) of "goods or household stuff," Matt. 12:29 and **Mark 3:27**, "goods"; Luke 17:31, RV, "goods" (KJV, "stuff"); (c) of "persons," (1) for the service of God, Acts 9:15, "a (chosen) vessel"; 2 Tim. 2:21, "a vessel (unto honor)"; (2) the "subjects" of divine wrath, Rom. 9:22; (3) the "subjects" of divine mercy, Rom. 9:23; (4) the human frame, 2 Cor. 4:7; perhaps 1 Thess. 4:4; (5) a husband and wife, 1 Pet. 3:7.

3:28 Verily I say unto you, All sins shall be forgiven unto the sons of men, and blasphemies wherewith soever they shall blaspheme:

Sins *hamartema* (265), denotes "an act of disobedience to divine law"; plural in **Mark 3:28**; Rom. 3:25; 2 Pet. 1:9, in some texts; sing. in **Mark 3:29** (some mss. have *krisis,* KJV, "damnation"); 1 Cor. 6:18.

Blasphemies *see Mark 2:7.*

3:29 But he that shall blaspheme against the Holy Ghost hath never forgiveness, but is in danger of eternal damnation:

He that *hos* (3739), the relative pronoun "who," is sometimes rendered "he that," e.g., Matt. 10:38; with the particle *an,* expressing possibility, uncertainty or a condition, signifying "whosoever," **Mark 3:29**, KJV (RV, "whosoever"); **4:25** and **9:40** (with *an,* in the best mss.).

Holy Ghost The "Holy Spirit" is spoken of under various titles in the NT ("Spirit" and "Ghost" are renderings of the same word, *pneuma;* the advantage of the rendering "Spirit" is that it can always be used, whereas "Ghost" always requires the word "Holy" prefixed). In the following list the omission of the definite article marks its omission in the original: "Spirit, Matt. 22:43; Eternal Spirit, Heb. 9:14; the Spirit, Matt. 4:1; Holy Spirit, Matt. 1:18; the Holy Spirit, Matt. 28:19; the Spirit, the Holy, Matt. 12:32; the Spirit of promise, the Holy, Eph. 1:13; Spirit of God, Rom. 8:9; Spirit of (the) living God, 2 Cor. 3:3; the Spirit of God, 1 Cor. 2:11; the Spirit of our God, 1 Cor. 6:11; the Spirit of God, the Holy, Eph. 4:30; the Spirit of glory and of God, 1 Pet. 4:14; the Spirit of Him that raised up Jesus from the dead (i.e., God), Rom. 8:11; the Spirit of your Father, Matt. 10:20; the Spirit of His Son, Gal. 4:6; Spirit of (the) Lord, Acts 8:39; the Spirit of (the) Lord, Acts 5:9; (the) Lord, (the) Spirit, 2 Cor. 3:18; the Spirit of Jesus, Acts 16:7; Spirit of Christ, Rom. 8:9; the Spirit of Jesus Christ, Phil. 1:19; Spirit of adoption, Rom. 8:15; the Spirit of truth, John 14:17; the Spirit of life, Rom. 8:2; the Spirit of grace, Heb. 10:29."

The use or absence of the article in the original where the "Holy Spirit" is spoken of cannot always be decided by grammatical rules, nor can the presence or absence of the article alone determine whether the reference is to the "Holy Spirit." Examples where the Person is meant when the article is absent are Matt. 22:43 (the article is used in **Mark 12:36**); Acts 4:25, RV (absent in some texts); 19:2, 6; Rom. 14:17; 1 Cor. 2:4; Gal. 5:25 (twice); 1 Pet. 1:2. Sometimes the absence is to be accounted for by the fact that *Pneuma* (like *Theos*) is substantially a proper name, e.g., in John 7:39. As a general rule the article is present where the subject of the teaching is the Personality of the Holy Spirit, e.g., John 14:26, where He is spoken of in distinction from the Father and the Son. See also 15:26 and cf. Luke 3:22. In Gal. 3:3, in the phrase "having begun in the Spirit," it is difficult to say whether the reference is to the "Holy Spirit" or to the quickened spirit of the believer; that it possibly refers to the latter is not to be determined by the absence of the article, but by the contrast with "the flesh"; on the other hand, the contrast may be between the "Holy Spirit" who in the believer sets His seal on the perfect work of Christ, and the flesh which seeks to better itself by works of its own. There is no preposition before either noun, and if the reference is to the quickened spirit it cannot be dissociated from the operation of the "Holy Spirit." In Gal. 4:29 the phrase "after the Spirit" signifies "by supernatural power," in contrast to "after the flesh," i.e., "by natural power," and the reference must be to the "Holy Spirit"; so in 5:17. The full title with the article before both *pneuma* and *hagios* (the "resumptive" use of the article), lit., "the Spirit the Holy," stresses the character of the Person, e.g., Matt. 12:32; **Mark 3:29**; **12:36**; **13:11**; Luke 2:26; 10:21 (RV); John 14:26; Acts 1:16; 5:3; 7:51; 10:44, 47;

13:2; 15:28; 19:6; 20:23, 28; 21:11; 28:25; Eph. 4:30; Heb. 3:7; 9:8; 10:15.

Never The phrase *eis ton aiona*, "for ever" (not to be rendered literally, "unto the age"), preceded by the double negative *ou me*, denotes "never," John 4:14; 8:51-52; 10:28; 11:26; 13:8; so, preceded by *ouk*, "not," in **Mark 3:29**.

Forgiveness *aphesis* (859), denotes "a dismissal, release"; it is used of the remission of sins, and translated "forgiveness" in **Mark 3:29**; Eph. 1:7; Col. 1:14, and in the KJV of Acts 5:31; 13:38; 26:18, in each of which the RV has "remission." Eleven times it is followed by "of sins," and once by "of trespasses." It is never used of the remission of sins in the Sept., but is especially connected with the Year of Jubilee (Lev. 25:10, etc.). Cf. the RV of Luke 4:18, "release" (KJV, "liberty"). For the significance in connection with remission of sins and the propitiatory sacrifice of Christ, see the different word *paresis*, "a passing over, a remission," of sins committed under the old covenant, Rom. 3:25. The RV should be used here. This passing over, or by, was neither forgetting nor "forgiving"; it was rather a suspension of the just penalty; cf. Acts 17:30, "the times of ignorance God overlooked," RV; see also, e.g., Ps. 78:38.

Danger *enochos* (1777), lit., "held in, contained in" (*en*, "in," *echo*, "to have, hold"), hence, "bound under obligation to, liable to, subject to," is used in the sense of being in "danger" of the penal effect of a misdeed, i.e.. in a forensic sense, signifying the connection of a person with (a) his crime, "guilty of an eternal sin," **Mark 3:29**, RV; (b) the trial or tribunal, as a result of which sentence is passed, Matt. 5:21-22, "the judgment," "the council"; *enochos* here has the obsolete sense of control (J. Hastings); (c) the penalty itself, 5:22, "the hell of fire," and, with the translation "worthy" (KJV, "guilty"), of the punishment determined to be inflicted on Christ, Matt. 26:66 and **Mark 14:64**, "death"; (d) the person or thing against whom or which the offense is committed, 1 Cor. 11:27, "guilty," the crime being against "the body and blood of the Lord"; Jas. 2:10, "guilty" of an offense against all the Law, because of a breach of one commandment.

Eternal *aionios* (166), "describes duration, either undefined but not endless, as in Rom. 16:25; 2 Tim. 1:9; Titus 1:2; or undefined because endless as in Rom. 16:26, and the other sixty-six places in the NT.

"The predominant meaning of *aionios*, that in which it is used everywhere in the NT, save the places noted above, may be seen in 2 Cor. 4:18, where it is set in contrast with *proskairos*, lit., 'for a season,' and in Philem. 15, where only in the NT it is used without a noun. Moreover it is used of persons and things which are in their nature endless, as, e.g., of God, Rom. 16:26; of His power, 1 Tim. 6:16, and of His glory, 1 Pet. 5:10; of the Holy Spirit, Heb. 9:14; of the redemption effected by Christ, Heb. 9:12, and of the consequent salvation of men, 5:9, as well as of His future rule, 2 Pet. 1:11, which is elsewhere declared to be without end, Luke 1:33; of the life received by those who believe in Christ, John 3:16, concerning whom He said, 'they shall never perish,' 10:28, and of the resurrection body, 2 Cor. 5:1, elsewhere said to be 'immortal,' 1 Cor. 15:53, in which that life will be finally realized, Matt. 25:46; Titus 1:2. *Aionios* is also used of the sin that 'hath never forgiveness,' **Mark 3:29**, and of the judgment of God, from which there is no appeal, Heb. 6:2, and of the fire, which is one of its instruments, Matt. 18:8; 25:41; Jude 7, and which is elsewhere said to be 'unquenchable,' **Mark 9:43**. The use of *aionios* here shows that the punishment referred to in 2 Thess. 1:9, is no temporary, but final, and, accordingly, the phraseology shows that its purpose is not remedial but retributive."

Aionios is set in contrast with *proskairos*, lit., "for a season," 2 Cor. 4:18. It is used of that which in nature is endless, as, e.g., of God, Rom. 16:26, His power, 1 Tim. 6:16, His glory, 1 Pet. 5:10, the Holy Spirit, Heb. 9:14, redemption, Heb. 9:12, salvation, 5:9, life in Christ, John 3:16, the resurrection body, 2 Cor. 5:1, the future rule of Christ, 2 Pet. 1:11, which is declared to be without end, Luke 1:33, of sin that never has forgiveness, **Mark 3:29**, the judgment of God, Heb. 6:2, and of fire, one of its instruments, Matt. 18:8; 25:41; Jude 7.

3:30-31 Because they said, He hath an unclean spirit.

There came then his brethren and his mother, and, standing without, sent unto him, calling him.

Standing *steko* (4739), a late present tense from *hesteka*, the perfect of *histemi*, is used (a) literally, **Mark 3:31**; **11:25**; John 1:26, in the best texts (in some texts, Rev. 12:4); (b) figuratively, Rom. 14:4, where the context indicates the meaning "standeth upright" rather than that of acquittal; of "standing fast," 1 Cor. 16:13, "in the faith," i.e., by adherence to it; Gal. 5:1, in freedom from legal bondage; Phil. 1:27, "in one spirit"; Phil. 4:1 and 1 Thess. 3:8, "in the Lord," i.e., in the willing subjection to His authority; 2 Thess. 2:15, in the apostle's teaching; some mss. have it in John 8:44, the most authentic have *histemi*, RV, "stood" (KJV, "abode").

3:32-34 And the multitude sat about him, and they said unto him, Behold, thy mother and thy brethren without seek for thee.

And he answered them, saying, Who is my mother, or my brethren?

And he looked round about on them which sat about him, and said, Behold my mother and my brethren!

Looked *see Mark 3:5.*

Round about *kuklo* (2945), the dative case of the noun *kuklos*, "a ring," is used as an adverb, and translated "round about" in **Mark 3:34**, KJV (RV, "round"); **6:6, 36**; Luke 9:12; Rom. 15:19; Rev. 4:6; 7:11.

Mother *meter* (3384), is used (a) of the natural relationship, e.g., Matt. 1:18; 2 Tim. 1:5; (b) figuratively, (1) of "one who takes the place of a mother," Matt. 12:49, 50; **Mark 3:34, 35**; John 19:27; Rom. 16:13; 1 Tim. 5:2; (2) of "the heavenly and spiritual Jerusalem," Gal. 4:26, which is "free" (not bound by law imposed externally, as under the Law of Moses), "which is our mother" (RV), i.e., of Christians, the metropolis, mother-city, used allegorically, just as the capital of a country is "the seat of its government, the center of its activities, and the place where the national characteristics are most fully expressed"; (3) symbolically, of "Babylon," Rev. 17:5, as the source from which has proceeded the religious harlotry of mingling pagan rites and doctrines with the Christian faith.

3:35 For whosoever shall do the will of God, the same is my brother, and my sister, and mother.

Will *thelema* (2307), signifies (a) objectively, "that which is willed, of the will of God," e.g., Matt. 18:14; Mark 3:35, the fulfilling being a sign of spiritual relationship to the Lord, John 4:34; 5:30; 6:39, 40; Acts 13:22, plural, "my desires"; Rom. 2:18; 12:2, lit., "the will of God, the good and perfect and acceptable"; here the repeated article is probably resumptive, the adjectives describing the will, as in the Eng. versions; Gal. 1:4; Eph. 1:9; 5:17, "of the Lord"; Col. 1:9; 4:12; 1 Thess. 4:3; 5:18, where it means "the gracious design," rather than "the determined resolve"; 2 Tim. 2:26, which should read "which have been taken captive by him" [(*autou*), i.e., by the Devil; the RV, "by the Lord's servant" is an interpretation; it does not correspond to the Greek] unto His (*ekeinou*) will" (i.e., "God's will"; the different pronoun refers back to the subject of the sentence, viz., God); Heb. 10:10; Rev. 4:11, RV, "because of Thy will"; of human will, e.g., 1 Cor. 7:37; (b) subjectively, the "will" being spoken of as the emotion of being desirous, rather than as the thing "willed"; of the "will" of God, e.g., Rom. 1:10; 1 Cor. 1:1; 2 Cor. 1:1; 8:5; Eph. 1:1, 5, 11; Col. 1:1; 2 Tim. 1:1; Heb. 10:7, 9, 36; 1 John 2:17; 5:14; of human "will," e.g., John 1:13; Eph. 2:3, "the desires of the flesh"; 1 Pet. 4:3 (in some texts); 2 Pet. 1:21.

Sister *adelphe* (79), is used (a) of natural relationship, e.g., Matt. 19:29; of the "sisters" of Christ, the children of Joseph and Mary after the virgin birth of Christ, e.g., Matt. 13:56; (b) of "spiritual kinship" with Christ, an affinity marked by the fulfillment of the will of the Father, Matt. 12:50; **Mark 3:35**; of spiritual relationship based upon faith in Christ, Rom. 16:1; 1 Cor. 7:15; 9:5, KJV and RV marg.; Jas. 2:15; Philem. 2, RV.

Mother *see Mark 3:34.*

Chapter 4

4:1 And he began again to teach by the sea side: and there was gathered unto him a great multitude, so that he entered into a ship, and sat in the sea; and the whole multitude was by the sea on the land.

Entered *embaino* (1684), "to go in" (*en*, "in"), is used only in the Gospels, of "entering" a boat, Matt. 8:23; 9:1; 13:2; 14:22, 32; 15:39; **Mark 4:1; 5:18; 6:45; 8:10, 13**; Luke 5:3; 8:22, 37; John 6:17, (in some mss., in v. 22), 24, RV, "got into the boats," for KJV, "took shipping"; 21:3; Acts 21:6 (in the best mss.); of stepping into water, John 5:4 (RV omits the verb).

Sat *see* **Sitting** at *Mark 2:14.*

Whole *pleistos* (4118), the superlative degree of *polus*, is used (a) as an adjective in Matt. 11:20; 21:8, RV, "(the) most part of" (KJV, "a very great"); (b) in the neuter, with the article, adverbially, "at the most," 1 Cor. 14:27; (c) as an elative (i.e., intensively) in **Mark 4:1** (in the best mss.; some have *polus*), "a very great (multitude)."

Land *ge* (1093), in one of its usages, denotes (a) "land" as distinct from sea or other water, e.g., **Mark 4:1; 6:47**; Luke 5:3; John 6:21; (b) "land" as subject to cultivation, e.g., Luke 14:35; (c) "land" as describing a country or region, e.g., Matt. 2:20, 21; 4:15; Luke 4:25; in 23:44, RV, "(the whole) land," KJV, "(all the) earth"; Acts 7:29; Heb. 11:9, RV, "a land (not his own)," KJV "a (strange) country;" Jude 5. In Acts 7:11 the KJV follows a reading of the noun with the definite article which necessitates the insertion of "land."

4:2 And he taught them many things by parables, and said unto them in his doctrine,

Doctrine *didache* (1322), denotes "teaching," either (a) that which is taught, e.g., Matt. 7:28, KJV, "doctrine," RV, "teaching"; Titus 1:9, RV; Rev. 2:14-15, 24, or (b) the act of teaching, instruction, e.g., **Mark 4:2**, KJV, "doctrine," RV, "teaching" the RV has "the doctrine" in Rom. 16:17.

4:3 Hearken; Behold, there went out a sower to sow:

Hearken *akouo* (191), "to hear," is rendered "hearken" in the KJV and RV, in **Mark 4:3**; Acts 4:19; 7:2; 15:13; Jas. 2:5; in the RV only, in Acts 3:22, 23; 13:16 (KJV, "give audience"); 15:12, "hearkened" (KJV "gave audience").

4:4 And it came to pass, as he sowed, some fell by the way side, and the fowls of the air came and devoured it up.

Devoured *katesthio and kataphago* (2719), *kata*, "down," intensive, signifies (a) "to consume by eating, to devour," said of birds, Matt. 13:4; **Mark 4:4**; Luke 8:5; of the Dragon, Rev. 12:4; of a prophet, "eating" up a book, suggestive of spiritually "eating" and digesting its contents, Rev. 10:9 (cf. Ezek. 2:8; 3:1-3; Jer. 15:16); (b) metaphorically, "to squander, to waste," Luke 15:30; "to consume" one's physical powers by emotion, John 2:17; "to devour" by forcible appropriation, as of widows' property, Matt. 23:14 (KJV only); **Mark 12:40**; "to demand maintenance," as false apostles did to the church at Corinth, 2 Cor. 11:20; "to exploit or prey on one another," Gal. 5:15, where "bite ... devour ... consume" form a climax, the first two describing a process, the last the act of swallowing down; to "destroy" by fire, Rev. 11:5; 20:9.

4:5 And some fell on stony ground, where it had not much earth; and immediately it sprang up, because it had no depth of earth:

Stony *petrodes* (4075), "rock-like" (*petra*, "a rock," *eidos*, "a form, appearance"), is used of "rock" underlying shallow soil, Matt. 13:5, 20, RV, "the rocky places" (KJV, "stony places"); **Mark 4:5**, RV, "the rocky ground" (KJV, "stony ground"); v. **16**, RV, "rocky places" (KJV, "stony ground").

Sprang *ex* (1816), *ek* or *ex*, "out," and *anatello*, is used of the "springing" up of seeds, Matt. 13:5; **Mark 4:5**.

Depth *bathos* (899), is used (a) naturally, in Matt. 13:5, "deepness"; **Mark 4:5**, KJV, "depth," RV, "deepness"; Luke 5:4, of "deep" water; Rom. 8:39 (contrasted with *hupsoma*, "height"); (b) metaphorically, in Rom. 11:33, of God's wisdom and knowledge; in 1 Cor. 2:10, of God's counsels; in Eph. 3:18, of the dimensions of the sphere of the activities of God's counsels, and of the love of Christ which occupies that sphere; in 2 Cor. 8:2, of "deep" poverty; some mss. have it in Rev. 2:24.

4:6 But when the sun was up, it was scorched; and because it had no root, it withered away.

Up *anatello* (393), "to arise," is used especially of things in the natural creation, e.g., "the rising" of the sun, moon and stars; metaphorically, of light, in Matt. 4:16, "did spring up"; of the sun, Matt. 5:45; 13:6 (RV); **Mark 4:6**; Jas. 1:11; in **Mark 16:2** the RV has "when the sun was risen," keeping to the verb form, for the KJV, "at the rising of"; of a cloud, Luke 12:54; of the day-star, 2 Pet. 1:19; in Heb. 7:14 metaphorically, of the Incarnation of Christ: "Our Lord hath sprung out of Judah," more lit., "Our Lord hath arisen out of Judah," as of the rising of the light of the sun.

Scorched *kaumatizo* (2739), "to scorch" (from *kauma*, "heat"), is used (a) of seed that had not much earth, Matt. 13:6; **Mark 4:6**; (b) of men, stricken retributively by the sun's heat, Rev. 16:8, 9.

Root *rhiza* (4491), is used (a) in the natural sense, Matt. 3:10; 13:6, 21; **Mark 4:6, 17, 11:20**; Luke 3:9; 8:13; (b) metaphorically (1) of "cause, origin, source," said of persons, ancestors, Rom. 11:16, 17, 18 (twice); of things, evils, 1 Tim. 6:10, RV, of the love of money as a "root" of all "kinds of evil" (marg., "evils", KJV, "evil"); bitterness, Heb. 12:15; (2) of that which springs from a "root," a shoot, said of offspring, Rom. 15:12; Rev. 5:5; 22:16.

Wither *see* Withered at *Mark 3:1*.

4:7 And some fell among thorns, and the thorns grew up, and choked it, and it yielded no fruit.

Some In the following *alloi*, "others" ("some" in the KJV), is translated "others" in the RV, Matt. 13:5, 7; **Mark 4:7** ("other"); **8:28**; Luke 9:19; John 9:9. Followed by a correlative expression it denotes "some," e.g., Acts 19:32; 21:34.

Grew *anabaino* (305), "to ascend," when used of plants, signifies "to grow up," **Mark 4:7, 32**; in **4:8**, of seed, "growing up," RV, KJV, "that sprang up."

Choked *sumpnigo* (4846), gives the suggestion of "choking together" (*sun*, "with"), i.e., by crowding, Matt. 13:22; **Mark 4:7, 19**; Luke 8:14. It is used in Luke 8:42, of the crowd that thronged the Lord, almost, so to speak, to suffocation.

Yielded *didomi* (1325), "to give," is used with various meanings according to the context; it is said, e.g., of seed "yielding fruit," **Mark 4:7, 8**; of "giving" (i.e., exercising) diligence, Luke 12:58; of giving lots, Acts 1:26, RV (KJV, "gave forth"); of "rendering" vengeance, 2 Thess. 1:8; of "striking or smiting" Christ, John 18:22 (lit., "gave a blow") and 19:3 (lit., "they gave Him blows"); of "putting" a ring on the hand, Luke 15:22; of Paul's "adventuring" himself into a place, Acts 19:31. (In Rev. 17:13 some mss. have *diadidomi*, "to divide").

4:8 And other fell on good ground, and did yield fruit that sprang up and increased; and brought forth, some thirty, and some sixty, and some an hundred.

Yield *see* Yielded at *Mark 4:7*.

Sprang *anabaino* (305), "to go up," is rendered "sprang up" in Matt. 13:7, KJV, of thorns, and **Mark 4:8**, of seed (RV, "grew up").

Increased *auxano* (837), "to grow or increase," of the growth of that which lives, naturally or spiritually, is used (a) transitively, signifying to make to increase, said of giving the increase, 1 Cor. 3:6, 7; 2 Cor. 9:10, the effect of the work of God, according to the analogy of His operations in nature; "to grow, become greater," e.g., of plants and fruit, Matt. 6:28; used in the passive voice in 13:32 and **Mark 4:8**, "increase"; in the active in Luke 12:27; 13:19; of the body, Luke 1:80; 2:40; of Christ, John 3:30, "increase"; of the work of the gospel of God, Acts 6:7, "increased"; 12:24; 19:20; of people, Acts 7:17; of faith, 2 Cor. 10:15 (passive voice), RV, "growth" (KJV, "is increased"); of believers individually, Eph. 4:15; Col. 1:6, RV, 10 (passive voice), "increasing"; 1 Pet. 2:2; 2 Pet. 3:18; of the church, Col. 2:19; of churches, Eph. 2:21.

Brought *phero* (5342), "to bear, or carry," is used also of "bearing or bringing forth fruit," **Mark 4:8**; John 15:5, etc. To bring is the most frequent meaning.

Thirty *triakonta* (5144), is usually rendered "thirty," e.g., Matt. 13:23; "thirtyfold," in Matt. 13:8, KJV only; in **Mark 4:8**, RV only; in **Mark 4:20**, KJV and RV.

Sixty *hexekonta* (1835), occurs in Matt. 13:8, RV (KJV, "sixty-fold"); 13:23; **Mark 4:8**, where the RV and KJV reverse the translation, as in Matt. 13:8, while in **Mark 4:20** the RV has "sixtyfold," KJV, "sixty"; in Rev. 13:18, RV, "sixty" (KJV, "threescore"). It is rendered "threescore" in Luke 24:13; 1 Tim. 5:9; Rev. 11:3; 12:6.

Hundred *hekaton* (1540), an indeclinable numeral, denotes "a hundred," e.g., Matt. 18:12, 28; it also signifies "a hundredfold," Matt. 13:8, 23, and the RV in the corresponding passage, **Mark 4:8, 20** (for KJV, "hundred"), signifying the complete productiveness of sown seed. In the passage in Mark the phrase is, lit., "in thirty and in sixty and in a hundred." In **Mark 6:40** it is used with the preposition *kata*, in the phrase "by hundreds." It is followed by other numerals in John 21:11; Acts 1:15; Rev. 7:4; 14:1, 3; 21:17.

4:9-10 And he said unto them, He that hath ears to hear, let him hear.

And when he was alone, they that were about him with the twelve asked of him the parable.

Alone *kata monas* (2651), signifies "apart, in private, alone," **Mark 4:10**; Luke 9:18. Some texts have the phrase as one word.

4:11 And he said unto them, Unto you it is given to know the mystery of the kingdom of God: but unto them that are without, all *these* things are done in parables:

Mystery *musterion* (3466), primarily that which is known to the *mustes*, "the initiated" (from *mueo*, "to initiate into the mysteries"; cf. Phil. 4:12, *mueomai*, "I have learned the secret," RV). In the NT it denotes, not the mysterious (as with the Eng. word), but that which, being outside the range of unassisted natural apprehension, can be made known only by divine revelation, and is made known in a manner and at a time appointed by God, and to those only who are illumined by His Spirit. In the ordinary sense a "mystery" implies knowledge withheld; its Scriptural significance is truth revealed. Hence the terms especially associated with the subject are "made known," "manifested," "revealed," "preached," "understand," "dispensation." The definition given above may be best illustrated by the following passage: "the mystery which hath been hid from all ages and generations: but now hath it been manifested to His saints" (Col. 1:26, RV). "It is used of ...: (a) spiritual truth generally, as revealed in the gospel, 1 Cor. 13:2; 14:2 [cf. 1 Tim. 3:9]. Among the ancient Greeks 'the mysteries' were religious rites and ceremonies practiced by secret societies into which anyone who so desired might be received. Those who were initiated into these 'mysteries' became possessors of certain knowledge, which was not imparted to the uninitiated, and were called 'the perfected,' cf. 1 Cor. 2:6-16 where the Apostle has these 'mysteries' in mind and presents the gospel in contrast thereto; here 'the perfected' are, of course the believers, who alone can perceive the things revealed; (b) Christ, who is God Himself revealed under the conditions of human life, Col. 2:2; 4:3, and submitting even to death, 1 Cor. 2:1 [in some mss., for *marturion*, testimony], 7, but raised from among the dead, 1 Tim. 3:16, that the will of God to coordinate the universe in Him, and subject it to Him, might in due time be accomplished, Eph. 1:9 (cf. Rev. 10:7), as is declared in the gospel, Rom. 16:25; Eph. 6:19; (c) the Church, which is Christ's Body, i.e., the union of redeemed men with God in Christ, Eph. 5:32 [cf. Col. 1:27]; (d) the rapture into the presence of Christ of those members of the Church which is His Body who shall be alive on the earth at His Parousia, 1 Cor. 15:51; (e) the operation of those hidden forces that either retard or accelerate the Kingdom of Heaven (i.e., of God), Matt. 13:11; **Mark 4:11**; (f) the cause of the present condition of Israel, Rom. 11:25; (g) the spirit of disobedience to God, 2 Thess. 2:7; Rev. 17:5, 7, cf. Eph. 2:2."

Kingdom *see Mark 3:24.*

4:12 That seeing they may see, and not perceive; and hearing they may hear, and not understand; lest at any time they should be converted, and *their* sins should be forgiven them.

Perceive *eidon* (3708), (akin to *oida*, "to know"), an aorist form used to supply that tense of *horao*, "to see," is translated "to perceive" in Matt. 13:14; **Mark 4:12**; Acts 28:26; in Luke 9:47, KJV (RV, "saw"); in Acts 14:9, KJV, "perceiving" (RV, "seeing").

Lest *me pote* (3379), lit., "lest ever," "lest haply," e.g., Luke 14:29, of laying a foundation, with the possibility of being unable to finish the building; Acts 5:39, of the possibility of being found fighting against God; Heb. 3:2, RV, "lest haply," of the possibility of having an evil heart of unbelief. The RV usually has "lest haply" (KJV "lest at any time"), e.g., Matt. 4:6; 5:25; 13:15; **Mark 4:12**; Luke 4:11; 21:34; Heb. 2:1; in Matt. 25:9, the RV has "peradventure"; in 2 Tim. 2:25, KJV and RV, have "if peradventure"; in John 7:26 the RV has "Can it be that," for the word "Do" in the KJV.

Converted *epistrepho* (1994), "to turn about, turn towards" (*epi*, "towards" and *strepho*), is used transitively, and so rendered "convert" (of causing a person to turn) in Jas. 5:19-20. Elsewhere, where the KJV translates this verb, either in the middle voice and intransitive use, or the passive, the RV adheres to the middle voice significance, and translates by "turn again," Matt. 13:15; **Mark 4:12**; Luke 22:32; Acts 3:19; 28:27.

4:13 And he said unto them, Know ye not this parable? and how then will ye know all parables?

Know *oida* (1492), from the same root as *eidon*, "to see," is a perfect tense with a present meaning, signifying, primarily, "to have seen or perceived"; hence, "to know, to have knowledge of," whether absolutely, as in divine knowledge, e.g., Matt. 6:8, 32; John 6:6, 64; 8:14; 11:42; 13:11; 18:4; 2 Cor. 11:31; 2 Pet. 2:9; Rev. 2:2, 9, 13, 19; 3:1, 8, 15; or in the case of human "knowledge," to know from observation, e.g., 1 Thess. 1:4, 5; 2:1; 2 Thess. 3:7.

The differences between *ginosko* and *oida* demand consideration: (a) *ginosko*, frequently suggests inception or progress in "knowledge," while *oida* suggests fullness of "knowledge," e.g., John 8:55, "ye have not known Him" (*ginosko*), i.e., begun to "know," "but I know Him" (*oida*), i.e., "know Him perfectly"; 13:7, "What I do thou knowest not now," i.e. Peter did not yet perceive (*oida*) its significance, "but thou shalt understand," i.e., "get to know (*ginosko*), hereafter"; 14:7, "If ye had known Me" (*ginosko*), i.e., "had definitely come to know Me," "ye would have known My Father also" (*oida*), i.e., "would have had perception of": "from henceforth ye know Him" (*ginosko*), i.e., having unconsciously been coming to the Father, as the One who was in Him, they would now consciously be in the constant and progressive experience of "knowing" Him; in **Mark 4:13**, "Know ye not (*oida*) this parable? and how shall ye know (*ginosko*) all the parables?" (RV), i.e., "Do ye not understand this parable? How shall ye come to perceive all ...," the intimation being that the first parable is a leading and testing one; (b) while *ginosko* frequently implies an active relation between the one who "knows" and the person or thing "known", *oida* expresses the fact that the object has simply come within the scope of the "knower's" perception; thus in Matt. 7:23 "I never knew you" (*ginosko*) suggests "I have never been in approving connection with you," whereas in 25:12, "I know you not" (*oida*) suggests "you stand in no relation to Me."

4:14-15 The sower soweth the word.

And these are they by the way side, where the word is sown; but when they have heard, Satan cometh immediately, and taketh away the word that was sown in their hearts.

Satan *see Mark 1:13.*

4:16 And these are they likewise which are sown on stony ground; who, when they have heard the word, immediately receive it with gladness;

Likewise *homoios* (3668), akin to the adjective *homoios*, "like," signifies in "like manner, equally"; in the following the RV has "in like manner" for KJV, "likewise"; Matt. 27:41; **Mark 4:16**; Luke 10:32; 13:3; 16:25; John 5:19; (Heb. 9:21); Jas. 2:25; 1 Pet. 3:1, 7; Rev. 8:12; in Rev. 2:15 the KJV "which thing I hate" translates a variant reading (*ho miso*).

Stony *see Mark 4:5.*

Ground In **Mark 4:16** the RV rightly has "rocky places" (*petrodes*) for KJV, "stony ground."

Receive *lambano* (2983), denotes either "to take" or "to receive," (I) literally, (a) without an object, in contrast to asking, e.g., Matt. 7:8; **Mark 11:24**, RV, "have received" (the original has no object); (b) in contrast to giving, e.g., Matt. 10:8; Acts 20:35; (c) with objects, whether things, e.g., **Mark 10:30**; Luke 18:30, in the best mss.; John 13:30; Acts 9:19, RV, "took" (KJV, "received"); 1 Cor. 9:25, RV, "receive" (KJV, "obtain"); or persons, e.g., John 6:21; 13:20; 16:14, RV, "take"; 2 John 10; in **Mark 14:65**, RV, "received (Him with blows of their hands)"; this has been styled a vulgarism; (II) metaphorically, of the word of God, Matt. 13:20; **Mark 4:16**; the sayings of Christ, John 12:48; the witness of Christ, John 3:11; a hundredfold in this life, and eternal life in the world to come, **Mark 10:30**; mercy, Heb. 4:16, RV, "may receive" (KJV, "may obtain"); a person (*prosopon*), Luke 20:21, "acceptest," and Gal. 2:6, "accepteth," an expression used in the OT either in the sense of being gracious or kind to a person, e.g., Gen. 19:21; 32:20, or (negatively) in the sense of being impartial, e.g., Lev. 19:15; Deut. 10:17; this latter is the meaning in the two NT passages just mentioned. *Lambano* and *prosopon* are combined in the nouns *prosopolempsia*, "respect of persons," and *prosopolemptes*, "respecter of persons," and in the verb *prosopolempto*, "to have respect of persons."

Gladness *chara* (5479), "joy, delight" (akin to *chairo*, "to rejoice"), is found frequently in Matthew and Luke, and especially in John, once in Mark (**4:16**, RV, "joy," KJV, "gladness"); it is absent from 1 Cor. (though the verb is used three times), but is frequent in 2 Cor., where the noun is used five times, and the verb eight times, suggestive of the apostle's relief in comparison with the circumstances of the 1st Epistle; in Col. 1:11, KJV, "joyfulness," RV, "joy." The word is sometimes used, by metonymy, of the occasion or cause of "joy," Luke 2:10 (lit., "I announce to you a great joy"); in 2 Cor. 1:15, in some mss., for *charis*, "benefit"; Phil. 4:1, where the readers are called the apostle's "joy"; so 1 Thess. 2:19, 20; Heb. 12:2, of the object of Christ's "joy"; Jas. 1:2, where it is connected with falling into trials; perhaps also in Matt. 25:21, 23, where some regard it as signifying, concretely, the circumstances attending cooperation in the authority of the Lord.

4:17 And have no root in themselves, and so endure but for a time: afterward, when affliction or persecution ariseth for the word's sake, immediately they are offended.

Root *see Mark 4:6.*

Time *proskairos*, rendered "for a time" in **Mark 4:17**, KJV.

Afterward *eita* (1534), denotes sequence (a) "of time, then, next," **Mark 4:17**, RV, "then"; **4:28**, in some texts; **8:25**, RV, "then" (KJV, "after that"); Luke 8:12; John 13:5; 19:27; 20:27; in some texts in 1 Cor. 12:28; 1 Cor. 15:5, 7, 24; 1 Tim. 2:13; 3:10; Jas. 1:15; (b) In argument, Heb. 12:9, "furthermore."

Affliction *thlipsis* (2347), primarily means "a pressing, pressure," anything which burdens the spirit. In two passages in Paul's Epistles it is used of future retribution, in the way of "affliction," Rom. 2:9; 2 Thess. 1:6. In Matt. 24:9, the KJV renders it as a verb, "to be afflicted," (RV, "unto tribulation"). It is coupled with *stenochoria*, "anguish," in Rom. 2:9; 8:35; with *ananke*, "distress," 1 Thess. 3:7; with *diogmos*, "persecution," Matt. 13:21; **Mark 4:17**; 2 Thess. 1:4. It is used of the calamities of war, Matt. 24:21, 29; **Mark 13:19, 24**; of want, 2 Cor. 8:13, lit., "distress for you"; Phil. 4:14 (cf. 1:16); Jas. 1:27; of the distress of woman in childbirth, John 16:21; of persecution, Acts 11:19; 14:22; 20:23; 1 Thess. 3:3, 7; Heb. 10:33; Rev. 2:10; 7:14; of the "afflictions" of Christ, from which (His vicarious sufferings apart) his followers must not shrink, whether sufferings of body or mind, Col. 1:24; of sufferings in general, 1 Cor. 7:28; 1 Thess. 1:6, etc.

Persecution *diogmos* (1375) occurs in Matt. 13:21; **Mark 4:17**; **10:30**; Acts 8:1; 13:50; Rom. 8:35; 2 Cor. 12:10; 2 Thess. 1:4; 2 Tim. 3:11, twice. In the Sept., Prov. 11:19; Lam. 3:19.

Ariseth *ginomai* (1096), "to become, to take place," is sometimes suitably translated "arise"; e.g., Matt. 8:24; **Mark 4:37**, "there arose a great tempest." So of the arising of persecution, Matt. 13:21; **Mark 4:17**; this might be translated "taketh place"; of a tumult, Matt. 27:24, RV, "arising," for KJV, "made"; of a flood,

Luke 6:48; a famine, 15:14; a questioning, John 3:25; a murmuring, Acts 6:1; a tribulation, 11:19 (RV); a stir in the city, 19:23; a dissension, 23:7; a great clamor, v. 9.

4:18-19 And these are they which are sown among thorns; such as hear the word,

And the cares of this world, and the deceitfulness of riches, and the lusts of other things entering in, choke the word, and it becometh unfruitful.

Cares *merimna* (3308), probably connected with *merizo*, "to draw in different directions, distract," hence signifies "that which causes this, a care, especially an anxious care," Matt. 13:22; **Mark 4:19**; Luke 8:14; 21:34; 2 Cor. 11:28 (RV, "anxiety for"), 1 Pet. 5:7 (RV, "anxiety").

Deceitfulness *apate* (539), "deceit or deceitfulness" (akin to *apatao*, "to cheat, deceive, beguile"), that which gives a false impression, whether by appearance, statement or influence, is said of riches, Matt. 13:22; **Mark 4:19**; of sin, Heb. 3:13. The phrase in Eph. 4:22, "deceitful lusts," KJV, "lusts of deceit," RV, signifies lusts excited by "deceit," of which "deceit" is the source of strength, not lusts "deceitful" in themselves. In 2 Thess. 2:10, "all deceit of unrighteousness," RV, signifies all manner of unscrupulous words and deeds designed to "deceive" (see Rev. 13:13-15). In Col. 2:8, "vain deceit" suggests that "deceit" is void of anything profitable.

Riches *ploutos* (4149), is used in the singular (I) of material "riches," used evilly, Matt. 13:22: **Mark 4:19**; Luke 8:14; 1 Tim. 6:17; Jas. 5:2; Rev. 18:17; (II) of spiritual and moral "riches," (a) possessed by God and exercised towards men, Rom. 2:4, "of His goodness and forbearance and longsuffering"; 9:23 and Eph. 3:16, "of His glory" (i.e., of its manifestation in grace towards believers); Rom. 11:33, of His wisdom and knowledge; Eph. 1:7 and 2:7, "of His grace"; 1:18, "of the glory of His inheritance in the saints"; 3:8, "of Christ"; Phil. 4:19, "in glory in Christ Jesus," RV; Col. 1:27, "of the glory of this mystery ... Christ in you, the hope of glory"; (b) to be ascribed to Christ, Rev. 5:12; (c) of the effects of the gospel upon the Gentiles, Rom. 11:12 (twice); (d) of the full assurance of understanding in regard to the mystery of God, even Christ, Col. 2:2, RV; (e) of the liberality of the churches of Macedonia, 2 Cor. 8:2 (where "the riches" stands for the spiritual and moral value of their liberality); (f) of "the reproach of Christ" in contrast to this world's treasures, Heb. 11:26.

Other *loipos* (3062), signifies "remaining, the rest." It is translated "other," or "others," e.g., in Matt. 25:11: **Mark 4:19**; Luke 18:9; 24:10 (in v. 9, "the rest"); but in Luke 8:10; Acts 28:9; Rom. 1:13; 1 Cor. 9:5; Eph. 2:3; 1 Thess. 4:13; 5:6; 1 Tim. 5:20, e.g., the RV renders this word "the rest" (KJV, "other" or "others"); in Eph. 4:17, some mss. have *loipa*, neuter plural, KJV, "other (Gentiles)."

Entering *see* **Entered** at *Mark 1:21*.

Choke *see* **Choked** at *Mark 4:7*.

Unfruitful *akarpos* (175), "unfruitful," is used figuratively (a) of "the word of the Kingdom," rendered "unfruitful" in the case of those influenced by the cares of the world and the deceitfulness of riches, Matt. 13:22; **Mark 4:19**; (b) of the understanding of one praying with a "tongue," which effected no profit to the church without an interpretation of it, 1 Cor. 14:14; (c) of the works of darkness, Eph. 5:11; (d) of believers who fail "to maintain good works," indicating the earning of one's living so as to do good works to others, Titus 3:14; of the effects of failing to supply in one's faith the qualities of virtue, knowledge, temperance, patience, godliness, love of the brethren, and love, 2 Pet. 1:8. In Jude 12 it is rendered "without fruit," of ungodly men, who oppose the gospel while pretending to uphold it, depicted as "autumn trees." In the Sept., Jer. 2:6.

4:20 And these are they which are sown on good ground; such as hear the word, and receive *it*, and bring forth fruit, some thirtyfold, some sixty, and some an hundred.

Such as "Such as" is a rendering of certain relative pronouns: *hoios*, "what sort of," e.g., Matt. 24:21; 2 Cor. 12:20 (twice); Rev. 16:18; *hostis*, "whoever," e.g., **Mark 4:20**; *hopoios*, "of what sort," preceded by *toioutos*, "of such a sort," Acts 26:29.

Receive *paradechomai* (3858), "to receive or admit with approval" (*para*, "beside"), is used (a) of persons, Acts 15:4; Heb. 12:6; (b) of things, **Mark 4:20**, KJV, "receive" (RV, "accept"); Acts 16:21; 22:18; 1 Tim. 5:9. In the Sept., Ex. 23:1; Prov. 3:12.

Bring forth *euphoreo* (2164), "to bear well, be productive," "brought forth plentifully," Luke 12:16. Cf. *karpophoreo*, **Mark 4:20**, RV "bear"; so, Col. 1:6.

Fruit *karpophoreo* (2592), "to bear or bring forth fruit," is used (a) in the natural sense, of the "fruit of the earth," **Mark 4:28**; (b) metaphorically, of conduct, or that which takes effect in conduct, Matt. 13:23; **Mark 4:20**; Luke 8:15; Rom. 7:4, 5 (the latter, of evil "fruit," borne "unto death," of activities resulting from a state of alienation from God); Col. 1:6 in the middle voice; Col. 1:10.

Thirtyfold *see* Thirty at *Mark 4:8.*

Sixty *see Mark 4:8.*

Hundred *see Mark 4:8.*

4:21 And he said unto them, Is a candle brought to be put under a bushel, or under a bed? and not to be set on a candlestick?

Candle *luchnos* (3088), frequently mistranslated "candle," is a portable "lamp" usually set on a stand; the word is used literally, Matt. 5:15; **Mark 4:21**; Luke 8:16; 11:33, 36; 15:8; Rev. 18:23; 22:5; (b) metaphorically, of Christ as the Lamb, Rev. 21:23, RV, "lamp" (KJV, "light"); of John the Baptist, John 5:35, RV, "the lamp" (KJV, "a ... light"); of the eye, Matt. 6:22, and Luke 11:34, RV, "lamp"; of spiritual readiness, Luke 12:35, RV, "lamps"; of "the word of prophecy," 2 Pet. 1:19, RV, "lamp."

"In rendering *luchnos* and *lampas* our translators have scarcely made the most of the words at their command. Had they rendered *lampas* by 'torch' not once only (John 18:3), but always, this would have left 'lamp,' now wrongly appropriated by lampas, disengaged. Altogether dismissing 'candle,' they might then have rendered *luchnos* by 'lamp' wherever it occurs. At present there are so many occasions where 'candle' would manifestly be inappropriate, and where, therefore, they are obliged to fall back on 'light,' that the distinction between *phos* and *luchnos* nearly, if not quite, disappears in our Version. The advantages of such a re-distribution of the words would be many. In the first place, it would be more accurate. *Luchnos* is not a 'candle' ('*candela,*' from '*candeo,*' the white wax light, and then any kind of taper), but a hand-lamp, fed with oil. Neither is *lampas* a 'lamp,' but a 'torch'" (Trench *Syn.*, Sec.xlvi).

Brought In **Mark 4:21**, *erchomai*, "to come," is translated "is brought," lit., "(does a lamp) come."

Put *tithemi* (5087), "to place, lay, set, put," is translated "to put" in Matt. 5:15; 12:18; in Matt. 22:44, RV, "put (underneath Thy feet)"; **Mark 4:21** (1st part), in the 2nd part, RV, "put" (in some texts, KJV "set"); **10:16**, KJV (RV, "laying"); Luke 8:16 (1st part); 2nd part, RV (KJV, "setteth"); 11:33; John 19:19; Acts 1:7, KJV (RV, "set"); 4:3; 5:18, 25; 12:4; Rom. 14:13; 1 Cor. 15:25; 2 Cor. 3:13; 1 Tim. 1:12, KJV (RV, "appointing"); Rev. 11:9, KJV (RV, "laid").

Bushel *modios* (3426), was a dry measure containing about a peck, Matt. 5:15; **Mark 4:21**; Luke 11:33.

Bed *kline* (2825), akin to *klino*, "to lean" (Eng., "recline, incline," etc.), "a bed," e.g., **Mark 7:30**, also denotes a "couch" for reclining at meals, **Mark 4:21**, or a "couch" for carrying the sick, Matt. 9:2, 6. The metaphorical phrase "to cast into a bed," Rev. 2:22, signifies to afflict with disease (or possibly, to lay on a bier). In **Mark 7:4** the KJV curiously translates the word "tables" (marg., "beds"), RV, marg. only, "couches."

Set *tithemi* (5087), "to put, to place," is translated "to set" in Acts 1:7, of times and seasons (KJV, "put"); Acts 13:47; Rev. 10:2; "setteth on" (of wine) in John 2:10, RV (KJV, "doth set forth"); in the KJV of **Mark 4:21** (2nd part) and in Luke 8:16 it is rendered "set" (RV, "put"), of a lamp. In **Mark 4:30** it is used of "setting" forth by parable the teaching concerning the kingdom of God, RV, "shall we set (it) forth" (KJV, "compare").

Candlestick *luchnia* (3087), is mistranslated "candlestick" in every occurrence in the KJV and in certain places in the RV; the RV has "stand" in Matt. 5:15; **Mark 4:21**; Luke 8:16; 11:33; "candlestick" in Heb. 9:2; Rev. 1:12, 13, 20 (twice); 2:1, 5; 11:4; the RV marg., gives "lampstands" in the passages in Rev., but not in Heb. 9:2.

4:22 For there is nothing hid, which shall not be manifested; neither was any thing kept secret, but that it should come abroad.

Hid *kruptos* (2927), "hidden, secret," is translated "hid" in Matt. 10:26; **Mark 4:22**; Luke 8:17, RV, for KJV, "secret"; 12:2 (last part); in 1 Cor. 4:5, "hidden (things of darkness)"; 2 Cor. 4:2, "hidden (things of shame)"; 1 Pet. 3:4, "hidden (man of the heart)."

Kept secret *apokruphos* (614), "hidden away from" (cf. Eng., "apocryphal"), is translated, "made (KJV, kept) secret," in **Mark 4:22**; in Luke 8:17, RV, "secret," for KJV, "hid"; in Col. 2:3, RV, "hidden," KJV, "hid."

4:23 If any man have ears to hear, let him hear.

Hear *akouo* (191), the usual word denoting "to hear," is used (a) intransitively, e.g., Matt. 11:15; **Mark 4:23**; (b) transitively when the object is expressed, sometimes in the accusative case, sometimes in the genitive. Thus in Acts 9:7, "hearing the voice," the noun "voice" is in the partitive genitive case [i.e., hearing (something) of], whereas in 22:9, "they heard not the voice," the construction is with the accusative. This removes the idea of any contradiction. The former indicates a "hearing" of the sound, the latter indicates the meaning or

"Do not think of the faults of others but of what is good in them and faulty in yourself."

ST. TERESA OF AVILA

message of the voice (this they did not hear). "The former denotes the sensational perception, the latter (the accusative case) the thing perceived" (Cremer). In John 5:25, 28, the genitive case is used, indicating a "sensational perception" that the Lord's voice is sounding; in 3:8, of "hearing" the wind, the accusative is used, stressing "the thing perceived."

4:24 And he said unto them, Take heed what ye hear: with what measure ye mete, it shall be measured to you: and unto you that hear shall more be given.

Heed *blepo* (991), "to look," see, usually implying more especially an intent, earnest contemplation, is rendered "take heed" in Matt. 24:4; **Mark 4:24**; **13:5**, **9**, **23**, **33**; Luke 8:18; 21:8; 1 Cor. 3:10; 8:9; 10:12; Gal. 5:15; Col. 2:8 (KJV, "beware"); 4:17; Heb. 3:12.

Measure *metron* (3358), denotes "that which is used for measuring, a measure," (a) of "a vessel," figuratively, Matt. 23:32; Luke 6:38 (twice); in John 3:34, with the preposition *ek*, "(He giveth not the Spirit) by measure," RV (which is a necessary correction; the italicized words "*unto him*," KJV, detract from the meaning). Not only had Christ the Holy Spirit without "measure," but God so gives the Spirit through Him to others. It is the ascended Christ who gives the Spirit to those who receive His testimony and set their seal to this, that God is true. The Holy Spirit is imparted neither by degrees, nor in portions, as if He were merely an influence, He is bestowed personally upon each believer, at the time of the New Birth; (b) of "a graduated rod or rule for measuring," figuratively, Matt. 7:2; **Mark 4:24**; literally, Rev. 21:15 (in the best mss.; see the RV); v. 17.

Mete, Measured *metreo* (3354), "to measure," is used (a) of space, number, value, etc., Rev. 11:1, 2; 21:15, 16, 17; metaphorically, 2 Cor. 10:12; (b) in the sense of "measuring" out, giving by "measure," Matt. 7:2, "ye mete"; **Mark 4:24**; in some mss. in Luke 6:38.

Given *prostithemi* (4369), lit., "to put in addition" (*pros*, "to," *tithemi*, "to put"), "to give more," is translated "shall more be given," in **Mark 4:24** (passive voice).

4:25 For he that hath, to him shall be given: and he that hath not, from him shall be taken even that which he hath.

He that *see Mark 3:29.*

4:26 And he said, So is the kingdom of God, as if a man should cast seed into the ground;

Seed *sporos* (4703), properly "a sowing," denotes "seed sown," (a) natural, **Mark 4:26**, **27**; Luke 8:5, 11 (the natural being figuratively applied to the Word of God); 2 Cor. 9:10 (1st part); (b) metaphorically of material help to the needy, 2 Cor. 9:10 (2nd part), RV, "(your) seed for sowing" (KJV, "seed sown").

Ground *see* **Land** at *Mark 4:1.*

4:27 And should sleep, and rise night and day, and the seed should spring and grow up, he knoweth not how.

Night *nux* (3571), is used (I) literally, (a) of "the alternating natural period to that of the day," e.g., Matt. 4:2; 12:40; 2 Tim. 1:3; Rev. 4:8; (b) of "the period of the absence of light," the time in which something takes place, e.g., Matt. 2:14 (27:64), in some mss.); Luke 2:8; John 3:2 (7:50, in some mss.); Acts 5:19; 9:25; (c) of "point of time," e.g., Matt. 14:27 (in some mss.), 30; Luke 12:20; Acts 27:23; (d) of "duration of time," e.g., Luke 2:37; 5:5; Acts 20:31; 26:7 (note the difference in the phrase in **Mark 4:27**); (II) metaphorically, (a) of "the period of man's alienation from God," Rom. 13:12; 1 Thess. 5:5, lit., "not of night," where "of" means 'belonging to;' cf. "of the Way," Acts 9:2; "of shrinking back" and "of faith," Heb. 10:39, marg.; (b) of "death," as the time when work ceases, John 9:4.

Seed *see Mark 4:26.*

Spring *blastano* (985), "to bud," is said of Aaron's rod, Heb. 9:14; "spring up," Matt. 13:26, and **Mark 4:27**; elsewhere, in Jas. 5:18.

Grow *mekunomai* (3373), "to grow long, lengthen, extend" (from *mekos*, "length"), is used of the "growth" of plants, in **Mark 4:27**.

4:28 For the earth bringeth forth fruit of herself; first the blade, then the ear, after that the full corn in the ear.

Fruit *see Mark 4:20.*

Herself *automatos* (844), from *autos*, "self," and a root *ma*–, signifying "desire," denotes of oneself, moved by one's own impulse. It occurs in **Mark 4:28**, of the power of the earth to produce plants and fruits of itself; Acts 12:10, of the door which opened of its own accord. In the Sept., Lev. 25:5, "spontaneous produce"; v. 11, "produce that comes of itself"; Josh. 6:5; 2 Kings 19:29, "(that which groweth) of itself"; Job 24:24, of an ear of corn "(falling off) of itself (from the stalk)."

Then *see* Afterward at *Mark 4:17*.

Ear *see* Ears at *Mark 2:23*.

Full *pleres* (4134), denotes "full," (a) in the sense of "being filled," materially, Matt. 14:20; 15:37; **Mark 8:19** (said of baskets "full" of bread crumbs); of leprosy, Luke 5:12; spiritually, of the Holy Spirit, Luke 4:1; Acts 6:3; 7:55; 11:24; grace and truth, John 1:14; faith, Acts 6:5; grace and power, 6:8; of the effects of spiritual life and qualities, seen in good works, Acts 9:36; in an evil sense, of guile and villany, Acts 13:10; wrath, 19:28; (b) in the sense of "being complete," "full corn in the ear," **Mark 4:28**; of a reward hereafter, 2 John 8.

Corn *sitos* (4621), "wheat, corn"; in the plural, "grain," is translated "corn" in **Mark 4:28**; "wheat," Matt. 3:12; 13:25, 29-30; Luke 3:17; 12:18 (some mss. have *genemata*, "fruits," here); 16:7; 22:31; John 12:24; Acts 27:38; 1 Cor. 15:37; Rev. 6:6; 18:13.

4:29 But when the fruit is brought forth, immediately he putteth in the sickle, because the harvest is come.

Brought forth *paradidomi* (3860), "to give over, commit, deliver," etc., also signifies "to permit"; in **Mark 4:29**, of the "ripe" condition of corn, RV, and KJV marg., "is ripe"; RV marg., "alloweth" (the nearest rendering); KJV, "is brought forth."

Putteth *apostello* (649), "to send forth" (*apo*, "from or forth," *stello*, "to send"), is said of using the sickle, **Mark 4:29**, RV, "he putteth forth," marg., "sendeth forth" (KJV, putteth in).

Sickle *drepanon* (1407), "a pruning hook, a sickle" (akin to *drepo*, "to pluck"), occurs in **Mark 4:29**; Rev. 14:14, 15, 16, 17, 18 (twice), 19.

Harvest *therismos* (2326), akin to *therizo*, "to reap," is used (a) of "the act of harvesting," John 4:35; (b) "the time of harvest," figuratively, Matt. 13:30, 39; **Mark 4:29**; (c) "the crop," figuratively, Matt. 9:37, 38; Luke 10:2; Rev. 14:15. The beginning of "harvest" varied according to natural conditions, but took place on the average about the middle of April in the eastern lowlands of Palestine, in the latter part of the month in the coast plains and a little later in high districts. Barley "harvest" usually came first and then wheat. "Harvesting" lasted about seven weeks, and was the occasion of festivities.

Come *paristemi* (3936), "to stand by or near, to be at hand" (*para*, "near"), is translated "is come," of the arrival of harvest, **Mark 4:29**.

4:30 And he said, Whereunto shall we liken the kingdom of God? or with what comparison shall we compare it?

Liken *homoioo* (3666), "to make like," is used (a) especially in the parables, with the significance of comparing, "likening," or, in the passive voice, "being likened," Matt. 7:24, 26; 11:16; 13:24; 18:23; 22:2 (RV, "likened"); 25:1; **Mark 4:30**; Luke 7:31; 13:18, RV, "liken" (KJV, "resemble"); v. 20; in several of these instances the point of resemblance is not a specific detail, but the whole circumstances of the parable; (b) of making "like," or, in the passive voice, of being made or becoming "like," Matt. 6:8; Acts 14:11, "in the likeness of (men)," lit., "being made like" (aorist participle, passive); Rom. 9:29; Heb. 2:17, of Christ in being "made like" unto His brethren, i.e., in partaking of human nature, apart from sin (cf. v. 14).

Comparison, Compare *paraballo* (3846), "to place side by side, to set forth," and the noun *parabole* (Eng., "parable"), occur in **Mark 4:30**, RV, "In what parable shall we set it forth?," KJV, "with what comparison shall we compare it."

4:31 *It is* like a grain of mustard seed, which, when it is sown in the earth, is less than all the seeds that be in the earth:

Like *hos* (5613), used as a relative adverb of manner, means "as, like as," etc. and is translated "like," e.g., in Matt. 6:29; **Mark 4:31**; Luke 12:27; in Acts 3:22 and 7:37 (see RV, marg.); in 8:32 (2nd part), RV, "as" (KJV, "like"); Rev. 2:18, RV (the rendering should have been "as" here); 18:21, RV, "as it were" (KJV, "like"); 21:11, 2nd part (ditto).

Grain *kokkos* (2848), denotes "a grain," Matt. 13:31; 17:20; **Mark 4:31**; Luke 13:19; 17:6; John 12:24 (KJV, "corn"); 1 Cor. 15:37 (where the RV has "a ... grain," to distinguish it from "grain" in general).

Mustard *sinapi* (4615), a word of Egyptian origin, is translated "mustard seed" in the NT. "The conditions to be fulfilled by the mustard are that it should be a familiar plant, with a very small seed, Matt. 17:20; Luke 17:6, sown in the earth, growing larger than garden herbs, Matt. 13:31, having large branches, **Mark 4:31**, ... attractive to birds, Luke 13:19 [RV, '(became) a tree']. The cultivated mustard is *sinapis nigra*. The seed is well known for its minuteness. The mustards are annuals, reproduced with extraordinary rapidity ... In fat soil they often attain a height of 10 or 12 feet, and have branches which attract passing birds" (A. E. Post, in *Hastings Bib. Dic.*).

As the parable indicates, Christendom presents a sort of Christianity that has become conformed to the principles and ways of the world, and the world has favored this debased Christianity. Contrast the testimony of the NT, e.g., in John 17:14; Gal. 6:14; 1 Pet. 2:11; 1 John 3:1.

Less *mikroteros* (3398), is used of (a) size, Matt. 13:32, KJV, "the least," RV, "less;" **Mark 4:31**; (b) estimation, Matt. 11:11 and Luke 7:28, KJV, "least," RV, "but little," marg., "lesser" (in the kingdom of heaven), those in the kingdom itself being less than John the Baptist; Luke 9:48.

4:32 But when it is sown, it groweth up, and becometh greater than all herbs, and shooteth out great branches; so that the fowls of the air may lodge under the shadow of it.

Groweth *see* Grew at *Mark 4:7*.

Herbs *lachanon* (3001), denotes "a garden herb, a vegetable" (from *lachaino*, "to dig"), in contrast to wild plants, Matt. 13:32; **Mark 4:32**; Luke 11:42; Rom. 14:2.

Shooteth In **Mark 4:32**, KJV, *poieo*, "to do, make," is rendered "shooteth out," RV, "putteth out."

Branches *klados* (2798), from *klao*, "to break" (cf. *klasma*, "a broken piece"), properly a young tender shoot, "broken off" for grafting, is used for any kind of branch, Matt. 13:32; 21:8; 24:32; **Mark 4:32**; **13:28**; Luke 13:19; the descendants of Israel, Rom. 11:16-19, 21.

May *dunamai* (1410), "to be able, have power," whether by personal ability, permission, or opportunity, is sometimes rendered "may" or "might," e.g., Matt. 26:9; **Mark 14:5**; Acts 17:19; 1 Thess. 2:6. In the following the RV substitutes "can," "canst," "couldst," for the KJV, e.g., Matt. 26:42; **Mark 4:32**; **14:7**; Luke 16:2; Acts 24:11; 25:11; 27:12; 1 Cor. 7:21; 14:31 (here the alteration is especially important, as not permission for all to prophesy, but ability to do so, is the meaning); Eph. 3:4. In the following the RV substitutes the verb "to be able," Acts 19:40; 24:8; Rev. 13:17.

Lodge *kataskenoo* (2681), "to pitch one's tent" (*kata*, "down," *skene*, "a tent"), is rendered "to lodge," of birds, in Matt. 13:32; **Mark 4:32**; Luke 13:19. In Acts 2:26, it is used of the body of the Lord in the tomb, as dwelling in hope, RV, "shall dwell" (marg., "tabernacle"), KJV, "shall rest." Cf. *katoskenosis*, "a roosting place."

Shadow *skia* (4639), is used (a) of "a shadow," caused by the interception of light, **Mark 4:32**; Acts 5:15; metaphorically of the darkness and spiritual death of ignorance, Matt. 4:16; Luke 1:79; (b) of "the image" or "outline" cast by an object, Col. 2:17, of ceremonies under the Law; of the tabernacle and its appurtenances and offerings, Heb. 8:5; of these as appointed under the Law, Heb. 10:1.

4:33-34 And with many such parables spake he the word unto them, as they were able to hear *it*.

But without a parable spake he not unto them: and when they were alone, he expounded all things to his disciples.

Alone The phrase *kat' idian*, **Mark 4:34**, signifies "in private," "privately," RV (KJV, "when they were alone").

Expounded *epiluo* (1956), primarily, "to loose, release," a strengthened form of *luo*, "to loose," signifies "to solve, explain, expound," **Mark 4:34**, "expounded"; in Acts 19:39, of settling a controversy, RV, "it shall be settled," for KJV, "it shall be determined." Cf. *epilusis*, "an interpretation," 2 Pet. 1:20.

4:35 And the same day, when the even was come, he saith unto them, Let us pass over unto the other side.

Day *see* Days at *Mark 1:13*.

Come *ginomai* (1096), "to become," signifies a change of condition, state or place, e.g., **Mark 4:35**. In Acts 27:33, the verb is used with *mello*, "to be about to," to signify the coming on of day.

Pass *dierchomai* (1330), denotes "to pass through or over," (a) of persons, e.g., Matt. 12:43, RV, "passeth (KJV, walketh) through"; **Mark 4:35**, KJV, "pass (RV, go) over"; Luke 19:1, 4; Heb. 4:14, RV, "passed through" (KJV "into"); Christ "passed through" the created heavens to the throne of God; (b) of things, e.g., Matt. 19:24, "to go through"; Luke 2:35, "shall pierce through" (metaphorically of a sword).

4:36 And when they had sent away the multitude, they took him even as he was in the ship. And there were also with him other little ships.

Sent In Matt. 13:36, KJV, *aphiemi*, "to leave," is translated "He sent ... away" (RV, "He left"); so in **Mark 4:36**, KJV, "they had sent away," RV, "leaving."

Even *hos* (5613), "as," in comparative sentences, is sometimes translated "even as," Matt. 15:28; **Mark 4:36**; Eph. 5:33; 1 Pet. 3:6 (KJV only); Jude 7.

Ship *see Mark 3:9*.

4:37 And there arose a great storm of wind, and the waves beat into the ship, so that it was now full.

Arose *see* Ariseth at *Mark 4:17*.

Storm *lailaps* (2978), "a hurricane, whirlwind," is rendered "storm" in **Mark 4:37**; Luke 8:23; 2 Pet. 2:17, RV (KJV, "tempest").

Waves *kuma* (2949), from *kuo*, "to be pregnant, to swell," is used (a) literally in the plural, Matt. 8:24; 14:24; **Mark 4:37** (Acts 27:41, in some mss.); (b) figuratively, Jude 13.

Beat *epiballo* (1911), "to cast upon, or lay hands upon," signifies to "beat" into, in **Mark 4:37**, of the action of the waves.

Full *gemizo* (1072), "to fill or load full," is used of a boat, **Mark 4:37** (RV, "was filling"); a sponge, **Mark 15:36** (cf. Matt. 27:48), a house, Luke 14:23; the belly, Luke 15:16; waterpots, John 2:1; baskets, 6:13; bowls, with fire, Rev. 8:5; the temple, with smoke, 15:8. Cf. *gemo*, "to be full."

4:38 And he was in the hinder part of the ship, asleep on a pillow: and they awake him, and say unto him, Master, carest thou not that we perish?

Hinder *prumna* (4403), the feminine form of the adjective *prumnos*, "hindmost," is rendered "stern" in Acts 27:29; and in the RV in v. 41 and **Mark 4:38**.

Part In **Mark 4:38** and Acts 27:41, KJV, *prumna*, "a stern", is translated "hinder part" (RV, "stern").

Pillow *proskephalaion* (4344), denotes "a pillow, a cushion for the head" (*pros*, "to," *kephale*, "a head"), **Mark 4:38** (RV, "cushion"). In the Sept., Ezek. 13:18.

Awake *diegeiro* (1326), is used of "awaking from natural sleep," Matt. 1:24; **Mark 4:38**; of the act of the disciples in "awaking" the Lord, Luke 8:24 (cf. *egeiro*, in Matt. 8:25); metaphorically, "of arousing the mind," 2 Pet. 1:13; 3:1.

Master *didaskalos* (1320), "a teacher" (from *didasko*, "to teach"), is frequently rendered "Master" in the four Gospels, as a title of address to Christ, e.g., Matt. 8:19; **Mark 4:38** (there are more instances in Luke than in the other Gospels); John 1:38, where it interprets "Rabbi"; 20:16, where it interprets "Rabboni." It is used by Christ of Himself in Matt. 23:8 and John 13:13-14; by others concerning Him, Matt. 17:24; 26:18; **Mark 5:35**; **14:14**; Luke 8:49; 22:11; John 11:28. In John 3:10, the Lord uses it in addressing Nicodemus, RV, "the teacher" (KJV, "a master"), where the article does not specify a particular "teacher," but designates the member of a class; for the class see Luke 2:46, "the doctors" (RV, marg., "teachers"). It is used of the relation of a disciple to his "master," in Matt. 10:24, 25; Luke 6:40. It is not translated "masters" in the rest of the NT, save in the KJV of Jas. 3:1 "(be not many) masters," where obviously the RV "teachers" is the meaning.

Carest *melei* (3199), the third person sing. of *melo*, used impersonally, signifies that "something is an object of care," especially the care of forethought and interest, rather than anxiety, Matt. 22:16; **Mark 4:38**; **12:14**; Luke 10:40; John 10:13; 12:6; Acts 18:17; 1 Cor. 9:9 (RV, "Is it for the oxen that God careth?" The KJV seriously misses the point. God does "care" for oxen, but there was a divinely designed significance in the OT passage, relating to the service of preachers of the gospel); 7:21; 1 Pet. 5:7.

"Jesus differs from all other teachers; they reach the ear, but he instructs the heart; they deal with the outward letter, but he imparts an inward taste for the truth."

CHARLES HADDON SPURGEON

4:39 And he arose, and rebuked the wind, and said unto the sea, Peace, be still. And the wind ceased, and there was a great calm.

Arose *diegeiro* (1326), a strengthened form of *egeiro* (*dia*, "through," intensive), signifies "to rouse, to awaken from sleep." The active voice is not used intransitively. In Matt. 1:24, RV, "Joseph arose from his sleep," the passive participle is, lit., "being aroused." In **Mark 4:39** (KJV, "he arose," RV, "he awoke"), the lit. rendering is "he being awakened." In John 6:18 the imperfect tense of the passive voice is used, and the rendering should be, "the sea was being aroused."

Rebuked *see Mark 1:25*.

Peace *see Mark 3:4*.

Still *phimoo* (5392), in the passive voice, is rendered "be still" in **Mark 4:39**.

"We are never nearer Christ than when we find ourselves lost in a holy amazement at His unspeakable love."

JOHN OWEN

Ceased *kopazo* (2869), "to cease through being spent with toil, to cease raging" (from *kopos*, "labor, toil," *kopiao*, "to labor"), is said of the wind only, Matt. 14:32; **Mark 4:39**; **6:51**.

Calm *galene* (1055), primarily signifies "calmness, cheerfulness" (from a root *gal–*, from which *gelao*, "to smile," is also derived, hence the "calm" of the sea, the smiling ocean being a favorite metaphor of the poets), Matt. 8:26; **Mark 4:39**; Luke 8:24.

4:40 And he said unto them, Why are ye so fearful? how is it that ye have no faith?

Fearful *deilos* (1169), "cowardly," "timid," is used in Matt. 8:26; **Mark 4:40**; Rev. 21:8 (here "the fearful" are first in the list of the transgressors).

4:41 And they feared exceedingly, and said one to another, What manner of man is this, that even the wind and the sea obey him?

Exceedingly *megas* (3173), is used (a) of external form, size, measure, e.g., of a stone, Matt. 27:60; fish, John 21:11; (b) of degree and intensity, e.g., of fear, **Mark 4:41**; wind, John 6:18; Rev. 6:13, RV, "great" (KJV, "mighty"); of a circumstance, 1 Cor. 9:11; 2 Cor. 11:15; in Rev. 5:2, 12, the RV has "great" (KJV, "loud"), of a voice; (c) of rank, whether of persons, e.g., God, Titus 2:13; Christ as a "great Priest," Heb. 10:21, RV; Diana, Acts 19:27, Simon Magus, Acts 8:9 "(some) great one"; in the plural "great ones," Matt. 20:25; **Mark 10:42**, those who hold positions of authority in gentile nations; or of things, e.g., a mystery, Eph. 5:32. Some mss. have it in Acts 8:8, of joy. In **Mark 4:41**, "they feared exceedingly" is, lit., "they feared a great fear."

Manner In Luke 24:17, KJV, the pronoun *tis*, "who, what," in the plural (RV, "what") is translated "what manner of"; similarly, in the singular in **Mark 4:41**; Luke 8:25 (RV, "who"), John 7:36.

Obey *see Mark 1:27.*

Chapter 5

5:1 And they came over unto the other side of the sea, into the country of the Gadarenes.

Side *peran* (4008), an adverb, signifying "beyond, on the other side," is used (a) as a preposition and translated "on the other side of," e.g., in **Mark 5:1**; Luke 8:22; John 6:1, RV; 6:22, 25; (b) as a noun with the article, e.g., Matt. 8:18, 28; 14:22; 16:5.

Country *see* Land at *Mark 1:5.*

5:2 And when he was come out of the ship, immediately there met him out of the tombs a man with an unclean spirit,

Met *apantao* (528), "to go to meet, to meet" (*apo*, "from," *antao*, "to meet with, come face to face with"), is used in **Mark 14:13** and Luke 17:12. Some mss. have this verb in Matt. 28:9; **Mark 5:2**; Luke 14:31; John 4:51; Acts 16:16.

Tombs *mnemeion* (3419), is almost invariably rendered "tomb" or "tombs" in the RV, never "grave," sometimes "sepulchre"; in the KJV, "tomb" in Matt. 8:28; 27:60; **Mark 5:2**; **6:29**.

Unclean spirit *daimonion* (1140), not a diminutive of *daimon*, but the neuter of the adjective *daimonios*, pertaining to a demon, is also mistranslated "devil," "devils." In Acts 17:18, it denotes an inferior pagan deity. "Demons" are the spiritual agents acting in all idolatry. The idol itself is nothing, but every idol has a "demon" associated with it who induces idolatry, with its worship and sacrifices, 1 Cor. 10:20-21; Rev. 9:20; cf. Deut. 32:17; Isa. 13:21; 34:14; 65:3, 11. They disseminate errors among men, and seek to seduce believers, 1 Tim. 4:1. As seducing spirits they deceive men into the supposition that through mediums (those who have "familiar spirits," Lev. 20:6, 27, e.g.) they can converse with deceased human beings. Hence the destructive deception of spiritism, forbidden in Scripture, Lev. 19:31; Deut. 18:11; Isa. 8:19. "Demons" tremble before God, Jas. 2:19; they recognized Christ as Lord and as their future Judge, Matt. 8:29; Luke 4:41. Christ cast them out of human beings by His own power. His disciples did so in His name, and by exercising faith, e.g., Matt. 17:20.

Acting under Satan (cf. Rev. 16:13-14), "demons" are permitted to afflict with bodily disease, Luke 13:16. Being unclean they tempt human beings with unclean thoughts, Matt. 10:1; **Mark 5:2; 7:25**; Luke 8:27-29; Rev. 16:13; 18:2, e.g. They differ in degrees of wickedness, Matt. 12:45. They will instigate the rulers of the nations at the end of this age to make war against God and His Christ, Rev. 16:14.

5:3 Who had *his* dwelling among the tombs; and no man could bind him, no, not with chains:

Dwelling *katoikesis* (2731), "a dwelling, a habitation," is used in **Mark 5:3**.

Tombs *mnema* (3418), rendered "tombs" in **Mark 5:3, 5**; Luke 8:27, signified "a memorial" or "record of a thing or a dead person," then "a sepulchral monument," and hence "a tomb"; it is rendered "graves" in the KJV of Rev. 11:9 (RV, "a tomb"); "tomb" or "tombs," **Mark 5:3, 5** and **16:2** (KJV, "sepulchre"); Luke 8:27; Acts 2:29 and 7:16 (KJV, "sepulchre").

Chains *halusis* (254), denotes "a chain or bond for binding the body, or any part of it (the hands or feet)." Some derive the word from *a*, negative, and *luo*, "to loose," i.e., "not to be loosed"; others from a root connected with a word signifying "to restrain." It is used in **Mark 5:3-4**; Luke 8:29; Acts 12:6-7; 21:33; 28:20; Eph. 6:20; 2 Tim. 1:16; Rev. 20:1.

5:4 Because that he had been often bound with fetters and chains, and the chains had been plucked asunder by him, and the fetters broken in pieces: neither could any *man* tame him.

Fetters *pede* (3976), "a fetter" (akin to *peza*, "the instep," and *pous*, "a foot"; cf. Eng. prefix *ped*–), occurs in **Mark 5:4** and Luke 8:29.

Plucked *diaspao* (1288), "to tear asunder," is translated "rent asunder" in **Mark 5:4**, RV (KJV, "plucked asunder"); for Acts 23:10.

Broken *suntribo* (4937), lit., "to rub together," and so "to shatter, shiver, break in pieces by crushing," is said of the bruising of a reed, Matt. 12:20; the "breaking" of fetters in pieces, **Mark 5:4**; the "breaking" of an alabaster cruse, **Mark 14:3**; an earthenware vessel, Rev. 2:27; of the physical bruising of a person possessed by a demon, Luke 9:39; concerning Christ, "a bone of Him shall not be broken," John 19:36; metaphorically of the crushed condition of a "broken-hearted" person, Luke 4:18 (KJV only); of the eventual crushing of Satan, Rom. 16:20. This verb is frequent in the Sept. in the passive voice, e.g., Ps. 51:17; Isa. 57:15, of a contrite heart, perhaps a figure of stones made smooth by being rubbed together in streams. Cf. *suntrimma*, "destruction."

Could *ischuo* (2480), "to have strength," is so rendered in **Mark 5:4**, RV (KJV, "could"); in Luke 16:3, RV, "I have not strength to" (KJV, "I cannot").

Tame *damazo* (1150), "to subdue, tame," is used (a) naturally in **Mark 5:4** and Jas. 3:7 (twice); (b) metaphorically, of the tongue, in Jas. 3:8. In the Sept., Dan. 2:40.

5:5 And always, night and day, he was in the mountains, and in the tombs, crying, and cutting himself with stones.

Always *diapantos* (1275), is, lit., "through all," i.e., through all time, (*dia*, "through," *pas*, "all"). In the best texts the words are separated. The phrase, which is used of the time throughout which a thing is done, is sometimes rendered "continually," sometimes "always"; "always" or "alway" in **Mark 5:5**; Acts 10:2; 24:16; Rom. 11:10; "continually" in Luke 24:53; Heb. 9:6; 13:15, the idea being that of a continuous practice carried on without being abandoned.

Mountains *oros* (3735), is used (a) without specification, e.g., Luke 3:5 (distinct from *bounos*, "a hill"); John 4:20; (b) of "the Mount of Transfiguration," Matt. 17:1, 9; **Mark 9:2, 9**; Luke 9:28, 37 (KJV, "hill"); 2 Pet. 1:18; (c) of "Zion," Heb. 12:22; Rev. 14:1; (d) of "Sinai," Acts 7:30, 38; Gal. 4:24, 25; Heb. 8:5; 12:20; (e) of "the Mount of Olives," Matt. 21:1; 24:3; **Mark 11:1; 13:3**; Luke 19:29, 37; 22:39; John 8:1; Acts 1:12; (f) of "the hill districts as distinct from the lowlands," especially of the hills above the Sea of Galilee, e.g., Matt. 5:1; 8:1; 18:12; **Mark 5:5**; (g) of "the mountains on the east of Jordan" and "those in the land of Ammon" and "the region of Petra," etc., Matt. 24:16; **Mark 13:14**; Luke 21:21; (h) proverbially, "of overcoming difficulties, or accomplishing great things," 1 Cor. 13:2; cf. Matt. 17:20; 21:21; **Mark 11:23**; (i) symbolically, of "a series of the imperial potentates of the Roman dominion, past and future," Rev. 17:9.

Tombs *see Mark 5:3.*

Cutting *katakopto* (2629), lit., to cut down, cut in pieces" (*kata*, "down," intensive), **Mark 5:5**, of the demoniac.

5:6 But when he saw Jesus afar off, he ran and worshipped him,

Afar *makrothen* (3113), also from *makros*, signifies "afar off, from far," Matt. 26:58; 27:55, etc. It is used with *apo*, "from," in **Mark 5:6; 14:54; 15:40**, etc.; outside the Synoptists, three times, Rev. 18:10, 15, 17.

5:7 And cried with a loud voice, and said, What have I to do with thee, Jesus, *thou* Son of the most high God? I adjure thee by God, that thou torment me not.

Have *see 1:24.*

Most high *hupsistos* (5310), "most high," is a superlative degree, the positive not being in use; it is used of God in Luke 1:32, 35, 76; 6:35, in each of which the RV has "the most High," for KJV, "the highest", KJV and RV in **Mark 5:7**; Luke 8:28; Acts 7:48; 16:17; Heb. 7:1.

Adjure *horkizo* (3726), "to cause to swear, to lay under the obligation of an oath" (*horkos*, **Mark 5:7**; Acts 19:13), is connected with the Heb. word for a thigh, cf. Gen. 24:2, 9; 47:29. Some mss. have this word in 1 Thess. 5:27. The synonymous verb *omnumi* signifies "to make an oath, to declare or promise with an oath." See, e.g., **Mark 6:23**, in contrast to **5:7** (*horkizo*).

Torment *basanizo* (928), is translated "to torment," (a) of sickness, Matt. 8:6; (b) of the doom of evil spirits, **Mark 5:7**; Luke 8:28; (c) of retributive judgments upon impenitent mankind at the close of this age, Rev. 9:5; 11:10; (d) upon those who worship the Beast and his image and receive the mark of his name, 14:10; (e) of the doom of Satan and his agents, 20:10.

5:8-9 For he said unto him, Come out of the man, *thou* unclean spirit.

And he asked him, What *is* thy name? And he answered, saying, My name *is* Legion: for we are many.

Thy One of the oblique cases of *su*, "thou"; *sou*, "of thee," e.g., Matt. 1:20; 7:3 (2nd part), "thine own"; *soi*, "to thee," e.g., **Mark 5:9**; with *meno*, "to remain," Acts 5:4 (1st part), "thine own," lit., "remain to thee"; in Matt. 26:18, *pros se*, "at thy house," lit., "with thee".

Legion *legion* (3003), otherwise spelled *legeon*, "a legion," occurs in Matt. 26:53, of angels; in **Mark 5:9, 15**, and Luke 8:30, of demons. Among the Romans a "legion" was primarily a chosen (*lego*, "to choose") body of soldiers divided into ten cohorts, and numbering from 4,200 to 6,000 men. In the time of our Lord it formed a complete army of infantry and cavalry, of upwards of 5,000 men. The "legions" were not brought into Judea till the outbreak of the Jewish war (AD 66), as they were previously employed in the frontier provinces of the Empire. Accordingly in its NT use the word has its other and more general significance "of a large number."

5:10 And he besought him much that he would not send them away out of the country.

Send *apostello* (649), lit., "to send forth" (*apo*, "from"), akin to *apostolos*, "an apostle," denotes (a) "to send on service, or with a commission." (1) of persons; Christ, sent by the Father, Matt. 10:40; 15:24; 21:37; **Mark 9:37; 12:6**; Luke 4:18, 43; 9:48; 10:16; John 3:17; 5:36, 38; 6:29, 57; 7:29; 8:42; 10:36; 11:42; 17:3, 8, 18 (1st part), 21, 23, 25; 20:21; Acts 3:20 (future); 3:26; 1 John 4:9, 10, 14; the Holy Spirit, Luke 24:49; 1 Pet. 1:12; Rev. 5:6; Moses, Acts 7:35; John the Baptist, John 1:6; 3:28; disciples and apostles, e.g., Matt. 10:16; **Mark 11:1**; Luke 22:8; John 4:38; 17:18 (2nd part); Acts 26:17; servants, e.g., Matt. 21:34; Luke 20:10; officers and officials, **Mark 6:27**; John 7:32; Acts 16:35; messengers, e.g., Acts 10:8, 17, 20; 15:27; evangelists, Rom. 10:15; angels, e.g., Matt. 24:31; **Mark 13:27**; Luke 1:19, 26; Heb. 1:14; Rev. 1:1; 22:6; demons, **Mark 5:10**; (2) of things, e.g., Matt. 21:3; **Mark 4:29**, RV, marg., "sendeth forth," text, "putteth forth" (KJV, "... in"); Acts 10:36; 11:30; 28:28; (b) "to send away, dismiss," e.g., **Mark 8:26; 12:3**; Luke 4:18, "to set (at liberty)."

Country *see* **Land** at *Mark 1:5.*

5:11 Now there was there nigh unto the mountains a great herd of swine feeding.

Herd *agele* (34), from *ago*, "to lead," is used, in the NT, only of swine, Matt. 8:30, 31, 32; **Mark 5:11, 13**; Luke 8:32, 33.

Swine *choiros* (5519), "a swine," is used in the plural, in the Synoptic Gospels only, Matt. 7:6; 8:30, 31, 32; **Mark 5:11, 13, 16**; Luke 8:32, 33; Luke 15:15, 16. It does not occur in the OT.

Nigh In **Mark 5:11**, KJV, *pros*, "towards, on the side of," is translated "nigh unto (the mountain)," RV, "on (the mountain) side"; the swine were not simply "near" the mountain.

Feeding *bosko* (1006), "to feed," is primarily used of a herdsman (from *boo*, "to nourish," the special function being to provide food; the root is *bo*, found in *boter*, "a herdsman or herd," and *botane*, "fodder, pasture"), its uses are (a) literal, Matt. 8:30; in v. 33, the RV corrects the KJV, "they that kept," to "they that fed," as in **Mark 5:14** (KJV and RV) and Luke 8:34; in **Mark 5:11** and Luke 8:32, "feeding"; Luke 15:15; (b) metaphorical, of spiritual ministry, John 21:15, 17.

5:12 And all the devils besought him, saying, Send us into the swine, that we may enter into them.

Send *pempo* (3992), "to send," is used (a) of persons: Christ, by the Father, Luke 20:13; John 4:34; 5:23, 24, 30, 37; 6:38, 39, (40), 44; 7:16, 18, 28, 33; 8:16, 18, 26, 29; 9:4; 12:44, 45, 49; 13:20 (2nd part); 14:24; 15:21; 16:5; Rom. 8:3; the Holy Spirit, John 14:26; 15:26; 16:7; Elijah, Luke 4:26; John the Baptist, John 1:33; disciples and apostles, e.g., Matt. 11:2; John 20:21; servants, e.g., Luke 20:11, 12; officials, Matt. 14:10; messengers, e.g., Acts 10:5, 32, 33; 15:22, 25; 2 Cor. 9:3, Eph. 6:22; Phil. 2:19, 23, 25; 1 Thess. 3:2, 5; Titus 3:12; a prisoner, Acts 25:25, 27; potentates, by God, 1 Pet. 2:14; an angel, Rev. 22:16, demons, **Mark 5:12**; (b) of things, Acts 11:29; Phil. 4:16; 2 Thess. 2:11; Rev. 1:11; 11:10; 14:15, 18, RV, "send forth" (KJV, "thrust in").

5:13 And forthwith Jesus gave them leave. And the unclean spirits went out, and entered into the swine: and the herd ran violently down a steep place into the sea, (they were about two thousand;) and were choked in the sea.

Forthwith *eutheos* (2112), "at once, straightway" (from the adjective, *euthus*, "straight"), is translated "forthwith," in the KJV of Matt. 13:5; 26:49; (it occurs in some mss. in **Mark 5:13**; the RV omits it); Acts 12:10; 21:30 (RV, "straightway," in each place).

Leave *epitrepo* (2010), lit. denotes "to turn to" (*epi*, "upon, to," *trepo*, "to turn"), and so (a) "to commit, entrust" (not in NT); (b) "to permit, give leave, send," of Christ's permission to the unclean spirits to enter the swine, **Mark 5:13**; in Luke 8:32, RV, "give ... leave," "gave ... leave" (KJV, "suffer" and "suffered"); in John 19:38, of Pilate's permission to Joseph to take away the body of the Lord; in Acts 21:39, of Paul's request to the chief captain to permit him to address the people, RV, "give ... leave" (for KJV, "suffer"); in 21:40, "he had given him leave" (KJV, "... licence").

Swine *see Mark 5:11.*

Herd *see Mark 5:11.*

Ran *hormao*, "to set in motion, urge on," but intransitively, "to hasten on, rush," is always translated "to rush" in the RV; KJV, "ran violently," Matt. 8:32; **Mark 5:13**; Luke 8:33; "ran," Acts 7:57; "rushed", 19:29.

Steep *kremnos* (2911), "a steep bank" (akin to *kremannumi*, "to hang"), occurs in Matt. 8:32; **Mark 5:13**; Luke 8:33, RV, "the steep" (KJV, "a steep place"). In the Sept., 2 Chron. 25:12.

About *hos* (5613), usually means "as." Used with numerals it signifies "about," e.g., **Mark 5:13**; **8:9**; John 1:40; 6:19; 11:18; Acts 1:15; Rev. 8:1.

Thousand The following compounds represent different multiples of a thousand: *dischilioi*, 2,000, **Mark 5:13**; *trischilioi*, 3,000, Acts 2:41; *tetrakischilioi*, 4,000, Matt. 15:38; 16:10; **Mark 8:9, 20**; Acts 21:35; *pentakischilioi*, 5,000, Matt. 14:21; 16:9; **Mark 6:44**; **8:9**; Luke 9:14; John 6:10; *heplakischilioi*, 7,000, Rom. 11:4.

Choked *pnigo* (4155), is used, in the passive voice, of "perishing by drowning," **Mark 5:13**; in the active, "to seize a person's throat, to throttle," Matt. 18:28

5:14 And they that fed the swine fled, and told *it* in the city, and in the country. And they went out to see what it was that was done.

Fed *see* Feeding at *Mark 5:11.*

Country *agros* (68), denotes "a field, especially a cultivated field"; hence, "the country" in contrast to the town (Eng., "agrarian, agriculture"), e.g., **Mark 5:14**, **6:36**; **15:21**; **16:12**; Luke 8:34; 9:12 (plural, lit., "fields"); 23:26; a piece of ground, e.g., **Mark 10:29**; Acts 4:37.

5:15 And they come to Jesus, and see him that was possessed with the devil, and had the legion, sitting, and clothed, and in his right mind: and they were afraid.

Possessed with the devil *see* Possessed with devils at *Mark 1:32.*

Legion *see Mark 5:9.*

Clothed *himatizo* (2439), means "to put on raiment," **Mark 5:15**; Luke 8:35.

Mind *sophroneo* (4993), signifies (a) "to be of sound mind," or "in one's right mind, sober-minded" (*sozo*, "to save," *phren*, "the mind"), **Mark 5:15** and Luke 8:35, "in his right mind"; 2 Cor. 5:13, RV, "we are of sober mind" (KJV, "we be sober"); (b) "to be temperate, self-controlled," Titus 2:6, "to be sober-minded"; 1 Pet. 4:7, RV, "be ye ... of sound mind" (KJV, "be ye sober"). See also Rom. 12:3.

5:16 And they that saw *it* told them how it befell to him that was possessed with the devil, and *also* concerning the swine.

Told *diegeomai* (1334), "to conduct a narration through to the end" (*dia*, "through," intensive, *hegeomai*, "to lead"), hence denotes "to recount, to relate in full," **Mark 5:16**; Luke 8:39; 9:10; Acts 8:33; 9:27; 12:17; in **Mark 9:9** and Heb. 11:32, "tell.

Befell *ginomai* (1096), "to become," is rendered "befell" in **Mark 5:16**; "hath befallen" in Rom. 11:25, RV, for KJV, "is happened to"; so the RV in 2 Cor. 1:8; 2 Tim. 3:11.

Swine *see Mark 5:11.*

5:17 And they began to pray him to depart out of their coasts.

Pray *parakaleo*, "to call to one's aid," is rendered by the verb "to pray" in the KJV in the following: Matt. 26:53 (RV, "beseech"); so **Mark 5:17, 18**; Acts 16:9; in 24:4, RV, "intreat"; in 27:34, RV, "beseech."

Coasts *horion* (3725), "the border of a country or district" (cf. Eng., "horizon"), is always used in the plural. The KJV has "coasts," but "borders" in Matt. 4:13; the RV always "borders," Matt. 2:16; 4:13; 8:34; 15:22, 39; 19:1; **Mark 5:17; 7:31** (twice); **10:1**; Acts 13:50. In some of these it signifies territory.

5:18 And when he was come into the ship, he that had been possessed with the devil prayed him that he might be with him.

Come *embaino* (1684), "to go into," is rendered, in **Mark 5:18**, KJV, "was come into," RV, "was entering."

Possessed with the devil *see* **Possessed with devils** at *Mark 1:32*.

Prayed *see* **Pray** at *Mark 5:17*.

5:19 Howbeit Jesus suffered him not, but saith unto him, Go home to thy friends, and tell them how great things the Lord hath done for thee, and hath had compassion on thee.

Suffered *see Mark 1:34*.

Thy The possessive pronoun *sos*, and its inflections, e.g., Matt. 7:3 (1st part); it is used as a noun with the article, in the phrases *to son*, "that which is thine," Matt. 20:14; 25:25, "thine own"; *hoi soi*, "thy friends," **Mark 5:19**; *ta sa*, "thy goods," Luke 6:30, lit., "the thine".

Friends In **Mark 5:19**, "thy friends" represents the phrase *hoitsoi*, lit., "the (ones) to thee," i.e., "thine own."

Great *hosos* (3745), "how much, how many," is used in the neuter plural to signify how great things, **Mark 5:19, 20**; Luke 8:39 (twice); Acts 9:16, KJV (RV, "how many things"); in Rev. 21:16 (in the best mss.), "as great as," RV (KJV, "as large as," said of length).

Lord *kurios* (2962), properly an adjective, signifying "having power" (*kuros*) or "authority," is used as a noun, variously translated in the NT, "'Lord,' 'master,' 'Master,' 'owner,' 'Sir,' a title of wide significance, occurring in each book of the NT save Titus and the Epistles of John. It is used (a) of an owner, as in Luke 19:33, cf. Matt. 20:8; Acts 16:16; Gal. 4:1; or of one who has the disposal of anything, as the Sabbath, Matt. 12:8; (b) of a master, i.e., one to whom service is due on any ground, Matt. 6:24; 24:50; Eph. 6:5; (c) of an Emperor or King, Acts 25:26; Rev. 17:14 ... (f) as a title of courtesy addressed to a stranger, John 12:21; 20:15; Acts 16:30; from the outset of His ministry this was a common form of address to the Lord Jesus, alike by the people, Matt. 8:2; John 4:11, and by His disciples, Matt. 8:25; Luke 5:8; John 6:68; (g) *kurios* is the Sept. and NT representative of Heb. Jehovah ('LORD' in Eng. versions), see Matt. 4:7; Jas. 5:11, e.g., of *adon*, Lord, Matt. 22:44, and of *Adonay*, Lord, 1:22; it also occurs for *Elohim*, God, 1 Pet. 1:25.

"Christ Himself assumed the title, Matt. 7:21, 22; 9:38; 22:41-45; **Mark 5:19** (cf. Ps. 66:16; the parallel passage, Luke 8:39, has 'God'); Luke 19:31; John 13:13, apparently intending it in the higher senses of its current use, and at the same time suggesting its OT associations. His purpose did not become clear to the disciples until after His resurrection, and the revelation of His Deity consequent thereon. Thomas, when he realized the significance of the presence of a mortal wound in the body of a living man, immediately joined with it the absolute title of Deity, saying, 'My Lord and my God,' John 20:28. Thereafter, except in Acts 10:4 and Rev. 7:14, there is no record that *kurios* was ever again used by believers in addressing any save God and the Lord Jesus; cf. Acts 2:47 with 4:29, 30.

Compassion *eleeo* (1653), "to have mercy (*eleos*, "mercy"), to show kindness, by beneficence, or assistance," is translated "have compassion" in Matt. 18:33 (KJV); **Mark 5:19** and Jude 22.

5:20 And he departed, and began to publish in Decapolis how great things Jesus had done for him: and all *men* did marvel.

Publish *see Mark 1:45*.

Great *see Mark 5:19*.

5:21 And when Jesus was passed over again by ship unto the other side, much people gathered unto him: and he was nigh unto the sea.

Passed over *diaperao* (1276), "to pass over, to cross over" (*dia*, "through," *perao*, "to pass": akin to this are *peran*, "across," *peras*, "a boundary," Latin, *porta*, "a gate," Eng., "portal, port," etc.), is translated by the verb "to cross" in the RV, but differently in the KJV; in Matt. 9:1; **Mark 5:21; 6:53** (KJV, "passed"); Matt. 14:34 (KJV, "were gone"); Luke 16:26 (KJV, "neither can they pass"); Acts 21:2 (KJV, "sailing"). In the Sept., Deut. 30:13; Isa. 23:2.

Nigh *para* (3844), "beside, alongside of," is translated "nigh unto" in

Matt. 15:29; in **Mark 5:21**, RV, "by" (KJV, "nigh unto").

5:22 And, behold, there cometh one of the rulers of the synagogue, Jairus by name; and when he saw him, he fell at his feet,

Rulers of the synagogue *archisunagogos* (752), denotes "the administrative official," with the duty of preserving order and inviting persons to read or speak in the assembly, **Mark 5:22, 35, 36, 38**; Luke 8:49; 13:14; Acts 13:15; "chief ruler" (KJV) in Acts 18:8, 17.

Fell *pipto* (4098), "to fall," is used (a) of descent, to "fall" down from, e.g., Matt. 10:29; 13:4; (b) of a lot, Acts 1:26; (c) of "falling" under judgment, Jas. 5:12 (cf. Rev. 18:2, RV); (d) of persons in the act of prostration, to prostrate oneself, e.g., Matt. 17:6; John 18:6; Rev. 1:17; in homage and worship, e.g., Matt. 2:11; **Mark 5:22**; Rev. 5:14; 19:4; (e) of things, "falling" into ruin, or failing, e.g., Matt. 7:25; Luke 16:17, RV, "fall," for KJV, "fail"; Heb. 11:30; (f), of "falling" in judgment upon persons, as of the sun's heat, Rev. 7:16, RV, "strike," KJV, "light"; of a mist and darkness, Acts 13:11 (some mss. have *epipipto*); (g) of persons, in "falling" morally or spiritually, Rom. 14:4; 1 Cor. 10:8, 12; Rev. 2:5.

5:23 And besought him greatly, saying, My little daughter lieth at the point of death: *I pray thee*, come and lay thy hands on her, that she may be healed; and she shall live.

Greatly *see* Much at *Mark 1:45*.

Daughter *thugatrion* (2365), denotes "a little daughter," **Mark 5:23; 7:25**.

Death The phrase *eschatos echo*, lit., "to have extremely," i.e., "to be in extremity," *in extremis*, "at the last (gasp), to be at the point of death," is used in **Mark 5:23**.

Lay *epitithemi* (2007), "to add to, lay upon," etc., is used of "laying" hands on the sick, for healing, Matt. 9:18; 19:13, RV, "lay" (KJV, "put"); 19:15; **Mark 5:23; 6:5; 7:32; 8:23**, RV, "laid" (KJV, "put"); so in v. **25**; **16:18**; Luke 4:40; 13:13; Acts 6:6; 8:17, 19; 9:12 and 17, RV, "laying" (KJV, "putting"); 13:3; 19:6; 28:8; in some mss. in Rev. 1:17; of "laying" hands on a person by way of public recognition, 1 Tim. 5:22; of a shepherd's "laying" a sheep on his shoulders, Luke 15:5; "of laying" the cross on Christ's shoulders, Luke 23:26; of "laying" on stripes, Acts 16:23; wood on a fire, 28:3; metaphorically, of "laying" burden's on men's shoulders, Matt. 23:4; similarly of "giving" injunctions, Acts 15:28 (cf. "put ... upon" in v. 10).

Healed *sozo* (4982), "to save," is translated by the verb "to heal" in the KJV of **Mark 5:23** and Luke 8:36 (RV, "to make whole"; so KJV frequently); the idea is that of saving from disease and its effects.

Live *zao* (2198), "to live, be alive," is used in the NT of "(a) God, Matt. 16:16; John 6:57; Rom. 14:11; (b) the Son in Incarnation, John 6:57; (c) the Son in Resurrection, John 14:19; Acts 1:3; Rom. 6:10; 2 Cor. 13:4; Heb. 7:8; (d) spiritual life, John 6:57; Rom. 1:17; 8:13b; Gal. 2:19, 20; Heb. 12:9; (e) the present state of departed saints, Luke 20:38; 1 Pet. 4:6; (f) the hope of resurrection, 1 Pet. 1:3; (g) the resurrection of believers, 1 Thess. 5:10; John 5:25; Rev. 20:4, and of unbelievers, v. 5, cf. v. 13; (h) the way of access to God through the Lord Jesus Christ, Heb. 10:20; (i) the manifestation of divine power in support of divine authority, 2 Cor. 13:4b; cf. 12:10, and 1 Cor. 5:5; (j) bread, figurative of the Lord Jesus, John 6:51; (k) a stone, figurative of the Lord Jesus, 1 Pet. 2:4; (l) water, figurative of the Holy Spirit, John 4:10; 7:38; (m) a sacrifice, figurative of the believer, Rom. 12:1; (n) stones, figurative of the believer, 1 Pet. 2:5; (o) the oracles, *logion*, Acts 7:38, and word, *logos*, Heb. 4:12; 1 Pet. 1:23, of God; (p) the physical life of men, 1 Thess. 4:15; Matt. 27:63; Acts 25:24; Rom. 14:9; Phil. 1:21 (in the infinitive mood used as a noun with the article, 'living'), 22; 1 Pet. 4:5; (q) the maintenance of physical life, Matt. 4:4; 1 Cor. 9:14; (r) the duration of physical life, Heb. 2:15; (s) the enjoyment of physical life, 1 Thess. 3:8; (t) the recovery of physical life from the power of disease, **Mark 5:23**; John 4:50; (u) the recovery of physical life from the power of death, Matt. 9:18; Acts 9:41; Rev. 20:5; (v) the course, conduct, and character of men, (1) good, Acts 26:5; 2 Tim. 3:12; Titus 2:12; (2) evil, Luke 15:13; Rom. 6:2; 8:13a; 2 Cor. 5:15b; Col. 3:7; (3) undefined, Rom. 7:9; 14:7; Gal. 2:14; (w) restoration after alienation, Luke 15:32."

5:24 And *Jesus* went with him; and much people followed him, and thronged him.

Much *polus* (4183), is used (a) as an adjective of degree, e.g., Matt. 13:5, "much (earth)"; Acts 26:24, "much (learning)"; in v. 29, in the answer to Agrippa's "with but little persuasion," some texts have *pollo* (some *megalo*, "with great"), RV, "(whether with little or) with much"; of number, e.g., **Mark 5:24**, RV, "a great (multitude)," KJV, "much (people)"; so Luke 7:11; John 12:12; Rev. 19:1, etc.; (b) in the neuter singular form (*polu*), as a noun, e.g., Luke 16:10 (twice); in the plural (*polla*), e.g., Rom. 16:6, 12, "(labored) much," lit., "many things"; (c) adverbially, in the neuter singular, e.g., Acts 18:27; James 5:16; Matt. 26:9 (a genitive of price); in the plural, e.g., **Mark 5:43**, RV, "much" (KJV, "straitly"); **Mark 9:26**, RV, "much" (KJV, "sore"); John 14:30; and with the article, Acts 26:24; Rom. 15:22; 1 Cor. 16:19; Rev. 5:4.

Thronged *sunthlibo* (4918), "to press together," on all sides (*sun*, "together," and *thlibo*), a strengthened form, is used in **Mark 5:24, 31**.

5:25 And a certain woman, which had an issue of blood twelve years,

Issue *rhusis* (4511), "a flowing" (akin to *rheo*, "to flow"), "an issue," is used in **Mark 5:25**; Luke 8:43, 44.

Blood In **Mark 5:25** and Luke 8:43, different constructions are used, the translations respectively being "having a flowing of blood" and "being in (i.e., with) a flowing of blood."

5:26 And had suffered many things of many physicians, and had spent all that she had, and was nothing bettered, but rather grew worse,

Suffered *pascho* (3958), "to suffer," is used (I) of the "sufferings" of Christ (a) at the hands of men, e.g., Matt. 16:21; 17:12; 1 Pet. 2:23; (b) in His expiatory and vicarious sacrifice for sin, Heb. 9:26; 13:12; 1 Pet. 2:21; 3:18; 4:1; (c) including both (a) and (b), Luke 22:15; 24:26, 46; Acts 1:3, "passion"; 3:18; 17:3; Heb. 5:8; (d) by the antagonism of the evil one, Heb. 2:18; (II) of human "suffering" (a) of followers of Christ, Acts 9:16; 2 Cor. 1:6; Gal. 3:4; Phil. 1:29; 1 Thess. 2:14; 2 Thess. 1:5; 2 Tim. 1:12; 1 Pet. 3:14, 17; 5:10; Rev. 2:10; in identification with Christ in His crucifixion, as the spiritual ideal to be realized, 1 Pet. 4:1; in a wrong way, 4:15; (b) of others, physically, as the result of demoniacal power, Matt. 17:15, RV, "suffereth (grievously)," KJV, "is (sore) vexed"; cf. **Mark 5:26**; in a dream, Matt. 27:19; through maltreatment, Luke 13:2; 1 Pet. 2:19, 20; by a serpent (negatively), Acts 28:5, RV, "took" (KJV, "felt"); (c) of the effect upon the whole body through the "suffering" of one member, 1 Cor. 12:26, with application to a church.

Physicians *see* **Physician** at *Mark 2:17.*

Spent *dapanao* (1159), denotes (a) "to expend, spend," **Mark 5:26**: 2 Cor. 12:15 (1st part); (b) "to consume, squander," Luke 15:14; Jas. 4:3.

Had In **Mark 5:26**, "all that she had" is, lit., "all the (things) with her."

Bettered *opheleo* (5623), in the active voice signifies "to help, to succor, to be of service"; in the passive "to receive help, to derive profit or advantage"; in **Mark 5:26**, "was (nothing) bettered," of the woman who had an issue of blood.

Grew *erchomai* (2064), "to come or go," is translated "grew (worse)," in **Mark 5:26**.

Worse *see Mark 2:21.*

5:27 When she had heard of Jesus, came in the press behind, and touched his garment.

Press *see Mark 2:4.*

Behind *opisthen* (3693), "behind," is used only of place, e.g., Matt. 9:20; **Mark 5:27**; Luke 8:44; Rev. 4:6; as a preposition, Matt. 15:23 ("after"), and Luke 23:26; in Rev. 5:1, RV, "on the back"; KJV, "backside."

5:28-29 For she said, If I may touch but his clothes, I shall be whole. And straightway the fountain of her blood was dried up; and she felt in *her* body that she was healed of that plague.

Fountain *pege* (4077), "a spring or fountain," is used of (a) "an artificial well," fed by a spring, John 4:6; (b) metaphorically (in contrast to such a well), "the indwelling Spirit of God," 4:14; (c) "springs," metaphorically in 2 Pet. 2:17, RV, for KJV, "wells"; (d) "natural fountains or springs," Jas. 3:11, 12; Rev. 8:10; 14:7; 16:4; (e) metaphorically, "eternal life and the future blessings accruing from it," Rev. 7:17; 21:6; (f) "a flow of blood," **Mark 5:29**.

Dried *xeraino* (3583), "to dry, dry up, make dry, wither," is translated "dried" (of physical infirmity), in **Mark 5:29**; of a tree, in the KJV of **Mark 11:20** (RV, "withered away"); of water, in Rev. 16:12. It is translated "ripe" (RV, "overripe") in Rev. 14:15, of a harvest (used figuratively of the gathered nations against Jerusalem at the end of this age); "pineth away," in **Mark 9:18**.

Felt *ginosko* (1097), "to know, perceive," is translated "she felt (in her body)," of the woman with the issue of blood, **Mark 5:29**, i.e., she became aware of the fact.

Plague *see* **Plagues** at *Mark 3:10.*

5:30 And Jesus, immediately knowing in himself that virtue had gone out of him, turned him about in the press, and said, Who touched my clothes?

Press *see Mark 2:4.*

Knowing *epiginosko* (1921), "to gain a full knowledge of, to become fully acquainted with," is translated "to perceive" in **Mark 5:30**, RV (KJV, "knowing"); Luke 1:22; 5:22; Acts 19:34, RV (KJV, "knew").

Virtue In the KJV of **Mark 5:30**; Luke 6:19; 8:46, *dunamis*, "power" (RV), is rendered "virtue."

Turned *epistrepho* (1994), is used (a) transitively, "to make to turn towards" (*epi*), Luke 1:16, 17; Jas. 5:19, 20 (to convert); (b) intransitively, "to turn oneself round," e.g., in the passive voice, **Mark 5:30**; in the active voice, Matt. 13:15, RV, "turn again" (KJV, "be converted"); Acts 11:21; 14:15; 15:19; 1 Thess. 1:9, "ye turned," the aorist tense indicating an immediate and decisive change, consequent upon a deliberate choice; conversion is a voluntary act in response to the presentation of truth.

5:31 And his disciples said unto him, Thou seest the multitude thronging thee, and sayest thou, Who touched me?

Thronging *see* Thronged at *Mark 5:24*.

5:32 And he looked round about to see her that had done this thing.

Looked *see Mark 3:5*.

5:33 But the woman fearing and trembling, knowing what was done in her, came and fell down before him, and told him all the truth.

Trembling *tremo* (5141), "to tremble, especially with fear," is used in **Mark 5:33**; Luke 8:47 (Acts 9:6, in some mss.); 2 Pet. 2:10, RV, "they tremble (not)," KJV, "they are (not) afraid."

Fell *see Mark 3:11*.

5:34 And he said unto her, Daughter, thy faith hath made thee whole; go in peace, and be whole of thy plague.

Whole *see Mark 3:5*.

Peace *eirene* (1515), "occurs in each of the books of the NT, save 1 John and save in Acts 7:26 ['(at) one again'] it is translated "peace" in the RV. It describes (a) harmonious relationships between men, Matt. 10:34; Rom. 14:19; (b) between nations, Luke 14:32; Acts 12:20; Rev. 6:4; (c) friendliness, Acts 15:33; 1 Cor. 16:11; Heb. 11:31; (d) freedom from molestation, Luke 11:21; 19:42; Acts 9:31 (RV, 'peace,' KJV, 'rest'); 16:36; (e) order, in the State, Acts 24:2 (RV, 'peace,' KJV, 'quietness'); in the churches, 1 Cor. 14:33; (f) the harmonized relationships between God and man, accomplished through the gospel, Acts 10:36; Eph. 2:17; (g) the sense of rest and contentment consequent thereon, Matt. 10:13; **Mark 5:34**; Luke 1:79; 2:29; John 14:27; Rom. 1:7; 3:17; 8:6; in certain passages this idea is not distinguishable from the last, Rom. 5:1."

Plague *see* Plagues at *Mark 3:10*.

5:35 While he yet spake, there came from the ruler of the synagogue's *house certain* which said, Thy daughter is dead: why troublest thou the Master any further?

Ruler of the synagogue *see* Rulers of the synagogue at *Mark 5:22*.

Troublest *skullo* (4660), primarily "to flay," hence, "to vex, annoy" ("there was a time when the Greek, in thus speaking, compared his trouble to the pains of flaying alive" (Moulton, *Proleg.*, p. 89), is used in the active voice in **Mark 5:35**; Luke 8:49; in the passive voice, Matt. 9:36, in the best texts, RV, "they were distressed" (some have *ekluo*, KJV, "they fainted"); in the middle voice, Luke 7:6, "trouble (not thyself)." The word is frequent in the papyri.

Master *see Mark 4:38*.

Further *eti* (2089), "yet, still, further," is used (a) of time, most usually translated "yet," e.g., Matt. 12:46; or negatively, "any more," "no more," e.g., Heb. 8:12; (b) of degree, translated "further," or "any further," Matt. 26:65; **Mark 5:35; 14:63**; Luke 22:71; Heb. 7:11 in Acts 21:28, RV, "moreover" (KJV, "further").

5:36 As soon as Jesus heard the word that was spoken, he saith unto the ruler of the synagogue, Be not afraid, only believe.

Heard *parakouo* (3878), primarily signifies "to overhear, hear amiss or imperfectly"; then (in the NT) "to hear without taking heed, to neglect to hear," Matt. 18:17 (twice); in **Mark 5:36** the best mss. have this verb, which the RV renders "not heeding" (marg., "overhearing"); KJV, "hearing." It seems obvious that the Lord paid no attention to those from the ruler's house and their message that his daughter was dead. Cf. the noun *parakoe*, "disobedience."

Ruler of the synagogue *see* Rulers of the synagogue at *Mark 5:22*.

5:37 And he suffered no man to follow him, save Peter, and James, and John the brother of James.

Suffered *see Mark 1:34*.

Follow *sunakoloutheo* (4870), "to follow along with, to accompany a leader" (*sun*, "with," and *akoloutheo*), is given its true rendering in the RV of **Mark 5:37**, "He suffered no man to follow with Him"; in **14:51**, of the young man who "followed with" Christ (inferior mss. have *akoloutheo* here); Luke 23:49, of the women who "followed with" Christ from Galilee.

5:38 And he cometh to the house of the ruler of the synagogue, and seeth the tumult, and them that wept and wailed greatly.

Ruler of the synagogue *see* Rulers of the synagogue at *Mark 5:22*.

Tumult *thorubos* (2351), "a noise, uproar, tumult," is rendered "tumult" in Matt. 27:24 and **Mark 5:38**; in Matt. 26:5, RV (KJV, "uproar"), so in **Mark 14:2**; in Acts 20:1, "uproar," KJV and RV; in 24:18, "tumult"; in 21:34, KJV, "tumult" (RV, "uproar").

Wept *klaio* (2799), is used of "any loud expression of grief," especially in mourning for the dead, Matt. 2:18; **Mark 5:38**, **39**; **16:10**; Luke 7:13; 8:52 (twice); John 11:31, 33 (twice); 20:11 (twice), 13, 15; Acts 9:39; otherwise, e.g., in exhortations, Luke 23:28; Rom. 12:15; Jas. 4:9; 5:1; negatively, "weep not," Luke 7:13; 8:52; 23:28; Rev. 5:5 (cf. Acts 21:13); in 18:9, RV, "shall weep" (KJV, "bewail").

Wailed *alalazo* (214), an onomatopoeic word, from the battle-cry, *alala*, is used of "raising the shout of battle," Josh. 6:20; hence, "to make a loud cry or shout," e.g., Ps. 47:1; "to wail," Jer. 29:2; in the NT, in **Mark 5:38**, of wailing mourners; in 1 Cor. 13:1, of the "clanging" of cymbals (KJV, "tinkling").

Greatly *see* Much at *Mark 1:45*.

5:39 And when he was come in, he saith unto them, Why make ye this ado, and weep? the damsel is not dead, but sleepeth.

Ado *thorubeo* (2350), "to make an uproar, to throw into confusion, or to wail tumultuously," is rendered "make ... ado," in **Mark 5:39**; elsewhere in Matt. 9:23; Acts 17:5; 20:10.

Weep *see* Wept at *Mark 5:38*.

Damsel *paidion* (3813), a diminutive of *pais*, denotes "a young child (male or female)" in the KJV of **Mark 5:39-41** (1st line); the RV corrects "damsel" to "child," so as to distinguish between the narrative of facts, and the homely address to the little girl herself, in which, and in the following sentence, *korasion* is used.

Sleepeth *katheudo* (2518), "to go to sleep," is chiefly used of natural "sleep," and is found most frequently in the Gospels, especially Matthew and Luke. With reference to death it is found in the Lord's remark concerning Jairus' daughter, Matt. 9:24; **Mark 5:39**; Luke 8:52. In the epistles of Paul it is used as follows: (a) of natural "sleep," e.g., 1 Thess. 5:7; (b) of carnal indifference to spiritual things on the part of believers, Eph. 5:14; 1 Thess. 5:6, 10 (as in **Mark 13:36**), a condition of insensibility to divine things involving conformity to the world.

5:40 And they laughed him to scorn. But when he had put them all out, he taketh the father and the mother of the damsel, and them that were with him, and entereth in where the damsel was lying.

Laughed *katagelao* (2606), denotes "to laugh scornfully at," signifies derisive laughter, Matt. 9:24; **Mark 5:40**; Luke 8:53. Cf. *ekmukterizo*, "to deride."

Put *ekballo* (1544), "to cast out," is translated "to put forth or out" in Matt. 9:25; **Mark 5:40** (Luke 8:54 in some mss.); John 10:4; Acts 9:40.

Entereth *see* Entered at *Mark 1:21*.

Lying In **Mark 5:40**, some mss. have the verb *anakeimai*, "to be laid up," translated "was lying," KJV. In the most authentic the word is absent.

5:41 And he took the damsel by the hand, and said unto her, Talitha cumi; which is, being interpreted, Damsel, I say unto thee, arise.

Took *see Mark 1:31*.

Damsel *korasion* (2877), a diminutive of *kore*, "a girl," denotes "a little girl" (properly a colloquial word, often used disparagingly, but not so in later writers); in the NT it is used only in familiar conversation, Matt. 9:24-25 (KJV, "maid"); 14:11; **Mark 5:41-42**; **6:22**, **28**.

Talitha *taleitha or talitha* (5008), an Aramaic feminine meaning "maiden," **Mark 5:41**, has been variously transliterated in the NT Greek mss. *Koumi* or *Koum* (Heb. and Aram., *qum*, "arise"), which follows, is interpreted by, "I say unto thee, arise." *Koum* is the better attested word; so in the Talmud, where this imperative occurs "seven times in one page" (Edersheim, *Life and Times of Jesus*, i, p. 631).

Interpreted *methermeneuo* (3177), "to change or translate from one language to another, to interpret," is always used in the passive voice in the NT, "being interpreted," of interpreting the names, Immanuel, Matt. 1:23; Golgotha, **Mark 15:22**; Barnabas, Acts 4:36; in Acts 13:8, of Elymas, the verb is rendered "is ... by interpretation," lit., "is interpreted"; it is used of interpreting or translating sentences in **Mark 5:41**; **15:34**; in the best mss., John 1:38 (Rabbi, interpreted as "Master"); v. 41 (Messiah, interpreted as "Christ").

Arise *egeiro* (1453), is frequently used in the NT in the sense of "raising" (active voice), or "rising" (middle and passive voices): (a) from sitting, lying, sickness, e.g., Matt. 2:14; 9:5, 7, 19; Jas. 5:15; Rev. 11:1; (b) of causing to appear, or, in the passive, appearing, or raising up so as to occupy a place in the midst of people, Matt. 3:9; 11:11; **Mark 13:22**; Acts 13:22. It is thus said of Christ in Acts 13:23; (c) of rousing, stirring up, or "rising" against, Matt. 24:7; **Mark 13:8**; (d) of "raising buildings," John 2:19-20; (e) of "raising or rising" from the dead; (1) of Christ, Matt. 16:21; and frequently elsewhere (but not in Phil., 2 Thess., 1 Tim., Titus, Jas., 2 Pet., 1, 2, 3 John, and Jude); (2) of Christ's "raising" the dead, Matt. 11:5; **Mark 5:41**; Luke 7:14; John 12:1, 9, 17; (3) of the act of the disciples, Matt. 10:8; (4) of the resurrection of believers, Matt. 27:52; John 5:21; 1 Cor. 15:15-16, 29, 32, 35, 42-44 52; 2 Cor. 1:9; 4:14; of unbelievers, Matt. 12:42. *Egeiro* stands in contrast to *anistemi* (when used with reference to resurrection) in this respect, that *egeiro* is frequently used both in the transitive sense of "raising up" and the intransitive of "rising," whereas *anistemi* is comparatively infrequent in the transitive use.

5:42 And straightway the damsel arose, and walked; for she was *of the age* of twelve years. And they were astonished with a great astonishment.

Age In **Mark 5:42**, RV, the verb *eimi*, "to be," with the phrase "of twelve years" is translated "was ... old" (KJV, "was *of the age* of").

Years *etos* (2094), is used (a) to mark a point of time at or from which events take place, e.g., Luke 3:1 (dates were frequently reckoned from the time when a monarch began to reign); Gal. 3:17; ... (b) to mark a space of time, e.g., Matt. 9:20; Luke 12:19; 13:11; John 2:20; Acts 7:6, where the 400 "years" mark not merely the time that Israel was in bondage in Egypt, but the time that they sojourned or were strangers there (the RV puts a comma after the word "evil"); the Genevan Version renders Gen. 15:13 "thy posterity shall inhabit a strange land for 400 years"; Heb. 3:17; Rev. 20:2-7; (c) to date an event from one's birth, e.g., **Mark 5:42**; Luke 2:42; 3:23; John 8:57; Acts 4:22; 1 Tim. 5:9; (d) to mark recurring events, Luke 2:41 (with *kata*, used distributively); 13:7; (e) of an unlimited number, Heb. 1:12.

Astonished, Astonishment *ekstasis* (1611), is, lit., "a standing out" (*ek*, "out of," *stasis*, "a standing"). Eng. "ecstasy" is a transliteration. It is translated "amazement" in Acts 3:10. It was said of any displacement, and especially, with reference to the mind, of that alteration of the normal condition by which the person is thrown into a state of surprise or fear, or both; or again, in which a person is so transported out of his natural state that he falls into a trance, Acts 10:10; 11:5; 22:17. As to the other meaning, the RV has "amazement" in **Mark 5:42** and Luke 5:26, but "astonishment" in **Mark 16:8**.

5:43 And he charged them straitly that no man should know it; and commanded that something should be given her to eat.

Charged *diastellomai* (1291), lit., "to draw asunder" (*dia*, "asunder," *stello*, "to draw"), signifies "to admonish, order, charge," Matt. 16:20; **Mark 5:43; 7:36** (twice); **8:15; 9:9**. In Acts 15:24 it is translated "gave commandment"; in Heb. 12:20, KJV, "commanded," RV, "enjoined."

Straitly *see* ***Mark 3:12***.

Commanded *epo* (2036), denotes "to speak" (connected with eipon, "to say"); hence, among various renderings, "to bid, command," Matt. 4:3; **Mark 5:43; 8:7**; Luke 4:3; 19:15.

Chapter 6

6:1 And he went out from thence, and came into his own country; and his disciples follow him.

Country *patris* (3968), primarily signifies "one's fatherland, native country, of one's own town," Matt. 13:54, 57; **Mark 6:1**, 4; Luke 4: 23-24; John 4:44; Heb. 11:14.

6:2 And when the sabbath day was come, he began to teach in the synagogue: and many hearing *him* were astonished, saying, From whence hath this *man* these things? and what wisdom *is* this which is given unto him, that even such mighty works are wrought by his hands?

Sabbath In Matt. 12:1 and 11, where the plural is used, the KJV (as the RV) rightly has the singular, "the sabbath day"; in v. 5 the KJV has the plural. Where the singular is used the RV omits the word "day," v. 2; 24:20; **Mark 6:2**; Luke 6:1 ("on a sabbath"); 14:3; John 9:14 ("it was the sabbath on the day when ..."). As to the use or omission of the article the omission does not always require the rendering "a sabbath"; it is absent, e.g., in Matt. 12:2.

Wisdom *sophia* (4678), is used with reference to (a) God, Rom. 11:33; 1 Cor. 1:21, 24; 2:7; Eph. 3:10; Rev. 7:12; (b) Christ, Matt. 13:54; **Mark**

6:2; Luke 2:40, 52; 1 Cor. 1:30; Col. 2:3; Rev. 5:12; (c) "wisdom" personified, Matt. 11:19; Luke 7:35; 11:49; (d) human "wisdom" (1) in spiritual things, Luke 21:15; Acts 6:3, 10; 7:10; 1 Cor. 2:6 (1st part); 12:8; Eph. 1:8, 17; Col. 1:9, RV, "(spiritual) wisdom," 28; 3:16; 4:5; Jas. 1:5; 3:13, 17; 2 Pet. 3:15; Rev. 13:18; 17:9; (2) in the natural sphere, Matt. 12:42; Luke 11:31; Acts 7:22; 1 Cor. 1:17, 19, 20, 21 (twice), 22; 2:1, 4, 5, 6 (2nd part), 13; 3:19; 2 Cor. 1:12; Col. 2:23; (3) in its most debased form, Jas. 3:15, "earthly, sensual, devilish" (marg., "demoniacal").

Works *ginomai* (1096), "to become, take place," is rendered "wrought" in **Mark 6:2**; Acts 5:12, "were … wrought."

6:3 Is not this the carpenter, the son of Mary, the brother of James, and Joses, and of Juda, and Simon? and are not his sisters here with us? And they were offended at him.

Carpenter *tekton* (5405), denotes any craftsman, but especially a worker in wood, a carpenter, Matt. 13:55; **Mark 6:3**.

Offended *skandalizo* (4624), from *skandalon*, signifies "to put a snare or stumblingblock in the way," always metaphorically in the NT, in the same ways as the noun, which see. It is used 14 times in Matthew, 8 in Mark, twice in Luke, twice in John; elsewhere in 1 Cor. 8:13 (twice) and 2 Cor. 11:29. It is absent in the most authentic mss. in Rom. 14:21. The RV renders it by the verb "to stumble," or "cause to stumble," in every place save the following, where it uses the verb "to offend," Matt. 13:57; 15:12; 26:31, 33; **Mark 6:3**; **14:27, 29**.

6:4 But Jesus said unto them, A prophet is not without honour, but in his own country, and among his own kin, and in his own house.

Prophet *prophetes* (4396), "one who speaks forth or openly", "a proclaimer of a divine message," denoted among the Greeks an interpreter of the oracles of the gods.

In the Sept. it is the translation of the word *roeh*, "a seer"; 1 Sam. 9:9, indicating that the "prophet" was one who had immediate intercourse with God. It also translates the word *nabhi*, meaning "either one in whom the message from God springs forth" or "one to whom anything is secretly communicated." Hence, in general, "the prophet" was one upon whom the Spirit of God rested, Num. 11:17-29, one, to whom and through whom God speaks, Num. 12:2; Amos 3:7, 8. In the case of the OT prophets their messages were very largely the proclamation of the divine purposes of salvation and glory to be accomplished in the future; the "prophesying" of the NT "prophets" was both a preaching of the divine counsels of grace already accomplished and the foretelling of the purposes of God in the future.

In the NT the word is used (a) of "the OT prophets," e.g., Matt. 5:12; **Mark 6:15**; Luke 4:27; John 8:52; Rom. 11:3; (b) of "prophets in general," e.g., Matt. 10:41; 21:46; **Mark 6:4**; (c) of "John the Baptist," Matt. 21:26; Luke 1:76; (d) of "prophets in the churches," e.g., Acts 13:1; 15:32; 21:10; 1 Cor. 12:28, 29; 14:29, 32, 37; Eph. 2:20; 3:5; 4:11; (e) of "Christ, as the aforepromised Prophet," e.g., John 1:21; 6:14; 7:40; Acts 3:22; 7:37, or, without the article, and, without reference to the Old Testament, **Mark 6:15**; Luke 7:16; in Luke 24:19 it is used with *aner*, "a man"; John 4:19; 9:17; (f) of "two witnesses" yet to be raised up for special purposes, Rev. 11:10, 18; (g) of "the Cretan poet Epimenides," Titus 1:12; (h) by metonymy, of "the writings of prophets," e.g., Luke 24:27; Acts 8:28.

Without honor *atimos* (820), without honor (*a*, negative, or privative, *time*, "honor"), "despised," is translated "without honor" in Matt. 13:57; **Mark 6:4**; "dishonor" in 1 Cor. 4:10, RV (KJV, "despised"). The comparative degree *atimoteros* is used in the best mss. in 1 Cor. 12:23, "less honorable."

Country *see Mark 6:1*.

Kin *sungeneus* (4773), is used in **Mark 6:4**, "kin," and Luke 2:44, "kinsfolk."

6:5 And he could there do no mighty work, save that he laid his hands upon a few sick folk, and healed *them*.

Mighty works *dunamis* (1411), "power," (a) used relatively, denotes "inherent ability, capability, ability to perform anything," e.g., Matt. 25:15, "ability"; Acts 3:12, "power"; 2 Thess. 1:7, RV, "(angels) of His power" (KJV, "mighty"); Heb. 11:11, RV, "power" (KJV, "strength"); (b) used absolutely, denotes (1) "power to work, to carry something into effect," e.g., Luke 24:49; (2) "power in action," e.g., Rom. 1:16; 1 Cor. 1:18; it is translated "might" in the KJV of Eph. 1:21 (RV, "power"); so 3:16; Col. 1:11 (1st clause); 2 Pet. 2:11; in Rom. 15:19, KJV, this noun is rendered "mighty"; RV, "(in the) power of signs." The RV consistently avoids the rendering "might" for *dunamis;* the usual rendering is "power." Under this heading comes the rendering "mighty works," e.g., Matt. 7:22, RV (KJV, "wonderful works"); 11:20-23; singular number in **Mark 6:5**; in Matt. 14:2 and **Mark 6:14** the RV has "powers"; in 2 Cor. 12:12, RV, "mighty works" (KJV, "mighty deeds").

Laid *see* Lay at *Mark 5:23*.

Sick *arrhostos* (732), "feeble, sickly" (*a*, negative, *rhonnumi*, "to be strong"), is translated "sick" in Matt. 14:14; **Mark 16:18**; "sick folk" in **Mark 6:5**; "that were sick" in **6:13**; "sickly" in 1 Cor. 11:30, here also of the physical state. In the Sept., 1 Kings 14:5; Mal. 1:8.

6:6 And he marvelled because of their unbelief. And he went round about the villages, teaching.

Unbelief The negative noun *apistia*, "unbelief," is used twice in Matthew (13:58); 17:20), three times in Mark (**6:6**; **9:24**; **16:14**), four times in Romans (3:3; 4:20; 11:20, 23); elsewhere in 1 Tim. 1:13 and Heb. 3:12, 19.

Went *periago* (4013), "to lead about," as in 1 Cor. 9:5, is used intransitively with the meaning "to go about"; "went about," Matt. 4:23, 9:35; **Mark 6:6**; Acts 13:11; in Matt. 23:15, "ye compass."

Round about *see Mark 3:34*.

6:7 And he called *unto him* the twelve, and began to send them forth by two and two; and gave them power over unclean spirits;

Two In the following phrases the numeral is used distributively: (a) *ana duo*, "two apiece," John 2:6 (in some mss., Luke 9:3); in Luke 10:1, "two and two" ("by twos"); (b) *kata duo*, "by two," 1 Cor. 14:27; (c) *duo duo*, "by two and two," lit., "two (and) two," **Mark 6:7** (not a Hebraism; the form of expression is used in the papyri); (d) *eis duo*, "into two," "in twain," Matt. 27:51 and **Mark 15:38**.

6:8 And commanded them that they should take nothing for *their* journey, save a staff only; no scrip, no bread, no money in *their* purse:

Commanded *parangello* (3853), "to announce beside" (*para*, "beside," *angello*, "to announce"), "to pass on an announcement," hence denotes "to give the word, order, give a charge, command", e.g., **Mark 6:8**; Luke 8:29; 9:21; Acts 5:28; 2 Thess. 3:4, 6, 10, 12.

Journey *hodos* (3598), "a way, path, road," used of a traveler's way, a "journey," is rendered "journey" in Matt. 10:13; **Mark 6:8**; Luke 2:44, "a day's journey" (probably to Beeroth, six miles north of Jerusalem); 9:3; 11:6; Acts 1:12, "a Sabbath day's journey," i.e., the journey which a Jew was allowed to take on the Sabbath, viz., about 2,000 yards or cubits (estimates vary). The regulation was not a Mosaic enactment, but a rabbinical tradition, based upon an exposition of Exod. 16:29, and a comparison of the width of the suburb of a Levitical city as enjoined in Num. 35:4, 5, and the distance between the ark and the people at the crossing of the Jordan, Josh. 3:4. In regard to Acts 1:12, there is no discrepancy between this and Luke 24:50, where the RV rightly translates by "over against Bethany," which does not fix the exact spot of the Ascension.

Staff *rhabdos* (4464), "a staff, rod, scepter," is used (a) of Aaron's "rod," Heb. 9:4; (b) a staff used on a journey, Matt. 10:10, RV, "staff" (KJV, "staves"); so Luke 9:3; **Mark 6:8**, "staff"; Heb. 11:21, "staff"; (c) a ruler's staff, a "scepter," Heb. 1:8 (twice); elsewhere a "rod," Rev. 2:27; 12:5; 19:15; (d) a "rod" for chastisement (figuratively), 1 Cor. 4:21; (e) a measuring rod, Rev. 11:1.

> *"When I have any money, I get rid of it as quickly as possible, lest it find a way into my heart."*
>
> JOHN WESLEY

Scrip *pera* (4082), "a traveler's leather bag or pouch for holding provisions," is translated "wallet" in the RV (KJV, "scrip"), Matt. 10:10; **Mark 6:8**; Luke 9:3; 10:4; 22:35, 36. Deissmann (*Light from the Ancient East*) regards it as an alms-bag.

Money *chalkos* (5475), primarily, "copper," became used for metals in general, later was applied to bronze, a mixture of copper and tin, then, by metonymy, to any article made of these metals, e.g., money, Matt. 10:9; **Mark 6:8**; **12:41**, or a sounding instrument, 1 Cor. 13:1, figurative of a person destitute of love. See Rev. 18:12.

Purse *zone*, "a girdle or belt," also served as "a purse for money," Matt. 10:9; **Mark 6:8**.

6:9 But *be* shod with sandals; and not put on two coats.

Shod *hupodeo* (5265), *hupo*, "under," with *deo*, "to bind underneath," is used of binding of sandals, Acts 12:8; rendered "shod" in **Mark 6:9** and Eph. 6:15

Sandals *sandalion* (4547), a diminutive of *sandalon*, probably a Persian word, **Mark 6:9**; Acts 12:8. The "sandal" usually had a wooden sole bound on by straps round the instep and ankle.

Put *enduo* (1746), used in the middle voice, of "putting" on oneself, or on another, is translated "to put on" (a) literally, Matt. 6:25; 27:31; **Mark 6:9; 15:20**; Luke 12:22; 15:22; (b) metaphorically, of "putting" on the armor of light, Rom. 13:12; the Lord Jesus Christ, 13:14; Christ, Gal. 3:27; incorruption and immortality (said of the body of the believer), 1 Cor. 15:53, 54; the new man, Eph. 4:24; Col. 3:10; the whole armor of God, Eph. 6:11; the breastplate of righteousness, 6:14, RV; the breastplate of faith and love, 1 Thess. 5:8; various Christian qualities, Col. 3:12.

6:10 And he said unto them, In what place soever ye enter into an house, there abide till ye depart from that place.

Place In the following the RV gives the correct meaning: in **Mark 6:10**, *ekeithen*, "thence" (KJV, "from that place"); in Heb. 2:6 and 4:4, *pou*, "somewhere" (KJV, "in a certain place"); in Matt. 12:6, *hode*, "here" (KJV, "in this place"); in **Mark 6:10**, *hopou ean*, "wheresoever" (KJV, "in what place soever").

6:11 And whosoever shall not receive you, nor hear you, when ye depart thence, shake off the dust under your feet for a testimony against them. Verily I say unto you, It shall be more tolerable for Sodom and Gomorrha in the day of judgment, than for that city.

Receive *dechomai* (1209), "to receive by deliberate and ready reception of what is offered," is used of (a) taking with the hand, taking hold, taking hold of or up, e.g., Luke 2:28, RV, "he received (Him)," KJV, "took he (Him) up"; 16:6, 7; 22:17; Eph. 6:17; (b) "receiving," said of a place "receiving" a person, of Christ into the Heavens, Acts 3:21; or of persons in giving access to someone as a visitor, e.g., John 4:45; 2 Cor. 7:15; Gal. 4:14; Col. 4:10; by way of giving hospitality, etc., e.g., Matt. 10:14, 40 (four times), 41 (twice); 18:5; **Mark 6:11; 9:37**; Luke 9:5, 48, 53; 10:8, 10; 16:4; v. 9, of reception, "into the eternal tabernacles," said of followers of Christ who have used "the mammon of unrighteousness" to render assistance to ("make ... friends of") others; of Rahab's reception of the spies, Heb. 11:31; of the reception, by the Lord, of the spirit of a departing believer, Acts 7:59; of "receiving" a gift, 2 Cor. 8:4 (in some mss.; RV follows those which omit it); of the favorable reception of testimony and teaching, etc., Luke 8:13; Acts 8:14; 11:1; 17:11; 1 Cor. 2:14; 2 Cor. 8:17; 1 Thess. 1:6; 2:13, where *paralambano* is used in the 1st part, "ye received," *dechomai* in the 2nd part, "ye accepted," RV (KJV, "received"), the former refers to the ear, the latter, adding the idea of appropriation, to the heart; Jas. 1:21; in 2 Thess. 2:10, "the love of the truth," i.e., love for the truth; cf. Matt. 11:14, "if ye are willing to receive it," an elliptical construction frequent in Greek writings; of "receiving," by way of bearing with, enduring, 2 Cor. 11:16; of "receiving" by way of getting, Acts 22:5; 28:21, of becoming partaker of benefits, **Mark 10:15**; Luke 18:17; Acts 7:38; 2 Cor. 6:1; 11:4 (last clause "did accept": cf. *lambano* in previous clauses); Phil. 4:18.

Depart *ekporeuo* (1607), *ek*, "from," in the middle and passive, "to proceed from or forth," more expressive of a definite course than simply "to go forth," is translated "go forth," in **Mark 6:11**; "went out" in Matt. 20:29, RV (KJV, "departed"); both have "depart" in Acts 25:4. It is frequently translated by the verb "to proceed," and is often best so rendered, e.g., in Rev. 9:17-18, RV, for KJV, issued.

Shake *ektinasso* (1621), "to shake out," is used of "shaking off" the dust from the feet, Matt. 10:14; **Mark 6:11**; Acts 13:51; of "shaking out" one's raiment, Acts 18:6.

Dust *chous, or choos* (5522), from *cheo*, "to pour," primarily, "earth dug out, an earth heap," then, "loose earth or dust," is used in **Mark 6:11** and Rev. 18:19.

Under *hupokato* (5270), an adverb signifying "under," is used as a preposition and rendered "under" in **Mark 6:11; 7:28**; Luke 8:16; Heb. 2:8; Rev. 5:3, 13; 6:9; 12:1; "underneath" in Matt. 22:44, RV (**Mark 12:36** in some mss.); John 1:50, RV (KJV, "under").

Tolerable *anektos* (414), (akin to *anecho*, in the middle voice, "to endure,") is used in its comparative form, *anektoteros*, in Matt. 10:15; 11:22, 24; Luke 10:12, 14; some texts have it in **Mark 6:11**.

6:12-13 And they went out, and preached that men should repent.

And they cast out many devils, and anointed with oil many that were sick, and healed *them*.

Anointed *aleipho* (218), is a general term used for "an anointing" of any kind, whether of physical refreshment after washing, e.g., in the Sept. of Ruth 3:3; 2 Sam. 12:20; Dan. 10:3; Micah 6:15; in the NT, Matt. 6:17; Luke 7:38, 46; John 11:2; 12:3; or of the sick, **Mark 6:13**; Jas. 5:14; or a dead body, **Mark 16:1**. The material used was either oil, or ointment, as in Luke 7:38, 46. In the Sept. it is also used of "anointing" a pillar, Gen. 31:13, or captives, 2 Chron. 28:15, or of daubing a wall with mortar, Ezek. 13:10-12, 14-15; and, in the sacred sense, of "anointing" priests, in Exod. 40:15 (twice), and Num. 3:3.

Oil *elaion* (1637), "olive oil," is mentioned over 200 times in the Bible. Different kinds were known in Palestine. The "pure," RV (KJV, "beaten"), mentioned in Exod. 27:20; 29:40; Lev. 24:2; Num. 28:5 (now known as virgin oil), extracted by pressure, without heat, is called "golden" in Zech. 4:12. There were also inferior kinds. In the NT the uses mentioned were (a) for lamps, in which the "oil" is a symbol of the Holy Spirit, Matt. 25:3-4, 8; (b) as a medicinal agent, for healing, Luke 10:34; (c) for anointing at feasts, Luke 7:46; (d) on festive occasions, Heb. 1:9, where the reference is probably to the consecration of kings; (e) as an accompaniment of miraculous power, **Mark 6:13**, or of the prayer of faith, Jas. 5:14. For its general use in commerce, see Luke 16:6; Rev. 6:6; 18:13.

Sick *see Mark 6:5.*

6:14 And king Herod heard *of him*; (for his name was spread abroad:) and he said, That John the Baptist was risen from the dead, and therefore mighty works do shew forth themselves in him.

Spread In **Mark 6:14**, KJV, *ginomai*, "to become," with *phaneros*, "manifest," is translated "had spread abroad" (RV, "had become known").

Mighty works *see Mark 6:5.*

Shew *energeo*, Matt. 14:2 and **Mark 6:14**, "work".

6:15 Others said, That it is Elias. And others said, That it is a prophet, or as one of the prophets.

Prophet *see Mark 6:4.*

6:16 But when Herod heard *thereof*, he said, It is John, whom I beheaded: he is risen from the dead.

Beheaded *apokephalizo* (607), *apo*, "from, off," *kephale*, "a head," is found in Matt. 14:10; **Mark 6:16, 27**; Luke 9:9.

6:17 For Herod himself had sent forth and laid hold upon John, and bound him in prison for Herodias' sake, his brother Philip's wife: for he had married her.

Hold *see Mark 3:21.*

Prison *phulake* (5438), denotes a "prison," e.g., Matt. 14:10; **Mark 6:17**; Acts 5:19; 2 Cor. 11:23; in 2 Cor. 6:5 and Heb. 11:36 it stands for the condition of imprisonment; in Rev. 2:10; 18:2, "hold" (twice, RV, marg., "prison"; in the 2nd case, KJV, "cage"); 20:7.

Married *gameo* (1060), "to marry," is used (a) of "the man," Matt. 5:32; 19:9, 10; 22:25 (RV; KJV, "married a wife"); v. 30; 24:38; **Mark 6:17; 10:11; 12:25**; Luke 14:20; 16:18; 17:27, RV, "married" (KJV, "married wives"); 20:34, 35; 1 Cor. 7:28 (1st part); v. 33; (b) of "the woman," in the active voice, **Mark 10:12**; 1 Cor. 7:28 (last part); ver. 34; 1 Tim. 5:11, 14; in the passive voice, 1 Cor. 7:39; (c) of "both sexes," 1 Cor. 7:9, 10, 36; 1 Tim. 4:3.

6:18-19 For John had said unto Herod, It is not lawful for thee to have thy brother's wife.

Therefore Herodias had a quarrel against him, and would have killed him; but she could not:

Had a quarrel against *enecho* (1758), "to hold in," is said (a) of being "entangled" in a yoke of bondage, such as Judaism, Gal. 5:1. Some mss. have the word in 2 Thess. 1:4, the most authentic have *anecho*, "to endure"; (b) with the meaning to set oneself against, be urgent against, said of the plotting of Herodias against John the Baptist, **Mark 6:19**, RV, "set herself against," KJV, "had a quarrel against"; of the effort of the scribes and Pharisees to provoke the Lord to say something which would provide them with a ground of accusation against Him, Luke 11:53, RV, "to press upon," marg., "to set themselves vehemently against," KJV, "to urge."

6:20 For Herod feared John, knowing that he was a just man and an holy, and observed him; and when he heard him, he did many things, and heard him gladly.

Feared *phobeo* (5399), in earlier Greek, "to put to flight," in the NT is always in the passive voice, with the meanings either (a) "to fear, be afraid," its most frequent use, e.g., Acts 23:10, according to the best mss.; or (b) "to show reverential fear," (1) of men, **Mark 6:20**; Eph. 5:33, RV, "fear," for KJV, "reverence"; (2) of God, e.g., Acts 10:2, 22; 13:16, 26; Col. 3:22 (RV, "the Lord"); 1 Pet. 2:17; Rev. 14:7; 15:4; 19:5; (a) and (b) are combined in Luke 12:4, 5, where Christ warns His followers not to be afraid of men, but to "fear" God.

Just *dikaios* (1342), signifies "just," without prejudice or partiality, e.g., of the judgment of God, 2 Thess. 1:5, 6; of His judgments, Rev. 16:7; 19:2; of His character as Judge, 2 Tim. 4:8; Rev. 16:5; of His ways and doings, Rev. 15:3. In the following the RV substitutes "righteous" for the KJV "just"; Matt. 1:19; 13:49; 27:19, 24; **Mark 6:20**; Luke 2:25; 15:7; 20:20; 23:50; John 5:30; Acts 3:14; 7:52; 10:22; 22:14; Rom. 1:17; 7:12; Gal. 3:11; Heb. 10:38; Jas. 5:6; 1 Pet. 3:18; 2 Pet. 2:7; 1 John 1:9; Rev. 15:3.

Observed *suntereo* (4933), denotes "to preserve, keep safe, keep close," in Luke 2:19, as in v. 51, of the mother of Jesus in regard to the words of the shepherds; in **Mark 6:20** it is used of Herod's preservation of John the Baptist from Herodias, RV, "kept (him) safe," KJV, "observed (him)" (marg., "kept"); in Matt. 9:17 (in some mss., Luke 5:38), of the preservation of wineskins.

Many In **Mark 6:20** the RV, following the mss. which have *aporeo*, "to be perplexed," translates *polla* by "much", some mss. have *poieo*, "to do"; hence KJV, "did many things."

Gladly *hedeos* (2234), "gladly" (from *hedus*, "sweet"), is used in **Mark 6:20**; **12:37**; 2 Cor. 11:19.

6:21 And when a convenient day was come, that Herod on his birthday made a supper to his lords, high captains, and chief *estates* of Galilee;

Convenient *eukairos* (2121), lit., "well-timed" (*eu*, "well," *kairos*, "a time, season"), hence signifies "timely, opportune, convenient"; it is said of a certain day, **Mark 6:21**; elsewhere, Heb. 4:16, "in time of need." Cf. *eukairia*, "opportunity," Matt. 26:16; Luke 22:6; *eukaireo*, "to have opportunity," **Mark 6:31**; Acts 17:21 ("they spent their time," marg. "had leisure for nothing else"); 1 Cor. 16:12.

Birthday *genesia* (1077), a neuter plural (akin to *genesis*, "lineage," from *ginomai*), primarily denoted "the festivities of a birthday, a birthday feast," though among the Greeks it was also used of a festival in commemoration of a deceased friend. It is found in Matt. 14:6 and **Mark 6:21**. Some have regarded it as the day of the king's accession, but this meaning is not confirmed in Greek writings.

Supper *deipnon* (1173), denotes (a) "the chief meal of the day," dinner or supper, taken at or towards evening; in the plural "feasts," Matt. 23:6; **Mark 6:21**; **12:39**; Luke 20:46; otherwise translated "supper," Luke 14:12, 16, 17, 24; John 12:2; 13:2, 4; 21:20; 1 Cor. 11:21 (of a social meal); (b) "the Lord's Supper," 1 Cor. 11:20; (c) "the supper or feast" which will celebrate the marriage of Christ with His spiritual Bride, at the inauguration of His Kingdom, Rev. 19:9; (d) figuratively, of that to which the birds of prey will be summoned after the overthrow of the enemies of the Lord at the termination of the war of Armageddon, 19:17 (cf. Ezek. 39:4, 17-20).

Lords *megistan* (3175), akin to *megistos*, "greatest," the superlative degree of *megas*, "great," denotes "chief men, nobles", it is rendered "lords" in **Mark 6:21**, of nobles in Herod's entourage; "princes" in Rev. 6:15 and 18:23, RV (KJV, "great men").

Captains *chiliarchos* (5506), denoting "a commander of 1000 soldiers" (from *chilios*, "a thousand," and *archo*, "to rule"), was the Greek word for the Persian vizier, and for the Roman military tribune, the commander of a Roman cohort, e.g., John 18:12; Acts 21:31-33, 37. One such commander was constantly in charge of the Roman garrison in Jerusalem. The word became used also for any military commander, e.g., a "captain" or "chief captain," **Mark 6:21**; Rev. 6:15; 19:18.

Chief *protos* (4413), denotes "the first," whether in time or place. It is translated "chief" in **Mark 6:21**, RV, of men of Galilee, in Acts 13:50, of men in a city; in 28:7, of the "chief" man in the island of Melita; in 17:4, of "chief" women in a city; in 28:17, of Jews; in 1 Tim. 1:15-16, of a sinner. In the following, where the KJV has "chief," or "chiefest," the RV renderings are different: Matt. 20:27 and **Mark 10:44**, "first"; Luke 19:47 and Acts 25:2, "principal men"; Acts 16:12, said of Philippi, "the first (city) of the district," RV, for incorrect KJV, "the chief city of that part of Macedonia." Amphipolis was the "chief" city of that part. *Protos* here must mean the first in the direction in which the apostle came.

Estates In **Mark 6:21** *protos*, lit., "first," is rendered "chief estates," KJV, RV, "the chief men," i.e., the men to whom belongs the dignity.

6:22 And when the daughter of the said Herodias came in, and danced, and pleased Herod and them that sat with him, the king said unto the damsel, Ask of me whatsoever thou wilt, and I will give *it* thee.

Daughter *see* Damsel at *Mark 5:41*.

Said In **Mark 6:22**, KJV, *autes*, "herself," RV, is rendered "the said."

Danced *orcheo* (3738), (cf. Eng., "orchestra"), probably originally signified "to lift up," as of the feet; hence, "to leap with regularity of motion." It is always used in the middle voice, Matt. 11:17; 14:6; **Mark 6:22**; Luke 7:32. The performance by the daughter of Herodias is the only clear instance of artistic dancing, a form introduced from Greek customs.

Pleased *aresko* (700), signifies (a) "to be pleasing to, be acceptable to," Matt. 14:6; **Mark 6:22**; Acts 6:5; Rom. 8:8; 15:2; 1 Cor. 7:32-34; Gal. 1:10; 1 Thess. 2:15; 4:1 (where the preceding *kai*, "and," is epexegetical, "even," explaining the "walking," i.e., Christian manner of life as "pleasing" God; in Gen. 5:22, where the Hebrew has "Enoch walked with God," the Sept. has "Enoch pleased God"; cf. Mic. 6:8; Heb. 11:5); 2 Tim. 2:4; (b) "to endeavor to please," and so, "to render service," doing so evilly in one's own interests, Rom. 15:1, which Christ did not, v. 3; or unselfishly, 1 Cor. 10:33; 1 Thess. 2:4.

Sat In John 12:2, RV, *anakeimai*, "to recline at table," is translated "sat at meat" (KJV, "sat at the table"); in **Mark 6:26**, RV, according to the best mss., "sat at meat," some have *sunanakeimai* (KJV, "sat with him"); in **Mark 6:22**, RV, *sunanakeimai*, "to recline at table together," is translated "that sat at meat with him." See also **2:15**.

6:23 And he sware unto her, Whatsoever thou shalt ask of me, I will give *it* thee, unto the half of my kingdom.

Sware *omnumi or omnuo* (3660), is used of "affirming or denying by an oath," e.g., Matt. 26:74; **Mark 6:23**; Luke 1:73; Heb. 3:11, 18; 4:3; 7:21; accompanied by that by which one swears, e.g., Matt. 5:34, 36; 23:16; Heb. 6:13, 16; Jas. 5:12; Rev. 10:6.

Half *hemisus* (2255), an adjective, is used (a) as such in the neuter plural, in Luke 19:8, lit., "the halves (of my goods)"; (b) as a noun, in the neuter sing., "the half," **Mark 6:23**; "half (a time)," Rev. 12:14; "a half," 11:9, 11, RV.

6:24-25 And she went forth, and said unto her mother, What shall I ask? And she said, The head of John the Baptist.

And she came in straightway with haste unto the king, and asked, saying, I will that thou give me by and by in a charger the head of John the Baptist.

Straightway *exautes* (1824), "at once" (from, *ek*, "out of," and *autes*, the genitive case of *autos*, "self or very," agreeing with "hour" understood, i.e., "from that very hour"), is translated "forthwith" in the RV in **Mark 6:25** (KJV, "by and by"); Acts 10:33 (KJV, "immediately"); 11:11 (ditto); 21:32 (ditto); 23:30 (KJV, "straightway"); Phil. 2:23 (KJV, "presently"). The word is frequent in the period of the *koine* Greek.

Haste *spoude* (4710), "earnestness, zeal," or sometimes "the haste accompanying this," **Mark 6:25**; Luke 1:39, is translated "diligence" in Rom. 12:8; in v. 11, KJV, "business" (RV, "diligence"); in 2 Cor. 8:7, KJV, "diligence," RV, "earnestness"; both have "diligence" in Heb. 6:11; 2 Pet. 1:5; Jude 3; in 2 Cor. 7:11, 12, RV, "earnest care," KJV, "carefulness," and "care."

Charger *pinax* (4094), primarily "a board or plank," came to denote various articles of wood; hence, "a wooden trencher, charger," Matt. 14:8, 11; **Mark 6:25, 28**; Luke 11:39.

6:26 And the king was exceeding sorry; *yet* for his oath's sake, and for their sakes which sat with him, he would not reject her.

Sorry *perilupos* (4036), is translated "exceeding sorry" in **Mark 6:26**.

Oath *horkos* (3727), is primarily equivalent to *herkos*, "a fence, an enclosure, that which restrains a person"; hence, "an oath." The Lord's command in Matt. 5:33 was a condemnation of the minute and arbitrary restrictions imposed by the scribes and Pharisees in the matter of adjurations, by which God's Name was profaned. The injunction is repeated in Jas. 5:12. The language of the apostle Paul, e.g., in Gal. 1:20 and 1 Thess. 5:27 was not inconsistent with Christ's prohibition, read in the light of its context. Contrast the "oaths" mentioned in Matt. 14:7, 9; 26:72; **Mark 6:26**.

Sat *see Mark 6:22*.

Reject *atheteo* (114), properly, "to do away" with what has been laid down, to make *atheton* (i.e., "without place," *a*, negative, *tithemi*, "to place"), hence, besides its meanings "to set aside, make void, nullify, disannul," signifies "to reject"; in **Mark 6:26**, regarding Herod's pledge to Salome, it almost certainly has the meaning "to break faith with" (cf. the Sept. of Jer. 12:6, and Lam. 1:2, "dealt treacherously"). Moulton and Milligan illustrate this meaning from the papyri. Field suggests "disappoint." In **Mark 7:9** "ye reject (the commandment)" means "ye set aside"; in Luke 7:30, "ye reject" may have the meaning of "nullifying or making void the counsel of God"; in Luke 10:16 (four times), "rejecteth," RV (KJV, "despiseth"); "rejecteth" in John 12:48; "reject" in 1 Cor. 1:19 (KJV, "bring to nothing"); 1 Thess. 4:8, "to despise," where the reference is to the charges in v. 2; in 1 Tim. 5:12, RV, "have rejected" (KJV, "have cast off").

6:27 And immediately the king sent an executioner, and commanded his head to be brought: and he went and beheaded him in the prison,

Sent *see* Send at *Mark 5:10*.

Executioner *spekoulator* (4688), Latin, *speculator*, primarily denotes "a lookout officer," or "scout," but, under the emperors, "a member of the bodyguard"; these were employed as messengers, watchers and executioners; ten such officers were attached to each legion; such a guard was employed by Herod Antipas, **Mark 6:27**, RV, "a soldier of his guard" (KJV, "executioner").

Commanded *see* Commandeth at *Mark 1:27.*

Beheaded *see Mark 6:16.*

6:28 And brought his head in a charger, and gave it to the damsel: and the damsel gave it to her mother.

Charger *see Mark 6:25.*

Damsel *see Mark 5:41.*

6:29 And when his disciples heard *of it*, they came and took up his corpse, and laid it in a tomb.

Corpse *ptoma* (4430), denotes, lit., "a fall" (akin to *pipto*, "to fall"); hence, "that which is fallen, a corpse," Matt. 14:12; 24:28, "carcase"; **Mark 6:29; 15:45**, "corpse"; Rev. 11:8-9, "dead bodies" (Gk., "carcase," but plural in the 2nd part of v. 9).

Laid *tithemi* (5087), "to put, place, set," frequently signifies "to lay," and is used of (a) "laying" a corpse in a tomb, Matt. 27:60; **Mark 6:29; 15:47; 16:6**; Luke 23:53, 55; John 11:34; 19:41, 42; 20:2, 13, 15; Acts 7:16; 13:29; Rev. 11:9, RV, "to be laid" (KJV, "to be put"); in an upper chamber, Acts 9:37; (b) "laying" the sick in a place, **Mark 6:56**; Luke 5:18; Acts 3:2; 5:15; (c) "laying" money at the apostles' feet, Acts 4:35, 37; 5:2; (d) Christ's "laying" His hands upon children, **Mark 10:16**, RV, "laying" (KJV, "put"); upon John, Rev. 1:17 (in the best mss.); (e) "laying" down one's life, (1) of Christ, John 10:11, RV, "layeth down" (KJV, "giveth"); vv. 17, 18 (twice); 1 John 3:16; (2) of Peter for Christ's sake, John 13:37, 38; (3) of Christ's followers, on behalf of others, 1 John 3:16; (4) of anyone, for his friends, John 15:13; (f) "laying" up sayings in one's heart, Luke 1:66 (middle voice, in the sense of "for themselves"); in 9:44, of letting Christ's words "sink" (middle voice, in the sense of "for oneself"; KJV, "sink down") into the ears; (g) "laying" a foundation (1) literally, Luke 6:48; 14:29; (2) metaphorically, of Christ in relation to an assembly, 1 Cor. 3:10, 11; (h) in "laying" Christ as a "stone of stumbling" for Israel, Rom. 9:33; (i) Christ's "laying" aside His garments, John 13:4; (j) Christians, in "laying" money in store for the help of the needy, 1 Cor. 16:2 (lit., "let him put"); (k) "depositing" money, Luke 19:21, 22.

Tomb *see* Tombs at *Mark 5:2.*

6:30 And the apostles gathered themselves together unto Jesus, and told him all things, both what they had done, and what they had taught.

What Other words are (a) *hoios*, "of what kind," e.g., 2 Cor. 10:11, RV (KJV, "such as"); 1 Thess. 1:5, "what manner of men"; 2 Tim. 3:11 (twice), lit., "what sorts of things," "what sorts of persecutions"; (b) *poios*, "what sort of," e.g., Matt. 21:23, 24, 27; 24:42, 43; Luke 5:19; 6:32-34; 20:2, 8; 24:19; John 12:33, "what manner of"; so in 18:32; 21:19; Rom. 3:27; 1 Cor. 15:35; in Jas. 4:14, "what"; 1 Pet. 2:20 and Rev. 3:3 (ditto); 1 Pet. 1:11, "what manner of"; (c) *hopoios*, "what sort of," 1 Cor. 3:13; "what manner of," 1 Thess. 1:9; (d) *hosos*, "how great," **Mark 6:30** (twice), RV, "whatsoever"; Acts 15:12; Rom. 3:19, "what things soever"; Jude 10 (1st part), "what soever things," RV; (2nd part) "what"; (e) *posos*, "how great, how much," 2 Cor. 7:11, "what (earnest care)," RV (*posos* here stands for the repeated words in the Eng. versions, the adjective not being repeated in the original); (f) *hostis*, "what (things)," Phil. 3:7; (g) in Matt. 26:40, *houtos*, "thus, so," is used as an exclamatory expression, translated "What" (in a word immediately addressed by the Lord to Peter), lit., "So"; (h) *potapos*, rendered "what" in **Mark 13:1** (2nd part), KJV; (i) in 1 Cor. 6:16, 19, KJV, the particle *e*, "or" (RV), is rendered "What?"; in 1 Cor. 14:36, KJV and RV, "what?" (j) in 1 Cor. 11:22, *gar*, "in truth, indeed," has its exclamatory use "What."

6:31 And he said unto them, Come ye yourselves apart into a desert place, and rest a while: for there were many coming and going, and they had no leisure so much as to eat.

Yourselves (1) These are most frequently the translations of various inflections of a verb; sometimes of the article before a nominative used as a vocative, e.g., Rev. 18:20, "ye saints, and ye apostles, and ye prophets" (lit., "the saints, etc."). When the 2nd person plural pronouns are used separately from a verb, they are usually one or other of the forms of *humeis*, the plural of *su*, "thou," and are frequently emphatic, especially when they are subjects of the verb, an emphasis always to be noticed, e.g., Matt. 5:13, 14, 48; 6:9, 19, 20; **Mark 6:31, 37**; John 15:27a; Rom. 1:6; 1 Cor. 3:17, 23; Gal. 3:28, 29a; Eph. 1:13a; 2:8; 2:11, 13; Phil. 2:18; Col. 3:4, 7a; 4:1; 1 Thess. 1:6; 2:10, 19, 20; 3:8; 2 Thess. 3:13; Jas. 5:8; 1 Pet. 2:9a; 1 John 2:20, 24 (1st and 3rd occurrences), 27a; 4:4; Jude 17, 20. (2) The addition of *autoi*, "yourselves," to the pronoun marks especial emphasis, e.g., **Mark 6:31**; John 3:28; 1 Cor. 11:13; 1 Thess. 4:9. Sometimes *autoi* is used without the pronoun, e.g., Luke 11:46, 52; Acts 2:22; 20:34; 1 Thess. 2:1; 3:3; 5:2; 2 Thess. 3:7; Heb. 13:3.

Rest *anapauo* (373), in the active voice, signifies "to give intermission from labor, to give rest, to refresh," Matt. 11:28; 1 Cor. 16:18, "have refreshed"; Philem. 20, "refresh"; passive voice, "to be rested, refreshed," 2 Cor. 7:13, "was refreshed"; Philem. 7, "are refreshed"; in the middle voice, "to take or enjoy rest," Matt. 26:45; **Mark 6:31**; **14:41**; Luke 12:19, "take thine ease"; 1 Pet. 4:14; Rev. 6:11; 14:13. In the papyri it is found as an agricultural term, e.g., of giving land "rest" by sowing light crops upon it. In inscriptions it is found on gravestones of Christians, followed by the date of death (Moulton and Milligan).

Leisure *eukaireo* (2119), "to have leisure or opportunity" (*eu*, "well," *kairos*, "a time or season"), is translated "they had ... leisure" in **Mark 6:31**; in Acts 17:21, "spent their time" (RV, marg., "had leisure for"); in 1 Cor. 16:12, "he shall have opportunity," RV (KJV, "... convenient time"). This verb differs from *scholazo*, "to have leisure"; it stresses the opportunity of doing something, whereas *scholazo* stresses the "leisure" for engaging in it, e.g., 1 Cor. 7:5, "(that) ye may give yourselves to."

Much *see Mark 2:2*.

6:32-33 And they departed into a desert place by ship privately. And the people saw them departing, and many knew him, and ran afoot thither out of all cities, and outwent them, and came together unto him.

Ran *suntrecho* (4936), "to run together with" (*sun*, "with"), is used (a) literally, **Mark 6:33**; Acts 3:11; (b) metaphorically, 1 Pet. 4:4, of "running" a course of evil with others. In the Sept., Ps. 50:18.

Afoot *poderes* (4158), signifies "reaching to the feet," from *pous*, and *aro*, "to fit," and is said of a garment, Rev. 1:13. In the Sept. it is used of the high priest's garment, e.g., Ex. 28:4. *pezos* (3978), an adjective, "on foot," is used in one of its forms as an adverb in Matt. 14:3, and **Mark 6:33**, in each place signifying "by land," in contrast to by sea. Cf. *pezeuo*, "to go on foot," Acts 20:3, RV, "to go by land" (marg., "on foot").

Outwent *proerchomai* (4281), "to go forward, go in advance, outgo," is used of time in **Mark 6:33**, "outwent," of the people who in their eagerness reached a spot earlier than Christ and His disciples.

6:34 And Jesus, when he came out, saw much people, and was moved with compassion toward them, because they were as sheep not having a shepherd: and he began to teach them many things.

Compassion *see Mark 1:41*.

Sheep *probaton* (4263), from *probaino*, "to go forward," i.e., of the movement of quadrupeds, was used among the Greeks of small cattle, sheep and goats; in the NT, of "sheep" only (a) naturally, e.g., Matt. 12:11, 12; (b) metaphorically, of those who belong to the Lord, the lost ones of the house of Israel, Matt. 10:6; of those who are under the care of the Good Shepherd, e.g., Matt. 26:31; John 10:1, lit., "the fold of the sheep," and vv. 2-27; 21:16, 17 in some texts; Heb. 13:20; of those who in a future day, at the introduction of the millennial kingdom, have shown kindness to His persecuted earthly people in their great tribulation, Matt. 25:33; of the clothing of false shepherds, Matt. 7:15; (c) figuratively, by way of simile, of Christ, Acts 8:32; of the disciples, e.g., Matt. 10:16; of true followers of Christ in general, Rom. 8:36; of the former wayward condition of those who had come under His Shepherd care, 1 Pet. 2:25; of the multitudes who sought the help of Christ in the days of His flesh, Matt. 9:36; **Mark 6:34**.

"With infinite love and compassion our Lord understood the human predicament. He had deep empathy with people; he saw their needs, their weaknesses, their desires, and their hurt. He understood and was concerned for people. Every word he spoke was uttered because he saw a need for that word in some human life."

CHARLES L. ALLEN

Shepherd *poimen* (4166), is used (a) in its natural significance, Matt. 9:36; 25:32; **Mark 6:34**; Luke 2:8, 15, 18, 20; John 10:2, 12; (b) metaphorically of Christ, Matt. 26:31; **Mark 14:27**; John 10:11, 14, 16; Heb. 13:20; 1 Pet. 2:25; (c) metaphorically of those who act as pastors in the churches, Eph. 4:11.

6:35 And when the day was now far spent, his disciples came unto him, and said, This is a desert place, and now the time *is* far passed:

Day In **Mark 6:35**, the clause "the day was far spent" is, lit., "a much hour (i.e., a late hour) having become," or, perhaps, "many an hour having become," i.e., many hours having passed. In the end of the v., RV, "day," for KJV, "time."

Spent *ginomai* (1096), "to become, occur," is rendered "was far spent" in **Mark 6:35**, lit., "much hour (i.e., many an hour) having taken place;" *polus*, much, is rendered "far spent" twice in **Mark 6:35**, RV.

Time *hora* (5610), primarily, "any time or period fixed by nature," is translated "time" in Matt. 14:15; Luke 14:17; Rom. 13:11, "high time"; in the following the RV renders it "hour," for KJV, "time," Matt. 18:1; Luke 1:10; John 16:2, 4, 25; 1 John 2:18 (twice); Rev. 14:15; in **Mark 6:35**, RV, "day"; in 1 Thess. 2:17, RV, "a short (season)," lit., "(the season, KJV, 'time') of an hour."

Passed In **Mark 6:35**; KJV, "the time is far passed" (RV, "the day is ... far spent") is, lit., "the hour is much (*polus*)."

6:36 Send them away, that they may go into the country round about, and into the villages, and buy themselves bread: for they have nothing to eat.

Send *apoluo* (630), "to set free, to let go," is translated "to send away" in Matt. 14:15, 22, 23; **Mark 6:36, 45**; **8:3, 9**; Luke 8:38; Acts 13:3, where the "sending" is not that of commissioning, but of letting go, intimating that they would gladly have retained them (contrast *ekpempo*, the act of commissioning by the Holy Spirit in v. 4).

Country *see Mark 5:14.*

Round about *see Mark 3:34.*

6:37 He answered and said unto them, Give ye them to eat. And they say unto him, Shall we go and buy two hundred pennyworth of bread, and give them to eat?

Ye *see 6:31.*

Two hundred *diakosioi* (1250), occurs in **Mark 6:37**; John 6:7; 21:8; Acts 23:23 (twice); 27:37, "two hundred (threescore and sixteen)"; Rev. 11:3, "(a thousand) two hundred (and threescore)"; so 12:6.

Pennyworth *denarion* (1220), a Roman coin, a *denarius*, a little less than the value of the Greek *drachme*, now estimated as amounting to about 9½d. in the time of our Lord, occurs in the singular, e.g., Matt. 20:2; 22:19; **Mark 12:15**; Rev. 6:6; in the plural, e.g., Matt. 18:28; **Mark 14:5**; Luke 7:41; 10:35; John 12:5; "pennyworth" in **Mark 6:37** and John 6:7, lit., "(loaves of two hundred) pence." Considering the actual value, "shilling" would have been a more accurate translation, as proposed by the American translators, retaining "penny" for the *as*, and "farthing" for the *quadrans*.

6:38 He saith unto them, How many loaves have ye? go and see. And when they knew, they say, Five, and two fishes.

Many *posos* (4214), "how much, how great, how many," has the last meaning in Matt. 15:34; 16:9, 10; 27:13 ("how many things"); **Mark 6:38**; **8:5, 19, 20**; **15:4** ("how many things); Luke 15:17; Acts 21:20.

Fish *ichthus* (2486), denotes "a fish," Matt. 7:10; **Mark 6:38**, etc.; apart from the Gospels, only in 1 Cor. 15:39.

See *horao* (3708), with its aorist form *eidon*, "to see" (in a few places the KJV uses the verb "to behold"), is said (a) of bodily vision, e.g., **Mark 6:38**; John 1:18, 46; (b) of mental perception, e.g., Rom. 15:21; Col. 2:18; (c) of taking heed, e.g., Matt. 8:4; 1 Thess. 5:15; (d) of experience, as of death, Luke 2:26; Heb. 11:5; life, John 3:36; corruption, Acts 2:27; (e) of caring for, Matt. 27:4; Acts 18:15 (here the form *opsomai* is used).

6:39 And he commanded them to make all sit down by companies upon the green grass.

Commanded *see* **Commandeth** at *Mark 1:27.*

Sit *anaklino* (347), "to cause to recline, make to sit down," is used in the active voice, in Luke 12:37 (also in 2:7, of "laying" the infant Christ in the manger); in the passive, Matt. 8:11; 14:19; **Mark 6:39** (in the best texts); in some texts, Luke 7:36 and 9:15; 13:29.

Companies *sumposion* (4849), lit. "denotes a drinking together (*sun*, "with," *pino*, "to drink"), a drinking-party"; hence, by metonymy, "any table party or any company arranged as a party." In **Mark 6:39** the noun is repeated, in the plural, by way of an adverbial and distributive phrase, *sumposia sumposia*, lit., "companies-companies" (i.e., by companies).

Green *chloros* (5515), akin to *chloe*, "tender foliage" (cf. the name "Chloe," 1 Cor. 1:11, and Eng., "chlorine"), denotes (a) "pale green," the color of young grass, **Mark 6:39**; Rev. 8:7; 9:4, "green thing"; hence, (b) "pale," Rev. 6:8, the color of the horse whose rider's name is Death.

Grass *chortos* (5528), primarily denoted "a feeding enclosure" (whence Latin *hortus*, "a garden"; Eng.. "yard," and "garden"); then, "food," especially grass for feeding cattle; it is translated "grass" in Matt. 6:30; 14:19; **Mark 6:39** (where "the green grass" is the first evidence of early spring); Luke 12:28; John 6:10; Jas. 1:10, 11; 1 Pet. 1:24; Rev. 8:7; 9:4; "blade" in Matt. 13:26; **Mark 4:28**; "hay" in 1 Cor. 3:12, used figuratively. In Palestine or Syria there are 90 genera and 243 species of grass.

6:40 And they sat down in ranks, by hundreds, and by fifties.

Ranks *prasia* (4237), "a garden bed or plot" (probably from *prason*, "a leek"), is used metaphorically in **Mark 6:40** of "ranks" of persons arranged in orderly groups.

Hundreds *see* **Hundred** at *Mark 4:8*.

Sat *anapipto* (377), "to fall back" (*ana*, "back," *pipto*, "to fall"), denotes, in the NT, "to recline for a repast," Matt. 15:35; **Mark 6:40**; **8:6**; Luke 11:37; 14:10; 17:7; 22:14; John 6:10 (twice); 13:12; in John 13:25 and 21:20 it is used of leaning on the bosom of Christ. In the Sept., Gen. 49:9.

Fifties *pentekonta* (4004), is found in Luke 7:41; 16:6; John 8:57; 21:11; Acts 13:20; in **Mark 6:40** with *kata* (in the most authentic mss.), according to, "by fifties"; in Luke 9:14, with *ana*, "up," used distributively, "fifty each," RV (Luke adds *hosei*, "about").

6:41 And when he had taken the five loaves and the two fishes, he looked up to heaven, and blessed, and brake the loaves, and gave *them* to his disciples to set before them; and the two fishes divided he among them all.

Brake *kataklao* (2622), *kata*, "down," and *klao*, is used in **Mark 6:41** and Luke 9:16, of Christ's "breaking" loaves for the multitudes.

Set *paratithemi* (3908), "to place beside" (*para*, "beside," and *tithemi*), "to set forth," of a parable, Matt. 13:24, RV (KJV, "put forth"); "to set before," of food, **Mark 6:41**; **8:6** (twice), 7; Luke 9:16; 10:8; 11:6; Acts 16:34; 1 Cor. 10:27.

Divided *see Mark 3:24*.

6:42-43 And they did all eat, and were filled.

And they took up twelve baskets full of the fragments, and of the fishes.

Baskets *kophinos* (2894), was "a wicker basket," originally containing a certain measure of capacity, Matt. 14:20; 16:9; **Mark 6:43** (RV, "basketfuls"); **8:19**; Luke 9:17; 13:8 in some mss.; John 6:13.

Full *see* **Filled** at *Mark 2:21*.

Fragments *klasma* (2801), "a broken piece" (from *klao*, "to break") is used of the broken pieces from the feeding of the multitudes, RV, "broken pieces," KJV, "fragments," Matt. 14:20; **Mark 6:43**; **8:19**, **20**; Luke 9:17; John 6:12, 13; in Matt. 15:37 and **Mark 8:8**, RV, "broken pieces" (KJV, "broken meat").

6:44 And they that did eat of the loaves were about five thousand men.

Thousand *see Mark 5:13*.

6:45 And straightway he constrained his disciples to get into the ship, and to go to the other side before unto Bethsaida, while he sent away the people.

Constrained *anankazo* (315), denotes "to put constraint upon (from *ananke*, 'necessity'), to constrain, whether by threat, entreaty, force or persuasion"; Christ "constrained" the disciples to get into a boat, Matt. 14:22; **Mark 6:45**; the servants of the man who made a great supper were to constrain people to come in, Luke 14:23 (RV, "constrain"); Saul of Tarsus "strove" to make saints blaspheme, Acts 26:11, RV (KJV, "compelled"); Titus, though a Greek, was not "compelled" to be circumcised, Gal. 2:3, as Galatian converts were, 6:12, RV; Peter was "compelling" Gentiles to live as Jews, Gal. 2:14; Paul was "constrained" to appeal to Caesar, Acts 28:19, and was "compelled" by the church at Corinth to become foolish in speaking of himself, 2 Cor. 12:11.

While The conjunction *heos*, "until," etc., has the meaning "while" in Matt. 14:22; **Mark 6:45**; **14:32**; in some texts, John 9:4; 12:35, 36; with *hotou*, "whatever" (an oblique case, neuter, of *hostis*, "whoever"), "whiles," Matt. 5:25.

Sent *see* **Send** at *Mark 6:36*.

6:46 And when he had sent them away, he departed into a mountain to pray.

Departed *apotasso* (657), is used in the middle voice to signify "to bid adieu to a person." It primarily means "to set apart, separate" (*apo*, "from," *tasso*, "to set, arrange"); then, "to take leave of, to bid farewell to," **Mark 6:46** (RV); Luke 9:61; "to give parting instructions to," Acts 18:18, 21; 2 Cor. 2:13; "to forsake, renounce," Luke 14:33.

6:47 And when even was come, the ship was in the midst of the sea, and he alone on the land.

Land *see Mark 4:1.*

6:48 And he saw them toiling in rowing; for the wind was contrary unto them: and about the fourth watch of the night he cometh unto them, walking upon the sea, and would have passed by them.

Toiling *basanizo* (928), primarily, "to rub on the touchstone, to put to the test," then, "to examine by torture" (*basanos,* "touchstone, torment"), hence denotes "to torture, torment, distress"; in the passive voice it is rendered "toiling" in **Mark 6:48**, KJV (RV, "distressed").

Rowing *elauno* (1643), signifies "to drive, impel, urge on." It is used of "rowing," **Mark 6:48** and John 6:19; of the act of a demon upon a man, Luke 8:29; of the power of winds upon ships, Jas. 3:4; and of storms upon mists, 2 Pet. 2:17, KJV, "carried," RV, "driven."

Contrary *enantios* (1727), "over against" (*en,* "in," *antios,* "against"), is used primarily of place, **Mark 15:39**; of an opposing wind, Matt. 14:24; **Mark 6:48**; Acts 27:4; metaphorically, opposed as an adversary, antagonistic, Acts 26:9; 1 Thess. 2:15; Titus 2:8; Acts 28:17, "against."

Fourth *tessares* (5064), "four," is not found in the NT outside the Gospels, the Acts and Revelation; in the last it is very frequent. *Tetartos,* "fourth," is found in Matt. 14:25; **Mark 6:48** and seven times in Revelation; also in Acts 10:30, "four days ago," lit., "from a fourth day." *Dekatessares,* "fourteen" (lit., "ten-four"), is found in Matt. 1:17; 2 Cor. 12:2; Gal. 2:1; *tessareskaidekatos,* "fourteenth" (lit., "four-and-tenth"), Acts 27:27, 33; *tetrakosia,* "four hundred," Acts 5:36; 7:6; 13:20; Gal. 3:17. In Acts 7:6 the 400 years refers to Abraham's descendants and to the sojourning and the bondage. This agrees with Gen. 15:13. In Exod. 12:40 the 430 years dates from the call of Abraham himself. Likewise the giving of the Law was 430 years from the promise in Gen. 12:3, which agrees with Gal. 3:17. In John 11:39 *tetartaios,* lit., "a fourth day (one)," is rendered "four days."

Watch *phulake* (5438), is used (a) with the meaning "a watch," actively, "a guarding," Luke 2:8, lit., "(keeping, *phulasso*) watches"; (b) of "the time during which guard was kept by night, a watch of the night," Matt. 14:25; 24:43; **Mark 6:48**; Luke 12:38.

Sea *thalassa* (2281), is used chiefly literally, e.g., "the Red Sea," Acts 7:36; 1 Cor. 10:1; Heb. 11:29; the "sea" of Galilee or Tiberias, Matt. 4:18; 15:29; **Mark 6:48, 49**, where the acts of Christ testified to His deity; John 6:1; 21:1; in general, e.g., Luke 17:2; Acts 4:24; Rom. 9:27; Rev. 16:3; 18:17; 20:8, 13; 21:1; in combination with *pelagos,* Matt. 18:6.

Passed *parerchomai* (3928), from *para,* "by," *erchomai,* "to come" or "go," denotes (I) literally, "to pass, pass by," (a) of persons, Matt. 8:28; **Mark 6:48**; Luke 18:37; Acts 16:8; (b) of things, Matt. 26:39, 42; of time, Matt. 14:15; **Mark 14:35**; Acts 27:9, KJV, "past" (RV, "gone by"); 1 Pet. 4:3; (II) metaphorically, (a) "to pass away, to perish," Matt. 5:18; 24:34, 35; **Mark 13:30, 31**; Luke 16:17; 21:32, 33; 2 Cor. 5:17; Jas. 1:10; 2 Pet. 3:10; (b) "to pass by, disregard, neglect, pass over," Luke 11:42; 15:29, "transgressed." For the meaning "to come forth or come," see Luke 12:37; 17:7, RV (Acts 24:7 in some mss.).

6:49 But when they saw him walking upon the sea, they supposed it had been a spirit, and cried out:

Sea *see Mark 6:48.*

Suppose *dokeo* (1380), "to be of opinion," is translated "to suppose" in **Mark 6:49**; Luke 24:37; John 20:15; Acts 27:13; in the following, KJV "suppose," RV, "think," Luke 12:51; 13:2; Heb. 10:29. It is most frequently rendered "to think," always in Matthew; always in John, except 11:31, "supposing," RV [where the best texts have this verb (for *lego,* KJV, "saying")], and 20:15.

Spirit *phantasma* (5326), "a phantasm or phantom" (from *phaino,* "to appear"), is translated "apparition" in the RV of Matt. 14:26 and **Mark 6:49** (KJV, "spirit"). In the Sept., Job 20:8; Isa. 28:7.

Cried *see Mark 1:23.*

6:50 For they all saw him, and were troubled. And immediately he talked with them, and saith unto them, Be of good cheer: it is I; be not afraid.

Troubled *tarosso* (5015), is used (1) in a physical sense, John 5:7 (in some mss. v. 4), (2) metaphorically, (a) of the soul and spirit of the Lord, John 11:33, where the true rendering is "He troubled Himself"; (b) of the hearts of disciples, 14:1, 27; (c) of the minds of those in fear or perplexity, Matt. 2:3; 14:26; **Mark 6:50**; Luke 1:12; 24:38; 1 Pet. 3:14; (d) of subverting the souls of believers, by evil doctrine, Acts 15:24; Gal. 1:7; 5:10; (e) of stirring up a crowd, Acts 17:8; v. 13 in the best texts, "troubling (the multitudes)," RV.

Talked *laleo* (2980), "to speak, say," is always translated "to speak" in the RV, where the KJV renders it by "to talk," Matt. 12:46; **Mark 6:50**; Luke 24:32; John 4:27 (twice); 9:37; 14:30; Acts 26:31; Rev. 4:1; 17:1; 21:9, 15. The RV rendering is preferable; the idea of "chat" or "chatter" is entirely foreign to the NT, and should never be regarded as the meaning in 1 Cor. 14:34, 35.

Saith *lego* (3004), primarily "to pick out, gather," chiefly denotes "to say, speak, affirm," whether of actual speech, e.g., Matt. 11:17, or of unspoken thought, e.g., Matt. 3:9, or of a message in writing, e.g., 2 Cor. 8:8. The 2nd aorist form *eipon* is used to supply that tense, which is lacking in *lego*. Concerning the phrase "he answered and said," it is a well known peculiarity of Hebrew narrative style that a speech is introduced, not simply by "and he said," but by prefixing "and he answered" (*apokrinomai*, with *eipon*). In Matt. 14:27, "saying," and **Mark 6:50**, "and saith," emphasis is perhaps laid on the fact that the Lord, hitherto silent as He moved over the lake, then addressed His disciples. That the phrase sometimes occurs where no explicit question has preceded (e.g., Matt. 11:25; 17:4; 28:5; **Mark 11:14**; **12:35**; Luke 13:15; 14:3; John 5:17, 19), illustrates the use of the Hebrew idiom.

Cheer *tharseo* (2293), "to be of good courage, of good cheer" (*tharsos*, "courage, confidence"), is used only in the imperative mood, in the NT; "be of good cheer," Matt. 9:2, 22; 14:27; **Mark 6:50**; **10:49**; Luke 8:48; John 16:33; Acts 23:11.

6:51 And he went up unto them into the ship; and the wind ceased: and they were sore amazed in themselves beyond measure, and wondered.

Ceased *see Mark 4:39.*

Sore *lian* (3029), "very, exceedingly," is translated "sore" in **Mark 6:51** (of amazement).

Measure In **Mark 6:51**, some mss. have the phrase *ek perissou*, "beyond measure" (KJV).

6:52 For they considered not *the miracle* of the loaves: for their heart was hardened.

Considered *suniemi*, "to understand," is translated "considered" in **Mark 6:52** (KJV), RV, "understood."

Hardened *poroo* (4456), "to make hard, callous, to petrify," is used metaphorically, of the heart, **Mark 6:52**; **8:17**; John 12:40; of the mind (or thoughts), 2 Cor. 3:14, of those in Israel who refused the revealed will and ways of God in the gospel, as also in Rom. 11:7, RV, "hardened" (KJV, "blinded"), in both places.

6:53 And when they had passed over, they came into the land of Gennesaret, and drew to the shore.

Passed over *see Mark 5:21.*

Drew In **Mark 6:53**, *prosormizo*, "to bring a ship (or boat) to anchor, cast anchor, land at a place" (*pros*, "to," *hormizo*, "to moor, bring to anchorage"), is translated "moored to the shore," in the RV, for KJV, "drew."

6:54-55 And when they were come out of the ship, straightway they knew him,

And ran through that whole region round about, and began to carry about in beds those that were sick, where they heard he was.

Ran *peritrecho* (4063), "to run about," is used in **Mark 6:55**, RV, "ran round about" (KJV, "ran through").

Region *see Mark 1:28.*

Carry *periphero* (4064), "about," signifies "to carry about, or bear about," and is used literally, of carrying the sick **Mark 6:55**, or of physical sufferings endured in fellowship with Christ, 2 Cor. 4:10; metaphorically, of being "carried" about by different evil doctrines, Eph. 4:14; Heb. 13:9; Jude 12.

Beds *see* Bed at *Mark 2:4.*

Sick *see* Diseased at *Mark 1:32.*

6:56 And whithersoever he entered, into villages, or cities, or country, they laid the sick in the streets, and besought him that they might touch if it were but the border of his garment: and as many as touched him were made whole.

Entered *see Mark 1:21.*

Laid *see Mark 6:29.*

Sick *astheneo* (770), lit., "to be weak, feeble" (*a*, negative, *sthenos*, "strength"), is translated "to be sick," e.g., in Matt. 10:8, "(the) sick"; 25:36; v. 39 in the best texts; **Mark 6:56**; Luke 4:40; 7:10 (RV omits the word); 9:2; John 4:46; 5:3, RV (KJV, "impotent folk"); v. 7; 6:2, RV (KJV, "were diseased"); 11:1-3, 6; Acts 9:37; 19:12; Phil. 2:26, 27; 2 Tim. 4:20; Jas. 5:14.

Streets *agora* (58), primarily "an assembly," or, in general, "an open space in a town" (akin to *ageiro*, "to bring together"), became applied, according to papyri evidences, to a variety of things, e.g., "a judicial assembly," "a market," or even "supplies, provisions" (Moulton and Milligan, *Vocab.*). In the NT it denotes "a place of assembly, a public place or forum, a marketplace." A variety of circumstances, connected with it as a public gathering place, is mentioned, e.g., business dealings such as the hiring of laborers, Matt. 20:3; the buying and selling of goods, **Mark 7:4** (involving risk of pollution); the games of children, Matt. 11:16; Luke 7:32; exchange of greetings, Matt. 23:7; **Mark 12:38**; Luke 11:43; 20:46; the holding of trials, Acts 16:19; public discussions, Acts 17:17. **Mark 6:56** records the bringing of the sick there. The word always carries with it the idea of publicity, in contrast to private circumstances. The RV always translates it "marketplace" or in the plural. The KJV sometimes changes the rendering to "markets" and translates it "streets" in **Mark 6:56**.

Streets *plateia* (4113), grammatically the feminine of *platus*, "broad," is used as a noun (*hodos*, "a way," being understood, i.e., "a broad way"), "a street," Matt. 6:5; 12:19 (in some texts, **Mark 6:56**); Luke 10:10; 13:26; 14:21; Acts 5:15; Rev. 11:8; 21:21; 22:2.

Border *kraspedon* (2899), was primarily "the extremity or prominent part of a thing, an edge"; hence "the fringe of a garment, or a little fringe," hanging down from the edge of the mantle or cloak. The Jews had these attached to their mantles to remind them of the Law, according to Num. 15:38-39; Deut. 22:12; Zech. 8:23. This is the meaning in Matt. 23:5. In Matt. 9:20; 14:36; **Mark 6:56**; Luke 8:44, it is used of the border of Christ's garment (KJV "hem," in the first two places).

Chapter 7

7:1 Then came together unto him the Pharisees, and certain of the scribes, which came from Jerusalem.

Came *sunago*, "to gather together," is always so rendered in RV, e.g., Matt. 27:62; **Mark 7:1**; Luke 22:66; Acts 13:44; 15:6; 20:7.

7:2 And when they saw some of his disciples eat bread with defiled, that is to say, with unwashen, hands, they found fault.

Unwashen *aniptos* (449), "unwashed" (*a*, negative, *nipto*, "to wash"), occurs in Matt. 15:20; **Mark 7:2** (v. **5** in some mss.).

Defiled *koinos* (2834), denotes (a) "common, belonging to several" (Lat., *communis*), said of things had in common, Acts 2:44; 4:32; of faith, Titus 1:4; of salvation, Jude 3; it stands in contrast to *idios*, "one's own"; (b) "ordinary, belonging to the generality, as distinct from what is peculiar to the few", hence the application to religious practices of Gentiles in contrast with those of Jews; or of the ordinary people in contrast with those of the Pharisees; hence the meaning "unhallowed, profane," Levitically unclean (Lat., *profanus*), said of hands, **Mark 7:2** (KJV, "defiled,") RV marg., "common"; of animals, ceremonially unclean, Acts 10:14; 11:8; of a man, 10:28; of meats, Rom. 14:14, "unclean"; of the blood of the covenant, as viewed by an apostate, Heb. 10:29, "unholy" (RV, marg., "common"); of everything unfit for the holy city, Rev. 21:27, RV, "unclean" (marg., "common"). Some mss. have the verb here.

Fault *memphomai* (3201), "to blame," is translated "to find fault" in Rom. 9:19 and Heb. 8:8. Some mss. have the verb in **Mark 7:2**.

7:3 For the Pharisees, and all the Jews, except they wash *their* hands oft, eat not, holding the tradition of the elders.

Jews *ioudaios* (2453), is used (a) adjectivally, with the lit. meaning, "Jewish," sometimes with the addition of *aner*, "a man," Acts 10:28; 22:3; in 21:39 with *anthropos*, in some mss. (a man in the generic sense); the best mss. omit the phrase here; in 13:6, lit., "a Jewish false-prophet"; in John 3:22, with the word *chora*, "land" or "country," signifying "Judean," lit., "Judean country"; used by metonymy for the people of the country; (b) as a noun, "a Jew, Jews," e.g., Matt. 2:2; **Mark 7:3**. The name "Jew" is primarily tribal (from Judah). It is first found in 2 Kings 16:6, as distinct from Israel, of the northern kingdom. After the Captivity it was chiefly used to distinguish the race from Gentiles, e.g., John 2:6; Acts 14:1; Gal. 2:15, where it denotes Christians of "Jewish" race; it distinguishes Jews from Samaritans, in John 4:9; from proselytes, in Acts 2:10.

Wash *nipto* (3538), is chiefly used of "washing part of the body," John 13:5-6, 8 (twice, figuratively in 2nd clause), 12, 14 (twice); in 1 Tim. 5:10, including the figurative sense; in the middle voice, to wash oneself, Matt. 6:17; 15:2; **Mark 7:3**; John 9:7, 11, 15; 13:10. For the corresponding noun.

Oft *pugme* (4435), the dative case of *pugme*, "a fist," lit. means "with the fist" (one hand being rubbed with the clenched fist of the other), a metaphorical expression for "thoroughly," in contrast to what is superficial; **Mark 7:3**, RV and KJV marg., "diligently" (KJV, text, "oft").

It also signified "boxing" (not in the NT); cf. *puktes* and *pugmachos*, "a boxer" (Lat., *pugnus* and *pugno*; Eng., "pugilist"). In the Sept., Exod. 21:18; Isa. 58:4.

Holding *see* Hold at *Mark 3:21*.

Tradition *paradosis* (3862), "a handing down or on" (akin to *paradidomi*, "to hand over, deliver"), denotes "a tradition," and hence, by metonymy, (a) "the teachings of the rabbis," interpretations of the Law, which was thereby made void in practice, Matt. 15:2, 3, 6; **Mark 7:3, 5, 8, 9, 13**; Gal. 1:14; Col. 2:8; (b) of "apostolic teaching," 1 Cor. 11:2, RV, "traditions" (KJV, "ordinances"), of instructions concerning the gatherings of believers (instructions of wider scope than ordinances in the limited sense); in 2 Thess. 2:15, of Christian doctrine in general, where the apostle's use of the word constitutes a denial that what he preached originated with himself, and a claim for its divine authority (cf. *paralambano*, "to receive," 1 Cor. 11:23; 15:3); in 2 Thess. 3:6, it is used of instructions concerning everyday conduct.

Elders *presbuteros* (4245), an adjective, the comparative degree of *presbus*, "an old man, an elder," is used (a) of age, whether of the "elder" of two persons, Luke 15:25, or more, John 8:9, "the eldest", or of a person advanced in life, a senior, Acts 2:17; in Heb. 11:2, the "elders" are the forefathers in Israel so in Matt. 15:2; **Mark 7:3, 5** the feminine of the adjective is used of "elder" women in the churches, 1 Tim. 5:2, not in respect of position but in seniority of age; (b) of rank or positions of responsibility, (1) among Gentiles, as in the Sept. of Gen. 50:7; Num. 22:7, (2) in the Jewish nation, firstly, those who were the heads or leaders of the tribes and families, as of the seventy who assisted Moses, Num. 11:16; Deut. 27:1, and those assembled by Solomon; secondly, members of the Sanhedrin, consisting of the chief priests, "elders" and scribes, learned in Jewish law, e.g., Matt. 16:21; 26:47; thirdly, those who managed public affairs in the various cities, Luke 7:3; (3) in the Christian churches those who, being raised up and qualified by the work of the Holy Spirit, were appointed to have the spiritual care of, and to exercise oversight over, the churches. To these the term "bishops," *episkopoi*, or "overseers," is applied (see Acts 20, v. 17 with v. 28, and Titus 1:5 and 7), the latter term indicating the nature of their work *presbuteroi* their maturity of spiritual experience. The divine arrangement seen throughout the NT was for a plurality of these to be appointed in each church, Acts 14:23; 20:17; Phil. 1:1; 1 Tim. 5:17; Titus 1:5. The duty of "elders" is described by the verb *episkopeo*. They were appointed according as they had given evidence of fulfilling the divine qualifications, Titus 1:6 to 9; cf. 1 Tim. 3:1-7 and 1 Pet. 5:2; (4) the twenty-four "elders" enthroned in heaven around the throne of God, Rev. 4:4, 10; 5:5-14; 7:11, 13; 11:16; 14:3; 19:4. The number twenty-four is representative of earthly conditions. The word "elder" is nowhere applied to angels.

7:4 And *when they come* from the market, except they wash, they eat not. And many other things there be, which they have received to hold, *as* the washing of cups, and pots, brasen vessels, and of tables.

Market *see* Streets at *Mark 6:56*.

Wash *rhantizo* (4472), "to sprinkle," is used in the middle voice in **Mark 7:4**, in some ancient texts, of the acts of the Pharisees in their assiduous attention to the cleansing of themselves after coming from the market place (some texts have *baptizo* here).

Received *paralambano* (3880), "to receive from another" (*para*, "from beside"), or "to take," signifies "to receive," e.g., in **Mark 7:4**; John 1:11; 14:3; 1 Cor. 11:23; 15:1, 3; Gal. 1:9, 12; Phil. 4:9; Col. 2:6; 4:17; 1 Thess. 2:13 (1st part); 4:1; 2 Thess. 3:6; Heb. 12:28.

Hold *see Mark 3:21*.

Washing *baptismos* (909), denotes "the act of washing, ablution," with special reference to purification, **Mark 7:4** (in some texts, v. **8**); Heb. 6:2, "baptisms"; 9:10, "washings."

Pots *xestes* (3582), was a Sicilian corruption of the Latin liquid measure *sextarius*, about a pint; in **Mark 7:4** (v. **8** also in some mss.) it denotes "a pitcher," of wood or stone.

Brasen *chalkion* (5473), is used in **Mark 7:4** of "brazen vessels."

Tables Some texts have the word *kline*, "a couch," in **Mark 7:4** (KJV, "tables").

7:5 Then the Pharisees and scribes asked him, Why walk not thy disciples according to the tradition of the elders, but eat bread with unwashen hands?

Then *epeita* (1899), "thereupon, thereafter," then (in some texts, **Mark 7:5**; *kai*, "and," in the best); Luke 16:7; John 11:7; 1 Cor. 12:28, RV, "then" (KJV, "after that"); 15:6 and 7 (ditto); v. 23, RV, KJV, "afterward"; v. 46; Gal. 1:18; v. 21, RV (KJV, "afterwards"), 2:1; 1 Thess. 4:17; Heb. 7:2, RV (KJV, "after that"); v. 27; Jas. 3:17; 4:14.

Walk *peripateo* (4043), is used (a) physically, in the Synoptic Gospels (except **Mark 7:5**); always in the

Acts except in 21:21; never in the Pauline Epistles, nor in those of John; (b) figuratively, "signifying the whole round of the activities of the individual life, whether of the unregenerate, Eph. 4:17, or of the believer, 1 Cor. 7:17; Col. 2:6. It is applied to the observance of religious ordinances, Acts 21:21; Heb. 13:9, marg., as well as to moral conduct. The Christian is to walk in newness of life, Rom. 6:4, after the spirit, 8:4, in honesty, 13:13, by faith, 2 Cor. 5:7, in good works, Eph. 2:10, in love, 5:2, in wisdom, Col. 4:5, in truth, 2 John 4, after the commandments of the Lord, v. 6. And, negatively, not after the flesh, Rom. 8:4; not after the manner of men, 1 Cor. 3:3; not in craftiness, 2 Cor. 4:2; not by sight, 5:7; not in the vanity of the mind, Eph. 4:17; not disorderly, 2 Thess. 3:6."

Tradition *see* ***Mark*** *7:3.*

Elders *see* ***Mark*** *7:3.*

Unwashen *see* ***Mark*** *7:2.*

7:6 He answered and said unto them, Well hath Esaias prophesied of you hypocrites, as it is written, This people honoureth me with *their* lips, but their heart is far from me.

Hypocrites *hupokrites* (5273), corresponding to the above, primarily denotes "one who answers"; then, "a stage-actor"; it was a custom for Greek and Roman actors to speak in large masks with mechanical devices for augmenting the force of the voice; hence the word became used metaphorically of "a dissembler, a hypocrite." It is found only in the Synoptists, and always used by the Lord, fifteen times in Matthew; elsewhere, **Mark 7:6**; Luke 6:42; 11:44 (in some mss.); 12:56; 13:15.

Honoureth *timao* (5091), "to honor," is used of (a) valuing Christ at a price, Matt. 27:9; (b) "honoring" a person: (1) the "honor" done by Christ to the Father, John 8:49; (2) "honor" bestowed by the Father upon him who serves Christ, John 12:26; (3) the duty of all to "honor" the Son equally with the Father, 5:23; (4) the duty of children to "honor" their parents, Matt. 15:4; 19:19; **Mark 7:10**; **10:19**; Luke 18:20; Eph. 6:2; (5) the duty of Christians to "honor" the king, and all men, 1 Pet. 2:17; (6) the respect and material assistance to be given to widows "that are widows indeed," 1 Tim. 5:3; (7) the "honor" done to Paul and his companions by the inhabitants of Melita, Acts 28:10; (8) mere lip profession of "honor" to God, Matt. 15:8; **Mark 7:6**.

Lips *cheilos* (5491), is used (a) of the organ of speech, Matt. 15:8 and **Mark 7:6**, where "honoring with the lips," besides meaning empty words, may have reference to a Jewish custom of putting to the mouth the tassel of the tallith (the woollen scarf wound round the head and neck during prayer), as a sign of acceptance of the Law from the heart; Rom. 3:13; 1 Cor. 14:21 (from Isa. 28:11, 12, speaking of the Assyrian foe as God's message to disobedient Israel); Heb. 13:15; 1 Pet. 3:10; (b) metaphorically, of "the brink or edge of things," as of the sea shore, Heb. 11:12, lit., "the shore (of the sea)."

Far *porro* (4206), is used (a) literally, Luke 14:32, "a great way off"; the comparative degree *porroteron*, "further," is used in 24:28; (b) metaphorically, of the heart in separation from God, Matt. 15:8; **Mark 7:6**. Cf. *porrothen*, "afar off".

7:7 Howbeit in vain do they worship me, teaching *for* doctrines the commandments of men.

Vain *maten* (3155), properly the accusative case of *mate*, "a fault, a folly," signifies "in vain, to no purpose," Matt. 15:9; **Mark 7:7**.

Worship *sebomai* (4576), "to revere," stressing the feeling of awe or devotion, is used of "worship" (a) to God, Matt. 15:9; **Mark 7:7**; Acts 16:14; 18:7, 13; (b) to a goddess, Acts 19:27.

Doctrines *didaskalia* (1319), denotes (a) "that which is taught, doctrine," Matt. 15:9; **Mark 7:7**; Eph. 4:14; Col. 2:22; 1 Tim. 1:10; 4:1, 6; 6:1, 3; 2 Tim. 4:3; Titus 1:9 ("doctrine," in last part of verse); 2:1, 10; (b) "teaching, instruction," Rom. 12:7, "teaching"; 15:4, "learning", 1 Tim. 4:13, KJV, "doctrine," RV, "teaching"; v. 16, KJV, "the doctrine," RV, (correctly) "thy teaching;" 5:17, KJV, "doctrine," RV "teaching"; 2 Tim. 3:10, 16 (ditto); Titus 2:7, "thy doctrine."

Commandments *entalma* (1778) marks more especially "the thing commanded, a commission"; in Matt. 15:9; **Mark 7:7**; Col. 2:22, RV, "precepts," KJV, "commandments."

7:8 For laying aside the commandment of God, ye hold the tradition of men, *as* the washing of pots and cups: and many other such like things ye do.

Laying In **Mark 7:8**, KJV, *aphiemi*, "to leave," is translated "laying aside" (RV, "ye leave").

Hold *see* ***Mark*** *3:21.*

Tradition *see* ***Mark*** *7:3.*

Washing *see* ***Mark*** *7:4.*

Pots *see* ***Mark*** *7:4.*

7:9 And he said unto them, Full well ye reject the commandment of God, that ye may keep your own tradition.

Reject *see Mark 6:26.*

Tradition *see Mark 7:3.*

7:10 For Moses said, Honour thy father and thy mother; and, Whoso curseth father or mother, let him die the death:

Honour *see* Honoureth at *Mark 7:6.*

Curseth *kakologeo* (2551), "to speak evil" (*kakos*, "evil," *lego*, "to speak"), is translated by the verb "to curse" in Matt. 15:4, and **Mark 7:10**, "to speak evil of father and mother," not necessarily "to curse," is what the Lord intended (RV). KJV and RV have the verb "to speak evil" in **Mark 9:39** and Acts 19:9.

Die *teleutao* (5053), "to end" (from *telos*, "an end"), hence, "to end one's life," is used (a) of the "death" of the body, Matt. 2:19; 9:18; 15:4, where "die the death" means "surely die," RV, marg., lit., "let him end by death"; **Mark 7:10**; Matt. 22:25, "deceased"; Luke 7:2; John 11:39, some mss. have verb *thnesko* here; Acts 2:29; 7:15; Heb. 11:22 (RV, "his end was nigh"); (b) of the gnawings of conscience in self reproach, under the symbol of a worm, **Mark 9:48** (vv. **44** and **46**, KJV).

7:11 But ye say, If a man shall say to his father or mother, *It is* Corban, that is to say, a gift, by whatsoever thou mightest be profited by me; *he shall be free*.

Corban *korban* (2878), signifies (a) "an offering," and was a Hebrew term for any sacrifice, whether by the shedding of blood or otherwise; (b) "a gift offered to God," **Mark 7:11**. Jews were much addicted to rash vows; a saying of the rabbis was, "It is hard for the parents, but the law is clear, vows must be kept." The Sept. translates the word by *doron*, "a gift."

Say The phrase *tout' esti* (i.e., *touto esti*), "that is," is so translated in Matt. 27:46, RV (KJV, "that is to say"); so Acts 1:19; in Heb. 9:11 and 10:20, KJV and RV, "that is to say"; in **Mark 7:11** the phrase is *ho esti*, lit., "which is"; the phrase *ho legetai*, lit., "which is said," John 1:38 and 20:16, is rendered "which is to say."

Gift *doron* (1435), akin to *didomi*, "to give," is used (a) of "gifts" presented as an expression of honor, Matt. 2:11; (b) of "gifts" for the support of the temple and the needs of the poor, Matt. 15:5; **Mark 7:11**; Luke 21:1, 4; (c) of "gifts" offered to God, Matt. 5:23, 24; 8:4; 23.18, 19, Heb. 5:1; 8:3, 4; 9:9; 11:4; (d) of salvation by grace as the "gift" of God, Eph. 2:8; (e) of "presents" for mutual celebration of an occasion, Rev. 11:10.

Profited *opheleo* (5623), is translated "to profit" in Matt. 15:5; 16:26; **Mark 7:11**; **8:36**; Luke 9:25, RV; John 6:63; Rom. 2:25; 1 Cor. 13:3; 14:6; Gal. 5:2; Heb. 4:2; 13:9.

Free In Matt. 15:6 and **Mark 7:11**, the words "he shall be free," KJV, have nothing to represent them in the Greek.

7:12 And ye suffer him no more to do ought for his father or his mother;

No more *ouketi* (3765), "no more, no longer," is rendered "no longer" in the RV of **Mark 7:12** (KJV, "no more"); John 15:15, RV (KJV, "henceforth not"); Rom. 14:15, RV (KJV, "now ... not"); Gal. 2:20, RV (KJV, "yet not"), Gal. 3:25; 4:7 (KJV, "no more"); Philem. 16 (KJV, "not now").

7:13 Making the word of God of none effect through your tradition, which ye have delivered: and many such like things do ye.

Word *logos* (3056), denotes "the expression of thought"—not the mere name of an object—(a) as embodying a conception or idea, e.g., Luke 7:7; 1 Cor. 14:9, 19; (b) a saying or statement, (1) by God, e.g., John 15:25; Rom. 9:9; 9:28, RV, "word" (KJV, "work"); Gal. 5:14; Heb. 4:12; (2) by Christ, e.g., Matt. 24:35 (plur.); John 2:22; 4:41; 14:23 (plur.); 15:20. In connection with (1) and (2) the phrase "the word of the Lord," i.e., the revealed will of God (very frequent in the OT), is used of a direct revelation given by Christ, 1 Thess. 4:15; of the gospel, Acts 8:25; 13:49; 15:35, 36; 16:32; 19:10; 1 Thess. 1:8; 2 Thess. 3:1; in this respect it is the message from the Lord, delivered with His authority and made effective by His power (cf. Acts 10:36); for other instances relating to the gospel see Acts 13:26; 14:3; 15:7; 1 Cor. 1:18, RV; 2 Cor. 2:17; 4:2; 5:19; 6:7; Gal. 6:6; Eph. 1:13; Phil. 2:16; Col. 1:5; Heb. 5:13; sometimes it is used as the sum of God's utterances, e.g., **Mark 7:13**; John 10:35; Rev. 1:2, 9; (c) discourse, speech, of instruction, etc., e.g., Acts 2:40; 1 Cor. 2:13; 12:8; 2 Cor. 1:18; 1 Thess. 1:5; 2 Thess. 2:15; Heb. 6:1, RV, marg.; doctrine, e.g., Matt. 13:20; Col. 3:16; 1 Tim. 4:6; 2 Tim. 1:13; Titus 1:9; 1 John 2:7;

Of none effect *akuroo* (208), signifies "to render void, deprive of force and authority" (from *a*, negative, and *kuros*, "might, authority"; *kurios*, "a lord," is from the same root), the opposite to *kuroo*, "to confirm". It is used of making "void" the Word of God, Matt. 15:6; **Mark 7:13** (KJV, "making of none effect"), and of the promise of God to Abraham as not being deprived of authority by the Law 430 years after, Gal. 3:17, "disannul." *Kuroo* is used in v. 15.

Tradition *see Mark 7:3.*

Like *paromoios* (3946), "much like," is used in **Mark 7:13**, in the neuter plural, "(many such) like things."

7:14 And when he had called all the people *unto him*, he said unto them, Hearken unto me every one *of you*, and understand:

One In **Mark 7:14**, KJV, the plural of *pas*, "all" (so RV), is translated "every one"; in Matt. 5:28, KJV, *pas*, with the article, is translated "whosoever" (RV "every one who").

7:15 There is nothing from without a man, that entering into him can defile him: but the things which come out of him, those are they that defile the man.

From without *exothen* (1855), an adverb formed from *exo*, "without," properly signifies "from without," **Mark 7:18** (in v. **15** it is used as a preposition); with the article it is equivalent to a noun, "the outside," Matt. 23:25; Luke 11:39; in v. 40, RV, "the outside" (KJV, "that which is without").

Entering *see* Entered at *Mark 1:21*.

Come *ekporeuo* (1607), in the middle voice, "to come forth" (*ek*, "out of"), **Mark 7:15, 20**; John 5:29. Rendered "proceed" in the RV of **Mark 7:15, 20, 23** (KJV, "come").

Come out of *ekporeuomai* (1607), "to go forth," is translated "to proceed out of" in Matt. 4:4; 15:11, RV; 15:18; **Mark 7:15**, RV; **7:20**, RV; **7:21**; **7:23**, RV; Luke 4:22; John 15:26; Eph. 4:29; Rev. 1:16, RV; 4:5; 9:17, 18, RV (KJV, "issued"); 11:5; 19:15, RV; 19:21, KJV (RV, "came forth"); 22:1.

Defile *koinoo* (2840), denotes (a) "to make common"; hence, in a ceremonial sense, "to render unholy, unclean, to defile," Matt. 15:11, 18, 20; **Mark 7:15, 18, 20, 23**; Acts 21:28 (RV, "defiled"; KJV, "polluted"); Heb. 9:13 (RV, "them that have been defiled," KJV, "the unclean"); (b) "to count unclean," Acts 10:15; 11:9. In Rev. 21:27, some mss. have this verb, "defileth"; the most authentic have the adjective, *koinos*, "unclean." *See also* Defiled at *Mark 7:2*.

7:16-17 If any man have ears to hear, let him hear.

And when he was entered into the house from the people, his disciples asked him concerning the parable.

Parable *see* Parables at *Mark 3:23*.

7:18 And he saith unto them, Are ye so without understanding also? Do ye not perceive, that whatsoever thing from without entereth into the man, *it* cannot defile him;

Understanding *asunetos* (801), "without understanding or discernment" (*a*, negative, *sunetos*, "intelligent, understanding"), is translated "without understanding" in Matt. 15:16; **Mark 7:18**; Rom. 1:31; 10:19, RV, "void of understanding" (KJV, "foolish"); in Rom. 1:21, RV, "senseless" (KJV, "foolish").

Perceive *noeo* (3539), "to perceive with the mind, to understand," is translated "to perceive" in Matt. 15:17, RV (KJV, "understand"); so 16:9, 11; John 12:40; Rom. 1:20; Eph. 3:4; in **Mark 7:18** and **8:17**, KJV and RV, "perceive."

Without *see Mark 7:15*.

Entereth *see* Entered at *Mark 1:21*.

Defile *see Mark 7:15*.

7:19 Because it entereth not into his heart, but into the belly, and goeth out into the draught, purging all meats?

Draught *aphedron* (856), "a latrine, a sink, drain," is found in Matt. 15:17 and **Mark 7:19**.

Purging *kathakizo* (2511), signifies (1) "to make clean, to cleanse" (a) from physical stains and dirt, as in the case of utensils, Matt. 23:25 (figuratively in verse 26); from disease, as of leprosy, Matt. 8:2; (b) in a moral sense, from the defilement of sin, Acts 15:9; 2 Cor. 7:1; Heb. 9:14; Jas. 4:8, "cleanse" from the guilt of sin, Eph. 5:26; 1 John 1:7; (2) "to pronounce clean in a Levitical sense," **Mark 7:19**, RV; Acts 10:15; 11:9; "to consecrate by cleansings," Heb. 9:22, 23; 10:2.

Meats *broma* (1033), "food" (akin to *bibrosko*, "to eat," John 6:13), solid food in contrast to milk, is translated "food" in Matt. 14:15, RV (KJV, "victuals"); "meats," **Mark 7:19**; 1 Cor. 6:13 (twice); 1 Tim. 4:3; Heb. 9:10; 13:9; "meat," John 4:34; Rom. 14:15 (twice), 20; 1 Cor. 3:2; 8:8, 13; 10:3; "food," RV, for KJV, "meat," Luke 3:11; 9:13.

7:20 And he said, That which cometh out of the man, that defileth the man.

Cometh *see* Come at *Mark 7:15*.

Defileth *see* Defile at *Mark 7:15*.

7:21 For from within, out of the heart of men, proceed evil thoughts, adulteries, fornications, murders,

Within This is a translation of (a) *entos*; in Luke 17:21 the RV marg., "in the midst of," is to be preferred; the kingdom of God was not in the hearts of the Pharisees; (b) *en*, "of thinking or saying within oneself," e.g., Luke 7:39, 49 (marg., "among"); locally, e.g., Luke 19:44; (c) *esothen*, 2 Cor. 7:5; Rev. 4:8; 5:1; "from within," **Mark 7:21, 23**; Luke

11:7; "within," Matt. 23:25; Luke 11:40, RV, "inside"; in Matt. 23:27, 28, RV, "inwardly"; (d) *eso*, John 20:26; Acts 5:23; 1 Cor. 5:12 (i.e., "within" the church); (e) *pros*, to, or with, in **Mark 14:4**, KJV, "within" (RV, "among"); (f) *dia*, "through," rendered "within (three days)" in **Mark 14:58**, KJV (RV, "in," looking through the time to the event, and in keeping with the metaphor of building); (g) *esoteros*, Heb. 6:19, the comparative degree of *eso*, used with the article translated "that within," lit., "the inner (part of the veil)," i.e., "inside"; (h) in Luke 11:41, RV, *eneimi*, "to be in," is rendered "are within" (KJV, "ye have").

Proceed *see* **Come out of** at *Mark 7:15*.

Evil *kakos* (2556), stands for "whatever is evil in character, base," in distinction (wherever the distinction is observable) from *poneros*, which indicates "what is evil in influence and effect, malignant." *Kakos* is the wider term and often covers the meaning of *poneros*. *Kakos* is antithetic to *kalos*, "fair, advisable, good in character," and to *agathos*, "beneficial, useful, good in act"; hence it denotes what is useless, incapable, bad; *poneros* is essentially antithetic to *chrestos*, "kind, gracious, serviceable"; hence it denotes what is destructive, injurious, evil. As evidence that *poneros* and *kakos* have much in common, though still not interchangeable, each is used of thoughts, cf. Matt. 15:19 with **Mark 7:21**; of speech, Matt. 5:11 with 1 Pet. 3:10; of actions, 2 Tim. 4:18 with 1 Thess. 5:15; of man, Matt. 18:32 with 24:48.

The use of *kakos* may be broadly divided as follows: (a) of what is morally or ethically "evil," whether of persons, e.g., Matt. 21:41; 24:48; Phil. 3:2; Rev. 2:2, or qualities, emotions, passions, deeds, e.g., **Mark 7:21**; John 18:23, 30; Rom. 1:30; 3:8; 7:19, 21; 13:4; 14:20; 16:19; 1 Cor. 13:5; 2 Cor. 13:7; 1 Thess. 5:15; 1 Tim. 6:10; 2 Tim. 4:14; 1 Pet. 3:9, 12; (b) of what is injurious, destructive, baneful, pernicious, e.g., Luke 16:25; Acts 16:28; 28:5; Titus 1:12; Jas. 3:8; Rev. 16:2, where *kakos* and *poneros* come in that order, "noisome and grievous."

Thoughts *dialogismos* (1261), "reasoning," is translated "thoughts" in Matt. 15:19; **Mark 7:21**; Luke 2:35; 6:8; in 5:22, KJV, RV, "reasonings"; in 9:47, KJV, RV, "reasoning," and 24:38, KJV, RV, "reasonings"; so 1 Cor. 3:20; in Luke 9:46, KJV and RV, "reasoning"; "thoughts" in Jas. 2:4, KJV and RV.

Adulteries *moicheia* (3430), "adultery," is found in Matt. 15:19; **Mark 7:21**; John 8:3 (KJV only).

Fornications *porneia* (4202), is used (a) of "illicit sexual intercourse," in John 8:41; Acts 15:20, 29; 21:25; 1 Cor. 5:1; 6:13, 18; 2 Cor. 12:21; Gal. 5:19; Eph. 5:3; Col. 3:5; 1 Thess. 4:3; Rev. 2:21; 9:21; in the plural in 1 Cor. 7:2; in Matt. 5:32 and 19:9 it stands for, or includes, adultery; it is distinguished from it in 15:19 and **Mark 7:21**; (b) metaphorically, of "the association of pagan idolatry with doctrines of, and professed adherence to, the Christian faith," Rev. 14:8; 17:2, 4; 18:3; 19:2; some suggest this as the sense in 2:21.

Murders *phonos* (5408), is used (a) of a special act, **Mark 15:7**; Luke 23:19, 25; (b) in the plural, of "murders" in general, Matt. 15:19; **Mark 7:21** (Gal. 5:21, in some inferior mss.); Rev. 9:21; in the singular, Rom. 1:29; (c) in the sense of "slaughter," Heb. 11:37, "they were slain with the sword," lit., "(they died by) slaughter (of the sword)"; in Acts 9:1, "slaughter."

"Put everything you have into the care of your heart, for it determines what your life amounts to."

DALLAS WILLARD

7:22 Thefts, covetousness, wickedness, deceit, lasciviousness, an evil eye, blasphemy, pride, foolishness:

Thefts *klope* (2829), akin to *klepto*, "to steal," is used in the plural in Matt. 15:19; **Mark 7:22**.

Covetousness *pleonexia* (4124), "covetousness," lit., "a desire to have more" (*pleon*, "more," *echo*, "to have"), always in a bad sense, is used in a general way in **Mark 7:22** (plural, lit., "covetings," i.e., various ways in which "covetousness" shows itself); Rom. 1:29; Eph. 5:3; 1 Thess. 2:5. Elsewhere it is used, (a) of material possessions, Luke 12:15; 2 Pet. 2:3; 2 Cor. 9:5 (RV, "extortion"), lit., "as (a matter of) extortion" i.e., a gift which betrays the giver's unwillingness to bestow what is due; (b) of sensuality, Eph. 4:19, "greediness"; Col. 3:5 (where it is called "idolatry"); 2 Pet. 2:14 (KJV, "covetous practices").

Wickedness *poneros* (4190), akin to *ponos*, "labor, toil," denotes "evil that causes labor, pain, sorrow, malignant evil"; it is used (a) with the meaning bad, worthless, in the physical sense, Matt. 7:17-18; in the moral or ethical sense, "evil," wicked; of persons, e.g., Matt. 7:11; Luke 6:45; Acts 17:5; 2 Thess. 3:2; 2 Tim. 3:13; of "evil" spirits, e.g., Matt.

12:45; Luke 7:21; Acts 19:12-13, 15-16; of a generation, Matt. 12:39, 45; 16:4; Luke 11:29; of things, e.g., Matt. 5:11; 6:23; 20:15; **Mark 7:22**; Luke 11:34; John 3:19; 7:7; Acts 18:14; Gal. 1:4; Col. 1:21; 1 Tim. 6:4; 2 Tim. 4:18; Heb. 3:12; 10:22; Jas. 2:4; 4:16; 1 John 3:12; 2 John 11; 3 John 10; (b) with the meaning toilsome, painful, Eph. 5:16; 6:13; Rev. 16:2. Cf. *poneria*, "iniquity, wickedness."

Deceit *dolos* (1388), primarily "a bait, snare"; hence, "craft, deceit, guile," is translated "deceit" in **Mark 7:22**; Rom. 1:29.

Lasciviousness *aselgeia* (766), denotes "excess, licentiousness, absence of restraint, indecency, wantonness"; "lasciviousness" in **Mark 7:22**, one of the evils that proceed from the heart; in 2 Cor. 12:21, one of the evils of which some in the church at Corinth had been guilty; in Gal. 5:19, classed among the works of the flesh; in Eph. 4:19, among the sins of the unregenerate who are "past feeling"; so in 1 Pet. 4:3; in Jude 4, of that into which the grace of God had been turned by ungodly men; it is translated "wantonness" in Rom. 13:13, one of the sins against which believers are warned; in 2 Pet. 2:2, according to the best mss., "lascivious (doings)," RV (the KJV "pernicious ways" follows those texts which have *apoleiais*); in v. 7, RV, "lascivious (life)," KJV, "filthy (conversation)," of the people of Sodom and Gomorrah; in 2:18, RV, "lasciviousness" (KJV, "wantonness"), practiced by the same persons as mentioned in Jude. The prominent idea is shameless conduct. Some have derived the word from *a*, negative, and *selge*, "a city in Pisidia." Others, with similar improbability, trace it to *a*, negative, and *selgo*, or *thelgo*, "to charm."

Eye *ophthalmos* (3788), akin to *opsis*, "sight," probably from a root signifying "penetration, sharpness" (Curtius, Gk. Etym.) (cf. Eng., "ophthalmia," etc.), is used (a) of the physical organ, e.g., Matt. 5:38; of restoring sight, e.g., Matt. 20:33; of God's power of vision, Heb. 4:13; 1 Pet. 3:12; of Christ in vision, Rev. 1:14; 2:18; 19:12; of the Holy Spirit in the unity of Godhood with Christ, Rev. 5:6; (b) metaphorically, of ethical qualities, evil, Matt. 6:23; **Mark 7:22** (by metonymy, for envy); singleness of motive, Matt. 6:22; Luke 11:34; as the instrument of evil desire, "the principal avenue of temptation," 1 John 2:16; of adultery, 2 Pet. 2:14; (c) metaphorically, of mental vision, Matt. 13:15; John 12:40; Rom. 11:8; Gal. 3:1, where the metaphor of the "evil eye" is altered to a different sense from that of bewitching (the posting up or placarding of an "eye" was used as a charm, to prevent mischief); by gospel-preaching Christ had been, so to speak, placarded before their "eyes"; the question may be paraphrased, "What evil teachers have been malignly fascinating you?"; Eph. 1:18, of the "eyes of the heart," as a means of knowledge.

Blasphemy *blasphemia* (988), either from *blax*, "sluggish, stupid," or, probably, from *blapto*, "to injure," and *pheme*, "speech," (Eng. "blasphemy") is so translated thirteen times in the RV, but "railing" in Matt. 15:19; **Mark 7:22**; Eph. 4:31; Col. 3:8; 1 Tim. 6:4; Jude 9. The word "blasphemy" is practically confined to speech defamatory of the Divine Majesty.

Pride *huperephania* (5243), "pride," **Mark 7:22**.

Foolishness *aphrosune* (877), "senselessness," is translated "foolishness" in **Mark 7:22**; 2 Cor. 11:1, 17, 21, "foolishness," RV (KJV, "folly" and "foolishly").

7:23 All these evil things come from within, and defile the man.

Evil *poneros* (4190), the adjective, is used as a noun, (a) of Satan as the "evil" one, Matt. 5:37; 6:13; 13:19, 38; Luke 11:4 (in some texts); John 17:15; Eph. 6:16; 2 Thess. 3:3; 1 John 2:13-14; 3:12; 5:18-19; (b) of human beings, Matt. 5:45; (probably v. 39); 13:49; 22:10; Luke 6:35; 1 Cor. 5:13; (c) neuter, "evil (things)," Matt. 9:4; 12:35; **Mark 7:23**; Luke 3:19; "that which is evil," Luke 6:45; Rom. 12:9; Acts 28:21, "harm."

Come *see* ***Mark 7:15***.

Within *see* ***Mark 7:21***.

Defile *see* ***Mark 7:15***.

7:24 And from thence he arose, and went into the borders of Tyre and Sidon, and entered into an house, and would have no man know *it*: but he could not be hid.

Borders *methorion* (3181), is found, in some mss., in **Mark 7:24**.

Know *ginosko* (1097), signifies "to be taking in knowledge, to come to know, recognize, understand," or "to understand completely," e.g., **Mark 13:28, 29**; John 13:12; 15:18; 21:17; 2 Cor. 8:9; Heb. 10:34; 1 John 2:5; 4:2, 6 (twice), 7, 13; 5:2, 20; in its past tenses it frequently means "to know in the sense of realizing," the aorist or point tense usually indicating definiteness, Matt. 13:11; **Mark 7:24**; John 7:26; in 10:38 "that ye may know (aorist tense) and understand, (present tense)"; 19:4; Acts 1:7; 17:19; Rom. 1:21; 1 Cor. 2:11 (2nd part), 14; 2 Cor. 2:4; Eph. 3:19; 6:22; Phil. 2:19; 3:10; 1 Thess. 3:5; 2 Tim. 2:19; Jas. 2:20; 1 John 2:13 (twice), 14; 3:6; 4:8; 2 John

1; Rev. 2:24; 3:3, 9. In the passive voice, it often signifies "to become known," e.g., Matt. 10:26; Phil. 4:5. In the sense of complete and absolute understanding on God's part, it is used, e.g., in Luke 16:15; John 10:15 (of the Son as well as the Father); 1 Cor. 3:20. In Luke 12:46, KJV, it is rendered "he is ... aware."

Hid *lanthano* (2990), "to escape notice, to be hidden from," is rendered "(could not) be hid" in **Mark 7:24**, of Christ; "was (not) hid," Luke 8:47, of the woman with the issue of blood; "is hidden," Acts 26:26, of the facts concerning Christ; the sentence might be rendered "none of these things has escaped the king's notice."

7:25 For a *certain* woman, whose young daughter had an unclean spirit, heard of him, and came and fell at his feet:

Young In **Mark 7:25**, KJV, *thugatrion*, a diminutive of *thugater*, "a daughter," is rendered "young (RV, 'little') daughter."

Daughter *see Mark 5:23.*

Unclean spirit *see Mark 5:2.*

Fell *see Mark 3:11.*

7:26 The woman was a Greek, a Syrophenician by nation; and she besought him that he would cast forth the devil out of her daughter.

Syrophoenician *surophoinikissa or surophunissa* (4949), occurs in **Mark 7:26** as the national name of a woman called "a Canaanitish woman" in Matt. 15:22, i.e., not a Jewess but a descendant of the early inhabitants of the coastland of Phoenicia. The word probably denoted a Syrian residing in Phoenicia proper. There is a tradition that the woman's name was Justa and her daughter Bernice (*Clementine Homilies*, ii:19; iii:73). In Acts 21:2, 3, the two parts of the term are used interchangeably.

Nation *genos* (1085), akin to *ginomai*, "to become," denotes (a) "a family," Acts 4:6, "kindred;" 7:13, RV, "race" (KJV, "kindred"); 13:26, "stock"; (b) "an offspring," Acts 17:28; Rev. 22:16; (c) "a nation, a race," **Mark 7:26**, RV, "race" (KJV, "nation"); Acts 4:36, RV "(a man of Cyprus) by race," KJV, "of the country (of Cyprus);" *genos* does not mean "a country;" the word here signifies "parentage" (Jews had settled in Cyprus from, or even before, the reign of Alexander the Great); 7:19, RV, "race" (KJV, "kindred"); 18:2, 24, RV, "by race" (KJV, "born"); 2 Cor. 11:26, "countrymen"; Gal. 1:14, RV, "countrymen" (KJV, "nation"); Phil. 3:5, "stock"; 1 Pet. 2:9, RV, "race" (KJV, "generation"); (d) "a kind, sort, class," Matt. 13:47, "kind"; in some mss. in 17:21, KJV, "kind;" **Mark 9:29**, "kind"; 1 Cor. 12:10, 28, "kinds" (KJV, "diversities"); 14:10 (ditto).

7:27 But Jesus said unto her, Let the children first be filled: for it is not meet to take the children's bread, and to cast *it* unto the dogs.

Let *aphiemi* (863), frequently denotes "to let, suffer, permit," e.g., Matt. 5:40 (translated "let ... have"); 7:4; 13:30; 15:14; 27:49 and **Mark 15:36**, RV, "let be," probably short for "let us see"; **Mark 7:27; 11:6** ("let ... go"); **14:6** ("let ... alone"); so Luke 13:8; John 11:48; in Acts 5:38 (where some mss. have *eao*, "to permit, let, suffer"); in John 11:44 and 18:8 ("let"); 1 Cor. 7:11, 12, RV, "let ... leave," KJV, "let ... put away"; 7:13 ("let ... leave").

Meet *kalos* (2570), "good," is translated "meet" in Matt. 15:26 and **Mark 7:27**.

Dogs *kunarion* (2952), "a little dog, a puppy," is used in Matt. 15:26-27; **Mark 7:27, 28**.

7:28 And she answered and said unto him, Yes, Lord: yet the dogs under the table eat of the children's crumbs.

Yes *nai* (3483), a particle of affirmation, is used (a) in answer to a question, Matt. 9:28; 11:9; 13:51; 17:25; 21:16; Luke 7:26; John 11:27; 21:15, 16; Acts 5:8; 22:27; Rom. 3:29; (b) in assent to an assertion, Matt. 15:27, RV (KJV, "truth"); **Mark 7:28**; Rev. 14:13; 16:7, RV (KJV, "even so"); (c) in confirmation of an assertion, Matt. 11:26 and Luke 10:21, RV (KJV, "even so"); Luke 11:51, RV (KJV, "verily"); 12:5; Phil. 4:3 (in the best texts); Philem. 20; (d) in solemn asseveration, Rev. 1:7 (KJV and RV, "even so"); 22:20, RV (KJV, "surely"); (e) in repetition for emphasis, Matt. 5:37; 2 Cor. 1:17; Jas. 5:12; (f) singly in contrast to *ou*, "nay," 2 Cor. 1:18, 19 (twice), 20, "(the) yea," RV.

Dogs *see Mark 7:27.*

Under *see Mark 6:11.*

Table *trapeza* (5132), is used of (a) "a dining table," Matt. 15:27; **Mark 7:28**; Luke 16:21; 22:21, 30; (b) "the table of shewbread," Heb. 9:2; (c) by metonymy, of "what is provided on the table" (the word being used of that with which it is associated), Acts 16:34; Rom. 11:9 (figurative of the special privileges granted to Israel and centering in Christ); 1 Cor. 10:21 (twice), "the Lord's table," denoting all that is provided for believers in Christ on the ground of His death (and thus expressing something more comprehensive than the Lord's Supper); "the table of demons," denoting all that is partaken of by idolaters as the result of the influence of demons in connection with their sacrifices; (d) "a moneychanger's table," Matt. 21:12; **Mark 11:15**; John 2:15; (e) "a bank," Luke 19:23 (cf. *trapezites*); (f) by metonymy for "the distribution of money," Acts 6:2.

Crumbs *psichion* (5589), "a small morsel," a diminutive of *psix*, "a bit, or crumb", of bread or meat, it is used in Matt. 15:27 and **Mark 7:28**; some mss. have it in Luke 16:21.

7:29 And he said unto her, For this saying go thy way; the devil is gone out of thy daughter.

Saying *logos* (3056), "a word," as embodying a conception or idea, denotes among its various meanings, "a saying, statement or declaration," uttered (a) by God; RV, "word" or "words" (KJV, "saying"), e.g., in John 8:55; Rom. 3:4; Rev. 19:9; 22:6, 7, 9, 10; (b) by Christ, e.g., **Mark 8:32**; **9:10**; **10:22**; Luke 9:28; John 6:60; 21:23; the RV appropriately substitutes "word" or "words" for KJV, "saying" or "sayings," especially in John's Gospel, e.g. 7:36, 40; 8:51, 52; 10:19; 14:24; 15:20; 18:9, 32; 19:13; (c) by an angel, Luke 1:29; (d) by OT prophets, John 12:38 (RV, "word"); Rom. 13:9 (ditto); 1 Cor. 15:54; (e) by the apostle Paul in the Pastoral Epp., 1 Tim. 1:15; 3:1; 4:9; 2 Tim. 2:11; Titus 3:8; (f) by other men, **Mark 7:29**; Acts 7:29; John 4:37 (in general).

7:30 And when she was come to her house, she found the devil gone out, and her daughter laid upon the bed.

Laid *ballo* (906), "to cast, throw, place, put," is used in the passive voice signifying "to be laid," e.g., **Mark 7:30**; Luke 16:20.

Bed *see* ***Mark 4:21***.

7:31 And again, departing from the coasts of Tyre and Sidon, he came unto the sea of Galilee, through the midst of the coasts of Decapolis.

Coasts *see* ***Mark 5:17***.

7:32 And they bring unto him one that was deaf, and had an impediment in his speech; and they beseech him to put his hand upon him.

Deaf *kophos* (2974), akin to *kopto*, "to beat," and *kopiao*, "to be tired" (from a root *kop*–, "to cut"), signifies "blunted, dull," as of a weapon; hence, "blunted in tongue, dumb," Matt. 9:32, etc.; "in hearing, deaf," Matt. 11:5; **Mark 7:32**, **37**; **9:25**; Luke 7:22.

Impediment *mogilalos* (3424), denotes "speaking with difficulty" (*mogis*, "hardly," *laleo*, "to talk"), "stammering," **Mark 7:32**; some mss. have *moggilalos*, "thick-voiced" (from *moggos*, "with a hoarse, hollow voice"). In the Sept., Isa. 35:6 "(the tongue) of stammerers."

Put *epitithemi* (2007), "to put on, upon," is so rendered in Matt. 19:13, KJV (RV, "lay"); so **Mark 7:32**; **8:25**; Matt. 21:7; 27:29; John 9:15; 19:2 (1st part); Acts 9:12 (RV, "laying ... on"); 15:10. *See also* **Lay** at *Mark 5:23*.

7:33 And he took him aside from the multitude, and put his fingers into his ears, and he spit, and touched his tongue;

Took *apolambano* (618), besides its common meaning, "to receive," denotes "to take apart or aside," **Mark 7:33**, middle voice. It is frequent in the papyri, and, in the sense of separation or drawing aside, is illustrated in a message of sorrow, concerning the nonarrival of one who with others had been "shut up" as recluses in a temple (Moulton and Milligan, *Vocab.*).

Put *see* **Putteth, Put** *at* ***Mark 2:22***.

Fingers *daktulos* (1147), Matt. 23:4; **Mark 7:33**; Luke 11:46; 16:24; John 8:6; 20:25, 27, is used metaphorically in Luke 11:20, for the power of God, the effects of which are made visible to men (cf. Matt. 12:28, "by the Spirit of God"; cf. also Exod. 8:19).

Spit *ptuo* (4429), "to spit," occurs in **Mark 7:33**; **8:23**; John 9:6. In the Sept., Num. 12:14.

Tongue *glossa* (1100), is used of (1) the "tongues ... like as of fire" which appeared at Pentecost; (2) "the tongue," as an organ of speech, e.g., **Mark 7:33**; Rom. 3:13; 14:11; 1 Cor. 14:9; Phil. 2:11; Jas. 1:26; 3:5, 6, 8; 1 Pet. 3:10; 1 John 3:18; Rev. 16:10; (3) (a) "a language," coupled with *phule*, "a tribe," *laos*, "a people," *ethnos*, "a nation," seven times in Revelation, 5:9; 7:9; 10:11; 11:9; 13:7; 14:6; 17:15; (b) "the supernatural gift of speaking in another language without its having been learnt"; Acts 2:4-13; 1 Cor. chapters 12 and 14.

7:34 And looking up to heaven, he sighed, and saith unto him, Ephphatha, that is, Be opened.

Sighed *stenazo* (4727), "to groan" (of an inward, unexpressed feeling of sorrow), is translated "with grief" in Heb. 13:17 (marg. "groaning"). It is rendered "sighed" in **Mark 7:34**; "groan," in Rom. 8:23; 2 Cor. 5:2, 4; "murmur," in Jas. 5:9, RV (KJV, "grudge").

Ephphatha *ephphatha* is an Aramaic word signifying "to open," used in the imperative mood, "be opened," **Mark 7:34**; while the application in this case was to the ears, the tongue was remedially affected.

Opened *dianoigo* (1272), "to open up completely" (*dia*, "through," intensive, and *anoigo*), is used (a) literally, Luke 2:23; Acts 7:56, in the best mss.; (b) metaphorically, of the eyes, **Mark 7:34**; Luke 24:31; of the Scriptures, v. 32 and Acts 17:3; of the mind, Luke 24:45, RV (KJV, "understanding"); of the heart, Acts 16:14.

7:35 And straightway his ears were opened, and the string of his tongue was loosed, and he spake plain.

Ears *akoe* (189), denotes (a) "the sense of hearing," 1 Cor. 12:17; 2 Pet. 2:8; a combination of verb and noun is used in phrases which have been termed Hebraic as they express somewhat literally an OT phraseology, e.g., "By hearing ye shall hear," Matt. 13:14; Acts 28:26, RV, a mode of expression conveying emphasis; (b) "the organ of hearing," **Mark 7:35**, "ears"; Luke 7:1, RV, "ears," for KJV, "audience"; Acts 17:20; 2 Tim. 4:3, 4; Heb. 5:11, "dull of hearing," lit., "dull as to ears"; (c) "a thing heard, a message or teaching," John 12:38, "report"; Rom. 10:16; 1 Thess. 2:13, "the word of the message," lit. "the word of hearing" (KJV, "which ye heard"); Heb. 4:2, "the word of hearing," RV, for KJV, "the word preached"; in a somewhat similar sense, "a rumor, report," Matt. 4:24; 14:1; **Mark 1:28**, KJV, "fame," RV, "report"; Matt. 24:6; **Mark 13:7**, "rumors (of wars)"; (d) "the receiving of a message," Rom. 10:17, something more than the mere sense of "hearing"; so with the phrase "the hearing of faith," Gal. 3:2, 5, which it seems better to understand so than under (c).

Opened *anoigo* (455), is used (1) transitively, (a) literally, of "a door or gate," e.g., Acts 5:19; graves, Matt. 27:52; a sepulchre, Rom. 3:13; a book, e.g., Luke 4:17; Rev. 5:2-5; 10:8; the seals of a roll, e.g., Rev. 5:9; 6:1; the eyes, Acts 9:40; the mouth of a fish, Matt. 17:27; "the pit of the abyss," Rev. 9:2, RV; heaven and the heavens, Matt. 3:16; Luke 3:21; Acts 10:11; Rev. 19:11; "the temple of the tabernacle of the testimony in heaven," Rev. 15:5; by metonymy, for that which contained treasures, Matt. 2:11; (b) metaphorically, e.g., Matt. 7:7-8; 25:11; Rev. 3:7; Hebraistically, "to open the mouth," of beginning to speak, e.g., Matt. 5:2; 13:35; Acts 8:32, 35; 10:34; 18:14; Rev. 13:6 (cf., e.g., Num. 22:28; Job. 3:1; Isa. 50:5); and of recovering speech, Luke 1:64; of the earth "opening," Rev. 12:16; of the "opening" of the eyes, Acts 26:18; the ears, **Mark 7:35**; (2) intransitively (perfect tense, active, in the Greek), (a) literally, of "the heaven," John 1:51, RV, "opened;" (b) metaphorically, of "speaking freely," 2 Cor. 6:11.

String *desmos* (1199), "a band, fetter, anything for tying" (from *deo*, "to bind, fasten with chains, etc."), is sometimes translated "band," sometimes "bond"; "bands," in Luke 8.29; Acts 16:26; 22:30, KJV only. In the case of the deaf man who had an impediment in his speech, whom the Lord took aside, **Mark 7:35**, the KJV says "the string of his tongue was loosed"; the RV, more literally, "the bond of his tongue.

Plain *orthos* (3723), "rightly" (from *orthos*, "straight"), is translated "plain," in **Mark 7:35**, of restored speech.

7:36 And he charged them that they should tell no man: but the more he charged them, so much the more a great deal they published *it*;

Charged *see Mark 5:43.*

More *mallon* (3123), the comparative degree of *mala*, "very, very much," is used (a) of increase, "more," with qualifying words, with *pollo*, "much," e.g., **Mark 10:48**, "the more (a great deal)"; Rom. 5:15, 17, "(much) more"; Phil. 2:12 (ditto); with *poso*, "how much," e.g., Luke 12:24; Rom. 11:12; with *tosouto*, "by so much," Heb. 10:25; (b) without a qualifying word, by way of comparison, "the more," e.g., Luke 5:15, "so much the more"; John 5:18, "the more"; Acts 5:14 (ditto); Phil. 1:9; 1 Thess. 4:1, 10, "more and more"; 2 Pet. 1:10, RV, "the more" (KJV, "the rather"); in Acts 20:35, by a periphrasis, it is translated "more (blessed)"; in Gal. 4:27, "more (than)," lit., "rather (than)"; (c) with qualifying words, similarly to (a), e.g., **Mark 7:36**.

Great In **Mark 7:36**, "so much the more a great deal" translates a phrase lit. signifying "more abundantly"; in **10:48** "the more a great deal" translates a phrase lit. signifying "more by much."

Published *see* **Publish** at *Mark 1:45.*

7:37 And were beyond measure astonished, saying, He hath done all things well: he maketh both the deaf to hear, and the dumb to speak.

Beyond measure *huperperissos* (5249), signifies "exceeding abundantly," **Mark 7:37**.

Deaf *see Mark 7:32.*

Dumb *alolos* (216), lit., "speechless" (*a*, negative, and *laleo*, "to speak"), is found in **Mark 7:37**; **9:17**, **25**. In the Sept., Ps. 38:13.

Chapter 8

8:1 In those days the multitude being very great, and having nothing to eat, Jesus called his disciples *unto him*, and saith unto them,

Very In **Mark 8:1** some texts have *pampollou*, "very great," KJV (from *pas*, "all," *polus*, "much"), RV, "a great (*pollou*) multitude" (after *palin*, "again").

8:2 I have compassion on the multitude, because they have now been with me three days, and have nothing to eat:

Compassion *see Mark 1:41.*

Been with *prosmeno* (4357), "to remain with," "to continue with a person," is said of the people with Christ, Matt. 15:32; **Mark 8:2** (KJV, "been with"); of "continuing" in supplications and prayers, 1 Tim. 5:5.

8:3 And if I send them away fasting to their own houses, they will faint by the way: for divers of them came from far.

Send *see Mark 6:36.*

Fasting *nestis* (3523), "not eating", "fasting," is used of lack of food, Matt. 15:32; **Mark 8:3.**

Houses *oikos* (3624), "a house, dwelling," is used with the preposition *eis*, "unto," with the meaning "to home," lit., "to a house," in **Mark 8:3**, RV, "to (their) home," KJV, "to (their own) houses"; so **8:26**, "to (his) home"; Luke 15:6, "home," lit., "into the house."

Faint *ekluo* (1590), denotes (a) "to loose, release" (*ek*, "out," *luo*, "to loose"); (b) "to unloose," as a bowstring, "to relax," and so, "to enfeeble," and is used in the passive voice with the significance "to be faint, grow weary," (1) of the body, Matt. 15:32; (some mss. have it in 9:36); **Mark 8:3**; (2) of the soul, Gal. 6:9 (last clause), in discharging responsibilities in obedience to the Lord; in Heb. 12:3, of becoming weary in the strife against sin; in v. 5, under the chastening hand of God. It expresses the opposite of *anazonnumi*, "to gird up," 1 Pet. 1:13.

Divers The pronoun *tines*, "some" (the plural of *tis*, "someone"), is translated "divers" in the KJV of **Mark 8:3** and Acts 19:9; RV, "some."

Far *makrothen* (3113), from "far," **Mark 8:3.**

8:4 And his disciples answered him, From whence can a man satisfy these *men* with bread here in the wilderness?

Man *tis* (5100), "some one, a certain one," is rendered "a man," "a certain man," e.g., in Matt. 22:24; **Mark 8:4**, KJV (RV, "one"); **12:19**; John 3:3, 5; 6:50; 14:23; 15:6, 13; Acts 13:41, KJV (RV, "one"); 1 Cor. 4:2; 1 Tim. 1:8; 2 Tim. 2:5, 21; Jas. 2:14, 18; 1 Pet. 2:19; 1 John 4:20.

Satisfy *chortazo* (5526), "to fill or satisfy with food," is translated "satisfy" in **Mark 8:4**, KJV (RV, "to fill").

Wilderness *eremia* (2047), primarily "a solitude, an uninhabited place," in contrast to a town or village, is translated "deserts" in Heb. 11:38; "the wilderness" in Matt. 15:33, KJV, "a desert place," RV; so in **Mark 8:4**; "wilderness" in 2 Cor. 11:26. It does not always denote a barren region, void of vegetation; it is often used of a place uncultivated, but fit for pasturage.

8:5 And he asked them, How many loaves have ye? And they said, Seven.

Many *see Mark 6:38.*

8:6 And he commanded the people to sit down on the ground: and he took the seven loaves, and gave thanks, and brake, and gave to his disciples to set before *them*; and they did set *them* before the people.

Sit *see* Sat at *Mark 6:40.*

Ground *ge* (1093), "the earth, land," etc., often denotes "the ground," e.g., Matt. 10:29; **Mark 8:6.**

Brake *klao* or *klazo* (2806), "to break, to break off pieces," is used of "breaking bread," (a) of the Lord's act in providing for people, Matt. 14:19; 15:36; **Mark 8:6, 19**; (b) of the "breaking of bread" in the Lord's Supper, Matt. 26:26; **Mark 14:22**; Luke 22:19; Acts 20:7; 1 Cor. 10:16; 11:24; (c) of an ordinary meal, Acts 2:46; 20:11; 27:35; (d) of the Lord's act in giving evidence of His resurrection, Luke 24:30.

Set *see Mark 6:41.*

Thanks *eucharisteo* (2168), "to give thanks," (a) is said of Christ, Matt. 15:36; 26:27; **Mark 8:6; 14:23**; Luke 22:17, 19; John 6:11, 23; 11:41; 1 Cor. 11:24; (b) of the Pharisee in Luke 18:11 in his selfcomplacent prayer; (c) is used by Paul at the beginning of all his epistles, except 2 Cor. (see, however, *eulogetos* in 1:3), Gal., 1 Tim., 2 Tim., and Titus ... "Thanksgiving" is the expression of joy Godward, and is therefore the fruit of the Spirit (Gal. 5:22); believers are encouraged to abound in it.

8:7 And they had a few small fishes: and he blessed, and commanded to set them also before *them*.

Fishes *ichthudion* (2485), "a little fish," Matt. 15:34; **Mark 8:7.**

Commanded *see Mark 5:43.*

8:8 So they did eat, and were filled: and they took up of the broken *meat* that was left seven baskets.

Meat In Matt. 15:37 and **Mark 8:8**, the KJV translates the plural of *klasma*, "a broken piece" (from *klao*, "to break"), "broken meat" (RV, "broken pieces").

Left In **Mark 8:8**, *perisseuma*, "an abundance," is used in the plural, RV, "(of broken pieces) that remained over" (KJV "that was left").

Baskets *spuris* (4711), or *sphuris*, signifies "something round, twisted or folded together" (connected with *speira*, "anything rolled into a circle"; Eng., "sphere"); hence a reed basket, plaited, a capacious kind of hamper, sometimes large enough to hold a man, Matt. 15:37; 16:10; **Mark 8:8, 20** (RV, "basketfuls"); Acts 9:25.

8:9 And they that had eaten were about four thousand: and he sent them away.

About *see Mark 5:13.*

Thousand *see Mark 5:13.*

Sent *see* Send at *Mark 6:36.*

8:10 And straightway he entered into a ship with his disciples, and came into the parts of Dalmanutha.

Entered *see Mark 4:1.*

Parts *meros* (3313), denotes (a) "a part, portion," of the whole, e.g., John 13:8; Rev. 20:6; 22:19; hence, "a lot" or "destiny," e.g., Rev. 21:8; in Matt. 24:51 and Luke 12:46, "portion"; (b) "a part" as opposite to the whole, e.g., Luke 11:36; John 19:23; 21:6, "side"; Acts 5:2; 23:6; Eph. 4:16; Rev. 16:19; a party, Acts 23:9; the divisions of a province, e.g., Matt. 2:22; Acts 2:10; the regions belonging to a city, e.g., Matt. 15:21, RV, "parts" (KJV, "coasts"); 16:13 (ditto); **Mark 8:10**, KJV and RV, "parts"; "the lower parts of the earth," Eph. 4:9; this phrase means the regions beneath the earth; (c) "a class," or "category" (with *en*, in, "in respect of"), Col. 2:16; "in this respect," 2 Cor. 3:10; 9:3, RV (KJV, "in this behalf").

8:11 And the Pharisees came forth, and began to question with him, seeking of him a sign from heaven, tempting him.

Question *see* Questioned at *Mark 1:27.*

8:12 And he sighed deeply in his spirit, and saith, Why doth this generation seek after a sign? verily I say unto you, There shall no sign be given unto this generation.

Sighed *anastenazo* (389), "to sigh deeply," occurs in **Mark 8:12**. In the Sept., Lam. 1:4.

Deeply In **Mark 8:12**, "He sighed deeply" represents *anastenazo*, "to fetch a deep-drawn sigh" (*ana*, "up," *stenazo*, "to sigh or groan").

Seek *epizeteo* (1934), "to seek after" (directive, *epi*, "towards") is always rendered in the RV, by some form of the verb "to seek," Acts 13:7, "sought" (KJV, "desired"); 19:39, "seek" (KJV, "inquire"); Phil. 4:17, "seek for" (KJV, "desire"), twice; elsewhere, Matt. 6:32; 12:39; 16:4; **Mark 8:12** (in some texts); Luke 12:30; Acts 12:19; Rom. 11:7; Heb. 11:14; 13:14.

8:13 And he left them, and entering into the ship again departed to the other side.

Left *see* Forsook at *Mark 1:18.*

Entering *see* Entered at *Mark 4:1.*

8:14 Now *the disciples* had forgotten to take bread, neither had they in the ship with them more than one loaf.

Forgotten *epilanthanomai* (1950), "to forget, or neglect," is said (a) negatively of God, indicating His remembrance of sparrows, Luke 12:6, and of the work and labor of love of His saints, Heb. 6:10; (b) of the disciples regarding taking bread, Matt. 16:5: **Mark 8:14**; (c) of Paul regarding "the things which are behind," Phil. 3:13; (d) of believers, as to showing love to strangers, Heb. 13:2, RV, and as to doing good and communicating, v. 16; (e) of a person who after looking at himself in a mirror, forgets what kind of person he is, Jas. 1:24.

More Various uses of the word "more" occur in connection with other words, especially in the comparative degree. The phrase "more than" translates certain prepositions and particles: in Rom. 1:25, KJV, *para*, "beside, compared with," is translated "more than" (RV, "rather than"): cf. Rom. 12:3, *huper*, "over, above," "more than," in Matt. 10:37 (twice); in Philem. 21, KJV, "more than" (RV, "beyond"). In **Mark 14:5**, KJV, *epano*, "above," is translated "more than" (RV, "above"). In Luke 15:7 the particle *e*, "than," is necessarily rendered "more than"; cf. Luke 17:2 and 1 Cor. 14:19, "rather than." In **Mark 8:14**, the conjunction *ei*, "if," with the negative *me*, lit., "if not," signifying "except," is translated "more than (one loaf)."

8:15 And he charged them, saying, Take heed, beware of the leaven of the Pharisees, and *of* the leaven of Herod.

Charged *see Mark 5:43.*

Heed *horao* (3708), "to see," usually expressing the sense of vision, is rendered "take heed" in Matt. 16:6; 18:10, KJV (RV, "see"); **Mark 8:15**; Luke 12:15; Acts 22:26 (KJV only).

Beware *blepo* (991), "to see," is applied to mental vision, and is sometimes used by way of warning "to take heed" against an object, **Mark 8:15**; **12:38**; Acts 13:40; Phil. 3:2 (three times); in Col. 2:8, RV, "take heed," marg., "see whether."

Leaven *zume* (2219), "leaven, sour dough, in a high state of fermentation," was used in general in making bread ... In the OT "leaven" is not used in a metaphorical sense. In the NT it is used (a) metaphorically (1) of corrupt doctrine, Matt. 13:33 and Luke 13:21, of error as mixed with the truth (there is no valid reason for regarding the symbol here differently from its application elsewhere in the NT); Matt. 16:6, 11; **Mark 8:15** (1st part); Luke 12:1; that the kingdom of heaven is likened to "leaven," does not mean that the kingdom is "leaven." The same statement, as made in other parables, shows that it is the whole parable which constitutes the similitude of the kingdom; the history of Christendom confirms the fact that the pure meal of the doctrine of Christ has been adulterated with error; (2) of corrupt practices, **Mark 8:15** (2nd part), the reference to the Herodians being especially applied to their irreligion; 1 Cor. 5:7, 8; (b) literally in Matt. 16:12, and in the general statements in 1 Cor. 5:6 and Gal. 5:9, where the implied applications are to corrupt practice and corrupt doctrine respectively.

8:16 And they reasoned among themselves, saying, *It is* because we have no bread.

Reasoned *see* Reasoning at *Mark 2:6*.

Themselves Regarding *allelon*, "of one another," and its other forms, the RV substitutes "one another" for the KJV "themselves" in **Mark 8:16**; **9:34**; Luke 4:36; John 6:52; 11:56; 16:17; 19:24; Acts 26:31; 28:4; Rom. 2:15, but adheres to the rendering "themselves" in **Mark 15:31**; Acts 4:15; 28:25.

8:17 And when Jesus knew *it*, he saith unto them, Why reason ye, because ye have no bread? perceive ye not yet, neither understand? have ye your heart yet hardened?

Knew *ginosko* (1097), "to know by experience and observation," is translated "to perceive" in Matt. 12:15, RV (KJV, "knew"); 16:8; 21:45; 22:18; 26:10, RV, (KJV, "understood"); **Mark 8:17**; **12:12** and **15:10**, RV (KJV, "knew"); so Luke 9:11; 18:34; in Luke 7:39, RV (KJV, "known"); 20:19; John 6:15; 8:27, RV (KJV, "understood"); 16:19, RV (KJV, "knew"); Acts 23:6; Gal. 2:9; in 1 John 3:16, KJV, "perceive" (RV, "know," perfect tense, lit., "we have perceived," and therefore "know").

Reason *see* Reasoning at *Mark 2:6*.

Perceive *see Mark 7:18*.

Hardened *see Mark 6:52*.

8:18 Having eyes, see ye not? and having ears, hear ye not? and do ye not remember?

Ears *ous* (3775), Latin *auris*, is used (a) of the physical organ, e.g., Luke 4:21; Acts 7:57; in Acts 11:22, in the plural with *akouo*, "to hear," lit., "was heard into the ears of someone," i.e., came to the knowledge of, similarly, in the singular, Matt. 10:27, in familiar private conversation; in Jas. 5:4 the phrase is used with *eiserchomai*, "to enter into"; in Luke 1:44, with *ginomai*, "to become, to come"; in Luke 12:3, with *lalein*, "to speak" and *pros*, "to", (b) metaphorically, of the faculty of perceiving with the mind, understanding and knowing, Matt. 13:16; frequently with *akouo*, "to hear," e.g., Matt. 11:15; 13:9, 43; Rev. 2 and 3, at the close of each of the messages to the churches, in Matt. 13:15 and Acts 28:27, with *bareos*, "heavily," of being slow to understand and obey; with a negative in **Mark 8:18**; Rom. 11:8; in Luke 9:44 the lit. meaning is "put those words into your ears," i.e., take them into your mind and keep them there, in Acts 7:51 it is used with *aperitmetos*, "uncircumcised." As seeing is metaphorically associated with conviction, so hearing is with obedience (*hupakoe*, lit., "hearing under"; the Eng., "obedience" is etymologically "hearing over against," i.e., with response in the hearer).

Remember *mnemoneuo* (3421), signifies "to call to mind, remember"; it is used absolutely in **Mark 8:18**; everywhere else it has an object, (a) persons, Luke 17:32; Gal. 2:10; 2 Tim. 2:8, where the RV rightly has "remember Jesus Christ, risen from the dead"; Paul was not reminding Timothy (nor did he need to) that Christ was raised from the dead (KJV), what was needful for him was to "remember" (to keep in mind) the One who rose, the Source and Supplier of all his requirements; (b) things, e.g., Matt. 16:9; John 15:20; 16:21; Acts 20:35; Col. 4:18; 1 Thess. 1:3; 2:9; Heb. 11:15, "had been mindful of"; 13:7; Rev. 18:5; (c) a clause, representing a circumstance, etc., John 16:4; Acts 20:31; Eph. 2:11; 2 Thess. 2:5; Rev. 2:5; 3:3; in Heb. 11:22 it signifies "to make mention of."

8:19 When I brake the five loaves among five thousand, how many baskets full of fragments took ye up? They say unto him, Twelve.

Brake *see Mark 8:6.*

Many *see Mark 6:38.*

Baskets *see Mark 6:43.*

Full *see Mark 4:28.*

Fragments *see Mark 6:43.*

8:20 And when the seven among four thousand, how many baskets full of fragments took ye up? And they said, Seven.

Thousand *see Mark 5:13.*

Many *see Mark 6:38.*

Baskets *see Mark 8:8.*

Fragments *see Mark 6:43.*

8:21-23 And he said unto them, How is it that ye do not understand?

And he cometh to Bethsaida; and they bring a blind man unto him, and besought him to touch him.

And he took the blind man by the hand, and led him out of the town; and when he had spit on his eyes, and put his hands upon him, he asked him if he saw ought.

Took *epilambano* (1949), in the middle voice, "to lay hold of, take hold of," is used literally, e.g., **Mark 8:23**; Luke 9:47; 14:4; metaphorically, e.g., Heb. 8:9, "(I) took them (by the hand)."

Led *exago* (1806), "to lead out," is rendered by the verb "to lead, out or forth," in **Mark 15:20** (in some mss. in **8:23**, the best have *ekphero*, "to bring out)"; Luke 24:50; John 10:3; Acts 7:36, 40 (KJV "brought"), and 13:17, RV; Acts 21:38; Heb. 8:9.

Town *kome* (2968), "a village," or "country town without walls." The RV always renders this "village" or "villages," KJV, "town" or "towns," Matt. 10:11; **Mark 8:23, 26** (twice), **27**; Luke 5:17; 9:6, 12; John 7:42; 11:1, 30.

Spit *see Mark 7:33.*

Eyes *omma* (3659), "sight," is used in the plural in Matt. 20:34; **Mark 8:23**. The writers may have changed the word with a view to distinguishing the simple desire of the blind man from the tender act of the Lord Himself.

8:24 And he looked up, and said, I see men as trees, walking.

Looked *anablepo* (308), denotes (a) "to look up," e.g., Matt. 14:19; **Mark 8:24** (in some mss. v. **25**); (b) "to recover sight," e.g., Matt. 11:5; 20:34, RV, "received their sight"; John 9:11. Cf. *anablepsis*, "recovering of sight," Luke 4:18.

8:25 After that he put *his* hands again upon his eyes, and made him look up: and he was restored, and saw every man clearly.

Put *see Mark 7:32.*

Eyes *see Mark 8:23.*

Look *see* Looked at *Mark 8:24.*

Restored *see Mark 3:5.*

Saw *emblepo* (1689), "to look at," used of earnestly looking, is translated "saw" in **Mark 8:25** (last part); "could (not) see" in Acts 22:11.

Every *hapas* (537), signifies "all, the whole, altogether"; it is translated "every one" in Acts 5:16, where it occurs in the plural. In **Mark 8:25**, the KJV, "every man" translates the text with the masculine plural; the best mss. have the neuter plural, RV, "all things."

Clearly *telaugos* (5081), from *tele*, "afar," and *auge*, "radiance," signifies "conspicuously, or clearly," **Mark 8:25**, of the sight imparted by Christ to one who had been blind. Some mss. have *delaugos*, "clearly" (*delos*, "clear").

8:26 And he sent him away to his house, saying, Neither go into the town, nor tell *it* to any in the town.

House *see* Houses at *Mark 8:3.*

Town *see Mark 8:23.*

8:27 And Jesus went out, and his disciples, into the towns of Caesarea Philippi: and by the way he asked his disciples, saying unto them, Whom do men say that I am?

Towns *see* Town at *Mark 8:23.*

8:28 And they answered, John the Baptist: but some *say*, Elias; and others, One of the prophets.

Some *see Mark 4:7.*

8:29-30 And he saith unto them, But whom say ye that I am? And Peter answereth and saith unto him, Thou art the Christ.

And he charged them that they should tell no man of him.

Charged *see Mark 3:12.*

8:31 And he began to teach them, that the Son of man must suffer many things, and be rejected of the elders, and *of* the chief priests, and scribes, and be killed, and after three days rise again.

Rejected *apodokimazo* (593), "to reject" as the result of examination and disapproval (*apo*, "away from," *dokimazo*, "to approve"), is used (a) of the "rejection" of Christ by the elders and chief priests of the Jews,

Matt. 21:42; **Mark 8:31**; **12:10**; Luke 9:22; 20:17; 1 Pet. 2:4, 7 (KJV, "disallowed"); by the Jewish people, Luke 17:25; (b) of the "rejection" of Esau from inheriting "the blessing," Heb. 12:17. Cf. and contrast *exoutheneo*, Acts 4:11.

Chief *archiereus* (749), "a chief priest, high priest" (*arche*, "first," *hiereus*, "a priest"), is frequent in the Gospels, Acts and Hebrews, but there only in the NT. It is used of Christ, e.g., in Heb. 2:17; 3:1; of "chief" priests, including ex-high-priests and members of their families, e.g., Matt. 2:4; **Mark 8:31**.

Scribes *see Mark 1:22*.

Rise *see* Rising at *Mark 1:35*.

8:32 And he spake that saying openly. And Peter took him, and began to rebuke him.

Saying *see Mark 7:29*.

Openly *parrhesia* (3954), "freedom of speech, boldness," is used adverbially in the dative case and translated "openly" in **Mark 8:32**, of a saying of Christ; in John 7:13, of a public statement; in 11:54, of Christ's public appearance; in 7:26 and 18:20, of His public testimony; preceded by the preposition *en*, "in," John 7:4, lit., "in boldness" (cf. v. 10, RV, "publicly).

Took *proslambano* (4355), "to take to oneself" (*pros*), is used of food, Acts 27:33-36; of persons, of Peter's act toward Christ, Matt. 16:22; **Mark 8:32**; for evil purposes, Acts 17:5; for good purposes, 18:26.

Rebuke *see* Rebuked at *Mark 1:25*.

8:33 But when he had turned about and looked on his disciples, he rebuked Peter, saying, Get thee behind me, Satan: for thou savourest not the things that be of God, but the things that be of men.

Rebuked *see Mark 1:25*.

Get *hupago* (5217), "to go away, withdraw," is rendered "get," "get ... hence," in Matt. 4:10; 16:23; **Mark 8:33**; some mss. have it in Luke 4:8.

Satan *see Mark 1:13*.

Savourest In the KJV of Matt. 16:23 and **Mark 8:33**, *phroneo*, "to think, to mind," is translated "thou savorest" (RV, "thou mindest").

God *theos* (2316), (I) in the polytheism of the Greeks, denoted "a god or deity," e.g., Acts 14:11; 19:26; 28:6; 1 Cor. 8:5; Gal. 4:8. (II) (a) Hence the word was appropriated by Jews and retained by Christians to denote "the one true God." In the Sept. *theos* translates (with few exceptions) the Hebrew words *Elohim* and *Jehovah*, the former indicating His power and preeminence, the latter His unoriginated, immutable, eternal and self-sustained existence.

In the NT, these and all the other divine attributes are predicated of Him. To Him are ascribed, e.g., His unity, or monism, e.g., **Mark 12:29**; 1 Tim. 2:5; self-existence, John 5:26; immutability, Jas. 1:17; eternity, Rom. 1:20; universality, Matt. 10:29; Acts 17:26-28; almighty power, Matt. 19:26; infinite knowledge, Acts 2:23; 15:18; Rom. 11:33, creative power, Rom. 11:36; 1 Cor. 8:6; Eph. 3:9; Rev. 4:11; 10:6; absolute holiness, 1 Pet. 1:15; 1 John 1:5; righteousness, John 17:25; faithfulness, 1 Cor. 1:9; 10:13; 1 Thess. 5:24; 2 Thess. 3:3; 1 John 1:9; love, 1 John 4:8, 16; mercy, Rom. 9:15, 18; truthfulness, Titus 1:2; Heb. 6:18.

(b) The divine attributes are likewise indicated or definitely predicated of Christ, e.g., Matt. 20:18-19; John 1:1-3; 1:18, RV, marg.; 5:22-29; 8:58; 14:6; 17:22-24; 20:28; Rom. 1:4; 9:5; Phil. 3:21; Col. 1:15; 2:3; Titus 2:13, RV; Heb. 1:3; 13:8; 1 John 5:20; Rev. 22:12, 13.

(c) Also of the Holy Spirit, e.g., Matt. 28:19; Luke 1:35; John 14:16; 15:26; 16:7-14; Rom. 8:9, 26; 1 Cor. 12:11; 2 Cor. 13:14.

... (e) In the following the nominative case is used for the vocative, and always with the article; **Mark 15:34**; Luke 18:11, 13; John 20:28; (Acts 4:24 in some mss.); Heb. 1:8; 10:7.

(f) The phrase "the things of God" (translated literally or otherwise) stands for (1) His interests, Matt. 16:23; **Mark 8:33**; (2) His counsels, 1 Cor. 2:11; (3) things which are due to Him, Matt. 22:21; **Mark 12:17**; Luke 20:25. The phrase "things pertaining to God," Rom. 15:17; Heb. 2:17; 5:1, describes, in the Heb. passages, the sacrificial service of the priest; in the Rom. passage the gospel ministry as an offering to God.

"Jesus invited us, not to a picnic, but to a pilgrimage; not to a frolic, but to a fight. He offered us, not an excursion, but an execution. Our Savior said that we would have to be ready to die to self, sin, and the world."

BILLY GRAHAM

8:34 And when he had called the people *unto him* with his disciples also, he said unto them, Whosoever will come after me, let him deny himself, and take up his cross, and follow me.

Will *thelo* (2309), usually expresses "desire" or "design"; it is most frequently translated by "will" or "would"; see especially Rom. 7:15, 16, 18-21. In 1 Tim. 2:4, RV, "willeth" signifies the gracious "desire" of God for all men to be saved; not all are "willing" to accept His condition, depriving themselves either by the self-established criterion of their perverted reason, or because of their self-indulgent preference for sin. In John 6:21, the KJV renders the verb "willingly" (RV, "they were willing"); in 2 Pet. 3:5, KJV, the present participle is translated "willingly" (RV, "wilfully"). The following are RV renderings for the KJV, "will": Matt. 16:24, 25, "would"; "wouldest," 19:21 and 20:21; "would," 20:26, 27; **Mark 8:34, 35; 10:43, 44**; "would fain," Luke 13:31; "would," John 6:67; "willeth," 7:17; in 8:44, "it is your will (to do)"; "wouldest," Rom. 13:3; "would," 1 Cor. 14:35 and 1 Pet. 3:10.

Deny *aparneomai* (533), means (a) "to deny utterly," to abjure, to affirm that one has no connection with a person, as in Peter's denial of Christ, Matt. 26:34-35, 75; **Mark 14:30-31, 72**; Luke 22:34, 61 (some mss. have it in John 13:38). This stronger form is used in the Lord's statements foretelling Peter's "denial," and in Peter's assurance of fidelity; the simple verb (*arneomai*) is used in all the records of his actual denial. The strengthened form is the verb used in the Lord's warning as to being "denied" in the presence of the angels, Luke 12:9; in the preceding clause, "he that denieth Me," the simple verb *arneomai* is used; the rendering therefore should be "he that denieth Me in the presence of men, shall be utterly denied in the presence of the angels of God"; (b) "to deny oneself" as a follower of Christ, Matt. 16:24; **Mark 8:34**; Luke 9:23.

Follow *akoloutheo* (190), to be an *akolouthos*, "a follower," or "companion" (from the prefix *a*, here expressing "union, likeness," and *keleuthos*, "a way"; hence, "one going in the same way"), is used (a) frequently in the literal sense, e.g., Matt. 4:25; (b) metaphorically, of "discipleship," e.g., **Mark 8:34; 9:38; 10:21**. It is used 77 times in the Gospels, of "following" Christ, and only once otherwise, **Mark 14:13**.

8:35 For whosoever will save his life shall lose it; but whosoever shall lose his life for my sake and the gospel's, the same shall save it.

Will *see Mark 8:34.*

8:36 For what shall it profit a man, if he shall gain the whole world, and lose his own soul?

Profit *see* Profited at *Mark 7:11.*

Gain *kerdaino* (2770), signifies (I) literally, (a) "to gain something," Matt. 16:26; 25:16 (in the best mss.), 17, 20, 22; **Mark 8:36**; Luke 9:25; (b) "to get gain, make a profit," Jas. 4:13; (II) metaphorically, (a) "to win persons," said (1) of "gaining" an offending brother who by being told privately of his offense, and by accepting the representations, is won from alienation and from the consequences of his fault, Matt. 18:15; (2) of winning souls into the kingdom of God by the gospel, 1 Cor. 9:19, 20 (twice), 21, 22, or by godly conduct, 1 Pet. 3:1 (RV, "gained"); (3) of so practically appropriating Christ to oneself that He becomes the dominating power in and over one's whole being and circumstances, Phil. 3:8 (RV, "gain"); (b) "to gain things," said of getting injury and loss, Acts 27:21, RV, "gotten."

Whole *holos* (3650), signifies "whole," (a) with a noun, e.g., Matt. 5:29, 30; **Mark 8:36; 15:1, 16, 33**; Luke 11:36 (1st part), though *holon* may here be used adverbially with *photeinon*, "wholly light" [as in the 2nd part, RV, "wholly (full of light)"]; John 11:50; 1 Cor. 12:17 (1st part); 1 John 2:2; 5:19; (b) absolutely, as a noun, e.g., Matt. 13:33; 1 Cor. 12:17 (2nd part).

Lose *zemioo* (2210), "to damage" (akin to *zemia*, "damage," e.g., Acts 27:10, 21), is used in the NT, in the passive voice, signifying "to suffer loss, forfeit, lose," Matt. 16:26; **Mark 8:36**, of losing one's soul or life; Luke 9:25, RV, "forfeit (his own self)," KJV, "be cast away"; 1 Cor. 3:15, "he shall suffer loss," i.e., at the Judgment-Seat of Christ (see v. 13 with 2 Cor. 5:10); 2 Cor. 7:9, "(that) ye might suffer loss," RV (KJV, "might receive damage"); though the apostle did regret the necessity of making them sorry by his letter, he rejoiced that they were made sorry after a godly sort, and that they thus suffered no spiritual loss, which they would have done had their sorrow been otherwise than after a godly manner; in Phil. 3:8, "I suffered the loss (of all things)," RV, i.e., of all things which he formerly counted gain (especially those in verses 5 and 6, to which the article before "all things" points).

8:37 Or what shall a man give in exchange for his soul?

Exchange *antallagma* (465), "the price received as an equivalent of, or in exchange for, an article, an exchange" (*anti*, "instead of," *allasso*, "to change," akin to *allos*, "another"), hence denotes the price at which the "exchange" is effected,

Matt. 16:26; **Mark 8:37**. Connected with this is the conception of atonement, as in the word *lutron*, "a ransom." Cf *allagma* in the Sept., e.g., in Isa. 43:3.

8:38 Whosoever therefore shall be ashamed of me and of my words in this adulterous and sinful generation; of him also shall the Son of man be ashamed, when he cometh in the glory of his Father with the holy angels.

Ashamed *epaischunomai* (1870), is said of being "ashamed" of persons, **Mark 8:38**; Luke 9:26; the gospel, Rom. 1:16; former evil doing, Rom. 6:21; "the testimony of our Lord," 2 Tim. 1:8; suffering for the gospel, v. 12; rendering assistance and comfort to one who is suffering for the gospel's sake, v. 16. It is used in Heb., of Christ in calling those who are sanctified His brethren, 2:11, and of God in His not being "ashamed" to be called the God of believers, 11:16. In the Sept., in Job 34:19; Ps. 119:6; Isa. 1:29.

My *emos* (1699), a possessive adjective of the first person, often used as a possessive pronoun with greater emphasis than the oblique forms of *ego*, a measure of stress which should always be observed; it denotes (I) subjectively, (a) "what I possess," e.g., John 4:34; 7:16 (1st part); 13:35; 1 Cor. 16:21; Gal. 6:11; Col. 4:18 (1st clause); as a pronoun, absolutely (i.e., not as an adjective), e.g., Matt. 20:15; 25:27; Luke 15:31, RV, "(all that is) mine," KJV, "(all that) I have"; John 16:14, 15; 17:10; (b) "proceeding from me," e.g., **Mark 8:38**; John 7:16 (2nd part); 8:37 (here the repetition of the article with the pronoun, after the article with the noun, lends special stress to the pronoun; more lit., "the word, that which is mine"); so in John 15:12. Such instances are to be distinguished from the less emphatic order where the pronoun comes between the article and the noun, as in John 7:16, already mentioned; (c) in the phrase "it is mine" (i.e., "it rests with me"), e.g., Matt. 20:23; **Mark 10:40**; (II) objectively, "pertaining or relating to me": (a) "appointed for me," e.g., John 7:6, "My time" (with the repeated article and special stress just referred to); (b) equivalent to an objective genitive ("of me"), e.g., Luke 22:19, "(in remembrance) of Me" (lit., "in My remembrance"); so 1 Cor. 11:24.

Adulterous *moichalis* (3428), "an adulteress," is used (a) in the natural sense, 2 Pet. 2:14; Rom. 7:3; (b) in the spiritual sense, Jas. 4:4; here the RV rightly omits the word "adulterers." It was added by a copyist. As in Israel the breach of their relationship with God through their idolatry, was described as "adultery" or "harlotry" (e.g., Ezek. 16:15, etc.; 23:43), so believers who cultivate friendship with the world, thus breaking their spiritual union with Christ, are spiritual "adulteresses," having been spiritually united to Him as wife to husband, Rom. 7:4. It is used adjectivally to describe the Jewish people in transferring their affections from God, Matt. 12:39; 16:4; **Mark 8:38**. In 2 Pet. 2:14, the lit. translation is "full of an adulteress" (RV, marg.).

Sinful *hamartolos* (268), an adjective, akin to *hamartano*, "to sin," is used as an adjective, "sinful" in **Mark 8:38**; Luke 5:8; 19:7 (lit., "a sinful man"); 24:7; John 9:16, and 24 (lit., "a man sinful"); Rom. 7:13. Elsewhere it is used as a noun.

Holy *hagios* (40), from the same root as *hagnos* (found in *hazo*, "to venerate"), fundamentally signifies "separated" (among the Greeks, dedicated to the gods), and hence, in Scripture in its moral and spiritual significance, separated from sin and therefore consecrated to God, sacred.

The adjective is also used of the outer part of the tabernacle, Heb. 9:2 (RV, "the holy place"); of the inner sanctuary, 9:3, RV, "the Holy of Holies"; 9:4, "a holy place," RV; v. 25 (plural), of the presence of God in heaven, where there are not two compartments as in the tabernacle, all being "the holy place"; 9:8, 12 (neuter plural); 10:19, "the holy place," RV (KJV, "the holiest," neut. plural); of the city of Jerusalem. Rev. 11:2; its temple, Acts 6:13; of the faith. Jude 20; of the greetings of saints, 1 Cor. 16:20; of angels, e.g., **Mark 8:38**; of apostles and prophets, Eph. 3:5; of the future heavenly Jerusalem, Rev. 21:2, 10; 22:19.

Angels *angelos* (32), "a messenger" (from *angello*, "to deliver a message"), sent whether by God or by man or by Satan, "is also used of a guardian or representative in Rev. 1:20, cf. Matt. 18:10; Acts 12:15 (where it is better understood as 'ghost'), but most frequently of an order of created beings, superior to man, Heb. 2:7; Ps. 8:5, belonging to Heaven, Matt. 24:36; **Mark 12:25**, and to God, Luke 12:8, and engaged in His service, Ps. 103:20. "Angels" are spirits, Heb. 1:14, i.e., they have not material bodies as men have; they are either human in form, or can assume the human form when necessary, cf. Luke 24:4, with v. 23, Acts 10:3 with v. 30. "They are called 'holy' in **Mark 8:38**, and 'elect,' 1 Tim. 5:21, in contrast with some of their original number, Matt. 25:41, who 'sinned,' 2 Pet. 2:4, 'left their proper habitation,' Jude 6, *oiketerion*, a word which occurs again, in the NT, only in 2 Cor. 5:2. Angels are always spoken of in the masculine gender, the feminine form of the word does not occur."

Chapter 9

9:1 And he said unto them, Verily I say unto you, That there be some of them that stand here, which shall not taste of death, till they have seen the kingdom of God come with power.

Here *hode* (5602), an adverb signifying (a) "here" (of place), e.g., Matt. 12:6; **Mark 9:1**; used with the neuter plural of the article, Col. 4:9, "(all) things (that are done) here," lit., "(all) the (things) here"; in Matt. 24:23, *hode* is used in both parts, hence the RV, "Lo, here (is the Christ, or) Here"; in **Mark 13:21** *hode* is followed by *ekei*, "there." The word is used metaphorically in the sense of "in this circumstance," or connection, in 1 Cor. 4:2; Rev. 13:10, 18; 14:12; 17:9.

Taste *geuo* (1089), "to make to taste," is used in the middle voice, signifying "to taste" (a) naturally, Matt. 27:34; Luke 14:24; John 2:9; Col. 2:21; (b) metaphorically, of Christ's "tasting" death, implying His personal experience in voluntarily undergoing death, Heb. 2:9; of believers (negatively) as to "tasting" of death, Matt. 16:28; **Mark 9:1**; Luke 9:27; John 8:52; of "tasting" the heavenly gift (different from receiving it), Heb. 6:4; "the good word of God, and the powers of the age to come," 6:5; "that the Lord is gracious," 1 Pet. 2:3.

9:2 And after six days Jesus taketh *with him* Peter, and James, and John, and leadeth them up into an high mountain apart by themselves: and he was transfigured before them.

Six *hex* (1803), whence Eng. prefix, "hex"-, is used separately from other numerals in Matt. 17:1; **Mark 9:2**; Luke 4:25; 13:14; John 2:6; 12:1; Acts 11:12; 18:11; Jas. 5:17; Rev. 4:8. It sometimes suggests incompleteness, in comparison with the perfect number seven.

Taketh *paralambano* (3880), besides its meaning "to receive," denotes "to take to (or with) oneself," of "taking" a wife, e.g., Matt. 1:20, 24; of "taking" a person or persons with one, e.g., Matt. 2:13, 14, 20, 21; 4:5, 8; of demons, 12:45; of Christ and His disciples, 17:1; 20:17; **Mark 9:2; 10:32; 14:33**; of witnesses, Matt. 18:16; of the removal of persons from the earth in judgment, when "the Son of Man is revealed," Matt. 24:40, 41; Luke 17:34, 35 (cf. the means of the removal of corruption, in v. 37); of the "taking" of Christ by the soldiers for scourging, Matt. 27:27, RV, and to crucifixion, John 19:16; see also Acts 15:39; 16:33; 21:24, 26, 32; 23:18.

Leadeth *anaphero* (399), "to carry or lead up," is translated "leadeth ... up" in the KJV of **Mark 9:2** (RV "bringeth ... up").

High *hupselos* (5308), "high, lofty," is used (a) naturally, of mountains, Matt. 4:8; 17:1; **Mark 9:2**; Rev. 21:10; of a wall, Rev. 21:12; (b) figuratively, of the arm of God, Acts 13:17; of heaven, "on high," plural, lit., "in high (places)," Heb. 1:3; (c) metaphorically, Luke 16:15, RV, "exalted" (KJV, "highly esteemed"); Rom. 11:20, in the best texts, "high-minded" [lit., "mind (not) high things"]; 12:16.

Mountain *see* **Mountains** at *Mark 5:5*.

Transfigured *metamorphoo* (3339), "to change into another form" (*meta*, implying change, and *morphe*, "form:"), is used in the passive voice (a) of Christ's "transfiguration," Matt. 17:2; **Mark 9:2**; Luke (in **9:29**) avoids this term, which might have suggested to gentile readers the metamorphoses of heathen gods, and uses the phrase *egeneto heteron*, "was altered", lit., "became (*ginomai*) different (*heteros*)"; (b) of believers, Rom. 12:2, "be ye transformed," the obligation being to undergo a complete change which, under the power of God, will find expression in character and conduct; *morphe* lays stress on the inward change, *schema* (see the preceding verb in that verse, *suschematizo*) lays stress on the outward; the present continuous tenses indicate a process; 2 Cor. 3:18 describes believers as being "transformed (RV) into the same image" (i.e., of Christ in all His moral excellencies), the change being effected by the Holy Spirit.

9:3 And his raiment became shining, exceeding white as snow; so as no fuller on earth can white them.

Raiment For *himation*, rendered "raiment" in Matt. 17:2, KJV (RV, "garments"), so Matt. 27:31; **Mark 9:3**; Luke 23:34; John 19:24; Acts 22:20; Rev. 3:5, 18; 4:4; KJV and RV, Acts 18:6. *Himatismos* is rendered "raiment" in Luke 9:29; *enduma* in Matt. 3:4; 6:25, 28; 28:3 and Luke 12:23. For *esthes*, translated "raiment" in Jas. 2:2 (2nd part), KJV.

Shining *stilbo* (4744), "to shine, glisten," is used in **Mark 9:3** of the garments of Christ at His transfiguration, RV, "glistering," KJV, "shining." Cf. *exastrapto*, "dazzling," in Luke 9:29, RV.

Exceeding *lian* (3029), "very, exceedingly," is translated "exceeding" in Matt. 2:16; 4:8; 8:28; **Mark 9:3**; Luke 23:8.

White *leukos* (3022), is used of (a) clothing (sometimes in the sense of "bright"), Matt. 17:2; 28:3; **Mark 9:3; 16:5**; Luke 9:29; John 20:12;

Acts 1:10; symbolically, Rev. 3:4, 5, 18; 4:4; 6:11; 7:9, 13; 19:14 (2nd part); (b) hair, Matt. 5:36; Christ's head and hair (in a vision; cf. Dan. 7:9), Rev. 1:14 (twice); ripened grain, John 4:35; a stone, Rev. 2:17, an expression of the Lord's special delight in the overcomer, the new name on it being indicative of a secret communication of love and joy; a horse (in a vision), 6:2; 19:11-14 (1st part); a cloud, 14:14; the throne of God, 20:11.

Snow *chion* (5510), occurs in Matt. 28:3; Rev. 1:14. Some mss. have it in **Mark 9:3** (KJV).

Fuller *gnapheus* (102), akin to *knapto*, "to card wool," denotes "a cloth-carder, or dresser" (*gnaphos*, "the prickly teasel-cloth"; hence, "a carding comb"); it is used of the raiment of the Lord in **Mark 9:3**.

9:4 And there appeared unto them Elias with Moses: and they were talking with Jesus.

Talking with *sullaleo* (4814), "to speak with" (*sun*), is translated "to talk with," Matt. 17:3; **Mark 9:4**; Luke 9:30.

9:5 And Peter answered and said to Jesus, Master, it is good for us to be here: and let us make three tabernacles; one for thee, and one for Moses, and one for Elias.

Master *rabbei* or *rabbi* (4461), from a word *rab*, primarily denoting "master" in contrast to a slave; this with the added pronominal suffix signified "my master" and was a title of respect by which teachers were addressed. The suffix soon lost its specific force, and in the NT the word is used as courteous title of address. It is applied to Christ in Matt. 26:25, 49; **Mark 9:5; 11:21; 14:45**; John 1:38 (where it is interpreted as *didaskalos*, "master," marg., "teacher" (see also "Rabboni" in John 20:16); v. 49; 3:2; 4:31; 6:25; 9:2; 11:8; to John the Baptist in John 3:26. In Matt. 23:7, 8, Christ forbids his disciples to covet or use it. In the latter verse it is again explained as *didaskalos*, "master" (some mss. have *kathegetes*, "a guide").

Tabernacles *skene* (4633), "a tent, booth, tabernacle," is used of (a) tents as dwellings, Matt. 17:4; **Mark 9:5**; Luke 9:33; Heb. 11:9, KJV, "tabernacles" (RV, "tents"); (b) the Mosaic tabernacle, Acts 7:44; Heb. 8:5; 9:1 (in some mss.); 9:8, 21, termed "the tent of meeting," RV (i.e., where the people were called to meet God), a preferable description to "the tabernacle of the congregation," as in the KJV in the OT; the outer part 9:2, 6; the inner sanctuary, 9:3; (c) the heavenly prototype, Heb. 8:2; 9:11; Rev. 13:6; 15:5; 21:3 (of its future descent); (d) the eternal abodes of the saints, Luke 16:9, RV, "tabernacles" (KJV, "habitations"); (e) the Temple in Jerusalem, as continuing the service of the tabernacle, Heb. 13:10; (f) the house of David, i.e., metaphorically of his people, Acts 15:16; (g) the portable shrine of the god Moloch, Acts 7:43.

9:6 For he wist not what to say; for they were sore afraid.

Wist *oida* (1492), "to know," in the pluperfect tense (with imperfect meaning) is rendered "wist" (the past tense of the verb "to wit": cf. WOT) in **Mark 9:6; 14:40**; Luke 2:49; John 5:13; Acts 12:9; 23:5.

Sore In **Mark 9:6**, *ekphobos* is rendered "sore afraid."

Afraid *ekphobos* (1630), signifies "frightened outright," Heb. 12:21 (with *eimi*, "I am"), "I exceedingly fear"; **Mark 9:6**, "sore afraid."

9:7 And there was a cloud that overshadowed them: and a voice came out of the cloud, saying, This is my beloved Son: hear him.

Overshadowed *episkiazo* (1982), "to throw a shadow upon" (*epi*, "over," *skia*, "a shadow"), "to overshadow," is used (a) of the bright cloud at the Transfiguration, Matt. 17:5; **Mark 9:7**; Luke 9:34; (b) metaphorically of the power of "the Most High" upon the Virgin Mary, Luke 1:35; (c) of the apostle Peter's shadow upon the sick, Acts 5:15.

9:8 And suddenly, when they had looked round about, they saw no man any more, save Jesus only with themselves.

Looked *see Mark 3:5.*

9:9 And as they came down from the mountain, he charged them that they should tell no man what things they had seen, till the Son of man were risen from the dead.

Mountain *see* Mountains at *Mark 5:5.*

Charged *see Mark 5:43.*

Tell *diegeomai* (1334), is rendered "to tell," in the KJV and RV, in **Mark 9:9**; Heb. 11:32.

Risen *see* Rising at *Mark 1:35.*

9:10 And they kept that saying with themselves, questioning one with another what the rising from the dead should mean.

Kept *krateo* (2902), "to be strong, get possession of, hold fast," is used in **Mark 9:10**, "(and) they kept (the saying)," i.e., they held fast to the Lord's command to refrain from telling what they had seen in the mount of Transfiguration.

Saying *see Mark 7:29.*

Questioning *see* Questioned at *Mark 1:27.*

One ... another In **Mark 9:10**, KJV, *pros heautous*, "among yourselves" (RV), is translated "one with another."

9:11-12 And they asked him, saying, Why say the scribes that Elias must first come?

And he answered and told them, Elias verily cometh first, and restoreth all things; and how it is written of the Son of man, that he must suffer many things, and be set at nought.

Verily *see* Indeed at *Mark 1:8.*

Restoreth *see* Restored at *Mark 3:5.*

Nought *exoudeneo* or *exoudenoo* (1847), is virtually the same word (*outhen* being another form of *ouden*, "nothing"), i.e., "to treat as nothing" (*ex*, intensive), and is translated "be set at nought" in **Mark 9:12**.

9:13 But I say unto you, That Elias is indeed come, and they have done unto him whatsoever they listed, as it is written of him.

Listed *thelo* (2309), "to will, wish," is translated by the verb "to list" in Matt. 17:12; **Mark 9:13**; John 3:8.

9:14 And when he came to *his* disciples, he saw a great multitude about them, and the scribes questioning with them.

Questioning *see* Questioned at *Mark 1:27.*

9:15 And straightway all the people, when they beheld him, were greatly amazed, and running to *him* saluted him.

Amazed *ekthambeo* (1568), is found in Mark's Gospel only; in **9:15**, "were greatly amazed"; in **14:33**, KJV, "were sore amazed"; in **16:5**, RV, "were amazed," KJV, "were affrighted"; in v. **6**, RV, "be not amazed," KJV, "be not affrighted."

Running *prostrecho* (4370), "to run to," is used in **Mark 9:15**; **10:17**; Acts 8:30.

9:16 And he asked the scribes, What question ye with them?

Question *see* Questioned at *Mark 1:27.*

9:17 And one of the multitude answered and said, Master, I have brought unto thee my son, which hath a dumb spirit;

Dumb *see Mark 7:37.*

9:18 And wheresoever he taketh him, he teareth him: and he foameth, and gnasheth with his teeth, and pineth away: and I spake to thy disciples that they should cast him out; and they could not.

Taketh *katalambano* (2638), properly signifies "to lay hold of"; then, "to lay hold of so as to possess as one's own, to appropriate." Hence it has the same twofold meaning as the Eng. "to apprehend"; (a), "to seize upon, take possession of," (1) with a beneficial effect, as of "laying hold" of the righteousness which is of faith, Rom. 9:30 (not there a matter of attainment, as in the Eng. versions, but of appropriation); of the obtaining of a prize, 1 Cor. 9:24 (RV, "attain"); of the apostle's desire "to apprehend," or "lay hold of," that for which he was apprehended by Christ, Phil. 3:12-13; (2) with a detrimental effect, e.g., of demon power, **Mark 9:18**; of human action in seizing upon a person, John 8:3-4; metaphorically, with the added idea of overtaking, of spiritual darkness in coming upon people, John 12:35; of the Day of the Lord, in suddenly coming upon unbelievers as a thief, 1 Thess. 5:4; (b), "to lay hold of" with the mind, to understand, perceive, e.g., metaphorically, of darkness with regard to light, John 1:5, though possibly here the sense is that of (a) as in 12:35; of mental perception, Acts 4:13; 10:34; 25:25; Eph. 3:18.

Teareth *rhegnumi* (4486), "to tear, rend, break," is used of the action of a demon upon a human victim, **Mark 9:18**, "dasheth ... down," RV; (KJV, marg.; KJV, text, "teareth"); Luke 9:42, RV, "dashed ... down" (KJV, "threw ... down").

Foameth *aphrizo* (875), denotes "to foam at the mouth" **Mark 9:18, 20**.

Gnasheth *trizo* (5149), primarily used of the sounds of animals, "to chirp, cry, squeak," came to signify "to grind or gnash with the teeth," **Mark 9:18**.

Teeth *odous* (3599), is used in the sing. in Matt. 5:38 (twice); elsewhere in the plural, of "the gnashing of teeth," the gnashing being expressive of anguish and indignation, Matt. 8:12; 13:42, 50; 22:13; 24:51; 25:30; **Mark 9:18**; Luke 13:28; Acts 7:54; in Rev. 9:8, of the beings seen in a vision and described as locusts.

Pineth away *xeraino* (3583), "to dry up, wither," is rendered "pineth away" in **Mark 9:18**. *See also* Dried at *Mark 5:29.*

9:19 He answereth him, and saith, O faithless generation, how long shall I be with you? how long shall I suffer you? bring him unto me.

Faithless *apistos* (571), is used with meanings: (a) "untrustworthy," not worthy of confidence or belief, is said of things "incredible," Acts 26:8 (b) "unbelieving, distrustful," used as a noun, "unbeliever," Luke 12:46; 1 Tim. 5:8 (RV, for KJV, "infidel"); in Titus 1:15 and Rev. 21:8, "unbelieving"; "faithless" in Matt. 17:17; **Mark 9:19**; Luke 9:41; John 20:27. The word is most frequent in 1 and 2 Corinthians. (In the Sept., Prov. 17:6; 28:25; Isa. 17:10.).

Generation *genea* (1074), connected with *ginomai*, "to become," primarily signifies "a begetting, or birth"; hence, that which has been begotten, a family; or successive members of a genealogy, Matt. 1:17, or of a race of people, possessed of similar characteristics, pursuits, etc., (of a bad character) Matt. 17:17; **Mark 9:19**; Luke 9:41; 16:8; Acts 2:40; or of the whole multitude of men living at the same time, Matt. 24:34; **Mark 13:30**; Luke 1:48; 21:32; Phil. 2:15, and especially of those of the Jewish race living at the same period, Matt. 11:16, etc. Transferred from people to the time in which they lived, the word came to mean "an age," i.e., a period ordinarily occupied by each successive generation, say, of thirty or forty years, Acts 14:16; 15:21; Eph. 3:5; Col. 1:26; see also, e.g., Gen. 15:16.

9:20 And they brought him unto him: and when he saw him, straightway the spirit tare him; and he fell on the ground, and wallowed foaming.

Tare In **Mark 9:20** and Luke 9:42, the RV renders the verb *susparasso* "tare (him) grievously," the adverb bringing out the intensive force of the prefix *su-* (i.e., *sun*); the meaning may be "threw violently to the ground." *See also* Torn at *Mark 1:26*.

Wallowed *kulio* (2947), in the active voice denotes "to roll, roll along"; in the middle voice in **Mark 9:20**, rendered "wallowed."

Foaming *see* Foameth at *Mark 9:18*.

9:21 And he asked his father, How long is it ago since this came unto him? And he said, Of a child.

Long *posos* (4214), "how much," is used with *chronos*, in **Mark 9:21**, "how long time," RV (KJV, "how long ago").

Child The adverb *paidiothen*, "from (or of) a child," is found in **Mark 9:21**.

9:22 And ofttimes it hath cast him into the fire, and into the waters, to destroy him: but if thou canst do any thing, have compassion on us, and help us.

Compassion *see Mark 1:41*.

Help *boetheo* (997), "to come to the aid of anyone, to succour," is used in Matt. 15:25; **Mark 9:22, 24**; Acts 16:9; 21:28; 2 Cor. 6:2, "did I succour"; Heb. 2:18, "to succour"; Rev. 12:16.

9:23 Jesus said unto him, If thou canst believe, all things *are* possible to him that believeth.

Possible *dunatos* (1415), "strong, mighty, powerful, able (to do)," in its neuter form signifies "possible," Matt. 19:26; 24:24; 26:39; **Mark 9:23; 10:27; 13:22; 14:35, 36**; Luke 18:27; Acts 2:24; 20:16 (27:39, in some mss; *dunamai*, "to be able," in the most authentic, RV, "they could"); Rom. 12:18; Gal. 4:15.

9:24 And straightway the father of the child cried out, and said with tears, Lord, I believe; help thou mine unbelief.

Child *see* Damsel at *Mark 5:39*.

Tears *dakruon* or *dakru* (1144), akin to *dakruo*, "to weep," is used in the plural, **Mark 9:24**; Luke 7:38, 44 (with the sense of washing therewith the Lord's feet); Acts 20:19, 31; 2 Cor. 2:4; 2 Tim. 1:4; Heb. 5:7; 12:17; Rev. 7:17; 21:4.

Believe *see* Unbelief at *Mark 6:6*.

Help *see Mark 9:22*.

9:25 When Jesus saw that the people came running together, he rebuked the foul spirit, saying unto him, *Thou* dumb and deaf spirit, I charge thee, come out of him, and enter no more into him.

Running together *episuntrecho* (1998), "to run together again," occurs in **Mark 9:25**.

Rebuked *see Mark 1:25*.

Foul *akathartos* (169), denotes "unclean, impure" (*a*, negative, and *kathairo*, "to purify"), (a) ceremonially, e g., Acts 10:14, 28; (b) morally, always, in the Gospels, of unclean spirits; it is translated "foul" in the KJV of **Mark 9:25** and Rev. 18:2, but always "unclean" in the RV. Since the word primarily had a ceremonial significance, the moral significance is less prominent as applied to a spirit, than when *poneros*, "wicked," is so applied. Cf. *akatharsia*, "uncleanness."

Dumb *see Mark 7:37*.

Deaf *see Mark 7:32*.

Charge *epitasso*, "to command," is so translated in **Mark 9:25**, RV, for the KJV, "charge."

9:26 And *the spirit* cried, and rent him sore, and came out of him: and he was as one dead; insomuch that many said, He is dead.

Rent In **Mark 9:26**, KJV, *sparasso*, "to tear" (RV), is rendered "rent."

Sore In **Mark 9:26**, KJV, *polla*, "much" (RV), the neuter plur. of *polus*, used as an adverb, is translated "sore."

One In **Mark 9:26** *nekros*, "dead," is translated "one dead."

Many *polus* (4183), "much, many great," is used especially of number when its significance is "many," e.g., Matt. 8:30; 9:10; 13:17; so the RV of Matt. 12:15, where some mss. follow the word by *ochloi*, "multitudes"; 1 Cor. 12:12; Rev. 1:15; it is more frequently used as a noun, "many (persons)," e.g., Matt. 3:7; 7:22; 22:14; with the article, "the many," e.g., Matt. 24:12, RV; **Mark 9:26**, RV, "the more part" (KJV "many"); Rom. 5:15, 19 (twice), RV; 12:5; 1 Cor. 10:17; v. 33, RV; so 2 Cor. 2:17; in 1 Cor. 11:30, RV, "not a few." In Luke 12:47 it is translated "many stripes," the noun being understood.

9:27 But Jesus took him by the hand, and lifted him up; and he arose.

Took *see Mark 1:31.*

Lifted *see Mark 1:31.*

9:28-29 And when he was come into the house, his disciples asked him privately, Why could not we cast him out?

And he said unto them, This kind can come forth by nothing, but by prayer and fasting.

Kind *see* Nation at *Mark 7:26.*

Fasting *nesteia* (3521), "a fasting, fast" (from *ne*, a negative prefix, and *esthio*, "to eat"), is used (a) of voluntary abstinence from food, Luke 2:37; Acts 14:23 (some mss. have it in Matt. 17:21 and **Mark 9:29**); "fasting" had become a common practice among Jews, and was continued among Christians; in Acts 27:9, "the Fast" refers to the Day of Atonement, Lev. 16:29; that time of the year would be one of dangerous sailing; (b) of involuntary abstinence (perhaps voluntary is included), consequent upon trying circumstances, 2 Cor. 6:5; 11:27.

9:30 And they departed thence, and passed through Galilee; and he would not that any man should know *it*.

Thence *ekeithen* (1564), is used (a) of place, e.g., Matt. 4:21, "from thence"; 5.26, in Acts 20:13, "there"; often preceded by *kai*, written *kakeithen*, e.g., **Mark 9:30** and Luke 11:53 (in the best texts); Acts 7:4; 14:26; (b) of time, Acts 13:21, "and afterward."

Passed *see* Pass at *Mark 2:23.*

9:31 For he taught his disciples, and said unto them, The Son of man is delivered into the hands of men, and they shall kill him; and after that he is killed, he shall rise the third day.

Delivered *see* Put in at *Mark 1:14.*

Rise *see* Rising at *Mark 1:35.*

Third *tritos* (5154), is used (a) as a noun, e.g., Luke 20:12, 31; in Rev. 8:7-12 and 9:15, 18, "the third part," lit., "the third"; (b) as an adverb, with the article, "the third time," e.g., **Mark 14:41**; John 21:17 (twice); without the article, lit., "a third time," e.g., John 21:14; 2 Cor. 12:14; 13:1; in enumerations, in Matt. 26:44, with *ek*, "from," lit., "from the third time" (the *ek* indicates the point of departure, especially in a succession of events, cf. John 9:24; 2 Pet. 2:8); absolutely, in the accusative neuter, in 1 Cor. 12:28, "thirdly"; (c) as an adjective (its primary use), e.g., in the phrase the third heaven, 2 Cor. 12:2; in the phrase "the third hour," Matt. 20:3; **Mark 15:25**; Acts 2:15 ("... of the day"); 23:23 ("... of the night"); in a phrase with *hemera*, "a day," "on the third day" (i.e., "the next day but one"), e.g., Matt. 16:21; Luke 24:46; Acts 10:40; in this connection the idiom "three days and three nights," Matt. 12:40, is explained by ref. to 1 Sam. 30:12, 13, and Esth. 4:16 with 5:1; in **Mark 9:31** and **10:34**, the RV, "after three days," follows the texts which have this phrase, the KJV, "the third day," those which have the same phrase as in Matt. 16:21, etc.

9:32 But they understood not that saying, and were afraid to ask him.

Understood not *agnoeo* (50), signifies (a) "to be ignorant, not to know," either intransitively, 1 Cor. 14:38 (in the 2nd occurrence in this verse, the RV text translates the active voice, the margin the passive); 1 Tim. 1:13, lit., "being ignorant (I did it)"; Heb. 5:2, "ignorant"; or transitively, 2 Pet. 2:12, KJV, "understand not," RV, "are ignorant (of)"; Acts 13:27, "knew (Him) not"; 17:23, RV, "(what ye worship) in ignorance," for KJV, "(whom ye) ignorantly (worship)," lit., "(what) not knowing (ye worship)"; also rendered by the verb "to be ignorant that," or "to be ignorant of," Rom. 1:13; 10:3; 11:25; 1 Cor. 10:1; 12:1; 2 Cor. 1:8; 2:11; 1 Thess. 4:13; to know not, Rom. 2:4; 6:3; 7:1; to be unknown (passive voice), 2 Cor. 6:9; Gal. 1:22; (b) "not to understand," **Mark 9:32**; Luke 9:45.

Saying *rhema* (4487), "that which is said, a word," is rendered "saying" or "sayings" in **Mark 9:32**; Luke 1:65; 2:17, 50, 51; 7:1; 9:45 (twice); 18:34.

9:33 And he came to Capernaum: and being in the house he asked them, What was it that ye disputed among yourselves by the way?

Disputed *dialogizomai* (1260), "to bring together different reasons, to reckon them up, to reason, discuss," in **Mark 9:33** is translated "ye disputed among yourselves," KJV; RV, "were reasoning."

9:34 But they held their peace: for by the way they had disputed among themselves, who *should be* the greatest.

Peace *see* Held their peace at *Mark 3:4.*

Disputed *dialegomai* (1256), primarily signifies "to think different things with oneself, to ponder"; then, with other persons, "to converse, argue, dispute"; it is translated "to dispute" in **Mark 9:34**, the RV and KJV "had disputed" is somewhat unsuitable here, for the delinquency was not that they had wrangled, but that they had reasoned upon the subject at all; in Acts 17:17, KJV (RV, "reasoned," as in the KJV of 10:4, 19), in 19:8-9 (RV, "reasoning"); in 24:12, "disputing"; in Jude 9, "disputed."

Themselves *see Mark 8:16.*

Greatest *meizon* (3187), is sometimes translated "greatest"; besides the two cases where the RV corrects the KJV, "greatest" to "greater" (Matt. 13:32 and Luke 22:26), the RV itself has "greatest" for this comparative in the following, and relegates "greater" to the margin, Matt. 18:1, 4; 23:11; **Mark 9:34**; Luke 9:46; 22:24.

9:35 And he sat down, and called the twelve, and saith unto them, If any man desire to be first, *the same* shall be last of all, and servant of all.

Last *eschatos* (2078), "last, utmost, extreme," is used (a) of place, e.g., Luke 14:9, 10, "lowest;" Acts 1:8 and 13:47, "uttermost part;" (b) of rank, e.g., **Mark 9:35**; (c) of time, relating either to persons or things, e.g., Matt. 5:26, "the last (farthing)," RV (KJV, "uttermost"); Matt. 20:8, 12, 14; **Mark 12:6, 22**; 1 Cor. 4:9, of apostles as "last" in the program of a spectacular display; 1 Cor. 15:45, "the last Adam"; Rev. 2:19; of the "last" state of persons, Matt. 12:45, neuter plural, lit., "the last (things)"; so Luke 11:26; 2 Pet. 2:20, RV, "the last state" (KJV, "the latter end"); of Christ as the Eternal One, Rev. 1:17 (in some mss. v. 11); 2:8; 22:13; and in eschatological phrases.

Servant *diakonos* (1249), (Eng., "deacon"), primarily denotes a "servant," whether as doing servile work, or as an attendant rendering free service, without particular reference to its character. The word is probably connected with the verb *dioko*, "to hasten after, pursue" (perhaps originally said of a runner). "It occurs in the NT of domestic servants, John 2:5, 9; the civil ruler, Rom. 13:4; Christ, Rom. 15:8; Gal. 2:17; the followers of Christ in relation to their Lord, John 12:26; Eph. 6:21; Col. 1:7; 4:7; the followers of Christ in relation to one another, Matt. 20:26; 23:11, **Mark 9:35**; **10:43**; the servants of Christ in the work of preaching and teaching, 1 Cor. 3:5; 2 Cor. 3:6; 6:4; 11:23; Eph. 3:7; Col. 1:23, 25; 1 Thess. 3:2; 1 Tim. 4:6; those who serve in the churches, Rom. 16:1 (used of a woman here only in NT); Phil. 1:1; 1 Tim. 3:8, 12; false apostles, servants of Satan, 2 Cor. 11:15. Once *diakonos* is used where, apparently, angels are intended, Matt. 22:13; in v. 3, where men are intended, *doulos* is used."

9:36 And he took a child, and set him in the midst of them: and when he had taken him in his arms, he said unto them,

Set *histemi* (2476), "to cause to stand," is translated "to set" in Matt. 4:5 (aorist tense in the best texts; some have the present, as in KJV); 18:2; 25:33; **Mark 9:36**; Luke 4:9; 9:47; John 8:3; Acts 4:7; 5:27; 6:6; v. 13, "set up"; 22:30; in Jude 24, RV, "to set" (KJV, "to present").

Arms *enankalizomai*, "to take into the arms, to embrace," is used in **Mark 9:36** and **10:16**, of the tenderness of Christ towards little children.

9:37 Whosoever shall receive one of such children in my name, receiveth me: and whosoever shall receive me, receiveth not me, but him that sent me.

Receive *see Mark 6:11.*

Sent *see* Send at *Mark 5:10.*

9:38 And John answered him, saying, Master, we saw one casting out devils in thy name, and he followeth not us: and we forbad him, because he followeth not us.

Followeth *see* Follow at *Mark 8:34.*

9:39 But Jesus said, Forbid him not: for there is no man which shall do a miracle in my name, that can lightly speak evil of me.

Lightly *tachu* (5035), the neuter of *tachus*, "swift, quick," signifies "quickly," Matt. 5:25; 28:7, 8; **Mark 9:39**, RV (KJV, "lightly"); Luke 15:22; John 11:29; Rev. 2:16 (v. 5 in some mss.); 3:11; 11:14; 22:7, 12, 20.

9:40 For he that is not against us is on our part.

He that *see Mark 3:29.*

Part In **Mark 9:40**, KJV, the preposition *huper*, "on behalf of," is translated "on (our) part," RV, "for (us)."

9:41 For whosoever shall give you a cup of water to drink in my name, because ye belong to Christ, verily I say unto you, he shall not lose his reward.

Drink *potizo* (4222), "to give to drink, to make to drink," is used in the material sense, in Matt. 10:42, 25:35, 37, 42 (here of "ministering" to those who belong to Christ and thus doing so virtually to Him); 27:48; **Mark 9:41**; **15:36**; Luke 13:15 ("to watering"); Rom. 12:20; 1 Cor. 3:7-8.

Name In **Mark 9:41**, the use of the phrase *en* with the dative case of *onoma* (as in the best mss.) suggests the idea of "by reason of" or "on the ground of" (i.e., "because ye are My disciples"); 1 Pet. 4:16, RV, "in this Name" (KJV, "on this behalf"), may be taken in the same way.

Belong This word represents a phrase consisting of *eimi*, "to be," with or without a preposition and a noun, and usually best rendered, as in the RV, by the verb "to be," **Mark 9:41**, lit., "ye are of Christ"; Luke 23:7 and Heb. 5:14; cf. Rom. 12:19, "belongeth unto Me," RV.

Christ *christos* (5547), "anointed," translates, in the Sept., the word "Messiah," a term applied to the priests who were anointed with the holy oil, particularly the high priest, e.g., Lev. 4:3, 5, 16. The prophets are called *hoi christoi Theou*, "the anointed of God," Ps. 105:15. A king of Israel was described upon occasion as *christos tou Kuriou*, "the anointed of the Lord," 1 Sam. 2:10, 35; 2 Sam. 1:14; Ps. 2:2; 18:50; Hab. 3:13; the term is used even of Cyrus, Isa. 45:1. The title *ho Christos*, "the Christ," is not used of Christ in the Sept. version of the inspired books of the OT. In the NT the word is frequently used with the article, of the Lord Jesus, as an appellative rather than a title, e.g., Matt. 2:4; Acts 2:31; without the article, Luke 2:11; 23:2; John 1:41. Three times the title was expressly accepted by the Lord Himself, Matt. 16:17; **Mark 14:61-62**; John 4:26. It is added as an appellative to the proper name "Jesus," e.g., John 17:3, the only time when the Lord so spoke of Himself; Acts 9:34; 1 Cor. 3:11; 1 John 5:6. It is distinctly a proper name in many passages, whether with the article, e.g., Matt. 1:17; 11:2; Rom. 7:4, 9:5; 15:19; 1 Cor. 1:6, or without the article, **Mark 9:41**; Rom. 6:4; 8:9, 17; 1 Cor. 1:12; Gal. 2:16. The single title Christos is sometimes used without the article to signify the One who by His Holy Spirit and power indwells believers and molds their character in conformity to His likeness, Rom. 8:10; Gal. 2:20; 4:19; Eph. 3:17. As to the use or absence of the article, the title with the article specifies the Lord Jesus as "the Christ"; the title without the article stresses His character and His relationship with believers. Again, speaking generally, when the title is the subject of a sentence it has the article; when it forms part of the predicate the article is absent.

Reward *misthos* (3408), primarily "wages, hire," and then, generally, "reward," (a) received in this life, Matt. 5:46; 6:2, 5, 16; Rom. 4:4; 1 Cor. 9:17, 18; of evil "rewards," Acts 1:18; (b) to be received hereafter, Matt. 5:12; 10:41 (twice), 42; **Mark 9:41**; Luke 6:23, 35; 1 Cor. 3:8, 14; 2 John 8; Rev. 11:18; 22:12.

9:42 And whosoever shall offend one of *these* little ones that believe in me, it is better for him that a millstone were hanged about his neck, and he were cast into the sea.

Little *mikros* (3398), "little, small" (the opposite of *megos*, "great"), is used (a) of persons, with regard to (1) station, or age, in the singular, **Mark 15:40**, of James "the less" (RV marg., "little"), possibly referring to age; Luke 19:3; in the plural, "little" ones, Matt. 18:6, 10, 14; **Mark 9:42**; (2) rank or influence, e.g., Matt. 10:42; Acts 8:10; 26:22, "small," as in Rev. 11:18; 13:16; 19:5, 18; 20:12; (b) of things, with regard to (1) size, e.g., Jas. 3:5; (2) quantity, Luke 12:32; 1 Cor. 5:6; Gal. 5:9; Rev. 3:8; (3) time, John 7:33; 12:35; Rev. 6:11; 20:3.

Millstone *mulos* (3458), denotes "a handmill," consisting of two circular stones, one above the other, the lower being fixed. From the center of the lower a wooden pin passes through a hole in the upper, into which the grain is thrown, escaping as flour between the stones and falling on a prepared material below them. The handle is inserted into the upper stone near the circumference. Small stones could be turned by one woman (millgrinding was a work deemed fit only for women and slaves; cf. Judg. 16:21); larger ones were turned by two or more. Still larger ones were turned by an ass (*onikos*), Matt. 18:6, RV, "a great millstone" (marg., "a millstone turned by an ass"), indicating the immediate and overwhelming drowning of one who causes one young believer to stumble; **Mark 9:42** (where some mss. have *lithos mulikos*, "a stone of a mill," as in Luke 17:2); Rev. 18:22 (some mss. have it in v. 21).

Hanged *perikeimai* (4029), signifies "to lie round" (*peri*, "around," *keimai*, "to lie"); then, "to be hanged round," said of "a great millstone" (lit., "a millstone turned by an ass"), **Mark 9:42**, RV, and marg., to be "hung" round the neck of him who causes one of Christ's "little ones" to stumble; in Luke 17:2, "a millstone."

Neck *trachelos* (5137), is used (a) literally, Matt. 18:6; **Mark 9:42**; Luke 17:2; of "embracing," Luke 15:20; Acts 20:37; (b) metaphorically, in Acts 15:10, of "putting a yoke upon": Rom. 16:4, singular in the original, "(laid down their) neck," indicating the figurative use of the term rather than the literal. Prisca and Aquila in some way had risked their lives for the apostle (the phrase is found with this significance in the papyri).

9:43 And if thy hand offend thee, cut it off: it is better for thee to enter into life maimed, than having two hands to go into hell, into the fire that never shall be quenched:

Cut *apokopto* (609), "to cut off, or cut away," is used (a) literally, of members of the body, **Mark 9:43, 45**; John 18:10, 26; of ropes, Acts 27:32; (b) metaphorically, in the middle voice, of "cutting off oneself," to excommunicate, Gal. 5:12, of the Judaizing teachers, with a reference, no doubt, to circumcision.

Maimed *kullos* (2948), denotes "crooked crippled" (akin to *kulio*, "to roll"); in Matt. 15:30, 31, translated "maimed"; so in 18:8, KJV (RV, "halt") and **Mark 9:43** (KJV and RV).

Hell *geenna* (1067), represents the Hebrew Ge-Hinnom (the valley of Tophet) and a corresponding Aramaic word; it is found twelve times in the NT, eleven of which are in the Synoptists, in every instance as uttered by the Lord Himself. He who says to his brother, Thou fool, will be in danger of "the hell of fire," Matt. 5:22; it is better to pluck out (a metaphorical description of irrevocable law) an eye that causes its possessor to stumble, than that his "whole body be cast into hell," v. 29; similarly with the hand, v. 30; in Matt. 18:8, 9, the admonitions are repeated, with an additional mention of the foot; here, too, the warning concerns the person himself (for which obviously the "body" stands in chapt. 5); in v. 8, "the eternal fire" is mentioned as the doom, the character of the region standing for the region itself, the two being combined in the phrase "the hell of fire," v. 9. To the passage in Matt. 18, that in **Mark 9:43-47**, is parallel; here to the word "hell" are applied the extended descriptions "the unquenchable fire" and "where their worm dieth not and the fire is not quenched."

Fire *pur* (4442), is used (besides its ordinary natural significance) of the "fire" of Hell, to be endured by the ungodly hereafter, Matt. 5:22; 13:42, 50; 18:8, 9; 25:41; **Mark 9:43, 48**; Luke 3:17.

Quenched *asbestos* (762), "not quenched," is used of the doom of persons described figuratively as "chaff," Matt. 3:12 and Luke 3:17, "unquenchable"; of the fire of Gehenna, **Mark 9:43**, RV, "unquenchable fire" (in some mss. v. **45**). In the Sept., Job 20:26.

9:44 Where their worm dieth not, and the fire is not quenched.

Worm *skolex* (4663), "a worm which preys upon dead bodies," is used metaphorically by the Lord in **Mark 9:48**; in some mss. vv. **44, 46**, cf. Isa. 66:24. The statement signifies the exclusion of the hope of restoration, the punishment being eternal.

Dieth *see* Die at *Mark 7:10.*

Quenched *sbennumi* (4570), is used of "quenching" fire or things on fire, Matt. 12:20, quoted from Isa. 42:3, figurative of the condition of the feeble; Heb. 11:34; in the passive voice, Matt. 25:8, of torches, RV, "are going out," lit., "are being quenched"; of the retributive doom hereafter of sin unrepented of and unremitted in this life, **Mark 9:48** (in some mss. in vv. **44, 46**).

9:45 And if thy foot offend thee, cut it off: it is better for thee to enter halt into life, than having two feet to be cast into hell, into the fire that never shall be quenched:

Cut *see Mark 9:43.*

Halt *cholos* (5560), "lame," is translated "halt" in Matt. 18:8; **Mark 9:45**; John 5:3, in Acts 14:8, "cripple"; in Luke 14:21, KJV, "halt," RV, "lame"; elsewhere, "lame," Matt. 11:5; 15:30, 31; 21:14: Luke 7:22; 14:13; Acts 3:2; 8:7; Heb. 12:13; some mss. have it in Acts 3:11 (KJV, "the lame man"), RV, "he," translating *autou*, as in the best texts.

Quenched *see Mark 9:43.*

9:46 Where their worm dieth not, and the fire is not quenched.

Worm *see Mark 9:44.*

Dieth *see* Die at *Mark 7:10.*

Quenched *see Mark 9:44.*

9:47 And if thine eye offend thee, pluck it out: it is better for thee to enter into the kingdom of God with one eye, than having two eyes to be cast into hell fire:

Pluck In **Mark 9:47**, KJV, *ekballo*, "to cast out" (RV), is translated "pluck ... out."

With one eye *monophthalmos* (3442), "one-eyed, deprived of one eye," is used in the Lord's warning in Matt. 18:9; **Mark 9:47**.

9:48 Where their worm dieth not, and the fire is not quenched.

Worm *see Mark 9:44.*

Dieth *see* Die at *Mark 7:10.*

Fire *see Mark 9:43.*

Quenched *see Mark 9:44.*

9:49 For every one shall be salted with fire, and every sacrifice shall be salted with salt.

Every *pas* (3956), signifies with nouns without the article, "every one" of the class denoted by the noun connected with *pas*, e.g., Matt. 3:10, "every tree"; **Mark 9:49**, "every sacrifice"; see also John 2:10; Acts 2:43; Rom. 2:9; Eph. 1:21; 3:15; 2 Thess. 2:4; 2 Tim. 3:16, RV.

Salted, Salt *halas* (251), a late form of *hals* (found in some mss. in **Mark 9:49**), is used (a) literally in Matt. 5:13 (2nd part); **Mark 9:50** (1st part, twice); Luke 14:34 (twice); (b) metaphorically, of "believers," Matt. 5:13 (1st part); of their "character and condition," **Mark 9:50** (2nd part); of "wisdom" exhibited in their speech, Col. 4:6. Being possessed of purifying, perpetuating and antiseptic qualities, "salt" became emblematic of fidelity and friendship among eastern nations. To eat of a person's "salt" and so to share his hospitality is still regarded thus among the Arabs. So in Scripture, it is an emblem of the covenant between God and His people, Num. 18:19; 2 Chron. 13:5; so again when the Lord says "Have salt in yourselves, and be at peace one with another" (**Mark 9:50**). In the Lord's teaching it is also symbolic of that spiritual health and vigor essential to Christian virtue and counteractive of the corruption that is in the world, e.g., Matt. 5:13, see (b) above. Food is seasoned with "salt"; every meal offering was to contain it, and it was to be offered with all offerings presented by Israelites, as emblematic of the holiness of Christ, and as betokening the reconciliation provided for man by God on the ground of the death of Christ, Lev. 2:13. To refuse God's provision in Christ and the efficacy of His expiatory sacrifice is to expose oneself to the doom of being "salted with fire," **Mark 9:49**. While "salt" is used to fertilize soil, excess of it on the ground produces sterility (e.g., Deut. 29:23; Judg. 9:45; Jer. 17:6; Zeph. 2:9).

Sacrifice *thusia* (2378), primarily denotes "the act of offering"; then, objectively, "that which is offered" (a) of idolatrous "sacrifice," Acts 7:41; (b) of animal or other "sacrifices," as offered under the Law, Matt. 9:13; 12:7; **Mark 9:49**; **12:33**; Luke 2:24; 13:1; Acts 7:42; 1 Cor. 10:18; Heb. 5:1; 7:27 (RV, plural); 8:3; 9:9; 10:1, 5, 8 (RV, plural), 11; 11:4.

9:50 Salt *is* good: but if the salt have lost his saltness, wherewith will ye season it? Have salt in yourselves, and have peace one with another.

Salt *see* Salted, Salt at *Mark 9:49.*

Saltness *analos* (358), denotes "saltless," insipid, **Mark 9:50**, "have lost its saltness," lit., "have become (*ginomai*) saltless (*analos*)"; cf. *moraino* in Luke 14:34.

Season *artuo* (741), "to arrange, make ready" (cf. *artios*, "fitted"), is used of "seasoning," **Mark 9:50**; Luke 14:34; Col. 4:6.

Yourselves The reflexive pronoun "yourselves" represents the various plural forms of the reflexive pronoun *heautou* (frequently governed by some preposition), e.g., Matt. 3:9; 16:8; 23:31; 25:9; **Mark 9:50**; Luke 3:8; 12:33, 57; 16:9; 21:30, "of your own selves"; 21:34; Acts 5:35; in Rom. 11:25, "in your own (conceits)," lit., "in (*en;* some texts have *para*, 'among') yourselves"; so 12:16 (with *para*); 1 Pet. 4:8; Jude 20, 21; in Eph. 5:19, RV, "one to another" (KJV, and RV marg., "to yourselves").

Peace *eireneuo* (1514), primarily, "to bring to peace, reconcile," denotes in the NT, "to keep peace or to be at peace": in **Mark 9:50**, RV, the Lord bids the disciples "be at peace" with one another, gently rebuking their ambitious desires; in Rom. 12:18 (RV, "be at peace," KJV, "live peaceably") the limitation "if it be possible, as much as in you lieth," seems due to the phrase "with all men," but is not intended to excuse any evasion of the obligation imposed by the command; in 2 Cor. 13:11 it is rendered "live in peace," a general exhortation to believers; in 1 Thess. 5:13, "be at peace (among yourselves)."

Chapter 10

10:1 And he arose from thence, and cometh into the coasts of Judaea by the farther side of Jordan: and the people resort unto him again; and, as he was wont, he taught them again.

Coasts *see Mark 5:17.*

Resort *sumporeuomai* (4848), "to go together with" (*sun*, "with"), is used in **Mark 10:1**, RV, "come together" (KJV, "resort"); Luke 7:11; 14:25; 24:15.

Wont *etho* (1486), "to be accustomed," is used in the pluperfect tense (with imperfect meaning), *eiotha*, rendered "was wont" in Matt. 27:15; **Mark 10:1**.

10:2 And the Pharisees came to him, and asked him, Is it lawful for a man to put away *his* wife? tempting him.

Put *apoluo* (630), "to let loose from, let go free" (*apo*, "from," *luo*, "to loose"), is translated "is divorced" in the KJV of Matt. 5:32 (RV, "is put away"); it is further used of "divorce" in Matt. 1:19; 19:3, 7-9; **Mark 10:2, 4, 11**; Luke 16:18. The Lord also used it of the case of a wife putting away her husband, **Mark 10:12**, a usage among Greeks and Romans, not among Jews.

10:3 And he answered and said unto them, What did Moses command you?

Command *entello* (1781), signifies "to enjoin upon, to charge with"; it is used in the Middle Voice in the sense of commanding, Matt. 19:7; 28:20; **Mark 10:3**; **13:34**; John 8:5; 15:14, 17; Acts 13:47; Heb. 9:20; 11:22, "gave commandment."

10:4 And they said, Moses suffered to write a bill of divorcement, and to put *her* away.

Suffered *epitrepo* (2010), is rendered "to suffer" in KJV and RV in Matt. 8:21; **Mark 10:4**; Luke 9:59; Acts 28:16; RV only, Luke 9:61 (KJV, "let"); KJV only, Acts 21:39; in some texts, Matt. 8:31, KJV only.

Write *see* Written at *Mark 1:2*.

Bill *biblion* (975), primarily "a small book, a scroll, or any sheet on which something has been written"; hence, in connection with *apostasion*, "divorce," signifies "a bill of divorcement," Matt. 19:7 (KJV, "writing"); **Mark 10:4**.

Divorcement *apostasion* (647), primarily, "a defection," lit., "a standing off" (*apo*, "from," *stasis*, "a standing"; cf. *aphistemi*, "to cause to withdraw"), denotes, in the NT, "a writing or bill of divorcement," Matt. 5:31; 19:7; **Mark 10:4**. In Sept., Deut. 24:3; Isa. 50:1; Jer. 3:8.

Put *see Mark 10:2*.

10:5 And Jesus answered and said unto them, For the hardness of your heart he wrote you this precept.

Hardness of heart *sklerokardia* (4641), "hardness of heart" (*skleros*, "hard," and *kardia*), is used in Matt. 19:8; **Mark 10:5**; **16:14**. In the Sept., Deut. 10:16; Jer. 4:4.

Wrote *see* Written at *Mark 1:2*.

Precept *entole* (1785), "a commandment," is translated "precept" in **Mark 10:5** (RV, "commandment"); so Heb. 9:19.

10:6 But from the beginning of the creation God made them male and female.

Male *arsen* or *arren* (730), is translated "men" in Rom. 1:27 (three times); "man child" in Rev. 12:5 (v. 13 in some mss.); "male" in Matt. 19:4; **Mark 10:6**; Luke 2:23; Gal. 3:28, "(there can be no) male (and female)," RV, i.e., sex distinction does not obtain in Christ; sex is no barrier either to salvation or the development of Christian graces.

Female *thelus* (2338), an adjective (from *thele*, "a breast"), is used in the form *thelu* (grammatically neuter) as a noun, "female," in Matt. 19:4; **Mark 10:6**; Gal. 3:28; in the feminine form *theleia*, in Rom. 1:26, "women"; v. 27 "woman."

10:7 For this cause shall a man leave his father and mother, and cleave to his wife;

Leave *kataleipo* (2641), a strengthened form of *leipo*, "to leave," signifies (a) "to leave, to leave behind," e.g., Matt. 4:13; (b) "to leave remaining, reserve," e.g., Luke 10:40; (c) "to forsake," in the sense of abandoning, translated "to forsake" in the RV of Luke 5:28 and Acts 6:2; in Heb. 11:27 and 2 Pet. 2:15, KJV and RV. In this sense it is translated "to leave," in **Mark 10:7**; **14:52**; Luke 15:4; Eph. 5:31.

Cleave *proskollao* (4347), "to stick to," is used in the passive voice, reflexively, in a metaphorical sense, with the meanings (a) "to join oneself to," in Acts 5:36; (b) "to cleave to," of the husband with regard to the wife, Matt. 19:5; **Mark 10:7**; in Eph. 5:31, KJV, "shall cleave to" (KJV, "shall be joined to").

10:8 And they twain shall be one flesh: so then they are no more twain, but one flesh.

Twain, Two *duo* (1417), is rendered "twain" in Matt. 5:41; 19:5, 6; 21:31; 27:21, 51; **Mark 10:8** (twice); **15:38**; in 1 Cor. 6:16 and Eph. 5:31, RV (KJV, "two"); Eph. 2:15; in Rev. 19:20, RV (KJV, "both").

10:9 What therefore God hath joined together, let not man put asunder.

Joined *su(n)zeugnumi* (4801), "to yoke together" (*sun*, "with," *zugos*, "a yoke"), is used metaphorically of union in wedlock, in Matt. 19:6; **Mark 10:9**.

Put *chorizo* (5563), "to separate, divide" (cf. *choris*, "apart, separate from"), is translated "to put asunder" in Matt. 19:6; **Mark 10:9**, of "putting" away a wife.

10:10-11 And in the house his disciples asked him again of the same *matter*.

And he saith unto them, Whosoever shall put away his wife, and marry another, committeth adultery against her.

Put *see Mark 10:2.*

Marry *see* Married at *Mark 6:17.*

Adultery *moichao* (3429), used in the middle voice in the NT, is said of men in Matt. 5:32; 19:9; **Mark 10:11**; of women in **Mark 10:12**.

10:12 And if a woman shall put away her husband, and be married to another, she committeth adultery.

Put *see Mark 10:2.*

Husband *aner* (435), denotes, in general, "a man, an adult male" (in contrast to *anthropos*, which generically denotes "a human being, male or female"); it is used of man in various relations, the context deciding the meaning; it signifies "a husband," e.g., Matt. 1:16, 19; **Mark 10:12**; Luke 2:36; 16:18; John 4:16, 17, 18; Rom. 7:23.

Married *see Mark 6:17.*

Adultery *see Mark 10:11.*

10:13 And they brought young children to him, that he should touch them: and *his* disciples rebuked those that brought *them*.

Brought *prosphero* (4374), means (a) "to bring (in addition)," Matt. 25:20; "to bring unto," Matt. 5:23 (RV, "art offering"); **Mark 10:13**; (b) to offer, Matt. 5:24.

Young In **Mark 10:13**, KJV, *paidion*, in the neuter plural, is rendered "young (RV, 'little') children."

Rebuked *see Mark 1:25.*

10:14 But when Jesus saw *it*, he was much displeased, and said unto them, Suffer the little children to come unto me, and forbid them not: for of such is the kingdom of God.

Displeased *aganakteo* (23), from *agan*, "much," and *achomai*, "to grieve," primarily meant "to feel a violent irritation, physically"; it was used, too, of the fermenting of wine hence, metaphorically, "to show signs of grief, to be displeased, to be grieved, vexed"; it is translated "sore displeased" in Matt. 21:15, KJV; "much displeased," in **Mark 10:14, 41**; the RV always renders it "to be moved with, or to have, indignation," as the KJV elsewhere, Matt. 20:24; 26:8; **Mark 14:4**; Luke 13:14.

Suffer *see* Suffered at *Mark 1:34.*

10:15 Verily I say unto you, Whosoever shall not receive the kingdom of God as a little child, he shall not enter therein.

Receive *see Mark 6:11.*

10:16 And he took them up in his arms, put *his* hands upon them, and blessed them.

Arms *see Mark 9:36.*

Put *see Mark 4:21.*

10:17 And when he was gone forth into the way, there came one running, and kneeled to him, and asked him, Good Master, what shall I do that I may inherit eternal life?

Running *see Mark 9:15.*

Kneeled *see* Kneeling at *Mark 1:40.*

Master "The form *epistata* ... alongside of the commoner *didaskale* is ... a Greek synonym for the latter, and both are to be traced back to the Aramaic *rabbei*." Christ forbade His disciples to allow themselves to be called *rabbi*, "on the ground that He alone was their Master, Matt. 23:8. In reference to Himself the designation was expressive of the real relation between them. The form of address 'Good Master' He, however, refused to allow, **Mark 10:17, 18** ... in the mouth of the speaker it was mere insolent flattery ... the Lord was unwilling that anyone should thoughtlessly deal with such an epithet; and here, as always, the honor due to the Father was the first consideration with Him.... The primitive community never ventured to call Jesus 'Our Teacher' after He had been exalted to the Throne of God. The title *rabbi*, expressing the relation of the disciple to the teacher, vanished from use; and there remained only the designation *maran*, the servant's appropriate acknowledgement of his Lord" (Dalman).

Inherit *kleronomeo* (2816), strictly means "to receive by lot" (*kleros*, "a lot," *nemomai*, "to possess"); then, in a more general sense, "to possess oneself of, to receive as one's own, to obtain." The following list shows how in the NT the idea of inheriting broadens out to include all spiritual good provided through and in Christ, and particularly all that is contained in the hope grounded on the promises of God. The verb is used of the reward (in the coming age, **Mark 10:30**) of the acknowledgment of the paramountcy of the claims of Christ, Matt. 19:29. In the three accounts given of this incident, see **Mark 10:17-31**; Luke 18:18-30, the words of the question put to the Lord are, in Matthew, "that I may have," in Mark and Luke, "that I may inherit." In the report of the Lord's word to Peter in reply to his subsequent question, Matthew has "inherit eternal life," while Mark and Luke have "receive eternal life." It seems to follow that the meaning of the word "inherit" is here ruled by the words "receive" and "have," with which it is interchanged in each of the three Gospels, i.e., the less common word "inherit" is to be regarded as equivalent to the more common words "receive" and "have." Cf. Luke 10:25:

10:18 And Jesus said unto him, Why callest thou me good? *there is* none good but one, *that is*, God.

One *see* Only at *Mark 2:7*.

Good *agathos* (18), describes that which, being "good" in its character or constitution, is beneficial in its effect; it is used (a) of things physical, e.g., a tree, Matt. 7:17; ground, Luke 8:8; (b) in a moral sense, frequently of persons and things. God is essentially, absolutely and consummately "good," Matt. 19:17; **Mark 10:18**; Luke 18:19. To certain persons the word is applied in Matt. 20:15; 25:21, 23; Luke 19:17; 23:50; John 7:12; Acts 11:24; Titus 2:5; in a general application, Matt. 5:45; 12:35; Luke 6:45; Rom. 5:7; 1 Pet. 2:18.

10:19 Thou knowest the commandments, Do not commit adultery, Do not kill, Do not steal, Do not bear false witness, Defraud not, Honour thy father and mother.

Adultery *moicheuo* (3431), is used in Matt. 5:27-28, 32; 19:18; **Mark 10:19**; Luke 16:18; 18:20; John 8:4; Rom. 2:22; 13:9; Jas. 2:11; in Rev. 2:22, metaphorically, of those who are by a Jezebel's solicitations drawn away to idolatry.

Kill *phoneuo* (5407), "to murder," akin to *phoneus*, "a murderer," is always rendered by the verb "to kill" (except in Matt. 19:18, KJV, "do ... murder," and in Matt. 23:35, KJV and RV, "ye slew"); Matt. 5:21 (twice); 23:31; **Mark 10:19**; Luke 18:20; Rom. 13:9; Jas. 2:11 (twice); 4:2; 5:6.

Steal *klepto* (2813), "to steal," akin to *kleptes*, "a thief" (cf. Eng., "kleptomania"), occurs in Matt. 6:19, 20; 19:18; 27:64; 28:13; **Mark 10:19**; Luke 18:20; John 10:10; Rom. 2:21 (twice); 13:9; Eph. 4:28 (twice).

False witness *pseudomartureo* (5576), "to bear false witness" (*pseudes*, "false"), occurs in Matt. 19:18; **Mark 10:19**; **14:56, 57**; Luke 18:20; in some texts, Rom. 13:9.

Defraud *apostereo* (650), signifies "to rob, despoil, defraud," **Mark 10:19**; 1 Cor. 6:8; 7:5 (of that which is due to the condition of natural relationship of husband and wife); in the middle voice, "to allow oneself to be defrauded," 1 Cor. 6:7; in the passive voice, "bereft," 1 Tim. 6:5, RV, with reference to the truth, with the suggestion of being retributively "robbed" of the truth, through the corrupt condition of the mind. Some mss. have this verb in Jas. 5:4 for *aphustereo*, "to keep back by fraud." In the Sept., Exod. 21:10; in some mss, Deut. 24:14.

Honour *see* Honoureth at *Mark 7:6*.

10:20 And he answered and said unto him, Master, all these have I observed from my youth.

Observed *phulasso* (5442), denotes (a) "to guard, watch, keep watch," e.g., Luke 2:8; in the passive voice, 8:29; (b) "to keep by way of protection," e.g., Luke 11:21; John 12:25; 17:12 (2nd part); (c) metaphorically, "to keep a law precept," etc., e.g., Matt. 19:20 and Luke 18:21, "have observed"; Luke 11:28; John 12:47 (in the best mss.); Acts 7:53; 16:4; 21:24; Rom. 2:26; Gal. 6:13; 1 Tim. 5:21 ("observe"); in the middle voice, **Mark 10:20** ("have observed"); (d) in the middle voice, "to keep oneself from," Acts 21:25; elsewhere translated by the verb "to beware."

Youth *neotes* (3503), from *neos*, "new," occurs in **Mark 10:20**; Luke 18:21; Acts 26:4; 1 Tim. 4:12 (in some mss., Matt. 19:20).

10:21 Then Jesus beholding him loved him, and said unto him, One thing thou lackest: go thy way, sell whatsoever thou hast, and give to the poor, and thou shalt have treasure in heaven: and come, take up the cross, and follow me.

Beholding *see* Saw at *Mark 8:25*.

Lackest *hustereo* (5302), "to come or be behind," is used in the sense of "lacking" certain things, Matt. 19:20; **Mark 10:21** ("one thing"; in Luke 18:22); Luke 22:35; in the sense of being inferior, 1 Cor. 12:24 (middle voice). Elsewhere it is translated in various ways.

Poor *ptochos* (4434), has the broad sense of "poor," (a) literally, e.g., Matt. 11:5; 26:9, 11; Luke 21:3 (with stress on the word, "a conspicuously poor widow"); John 12:5, 6, 8; 13:29; Jas. 2:2, 3, 6; the "poor" are constantly the subjects of injunctions to assist them, Matt. 19:21; **Mark 10:21**; Luke 14:13, 21; 18:22; Rom. 15:26; Gal. 2:10; (b) metaphorically, Matt. 5:3; Luke 6:20; Rev. 3:17.

Treasure *thesauros* (2344), denotes (1) "a place of safe keeping" (possibly akin to *tithemi*, "to put"), (a) "a casket," Matt. 2:11; (b) "a storehouse," Matt. 13:52; used metaphorically of the heart, Matt. 12:35, twice (RV, "out of his treasure"); Luke 6:45; (2) "a treasure," Matt. 6:19, 20, 21; 13:44; Luke 12:33, 34; Heb. 11:26; "treasure" (in heaven or the heavens), Matt. 19:21; **Mark 10:21**; Luke 18:22; in these expressions (which are virtually equivalent to that in Matt. 6:1, "with your Father which is in Heaven") the promise does not simply refer to the present life, but looks likewise to the hereafter; in 2 Cor. 4:7 it is used of "the light of the knowledge of the glory of God in the face of Jesus Christ," descriptive of the gospel, as deposited in the earthen vessels of the persons who proclaim it (cf. v. 4); in Col. 2:3, of the wisdom and knowledge hidden in Christ.

Come *deuro*, "hither, here," is used (sometimes with verbs of motion) in the singular number, in calling a person to come, Matt. 19:21; **Mark 10:21**; Luke 18:22; John 11:43; Acts 7:3, 34; Rev. 17:1; 21:9. It has a plural, *deute*, frequent in the Gospels; elsewhere in Rev. 19:17. In the following the RV *has a different rendering:*

Follow *see Mark 8:34.*

10:22 And he was sad at that saying, and went away grieved: for he had great possessions.

Sad *stugnazo* (4768), "to have a gloomy, somber appearance" (akin to *stugnos*, "somber, gloomy," from a root *stug–*, "to hate"; cf. *stugetos*, "hateful," Titus 3:3), is said of the human countenance, **Mark 10:22**, RV, "his countenance fell" (KJV, "he was sad"); of the sky, Matt. 16:3, "lowring." In the Sept., Ezek. 27:35; 28:19; 32:10.

Saying *see Mark 7:29.*

Grieved *lupeo* (3076), denotes (a), in the active voice, "to cause pain, or grief, to distress, grieve," e.g., 2 Cor. 2:2 (twice, active and passive voices); v. 5 (twice), RV, "hath caused sorrow" (KJV, "have caused grief," and "grieved"); 7:8, "made (you) sorry"; Eph. 4:30, of grieving the Holy Spirit of God (as indwelling the believer); (b) in the passive voice, "to be grieved, to be made sorry, to be sorry, sorrowful," e.g., Matt. 14:9, RV, "(the king) was grieved" (KJV, "was sorry"); **Mark 10:22**, RV, "(went away) sorrowful" (KJV, "grieved"); John 21:17, "(Peter) was grieved", Rom. 14:15, "(if ... thy brother) is grieved"; 2 Cor. 2:4, "(not that) ye should be made sorry," RV, KJV, "ye should be grieved."

Possessions *ktema* (2933), denotes "a possession, property," Matt. 19:22; **Mark 10:22**; Acts 2:45; 5:1.

10:23 And Jesus looked round about, and saith unto his disciples, How hardly shall they that have riches enter into the kingdom of God!

Looked *see Mark 3:5.*

Hardly *duskolos* (1423), the adverbial form, is used in Matt. 19:23; **Mark 10:23**; Luke 18:24 of the danger of riches.

Riches *chrema* (5536), lit., "a thing that one uses" (akin to *chraomai* "to use"), hence, (a) "wealth, riches," **Mark 10:23, 24**; Luke 18:24; (b) "money," Acts 4:37, singular number, "a sum of money"; plural in 8:18, 20; 24:26.

10:24 And the disciples were astonished at his words. But Jesus answereth again, and saith unto them, Children, how hard is it for them that trust in riches to enter into the kingdom of God!

Astonished *see* **Amazed** at *Mark 1:27.*

Hard *duskolos* (1422), primarily means "hard to satisfy with food" (*dus*, a prefix like Eng., *un–* or *mis–*, indicating "difficulty, opposition, injuriousness," etc., the opposite of, *eu*, "well," and *kolon*, "food"); hence, "difficult," **Mark 10:24**, of the "difficulty," for those who trust in riches, to enter into the Kingdom of God.

Trust *peitho* (3982), intransitively, in the perfect and pluperfect active, "to have confidence, trust," is rendered "to trust" in Matt. 27:43; **Mark 10:24**; Luke 11:22; 18:9; 2 Cor. 1:9; 10:7; Phil, 2:24; 3:4, KJV (RV, "to have confidence"); Heb. 2:13; in the present middle, Heb. 13:18, KJV (RV, "are persuaded").

Riches *see Mark 10:23.*

10:25 It is easier for a camel to go through the eye of a needle, than for a rich man to enter into the kingdom of God.

Easier *see Mark 2:9.*

Eye *trumalia* (5168), is used of the "eye" of a needle, **Mark 10:25** (from *trume*, "a hole," *truo*, "to wear away") Cf. *trema*, "a hole, perforation," Matt. 19:24 (some texts have *trupema*, "a hole," from *trupao*, "to bore a hole") and Luke 18:25, as in the most authentic mss. (some texts have *trumalia* here).

Needle *rhaphis* (4476), from *rhapto*, "to sew," occurs in Matt. 19:24; **Mark 10:25**.

Rich man *plousios* (4145), "rich, wealthy," is used (I) literally, (a) adjectivally (with a noun expressed separately) in Matt. 27:57; Luke 12:16; 14:12; 16:1, 19; (without a noun), 18:23; 19:2; (b) as a noun, singular, a "rich" man (the noun not being expressed), Matt.

19:23, 24; **Mark 10:25**; **12:41**; Luke 16:21, 22; 18:25; Jas. 1:10, 11, "the rich," "the rich (man)"; plural, **Mark 12:41**, lit., "rich (ones)"; Luke 6:24 (ditto); 21:1; 1 Tim. 6:17, "(them that are) rich," lit., "(the) rich"; Jas. 2:6, RV, "the rich"; 5:1, RV, "ye rich"; Rev. 6:15 and 13:16, RV, "the rich"; (II) metaphorically, of God, Eph. 2:4 ("in mercy"); of Christ, 2 Cor. 8:9; of believers, Jas. 2:5, RV, "(*to be*) rich (in faith)"; Rev. 2:9, of spiritual "enrichment" generally; 3:17, of a false sense of "enrichment."

10:26 And they were astonished out of measure, saying among themselves, Who then can be saved?

Out of measure *perissos* (4057), is used in Matt. 27:23, RV, "exceedingly," for KJV, "the more"; **Mark 10:26**, RV, "exceedingly," for KJV, "out of measure"; in Acts 26:11, "exceedingly." In **Mark 15:14**, the most authentic mss. have this word (RV, "exceedingly") for *perissoteros* (KJV, "the more exceedingly")

10:27 And Jesus looking upon them saith, With men *it is* impossible, but not with God: for with God all things are possible.

Looking *emblepo* (1689), to look at, is translated "to look upon" in **Mark 10:27**; **14:67**; Luke 22:61; John 1:36. This verb implies a close, penetrating "look," as distinguished from *epiblepo* and *epeidon*.

Impossible *adunatos* (102), from *a*, negative, and *dunatos*, "able, strong," is used (a) of persons, Acts 14:8, "impotent"; figuratively, Rom. 15:1, "weak"; (b) of things, "impossible," Matt. 19:26; **Mark 10:27**; Luke 18:27; Heb. 6:4, 18; 10:4; 11:6; in Rom. 8:3, "for what the Law could not do," is, more lit., "the inability of the law"; the meaning may be either "the weakness of the Law," or "that which was impossible for the Law"; the latter is perhaps preferable; literalism is ruled out here, but the sense is that the Law could neither justify nor impart life.

Possible *see Mark 9:23*.

10:28 Then Peter began to say unto him, Lo, we have left all, and have followed thee.

Left *see* Forsook at *Mark 1:18*.

10:29 And Jesus answered and said, Verily I say unto you, There is no man that hath left house, or brethren, or sisters, or father, or mother, or wife, or children, or lands, for my sake, and the gospel's,

Left *see* Forsook at *Mark 1:18*.

Lands *agros* (68), "a field," or "piece of ground," or "the country" as distinct from the town, is translated "lands" in Matt. 19:29; **Mark 10:29**, **30**; Acts 4:37.

10:30 But he shall receive an hundredfold now in this time, houses, and brethren, and sisters, and mothers, and children, and lands, with persecutions; and in the world to come eternal life.

Receive *see Mark 4:16*.

Hundredfold *hekatontaplasion* (1542), an adjective, denotes "a hundredfold," **Mark 10:30**; Luke 8:8; the best mss. have it in Matt. 19:29 for *pollaplasion*, "many times more." See the RV margin.

Time *kairos* (2540), primarily "due measure, due proportion," when used of "time," signified "a fixed or definite period, a season," sometimes an opportune or seasonable "time," e.g., Rom. 5:6, RV, "season"; Gal. 6:10, "opportunity." In **Mark 10:30** and Luke 18:30, "this time" (*kairos*), i.e., "in this lifetime," is contrasted with "the coming age." In 1 Thess. 5:1, "the times and the seasons," "times" (*chronos*) refers to the duration of the interval previous to the Parousia of Christ and the length of "time" it will occupy, as well as other periods; "seasons" refers to the characteristics of these periods.

Lands *see Mark 10:29*.

Persecutions *see* Persecution at *Mark 4:17*.

10:31-32 But many *that are* first shall be last; and the last first.
And they were in the way going up to Jerusalem; and Jesus went before them: and they were amazed; and as they followed, they were afraid. And he took again the twelve, and began to tell them what things should happen unto him,

Amazed *see Mark 1:27*.

Took *see* Taketh at *Mark 9:2*.

Should *mello* (3195), "to be about to," e.g., **Mark 10:32**, RV, "were to"; Luke 19:11, RV, "was to"; "should" in 22:23; 24:21; John 6:71; 7:39, RV, "were to"; 11:51; 12:4, 33; 18:32; Acts 11:28; 23:27, RV, "was about (to be slain)"; 1 Thess. 3:4, RV, "are to"; Rev. 6:11.

Happen *sumbaino* (4819), lit., "to go or come together" (*sun*, "with," *baino*, "to go"), signifies "to happen together," of things or events, **Mark 10:32**; Luke 24:14; Acts 3:10; 1 Cor. 10:11; 1 Pet. 4:12; 2 Pet. 2:22; "befell" in Acts 20:19; in Acts 21:35, "so it was."

10:33 *Saying*, Behold, we go up to Jerusalem; and the Son of man shall be delivered unto the chief priests, and unto the

scribes; and they shall condemn him to death, and shall deliver him to the Gentiles:

Scribes *see Mark 1:22.*

10:34 And they shall mock him, and shall scourge him, and shall spit upon him, and shall kill him: and the third day he shall rise again.

Mock *empaizo* (1702), a compound of *paizo*, "to play like a child" (*pais*), "to sport, jest," prefixed by *en*, "in" or "at," is used only in the Synoptists, and, in every instance, of the "mockery" of Christ, except in Matt. 2:16 (there in the sense of deluding, or deceiving, of Herod by the wise men) and in Luke 14:29, of ridicule cast upon the one who after laying a foundation of a tower is unable to finish it. The word is used (a) prophetically by the Lord, of His impending sufferings, Matt. 20:19; **Mark 10:34**; Luke 18:32; (b) of the actual insults inflicted upon Him by the men who had taken Him from Gethsemane, Luke 22:63; by Herod and his soldiers, Luke 23:11; by the soldiers of the governor, Matt. 27:29, 31; **Mark 15:20**; Luke 23:36; by the chief priests, Matt. 27:41; **Mark 15:31**.

Scourge In John 19:1 the "scourging" of Christ is described by *mastigoo* (3146), as also in His prophecy of His sufferings, Matt. 20:19; **Mark 10:34**; Luke 18:33. In Acts 22:25 the similar punishment about to be administered to Paul is described by *mastizo* (3147) (the "scourging" of Roman citizens was prohibited by the Porcian law of 197 BC).

Spit *emptuo* (1716), "to spit upon," occurs in Matt. 26:67; 27:30; **Mark 10:34**; **14:65**; **15:19**; Luke 18:32. In the Sept., Num. 12:14, in some texts; Deut. 25:9.

Third *see 9:31.* In **Mark 9:31** and **10:34** the best texts have *meta treis hemeras*, "after three days," which idiomatically expresses the same thing as *te tritehemera*, "on the third day," which some texts have here, as, e.g., the phrase "the third day" in Matt. 17:23; 20:19; Luke 9:22; 18:33, where the repetition of the article lends stress to the number, lit., "the day the third"; 24:7, 46; Acts 10:40.

Rise *see* Rising at *Mark 1:35.*

10:35 And James and John, the sons of Zebedee, come unto him, saying, Master, we would that thou shouldest do for us whatsoever we shall desire.

Come *prosporeuomai* (4365), in **Mark 10:35**, is translated "come near unto."

10:36-37 And he said unto them, What would ye that I should do for you?

They said unto him, Grant unto us that we may sit, one on thy right hand, and the other on thy left hand, in thy glory.

Grant *didomi* (1325), "to give," is rendered "grant" in **Mark 10:37**; Luke 1:74; Acts 4:29; 11:18; 14:3.

Right *dexios* (1188), an adjective, used (a) of "the right" as opposite to the left, e.g., Matt. 5:29, 30; Rev. 10:5, RV, "right hand"; in connection with armor (figuratively), 2 Cor. 6:7; with *en*, followed by the dative plural, **Mark 16:5**; with *ek*, and the genitive plural, e.g., Matt. 25:33, 34; Luke 1:11; (b) of giving the "right hand" of fellowship, Gal. 2:9, betokening the public expression of approval by leaders at Jerusalem of the course pursued by Paul and Barnabas among the Gentiles; the act was often the sign of a pledge, e.g., 2 Kings 10:15; 1 Chron. 29:24, marg.; Ezra 10:19; Ezek. 17:18; figuratively, Lam. 5:6; it is often so used in the papyri; (c) metaphorically of "power" or "authority," Acts 2:33; with *ek*, signifying "on," followed by the genitive plural, Matt. 26:64; **Mark 14:62**; Heb. 1:13; (d) similarly of "a place of honor in the messianic kingdom," Matt. 20:21; **Mark 10:37**.

Left *aristeros* (710), is used (a) of the "left" hand, in Matt. 6:3, the word "hand" being understood; in connection with the armor of righteousness, in 2 Cor. 6:7, "(on the right hand and) on the left," lit., "(of the weapons ... the right and) the left"; (b) in the phrase "on the left," formed by *ex* (for *ek*), "from," and the genitive plural of this adjective, **Mark 10:37**; Luke 23:33.

10:38 But Jesus said unto them, Ye know not what ye ask: can ye drink of the cup that I drink of? and be baptized with the baptism that I am baptized with?

Drink *pino* (4095), "to drink," is used chiefly in the Gospels and in 1 Cor., whether literally (most frequently), or figuratively, (a) of "drinking" of the blood of Christ, in the sense of receiving eternal life, through His death, John 6:53-54, 56; (b) of "receiving" spiritually that which refreshes, strengthens and nourishes the soul, John 7:37; (c) of "deriving" spiritual life from Christ, John 4:14, as Israel did typically, 1 Cor. 10:4; (d) of "sharing" in the sufferings of Christ humanly inflicted, Matt. 20:22-23; **Mark 10:38-39**; (e) of "participating" in the abominations imparted by the corrupt religious and commercial systems emanating from Babylon, Rev. 18:3; (f) of "receiving" divine judgment, through partaking unworthily of the Lord's Supper, 1 Cor. 11:29; (g) of "experiencing" the wrath of God, Rev. 14:10; 16:6; (h) of the earth's "receiving" the benefits of rain, Heb. 6:7.

Cup *poterion* (4221), a diminutive of *poter*, denotes, primarily, a "drinking vessel"; hence, "a cup" (a) literal, as, e.g., in Matt. 10:42. The "cup" of blessing, 1 Cor. 10:16, is so named from the third (the fourth according to Edersheim) "cup" in the Jewish Passover feast, over which thanks and praise were given to God. This connection is not to be rejected on the ground that the church at Corinth was unfamiliar with Jewish customs. That the contrary was the case, see 5:7; (b) figurative, of one's lot or experience, joyous or sorrowful (frequent in the Psalms; cf. Ps. 116:18, "cup of salvation"); in the NT it is used most frequently of the sufferings of Christ, Matt. 20:22-23; 26:39; **Mark 10:38-39**; **14:36**; Luke 22:42; John 18:11; also of the evil deeds of Babylon, Rev. 17:4; 18:6; of divine punishments to be inflicted, Rev. 14:10; 16:19. Cf. Ps. 11:6; 75:8; Isa. 51:17; Jer. 25:15; Ezek. 23:32-34; Zech. 12:2.

Baptized, Baptism *baptisma* (908), "baptism," consisting of the processes of immersion, submersion and emergence (from *bapto*, "to dip"), is used (a) of John's "baptism," (b) of Christian "baptism"; (c) of the overwhelming afflictions and judgments to which the Lord voluntarily submitted on the cross, e.g., Luke 12:50; (d) of the sufferings His followers would experience, not of a vicarious character, but in fellowship with the sufferings of their Master. Some mss. have the word in Matt. 20:22-23; it is used in **Mark 10:38-39**, with this meaning.

10:39-40 And they said unto him, We can. And Jesus said unto them, Ye shall indeed drink of the cup that I drink of; and with the baptism that I am baptized withal shall ye be baptized:

But to sit on my right hand and on my left hand is not mine to give; but *it shall be given to them* for whom it is prepared.

My *see* ***Mark 8:38***.

Left *euonumos* (2176), lit., "of good name," or "omen" (*eu*, "well," *onoma*, "a name"), a word adopted to avoid the ill-omen attaching to the "left" (omens from the "left" being unlucky, but a good name being desired for them, cf. *aristeros*, lit., "better of two," euphemistic for the ill-omened *laios* and *skaios*; cf, too, the Eng., "sinister," from the Latin word meaning "left"), is used euphemistically, either (a) simply as an adjective in Rev. 10:2, of the "left" foot; in Acts 21:3, "on the left" (lit., "left"); or (b) with the preposition *ex* (for *ek*), signifying "on the left hand," Matt. 20:21, 23; 25:33, 41; 27:38; **Mark 10:40**; **15:27**.

10:41 And when the ten heard *it*, they began to be much displeased with James and John.

Displeased *see* ***Mark 10:14***.

10:42 But Jesus called them *to him*, and saith unto them, Ye know that they which are accounted to rule over the Gentiles exercise lordship over them; and their great ones exercise authority upon them.

Accounted *dokeo* (1380), primarily, "to be of opinion, think, suppose," also signifies "to seem, be accounted, reputed," translated "accounted" in **Mark 10:42**; Luke 22:24. It is not used ironically here, nor in Gal. 2:2, 6, 9, "those who were of repute."

Rule *archo* (756), in the active voice denotes "to rule," **Mark 10:42** and Rom. 15:12, RV, "to rule" (KJV, "to reign").

Great *see* **Exceedingly** at ***Mark 4:41***.

Exercise The following verbs contain in translation the word "exercise" but belong to other headings: *exousiazo*, "to exercise authority over," Luke 22:25 (*exousia*, "authority"); in the first part of this verse, the verb *kurieuo*, "to be lord," is translated "exercise lordship," KJV (RV, "have lordship"); *katexousiazo*, a strengthened form of the preceding (*kata*, "down," intensive), Matt. 20:25; **Mark 10:42**, "exercise authority" (in the first part of these verses the synonymous verb *katakurieuo*, is rendered "lord it," RV, for KJV, "exercise dominion," and "exercise lordship," respectively); *episkopeo*, "to look over or upon" (*epi*, "over," *skopeo*, "to look"), "to care for," 1 Pet. 5:2 (absent in some mss.), RV, "exercising the oversight," for KJV "taking, etc."

Lordship *katakurieuo* (2634), "to exercise, or gain, dominion over, to lord it over," is used of (a) the "lordship" of gentile rulers, Matt. 20:25, KJV, "exercise dominion," RV, "lord it", **Mark 10:42**, KJV, "exercise lordship," RV, "lord it"; (b) the power of demons over men, Acts 19:16, KJV, "overcame," RV, "mastered"; (c) of the evil of elders in "lording" it over the saints under their spiritual care, 1 Pet. 5:3.

Authority *katexousiazo* (2175), "to exercise authority upon," is used in Matt. 20:25, and **Mark 10:42**.

10:43 But so shall it not be among you: but whosoever will be great among you, shall be your minister:

Will *see* ***Mark 8:34***.

Minister *diakonos* (1249), "a servant, attendant, minister, deacon," is translated "minister" in **Mark 10:43**; Rom. 13:4 (twice); 15:8; 1 Cor. 3:5; 2 Cor. 3:6; 6:4; 11:15 (twice); Gal. 2:17; Eph. 6:21; Col. 1:7, 23, 25; 4:7; 1 Thess. 3:2; 1 Tim. 4:6.

10:44 And whosoever of you will be the chiefest, shall be servant of all.

Will *see Mark 8:34.*

Chiefest *see* Chief at *Mark 6:21.*

10:45 For even the Son of man came not to be ministered unto, but to minister, and to give his life a ransom for many.

Ministered *see Mark 1:13.*

Life *psuche* (5590), besides its meanings, "heart, mind, soul," denotes "life" in two chief respects, (a) "breath of life, the natural life," e.g., Matt. 2:20; 6:25; **Mark 10:45**; Luke 12:22; Acts 20:10; Rev. 8:9; 12:11 (cf. Lev. 17:11; Esth. 8:11); (b) "the seat of personality," e.g., Luke 9:24, explained in v. 25 as "own self."

Ransom *lutron* (3383), lit., "a means of loosing" (from *luo*, "to loose"), occurs frequently in the Sept., where it is always used to signify "equivalence." Thus it is used of the "ransom" for a life, e.g., Exod. 21:30, of the redemption price of a slave, e.g., Lev. 19:20, of land, 25:24, of the price of a captive, Isa. 45:13. In the NT it occurs in Matt. 20:28 and **Mark 10:45**, where it is used of Christ's gift of Himself as "a ransom for many." Some interpreters have regarded the "ransom" price as being paid to Satan; others, to an impersonal power such as death, or evil, or "that ultimate necessity which has made the whole course of things what it has been." Such ideas are largely conjectural, the result of an attempt to press the details of certain Old Testament illustrations beyond the actual statements of New Testament doctrines.

10:46 And they came to Jericho: and as he went out of Jericho with his disciples and a great number of people, blind Bartimaeus, the son of Timaeus, sat by the highway side begging.

Great *hikanos* (2425), lit., "reaching to" (from *hikano*, "to reach"), denotes "sufficient, competent, fit," and is sometimes rendered "great," e.g., of number (of people), **Mark 10:46**; of degree (of light), Acts 22:6.

Number *ochlos* (3793), "a multitude," is translated "number" in Luke 6:17, RV (KJV, "multitude"); in **Mark 10:46** and Acts 1:15 the renderings are reversed.

Highway side *hodos* (3598), "a way, path, road," is rendered "highways" in Matt. 22:10; Luke 14:23; in **Mark 10:46**, RV, "way side," KJV, "highway side"; in Matt. 22:9, the word is used with *diexodoi* ("ways out through"), and the phrase is rightly rendered in the RV, "the partings of the highways" (i.e., the crossroads), KJV, "the highways."

Begging *prosaiteo* (4319), lit., "to ask besides" (*pros*, "towards," used intensively, and *aiteo*), "to ask earnestly, to importune, continue asking," is said of the blind beggar in John 9:8. In **Mark 10:46** and Luke 18:35 certain mss. have this verb; the most authentic have *prosaites*, "a beggar," a word used in John 9:8, as well as the verb (see the RV).

10:47-48 And when he heard that it was Jesus of Nazareth, he began to cry out, and say, Jesus, *thou* Son of David, have mercy on me.

> *"The strangest truth of the Gospel is that redemption comes through suffering."*
>
> MILO L. CHAPMAN

And many charged him that he should hold his peace: but he cried the more a great deal, *Thou* Son of David, have mercy on me.

Charged *see Mark 3:12.*

Peace *see Mark 3:4.*

More *see Mark 7:36.*

Great *see Mark 7:36.*

10:49 And Jesus stood still, and commanded him to be called. And they call the blind man, saying unto him, Be of good comfort, rise; he calleth thee.

Comfort *see* Cheer at *Mark 6:50.*

10:50 And he, casting away his garment, rose, and came to Jesus.

Casting *apoballo* (577), "to throw off from, to lay aside, to cast away," Mark 10:50; Heb. 10:35.

10:51 And Jesus answered and said unto him, What wilt thou that I should do unto thee? The blind man said unto him, Lord, that I might receive my sight.

Lord *rabbounei or rabboni* (4462), was an Aramaic form of a title almost entirely applied to the president of the Sanhedrin, if such was a descendant of Hillel. It was even more respectful than Rabbi, and signified "My great master"; in its use in the NT the pronominal force of the suffix is apparently retained (contrast Rabbi above); it is found in **Mark 10:51** in the best texts, RV, "Rabboni" (KJV, "Lord"), addressed to Christ by blind Bartimaeus, and in John 20:16 by Mary Magdalene, where it is interpreted by *didaskalos*, "Master" (marg., "Teacher").

Sight *anablepo* (308), "to look up," also denotes "to receive or recover sight," e.g., Matt. 11:5; 20:34; **Mark 10:51, 52**; Luke 18:41-43; John 9:11, 15, 18 (twice); Acts 9:12, 17, 18; 22:13.

10:52 And Jesus said unto him, Go thy way; thy faith hath made thee whole. And immediately he received his sight, and followed Jesus in the way.

Sight *see 10:51.*

Chapter 11

11:1 And when they came nigh to Jerusalem, unto Bethphage and Bethany, at the mount of Olives, he sendeth forth two of his disciples,

Mount *see* Mountains at *Mark 5:5.*

Olives (Olive Berries), Olive Tree *elaia* (1636), denotes (a) "an olive tree," Rom. 11:17, 24; Rev. 11:4 (plural); the Mount of Olives was so called from the numerous olive trees there, and indicates the importance attached to such; the Mount is mentioned in the NT in connection only with the Lord's life on earth, Matt. 21:1; 24:3; 26:30; **Mark 11:1; 13:3; 14:26**; Luke 19:37; 22:39; John 8:1; (b) "an olive," Jas. 3:12, RV (KJV, "olive berries").

Sendeth *see* Send at *Mark 5:10.*

11:2 And saith unto them, Go your way into the village over against you: and as soon as ye be entered into it, ye shall find a colt tied, whereon never man sat; loose him, and bring *him*.

Over against *katenanti* (2713), lit., "down over against," is used (a) of locality, e.g., **Mark 11:2; 13:3**; Luke 19:30; (b) as "in the sight of," Rom. 4:17; in most mss. in 2 Cor. 2:17; 12:19.

Entered *see Mark 1:21.*

Tied *deo* (1210), "to bind," is rendered "to tie" in Matt. 21:2; **Mark 11:2, 4**; Luke 19:30.

Man *see Mark 3:3.*

Sat *kathizo* (2523), is used (a) transitively, "to make sit down," Acts 2:30; (b) intransitively, "to sit down," e.g., Matt. 5:1, RV, "when (He) had sat down" (KJV, "was set"); 19:28; 20:21, 23; 23:2; 25:31; 26:36; **Mark 11:2, 7; 12:41**; Luke 14:28, 31; 16:6; John 19:13; Acts 2:3 (of the tongues of fire); 8:31; 1 Cor. 10:7; 2 Thess. 2:4, "he sitteth," aorist tense, i.e., "he takes his seat" (as, e.g., in **Mark 16:19**); Rev. 3:21 (twice), RV, "to sit down" and "sat down"; 20:4.

11:3 And if any man say unto you, Why do ye this? say ye that the Lord hath need of him; and straightway he will send him hither.

Hither *hode* (5602), primarily an adverb of manner then, of place, (a) of "motion" or "direction towards a place," e.g., Matt. 8:29; **Mark 11:3**; Luke 9:41; John 6:25; (b) of "position."

11:4 And they went their way, and found the colt tied by the door without in a place where two ways met; and they loose him.

Way *aperchomai*, "to go away," is rendered "to go one's way," e.g., Matt. 13:25; 20:4; **Mark 11:4; 12:12**; Luke 19:32; John 11:46; Acts 9:17; Jas. 1:24.

Tied *see Mark 11:2.*

Place For *amphodon*, rendered "a place where two ways met," **Mark 11:4** (RV, "the open street").

Ways *amphodon* (296), properly "a way around" (*amphi*, "around," *hodos*, "a way"), occurs in **Mark 11:4**, RV, "the open street" (KJV, "where two ways met").

11:5-6 And certain of them that stood there said unto them, What do ye, loosing the colt? And they said unto them even as Jesus had commanded: and they let them go.

Even as *kathos* (2531), "according as," is frequently translated "even as," e.g., **Mark 11:6**; Luke 1:2; 1 Thess. 5:11.

Let *see Mark 7:27.*

11:7 And they brought the colt to Jesus, and cast their garments on him; and he sat upon him.

Cast *epiballo* (1911), "to cast on, or upon," is used in this sense in **Mark 11:7** and 1 Cor. 7:35.

Sat *see Mark 11:2.*

11:8 And many spread their garments in the way: and others cut down branches off the trees, and strawed *them* in the way.

Spread, Strawed *stronnumi* (4766), or *stronnuo*, "to spread," is used of "furnishing a room," **Mark 14:15**;

Luke 22:12; of "making a bed," Acts 9:34; in Matt. 21:8; **Mark 11:8**, "spread" (KJV, "strawed," twice).

Cut *kopto* (2875), denotes "to cut by a blow," e.g., branches, Matt. 21:8; **Mark 11:8**.

Branches *stoibas or stibas* (4746), from *steibo*, "to tread on," primarily denoted "a layer of leaves, reeds, twigs or straw, serving for a bed"; then "a branch full of leaves, soft foliage," which might be used in making a bed, or for treading upon, **Mark 11:8**.

11:9 And they that went before, and they that followed, cried, saying, Hosanna; Blessed *is* he that cometh in the name of the Lord:

Hosanna *hosanna* (5614), in the Hebrew, means "save, we pray." The word seems to have become an utterance of praise rather than of prayer, though originally, probably, a cry for help. The people's cry at the Lord's triumphal entry into Jerusalem (Matt. 21:9, 15; **Mark 11:9, 10**; John 12:13) was taken from Ps. 118, which was recited at the Feast of Tabernacles in the great Hallel (Psalms 113 to 118) in responses with the priest, accompanied by the waving of palm and willow branches. "The last day of the feast" was called "the great Hosanna"; the boughs also were called "hosannas."

11:10 Blessed *be* the kingdom of our father David, that cometh in the name of the Lord: Hosanna in the highest.

Hosanna *see* ***Mark 11:9***.

Highest *hupsistos* (5310), is used in the plural in the phrase "in the highest," i.e., in the "highest" regions, the abode of God, Matt. 21:9; **Mark 11:10**; Luke omits the article, Luke 2:14; 19:38; for its use as a title of God.

11:11 And Jesus entered into Jerusalem, and into the temple: and when he had looked round about upon all things, and now the eventide was come, he went out unto Bethany with the twelve.

Temple *hieron* (2411), the neuter of the adjective *hieros*, "sacred," is used as a noun denoting "a sacred place, a temple," that of Artemis (Diana), Acts 19:27; that in Jerusalem, **Mark 11:11**, signifying the entire building with its precincts, or some part thereof, as distinct from the *naos*, "the inner sanctuary"; apart from the Gospels and Acts, it is mentioned only in 1 Cor. 9:13. Christ taught in one of the courts, to which all the people had access. *Hieron* is never used figuratively. The Temple mentioned in the Gospels and Acts was begun by Herod in 20 BC, and destroyed by the Romans in AD 70.

Looked *see* ***Mark 3:5***.

Eventide *opse* (3796), "long after, late, late in the day, at evening" (in contrast to *proi*, "early," e.g., Matt. 20:1), is used practically as a noun in **Mark 11:11**, lit., "the hour being at eventide"; **11:19**; **13:35**; in Matt. 28:1 it is rendered "late on," RV, for KJV, "in the end of." Here, however, the meaning seems to be "after," a sense in which the word was used by late Greek writers. In the Sept., Gen. 24:11; Exod. 30:8; Jer. 2:23; Isa. 5:11. *See also* Even at ***Mark 1:32***.

11:12-13 And on the morrow, when they were come from Bethany, he was hungry:

And seeing a fig tree afar off having leaves, he came, if haply he might find any thing thereon: and when he came to it, he found nothing but leaves; for the time of figs was not *yet*.

Fig tree *suke or sukea* (4808), "a fig tree," is found in Matt. 21:19, 20, 21; 24:32; **Mark 11:13, 20, 21**; **13:28**; Luke 13:6, 7; 21:29; John 1:48, 50, Jas. 3:12; Rev. 6:13. A "fig tree" with leaves must have young fruits already, or it will be barren for the season. The first figs ripen in late May or early June. The tree in **Mark 11:13** should have had fruit, unripe indeed, but existing. In some lands "fig trees" bear the early fruit under the leaves and the later fruit above the leaves. In that case the leaves were a sign that there should have been fruit, unseen from a distance, underneath the leaves. The condemnation of this fig tree lay in the absence of any sign of fruit.

Leaves *phullon* (5444), "a leaf" (originally *phulion*, Lat., *folium*, Eng., "folio," "foliaceous," "foliage," "foliate," "folious," etc.), is found in Matt. 21:19; 24:32; **Mark 11:13** (twice); **13:28**; Rev. 22:2.

Time *kairos* (2540), primarily, "due measure, fitness, proportion," is used in the NT to signify "a season, a time, a period" possessed of certain characteristics, frequently rendered "time" or "times"; in the following the RV substitutes "season" for the KJV "time," thus distinguishing the meaning from *chronos*: Matt. 11:25; 12:1; 14:1; 21:34; **Mark 11:13**; Acts 3:19; 7:20; 17:26; Rom. 3:26; 5:6; 9:9; 13:11; 1 Cor. 7:5; Gal. 4:10; 1 Thess. 2:17, lit., "for a season (of an hour)", 2 Thess. 2:6; in Eph. 6:18, "at all seasons" (KJV, "always"); in Titus 1:3, "His own seasons" (marg., "its"; KJV, "in due times"); in the preceding clause *chronos* is used.

11:14 And Jesus answered and said unto it, No man eat fruit of thee hereafter for ever. And his disciples heard *it*.

Said *see* Saith at *Mark 6:50.*

Hereafter Negatively, "henceforth ... not" (or "no more") translates one or other of the negative adverbs *ouketi* and *meketi*, "no longer," e.g., Acts 4:17, KJV, and RV, "henceforth (to no man)"; in the following the RV has "no longer" for the KJV, "henceforth" (with a negative), John 15:15; Rom. 6:6; 2 Cor. 5:15; Eph. 4:17; in 2 Cor. 5:16 (last part), RV, "no more"; in Matt. 21:19 and **Mark 11:14**, "no (fruit ...) henceforward"; KJV in the latter, "hereafter."

11:15 And they come to Jerusalem: and Jesus went into the temple, and began to cast out them that sold and bought in the temple, and overthrew the tables of the moneychangers, and the seats of them that sold doves;

Overthrew *katastrepho* (2690), primarily "to turn down" or "turn over," as, e.g., the soil, denotes to "overturn, overthrow," Matt. 21:12; **Mark 11:15**; in Acts 15:16, passive voice, "ruins," lit., "the overthrown (things) of it" (some mss. have *kataskapto*, "to dig down").

Tables *trapeza* (5132), primarily "a table," denotes (a) an eating-table, e.g., Matt. 15:27; (b) food, etc. placed on "a table," Acts 6:2; 16:34; (c) "a feast, a banquet," 1 Cor. 10:21; (d) "the table or stand" of a moneychanger, where he exchanged money for a fee, or dealt with loans and deposits, Matt. 21:12; **Mark 11:15**; Luke 19:23; John 2:15. *See also* Table at *Mark 7:28.*

Moneychangers *kollubistes* (2855), from *kollubos* (lit., "clipped"), "a small coin or rate of change" (*koloboo* signifies "to cut off, to clip, shorten," Matt. 24:22), denotes "a money-changer," lit., money-clipper, Matt. 21:12; **Mark 11:15**; John 2:15.

Seats *kathedra* (2515), from *kata*, "down," and *hedra*, "a seat," denotes "a seat" (Eng., "cathedral"), "a chair," Matt. 21:12; **Mark 11:15**; of teachers, Matt. 23:2.

Doves *see* Dove at *Mark 1:10.*

11:16 And would not suffer that any man should carry *any* vessel through the temple.

Suffer *see* Suffered at *Mark 1:34.*

Carry ... through *diaphero* (1308), used (a) transitively, means "to carry through" or "about" (*dia*, "through," *phero*, "to carry"), **Mark 11:16** ("carry ... through"); Acts 13:49; 27:27 ("driven to and fro"); (b) intransitively, (1) "to differ," Rom. 2:18; Gal. 2:6; Phil. 1:10; (2) "to excel, be better," e.g., Matt. 6:26; 10:31 ("of more value"); 12:12; Luke 12:7, 24; 1 Cor. 15:41; Gal. 4:1; some would put Rom. 2:18 and Phil. 1:10 here (see marg.).

Vessel *see* Goods at *Mark 3:27.*

11:17 And he taught, saying unto them, Is it not written, My house shall be called of all nations the house of prayer? but ye have made it a den of thieves.

Den *spelaion* (4693), "a grotto, cavern, den" (Lat., *spelunca*), "cave," John 11:38, is said of the grave of Lazarus; in the RV in Heb. 11:38 and Rev. 6:15 (KJV, "dens"); in the Lord's rebuke concerning the defilement of the Temple, Matt. 21:13; **Mark 11:17**; Luke 19:46, "den" is used.

11:18 And the scribes and chief priests heard *it*, and sought how they might destroy him: for they feared him, because all the people was astonished at his doctrine.

Scribes *see Mark 1:22.*

Sought *zeteo* (2212), signifies (a) "to seek, to seek for," e.g., Matt. 7:7, 8; 13:45; Luke 24:5; John 6:24; of plotting against a person's life, Matt. 2:20; Acts 21:31; Rom. 11:3; metaphorically, to "seek" by thinking, to "seek" how to do something, or what to obtain, e.g., **Mark 11:18**; Luke 12:29; to "seek" to ascertain a meaning, John 16:19, "do ye inquire"; to "seek" God, Acts 17:27, RV; Rom. 10:20; (b) "to seek or strive after, endeavor, to desire," e.g., Matt. 12:46, 47, RV, "seeking" (KJV, "desiring"); Luke 9:9, RV, "sought" (KJV, "desired"); John 7:19, RV, "seek ye" (KJV, "go ye about"); so v. 20; Rom. 10:3, RV, "seeking" (KJV, "going about"); of "seeking" the kingdom of God and His righteousness, in the sense of coveting earnestly, striving after, Matt. 6:33; "the things that are above," Col. 3:1; peace, 1 Pet. 3:11; (c) "to require or demand," e.g., **Mark 8:12**; Luke 11:29; 1 Cor. 4:2, "it is required"; 2 Cor. 13:3, "ye seek."

11:19 And when even was come, he went out of the city.

Even *see* Eventide at *Mark 11:11.*

11:20 And in the morning, as they passed by, they saw the fig tree dried up from the roots.

In the morning *see Mark 1:35.*

Passed *see* Pass at *Mark 2:23.*

Fig tree *see Mark 11:13.*

Dried *see Mark 5:29. See also* Withered at *Mark 3:1.*

Roots *see* Root at *Mark 4:6.*

11:21 And Peter calling to remembrance saith unto him, Master, behold, the fig tree which thou cursedst is withered away.

Remembrance *anamimnesko* (363), *ana*, signifies in the active voice "to remind, call to one's mind," 1 Cor. 4:17, "put (KJV, bring) … into remembrance"; so 2 Tim. 1:6; in the passive voice, "to remember, call to (one's own) mind," **Mark 11:21**, "calling to remembrance"; **14:72**, "called to mind"; 2 Cor. 7:15, "remembereth"; Heb. 10:32, "call to remembrance."

Master *see Mark 9:5.*

Fig tree *see Mark 11:13.*

Cursedst *kataraomai* (2672), primarily signifies "to pray against, to wish evil against a person or thing"; hence "to curse," Matt. 25:41; **Mark 11:21**; Luke 6:28; Rom. 12:14; Jas. 3:9. Some mss. have it in Matt. 5:44.

11:22-23 And Jesus answering saith unto them, Have faith in God.

For verily I say unto you, That whosoever shall say unto this mountain, Be thou removed, and be thou cast into the sea; and shall not doubt in his heart, but shall believe that those things which he saith shall come to pass; he shall have whatsoever he saith.

Mountain *see* Mountains at *Mark 5:5.*

Removed In Matt. 21:21 and **Mark 11:23**, *airo*, "to lift, take up," is translated "be thou removed" (RV, "be thou taken up").

Doubt *diakrino* (1252), lit., "to separate throughout, to make a distinction," Acts 15:9, RV, is translated "to make to differ," in 1 Cor. 4:7. In Jude 22, where the middle voice is used, the KJV has "making a difference"; the RV, adopting the alternative reading, the accusative case, has "who are in doubt," a meaning found in Matt. 21:21; **Mark 11:23**; Acts 10:20; Rom. 14:23; Jas. 1:6; 2:4.

Heart *see* Hearts at *Mark 2:6.*

11:24 Therefore I say unto you, What things soever ye desire, when ye pray, believe that ye receive *them*, and ye shall have *them*.

Pray "Prayer is properly addressed to God the Father, Matt. 6:6; John 16:23; Eph. 1:17; 3:14, and the Son, Acts 7:59; 2 Cor. 12:8; but in no instance in the NT is prayer addressed to the Holy Spirit distinctively, for whereas the Father is in Heaven, Matt. 6:9, and the Son is at His right hand, Rom. 8:34, the Holy Spirit is in and with the believers, John 14:16, 17.

"Prayer is to be offered in the Name of the Lord Jesus, John 14:13, that is, the prayer must accord with His character, and must be presented in the same spirit of dependence and submission that marked Him, Matt. 11:26; Luke 22:42.

"The Holy Spirit, being the sole interpreter of the needs of the human heart, makes His intercession therein; and inasmuch as prayer is impossible to man apart from His help, Rom. 8:26, believers are exhorted to pray at all seasons in the Spirit, Eph. 6:18; cf. Jude 20, and Jas. 5:16, the last clause of which should probably be read 'the inwrought [i.e., by the Holy Spirit] supplication of righteous man availeth much' (or 'greatly prevails' *ischuo*, as in Acts 19:16, 20).

"Faith is essential to prayer, Matt. 21:22; **Mark 11:24**; Jas. 1:5-8, for faith is the recognition of, and the committal of ourselves and our matters to, the faithfulness of God."

Receive *see Mark 4:16.*

11:25 And when ye stand praying, forgive, if ye have ought against any: that your Father also which is in heaven may forgive you your trespasses.

Have *see* Next at *Mark 1:38.*

Stand *see* Standing at *Mark 3:31.*

Trespasses *paraptoma* (3900), primarily "a false step, a blunder" (akin to *parapipto*, "to fall away," Heb. 6:6), lit., "a fall beside," used ethically, denotes "a trespass," a deviation, from uprightness and truth, Matt. 6:14, 15 (twice); 18:35, in some mss.; **Mark 11:25, 26**; in Romans the RV substitutes "trespass" and "trespasses" for KJV, "offense" and "offenses," 4:25, "for (i.e., because of) our trespasses"; 5:15 (twice), where the trespass is that of Adam (in contrast to the free gift of righteousness, v. 17, a contrast in the nature and the effects); 5:16, where "of many trespasses" expresses a contrast of quantity; the condemnation resulted from one "trespass," the free gift is "of (*ek*, expressing the origin, and throwing stress upon God's justifying grace in Christ) many trespasses"; v. 17, introducing a contrast between legal effects and those of divine grace; v. 18, where the RV, "through one trespass," is contrasted with "one act of righteousness"; this is important, the difference is not between one man's "trespass" and Christ's righteousness (as KJV), but between two acts, that of Adam's "trespass" and the vicarious death of Christ; v. 20; in **2 Cor.** 5:19, KJV and RV, "trespasses"; in Eph. 1:7, RV, "trespasses" (KJV, "sins"); in 2:1, RV, "(dead through your) trespasses," KJV, "(dead in) trespasses"; 2:5, RV, "(dead through our) trespasses," KJV, "(dead in)

"The man who is truly forgiven and knows it, is a man who forgives."

MARTYN LLOYD-JONES

sins"; so Col. 2:13 (1st part); in the 2nd part, KJV and RV, "trespasses."

11:26 But if ye do not forgive, neither will your Father which is in heaven forgive your trespasses.

Trespasses *see Mark 11:25.*

11:27 And they come again to Jerusalem: and as he was walking in the temple, there come to him the chief priests, and the scribes, and the elders,

Scribes *see Mark 1:22.*

11:28-29 And say unto him, By what authority doest thou these things? and who gave thee this authority to do these things?

And Jesus answered and said unto them, I will also ask of you one question, and answer me, and I will tell you by what authority I do these things.

Question *logos* (3056), "a word," is translated "question" in Matt. 21:24 (KJV, "thing"); in **Mark 11:29** (RV, marg., "word") and Luke 20:3, KJV, "one thing:" there is no word in the original for "one," hence the RV, "a question."

Tell *eiro* (3004), is rendered "to tell" in Matt. 21:24; **Mark 11:29**; John 14:29; Rev. 17:7.

11:30-31 The baptism of John, was *it* from heaven, or of men? answer me.

And they reasoned with themselves, saying, If we shall say, From heaven; he will say, Why then did ye not believe him?

Reasoned *see* Reasoning at *Mark 2:6.*

11:32 But if we shall say, Of men; they feared the people: for all *men* counted John, that he was a prophet indeed.

Counted *echo* (2192), "to have, to hold"; then, "to hold in the mind, to regard, to count," has this significance in Matt. 14:5, "they counted Him as a prophet"; Philem. 17, "If then thou countest me a partner"; **Mark 11:32**, KJV, (RV, "hold"); Acts 20:24, KJV. *See also* **Next** at ***Mark 1:38.***

Indeed *ontos* (3689), an adverb from *on*, the present participle of *eimi*, "to be," denotes "really, actually"; it is translated "indeed" in **Mark 11:32** (RV, "verily"); Luke 24:34; John 8:36; 1 Cor. 14:25, RV (KJV "of a truth"); 1 Tim. 5:3, 5, 16; 6:15, RV, where some mss. have *aionios*, "eternal" (KJV); in Gal. 3:21, "verily."

11:33 And they answered and said unto Jesus, We cannot tell. And Jesus answering saith unto them, Neither do I tell you by what authority I do these things.

Cannot *oida* (1492), "to know by perception," is the word in Pilate's remark "make it as sure as ye can" (marg. "sure, as ye know"), Matt. 27:65. The phrases "cannot tell," "canst not tell," etc., are in the RV rendered "know not," etc., Matt. 21:27; **Mark 11:33**; Luke 20:7; John 3:8; 8:14; 16:18; 2 Cor. 12:2-3.

Tell *In* the following, *oida*, "to know," is translated "tell" in the KJV (RV, "know"), Matt. 21:27; **Mark 11:33**; Luke 20:7; John 3:8; 8:14; 16:18; 2 Cor. 12:2.

Chapter 12

12:1 And he began to speak unto them by parables. A *certain* man planted a vineyard, and set an hedge about *it*, and digged *a place for* the winefat, and built a tower, and let it out to husbandmen, and went into a far country.

Planted *phuteuo* (5452), "to plant," is used (a) literally, Matt. 21:33; **Mark 12:1**; Luke 13:6; 17:6, 28; 20:9; 1 Cor. 9:7; (b) metaphorically Matt. 15:13; 1 Cor. 3:6, 7, 8.

Set *peritithemi* (4060), "to place or put around," is translated "to set about" (of a hedge) in **Mark 12:1**.

Hedge *phragmos* (5418), denotes any sort of fence, hedge, palings or wall (akin to *phrasso*, "to fence in, stop"). It is used (a) in its literal sense, in Matt. 21:33, lit. "(he put) a hedge (around)"; **Mark 12:1**; Luke 14:23; (b) metaphorically, of the "partition" which separated Gentile from Jew, which was broken down by Christ through the efficacy of His expiatory sacrifice, Eph. 2:14.

Digged *orusso* (3736), "to dig, dig up soil, dig a pit," is said of a place for a winepress, Matt. 21:33; **Mark 12:1**; of "digging" a pit for hiding something, Matt. 25:15.

Wine-vat *hupolenion* (5276), was "a vessel" or "trough" beneath the press itself (*hupo*, "beneath," and *lenos*), for receiving the juice, **Mark 12:1**, RV, "a pit for the winepress." In the Sept., Isa. 16:10; Joel 3:13; Hag. 2:16; Zech. 14:10.

Tower *purgos* (4444), is used of "a watchtower in a vineyard," Matt. 21:33; **Mark 12:1**; probably, too, in Luke 14:28 (cf. Isa. 5:2); in Luke 13:4, of the "tower in Siloam," the modern Silwan, which is built on a steep escarpment of rock.

Let ... out *ekdidomi* (1554), primarily, "to give out, give up, surrender" (*ek*, "out, from," *didomi*, "to give"), denotes "to let out for hire"; in the NT it is used, in the middle voice, with the meaning "to let out to one's advantage," in the parable of the husbandman and his vineyard, Matt. 21:33, 41; **Mark 12:1**; Luke 20:9, KJV, "let ... forth"; RV, "let out."

Husbandmen *georgos* (1092), from *ge*, "land, ground," and *ergo* (or *erdo*), "to do" (Eng., "George"), denotes (a) "a husbandman," a tiller of the ground, 2 Tim. 2:6; Jas. 5:7; (b) "a vinedresser," Matt. 21:33-35, 38, 40, 41; **Mark 12:1, 2, 7, 9**; Luke 20:9, 10, 14, 16; John 15:1, where Christ speaks of the Father as the "Husbandman," Himself as the Vine, His disciples as the branches, the object being to bear much fruit, life in Christ producing the fruit of the Spirit, i.e., character and ways in conformity to Christ.

Far In the following the verb *apodemeo*, "to go abroad," is rendered, in the KJV, "to go into a far country," RV, "to go into another country," Matt. 21:33; 25:14; **Mark 12:1**; in Matt. 25:15, RV, "he went on his journey" (KJV, "took, etc."). In Luke 15:13 the KJV and RV have "took (his) journey into a far country"; in Luke 20:9, RV, "another country," for KJV, "a far country." The adjective *apodemos* in **Mark 13:34** is rendered in the KJV, "taking a far journey," RV, "sojourning in another country."

Country *apodemeo* (589), signifies "to go or travel into a far country," lit., "to be away from one's people" (*apo*, "from," *demos*, "a people"), Matt. 21:33; 25:14; in v. 15 the verb is translated in the RV, "went on his journey" (KJV, "took his journey"); **Mark 12:1**; Luke 20:9, "went into another country," RV. In Luke 15:13 both versions translate by "took his journey" ("into a far country" being separately expressed). Cf. *apodemos*, lit., "away from one's own people, gone abroad," **Mark 13:34**.

12:2 And at the season he sent to the husbandmen a servant, that he might receive from the husbandmen of the fruit of the vineyard.

Husbandmen *see Mark 12:1.*

12:3 And they caught *him*, and beat him, and sent *him* away empty.

Caught *lambano* (2983), "to receive," is once used of "catching" by fraud, circumventing, 2 Cor. 12:16. In Matt. 21:39 and **Mark 12:3**, RV "took," for KJV "caught."

Beat *dero* (1194), from a root *der—*, "skin" (*derma*, "a skin," cf. Eng., "dermatology"), primarily "to flay," then "to beat, thrash or smite," is used of the treatment of the servants of the owner of the vineyard by the husbandmen, in the parable in Matt. 21:35; **Mark 12:3, 5**; Luke 20:10-11; of the treatment of Christ, Luke 22:63, RV, "beat," for KJV, "smote"; John 18:23; of the followers of Christ, in the synagogues, **Mark 13:9**; Acts 22:19; of the punishment of unfaithful servants, Luke 12:47-48; of the "beating" of apostles by the High Priest and the Council of the Sanhedrin, Acts 5:40; by magistrates, 16:37. The significance of flogging does not always attach to the word; it is used of the infliction of a single blow, John 18:23; 2 Cor. 11:20, and of "beating" the air, 1 Cor. 9:26. The usual meaning is that of "thrashing or cudgelling," and when used of a blow it indicates one of great violence.

Sent *see* Send at *Mark 5:10.*

Empty *kenos* (2756), expresses the "hollowness" of anything, the "absence" of that which otherwise might be possessed. It is used literally, **Mark 12:3**; Luke 1:53; 20:10-11.

12:4 And again he sent unto them another servant; and at him they cast stones, and wounded *him* in the head, and sent *him* away shamefully handled.

Shamefully *atimazo* (818), signifies "to dishonor, treat shamefully, insult," whether in word, John 8:49, or deed, **Mark 12:4**; Luke 20:11, RV "handled (him) shamefully," (RV "entreated ... shamefully"); Rom. 1:24; 2:23, "dishonorest;" Jas. 2:6, RV, "ye have dishonored (the poor)," (KJV, "despised"); in the passive voice, to suffer dishonor, Acts 5:41 (KJV, "suffer shame"). *atimao* is found in some mss. in **Mark 12:4**.

Handled *atimazo* (818), "to dishonor, insult," is rendered "handled shamefully" in **Mark 12:4**. Some mss. have the alternative verb *atimao*.

Wounded ... in the head *kephalioo, or kephalioo* (2775), from *kephalion*, a diminutive of *kephale*, usually meant "to sum up, to bring under heads"; in **Mark 12:4** it is used for "wounding on the head," the only place where it has this meaning.

12:5 And again he sent another; and him they killed, and many others; beating some, and killing some.

Beating *see* Beat at *Mark 12:3.*

12:6 Having yet therefore one son, his wellbeloved, he sent him also last unto them, saying, They will reverence my son.

Sent *see* Send at *Mark 5:10.*

Last *see Mark 9:35.*

Reverence *entrepo* (1788), lit., "to turn in" (i.e., upon oneself), "to put to shame," denotes, when used in the passive voice, "to feel respect for, to show deference to, to reverence," Matt. 21:37; **Mark 12:6**; Luke 20:13; Heb. 12:9.

12:7 But those husbandmen said among themselves, This is the heir; come, let us kill him, and the inheritance shall be ours.

Husbandmen *see Mark 12:1.*

Heir *kleronomos* (2818), lit. denotes "one who obtains a lot or portion (*kleros*, "a lot," *nemomai*, "to possess"), especially of an inheritance. The NT usage may be analyzed as under: "(a) the person to whom property is to pass on the death of the owner, Matt. 21:38; **Mark 12:7**; Luke 20:14; Gal. 4:1; (b) one to whom something has been assigned by God, on possession of which, however, he has not yet entered, as Abraham, Rom. 4:13, 14; Heb. 6:17; Christ, Heb. 1:2; the poor saints, Jas. 2:5; (c) believers, inasmuch as they share in the new order of things to be ushered in at the return of Christ, Rom. 8:17; Gal. 3:29; 4:7; Titus 3:7; (d) one who receives something other than by merit, as Noah, Heb. 11:7."

Inheritance *kleronomia* (2817), "a lot," properly "an inherited property, an inheritance." "It is always rendered inheritance in NT, but only in a few cases in the Gospels has it the meaning ordinarily attached to that word in English, i.e., that into possession of which the heir enters only on the death of an ancestor. The NT usage may be set out as follows: (a) that property in real estate which in ordinary course passes from father to son on the death of the former, Matt. 21:38; **Mark 12:7**; Luke 12:13; 20:14; (b) a portion of an estate made the substance of a gift, Acts 7:5; Gal. 3:18, which also is to be included under (c); (c) the prospective condition and possessions of the believer in the new order of things to be ushered in at the return of Christ, Acts 20:32; Eph. 1:14; 5:5; Col. 3:24; Heb. 9:15; 1 Pet. 1:4; (d) what the believer will be to God in that age, Eph. 1:18."

Ours This usually translates *hemon*, the genitive of *hemeis*, "we," lit., "of us," e.g., Matt. 6:9, 11-12. It is translated "ours," e.g., in **Mark 12:7**; Luke 20:14; 1 Cor. 1:2; 2 Cor. 1:14.

12:8-9 And they took him, and killed *him*, and cast *him* out of the vineyard.

What shall therefore the lord of the vineyard do? he will come and destroy the husbandmen, and will give the vineyard unto others.

Husbandmen *see Mark 12:1.*

12:10 And have ye not read this scripture; The stone which the builders rejected is become the head of the corner:

Scripture *graphe* (1124), akin to *grapho*, "to write" (Eng., "graph," "graphic," etc.), primarily denotes "a drawing, painting"; then "a writing," (a) of the OT Scriptures, (1) in the plural, the whole, e.g., Matt. 21:42; 22:29; John 5:39; Acts 17:11; 18:24; Rom. 1:2, where "the prophets" comprises the OT writers in general; 15:4; 16:26, lit., "prophetic writings," expressing the character of all the Scriptures; (2) in the singular in reference to a particular passage, e.g., **Mark 12:10**; Luke 4:21; John 2:22; 10:35 (though applicable to all); 19:24, 28, 36, 37; 20:9; Acts 1:16; 8:32, 35; Rom. 4:3; 9:17; 10:11; 11:2; Gal. 3:8, 22; 4:30; 1 Tim. 5:18, where the 2nd quotation is from Luke 10:7, from which it may be inferred that the apostle included Luke's Gospel as "Scripture" alike with Deuteronomy, from which the first quotation is taken; in reference to the whole, e.g., Jas. 4:5 (see RV, a separate rhetorical question from the one which follows); in 2 Pet. 1:20, "no prophecy of Scripture," a description of all, with special application to the OT in the next verse; (b) of the OT Scriptures (those accepted by the Jews as canonical) and all those of the NT which were to be accepted by Christians as authoritative, 2 Tim. 3:16; these latter were to be discriminated from the many forged epistles and other religious "writings" already produced and circulated in Timothy's time. Such discrimination would be directed by the fact that "every Scripture," characterized by inspiration of God, would be profitable for the purposes mentioned; so the RV. The KJV states truth concerning the completed canon of Scripture, but that was not complete when the apostle wrote to Timothy.

Builders *oikodomeo* (3618), lit., "to build a house," usually signifies "to build," whether literally, or figuratively; the present participle, lit., "the (ones) building," is used as a noun, "the builders," in Matt. 21:42; **Mark 12:10**; Luke 20:17; Acts 4:11 (in some mss.; the most authentic have the noun *oikodomos;*) 1 Pet. 2:7.

Rejected *see Mark 8:31.*

Corner *gonia* (1137), "an angle" (Eng., "coign"), signifies (a) "an external angle," as of the "corner" of a street,

Matt. 6:5; or of a building, 21:42; **Mark 12:10**; Luke 20:17; Acts 4:11; 1 Pet. 2:7, "the corner stone or headstone of the corner"; or the four extreme limits of the earth, Rev. 7:1; 20:8; (b) "an internal corner," a secret place, Acts 26:26.

12:11 This was the Lord's doing, and it is marvellous in our eyes?

Doing *ginomai* (1096), "to become," is sometimes translated "do" or "done," e.g., Luke 4:23, "done (at Capernaum)," followed by *poieo* in the next clause. In Matt. 21:42 and **Mark 12:11**, this verb is translated, in the KJV, "(the Lord's) doing"; RV, "this was from the Lord."

Marvellous *thaumastos* (2298), "marvelous," is said (a) of the Lord's doing in making the rejected Stone the Head of the corner, Matt. 21:42; **Mark 12:11**; (b) of the erstwhile blind man's astonishment that the Pharisees knew not from whence Christ had come, and yet He had given him sight, John 9:30, RV, "the marvel," KJV, "a marvelous thing"; (c) of the spiritual light into which believers are brought, 1 Pet. 2:9; (d) of the vision of the seven angels having the seven last plagues, Rev. 15:1; (e) of the works of God, 15:3.

12:12 And they sought to lay hold on him, but feared the people: for they knew that he had spoken the parable against them: and they left him, and went their way.

Hold *see Mark 3:21.*

But *kai*: Occasionally *kai* tends towards an *adversative* meaning, expressing a contrast, "yet," almost the equivalent of *alla,* "but"; see, e.g., **Mark 12:12**, "yet they feared"; Luke 20:19; John 18:28, "yet they themselves entered not." Some take it in this sense in Rom. 1:13, where, however, it may be simply parenthetic. Sometimes in the English versions the "yet" has been added in italics, as in 2 Cor. 6:8, 9, 10.

Left *see* **Forsook** at *Mark 1:18.*

Way *see Mark 11:4.*

12:13 And they send unto him certain of the Pharisees and of the Herodians, to catch him in *his* words.

Catch *agreuo* (4), "to take by hunting" (from *agra,* "a hunt, a catch"), is used metaphorically, of the Pharisees and Herodians in seeking to catch Christ in His talk, **Mark 12:13**.

Words *logos* (3056), a word, is translated "talk" in Matt. 22:15; **Mark 12:13**.

12:14 And when they were come, they say unto him, Master, we know that thou art true, and carest for no man: for thou regardest not the person of men, but teachest the way of God in truth: Is it lawful to give tribute to Caesar, or not?

True *alethes* (227), primarily, "unconcealed, manifest" (*a,* negative, *letho,* "to forget," = *lanthano,* "to escape notice"), hence, actual, "true to fact," is used (a) of persons, "truthful," Matt. 22:16; **Mark 12:14**; John 3:33; 7:18; 8:26; Rom. 3:4; 2 Cor. 6:8; (b) of things, "true," conforming to reality, John 4:18, "truly," lit., "true"; 5:31, 32; in the best texts, 6:55 (twice), "indeed"; 8:13, 14 (v. 16 in some texts), 17; 10:41; 19:35; 21:24; Acts 12:9; Phil. 4:8; Titus 1:13; 1 Pet. 5:12; 2 Pet. 2:22; 1 John 2:8, 27; 3 John 12.

Carest *see Mark 4:38.*

Regardest *blepo* (991), "to behold, look, perceive, see," has the sense of "regarding" by way of partiality, in Matt. 22:16 and **Mark 12:14**.

Person *prosopon* (4383), is translated "person" or "persons" in Matt. 22:16; **Mark 12:14**; Luke 20:21; 2 Cor. 1:11; 2 Cor. 2:10; Gal. 2:6; Jude 16, lit., "(admiring, or showing respect of) persons," RV.

Truth *aletheia* (225), "truth," is used (a) objectively, signifying "the reality lying at the basis of an appearance; the manifested, veritable essence of a matter" (Cremer), e.g., Rom. 9:1; 2 Cor. 11:10; especially of Christian doctrine, e.g., Gal. 2:5, where "the truth of the Gospel" denotes the "true" teaching of the Gospel, in contrast to perversions of it; Rom. 1:25, where "the truth of God" may be "the truth concerning God" or "God whose existence is a verity"; but in Rom. 15:8 "the truth of God" is indicative of His faithfulness in the fulfillment of His promises as exhibited in Christ; the word has an absolute force in John 14:6; 17:17; 18:37, 38; in Eph. 4:21, where the RV, "even as truth is in Jesus," gives the correct rendering, the meaning is not merely ethical "truth," but "truth" in all its fullness and scope, as embodied in Him; He was the perfect expression of the truth; this is virtually equivalent to His statement in John 14:6; (b) subjectively, "truthfulness," "truth," not merely verbal, but sincerity and integrity of character, John 8:44; 3 John 3, RV; (c) in phrases, e.g., "in truth" (*epi,* "on the basis of"), **Mark 12:14**; Luke 20:21; with *en,* "in," 2 Cor. 6:7; Col. 1:6; 1 Tim. 2:7, RV (KJV, "in … verity"), 1 John 3:18; 2 John 1, 3, 4.

Tribute *kensos* (2778), Lat. and Eng., "census," denotes "a poll tax," Matt. 17:25; 22:17, 19; **Mark 12:14**.

12:15 Shall we give, or shall we not give? But he, knowing their hypocrisy, said unto them, Why tempt ye me? bring me a penny, that I may see *it*.

Hypocrisy *hupokrisis* (5272), primarily denotes "a reply, an answer" (akin to *hupokrinomai*, "to answer"); then, "play-acting," as the actors spoke in dialogue; hence, "pretence, hypocrisy"; it is translated "hypocrisy" in Matt. 23:28; **Mark 12:15**; Luke 12:1; 1 Tim. 4:2; the plural in 1 Pet. 2:1. For Gal. 2:13 and *anupokritos*, "without hypocrisy," in Jas. 3:17.

Penny *see* Pennyworth at *Mark 6:37*.

12:16 And they brought *it*. And he saith unto them, Whose *is* this image and superscription? And they said unto him, Caesar's.

Image *eikon* (1504), denotes "an image"; the word involves the two ideas of representation and manifestation. "The idea of perfection does not lie in the word itself, but must be sought from the context" (Lightfoot); the following instances clearly show any distinction between the imperfect and the perfect likeness. The word is used of an "image" or a coin (not a mere likeness), Matt. 22:20; **Mark 12:16**; Luke 20:24; so of a statue or similar representation (more than a resemblance), Rom. 1:23; Rev. 13:14, 15 (thrice); 14:9, 11; 15:2; 16:2; 19:20; 20:4; of the descendants of Adam as bearing his image, 1 Cor. 15:49, each a representation derived from the prototype. As to synonymous words, *homoioma*, "likeness," stresses the resemblance to an archetype, though the resemblance may not be derived, whereas *eikon* is a "derived likeness"; *eidos*, "a shape, form," is an appearance, "not necessarily based on reality"; *skia*, is "a shadowed resemblance"; *morphe* is "the form, as indicative of the inner being" (Abbott-Smith).

Superscription *epigraphe* (1923), lit., "an overwriting" (*epi*, "over," *grapho*, "to write") (the meaning of the anglicized Latin word "superscription"), denotes "an inscription, a title." On Roman coins the emperor's name was inscribed, Matt. 22:20; **Mark 12:16**; Luke 20:24. In the Roman Empire, in the case of a criminal on his way to execution, a board on which was inscribed the cause of his condemnation, was carried before him or hung round his neck; the inscription was termed a "title" (*titlos*). The four Evangelists state that at the crucifixion of Christ the title was affixed to the cross, Mark (**15:26**), and Luke (23:38), call it a "superscription"; Mark says it was "written over" (*epigrapho*, the corresponding verb). Matthew calls it "His accusation"; John calls it "a title" (a technical term). The wording varies: the essential words are the same, and the variation serves to authenticate the narratives, showing that there was no consultation leading to an agreement as to the details.

12:17 And Jesus answering said unto them, Render to Caesar the things that are Caesar's, and to God the things that are God's. And they marvelled at him.

Render *apodidomi* (591), "to give up or back," is translated "to render," (a) of righteous acts, (1) human, Matt. 21:41; 22:21; **Mark 12:17**; Luke 16:2, RV (KJV, "give"); Luke 20:25; Rom. 13:7, 1 Cor. 7:3; (2) divine, Matt. 16:27, RV, "shall render" (KJV, "shall reward"), an important RV change; Rom. 2:6; 2 Tim. 4:14, RV (KJV, "reward"); Rev. 18:6 (ditto); 22:12, RV (KJV, "give"); (b) of unrighteous acts, Rom. 12:17, RV (KJV, "recompense"); 1 Thess. 5:15; 1 Pet. 3:9.

God *see Mark 8:33*.

Marvelled *ekthaumazo* (1537), is found in the best mss. in **Mark 12:17**, RV, "wondered greatly."

12:18 Then come unto him the Sadducees, which say there is no resurrection; and they asked him, saying,

Resurrection *anastasis* (386), denotes (I) "a raising up," or "rising" (*ana*, "up," and *histemi*, "to cause to stand"), Luke 2:34, "the rising up"; the KJV "again" obscures the meaning; the Child would be like a stone against which many in Israel would stumble while many others would find in its strength and firmness a means of their salvation and spiritual life; (II) of "resurrection" from the dead, (a) of Christ, Acts 1:22; 2:31; 4:33; Rom. 1:4; 6:5; Phil. 3:10; 1 Pet. 1:3; 3:21; by metonymy, of Christ as the Author of "resurrection," John 11:25; (b) of those who are Christ's at His Parousia, Luke 14:14, "the resurrection of the just"; Luke 20:33, 35, 36; John 5:29 (1st part), "the resurrection of life"; 11:24; Acts 23:6; 24:15 (1st part); 1 Cor. 15:21, 42; 2 Tim. 2:18; Heb. 11:35 (2nd part); Rev. 20:5, "the first resurrection"; hence the insertion of "is" stands for the completion of this "resurrection," of which Christ was "the firstfruits"; 20:6; (c) of "the rest of the dead," after the Millennium (cf. Rev. 20:5); John 5:29 (2nd part), "the resurrection of judgment"; Acts 24:15 (2nd part), "of the unjust"; (d) of those who were raised in more immediate connection with Christ's "resurrection," and thus had part already in the first "resurrection," Acts 26:23 and Rom. 1:4 (in each of which "dead" is plural; see Matt. 27:52); (e) of the "resurrection" spoken of in general terms, Matt. 22:23; **Mark 12:18**; Luke 20:27; Acts 4:2; 17:18; 23:8;

24:21; 1 Cor. 15:12, 13; Heb. 6:2; (f) of those who were raised in OT times, to die again, Heb. 11:35 (1st part), lit., "out of resurrection."

12:19 Master, Moses wrote unto us, If a man's brother die, and leave *his* wife *behind him*, and leave no children, that his brother should take his wife, and raise up seed unto his brother.

Man *see Mark 8:4.*

Leave *see* Forsook at *Mark 1:18.*

Raise *exanistemi* (1817), is used of "raising" up seed, **Mark 12:19**; Luke 20:28; elsewhere, Acts 15:5, "to rise up."

12:20 Now there were seven brethren: and the first took a wife, and dying left no seed.

Now *oun* (3767), "therefore, so then," is sometimes used in continuing a narrative, e.g., Acts 1:18; 1 Cor. 9:25; or resuming it after a digression, usually rendered "therefore," e.g., Acts 11:19; 25:1, RV (KJV, "now"). In the following it is absent from the best mss., **Mark 12:20**; Luke 10:36; John 16:19; 18:24; 19:29.

12:21-22 And the second took her, and died, neither left he any seed: and the third likewise.
And the seven had her, and left no seed: last of all the woman died also.

Had In **Mark 12:22**, in some mss., *lambano*, "to take" or "receive," is translated "had," in the statement "the seven had her"; in Acts 25:16, RV, "have had" (KJV, "have"); in Heb. 11:36, "had."

Last *see Mark 9:35.*

12:23-24 In the resurrection therefore, when they shall rise, whose wife shall she be of them? for the seven had her to wife.
And Jesus answering said unto them, Do ye not therefore err, because ye know not the scriptures, neither the power of God?

Err *planao* (4105), in the active voice, signifies "to cause to wander, lead astray, deceive" (*plane*, "a wandering"; cf. Eng., "planet"); in the passive voice, "to be led astray, to err." It is translated "err," in Matt. 22:29; **Mark 12:24, 27**; Heb. 3:10; Jas. 1:16 (KJV, "do not err," RV, "be not deceived"); 5:19.

12:25 For when they shall rise from the dead, they neither marry, nor are given in marriage; but are as the angels which are in heaven.

Marry *see* Married at *Mark 6:17.*

Marriage *gamizo* (1061), "to give in marriage," is used in the passive voice in Matt. 22:30 (2nd clause), some mss. have *ekgamizo* here; **Mark 12:25** (*gamisko* in some mss.); Luke 17:27 (*ekgamizo* in some mss.); 20:35 (last word), passive (*gamisko* and *ekgamisko* in some mss.); in the active voice Matt. 24:38 (*gamisko* and *ekgamizo* in some mss.); further, of giving a daughter in "marriage," 1 Cor. 7:38 (twice), RV (*ekgamizo* in some mss.), which, on the whole, may be taken as the meaning. In this part of the Epistle, the apostle was answering a number of questions on matters about which the church at Corinth had written to him, and in this particular matter the formal transition from "marriage" in general to the subject of giving a daughter in "marriage," is simple. Eastern customs naturally would involve the inclusion of the latter in the inquiry and the reply.

Angels *see Mark 8:38.*

12:26 And as touching the dead, that they rise: have ye not read in the book of Moses, how in the bush God spake unto him, saying, I *am* the God of Abraham, and the God of Isaac, and the God of Jacob?

Rise *see* Lifted at *Mark 1:31.*

Book *biblos* (976), (Eng. "Bible") was the inner part, or rather the cellular substance, of the stem of the papyrus (Eng. "paper"). It came to denote the paper made from this bark in Egypt, and then a written "book," roll, or volume. It is used in referring to "books" of Scripture, the "book," or scroll, of Matthew's Gospel, Matt. 1:1; the Pentateuch, as the "book" of Moses, **Mark 12:26**; Isaiah, as "the book of the words of Isaiah," Luke 3:4; the Psalms, Luke 20:42 and Acts 1:20; "the prophets," Acts 7:42; to "the Book of Life," Phil. 4:3; Rev. 3:5; 20:15. Once only it is used of secular writings, Acts 19:19.

Bush *batos* (942), denotes "a bramble bush," as in Luke 6:44. In **Mark 12:26** and Luke 20:37 the phrase "in the place concerning the Bush" signifies in that part of the book of Exodus concerning it. See also Acts 7:30, 35.

12:27 He is not the God of the dead, but the God of the living: ye therefore do greatly err.

Greatly *see* Much at *Mark 1:45.*

Err *see Mark 12:24.*

12:28 And one of the scribes came, and having heard them reasoning together, and perceiving that he had answered them well, asked him, Which is the first commandment of all?

Perceiving In **Mark 12:28** the best mss. have *oida*, "to know" (so RV), for *eidon*, "to see, perceive" (KJV).

Asked *see* Questioned at *Mark 1:27*.

12:29 And Jesus answered him, The first of all the commandments *is*, Hear, O Israel; The Lord our God is one Lord:

God *see Mark 8:33*.

12:30 And thou shalt love the Lord thy God with all thy heart, and with all thy soul, and with all thy mind, and with all thy strength: this *is* the first commandment.

Mind *dianoia* (1271), lit. "a thinking through, or over, a meditation, reflecting," signifies (a) "the faculty of knowing, understanding, or moral reflection," (1) with an evil significance, a consciousness characterized by a perverted moral impulse, Eph. 2:3 (plural); 4:18; (2) with a good significance, the faculty renewed by the Holy Spirit, Matt. 22:37; **Mark 12:30**; Luke 10:27; Heb. 8:10; 10:16; 1 Pet. 1:13; 1 John 5:20; (b) "sentiment, disposition" (not as a function but as a product); (1) in an evil sense, Luke 1:51, "imagination"; Col. 1:21; (2) in a good sense, 2 Pet. 3:1.

Strength *ischus* (2479), denotes "might, strength, power," (a) inherent and in action as used of God, Eph. 1:19, RV, "(the strength, *kratos*, of His) might," KJV, "(His mighty) power," i.e., power (over external things) exercised by strength; Eph. 6:10, "of His might"; 2 Thess. 1:9, RV, "(from the glory) of His might" (KJV "power"); Rev. 5:12, RV, "might" (KJV, "strength"); 7:12, "might"; (b) as an endowment, said (1) of angels, 2 Pet. 2:11; here the order is RV "might and power," which better expresses the distinction than the KJV, "power and might"; in some mss. in Rev. 18:2 it is said of the voice of an angel; the most authentic mss. have the adjective *ischuros*, "mighty"; (2) of men, **Mark 12:30, 33**; Luke 10:27 (RV and KJV, "strength," in all three verses); 1 Pet. 4:11, RV, "strength" (KJV, "ability"). Either "strength" or "might" expresses the true significance of *ischus*.

12:31 And the second *is* like, *namely* this, Thou shalt love thy neighbour as thyself. There is none other commandment greater than these.

Neighbour *plesion* (4139), the neuter of the adjective *plesios* (from *pelas*, "near"), is used as an adverb accompanied by the article, lit., "the (one) near"; hence, one's "neighbor." There were no farmhouses scattered over the agricultural areas of Palestine; the populations, gathered in villages, went to and fro to their toil. Hence domestic life was touched at every point by a wide circle of neighborhood. The terms for neighbor were therefore of a very comprehensive scope. This may be seen from the chief characteristics of the privileges and duties of neighborhood as set forth in Scripture, (a) its helpfulness, e.g., Prov. 27:10; Luke 10:36; (b) its intimacy, e.g., Luke 15:6, 9; Heb. 8:11; (c) its sincerity and sanctity, e.g., Ex. 22:7, 10; Prov. 3:29; 14:21; Rom. 13:10; 15:2; Eph. 4:25; Jas. 4:12. The NT quotes and expands the command in Lev. 19:18, "to love one's neighbor as oneself"; see, e.g., Matt. 5:43; 19:19; 22:39; **Mark 12:31, 33**; Luke 10:27; Gal. 5:14; Jas. 2:8. See also Acts 7:27.

12:32 And the scribe said unto him, Well, Master, thou hast said the truth: for there is one God; and there is none other but he:

Well *kalos* (2573), "finely" (akin to *kalos*, "good, fair"), is usually translated "well," indicating what is done rightly, in the Epistles it is most frequent in 1 Tim. (3:4, 12, 13; 5:17); twice it is used as an exclamation of approval, **Mark 12:32**; Rom. 11:20; the comparative degree *kallion*, "very well," occurs in Acts 25:10.

But *plen* (4133), an adverb, most frequently signifying "yet, howbeit," or "only," sometimes has the meaning "except (that)," "save (that)," Acts 20:23; Phil. 1:18, RV, "only that," for KJV, "notwithstanding." It is also used as a preposition, signifying "except, save," **Mark 12:32**, "but"; John 8:10, "but" (KJV only); Acts 8:1, "except"; Acts 15:28, "than"; 27:22, "but (only)."

12:33 And to love him with all the heart, and with all the understanding, and with all the soul, and with all the strength, and to love *his* neighbour as himself, is more than all whole burnt offerings and sacrifices.

Understanding *sunesis* (4907), akin to *suniemi*, "to set together, to understand," denotes (a) "the understanding, the mind or intelligence," **Mark 12:33**; (b) "understanding, reflective thought," Luke 2:47; 1 Cor. 1:19, RV, "prudence", Eph. 3:4, RV (KJV, "knowledge"); Col. 1:9; 2:2; 2 Tim. 2:7.

Strength *see Mark 12:30*.

Neighbour *see Mark 12:31*.

Burnt offerings *holokautoma* (3646), denotes "a whole burnt offering" (*holos*, "whole," *kautos*, for *kaustos*, a verbal adjective from *kaio*, "to burn"), i.e., "a victim," the whole of which is burned, as in Ex. 30:20; Lev. 5:12; 23:8, 25, 27. It is used in **Mark 12:33**, by the scribe who questioned the Lord as to the first commandment in the Law and in Heb. 10:6, 8, RV "whole burnt offerings."

Sacrifices *see* Sacrifice at *Mark 9:49*.

12:34 And when Jesus saw that he answered discreetly, he said unto him, Thou art not far from the kingdom of God. And no man after that durst ask him *any question*.

Discreetly *nounechos* (3562), lit., "mindpossessing" (*nous*, "mind, understanding," *echo*, "to have"), hence denotes "discreetly, sensibly prudently," Mark 12:34.

Far *makran* (3112), properly a feminine form of the adjective above, denotes "a long way, far," (a) literally, Matt. 8:30, RV, "afar off." Luke 7:6; 15:20, RV, "afar off"; John 21:8; Acts 17:27; 22:21; (b) metaphorically, "far (from the kingdom of God)," **Mark 12:34**; in spiritual darkness, Acts 2:39; Eph. 2:13, 17.

Durst *tolmao* (5111), signifies "to dare," (a) in the sense of not dreading or shunning through fear, Matt. 22:46; **Mark 12:34**; **Mark 15:43**, "boldly," lit., "having dared, went in"; Luke 20:40; John 21:12; Acts 5:13; 7:32; Rom. 15:18; 2 Cor. 10:2, RV, "show courage," (KJV, "be bold"); 10:12, RV, "are (not) bold", 11:21; Phil. 1:14, "are bold"; Jude 9; (b) in the sense of bearing, enduring, bringing oneself to do a thing, Rom. 5:7; 1 Cor. 6:1. Cf. *apotolmao*, "to be very bold," Rom. 10:20.

12:35 And Jesus answered and said, while he taught in the temple, How say the scribes that Christ is the Son of David?

Answered *apokrinomai* (611), signifies either "to give an answer to a question" (its more frequent use) or "to begin to speak," but always where something has preceded, either statement or act to which the remarks refer, e.g., Matt. 11:25; Luke 14:3; John 2:18. The RV translates by "answered," e.g., Matt. 28:5; **Mark 12:35**; Luke 3:16, where some have suggested "began to say" or "uttered solemnly," whereas the speaker is replying to the unuttered thought or feeling of those addressed by him.

Say *see* Saith at *Mark 6:50*.

12:36 For David himself said by the Holy Ghost, The Lord said to my Lord, Sit thou on my right hand, till I make thine enemies thy footstool.

Holy Ghost *see Mark 3:29*.

Make *tithemi* (5087), "to put," is used in Matt. 22:44; **Mark 12:36**; Luke 20:43; Acts 2:35; 1 Cor. 9:18 (of making the gospel without charge); Heb. 1:13; 10:13; 2 Pet. 2:6; Acts 20:28; Rom. 4:17.

Enemies *echthros* (2190), an adjective, primarily denoting "hated" or "hateful" (akin to *echthos*, "hate"; perhaps associated with *ekos*, "outside"), hence, in the active sense, denotes "hating, hostile"; it is used as a noun signifying an "enemy," adversary, and is said (a) of the Devil, Matt. 13:39; Luke 10:19; (b) of death, 1 Cor. 15:26; (c) of the professing believer who would be a friend of the world, thus making himself an enemy of God, Jas. 4:4; (d) of men who are opposed to Christ, Matt. 13:25, 28; 22:44; **Mark 12:36**; Luke 19:27; 20:43; Acts 2:35; Rom. 11:28; Phil. 3:18; Heb. 1:13; 10:13; or to His servants, Rev. 11:5, 12; to the nation of Israel, Luke 1:71, 74; 19:43; (e) of one who is opposed to righteousness, Acts 13:10; (f) of Israel in its alienation from God, Rom. 11:28; (g) of the unregenerate in their attitude toward God, Rom. 5:10; Col. 1:21; (h) of believers in their former state, 2 Thess. 3:15; (i) of foes, Matt. 5:43-44; 10:36; Luke 6:27, 35; Rom. 12:20; 1 Cor. 15:25; of the apostle Paul because he told converts "the truth," Gal. 4:16. Cf. *echthra*, "enmity".

Footstool *hupopodion* (5286), from *hupo*, "under," and *pous*, "a foot," is used (a) literally in Jas. 2:3, (b) metaphorically, of the earth as God's "footstool," Matt. 5:35; of the foes of the Lord, Matt. 22:44 (in some mss.); **Mark 12:36**, "underneath" (in some mss.), Luke 20:43; Acts 2:35; 7:49; Heb. 1:13; 10:13. The RV, adhering to the literal rendering, translates the phrase "the footstool of My (Thy, His) feet," for the KJV, "My (etc.) footstool," but in Matt. 22:44, "(till I put Thine enemies) underneath thy feet."

12:37 David therefore himself calleth him Lord; and whence is he *then* his son? And the common people heard him gladly.

Common *polus*, used of number, signifies "many, numerous"; used of space, it signifies "wide, far reaching"; hence, with the article it is said of a multitude as being numerous; it is translated "common" (people) in **Mark 12:37** (see the RV, marg.). It does not, however, mean the ordinary folk, but the many folk.

Gladly *see Mark 6:20*.

12:38 And he said unto them in his doctrine, Beware of the scribes, which love to go in long clothing, and *love* salutations in the marketplaces,

Beware *see Mark 8:15*.

Love In **Mark 12:38**, KJV, *thelo*, "to wish," is translated "love" (RV, "desire").

Go *peripateo*, "to walk," **Mark 12:38**, RV, "walk" (KJV "go").

Clothing *stole* (4749), (Eng., "stole"), denotes any "stately robe," a long garment reaching to the feet or with a train behind. It is used of the long clothing in which the scribes walked, making themselves conspicuous in the eyes of men, **Mark 12:38**; Luke 20:46; of the robe worn by the young man in the Lord's tomb, **Mark 16:5**; of the best or, rather, the chief robe, which was brought out for the returned prodigal, Luke 15:22; five times in Revelation, as to glorified saints, 6:11; 7:9, 13-14; 22:14. In the Sept. it is used of the holy garments of the priests, e.g., Exod. 28:2; 29:21; 31:10.

Salutations *aspamos* (783), a salutation, is always so rendered in the RV; KJV, "greetings" in Matt. 23:7; Luke 11:43; 20:46, it is used (a) orally in those instances and in **Mark 12:38**; Luke 1:29, 41, 44; (b) in written salutations, 1 Cor. 16:21; Col. 4:18; 2 Thess. 3:17.

Marketplaces *see* **Streets** at *Mark 6:56*.

12:39 And the chief seats in the synagogues, and the uppermost rooms at feasts:

Chief seats *protokathedria* (4410), "the first seat," "a sitting in the first or chief seat" (*protos*, "first," *kathedra*, "a seat"), is found in Matt. 23:6; **Mark 12:39**; Luke 11:43; 20:46.

Uppermost In Luke 11:43 *protokathedria*, "a chief seat," is translated "uppermost seats," KJV (RV, "chief seats"). In Matt. 23:6 and **Mark 12:39**, KJV, *protoklisia*, "a chief place," is translated "uppermost rooms" (RV, "chief place" and "chief places").

Rooms *protoklisia* (4411), "the chief reclining place at table," is rendered "uppermost rooms," in Matt. 23:6, KJV (RV, "chief place"); in **Mark 12:39**, "uppermost rooms," KJV (RV, "chief places"); in Luke 14:7, "chief rooms," KJV (RV, "chief seats"); in v. 8, KJV, "highest room" (RV, "chief seat"); in 20:46, KJV, "highest seats" (RV, "chief seats").

Feasts *see* **Supper** at *Mark 6:21*.

12:40 Which devour widows' houses, and for a pretence make long prayers: these shall receive greater damnation.

Devour *see* **Devoured** at *Mark 4:4*.

Widows *chera* (5503), Matt. 28:13 (in some texts); **Mark 12:40, 42, 43**; Luke 2:37; 4:25, 26, lit., "a woman, a widow"; 7:12; 18:3, 5; 20:47; 21:2, 3; Acts 6:1; 9:39, 41; 1 Tim. 5:3 (twice), 4, 5, 11, 16 (twice); Jas. 1:27; 1 Tim. 5:9 refers to elderly "widows" (not an ecclesiastical "order"), recognized, for relief or maintenance by the church (cf. vv. 3, 16), as those who had fulfilled the conditions mentioned; where relief could be ministered by those who had relatives that were "widows" (a likely circumstance in large families), the church was not to be responsible; there is an intimation of the tendency to shelve individual responsibility at the expense of church funds. In Rev. 18:7, it is used figuratively of a city forsaken.

Houses *oikia* (3614), in Attic law *oikos* denoted the whole estate, *oikia* stood for the dwelling only; this distinction was largely lost in later Greek. In the NT it denotes (a) "a house, a dwelling," e.g., Matt. 2:11; 5:15; 7:24-27; 2 Tim. 2:20; 2 John 10; it is not used of the Tabernacle or the Temple; (b) metaphorically, the heavenly abode, spoken of by the Lord as "My Father's house," John 14:2, the eternal dwelling place of believers; the body as the dwelling place of the soul, 2 Cor. 5:1; similarly the resurrection body of believers (*id.*); property, e.g., **Mark 12:40**; by metonymy, the inhabitants of a house, a household, e.g., Matt. 12:25; John 4:53; 1 Cor. 16:15.

Pretence *prophasis* (4392), either from *pro*, "before," and *phaino*, "to cause to appear, shine," or, more probably, from *pro*, and *phemi*, "to say," is rendered "cloke" (of covetousness) in 1 Thess. 2:5; "excuse" in John 15:22 (KJV "cloke"); "pretense" in Matt. 23:14; **Mark 12:40**; Luke 20:47 (KJV "show"); Phil. 1:18; "color" in Acts 27:30. It signifies the assuming of something so as to disguise one's real motives.

Long *makros* (3117), is used of "long prayers" (Matt. 23:14, in some mss.), **Mark 12:40**; Luke 20:47. It denotes "far" in Luke 15:13; 19:12.

Greater *perissoteros* (4055), is translated as follows: in Matt. 11:9, and Luke 7:26, RV, "much more" (KJV, "more"); in **Mark 12:40**, "greater"; in Luke 12:4, 48, "more"; in 1 Cor. 12:23-24, "more abundant"; in 2 Cor. 2:7, "overmuch"; in 2 Cor. 10:8, RV, "abundantly"; KJV, "more."

Damnation *krima* (2917), denotes (a) "the sentence pronounced, a verdict, a condemnation, the decision resulting from an investigation," e.g., **Mark 12:40**; Luke 23:40; 1 Tim. 3:6; Jude 4; (b) "the process of judgment leading to a decision," 1 Pet. 4:17 ("judgment"), where *krisis* might be expected. In Luke 24:20, "to be condemned" translates the phrase *eis krima*, "unto condemnation" (i.e., unto the pronouncement of the sentence of "condemnation"). For the rendering "judgment," see, e.g., Rom. 11:33; 1 Cor. 11:34; Gal. 5:10; Jas. 3:1. In these (a) the process leading to a decision and (b) the pronouncement of the decision, the verdict, are to be distinguished. In 1 Cor. 6:7 the word means a matter for judgment, a lawsuit.

12:41 And Jesus sat over against the treasury, and beheld how the people cast money into the treasury: and many that were rich cast in much.

Sat *see Mark 11:2.*

Treasury *gazophulakion* (1049), from *gaza*, "a treasure," *phulake*, "a guard," is used by Josephus for a special room in the women's court in the Temple in which gold and silver bullion was kept. This seems to be referred to in John 8:20; in **Mark 12:41** (twice), **43** and Luke 21:1 it is used of the trumpet-shaped or ram's-horn-shaped chests, into which the temple offerings of the people were cast. There were 13 chests, six for such gifts in general, seven for distinct purposes.

Money *see Mark 6:8.*

Rich *see Mark 10:25.*

12:42 And there came a certain poor widow, and she threw in two mites, which make a farthing.

Widow *see* Widows at *Mark 12:40.*

Threw *ballo* (906), "to cast, to throw," is rendered "to throw" in **Mark 12:42**, KJV (RV, "cast"); so Acts 22:23 (2nd part); "to throw down," Rev. 18:21 (2nd part), KJV (RV, "cast down").

Mites *lepton* (3016), the neuter of the adjective *leptos*, signifying, firstly, "peeled," then, "fine, thin, small, light," became used as a noun, denoting a small copper coin, often mentioned in the Mishna as proverbially the smallest Jewish coin. It was valued at 1/8th of the Roman *as*, and the 1/128th part of the *denarius*: its legal value was about one third of an English farthing; **Mark 12:42** lit. reads "two *lepta*, which make a *kodrantes* (a *quadrans*)"; in Luke 12:59 "the last *lepton*" corresponds in effect to Matt. 5:26, "the uttermost *kodrantes*," "farthing"; elsewhere, Luke 21:2.

Make *eimi* (1510), "to be," is translated "make" in **Mark 12:42**, lit., "which is (a farthing)."

Farthing *kodrantes* (2835), was the Latin *quadrans*, "the fourth part of an as", about two thirds of a farthing, Matt. 5:26; **Mark 12:42**.

12:43 And he called *unto him* his disciples, and saith unto them, Verily I say unto you, That this poor widow hath cast more in, than all they which have cast into the treasury:

Widow *see* Widows at *Mark 12:40.*

More *pleion* (4119), the comparative degree of *polus*, "much," is used (a) as an adjective, e.g., John 15:2; Acts 24:11, RV, "(not) more (than)" (KJV, "yet but"); Heb. 3:3; (b) as a noun, or with a noun understood, e.g., Matt. 20:10; **Mark 12:43**; Acts 19:32 and 27:12, "the more part"; 1 Cor. 9:19; (c) as an adverb, Matt. 5:20, "shall exceed," lit., "(shall abound) more (than)"; 26:53; Luke 9:13.

Treasury *see Mark 12:41.*

12:44 For all *they* did cast in of their abundance; but she of her want did cast in all that she had, *even* all her living.

Abundance *perisseuo* (4052), is used intransitively "of exceeding a certain number, or measure, to be over, to remain," of the fragments after feeding the multitude (cf. *perisseuma*), Luke 9:17; John 6:12-13; "to exist in abundance"; as of wealth, Luke 12:15; 21:4; of food, 15:17. In this sense it is used also of consolation, 2 Cor. 1:5, of the effect of a gift sent to meet the need of saints, 2 Cor. 9:12; of rejoicing, Phil. 1:26; of what comes or falls to the lot of a person in large measure, as of the grace of God and the gift by the grace of Christ, Rom. 5:15, of the sufferings of Christ, 2 Cor. 1:5. In **Mark 12:44** and Luke 21:4, the RV has "superfluity."

Living *bios* (979), (cf. Eng. words beginning with *bio*), is used in three respects (a) of "the period or duration of life," e.g., in the KJV of 1 Pet. 4:3, "the time past of our life" (the RV follows the mss. which omit "of our life"); Luke 8:14; 2 Tim. 2:4; (b) of "the manner of life, life in regard to its moral conduct," 1 Tim. 2:2; 1 John 2:16; (c) of "the means of life, livelihood, maintenance, living," **Mark 12:44**; Luke 8:43; 15:12, 30; 21:4; 1 John 3:17, "goods," RV (KJV, "good").

Chapter 13

13:1 And as he went out of the temple, one of his disciples saith unto him, Master, see what manner of stones and what buildings *are here*!

What *see Mark 6:30.*

Manner *potapos* (4217), primarily, "from what country," then, "of what sort," is rendered "what manner of man," Matt. 8:27: so 2 Pet. 3:11; **Mark 13:1** (twice); Luke 1:29; 7:39; 1 John 3:1.

Buildings *oikodome* (3619), "a building, or edification," is used (a) literally, e.g., Matt. 24:1; **Mark 13:1-2**; (b) figuratively, e.g., Rom. 14:19 (lit., "the things of building up"); 15:2 of a local church as a spiritual building, 1 Cor. 3:9, or the whole church, the body of Christ, Eph. 2:21. It expresses the strengthening effect of teaching, 1 Cor. 14:3, 5, 12, 26; 2 Cor. 10:8; 12:19; 13:10, or other ministry, Eph. 4:12, 16, 29 (the idea conveyed is progress resulting from patient effort). It is also used of the believer's resurrection body, 2 Cor. 5:1.

13:2 And Jesus answering said unto him, Seest thou these great buildings? there shall not be left one stone upon another, that shall not be thrown down.

Thrown down *kataluo* (2647), "to destroy utterly, to overthrow completely," is rendered "destroy," in Matt. 5:17, twice, of the Law; Matt. 24:2; 26:61; 27:40; **Mark 13:2**; **14:58**; **15:29**; Luke 21:6, of the Temple; in Acts 6:14, of Jerusalem; in Gal. 2:18, of the Law as a means of justification; in Rom. 14:20 (KJV, "destroy," RV, "overthrow"), of the marring of a person's spiritual well-being; in Acts 5:38 and 39 (RV, "overthrow") of the failure of purposes; in 2 Cor. 5:1, of the death of the body ("dissolved").

One ... another In Matt. 24:2; **Mark 13:2**; Luke 19:44, and 21:6, "one (stone upon) another" is, lit., "stone upon stone."

13:3 And as he sat upon the mount of Olives over against the temple, Peter and James and John and Andrew asked him privately,

Mount *see* Mountains at *Mark 5:5.*

Olives *see Mark 11:1.*

13:4 Tell us, when shall these things be? and what *shall be* the sign when all these things shall be fulfilled?

Shall *mello* (3195), "to be about (to be or do)," is used of purpose, certainty, compulsion or necessity. It is rendered simply by "shall" or "should" (which frequently represent elsewhere part of the future tense of the verb) in the following (the RV sometimes translates differently, as noted): Matt. 16:27 (1st part), lit., "is about to come"; 17:12, 22; 20:22, RV, "am about"; 24:6; **Mark 13:4** (2nd part), RV, "are about"; Luke 9:44; 21:7 (2nd part), RV, "are about"; v. 36; Acts 23:3; 24:15; 26:2, RV, "I am (to)"; Rom. 4:24; 8:13 (1st part), RV, "must"; v. 18; 2 Tim. 4:1; Heb. 1:14; 10:27; Jas. 2:12, RV, "are to"; 1 Pet. 5:1; Rev. 1:19; 2:10 (1st and 2nd parts), RV, "art about," "is about"; 3:10, RV, "is (to)"; 17:8 (1st part), RV, "is about."

Sign *semeion* (4592), "a sign, mark, indication, token," is used (a) of that which distinguished a person or thing from others, e.g., Matt. 26:48; Luke 2:12; Rom. 4:11; 2 Cor. 12:12 (1st part); 2 Thess. 3:17, "token," i.e., his autograph attesting the authenticity of his letters; (b) of a "sign" as a warning or admonition, e.g., Matt. 12:39, "the sign of (i.e., consisting of) the prophet Jonas"; 16:4; Luke 2:34; 11:29, 30; (c) of miraculous acts (1) as tokens of divine authority and power, e.g., Matt. 12:38, 39 (1st part); John 2:11, RV, "signs"; 3:2 (ditto); 4:54, "(the second) sign," RV; 10:41 (ditto); 20:30; in 1 Cor. 1:22, "the Jews ask for signs," RV, indicates that the Apostles were met with the same demand from Jews as Christ had been: "signs were vouchsafed in plenty, signs of God's power and love, but these were not the signs which they sought.... They wanted signs of an outward Messianic Kingdom, of temporal triumph, of material greatness for the chosen people.... With such cravings the Gospel of a 'crucified Messiah' was to them a stumblingblock indeed" (Lightfoot); 1 Cor. 14:22; (2) by demons, Rev. 16:14; (3) by false teachers or prophets, indications of assumed authority, e.g., Matt. 24:24; **Mark 13:22**; (4) by Satan through his special agents, 2 Thess. 2:9; Rev. 13:13, 14; 19:20; (d) of tokens portending future events, e.g., Matt. 24:3, where "the sign of the Son of Man" signifies, subjectively, that the Son of Man is Himself the "sign" of what He is about to do; **Mark 13:4**; Luke 21:7, 11, 25; Acts 2:19; Rev. 12:1, RV; 12:3, RV; 15:1.

Fulfilled *sunteleo* (4931), "to end together, bring quite to an end" (*sun*, "together," intensive, *telos*, "an end"), is said (a) of the "completion" of a period of days, Luke 4:2; Acts 21:27; (b) of "completing" something; some mss. have it in Matt. 7:28, of the Lord, in ending His discourse (the best mss. have *teleo*, "to finish"); of God, in finishing a work, Rom. 9:28, in making a new covenant, Heb. 8:8, marg., "accomplish"; of the fulfillment of things foretold, **Mark 13:4**; of the Devil's temptation of the Lord, Luke 4:13.

13:5 And Jesus answering them began to say, Take heed lest any *man* deceive you:

Heed *see Mark 4:24.*

Lest *me* (3361), a negative particle, often used as a conjunction, is frequently translated "lest," e.g., **Mark 13:36** (in v. **5**, RV, "that no," for KJV, "lest"); Acts 13:40; 23:10.

Deceive *planao* (4105), "to lead astray" (akin to *plane*, "a wandering"), is translated "lead ... astray," metaphorically, in Matt. 24:4, 5, 11 and **Mark 13:5, 6** (KJV, "deceive").

13:6 For many shall come in my name, saying, I am *Christ*; and shall deceive many.

Deceive *see Mark 13:5.*

13:7 And when ye shall hear of wars and rumours of wars, be ye not troubled: for *such things* must needs be; but the end *shall* not *be* yet.

Hear *see* Ears at *Mark 7:35*.

Rumours *akoe* (189), "a hearing," is translated "rumour" in Matt. 24:6; Mark 13:7.

Troubled *throeo* (2360), "to make an outcry" (*throos*, "a tumult"), is used in the passive voice, Matt. 24:6; Mark 13:7; Luke 24:37; 2 Thess. 2:2. In the Sept., Song of Sol. 5:4.

Needs *dei* (1163), an impersonal verb, signifying "it is necessary," is rendered "must needs" in Mark 13:7; John 4:4; Acts 1:16, KJV (RV, "it was needful"); 17:3, KJV (RV, "it behoved"); (in some mss. in Acts 21:22); 2 Cor. 11:30; 12:1; in Acts 15:5, "it was needful."

13:8 For nation shall rise against nation, and kingdom against kingdom: and there shall be earthquakes in divers places, and there shall be famines and troubles: these *are* the beginnings of sorrows.

Rise *see* Arise at *Mark 5:41*.

Earthquakes *seismos* (4578), "a shaking, a shock," from *seio*, "to move to and fro, to shake," chiefly with the idea of concussion (Eng., "seismic," "seismology," "seismometry"), is used (a) of a "tempest" in the sea, Matt. 8:24; (b) of "earthquakes," Matt. 24:7; 27:54; 28:2; Mark 13:8; Luke 21:11; Acts 16:26; Rev. 6:12; 8:5; 11:13 (twice), 19; 16:18 (twice).

Divers The phrase *kata topous*, lit., "throughout places" (*kata*, "down, or throughout," in a distributive sense, *topos*, "a place"), is translated "in divers places," in Matt. 24:7; Mark 13:8 and Luke 21:11.

Famines *limos* (3042), is translated "hunger" in Luke 15:17; 2 Cor. 11:27; elsewhere it signifies "a famine," and is so translated in each place in the RV; the KJV has the word "dearth" in Acts 7:11 and 11:28, and "hunger" in Rev. 6:8; the RV "famine" is preferable there; see Matt. 24:7; Mark 13:8; Luke 4:25; 15:14; 21:11; Rom. 8:35; Rev. 18:8.

Troubles In some mss. *tarache*, "an agitation, disturbance, trouble," is found in Mark 13:8 (plur.) and John 5:4 (RV omits).

Sorrows *odin* (5604), "a birth-pang, travail, pain," "sorrows," Matt. 24:8; Mark 13:8.

13:9 But take heed to yourselves: for they shall deliver you up to councils; and in the synagogues ye shall be beaten: and ye shall be brought before rulers and kings for my sake, for a testimony against them.

Heed *see Mark 4:24*.

Councils *sunedrion* (4892), properly, "a settling together" (*sun*, "together," *hedra*, "a seat"), hence, (a) "any assembly or session of persons deliberating or adjusting," as in the Sept. of Ps. 26:4 (lit., "with a council of vanity"); Prov. 22:10; Jer. 15:17, etc.; in the NT, e.g., Matt. 10:17; Mark 13:9; John 11:47, in particular, it denoted (b) "the Sanhedrin," the Great Council at Jerusalem, consisting of 71 members, namely, prominent members of the families of the high priest, elders and scribes. The Jews trace the origin of this to Num. 11:16. The more important causes came up before this tribunal. The Roman rulers of Judea permitted the Sanhedrin to try such cases, and even to pronounce sentence of death, with the condition that such a sentence should be valid only if confirmed by the Roman procurator. In John 11:47, it is used of a meeting of the Sanhedrin; in Acts 4:15, of the place of meeting.

> *"Christ hath told us He will come, but not when, that we might never put off our clothes, or put out the candle."*
>
> WILLIAM GURNALL

Beaten *see* Beat at *Mark 12:3*.

Brought In Mark 13:9, the verb translated "be brought," KJV, is *histemi*, "to stand" (RV); in Acts 27:24, *paristemi*, "to stand before" (KJV, "be brought before").

Rulers *hegemon* (2232), is a term used (a) for "rulers" generally, Mark 13:9; 1 Pet. 2:14; translated "princes" (i.e., leaders) in Matt. 2:6; (b) for the Roman procurators, referring, in the Gospels to Pontius Pilate, e.g., Matt. 27:2; Luke 20:20 (so designated by Tacitus, *Annals*, xv. 44); to Felix, Acts 23:26. Technically the procurator was a financial official under a proconsul or propretor, for collecting the imperial revenues, but entrusted also with magisterial powers for decisions of questions relative to the revenues. In certain provinces, of which Judea was one (the procurator of which was dependent on the legate of Syria), he was the general administrator and supreme judge, with sole power of life and death. Such a governor was a person of high social standing. Felix, however, was an ex-slave, a freedman, and his appointment to Judea could not but be regarded by the Jews as an insult to the nation. The headquarters of the governor of Judea

"The perseverance of the saints is only possible because of the perseverance of God."

J. OSWALD SANDERS

was Caesarea, which was made a garrison town. For *anthupatos*, "a proconsul."

13:10 And the gospel must first be published among all nations.

Published *see* Publish at *Mark 1:45*.

13:11 But when they shall lead *you*, and deliver you up, take no thought beforehand what ye shall speak, neither do ye premeditate: but whatsoever shall be given you in that hour, that speak ye: for it is not ye that speak, but the Holy Ghost.

Lead *ago* (71), "to bear, bring, carry, lead," is translated by the verb "to lead," e.g., in **Mark 13:11**; Luke 4:1; 4:9, RV; 4:29; 22:54; 23:1, KJV only; 23:32; John 18:28 (present tense, RV), Acts 8:32; metaphorically in Rom. 2:4, of the goodness of God; 8:14 and Gal. 5:18, of the Spirit of God; 1 Cor. 12:2, of the powers of darkness instigating to idolatry; 2 Tim. 3:6, of divers lusts (in some mss., *aichmaloteuo*). In Luke 24:21 *ago* is used of the passing (or spending) of a day, and translated "it is (now the third day)"; here the verb is probably to be taken impersonally, according to idiomatic usage, in the sense "there is passing the third day."

Meditate *promeletao* (4304), "to premeditate," is used in Luke 21:14. In the corresponding passage in **Mark 13:11**, the most authentic mss. have the verb *promerimnao*, "to be anxious beforehand" (RV). The KJV rendering of *meletao*, "to care for," occurs in some mss. in **Mark 13:11**, "(neither) do ye premeditate." It is absent from the best mss.

Holy Ghost *see Mark 3:29*.

13:12 Now the brother shall betray the brother to death, and the father the son; and children shall rise up against *their* parents, and shall cause them to be put to death.

Death *thanatoo* (2289), "to put to death," in Matt. 10:21; **Mark 13:12**; Luke 21:16, is translated "shall ... cause (them) to be put to death," lit., "shall put (them) to death" (RV marg.). It is used of the death of Christ in Matt. 26:59; 27:1; **Mark 14:55** and 1 Pet. 3:18. In Rom. 7:4 (passive voice) it is translated "ye ... were made dead," RV (for KJV, "are become"), with reference to the change from bondage to the Law to union with Christ; in 8:13, "mortify" (marg., "make to die"), of the act of the believer in regard to the deeds of the body; in 8:36, "are killed"; so in 2 Cor. 6:9.

Rise *epanistamai*, "to rise up against," occurs in Matt. 10:21; **Mark 13:12**.

Parents *goneus* (1118), "a begetter, a father" (akin to *ginomai*, "to come into being, become"), is used in the plural in the NT, Matt. 10:21; **Mark 13:12**; six times in Luke (in Luke 2:43, RV, "His parents," KJV, "Joseph and His mother"); six in John; elsewhere, Rom. 1:30; 2 Cor. 12:14 (twice); Eph. 6:1; Col. 3:20; 2 Tim. 3:2.

13:13 And ye shall be hated of all *men* for my name's sake: but he that shall endure unto the end, the same shall be saved.

Sake *see* Surnamed at *Mark 3:16*.

Endure *hupomeno* (5278), denotes "to abide under, to bear up courageously" (under suffering), Matt. 10:22; 24:13; **Mark 13:13**; Rom. 12:12, translated "patient"; 1 Cor. 13:7; 2 Tim. 2:10, 12 (KJV, "suffer"); Heb. 10:32; 12:2-3, 7; Jas. 1:12; 5:11; 1 Pet. 2:20, "ye shall take it patiently." It has its other significance, "to tarry, wait for, await," in Luke 2:43; Acts 17:14 (in some mss., Rom. 8:24).

13:14 But when ye shall see the abomination of desolation, spoken of by Daniel the prophet, standing where it ought not, (let him that readeth understand,) then let them that be in Judaea flee to the mountains:

Abomination *bdelugma* (946), denotes an "object of disgust, an abomination." This is said of the image to be set up by Antichrist, Matt. 24:15; **Mark 13:14**; of that which is highly esteemed amongst men, in contrast to its real character in the sight of God, Luke 16:15. The constant association with idolatry suggests that what is highly esteemed among men constitutes an idol in the human heart. In Rev. 21:27, entrance is forbidden into the Holy City on the part of the unclean, or one who "maketh an abomination and a lie." It is also used of the contents of the golden cup in the hand of the evil woman described in Rev. 17:4, and of the name ascribed to her in the following verse.

Desolation *eremosis* (2050), denotes "desolation," (a) in the sense of "making desolate," e.g., in the phrase "the abomination of desolation," Matt. 24:15; **Mark 13:14**; the genitive is objective, "the abomination that makes desolate"; (b) with stress upon the effect of the process, Luke 21:20, with reference to the "desolation" of Jerusalem.

Spoken *eiro* (3004), has a 1st aorist, passive participle *rhethen*, "spoken" or "spoken of," used in Matt. 1:22; 2:15, 17, 23; 3:3; 4:14; 8:17; 12:17; 13:35; 21:4; 22:31; 24:15; 27:9 (in some texts in 27:35 and **Mark 13:14**).

Mountains *see Mark 5:5.*

13:15 And let him that is on the housetop not go down into the house, neither enter *therein*, to take any thing out of his house:

Housetop *doma* (1430), akin to *demo*, "to build," denotes a housetop. The housetop was flat, and guarded by a low parapet wall (see Deut. 22:8). It was much frequented and used for various purposes, e.g., for proclamations, Matt. 10:27; Luke 12:3; for prayer, Acts 10:9. The house was often built round a court, across the top of which cords were fixed from the parapet walls for supporting a covering from the heat. The housetop could be reached by stairs outside the building; the paralytic in Luke 5:19 could be let down into the court or area by rolling back the covering. External flight from the housetop in time or danger is enjoined in Matt. 24:17; **Mark 13:15**; Luke 17:31.

13:16 And let him that is in the field not turn back again for to take up his garment.

Turn *epistrepho* (1994), "to turn about," or "towards," is translated "to return" in Matt. 12:44; 24:18; **Mark 13:16**, RV (KJV, "turn back again"); Luke 2:39; 8:55, RV (KJV, "came again"); 17:31; Acts 15:36, RV (KJV, "go again").

Back *opiso* (3694), connected with *hepomai*, "to follow," is used adverbially, of place, with the meaning "back," "backward," in the phrase *eis ta opiso*, lit., "unto the things behind," in **Mark 13:16**; Luke 9:62; 17:31; John 6:66; 18:6; 20:14. Cf. Phil. 3:13, "the things which are behind.

13:17 But woe to them that are with child, and to them that give suck in those days!

Woe *ouai* (3759), an interjection, is used (a) in denunciation, Matt. 11:21; 18:7 (twice); eight times in ch. 23; 24:19; 26:24; **Mark 13:17**; **14:21**; Luke 6:24, 25 (twice), 26; 10:13; six times in ch. 11; 17:1; 21:23; 22:22; 1 Cor. 9:16; Jude 11; Rev. 8:13 (thrice); 12:12; as a noun, Rev. 9:12 (twice); 11:14 (twice); (b) in grief, "alas," Rev. 18:10, 16, 19 (twice in each).

Suck *thelazo* (2337), from *thele*, "a breast," is used (a) of the mother, "to suckle," Matt. 24:19; **Mark 13:17**; Luke 21:23; in some texts in 23:29 (the best have *trepho*); (b) of the young, "to suck," Matt. 21:16, "sucklings"; Luke 11:27.

13:18 And pray ye that your flight be not in the winter.

Flight *phuge* (5437), akin to *pheugo*, is found in Matt. 24:20. Some inferior mss. have it in **Mark 13:18**.

Winter *cheimon* (5494), denotes "winter," in Matt. 24:20; **Mark 13:18**; John 10:22; 2 Tim. 4:21.

13:19 For *in* those days shall be affliction, such as was not from the beginning of the creation which God created unto this time, neither shall be.

Affliction *see Mark 4:17.*

Creation *ktizo* (2936), used among the Greeks to mean the founding of a place, a city or colony, signifies, in Scripture, "to create," always of the act of God, whether (a) in the natural creation, **Mark 13:19**; Rom. 1:25 (where the title "The Creator" translates the article with the aorist participle of the verb); 1 Cor. 11:9; Eph. 3:9; Col. 1:16; 1 Tim. 4:3; Rev. 4:11; 10:6, or (b) in the spiritual creation, Eph. 2:10, 15; 4:24; Col. 3:10.

Time In 1 Cor. 16:12, KJV, *nun*, "now" (RV), is rendered "at this time"; in Acts 24:25, the phrase *to nun echon*, lit., "the now having," is rendered "at this time" (the verb is adjectival); the phrase is more expressive than the simple "now." Cf. *heos tou nun*, "until now," Matt. 24:21 and **Mark 13:19**, RV, KJV, "unto (this time)."

13:20 And except that the Lord had shortened those days, no flesh should be saved: but for the elect's sake, whom he hath chosen, he hath shortened the days.

Elect *eklektos* (1588), lit. signifies "picked out, chosen" (*ek*, "from," *lego*, "to gather, pick out"), and is used of (a) Christ, the "chosen" of God, as the Messiah, Luke 23:35, and metaphorically as a "living Stone," "a chief corner Stone," 1 Pet. 2:4, 6; some mss. have it in John 1:34, instead of *huios*, "Son"; (b) angels, 1 Tim. 5:21, as "chosen" to be of especially high rank in administrative association with God, or as His messengers to human beings, doubtless in contrast to fallen angels (see 2 Pet. 2:4 and Jude 6); (c) believers (Jews or Gentiles), Matt. 24:22, 24, 31; **Mark 13:20**, **22**, **27**; Luke 18:7; Rom. 8:33; Col. 3:12; 2 Tim. 2:10; Titus 1:1; 1 Pet. 1:1; 2:9 (as a spiritual race); Matt. 20:16; 22:14 and Rev. 17:14, "chosen"; individual believers are so mentioned in Rom. 16:13; 2 John 1, 13.

Chosen *eklego* (1586), "to pick out, select," means, in the middle voice, "to choose for oneself," not necessarily implying the rejection of what is not chosen, but "choosing" with the subsidiary ideas of kindness or favor or love, **Mark 13:20**; Luke 6:13; 9:35 (RV); 10:42; 14:7; John 6:70; 13:18; 15:16, 19; Acts 1:2, 24; 6:5; 13:17; 15:22, 25; in 15:7 it is rendered "made choice"; 1 Cor. 1:27-28; Eph. 1:4; Jas. 2:5.

Shortened *koloboo* (2856), denotes "to cut off, amputate" (*kolobos*, "docked"); hence, "to curtail, shorten," said of the "shortening" by God of the time of the great tribulation, Matt. 24:22 (twice); **Mark 13:20** (twice). In the Sept., 2 Sam. 4:12.

13:21 And then if any man shall say to you, Lo, here *is* Christ; or, lo, *he is* there; believe *him* not:

Here *see Mark 9:1.*

13:22 For false Christs and false prophets shall rise, and shall shew signs and wonders, to seduce, if *it were* possible, even the elect.

Christs (false) *pseudochristos* (5580), denotes "one who falsely lays claim to the name and office of the Messiah," Matt. 24:24; **Mark 13:22**. The false Christ does not deny the existence of Christ, he trades upon the expectation of His appearance, affirming that he is the Christ. The Antichrist denies the existence of the true God (Trench, *Syn.* Sec. xxx).

Prophets *pseudoprophetes* (5578), "a false prophet," is used of such (a) in OT times, Luke 6:26; 2 Pet. 2:1; (b) in the present period since Pentecost, Matt. 7:15; 24:11, 24; **Mark 13:22**; Acts 13:6; 1 John 4:1; (c) with reference to a false "prophet" destined to arise as the supporter of the "Beast" at the close of this age, Rev. 16:13; 19:20; 20:10 (himself described as "another beast," 13:11).

Rise *see* **Arise** at ***Mark 5:41.***

Shew *poieo* (4160), "to make, to do," is translated, "He hath showed" in Luke 1:51; "to show (mercy)," v. 72, RV (KJV, "perform"); "showed (mercy)," 10:37; John 6:30, KJV, "showest Thou," RV, "doest Thou (for a sign)"; Acts 7:36, KJV, "showed," RV, "wrought"; Jas. 2:13, "showed (no mercy)"; in **Mark 13:22** in the best texts (some have *didomi*), "shall show (signs)."

Signs *see* **Sign** at ***Mark 13:4.***

Wonders *teras* (5059), "something strange," causing the beholder to marvel, is always used in the plural, always rendered "wonders," and generally follows *semeia*, "signs"; the opposite order occurs in Acts 2:22, 43; 6:8, RV; 7:36; in Acts 2:19 "wonders" occurs alone. A sign is intended to appeal to the understanding, a "wonder" appeals to the imagination, a power (*dunamis*) indicates its source as supernatural. "Wonders" are manifested as divine operations in thirteen occurrences (9 times in Acts); three times they are ascribed to the work of Satan through human agents, Matt. 24:24; **Mark 13:22** and 2 Thess. 2:9.

Seduce *apoplanao* (635), "to cause to go astray," is used metaphorically of "leading into error," **Mark 13:22**, RV, "lead astray" (KJV, "seduce"); passive voice in 1 Tim. 6:10 (KJV, "erred").

Possible *see Mark 9:23.*

Elect *see Mark 13:20.*

13:23 But take ye heed: behold, I have foretold you all things.

Heed *see Mark 4:24.*

Behold *blepo* (991), is also used of (a) bodily and (b) mental vision, (a) "to perceive," e.g., Matt. 13:13; (b) "to take heed," e.g., **Mark 13:23, 33**; it indicates greater vividness than *horao*, expressing a more intent, earnest contemplation; in Luke 6:41, of "beholding" the mote in a brother's eye; Luke 24:12, of "beholding" the linen clothes in the empty tomb; Acts 1:9, of the gaze of the disciples when the Lord ascended. The greater earnestness is sometimes brought out by the rendering "regardest," Matt. 22:16.

Foretold *prolego* (4302), with the aorist form *proeipon*, and a perfect form *proeireka* (from *proereo*), signifies (1) "to declare openly" or "plainly," or "to say" or "tell beforehand" (*pro*, "before," *lego*, "to say"), translated in 2 Cor. 13:2 (in the first sentence), RV, "I have said beforehand," KJV, "I told ... before", in the next sentence, KJV, "I foretell," RV, "I do say beforehand" (marg., "plainly"); not prophecy is here in view, but a warning given before and repeated; (2) "to speak before, of prophecy," as "foretelling" the future, **Mark 13:23**, KJV, "have foretold," RV, "have told ... beforehand"; Acts 1:16 (of the prophecy concerning Judas); Rom. 9:29; 2 Pet. 3:2; Jude 17; some inferior mss. have it in Heb. 10:15.

13:24 But in those days, after that tribulation, the sun shall be darkened, and the moon shall not give her light,

Tribulation *see* **Affliction** at ***Mark 4:17.***

Sun *helios* (2246), whence Eng. prefix "helio–," is used (a) as a means of the natural benefits of light and heat, e.g., Matt. 5:45, and power, Rev. 1:16; (b) of its qualities of brightness and glory, e.g., Matt.

13:43; 17:2; Acts 26:13; 1 Cor. 15:41; Rev. 10:1; 12:1; (c) as a means of destruction, e.g., Matt. 13:6; Jas. 1:11; of physical misery, Rev. 7:16; (d) as a means of judgment, e.g., Matt. 24:29; **Mark 13:24**; Luke 21:25; 23:45; Acts 2:20; Rev. 6:12; 8:12; 9:2; 16:8.

Darkened *skotizo* (4654), "to deprive of light, to make dark," is used in the NT in the passive voice only, (a) of the heavenly bodies, Matt. 24:29; **Mark 13:24**; Rev. 8:12; (b) metaphorically, of the mind, Rom. 1:21; 11:10; (some mss. have it in Luke 23:45).

Moon *selene* (4582), from *selas*, "brightness" (the Heb. words are *yareach*, "wandering," and *lebanah*, "white"), occurs in Matt. 24:29; **Mark 13:24**; Luke 21:25; Acts 2:20; 1 Cor. 15:41; Rev. 6:12; 8:12; 12:1; 21:23. In Rev. 12:1, "the moon under her feet" is suggestive of derived authority, just as her being clothed with the sun is suggestive of supreme authority, everything in the symbolism of the passage centers in Israel. In 6:12 the similar symbolism of the sun and "moon" is suggestive of the supreme authority over the world, and of derived authority, at the time of the execution of divine judgments upon nations at the close of the present age.

Light *phengos* (5338), "brightness, luster," is used of the "light" of the moon, Matt. 24:29; **Mark 13:24**; of a lamp, Luke 11:33 (some mss. have *phos*, here).

13:25 And the stars of heaven shall fall, and the powers that are in heaven shall be shaken.

Stars *aster* (792), "a star," Matt. 2:2–10; 24:29; **Mark 13:25**; 1 Cor. 15:41; Rev. 6:13; 8:10-12; 9:1; 12:1, 4, is used metaphorically, (a) of Christ, as "the morning star," figurative of the approach of the day when He will appear as the "sun of righteousness," to govern the earth in peace, an event to be preceded by the rapture of the Church, Rev. 2:28; 22:16, the promise of the former to the overcomer being suggestive of some special personal interest in Himself and His authority; (b) of the angels of the seven churches, Rev. 1:16, 20; 2:1; 3:1; (c) of certain false teachers, described as "wandering stars," Jude 13, as if the "stars," intended for light and guidance, became the means of deceit by irregular movements.

Fall *ekpipto* (1601), "to fall out of," is used in the NT, literally, of flowers that wither in the course of nature, Jas. 1:11; 1 Pet. 1:24; of a ship not under control, Acts 27:17, 26, 29, 32; of shackles loosed from a prisoner's wrist, 12:7; figuratively, of the Word of God (the expression of His purpose), which cannot "fall" away from the end to which it is set, Rom. 9:6; of the believer who is warned lest he "fall" away from the course in which he has been confirmed by the Word of God, 2 Pet. 3:17." So of those who seek to be justified by law, Gal. 5:4, "ye are fallen away from grace." Some mss. have this verb in **Mark 13:25**; so in Rev. 2:5.

Heaven *ouranos* (3772), probably akin to *ornumi*, "to lift, to heave," is used in the NT (a) of "the aerial heavens," e.g., Matt. 6:26; 8:20; Acts 10:12; 11:6 (RV, "heaven," in each place, KJV, "air"); Jas. 5:18; (b) "the sidereal," e.g., Matt. 24:29, 35; **Mark 13:25, 31**; Heb. 11:12, RV, "heaven," KJV, "sky"; Rev. 6:14; 20:11 ... (c) "the eternal dwelling place of God," Matt. 5:16; 12:50; Rev. 3:12; 11:13; 16:11; 20:9. From thence the Son of God descended to become incarnate, John 3:13, 31; 6:38, 42. In His ascension Christ "passed through the heavens," Heb. 4:14, RV; He "ascended far above all the heavens," Eph. 4:10, and was "made higher than the heavens," Heb. 7:26; He "sat down on the right hand of the throne of the Majesty in the heavens," Heb. 8:1; He is "on the right hand of God," having gone into heaven, 1 Pet. 3:22. Since His ascension it is the scene of His present life and activity, e.g., Rom. 8:34; Heb. 9:24. From thence the Holy Spirit descended at Pentecost, 1 Pet. 1:12. It is the abode of the angels, e.g., Matt. 18:10; 22:30; cf. Rev. 3:5.

Shaken *saleuo* (4531), "to agitate, shake," primarily of the action of stormy winds, waves, etc., is used literally, of a reed, Matt. 11:7; Luke 7:24; a vessel, "shaken" in filling, Luke 6:38; a building, Luke 6:48; Acts 4:31; 16:26; the natural forces of the heavens and heavenly bodies, Matt. 24:29; **Mark 13:25**; Luke 21:26; the earth, Heb. 12:26, "shook."

13:26-27 And then shall they see the Son of man coming in the clouds with great power and glory.

And then shall he send his angels, and shall gather together his elect from the four winds, from the uttermost part of the earth to the uttermost part of heaven.

Send *see Mark 5:10.*

Gather *see* Gathered at *Mark 1:33.*

Elect *see Mark 13:20.*

Winds *anemos* (417), besides its literal meaning, is used metaphorically in Eph. 4:14, of variable teaching. In Matt. 24:31 and **Mark 13:27** the four "winds" stand for the four cardinal points of the compass; so in Rev. 7:1, "the four winds of the earth" (cf. Jer. 49:36; Dan. 7:2); the contexts indicate that these

"The primitive church thought more about the Second Coming of Jesus Christ than about death or about heaven. The early Christians were looking not for a cleft in the ground called a grave but for a cleavage in the sky called Glory. They were watching not for the undertaker but for the uppertaker."

ALEXANDER MACLAREN

are connected with the execution of divine judgments. Deissmann (*Bible Studies*) and Moulton and Milligan (*Vocab.*) illustrate the phrase from the papyri.

13:28 Now learn a parable of the fig tree; When her branch is yet tender, and putteth forth leaves, ye know that summer is near:

Learn *manthano* (3129), denotes "to learn" (akin to *mathetes*, "a disciple"), "to increase one's knowledge," or "be increased in knowledge," frequently "to learn by inquiry, or observation," e.g., Matt. 9:13; 11:29; 24:32; **Mark 13:28**; John 7:15; Rom. 16:17; 1 Cor. 4:6; 14:35; Phil. 4:9; 2 Tim. 3:14; Rev. 14:3; said of "learning" Christ, Eph. 4:20, not simply the doctrine of Christ, but Christ Himself, a process not merely of getting to know the person but of so applying the knowledge as to walk differently from the rest of the Gentiles.

Fig tree *see Mark 11:13.*

Branch *see* Branches at *Mark 4:32.*

Tender *hapalos* (527), "soft, tender," is used of the branch of a tree, Matt. 24:32; **Mark 13:28.**

Putteth *ekphuo* (1631), "to cause to grow out, put forth" (*ek*, "out," *phuo*, "to bring forth, produce, beget"), is used of the leaves of a tree, Matt. 24:32; **Mark 13:28**, "putteth forth."

Leaves *see Mark 11:13.*

Know *see Mark 7:24.*

Summer *theros* (2330), akin to *thero*, "to heat," occurs in Matt. 24:32; **Mark 13:28**; Luke 21:30.

Near *engus* (1451), "nigh" or "near," is translated in both ways in Matt. 24:32-33 and **Mark 13:28-29**, KJV (RV, "nigh" in both); in Acts 1:12, with *echon*, present participle neuter of *echo*, "to have," RV, "nigh unto ... off" (KJV, "from").

13:29 So ye in like manner, when ye shall see these things come to pass, know that it is nigh, *even* at the doors.

Manner In **Mark 13:29**, KJV, *kai*, "also" (so RV), is translated "in like manner."

Know *see Mark 7:24.*

Doors *thura* (2374), "a door, gate" (Eng., "door" is connected), is used (a) literally, e.g., Matt. 6:6; 27:60; (b) metaphorically, of Christ, John 10:7, 9; of faith, by acceptance of the gospel, Acts 14:27; of "openings" for preaching and teaching the Word of God, 1 Cor. 16:9; 2 Cor. 2:12; Col. 4:3; Rev. 3:8; of "entrance" into the Kingdom of God, Matt. 25:10; Luke 13:24-25; of Christ's "entrance" into a repentant believer's heart, Rev. 3:20; of the nearness of Christ's second advent, Matt. 24:33; **Mark 13:29**; cf. Jas. 5:9; of "access" to behold visions relative to the purposes of God, Rev. 4:1.

13:30 Verily I say unto you, that this generation shall not pass, till all these things be done.

Generation *see Mark 9:19.*

Pass *see* Passed at *Mark 6:48.*

13:31 Heaven and earth shall pass away: but my words shall not pass away.

Heaven *see Mark 13:25.*

Pass *see* Passed at *Mark 6:48.*

13:32-33 But of that day and *that* hour knoweth no man, no, not the angels which are in heaven, neither the Son, but the Father.

Take ye heed, watch and pray: for ye know not when the time is.

Heed *see Mark 4:24.*

Watch *agrupneo* (69), "to be sleepless" (from *agreuo*, "to chase," and *hupnos*, "sleep"), is used metaphorically, "to be watchful," in **Mark 13:33**; Luke 21:36; Eph. 6:18; Heb. 13:17. The word expresses not mere wakefulness, but the "watchfulness" of those who are intent upon a thing.

13:34 *For the Son of man is* as a man taking a far journey, who left his house, and gave

authority to his servants, and to every man his work, and commanded the porter to watch.

Far *see Mark 12:1.*

Journey For the adjective *apodemos*, **Mark 13:34**, KJV, "taking a far journey," RV, "sojourning in another country."

Left *see* Forsook at *Mark 1:18.*

Authority *exousia* (1849), denotes "authority" (from the impersonal verb *exesti*, "it is lawful"). From the meaning of "leave or permission," or liberty of doing as one pleases, it passed to that of "the ability or strength with which one is endued," then to that of the "power of authority," the right to exercise power, e.g., Matt. 9:6; 21:23; 2 Cor. 10:8; or "the power of rule or government," the power of one whose will and commands must be obeyed by others, e.g., Matt. 28:18; John 17:2; Jude 25; Rev. 12:10; 17:13; more specifically of apostolic "authority," 2 Cor. 10:8; 13:10; the "power" of judicial decision, John 19:10; of "managing domestic affairs," **Mark 13:34**.

Work *ergon* (2041), denotes (I) "work, employment, task," e.g., **Mark 13:34**; John 4:34; 17:4; Acts 13:2; Phil. 2:30; 1 Thess. 5:13; in Acts 5:38 with the idea of enterprise; (II) "a deed, act," (a) of God, e.g., John 6:28, 29; 9:3; 10:37; 14:10; Acts 13:41; Rom. 14:20; Heb. 1:10; 2:7; 3:9; 4:3, 4, 10; Rev. 15:3; (b) of Christ, e.g., Matt. 11:2; especially in John, 5:36; 7:3, 21; 10:25, 32, 33, 38; 14:11, 12; 15:24; Rev. 2:26; (c) of believers, e.g., Matt. 5:16; **Mark 14:6**; Acts 9:36; Rom. 13:3; Col. 1:10; 1 Thess. 1:3, "work of faith," here the initial act of faith at conversion (turning to God, v. 9); in 2 Thess. 1:11, "*every* work of faith," RV, denotes every activity undertaken for Christ's sake; 2:17; 1 Tim. 2:10; 5:10; 6:18; 2 Tim. 2:21; 3:17; Titus 2:7, 14; 3:1, 8, 14; Heb. 10:24; 13:21; frequent in James, as the effect of faith [in 1:25, KJV, "(a doer) of the work," RV, "(a doer) that worketh"]; 1 Pet. 2:12; Rev. 2:2 and in several other places in chs. 2 and 3; 14:13; (d) of unbelievers, e.g., Matt. 23:3, 5; John 7:7; Acts 7:41 (for idols); Rom. 13:12; Eph. 5:11; Col. 1:21; Titus 1:16 (1st part); 1 John 3:12; Jude 15, RV; Rev. 2:6, RV; of those who seek justification by works, e.g., Rom. 9:32; Gal. 3:10; Eph. 2:9; described as the works of the law, e.g., Gal. 2:16; 3:2, 5; dead works, Heb. 6:1; 9:14; (e) of Babylon, Rev. 18:6; (f) of the Devil, John 8:41; 1 John 3:8.

Commanded *see* Command at *Mark 10:3.*

Porter *thuroros* (2377), "a doorkeeper" (*thura*, "a door," *ouros*, "a guardian"), is translated "porter" in **Mark 13:34**; John 10:3; it is used of a female in John 18:16, 17, translated "(her) that kept the door." In the Sept., 2 Sam. 4:6; 2 Kings 7:11; Ezek. 44:11.

13:35 Watch ye therefore: for ye know not when the master of the house cometh, at even, or at midnight, or at the cock-crowing, or in the morning:

Master *kurios* (2962), "a lord, one who exercises power," is translated "masters" in Matt. 6:24; 15:27; **Mark 13:35**; Luke 16:13; Acts 16:16, 19; Rom. 14:4, KJV (RV, "lord"); Eph. 6:5, 9 (twice), the 2nd time of Christ; so in Col. 3:22; 4:1.

Even *see* Eventide at *Mark 11:11.*

Midnight *mesonuktion* (3317), an adjective denoting "at, or of, midnight," is used as a noun in **Mark 13:35**; Luke 11:5; Acts 16:25; 20:7.

Cock-crowing *alektorophonia* (219), denotes "cock-crowing" (*alektor*, and *phone*, "a sound"), **Mark 13:35**. There were two "cockcrowings," one after midnight, the other before dawn. In these watches the Jews followed the Roman method of dividing the night. The first "cock-crowing" was at the third watch of the night. That is the one mentioned in **Mark 13:35**. Mark mentions both; see **14:30**. The latter, the second, is that referred to in the other Gospels and is mentioned especially as "the cock-crowing."

Morning *see 1:35.*

13:36-37 Lest coming suddenly he find you sleeping.

And what I say unto you I say unto all, Watch.

Lest *see Mark 13:5.*

Suddenly *exaiphnes* (1810), a strengthened form, occurs in **Mark 13:36**; Luke 2:13; 9:39; Acts 9:3; 22:6.

Sleeping *see* Sleepeth at *Mark 5:39.*

"He who loves the coming of the Lord is not he who affirms it is far off, nor is it he who says it is near. It is he who, whether it be far or near, awaits it with sincere faith, steadfast hope, and fervent love."

ST. AUGUSTINE OF HIPPO

Chapter 14

14:1 After two days was *the feast* of the passover, and of unleavened bread: and the chief priests and the scribes sought how they might take him by craft, and put *him* to death.

And *kai:* The *epexegetic* or *explanatory* use. This may be represented by the expressions "namely," "again," "and indeed," "that is to say"; it is usually translated by "and." In such cases not merely an addition is in view ... In **Mark 14:1**, "and the unleavened bread" is perhaps an instance, since the Passover feast is so defined in Luke 22:1.

Bread *azumos* (106), denotes "unleavened bread," i.e., without any process of fermentation; hence, metaphorically, "of a holy, spiritual condition," 1 Cor. 5:7, and of "sincerity and truth" (v. 8). With the article it signifies the feast of unleavened bread, Matt. 26:17; **Mark 14:1, 12**; Luke 22:1, 7; Acts 12:3; 20:6.

Take *see* **Took** at *Mark 1:31*.

Craft *dolos* (1388), primarily, "a bait," hence, "fraud, guile, deceit," is rendered "craft" in the KJV of **Mark 14:1** (RV "subtilty").

Put ... to death *apokteino* (615), to kill, is so translated in the RV, for the KJV, "put to death," in **Mark 14:1**; Luke 18:33; in John 11:53; 12:10 and 18:31, RV, "put to death."

14:2 But they said, Not on the feast *day*, lest there be an uproar of the people.

Feast In **Mark 14:2** and John 2:23 the KJV translates *heorte* by "feast day" (RV, "feast").

Lest *mepote or me pote* (3379), denotes "lest ever, lest perhaps, lest at any time," e.g., Matt. 4:6; "lest haply," Matt. 7:6, RV (KJV, "lest"), and in 13:15 (KJV, "lest at any time"); in 25:9, RV, "peradventure" (KJV, "lest"). The RV does not translate this simply by "lest," as in the KJV; see further, e.g., in Matt. 27:64; **Mark 14:2**; Luke 12:58; the addition of *pote* requires the fuller rendering.

Tumult *see* **Uproar** at *Mark 5:38*.

14:3 And being in Bethany in the house of Simon the leper, as he sat at meat, there came a woman having an alabaster box of ointment of spikenard very precious; and she brake the box, and poured *it* on his head.

Leper *see Mark 1:40*.

Sat *see Mark 2:15*.

Box *alabastron* (211), "an alabaster vessel," is translated in the KJV of Matt. 26:7; **Mark 14:3**; Luke 7:37, "box." "Cruse," RV, is a more suitable rendering than "box"; Matt. 26:7; **Mark 14:3**; Luke 7:37. The breaking refers to the seal, not to the box or cruse.

Ointment *muron* (3464), a word derived by the ancients from *muro*, "to flow," or from *murra*, "myrrh-oil" (it is probably of foreign origin). The "ointment" is mentioned in the NT in connection with the anointing of the Lord on the occasions recorded in Matt. 26:7, 9, 12; **Mark 14:3-4**; Luke 7:37-38, 46; John 11:2; 12:3 (twice), 5. The alabaster cruse mentioned in the passages in Matthew, Mark and Luke was the best of its kind, and the spikenard was one of the costliest of perfumes. "Ointments" were used in preparing a body for burial, Luke 23:56 ("ointments"). Of the act of the woman mentioned in Matt. 26:6-13, the Lord said, "she did it to prepare Me for burial"; her devotion led her to antedate the customary ritual after death, by showing both her affection and her understanding of what was impending. For the use of the various kinds of "ointments" as articles of commerce, see Rev. 18:13.

Spikenard *nardos* (3487), is derived, through the Semitic languages (Heb. *nerd*, Syriac *nardin*), from the Sanskrit *nalada*, "a fragrant oil," procured from the stem of an Indian plant. The Arabs call it the "Indian spike." The adjective *pistikos* is attached to it in the NT, **Mark 14:3**; John 12:3; *pistikos*, if taken as an ordinary Greek word, would signify "genuine." There is evidence, however, that it was regarded as a technical term. It has been suggested that the original reading was *pistakes*, i.e., the *Pistacia Terebinthus*, which grows in Cyprus, Syria, Palestine, etc., and yields a resin of very fragrant odor, and in such inconsiderable quantities as to be very costly.

Precious *poluteles* (4185), "very expensive," translated "very precious" in **Mark 14:3**, KJV (RV, "very costly).

Brake *see* **Broken** at *Mark 5:4*.

Poured *katacheo* (2708), "to pour down upon" (*kata*, "down," *cheo*, "to pour"), is used in Matt. 26:7 and **Mark 14:3**, of ointment.

14:4 And there were some that had indignation within themselves, and said, Why was this waste of the ointment made?

Indignation *see* **Displeased** at *Mark 10:14*.

Within *see Mark 7:21*.

Waste *apoleia* (684), indicating "loss of well-being, not of being," is used of things, signifying their waste, or ruin; of ointment, Matt. 26:8; **Mark 14:4**; of money, Acts 8:20 ("perish").

Trouble *diaponeo* (1278), denotes "to work out with toil," hence, "to be sore troubled"; so the RV in Acts 4:2 and 16:18 (KJV, "grieved"); **Mark 14:4** in some texts.

14:5 For it might have been sold for more than three hundred pence, and have been given to the poor. And they murmured against her.

Might *see* May at *Mark 4:32*.

Sold *piprasko* (4097), from an earlier form, *perao*, "to carry across the sea for the purpose of selling or to export," is used (a) literally, Matt. 13:46; 18:25; 26:9; **Mark 14:5**; John 12:5; Acts 2:45; 4:34; 5:4; (b) metaphorically, Rom. 7:14, "sold under sin," i.e., as fully under the domination of sin as a slave is under his master; the statement evinces an utter dissatisfaction with such a condition; it expresses, not the condemnation of the unregenerate state, but the evil of bondage to a corrupt nature, involving the futility of making use of the Law as a means of deliverance.

More *epano* (1883), *epi*, "over," *ano*, "above," is used frequently as a preposition with a noun; adverbially, of number, e.g., **Mark 14:5**, RV; 1 Cor. 15:6. See also 8:14.

Three hundred *triakosioi* (5145), occurs in **Mark 14:5** and John 12:5.

Pence *see* Pennyworth at *Mark 6:37*.

Murmured *embrimaomai* (1690), is rendered "murmured against" in **Mark 14:5**; it expresses indignant displeasure.

14:6 And Jesus said, Let her alone; why trouble ye her? she hath wrought a good work on me.

Let alone *aphiemi* (863), signifies "to send away, set free"; also "to let alone," Matt. 15:14; **Mark 14:6**; Luke 13:8; John 11:48; 12:7 (RV, "suffer her"); in Acts 5:38 some texts have *easate* from *eao*, "to permit." *See also* Let at *Mark 7:27*.

Trouble *kopos* (2873), "a striking, beating," then, "laborious toil, trouble," used with *parecho*, "to furnish, to supply," is rendered "to trouble" (lit., "to give trouble to"), in Matt. 26:10; **Mark 14:6**; Luke 11:7; 18:5; Gal. 6:17; the meaning is to embarrass a person by distracting his attention, or to give occasion for anxiety. In the last passage the apostle expresses his determination not to allow the Judaizing teachers to distract him any further.

Wrought, Work *see* Work at *Mark 13:34*.

14:7 For ye have the poor with you always, and whensoever ye will ye may do them good: but me ye have not always.

May *see Mark 4:32*.

Good In **Mark 14:7**, the two words *eu*, "well," and *poieo*, "to do," are in some mss. treated as one verb *eupoieo*, "to do good."

14:8 She hath done what she could: she is come aforehand to anoint my body to the burying.

Could *echo* (2192), "to have," is rendered "could" in **Mark 14:8**, "she hath done what she could," lit., "she hath done what she had."

Come aforehand *prolambano* (4301), "to anticipate" (*pro*, "before," *lambano*, "to take"), is used of the act of Mary, in **Mark 14:8**; of forestalling the less favored at a social meal, 1 Cor. 11:21; of being "overtaken" in any trespass, Gal. 6:1, where the meaning is not that of detecting a person in the act, but of his being caught by the trespass, through his being off his guard (see 5:21 and contrast the premeditated practice of evil in 5:26). The modern Greek version is "even if a man, through lack of circumspection, should fall into any sin."

Anoint *murizo* (3462), is used of "anointing" the body for burial, in **Mark 14:8**.

Burying *entaphiasmos* (1780), lit. "an entombing" (from *en*, "in," *taphos*, "a tomb"), "burying," occurs in **Mark 14:8**; John 12:7.

14:9 Verily I say unto you, Wheresoever this gospel shall be preached throughout the whole world, *this* also that she hath done shall be spoken of for a memorial of her.

Preached *see* Publish at *Mark 1:45*.

Memorial *mnemosunon* (3422), denotes "a memorial," that which keeps alive the memory of someone or something (from *mnemon*, "mindful"), Matt. 26:13; **Mark 14:9**; Acts 10:4.

14:10-11 And Judas Iscariot, one of the twelve, went unto the chief priests, to betray him unto them.

And when they heard *it*, they were glad, and promised to give him money. And he sought how he might conveniently betray him.

Glad *chairo* (5463), is the usual word for "rejoicing, being glad"; it is rendered by the verb "to be glad" in **Mark 14:11**; Luke 15:32; 22:5; 23:8; John 8:56; 11:15; 20:20; Acts 11:23; 13:48; in the following the RV has "to rejoice" for KJV, "to be glad," Rom. 16:19; 1 Cor. 16:17; 2 Cor. 13:9; 1 Pet. 4:13; Rev. 19:7.

Promised *epangello* (1861), "to announce, proclaim," has in the

NT the two meanings "to profess" and "to promise," each used in the middle voice; "to promise" (a) of "promises" of God, Acts 7:5; Rom. 4:21; in Gal. 3:19, passive voice; Titus 1:2; Heb. 6:13; 10:23; 11:11; 12:26; Jas. 1:12; 2:5; 1 John 2:25; (b) made by men, **Mark 14:11**; 2 Pet. 2:19.

Money *argurion* (694), properly, "a piece of silver," denotes (a) "silver," e.g., Acts 3:6; (b) a "silver coin," often in the plural, "pieces of silver," e.g., Matt. 26:15; so 28:12, where the meaning is "many, (*hikanos*) pieces of silver"; (c) "money"; it has this meaning in Matt. 25:18, 27; 28:15; **Mark 14:11**; Luke 9:3; 19:15, 23; 22:5; Acts 8:20 (here the RV has "silver").

Conveniently *eukairos* (2122), "conveniently," **Mark 14:11**, is used elsewhere in 2 Tim. 4:2, "in season."

14:12 And the first day of unleavened bread, when they killed the passover, his disciples said unto him, Where wilt thou that we go and prepare that thou mayest eat the passover?

Bread *see Mark 14:1.*

Killed *thuo* (2380), primarily denotes "to offer firstfruits to a god"; then (a) "to sacrifice by slaying a victim," Acts 14:13, 18, to do sacrifice; 1 Cor. 10:20, to sacrifice; 1 Cor. 5:7, "hath been sacrificed," of the death of Christ as our Passover; (b) "to slay, kill," Matt. 22:4; **Mark 14:12**; Luke 15:23, 27, 30; 22:7; John 10:10; Acts 10:13; 11:7.

Passover *pascha* (3957), the Greek spelling of the Aramaic word for the Passover, from the Hebrew *pasach*, "to pass over, to spare," a feast instituted by God in commemoration of the deliverance of Israel from Egypt, and anticipatory of the expiatory sacrifice of Christ. The word signifies (I) "the Passover Feast," e.g., Matt. 26:2; John 2:13, 23; 6:4; 11:55; 12:1; 13:1; 18:39; 19:14; Acts 12:4; Heb. 11:28; (II) by metonymy, (a) "the Paschal Supper," Matt. 26:18, 19; **Mark 14:16**; Luke 22:8, 13; (b) "the Paschal lamb," e.g., **Mark 14:12** (cf. Exod. 12:21); Luke 22:7; (c) "Christ Himself," 1 Cor. 5:7.

14:13 And he sendeth forth two of his disciples, and saith unto them, Go ye into the city, and there shall meet you a man bearing a pitcher of water: follow him.

Meet *see* **Met** at *Mark 5:2.*

Bearing *bastazo* (941), signifies "to support as a burden." It is used with the meaning (a) "to take up," as in picking up anything stones, John 10:31; (b) "to carry" something, Matt. 3:11; **Mark 14:13**; Luke 7:14; 22:10; Acts 3:2; 21:35; Rev. 17:7; "to carry" on one's person, Luke 10:4; Gal. 6:17; in one's body, Luke 11:27; "to bear" a name in testimony, Acts 9:15; metaphorically, of a root "bearing" branches, Rom. 11:18.

Pitcher *keramion* (2765), "an earthen vessel" (*keramos*, "potter's clay"), "a jar" or "jug," occurs in **Mark 14:13**; Luke 22:10.

Follow *see Mark 8:34.*

14:14 And wheresoever he shall go in, say ye to the goodman of the house, The Master saith, Where is the guestchamber, where I shall eat the passover with my disciples?

Goodman *oikodespotes* (3617), denotes "the master of a house" (*oikos*, "a house," *despotes*, "a master"), "a householder." It occurs only in the Synoptists, and there 12 times. It is rendered "goodman" in Luke 22:11, where "of the house" is put separately; in Matt. 20:11, where the KJV has "the goodman of the house" for the one word, the RV renders it by "householder," as in v. 1; in 24:43, "master"; so in Luke 12:39; in **Mark 14:14**, both have "the goodman of the house."

Master *see Mark 4:38.*

Guest-chamber *kataluma* (2646), akin to *kataluo*, signifies (a) "an inn, lodging-place," Luke 2:7; (b) "a guest-room," **Mark 14:14**; Luke 22:11. The word lit. signifies "a loosening down" (*kata*, "down," *luo*, "to loose"), used of the place where travelers and their beasts untied their packages, girdles and sandals.

14:15 And he will shew you a large upper room furnished *and* prepared: there make ready for us.

Large *megas* (3173), "great, large, of physical magnitude," is translated "large" in **Mark 14:15** and Luke 22:12, of the upper room.

Room *anagaion* or *anogeon* (508), "an upper room" (*ana*, "above," *ge*, "ground"), occurs in **Mark 14:15**; Luke 22:12, "a chamber," often over a porch, or connected with the roof, where meals were taken and privacy obtained.

Furnished *see* **Spread, Strawed** at *Mark 11:8.*

Prepared *hetoimazo* (2090), "to prepare, make ready," is used (I) absolutely, e.g., **Mark 14:15**; Luke 9:52; (II) with an object, e.g., (a) of those things which are ordained (1) by God, such as future positions of authority, Matt. 20:23; the coming Kingdom, 25:34; salvation personified in Christ, Luke 2:31; future blessings, 1 Cor. 2:9; a city, Heb. 11:16; a place of refuge for the Jewish remnant, Rev. 12:6; Divine judgments on the world, Rev. 8:6;

9:7, 15; 16:12; eternal fire, for the Devil and his angels, Matt. 25:41; (2) by Christ: a place in Heaven for His followers, John 14:2, 3; (b) of human "preparation" for the Lord, e.g., Matt. 3:3; 26:17, 19; Luke 1:17 ("make ready"), 76; 3:4, KJV (RV, "make ye ready"); 9:52 ("to make ready"); 23:56; Rev. 19:7; 21:2; in 2 Tim. 2:21, of "preparation" of oneself for "every good work"; (c) of human "preparations" for human objects, e.g., Luke 12:20, RV, "thou hast prepared" (KJV, "provided"); Acts 23:23; Philem. 22.

Ready *hetoimos* (2092), "prepared, ready" (akin to *hetoimasia*, "preparation"), is used (a) of persons, Matt. 24:44; 25:10; Luke 12:40; 22:33; Acts 23:15, 21; Titus 3:1; 1 Pet. 3:15; (b) of things, Matt. 22:4 (2nd part), 8; **Mark 14:15**, RV, "ready" (KJV, "prepared"); Luke 14:17; John 7:6; 2 Cor. 9:5; 10:16, RV, "things ready" (KJV, "things made ready"); 1 Pet. 1:5.

14:16 And his disciples went forth, and came into the city, and found as he had said unto them: and they made ready the passover.

Passover *see Mark 14:12.*

14:17-18 And in the evening he cometh with the twelve.

And as they sat and did eat, Jesus said, Verily I say unto you, One of you which eateth with me shall betray me.

Sat *anakeimai* (345), "to recline at table" (*ana*, "up" *keimai*, "to lie"), is rendered "to sit at meat" in Matt. 9:10 (RV, marg., "reclined"); 26:7; 26:20, RV, "He was sitting at meat" (KJV, "He sat down"); **Mark 16:14**; in some mss. Luke 7:37; 22:27 (twice); in **Mark 14:18**, "sat"; in John 6:11, "were set down"; John 12:2 in the best texts.

14:19 And they began to be sorrowful, and to say unto him one by one, *Is* it I? and another said, *Is* it I?

One *see* Only at *Mark 2:7.*

14:20 And he answered and said unto them, *It is* one of the twelve, that dippeth with me in the dish.

Dippeth *embapto* (1686), "to dip into," is used of the act of Judas in "dipping" his hand with that of Christ in the dish, Matt. 26:23; **Mark 14:20**.

Dish *trublion* (5165), denotes "a bowl," somewhat deep, Matt. 26:23; **Mark 14:20**; among the Greeks it was a measure in medical prescriptions.

14:21 The Son of man indeed goeth, as it is written of him: but woe to that man by whom the Son of man is betrayed! good were it for that man if he had never been born.

Woe *see Mark 13:17.*

Never In **Mark 14:21**, KJV, the negative particle *ouk*, "not," is translated "never" (RV, "not"); the negative particle *me*, "not" (which suggests nonexistence when the existence was after all possible, or even probable, in contrast to *ou*, which implies nonexistence absolutely), is translated "never" in John 7:15, KJV and RV.

14:22 And as they did eat, Jesus took bread, and blessed, and brake *it*, and gave to them, and said, Take, eat: this is my body.

Brake *see Mark 8:6.*

Gave *epididomi* (1929), signifies (a) "to give by handing, to hand" (*epi*, "over"), e.g., Matt. 7:9, 10; Luke 4:17; 24:30, here of the Lord's act in "handing" the broken loaf to the two at Emmaus, an act which was the means of the revelation of Himself as the crucified and risen Lord; the simple verb is used of His "handing" the bread at the institution of the Lord's Supper, Matt. 26:26; **Mark 14:22**; Luke 22:19; this meaning of the verb *epididomi* is found also in Acts 15:30, "they delivered"; (b) "to give in, give way," Acts 27:15, RV, "we gave way to it."

14:23 And he took the cup, and when he had given thanks, he gave *it* to them: and they all drank of it.

Thanks *see Mark 8:6.*

14:24 And he said unto them, This is my blood of the new testament, which is shed for many.

Shed *ekchuno*, or *ekchunno* (1632), is used of the voluntary giving up of His life by Christ through the "shedding" of His blood in crucifixion as an atoning sacrifice, Matt. 26:28; **Mark 14:24**; Luke 22:20, KJV, "is shed," RV, "is poured out"; these passages do not refer to the effect of the piercing of His side (which took place after His death); of the murder of servants of God, Matt. 23:35; Luke 11:50; Acts 22:20 (in the best texts); of the love of God in the hearts of believers through the Holy Spirit, Rom. 5:5. For the "pouring out" of the Holy Spirit, Acts 10:45.

14:25 Verily I say unto you, I will drink no more of the fruit of the vine, until that day that I drink it new in the kingdom of God.

No more *ouketi* (3765), a negative adverb of time, signifies "no longer, no more" (*ou*, "not," *k*, euphonic, *eti* "longer"), denying absolutely and directly, e.g., Matt. 19:6; John 4:42, "now ... not"; 6:66; Acts 20:25, 38;

2 Cor. 1:23, KJV, "not as yet"; Eph. 2:19; with another negative, to strengthen the negation, e.g., Matt. 22:46; **Mark 14:25**; **15:5**, RV, "no more (anything)," KJV, "yet ... no (thing)"; Acts 8:39; Rev. 18:11, 14.

Fruit *genema* (1096), from *ginomai*, "to come into being," denotes "fruit" (a) as the produce of the earth, e.g., the vine; in the following the best mss. have this noun, Matt. 26:29; **Mark 14:25**; Luke 22:18; [12:18 in some mss.]; (b) metaphorically, as "the fruits of ... righteousness" (i.e., of material ministrations to the needy), 2 Cor. 9:10.

New *see Mark 2:22*.

Kingdom *see Mark 3:24*.

14:26 And when they had sung an hymn, they went out into the mount of Olives.

Hymn *humneo* (5214), is used (a) transitively, Matt. 26:30; **Mark 14:26**, where the "hymn" was that part of the Hallel consisting of Psalms 113-118; (b) intransitively, where the verb itself is rendered "to sing praises" or "praise," Acts 16:25; Heb. 2:12. The Psalms are called, in general, "hymns," by Philo; Josephus calls them "songs and hymns."

Olives *see Mark 11:1*.

14:27 And Jesus saith unto them, All ye shall be offended because of me this night: for it is written, I will smite the shepherd, and the sheep shall be scattered.

Offended *see Mark 6:3*.

Smite *patasso* (3960), "to strike, smite," is used (I) literally, of giving a blow with the hand, or fist or a weapon, Matt. 26:51, RV, "smote" (KJV, "struck"); Luke 22:49, 50; Acts 7:24; 12:7; (II) metaphorically, (a) of judgment meted out to Christ, Matt. 26:31; **Mark 14:27**; (b) of the infliction of disease, by an angel, Acts 12:23; of plagues to be inflicted upon men by two divinely appointed witnesses, Rev. 11:6; (c) of judgment to be executed by Christ upon the nations, Rev. 19:15, the instrument being His Word, described as a sword.

Shepherd *see Mark 6:34*.

Scattered *diaskorpizo* (1287), "to scatter abroad," is rendered "to scatter" in Matt. 25:24, 26, RV (KJV, "strawed"); 26:31; **Mark 14:27**; Luke 1:51; John 11:52; Acts 5:37, RV.

14:28-29 But after that I am risen, I will go before you into Galilee.
But Peter said unto him, Although all shall be offended, yet *will* not I.

But *see* **And** at *Mark 1:27*.

Offended *see Mark 6:3*.

Yet *alla*, but, marking antithesis or transition, e.g., **Mark 14:29**; 1 Cor. 4:4, 15; 9:2.

14:30 And Jesus saith unto him, Verily I say unto thee, That this day, *even* in this night, before the cock crow twice, thou shalt deny me thrice.

This day *semeron* (4594), an adverb (the Attic form is *temeron*), akin to *hemera*, a day, with the prefix *t* originally representing a pronoun. It is used frequently in Matthew, Luke and Acts; in the last it is always rendered "this day"; also in Heb. 1:5, and the RV of 5:5 (KJV, "to day") in the same quotation; "today" in 3:7, 13, 15; 4:7 (twice); 13:8; also Jas. 4:13. The clause containing *semeron* is sometimes introduced by the conjunction *hoti*, "that," e.g., **Mark 14:30**; Luke 4:21; 19:9; sometimes without the conjunction, e.g., Luke 22:34; 23:43, where "today" is to be attached to the next statement, "shalt thou be with Me"; there are no grammatical reasons for the insistence that the connection must be with the statement "Verily I say unto thee," nor is such an idea necessitated by examples from either the Sept. or the NT; the connection given in the KJV and RV is right.

Cock *alektor* (220), "a cock," perhaps connected with a Hebrew phrase for the oncoming of the light, is found in the passages concerning Peter's denial of the Lord, Matt. 26:34, 74-75; **Mark 14:30**, **68**, **72**; Luke 22:34, 60-61; John 13:38; 18:27. *See also* **Cock-Crowing** at *Mark 13:35*.

Twice *dis* (1364), occurs in **Mark 14:30**, **72**; Luke 18:12; Jude 12; combined with *muriades*, "ten thousand," in Rev. 9:16; rendered "again" in Phil. 4:16 and 1 Thess. 2:18.

Deny *see Mark 8:34*.

14:31 But he spake the more vehemently, If I should die with thee, I will not deny thee in any wise. Likewise also said they all.

Vehemently *ekperissos* (1537 and 4053), formed from *ek*, "out of," and the adverb *perissos*, "exceedingly, the more," is found in **Mark 14:31**, in the best texts (some have *ek perissou*, the genitive case of the adjective *perissos*, "more"), RV, "exceeding vehemently" (KJV, "the more vehemently"), of Peter's protestation of loyalty; the RV gives the better rendering.

Die *sunapothnesko* (4880), "to die with, to die together," is used of association in physical "death," **Mark 14:31**; in 2 Cor. 7:3, the apostle declares that his love to the saints makes separation impossible, whether in life or in "death." It is used once of association spiritually with Christ in His "death," 2 Tim. 2:11.

Likewise *hosautos* (5615), a strengthened form of *hos*, "thus," signifies "just so, likewise, in like manner," e.g., 1 Tim. 2:9; in the following the RV has "in like manner," for KJV, "likewise"; **Mark 14:31**; Luke 22:20; Rom. 8:26; 1 Tim. 3:8; 5:25; in Luke 20:31 the RV has "likewise," KJV, "in like manner."

14:32 And they came to a place which was named Gethsemane: and he saith to his disciples, Sit ye here, while I shall pray.

Place *chorion* (5564), "a region" (a diminutive of *chora*, "a land, country"), is used of Gethsemane, Matt. 26:36; **Mark 14:32**.

Named *see* Surnamed at *Mark 3:16*.

While *see Mark 6:45*.

14:33 And he taketh with him Peter and James and John, and began to be sore amazed, and to be very heavy;

Taketh *see Mark 9:2*.

Sore amazed *see* Amazed at *Mark 9:15*.

Heavy *ademoneo* (85), "to be troubled, much distressed," is used of the Lord's sorrow in Gethsemane, Matt. 26:37; **Mark 14:33**, KJV, "to be very heavy," RV, "to be sore troubled"; of Epaphroditus, because the saints at Philippi had received news of his sickness, Phil. 2:26, KJV, "was full of heaviness," RV, "was sore troubled."

14:34 And saith unto them, My soul is exceeding sorrowful unto death: tarry ye here, and watch.

Sorrowful *see* Sorry at *Mark 6:26*.

Tarry *meno* (3306), "to abide," is translated by the verb "to abide," in the RV, for KJV, "to tarry," in Matt. 26:38; **Mark 14:34**; Luke 24:29; John 4:40; Acts 9:43; 18:20; the RV retains the verb "to tarry" in John 21:22, 23; in Acts 20:5, KJV, "tarried" (RV, "were waiting"). Some mss. have it in Acts 20:15 (KJV, "tarried").

14:35 And he went forward a little, and fell on the ground, and prayed that, if it were possible, the hour might pass from him.

Little *mikron* (3397), is used adverbially (a) of distance, Matt. 26:39; **Mark 14:35**; (b) of quantity, 2 Cor. 11:1, 16; (c) of time, Matt. 26:73, "a while"; **Mark 14:70**; John 13:33, "a little while", 14:19; 16:16-9; Heb. 10:37, with the repeated *hoson*, "how very," lit., "a little while, how little, how little."

Possible *see Mark 9:23*.

Pass *see* Passed at *Mark 6:48*.

14:36 And he said, Abba, Father, all things *are* possible unto thee; take away this cup from me: nevertheless not what I will, but what thou wilt.

Abba *abba* (5), is an Aramaic word, found in **Mark 14:36**; Rom. 8:15 and Gal. 4:6. In the Gemara (a Rabbinical commentary on the Mishna, the traditional teaching of the Jews) it is stated that slaves were forbidden to address the head of the family by this title. It approximates to a personal name, in contrast to "Father," with which it is always joined in the NT. This is probably due to the fact that, *abba* having practically become a proper name, Greek-speaking Jews added the Greek word *pater*, "father," from the language they

"I do not think that prayer is ever evasion, that prayer saves us from having to face things that we do not want to face and that are going to hurt if we face them. Jesus in Gethsemane discovered that there was no evasion of the cross."

WILLIAM BARCLAY

used. *Abba* is the word framed by the lips of infants, and betokens unreasoning trust; "father" expresses an intelligent apprehension of the relationship. The two together express the love and intelligent confidence of the child.

Possible *see Mark 9:23*.

Take away *paraphero* (3911), "to bear away" (*para*, "aside," *phero*, "to bear"), "remove," is rendered "take away" in **Mark 14:36**, KJV, RV, "remove," as in Luke 22:42.

Cup *see Mark 10:38*.

14:37 And he cometh, and findeth them sleeping, and saith unto Peter, Simon, sleepest thou? couldest not thou watch one hour?

"I have a great need for Christ; I have a great Christ for my need."

CHARLES HADDON SPURGEON

Couldest *ischuo* (2480), "to have strength," is translated in **Mark 14:37** "couldest thou not."

14:38 Watch ye and pray, lest ye enter into temptation. The spirit truly *is* ready, but the flesh *is* weak.

Temptation *peirasmos* (3986), is used of (1) "trials" with a beneficial purpose and effect, (a) of "trials" or "temptations," divinely permitted or sent, Luke 22:28; Acts 20:19; Jas. 1:2; 1 Pet. 1:6; 4:12, RV, "to prove," KJV, "to try"; 2 Pet. 2:9 (singular); Rev. 3:10, RV, "trial" (KJV, "temptation"); in Jas. 1:12, "temptation" apparently has meanings (1) and (2) combined and is used in the widest sense; (b) with a good or neutral significance, Gal. 4:14, of Paul's physical infirmity, "a temptation" to the Galatian converts, of such a kind as to arouse feelings of natural repugnance; (c) of "trials" of a varied character, Matt. 6:13 and Luke 11:4, where believers are commanded to pray not to be led into such by forces beyond their own control; Matt. 26:41; **Mark 14:38**; Luke 22:40, 46, where they are commanded to watch and pray against entering into "temptations" by their own carelessness or disobedience; in all such cases God provides "the way of escape," 1 Cor. 10:13 (where *peirasmos* occurs twice). (2) Of "trial" definitely designed to lead to wrong doing, "temptation," Luke 4:13; 8:13; 1 Tim. 6:9; (3) of "trying" or challenging God, by men, Heb. 3:8.

Ready *prothumos* (4289), "predisposed, willing" (akin to *prothumia*), is translated "ready" in Rom. 1:15, expressive of willingness, eagerness: in **Mark 14:38**, RV, "willing" (KJV, "ready"); in Matt. 26:41. "willing."

Weak *asthenes* (772), lit., "strengthless", is translated "weak," (a) of physical "weakness," Matt. 26:41; **Mark 14:38**; 1 Cor. 1:27; 4:10; 11:30 (a judgment upon spiritual laxity in a church); 2 Cor. 10:10; 1 Pet. 3:7 (comparative degree); (b) in the spiritual sense, said of the rudiments of Jewish religion, in their inability to justify anyone, Gal. 4:9; of the Law, Heb. 7:18; in Rom. 5:6, RV, "weak" (KJV, "without strength"), of the inability of man to accomplish his salvation; (c) morally or ethically, 1 Cor. 8:7, 10; 9:22; (d) rhetorically, of God's actions according to the human estimate, 1 Cor. 1:25, "weakness," lit., "the weak things of God."

14:39 And again he went away, and prayed, and spake the same words.

Same *autos* (846), denotes "the same" when preceded by the article, and either with a noun following, e.g., **Mark 14:39**; Phil. 1:30; 1 Cor. 12:4, or without, e.g., Matt. 5:46, 47; Rom. 2:1; Phil. 2:2; 3:1; Heb. 1:12; 13:8. It is thus to be distinguished from uses as a personal and a reflexive pronoun.

14:40 And when he returned, he found them asleep again, (for their eyes were heavy,) neither wist they what to answer him.

Returned *hupostrepho* (5290), "to turn behind," or "back" (*hupo*, "under"), is translated "to return" (in some texts in **Mark 14:40**) in Luke 1:56; 2:20, 43; v. 45, RV (KJV, "turned back again"), 4:1, 14; 7:10; 8:37; 10:17; 11:24, KJV (RV, "I will turn back"); 17:18; 19:12; 23:48, 56; Acts 1:12; 12:25; 13:13; 13:34; 20:3; 21:6; 22:17, RV (KJV, "was come again"); 23:32; Gal. 1:17; Heb. 7:1.

Were heavy *bareo* (916), is used of the effect of drowsiness, "were heavy," Matt. 26:43; **Mark 14:40**; Luke 9:32; of the effects of gluttony, Luke 21:34 ("overcharged"); of the believer's present physical state in the body, 2 Cor. 5:4; of persecution, 2 Cor. 1:8; of a charge upon material resources, 1 Tim. 5:16 (RV).

Wist *see Mark 9:6.*

14:41 And he cometh the third time, and saith unto them, Sleep on now, and take *your* rest: it is enough, the hour is come; behold, the Son of man is betrayed into the hands of sinners.

Third *see Mark 9:31.*

Now *loipon* (3063), the neuter of *loipos*, "the rest, from now," is used adverbially with the article and translated "now" in **Mark 14:41**.

Rest *see Mark 6:31.*

Enough *apecho* (568), lit., "to hold off from, to have off or out" (*apo*, "from," *echo*, "to have"), i.e., "to have in full, to have received," is used impersonally in **Mark 14:41**, "it is enough," in the Lord's words to His slumbering disciples in Gethsemane. It is difficult, however, to find examples of this meaning in Greek usage of the word, and *apecho* may here refer, in its commercial significance, to Judas (who is mentioned immediately afterwards), with the meaning "he hath received" (his payment); cf. the same use in Matt. 6:2, 5, 16.

14:42 Rise up, let us go; lo, he that betrayeth me is at hand.

Go *see Mark 1:38.*

14:43-44 And immediately, while he yet spake, cometh Judas, one of the twelve, and with him a great multitude with swords and staves, from the chief priests and the scribes and the elders.

And he that betrayed him had given them a token, saying, Whomsoever I shall kiss, that same is he; take him, and lead *him* away safely.

Token *sussemon* (4953), "a fixed sign or signal, agreed upon with others" (*sun*, "with"), is used in **Mark 14:44**, "a token." In the Sept., Judg. 20:38, 40; Isa. 5:26; 49:22; 62:10.

Kiss *phileo* (5368), "to love," signifies "to kiss," in Matt. 26:48; **Mark 14:44**; Luke 22:47.

Take *see* Took at *Mark 1:31.*

Lead *apago* (520), "to lead away" (*apo*, "away"), is used of a way "leading" to destruction, Matt. 7:13, to life, v. 14; of those who "led" Christ away from Gethsemane, **Mark 14:44**; in some mss., John 18:13, to Annas; to Caiaphas, Matt. 26:57; **Mark 14:53**; to Pilate, Matt. 27:2; to the Praetorium, **Mark 15:16**; to crucifixion, Matt. 27:31; Luke 23:26; in some mss. John 19:16; of "leading" an animal away to watering, Luke 13:15; of being "led" away to idolatry, 1 Cor. 12:2, RV, "led away" (KJV, "carried away"). Some mss. have it in Acts 24:7 (KJV, "took away"). It is translated "bring" in 23:17. In 12:19 it signifies "to put to death."

Safely *asphalos* (806), means (a) "safely," **Mark 14:44**; Acts 16:23; (b) "assuredly," Acts 2:36; the knowledge there enjoined involves freedom from fear of contradiction, with an intimation of the impossibility of escape from the effects.

14:45 And as soon as he was come, he goeth straightway to him, and saith, Master, master; and kissed him.

Master *see Mark 9:5.*

Kissed *kataphileo* (2705), denotes "to kiss fervently"; the stronger force of this verb has been called in question, but the change from *phileo* to *kataphileo* in Matt. 26:49 and **Mark 14:45** can scarcely be without significance, and the act of the traitor was almost certainly more demonstrative than the simple kiss of salutation. So with the kiss of genuine devotion, Luke 7:38, 45; 15:20; Acts 20:37, in each of which this verb is used.

14:46 And they laid their hands on him, and took him.

Took *see Mark 1:31.*

14:47 And one of them that stood by drew a sword, and smote a servant of the high priest, and cut off his ear.

Stood *paristemi* (3936), intransitively, denotes "to stand by or beside," **Mark 14:47, 69, 70; 15:35, 39** (RV, "stood by"); Luke 19:24; John 18:22; 19:26; Acts 1:10; 9:39; 23:2, 4; 27:23; in 27:24, "stand before"; in 4:10, "doth ... stand here"; in Luke 1:19, "stand"; Rom. 14:10, "we shall ... stand before" (middle voice); 2 Tim. 4:17, RV, "stood by" (KJV, "... with").

Drew *spao* (4685), "to draw or pull," is used, in the middle voice of "drawing" a sword from its sheath, **Mark 14:47**; Acts 16:27.

Smote *paio* (3817), signifies "to strike or smite" (a) with the hand or fist, Matt. 26:68; Luke 22:64; (b) with a sword, **Mark 14:47**; John 18:10, KJV (RV, "struck"); (c) with a sting, Rev. 9:5, "striketh."

Cut *aphaireo* (851), "to take away, remove," is translated "cut off" in **Mark 14:47**, KJV, and Luke 22:50, and "smote off" in Matt. 26:51; RV, "struck off" in each place.

Ear *otion* (5621), a diminutive, but without the diminutive force, it being a common tendency in everyday speech to apply a diminutive form to most parts of the body, is used in Matt. 26:51; **Mark 14:47** (in some mss.); Luke 22:51; John 18:10 (in some mss.) and v. 26, all with reference to the "ear" of Malchus. The most authentic mss. have the alternative diminutive *otarion*, in **Mark 14:47** and John 18:10.

14:48 And Jesus answered and said unto them, Are ye come out, as against a thief, with swords and *with* staves to take me?

Take *sullambano* (4815), lit., "to take together" (*sun*, "with," *lambano*, "to take or lay hold of"), chiefly signifies "to seize as a prisoner"; in the following the RV substitutes the more suitable and forceful verb, "to seize," for KJV, "to take": Matt. 26:55; **Mark 14:48**; Luke 22:54; John 18:12; Acts 12:3; 23:27; 26:21; in Acts 1:16, RV and KJV, "took."

14:49 I was daily with you in the temple teaching, and ye took me not: but the scriptures must be fulfilled.

Took *see Mark 1:31.*

Must In **Mark 14:49**, KJV, the conjunction *hina* with the subjunctive mood, "in order that," is represented by "must" (RV, "that ... might").

14:50 And they all forsook him, and fled.

Forsook *see Mark 1:18.*

14:51 And there followed him a certain young man, having a linen cloth cast about *his* naked *body*; and the young men laid hold on him:

Followed *see* Followed at *Mark 5:37.*

Certain The indefinite pronoun *tis* signifies "anyone, some one, a certain one"; the neuter, *ti*, "a certain thing," e.g., Matt. 20:20; **Mark 14:51**.

Young *neaniskos* (3495), "a youth, a young man," occurs in Matt. 19:20, 22; **Mark 14:51** (1st part; RV omits in 2nd part); **16:5**; Luke 7:14; Acts 2:17; 5:10 (i.e., attendants); 23:18 (in the best texts), 22; 1 John 2:13, 14, of the second branch of the spiritual family.

Linen cloth *sindon* (4616), was "a fine linen cloth, an article of domestic manufacture" (Prov. 31:24) used (a) as a garment or wrap, the "linen cloth" of **Mark 14:51**, **52**; (b) as shrouds or winding sheets, Matt. 27:59; **Mark 15:46**, RV, "linen cloth," for KJV, "linen"; Luke 23:53 (ditto). In the Sept., Judg. 14:2, "(thirty) sheets"; Prov. 31:24. The Mishna (the great collection of legal decisions by the ancient Rabbis) records that the material was sometimes used for curtains.

Cast *periballo* (4016), "to cast about, or around," is used in 23 of its 24 occurrences, of putting on garments, clothing, etc.; it is translated "cast about" in **Mark 14:51**; Acts 12:8, in Luke 19:43, used of "casting" up a bank or palisade against a city (see RV and marg.), KJV, "shall cast a trench about thee."

Naked *gumnos* (1131), signifies (a) "unclothed," **Mark 14:52**; in v. **51** it is used as a noun ("*his*" and "*body*" being italicized); (b) "scantily or poorly clad," Matt. 25:36, 38, 43, 44; Acts 19:16 (with torn garments); Jas. 2:15; (c) "clad in the under-garment only" (the outer being laid aside), John 21:7; (d) metaphorically, (1) of "a bare seed," 1 Cor. 15:37; (2) of "the soul without the body," 2 Cor. 5:3; (3) of "things exposed to the allseeing eye of God," Heb. 4:13; (4) of "the carnal condition of a local church," Rev. 3:17; (5) of "the similar state of an individual," 16:15; (6) of "the desolation of religious Babylon," 17:16.

Hold *see Mark 3:21.*

14:52 And he left the linen cloth, and fled from them naked.

Left *see* Leave at *Mark 10:7.*

Linen cloth *see Mark 14:51.*

Naked *see Mark 14:51.*

14:53 And they led Jesus away to the high priest: and with him were assembled all the chief priests and the elders and the scribes.

Led *see* Lead at *Mark 14:44.*

Assembled *sunerchomai* (4905), "to come together" (*sun*, "together," *erchomai* "to come"), is once rendered "assemble," **Mark 14:53**, KJV. It is frequently used of "coming together," especially of the "gathering" of a local church, 1 Cor. 11:17-18, 20, 33-34; 14:23, 26; it is rendered "resorted" in Acts 16:13, KJV, where the RV adheres to the lit. rendering, "came together."

14:54 And Peter followed him afar off, even into the palace of the high priest: and he sat with the servants, and warmed himself at the fire.

Afar *see Mark 5:6.*

Palace *aule* (833), primarily, "an uncovered space around a house, enclosed by a wall, where the stables were," hence was used to describe (a) "the courtyard of a house"; in the OT it is used of the "courts" of the tabernacle and Temple; in this sense it is found in the NT in Rev. 11:2; (b) "the courts in the dwellings of well-to-do folk," which usually had two, one exterior, between the door and the street (called the *proaulion*, or "porch," **Mark 14:68**.), the other, interior, surrounded by the buildings of the dwellings, as in Matt. 26:69 (in contrast to the room where the judges were sitting); **Mark 14:66**; Luke 22:55; KJV, "hall"; RV "court" gives the proper significance, Matt. 26:3, 58; **Mark 14:54**; **15:16** (RV, "Praetorium"); Luke 11:21; John 18:15. It is here to be distinguished from the Praetorium, translated "palace." For the other meaning "sheepfold," John 10:1, 16.

Sat with *sunkathemai* (4775), "to sit with," occurs in **Mark 14:54**; Acts 26:30. In the Sept., Ps. 101:6, "dwell."

Servants *huperetes* (5257), is translated "officer," with the following applications, (a) to a magistrate's attendant, Matt. 5:25; (b) to officers of the synagogue, or officers or bailiffs of the Sanhedrin, Matt. 26:58; **Mark 14:54**, **65**; John 7:32, 45-46; 18:3, 12, 18, 22; 19:6; Acts 5:22, 26.

Warmed *thermaino* (2328), "to warm, heat" (Eng. "thermal," etc.), when used in the middle voice, signifies "to warm oneself," **Mark 14:54**, **67**; John 18:18 (twice), 25; Jas. 2:16.

Fire In **Mark 14:54**, the italicized phrase "of the fire" is added in the Eng. versions to indicate the light as coming from the "fire."

14:55 And the chief priests and all the council sought for witness against Jesus to put him to death; and found none.

Witness *marturia* (3141), "testimony, a bearing witness," is translated "witness" in **Mark 14:55, 56, 59**; Luke 22:71; John 1:7, 19 (RV); 3:11, 32 and 33 (RV); 5:31, 32, 34 (RV), 36; RV in 8:13, 14, 17; 19:35; 21:24; KJV in Titus 1:13; KJV and RV in 1 John 5:9 (thrice), 10a; RV in 10b, 11; 3 John 12.

Death *see Mark 13:12.*

14:56 For many bare false witness against him, but their witness agreed not together.

Witness *see Mark 14:55.*

Agreed *isos* (2470), "equal," is used with the verb to be, signifying "to agree," **Mark 14:56, 59**, lit., "their thought was not equal one with the other.

14:57 And there arose certain, and bare false witness against him, saying,

False witness *see Mark 10:19.*

14:58 We heard him say, I will destroy this temple that is made with hands, and within three days I will build another made without hands.

Destroy *see* Thrown down at *Mark 13:2.*

Within *see Mark 7:21.*

With hands *cheiropoietos* (5499), "made by hand," of human handiwork (*cheir*, and *poieo*, "to make"), is said of the temple in Jerusalem, **Mark 14:58**; temples in general, Acts 7:48 (RV, "houses"); 17:24; negatively, of the heavenly and spiritual tabernacle, Heb. 9:11; of the holy place in the earthly tabernacle, v. 24; of circumcision, Eph. 2:11. In the Sept., of idols, Lev. 26:1, 30; Isa. 2:18; 10:11; 16:12; 19:1; 21:9; 31:7; 46:6.

Without hands *acheiropoietos* (886), "not made by hands," is said of an earthly temple, **Mark 14:58**; of the resurrection body of believers, metaphorically as a house, 2 Cor. 5:1; metaphorically, of spiritual circumcision, Col. 2:11. This word is not found in the Sept.

14:59 But neither so did their witness agree together.

Witness *see Mark 14:55.*

Agree *see* Agreed at *Mark 14:56.*

14:60 And the high priest stood up in the midst, and asked Jesus, saying, Answerest thou nothing? what *is it which* these witness against thee?

Stood *anistemi* (450), "to raise," intransitively, "to rise," is translated "to stand up" in Matt. 12:41, RV; **Mark 14:60**; Luke 4:16; 10:25; Acts 1:15; 5:34; 10:26; 11:28; 13:16; in 14:10, "stand upright."

Midst *see* Forth at *Mark 3:3.*

Witness *katamartureo* (2649), denotes "to witness against" (*kata*), Matt. 26:62; 27:13; **Mark 14:60** (in some mss., 15:4, for *kategoreo*, "to accuse," RV).

14:61 But he held his peace, and answered nothing. Again the high priest asked him, and said unto him, Art thou the Christ, the Son of the Blessed?

Peace *see Mark 3:4.*

Christ *see Mark 9:41.*

Blessed *eulogetos* (2128), means "blessed, praised"; it is applied only to God, **Mark 14:61**; Luke 1:68; Rom. 1:25; 9:5; 2 Cor. 1:3; 11:31; Eph. 1:3; 1 Pet. 1:3. In the Sept. it is also applied to man, e.g., in Gen. 24:31; 26:29; Deut. 7:14; Judg. 17:2; Ruth 2:20; 1 Sam. 15:13.

14:62 And Jesus said, I am: and ye shall see the Son of man sitting on the right hand of power, and coming in the clouds of heaven.

Right *see Mark 10:37.*

Power *see* Mighty works at *Mark 6:5.*

14:63 Then the high priest rent his clothes, and saith, What need we any further witnesses?

Rent *diarrhesso*, or *diaresso* (1284), a late form of *diarrhegnumi*, "to break asunder, rend," is used of "rending" one's garments, Matt. 26:65; **Mark 14:63**; Acts 14:14.

Clothes *chiton* (5509), denotes "the inner vest or undergarment," and is to be distinguished, as such, from the *himation*. The distinction is made, for instance, in the Lord's command in Matt. 5:40: "If any man would go to law with thee, and take away thy coat (*chiton*), (*himation*) also." The order is reversed in Luke 6:29, and the difference lies in this, that in Matt. 5:40 the Lord is referring to a legal process, so the claimant is supposed to claim the inner garment, the less costly. The defendant is to be willing to let him have the more valuable one too ... The high priest, in rending his clothes after the reply the Lord gave him in answer to his challenge, rent his undergarments (*chiton*), the more forcibly to express his assumed horror and indignation, **Mark 14:63**. In Jude 23, "the garment spotted by the flesh" is the *chiton*, the metaphor of the undergarment being appropriate; for it would be that which was brought into touch with the pollution of the flesh.

Need *chreia* (5532), denotes "a need," in such expressions as "there is a need"; or "to have need of" something, e.g., Matt. 3:14; 6:8; 9:12, RV, "(have no) need," KJV, "need (not)," the RV adheres to the noun form; so in 14:16; **Mark 14:63**; Luke 5:31; 22:71; Eph. 4:28; 1 Thess. 4:9; in the following, however, both RV and KJV use the verb form, "to need" (whereas the original has the verb *echo*, "to have," with the noun *chreia* as the object, as in the instances just mentioned): Luke 15:7; John 2:25; 13:10; 16:30; 1 Thess. 1:8; 1 John 2:27; Rev. 22:5; in all these the verb "to have" could well have been expressed in the translation.

Further *see* ***Mark 5:35.***

Witnesses *martus or martur* (3144), (whence Eng., "martyr," one who bears "witness" by his death) denotes "one who can or does aver what he has seen or heard or knows"; it is used (a) of God, Rom. 1:9; 2 Cor. 1:23; Phil. 1:8; 1 Thess. 2:5, 10 (2nd part); (b) of Christ, Rev. 1:5; 3:14; (c) of those who "witness" for Christ by their death, Acts 22:20; Rev. 2:13; Rev. 17:6; (d) of the interpreters of God's counsels, yet to "witness" in Jerusalem in the times of the Antichrist, Rev. 11:3; (e) in a forensic sense, Matt. 18:16; 26:65; **Mark 14:63**; Acts 6:13; 7:58; 2 Cor. 13:1; 1 Tim. 5:19; Heb. 10:28; (f) in a historical sense, Luke 11:48; 24:48; Acts 1:8, 22; 2:32; 3:15; 5:32; 10:39, 41; 13:31; 22:15; 26:16; 1 Thess. 2:10 (1st part); 1 Tim. 6:12; 2 Tim. 2:2; Heb. 12:1, "(a cloud) of witnesses," here of those mentioned in ch. 11, those whose lives and actions testified to the worth and effect of faith, and whose faith received "witness" in Scripture; 1 Pet. 5:1.

14:64 Ye have heard the blasphemy: what think ye? And they all condemned him to be guilty of death.

Think *phaino* (5316), in the passive voice, "to appear," is rendered "(what) think (ye)" in **Mark 14:64**, lit., "what does it appear to you."

Condemned *katakrino* (2632), a strengthened form of *krino*, signifies "to give judgment against, pass sentence upon"; hence, "to condemn," implying (a) the fact of a crime, e.g., Rom. 2:1; 14:23; 2 Pet. 2:6; some mss. have it in Jas. 5:9; (b) the imputation of a crime, as in the "condemnation" of Christ by the Jews, Matt. 20:18; **Mark 14:64**. It is used metaphorically of "condemning" by a good example, Matt. 12:41-42; Luke 11:31-32; Heb. 11:7. In Rom. 8:3, God's "condemnation" of sin is set forth in that Christ, His own Son, sent by Him to partake of human nature (sin apart) and to become an offering for sin, died under the judgment due to our sin.

Guilty *enochos* (1777), "held in, bound by," is translated "worthy (of death)" in Matt. 26:66 and **Mark 14:64**, RV (marg., "liable to"; KJV, "guilty").

14:65 And some began to spit on him, and to cover his face, and to buffet him, and to say unto him, Prophesy: and the servants did strike him with the palms of their hands.

Spit *see* ***Mark 10:34.***

Cover *perikalupto* (4028), "to cover around" (*peri*, "around"), e.g., the face, and so, to blindfold, is translated "cover" in **Mark 14:65**, "blindfold" in Luke 22:64. In Heb. 9:4, it signifies "to overlay."

Buffet *kolaphizo* (2852), signifies "to strike with clenched hands, to buffet with the fist" (*kolaphos*, "a fist"), Matt. 26:67; **Mark 14:65**; 1 Cor. 4:11; 2 Cor. 12:7; 1 Pet. 2:20.

Servants *see* ***Mark 14:54.***

Strike *rhapisma* (4475), (a) "a blow with a rod or staff," (b) "a blow with the hand, a slap or cuff," is found in three places; of the maltreatment of Christ by the officials or attendants of the high priest, **Mark 14:65**, RV, "received (according to the most authentic mss.) Him with blows of their hands," (KJV, "did strike Him with the palms of their hands"); that they received, or took, Him would indicate their rough handling of Him; John 18:22 and 19:3; in all three places the RV marg. gives the meaning (a), as to the use of a rod. So with the corresponding verb *rhapizo*, in Matt. 26:67. The soldiers subsequently beat Him with a reed, 27:30, where *tupto*, "to beat," is used; *rhapizo* occurs elsewhere in Matt. 5:39.

Palms (of the hand) For *rhapisma*, "a blow," with *didomi*, "to give," translated "did strike (and, struck) ... with the palm of his hand" (KJV, in **Mark 14:65**; John 18:22).

14:66 And as Peter was beneath in the palace, there cometh one of the maids of the high priest:

Beneath *kato* (2736), signifies (a) "down, downwards," Matt. 4:6; Luke 4:9; John 8:6, 8; Acts 20:9; (b) "below, beneath," of place, **Mark 14:66**; the realms that lie below in contrast to heaven, John 8:23; the earth, as contrasted with the heavens, Acts 2:19; with *heos*, "unto," Matt. 27:51; **Mark 15:38**. The comparative degree, *katotero*, "under," is used in Matt. 2:16.

Palace *see* ***Mark 14:54.***

Maids *paidiske* (3814), is translated "maid," "maids," in the KJV and RV in **Mark 14:66, 69**; Luke 22:56, in the RV (KJV, "damsel"), in Matt. 26:69; John 18:17; Acts 12:13; 16:16; in Luke 12:45, "maidservants" (KJV "maidens"); in Gal. 4:22, 23, 30, 31, RV, "handmaid" (KJV, "bondmaid" or "bondwoman").

14:67 And when she saw Peter warming himself, she looked upon him, and said, And thou also wast with Jesus of Nazareth.

Warming *see* Warmed at *Mark 14:54.*

Looked *see* Looking at *Mark 10:27.*

14:68 But he denied, saying, I know not, neither understand I what thou sayest. And he went out into the porch; and the cock crew.

Know *epistamai* (1987), "to know, know of, understand" (probably an old middle voice form of *ephistemi*, "to set over"), is used in **Mark 14:68**, "understand," which follows *oida* "I (neither) know"; most frequently in the Acts, 10:28; 15:7; 18:25; 19:15, 25; 20:18; 22:19; 24:10; 26:26; elsewhere, 1 Tim. 6:4; Heb. 11:8; Jas. 4:14; Jude 10.

Understand *epistamai* (1987), "to know well," is rendered "to understand" in **Mark 14:68**; Jude 10, RV, 2nd clause (KJV, "know").

Porch *proaulion* (4259), "the exterior court" or "vestibule," between the door and the street, in the houses of well-to-do folk, **Mark 14:68**, "porch" (RV marg., "forecourt").

Cock *see Mark 14:30.*

14:69 And a maid saw him again, and began to say to them that stood by, This is *one* of them.

Maid *see* Maids at *Mark 14:66.*

Stood *see Mark 14:47.*

14:70 And he denied it again. And a little after, they that stood by said again to Peter, Surely thou art *one* of them: for thou art a Galilaean, and thy speech agreeth *thereto*.

Denied *arneomai* (720), signifies (a) "to say ... not, to contradict," e.g., **Mark 14:70**; John 1:20; 18:25, 27; 1 John 2:22; (b) "to deny" by way of disowning a person, as, e.g., the Lord Jesus as master, e.g., Matt. 10:33; Luke 12:9; John 13:38 (in the best mss.); 2 Tim. 2:12; or, on the other hand, of Christ Himself, "denying" that a person is His follower, Matt. 10:33; 2 Tim. 2:12; or to "deny" the Father and the Son, by apostatizing and by disseminating pernicious teachings, to "deny" Jesus Christ as master and Lord by immorality under a cloak of religion, 2 Pet. 2:1; Jude 4; (c) "to deny oneself," either in a good sense, by disregarding one's own interests, Luke 9:23, or in a bad sense, to prove false to oneself, to act quite unlike oneself, 2 Tim. 2:13; (d) to "abrogate, forsake, or renounce a thing," whether evil, Titus 2:12, or good, 1 Tim. 5:8; 2 Tim. 3:5; Rev. 2:13; 3:8; (e) "not to accept, to reject" something offered, Acts 3:14; 7:35, "refused"; Heb. 11:24 "refused."

Little *see Mark 14:35.*

Stood *see Mark 14:47.*

Surely *alethos* (230), "truly, surely," is rendered "of a truth" in Matt. 14:33; 26:73 and **Mark 14:70**, RV, (KJV, "surely"); Luke 9:27; 12:44; 21:3; John 6:14; 7:40; 17:8, RV, "of a truth (KJV, surely); Acts 12:11, RV (KJV, "of a surety"); "in truth," 1 Thess. 2:13; "truly," Matt. 27:54; **Mark 15:39**.

Speech *lalia* (2981), akin to *laleo*, denotes "talk, speech," (a) of "a dialect," Matt. 26:73; **Mark 14:70**; (b) "utterances," John 4:42, RV, "speaking" (KJV, "saying"); 8:43.

Agreed *sumphonos*, "harmonious, agreeing," is used only with the preposition *ek* in the phrase *ek sumphonou*, "by consent," lit., "out of agreement," 1 Cor. 7:5. In **Mark 14:70** some texts have the verb *homoiazo*, "agreeth," KJV.

14:71 But he began to curse and to swear, *saying*, I know not this man of whom ye speak.

Curse *anathematizo* (332), signifies "to declare anathema," i.e., "devoted to destruction, accursed, to curse," **Mark 14:71**, or "to bind by a curse," Acts 23:12, 14, 21.

14:72 And the second time the cock crew. And Peter called to mind the word that Jesus said unto him, Before the cock crow twice, thou shalt deny me thrice. And when he thought thereon, he wept.

Second *deuteros* (1208), denotes "second in order" with or without the idea of time, e.g., Matt. 22:26, 39; 2 Cor. 1:15; Rev. 2:11; in Rev. 14:8, RV only ("a second angel"); it is used in the neuter, *deuteron*, adverbially, signifying a "second" time, e.g., John 3:4; 21:16; Acts 7:13; Rev. 19:3, RV (KJV, "again"); Jude 5, "afterward" (RV, marg., "the second time"); used with *ek* ("of") idiomatically, the preposition signifying "for (the second time)," **Mark 14:72**; John 9:24 and Acts 11:9, RV (KJV, "again"); Heb. 9:28; in 1 Cor. 12:28, KJV, "secondarily," RV, "secondly."

Cock *see Mark 14:30.*

Mind *anamimnesko* (363), "to remind, call to remembrance" (*ana*, "up," *mimnesko*, "to remind"), is translated "called to mind," in **Mark 14:72** (passive voice).

Deny *see Mark 8:34.*

Twice *see Mark 14:30.*

Thought *epiballo* (1911), "to throw oneself upon," is used metaphorically in **Mark 14:72**, "when he thought thereon (he wept)," lit., "thinking thereon," but "to think" is an exceptional sense of the word; hence various suggestions have been made. Field, following others, adopts the meaning "putting (his garment) over (his head)," as an expression of grief. Others regard it as having here the same meaning as *archomai*, "to begin" (at an early period, indeed, *archomai* was substituted in the text for the authentic *epiballo*); Moulton confirms this from a papyrus writing. Another suggestion is to understand it as with *dianouan*, mind, i.e., "casting his mind thereon."

Chapter 15

15:1 And straightway in the morning the chief priests held a consultation with the elders and scribes and the whole council, and bound Jesus, and carried *him* away, and delivered *him* to Pilate.

In the morning *see Mark 1:35.*

Held In **Mark 15:1**, some mss. have the verb *poieo*, "to make," rendered "held (a consultation)"; the most authentic have *hetoimazo*, "to prepare," also translated "held."

Consultation *sumboulion* (4824), a word of the Graeco-Roman period, "counsel, advice," is translated "consultation" in **Mark 15:1** (with *poieo*, "to make"), "to hold a consultation"; elsewhere "counsel" in the RV, except in Acts 25:12, where, by metonymy, it means a "council."

Whole *see Mark 8:36.*

15:2-4 And Pilate asked him, Art thou the King of the Jews? And he answering said unto him, Thou sayest *it*.

And the chief priests accused him of many things: but he answered nothing.

And Pilate asked him again, saying, Answerest thou nothing? behold how many things they witness against thee.

Accused *kategoreo* (2723), "to speak against, accuse," is used (a) in a general way, "to accuse," e.g., Luke 6:7, RV, "how to accuse"; Rom. 2:15; Rev. 12:10; (b) before a judge, e.g., Matt. 12:10; **Mark 15:4** (RV, "witness against"); Acts 22:30; 25:16. In Acts 24:19, RV renders it "make accusation," for the KJV, "object."

Many *see Mark 6:38.*

15:5 But Jesus yet answered nothing; so that Pilate marvelled.

Yet ... nothing *ouketi*, "no longer," **Mark 15:5**, KJV, "yet ... nothing" (RV, "no more ... anything"); 2 Cor. 1:23, KJV, "not as yet", "yet not," e.g. Gal. 2:20, KJV.

15:6 Now at *that* feast he released unto them one prisoner, whomsoever they desired.

Released *apoluo* (630), "to loose from," is translated "to release" in Matt. 18:27, RV (KJV, "loosed"); 27:15, 17, 21, 26; **Mark 15:6, 9, 11, 15**; Luke 6:37 (twice), RV (KJV, "forgive" and "ye shall be forgiven"); 23:16 (v. 17, in some mss.), 18, 20, 25; 23:22, RV (KJV, "let ... go"); John 18:39 (twice); 19:10; in 19:12, in the 1st part, KJV and RV; in the 2nd part, RV, "release" (KJV, "let ... go"); so in Acts 3:13.

Prisoner *desmios* (1198), an adjective, primarily denotes "binding, bound," then, as a noun, "the person bound, a captive, prisoner" (akin to *deo*, "to bind"), Matt. 27:15, 16; **Mark 15:6**; Acts 16:25, 27; 23:18; 25:14, RV (KJV, "in bonds"), 27; 28:16, 17; Eph. 3:1; 4:1; 2 Tim. 1:8; Philem. 1, 9; in Heb. 10:34 and 13:3, "in bonds."

Whomsoever Some texts in **Mark 15:6** have *hosper*, a strengthened form of *hos*, KJV, "whomsoever."

15:7 And there was *one* named Barabbas, *which lay* bound with them that had made insurrection with him, who had committed murder in the insurrection.

Named In Matt. 9:9 and **Mark 15:7**, KJV, the verb *lego*, "to speak, to call by name," is rendered "named" (RV, "called").

Insurrection *stasis* (4714), akin to *histemi*, "to make to stand," denotes (a) primarily, "a standing or place," Heb. 9:8; (b) "an insurrection, sedition," translated "insurrection" in **Mark 15:7**; "insurrections" in Acts 24:5, RV (KJV, "sedition"); in Luke 23:19, 25 (KJV "sedition"), "riot," Acts 19:40, RV (KJV, "uproar"); (c) "a dissension," Acts 15:2; in Acts 23:7, 10, "dissension."

Who These are usually the translations of forms of the relative pronoun *hos*, or of the interrogative pronoun *tis;* otherwise of *hostis*, "whoever," usually of a more general subject than *hos*, e.g., **Mark 15:7**; Luke 23:19; Gal. 2:4; *hosos*, "as many as," Heb. 2:15; in Acts 13:7, KJV, *houtos*, "this (man)," is translated "who," RV, "the same."

Committed *poieo* (4160), "to do, cause, etc.," sometimes signifies "to commit, of any act, as of murder," **Mark 15:7**; sin, John 8:34; 2 Cor. 11:7; Jas. 5:15.

Murder *see* **Murders** at *Mark 7:21.*

15:8 And the multitude crying aloud began to desire *him to do* as he had ever done unto them.

Crying *anaboao* (310), "to lift up the voice, cry out," is said of Christ at the moment of His death, a testimony to His supernatural power in giving up His life, Matt. 27:46; in some mss. in **Mark 15:8**, of the shouting of a multitude; in some mss. in Luke 9:38, of the "crying" out of a man in a company.

Ever *aei* (104), "ever," is used (a) of continuous time, signifying "unceasingly, perpetually," Acts 7:51; 2 Cor. 4:11; 6:10; Titus 1:12; Heb. 3:10; (b) of successive occurrences, signifying "on every occasion," 1 Pet. 3:15; 2 Pet. 1:12. Some texts have the word in **Mark 15:8**.

15:9 But Pilate answered them, saying, Will ye that I release unto you the King of the Jews?

Release *see* Released at *Mark 15:6*.

15:10 For he knew that the chief priests had delivered him for envy.

Knew *see Mark 8:17*.

Envy *phthonos* (5355), "envy," is the feeling of displeasure produced by witnessing or hearing of the advantage or prosperity of others; this evil sense always attaches to this word, Matt. 27:18; **Mark 15:10**; Rom. 1:29; Gal. 5:21; Phil. 1:15; 1 Tim. 6:4; Titus 3:3; 1 Pet. 2:1; so in Jas. 4:5, where the question is rhetorical and strongly remonstrative, signifying that the Spirit (or spirit) which God made to dwell in us was certainly not so bestowed that we should be guilty of "envy."

15:11 But the chief priests moved the people, that he should rather release Barabbas unto them.

Moved *anaseio* (383), primarily denotes "to shake back or out, move to and fro"; then, "to stir up," used metaphorically in **Mark 15:11**, RV, "stirred ... up" (KJV, "moved"), and Luke 3:14; 23:5.

Release *see* Released at *Mark 15:6*.

15:12-13 And Pilate answered and said again unto them, What will ye then that I shall do *unto him* whom ye call the King of the Jews?

And they cried out again, Crucify him.

Cried out *krazo* (2896), "to cry out," an onomatopoeic word, used especially of the "cry" of the raven; then, of any inarticulate cries, from fear, pain, etc.; of the "cry" of a Canaanitish woman, Matt. 15:22 (so the best mss., instead of *kraugazo*); of the shouts of the children in the Temple, Matt. 21:15; of the people who shouted for Christ to be crucified, 27:23; **Mark 15:13-14**; of the "cry" of Christ on the Cross at the close of His sufferings, Matt. 27:50; **Mark 15:39**.

15:14 Then Pilate said unto them, Why, what evil hath he done? And they cried out the more exceedingly, Crucify him.

Exceedingly *see* Out of measure at *Mark 10:26*.

15:15 And *so* Pilate, willing to content the people, released Barabbas unto them, and delivered Jesus, when he had scourged *him*, to be crucified.

Willing *boulomai* (1014), in **Mark 15:15**, RV, is translated "wishing" (KJV, "willing"); so 2 Pet. 3:9; in Acts 25:22, RV, "could wish" (KJV, "would").

Content *hikanos* (2425), "sufficient," used with *poieo*, "to do," in **Mark 15:15**, is translated "to content (the multitude)," i.e., to do sufficient to satisfy them.

Released *see Mark 15:6*.

Scourged *phragelloo* (5417), (Latin, *flagello;* Eng., "flagellate"), is the word used in Matt. 27:26, and **Mark 15:15**, of the "scourging" endured by Christ and administered by the order of Pilate. Under the Roman method of "scourging," the person was stripped and tied in a bending posture to a pillar, or stretched on a frame. The "scourge" was made of leather thongs, weighted with sharp pieces of bone or lead, which tore the flesh of both the back and the breast (cf. Ps. 22:17). Eusebius (*Chron.*) records his having witnessed the suffering of martyrs who died under this treatment.

15:16 And the soldiers led him away into the hall, called Praetorium; and they call together the whole band.

Soldiers *stratiotes* (4757), "a soldier," is used (a) in the natural sense, e.g., Matt. 8:9; 27:27; 28:12; **Mark 15:16**; Luke 7:8; 23:36; six times in John; thirteen times in Acts; not again in the NT; (b) metaphorically of one who endures hardship in the cause of Christ, 2 Tim. 2:3.

Led *see* Lead at *Mark 14:44*.

Hall *aule* (833), "a court," most frequently the place where a governor dispensed justice, is rendered "hall" in **Mark 15:16** and Luke 22:55, KJV (RV, "court").

Praetorium *praitorion* (4232), is translated "common hall" in Matt. 27:27, KJV (RV, "palace"); "Praetorium" in **Mark 15:16**; "hall of judgment" or "judgment hall" in John 18:28, 33; 19:9; Acts 23:35 (RV, "palace," in each place); "praetorian guard," Phil. 1:13 (KJV, "palace").

Called *sunkaleo* (4779), signifies "to call together," **Mark 15:16**; Luke 9:1; 15:6, 9; 23:13; Acts 5:21; 10:24; 28:17.

Whole *see Mark 8:36.*

15:17 And they clothed him with purple, and platted a crown of thorns, and put it about his *head,*

Clothed *endidusko* (1737); the termination,–*sko* suggests the beginning or progress of the action. The verb is used in the middle voice in Luke 16:19 (of a rich man). Some mss. have it in 8:27, for *enduo* (of a demoniac). In **Mark 15:17** the best texts have this verb.

Purple *porphura* (4209), originally denoted the "purple-fish," then, "purple dye" (extracted from certain shell fish): hence, "a purple garment," **Mark 15:17, 20**; Luke 16:19; Rev. 18:12.

Platted *pleko* (4120), "to weave, twist, plait," is used of the crown of thorns inflicted on Christ, Matt. 27:29; **Mark 15:17**; John 19:2.

Crown *stephanos* (4735), primarily, "that which surrounds, as a wall or crowd" (from *stepho*, "to encircle"), denotes (a) "the victor's crown," the symbol of triumph in the games or some such contest; hence, by metonymy, a reward or prize; (b) "a token of public honor" for distinguished service, military prowess, etc., or of nuptial joy, or festal gladness, especially at the parousia of kings. It was woven as a garland of oak, ivy, parsley, myrtle, or olive, or in imitation of these in gold. In some passages the reference to the games is clear, 1 Cor. 9:25; 2 Tim. 4:8 ("crown of righteousness"); it may be so in 1 Pet. 5:4, where the fadeless character of "the crown of glory" is set in contrast to the garlands of earth. In other passages it stands as an emblem of life, joy, reward and glory, Phil. 4:1; 1 Thess. 2:19; Jas. 1:12 ("crown of life"); Rev. 2:10 (ditto); 3:11; 4:4, 10: of triumph, 6:2; 9:7; 12:1; 14:14. It is used of "the crown of thorns" which the soldiers plaited and put on Christ's head, Matt. 27:29; **Mark 15:17**; John 19:2, 5. At first sight this might be taken as an alternative for *diadema*, "a kingly crown", but considering the blasphemous character of that masquerade, and the materials used, obviously *diadema* would be quite unfitting and the only alternative was *stephanos.*

Thorns *akanthinos* (174), "of thorns," is used in **Mark 15:17** and John 19:5. In the Sept., Isa. 34:13.

Put *peritithemi* (4060), "to put around or on," is so used in Matt. 27:28; **Mark 15:17**, RV, "put on" (KJV, "... about"); **15:36**; John 19:29.

15:18 And began to salute him, Hail, King of the Jews!

Hail *chairo* (5463), "to rejoice," is used in the imperative mood, (a) as a salutation, only in the Gospels; in this respect it is rendered simply "hail," in mockery of Christ, Matt. 26:49; 27:29; **Mark 15:18**; John 19:3; (b) as a greeting, by the angel Gabriel to Mary, Luke 1:28, and, in the plural, by the Lord to the disciples after His resurrection, Matt. 28:9.

15:19 And they smote him on the head with a reed, and did spit upon him, and bowing *their* knees worshipped him.

Smote *tupto* (5180), from a root *tup*–, meaning "a blow," (*tupos*, "a figure or print:" (Eng., "type") denotes "to smite, strike, or beat," usually not with the idea of giving a thrashing as with *dero*. It frequently signifies a "blow" of violence, and, when used in a continuous tense, indicates a series of "blows." In Matt. 27:30 the imperfect tense signifies that the soldiers kept on striking Christ on the head. So **Mark 15:19**. The most authentic mss. omit it in Luke 22:64. In that verse the word *paio*, "to smite," is used of the treatment given to Christ (*dero* in the preceding verse). The imperfect tense of the verb is again used in Acts 18:17, of the beating given to Sosthenes. Cf. Acts 21:32, which has the present participle. It is used in the metaphorical sense of "wounding," in 1 Cor. 8:12.

Reed *kalamos* (2563), denotes (a) "the reed" mentioned in Matt. 11:7; 12:20; Luke 7:24, the same as the Heb., *qaneh* (among the various reeds in the OT), e.g., Isa. 42:3, from which Matt. 12:20 is quoted (cf. Job 40:21; Ezek. 29:6, "a reed with jointed, hollow stalk"); (b) "a reed staff, staff," Matt. 27:29, 30, 48; **Mark 15:19, 36** (cf. *rhabdos*, "a rod"; in 2 Kings 18:21, *rhabdos kalamine*); (c) "a measuring reed or rod," Rev. 11:1; 21:15, 16; (d) "a writing reed, a pen," 3 John 13.

Spit *see Mark 10:34.*

Bowing *tithemi* (5087), "to put, or place," is said of the soldiers who mockingly bowed their knees to Christ, **Mark 15:19**.

Knees *gonu* (1119), "a knee" (Latin, *genu*), is used (a) metaphorically in Heb. 12:12, where the duty enjoined is that of "courageous self-recovery in God's strength;" (b) literally, of the attitude of a suppliant, Luke 5:8; Eph. 3:14; of veneration, Rom. 11:4; 14:11; Phil. 2:10; in mockery, **Mark 15:19**.

15:20 And when they had mocked him, they took off the purple from him, and put his own clothes on him, and led him out to crucify him.

Mocked *see* Mock at *Mark 10:34.*

Took off *ekduo* (1562), "to take off, strip off," is used especially of clothes, and rendered "to strip" in Matt. 27:28 (some mss. have *enduo*, "to clothe"), and Luke 10:30, to take off, Matt. 27:31; **Mark 15:20**; figuratively, 2 Cor. 5:4, "unclothed" (middle voice), of putting off the body at death (the believer's state of being unclothed does not refer to the body in the grave but to the spirit, which awaits the "body of glory" at the resurrection).

Purple *see Mark 15:17.*

Put *see Mark 6:9.*

Led *see Mark 8:23.*

15:21 And they compel one Simon a Cyrenian, who passed by, coming out of the country, the father of Alexander and Rufus, to bear his cross.

Compel *angareuo* (29), "to dispatch as an *angaros*" (a Persian courier kept at regular stages with power of impressing men into service), and hence, in general, "to impress into service," is used of "compelling" a person to go a mile, Matt. 5:41; of the impressing of Simon to bear Christ's cross, Matt. 27:32; **Mark 15:21**.

Country *see Mark 5:14.*

15:22 And they bring him unto the place Golgotha, which is, being interpreted, The place of a skull.

Interpreted *see Mark 5:41.*

Skull *kranion* (2898), Lat., *cranium* (akin to *kara*, "the head"), is used of the scene of the Crucifixion, Matt. 27:33; **Mark 15:22**; John 19:17; in Luke 23:33, RV, "(the place which is called) The skull," KJV, "Calvary" (from Latin *calvaria*, "a skull": marg., "the place of a skull"). The locality has been identified by the traces of the resemblance of the hill to a "skull." In the Sept., Judg. 9:53; 2 Kings 9:35.

15:23 And they gave him to drink wine mingled with myrrh: but he received *it* not.

Mingled For the verb *smurnizo*, "to mingle with myrrh," **Mark 15:23**.

Myrrh *smurnizo* (4669), is used transitively in the NT, with the meaning "to mingle or drug with myrrh," **Mark 15:23**; the mixture was doubtless offered to deaden the pain (Matthew's word "gall" suggests that "myrrh" was not the only ingredient). Christ refused to partake of any such means of alleviation; He would retain all His mental power for the complete fulfillment of the Father's will.

15:24 And when they had crucified him, they parted his garments, casting lots upon them, what every man should take.

Parted *diamerizo* (1266), "to part among, to distribute," is translated by the verb "to part" (a) in the middle voice, with reference to the Lord's garments, Matt. 27:35, 1st part (in some mss., 2nd part); **Mark 15:24**; Luke 23:34; John 19:24; (b) in the active voice, of "the proceeds of the sale of possessions and goods," Acts 2:45; (c) in the passive voice in Acts 2:3, of the "parting asunder" (RV) of tongues like fire (KJV, "cloven").

Lots *kleros* (2819), denotes (a) an object used in casting or drawing lots, which consisted of bits, or small tablets, of wood or stone (the probable derivation is from *klao*, "to break"); these were sometimes inscribed with the names of persons, and were put into a receptacle or a garment ("a lap," Prov. 16:33), from which they were cast, after being shaken together; he whose "lot" first fell out was the one chosen. The method was employed in a variety of circumstances, e.g., of dividing or assigning property, Matt. 27:35; **Mark 15:24**; Luke 23:34; John 19:24 (cf., e.g., Num. 26:55); of appointing to office, Acts 1:26 (cf. e.g., 1 Sam. 10:20); for other occurrences in the OT, see, e.g., Josh. 7:14 (the earliest instance in Scripture), Lev. 16:7-10; Esth. 3:7; 9:24; (b) "what is obtained by lot, an allotted portion," e.g., of the ministry allotted to the apostles, Acts 1:17, RV, "portion," marg., "lot" (KJV, "part"); in some mss. v. 25, KJV, "part" (the RV follows those which have *topos*, "place).

Every The pronoun *tis*, "anyone," is rendered "any" in Acts 2:45, RV, for the incorrect KJV, "every." In **Mark 15:24**, the interrogative form is rendered "what each (should take)" (KJV, "every man"), lit., "who (should take) what."

15:25 And it was the third hour, and they crucified him.

Third *see Mark 9:31.*

15:26 And the superscription of his accusation was written over, THE KING OF THE JEWS.

Superscription *see Mark 12:16.*

Accusation *aitia* (156), probably has the primary meaning of "a cause, especially an occasion of something evil, hence a charge, an accusation." It is used in a forensic sense, of (a) an accusation, Acts 25:18 (RV, "charge"), 27; (b) a crime, Matt. 27:37; **Mark 15:26**, John 18:38; 19:4, 6; Acts 13:28; 23:28; 28:18.

Written over *epigrapho* (1924), is rendered "to write over or upon" (*epi*) in **Mark 15:26**; figuratively, on the heart, Heb. 8:10; 10:16; on the gates of the heavenly Jerusalem, Rev. 21:12.

15:27 And with him they crucify two thieves; the one on his right hand, and the other on his left.

Thieves *lestes* (3027), "a robber, brigand" (akin to *leia*, "booty"), "one who plunders openly and by violence" (in contrast to *kleptes*, "a thief"), is always translated "robber" or "robbers" in the RV, as the KJV in John 10:1, 8, 18:40; 2 Cor. 11:26; the KJV has "thief" or "thieves" in Matt. 21:13, and parallel passages; 26:55, and parallel passages; 27:38, 44 and **Mark 15:27**; Luke 10:30, 36; but "thief" is the meaning of *kleptes*.

Left *see* ***Mark 10:37.***

15:28 And the scripture was fulfilled, which saith, And he was numbered with the transgressors.

Numbered Some mss. have verse **Mark 15:28** (KJV), *logizomai*, "to reckon," translated "He was numbered."

Transgressors *anomos* (459), "without law" (*a*-, negative), is translated "transgressors" in Luke 22:37 (in some texts, **Mark 15:28**), in a quotation from Isa. 53:12.

15:29 And they that passed by railed on him, wagging their heads, and saying, Ah, thou that destroyest the temple, and buildest *it* in three days,

Passed *see* Pass at *Mark 2:23.*

Railed *blasphemeo* (987), "to blaspheme, rail, revile," is translated "to rail at, or on," in Matt. 27:39, RV (KJV, "reviled"); **Mark 15:29**; Luke 23:39; 2 Pet. 2:10, RV (KJV, "to speak evil of"); 2:12, RV (KJV, "speak evil of"). Cf. *loidoreo*, "to revile."

Wagging *kineo* (2795), "to set in motion, move" (hence, e.g., Eng. "kinematics," "kinetics," "cinema"), is used (a) of wagging the head, Matt. 27:39; **Mark 15:29**; (b) of the general activity of the human being, Acts 17:28; (c) of the "moving" of mountains, Rev. 6:14, in the sense of removing, as in Rev. 2:5, of removing a lampstand (there figuratively of causing a local church to be discontinued); (d) figuratively, of exciting, stirring up feelings and passions, Acts 21:30 (passive voice); 24:5, "a mover"; (e) of "moving burdens," Matt. 23:4. Cf. *sunkineo*, "to stir up," Acts 6:12.

Ah! *oua* (3758), an interjection of derision and insult, is translated "Ha!" in **Mark 15:29**, RV.

Destroyest *see* Thrown down at *Mark 13:2.*

15:30-31 Save thyself, and come down from the cross.

Likewise also the chief priests mocking said among themselves with the scribes, He saved others; himself he cannot save.

Mocking *see* Mock at *Mark 10:34.*

Themselves *see* *Mark 8:16.*

15:32 Let Christ the King of Israel descend now from the cross, that we may see and believe. And they that were crucified with him reviled him.

King *basileus* (935), "a king" (cf. Eng., "Basil"), e.g., Matt. 1:6, is used of the Roman emperor in 1 Pet. 2:13, 17 (a command of general application); this reference to the emperor is illustrated frequently in the *Koine*; of Herod the Tetrarch (used by courtesy), Matt. 14:9; of Christ, as the "King" of the Jews, e.g., Matt, 2:2; 27:11, 29, 37; as the "King" of Israel, **Mark 15:32**; John 1:49; 12:13; as "King of kings," Rev. 17:14; 19:16; as "the King" in judging nations and men at the establishment of the millennial kingdom, Matt. 25:34, 40; of God, "the great King," Matt. 5:35; "the King eternal, incorruptible, invisible," 1 Tim. 1:17; "King of kings," 1 Tim. 6:15; "King of the ages," Rev. 15:3, RV (KJV, "saints"). Christ's "kingship" was predicted in the OT, e.g., Ps. 2:6, and in the NT, e.g., Luke 1:32, 33; He came as such, e.g., Matt. 2:2; John 18:37; was rejected and died as such, Luke 19:14; Matt. 27:37; is now a "King" Priest, after the order of Melchizedek, Heb. 5:6; 7:1, 17; and will reign for ever and ever, Rev. 11:15.

Descend *katabaino* (2597), "to go down" (*kata*, "down," *baino*, "to go"), used for various kinds of motion on the ground (e.g., going, walking, stepping), is usually translated "to descend." The RV uses the verb "to come down," for KJV, "descend," in **Mark 15:32**; Acts 24:1; Rev. 21:10.

Cross *sustauroo* (4957), "to crucify with" (*su*-, "for," *sun*, "with"), is used (a) of actual "crucifixion" in company with another, Matt. 27:44; **Mark 15:32**; John 19:32; (b) metaphorically, of spiritual identification with Christ in His death, Rom. 6:6, and Gal. 2:20.

Reviled *oneidizo* (3679), signifies (a) in the active voice, "to reproach, upbraid," Matt. 5:11, RV, "shall reproach" (KJV, "shall revile"); 11:20, "to upbraid"; 27:44, RV, "cast ... reproach" [KJV, "cast ... in (His) teeth"]; **Mark 15:32** RV, "reproached" (KJV, "reviled"); **16:14** "upbraided"; Luke 6:22 "shall reproach", Rom. 15:3; Jas. 1:5, "upbraideth"; (b) in the passive voice, "to suffer reproach, be reproached," 1 Tim. 4:10 (in some mss. in the 2nd part); 1 Pet. 4:14.

15:33 And when the sixth hour was come, there was darkness over the whole land until the ninth hour.

Whole *see Mark 8:36.*

Ninth *enatos* or *ennatos* (1766), is found in reference (a) to "the ninth hour" (3 o'clock, p.m.) in Matt. 20:5; 27:45-46; **Mark 15:33-34**; Luke 23:44; Acts 3:1; 10:3, 30; (b) to "the topaz" as the "ninth" foundation of the city wall in the symbolic vision in Rev. 21 (v. 20).

15:34 And at the ninth hour Jesus cried with a loud voice, saying, Eloi, Eloi, lama sabachthani? which is, being interpreted, My God, my God, why hast thou forsaken me?

Cried *see* Crying at *Mark 1:3.*

Lama *lama* (2982), is the Hebrew word for "Why?" (the variant *lema* is the Aramaic form), Matt. 27:46; **Mark 15:34**.

Sabachthani *sabachthanei* (4518), an Aramaic word signifying "Thou hast forsaken Me," is recorded as part of the utterance of Christ on the cross, Matt. 27:46; **Mark 15:34**, a quotation from Ps. 22:1. Recently proposed renderings which differ from those of the KJV and RV have not been sufficiently established to require acceptance.

Interpreted *see Mark 5:41.*

God *see Mark 8:33.*

Forsaken *enkataleipo* (1459), denotes (a) "to leave behind, among, leave surviving," Rom. 9:29; (b) "to forsake, abandon, leave in straits, or helpless," said by, or of, Christ, Matt. 27:46; **Mark 15:34**; Acts 2:27, 31; of men, 2 Cor. 4:9; 2 Tim. 4:10, 16; by God, Heb. 13:5; of things, by Christians (negatively), Heb. 10:25.

15:35 And some of them that stood by, when they heard *it*, said, Behold, he calleth Elias.

Stood *see Mark 14:47.*

15:36 And one ran and filled a spunge full of vinegar, and put *it* on a reed, and gave him to drink, saying, Let alone; let us see whether Elias will come to take him down.

Filled *see* Full at *Mark 4:37.*

Spunge *spongos* (4699), was the medium by which vinegar was carried to the mouth of Christ on the cross, Matt. 27:48; **Mark 15:36**; John 19:29.

Vinegar *see* Wine at *Mark 15:23.*

Put *see Mark 15:17.*

Reed *see Mark 15:19.*

Drink *see Mark 9:41.*

Let *see Mark 7:27.*

Take ... down *kathaireo* (2507), lit. signifies "to take down" (*kata*, "down," *haireo*, "to take"), the technical term for "removing a body after crucifixion," e.g., **Mark 15:36**; hence, "to pull down, demolish"; in Acts 19:27, according to the most authentic mss., the translation is (as the RV) "that she (Diana) should even be deposed from her magnificence" (possibly, in the partitive sense of the genitive, "destroyed from, or diminished in, somewhat of her magnificence").

15:37 And Jesus cried with a loud voice, and gave up the ghost.

Cried *aphiemi* (863), "to send forth," is used of "uttering" a cry, **Mark 15:37**, of Christ's final "utterance" on the cross, RV, "uttered" (KJV, "cried").

Ghost *ekpneo* (1606), lit., "to breathe out" (*ek*, "out," *pneo*, "to breathe"), "to expire," is used in the NT, without an object, "soul" or "life" being understood, **Mark 15:37, 39**, and Luke 23:46, of the death of Christ. In Matt. 27:50 and John 19:30, where different verbs are used, the act is expressed in a way which stresses it as of His own volition: in the former, "Jesus ... yielded up His spirit (*pneuma*); in the latter, "He gave up His spirit."

15:38 And the veil of the temple was rent in twain from the top to the bottom.

Veil *katapetasma* (2665), lit., "that which is spread out" (*petannumi*) "before" (*kata*), hence, "a veil," is used (a) of the inner "veil" of the tabernacle, Heb. 6:19; 9:3; (b) of the corresponding "veil" in the Temple, Matt. 27:51; **Mark 15:38**; Luke 23:45; (c) metaphorically of the "flesh" of Christ, Heb. 10:20, i.e., His body which He gave up to be crucified, thus by His expiatory death providing a means of the spiritual access of believers, the "new and living way," into the presence of God.

Rent *see* Opened at *Mark 1:10.*

Twain *see Mark 10:8.*

From the top *anothen* (509), "from above," is used of place, (a) with the meaning "from the top," Matt. 27:51; **Mark 15:38**, of the temple veil; in John 19:23, of the garment of Christ, lit., "from the upper parts" (plural); (b) of things which come from heaven, or from God in Heaven, John 3:31; 19:11; Jas. 1:17; 3:15, 17. It is also used in the sense of "again."

To *see* Beneath at *Mark 14:66.*

15:39 And when the centurion, which stood over against him, saw that he so cried out, and gave up the ghost, he said, Truly this man was the Son of God.

Centurion *kenturion* (2760), is a Greek transliteration of the Latin *centurio*, **Mark 15:39, 44-45**. There were ten "centurions" to a cohort when the numbers were complete. There were several at Jerusalem under the chief captain mentioned in Acts 21:31.

Stood *see Mark 14:47*.

Against *see* Contrary at *Mark 6:48*.

Cried *see Mark 15:13*.

Ghost *see Mark 15:37*.

Truly *see* Surely at *Mark 14:70*.

15:40 There were also women looking on afar off: among whom was Mary Magdalene, and Mary the mother of James the less and of Joses, and Salome;

Looking *theoreo* (2334), "to look at, gaze at, behold," is translated "looking on" in **Mark 15:40**, KJV (RV, "beholding").

Afar *see Mark 5:6*.

Less *see* Little at *Mark 9:42*.

15:41 (Who also, when he was in Galilee, followed him, and ministered unto him;) and many other women which came up with him unto Jerusalem.

Ministered *see Mark 1:13*.

Came *sunanabaino* (4872), "to come up with" (*sun*, "with," *ana*, "up"), is used in **Mark 15:41**; Acts 13:31.

15:42 And now when the even was come, because it was the preparation, that is, the day before the sabbath,

Preparation *paraskeue* (3904), denotes "preparation, equipment." The day on which Christ died is called "the Preparation" in **Mark 15:42** and John 19:31; in John 19:42 "the Jews' Preparation," RV; in 19:14 it is described as "the Preparation of the Passover"; in Luke 23:54, RV, "the day of the Preparation (and the Sabbath drew on)." The same day is in view in Matt. 27:62, where the events recorded took place on "the day after the Preparation" (RV). The reference would be to the 6th day of the week. The title arose from the need of preparing food, etc., for the Sabbath. Apparently it was first applied only to the afternoon of the 6th day; later, to the whole day. In regard to the phraseology in John 19:14, many hold this to indicate the "preparation" for the paschal feast. It probably means "the Preparation day," and thus falls in line with the Synoptic Gospels. In modern Greek and ecclesiastical Latin, *Parasceve* = Friday.

Sabbath *prosabbaton* (4315), signifies "the day before the sabbath," **Mark 15:42**; some mss. have *prin*, "before," with *sabbaton* separately).

15:43 Joseph of Arimathaea, an honourable counsellor, which also waited for the kingdom of God, came, and went in boldly unto Pilate, and craved the body of Jesus.

Honourable *euschemon* (2158), "elegant in figure, well formed, graceful," is used in 1 Cor. 12:24, of parts of the body; in 1 Cor. 7:35 RV, "(that which is) seemly," KJV, "comely"; "honourable," **Mark 15:43**; Acts 13:50; 17:12.

Counsellor *bouleutes* (1010), Joseph of Arimathaea is described as "a councillor of honorable estate," **Mark 15:43**, RV; cf. Luke 23:50 (not as KJV, "counsellor").

Waited *prosdechomai* (4327), "to look for" with a view to favorable reception, is rendered "to wait for" in **Mark 15:43**; Luke 2:25; 12:36; 23:51.

Craved The word "crave," found in the KJV of **Mark 15:43**, translates the verb *aiteo*, "to ask" (RV, "asked for").

15:44 And Pilate marvelled if he were already dead: and calling *unto him* the centurion, he asked him whether he had been any while dead.

Centurion *see Mark 15:39*.

While In **Mark 15:44** *palai*, "long ago," is rendered "any while."

15:45 And when he knew *it* of the centurion, he gave the body to Joseph.

Knew *ginosko* (1097), "to know by observation and experience," is translated "to learn," in the RV of **Mark 15:45**; John 12:9.

Gave *doreo* (1433), "to present, bestow," is rendered "granted" in **Mark 15:45**, RV (KJV, "gave"); in 2 Pet. 1:3, 4, "hath granted," "He hath granted," RV (KJV, "hath given" and "are given"); in each place middle voice.

Body *see* Corpse at *Mark 6:29*.

15:46 And he bought fine linen, and took him down, and wrapped him in the linen, and laid him in a sepulchre which was hewn out of a rock, and rolled a stone unto the door of the sepulchre.

Linen *see* Linen cloth at *Mark 14:51*.

Took *see* Take at *Mark 15:36*.

Wrapped *eneileo* (1750), "to roll in, wind in," is used in **Mark 15:46**, of "winding" the cloth around the Lord's body, RV, "wound" (KJV, "wrapped").

Laid *katatithemi* (2698), "to lay down" (*kata*), is used in **Mark 15:46** of the act of Joseph of Arimathaea in "laying" Christ's body in the tomb.

Sepulchre *see* Tombs at *Mark 5:3*.

Hewn *latomeo* (2998), signifies "to hew out stones" (from *latomos*, "a stone-cutter"; *las*, "a stone," *temno*, "to cut"), and is used of the sepulchre which Joseph of Arimathaea had "hewn" out of a rock for himself, where the body of the Lord was buried, Matt. 27:60; **Mark 15:46**.

Rock *petra* (4073), denotes "a mass of rock," as distinct from *petros*, "a detached stone or boulder," or a stone that might be thrown or easily moved. For the nature of *petra*, see Matt. 7:24, 25; 27:51, 60; **Mark 15:46**; Luke 6:48 (twice), a type of a sure foundation (here the true reading is as in the RV, "because it had been well builded"); Rev. 6:15, 16 (cf. Isa. 2:19ff.; Hos. 10:8); Luke 8:6, 13, used illustratively; 1 Cor. 10:4 (twice), figuratively, of Christ; in Rom. 9:33 and 1 Pet. 2:8, metaphorically, of Christ; in Matt. 16:18, metaphorically, of Christ and the testimony concerning Him; here the distinction between *petra*, concerning the Lord Himself, and *Petros*, the apostle, is clear.

Rolled *proskulio* (4351), "to roll up or to" (*pros*), is used in Matt. 27:60; **Mark 15:46**, of the sepulchre stone.

15:47 And Mary Magdalene and Mary *the mother* of Joses beheld where he was laid.

Beheld *theoreo* (2334), from *theoros*, "a spectator," is used of one who looks at a thing with interest and for a purpose, usually indicating the careful observation of details; see, e.g., **Mark 15:47**; Luke 10:18; 23:35; John 20:6 (RV, "beholdeth," for KJV, "seeth"); so in verses 12 and 14; "consider," in Heb. 7:4. It is used of experience, in the sense of partaking of, in John 8:51; 17:24. Cf. *theoria*, "sight," Luke 23:48, only.

Laid *see Mark 6:29*.

Chapter 16

16:1 And when the sabbath was past, Mary Magdalene, and Mary the *mother* of James, and Salome, had bought sweet spices, that they might come and anoint him.

Past *diaginomai* (1230), *dia*, "through," used of time, denotes "to intervene, elapse, pass," **Mark 16:1**, "was past"; Acts 25:13, RV, "were passed"; 27:9, "was spent."

Mother In **Mark 16:1** the article, followed by the genitive case of the name "James," the word "mother" being omitted, is an idiomatic mode of expressing the phrase "the mother of James."

Spices *aroma* (759), "spice," occurs in **Mark 16:1**, RV "spices" (KJV, "sweet spice"); Luke 23:56; 24:1; John 19:40. A papyrus document has it in a list of articles for a sacrifice.

Anoint *see* Anointed at *Mark 6:13*.

16:2 And very early in the morning the first *day* of the week, they came unto the sepulchre at the rising of the sun.

Very The adverb *lian* is translated "very" in **Mark 16:2**; 2 Cor. 11:5; 12:11.

Early *proi* (4404), "early in the day, at morn," is derived from *pro*, "before." In **Mark 16:2**, KJV, it is translated "early in the morning"; in **Mark 16:9** and John 18:28; 20:1, "early"; in Matt. 16:3; 20:1; 21:18; **Mark 1:35**; **11:20**; **13:35**; **15:1**, "in the morning"; in Acts 28:23, "(from) morning."

Morning *see Mark 1:35*.

Week *sabbaton* (4521), is used (a) in the plural in the phrase "the first day of the week," Matt. 28:1; **Mark 16:2**, **9**; Luke 24:1; John 20:1, 19; Acts 20:7; 1 Cor. 16:2; (b) in the singular, Luke 18:12, "twice in the week," lit., "twice of the sabbath," i.e., twice in the days after the sabbath.

Sepulchre *see* Tombs at *Mark 5:3*.

Rising *see Mark 9:10*.

16:3 And they said among themselves, Who shall roll us away the stone from the door of the sepulchre?

Roll *apokulio* or *apokulizo* (617), "to roll away" (*apo*, "from," *kulio*, "to roll"; cf. Eng., "cylinder," etc.), is used of the sepulchre stone, Matt. 28:2; **Mark 16:3** (v. **4** in some mss.); Luke 24:2. In the Sept., Gen. 29:3, 8, 10.

16:4 And when they looked, they saw that the stone was rolled away: for it was very great.

Rolled *anakulio* (303 and 2947), "to roll up or back" (*ana*), is found in the best texts, in **Mark 16:4**. *See also* Roll at *Mark 16:3*.

Very *sphodra* (4970), properly the neuter plural of *sphodros*, "excessive, violent" (from a root indicating restlessness), signifies "very, very much, exceedingly," Matt. 2:10; 17:6, "sore"; 17:23; 18:31, RV, "exceeding," for KJV, "very"; 19:25; 26:22; 27:54, RV, "exceedingly" for KJV, "greatly"; **Mark 16:4**, "very"; Luke 18:23 (ditto); Acts 6:7, RV, "exceedingly," for KJV, greatly; Rev. 16:21.

"Jesus has forced open a door that had been locked since the death of the first man. He has met, fought, and beaten the King of Death. Everything is different because he has done so."

C. S. LEWIS

16:5 And entering into the sepulchre, they saw a young man sitting on the right side, clothed in a long white garment; and they were affrighted.

Young *see Mark 14:51.*

White *see Mark 9:3.*

Garment *stole* (4749), is translated "robe" in **Mark 16:5**, RV (KJV, "garment"); "long robes" in Luke 20:46.

Right *see Mark 10:37.*

Affrighted *see* Amazed at *Mark 9:15.*

16:6 And he saith unto them, Be not affrighted: Ye seek Jesus of Nazareth, which was crucified: he is risen; he is not here: behold the place where they laid him.

Affrighted *see* Amazed at *Mark 9:15.*

Laid *see Mark 6:29.*

16:7-8 But go your way, tell his disciples and Peter that he goeth before you into Galilee: there shall ye see him, as he said unto you.

And they went out quickly, and fled from the sepulchre; for they trembled and were amazed: neither said they any thing to any *man*; for they were afraid.

Amazed *see* Astonished, Astonishment at *Mark 5:42.*

Trembled *tromos* (5156), "a trembling," occurs in **Mark 16:8**, RV, "trembling (... had come upon them)"; 1 Cor. 2:3; 2 Cor. 7:15; Eph. 6:5; Phil. 2:12.

16:9 Now when *Jesus* was risen early the first *day* of the week, he appeared first to Mary Magdalene, out of whom he had cast seven devils.

Early *see Mark 16:2.*

First *protos* (4413), the superlative degree of *pro*, "before," is used (I) "of time or place," (a) as a noun, e.g., Luke 14:18; Rev. 1:17; opposite to "the last," in the neuter plural, Matt. 12:45; Luke 11:26; 2 Pet. 2:20; in the neuter singular, opposite to "the second," Heb. 10:9; in 1 Cor. 15:3, *en protois*, lit., "in the first (things, or matters)" denotes "first of all"; (b) as an adjective, e.g., **Mark 16:9**, used with "day" understood, lit., "the first (day) of (i.e., after) the Sabbath," in which phrase the "of" is objective, not including the Sabbath, but following it; in John 20:4, 8; Rom. 10:19, e.g., equivalent to an English adverb; in John 1:15, lit., "first of me," i.e., "before me" (of superiority); (II) "of rank or dignity."

Week *see Mark 16:2.*

Appeared *phaino* (5316), signifies, in the active voice, "to shine"; in the passive, "to be brought forth into light, to become evident, to appear." In Rom. 7:13, concerning sin, the RV has "might be shewn to be," for KJV, "appear." It is used of the "appearance" of Christ to the disciples, **Mark 16:9**; of His future "appearing" in glory as the Son of Man, spoken of as a sign to the world, Matt. 24:30; there the genitive is subjective, the sign being the "appearing" of Christ Himself; of Christ as the light, John 1:5; of John the Baptist, 5:35; of the "appearing" of an angel of the Lord, either visibly, Matt. 1:20, or in a dream, 2:13; of a star, 2:7; of men who make an outward show, Matt. 6:5; 6:18 (see the RV); 23:27-28; 2 Cor. 13:7; of tares, Matt. 13:26; of a vapor, Jas. 4:14; of things physical in general, Heb. 11:3; used impersonally in Matt. 9:33, "it was never so seen"; also of what appears to the mind, and so in the sense of to think, **Mark 14:64**, or to seem, Luke 24:11 (RV, "appeared").

16:10 *And* she went and told them that had been with him, as they mourned and wept.

Mourned *pentheo* (3996), "to mourn for, lament," is used (a) of mourning in general, Matt. 5:4; 9:15; Luke 6:25; (b) of sorrow for the death of a loved one, **Mark 16:10**; (c) of "mourning" for the overthrow of Babylon and the Babylonish system, Rev. 18:11, 15, RV, "mourning" (KJV, "wailing"); v. 19 (ditto); (d) of sorrow for sin or for condoning it, Jas. 4:9; 1 Cor. 5:2; (e) of grief for those in a local church who show no repentance for evil committed, 2 Cor. 12:21, RV, "mourn" (KJV, "bewail"). Trench points out that *pentheo* is often joined with *klaio*, "to weep," 2 Sam. 19:1; **Mark 16:10**; Jas. 4:9; Rev. 18:15, indicating that *pentheo* is used especially of external manifestation of grief (as with *kopto* and *threneo*), in contrast to *lupeomai* which may be used of inward grief (*Syn.* Sec.xlv);

though in Classical Greek *pentheo* was used of grief without violent manifestations (Grimm-Thayer).

Wept *see Mark 5:38.*

16:11 And they, when they had heard that he was alive, and had been seen of her, believed not.

Seen *theaomai* (2300), "to view attentively, to see with admiration, desire, or regard," stresses more especially the action of the person beholding; it is used in Matt. 11:7 (RV, "to behold"), while *idein*, the infinitive of *eidon*, is used in the questions in the next two verses; in verse 7 the interest in the onlooker is stressed, in vv. 8, 9, the attention is especially directed to the object "seen." The verb is translated "to see" in the KJV and RV of Matt. 6:1; **Mark 16:11, 14**; John 6:5; Acts 8:18 (in some mss.); 21:27; Rom. 15:24; elsewhere, for the KJV, "to see," the RV uses the verb "to behold," bringing out its force more suitably.

Believed not *apisteo* (569), "to be unbelieving" (*a*, negative, *pistis*, "faith"; cf. *apistos*, "unbelieving"), is translated "believed not," etc., in the KJV (except in 1 Pet. 2:7, "be disobedient"); "disbelieve" (or "disbelieved") in the RV, in **Mark 16:11, 16**; Luke 24:11, 41; Acts 28:24; "disbelieve" is the best rendering, implying that the unbeliever has had a full opportunity of believing and has rejected it; some mss. have *apeitheo*, "to be disobedient," in 1 Pet. 2:7; Rom. 3:3, RV, "were without faith"; 2 Tim. 2:13, RV, "are faithless."

16:12 After that he appeared in another form unto two of them, as they walked, and went into the country.

Appeared *phaneroo* (5319), "to make visible, clear, manifest," known, is used especially in the writings of the apostles John and Paul, occurring 9 times in the Gospel, 9 times in 1 John, 2 in Rev.; in the Pauline Epistles (including Heb.) 24 times; in the other Gospels, only in Mark, 3 times; elsewhere in 1 Pet. 1:20; 5:4.

The true meaning is "to uncover, lay bare, reveal." The following are variations in the rendering, which should be noted: **Mark 16:12, 14** (RV, "was manifested," KJV, "appeared"); John 21:1 (RV, "manifested," KJV, "shewed"; cf. v. 14); Rom. 1:19 (RV, "manifested," KJV, "hath shewed"); 2 Cor. 3:3 (RV, "being made manifest," KJV, "are manifestly declared"); 2 Cor. 5:10; 7:12 and Rev. 3:18 (RV, "be made manifest," KJV, "appear"); 2 Cor. 11:6 (RV, "we have made it manifest," KJV, "we have been throughly made manifest"); Col. 1:26 (RV "hath it been manifested," KJV, "is made manifest"); 3:4 (RV, "be manifested," KJV, "appear"; so 1 Pet. 5:4); 1 Tim. 3:16 (RV, "was manifested," KJV, "was manifest"); 2 Tim. 1:10 (RV, "hath ... been manifested," KJV, "is ... made manifest"; cf. Rom. 16:26, 2 Cor. 4:10, 11; 1 Pet. 1:20); Heb. 9:26 (RV, "hath He been manifested," KJV, "hath He appeared"); 1 John 2:28; 3:2 (RV, "is ... made manifest," KJV, "doth appear").

Form *morphe* (3444), denotes "the special or characteristic form or feature" of a person or thing; it is used with particular significance in the NT, only of Christ, in Phil. 2:6, 7, in the phrases "being in the form of God," and "taking the form of a servant." An excellent definition of the word is that of Gifford: "*morphe* is therefore properly the nature or essence, not in the abstract, but as actually subsisting in the individual, and retained as long as the individual itself exists.... Thus in the passage before us *morphe Theou* is the Divine nature actually and inseparably subsisting in the Person of Christ.... For the interpretation of 'the form of God' it is sufficient to say that (1) it includes the whole nature and essence of Deity, and is inseparable from them, since they could have no actual existence without it; and (2) that it does not include in itself anything 'accidental' or separable, such as particular modes of manifestation, or conditions of glory and majesty, which may at one time be attached to the 'form,' at another separated from it.... The true meaning of *morphe* in the expression 'form of God' is confirmed by its recurrence in the corresponding phrase, 'form of a servant.' It is universally admitted that the two phrases are directly antithetical, and that 'form' must therefore have the same sense in both."

The definition above mentioned applies to its use in **Mark 16:12**, as to the particular ways in which the Lord manifested Himself.

Country *see Mark 5:14.*

16:13 And they went and told *it* unto the residue: neither believed they them.

Residue In **Mark 16:13**, KJV, the plural of *loipos*, "left," is translated "residue" (RV, "rest").

16:14 Afterward he appeared unto the eleven as they sat at meat, and upbraided them with their unbelief and hardness of heart, because they believed not them which had seen him after he was risen.

Afterward *husteron* (5305), "afterwards," with the suggestion of at length, is found in Matt. 4:2; 21:29,

32, 37 (KJV, "last of all"); 22:27; 25:11; 26:60 (KJV, "at the last"), **Mark 16:14**; Luke 4:2; 20:32 (KJV, "last"), John 13:36; Heb. 12:11.

Appeared *see Mark 16:12.*

Eleven *hendeka* (1733), lit., "one ten" (Lat., *undecim*), is used only of the eleven apostles remaining after the death of Judas Iscariot, Matt. 28:16; **Mark 16:14**; Luke 24:9, 33; Acts 1:26; 2:14.

Sat *see Mark 14:18.*

Upbraided *see* Reviled at *Mark 15:32.*

Unbelief *see Mark 6:6.*

Hardness of heart *see Mark 10:5.*

Seen *see Mark 16:11.*

16:15 And he said unto them, Go ye into all the world, and preach the gospel to every creature.

Preach *see* Publish at *Mark 1:45.*

Creature *ktisis* (2937), primarily "the act of creating," or "the creative act in process," has this meaning in Rom. 1:20 and Gal. 6:15. Like the English word "creation," it also signifies the product of the "creative" act, the "creature," as in **Mark 16:15**, RV; Rom. 1:25; 8:19; Col. 1:15, etc.; in Heb. 9:11, KJV, "building." In **Mark 16:15** and Col. 1:23 its significance has special reference to mankind in general. As to its use in Gal. 6:15 and 2 Cor. 5:17, in the former, apparently, "the reference is to the creative act of God, whereby a man is introduced into the blessing of salvation, in contrast to circumcision done by human hands, which the Judaizers claimed was necessary to that end. In 2 Cor. 5:17 the reference is to what the believer is in Christ; in consequence of the creative act he has become a new creature." *Ktisis* is once used of human actions, 1 Pet. 2:13, "ordinance" (marg., "creation").

16:16 He that believeth and is baptized shall be saved; but he that believeth not shall be damned.

Believeth not *see* Believed not at *Mark 16:11.*

16:17 And these signs shall follow them that believe; In my name shall they cast out devils; they shall speak with new tongues;

Follow *parakoloutheo* (3877), lit. signifying "to follow close up, or side by side," hence, "to accompany, to conform to" (*para*, "beside," and *akoloutheo*), is used of signs accompanying "them that believe," **Mark 16:17**; of tracing the course of facts, Luke 1:3, RV; of "following" the good doctrine, 1 Tim. 4:6, RV (KJV, "attained"); similarly of "following" teaching so as to practice it, 2 Tim. 3:10, RV, "didst follow" (KJV, "hast fully known").

Name *see* Surnamed at *Mark 3:16.*

New *see Mark 2:22.*

16:18 They shall take up serpents; and if they drink any deadly thing, it shall not hurt them; they shall lay hands on the sick, and they shall recover.

Serpents *ophis* (3789), the characteristics of the "serpent" as alluded to in Scripture are mostly evil (though Matt. 10:16 refers to its caution in avoiding danger); its treachery, Gen. 49:17; 2 Cor. 11:3; its venom, Ps. 58:4; 1 Cor. 10:9; Rev. 9:19; its skulking, Job 26:13; its murderous proclivities, e.g., Ps. 58:4; Prov. 23:32; Eccl. 10:8, 11; Amos 5:19; **Mark 16:18**; Luke 10:19; the Lord used the word metaphorically of the scribes and Pharisees, Matt. 23:33 (cf. *echidna*, "viper," in Matt. 3:7; 12:34). The general aspects of its evil character are intimated in the Lord's rhetorical question in Matt. 7:10 and Luke 11:11. Its characteristics are concentrated in the archadversary of God and man, the Devil, metaphorically described as the serpent, 2 Cor. 11:3; Rev. 12:9, 14, 15; 20:2. The brazen "serpent" lifted up by Moses was symbolical of the means of salvation provided by God, in Christ and His vicarious death under the divine judgment upon sin, John 3:14. While the living "serpent" symbolizes sin in its origin, hatefulness, and deadly effect, the brazen "serpent" symbolized the bearing away of the curse and the judgment of sin; the metal was itself figurative of the righteousness of God's judgment.

Deadly *thanasimos* (2286), from *thanatos*, "belonging to death, or partaking of the nature of death," is used in **Mark 16:18**.

Hurt *blapto* (984), signifies "to injure, mar, do damage to," **Mark 16:18**, "shall (in no wise) hurt (them)"; Luke 4:35, "having done (him no) hurt," RV. *Adikeo* stresses the unrighteousness of the act, *blapto* stresses the injury done.

Lay *see Mark 5:23.*

Sick *see Mark 6:5.*

Recover In **Mark 16:18**, the phrase *echo kalos*, lit., "to have well," i.e., "to be well," is rendered "they shall recover."

16:19 So then after the Lord had spoken unto them, he was received up into heaven, and sat on the right hand of God.

Lord *see* Jesus at *Mark 1:1.*

Received *analambano* (353), "to take up" (*ana*), "to take to oneself, receive," is rendered "to receive" in **Mark 16:19**; Acts 1:2, 11, 22, RV, "He was received up" (KJV, "taken"); 10:16; 1 Tim. 3:16.

Sat *see Mark 11:2.*

16:20 And they went forth, and preached every where, the Lord working with *them*, and confirming the word with signs following. Amen.

Preached *see* Publish at *Mark 1:45.*

Every where *see* Abroad at *Mark 1:28.*

Lord *see* Jesus at *Mark 1:1.*

Working *sunergeo* (4903), "to work with or together" (*sun*), occurs in **Mark 16:20**; Rom. 8:28, "work together"; 1 Cor. 16:16, "helpeth with"; 2 Cor. 6:1, "workers together," present participle, "working together"; the "*with Him*" represents nothing in the Greek; Jas. 2:22, "wrought with."

Confirming *bebaioo* (950), "to make firm, establish, make secure" (the connected adjective *bebaios* signifies "stable, fast, firm"), is used of "confirming" a word, **Mark 16:20**; promises, Rom. 15:8; the testimony of Christ, 1 Cor. 1:6; the saints by the Lord Jesus Christ, 1 Cor. 1:8; the saints by God, 2 Cor. 1:21 ("stablisheth"); in faith, Col. 2:7; the salvation spoken through the Lord and "confirmed" by the apostles, Heb. 2:3; the heart by grace, Heb. 13:9 ("stablished").

Following *epakoloutheo* (1872), "to follow after, clowing" good works, 1 Tim. 5:10; of sins "following" after those who are guilty of them, 5:24; of "following" the steps of Christ, 1 Pet. 2:21.

"The Spirit of Christ is the spirit of missions, and the nearer we get to him, the more intensely missionary we must become."

HENRY MARTYN

Luke

Chapter 1

1:1 Forasmuch as many have taken in hand to set forth in order a declaration of those things which are most surely believed among us,

Taken in hand *epicheireo* (2021), lit., "to put the hand to" (*epi*, "to," *cheir*, "the hand"), "to take in hand, undertake," occurs in **Luke 1:1**, "have taken in hand"; in Acts 9:29, "they went about"; in 19:13, "took upon them."

Set *anatassomai* (392), "to arrange in order, draw up in order," occurs in **Luke 1:1**, KJV, "to set forth in order," RV, "to draw up."

Order *anatassomai* (392), "to arrange in order" (*ana*, "up," and the middle voice of *tasso*, "to arrange"), is used in **Luke 1:1**, KJV, "to set forth in order" (RV, "to draw up"); the probable meaning is to bring together and so arrange details in "order."

Declaration *diegesis* (1335), translated "a declaration" in the KJV of **Luke 1:1**, denotes a "narrative," RV (akin to *diegeomai*, "to set out in detail, recount, describe"). In the Sept., Judg. 7:15; Hab. 2:6.

Things *pragma* (4229), akin to *prasso*, "to do," denotes (a) "that which has been done, a deed," translated "matters" in **Luke 1:1**, RV (KJV, "things"); "matter" in 2 Cor. 7:11; (b) "that which is being done, an affair," translated "matter" in Rom. 16:2, RV (KJV, "business"); 1 Cor. 6:1, in a forensic sense, "a lawsuit" (frequently found with this meaning in the papyri); 1 Thess. 4:6, "in the matter," i.e., the "matter" under consideration, which, as the preceding words show, is here the sin of adultery.

Surely believed *plerophoreo* (4135), "to bring in full measure," from *pleroo*, and *phoreo*, "to bring"; hence, "to fulfill," of circumstances relating to Christ, **Luke 1:1**, RV, "have been fulfilled" (KJV "are most surely believed"); of evangelical ministry, 2 Tim. 4:5, "fulfill" (KJV, "make full proof"); so in v. 17, RV, "fully proclaimed" (KJV, "fully known").

1:2 Even as they delivered them unto us, which from the beginning were eyewitnesses, and ministers of the word;

Even as *kathos* (2531), "according as," is frequently translated "even as," e.g., Mark 11:6; **Luke 1:2**; 1 Thess. 5:11.

Eyewitnesses *autoptes* (845), signifies "seeing with one's own eyes" (*autos*, "self," and a form, *optano*, "to see"), **Luke 1:2**.

1:3 It seemed good to me also, having had perfect understanding of all things from the very first, to write unto thee in order, most excellent Theophilus,

Seemed *dokeo* (1380), denotes (a) "to be of opinion" (akin to *doxa*, "opinion"), e.g., **Luke 8:18**, RV, "thinketh" (KJV, "seemeth"); so 1 Cor. 3:18; to think, suppose, Jas. 1:26, RV, "thinketh himself (KJV, "seem"); (b) "to seem, to be reputed," e.g., Acts 17:18; 1 Cor. 11:16; 12:22; 2 Cor. 10:9; Heb. 4:1; 12:11; (c) impersonally (1) to think, (2) to "seem" good, **Luke 1:3**; Acts 15:22, RV, "it seemed good" (KJV, "it pleased"); 15:25, 28 (v. 34 in some mss.); in Heb. 12:10, the neuter of the present participle is used with the article, lit., "the (thing) seeming good," RV, "(as) seemed good," KJV, "after (their own) pleasure."

Having had … understanding *parakoloutheo* (3877), "to follow up," is used of investigating or "tracing" a course of events, **Luke 1:3**, where the writer, humbly differentiating himself from those who possessed an essential apostolic qualification, declares that he "traced the course of all things" (RV) about which he was writing (KJV, "having had … understanding, etc.").

Perfect *akribos* (199), is correctly translated in the RV of **Luke 1:3**, "having traced the course of all things accurately" (KJV, "having had perfect understanding"). It is used in Matt. 2:8, of Herod's command to the wise men as to searching for the young Child (RV, "carefully"; KJV, "diligently"); in Acts 18:25, of Apollos' teaching of "the things concerning Jesus" (RV, "carefully"; KJV, "diligently"); in Eph. 5:15, of the way in which believers are to walk (RV, "carefully"; KJV, "circumspectly"); in 1 Thess. 5:2, of the knowledge gained by the saints through the apostle's teaching concerning the Day of the Lord (RV and KJV, "perfectly"). The word expresses that "accuracy" which is the outcome of carefulness. It is connected with *akros*, "pointed." This word and its other grammatical forms, *akribeia, akribes, akribesteron* and *akriboo*, are used especially by Luke, who employs them eight times out of the thirteen in the NT; Matthew uses them three times, Paul twice.

First *anothen* (509), "from above," is rendered "from the first" in **Luke 1:3**, RV, it may mean "from their beginning, or source."

Order *kathexes* (2517), a strengthened form, denotes "afterward," or "in order," **Luke 1:3**; **8:1**; Acts 3:24; 11:4; 18:23.

Excellent *kratistos* (2903), "mightiest, noblest, best," the superlative degree of *kratus*, "strong" (cf. *kratos*, "strength"), is used as a title of honor and respect, "most excellent," **Luke 1:3** (Theophilus was quite possibly a man of high rank); Acts 23:26; 24:3 and 26:25, RV, for KJV, "most noble."

1:4 That thou mightest know the certainty of those things, wherein thou hast been instructed.

Certainty *asphaleia* (803), primarily, "not liable to fall, steadfast, firm," hence denoting "safety," Acts 5:23, and 1 Thess. 5:3, has the further meaning, "certainty," **Luke 1:4**.

Things *logos* (3056), "a word, an account," etc., is translated "thing" in Matt. 21:24, KJV (1st part), and **Luke 20:3**, KJV, RV, "question" (in Matt. 21:24, 2nd part, "these things" translates *tauta*, the neut. plur. of *houtos*, "this"); **Luke 1:4**; Acts 5:24, KJV (RV, "words").

Instructed *katecheo* (2727), "to teach orally, inform, instruct," is translated by the verb "to instruct" in **Luke 1:4**; Acts 18:25 (RV marg., "taught by word of mouth"); Rom. 2:18; 1 Cor. 14:19, RV (KJV, "teach").

1:5 There was in the days of Herod, the king of Judaea, a certain priest named Zacharias, of the course of Abia: and his wife *was* of the daughters of Aaron, and her name *was* Elisabeth.

Judaea *ioudaios* (2453), is used (a) adjectivally, with the lit. meaning, "Jewish," sometimes with the addition of *aner*, "a man," Acts 10:28; 22:3; in 21:39 with *anthropos*, in some mss. (a man in the generic sense); the best mss. omit the phrase here; in 13:6, lit., "a Jewish false-prophet"; in John 3:22, with the word *chora*, "land" or "country," signifying "Judean," lit., "Judean country"; used by metonymy for the people of the country; (b) as a noun, "a Jew, Jews," e.g., Matt. 2:2; Mark 7:3. The name "Jew" is primarily tribal (from Judah). It is first found in 2 Kings 16:6, as distinct from Israel, of the northern kingdom. After the Captivity it was chiefly used to distinguish the race from Gentiles, e.g., John 2:6; Acts 14:1; Gal. 2:15, where it denotes Christians of "Jewish" race; it distinguishes Jews from Samaritans, in John 4:9; from proselytes, in Acts 2:10. The word is most frequent in John's Gospel and the Acts; in the former "it especially denotes the typical representatives of Jewish thought contrasted with believers in Christ ... or with other Jews of less pronounced opinions, e.g., John 3:25; 5:10; 7:13; 9:22" (Lukyn Williams, in *Hastings' Bib. Dic.*); such representatives were found, generally, in opposition to Christ; in the Acts they are chiefly those who opposed the apostles and the gospel. In Rom. 2:28, 29 the word is used of ideal "Jews," i.e., "Jews" in spiritual reality, believers, whether "Jews" or Gentiles by natural birth. The feminine, "Jewess," is found in Acts 16:1; 24:24. It also denotes Judea, e.g., Matt. 2:1; **Luke 1:5**; John 4:3, the word "country" being understood [cf. (a) above]. In **Luke 23:5** and John 7:1, where the KJV has "Jewry," the RV translates it as usual, "Judea."

Priest *hiereus* (2409), "one who offers sacrifice and has the charge of things pertaining thereto," is used (a) of a "priest" of the pagan god Zeus, Acts 14:13; (b) of Jewish "priests," e.g., Matt. 8:4; 12:4, 5; **Luke 1:5**, where allusion is made to the 24 courses of "priests" appointed for service in the Temple (cf. 1 Chron. 24:4ff.); John 1:19; Heb. 8:4; (c) of believers, Rev. 1:6; 5:10; 20:6. Israel was primarily designed as a nation to be a kingdom of "priests," offering service to God, e.g., Ex. 19:6, the Israelites having renounced their obligations, Ex. 20:19, the Aaronic priesthood was selected for the purpose, till Christ came to fulfil His ministry in offering up Himself; since then the Jewish priesthood has been abrogated, to be resumed nationally, on behalf of Gentiles, in the millennial kingdom, Is. 61:6; 66:21.

Course *ephemeria* (2183), primarily, "daily service," as, e.g., in the Sept. of 2 Chron. 13:11 (from *epi*, "upon, or by," *hemera*, "a day," Eng., "ephemeral"), hence denoted a "class," or "course," into which the priests were divided for the daily service in the Temple, each "class" serving for seven days (see 1 Chron. 9:25). In the NT it is used in **Luke 1:5, 8**.

Daughters *thugater* (2364), "a daughter," (etymologically, Eng., "daughter" is connected), is used of (a) the natural relationship (frequent in the Gospels); (b) spiritual relationship to God, 2 Cor. 6:18, in the sense of the practical realization of acceptance with, and the approval of, God (cf. Isa. 43:6), the only place in the NT where it applies to spiritual relationship; (c) the inhabitants of a city or region, Matt. 21:5; John 12:15 ("of Zion"); cf. Isa. 37:22; Zeph. 3:14 (Sept.); (d) the women who followed Christ to Calvary, **Luke 23:28**; (e) women of Aaron's posterity, **Luke 1:5**; (f) a female descendant of Abraham, **Luke 13:16**.

1:6 And they were both righteous before God, walking in all the commandments and ordinances of the Lord blameless.

Righteous *dikaios* (1342), was first used of persons observant of *dike*, "custom, rule, right," especially in the fulfillment of duties towards gods and men, and of things that were in accordance with right. The Eng. word "righteous" was formerly spelt "rightwise," i.e., (in a) straight way. In the NT it denotes "righteous," a state of being right, or right conduct, judged whether by the divine standard, or according to human standards, of what is right. Said of God, it designates the perfect agreement between His nature and His acts (in which He is the standard for all men). It is used (1) in the broad sense, of persons: (a) of God, e.g., John 17:25; Rom. 3:26; 1 John 1:9; 2:29; 3:7; (b) of Christ, e.g., Acts 3:14; 7:52; 22:14; 2 Tim. 4:8; 1 Pet. 3:18; 1 John 2:1; (c) of men, Matt. 1:19; **Luke 1:6**; Rom. 1:17; 2:13; 5:7. (2) of things; blood (metaphorical), Matt. 23:35; Christ's judgment, John 5:30; any circumstance, fact or deed, Matt. 20:4 (v. 7, in some mss.); **Luke 12:57**; Acts 4:19; Eph. 6:1; Phil. 1:7; 4:8; Col. 4:1; 2 Thess. 1:6; "the commandment" (the Law), Rom. 7:12; works, 1 John 3:12, the ways of God, Rev. 15:3.

Walking *poreuo* (4198), is used in the middle voice and rendered "to walk" in **Luke 1:6**, of the general activities of life; so in **Luke 13:33**, KJV, "walk" (RV, "go on My way"); Acts 9:31; 14:16; 1 Pet. 4:3; 2 Pet. 2:10; Jude 16, 18.

Ordinances *dikaioma* (1345), has three distinct meanings, and seems best described comprehensively as "a concrete expression of righteousness"; it is a declaration that a person or thing is righteous, and hence, broadly speaking, it represents the expression and effect of *dikaiosis*. It signifies (a) "an ordinance," **Luke 1:6**; Rom. 1:32, RV, "ordinance," i.e., what God has declared to be right, referring to His decree of retribution (KJV, "judgment"); Rom. 2:26, RV, "ordinances of the Law" (i.e., righteous requirements enjoined by the Law); so 8:4, "ordinance of the Law," i.e., collectively, the precepts of the Law, all that it demands as right; in Heb. 9:1, 10, ordinances connected with the tabernacle ritual; (b) "a sentence of acquittal," by which God acquits men of their guilt, on the conditions (1) of His grace in Christ, through His expiatory sacrifice, (2) the acceptance of Christ by faith, Rom. 5:16; (c) "a righteous act," Rom. 5:18, "(through one) act of righteousness," RV, not the act of "justification," nor the righteous character of Christ (as suggested by the KJV: *dikaioma* does not signify character, as does *dikaiosune*, righteousness), but the death of Christ, as an act accomplished consistently with God's character and counsels.

Blameless *amemptos* (273), related to *memphomai*, is translated "unblameable" in 1 Thess. 3:13; "blameless," in **Luke 1:6**; Phil. 2:15; 3:6; "faultless" in Heb. 8:7.

1:7 And they had no child, because that Elisabeth was barren, and they both were *now* well stricken in years.

Because *kathoti* (2530), from *kata*, "according to," and *hoti*, "that," lit., "because that," **Luke 1:7**; **19:9**; Acts 2:24, is translated "according as" in Acts 2:45, RV (KJV, "as") and in 4:35; "inasmuch as," 17:31.

Barren *steiros* (4723), from a root *ster-* meaning "hard, firm" (hence Eng., "sterile"), signifies "barren, not bearing children," and is used with the natural significance three times in the Gospel of Luke, **1:7, 36**; **23:29**; and with a spiritual significance in Gal. 4:27, in a quotation from Isa. 54:1. The circumstances of Sarah and Hagar, which Isaiah no doubt had in mind, are applied by the apostle to the contrast between the works of the Law and the promise by grace.

Stricken *probaino* (4260), "to go forward," is used metaphorically of age, in **Luke 1:7, 18**, with the phrases "in their (her) days," translated "well stricken in years" (see marg.); in **2:36**, "of a great age" (marg., "advanced in many days").

Years In **Luke 1:7, 18**, *hemera*, "a day," is rendered "years."

1:8 And it came to pass, that while he executed the priest's office before God in the order of his course,

Executed *hierateuo* (2407), "to be a priest, to officiate as such," is translated "executed the priest's office," in **Luke 1:8**. It occurs frequently in the Sept., and in inscriptions. Cf. *hierateuma*, "priesthood," 1 Pet. 2:5, 9, *hierateia*, "a priest's office," **Luke 1:9**; Heb. 7:5, *hiereus*, "a priest," and *hieros*, "sacred."

Priest's office *hierateuo* (2407), signifies "to officiate as a priest," **Luke 1:8**, "he executed the priest's office."

Before *enanti* (1725), an adverb, used as a preposition, "before," **Luke 1:8**; "in the judgment of," Acts 8:21. Some texts have the word in Acts 7:10.

Order *taxis* (5010), "an arranging, arrangement, order" (akin to *tasso*, "to arrange, draw up in order"), is used in **Luke 1:8** of the fixed succession of the course of the priests; of due "order," in contrast to confusion, in the gatherings of a local church, 1 Cor. 14:40; of the general condition of such, Col. 2:5 (some give it a military significance here); of the divinely appointed character or nature of a priesthood, of Melchizedek, as foreshadowing that of Christ, Heb. 5:6, 10; 6:20; 7:11 (where also the character of the Aaronic priesthood is set in contrast); 7:17 (in some mss, v. 21).

Course *see **Luke 1:5**.*

1:9 According to the custom of the priest's office, his lot was to burn incense when he went into the temple of the Lord.

Priest's office *hierateia* (2405), "a priesthood," denotes the priest's office, **Luke 1:9**; Heb. 7:5, RV, "priest's office." *See also **Luke 1:8**.*

Lot *lanchano* (2975), denotes (a) "to draw lots," John 19:24; (b) "to obtain by lot, to obtain," **Luke 1:9**, "his lot was," lit., "he received by lot," i.e., by divine appointment; Acts 1:17, of the portion "allotted" by the Lord to His apostles in their ministry; 2 Pet. 1:1, "that have obtained (a like precious faith)," i.e., by its being "allotted" to them, not by acquiring it for themselves, but by divine grace (an act independent of human control, as in the casting of "lots").

Burn incense *thumiao* (2370), "to burn incense," is found in **Luke 1:9**.

Temple *naos* (3485), "a shrine or sanctuary," was used (a) among the heathen, to denote the shrine containing the idol, Acts 17:24; 19:24 (in the latter, miniatures); (b) among the Jews, the sanctuary in the "Temple," into which only the priests could lawfully enter, e.g., **Luke 1:9, 21, 22**; Christ, as being of the tribe of Judah, and thus not being a priest while upon the earth (Heb. 7:13, 14; 8:4), did not enter the *naos*; (c) by Christ metaphorically, of His own physical body, John 2:19, 21; (d) in apostolic teaching, metaphorically, (1) of the church, the mystical body of Christ, Eph. 2:21; (2) of a local church, 1 Cor. 3:16, 17; 2 Cor. 6:16; (3) of the present body of the individual believer, 1 Cor. 6:19; (4) of the "Temple" seen in visions in Revelation, 3:12; 7:15; 11:19; 14:15, 17; 15:5, 6, 8; 16:1, 17; (5) of the Lord God Almighty and the Lamb, as the "Temple" of the new and heavenly Jerusalem, Rev. 21:22.

1:10 And the whole multitude of the people were praying without at the time of incense.

Multitude *plethos* (4128), lit., "a fullness," hence, "a large company, a multitude," is used (a) of things: of fish, **Luke 5:6**; John 21:6; of sticks ("bundle"), Acts 28:3; of stars and of sand, Heb. 11:12; of sins, Jas. 5:20; 1 Pet. 4:8; (b) of persons, (1) a "multitude": of people, e.g., Mark 3:7, 8; **Luke 6:17**; John 5:3; Acts 14:1; of angels, **Luke 2:13**; (2) with the article, the whole number, the "multitude," the populace, e.g., **Luke 1:10**; **8:37**; Acts 5:16; 19:9; 23:7; a particular company, e.g., of disciples, **Luke 19:37**; Acts 4:32; 6:2, 5; 15:30; of elders, priests, and scribes, 23:7; of the apostles and the elders of the Church in Jerusalem, Acts 15:12.

Time *hora* (5610), whence Lat., *hora*, Eng., "hour," primarily denoted any time or period, expecially a season. In the NT it is used to denote (a) "a part of the day," especially a twelfth part of day or night, an "hour," e.g., Matt. 8:13; Acts 10:3, 9; 23:23; Rev. 9:15; in 1 Cor. 15:30, "every hour" stands for "all the time"; in some passages it expresses duration, e.g., Matt. 20:12; 26:40; **Luke 22:59**; inexactly, in such phrases as "for a season," John 5:35; 2 Cor. 7:8; "for an hour," Gal. 2:5; "for a short season," 1 Thess. 2:17, RV (KJV, "for a short time," lit., "for the time of an hour"); (b) "a period more or less extended," e.g., 1 John 2:18, "it is the last hour," RV; (c) "a definite point of time," e.g., Matt. 26:45, "the hour is at hand"; **Luke 1:10**; **10:21**; **14:17**, lit., "at the hour of supper"; Acts 16:18; 22:13; Rev. 3:3; 11:13; 14:7; a point of time when an appointed action is to begin, Rev. 14:15; in Rom. 13:11, "it is high time," lit., "it is already an hour," indicating that a point of time has come later than would have been the case had responsibility been realized. In 1 Cor. 4:11, it indicates a point of time previous to which certain circumstances have existed.

Incense *thumiama* (2368), denotes "fragrant stuff for burning, incense" (from *thuo*, "to offer in sacrifice"), **Luke 1:10**, **11**; in the plural, Rev. 5:8 and 18:13, RV (KJV, "odors"); 8:3, 4, signifying "frankincense" here. In connection with the tabernacle, the "incense" was to be prepared from stacte, onycha, and galbanum, with pure frankincense, an equal weight of each; imitation for private use was forbidden, Exod. 30:34-38. Cf. *thumiaterion*, "a censer," Heb. 9:4, and *libanos*, "frankincense," Rev. 18:13.

1:11 And there appeared unto him an angel of the Lord standing on the right side of the altar of incense.

Incense *see Luke 1:10.*

Right *dexios* (1188), an adjective, used (a) of "the right" as opposite to the left, e.g., Matt. 5:29, 30; Rev. 10:5, RV, "right hand"; in connection with armor (figuratively), 2 Cor. 6:7; with *en*, followed by the dative plural, Mark 16:5; with *ek*, and the genitive plural, e.g., Matt. 25:33, 34; **Luke 1:11**; (b) of giving the "right hand" of fellowship, Gal. 2:9, betokening the public expression of approval by leaders at Jerusalem of the course pursued by Paul and Barnabas among the Gentiles; the act was often the sign of a pledge, e.g., 2 Kings 10:15; 1 Chron. 29:24, marg.; Ezra 10:19; Ezek. 17:18; figuratively, Lam. 5:6; it is often so used in the papyri; (c) metaphorically of "power" or "authority," Acts 2:33; with *ek*, signifying "on," followed by the genitive plural, Matt. 26:64; Mark 14:62; Heb. 1:13; (d) similarly of "a place of honor in the messianic kingdom," Matt. 20:21; Mark 10:37.

Altar *thuciasterion* (2379), probably the neuter of the adjective *thuciaterioc*, is derived from *thuciazo*, "to sacrifice." Accordingly it denotes an "altar" for the sacrifice of victims, though it was also used for the "altar" of incense, e.g., **Luke 1:11**. In the NT this word is reserved for the "altar" of the true God, Matt. 5:23-24; 23:18-20, 35; **Luke 11:51**; 1 Cor. 9:13; 10:18, in contrast to *bomos*. In the Sept. *thuciasterion* is mostly, but not entirely, used for the divinely appointed altar; it is used for idol "altars," e.g., in Judg. 2:2; 6:25; 2 Kings 16:10.

1:12 And when Zacharias saw *him*, he was troubled, and fear fell upon him.

Troubled *tarosso* (5015), akin to *tarache*, is used (1) in a physical sense, John 5:7 (in some mss. v. 4), (2) metaphorically, (a) of the soul and spirit of the Lord, John 11:33, where the true rendering is "He troubled Himself"; (b) of the hearts of disciples, 14:1, 27; (c) of the minds of those in fear or perplexity, Matt. 2:3; 14:26; Mark 6:50; **Luke 1:12**; **24:38**; 1 Pet. 3:14; (d) of subverting the souls of believers, by evil doctrine, Acts 15:24; Gal. 1:7; 5:10; (e) of stirring up a crowd, Acts 17:8; v. 13 in the best texts, "troubling (the multitudes)," RV.

Fell *epipipto* (1968), "to fall upon," is used (a) literally, Mark 3:10, "pressed upon"; Acts 20:10, 37; (b) metaphorically, of fear, **Luke 1:12**; Acts 19:17; Rev. 11:11; reproaches, Rom. 15:3; of the Holy Spirit, Acts 8:16; 10:44; 11:15.

1:13 But the angel said unto him, Fear not, Zacharias: for thy prayer is heard; and thy wife Elisabeth shall bear thee a son, and thou shalt call his name John.

Prayer *deesis* (1162), primarily "a wanting, a need," then, "an asking, entreaty, supplication," in the NT is always addressed to God and always rendered "supplication" or "supplications" in the RV; in the KJV "prayer," or "prayers," in **Luke 1:13**; **2:37**; **5:33**; Rom. 10:1; 2 Cor. 1:11; 9:14; Phil. 1:4 (in the 2nd part, "request"); 1:19; 2 Tim. 1:3; Heb. 5:7; Jas. 5:16; 1 Pet. 3:12.

Heard *eisakouo* (1522), "to listen to," has two meanings, (a) "to hear and to obey," 1 Cor. 14:21, "they will not hear"; (b) "to hear so as to answer," of God's answer to prayer, Matt. 6:7; **Luke 1:13**; Acts 10:31; Heb. 5:7.

Bear *gennao* (1080), "to beget," in the passive voice, "to be born," is chiefly used of men "begetting" children, Matt. 1:2-16; more rarely of women "begetting" children, **Luke 1:13**, **57**, "brought forth"; **23:29**; John 16:21, "is delivered of," and of the child, "is born." In Gal. 4:24, it is used allegorically, to contrast Jews under bondage to the Law, and spiritual Israel, KJV, "gendereth," RV, "bearing children," to contrast the natural birth of Ishmael and the supernatural birth of Isaac. In Matt. 1:20 it is used of conception, "that which is conceived in her." It is used of the act of God in the birth of Christ, Acts 13:33; Heb. 1:5; 5:5, quoted from Psalm 2:7, none of which indicate that Christ became the Son of God at His birth.

1:14 And thou shalt have joy and gladness; and many shall rejoice at his birth.

Gladness *agalliasis* (20), "exultation, exuberant joy," is translated "gladness" in **Luke 1:14**; Acts 2:6; Heb. 1:9; "joy" in **Luke 1:44**; "exceeding joy" in Jude 24. It indicates a more exultant "joy" than *chara*. In the Sept. this word is found chiefly in the Psalms, where it denotes "joy" in God's redemptive work, e.g., 30:5; 42:4; 45:7, 15.

Rejoice *chairo* (5463), "to rejoice," is most frequently so translated. As to this verb, the following are grounds and occasions for "rejoicing," on the part of believers: in the Lord, Phil. 3:1; 4:4; His incarnation, **Luke 1:14**; His power, **Luke 13:17**; His presence with the Father, John 14:28; His presence with them, John 16:22; 20:20; His ultimate triumph, 8:56; hearing the gospel, Acts 13:48; their salvation, Acts 8:39; receiving the Lord, **Luke 19:6**; their enrollment in Heaven, **Luke 10:20**; their liberty in Christ, Acts 15:31; their hope, Rom. 12:12 (cf. Rom. 5:2; Rev. 19:7); their prospect of reward, Matt. 5:12; the obedience and godly conduct of fellow believers, Rom. 16:19, RV, "I rejoice" (KJV, "I am glad"); 2 Cor. 7:7, 9; 13:9; Col. 2:5; 1 Thess. 3:9; 2 John 4; 3 John 3; the proclamation of Christ, Phil. 1:18; the gospel harvest, John 4:36; suffering with Christ, Acts 5:41; 1 Pet. 4:13; suffering in the cause of the gospel, 2 Cor. 13:9 (1st part); Phil. 2:17 (1st part); Col. 1:24; in persecutions, trials and afflictions, Matt. 5:12; **Luke 6:23**; 2 Cor. 6:10; the manifestation of grace, Acts 11:23; meeting with fellow believers, 1 Cor. 16:17, RV, "I rejoice"; Phil. 2:28; receiving tokens of love and fellowship, Phil. 4:10; the "rejoicing" of others, Rom. 12:15; 2 Cor. 7:13; learning of the well-being of others, 2 Cor. 7:16.

Birth *gennesis* (1083), "a birth, begetting, producing" (related to *gennao*, "to beget"), is used in Matt. 1:18 and **Luke 1:14**. Some mss. have *genesis*, "lineage, birth" (from *ginomai*, "to become").

1:15 For he shall be great in the sight of the Lord, and shall drink neither wine nor strong drink; and he shall be filled with the Holy Ghost, even from his mother's womb.

Drink *sikera* (4608), is "a strong, intoxicating drink," made from any sweet ingredients, whether grain, vegetables, or the juice of fruits, or a decoction of honey; "strong drink," **Luke 1:15**. In the Sept., Lev. 10:9; Num. 6:3; 28:7; Deut. 14:26; 29:6; Isa. 5:11, 22; 24:9; 28:7; 29:9.

Filled *pimplemi* (4130), and *pletho* (4130), lengthened forms of *pleo*, "to fill" (*pletho* supplies certain tenses of *pimplemi*), is used (1) of things; boats, with fish, **Luke 5:7**; a sponge, with vinegar, Matt. 27:48 (some mss. have this verb in John 19:29); a city, with confusion, Acts 19.29; a wedding, with guests, Matt. 22:10; (2) of persons (only in Luke's writings): (a) with the Holy Spirit, **Luke 1:15, 41, 67**; Acts 2:4; 4:8, 31; 9:17; 13:9; (b) with emotions: wrath, **Luke 4:28**; fear, **5:26**; madness, **6:11**; wonder, amazement, Acts 3:10; jealousy, 5:17, RV, for KJV, "indignation," and 13:45 (KJV, "envy").

Even *eti* (2089), an adverb, "as yet, still," is rendered "even" in **Luke 1:15**.

Womb *koilia* (2836), denotes "the womb," Matt. 19:12; **Luke 1:15, 41, 42, 44; 2:21; 11:27; 23:29**; John 3:4; Acts 3:2; 14:8; Gal. 1:15.

1:16 And many of the children of Israel shall he turn to the Lord their God.

Turn *epistrepho* (1994), is used (a) transitively, "to make to turn towards" (*epi*), **Luke 1:16, 17**; Jas. 5:19, 20 (to convert); (b) intransitively, "to turn oneself round," e.g., in the passive voice, Mark 5:30; in the active voice, Matt. 13:15, RV, "turn again" (KJV, "be converted"); Acts 11:21; 14:15; 15:19; 1 Thess. 1:9, "ye turned," the aorist tense indicating an immediate and decisive change, consequent upon a deliberate choice; conversion is a voluntary act in response to the presentation of truth.

1:17 And he shall go before him in the spirit and power of Elias, to turn the hearts of the fathers to the children, and the disobedient to the wisdom of the just; to make ready a people prepared for the Lord.

Go *proerchomai* (4281), "to go before, precede, go forward or farther" (*pro*, "before"), is used of (a) place, e.g., Matt. 26:39; Acts 12:10, "passed on through"; (b) time, **Luke 1:17**; Acts 20:5, 13; 2 Cor. 9:5.

Before *enopion* (1799), from *en*, "in," and *ops*, "the eye," is the neuter of the adjective *enopios*, and is used prepositionally, (a) of place, that which is before or opposite a person, "towards which he turns his eyes," e.g., **Luke 1:19**; Acts 4:10; 6:6; Rev. 1:4; 4-10; 7:15; (b) in metaphorical phrases after verbs of motion, **Luke 1:17**; **12:9**; Acts 9:15, etc.; signifying "in the mind or soul of persons," **Luke 12:6**; Acts 10:31; Rev. 16:19; (c) "in one's sight or hearing," **Luke 24:43**; John 20:30; 1 Tim. 6:12; metaphorically, Rom. 14:22; especially in Gal. 1:20; 1 Tim. 5:21; 6:13; 2 Tim. 2:14; 4:1; before, as "having a person present to the mind," Acts 2:25; Jas. 4:10; "in the judgment of a person," **Luke 16:15**; **24:11**, RV, "in their sight," for KJV, "to"; Acts 4:19; Rom. 3:20; 12:17; 2 Cor. 8:21; 1 Tim. 2:3; "in the approving sight of God," **Luke 1:75**; Acts 7:46; 10:33; 2 Cor. 4:2; 7:12.

Spirit *pneuma* (4151), primarily denotes "the wind" (akin to *pneo*, "to breathe, blow"); also "breath"; then, especially "the spirit," which, like the wind, is invisible, immaterial and powerful. The NT uses of the word may be analyzed approximately as follows: "(a) the wind, John 3:8 (where marg. is, perhaps, to be preferred); Heb. 1:7; cf. Amos 4:13, Sept.; (b) the breath, 2 Thess. 2:8; Rev. 11:11; 13:15; cf. Job 12:10, Sept.; (c) the immaterial, invisible part of man, **Luke 8:55**; Acts 7:59; 1 Cor. 5:5; Jas. 2:26; cf. Eccl. 12:7, Sept.; (d) the disembodied (or 'unclothed,' or 'naked,' 2 Cor. 5:3, 4) man, **Luke 24:37**, **39**; Heb. 12:23; 1 Pet. 4:6; (e) the resurrection body, 1 Cor. 15:45; 1 Tim. 3:16; 1 Pet. 3:18; (f) the sentient element in man, that by which he perceives, reflects, feels, desires, Matt. 5:3; 26:41; Mark 2:8; **Luke 1:47**, **80**; Acts 17:16; 20:22; 1 Cor. 2:11; 5:3, 4; 14:4, 15; 2 Cor. 7:1; cf. Gen. 26:35; Isa. 26:9; Ezek. 13:3; Dan. 7:15; (g) purpose, aim, 2 Cor. 12:18; Phil. 1:27; Eph. 4:23; Rev. 19:10; cf. Ezra 1:5; Ps. 78:8; Dan. 5:12; (h) the equivalent of the personal pronoun, used for emphasis and effect: 1st person, 1 Cor. 16:18; cf. Gen. 6:3; 2nd person, 2 Tim. 4:22; Philem. 25; cf. Ps. 139:7; 3rd person, 2 Cor. 7:13; cf. Isa. 40:13; (i) character, **Luke 1:17**; Rom. 1:4; cf. Num. 14:24; (j) moral qualities and activities: bad, as of bondage as of a slave, Rom. 8:15; cf. Isa. 61:3; stupor, Rom. 11:8; cf. Isa. 29:10; timidity, 2 Tim. 1:7; cf. Josh. 5:1; good, as of adoption, i.e., liberty as of a son, Rom. 8:15; cf. Ps. 51:12; meekness, 1 Cor. 4:21; cf. Prov. 16:19; faith, 2 Cor. 4:13; quietness, 1 Pet. 3:4; cf. Prov. 14:29; (k) the Holy Spirit, e.g., Matt. 4:1; **Luke 4:18**; (l) 'the inward man' (an expression used only of the believer, Rom. 7:22; 2 Cor. 4:16; Eph. 3:16); the new life, Rom. 8:4-6, 10, 16; Heb. 12:9; cf. Ps. 51:10; (m) unclean spirits, demons, Matt. 8:16; **Luke 4:33**; 1 Pet. 3:19; cf. 1 Sam. 18:10; (n) angels, Heb. 1:14; cf. Acts 12:15; (o) divine gift for service, 1 Cor. 14:12, 32; (p) by metonymy, those who claim to be depositories of these gifts, 2 Thess. 2:2; 1 John 4:1-3; (q) the significance, as contrasted with the form, of words, or of a rite, John 6:63; Rom. 2:29; 7:6; 2 Cor. 3:6; (r) a vision, Rev. 1:10; 4:2; 17:3; 21:10."

Turn *see **Luke 1:16**.*

Disobedient *apeithes* (545), signifies "unwilling to be persuaded, spurning belief, disobedient," **Luke 1:17**; Acts 26:19; Rom. 1:30; 2 Tim. 3:2; Titus 1:16; 3:3.

Wisdom *phronesis* (5428), "understanding, prudence," i.e., a right use of *phren*, "the mind," is translated "wisdom" in **Luke 1:17**.

Make ready *hetoimazo* (2090), "to prepare, make ready," is used (I) absolutely, e.g., Mark 14:15; **Luke 9:52**; (II) with an object, e.g., (a) of those things which are ordained (1) by God, such as future positions of authority, Matt. 20:23; the coming Kingdom, 25:34; salvation personified in Christ, **Luke 2:31**; future blessings, 1 Cor. 2:9; a city, Heb. 11:16; a place of refuge for the Jewish remnant, Rev. 12:6; Divine judgments on the world, Rev. 8:6; 9:7, 15; 16:12; eternal fire, for the Devil and his angels, Matt. 25:41; (2) by Christ: a place in Heaven for His followers, John 14:2, 3; (b) of human "preparation" for the Lord, e.g., Matt. 3:3; 26:17, 19; **Luke 1:17** ("make ready"), **76**; **3:4**, KJV (RV, "make ye ready"); **9:52** ("to make ready"); **23:56**; Rev. 19:7; 21:2; in 2 Tim. 2:21, of "preparation" of oneself for "every good work"; (c) of human "preparations" for human objects, e.g., **Luke 12:20**, RV, "thou hast prepared" (KJV, "provided"); Acts 23:23; Philem. 22.

Prepared *kataskeuazo* (2680), "to prepare, make ready" (*kata*, used intensively, *skeue*, "equipment"), is so translated in Matt. 11:10; Mark 1:2; **Luke 1:17**; **7:27**; Heb. 9:2, RV (KJV, "made"); 9:6, RV (KJV, "were ... ordained"); 11:7; 1 Pet. 3:20.

1:18 And Zacharias said unto the angel, Whereby shall I know this? for I am an old man, and my wife well stricken in years.

Old *presbutes* (4246), "an old man," **Luke 1:18**, is translated "aged" in Titus 2:2; Philem. 9 (for this, however, see the RV marg.)

Stricken *see **Luke 1:7**.*

Years *hemera* (2250), "a day," is used of (a) the period of natural light, Gen. 1:5; Prov. 4:18; Mark 4:35; (b) the same, but figuratively, for a period of opportunity for service, John 9:4; Rom. 13:13; (c) one period of alternate light and darkness, Gen. 1:5; Mark 1:13; (d) a period of undefined length marked by certain characteristics, such as "the day of small things," Zech. 4:10; of perplexity and distress, Isa. 17:11; Obad. 12-14; of prosperity and of adversity, Ecc. 7:14; of trial or testing, Ps. 95:8; of salvation, Isa. 49:8; 2 Cor. 6:2; cf. **Luke 19:42**; of evil, Eph. 6:13; of wrath and revelation of the judgments of God, Rom. 2:5; (e) an appointed time, Ecc. 8:6; Eph. 4:30; (f) a notable defeat in battle, etc., Isa. 9:4; Psa. 137:7; Ezek. 30:9; Hos. 1:11; (g) by metonymy = "when," "at the time when"; (1), of the past, Gen. 2:4; Num. 3:13; Deut. 4:10, (2), of the future, Gen. 2:17; Ruth 4:5; Matt. 24:50; **Luke 1:20**; (h) a judgment or doom, Job 18:20. (i) of a time of life, **Luke 1:17-18** ("years"). *See also **Luke 1:7**.*

1:19 And the angel answering said unto him, I am Gabriel, that stand in the presence of God; and am sent to speak unto thee, and to shew thee these glad tidings.

Stand *paristemi* (3936), intransitively, denotes "to stand by or beside" (*para*, "by," and *histemi*), Mark 14:47, 69, 70; 15:35, 39 (RV, "stood by"); **Luke 19:24**; John 18:22; 19:26; Acts 1:10; 9:39; 23:2, 4; 27:23; in 27:24, "stand before"; in 4:10, "doth ... stand here"; in **Luke 1:19**, "stand"; Rom. 14:10, "we shall ... stand before" (middle voice); 2 Tim. 4:17, RV, "stood by" (KJV, "... with").

Presence *enopion* (1799), is translated "in the presence of" in **Luke 1:19**; **13:26**; **14:10**; **15:10**; John 20:30; Rev. 14:10 (twice); in 1 Cor. 1:29 KJV, "in His presence" (RV, "before God"). *See also* **Before** at *Luke 1:17*.

Sent *apostello* (649), lit., "to send forth" (*apo*, "from"), akin to *apostolos*, "an apostle," denotes (a) "to send on service, or with a commission," (1) of persons; Christ, sent by the Father, Matt. 10:40; 15:24; 21:37; Mark 9:37; 12:6; **Luke 4:18**, **43**; **9:48**; **10:16**; John 3:17; 5:36, 38; 6:29, 57; 7:29; 8:42; 10:36; 11:42; 17:3, 8, 18 (1st part), 21, 23, 25; 20:21; Acts 3:20 (future); 3:26; 1 John 4:9, 10, 14; the Holy Spirit, **Luke 24:49** (in some texts); 1 Pet. 1:12; Rev. 5:6; Moses, Acts 7:35; John the Baptist, John 1:6; 3:28; disciples and apostles, e.g., Matt. 10:16; Mark 11:1; **Luke 22:8**; John 4:38; 17:18 (2nd part); Acts 26:17; servants, e.g., Matt. 21:34; **Luke 20:10**; officers and officials, Mark 6:27; John 7:32; Acts 16:35; messengers, e.g., Acts 10:8, 17, 20; 15:27; evangelists, Rom. 10:15; angels, e.g., Matt. 24:31; Mark 13:27; **Luke 1:19**, **26**; Heb. 1:14; Rev. 1:1; 22:6; demons, Mark 5:10; (2) of things, e.g., Matt. 21:3; Mark 4:29, RV, marg., "sendeth forth," text, "putteth forth" (KJV, "... in"); Acts 10:36; 11:30; 28:28; (b) "to send away, dismiss," e.g., Mark 8:26; 12:3; **Luke 4:18**, "to set (at liberty)."

Glad tidings *euangelizo* (2097), is used of any message designed to cheer those who receive it; it is rendered "to bring, declare, preach," or "show good or glad tidings," e.g., **Luke 1:19**; **2:10**; **3:18**, RV; **4:43**, RV; **7:22**, RV; **8:1**; Acts 8:12 and 10:36, RV; 14:15, RV; in 1 Thess. 3:6, "brought us glad (KJV, good) tidings"; in Heb. 4:2, RV, "we have had good tidings preached"; similarly, 4:6; in 1 Pet. 1:25 *rhema*, "a word," is coupled with this verb, "the word of good tidings which was preached," RV (KJV, "the word which by the gospel is preached"). In **Luke 4:18** the RV "to preach good tidings" gives the correct quotation from Isaiah, rather than the KJV "to preach the Gospel." In the Sept. the verb is used of any message intended to cheer the hearers, e.g. 1 Sam. 31:9; 2 Sam. 1:20.

1:20 And, behold, thou shalt be dumb, and not able to speak, until the day that these things shall be performed, because thou believest not my words, which shall be fulfilled in their season.

Dumb *siopao* (4623), "to be silent or still, to keep silence" (from *siope*, "silence"), is translated "to hold one's peace," in Matt. 20:31; 26:63; Mark 3:4; 9:34; 10:48; 14:61; **Luke 19:40**; Acts 18:9; in the Lord's command to the sea, in Mark 4:39, it is translated "peace"; in **Luke 1:20**, RV, "thou shalt be silent" (KJV, "dumb").

Performed In **Luke 1:20**, KJV, *ginomai* "to come to pass" (RV), is translated "shall be performed."

Season *kairos* (2540), primarily, "due measure, fitness, proportion," is used in the NT to signify "a season, a time, a period" possessed of certain characteristics, frequently rendered "time" or "times"; in the following the RV substitutes "season" for the KJV "time," thus distinguishing the meaning from *chronos*: Matt. 11:25; 12:1; 14:1; 21:34; Mark 11:13; Acts 3:19; 7:20; 17:26; Rom. 3:26; 5:6; 9:9; 13:11; 1 Cor. 7:5; Gal. 4:10; 1 Thess. 2:17, lit., "for a season (of an hour)", 2 Thess. 2:6; in Eph. 6:18, "at all seasons" (KJV, "always"); in Titus 1:3, "His own seasons" (marg., "its"; KJV, "in due times"); in the preceding clause *chronos* is used. The characteristics of a period are exemplified in the use of the term with regard, e.g. to harvest, Matt. 13:30; reaping, Gal. 6:9; punishment, Matt. 8:29; discharging duties, **Luke 12:42**; opportunity for doing anything, whether good, e.g., Matt. 26:18; Gal. 6:10 ("opportunity"); Eph. 5:16; or evil, e.g., Rev. 12:12; the fulfillment of prophecy, **Luke 1:20**; Acts 3:19; 1 Pet. 1:11; a time suitable for a purpose, **Luke 4:13**, lit., "until a season"; 2 Cor. 6:2. *See also* **Years** at *Luke 1:18*.

1:21 And the people waited for Zacharias, and marvelled that he tarried so long in the temple.

People *laos* (2992), is used of (a) "the people at large," especially of people assembled, e.g., Matt. 27:25; **Luke 1:21**; **3:15**; Acts 4:27; (b) "a people of the same race and language," e.g., Rev. 5:9; in the plural, e.g., **Luke 2:31**; Rom. 15:11; Rev. 7:9; 11:9; especially of Israel, e.g., Matt. 2:6; 4:23; John 11:50; Acts 4:8; Heb. 2:17; in distinction from their rulers and priests, e.g., Matt. 26:5; **Luke 20:19**; Heb. 5:3; in distinction from Gentiles, e.g., Acts 26:17, 23; Rom. 15:10; (c) of Christians as the people of God, e.g., Acts 15:14; Titus 2:14; Heb. 4:9; 1 Pet. 2:9.

Waited *prosdokao* (4328), "to await," is rendered "to wait for" in **Luke 1:21**; **8:40**; Acts 10:24; in 27:33, RV "ye wait" (KJV, "have tarried").

Tarried *chronizo* (5549), from *chronos*, "time," lit. means "to while away time," i.e., by way of lingering, tarrying, "delaying"; "delayeth," Matt. 24:48; **Luke 12:45**, "tarried," Matt. 25:5; "tarried so long," **Luke 1:21**; "will (not) tarry," Heb. 10:37.

So long In Acts 27:33 and Heb. 3:13 *achri* (or *achris*) followed by *hou*, the genitive case of the relative pronoun *hos*, lit., "until which," is rendered "while"; cf. *en ho*, in Mark 2:19; **Luke 5:34**; John 5:7; *en to*, in **Luke 1:21**, RV, "while"; in Heb. 3:15, "while it is said," is, lit., "in the being said" (*en*, with the article and the pres. infin., passive of *lego*); so, e.g., in Matt. 13:25

Temple *see* ***Luke 1:9***.

1:22 And when he came out, he could not speak unto them: and they perceived that he had seen a vision in the temple: for he beckoned unto them, and remained speechless.

Perceived *epiginosko* (1921), a strengthened form, "to gain a full knowledge of, to become fully acquainted with," is translated "to perceive" in Mark 5:30, RV (KJV, "knowing"); **Luke 1:22**; **5:22**; Acts 19:34, RV (KJV, "knew").

Vision *optasia* (3701), (a late form of *opsis*, "the act of seeing"), from *optano*, "to see, a coming into view," denotes a "vision" in **Luke 1:22**; **24:23**; Acts 26:19; 2 Cor. 12:1.

Temple *see* ***Luke 1:9***.

Beckoned *dianeuo* (1269), "to express one's meaning by a sign," is said of the act of Zacharias, **Luke 1:22** (RV, "continued making signs," for KJV, "beckoned"). In Sept., Ps. 35:19, "wink."

Remained *diameno* (1265), "to continue throughout," i.e., without interruption, is said of the dumbness of Zacharias, **Luke 1:22**, KJV, "remained"; of the "continuance" of the disciples with Christ, **Luke 22:28**; of the permanency of the truth of the gospel with churches, Gal. 2:5; of the unchanged course of things, 2 Pet. 3:4; of the eternal permanency of Christ, Heb. 1:11.

1:23 And it came to pass, that, as soon as the days of his ministration were accomplished, he departed to his own house.

Ministration *leitourgia* (3009), akin to *leitourgos*, to which the meanings of *leitourgia* correspond, is used in the NT of "sacred ministrations," (a) priestly, **Luke 1:23**; Heb. 8:6; 9:21; (b) figuratively, of the practical faith of the members of the church at Philippi regarded as priestly sacrifice, upon which the apostle's lifeblood might be poured out as a libation, Phil. 2:17; (c) of the "ministration" of believers one to another, regarded as priestly service, 2 Cor. 9:12; Phil. 2:30.

Accomplished *pletho* (4130), "to fulfill," is translated "accomplished" in the KJV of **Luke 1:23**; **2:6**, **21-22** (RV, "fulfilled").

1:24 And after those days his wife Elisabeth conceived, and hid herself five months, saying,

Conceived *sullambano* (4815), lit., "to take together" (*sun*, "with," *lambano*, "to take or receive"), is used (a) of a woman, to "conceive," **Luke 1:24**, **31**, **36**; in the passive voice. **Luke 2:21**; (b) metaphorically, of the impulse of lust in the human heart, enticing to sin, Jas. 1:15.

Hid *perikrupto* (4032), signifies "to hide by placing something around, to conceal entirely, to keep hidden," **Luke 1:24**.

Months *men* (3376), connected with *mene*, "the moon," akin to a Sanskrit root *ma-*, "to measure" (the Sanskrit *masa* denotes both moon and month, cf. e.g., Lat. *mensis*, Eng., "moon" and "month," the moon being in early times the measure of the "month"). The interval between the 17th day of the second "month" (Gen. 7:11) and the 17th day of the seventh "month," is said to be 150 days (8:3, 4), i.e., five months of 30 days each; hence the year would be 360 days (cf. Dan. 7:25; 9:27; 12:7 with Rev. 11:2-3; 12:6, 14; 13:5; whence we conclude that 3 ½ years or 42 months = 1260 days, i.e., one year = 60 days); this was the length of the old Egyptian year; later, five days were added to correspond to the solar year. The Hebrew year was as nearly solar as was compatible with its commencement, coinciding with the new moon, or first day of the "month." This was a regular feast day, Num. 10:10; 28:11-14; the Passover coincided with the full moon (the 14th of the month Abib). Except in Gal. 4:10; Jas. 5:17; Rev. 9:5, 10, 15; 11:2; 13:5; 22:2, the word is found only in Luke's writings, **Luke 1:24**, **26**, **36**, **56**; **4:25**; Acts 7:20; 18:11; 19:8; 20:3; 28:11, examples of Luke's care as to accuracy of detail.

1:25 Thus hath the Lord dealt with me in the days wherein he looked on *me*, to take away my reproach among men.

Thus *houtos* or *houto* (3779), "in this way, so, thus," is used (a) with reference to what precedes, e.g., **Luke 1:25**; **2:48**; (b) with reference to what follows, e.g., **Luke 19:31**, rendered "on this wise," in Matt. 1:18; John 21:1, and before quotations, Acts 7:6; 13:34; Rom. 10:6, KJV (RV, "thus"); Heb. 4:4; (c) marking intensity, rendered "so," e.g., Gal. 1:6;

Heb. 12:21; Rev. 16:18; (d) in comparisons, rendered "so," e.g., **Luke 11:30**; Rom. 5:15.

Dealt with *poieo* (4160), "to do," used to describe almost any act, whether complete or repeated, like the Eng. "do," is translated to deal with, in **Luke 2:48**. In **Luke 1:25**, KJV, "hath dealt with (me)," the RV, adhering to the ordinary meaning, translates by "hath done unto (me)."

Looked *epeidon* (1896), denotes "to look upon" (*epi*, "upon"), (a) favorably, **Luke 1:25** (b) unfavorably, in Acts 4:29.

Take *aphaireo* (851), "to take away" (*apo*), is used with this meaning in **Luke 1:25**; **10:42**; **16:3**; Rom. 11:27, of the "removal" of the sins of Israel; Heb. 10:4, of the impossibility of the "removal" of sins by offerings under the Law; in Rev. 22:19 (twice).

Reproach *oneidos* (3681), is used in **Luke 1:25** in the concrete sense of "a matter of reproach, a disgrace." To have no children was, in the Jewish mind, more than a misfortune, it might carry the implication that this was a divine punishment for some secret sin. Cf. Gen. 30:1; 1 Sam. 1:6-10.

1:26 And in the sixth month the angel Gabriel was sent from God unto a city of Galilee, named Nazareth,

Sixth *hektos* (1623), is used (a) of a month, **Luke 1:26**, **36**; (b) an hour, Matt. 20:5; 27:45 and parallel passages; John 4:6; (c) an angel, Rev. 9:13, 14; 16:12; (d) a seal of a roll, in vision, Rev. 6:12; (e) of the "sixth" precious stone, the sardius, in the foundations of the wall of the heavenly Jerusalem, Rev. 21:20.

Month *see* Months at *Luke 1:24*.

Sent *see Luke 1:19*.

1:27 To a virgin espoused to a man whose name was Joseph, of the house of David; and the virgin's name *was* Mary.

Virgin *parthenos* (3933), is used (a) of "the Virgin Mary," Matt. 1:23; **Luke 1:27**; (b) of the ten "virgins" in the parable, Matt. 25:1, 7, 11; (c) of the "daughters" of Philip the evangelist, Acts 21:9; (d) those concerning whom the apostle Paul gives instructions regarding marriage, 1 Cor. 7:25, 28, 34; in vv. 36, 37, 38, the subject passes to that of "virgin *daughters*" (RV), which almost certainly formed one of the subjects upon which the church at Corinth sent for instructions from the apostle; one difficulty was relative to the discredit which might be brought upon a father (or guardian), if he allowed his daughter or ward to grow old unmarried. The interpretation that this passage refers to a man and woman already in some kind of relation by way of a spiritual marriage and living together in a vow of virginity and celibacy, is untenable if only in view of the phraseology of the passage; (e) figuratively, of "a local church" in its relation to Christ, 2 Cor. 11:2; (f) metaphorically, of "chaste persons," Rev. 14:4.

Espoused *mnesteuo* (3423), "to woo and win, to espouse or promise in marriage," is used in the passive voice in Matt. 1:18; **Luke 1:27**; **2:5**, all with reference to the Virgin Mary, RV, "betrothed," for KJV, "espoused," in each case.

House *oikos* (3624), denotes (a) "a house, a dwelling," e.g., Matt. 9:6, 7; 11:8; it is used of the Tabernacle, as the House of God, Matt. 12:4, and the Temple similarly, e.g., Matt. 21:13; **Luke 11:51**, KJV, "temple," RV, "sanctuary"; John 2:16, 17; called by the Lord "your house" in Matt. 23:38 and **Luke 13:35** (some take this as the city of Jerusalem); metaphorically of Israel as God's house, Heb. 3:2, 5, where "his house" is not Moses', but God's; of believers, similarly, v. 6, where Christ is spoken of as "over God's House" (the word "own" is rightly omitted in the RV); Heb. 10:21; 1 Pet. 2:5; 4:17; of the body, Matt. 12:44; **Luke 11:24**; (b) by metonymy, of the members of a household or family, e.g., **Luke 10:5**; Acts 7:10; 11:14; 1 Tim. 3:4, 5, 12; 2 Tim. 1:16; 4:19, RV (KJV, "household"); Titus 1:11 (plural); of a local church, 1 Tim. 3:15; of the descendants of Jacob (Israel) and David, e.g., Matt. 10:6; **Luke 1:27**, **33**; Acts 2:36; 7:42.

1:28 And the angel came in unto her, and said, Hail, *thou that art* highly favoured, the Lord *is* with thee: blessed *art* thou among women.

Hail *chairo* (5463), "to rejoice," is used in the imperative mood, (a) as a salutation, only in the Gospels; in this respect it is rendered simply "hail," in mockery of Christ, Matt. 26:49; 27:29; Mark 15:18; John 19:3; (b) as a greeting, by the angel Gabriel to Mary, **Luke 1:28**, and, in the plural, by the Lord to the disciples after His resurrection, Matt. 28:9.

Favoured *charitoo* (5487), to endow with *charis*, primarily signified "to make graceful or gracious," and came to denote, in Hellenistic Greek, "to cause to find favor," **Luke 1:28**, "highly favored" (marg., "endued with grace"); in Eph. 1:6, it is translated "made ... accepted," KJV, "freely bestowed," RV (lit., "graced"); it does not here mean to endue with grace. Grace implies more than favor; grace is a free gift, favor may be deserved or gained.

1:29 And when she saw *him*, she

was troubled at his saying, and cast in her mind what manner of salutation this should be.

Troubled *diatarasso* (1298), "to agitate greatly," is used of the Virgin Mary, **Luke 1:29**.

Saying *logos* (3056), "a word," as embodying a conception or idea, denotes among its various meanings, "a saying, statement or declaration," uttered (a) by God; RV, "word" or "words" (KJV, "saying"), e.g., in John 8:55; Rom. 3:4; Rev. 19:9; 22:6, 7, 9, 10; (b) by Christ, e.g., Mark 8:32; 9:10; 10:22; **Luke 9:28**; John 6:60; 21:23; the RV appropriately substitutes "word" or "words" for KJV, "saying" or "sayings," especially in John's Gospel, e.g. 7:36, 40; 8:51, 52; 10:19; 14:24; 15:20; 18:9, 32; 19:13; (c) by an angel, **Luke 1:29**; (d) by OT prophets, John 12:38 (RV, "word") Rom. 13:9 (ditto); 1 Cor. 15:54; (e) by the apostle Paul in the Pastoral Epp., 1 Tim. 1:15; 3:1; 4:9; 2 Tim. 2:11; Titus 3:8; (f) by other men, Mark 7:29; Acts 7:29; John 4:37 (in general).

Cast *dialogizomai* (1260), "to bring together different reasons and reckon them up, to reason," is used in the NT (a) chiefly of thoughts and considerations which are more or less objectionable, e.g., of the disciples who "reasoned" together, through a mistaken view of Christ's teaching regarding leaven, Matt. 16:7, 8 and Mark 8:16, 17; of their "reasoning" as to who was the greatest among them, Mark 9:33, RV, "were ye reasoning," KJV, "ye disputed"; of the scribes and Pharisees in criticizing Christ's claim to forgive sins, Mark 2:6, 8 (twice) and **Luke 5:21, 22**; of the chief priests and elders in considering how to answer Christ's question regarding John's baptism, Matt. 21:25; Mark 11:31 (some mss. have *logizomai*, here, which is nowhere else rendered "to reason"); of the wicked husbandmen, and their purpose to murder the heir and seize his inheritance, **Luke 20:14**; of the rich man who "reasoned" within himself, RV (KJV, "thought"), as to where to bestow his fruits, **Luke 12:17** (some mss. have it in John 11:50, the best have *logizomai*); (b) of considerations not objectionable, **Luke 1:29**, "cast in (her) mind"; **3:15**, RV, and KJV, marg., "reasoned" (KJV, "mused").

Manner *potapos* (4217), primarily, "from what country," then, "of what sort," is rendered "what manner of man," Matt. 8:27: so 2 Pet. 3:11; Mark 13:1 (twice); **Luke 1:29**; **7:39**; 1 John 3:1.

Salutation *aspamos* (783), a salutation, is always so rendered in the RV; KJV, "greetings" in Matt. 23:7; **Luke 11:43**; **20:46**, it is used (a) orally in those instances and in Mark 12:38; **Luke 1:29, 41, 44**; (b) in written salutations, 1 Cor. 16:21; Col. 4:18; 2 Thess. 3:17.

1:30 And the angel said unto her, Fear not, Mary: for thou hast found favour with God.

Found *heurisko* (2147), denotes (a) "to find," either with previous search, e.g., Matt. 7:7, 8, or without, e.g., Matt. 27:32; in the passive voice, of Enoch's disappearance, Heb. 11:5; of mountains, Rev. 16:20; of Babylon and its occupants, 18:21, 22; (b) metaphorically, "to find out by enquiry," or "to learn, discover," e.g., **Luke 19:48**; John 18:38; 19:4, 6; Acts 4:21; 13:28; Rom. 7:10; Gal. 2:17, which indicates "the surprise of the Jew" who learned for the first time that before God he had no moral superiority over the Gentiles whom he superciliously dubbed "sinners," while he esteemed himself to be "righteous"; 1 Pet. 1:7; Rev. 5:4; (c) in the middle voice, "to find for oneself, gain, procure, obtain," e.g., Matt. 10:39; 11:29, "ye shall find (rest)"; **Luke 1:30**; Acts 7:46; 2 Tim. 1:18.

Favour *charis* (5485), denotes (a) objectively, "grace in a person, graciousness," (b) subjectively, (1) "grace on the part of a giver, favor, kindness," (2) "a sense of favor received, thanks." It is rendered "favor" in **Luke 1:30**; **2:52**; Acts 2:47; 7:10, 46; 24:27 and 25:9, RV (for KJV, "pleasure"); 25:3.

1:31 And, behold, thou shalt conceive in thy womb, and bring forth a son, and shalt call his name JESUS.

Conceive *see* **Conceived** at **Luke** ***1:24***.

Womb *gaster* (1064), is rendered "womb" in **Luke 1:31**.

1:32 He shall be great, and shall be called the Son of the Highest: and the Lord God shall give unto him the throne of his father David:

Son *The Son of God* In this title the word "Son" is used sometimes (a) of relationship, sometimes (b) of the expression of character. "Thus, e.g., when the disciples so addressed Him, Matt. 14:33; 16:16; John 1:49, when the centurion so spoke of Him, Matt. 27:54, they probably meant that (b) He was a manifestation of God in human form. But in such passages as **Luke 1:32, 35**; Acts 13:33, which refer to the humanity of the Lord Jesus, ... the word is used in sense (a).

"The Lord Jesus Himself used the full title on occasion, John 5:25; 9:35 [some mss. have 'the Son of Man'; see RV marg.]; 11:4, and on the more frequent occasions on which He spoke of Himself as 'the Son,' the words are to be understood as an abbreviation of 'the Son of God,' not of 'The Son of Man'; this latter He always expressed in full; see **Luke 10:22**; John 5:19, etc.

"John uses both the longer and shorter forms of the title in his Gospel, see 3:16-18; 20:31, e.g., and in his Epistles; cf. Rev. 2:18. So does the writer of Hebrews, 1:2; 4:14; 6:6, etc. An eternal relation subsisting between the Son and the Father in the Godhead is to be understood. That is to say, the Son of God, in His eternal relationship with the Father, is not so entitled because He at any time began to derive His being from the Father (in which case He could not be co-eternal with the Father), but because He is and ever has been the expression of what the Father is; cf. John 14:9, 'he that hath seen Me hath seen the Father.' The words of Heb. 1:3, 'Who being the effulgence of His (God's) glory, and the very image of His (God's) substance' are a definition of what is meant by 'Son of God.' Thus absolute Godhead, not Godhead in a secondary or derived sense, is intended in the title."

"The Son is the eternal object of the Father's love, John 17:24, and the sole Revealer of the Father's character, John 1:14; Heb. 1:3. The words, 'Father' and 'Son,' are never in the NT so used as to suggest that the Father existed before the Son; the Prologue to the Gospel according to John distinctly asserts that the Word existed 'in the beginning,' and that this Word is the Son, Who 'became flesh and dwelt among us.'"

The declaration "Thou art My Son, this day have I begotten Thee," Ps. 2:7, quoted in Acts 13:33; Heb. 1:5; 5:5, refers to the birth of Christ, not to His resurrection. In Acts 13:33 the verb "raise up" is used of the raising up of a person to occupy a special position in the nation, as of David in verse 22 (so of Christ as a Prophet in 3:22 and 7:37). The word "again" in the KJV in v. 33 represents nothing in the original. The RV rightly omits it. In v. 34 the statement as to the resurrection of Christ receives the greater stress in this respect through the emphatic contrast to that in v. 33 as to His being raised up in the nation, a stress imparted by the added words "from the dead." Accordingly v. 33 speaks of His incarnation, v. 34 of His resurrection.

Son of Man In the NT this is a designation of Christ, almost entirely confined to the Gospels. Elsewhere it is found in Acts 7:56, the only occasion where a disciple applied it to the Lord and in Rev. 1:13; 14:14 (see below). "Son of Man" is the title Christ used of Himself; John 12:34 is not an exception, for the quotation by the multitude was from His own statement. The title is found especially in the Synoptic Gospels. The occurrences in John's Gospel, 1:51; 3:13, 14; 5:27; 6:27, 53, 62; 8:28 (9:35 in some texts); 12:23, 34 (twice); 13:31, are not parallel to those in the Synoptic Gospels. In the latter the use of the title falls into two groups, (a) those in which it refers to Christ's humanity, His earthly work, sufferings and death, e.g., Matt. 8:20; 11:19; 12:40; 26:2, 24; (b) those which refer to His glory in resurrection and to that of His future advent, e.g., Matt. 10:23; 13:41; 16:27, 28; 17:9; 24:27, 30 (twice), 37, 39, 44.

While it is a messianic title it is evident that the Lord applied it to Himself in a distinctive way, for it indicates more than Messiahship, even universal headship on the part of One who is Man. It therefore stresses His manhood, manhood of a unique order in comparison with all other men, for He is declared to be of heaven, 1 Cor. 15:47, and even while here below, was "the Son of Man, which is in Heaven," John 3:13. As the "Son of Man" He must be appropriated spiritually as a condition of possessing eternal life, John 6:53. In His death, as in His life, the glory of His Manhood was displayed in the absolute obedience and submission to the will of the Father (12:23; 13:31), and, in view of this, all judgment has been committed to Him, who will judge in full understanding experimentally of human conditions, sin apart, and will exercise the judgment as sharing the nature of those judged, John 5:22, 27. Not only is He man, but He is "Son of Man," not by human generation but, according to the Semitic usage of the expression, partaking of the characteristics (sin apart) of manhood belonging to the category of mankind. Twice in Revelation, 1:13 and 14:14, He is described as "One like unto a Son of man," RV (KJV, "... the Son of Man"), cf. Dan. 7:13. He who was thus seen was indeed the "Son of Man," but the absence of the article in the original serves to stress what morally characterizes Him as such. Accordingly in these passages He is revealed, not as the Person known by the title, but as the One who is qualified to act as the Judge of all men. He is the same Person as in the days of His flesh, still continuing His humanity with His Deity. The phrase "like unto" serves to distinguish Him as there seen in His glory and majesty in contrast to the days of His humiliation.

Highest *hupsistos* (5310), "most high," is a superlative degree, the positive not being in use; it is used of God in **Luke 1:32, 35, 76; 6:35**, in each of which the RV has "the most High," for KJV, "the highest", KJV and RV in Mark 5:7; **Luke 8:28**; Acts 7:48; 16:17; Heb. 7:1.

Throne *thronos* (2362), "a throne, a seat of authority," is used of the "throne" (a) of God, e.g., Heb. 4:16, "the throne of grace," i.e., from which grace proceeds; 8:1; 12:2; Rev. 1:4; 3:21 (2nd part); 4:2 (twice); 5:1; frequently in Rev.; in 20:12, in the best texts, "the throne" (some have *Theos*, "God," KJV); cf. 21:3; Matt. 5:34; 23:22; Acts 7:49; (b) of Christ, e.g. Heb. 1:8; Rev. 3:21 (1st part); 22:3; His seat of authority in the Millennium, Matt. 19:28 (1st part); (c) by metonymy for angelic powers, Col. 1:16; (d) of the Apostles in millennial authority, Matt. 19:28 (2nd part); **Luke 22:30**; (e) of the elders in the heavenly vision, Rev. 4:4 (2nd and 3rd parts), RV, "thrones" (KJV, "seats"); so 11:16; (f) of David, **Luke 1:32**; Acts 2:30; (g) of Satan, Rev. 2:13, RV, "throne" (KJV, "seat"); (h) of "the beast," the final and federal head of the revived Roman Empire, Rev. 13:2; 16:10.

1:33 And he shall reign over the house of Jacob for ever; and of his kingdom there shall be no end.

Reign *basileuo* (936), "to reign," is used (I) literally, (a) of God, Rev. 11:17; 19:6, in each of which the aorist tense (in the latter, translated "reigneth") is "ingressive," stressing the point of entrance; (b) of Christ, **Luke 1:33**; 1 Cor. 15:25; Rev. 11:15; as rejected by the Jews, **Luke 19:14, 27**; (c) of the saints, hereafter, 1 Cor. 4:8 (2nd part), where the apostle, casting a reflection upon the untimely exercise of authority on the part of the church at Corinth, anticipates the due time for it in the future; Rev. 5:10; 20:4, where the aorist tense is not simply of a "point" character, but "constative," that is, regarding a whole action as having occurred, without distinguishing any steps in its progress (in this instance the aspect is future); v. 6; 22:5; (d) of earthly potentates, Matt. 2:22; 1 Tim. 6:15, where "kings" is, lit., "them that reign"; (II), metaphorically, (a) of believers, Rom. 5:17, where "shall reign in life" indicates the activity of life in fellowship with Christ in His sovereign power, reaching its fullness hereafter; 1 Cor. 4:8 (1st part), of the carnal pride that laid claim to a power not to be exercised until hereafter; (b) of divine grace, Rom. 5:21; (c) of sin, Rom. 5:21; 6:12; (d) of death, Rom. 5:14, 17.

House *see Luke 1:27.*

End *telos* (5056), signifies (a) "the limit," either at which a person or thing ceases to be what he or it was up to that point, or at which previous activities were ceased, 2 Cor. 3:13; 1 Pet. 4:7; (b) "the final issue or result" of a state or process, e.g., **Luke 1:33**; in Rom. 10:4, Christ is described as "the end of the Law unto righteousness to everyone that believeth"; this is best explained by Gal. 3:23-26; cf. Jas. 5:11; the following more especially point to the issue or fate of a thing, Matt. 26:58; Rom. 6:21; 2 Cor. 11:15; Phil. 3:19; Heb. 6:8; 1 Pet. 1:9; (c) "a fulfillment," **Luke 22:37**, KJV, "(have) an end"; (d) "the utmost degree" of an act, as of the love of Christ towards His disciples, John 13:1; (e) "the aim or purpose" of a thing, 1 Tim. 1:5; (f) "the last" in a succession or series, Rev. 1:8 (KJV, only, "ending"); 21:6; 22:13.

1:34 Then said Mary unto the angel, How shall this be, seeing I know not a man?

Know *ginosko* (1097), signifies "to be taking in knowledge, to come to know, recognize, understand," or "to understand completely," e.g., Mark 13:28, 29; John 13:12; 15:18; 21:17; 2 Cor. 8:9; Heb. 10:34; 1 John 2:5; 4:2, 6 (twice), 7, 13; 5:2, 20; in its past tenses it frequently means "to know in the sense of realizing," the aorist or point tense usually indicating definiteness, Matt. 13:11; Mark 7:24; John 7:26; in 10:38, "that ye may know (aorist tense) and understand (present tense)"; 19:4; Acts 1:7; 17:19; Rom. 1:21; 1 Cor. 2:11 (2nd part), 14; 2 Cor. 2:4; Eph. 3:19; 6:22; Phil. 2:19; 3:10; 1 Thess. 3:5; 2 Tim. 2:19; Jas. 2:20; 1 John 2:13 (twice), 14; 3:6; 4:8; 2 John 1; Rev. 2:24; 3:3, 9. In the passive voice, it often signifies "to become known," e.g., Matt. 10:26; Phil. 4:5. In the sense of complete and absolute understanding on God's part, it is used, e.g., in **Luke 16:15**; John 10:15 (of the Son as well as the Father); 1 Cor. 3:20. In **Luke 12:46**, KJV, it is rendered "he is ... aware." The verb is also used to convey the thought of connection or union, as between man and woman, Matt. 1:25; **Luke 1:34**.

1:35 And the angel answered and said unto her, The Holy Ghost shall come upon thee, and the power of the Highest shall overshadow thee: therefore also that holy thing which shall be born of thee shall be called the Son of God.

Holy *hagios* (40), fundamentally signifies "separated" (among the Greeks, dedicated to the gods), and hence, in Scripture in its moral and spiritual significance, separated from sin and therefore consecrated to God, sacred.

(a) It is predicated of God (as the absolutely "Holy" One, in His purity, majesty and glory): of the Father, e.g., **Luke 1:49**; John 17:11; 1 Pet. 1:15, 16; Rev. 4:8; 6:10; of the Son, e.g., **Luke 1:35**; Acts 3:14; 4:27,

30; 1 John 2:20; of the Spirit, e.g., Matt. 1:18 and frequently in all the Gospels, Acts, Romans, 1 and 2 Cor., Eph., 1 Thess.; also in 2 Tim. 1:14; Titus 3:5; 1 Pet. 1:12; 2 Pet. 1:21; Jude 20.

(b) It is used of men and things in so far as they are devoted to God. Indeed the quality, as attributed to God, is often presented in a way which involves divine demands upon the conduct of believers. These are called *hagioi*, "saints," i.e., "sanctified" or "holy" ones.

This sainthood is not an attainment, it is a state into which God in grace calls men; yet believers are called to sanctify themselves (consistently with their calling, 2 Tim. 1:9), cleansing themselves from all defilement, forsaking sin, living a "holy" manner of life, 1 Pet. 1:15; 2 Pet. 3:11, and experiencing fellowship with God in His holiness. The saints are thus figuratively spoken of as "a holy temple", 1 Cor. 3:17 (a local church); Eph. 2:21 (the whole Church), cp. 5:27; "a holy priesthood," 1 Pet. 2:5; "a holy nation," 2:9.

"It is evident that *hagios* and its kindred words ... express something more and higher than *hieros*, sacred, outwardly associated with God; ... something more than *semnos*, worthy, honorable; something more than *hagnos*, pure, free from defilement. *Hagios* is ... more comprehensive.... It is characteristically godlikeness" (G. B. Stevens, in Hastings' *Bib. Dic.*).

The adjective is also used of the outer part of the tabernacle, Heb. 9:2 (RV, "the holy place"); of the inner sanctuary, 9:3, RV, "the Holy of Holies"; 9:4, "a holy place," RV; v. 25 (plural), of the presence of God in heaven, where there are not two compartments as in the tabernacle, all being "the holy place"; 9:8, 12 (neuter plural); 10:19, "the holy place," RV (KJV, "the holiest," neut. plural); of the city of Jerusalem. Rev. 11:2; its temple, Acts 6:13; of the faith. Jude 20; of the greetings of saints, 1 Cor. 16:20; of angels, e.g., Mark 8:38; of apostles and prophets, Eph. 3:5; of the future heavenly Jerusalem, Rev. 21:2, 10; 22:19.

See also **Holy Ghost** at ***Luke 2:26***.

Come *eperchomai* (1904), "to come or go upon" (*epi*, "upon"), e.g., **Luke 1:35**; in **Luke 21:26**, used of "coming" events, suggesting their certainty; in Eph. 2:7, said of the "oncoming" of the ages; in Acts 14:19, of Jews coming to (lit., "upon") a place.

Highest *see* ***Luke 1:32***.

Overshadow *episkiazo* (1982), "to throw a shadow upon" (*epi*, "over," *skia*, "a shadow"), "to overshadow," is used (a) of the bright cloud at the Transfiguration, Matt. 17:5; Mark 9:7; **Luke 9:34**; (b) metaphorically of the power of "the Most High" upon the Virgin Mary, **Luke 1:35**; (c) of the apostle Peter's shadow upon the sick, Acts 5:15.

Son *see* ***Luke 1:32***.

God *theos* (2316), (I) in the polytheism of the Greeks, denoted "a god or deity," e.g., Acts 14:11; 19:26; 28:6; 1 Cor. 8:5; Gal. 4:8.

(II) (a) Hence the word was appropriated by Jews and retained by Christians to denote "the one true God." In the Sept. *theos* translates (with few exceptions) the Hebrew words *Elohim* and *Jehovah*, the former indicating His power and preeminence, the latter His unoriginated, immutable, eternal and self-sustained existence. In the NT, these and all the other divine attributes are predicated of Him. To Him are ascribed, e.g., His unity, or monism, e.g., Mark 12:29; 1 Tim. 2:5; self-existence, John 5:26; immutability, Jas. 1:17; eternity, Rom. 1:20; universality, Matt. 10:29; Acts 17:26-28; almighty power, Matt. 19:26; infinite knowledge, Acts 2:23; 15:18; Rom. 11:33, creative power, Rom. 11:36; 1 Cor. 8:6; Eph. 3:9; Rev. 4:11; 10:6; absolute holiness, 1 Pet. 1:15; 1 John 1:5; righteousness, John 17:25; faithfulness, 1 Cor. 1:9; 10:13; 1 Thess. 5:24; 2 Thess. 3:3; 1 John 1:9; love, 1 John 4:8, 16; mercy, Rom. 9:15, 18; truthfulness, Titus 1:2; Heb. 6:18.

(b) The divine attributes are likewise indicated or definitely predicated of Christ, e.g., Matt. 20:18-19; John 1:1-3; 1:18, RV, marg.; 5:22-29; 8:58; 14:6; 17:22-24; 20:28; Rom. 1:4; 9:5; Phil. 3:21; Col. 1:15; 2:3; Titus 2:13, RV; Heb. 1:3; 13:8; 1 John 5:20; Rev. 22:12, 13.

(c) Also of the Holy Spirit, e.g., Matt. 28:19; **Luke 1:35**; John 14:16; 15:26; 16:7-14; Rom. 8:9, 26; 1 Cor. 12:11; 2 Cor. 13:14.

(d) *Theos* is used (1) with the definite article, (2) without (i.e., as an anarthrous noun). "The English may or may not have need of the article in translation. But that point cuts no figure in the Greek idiom. Thus in Acts 27:23 ('the God whose I am,' RV) the article points out the special God whose Paul is, and is to be preserved in English. In the very next verse (*ho theos*) we in English do not need the article" (A. T. Robertson, *Gram. of Greek, NT*, p. 758).

(e) In the following the nominative case is used for the vocative, and always with the article; Mark 15:34; **Luke 18:11, 13**; John 20:28; (Acts 4:24 in some mss.); Heb. 1:8; 10:7.

(f) The phrase "the things of God" (translated literally or otherwise) stands for (1) His interests, Matt. 16:23; Mark 8:33; (2) His counsels, 1 Cor. 2:11; (3) things which are due to Him, Matt. 22:21; Mark 12:17; **Luke 20:25**. The phrase "things pertaining to God," Rom. 15:17; Heb. 2:17; 5:1, describes, in the Heb. passages, the sacrificial service of the priest; in the Rom. passage the gospel ministry as an offering to God.

1:36 And, behold, thy cousin Elisabeth, she hath also conceived a son in her old age: and this is the sixth month with her, who was called barren.

Cousin *sungenis* (4773), in **Luke 1:36** (so in the most authentic mss.) and *sungenes* in v. **58** (plural), KJV, "cousin" and "cousins," respectively signify "kinswoman" and "kinsfolk," (RV); so the RV and KJV in **2:44** and **21:16**. The word lit. signifies "born with," i.e., of the same stock, or descent; hence "kinsman, kindred." *See also* **Cousins** at *Luke 1:58.*

Conceived *see Luke 1:24.*

Old *geras* (1094), "old age," occurs in **Luke 1:36**.

Sixth *see Luke 1:26.*

Month *see* Months at *Luke 1:24.*

Barren *see Luke 1:7.*

1:37 For with God nothing shall be impossible.

Impossible *adunateo* (101), signifies "to be impossible," "unable"; in the NT it is used only of things, Matt. 17:20, "(nothing) shall be impossible (unto you)"; **Luke 1:37**. KJV "(with God nothing) shall be impossible"; RV, "(no word from God – a different construction in the best mss.) shall be void of power"; *rhema* may mean either "word" or "thing" (i.e., fact). In the Sept. the verb is always used of things and signifies either to be "impossible" or to be impotent, e.g., Gen. 18:14; Lev. 25:35, "he fail"; Deut. 17:8; Job 4:4, "feeble"; 42:2; Dan. 4:6; Zech. 8:6.

1:38 And Mary said, Behold the handmaid of the Lord; be it unto me according to thy word. And the angel departed from her.

Handmaid *doulos* (1401), from *deo,* "to bind," "a slave," originally the lowest term in the scale of servitude, came also to mean "one who gives himself up to the will of another," e.g., 1 Cor. 7:23; Rom. 6:17, 20, and became the most common and general word for "servant," as in Matt. 8:9, without any idea of bondage. In calling himself, however, a "bondslave of Jesus Christ," e.g., Rom. 1:1, the apostle Paul intimates (1) that he had been formerly a "bondslave" of Satan, and (2) that, having been bought by Christ, he was now a willing slave, bound to his new Master. The feminine, *doule,* signifies "a handmaid," **Luke 1:38, 48**; Acts 2:18.

Word *rhema* (4487), denotes "that which is spoken, what is uttered in speech or writing"; in the singular, "a word," e.g., Matt. 12:36; 27:14; 2 Cor. 12:4; 13:1; Heb. 12:19; in the plural, speech, discourse, e.g., John 3:34; 8:20; Acts 2:14; 6:11, 13; 11:14; 13:42; 26:25; Rom. 10:18; 2 Pet. 3:2; Jude 17; it is used of the gospel in Rom. 10:8 (twice), 17, RV, "the word of Christ" (i.e., the "word" which preaches Christ); 10:18; 1 Pet. 1:25 (twice); of a statement, command, instruction, e.g., Matt. 26:75; **Luke 1:37**, RV, "(no) word (from God shall be void of power)", v. **38**; Acts 11:16; Heb. 11:3. The significance of *rhema* (as distinct from *logos*) is exemplified in the injunction to take "the sword of the Spirit, which is the word of God," Eph. 6:17; here the reference is not to the whole Bible as such, but to the individual scripture which the Spirit brings to our remembrance for use in time of need, a prerequisite being the regular storing of the mind with Scripture.

1:39 And Mary arose in those days, and went into the hill country with haste, into a city of Juda;

Hill *oreinos* (3714), an adjective meaning "mountainous, hilly," is used in the feminine, *oreine,* as a noun, and rendered "hill country" in **Luke 1:39, 65**.

Country *oreinos* (3714), "hilly" (from *oros,* "a hill, mountain"), is translated "hill country" in **Luke 1:39, 65**.

Haste *spoude* (4710), denotes (a) "haste, speed," accompanied by "with," Mark 6:25; **Luke 1:39**; (b) "zeal, diligence, earnestness".

1:40-41 And entered into the house of Zacharias, and saluted Elisabeth.

And it came to pass, that, when Elisabeth heard the salutation of Mary, the babe leaped in her womb; and Elisabeth was filled with the Holy Ghost:

Salutation *see Luke 1:29.*

Babe *brephos* (1025), denotes (a) "an unborn child," as in **Luke 1:41, 44**; (b) "a newborn child, or an infant still older," **Luke 2:12, 16; 18:15**; Acts 7:19; 2 Tim. 3:15; 1 Pet. 2:2.

Leaped *skirtao* (4640), "to leap," is found in **Luke 1:41, 44** and **6:23**, there translated "leap for joy"; in **1:44** the words "for joy" are expressed separately.

Womb *see Luke 1:15.*

Filled *see Luke 1:15.*

1:42 And she spake out with a

loud voice, and said, Blessed *art* thou among women, and blessed *is* the fruit of thy womb.

Spake *krauge* (2906), an onomatopoeic word, is used in Matt. 25:6; **Luke 1:42** (some mss. have *phone*); Acts 23:9, RV, "clamor"; Eph. 4:31, "clamor"; Heb. 5:7; Rev. 21:4, "crying." Some mss. have it in Rev. 14:18 (the most authentic have *phone*).

Voice In **Luke 1:42** (1st part), KJV, *anaphoneo*, "to lift up one's voice," is rendered "spake out," RV, "lifted up (her) voice." From *phone* (5456), "a sound," which is used of the voice (a) of God, Matt. 3:17; John 5:37; 12:28, 30; Acts 7:31; 10:13, 15; 11:7, 9; Heb. 3:7, 15; 4:7; 12:19, 26; 2 Pet. 1:17, 18; Rev. 18:4; 21:3; (b) of Christ, (1) in the days of His flesh, Matt. 12:19 (negatively); John 3:29; 5:25; 10:3, 4, 16, 27; 11:43; 18:37; (2) on the cross, Matt. 27:46, and parallel passages; (3) from heaven, Acts 9:4, 7; 22:7, 9, 14; 26:14; Rev. 1:10, 12 (here, by metonymy, of the speaker), 15; 3:20; (4) at the resurrection "to life," John 5:28; 1 Thess. 4:16, where "the voice of the archangel" is, lit., "a voice of an archangel," and probably refers to the Lord's voice as being of an archangelic character; (5) at the resurrection to judgment, John 5:28 [not the same event as (4)]; (c) of human beings on earth, e.g., Matt. 2:18; 3:3; **Luke 1:42**, in some texts, KJV, "voice", and frequently in the Synoptists; (d) of angels, Rev. 5:11, and frequently in Revelation; (e) of the redeemed in heaven, e.g., Rev. 6:10; 18:22; 19:1, 5; (f) of a pagan god, Acts 12:22; (g) of things, e.g., wind, John 3:8, RV, "voice" (KJV, "sound").

Fruit *karpos* (2590), "fruit," is used (I) of the fruit of trees, fields, the earth, that which is produced by the inherent energy of a living organism, e.g., Matt. 7:17; Jas. 5:7, 18; plural, e.g., in **Luke 12:17** and 2 Tim. 2:6; of the human body, **Luke 1:42**; Acts 2:30; (II) metaphorically, (a) of works or deeds, "fruit" being the visible expression of power working inwardly and invisibly, the character of the "fruit" being evidence of the character of the power producing it, Matt. 7:16. As the visible expressions of hidden lusts are the works of the flesh, so the invisible power of the Holy Spirit in those who are brought into living union with Christ (John 15:2-8, 16) produces "the fruit of the Spirit," Gal. 5:22, the singular form suggesting the unity of the character of the Lord as reproduced in them, namely, "love, joy, peace, longsuffering, kindness, goodness, faithfulness, meekness, temperance," all in contrast with the confused and often mutually antagonistic "works of the flesh."

Womb *see* ***Luke 1:15.***

1:43-44 And whence *is* this to me, that the mother of my Lord should come to me?

For, lo, as soon as the voice of thy salutation sounded in mine ears, the babe leaped in my womb for joy.

Salutation *see* ***Luke 1:29.***

Sounded In **Luke 1:44**, KJV, *ginomai*, "to become," is rendered "sounded" (RV, "came").

Ears *ous* (3775), Latin *auris*, is used (a) of the physical organ, e.g., **Luke 4:21**; Acts 7:57; in Acts 11:22, in the plural with *akouo*, "to hear," lit., "was heard into the ears of someone," i.e., came to the knowledge of, similarly, in the singular, Matt. 10:27, in familiar private conversation; in Jas. 5:4 the phrase is used with *eiserchomai*, "to enter into"; in **Luke 1:44**, with *ginomai*, "to become, to come"; in **Luke 12:3**, with *lalein*, "to speak" and *pros*, "to", (b) metaphorically, of the faculty of perceiving with the mind, understanding and knowing, Matt. 13:16; frequently with *akouo*, "to hear," e.g., Matt. 11:15; 13:9, 43; Rev. 2 and 3, at the close of each of the messages to the churches, in Matt. 13:15 and Acts 28:27, with *bareos*, "heavily," of being slow to understand and obey; with a negative in Mark 8:18; Rom. 11:8; in **Luke 9:44** the lit. meaning is "put those words into your ears," i.e., take them into your mind and keep them there, in Acts 7:51 it is used with *aperitmetos*, "uncircumcised." As seeing is metaphorically associated with conviction, so hearing is with obedience (*hupakoe*, lit., "hearing under"; the Eng., "obedience" is etymologically "hearing over against," i.e., with response in the hearer).

Babe *see* ***Luke 1:41.***

Leaped *see* ***Luke 1:41.***

Womb *see* ***Luke 1:15.***

Joy *see* Gladness at *Luke 1:14.*

1:45 And blessed *is* she that believed: for there shall be a performance of those things which were told her from the Lord.

Performance *teleiosis* (5050), denotes "a fulfillment, completion, perfection, an end accomplished as the effect of a process," Heb. 7:11; in **Luke 1:45**, RV, "fulfillment" (KJV, "performance").

Told *laleo* (2980), is usually rendered "to speak," in the RV (for KJV, "to tell"), e.g., Matt. 26:13; **Luke 1:45**; **2:17, 18, 20**; Acts 11:14; 27:25; but RV and KJV, "to tell" in John 8:40; Acts 9:6; 22:10.

1:46 And Mary said, My soul doth magnify the Lord,

Soul *psuche* (5590), denotes "the breath, the breath of life," then "the soul," in its various meanings. The NT uses "may be analyzed approximately as follows:

(a) the natural life of the body, Matt. 2:20; **Luke 12:22**; Acts 20:10; Rev. 8:9; 12:11; cf. Lev. 17:11; 2 Sam. 14:7; Esth. 8:11; (b) the immaterial, invisible part of man, Matt. 10:28; Acts 2:27; cf. 1 Kings 17:21; (c) the disembodied (or "unclothed" or "naked," 2 Cor. 5:3, 4) man, Rev. 6:9; (d) the seat of personality, **Luke 9:24**, explained as = "own self," v. **25**; Heb. 6:19; 10:39; cf. Isa. 53:10 with 1 Tim. 2:6; (e) the seat of the sentient element in man, that by which he perceives, reflects, feels, desires, Matt. 11:29; **Luke 1:46**; **2:35**; Acts 14:2, 22; cf. Ps. 84:2; 139:14; Isa. 26:9; (f) the seat of will and purpose, Matt. 22:37; Acts 4:32; Eph. 6:6; Phil. 1:27; Heb. 12:3; cf. Num. 21:4; Deut. 11:13; (g) the seat of appetite, Rev. 18:14; cf. Ps. 107:9; Prov. 6:30; Isa. 5:14 ("desire"); 29:8; (h) persons, individuals, Acts 2:41, 43; Rom. 2:9; Jas. 5:20; 1 Pet. 3:20; 2 Pet. 2:14; cf. Gen. 12:5; 14:21 ("persons"); Lev. 4:2 ('any one');Ezek. 27:13; of dead bodies, Num. 6:6, lit., "dead soul"; and of animals, Lev. 24:18, lit., "soul for soul"; (i) the equivalent of the personal pronoun, used for emphasis and effect:—1st person, John 10:24 ("us"); Heb. 10:38; cf. Gen. 12:13; Num. 23:10; Jud. 16:30; Ps. 120:2 ("me"); 2nd person, 2 Cor. 12:15; Heb. 13:17; Jas. 1:21; 1 Pet. 1:9; 2:25; cf. Lev. 17:11; 26:15; 1 Sam. 1:26; 3rd person, 1 Pet. 4:19; 2 Pet. 2:8; cf. Exod. 30:12; Job 32:2, Heb. "soul," Sept. "self"; (j) an animate creature, human or other, 1 Cor. 15:45; Rev. 16:3; cf. Gen. 1:24; 2:7, 19; (k) "the inward man," the seat of the new life, **Luke 21:19** (cf. Matt. 10:39); 1 Pet. 2:11; 3 John 2.

"The language of Heb. 4:12 suggests the extreme difficulty of distinguishing between the soul and the spirit, alike in their nature and in their activities. Generally speaking the spirit is the higher, the soul the lower element. The spirit may be recognized as the life principle bestowed on man by God, the soul as the resulting life constituted in the individual, the body being the material organism animated by soul and spirit....

"Body and soul are the constituents of the man according to Matt. 6:25; 10:28; **Luke 12:20**; Acts 20:10; body and spirit according to **Luke 8:55**; 1 Cor. 5:3; 7:34; Jas. 2:26. In Matt. 26:38 the emotions are associated with the soul, in John 13:21 with the spirit; cf. also Ps. 42:11 with 1 Kings 21:5. In Ps. 35:9 the soul rejoices in God, in **Luke 1:47** the spirit."

Magnify *megaluno* (3170), "to make great" (*megas*), is translated "to magnify" in **Luke 1:46**; in v. **58**, RV, "had magnified (His mercy)," KJV, "had shewed great (mercy)"; Acts 5:13; 10:46; 19:17; 2 Cor. 10:15, RV (KJV, "we shall be enlarged"), i.e., by their faith in its practical effect he will be so assisted as to enlarge the scope of his gospel ministry and carry its message to regions beyond them; in Phil. 1:20, of the "magnifying" of Christ by him in his body, i.e., in all his activities and ways. In Matt. 23:5, it signifies "to enlarge."

1:47 And my spirit hath rejoiced in God my Saviour.

Spirit *see Luke 1:17. See also* **Soul** at *Luke 1:46*.

Rejoiced *agalliao* (21), "to rejoice greatly, to exult," is used, (I) in the active voice, of "rejoicing" in God, **Luke 1:47**; in faith in Christ, 1 Pet. 1:8, RV (middle voice in some mss.), "ye rejoice greatly"; in the event of the marriage of the Lamb, Rev. 19:7, "be exceeding glad," RV; (II) in the middle voice, (a) of "rejoicing" in persecutions, Matt. 5:12 (2nd part); in the light of testimony for God, John 5:35; in salvation received through the gospel, Acts 16:34, "he rejoiced greatly," RV; in salvation ready to be revealed, 1 Pet. 1:6; at the revelation of His glory, 1 Pet. 4:13, "with exceeding joy," lit., "ye may rejoice exulting"; (b) of Christ's "rejoicing" (greatly) "in the Holy Spirit," **Luke 10:21**, RV; said of His praise, as foretold in Ps. 16:9, quoted in Acts 2:26 (which follows the Sept., "My tongue"); (c) of Abraham's "rejoicing," by faith, to see Christ's day, John 8:56.

Saviour *soter* (4990), "a savior, deliverer, preserver," is used (a) of God, **Luke 1:47**; 1 Tim. 1:1; 2:3; 4:10 (in the sense of "preserver," since He gives "to all life and breath and all things"); Titus 1:3; 2:10; 3:4; Jude 25; (b) of Christ, **Luke 2:11**; John 4:42; Acts 5:31; 13:23 (of Israel); Eph. 5:23 (the sustainer and preserver of the church, His "body"); Phil. 3:20 (at His return to receive the Church to Himself); 2 Tim. 1:10 (with reference to His incarnation, "the days of His flesh"); Titus 1:4 (a title shared, in the context, with God the Father); 2:13, RV, "our great God and Savior Jesus Christ," the pronoun "our," at the beginning of the whole clause, includes all the titles; Titus 3:6; 2 Pet. 1:1, "our God and Savior Jesus Christ"; RV, where the pronoun "our," coming immediately in connection with "God," involves the inclusion of both titles as referring to Christ, just as in the parallel in v. 11, "our Lord and Savior Jesus Christ" (KJV and RV); these passages are therefore a testimony to His deity; 2 Pet. 2:20; 3:2, 18; 1 John 4:14.

1:48 For he hath regarded the low estate of his handmaiden: for, behold, from henceforth all generations shall call me blessed.

Regarded *epiblepo* (1914), "to look upon" (*epi*, "upon"), is used in the NT of favorable regard, **Luke 1:48**, RV, "he hath looked upon" (KJV, "hath regarded"), of the low estate of the Virgin Mary; in **9:38**, in a request to the Lord to "look" upon an afflicted son; in Jas. 2:3, RV, "ye have regard" (KJV, "... respect"), of having a partial regard for the well-to-do.

Low *tapeinosis* (5014), "abasement, humiliation, low estate," is translated "low estate" in **Luke 1:48**; in Jas. 1:10, "that he is made low," lit., "in his abasement."

Estate *tapeinosis* (5014), denotes "abasement, humiliation, low estate" (from *tapeinos*, "lowly"), **Luke 1:48**, "low estate"; Acts 8:33, "humiliation"; Phil. 3:21, RV, "of humiliation," for KJV, "vile"; Jas. 1:10, "is made low," lit., "in his low estate.

Handmaiden *see* **Handmaid** at *Luke 1:38.*

Henceforth Positively, "henceforth" stands for the following: (a) *ap' arti* (i.e., *apo arti*), lit., "from now," e.g., Matt. 26:64; **Luke 22:69**; John 13:19, RV, and KJV marg., "from henceforth"; Rev. 14:13 (where *aparti* is found as one word in the best mss.); (b) *to loipon*, lit., "(for) the remaining (time)," Heb. 10:13; *tou loipou*, Gal. 6:17; (c) *apo tou nun*, lit., "from the now," e.g., **Luke 1:48**; **5:10**; **12:52**; Acts 18:6; 2 Cor. 5:16 (1st part).

Generations *genea* (1074), connected with *ginomai*, "to become," primarily signifies "a begetting, or birth"; hence, that which has been begotten, a family; or successive members of a genealogy, Matt. 1:17, or of a race of people, possessed of similar characteristics, pursuits, etc., (of a bad character) Matt. 17:17; Mark 9:19; **Luke 9:41**; **16:8**; Acts 2:40; or of the whole multitude of men living at the same time, Matt. 24:34; Mark 13:30; **Luke 1:48**; **21:32**; Phil. 2:15, and especially of those of the Jewish race living at the same period, Matt. 11:16, etc. Transferred from people to the time in which they lived, the word came to mean "an age," i.e., a period ordinarily occupied by each successive generation, say, of thirty or forty years, Acts 14:16; 15:21; Eph. 3:5; Col. 1:26; see also, e.g., Gen. 15:16. In Eph. 3:21 *genea* is combined with *aion* in a remarkable phrase in a doxology: "Unto Him be the glory in the church and in Christ Jesus, unto all generations for ever and ever (wrongly in KJV 'all ages, world without end')." The word *genea* is to be distinguished from *aion*, as not denoting a period of unlimited duration.

Blessed *makarizo* (3106), from a root *mak–*, meaning "large, lengthy," found also in *makros*, "long," *mekos*, "length," hence denotes "to pronounce happy, blessed," **Luke 1:48** and Jas. 5:11.

1:49 For he that is mighty hath done to me great things; and holy *is* his name.

Mighty *dunatos* (1415), "powerful, mighty," is used, with that significance, (1) of God, **Luke 1:49**, "mighty"; Rom. 9:22, "power" (here the neuter of the adjective is used with the article, as a noun, equivalent to *dunamis*); frequently with the meaning "able"; (2) of Christ, regarded as a prophet, **Luke 24:19** ("in deed and word"); (3) of men: Moses, Acts 7:22 ("in his words and works"); Apollos, 18:24, "in the Scriptures"; of those possessed of natural power, 1 Cor. 1:26; of those possessed of spiritual power, 2 Cor. 10:4. For the shades of meaning in the translation "strong," see Rom. 15:1; 2 Cor. 12:10; 13:9.

Great In **Luke 1:49** some texts have *megaleia*, "great things"; the best have *megas* (3173).

Holy *see Luke 1:35.*

Name *onoma* (3686), is used (I) in general of the "name" by which a person or thing is called, e.g., Mark 3:16, 17, "(He) surnamed," lit., "(He added) the name"; 14:32, lit., "(of which) the name (was)"; **Luke 1:63**; John 18:10, sometimes translated "named," e.g., **Luke 8:5**, "named (Zacharias)," lit., "by name"; in the same verse, "named (Elizabeth)," lit., "the name of her," an elliptical phrase, with "was" understood; Acts 8:9, RV, "by name," 10:1; the "name" is put for the reality in Rev. 3:1; in Phil. 2:9, the "Name" represents "the title and dignity" of the Lord, as in Eph. 1:21 and Heb. 1:4;

(II) for all that a "name" implies, of authority, character, rank, majesty, power, excellence, etc., of everything that the "name" covers: (a) of the "Name" of God as expressing His attributes, etc., e.g., Matt. 6:9; **Luke 1:49**; John 12:28; 17:6, 26; Rom. 15:9; 1 Tim. 6:1; Heb. 13:15; Rev. 13:6; (b) of the "Name" of Christ, e.g., Matt. 10:22; 19:29; John 1:12; 2:23; 3:18; Acts 26:9; Rom. 1:5; Jas. 2:7; 1 John 3:23; 3 John 7; Rev. 2:13; 3:8; also the phrases rendered "in the name"; these may be analyzed as follows: (1) representing the authority of Christ, e.g., Matt. 18:5 (with *epi*, "on the ground of My authority"); so Matt. 24:5 (falsely) and parallel passages; as substantiated by the Father, John 14:26; 16:23 (last clause), RV; (2) in the power of (with *en*, "in"), e.g., Mark 16:17; **Luke 10:17**; Acts 3:6; 4:10; 16:18; Jas. 5:14; (3) in acknowledgement or confession of, e.g., Acts 4:12; 8:16; 9:27, 28; (4) in recognition of the authority of (sometimes combined with the thought of relying or resting on), Matt. 18:20; cf. 28:19; Acts 8:16; 9:2 (*eis*, "into"); John 14:13; 15:16; Eph. 5:20; Col. 3:17; (5) owing to the fact that one is called by Christ's "Name" or is identified with Him, e.g. 1 Pet. 4:14 (with *en*, "in"); with *heneken*, "for the sake of," e.g., Matt. 19:29; with *dia*, "on account of," Matt. 10:22; 24:9; Mark 13:13; **Luke 21:17**; John 15:21; 1 John 2:12; Rev. 2:3.

1:50 And his mercy *is* on them that fear him from generation to generation.

Mercy *eleos* (1656), "is the outward manifestation of pity; it assumes need on the part of him who receives it, and resources adequate to meet the need on the part of him who shows it. It is used (a) of God, who is rich in mercy, Eph. 2:4, and who has provided salvation for all men, Titus 3:5, for Jews, **Luke 1:72**, and Gentiles, Rom. 15:9. He is merciful to those who fear him, **Luke 1:50**, for they also are compassed with infirmity, and He alone can succor them. Hence they are to pray boldly for mercy, Heb. 4:16, and if for themselves, it is seemly that they should ask for mercy for one another, Gal. 6:16; 1 Tim. 1:2. When God brings His salvation to its issue at the Coming of Christ, His people will obtain His mercy, 2 Tim. 1:16; Jude 21; (b) of men; for since God is merciful to them, He would have them show mercy to one another, Matt. 9:13; 12:7; 23:23; **Luke 10:37**; Jas. 2:13.

1:51 He hath shewed strength with his arm; he hath scattered the proud in the imagination of their hearts.

Shewed *poieo* (4160), "to make, to do," is translated, "He hath showed" in **Luke 1:51**; "to show (mercy)," v. **72**, RV (KJV, "perform"); "showed (mercy)," **10:37**; John 6:30, KJV, "showest Thou," RV, "doest Thou (for a sign)"; Acts 7:36, KJV, "showed," RV, "wrought"; Jas. 2:13, "showed (no mercy)"; in Mark 13:22 in the best texts (some have *didomi*), "shall show (signs)."

Strength *krotos* (2904), "force, might," is rendered "strength" in **Luke 1:51**, RV and KJV; RV, "strength" (KJV, "power") in Eph. 1:19 and 6:10.

Arm *brachion* (1023), "the shorter part of the arm, from the shoulder to the elbow," is used metaphorically to denote strength, power, and always in the NT of the power of God, **Luke 1:51**; John 12:38; Acts 13:17; frequently so in the OT, especially in Deuteronomy, the Psalms and Isaiah; see, e.g., Deut. 4:34; 5:15; Ps. 44:3; 71:18, where "strength" is, lit., "arm"; 77:15; Isa. 26:11, where "hand" is, lit., "arm"; 30:30; 40:10-11, etc.

Scattered *diaskorpizo* (1287), signifies "to scatter abroad," in Matt. 26:31; Mark 14:27, metaphorically of sheep; in **Luke 1:51**, of the proud; in John 11:52, of the "scattering" of the children of God; in Acts 5:37, of the followers of Judas of Galilee (KJV, "were dispersed"); cf. of "scattering" grain by winnowing, Matt. 25:24, 26; in **Luke 15:13** and **16:1**, it signifies "to waste."

Proud *huperephanos* (5244), signifies "showing oneself above others, preeminent" (*huper*, "above," *phainomai*, "to appear, be manifest"); it is always used in Scripture in the bad sense of "arrogant, disdainful, proud," **Luke 1:51**; Rom: 1:30; 2 Tim. 3:2; Jas. 4:6; 1 Pet. 5:5.

Imagination *dianoia* (1271), lit. "a thinking through, or over, a meditation, reflecting," signifies (a) "the faculty of knowing, understanding, or moral reflection," (1) with an evil significance, a consciousness characterized by a perverted moral impulse, Eph. 2:3 (plural); 4:18; (2) with a good significance, the faculty renewed by the Holy Spirit, Matt. 22:37; Mark 12:30; **Luke 10:27**; Heb. 8:10; 10:16; 1 Pet. 1:13; 1 John 5:20; (b) "sentiment, disposition" (not as a function but as a product); (1) in an evil sense, **Luke 1:51**, "imagination"; Col. 1:21; (2) in a good sense, 2 Pet. 3:1.

Hearts *kardia* (2588), "the heart" (Eng., "cardiac," etc.), the chief organ of physical life ("for the life of the flesh is in the blood," Lev. 17:11), occupies the most important place in the human system. By an easy transition the word came to stand for man's entire mental and moral activity, both the rational and the emotional elements. In other words, the heart is used figuratively for the hidden springs of the personal life. "The Bible describes human depravity as in the 'heart,' because sin is a principle which has its seat in the center of man's inward life, and then 'defiles' the whole circuit of his action, Matt. 15:19, 20. On the other hand, Scripture regards the heart as the sphere of Divine influence, Rom. 2:15; Acts 15:9... The heart, as lying deep within, contains 'the hidden man,' 1 Pet. 3:4, the real man. It represents the true character but conceals it" (J. Laidlaw, in *Hastings' Bible Dic.*).

As to its usage in the NT it denotes (a) the seat of physical life, Acts 14:17; Jas. 5:5; (b) the seat of moral nature and spiritual life, the seat of grief, John 14:1; Rom. 9:2; 2 Cor. 2:4; joy, John 16:22; Eph. 5:19; the desires, Matt. 5:28; 2 Pet. 2:14;

the affections, **Luke 24:32**; Acts 21:13; the perceptions, John 12:40; Eph. 4:18; the thoughts, Matt. 9:4; Heb. 4:12; the understanding, Matt. 13:15; Rom. 1:21; the reasoning powers, Mark 2:6; **Luke 24:38**; the imagination, **Luke 1:51**; conscience, Acts 2:37; 1 John 3:20; the intentions, Heb. 4:12, cf. 1 Pet. 4:1; purpose, Acts 11:23; 2 Cor. 9:7; the will, Rom. 6:17; Col. 3:15; faith, Mark 11:23; Rom. 10:10; Heb. 3:12. The heart, in its moral significance in the OT, includes the emotions, the reason and the will.

1:52 He hath put down the mighty from *their* seats, and exalted them of low degree.

Put *kathaireo* (2507), "to take down, put down," is rendered "He hath put down" in **Luke 1:52**.

Mighty *dunastes* (1413), akin to *dunamis*, "power," (Eng., "dynasty,") signifies "a potentate, a high officer"; in Acts 8:27, of a high officer, it is rendered "of great authority"; in **Luke 1:52**, RV, "princes," (KJV, "the mighty"); in 1 Tim. 6:15 it is said of God ("Potentate").

Exalted *hupsoo* (5312), "to lift up" (akin to *hupsos*, "height"), is used (a) literally of the "lifting" up of Christ in His crucifixion, John 3:14; 8:28; 12:32, 34; illustratively, of the serpent of brass, John 3:14; (b) figuratively, of spiritual privileges bestowed on a city, Matt. 11:23; **Luke 10:15**; of "raising" to dignity and happiness, **Luke 1:52**; Acts 13:17; of haughty self-exaltation, and, contrastingly, of being "raised" to honor, as a result of self-humbling, Matt. 23:12; **Luke 14:11**; **18:14**; of spiritual "uplifting" and revival, Jas. 4:10; 1 Pet. 5:6; of bringing into the blessings of salvation through the gospel, 2 Cor. 11:7; (c) with a combination of the literal and metaphorical, of the "exaltation" of Christ by God the Father, Acts 2:33; 5:31.

Low degree *tapeinos* (5011), primarily "that which is low, and does not rise far from the ground," as in the Sept. of Ezek. 17:24, hence, metaphorically, signifies "lowly, of no degree." So the RV in 2 Cor. 10:1. Cf. **Luke 1:52** and Jas. 1:9, "of low degree." Cf. *tapeinophrosune*, "lowliness of mind," and *tapeinoo*, "to humble."

1:53 He hath filled the hungry with good things; and the rich he hath sent empty away.

Filled *empiplemi* (1705), or *empletho*, "to fill full, to satisfy," is used (a) of "filling" the hungry, **Luke 1:53**; John 6:12; of the abundance of the rich, **Luke 6:25**; (b) metaphorically, of a company of friends, Rom. 15:24, RV, "satisfied," for KJV, "filled."

Good *agathos* (18), describes that which, being "good" in its character or constitution, is beneficial in its effect; it is used (a) of things physical, e.g., a tree, Matt. 7:17; ground, **Luke 8:8**; (b) in a moral sense, frequently of persons and things. God is essentially, absolutely and consummately "good," Matt. 19:17; Mark 10:18; **Luke 18:19**. To certain persons the word is applied in Matt. 20:15; 25:21, 23; **Luke 19:17**; **23:50**; John 7:12; Acts 11:24; Titus 2:5; in a general application, Matt. 5:45; 12:35; **Luke 6:45**; Rom. 5:7; 1 Pet. 2:18.

The neuter plural is also used of material "goods," riches, etc., **Luke 1:53**; **12:18, 19**; **16:25**; Gal. 6:6 (of temporal supplies); in Rom. 10:15; Heb. 9:11; 10:1, the "good" things are the benefits provided through the sacrifice of Christ, in regard both to those conferred through the gospel and to those of the coming messianic kingdom.

Rich *plouteo* (4147), "to be rich," in the aorist or point tense, "to become rich," is used (a) literally, **Luke 1:53**, "the rich," present participle, lit., "(ones or those) being rich"; 1 Tim. 6:9, 18; Rev. 18:3, 15, 19 (all three in the aorist tense); (b) metaphorically, of Christ, Rom. 10:12 (the passage stresses the fact that Christ is Lord; see v. 9, and the RV); of the "enrichment" of believers through His poverty, 2 Cor. 8:9 (the aorist tense expressing completeness, with permanent results); so in Rev. 3:18, where the spiritual "enrichment" is conditional upon righteousness of life and conduct; of a false sense of "enrichment," 1 Cor. 4:8 (aorist), RV, "ye are become rich" (KJV, "ye are rich"); Rev. 3:17 (perfect tense, RV, "I ... have gotten riches," KJV, "I am ... increased with goods"); of not being "rich" toward God, **Luke 12:21**.

Sent *exapostello* (1821), denotes (a) "to send forth": of the Son by God the Father, Gal. 4:4; of the Holy Spirit, 4:6; **Luke 24:49** in the best texts; an angel, Acts 12:11; the ancestors of Israel, Acts 7:12; Paul to the Gentiles, 22:21; of the word of salvation, 13:26; (b) "to send away," **Luke 1:53**; **20:10, 11**; Acts 9:30; 11:22; 17:14.

Empty *kenos* (2756), expresses the "hollowness" of anything, the "absence" of that which otherwise might be possessed. It is used (a) literally, Mark 12:3; **Luke 1:53**; **20:10-11**; (b) metaphorically, of imaginations, Acts 4:25; of words which convey erroneous teachings, Eph. 5:6; of deceit, Col. 2:8; of a person whose professed faith is not accompanied by works, Jas. 2:20; negatively, concerning the grace of God, 1 Cor. 15:10; of refusal to receive it, 2 Cor. 6:1; of faith, 1 Cor. 15:14; of preaching (id.); and other forms of Christian activity and labor, 1 Cor. 15:58; Gal. 2:2; Phil. 2:16; 1 Thess. 2:1; 3:5. The synonymous word *mataios*, "vain," signifies "void" of result, it marks the aimlessness of anything. The vain (*kenos*) man in Jas. 2:20 is one who is "empty" of divinely imparted wisdom; in 1:26 the vain (mataios) religion is one that produces nothing profitable. *Kenos* stresses the absence of quality, *mataios*, the absence of useful aim or effect. Cf. the corresponding adverb *kenos*, "in vain," in Jas. 4:5, the noun *kenodoxia*, "vainglory," Phil. 2:3, the adjective *kenodoxos*, "vainglorious," Gal. 5:26, and the noun *kenophonia*, "vain," or "empty," babblings, 1 Tim. 6:20; 2 Tim. 2:16.

1:54 He hath holpen his servant Israel, in remembrance of *his* mercy;

Holpen *antilambano* (482), lit., "to take instead of, or in turn," is used in the middle voice, and rendered "He hath holpen" in **Luke 1:54**; "to help," RV, "to support," KJV, in Acts 20:35; its other meaning, to partake of, is used of partaking of things, 1 Tim. 6:2, "that partake of," for KJV, "partakers of."

Servant *pais* (3816), also denotes "an attendant"; it is translated "servant" (a) of natural conditions, in Matt. 8:6, 8, 13; 14:2; **Luke 7:7** ("menservants" in **12:45**); **15:26**; (b) of spiritual relation to God, (1) of Israel, **Luke 1:54**; (2) of David, **Luke 1:69**; Acts 4:25; (3) of Christ, so declared by God the Father, Matt. 12:18; spoken of in prayer, Acts 4:27, 30, RV (KJV, "child"); the argument advanced by Dalman for the rendering "Child" in these passages, is not sufficiently valid as against the RV, "Servant" in Acts 4, and the KJV and RV in Matt. 12 (cf. e.g., the use of *pais* in the Sept. of Gen. 41:38; Jer. 36:24). The Matt. 12 passage by direct quotation, and the Acts 4 passages by implication, refer to the ideal "Servant of Jehovah" (Sept., *pais Kuriou*), of Isa. 42:1 and following passages, thus identifying the Servant with the Lord Jesus; for the same identification, cf. Acts 8:35.

Remembrance *mimnesko* (3403), from the older form *mnaomai*, in the active voice signifies "to remind"; in the middle voice, "to remind oneself of," hence, "to remember, to be mindful of"; the later form is found only in the present tense, in Heb. 2:6, "are mindful of," and 13:3, "remember"; the perfect tense in 1 Cor. 11:2 and in 2 Tim. 1:4 (RV, "remembering," KJV, "being mindful of"), is used with a present meaning. RV variations from the KJV are, in **Luke 1:54**, RV, "that He might remember" (KJV, "in remembrance of"); 2 Pet. 3:2, "remember" (KJV, "be mindful of"); Rev. 16:19 (passive voice), "was remembered" (KJV, "came in remembrance"). The passive voice is used also in Acts 10:31, KJV and RV, "are had in remembrance."

1:55-56 As he spake to our fathers, to Abraham, and to his seed for ever.

And Mary abode with her about three months, and returned to her own house.

Months *see **Luke 1:24**.*

Returned *hupostrepho* (5290), "to turn behind," or "back" (*hupo*, "under"), is translated "to return" (in some texts in Mark 14:40) in **Luke 1:56**; **2:20**, **43**; v. **45**, RV (KJV, "turned back again"), **4:1**, **14**; **7:10**; **8:37**; **10:17**; **11:24**, KJV (RV, "I will turn back"); **17:18**; **19:12**; **23:48**, **56**; Acts 1:12; 12:25; 13:13; 13:34; 20:3; 21:6; 22:17, RV (KJV, "was come again"); 23:32; Gal. 1:17; Heb. 7:1.

1:57 Now Elisabeth's full time came that she should be delivered; and she brought forth a son.

Brought forth *gennao* (1080), "to beget," translated "brought forth" in **Luke 1:57**. *See also* **Bear** at ***Luke 1:13***. Also, *tikto* (5088), "to bring forth," **Luke 1:57**; John 16:21; Heb. 11:11; Rev. 12:2, 4, or, "to be born," said of the Child, Matt. 2:2; **Luke 2:11**, is used metaphorically in Jas. 1:15, of lust as bringing forth sin.

1:58 And her neighbours and her cousins heard how the Lord had shewed great mercy upon her; and they rejoiced with her.

Neighbours *perioikos* (4040), an adjective, lit., "dwelling around" (*peri*, "around," *oikos*, "a dwelling"), is used as a noun in **Luke 1:58**, "neighbors".

Cousins *sungenes* (4773), primarily denoting "congenital, natural, innate" (*sun*, "with," *genos*, "a family, race, offspring"), then, "akin to," is used as a noun, denoting (a) of "family relationship, kin, a kinsman, kinsfolk(s)," **Luke 1:58**, RV, "kinsfolk" (KJV, "cousins"); **14:12**; **21:16**; John 18:26; Acts 10:24; (b) of "tribal or racial kinship, fellow nationals," Rom. 9:3; 16:7, 11, 21. *See also* **Cousin** at ***Luke 1:36***.

Shewed In **Luke 1:58**, KJV, *megaluno*, to magnify (RV), is rendered "shewed great."

Great In **Luke 1:58**, the verb *megaluno*, "to magnify, make great," is rendered "had magnified (His mercy)," RV [KJV, "had shewed great (mercy)"]. *See also* **Magnify** at ***Luke 1:46***.

Rejoiced *sunchairo* (4796), "to rejoice with," is used of "rejoicing" together in the recovery of what was lost, **Luke 15:6, 9**; in suffering in the cause of the gospel, Phil. 2:17 (2nd part), 18; in the joy of another, **Luke 1:58**; in the honor of fellow believers, 1 Cor. 12:26; in the triumph of the truth, 1 Cor. 13:6, RV, "rejoiceth with."

1:59 And it came to pass, that on the eighth day they came to circumcise the child; and they called him Zacharias, after the name of his father.

Eighth *ogdoos* (3590), "eighth" (connected with the preceding), is used in **Luke 1:59**; Acts 7:8; 2 Pet. 2:5; Rev. 17:11; 21:20.

Circumcise *peritemno* (4059), "to circumcise," is used (a) lit., e.g., **Luke 1:59**; **2:21**; of receiving circumcision, Gal. 5:2-3; 6:13, RV; (b) metaphorically, of spiritual circumcision, Col. 2:11.

1:60-61 And his mother answered and said, Not *so*; but he shall be called John.

And they said unto her, There is none of thy kindred that is called by this name.

Kindred *sungeneia* (4772), primarily denotes "kinship"; then, "kinsfolk, kindred" (cf. *sungenes*, "a kinsman"), **Luke 1:61**; Acts. 7:3, 14.

1:62 And they made signs to his father, how he would have him called.

Signs *enneuo* (1770), "to nod to" (*en*, "in," *neuo*, "to nod"), denotes "to make a sign to" in **Luke 1:62**. In the Sept., Prov. 6:13; 10:10.

1:63 And he asked for a writing table, and wrote, saying, His name is John. And they marvelled all.

Writing table *pinakidion* (4093), occurs in **Luke 1:63**, a diminutive of *pinakis*, "a tablet," which is a variant reading here.

Wrote *grapho* (1125), is used (a) of "forming letters" on a surface or writing material, John 8:6; Gal. 6:11, where the apostle speaks of his having "written" with large letters in his own hand, which not improbably means that at this point he took the pen from his amanuensis and finished the epistle himself; this is not negatived by the fact that the verb is in the aorist or past definite tense, lit., "I wrote," for in Greek idiom the writer of a letter put himself beside the reader and spoke of it as having been "written" in the past; in Eng. we should say "I am writing," taking our point of view from the time at which we are doing it; cf. Philem. 19 ... possibly the apostle, in Galatians, was referring to his having "written" the body of the epistle but the former alternative seems the more likely; in 2 Thess. 3:17 he says that the closing salutation is written by his own hand and speaks of it as "the token in every epistle" which some understand as a purpose for the future rather than a custom; see, however, 1 Cor. 16:21 and Col. 4:18. The absence of the token from the other epistles of Paul can be explained differently, their authenticity not being dependent upon this; (b) "to commit to writing, to record," e.g., **Luke 1:63**; John 19:21, 22; it is used of Scripture as a standing authority, "it is written," e.g., Mark 1:2; Rom. 1:17 (cf. 2 Cor. 4:13); (c) of "writing directions or giving information," e.g., Rom. 10:5, "(Moses) writeth," RV (KJV, "describeth"); 15:15; 2 Cor. 7:12; (d) of "that which contained a record or message," e.g., Mark 10:4, 5; John 19:19; 21:25; Acts 23:25.

Name *see* ***Luke 1:49***.

1:64 And his mouth was opened immediately, and his tongue *loosed*, and he spake, and praised God.

Mouth *stoma* (4750), akin to *stomachos* (which originally meant "a throat, gullet"), is used (a) of "the mouth" of man, e.g., Matt. 15:11; of animals, e.g., Matt. 17:27; 2 Tim. 4:17 (figurative); Heb. 11:33; Jas. 3:3; Rev. 13:2 (2nd occurrence); (b) figuratively of "inanimate things," of the "edge" of a sword, **Luke 21:24**; Heb. 11:34; of the earth, Rev. 12:16; (c) figuratively, of the "mouth," as the organ of speech, (1) of Christ's words, e.g., Matt. 13:35; **Luke 11:54**; Acts 8:32; 22:14; 1 Pet. 2:22; (2) of human, e.g., Matt. 18:16; 21:16; **Luke 1:64**; Rev. 14:5; as emanating from the heart, Matt. 12:34; Rom. 10:8, 9; of prophetic ministry through the Holy Spirit, **Luke 1:70**; Acts 1:16; 3:18; 4:25; of the destructive policy of two world potentates at the end of this age, Rev. 13:2, 5, 6; 16:13 (twice); of shameful speaking, Eph. 4:29 and Col. 3:8; (3) of the Devil speaking as a dragon or serpent, Rev. 12:15, 16; 16:13; (d) figuratively, in the phrase "face to face" (lit., "mouth to mouth"), 2 John 12; 3 John 14; (e) metaphorically, of "the utterances of the Lord, in judgment," 2 Thess. 2:8; Rev. 1:16; 2:16; 19:15, 21; of His judgment upon a local church for its lukewarmness, Rev. 3:16; (f) by metonymy, for "speech," Matt. 18:16; **Luke 19:22**; **21:15**; 2 Cor. 13:1.

Opened *anoigo* (455), is used (1) transitively, (a) literally, of "a door or gate," e.g., Acts 5:19; graves, Matt. 27:52; a sepulchre, Rom. 3:13; a book, e.g., **Luke 4:17**; Rev. 5:2-5; 10:8; the seals of a roll, e.g., Rev. 5:9; 6:1; the eyes, Acts 9:40; the mouth of a fish, Matt. 17:27; "the pit of the abyss," Rev. 9:2, RV; heaven and the heavens, Matt. 3:16; **Luke 3:21**; Acts 10:11; Rev. 19:11; "the temple of the tabernacle of the testimony in heaven," Rev. 15:5; by metonymy, for that which contained treasures, Matt. 2:11; (b) metaphorically, e.g., Matt. 7:7-8; 25:11; Rev. 3:7; Hebraistically, "to open the mouth," of beginning to speak, e.g., Matt. 5:2; 13:35; Acts 8:32, 35; 10:34; 18:14; Rev. 13:6 (cf., e.g., Num. 22:28; Job. 3:1; Isa. 50:5); and of recovering speech, **Luke 1:64**; of the earth "opening," Rev. 12:16; of the "opening" of the eyes, Acts 26:18; the ears, Mark 7:35 (in the best mss.); (2) intransitively (perfect tense, active, in the Greek), (a) literally, of "the heaven," John 1:51, RV, "opened;" (b) metaphorically, of "speaking freely," 2 Cor. 6:11.

Immediately *parachrema* (3916), lit., "with the matter (or business) itself" (*para*, "with," *chrema*, "a business," or "event"), and so, "immediately," Matt. 21:19 (KJV, "presently"), 20; **Luke 1:64; 4:39; 5:25; 8:44, 47, 55; 13:13; 18:43; 19:11; 22:60**; Acts 3:7; 5:10; 12:23; 13:11; 16:26, 33; it is thus used by Luke only, save for the two instances in Matthew. It is also rendered "presently," "soon," "straightway."

Praised *eulogeo* (2127), lit., "to speak well of" (*eu*, "well," *logos*, "a word"), signifies, (a) "to praise, to celebrate with praises," of that which is addressed to God, acknowledging His goodness, with desire for His glory, **Luke 1:64; 2:28; 24:51, 53**; Jas. 3:9; (b) "to invoke blessings upon a person," e.g., **Luke 6:28**; Rom. 12:14. The present participle passive, "blessed, praised," is especially used of Christ in Matt. 21:9; 23:39, and the parallel passages; also in John 12:13; (c) "to consecrate a thing with solemn prayers, to ask God's blessing on a thing," e.g., **Luke 9:16**; 1 Cor. 10:16; (d) "to cause to prosper, to make happy, to bestow blessings on," said of God, e.g., in Acts 3:26; Gal. 3:9; Eph. 1:3. Cf. the synonym *aineo*, "to praise."

1:65 And fear came on all that dwelt round about them: and all these sayings were noised abroad throughout all the hill country of Judaea.

Dwelt *see* Neighbours at *Luke 1:58.*

Sayings *rhema* (4487), "that which is said, a word," is rendered "saying" or "sayings" in Mark 9:32; **Luke 1:65; 2:17, 50, 51; 7:1; 9:45** (twice); **18:34.**

Noised *dialaleo* (1255), signifies "to speak with anyone" (*dia*, "by turns," *laleo*, "to speak"), **Luke 6:11**; in **1:65**, "to talk over, to noise abroad." The idea that *laleo* and its compounds bear no reference to the word spoken or the sentiment, is unfounded.

Hill *see Luke 1:39.*

Country *see Luke 1:39.*

1:66 And all they that heard *them* laid *them* up in their hearts, saying, What manner of child shall this be! And the hand of the Lord was with him.

Laid *tithemi* (5087), "to put, place, set," frequently signifies "to lay," and is used of (a) "laying" a corpse in a tomb, Matt. 27:60; Mark 6:29; 15:47; 16:6; **Luke 23:53, 55**; John 11:34; 19:41, 42; 20:2, 13, 15; Acts 7:16; 13:29; Rev. 11:9, RV, "to be laid" (KJV, "to be put"); in an upper chamber, Acts 9:37; (b) "laying" the sick in a place, Mark 6:56; **Luke 5:18**; Acts 3:2; 5:15; (c) "laying" money at the apostles' feet, Acts 4:35, 37; 5:2; (d) Christ's "laying" His hands upon children, Mark 10:16, RV, "laying" (KJV, "put"); upon John, Rev. 1:17 (in the best mss.); (e) "laying" down one's life, (1) of Christ, John 10:11, RV, "layeth down" (KJV, "giveth"); vv. 17, 18 (twice); 1 John 3:16; (2) of Peter for Christ's sake, John 13:37, 38; (3) of Christ's followers, on behalf of others, 1 John 3:16; (4) of anyone, for his friends, John 15:13; (f) "laying" up sayings in one's heart, **Luke 1:66** (middle voice, in the sense of "for themselves"); in **9:44**, of letting Christ's words "sink" (middle voice, in the sense of "for oneself"; KJV, "sink down") into the ears; (g) "laying" a foundation (1) literally, **Luke 6:48; 14:29**; (2) metaphorically, of Christ in relation to an assembly, 1 Cor. 3:10, 11; (h) in "laying" Christ as a "stone of stumbling" for Israel, Rom. 9:33; (i) Christ's "laying" aside His garments, John 13:4; (j) Christians, in "laying" money in store for the help of the needy, 1 Cor. 16:2 (lit., "let him put"); (k) "depositing" money, **Luke 19:21, 22.**

Manner In **Luke 1:66**, KJV, *ara*, "then" (so RV), is rendered freely "(what) manner."

Hand *cheir* (5495), "the hand" (cf. Eng., "chiropody"), is used, besides its ordinary significance, (a) in the idiomatic phrases, "by the hand of," "at the hand of," etc., to signify "by the agency of," Acts 5:12; 7:35; 17:25; 14:3; Gal. 3:19 (cf. Lev. 26:46); Rev. 19:2; (b) metaphorically, for the power of God, e.g., **Luke 1:66; 23:46**; John 10:28, 29; Acts 11:21; 13:11; Heb. 1:10; 2:7; 10:31; (c) by metonymy, for power, e.g., Matt. 17:22; **Luke 24:7**; John 10:39; Acts 12:11.

1:67 And his father Zacharias was filled with the Holy Ghost, and prophesied, saying,

Filled *see Luke 1:15.*

1:68 Blessed *be* the Lord God of Israel; for he hath visited and redeemed his people,

Blessed *eulogetos* (2128), means "blessed, praised"; it is applied only to God, Mark 14:61; **Luke 1:68**; Rom. 1:25; 9:5; 2 Cor. 1:3; 11:31; Eph. 1:3; 1 Pet. 1:3. In the Sept. it is also applied to man, e.g., in Gen. 24:31; 26:29; Deut. 7:14; Judg. 17:2; Ruth 2:20; 1 Sam. 15:13.

Visited *episkeptomai* (1980), primarily, "to inspect" (a late form of *episkopeo*, "to look upon, care for, exercise oversight"), signifies (a) "to visit" with help, of the act of God, **Luke 1:68**, **78**; **7:16**; Acts 15:14; Heb. 2:6; (b) "to visit" the sick and afflicted, Matt. 25:36, 43; Jas. 1:27; (c) "to go and see," "pay a visit to," Acts 7:23; 15:36; (d) "to look out" certain men for a purpose, Acts 6:3

Redeemed *lutrosis* (30), "a redemption," is used (a) in the general sense of "deliverance," of the nation of Israel, **Luke 1:68** RV, "wrought redemption"; **2:38**; (b) of "the redemptive work" of Christ, Heb. 9:12, bringing deliverance through His death, from the guilt and power of sin. In the Sept., Lev. 25:29, 48; Num. 18:16; Judg. 1:15; Ps. 49:8; 111:9; 130:7; Isa. 63:4.

1:69 And hath raised up an horn of salvation for us in the house of his servant David;

Raised *egeiro* (1453), is used (a) of "raising" the dead, active and passive voices, e.g. of the resurrection of Christ, Matt. 16:21; 17:23; 20:19, RV; 26:32, RV, "(after) I am raised up" (KJV, "... risen again"); **Luke 9:22**; **20:37**; John 2:19; Acts 3:15; 4:10 [not 5:30, see (c) below]; 10:40 [not 13:23 in the best texts, see (c) below]; 13:30, 37; Rom. 4:24, 25; 6:4, 9; 7:4; 8:11 (twice); 8:34, RV; 10:9; 1 Cor. 6:14 (1st part); 15:13, 14, RV; 15:15 (twice), 16, 17; 15:20, RV; 2 Cor. 4:14; Gal. 1:1; Eph. 1:20; Col. 2:12; 1 Thess. 1:10; 1 Pet. 1:21; in 2 Tim. 2:8, RV, "risen"; (b) of the resurrection of human beings, Matt. 10:8; 11:5; Matt. 27:52, RV (KJV, "arose"); Mark 12:26, RV; **Luke 7:22**; John 5:21; 12:1, 9, 17; Acts 26:8; 1 Cor. 15:29 and 32, RV; 15:35, 42, 43 (twice), 44, 52; 2 Cor. 1:9; 4:14; Heb. 11:19; (c) of "raising" up a person to occupy a place in the midst of a people, said of Christ, Acts 5:30; in 13:23, KJV only (the best texts have *ago*, to bring, RV, "hath ... brought"); of David, Acts 13:22; (d) metaphorically, of a horn of salvation, **Luke 1:69**; (e) of children, from stones, by creative power, **Luke 3:8**; (f) of the Temple, as the Jews thought, John 2:20, RV, "wilt Thou raise (it) up" (KJV, "rear"); (g) of "lifting" up a person, from physical infirmity, Mark 1:31, RV, "raised ... up" (KJV, "lifted"); so 9:27; Acts 3:7; 10:26, RV (KJV, "took"); Jas. 5:15, "shall raise ... up"; (h) metaphorically, of "raising" up affliction, Phil. 1:17, RV (in the best texts; the KJV, v. 16, following those which have *epiphero*, has "to add").

Horn *keras* (2768), "a horn," is used in the plural, as the symbol of strength, (a) in the apocalyptic visions; (1) on the head of the Lamb as symbolic of Christ, Rev. 5:6; (2) on the heads of beasts as symbolic of national potentates, Rev. 12:3; 13:1, 11; 17:3, 7, 12, 16 (cf. Dan. 7:8; 8:9; Zech. 1:18, etc.); (3) at the corners of the golden altar, Rev. 9:13 (cf. Exod. 30:2; the horns were of one piece with the altar, as in the case of the brazen altar, 27:2, and were emblematic of the efficacy of the ministry connected with it); (b) metaphorically, in the singular, "a horn of salvation," **Luke 1:69** (a frequent metaphor in the OT, e.g., Ps. 18:2; cf. 1 Sam. 2:10; Lam. 2:3).

Salvation *soteria* (4991), denotes "deliverance, preservation, salvation." "Salvation" is used in the NT (a) of material and temporal deliverance from danger and apprehension, (1) national, **Luke 1:69**, **71**; Acts 7:25, RV marg., "salvation" (text, "deliverance"); (2) personal, as from the sea, Acts 27:34; RV, "safety" (KJV, "health"); prison, Phil. 1:19; the flood, Heb. 11:7; (b) of the spiritual and eternal deliverance granted immediately by God to those who accept His conditions of repentance and faith in the Lord Jesus, in whom alone it is to be obtained, Acts 4:12, and upon confession of Him as Lord, Rom. 10:10; for this purpose the gospel is the saving instrument, Rom. 1:16; Eph. 1:13; (c) of the present experience of God's power to deliver from the bondage of sin, e.g., Phil. 2:12, where the special, though not the entire, reference is to the maintenance of peace and harmony; 1 Pet. 1:9; this present experience on the part of believers is virtually equivalent to sanctification; for this purpose, God is able to make them wise, 2 Tim. 3:15; they are not to neglect it, Heb. 2:3; (d) of the future deliverance of believers at the Parousia of Christ for His saints, a salvation which is the object of their confident hope, e.g., Rom. 13:11; 1 Thess. 5:8, and v. 9, where "salvation" is assured to them, as being deliverance from the wrath of God destined to be executed upon the ungodly at the end of this age (see 1 Thess. 1:10); 2 Thess. 2:13; Heb. 1:14; 9:28; 1 Pet. 1:5; 2 Pet. 3:15; (e) of the deliverance of the nation of Israel at the second advent of Christ at the time of "the epiphany (or shining forth) of His Parousia" (2 Thess. 2:8); **Luke 1:71**; Rev. 12:10; (f) inclusively, to sum up all the blessings bestowed by God on men in Christ through the Holy Spirit, e.g., 2 Cor. 6:2; Heb. 5:9; 1 Pet. 1:9, 10; Jude 3; (g) occasionally, as standing virtually for the Savior, e.g., **Luke 19:9**; cf. John 4:22; (h) in ascriptions of praise to God, Rev. 7:10, and as that which it is His prerogative to bestow, 19:1 (RV).

Servant *see Luke 1:54.*

1:70 As he spake by the mouth of his holy prophets, which have been since the world began:

Mouth *see Luke 1:64.*

Began In the following passages the KJV faulty translations, "since the world began," etc., are rightly rendered in the RV by "before times eternal" and similar phrases, Rom. 16:25; Eph. 3:9; 2 Tim. 1:9; Titus 1:2. The alteration has not been made, however, in **Luke 1:70**; John 9:32; Acts 3:21; 15:18.

1:71 That we should be saved from our enemies, and from the hand of all that hate us;

Saved *see* Salvation at *Luke 1:69.*

Enemies *echthros* (2190), an adjective, primarily denoting "hated" or "hateful" (akin to *echthos*, "hate"; perhaps associated with *ekos*, "outside"), hence, in the active sense, denotes "hating, hostile"; it is used as a noun signifying an "enemy," adversary, and is said (a) of the Devil, Matt. 13:39; **Luke 10:19**; (b) of death, 1 Cor. 15:26; (c) of the professing believer who would be a friend of the world, thus making himself an enemy of God, Jas. 4:4; (d) of men who are opposed to Christ, Matt. 13:25, 28; 22:44; Mark 12:36; **Luke 19:27**; **20:43**; Acts 2:35; Rom. 11:28; Phil. 3:18; Heb. 1:13; 10:13; or to His servants, Rev. 11:5, 12; to the nation of Israel, **Luke 1:71**, **74**; **19:43**; (e) of one who is opposed to righteousness, Acts 13:10; (f) of Israel in its alienation from God, Rom. 11:28; (g) of the unregenerate in their attitude toward God, Rom. 5:10; Col. 1:21; (h) of believers in their former state, 2 Thess. 3:15; (i) of foes, Matt. 5:43-44; 10:36; **Luke 6:27**, **35**; Rom. 12:20; 1 Cor. 15:25; of the apostle Paul because he told converts "the truth," Gal. 4:16. Cf. *echthra*, "enmity".

1:72 To perform the mercy *promised* to our fathers, and to remember his holy covenant;

Perform *poieo* (4160), "to do," is translated "to perform" in Rom. 4:21; in **Luke 1:72**, KJV (RV, "to show"). *See also* **Shewed** at *Luke 1:51.*

Mercy *see Luke 1:50.*

Covenant *diatheke* (1242), primarily signifies "a disposition of property by will or otherwise." In its use in the Sept., it is the rendering of a Hebrew word meaning a "covenant" or agreement (from a verb signifying "to cut or divide," in allusion to a sacrificial custom in connection with "covenant-making," e.g., Gen. 15:10, "divided," Jer. 34:18-19). In contradistinction to the English word "covenant" (lit., "a coming together"), which signifies a mutual undertaking between two parties or more, each binding himself to fulfill obligations, it does not in itself contain the idea of joint obligation, it mostly signifies an obligation undertaken by a single person ... "The NT uses of the word may be analyzed as follows: (a) a promise or undertaking, human or divine, Gal. 3:15; (b) a promise or undertaking on the part of God, **Luke 1:72**; Acts 3:25; Rom. 9:4; 11:27; Gal. 3:17; Eph. 2:12; Heb. 7:22; 8:6, 8, 10; 10:16; (c) an agreement, a mutual undertaking, between God and Israel, see Deut. 29-30 (described as a 'commandment,' Heb. 7:18, cf. v. 22); Heb. 8:9; 9:20; (d) by metonymy, the token of the covenant, or promise, made to Abraham, Acts 7:8, (e) by metonymy, the record of the covenant, 2 Cor. 3:14; Heb. 9:4; cf. Rev. 11:19; (f) the basis, established by the death of Christ, on which the salvation of men is secured, Matt. 26:28; Mark 14:24; **Luke 22:20**; 1 Cor. 11:25; 2 Cor. 3:6; Heb. 10:29; 12:24; 13:20. This covenant is called the 'new,' Heb. 9:15, the 'second,' 8:7, the 'better,' 7:22."

1:73 The oath which he sware to our father Abraham,

Oath *horkos* (3727), is primarily equivalent to *herkos*, "a fence, an enclosure, that which restrains a person"; hence, "an oath." The Lord's command in Matt. 5:33 was a condemnation of the minute and arbitrary restrictions imposed by the scribes and Pharisees in the matter of adjurations, by which God's Name was profaned. The injunction is repeated in Jas. 5:12. The language of the apostle Paul, e.g., in Gal. 1:20 and 1 Thess. 5:27 was not inconsistent with Christ's prohibition, read in the light of its context. Contrast the "oaths" mentioned in Matt. 14:7, 9; 26:72; Mark 6:26. Heb. 6:16 refers to the confirmation of a compact among men, guaranteeing the discharge of liabilities; in their disputes "the oath is final for confirmation." This is referred to in order to illustrate the greater subject of God's "oath" to Abraham, confirming His promise; cf. **Luke 1:73**; Acts 2:30.

Sware *omnumi* or *omnuo* (3660), is used of "affirming or denying by an oath," e.g., Matt. 26:74; Mark 6:23; **Luke 1:73**; Heb. 3:11, 18; 4:3; 7:21; accompanied by that by which one swears, e.g., Matt. 5:34, 36; 23:16; Heb. 6:13, 16; Jas. 5:12; Rev. 10:6.

1:74 That he would grant unto us, that we being delivered out of the hand of our enemies might serve him without fear,

Grant *didomi* (1325), "to give," is rendered "grant" in Mark 10:37; **Luke 1:74**; Acts 4:29; 11:18; 14:3.

Delivered *rhuomai* (4506), "to rescue from, to preserve from," and so, "to deliver," the word by which it is regularly translated, is largely synonymous with *sozo*, "to save," though the idea of "rescue from" is predominant in *rhuomai* (see Matt. 27:43), that of "preservation from," in *sozo*. In Rom. 11:26 the present participle is used with the article, as a noun, "the Deliverer." This is the construction in 1 Thess. 1:10, where Christ is similarly spoken of. Here the KJV wrongly has "which delivered" (the tense is not past); RV, "which delivereth"; the translation might well be (as in Rom. 11:26), "our Deliverer," that is, from the retributive calamities with which God will visit men at the end of the present age. From that wrath believers are to be "delivered." The verb is used with *apo*, "away from," in Matt. 6:13; **Luke 11:4** (in some mss.); so also in **11:4**; Rom. 15:31; 2 Thess. 3:2; 2 Tim. 4:18; and with *ek*, "from, out of," in **Luke 1:74**; Rom. 7:24; 2 Cor. 1:10; Col. 1:13, from bondage; in 2 Pet. 2:9, from temptation, in 2 Tim. 3:11, from persecution; but *ek* is used of ills impending, in 2 Cor. 1:10; in 2 Tim. 4:17, *ek* indicates that the danger was more imminent than in v. 18, where *apo* is used. Accordingly the meaning "out of the midst of" cannot be pressed in 1 Thess. 1:10.

Enemies *see* ***Luke 1:71***.

Serve *latreuo* (3000), primarily "to work for hire" (akin to *latris*, "a hired servant"), signifies (1) to worship, (2) to "serve"; in the latter sense it is used of service (a) to God, Matt. 4:10; **Luke 1:74** ("without fear"); **4:8**; Acts 7:7; 24:14, RV, "serve" (KJV, "worship"); 26:7; 27:23; Rom. 1:9 ("with my spirit"); 2 Tim. 1:3; Heb. 9:14; 12:28, KJV, "we may serve," RV, "we may offer service"; Rev. 7:15; (b) to God and Christ ("the Lamb"), Rev. 22:3; (c) in the tabernacle, Heb. 8:5, RV; 13:10; (d) to "the host of heaven," Acts 7:42, RV, "to serve" (KJV, "to worship"); (e) to "the creature," instead of the Creator, Rom. 1:25, of idolatry.

Without fear *aphobos* (880), denotes "without fear," and is said of serving the Lord, **Luke 1:74**; of being among the Lord's people as His servant, 1 Cor. 16:10; of ministering the Word of God, Phil. 1:14; of the evil of false spiritual shepherds, Jude 12. In the Sept., Prov. 1:33.

1:75 In holiness and righteousness before him, all the days of our life.

Holiness *hosiotes* (3742), denoting that quality of "holiness" which is manifested in those who have regard equally to grace and truth; it involves a right relation to God; it is used in **Luke 1:75** and Eph. 4:24, and in each place is associated with righteousness.

Before *see* ***Luke 1:17***.

1:76 And thou, child, shalt be called the prophet of the Highest: for thou shalt go before the face of the Lord to prepare his ways;

Thou Frequently this forms part of the translation of a verb in the 2nd person, singular. Otherwise it translates (a) the pronoun *su*, used for emphasis or contrast, e.g., John 1:19, 21 (twice), 25, 42 (twice); 8:5, 13, 25, 33, 48, 52, 53; Acts 9:5; in addressing a person or place, e.g., Matt. 2:6; **Luke 1:76**; John 17:5; perhaps also in the phrase *su eipas*, "thou hast said," e.g., Matt. 26:64 (sometimes without emphasis, e.g., Acts 13:33); (b) in the oblique cases, e.g., the dative *soi*, lit., "to thee," e.g., Matt. 17:25, "what thinkest thou?" (lit., "what does it seem to thee?"); (c) *autos*, "self," e.g., **Luke 6:42**; Acts 21:24, "thou thyself"; (d) the reflexive pronoun, *seauton*, Rom. 2:19, "thou thyself."

Prophet *prophetes* (4396), "one who speaks forth or openly", "a proclaimer of a divine message," denoted among the Greeks an interpreter of the oracles of the gods. In the Sept. it is the translation of the word *roeh*, "a seer"; 1 Sam. 9:9, indicating that the "prophet" was one who had immediate intercourse with God. It also translates the word *nabhi*, meaning "either one in whom the message from God springs forth" or "one to whom anything is secretly communicated." Hence, in general, "the prophet" was one upon whom the Spirit of God rested, Num. 11:17-29, one, to whom and through whom God speaks, Num. 12:2; Amos 3:7, 8. In the case of the OT prophets their messages were very largely the proclamation of the divine purposes of salvation and glory to be accomplished in the future; the "prophesying" of the NT "prophets" was both a preaching of the divine counsels of grace already accomplished and the foretelling of the purposes of God in the future. In the NT the word is used (a) of "the OT prophets," e.g., Matt. 5:12; Mark 6:15; **Luke 4:27**; John 8:52; Rom. 11:3; (b) of "prophets in general," e.g., Matt. 10:41; 21:46; Mark 6:4; (c) of "John the Baptist," Matt. 21:26; **Luke 1:76**; (d) of "prophets in the churches," e.g., Acts 13:1; 15:32; 21:10; 1 Cor. 12:28, 29; 14:29, 32, 37; Eph. 2:20; 3:5; 4:11; (e) of "Christ, as the aforepromised Prophet," e.g., John 1:21; 6:14; 7:40; Acts 3:22; 7:37, or, without the article, and, without reference to the Old Testament, Mark 6:15; **Luke 7:16**;

in **Luke 24:19** it is used with *aner*, "a man"; John 4:19; 9:17; (f) of "two witnesses" yet to be raised up for special purposes, Rev. 11:10, 18; (g) of "the Cretan poet Epimenides," Titus 1:12; (h) by metonymy, of "the writings of prophets," e.g., **Luke 24:27**; Acts 8:28.

Highest *see* ***Luke 1:32***.

Go *proporeuomai* (4313), "to go before," is used in **Luke 1:76** and Acts 7:40.

Prepare *see* **Make ready** at ***Luke 1:17***.

1:77 To give knowledge of salvation unto his people by the remission of their sins,

Knowledge *gnosis* (1108), primarily "a seeking to know, an enquiry, investigation," denotes, in the NT, "knowledge," especially of spiritual truth; it is used (a) absolutely, in **Luke 11:52**; Rom. 2:20; 15:14; 1 Cor. 1:5; 8:1 (twice), 7, 10, 11; 13:2, 8; 14:6; 2 Cor. 6:6; 8:7; 11:6; Eph. 3:19; Col. 2:3; 1 Pet. 3:7; 2 Pet. 1:5, 6; (b) with an object: in respect of (1) God, 2 Cor. 2:14; 10:5; (2) the glory of God, 2 Cor. 4:6; (3) Christ Jesus, Phil. 3:8; 2 Pet. 3:18; (4) salvation, **Luke 1:77**; (c) subjectively, of God's "knowledge," Rom. 11:33; the word of "knowledge," 1 Cor. 12:8; "knowledge" falsely so called, 1 Tim. 6:20.

Remission *aphesis* (859), "a dismissal, release" (from *aphiemi*), is used of the forgiveness of sins and translated "remission" in Matt. 26:28; Mark 1:4; **Luke 1:77**; **3:3**; **24:47**; Acts 2:38; 5:31 (KJV, "forgiveness"); 10:43; 13:38, RV (KJV, "forgiveness"); 26:18 (ditto); Heb. 9:22; 10:18.

1:78 Through the tender mercy of our God; whereby the dayspring from on high hath visited us,

Tender *splanchnon* (4698), always in the plural, properly denotes "the physical organs of the intestines," and is once used in this respect, Acts 1:18. The RV substitutes the following for the word "bowels": "affections," 2 Cor. 6:12; "affection," 2 Cor. 7:15; "tender mercies," Phil. 1:8; 2:1; "a heart (of compassion)," Col. 3:12; "heart," Philem. 12, 20; "hearts," Philem. 7; "compassion," 1 John 3:17. The word is rendered "tender" in the KJV and RV of **Luke 1:78**, in connection with the word mercy.

Dayspring *anatole* (395), lit., "a rising up" (cf. *anatello*, "to cause to rise"), is used of the rising of the sun and stars; it chiefly means the east, as in Matt. 2:1, etc.; rendered "dayspring" in **Luke 1:78**. Its other meaning, "a shoot," is found in the Sept. in Jer. 23:5; Zech. 6:12. See also the margin of **Luke 1:78**, "branch." Elsewhere it denotes the "east," as the quarter of the sun's rising, Matt. 2:1-2, 9; 8:11; 24:27; **Luke 13:29**; Rev. 7:2; 16:12; 21:13. The "east" in general stands for that side of things upon which the rising of the sun gives light. In the heavenly city itself, Rev. 21:13, the reference to the "east" gate points to the outgoing of the influence of the city "eastward."

On high *hupsos* (5311), "height," is used with *ex* (*ek*) "from," in the phrase "on high," **Luke 1:78**; **24:49**; with *eis*, "in" or "into," Eph. 4:8.

Visited *see* ***Luke 1:68***.

1:79 To give light to them that sit in darkness and *in* the shadow of death, to guide our feet into the way of peace.

Light *epiphaino* (2014), transitively, "to show forth" (*epi*, "upon," *phaino*, "to cause to shine"), is used intransitively and metaphorically in **Luke 1:79**, and rendered "to give light," KJV (RV, "to shine upon").

Sit *kathemai* (2521), is used (a) of the natural posture, e.g., Matt. 9:9, most frequently in Revelation, some 32 times; frequently in the Gospels and Acts; elsewhere only in 1 Cor. 14:30; Jas. 2:3 (twice); and of Christ's position of authority on the throne of God, Col. 3:1, KJV, "sitteth" (RV, "is, seated"); Heb. 1:13 (cf. Matt. 22:44; 26:64 and parallel passages in Mark and Luke, and Acts 2:34); often as antecedent or successive to, or accompanying, another act (in no case a superfluous expression), e.g., Matt. 15:29; 27:36; Mark 2:14; 4:1; (b) metaphorically in Matt. 4:16 (twice); **Luke 1:79**; of inhabiting a place (translated "dwell"), **Luke 21:35**; Rev. 14:6, RV marg., "sit" (in the best texts: some have *katoikeo*, "to dwell").

Darkness *skotos* (4655), a neuter noun frequent in the Sept., is used in the NT (a) of "physical darkness," Matt. 27:45; 2 Cor. 4:6; (b) of "intellectual darkness," Rom. 2:19; (c) of "blindness," Acts 13:11; (d) by metonymy, of the "place of punishment," e.g., Matt. 8:12; 2 Pet. 2:17; Jude 13; (e) metaphorically, of "moral and spiritual darkness," e.g., Matt. 6:23; **Luke 1:79**; **11:35**; John 3:19; Acts 26:18; 2 Cor. 6:14; Eph. 6:12; Col. 1:13; 1 Thess. 5:4-5; 1 Pet. 2:9; 1 John 1:6; (f) by metonymy, of "those who are in moral or spiritual darkness," Eph. 5:8; (g) of "evil works," Rom. 13:12; Eph. 5:11; (h) of the "evil powers that dominate the world," **Luke 22:53**; (i) "of secrecy." While *skotos* is used more than twice as many times as *skotia* in the NT, the apostle John uses *skotos* only once, 1 John 1:6, but *skotia* 15 times out of the 18.

Shadow *skia* (4639), is used (a) of "a shadow," caused by the interception of light, Mark 4:32; Acts 5:15; metaphorically of the darkness and spiritual death of ignorance, Matt. 4:16; **Luke 1:79**; (b) of "the image" or "outline" cast by an object, Col. 2:17, of ceremonies under the Law; of the tabernacle and its appurtenances and offerings, Heb. 8:5; of these as appointed under the Law, Heb. 10:1.

Guide *kateuthuno* (2720), "to make straight" (*kata*, "down," intensive, *euthus*, "straight," *euthuno*, "to straighten"), is translated "guide" in **Luke 1:79**, of the Lord's "guidance" of the feet of His people; "direct," in 1 Thess. 3:11, of His "directing" the way of His servants; in 2 Thess. 3:5, of His "directing" the hearts of His saints into the love of God.

Feet *pous* (4228), besides its literal meaning, is used, by metonymy, of "a person in motion," **Luke 1:79**; Acts 5:9; Rom. 3:15; 10:15; Heb. 12:13. It is used in phrases expressing subjection, 1 Cor. 15:27, RV; of the humility and receptivity of discipleship, **Luke 10:39**; Acts 22:3; of obeisance and worship, e.g., Matt. 28:9; of scornful rejection, Matt. 10:14; Acts 13:51. Washing the "feet" of another betokened the humility of the service and the comfort of the guest, and was a feature of hospitality, **Luke 7:38**; John 13:5; 1 Tim. 5:10 (here figuratively).

Way *hodos* (3598), denotes (a) "a natural path, road, way," frequent in the Synoptic Gospels; elsewhere, e.g., Acts 8:26; 1 Thess. 3:11; Jas. 2:25; Rev. 16:12; (b) "a traveler's way"; (c) metaphorically, of "a course of conduct," or "way of thinking," e.g., of righteousness, Matt. 21:32; 2 Pet. 2:21; of God, Matt. 22:16, and parallels, i.e., the "way" instructed and approved by God; so Acts 18:26 and Heb. 3:10, "My ways" (cf. Rev. 15:3); of the Lord, Acts 18:25; "that leadeth to destruction," Matt. 7:13; "… unto life," 7:14; of peace, **Luke 1:79**; Rom. 3:17; of Paul's "ways" in Christ, 1 Cor. 4:17 (plural); "more excellent" (of love), 1 Cor. 12:31; of truth, 2 Pet. 2:2; of the right "way," 2:15; of Balaam (*id.*), of Cain, Jude 11; of a "way" consisting in what is from God, e.g., of life, Acts 2:28 (plural); of salvation, Acts 16:17; personified, of Christ as the means of access to the Father, John 14:6; of the course followed and characterized by the followers of Christ, Acts 9:2; 19:9, 23; 24:22.

Peace *eirene* (1515), "occurs in each of the books of the NT, save 1 John and save in Acts 7:26 ['(at) one again'] it is translated "peace" in the RV. It describes (a) harmonious relationships between men, Matt. 10:34; Rom. 14:19; (b) between nations, **Luke 14:32**; Acts 12:20; Rev. 6:4; (c) friendliness, Acts 15:33; 1 Cor. 16:11; Heb. 11:31; (d) freedom from molestation, **Luke 11:21**; **19:42**; Acts 9:31 (RV, 'peace,' KJV, 'rest'); 16:36; (e) order, in the State, Acts 24:2 (RV, 'peace,' KJV, 'quietness'); in the churches, 1 Cor. 14:33; (f) the harmonized relationships between God and man, accomplished through the gospel, Acts 10:36; Eph. 2:17; (g) the sense of rest and contentment consequent thereon, Matt. 10:13; Mark 5:34; **Luke 1:79**; **2:29**; John 14:27; Rom. 1:7; 3:17, 8:6; in certain passages this idea is not distinguishable from the last, Rom. 5:1."

"The God of peace" is a title used in Rom. 15:33; 16:20; Phil. 4:9; 1 Thess. 5:23; Heb. 13:20; cf. 1 Cor. 14:33; 2 Cor. 13:11. The corresponding Heb. word *shalom* primarily signifies "wholeness": see its use in Josh. 8:31, "unhewn"; Ruth 2:12, "full"; Neh. 6:15, "finished"; Isa. 42:19, marg., "made perfect." Hence there is a close connection between the title in 1 Thess. 5:23 and the word *holokleros*, "entire," in that verse. In the Sept. *shalom* is often rendered by *soteria*, "salvation, e.g., Gen. 26:31; 41:16; hence the "peace-offering" is called the "salvation offering." Cf. **Luke 7:50**; **8:48**. In 2 Thess. 3:16, the title "the Lord of peace" is best understood as referring to the Lord Jesus. In Acts 7:26, "would have set them at one" is, lit., "was reconciling them (conative imperfect tense, expressing an earnest effort) into peace."

1:80 And the child grew, and waxed strong in spirit, and was in the deserts till the day of his shewing unto Israel.

Grew *auxano* (837), "to grow or increase," of the growth of that which lives, naturally or spiritually, is used transitively, signifying to make to increase, said of giving the increase, 1 Cor. 3:6, 7; 2 Cor. 9:10, the effect of the work of God, according to the analogy of His operations in nature; "to grow, become greater," e.g. of plants and fruit, Matt. 6:28; used in the passive voice in 13:32 and Mark 4:8, "increase"; in the active in **Luke 12:27**; **13:19**; of the body, **Luke 1:80**; **2:40**; of Christ, John 3:30, "increase"; of the work of the gospel of God, Acts 6:7, "increased"; 12:24; 19:20; of people, Acts 7:17; of faith, 2 Cor. 10:15 (passive voice), RV, "groweth" (KJV, "is increased"); of believers individually, Eph. 4:15; Col. 1:6, RV, 10 (passive voice), "increasing"; 1 Pet. 2:2; 2 Pet. 3:18; of the church, Col. 2:19; of churches, Eph. 2:21.

Strong *krataioo* (2901), "to strengthen" (akin to *kratos*, "strength"), is rendered (a) "to wax strong," **Luke 1:80**; **2:40**; "be strong," 1 Cor. 16:13, lit., "be strengthened"; "to be strengthened," Eph. 3:16 (passive voice in each place).

Spirit *see* ***Luke 1:17***.

Shewing *anadeixis* (323), "a shewing forth" (*ana*, "up or forth," and *deiknumi*, "to show"), is translated "showing" in **Luke 1:80**.

CHAPTER 2

2:1 And it came to pass in those days, that there went out a decree from Caesar Augustus, that all the world should be taxed.

Decree *dogma* (1378), transliterated in English, primarily denoted "an opinion or judgment" (from *dokeo*, "to be of opinion"), hence, an "opinion expressed with authority, a doctrine, ordinance, decree"; "decree," **Luke 2:1**; Acts 16:4; 17:7; in the sense of ordinances, Eph. 2:15; Col. 2:14.

World *oikoumene* (3625), "the inhabited earth", is used (a) of the whole inhabited world, Matt. 24:14; **Luke 4:5**; **21:26**; Rom. 10:18; Heb. 1:6; Rev. 3:10; 16:14; by metonymy, of its inhabitants, Acts 17:31; Rev. 12:9; (b) of the Roman Empire, the world as viewed by the writer or speaker, **Luke 2:1**; Acts 11:28; 24:5; by metonymy, of its inhabitants, Acts 17:6; 19:27; (c) the inhabited world in a coming age, Heb. 2:5.

Taxed *apographo* (583), primarily signifies "to write out, to copy"; then, "to enroll, to inscribe," as in a register. It is used of a census, **Luke 2:1**, RV, "be enrolled," for KJV, "be taxed"; in the middle voice, vv. **3**, **5**, to enroll oneself, KJV, "be taxed." Confirmation that this census (not taxation) was taken in the dominions of the Roman Empire is given by the historians Tacitus and Suetonius. Augustus himself drew up a sort of Roman Doomsday Book, a rationarium, afterwards epitomized into a breviarium, to include the allied kingdoms, appointing twenty commissioners to draw up the lists. In Heb. 12:23 the members of the church of the firstborn are said to be "enrolled," RV.

2:2 (*And* this taxing was first made when Cyrenius was governor of Syria.)

Taxing *apographe* (582), primarily denotes "a written copy," or, as a law term, "a deposition"; then, "a register, census, enrollment," **Luke 2:2**; Acts 5:37, RV, for KJV, "taxing." Luke's accuracy has been vindicated, as against the supposed inconsistency that as Quirinius was governor of Syria in AD 6, ten years after the birth of Christ, the census, as "the first" (RV), could not have taken place. At the time mentioned by Luke, Cilicia, of which Quirinius was governor, was separated from Cyprus and joined to Syria. His later direct governorship of Syria itself accounts for the specific inclusion of, and reference to, his earlier connection with that province. Justin Martyr, a native of Palestine, writing in the middle of the 2nd century, asserts thrice that Quirinius was present in Syria at the time mentioned by Luke (see Apol., 1:34, 46; Trypho 78). Noticeable, too, are the care and accuracy taken by Luke in his historical details, **1:3**, RV. As to charges made against Luke's accuracy, Moulton and Milligan say as follows: "The deduction so long made ... about the census apparently survives the demonstration that the blunder lay only in our lack of information: the microbe is not yet completely expelled. Possibly the salutary process may be completed by our latest inscriptional evidence that Quirinius was a legate in Syria for census purposes in 8-6 BC."

Governor *hegemoneuo* (2230), to be a *hegemon*, "to lead the way," came to signify to be "a governor of a province"; it is used of Quirinius, governor of Syria, **Luke 2:2**, RV, of Pontius Pilate, governor of Judea, **3:1**. In the first clause of this verse the noun *hegemonia*, "a rule or sovereignty," is translated "reign"; Eng., "hegemony."

2:3 And all went to be taxed, every one into his own city.

Taxed *see Luke 2:1*.

2:4 And Joseph also went up from Galilee, out of the city of Nazareth, into Judaea, unto the city of David, which is called Bethlehem; (because he was of the house and lineage of David:)

Lineage *patria* (3965), primarily "an ancestry, lineage," signifies in the NT "a family or tribe" (in the Sept. it is used of related people, but narrower than *phule*, "a tribe," e.g., Exod. 12:3; Num. 32:28); it is used of the "family" of David, **Luke 2:4**, RV, for KJV, "lineage"; in the wider sense of "nationalities, races," Acts 3:25, RV, "families," for KJV, "kindreds"; in Eph. 3:15, RV, "every family," for KJV, "the whole family," the reference being to all those who are spiritually related to God the Father, He being the Author of their spiritual relationship to Him as His children, they being united to one another in "family" fellowship (*patria* is akin to *pater*, "a father"); Luther's translation, "all who bear the name of children," is advocated by Cremer, p. 474. The phrase, however, is lit., "every family."

2:5 To be taxed with Mary his espoused wife, being great with child.

Taxed *see Luke 2:1*.

Espoused *see Luke 1:27*.

Child *enkuos* (1471), denotes "great with child" (*en*, "in," and *kuo*, "to conceive"), **Luke 2:5**.

2:6 And so it was, that, while they were there, the days were accomplished that she should be delivered.

Accomplished *see Luke 1:23.*

2:7 And she brought forth her firstborn son, and wrapped him in swaddling clothes, and laid him in a manger; because there was no room for them in the inn.

Firstborn *prototokos* (4416), "firstborn" (from *protos*, "first," and *tikto*, "to beget"), is used of Christ as born of the Virgin Mary, **Luke 2:7**; further, in His relationship to the Father, expressing His priority to, and preeminence over, creation, not in the sense of being the "first" to be born. It is used occasionally of superiority of position in the OT, see Exod. 4:22; Deut. 21:16, 17, the prohibition being against the evil of assigning the privileged position of the "firstborn" to one born subsequently to the "first" child. The five passages in the NT relating to Christ may be set forth chronologically thus: (a) Col. 1:15, where His eternal relationship with the Father is in view, and the clause means both that He was the "Firstborn" before all creation and that He Himself produced creation (the genitive case being objective, as v. 16 makes clear); (b) Col. 1:18 and Rev. 1:5, in reference to His resurrection; (c) Rom. 8:29, His position in relationship to the church; (d) Heb. 1:6, RV, His second advent (the RV "when He again bringeth in," puts "again" in the right place, the contrast to His first advent, at His birth, being implied); cf. Ps. 89:27.

Swaddling clothes *sparganoo* (4683), "to swathe" (from *sparganon*, "a swathing band"), signifies "to wrap in swaddling clothes" in **Luke 2:7**, **12**. The idea that the word means "rags" is without foundation. In the Sept., Job 38:9; Ezek. 16:4.

Laid *anaklino* (347), "to cause to recline, make to sit down," is used in the active voice, in **Luke 12:37** (also in **2:7**, of "laying" the infant Christ in the manger); in the passive, Matt. 8:11; 14:19; Mark 6:39 (in the best texts); in some texts, **Luke 7:36** and **9:15**; **13:29**.

Manger *phatne* (5336), "a manger," **Luke 2:7**, **12**, **16**, also denotes "a stall," **13:15**. So in the Sept., the word denoted not only a "manger" but, by metonymy, the stall or crib (Prov. 14:4) containing the "manger."

Room *topos* (5117), (Eng., "topic," "topography," etc.) is used of "a region" or "locality," frequently in the Gospels and Acts, in **Luke 2:7** and **14:22**, "room"; of a place which a person or thing occupies, a couch at table, e.g., **Luke 14:9**, **10**, RV, "place" (KJV, "room"); of the destiny of Judas Iscariot, Acts 1:25; of the condition of the "unlearned" or nongifted in a church gathering, 1 Cor. 14:16, RV, "place"; the sheath of a sword, Matt. 26:52; a place in a book, **Luke 4:17**; see also Rev. 2:5; 6:14; 12:8; metaphorically, of "condition, occasion, opportunity" Acts 25:16, RV, "opportunity" (KJV, "license"); Rom. 12:19; Eph. 4:27.

Inn *kataluma* (2646), akin to *kataluo*, signifies (a) "an inn, lodging-place," **Luke 2:7**; (b) "a guest-room," Mark 14:14; **Luke 22:11**. The word lit. signifies "a loosening down" (*kata*, "down," *luo*, "to loose"), used of the place where travelers and their beasts untied their packages, girdles and sandals. "In the East, no figure is more invested with chivalry than the guest. In his own right he cannot cross the threshold, but when once he is invited in, all do him honor and unite in rendering service; cf. Gen. 18:19; Judg. 19:9, 15." These two passages in the NT "concern a room in a private house, which the owner readily placed at the disposal of Jesus and His disciples for the celebration of the Passover ... At the festivals of Passover, Pentecost and Tabernacles the people were commanded to repair to Jerusalem; and it was a boast of the Rabbis that, notwithstanding the enormous crowds, no man could truthfully say to his fellow, 'I have not found a fire where to roast my paschal lamb in Jerusalem,' or 'I have not found a bed in Jerusalem to lie in,' or 'My lodging is too strait in Jerusalem.'"

2:8 And there were in the same country shepherds abiding in the field, keeping watch over their flock by night.

Country *chora* (5561), properly denotes "the space lying between two limits or places"; accordingly it has a variety of meanings: "country," Matt. 2:12; 8:28; Mark 1:5, RV (KJV, "land"); 5:1, 10; **Luke 2:8**; **8:26**; **15:13-14**, RV (KJV, "land"), **15**; **19:12**; **21:21**; Acts 10:39, RV (KJV, "land"); 12:20; 26:20, RV (KJV, "coasts"); 27:27; in Mark 6:55 (in the best mss.) and Acts 18:23, RV, region.

Shepherds *poimen* (4166), is used (a) in its natural significance, Matt. 9:36; 25:32; Mark 6:34; **Luke 2:8**, **15**, **18**, **20**; John 10:2, 12; (b) metaphorically of Christ, Matt. 26:31; Mark 14:27; John 10:11, 14, 16; Heb. 13:20; 1 Pet. 2:25; (c) metaphorically of those who act as pastors in the churches, Eph. 4:11.

Abiding *agrauleo* (63), "to lodge in a fold in a field" (*agros*, "a field," *aule*, "a fold"), is used in **Luke 2:8**.

"There were only a few shepherds at the first Bethlehem. The ox and the ass understood more of the first Christmas than the high priests in Jerusalem. And it is the same today."

THOMAS MERTON

Keeping *phulasso* (5442), denotes (a) "to guard, watch, keep watch," e.g., **Luke 2:8**; in the passive voice, **8:29**; (b) "to keep by way of protection," e.g., **Luke 11:21**; John 12:25; 17:12 (2nd part); (c) metaphorically, "to keep a law precept," etc., e.g., Matt. 19:20 and **Luke 18:21**, "have observed"; **Luke 11:28**; John 12:47 (in the best mss.); Acts 7:53; 16:4; 21:24; Rom. 2:26; Gal. 6:13; 1 Tim. 5:21 ("observe"); in the middle voice, Mark 10:20 ("have observed"); (d) in the middle voice, "to keep oneself from," Acts 21:25; elsewhere translated by the verb "to beware."

Watch *phulake* (5438), is used (a) with the meaning "a watch," actively, "a guarding," **Luke 2:8**, lit., "(keeping, *phulasso*) watches"; (b) of "the time during which guard was kept by night, a watch of the night," Matt. 14:25; 24:43; Mark 6:48; **Luke 12:38**.

Flock *poimne* (4167), akin to *poimen*, "a shepherd," denotes "a flock" (properly, of sheep), Matt. 26:31; **Luke 2:8**; 1 Cor. 9:7; metaphorically, of Christ's followers, John 10:16, RV, for the erroneous KJV, "fold." What characterizes Christ's sheep is listening to His voice, and the "flock" must be one as He is one.

Night *nux* (3571), is used (I) literally, (a) of "the alternating natural period to that of the day," e.g., Matt. 4:2; 12:40; 2 Tim. 1:3; Rev. 4:8; (b) of "the period of the absence of light," the time in which something takes place, e.g., Matt. 2:14 (27:64), in some mss.); **Luke 2:8**; John 3:2 (7:50, in some mss.); Acts 5:19; 9:25; (c) of "point of time," e.g., Matt. 14:27 (in some mss.), 30; **Luke 12:20**; Acts 27:23; (d) of "duration of time," e.g., **Luke 2:37**; **5:5**; Acts 20:31; 26:7 (note the difference in the phrase in Mark 4:27); (II) metaphorically, (a) of "the period of man's alienation from God," Rom. 13:12; 1 Thess. 5:5, lit., "not of night," where "of" means 'belonging to;' cf. "of the Way," Acts 9:2; "of shrinking back" and "of faith," Heb. 10:39, marg.; (b) of "death," as the time when work ceases, John 9:4.

2:9 And, lo, the angel of the Lord came upon them, and the glory of the Lord shone round about them: and they were sore afraid.

Came *ephistemi* (2186), signifies "to stand by or over" (*epi*, "upon"), **Luke 2:9**, RV; Acts 12:7 "before," Acts 11:11; to come upon, **Luke 20:1** (here with the idea of suddenness); Acts 4:1; 6:12; 23:27; 1 Thess. 5:3; "coming up," of the arrival of Anna at the Temple, **Luke 2:38**; "came up to (Him)," of Martha, **Luke 10:40**; "is come," 2 Tim. 4:6 (probably with the same idea as in **Luke 20:1**). The RV is significant in all these places. Used intransitively, it also denotes: **Luke 4:39**, "stood over"; **24:4** and Acts 23:11, "stood by"; Acts 10:17, "stood"; 22:13, "standing by (me)," RV; so v. 20, KJV and RV.

Glory *doxa* (1391), "glory" (from *dokeo*, "to seem"), primarily signifies an opinion, estimate, and hence, the honor resulting from a good opinion. It is used (I) (a) of the nature and acts of God in self-manifestation, i.e., what He essentially is and does, as exhibited in whatever way he reveals Himself in these respects, and particularly in the person of Christ, in whom essentially His "glory" has ever shone forth and ever will do, John 17:5, 24; Heb. 1:3; it was exhibited in the character and acts of Christ in the days of His flesh, John 1:14; John 2:11; at Cana both His grace and His power were manifested, and these constituted His "glory", so also in the resurrection of Lazarus 11:4, 40; the "glory" of God was exhibited in the resurrection of Christ, Rom. 6:4, and in His ascension and exaltation, 1 Pet. 1:21, likewise on the Mount of Transfiguration, 2 Pet. 1:17. In Rom. 1:23 His "everlasting power and Divinity" are spoken of as His "glory," i.e., His attributes and power as revealed through creation; in Rom. 3:23 the word denotes the manifested perfection of His character, especially His righteousness, of which all men fall short; in Col. 1:11 "the might of His glory" signifies the might which is characteristic of His "glory"; in Eph. 1:6, 12, 14, "the praise of the glory of His grace" and "the praise of His glory" signify the due acknowledgement of the exhibition of His attributes and ways; in Eph. 1:17, "the Father of glory" describes Him as the source from whom all divine splendor and perfection proceed in their manifestation, and to whom they belong; (b) of the character and ways of God as exhibited through

Christ to and through believers, 2 Cor. 3:18 and 4:6; (c) of the state of blessedness into which believers are to enter hereafter through being brought into the likeness of Christ, e.g., Rom. 8:18, 21; Phil. 3:21 (RV, "the body of His glory"); 1 Pet. 5:1, 10; Rev. 21:11; (d) brightness or splendor, (1) supernatural, emanating from God (as in the *shekinah* "glory," in the pillar of cloud and in the Holy of Holies, e.g., Exod. 16:10; 25:22), **Luke 2:9**; Acts 22:11; Rom. 9:4; 2 Cor. 3:7; Jas. 2:1; in Titus 2:13 it is used of Christ's return, "the appearing of the glory of our great God and Savior Jesus Christ" (RV); cf. Phil. 3:21, above; (2) natural, as of the heavenly bodies, 1 Cor. 15:40, 41; (II) of good reputation, praise, honor, **Luke 14:10** (RV, "glory," for KJV, "worship"); John 5:41 (RV, "glory," for KJV, "honor"); 7:18; 8:50; 12:43 (RV, "glory," for KJV, "praise"); 2 Cor. 6:8 (RV, "glory," for KJV "honor"); Phil. 3:19; Heb. 3:3; in 1 Cor. 11:7, of man as representing the authority of God, and of woman as rendering conspicuous the authority of man; in 1 Thess. 2:6, "glory" probably stands, by metonymy, for material gifts, an honorarium, since in human estimation "glory" is usually expressed in things material. The word is used in ascriptions of praise to God, e.g.. **Luke 17:18**; John 9:24, RV, "glory" (KJV, "praise"); Acts 12:23; as in doxologies (lit., "glory-words"), e.g., **Luke 2:14**; Rom. 11:36; 16:27; Gal. 1:5; Rev. 1:6.

Shone *perilampo* (4034), "to shine around" (*peri*, "around," and *lampo*), is used in **Luke 2:9**, "shone round about," of the glory of the Lord; so in Acts 26:13, of the light from Heaven upon Saul of Tarsus.

Sore In **Luke 2:9** *megas*, "great," is used with *phobos*, "fear," as the object of the verb "to fear," "(they were) sore (afraid)," lit., "(they feared) a great (fear)."

2:10 And the angel said unto them, Fear not: for, behold, I bring you good tidings of great joy, which shall be to all people.

Tidings *see* Glad tidings *Luke 1:19*.

Joy *chara* (5479), "joy, delight" (akin to *chairo*, "to rejoice"), is found frequently in Matthew and Luke, and especially in John, once in Mark (4:16, RV, "joy," KJV, "gladness"); it is absent from 1 Cor. (though the verb is used three times), but is frequent in 2 Cor., where the noun is used five times, and the verb eight times, suggestive of the apostle's relief in comparison with the circumstances of the 1st Epistle; in Col. 1:11, KJV, "joyfulness," RV, "joy." The word is sometimes used, by metonymy, of the occasion or cause of "joy," **Luke 2:10** (lit., "I announce to you a great joy"); in 2 Cor. 1:15, in some mss., for *charis*, "benefit"; Phil. 4:1, where the readers are called the apostle's "joy"; so 1 Thess. 2:19, 20; Heb. 12:2, of the object of Christ's "joy"; Jas. 1:2, where it is connected with falling into trials; perhaps also in Matt. 25:21, 23, where some regard it as signifying, concretely, the circumstances attending cooperation in the authority of the Lord.

2:11 For unto you is born this day in the city of David a Saviour, which is Christ the Lord.

Born *see* Brought forth at *Luke 1:57*.

Saviour *see* *Luke 1:47*.

Christ *christos* (5547), "anointed," translates, in the Sept., the word "Messiah," a term applied to the priests who were anointed with the holy oil, particularly the high priest, e.g., Lev. 4:3, 5, 16. The prophets are called *hoi christoi Theou*, "the anointed of God," Ps. 105:15. A king of Israel was described upon occasion as *christos tou Kuriou*, "the anointed of the Lord," 1 Sam. 2:10, 35; 2 Sam. 1:14; Ps. 2:2; 18:50; Hab. 3:13; the term is used even of Cyrus, Isa. 45:1. The title *ho Christos*, "the Christ," is not used of Christ in the Sept. version of the inspired books of the OT. In the NT the word is frequently used with the article, of the Lord Jesus, as an appellative rather than a title, e.g., Matt. 2:4; Acts 2:31; without the article, **Luke 2:11**; **23:2**; John 1:41. Three times the title was expressly accepted by the Lord Himself, Matt. 16:17; Mark 14:61-62; John 4:26.

2:12 And this *shall* be a sign unto you; Ye shall find the babe wrapped in swaddling clothes, lying in a manger.

Sign *semeion* (4592), "a sign, mark, indication, token," is used (a) of that which distinguished a person or thing from others, e.g., Matt. 26:48; **Luke 2:12**; Rom. 4:11; 2 Cor. 12:12 (1st part); 2 Thess. 3:17, "token," i.e., his autograph attesting the authenticity of his letters; (b) of a "sign" as a warning or admonition, e.g., Matt. 12:39, "the sign of (i.e., consisting of) the prophet Jonas"; 16:4; **Luke 2:34**; **11:29**, **30**; (c) of miraculous acts (1) as tokens of divine authority and power, e.g., Matt. 12:38, 39 (1st part); John 2:11, RV, "signs"; 3:2 (ditto); 4:54, "(the second) sign," RV; 10:41 (ditto); 20:30; in 1 Cor. 1:22, "the Jews ask for signs," RV, indicates that the Apostles were met with the same demand from Jews as Christ had been: "signs were vouchsafed in plenty, signs of God's power and love, but these were not the signs which they sought.... They wanted signs of an outward Messianic

Kingdom, of temporal triumph, of material greatness for the chosen people.... With such cravings the Gospel of a 'crucified Messiah' was to them a stumblingblock indeed" (Lightfoot); 1 Cor. 14:22; (2) by demons, Rev. 16:14; (3) by false teachers or prophets, indications of assumed authority, e.g., Matt. 24:24; Mark 13:22; (4) by Satan through his special agents, 2 Thess. 2:9; Rev. 13:13, 14; 19:20; (d) of tokens portending future events, e.g., Matt. 24:3, where "the sign of the Son of Man" signifies, subjectively, that the Son of Man is Himself the "sign" of what He is about to do; Mark 13:4; **Luke 21:7, 11, 25**; Acts 2:19; Rev. 12:1, RV; 12:3, RV; 15:1.

Babe *see Luke 1:41*.

Swaddling clothes *see Luke 2:7*.

Lying *keimai* (2749), "to be laid, to lie," used as the passive voice of *tithemi*, "to lay", is said (a) of the Child Jesus, **Luke 2:12, 16**; (b) of the dead body of the Lord, Matt. 28:6; John 20:12; in **Luke 23:53**, "had ... lain," RV, KJV, "was laid," in the tomb as hitherto empty; (c) of the linen cloths, John 20:5, 6, 7; (d) figuratively of a veil as "lying" upon the hearts of the Jews, 2 Cor. 3:15, RV, "lieth" (KJV, "is"); (e) metaphorically, of the world as "lying" in the evil one, 1 John 5:19, RV; (f) of the heavenly city, Rev. 21:16.

Manger *see Luke 2:7*.

2:13 And suddenly there was with the angel a multitude of the heavenly host praising God, and saying,

Suddenly *exaiphnes* (1810), a strengthened form, occurs in Mark 13:36; **Luke 2:13**; **9:39**; Acts 9:3; 22:6.

Multitude *see Luke 1:10*.

Heavenly *ouranios* (3770), signifying "of heaven, heavenly," is used (a) as an appellation of God the Father, Matt. 6:14, 26, 32, "your heavenly Father"; 15:13, "My heavenly Father"; (b) as descriptive of the holy angels, **Luke 2:13**; (c) of the vision seen by Paul, Acts 26:19.

Host *stratia* (4756), "an army," is used of angels, **Luke 2:13**; of stars, Acts 7:42; some mss. have it instead of *strateia*, in 2 Cor. 10:4 ("warfare"). Cf. *strateuma*, "an army."

Praising *aineo* (134), "to speak in praise of, to praise," is always used of "praise" to God, (a) by angels, **Luke 2:13**; (b) by men, **Luke 2:20**; **19:37**; **24:53**; Acts 2:20, 47; 3:8, 9; Rom. 15:11; Rev. 19:5.

2:14 Glory to God in the highest, and on earth peace, good will toward men.

Glory *see Luke 2:9*.

Highest *hupsistos* (5310), is used in the plural in the phrase "in the highest," i.e., in the "highest" regions, the abode of God, Matt. 21:9; Mark 11:10; Luke omits the article, **Luke 2:14**; **19:38**; for its use as a title of God.

Good will *eudokia* (2107), lit., "good pleasure" (*eu*, "well," *dokeo*, "to seem"), implies a gracious purpose, a good object being in view, with the idea of a resolve, showing the willingness with which the resolve is made. It is often translated "good pleasure," e.g., Eph. 1:5, 9; Phil. 2:13; in Phil. 1:15, "good will"; in Rom. 10:1, "desire," (marg., "good pleasure"); in 2 Thess. 1:11, RV, "desire," KJV and RV, marg., "good pleasure." It is used of God in Matt. 11:26 ("well pleasing," RV, for KJV, "seemed good"); **Luke 2:14**, RV, "men in whom He is well pleased," lit., "men of good pleasure" (the construction is objective); **10:21**; Eph. 1:5, 9; Phil. 2:13.

2:15 And it came to pass, as the angels were gone away from them into heaven, the shepherds said one to another, Let us now go even unto Bethlehem, and see this thing which is come to pass, which the Lord hath made known unto us.

Shepherds *see Luke 2:8*.

Now *de* (1211), a consecutive particle, giving stress to the word or words to which it is attached, sometimes with hardly any exact Eng. equivalent, is translated "now" in **Luke 2:15**, in the words of the shepherds; in Acts 15:36, RV (KJV, "and"). Some mss. have it in 2 Cor. 12:1; see RV marg.

Thing *rhema* (4487), "a saying, word," is translated "thing" in **Luke 2:15**; v. **19**, KJV (RV, "saying"); in Acts 5:32, "things."

Known *gnorizo* (1107), signifies (a) "to come to know, discover, know," Phil. 1:22, "I wot (not)," i.e., "I know not," "I have not come to know" (the RV, marg. renders it, as under (b), "I do not make known"); (b) "to make known," whether (I) communicating things before "unknown," **Luke 2:15, 17**; in the latter some mss. have the verb *diagnorizo* (hence the KJV, "made known abroad"); John 15:15, "I have made known"; 17:26; Acts 2:28; 7:13 (1st part); Rom. 9:22, 23; 16:26 (passive voice); 2 Cor. 8:1, "we make known (to you)," RV, KJV, "we do (you) to wit"; Eph. 1:9; 3:3, 5, 10 (all three in the passive voice); 6:19, 21; Col. 1:27; 4:7, 9, "shall make known" (KJV, "shall declare"); 2 Pet. 1:16; or (II) reasserting things already "known," 1 Cor. 12:3, "I give (you) to understand" (the apostle reaffirms what they knew); 15:1, of the gospel; Gal. 1:11 (he reminds them of what they well knew, the ground of his claim to apostleship); Phil. 4:6 (passive voice), of requests to God.

2:16 And they came with haste, and found Mary, and Joseph, and the babe lying in a manger.

Haste *speudo* (4692), denotes (a) intransitively, "to hasten," **Luke 2:16**, "with haste," lit., "(they came) hastening"; **Luke 19:5, 6**; Acts 20:16; 22:18; (b) transitively, "to desire earnestly," 2 Pet. 3:12, RV, "earnestly desiring" (marg., "hastening"), KJV, "hasting" (the day of God), i.e., in our practical fellowship with God as those who are appointed by Him as instruments through prayer and service for the accomplishment of His purposes, purposes which will be unthwartably fulfilled both in time and manner of accomplishment. In this way the earnest desire will find its fulfillment.

Found *aneurisko* (429), "to find out" (by search), "discover," implying diligent searching, is used in **Luke 2:16**, of the shepherds in searching for and "finding" Mary and Joseph and the Child; in Acts 21:4, of Paul and his companions, in searching for and "finding" "the disciples" at Tyre.

Babe *see Luke 1:41.*

Lying *see Luke 2:12.*

Manger *see Luke 2:7.*

2:17 And when they had seen *it*, they made known abroad the saying which was told them concerning this child.

Known *see Luke 2:15.*

Saying *see* Sayings at Luke *1:65.*

Told *see Luke 1:45.*

2:18 And all they that heard *it* wondered at those things which were told them by the shepherds.

Told *see Luke 1:45.*

Shepherds *see Luke 2:8.*

2:19 But Mary kept all these things, and pondered *them* in her heart.

Kept *suntereo* (4933), denotes "to preserve, keep safe, keep close" (*sun*, "together with," used intensively, and *tereo*), in **Luke 2:19**, as in v. **51**, of the mother of Jesus in regard to the words of the shepherds; in Mark 6:20 it is used of Herod's preservation of John the Baptist from Herodias, RV, "kept (him) safe," KJV, "observed (him)" (marg., "kept"); in Matt. 9:17 (in some mss., **Luke 5:38**), of the preservation of wineskins.

Things *see* Thing at *Luke 2:15.*

Pondered *sumballo* (4820), "to throw together, confer," etc., has the meaning "to ponder," i.e., "to put one thing with another in considering circumstances," in **Luke 2:19**.

2:20 And the shepherds returned, glorifying and praising God for all the things that they had heard and seen, as it was told unto them.

Shepherds *see Luke 2:8.*

Returned *see Luke 1:56.*

Told *see Luke 1:45.*

2:21 And when eight days were accomplished for the circumcising of the child, his name was called JESUS, which was so named of the angel before he was conceived in the womb.

Eight *okto* (3638), "eight" (Lat., *octo, octavus;* cf. Eng., "octagon," "octave," "octavo," "October," etc.), is used in **Luke 2:21**; **9:28**; John 20:26; Acts 9:33; 25:6; 1 Pet. 3:20; in composition with other numerals, *okto kai deka*, lit., "eight and ten, eighteen," **Luke 13:4, 11, 16**; *triakonta kai okto*, "thirty and eight," John 5:5.

"The simple shepherds heard the voice of an angel and found their Lamb; the wise men saw the light of a star and found their Wisdom."

FULTON JOHN SHEEN

Accomplished *see Luke 1:23.*

Circumcising *see* Circumcise at *Luke 1:59.*

Named In **Luke 19:2**, KJV, *kaleo*, "to call" (with the dative case of *onoma*, "by name"), is translated "named" (RV, "called by name"); in **Luke 2:21**, KJV, the verb alone is rendered "named" (RV, "called").

Conceived *see Luke 1:24.*

Womb *see Luke 1:15.*

2:22 And when the days of her purification according to the law of Moses were accomplished, they brought him to Jerusalem, to present *him* to the Lord;

Purification *katharismos* (2512), denotes "cleansing," (a) both the action and its results, in the Levitical sense, Mark 1:44; **Luke 2:22**, "purification"; **5:14**, "cleansing"; John 2:6; 3:25, "purifying"; (b) in the moral sense, from sins, Heb. 1:3; 2 Pet. 1:9, RV, "cleansing.

Brought *anago* (321), "to lead or bring up to," **Luke 2:22**; Acts 9:39, etc.; "to bring forth," Acts 12:4; "to bring again," Heb. 13:20; "to bring up again," Rom. 10:7.

"The pulse of prayer is praise. The heart of prayer is gratitude. The voice of prayer is obedience. The arm of prayer is service."

WILLIAM ARTHUR WARD

Present *paristemi* (3936), denotes, when used transitively, "to place beside" (*para*, "by," *histemi*, "to set"), "to present," e.g., **Luke 2:22**; Acts 1:3, "He shewed (Himself)"; 9:41; 23:33; Rom. 6:13 (2nd part), RV, "present," KJV "yield"; so 6:19 (twice); 12:1; 2 Cor. 4:14; 11:2; Eph. 5:27; Col. 1:22, 28; 2 Tim. 2:15, RV (KJV, "shew").

2:23 (As it is written in the law of the Lord, Every male that openeth the womb shall be called holy to the Lord;)

Male *arsen* or *arren* (730), is translated "men" in Rom. 1:27 (three times); "man child" in Rev. 12:5 (v. 13 in some mss.); "male" in Matt. 19:4; Mark 10:6; **Luke 2:23**; Gal. 3:28, "(there can be no) male (and female)," RV, i.e. sex distinction does not obtain in Christ; sex is no barrier either to salvation or the development of Christian graces.

Openeth *dianoigo* (1272), "to open up completely," is used (a) literally, **Luke 2:23**; Acts 7:56, in the best mss.; (b) metaphorically, of the eyes, Mark 7:34; **Luke 24:31**; of the Scriptures, v. **32** and Acts 17:3; of the mind, **Luke 24:45**, RV (KJV, "understanding"); of the heart, Acts 16:14.

Womb *metra* (3388), the matrix (akin to meter "a mother"), occurs in **Luke 2:23**; Rom. 4:19.

2:24 And to offer a sacrifice according to that which is said in the law of the Lord, A pair of turtledoves, or two young pigeons.

Offer *didomi* (1325), to give, is translated "to offer" in **Luke 2:24**; in Rev. 8:3, KJV, "offer" (RV, "add;" marg., "give").

Sacrifice *thusia* (2378), primarily denotes "the act of offering"; then, objectively, "that which is offered" (a) of idolatrous "sacrifice," Acts 7:41; (b) of animal or other "sacrifices," as offered under the Law, Matt. 9:13; 12:7; Mark 9:49; 12:33; **Luke 2:24**; **13:1**; Acts 7:42; 1 Cor. 10:18; Heb. 5:1; 7:27 (RV, plural); 8:3; 9:9; 10:1, 5, 8 (RV, plural), 11; 11:4; (c) of Christ, in His "sacrifice" on the cross, Eph. 5:2; Heb. 9:23, where the plural antitypically comprehends the various forms of Levitical "sacrifices" in their typical character; 9:26; 10:12, 26; (d) metaphorically, (1) of the body of the believer, presented to God as a living "sacrifice," Rom. 12:1; (2) of faith, Phil. 2:17; (3) of material assistance rendered to servants of God, Phil. 4:18; (4) of praise, Heb, 13:15; (5) of doing good to others and communicating with their needs, Heb. 13:16; (6) of spiritual "sacrifices" in general, offered by believers as a holy priesthood, 1 Pet. 2:5.

Pair *zeugos* (2201), "a yoke" (akin to *zeugnumi*, "to yoke"), is used (a) of beasts, **Luke 14:19**; (b) of a pair of anything; in **Luke 2:24**, of turtledoves.

Turtledoves *trugon* (5167), denotes "a turtledove" (from *truzo*, "to murmur, to coo"), **Luke 2:24**.

Young *nossos* or *neossos* (3502), "a young bird," is translated "young" in **Luke 2:24**. Cf. *nossia*, "a brood," **Luke 13:34**, and the noun *nossion*, used in the neuter plural, *nossia*, in Matt. 23:37, "chickens"; *nossion* is the diminutive of *nossos*.

Pigeons *peristera* (4058), denotes "a dove or pigeon," Matt. 3:16; 10:16 (indicating its proverbial harmlessness); 21:12; Mark 1:10; 11:15; **Luke 2:24** ("pigeons"); **3:22**; John 1:32; 2:14, 16.

2:25 And, behold, there was a man in Jerusalem, whose name *was* Simeon; and the same man *was* just and devout, waiting for the consolation of Israel: and the Holy Ghost was upon him.

Just *dikaios* (1342), signifies "just," without prejudice or partiality, e.g., of the judgment of God, 2 Thess. 1:5, 6; of His judgments, Rev. 16:7; 19:2; of His character as Judge, 2 Tim. 4:8; Rev. 16:5; of His ways and doings, Rev. 15:3. In the following the RV substitutes "righteous" for the KJV "just"; Matt. 1:19; 13:49; 27:19, 24; Mark 6:20; **Luke 2:25**; **15:7**; **20:20**; **23:50**; John 5:30; Acts 3:14; 7:52; 10:22; 22:14; Rom. 1:17; 7:12; Gal. 3:11; Heb. 10:38; Jas. 5:6; 1 Pet. 3:18; 2 Pet. 2:7; 1 John 1:9; Rev. 15:3.

Devout *eulabes* (2126), lit., "taking hold well" (*eu*, "well," *lambano*, "to take hold"), primarily, "cautious," signifies in the NT, "careful as to the realization of the presence and claims of God, reverencing God, pious, devout", in **Luke 2:25**

it is said of Simeon, in Acts 2:5, of certain Jews; in 8:2, of those who bore Stephen's body to burial; of Ananias, 22:12. "In that mingled fear and love which, combined, constitute the piety of man toward God, the Old Testament placed its emphasis on the fear, the New places it on the love (though there was love in the fear of God's saints then, as there must be fear in their love now)," Trench, *Syn.*, Sec.xlviii.

Waiting *prosdechomai* (4327), "to look for" with a view to favorable reception, is rendered "to wait for" in Mark 15:43; **Luke 2:25**; **12:36**; **23:51**.

Consolation *paraklesis* (3874), means "a calling to one's side" (*para*, "beside," *kaleo*, "to call"); hence, either "an exhortation, or consolation, comfort," e.g., **Luke 2:25** (here "looking for the consolation of Israel" is equivalent to waiting for the coming of the Messiah); **6:24**; Acts 9:31; Rom. 15:4-5; 1 Cor. 14:3, "exhortation"; 2 Cor. 1:3, 4-7; 7:4, 7, 13; 2 Thess. 2:16; Philem. 7. In 2 Thess. 2:16 it combines encouragement with alleviation of grief. The RV changes "consolation" into "comfort," except in **Luke 2:25**; **6:24**; Acts 15:31; in Heb. 6:18, "encouragement"; in Acts 4:36, "exhortation," RV (KJV, "consolation").

2:26 And it was revealed unto him by the Holy Ghost, that he should not see death, before he had seen the Lord's Christ.

Revealed *chrematizo* (5537), "to give divine admonition, instruction, revelation," is translated "it had been revealed," in **Luke 2:26**.

Holy Ghost The "Holy Spirit" is spoken of under various titles in the NT ("Spirit" and "Ghost" are renderings of the same word, *pneuma;* the advantage of the rendering "Spirit" is that it can always be used, whereas "Ghost" always requires the word "Holy" prefixed.) In the following list the omission of the definite article marks its omission in the original (concerning this see below): "Spirit, Matt. 22:43; Eternal Spirit, Heb. 9:14; the Spirit, Matt. 4:1; Holy Spirit, Matt. 1:18; the Holy Spirit, Matt. 28:19; the Spirit, the Holy, Matt. 12:32; the Spirit of promise, the Holy, Eph. 1:13; Spirit of God, Rom. 8:9; Spirit of (the) living God, 2 Cor. 3:3; the Spirit of God, 1 Cor. 2:11; the Spirit of our God, 1 Cor. 6:11; the Spirit of God, the Holy, Eph. 4:30; the Spirit of glory and of God, 1 Pet. 4:14; the Spirit of Him that raised up Jesus from the dead (i.e., God), Rom. 8:11; the Spirit of your Father, Matt. 10:20; the Spirit of His Son, Gal. 4:6; Spirit of (the) Lord, Acts 8:39; the Spirit of (the) Lord, Acts 5:9; (the) Lord, (the) Spirit, 2 Cor. 3:18; the Spirit of Jesus, Acts 16:7; Spirit of Christ, Rom. 8:9; the Spirit of Jesus Christ, Phil. 1:19; Spirit of adoption, Rom. 8:15; the Spirit of truth, John 14:17; the Spirit of life, Rom. 8:2; the Spirit of grace, Heb. 10:29."

The use or absence of the article in the original where the "Holy Spirit" is spoken of cannot always be decided by grammatical rules, nor can the presence or absence of the article alone determine whether the reference is to the "Holy Spirit." Examples where the Person is meant when the article is absent are Matt. 22:43 (the article is used in Mark 12:36); Acts 4:25, RV (absent in some texts); 19:2, 6; Rom. 14:17; 1 Cor. 2:4; Gal. 5:25 (twice); 1 Pet. 1:2. Sometimes the absence is to be accounted for by the fact that *Pneuma* (like *Theos*) is substantially a proper name, e.g., in John 7:39. As a general rule the article is present where the subject of the teaching is the Personality of the Holy Spirit, e.g., John 14:26, where He is spoken of in distinction from the Father and the Son. See also 15:26 and cf. **Luke 3:22**.

In Gal. 3:3, in the phrase "having begun in the Spirit," it is difficult to say whether the reference is to the "Holy Spirit" or to the quickened spirit of the believer; that it possibly refers to the latter is not to be determined by the absence of the article, but by the contrast with "the flesh"; on the other hand, the contrast may be between the "Holy Spirit" who in the believer sets His seal on the perfect work of Christ, and the flesh which seeks to better itself by works of its own. There is no preposition before either noun, and if the reference is to the quickened spirit it cannot be dissociated from the operation of the "Holy Spirit." In Gal. 4:29 the phrase "after the Spirit" signifies "by supernatural power," in contrast to "after the flesh," i.e., "by natural power," and the reference must be to the "Holy Spirit"; so in 5:17.

The full title with the article before both *pneuma* and *hagios* (the "resumptive" use of the article), lit., "the Spirit the Holy," stresses the character of the Person, e.g., Matt. 12:32; Mark 3:29; 12:36; 13:11; **Luke 2:26**; **10:21** (RV); John 14:26; Acts 1:16; 5:3; 7:51; 10:44, 47; 13:2; 15:28; 19:6; 20:23, 28; 21:11; 28:25; Eph. 4:30; Heb. 3:7; 9:8; 10:15.

See *horao* (3708), with its aorist form *eidon*, "to see" (in a few places the KJV uses the verb "to behold"), is said (a) of bodily vision, e.g., Mark 6:38; John 1:18, 46; (b) of mental perception, e.g., Rom. 15:21; Col. 2:18; (c) of taking heed, e.g., Matt. 8:4; 1 Thess. 5:15; (d) of experience, as of death, **Luke 2:26**; Heb. 11:5; life, John 3:36; corruption, Acts 2:27; (e) of caring for, Matt. 27:4; Acts 18:15 (here the form *opsomai* is used).

2:27 And he came by the Spirit into the temple: and when the parents brought in the child Jesus, to do for him after the custom of the law,

Brought *eisago* (1521), "to bring in, into," **Luke 2:27**, etc.

Custom *ethizo* (1480), signifies "to accustom," or in the passive voice, "to be accustomed." In the participial form it is equivalent to a noun, "custom," **Luke 2:27**.

2:28 Then took he him up in his arms, and blessed God, and said,

Took *dechomai* (1209), "to receive by deliberate and ready reception of what is offered," is used of (a) taking with the hand, taking hold, taking hold of or up, e.g., **Luke 2:28**, RV, "he received (Him)," KJV, "took he (Him) up"; **16:6**, **7**; **22:17**; Eph. 6:17; (b) "receiving," said of a place "receiving" a person, of Christ into the Heavens, Acts 3:21; or of persons in giving access to someone as a visitor, e.g., John 4:45; 2 Cor. 7:15; Gal. 4:14; Col. 4:10; by way of giving hospitality, etc., e.g., Matt. 10:14, 40 (four times), 41 (twice); 18:5; Mark 6:11; 9:37; **Luke 9:5**, **48**, **53**; **10:8**, **10**; **16:4**; v. **9**, of reception, "into the eternal tabernacles," said of followers of Christ who have used "the mammon of unrighteousness" to render assistance to ("make ... friends of") others; of Rahab's reception of the spies, Heb. 11:31; of the reception, by the Lord, of the spirit of a departing believer, Acts 7:59; of "receiving" a gift, 2 Cor. 8:4 (in some mss.; RV follows those which omit it); of the favorable reception of testimony and teaching, etc., **Luke 8:13**; Acts 8:14; 11:1; 17:11; 1 Cor. 2:14; 2 Cor. 8:17; 1 Thess. 1:6; 2:13, where *paralambano* is used in the 1st part, "ye received," *dechomai* in the 2nd part, "ye accepted," RV (KJV, "received"), the former refers to the ear, the latter, adding the idea of appropriation, to the heart; Jas. 1:21; in 2 Thess. 2:10, "the love of the truth,:" i.e., love for the truth; cf. Matt. 11:14, "if ye are willing to receive it," an elliptical construction frequent in Greek writings; of "receiving," by way of bearing with, enduring, 2 Cor. 11:16; of "receiving" by way of getting, Acts 22:5; 28:21, of becoming partaker of benefits, Mark 10:15; **Luke 18:17**; Acts 7:38; 2 Cor. 6:1; 11:4 (last clause "did accept": cf. *lambano* in previous clauses); Phil. 4:18.

Arms *ankale* (43), used in the plural, in **Luke 2:28**, originally denoted "the curve, or the inner angle, of the arm." The word is derived from a term signifying "to bend, to curve"; the Eng. "angle" is connected.

Blessed *see* **Praised** at *Luke 1:64*.

2:29 Lord, now lettest thou thy servant depart in peace, according to thy word:

Lord *despotes* (1203), "a master, lord, one who possesses supreme authority," is used in personal address to God in **Luke 2:29**; Acts 4:24; Rev. 6:10; with reference to Christ, 2 Pet. 2:1; Jude 4; elsewhere it is translated "master," "masters," 1 Tim. 6:1, 2; 2 Tim. 2:21 (of Christ); Titus 2:9; 1 Pet. 2:18.

Depart *apoluo* (630), "to loose from" (*apo*), in the middle voice, signifies "to depart," **Luke 2:29**; Acts 23:22, RV, "let go"; 28:25.

Peace *see Luke 1:79*.

2:30 For mine eyes have seen thy salvation,

Salvation *soterion* (4992), the neuter of the adjective, is used as a noun in **Luke 2:30**; **3:6**, in each of which it virtually stands for the Savior; in Acts 28:28; in Eph. 6:17, where the hope of "salvation" is metaphorically described as "a helmet."

2:31 Which thou hast prepared before the face of all people;

Prepared *see* **Make ready** at *Luke 1:17*.

People *see Luke 1:21*.

2:32 A light to lighten the Gentiles, and the glory of thy people Israel.

Lighten *apokalupsis* (602), "an uncovering" (akin to *apokalupto*), "is used in the NT of (a) the drawing away by Christ of the veil of darkness covering the Gentiles, **Luke 2:32**; cf. Isa. 25:7; (b) 'the mystery,' the purpose of God in this age, Rom. 16:25; Eph. 3:3; (c) the communication of the knowledge of God to the soul, Eph. 1:17; (d) an expression of the mind of God for the instruction of the church, 1 Cor. 14:6, 26, for the instruction of the Apostle Paul, 2 Cor. 12:1, 7; Gal. 1:12, and for his guidance, Gal. 2:2; (e) the Lord Jesus Christ, to the saints at His Parousia, 1 Cor. 1:7, RV (KJV, 'coming'); 1 Pet. 1:7, RV (KJV, 'appearing'), 13; 4:13; (f) the Lord Jesus Christ when He comes to dispense the judgments of God, 2 Thess. 1:7; cf. Rom. 2:5; (g) the saints, to the creation, in association with Christ in His glorious reign, Rom. 8:19, RV, 'revealing' (KJV, 'manifestation'); (h) the symbolic forecast of the final judgments of God, Rev. 1:1 (hence the Greek title of the book, transliterated 'Apocalypse' and translated 'Revelation')."

2:33 And Joseph and his mother marvelled at those things which were spoken of him.

Marvelled *thaumazo* (2296), signifies "to wonder at, marvel"; the following are RV differences from the KJV: **Luke 2:33**, "were marveling" for "marveled"; **Luke 8:25** and **11:14**, "marveled" for "wondered"; **9:43**, "were marveling" for "wondered"; 2 Thess. 1:10, "marveled at" for "admired" (of the person of Christ at the time of the shining forth of His Parousia, at the Second Advent).

2:34 And Simeon blessed them, and said unto Mary his mother, Behold, this *child* is set for the fall and rising again of many in Israel; and for a sign which shall be spoken against;

This *houtos*, which is used (a) as a noun, "this one," followed by no noun, e.g., Matt. 3:17; translated in **Luke 2:34**, "this *child*"; in 1 Cor. 5:3, RV, "this thing." (KJV, "this deed").

Set *keimai* (2749), "to lie, to be laid" (used as the passive voice of *tithemi*), is translated "to be set," e.g., in Matt. 5:14 (of a city); **Luke 2:34** (of Christ); John 2:6 (of waterpots); 19:29 (of a vessel of vinegar); Phil. 1:16, RV (v. 17, KJV) (of the apostle Paul); Rev. 4:2 (of the throne in heaven).

Fall *ptosis* (4431), "a fall," is used (a) literally, of the "overthrow of a building," Matt. 7:27; (b) metaphorically, **Luke 2:34**, of the spiritual "fall" of those in Israel who would reject Christ; the word "again" in the KJV of the next clause is misleading; the "rising up" (RV) refers to those who would acknowledge and receive Him, a distinct class from those to whom the "fall" applies. The "fall" would be irretrievable, cf. (a); such a lapse as Peter's is not in view.

Rising *anastasis* (386), denotes (I) "a raising up," or "rising" (*ana*, "up," and *histemi*, "to cause to stand"), **Luke 2:34**, "the rising up"; the KJV "again" obscures the meaning; the Child would be like a stone against which many in Israel would stumble while many others would find in its strength and firmness a means of their salvation and spiritual life; (II) of "resurrection" from the dead, (a) of Christ, Acts 1:22; 2:31; 4:33; Rom. 1:4; 6:5; Phil. 3:10; 1 Pet. 1:3; 3:21; by metonymy, of Christ as the Author of "resurrection," John 11:25; (b) of those who are Christ's at His Parousia, **Luke 14:14**, "the resurrection of the just"; **Luke 20:33, 35, 36**; John 5:29 (1st part), "the resurrection of life"; 11:24; Acts 23:6; 24:15 (1st part); 1 Cor. 15:21, 42; 2 Tim. 2:18; Heb. 11:35 (2nd part); Rev. 20:5, "the first resurrection"; hence the insertion of "is" stands for the completion of this "resurrection," of which Christ was "the firstfruits"; 20:6; (c) of "the rest of the dead," after the Millennium (cf. Rev. 20:5); John 5:29 (2nd part), "the resurrection of judgment"; Acts 24:15 (2nd part), "of the unjust"; (d) of those who were raised in more immediate connection with Christ's "resurrection," and thus had part already in the first "resurrection," Acts 26:23 and Rom. 1:4 (in each of which "dead" is plural; see Matt. 27:52); (e) of the "resurrection" spoken of in general terms, Matt. 22:23; Mark 12:18; **Luke 20:27**; Acts 4:2; 17:18; 23:8; 24:21; 1 Cor. 15:12, 13; Heb. 6:2; (f) of those who were raised in OT times, to die again, Heb. 11:35 (1st part), lit., "out of resurrection."

Sign *see* ***Luke 2:12***.

Spoken against *antilego* (483), "to speak against," is so rendered in **Luke 2:34**; John 19:12; Acts 13:45, KJV (RV, "contradicted"); 28:19, 22.

2:35 (Yea, a sword shall pierce through thy own soul also,) that the thoughts of many hearts may be revealed.

Yea *kai* (2532), "and, even," is rendered "yea," e.g., **Luke 2:35**; John 16:32; 1 Cor. 2:10; 2 Cor. 8:3; in Acts 7:43, KJV (RV, "and").

Sword *rhomphaia* (4501), a word of somewhat doubtful origin, denoted "a Thracian weapon of large size," whether a sword or spear is not certain; it occurs (a) literally in Rev. 6:8; (b) metaphorically, as the instrument of anguish, **Luke 2:35**; of judgment, Rev. 1:16; 2:12, 16; 19:15, 21, probably figurative of the Lord's judicial utterances.

Pierce *dierchomai* (1330), "to go through," is translated "shall pierce through" in **Luke 2:35**.

dierchomai also denotes "to pass through or over," (a) of persons, e.g., Matt. 12:43, RV, "passeth (KJV, walketh) through"; Mark 4:35, KJV, "pass (RV, go) over"; **Luke 19:1, 4**; Heb. 4:14, RV, "passed through" (KJV "into"); Christ "passed through" the created heavens to the throne of God; (b) of things, e.g., Matt. 19:24, "to go through."

Soul *see* ***Luke 1:46***.

Thoughts *dialogismos* (1261), "reasoning," is translated "thoughts" in Matt. 15:19; Mark 7:21; **Luke 2:35**; **6:8**; in **5:22**, KJV, RV, "reasonings"; in **9:47**, KJV, RV, "reasoning," and **24:38**, KJV, RV, "reasonings"; so 1 Cor. 3:20; in **Luke 9:46**, KJV and RV, "reasoning"; "thoughts" in Jas. 2:4, KJV and RV. *See also* ***Luke 5:22***.

Revealed *apokalupto* (601), signifies "to uncover, unveil" (*apo*, "from," *kalupto*, "to cover"); both verbs are used in Matt. 10:26; in **Luke 12:2**, *apokalupto* is set in contrast to *sunkalupto*, "to cover up, cover completely." "The NT occurrences of this word fall under two heads, subjective and objective. The subjective use is that in which something is presented to the mind directly, as, (a) the meaning of the acts of God, Matt. 11:25; **Luke 10:21**; (b) the secret of the Person of the Lord Jesus, Matt. 16:17; John 12:38; (c) the character of God as Father, Matt. 11:27; **Luke 10:22**; (d) the will of God for the conduct of His children, Phil. 3:15; (e) the mind of God to the prophets of Israel, 1 Pet. 1:12, and of the Church, 1 Cor. 14:30; Eph. 3:5.

"The objective use is that in which something is presented to the senses, sight or hearing, as, referring to the past, (f) the truth declared to men in the gospel, Rom. 1:17; 1 Cor. 2:10; Gal. 3:23; (g) the Person of Christ to Paul on the way to Damascus, Gal. 1:16; (h) thoughts before hidden in the heart, **Luke 2:35**; referring to the future, (i) the coming in glory of the Lord Jesus, **Luke 17:30**; (j) the salvation and glory that await the believer, Rom. 8:18; 1 Pet. 1:5; 5:1; (k) the true value of service, 1 Cor. 3:13; (l) the wrath of God (at the Cross, against sin, and, at the revelation of the Lord Jesus, against the sinner), Rom. 1:18; (m) the Lawless One, 2 Thess. 2:3, 6, 8."

2:36 And there was one Anna, a prophetess, the daughter of Phanuel, of the tribe of Aser: she was of a great age, and had lived with an husband seven years from her virginity;

Prophetess *prophetis* (4398), the feminine of *prophetes*, is used of Anna, **Luke 2:36**; of the self-assumed title of "the woman Jezebel" in Rev. 2:20.

Tribe *phule* (5443), "a company of people united by kinship or habitation, a clan, tribe," is used (a) of the peoples of the earth, Matt. 24:30; in the following the RV has "tribe(-s)" for KJV, "kindred(-s)," Rev. 1:7; 5:9; 7:9; 11:9; 13:7; 14:6; (b) of the "tribes" of Israel, Matt. 19:28; **Luke 2:36**; **22:30**; Acts 13:21; Rom. 11:1; Phil. 3:5; Heb. 7:13, 14; Jas. 1:1; Rev. 5:5; 7:4-8; 21:12.

Age *hemera* (2250), "a day," is rendered "age" in **Luke 2:36**, "of a great age" (lit., "advanced in many days"). In **Luke 3:23** there is no word in the original corresponding to age. The phrase is simply "about thirty years." *See also* **Stricken** at ***Luke 1:7.***

Husband *aner* (435), denotes, in general, "a man, an adult male" (in contrast to *anthropos*, which generically denotes "a human being, male or female"); it is used of man in various relations, the context deciding the meaning; it signifies "a husband," e.g., Matt. 1:16, 19; Mark 10:12; **Luke 2:36**; **16:18**; John 4:16, 17, 18; Rom. 7:23.

Virginity *parthenia* (3932) occurs in **Luke 2:36**. In the Sept., Jer. 3:4.

2:37 And she *was* a widow of about fourscore and four years, which departed not from the temple, but served *God* with fastings and prayers night and day.

Widow *chera* (5503), Matt. 28:13 (in some texts); Mark 12:40, 42, 43; **Luke 2:37**; **4:25, 26**, lit., "a woman, a widow"; **7:12**; **18:3**, **5**; **20:47**; **21:2**, **3**; Acts 6:1; 9:39, 41; 1 Tim. 5:3 (twice), 4, 5, 11, 16 (twice); Jas. 1:27; 1 Tim. 5:9 refers to elderly "widows" (not an ecclesiastical "order"), recognized, for relief or maintenance by the church (cf. vv. 3, 16), as those who had fulfilled the conditions mentioned; where relief could be ministered by those who had relatives that were "widows" (a likely circumstance in large families), the church was not to be responsible; there is an intimation of the tendency to shelve individual responsibility at the expense of church funds. In Rev. 18:7, it is used figuratively of a city forsaken.

Fourscore *ogdoekonta* (3589), from *ogdoos*, "eighth," is found in **Luke 2:37**; **16:7**.

Departed *aphistemi* (868), in the active voice, used transitively, signifies "to cause to depart, to cause to revolt," Acts 5:37; used intransitively, "to stand off, or aloof, or to depart from anyone," **Luke 4:13**; **13:27**; Acts 5:38 ("refrain from"); 12:10; 15:38; 19:9; 22:29; 2 Cor. 12:8; metaphorically, "to fall away," 2 Tim. 2:19; in the middle voice, "to withdraw or absent oneself from," **Luke 2:37**; to "apostatize," **Luke 8:13**; 1 Tim. 4:1; Heb. 3:12, RV, "falling away."

Served In **Luke 2:37** the RV has "worshiping," for KJV, "served"; in Heb. 9:9, "the worshiper," for KJV, "that did the service."

Fastings *nesteia* (3521), "a fasting, fast" (from *ne*, a negative prefix, and *esthio*, "to eat"), is used (a) of voluntary abstinence from food, **Luke 2:37**; Acts 14:23 (some mss. have it in Matt. 17:21 and Mark 9:29); "fasting" had become a common practice among Jews, and was continued among Christians; in Acts 27:9, "the Fast" refers to the Day of Atonement, Lev. 16:29; that time of the year would be one of dangerous sailing; (b) of involuntary abstinence (perhaps voluntary is included), consequent upon trying circumstances, 2 Cor. 6:5; 11:27.

Prayers *see* **Prayer** at ***Luke 1:13.***

Night *see* ***Luke 2:8.***

2:38 And she coming in that instant gave thanks likewise unto the Lord, and spake of him to all them that looked for redemption in Jerusalem.

Coming *see* **Came** at ***Luke 2:9.***

Instant The word *hora*, "an hour," is translated "instant" in **Luke 2:38**, KJV; the RV renders it "hour."

Looked *prosdechomai* (4327), "to receive favorably," also means "to expect," and is rendered "to look for," e.g., in **Luke 2:38**; **23:51**; Acts 24:15, RV (KJV, "allow"); Titus 2:13; Jude 21.

Redemption *see* Redeemed at *Luke 1:68*.

2:39 And when they had performed all things according to the law of the Lord, they returned into Galilee, to their own city Nazareth.

Performed *teleo* (5055), "to finish, to bring to an end" (*telos*, "an end"), frequently signifies, not merely to terminate a thing, but to carry out a thing to the full. It is used especially in Revelation, where it occurs eight times, and is rendered "finish" in 10:7; 11:7, and in the RV of 15:1, which rightly translates it "(in them) is finished (the wrath of God)." So in v. 8; in 17:17, RV, "accomplish," and "finish" in 20:3, 5, 7; in **Luke 2:39**, RV, "accomplish," for KJV, performed.

Returned *epistrepho* (1994), "to turn about," or "towards," is translated "to return" in Matt. 12:44; 24:18; Mark 13:16, RV (KJV, "turn back again"); **Luke 2:39**; **8:55**, RV (KJV, "came again"); **17:31**; Acts 15:36, RV (KJV, "go again").

2:40 And the child grew, and waxed strong in spirit, filled with wisdom: and the grace of God was upon him.

Grew *see Luke 1:80*.

Strong *see Luke 1:80*.

Filled *pleroo* (4137), denotes (I) "to make full, to fill to the full"; in the passive voice, "to be filled, made full"; it is used (1) of things: a net, Matt. 13:48; a building, John 12:3; Acts 2:2; a city, Acts 5:28; needs, Phil. 4:19, KJV "supply," RV, "fulfill"; metaphorically, of valleys, **Luke 3:5**; figuratively, of a measure of iniquity, Matt. 23:32; (2) of persons: (a) of the members of the church, the body of Christ, as filled by Him, Eph. 1:23 ("all things in all the members"); 4:10; in 3:19, of their being filled "into" (*eis*), RV, "unto," KJV, "with" (all the fullness of God); of their being "made full" in Him, Col. 2:10 (RV, for KJV, "complete"); (b) of Christ Himself: with wisdom, in the days of His flesh, **Luke 2:40**; with joy, in His return to the Father, Acts 2:28; (c) of believers: with the Spirit, Eph. 5:18; with joy, Acts 13:52; 2 Tim. 1:4; with joy and peace, Rom. 15:13; with knowledge, Rom. 15:14; with comfort, 2 Cor. 7:4; with the fruits of righteousness, Phil. 1:11 (Gk. "fruit"); with the knowledge of God's will, Col. 1:9; with abundance through material supplies by fellow believers, Phil. 4:18; (d) of the hearts of believers as the seat of emotion and volition, John 16:6 (sorrow); Acts 5:3 (deceitfulness); (e) of the unregenerate who refuse recognition of God, Rom. 1:29; (II) "to accomplish, complete, fulfill.

Wisdom *sophia* (4678), is used with reference to (a) God, Rom. 11:33; 1 Cor. 1:21, 24; 2:7; Eph. 3:10; Rev. 7:12; (b) Christ, Matt. 13:54; Mark 6:2; **Luke 2:40, 52**; 1 Cor. 1:30; Col. 2:3; Rev. 5:12; (c) "wisdom" personified, Matt. 11:19; **Luke 7:35**; **11:49**; (d) human "wisdom" (1) in spiritual things, **Luke 21:15**; Acts 6:3, 10; 7:10; 1 Cor. 2:6 (1st part); 12:8; Eph. 1:8, 17; Col. 1:9, RV, "(spiritual) wisdom," 28; 3:16; 4:5; Jas. 1:5; 3:13, 17; 2 Pet. 3:15; Rev. 13:18; 17:9; (2) in the natural sphere, Matt. 12:42; **Luke 11:31**; Acts 7:22; 1 Cor. 1:17, 19, 20, 21 (twice), 22; 2:1, 4, 5, 6 (2nd part), 13; 3:19; 2 Cor. 1:12; Col. 2:23; (3) in its most debased form, Jas. 3:15, "earthly, sensual, devilish" (marg., "demoniacal").

Grace *charis* (5485), has various uses, (a) objective, that which bestows or occasions pleasure, delight, or causes favorable regard; it is applied, e.g., to beauty, or gracefulness of person, **Luke 2:40**; act, 2 Cor. 8:6, or speech, **Luke 4:22**, RV, "words of grace" (KJV, "gracious words"); Col. 4:6; (b) subjective, (1) on the part of the bestower, the friendly disposition from which the kindly act proceeds, graciousness, loving-kindness, goodwill generally, e.g., Acts 7:10; especially with reference to the divine favor or "grace," e.g., Acts 14:26; in this respect there is stress on its freeness and universality, its spontaneous character, as in the case of God's redemptive mercy, and the pleasure or joy He designs for the recipient; thus it is set in contrast with debt, Rom. 4:4, 16, with works, 11:6, and with law, John 1:17; see also, e.g., Rom. 6:14, 15; Gal. 5:4; (2) on the part of the receiver, a sense of the favor bestowed, a feeling of gratitude, e.g., Rom. 6:17 ("thanks"); in this respect it sometimes signifies "to be thankful," e.g., **Luke 17:9** ("doth he thank the servant?" lit., "hath he thanks to"); 1 Tim. 1:12; (c) in another objective sense, the effect of "grace," the spiritual state of those who have experienced its exercise, whether (1) a state of "grace," e.g., Rom. 5:2; 1 Pet. 5:12; 2 Pet. 3:18, or (2) a proof thereof in practical effects, deeds of "grace," e.g., 1 Cor. 16:3, RV, "bounty" (KJV, "liberality"); 2 Cor. 8:6, 19 (in 2 Cor. 9:8 it means the sum of earthly blessings); the power and equipment for ministry, e.g., Rom. 1:5; 12:6; 15:15; 1 Cor. 3:10; Gal. 2:9; Eph. 3:2, 7.

2:41 Now his parents went to Jerusalem every year at the feast of the passover.

Every The preposition *kata*, "down," is sometimes found governing a noun, in the sense of "every," e.g., **Luke 2:41**, "every year"; **16:19**, "every day"; Heb. 9:25, "every year" (RV, "year by year"); so 10:3. This construction sometimes signifies "in every ...," e.g., Acts 14:23, "in every church"; 15:21, "in every city"; so 20:23; Titus 1:5; Acts 22:19, "in every synagogue" (plural); Acts 8:3 "(into) every house." In **Luke 8:1** the phrase means "throughout every city," as in the KJV; in v. **4** "of every city," RV. In Acts 5:42 the RV renders *kat' oikon* "at home," for KJV, "in every house"; in 2:46, for KJV, "from house to house" (marg., "at home"). In Acts 15:21 (last part) the adjective *pas*, "all," is placed between the preposition and the noun for the sake of emphasis. In Acts 26:11, *kata*, followed by the plural of *pas* and the article before the noun, is rendered "in all the synagogues," RV, for KJV, "in every synagogue." The presence of the article confirms the RV.

Year *etos* (2094), is used (a) to mark a point of time at or from which events take place, e.g., **Luke 3:1** (dates were frequently reckoned from the time when a monarch began to reign); in Gal. 3:17 the time of the giving of the Law is stated as 430 "years" after the covenant of promise given to Abraham; there is no real discrepancy between this and Ex. 12:40; the apostle is not concerned with the exact duration of the interval, it certainly was not less than 430 "years"; the point of the argument is that the period was very considerable; Gal. 1:18 and 2:1 mark events in Paul's life; as to the former the point is that three "years" elapsed before he saw any of the apostles; in 2:1 the 14 "years" may date either from his conversion or from his visit to Peter mentioned in 1:18; the latter seems the more natural (for a full discussion of the subject see *Notes on Galatians* by Hogg and Vine, pp. 55ff.); (b) to mark a space of time, e.g., Matt. 9:20; **Luke 12:19**; **13:11**; John 2:20; Acts 7:6, where the 400 "years" mark not merely the time that Israel was in bondage in Egypt, but the time that they sojourned or were strangers there (the RV puts a comma after the word "evil"); the Genevan Version renders Gen. 15:13 "thy posterity shall inhabit a strange land for 400 years"; Heb. 3:17; Rev. 20:2-7; (c) to date an event from one's birth, e.g., Mark 5:42; **Luke 2:42**; **3:23**; John 8:57; Acts 4:22; 1 Tim. 5:9; (d) to mark recurring events, **Luke 2:41** (with *kata*, used distributively); **13:7**; (e) of an unlimited number, Heb. 1:12.

2:42 And when he was twelve years old, they went up to Jerusalem after the custom of the feast.

Years *see* Year at *Luke 2:41.*

Custom *ethos* (1485), denotes (a) "a custom, usage, prescribed by law," Acts 6:14; 15:1; 25:16; "a rite or ceremony," **Luke 2:42**; (b) a "custom, habit, manner," **Luke 22:39**; John 19:40; Heb. 10:25 (KJV, "manner").

2:43 And when they had fulfilled the days, as they returned, the child Jesus tarried behind in Jerusalem; and Joseph and his mother knew not *of it*.

Fulfilled *teleioo* (5048), "to bring to an end, fulfill," is rendered "to fulfill," of days. **Luke 2:43**; of the Scripture, John 19:28.

Returned *see Luke 1:56.*

Child *pais* (3816), signifies (a) "a child in relation to descent," (b) "a boy or girl in relation to age," (c) "a servant, attendant, maid, in relation to condition." As an instance of (a) see Matt. 21:15, "children," and Acts 20:12 (RV, "lad"). In regard to (b) the RV has "boy" in Matt. 17:18 and **Luke 9:42**. In **Luke 2:43** it is used of the Lord Jesus. In regard to (c), see Matt. 8:6, 8, 13, etc. As to (a) note Matt. 2:16, RV, male children.

Tarried behind *hupomeno* (5278), lit., "to abide under" (*hupo*, "under"), signifies "to remain in a place instead of leaving it, to stay behind," e.g., **Luke 2:43**; Acts 17:14; or "to persevere," Matt. 10:22; 24:13; Mark 13:13; in each of which latter it is used with the phrase "unto the end"; or "to endure bravely and trustfully," e.g., Heb. 12:2-3, 7, suggesting endurance under what would be burdensome. See also Jas. 1:12; 5:11; 1 Pet. 2:20. Cf., *makrothumeo*, "to be longsuffering."

2:44 But they, supposing him to have been in the company, went a day's journey; and they sought him among *their* kinsfolk and acquaintance.

Company *sunodia* (4923), lit., "a way or journey together" (*sun*, "with," *hodos*, "a way"), denotes, by metonymy, "a company of travelers"; in **Luke 2:44**, of the company from which Christ was missed by Joseph and Mary (Eng., synod).

Journey *hodos* (3598), "a way, path, road," used of a traveler's way, a "journey," is rendered "journey" in Matt. 10:13; Mark 6:8; **Luke 2:44**, "a day's journey" (probably to Beeroth, six miles north of Jerusalem); **9:3**; **11:6**; Acts 1:12, "a Sabbath day's journey," i.e., the journey which a Jew was allowed to take on the Sabbath, viz., about 2,000 yards or cubits (estimates vary). The regulation was not a Mosaic enactment, but a rabbinical tradition, based upon an exposition of Exod. 16:29, and a comparison of the width of the suburb of a Levitical city as enjoined in Num. 35:4, 5, and the distance between the ark and the people at the crossing of the Jordan, Josh. 3:4.

Sought *anazeteo* (327), "to seek carefully," is used of searching for human beings, difficulty in the effort being implied **Luke 2:44, 45**, Acts 11:25; numerous illustrations of this particular meaning in the papyri are given by Moulton and Milligan. In the Sept., Job 3:4; 10:6.

Kinsfolk *sungeneus* (4773), is used in Mark 6:4, "kin," and **Luke 2:44**, "kinsfolk." *See also* **Cousin** at ***Luke 1:36***.

Acquaintance *gnostos* (1110), from *ginosko*, "to know," signifies "known, or knowable"; hence, "one's acquaintance"; it is used in this sense, in the plural, in **Luke 2:44** and **23:49**.

2:45 And when they found him not, they turned back again to Jerusalem, seeking him.

Turned *hupostrepho* (5290), is used intransitively of "turning back, behind" (*hupo*), e.g., **Luke 17:15**, "turned back"; in **2:45**, RV, "returned". *See also* **Returned** at ***Luke 1:56***.

Seeking *see* **Sought** at ***Luke 2:44***.

2:46 And it came to pass, that after three days they found him in the temple, sitting in the midst of the doctors, both hearing them, and asking them questions.

Sitting *kathezomai* (2516), "to sit (down)," is used in Matt. 26:55; **Luke 2:46**; John 4:6; 11:20; 20:12; Acts 6:15.

Doctors *didaskalos* (1320), "a teacher" (from *didasko*, "to teach"), is frequently rendered "Master" in the four Gospels, as a title of address to Christ, e.g., Matt. 8:19; Mark 4:38 (there are more instances in Luke than in the other Gospels); John 1:38, where it interprets "Rabbi"; 20:16, where it interprets "Rabboni." It is used by Christ of Himself in Matt. 23:8 and John 13:13-14; by others concerning Him, Matt. 17:24; 26:18; Mark 5:35; 14:14; **Luke 8:49**; **22:11**; John 11:28. In John 3:10, the Lord uses it in addressing Nicodemus, RV, "the teacher" (KJV, "a master"), where the article does not specify a particular "teacher," but designates the member of a class; for the class see **Luke 2:46**, "the doctors" (RV, marg., "teachers"). It is used of the relation of a disciple to his "master," in Matt. 10:24, 25; **Luke 6:40**. It is not translated "masters" in the rest of the NT, save in the KJV of Jas. 3:1 "(be not many) masters," where obviously the RV "teachers" is the meaning.

Asking *eperotao* (1905), is frequently used in the Synoptic Gospels, but only twice in the Gospel of John, 18:7, 21. In Rom. 10:20 it is rendered "asked of" (KJV, "asked after"). The more intensive character of the "asking" may be observed in **Luke 2:46**; **3:14**; **6:9**; **17:20**; **20:21**, **27**, **40**; **22:64**, **23:3**, **6**, **9**. In Matt. 16:1, it virtually signifies to demand (its meaning in later Greek).

Questions *eperotao* (1905), "to ask," is translated "asked ... a question," in Matt. 22:35, 41; in **Luke 2:46**, "asking ... questions"; "questioned" in **Luke 23:9**.

2:47 And all that heard him were astonished at his understanding and answers.

Understanding *sunesis* (4907), akin to *suniemi*, "to set together, to understand," denotes (a) "the understanding, the mind or intelligence," Mark 12:33; (b) "understanding, reflective thought," **Luke 2:47**; 1 Cor. 1:19, RV, "prudence", Eph. 3:4, RV (KJV, "knowledge"); Col. 1:9; 2:2; 2 Tim. 2:7.

Answers *apokrisis* (612), lit., "a separation or distinction," is the regular word for "answer," **Luke 2:47**; **20:26**; John 1:22 and 19:9.

2:48 And when they saw him, they were amazed: and his mother said unto him, Son, why hast thou thus dealt with us? behold, thy father and I have sought thee sorrowing.

Amazed *ekplesso* (1605), from *ek*, "out of," *plesso*, "to strike," lit., "to strike out," signifies "to be exceedingly struck in mind, to be astonished" (*ek*, intensive). The English "astonish" should be used for this verb, and "amaze" for *existemi*, as in the RV; see Matt. 19:25; **Luke 2:48**; **9:43**.

Thus *see* ***Luke 1:25***.

Dealt with *see* ***Luke 1:25***.

Sorrowing *odunao* (3600), in the middle and passive voices, signifies "to suffer pain, be in anguish, be greatly distressed" (akin to *odune*, "pain, distress"); it is rendered "sorrowing" in **Luke 2:48**; in **16:24-25**, RV, "in anguish," for KJV, "tormented"; in Acts 20:38, "sorrowing."

2:49 And he said unto them, How is it that ye sought me? wist ye not that I must be about my Father's business?

Wist *oida* (1492), "to know," in the pluperfect tense (with imperfect meaning) is rendered "wist" (the past tense of the verb "to wit") in Mark 9:6; 14:40; **Luke 2:49**; John 5:13; Acts 12:9; 23:5.

Must *dei* (1163), an impersonal verb, signifying "it is necessary" or "one must," "one ought," is found most frequently in the Gospels, Acts and Revelation, and is used (a) of a necessity lying in the nature of the case, e.g., John 3:30; 2 Tim. 2:6; (b) of necessity brought about by circumstances, e.g., Matt. 26:35, RV, "must," KJV, "should"; John 4:4; Acts 27:21, "should"; 2 Cor. 11:30; in the case of Christ, by reason of the Father's will, e.g., **Luke 2:49**; **19:5**; (c) of necessity as to what is required that something may be brought about, e.g., **Luke 12:12**, "ought"; John 3:7; Acts 9:6; 1 Cor. 11:19; Heb. 9:26; (d) of a necessity of law, duty, equity, e.g., Matt. 18:33, "shouldest"; 23:23, "ought"; **Luke 15:32**, "it was meet"; Acts 15:5, "it is needful" (RV); Rom. 1:27, RV, "was due," KJV, "was meet" (of a recompense due by the law of God); frequently requiring the rendering "ought," e.g., Rom. 8:26; 12:3; 1 Cor. 8:2; (e) of necessity arising from the determinate will and counsel of God, e.g., Matt. 17:10; 24:6; 26:54; 1 Cor. 15:53, especially regarding the salvation of men through the death, resurrection and ascension of Christ, e.g., John 3:14; Acts 3:21; 4:12.

Business *idios* (2398), expresses "what is one's own" (hence, Eng. "idiot," in a changed sense, lit., "a person with his own opinions"); the neuter plural with the artide (*ta idia*) signifies "one's own things." In 1 Thess. 4:11, the noun is not expressed in the original but is supplied in the English versions by "business," "your own business." For the same phrase, otherwise expressed, see John 1:11, "His own (things)"; 16:32 and 19:27, "his own (home)"; Acts 21:6, "home." In **Luke 2:49**, the phrase "in My Father's house" (RV), "about My Father's business" (KJV), is, lit., "in the (things, the neuter plural of the article) of My Father."

2:50 And they understood not the saying which he spake unto them.

Saying *see* Sayings at *Luke 1:65.*

2:51 And he went down with them, and came to Nazareth, and was subject unto them: but his mother kept all these sayings in her heart.

Subject *hupotasso* (5293), primarily a military term, "to rank under" (*hupo*, "under," *tasso*, "to arrange"), denotes (a) "to put in subjection, to subject," Rom. 8:20 (twice); in the following, the RV, has to subject for KJV, "to put under," 1 Cor. 15:27 (thrice), 28 (3rd clause); Eph. 1:22; Heb. 2:8 (4th clause); in 1 Cor. 15:28 (1st clause), for KJV "be subdued"; in Phil. 3:21, for KJV, "subdue"; in Heb. 2:5, KJV, "hath ... put in subjection"; (b) in the middle or passive voice, to subject oneself, to obey, be subject to, **Luke 2:51**; **10:17, 20**; Rom. 8:7; 10:3, RV, "did (not) subject themselves" [KJV, "have (not) submitted themselves"]; 13:1, 5; 1 Cor. 14:34, RV, "be in subjection" (KJV, "be under obedience"); 15:28 (2nd clause); 16:16 RV, "be in subjection" (KJV, "submit, etc."); so Col. 3:18; Eph. 5:21, RV, "subjecting yourselves" (KJV, "submitting, etc."); v. 22, RV in italics, according to the best texts; v. 24, "is subject"; Titus 2:5, 9, RV, "be in subjection" (KJV, "be obedient"); 3:1, RV, "to be in subjection" (KJV, "to be subject"); Heb. 12:9, "be in subjection"; Jas. 4:7, RV, "be subject" (KJV, "submit yourselves"); so 1 Pet. 2:13; v. 18, RV, "be in subjection"; so 3:1, KJV and RV; v. 5, similarly; 3:22, "being made subject"; 5:5, RV, "be subject" (KJV, "submit yourselves"); in some texts in the 2nd part, as KJV.

Kept *diatereo* (1301), "to keep carefully," is said of "the mother of Jesus," in keeping His sayings in her heart, **Luke 2:51**, and of the command of the apostles and elders in Jerusalem to gentile converts in the churches to "keep" themselves from the evils mentioned in Acts 15:29. *See also* ***Luke 2:19.***

Sayings *see Luke 1:65.*

2:52 And Jesus increased in wisdom and stature, and in favour with God and man.

Increased *prokopto* (4278), is translated by the verb "to increase" in **Luke 2:52** and in the KJV of 2 Tim. 2:16 (RV, "will proceed further").

Wisdom *see Luke 2:40.*

Stature *helikia* (2244), primarily "an age," as a certain length of life, came to mean (a) "a particular time of life," as when a person is said to be "of age," John 9:21, 23, or beyond a certain stage of life, Heb. 11:11; (b) elsewhere only "of stature," e.g., Matt. 6:27; **Luke 2:52**; **12:25**; **19:3**; Eph. 4:13. Some regard Matt. 6:27 and **Luke 12:25** as coming under (a). It is to be distinguished from *aion* and *genea*, since it has to do simply with matters relating to an individual, either his time of life or his height.

Favour *see Luke 1:30.*

Chapter 3

3:1 Now in the fifteenth year of the reign of Tiberius Caesar, Pontius Pilate being governor of Judaea, and Herod being tetrarch of Galilee, and his brother Philip tetrarch of Ituraea and of the region of Trachonitis, and Lysanias the tetrarch of Abilene,

Fifteenth The corresponding ordinal numeral *pentekaidekatos*, "fifteenth" (lit., "five and tenth") is found in **Luke 3:1**, where Luke dates the reign of Tiberias from the period of his joint rule with Augustus.

Year *see Luke 2:41*.

Reign In **Luke 3:1**, *hegemonia*, "rule," is rendered "reign."

Governor *see Luke 2:2*.

Tetrarch *tetraarcheo* or *tetrarcheo* (5075), "to be a tetrarch," occurs in **Luke 3:1** (thrice), of Herod Antipas, his brother Philip and Lysanias. Antipas and Philip each inherited a fourth part of his father's dominions. Inscriptions bear witness to the accuracy of Luke's details.

Region *chora* (5561), "a space lying between two limits, a country, land," is translated "region" in Matt. 4:16; **Luke 3:1**; Acts 8:1; 13:49; 16:6; 18:23, RV. In the last three passages it has the technical sense of a subdivision of a Roman province, Lat. *regio*. It is also used with the meaning "land," (a) of a country, region, e.g., Mark 1:5; **Luke 15:14**; (b) of property, **Luke 12:16**, "ground."

3:2 Annas and Caiaphas being the high priests, the word of God came unto John the son of Zacharias in the wilderness.

Priests *archiereus* (749), designates ... "the high priests" of the Levitical order, frequently called "chief priests" in the NT, and including "ex-high priests" and members of "high priestly" families, e.g., Matt. 2:4; 16:21; 20:18; 21:15; in the singular, a "high priest," e.g., Abiathar, Mark 2:26; Annas and Caiaphas, **Luke 3:2**, where the RV rightly has "in the high priesthood of A. and C." (cf. Acts 4:6). As to the combination of the two in this respect, Annas was the "high priest" from AD 7-14, and, by the time referred to, had been deposed for some years; his son-in-law, Caiaphas, the fourth "high priest" since his deposition, was appointed about AD 24. That Annas was still called the "high priest" is explained by the facts (1) that by the Mosaic law the high priesthood was held for life, Num. 35:25; his deposition was the capricious act of the Roman procurator, but he would still be regarded legally and religiously as "high priest" by the Jews; (2) that he probably still held the office of deputy-president of the Sanhedrin (cf. 2 Kings 25:18); (3) that he was a man whose age, wealth and family connections gave him a preponderant influence, by which he held the real sacerdotal power; indeed at this time the high priesthood was in the hands of a clique of some half dozen families; the language of the writers of the Gospels is in accordance with this, in attributing the high priesthood rather to a caste than a person; (4) the "high priests" were at that period mere puppets of Roman authorities who deposed them at will, with the result that the title was used more loosely than in former days.

The divine institution of the priesthood culminated in the "high priest," it being his duty to represent the whole people, e.g., Lev. 4:15, 16; ch. 16. The characteristics of the Aaronic "high priests" are enumerated in Heb. 5:1-4; 8:3; 9:7, 25; in some mss., 10:11 (RV, marg.); 13:11.

3:3 And he came into all the country about Jordan, preaching the baptism of repentance for the remission of sins;

Country *perichoros* (4066), *peri*, "around," and *chora*, signifies "country round about," **Luke 8:37**; "country about," **Luke 3:3**, KJV (RV, "region round about"); in Matt. 14:35 and **Luke 4:37**, KJV, "country round about" (RV, "region round about"); Matt. 3:5; Mark 1:28; **Luke 4:14**; **7:17**; Acts 14:6.

Remission *see Luke 1:77*.

3:4 As it is written in the book of the words of Esaias the prophet, saying, The voice of one crying in the wilderness, Prepare ye the way of the Lord, make his paths straight.

Book *biblos* (976), (Eng. "Bible") was the inner part, or rather the cellular substance, of the stem of the papyrus (Eng. "paper"). It came to denote the paper made from this bark in Egypt, and then a written "book," roll, or volume. It is used in referring to "books" of Scripture, the "book," or scroll, of Matthew's Gospel, Matt. 1:1; the Pentateuch, as the "book" of Moses, Mark 12:26; Isaiah, as "the book of the words of Isaiah," **Luke 3:4**; the Psalms, **Luke 20:42** and Acts 1:20; "the prophets," Acts 7:42; to "the Book of Life," Phil. 4:3; Rev. 3:5; 20:15. Once only it is used of secular writings, Acts 19:19.

Crying *boao* (994), signifies (a) "to raise a cry," whether of joy, Gal. 4:27, or vexation, Acts 8:7; (b) "to speak with a strong voice," Matt. 3:3; Mark 1:3; 15:34; **Luke 3:4**; **9:38** (some mss. have *anaboao* here); John 1:23; Acts 17:6; 25:24 (some mss. have *epiboao* here); (c) "to cry out for help," **Luke 18:7, 38.**

Prepare *see* **Make ready** at *Luke 1:17.*

Paths *tribos* (5147), "a beaten track" (akin to *tribo*, "to rub, wear down"), "a path," is used in Matt. 3:3; Mark 1:3; **Luke 3:4.**

Straight *euthus* (2117), "direct, straight, right," is translated "straight," figuratively, of the paths of the Lord, Matt. 3:3; Mark 1:3; **Luke 3:4**; in v. **5** of the rectification of the crooked, with reference to moral transformation; in Acts 9:11, the name of a street in Damascus, still one of the principal thoroughfares.

3:5 Every valley shall be filled, and every mountain and hill shall be brought low; and the crooked shall be made straight, and the rough ways *shall be* made smooth;

Valley *pharanx* (5327), denotes "a ravine or valley," sometimes figurative of "a condition of loneliness and danger" (cf. Ps. 23:4); the word occurs in **Luke 3:5** (from the Sept. of Isa. 40:4).

Filled *see Luke 2:40.*

Mountain *oros* (3735), is used (a) without specification, e.g., **Luke 3:5** (distinct from *bounos*, "a hill"); John 4:20; (b) of "the Mount of Transfiguration," Matt. 17:1, 9; Mark 9:2, 9; **Luke 9:28, 37** (KJV, "hill"); 2 Pet. 1:18; (c) of "Zion," Heb. 12:22; Rev. 14:1; (d) of "Sinai," Acts 7:30, 38; Gal. 4:24, 25; Heb. 8:5; 12:20; (e) of "the Mount of Olives," Matt. 21:1; 24:3; Mark 11:1; 13:3; **Luke 19:29, 37; 22:39**; John 8:1; Acts 1:12; (f) of "the hill districts as distinct from the lowlands," especially of the hills above the Sea of Galilee, e.g., Matt. 5:1; 8:1; 18:12; Mark 5:5; (g) of "the mountains on the east of Jordan" and "those in the land of Ammon" and "the region of Petra," etc., Matt. 24:16; Mark 13:14; **Luke 21:21**; (h) proverbially, "of overcoming difficulties, or accomplishing great things," 1 Cor. 13:2; cf. Matt. 17:20; 21:21; Mark 11:23; (i) symbolically, of "a series of the imperial potentates of the Roman dominion, past and future," Rev. 17:9.

Hill *bounos* (1015), "a mound, heap, height," is translated "hill" in **Luke 3:5**, "hills" in **23:30.**

Brought low *tapeinoo* (5013), signifies "to make low, bring low," (a) of bringing to the ground, making level, reducing to a plain, as in **Luke 3:5**; (b) metaphorically in the active voice, to bring to a humble condition, "to abase," 2 Cor. 11:7, and in the passive, "to be abased," Phil. 4:12; in Matt. 23:12; **Luke 14:11; 18:14**, the KJV has "shall be abased," the RV "shall be humbled." It is translated "humble yourselves" in the middle voice sense in Jas. 4:10; 1 Pet. 5:6; "humble," in Matt. 18:4; 2 Cor. 12:21 and Phil. 2:8. Cf., *tapeinos*, "lowly," *tapeinosis*, "humiliation," and *tapeinophrosune*, "humility."

Crooked *skolios* (4646), "curved, crooked," was especially used (a) of a way, **Luke 3:5**, with spiritual import (see Prov. 28:18, Sept.); it is set in contrast to *orthos* and *euthus*, "straight"; (b) metaphorically, of what is morally "crooked," perverse, froward, of people belonging to a particular generation, Acts 2:40 (KJV, "untoward"); Phil. 2:15; of tyrannical or unjust masters, 1 Pet. 2:18, "froward"; in this sense it is set in contrast to *agathos*, "good."

Made In **Luke 3:5**, KJV (3rd statement), the future tense of *eimi*, "to be," is translated "shall be made" (RV, "shall become"); in the next sentence there is nothing in the original representing "*shall be* made".

Straight *see Luke 3:4.*

Rough *trachus* (5138), "rough, uneven," is used of paths, **Luke 3:5**; of rocky places, Acts 27:29.

Smooth *leois* (3006), "smooth," occurs in **Luke 3:5**, figurative of the change in Israel from self-righteousness, pride and other forms of evil, to repentance, humility and submission. In the Sept., Gen. 27:11; 1 Sam. 17:40; Prov. 2:20; 12:13; 26:23; Isa. 40:4.

3:6 And all flesh shall see the salvation of God.

Salvation *see Luke 2:30.*

3:7 Then said he to the multitude that came forth to be baptized of him, O generation of vipers, who hath warned you to flee from the wrath to come?

Generation *gennema* (1081), akin to *gennao*, "to beget," denotes "the offspring of men and animals," Matt. 3:7; 12:34; 23:33; **Luke 3:7**, RV, "offspring" (KJV, "generation").

Vipers *echidna* (2191), is probably a generic term for "poisonous snakes." It is rendered "viper" in the NT, (a) of the actual creature, Acts 28:3; (b) metaphorically in Matt. 3:7; 12:34; 23:33; **Luke 3:7.**

Warned *hupodeiknumi* (5263), primarily, "to show secretly" (*hupo*, "under," *deiknumi*, "to show"), "to show by tracing out"; hence, "to teach, to show by example," Acts 20:35, RV, "I gave you an example," for KJV, "I showed you." Elsewhere, "to warn," Matt. 3:7; **Luke 3:7; 12:5**, RV, for KJV, "forewarn"; "to show," **Luke 6:47**; Acts 9:16.

Wrath *orge* (3709), originally any "natural impulse, or desire, or disposition," came to signify "anger," as the strongest of all passions. It is used of the wrath of man, Eph. 4:31; Col. 3:8; 1 Tim. 2:8; Jas. 1:19-20; the displeasure of human governments, Rom. 13:4-5; the sufferings of the Jews at the hands of the Gentiles, **Luke 21:23**; the terrors of the Law, Rom. 4:15; "the anger" of the Lord Jesus, Mark 3:5; God's "anger" with Israel in the wilderness, in a quotation from the OT, Heb. 3:11; 4:3; God's present "anger" with the Jews nationally, Rom. 9:22; 1 Thess. 2:16; His present "anger" with those who disobey the Lord Jesus in His gospel, John 3:36; God's purposes in judgment, Matt. 3:7; **Luke 3:7**; Rom. 1:18; 2:5, 8; 3:5; 5:9; 12:19; Eph. 2:3; 5:6; Col. 3:6; 1 Thess. 1:10; 5:9.

3:8 Bring forth therefore fruits worthy of repentance, and begin not to say within yourselves, We have Abraham to *our* father: for I say unto you, That God is able of these stones to raise up children unto Abraham.

Worthy *axios* (514), has the meaning of being of "weight, value, worth"; also "befitting, becoming, right on the ground of fitness," e.g., Matt. 3:8, KJV, "meet" (RV, "worthy"); so Acts 26:20; **Luke 3:8** ("worthy"); **23:41** ("due reward").

Repentance *metanoia* (3341), "afterthought, change of mind, repentance," is used of "repentance" from sin or evil, except in Heb. 12:17, where the word "repentance" seems to mean, not simply a change of Isaac's mind, but such a change as would reverse the effects of his own previous state of mind. Esau's birthright-bargain could not be recalled; it involved an irretrievable loss. As regards "repentance" from sin, (a) the requirement by God on man's part is set forth, e.g., in Matt. 3:8; **Luke 3:8**; Acts 20:21; 26:20; (b) the mercy of God in giving "repentance" or leading men to it is set forth, e.g., in Acts 5:31; 11:18; Rom. 2:4; 2 Tim. 2:25. The most authentic mss. omit the word in Matt. 9:13 and Mark 2:17, as in the RV.

Yourselves The reflexive pronoun "yourselves" represents the various plural forms of the reflexive pronoun *heautou* (frequently governed by some preposition), e.g., Matt. 3:9; 16:8; 23:31; 25:9; Mark 9:50; **Luke 3:8**; **12:33**, **57**; **16:9**; **21:30**, "of your own selves"; **21:34**; Acts 5:35; in Rom. 11:25, "in your own (conceits)," lit., "in (*en;* some texts have *para,* 'among') yourselves"; so 12:16 (with *para*); 1 Pet. 4:8; Jude 20, 21; in Eph. 5:19, RV, "one to another" (KJV, and RV marg., "to yourselves").

Raise *see* **Raised** at ***Luke 1:69***.

3:9 And now also the axe is laid unto the root of the trees: every tree therefore which bringeth not forth good fruit is hewn down, and cast into the fire.

Axe *axine* (513), "an axe," akin to *agnumi*, "to break," is found in Matt. 3:10 and **Luke 3:9**.

Laid *keimai* (2749), "to be laid, to lie," is used as the passive voice of *tithemi*, "to put," and is translated by some part of the verb "to be laid" in Matt. 3:10 and **Luke 3:9**, of an axe; **Luke 12:19**, of goods; John 21:9, where the verb has been omitted from the translation, after the words "a fire of coals"; 1 Cor. 3:11, of Christ, as a foundation.

Root *rhiza* (4491), is used (a) in the natural sense, Matt. 3:10; 13:6, 21; Mark 4:6, 17, 11:20; **Luke 3:9**; **8:13**; (b) metaphorically (1) of "cause, origin, source," said of persons, ancestors, Rom. 11:16, 17, 18 (twice); of things, evils, 1 Tim. 6:10, RV, of the love of money as a "root" of all "kinds of evil" (marg., "evils", KJV, "evil"); bitterness, Heb. 12:15; (2) of that which springs from a "root," a shoot, said of offspring, Rom. 15:12; Rev. 5:5; 22:16.

Hewn *ekkopto* (1581), lit., "to cut or strike out," "to cut down," is used (a) literally, Matt. 5:30 (in 3:10 and 7:19 and **Luke 3:9**, "hewn down"); 18:8; **Luke 13:7**, **9**; (b) metaphorically, of "cutting off" from spiritual blessing, Rom. 11:22, 24; of depriving persons of an occasion for something 2 Cor. 11:12.

3:10-11 And the people asked him, saying, What shall we do then?

He answereth and saith unto them, He that hath two coats, let him impart to him that hath none; and he that hath meat, let him do likewise.

Impart *metadidomi* (3330), "to give a share of, impart" (*meta*, "with"), as distinct from "giving." The apostle Paul speaks of "sharing" some spiritual gift with Christians at Rome, Rom. 1:11, "that I may impart," and exhorts those who minister in things temporal, to do so as "sharing," and that generously, 12:8, "he that giveth"; so in Eph. 4:28; **Luke 3:11**; in 1 Thess. 2:8 he speaks of himself and his fellow missionaries as having been well pleased to impart to the converts both God's gospel and their own souls (i.e., so "sharing" those with them as to spend themselves and spend out their lives for them).

Meat *broma* (1033), "food" (akin to *bibrosko*, "to eat," John 6:13), solid food in contrast to milk, is translated "food" in Matt. 14:15, RV (KJV, "victuals"); "meats," Mark 7:19; 1 Cor. 6:13 (twice); 1 Tim. 4:3; Heb. 9:10; 13:9; "meat," John 4:34; Rom.

14:15 (twice), 20; 1 Cor. 3:2; 8:8, 13; 10:3; "food," RV, for KJV, "meat," **Luke 3:11**; **9:13**.

3:12 Then came also publicans to be baptized, and said unto him, Master, what shall we do?

Publicans *telones* (5057), primarily denoted "a farmer of the tax" (from *telos*, "toll, custom, tax"), then, as in the NT, a subsequent subordinate of such, who collected taxes in some district, "a tax gatherer"; such were naturally hated intensely by the people; they are classed with "sinners," Matt. 9:10, 11; 11:9; Mark 2:15, 16; **Luke 5:30**; **7:34**; **15:1**; with harlots, Matt. 21:31, 32; with "the Gentile," Matt. 18:17; some mss. have it in Matt. 5:47, the best have *ethnikoi*, "Gentiles." See also Matt. 5:46; 10:3; **Luke 3:12**; **5:27**, **29**; **7:29**; **18:10**, **11**, **13**.

3:13 And he said unto them, Exact no more than that which is appointed you.

Exact *prasso* (4238), "to practice," has the special meaning "extort" in **Luke 3:13**, RV (KJV, "exact"). In **Luke 19:23** it is translated "required"; it may be that the master, in addressing the slothful servant, uses the word "extort" or "exact" (as in **3:13**), in accordance with the character attributed to him by the servant.

Appointed *diatasso* (1299), frequently denotes "to arrange, appoint, prescribe," e.g., of what was "appointed" for tax collectors to collect, **Luke 3:13**; of the tabernacle, as "appointed" by God for Moses to make, Acts 7:44; of the arrangements "appointed" by Paul with regard to himself and his travelling companions, Acts 20:13; of what the apostle "ordained" in all the churches in regard to marital conditions, 1 Cor. 7:17; of what the Lord "ordained" in regard to the support of those who proclaimed the gospel, 1 Cor. 9:14; of the Law as divinely "ordained," or administered, through angels, by Moses, Gal. 3:19.

3:14 And the soldiers likewise demanded of him, saying, And what shall we do? And he said unto them, Do violence to no man, neither accuse *any* falsely; and be content with your wages.

Soldiers *strateuo* (4754), always in the middle voice in the NT, is used (a) literally of "serving as a soldier," **Luke 3:14**, "soldiers" (RV, marg., "soldiers on service," present participle); 1 Cor. 9:7, RV, "(what) soldier ... serveth," KJV, "(who) goeth a warfare"; 2 Tim. 2:4, RV, "soldier on service," KJV, "man that warreth," lit., "serving as a soldier"; (b) metaphorically, of "spiritual conflict".

Likewise *kai* (2532), "and, even," is translated "likewise" in the KJV and RV of Matt. 20:10 (last *kai* in the verse), more lit., "even they"; elsewhere the RV has "also," for the KJV, "likewise," Matt. 18:35; 24:33; **Luke 3:14**; **17:10**; **19:19**; **21:31**; Acts 3:24; 1 Cor. 14:9; Col. 4:16; 1 Pet. 4:1; in Matt. 21:24, the KJV has "in like wise" (RV, "likewise").

Demanded *see* Asking at *Luke 2:46*.

Violence *diaseio* (1286), "to shake violently," is used in **Luke 3:14**, "do violence," including intimidation. In the Sept., Job 4:14.

Accuse *sukophanteo* (4811), (Eng., "sycophant") means (a) "to accuse wrongfully"; **Luke 3:14** (KJV and RV, margin); RV, "exact wrongfully"; (b) "to exact money wrongfully, to take anything by false accusation," **Luke 19:8**, and the RV text of **3:14**. It is more frequently found in the Sept.; see Gen. 43:18, "to inform against"; Lev. 19:11, "neither shall each falsely accuse his neighbor"; Job 35:9, "they that are oppressed by false accusation"; Ps. 119:122, "let not the proud accuse me falsely"; Prov. 14:31 and 22:16, "he that oppresses the needy by false accusation."

Content *arkeo* (174), primarily signifies "to be sufficient, to be possessed of sufficient strength, to be strong, to be enough for a thing"; hence, "to defend, ward off"; in the middle voice, "to be satisfied, contented with," **Luke 3:14**, with wages; 1 Tim. 6:8, with food and raiment; Heb. 13:5, with "such things as ye have"; negatively of Diotrephes, in 3 John 10, "not content therewith."

Wages *opsonion* (3800), denotes (a) "soldier's pay," **Luke 3:14**; 1 Cor. 9:7 ("charges"); (b) in general, "hire, wages of any sort," used metaphorically, Rom. 6:23, of sin; 2 Cor. 11:8, of material support which Paul received from some of the churches which he had established and to which he ministered in spiritual things; their support partly maintained him at Corinth, where he forebore to receive such assistance (vv. 9, 10).

3:15 And as the people were in expectation, and all men mused in their hearts of John, whether he were the Christ, or not;

People *see Luke 1:21*.

Expectation *prosdokao* (4328), "to watch toward, to look for, expect" (*pros*, "toward," *dokeo*, "to think": *dokao* "does not exist"), is translated "expecting" in Matt. 24:50 and **Luke 12:46**, RV (KJV, "looketh for"); **Luke 3:15**, "were in expectation"; Acts 3:5, "expecting" (KJV and RV); 28:6 (twice), "expected that," RV

(KJV, "looked when") and "when they were long in expectation" (KJV, "after they had looked a great while").

Mused *see* Cast at *Luke 1:29*.

Whether *mepote* (3379), often written as two words, usually signifies "lest ever, lest haply, haply"; in indirect questions, "if haply" or "whether haply," e.g., **Luke 3:15**, RV; in Matt. 25:9, RV, "peradventure" (KJV, "lest"); "if peradventure," in 2 Tim. 2:25.

3:16 John answered, saying unto *them* all, I indeed baptize you with water; but one mightier than I cometh, the latchet of whose shoes I am not worthy to unloose: he shall baptize you with the Holy Ghost and with fire:

Answered *apokrinomai* (611), signifies either "to give an answer to a question" (its more frequent use) or "to begin to speak," but always where something has preceded, either statement or act to which the remarks refer, e.g., Matt. 11:25; **Luke 14:3**; John 2:18. The RV translates by "answered," e.g., Matt. 28:5; Mark 12:35; **Luke 3:16**, where some have suggested "began to say" or "uttered solemnly," whereas the speaker is replying to the unuttered thought or feeling of those addressed by him.

Baptize *baptizo* (907), "to baptize," primarily a frequentative form of *bapto*, "to dip," was used among the Greeks to signify the dyeing of a garment, or the drawing of water by dipping a vessel into another, etc. Plutarchus uses it of the drawing of wine by dipping the cup into the bowl (*Alexis*, 67) and Plato, metaphorically, of being overwhelmed with questions (*Euthydemus*, 277 D).

It is used in the NT in **Luke 11:38** of washing oneself (as in 2 Kings 5:14, "dipped himself," Sept.); see also Isa. 21:4, lit., "lawlessness overwhelms me." In the early chapters of the four Gospels and in Acts 1:5; 11:16; 19:4, it is used of the rite performed by John the Baptist who called upon the people to repent that they might receive remission of sins. Those who obeyed came "confessing their sins," thus acknowledging their unfitness to be in the Messiah's coming kingdom. Distinct from this is the "baptism" enjoined by Christ, Matt. 28:19, a "baptism" to be undergone by believers, thus witnessing to their identification with Him in death, burial and resurrection, e.g., Acts 19:5; Rom. 6:3-4; 1 Cor. 1:13-17; 12:13; Gal. 3:27; Col. 2:12. The phrase in Matt. 28:19, "baptizing them into the Name" (RV; cf. Acts 8:16, RV), would indicate that the "baptized" person was closely bound to, or became the property of, the one into whose name he was "baptized."

... The verb is used metaphorically also in two distinct senses: firstly, of "baptism" by the Holy Spirit, which took place on the Day of Pentecost; secondly, of the calamity which would come upon the nation of the Jews, a "baptism" of the fire of divine judgment for rejection of the will and word of God, Matt. 3:11; **Luke 3:16**.

Mightier *ischuroteros* (2478), "stronger, mightier," the comparative degree of *ischuros*, is translated "mightier" in Matt. 3:11; Mark 1:7; **Luke 3:16**; "stronger" in **Luke 11:22**; 1 Cor. 1:25; 10:22.

Latchet *himas* (2438), denotes "a thong, strap," whether for binding prisoners, Acts 22:25, "(the) thongs," or for fastening sandals, Mark 1:7; **Luke 3:16**; John 1:27. "Among the Orientals everything connected with the feet and shoes is defiled and debasing, and the stooping to unfasten the dusty latchet is the most insignificant in such service" (Mackie, in *Hastings' Bib. Dic.*).

Worthy *hikanos* (2425), "sufficient," is translated "worthy" in this sense in Matt. 3:11 (marg., "sufficient"); so 8:8; Mark 1:7; **Luke 3:16**; **7:6**.

Unloose *luo* (3089), "to loose," is rendered "to unloose" in Mark 1:7; **Luke 3:16**; John 1:27; in Acts 13:25, RV.

Fire *pur* (4442), (akin to which are *pura*, and *puretos*, "a fever," Eng., "fire," etc.) is used (besides its ordinary natural significance):

(a) of the holiness of God, which consumes all that is inconsistent therewith, Heb. 10:27; 12:29; cf. Rev. 1:14; 2:18; 10:1; 15:2; 19:12; similarly of the holy angels as His ministers, Heb. 1:7; in Rev. 3:18 it is symbolic of that which tries the faith of saints, producing what will glorify the Lord;

(b) of the divine judgment, testing the deeds of believers, at the judgment seat of Christ. 1 Cor. 3:13 and 15;

(c) of the fire of divine judgment upon the rejectors of Christ, Matt. 3:11 (where a distinction is to be made between the baptism of the Holy Spirit at Pentecost and the "fire" of divine retribution; Acts 2:3 could not refer to baptism): **Luke 3:16**;

(d) of the judgments of God at the close of the present age previous to the establishment of the kingdom of Christ in the world, 2 Thess. 1:8; Rev. 18:8;

(e) of the "fire" of Hell, to be endured by the ungodly hereafter, Matt. 5:22; 13:42, 50; 18:8, 9; 25:41; Mark 9:43, 48; **Luke 3:17**;

(f) of human hostility both to the Jews and to Christ's followers, **Luke 12:49**;

(g) as illustrative of retributive judgment upon the luxurious and tyrannical rich, Jas. 5:3; (h) of the future overthrow of the Babylonish religious system at the hands of the Beast and the nations under him, Rev. 17:16; (i) of turning the heart of an enemy to repentance by repaying his unkindness by kindness, Rom. 12:20; (j) of the tongue, as governed by a "fiery" disposition and as exercising a destructive influence over others, Jas. 3:6.; (k) as symbolic of the danger of destruction, Jude 23.

3:17 Whose fan *is* in his hand, and he will throughly purge his floor, and will gather the wheat into his garner; but the chaff he will burn with fire unquenchable.

Fan *ptuon* (4425), denotes "a winnowing shovel or fan," with which grain is thrown up against the wind, in order to separate the chaff, Matt. 3:12; **Luke 3:17**.

Purge *diakathairo* (1223 and 2508), "to cleanse thoroughly," is translated "will throughly purge" in **Luke 3:17**, KJV (RV, "thoroughly to cleanse"; less authentic mss. have *diakatharizo*).

Floor *halon* (257), "a threshing floor," is so translated in Matt. 3:12, and **Luke 3:17**, RV (KJV, "floor"), perhaps by metonymy for the grain.

Wheat *sitos* (4621), "wheat, corn"; in the plural, "grain," is translated "corn" in Mark 4:28; "wheat," Matt. 3:12; 13:25, 29-30; **Luke 3:17**; **12:18** (some mss. have *genemata*, "fruits," here); **16:7**; **22:31**; John 12:24; Acts 27:38; 1 Cor. 15:37; Rev. 6:6; 18:13.

Garner *apotheke* (596), lit., "a place where anything is stored" (Eng., "apothecary"), hence denoted a garner, granary, barn, Matt. 3:12; 6:26; 13:30; **Luke 3:17**; **12:18, 24**.

Chaff *achuron* (892), "chaff, the stalk of the grain from which the kernels have been beaten out, or the straw broken up by a threshing machine," is found in Matt. 3:12 and **Luke 3:17**.

Burn *katakaio* (2618), signifies "to burn up, burn utterly," as of chaff, Matt. 3:12; **Luke 3:17**; tares, Matt. 13:30, 40; the earth and its works, 2 Pet. 3:10; trees and grass, Rev. 8:7. This form should be noted in Acts 19:19; 1 Cor. 3:15; Heb. 13:11, Rev. 17:16. In each place the full rendering "burn utterly" might be used, as in Rev. 18:8.

Fire *see* ***Luke 3:16***.

Unquenchable *asbestos* (762), "not quenched," is used of the doom of persons described figuratively as "chaff," Matt. 3:12 and **Luke 3:17**, "unquenchable"; of the fire of Gehenna, Mark 9:43, RV, "unquenchable fire" (in some mss. v. 45). In the Sept., Job 20:26.

3:18 And many other things in his exhortation preached he unto the people.

Preached *see* **Glad tidings** at *Luke 1:19*.

3:19 But Herod the tetrarch, being reproved by him for Herodias his brother Philip's wife, and for all the evils which Herod had done,

Tetrarch *tetraarches* or *tetrarches* (5076), denotes "one of four rulers" (*tetra*, "four," *arche*, "rule"), properly, "the governor of the fourth part of a region"; hence, "a dependent princeling," or "any petty ruler" subordinate to kings or ethnarchs; in the NT, Herod Antipas, Matt. 14:1; **Luke 3:19**; **9:7**; Acts 13:1.

Reproved *elencho* (1651), signifies (a) "to convict, confute, refute," usually with the suggestion of putting the convicted person to shame; see Matt. 18:15, where more than telling the offender his fault is in view; it is used of "convicting" of sin, John 8:46; 16:8; gainsayers in regard to the faith, Titus 1:9; transgressors of the Law, Jas. 2:9; some texts have the verb in John 8:9; (b) "to reprove," 1 Cor. 14:24, RV (for KJV, "convince"), for the unbeliever is there viewed as being reproved for, or "convicted" of, his sinful state; so in **Luke 3:19**; it is used of reproving works, John 3:20; Eph. 5:11, 13; 1 Tim. 5:20; 2 Tim. 4:2; Titus 1:13; 2:15; all these speak of reproof by word of mouth. In Heb. 12:5 and Rev. 3:19, the word is used of reproving by action.

Evils *poneros* (4190), the adjective, is used as a noun, (a) of Satan as the "evil" one, Matt. 5:37; 6:13; 13:19, 38; **Luke 11:4** (in some texts); John 17:15; Eph. 6:16; 2 Thess. 3:3; 1 John 2:13-14; 3:12; 5:18-19; (b) of human beings, Matt. 5:45; (probably v. 39); 13:49; 22:10; **Luke 6:35**; 1 Cor. 5:13; (c) neuter, "evil (things)," Matt. 9:4; 12:35; Mark 7:23; **Luke 3:19**; "that which is evil," **Luke 6:45**; Rom. 12:9; Acts 28:21, "harm." *See also* **Evil** at *Luke 6:45*.

3:20 Added yet this above all, that he shut up John in prison.

Yet *kai*, "and, even, also," "yet" in **Luke 3:20**; in Gal. 3:4, *ei ge kai*, KJV, "if ... yet" (RV, "if ... indeed").

Shut *katakleio* (2623), lit., to shut down" (the *kata* has, however, an intensive use), signifies "to shut up in confinement," **Luke 3:20**; Acts 26:10. In the Sept., Jer. 32:3.

3:21 Now when all the people were baptized, it came to pass, that Jesus also being baptized, and praying, the heaven was opened,

Opened *see* ***Luke 1:64***.

"The cross of Jesus Christ and his baptism express the same thing. Our Lord was not a martyr; he was not merely a good man; he was God Incarnate. He came down to the lowest reach of creation in order to bring back the whole human race to God, and in order to do this he must take upon him, as representative man, the whole massed sin of the race."

OSWALD CHAMBERS

3:22 And the Holy Ghost descended in a bodily shape like a dove upon him, and a voice came from heaven, which said, Thou art my beloved Son; in thee I am well pleased.

Holy Ghost *see Luke 2:26.*

Bodily *somatikos* (4984), "bodily," is used in **Luke 3:22**, of the Holy Spirit in taking a bodily shape; in 1 Tim. 4:8 of bodily exercise.

Shape *eidos* (1491), lit., "that which is seen" (*eidon*, "to see"), "an appearance or external form," is rendered "form" in the RV of **Luke 3:22**, of the Holy Spirit's appearance at the baptism of Christ; in John 5:37, in the Lord's testimony concerning the Father; in **Luke 9:29** it is said of Christ Himself; it is translated "sight" in 2 Cor. 5:7, the Christian being guided by what he knows to be true, though unseen; in 1 Thess. 5:22 Christians are exhorted to abstain from "every form of evil," RV (the KJV, "appearance" is inadequate), i.e., from every kind of evil.

Like In the following the most authentic mss. have *hos*, "as," for *hosei*, "like," in the KJV; Mark 1:10; **Luke 3:22**; John 1:32; Rev. 1:14.

Dove *see* Turtledoves at *Luke 2:24.*

3:23 And Jesus himself began to be about thirty years of age, being (as was supposed) the son of Joseph, which was *the son* of Heli,

Began *archomai* (756), denotes "to begin." In **Luke 3:23** the present participle is used in a condensed expression, lit., "And Jesus Himself was beginning about thirty years." Some verb is to be supplied in English. The RV has "when He began to teach, was about thirty years of age." The meaning seems to be that He was about thirty years when He "began" His public career (cf. Acts 1:1). The KJV has "began to be about thirty years of age." In Acts 11:4 the RV suitably has "began, and expounded," instead of "from the beginning."

About *hosei* (5616), "as if," before numerals, denotes "about, nearly, something like," with perhaps an indication of greater indefiniteness, e.g., Matt. 14:21; **Luke 3:23**; **9:14**, **28**; Acts 2:41; with a measure of space, **Luke 22:41**, "about a stone's cast."

Years *see* Year at *Luke 2:41.*

Age *see Luke 2:36.*

Supposed *nomizo* (3543), "to consider, suppose, think," is rendered "to suppose" in Matt. 20:10; **Luke 3:23**; Acts 7:25; 14:19; 16:27; 21:29; 1 Tim. 6:5; in 1 Cor. 7:26, KJV (RV, "I think"); in Acts 16:13, the RV adheres to the meaning "to suppose," "(where) we supposed (there was a place of prayer)"; this word also signifies "to practice a custom" (*nomos*) and is commonly so used by Greek writers. Hence the KJV, "was wont (to be made)"; it is rendered "to think" in Matt. 5:17; 10:34; Acts 8:20; 17:29; 1 Cor. 7:36.

3:24-38 Which was *the son* of Matthat, which was *the son* of Levi, which was *the son* of Melchi, which was *the son* of Janna, which was *the son* of Joseph,

Which was *the son* of Mattathias, which was *the son* of Amos, which was *the son* of Naum, which was *the son* of Esli, which was *the son* of Nagge,

Which was *the son* of Maath, which was *the son* of Mattathias, which was *the son* of Semei, which was *the son* of Joseph, which was *the son* of Juda,

Which was *the son* of Joanna, which was *the son* of Rhesa, which was *the son* of Zorobabel, which was *the son* of Salathiel, which was *the son* of Neri,

Which was *the son* of Melchi, which was *the son* of Addi, which was *the son* of Cosam, which was *the son* of Elmodam, which was *the son* of Er,

Which was *the son* of Jose, which was *the son* of Eliezer, which was *the son* of Jorim, which was *the son* of Matthat, which was *the son* of Levi,

Which was *the son* of Simeon,

which was *the son* of Juda,
which was *the son* of Joseph,
which was *the son* of Jonan,
which was *the son* of Eliakim,
Which was *the son* of Melea,
which was *the son* of Menan,
which was *the son* of Mattatha,
which was *the son* of Nathan,
which was *the son* of David,
Which was *the son* of Jesse,
which was *the son* of Obed,
which was *the son* of Booz,
which was *the son* of Salmon,
which was *the son* of Naasson,
Which was *the son* of Aminadab, which was *the son* of Aram, which was *the son* of Esrom, which was *the son* of Phares, which was *the son* of Juda,
Which was *the son* of Jacob,
which was *the son* of Isaac,
which was *the son* of Abraham,
which was *the son* of Thara,
which was *the son* of Nachor,
Which was *the son* of Saruch,
which was *the son* of Ragau,
which was *the son* of Phalec,
which was*the son* of Heber,
which was *the son* of Sala,
Which was *the son* of Cainan,
which was *the son* of Arphaxad,
which was *the son* of Sem,
which was *the son* of Noe,
which was *the son* of Lamech,
Which was *the son* of Mathusala, which was *the son* of Enoch, which was *the son* of Jared, which was *the son* of Maleleel, which was *the son* of Cainan,
Which was *the son* of Enos,
which was *the son* of Seth,
which was *the son* of Adam,
which was *the son* of God.

Jose *iesous* (2424), i.e. also Jesus, is a transliteration of the Heb. "Joshua," meaning "Jehovah is salvation," i.e., "is the Savior," "a common name among the Jews," e.g., Ex. 17:9; **Luke 3:29** (RV); Col. 4:11. It was given to the Son of God in Incarnation as His personal name, in obedience to the command of an angel to Joseph, the husband of His Mother, Mary, shortly before He was born, Matt. 1:21. By it He is spoken of throughout the Gospel narratives generally, but not without exception, as in Mark 16:19, 20; **Luke 7:13**, and a dozen other places in that Gospel, and a few in John.

"'Jesus Christ' occurs only in Matt. 1:1, 18; 16:21, marg.; Mark 1:1; John 1:17; 17:3. In Acts the name 'Jesus' is found frequently. 'Lord Jesus' is the normal usage, as in Acts 8:16; 19:5, 17; see also the reports of the words of Stephen, 7:59, of Ananias, 9:17, and of Paul, 16:31; though both Peter, 10:36, and Paul, 16:18, also used 'Jesus Christ.' "

Chapter 4

4:1 And Jesus being full of the Holy Ghost returned from Jordan, and was led by the Spirit into the wilderness,

Full *pleres* (4134), denotes "full," (a) in the sense of "being filled," materially, Matt. 14:20; 15:37; Mark 8:19 (said of baskets "full" of bread crumbs); of leprosy, **Luke 5:12**; spiritually, of the Holy Spirit, **Luke 4:1**; Acts 6:3; 7:55; 11:24; grace and truth, John 1:14; faith, Acts 6:5; grace and power, 6:8; of the effects of spiritual life and qualities, seen in good works, Acts 9:36; in an evil sense, of guile and villany, Acts 13:10; wrath, 19:28; (b) in the sense of "being complete," "full corn in the ear," Mark 4:28; of a reward hereafter, 2 John 8.

Holy Ghost *see **Luke 2:26**.*

Returned *see **Luke 1:56**.*

Led *ago* (71), "to bear, bring, carry, lead," is translated by the verb "to lead," e.g., in Mark 13:11; **Luke 4:1**; **4:9**, RV; **4:29**; **22:54**; **23:1**, KJV only; **23:32**; John 18:28 (present tense, RV), Acts 8:32; metaphorically in Rom. 2:4, of the goodness of God; 8:14 and Gal. 5:18, of the Spirit of God; 1 Cor. 12:2, of the powers of darkness instigating to idolatry; 2 Tim. 3:6, of divers lusts (in some mss., *aichmaloteuo*). In **Luke 24:21** *ago* is used of the passing (or spending) of a day, and translated "it is (now the third day)"; here the verb is probably to be taken impersonally, according to idiomatic usage, in the sense "there is passing the third day."

4:2 Being forty days tempted of the devil. And in those days he did eat nothing: and when they were ended, he afterward hungered.

Ended *sunteleo* (4931), signifies (a) "to bring to an end, finish completely" (*sun*, "together," imparting a perfective significance to *teleo*), Matt. 7:28 (in some mss.); **Luke 4:2**, **13**; Acts 21:27, RV, "completed"; (b) "to bring to fulfillment," Mark 13:4; Rom. 9:28; (c) "to effect, make," Heb. 8:8.

Afterward *husteron* (5305), "afterwards," with the suggestion of at length, is found in Matt. 4:2; 21:29, 32, 37 (KJV, "last of all"); 22:27; 25:11; 26:60 (KJV, "at the last"), Mark 16:14; **Luke 4:2**; **20:32** (KJV, "last"), John 13:36; Heb. 12:11.

4:3 And the devil said unto him, If thou be the Son of God, command this stone that it be made bread.

Command *epo* (2036), denotes "to speak" (connected with *eipon*, "to say"); hence, among various renderings, "to bid, command," Matt. 4:3; Mark 5:43; 8:7; **Luke 4:3**; **19:15**.

4:4-5 And Jesus answered him, saying, It is written, That man shall not live by bread alone, but by every word of God.

And the devil, taking him up into an high mountain, shewed unto him all the kingdoms of the world in a moment of time.

Taking *anago* (321), "to lead up" (*ana*, "up"), is used of Christ in being "led" up by the Spirit into the wilderness, Matt. 4:1; **Luke 4:5** (KJV, "taking up"); by the elders of the people into their council, **Luke 22:66**, "led away."

Kingdoms *basileia* (932), is primarily an abstract noun, denoting "sovereignty, royal power, dominion," e.g., Rev. 17:18, translated "(which) reigneth," lit., "hath a kingdom" (RV marg.); then, by metonymy, a concrete noun, denoting the territory or people over whom a king rules, e.g., Matt. 4:8; Mark 3:24. It is used especially of the "kingdom" of God and of Christ.

"The Kingdom of God is (a) the sphere of God's rule, Ps. 22:28; 145:13; Dan. 4:25; **Luke 1:52**; Rom. 13:1, 2. Since, however, this earth is the scene of universal rebellion against God, e.g., **Luke 4:5, 6**; 1 John 5:19; Rev. 11:15-18, the "kingdom" of God is (b) the sphere in which, at any given time, His rule is acknowledged. God has not relinquished His sovereignty in the face of rebellion, demoniac and human, but has declared His purpose to establish it, Dan. 2:44; 7:14; 1 Cor. 15:24, 25. Meantime, seeking willing obedience, He gave His law to a nation and appointed kings to administer His "kingdom" over it, 1 Chron. 28:5. Israel, however, though declaring still a nominal allegiance shared in the common rebellion, Isa. 1:2-4, and, after they had rejected the Son of God, John 1:11 (cf. Matt. 21:33-43), were "cast away," Rom. 11:15, 20, 25. Henceforth God calls upon men everywhere, without distinction of race or nationality, to submit voluntarily to His rule. Thus the "kingdom" is said to be "in mystery" now, Mark 4:11, that is, it does not come within the range of the natural powers of observation, **Luke 17:20**, but is spiritually discerned, John 3:3 (cf. 1 Cor. 2:14). When, hereafter, God asserts His rule universally, then the "kingdom" will be in glory, that is, it will be manifest to all; cf. Matt. 25:31-34; Phil. 2:9-11; 2 Tim. 4:1, 18.

World *see Luke 2:1.*

Moment *stigme* (4743), "a prick, a point" (akin to *stizo*, "to prick"), is used metaphorically in **Luke 4:5**, of a "moment," with *chronos*, "a moment (of time)."

Time *chronos* (5550), whence Eng. words beginning with "chron-", denotes "a space of time," whether short, e.g., Matt. 2:7; **Luke 4:5**, or long, e.g., **Luke 8:27**; **20:9**; or a succession of "times," shorter, e.g., Acts 20:18, or longer, e.g., Rom. 16:25, RV, "times eternal"; or duration of "time," e.g., Mark 2:19, 2nd part, RV, "while" (KJV, "as long as"), lit., "for whatever time."

Broadly speaking, *chronos* expresses the duration of a period, *kairos* stresses it as marked by certain features; thus in Acts 1:7, "the Father has set within His own authority" both the times (*chronos*), the lengths of the periods, and the "seasons" (*kairos*), epochs characterized by certain events; in 1 Thess. 5:1, "times" refers to the length of the interval before the Parousia takes place (the presence of Christ with the saints when He comes to receive them to Himself at the Rapture), and to the length of time the Parousia will occupy; "seasons" refers to the special features of the period before, during, and after the Parousia.

Chronos marks quantity, *kairos*, quality. Sometimes the distinction between the two words is not sharply defined as, e.g., in 2 Tim. 4:6, though even here the apostle's "departure" signalizes the time (*kairos*). The words occur together in the Sept. only in Dan. 2:21 and Eccl. 3:1. *Chronos* is rendered "season" in Acts 19:22, KJV (RV, "a while); 20:18 (RV, "all the time"); Rev. 6:11, KJV (RV, "time"); so 20:3. In **Luke 23:8** it is used with *hikanos* in the plural, RV, "(of a long) time," more lit., "(for a sufficient number) of times."

In Rev. 10:6 *chronos* has the meaning "delay" (RV, marg.), an important rendering for the understanding of the passage (the word being akin to *chronizo*, "to take time, to linger, delay," Matt. 24:48; **Luke 12:45**).

4:6 And the devil said unto him, All this power will I give thee, and the glory of them: for that is delivered unto me; and to whomsoever I will I give it.

Power *exousia* (1849), denotes "authority" (from the impersonal verb *exesti*, "it is lawful"). From the meaning of "leave or permission," or liberty of doing as one pleases, it passed to that of "the ability or strength with which one is endued," then to that of the "power of authority," the right to exercise power, e.g., Matt. 9:6; 21:23; 2 Cor. 10:8; or "the power of rule or government," the power of one whose will and commands must be obeyed by others, e.g., Matt. 28:18; John 17:2; Jude 25; Rev. 12:10; 17:13; more specifically of apostolic "authority," 2 Cor. 10:8; 13:10; the "power" of judicial decision, John 19:10; of "managing domestic affairs," Mark 13:34. By metonymy, or name-change (the substitution of a suggestive word for the name of the thing meant), it stands for "that which is subject to authority or rule," **Luke 4:6** (RV, "authority," for the KJV "power"); or, as with the English "authority," "one who possesses authority, a ruler, magistrate," Rom. 13:1-3; **Luke 12:11**; Titus 3:1; or "a spiritual potentate," e.g., Eph. 3:10; 6:12; Col. 1:16; 2:10, 15; 1 Pet. 3:22. The RV usually translates it "authority." In 1 Cor. 11:10 it is used of the veil with which a woman is required to cover herself in an assembly or church, as a sign of the Lord's "authority" over the church.

4:7-8 If thou therefore wilt worship me, all shall be thine.
And Jesus answered and said unto him, Get thee behind me, Satan: for it is written, Thou shalt worship the Lord thy God, and him only shalt thou serve.

Get *hupago* (5217), "to go away, withdraw," is rendered "get," "get ... hence," in Matt. 4:10; 16:23; Mark 8:33; some mss. have it in **Luke 4:8**.

Satan *satanas* (4567), a Greek form derived from the Aramaic (Heb., *Satan*), "an adversary," is used (a) of an angel of Jehovah in Num. 22:22 (the first occurrence of the Word in the OT); (b) of men, e.g., 1 Sam. 29:4; Ps. 38:20; 71:13; four in Ps. 109; (c) of "Satan," the Devil, some seventeen or eighteen times in the OT; in Zech. 3:1, where the name receives its interpretation, "to be (his) adversary," RV (see marg.; KJV, "to resist him").

In the NT the word is always used of "Satan," the adversary (a) of God and Christ, e.g., Matt. 4:10; 12:26; Mark 1:13; 3:23, 26; 4:15; **Luke 4:8** (in some mss.); **11:18**; **22:3**; John 13:27; (b) of His people, e.g., **Luke 22:31**; Acts 5:3; Rom. 16:20; 1 Cor. 5:5; 7:5; 2 Cor. 2:11; 11:14; 12:7; 1 Thess. 2:18; 1 Tim. 1:20; 5:15; Rev. 2:9, 13 (twice), 24; 3:9; (c) of mankind, **Luke 13:16**; Acts 26:18; 2 Thess. 2:9; Rev. 12:9; 20:7.

His doom, sealed at the Cross, is foretold in its stages in **Luke 10:18**; Rev. 20:2, 10. Believers are assured of victory over him, Rom. 16:20.

"Satan" is not simply the personification of evil influences in the heart, for he tempted Christ, in whose heart no evil thought could ever have arisen (John 14:30; 2 Cor. 5:21; Heb. 4:15); moreover his personality is asserted in both the OT and the NT, and especially in the latter, whereas if the OT language was intended to be figurative, the NT would have made this evident.

Serve *see Luke 1:74.*

4:9 And he brought him to Jerusalem, and set him on a pinnacle of the temple, and said unto him, If thou be the Son of God, cast thyself down from hence:

Brought *see* Led at *Luke 4:1.*

Set *histemi* (2476), "to cause to stand," is translated "to set" in Matt. 4:5 (aorist tense in the best texts; some have the present, as in KJV); 18:2; 25:33; Mark 9:36; **Luke 4:9**; **9:47**; John 8:3; Acts 4:7; 5:27; 6:6; v. 13, "set up"; 22:30; in Jude 24, RV, "to set" (KJV, "to present").

Pinnacle *pterugion* (4419), denotes (a) "a little wing" (diminutive of *pterux*, "a wing"); (b) "anything like a wing, a turret, battlement," of the temple in Jerusalem, Matt. 4:5 and **Luke 4:9** (of the *hieron*, "the entire precincts," or parts of the main building, as distinct from the *naos*, "the sanctuary"). This "wing" has been regarded (1) as the apex of the sanctuary, (2) the top of Solomon's porch, (3) the top of the Royal Portico, which Josephus describes as of tremendous height (*Antiq.* xv. 11.5). It is used in the Sept. of the fins of fishes, e.g. Lev. 11:9-12; of the part of a dress, hanging down in the form of a wing, Ruth 3:9; 1 Sam. 24:5.

Down *kato* (2736), signifies (a) "down, downwards," Matt. 4:6; **Luke 4:9**; John 8:6, 8; Acts 20:9; (b) "below, beneath," of place, Mark 14:66; the realms that lie below in contrast to heaven, John 8:23; the earth, as contrasted with the heavens, Acts 2:19; with *heos*, "unto," Matt. 27:51; Mark 15:38. The comparative degree, *katotero*, "under," is used in Matt. 2:16.

Hence *enteuthen* (1782), is used (a) of place, "hence," or "from hence," **Luke 4:9**; **13:31**; John 2:16; 7:3; 14:31; 18:36; in John 19:18, "on either side (one)," lit., "hence and hence"; in Rev. 22:2, it is contrasted with *ekeithen*, "thence," RV, "on this side ... on that" (KJV, "on either side"), lit. "hence ... thence"; (b) causal; Jas. 4:1, "(come they not) hence," i.e., "owing to."

4:10 For it is written, He shall give his angels charge over thee, to keep thee:

Charge *entellomai* (1781), to order, command, enjoin (from *en*, in, used intensively, and *teleo*, to fulfil), is translated by the verb to give charge, Matt. 4:6; 17:9 (AV); **Luke 4:10**.

Keep *diaphulasso* (1314), a strengthened form (*dia*, "through," used intensively), "to guard carefully, defend," is found in **Luke 4:10** (from the Sept. of Ps. 91:11), RV, "to guard" (KJV, "to keep").

4:11 And in *their* hands they shall bear thee up, lest at any time thou dash thy foot against a stone.

Lest *me pote* (3379), lit., "lest ever," "lest haply," e.g., **Luke 14:29**, of laying a foundation, with the possibility of being unable to finish the building; Acts 5:39, of the possibility of being found fighting against God; Heb. 3:2, RV, "lest haply," of the possibility of having an evil heart of unbelief. The RV usually has "lest haply" (KJV "lest at any time"), e.g., Matt. 4:6; 5:25; 13:15; Mark 4:12; **Luke 4:11**; **21:34**; Heb. 2:1; in Matt. 25:9, the RV has "peradventure"; in 2 Tim. 2:25, KJV and RV, have "if peradventure"; in John 7:26 the RV has "Can it be that," for the word "Do" in the KJV.

Dash *proskopto* (4350), denotes "to beat upon or against, to strike against, dash against" (*pros*, "to or against," *kopto*, "to strike, beat"); hence, of the foot, to stumble, "dash" (KJV and RV), Matt. 4:6; **Luke 4:11**.

4:12 And Jesus answering said unto him, It is said, Thou shalt not tempt the Lord thy God.

Tempt *ekpeirazo* (1598), an intensive form, is used in Christ's quotation from Deut. 6:16, in reply to the Devil, Matt. 4:7; **Luke 4:12**; so in 1 Cor. 10:9, RV, "the Lord" (KJV, "Christ"); of the lawyer who "tempted" Christ, **Luke 10:25**. In the Sept., Deut. 6:16; 8:2, 16; Ps. 78:15. Cf. *dokimazo*.

4:13 And when the devil had ended all the temptation, he departed from him for a season.

Ended *see Luke 4:2*.

Temptation *peirasmos* (3986), is used of (1) "trials" with a beneficial purpose and effect, (a) of "trials" or "temptations," divinely permitted or sent, **Luke 22:28**; Acts 20:19; Jas. 1:2; 1 Pet. 1:6; 4:12, RV, "to prove," KJV, "to try"; 2 Pet. 2:9 (singular); Rev. 3:10, RV, "trial" (KJV, "temptation"); in Jas. 1:12, "temptation" apparently has meanings (1) and (2) combined and is used in the widest sense; (b) with a good or neutral significance, Gal. 4:14, of Paul's physical infirmity, "a temptation" to the Galatian converts, of such a kind as to arouse feelings of natural repugnance; (c) of "trials" of a varied character, Matt. 6:13 and **Luke 11:4**, where believers are commanded to pray not to be led into such by forces beyond their own control; Matt. 26:41; Mark 14:38; **Luke 22:40**, **46**, where they are commanded to watch and pray against entering into "temptations" by their own carelessness or disobedience; in all such cases God provides "the way of escape," 1 Cor. 10:13 (where *peirasmos* occurs twice). (2) Of "trial" definitely designed to lead to wrong doing, "temptation," **Luke 4:13**; **8:13**; 1 Tim. 6:9; (3) of "trying" or challenging God, by men, Heb. 3:8.

Departed *see Luke 2:37*.

Season *see Luke 1:20*.

4:14 And Jesus returned in the power of the Spirit into Galilee: and there went out a fame of him through all the region round about.

Returned *see Luke 1:56*.

Fame *pheme* (5345), originally denoted "a divine voice, an oracle"; hence, "a saying or report" (akin to *phemi*, "to say," from a root meaning "to shine, to be clear"; hence, Lat., *fama*, Eng., "fame"), is rendered "fame" in Matt. 9:26 and **Luke 4:14**.

Region *see* Country at *Luke 3:3*.

4:15-16 And he taught in their synagogues, being glorified of all.

"The Spirit-filled life is no mystery revealed to a select few, no goal difficult of attainment. To trust and to obey is the substance of the whole matter."

VICTOR RAYMOND EDMAN

And he came to Nazareth, where he had been brought up: and, as his custom was, he went into the synagogue on the sabbath day, and stood up for to read.

Brought *trepho* (5142), signifies (a) "to make to grow, bring up, rear," **Luke 4:16**, "brought up"; (b) "to nourish, feed," Matt. 6:26; 25:37; **Luke 12:24**; Acts 12:20; Rev. 12:6, 14; of a mother, "to give suck," **Luke 23:29** (some mss. here have *thelazo*, "to suckle"); "to fatten," as of fattening animals, Jas. 5:5, "ye have nourished (your hearts)."

Custom *etho* (1486), "to be accustomed," is used in the passive participle as a noun, signifying "a custom," **Luke 4:16**; Acts 17:2 (KJV, "manner"; RV, "custom"); in Matt. 17:15 and Mark 10:1, "was wont."

Stood *anistemi* (450), "to raise," intransitively, "to rise," is translated "to stand up" in Matt. 12:41, RV; Mark 14:60; **Luke 4:16**; **10:25**; Acts 1:15; 5:34; 10:26; 11:28; 13:16; in 14:10, "stand upright."

Read *anaginosko* (314), primarily, "to know certainly, to know again, recognize" (*ana*, "again," *ginosko*, "to know"), is used of "reading" written characters, e.g., Matt. 12:3, 5; 21:16; 24:15; of the private "reading" of Scripture, Acts 8:28, 30, 32; of the public "reading" of Scripture, **Luke 4:16**; Acts 13:27; 15:21; 2 Cor. 3:15; Col. 4:16 (thrice); 1 Thess. 5:27; Rev. 1:3. In 2 Cor. 1:13 there is a purposive play upon words; firstly, "we write none other things unto you, than what ye read (*anaginosko*)" signifies that there is no hidden or mysterious meaning in his epistles; whatever doubts may have arisen and been expressed in this respect, he means what he says; then follows the similar verb *epiginosko*, "to acknowledge," "or even acknowledge, and I hope ye will acknowledge unto the end." The *paronomasia* can hardly be reproduced in English. Similarly, in 3:2 the verb *ginosko*, "to know," and *anaginosko*, "to read," are put in that order, and metaphorically applied to the church at Corinth as being an epistle, a message to the world, written by the apostle and his fellow missionaries, through their ministry of the gospel and the consequent change in the lives of the converts, an epistle "known and read of all men." For other instances of *paronomasia* see, e.g., Rom. 12:3, *phroneo, huperphroneo, sophroneo;* 1 Cor. 2:13, 14, *sunkrino, anakrino;* 2 Thess. 3:11, *ergazomai*, and *periergazomai;* 1 Cor. 7:31, *chraomai* and *katachraomai;* 11:31, *diakrino* and *krino;* 12:2, *ago* and *apago;* Phil. 3:2, 3, *katatome* and *peritome.*

4:17 And there was delivered unto him the book of the prophet Esaias. And when he had opened the book, he found the place where it was written,

Delivered *epididomi* (1929), signifies (a) "to give by handing, to hand" (*epi*, "over"), e.g., Matt. 7:9, 10; **Luke 4:17**; **24:30**, here of the Lord's act in "handing" the broken loaf to the two at Emmaus, an act which was the means of the revelation of Himself as the crucified and risen Lord; the simple verb is used of His "handing" the bread at the institution of the Lord's Supper, Matt. 26:26; Mark 14:22; **Luke 22:19**; this meaning of the verb *epididomi* is found also in Acts 15:30, "they delivered"; (b) "to give in, give way," Acts 27:15, RV, "we gave way to it."

Book *biblion* (975), a diminutive, had in Hellenistic Greek almost lost its diminutive force and was ousting *biblos* in ordinary use; it denotes "a scroll or a small book." It is used in **Luke 4:17**, **20**, of the "book" of Isaiah; in John 20:30, of the Gospel of John; in Gal. 3:10 and Heb. 10:7, of the whole of the OT; in Heb. 9:19, of the "book" of Exodus; in Rev. 1:11; 22:7, 9-10, 18 (twice), 19, of Revelation; in John 21:25 and 2 Tim. 4:13, of "books" in general; in Rev. 13:8; 17:8; 20:12; 21:27, of the "Book" of Life; in Rev. 20:12, of other "books" to be opened in the Day of Judgment, containing, it would seem, the record of human deeds. In Rev. 5:1-9 the "Book" represents the revelation of God's purposes and counsels concerning the world. So with the "little book" in Rev. 10:8. In 6:14 it is used of a scroll, the rolling up of which illustrates the removal of the heaven. In Matt. 19:7 and Mark 10:4 the word is used of a bill of divorcement.

Opened *anaptusso* (380), "to unroll" (*ana*, "back," *ptusso*, "to roll"), is found in some mss. in **Luke 4:17** (of the roll of Isaiah), and translated "He had opened" (KJV). *See also* ***Luke 1:64***.

Pace *see* **Room** at ***Luke 2:7***.

4:18 The Spirit of the Lord *is* upon me, because he hath anointed me to preach the gospel to the poor; he hath sent me to heal the brokenhearted, to preach deliverance to the captives, and recovering of sight to the blind, to set at liberty them that are bruised,

Spirit *see* ***Luke 1:17***.

Anointed *chrio* (5548), is confined to "sacred and symbolical anointings"; of Christ as the "Anointed" of God, **Luke 4:18**; Acts 4:27; 10:38, and Heb. 1:9, where it is used metaphorically in connection with "the oil of gladness." The title Christ signifies "The Anointed One," The word (*Christos*) is rendered "(His) Anointed" in Acts 4:26, RV. Once it is said of believers, 2 Cor. 1:21. *Chrio* is very frequent in the Sept., and is used of kings, 1 Sam. 10:1, and priests, Ex. 28:41, and prophets, 1 Kings 19:16. Among the Greeks it was used in other senses than the ceremonial, but in the Scriptures it is not found in connection with secular matters.

Preach *kerusso* (2784), signifies (a) "to be a herald," or, in general, "to proclaim," e.g., Matt. 3:1; Mark 1:45, "publish"; in **Luke 4:18**, RV, "to proclaim," KJV, "to preach"; so verse **19**; **Luke 12:3**; Acts 10:37; Rom. 2:21; Rev. 5:2. In 1 Pet. 3:19 the probable reference is, not to glad tidings (which there is no real evidence that Noah preached, nor is there evidence that the spirits of antediluvian people are actually "in prison"), but to the act of Christ after His resurrection in proclaiming His victory to fallen angelic spirits; (b) "to preach the gospel as a herald," e.g., Matt. 24:14; Mark 13:10, RV, "be preached" (KJV, "be published"); 14:9; 16:15, 20; **Luke 8:1**; **9:2**; **24:47**; Acts 8:5;

19:13; 28:31; Rom. 10:14, present participle, lit., "(one) preaching," "a preacher"; 10:15 (1st part); 1 Cor. 1:23; 15:11, 12; 2 Cor. 1:19; 4:5; 11:4; Gal. 2:2; Phil. 1:15; Col. 1:23; 1 Thess. 2:9; 1 Tim. 3:16; (c) "to preach the word," 2 Tim. 4:2 (of the ministry of the Scriptures, with special reference to the gospel).

Sent *see* ***Luke 1:19***.

Heal *iaomai* (2390), "to heal," is used (a) of physical treatment 22 times; in Matt. 5:28, KJV, "made whole," RV, "healed"; so in Acts 9:34; (b) figuratively, of spiritual "healing," Matt. 13:15; John 12:40; Acts 28:27; Heb. 12:13; 1 Pet. 2:24; possibly, Jas. 5:16 includes both (a) and (b); some mss. have the word, with sense (b), in **Luke 4:18**. Apart from this last, Luke, the physician, uses the word a number of times (inc. **5:17**; **9:2**).

Brokenhearted *suntribo* (4937), lit., "to rub together," and so "to shatter, shiver, break in pieces by crushing," is said of the bruising of a reed, Matt. 12:20; the "breaking" of fetters in pieces, Mark 5:4; the "breaking" of an alabaster cruse, Mark 14:3; an earthenware vessel, Rev. 2:27; of the physical bruising of a person possessed by a demon, **Luke 9:39**; concerning Christ, "a bone of Him shall not be broken," John 19:36; metaphorically of the crushed condition of a "broken-hearted" person, **Luke 4:18** (KJV only); of the eventual crushing of Satan, Rom. 16:20. This verb is frequent in the Sept. in the passive voice, e.g., Ps. 51:17; Isa. 57:15, of a contrite heart, perhaps a figure of stones made smooth by being rubbed together in streams. Cf. *suntrimma*, "destruction."

Captives *aichmalotos* (164), lit., "one taken by the spear" (from *aichme*, "a spear," and *halotos*, a verbal adjective, from *halonai*, "to be captured"), hence denotes "a captive," **Luke 4:18**.

"If people ask, 'Why did he not appear by means of other parts of creation, and use some nobler instrument, as the sun or moon or stars or fire or air, instead of man merely?' let them know that the Lord came not to make a display, but to teach and heal those who were suffering."

ST. ATHANASIUS OF ALEXANDRIA

Sight *anablepsis* (309), denotes "recovering of sight" (*ana*, "again," *blepo*, "to see"), **Luke 4:18**. In the Sept, Isa. 61:1. In **Luke 7:21**, the infinitive mood of *blepo*, "to see," is used as a noun, "(He bestowed, KJV, 'gave') sight." In Acts 9:9 it is used in the present participle with *me*, "not," "without sight" (lit., "not seeing"). In Heb. 12:21 *phantazomai*, "to make visible," is used in the present participle as a noun, with the article, "(the) sight." (4) In **Luke 21:11**, KJV, *phobetron* (or *phobethron*), plur., is translated "fearful sights" (RV, "terrors").

Set *apostello* (649), "to send away," is translated "to set at liberty" in **Luke 4:18**.

Liberty *aphesis* (859), "dismissal, release, forgiveness," is rendered "liberty" in the KJV of **Luke 4:18**, RV, "release."

Bruised *thrauo* (2352), "to smite through, shatter," is used in **Luke 4:18**, "them that are bruised," i.e., broken by calamity.

4:19 To preach the acceptable year of the Lord.

Preach *kerusso* (2784), is translated "to proclaim" in the RV, for KJV, "to preach," in Matt. 10:27; **Luke 4:19**; Acts 8:5; 9:20. *See also* ***Luke 4:18***.

Acceptable *dektos* (1184), denotes "a person or thing who has been regarded favorably," **Luke 4:19, 24**; Acts 10:35; 2 Cor. 6:2; Phil. 4:18.

Year *eniautos* (1763), originally "a cycle of time," is used (a) of a particular time marked by an event, e.g., **Luke 4:19**; John 11:49, 51; 18:13; Gal. 4:10; Rev. 9:15; (b) to mark a space of time, Acts 11:26; 18:11; Jas. 4:13; 5:17; (c) of that which takes place every year, Heb. 9:7; with *kata*, Heb. 9:25; 10:1, 3.

4:20 And he closed the book, and he gave *it* again to the minister, and sat down. And the eyes of all them that were in the synagogue were fastened on him.

Closed *ptusso* (4428), "to fold, double up," is used of a scroll of parchment, **Luke 4:20**. Cf. *anaptusso*, "to open up," v. **17**.

Book *see* ***Luke 4:17***.

Minister *huperetes* (5257), properly "an under rower" (*hupo*, "under," *eretes*, "a rower"), as distinguished from *nautes*, "a seaman" (a meaning which lapsed from the word), hence came to denote "any subordinate acting under another's direction"; in **Luke 4:20**, RV, "attendant," KJV, "minister," it signifies the attendant at the synagogue service; in Acts 13:5, it is said of John Mark, RV, "attendant," KJV, "minister;" in Acts 26:16, "a minister," it is said of Paul as a servant of Christ in the gospel; so in 1 Cor. 4:1, where the apostle associates others with himself, as Apollos and Cephas, as "ministers of Christ."

Fastened *atenizo* (816), from *atenes*, "strained, intent," and *teino*, "to stretch, strain" (from a root *ten-*, seen in Eng., "tension, tense," etc.), signifies "to look fixedly, gaze, fasten one's eyes upon," and is found twelve times in the writings of Luke (ten in the Acts), out of its fourteen occurrences. It always has a strongly intensive meaning, and is translated "to fasten the eyes upon" in the KJV and RV in **Luke 4:20**; Acts 3:4; 11:6; so in the RV, where the KJV has different renderings, in Acts 6:15 (for KJV, "looking steadfastly"); 10:4 ("looked"); 13:9 ("set his eyes"); 14:9 ("steadfastly beholding"). In Acts 7:55, both have "looked up steadfastly." In the following the RV also varies the translation, **Luke 22:56**; Acts 1:10; 3:12; 23:1; 2 Cor. 3:7, 13.

4:21 And he began to say unto them, This day is this scripture fulfilled in your ears.

This day *semeron* (4594), an adverb (the Attic form is *temeron*), akin to *hemera*, a day, with the prefix *t* originally representing a pronoun. It is used frequently in Matthew, Luke and Acts; in the last it is always rendered "this day"; also in Heb. 1:5, and the RV of 5:5 (KJV, "to day") in the same quotation; "today" in 3:7, 13, 15; 4:7 (twice); 13:8; also Jas. 4:13. The clause containing *semeron* is sometimes introduced by the conjunction *hoti*, "that," e.g., Mark 14:30; **Luke 4:21**; **19:9**; sometimes without the conjunction, e.g., **Luke 22:34**; **23:43**, where "today" is to be attached to the next statement, "shalt thou be with Me"; there are no grammatical reasons for the insistence that the connection must be with the statement "Verily I say unto thee," nor is such an idea necessitated by examples from either the Sept. or the NT; the connection given in the KJV and RV is right. In Rom. 11:8 and 2 Cor. 3:14, 15, the lit. rendering is "unto the today day," the emphasis being brought out by the RV, "unto (until) this very day." In Heb. 4:7, the "today" of Ps. 95:7 is evidently designed to extend to the present period of the Christian faith.

Scripture *graphe* (1124), akin to *grapho*, "to write" (Eng., "graph," "graphic," etc.), primarily denotes "a drawing, painting"; then "a writing," (a) of the OT Scriptures, (1) in the plural, the whole, e.g., Matt. 21:42; 22:29; John 5:39; Acts 17:11; 18:24; Rom. 1:2, where "the prophets" comprises the OT writers in general; 15:4; 16:26, lit., "prophetic writings," expressing the character of all the Scriptures; (2) in the singular in reference to a particular passage, e.g., Mark 12:10; **Luke 4:21**; John 2:22; 10:35 (though applicable to all); 19:24, 28, 36, 37; 20:9; Acts 1:16; 8:32, 35; Rom. 4:3; 9:17; 10:11; 11:2; Gal. 3:8, 22; 4:30; 1 Tim. 5:18, where the 2nd quotation is from **Luke 10:7**, from which it may be inferred that the apostle included Luke's Gospel as "Scripture" alike with Deuteronomy, from which the first quotation is taken; in reference to the whole, e.g. Jas. 4:5 (see RV, a separate rhetorical question from the one which follows); in 2 Pet. 1:20, "no prophecy of Scripture," a description of all, with special application to the OT in the next verse; (b) of the OT Scriptures (those accepted by the Jews as canonical) and all those of the NT which were to be accepted by Christians as authoritative, 2 Tim. 3:16; these latter were to be discriminated from the many forged epistles and other religious "writings" already produced and circulated in Timothy's time. Such discrimination would be directed by the fact that "every Scripture," characterized by inspiration of God, would be profitable for the purposes mentioned; so the RV. The KJV states truth concerning the completed canon of Scripture, but that was not complete when the apostle wrote to Timothy.

Fulfilled *pleroo* (4137), signifies (1) "to fill"; (2) "to fulfill, complete," (a) of time, e.g., Mark 1:15; **Luke 21:24**; John 7:8 (KJV, "full come"); Acts 7:23, RV, "he was wellnigh forty years old" (KJV, "was full," etc.), lit., "the time of forty years was fulfilled to him"; v. 30, KJV, "were expired"; 9:23; 24:27 (KJV, "after two years"; RV, "when two years were fulfilled"); (b) of number, Rev. 6:11; (c) of good pleasure, 2 Thess. 1:11; (d) of joy, Phil. 2:2; in the passive voice, "to be fulfilled," John 3:29 and 17:13; in the following the verb is rendered "fulfilled" in the RV, for the KJV, "full," John 15:11; 16:24; 1 John 1:4; 2 John 12; (e) of obedience, 2 Cor. 10:6; (f) of works, Rev. 3:2; (g) of the future Passover, **Luke 22:16**; (h) of sayings, prophecies, etc., e.g., Matt. 1:22 (twelve times in Matt., two in Mark, four in Luke, eight in John, two in Acts); Jas. 2:23; in Col. 1:25 the word signifies to preach "fully," to complete the ministry of the Gospel appointed.

Ears *see* ***Luke 1:44***.

4:22 And all bare him witness, and wondered at the gracious words which proceeded out of his mouth. And they said, Is not this Joseph's son?

Witness *martureo* (3140), denotes (I) "to be a *martus*," or "to bear witness to," sometimes rendered "to testify"; it is used of the witness (a) of God the Father to Christ, John 5:32, 37; 8:18 (2nd part); 1 John 5:9, 10; to others, Acts 13:22; 15:8; Heb. 11:2, 4 (twice), 5, 39; (b) of Christ, John 3:11, 32; 4:44; 5:31; 7:7; 8:13, 14, 18 (1st part); 13:21; 18:37; Acts 14:3; 1 Tim. 6:13; Rev. 22:18, 20; of the Holy Spirit, to Christ, John 15:26; Heb. 10:15; 1 John 5:7, 8, RV ...; (c) of the Scriptures, to Christ, John 5:39; Heb. 7:8, 17; (d) of the works of Christ, to Himself, and of the circumstances connected with His death, John 5:36; 10:25; 1 John 5:8; (e) of prophets and apostles, to the righteousness of God, Rom. 3:21; to Christ, John 1:7, 8, 15, 32, 34; 3:26; 5:33, RV; 15:27; 19:35; 21:24; Acts 10:43; 23:11; 1 Cor. 15:15; 1 John 1:2; 4:14; Rev. 1:2; to doctrine, Acts 26:22 (in some texts, so KJV); to the Word of God, Rev. 1:2; (f) of others, concerning Christ, **Luke 4:22**; John 4:39; 12:17; (g) of believers to one another, John 3:28; 2 Cor. 8:3; Gal. 4:15; Col. 4:13; 1 Thess. 2:11 (in some texts); 3 John 3, 6, 12 (2nd part); (h) of the apostle Paul concerning Israel, Rom. 10:2; (i) of an angel, to the churches, Rev. 22:16; (j) of unbelievers, concerning themselves, Matt. 23:31; concerning Christ, John 18:23; concerning others, John 2:25; Acts 22:5; 26:5; (II) "to give a good report, to approve of," Acts 6:3; 10:22; 16:2; 22:12; 1 Tim. 5:10; 3 John 12 (1st part); some would put **Luke 4:22** here.

Gracious *see* Grace at *Luke 2:40*.

Proceeded *ekporeuomai* (1607), "to go forth," is translated "to proceed out of" in Matt. 4:4; 15:11, RV; 15:18; Mark 7:15, RV; 7:20, RV; 7:21; 7:23, RV; **Luke 4:22**; John 15:26; Eph. 4:29; Rev. 1:16, RV; 4:5; 9:17, 18, RV (KJV, "issued"); 11:5; 19:15, RV; 19:21, KJV (RV, "came forth"); 22:1.

4:23 And he said unto them, Ye will surely say unto me this proverb, Physician, heal thyself: whatsoever we have heard done in Capernaum, do also here in thy country.

Surely *pantos* (3843), when used without a negative, signifies "wholly, entirely, by all means," Acts 18:21 (KJV); 1 Cor. 9:22; "altogether," 1 Cor. 9:10; "no doubt, doubtless," **Luke 4:23**, RV (KJV, "surely"); Acts 28:4. In 21:22 it is translated "certainly," RV, for KJV, "needs" (lit., "by all means"). With a negative it signifies "in no wise," Rom. 3:9; 1 Cor. 5:10; 16:12 (at all).

Say *eiro* (3004), an obsolete verb, has the future tense *ereo*, used, e.g., in Matt. 7:4; **Luke 4:23** (2nd part); **13:25** (last part); Rom. 3:5; 4:1; 6:1; 7:7 (1st part); 8:31; 9:14, 19, 20, 30; 11:19; 1 Cor. 15:35; 2 Cor. 12:6; Jas. 2:18. The perfect is used, e.g., in John 12:50.

Proverb *parabole* (3850), lit. denotes "a placing beside" (akin to *paraballo*, "to throw" or "lay beside, to compare"). It signifies "a placing of one thing beside another" with a view to comparison (some consider that the thought of comparison is not necessarily contained in the word). In the NT it is found outside the Gospels, only in Heb. 9:9 and 11:19. It is generally used of a somewhat lengthy utterance or narrative drawn from nature or human circumstances, the object of which is to set forth a spiritual lesson, e.g., those in Matt. 13 and Synoptic parallels; sometimes it is used of a short saying or proverb, e.g., Matt. 15:15; Mark 3:23; 7:17; **Luke 4:23**; **5:36**; **6:39**. It is the lesson that is of value; the hearer must catch the analogy if he is to be instructed (this is true also of a proverb). Such a narrative or saying, dealing with earthly things with a spiritual meaning, is distinct from a fable, which attributes to things what does not belong to them in nature. Christ's "parables" most frequently convey truths connected with the subject of the kingdom of God. His withholding the meaning from His hearers as He did from the multitudes, Matt. 13:34, was a divine judgment upon the unworthy. Two dangers are to be avoided in seeking to interpret the "parables" in Scripture, that of ignoring the important features, and that of trying to make all the details mean something.

Physician *iatros* (2395), akin to *iaomai*, "to heal," "a physician," occurs in Matt. 9:12; Mark 2:17; 5:26; **Luke 4:23**; **5:31** (in some mss., **8:43**); Col. 4:14.

Heal *therapeuo* (2323) primarily signifies "to serve as a *therapon*, an attendant"; then, "to care for the sick, to treat, cure, heal" (Eng., "therapeutics"). It is chiefly used in Matthew and Luke (**6:7**; **10:9**; **14:3**), once in John (5:10), and, after the Acts, only in Rev. 13:3 and 12.

Done *ginomai* (1096), "to become," is sometimes translated "do" or "done," e.g., **Luke 4:23**, "done (at Capernaum)," followed by *poieo* in the next clause. In Matt. 21:42 and Mark 12:11, this verb is translated, in the KJV, "(the Lord's) doing"; RV, "this was from the Lord."

Country *patris* (3968), primarily signifies "one's fatherland, native country, of one's own town," Matt. 13:54, 57; Mark 6:1, 4; **Luke 4:23-24**; John 4:44; Heb. 11:14.

4:24 And he said, Verily I say unto you, No prophet is accepted in his own country.

Accepted *see* Acceptable at *Luke 4:19*.

4:25 But I tell you of a truth, many widows were in Israel in the days of Elias, when the heaven was shut up three years and six months, when great famine was throughout all the land;

Widows *see* Widow at *Luke 2:37*.

Shut *kleio* (2808), is used (a) of things material, Matt. 6:6; 25:10; **Luke 11:7**; John 20:19, 26; Acts 5:23; 21:30; Rev. 20:3; figuratively, 21:25; (b) metaphorically, of the kingdom of heaven, Matt. 23:13; of heaven, with consequences of famine, **Luke 4:25**; Rev. 11:6; of compassion, 1 John 3:17, RV (KJV, "bowels *of compassion*"); of the blessings accruing from the promises of God regarding David, Rev. 3:7; of a door for testimony, 3:8.

Six *hex* (1803), whence Eng. prefix, "hex"-, is used separately from other numerals in Matt. 17:1; Mark 9:2; **Luke 4:25**; **13:14**; John 2:6; 12:1; Acts 11:12; 18:11; Jas. 5:17; Rev. 4:8. It sometimes suggests incompleteness, in comparison with the perfect number seven.

Months *see Luke 1:24*.

Famine *limos* (3042), is translated "hunger" in **Luke 15:17**; 2 Cor. 11:27; elsewhere it signifies "a famine," and is so translated in each place in the RV; the KJV has the word "dearth" in Acts 7:11 and 11:28, and "hunger" in Rev. 6:8; the RV "famine" is preferable there; see Matt. 24:7; Mark 13:8; **Luke 4:25**; **15:14**; **21:11**; Rom. 8:35; Rev. 18:8.

Land *ge* (1093), denotes (a) "land," as subject to cultivation, e.g., **Luke 14:35**; in 1 Cor. 15:47 it is said of the "earthly" material of which "the first man" was made, suggestive of frailty; (b) "land" as distinct from sea or other water, e.g., Mark 4:1; 6:47; **Luke 5:3**; John 6:21; (c) "the inhabited earth," e.g., **Luke 21:35**; Acts 1:8; 8:33; 10:12; 11:6; 17:26; 22:22; Heb. 11:13; Rev. 13:8. In the following the phrase "on the earth" signifies "among men," **Luke 12:49**; **18:8**; John 17:4, (d) "a country, territory," e.g. **Luke 4:25**; John 3:22; in **23:44**, RV, "(the whole) land," KJV, "(all the) earth"; Acts 7:29; Heb. 11:9, RV, "a land (not his own)," KJV "a (strange) country;" Jude 5; (e) "the ground," e.g., Matt. 10:29; Mark 4:26, RV, "(upon the) earth," for KJV, "(into the) ground."

4:26 But unto none of them was Elias sent, save unto Sarepta, *a city* of Sidon, unto a woman *that was* a widow.

Sent *pempo* (3992), "to send," is used (a) of persons: Christ, by the Father, **Luke 20:13**; John 4:34; 5:23, 24, 30, 37; 6:38, 39, (40), 44; 7:16, 18, 28, 33; 8:16, 18, 26, 29; 9:4; 12:44, 45, 49; 13:20 (2nd part); 14:24; 15:21; 16:5; Rom. 8:3; the Holy Spirit, John 14:26; 15:26; 16:7; Elijah, **Luke 4:26**; John the Baptist, John 1:33; disciples and apostles, e.g., Matt. 11:2; John 20:21; servants, e.g., **Luke 20:11, 12**; officials, Matt. 14:10; messengers, e.g., Acts 10:5, 32, 33; 15:22, 25; 2 Cor. 9:3, Eph. 6:22; Phil. 2:19, 23, 25; 1 Thess. 3:2, 5; Titus 3:12; a prisoner, Acts 25:25, 27; potentates, by God, 1 Pet. 2:14; an angel, Rev. 22:16, demons, Mark 5:12; (b) of things, Acts 11:29; Phil. 4:16; 2 Thess. 2:11; Rev. 1:11; 11:10; 14:15, 18, RV, "send forth" (KJV, "thrust in").

Save The conjunction *ei*, "if," with the negative *me*, "not," is translated "but only" in **Luke 4:26**, RV (KJV, "save"); **4:27** (KJV, "saving"); "only" in 1 Cor. 7:17 (KJV, "but"); in some mss. in Acts 21:25 (KJV "save only").

Woman *gune* (1135), is used of a "woman" unmarried or married, e.g., Matt. 11:11; 14:21; **Luke 4:26**, of a "widow"; Rom. 7:2; in the vocative case, used in addressing a "woman," it is a term not of reproof or severity, but of endearment or respect, Matt. 15:28; John 2:4, where the Lord's words to His mother at the wedding in Cana, are neither rebuff nor rebuke. The question is, lit., "What to Me and to thee?" and the word "woman," the term of endearment, follows this. The meaning is "There is no obligation on Me or you, but love will supply the need." She confides in Him, He responds to her faith. There was lovingkindness in both hearts. His next words about "His hour" suit this; they were not unfamiliar to her. Cana is in the path to Calvary; Calvary was not yet, but it made the beginning of signs possible. See also **4:21; 19:26**.

Widow *see Luke 2:37*.

4:27 And many lepers were in Israel in the time of Eliseus the prophet; and none of them was cleansed, saving Naaman the Syrian.

Lepers *lepros* (3015), an adjective, primarily used of "psoriasis," characterized by an eruption of rough scaly patches; later, "leprous," but chiefly used as a noun, "a leper," Matt. 8:2; 10:8; 11:5; Mark 1:40; **Luke 4:27**; **7:22**; **17:12**; especially of Simon, mentioned in Matt. 26:6; Mark 14:3.

Time In **Luke 4:27**, the preposition *epi* signifies "in the time of."

Prophet *see Luke 1:76*.

Saving In **Luke 4:27** and Rev. 2:17, KJV, *ei me* (lit., "if not"), is translated "saving" (RV, "but only" and "but"). *See also* **Save** at ***Luke 4:26.***

4:28 And all they in the synagogue, when they heard these things, were filled with wrath,

Filled *see* ***Luke 1:15.***

Wrath *thumos* (2372), "hot anger, passion," is translated "wrath" in **Luke 4:28**; Acts 19:28; Rom. 2:8, RV; Gal. 5:20; Eph. 4:31; Col. 3:8; Heb. 11:27; Rev. 12:12; 14:8, 10, 19; 15:1, 7; 16:1; 18:3; "wraths" in 2 Cor. 12:20; "fierceness" in Rev. 16:19; 19:15.

4:29 And rose up, and thrust him out of the city, and led him unto the brow of the hill whereon their city was built, that they might cast him down headlong.

Rose *anistemi* (450), "to stand up or to make to stand up," according as its use is intransitive or transitive (*ana*, "up," *histemi*, "to stand"), is used (a) of a physical change of position, e.g., of "rising" from sleep, Mark 1:35; from a meeting in a synagogue, **Luke 4:29**; of the illegal "rising" of the high priest in the tribunal in Matt. 26:62; of an invalid "rising" from his couch, **Luke 5:25**; the "rising" up of a disciple from his vocation to follow Christ, **Luke 5:28**; cf. John 11:31; "rising" up from prayer, **Luke 22:45**; of a whole company, Acts 26:30; 1 Cor. 10:7; (b) metaphorically, of "rising" up antagonistically against persons, e.g. of officials against people, Acts 5:17; of a seditious leader, 5:36, of the "rising" up of Satan, Mark 3:26; of false teachers, Acts 20:30; (c) of "rising" to a position of preeminence or power; e.g., of Christ as a prophet, Acts 3:22; 7:37; as God's servant in the midst of the nation of Israel, Acts 3:26; as the Son of God in the midst of the nation, 13:33 (not here of resurrection, but with reference to the Incarnation: the KJV "again" has nothing corresponding to it in the original, it was added as a misinterpretation: the mention of His resurrection is in the next verse, in which it is stressed by way of contrast and by the addition, "from the dead"); as a priest, Heb. 7:11, 15; as king over the nations, Rom. 15:12; (d) of a spiritual awakening from lethargy, Eph. 5:14; (e) of resurrection from the dead: (1) of the resurrection of Christ, Matt. 17:9; 20:19; Mark 8:31; 9:9-10, 31; 10:34; **Luke 18:33**; **24:7, 46**; John 20:9; Acts 2:24, 32; 10:41; 13:34; 17:3, 31; 1 Thess. 4:14; (2) of believers, John 6:39-40, 44, 54; 11:24; 1 Thess. 4:16; of unbelievers, Matt. 12:41.

Thrust *ekballo* (1544), "to cast out," is rendered "thrust ... out" in **Luke 4:29**, KJV (RV, "cast ... forth"); so **13:28** and Acts 16:37.

Led *see* ***Luke 4:1.***

Brow *ophrus* (3790), "an eyebrow," stands for "the brow of a hill," **Luke 4:29**, from the resemblance to an eyebrow, i.e., a ridge with an overhanging bank.

Hill *oros* (3735), "a hill or mountain," is translated "hill" in Matt. 5:14; **Luke 4:29**; "mountain" in **Luke 9:37**, RV, KJV, "hill" (of the mount of transfiguration) as in v. **28**.

Built *oikodomeo* (3618), lit., "to build a house" (*oikos*, "a house," *domeo*, "to build"), hence, to build anything, e.g., Matt. 7:24; **Luke 4:29**; **6:48**, RV, "well builded" (last clause of verse); John 2:20; is frequently used figuratively, e.g., Acts 20:32; Gal. 2:18; especially of edifying, Acts 9:31; Rom. 15:20; 1 Cor. 10:23; 14:4; 1 Thess. 5:11 (RV). In 1 Cor. 8:10 it is translated "emboldened" (marg., "builded up"). The participle with the article (equivalent to a noun) is rendered "builder," Matt. 21:42; Acts 4:11; 1 Pet. 2:7.

Cast ... headlong *katakremnizo* (2630), "to throw over a precipice" (*kremnos*), "cast down headlong," is rendered "throw ... down" in **Luke 4:29** (KJV, "cast ... down headlong").

4:30 But he passing through the midst of them went his way,

Midst *mesos* (3319), an adjective denoting "middle, in the middle or midst," is used in the following, in which the English requires a phrase, and the adjectival rendering must be avoided: **Luke 22:55**, "Peter sat in the midst of them," lit., "a middle one of (them)"; **Luke 23:45**, of the rending of the veil "in the midst"; here the adjective idiomatically belongs to the verb "was rent," and is not to be taken literally, as if it meant "the middle veil"; John 1:26, "in the midst of you (standeth One)," RV (lit., "a middle One"); Acts 1:18, where the necessity of avoiding the lit. rendering is obvious. Cf. the phrases "at midday," "at midnight." *Mesos* is used adverbially, in prepositional phrases, (a) *ana m.*, e.g., 1 Cor. 6:5, "between"; Matt. 13:25, "among"; Rev. 7:17, "in the midst"; (b) *dia m.*, e.g., **Luke 4:30**; **17:11**, "through the midst"; (c) *en m.*, **Luke 10:3**, RV, "in the midst," KJV, "among"; so **22:27**; 1 Thess. 2:7; with the article after *en*, e.g., Matt. 14:6, RV, "in the midst," KJV, "before"; (d) *eis m.*, Mark 14:60, "in the midst"; with the article, e.g., Mark 3:3, "forth" (lit., "into the midst"); (e) *ek m.*, "out of the way," lit., "out of the midst," Col. 2:14; 2 Thess. 2:7, where, however, removal is not necessarily in view;

there is no accompanying verb signifying removal, as in each of the other occurrences of the phrase; with the article, e.g., 1 Cor. 5:2; 2 Cor. 6:17; (f) *kata m.*, Acts 27:27, "about mid(night)."

4:31-33 And came down to Capernaum, a city of Galilee, and taught them on the sabbath days.

And they were astonished at his doctrine: for his word was with power.

And in the synagogue there was a man, which had a spirit of an unclean devil, and cried out with a loud voice,

Spirit *see Luke 1:17.*

Cried *anakrazo* (349), signifies "to cry out loudly," Mark 1:23; 6:49; **Luke 4:33**; **8:28**; **23:18**.

4:34 Saying, Let *us* alone; what have we to do with thee, *thou* Jesus of Nazareth? art thou come to destroy us? I know thee who thou art; the Holy One of God.

Let us alone *ea* (1436), an interjection of surprise, fear and anger, was the ejaculation of the man with the spirit of an unclean demon, **Luke 4:34**, RV; the KJV renders it "Let us alone" (see RV, marg.).

Have In Matt. 27:19, "Have thou nothing to do with that righteous man" translates what is lit. "nothing to thee and that righteous man," the verb being omitted. Similarly with the phrase, "What have I to do with thee?" lit., "what (is) to me and thee?" Mark 5:7; **Luke 8:28**; John 2:4, where Westcott translates it "What is there to Me and to thee?"; Ellicott, "What is that to Me and to thee," i.e., "What is My concern and thine in the matter?" There is certainly nothing disparaging in the question. On the contrary, it answers what must have been the thought in Mary's heart, and suggests that while there is no obligation either on Him or her, yet the need is a case for rendering help. For the construction with the plural pronoun see Matt. 8:29; Mark 1:24; **Luke 4:34**.

4:35 And Jesus rebuked him, saying, Hold thy peace, and come out of him. And when the devil had thrown him in the midst, he came out of him, and hurt him not.

Rebuked *epitimao* (2008), primarily, "to put honor upon," then, "to adjudge," hence signifies "to rebuke." Except for 2 Tim. 4:2 and Jude 9, it is confined in the NT to the Synoptic Gospels, where it is frequently used of the Lord's rebukes to (a) evil spirits, e.g., Matt. 17:18; Mark 1:25; 9:25; **Luke 4:35**, **41**; **9:42**; (b) winds, Matt. 8:26; Mark 4:39; **Luke 8:24**; (c) fever, **Luke 4:39**; (d) disciples, Mark 8:33; **Luke 9:55**; contrast **Luke 19:39**. For rebukes by others see Matt. 16:22; 19:13; 20:31; Mark 8:32; 10:13; 10:48, RV, "rebuked" (KJV, "charged"); **Luke 17:3**; **18:15**, **39**; **23:40**.

Hold ... peace *phimoo* (5392), "to muzzle," is used metaphorically in the passive voice, in Mark 1:25 and **Luke 4:35**, "hold thy peace"; in Mark 4:39, "be still."

Thrown *rhipto* (4496), denotes "to throw with a sudden motion, to jerk, cast forth"; "cast down," Matt. 15:30 and 27:5; "thrown down," **Luke 4:35**; "thrown," **17:2** (KJV, "cast"); [*rhipteo* in Acts 22:23 (KJV, "cast off"), of the "casting" off of clothes (in the next sentence *ballo* is used of "casting" dust into the air)]; in 27:19 "cast out," of the tackling of a ship, in v. 29 "let go" (KJV, "cast"), of anchors; in Matt. 9:36, "scattered," said of sheep.

Hurt *blapto* (984), signifies "to injure, mar, do damage to," Mark 16:18, "shall (in no wise) hurt (them)"; **Luke 4:35**, "having done (him no) hurt," RV. *Adikeo* stresses the unrighteousness of the act, *blapto* stresses the injury done.

4:36 And they were all amazed, and spake among themselves, saying, What a word *is* this! for with authority and power he commandeth the unclean spirits, and they come out.

Amazed *thambos* (2285), "amazement, wonder," is probably connected with a root signifying "to render immovable"; it is frequently associated with terror as well as astonishment, as with the verb in Acts 9:6. It occurs in **Luke 4:36**; **5:9**; Acts 3:10.

Spake *sullaleo* (4814), "to speak together with" (*sun*, "with," *laleo*, "to speak"), is translated "conferred" in Acts 25:12; elsewhere of talking with Matt. 17:3; Mark 9:4; **Luke 4:36**; **9:30**; "communed" in **Luke 22:4**.

Themselves Regarding *allelon*, "of one another," and its other forms, the RV substitutes "one another" for the KJV "themselves" in Mark 8:16; 9:34; **Luke 4:36**; John 6:52; 11:56; 16:17; 19:24; Acts 26:31; 28:4; Rom. 2:15, but adheres to the rendering "themselves" in Mark 15:31; Acts 4:15; 28:25.

Commandeth *epitasso* (2004), signifies to appoint over, put in charge (*epi*, "over," *tasso*, "to appoint"); then, "to put upon one as a duty, to enjoin," Mark 1:27; 6:27, 39; 9:25; **Luke 4:36**; **8:25**, **31**; **14:22**; Acts 23:2; Philem. 8.

4:37 And the fame of him went out into every place of the country round about.

Fame *echos*, "a noise, report, sound," is translated "rumor," in the RV of **Luke 4:37**, for KJV, "fame"; "sound" in Acts 2:2; Heb. 12:19.

Country *see Luke 3:3*.

4:38 And he arose out of the synagogue, and entered into Simon's house. And Simon's wife's mother was taken with a great fever; and they besought him for her.

Wife's mother *penthera* (3994), denotes "a mother-in-law," Matt. 8:14; 10:35; Mark 1:30; **Luke 4:38**; **12:53** (twice).

Taken *sunecho* (4912), "to hold together, confine, secure, to hold fast" (*echo*, "to have or hold"), "to constrain," is said (a) of the effect of the word of the Lord upon Paul, Acts 18:5 (KJV, "was pressed in spirit," RV, "was constrained by the word"); of the effect of the love of Christ, 2 Cor. 5:14; (b) of being taken with a disease, Matt. 4:24; **Luke 4:38**; Acts 28:8; with fear, **Luke 8:37**; (c) of thronging or holding in a person, **Luke 8:45**; being straitened, **Luke 12:50**; being in a strait betwixt two, Phil. 1:23; keeping a city in on every side, **Luke 19:43**; keeping a tight hold on a person, as the men who seized the Lord Jesus did, after bringing Him into the High Priest's house, **Luke 22:63**; (d) of stopping the ears in refusal to listen, Acts 7:57. Luke uses the word nine times out of its twelve occurrences in the NT.

Fever *puretos* (4446), "feverish heat" (from *pur*, "fire"), hence, "a fever," occurs in Matt. 8:15; Mark 1:31; John 4:52; Acts 28:8; in **Luke 4:38**, with *megas*, "great, a high fever"; v. **39**. Luke, as a physician, uses the medical distinction by which the ancients classified fevers into great and little. In the Sept., Deut. 28:22.

4:39 And he stood over her, and rebuked the fever; and it left her: and immediately she arose and ministered unto them.

Stood *see* Came at *Luke 2:9*.

Rebuked *see Luke 4:35*.

Fever *see Luke 4:38*.

Immediately *see Luke 1:64*.

Ministered *diakoneo* (1247), signifies "to be a servant, attendant, to serve, wait upon, minister." In the following it is translated "to minister," except where "to serve" is mentioned: it is used (a) with a general significance, e.g., Matt. 4:11; 20:28; Mark 1:13; 10:45; John 12:26 ("serve," twice); Acts 19:22; Philem. 13; (b) of waiting at table, "ministering" to the guests, Matt. 8:15; **Luke 4:39**; **8:3**; **12:37**; **17:8**, "serve"; **22:26**, "serve," v. **27**, "serveth," twice; the 2nd instance, concerning the Lord, may come under (a); so of women preparing food, etc., Mark 1:31; **Luke 10:40**, "serve"; John 12:2, "served"; (c) of relieving one's necessities, supplying the necessaries of life, Matt. 25:44; 27:55; Mark 15:41; Acts 6:2, "serve"; Rom. 15:25; Heb. 6:10; more definitely in connection with such service in a local church, 1 Tim. 3:10, 13 [there is nothing in the original representing the word "office"; RV, "let them serve as deacons," "they that have served (well) as deacons"]; (d) of attending, in a more general way, to anything that may serve another's interests, as of the work of an amanuensis, 2 Cor. 3:3 (metaphorical): of the conveyance of material gifts for assisting the needy, 2 Cor. 8:19, 20, RV, "is ministered" (KJV, "is administered"); of a variety of forms of service, 2 Tim. 1:18; of the testimony of the OT prophets, 1 Pet. 1:12; of the ministry of believers one to another in various ways, 1 Pet. 4:10, 11.

4:40 Now when the sun was setting, all they that had any sick with divers diseases brought them unto him; and he laid his hands on every one of them, and healed them.

Setting *duno* (1416), "to sink into," is used of the "setting" of the sun, Mark 1:32, "did set"; **Luke 4:40**, "was setting." The sun, moon and stars were conceived of as sinking into the sea when they set.

Sick *astheneo* (770), lit., "to be weak, feeble" (*a*, negative, *sthenos*, "strength"), is translated "to be sick," e.g., in Matt. 10:8, "(the) sick"; 25:36; v. 39 in the best texts; Mark 6:56; **Luke 4:40**; **7:10** (RV omits the word); **9:2**; John 4:46; 5:3, RV (KJV, "impotent folk"); v. 7; 6:2, RV (KJV, "were diseased"); 11:1-3, 6; Acts 9:37; 19:12; Phil. 2:26, 27; 2 Tim. 4:20; Jas. 5:14.

Divers *poikilos* (4164), denotes "parti-colored, variegated" (*poikillo* means "to make gay": the root of the first syllable is *pik-*, found in Eng., "picture"), hence "divers," Matt. 4:24; Mark 1:34; **Luke 4:40**; 2 Tim. 3:6; Titus 3:3; Heb. 2:4 (RV, "manifold"), 13:9; Jas. 1:2 (RV, "manifold"); in 1 Pet. 1:6 and 4:10, "manifold," both KJV and RV.

Diseases *nosos* (3554), akin to Lat. *nocere*, "to injure" (Eng., "nosology"), is the regular word for "disease, sickness," Matt. 4:23; 8:17; 9:35; 10:1, RV, "disease," KJV, "sickness"; in Matt. 4:24; Mark 1:34; **Luke 4:40**; **6:17**; **9:1**; Acts 19:12, KJV and RV render it "diseases." In **Luke 7:21**, KJV has "infirmities." The most authentic mss. omit the word in Mark 3:15.

Laid *epitithemi* (2007), "to add to, lay upon," etc., is used of "laying" hands on the sick, for healing, Matt. 9:18; 19:13, RV, "lay" (KJV, "put"); 19:15; Mark 5:23; 6:5; 7:32; 8:23, RV, "laid" (KJV, "put"); so in v. 25; 16:18; **Luke 4:40**; **13:13**; Acts 6:6; 8:17, 19; 9:12 and 17, RV, "laying" (KJV, "putting"); 13:3; 19:6; 28:8; in some mss. in Rev. 1:17; of "laying" hands on a person by way of public recognition, 1 Tim. 5:22; of a shepherd's "laying" a sheep on his shoulders, **Luke 15:5**; "of laying" the cross on Christ's shoulders, **Luke 23:26**; of "laying" on stripes, Acts 16:23; wood on a fire, 28:3; metaphorically, of "laying" burden's on men's shoulders, Matt. 23:4; similarly of "giving" injunctions, Acts 15:28 (cf. "put ... upon" in v. 10).

Every *hekastos* (1538), "each" or "every," is used of any number separately, either (a) as an adjective qualifying a noun, e.g., **Luke 6:44**; John 19:23; Heb. 3:13, where "day by day," is, lit., "according to each day"; or, more emphatically with *heis*, "one," in Matt. 26:22; **Luke 4:40**; **16:5**; Acts 2:3, 6, 20:31; 1 Cor. 12:18; Eph. 4:7, 16, RV, "each (several)," for KJV, "every"; Col. 4:6; 1 Thess. 2:11; 2 Thess. 1:3; (b) as a distributive pronoun, e.g., Acts 4:35; Rom. 2:6; Gal. 6:4; in Phil. 2:4, it is used in the plural; some mss. have it thus in Rev. 6:11. The repetition in Heb. 8:11 is noticeable "every man" (i.e., everyone). Prefixed by the preposition *ana*, "apiece" (a colloquialism), it is used, with stress on the individuality, in Rev. 21:21, of the gates of the heavenly city, "each one of the several," RV; in Eph. 5:33, preceded by *kath' hena*, "by one," it signifies "each (one) his own."

One *heis* (1520), the first cardinal numeral, masculine (feminine and neuter nominative forms are *mia* and *hen*, respectively), is used to signify (1) (a) "one" in contrast to many, e.g., Matt. 25:15; Rom. 5:18, RV, "(through) one (trespass)," i.e., Adam's transgression, in contrast to the "one act of righteousness," i.e., the death of Christ (not as KJV, "the offense of one," and "the righteousness of one"); (b) metaphorically, "union" and "concord," e.g., John 10:30; 11:52; 17:11, 21-22; Rom. 12:4-5; Phil. 1:27; (2) emphatically, (a) a single ("one"), to the exclusion of others, e.g., Matt. 21:24; Rom. 3:10; 1 Cor. 9:24; 1 Tim. 2:5 (twice); (b) "one, alone," e.g., Mark 2:7, RV (KJV, "only"); 10:18; **Luke 18:19**; (c) "one and the same," e.g., Rom. 3:30, RV, "God is one," i.e., there is not "one" God for the Jew and one for the Gentile; cf. Gal. 3:20, which means that in a promise there is no other party; 1 Cor. 3:8; 11:5; 12:11; 1 John 5:8 (lit., "and the three are into one," i.e., united in "one" and the same witness); (3) a certain "one," in the same sense as the indefinite pronoun *tis*, e.g., Matt. 8:19, RV, "a (scribe)," marg., "one (scribe)," KJV, "a certain (scribe)"; 19:16, "one;" in Rev. 8:13, RV marg., "one (eagle)"; *heis tis* are used together in **Luke 22:50**; John 11:49; this occurs frequently in the papyri (Moulton, *Prol.*, p. 96); (4) distributively, with *hekastos*, "each," i.e., "every one," e.g., **Luke 4:40**; Acts 2:6, "every man" (lit., "every one"); in the sense of "one ... and one," e.g., John 20:12; or "one" ... followed by *allos* or *heteros*, "the other," e.g., Matt. 6:24; or by a second *heis*, e.g., Matt. 24:40, RV, "one"; John 20:12; in Rom. 12:5 *heis* is preceded by *kata* (*kath'* in the sense of "severally (members) one (of another)," RV (KJV, "every one ... one"); cf. Mark 14:19; in 1 Thess. 5:11 the phrase in the 2nd part, "each other," RV (KJV, "one another"), is, lit., "one the one"; (5) as an ordinal number, equivalent to *protos*, "first," in the phrase "the first day of the week," lit. and idiomatically, "one of sabbaths," signifying "the first day after the sabbath," e.g., Matt. 28:1; Mark 16:2; Acts 20:7; 1 Cor. 16:2. Moulton remarks on the tendency for certain cardinal numerals to replace ordinals (*Prol.*, p. 96).

4:41 And devils also came out of many, crying out, and saying, Thou art Christ the Son of God. And he rebuking *them* suffered them not to speak: for they knew that he was Christ.

Devils *daimonion* (1140), not a diminutive of *daimon*, but the neuter of the adjective *daimonios*, pertaining to a demon, is also mistranslated "devil," "devils." In Acts 17:18, it denotes an inferior pagan deity. "Demons" are the spiritual agents acting in all idolatry. The idol itself is nothing, but every idol has a "demon" associated with it who induces idolatry, with its worship and sacrifices, 1 Cor. 10:20-21; Rev. 9:20; cf. Deut. 32:17; Isa. 13:21; 34:14; 65:3, 11. They disseminate errors among men, and seek to seduce believers, 1 Tim. 4:1. As seducing spirits they deceive men into the supposition that through mediums (those who have "familiar spirits," Lev. 20:6, 27, e.g.) they can converse with deceased human beings. Hence the destructive deception of spiritism, forbidden in Scripture, Lev. 19:31; Deut. 18:11; Isa. 8:19. "Demons" tremble before God, Jas. 2:19; they recognized Christ as Lord and as their future Judge, Matt. 8:29; **Luke 4:41**. Christ cast them out of human beings by His own power. His disciples did so in His name, and by exercising faith, e.g., Matt. 17:20. Acting under Satan (cf. Rev. 16:13-14), "demons" are permitted to afflict with bodily disease, **Luke 13:16**. Being unclean they tempt human beings with unclean thoughts, Matt. 10:1; Mark 5:2; 7:25; **Luke 8:27-29**; Rev. 16:13; 18:2, e.g. They differ in degrees of wickedness, Matt. 12:45. They will instigate the rulers of the nations at the end of this age to make war against God and His Christ, Rev. 16:14.

Crying *kraugazo* (2905), a stronger form, "to make a clamor or outcry," is used in Matt. 12:19, in a prophecy from Isaiah of Christ; in **Luke 4:41** (in the best mss., instead of *krazo*); John 11:43; 12:13 (in the best mss.); 18:40; 19:6, 12, 19:15; Acts 22:23.

Rebuking *see* Rebuked at *Luke 4:35*.

Suffered *eao* (1439), "to let, permit," is translated "to suffer" in Matt. 24:43; **Luke 4:41**; **22:51**; Acts 14:16; 16:7; 19:30; 28:4; 1 Cor. 10:13.

4:42 And when it was day, he departed and went into a desert place: and the people sought him, and came unto him, and stayed him, that he should not depart from them.

Departed *exerchomai* (1831), denotes "to come out, or go out of, to go forth." It is frequently translated by the verb "to depart," e.g., Matt. 9:31; in **Luke 4:42**, for the KJV, "He departed and went," the RV has "He came out and went"; in **9:6** the KJV and RV agree.

Stayed *katecho* (2722), "to hold fast, hold back," is used in the sense of detaining in **Luke 4:42**, "would have stayed (Him)," RV.

Depart *poreuo* (4198), akin to *poros*, "a passage," in the middle voice signifies "to go on one's way, to depart from one place to another." In some places, where the KJV has the verb "to depart," the RV translates by "to go one's way," e.g., Matt. 2:9, "went their way"; 11:7; 24:1, "was going on His way." In the following the RV has the verb "to go," for the KJV "depart," **Luke 4:42** (latter part of verse); **13:31**; John 16:7; 2 Tim. 4:10. In **Luke 21:8**, "go (after)," is said of disciples or partisans. In some places both KJV and RV translate by the verb "to depart," e.g., Matt. 19:15; 25:41; Acts 5:41; Acts 22:21. This verb is to be distinguished from others signifying "to go." It is best rendered, as often as possible, "to go on one's way."

4:43-44 And he said unto them, I must preach the kingdom of God to other cities also: for therefore am I sent.

And he preached in the synagogues of Galilee.

Preach *see* Glad tidings at *Luke 1:19*.

Other *heteros* (2087), indicates either numerical distinction, e.g., **Luke 4:43**; **5:7**; or generic distinction, different in character, etc., e.g., **Luke 9:29**, "(the fashion of His countenance) was altered," lit., "became other"; **23:32**, "two others, (malefactors)," RV, where the plural serves to make the necessary distinction between them and Christ; Acts 2:4; 19:39 ("other matters"); 1 Cor. 14:21, KJV, "other" (RV, "strange"); 2 Cor. 11:4 (2nd and 3rd parts, RV, "different"; in the 1st clause, *allos*, "another").

Sent *see Luke 1:19*.

Chapter 5

5:1 And it came to pass, that, as the people pressed upon him to hear the word of God, he stood by the lake of Gennesaret,

Pressed *epikeimai* (1945), denotes "to be placed on, to lie on," (a) literally, as of the stone on the sepulchre of Lazarus, John 11:38; of the fish on the fire of coals, 21:9; (b) figuratively, of a tempest (to press upon), Acts 27:20; of a necessity laid upon the apostle Paul, 1 Cor. 9:16; of the pressure of the multitude upon Christ to hear Him, **Luke 5:1**, "pressed upon"; of the insistence of the chief priests, rulers and people that Christ should be crucified, **Luke 23:23**, "were instant"; of carnal ordinances "imposed" under the Law until a time of reformation, brought in through the High Priesthood of Christ, Heb. 9:10.

Lake *limne* (3041), "a lake," is used (a) in the Gospels, only by Luke, of the Sea of Galilee, **Luke 5:2**; **8:22**, **23**, **33**, called Gennesaret in **5:1** (Matthew and Mark use *thalassa*, "a sea"); (b) of the "lake" of fire, Rev. 19:20; 20:10, 14, 15; 21:8.

5:2 And saw two ships standing by the lake: but the fishermen were gone out of them, and were washing *their* nets.

Lake *see Luke 5:1*.

Fishermen *halieus* (231), "a fisherman, fisher" (from *hals*, "the sea"), occurs in Matt. 4:18, 19; Mark 1:16, 17; **Luke 5:2**.

Gone *apobaino* (576), "to go away or from," is translated "had gone out," in **Luke 5:2**, i.e., disembarked.

Washing *pluno* (4150), is used of "washing inanimate objects," e.g., "nets," **Luke 5:2** (some texts have *apopluno*); of "garments," figuratively, Rev. 7:14; 22:14 (in the best texts; the KJV translates those which have the verb *poieo*, "to do," followed by *tas entolas autou*, "His commandments").

Nets *diktuon* (1350), a general term for a "net" (from an old verb *diko*, "to cast": akin to *diskos*, "a quoit"), occurs in Matt. 4:20-21; Mark 1:18-19; **Luke 5:2**, **4-6**; John 21:6, 8, 11 (twice). In the Sept. it was used for a "net" for catching birds, Prov. 1:17, in other ways, e.g., figuratively of a snare, Job 18:8; Prov. 29:5.

5:3 And he entered into one of the ships, which was Simon's, and prayed him that he would thrust out a little from the land. And he sat down, and taught the people out of the ship.

Entered *embaino* (1684), "to go in" (*en*, "in"), is used only in the Gospels, of "entering" a boat, Matt. 8:23; 9:1; 13:2; 14:22, 32; 15:39; Mark 4:1; 5:18; 6:45; 8:10, 13; **Luke 5:3**; **8:22, 37**; John 6:17, (in some mss., in v. 22), 24, RV, "got into the boats," for KJV, "took shipping"; 21:3; Acts 21:6 (in the best mss.); of stepping into water, John 5:4 (RV omits the verb).

Land *see Luke 4:25.*

Thrust *epanago* (1877), "to lead up upon," is used as a nautical term with *ploion*, "a ship," understood, denoting "to put out to sea," translated in **Luke 5:3**, put out, RV (KJV, "thrust out"); in v. **4**, for KJV, "launch." For the nonnautical significance "to return," see Matt. 21:18. In the Sept., Zech. 4:12, "that communicate with (the golden oil vessels)."

Little *oligon* (3641), is used adverbially of (a) time, Mark 6:31, "a while;" 1 Pet. 1:6, RV, "a little while (KJV, "a season"); 5:10, RV, "a little while" (KJV, "a while"); Rev. 17:10, RV, "a little while" (KJV, "a short space"); (b) space, Mark 1:19; **Luke 5:3**; (c) extent, with the preposition *pros*, "for," in 1 Tim. 4:8, RV, "(for) a little" (KJV and RV marg., "little"), where, while the phrase might refer to duration (as KJV marg.), yet the antithesis "for all things" clearly indicates extent, i.e., "physical training is profitable towards few objects in life."

5:4 Now when he had left speaking, he said unto Simon, Launch out into the deep, and let down your nets for a draught.

Left *pauo* (3973), "to stop, to make an end," is used chiefiy in the middle voice in the NT, signifying "to come to an end, to take one's rest, a willing cessation" (in contrast to the passive voice which denotes a forced cessation), **Luke 5:4**, of a discourse; **8:24**, of a storm, **11:1**, of Christ's prayer; Acts 5:42, of teaching and preaching; 6:13, of speaking against; 13:10, of evil doing; 20:1, of an uproar; 20:31, of admonition; 21:32, of a scourging; 1 Cor. 13:8, of tongues; Eph. 1:16, of giving thanks; Col. 1:9, of prayer; Heb. 10:2, of sacrifices; 1 Pet. 4:1, of "ceasing" from sin. It is used in the active voice in 1 Pet. 3:10, "let him cause his tongue to cease from evil."

Launch *see* Thrust at *Luke 5:3.*

Deep *bathos* (899), is used (a) naturally, in Matt. 13:5, "deepness"; Mark 4:5, KJV, "depth," RV, "deepness"; **Luke 5:4**, of "deep" water; Rom. 8:39 (contrasted with *hupsoma*, "height"); (b) metaphorically, in Rom. 11:33, of God's wisdom and knowledge; in 1 Cor. 2:10, of God's counsels; in Eph. 3:18, of the dimensions of the sphere of the activities of God's counsels, and of the love of Christ which occupies that sphere; in 2 Cor. 8:2, of "deep" poverty; some mss. have it in Rev. 2:24.

Let down *chalao* (5465), "to slacken, loosen, let loose," denotes in the NT, "to let down, to lower"; it is used with reference to (a) the paralytic, in Mark 2:4; (b) Saul of Tarsus, Acts 9:25, "lowering"; 2 Cor. 11:33, "was I let down" (passive voice); (c) nets, **Luke 5:4, 5** (in the latter, RV, "nets"; KJV, "net"); (d) the gear of a ship, Acts 27:17, RV, "they lowered (the gear)," KJV, "they strake (sail)"; (e) a ship's boat, v. 30, RV, "lowered" (KJV, "let down").

Nets *see Luke 5:2.*

Draught *agra* (61), "a hunting, catching" (from *ago*, "to lead"), is used only in connection with fishing. In **Luke 5:4** it signifies the act of catching fish; in v. **9** it stands for the catch itself.

5:5 And Simon answering said unto him, Master, we have toiled all the night, and have taken nothing: nevertheless at thy word I will let down the net.

Master *epistates* (1988), denotes "a chief, a commander, overseer master." It is used by the disciples in addressing the Lord, in recognition of His authority rather than His instruction; it occurs only in **Luke 5:5**; **8:24, 45**; **9:33, 49**; **17:13**. In the Sept., 2 Kings 25:19; 2 Chron. 31:12; Jer. 36:26; 52:25.

Toiled *kopiao* (2872), "to be weary, to labor," is rendered "to toil" in Matt. 6:28; **Luke 5:5** (**12:27**), in some mss.); in 1 Cor. 4:12, RV (KJV, "we labor").

All *holos* (3650), "the whole, all," is most frequently used with the article followed by a noun, e.g., Matt. 4:23. It is used with the article alone, in John 7:23, "every whit"; Acts 11:26; 21:31; 28:30; Titus 1:11; **Luke 5:5**, in the best texts.

Night *see Luke 2:8* Night.

Let down *see Luke 5:4.*

5:6 And when they had this done, they inclosed a great multitude of fishes: and their net brake.

Inclosed *sunkleio* (4788), "to shut together, shut in on all sides" (*sun*, "with," *kleio*, "to shut"), is used of a catch of fish, **Luke 5:6**; metaphorically in Rom. 11:32, of God's dealings with Jew and Gentile, in that He has "shut up (KJV, concluded) all unto disobedience, that He might have mercy upon all." There is no intimation in this of universal salvation. The meaning, from the context, is that God has ordered that all should be convicted of disobedience without escape by human merit, that He might display His mercy, and has offered the gospel without national distinction, and that when Israel is restored, He will, in the resulting Millennium, show His mercy to all nations. The word "all" with reference to Israel, is to be viewed in the light of v. 26, and, in reference to the Gentiles, in the light of vv. 12-25; in Gal. 3:22, 23 ("the Scripture hath shut up all things under sin"), the apostle shows that, by the impossibility of being justified by keeping the Law, all, Jew and Gentile, are under sin, so that righteousness might be reckoned to all who believe.

Great *polus* (4183), "much, many, great," is used of number, e.g., **Luke 5:6**; Acts 11:21; degree, e.g., of harvest, Matt. 9:37; mercy, 1 Pet. 1:3, RV "great" (KJV, "abundant"); glory, Matt. 24:30; joy, Philem. 7, RV, "much" (KJV, "great"); peace, Acts 24:2. The best mss. have it in Acts 8:8 (RV, "much"), of joy.

Multitude *see Luke 1:10.*

Brake *diarrhegnumi* (1284), "to burst asunder, to rend, cleave," is said of the rending of garments, Matt. 26:65; Mark 14:63; Acts 14:14; of the "breaking" of a net, **Luke 5:6**; of fetters, **8:29**.

5:7 And they beckoned unto *their* partners, which were in the other ship, that they should come and help them. And they came, and filled both the ships, so that they began to sink.

Beckoned *kataneuo* (2656), is used of the fishermen-partners in **Luke 5:7**, "beckoned."

Partners *metochos* (3353), an adjective, signifying "having with, sharing," is used as a noun, "partners" in **Luke 5:7**.

Other *see Luke 4:43.*

Help *sullambano* (4815), "to assist, take part with" (*sun*, "with," and *lambano*), is used, in the middle voice, of rendering help in what others are doing, **Luke 5:7**, of bringing in a catch of fish; in Phil. 4:3, in an appeal to Synzygus ("yokefellow") to help Euodia and Syntyche (v. 2).

Filled *see Luke 1:15.*

Sink *buthizo* (1036), "to plunge into the deep, to sink" (*buthos*, "bottom, the deep, the sea"), akin to *bathos*, "depth," and *abussos*, "bottomless," and Eng., "bath," is used in **Luke 5:7** of the "sinking" of a boat; metaphorically in 1 Tim. 6:9, of the effect of foolish and hurtful lusts, which "drown men in destruction and perdition."

5:8 When Simon Peter saw *it*, he fell down at Jesus' knees, saying, Depart from me; for I am a sinful man, O Lord.

Fell *prospipto* (4363), "to fall towards anything" (*pros*, "towards"), "to strike against," is said of "wind," Matt. 7:25; it also signifies to "fall" down at one's feet, "fall" prostrate before, Mark 3:11; 5:33; 7:25; **Luke 5:8**; **8:28**, **47**; Acts 16:29.

Knees *gonu* (1119), "a knee" (Latin, *genu*), is used (a) metaphorically in Heb. 12:12, where the duty enjoined is that of "courageous self-recovery in God's strength;" (b) literally, of the attitude of a suppliant, **Luke 5:8**; Eph. 3:14; of veneration, Rom. 11:4; 14:11; Phil. 2:10; in mockery, Mark 15:19.

Sinful *hamartolos* (268), an adjective, akin to *hamartano*, "to sin," is used as an adjective, "sinful" in Mark 8:38; **Luke 5:8**; **19:7** (lit., "a sinful man"); **24:7**; John 9:16, and 24 (lit., "a man sinful"). Elsewhere it is used as a noun. The noun is frequently found in a common phrase in sepulchral epitaphs in the S.W. of Asia Minor, with the threat against any desecrator of the tomb, "let him be as a sinner before the subterranean gods" (Moulton and Milligan).

Man *aner* (435), is never used of the female sex; it stands (a) in distinction from a woman, Acts 8:12; 1 Tim. 2:12; as a husband, Matt. 1:16; John 4:16; Rom. 7:2; Titus 1:6; (b) as distinct from a boy or infant, 1 Cor. 13:11; metaphorically in Eph. 4:13; (c) in conjunction with an adjective or noun, e.g., **Luke 5:8**, lit., "a man, a sinner"; **24:19**, lit., "a man, a prophet"; often in terms of address, e.g., Acts 1:16; 13:15, 26; 15:7, 13, lit., "men, brethren"; with gentilic or local names (virtually a title of honor), e.g., Acts 2:14; 22:3, lit., "Judean men," "a Judean man"; 3:12; 5:35, lit., "Israelite men"; 17:22, "Athenian men"; 19:35, lit., "Ephesian men"; in Acts 14:15 it is used in addressing a company of "men," without any descriptive term. In this verse, however, the distinction between *aner* and *anthropos* (2nd part) is noticeable; (d) in general, "a man, a male person" (used like the pronoun *tis*), "a man" (i.e., a certain "man"), e.g., **Luke 8:41**; in the plural, Acts 6:11.

Lord *kurios* (2962), properly an adjective, signifying "having power" (*kuros*) or "authority," is used as a noun, variously translated in the NT, "'Lord,' 'master,' 'Master,' 'owner,' 'Sir,' a title of wide significance, occurring in each book of the NT save Titus and the Epistles of John. It is used (a) of an owner, as in **Luke 19:33**, cf. Matt. 20:8; Acts 16:16; Gal. 4:1; or of one who has the disposal of anything, as the Sabbath, Matt. 12:8; (b) of a master, i.e., one to whom service is due on any ground, Matt. 6:24; 24:50; Eph. 6:5; (c) of an Emperor or King, Acts 25:26; Rev. 17:14; (d) of idols, ironically, 1 Cor. 8:5, cf. Isa. 26:13; (e) as a title of respect addressed to a father, Matt. 21:30, a husband, 1 Pet. 3:6, a master, Matt. 13:27; **Luke 13:8**, a ruler, Matt. 27:63, an angel, Acts 10:4; Rev. 7:14; (f) as a title of courtesy addressed to a stranger, John 12:21; 20:15; Acts 16:30; from the outset of His ministry this was a common form of address to the Lord Jesus, alike by the people, Matt. 8:2; John 4:11, and by His disciples, Matt. 8:25; **Luke 5:8**; John 6:68; (g) *kurios* is the Sept. and NT representative of Heb. Jehovah ('LORD' in Eng. versions), see Matt. 4:7; Jas. 5:11, e.g., of *adon*, Lord, Matt. 22:44, and of *Adonay*, Lord, 1:22; it also occurs for *Elohim*, God, 1 Pet. 1:25.

"Thus the usage of the word in the NT follows two main lines: one - *a-f*, customary and general, the other, *g*, peculiar to the Jews, and drawn from the Greek translation of the OT.

"Christ Himself assumed the title, Matt. 7:21, 22; 9:38; 22:41-45; Mark 5:19 (cf. Ps. 66:16; the parallel passage, **Luke 8:39**, has 'God'); **Luke 19:31**; John 13:13, apparently intending it in the higher senses of its current use, and at the same time suggesting its OT associations.

"His purpose did not become clear to the disciples until after His resurrection, and the revelation of His Deity consequent thereon. Thomas, when he realized the significance of the presence of a mortal wound in the body of a living man, immediately joined with it the absolute title of Deity, saying, 'My Lord and my God,' John 20:28. Thereafter, except in Acts 10:4 and Rev. 7:14, there is no record that *kurios* was ever again used by believers in addressing any save God and the Lord Jesus; cf Acts 2:47 with 4:29, 30.

... "Though John does not use 'Lord' in his Epistles, and though, like the other Evangelists, he ordinarily uses the personal Name in his narrative, yet he occasionally speaks of Him as 'the Lord,' John 4:1; 6:23; 11:2; 20:20; 21:12.

"The full significance of this association of Jesus with God under the one appellation, 'Lord,' is seen when it is remembered that these men belonged to the only monotheistic race in the world. To associate with the Creator one known to be a creature, however exalted, though possible to Pagan philosophers, was quite impossible to a Jew.

"It is not recorded that in the days of His flesh any of His disciples either addressed the Lord, or spoke of Him, by His personal Name. Where Paul has occasion to refer to the facts of the gospel history he speaks of what the Lord Jesus said, Acts 20:35, and did, 1 Cor. 11:23, and suffered, 1 Thess. 2:15; 5:9, 10. It is our Lord Jesus who is coming, 1 Thess. 2:19, etc. In prayer also the title is given, 3:11; Eph. 1:3; the sinner is invited to believe on the Lord Jesus, Acts 16:31; 20:21, and the saint to look to the Lord Jesus for deliverance, Rom. 7:24, 25, and in the few exceptional cases in which the personal Name stands alone a reason is always discernible in the immediate context.

"The title 'Lord,' as given to the Savior, in its full significance rests upon the resurrection, Acts 2:36; Rom. 10:9; 14:9, and is realized only in the Holy Spirit, 1 Cor. 12:3."

5:9 For he was astonished, and all that were with him, at the draught of the fishes which they had taken:

Astonished *periecho* (4023), lit., "to have round" (*peri*, "around," *echo*, "to have"), means "to encompass, enclose, contain," as a writing contains details, 1 Pet. 2:6. Some mss. have it in Acts 23:25, lit., "having this form" (the most authentic have *echo*, "to have"). For the secondary meaning, "amazed" (KJV, "astonished"), **Luke 5:9** (lit., "amazement encompassed," i.e., seized, him). *See also* **Amazed** at *Luke 4:36*.

Draught *see Luke 5:4*.

Taken *sullambano* (4815), "to seize, take," is rendered "to take" in Matt. 26:55 and Mark 14:48, KJV (RV, "seize"); **Luke 5:9**; Acts 1:16; in 12:3 and 23:27, KJV (RV, "seize").

5:10 And so *was* also James, and John, the sons of Zebedee, which were partners with Simon. And Jesus said unto Simon, Fear not; from henceforth thou shalt catch men.

So It translates *homoios*, "likewise," e.g., in **Luke 5:10**; *oun*, "therefore," e.g., John 4:40, 53.

Partners *koinonos* (2844), an adjective, signifying "having in common" (*koinos*), is used as a noun, "partners" in **Luke 5:10**, "partner" in 2 Cor. 8:23; Philem. 17 (in spiritual life and business).

Henceforth *see Luke 1:48*.

Catch *zogreo* (2221), lit. signifies "to take men alive" (from *zoos*, "alive," and *agreuo*, "to hunt or catch"), **Luke 5:10** (marg. "take alive"), there of the effects of the work of the gospel; in 2 Tim. 2:26 it is said of the power of Satan to lead men astray. The verse should read "and that they may recover themselves out of the snare of the Devil (having been taken captive by him), unto the will of God." This is the probable meaning rather than "to take alive or for life."

Men *anthropos* (444), is used (a) generally, of "a human being, male or female," without reference to sex or nationality, e.g., Matt. 4:4; 12:35; John 2:25; (b) in distinction from God, e.g., Matt. 19:6; John 10:33; Gal. 1:11; Col. 3:23; (c) in distinction from animals, etc., e.g., **Luke 5:10**; (d) sometimes, in the plural, of "men and women," people, e.g., Matt. 5:13, 16; in Mark 11:2 and 1 Tim. 6:16, lit., "no one of men"; (e) in some instances with a suggestion of human frailty and imperfection, e.g., 1 Cor. 2:5; Acts 14:15 (2nd part); (f) in the phrase translated "after man," "after the manner of men," "as a man" (KJV), lit. "according to (*kata*) man," is used only by the apostle Paul, of "(1) the practices of fallen humanity 1 Cor. 3:3; (2) anything of human origin, Gal. 1:11; (3) the laws that govern the administration of justice among men, Rom. 3:5; (4) the standard generally accepted among men, Gal. 3:15; (5) an illustration not drawn from Scripture, 1 Cor. 9:8; (6) probably = 'to use a figurative expression' (see KJV, marg.), i.e., to speak evil of men with whom he had contended at Ephesus as 'beasts' (cf. 1 Cor. 4:6), 1 Cor. 15:32...

(j) as equivalent simply to "a person," or "one," whether "man" or woman, e.g., Acts 19:16; Rom. 3:28; Gal. 2:16; Jas. 1:19; 2:24; 3:8 (like the pronoun *tis*, "someone"; *tis* is rendered "man" in Matt. 8:28); or, again (as *tis* sometimes signifies), "a man," e.g., Matt. 17:14; **Luke 13:19**.

(k) definitely, with the article, of some particular person, Matt. 12:13; Mark 3:3, 5; or with the demonstrative pronoun and the article, e.g., Matt. 12:45; **Luke 14:30**.

5:11 And when they had brought their ships to land, they forsook all, and followed him.

Brought *katago* (2609), "to bring down," Acts 9:30; 22:30; 23:15, 20; Rom. 10:6; "to bring forth," Acts 23:28; of boats, "to bring to land," **Luke 5:11**.

Forsook *aphiemi* (863), sometimes has the significance of "forsaking," Mark 1:18; 14:50 (RV, "left"); so **Luke 5:11**.

5:12 And it came to pass, when he was in a certain city, behold a man full of leprosy: who seeing Jesus fell on *his* face, and besought him, saying, Lord, if thou wilt, thou canst make me clean.

Certain The rendering "certain," is frequently changed in the RV, or omitted, e.g., **Luke 5:12**; **8:22**; Acts 23:17; Heb. 2:6; 4:4.

Behold *kai* Occasionally it has almost the sense of *hoti*, "that," e.g., Matt. 26:15 (first part); Mark 14:40 (last part); **Luke 5:12**, **17**, where, if the *kai* had been translated, the clause might be rendered "that, behold, a man ... ," lit., "and behold ... "; so v. **17**; in **12:15**, "take heed that ye keep."

Full *see* ***Luke 4:1***.

Leprosy *lepra* (3014), akin to *lepros*, is mentioned in Matt. 8:3; Mark 1:42; **Luke 5:12**, **13**. In the removal of other maladies the verb "to heal" (*iaomai*) is used, but in the removal of "leprosy," the verb "to cleanse" (*katharizo*), save in the statement concerning the Samaritan, **Luke 17:15**, "when he saw that he was healed." Matt. 10:8 and **Luke 4:27** indicate that the disease was common in the nation. Only twelve cases are recorded in the NT, but these are especially selected. For the Lord's commands to the leper mentioned in Matthew 8 and to the ten in **Luke 17**, see Lev. 14:2-32.

Besought *deomai* (1189), "to desire, to long for," usually representing the word "need," is sometimes translated "beseech," e.g., **Luke 5:12**; Acts 21:39; 2 Cor. 10:2; Gal. 4:12. It is used of prayer to God, in Matt. 9:38; **Luke 10:2**; **21:36**; **22:32**; Acts 4:31; 8:22, 24; 10:2; Rom. 1:10; 1 Thess. 3:10.

5:13 And he put forth *his* hand, and touched him, saying, I will: be thou clean. And immediately the leprosy departed from him.

Put forth *ekteino* (1614), "to stretch out or forth," is so rendered in Matt. 12:13 (twice), 49; 14:31; 26:51; Mark 3:5 (twice), **Luke 6:10**; in Matt. 8:3; Mark 1:41 and **Luke 5:13**, RV (KJV, "put forth"); **Luke 22:53**; John 21:18; Acts 4:30; 26:1. For Acts 27:30

Leprosy *see* Lepers at ***Luke 4:27***.

5:14 And he charged him to tell no man: but go, and shew thyself to the priest, and offer for thy cleansing, according as Moses commanded, for a testimony unto them.

Charged *parangello* (3853), lit., "to announce beside" (*para*, "beside," *angello*, "to announce"), "to hand on an announcement from one to another," usually denotes "to command, to charge," **Luke 5:14**; **8:56**; 1 Cor. 7:10 (KJV, "command"),

"Jesus Christ served others first; he spoke to those to whom no one spoke; he dined with the lowest members of society; he touched the untouchable. He had no throne, no crown, no bevy of servants or armored guards. A borrowed manger and a borrowed tomb framed his early life."

CHARLES W. COLSON

"give charge," RV; 11:17, "in giving you this charge," RV; 1 Tim. 1:3; 6:13, RV, and 6:17. It is rendered by the verb "to charge" in the RV of Acts 1:4; 4:18; 5:28; 15:5; 1 Thess. 4:11.

Cleansing *katharismos* (2512), is rendered "a cleansing," Mark 1:44; **Luke 5:14**; in Heb. 1:3, RV, "purification." *See also* **Purification** at *Luke 2:22*.

Commanded *prostasso* (4367), denotes "to arrange or set in order towards" (*pros*, "towards," *tasso*, "to arrange"); hence "to prescribe, give command," Matt. 1:24; 8:4; Mark 1:44; **Luke 5:14**; Acts 10:33, 48.

5:15 But so much the more went there a fame abroad of him: and great multitudes came together to hear, and to be healed by him of their infirmities.

More *mallon* (3123), the comparative degree of *mala*, "very, very much," is used (a) of increase, "more," with qualifying words, with *pollo*, "much," e.g., Mark 10:48, "the more (a great deal)"; Rom. 5:15, 17, "(much) more"; Phil. 2:12 (ditto); with *poso*, "how much," e.g., **Luke 12:24**; Rom. 11:12; with *tosouto*, "by so much," Heb. 10:25; (b) without a qualifying word, by way of comparison, "the more," e.g., **Luke 5:15**, "so much the more"; John 5:18, "the more"; Acts 5:14 (ditto); Phil. 1:9; 1 Thess. 4:1, 10, "more and more"; 2 Pet. 1:10, RV; "the more" (KJV, "the rather"); in Acts 20:35, by a periphrasis, it is translated "more (blessed)"; in Gal. 4:27, "more (than)," lit., "rather (than)"; (c) with qualifying words, similarly to (a), e.g., Mark 7:36.

Fame *logos* (3056), "a word," is translated "report," i.e., "a story, narrative"; in **Luke 5:15** (KJV, "fame"); **7:17** (KJV, "rumor"); Acts 11:22 (KJV, "tidings").

5:16 And he withdrew himself into the wilderness, and prayed.

Withdrew *hupochoreo* (5298), "to go back, retire" (*hupo*, "under," suggesting privacy), **Luke 5:16**; **9:10**, KJV, "went aside" (RV, "withdrew apart").

Wilderness *eremos* (2048), used as a noun, has the same meaning as *eremia*, in **Luke 5:16** and **8:29**, RV, "deserts," for KJV, "wilderness"; in Matt. 24:26 and John 6:31, RV, "wilderness," for KJV, "desert." As an adjective, it denotes (a), with reference to persons, "deserted," desolate, deprived of the friends and kindred, e.g. of a woman deserted by a husband, Gal 4:21; (b) so of a city, as Jerusalem, Matt. 23:38; or uninhabited places, "desert," e.g., Matt. 14:13, 15; Acts 8:26; in Mark 1:35, RV, "desert," for KJV, solitary.

5:17 And it came to pass on a certain day, as he was teaching, that there were Pharisees and doctors of the law sitting by, which were come out of every town of Galilee, and Judaea, and Jerusalem: and the power of the Lord was *present* to heal them.

And *see* **Behold** at *Luke 5:12*.

Doctors of the law *nomodidaskalos* (3547), "a teacher of the Law," with reference to the teachers of the Mosaic Law, **Luke 5:17**; Acts 5:34; also of those who went about among Christians, professing to be instructors of the Law, 1 Tim. 1:7.

Town *kome* (2968), "a village," or "country town without walls." The RV always renders this "village" or "villages," KJV, "town" or "towns," Matt. 10:11; Mark 8:23, 26 (twice), 27; **Luke 5:17**; **9:6**, **12**; John 7:42; 11:1, 30.

Heal *see* *Luke 4:18*.

5:18 And, behold, men brought in a bed a man which was taken with a palsy: and they sought *means* to bring him in, and to lay *him* before him.

Brought *eisphero* (1533), denotes "to bring to," Acts 17:20; "to bring into," **Luke 5:18**, **19**; 1 Tim. 6:7; Heb. 13:11.

Bed *klinidion* (2826), "a small bed," a diminutive form of *kline*, "a bed" (from *klino*, "to incline, recline"), is used in **Luke 5:19**, **24** of the "bed" (kline, in v. **18**) on which the palsied man was brought.

Palsy *paraluo* (3886), lit., "to loose from the side," hence, "to set free," is used in the passive voice of "being enfeebled by a paralytic stroke, palsied," **Luke 5:18**, RV, "palsied" (KJV, "taken with a palsy"); **5:24** (ditto), in the best mss.; Acts 8:7 (ditto); 9:33, RV, "he was palsied" (KJV, "was sick of the palsy"); Heb. 12:12, RV, "palsied (knees)," KJV, "feeble."

Means In **Luke 5:18** the KJV adds the word "means" in italics.

Lay *see* Laid at *Luke 1:66*.

5:19 And when they could not find by what *way* they might bring him in because of the multitude, they went upon the housetop, and let him down through the tiling with *his* couch into the midst before Jesus.

What Other words are (a) *hoios*, "of what kind," e.g., 2 Cor. 10:11, RV (KJV, "such as"); 1 Thess. 1:5, "what manner of men"; 2 Tim. 3:11 (twice), lit., "what sorts of things," "what sorts of persecutions"; (b) *poios*, "what sort of," e.g., Matt. 21:23, 24, 27; 24:42, 43; **Luke 5:19**; **6:32-34**; **20:2**, **8**; **24:19**; John 12:33, "what manner of"; so in 18:32; 21:19; Rom. 3:27; 1 Cor. 15:35; in Jas. 4:14, "what"; 1 Pet. 2:20 and Rev. 3:3 (ditto); 1 Pet. 1:11, "what manner of"; (c) *hopoios*, "what sort of," 1 Cor. 3:13; "what manner of," 1 Thess. 1:9; (d) *hosos*, "how great," Mark 6:30 (twice), RV, "whatsoever"; Acts 15:12; Rom. 3:19, "what things soever"; Jude 10 (1st part), "what soever things," RV; (2nd part) "what"; (e) *posos*, "how great, how much," 2 Cor. 7:11, "what (earnest care)," RV (posos here stands for the repeated words in the Eng. versions, the adjective not being repeated in the original); (f) *hostis*, "what (things)," Phil. 3:7; (g) in Matt. 26:40, *houtos*, "thus, so," is used as an exclamatory expression, translated "What" (in a word immediately addressed by the Lord to Peter), lit., "So"; (h) for *potapos*, rendered "what" in Mark 13:1 (2nd part), KJV; (i) in 1 Cor. 6:16, 19, KJV, the particle *e*, "or" (RV), is rendered "What?"; in 1 Cor. 14:36, KJV and RV, "what?" (j) in 1 Cor. 11:22, *gar*, "in truth, indeed," has its exclamatory use "What."

Way In **Luke 5:19** and **19:4** the noun is not expressed in the original, but is understood.

Bring *see* Brought at *Luke 5:18*.

Housetop *doma* (1430), akin to *demo*, "to build," denotes a housetop. The housetop was flat, and guarded by a low parapet wall (see Deut. 22:8). It was much frequented and used for various purposes, e.g., for proclamations, Matt. 10:27; **Luke 12:3**; for prayer, Acts 10:9. The house was often built round a court, across the top of which cords were fixed from the parapet walls for supporting a covering from the heat. The housetop could be reached by stairs outside the building; the paralytic in **Luke 5:19** could be let down into the court or area by rolling back the covering. External flight from the housetop in time or danger is enjoined in Matt. 24:17; Mark 13:15; **Luke 17:31**.

Let ... down *kathiemi* (2524), "to send," or "let down" (*kata*, "down," *hiemi*, "to send"), is translated "to let down," with reference to (a) the paralytic in **Luke 5:19**; (b) Saul of Tarsus, Acts 9:25; (c) the great sheet in Peter's vision, 10:11 and 11:5.

Tiling *keramos* (2766), "potter's clay," or "an earthen vessel," denotes in the plural "tiles" in **Luke 5:19**, RV, KJV, "tiling." In the Sept., 2 Sam. 17:25.

Couch *see* Bed at *Luke 5:18*.

5:20 And when he saw their faith, he said unto him, Man, thy sins are forgiven thee.

Forgiven *aphiemi* (863), primarily, "to send forth, send away" (*apo*, "from," *hiemi*, "to send"), denotes, besides its other meanings, "to remit or forgive" (a) debts, Matt. 6:12; 18:27, 32, these being completely cancelled; (b) sins, e.g., Matt. 9:2, 5, 6; 12:31, 32; Acts 8:22 ("the thought of thine heart"); Rom. 4:7; Jas. 5:15; 1 John 1:9; 2:12. In this latter respect the verb, like its corresponding noun, firstly signifies the remission of the punishment due to sinful conduct, the deliverance of the sinner from the penalty divinely, and therefore righteously, imposed; secondly, it involves the complete removal of the cause of offense; such remission is based upon the vicarious and propitiatory sacrifice of Christ. In the OT atoning sacrifice and "forgiveness" are often associated, e.g., Lev. 4:20, 26. The verb is used in the NT with reference to trespasses (*paraptoma*), e.g., Matt. 6:14, 15; sins (*hamartia*), e.g., **Luke 5:20**; debts (*opheilema*), Matt. 6:12; (*opheile*), 18:32; (*daneion*), 18:27; the thought (*dianoia*) of the heart, Acts 8:22. Cf. *kalupto*, "to cover," 1 Pet. 4:8; Jas. 5:20; and *epikalupto*, "to cover over," Rom. 4:7, representing the Hebrew words for "atonement." Human "forgiveness" is to be strictly analogous to divine "forgiveness," e.g., Matt. 6:12. If certain conditions are fulfilled, there is no limitation to Christ's law of "forgiveness," Matt. 18:21, 22. The conditions are repentance and confession, Matt. 18:15-17; **Luke 17:3**.

5:21 And the scribes and the Pharisees began to reason, saying, Who is this which speaketh blasphemies? Who can forgive sins, but God alone?

Scribes *grammateus* (1122), from *gramma,* "a writing," denotes "a scribe, a man of letters, a teacher of the law"; the "scribes" are mentioned frequently in the Synoptists, especially in connection with the Pharisees, with whom they virtually formed one party (see **Luke 5:21**), sometimes with the chief priests, e.g., Matt. 2:4; Mark 8:31; 10:33; 11:18, 27; **Luke 9:22**. They are mentioned only once in John's Gospel, 8:3, three times in the Acts, 4:5; 6:12; 23:9; elsewhere only in 1 Cor. 1:20, in the singular. They were considered naturally qualified to teach in the synagogues, Mark 1:22. They were ambitious of honor, e.g., Matt. 23:5–11, which they demanded especially from their pupils, and which was readily granted them, as well as by the people generally. Like Ezra (Ezra 7:12), the "scribes" were found originally among the priests and Levites. The priests being the official interpreters of the Law, the "scribes" ere long became an independent company; though they never held political power, they became leaders of the people. Their functions regarding the Law were to teach it, develop it, and use it in connection with the Sanhedrin and various local courts. They also occupied themselves with the sacred writings both historical and didactic. They attached the utmost importance to ascetic elements, by which the nation was especially separated from the Gentiles. In their regime piety was reduced to external formalism. Only that was of value which was governed by external precept. Life under them became a burden; they themselves sought to evade certain of their own precepts, Matt. 23:16ff.; **Luke 11:46**; by their traditions the Law, instead of being a help in moral and spiritual life, became an instrument for preventing true access to God, **Luke 11:52**. Hence the Lord's stern denunciations of them and the Pharisees. *See also* **Doctors of the law** at *Luke 5:17*.

Reason *see* **Cast** at *Luke 1:29*.

5:22 But when Jesus perceived their thoughts, he answering said unto them, What reason ye in your hearts?

Perceived *see Luke 1:22*.

Thoughts *dialogismos* (126), "a thought, reasoning, inward questioning," is translated "reasoning" or "reasonings" in **Luke 5:22**, RV (KJV, "thoughts"); **9:46**; v. 47, RV (KJV, "thoughts"); **24:38** (KJV, "thoughts"); Rom. 1:21 (KJV, "imaginations"); 1 Cor. 3:20 (KJV, "thoughts"). *See also Luke 2:35*.

Reason *See* **Cast** at *Luke 1:29*.

5:23 Whether is easier, to say, Thy sins be forgiven thee; or to say, Rise up and walk?

Easier *eukopoteros* (2123), the comparative degree of *eukopos*, "easy, with easy labor" (*eu*, "well," *kopos*, "labor"), hence, of that which is "easier to do," is found in the Synoptics only, Matt. 9:5; 19:24; Mark 2:9; 10:25; **Luke 5:23**; **16:17**; **18:25**.

5:24 But that ye may know that the Son of man hath power upon earth to forgive sins, (he said unto the sick of the palsy,) I say unto thee, Arise, and take up thy couch, and go into thine house.

Son of man *see* **Son** at *Luke 1:32*.

Palsy *paralutikos* (3885), "paralytic, sick of the palsy," is found in Matt. 4:24 (RV, "palsied"); 8:6; 9:2 (twice), 6; Mark 2:3, 4, 5, 9, 10; in some mss. **Luke 5:24**. *See also Luke 5:18*.

Couch *see* **Bed** at *Luke 5:18*.

5:25 And immediately he rose up before them, and took up that whereon he lay, and departed to his own house, glorifying God.

Immediately *see Luke 1:64*.

Rose *see Luke 4:29*.

Lay *katakeimai* (2621), "to lie down," is used of the sick, Mark 1:30; 2:4; **Luke 5:25**; John 5:3, 6; Acts 28:8; in Acts 9:33 it is rendered "had kept (his bed)," lit., "lying (on a bed)."

5:26 And they were all amazed, and they glorified God, and were filled with fear, saying, We have seen strange things to day.

Amazed *ekstasis* (1611), is, lit., "a standing out" (*ek*, "out of," *stasis*, "a standing"). Eng. "ecstasy" is a transliteration. It is translated "amazement" in Acts 3:10. It was said of any displacement, and especially, with reference to the mind, of that alteration of the normal condition by which the person is thrown into a state of surprise or fear, or both; or again, in which a person is so transported out of his natural state that he falls into a trance, Acts 10:10; 11:5; 22:17. As to the other meaning, the RV has "amazement" in Mark 5:42 and **Luke 5:26**, but "astonishment" in Mark 16:8.

Filled *see Luke 1:15*.

Strange *paradoxos* (3861), "contrary to received opinion" (*para*, "beside," *doxa*, "opinion"; Eng. "paradox," "-ical"), is rendered "strange things" in **Luke 5:26**.

5:27 And after these things he went forth, and saw a publican, named Levi, sitting at the receipt of custom: and he said unto him, Follow me.

Publican *see* Publicans at *Luke 3:12*.

Custom *telonion* (5058), denotes "a custom-house," for the collection of the taxes, Matt. 9:9; Mark 2:14; **Luke 5:27** (RV, "place of toll").

5:28 And he left all, rose up, and followed him.

Left *kataleipo* (2641), a strengthened form of *leipo*, "to leave," signifies (a) "to leave, to leave behind," e.g., Matt. 4:13; (b) "to leave remaining, reserve," e.g., **Luke 10:40**; (c) "to forsake," in the sense of abandoning, translated "to forsake" in the RV of **Luke 5:28** and Acts 6:2; in Heb. 11:27 and 2 Pet. 2:15, KJV and RV. In this sense it is translated "to leave," in Mark 10:7; 14:52; **Luke 15:4**; Eph. 5:31.

Rose *see Luke 4:29*.

5:29 And Levi made him a great feast in his own house: and there was a great company of publicans and of others that sat down with them.

Feast *doche* (1403), "a reception feast, a banquet" (from dechomai, "to receive"), **Luke 5:29**; **14:13** (see v. 12).

Publicans *see* **Luke 3:12**.

Sat *katakeimai* (2621), "to lie down" (*kata*, "down," and *keimai*), is used of "reclining at a meal," Mark 2:15; 14:3; **Luke 5:29**, RV, "were sitting at meat" (KJV, "sat down"); **7:37** (in the best texts); 1 Cor. 8:10.

5:30 But their scribes and Pharisees murmured against his disciples, saying, Why do ye eat and drink with publicans and sinners?

Murmured *gonguzo* (1111), "to mutter, murmur, grumble, say anything in a low tone" (Eng., "gong"), an onomatopoeic word, representing the significance by the sound of the word, as in the word "murmur" itself, is used of the laborers in the parable of the householder, Matt. 20:11; of the scribes and Pharisees, against Christ, **Luke 5:30**; of the Jews, John 6:41, 43, of the disciples, 6:61; of the people, 7:32 (of debating secretly); of the Israelites, 1 Cor. 10:10 (twice), where it is also used in a warning to believers. In the papyri it is used of the "murmuring" of a gang of workmen, also in a remark interposed, while the Emperor (late 2nd cent. AD) was interviewing a rebel, that the Romans were then "murmuring" (Moulton and Milligan, Vocab.).

Publicans *see Luke 3:12*.

5:31 And Jesus answering said unto them, They that are whole need not a physician; but they that are sick.

Whole *hugiaino* (5198), "to be in good health," is rendered "they that are whole" in **Luke 5:31**; "whole" in **7:10** (present participle); "wholesome" in 1 Tim. 6:3, KJV (RV, "sound"; marg., "healthful").

Need *chreia* (5532), denotes "a need," in such expressions as "there is a need"; or "to have need of" something, e.g., Matt. 3:14; 6:8; 9:12, RV, "(have no) need," KJV, "need (not)," the RV adheres to the noun form; so in 14:16; Mark 14:63; **Luke 5:31**; **22:71**; Eph. 4:28; 1 Thess. 4:9; in the following, however, both RV and KJV use the verb form, "to need" (whereas the original has the verb echo, "to have," with the noun chreia as the object, as in the instances just mentioned): **Luke 15:7**; John 2:25; 13:10; 16:30; 1 Thess. 1:8; 1 John 2:27; Rev. 22:5; in all these the verb "to have" could well have been expressed in the translation. In **Luke 10:42** it is translated "needful," where the "one thing" is surely not one dish, or one person, but is to be explained according to Matt. 6:33 and 16:26. In Eph. 4:29, for the KJV, "(to) the use (of edifying)," the RV more accurately has "(for edifying) as the need may be," marg., "the building up of the need," i.e., "to supply that which needed in each case"; so Westcott, who adds "The need represents a gap in the life which the wise word 'builds up,' fills up solidly and surely." In Phil. 4:19 the RV has "every need of yours" (KJV, "all your need"); in 1 Thess. 4:12, RV, "need" (KJV, "lack"); in Acts 28:10, RV, "(such things) as we needed" (KJV, "as were necessary"), lit., "the things for the needs (plural)."

Physician *see Luke 4:23*.

Sick *kakos* (2560), "badly, evilly," is used in the physical sense, "to be sick," e.g., Matt. 4:24; Mark 1:32, 34; **Luke 5:31**. In Matt. 21:41 this adverb is used with the adjective, "He will miserably destroy those miserable men," more lit., "He will evilly destroy those men (evil as they are)," with stress on the adjective; in the moral sense, "to speak evilly," John 18:23; Acts 23:5; to ask evilly, Jas. 4:3.

5:32-33 I came not to call the righteous, but sinners to repentance.

And they said unto him, Why do the disciples of John fast often, and make prayers, and likewise *the disciples* of the Pharisees; but thine eat and drink?

Fast *nesteuo* (3522), "to fast, to abstain from eating," is used of voluntary "fasting," Matt. 4:2; 6:16, 17, 18; 9:14, 15; Mark 2:18, 19, 20; **Luke 5:33, 34, 35**; **18:12**; Acts 13:2, 3. Some of these passages show that teachers to whom scholars or disciples were attached gave them special instructions as to "fasting." Christ taught the need of purity and simplicity of motive. The answers of Christ to the questions of the disciples of John and of the Pharisees reveal His whole purpose and method. No doubt He and His followers observed such a fast as that on the Day of Atonement, but He imposed no frequent "fasts" in addition. What He taught was suitable to the change of character and purpose which He designed for His disciples. His claim to be the Bridegroom, Matt. 9:15, and the reference there to the absence of "fasting," virtually involved a claim to be the Messiah (cf. Zech. 8:19). Some mss. have the verb in Acts 10:30.

Often *pukna* (4437), the neuter plural of *puknos*, used adverbially, is translated "often" in **Luke 5:33**.

Prayers *see* Prayer at *Luke 1:13*.

Likewise *homoios* (3668), "in like manner" (from the adjective *homoios*), is rendered "likewise" in the KJV of Matt. 22:26; 27:41, **Luke 10:32**; **16:25**; John 5:19; Jas. 2:25; 1 Pet. 3:1, 7; Jude 8; Rev. 8:12 (in all these the RV has "in like manner"); in the following, KJV and RV have "likewise"; Matt. 26:35; **Luke 5:33**; **6:31**; **10:37**; **17:28**, **31**; **22:36**; John 6:11; 21:13; Rom. 1:27; 1 Pet. 5:5.

5:34 And he said unto them, Can ye make the children of the bridechamber fast, while the bridegroom is with them?

Make *poieo* (4160), "to do, to make," is used in the ... sense (a) of constructing or producing anything, of the creative acts of God, e.g., Matt. 19:4 (2nd part); Acts 17:24; of the acts of human beings, e.g., Matt. 17:4; Acts 9:39; (b) with nouns denoting a state or condition, to be the author of, to cause, e.g., peace, Eph. 2:15; Jas. 3:18; stumbling blocks, Rom. 16:17; (c) with nouns involving the idea of action (or of something accomplished by action), so as to express the idea of the verb more forcibly (the middle voice is commonly used in this respect, suggesting the action as being of special interest to the doer); for the active voice see, e.g., Mark 2:23, of "making" one's way, where the idea is not that the disciples "made" a path through the standing corn, but simply that they went, the phrase being equivalent to going, "(they began) as they went (to pluck the ears)"; other instances of the active are Rev. 13:13, 14; 16:14; 19:20; for the middle voice (the dynamic or subjective middle), see, e.g., John 14:23, "will make Our abode"; in Acts 20:24, "none of these things move me," lit., "I make account of none of these things"; 25:17, "I made no delay," RV, Rom. 15:26; Eph. 4:16; Heb. 1:2; 2 Pet. 1:10; (d) to "make" ready or prepare, e.g., a dinner, **Luke 14:12**; a supper, John 12:2; (e) to acquire, provide a thing for oneself, Matt. 25:16; **Luke 19:18**; (f) to render or "make" one or oneself anything, or cause a person or thing to become something, e.g., Matt. 4:19; 12:16, "make (Him known)"; John 5:11, 15, to "make" whole; 16:2, lit., "they shall make (you put out of the synagogue)"; Eph. 2:14; Heb. 1:7; to change one thing into another, Matt. 21:13; John 2:16; 4:46; 1 Cor. 6:15; (g) to constitute one anything, e.g., Acts 2:36, (h) to declare one or oneself anything, John 5:18, "making (Himself equal with God)"; 8:53; 10:33; 19:7, 12; 1 John 1:10; 5:10; (i) to "make" one do a thing, e.g., **Luke 5:34**; John 6:10; Rev. 3:9.

Bridechamber *numphon* (3567), signifies (a) "the room or dining hall in which the marriage ceremonies were held," Matt. 22:10; some mss. have *gamos*, "a wedding," here; (b) "the chamber containing the bridal bed," "the sons of the bridechamber" being the friends of the bridegroom, who had the charge of providing what was necessary for the nuptials, Matt. 9:15; Mark 2:19; **Luke 5:34**.

Fast *see Luke 5:33*.

While *see* So long at *Luke 1:21*.

5:35 But the days will come, when the bridegroom shall be taken away from them, and then shall they fast in those days.

Taken *apairo* (522), "to lift off," is used, in the passive voice, of Christ, metaphorically as the Bridegroom of His followers, Matt. 9:15; Mark 2:20; **Luke 5:35**.

Fast *see Luke 5:33*.

5:36 And he spake also a parable unto them; No man putteth a piece of a new garment upon an old; if otherwise, then both the new maketh a rent, and the piece that was *taken* out of the new agreeth not with the old.

Parable *see* Proverb at *Luke 4:23*.

Putteth *epiballo* (1911), "to put to or unto," is so translated in Matt. 9:16; **Luke 5:36**; **9:62**; in Acts 12:1, RV, "put forth (his hands)," KJV, "stretched forth."

Piece *epiblema* (1915), primarily denotes "that which is thrown over, a cover" (*epi*, "over," *ballo*, "to throw"); then, "that which is put on, or sewed on, to cover a rent, a patch," Matt. 9:16; Mark 2:21; in the next sentence, RV, "that which should fill" (KJV, "the new piece that filled"), there is no word representing "piece" (lit., "the filling," *pleroma*); **Luke 5:36**.

Old *palaios* (3820), (Eng., "paleontology," etc.), "of what is of long duration, old in years," etc., a garment, wine (in contrast to *neos*), Matt. 9:16-17; Mark 2:21-22 (twice); **Luke 5:36-37, 39** (twice); of the treasures of divine truth, Matt. 13:52 (compared with *kainos*); of what belongs to the past, e.g., the believer's former self before his conversion, his "old man," "old" because it has been superseded by that which is new, Rom. 6:6; Eph. 4:22 (in contrast to *kainos*); Col. 3:9 (in contrast to *neos*); of the covenant in connection with the Law, 2 Cor. 3:14; of leaven, metaphorical of moral evil, 1 Cor. 5:7, 8 (in contrast to *neos*); of that which was given long ago and remains in force, an "old" commandment, 1 John 2:7 (twice), that which was familiar and well known in contrast to that which is fresh (*kainos*).

Otherwise The phrase *ei*, "if," *de*, "but," mege, "not indeed," i.e., "but if not indeed," is translated "otherwise" in the KJV of Matt. 6:1; **Luke 5:36** (RV, "else," in each place); in 2 Cor. 11:16, KJV, "if otherwise" (RV, "but if ye do").

Rent *schizo* (4977), "to split, rend open," translated "to rend" in Matt. 27:51 (twice); Mark 1:10, RV, "rent asunder" (KJV, "open"); 15:38; **Luke 5:36**, RV, "rendeth (from)"; the KJV follows the mss. which omit it in the 1st part of this verse; **23:45**; John 19:24; 21:11, RV, "rent" (KJV, "broken"), of a net.

Agreeth *sumphoneo* (4856), lit., "to sound together" (*sun*, "together," *phone*, "a sound"), i.e., "to be in accord, primarily of musical instruments," is used in the NT of the "agreement" (a) of persons concerning a matter, Matt. 18:19; 20:2, 13; Acts 5:9; (b) of the writers of Scripture, Acts 15:15; (c) of things that are said to be congruous in their nature, **Luke 5:36**.

5:37 And no man putteth new wine into old bottles; else the new wine will burst the bottles, and be spilled, and the bottles shall perish.

Putteth *ballo* (906), "to throw, cast, put," is translated "to put," in Matt. 9:17 (twice); 25:27; 27:6; Mark 2:22; 7:33; **Luke 5:37**; John 5:7; 12:6; 13:2 (of "putting" into the heart by the Devil), 18.11 (of "putting" up a sword); 20:25 (RV twice, KJV, "put" and "thrust"); v. 27, RV; Jas. 3:3; Rev. 2:24 (RV, "cast").

New *neos* (3501), signifies "new" in respect of time, that which is recent; it is used of the young, and so translated, especially the comparative degree "younger"; accordingly what is *neos* may be a reproduction of the old in quality or character. *Neos* and *kainos* are sometimes used of the same thing, but there is a difference, as already indicated. Thus the "new man" in Eph. 2:15 (*kainos*) is "new" in differing in character; so in 4:24; but the "new man" in Col. 3:10 (*neos*) stresses the fact of the believer's "new" experience, recently begun, and still proceeding. "The old man in him ... dates as far back as Adam; a new man has been born, who therefore is fitly so called" [i.e., *neos*], Trench, Syn. Sec.lx. The "New" Covenant in Heb. 12:24 is "new" (*neos*) compared with the Mosaic, nearly fifteen hundred years before; it is "new" (*kainos*) compared with the Mosaic, which is old in character, ineffective, 8:8, 13; 9:15. The "new" wine of Matt. 9:17; Mark 2:22; **Luke 5:37-39**, is *neos*, as being of recent production; the "new" wine of the kingdom, Matt. 26:29; Mark 14:25, is *kainos*, since it will be of a different character from that of this world. The rendering "new" (*neos*) is elsewhere used metaphorically in 1 Cor. 5:7, "a new lump."

Wine *oinos* (3631), is the general word for "wine." The mention of the bursting of the wineskins, Matt. 9:17; Mark 2:22; **Luke 5:37**, implies fermentation. See also Eph. 5:18 (cf. John 2:10; 1 Tim. 3:8; Titus 2:3). In Matt. 27:34, the RV has "wine" (KJV, "vinegar," translating the inferior reading *oxos*). The drinking of "wine" could be a stumbling block and the apostle enjoins abstinence in this respect, as in others, so as to avoid giving an occasion of stumbling to a brother, Rom. 14:21. Contrast 1 Tim. 5:23, which has an entirely different connection. The word is used metaphorically (a) of the evils ministered to the nations by religious Babylon, 14:8; 17:2; 18:3; (b) of the contents of the cup of divine wrath upon the nations and Babylon, Rev. 14:10; 16:19; 19:15.

Bottles *askos* (779), "a leather bottle, wineskin," occurs in Matt. 9:17 (four times); Mark 2:22 (four times); **Luke 5:37** (three times), **38**; in each place, RV, "wineskins" or "skins," for KJV, "bottles." A whole goatskin, for example, would be used with the apertures bound up, and when filled, tied at the neck. They were tanned with acacia bark and left hairy on the outside. New wines, by fermenting, would rend old skins (cf. Josh. 9:13; Job 32:19). Hung in the smoke to dry, the skin-bottles become shriveled (see Ps. 119:83).

Burst *rhegnumi* (4486), "to tear, rend, as of garments, etc.," is translated "break" in the KJV, of Matt. 9:17, of wine-skins (RV, "burst"); as in Mark 2:22 and **Luke 5:37**.; "break forth" in Gal. 4:27.

Spilled *ekchunno* (or *ekchuno*) (1632), "to pour out, shed," is rendered "be spilled" in **Luke 5:37**.

Perish *apollumi* (622), a strengthened form of *ollumi*, signifies "to destroy utterly"; in middle voice, "to perish." The idea is not extinction but ruin, loss, not of being, but of well-being. This is clear from its use, as, e.g., of the marring of wine skins, **Luke 5:37**; of lost sheep, i.e., lost to the shepherd, metaphorical of spiritual destitution, **Luke 15:4**, **6**, etc.; the lost son, **15:24**; of the perishing of food, John 6:27; of gold, 1 Pet. 1:7. So of persons, Matt. 2:13, "destroy"; 8:25, "perish"; 22:7; 27:20; of the loss of well-being in the case of the unsaved hereafter, Matt. 10:28; **Luke 13:3**, **5**; John 3:16 (v. 15 in some mss.); 10:28; 17:12; Rom. 2:12; 1 Cor. 15:18; 2 Cor. 2:15, "are perishing"; 4:3; 2 Thess. 2:10; Jas. 4:12; 2 Pet. 3:9.

5:38 But new wine must be put into new bottles; and both are preserved.

New *kainos* (2537), denotes "new," of that which is unaccustomed or unused, not "new" in time, recent, but "new" as to form or quality, of different nature from what is contrasted as old. " 'The new tongues,' *kainos*, of Mark 16:17 are the 'other tongues,' *heteros*, of Acts 2:4. These languages, however, were 'new' and 'different,' not in the sense that they had never been heard before, or that they were new to the hearers, for it is plain from v. 8 that this is not the case; they were new languages to the speakers, different from those in which they were accustomed to speak.

"The new things that the Gospel brings for present obedience and realization are: a new covenant, Matt. 26:28 in some texts; a new commandment, John 13:34; a new creative act, Gal. 6:15; a new creation, 2 Cor. 5:17; a new man, i.e., a new character of manhood, spiritual and moral, after the pattern of Christ, Eph. 4:24; a new man, i.e., 'the Church which is His (Christ's) body,' Eph. 2:15.

"The new things that are to be received and enjoyed hereafter are: a new name, the believer's, Rev. 2:17; a new name, the Lord's, Rev. 3:12; a new song, Rev. 5:9; a new Heaven and a new Earth, Rev. 21:1; the new Jerusalem, Rev. 3:12; 21:2; 'And He that sitteth on the Throne said, Behold, I make all things new,' Rev. 21:5."

Kainos is translated "fresh" in the RV of Matt. 9:17; Mark 2:22 (in the best texts) and **Luke 5:38**, of wineskins. Cf. *kainotes*, "newness."

Put *bleteos* (992) (a gerundive form from *ballo*), meaning "(that which) one must put," is found in **Luke 5:38**, and, in some mss., Mark 2:22.

New *neos* (3501), "new" (in respect of time, as distinct from kainos, "new," in respect of quality), is translated "fresh" in the RV of Matt. 9:17; Mark 2:22; **Luke 5:38**, with reference to wineskins.

Bottles *see Luke 5:37*.

Preserved *see* **Kept** at *Luke 2:19*.

5:39 No man also having drunk old *wine* straightway desireth new: for he saith, The old is better.

Old *see Luke 5:36*.

Better *chrestos* (5543), primarily signifies "fit for use, able to be used" (akin to *chraomai*, "to use"), hence, "good, virtuous, mild, pleasant" (in contrast to what is hard, harsh, sharp, bitter). It is said (a) of the character of God as "kind, gracious," **Luke 6:35**; 1 Pet. 2:3; "good," Rom. 2:4, where the neuter of the adjective is used as a noun, "the goodness" (cf. the corresponding noun *chrestotes*, "goodness," in the same verse); of the yoke of Christ, Matt. 11:30, "easy" (a suitable rendering would be "kindly"); (c) of believers, Eph. 4:32; (d) of things, as wine, **Luke 5:39**, RV, "good," for KJV, "better" (cf. Jer. 24:3, 5, of figs); (e) ethically, of manners, 1 Cor. 15:33.

Chapter 6

6:1 And it came to pass on the second sabbath after the first, that he went through the corn fields; and his disciples plucked the ears of corn, and did eat, rubbing *them* in *their* hands.

Second In **Luke 6:1**, the KJV translates those mss. which have *deuteroprotos*, lit., "secondfirst," said of a sabbath (see RV marg.).

Sabbath *sabbaton* (4521), or *sabbata:* the latter, the plural form, was transliterated from the Aramaic word, which was mistaken for a plural; hence the singular, *sabbaton*, was formed from it. The root means "to cease, desist" (Heb., *shabath*; cf. Arab., *sabata*, "to intercept, interrupt"); the doubled *b* has an intensive force, implying a complete cessation or a making to cease, probably the former. The idea is not that of relaxation or refreshment, but cessation from activity. In Matt. 12:1 and 11, where the plural is used, the KJV (as the RV) rightly has the singular, "the sabbath day"; in v. 5 the KJV has the plural. Where the singular is used the RV omits the word "day," v. 2; 24:20; Mark 6:2; **Luke 6:1** ("on a sabbath"); **14:3**; John 9:14 ("it was the sabbath on the day when ..."). As to the use or omission of the article the omission does not always require the rendering "a sabbath"; it is absent, e.g., in Matt. 12:2. The observation of the seventh day of the week, enjoined upon Israel, was a sign between God and His earthly people, based upon the fact that after the six days of creative operations He rested, Exod. 31:16, 17, with 20:8-11. The OT regulations were developed and systematized to such an extent that they became a burden upon the people (who otherwise rejoiced in the rest provided) and a byword for absurd extravagance. Two treatises of the Mishna (the *Shabbath* and *Erubin*) are entirely occupied with regulations for the observance; so with the discussions in the Gemara, on rabbinical opinions. The effect upon current opinion explains the antagonism roused by the Lord's cures wrought on the "Sabbath," e.g., Matt. 12:9-13; John 5:5-16, and explains the fact that on a "Sabbath" the sick were brought to be healed after sunset, e.g., Mark 1:32. According to rabbinical ideas, the disciples, by plucking ears of corn (Matt. 12:1; Mark 2:23), and rubbing them (**Luke 6:1**), broke the "sabbath" in two respects: for to pluck was to reap, and to rub was to thresh. The Lord's attitude towards the "sabbath" was by way of freeing it from these vexatious traditional accretions by which it was made an end in itself, instead of a means to an end (Mark 2:27).

Went *diaporeuomai* (1279), "to go through," "to pass across," is translated "to go through," in **Luke 6:1**; **13:22**, "went on His way through," RV; Acts 16:4; "going by" in **Luke 18:36**, RV (KJV, "pass by"); "in my journey" in Rom. 15:24 (2nd part).

Corn fields *sporimos* (4702), lit., "sown, or fit for sowing" (*speiro* "to sow, scatter seed"), denotes, in the plural, "sown fields, fields of grain, cornfields," Matt. 12:1, RV; Mark 2:23; **Luke 6:1** (cf. *spora*, 1 Pet. 1:23, and *sporos*, "seed").

Plucked *tillo* (5089), is used of "plucking off ears of corn," Matt. 12:1; Mark 2:23; **Luke 6:1**. In the Sept., Isa. 18:7.

Ears of corn *stachus* (4719), is found in Matt. 12:1; Mark 2:23; 4:28 ("ear," twice); **Luke 6:1**. The first part of the word is derived from the root *sta-* found in parts of the verb *histemi*, "to cause to stand." It is used as a proper name in Rom. 16:9.

Rubbing *psocho* (5597), "to rub, to rub to pieces," is used in **Luke 6:1**.

6:2-3 And certain of the Pharisees said unto them, Why do ye that which is not lawful to do on the sabbath days?

And Jesus answering them said, Have ye not read so much as this, what David did, when himself was an hungred, and they which were with him;

Much The negatives *oude* and *mede*, "not even" (RV) are translated "not so much as" in the KJV in Mark 2:2; **Luke 6:3** and 1 Cor. 5:1; in the following the RV and KJV translate them "not so much as," Mark 3:20 (some mss. have *mete*, with the same meaning); Acts 19:2; in Mark 6:31 "no (leisure) so much as."

6:4 How he went into the house of God, and did take and eat the shewbread, and gave also to them that were with him; which it is not lawful to eat but for the priests alone?

Shewbread The phrase rendered "the shewbread" is formed by the combination of the nouns *prothesis*, "a setting forth" (*pro*, "before," *tithemi*, "to place") and *artos*, "a loaf" (in the plural), each with the article, Matt. 12:4; Mark 2:26 and **Luke 6:4**, lit., "the loaves of the setting forth"; in Heb. 9:2, lit., "the setting forth of the loaves." The corresponding OT phrases are lit., "bread of the face," Exod. 25:30, i.e., the presence, referring to the Presence of God (cf. Isa. 63:9 with Exod. 33:14, 15); "the bread of ordering," 1 Chron. 9:32, marg. In Num. 4:7 it is called "the continual bread"; in 1 Sam. 21:4, 6, "holy bread" (KJV, "hallowed"). In the Sept. of 1 Kings 7:48, it is called "the bread of the offering" (*prosphora*, "a bearing towards"). The twelve loaves, representing the tribes of Israel, were set in order every Sabbath day before the Lord, "on the behalf of the children," Lev. 24:8, RV (marg., and KJV, "from"), "an everlasting covenant." The loaves symbolized the fact that on the basis of the sacrificial atonement of the Cross, believers are accepted before God, and nourished by Him in the person of Christ. The showbread was partaken of by the priests, as representatives of the nation. Priesthood now being coextensive with all who belong to Christ, 1 Pet. 2:5, 9, He, the Living Bread, is the nourishment of all, and where He is, there, representatively, they are.

6:5-6 And he said unto them, That the Son of man is Lord also of the sabbath.

And it came to pass also on another sabbath, that he entered into the synagogue and taught: and there was a man whose right hand was withered.

Withered *xeros* (3584), is used (a) naturally, of "dry" land, Heb. 11:29; or of land in general, Matt. 23:15, "land"; or of physical infirmity, "withered," Matt. 12:10; Mark 3:3; **Luke 6:6**, 8; John 5:3; (b) figuratively, in **Luke 23:31**, with reference to the spiritual "barrenness" of the Jews, in contrast to the character of the Lord. Cf. Ps. 1:3; Isa. 56:3; Ezek. 17:24; 20:47.

6:7 And the scribes and Pharisees watched him, whether he would heal on the sabbath day; that they might find an accusation against him.

Watched *paratereo* (3906), "to observe," especially with sinister intent, is rendered "to watch" in Mark 3:2; **Luke 6:7**; **14:1**; **20:20**; Acts 9:24.

Heal *see Luke 4:23.*

Accusation *kategoreo* (2723), "to speak against, accuse," is used (a) in a general way, "to accuse," e.g., **Luke 6:7**, RV, "how to accuse"; Rom. 2:15; Rev. 12:10; (b) before a judge, e.g., Matt. 12:10; Mark 15:4 (RV, "witness against"); Acts 22:30; 25:16. In Acts 24:19, RV renders it "make accusation," for the KJV, "object."

6:8 But he knew their thoughts, and said to the man which had the withered hand, Rise up, and stand forth in the midst. And he arose and stood forth.

Thoughts *see Luke 2:35.*

Withered *see Luke 6:6.*

Stand, Stood *histemi* (2476), (a) transitively, denotes "to cause to stand, to set"; in the passive voice, "to be made to stand," e.g., Matt. 2:9, lit., "was made to stand"; so **Luke 11:18**; **19:8** (Col. 4:12 in some mss.); in Rev. 13:1 the RV follows the best texts, "he stood" (not as KJV, "I stood"); the reference is to the Dragon. In the middle voice, "to take one's stand, place oneself," e.g., Rev. 18:15; (b) intransitively, in the 2nd aorist and perfect active, "to stand, stand by, stand still," e.g., Matt. 6:5; 20:32, "stood still"; in **Luke 6:8**, "stand forth" and "stood forth"; metaphorically, "to stand firm," John 8:44 (negatively), in the truth; Rom. 5:2, in grace; 1 Cor. 15:1, in the gospel; Rom. 11:20, "by thy faith," RV; 2 Cor. 1:24, "by faith" (marg., "by your faith"); of steadfastness, 1 Cor. 7:37; Eph. 6:11, 13, 14; Col. 4:12.

6:9 Then said Jesus unto them, I will ask you one thing; Is it lawful on the sabbath days to do good, or to do evil? to save life, or to destroy *it*?

Ask *see* **Asking** at *Luke 2:46.*

Good *agathopoieo* (15), "to do," is used (a) in a general way, "to do well," 1 Pet. 2:15, 20; 3:6, 17; 3 John 11; (b) with pointed reference "to the benefit of another," **Luke 6:9**, **33**, **35**; in Mark 3:4 the parts of the word are separated in some mss. Some mss. have it in Acts 14:17. Cf. the noun *agathopoiia*, "well-doing," 1 Pet. 4:19, and the adjective *agathopoios*, "doing well," 1 Pet. 2:14.

Evil *kakopoieo* (2554), signifies "to do evil," Mark 3:4 (RV, "to do harm"); so, **Luke 6:9**; in 3 John 11, "doeth evil"; in 1 Pet. 3:17, "evil doing."

6:10 And looking round about upon them all, he said unto the man, Stretch forth thy hand. And he did so: and his hand was restored whole as the other.

Looking *periblepo* (4017), "to look about, or round about, on," is used in the middle voice, Mark 3:5, 34, 5:32; 9:8; 10:23; 11:11; **Luke 6:10**.

Stretch *see* **Put forth** at *Luke 5:13.*

Restored *apokathistemi or the alternative form apokathistano* (600), is used (a) of "restoration" to a former condition of health, Matt. 12:13; Mark 3:5; 8:25; **Luke 6:10**; (b) of the divine "restoration" of Israel and conditions affected by it, including the renewal of the covenant broken by them, Matt. 17:11; Mark 9:12; Acts 1:6; (c) of "giving" or "bringing" a person back, Heb. 13:19. In the papyri it is used of financial restitution, of making good the breaking of a stone by a workman by his substituting another, of the reclamation of land, etc. (Moulton and Milligan).

Whole *hugies* (5199), (cf. Eng., "hygiene") is used especially in the Gospels of making sick folk "whole," Matt. 12:13; 15:31; Mark 3:5; 5:34; **Luke 6:10**; John 5:4, 6, 9, 11, 14, 15; 7:23; also Acts 4:10; of "sound (speech)," Titus 2:8.

6:11 And they were filled with madness; and communed one with another what they might do to Jesus.

Filled *see Luke 1:15.*

Madness *anoia* (454), lit. signifies "without understanding" (*a*, negative, *nous*, "mind"); hence, "folly," or, rather, "senselessness," 2 Tim. 3:9; in **Luke 6:11** it denotes violent or mad rage, "madness." Cf. *anoetos*, "foolish."

Communed *see* **Noised** at *Luke 1:65.*

6:12 And it came to pass in those days, that he went out into a mountain to pray, and continued all night in prayer to God.

Continued *dianuktereuo* (1273), "to pass the night through" (*dia*, "through," *nux*, "a night"), "to continue all night," is found in **Luke 6:12**, of the Lord in spending all night in prayer.

Prayer *proseuche* (4335), denotes (a) "prayer" (to God), the most frequent term, e.g., Matt. 21:22; **Luke**

6:12, where the phrase is not to be taken literally as if it meant, "the prayer of God" (subjective genitive), but objectively, "prayer to God." In Jas. 5:17, "He prayed fervently," RV, is, lit., "he prayed with prayer" (a Hebraistic form).

6:13 And when it was day, he called *unto him* his disciples: and of them he chose twelve, whom also he named apostles;

Called *prosphoneo* (4377), "to address, call to," is rendered "spake unto" (or "to") in **Luke 23:20**; Acts 21:40; 22:2; "to call unto" (or "to") in Matt. 11:16; **Luke 6:13**, **7:32**, **13:12**.

Chose *eklego* (1586), "to pick out, select," means, in the middle voice, "to choose for oneself," not necessarily implying the rejection of what is not chosen, but "choosing" with the subsidiary ideas of kindness or favor or love, Mark 13:20; **Luke 6:13**; **9:35** (RV); **10:42**; **14:7**; John 6:70; 13:18; 15:16, 19; Acts 1:2, 24; 6:5; 13:17; 15:22, 25; in 15:7 it is rendered "made choice"; 1 Cor. 1:27-28; Eph. 1:4; Jas. 2:5.

Named *onomazo* (3687), denotes (a) "to name," "mention," or "address by name," Acts 19:13, RV, "to name" (KJV, "to call"); in the passive voice, Rom. 15:20; Eph. 1:21; 5:3; to make mention of the "Name" of the Lord in praise and worship, 2 Tim. 2:19; (b) "to name, call, give a name to," **Luke 6:13**, **14**; passive voice, 1 Cor. 5:11, RV, "is named" (KJV, "is called"); Eph. 3:15 (some mss. have the verb in this sense in Mark 3:14 and 1 Cor. 5:1).

Apostles *apostolos* (652), is, lit., "one sent forth" (*apo*, "from," *stello*, "to send"). "The word is used of the Lord Jesus to describe His relation to God, Heb. 3:1; see John 17:3. The twelve disciples chosen by the Lord for special training were so called, **Luke 6:13**; **9:10**. Paul, though he had seen the Lord Jesus, 1 Cor. 9:1; 15:8, had not 'companied with' the Twelve 'all the time' of His earthly ministry, and hence was not eligible for a place among them, according to Peter's description of the necessary qualifications, Acts 1:22. Paul was commissioned directly, by the Lord Himself, after His Ascension, to carry the gospel to the Gentiles.

"The word has also a wider reference. In Acts 14:4, 14, it is used of Barnabas as well as of Paul; in Rom. 16:7 of Andronicus and Junias. In 2 Cor. 8:23 (RV, margin) two unnamed brethren are called 'apostles of the churches'; in Phil. 2:25 (RV, margin) Epaphroditus is referred to as 'your apostle.' It is used in 1 Thess. 2:6 of Paul, Silas and Timothy, to define their relation to Christ."

6:14 Simon, (whom he also named Peter,) and Andrew his brother, James and John, Philip and Bartholomew,

Named *see Luke 6:13.*

6:15 Matthew and Thomas, James the *son* of Alphaeus, and Simon called Zelotes,

Zelotes *zelotes* (2207), is used adjectivally, of "being zealous" (a) "of the Law," Acts 21:20; (b) "toward God," lit., "of God," 22:3, RV, "for God"; (c) "of spiritual gifts," 1 Cor. 14:12, i.e., for exercise of spiritual gifts (lit., "of spirits," but not to be interpreted literally); (d) "for (KJV, 'of') the traditions of my fathers," Gal. 1:14, of Paul's loyalty to Judaism before his conversion; (e) "of good works," Titus 2:14. The word is, lit., "a zealot," i.e., "an uncompromising partisan." The "Zealots" was a name applied to an extreme section of the Pharisees, bitterly antagonistic to the Romans. Josephus (*Antiq.* xviii. 1. 1, 6; *B.J.* ii. 8. 1) refers to them as the "fourth sect of Jewish philosophy" (i.e., in addition to the Pharisees, Sadducees, and Essenes), founded by Judas of Galilee (cf. Acts 5:37). After his rebellion in AD 6, the Zealots nursed the fires of revolt, which, bursting out afresh in AD 66, led to the destruction of Jerusalem in 70. To this sect Simon, one of the apostles, had belonged, **Luke 6:15**; Acts 1:13. The equivalent Hebrew and Aramaic term was "Cananaean" (Matt. 10:4); this is not connected with Canaan, as the KJV "Canaanite" would suggest, but is derived from Heb. *qanna*, "jealous."

6:16 And Judas *the brother* of James, and Judas Iscariot, which also was the traitor.

Brother In **Luke 6:16** and Acts 1:13, the RV has "son," for KJV, "brother."

Traitor *prodotes* (4273), denotes "a betrayer, traitor"; the latter term is assigned to Judas, virtually as a title, in **Luke 6:16**; in 2 Tim. 3:4 it occurs in a list of evil characters, foretold as abounding in the last days.

6:17 And he came down with them, and stood in the plain, and the company of his disciples, and a great multitude of people out of all Judaea and Jerusalem, and from the sea coast of Tyre and Sidon, which came to hear him, and to be healed of their diseases;

Plain In **Luke 6:17**, RV, *topos*, with *pedinos*, "level," is translated "level place" (KJV, "plain").

Disciples *mathetes* (3101), lit., "a learner" (from *manthano*, "to learn," from a root *math*–, indicating thought accompanied by endeavor), in contrast to *didaskalos*, "a teacher"; hence it denotes "one who follows one's teaching," as the "disciples" of John, Matt. 9:14; of the Pharisees, Matt. 22:16; of Moses, John 9:28; it is used of the "disciples" of Jesus (a) in a wide sense, of Jews who became His adherents, John 6:66; **Luke 6:17**, some being secretly so, John 19:38; (b) especially of the twelve apostles, Matt. 10:1; **Luke 22:11**, e.g.; (c) of all who manifest that they are His "disciples" by abiding in His Word, John 8:31, cf. 13:35; 15:8; (d) in the Acts, of those who believed upon Him and confessed Him, 6:1-2, 7; 14:20, 22, 28; 15:10; 19:1, etc. A "disciple" was not only a pupil, but an adherent; hence they are spoken of as imitators of their teacher; cf. John 8:31; 15:8.

Multitude *ochlos* (3793), is used frequently in the four Gospels and the Acts; elsewhere only in Rev. 7:9; 17:15; 19:1, 6; it denotes (a) "a crowd or multitude of persons, a throng," e.g., Matt. 14:14, 15; 15:33; often in the plural, e.g., Matt. 4:25; 5:1; with *polus*, "much" or "great," it signifies "a great multitude," e.g., Matt. 20.29, or "the common people," Mark 12:37, perhaps preferably "the mass of the people." Field supports the meaning in the text, but either rendering is suitable. The mass of the people was attracted to Him (for the statement "heard Him gladly," cf. what is said in Mark 6:20 of Herod Antipas concerning John the Baptist); in John 12:9, "the common people," RV, stands in contrast with their leaders (v. 10); Acts 24:12, RV, "crowd"; (b) "the populace, an unorganized multitude," in contrast to *demos*, "the people as a body politic," e.g., Matt. 14:5; 21:26; John 7:12 (2nd part); (c) in a more general sense, "a multitude or company," e.g., **Luke 6:17**, RV, "a (great) multitude (of His disciples)," KJV, "the company"; Acts 1:15, "a multitude (of persons)," RV, KJV, "the number (of names)"; Acts 24:18, RV, "crowd" (KJV, "multitude"). *See also* ***Luke 1:10***.

Sea coast *paralios* (3882), "by the sea" (*para*, "by," *hals*, "salt"), hence denotes "a sea coast," **Luke 6:17**. In the Sept., Gen. 49:13; Deut. 1:7; 33:19; Josh. 9:1; 11:3 (twice); Job 6:3; Isa. 9:1.

Diseases *see* ***Luke 4:40***.

6:18 And they that were vexed with unclean spirits: and they were healed.

Vexed *enochleo* (1776), from *en*, "in," *ochlos*, "a throng, crowd," is used in Heb. 12:15 of a root of bitterness; in **Luke 6:18** (in the best texts; some have *ochleo*), RV, "were troubled" (KJV, "were vexed").

6:19 And the whole multitude sought to touch him: for there went virtue out of him, and healed *them* all.

Virtue In the KJV of Mark 5:30; **Luke 6:19**; **8:46**, *dunamis*, "power" (RV), is rendered "virtue."

6:20 And he lifted up his eyes on his disciples, and said, Blessed *be ye* poor: for yours is the kingdom of God.

Lifted *epairo* (1869), "to lift up, raise," is used of "lifting" up the eyes, Matt. 17:8; **Luke 6:20**; **16:23**, **18:13**; John 4:35; 6:5; 17:1; the head, **Luke 21:28**; the hands, **Luke 24:50**; 1 Tim. 2:8; the voice, **Luke 11:27**; Acts 2:14; 14:11; 22:22; a foresail, Acts 27:40 ("hoisting," RV); metaphorically, of the heel, John 13:18, as of one "lifting" up the foot before kicking; the expression indicates contempt and violence; in the passive voice, Acts 1:9, of Christ's ascension, "was taken up"; 2 Cor. 10:5, "is exalted" (with pride); 11:20, "exalteth himself."

Blessed *makarios* (3107), is used in the beatitudes in Matt. 5 and **Luke 6**, is especially frequent in the Gospel of Luke, and is found seven times in Revelation, 1:3; 14:13; 16:15; 19:9; 20:6; 22:7, 14. It is said of God twice, 1 Tim. 1:11; 6:15. In the beatitudes the Lord indicates not only the characters that are "blessed," but the nature of that which is the highest good.

Poor *ptochos* (4434), has the broad sense of "poor," (a) literally, e.g., Matt. 11:5; 26:9, 11; **Luke 21:3** (with stress on the word, "a conspicuously poor widow"); John 12:5, 6, 8; 13:29; Jas. 2:2, 3, 6; the "poor" are constantly the subjects of injunctions to assist them, Matt. 19:21; Mark 10:21; **Luke 14:13**, **21**; **18:22**; Rom. 15:26; Gal. 2:10; (b) metaphorically, Matt. 5:3; **Luke 6:20**; Rev. 3:17.

Yours The possessive pronoun, *humeteros*, "your," is used in **Luke 6:20**; John 7:6; 8:17; 15:20; Acts 27:34; Rom. 11:31; 1 Cor. 15:31; 16:17; 2 Cor. 8:8; Gal. 6:13; in **Luke 16:12**, "your own."

6:21 Blessed *are ye* that hunger now: for ye shall be filled. Blessed *are ye* that weep now: for ye shall laugh.

Hunger *peinao* (3983), "to hunger, be hungry, hungered," is used (a) literally, e.g., Matt. 4:2; 12:1; 21:18; Rom. 12:20; 1 Cor. 11:21, 34; Phil. 4:12; Rev. 7:16; Christ identifies Himself with His saints in speaking of Himself as suffering in their sufferings in this and other respects, Matt. 25:35, 42; (b) metaphorically, Matt. 5:6; **Luke 6:21**, **25**; John 6:35.

Filled *chortazo* (5526), "to fill or satisfy with food," e.g., Matt. 15:33; Phil. 4:12, is used metaphorically in Matt. 5:6; **Luke 6:21**.

Laugh *gelao* (1070), "to laugh," is found in **Luke 6:21, 25**. This signifies loud laughter in contrast to demonstrative weeping.

6:22 Blessed are ye, when men shall hate you, and when they shall separate you *from their company*, and shall reproach *you*, and cast out your name as evil, for the Son of man's sake.

Hate *miseo* (3404), "to hate," is used especially (a) of malicious and unjustifiable feelings towards others, whether towards the innocent or by mutual animosity, e.g., Matt. 10:22; 24:10; **Luke 6:22, 27; 19:14**; John 3:20, of "hating" the light (metaphorically); 7:7; 15:18, 19, 23-25; Titus 3:3; 1 John 2:9, 11; 3:13, 15; 4:20; Rev. 18:2, where "hateful" translates the perfect participle passive voice of the verb, lit., "hated," or "having been hated"; (b) of a right feeling of aversion from what is evil; said of wrongdoing, Rom. 7:15; iniquity, Heb. 1:9; "the garment (figurative) spotted by the flesh," Jude 23; "the works of the Nicolaitans," Rev. 2:6 (and v. 15, in some mss.; see the KJV); (c) of relative preference for one thing over another, by way of expressing either aversion from, or disregard for, the claims of one person or thing relatively to those of another, Matt. 6:24, and **Luke 16:13**, as to the impossibility of serving two masters; **Luke 14:26**, as to the claims of parents relatively to those of Christ; John 12:25, of disregard for one's life relatively to the claims of Christ; Eph. 5:29, negatively, of one's flesh, i.e. of one's own, and therefore a man's wife as one with him.

Separate *aphorizo* (873), "to mark off by bounds" (*apo*, "from," *horizo*, "to determine"; *horos*, "a limit"), "to separate," is used of "(a) the Divine action in setting men apart for the work of the gospel, Rom. 1:1; Gal. 1:15; (b) the Divine judgment upon men, Matt. 13:49; 25:32; (c) the separation of Christians from unbelievers, Acts 19:9; 2 Cor. 6:17; (d) the separation of believers by unbelievers, **Luke 6:22**; (e) the withdrawal of Christians from their brethren, Gal. 2:12. In (c) is described what the Christian must do, in (d) what he must be prepared to suffer, and in (e) what he must avoid."

Company *aphorizo*, "to separate," is translated "separate (you) from (their) company," in **Luke 6:22**, the latter part being added in italics to supply the meaning of excommunication.

Reproach *oneidizo* (3679), signifies (a), in the active voice, "to reproach, upbraid," Matt. 5:11, RV, "shall reproach" (KJV, "shall revile"); 11:20, "to upbraid"; 27:44, RV, "cast ... reproach" [KJV, "cast ... in (His) teeth"]; Mark 15:32 RV, "reproached" (KJV, "reviled"); 16:14 "upbraided"; **Luke 6:22** "shall reproach", Rom. 15:3; Jas. 1:5, "upbraideth"; (b) in the passive voice, "to suffer reproach, be reproached," 1 Tim. 4:10 (in some mss. in the 2nd part); 1 Pet. 4:14.

6:23 Rejoice ye in that day, and leap for joy: for, behold, your reward *is* great in heaven: for in the like manner did their fathers unto the prophets.

Rejoice *see Luke 1:14.*

Leap *see* Leaped at *Luke 1:41.*

Reward *misthos* (3408), primarily "wages, hire," and then, generally, "reward," (a) received in this life, Matt. 5:46; 6:2, 5, 16; Rom. 4:4; 1 Cor. 9:17, 18; of evil "rewards," Acts 1:18; (b) to be received hereafter, Matt. 5:12; 10:41 (twice), 42; Mark 9:41; **Luke 6:23, 35**; 1 Cor. 3:8, 14; 2 John 8; Rev. 11:18; 22:12.

Manner In the following the phrase *kata tauta*, or *kata ta auta*, lit., "according to the same things," is translated "in (the) like (RV, same) manner," **Luke 6:23**; v. **26**, RV (KJV, "so"); **17:30**, RV, "after the same manner" (KJV, "even thus").

6:24 But woe unto you that are rich! for ye have received your consolation.

Woe *ouai* (3759), an interjection, is used (a) in denunciation, Matt. 11:21; 18:7 (twice); eight times in ch. 23; 24:19; 26:24; Mark 13:17; 14:21; **Luke 6:24, 25** (twice), **26; 10:13**; six times in **ch. 11; 17:1; 21:23; 22:22**; 1 Cor. 9:16; Jude 11; Rev. 8:13 (thrice); 12:12; as a noun, Rev. 9:12 (twice); 11:14 (twice); (b) in grief, "alas," Rev. 18:10, 16, 19 (twice in each).

Rich *plousios* (4145), "rich, wealthy," is used (I) literally, (a) adjectivally (with a noun expressed separately) in Matt. 27:57; **Luke 12:16; 14:12; 16:1, 19**; (without a noun), **18:23; 19:2**; (b) as a noun, singular, a "rich" man (the noun not being expressed), Matt. 19:23, 24; Mark 10:25; 12:41; **Luke 16:21, 22; 18:25**; Jas. 1:10, 11, "the rich," "the rich (man)"; plural, Mark 12:41, lit., "rich (ones)"; **Luke 6:24** (ditto); **21:1**; 1 Tim. 6:17, "(them that are) rich," lit., "(the) rich"; Jas. 2:6, RV, "the rich"; 5:1, RV, "ye rich"; Rev. 6:15 and 13:16, RV, "the rich"; (II) metaphorically, of God, Eph. 2:4 ("in mercy"); of Christ, 2 Cor. 8:9; of believers, Jas. 2:5, RV, "(*to be*) rich (in faith)"; Rev. 2:9, of spiritual "enrichment" generally; 3:17, of a false sense of "enrichment."

Have received *apecho* (568), denotes (a) transitively, "to have in full, to have received"; so the RV in Matt. 6:2, 5, 16 (for KJV, "they have"); **Luke 6:24**, KJV, and RV; in all these instances the present tense (to which the KJV incorrectly adheres in the Matt. 6 verses) has a perfective force, consequent upon the combination with the prefix *apo* ("from"), not that it stands for the perfect tense, but that it views the action in its accomplished result; so in Phil. 4:18, where the KJV and RV translate it "I have"; in Philem. 15, "(that) thou shouldest have (him for ever)," KJV, "shouldest receive"; (b) intransitively, "to be away, distant," used with *porro*, "far," Matt. 15:8; Mark 7:6; with *makran*, "far off, afar," **Luke 7:6**; **15:20**; without an accompanying adverb, **Luke 24:13**, "which was from."

Consolation *see Luke 2:25.*

6:25 Woe unto you that are full! for ye shall hunger. Woe unto you that laugh now! for ye shall mourn and weep.

Woe *see Luke 6:24.*

Full *see* Filled at *Luke 1:53.*

Hunger *see Luke 6:21.*

Laugh *see Luke 6:21.*

Mourn *pentheo* (3996), "to mourn for, lament," is used (a) of mourning in general, Matt. 5:4; 9:15; **Luke 6:25**; (b) of sorrow for the death of a loved one, Mark 16:10; (c) of "mourning" for the overthrow of Babylon and the Babylonish system, Rev. 18:11, 15, RV, "mourning" (KJV, "wailing"); v. 19 (ditto); (d) of sorrow for sin or for condoning it, Jas. 4:9; 1 Cor. 5:2; (e) of grief for those in a local church who show no repentance for evil committed, 2 Cor. 12:21, RV, "mourn" (KJV, "bewail").

6:26 Woe unto you, when all men shall speak well of you! for so did their fathers to the false prophets.

Woe *see Luke 6:24.*

So *see* **Manner** at *Luke 6:23.*

False prophets *pseudoprophetes* (5578), "a false prophet," is used of such (a) in OT times, **Luke 6:26**; 2 Pet. 2:1; (b) in the present period since Pentecost, Matt. 7:15; 24:11, 24; Mark 13:22; Acts 13:6; 1 John 4:1; (c) with reference to a false "prophet" destined to arise as the supporter of the "Beast" at the close of this age, Rev. 16:13; 19:20; 20:10 (himself described as "another beast," 13:11).

6:27 But I say unto you which hear, Love your enemies, do good to them which hate you,

Enemies *see Luke 1:71.*

Hate *see Luke 6:22.*

6:28 Bless them that curse you, and pray for them which despitefully use you.

Bless *see* Praised at *Luke 1:64.*

Curse *kataraomai* (2672), primarily signifies "to pray against, to wish evil against a person or thing"; hence "to curse," Matt. 25:41; Mark 11:21; **Luke 6:28**; Rom. 12:14; Jas. 3:9. Some mss. have it in Matt. 5:44.

Despitefully use *epereazo* (1908), is found in some mss. in Matt. 5:44, and translated "despitefully use," KJV (the RV follows the mss. which omit the sentence). In the corresponding passage in **Luke 6:28**, the KJV and RV have "despitefully use"; in 1 Pet. 3:16, KJV, "falsely accuse," RV, "revile."

6:29 And unto him that smiteth thee on the *one* cheek offer also the other; and him that taketh away thy cloke forbid not *to take thy* coat also.

Smiteth *tupto* (5180), "to strike, smite, beat," is rendered "to smite" in Matt. 24:49, KJV (RV, "beat"); 27:30; Mark 15:19; **Luke 6:29**; **18:13**; in some texts in **22:64** (1st part: RV omits); **23:48**; Acts 23:2, 3 (twice).

Cheek *siagon* (4600), primarily denotes "the jaw, the jaw-bone"; hence "cheek," Matt. 5:39; **Luke 6:29**.

Offer *parecho* (3930), "to furnish, offer, present, supply," is used in **Luke 6:29**, of "offering" the other cheek to be smitten after receiving a similar insult; for the KJV marg., in Acts 17:31.

Forbid *koluo* (2967), "to hinder, restrain, withhold, forbid" (akin to *kolos*, "docked, lopped, clipped"), is most usually translated "to forbid," often an inferior rendering to that of hindering or restraining, e.g., 1 Thess. 2:16; **Luke 23:2**; 2 Pet. 2:16, where the RV has "stayed"; in Acts 10:47 "forbid." In **Luke 6:29**, the RV has "withhold not (thy coat also)."

Coat *chiton* (5509), denotes "the inner vest or undergarment," and is to be distinguished, as such, from the *himation*. The distinction is made, for instance, in the Lord's command in Matt. 5:40: "If any man would go to law with thee, and take away thy coat (*chiton*), (*himation*) also." The order is reversed in **Luke 6:29**, and the difference lies in this, that in Matt. 5:40 the Lord is referring to a legal process, so the claimant is supposed to claim the inner garment, the less costly. The defendant is to be willing to let him have the more valuable one too. In the passage in Luke an act of violence is in view, and there is no mention of going to law. So the outer garment is the first one which would be seized.

6:30 Give to every man that asketh of thee; and of him that taketh away thy goods ask *them* not again.

Asketh *apaiteo* (523), "to ask back, demand back" (*apo*, "from," or "back," *aiteo*, "to ask"), is translated "shall be required" in **Luke 12:20**, lit. "do they require," in the impersonal sense; elsewhere, **Luke 6:30**, "to ask again." It is used in the papyri frequently in the sense of "demanding, making demands."

Thy goods The possessive pronoun *sos*, and its inflections, e.g., Matt. 7:3 (1st part); it is used as a noun with the article, in the phrases *to son*, "that which is thine," Matt. 20:14; 25:25, "thine own"; *hoi soi*, "thy friends," Mark 5:19; *ta sa*, "thy goods," **Luke 6:30**, lit., "the thine".

6:31 And as ye would that men should do to you, do ye also to them likewise.

Likewise *see Luke 5:33.*

6:32 For if ye love them which love you, what thank have ye? for sinners also love those that love them.

What *see Luke 5:19.*

Thank *charis* (5485), is rendered "thank" in **Luke 6:32**, **33**, **34**; in **17:9**, "doth he thank" is lit., "hath he thanks to"; it is rendered "thanks (be to God)" in Rom. 6:17, RV (KJV, "God be thanked"); "thanks" in 1 Cor. 15:57; in 1 Tim. 1:12 and 2 Tim. 1:3, "I thank" is, lit., "I have thanks"; "thankworthy," 1 Pet. 2:19, KJV (RV, "acceptable").

6:33 And if ye do good to them which do good to you, what thank have ye? for sinners also do even the same.

Good *see Luke 6:9.*

Thank *see Luke 6:32.*

Even *kai* (2532), a conjunction, is usually a mere connective, meaning "and"; it frequently, however, has an ascensive or climactic use, signifying "even," the thing that is added being out of the ordinary, and producing a climax. The determination of this meaning depends on the context. Examples are Matt. 5:46-47; Mark 1:27; **Luke 6:33** (RV); **10:17**; John 12:42; Gal. 2:13, 17, where "also" should be "even"; Eph. 5:12. Examples where the RV corrects the KJV "and" or "also," by substituting "even," are **Luke 7:49**, Acts 17:28; Heb. 11:11; in 1 John 4:3 the RV rightly omits "even." When followed by "if" or "though," *kai* often signifies "even," e.g., Matt. 26:35; John 8:14. So sometimes when preceded by "if," e.g., 1 Cor. 7:11, where "but and if" should be "but even if." The epexegetic or explanatory use of *kai* followed by a noun in apposition, and meaning "namely," or "even" is comparatively rare. Winer's cautionary word needs heeding, that "this meaning has been introduced into too many passages" (Gram. of the NT, p. 546.). Some think it has this sense in John 3:5, "water, even the Spirit," and Gal. 6:16, "even the Israel of God."

6:34 And if ye lend *to them* of whom ye hope to receive, what thank have ye? for sinners also lend to sinners, to receive as much again.

Lend *daneizo* (1155), in the active voice signifies "to lend money," as in **Luke 6:34-35**, in the middle voice, "to have money lent to oneself, to borrow," Matt. 5:42. Cf. *dan(e)ion*, "a debt," Matt. 18:27, and *dan(e)istes*, "a creditor," **Luke 7:41**.

Receive *apolambano* (618), signifies "to receive from another," (a) to "receive" as one's due (for **Luke 18:30**, see *lambano* [at **Luke 18:30**]); **Luke 23:41**; Rom. 1:27; Col. 3:24; 2 John 8; (b) without the indication of what is due, **Luke 16:25**; Gal. 4:5 (in some mss. 3 John 8); (c) to receive back, **Luke 6:34** (twice); **15:27**. For its other meaning, "to take apart," Mark 7:33.

Thank *see Luke 6:32.*

Much In **Luke 6:34** the phrase *ta isa*, lit., "the equivalent (things)," is translated "as much" (of lending, to receive back the equivalent).

6:35 But love ye your enemies, and do good, and lend, hoping for nothing again; and your reward shall be great, and ye shall be the children of the Highest: for he is kind unto the unthankful and *to* the evil.

Enemies *see Luke 1:71.*

Good *see Luke 6:9.*

Lend *see Luke 6:34.*

Nothing *apelpizo* (560), lit., "to hope away" (*apo*, "away from," *elpizo*, "to hope"). i.e., "to give up in despair, to despair," is used in **Luke 6:35**, RV, "nothing despairing," i.e., without anxiety as to the result, or not "despairing" of the recompense from God; this is probably the true meaning; KJV, "hoping for nothing again." The marg., "of no man," is to be rejected.

Reward *see Luke 6:23.*

Children *huios* (5207), primarily signifies the relation of offspring to parent (see John 9:18-20; Gal. 4:30). It is often used metaphorically of prominent moral characteristics. "It is used in the NT of (a) male offspring, Gal. 4:30; (b) legitimate, as opposed to illegitimate offspring, Heb. 12:8; (c) descendants, without reference to sex, Rom. 9:27; (d) friends attending a wedding, Matt. 9:15; (e) those who enjoy certain privileges, Acts 3:25; (f) those who act in a certain way, whether evil, Matt. 23:31, or good, Gal. 3:7; (g) those who manifest a certain character, whether evil, Acts 13:10; Eph. 2:2, or good, **Luke 6:35**; Acts 4:36; Rom. 8:14; (h) the destiny that corresponds with the character, whether evil, Matt. 23:15; John 17:12; 2 Thess. 2:3, or good, **Luke 20:36**; (i) the dignity of the relationship with God whereinto men are brought by the Holy Spirit when they believe on the Lord Jesus Christ, Rom. 8:19; Gal. 3:26....

"As to moral characteristics, the following phrases are used: (a) sons of God, Matt. 5:9, 45; **Luke 6:35**; (b) sons of the light, **Luke 16:8**; John 12:36; (c) sons of the day, 1 Thess. 5:5; (d) sons of peace, **Luke 10:6**; (e) sons of this world, **Luke 16:8**; (f) sons of disobedience, Eph. 2:2; (g) sons of the evil one, Matt. 13:38, cf. 'of the Devil,' Acts 13:10; (h) son of perdition, John 17:12; 2 Thess. 2:3. It is also used to describe characteristics other than moral, as: (i) sons of the resurrection, **Luke 20:36**; (j) sons of the Kingdom, Matt. 8:12; 13:38; (k) sons of the bridechamber, Mark 2:19; (l) sons of exhortation, Acts 4:36; (m) sons of thunder, Boanerges, Mark 3:17."

Highest *see Luke 1:32.*

Kind *chrestos* (5543), "serviceable, good, pleasant" (of things), "good, gracious, kind" (of persons), is translated "kind" in **Luke 6:35**, of God; in Eph. 4:32, enjoined upon believers. *See also* **Better** at *Luke 5:39.*

Unthankful *acharistos* (884), denotes "ungrateful, thankless" (*charis*, "thanks"), **Luke 6:35**; 2 Tim. 3:2.

Evil *see* Evils at *Luke 3:19.*

6:36 Be ye therefore merciful, as your Father also is merciful.

Merciful *oiktirmon* (3629), "pitiful, compassionate for the ills of others," is used twice in **Luke 6:36**, "merciful" (of the character of God, to be expressed in His people); Jas. 5:11, RV, "merciful," KJV, "of tender mercy."

6:37 Judge not, and ye shall not be judged: condemn not, and ye shall not be condemned: forgive, and ye shall be forgiven:

Condemn, Condemned *katadikazo* (2613), signifies "to exercise right or law against anyone"; hence, "to pronounce judgment, to condemn" (*kata*, "down, or against," *dike*, "justice"), Matt. 12:7, 37; **Luke 6:37**; Jas. 5:6.

Forgive, Forgiven *apoluo* (630), signifies "to set free, release, loose" (*apo*, "from," *luo*, "to loose"), e.g., **Luke 13:12**; John 19:10; it is translated "to release" in Matt. 18:27, RV (KJV, "loosed"); 27:15, 17, 21, 26; Mark 15:6, 9, 11, 15; **Luke 6:37** (twice), RV (KJV, "forgive" and "ye shall be forgiven"); **23:16** (v. **17**, in some mss.), **18**, **20**, **25**; **23:22**, RV (KJV, "let ... go"); John 18:39 (twice); 19:10; in 19:12, in the 1st part, KJV and RV; in the 2nd part, RV, "release" (KJV, "let ... go"); so in Acts 3:13; to release, dismiss, send away, translated "to let go," e.g., in **Luke 14:4**; in some mss. **22:68**; in **Luke 23:22**; in Acts 4:21, "they let ... go"; in v. 23 (passive voice), "being let go"; 5:40; in 15:33, KJV, "let go" (RV, "dismissed"); 16:35, 36; 17:9; in 23:22, RV, "let ... go" (KJV, "let ... depart"); in 28:18, KJV, "let ... go" (RV, "set ... at liberty").

6:38 Give, and it shall be given unto you; good measure, pressed down, and shaken together, and running over, shall men give into your bosom. For with the same measure that ye mete withal it shall be measured to you again.

Measure *metron* (3358), denotes (I) "that which is used for measuring, a measure," (a) of "a vessel," figuratively, Matt. 23:32; **Luke 6:38** (twice); in John 3:34, with the preposition *ek*, "(He giveth not the Spirit) by measure," RV (which is a necessary correction; the italicized words "*unto him*," KJV, detract from the meaning). Not only had Christ the Holy Spirit without "measure," but God so gives the Spirit through Him to others. It is the ascended Christ who gives the Spirit to those who receive His testimony and set their seal to this, that God is true. The Holy Spirit is imparted neither by degrees, nor in portions, as if He were merely an influence, He is bestowed personally upon each believer, at the time of the New Birth; (b) of "a graduated rod or rule for measuring," figuratively, Matt. 7:2; Mark 4:24; literally, Rev. 21:15 (in the best mss.; see the RV); v. 17; (II) "that which is measured, a determined extent, a portion measured off," Rom. 12:3; 2 Cor. 10:13 (twice); Eph. 4:7, "(according to the) measure (of the gift of Christ)"; the gift of grace is "measured" and given according to the will of Christ; whatever the endowment, His is the bestowment and the adjustment; v. 13, "the measure (of the stature of the fullness of Christ)," the standard of spiritual stature being the fullness which is essentially Christ's; v. 16, "(according to the working in due) measure (of each several part)," i.e., according to the effectual working of the ministration rendered in due "measure" by every part.

Pressed *piezo* (4085), "to press down together," is used in **Luke 6:38**, "pressed down," of the character of the measure given in return for giving. In the Sept., Mic. 6:15.

Shaken *saleuo* (4531), "to agitate, shake," primarily of the action of stormy winds, waves, etc., is used (a) literally, of a reed, Matt. 11:7; **Luke 7:24**; a vessel, "shaken" in filling, **Luke 6:38**; a building, **Luke 6:48**; Acts 4:31; 16:26; the natural forces of the heavens and heavenly bodies, Matt. 24:29; Mark 13:25; **Luke 21:26**; the earth, Heb. 12:26, "shook"; (b) metaphorically, (1) of "shaking" so as to make insecure, Heb. 12:27 (twice); (2) of casting down from a sense of security, Acts 2:25, "I should (not) be moved"; (3) to stir up (a crowd), Acts 17:13; (4) to unsettle, 2 Thess. 2:2, "(to the end that) ye be not (quickly) shaken (from your mind)," i.e., from their settled conviction and the purpose of heart begotten by it, as to the return of Christ before the Day of the Lord begins; the metaphor may be taken from the loosening of a ship from its moorings by a storm.

Running over *huperekchunno* (5240), a late form of *huperekcheo*, "to overflow," is rendered "running over" in **Luke 6:38**.

Bosom *kolpos* (2859), signifies (a) "the front of the body between the arms"; hence, to recline in the "bosom" was said of one who so reclined at table that his head covered, as it were, the "bosom" of the one next to him, John 13:23. Hence, figuratively, it is used of a place of blessedness with another, as with Abraham in paradise, **Luke 16:22-23** (plural in v. **23**), from the custom of reclining at table in the "bosom," a place of honor; of the Lord's eternal and essential relation with the Father, in all its blessedness and affection as intimated in the phrase, "The Only-begotten Son, which is in the bosom of the Father" (John 1:18); (b) "of the bosom of a garment, the hollow formed by the upper forepart of a loose garment, bound by a girdle and used for carrying or keeping things"; thus figuratively of repaying one liberally, **Luke 6:38**; cf. Isa. 65:6; Jer. 39:18; (c) "of an inlet of the sea," because of its shape, like a bosom, Acts 27:39.

Measured *antimetreo* (488), "to measure in return," is used in the passive voice, and found in some mss. in Matt. 7:2; in **Luke 6:38** the most authentic have this verb. It is not found in the Sept.

6:39 And he spake a parable unto them, Can the blind lead the blind? shall they not both fall into the ditch?

Parable *see* Proverb at *Luke 4:23*.

Lead *hodegeo* (3594), "to lead the way," is used (a) literally, RV, "guide" (KJV, "lead"), of "guiding" the blind, in Matt. 15:14; **Luke 6:39**; of "guiding" unto fountains of waters of life, Rev. 7:17; (b) figuratively, in John 16:13, of "guidance" into the truth by the Holy Spirit; in Acts 8:31, of the interpretation of Scripture.

Fall *empipto* (1706), "to fall into, or among" (*en*, "in," and *pipto*), is used (a) literally, Matt. 12:11; **Luke 6:39** (some mss. have *pipto* here); **10:36**; some mss. have it in **14:5**; (b) metaphorically, into condemnation, 1 Tim. 3:6; reproach, 3:7; temptation and snare, 6:9; the hands of God in judgment, Heb. 10:13.

Ditch *bothunos* (999), any kind of "deep hole or pit" (probably connected with *bathos*, "deep"), is translated "ditch" in the KJV of Matt. 15:14 and **Luke 6:39**, RV, "pit" in each place, as in both versions of Matt. 12:11.

6:40 The disciple is not above his master: but every one that is perfect shall be as his master.

Master *see* Doctors at *Luke 2:46*.

Perfect *katartizo* (2675), "to render fit, complete" (*artios*), "is used of mending nets, Matt. 4:21; Mark 1:19, and is translated 'restore' in Gal. 6:1. It does not necessarily imply, however, that that to which it is applied has been damaged, though it may do so, as in these passages; it signifies, rather, right ordering and arrangement, Heb. 11:3, 'framed;' it points out the path of progress, as in Matt. 21:16; **Luke 6:40**; cf. 2 Cor. 13:9; Eph. 4:12, where corresponding nouns occur. It indicates the close relationship between character and destiny, Rom. 9:22, 'fitted.' It expresses the pastor's desire for the flock, in prayer, Heb. 13:21, and in exhortation, 1 Cor. 1:10, RV, 'perfected' (KJV, 'perfectly joined'); 2 Cor. 13:11, as well as his conviction of God's purpose for them, 1 Pet. 5:10. It is used of the Incarnation of the Word in Heb. 10:5, 'prepare,' quoted from Ps. 40:6 (Sept.), where it is apparently intended to describe the unique creative act involved in the Virgin Birth, **Luke 1:35**. In 1 Thess. 3:10 it means to supply what is necessary, as the succeeding words show."

6:41 And why beholdest thou the mote that is in thy brother's eye, but perceivest not the beam that is in thine own eye?

Beholdest *blepo* (991), is also used of (a) bodily and (b) mental vision, (a) "to perceive," e.g., Matt. 13:13; (b) "to take heed," e.g., Mark 13:23, 33; it indicates greater vividness than *horao*, expressing a more intent, earnest contemplation; in **Luke 6:41**, of "beholding" the mote in a brother's eye; **Luke 24:12**, of "beholding" the linen clothes in the empty tomb; Acts 1:9, of the gaze of the disciples when the Lord ascended. The greater earnestness is sometimes brought out by the rendering "regardest," Matt. 22:16.

Mote *karphos* (2595), "a small, dry stalk, a twig, a bit of dried stick" (from *karpho*, "to dry up"), or "a tiny straw or bit of wool," such as might fly into the eye, is used metaphorically of a minor fault, Matt. 7:3, 4, 5; **Luke 6:41, 42** (twice), in contrast with *dokos*, "a beam supporting the roof of a building". In the Sept., Gen. 8:11.

Perceivest *katanoeo* (2657), "to perceive clearly," "to understand fully, consider closely," is used of not "considering" thoroughly the beam in one's own eye, Matt. 7:3 and **Luke 6:41** (KJV, "perceivest"); of carefully "considering" the ravens, **Luke 12:24**; the lilies, v. 27; of Peter's full "consideration" of his vision, Acts 11:6; of Abraham's careful "consideration" of his own body, and Sarah's womb, as dead, and yet accepting by faith God's promise, Rom. 4:19 (RV); of "considering" fully the Apostle and High Priest of our confession, Heb. 3:1; of thoughtfully "considering" one another to provoke unto love and good works, Heb. 10:24. It is translated by the verbs "behold," Acts 7:31-32; Jas. 1:23-24; "perceive," **Luke 20:23**; "discover," Acts 27:39.

Beam *dokos* (1385), "a beam," is perhaps etymologically connected with the root *dek-*, seen in the word *dechomai*, "to receive," "beams" being received at their ends into walls or pieces of timber. The Lord used it metaphorically, in contrast to a mote, "of a great fault, or vice," Matt. 7:3-5; **Luke 6:41-42**.

6:42 Either how canst thou say to thy brother, Brother, let me pull out the mote that is in thine eye, when thou thyself beholdest not the beam that is in thine own eye? Thou hypocrite, cast out first the beam out of thine own eye, and then shalt thou see clearly to pull out the mote that is in thy brother's eye.

Either *e* (2228), is a disjunctive particle. One of its uses is to distinguish things which exclude each other, or one of which can take the place of another. It is translated "either" in Matt. 6:24; 12:33; **Luke 16:13**; Acts 17:21; 1 Cor. 14:6. The RV rightly omits it in **Luke 6:42**, and translates it by "or" in **Luke 15:8**; Phil. 3:12 and Jas. 3:12.

Pull *ekballo*, "to cast out," is translated "to pull out" in Matt. 7:4 and **Luke 6:42** (twice), KJV (RV, "cast out").

Mote *see* ***Luke 6:41***.

Thou *see* ***Luke 1:76***.

Thyself *autos* (846), "he," also means "self," in the reflexive pronouns "myself, thyself, himself," etc., expressing distinction, exclusion, etc.; it is usually emphatic in the nominative case, e.g., **Luke 6:42**; **11:4**; John 18:28; Rom. 8:16, RV, "Himself."

Hypocrite *hupokrites* (5273), primarily denotes "one who answers"; then, "a stage-actor"; it was a custom for Greek and Roman actors to speak in large masks with mechanical devices for augmenting the force of the voice; hence the word became used metaphorically of "a dissembler, a hypocrite." It is found only in the Synoptists, and always used by the Lord, fifteen times in Matthew; elsewhere, Mark 7:6; **Luke 6:42**; **11:44** (in some mss.); **12:56**; **13:15**.

See *diablepo* (1227), "to see clearly," is used in Matt. 7:5; **Luke 6:42**; in Mark 8:25, RV, "he looked steadfastly."

Clearly For *diablepo*, "to see clearly," Matt. 7:5; **Luke 6:42**, and *kathorao*, ditto, Rom. 1:20.

6:43 For a good tree bringeth not forth corrupt fruit; neither doth a corrupt tree bring forth good fruit.

Tree *dendron* (1186), "a living, growing tree" (cf. Eng., "rhododendron," lit., "rose tree"), known by the fruit it produces, Matt. 12:33; **Luke 6:44**; certain qualities are mentioned in the NT; "a good tree," Matt. 7:17, 18; 12:33; **Luke 6:43**; "a corrupt tree" (ditto); in Jude 12, metaphorically, of evil teachers, "autumn trees (KJV, 'trees whose fruit withereth') without fruit, twice dead, plucked up by the roots," RV; in **Luke 13:19** in some texts, "a great tree," KJV (RV, "a tree"); in **Luke 21:29** "the fig tree" is illustrative of Israel, "all the trees" indicating gentile nations.

Neither *palin* (3825), the regular word for "again," is used chiefly in two senses, (a) with reference to repeated action; (b) rhetorically, in the sense of "moreover" or "further," indicating a statement to be added in the course of an argument, e.g., Matt. 5:33; or with the meaning "on the other hand, in turn," **Luke 6:43**; 1 Cor. 12:21; 2 Cor. 10:7; 1 John 2:8. In the first chapter of Hebrews, v. 5, *palin* simply introduces an additional quotation; in v. 6 this is not so. There the RV rightly puts the word "again" in connection with "He bringeth in the firstborn into the world," "When He again bringeth, etc." That is to say, *palin* is here set in contrast to the time when God *first* brought His Son into the world. This statement, then, refers to the future second advent of Christ. The word is used far more frequently in the Gospel of John than in any other book in the New Testament.

Corrupt *sapros* (4550), "corrupt, rotten" (akin to *sepo*, "to rot"), primarily, of vegetable and animal substances, expresses what is of poor quality, unfit for use, putrid. It is said of a tree and its fruit, Matt. 7:17-18; 12:33; **Luke 6:43**; of certain fish, Matt. 13:48 (here translated "bad"); of defiling speech, Eph. 4:29.

6:44 For every tree is known by his own fruit. For of thorns men do not gather figs, nor of a bramble bush gather they grapes.

Every *see Luke 4:40.*

Tree *see Luke 6:43.*

Thorns *akantha* (173), "a brier, a thorn" (from *ake*, "a point"), is always used in the plural in the NT, Matt. 7:16 and parallel passage in **Luke 6:44**; Matt. 13:7 (twice), 22 and parallels in Mark and Luke; in Matt. 27:29 and John 19:2, of the crown of "thorns" placed on Christ's head in mock imitation of the garlands worn by emperors. They were the effects of the divine curse on the ground (Gen. 3:18; contrast Isa. 55:13). The "thorns" of the crown plaited by the soldiers, are usually identified with those of the *Zizyphus spina Christi*, some 20 feet high or more, fringing the Jordan and abundant in Palestine; its twigs are flexible. Another species, however, the Arabian *qundaul*, crowns of which are plaited and sold in Jerusalem as representatives of Christ's crown, seems likely to be the one referred to. The branches are easily woven and adapted to the torture intended. The word *akantha* occurs also in Heb. 6:8.

Gather *sullego* (4816), "to collect, gather up or out" (*sun*, "with" *lego*, "to pick out"), is said of "gathering" grapes and figs, Matt. 7:16; **Luke 6:44**; tares, Matt. 13:28, 29, 30, 40; good fish, 13:48; "all things that cause stumbling, and them that do iniquity," 13:41.

Figs *sukon* (4810), denotes "the ripe fruit of a *suke*, a fig-tree," Matt. 7:16; Mark 11:13; **Luke 6:44**; Jas. 3:12.

Bush *batos* (942), denotes "a bramble bush," as in **Luke 6:44**. In Mark 12:26 and **Luke 20:37** the phrase "in the place concerning the Bush" signifies in that part of the book of Exodus concerning it. See also Acts 7:30, 35.

Gather *trugao* (5166), signifies "to gather in," of harvest, vintage, ripe fruits (*truge* denotes "fruit," etc., gathered in autumn), **Luke 6:44**, of grapes (last part of v.); metaphorically, of the clusters of "the vine of the earth," Rev. 14:18; of that from which they are "gathered," v. 19.

Grapes *staphule* (4718), denotes "a bunch of grapes, or a grape," Matt. 7:16; **Luke 6:44**; Rev. 14:18. It is to be distinguished from *omphax*, "an unripe grape" (not in NT), e.g., in the Sept. of Job 15:33, and from *botrus*, "a cluster," used together with *staphule* in Rev. 14:18.

6:45 A good man out of the good treasure of his heart bringeth forth that which is good; and an evil man out of the evil treasure of his heart bringeth forth that which is evil: for of the abundance of the heart his mouth speaketh.

Good *see Luke 1:53.*

Treasure *thesauros* (2344), denotes (1) "a place of safe keeping" (possibly akin to *tithemi*, "to put"), (a) "a casket," Matt. 2:11; (b) "a storehouse," Matt. 13:52; used metaphorically of the heart, Matt. 12:35, twice (RV, "out of his treasure"); **Luke 6:45**; (2) "a treasure," Matt. 6:19, 20, 21; 13:44; **Luke 12:33, 34**; Heb. 11:26; "treasure" (in heaven or the heavens), Matt. 19:21; Mark 10:21; **Luke 18:22**; in these expressions (which are virtually equivalent to that in Matt. 6:1, "with your Father which is in Heaven") the promise does not simply refer to the present life, but looks likewise to the hereafter; in 2 Cor. 4:7 it is used of "the light of the knowledge of the glory of God in the face of Jesus Christ," descriptive of the gospel, as deposited in the earthen vessels of the persons who proclaim it (cf. v. 4); in Col. 2:3, of the wisdom and knowledge hidden in Christ.

Bringeth *prophero* (4393), denotes "to bring forth," **Luke 6:45**, twice.

Evil *poneros* (4190), akin to *ponos*, "labor, toil," denotes "evil that causes labor, pain, sorrow, malignant evil"; it is used (a) with the meaning bad, worthless, in the physical sense, Matt. 7:17-18; in the moral or ethical sense, "evil," wicked; of persons, e.g., Matt. 7:11; **Luke 6:45**; Acts 17:5; 2 Thess. 3:2; 2 Tim. 3:13; of "evil" spirits, e.g., Matt. 12:45; **Luke 7:21**; Acts 19:12-13, 15-16; of a generation, Matt. 12:39, 45; 16:4; **Luke 11:29**; of things, e.g., Matt. 5:11; 6:23; 20:15; Mark 7:22; **Luke 11:34**; John 3:19; 7:7; Acts 18:14; Gal. 1:4; Col. 1:21; 1 Tim. 6:4; 2 Tim. 4:18; Heb. 3:12; 10:22; Jas. 2:4; 4:16; 1 John 3:12; 2 John 11; 3 John 10; (b) with the meaning toilsome, painful, Eph. 5:16; 6:13; Rev. 16:2. Cf. *poneria*, "iniquity, wickedness." *See also* **Evils** at ***Luke 3:19***.

Abundance *perisseuma* (4051), denotes "abundance" in a slightly more concrete form, 2 Cor. 8:13-14, where it stands for the gifts in kind supplied by the saints. In Matt. 12:34 and **Luke 6:45** it is used of the "abundance" of the heart; in Mark 8:8, of the broken pieces left after feeding the multitude "that remained over" (KJV "that was left"). In the Sept., Eccl. 2:15.

6:46-47 And why call ye me, Lord, Lord, and do not the things which I say?

Whosoever cometh to me, and heareth my sayings, and doeth them, I will shew you to whom he is like:

Shew *hupodeiknumi* (5263), primarily, "to show secretly (*hupo*, 'under'), or by tracing out," hence, "to make known, warn," is translated "to show" in **Luke 6:47**; Acts 9:16; in 20:35, KJV (RV, "I gave ... an example").

Like *homoios* (3664), "like, resembling, such as, the same as," is used (a) of appearance or form John 9:9; Rev. 1:13, 15; 2:18; 4:3 (twice), 6, 7; 9:7 (twice), 10, 19; 11:1; 13:2, 11; 14:14; (b) of ability, condition, nature, Matt. 22:39; Acts 17:29; Gal. 5:21, "such like," lit., "and the (things) similar to these"; 1 John 3:2; Rev. 13:4; 18:18; 21:11, 18; (c) of comparison in parables, Matt. 13:31, 33, 44, 45, 47; 20:1; **Luke 13:18, 19, 21**; (d) of action, thought, etc. Matt. 11:16; 13:52; **Luke 6:47, 48, 49; 7:31, 32; 12:36**; John 8:55; Jude 7.

6:48 He is like a man which built an house, and digged deep, and laid the foundation on a rock: and when the flood arose, the stream beat vehemently upon that house, and could not shake it: for it was founded upon a rock.

Like *see Luke 6:47.*

Built *see Luke 4:29.*

Digged *skapto* (4626), primarily, "to dig, by way of hollowing out," hence, denotes "to dig." The root *skap* is seen in *skapane*, "a spade," *skapetos*, "a ditch," *skaphe*, "a boat," and in Eng., "scoop, skiff, and ship" (i.e., something hollowed out). The verb is found in **Luke 6:48; 13:8; 16:3**.

Deep *bathuno* (900), "to deepen, make deep," is used in **Luke 6:48** (KJV, "digged deep"). The original has two separate verbs, *skapto*, "to dig," and *bathuno*; the RV therefore has "digged and went deep."

Laid *see Luke 1:66.*

Foundation *themelios*, or *themelion* (2310), is properly an adjective denoting "belonging to a foundation" (connected with *tithemi*, "to place"). It is used (1) as a noun, with *lithos*, "a stone," understood, in **Luke 6:48, 49; 14:29**; Heb. 11:10; Rev. 21:14, 19; (2) as a neuter noun in Acts 16:26, and metaphorically, (a) of "the ministry of the gospel and the doctrines of the faith," Rom. 15:20; 1 Cor. 3:10, 11, 12; Eph. 2:20, where the "of" is not subjective (i.e., consisting of the apostles and prophets), but objective, (i.e., laid by the apostles, etc.); so in 2 Tim. 2:19, where "the foundation of God" is "the foundation laid by God," – not the Church (which is not a "foundation"), but Christ Himself, upon whom the saints are built; Heb. 6:1; (b) "of good works, 1 Tim. 6:19.

Rock *petra* (4073), denotes "a mass of rock," as distinct from *petros*, "a detached stone or boulder," or a stone that might be thrown or easily moved. For the nature of *petra*, see Matt. 7:24, 25; 27:51, 60; Mark 15:46; **Luke 6:48** (twice), a type of a sure foundation (here the true reading is as in the RV, "because it had been well builded"); Rev. 6:15, 16 (cf. Isa. 2:19ff.; Hos. 10:8); **Luke 8:6, 13**, used illustratively; 1 Cor. 10:4 (twice), figuratively, of Christ; in Rom. 9:33 and 1 Pet. 2:8, metaphorically, of Christ; in Matt. 16:18, metaphorically, of Christ and the testimony concerning Him; here the distinction between *petra*, concerning the Lord Himself, and *Petros*, the apostle, is clear.

Arose *ginomai* (1096), "to become, to take place," is sometimes suitably translated "arise"; e.g., Matt. 8:24; Mark 4:37, "there arose a great tempest." So of the arising of persecution, Matt. 13:21; Mark 4:17; this might be translated "taketh place"; of a tumult, Matt. 27:24, RV, "arising," for KJV, "made"; of a flood, **Luke 6:48**; a famine, **15:14**; a questioning, John 3:25; a murmuring, Acts 6:1; a tribulation, 11:19 (RV); a stir in the city, 19:23; a dissension, 23:7; a great clamor, v. 9.

Stream *potamos* (4215), denotes (a) "a stream," **Luke 6:48, 49**; (b) "a flood or floods," Matt. 7:25, 27; (c) "a river," natural, Matt. 3:6, RV; Mark 1:5; Acts 16:13; 2 Cor. 11:26, RV (KJV, "waters"); Rev. 8:10; 9:14; 16:4, 12; symbolical, Rev. 12:15 (1st part), RV, "river" (KJV, "flood"); so v. 16; 22:1, 2 (cf. Gen. 2:10; Ezek. 47); figuratively, John 7:38, "the effects of the operation of the Holy Spirit in and through the believer."

Beat vehemently *prosregnumi* (4366), "to break upon," is translated "beat vehemently upon, or against" (*pros*, "upon," *rhegnumi*, "to break"), in **Luke 6:48-49**, of the violent action of a flood (RV, "brake").

Shake *see* Shaken at *Luke 6:38.*

6:49 But he that heareth, and doeth not, is like a man that without a foundation built an house upon the earth; against which the stream did beat

vehemently, and immediately it fell; and the ruin of that house was great.

Like *see Luke 6:47.*

Foundation *see Luke 6:48.*

Stream *see Luke 6:48.*

Beat vehemently *see Luke 6:48.*

Ruin *rhegma* (4485), akin to *rhegnumi*, "to break," denotes "a cleavage, fracture" (so in the Sept., e.g., 1 Kings 11:30, 31); by metonymy, that which is broken, "a ruin," **Luke 6:49**.

Chapter 7

7:1 Now when he had ended all his sayings in the audience of the people, he entered into Capernaum.

Ended *pleroo* (4137), (a) "to fill," (b) "to fulfill, complete, end," is translated "had ended" in **Luke 7:1**; "were ended" (passive) in Acts 19:21.

Sayings *see Luke 1:65.*

Audience *akoe* (189), "hearing," akin to *akouo*, "to hear," denotes (a) the sense of "hearing," e.g., 1 Cor. 12:17; 2 Pet. 2:8; (b) that which is "heard," a report, e.g., Matt. 4:24; (c) the physical organ, Mark 7:35, standing for the sense of "hearing"; so in **Luke 7:1**, RV, for KJV, "audience"; Acts 17:20; 2 Tim. 4:3-4 (in v. 3, lit., "being tickled as to the ears"); (d) a message or teaching, John 12:38; Rom. 10:16-17; Gal. 3:2, 5; 1 Thess. 2:13; Heb. 4:2, RV, "(the word) of hearing," for KJV, "(the word) preached."

7:2 And a certain centurion's servant, who was dear unto him, was sick, and ready to die.

Dear *entimos* (1784), "held in honor" (*time*), "precious, dear," is found in **Luke 7:2**, of the centurion's servant; **14:8**, "more honorable"; Phil. 2:29, "honor" (KJV, "reputation"), of devoted servants of Christ, in 1 Pet. 2:4, 6, "precious," of stones, metaphorically.

Sick *see Luke 5:31.*

Ready *mello* (3195), "to be about to," is translated "to be ready" in 2 Pet. 1:12, RV, where the future indicates that the apostle will be prepared, as in the past and the present, to remind his readers of the truths they know (some mss. have *ouk ameleso*, "I will not be negligent," KJV; cf., however, v. 15. Field, in *Notes on the Translation of the NT*, suggests that the true reading is *meleso*, the future of *melo*, "to be a care, or an object of care"); in Rev. 3:2, RV, "were ready" (some texts have the present tense, as in the KJV). Elsewhere, where the KJV has the rendering to be ready, the RV gives renderings in accordance with the usual significance as follows: **Luke 7:2**, "was ... at the point of"; Acts 20:7, "intending"; Rev. 12:4, "about (to)."

Die *teleutao* (5053), "to end" (from *telos*, "an end"), hence, "to end one's life," is used (a) of the "death" of the body, Matt. 2:19; 9:18; 15:4, where "die the death" means "surely die," RV, marg., lit., "let him end by death"; Mark 7:10; Matt. 22:25, "deceased"; **Luke 7:2**; John 11:39; Acts 2:29; 7:15; Heb. 11:22 (RV, "his end was nigh"); (b) of the gnawings of conscience in self reproach, under the symbol of a worm, Mark 9:48 (vv. 44 and 46, KJV).

7:3 And when he heard of Jesus, he sent unto him the elders of the Jews, beseeching him that he would come and heal his servant.

Elders *presbuteros* (4245), an adjective, the comparative degree of *presbus*, "an old man, an elder," is used (a) of age, whether of the "elder" of two persons, **Luke 15:25**, or more, John 8:9, "the eldest", or of a person advanced in life, a senior, Acts 2:17; in Heb. 11:2, the "elders" are the forefathers in Israel so in Matt. 15:2; Mark 7:3, 5 the feminine of the adjective is used of "elder" women in the churches, 1 Tim. 5:2, not in respect of position but in seniority of age; (b) of rank or positions of responsibility, (1) among Gentiles, as in the Sept. of Gen. 50:7; Num. 22:7, (2) in the Jewish nation, firstly, those who were the heads or leaders of the tribes and families, as of the seventy who assisted Moses, Num. 11:16; Deut. 27:1, and those assembled by Solomon; secondly, members of the Sanhedrin, consisting of the chief priests, "elders" and scribes, learned in Jewish law, e.g., Matt. 16:21; 26:47; thirdly, those who managed public affairs in the various cities, **Luke 7:3**; (3) in the Christian churches those who, being raised up and qualified by the work of the Holy Spirit, were appointed to have the spiritual care of, and to exercise oversight over, the churches. To these the term "bishops," *episkopoi*, or "overseers," is applied (see Acts 20, v. 17 with v. 28, and Titus 1:5 and 7), the latter term indicating the nature of their work *presbuteroi* their maturity of spiritual experience. The divine arrangement seen throughout the NT was for a plurality of these to be appointed in each church, Acts 14:23; 20:17; Phil. 1:1; 1 Tim. 5:17; Titus 1:5. The duty of "elders" is described by the verb *episkopeo*. They were appointed according as they had given evidence of fulfilling the divine qualifications, Titus 1:6 to 9; cf. 1 Tim. 3:1-7 and 1 Pet. 5:2; (4) the twenty-four "elders" enthroned in heaven around the throne of God, Rev. 4:4, 10; 5:5-14; 7:11, 13; 11:16; 14:3; 19:4. The number twenty-four is representative of earthly conditions. The word "elder" is nowhere applied to angels.

Heal *diasozo* (1295), "to bring safely through," is used (a) of the healing of the sick by the Lord, Matt. 14:36, RV, "were made whole" (KJV adds "perfectly"); **Luke 7:3**; (b) of bringing "safe" to a destination, Acts 23:24; (c) of keeping a person "safe," 27:43; (d) of escaping through the perils of shipwreck, 27:44; 28:1, 4, passive voice; (e) through the Flood, 1 Pet. 3:20. In 2 Pet. 2:5, KJV, *phulasso*, "to guard, keep, preserve," is translated "saved" (RV, "preserved"). In **Luke 17:33** some mss. have *sozo* (KJV, "save"). For "save alive," **Luke 17:33**, RV.

7:4 And when they came to Jesus, they besought him instantly, saying, That he was worthy for whom he should do this:

Instantly *spoudaios* (4709), "earnestly, diligently," is rendered "instantly" in **Luke 7:4**, KJV (RV, "earnestly").

Worthy *axios* (514), "of weight, worth, worthy," is said of persons and their deeds: (a) in a good sense, e.g., Matt. 10:10, 11, 13 (twice), 37 (twice), 38; 22:8; **Luke 7:4**; **10:7**; **15:19**, **21**; John 1:27; Acts 13:25; 1 Tim. 5:18; 6:1; Heb. 11:38; Rev. 3:4; 4:11; 5:2, 4, 9, 12; (b) in a bad sense, **Luke 12:48**; **23:15**; Acts 23:29; 25:11, 25; 26:31; Rom. 1:32; Rev. 16:6.

Do *parecho* (3930), lit. means "to hold near" (*para*, "beside," and *echo*, "to have"), i.e., "to present, offer, supply." It is translated "do for" in **Luke 7:4**. (1) In Phil. 2:13 *energeo*, "to work," is translated "to do," KJV; RV, "to work." (2) In **Luke 13:32** *apoteleo*, "to complete, perform," is translated "I ... do," KJV; RV, "I perform" (some mss. have *epiteleo* here). (3) In Acts 15:36, *echo*, "to have, to hold," sometimes used to express the condition in which a person is, how he is faring, is translated "(how) they do," KJV; RV, "how they fare." It is often used of a physical condition, e.g., Matt. 4:24. (4) In Acts 25:9 *katatithemi*, "to deposit, or lay up, for future use, to lay up favor for oneself with a person," is translated "to do (the Jews a pleasure)," KJV; RV, "to gain (favor with the Jews)." (5) In John 16:2 *prosphero*, "to bring near, offer, present," is translated "doeth (service)," KJV; RV, "offereth (service)." (6) In Heb. 4:13 the phrase *hemin ho logos*, rendered "(with whom) we have to do," is, lit., "(with whom is) the account to us." (7) In 1 Cor. 13:10, *katargeo*, "to render inactive, abolish," so is translated "shall be done away"; 2 Cor. 3:7, KJV, "was to be done away," RV, "was passing away."

7:5 For he loveth our nation, and he hath built us a synagogue.

Nation *ethnos* (1484), originally "a multitude," denotes (a) "a nation" or "people," e.g., Matt. 24:7; Acts 10:35; the Jewish people, e.g., **Luke 7:5**; **23:2**; John 11:48, 50-52; Acts 10:22; 24:2, 10, 17; in Matt. 21:43, the reference is to Israel in its restored condition, (b) in the plural "the nations" as distinct from Israel.

7:6 Then Jesus went with them. And when he was now not far from the house, the centurion sent friends to him, saying unto him, Lord, trouble not thyself: for I am not worthy that thou shouldest enter under my roof:

Was When not part of another verb, or phrase, these translate *eimi*, "to be," e.g., Matt. 1:18, or the following: (a) *ginomai*, "to become," e.g., Matt. 8:26; (b) *huparcho*, "to exist," especially when referring to an already existing condition, e.g., **Luke 8:41**; Acts 5:4 (2nd part); 16:3; 27:12; Rom. 4:19, KJV, "when he was" (RV, "he being"); (c) *echo*, "to have," e.g., Acts 12:15; (d) *apecho*, "to be away, to be distant," e.g., **Luke 7:6**; **24:13**; (e) *mello*, "to be about to," e.g., **Luke 19:4**; Acts 21:27, 37, KJV (RV, "was about to"); (f) *sumbaino*, "to come to pass, happen," e.g., Acts 21:35; (g) in Gal. 4:28, the preposition *kata*, "according to," is rendered "was," in the phrase "as Isaac was," lit., "like Isaac"; as Isaac's birth came by divine interposition, so does the spiritual birth of every believer.

Far *makran* (3112), denotes "a long way, far," (a) literally, Matt. 8:30, RV, "afar off." **Luke 7:6**; **15:20**, RV, "afar off"; John 21:8; Acts 17:27; 22:21; (b) metaphorically, "far (from the kingdom of God)," Mark 12:34; in spiritual darkness, Acts 2:39; Eph. 2:13, 17. *See also* **Have received** at *Luke 6:24*.

Friends *philos* (5384), primarily an adjective, denoting "loved, dear, or friendly," became used as a noun, (a) masculine, Matt. 11:19; fourteen times in Luke (once feminine, **15:9**); six in John; three in Acts; two in James, 2:23, "the friend of God"; 4:4, "a friend of the world"; 3 John 14 (twice); (b) feminine, **Luke 15:9**, "her friends."

Trouble *skullo* (4660), primarily "to flay," hence, "to vex, annoy" ("there was a time when the Greek, in thus speaking, compared his trouble to the pains of flaying alive," Moulton, *Proleg.*, p. 89), is used in the active voice in Mark 5:35; **Luke 8:49**; in the passive voice, Matt. 9:36, in the best texts, RV, "they were distressed" (some have *ekluo*, KJV, "they fainted"); in the middle voice,

Luke 7:6, "trouble (not thyself)." The word is frequent in the papyri.

Worthy *see Luke 3:16*.

Roof *stege* (4721), "a covering" (*stego*, "to cover"), denotes "a roof," Mark 2:4; said of entering a house, Matt. 8:8; **Luke 7:6**.

7:7 Wherefore neither thought I myself worthy to come unto thee: but say in a word, and my servant shall be healed.

Myself *emautou* (1683), a reflexive pronoun, of the first person, lit., "of myself," is used (a) frequently after various prepositions, e.g., *hupo*, "under," Matt. 8:9; **Luke 7:8**; RV, "under myself"; *peri*, "concerning," John 5:31; 8:14, 18; Acts 24:10; *apo*, "from," John 5:30; 7:17, RV, "from" (KJV, "of," which is ambiguous); so v. 28; 8:28, 42; 10:18; 14:10 (RV, "from"); *pros*, "unto," John 12:32, RV, "unto Myself"; 14:3; Philem. 13, "with me"; *eis*, "to," 1 Cor. 4:6; *huper*, "on behalf of," 2 Cor. 12:5; *ek* (*ex*), "out of," or "from," John 12:49, RV, "from Myself"; (b) as the direct object of a verb, **Luke 7:7**; John 8:54; 14:21; 17:19; Acts 26:2; 1 Cor. 4:3; 9:19; 2 Cor. 11:7, 9; Gal. 2:18; Phil. 3:13; (c) in other oblique cases of the pronoun, without a preposition, e.g., Acts 20:24, "unto" (or to); 26:9, "with" (or "to"); Rom. 11:4, RV, "for" (KJV, "to"); 1 Cor. 4:4, RV, "against myself" (KJV, inaccurately, "by"); in all these instances the pronoun is in the dative case; in 1 Cor. 10:33, "mine own" (the genitive case); in 1 Cor. 7:7, "I myself" (the accusative case).

Worthy *axioo* (515), "to think or count worthy," is used (1) of the estimation formed by God (a) favorably, 2 Thess. 1:11, "may count (you) worthy (of your calling)," suggestive of grace (it does not say "may make you worthy"); Heb. 3:3, "of more glory," of Christ in comparison with Moses; (b) unfavorably, 10:29, "of how much sorer punishment"; (2) by a centurion (negatively) concerning himself, **Luke 7:7**; (3) by a church, regarding its elders, 1 Tim. 5:17, where "honor" stands probably for "honorarium," i.e., "material support."

Word *logos* (3056), denotes (I) "the expression of thought" – not the mere name of an object – (a) as embodying a conception or idea, e.g., **Luke 7:7**; 1 Cor. 14:9, 19; (b) a saying or statement, (1) by God, e.g., John 15:25; Rom. 9:9; 9:28, RV, "word" (KJV, "work"); Gal. 5:14; Heb. 4:12; (2) by Christ, e.g., Matt. 24:35 (plur.); John 2:22; 4:41; 14:23 (plur.); 15:20. In connection with (1) and (2) the phrase "the word of the Lord," i.e., the revealed will of God (very frequent in the OT), is used of a direct revelation given by Christ, 1 Thess. 4:15; of the gospel, Acts 8:25; 13:49; 15:35, 36; 16:32; 19:10; 1 Thess. 1:8; 2 Thess. 3:1; in this respect it is the message from the Lord, delivered with His authority and made effective by His power (cf. Acts 10:36); for other instances relating to the gospel see Acts 13:26; 14:3; 15:7; 1 Cor. 1:18, RV; 2 Cor. 2:17; 4:2; 5:19; 6:7; Gal. 6:6; Eph. 1:13; Phil. 2:16; Col. 1:5; Heb. 5:13; sometimes it is used as the sum of God's utterances, e.g., Mark 7:13; John 10:35; Rev. 1:2, 9; (c) discourse, speech, of instruction, etc., e.g., Acts 2:40, 1 Cor. 2:13; 12:8; 2 Cor. 1:18; 1 Thess. 1:5; 2 Thess. 2:15; Heb. 6:1, RV, marg.; doctrine, e.g., Matt. 13:20; Col. 3:16; 1 Tim. 4:6; 2 Tim. 1:13; Titus 1:9; 1 John 2:7;

(II) "The Personal Word," a title of the Son of God; this identification is substantiated by the statements of doctrine in John 1:1-18, declaring in verses 1 and 2 (1) His distinct and superfinite Personality, (2) His relation in the Godhead (*pros*, "with," not mere company, but the most intimate communion), (3) His deity; in v. 3 His creative power; in v. 14 His incarnation ("became flesh," expressing His voluntary act; not as KJV, "was made"), the reality and totality of His human nature, and His glory "as of the only begotten from the Father," RV (marg., "an only begotten from a father"), the absence of the article in each place lending stress to the nature and character of the relationship.

Servant *see Luke 1:54*.

7:8 For I also am a man set under authority, having under me soldiers, and I say unto one, Go, and he goeth; and to another, Come, and he cometh; and to my servant, Do this, and he doeth *it*.

Set *tasso* (5021), "to arrange, assign, order," is translated "set (under authority)" in **Luke 7:8**. In 1 Cor. 16:15, RV, "have set (themselves)," KJV, "addicted."

Me *see* **Myself** at *Luke 7:7*.

Soldiers *stratiotes* (4757), "a soldier," is used (a) in the natural sense, e.g., Matt. 8:9; 27:27; 28:12; Mark 15:16; **Luke 7:8; 23:36**; six times in John; thirteen times in Acts; not again in the NT; (b) metaphorically of one who endures hardship in the cause of Christ, 2 Tim. 2:3.

One The pronoun *houtos* is sometimes translated "this one," e.g., **Luke 7:8**.

7:9 When Jesus heard these things, he marvelled at him, and turned him about, and said unto the people that followed him, I say unto you, I have not found so great faith, no, not in Israel.

Great *tosoutos* (5118), "so great, so many, so much," of quantity, size, etc., is rendered "so great," in Matt. 8:10, and **Luke 7:9**, of faith; Matt. 15:33, of a multitude; Heb. 12:1, of a cloud of witnesses; Rev. 18:17, of riches.

7:10 And they that were sent, returning to the house, found the servant whole that had been sick.

Returning *see* Returned at *Luke 1:56*.

Whole *see Luke 5:31*.

Sick *see Luke 4:40*.

7:11 And it came to pass the day after, that he went into a city called Nain; and many of his disciples went with him, and much people.

Day In 2 Thess. 2:3, "that day shall not come" (KJV) translates nothing in the original; it is inserted to supply the sense (see the RV); cf. **Luke 7:11** (RV, "soon afterwards"); 1 Cor. 4:13 (RV, "even until now").

After *hexes* (1836), denotes "after" with the significance of a succession of events, an event following next in order after another, **Luke 7:11**; **9:37**; Acts 21:1; 25:17; 27:18.

Went *sumporeuomai* (4848), "to go together with" (*sun*, "with"), is used in Mark 10:1, RV, "come together" (KJV, "resort"); **Luke 7:11**; **14:25**; **24:15**.

Much *polus* (4183), is used (a) as an adjective of degree, e.g., Matt. 13:5, "much (earth)"; Acts 26:24, "much (learning)"; in v. 29, in the answer to Agrippa's "with but little persuasion," some texts have *pollo* (some *megalo*, "with great"), RV, "(whether with little or) with much"; of number, e.g., Mark 5:24, RV, "a great (multitude)," KJV, "much (people)"; so **Luke 7:11**; John 12:12; Rev. 19:1, etc.; (b) in the neuter singular form (*polu*), as a noun, e.g., **Luke 16:10** (twice); in the plural (*polla*), e.g., Rom. 16:6, 12, "(labored) much," lit., "many things"; (c) adverbially, in the neuter singular, e.g., Acts 18:27; James 5:16; Matt. 26:9 (a genitive of price); in the plural, e.g., Mark 5:43, RV, "much" (KJV, "straitly"); Mark 9:26, RV, "much" (KJV, "sore"); John 14:30; and with the article, Acts 26:24; Rom. 15:22; 1 Cor. 16:19; Rev. 5:4.

7:12 Now when he came nigh to the gate of the city, behold, there was a dead man carried out, the only son of his mother, and she was a widow: and much people of the city was with her.

Came nigh *engizo* (1448), "to come near draw nigh" (akin to *engus*, "near"), is translated by the verb "draw near or nigh," in the RV, **Luke 12:33**, KJV, "approacheth"; Heb. 10:25, KJV, "approaching"; **Luke 18:35**; **19:29**, **37**; Acts 22:6, KJV, "was come nigh"; **Luke 7:12** "came nigh"; Acts 9:3, "came near."

Gate *pule* (4439), is used (a) literally, for a larger sort of "gate," in the wall either of a city or palace or temple, **Luke 7:12**, of Nain (burying places were outside the "gates" of cities); Acts 3:10; 9:24; 12:10; Heb. 13:12; (b) metaphorically, of the "gates" at the entrances of the ways leading to life and to destruction, Matt. 7:13, 14; some mss. have *pule*, for *thura*, "a door," in **Luke 13:24** (see the RV); of the "gates" of Hades, Matt. 16:18, than which nothing was regarded as stronger. The importance and strength of "gates" made them viewed as synonymous with power. By metonymy, the "gates" stood for those who held government and administered justice there.

Carried *ekkomizo* (1580), "to carry out," is found in **Luke 7:12**.

Only *monogenes* (3439), "only begotten," has the meaning "only," of human offspring, in **Luke 7:12**; **8:42**; **9:38**; the term is one of endearment, as well as of singleness.

Widow *see Luke 2:37*.

Much *hikanos* (2425), "enough, much, many," is translated "much," e.g., in **Luke 7:12** (in some mss. Acts 5:37; see the RV); Acts 11:24, 26; 19:26; 27:9.

7:13 And when the Lord saw her, he had compassion on her, and said unto her, Weep not.

Lord *see* Jose at *Luke 3:29*.

Compassion *splanchnizomai* (4697), "to be moved as to one's inwards (*splanchna*), to be moved with compassion, to yearn with compassion," is frequently recorded of Christ towards the multitude and towards individual sufferers, Matt. 9:36; 14:14; 15:32; 18:27; 20:34; Mark 1:41; 6:34; 8:2; 9:22 (of the appeal of a father for a demon-possessed son); **Luke 7:13**; **10:33**; of the father in the parable of the Prodigal Son, 15:20. (Moulton and Milligan consider the verb to have been coined in the Jewish dispersion).

Weep *klaio* (2799), is used of "any loud expression of grief," especially in mourning for the dead, Matt. 2:18; Mark 5:38, 39; 16:10; **Luke 7:13**; **8:52** (twice); John 11:31, 33 (twice); 20:11 (twice), 13, 15; Acts 9:39; otherwise, e.g., in exhortations, **Luke 23:28**; Rom. 12:15; Jas. 4:9; 5:1; negatively, "weep not," **Luke 7:13**; **8:52**; **23:28**; Rev. 5:5 (cf. Acts 21:13); in 18:9, RV, "shall weep" (KJV, "bewail").

7:14 And he came and touched the bier: and they that bare *him* stood still. And he said, Young man, I say unto thee, Arise.

Bier *soros* (4673), originally denoted a receptacle for containing the bones of the dead, "a cinerary urn"; then "a coffin," Gen. 50:26; Job 21:32; then, "the funeral couch or bier" on which the Jews bore their dead to burial, **Luke 7:14**.

Bare *bastazo* (941), signifies "to support as a burden." It is used with the meaning (a) "to take up," as in picking up anything, stones, John 10:31; (b) "to carry" something, Matt. 3:11; Mark 14:13; **Luke 7:14; 22:10**; Acts 3:2; 21:35; Rev. 17:7; "to carry" on one's person, **Luke 10:4**; Gal. 6:17; in one's body, **Luke 11:27**; "to bear" a name in testimony, Acts 9:15; metaphorically, of a root "bearing" branches, Rom. 11:18; (c) "to bear" a burden, whether physically, as of the cross, John 19:17, or metaphorically in respect of sufferings endured in the cause of Christ, **Luke 14:27**; Rev. 2:3; it is said of physical endurance, Matt. 20:12; of sufferings "borne" on behalf of others, Matt. 8:17; Rom. 15:1; Gal. 6:2; of spiritual truths not able to be "borne," John 16:12; of the refusal to endure evil men, Rev. 2:2; of religious regulations imposed on others, Acts 15:10; of the burden of the sentence of God to be executed in due time, Gal. 5:10; of the effect at the judgment seat of Christ, to be "borne" by the believer for failure in the matter of discharging the obligations of discipleship, Gal. 6:5; (d) to "bear" by way of carrying off, John 12:6; 20:15.

Young *neaniskos* (3495), "a youth, a young man," occurs in Matt. 19:20, 22; Mark 14:51 (1st part; RV omits in 2nd part); 16:5; **Luke 7:14**; Acts 2:17; 5:10 (i.e., attendants); 23:18 (in the best texts), 22; 1 John 2:13, 14, of the second branch of the spiritual family.

Arise *egeiro* (1453), is frequently used in the NT in the sense of "raising" (active voice), or "rising" (middle and passive voices): (a) from sitting, lying, sickness, e.g., Matt. 2:14; 9:5, 7, 19; Jas. 5:15; Rev. 11:1; (b) of causing to appear, or, in the passive, appearing, or raising up so as to occupy a place in the midst of people, Matt. 3:9; 11:11; Mark 13:22; Acts 13:22. It is thus said of Christ in Acts 13:23; (c) of rousing, stirring up, or "rising" against, Matt. 24:7; Mark 13:8; (d) of "raising buildings," John 2:19-20; (e) of "raising or rising" from the dead; (1) of Christ, Matt. 16:21; and frequently elsewhere (but not in Phil., 2 Thess., 1 Tim., Titus, Jas., 2 Pet., 1, 2, 3 John, and Jude); (2) of Christ's "raising" the dead, Matt. 11:5; Mark 5:41; **Luke 7:14**; John 12:1, 9, 17; (3) of the act of the disciples, Matt. 10:8; (4) of the resurrection of believers, Matt. 27:52; John 5:21; 1 Cor. 15:15-16, 29, 32, 35, 42-44, 52; 2 Cor. 1:9; 4:14; of unbelievers, Matt. 12:42. *Egeiro* stands in contrast to *anistemi* (when used with reference to resurrection) in this respect, that *egeiro* is frequently used both in the transitive sense of "raising up" and the intransitive of "rising," whereas *anistemi* is comparatively infrequent in the transitive use.

7:15 And he that was dead sat up, and began to speak. And he delivered him to his mother.

Sat *anakathizo* (339), "to set up," is used intransitively, "to sit up," of two who were raised from the dead, **Luke 7:15**; Acts 9:40.

Delivered *didomi* (1325), "to give," is translated "delivered" in **Luke 7:15**; RV, "gave"; so **19:13**.

7:16 And there came a fear on all: and they glorified God, saying, That a great prophet is risen up among us; and, That God hath visited his people.

Came *lambano* (2983), "to take, lay hold of," besides its literal sense, e.g., Matt. 5:40; 26:26, 27, is used metaphorically, of fear, in "taking" hold of people, **Luke 7:16**, RV (KJV, "came ... on"); of sin in "finding (occasion)," RV (KJV, "taking"), Rom. 7:8, 11, where sin is viewed as the corrupt source of action, an inward element using the commandment to produce evil effects; of the power of temptation, 1 Cor. 10:13; of "taking" an example, Jas. 5:10; of "taking" peace from the earth, Rev. 6:4; of Christ in "taking" the form of a servant, Phil. 2:7; of "taking" rightful power (by the Lord, hereafter), Rev. 11:17.

Prophet *see* ***Luke 1:76***.

Visited *see* ***Luke 1:68***.

7:17 And this rumour of him went forth throughout all Judaea, and throughout all the region round about.

Rumour *see* Fame at ***Luke 5:15***.

Region *see* Country at ***Luke 3:3***.

7:18-21 And the disciples of John shewed him of all these things.

And John calling *unto him* two of his disciples sent *them* to Jesus, saying, Art thou he that should come? or look we for another?

When the men were come unto him, they said, John Baptist hath sent us unto thee, saying, Art thou he that should come? or look we for another?

And in that same hour he cured many of *their* infirmities

and plagues, and of evil spirits; and unto many *that were* blind he gave sight.

Cured *therapeuo* (2323), (Eng., "therapeutics," etc.), denotes (a) primarily, "to serve" (cf. *therapeia* and *therapon*), Acts 17:25 (KJV, "worshiped"); then, (b) "to heal, restore to health, to cure"; it is usually translated "to heal," but "cure" in Matt. 17:16, 18; **Luke 7:21**; **9:1**; John 5:10; Acts 28:9, RV.

Infirmities *see* Diseases at *Luke 4:40*.

Plagues *mastix* (3148), "a whip, scourge," Acts 22:24, "by scourging"; Heb. 11:36, "scourgings," is used metaphorically of "disease" or "suffering," Mark 3:10; 5:29, 34; **Luke 7:21**.

Evil *poneros* (4190), connected with *ponos*, "labor," expresses especially the "active form of evil." It is used, e.g., of thoughts, Matt. 15:19 (cf. *kakos*, in Mark 7:21); of speech, Matt. 5:11 (cf. *kakos*, in 1 Pet. 3:10); of acts 2 Tim. 4:18. Where *kakos* and *poneros* are put together, *kakos* is always put first and signifies "bad in character, base," *poneros*, "bad in effect, malignant": see 1 Cor. 5:8, and Rev. 16:2. *Kakos* has a wider meaning, *poneros* a stronger meaning. *Poneros* alone is used of Satan and might well be translated "the malignant one," e.g., Matt. 5:37 and five times in 1 John (2:13-14; 3:12; 5:18-19, RV); of demons, e.g., **Luke 7:21**. Once it is translated bad, Matt. 22:10. *See also Luke 6:45*.

Gave *charizomai* (5483), primarily denotes "to show favor or kindness," as in Gal. 3:18, RV, "hath granted" (KJV, "gave"); then, to "give" freely, bestow graciously; in this sense it is used almost entirely of that which is "given" by God, Acts 27:24, "God hath granted thee all them that sail with thee" (RV); in Rom. 8:32, "shall ... freely give"; 1 Cor. 2:12, "are freely given"; Phil. 1:29, "it hath been granted" (said of believing on Christ and suffering for Him); 2:9, "hath given" (said of the name of Jesus as "given" by God); Philem. 22, "I shall be granted unto you" (RV). In **Luke 7:21**, it is said in regard to the blind, upon whom Christ "bestowed" sight (RV). The only exceptions, in this sense of the word, as to divinely imparted "gifts," are Acts 3:14, of the "granting" of Barabbas by Pilate to the Jews, and Acts 25:11, 16, of the "giving" up of a prisoner to his accusers or to execution.

Sight *see Luke 4:18*.

7:22 Then Jesus answering said unto them, Go your way, and tell John what things ye have seen and heard; how that the blind see, the lame walk, the lepers are cleansed, the deaf hear, the dead are raised, to the poor the gospel is preached.

Go *poreuomai* (4198), "to go on one's way, to proceed from one place to another" (from *poros*, "a passage, a ford," Eng., "pore"), is always used in the middle voice in the NT and the Sept., and is the most frequent verb signifying "to go"; it is more distinctly used to indicate procedure or course than the verb *eimi*, "to go" (not found in the NT). It is often rendered "go thy (your) way," in Oriental usage the customary dismissal, marking the close of a case in court. Hence, in ordinary parlance, marking the end of a conversation, etc., e.g., **Luke 7:22**; **17:19**; John 4:50; Acts 9:15; 24:25; cf. Dan. 12:9; in Rom. 15:24 (1st part), RV, "go" (KJV, "take my journey"); in Acts 9:3 and 26:13, journeyed (KJV and RV).

See *anablepo* (308), "to look up," is translated "see," of the blind, in **Luke 7:22**, KJV (RV, "receive their sight").

Lame *cholos* (5560), "lame," is translated "halt" in Matt. 18:8; Mark 9:45; John 5:3, in Acts 14:8, "cripple"; in **Luke 14:21**, KJV, "halt," RV, "lame"; elsewhere, "lame," Matt. 11:5; 15:30, 31; 21:14: **Luke 7:22**; **14:13**; Acts 3:2; 8:7; Heb. 12:13; some mss. have it in Acts 3:11 (KJV, "the lame man"), RV, "he," translating *autou*, as in the best texts.

Lepers *see Luke 4:27*.

Deaf *kophos* (2974), akin to *kopto*, "to beat," and *kopiao*, "to be tired" (from a root *kop-*, "to cut"), signifies "blunted, dull," as of a weapon; hence, "blunted in tongue, dumb," Matt. 9:32, etc.; "in hearing, deaf," Matt. 11:5; Mark 7:32, 37; 9:25; Luke 7:22.

Raised *see Luke 1:69*.

Gospel *euangelizo* (2097), "to bring or announce glad tidings" (Eng., "evangelize"), is used (a) in the active voice in Rev. 10:7 ("declared") and 14:6 ("to proclaim," RV, KJV, "to preach"); (b) in the passive voice, of matters to be proclaimed as "glad tidings," **Luke 16:16**; Gal. 1:11; 1 Pet. 1:25; of persons to whom the proclamation is made, Matt. 11:5; **Luke 7:22**; Heb. 4:2, 6; 1 Pet. 4:6; (c) in the middle voice, especially of the message of salvation, with a personal object, either of the person preached, e.g., Acts 5:42; 11:20; Gal. 1:16, or, with a preposition, of the persons evangelized, e.g., Acts 13:32, "declare glad tidings"; Rom. 1:15; Gal. 1:8; with an impersonal object, e.g., "the word," Acts 8:4; "good tidings," 8:12; "the word of the Lord," 15:35; "the gospel," 1 Cor. 15:1; 2 Cor. 11:7; "the faith," Gal. 1:23; "peace," Eph. 2:17; "the unsearchable riches of Christ, 3:8.

Preached *see* **Glad tidings** at ***Luke 1:19***.

7:23-24 And blessed is *he*, whosoever shall not be offended in me.

And when the messengers of John were departed, he began to speak unto the people concerning John, What went ye out into the wilderness for to see? A reed shaken with the wind?

Messengers *angelos* (32), "a messenger, an angel, one sent," is translated "messenger," of John the Baptist, Matt. 11:10; Mark 1:2; **Luke 7:27**; in the plural, of John's "messengers," **7:24**; of those whom Christ sent before Him when on His journey to Jerusalem, **9:52**; of Paul's "thorn in the flesh," "a messenger of Satan," 2 Cor. 12:7; of the spies as received by Rahab, Jas. 2:25.

Reed *kalamos* (2563), denotes (a) "the reed" mentioned in Matt. 11:7; 12:20; **Luke 7:24**, the same as the Heb., *qaneh* (among the various reeds in the OT), e.g., Isa. 42:3, from which Matt. 12:20 is quoted (cf. Job 40:21; Ezek. 29:6, "a reed with jointed, hollow stalk"); (b) "a reed staff, staff," Matt. 27:29, 30, 48; Mark 15:19, 36 (cf. *rhabdos*, "a rod"; in 2 Kings 18:21, *rhabdos kalamine*); (c) "a measuring reed or rod," Rev. 11:1; 21:15, 16; (d) "a writing reed, a pen," 3 John 13.

Shaken *see Luke 6:38*.

7:25 But what went ye out for to see? A man clothed in soft raiment? Behold, they which are gorgeously apparelled, and live delicately, are in kings' courts.

Clothed *amphiennumi* (294), "to put clothes round" (*amphi*, "around," *hennumi*, "to clothe"), "to invest," signifies, in the middle voice, to put clothing on oneself, e.g., Matt. 6:30; 11:8; **Luke 7:25**; **12:28**.

Soft *malakos* (3120), "soft, soft to the touch" (Lat., *mollis*, Eng., "mollify," "emollient," etc.), is used (a) of raiment, Matt. 11:8 (twice); **Luke 7:25**; (b) metaphorically, in a bad sense, 1 Cor. 6:9, "effeminate," not simply of a male who practices forms of lewdness, but persons in general, who are guilty of addiction to sins of the flesh, voluptuous.

Raiment *himatismos* (2441), in form a collective word, denoting "vesture, garments," is used generally of "costly or stately raiment," the apparel of kings, of officials, etc. See **Luke 7:25**, where "gorgeously apparelled" is, lit., "in gorgeous vesture." See also Acts 20:33 and 1 Tim. 2:9, "costly raiment." This is the word used of the Lord's white and dazzling raiment on the Mount of Transfiguration, **Luke 9:29**. It is also used of His *chiton*, for which the soldiers cast lots, John 19:23-24, "vesture"; in Matt. 27:35 it is also translated vesture.

Gorgeously *endoxos* (1741), signifies (a) "held in honor" (*en*, "in," *doxa*, "honor"), "of high repute," 1 Cor. 4:10, RV "have glory" (KJV, "are honorable"); (b) "splendid, glorious," said of apparel, **Luke 7:25**, "gorgeously"; of the works of Christ, **13:17**; of the church, Eph. 5:27.

Apparelled *himatismos* (2441), a collective word, is translated "apparelled" in **Luke 7:25**, and preceded by *en*, "in," lit., "in apparel."

Live *huparcho* (5225), "to be in existence, to be," is translated "live (delicately)" in **Luke 7:25**.

Delicately *truphe* (5172), is used with *en*, in the phrase *en truphe*, "luxuriously," "delicately," **Luke 7:25**, and denotes effeminacy, softness; "to revel" in 2 Pet. 2:13 (KJV, "riot"), lit., "counting reveling in the day time a pleasure."

Kings *basileios* (934), denoting "royal," as in 1 Pet. 2:9, is used in the plural, of the courts or palaces of kings, **Luke 7:25**, "kings' courts"; a possible meaning is "among royal courtiers or persons."

Court *basileion* (933), an adjective meaning "royal," signifies, in the neuter plural, "a royal palace," translated "kings' courts" in **Luke 7:25**; in the singular, 1 Pet. 2:9, "royal."

7:26 But what went ye out for to see? A prophet? Yea, I say unto you, and much more than a prophet.

Yea *nai* (3483), a particle of affirmation, is used (a) in answer to a question, Matt. 9:28; 11:9; 13:51; 17:25; 21:16; **Luke 7:26**; John 11:27; 21:15, 16; Acts 5:8; 22:27; Rom. 3:29; (b) in assent to an assertion, Matt. 15:27, RV (KJV, "truth"); Mark 7:28; Rev. 14:13; 16:7, RV (KJV, "even so"); (c) in confirmation of an assertion, Matt. 11:26 and **Luke 10:21**, RV (KJV, "even so"); **Luke 11:51**, RV (KJV, "verily"); **12:5**; Phil. 4:3 (in the best texts); Philem. 20; (d) in solemn asseveration, Rev. 1:7 (KJV and RV, "even so"); 22:20, RV (KJV, "surely"); (e) in repetition for emphasis, Matt. 5:37; 2 Cor. 1:17; Jas. 5:12; (f) singly in contrast to *ou*, "nay," 2 Cor. 1:18, 19 (twice), 20, "(the) yea," RV.

More *perissoteros* (4055), is translated as follows: in Matt. 11:9, and **Luke 7:26**, RV, "much more" (KJV, "more"); in Mark 12:40, "greater"; in **Luke 12:4**, **48**, "more"; in 1 Cor. 12:23-24, "more abundant"; in 2 Cor. 2:7, "overmuch"; in 2 Cor. 10:8, RV, "abundantly"; KJV, "more."

7:27 This is *he*, of whom it is written, Behold, I send my messenger before thy face, which shall prepare thy way before thee.

Messenger *see* Messengers at *Luke 7:24.*

Prepare *see* Make ready at *Luke 1:17.*

7:28 For I say unto you, Among those that are born of women there is not a greater prophet than John the Baptist: but he that is least in the kingdom of God is greater than he.

Born *gennetos* (1084), "born" (related to *gennao*), is used in Matt. 11:11 and **Luke 7:28** in the phrase "born of women," a periphrasis for "men," and suggestive of frailty.

Least *mikroteros* (3398), is used of (a) size, Matt. 13:32, KJV, "the least," RV, "less;" Mark 4:31; (b) estimation, Matt. 11:11 and **Luke 7:28**, KJV, "least," RV, "but little," marg., "lesser" (in the kingdom of heaven), those in the kingdom itself being less than John the Baptist; **Luke 9:48**.

7:29 And all the people that heard *him*, and the publicans, justified God, being baptized with the baptism of John.

Publicans *see Luke 3:12.*

Justified *dikaioo* (1344), primarily "to deem to be right," signifies, in the NT, (a) "to show to be right or righteous"; in the passive voice, to be justified, Matt. 11:19; **Luke 7:35**; Rom. 3:4; 1 Tim. 3:16; (b) "to declare to be righteous, to pronounce righteous," (1) by man, concerning God, **Luke 7:29** (see Rom. 3:4, above); concerning himself, **Luke 10:29**; **16:15**; (2) by God concerning men, who are declared to be righteous before Him on certain conditions laid down by Him.

7:30 But the Pharisees and lawyers rejected the counsel of God against themselves, being not baptized of him.

Lawyers *nomikos* (3544), an adjective, "learned in the law," is used as a noun, "a lawyer," Matt. 22:35; **Luke 7:30**; **10:25**; **11:45**, **46**, **52** (v. **53** in some mss.); **14:3**; Titus 3:13, where Zenas is so named. As there is no evidence that he was one skilled in Roman jurisprudence, the term may be regarded in the usual NT sense as applying to one skilled in the Mosaic Law. The usual name for a scribe is *grammateus*, a man of letters; for a doctor of the law, *nomodidaskalos*, "A comparison of **Luke 5:17** with v. **21** and Mark 2:6 and Matt. 9:3 shows that the three terms were used synonymously, and did not denote three distinct classes. The scribes were originally simply men of letters, students of Scripture, and the name first given to them contains in itself no reference to the law; in course of time, however, they devoted themselves mainly, though by no means exclusively, to the study of the law. They became jurists rather than theologians, and received names which of themselves called attention to that fact. Some would doubtless devote themselves more to one branch of activity than to another; but a 'lawyer' might also be a 'doctor,' and the case of Gamaliel shows that a 'doctor' might also be a member of the Sanhedrin, Acts 5:34" (Eaton, in *Hastings' Bib. Dic.*).

Rejected *atheteo* (114), properly, "to do away" with what has been laid down, to make *atheton* (i.e., "without place," *a*, negative, *tithemi*, "to place"), hence, besides its meanings "to set aside, make void, nullify, disannul," signifies "to reject"; in Mark 6:26, regarding Herod's pledge to Salome, it almost certainly has the meaning "to break faith with" (cf. the Sept. of Jer. 12:6, and Lam. 1:2, "dealt treacherously"). Moulton and Milligan illustrate this meaning from the papyri. Field suggests "disappoint." In Mark 7:9 "ye reject (the commandment)" means "ye set aside"; in **Luke 7:30**, "ye reject" may have the meaning of "nullifying or making void the counsel of God"; in **Luke 10:16** (four times), "rejecteth," RV (KJV, "despiseth"); "rejecteth" in John 12:48; "reject" in 1 Cor. 1:19 (KJV, "bring to nothing"); 1 Thess. 4:8, "to despise," where the reference is to the charges in v. 2; in 1 Tim. 5:12 RV, "have rejected" (KJV, "have cast off").

Counsel *boule* (1012), from a root meaning "a will," hence "a counsel, a piece of advice," is to be distinguished from *gnome; boule* is the result of determination, *gnome* is the result of knowledge. *Boule* is everywhere rendered by "counsel" in the RV except in Acts 27:12, "advised," lit., "gave counsel." In Acts 13:36 the KJV wrongly has "by the will of God fell on sleep"; the RV, "after he had served the counsel of God, fell on sleep." The word is used of the counsel of God, in **Luke 7:30**; Acts 2:23; 4:28; 13:36; 20:27; Eph. 1:11; Heb. 6:17; in other passages, of the counsel of men, **Luke 23:51**; Acts 27:12, 42; 1 Cor. 4:5.

7:31 And the Lord said, Whereunto then shall I liken the men of this generation? and to what are they like?

Liken *homoioo* (3666), "to make like," is used (a) especially in the parables, with the significance of comparing, "likening," or, in the passive voice, "being likened," Matt. 7:24, 26; 11:16; 13:24; 18:23; 22:2 (RV, "likened"); 25:1; Mark 4:30; **Luke 7:31**; **13:18**, RV, "liken" (KJV, "resemble"); v. **20**; in several of these instances the point of resemblance is not a specific detail, but the whole circumstances of the parable; (b) of making "like," or, in the passive voice, of being made or becoming "like," Matt. 6:8; Acts 14:11, "in the likeness of (men)," lit., "being made like" (aorist participle, passive); Rom. 9:29; Heb. 2:17, of Christ in being "made like" unto His brethren, i.e., in partaking of human nature, apart from sin (cf. v. 14).

Like *see* ***Luke 6:47.***

7:32 They are like unto children sitting in the marketplace, and calling one to another, and saying, We have piped unto you, and ye have not danced; we have mourned to you, and ye have not wept.

Like *see* ***Luke 6:47.***

Marketplace *agora* (58), primarily "an assembly," or, in general, "an open space in a town" (akin to *ageiro*, "to bring together"), became applied, according to papyri evidences, to a variety of things, e.g., "a judicial assembly," "a market," or even "supplies, provisions" (Moulton and Milligan, *Vocab.*). In the NT it denotes "a place of assembly, a public place or forum, a marketplace." A variety of circumstances, connected with it as a public gathering place, is mentioned, e.g., business dealings such as the hiring of laborers, Matt. 20:3; the buying and selling of goods, Mark 7:4 (involving risk of pollution); the games of children, Matt. 11:16; **Luke 7:32**; exchange of greetings, Matt. 23:7; Mark 12:38; **Luke 11:43**; **20:46**; the holding of trials, Acts 16:19; public discussions, Acts 17:17. Mark 6:56 records the bringing of the sick there. The word always carries with it the idea of publicity, in contrast to private circumstances.

The RV always translates it "marketplace" or in the plural. The KJV sometimes changes the rendering to "markets" and translates it "streets" in Mark 6:56.

Calling *see* **Called** at ***Luke 6:13.***

One another This translates a number of words and phrases, (a) *allelon*, a reciprocal pronoun in the genitive plural, signifying "of, or from, one another" (akin to *allos*, "another"), e.g., Matt. 25:32; John 13:22; Acts 15:39; 19:38; 1 Cor. 7:5; Gal. 5:17; the accusative *allelous* denotes "one another," e.g., Acts 7:26, lit., "why do ye wrong one another?"; 2 Thess. 1:3, RV; in Eph. 4:32 and Col. 3:13, e.g., RV, "each other"; in 1 Thess. 5:15, "one (toward) another," RV; the dative *allelois* denotes "one to another," e.g., **Luke 7:32**; (b) different forms of the plural of *heautou*, "of himself," used as a reciprocal pronoun, e.g., Eph. 5:19, RV, "one to another" (KJV, and RV marg., "to yourselves").

Piped *auleo* (832), "to play on an *aulos*," is used in Matt. 11:17; **Luke 7:32**; 1 Cor. 14:7 (2nd part).

Danced *orcheo* (3738), (cf. Eng., "orchestra"), probably originally signified "to lift up," as of the feet; hence, "to leap with regularity of motion." It is always used in the middle voice, Matt. 11:17; 14:6; Mark 6:22; **Luke 7:32**. The performance by the daughter of Herodias is the only clear instance of artistic dancing, a form introduced from Greek customs.

Mourned *threneo* (2354), "to lament, wail" (akin to *threnos*, "a lamentation, a dirge"), is used (a) in a general sense, of the disciples during the absence of the Lord, John 16:20, "lament"; (b) of those who sorrowed for the sufferings and the impending crucifixion of the Lord, **Luke 23:27**, "lamented"; the preceding word is *kopto*; (c) of "mourning" as for the dead, Matt. 11:17, RV, "wailed" (KJV, "have mourned"); **Luke 7:32** (ditto).

7:33-34 For John the Baptist came neither eating bread nor drinking wine; and ye say, He hath a devil.

The Son of man is come eating and drinking; and ye say, Behold a gluttonous man, and a winebibber, a friend of publicans and sinners!

Gluttonous *phagos* (5314), akin to *phago*, "to eat," a form used for the aorist or past tense of *esthio*, denotes "a glutton," Matt. 11:19; **Luke 7:34**.

Winebibber *oinopotes* (3630), "a wine drinker" (*oinos*, and *potes*, "a drinker"), is used in Matt. 11:19; **Luke 7:34**. In the Sept., Prov. 23:20.

Publicans *see* ***Luke 3:12.***

7:35 But wisdom is justified of all her children.

Wisdom *see* ***Luke 2:40.***

Justified *see* ***Luke 7:29.***

7:36 And one of the Pharisees desired him that he would eat with him. And he went into the Pharisee's house, and sat down to meat.

Desired *erotao* (2065), more frequently suggests that the petitioner is on a footing of equality or familiarity with the person whom he requests. It is used of a king in making request from another king, **Luke 14:32**; of the Pharisee who "desired" Christ that He would eat with him, an indication of the inferior conception he had of Christ, **Luke 7:36**; cf. **11:37**; John 9:15; 18:19.

In this respect it is significant that the Lord Jesus never used *aiteo* in the matter of making request to the Father. "The consciousness of His equal dignity, of His potent and prevailing intercession, speaks out in this, that as often as He asks, or declares that He will ask anything of the Father, it is always *erotao*, an asking, that is, upon equal terms, John 14:16; 16:26; 17:9, 15, 20, never *aiteo*, that He uses. Martha, on the contrary, plainly reveals her poor unworthy conception of His person, that … she ascribes that *aiteo* to Him which He never ascribes to Himself, John 11:22" (Trench, *Syn.* Sec. xl). In passages where both words are used, the distinction should be noticed, even if it cannot be adequately represented in English. In John 16:23, "in that day ye shall ask Me nothing," the verb is *erotao*, whereas in the latter part of the verse, in the sentence, "If ye shall ask anything of the Father," the verb is *aiteo*. The distinction is brought out in the RV margin, which renders the former clause "Ye shall ask Me no question," and this meaning is confirmed by the fact that the disciples had been desirous of "asking" Him a question (*erotao*, v. 19).

Sat *kataklino* (2625), is used only in connection with meals, in the active voice, "to make recline," **Luke 9:14, 15** (in the best texts); in the passive voice, "to recline," **Luke 7:36** (in the best texts), "sat down to meat"; **14:8**; **24:30** (RV, "had sat down … to meat"). *See also* **Laid** at *Luke 2:7*.

7:37 And, behold, a woman in the city, which was a sinner, when she knew that *Jesus* sat at meat in the Pharisee's house, brought an alabaster box of ointment,

Sinner *hamartolos* (268), lit., "one who misses the mark" (a meaning not to be pressed), is an adjective, most frequently used as a noun; it is the most usual term to describe the fallen condition of men; it is applicable to all men, Rom. 5:8, 19. In the Synoptic Gospels the word is used not infrequently, by the Pharisees, of publicans (tax collectors) and women of ill repute, e.g., "a woman which was in the city, a sinner," **Luke 7:37**; "a man that is a sinner," **19:7**. In Gal. 2:15, in the clause "not sinners of the Gentiles," the apostle is taking the Judaizers on their own ground, ironically reminding them of their claim to moral superiority over Gentiles; he proceeds to show that the Jews are equally sinners with Gentiles.

Knew *epiginosko* (1921), denotes (a) "to observe, fully perceive, notice attentively, discern, recognize" (*epi*, "upon," and *ginosko*); it suggests generally a directive, a more special, recognition of the object "known" than does *ginosko*; it also may suggest advanced "knowledge" or special appreciation; thus, in Rom. 1:32, "knowing the ordinance of God" (*epiginosko*) means "knowing full well," whereas in verse 21 "knowing God" (*ginosko*) simply suggests that they could not avoid the perception. Sometimes *epiginosko* implies a special participation in the object "known," and gives greater weight to what is stated; thus in John 8:32, "ye shall know the truth," *ginosko* is used, whereas in 1 Tim. 4:3, "them that believe and know the truth," *epiginosko* lays stress on participation in the truth. Cf. the stronger statement in Col. 1:6 (*epiginosko*) with that in 2 Cor. 8:9 (*ginosko*), and the two verbs in 1 Cor. 13:12, "now I know in part (*ginosko*); but then shall I know (*piginosko*) even as also I have been known (*epiginosko*)," "a knowledge" which perfectly unites the subject with the object; (b) "to discover, ascertain, determine," e.g., **Luke 7:37**; **23:7**; Acts 9:30; 19:34; 22:29; 24:11; 28:1; hence the RV, "take knowledge." J. Armitage Robinson (on Ephesians) points out that *epignosis* is "knowledge directed towards a particular object, perceiving, discerning," whereas *gnosis* is knowledge in the abstract.

Sat *anakeimai* (345), "to recline at table" (*ana*, "up" *keimai*, "to lie"), is rendered "to sit at meat" in Matt. 9:10 (RV, marg., "reclined"); 26:7; 26:20, RV, "He was sitting at meat" (KJV, "He sat down"); Mark 16:14; in some mss. **Luke 7:37; 22:27** (twice); in Mark 14:18, "sat"; in John 6:11, "were set down"; John 12:2 in the best texts. *See also* ***Luke 5:29***.

Brought *komizo* (2865), denotes "to bear, carry," e.g., **Luke 7:37**; in the middle voice, "to bear for oneself," hence (a) "to receive," Heb. 10:36; 11:13 (in the best texts; some have *lambano*), 39; 1 Pet. 1:9; 5:4; in some texts in 2 Pet. 2:13 (in the best mss. *adikeomai*, "suffering wrong," RV); (b) "to receive back, recover," Matt. 25:27; Heb. 11:19; metaphorically, of requital, 2 Cor. 5:10; Col. 3:25, of "receiving back again" by the believer at the judgment seat of Christ hereafter, for wrong done in this life; Eph. 6:8, of "receiving," on the same occasion, "whatsoever good thing each one doeth," RV.

Box *alabastron* (211), "an alabaster vessel," is translated in the KJV of Matt. 26:7; Mark 14:3; **Luke 7:37**, "box," RV, "cruse." The breaking refers to the seal, not to the box or cruse.

Ointment *muron* (3464), a word derived by the ancients from *muro*, "to flow," or from *murra*, "myrrh-oil" (it is probably of foreign origin). The "ointment" is mentioned in the NT in connection with the anointing of the Lord on the occasions recorded in Matt. 26:7, 9, 12; Mark

14:3-4; **Luke 7:37-38, 46**; John 11:2; 12:3 (twice), 5. The alabaster cruse mentioned in the passages in Matthew, Mark and Luke was the best of its kind, and the spikenard was one of the costliest of perfumes. "Ointments" were used in preparing a body for burial, **Luke 23:56** ("ointments"). Of the act of the woman mentioned in Matt. 26:6-13, the Lord said, "she did it to prepare Me for burial"; her devotion led her to antedate the customary ritual after death, by showing both her affection and her understanding of what was impending. For the use of the various kinds of "ointments" as articles of commerce, see Rev. 18:13.

7:38 And stood at his feet behind *him* weeping, and began to wash his feet with tears, and did wipe *them* with the hairs of her head, and kissed his feet, and anointed *them* with the ointment.

Feet *see Luke 1:79.*

Wash *brecho* (1026), signifies (a) "to wet," **Luke 7:38, 44**, RV (KJV, to wash); (b) "to send rain," Matt. 5:45; to rain, **Luke 17:29** (of fire and brimstone); Jas. 5:17, used impersonally (twice); Rev. 11:6, where *huetos* is used as the subject, lit., "(that) rain rain (not)."

Tears *dakruon* or *dakru* (1144), akin to *dakruo*, "to weep," is used in the plural, Mark 9:24; **Luke 7:38, 44** (with the sense of washing therewith the Lord's feet); Acts 20:19, 31; 2 Cor. 2:4; 2 Tim. 1:4; Heb. 5:7; 12:17; Rev. 7:17; 21:4.

Wipe *ekmasso* (1591), "to wipe out" (*ek*), "wipe dry," is used of "wiping" tears from Christ's feet, **Luke 7:38, 44**; John 11:2; 12:3; of Christ's "wiping" the disciples' feet, John 13:5.

Hairs *thrix* (2359), denotes the "hair," whether of beast, as of the camel's "hair" which formed the raiment of John the Baptist, Matt. 3:4; Mark 1:6; or of man. Regarding the latter (a) it is used to signify the minutest detail, as that which illustrates the exceeding care and protection bestowed by God upon His children, Matt. 10:30; **Luke 12:7; 21:18**; Acts 27:34; (b) as the Jews swore by the "hair," the Lord used the natural inability to make one "hair" white or black, as one of the reasons for abstinence from oaths, Matt. 5:36; (c) while long "hair" is a glory to a woman, and to wear it loose or dishevelled is a dishonor, yet the woman who wiped Christ's feet with her "hair" (in place of the towel which Simon the Pharisee omitted to provide), despised the shame in her penitent devotion to the Lord (slaves were accustomed to wipe their masters' feet), **Luke 7:38, 44** (RV, "hair"); see also John 11:2; 12:3; (d) the dazzling whiteness of the head and "hair" of the Son of Man in the vision of Rev. 1 (v. 14) is suggestive of the holiness and wisdom of "the Ancient of Days"; (e) the long "hair" of the spirit-beings described as locusts in Rev. 9:8 is perhaps indicative of their subjection to their satanic master (cf. 1 Cor. 11:10, RV); (f) Christian women are exhorted to refrain from adorning their "hair" for outward show, 1 Pet. 3:3.

Kissed *kataphileo* (2705), denotes "to kiss fervently"; the stronger force of this verb has been called in question, but the change from *phileo* to *kataphileo* in Matt. 26:49 and Mark 14:45 can scarcely be without significance, and the act of the traitor was almost certainly more demonstrative than the simple kiss of salutation. So with the kiss of genuine devotion, **Luke 7:38, 45; 15:20**; Acts 20:37, in each of which this verb is used.

Anointed *aleipho* (218), is a general term used for "an anointing" of any kind, whether of physical refreshment after washing, e.g., in the Sept. of Ruth 3:3; 2 Sam. 12:20; Dan. 10:3; Micah 6:15; in the NT, Matt. 6:17; **Luke 7:38, 46**; John 11:2; 12:3; or of the sick, Mark 6:13; Jas. 5:14; or a dead body, Mark 16:1. The material used was either oil or ointment, as in **Luke 7:38, 46**. In the Sept. it is also used of "anointing" a pillar, Gen. 31:13, or captives, 2 Chron. 28:15, or of daubing a wall with mortar, Ezek. 13:10-12, 14-15; and, in the sacred sense, of "anointing" priests, in Exod. 40:15 (twice), and Num. 3:3.

7:39 Now when the Pharisee which had bidden him saw *it*, he spake within himself, saying, This man, if he were a prophet, would have known who and what manner of woman *this is* that toucheth him: for she is a sinner.

Within This is a translation of (a) *entos*; in **Luke 17:21** the RV marg., "in the midst of," is to be preferred; the kingdom of God was not in the hearts of the Pharisees; (b) *en*, "of thinking or saying within oneself," e.g., **Luke 7:39, 49** (marg., "among"); locally, e.g., **Luke 19:44**; (c) *esothen*, 2 Cor. 7:5; Rev. 4:8; 5:1; "from within," Mark 7:21, 23; **Luke 11:7**; "within," Matt. 23:25; **Luke 11:40**, RV, "inside"; in Matt. 23:27, 28, RV, "inwardly"; (d) *eso*, John 20:26; Acts 5:23; 1 Cor. 5:12 (i.e., "within" the church); (e) *pros*, to, or with, in Mark 14:4, KJV, "within" (RV, "among"); (f) *dia*, "through," rendered "within (three days)" in Mark 14:58, KJV (RV, "in," looking through the time to the event, and in keeping with the metaphor of building); (g) *esoteros*, Heb. 6:19, the comparative degree of *eso*, used with the article translated "that within," lit., "the inner (part of the veil)," i.e., "inside"; (h) in **Luke 11:41**, RV, *eneimi*, "to be in," is rendered "are within" (KJV, "ye have").

Manner *see* ***Luke 1:29***.

Known *ginosko* (1097), "to know by experience and observation," is translated "to perceive" in Matt. 12:15, RV (KJV, "knew"); 16:8; 21:45; 22:18; 26:10, RV, (KJV, "understood"); Mark 8:17; 12:12 and 15:10, RV (KJV, "knew"); so **Luke 9:11**; **18:34**; in **Luke 7:39**, RV (KJV, "known"); **20:19** (*katanoeo* in v. **23**); John 6:15; 8:27, RV (KJV, "understood"); 16:19, RV (KJV, "knew"); Acts 23:6; Gal. 2:9; in 1 John 3:16, KJV, "perceive" (RV, "know," perfect tense, lit., "we have perceived," and therefore "know").

7:40 And Jesus answering said unto him, Simon, I have somewhat to say unto thee. And he saith, Master, say on.

Somewhat The indefinite pronoun *tis* in its singular or plural forms, frequently means "some," "some one" (translated "some man," in the KJV, e.g., of Acts 8:31; 1 Cor. 15:35), or "somebody," **Luke 8:46**; the neuter plural denotes "some things" in 2 Pet. 3:16; the singular denotes "something," e.g., **Luke 11:54**; John 13:29 (2nd part); Acts 3:5; 23:18; Gal. 6:3, where the meaning is "anything," as in 2:6, "somewhat." It is translated "somewhat," in the more indefinite sense, in **Luke 7:40**; Acts 23:20; 25:26; 2 Cor. 10:8; Heb. 8:3.

Say In **Luke 7:40** and Acts 13:15, the imperative mood of *eipon* and *lego*, respectively, is rendered "say on."

7:41 There was a certain creditor which had two debtors: the one owed five hundred pence, and the other fifty.

Creditor *danistes* or *daneistes* (1157), denotes a moneylender), translated "lender" in **Luke 7:41**, RV (KJV, "creditor"). In the Sept., 2 Kings 4:1; Ps. 109:11; Prov. 29:13. *See also* **Lend** at ***Luke 6:34***.

Debtors *chreopheiletes* (5533), lit., "a debt-ower," is found in **Luke 7:41**, of the two "debtors" mentioned in the Lord's parable addressed to Simon the Pharisee, and in **16:5**, of the "debtors" in the parable of the unrighteous steward. This parable indicates a system of credit in the matter of agriculture. In the Sept., Job 31:37, "having taken nothing from the debtor"; Prov. 29:13, "when the creditor and the debtor meet together."

Owed *opheilo* (3784), "to owe, to be a debtor" (in the passive voice, "to be owed, to be due"), is translated by the verb "to owe" in Matt. 18:28 (twice); **Luke 7:41**; **16:5**, **7**; Rom. 13:8; in 15:27, RV, "they (gentile converts) owe it" (KJV, "it is their duty"); Philem. 18.

Five *pente* (4002), is derived by some from words suggesting the fingers of a hand, or a fist. The word is frequent in the Gospels. *Pentakis*, "five times," is found in 2 Cor. 11:24; *pentakosioi*, "five hundred," in **Luke 7:41**; 1 Cor. 15:6; *pentakischilioi*, "five thousand" (*chilios*, "a thousand"), in Matt. 14:21; 16:9 and corresponding passages.

Pence *denarion* (1220), a Roman coin, a *denarius*, a little less than the value of the Greek *drachme*, now estimated as amounting to about 9½d. in the time of our Lord, occurs in the singular, e.g., Matt. 20:2; 22:19; Mark 12:15; Rev. 6:6; in the plural, e.g., Matt. 18:28; Mark 14:5; **Luke 7:41**; **10:35**; John 12:5; "pennyworth" in Mark 6:37 and John 6:7, lit., "(loaves of two hundred) pence." Considering the actual value, "shilling" would have been a more accurate translation, as proposed by the American translators, retaining "penny" for the *as*, and "farthing" for the *quadrans*.

Fifty *pentekonta* (4004), is found in **Luke 7:41**; **16:6**; John 8:57; 21:11; Acts 13:20; in Mark 6:40 with *kata* (in the most authentic mss.), according to, "by fifties"; in **Luke 9:14**, with *ana*, "up," used distributively, "fifty each," RV (Luke adds *hosei*, "about").

7:42 And when they had nothing to pay, he frankly forgave them both. Tell me therefore, which of them will love him most?

Nothing *me* (3361), "not," is translated "nothing" in John 6:39 in a clause expressing purpose; in the KJV of **Luke 7:42** (RV, "not"), in a temporal clause.

Frankly In **Luke 7:42**, the verb *charizomai*, "to forgive" (as a matter of grace), is rendered "frankly forgave," so as to bring out the force of the grace in the action. Older versions had "forgave," and to this the RV returns.

Forgave *charizomai* (5483), "to bestow a favor unconditionally," is used of the act of "forgiveness," whether divine, Eph. 4:32; Col. 2:13; 3:13; or human, **Luke 7:42**, **43** (debt); 2 Cor. 2:7, 10; 12:13; Eph. 4:32 (1st mention). Paul uses this word frequently ... in Rom. 4:7, in this sense of the word.

Most *pleion* (4119), the neuter of *pleion*, "more," is used adverbially and translated "most" (of degree) in **Luke 7:42** (without the article); in v. **43** (with the article, "the most"); 1 Cor. 10:5, RV, "most" (KJV, "many"); Phil. 1:14 (ditto).

7:43 Simon answered and said, I suppose that *he*, to whom he forgave most. And he said unto him, Thou hast rightly judged.

Suppose *hupolambano* (5274), signifies (a) "to take or bear up from beneath," Acts 1:9; (b) "to receive," 3 John 8; (c) "to suppose," **Luke 7:43**; Acts 2:15; (d) "to catch up (in speech), to answer," **Luke 10:30**; in sense (d) it indicates that a person follows what another has said, either by controverting or supplementing it.

Forgave *see* **Luke** *7:42.*

Most *see* **Luke** *7:42.*

Judged *krino* (2919), primarily denotes "to separate, select, choose"; hence, "to determine," and so "to judge, pronounce judgment." "The uses of this verb in the NT may be analyzed as follows: (a) to assume the office of a judge, Matt. 7:1; John 3:17; (b) to undergo process of trial, John 3:18; 16:11; 18:31; Jas. 2:12; (c) to give sentence, Acts 15:19; 16:4; 21:25; (d) to condemn, John 12:48; Acts 13:27; Rom. 2:27; (e) to execute judgment upon, 2 Thess. 2:12; Acts 7:7; (f) to be involved in a lawsuit, whether as plaintiff, Matt. 5:40; 1 Cor. 6:1; or as defendant, Acts 23:6; (g) to administer affairs, to govern, Matt. 19:28; cf. Judg. 3:10; (h) to form an opinion, **Luke 7:43**; John 7:24; Acts 4:19; Rom. 14:5; (i) to make a resolve, Acts 3:13; 20:161 Cor. 2:2."

Rightly *orthos* (3723), "rightly" (akin to *orthos*, "straight, direct"), is translated "plain" in Mark 7:35; in **Luke 7:43** and **20:21**, "rightly"; in **Luke 10:28**, "right."

7:44 And he turned to the woman, and said unto Simon, Seest thou this woman? I entered into thine house, thou gavest me no water for my feet: but she hath washed my feet with tears, and wiped them *with* the hairs of her head.

Washed *see* Wash at **Luke** *7:38.*

Tears *see* **Luke** *7:38.*

Wiped *see* Wipe at **Luke** *7:38.*

Hairs *see* **Luke** *7:38.*

7:45 Thou gavest me no kiss: but this woman since the time I came in hath not ceased to kiss my feet.

Kiss *philema* (5370), "a kiss," **Luke 7:45**; **22:48**, was a token of Christian brotherhood, whether by way of welcome or farewell, "a holy kiss," Rom. 16:16; 1 Cor. 16:20; 2 Cor. 13:12; 1 Thess. 5:26, "holy" (*hagios*), as free from anything inconsistent with their calling as saints (*hagioi*); "a kiss of love," 1 Pet. 5:14. There was to be an absence of formality and hypocrisy, a freedom from prejudice arising from social distinctions, from discrimination against the poor, from partiality towards the well-to-do. In the churches masters and servants would thus salute one another without any attitude of condescension on the one part or disrespect on the other. The "kiss" took place thus between persons of the same sex. In the "Apostolic Constitutions," a writing compiled in the 4th century, AD, there is a reference to the custom whereby men sat on one side of the room where a meeting was held and women on the other side of the room (as is frequently the case still in parts of Europe and Asia), and the men are bidden to salute the men, and the women the women, with "the kiss of the Lord."

Ceased *dialeipo* (1257), lit., "to leave between," i.e., "to leave an interval, whether of space or time" (*dia*, "between," *leipo*, "to leave"); hence, "to intermit, desist, cease," in **Luke 7:45** is used of the kissing of the Lord's feet.

"The man who is truly forgiven and knows it, is a man who forgives."

DAVID MARTYN LLOYD-JONES

Kiss *see* Kissed at **Luke** *7:38.*

7:46 My head with oil thou didst not anoint: but this woman hath anointed my feet with ointment.

Oil *elaion* (1637), "olive oil," is mentioned over 200 times in the Bible. Different kinds were known in Palestine. The "pure," RV (KJV, beaten), mentioned in Exod. 27:20; 29:40; Lev. 24:2; Num. 28:5 (now known as virgin oil), extracted by pressure, without heat, is called "golden" in Zech. 4:12. There were also inferior kinds. In the NT the uses mentioned were (a) for lamps, in which the "oil" is a symbol of the Holy Spirit, Matt. 25:3-4, 8; (b) as a medicinal agent, for healing, **Luke 10:34**; (c) for anointing at feasts, **Luke 7:46**; (d) on festive occasions, Heb. 1:9, where the reference is probably to the consecration of kings; (e) as an accompaniment of miraculous power, Mark 6:13, or of the prayer of faith, Jas. 5:14. For its general use in commerce, see **Luke 16:6**; Rev. 6:6; 18:13.

Anoint, Anointed *see* **Luke** *7:38.*

Ointment *See* **Luke** *7:37. Muron* denotes "ointment." The distinction between this and *elaion*, "oil," is observable in Christ's reproof of the Pharisee who, while desiring Him to eat with him, failed in the ordinary marks of courtesy; "My head with oil (*elaion*) thou didst not anoint, but she hath anointed My feet with ointment" (*muron*), Luke 7:46.

7:47 Wherefore I say unto thee, Her sins, which are many, are forgiven; for she loved much: but to whom little is forgiven, *the same* loveth little.

Wherefore *charin* with *hou*, the genitive case, neuter of *hos*, "for the sake of what," **Luke 7:47**.

7:48-49 And he said unto her, Thy sins are forgiven.
And they that sat at meat with him began to say within themselves, Who is this that forgiveth sins also?

Sat *sunanakeimai* (4873), "to recline at table with or together," "to sit at meat or at table with," occurs in Matt. 9:10, "sat down"; 14:9; Mark 2:15, RV, "sat down with" (KJV, "sat ... together with"); 6:22; **Luke 7:49**; **14:10**, **15**; John 12:2 (in some texts).

Within *see Luke 7:39*.

Also *see* Even at *Luke 6:33*.

7:50 And he said to the woman, Thy faith hath saved thee; go in peace.

Peace *see Luke 1:79*.

Chapter 8

8:1 And it came to pass afterward, that he went throughout every city and village, preaching and shewing the glad tidings of the kingdom of God: and the twelve *were* with him,

Afterward *see* Order at *Luke 1:3*.

Went *diodeuo* (1353), "to travel throughout or along" (*dia*, "through," *hodos*, "a way"), is used in **Luke 8:1**, of "going throughout" (KJV) or "about through" (RV) cities and villages; of "passing through" towns, Acts 17:1.

Every *see Luke 2:41*.

Preaching *see* Preach at *Luke 4:18*.

Glad tidings *see Luke 1:19*.

8:2-3 And certain women, which had been healed of evil spirits and infirmities, Mary called Magdalene, out of whom went seven devils,
And Joanna the wife of Chuza Herod's steward, and Susanna, and many others, which ministered unto him of their substance.

Ministered *see Luke 4:39*.

Steward *epitropos* (2012), lit., "one to whose care something is committed" (*epi*, "upon," *trepo*, "to turn" or "direct"), is rendered "guardians" in Gal. 4:2, RV, KJV, "tutors" (in Matt. 20:8 and **Luke 8:3**, "steward"). "The corresponding verb, *epitrepo*, is translated "permit, give leave, suffer"; see 1 Cor. 14:34; 16:7; 1 Tim. 2:12, e.g., ... An allied noun, *epitrope*, is translated "commission" in Acts 26:12 and refers to delegated authority over persons. This usage of cognate words suggests that the *epitropos* was a superior servant responsible for the persons composing the household, whether children or slaves."

Substance *huparchonta* (5224), the neuter plural of the present participle of *huparcho*, "to be in existence," is used as a noun with the article, signifying one's "goods," and translated "substance" in **Luke 8:3**.

8:4 And when much people were gathered together, and were come to him out of every city, he spake by a parable:

Gathered In **Luke 8:4**, KJV (*suneimi*, "to come together") as "were gathered together" (see RV).

Come *epiporeuomai* (1975), "to travel or journey to a place" (*epi*, "to," *poreuomai*, "to go"), is translated "resorted" in **Luke 8:4**, RV (KJV, "were come").

Out of In **Luke 8:4**, KJV, the phrase *kata polin* is translated "out of every city" (RV, "of every city," to be taken in connection with "they").

Every *see Luke 2:41*.

8:5 A sower went out to sow his seed: and as he sowed, some fell by the way side; and it was trodden down, and the fowls of the air devoured it.

Seed *sporos* (4703), properly "a sowing," denotes "seed sown," (a) natural, Mark 4:26, 27; **Luke 8:5**, **11** (the natural being figuratively applied to the Word of God); 2 Cor. 9:10 (1st part); (b) metaphorically of material help to the needy, 2 Cor. 9:10 (2nd part), RV, "(your) seed for sowing" (KJV, "seed sown").

Trodden *katapateo* (2662), "to tread down, trample under foot," is used (a) literally, Matt. 5:13; 7:6; **Luke 8:5**; **12:1**; (b) metaphorically, of "treading under foot" the Son of God, Heb. 10:29, i.e., turning away from Him, to indulge in willful sin.

Devoured *katesthio* and *kataphago* (2719), signifies (a) "to consume by eating, to devour," said of birds, Matt. 13:4; Mark 4:4; **Luke 8:5**; of the Dragon, Rev. 12:4; of a prophet, "eating" up a book, suggestive of spiritually "eating" and digesting its contents, Rev. 10:9 (cf. Ezek. 2:8; 3:1-3; Jer. 15:16); (b) metaphorically, "to squander, to waste," **Luke 15:30**; "to consume" one's physical powers by emotion, John 2:17; "to devour" by forcible appropriation, as of widows' property, Matt. 23:14 (KJV only); Mark 12:40; "to demand maintenance," as false apostles did to the church at Corinth, 2 Cor. 11:20; "to exploit or prey on one another," Gal. 5:15, where "bite ... devour ... consume" form a climax, the first two describing a process, the last the act of swallowing down; to "destroy" by fire, Rev. 11:5; 20:9.

8:6 And some fell upon a rock; and as soon as it was sprung up, it withered away, because it lacked moisture.

Fell *katapipto* (2667), "to fall down," is used in **Luke 8:6** (in the best mss.); Acts 26:14; 28:6.

Rock *see Luke 6:48.*

Sprung *phuo* (5453), used transitively, "to bring forth, produce," denotes, in the passive voice, "to spring up, grow," of seed, **Luke 8:6, 8**, KJV, "was sprung up" and "sprang up" (RV, "grew"); in the active voice, intransitively, in Heb. 12:15, of a root of bitterness.

Withered *xeraino* (3583), "to dry up, parch, wither," is translated "to wither," (a) of plants, Matt. 13:6; 21:19, 20; Mark 4:6; 11:20, RV (KJV, "dried up"), 21; **Luke 8:6**; John 15:6; Jas. 1:11; 1 Pet. 1:24; (b) of members of the body, Mark 3:1, and, in some texts, 3.

Moisture *ikmas* (2429), "moisture" (probably from an Indo-European root *sik–* indicating "wet"), is used in **Luke 8:6**. In the Sept., Job 26:14; Jer. 17:8.

8:7 And some fell among thorns; and the thorns sprang up with it, and choked it.

Sprang *sumphuo* (4855), "to cause to grow together," occurs in **Luke 8:7**, RV, "grew with," KJV, "sprang up with."

Choked *apopnigo* (638), a strengthened form (*apo*, "from," intensive; cf. Eng., "to choke off"), is used metaphorically, of "thorns crowding out seed sown and preventing its growth," Matt. 13:7; **Luke 8:7**. It is Luke's word for "suffocation by drowning," **Luke 8:33** (Cf. Mark 5:13).

8:8 And other fell on good ground, and sprang up, and bare fruit an hundredfold. And when he had said these things, he cried, He that hath ears to hear, let him hear.

Good *see Luke 1:53.*

Sprang *see* Sprung at *Luke 8:6.*

Bare *poieo* (4160), "to do," sometimes means "to produce, bear," **Luke 8:8; 13:9**; Jas. 3:12 (KJV, "bear," RV, "yield"); Rev. 22:2.

Hundredfold *hekatontaplasion* (1542), an adjective, denotes "a hundredfold," Mark 10:30; **Luke 8:8**; the best mss. have it in Matt. 19:29 for *pollaplasion*, "many times more." See the RV margin.

Cried *phoneo* (5455), "to utter a loud sound or cry," whether of animals, e.g., Matt. 26:34; or persons, **Luke 8:8; 16:24**; this is the word which Luke uses to describe the "cry" of the Lord at the close of His sufferings on the cross, **Luke 23:46**; also, e.g., Acts 16:28; Rev. 14:18.

8:9-10 And his disciples asked him, saying, What might this parable be?

And he said, Unto you it is given to know the mysteries of the kingdom of God: but to others in parables; that seeing they might not see, and hearing they might not understand.

Others *loipos* (3062), signifies "remaining, the rest." It is translated "other," or "others," e.g., in Matt. 25:11: Mark 4:19; **Luke 18:9; 24:10** (in v. 9, "the rest"); but in **Luke 8:10**; Acts 28:9; Rom. 1:13; 1 Cor. 9:5; Eph. 2:3; 1 Thess. 4:13; 5:6; 1 Tim. 5:20, e.g., the RV renders this word "the rest" (KJV, "other" or "others"); KJV, "other" in **Luke 18:11**; Acts 17:9; Rom. 1:13; 2 Cor. 12:13; 13:2; Gal. 2:13; Phil. 1:13; 4:3); the neut. plur., lit., "remaining things," is used in **Luke 12:26**; 1 Cor. 11:34; in Eph. 4:17, some mss. have *loipa*, neuter plural, KJV, "other (Gentiles)."

8:11 Now the parable is this: The seed is the word of God.

Seed *see Luke 8:5.*

8:12 Those by the way side are they that hear; then cometh the devil, and taketh away the word out of their hearts, lest they should believe and be saved.

Then *eita* (1534), denotes sequence (a) "of time, then, next," Mark 4:17, RV, "then"; 4:28, in some texts; 8:25, RV, "then" (KJV, "after that"); **Luke 8:12**; John 13:5; 19:27; 20:27; in some texts in 1 Cor. 12:28; 1 Cor. 15:5, 7, 24; 1 Tim. 2:13; 3:10; Jas. 1:15; (b) In argument, Heb. 12:9, "furthermore."

8:13 They on the rock *are they*, which, when they hear, receive the word with joy; and these have no root, which for a while believe, and in time of temptation fall away.

Rock *see Luke 6:48.*

Receive *see* Took at *Luke 2:28.*

Root *see Luke 3:9.*

While *chronos,* "time," is rendered "while" in **Luke 18:4**; John 7:33; 12:35 (1st part); 1 Cor. 16:7; *kairos,* "a season," "a while," **Luke 8:13**; in Acts 19:22, RV, "while" (KJV, "season"); for the different meanings of these words.

Temptation *see Luke 4:13.*

Fall away *see* Departed at *Luke 2:37.*

8:14 And that which fell among thorns are they, which, when they have heard, go forth, and are choked with cares and riches and pleasures of *this* life, and bring no fruit to perfection.

Go forth In **Luke 8:14**, KJV, *poreuomai,* "to go on one's way" (RV), is rendered "go forth"; in **13:33**, KJV, "walk" (RV, "go on my way"); in Matt. 24:1, KJV, it is rendered "departed" (RV, "was going on his way").

Choked *sumpnigo* (4846), gives the suggestion of "choking together" (*sun,* "with"), i.e., by crowding, Matt. 13:22; Mark 4:7, 19; **Luke 8:14**. It is used in **Luke 8:42**, of the crowd that thronged the Lord, almost, so to speak, to suffocation.

Cares *merimna* (3308), probably connected with *merizo,* "to draw in different directions, distract," hence signifies "that which causes this, a care, especially an anxious care," Matt. 13:22; Mark 4:19; **Luke 8:14**; **21:34**; 2 Cor. 11:28 (RV, "anxiety for"), 1 Pet. 5:7 (RV, "anxiety").

Riches *ploutos* (4149), is used in the singular (I) of material "riches," used evilly, Matt. 13:22; Mark 4:19; **Luke 8:14**; 1 Tim. 6:17; Jas. 5:2; Rev. 18:17; (II) of spiritual and moral "riches," (a) possessed by God and exercised towards men, Rom. 2:4, "of His goodness and forbearance and longsuffering"; 9:23 and Eph. 3:16, "of His glory" (i.e., of its manifestation in grace towards believers); Rom. 11:33, of His wisdom and knowledge; Eph. 1:7 and 2:7, "of His grace"; 1:18, "of the glory of His inheritance in the saints"; 3:8, "of Christ"; Phil. 4:19, "in glory in Christ Jesus," RV; Col. 1:27, "of the glory of this mystery ... Christ in you, the hope of glory"; (b) to be ascribed to Christ, Rev. 5:12; (c) of the effects of the gospel upon the Gentiles, Rom. 11:12 (twice); (d) of the full assurance of understanding in regard to the mystery of God, even Christ, Col. 2:2, RV; (e) of the liberality of the churches of Macedonia, 2 Cor. 8:2 (where "the riches" stands for the spiritual and moral value of their liberality); (f) of "the reproach of Christ" in contrast to this world's treasures, Heb. 11:26.

Pleasures *hedone* (2237), "pleasure," is used of the gratification of the natural desire or sinful desires (akin to *hedormai,* "to be glad," and *hedeos,* "gladly"), **Luke 8:14**; Titus 3:3; Jas. 4:1, 3, RV, "pleasures" (KJV, "lusts"); in the singular, 2 Pet. 2:13.

Life *bios* (979), (cf. Eng. words beginning with *bio*), is used in three respects (a) of "the period or duration of life," e.g., in the KJV of 1 Pet. 4:3, "the time past of our life" (the RV follows the mss. which omit "of our life"); **Luke 8:14**; 2 Tim. 2:4; (b) of "the manner of life, life in regard to its moral conduct," 1 Tim. 2:2; 1 John 2:16; (c) of "the means of life, livelihood, maintenance, living," Mark 12:44; **Luke 8:43**; **15:12**, **30**; **21:4**; 1 John 3:17, "goods," RV (KJV, "good").

Perfection *telesphoreo* (5052), "to bring to a completion" or "an end in view" (*telos,* "an end," *phero,* "to bear"), is said of plants, **Luke 8:14**.

8:15 But that on the good ground are they, which in an honest and good heart, having heard the word, keep *it*, and bring forth fruit with patience.

Good *kalos* (2570), denotes that which is intrinsically "good," and so, "goodly, fair, beautiful," as (a) of that which is well adapted to its circumstances or ends, e.g., fruit, Matt. 3:10; a tree, 12:33; ground, 13:8, 23; fish, 13:48; the Law, Rom. 7:16; 1 Tim. 1:8; every creature of God, 1 Tim. 4:4; a faithful minister of Christ and the doctrine he teaches, 4:6; (b) of that which is ethically good, right, noble, honorable e.g., Gal. 4:18; 1 Tim. 5:10, 25; 6:18; Titus 2:7, 14; 3:8, 14. The word does not occur in Revelation, nor indeed after 1 Peter. *Kalos* and *agathos* occur together in **Luke 8:15**, an "honest" (*kalos*) heart [*see* **Honest** at *Luke 8:15*], i.e., the attitude of which is right towards God; a "good" (*agathos*) heart, i.e., one that, instead of working ill to a neighbor, acts beneficially towards him. In Rom. 7:18, "in me ... dwelleth no good thing" (*agathos*) signifies that in him is nothing capable of doing "good," and hence he lacks the power "to do that which is good" (*kalos*). In 1 Thess. 5:15, "follow after that which is good" (*agathos*), the "good" is that which is beneficial; in v. 21, "hold fast that which is good (*kalos*)," the "good" describes the intrinsic value of the teaching.

Honest *kalos* (2570), "good,

admirable, becoming," has also the ethical meaning of what is "fair, right, honorable, of such conduct as deserves esteem"; it is translated "honest" [cf. Latin *honestus* (from *honos*, "honor")], which has the same double meaning as "honest" in the KJV, namely, regarded with honor, honorable, and bringing honor, becoming; in **Luke 8:15** (KJV and RV), "an honest and good (*agathos*) heart" [*see* **Good** at ***Luke 8:15***]; Rom. 12:17; 2 Cor. 8:21 and 13:7, RV, "honorable" (KJV, "honest"), of things which are regarded with esteem; in 1 Pet. 2:12, of behavior, RV, "seemly," KJV, "honest" (i.e., becoming).

Keep In **Luke 8:15** and 1 Cor. 11:2, *katecho*, "to hold fast" (a strengthened form of *echo*), is translated "hold fast," RV, KJV, "keep;" in 15:2, RV, "hold fast," KJV, "keep in memory."

Fruit *karpophoreo* (2592), "to bear or bring forth fruit," is used (a) in the natural sense, of the "fruit of the earth," Mark 4:28; (b) metaphorically, of conduct, or that which takes effect in conduct, Matt. 13:23; Mark 4:20; **Luke 8:15**; Rom. 7:4, 5 (the latter, of evil "fruit," borne "unto death," of activities resulting from a state of alienation from God); Col. 1:6 in the middle voice; Col. 1:10.

Patience *hupomone* (5281), lit., "an abiding under" (*hupo*, "under," *meno*, "to abide"), is almost invariably rendered "patience." "Patience, which grows only in trial, Jas. 1:3 may be passive, i.e., = "endurance," as, (a) in trials, generally, **Luke 21:19** (which is to be understood by Matt. 24:13), cf. Rom. 12:12; Jas. 1:12; (b) in trials incident to service in the gospel, 2 Cor. 6:4; 12:12; 2 Tim. 3:10; (c) under chastisement, which is trial viewed as coming from the hand of God our Father, Heb. 12:7; (d) under undeserved affliction, 1 Pet. 2:20; or active, i.e. = "persistence, perseverance," as (e) in well doing, Rom. 2:7 (KJV, "patient continuance"); (f) in fruit bearing, **Luke 8:15**; (g) in running the appointed race, Heb. 12:1.

"Patience perfects Christian character, Jas. 1:4, and fellowship in the patience of Christ is therefore the condition upon which believers are to be admitted to reign with Him, 2 Tim. 2:12; Rev. 1:9. For this patience believers are 'strengthened with all power,' Col. 1:11, 'through His Spirit in the inward man,' Eph. 3:16."

8:16 No man, when he hath lighted a candle, covereth it with a vessel, or putteth *it* under a bed; but setteth *it* on a candlestick, that they which enter in may see the light.

Lighted *hapto* is used of "lighting a lamp," in **Luke 8:16**; **11:33**; **15:8**.

Candle *luchnos* (3088), frequently mistranslated "candle," is a portable "lamp" usually set on a stand; the word is used literally, Matt. 5:15; Mark 4:21; **Luke 8:16**; **11:33, 36**; **15:8**; Rev. 18:23; 22:5; metaphorically, of Christ as the Lamb, Rev. 21:23, RV, "lamp" (KJV, "light"); of John the Baptist, John 5:35, RV, "the lamp" (KJV, "a ... light"); of the eye, Matt. 6:22, and **Luke 11:34**, RV, "lamp"; of spiritual readiness, **Luke 12:35**, RV, "lamps"; of "the word of prophecy," 2 Pet. 1:19, RV, "lamp."

Covereth *kalupto* (2572), signifies "to cover," Matt. 8:24; 10:26; **Luke 8:16**; **23:30**; Jas. 5:20 (RV); 1 Pet. 4:8; to veil, in 2 Cor. 4:3 (RV; KJV, "hid").

Vessel *skeuos* (4632), is used (a) of "a vessel or implement" of various kinds, Mark 11:16; **Luke 8:16**; John 19:29; Acts 10:11, 16; 11:5; 27:17 (a sail); Rom. 9:21; 2 Tim. 2:20; Heb. 9:21; Rev. 2:27; 18:12; (b) of "goods or household stuff," Matt. 12:29 and Mark 3:27, "goods"; **Luke 17:31**, RV, "goods" (KJV, "stuff"); (c) of "persons," (1) for the service of God, Acts 9:15, "a (chosen) vessel"; 2 Tim. 2:21, "a vessel (unto honor)"; (2) the "subjects" of divine wrath, Rom. 9:22; (3) the "subjects" of divine mercy, Rom. 9:23; (4) the human frame, 2 Cor. 4:7; perhaps 1 Thess. 4:4; (5) a husband and wife, 1 Pet. 3:7; of the wife, probably, 1 Thess. 4:4.

Putteth, Setteth *tithemi* (5087), "to place, lay, set, put," is translated "to put" in Matt. 5:15; 12:18; in Matt. 22:44, RV, "put (underneath Thy feet)"; Mark 4:21 (1st part), in the 2nd part, RV, "put" (KJV, "set"); 10:16, KJV (RV, "laying"); **Luke 8:16** (1st part); 2nd part, RV (KJV, "setteth"); **11:33**; John 19:19; Acts 1:7, KJV (RV, "set"); 4:3; 5:18, 25; 12:4; Rom. 14:13; 1 Cor. 15:25; 2 Cor. 3:13; 1 Tim. 1:12, KJV (RV, "appointing"); Rev. 11:9, KJV (RV, "laid").

Under *hupokato* (5270), an adverb signifying "under," is used as a preposition and rendered "under" in Mark 6:11; 7:28; **Luke 8:16**; Heb. 2:8; Rev. 5:3, 13; 6:9; 12:1; "underneath" in Matt. 22:44, RV (Mark 12:36 in some mss.); John 1:50, RV (KJV, "under").

Candlestick *luchnia* (3087), is mistranslated "candlestick" in every occurrence in the KJV and in certain places in the RV; the RV has "stand" in Matt. 5:15; Mark 4:21; **Luke 8:16**; **11:33**; "candlestick" in Heb. 9:2; Rev. 1:12, 13, 20 (twice); 2:1, 5; 11:4; the RV marg., gives "lampstands" in the passages in Rev., but not in Heb. 9:2.

Enter *eisporeuomai* (1531), "to go into," found only in the Synoptists and Acts, is translated "to enter," in the RV of Mark 1:21; 6:56; 11:2; **Luke**

8:16; **11:33** (KJV, "come in"); **19:30** (KJV, "at your entering"); **22:10**; in the following the RV has the verb "to go," for the KJV, "to enter," Matt. 15:17; Mark 5:40; 7:15, 18-19; in Acts 28:30, "went," KJV, "came"; in 9:28, RV, "going," KJV, "coming"; in the following both KJV and RV have the verb "to enter," Mark 4:19; **Luke 18:24** (in the best mss.); Acts 3:2; 8:3.

8:17 For nothing is secret, that shall not be made manifest; neither *any thing* hid, that shall not be known and come abroad.

Nothing *ou* (3756), "not," is translated "nothing" in **Luke 8:17**; **11:6**; 1 Cor. 9:16; 2 Cor. 8:15 (in each case, an absolute and direct negative).

Secret *kruptos* (2927), "secret, hidden" (akin to *krupto*, "to hide"), Eng., "crypt," "cryptic," etc., "hidden, secret," is translated "hid" in Matt. 10:26; Mark 4:22; **Luke 8:17**, RV, for KJV, "secret"; **12:2** (last part); in 1 Cor. 4:5, "hidden (things of darkness)"; 2 Cor. 4:2, "hidden (things of shame)"; 1 Pet. 3:4, "hidden (man of the heart)"; in the neuter, with *en*, "in," as an adverbial phrase, "in secret," with the article, Matt. 6:4, 6 (twice in each v.), without the article, John 7:4, 10; 18:20; in the neuter plural, with the article, "the secrets (of men)," Rom. 2:16; of the heart, 1 Cor. 14:25; in **Luke 11:33**, KJV, "a secret place" (RV, "cellar").

Manifest *phaneros* (5318), "open to sight, visible, manifest" (the root *phan*–, signifying "shining," exists also in *emphanes*), is translated "manifest" in **Luke 8:17**; Acts 4:16; 7:13, RV (KJV, "known"); Rom. 1:19; 1 Cor. 3:13; 11:19; 14:25; Gal. 5:19; Phil. 1:13; 1 Tim. 4:15 (KJV "appear"); 1 John 3:10.

Hid *apokruphos* (614), "hidden away from" (cf Eng., "apocryphal"), is translated, "made (KJV, kept) secret," in Mark 4:22; in **Luke 8:17**, RV, "secret," for KJV, "hid"; in Col. 2:3, RV, "hidden," KJV, "hid."

8:18 Take heed therefore how ye hear: for whosoever hath, to him shall be given; and whosoever hath not, from him shall be taken even that which he seemeth to have.

Heed *blepo* (991), "to look," see, usually implying more especially an intent, earnest contemplation, is rendered "take heed" in Matt. 24:4; Mark 4:24; 13:5, 9, 23, 33; **Luke 8:18**; **21:8**; 1 Cor. 3:10; 8:9; 10:12; Gal. 5:15; Col. 2:8 (KJV, "beware"); 4:17; Heb. 3:12.

Seemeth *see* **Seemed** at *Luke 1:3*.

8:19 Then came to him *his* mother and his brethren, and could not come at him for the press.

Came *suntunchano* (4940), "to meet with" (*sun*, "with," and *tunchano*, "to reach"), is rendered "to come at" in **Luke 8:19** (of the efforts of Christ's mother and brethren to get at Him through a crowd).

Press *ochlos* (3793), "a confused throng," is usually translated "multitude." The RV translates it "crowd" (KJV, "press" in some) in Matt. 9:23, 25; Mark 2:4; 3:9; 5:27, 30; **Luke 8:19**; **19:3**; Acts 21:34-35; 24:12, 18.

8:20-22 And it was told him *by certain* which said, Thy mother and thy brethren stand without, desiring to see thee.

And he answered and said unto them, My mother and my brethren are these which hear the word of God, and do it.

Now it came to pass on a certain day, that he went into a ship with his disciples: and he said unto them, Let us go over unto the other side of the lake. And they launched forth.

Certain *see Luke 5:12*.

Went *embaino*, "to enter," Matt. 13:2 and **Luke 8:22**, RV, "entered" (KJV, "went into"); in v. **37** (KJV, "went up into"); *apoluo*, "to set free," **Luke 23:22** and John 19:12, RV, "release" (KJV, "let ... go"); Acts 15:33, RV, "dismissed" (KJV, ditto); Acts 28:18, RV, "set at liberty" (KJV, ditto). *See also* **Entered** at *Luke 5:3*.

Side *peran* (4008), an adverb, signifying "beyond, on the other side," is used (a) as a preposition and translated "on the other side of," e.g., in Mark 5:1; **Luke 8:22**; John 6:1, RV; 6:22, 25; (b) as a noun with the article, e.g., Matt. 8:18, 28; 14:22; 16:5.

Lake *see Luke 5:1*.

Launched *anago* (321), "to bring up" (*ana*, "up," *ago*, "to lead"), is used in the middle voice as a nautical term signifying "to put to sea"; it is translated "launch forth" in **Luke 8:22**; "set sail" in Acts 13:13, RV (KJV, "loosed"); similarly in 16:11; in 18:21, for KJV, "sailed"; similarly in 20:3, 13; in 21:1, RV, "set sail," (KJV, "launched"), and in v. 2, for KJV, "set forth"; in 27:2 and 4 the RV has the verb "to put to sea," for KJV "to launch"; in v. 12 for KJV, "depart"; in v. 21, RV, "set sail" (KJV, "loosed"); in 28:10, 11, "sailed" and "set sail" (KJV, "departed").

8:23 But as they sailed he fell asleep: and there came down a storm of wind on the lake; and they were filled *with water*, and were in jeopardy.

Sailed *pleo* (4126), "to sail," occurs in **Luke 8:23**; Acts 21:3; 27:2, 6, 24; Rev. 18:17, RV, "saileth."

Asleep *aphupnoo* (879), "to fall asleep"

(*apo*, "away"), is used of natural "sleep," **Luke 8:23**, of the Lord's falling "asleep" in the boat on the lake of Galilee.

Came *sumpleroo* (4845), "to fill completely" (*sun*, "with," intensive), is used, in the passive voice, of time to be fulfilled or completed, **Luke 9:51**, "the days were well-nigh come"; Acts 2:1, "the day ... was now come" (KJV "was fully come"). In **Luke 8:23**, it is used in the active voice, of the filling of a boat in a storm.

Storm *lailaps* (2978), "a hurricane, whirlwind," is rendered "storm" in Mark 4:37; **Luke 8:23**; 2 Pet. 2:17, RV (KJV, "tempest").

Lake *see Luke 5:1.*

Filled *sumpleroo* (4845), "to fill completely," is used in the passive voice (a) of a boat filling with water, and, by metonymy, of the occupants themselves, **Luke 8:23** (RV, "were filling"); (b) of "fulfilling," with regard to time, "when the days were well-nigh come," RV, for KJV, "when the time was come" (RV, marg., "were being fulfilled"), **Luke 9:51**; Acts 2:1, see RV, marg. In the Sept., Jer. 25:12.

Jeopardy *kinduneuo* (2793), properly signifies "to run a risk, face danger," but is used in the NT in the sense of "being in danger, jeopardy," Acts 19:27, 40. It is translated "were in jeopardy" in **Luke 8:23**, and "stand we in jeopardy," 1 Cor. 15:30.

8:24 And they came to him, and awoke him, saying, Master, master, we perish. Then he arose, and rebuked the wind and the raging of the water: and they ceased, and there was a calm.

Awoke *diegeiro* (1326), is used of "awaking from natural sleep," Matt. 1:24; Mark 4:38; of the act of the disciples in "awaking" the Lord, **Luke 8:24** (cf. *egeiro*, in Matt. 8:25); metaphorically, "of arousing the mind," 2 Pet. 1:13; 3:1.

Master *see Luke 5:5.*

Rebuked *see Luke 4:35.*

Raging *kludon* (2830), "a billow, surge" (akin to *kluzo*, "to wash over," said of the sea; cf. *kludonizomai*, "to be tossed by the waves," Eph. 4:14), is translated "raging" in **Luke 8:24**; in Jas. 1:6, RV, "surge" (KJV, "wave").

Ceased *see* **Left** at *Luke 5:4.*

Calm *galene* (1055), primarily signifies "calmness, cheerfulness" (from a root *gal–*, from which *gelao*, "to smile," is also derived, hence the "calm" of the sea, the smiling ocean being a favorite metaphor of the poets), Matt. 8:26; Mark 4:39; **Luke 8:24**.

8:25 And he said unto them, Where is your faith? And they being afraid wondered, saying one to another, What manner of man is this! for he commandeth even the winds and water, and they obey him.

Wondered *see* **Marvelled** at *Luke 2:33.*

Manner In **Luke 24:17**, KJV, the pronoun *tis*, "who, what," in the plural (RV, "what") is translated "what manner of"; similarly, in the singular in Mark 4:41; **Luke 8:25** (RV, "who"), John 7:36.

Commandeth *see Luke 4:36.*

Obey *hupakouo* (5219), "to listen, attend" (as in Acts 12:13), and so, "to submit, to obey," is used of "obedience" (a) to God, Heb. 5:9; 11:8; (b) to Christ, by natural elements, Matt. 8:27; Mark 1:27; 4:41; **Luke 8:25**; (c) to disciples of Christ, **Luke 17:6**; (d) to the faith, Acts 6:7; the gospel, Rom. 10:16; 2 Thess. 1:8; Christian doctrine, Rom. 6:17 (as to a form or mold of teaching); (e) to apostolic injunctions, Phil. 2:12; 2 Thess. 3:14; (f) to Abraham by Sarah, 1 Pet. 3:6; (g) to parents by children, Eph. 6:1; Col. 3:20; (h) to masters by servants, Eph. 6:5; Col. 3:22; (i) to sin, Rom. 6:12; (j) in general, Rom. 6:16.

8:26 And they arrived at the country of the Gadarenes, which is over against Galilee.

Arrived *katapleo* (2668), denotes "to sail down" (*kata*, "down," *pleo*, "to sail"), i.e., from the high sea to the shore, **Luke 8:26**.

Country *see Luke 2:8.*

8:27 And when he went forth to land, there met him out of the city a certain man, which had devils long time, and ware no clothes, neither abode in *any* house, but in the tombs.

Met *hupantao* (5221), "to go to meet, to meet," is used in Matt. 8:28; **Luke 8:27**; John 11:20, 30, and, in the most authentic mss., in Matt. 28:9; Mark 5:2; **Luke 14:31** (of meeting in battle); John 4:51; 12:18 and Acts 16:16.

Devils *see Luke 4:41.*

Long *hikanos* (2425), "sufficient, much, long," is used with *chronos*, "time," in **Luke 8:27**; in **20:9** and **23:8** (KJV, "season") the plural is used, lit., "long times"; Acts 8:11; 14:3.

Time *see Luke 4:5.*

Ware *endidusko* (1737), "to put on," is used in the active voice in Mark 15:17 (in good mss.); in **Luke 8:27** (middle voice), in some texts. For **Luke 16:19**. *Enduo* (1746), (Eng., "endue"), signifies "to enter into, get into," as into clothes, "to put on," e.g., Mark 1:6; **Luke 8:27** (in the best mss.); **24:49** (KJV, "endued"); 2 Cor. 5:3; Rev. 1:13; 19:14.

Tombs *mnema* (3418), signified "a memorial" or "record of a thing or a dead person," then "a sepulchral monument," and hence "a tomb"; it is rendered "graves" in the KJV of Rev. 11:9 (RV, "a tomb"); "tomb" or "tombs," Mark 5:3, 5 (some mss. have *mnemeion*, as in 15:46, KJV, "sepulchre") and 16:2 (KJV, "sepulchre"); **Luke 8:27**; Acts 2:29 and 7:16 (KJV, "sepulchre").

8:28 When he saw Jesus, he cried out, and fell down before him, and with a loud voice said, What have I to do with thee, Jesus, *thou* Son of God most high? I beseech thee, torment me not.

Cried *see Luke 4:33.*

Fell *see Luke 5:8.*

Have *see Luke 4:34.*

High *see* **Highest** at *Luke 1:32.*

Torment *basanizo* (928), is translated "to torment," (a) of sickness, Matt. 8:6; (b) of the doom of evil spirits, Mark 5:7; **Luke 8:28**; (c) of retributive judgments upon impenitent mankind at the close of this age, Rev. 9:5; 11:10; (d) upon those who worship the Beast and his image and receive the mark of his name, 14:10; (e) of the doom of Satan and his agents, 20:10.

8:29 (For he had commanded the unclean spirit to come out of the man. For oftentimes it had caught him: and he was kept bound with chains and in fetters; and he brake the bands, and was driven of the devil into the wilderness.)

Commanded *parangello* (3853), "to announce beside" (*para*, "beside," *angello*, "to announce"), "to pass on an announcement," hence denotes "to give the word, order, give a charge, command", e.g., Mark 6:8; **Luke 8:29**; **9:21**; Acts 5:28; 2 Thess. 3:4, 6, 10, 12.

Oftentimes In **Luke 8:29**, the phrase *pollois chronois*, lit., "many times," is translated "oftentimes" (RV marg., "of a long time").

Caught *sunarpazo* (4884), *sun*, used intensively, and *harpazo*, "to snatch, to seize, to keep a firm grip of," is used only by Luke, and translated "caught" in the KJV of **Luke 8:29**, of demon-possession; in Acts 6:12, of the act of the elders and scribes in seizing Stephen, RV, more suitably, "seized." So in Acts 19:29. In 27:15, it is used of the effects of wind upon a ship.

Kept *phulasso* (5442), "to guard, watch, keep," is rendered by the verb "to guard" in the RV (KJV, "to keep") of **Luke 11:21**; John 17:12; Acts 12:4; 28:16; 2 Thess. 3:3; 1 Tim. 6:20; 2 Tim. 1:12, 14; 1 John 5:21; Jude 24. In **Luke 8:29**, "was kept under guard, RV (KJV, kept). *See also* **Keeping** at *Luke 2:8.*

Bound *desmeuo* or *desmeo* (1195), signifies "to put in fetters or any kind of bond," **Luke 8:29**; Acts 22:4, or "to bind a burden upon a person," Matt. 23:4.

Chains *halusis* (254), denotes "a chain or bond for binding the body, or any part of it (the hands or feet)." Some derive the word from *a*, negative, and *luo*, "to loose," i.e., "not to be loosed"; others from a root connected with a word signifying "to restrain." It is used in Mark 5:3-4; **Luke 8:29**; Acts 12:6-7; 21:33; 28:20; Eph. 6:20; 2 Tim. 1:16; Rev. 20:1.

Fetters *pede* (3976), "a fetter" (akin to *peza*, "the instep," and *pous*, "a foot"; cf. Eng. prefix *ped-*), occurs in Mark 5:4 and **Luke 8:29**.

Brake *see Luke 5:6.*

Bands *desmos* (1199), from *deo*, "to bind", is usually found in the plural, either masculine or neuter; (a) it stands thus for the actual "bonds" which bind a prisoner, as in **Luke 8:29**; Acts 16:26; 20:23 (the only three places where the neuter plural is used); 22:30; (b) the masculine plural stands frequently in a figurative sense for "a condition of imprisonment," Phil. 1:7, 13, i.e., "so that my captivity became manifest as appointed for the cause of Christ"; verses 14, 16; Col. 4:18; 2 Tim. 2:9; Philem. 10, 13; Heb. 10:34. In Mark 7:35 "the bond (KJV, string)" stands metaphorically for "the infirmity which caused an impediment in his speech." So in **Luke 13:16**, of the infirmity of the woman who was bowed together.

Driven *elauno* (1643), signifies "to drive, impel, urge on." It is used of "rowing," Mark 6:48 and John 6:19; of the act of a demon upon a man, **Luke 8:29**; of the power of winds upon ships, Jas. 3:4; and of storms upon mists, 2 Pet. 2:17, KJV, "carried," RV, "driven."

Wilderness *see Luke 5:16.*

8:30 And Jesus asked him, saying, What is thy name? And he said, Legion: because many devils were entered into him.

Legion *legion* (3003), otherwise spelled *legeon*, "a legion," occurs in Matt. 26:53, of angels; in Mark 5:9, 15, and **Luke 8:30**, of demons. Among the Romans a "legion" was primarily a chosen (*lego*, "to choose") body of soldiers divided into ten cohorts, and numbering from 4,200 to 6,000 men (Gk. *speira*). In the time of our Lord it formed a complete army of infantry and cavalry, of upwards of 5,000 men. The "legions" were not brought into Judea till the outbreak of the Jewish war (AD 66), as they were previously employed in the frontier provinces of the Empire. Accordingly in its NT use the word has its other and more general significance "of a large number."

8:31 And they besought him that he would not command them to go out into the deep.

Besought *parakaleo* (3870), "to beseech, comfort, exhort," is rendered by the verb "to intreat" in **Luke 8:31**, RV, "intreated" (KJV, "besought"); **15:28**; Acts 9:38, RV, "intreating" (KJV, "desiring"); 28:20, RV (KJV, "called for"); 1 Cor. 4:13; 2 Cor. 9:5, RV (KJV, "exhort"); 10:1, RV (KJV, "beseech"); 1 Tim. 5:1, KJV (RV, "exhort").

Command *see* Commandeth at *Luke 4:36*.

Deep *abussos* (12), "bottomless" (from *a*, intensive, and *bussos*, "a depth"; akin to *bathus*, "deep"; Eng., "bath"), is used as a noun denoting the abyss (KJV, "bottomless pit"). It describes an immeasurable depth, the underworld, the lower regions, the abyss of Sheol. In Rom. 10:7, quoted from Deut. 30:13, the abyss (the abode of the lost dead) is substituted for the sea (the change in the quotation is due to the facts of the death and resurrection of Christ); the KJV has "deep" here and in **Luke 8:31**; the reference is to the lower regions as the abode of demons, out of which they can be let loose, Rev. 11:7; 17:8, it is found seven times in Revelation, 9:1-2, 11; 11:7; 17:8; 20:1, 3; in 9:1, 2 the RV has "the pit of the abyss."

8:32 And there was there an herd of many swine feeding on the mountain: and they besought him that he would suffer them to enter into them. And he suffered them.

Herd *agele* (34), from *ago*, "to lead," is used, in the NT, only of swine, Matt. 8:30, 31, 32; Mark 5:11, 13; **Luke 8:32, 33**.

Many *hikanos* (2425), "sufficient," when used of number sometimes signifies "many," suggesting a sufficient number, (a) with nouns, **Luke 8:32**; **23:9**; Acts 9:23, 43; 20:8; 27:7; (b) absolutely, some noun being understood, e.g., Acts 12:12; 14:21; 19:19; 1 Cor. 11:30.

Swine *choiros* (5519), "a swine," is used in the plural, in the Synoptic Gospels only, Matt. 7:6; 8:30, 31, 32; Mark 5:11, 13, 16; **Luke 8:32, 33**; **Luke 15:15, 16**. It does not occur in the OT.

Feeding *bosko* (1006), "to feed," is primarily used of a herdsman (from *boo*, "to nourish," the special function being to provide food; the root is *bo*, found in *boter*, "a herdsman or herd," and *botane*, "fodder, pasture"), its uses are (a) literal, Matt. 8:30; in v. 33, the RV corrects the KJV, "they that kept," to "they that fed," as in Mark. 5:14 (KJV and RV) and **Luke 8:34**; in Mark 5:11 and **Luke 8:32**, "feeding"; **Luke 15:15**; (b) metaphorical, of spiritual ministry, John 21:15, 17.

Suffer *epitrepo* (2010), lit. denotes "to turn to" (*epi*, "upon, to," *trepo*, "to turn"), and so (a) "to commit, entrust" (not in NT); (b) "to permit, give leave, send," of Christ's permission to the unclean spirits to enter the swine, Mark 5:13; in **Luke 8:32**, RV, "give ... leave," "gave ... leave" (KJV, "suffer" and "suffered"); in John 19:38, of Pilate's permission to Joseph to take away the body of the Lord; in Acts 21:39, of Paul's request to the chief captain to permit him to address the people, RV, "give ... leave" (for KJV, "suffer"); in 21:40, "he had given him leave" (KJV, "... licence"); (c) In the sense of taking leave of, bidding farewell to.

8:33 Then went the devils out of the man, and entered into the swine: and the herd ran violently down a steep place into the lake, and were choked.

Swine *see Luke 8:32*.

Herd *see Luke 8:32*.

Ran *hormao*, "to set in motion, urge on," but intransitively, "to hasten on, rush," is always translated "to rush" in the RV; KJV, "ran violently," Matt. 8:32; Mark 5:13; **Luke 8:33**; "ran," Acts 7:57; "rushed", 19:29.

Steep *kremnos* (2911), "a steep bank" (akin to *kremannumi*, "to hang"), occurs in Matt. 8:32; Mark 5:13; **Luke 8:33**, RV, "the steep" (KJV, "a steep place"). In the Sept., 2 Chron. 25:12.

Lake *see Luke 5:1*.

Choked *see Luke 8:7*.

8:34 When they that fed *them* saw what was done, they fled, and went and told *it* in the city and in the country.

Fed *see* Feeding at *Luke 8:32*.

Country *agros* (68), denotes "a field, especially a cultivated field"; hence, "the country" in contrast to the town (Eng., "agrarian, agriculture"), e.g., Mark 5:14, 6:36; 15:21; 16:12; **Luke 8:34**; **9:12** (plural, lit., "fields"); **23:26**; a piece of ground, e.g., Mark 10:29; Acts 4:37.

8:35 Then they went out to see what was done; and came to Jesus, and found the man,

out of whom the devils were departed, sitting at the feet of Jesus, clothed, and in his right mind: and they were afraid.

Clothed *himatizo* (2439), means "to put on raiment," Mark 5:15; **Luke 8:35.**

Mind *sophroneo* (4993), signifies (a) "to be of sound mind," or "in one's right mind, sober-minded" (*sozo*, "to save," *phren*, "the mind"), Mark 5:15 and **Luke 8:35**, "in his right mind"; 2 Cor. 5:13, RV, "we are of sober mind" (KJV, "we be sober"); (b) "to be temperate, self-controlled," Titus 2:6, "to be sober-minded"; 1 Pet. 4:7, RV, "be ye ... of sound mind" (KJV, "be ye sober"). See also Rom. 12:3.

8:36 They also which saw *it* told them by what means he that was possessed of the devils was healed.

Means *pos* (4459), an interrogative adverb, "how, in what way," **Luke 8:36**, KJV, "by what means," RV, "how"; so John 9:21.

Possessed of the devils *daimonizomai* (1139), signifies "to be possessed of a demon, to act under the control of a demon." Those who were thus afflicted expressed the mind and consciousness of the "demon" or "demons" indwelling them, e.g., **Luke 8:28**. The verb is found chiefly in Matt. and Mark; Matt. 4:24; 8:16, 28, 33; 9:32; 12:22; 15:22; Mark 1:32; 5:15-16, 18; elsewhere in **Luke 8:36** and John 10:21, "him that hath a devil (demon)."

Healed *sozo* (4982), "to save," is translated by the verb "to heal" in the KJV of Mark 5:23 and **Luke 8:36** (RV, "to make whole"; so KJV frequently); the idea is that of saving from disease and its effects.

8:37 Then the whole multitude of the country of the Gadarenes round about besought him to depart from them; for they were taken with great fear: and he went up into the ship, and returned back again.

Multitude *see Luke 1:10.*

Country *see Luke 3:3.*

Besought *see Luke 4:38.*

Taken *see Luke 4:38.*

Went *see Luke 8:22. See also* Entered at *Luke 5:3.*

Returned *see Luke 1:56.*

8:38 Now the man out of whom the devils were departed besought him that he might be with him: but Jesus sent him away, saying,

Might The phrases "may be," "might be," are frequently the rendering of the verb "to be," in the subjunctive or optative moods, preceded by a conjunction introducing a condition, or expressing a wish or purpose, e.g., Matt. 6:4; John 14:3; 17:11. Sometimes the phrase translates simply the infinitive mood of the verb *eimi*, "to be," e.g., **Luke 8:38**, lit., "to be (with Him)"; so the RV in 2 Cor. 5:9; in 2 Cor. 9:5, "that (the same) might be," lit., "(the same) to be."

Sent *apoluo* (630), "to set free, to let go," is translated "to send away" in Matt. 14:15, 22, 23; Mark 6:36, 45; 8:3, 9; **Luke 8:38**; Acts 13:3, where the "sending" is not that of commissioning, but of letting go, intimating that they would gladly have retained them (contrast *ekpempo*, the act of commissioning by the Holy Spirit in v. 4).

8:39 Return to thine own house, and shew how great things God hath done unto thee. And he went his way, and published throughout the whole city how great things Jesus had done unto him.

Shew *diegeomai* (1334), "to conduct a narration through to the end" (*dia*, "through," intensive, *hegeomai*, "to lead"), hence denotes "to recount, to relate in full," Mark 5:16; **Luke 8:39; 9:10**; Acts 8:33; 9:27; 12:17; in Mark 9:9 and Heb. 11:32, "tell.

Great *hosos* (3745), "how much, how many," is used in the neuter plural to signify how great things, Mark 5:19, 20; **Luke 8:39** (twice); Acts 9:16, KJV (RV, "how many things"); in Rev. 21:16 (in the best mss.), "as great as," RV (KJV, "as large as," said of length).

Published *kerusso* (2784), "to be a herald, to proclaim, preach," is translated "to publish" in Mark 1:45; 5:20; 7:36; 13:10, KJV (RV, "preached"); **Luke 8:39.**

Jesus *see* Lord at *Luke 5:8.*

8:40 And it came to pass, that, when Jesus was returned, the people *gladly* received him: for they were all waiting for him.

Received *apodechomai* (588), "to welcome, to accept gladly" (*apo*, "from"), "to receive without reserve," is used (a) literally, **Luke 8:40**, RV, "welcomed"; **9:11** (in the best texts); Acts 18:27; 21:17; 28:30; (b) metaphorically, Acts 2:41; 24:3, "we accept," in the sense of acknowledging, the term being used in a tone of respect.

Waiting *see* Waited at *Luke 1:21.*

8:41 And, behold, there came a man named Jairus, and he was a ruler of the synagogue: and he fell down at Jesus' feet, and besought him that he would come into his house:

Man *see Luke 5:8.*

Was *see Luke 7:6.*

Ruler *archon* (758), the present participle of the verb *archo*, "to rule"; denotes "a ruler, a prince." It is used as follows ("p" denoting "prince," or "princes"; "r," "ruler" or "rulers"): (a) of Christ, as "the Ruler (KJV, Prince) of the kings of the earth," Rev. 1:5; (b) of rulers of nations, Matt. 20:25, RV, "r," KJV, "p"; Acts 4:26, "r"; 7:27, "r"; 7:35, "r" (twice); (c) of judges and magistrates, Acts 16:19, "r"; Rom. 13:3, "r"; (d) of members of the Sanhedrin, **Luke 14:1**, RV, "r" (KJV, "chief"); **23:13, 35**, "r"; so **24:20**, John 3:1; 7:26, 48; 12:42, RV, "r" (KJV, "chief r."); "r" in Acts 3:17; 4:5, 8; 13:27; 14:5; (e) of rulers of synagogues, Matt. 9:18, 23, "r"; so **Luke 8:41**; **18:18**; (f) of the Devil, as "prince" of this world, John 12:31; 14:30; 16:11; of the power of the air, Eph. 2:2, "the air" being that sphere in which the inhabitants of the world live and which, through the rebellious and godless condition of humanity, constitutes the seat of his authority; (g) of Beelzebub, the "prince" of the demons, Matt. 9:24; 12:24; Mark 3:22; **Luke 11:15**.

Synagogue In **Luke 8:41**, "ruler of the synagogue" represents *archon*, "ruler," followed by the genitive case of the article and *sunagoge*.

8:42 For he had one only daughter, about twelve years of age, and she lay a dying. But as he went the people thronged him.

Only *see Luke 7:12.*

Thronged *sumpnigo* (4846), "to choke," is used of "thronging" by a crowd, **Luke 8:42**. *See also* Choked at *Luke 8:14.*

8:43 And a woman having an issue of blood twelve years, which had spent all her living upon physicians, neither could be healed of any,

Issue *rhusis* (4511), "a flowing" (akin to *rheo*, "to flow"), "an issue," is used in Mark 5:25; **Luke 8:43, 44**.

Blood In Mark 5:25 and **Luke 8:43**, different constructions are used, the translations respectively being "having a flowing of blood" and "being in (i.e., with) a flowing of blood."

Spent *prosanalisko* (4321), "to spend besides," a strengthened form of *analisko*, "to expend, consume", occurs in most texts in **Luke 8:43**.

Living *see* Life at *Luke 8:14.*

Physicians *see* Physician at *Luke 4:23.*

8:44 Came behind *him*, and touched the border of his garment: and immediately her issue of blood stanched.

Behind *opisthen* (3693), "behind," is used only of place, e.g., Matt. 9:20; Mark 5:27; **Luke 8:44**; Rev. 4:6; as a preposition, Matt. 15:23 ("after"), and **Luke 23:26**; in Rev. 5:1, RV, "on the back"; KJV, "backside."

Border *kraspedon* (2899), was primarily "the extremity or prominent part of a thing, an edge"; hence "the fringe of a garment, or a little fringe," hanging down from the edge of the mantle or cloak. The Jews had these attached to their mantles to remind them of the Law, according to Num. 15:38-39; Deut. 22:12; Zech. 8:23. This is the meaning in Matt. 23:5. In Matt. 9:20; 14:36; Mark 6:56; **Luke 8:44**, it is used of the border of Christ's garment (KJV "hem," in the first two places).

Immediately *see Luke 1:64.*

Issue *see Luke 8:43.*

Stanched *histemi* (2476), transitively, "to cause to stand," is used intransitively ("to stand still") in **Luke 8:44**, translated "stanched."

8:45 And Jesus said, Who touched me? When all denied, Peter and they that were with him said, Master, the multitude throng thee and press *thee*, and sayest thou, Who touched me?

Master *see Luke 5:5.*

Throng *sunecho* (4912), for the significance of this in Acts 18:5, "was constrained by the word," RV, i.e., Paul felt the urge of the word of his testimony to the Jews in Corinth. It is used with *apothlibo* in **Luke 8:45**, RV, "press" (KJV, "throng"). *See also* Taken at *Luke 4:38.*

Press *apothlibo* (598), a strengthened form of *thlibo*, "to throng" (*apo*, intensive), is used in **Luke 8:45**, RV, "crush," for KJV, "press," of the multitude who were pressing around Christ (cf. the preceding word *sunecho*, "to press"). In the Sept., Num. 22:25.

8:46 And Jesus said, Somebody hath touched me: for I perceive that virtue is gone out of me.

Somebody *see* Somewhat at *Luke 7:40.*

Virtue *see Luke 6:19.*

8:47 And when the woman saw that she was not hid, she came trembling, and falling down before him, she declared unto him before all the people for what cause she had touched him, and how she was healed immediately.

Hid *lanthano* (2990), "to escape notice, to be hidden from," is rendered "(could not) be hid" in Mark 7:24, of Christ; "was (not) hid," **Luke 8:47**, of the woman with the issue of blood; "is hidden," Acts 26:26, of the facts concerning Christ; the sentence might be rendered "none of these things has escaped the king's notice."

Trembling *tremo* (5141), "to tremble, especially with fear," is used in Mark 5:33; **Luke 8:47** (Acts 9:6, in some mss.); 2 Pet. 2:10, RV, "they tremble (not)," KJV, "they are (not) afraid."

Falling *see* Fell at *Luke 5:8*.

Declared *apangello* (518), signifies "to announce or report from a person or place" (*apo*, "from"); hence, "to declare, publish"; it is rendered "declare" in **Luke 8:47**; Heb. 2:12; 1 John 1:3. It is very frequent in the Gospels and Acts; elsewhere, other than the last two places mentioned, only in 1 Thess. 1:9 and 1 John 1:2.

Immediately *see Luke 1:64*.

8:48 And he said unto her, Daughter, be of good comfort: thy faith hath made thee whole; go in peace.

Comfort *tharseo* (2293), "to be of good courage, of good cheer" (*tharsos*, "courage, confidence"), is used only in the imperative mood, in the NT; "be of good cheer," Matt. 9:2, 22; 14:27; Mark 6:50; 10:49; **Luke 8:48**; John 16:33; Acts 23:11.

Made ... whole *sozo* (4982), "to save," is used (as with the noun *soteria*, "salvation") (a) of material and temporal deliverance from danger, suffering, etc., e.g., Matt. 8:25; Mark 13:20; **Luke 23:35**; John 12:27; 1 Tim. 2:15; 2 Tim. 4:18 (KJV, "preserve"); Jude 5; from sickness, Matt. 9:22, "made ... whole" (RV, marg., "saved"); so Mark 5:34; **Luke 8:48**; Jas. 5:15; (b) of the spiritual and eternal salvation granted immediately by God to those who believe on the Lord Jesus Christ, e.g., Acts 2:47, RV "(those that) were being saved"; 16:31; Rom. 8:24, RV, "were we saved"; Eph. 2:5, 8; 1 Tim. 2:4; 2 Tim. 1:9; Titus 3:5; of human agency in this, Rom. 11:14; 1 Cor. 7:16; 9:22; (c) of the present experiences of God's power to deliver from the bondage of sin, e.g., Matt. 1:21; Rom. 5:10; 1 Cor. 15:2; Heb. 7:25; Jas. 1:21; 1 Pet. 3:21; of human agency in this, 1 Tim. 4:16; (d) of the future deliverance of believers at the second coming of Christ for His saints, being deliverance from the wrath of God to be executed upon the ungodly at the close of this age and from eternal doom, e.g., Rom. 5:9; (e) of the deliverance of the nation of Israel at the second advent of Christ, e.g., Rom. 11:26; (f) inclusively for all the blessings bestowed by God on men in Christ, e.g., **Luke 19:10**; John 10:9; 1 Cor. 10:33; 1 Tim. 1:15; (g) of those who endure to the end of the time of the Great Tribulation, Matt. 10:22; Mark 13:13; (h) of the individual believer, who, though losing his reward at the judgment seat of Christ hereafter, will not lose his salvation, 1 Cor. 3:15; 5:5; (i) of the deliverance of the nations at the Millennium, Rev. 21:24 (in some mss.).

Peace *see Luke 1:79*.

8:49 While he yet spake, there cometh one from the ruler of the synagogue's *house*, saying to him, Thy daughter is dead; trouble not the Master.

Ruler of the synangogue *archisunagogos* (752), denotes "the administrative official," with the duty of preserving order and inviting persons to read or speak in the assembly, Mark 5:22, 35, 36, 38; **Luke 8:49**; **13:14**; Acts 13:15; "chief ruler" (KJV) in Acts 18:8, 17.

Trouble *see Luke 7:6*.

Master *see* Doctors at *Luke 2:46*.

8:50-51 But when Jesus heard *it*, he answered him, saying, Fear not: believe only, and she shall be made whole.

And when he came into the house, he suffered no man to go in, save Peter, and James, and John, and the father and the mother of the maiden.

Suffered *aphiemi* (863), "to send away," signifies "to permit, suffer," in Matt. 3:15 (twice); Matt. 19:14; 23:13; Mark 1:34; 5:19, 37; 10:14; 11:16; **Luke 8:51**; **12:39**, KJV (RV, "left"); **18:16**; John 12:7, RV, KJV and RV marg., "let (her) alone"; Rev. 11:9.

Go in *eiserchomai* (1525), "to come into" (*eis*, "in," *erchomai*, "to come"), is frequently rendered "entered" in the RV for KJV, "went into," e.g., Matt. 9:25; 21:12; or "go in," e.g., Matt. 7:13; **Luke 8:51**; "go," **Luke 18:25**; "was coming in," Acts 10:25.

Maiden *pais* (3816), "a child," denotes "a maid" or "maiden" in **Luke 8:51** and **54**, RV, "maiden in both places."

8:52 And all wept, and bewailed her: but he said, Weep not; she is not dead, but sleepeth.

Wept *see* Weep at *Luke 7:13*.

Bewailed *kopto* (2875), primarily, "to beat, smite"; then, "to cut off," Matt. 21:8; Mark 11:8, is used in the middle voice, of beating oneself, beating the breast, as a token of grief; hence, "to bewail," Matt. 11:17 (RV, "mourn," for KJV, "lament"); 24:30, "mourn"; Rev. 1:7 (RV, "mourn"; KJV, "wail"); in **Luke 8:52**; **23:27** "bewail"; in Rev. 18:9, "wail" (for KJV, "lament"). Cf. *kopetos*, "lamentation," Acts 8:2.

Sleepeth *katheudo* (2518), "to go to sleep," is chiefly used of natural "sleep," and is found most frequently in the Gospels, especially Matthew and Luke. With reference to death it is found in the Lord's remark concerning Jairus' daughter, Matt. 9:24; Mark 5:39; **Luke 8:52**. In the epistles of Paul it is used as follows: (a) of natural "sleep," e.g., 1 Thess. 5:7; (b) of carnal indifference to spiritual things on the part of believers, Eph. 5:14; 1 Thess. 5:6, 10 (as in Mark 13:36), a condition of insensibility to divine things involving conformity to the world (cf. *hupnos*).

8:53 And they laughed him to scorn, knowing that she was dead.

Laughed *katagelao* (2606), denotes "to laugh scornfully at," and signifies derisive laughter, Matt. 9:24; Mark 5:40; **Luke 8:53**. Cf. *ekmukterizo*, "to deride."

8:54 And he put them all out, and took her by the hand, and called, saying, Maid, arise.

Put *ekballo* (1544), "to cast out," is translated "to put forth or out" in Matt. 9:25; Mark 5:40 (**Luke 8:54** in some mss.); John 10:4; Acts 9:40.

Took *krateo* (2902), "to take hold of, get possession of," is translated "to take" in Matt. 9:25; 22:6; 26:4; Mark 1:31; 5:41; 9:27; 14:1, 44, 46, 49; **Luke 8:54**; Acts 24:6.

Maid *see* **Maiden** at *Luke 8:51*.

8:55 And her spirit came again, and she arose straightway: and he commanded to give her meat.

Spirit *see Luke 1:17. See also* **Soul** at *Luke 1:46*.

Came again *see* **Returned** at *Luke 2:39*.

Straightway *see* **Immediately** at *Luke 1:64*.

Commanded *diatasso* (1299), signifies "to set in order, appoint, command," Matt. 11:1; **Luke 8:55**; **17:9-10**; Acts 18:2; 23:31; "gave order," 1 Cor. 16:1, RV. So in Acts 24:23, where it is in the middle voice.

Meat *phago* (5315), "to eat," is used as a noun, in the infinitive mood, and translated "meat" in Matt. 25:35, 42 (lit., "to eat"); in **Luke 8:55** the RV translates it literally, "to eat" (KJV, "meat").

8:56 And her parents were astonished: but he charged them that they should tell no man what was done.

Charged *see Luke 5:14*.

Chapter 9

9:1 Then he called his twelve disciples together, and gave them power and authority over all devils, and to cure diseases.

Called *sunkaleo* (4779), signifies "to call together," Mark 15:16; **Luke 9:1**; **15:6**, **9**; **23:13**; Acts 5:21; 10:24; 28:17.

Cure *see* **Cured** at *Luke 7:21*.

Diseases *see Luke 4:40*.

9:2 And he sent them to preach the kingdom of God, and to heal the sick.

Preach *see Luke 4:18*.

Heal *see Luke 4:18*.

Sick *asthenes* (772), lit., "without strength," hence, "feeble, weak," is used of "bodily debility," Matt. 25:43, 44; some texts have it in **Luke 9:2** (the best omit it, the meaning being "to heal" in general); **10:9**; Acts 5:15, 16; in 4:9 it is rendered "impotent." *See also Luke 4:40*.

9:3 And he said unto them, Take nothing for *your* journey, neither staves, nor scrip, neither bread, neither money; neither have two coats apiece.

Journey *see Luke 2:44*.

Staves *rhabdos* (4464), "a staff, rod, scepter," is used (a) of Aaron's "rod," Heb. 9:4; (b) a staff used on a journey, Matt. 10:10, RV, "staff" (KJV, "staves"); so **Luke 9:3**; Mark 6:8, "staff"; Heb. 11:21, "staff"; (c) a ruler's staff, a "scepter," Heb. 1:8 (twice); elsewhere a "rod," Rev. 2:27; 12:5; 19:15; (d) a "rod" for chastisement (figuratively), 1 Cor. 4:21; (e) a measuring rod, Rev. 11:1.

Scrip *pera* (4082), "a traveler's leather bag or pouch for holding provisions," is translated "wallet" in the RV (KJV, "scrip"), Matt. 10:10; Mark 6:8; **Luke 9:3**; **10:4**; **22:35**, **36**. Deissmann (*Light from the Ancient East*) regards it as an alms-bag.

Money *argurion* (694), properly, "a piece of silver," denotes (a) "silver," e.g., Acts 3:6; (b) a "silver coin," often in the plural, "pieces of silver," e.g., Matt. 26:15; so 28:12, where the meaning is "many, (*hikanos*) pieces of silver"; (c) "money"; it has this meaning in Matt. 25:18, 27; 28:15; Mark 14:11; **Luke 9:3**; **19:15**, **23**; **22:5**; Acts 8:20 (here the RV has "silver").

Two In the following phrases the numeral is used distributively: (a) *ana duo*, "two apiece," John 2:6 (in some mss., **Luke 9:3**); in **Luke 10:1**, "two and two" ("by twos"); (b) *kata duo*, "by two," 1 Cor. 14:27; (c) *duo duo*, "by two and two," lit., "two (and) two," Mark 6:7 (not a Hebraism; the form of expression is used in the papyri); (d) *eis duo*, "into two," "in twain," Matt. 27:51 and Mark 15:38.

Apiece *ana* (303), used with numerals or measures of quantity with a distributive force, is translated "apiece" in **Luke 9:3**, "two coats apiece," KJV; in John 2:6, "two or three firkins apiece." In Matt. 20:9-10, "every man a penny," is a free rendering for "a penny apiece"; in **Luke 9:14**, the RV adds "each" to translate the *ana*, in **10:1**, *ana duo* is "two by two." See Rev. 4:8, "each."

9:4-5 And whatsoever house ye enter into, there abide, and thence depart.

And whosoever will not receive you, when ye go out of that city, shake off the very dust from your feet for a testimony against them.

Whosoever *hosos* (3745), "how much, how many, how great, as much as, as many as," is translated "as many as," e.g., in Matt. 14:36; Mark 3:10; **Luke 9:5**, RV (KJV, "whosoever"); Acts 2:39; in 9:16, RV, "how many things" (KJV, "how great things"); in Rom. 6:3 the RV renders it by "all we who" (KJV, "so many of us as"), a necessary alteration, not singling out some believers from others, as if some were not baptized, but implying what was recognized as true of all (see Acts 18:8); in 2 Cor. 1:20, RV, "how many soever be" (KJV, "all").

Receive *see* **Took** at *Luke 2:28*.

Shake *apotinasso* (660), "to shake off" (*apo*, "from," *tinasso*, "to shake"), is used in **Luke 9:5**, of dust from the feet; Acts 28:5, of a viper from the hand. In the Sept., Judg. 16:20; 1 Sam. 10:2; Lam. 2:7.

Dust *koniortos* (2868), "raised or flying dust" (*konia*, "dust," *ornumi*, "to stir up"), is found in Matt. 10:14; **Luke 9:5; 10:11**; Acts 13:51; 22:23.

9:6 And they departed, and went through the towns, preaching the gospel, and healing every where.

Departed *see Luke 4:42*.

Towns *see* **Town** at *Luke 5:17*.

Every where *pantachou* (3837), is translated "everywhere" in Mark 1:28, RV, of the report throughout Galilee concerning Christ; in Mark 16:20, of preaching; **Luke 9:6**, of healing; Acts 17:30, of a divine command for repentance; 28:22, of disparagement of Christians; 1 Cor. 4:17, of apostolic teaching; in Acts 24:3, it is rendered "in all places." In the Sept., Isa. 42:22.

9:7 Now Herod the tetrarch heard of all that was done by him: and he was perplexed, because that it was said of some, that John was risen from the dead;

Tetrarch *see Luke 3:19*.

By For *hupo*, "by," see the RV of Matt. 1:22; 2:16; 11:27; **Luke 9:7**; Acts 15:4; 1 Cor. 14:24; 2 Cor. 8:19; Phil. 3:12.

Perplexed *diaporeo* (1280), signifies "to be thoroughly perplexed," with a perplexity amounting to despair, Acts 2:12; 5:24 and 10:17, KJV, "were in doubt," "doubted," RV, "were (was) perplexed." See also **Luke 9:7** (some mss. have it in **Luke 24:4**).

9:8 And of some, that Elias had appeared; and of others, that one of the old prophets was risen again.

Old *archaios* (744), "original, ancient" (from *arche*, "a beginning": Eng., "archaic," "archaeology," etc.), is used (a) of persons belonging to a former age, "(to) them of old time," Matt. 5:21, 33, RV; in some mss. v. 27; the RV rendering is right; not ancient teachers are in view; what was said to them of old time was "to be both recognized in its significance and estimated in its temporary limitations, Christ intending His words to be regarded not as an abrogation, but a deepening and fulfilling" (Cremer); of prophets, **Luke 9:8, 19**; (b) of time long gone by, Acts 15:21; (c) of days gone by in a person's experience, Acts 15:7, "a good while ago," lit., "from old (days)," i.e., from the first days onward in the sense of originality, not age; (d) of Mnason, "an early disciple," Acts 21:16, RV, not referring to age, but to his being one of the first who had accepted the gospel from the beginning of its proclamation; (e) of things which are "old" in relation to the new, earlier things in contrast to things present, 2 Cor. 5:17, i.e., of what characterized and conditioned the time previous to conversion in a believer's experience, RV, "they are become new," i.e., they have taken on a new complexion and are viewed in an entirely different way; (f) of the world (i.e., the inhabitants of the world) just previous to the Flood, 2 Pet. 2:5; (g) of the Devil, as "that old serpent," Rev. 12:9; 20:2, "old," not in age, but as characterized for a long period by the evils indicated.

9:9 And Herod said, John have I beheaded: but who is this, of whom I hear such things? And he desired to see him.

Beheaded *apokephalizo* (607), *apo*, "from, off," *kephale*, "a head," is found in Matt. 14:10; Mark 6:16, 27; **Luke 9:9**.

Desired *zeteo* (2212), signifies (a) "to seek, to seek for," e.g., Matt. 7:7, 8; 13:45; **Luke 24:5**; John 6:24; of plotting against a person's life, Matt. 2:20; Acts 21:31; Rom. 11:3; metaphorically, to "seek" by thinking, to "seek" how to do something, or what to obtain, e.g., Mark 11:18; **Luke 12:29**; to "seek" to ascertain a meaning, John 16:19, "do ye inquire"; to "seek" God, Acts 17:27, RV; Rom. 10:20; (b) "to seek or strive after, endeavor, to desire," e.g., Matt. 12:46, 47, RV, "seeking" (KJV, "desiring"); **Luke 9:9**, RV, "sought" (KJV, "desired"); John 7:19, RV, "seek ye" (KJV, "go ye about"); so v. 20; Rom. 10:3, RV, "seeking" (KJV, "going about"); of "seeking" the kingdom of God and His righteousness, in the sense of coveting earnestly, striving after, Matt. 6:33; "the things that are above," Col. 3:1; peace, 1 Pet. 3:11; (c) "to require or demand," e.g., Mark 8:12; **Luke 11:29**; 1 Cor. 4:2, "it is required"; 2 Cor. 13:3, "ye seek."

9:10 And the apostles, when they were returned, told him all that they had done. And he took them, and went aside privately into a desert place belonging to the city called Bethsaida.

Apostles *see Luke 6:13.*

Told *see* Published at *Luke 8:39.*

All *hosa* (3745), the neuter plural of *hosos*, "as much as," chiefly used in the plural, is sometimes rendered "all that," e.g., Acts 4:23; 14:27. It really means "whatsoever things." See **Luke 9:10**, RV, "what things."

Went *see* Withdrew at *Luke 5:16.*

9:11 And the people, when they knew *it*, followed him: and he received them, and spake unto them of the kingdom of God, and healed them that had need of healing.

"Jesus came to save persons, not just souls. He came to help the suffering in whatever way they were suffering. Sickness of the body was part of the kingdom of Satan he had come to destroy."

FRANCIS MACNUTT

Knew *see* Known at *Luke 7:39.*

Received *see Luke 8:40.*

Healed, Healing *therapeia* (2322), primarily denotes "care, attention," **Luke 12:42**; then, "medical service, healing" (Eng., "therapy"), **Luke 9:11**; Rev. 22:2, of the effects of the leaves of the tree of life, perhaps here with the meaning "health."

9:12 And when the day began to wear away, then came the twelve, and said unto him, Send the multitude away, that they may go into the towns and country round about, and lodge, and get victuals: for we are here in a desert place.

Wear *klino* (2827), "to incline, to bow down," is used of the women who in their fright "bowed" their faces to the earth at the Lord's empty tomb, **Luke 24:5**; of the act of the Lord on the cross immediately before giving up His Spirit. What is indicated in the statement "He bowed His head," is not the helpless dropping of the head after death, but the deliberate putting of His head into a position of rest, John 19:30. The verb is deeply significant here. The Lord reversed the natural order. The same verb is used in His statement in Matt. 8:20 and **Luke 9:58**, "the Son of Man hath not where to lay His head." It is used, too, of the decline of day, **Luke 9:12**; **24:29**; of turning enemies to flight, Heb. 11:34.

Towns *see* Town at *Luke 5:17.*

Country *see Luke 8:34.*

Round about *kuklo* (2945), the dative case of the noun *kuklos*, "a ring," is used as an adverb, and translated "round about" in Mark 3:34, KJV (RV, "round"); 6:6, 36; **Luke 9:12**; Rom. 15:19; Rev. 4:6; 7:11.

Lodge *kataluo* (2647), "to destroy utterly, to overthrow completely," is rendered "destroy," in Matt. 5:17, twice, of the Law; Matt. 24:2; 26:61; 27:40; Mark 13:2; 14:58; 15:29; **Luke 21:6**, of the Temple; in Acts 6:14, of Jerusalem; in Gal. 2:18, of the Law as a means of justification; in Rom. 14:20 (KJV, "destroy," RV, "overthrow"), of the marring of a person's spiritual well-being; in Acts 5:38 and 39 (RV, "overthrow") of the failure of purposes; in 2 Cor. 5:1, of the death of the body ("dissolved"). In one of its meanings, it signifies "to unloose" (*kata*, "down," *luo*, "to loose"), "unyoke," as of horses, etc., hence intransitively, "to take up one's quarters, to lodge," **Luke 9:12**; **19:7**, RV, "to lodge" (KJV, "to be a guest").

Get *heurisko* (2147), "to find," is translated "get" in **Luke 9:12**, of victuals.

Victuals *episitismos* (1979), "provisions, food" (*epi*, "upon," *sitizo*, "to feed, nourish"; *sitos*, "food"), is translated "victuals" in **Luke 9:12**.

9:13 But he said unto them, Give ye them to eat. And they said, We have no more but five loaves and two fishes; except we should go and buy meat for all this people.

More *pleion* (4119), the comparative degree of *polus*, "much," is used (a) as an adjective, e.g., John 15:2; Acts 24:11, RV, "(not) more (than)" (KJV, "yet but"); Heb. 3:3; (b) as a noun, or with a noun understood, e.g., Matt. 20:10; Mark 12:43; Acts 19:32 and 27:12, "the more part"; 1 Cor. 9:19; (c) as an adverb, Matt. 5:20, "shall exceed," lit., "(shall abound) more (than)"; 26:53; **Luke 9:13**.

Meat *see Luke 3:11*.

9:14 For they were about five thousand men. And he said to his disciples, Make them sit down by fifties in a company.

About *see Luke 3:23*.

Thousand The following compounds represent different multiples of a thousand: *dischilioi*, 2,000, Mark 5:13; *trischilioi*, 3,000, Acts 2:41; *tetrakischilioi*, 4,000, Matt. 15:38; 16:10; Mark 8:9, 20; Acts 21:35; *pentakischilioi*, 5,000, Matt. 14:21; 16:9; Mark 6:44; 8:9; **Luke 9:14**; John 6:10; *heplakischilioi*, 7,000, Rom. 11:4.

Sit *see* Sat at *Luke 7:36*.

Fifties *see* Fifty at *Luke 7:41*.

Company *klisia* (2828), akin to *klino*, "to recline," primarily means "a place for lying down in, and hence a reclining company." It is found in the plural in **Luke 9:14**, corresponding to Mark's word *sumposia*, signifying "companies reclining at a meal."

9:15 And they did so, and made them all sit down.

Sit *see* Laid at *Luke 2:7*.

9:16 Then he took the five loaves and the two fishes, and looking up to heaven, he blessed them, and brake, and gave to the disciples to set before the multitude.

Blessed *see* Praised at *Luke 1:64*.

Brake *kataklao* (2622), is used in Mark 6:41 and **Luke 9:16**, of Christ's "breaking" loaves for the multitudes.

Set *paratithemi* (3908), "to place beside," "to set forth," of a parable, Matt. 13:24, RV (KJV, "put forth"); "to set before," of food, Mark 6:41; 8:6 (twice), 7; **Luke 9:16**; **10:8**; **11:6**; Acts 16:34; 1 Cor. 10:27.

9:17 And they did eat, and were all filled: and there was taken up of fragments that remained to them twelve baskets.

Fragments *klasma* (2801), "a broken piece" (from *klao*, "to break") is used of the broken pieces from the feeding of the multitudes, RV, "broken pieces," KJV, "fragments," Matt. 14:20; Mark 6:43; 8:19, 20; **Luke 9:17**; John 6:12, 13; in Matt. 15:37 and Mark 8:8, RV, "broken pieces" (KJV, "broken meat").

Remained *perisseuo* (4052), is used intransitively (a) "of exceeding a certain number, or measure, to be over, to remain," of the fragments after feeding the multitude (cf. *perisseuma*), **Luke 9:17**; John 6:12-13; "to exist in abundance"; as of wealth, **Luke 12:15**; **21:4**; of food, **15:17**. In this sense it is used also of consolation, 2 Cor. 1:5, of the effect of a gift sent to meet the need of saints, 2 Cor. 9:12; of rejoicing, Phil. 1:26; of what comes or falls to the lot of a person in large measure, as of the grace of God and the gift by the grace of Christ, Rom. 5:15, of the sufferings of Christ, 2 Cor. 1:5. In Mark 12:44 and **Luke 21:4**, the RV has "superfluity."

(b) "to redound to, or to turn out abundantly for something," as of the liberal effects of poverty, 2 Cor. 8:2; in Rom. 3:7, argumentatively of the effects of the truth of God, as to whether God's truthfulness becomes more conspicuous and His glory is increased through man's untruthfulness; of numerical increase, Acts 16:5.

(c) "to be abundantly furnished, to abound in a thing," as of material benefits, **Luke 12:15**; Phil. 4:18 of spiritual gifts; 1 Cor. 14:12, or "to be pre-eminent, to excel, to be morally better off," as regards partaking of certain meats; 1 Cor. 8:8, "are we the better", "to abound" in hope, Rom. 15:13; the work of the Lord, 1 Cor. 15:58; faith and grace, 2 Cor. 8:7; thanksgiving, Col. 2:7; walking so as to please God, Phil. 1:9; 1 Thess. 4:1, 10; of righteousness, Matt. 5:20; of the Gospel, as the ministration of righteousness 2 Cor. 3:9, "exceed."

Baskets *kophinos* (2894), was "a wicker basket," originally containing a certain measure of capacity, Matt. 14:20; 16:9; Mark 6:43 (RV, "basketfuls"); 8:19; **Luke 9:17**; **13:8** in some mss.; John 6:13.

9:18 And it came to pass, as he was alone praying, his disciples were with him: and he asked them, saying, Whom say the people that I am?

Alone *kata monas* (2651), signifies "apart, in private, alone," Mark 4:10; **Luke 9:18**. Some texts have the phrase as one word.

9:19 They answering said, John the Baptist; but some *say*, Elias; and others *say*, that one of the old prophets is risen again.

Some In the following *alloi*, "others" ("some" in the KJV), is translated "others" in the RV, Matt. 13:5, 7; Mark 4:7 ("other"); 8:28; **Luke 9:19**;

John 9:9. Followed by a correlative expression it denotes "some," e.g., Acts 19:32; 21:34.

Others *allos* (243), indicates numeral distinction of objects of similar character, and is used (a) absolutely, e.g., Matt. 20:3 (plural); (b) attached to a noun, e.g., Matt. 21:36; (c) with the article, e.g., Matt. 5:39; 1 Cor. 14:29 (plural, RV); in Matt. 13:5; **Luke 9:19**; John 9:9, e.g., RV, "others" (KJV, "some"); in Matt. 25:20, RV, "other" (KJV, "beside them ... more").

Old *see Luke 9:8.*

9:20-21 He said unto them, But whom say ye that I am? Peter answering said, The Christ of God.

And he straitly charged them, and commanded *them* to tell no man that thing;

Commanded *see Luke 8:29.*

9:22 Saying, The Son of man must suffer many things, and be rejected of the elders and chief priests and scribes, and be slain, and be raised the third day.

Rejected *apodokimazo* (593), "to reject" as the result of examination and disapproval (*apo*, "away from," *dokimazo*, "to approve"), is used (a) of the "rejection" of Christ by the elders and chief priests of the Jews, Matt. 21:42; Mark 8:31; 12:10; **Luke 9:22**; **20:17**; 1 Pet. 2:4, 7 (KJV, "disallowed"); by the Jewish people, **Luke 17:25**; (b) of the "rejection" of Esau from inheriting "the blessing," Heb. 12:17. Cf. and contrast *exoutheneo*, Acts 4:11.

Scribes *see Luke 5:21.*

Raised *see Luke 1:69.*

Third *treis* (5143), is regarded by many as a number sometimes symbolically indicating fullness of testimony or manifestation, as in the three persons in the Godhead, cf. 1 Tim. 5:19; Heb. 10:28; the mention in 1 John 5:7 is in a verse which forms no part of the original; no Greek ms. earlier than the 14th century contained it; no version earlier than the 5th cent. in any other language contains it, nor is it quoted by any of the Greek or Latin "Fathers" in their writings on the Trinity. That there are those who bear witness in Heaven is not borne out by any other Scripture. It must be regarded as the interpolation of a copyist. In Mark 9:31 and 10:34 the best texts have *meta treis hemeras*, "after three days," which idiomatically expresses the same thing as *te tritehemera*, "on the third day," which some texts have here, as, e.g., the phrase "the third day" in Matt. 17:23; 20:19; **Luke 9:22**; **18:33**, where the repetition of the article lends stress to the number, lit., "the day the third"; **24:7**, **46**; Acts 10:40.

9:23 And he said to *them* all, If any *man* will come after me, let him deny himself, and take up his cross daily, and follow me.

Deny *aparneomai* (533), a strengthened form with *apo*, "from," prefixed (Lat., *abnego*), means (a) "to deny utterly," to abjure, to affirm that one has no connection with a person, as in Peter's denial of Christ, Matt. 26:34-35, 75; Mark 14:30-31, 72; **Luke 22:34**, **61** (some mss. have it in John 13:38). This stronger form is used in the Lord's statements foretelling Peter's "denial," and in Peter's assurance of fidelity; the simple verb is used in all the records of his actual denial. The strengthened form is the verb used in the Lord's warning as to being "denied" in the presence of the angels, **Luke 12:9**; in the preceding clause, "he that denieth Me," the simple verb *arneomai* is used; the rendering therefore should be "he that denieth Me in the presence of men, shall be utterly denied in the presence of the angels of God"; (b) "to deny oneself" as a follower of Christ, Matt. 16:24; Mark 8:34; **Luke 9:23**.

> *"Being a Christian is more than just an instantaneous conversion – it is a daily process whereby you grow to be more and more like Christ."*
>
> BILLY GRAHAM

9:24 For whosoever will save his life shall lose it: but whosoever will lose his life for my sake, the same shall save it.

Life *psuche* (5590), besides its meanings, "heart, mind, soul," denotes "life" in two chief respects, (a) "breath of life, the natural life," e.g., Matt. 2:20; 6:25; Mark 10:45; **Luke 12:22**; Acts 20:10; Rev. 8:9; 12:11 (cf. Lev. 17:11; Esth. 8:11); (b) "the seat of personality," e.g., **Luke 9:24**, explained in v. **25** as "own self." *See also* **Soul** at *Luke 1:46.*

9:25 For what is a man advantaged, if he gain the whole world, and lose himself, or be cast away?

Advantaged *opheleo* (5623), signifies "to be useful, do good, profit," Rom. 2:25; with a negative, "to be of no use, to effect nothing,"

"If Jesus Christ be God and died for me, then no sacrifice can be too great for me to make for him."

C. T. STUDD

Matt. 27:24; John 6:63, "profiteth"; 12:19, "prevail"; in **Luke 9:25**, KJV, "(what is a man) advantaged?" RV, "profited."

Gain *kerdaino* (2770), signifies (I) literally, (a) "to gain something," Matt. 16:26; 25:16 (in the best mss.), 17, 20, 22; Mark 8:36; **Luke 9:25**; (b) "to get gain, make a profit," Jas. 4:13; (II) metaphorically, (a) "to win persons," said (1) of "gaining" an offending brother who by being told privately of his offense, and by accepting the representations, is won from alienation and from the consequences of his fault, Matt. 18:15; (2) of winning souls into the kingdom of God by the gospel, 1 Cor. 9:19, 20 (twice), 21, 22, or by godly conduct, 1 Pet. 3:1 (RV, "gained"); (3) of so practically appropriating Christ to oneself that He becomes the dominating power in and over one's whole being and circumstances, Phil. 3:8 (RV, "gain"); (b) "to gain things," said of getting injury and loss, Acts 27:21, RV, "gotten."

Lose *apollumi* (622), signifies (I) In the active voice, (a) "to destroy, destroy utterly, kill," e.g., Matt. 10:28; Mark 1:24; 9:22; (b) "to lose utterly," e.g., Matt. 10:42, of "losing" a reward; **Luke 15:4** (1st part), of "losing" a sheep; **Luke 9:25**, of "losing" oneself (of the "loss" of well-being hereafter); metaphorically, John 6:39, of failing to save; 18:9, of Christ's not "losing" His own; (II) in the middle voice (a) "to perish," of things, e.g., John 6:12 "(that nothing) be lost"; of persons, e.g., Matt. 8:25, "we perish;" of the "loss" of eternal life, usually (always in the RV) translated to perish, John 3:16; 17:12, KJV, "is lost," RV, "perished"; 2 Cor. 4:3, "are perishing," KJV, "are lost"; (b) "to be lost," e.g., **Luke 15:4** (2nd part), "which is lost"; metaphorically, from the relation between shepherd and flock, of spiritual destitution and alienation from God, Matt. 10:6, "(the) lost (sheep)" of the house of Israel; **Luke 19:10** (the perfect tense translated "lost" is here intransitive).

Himself *see* **Life** at ***Luke 9:24***.

Cast *zemioo* (2210), "to damage" (akin to *zemia*, "damage," e.g., Acts 27:10, 21), is used in the NT, in the passive voice, signifying "to suffer loss, forfeit, lose," Matt. 16:26; Mark 8:36, of losing one's soul or life; **Luke 9:25**, RV, "forfeit (his own self)," KJV, "be cast away"; 1 Cor. 3:15, "he shall suffer loss," i.e., at the Judgment-Seat of Christ (see v. 13 with 2 Cor. 5:10); 2 Cor. 7:9, "(that) ye might suffer loss," RV (KJV, "might receive damage"); though the apostle did regret the necessity of making them sorry by his letter, he rejoiced that they were made sorry after a godly sort, and that they thus suffered no spiritual loss, which they would have done had their sorrow been otherwise than after a godly manner; in Phil. 3:8, "I suffered the loss (of all things)," RV, i.e., of all things which he formerly counted gain (especially those in verses 5 and 6, to which the article before "all things" points).

9:26 For whosoever shall be ashamed of me and of my words, of him shall the Son of man be ashamed, when he shall come in his own glory, and *in his* Father's, and of the holy angels.

Ashamed *epaischunomai* (1870), (*epi*, "upon," intensive), is used only in the sense of being "ashamed" of persons, Mark 8:38; **Luke 9:26**; the gospel, Rom. 1:16; former evil doing, Rom. 6:21; "the testimony of our Lord," 2 Tim. 1:8; suffering for the gospel, v. 12; rendering assistance and comfort to one who is suffering for the gospel's sake, v. 16. It is used in Heb., of Christ in calling those who are sanctified His brethren, 2:11, and of God in His not being "ashamed" to be called the God of believers, 11:16. In the Sept., in Job 34:19; Ps. 119:6; Isa. 1:29.

9:27 But I tell you of a truth, there be some standing here, which shall not taste of death, till they see the kingdom of God.

Truth *alethos* (230), "truly, surely," is rendered "of a truth" in Matt. 14:33; 26:73 and Mark 14:70, RV, (KJV, "surely"); **Luke 9:27**; **12:44**; **21:3**; John 6:14; 7:40; 17:8, RV, "of a truth (KJV, surely); Acts 12:11, RV (KJV, "of a surety"); "in truth," 1 Thess. 2:13; "truly," Matt. 27:54; Mark 15:39.

Taste *geuo* (1089), "to make to taste," is used in the middle voice, signifying "to taste" (a) naturally, Matt. 27:34; **Luke 14:24**; John 2:9; Col. 2:21; (b) metaphorically, of Christ's "tasting" death, implying His personal experience in voluntarily undergoing death, Heb. 2:9; of believers (negatively) as to "tasting" of death, Matt. 16:28; Mark 9:1; **Luke 9:27**; John 8:52; of "tasting" the heavenly gift (different from receiving it), Heb. 6:4; "the good word of God, and the powers of the age to come," 6:5; "that the Lord is gracious," 1 Pet. 2:3.

9:28 And it came to pass about an eight days after these sayings, he took Peter and John and James, and went up into a mountain to pray.

About *see Luke 3:23.*

Eight *see Luke 2:21.*

Sayings *see* Saying at *Luke 1:29.*

Mountain *see Luke 3:5. See also* Hill at *Luke 4:29.*

9:29 And as he prayed, the fashion of his countenance was altered, and his raiment *was* white *and* glistering.

Fashion *eidos* (1491), "that which is seen, an appearance," is translated "fashion" in **Luke 9:29**, of the Lord's countenance at the Transfiguration.

Countenance *prosopon* (4383), is translated "countenance" in **Luke 9:29**; Acts 2:28, and in the KJV of 2 Cor. 3:7 (RV, "face"). *See also* Shape at *Luke 3:22.*

Altered *see* Other at *Luke 4:43.*

Raiment *see Luke 7:25.*

White *leukos* (3022), is used of (a) clothing (sometimes in the sense of "bright"), Matt. 17:2; 28:3; Mark 9:3; 16:5; **Luke 9:29**; John 20:12; Acts 1:10; symbolically, Rev. 3:4, 5, 18; 4:4; 6:11; 7:9, 13; 19:14 (2nd part); (b) hair, Matt. 5:36; Christ's head and hair (in a vision; cf. Dan. 7:9), Rev. 1:14 (twice); ripened grain, John 4:35; a stone, Rev. 2:17, an expression of the Lord's special delight in the overcomer, the new name on it being indicative of a secret communication of love and joy; a horse (in a vision), 6:2; 19:11-14 (1st part); a cloud, 14:14; the throne of God, 20:11.

Glistering *exastrapto* (1823), signifies "to flash like lightning, gleam, be radiant," in **Luke 9:29** of the Lord's raiment at His transfiguration, RV, "dazzling"; KJV, "glistering." In the Sept., Ezek. 1:4, 7; Nahum 3:3.

9:30 And, behold, there talked with him two men, which were Moses and Elias:

Talked *sullaleo* (4814), "to speak with" (*sun*), is translated "to talk with," Matt. 17:3; Mark 9:4; **Luke 9:30**. *See also* Spake at *Luke 4:36.*

9:31 Who appeared in glory, and spake of his decease which he should accomplish at Jerusalem.

Decease *exodos* (1841), (Eng., "exodus"), lit. signifies "a way out" (*ex*, "out," *hodos*, "a way"); hence, "a departure," especially from life, "a decease"; in **Luke 9:31**, of the Lord's death, "which He was about to accomplish"; in 2 Pet. 1:15, of Peter's death (marg., "departure" in each case); "departure" in Heb. 11:22, RV.

Accomplish *pleroo* (4137), "to fulfill, to complete, carry out to the full" (as well as to fill), is translated "perfect" in Rev. 3:2, KJV; RV, "I have found no works of thine fulfilled before My God"; "accomplish" in **Luke 9:31**.

9:32 But Peter and they that were with him were heavy with sleep: and when they were awake, they saw his glory, and the two men that stood with him.

Heavy *bareo* (916), is used of the effect of drowsiness, "were heavy," Matt. 26:43; Mark 14:40; **Luke 9:32**; of the effects of gluttony, **Luke 21:34** ("overcharged"); of the believer's present physical state in the body, 2 Cor. 5:4; of persecution, 2 Cor. 1:8; of a charge upon material resources, 1 Tim. 5:16 (RV).

Awake *diagregoreo* (1235), *dia*, intensive, *gregoreo*, "to watch," is used in **Luke 9:32**, RV, "were fully awake," KJV "were awake."

Stood *sunistemi* (4921), intransitively, denotes "to stand with" (*sun*), **Luke 9:32**; for 2 Pet. 3:5, KJV, standing.

9:33 And it came to pass, as they departed from him, Peter said unto Jesus, Master, it is good for us to be here: and let us make three tabernacles; one for thee, and one for Moses, and one for Elias: not knowing what he said.

Departed *diachorizo* (1316), lit., "to separate throughout" (*dia*), i.e., "completely," in the middle voice, "to separate oneself definitely from," is used in **Luke 9:33**, RV, "were parting from."

Master *see Luke 5:5.*

Tabernacles *skene* (4633), "a tent, booth, tabernacle," is used of (a) tents as dwellings, Matt. 17:4; Mark 9:5; **Luke 9:33**; Heb. 11:9, KJV, "tabernacles" (RV, "tents"); (b) the Mosaic tabernacle, Acts 7:44; Heb. 8:5; 9:1 (in some mss.); 9:8, 21, termed "the tent of meeting," RV (i.e., where the people were called to meet God), a preferable description to "the tabernacle of the congregation," as in the KJV in the OT; the outer part 9:2, 6; the inner sanctuary, 9:3; (c) the heavenly prototype, Heb. 8:2; 9:11; Rev. 13:6; 15:5; 21:3 (of its future descent); (d) the eternal abodes of the saints, **Luke**

16:9, RV, "tabernacles" (KJV, "habitations"); (e) the Temple in Jerusalem, as continuing the service of the tabernacle, Heb. 13:10; (f) the house of David, i.e., metaphorically of his people, Acts 15:16; (g) the portable shrine of the god Moloch, Acts 7:43.

9:34 While he thus spake, there came a cloud, and overshadowed them: and they feared as they entered into the cloud.

Overshadowed *see* Overshadow at *Luke 1:35.*

9:35 And there came a voice out of the cloud, saying, This is my beloved Son: hear him.

Beloved In **Luke 9:35**, the RV, translating from the most authentic mss., has "My chosen" (*eklego*), for KJV, "beloved" (*agapetos*); so in Philem. 2, "sister" (*adelphe*). *See also* Chose at *Luke 6:13.*

9:36 And when the voice was past, Jesus was found alone. And they kept *it* close, and told no man in those days any of those things which they had seen.

Past *ginomai* (1096), "to become, come to pass," is translated "was past" in **Luke 9:36**, KJV, and RV marg. (RV, "came"), of the voice of God the Father at the Transfiguration; "is past," 2 Tim. 2:18.

Close *sigao* (4601), signifies (a), used intransitively, "to be silent" (from *sige*, "silence"), translated "to hold one's peace," in **Luke 9:36**; **18:39**; **20:26**; Acts 12:17; 15:13 (in v. 12, "kept silence"; similarly rendered in 1 Cor. 14:28, 30, KJV, "hold his peace," 34); (b) used transitively, "to keep secret"; in the passive voice, "to be kept secret," Rom. 16:25, RV, "hath been kept in silence."

9:37 And it came to pass, that on the next day, when they were come down from the hill, much people met him.

Next *see* After at *Luke 7:11.*

Come *katerchomai* (2718), "to come down" (*kata*, "down"), e.g., **Luke 9:37**.

Hill *see Luke 4:29. See also* Mountain at *Luke 3:5.*

Met *sunantao* (4876), "to meet with," lit., "to meet together with" is used in **Luke 9:37** (in v. **18**, in some mss.); **22:10**; Acts 10:25; Heb. 7:1, 10; metaphorically in Acts 20:22 ("shall befall").

9:38 And, behold, a man of the company cried out, saying, Master, I beseech thee, look upon my son: for he is mine only child.

Cried *anaboao* (310), "to lift up the voice, cry out," is said of Christ at the moment of His death, a testimony to His supernatural power in giving up His life, Matt. 27:46; in some mss. in Mark 15:8, of the shouting of a multitude; in some mss. in **Luke 9:38**, of the "crying" out of a man in a company. *See also* Crying at *Luke 3:4.*

Look *see* Regarded at *Luke 1:48.*

Only *see Luke 7:12.*

Child *monogenes* (3439), lit., "only-begotten," is translated "only child" in **Luke 9:38**.

9:39 And, lo, a spirit taketh him, and he suddenly crieth out; and it teareth him that he foameth again, and bruising him hardly departeth from him.

Suddenly *see Luke 2:13.*

Teareth *sparasso* (4682), denotes "to tear, rend, convulse," Mark 1:26; 9:20 (in some mss.), 26, RV, "having ... torn" (KJV, "rent"); **Luke 9:39**. In the Sept., 2 Sam. 22:8, of the foundations of heaven; Jer. 4:18, of the heart.

Foameth *aphros* (876), "foam," occurs in **Luke 9:39**, where it is used with the preposition *meta*, "with," lit., "(teareth him) with (accompanied by) foam."

Bruising In **Luke 9:39**, RV, *suntribo*, "to break, bruise," is rendered "bruiseth sorely." *See also* **Bruised** at *Luke 4:18.*

Hardly *molis* (3433), "with difficulty, scarcely, hardly" (akin to *molos*, "toil"), is used as an alternative for *mogis*, and occurs in the most authentic mss. in **Luke 9:39**; it is rendered "hardly" in Acts 27:8, KJV.

Departeth *apochoreo* (672), "to depart from" (*apo*), is so translated in Matt. 7:23; **Luke 9:39**; Acts 13:13 (both KJV and RV). Some mss. have it in **Luke 20:20**.

9:40-41 And I besought thy disciples to cast him out; and they could not.

And Jesus answering said, O faithless and perverse generation, how long shall I be with you, and suffer you? Bring thy son hither.

Faithless *apistos* (571), (a) "untrustworthy," not worthy of confidence or belief, is said of things "incredible," Acts 26:8 (b) "unbelieving, distrustful," used as a noun, "unbeliever," **Luke 12:46**; 1 Tim. 5:8 (RV, for KJV, "infidel"); in Titus 1:15 and Rev. 21:8, "unbelieving"; "faithless" in Matt. 17:17; Mark 9:19; **Luke 9:41**; John 20:27. The word is most frequent in 1 and 2 Corinthians. (In the Sept., Prov. 17:6; 28:25; Isa. 17:10).

Perverse *diastrepho* (1294), "to distort, twist" (*dia*, "through," and *strepho*), is translated "to pervert" in **Luke 23:2** (*apostrepho* in v. **14**); Acts 13:10 [in v. 8, "to turn aside" (KJV, "away")]; in the perfect participle, passive voice, it is translated "perverse," lit., "turned aside, corrupted," in Matt. 17:17; **Luke 9:41**; Acts 20:30; Phil. 2:15.

Generation *see* Generations at *Luke 1:48.*

Hither *hode* (5602), primarily an adverb of manner then, of place, (a) of "motion" or "direction towards a place," e.g., Matt. 8:29; Mark 11:3; **Luke 9:41**; John 6:25; (b) of "position."

9:42 And as he was yet a coming, the devil threw him down, and tare *him*. And Jesus rebuked the unclean spirit, and healed the child, and delivered him again to his father.

Threw *rhegnumi* (4486), "to tear, rend, break," is used of the action of a demon upon a human victim, Mark 9:18, "dasheth ... down," RV; (KJV, marg.; KJV, text, "teareth"); **Luke 9:42**, RV, "dashed ... down" (KJV, "threw ... down").

Tare *susparasso* (4952), "to tear violently" (*sun*, "with," intensive), "convulse completely," is used in Mark 9:20, in the best texts; **Luke 9:42**.

Rebuked *see Luke 4:35.*

Child *see Luke 2:43.*

Delivered *apodidomi* (591), lit., "to give away," hence, "to give back or up," is used in Pilate's command for the Lord's body to be "given up," Matt. 27:58; in the sense of "giving back," of the Lord's act in giving a healed boy back to his father, **Luke** 9:42.

9:43 And they were all amazed at the mighty power of God. But while they wondered every one at all things which Jesus did, he said unto his disciples,

Amazed *see Luke 2:48.*

Mighty power *megaleiotes* (3168), denotes "splendor, magnificence" (from *megaleios*, "magnificent," mighty," Acts 2:11, *megas*, "great"), translated "magnificence" in Acts 19:27, of the splendor of the goddess Diana. In **Luke 9:43**, RV (KJV, "mighty power"); in 2 Pet. 1:16, "majesty." In the papyri writings it is frequent as a ceremonial title.

Wondered *see* Marvelled at *Luke 2:33.*

9:44 Let these sayings sink down into your ears: for the Son of man shall be delivered into the hands of men.

Sink *tithemi* (5087), "to put," is rendered "let ... sink" in **Luke 9:44**, RV ("let ... sink down," KJV). *See also* Laid at *Luke 1:66.*

Ears *see Luke 1:44.*

Shall *mello* (3195), "to be about (to be or do)," is used of purpose, certainty, compulsion or necessity. It is rendered simply by "shall" or "should" (which frequently represent elsewhere part of the future tense of the verb) in the following (the RV sometimes translates differently, as noted): Matt. 16:27 (1st part), lit., "is about to come"; 17:12, 22; 20:22, RV, "am about"; 24:6; Mark 13:4 (2nd part), RV, "are about"; **Luke 9:44**; **21:7** (2nd part), RV, "are about"; v. **36**; Acts 23:3; 24:15; 26:2, RV, "I am (to)"; Rom. 4:24; 8:13 (1st part), RV, "must"; v. 18; 2 Tim. 4:1; Heb. 1:14; 10:27; Jas. 2:12, RV "are to"; 1 Pet. 5:1; Rev. 1:19; 2:10 (1st and 2nd parts), RV, "art about," "is about"; 3:10, RV, "is (to)"; 17:8 (1st part), RV, "is about."

9:45 But they understood not this saying, and it was hid from them, that they perceived it not: and they feared to ask him of that saying.

Understood not *agnoeo* (50), "to be ignorant," is rendered "they understood not" in Mark 9:32; **Luke 9:45**; in 2 Pet. 2:12, KJV, RV, "they are ignorant of."

Saying *see* Sayings at *Luke 1:65.*

Hid *parakalupto* (3871), lit., "to cover with a veil," KJV, "hid," in **Luke 9:45**, "it was veiled from them".

Perceived *aisthanomai* (143), "to perceive, to notice, understand," is used in **Luke 9:45**, RV, "(that they should not) perceive," KJV, "(that) they perceived ... (not)."

9:46 Then there arose a reasoning among them, which of them should be greatest.

Arose *eiserchomai* (1525), lit., "to go in" (*eis*, "in," *erchomai*, "to go"), "to enter," is once rendered "arose," metaphorically, with reference to a reasoning among the disciples which of them should be the greatest, **Luke 9:46**.

Reasoning *see* Thoughts at *Luke 2:35; 5:22.*

Greatest *meizon* (3187), sometimes translated "greatest"; besides the two cases where the RV corrects the KJV, "greatest" to "greater" (Matt. 13:32 and **Luke 22:26**), the RV itself has "greatest" for this comparative in the following, and relegates "greater" to the margin Matt. 18:1, 4; 23:11; Mark 9:34; **Luke 9:46**; **22:24**.

9:47 And Jesus, perceiving the thought of their heart, took a child, and set him by him,

Perceiving *eidon* (3708), (akin to *oida*, "to know"), an aorist form used to supply that tense of *horao*, "to see," is translated "to perceive" in Matt. 13:14; Mark 4:12; Acts 28:26; in **Luke 9:47**, KJV (RV, "saw"); in Acts 14:9, KJV, "perceiving" (RV, "seeing").

Thought *see* Thoughts at *Luke 2:35; 5:22*.

Took *epilambano* (1949), in the middle voice, "to lay hold of, take hold of," is used literally, e.g., Mark 8:23; **Luke 9:47**; **14:4**; metaphorically, e.g., Heb. 8:9, "(I) took them (by the hand)": for other instances in each respect.

Set *see Luke 4:9*.

By In **Luke 9:47**, the preposition *para*, "by the side of," with the dative case of the pronoun *heautou*, is rendered "by His side," RV (KJV, "by Him").

9:48 And said unto them, Whosoever shall receive this child in my name receiveth me: and whosoever shall receive me receiveth him that sent me: for he that is least among you all, the same shall be great.

Receive *see* Took at *Luke 2:28*.

Sent *see Luke 1:19*.

He *houtos* (3778), "this, this person here," is always emphatic; it is used with this meaning, sometimes to refer to what precedes, e.g., Matt. 5:19, "he (shall be called great)"; John 6:46, "he (hath seen)"; often rendered "this," e.g., Rom. 9:9, or "this man," e.g., Matt. 27:58, RV; Jas. 1:25; "the same," e.g., **Luke 9:48**.

Least *see Luke 7:28*.

9:49 And John answered and said, Master, we saw one casting out devils in thy name; and we forbad him, because he followeth not with us.

Master *see Luke 5:5*.

9:50-51 And Jesus said unto him, Forbid *him* not: for he that is not against us is for us.

And it came to pass, when the time was come that he should be received up, he stedfastly set his face to go to Jerusalem,

Time In **Luke 9:51** and Acts 8:1, KJV, *hemera*, "a day," is translated "time," in the former, plural, RV, "the days"; in **Luke 23:7** (plural), RV "(in these) days," KJV, "(at that) time."

Come *see* Filled at *Luke 8:23*.

Received *anale(m)psis* (354), "a taking up," is used in **Luke 9:51** with reference to Christ's ascension; "that He should be received up" is, lit., "of the receiving up (of Him)."

Face *prosopon* (4383), denotes "the countenance," lit., "the part towards the eyes" (from *pros*, "towards," *ops*, "the eye"), and is used (a) of the "face," Matt. 6:16-17; 2 Cor. 3:7, 2nd part (KJV, "countenance"); in 2 Cor. 10:7, in the RV, "things that are before your face" (KJV, "outward appearance"), the phrase is figurative of superficial judgment; (b) of the look, i.e., the "face," which by its various movements affords an index of inward thoughts and feelings. e g., **Luke 9:51**, **53**; 1 Pet. 3:12; (c) the presence of a person, the "face" being the noblest part, e.g., Acts 3:13, RV, "before the face of," KJV, "in the presence of"; 5:41, "presence"; 2 Cor. 2:10, "person"; 1 Thess. 2:17 (first part), "presence"; 2 Thess. 1:9, RV, "face," KJV, "presence"; Rev. 12:14, "face"; (d) the person himself, e.g., Gal. 1:22; 1 Thess. 2:17 (second part); (e) the appearance one presents by his wealth or poverty, his position or state, Matt. 22:16; Mark 12:14; Gal. 2:6; Jude 16; (f) the outward appearance of inanimate things, Matt. 16:3; **Luke 12:56**; **21:35**; Acts 17:26. "To spit in a person's face" was an expression of the utmost scorn and aversion, e.g., Matt. 26:67 (cf. 27:30; Mark 10:34; **Luke 18:32**).

Set *sterizo* (4741), "to fix, make fast, to set" (from *sterix*, "a prop"), is used of "establishing" or "stablishing" (i.e., the confirmation) of persons; the apostle Peter was called by the Lord to "establish" his brethren, **Luke 22:32**, translated "strengthen"; Paul desired to visit Rome that the saints might be "established," Rom. 1:11; cf. Acts 8:23; so with Timothy at Thessalonica, 1 Thess. 3:2; the "confirmation" of the saints is the work of God, Rom. 16:25, "to stablish (you)"; 1 Thess. 3:13, "stablish (your hearts)"; 2 Thess. 2:17, "stablish them (in every good work and word)"; 1 Pet. 5:10, "stablish"; the means used to effect the "confirmation" is the ministry of the Word of God, 2 Pet. 1:12, "are established (in the truth which is with you)"; James exhorts Christians to "stablish" their hearts, Jas. 5:8; cf. Rev. 3:2, RV. The character of this "confirmation" may be learned from its use in **Luke 9:51**, "steadfastly set"; **16:26**, "fixed," and in the Sept. in Exod. 17:12, "stayed up" (also from its strengthened form *episterizo*, "to confirm," in Acts 14:22; 15:32, 41; in some mss. "to strengthen," in 18:23). Neither the laying on of hands nor the impartation of the Holy Spirit is mentioned in the NT in connection with either of these words, or with the synonymous verb *bebaioo* (see 1 Cor. 1:8; 2 Cor. 1:21, etc.).

9:52 And sent messengers before his face: and they went, and entered into a village of the Samaritans, to make ready for him.

Messengers *prodromos* (4274), an adjective signifying "running forward, going in advance," is used as a noun, of "those who were sent before to take observations," acting as scouts, especially in military matters; or of "one sent before a king" to see that the way was prepared, Isa. 40:3; (cf. **Luke 9:52**; and, of John the Baptist, Matt. 11:10, etc.). In the NT it is said of Christ in Heb. 6:20, as going in advance of His followers who are to be where He is, when He comes to receive them to Himself. In the Sept., Num. 13:21, "forerunners (of the grape)"; Isa. 28:4, "an early (fig)." *See also* ***Luke 7:24.***

Make ready *see* ***Luke 1:17.***

9:53 And they did not receive him, because his face was as though he would go to Jerusalem.

Receive *see* **Took** at ***Luke 2:28.***

Face *see* ***Luke 9:51.***

9:54 And when his disciples James and John saw *this*, they said, Lord, wilt thou that we command fire to come down from heaven, and consume them, even as Elias did?

Command *eipon* (3004), used as the aorist tense of *lego,* "to speak, to say," sometimes has the meaning of "commanding, or bidding," and is translated "bid," or "bade," e.g., in Matt. 16:12; 23:3; **Luke 10:40; 9:54,** KJV, "command," RV, "bid"; Acts 11:12; "bidding," Acts 22:24, RV.

Consume *analisko* (355), "to use up, spend up, especially in a bad sense, to destroy," is said of the destruction of persons, (a) literally, **Luke 9:54** and the RV marg. of 2 Thess. 2:8 (text, "shall slay"); (b) metaphorically, Gal. 5:15 "(that) ye be not consumed (one of another)."

9:55 But he turned, and rebuked them, and said, Ye know not what manner of spirit ye are of.

Rebuked *see* ***Luke 4:35.***

Manner *hoios* (3634), a relative pronoun, signifying "what sort of or manner of," is translated by the latter phrase in 1 Thess. 1:5; some mss. have it in **Luke 9:55,** as in KJV; the RV follows those in which it is absent.

9:56-58 For the Son of man is not come to destroy men's lives, but to save *them*. And they went to another village.

And it came to pass, that, as they went in the way, a certain *man* said unto him, Lord, I will follow thee whithersoever thou goest.

And Jesus said unto him, Foxes have holes, and birds of the air *have* nests; but the Son of man hath not where to lay *his* head.

Foxes *alopex* (258), is found in Matt. 8:20; **Luke 9:58;** metaphorically, of Herod, in **Luke 13:32.**

Holes *pholeos* (5454), "a lair, burrow, den or hole," is used of foxes in Matt. 8:20 and **Luke 9:58.**

Birds *peteinon* (4071), signifies "that which is able to fly, winged." It is connected with *ptenon* signifying "feathered, winged," which is used in 1 Cor. 15:39. Cf. *petomai* and *petaomai,* "to fly." In the Gospels the RV always translates it "birds," e.g., Matt. 6:26; but "fowls" in Acts 10:12; 11:6. The KJV unsuitably has "fowls," in the Gospels, except Matt. 8:20; 13:32; **Luke 9:58.**

Nests *kataskenosis* (2682), properly "an encamping, taking up one's quarters," then, "a lodging, abode" (*kata,* "down over," *skene,* "a tent"), is used of birds' "nests" in Matt. 8:20 and **Luke 9:58.** In the Sept., 1 Chron. 28:2, "the building"; Ezek. 37:27, "(My) tabernacle." The word *nossia,* signifying "a brood," **Luke 13:34,** used in the Sept. to denote a "nest," e.g., in Deut. 22:6; 32:11, signifies the actual receptacle built by birds in which to lay their eggs (having special reference to the prospective brood); but the word *kataskenosis,* used by the Lord, denotes "a resting or roosting place." This lends force to His comparison. Not only was He without a home, He had not even a lodging place (cf. *kataskenoo,* "to lodge," e.g., Matt. 13:32; Acts 2:26, RV marg., "shall tabernacle").

Lay *klino* (2827), "to make to bend, to bow," or "to make to lean, to rest," is used in Matt. 8:20 and **Luke 9:58,** in the Lord's statement, "the Son of man hath not where to lay His head"; it is significant that this verb is used in John 19:30 of the Lord's act at the moment of His death in placing His head into a position of rest, not a helpless drooping of the head as in all other cases of crucifixion. He reversed the natural order, by first reclining His head (indicative of His submission to His Father's will), and then "giving up His spirit." The rest He found not on earth in contrast to His creatures the foxes and birds, He found in this consummating act on the cross. *See also* **Wear** at ***Luke 9:12.***

9:59 And he said unto another, Follow me. But he said, Lord, suffer me first to go and bury my father.

Suffer *epitrepo* (2010), is rendered "to suffer" in KJV and RV in Matt. 8:21; Mark 10:4; **Luke 9:59;** Acts 28:16; RV only, **Luke 9:61** (KJV, "let"); KJV only, Acts 21:39; in some texts, Matt. 8:31, KJV only.

9:60 Jesus said unto him, Let the dead bury their dead: but go thou and preach the kingdom of God.

Preach *diangello* (1229), lit., "to announce through," hence, "to declare fully, or far and wide" (*dia*, "through"), is translated "declaring" in Acts 21:26, RV (KJV, "to signify"); in **Luke 9:60**, RV, "publish abroad" (for KJV, "preach"), giving the verb its fuller significance; so in Rom. 9:17, for KJV, "declared."

9:61 And another also said, Lord, I will follow thee; but let me first go bid them farewell, which are at home at my house.

Let *see* **Suffer** at *Luke 9:59.*

Bid ... farewell *apotasso* (657), is used in the middle voice to signify "to bid adieu to a person." It primarily means "to set apart, separate" (*apo*, "from," *tasso*, "to set, arrange"); then, "to take leave of, to bid farewell to," Mark 6:46 (RV); **Luke 9:61**; "to give parting instructions to," Acts 18:18, 21; 2 Cor. 2:13; "to forsake, renounce," **Luke 14:33**.

9:62 And Jesus said unto him, No man, having put his hand to the plough, and looking back, is fit for the kingdom of God.

Put *see* **Putteth** at *Luke 5:36.*

Plough *arotron* (723), from *aroo*, "to plough," occurs in **Luke 9:62**.

Looking *blepo* (991), primarily, "to have sight, to see," then, "observe, discern, perceive," frequently implying special contemplation, is rendered by the verb "to look" in **Luke 9:62**, "looking (back)"; John 13:22 "(the disciples) looked (one on another)"; Acts 1:9, RV, "were looking" (KJV, "beheld"); 3:4, "look (on us)"; 27:12, RV, looking," KJV, "that lieth (towards)," of the haven Phenix; Eph. 5:15, RV, "look (therefore carefully how ye walk)," KJV, "see (that ye walk circumspectly)"; Rev. 11:9 and 18:9, RV, "look upon" (KJV, "shall see").

Back *opiso* (3694), connected with *hepomai*, "to follow," is used adverbially, of place, with the meaning "back," "backward," in the phrase *eis ta opiso*, lit., "unto the things behind," in Mark 13:16; **Luke 9:62; 17:31**; John 6:66; 18:6; 20:14. Cf. Phil. 3:13, "the things which are behind.

Fit *euthetos* (2111), "ready for use, fit, well adapted," lit., "well placed" (*eu*, "well," *tithemi*, "to place"), is used (a) of persons, **Luke 9:62**, negatively, of one who is not fit for the kingdom of God; (b) of things, **Luke 14:35**, of salt that has lost its savor; rendered "meet" in Heb. 6:7, of herbs.

Chapter 10

10:1 After these things the Lord appointed other seventy also, and sent them two and two before his face into every city and place, whither he himself would come.

Appointed *anadeiknumi* (322), lit., "to show up, to show clearly," also signifies "to appoint to a position or a service"; it is used in this sense of the 70 disciples, **Luke 10:1**; for the meaning "show," see Acts 1:24.

Seventy *hebdomekonta* (1440), occurs in **Luke 10:1, 17**; in Acts 7:14 it precedes *pente*, "five," lit., "seventy-five," rendered "threescore and fifteen"; in 23:23 it is translated "threescore and ten"; in 27:37 it precedes *hex*, "six," lit., "seventy-six," rendered "threescore and sixteen."

Two *see Luke 9:3. See also* **Apiece** at *Luke 9:3.*

10:2 Therefore said he unto them, The harvest truly *is* great, but the labourers *are* few: pray ye therefore the Lord of the harvest, that he would send forth labourers into his harvest.

Harvest *therismos* (2326), akin to *therizo*, "to reap," is used (a) of "the act of harvesting," John 4:35; (b) "the time of harvest," figuratively, Matt. 13:30, 39; Mark 4:29; (c) "the crop," figuratively, Matt. 9:37, 38; **Luke 10:2**; Rev. 14:15. The beginning of "harvest" varied according to natural conditions, but took place on the average about the middle of April in the eastern lowlands of Palestine, in the latter part of the month in the coast plains and a little later in high districts. Barley "harvest" usually came first and then wheat. "Harvesting" lasted about seven weeks, and was the occasion of festivities.

Great *polus* (4183), "much," is rendered "plenteous" in Matt. 9:37, of a harvest of souls, and **Luke 10:2**, RV (KJV, "great").

Labourers *ergates* (2040), akin to *ergazomai*, "to work," and *ergon*, "work," denotes (a) "a field laborer, a husbandman," Matt. 9:37, 38; 20:1, 2, 8; **Luke 10:2** (twice); Jas. 5:4; (b) "a workman, laborer," in a general sense, Matt. 10:10; **Luke 10:7**; Acts 19:25; 1 Tim. 5:18; it is used (c) of false apostles and evil teachers, 2 Cor. 11:13; Phil. 3:2, (d) of a servant of Christ, 2 Tim. 2:15; (e) of evildoers, **Luke 13:27**.

Pray *see* **Besought** at *Luke 5:12.*

10:3 Go your ways: behold, I send you forth as lambs among wolves.

Lambs *aren* (704), a noun the nominative case of which is found only in early times occurs in **Luke 10:3**. In normal usage it was replaced by *arnion*, of which it is the equivalent.

Among *see* **Midst** at *Luke 4:30.*

Wolves *lukos* (3074), occurs in Matt. 10:16; **Luke 10:3**; John 10:12 (twice); metaphorically, Matt. 7:15; Acts 20:29.

10:4 Carry neither purse, nor scrip, nor shoes: and salute no man by the way.

Carry *see* Bare at *Luke 7:14*.

Purse *ballantion* (905), from *ballo*, "to cast," "a money-box or purse," is found in Luke's Gospel, four times, **10:4**; **12:33** (KJV, "bag"); **22:35-36**.

Scrip *see Luke 9:3*.

Salute *aspazomai* (782), lit. signifies "to draw to oneself"; hence, "to greet, salute, welcome," the ordinary meaning, e.g., in Rom. 16, where it is used 21 times. It also signifies "to bid farewell," e.g., Acts 20:1, RV, "took leave of" (KJV, "embraced"). A "salutation or farewell" was generally made by embracing and kissing (see **Luke 10:4**, which indicates the possibility of delay on the journey by frequent salutation). In Heb. 11:13 it is said of those who greeted the promises from afar, RV, "greeted," for KJV, "embraced." Cf. *aspasmos*, "a salutation."

10:5 And into whatsoever house ye enter, first say, Peace *be* to this house.

House *see Luke 1:27*.

First *proton* (4412), the neuter of the adjective *protos* (the superlative degree of *pro*, "before"), signifies "first, or at the first," (a) in order of time, e.g., **Luke 10:5**; John 18:13; 1 Cor. 15:46; 1 Thess. 4:16; 1 Tim. 3:10; (b) in enumerating various particulars, e.g., Rom. 3:2; 1 Cor. 11:18; 12:28; Heb. 7:2; Jas. 3:17. It is translated "before" in John 15:18.

10:6 And if the son of peace be there, your peace shall rest upon it: if not, it shall turn to you again.

Son *see* Children at *Luke 6:35*.

Rest *epanapauo* (1879), "to cause to rest," is used in the middle voice, metaphorically, signifying "to rest upon," in **Luke 10:6** and Rom. 2:17.

Turn *anakampto* (344), *ana*, "back," *kampto*, "to bend," is rendered "shall turn ... again," in **Luke 10:6**.

10:7 And in the same house remain, eating and drinking such things as they give: for the labourer is worthy of his hire. Go not from house to house.

Remain *meno* (3306), "to stay, abide," is frequently rendered "to remain," e.g., Matt. 11:23; **Luke 10:7**; John 1:33, KJV (RV, "abiding"); 9:41 (in 15:11, the best texts have the verb to be, see RV); 15:16, KJV (RV, "abide"); 19:31; Acts 5:4 (twice), RV, "whiles it remained, did it (not) remain (thine own)?"; 27:41; 1 Cor. 7:11; 15:6; 2 Cor. 3:11, 14; 9:9, KJV (RV, "abideth"); Heb. 12:27; 1 John 3:9.

Give In **Luke 10:7**, the phrase, lit., "the (things) by them," is rendered "such things as they give."

Labourer *see* Labourers at *Luke 10:2*.

Worthy *see Luke 7:4*.

Hire *misthos* (3408), denotes "wages, hire," Matt. 20:8; **Luke 10:7**; Jas. 5:4; in 1 Tim. 5:18; 2 Pet. 2:13; Jude 11, RV, "hire" (KJV, "reward"); in 2 Pet. 2:15, RV, "hire" (KJV, "wages").

Go *metabaino* (3327), "to go or pass over from one place to another," is translated "go" in **Luke 10:7**.

10:8 And into whatsoever city ye enter, and they receive you, eat such things as are set before you:

Receive *see* Took at *Luke 2:28*.

Set *see Luke 9:16*.

10:9 And heal the sick that are therein, and say unto them, The kingdom of God is come nigh unto you.

Heal *see Luke 4:23*.

Sick *see Luke 9:2*.

Come nigh *engizo* (1448), "to draw near, to approach," from *engus*, "near," is used (a) of place and position, literally and physically, Matt. 21:1; Mark 11:1; **Luke 12:33**; **15:25**; figuratively, of drawing near to God, Matt. 15:8; Heb. 7:19; Jas. 4:8; (b) of time, with reference to things that are imminent, as the kingdom of heaven, Matt. 3:2; 4:17; 10:7; the kingdom of God, Mark 1:15; **Luke 10:9**, **11**; the time of fruit, Matt. 21:34; the desolation of Jerusalem, **Luke 21:8**; redemption, **21:28**; the fulfillment of a promise, Acts 7:17; the Day of Christ in contrast to the present night of the world's spiritual darkness, Rom. 13:12; Heb. 10:25; the coming of the Lord, Jas. 5:8; the end of all things, 1 Pet. 4:7. It is also said of one who was drawing near to death, Phil. 2:30.

10:10 But into whatsoever city ye enter, and they receive you not, go your ways out into the streets of the same, and say,

Street *plateia* (4113), grammatically the feminine of *platus*, "broad," is used as a noun (*hodos*, "a way," being understood, i.e., "a broad way"), "a street," Matt. 6:5; 12:19 (in some texts, Mark 6:56); **Luke 10:10**; **13:26**; **14:21**; Acts 5:15; Rev. 11:8; 21:21; 22:2.

Receive *see* Took at *Luke 2:28*.

10:11 Even the very dust of your city, which cleaveth on

us, we do wipe off against you: notwithstanding be ye sure of this, that the kingdom of God is come nigh unto you.

Dust *see Luke 9:5.*

Cleaveth *kollao* (2853), primarily, "to glue or cement together," then, generally, "to unite, to join firmly," is used in the passive voice signifying "to join oneself to, to be joined to," **Luke 15:15**; Acts 5:13; 8:29; 9:26; 10:28, RV (KJV, "to keep company with"); 1 Cor. 6:16, 17; elsewhere, "to cleave to," **Luke 10:11**; Acts 17:34; Rom. 12:9.

Wipe *apomasso* (631), "to wipe off, wipe clean" (*apo*, "from," masso, "to touch, handle"), is used in the middle voice, of "wiping" dust from the feet, **Luke 10:11**.

Notwithstanding *plen*, "howbeit, yet, except that," in **Luke 10:11, 20**, and Phil. 1:18 (RV, "only that"); in 4:14, KJV, "notwithstanding" (RV, "howbeit").

Come nigh *see Luke 10:9.*

10:12 But I say unto you, that it shall be more tolerable in that day for Sodom, than for that city.

Tolerable *anektos* (414), (akin to *anecho*, in the middle voice) is used in its comparative form, *anektoteros*, in Matt. 10:15; 11:22, 24; **Luke 10:12, 14**; some texts have it in Mark 6:11.

10:13 Woe unto thee, Chorazin! woe unto thee, Bethsaida! for if the mighty works had been done in Tyre and Sidon, which have been done in you, they had a great while ago repented, sitting in sackcloth and ashes.

Woe *see Luke 6:24.*

Great In **Luke 10:13**, the adverb *palai*, "of old, long ago," is so rendered in the RV (KJV, "a great while ago").

Repented *metanoeo* (3340), lit., "to perceive afterwards" (*meta*, "after," implying "change," *noeo*, "to perceive"; *nous*, "the mind, the seat of moral reflection"), in contrast to *pronoeo*, "to perceive beforehand," hence signifies "to change one's mind or purpose," always, in the NT, involving a change for the better, an amendment, and always, except in **Luke 17:3, 4**, of "repentance" from sin. The word is found in the Synoptic Gospels (in Luke, nine times, **Luke 10:13; 11:32; 13:3, 5; 16:30; 17:3, 4**), in Acts five times, in Revelation twelve times, eight in the messages to the churches, 2:5 (twice), 16, 21 (twice), RV, "she willeth not to repent" (2nd part); 3:3, 19 (the only churches in those chapters which contain no exhortation in this respect are those at Smyrna and Philadelphia); elsewhere only in 2 Cor. 12:21.

Sackcloth *sakkos* (4526), "a warm material woven from goat's or camel's hair," and hence of a dark color, Rev. 6:12; Jerome renders it *saccus cilicinus* (being made from the hair of the black goat of Cilicia; the Romans called it *cilicium*); cf. Isa. 50:3; it was also used for saddlecloths, Josh. 9:4; also for making sacks, e.g., Gen. 42:25, and for garments worn as expressing mourning or penitence, Matt. 11:21; **Luke 10:13**, or for purposes of prophetic testimony, Rev. 11:3.

Ashes *spodos* (4700), "ashes", is found three times, twice in association with sackcloth, Matt. 11:21 and **Luke 10:13**, as tokens of grief (cf. Esth. 4:1, 3; Isa. 58:5; 61:3; Jer. 6:26; Jonah 3:6); of the ashes resulting from animal sacrifices, Heb. 9:13; in the OT, metaphorically, of one who describes himself as dust and "ashes," Gen. 18:27, etc.

10:14 But it shall be more tolerable for Tyre and Sidon at the judgment, than for you.

Tolerable *see Luke 10:12.*

10:15 And thou, Capernaum, which art exalted to heaven, shalt be thrust down to hell.

Exalted *see Luke 1:52.*

Thrust *katabibazo* (2601), in the active voice, "to cause to go down," is used in the passive in the sense of "being brought down," **Luke 10:15** (KJV, "thrust down"); "go down" in Matt. 11:23 (marg., "be brought down").

Hell *hades* (86), "the region of departed spirits of the lost" (but including the blessed dead in periods preceding the ascension of Christ). It has been thought by some that the word etymologically meant "the unseen" (from *a*, negative, and *eido*, "to see"), but this derivation is questionable; a more probable derivation is from *hado*, signifying "all-receiving." It corresponds to "Sheol" in the OT. In the KJV of the OT and NT; it has been unhappily rendered "hell," e.g., Ps. 16:10; or "the grave," e.g., Gen. 37:35; or "the pit," Num. 16:30, 33; in the NT the revisers have always used the rendering "hades"; in the OT, they have not been uniform in the translation, e.g. in Isa. 14:15 "hell" (marg., "Sheol"); usually they have "Sheol" in the text and "the grave" in the margin. It never denotes the grave, nor is it the permanent region of the lost; in point of time it is, for such, intermediate between decease and the doom of Gehenna. For the condition, see **Luke 16:23-31**. The word is used four times in the Gospels, and always by the Lord, Matt. 11:23;

16:18; **Luke 10:15**; **16:23**; it is used with reference to the soul of Christ, Acts 2:27, 31; Christ declares that He has the keys of it, Rev. 1:18; in Rev. 6:8 it is personified, with the signification of the temporary destiny of the doomed; it is to give up those who are therein, 20:13, and is to be cast into the lake of fire, v. 14.

10:16 He that heareth you heareth me; and he that despiseth you despiseth me; and he that despiseth me despiseth him that sent me.

Despiseth *see* Rejected at *Luke 7:30.*

Sent *see* *Luke 1:19.*

10:17 And the seventy returned again with joy, saying, Lord, even the devils are subject unto us through thy name.

Seventy *see* *Luke 10:1.*

Returned *see* *Luke 1:56.*

Even *kai* The *ascensive* use. This is somewhat similar to the epexegetic significance. It represents, however, an advance in thought upon what precedes and has the meaning "even." The context alone can determine the occurrences of this use. The following are some instances. In Matt. 5:46, 47, the phrases "even the publicans" and "even the Gentiles" represent an extension of thought in regard to the manner of reciprocity exhibited by those referred to, in comparison with those who, like the Pharisees, were considered superior to them. In Mark 1:27, "even the unclean spirits" represents an advance in the minds of the people concerning Christ's miraculous power, in comparison with the authority exercised by the Lord in less remarkable ways. So in **Luke 10:17**. In Acts 10:45, the *kai*, rendered "also," in the phrase "on the Gentiles also," seems necessary to be regarded in the same way, in view of the amazement manifested by those of the circumcision, and thus the rendering will be "even on the Gentiles was poured out the gift"; cf. 11:1. *See also* ***Luke 6:33.***

Subject *see* *Luke 2:51.*

Name *see* *Luke 1:49.*

10:18 And he said unto them, I beheld Satan as lightning fall from heaven.

Beheld *theoreo* (2334), from *theoros*, "a spectator," is used of one who looks at a thing with interest and for a purpose, usually indicating the careful observation of details; this marks the distinction from *blepo*; see, e.g., Mark 15:47; **Luke 10:18**; **23:35**; John 20:6 (RV, "beholdeth," for KJV, "seeth"); so in verses 12 and 14; "consider," in Heb. 7:4. It is used of experience, in the sense of partaking of, in John 8:51; 17:24. Cf. *theoria*, "sight," **Luke 23:48**, only.

Satan *see* *Luke 4:8.*

Lightning *astrape* (796), denotes (a) "lightning," Matt. 24:27; 28:3; **Luke 10:18**; **17:24**; in the plural, Rev. 4:5; 8:5; 11:19; 16:18; (b) "bright shining," or "shining brightness," **Luke 11:36**.

10:19 Behold, I give unto you power to tread on serpents and scorpions, and over all the power of the enemy: and nothing shall by any means hurt you.

Tread *pateo* (3961), is used (a) intransitively and figuratively, of "treading" upon serpents, **Luke 10:19**; (b) transitively, of "treading" on, down or under, of the desecration of Jerusalem by its foes, **Luke 21:24**; Rev. 11:2; of the avenging, by the Lord in Person hereafter, of this desecration and of the persecution of the Jews, in divine retribution, metaphorically spoken of as the "treading" of the winepress of God's wrath, Rev. 14:20; 19:15 (cf. Isa. 63:2, 3).

Serpents *ophis* (3789), the characteristics of the "serpent" as alluded to in Scripture are mostly evil (though Matt. 10:16 refers to its caution in avoiding danger); its treachery, Gen. 49:17; 2 Cor. 11:3; its venom, Ps. 58:4; 1 Cor. 10:9; Rev. 9:19; its skulking, Job 26:13; its murderous proclivities, e.g., Ps. 58:4; Prov. 23:32; Eccl. 10:8, 11; Amos 5:19; Mark 16:18; **Luke 10:19**; the Lord used the word metaphorically of the scribes and Pharisees, Matt. 23:33 (cf. *echidna*, "viper," in Matt. 3:7; 12:34). The general aspects of its evil character are intimated in the Lord's rhetorical question in Matt. 7:10 and **Luke 11:11**. Its characteristics are concentrated in the archadversary of God and man, the Devil, metaphorically described as the serpent, 2 Cor. 11:3; Rev. 12:9, 14, 15; 20:2. The brazen "serpent" lifted up by Moses was symbolical of the means of salvation provided by God, in Christ and His vicarious death under the divine judgment upon sin, John 3:14. While the living "serpent" symbolizes sin in its origin, hatefulness, and deadly effect, the brazen "serpent" symbolized the bearing away of the curse and the judgment of sin; the metal was itself figurative of the righteousness of God's judgment.

Scorpions *skorpios* (4651), akin to *skorpizo*, "to scatter" (which see), is a small animal (the largest of the several species is 6 in. long) like a lobster, but with a long tail, at the end of which is its venomous sting;

the pain, the position of the sting, and the effect are mentioned in Rev. 9:3, 5, 10. The Lord's rhetorical question as to the provision of a "scorpion" instead of an egg, **Luke 11:12**, is, firstly, an allusion to the egg-like shape of the creature when at rest; secondly, an indication of the abhorrence with which it is regarded. In **Luke 10:19**, the Lord's assurance to the disciples of the authority given them by Him to tread upon serpents and scorpions conveys the thought of victory over spiritually antagonistic forces, the powers of darkness, as is shown by His reference to the "power of the enemy" and by the context in vv. **17, 20**.

Enemy *see* Enemies at *Luke 1:71*.

Means The double negative *ou me*, i.e., "no not," "not at all," is translated "by no means," Matt. 5:26; in **Luke 10:19**, "by any means," KJV (RV, "in any wise"); **Luke 12:59**, RV, "by no means" (KJV, "not").

Hurt *adikeo* (91), signifies, intransitively, "to do wrong, do hurt, act unjustly" (*a*, negative, and *dike*, "justice"), transitively, "to wrong, hurt or injure a person." It is translated "to hurt" in the following: (a), intransitively, Rev. 9:19; (b) transitively, **Luke 10:19**; Rev. 2:11 (passive); 6:6; 7:2, 3; 9:4, 10; 11:5.

10:20 Notwithstanding in this rejoice not, that the spirits are subject unto you; but rather rejoice, because your names are written in heaven.

Notwithstanding *see Luke 10:11*.

Rejoice *see Luke 1:14*.

Subject *see Luke 2:51*.

Rather In **Luke 10:20**, KJV, "rather rejoice," there is no word in the original for "rather" (see the RV).

Written *engrapho* (1449), denotes "to write in," **Luke 10:20**; 2 Cor. 3:2, 3.

10:21 In that hour Jesus rejoiced in spirit, and said, I thank thee, O Father, Lord of heaven and earth, that thou hast hid these things from the wise and prudent, and hast revealed them unto babes: even so, Father; for so it seemed good in thy sight.

Hour *see* Time at *Luke 1:10*.

Rejoiced *see Luke 1:47*.

Spirit *see* Holy Ghost at *Luke 2:26*.

Thank *exomologeo* (1843), "to confess forth," i.e., "freely, openly," is used (a) "of a public acknowledgment or confession of sins," Matt. 3:6; Mark 1:5; Acts 19:18; Jas. 5:16; (b) "to profess or acknowledge openly," Matt. 11:25 (translated "thank," but indicating the fuller idea); Phil. 2:11 (some mss. have it in Rev. 3:5); (c) "to confess by way of celebrating, giving praise," Rom. 14:11; 15:9. In **Luke 10:21**, it is translated "I thank," the true meaning being "I gladly acknowledge." In **Luke 22:6** it signifies to consent (RV), for KJV, "promised."

Hid *apokrupto* (613), "to conceal from, to keep secret," is used metaphorically, in **Luke 10:21**, of truths "hidden" from the wise and prudent and revealed to babes; 1 Cor. 2:7, of God's wisdom; Eph. 3:9, of the mystery of the unsearchable riches of Christ, revealed through the gospel, Col. 1:26, of the mystery associated with the preceding.

Wise *sophos* (4680), is used of (a) God, Rom. 16:27; in 1 Tim. 1:17 and Jude 25 *sophos* is absent, in the best mss. (see the RV), the comparative degree, *sophoteros*, occurs in 1 Cor. 1:25, where "foolishness" is simply in the human estimate; (b) spiritual teachers in Israel, Matt. 23:34; (c) believers endowed with spiritual and practical wisdom, Rom. 16:19; 1 Cor. 3:10; 6:5; Eph. 5:15; Jas. 3:13; (d) Jewish teachers in the time of Christ, Matt. 11:25; **Luke 10:21**; (e) the naturally learned, Rom. 1:14, 22; 1 Cor. 1:19, 20, 26, 27; 3:15-20.

Prudent *sunetos* (4908), signifies "intelligent, sagacious, understanding" (akin to *suniemi*, "to perceive"), translated "prudent" in Matt. 11:25, KJV (RV, "understanding"); **Luke 10:21** (ditto); Acts 13:7, RV, "(a man) of understanding"; in 1 Cor. 1:19, "prudent," RV and KJV. Cf. *asunetos*, "without understanding."

Revealed *see Luke 2:35*.

Babes *nepios* (3516), lit., "without the power of speech," denotes "a little child," the literal meaning having been lost in the general use of the word. It is used (a) of "infants," Matt. 21:16; (b) metaphorically, of the unsophisticated in mind and trustful in disposition, Matt. 11:25 and **Luke 10:21**, where it stands in contrast to the wise; of those who are possessed merely of natural knowledge, Rom. 2:20; of those who are carnal, and have not grown, as they should have done, in spiritual understanding and power, the spiritually immature, 1 Cor. 3:1, those who are so to speak partakers of milk, and "without experience of the word of righteousness," Heb. 5:13; of the Jews, who, while the Law was in force, were in a state corresponding to that of childhood, or minority, just as the word "infant" is used of a minor, in English law, Gal. 4:3, "children"; of believers in an immature condition, impressionable and liable to be imposed upon instead of being in a state of spiritual maturity, Eph. 4:14, "children." "Immaturity" is always associated with this word.

Even so *nai* (3483), a particle of strong affirmation, "yea, verily, even so," is rendered "even so" in the KJV, "yea" in the RV, in Matt. 11:26; **Luke 10:21**; Rev. 16:7; both KJV and RV have it in Rev. 1:7; the most authentic mss. omit it in 22:20. *See also* Yea at *Luke 7:26*.

Good *eudokia* (2107), lit., "good pleasure," is rendered "well-pleasing" in Matt. 11:26 and **Luke 10:21**. *See also* Good will at *Luke 2:14*.

Sight *emprosthen* (1715), is used of place or position only; adverbially, signifying "in front," **Luke 19:28**; Phil. 3:13; Rev. 4:6; as a preposition, e.g., Matt. 5:24; John 10:4; with the meaning "in the sight of a person," e.g., Matt. 5:16; 6:1; 17:2; **Luke 19:27**; John 12:37; 1 Thess. 2:19, RV, "before"; KJV, "in the presence of"; Rev. 19:10, RV, "before," especially in phrases signifying in the sight of God, as God wills, Matt. 11:26; 18:14 (lit., "a thing willed before your Father," RV, marg.); **Luke 10:21**; in the sense of "priority of rank or position or dignity," John 1:15, 30 (in some texts, v. 27); in an antagonistic sense, "against," Matt. 23:13 (RV, marg., "before").

10:22 All things are delivered to me of my Father: and no man knoweth who the Son is, but the Father; and who the Father is, but the Son, and *he* to whom the Son will reveal *him*.

Son *see Luke 1:32*.

Will *boulomai* (1014), usually expresses the deliberate exercise of volition, and is rendered as follows in the RV, where the KJV has "will": Matt. 11:27 and **Luke 10:22**, "willeth"; Jas. 4:4, "would"; in Jas. 3:4, RV, "willeth" (KJV, "listeth"). In Jas. 1:18 the perfect participle is translated "of His own will," lit. "having willed."

Reveal *see* Revealed at *Luke 2:35*.

10:23-25 And he turned him unto *his* disciples, and said privately, Blessed *are* the eyes which see the things that ye see:

For I tell you, that many prophets and kings have desired to see those things which ye see, and have not seen *them*; and to hear those things which ye hear, and have not heard *them*.

And, behold, a certain lawyer stood up, and tempted him, saying, Master, what shall I do to inherit eternal life?

Lawyer *see* Doctors of the law at *Luke 5:17*.

Stood *see Luke 4:16*.

Tempted *see* Tempt at *Luke 4:12*.

Inherit *kleronomeo* (2816), strictly means "to receive by lot" (*kleros*, "a lot," *nemomai*, "to possess"); then, in a more general sense, "to possess oneself of, to receive as one's own, to obtain." The following list shows how in the NT the idea of inheriting broadens out to include all spiritual good provided through and in Christ, and particularly all that is contained in the hope grounded on the promises of God.

The verb is used of the following objects: "(a) birthright, that into the possession of which one enters in virtue of sonship, not because of a price paid or of a task accomplished, Gal. 4:30; Heb. 1:4; 12:17; (b) that which is received as a gift, in contrast with that which is received as the reward of law-keeping, Heb. 1:14; 6:12 ("through," i.e., "through experiences that called for the exercise of faith and patience,' but not 'on the ground of the exercise of faith and patience.'); (c) that which is received on condition of obedience to certain precepts, 1 Pet. 3:9, and of faithfulness to God amidst opposition, Rev. 21:7; (d) the reward of that condition of soul which forbears retaliation and self-vindication, and expresses itself in gentleness of behavior.... Matt. 5:5; (e) the reward (in the coming age, Mark 10:30) of the acknowledgment of the paramountcy of the claims of Christ, Matt. 19:29. In the three accounts given of this incident, see Mark 10:17-31; **Luke 18:18-30**, the words of the question put to the Lord are, in Matthew, "that I may have," in Mark and Luke, "that I may inherit." In the report of the Lord's word to Peter in reply to his subsequent question, Matthew has "inherit eternal life," while Mark and Luke have "receive eternal life." It seems to follow that the meaning of the word "inherit" is here ruled by the words "receive" and "have," with which it is interchanged in each of the three Gospels, i.e., the less common word "inherit" is to be regarded as equivalent to the more common words "receive" and "have." Cf. **Luke 10:25**; (f) the reward of those who have shown kindness to the "brethren" of the Lord in their distress, Matt. 25:34; (g) the kingdom of God, which the morally corrupt cannot "inherit," 1 Cor. 6:9, 10, the "inheritance" of which is likewise impossible to the present physical constitution of man, 1 Cor. 15:50; (h) incorruption, impossible of "inheritance" by corruption, 1 Cor. 15:50."

10:26-27 He said unto him, What is written in the law? how readest thou?

And he answering said, Thou shalt love the Lord thy God with all thy heart, and with all thy soul, and with all thy strength, and with all thy mind; and thy neighbour as thyself.

Love *phileo* (5368), is to be distinguished from *agapao* in this, that *phileo* more nearly represents "tender affection." The two words are used for the "love" of the Father for the Son, John 3:35 (*agapeo*), and 5:20 (*phileo*); for the believer, 14:21 (*agapeo*) and 16:27 (*phileo*); both, of Christ's "love" for a certain disciple, 13:23 (*agapeo*), and 20:2 (*phileo*). Yet the distinction between the two verbs remains, and they are never used indiscriminately in the same passage; if each is used with reference to the same objects, as just mentioned, each word retains its distinctive and essential character.

Phileo is never used in a command to men to "love" God; it is, however, used as a warning in 1 Cor. 16:22; *agapao* is used instead, e.g., Matt. 22:37; **Luke 10:27**; Rom. 8:28; 1 Cor. 8:3; 1 Pet. 1:8; 1 John 4:21. The distinction between the two verbs finds a conspicuous instance in the narrative of John 21:15-17. The context itself indicates that *agapao* in the first two questions suggests the "love" that values and esteems (cf. Rev. 12:11). It is an unselfish "love," ready to serve. The use of *phileo* in Peter's answers and the Lord's third question, conveys the thought of cherishing the Object above all else, of manifesting an affection characterized by constancy, from the motive of the highest veneration.

Again, to "love" (*phileo*) life, from an undue desire to preserve it, forgetful of the real object of living, meets with the Lord's reproof, John 12:25. On the contrary, to "love" life (*agapao*) as used in 1 Pet. 3:10, is to consult the true interests of living. Here the word *phileo* would be quite inappropriate.

Strength *ischus* (2479), connected with *ischo* and *echo*, "to have, to hold" (from the root *ech-*, signifying "holding"), denotes "ability, force, strength"; "ability" in 1 Pet. 4:11, KJV (RV, "strength"). In Eph. 1:19 and 6:10, it is said of the strength of God bestowed upon believers, the phrase "the power of His might" indicating strength afforded by power. In 2 Thess. 1:9, "the glory of His might" signifies the visible expression of the inherent personal power of the Lord Jesus. It is said of angels in 2 Pet. 2:11 (cf., Rev. 18:2, KJV, "mightily"). It is ascribed to God in Rev. 5:12 and 7:12. In Mark 12:30, 33, and **Luke 10:27** it describes the full extent of the power wherewith we are to love God.

Mind *see* Imagination at *Luke 1:51*.

Neighbour *plesion* (4139), the neuter of the adjective *plesios* (from *pelas*, "near"), is used as an adverb accompanied by the article, lit., "the (one) near"; hence, one's "neighbor." There were no farmhouses scattered over the agricultural areas of Palestine; the populations, gathered in villages, went to and fro to their toil. Hence domestic life was touched at every point by a wide circle of neighborhood. The terms for neighbor were therefore of a very comprehensive scope. This may be seen from the chief characteristics of the privileges and duties of neighborhood as set forth in Scripture, (a) its helpfulness, e.g., Prov. 27:10; **Luke 10:36**; (b) its intimacy, e.g., **Luke 15:6, 9**; Heb. 8:11; (c) its sincerity and sanctity, e.g., Ex. 22:7, 10; Prov. 3:29; 14:21; Rom. 13:10; 15:2; Eph. 4:25; Jas. 4:12. The NT quotes and expands the command in Lev. 19:18, "to love one's neighbor as oneself"; see, e.g., Matt. 5:43; 19:19; 22:39; Mark 12:31, 33; **Luke 10:27**; Gal. 5:14; Jas. 2:8. See also Acts 7:27.

10:28 And he said unto him, Thou hast answered right: this do, and thou shalt live.

Right *see* Rightly at *Luke 7:43*.

10:29 But he, willing to justify himself, said unto Jesus, And who is my neighbour?

Willing *thelo* (2309), "to will, to wish," implying volition and purpose, frequently a determination, is most usually rendered "to will." It is translated "to desire" in the RV of the following: Matt. 9:13; 12:7; Mark 6:19; **Luke 10:29**; **14:28**; **23:20**; Acts 24:27; 25:9; Gal. 4:17; 1 Tim. 5:11; Heb. 12:17; 13:18.

Justify *see* Justified at *Luke 7:29*.

And *kai* There is also the *inferential* use before a question, e.g., Mark 10:26, "then who can be saved?" RV. This is commonly expressed by the English "and," as in **Luke 10:29**; John 9:36.

Neighbour *see Luke 10:27*.

10:30 And Jesus answering said, A certain *man* went down from Jerusalem to Jericho, and fell among thieves, which stripped him of his raiment, and wounded *him*, and departed, leaving *him* half dead.

Answering *see* Answered at *Luke 7:43*.

Fell *peripipto* (4045), "to fall around" (*peri*, "around"), hence signifies to "fall" in with, or among, to light upon, come across, **Luke 10:30**, "among (robbers)"; Acts 27:41, KJV, "falling into," RV, "lighting upon," a part of a shore; Jas. 1:2, into temptation (i.e., trials).

Thieves *lestes* (3027), "a robber, brigand" (akin to *leia*, "booty"), "one who plunders openly and by violence" (in contrast to *kleptes*, "a thief"), is always translated "robber" or "robbers" in the RV, as the KJV in John 10:1, 8, 18:40;

2 Cor. 11:26; the KJV has "thief" or "thieves" in Matt. 21:13, and parallel passages; 26:55, and parallel passages; 27:38, 44 and Mark 15:27; **Luke 10:30, 36**; but "thief" is the meaning of *kleptes*.

Stripped *ekduo* (1562), "to take off, strip off," is used especially of clothes, and rendered "to strip" in Matt. 27:28 (some mss. have *enduo*, "to clothe"), and **Luke 10:30**, to take off, Matt. 27:31; Mark 15:20; figuratively, 2 Cor. 5:4, "unclothed" (middle voice), of putting off the body at death (the believer's state of being unclothed does not refer to the body in the grave but to the spirit, which awaits the "body of glory" at the resurrection).

Wounded *plege*, "a blow, a stroke," is used in **Luke 10:30** with *epitithemi* "to lay on," lit., "laid on blows," RV, "beat" (KJV, "wounded"). In Rev. 13:3, 12, *plege* is used with the genitive case of *thanatos*, "death," lit., "stroke of death," RV, "death stroke" (KJV, "deadly wound"); the rendering "wound" does not accurately give the meaning; in v. 14, with the genitive of *machaira*, "a sword," KJV, "wound" (RV, "stroke").

Leaving *aphiemi* (863), *apo*, "from," and *hiemi*, "to send," has three chief meanings, (a) "to send forth, let go, forgive"; (b) "to let, suffer, permit"; (c) "to leave, leave alone, forsake, neglect." It is translated by the verb "to leave" (c), in Matt. 4:11; 4:20, 22, and parallel passages; 5:24; 8:15, and parallel passages; 8:22, RV, "leave (the dead)," KJV, "let," and the parallel passage; 13:36, RV, "left (the multitude)," KJV, "sent ... away"; 18:12; 19:27, and parallel passages, RV, "we have left" (KJV, "we have forsaken"), so v. 29; 22:22, 25; 23:23, RV, "have left undone" (KJV, "have omitted," in the 1st part, "leave undone" in the second); 23:38, and the parallel passage; 24:2, 40, 41, and parallel passages; 26:56, RV, "left"; Mark 1:18, "left"; 1:31; 7:8, RV, "ye leave"; 8:13; 10:28, 29; 12:12, 19-22; 13:34; **Luke 10:30; 11:42** (in some mss.); **Luke 12:39**, RV "have left," KJV "have suffered"; John 4:3, 28, 52; 8:29; 10:12; 14:18, 27; 16:28, 32; Rom. 1:27; 1 Cor. 7:11, RV, "leave" (KJV "put away"); 7:13 (KJV and RV); Heb. 2:8; 6:1; Rev. 2:4.

Half dead *hemithanes* (2253), from *hemi*, "half," and *thnesko*, "to die," is used in **Luke 10:30**.

10:31 And by chance there came down a certain priest that way: and when he saw him, he passed by on the other side.

Chance *sunkuria* (4795), lit., "a meeting together with, a coincidence of circumstances, a happening," is translated "chance" in **Luke 10:31**. But concurrence of events is what the word signifies, rather than chance.

Passed *antiparerchomai* (492), denotes "to pass by opposite to," **Luke 10:31, 32**.

10:32 And likewise a Levite, when he was at the place, came and looked *on him*, and passed by on the other side.

Likewise *homoios* (3668), akin to the adjective *homoios*, "like," signifies in "like manner, equally"; in the following the RV has "in like manner" for KJV, "likewise"; Matt. 27:41; Mark 4:16; **Luke 10:32; 13:3; 16:25**; John 5:19; (Heb. 9:21); Jas. 2:25; 1 Pet. 3:1, 7; Rev. 8:12; in Rev. 2:15 the KJV "which thing I hate" translates a variant reading (*ho miso*). *See also* ***Luke 5:33***.

Passed *see* ***Luke 10:31***.

10:33 But a certain Samaritan, as he journeyed, came where he was: and when he saw him, he had compassion *on him*,

Journeyed *hodeuo* (3593), "to be on the way, journey" (from *hodos*, "a way"), the simplest form of the verbs denoting "to journey," is used in the parable of the good samaritan, **Luke 10:33**.

Compassion *see* ***Luke 7:13***.

10:34 And went to *him*, and bound up his wounds, pouring in oil and wine, and set him on his own beast, and brought him to an inn, and took care of him.

Bound *katadeo* (2611), "to bind or tie down, or bind up," is used in **Luke 10:34** of the act of the good Samaritan.

Wounds *trauma* (5134), "a wound," occurs in **Luke 10:34**.

Pouring *epicheo* (2022), "to pour upon" (*epi*), is used in **Luke 10:34**, of the oil and wine used by the good Samaritan on the wounds of him who had fallen among robbers.

Oil *see* ***Luke 7:46***.

Set *epibibazo* (1913), "to place upon," is used of causing persons to mount animals for riding, **Luke 10:34; 19:35**; Acts 23:24.

Beast *ktenos* (2934), primarily denotes "property" (the connected verb *ktaomai* means "to possess"); then, "property in flocks and herds." In Scripture it signifies, (a) a "beast" of burden, **Luke 10:34**; Acts 23:24, (b) "beasts" of any sort, apart from those signified by *therion*, 1 Cor. 15:39; Rev. 18:13, (c) animals for slaughter; this meaning is not found in the NT, but is very frequent in the Sept.

Inn *pandocheion* (3829), lit., "a place where all are received" (*pas*, "all," *dechomai*, "to receive"), denotes "a house for the reception of strangers," a *caravanserai*, translated "inn," in **Luke 10:34**, in the parable of the good samaritan. Cattle and beasts of burden could be sheltered there, and this word must thereby be distinguished from *pandocheus* in the next verse, "(the) host."

Care *epimeleomai* (1959), signifies "to take care of," involving forethought and provision (*epi* indicating "the direction of the mind toward the object cared for"), **Luke 10:34-35**, of the Good Samaritan's care for the wounded man, and in 1 Tim. 3:5, of a bishop's (or overseer's) care of a church – a significant association of ideas.

Luke 10:35 And on the morrow when he departed, he took out two pence, and gave *them* to the host, and said unto him, Take care of him; and whatsoever thou spendest more, when I come again, I will repay thee.

Morrow *aurion* (839), an adverb denoting "tomorrow," is used (a) with this meaning in Matt. 6:30; **Luke 12:28**; **13:32**, **33**; Acts 23:15 (in some mss.), 20; 25:22; 1 Cor. 15:32; Jas. 4:13, (b) with the word *hemera*, "day," understood (occurring thus in the papyri), translated as a noun, "(the) morrow," Matt. 6:34 (twice); **Luke 10:35**; Acts 4:3 (KJV, "next day"); 4:5; Jas. 4:14.

Took *ekballo* (1544), has the meaning "to bring or take out" in **Luke 10:35**, "took out (two pence)," a word perhaps chosen to express the wholeheartedness of the act (lit., "to throw out").

Pence *see Luke 7:41.*

Host *pandocheus* (3830), lit., "one who receives all" (*pas*, "all," *dechomai*, "to receive"), denotes "an innkeeper, host," **Luke 10:35**.

Whatsoever Frequently by the addition of the particle *an*, or the conjunction *ean*, "if," the phrase has the more general idea of "whatsoever," e.g., with *hos*, Matt. 10:11; with *hosos*, Matt. 17:12; with *hostis*, neuter form, **Luke 10:35**.

Spendest *prosdapanao* (4325), "to spend besides" (*pros*, and *dapanao*), is used in **Luke 10:35**, "thou spendest more."

Come *epanerchomai* (1880), "to come back again, return" (*epi*, "on," *ana*, "again"), **Luke 10:35**; **19:15**.

Repay *apodidomi* (591), "to give back," is translated "I will repay" in **Luke 10:35**.

10:36 Which now of these three, thinkest thou, was neighbour unto him that fell among the thieves?

Now *oun* (3767), "therefore, so then," is sometimes used in continuing a narrative, e.g. Acts 1:18; 1 Cor. 9:25; or resuming it after a digression, usually rendered "therefore," e.g., Acts 11:19; 25:1, RV (KJV, now). In the following it is absent from the best mss., Mark 12:20; **Luke 10:36**; John 16:19; 18:24; 19:29.

Neighbour *see Luke 10:27.*

Fell *see* **Fall** at *Luke 6:39.*

Thieves *see Luke 10:30.*

10:37 And he said, He that shewed mercy on him. Then said Jesus unto him, Go, and do thou likewise.

Shewed *see Luke 1:51.*

Mercy *see Luke 1:50.*

Likewise *see Luke 5:33.*

10:38 Now it came to pass, as they went, that he entered into a certain village: and a certain woman named Martha received him into her house.

Received *hupodechomai* (5264), denotes "to receive under one's roof" (*hupo*, "under"), "receive as a guest, entertain hospitably," **Luke 10:38**; **19:6**; Acts 17:7; Jas. 2:25.

10:39 And she had a sister called Mary, which also sat at Jesus' feet, and heard his word.

Sat *parakathezomai* (3869), "to sit down beside" (*para*), in a passive voice form, occurs in the best mss. in **Luke 10:39**. Some texts have the verb *parakathizo*, "to set beside," active form in middle sense.

Feet *see Luke 1:79.*

10:40 But Martha was cumbered about much serving, and came to him, and said, Lord, dost thou not care that my sister hath left me to serve alone? bid her therefore that she help me.

Cumbered *perispao* (4049), lit., "to draw around" (*peri*), "draw away, distract," is used in the passive voice in the sense of being overoccupied about a thing, to be "cumbered," **Luke 10:40**.

Serving *diakonia* (1248), is rendered "service" in Rom. 15:31, KJV; "serving" in **Luke 10:40**.

Came *see Luke 2:9.*

Care *melei* (3199), the third person sing. of *melo*, used impersonally, signifies that "something is an object of care," especially the care of forethought and interest, rather than anxiety, Matt. 22:16; Mark 4:38; 12:14; **Luke 10:40**; John 10:13; 12:6; Acts 18:17; 1 Cor. 9:9 (RV, "Is it for the oxen that God careth?" The KJV seriously misses the point. God does "care" for oxen, but there was a divinely designed significance in the OT passage, relating to the service of preachers of the gospel); 7:21; 1 Pet. 5:7.

Left *see* *Luke 5:28*.

Serve *diakoneo* (1247), "to minister" (akin to *diakonos*), "to render any kind of service," is translated "to serve," e.g., in **Luke 10:40; 12:37; 17:8; 22:26, 27** (twice). *See also* Ministered at *Luke 4:39*.

Bid *see* *Luke 9:54* Command.

Help *sunantizambano* (4878), signifies "to lake hold with at the side for assistance"; hence, "to take a share in, help in bearing, to help in general." It is used, in the middle voice in Martha's request to the Lord to bid her sister help her, **Luke 10:40**; and of the ministry of the Holy Spirit in helping our infirmities, Rom. 8:26. In the Sept., Exod. 18:22; Num. 11:17; Ps. 89:21.

10:41 And Jesus answered and said unto her, Martha, Martha, thou art careful and troubled about many things:

Careful *merimnao* (3309), signifies "to be anxious about, to have a distracting care," e.g., Matt. 6:25, 28, RV, "be anxious," for KJV, "take thought"; 10:19; **Luke 10:41** (RV, "anxious," for KJV, "careful"); **12:11** (RV, "anxious"); to be careful for, 1 Cor. 7:32-34; to have a care for, 1 Cor. 12:25; to care for, Phil. 2:20; "be anxious," Phil. 4:6, RV.

Troubled *thorubazo* (2351), "to disturb, to trouble," is used in **Luke 10:41**, in the best texts (in some, *turbazo*, with the same meaning).

10:42 But one thing is needful: and Mary hath chosen that good part, which shall not be taken away from her.

Needful *see* Need at *Luke 5:31*.

Chosen *see* Chose at *Luke 6:13*.

Part *meris* (3310), denotes (a) "a part" or "portion," **Luke 10:42**; Acts 8:21; 2 Cor. 6:15 (RV, "portion"); in Col. 1:12, "partakers," lit., "unto the part of"; (b) "a district" or "division," Acts 16:12, RV, "district" (KJV, "part").

Taken *see* Take at *Luke 1:25*.

Chapter 11

11:1 And it came to pass, that, as he was praying in a certain place, when he ceased, one of his disciples said unto him, Lord, teach us to pray, as John also taught his disciples.

Ceased *see* Left at *Luke 5:4*.

11:2 And he said unto them, When ye pray, say, Our Father which art in heaven, Hallowed be thy name. Thy kingdom come. Thy will be done, as in heaven, so in earth.

Hallowed *hagiazo* (37), "to make holy" (from *hagios*, "holy"), signifies to set apart for God, to sanctify, to make a person or thing the opposite of *koinos*, "common"; it is translated "Hallowed," with reference to the name of God the Father in the Lord's Prayer, Matt. 6:9; **Luke 11:2**.

Heaven In **Luke 11:2**, the KJV, "as in heaven," translates a phrase found in some mss.

11:3 Give us day by day our daily bread.

Daily *epiousios* (1967), is found in Matt. 6:11 and **Luke 11:3**. Some would derive the word from *epi*, "upon," and *eimi*, "to be," as if to signify "(bread) present," i.e., sufficient bread, but this formation is questionable. The same objection applies to the conjecture, that it is derived from *epi*, and *ousia*, and signifies "(bread) for sustenance." The more probable derivation is from *epi*, and *eimi*, "to go," (bread) for going on, i.e., for the morrow and after, or (bread) coming (for us). See the RV marg. This suits the added *semeron*, "to-day," i.e., the prayer is to be for bread that suffices for this day and next, so that the mind may conform to Christ's warning against anxiety for the morrow. Confirmation of this derivation is also to be found in the word *epious*, in the phrase "the next day," Acts 7:26; 16:11.

> *"Teach me to pray, pray thou thyself in me."*
>
> FRANÇOIS DE LA MOTHE FÉNELON

11:4 And forgive us our sins; for we also forgive every one that is indebted to us. And lead us not into temptation; but deliver us from evil.

One *see* Thyself at *Luke 6:42*.

Indebted *opheilo* (3784), "to owe, to be a debtor," is translated "is indebted" in **Luke 11:4**. Luke does not draw a parallel between our forgiving and God's; he speaks of God's forgiving sins, of our forgiving "debts," moral debts, probably not excluding material debts. Matthew speaks of our sins as *opheilemata*, "debts," and uses parallel terms. Ellicott and others suggest that Luke used a term more adapted to the minds of gentile readers. The inspired language provides us with both, as intended by the Lord.

Lead *eisphero* (1533), "to bring in, or into," is translated "lead (us not) into," in Matt. 6:13 and **Luke 11:4** (RV, "bring ... into"), of temptation.

Temptation *see Luke 4:13.*

Deliver *see* Delivered at *Luke 1:74.*

Evil *poneros* (4190), is translated "wicked" in the KJV and RV in Matt. 13:49; 18:32; 25:26; **Luke 19:22**; Acts 18:14; 1 Cor. 5:13; in the following the RV substitutes "evil" for KJV, "wicked": Matt. 12:45 (twice); 13:19; 16:4; **Luke 11:26**; Col. 1:21; 2 Thess. 3:2; and in the following, where Satan is mentioned as "the (or that) evil one": Matt. 13:38; Eph. 6:16; 1 John 2:13, 14; 3:12 (1st part); 5:18; in v. 19 for KJV, "wickedness"; he is so called also in KJV and RV in John 17:15; 2 Thess. 3:3; KJV only in **Luke 11:4**; in 3 John 10, KJV, the word is translated "malicious," RV, "wicked." *See also* Evils at *Luke 3:19.*

11:5 And he said unto them, Which of you shall have a friend, and shall go unto him at midnight, and say unto him, Friend, lend me three loaves;

Midnight *mesonuktion* (3317), an adjective denoting "at, or of, midnight," is used as a noun in Mark 13:35; **Luke 11:5**; Acts 16:25; 20:7.

Lend *kichremi* or *chrao* (5531), "to lend," is used in the aorist (or "point") tense, active voice, in **Luke 11:5**, in the request, "lend me three loaves." The radical sense of the verb is "to furnish what is needful" (akin to *chreia*, which means both "use" and "need," and to *chre*, "it is needful").

11:6 For a friend of mine in his journey is come to me, and I have nothing to set before him?

Journey *see Luke 2:44.*

Nothing *see Luke 8:17.*

Set *see Luke 9:16.*

11:7 And he from within shall answer and say, Trouble me not: the door is now shut, and my children are with me in bed; I cannot rise and give thee.

Within *see Luke 7:39.*

Trouble The noun *kopos*, "a striking, beating," then, "laborious toil, trouble," used with *parecho*, "to furnish, to supply," is rendered "to trouble" (lit., "to give trouble to"), in Matt. 26:10; Mark 14:6; **Luke 11:7**; **18:5**; Gal. 6:17; the meaning is to embarrass a person by distracting his attention, or to give occasion for anxiety. In the last passage the apostle expresses his determination not to allow the Judaizing teachers to distract him any further.

Now *ede* (2235), denotes "already, now already," "the subjective present, with a suggested reference to some other time, or to some expectation" (Thayer), e.g., Matt. 3:10; 14:24; **Luke 11:7**; John 6:17; Rom. 1:10; 4:19; 13:11; Phil. 4:10.

Shut *see Luke 4:25.*

Bed *koite* (2845), primarily "a place for lying down" (connected with *keimai*, "to lie"), denotes a "bed," **Luke 11:7**; the marriage "bed," Heb. 13:4; in Rom. 13:13, it is used of sexual intercourse. By metonymy, the cause standing for the effect, it denotes conception, Rom. 9:10.

11:8 I say unto you, Though he will not rise and give him, because he is his friend, yet because of his importunity he will rise and give him as many as he needeth.

Yet *ge*, a particle meaning "indeed," "yet," **Luke 11:8**.

Importunity *anaidia (or anaideia)* (335), denotes "shamelessness, importunity" (*a*, negative, *n*, euphonic, and *aidos*, "shame, modesty"), and is used in the Lord's illustration concerning the need of earnestness and perseverance in prayer, **Luke 11:8**. If shameless persistence can obtain a boon from a neighbor, then certainly earnest prayer will receive our Father's answer.

Needeth *chrezo* (5535), "to need, to have need of" (akin to *chre*, "it is necessary, fitting"), is used in Matt. 6:32; **Luke 11:8**; **12:30**; Rom. 16:2, RV, "may have need" (KJV, "hath need"); 2 Cor. 3:1.

11:9 And I say unto you, Ask, and it shall be given you; seek, and ye shall find; knock, and it shall be opened unto you.

Knock *krouo* (2925), "to strike, knock," is used in the NT of "knocking" at a door, (a) literally, **Luke 12:36**; Acts 12:13, 16; (b) figuratively, Matt. 7:7, 8; **Luke 11:9**, **10** (of importunity in dealing with God); **13:25**; Rev. 3:20.

11:10 For every one that asketh receiveth; and he that seeketh findeth; and to him that knocketh it shall be opened.

Knocketh *see* Knock at *Luke 11:9.*

11:11 If a son shall ask bread of any of you that is a father, will he give him a stone? or if *he ask* a fish, will he for a fish give him a serpent?

Serpent *see* Serpents at *Luke 10:19.*

11:12 Or if he shall ask an egg, will he offer him a scorpion?

Egg *oon* (5609), denotes "an egg" (Lat., *ovum*), **Luke 11:12**.

Offer In **Luke 11:12**, KJV, *epididomi*, "to give," is translated "will he offer" (RV, and KJV marg., "will he give").

Scorpion *see* Scorpions at **Luke** *10:19.*

11:13 If ye then, being evil, know how to give good gifts unto your children: how much more shall *your* heavenly Father give the Holy Spirit to them that ask him?

Then *oun* (3767), a particle expressing sequence or consequence, is rendered "then," e.g., Matt. 22:43; 27:22; **Luke 11:13**.

Gifts *doma* (1390), lends greater stress to the concrete character of the "gift," than to its beneficent nature, Matt. 7:11; **Luke 11:13**; Eph. 4:8; Phil. 4:17.

Heavenly In connection with (a), the word "heavenly," used of God the Father in **Luke 11:13**, represents the phrase *ex ouranou*, "from heaven."

11:14 And he was casting out a devil, and it was dumb. And it came to pass, when the devil was gone out, the dumb spake; and the people wondered.

Wondered *see* Marvelled at *Luke 2:33*.

11:15 But some of them said, He casteth out devils through Beelzebub the chief of the devils.

Chief *archon* (758), "a ruler," is rendered "chief" in the KJV of **Luke 14:1** (RV, "ruler"); "chief rulers," in John 12:42, RV, "rulers (of the people)," i.e., of members of the Sanhedrin; "chief," in **Luke 11:15** (RV, "prince"), in reference to Beelzebub, the prince of demons. *See also* Ruler at *Luke 8:41*.

11:16-17 And others, tempting *him*, sought of him a sign from heaven.

But he, knowing their thoughts, said unto them, Every kingdom divided against itself is brought to desolation; and a house *divided* against a house falleth.

Thoughts *dianoema* (1270), "a thought," occurs in **Luke 11:17**, where the sense is that of "machinations."

Divided *diamerizo* (1266), "to divide through," i.e., "completely, to divide up," is translated "to divide" in **Luke 11:17-18**; **12:52-53**; **22:17**; "parted" in Matt. 27:35; Mark 15:24; **Luke 23:34**; John 19:24; Acts 2:45; in Acts 2:3, KJV, "cloven," RV, "parting asunder."

Desolation *eremoo* (2049), signifies "to make desolate, lay waste." From the primary sense of "making quiet" comes that of "making lonely." It is used only in the passive voice in the NT; in Rev. 17:16, "shall make desolate" is, lit., "shall make her desolated"; in 18:17, 19, "is made desolate"; in Matt. 12:25 and **Luke 11:17**, "is brought to desolation."

11:18 If Satan also be divided against himself, how shall his kingdom stand? because ye say that I cast out devils through Beelzebub.

Satan *see Luke 4:8*.

Stand *see* Stand, Stood at *Luke 6:8*.

11:19 And if I by Beelzebub cast out devils, by whom do your sons cast *them* out? therefore shall they be your judges.

Judges *krites* (2923), "a judge" (from *krino*), is used (a) of God, Heb. 12:23, where the order in the original is "to a Judge who is God of all"; this is really the significance; it suggests that He who is the Judge of His people is at the same time their God; that is the order in 10:30; the word is also used of God in Jas. 4:12, RV; (b) of Christ, Acts 10:42; 2 Tim. 4:8; Jas. 5:9; (c) of a ruler in Israel in the times of the Judges, Acts 13:20; (d) of a Roman procurator, Acts 24:10; (e) of those whose conduct provides a standard of "judging," Matt. 12:27; **Luke 11:19**; (f) in the forensic sense, of one who tries and decides a case, Matt. 5:25 (twice); **Luke 12:14**; **12:58** (twice); **18:2**; **18:6** (lit., "the judge of unrighteousness," expressing subjectively his character); Acts 18:15; (g) of one who passes, or arrogates to himself, judgment on anything, Jas. 2:4 (see the RV); 4:11.

11:20 But if I with the finger of God cast out devils, no doubt the kingdom of God is come upon you.

Finger *daktulos* (1147), Matt. 23:4; Mark 7:33; **Luke 11:46**; **16:24**; John 8:6; 20:25, 27, is used metaphorically in **Luke 11:20**, for the power of God, the effects of which are made visible to men (cf. Matt. 12:28, "by the Spirit of God"; cf. also Exod. 8:19).

No doubt In **Luke 11:20**, the particle *ara*, KJV, "no doubt," means "then" (RV).

Come *phthano* (5348), denotes "to anticipate, to come sooner than expected," 1 Thess. 2:16, "is come upon," of divine wrath; cf. Rom. 9:31, "did not arrive at"; or to "come" in a different manner from what was expected, Matt. 12:28, "come upon"; **Luke 11:20**, of the kingdom of God; so of coming to a place, 2 Cor. 10:14.

11:21 When a strong man armed keepeth his palace, his goods are in peace:

Armed *kathoplizo* (2528), is an intensive form, "to furnish fully with arms," *kata,* "down," intensive, *hoplon,* "a weapon," **Luke 11:21**, lit., "a strong man fully armed." In the Sept., Jer. 46:9.

Keepeth *see* **Keeping** at *Luke 2:8. See also* **Kept** at *Luke 8:29.*

Palace *aule* (833), primarily, "an uncovered space around a house, enclosed by a wall, where the stables were," hence was used to describe (a) "the courtyard of a house"; in the OT it is used of the "courts" of the tabernacle and Temple; in this sense it is found in the NT in Rev. 11:2; (b) "the courts in the dwellings of well-to-do folk," which usually had two, one exterior, between the door and the street (called the *proaulion,* or "porch," Mark 14:68.), the other, interior, surrounded by the buildings of the dwellings, as in Matt. 26:69 (in contrast to the room where the judges were sitting); Mark 14:66; **Luke 22:55**; KJV, "hall"; RV "court" gives the proper significance, Matt. 26:3, 58; Mark 14:54; 15:16 (RV, "Praetorium"); **Luke 11:21**; John 18:15. It is here to be distinguished from the Praetorium, translated "palace." For the other meaning "sheepfold," John 10:1, 16.

His These translate (a) forms of pronouns (a frequent use: in 1 Pet. 2:24, "His own self"); the form *autou,* "his," becomes emphatic when placed between the article and the noun, e.g., 1 Thess. 2:19; Titus 3:5; Heb. 2:4 ... (b) *heautou,* "of himself, his own"; the RV rightly puts "his own," for the KJV, "his," in **Luke 11:21**; **14:26**; Rom. 4:19; 5:8, "His own (love)"; 1 Cor. 7:37; Gal. 6:8; Eph. 5:28, 33; 1 Thess. 2:11, 12; 4:4; in Rev. 10:7 the change has not been made; it should read "his own servants"; (c) *idios,* "one's own," "his own," in the RV, in Matt. 22:5; John 5:18; 2 Pet. 2:16; in Matt. 25:15, it is rendered "his several"; in John 19:27, "his own home," lit., "his own things"; in 1 Tim. 6:15, RV, "its own (times)," referring to the future appearing of Christ; in Heb. 4:10 (end of verse), both KJV and RV have "his," where it should be "his own"; so in Acts 24:23, for KJV and RV, "his"; in 1 Cor. 7:7, RV, "his own," KJV, "his proper"; (d) in Acts 17:28, the genitive case of the definite article, "His (offspring)," lit., "of the" (i.e., the one referred to, namely, God).

Goods The neuter plural of the present participle of *huparcho,* is used as a noun denoting "goods," in Matt. 24:47, KJV "his goods," RV, "that he hath"; "goods" in Matt. 25:14; **Luke 11:21**; **16:1**; **19:8**; 1 Cor. 13:3; in Heb. 10:34 (1st part).

Peace *see Luke 1:79.*

11:22 But when a stronger than he shall come upon him, and overcome him, he taketh from him all his armour wherein he trusted, and divideth his spoils.

Stronger *see* **Mightier** at *Luke 3:16.*

Armour *panoplia* (3833), (Eng., "panoply"), lit., "all armor, full armor," (*pas,* "all," *hoplon,* "a weapon"), is used (a) of literal "armor," **Luke 11:22**; (b) of the spiritual helps supplied by God for overcoming the temptations of the Devil, Eph. 6:11, 13. Among the Greeks the *panoplia* was the complete equipment used by heavily armed infantry.

Trusted *peitho* (3982), intransitively, in the perfect and pluperfect active, "to have confidence, trust," is rendered "to trust" in Matt. 27:43; Mark 10:24; **Luke 11:22**; **18:9**; 2 Cor. 1:9; 10:7; Phil, 2:24; 3:4, KJV (RV, "to have confidence"); Heb. 2:13; in the present middle, Heb. 13:18, KJV (RV, "are persuaded").

Divideth *diadidomi* (1239), lit., "to give through," (*dia,* "through," *didomi,* "to give"), as from one to another, "to deal out," is said of "distributing" to the poor, **Luke 18:22**; Acts 4:35, "distribution was made," or to a company of people, John 6:11. It is translated "divideth" in **Luke 11:22**. In Rev. 17:13 the most authentic mss. have the verb *didomi,* to give, instead of the longer form.

Spoils *skulon* (4661), used in the plural, denotes "arms stripped from a foe"; "spoils" in **Luke 11:22**.

11:23 He that is not with me is against me: and he that gathereth not with me scattereth.

Scattereth *skorpizo* (4650), "to scatter" (probably from a root, *skarp-,* signifying "to cut asunder," akin to *skorpios,* "a scorpion"), is used in Matt. 12:30; **Luke 11:23**; John 10:12; 16:32; in the RV of 2 Cor. 9:9, "scattered abroad" (KJV, "he hath dispersed abroad"), of one who liberally dispenses benefits.

11:24 When the unclean spirit is gone out of a man, he walketh through dry places, seeking rest; and finding none, he saith, I will return unto my house whence I came out.

Walketh *dierchomai* (1330), "to go through" (*dia*), is rendered "to walk through" in the KJV of Matt. 12:43 and **Luke 11:24** (RV, "passeth through").

Dry *anudros* (504), "waterless" (*a,* negative, *n,* euphonic, *hudor,* "water"), is rendered "dry" in Matt. 12:43, KJV, and **Luke 11:24** (RV, "waterless"); "without water" in 2 Pet. 2:17 and Jude 12.

Rest *anapausis* (372), "cessation, refreshment, rest" (*ana*, "up," *pauo*, "to make to cease"), the constant word in the Sept. for the Sabbath "rest," is used in Matt. 11:29; here the contrast seems to be to the burdens imposed by the Pharisees. Christ's "rest" is not a "rest" from work, but in work, "not the rest of inactivity but of the harmonious working of all the faculties and affections – of will, heart, imagination, conscience – because each has found in God the ideal sphere for its satisfaction and development" (J. Patrick, in *Hastings Bib. Dic.*); it occurs also in Matt. 12:43; **Luke 11:24**; Rev. 4:8, RV, "(they have no) rest" [KJV, "(they) rest (not)"], where the noun is the object of the verb *echo*, "to have"; so in 14:11.

Return *see* Returned at *Luke 1:56*.

House *see Luke 1:27*.

11:25 And when he cometh, he findeth *it* swept and garnished.

Swept *saroo* (4563), occurs in Matt. 12:44; **Luke 11:25**; **15:8**.

Garnished *kosmeo* (2885), primarily "to arrange, to put in order" (Eng., "cosmetic"), is used of furnishing a room, Matt. 12:44; **Luke 11:25**, and of trimming lamps, Matt. 25:7. Hence, "to adorn, to ornament," as of garnishing tombs, Matt. 23:29; buildings, **Luke 21:5**; Rev. 21:19; one's person, 1 Tim. 2:9; 1 Pet. 3:5; Rev. 21:2; metaphorically, of "adorning a doctrine, Titus 2:10.

11:26 Then goeth he, and taketh *to him* seven other spirits more wicked than himself; and they enter in, and dwell there: and the last *state* of that man is worse than the first.

Then *tote* (5119), a demonstrative adverb of time, denoting "at that time," is used (a) of concurrent events, e.g., Matt. 2:17; Gal. 4:8, "at that time"; v. 29, "then"; 2 Pet. 3:6, "(the world) that then was," lit., "(the) then (world)"; (b) of consequent events, "then, thereupon," e.g., Matt. 2:7; **Luke 11:26**; **16:16**, "[from (KJV, "since")] that time"; John 11:14; Acts 17:14; (c) of things future, e.g., Matt. 7:23; 24:30 (twice), 40; eight times in ch. 25; 1 Cor. 4:5; Gal. 6:4; 1 Thess. 5:3; 2 Thess. 2:8. It occurs 90 times in Matthew, more than in all the rest of the NT together.

Wicked *see* Evil at *Luke 11:4*.

Last *eschatos* (2078), "last, utmost, extreme," is used (a) of place, e.g., **Luke 14:9**, **10**, "lowest;" Acts 1:8 and 13:47, "uttermost part;" (b) of rank, e.g., Mark 9:35; (c) of time, relating either to persons or things, e.g., Matt. 5:26, "the last (farthing)," RV (KJV, "uttermost"); Matt. 20:8, 12, 14; Mark 12:6, 22; 1 Cor. 4:9, of apostles as "last" in the program of a spectacular display; 1 Cor. 15:45, "the last Adam"; Rev. 2:19; of the "last" state of persons, Matt. 12:45, neuter plural, lit., "the last (things)"; so **Luke 11:26**; 2 Pet. 2:20, RV, "the last state" (KJV, "the latter end"); of Christ as the Eternal One, Rev. 1:17 (in some mss. v. 11); 2:8; 22:13; in eschatological phrases as follows: (a) "the last day," a comprehensive term including both the time of the resurrection of the redeemed, John 6:39, 40, 44, 54 and 11:24, and the ulterior time of the judgment of the unregenerate, at the Great White Throne, John 12:48; (b) "the last days," Acts 2:17, a period relative to the supernatural manifestation of the Holy Spirit at Pentecost and the resumption of the divine interpositions in the affairs of the world at the end of the present age, before "the great and notable Day of the Lord," which will usher in the messianic kingdom; (c) in 2 Tim. 3:1, "the last days" refers to the close of the present age of world conditions; (d) in Jas. 5:3, the phrase "in the last days" (RV) refers both to the period preceding the Roman overthrow of the city and the land in AD 70, and to the closing part of the age in consummating acts of gentile persecution including "the time of Jacob's trouble" (cf. verses 7, 8); (e) in 1 Pet. 1:5, "the last time" refers to the time of the Lord's second advent; (f) in 1 John 2:18, "the last hour" (RV) and, in Jude 18, "the last time" signify the present age previous to the Second Advent.

Worse *cheiron* (5501), used as the comparative degree of *kakos*, "evil," describes (a) the condition of certain men, Matt. 12:45; **Luke 11:26**; 2 Pet. 2:20; (b) evil men themselves and seducers, 2 Tim. 3:13; (c) indolent men who refuse to provide for their own households, and are worse than unbelievers, 1 Tim. 5:8, RV; (d) a rent in a garment, Matt. 9:16; Mark 2:21; (e) an error, Matt. 27:64; (f) a person suffering from a malady, Mark 5:26; (g) a possible physical affliction, John 5:14; (h) a punishment, Heb. 10:29, "sorer."

First *protos* (4413), the superlative degree of *pro*, "before," is used "of time or place," (a) as a noun, e.g., **Luke 14:18**; Rev. 1:17; opposite to "the last," in the neuter plural, Matt. 12:45; **Luke 11:26**; 2 Pet. 2:20; in the neuter singular, opposite to "the second," Heb. 10:9; in 1 Cor. 15:3, *en protois*, lit., "in the first (things, or matters)" denotes "first of all"; (b) as an adjective, e.g., Mark 16:9, used with "day" understood, lit., "the first (day) of (i.e., after) the Sabbath," in which phrase the "of" is objective, not including the Sabbath, but following it; in John

20:4, 8; Rom. 10:19, e.g., equivalent to an English adverb; in John 1:15, lit., "first of me," i.e., "before me" (of superiority).

11:27 And it came to pass, as he spake these things, a certain woman of the company lifted up her voice, and said unto him, Blessed *is* the womb that bare thee, and the paps which thou hast sucked.

Lifted *see Luke 6:20.*

Womb *see Luke 1:15.*

Bare *see Luke 7:14.*

Paps *mastos* (3149), used in the plural, "paps," **Luke 11:27; 23:29**; Rev. 1:13, KJV, is preferably rendered "breasts," in the RV.

Sucked *thelazo* (2337), from *thele*, "a breast," is used (a) of the mother, "to suckle," Matt. 24:19; Mark 13:17; **Luke 21:23**; in some texts in **23:29** (the best have *trepho*); (b) of the young, "to suck," Matt. 21:16, "sucklings"; **Luke 11:27**.

11:28 But he said, Yea rather, blessed *are* they that hear the word of God, and keep it.

Yea *men oun* (3304), in some texts *menounge*, i.e., *men-oun-ge*, "yea rather," occurs, e.g., in **Luke 11:28**; in Rom. 10:18, "yea (KJV, yes) verily"; in Phil. 3:8, RV, "yea verily" (KJV, "yea doubtless").

Keep *see* Keeping at *Luke 2:8.*

11:29 And when the people were gathered thick together, he began to say, This is an evil generation: they seek a sign; and there shall no sign be given it, but the sign of Jonas the prophet.

Gathered *epathroizo* (1865), "to assemble besides" (*epi*), said of multitudes, **Luke 11:29**, is rendered "were gathering together" (middle voice), RV (KJV, "were gathered thick together").

Evil *see Luke 6:45.*

Seek *see* Desired at *Luke 9:9.*

Sign *see Luke 2:12.*

11:30 For as Jonas was a sign unto the Ninevites, so shall also the Son of man be to this generation.

Sign *see Luke 2:12.*

So *see* Thus at *Luke 1:25.*

11:31 The queen of the south shall rise up in the judgment with the men of this generation, and condemn them: for she came from the utmost parts of the earth to hear the wisdom of Solomon; and, behold, a greater than Solomon *is* here.

Queen *basilissa* (938), the feminine of *basileus*, "a king," is used (a) of the "Queen of Sheba," Matt. 12:42; **Luke 11:31**; of "Candace," Acts 8:27; (b) metaphorically, of "Babylon," Rev. 18:7.

South *notos* (3558), denotes (a) "the south wind," **Luke 12:55**; Acts 27:13; 28:13; (b) "south," as a direction, **Luke 13:29**; Rev. 21:13; (c) "the South," as a region, Matt. 12:42; **Luke 11:31**.

Condemn *katakrino* (2632), signifies "to give judgment against, pass sentence upon"; hence, "to condemn," implying (a) the fact of a crime, e.g., Rom. 2:1; 14:23; 2 Pet. 2:6; some mss. have it in Jas. 5:9; (b) the imputation of a crime, as in the "condemnation" of Christ by the Jews, Matt. 20:18; Mark 14:64. It is used metaphorically of "condemning" by a good example, Matt. 12:41-42; **Luke 11:31-32**; Heb. 11:7. In Rom. 8:3, God's "condemnation" of sin is set forth in that Christ, His own Son, sent by Him to partake of human nature (sin apart) and to become an offering for sin, died under the judgment due to our sin.

Utmost *peras* (4009), "a limit, boundary" (from *pera*, "beyond"), is used (a) of space, chiefly in the plural, Matt. 12:42, RV, "ends," for KJV, "uttermost parts"; so **Luke 11:31** (KJV, "utmost"); Rom. 10:18 (KJV and RV, "ends"); (b) of the termination of something occurring in a period, Heb. 6:16, RV, "final," for KJV, "an end," said of strife.

Parts *peras* (4009), "an end, boundary," is translated "utmost parts" in the KJV of Matt. 12:42 and **Luke 11:31**.

Wisdom *see Luke 2:40.*

11:32 The men of Nineve shall rise up in the judgment with this generation, and shall condemn it: for they repented at the preaching of Jonas; and, behold, a greater than Jonas *is* here.

Repented *see Luke 10:13.*

Preaching *kerugma* (2782), "a proclamation by a herald," denotes "a message, a preaching" (the substance of what is "preached" as distinct from the act of "preaching"), Matt. 12:41; **Luke 11:32**; Rom. 16:25; 1 Cor. 1:21; 2:4; 15:14; in 2 Tim. 4:17 and Titus 1:3, RV, "message," marg., "proclamation," KJV, "preaching." In the Sept., 2 Chron. 30:5; Prov. 9:3; Jonah 3:2.

11:33 No man, when he hath lighted a candle, putteth *it* in a secret place, neither under a bushel, but on a candlestick, that they which come in may see the light.

Lighted *see Luke 8:16.*

Candle *see Luke 8:16.*

Putteth *see* **Putteth, Setteth** at *Luke 8:16.*

Secret *see Luke 8:17.*

Bushel *modios* (3426), was a dry measure containing about a peck, Matt. 5:15; Mark 4:21; **Luke 11:33**.

Candlestick *see Luke 8:16.*

Come in *eisporeuomai* (1531), "to go in, enter," is never rendered by the verb "to come in," in the RV. See, e.g., **Luke 11:33**, "enter"; Acts 9:28, going in; 28:30, "went in." *See also* **Enter** at *Luke 8:16.*

Light *phengos* (5338), "brightness, luster," is used of the "light" of the moon, Matt. 24:29; Mark 13:24; of a lamp, **Luke 11:33** (some mss. have *phos*, here).

11:34 The light of the body is the eye: therefore when thine eye is single, thy whole body also is full of light; but when *thine eye* is evil, thy body also *is* full of darkness.

Light *see Luke 8:16.*

Eye *ophthalmos* (3788), akin to *opsis*, "sight," probably from a root signifying "penetration, sharpness" (Curtius, Gk. Etym.) (cf. Eng., "ophthalmia," etc.). is used (a) of the physical organ, e.g., Matt. 5:38; of restoring sight, e.g., Matt. 20:33; of God's power of vision, Heb. 4:13; 1 Pet. 3:12; of Christ in vision, Rev. 1:14; 2:18; 19:12; of the Holy Spirit in the unity of Godhood with Christ, Rev. 5:6; (b) metaphorically, of ethical qualities, evil, Matt. 6:23; Mark 7:22 (by metonymy, for envy); singleness of motive, Matt. 6:22; **Luke 11:34**; as the instrument of evil desire, "the principal avenue of temptation," 1 John 2:16; of adultery, 2 Pet. 2:14; (c) metaphorically, of mental vision, Matt. 13:15; John 12:40; Rom. 11:8; Gal. 3:1, where the metaphor of the "evil eye" is altered to a different sense from that of bewitching (the posting up or placarding of an "eye" was used as a charm, to prevent mischief); by gospel-preaching Christ had been, so to speak, placarded before their "eyes"; the question may be paraphrased, "What evil teachers have been malignly fascinating you?"; Eph. 1:18, of the "eyes of the heart," as a means of knowledge.

Single *haplous* (573), "simple, single," is used in a moral sense in Matt. 6:22 and **Luke 11:34**, said of the eye; "singleness" of purpose keeps us from the snare of having a double treasure and consequently a divided heart. The papyri provide instances of its use in other than the moral sense, e.g., of a marriage dowry, to be repaid pure and simple by a husband (Moulton and Milligan). In the Sept., Prov. 11:25.

Light *photeinos* (5460), from *phos*, "bright," is rendered "full of light" in Matt. 6:22; **Luke 11:34, 36** (twice), figuratively, of the single-mindedness of the eye, which acts as the lamp of the body; in Matt. 17:5, "bright," of a cloud.

Evil *see Luke 6:45.*

Darkness *skoteinos* (4652), "full of darkness, or covered with darkness," is translated "dark" in **Luke 11:36**; "full of darkness," in Matt. 6:23 and **Luke 11:34**, where the physical condition is figurative of the moral. The group of *skot-* words is derived from a root *ska-*, meaning "to cover." The same root is to be found in *skene*, "a tent".

11:35 Take heed therefore that the light which is in thee be not darkness.

Heed In **Luke 11:35**, KJV, *skopeo*, "to look," is translated "take heed (that)," RV, "look (whether)."

Darkness *see Luke 1:79.*

11:36 If thy whole body therefore *be* full of light, having no part dark, the whole shall be full of light, as when the bright shining of a candle doth give thee light.

Whole *holos* (3650), signifies "whole," (a) with a noun, e.g., Matt. 5:29, 30; Mark 8:36; 15:1, 16, 33; **Luke 11:36** (1st part), though *holon* may here be used adverbially with *photeinon*, "wholly light" [as in the 2nd part, RV, "wholly (full of light)"]; John 11:50; 1 Cor. 12:17 (1st part); 1 John 2:2; 5:19; (b) absolutely, as a noun, e.g., Matt. 13:33; 1 Cor. 12:17 (2nd part).

Light *see Luke 11:34.*

Part *meros* (3313), denotes (a) "a part, portion," of the whole, e.g., John 13:8; Rev. 20:6; 22:19; hence, "a lot" or "destiny," e.g., Rev. 21:8; in Matt. 24:51 and **Luke 12:46**, "portion"; (b) "a part" as opposite to the whole, e.g., **Luke 11:36**; John 19:23; 21:6, "side"; Acts 5:2; 23:6; Eph. 4:16; Rev. 16:19; a party, Acts 23:9; the divisions of a province, e.g., Matt. 2:22; Acts 2:10; the regions belonging to a city, e.g., Matt. 15:21, RV, "parts" (KJV, "coasts"); 16:13 (ditto); Mark 8:10, KJV and RV, "parts"; "the lower parts of the earth," Eph. 4:9; this phrase means the regions beneath the earth; (c) "a class," or "category" (with *en*, in, "in respect of"), Col. 2:16; "in this respect," 2 Cor. 3:10; 9:3, RV (KJV, "in this behalf").

Dark *see* **Darkness** at *Luke 11:34.*

Shining *astrape* (796), denotes (a) "lightning," (b) "bright shining," of a lamp, **Luke 11:36**. *See also* **Lightning** at *Luke 10:18.*

Candle *see Luke 8:16.*

Light *photizo* (5461), used (a) intransitively, signifies "to shine, give light," Rev. 22:5; (b) transitively, (1) "to illumine, to light, enlighten, to be lightened," **Luke 11:36**; Rev. 21:23; in the passive voice, Rev. 18:1; metaphorically, of spiritual enlightenment, John 1:9; Eph. 1:18; 3:9, "to make ... see;" Heb. 6:4; 10:32, "ye were enlightened," RV (KJV, "... illuminated"); (2) "to bring to light," 1 Cor. 4:5 (of God's act in the future); 2 Tim. 1:10 (of God's act in the past).

11:37 And as he spake, a certain Pharisee besought him to dine with him: and he went in, and sat down to meat.

Besought *see* Desired at *Luke 7:36.*

Dine *ariston* (712), primarily, "the first food," taken early in the morning before work; the meal in the Pharisee's house, in **Luke 11:37**, was a breakfast or early meal (see RV, marg.); the dinner was called *deipnon*. Later the breakfast was called *akratisma* (not in NT), and dinner, *ariston*, as in Matt. 22:4; **Luke 11:38; 14:12**.

Sat *anapipto* (377), "to fall back" (*ana*, "back," *pipto*, "to fall"), denotes, in the NT, "to recline for a repast," Matt. 15:35; Mark 6:40; 8:6; **Luke 11:37; 14:10; 17:7; 22:14**; John 6:10 (twice); 13:12; in John 13:25 and 21:20 it is used of leaning on the bosom of Christ. In the Sept., Gen. 49:9.

11:38 And when the Pharisee saw *it*, he marvelled that he had not first washed before dinner.

Washed *baptizo* (907), is rendered "washed" in **Luke 11:38**. *See also* Baptize at *Luke 3:16*.

Dinner *see* Dine at *Luke 11:37.*

11:39 And the Lord said unto him, Now do ye Pharisees make clean the outside of the cup and the platter; but your inward part is full of ravening and wickedness.

Now *nun* (3568), is used (a) of time, the immediate present, whether in contrast to the past, e.g., John 4:18; Acts 7:52, or to the future, e.g., John 12:27; Rom. 11:31; sometimes with the article, singular or plural, e.g., Acts 4:29; 5:38; (b) of logical sequence, often partaking also of the character of (a), "now therefore, now however," as it is, e.g., **Luke 11:39**; John 8:40; 9:41; 15:22, 24; 1 Cor. 5:11, RV marg., "as it is."

Outside *exothen* (1855), an adverb formed from *exo*, "without," properly signifies "from without," Mark 7:18 (in v. 15 it is used as a preposition); with the article it is equivalent to a noun, "the outside," Matt. 23:25; **Luke 11:39**; in v. **40**, RV, "the outside" (KJV, "that which is without").

Platter *pinax* (4094), primarily "a board or plank," came to denote various articles of wood; hence, "a wooden trencher, charger," Matt. 14:8, 11; Mark 6:25, 28; **Luke 11:39**.

Inward *esothen* (2081), an adverb denoting "from within," or "within," is used with the article, as a noun, of the inner being, the secret intents of the heart, which, the Lord declared, God made, as well as the visible physical frame, **Luke 11:40**. In v. **39**, it is rendered "inward part."

Full *gemo* (1073), "to be full, to be heavily laden with," was primarily used of a ship; it is chiefly used in the NT of evil contents, such as extortion and excess, Matt. 23:25; dead men's bones, v. 27; extortion and wickedness, **Luke 11:39**; cursing, Rom. 3:14; blasphemy, Rev. 17:3; abominations, v. 4; of divine judgments 15:7; 21:9; (RV, "laden," KJV, "full"); of good things, 4:6, 8; 5:8.

Ravening *harpage* (724), denotes "pillage, plundering, robbery, extortion" (akin to *harpazo*, "to seize, carry off by force," and *harpagmos*, "a thing seized, or the act of seizing"; from the root *arp*, seen in Eng., "rapacious"; an associated noun, with the same spelling, denoted a rake, or hook for drawing up a bucket); it is translated "extortion" in Matt. 23:25; **Luke 11:39**, RV, KJV, "ravening"; Heb. 10:34, "spoiling.

Wickedness *poneria* (4189), akin to *poneo*, "to toil" (cf. *poneros*, "bad, worthless"), denotes "wickedness," and is so translated in Matt. 22:18; Mark 7:22 (plural); **Luke 11:39**; Rom. 1:29; 1 Cor. 5:8; Eph. 6:12; in Acts 3:26, "iniquities." Cf. *kakia*, "evil."

11:40 *Ye* fools, did not he that made that which is without make that which is within also?

Fools *aphron* (878), signifies "without reason" (*a*, negative, *phren*, "the mind"), "want of mental sanity and sobriety, a reckless and inconsiderate habit of mind" (Hort), or "the lack of commonsense perception of the reality of things natural and spiritual ... or the imprudent ordering of one's life in regard to salvation" (G. Vos, in *Hastings' Bible Dic.*); it is mostly translated "foolish" or "foolish ones" in the RV; **Luke 11:40; 12:20**; Rom. 2:20; 1 Cor. 15:36; 2 Cor. 11:16 (twice), 19 (contrasted with *phronimos*, "prudent"); 12:6, 11; Eph. 5:17; 1 Pet. 2:15.

Without This is a translation of (a) *exo*, "outside," e.g., Matt. 12:46, 47;

"(them that are) without," 1 Cor. 5:12, 13; Col. 4:5; 1 Thess. 4:12 (the unregenerate); Heb. 13:11-13; (b) *exothen*, "from without," or "without," e.g., Mark 7:15, 18; **Luke 11:40**; 2 Cor. 7:5; 1 Tim. 3:7; as a preposition, Rev. 11:2; (c) *choris*, "apart from," frequently used as a preposition, especially in Hebrews [4:15; 7:7, 20, 21; 9:7, 18, 22, 28; 11:6; in 11:40, RV, "apart from" (KJV, "without"); 12:8, 14]; (d) *aneu*, like *choris*, but rarer, Matt. 10:29; Mark 13:2; 1 Pet. 3:1; 4:9; (e) *ater*, **Luke 22:6**, marg., "without (tumult)"; v. **35**; (f) *ektos*, "out of, outside," 1 Cor. 6:18; (g) *parektos*, "besides, in addition," 2 Cor. 11:28, "(those things that are) without," RV, marg., "(the things which) I omit," or "(the things that come) out of course." *See also* **Outside** at ***Luke 11:39***.

Within *see* ***Luke 7:39***. *See also* **Inward** at ***Luke 11:39***.

11:41 But rather give alms of such things as ye have; and, behold, all things are clean unto you.

Rather In **Luke 11:41** and **12:31**, KJV, *plen*, an adverb signifying "yet, howbeit," is translated "rather" (RV, "howbeit").

Alms *eleemosune* (1654), connected with *eleemon*, "merciful," signifies (a) "mercy, pity, particularly in giving alms," Matt. 6:1, 2-4; Acts 10:2; 24:17; (b) the benefaction itself, the "alms" (the effect for the cause), **Luke 11:41**; **12:33**; Acts 3:2-3, 10; 9:36, "alms-deeds"; 10:2, 4, 31.

Such In **Luke 11:41**, *ta enonta*, KJV, "such things as ye have," lit., "the (things) within" (*eneimi*, "to be in"), RV, "those things which are within" (KJV marg., "as you are able," RV, marg., "ye can"), perhaps signifying not outward things such as lustrations, but "what things ye have within your cups and platters," i.e., "your possessions."

Have For *eneimi*, **Luke 11:41**, "ye have."

Clean *katharos* (2513), "free from impure admixture, without blemish, spotless," is used (a) physically, e.g., Matt. 23:26; 27:59; John 13:10 (where the Lord, speaking figuratively, teaches that one who has been entirely "cleansed," needs not radical renewal, but only to be "cleansed" from every sin into which he may fall); 15:3; Heb. 10:22; Rev. 15:6; 19:8, 14; 21:18, 21; (b) in a Levitical sense, Rom. 14:20; Titus 1:15, "pure"; (c) ethically, with the significance free from corrupt desire, from guilt, Matt. 5:8; John 13:10-11; Acts 20:26; 1 Tim. 1:5; 3:9; 2 Tim. 1:3; 2:22; Titus 1:15; Jas. 1:27; blameless, innocent (a rare meaning for this word), Acts 18:6; (d) in a combined Levitical and ethical sense ceremonially, **Luke 11:41**, "all things are clean unto you."

11:42 But woe unto you, Pharisees! for ye tithe mint and rue and all manner of herbs, and pass over judgment and the love of God: these ought ye to have done, and not to leave the other undone.

Woe *see* ***Luke 6:24***.

Tithe *apodekatoo* (586), denotes (a) "to tithe" (*apo*, "from," *dekatos*, "tenth"), Matt. 23:23 (KJV, "pay tithe of"); **Luke 11:42**; in **Luke 18:12** (where the best texts have the alternative form *apodekateuo*), "I give tithes"; (b) "to exact tithes" from Heb. 7:5.

Mint *heduosmon* (2238), an adjective denoting sweet-smelling (*hedus*, "sweet," *osme*, "a smell"), is used as a neuter noun signifying "mint," Matt. 23:23; **Luke 11:42**.

Rue *peganon* (4076), a shrubby plant with yellow flowers and a heavy smell, cultivated for medicinal purposes, is mentioned in **Luke 11:42**.

Manner In Matt. 12:31; **Luke 11:42**; Rev. 18:12, KJV, *pas*, "every" (so RV), is translated "all manner."

Herbs *lachanon* (3001), denotes "a garden herb, a vegetable" (from *lachaino*, "to dig"), in contrast to wild plants, Matt. 13:32; Mark 4:32; **Luke 11:42**; Rom. 14:2.

Pass *parerchomai* (3928), from *para*, "by," *erchomai*, "to come" or "go," denotes (I) literally, "to pass, pass by," (a) of persons, Matt. 8:28; Mark 6:48; **Luke 18:37**; Acts 16:8; (b) of things, Matt. 26:39, 42; of time, Matt. 14:15; Mark 14:35; Acts 27:9, KJV, "past" (RV, "gone by"); 1 Pet. 4:3; (II) metaphorically, (a) "to pass away, to perish," Matt. 5:18; 24:34, 35; Mark 13:30, 31; **Luke 16:17**; **21:32, 33**; 2 Cor. 5:17; Jas. 1:10; 2 Pet. 3:10; (b) "to pass by, disregard, neglect, pass over," **Luke 11:42**; **15:29**, "transgressed." For the meaning "to come forth or come," see **Luke 12:37**; **17:7**, RV (Acts 24:7 in some mss.).

Judgment *krisis* (2920), (a) denotes "the process of investigation, the act of distinguishing and separating" (as distinct from *krima*); hence "a judging, a passing of judgment upon a person or thing"; it has a variety of meanings, such as judicial authority, John 5:22, 27; justice, Acts 8:33; Jas. 2:13; a tribunal, Matt. 5:21-22; a trial, John 5:24; 2 Pet. 2:4; a judgment, 2 Pet. 2:11; Jude 9; by metonymy, the standard of judgment, just dealing, Matt. 12:18, 20; 23:23; **Luke 11:42**; divine judgment executed, 2 Thess. 1:5; Rev. 16:7; (b) sometimes it has the meaning "condemnation," and is virtually equivalent to *krima*; see Matt. 23:33; John 3:19; Jas. 5:12, *hupo krisin*, "under judgment."

Leave *parerchomai* (3928), *para*, "by or away"), signifies (a) "to come or go forth, or arrive," e.g., **Luke 12:37; 17:7** (last part); Acts 24:7; (b) "to pass by," e.g., **Luke 18:37**; (c) "to neglect," e.g., **Luke 11:42**. *See also* Leaving at *Luke 10:30*.

Other *ekeinos* (1565), signifying "that one," implying remoteness as compared with *houtos*, "this," is translated "the other," e.g., in Matt. 23:23; **Luke 11:42; 18:14**.

Undone *pariemi* (3935), signifies (a) "to disregard, leave alone, leave undone," **Luke 11:42** (some mss. have *aphiemi*, here); (b) "to relax, loosen," and, in the passive voice, "to be relaxed, exhausted," said of hands that "hang" down in weakness, Heb. 12:12.

11:43 Woe unto you, Pharisees! for ye love the uppermost seats in the synagogues, and greetings in the markets.

Woe *see Luke 6:24*.

Uppermost seats *protokathedria* (4410), "a sitting in the first or chief seat" (*protos*, "first," *kathedra*, "a seat"), is found in Matt. 23:6; Mark 12:39; **Luke 11:43; 20:46**.

Greetings *see* Salutation at *Luke 1:29*.

Markets *see* Marketplace at *Luke 7:32*.

11:44 Woe unto you, scribes and Pharisees, hypocrites! for ye are as graves which appear not, and the men that walk over *them* are not aware *of them*.

Woe *see Luke 6:24*.

Hypocrites *see* Hypocrite at *Luke 6:42*.

Appear not *adelos* (82), denotes (a) "unseen"; with the article, translated "which appear not" (*a*, negative, *delos*, "evident"), **Luke 11:44**; (b) "uncertain, indistinct," 1 Cor. 14:8. In the Sept., Ps. 51:6.

11:45 Then answered one of the lawyers, and said unto him, Master, thus saying thou reproachest us also.

Lawyers *see* Doctors of the law at *Luke 5:17*.

Reproachest *hubrizo* (5195), used transitively, denotes "to outrage, treat insolently"; "to entreat shamefully" in Matt. 22:6, RV (KJV, "spitefully"); so in **Luke 18:32**, RV; in Acts 14:5 (KJV, "use despitefully"); in 1 Thess. 2:2, KJV and RV; in **Luke 11:45**, "reproachest." The word is much stronger than "to reproach"; the significance is "Thou insultest (even us)," i.e., who are superior to ordinary Pharisees. The lawyer's imputation was unjust; Christ's rebuke was not *hubris*, "insult." What He actually said was by way of "reproach" (*oneidizo*).

11:46 And he said, Woe unto you also, *ye* lawyers! for ye lade men with burdens grievous to be borne, and ye yourselves touch not the burdens with one of your fingers.

Woe *see Luke 6:24*.

Lawyers *see* Doctors of the law at *Luke 5:17*. *See also* Scribes at *Luke 5:21*.

Lade *phortizo* (5412), "to load" (akin to *phero*, "to bear"), is used in the active voice in **Luke 11:46**, "ye lade"; in the passive voice, metaphorically, in Matt. 11:28, "heavy laden." In the Sept., Ezek. 16:33.

Burdens *phortion* (5413), lit., "something carried" (from *phero*, "to bear"), is always used metaphorically (except in Acts 27:10, of the lading of a ship); of that which, though "light," is involved in discipleship of Christ, Matt. 11:30; of tasks imposed by the scribes, Pharisees and lawyers, Matt. 23:4; **Luke 11:46**; of that which will be the result, at the judgment-seat of Christ, of each believer's work, Gal. 6:5.

Grievous *dusbastaktos* (1419), "hard to be borne" (from *dus*, an inseparable prefix, like Eng. "mis-," and "un-," indicating "difficulty, injuriousness, opposition," etc., and *bastazo*, "to bear"), is used in **Luke 11:46** and, in some mss., in Matt. 23:4, "grievous to be borne"; in the latter the RV marg. has "many ancient authorities omit."

Yourselves The addition of *autoi*, "yourselves," to the pronoun marks especial emphasis, e.g., Mark 6:31; John 3:28; 1 Cor. 11:13; 1 Thess. 4:9. Sometimes *autoi* is used without the pronoun, e.g., **Luke 11:46, 52**; Acts 2:22; 20:34; 1 Thess. 2:1; 3:3; 5:2; 2 Thess. 3:7; Heb. 13:3.

Touch *prospsauo* (4379), "to touch upon, to touch slightly," occurs in **Luke 11:46**.

Fingers *see* Finger at *Luke 11:20*.

11:47 Woe unto you! for ye build the sepulchres of the prophets, and your fathers killed them.

Woe *see Luke 6:24*.

Sepulchres *mnemeion* (3419), primarily denotes "a memorial" (akin to *mnaomai*, "to remember"), then, "a monument" (the significance of the word rendered "tombs," KJV, "sepulchres," in **Luke 11:47**), anything done to preserve the memory of things and persons; it usually denotes a tomb, and is translated either "tomb" or "sepulchre" or "grave." Apart from the Gospels, it is found only in Acts 13:29. Among the Hebrews it was generally a cavern, closed by a door or stone, often decorated. Cf. Matt. 23:29.

11:48 Truly ye bear witness that ye allow the deeds of your fathers: for they indeed killed them, and ye build their sepulchres.

Witness *martus,* or *martur* (3144), (whence Eng., "martyr," one who bears "witness" by his death) denotes "one who can or does aver what he has seen or heard or knows"; it is used (a) of God, Rom. 1:9; 2 Cor. 1:23; Phil. 1:8; 1 Thess. 2:5, 10 (2nd part); (b) of Christ, Rev. 1:5; 3:14; (c) of those who "witness" for Christ by their death, Acts 22:20; Rev. 2:13; Rev. 17:6; (d) of the interpreters of God's counsels, yet to "witness" in Jerusalem in the times of the Antichrist, Rev. 11:3; (e) in a forensic sense, Matt. 18:16; 26:65; Mark 14:63; Acts 6:13; 7:58; 2 Cor. 13:1; 1 Tim. 5:19; Heb. 10:28; (f) in a historical sense, **Luke 11:48**; **24:48**; Acts 1:8, 22; 2:32; 3:15; 5:32; 10:39, 41; 13:31; 22:15; 26:16; 1 Thess. 2:10 (1st part); 1 Tim. 6:12; 2 Tim. 2:2; Heb. 12:1, "(a cloud) of witnesses," here of those mentioned in ch. 11, those whose lives and actions testified to the worth and effect of faith, and whose faith received "witness" in Scripture; 1 Pet. 5:1.

Allow *suneudokeo* (4909), "to consent or fully approve" (*sun,* "with," *eu,* "well," *dokeo,* "to think"), is translated "allow" in **Luke 11:48**; "was consenting" in Acts 8:1; 22:20.

11:49 Therefore also said the wisdom of God, I will send them prophets and apostles, and *some* of them they shall slay and persecute:

Also *kai* The particle *kai,* "and," chiefly used for connecting words, clauses and sentences (the copulative or connective use), not infrequently signifies "also." This is the *adjunctive,* or *amplificatory,* use, and it is to be distinguished from the purely copulative significance "and." A good illustration is provided in Matt. 8:9, in the words of the centurion, "I also am a man under authority." Other instances are Matt. 5:39, 40; 8:9; 10:18; 18:33; 20:4; **Luke 11:49**; **12:41**, **54**, **57**; **20:3**; John 5:26, "the Son also," RV; 7:3; 12:10; 14:1, 3, 7, 19; 15:9, 27; 17:24; Acts 11:17; Rom. 1:13; 6:11; 1 Cor. 7:3; 11:25; 15:30; Gal. 6:1; Phil. 4:12, "I know also," RV, 1 Thess. 3:12. In 1 Cor. 2:13 the *kai* phrase signifies "which are the very things we speak, with the like power of the Holy Spirit."

Wisdom *see* ***Luke 2:40***.

Slay *apokteino* (615), the usual word for "to kill," is so translated in the RV wherever possible (e.g., for KJV, "to slay," in **Luke 11:49**; Acts 7:52; Rev. 2:13; 9:15; 11:13; 19:21); in the following the verb "to kill" would not be appropriate, Rom. 7:11, "slew," metaphorically of sin, as using the commandment; Eph. 2:16, "having slain," said metaphorically of the enmity between Jew and Gentile.

Persecute *dioko* (1377), has the meanings (a) "to put to flight, drive away," (b) "to pursue," whence the meaning "to persecute," Matt. 5:10-12, 44; 10:23; 23:34; **Luke 11:49** (*ekdioko* in some mss.); **21:12**; John 5:16; 15:20 (twice); Acts 7:52; 9:4, 5, and similar passages; Rom. 12:14; 1 Cor. 4:12; 15:9; 2 Cor. 4:9, KJV (RV, "pursued"); Gal. 1:13, 23; 4:29; Gal. 5:11, RV, "am ... persecuted" (KJV, "suffer persecution"); so 6:12; Phil. 3:6; 2 Tim. 3:12, "shall suffer persecution"; Rev. 12:13. *ekdioko* (1559), to chase away, drive out" (*ek,* "out," *dioko,* "to pursue"), is used in 1 Thess. 2:15, RV, "drave out," KJV, "have persecuted." Some mss. have this verb for *dioko,* in **Luke 11:49**.

11:50 That the blood of all the prophets, which was shed from the foundation of the world, may be required of this generation;

Shed *ekchuno,* or *ekchunno* (1632) is used of the voluntary giving up of His life by Christ through the "shedding" of His blood in crucifixion as an atoning sacrifice, Matt. 26:28; Mark 14:24; **Luke 22:20**, KJV, "is shed," RV, "is poured out"; these passages do not refer to the effect of the piercing of His side (which took place after His death); of the murder of servants of God, Matt. 23:35; **Luke 11:50**; Acts 22:20 (in the best texts); of the love of God in the hearts of believers through the Holy Spirit, Rom. 5:5.

Foundation *katabole* (2602), lit., "a casting down," is used (a) of "conceiving seed," Heb. 11:11; (b) of "a foundation," as that which is laid down, or in the sense of founding; metaphorically, of "the foundation of the world"; in this respect two phrases are used, (1) "from the foundation of the world," Matt. 25:34 (in the most authentic mss. in 13:35 there is no phrase representing "of the world"); **Luke 11:50**; Heb. 4:3; 9:26; Rev. 13:8; 17:8; (2) "before the foundation of the world," John 17:24; Eph. 1:4; 1 Pet. 1:20. The latter phrase looks back to the past eternity.

Required *ekzeteo* (1567), "to seek out," also denotes "to demand, require," **Luke 11:50**, **51**, of executing vengeance for the slaughter of the prophets (cf. 2 Sam. 4:11; Ezek. 3:18).

11:51 From the blood of Abel unto the blood of Zacharias, which perished between the altar and the temple: verily I say unto you, It shall be required of this generation.

Between *metaxu* (3342), "in the midst, or between" (from *meta*, and *xun*, i.e., *sun*, "with"), is used as a preposition, (a) of mutual relation, Matt. 18:15; Acts 15:9; Rom. 2:15, RV, "one with another," lit., "between one another," for KJV, "the meanwhile"; (b) of place, Matt. 23:35; **Luke 11:51**; **16:26**; Acts 12:6; (c) of time, "meanwhile," John 4:31. In Acts 13:42, the KJV marg. has "in the week between," the literal rendering.

Altar *see Luke 1:11.*

Temple For *oikos*, rendered "temple," **Luke 11:51**, KJV. *See also* **House** at *Luke 1:27.*

Verily In **Luke 11:51**, KJV, *nai*, "yea" (RV), is translated "verily." *See also* **Yea** at *Luke 7:26.*

Required *see Luke 11:50.*

11:52 Woe unto you, lawyers! for ye have taken away the key of knowledge: ye entered not in yourselves, and them that were entering in ye hindered.

Woe *see Luke 6:24.*

Lawyers *see* **Doctors of the law** at *Luke 5:17. See also* **Scribes** at *Luke 5:21.*

Key *kleis* (2807), "a key," is used metaphorically (a) of "the keys of the kingdom of heaven," which the Lord committed to Peter, Matt. 16:19, by which he would open the door of faith, as he did to Jews at Pentecost, and to Gentiles in the person of Cornelius, acting as one commissioned by Christ, through the power of the Holy Spirit; he had precedence over his fellow disciples, not in authority, but in the matter of time, on the ground of his confession of Christ (v. 16); equal authority was committed to them (18:18); (b) of "the key of knowledge," **Luke 11:52**, i.e., knowledge of the revealed will of God, by which men entered into the life that pleases God; this the religious leaders of the Jews had presumptuously "taken away," so that they neither entered in themselves, nor permitted their hearers to do so; (c) of "the keys of death and of Hades," Rev. 1:18, RV, indicative of the authority of the Lord over the bodies and souls of men.

Knowledge *see Luke 1:77.*

Yourselves *see Luke 11:46.*

Hindered *koluo* (2967), "to hinder, forbid, restrain," is translated "to hinder" in **Luke 11:52**; Acts 8:36; Rom. 1:13, RV (KJV, "was let"); Heb. 7:23, RV (KJV, "were not suffered").

11:53 And as he said these things unto them, the scribes and the Pharisees began to urge *him* vehemently, and to provoke him to speak of many things:

Scribes *see* **Doctors of the law** at *Luke 5:17.*

Urge *enecho* (1758), "to hold in," is said (a) of being "entangled" in a yoke of bondage, such as Judaism, Gal. 5:1. Some mss. have the word in 2 Thess. 1:4, the most authentic have *anecho*, "to endure"; (b) with the meaning to set oneself against, be urgent against, said of the plotting of Herodias against John the Baptist, Mark 6:19, RV, "set herself against," KJV, "had a quarrel against"; of the effort of the scribes and Pharisees to provoke the Lord to say something which would provide them with a ground of accusation against Him, **Luke 11:53**, RV, "to press upon," marg., "to set themselves vehemently against," KJV, "to urge."

Vehemently *deinos* (1171), akin to *deos*, "fear," signifies (a) "terribly," Matt. 8:6, "grievously (tormented)"; (b) "vehemently," **Luke 11:53**.

Provoke *apostomatizo* (653), in classical Greek meant "to speak from memory, to dictate to a pupil" (*apo*, "from," *stoma*, "a mouth"); in later Greek, "to catechize"; in **Luke 11:53**, "to provoke (Him) to speak."

11:54 Laying wait for him, and seeking to catch something out of his mouth, that they might accuse him.

Laying in wait *enedreuo* (1748), "to lie in wait for, to lay wait for" (from *en*, "in," and *hedra*, "a seat"), occurs in **Luke 11:54**, "laying wait for"; Acts 23:21, "there lie in wait for."

Catch *thereuo* (2340), "to hunt or catch wild beasts" (*therion*, "a wild beast"), is used by Luke in **Luke 11:54**.

Something *see* **Somewhat** at *Luke 7:40.*

Mouth *see Luke 1:64.*

Chapter 12

12:1 In the mean time, when there were gathered together an innumerable multitude of people, insomuch that they trode one upon another, he began to say unto his disciples first of all, Beware ye of the leaven of the Pharisees, which is hypocrisy.

Time In **Luke 12:1**, "in the mean time" is a rendering of the phrase *en hois*, lit., "in which (things or circumstances)."

Gathered *episunago* (1996), "to gather together," suggesting stress upon the place at which the "gathering" is made (*epi*, "to"), is said of a hen and her chickens, Matt. 23:37; and so of the Lord's would-be protecting care of the people of Jerusalem, *id*, and **Luke 13:34**;

of the "gathering" together of the elect, Matt. 24:31; Mark 13:27; of the "gathering" together of a crowd, Mark 1:33; **Luke 12:1**.

Innumerable multitude *murias* (3461), denotes either "ten thousand," or, "indefinitely, a myriad, a numberless host," in the plural, Acts 19:19; lit. "five ten-thousands," Rev. 5:11; 9:16; in the following, used of vast numbers, **Luke 12:1**, KJV, "an innumerable multitude," RV, "the many thousands" (RV marg., "the myriads"); Acts 21:20, "thousands"; Heb. 12:22, "innumerable hosts"; Jude 14, "ten thousands" (RV, marg., in each place, "myriads"). Cf. the adjective *murios*, "ten thousand," Matt. 18:24; 1 Cor. 4:15; 14:19.

Trode *see* **Trodden** at *Luke 8:5*.

Beware *prosecho* (4337), lit., "to hold to" (*pros*, "to," *echo*, "to have, to hold"), hence, "to turn one's mind or attention to a thing by being on one's guard against it," is translated "beware" in Matt. 7:15; 10:17; 16:6, 11-12; **Luke 12:1**; **20:46**.

Leaven *zume* (2219), "leaven, sour dough, in a high state of fermentation," was used in general in making bread. It required time to fulfill the process. Hence, when food was required at short notice, unleavened cakes were used, e.g., Gen. 18:6; 19:3; Exod. 12:8. The Israelites were forbidden to use "leaven" for seven days at the time of Passover, that they might be reminded that the Lord brought them out of Egypt "in haste," Deut. 16:3, with Exod. 12:11; the unleavened bread, insipid in taste, reminding them, too, of their afflictions, and of the need of self-judgment, is called "the bread of affliction." "Leaven" was forbidden in all offerings to the Lord by fire, Lev. 2:11; 6:17. Being bred of corruption and spreading through the mass of that in which it is mixed, and therefore symbolizing the pervasive character of evil, "leaven" was utterly inconsistent in offerings which typified the propitiatory sacrifice of Christ. In the OT "leaven" is not used in a metaphorical sense. In the NT it is used (a) metaphorically (1) of corrupt doctrine, Matt. 13:33 and **Luke 13:21**, of error as mixed with the truth (there is no valid reason for regarding the symbol here differently from its application elsewhere in the NT); Matt. 16:6, 11; Mark 8:15 (1st part); **Luke 12:1**; that the kingdom of heaven is likened to "leaven," does not mean that the kingdom is "leaven." The same statement, as made in other parables, shows that it is the whole parable which constitutes the similitude of the kingdom; the history of Christendom confirms the fact that the pure meal of the doctrine of Christ has been adulterated with error; (2) of corrupt practices, Mark 8:15 (2nd part), the reference to the Herodians being especially applied to their irreligion; 1 Cor. 5:7, 8; (b) literally in Matt. 16:12, and in the general statements in 1 Cor. 5:6 and Gal. 5:9, where the implied applications are to corrupt practice and corrupt doctrine respectively.

Hypocrisy *hupokrisis* (5272), primarily denotes "a reply, an answer" (akin to *hupokrinomai*, "to answer"); then, "play-acting," as the actors spoke in dialogue; hence, "pretence, hypocrisy"; it is translated "hypocrisy" in Matt. 23:28; Mark 12:15; **Luke 12:1**; 1 Tim. 4:2; the plural in 1 Pet. 2:1. For Gal. 2:13 and *anupokritos*, "without hypocrisy," in Jas. 3:17.

12:2 For there is nothing covered, that shall not be revealed; neither hid, that shall not be known.

Covered *sunkalupto* (4780), lit., "to cover together"; the *sun-*, however, is intensive, and the verb signifies "to cover wholly, to cover up," **Luke 12:2**.

Revealed *see Luke 2:35*.

Hid *see Luke 8:17*.

12:3 Therefore whatsoever ye have spoken in darkness shall be heard in the light; and that which ye have spoken in the ear in closets shall be proclaimed upon the housetops.

Darkness *skotia* (4653), is used (a) of physical darkness, "dark," John 6:17, lit., "darkness had come on," and 20:1, lit., "darkness still being"; (b) of secrecy, in general, whether what is done therein is good or evil, Matt. 10:27; **Luke 12:3**; (c) of spiritual or moral "darkness," emblematic of sin, as a condition of moral or spiritual depravity, Matt. 4:16; John 1:5; 8:12; 12:35, 46; 1 John 1:5; 2:8-9, 11.

Ear *see* **Ears** at *Luke 1:44*.

Closets *tameion* (5009), denotes, firstly, "a store-chamber," then, "any private room, secret chamber," Matt. 6:6; RV, "inner chamber" (KJV, "closet"); 24:26, "inner (KJV, secret) chambers"; **Luke 12:3**, RV, ditto, for KJV, "closets"; it is used in **Luke 12:24** ("store-chamber") of birds.

Proclaimed *see* **Preach** at *Luke 4:18*.

Housetops *see* **Housetop** at *Luke 5:19*.

12:4 And I say unto you my friends, Be not afraid of them that kill the body, and after that have no more that they can do.

Friends *see Luke 7:6*.

Afraid *phobeo* (5399), in earlier Greek, "to put to flight," in the NT is always in the passive voice, with the meanings either (a) "to fear, be afraid," its most frequent use, e.g., Acts 23:10, according to the best mss.; or (b) "to show reverential fear," (1) of men, Mark 6:20; Eph. 5:33, RV, "fear," for KJV, "reverence"; (2) of God, e.g., Acts 10:2, 22; 13:16, 26; Col. 3:22 (RV, "the Lord"); 1 Pet. 2:17; Rev. 14:7; 15:4; 19:5; (a) and (b) are combined in **Luke 12:4, 5**, where Christ warns His followers not to be afraid of men, but to "fear" God.

Have *echo* (2192), the usual verb for "to have," is used with the following meanings: (a) "to hold, in the hand," etc., e.g., Rev. 1:16; 5:8; (b) "to hold fast, keep," **Luke 19:20**; metaphorically, of the mind and conduct, e.g., Mark 16:8; John 14:21; Rom. 1:28; 1 Tim. 3:9; 2 Tim. 1:13; (c) "to hold on, cling to, be next to," e.g., of accompaniment, Heb. 6:9, "things that accompany (salvation)," lit., "the things holding themselves of salvation" (RV, marg., "are near to"); of place, Mark 1:38, "next (towns)," lit., "towns holding nigh"; of time, e.g., **Luke 13:33**, "(the day) following," lit., "the holding (day)"; Acts 13:44; 20:15; 21:26; (d) "to hold, to count, consider, regard," e.g., Matt. 14:5; 21:46; Mark 11:32; **Luke 14:18**; Philem. 17; (e) "to involve," Heb. 10:35; Jas. 1:4; 1 John 4:18; (f) "to wear," of clothing, arms, etc., e.g., Matt. 3:4; 22:12; John 18:10; (g) "to be with child," of a woman, Mark 13:17; Rom. 9:10 (lit., "having conception"); (h) "to possess," the most frequent use, e.g., Matt. 8:20; 19:22; Acts 9:14; 1 Thess. 3:6; (i) of complaints, disputes, Matt. 5:23; Mark 11:25; Acts 24:19; Rev. 2:4, 20; (j) of ability, power, e.g., **Luke 12:4**; Acts 4:14 (lit., "had nothing to say"); (k) of necessity, e.g., **Luke 12:50**; Acts 23:17-19; (1) "to be in a certain condition," as of readiness, Acts 21:12 (lit., "I have readily"); of illness, Matt. 4:24, "all that were sick" (lit., "that had themselves sickly"); Mark 5:23, "lieth (lit., "hath herself") at the point of death"; Mark 16:18 "they shall recover" (lit., "shall have themselves well"), John 4:52, "he began to amend" (lit., "he had himself better"); of evil works, 1 Tim. 5:25, "they that are otherwise," (lit., "the things having otherwise"); to be so, e.g., Acts 7:1, "are these things so?" (lit., "have these things thus?"), of time, Acts 24:25, "for this time" (lit., "the thing having now").

More *perissoteron* (4054), the neuter of the comparative degree of *perissos*, "more abundant," is used a an adverb, "more," e.g., **Luke 12:4**; 2 Cor. 10:8, KJV (RV, "abundantly"); Heb. 7:15, RV, "more abundantly" (KJV, "far more"). *See also **Luke 7:26**.*

12:5 But I will forewarn you whom ye shall fear: Fear him, which after he hath killed hath power to cast into hell; yea, I say unto you, Fear him.

Forewarn In **Luke 12:5** the verb *hupodeiknumi*, "to shew, teach, make known," is translated "will warn" in the RV (KJV, "forewarn"). *See also* **Warned** at ***Luke 3:7***.

Fear *see* **Afraid** at ***Luke 12:4***.

Power *exousia* (1849), denotes "freedom of action, right to act"; used of God, it is absolute, unrestricted, e.g., **Luke 12:5** (RV marg., "authority"); in Acts 1:7 "right of disposal" is what is indicated; used of men, authority is delegated. Angelic beings are called "powers" in Eph. 3:10 (cf. 1:21); 6:12; Col. 1:16; 2:15 (cf. 2:10).

Cast *emballo* (1685), "to cast into," is used in **Luke 12:5**.

Hell *geenna* (1067), represents the Hebrew Ge-Hinnom (the valley of Tophet) and a corresponding Aramaic word; it is found twelve times in the NT, eleven of which are in the Synoptists, in every instance as uttered by the Lord Himself. He who says to his brother, Thou fool, will be in danger of "the hell of fire," Matt. 5:22; it is better to pluck out (a metaphorical description of irrevocable law) an eye that causes its possessor to stumble, than that his "whole body be cast into hell," v. 29; similarly with the hand, v. 30; in Matt. 18:8, 9, the admonitions are repeated, with an additional mention of the foot; here, too, the warning concerns the person himself (for which obviously the "body" stands in chapt. 5); in v. 8, "the eternal fire" is mentioned as the doom, the character of the region standing for the region itself, the two being combined in the phrase "the hell of fire," v. 9. To the passage in Matt. 18, that in Mark 9:43-47, is parallel; here to the word "hell" are applied the extended descriptions "the unquenchable fire" and "where their worm dieth not and the fire is not quenched." That God, "after He hath killed, hath power to cast into hell," is assigned as a reason why He should be feared with the fear that keeps from evil doing, **Luke 12:5**; the parallel passage to this in Matt. 10:28 declares, not the casting in, but the doom which follows, namely, the destruction (not the loss of being, but of well-being) of "both soul and body." In Matt. 23 the Lord denounces the scribes and Pharisees, who in proselytizing a person "make him two-fold more a son of hell" than themselves (v. 15), the phrase here being expressive of moral characteristics, and declares the impossibility of their escaping "the judgment of hell," v. 33. In Jas. 3:6 "hell" is described as the source of the evil done by misuse of the tongue; here the word stands for the powers of darkness, whose characteristics and destiny are those of "hell." For terms descriptive of "hell," see e.g., Matt. 13:42; 25:46; Phil. 3:19; 2 Thess. 1:9; Heb. 10:39; 2 Pet. 2:17; Jude 13; Rev. 2:11; 19:20; 20:6, 10, 14; 21:8.

Yea *see Luke 7:26.*

12:6 Are not five sparrows sold for two farthings, and not one of them is forgotten before God?

Sparrows *strouthion* (4765), a diminutive of *strouthos*, "a sparrow," occurs in Matt. 10:29, 31; **Luke 12:6, 7**.

Farthings *assarion* (787), a diminutive of the Latin *as*, was one-tenth of a drachma, or one-sixteenth of a Roman *denarius*, i.e., about three farthings, Matt. 10:29; **Luke 12:6**.

Forgotten *epilanthanomai* (1950), "to forget, or neglect," is said (a) negatively of God, indicating His remembrance of sparrows, **Luke 12:6**, and of the work and labor of love of His saints, Heb. 6:10; (b) of the disciples regarding taking bread, Matt. 16:5; Mark 8:14; (c) of Paul regarding "the things which are behind," Phil. 3:13; (d) of believers, as to showing love to strangers, Heb. 13:2, RV, and as to doing good and communicating, v. 16; (e) of a person who after looking at himself in a mirror, forgets what kind of person he is, Jas. 1:24.

Before *enopion* (1799), is translated "in the sight of" in the RV (for KJV, "before") in **Luke 12:6; 15:18; 16:15**; Acts 7:46; 10:33; 19:19; 1 Tim. 5:4, 21; 2 Tim. 2:14; 4:1; Rev. 13:12. The RV is more appropriate in most passages, as giving the real significance of the word. *See also Luke 1:17.*

12:7 But even the very hairs of your head are all numbered. Fear not therefore: ye are of more value than many sparrows.

Very In **Luke 12:7** the RV renders *kai* by "very" (for KJV, "even the very").

Hairs *see Luke 7:38.*

Numbered *arithmeo* (705), is found in Matt. 10:30; **Luke 12:7**; Rev. 7:9.

More value *diaphero* (1308), used intransitively, means "to differ, to excel," hence "to be of more value," Matt. 6:26, RV, "are (not) ye of (much) more value" (KJV, "better"); 12:12 and **Luke 12:24**, ditto; Matt. 10:31; **Luke 12:7**.

Sparrows *see Luke 12:6.*

12:8 Also I say unto you, Whosoever shall confess me before men, him shall the Son of man also confess before the angels of God:

Confess *homologeo* (3670), lit., "to speak the same thing" (*homos*, "same," *lego*, "to speak"), "to assent, accord, agree with," denotes, (a) "to confess, declare, admit," John 1:20; e.g., Acts 24:14; Heb. 11:13; (b) "to confess by way of admitting oneself guilty of what one is accused of, the result of inward conviction," 1 John 1:9; (c) "to declare openly by way of speaking out freely, such confession being the effect of deep conviction of facts," Matt. 7:23; 10:32 (twice) and **Luke 12:8** (see next par.); John 9:22; 12:42; Acts 23:8; Rom. 10:9-10 ("confession is made"); 1 Tim. 6:12 (RV); Titus 1:16; 1 John 2:23; 4:2, 15; 2 John 7 (in John's epistle it is the necessary antithesis to Gnostic doceticism); Rev. 3:5, in the best mss.; (d) "to confess by way of celebrating with praise," Heb. 13:15; (e) "to promise," Matt. 14:7. In Matt. 10:32 and **Luke 12:8** the construction of this verb with *en*, "in," followed by the dative case of the personal pronoun, has a special significance, namely, to "confess" in a person's name, the nature of the "confession" being determined by the context, the suggestion being to make a public "confession." Thus the statement, "every one … who shall confess Me (lit. "in Me," i.e., in My case) before men, him (lit., "in him," i.e., in his case) will I also confess before My Father … ," conveys the thought of "confessing" allegiance to Christ as one's Master and Lord, and, on the other hand, of acknowledgment, on His part, of the faithful one as being His worshipper and servant, His loyal follower; this is appropriate to the original idea in *homologeo* of being identified in thought or language.

Angels *angelos* (32), "a messenger" (from *angello*, "to deliver a message"), sent whether by God or by man or by Satan, "is also used of a guardian or representative in Rev. 1:20, cf. Matt. 18:10; Acts 12:15 (where it is better understood as 'ghost'), but most frequently of an order of created beings, superior to man, Heb. 2:7; Ps. 8:5, belonging to Heaven, Matt. 24:36; Mark 12:25, and to God, **Luke 12:8**, and engaged in His service, Ps. 103:20. "Angels" are spirits, Heb. 1:14, i.e., they have not material bodies as men have; they are either human in form, or can assume the human form when necessary, cf. **Luke 24:4**, with v. **23**, Acts 10:3 with v. 30."

12:9 But he that denieth me before men shall be denied before the angels of God.

Denieth, Denied *see* Deny at *Luke 9:23.*

Before *see Luke 1:17.*

12:10-11 And whosoever shall speak a word against the Son of man, it shall be forgiven him: but unto him that blasphemeth against the Holy Ghost it shall not be forgiven.

And when they bring you unto the synagogues, and *unto* magistrates, and powers, take ye no thought how or what thing ye shall answer, or what ye shall say:

Magistrates *arche* (746), "a rule, sovereignty," is rendered "rulers" in **Luke 12:11**, RV (KJV, "magistrates").

Powers *see* **Power** at *Luke 4:6*.

Thought *merimnao* (3309), denotes "to be anxious, careful." For the KJV, "to take thought," the RV substitutes "to be anxious" in Matt. 6:25, 27, 28, 31, 34; 10:19; **Luke 12:11, 22, 25, 26**. *See also* **Careful** at *Luke 10:41*.

Answer *apologeomai* (626), lit., "to talk oneself off from" (*apo*, "from," *lego*, "to speak"), "to answer by way of making a defense for oneself" (besides its meaning "to excuse," Rom. 2:15; 2 Cor. 12:19), is translated "answer" in **Luke 12:11; 21:14**; in Acts 19:33, KJV and RV both have "made defense"; in Acts 24:10; 25:8; 26:1-2, the RV has the verb to make a defense, for the KJV, "to answer," and in 26:24 for the KJV, "spake for himself."

12:12 For the Holy Ghost shall teach you in the same hour what ye ought to say.

Same Occasionally one of the forms of the pronoun *autos*, "self, same," is translated "very"; the RV rendering is sometimes "himself," etc., e.g., 1 Thess. 5:23, "(The God of peace) Himself"; see, however, John 14:11, "(the) very (works)"; Rom. 13:6 and Phil. 1:6, "(this) very (thing)"; Heb. 10:1, "(the) very (image)"; and the RV, "very" (KJV, "same") in **Luke 12:12; 20:19; 24:13, 33**; Acts 16:18; Rom. 9:17; Eph. 6:22.

Ought *see* **Must** at *Luke 2:49*.

12:13 And one of the company said unto him, Master, speak to my brother, that he divide the inheritance with me.

Divide *merizo* (3307), akin to *meros*, "a part, to part, divide into," in the middle voice means "to divide anything with another, to share with." The usual meaning is "to divide," Matt. 12:25, 26; Mark 3:24-26; 6:41; **Luke 12:13** (middle voice); Rom. 12:3, "hath dealt"; 1 Cor. 1:13; Heb. 7:2, RV (KJV, "gave a part"). Elsewhere with other meanings, 1 Cor. 7:17, 34; 2 Cor. 10:13.

Inheritance *kleronomia* (2817), "a lot," properly "an inherited property, an inheritance." "It is always rendered inheritance in NT, but only in a few cases in the Gospels has it the meaning ordinarily attached to that word in English, i.e., that into possession of which the heir enters only on the death of an ancestor. The NT usage may be set out as follows: (a) that property in real estate which in ordinary course passes from father to son on the death of the former, Matt. 21:38; Mark 12:7; **Luke 12:13; 20:14**; (b) a portion of an estate made the substance of a gift, Acts 7:5; Gal. 3:18, which also is to be included under (c); (c) the prospective condition and possessions of the believer in the new order of things to be ushered in at the return of Christ, Acts 20:32; Eph. 1:14; 5:5; Col. 3:24; Heb. 9:15; 1 Pet. 1:4; (d) what the believer will be to God in that age, Eph. 1:18."

12:14 And he said unto him, Man, who made me a judge or a divider over you?

Made *kathistemi* (2525), usually signifies "to appoint a person to a position." In this sense the verb is often translated "to make" or "to set," in appointing a person to a place of authority, e.g., a servant over a household, Matt. 24:45, 47; 25:21, 23; **Luke 12:42, 44**; a judge, **Luke 12:14**; Acts 7:27, 35; a governor, Acts 7:10; man by God over the work of His hands, Heb. 2:7. It is rendered "appoint," with reference to the so-called seven deacons in Acts 6:3. The RV translates it by "appoint" in Titus 1:5, instead of "ordain," of the elders whom Titus was to "appoint" in every city in Crete. Not a formal ecclesiastical ordination is in view, but the "appointment," for the recognition of the churches, of those who had already been raised up and qualified by the Holy Spirit, and had given evidence of this in their life and service. It is used of the priests of old, Heb. 5:1; 7:28; 8:3 (RV, "appointed").

Judge *dikastes* (1348), denotes "a judge" (from *dike*, "right, a judicial hearing, justice"; akin to *dikazo*, "to judge"), Acts 7:27, 35; some mss. have it in **Luke 12:14**; while *dikastes* is a forensic term, *krites* "gives prominence to the mental process" (Thayer). At Athens the *dikastes* acted as a juryman, the *krites* being the presiding "judge." *See also* **Judges** at *Luke 11:19*.

Divider *meristes* (3312), "a divider," is found in **Luke 12:14**.

12:15 And he said unto them, Take heed, and beware of covetousness: for a man's life consisteth not in the abundance of the things which he possesseth.

Heed *horao* (3708), "to see," usually expressing the sense of vision, is rendered "take heed" in Matt. 16:6; 18:10, KJV (RV, "see"); Mark 8:15; **Luke 12:15**; Acts 22:26 (KJV only).

And *see* **Behold** at *Luke 5:12*.

Beware *phulasso* (5442), "to guard, watch, keep," is used, in the middle voice, of being "on one's guard against" (the middle v. stressing personal interest in the action), **Luke 12:15**, "beware of," RV, "keep yourselves from," as in Acts 21:25; in 2 Tim. 4:15, "be thou ware"; in 2 Pet. 3:17, "beware."

Covetousness *pleonexia* (4124), "covetousness," lit., "a desire to have more" (*pleon*, "more," *echo*, "to have"), always in a bad sense, is used in a general way in Mark 7:22 (plural, lit., "covetings," i.e., various ways in which "covetousness" shows itself); Rom. 1:29, Eph. 5:3, 1 Thess. 2:5. Elsewhere it is used, (a) of material possessions, **Luke 12:15**; 2 Pet. 2:3; 2 Cor. 9:5 (RV, "extortion"), lit., "as (a matter of) extortion" i.e., a gift which betrays the giver's unwillingness to bestow what is due; (b) of sensuality, Eph. 4:19, "greediness"; Col. 3:5 (where it is called "idolatry"); 2 Pet. 2:14 (KJV, "covetous practices").

Consisteth *eimi* (1510), "to be," is rendered "consist" (lit., "is") in **Luke 12:15**.

Abundance *see* **Remained** at *Luke 9:17*.

Possesseth *huparcho* (5225), "to be in existence," and, in a secondary sense, "to belong to," is used with this meaning in the neuter plural of the present participle with the article signifying one's "possessions," "the things which he possesseth," **Luke 12:15**; Acts 4:32; in Heb. 10:34, RV, "possessions" (KJV, "goods").

12:16 And he spake a parable unto them, saying, The ground of a certain rich man brought forth plentifully

Ground *chora* (5561), "land, country," is used of property, "ground," in **Luke 12:16**, "the ground (of a certain rich man)." *See also* **Region** at *Luke 3:1*.

Rich *see Luke 6:24*.

Brought *euphoreo* (2164), "to bear well, be productive," "brought forth plentifully," **Luke 12:16**. Cf. *karpophoreo*, Mark 4:20, RV "bear"; so, Col. 1:6.

Plentifully This translates the prefix *eu* ("well") of the verb *euphoreo*, "to produce well," in **Luke 12:16**, "brought forth plentifully."

12:17 And he thought within himself, saying, What shall I do, because I have no room where to bestow my fruits?

Thought *see* **Cast** at *Luke 1:29*.

Room In **Luke 12:17**, KJV, *pou*, "anywhere" or "where," with a negative, is translated "no room" (RV, "not where").

Bestow *sunago* (4863), "to assemble" (*sun*, "together," *ago*, "to bring"), is used of the "gathering together" of people or things; in **Luke 12:17-18**, "bestow," with reference to the act of "gathering" one's goods; so in **Luke 15:13**, suggesting that the Prodigal, having "gathered" all his goods together, sold them off; in John 6:12, of "gathering" up fragments; in John 18:2, "resorted," with reference to the "assembling" of Christ with His disciples in the garden of Gethsemane, there in the passive voice (unsuitable, however, in an English translation). In Acts 11:26, the RV has "were gathered together (with the church)," for KJV, "assembled themselves" (possibly "they were hospitably entertained by"). The verb is not found in the most authentic mss. in Rev. 13:10.

Fruits *see* **Fruit** at *Luke 1:42*.

12:18 And he said, This will I do: I will pull down my barns, and build greater; and there will I bestow all my fruits and my goods.

Pull *kathaireo* (2507), "to take down," is translated "I will pull down" in **Luke 12:18**.

Barns *see* **Garner** at *Luke 3:17*.

Fruits *genema* (1096), from *ginomai*, "to come into being," denotes "fruit" (a) as the produce of the earth, e.g., the vine; in the following the best mss. have this noun, Matt. 26:29; Mark 14:25; **Luke 22:18**; (b) metaphorically, as "the fruits of ... righteousness" (i.e., of material ministrations to the needy), 2 Cor. 9:10. In **Luke 12:18** some mss. have *gennemata*, a mistake for *genemata*; the best have *sitos*, "corn."

Goods *see* **Good** at *Luke 1:53*.

12:19 And I will say to my soul, Soul, thou hast much goods laid up for many years; take thine ease, eat, drink, *and* be merry.

Goods *see* **Good** at *Luke 1:53*.

Laid *see Luke 3:9*.

Years *see* **Year** at *Luke 2:41*.

Ease *anapauo* (373), in the active voice, signifies "to give intermission from labor, to give rest, to refresh," Matt. 11:28; 1 Cor. 16:18, "have refreshed"; Philem. 20, "refresh"; passive voice, "to be rested, refreshed," 2 Cor. 7:13, "was refreshed"; Philem. 7, "are refreshed"; in the middle voice, "to take or enjoy rest," Matt. 26:45; Mark 6:31; 14:41; **Luke 12:19**, "take thine ease"; 1 Pet. 4:14; Rev. 6:11; 14:13. In the papyri it is found as an agricultural term, e.g., of giving land "rest" by sowing light crops upon it. In inscriptions it is found on gravestones of Christians, followed by the date of death (Moulton and Milligan).

Merry *euphraino* (2165), in the active voice, "to cheer, make glad," 2 Cor. 2:2, is used everywhere else in the passive voice, signifying, "to be happy, rejoice, make merry," and translated "to be merry" in **Luke 12:19; 15:23, 24, 29, 32**; in **16:19**, "fared (sumptuously)"; in Rev. 11:10, make merry.

12:20 But God said unto him, *Thou* fool, this night thy soul shall be required of thee: then whose shall those things be, which thou hast provided?

Fool *see* Fools at *Luke 11:40*.

Night *see Luke 2:8*.

Soul *see Luke 1:46*.

Required *see* Asketh at *Luke 6:30*.

Provided *hetoimazo* (2090), "to prepare," is translated "hast provided" in **Luke 12:20**, KJV. *See also* Make ready at *Luke 1:17*.

12:21 So *is* he that layeth up treasure for himself, and is not rich toward God.

Layeth *thesaurizo* (2343), "to lay up, store up" (akin to *thesauros*, "a treasury, a storehouse, a treasure"), is used of "laying" up treasures, on earth, Matt. 6:19; in Heaven, v. 20; in the last days, Jas. 5:3, RV, "ye have laid up your treasure" (KJV, "ye have heaped treasure together"); in **Luke 12:21**, "that layeth up treasure (for himself)"; in 1 Cor. 16:2, of money for needy ones (here the present participle is translated "in store," lit. "treasuring" or "storing," the "laying by" translating the preceding verb *tithemi*); in 2 Cor. 12:14, negatively, of children for parents; metaphorically, of "laying" up wrath, Rom. 2:5, "treasurest up." In 2 Pet. 3:7 the passive voice is used of the heavens and earth as "stored up" for fire, RV (marg., "stored" with fire), KJV, "kept in store."

Rich *see Luke 1:53*.

12:22 And he said unto his disciples, Therefore I say unto you, Take no thought for your life, what ye shall eat; neither for the body, what ye shall put on.

Thought *see Luke 12:11*.

Life *see Luke 9:24*. *See also* Soul at *Luke 1:46*.

Put on *enduo* (1746), used in the middle voice, of "putting" on oneself, or on another, is translated "to put on" (a) literally, Matt. 6:25; 27:31; Mark 6:9; 15:20; **Luke 12:22; 15:22**; (b) metaphorically, of "putting" on the armor of light, Rom. 13:12; the Lord Jesus Christ, 13:14; Christ, Gal. 3:27; incorruption and immortality (said of the body of the believer), 1 Cor. 15:53, 54; the new man, Eph. 4:24; Col. 3:10; the whole armor of God, Eph. 6:11; the breastplate of righteousness, 6:14, RV; the breastplate of faith and love, 1 Thess. 5:8; various Christian qualities, Col. 3:12.

12:23 The life is more than meat, and the body *is more* than raiment.

Meat *trophe* (5160), denotes "nourishment, food" (akin to *trepho*, "to rear, nourish, feed"); it is used literally, in the Gospels, Acts and Jas. 2:15; metaphorically, in Heb. 5:12, 14, RV, "(solid) food," KJV, "(strong) meat," i.e., deeper subjects of the faith than that of elementary instruction. The word is always rendered "food" in the RV, where the KJV has "meat"; e.g., Matt. 3:4; 6:25; 10:10; 24:45; **Luke 12:23**; John 4:8; Acts 2:46, "did take their food," RV (KJV, "did eat their meat"); 9:19, "took food"; 27:33, 34, 36. The KJV also has "food" in Acts 14:17 and Jas. 2:15.

Raiment *enduma* (1742), akin to *enduo*, denotes "anything put on, a garment of any kind." It was used of the clothing of ancient prophets, in token of their contempt of earthly splendor, 1 Kings 19:13; 2 Kings 1:8, RV; Zech. 13:4. In the NT it is similarly used of John the Baptist's raiment, Matt. 3:4: of raiment in general, Matt. 6:25, 28; **Luke 12:23**; metaphorically, of sheep's clothing, Matt. 7:15; of a wedding garment, 22:11-12; of the raiment of the angel at the tomb of the Lord after His resurrection, 28:3.

12:24 Consider the ravens: for they neither sow nor reap; which neither have storehouse nor barn; and God feedeth them: how much more are ye better than the fowls?

Consider *see* Perceivest at *Luke 6:41*.

Ravens *korax* (2876), "a raven" (perhaps onomatopoeic, representing the sound), occurs in the plural in **Luke 12:24**. The Heb. *oreb* and the Arabic *ghurab* are from roots meaning "to be black"; the Arabic root also has the idea of leaving home. Hence the evil omen attached to the bird. It is the first bird mentioned in the Bible, Gen. 8:7. Christ used the "ravens" to illustrate and enforce the lesson of God's provision and care.

Reap *therizo* (2325), "to reap" (akin to *theros*, "summer, harvest"), is used (a) literally, Matt. 6:26; 25:24, 26; **Luke 12:24; 19:21, 22**; Jas. 5:4 (2nd part), KJV, "have reaped"; (b) figuratively or in proverbial expressions, John 4:36 (twice), 37, 38, with immediate reference to bringing Samaritans into the kingdom of God, in regard to which the disciples would enjoy the fruits of what Christ Himself had been doing in Samaria; the Lord's words are, however, of a general application in respect of such service; in 1 Cor. 9:11, with reference to the right of the apostle and his fellow missionaries to receive material assistance from the church, a right which he forbore to exercise; in 2 Cor. 9:6 (twice), with reference to rendering material help to the needy, either "sparingly" or "bountifully," the "reaping" being proportionate to the sowing; in Gal. 6:7, 8 (twice), of "reaping" corruption, with special reference, according to the context, to that which is naturally shortlived transient (though the statement applies to every form of sowing to the flesh), and of "reaping" eternal life (characteristics and moral qualities being in view), as a result of sowing "to the Spirit," the reference probably being to the new nature of the believer, which is, however, under the controlling power of the Holy Spirit, v. 9, the "reaping" (the effect of well doing) being accomplished, to a limited extent, in this life, but in complete fulfillment at and beyond the judgment seat of Christ; diligence or laxity here will then produce proportionate results; in Rev. 14:15 (twice), 16, figurative of the discriminating judgment divinely to be fulfilled at the close of this age, when the wheat will be separated from the tares (see Matt. 13:30).

Storehouse *see* Closets at *Luke 12:3.*

Barn *see* Garner at *Luke 3:17.*

Feedeth *see* Brought at *Luke 4:16.*

More *see Luke 5:15.*

Better *see* More value at *Luke 12:7.*

12:25 And which of you with taking thought can add to his stature one cubit?

Thought *see Luke 12:11.*

Stature *see Luke 2:52.*

Cubit *pechus* (4083), denotes the forearm, i.e., the part between the hand and the elbowjoint; hence, "a measure of length," not from the wrist to the elbow, but from the tip of the middle finger to the elbow joint, i.e., about a foot and a half, or a little less than two feet, Matt. 6:27; **Luke 12:25**; John 21:8; Rev. 21:17.

12:26 If ye then be not able to do that thing which is least, why take ye thought for the rest?

Least *elachistos* (1646), "least," is a superlative degree formed from the word *elachus*, "little," the place of which was taken by *mikros* (the comparative degree being *elasson*, "less"); it is used of (a) size, Jas. 3:4; (b) amount; of the management of affairs, **Luke 16:10** (twice), **19:17**, "very little"; (c) importance, 1 Cor. 6:2, "smallest (matters)"; (d) authority: of commandments, Matt. 5:19; (e) estimation, as to persons, Matt. 5:19 (2nd part); 25:40, 45; 1 Cor. 15:9; as to a town, Matt. 2:6; as to activities or operations, **Luke 12:26**; 1 Cor. 4:3, "a very small thing."

Thought *see Luke 12:11.*

Rest *see* Others at *Luke 8:10.*

12:27 Consider the lilies how they grow: they toil not, they spin not; and yet I say unto you, that Solomon in all his glory was not arrayed like one of these.

Lilies *krinon* (2918), occurs in Matt. 6:28 and **Luke 12:27**; in the former the Lord speaks of "the lilies of the field"; the "lily" referred to was a flower of rich color, probably including the gladiolus and iris species. The former "grow among the grain, often overtopping it and illuminating the broad fields with their various shades of pinkish purple to deep violet purple and blue.... Anyone who has stood among the wheat fields of Galilee ... will see at once the appropriateness of our Savior's allusion. They all have a reedy stem, which, when dry, would make such fuel as is used in the ovens. The beautiful irises ... have gorgeous flowers, and would suit our Savior's comparison even better than the above. But they are plants of pasture grounds and swamps, and seldom found in grain fields. If, however, we understand by 'lilies of the field' simply wild lilies, these would also be included in the expression. Our Savior's comparison would then be like a 'composite photograph,' a reference to all the splendid colors and beautiful shapes of the numerous wild plants comprehended under the name 'lily'" (G. E. Post, in *Hastings' Bib. Dic.*).

Grow *see* Grew at *Luke 1:80.*

Toil *see* Toiled at *Luke 5:5.*

Spin *netho* (3514), "to spin," is found in Matt. 6:28 and **Luke 12:27**, of the lilies of the field.

Like *hos* (5613), used as a relative adverb of manner, means "as, like as," etc., and is translated "like," e.g., in Matt. 6:29; Mark 4:31; **Luke 12:27**; in Acts 3:22 and 7:37 (see RV, marg.); in 8:32 (2nd part), RV, "as" (KJV, "like"); Rev. 2:18, RV (the rendering should have been "as" here); 18:21, RV, "as it were" (KJV, "like"); 21:11, 2nd part (ditto).

12:28 If then God so clothe the grass, which is to day in the field, and to morrow is cast

into the oven; how much more *will he clothe* you, O ye of little faith?

Clothe *see* Clothed at *Luke 7:25*.

Grass *chortos* (5528), primarily denoted "a feeding enclosure" (whence Latin *hortus*, "a garden"; Eng.. "yard," and "garden"); then, "food," especially grass for feeding cattle; it is translated "grass" in Matt. 6:30; 14:19; Mark 6:39 (where "the green grass" is the first evidence of early spring); **Luke 12:28**; John 6:10; Jas. 1:10, 11; 1 Pet. 1:24; Rev. 8:7; 9:4; "blade" in Matt. 13:26; Mark 4:28; "hay" in 1 Cor. 3:12, used figuratively. In Palestine or Syria there are 90 genera and 243 species of grass.

Morrow *see Luke 10:35*.

Oven *klibanos* (2823), is mentioned in Matt. 6:30 and **Luke 12:28**. The form of "oven" commonly in use in the east indicates the kind in use as mentioned in Scripture. A hole is sunk in the ground about 3 feet deep and somewhat less in diameter. The walls are plastered with cement. A fire is kindled inside, the fuel being grass, or dry twigs, which heat the oven rapidly and blacken it with smoke and soot (see Lam. 5:10). When sufficiently heated the surface is wiped, and the dough is molded into broad thin loaves, placed one at a time on the wall of the "oven" to fit its concave inner circle. The baking takes a few seconds. Such ovens are usually outside the home, and often the same "oven" serves for several families (Lev. 26:26). An "oven" of this sort is doubtless referred to in Ex. 8:3 (see *Hastings' Bib. Dic.*).

Faith *oligopistos* (3640), lit., "little of faith" (*oligos*, "little," *pistis*, "faith"), is used only by the Lord, and as a tender rebuke, for anxiety, Matt. 6:30 and **Luke 12:28**; for fear, Matt. 8:26; 14:31; 16:8.

12:29 And seek not ye what ye shall eat, or what ye shall drink, neither be ye of doubtful mind.

Seek *see* Desired at *Luke 9:9*.

Doubtful *meteorizo* (3349), from *meteoros* (Eng., "meteor"), signifying "in mid air, raised on high," was primarily used of putting a ship out to sea, or of "raising" fortifications, or of the "rising" of the wind. In the Sept., it is used, e.g., in Micah 4:1, of the "exaltation" of the Lord's house; in Ezek. 10:16, of the "lifting" up of the wings of the cherubim; in Obad. 4, of the "mounting" up of the eagle; in the NT metaphorically, of "being anxious," through a "distracted" state of mind, of "wavering" between hope and fear, **Luke 12:29**, "neither be ye of doubtful mind" (KJV, marg., "live not in careful suspense"), addressed to those who have little faith. The interpretation "do not exalt yourselves" is not in keeping with the context.

12:30 For all these things do the nations of the world seek after: and your Father knoweth that ye have need of these things.

Seek *epizeteo* (1934), "to seek after" (directive, *epi*, "towards") is always rendered in the RV, by some form of the verb "to seek," Acts 13:7, "sought" (KJV, "desired"); 19:39, "seek" (KJV, "inquire"); Phil. 4:17, "seek for" (KJV, "desire"), twice; elsewhere, Matt. 6:32; 12:39; 16:4; Mark 8:12 (in some texts); **Luke 12:30**; Acts 12:19; Rom. 11:7; Heb. 11:14; 13:14.

Need *see* Needeth at *Luke 11:8*.

12:31 But rather seek ye the kingdom of God; and all these things shall be added unto you.

Rather *see Luke 11:41*.

12:32 Fear not, little flock; for it is your Father's good pleasure to give you the kingdom.

Little *mikros* (3398), "little, small" (the opposite of *megos*, "great"), is used (a) of persons, with regard to (1) station, or age, in the singular, Mark 15:40, of James "the less" (RV marg., "little"), possibly referring to age; **Luke 19:3**; in the plural, "little" ones, Matt. 18:6, 10, 14; Mark 9:42; (2) rank or influence, e.g., Matt. 10:42 (see context); Acts 8:10; 26:22, "small," as in Rev. 11:18; 13:16; 19:5, 18; 20:12; (b) of things, with regard to (1) size, e.g., Jas. 3:5; (2) quantity, **Luke 12:32**; 1 Cor. 5:6; Gal. 5:9; Rev. 3:8; (3) time, John 7:33; 12:35; Rev. 6:11; 20:3.

Flock *poimnion* (4168), is used in the NT only metaphorically, of a group of Christ's disciples, **Luke 12:32**; of local churches cared for by elders, Acts 20:28, 29; 1 Pet. 5:2, 3.

Pleasure *eudokeo* (2106), signifies (a) "to be well pleased, to think it good" [*eu*, "well," and *dokeo*], not merely an understanding of what is right and good as in *dokeo*, but stressing the willingness and freedom of an intention or resolve regarding what is good, e.g., **Luke 12:32**, "it is (your Father's) good pleasure"; so Rom. 15:26, 27, RV; 1 Cor. 1:21; Gal. 1:15; Col. 1:19; 1 Thess. 2:8, RV, "we were well pleased" (KJV, "we were willing"); this meaning is frequently found in the papyri in legal documents; (b) "to be well pleased with," or "take pleasure in," e.g., Matt. 3:17; 12:18; 17:5; 1 Cor. 10:5; 2 Cor. 12:10; 2 Thess. 2:12; Heb. 10:6, 8, 38; 2 Pet. 1:17.

12:33 Sell that ye have, and give alms; provide yourselves bags which wax not old, a treasure in the heavens that faileth not, where no thief approacheth, neither moth corrupteth.

Have *huparcho* (5225), "to be in existence, to be ready, at hand," is translated by the verb "to have" in Acts 3:6, lit., "silver and gold is not to me" (in the next clause, "such as I have," *echo* is used); 4:37, "having (land)," lit., "(land) being (to him)"; Matt. 19:21, "that (thou) hast," lit., "(things that) are (thine)," i.e., "thy belongings"; similarly **Luke 12:33**; **44**; **14:33**.

Alms *see Luke 11:41*.

Provide In **Luke 12:33**, KJV, *poieo*, "to make" (RV), is translated "provide."

Yourselves *see Luke 3:8*.

Bags *see* **Purse** at *Luke 10:4*.

Old *palaioo* (3822), denotes, in the active voice, "to make or declare old," Heb. 8:13 (1st part); in the passive voice, "to become old," of things worn out by time and use, **Luke 12:33**; Heb. 1:11, "shall wax old," lit., "shall be made old," i.e., worn out; in 8:13 (2nd part), RV, "is becoming old" (KJV "decayeth"); here and in the 1st part of the verse, the verb may have the meaning "to abrogate."

Treasure *see Luke 6:45*.

Faileth *anekleiptos* (413), "unfailing" (*a*, negative, and *ekleipo*), is rendered "that faileth not," in **Luke 12:33**. In a Greek document dated AD 42, some contractors undertake to provide "unfailing" heat for a bath during the current year (Moulton and Milligan, Vocab.).

Thief *kleptes* (2812), is used (a) literally, Matt. 6:19, 20; 24:43; **Luke 12:33, 39**; John 10:1, 10; 12:6; 1 Cor. 6:10; 1 Pet. 4:15; (b) metaphorically of "false teachers," John 10:8; (c) figuratively, (1) of the personal coming of Christ, in a warning to a local church, with most of its members possessed of mere outward profession and defiled by the world, Rev. 3:3; in retributive intervention to overthrow the foes of God, 16:15; (2) of the Day of the Lord, in divine judgment upon the world, 2 Pet. 3:10 and 1 Thess. 5:2, 4; in v. 2, according to the order in the original "the word 'night' is not to be read with 'the day of the Lord,' but with 'thief,' i.e., there is no reference to the time of the coming, only to the manner of it. To avoid ambiguity the phrase may be paraphrased, 'so comes as a thief in the night comes.' The use of the present tense instead of the future emphasizes the certainty of the coming.... The unexpectedness of the coming of the thief, and the unpreparedness of those to whom he comes, are the essential elements in the figure; cf. the entirely different figure used in Matt. 25:1-13."

Approacheth *see* **Come nigh** at *Luke 10:9*. *See also* **Came nigh** at *Luke 7:12*.

Moth *ses* (4597), denotes "a clothes moth," Matt. 6:19, 20; **Luke 12:33**. In Job 4:19 "crushed before the moth" alludes apparently to the fact that woolen materials, riddled by the larvae of "moths," become so fragile that a touch demolishes them. In Job 27:18 "He buildeth his house as a "moth" alludes to the frail covering which a larval "moth" constructs out of the material which it consumes. The rendering "spider" (marg.) seems an attempt to explain a difficulty.

Corrupteth *diaphtheiro* (1311), "to corrupt utterly, through and through," is said of men "corrupted in mind," whose wranglings result from the doctrines of false teachers, 1 Tim. 6:5 (the KJV wrongly renders it as an adjective, "corrupt"). It is translated "destroyeth" instead of "corrupteth," in the RV of **Luke 12:33**, of the work of a moth, in Rev. 8:9, of the effect of divine judgments hereafter upon navigation; in 11:18, of the divine retribution of destruction upon those who have destroyed the earth; in 2 Cor. 4:16 it is translated "is decaying," said of the human body.

12:34 For where your treasure is, there will your heart be also.

Treasure *see Luke 6:45*.

12:35 Let your loins be girded about, and *your* lights burning;

Loins *osphus* (3751), is used (a) in the natural sense in Matt. 3:4; Mark 1:6; (b) as "the seat of generative power," Heb. 7:5, 10; metaphorically in Acts 2:30; (c) metaphorically, (1) of girding the "loins" in readiness for active service for the Lord, **Luke 12:35**; (2) the same, with truth, Eph. 6:14, i.e., bracing up oneself so as to maintain perfect sincerity and reality as the counteractive in Christian character against hypocrisy and falsehood; (3) of girding the "loins" of the mind, 1 Pet. 1:13, RV, "girding," suggestive of the alertness necessary for sobriety and for setting one's hope perfectly on "the grace to be brought ... at the revelation of Jesus Christ" (the present participle, "girding," is introductory to the rest of the verse).

Girded *perizonnumi* (4024), "to gird around or about," is used (a) literally, of "girding" oneself for service, **Luke 12:37**; **17:8**; for rapidity of movement, Acts 12:8; (b) figuratively, of the condition for service on the part of the followers of Christ, **Luke 12:35**; Eph. 6:14; (c) emblematically, of Christ's priesthood, Rev. 1:13, indicative of majesty of attitude and action, the middle voice suggesting the particular interest taken by Christ in "girding" Himself thus; so of the action of the angels mentioned in 15:6.

Lights *see* Candle at *Luke 8:16.*

Burning *kaio* (2545), "to set fire to, to light"; in the passive voice, "to be lighted, to burn," Matt. 5:15; John 15:6; Heb. 12:18; Rev. 4:5; 8:8, 10; 19:20; 21:8; 1 Cor. 13:3, is used metaphorically of the heart, Luke **24:32**; of spiritual light, Luke **12:35**; John 5:35.

12:36 And ye yourselves like unto men that wait for their lord, when he will return from the wedding; that when he cometh and knocketh, they may open unto him immediately.

Like unto *see* Like at *Luke 6:47.*

Wait *see* Waiting at *Luke 2:25.*

Return *analuo* (360), "to depart" in Phil. 1:23, signifies "to return" in Luke **12:36**, used in a simile of the "return" of a lord for his servants after a marriage feast (RV).

Wedding *gamos* (1062), "a wedding," especially a wedding "feast" (akin to *gameo*, "to marry"); it is used in the plural in the following passages (the RV rightly has "marriage feast" for the KJV, "marriage," or "wedding"), Matt. 22:2, 3, 4, 9 (in verses 11, 12, it is used in the singular, in connection with the wedding garment); 25:10; Luke **12:36**; **14:8**; in the following it signifies a wedding itself, John 2:1, 2; Heb. 13:4; and figuratively in Rev. 19:7, of the marriage of the Lamb; in v. 9 it is used in connection with the supper, the wedding supper (or what in English is termed "breakfast"), not the wedding itself, as in v. 7.

Knock *see* Knock at Luke *11:9.*

12:37 Blessed *are* those servants, whom the lord when he cometh shall find watching: verily I say unto you, that he shall gird himself, and make them to sit down to meat, and will come forth and serve them.

Gird *see* Girded at *Luke 12:35.*

Sit *see* Laid at *Luke 2:7.*

Come *see* Pass at *Luke 11:42.*

Serve *see Luke 10:40. See also* Ministered at *Luke 4:39.*

12:38 And if he shall come in the second watch, or come in the third watch, and find *them* so, blessed are those servants.

Watch *see Luke 2:8.* In Luke **12:38** some mss. have the adjective *hesperinos*, "of the evening," lit., "in the evening watch."

12:39 And this know, that if the goodman of the house had known what hour the thief would come, he would have watched, and not have suffered his house to be broken through.

Goodman *oikodespotes* (3617), "a master of a house" (*oikos*, "a house," *despotes*, "a master"), is rendered "master of the house" in Matt. 10:25; Luke **13:25**, and **14:21**, where the context shows that the authority of the "householder" is stressed; in Matt. 24:43 and Luke **12:39**, the RV "master of the house" (KJV, "goodman of the house," does not give the exact meaning); "householder" is the rendering in both versions in Matt. 13:27, 52; 20:1; 21:33; so the RV in 20:11 (for KJV, "goodman of the house"); both have "goodman of the house" in Mark 14:14; in Luke **22:11**, "goodman."

Suffered *see Luke 8:51. See also* Leaving at *Luke 10:30.*

Thief *see Luke 12:33.*

Broken *diorusso* (1358), lit., "to dig through" (*dia*, "through," *orusso*, "to dig"), is used of the act of thieves in "breaking" into a house, Matt. 6:19, 20; 24:43; Luke **12:39**.

12:40 Be ye therefore ready also: for the Son of man cometh at an hour when ye think not.

Ready *hetoimos* (2092), "prepared, ready" (akin to *hetoimasia*, "preparation"), is used (a) of persons, Matt. 24:44; 25:10; Luke **12:40**; **22:33**; Acts 23:15, 21 (for 2 Cor. 10:6); Titus 3:1; 1 Pet. 3:15; (b) of things, Matt. 22:4 (2nd part), 8; Mark 14:15, RV, "ready" (KJV, "prepared"); Luke **14:17**; John 7:6; 2 Cor. 9:5; 10:16, RV, "things ready" (KJV, "things made ready"); 1 Pet. 1:5.

Luke 12:41 Then Peter said unto him, Lord, speakest thou this parable unto us, or even to all?

Even *see* Also at *Luke 11:49.*

12:42 And the Lord said, Who then is that faithful and wise steward, whom *his* lord shall make ruler over his household, to give *them their* portion of meat in due season?

Wise *phronimos* (5429), "prudent, sensible, practically wise," Matt. 7:24; 10:16; 24:45; 25:2, 4, 8, 9; Luke **12:42**; **16:8** (comparative degree, *phronimoteros*); 1 Cor. 10:15; in an evil sense, "wise (in your own conceits)," lit., "wise (in yourselves)," i.e., "judged by the standard of your self-complacency," Rom. 11:25; 12:16; ironically, 1 Cor. 4:10; 2 Cor. 11:19.

Steward *oikonomos* (3623), primarily denoted "the manager of a household or estate" (*oikos*, "a house," *nemo*, "to arrange"), "a steward" (such were usually slaves or freedmen), Luke **12:42**; **16:1**, **3**, **8**; 1 Cor. 4:2; Gal. 4:2, RV (KJV, "governors"); in Rom. 16:23, the "treasurer (RV) of a city; it is used metaphorically, in the wider sense, of a "steward" in general, (a) of preachers of the gospel and teachers of the Word of God, 1 Cor. 4:1; (b) of elders or bishops in churches, Titus 1:7; (c) of believers generally, 1 Pet. 4:10.

Make ruler *kathistemi* (2525), lit., to set down," "to appoint, constitute," is translated "to set" in Matt. 24:45, 47; 25:21, 23, RV (KJV, "made"); so **Luke 12:42, 44**; it is found in some mss. in Heb. 2:7, and translated "set over" (KJV). *See also* Made at *Luke 12:14*.

Household *therapeia* (2322), "service, care, attention," is also used in the collective sense of "a household," in **Luke 12:42**. *See also* Healed, Healing at *Luke 9:11*.

Portion of meat *sitometrion* (4620), a measured "portion of food" (*sitos*, "corn," *metreo*, "to measure"), is used in **Luke 12:42**, RV.

Due In the phrases "in due season" in Matt. 24:45; **Luke 12:42**; Rom. 5:6 (lit., "according to time"), and "in due time," 1 Pet. 5:6, there is no word representing "due" in the original, and the phrases are, lit., "in season," "in time."

Season *see Luke 1:20*.

12:43-44 Blessed *is* that servant, whom his lord when he cometh shall find so doing.

Of a truth I say unto you, that he will make him ruler over all that he hath.

Truth *see Luke 9:27*.

Make … ruler *see Make ruler* at *Luke 12:42*. *See also* Made at *Luke 12:14*.

Hath *see* Have at *Luke 12:33*.

12:45 But and if that servant say in his heart, My lord delayeth his coming; and shall begin to beat the menservants and maidens, and to eat and drink, and to be drunken;

> *"There is no portion of our time that is our time, and the rest God's; there is no portion of our money that is our money, and the rest God's money. It is all his; he made it all, gives it all, and he has simply trusted it to us for his service. A servant has two purses, the master's and his own, but we have only one."*
>
> ADOLPHE THEODORE MONOD

Delayeth *see* Tarried at *Luke 1:21*. *See also* Time at *Luke 4:5*.

Menservants *pais* (3816), "a child, boy, youth," also means "a servant, attendant"; in **Luke 12:45** it is used in the plural "menservants," in contrast to *paidiske*, "a maidservant." *See also* Servant at *Luke 1:54*.

Maidens *paidiske* (3814), is translated "maid," "maids," in the KJV and RV in Mark 14:66, 69; **Luke 22:56**, in the RV (KJV, "damsel"), in Matt. 26:69; John 18:17; Acts 12:13; 16:16; in **Luke 12:45**, "maidservants" (KJV "maidens"); in Gal. 4:22, 23, 30, 31, RV, "handmaid" (KJV, "bondmaid" or "bondwoman").

Eat *esthio* (2068), signifies "to eat" (as distinct from *pino*, "to drink"); it is a lengthened form from *edo* (Lat., *edo*; cf. Eng., "edible"); in Heb. 10:27, metaphorically, "devour"; it is said of the ordinary use of food and drink, 1 Cor. 9:7; 11:22; of partaking of food at table, e.g., Mark 2:16; of reveling, Matt. 24:49; **Luke 12:45**.

Drunken *methusko* (3182), signifies "to make drunk, or to grow drunk" (an inceptive verb, marking the process or the state), "to become intoxicated," **Luke 12:45**; Eph. 5:18; 1 Thess. 5:7*a*.

12:46 The lord of that servant will come in a day when he looketh not for *him*, and at an hour when he is not aware, and will cut him in sunder, and will appoint him his portion with the unbelievers.

Looketh *see* Expectation at *Luke 3:15*.

Aware *see* Know at *Luke 1:34*.

Cut *dichotomeo* (1371), lit., to cut into two parts" (*dicha*, "apart," *temno*, "to cut," *tome*, "a cutting"), Matt. 24:51, "to cut asunder," is used in **Luke 12:46**. Some take the reference to be to the mode of punishment by which criminals and captives were "cut" in two; others, on account of the fact that in these passages the delinquent is still surviving after the treatment, take the verb to denote "to cut up" by scourging, to scourge severely, the word being used figuratively. As to Matt. 24:51, it has been remarked that the "cutting asunder" was an appropriate punishment for one who had lived a double life. In both passages the latter part of the sentence applies to retribution beyond this life. In the Sept. the verb is used in Exod. 29:17 of the dividing of the ram as a whole burnt offering at the consecration of the priests. The corresponding noun is found in Gen. 15:11, 17; Ex. 29:17; Lev. 1:8; Ezek. 24:4.

Appoint *tithemi* (5087), "to put," is used of "appointment" to any form of service. Christ used it of His followers, John 15:16 (RV, "appointed," for KJV, "ordained"). "I set you" would be more in keeping with the metaphor of grafting. The verb is used by Paul of his service in the ministry of the gospel, 1 Tim. 1:12 (RV, "appointing" for "putting"); 2:7 (RV, "appointed" for "ordained"); and 2 Tim. 1:11 (RV, "appointing" for "putting"); of the overseers, or bishops, in the local church at Ephesus, as those "appointed" by the Holy Ghost, to tend the church of God, Acts 20:28 ("hath made"); of the Son of God, as appointed Heir of all things, Heb. 1:2. It is also used of "appointment" to punishment, as of the unfaithful servant, Matt. 24:51; **Luke 12:46**; of unbelieving Israel, 1 Pet. 2:8. Cf. 2 Pet. 2:6.

Portion *meros* (3313), "a part," is translated "portion" in Matt. 24:51; **Luke 12:46**; **15:12**. *See also* **Part** at *Luke 11:36*.

Unbelievers *apistos* (571), an adjective, is used as a noun, rendered "unbeliever" in 2 Cor. 6:15 and 1 Tim. 5:8, RV; plural in 1 Cor. 6:6 and 2 Cor. 6:14; KJV only, **Luke 12:46** (RV, "unfaithful"). *See also* Faithless at *Luke 9:41*.

12:47 And that servant, which knew his lord's will, and prepared not *himself*, neither did according to his will, shall be beaten with many *stripes*.

Beaten *dero* (1194), from a root *der-*, "skin" (*derma*, "a skin," cf. Eng., "dermatology"), primarily "to flay," then "to beat, thrash or smite," is used of the treatment of the servants of the owner of the vineyard by the husbandmen, in the parable in Matt. 21:35; Mark 12:3, 5; **Luke 20:10-11**; of the treatment of Christ, **Luke 22:63**, RV, "beat," for KJV, "smote"; John 18:23; of the followers of Christ, in the synagogues, Mark 13:9; Acts 22:19; of the punishment of unfaithful servants, **Luke 12:47-48**; of the "beating" of apostles by the High Priest and the Council of the Sanhedrin, Acts 5:40; by magistrates, 16:37. The significance of flogging does not always attach to the word; it is used of the infliction of a single blow, John 18:23; 2 Cor. 11:20, and of "beating" the air, 1 Cor. 9:26. The usual meaning is that of "thrashing or cudgelling," and when used of a blow it indicates one of great violence.

Many stripes *polus* (4183), "much, many great," is used especially of number when its significance is "many," e.g., Matt. 8:30; 9:10; 13:17; so the RV of Matt. 12:15, where some mss. follow the word by *ochloi*, "multitudes"; 1 Cor. 12:12; Rev. 1:15; it is more frequently used as a noun, "many (persons)," e.g., Matt. 3:7; 7:22; 22:14; with the article, "the many," e.g., Matt. 24:12, RV; Mark 9:26, RV, "the more part" (KJV "many"); Rom. 5:15, 19 (twice), RV; 12:5; 1 Cor. 10:17; v. 33, RV; so 2 Cor. 2:17; in 1 Cor. 11:30, RV, "not a few." In **Luke 12:47** it is translated "many stripes," the noun being understood.

12:48 But he that knew not, and did commit things worthy of stripes, shall be beaten with few *stripes*. For unto whomsoever much is given, of him shall be much required: and to whom men have committed much, of him they will ask the more.

Commit *paratithemi* (3908), signifies "to entrust, commit to one's charge," e.g., in **Luke 12:48**; 1 Tim. 1:18; 2 Tim. 2:2; 1 Pet. 4:19 (KJV, "commit the keeping").

Worthy *see Luke 7:4*.

Stripes *plege* (4127), "a blow, stripe, wound" (akin to *plesso*, "to strike," and *plektes*, "a striker"), is rendered "stripes" in **Luke 12:48** (the noun is omitted in the original in v. **47** and the 2nd part of v. **48**); Acts 16:23, 33; 2 Cor. 6:5; 11:23.

Much *see Luke 7:26*.

Required *zeteo* (2212), "to seek, seek after," also signifies "to require, demand," "shall be required," **Luke 12:48**; in 1 Cor. 4:2, "it is required (in stewards)."

12:49 I am come to send fire on the earth; and what will I, if it be already kindled?

Fire *see Luke 3:16*.

Earth *see* **Land** at *Luke 4:25*.

Kindled *anapto* (381), "to light up," is used (a) literally, in Jas. 3:5, "kindleth"; (b) metaphorically, in the passive voice, in **Luke 12:49**, of the "kindling" of the fire of hostility.

12:50 But I have a baptism to be baptized with; and how am I straitened till it be accomplished!

Have *see Luke 12:4*.

Baptism, Baptized *baptisma* (908), "baptism," consisting of the processes of immersion, submersion and emergence (from *bapto*, "to dip"), is used (a) of John's "baptism," (b) of Christian "baptism," (c) of the overwhelming afflictions and judgments to which the Lord voluntarily submitted on the cross, e.g., **Luke 12:50**; (d) of the sufferings His followers would experience, not of a vicarious character, but in fellowship with the sufferings of their Master. Some mss. have the word in Matt. 20:22-23; it is used in Mark 10:38-39, with this meaning.

Straitened *sunecho* (4912), "to hold together, constrain," is translated "I am in a strait" in Phil. 1:23 (passive voice), i.e., being restricted on both sides, under a pressure which prevents a definite choice; so in **Luke 12:50**, "(how) am I straitened," i.e., pressed in. *See also* **Taken** at *Luke 4:38*.

12:51 Suppose ye that I am come to give peace on earth? I tell you, Nay; but rather division:

Suppose *dokeo* (1380), "to be of opinion," is translated "to suppose" in Mark 6:49; **Luke 24:37**; John 20:15; Acts 27:13; in the following, KJV, "suppose," RV, "think," **Luke 12:51**; **13:2**; Heb. 10:29. It is most frequently rendered "to think," always in Matthew; always in John, except 11:31, "supposing," RV [where the best texts have this verb (for *lego*, KJV, "saying")], and 20:15.

Nay *ouchi* (3780), is used, e.g., in **Luke 12:51**; **13:3, 5**; **16:30**; Rom. 3:27.

Division *diamerismos* (1267), primarily, "a parting, distribution," denotes "a discussion, dissension, division or discord, breaking up as of family ties" (*dia*, "asunder," *meros*, "a part"), it is found in **Luke 12:51**, where it is contrasted with *eirene*, "peace."

12:52 For from henceforth there shall be five in one house divided, three against two, and two against three.

Henceforth *see Luke 1:48*.

Divided *see Luke 11:17*.

12:53 The father shall be divided against the son, and the son against the father; the mother against the daughter, and the daughter against the mother; the mother in law against her daughter in law, and the daughter in law against her mother in law.

Mother in law *see* **Wife's mother** at *Luke 4:38*.

Daughter in law *numphe* (3565), (Eng., "nymph"), denotes "a bride," John 3:29; also "a daughter-in-law, Matt. 10:35; **Luke 12:53**.

12:54 And he said also to the people, When ye see a cloud rise out of the west, straightway ye say, There cometh a shower; and so it is.

Also *see* **Luke** *11:49*.

Rise *anatello* (393), "to arise," is used especially of things in the natural creation, e.g., "the rising" of the sun, moon and stars; metaphorically, of light, in Matt. 4:16, "did spring up"; of the sun, Matt. 5:45; 13:6 (RV); Mark 4:6; Jas. 1:11; in Mark 16:2 the RV has "when the sun was risen," keeping to the verb form, for the KJV, "at the rising of"; of a cloud, **Luke 12:54**; of the day-star, 2 Pet. 1:19; in Heb. 7:14 metaphorically, of the Incarnation of Christ: "Our Lord hath sprung out of Judah," more lit., "Our Lord hath arisen out of Judah," as of the rising of the light of the sun.

West *dusme* (1424), "the quarter of the sun-setting" (*dusis*, "a sinking, setting"; *duno*, "to sink"), hence, "the west," occurs in Matt. 8:11; 24:27; **Luke 12:54** (some regard this as the sunset); **13:29**; Rev. 21:13.

Shower *ombros* (3655), denotes a "heavy shower, a storm of rain," **Luke 12:54**.

12:55 And when *ye see* the south wind blow, ye say, There will be heat; and it cometh to pass.

South *see Luke 11:31*.

Heat *kauson* (2742), denotes "a burning heat" (from *kaio*, "to burn"; cf. Eng., "caustic," "cauterize"), Matt. 20:12; **Luke 12:55** (KJV, "heat"), RV, in each place, "scorching heat" (marg. "hot wind"); in Jas. 1:11, "a burning heat," KJV, RV, "the scorching wind" like the sirocco. Cf. Amos 4:9, where the Sept. has *purosis*, "burning" (*pur*, "fire").

12:56 *Ye* hypocrites, ye can discern the face of the sky and of the earth; but how is it that ye do not discern this time?

Hypocrites *see* **Hypocrite** at *Luke 6:42*.

Discern *dokimazo* (1381), signifies "to test, prove, scrutinize," so as "to decide." It is translated "discern" in the KJV of **Luke 12:56**; RV, "interpret" (marg., "prove").

Face *see Luke 9:51*.

Sky *ouranos* (3772), denotes "the heaven." The RV always renders it "heaven." The KJV translates it "air" in Matt. 8:20. In the phrase "the fowls (or birds) of the heaven" the KJV always has "air"; "sky" in Matt. 16:2-3; **Luke 12:56**; in all other instances "heaven." The word is probably derived from a root meaning to cover or encompass.

12:57 Yea, and why even of yourselves judge ye not what is right?

And *see* **Also** at *Luke 11:49*.

Yourselves *see Luke 3:8*.

Right *dikaios* (1342), "just, righteous, that which is in accordance with" *dike*, "rule, right, justice," is translated "right" in Matt. 20:4; v. 7, KJV only (RV omits, according to the most authentic mss., the clause having been inserted from v. 4, to the detriment of the narrative); **Luke 12:57**; Acts 4:19; Eph. 6:1; Phil. 1:7, RV (KJV, "meet"); 2 Pet. 1:13 (KJV, "meet"). *See also* **Righteous** at *Luke 1:6*.

12:58 When thou goest with thine adversary to the magistrate, *as thou art* in the way, give diligence that thou mayest be delivered from him; lest he hale thee to the judge, and the judge deliver thee to the officer, and the officer cast thee into prison.

Adversary *antidikos* (476), firstly, "an opponent in a lawsuit," Matt. 5:25 (twice); **Luke 12:58**; **18:3**, is also used to denote "an adversary or an enemy," without reference to legal affairs, and this is perhaps its meaning in 1 Pet. 5:8, where it is used of the Devil. Some would regard the word as there used in a legal sense, since the Devil accuses men before God.

Magistrate *archon* (758), "a ruler," denotes, in **Luke 12:58**, "a local authority, a magistrate," acting in the capacity of one who received complaints, and possessing higher authority than the judge, to whom the "magistrate" remits the case.

Give *didomi* (1325), "to give," is used with various meanings according to the context; it is said, e.g., of seed "yielding fruit," Mark 4:7, 8; of "giving" (i.e., exercising) diligence, **Luke 12:58**; of giving lots, Acts 1:26, RV (KJV, "gave forth"); of "rendering" vengeance, 2 Thess. 1:8; of "striking or smiting" Christ, John 18:22 (lit., "gave a blow") and 19:3 (lit., "they gave Him blows"); of "putting" a ring on the hand, **Luke 15:22**; of Paul's "adventuring" himself into a place, Acts 19:31. (In Rev. 17:13 some mss. have *diadidomi*, "to divide".)

Diligence *ergasia* (2039), (a) lit., "a working" (akin to *ergon*, "work"), is indicative of a process, in contrast to the concrete, *ergon*, e.g., Eph. 4:19, lit., "unto a working" (RV marg., "to make a trade of"); contrast *ergon* in v. 12; (b) "business," Acts 19:25, RV (for KJV, "craft"); or gain got by "work," Acts 16:16, 19; 19:24; (c) endeavor, pains, "diligence," **Luke 12:58**.

Delivered *apallasso* (525), lit., "to change from" (*apo*, "from," *allasso*, "to change"), "to free from, release," is translated "might deliver" in Heb. 2:15; in **Luke 12:58**, it is used in a legal sense of being quit of a person, i.e., the opponent being appeased and withdrawing his suit. For its other meaning, "to depart," in Acts 19:12.

Lest *mepote* or *me pote* (3379), denotes "lest ever, lest perhaps, lest at any time," e.g., Matt. 4:6; "lest haply," Matt. 7:6, RV (KJV, "lest"), and in 13:15 (KJV, "lest at any time"); in 25:9, RV, "peradventure" (KJV, "lest"). The RV does not translate this simply by "lest," as in the KJV; see further, e.g., in Matt. 27:64; Mark 14:2; **Luke 12:58**; the addition of *pote* requires the fuller rendering.

Hale *katasuro* (2694), an intensive form, lit., "to pull down" (*kata*), hence, "to drag away," is used in **Luke 12:58**, of haling a person before a judge.

Judge *see* **Judges** at *Luke 11:19*.

Officer *praktor* (4233), lit., "one who does," or "accomplishes" (akin to *prasso*, "to do"), was used in Athens of one who exacts payment, a collector (the word is frequently used in the papyri of a public accountant); hence, in general, a court "officer," an attendant in a court of justice (so Deissmann); the word is used in **Luke 12:58** (twice). In the Sept., Isa. 3:12.

12:59 I tell thee, thou shalt not depart thence, till thou hast paid the very last mite.

Not *see* **Means** at *Luke 10:19*.

Very Sometimes it translates the conjunction *kai*, in the sense of "even," e.g., Matt. 10:30; in 24:24, KJV, "very" (RV, "even"); **Luke 12:59**.

Mite *lepton* (3016), the neuter of the adjective *leptos*, signifying, firstly, "peeled," then, "fine, thin, small, light," became used as a noun, denoting a small copper coin, often mentioned in the Mishna as proverbially the smallest Jewish coin. It was valued at 1/8th of the Roman *as*, and the 1/128th part of the *denarius*: its legal value was about one third of an English farthing; Mark 12:42 lit. reads "two *lepta*, which make a *kodrantes* (a *quadrans*)"; in **Luke 12:59** "the last *lepton*" corresponds in effect to Matt. 5:26, "the uttermost *kodrantes*," "farthing"; elsewhere **Luke 21:2**.

Chapter 13

13:1 There were present at that season some that told him of the Galilaeans, whose blood Pilate had mingled with their sacrifices.

Present *pareimi* (3918), signifies (a) "to be by, at hand or present," of persons, e.g., **Luke 13:1**; Acts 10:33; 24:19; 1 Cor. 5:3; 2 Cor. 10:2, 11; Gal. 4:18, 20; of things, John 7:6, of a particular season in the Lord's life on earth, "is (not yet) come," or "is not yet at hand"; Heb. 12:11, of chastening "(for the) present" (the neuter of the present participle, used as a noun); in 13:5 "such things as ye have" is, lit., "the things that are present"; 2 Pet. 1:12, of the truth "(which) is with (you)" (not as KJV, "the present truth," as if of special doctrines applicable to a particular time); in v. 9 "he that lacketh" is lit., "to whom are not present"; (b) "to have arrived or come," Matt. 26:50, "thou art come," RV; John 11:28; Acts 10:21; Col. 1:6.

Mingled *mignumi* (3396), "to mix, mingle" (from a root *mik*; Eng., "mix" is akin), is always in the NT translated "to mingle," Matt. 27:34; **Luke 13:1**; Rev. 8:7; 15:2.

Sacrifices *see* Sacrifice at *Luke 2:24*.

13:2 And Jesus answering said unto them, Suppose ye that these Galilaeans were sinners above all the Galilaeans, because they suffered such things?

Suppose *see Luke 12:51*.

Suffered *pascho* (3958), "to suffer," is used (I) of the "sufferings" of Christ (a) at the hands of men, e.g., Matt. 16:21; 17:12; 1 Pet. 2:23; (b) in His expiatory and vicarious sacrifice for sin, Heb. 9:26; 13:12; 1 Pet. 2:21; 3:18; 4:1; (c) including both (a) and (b), **Luke 22:15**; **24:26**, **46**; Acts 1:3, "passion"; 3:18; 17:3, Heb. 5:8; (d) by the antagonism of the evil one, Heb. 2:18; (II) of human "suffering" (a) of followers of Christ, Acts 9:16; 2 Cor. 1:6; Gal. 3:4; Phil. 1:29; 1 Thess. 2:14; 2 Thess. 1:5; 2 Tim. 1:12; 1 Pet. 3:14, 17; 5:10; Rev. 2:10; in identification with Christ in His crucifixion, as the spiritual ideal to be realized, 1 Pet. 4:1; in a wrong way, 4:15; (b) of others, physically, as the result of demoniacal power, Matt. 17:15, RV, "suffereth (grievously)," KJV, "is (sore) vexed"; cf. Mark 5:26; in a dream, Matt. 27:19; through maltreatment, **Luke 13:2**; 1 Pet. 2:19, 20; by a serpent (negatively), Acts 28:5, RV, "took" (KJV, "felt"); (c) of the effect upon the whole body through the "suffering" of one member, 1 Cor. 12:26, with application to a church.

13:3 I tell you, Nay: but, except ye repent, ye shall all likewise perish.

Nay *see Luke 12:51*.

Repent *see* Repented at *Luke 10:13*.

Likewise *see Luke 10:32*.

Perish *see Luke 5:37*.

13:4 Or those eighteen, upon whom the tower in Siloam fell, and slew them, think ye that they were sinners above all men that dwelt in Jerusalem?

Eighteen *see* Eight at *Luke 2:21*.

Tower *purgos* (4444), is used of "a watchtower in a vineyard," Matt. 21:33; Mark 12:1; probably, too, in **Luke 14:28** (cf. Isa. 5:2); in **Luke 13:4**, of the "tower in Siloam," the modern Silwan, which is built on a steep escarpment of rock.

Sinners *opheiletes* (3781), "one who owes anything to another," primarily in regard to money; in Matt. 18:24, "who owed" (lit., "one was brought, a debtor to him of ten thousand talents"). The slave could own property, and so become a "debtor" to his master, who might seize him for payment. It is used metaphorically, (a) of a person who is under an obligation, Rom. 1:14, of Paul, in the matter of preaching the gospel; in Rom. 8:12, of believers, to mortify the deeds of the body; in Rom. 15:27, of gentile believers, to assist afflicted Jewish believers; in Gal. 5:3, of those who would be justified by circumcision, to do the whole Law: (b) of those who have not yet made amends to those whom they have injured, Matt. 6:12, "our debtors"; of some whose disaster was liable to be regarded as a due punishment, **Luke 13:4** (RV, "offenders"; KJV, "sinners"; marg, "debtors").

13:5 I tell you, Nay: but, except ye repent, ye shall all likewise perish.

Nay *see Luke 12:51*.

Repent *see* Repented at *Luke 10:13*.

Perish *see Luke 5:37*.

13:6 He spake also this parable; A certain *man* had a fig tree planted in his vineyard; and he came and sought fruit thereon, and found none.

Fig tree *suke* or *sukea* (4808), "a fig tree," is found in Matt. 21:19, 20, 21; 24:32; Mark 11:13, 20, 21; 13:28; **Luke 13:6**, **7**; **21:29**; John 1:48, 50, Jas. 3:12; Rev. 6:13.

Planted *phuteuo* (5452), "to plant," is used (a) literally, Matt. 21:33; Mark 12:1; **Luke 13:6**; **17:6**, **28**; **20:9**; 1 Cor. 9:7; (b) metaphorically, Matt. 15:13; 1 Cor. 3:6, 7, 8.

13:7 Then said he unto the dresser of his vineyard, Behold, these three years I come seeking fruit on this fig tree, and find none: cut it down; why cumbereth it the ground?

Dresser *ampelourgos* (289), "a worker in a vineyard" (from *ampelos*, "a vine," and *ergon*), is rendered "vinedresser" in **Luke 13:7**, RV (KJV, "dresser of the vineyard").

Years *see* Year at *Luke 2:41*.

Fig tree *see Luke 13:6.*

Cut *see* Hewn at *Luke 3:9.*

Cumbereth *katargeo* (2673), lit., "to reduce to idleness or inactivity" (*kata*, "down," and *argos*, "idle"), is once rendered "cumber," Luke 13:7.

13:8 And he answering said unto him, Lord, let it alone this year also, till I shall dig about it, and dung *it*:

Lord *see Luke 5:8.*

Let ... alone *aphiemi* (863), frequently denotes "to let, suffer, permit," e.g., Matt. 5:40 (translated "let ... have"); 7:4; 13:30; 15:14; 27:49 and Mark 15:36, RV, "let be," probably short for "let us see" (Moulton and Milligan, *Vocab.*); Mark 7:27; 11:6 ("let ... go"); 14:6 ("let ... alone"); so **Luke 13:8**; John 11:48; in Acts 5:38 (where some mss. have *eao*, "to permit, let, suffer"); in John 11:44 and 18:8 ("let"); 1 Cor. 7:11, 12, RV, "let ... leave," KJV, "let ... put away"; 7:13 ("let ... leave").

Dig *see* Digged at *Luke 6:48.*

Dung *koprion* (2874), "manure," **Luke 13:8**, used in the plural with *ballo*, "to throw," is translated by the verb "to dung." Some mss. have the accusative case of the noun *kopria*, "a dunghill."

13:9 And if it bear fruit, *well*: and if not, *then* after that thou shalt cut it down.

Bear *see* Bare at *Luke 8:8.*

After that In **Luke 13:9**, RV, the phrase *eis* to *mellon*, lit., "unto the about to be" (*mello*, "to be about to"), is translated "thenceforth" (KJV, "after that").

Cut *see* Hewn at *Luke 3:9.*

13:10-11 And he was teaching in one of the synagogues on the sabbath.

And, behold, there was a woman which had a spirit of infirmity eighteen years, and was bowed together, and could in no wise lift up *herself*.

Infirmity *ostheneia* (769), lit., "want of strength" (*a*, negative, *sthenos*, "strength"), "weakness," indicating inability to produce results, is most frequently translated "infirmity," or "infirmities"; in Rom. 8:26, the RV has "infirmity" (KJV, "infirmities"); in 2 Cor. 12:5, 9, 10, "weaknesses" and in 11:30, "weakness" (KJV, "infirmities"); in **Luke 13:11** the phrase "a spirit of infirmity" attributes her curvature directly to satanic agency. The connected phraseology is indicative of trained medical knowledge on the part of the writer.

Eighteen *see* Eight at *Luke 2:21.*

Years *see* Year at *Luke 2:41.*

Bowed *sunkupto* (4794), "to bow together" (*sun*, "together with," *kupto*, "to bow"), is said, in **Luke 13:11**, of the woman crippled with a physical infirmity.

In no wise *panteles* (3838), the neuter of *panteles*, is used with the negative *me*, and with *eis to*, "unto the," in **Luke 13:11**, and translated "in no wise," lit., "not to the uttermost".

Lift *anakupto* (352), "to lift oneself up," is used (a) of the body, **Luke 13:11**; John 8:7, 10; (b) metaphorically, of the mind, to look up, to be elated, **Luke 21:28** (followed by *epairo*, "lift up"); an instance is found in the papyri in which a person speaks of the impossibility of ever looking up again in a certain place, for very shame (Moulton and Milligan, *Vocab.*). In the Sept., Job 10:15.

13:12 And when Jesus saw her, he called *her to him*, and said unto her, Woman, thou art loosed from thine infirmity.

Called *see Luke 6:13.*

Loosed *apoluo* (630), denotes (a) "to set free, release," translated "loosed" in **Luke 13:12**, of deliverance from an infirmity; in Matt. 18:27, KJV, "loosed" (RV, "released"), of a debtor; (b) "to let go, dismiss," e.g., Matt. 14:15, 22. *See also* Forgive, Forgiven at *Luke 6:37.*

13:13 And he laid *his* hands on her: and immediately she was made straight, and glorified God.

Laid *see Luke 4:40.*

Immediately *see Luke 1:64.*

Made straight *anorthoo* (461), "to set upright" (*ana*, "up," *orthos*, "straight"), is used of "lifting" up "hands that hang down," Heb. 12:12; of setting up a building, restoring ruins, Acts 15:16 (cf, e.g., 2 Sam. 7:13, 16; 1 Chron. 17:12; Jer. 10:12; often so used in the papyri); of the healing of the woman with a spirit of infirmity, **Luke 13:13**, "was made straight."

13:14 And the ruler of the synagogue answered with indignation, because that Jesus had healed on the sabbath day, and said unto the people, There are six days in which men ought to work: in them therefore come and be healed, and not on the sabbath day.

Ruler of the synagogue *see Luke 8:49.*

Indignation *aganakteo* (23), "to be indignant, to be moved with indignation" (from *agan*, "much," *achomai*, "to grieve"), is translated "were moved with indignation" of the ten disciples against James and John, Matt. 20:24; in Mark 10:41, RV (KJV, "they began to be much displeased"); in Matt. 21:15, of the chief priests and scribes, against Christ and the children, RV, "they were moved with indignation" (KJV, "they were sore displeased"); in 26:8, of the disciples against the woman who anointed Christ's feet, "they had indignation"; so Mark 14:4; in Mark 10:14, of Christ, against the disciples, for rebuking the children, "He was moved with indignation," RV (KJV, "he was much displeased"); in **Luke 13:14**, of the ruler of the synagogue against Christ for healing on the Sabbath, "being moved with indignation," RV, KJV, "(answered) with indignation."

Six *see Luke 4:25.*

13:15 The Lord then answered him, and said, *Thou* hypocrite, doth not each one of you on the sabbath loose his ox or *his* ass from the stall, and lead *him* away to watering?

Said *lego* (3004), primarily to pick out, gather," chiefly denotes "to say, speak, affirm," whether of actual speech, e.g., Matt. 11:17, or of unspoken thought, e.g., Matt. 3:9, or of a message in writing, e.g., 2 Cor. 8:8. The 2nd aorist form *eipon* is used to supply that tense, which is lacking in *lego*. Concerning the phrase "he answered and said," it is a well known peculiarity of Hebrew narrative style that a speech is introduced, not simply by "and he said," but by prefixing "and he answered" (*apokrinomai*, with *eipon*). In Matt. 14:27, "saying," and Mark 6:50, "and saith," emphasis is perhaps laid on the fact that the Lord, hitherto silent as He moved over the lake, then addressed His disciples. That the phrase sometimes occurs where no explicit question has preceded (e.g., Matt. 11:25; 17:4; 28:5; Mark 11:14; 12:35; **Luke 13:15**; **14:3**; John 5:17, 19), illustrates the use of the Hebrew idiom.

Hypocrite *see Luke 6:42.*

Ox *bous* (1016), denotes an "ox" or "a cow," **Luke 13:15**; **14:5**, **19**; John 2:14-15; 1 Cor. 9:9 (twice); 1 Tim. 5:18.

Stall *see* **Manger** at *Luke 2:7.*

Lead *apago* (520), "to lead away" (*apo*, "away"), is used of a way "leading" to destruction, Matt. 7:13, to life, v. 14; of those who "led" Christ away from Gethsemane, Mark 14:44; in some mss., John 18:13, to Annas; to Caiaphas, Matt. 26:57; Mark 14:53; to Pilate, Matt. 27:2; to the Praetorium, Mark 15:16; to crucifixion, Matt. 27:31; **Luke 23:26**; in some mss. John 19:16; of "leading" an animal away to watering, **Luke 13:15**; of being "led" away to idolatry, 1 Cor. 12:2, RV, "led away" (KJV, "carried away"). Some mss. have it in Acts 24:7 (KJV, "took away"). It is translated "bring" in 23:17. In 12:19 it signifies "to put to death."

Watering *potizo* (4222), "to give to drink," is used (a) naturally in **Luke 13:15**, "watering," with reference to animals; (b) figuratively, with reference to spiritual ministry to converts, 1 Cor. 3:6-8.

13:16 And ought not this woman, being a daughter of Abraham, whom Satan hath bound, lo, these eighteen years, be loosed from this bond on the sabbath day?

This *autos*; "he," rendered "this" in Matt. 11:14, lit., "he"; in John 12:7, KJV (RV, "it"); in the feminine, **Luke 13:16**.

Daughter *see* **Daughters** at *Luke 1:5.*

Satan *see Luke 4:8. See also* **Devils** at *Luke 4:41.*

Bound *deo* (1210), "to bind," is used (a) literally, of any sort of "binding," e.g., Acts 22:5; 24:27, (b) figuratively, of the Word of God, as not being "bound," 2 Tim. 2:9, i.e., its ministry, course and efficacy were not hindered by the bonds and imprisonment suffered by the apostle. A woman who was bent together, had been "bound" by Satan through the work of a demon, **Luke 13:16**. Paul speaks of himself, in Acts 20:22, as being "bound in the spirit," i.e. compelled by his convictions, under the constraining power of the Spirit of God, to go to Jerusalem. A wife is said to be "bound" to her husband, Rom. 7:2; 1 Cor. 7:39; and the husband to the wife, 1 Cor. 7:27. The Lord's words to the apostle Peter in Matt. 16:19, as to "binding," and to all the disciples in 18:18, signify, in the former case, that the apostle, by his ministry of the Word of Life, would keep unbelievers outside the kingdom of God, and admit those who believed. So with regard to 18:18, including the exercise of disciplinary measures in the sphere of the local church; the application of the rabbinical sense of forbidding is questionable.

Eighteen *see* **Eight** at *Luke 2:21.*

Loosed *luo* (3089), denotes (a) "to loose, unbind, release," (1) of things, e.g., in Acts 7:33, RV, "loose (the shoes)," KJV, "put off"; Mark 1:7; (2) of animals, e.g., Matt. 21:2; (3) of persons, e.g., John 11:44; Acts 22:30; (4) of Satan, Rev. 20:3, 7, and angels, Rev. 9:14, 15; (5) metaphorically, of one diseased, **Luke 13:16**; of the marriage tie, 1 Cor. 7:27; of release from sins, Rev. 1:5 (in the most authentic mss.); (b) "to loosen, break up, dismiss, dissolve, destroy"; in this sense it is translated "to loose" in Acts 2:24, of the pains of death; in Rev. 5:2, of the seals of a roll.

Bond *see* Bands at *Luke 8:29*.

13:17 And when he had said these things, all his adversaries were ashamed: and all the people rejoiced for all the glorious things that were done by him.

Adversaries *antikeimai* (480), is, lit., "to lie opposite to, to be set over against." In addition to its legal sense it signifies "to withstand"; the present participle of the verb with the article, which is equivalent to a noun, signifies "an adversary," e.g., **Luke 13:17**; **21:15**; 1 Cor. 16:9; Phil. 1:28; 1 Tim. 5:14. This construction is used of the Man of Sin, in 2 Thess. 2:4, and is translated "He that opposeth," where, adopting the noun form, we might render by "the opponent and self-exalter against...." In Gal. 5:17 it is used of the antagonism between the Holy Spirit and the flesh in the believer; in 1 Tim. 1:10, of anything, in addition to persons, that is opposed to the doctrine of Christ. In these two places the word is rendered "contrary to." In the Sept. it is used of Satan, Zech. 3:1, and of men, Job 13:24; Isa. 66:6.

Rejoiced *see* Rejoice at *Luke 1:14*.

Glorious *see* Gorgeously at *Luke 7:25*.

13:18 Then said he, Unto what is the kingdom of God like? and whereunto shall I resemble it?

Like *see Luke 6:47*.

13:19 It is like a grain of mustard seed, which a man took, and cast into his garden; and it grew, and waxed a great tree; and the fowls of the air lodged in the branches of it.

Like *see Luke 6:47*.

Grain *kokkos* (2848), denotes "a grain," Matt. 13:31; 17:20; Mark 4:31; **Luke 13:19**; **17:6**; John 12:24 (KJV, "corn"); 1 Cor. 15:37 (where the RV has "a ... grain," to distinguish it from "grain" in general).

Mustard *sinapi* (4615), a word of Egyptian origin, is translated "mustard seed" in the NT. "The conditions to be fulfilled by the mustard are that it should be a familiar plant, with a very small seed, Matt. 17:20; **Luke 17:6**, sown in the earth, growing larger than garden herbs, Matt. 13:31, having large branches, Mark 4:31, ... attractive to birds, **Luke 13:19** [RV, '(became) a tree']. The cultivated mustard is *sinapis nigra*. The seed is well known for its minuteness. The mustards are annuals, reproduced with extraordinary rapidity ... In fat soil they often attain a height of 10 or 12 feet, and have branches which attract passing birds" (A. E. Post, in *Hastings' Bib. Dic.*). The correct RV translation in Matt. 13:32, "greater than the herbs," for the KJV, "greatest among herbs" (the "mustard" is not a herb), should be noted. As the parable indicates, Christendom presents a sort of Christianity that has become conformed to the principles and ways of the world, and the world has favored this debased Christianity. Contrast the testimony of the NT, e.g., in John 17:14; Gal. 6:14; 1 Pet. 2:11; 1 John 3:1.

Man *see* Men at *Luke 5:10*.

Garden *kepos* (2779), "a garden," occurs in **Luke 13:19**, in one of the Lord's parables; in John 18:1, 26, of the garden of Gethsemane; in 19:41, of the garden near the place of the Lord's crucifixion.

Grew *see Luke 1:80*.

Waxed *ginomai* (1096), "to become," is translated "waxed" in **Luke 13:19**, KJV (RV, "became"); in Heb. 11:34, KJV and RV, "waxed".

Tree *see Luke 6:43*.

Lodged *kataskenoo* (2681), "to pitch one's tent" (*kata*, "down," *skene*, "a tent"), is rendered "to lodge," of birds, in Matt. 13:32; Mark 4:32; **Luke 13:19**. In Acts 2:26, it is used of the body of the Lord in the tomb, as dwelling in hope, RV, "shall dwell" (marg., "tabernacle"), KJV, "shall rest." Cf. *katoskenosis*, "a roosting place."

Branches *klados* (2798), from *klao*, "to break" (cf. *klasma*, "a broken piece"), properly a young tender shoot, "broken off" for grafting, is used for any kind of branch, Matt. 13:32; 21:8; 24:32; Mark 4:32; 13:28; **Luke 13:19**; the descendants of Israel, Rom. 11:16-19, 21.

13:20 And again he said, Whereunto shall I liken the kingdom of God?

Liken *see Luke 7:31*.

13:21 It is like leaven, which a woman took and hid in three measures of meal, till the whole was leavened.

Like *see Luke 6:47*.

Leaven *see Luke 12:1*.

Measures *saton* (4568), is a Hebrew dry measure (Heb., *seah*), about a peck and a half, Matt. 13:33; **Luke 13:21**; "three measures" would be the quantity for a baking (cf. Gen. 18:6; Judg. 6:19; 1 Sam. 1:24; the "ephah" of the last two passages was equal to three *sata*).

Meal *aleuron* (224), "meal" (akin to *aleuo*, "to grind," and therefore, lit., "what is ground"), occurs in Matt. 13:33; **Luke 13:21**.

Whole *see Luke 11:36.*

Leavened *zumoo* (2220), signifies "to leaven, to act as leaven," passive voice in Matt. 13:33 and **Luke 13:21**; active voice in 1 Cor. 5:6 and Gal. 5:9.

13:22 And he went through the cities and villages, teaching, and journeying toward Jerusalem.

Went *see Luke 6:1.*

Journeying In **Luke 13:22** the noun *poreia*, "a journey, a going," is used with the verb *poieo*, "to make," with the meaning "to journey," lit., "making (for Himself, middle voice) a way", "journeying." In Jas. 1:11, "ways."

13:23-24 Then said one unto him, Lord, are there few that be saved? And he said unto them,
Strive to enter in at the strait gate: for many, I say unto you, will seek to enter in, and shall not be able.

Strive *agonizomai* (75), "to contend" (Eng., "agonize"), is rendered "to strive" in **Luke 13:24**; 1 Cor. 9:25; Col. 1:29; 4:12, RV (KJV, "laboring fervently"). In 1 Tim. 4:10, the best texts have this verb (RV, "strive") for *oneidizomai*, "to suffer reproach," KJV.

Strait *stenos* (4728), from a root *sten-*, seen in *stenazo*, "to groan," *stenagmos*, "groaning" (Eng., "stenography," lit., "narrow writing"), is used figuratively in Matt. 7:13, 14, of the gate which provides the entrance to eternal life, "narrow" because it runs counter to natural inclinations, and "the way" is similarly characterized; so in **Luke 13:24** (where the more intensive word *agonizomai*, "strive," is used); RV, "narrow" (KJV, "strait") in each place. Cf. *stenochoreo*, "to be straitened," and *stenochoria*, "narrowness, anguish, distress."

Gate *thura* (2374), "a door, gate" (Eng., "door" is connected), is used (a) literally, e.g., Matt. 6:6; 27:60; (b) metaphorically, of Christ, John 10:7, 9; of faith, by acceptance of the gospel, Acts 14:27; of "openings" for preaching and teaching the Word of God, 1 Cor. 16:9; 2 Cor. 2:12; Col. 4:3; Rev. 3:8; of "entrance" into the Kingdom of God, Matt. 25:10; **Luke 13:24-25**; of Christ's "entrance" into a repentant believer's heart, Rev. 3:20; of the nearness of Christ's second advent, Matt. 24:33; Mark 13:29; cf. Jas. 5:9; of "access" to behold visions relative to the purposes of God, Rev. 4:1. *See also Luke 7:12.*

13:25 When once the master of the house is risen up, and hath shut to the door, and ye begin to stand without, and to knock at the door, saying, Lord, Lord, open unto us; and he shall answer and say unto you, I know you not whence ye are:

Master *see* Goodman at *Luke 12:39.*

Shut *apokleio* (608), to shut fast (*apo*, away from, and *kleio*), is used in **Luke 13:25**, expressing the impossibility of entrance after the closing.

Knock *see Luke 11:9.*

Saying, Say *see* Say at *Luke 4:23.*

13:26 Then shall ye begin to say, We have eaten and drunk in thy presence, and thou hast taught in our streets.

Presence *see Luke 1:19.*

Streets *see Luke 10:10.*

13:27 But he shall say, I tell you, I know you not whence ye are; depart from me, all *ye* workers of iniquity.

Depart *see* Departed at *Luke 2:37.*

Workers *ergates* (2040), is translated "workers" in **Luke 13:27** ("of iniquity"); 2 Cor. 11:13 ("deceitful"); Phil. 3:2 ("evil"); "workman," Matt. 10:10, KJV (RV, "laborer"); "workman," 2 Tim. 2:15; "workmen," Acts 19:25. *See also* **Labourers** at *Luke 10:2.*

Iniquity *adikia* (93), denotes "unrighteousness," lit., "unrightness" (*a*, negative, *dike*, "right"), a condition of not being right, whether with God, according to the standard of His holiness and righteousness, or with man, according to the standard of what man knows to be right by his conscience. In **Luke 16:8** and **18:6**, the phrases lit. are, "the steward of unrighteousness" and "the judge of injustice," the subjective genitive describing their character; in **18:6** the meaning is "injustice" and so perhaps in Rom. 9:14. The word is usually translated "unrighteousness," but is rendered "iniquity" in **Luke 13:27**; Acts 1:18; 8:23; 1 Cor. 13:6, KJV (RV, "unrighteousness"); so in 2 Tim. 2:19; Jas. 3:6.

13:28 There shall be weeping and gnashing of teeth, when ye shall see Abraham, and Isaac, and Jacob, and all the prophets, in the kingdom of God, and you *yourselves* thrust out.

Weeping *klauthmos* (2805), denotes "weeping, crying," Matt. 2:18; 8:12; 13:42, 50, RV (KJV, "wailing"); 22:13; 24:51; 25:30; **Luke 13:28**; Acts 20:37.

Gnashing *brugmos* (1030), denotes "gnashing" ("of teeth" being added), Matt. 8:12; 13:42, 50; 22:13; 24:51; 25:30; **Luke 13:28.**

Teeth *odous* (3599), is used in the sing. in Matt. 5:38 (twice); elsewhere in the plural, of "the gnashing of teeth," the gnashing being expressive of anguish and indignation, Matt. 8:12; 13:42, 50; 22:13; 24:51; 25:30; Mark 9:18; **Luke 13:28**; Acts 7:54; in Rev. 9:8, of the beings seen in a vision and described as locusts.

Thrust *see Luke 4:29.*

13:29 And they shall come from the east, and *from* the west, and from the north, and *from* the south, and shall sit down in the kingdom of God.

East *see* Dayspring at *Luke 1:78.*

West *see Luke 12:54.*

North *borras* (1005), primarily Boreas, the North Wind, came to denote the "north" (cf. "Borealis"), **Luke 13:29**; Rev. 21:13.

South *see Luke 11:31.*

Sit *see* Laid at *Luke 2:7.*

13:30-31 And, behold, there are last which shall be first, and there are first which shall be last.

The same day there came certain of the Pharisees, saying unto him, Get thee out, and depart hence: for Herod will kill thee.

Get *exerchomai* (1831), "to come or go out," is translated "get ... out" in **Luke 13:31**; Acts 7:3; 22:18.

Depart *see Luke 4:42.*

Hence *see Luke 4:9.*

Will *thelo* (2309), usually expresses "desire" or "design"; it is most frequently translated by "will" or "would"; see especially Rom. 7:15, 16, 18-21. In 1 Tim. 2:4, RV, "willeth" signifies the gracious "desire" of God for all men to be saved; not all are "willing" to accept His condition, depriving themselves either by the self-established criterion of their perverted reason, or because of their self-indulgent preference for sin. In John 6:21, the KJV renders the verb "willingly" (RV, "they were willing"); in 2 Pet. 3:5, KJV, the present participle is translated "willingly" (RV, "wilfully"). The following are RV renderings for the KJV, "will": Matt. 16:24, 25, "would"; "wouldest," 19:21 and 20:21; "would," 20:26, 27; Mark 8:34, 35; 10:43, 44; "would fain," **Luke 13:31**; "would," John 6:67; "willeth," 7:17; in 8:44, "it is your will (to do)"; "wouldest," Rom. 13:3; "would," 1 Cor. 14:35 and 1 Pet. 3:10.

13:32 And he said unto them, Go ye, and tell that fox, Behold, I cast out devils, and I do cures to day and to morrow, and the third *day* I shall be perfected.

Fox *see* Foxes at *Luke 9:58.*

Do *apoteleo* (658), "to bring to an end, accomplish," is translated "I perform" in **Luke 13:32**, RV (KJV, "I do"); in Jas. 1:15, it is used of sin, "fullgrown" RV (KJV, "finished"). *See also Luke 7:4.*

Cures *iasis* (2392), "a healing, a cure" (akin to *iaomai*, "to heal," and *iatros*, "a physician"), is used in the plural in **Luke 13:32**; in Acts 4:22, "healing", in 4:30 with the preposition *eis* "unto," lit., "unto healing," translated "heal."

Morrow *see Luke 10:35.*

Perfected *teleioo* (5048), "to bring to an end by completing or perfecting," is used (I) of "accomplishing"; (II) of "bringing to completeness," (a) of persons: of Christ's assured completion of His earthly course, in the accomplishment of the Father's will, the successive stages culminating in His death, **Luke 13:32**; Heb. 2:10, to make Him "perfect," legally and officially, for all that He would be to His people on the ground of His sacrifice; cf. 5:9; 7:28, RV, "perfected" (KJV, "consecrated"); of His saints, John 17:23, RV, "perfected" (KJV, "made perfect"); Phil. 3:12; Heb. 10:14; 11:40 (of resurrection glory); 12:23 (of the departed saints); 1 John 4:18, of former priests (negatively), Heb. 9:9; similarly of Israelites under the Aaronic priesthood, 10:1; (b) of things, Heb. 7:19 (of the ineffectiveness of the Law); Jas. 2:22 (of faith made "perfect" by works); 1 John 2:5, of the love of God operating through him who keeps His word; 4:12, of the love of God in the case of those who love one another; 4:17, of the love of God as "made perfect with" (RV) those who abide in God, giving them to be possessed of the very character of God, by reason of which "as He is, even so are they in this world."

13:33 Nevertheless I must walk to day, and to morrow, and the *day* following: for it cannot be that a prophet perish out of Jerusalem.

Walk *see* Walking at *Luke 1:6. See also* Go forth at *Luke 8:14.*

Morrow *see Luke 10:35.*

Following In **Luke 13:33**, the present participle, middle voice, of the verb *echo*, "to have, to be next," is used with the article, the word *hemera*, "a day," being understood, signifying "the day following." *See also* Have at *Luke 12:4.*

Cannot *endechomai* (1735), "to accept, admit, allow of," is used impersonally in **Luke 13:33**, "it can (not) be," i.e., it is not admissible.

13:34 O Jerusalem, Jerusalem, which killest the prophets, and stonest them that are sent unto thee; how often would I have

gathered thy children together, as a hen *doth gather* her brood under *her* wings, and ye would not!

Stonest *lithoboleo* (3036), "to pelt with stones," "to stone to death," occurs in Matt. 21:35; 23:37; **Luke 13:34** (John 8:5 in some mss.); Acts 7:58, 59; 14:5; Heb. 12:20.

Often *posakis* (4212), an interrogative numeral adverb, "how many times, how oft (or often)?" occurs in Matt. 18:21; 23:37; **Luke 13:34**.

Gathered, Gather *see* Gathered at *Luke 12:1*.

Children *see* Young at *Luke 2:24*.

Hen *ornis* (3733), "a bird," is used, in the NT, only of a "hen," Matt. 23:37; **Luke 13:34**.

Brood *nossia* (3555), primarily, "a nest," denotes "a brood," **Luke 13:34**. Some texts have *nossion* in the plural, as Matt. 23:37, "chicken."

Wings *pterux* (4420), is used of birds, Matt. 23:37; **Luke 13:34**; symbolically in Rev. 12:14, RV, "the two wings of the great eagle" (KJV, "two wings of a great eagle"), suggesting the definiteness of the action, the "wings" indicating rapidity and protection, an allusion, perhaps, to Exod. 19:4 and Deut. 32:11, 12; of the "living creatures" in a vision, Rev. 4:8; 9:9. Cf. *pterugion*, "a pinnacle." *See also* Nests at *Luke 9:58*.

13:35 Behold, your house is left unto you desolate: and verily I say unto you, Ye shall not see me, until *the time* come when ye shall say, Blessed *is* he that cometh in the name of the Lord.

House *see Luke 1:27*.

Desolate *eremos* (2048), is translated "desolate" in the Lord's words against Jerusalem, Matt. 23:38; some mss. have it in **Luke 13:35**; in reference to the habitation of Judas, Acts 1:20, and to Sarah, from whom, being barren, her husband had turned, Gal. 4:27.

Chapter 14

14:1 And it came to pass, as he went into the house of one of the chief Pharisees to eat bread on the sabbath day, that they watched him.

Chief *see Luke 11:15*.

Watched *see Luke 6:7*.

14:2 And, behold, there was a certain man before him which had the dropsy.

Dropsy *hudropikos* (5203), "dropsical, suffering from dropsy" (*hudrops*, "dropsy"), is found in **Luke 14:2**, the only instance recorded of the healing of this disease by the Lord.

14:3 And Jesus answering spake unto the lawyers and Pharisees, saying, Is it lawful to heal on the sabbath day?

Answering *see* Answered at *Luke 3:16*.

Lawyers *see* Doctors of the law at *Luke 5:17*.

Saying *see* Said at *Luke 13:15*.

Heal *see Luke 4:23*.

Sabbath *see Luke 6:1*.

14:4 And they held their peace. And he took *him*, and healed him, and let him go;

Peace *hesuchazo* (2270), "to be quiet, still, at rest," is said of Paul's friends in Caesarea, in "ceasing" to persuade him not to go to Jerusalem, Acts 21:14; it is used of silence (save in **Luke 23:56** and 1 Thess. 4:11) in **Luke 14:4** and Acts 11:18.

Took *see Luke 9:47*.

Let *see* Forgive, Forgiven at *Luke 6:37*.

14:5 And answered them, saying, Which of you shall have an ass or an ox fallen into a pit, and will not straightway pull him out on the sabbath day?

Ox *see Luke 13:15*.

Fallen *see* Fall at *Luke 6:39*.

Pit *phrear* (5421), "a well, dug for water" (distinct from *pege*, "a fountain"), denotes "a pit" in Rev. 9:1, 2, RV, "the pit (of the abyss)," "the pit," i.e., the shaft leading down to the abyss, KJV, "(bottomless) pit"; in **Luke 14:5**, RV, well (KJV, "pit"); in John 4:11, 12, "well."

Pull ... out *anaspao* (385), "to draw up," is used of "drawing" up an animal out of a pit, **Luke 14:5** (RV, "draw up"; KJV, "pull out"), and of the "drawing" up of the sheet into heaven, in the vision in Acts 11:10.

14:6 And they could not answer him again to these things.

Answer *antapokrinomai* (470), a strengthened form, "to answer by contradiction, to reply against," is found in **Luke 14:6** and Rom. 9:20.

14:7 And he put forth a parable to those which were bidden, when he marked how they chose out the chief rooms; saying unto them,

Put In **Luke 14:7**, KJV, *lego*, "to speak" (see RV), is translated "He put forth."

Bidden *kaleo* (2564), "to call," often means "to bid," in the sense of "invite," e.g., Matt. 22:3-4, 8, 9; **Luke 14:7-10, 13**, RV; Rev. 19:9, RV. *See also* Chose at *Luke 6:13*.

Marked *epecho* (1907), lit., "to hold upon" (*epi*, "upon," *echo*, "to hold"), signifies (like *parecho*) "to hold out," Phil. 2:16, of the word of life; then, "to hold one's mind towards, to observe," translated "marked" in **Luke 14:7**, of the Lord's observance of those who chose the chief seats.

Chief rooms *protoklisia* (4411), "the chief reclining place at table," is rendered "uppermost rooms," in Matt. 23:6, KJV (RV, "chief place"); in Mark 12:39, "uppermost rooms," KJV (RV, "chief places"); in **Luke 14:7**, "chief rooms," KJV (RV, "chief seats"); in **v. 8**, KJV, "highest room" (RV, "chief seat"); in **20:46**, KJV, "highest seats" (RV, "chief seats").

14:8 When thou art bidden of any *man* to a wedding, sit not down in the highest room; lest a more honourable man than thou be bidden of him;

Wedding *see Luke 12:36*.

Sit *see* Sat at *Luke 7:36*.

Honourable *see* Dear at *Luke 7:2*.

14:9 And he that bade thee and him come and say to thee, Give this man place; and thou begin with shame to take the lowest room.

"Nothing sets a person so much out of the devil's reach as humility."

JONATHAN EDWARDS

Place, Room *see* Room at *Luke 2:7*.

Shame *aischune* (152), "shame," signifies (a) subjectively, the confusion of one who is "ashamed" of anything, a sense of "shame," **Luke 14:9**; those things which "shame" conceals, 2 Cor. 4:2; (b) objectively, ignominy, that which is visited on a person by the wicked, Heb. 12:2; that which should arise from guilt, Phil. 3:19; (c) concretely, a thing to be "ashamed" of, Rev. 3:18; Jude 13, where the word is in the plural, lit., "basenesses," "disgraces."

Take *katecho* (2722), "to hold," is rendered "to take (the lowest place)" in **Luke 14:9**.

Lowest *eschatos* (2078), "last, utmost, lowest," is rendered "lowest" in **Luke 14:9, 10**, of the "lowest" place at a meal. *See also* Last at *Luke 11:26*.

14:10 But when thou art bidden, go and sit down in the lowest room; that when he that bade thee cometh, he may say unto thee, Friend, go up higher: then shalt thou have worship in the presence of them that sit at meat with thee.

Lowest *see Luke 14:9. See also* Last at *Luke 11:26*.

Room *see Luke 2:7*.

Go up *prosanabaino* (4320), "to go up higher" (*pros*, "towards"), is used of moving to a couch of greater honor at a feast, **Luke 14:10**.

Higher *anoteron* (511), the neuter of *anoteros*, "higher," the comparative of *ano*, is used as an adverb of place in **Luke 14:10**; for the meaning "above," in Heb. 10:8.

Worship In **Luke 14:10**, KJV, *doxa*, "glory" (RV), is translated "worship." *See also* Glory at *Luke 2:9*.

Presence *see Luke 1:19*.

Sit *see* Sat at *Luke 7:49*.

14:11 For whosoever exalteth himself shall be abased; and he that humbleth himself shall be exalted.

Exalteth *see* Exalted at *Luke 1:52*.

Abased, Humbleth *see* Brought low at *Luke 3:5*.

14:12 Then said he also to him that bade him, When thou makest a dinner or a supper, call not thy friends, nor thy brethren, neither thy kinsmen, nor *thy* rich neighbours; lest they also bid thee again, and a recompence be made thee.

Bade *antikaleo* (479), "to bid again, invite in turn," is found in **Luke 14:12**.

Makest *see* Make at *Luke 5:34*.

Supper *deipnon* (1173), denotes (a) "the chief meal of the day," dinner or supper, taken at or towards evening; in the plural "feasts," Matt. 23:6; Mark 6:21; 12:39; **Luke 20:46**; otherwise translated "supper," **Luke 14:12, 16, 17, 24**; John 12:2; 13:2, 4; 21:20; 1 Cor. 11:21 (of a social meal); (b) "the Lord's Supper," 1 Cor. 11:20; (c) "the supper or feast" which will celebrate the marriage of Christ with His spiritual Bride, at the inauguration of His Kingdom, Rev. 19:9; (d) figuratively, of that to which the birds of prey will be summoned after the overthrow of the enemies of the Lord at the termination of the war of Armageddon, 19:17 (cf. Ezek. 39:4, 17-20).

See also Feast at *Luke 5:29;* Dine at *Luke 11:37*.

Call *phoneo* (5455), "to sound" (Eng.,"phone"), is used of the crowing of a cock, e.g., Matt. 26:34; John 13:38; of "calling" out with a clear or loud voice, to cry out, e.g. Mark 1:26 (some mss. have *krazo* here), Acts 16:28; of "calling" to come to oneself, e.g., Matt. 20:32; **Luke 19:15**; of "calling" forth, as of Christ's call to Lazarus to come forth from the tomb, John 12:17; of inviting, e.g., **Luke 14:12**; of "calling" by name, with the implication of the pleasure taken in the possession of those "called," e.g., John 10:3; 13:13.

Friends *see* ***Luke 7:6.***

Kinsmen *see* **Cousins** at ***Luke 1:58.***

Rich *see* ***Luke 6:24.***

Neighbours *geiton* (1069), lit., "one living in the same land," denotes "a neighbor," always plural in the NT, **Luke 14:12; 15:6, 9**; John 9:5.

Recompence *antapodoma* (468), akin to *antapodidomi*, "to recompense," lit., "a giving back in return" (*anti*, "in return," *apo*, back, *didomi*, "to give"), a requital, recompence, is used (a) in a favorable sense, **Luke 14:12**; (b) in an unfavorable sense, Rom. 11:9, indicating that the present condition of the Jewish nation is the retributive effect of their transgressions, on account of which that which was designed as a blessing ("their table") has become a means of judgment.

14:13 But when thou makest a feast, call the poor, the maimed, the lame, the blind:

Feast *see* ***Luke 5:29.***

Call *see* **Bidden** at ***Luke 14:7.***

Poor *ptochos* (4434), an adjective describing "one who crouches and cowers," is used as a noun, "a beggar" (from *ptosso*, "to cower down or hide oneself for fear"), **Luke 14:13, 21** ("poor"); **16:20, 22**; as an adjective, "beggarly" in Gal. 4:9, i.e., poverty-stricken, powerless to enrich, metaphorically descriptive of the religion of the Jews. While *prosaites* is descriptive of a "beggar," and stresses his "begging," *ptochos* stresses his poverty-stricken condition. *See also* ***Luke 6:20.***

Maimed *anaperos, or anapeiros* (376), "crippled, maimed" (from *ana*, "up," and *peros*, "disabled in a limb"), is found in **Luke 14:13, 21.**

Lame *see* ***Luke 7:22.***

14:14 And thou shalt be blessed; for they cannot recompense thee: for thou shalt be recompensed at the resurrection of the just.

Cannot *echo* (2192), "to have," is translated "could" in Mark 14:8, lit., "she hath done what she had", in **Luke 14:14**, for the KJV, "cannot," the RV has "they have not wherewith"; in Acts 4:14, "could say nothing against" is, lit., "had nothing to say against"; in Heb. 6:13, "he could swear" is, lit., "He had (by none greater) to swear."

Recompense, Recompensed *antapodidomi* (467), "to give back as an equivalent, to requite, recompense" (the *anti* expressing the idea of a complete return), is translated "render" in 1 Thess. 3:9, here only in the NT of thanksgiving to God (cf. the Sept. of Ps. 116:12); elsewhere it is used of "recompense," "whether between men (but in that case only of good, not of evil), **Luke 14:14a**, or between God and evil-doers, Rom. 12:19, RV (KJV, "repay"); Heb. 10:30, cf. the noun in Rom. 11:9; or between God and those who do well, **Luke 14:14b**; Rom. 11:35, cf. the noun in Col. 3:24; in 2 Thess. 1:6 both reward and retribution are in view."

Resurrection *see* **Rising** at ***Luke 2:34.***

14:15 And when one of them that sat at meat with him heard these things, he said unto him, Blessed *is* he that shall eat bread in the kingdom of God.

Sat *see* ***Luke 7:49.***

14:16 Then said he unto him, A certain man made a great supper, and bade many:

Supper *see* ***Luke 14:12.***

14:17 And sent his servant at supper time to say to them that were bidden, Come; for all things are now ready.

Supper *see* ***Luke 14:12.***

Time *see* ***Luke 1:10.***

Ready *see* ***Luke 12:40.***

14:18 And they all with one *consent* began to make excuse. The first said unto him, I have bought a piece of ground, and I must needs go and see it: I pray thee have me excused.

Excuse, Excused *paraiteomai* (3868), besides the meanings "to beg from another," Mark 15:6 (in the best texts); "to entreat that ... not," Heb. 12:19; "to beg off, ask to be excused," **Luke 14:18, 19; 12:25**, is translated to reject in Titus 3:10, KJV.

First *see* ***Luke 11:26.***

Piece of ground In **Luke 14:18**, *agros*, "a field," is translated "a piece of ground," KJV, RV, a field.

Needs *ananke* (318), "a necessity, need," is translated "it must needs be" in Matt. 18:7, with the verb "to be" understood (according to the best mss.); in **Luke 14:18**, "I must needs" translates the verb *echo*, "to have," with this noun as the object, lit., "I have need"; in Rom. 13:5 "(ye) must needs," lit., "(it is) necessary (to be subject)."

Pray *erotao* (2065), "to ask," is translated by the verb to pray in **Luke 14:18, 19**; **16:27**; John 4:31; 14:16; 16:26; 17:9, 15, 20; in Acts 23:18, RV, "asked" (KJV "prayed"); in 1 John 5:16, RV, "should make request" (KJV "shall pray").

Have *see Luke 12:4.*

14:19 And another said, I have bought five yoke of oxen, and I go to prove them: I pray thee have me excused.

Yoke *zeugos* (2201), "a pair of animals," **Luke 14:19**. *See also* **Pair** at *Luke 2:24.*

Oxen *see* **Ox** at *Luke 13:15.*

Prove *dokimazo* (1381), "to test, prove," with the expectation of approving, is translated "to prove" in **Luke 14:19**; Rom. 12:2; 1 Cor. 3:13, RV (KJV, "shall try"); 11:28, RV (KJV, "examine"); 2 Cor. 8:8, 22; 13:5; Gal. 6:4; Eph. 5:10; 1 Thess. 2:4 (2nd part), RV (KJV, "trieth"); 5:21; 1 Tim. 3:10; in some mss., Heb. 3:9 (the most authentic have the noun *dokimasia*, "a proving"); 1 Pet. 1:7, RV (KJV, "tried"); 1 John 4:1, RV (KJV, "try").

Pray *see Luke 14:18.*

Excused *see* **Excuse, Excused** at *Luke 14:18.*

14:20 And another said, I have married a wife, and therefore I cannot come.

Married *gameo* (1060), "to marry," is used (a) of "the man," Matt. 5:32; 19:9, 10; 22:25 (RV; KJV, "married a wife"); v. 30; 24:38; Mark 6:17; 10:11; 12:25; **Luke 14:20**; **16:18**; **17:27**, RV, "married" (KJV, "married wives"); **20:34, 35**; 1 Cor. 7:28 (1st part); v. 33; (b) of "the woman," in the active voice, Mark 10:12; 1 Cor. 7:28 (last part); ver. 34; 1 Tim. 5:11, 14; in the passive voice, 1 Cor. 7:39; (c) of "both sexes," 1 Cor. 7:9, 10, 36; 1 Tim. 4:3.

14:21 So that servant came, and shewed his lord these things. Then the master of the house being angry said to his servant, Go out quickly into the streets and lanes of the city, and bring in hither the poor, and the maimed, and the halt, and the blind.

Shewed *apangello* ("to announce"), Matt. 11:4, "tell"; 12:18, "declare"; 28:11, "told"; **Luke 14:21**, "told"; Acts 26:20, "declared"; 28:21, "report"; 1 Thess. 1:9, "report"; 1 John 1:2, "declare".

Master *see* **Goodman** at *Luke 12:39.*

Angry *orgizo* (3710), "to provoke, to arouse to anger," is used in the middle voice in the eight places where it is found, and signifies "to be angry, wroth." It is said of individuals, in Matt. 5:22; 18:34; 22:7; **Luke 14:21**; **15:28**, and Eph. 4:26 (where a possible meaning is "be ye angry with yourselves"); of nations, Rev. 11:18; of Satan as the Dragon, 12:17.

Quickly *tacheos* (5030), is translated "quickly" in **Luke 14:21**; **16:6**; John 11:31, RV; "shortly" in 1 Cor. 4:19; Phil. 2:19, 24; 2 Tim. 4:9; with a suggestion of rashness in the following, Gal. 1:6, RV, "quickly" (KJV, "soon"); 2 Thess. 2:2; and 1 Tim. 5:22, "hastily," (KJV, "suddenly").

Streets *see Luke 10:10.*

Lanes *rhume* (4505), in earlier Greek meant "the force or rush or swing of a moving body" in later times, "a narrow road lane or street", it is translated "lanes" in **Luke 14:21**; "streets" in Matt. 6:2; "street" in Acts 9:11; 12:10. In the Sept., Isa. 15:3.

Poor *see Luke 14:13. See also Luke 6:20.*

Maimed *see Luke 14:13.*

Halt *see* **Lame** at *Luke 7:22.*

14:22 And the servant said, Lord, it is done as thou hast commanded, and yet there is room.

Commanded *see* **Commandeth** at *Luke 4:36.*

Room *see Luke 2:7.*

14:23 And the lord said unto the servant, Go out into the highways and hedges, and compel *them* to come in, that my house may be filled.

Highways *hodos* (3598), "a way, path, road," is rendered "highways" in Matt. 22:10; **Luke 14:23**; in Mark 10:46, RV, "way side," KJV, "highway side"; in Matt. 22:9, the word is used with *diexodoi* ("ways out through"), and the phrase is rightly rendered in the RV, "the partings of the highways" (i.e., the crossroads), KJV, "the highways."

Hedges *phragmos* (5418), denotes any sort of fence, hedge, palings or wall (akin to *phrasso*, "to fence in, stop"). It is used (a) in its literal sense, in Matt. 21:33, lit. "(he put) a hedge (around)"; Mark 12:1; **Luke 14:23**; (b) metaphorically, of the "partition" which separated Gentile from Jew, which was broken down by Christ through the efficacy of His expiatory sacrifice, Eph. 2:14.

Compel *anankazo* (315), denotes "to put constraint upon (from *ananke*, 'necessity'), to constrain, whether by threat, entreaty, force or persuasion"; Christ "constrained" the disciples to get into a boat, Matt. 14:22; Mark 6:45; the servants of the man who made a great supper were to constrain people to come in, **Luke 14:23** (RV, "constrain"); Saul of Tarsus "strove" to make saints blaspheme, Acts 26:11, RV (KJV, "compelled"); Titus, though a Greek, was not "compelled" to be circumcised, Gal. 2:3, as Galatian converts were, 6:12, RV; Peter was "compelling"

Gentiles to live as Jews, Gal. 2:14; Paul was "constrained" to appeal to Caesar, Acts 28:19, and was "compelled" by the church at Corinth to become foolish in speaking of himself, 2 Cor. 12:11.

Filled *gemizo* (1072), "to fill or load full," is used of a boat, Mark 4:37 (RV, "was filling"); a sponge, Mark 15:36, a house, **Luke 14:23**; the belly, **Luke 15:16**; waterpots, John 2:1; baskets, 6:13; bowls, with fire, Rev. 8:5; the temple, with smoke, 15:8. Cf. *gemo*, "to be full."

14:24 For I say unto you, That none of those men which were bidden shall taste of my supper.

Taste *see Luke 9:27.*

Supper *see Luke 14:12.*

14:25 And there went great multitudes with him: and he turned, and said unto them,

Went *see Luke 7:11.*

14:26 If any *man* come to me, and hate not his father, and mother, and wife, and children, and brethren, and sisters, yea, and his own life also, he cannot be my disciple.

Hate *see Luke 6:22.*

His *see Luke 11:21.*

Also *eti* (2089), "yet" or "further," is used (a) of time, (b) of degree, and in this sense is once translated "also," **Luke 14:26**, "his own life also." Here the meaning probably is "and, further, even his own life" (the force of the *kai* being "even"). No other particles mean "also."

14:27 And whosoever doth not bear his cross, and come after me, cannot be my disciple.

Bear *see* **Bare** at *Luke 7:14.*

14:28 For which of you, intending to build a tower, sitteth not down first, and counteth the cost, whether he have *sufficient* to finish *it*?

Intending *thelo* (2309), "to will, be willing, desire," is translated "intending" in **Luke 14:28**, KJV (RV, "desiring"). *See also* **Willing** at *Luke 10:29.*

Tower *see Luke 13:4.*

Sitteth *kathizo* (2523), is used (a) transitively, "to make sit down," Acts 2:30; (b) intransitively, "to sit down," e.g., Matt. 5:1, RV, "when (He) had sat down" (KJV, "was set"); 19:28; 20:21, 23; 23:2; 25:31; 26:36; Mark 11:2, 7; 12:41; **Luke 14:28, 31; 16:6**; John 19:13; Acts 2:3 (of the tongues of fire); 8:31; 1 Cor. 10:7; 2 Thess. 2:4, "he sitteth," aorist tense, i.e., "he takes his seat" (as, e.g., in Mark 16:19); Rev. 3:21 (twice), RV, "to sit down" and "sat down"; 20:4.

Counteth *psephizo* (5585), akin to *psephos*, "a stone," used in voting, occurs in **Luke 14:28**; Rev. 13:18.

Cost *dapane* (1160), "expense, cost" (from *dapto*, "to tear"; from a root *dap-* meaning "to divide"), is found in **Luke 14:28**, in the Lord's illustration of counting the "cost" of becoming His disciple. Cf. *dapanao*, "to spend."

Finish *apartismos* (535), is rendered "complete" in **Luke 14:28**, RV. *Apartismos* denotes "a completion," and the phrase is, lit., "unto a completion." The KJV has "to finish" (RV, "to complete").

14:29 Lest haply, after he hath laid the foundation, and is not able to finish *it*, all that behold *it* begin to mock him,

Lest In **Luke 14:29**, the conjunctive phrase *hina mepote*, "lest haply," is used. *See also Luke 4:11.*

Laid *see Luke 1:66.*

Foundation *see Luke 6:48.*

Finish *ekteleo* (1615), lit., "to finish out," i.e., "completely," is used in **Luke 14:29, 30**.

Mock *empaizo* (1702), a compound of *paizo*, "to play like a child" (*pais*), "to sport, jest," prefixed by *en*, "in" or "at," is used only in the Synoptists, and, in every instance, of the "mockery" of Christ, except in Matt. 2:16 (there in the sense of deluding, or deceiving, of Herod by the wise men) and in **Luke 14:29**, of ridicule cast upon the one who after laying a foundation of a tower is unable to finish it. The word is used (a) prophetically by the Lord, of His impending sufferings, Matt. 20:19; Mark 10:34; **Luke 18:32**; (b) of the actual insults inflicted upon Him by the men who had taken Him from Gethsemane, **Luke 22:63**; by Herod and his soldiers, **Luke 23:11**; by the soldiers of the governor, Matt. 27:29, 31; Mark 15:20; **Luke 23:36**; by the chief priests, Matt. 27:41; Mark 15:31.

14:30 Saying, This man began to build, and was not able to finish.

Man *see* **Men** at *Luke 5:10.*

Finish *see Luke 14:29.*

14:31 Or what king, going to make war against another king, sitteth not down first, and consulteth whether he be able with ten thousand to meet him that cometh against him with twenty thousand?

Make war against *sumballo* (4820), lit., "to throw together" (*sun*, "with," *ballo*, "to throw"), is used of "encountering" in war, **Luke 14:31**, RV, "to encounter ... (in war)," for KJV, "to make war against"; of meeting in order to discuss, in Acts 17:18, "encountered," of the philosophers in Athens and the apostle.

Sitteth *see Luke 14:28.*

Consulteth *bouleuo* (1011), used in the middle voice, means (a) "to consult," **Luke 14:31**; (b) "to resolve," John 12:10, KJV, "consulted"; RV, "took counsel."

Meet *apantao* (528), "to go to meet, to meet" (*apo*, "from," *antao*, "to meet with, come face to face with"), in Matt. 28:9; Mark 5:2; **Luke 14:31**; John 4:51; Acts 16:16. It is also used in Mark 14:13 and **Luke 17:12**. *See also* **Met** at *Luke 8:27.*

Twenty *eikosi* (1501), occurs in **Luke 14:31**; John 6:19; Acts 1:15; 27:28; 1 Cor. 10:8; of the "four and twenty" elders, in Rev. 4:4 (twice), 10; 5:8; 11:16; 19:4 (combined in one numeral with *tessares*, "four," in some mss.).

14:32 Or else, while the other is yet a great way off, he sendeth an ambassage, and desireth conditions of peace.

Way *porro* (4206), is used (a) literally, **Luke 14:32**, "a great way off"; the comparative degree *porroteron*, "further," is used in **24:28**; (b) metaphorically, of the heart in separation from God, Matt. 15:8; Mark 7:6. Cf. *porrothen*, "afar off".

Sendeth The "sending" of the Son by the Father was from the glory which He had with the Father into the world, by way of the Incarnation, not a "sending" out into the world after His birth, as if denoting His mission among and His manifestation to the people. "Hofmann, in support of his view that Jesus is called the Son of God only in virtue of His being born of man, vainly urges that the simple accusative after *apostello* also denotes what the Person is or becomes by being sent. What he states is true but only when the name of the object spoken of is chosen to correspond with the purposed mission, as e.g., in Mark 1:2; **Luke 14:32**; **19:14**. We can no more say, 'God sent Jesus that He should be His Son' than we can render 'he sent his servants,' Matt. 21:34, in this manner. That the Sonship of Christ is anterior to His mission to the world … is clear from John 16:28; cf. especially also the double accusative in 1 John 4:14, 'the Father sent the Son the Savior of the world.' The expression that Jesus is sent by God denotes the mission which He has to fulfill and the authority which backs Him" (Cremer, *Lexicon of NT Greek*).

Ambassage *presbeia* (4242), primarily, "age, eldership, rank," hence, "an embassy or ambassage," is used in **Luke 14:32**; in **19:14**, RV, "ambassage," for KJV, "message."

Desireth *see* **Desired** at *Luke 7:36.*

Conditions This translates the phrase *ta pros* in **Luke 14:32**, lit., "the (things) towards," i.e., the things relating to, or conditions of, (peace).

Peace *see Luke 1:79.*

14:33 So likewise, whosoever he be of you that forsaketh not all that he hath, he cannot be my disciple.

Likewise In Matt. 17:12 and Rom. 6:11, KJV, the adverb *houtos*, "thus, so," is translated "likewise" (RV, "so"); in **Luke 15:7** and **10**, KJV, "likewise," RV, "even so", in **Luke 14:33**, KJV, followed by *oun*, "therefore," it is rendered "so likewise" (RV, "so therefore").

Forsaketh *apotasso* (657), primarily, "to set apart" (*apo*, off, "from," *tasso*, "to arrange"), is used in the middle voice, meaning (a) "to take leave of," e.g., Mark 6:46, (b) "to renounce, forsake," **Luke 14:33**, KJV, "forsaketh," RV, "renounceth" ("all that he hath"). *See also* **Bid … farewell** at *Luke 9:61.*

Hath *see* **Have** at *Luke 12:33.*

14:34 Salt *is* good: but if the salt have lost his savour, wherewith shall it be seasoned?

Salt (*halas* (251), a late form of *hals* (found in some mss. in Mark 9:49), is used (a) literally in Matt. 5:13 (2nd part); Mark 9:50 (1st part, twice); **Luke 14:34** (twice); (b) metaphorically, of "believers," Matt. 5:13 (1st part); of their "character and condition," Mark 9:50 (2nd part); of "wisdom" exhibited in their speech, Col. 4:6. Being possessed of purifying, perpetuating and antiseptic qualities, "salt" became emblematic of fidelity and friendship among eastern nations. To eat of a person's "salt" and so to share his hospitality is still regarded thus among the Arabs. So in Scripture, it is an emblem of the covenant between God and His people, Num. 18:19; 2 Chron. 13:5; so again when the Lord says "Have salt in yourselves, and be at peace one with another" (Mark 9:50). In the Lord's teaching it is also symbolic of that spiritual health and vigor essential to Christian virtue and counteractive of the corruption that is in the world, e.g., Matt. 5:13, see (b) above. Food is seasoned with "salt"; every meal offering was to contain it, and it was to be offered with all offerings presented by Israelites, as emblematic of the holiness of Christ, and as betokening the reconciliation provided for man by God on the ground of the death of Christ, Lev. 2:13. To refuse God's provision in Christ and the efficacy of His expiatory sacrifice is to expose oneself to the doom of being "salted with fire," Mark 9:49. While "salt" is used to fertilize soil, excess of it on the ground produces sterility (e.g., Deut. 29:23; Judg. 9:45; Jer. 17:6; Zeph. 2:9).

Savour *moraino* (3471), primarily, "to be foolish," is used of salt that has lost its "savor," Matt. 5:13; **Luke 14:34**.

Seasoned *artuo* (741), "to arrange, make ready" (cf. *artios*, "fitted"), is used of "seasoning," Mark 9:50; **Luke 14:34**; Col. 4:6.

14:35 It is neither fit for the land, nor yet for the dunghill; *but* men cast it out. He that hath ears to hear, let him hear.

Fit *see* ***Luke 9:62.***

Land *see* ***Luke 4:25.***

Dunghill *kopria* (2874), "a dunghill," is found in **Luke 14:35**.

Chapter 15

15:1 Then drew near unto him all the publicans and sinners for to hear him.

Publicans *see* ***Luke 3:12.***

15:2 And the Pharisees and scribes murmured, saying, This man receiveth sinners, and eateth with them.

Murmured *diagonguzo* (1234), lit., "to murmur through" (*dia*, i.e., "through a whole crowd," or "among themselves"), is always used of indignant complaining, **Luke 15:2**; 19:7.

Receiveth *prosdechomai* (4327), "to receive to oneself, to receive favorably," also "to look for, wait for," is used of "receiving" in **Luke 15:2**; Rom. 16:2; Phil. 2:29.

Eateth *sunesthio* (4906), "to eat with" (*sun*, "with," and *esthio*), is found in **Luke 15:2**; Acts 10:41; 11:3; 1 Cor. 5:11; Gal. 2:12.

15:3-4 And he spake this parable unto them, saying, What man of you, having an hundred sheep, if he lose one of them, doth not leave the ninety and nine in the wilderness, and go after that which is lost, until he find it?

Lose *see* ***Luke 9:25.***

Leave *see* Left at ***Luke 5:28.***

Ninety *enenekonta*, or *ennen-* (1767), is found in Matt. 18:12-13; **Luke 15:4, 7**.

Lost *see* Perish at ***Luke 5:37.***

15:5 And when he hath found *it*, he layeth *it* on his shoulders, rejoicing.

Layeth *see* Laid at ***Luke 4:40.***

Shoulders *omos* (5606), occurs in Matt. 23:4 and **Luke 15:5**, and is suggestive (as in the latter passage) of strength and safety.

15:6 And when he cometh home, he calleth together *his* friends and neighbours, saying unto them, Rejoice with me; for I have found my sheep which was lost.

Home *oikos* (3624), "a house, dwelling," is used (a) with the preposition *eis*, "unto," with the meaning "to home," lit., "to a house," in Mark 8:3, RV, "to (their) home," KJV, "to (their own) houses"; so 8:26, "to (his) home"; **Luke 15:6**, "home," lit., "into the house"; (b) with the preposition *en*, "in," 1 Cor. 11:34, "(let him eat) at home"; 14:35, "(let them ask ...) at home"; (c) with the preposition *kata*, "down," Acts 2:46, "(breaking bread) at home," RV (KJV, "from house to house"); so in 5:42 (KJV, "in every house").

Calleth *see* Called at ***Luke 9:1.***

Friends *see* ***Luke 7:6.***

Neighbours *see* ***Luke 14:12.***

Rejoice *see* Rejoiced at ***Luke 1:58.***

Lost *see* Perish at ***Luke 5:37.***

15:7 I say unto you, that likewise joy shall be in heaven over one sinner that repenteth, more than over ninety and nine just persons, which need no repentance.

Likewise *see* ***Luke 14:33.***

More Various uses of the word "more" occur in connection with other words, especially in the comparative degree. The phrase "more than" translates certain prepositions and particles: in Rom. 1:25, KJV, *para*, "beside, compared with," is translated "more than" (RV, "rather than"): cf. Rom. 12:3, *huper*, "over, above," "more than," in Matt. 10:37 (twice); in Philem. 21, KJV, "more than" (RV, "beyond"). In Mark 14:5, KJV, *epano*, "above," is translated "more than" (RV, "above"). In **Luke 15:7** the particle *e*, "than," is necessarily rendered "more than"; cf. **Luke 17:2** and 1 Cor. 14:19, "rather than." In Mark 8:14, the conjunction *ei*, "if," with the negative *me*, lit., "if not," signifying "except," is translated "more than (one loaf)."

Ninety *see* ***Luke 15:4.***

Need *see* ***Luke 5:31.***

15:8 Either what woman having ten pieces of silver, if she lose one piece, doth not light a candle, and sweep the house, and seek diligently till she find *it*?

Either *see Luke 6:42.*

Pieces of silver, Piece *drachme* (1406), a *drachma,* firstly, "an Attic weight," as much as one can hold in the hand (connected with *drassomai,* "to grasp with the hand, lay hold of," 1 Cor. 3:19), then, "a coin," nearly equal to the Roman *denarius,* is translated "pieces of silver" in **Luke 15:8**, 1st part; "piece," 2nd part and v. 9.

Light *see* **Lighted** at *Luke 8:16.*

Candle *see Luke 8:16.*

Sweep *see* **Swept** at *Luke 11:25.*

Diligently *epimelos* (1960), from *epi* intensive, and an adverbial form of the impersonal verb *melei,* "it is a care," signifies "carefully, diligently," **Luke 15:8**.

15:9 And when she hath found *it*, she calleth *her* friends and *her* neighbours together, saying, Rejoice with me; for I have found the piece which I had lost.

Calleth *see* **Called** at *Luke 9:1.*

Friends *see Luke 7:6.*

Neighbours *see Luke 14:12.*

Rejoice *see* **Rejoiced** at *Luke 1:58.*

Piece *see* Pieces of silver, Piece at *Luke 15:8.*

15:10 Likewise, I say unto you, there is joy in the presence of the angels of God over one sinner that repenteth.

Likewise *see Luke 14:33.*

Presence *see Luke 1:19.*

15:11-12 And he said, A certain man had two sons:

And the younger of them said to *his* father, Father, give me the portion of goods that falleth *to me*. And he divided unto them *his* living.

Younger *neoteros* (3501), occurs in **Luke 15:12, 13; 22:26**; 1 Tim. 5:1 ("younger men"); 5:2, feminine; v. 11, "younger (widows)"; v. 14, "younger (*widows*)," RV, marg. and KJV, "younger (women)"; 1 Pet. 5:5. For Titus 2:6.

Portion *see Luke 12:46.*

Goods *ouisia* (3776), derived from a present participial form of *eimi,* "to be," denotes "substance, property," **Luke 15:12, 13**, RV, "substance," KJV, "goods" and "substance."

Falleth *epiballo* (1911), "to cast upon" (*epi,* "on," *ballo,* "to throw"), also signifies to "fall" to one's share, **Luke 15:12**, "that falleth." The phrase is frequently found in the papyri documents as a technical formula.

Divided *diaireo* (1244), lit., "to take asunder", "to divide into parts, to distribute," is found in **Luke 15:12** and 1 Cor. 12:11.

Living *see* **Life** at *Luke 8:14.*

15:13 And not many days after the younger son gathered all together, and took his journey into a far country, and there wasted his substance with riotous living.

Younger *see Luke 15:12.*

Gathered *sunago* (4863), "to gather or bring together," is said of (a) persons, e.g., Matt. 2:4; (b) things, e.g., Matt. 13:30; in **Luke 15:13** the idea is that of "gathering" his goods together for sale, i.e., "having sold off all." *See also* **Bestow** at *Luke 12:17.*

Journey *apodemeo* (589), denotes "to go on a journey to another country, go abroad," Matt. 21:33; 25:14, 15; Mark 12:1; **Luke 15:13**; **20:9**. The verb *apodemeo* is rendered, in the KJV, "to go into a far country," RV, "to go into another country," Matt. 21:33; 25:14; Mark 12:1; in Matt. 25:15, RV, "he went on his journey" (KJV, "took, etc."). In **Luke 15:13** the KJV and RV have "took (his) journey into a far country"; in **Luke 20:9**, RV, "another country," for KJV, "a far country." *See also* **Country** at *Luke 2:8.*

Far *makros* (3117), is used (a) of space and time, long, said of prayers (in some mss., Matt. 23:14), Mark 12:40; **Luke 20:47**; (b) of distance, "far, far" distant, **Luke 15:13; 19:12**.

Wasted *diaskorpizo* (1287), "to scatter abroad," is used metaphorically of "squandering property," **Luke 15:13; 16:1**. *See also* **Scattered** at *Luke 1:51.*

Substance *see* **Goods** at *Luke 15:12.*

Riotous *asotos* (811), "wastefully," is translated "with riotous living" in **Luke 15:13**; though the word does not necessarily signify "dissolutely," the parable narrative makes clear that this is the meaning here. In the Sept., Prov. 7:11.

Living *zao* (2198), "to live, be alive," is used in the NT of "(a) God, Matt. 16:16; John 6:57; Rom. 14:11; (b) the Son in Incarnation, John 6:57; (c) the Son in Resurrection, John 14:19; Acts 1:3; Rom. 6:10; 2 Cor. 13:4; Heb. 7:8; (d) spiritual life, John 6:57; Rom. 1:17; 8:13b; Gal. 2:19, 20; Heb. 12:9; (e) the present state of departed saints, **Luke 20:38**; 1 Pet. 4:6; (f) the hope of resurrection, 1 Pet. 1:3; (g) the resurrection of believers, 1 Thess. 5:10; John 5:25; Rev. 20:4, and of unbelievers, v. 5, cf. v. 13; (h) the way of access to God through the Lord Jesus Christ, Heb. 10:20; (i) the manifestation of divine power in support of divine authority, 2 Cor. 13:4b; cf. 12:10, and 1 Cor. 5:5; (j) bread, figurative of the Lord Jesus, John 6:51; (k) a stone, figurative of the Lord Jesus, 1 Pet. 2:4; (l) water, figurative of the Holy Spirit, John 4:10; 7:38; (m) a sacrifice, figurative of the believer, Rom. 12:1; (n) stones, figurative of the believer, 1 Pet. 2:5; (o) the oracles, *logion*, Acts 7:38, and word, *logos*, Heb. 4:12; 1 Pet. 1:23, of God; (p) the physical life of men, 1 Thess. 4:15; Matt. 27:63; Acts 25:24; Rom. 14:9; Phil. 1:21 (in the infinitive mood used as a noun with the article, 'living'), 22; 1 Pet. 4:5; (q) the maintenance of physical life, Matt. 4:4; 1 Cor. 9:14; (r) the duration of physical life, Heb. 2:15; (s) the enjoyment of physical life, 1 Thess. 3:8; (t) the recovery of physical life from the power of disease, Mark 5:23; John 4:50; (u) the recovery of physical life from the power of death, Matt. 9:18; Acts 9:41; Rev. 20:5; (v) the course, conduct, and character of men, (1) good, Acts 26:5; 2 Tim. 3:12; Titus 2:12; (2) evil, **Luke 15:13**; Rom. 6:2; 8:13a; 2 Cor. 5:15b; Col. 3:7; (3) undefined, Rom. 7:9; 14:7; Gal. 2:14; (w) restoration after alienation, **Luke 15:32**."

15:14 And when he had spent all, there arose a mighty famine in that land; and he began to be in want.

Spent *dapanao* (1159), denotes (a) "to expend, spend," Mark 5:26; 2 Cor. 12:15; (b) "to consume, squander," **Luke 15:14**; Jas. 4:3.

Arose *see* ***Luke 6:48.***

Mighty *ischuros* (2478), "strong, mighty," is usually translated "strong"; "mighty" in **Luke 15:14** (of a famine); Rev. 19:6 (of thunders); 19:18 (of men): in the following, where the KJV has "mighty," the RV substitutes "strong," 1 Cor. 1:27; Rev. 6:15 (KJV, "mighty men"); 18:10, 21; Heb. 11:34, RV, "(waxed) mighty" (KJV, "valiant").

Famine *see* ***Luke 4:25.***

Land *see* **Region** at ***Luke 3:1.***

Want *hustereo* (5302), signifies "to be in want," **Luke 15:14**; 2 Cor. 11:9 (1st occurrence); Phil. 4:12, RV (KJV "to suffer need"); in John 2:3, KJV, "wanted" (RV, "failed").

15:15 And he went and joined himself to a citizen of that country; and he sent him into his fields to feed swine.

Joined *see* **Cleaveth** at ***Luke 10:11.***

Citizen *polites* (4177), "a member of a city or state, or the inhabitant of a country or district," **Luke 15:15**, is used elsewhere in **Luke 19:14**; Acts 21:39, and, in the most authentic mss., in Heb. 8:11 (where some texts have *plesion*, "a neighbor"). Apart from Heb. 8:11, the word occurs only in the writings of Luke (himself a Greek).

Country *see* ***Luke 2:8.***

Fields *agros* (68), "a cultivated field," or "fields in the aggregate," e.g., Matt. 6:28; Mark 11:8 (some mss. here have *dendron*, "trees"); **Luke 15:15**.

Feed *see* **Feeding** at ***Luke 8:32.***

Swine *see* ***Luke 8:32.***

15:16 And he would fain have filled his belly with the husks that the swine did eat: and no man gave unto him.

Fain *epithumeo* (1937), has the same twofold meaning as the noun, namely (a) "to desire," used of the Holy Spirit against the flesh, Gal. 5:17; of the Lord Jesus, **Luke 22:15**, "I have desired;" of the holy angels, 1 Pet. 1:12; of good men, for good things, Matt. 13:17; 1 Tim. 3:1; Heb. 6:11; of men, for things without moral quality, **Luke 15:16**; **16:21**; **17:22**; Rev. 9:6; (b) of "evil desires," in respect of which it is translated "to lust" in Matt. 5:28; 1 Cor. 10:6; Gal. 5:17; Jas. 4:2; to covet, Acts 20:23; Rom. 7:7; 13:9. It is translated "would fain" in **Luke 15:16**, of the Prodigal Son.

Filled *see* ***Luke 14:23.***

Husks *keration* (2769), "a little horn" (a diminutive of *keras*, "a horn"), is used in the plural in **Luke 15:16**, of carob pods, given to swine, and translated "husks."

Swine *see* ***Luke 8:32.***

15:17 And when he came to himself, he said, How many hired servants of my father's have bread enough and to spare, and I perish with hunger!

Many *posos* (4214), "how much, how great, how many," has the last meaning in Matt. 15:34; 16:9, 10; 27:13 ("how many things"); Mark 6:38; 8:5, 19, 20; 15:4 ("how many things); **Luke 15:17**; Acts 21:20.

Hired servants *misthios* (3407), an adjective signifying "a hired servant," is used in **Luke 15:17**, **19** (in some texts, v. **21**).

Enough and to spare In **Luke 15:17** the verb *perisseuo*, "to have abundance," is translated "have enough and to spare." In Acts 27:38 the verb *korennumi*, "to satisfy," is translated "had eaten enough." *See also* **Remained** at ***Luke 9:17.***

Hunger *limos* (3042), has the meanings "famine" and "hunger"; "hunger" in **Luke 15:17**; 2 Cor. 11:27; in Rev. 6:8, RV, "famine" (KJV, "hunger"). *See also* **Famine** at ***Luke 4:25.***

15:18 I will arise and go to my father, and will say unto him, Father, I have sinned against heaven, and before thee,

"Reconciliation sounds a large theological term, but it simply means coming to ourselves and arising and going to our Father."
JOHN WOOD OMAN

Sinned *hamartano* (264), lit., "to miss the mark," is used in the NT (a) of "sinning" against God, (1) by angels, 2 Pet. 2:4; (2) by man, Matt. 27:4; **Luke 15:18, 21** (heaven standing, by metonymy, for God); John 5:14; 8:11; 9:2, 3; Rom. 2:12 (twice); 3:23; 5:12, 14, 16; 6:15; 1 Cor. 7:28 (twice), 36; 15:34; Eph. 4:26; 1 Tim. 5:20; Titus 3:11; Heb. 3:17; 10:26; 1 John 1:10; in 2:1 (twice), the aorist tense in each place, referring to an act of "sin"; on the contrary, in 3:6 (twice), 8, 9, the present tense indicates, not the committal of an act, but the continuous practice of "sin"; in 5:16 (twice) the present tense indicates the condition resulting from an act, "unto death" signifying "tending towards death"; (b) against Christ, 1 Cor. 8:12; (c) against man, (1) a brother, Matt. 18:15, RV, "sin" (KJV, "trespass"); v. 21; **Luke 17:3, 4**, RV, "sin" (KJV, "trespass"); 1 Cor. 8:12; (2) in **Luke 15:18, 21**, against the father by the Prodigal Son, "in thy sight" being suggestive of befitting reverence; (d) against Jewish law, the Temple, and Caesar, Acts 25:8, RV, "sinned" (KJV, "offended"); (e) against one's own body, by fornication, 1 Cor. 6:18; (f) against earthly masters by servants, 1 Pet. 2:20, RV, "(when) ye sin (and are buffeted for it)," KJV, "(when ye be buffeted) for your faults," lit., "having sinned."

Heaven *ouranos* (3772), probably akin to *ornumi*, "to lift, to heave," is used in the NT (a) of "the aerial heavens," e.g., Matt. 6:26; 8:20; Acts 10:12; 11:6 (RV, "heaven," in each place, KJV, "air"); Jas. 5:18; (b) "the sidereal," e.g., Matt. 24:29, 35; Mark 13:25, 31; Heb. 11:12, RV, "heaven," KJV, "sky"; Rev. 6:14; 20:11; they, (a) and (b), were created by the Son of God, Heb. 1:10, as also by God the Father, Rev. 10:6; (c) "the eternal dwelling place of God," Matt. 5:16; 12:50; Rev. 3:12; 11:13; 16:11; 20:9. From thence the Son of God descended to become incarnate, John 3:13, 31; 6:38, 42. In His ascension Christ "passed through the heavens," Heb. 4:14, RV; He "ascended far above all the heavens," Eph. 4:10, and was "made higher than the heavens," Heb. 7:26; He "sat down on the right hand of the throne of the Majesty in the heavens," Heb. 8:1; He is "on the right hand of God," having gone into heaven, 1 Pet. 3:22. Since His ascension it is the scene of His present life and activity, e.g., Rom. 8:34; Heb. 9:24. From thence the Holy Spirit descended at Pentecost, 1 Pet. 1:12. It is the abode of the angels, e.g., Matt. 18:10; 22:30; cf. Rev. 3:5 ... In the present life "heaven" is the region of the spiritual citizenship of believers, Phil. 3:20. The present "heavens," with the earth, are to pass away, 2 Pet. 3:10, "being on fire," v. 12 (see v. 7); Rev. 20:11, and new "heavens" and earth are to be created, 2 Pet. 3:13; Rev. 21:1, with Isa. 65:17, e.g. In **Luke 15:18, 21**, "heaven" is used, by metonymy, for God.

Before *see Luke 12:6.*

15:19 And am no more worthy to be called thy son: make me as one of thy hired servants.

More *ouketi* (3765), is translated "no more," e.g., in Matt. 19:6; **Luke 15:19, 21**; Acts 20:25, 38; Eph. 2:19.

Worthy *see Luke 7:4.*

Hired servants *see Luke 15:17.*

15:20 And he arose, and came to his father. But when he was yet a great way off, his father saw him, and had compassion, and ran, and fell on his neck, and kissed him.

Way For the KJV rendering of *makran* "a good (or great) way off," Matt. 8:30; **Luke 15:20**. *See also* **Have received** at *Luke 6:24;* **Far** at *Luke 7:6.*

Neck *trachelos* (5137), is used (a) literally, Matt. 18:6; Mark 9:42; **Luke 17:2**; of "embracing," **Luke 15:20**; Acts 20:37; (b) metaphorically, in Acts 15:10, of "putting a yoke upon": Rom. 16:4, singular in the original, "(laid down their) neck," indicating the figurative use of the term rather than the literal. Prisca and Aquila in some way had risked their lives for the apostle (the phrase is found with this significance in the papyri).

Kissed *see Luke 7:38.*

15:21 And the son said unto him, Father, I have sinned against heaven, and in thy sight, and am no more worthy to be called thy son.

Sinned *see Luke 15:18.*

Heaven *see Luke 15:18.*

More *see Luke 15:19.*

Worthy *see Luke 7:4.*

15:22 But the father said to his servants, Bring forth the best robe, and put *it* on him; and put a ring on his hand, and shoes on *his* feet:

Bring forth *ekphero* (1627), is used, literally, "of carrying something forth, or out," e.g., a garment, **Luke 15:22**; sick folk, Acts 5:15; a corpse, Acts 5:6; 9-10; of the impossibility of "carrying" anything out from this world at death, 1 Tim. 6:7. The most authentic mss. have this word in Mark 8:23, of the blind man, whom the Lord brought out of the village (RV). It is also used of the earth, in "bringing forth" produce, Heb. 6:8.

Best *protos* (4413), is one of two words translated "best" in the KJV, but the only one so rendered in the RV. In **Luke 15:22** "the best (robe)" is, lit., "the first (robe)," i.e., chief, principal, first in rank or quality.

Robe *stole* (4749), (Eng., "stole"), denotes any "stately robe," a long garment reaching to the feet or with a train behind. It is used of the long clothing in which the scribes walked, making themselves conspicuous in the eyes of men, Mark 12:38; **Luke 20:46**; of the robe worn by the young man in the Lord's tomb, Mark 16:5; of the best or, rather, the chief robe, which was brought out for the returned prodigal, **Luke 15:22**; five times in Revelation, as to glorified saints, 6:11; 7:9, 13-14; 22:14. In the Sept. it is used of the holy garments of the priests, e.g., Exod. 28:2; 29:21; 31:10.

Put . . . on *see* ***Luke 12:22***.

Put *didomi* (1325), "to give," is rendered "to put" in **Luke 15:22**, of the ring on the returned Prodigal's finger; 2 Cor. 8:16 and Rev. 17:17, of "putting" into the heart by God; Heb. 8:10, of laws into the mind (KJV, marg., "give"); 10:16, of laws on (RV; KJV, "into") the heart. *See also* Give at ***Luke 12:58***.

Ring *daktulios* **(1146), "a finger ring," occurs in** Luke 15:22. **15:23 And bring hither the fatted calf, and kill *it*; and let us eat, and be merry:**

Fatted *siteutos* (4618), "fed" (with grain), denotes "fatted," **Luke 15:23, 27, 30**.

Calf *moschos* (3448), primarily denotes "anything young," whether plants or the offspring of men or animals, the idea being that which is tender and delicate; hence "a calf, young bull, heifer," **Luke 15:23, 27, 30**; Heb. 9:12, 19; Rev. 4:7.

Kill *thuo* (2380), primarily denotes "to offer firstfruits to a god"; then (a) "to sacrifice by slaying a victim," Acts 14:13, 18, to do sacrifice; 1 Cor. 10:20, to sacrifice; 1 Cor. 5:7, "hath been sacrificed," of the death of Christ as our Passover; (b) "to slay, kill," Matt. 22:4; Mark 14:12; **Luke 15:23, 27, 30; 22:7**; John 10:10; Acts 10:13; 11:7.

Merry *see* ***Luke 12:19***.

15:24 For this my son was dead, and is alive again; he was lost, and is found. And they began to be merry.

Dead *nekros* (3498), is used of (a) the death of the body, cf. Jas. 2:26, its most frequent sense: (b) the actual spiritual condition of unsaved men, Matt. 8:22; John 5:25; Eph. 2:1, 5; 5:14; Phil. 3:11; Col. 2:13; cf. **Luke 15:24**: (c) the ideal spiritual condition of believers in regard to sin, Rom. 6:11: (d) a church in declension, inasmuch as in that state it is inactive and barren, Rev. 3:1: (e) sin, which apart from law cannot produce a sense of guilt, Rom. 7:8: (f) the body of the believer in contrast to his spirit, Rom. 8:10: (g) the works of the Law, inasmuch as, however good in themselves, Rom. 7:13, they cannot produce life, Heb. 6:1; 9:14: (h) the faith that does not produce works, Jas. 2:17, 26; cf. v. 20.

Alive *anazao* (326), "to live again" (*ana*, "and" *zao*, "to live"), "to regain life," is used of moral "revival," **Luke 15:24**, "is alive again"; (b) of sin, Rom. 7:9, "revived," lit., "lived again" i.e., it sprang into activity, manifesting the evil inherent in it; here sin is personified, by way of contrast to the man himself. Some mss. have it in Rom. 14:9, for *zao*, as in the RV, which italicizes "*again*."

Lost *see* Perish at ***Luke 5:37***.

Merry *see* ***Luke 12:19***.

15:25 Now his elder son was in the field: and as he came and drew nigh to the house, he heard musick and dancing.

Elder *see* Elders at ***Luke 7:3***.

Drew nigh *see* Come nigh at ***Luke 10:9***.

Musick *sumphonua* (4858), lit., "a sounding together" (Eng., "symphony"), occurs in **Luke 15:25**. In the Sept., Dan. 3:5, 7, 10, 15, for Aramaic *sumponya* (not in v. 7), itself a loan word from the Greek; translated "dulcimer" (RV, marg., "bagpipe").

Dancing *choros* (5525), (Eng., "chorus"), primarily denoted "an enclosure for dancing"; hence, "a company of dancers and singers." The supposition that the word is connected with *orcheo* by metathesis (i.e., change of place, of the letters *ch* and *o*) seems to be without foundation. The word is used in **Luke 15:25**.

15:26 And he called one of the servants, and asked what these things meant.

Servants *see* Servant at *Luke 1:54*.

Asked *punthanomai* (4441), "to inquire," is translated "inquired" in Matt. 2:4, and Acts 21:33, RV (KJV, "demanded"); in **Luke 15:26; 18:36** and Acts 4:7 (KJV, "asked"); "inquired" (KJV, "inquired") in John 4:52; "inquire" (KJV, "inquire") in Acts 23:20; in Acts 23:34 it denotes "to learn by inquiry," KJV, and RV, "when (he) understood"; elsewhere it is rendered by the verb "to ask," Acts 10:18, 29; 23:19.

Meant *eimi* (1510), "to be," in certain of its forms, has an explicative force, signifying "to denote, to import," e.g., Matt. 9:13; 12:7, "(what this) meaneth," lit. "(what this) is"; **Luke 18:36**, "meant" (lit., "might be"); Acts 10:17, "might mean," RV (lit., "might be"); in **Luke 15:26** the RV keeps to the verb "to be," "(what these things) might be" (KJV, "meant"). In Acts 2:12 the verb "to be" is preceded by *thelo*, "to will," and the phrase is translated "(what) meaneth (this)," lit., "(what) does (this) will to be?" in 17:20, lit., "(what do these things) will to be."

15:27 And he said unto him, Thy brother is come; and thy father hath killed the fatted calf, because he hath received him safe and sound.

Killed *see* Kill at *Luke 15:23*.

Fatted *see Luke 15:23*.

Calf *see Luke 15:23*.

Received *see* Receive at *Luke 6:34*.

Safe *hugiaino* (5198), "to be sound, healthy" (Eng., "hygiene," etc.), is translated "safe and sound" in **Luke 15:27**, lit., "being healthy."

Sound *hugiaino* (5198), "to be healthy, sound in health" (Eng., "hygiene," etc.), translated "safe and sound" in **Luke 15:27**, is used metaphorically of doctrine, 1 Tim. 1:10; 2 Tim. 4:3; Titus 1:9; 2:1; of words, 1 Tim. 6:3, RV (KJV, "wholesome," RV marg., "healthful"); 2 Tim. 1:13; "in the faith," Titus 1:13 (RV marg., "healthy"); "in faith," Titus 2:2 (RV marg., ditto).

15:28 And he was angry, and would not go in: therefore came his father out, and intreated him.

Angry *see Luke 14:21*.

Intreated *see* Besought at *Luke 8:31*.

15:29 And he answering said to *his* father, Lo, these many years do I serve thee, neither transgressed I at any time thy commandment: and yet thou never gavest me a kid, that I might make merry with my friends:

Many *tosoutos* (5118), "so great, so much, so many," (a) qualifying a noun, is rendered "these many (years)" in **Luke 15:29**; "so many," John 12:37; 1 Cor. 14:10; (b) without a noun, John 6:9; 21:11; Gal. 3:4, "so many things."

Serve *douleuo* (1398), "to serve as a *doulos*," is used (a) of serving God (and the impossibility of serving mammon also), Matt. 6:24 and **Luke 16:13**; Rom. 7:6; in the gospel, Phil. 2:22; (b) Christ, Acts 20:19; Rom. 12:11; 14:18; 16:18; Eph. 6:7; Col. 3:24; (c) the law of God, Rom. 7:25; (d) one another, Gal. 5:13, RV, "be servants to" (KJV, "serve"); (e) a father, **Luke 15:29** (with a suggestion of acting as a slave); (f) earthly masters, Matt. 6:24; **Luke 16:13**; 1 Tim. 6:2, RV, "serve"; (g) the younger by the elder, Rom. 9:12; (h) of being in bondage to a nation, Acts 7:7; Gal. 4:25, to the Romans, actually, though also spiritually to Judaizers; (i) to idols, Gal. 4:8, RV, "were in bondage" (KJV, "did service"); (j) to "the weak and beggarly rudiments," v. 9 (RV), "to be in bondage" (aorist tense in the best texts, suggesting "to enter into bondage"), i.e., to the religion of the Gentiles ("rudiments" being used in v. 3 of the religion of the Jews); (k) sin, Rom. 6:6, RV, "be in bondage" (KJV, "serve"); (l) "divers lusts and pleasures," Titus 3:3; (m) negatively, to any man – a proud and thoughtless denial by the Jews, John 8:33.

Transgressed *parerchomai* (3928), "to come by" (*para*, "by," *erchomai*, "to come"), "pass over," and hence, metaphorically, "to transgress," is so used in **Luke 15:29**. *See also* **Pass** at *Luke 11:42*.

Time *oudepote* (3763), from *oude*, "not even," and *pote*, "at any time," is used in definite negative statements, e.g., Matt. 7:23; 1 Cor. 13:8; Heb. 10:1, 11, or questions, e.g., Matt. 21:16, 42; in **Luke 15:29** (1st part), RV, "never" (KJV, "neither ... at any time"); KJV and RV, "never" (2nd part).

Kid *eriphos* (2056), denotes "a kid or goat," Matt. 25:32 (RV, marg., "kids"); **Luke 15:29**, "a kid"; some mss. have *eriphion* here, indicating a sneer on the part of the elder son, that his father had never given him even a tiny kid.

Merry *see Luke 12:19*.

Friends *see Luke 7:6*.

15:30 But as soon as this thy son was come, which hath devoured thy living with harlots, thou hast killed for him the fatted calf.

Devoured *see* ***Luke 8:5.***

Living *see* **Life** at ***Luke 8:14.***

Harlots *porne* (4204), "a prostitute, harlot" (from *pernemi*, "to sell"), is used (a) literally, in Matt. 21:31, 32, of those who were the objects of the mercy shown by Christ; in **Luke 15:30**, of the life of the Prodigal; in 1 Cor. 6:15, 16, in a warning to the Corinthian church against the prevailing licentiousness which had made Corinth a byword; in Heb. 11:31 and Jas. 2:25, of Rahab; (b) metaphorically, of mystic Babylon, Rev. 17:1, 5 (KJV, "harlots"), 15, 16; 19:2, RV, for KJV, "whore."

Killed *see* **Kill** at ***Luke 15:23.***

Fatted *see* ***Luke 15:23.***

Calf *see* ***Luke 15:23.***

15:31 And he said unto him, Son, thou art ever with me, and all that I have is thine.

Ever *pantote* (3842), "at all times, always" (akin to *pas*, "all"), is translated "ever" in **Luke 15:31**; John 18:20; 1 Thess. 4:17; 5:15; 2 Tim. 3:7; Heb. 7:25; "evermore" in John 6:34; in 1 Thess. 5:16, RV, "alway," for KJV, "evermore." It there means "on all occasions," as, e.g., in 1 Thess. 1:2; 3:6; 5:15; 2 Thess. 1:3, 11; 2:13.

All that I have *emos* (1699), a possessive adjective of the first person, often used as a possessive pronoun with greater emphasis than the oblique forms of *ego*, a measure of stress which should always be observed; it denotes (I) subjectively, (a) "what I possess," e.g., John 4:34; 7:16 (1st part); 13:35; 1 Cor. 16:21; Gal. 6:11; Col. 4:18 (1st clause); as a pronoun, absolutely (i.e., not as an adjective), e.g., Matt. 20:15; 25:27; **Luke 15:31**, RV, "(all that is) mine," KJV, "(all that) I have"; John 16:14, 15; 17:10; (b) "proceeding from me," e.g. Mark 8:38; John 7:16 (2nd part); 8:37 (here the repetition of the article with the pronoun, after the article with the noun, lends special stress to the pronoun; more lit., "the word, that which is mine"); so in John 15:12. Such instances are to be distinguished from the less emphatic order where the pronoun comes between the article and the noun, as in John 7:16, already mentioned; (c) in the phrase "it is mine" (i.e., "it rests with me"), e.g., Matt. 20:23; Mark 10:40; (II) objectively, "pertaining or relating to me": (a) "appointed for me," e.g., John 7:6, "My time" (with the repeated article and special stress just referred to); (b) equivalent to an objective genitive ("of me") e.g., **Luke 22:19**, "(in remembrance) of Me" (lit., "in My remembrance"); so 1 Cor. 11:24.

15:32 It was meet that we should make merry, and be glad: for this thy brother was dead, and is alive again; and was lost, and is found.

Meet *dei* (1163), an impersonal verb, "it is necessary, one must," is translated "It was meet," in **Luke 15:32**, in Rom. 1:27, KJV, "was meet" (RV, "was due"). *See also* **Must** at ***Luke 2:49.***

Merry *see* ***Luke 12:19.***

Glad *chairo* (5463), is the usual word for "rejoicing, being glad"; it is rendered by the verb "to be glad" in Mark 14:11; **Luke 15:32; 22:5; 23:8**; John 8:56; 11:15; 20:20; Acts 11:23; 13:48; in the following the RV has "to rejoice" for KJV, "to be glad," Rom. 16:19; 1 Cor. 16:17; 2 Cor. 13:9; 1 Pet. 4:13; Rev. 19:7.

Alive *see* **Living** at ***Luke 15:13.***

Chapter 16

16:1 And he said also unto his disciples, There was a certain rich man, which had a steward; and the same was accused unto him that he had wasted his goods.

Rich *see* ***Luke 6:24.***

Steward *see* ***Luke 12:42.***

Accused *diaballo* (1225), used in **Luke 16:1**, in the passive voice, lit. signifies "to hurl across" (*dia*, "through," *ballo*, "to throw"), and suggests a verbal assault. It stresses the act rather than the author, as in the case of *aitia* and *kategoria. Diabolos* is connected.

Wasted *see* ***Luke 15:13.*** *See also* **Scattered** at ***Luke 1:51.***

Goods *see* ***Luke 11:21.***

16:2 And he called him, and said unto him, How is it that I hear this of thee? give an account of thy stewardship; for thou mayest be no longer steward.

Give *apodidomi* (591), to give up or back," is translated "to render," (a) of righteous acts, (1) human, Matt. 21:41; 22:21; Mark 12:17; **Luke 16:2**, RV (KJV, "give"); **Luke 20:25**; Rom. 13:7, 1 Cor. 7:3; (2) divine, Matt. 16:27, RV, "shall render" (KJV, "shall reward"), an important RV change; Rom. 2:6; 2 Tim. 4:14, RV (KJV, "reward"); Rev. 18:6 (ditto); 22:12, RV (KJV, "give"); (b) of unrighteous acts. Rom. 12:17, RV (KJV, "recompense"); 1 Thess. 5:15; 1 Pet. 3:9.

Stewardship *oikonomia* (3622), is rendered "stewardship" in **Luke 16:2, 3, 4**, and in the RV in 1 Cor. 9:17.

Mayest *dunamai* (1410), "to be able, have power," whether by personal ability, permission, or opportunity, is sometimes rendered "may" or "might," e.g., Matt. 26:9; Mark 14:5; Acts 17:19; 1 Thess. 2:6. In the following the RV substitutes "can," "canst," "couldst," for the KJV, e.g., Matt. 26:42; Mark 4:32; 14:7; **Luke 16:2**; Acts 24:11; 25:11; 27:12; 1 Cor. 7:21; 14:31 (here the alteration is especially important, as not permission for all to prophesy, but ability to do so, is the meaning); Eph. 3:4. In the following the RV substitutes the verb "to be able," Acts 19:40; 24:8; Rev. 13:17.

Longer *eti* (2089), "yet, as yet, still," is translated "longer" in **Luke 16:2** (with separate negative); "any longer" in Rom. 6:2.

Steward *oikonomeo* (3621), signifies "to be a house steward," **Luke 16:2**. In the Sept., Ps. 112:5.

16:3 Then the steward said within himself, What shall I do? for my lord taketh away from me the stewardship: I cannot dig; to beg I am ashamed.

Steward *see Luke 12:42.*

Taketh *see* **Take** at *Luke 1:25.*

Cannot *ischuo* (2480), "to have strength," is so rendered in Mark 5:4, RV (KJV, "could"); in **Luke 16:3**, RV, "I have not strength to" (KJV, "I cannot").

Dig *see* **Digged** at *Luke 6:48.*

Beg *epaiteo* (1871), a strengthened form of *aiteo*, is used in **Luke 16:3**.

Ashamed *aischuno* (153), from *aischos*, "shame," always used in the passive voice, signifies (a) "to have a feeling of fear or shame which prevents a person from doing a thing," e.g., **Luke 16:3**; (b) "the feeling of shame arising from something that has been done," e.g., 2 Cor. 10:8; Phil. 1:20; 1 John 2:28, of the possibility of being "ashamed" before the Lord Jesus at His judgment seat in His Parousia with His saints; in 1 Pet. 4:16, of being ashamed of suffering as a Christian.

16:4 I am resolved what to do, that, when I am put out of the stewardship, they may receive me into their houses.

Resolved *ginosko* (1097), "to come to know, perceive, realize," is used in the 2nd aorist tense in **Luke 16:4**. "I am resolved," expressing the definiteness of the steward's realization, and his consequent determination of his course of action.

Put *methistemi* or *methistano* (3179), "to change, remove" (*meta*, implying "change," *histemi*, "to cause to stand"), is used of "putting" a man out of his stewardship, **Luke 16:4** (passive voice).

Stewardship *see Luke 16:2.*

Receive *see* **Took** at *Luke 2:28.*

16:5 So he called every one of his lord's debtors *unto him*, and said unto the first, How much owest thou unto my lord?

Every *see Luke 4:40.*

Debtors *see Luke 7:41.*

Owest *see* **Owed** at *Luke 7:41.*

16:6 And he said, An hundred measures of oil. And he said unto him, Take thy bill, and sit down quickly, and write fifty.

Measures *batos* (943), denotes a *bath*, a Jewish liquid measure (the equivalent of an *ephah*), containing between 8 and 9 gallons, **Luke 16:6**.

Oil *see Luke 7:46.*

Take *dechomai* (1209), "to receive," is rendered "take (thy bond, RV, KJV, bill)" in **Luke 16:6**, 7; "take (the helmet of salvation)," Eph. 6:17, suggesting a heartiness in the "taking." *See also* **Took** at *Luke 2:28.*

Bill *gramma* (1121), from *grapho*, "to write" (Eng., "graph, graphic," etc.), in **Luke 16:6**, KJV, is translated "bill." It lit. signifies that which is drawn, a picture; hence, a written document; hence, a "bill," or bond, or note of hand, showing the amount of indebtedness. In the passage referred to the word is in the plural, indicating perhaps, but not necessarily, various "bills." The bonds mentioned in rabbinical writings, were formal, signed by witnesses and the Sanhedrin of three, or informal, when only the debtor signed. The latter were usually written on wax, and easily altered.

Sit *see* **Sitteth** at *Luke 14:28.*

Quickly *see Luke 14:21.*

Fifty *see Luke 7:41.*

16:7 Then said he to another, And how much owest thou? And he said, An hundred measures of wheat. And he said unto him, Take thy bill, and write fourscore.

Then *epeita* (1899), "thereupon, thereafter," then (in some texts, Mark 7:5; *kai*, "and," in the best); **Luke 16:7**; John 11:7; 1 Cor. 12:28, RV, "then" (KJV, "after that"); 15:6 and 7 (ditto); v. 23, RV, KJV, "afterward"; v. 46 (ditto); Gal. 1:18; v. 21, RV (KJV, "afterwards"), 2:1; 1 Thess. 4:17; Heb. 7:2, RV (KJV, "after that"); v. 27; Jas. 3:17; 4:14.

Owest *see* **Owed** at *Luke 7:41.*

Measures *koros* (2884), denotes a *cor*, the largest Hebrew dry measure (ten *ephahs*), containing about 11 bushels, **Luke 16:7**; the hundred "measures" amounted to a very considerable quantity.

Wheat *see Luke 3:17.*

Take *see Luke 16:6. See also* Took at *Luke 2:28.*

Bill *see Luke 16:6.*

Fourscore *see Luke 2:37.*

16:8 And the lord commended the unjust steward, because he had done wisely: for the children of this world are in their generation wiser than the children of light.

Commended *epaineo* (1867), "to praise," is an intensive form of *aineo*, **Luke 16:8.** It is elsewhere translated by the verb "to praise," in the RV, Rom. 15:11; 1 Cor. 11:2, 17, 22.

Unjust For *adikeo*, "to be unrighteous," or "do unrighteousness," Rev. 22:11, RV, and *adikia*, "unrighteous," **Luke 16:8** and **18:6**, RV. *See also* **Iniquity** at *Luke 13:27.*

Steward *see Luke 12:42.*

Wisely *phronimos* (5430), "wisely," occurs in **Luke 16:8.**

Children *see Luke 6:35.*

World *aion* (165), "an age, a period of time," marked in the NT usage by spiritual or moral characteristics, is sometimes translated "world"; the RV marg. always has "age." The following are details concerning the world in this respect; its cares, Matt. 13:22; its sons, **Luke 16:8**; **20:34**; its rulers, 1 Cor. 2:6, 8; its wisdom, 1 Cor. 1:20; 2:6; 3:18; its fashion, Rom. 12:2; its character, Gal. 1:4; its god, 2 Cor. 4:4. The phrase "the end of the world" should be rendered "the end of the age," in most places; in 1 Cor. 10:11, KJV, "the ends (*tele*) of the world," RV, "the ends of the ages," probably signifies the fulfillment of the divine purposes concerning the ages in regard to the church the word indicates all that the successive periods contain; cf. 1:2.

Generation *see* Generations at *Luke 1:48.*

Wiser *see* Wise at *Luke 12:42.*

Light *phos* (5457), akin to *phao*, "to give light" (from roots *pha-* and *phan-*, expressing "light as seen by the eye," and, metaphorically, as "reaching the mind," whence *phaino*, "to make to appear," *phaneros*, "evident," etc.); cf. Eng., "phosphorus" (lit., "light-bearing"). "Primarily light is a luminous emanation, probably of force, from certain bodies, which enables the eye to discern form and color. Light requires an organ adapted for its reception (Matt. 6:22). Where the eye is absent, or where it has become impaired from any cause, light is useless. Man, naturally, is incapable of receiving spiritual light inasmuch as he lacks the capacity for spiritual things, 1 Cor. 2:14. Hence believers are called 'sons of light,' **Luke 16:8**, not merely because they have received a revelation from God, but because in the New Birth they have received the spiritual capacity for it.

16:9 And I say unto you, Make to yourselves friends of the mammon of unrighteousness; that, when ye fail, they may receive you into everlasting habitations.

Yourselves *see Luke 3:8.*

Friends *see Luke 7:6.*

Mammon *mamonas* (3126), a common Aramaic word for "riches," akin to a Hebrew word signifying "to be firm, steadfast" (whence "Amen"), hence, "that which is to be trusted"; Gesenius regards it as derived from a Heb. word signifying "treasure" (Gen. 43:23); it is personified in Matt. 6:24; **Luke 16:9**, **11**, **13**.

Fail *ekleipo* (1587), "to leave out" (*ek*, "out," *leipo*, "to leave"), used intransitively, means "to leave off, cease, fail"; it is said of the cessation of earthly life, **Luke 16:9**; of faith, **22:32**; of the light of the sun, **23:45** (in the best mss.); of the years of Christ, Heb. 1:12.

Receive *see* Took at *Luke 2:28.*

Habitations *skene* (4633), akin to *skenoo*, "to dwell in a tent or tabernacle," is rendered "habitations" in **Luke 16:9**, KJV (RV, "tabernacles") of the eternal dwelling places of the redeemed. *See also* **Tabernacles** at *Luke 9:33.*

16:10 He that is faithful in that which is least is faithful also in much: and he that is unjust in the least is unjust also in much.

Least *see Luke 12:26.*

Much *see Luke 7:11.*

Unjust *adikos* (94), not conforming to *dike*, "right," is translated "unrighteous" in **Luke 16:10** (twice), RV, 11; Rom. 3:5; 1 Cor. 6:1, RV; 6:9; Heb. 6:10; 1 Pet. 3:18, RV; 2 Pet. 2:9, RV.

16:11 If therefore ye have not been faithful in the unrighteous mammon, who will commit to your trust the true *riches*?

Mammon *see Luke 16:9.*

Commit to … trust *pisteuo* (4100), signifies "to entrust, commit to," **Luke 16:11**; 1 Tim. 1:11, "committed to (my) trust."

Your "Your" is most frequently the translation of *humon*, lit., "of you," the genitive plural of *su*, "thou, you"; it is translated "yours" in 1 Cor. 3:21, 22; in 8:9, "of yours"; 16:18; 2 Cor. 12:14. In the following the dative plural, *humin*, lit., "to you," is translated "your"; **Luke 16:11**, lit., "(who will entrust) to

"Money is emphasized in Scripture simply because our temptation to love it is inexplicably powerful."

ERWIN W. LUTZER

you"; in **21:15** "your adversaries" is, lit., "(those opposed) to you"; in 1 Cor. 6:5 and 15:34, KJV, "(I speak to) your (shame)," RV, "(I say *this* to move) you (to shame)," is, lit., "(I speak unto a shame) to you." The accusative plural, *humas*, preceded by *kata*, "according to," is rendered in Acts 18:15 "your own (law)," RV, KJV, "your (law)," lit., "(of the law) according to you," with emphasis and scorn; in Eph. 1:15 the same construction is used of faith, but *kata* here means "among," as in the RV, "(the faith ... which is) among you," KJV, "your (faith)"; in John 14:26 "He shall ... bring to your remembrance" is, lit., "He shall ... put you in mind of."

True *alethinos* (228), denotes "true" in the sense of real, ideal, genuine; it is used (a) of God, John 7:28; 17:3; 1 Thess. 1:9; Rev. 6:10; these declare that God fulfills the meaning of His Name; He is "very God," in distinction from all other gods, false gods (*alethes*, see John 3:33, signifies that He is veracious, "true" to His utterances, He cannot lie); (b) of Christ, John 1:9; 6:32; 15:1; 1 John 2:8; 5:20 (thrice); Rev. 3:7, 14; 19:11; His judgment, John 8:16 (in the best texts); (c) God's words, John 4:37; Rev. 19:9, 21:5; 22:6; (d) His ways, Rev. 15:3; (e) His judgments, Rev. 16:7; 19:2; (to His riches, **Luke 16:11**; (g) His worshipers, John 4:23; (h) their hearts, Heb. 10:22; (i) the witness of the apostle John, John 19:35; (j) the spiritual, antitypical tabernacle, Heb. 8:2; 9:24, not that the wilderness tabernacle was false, but that it was a weak and earthly copy of the heavenly.

16:12 And if ye have not been faithful in that which is another man's, who shall give you that which is your own?

Man's In **Luke 16:12**, KJV, *allotrios*, "belonging to another" (*allos*, "another"), here used as a pronoun, is translated "another man's" (RV, "another's"); so, as an adjective, in Rom. 14:4; 15:20; 2 Cor. 10:15, 16 (in this last the RV omits "man").

Your In **Luke 24:22**, "of our company" is, lit., "from among us." *Hemeteros*, a possessive pronoun, more emphatic than *hemeis*, is used in **Luke 16:12**, in the best mss. (some have *humeteros*, "your own"); Acts 2:11; 24:6, in some mss.; 26:5; 2 Tim. 4:15; Titus 3:14, "ours"; 1 John 1:3; 2:2, "ours." *See also* **Yours** at ***Luke 6:20***.

16:13 No servant can serve two masters: for either he will hate the one, and love the other; or else he will hold to the one, and despise the other. Ye cannot serve God and mammon.

Servant *oiketes* (3610), "a house servant" (*oikeo*, "to dwell," *oikos*, "a house"), is translated "servant" in **Luke 16:13** (RV marg., "household servant"); so Rom. 14:4 and 1 Pet. 2:18; in Acts 10:7, KJV and RV, "household servants."

Serve *see* ***Luke 15:29***.

Masters *kurios* (2962), "a lord, one who exercises power," is translated "masters" in Matt. 6:24; 15:27; Mark 13:35; **Luke 16:13**; Acts 16:16, 19; Rom. 14:4, KJV (RV, "lord"); Eph. 6:5, 9 (twice), the 2nd time of Christ; so in Col. 3:22; 4:1.

Either *see* ***Luke 6:42***.

Hate *see* ***Luke 6:22***.

Hold *antecho* (472), signifies in the middle voice, (a) "to hold firmly to, cleave to," of "holding" or cleaving to a person, Matt. 6:24; **Luke 16:13**; of "holding" to the faithful word, Titus 1:9, RV, KJV, "holding fast"; (b) "to support," 1 Thess. 5:14 (the weak).

Despise *kataphroneo* (2706), lit., "to think down upon or against anyone" (*kata*, "down," *phren*, "the mind"), hence signifies "to think slightly of, to despise," Matt. 6:24; 18:10; **Luke 16:13**; Rom. 2:4; 1 Cor. 11:22; 1 Tim. 4:12; 6:2; Heb. 12:2; 2 Pet. 2:10.

Mammon *see* ***Luke 16:9***.

16:14 And the Pharisees also, who were covetous, heard all these things: and they derided him.

Were *huparcho* (5225), primarily, "to make a beginning" (*hupo*, "under," *arche*, "a beginning"), denotes "to be, to be in existence," involving an "existence" or condition both previous to the circumstances mentioned and continuing after it. This is important in Phil. 2:6, concerning the deity of Christ. The phrase "being (existing) in the form (*morphe*, the essential and specific form and character) of God," carries with it the two facts of the antecedent Godhood of Christ, previous to His incarnation, and the continuance of His Godhood at and after the event of His Birth (see Gifford, on the Incarnation, pp. 11, sqq.). It is translated "exist" in 1 Cor. 11:18, RV, for KJV, "there be." Cf. **Luke 16:14; 23:50**; Acts 2:30; 3:2; 17:24; 22:3, etc.

Covetous *philarguros* (5366), lit., "money-loving," is rendered "covetous" in the KJV of **Luke 16:14** and 2 Tim. 3:2; RV, "lovers of money," the wider and due significance.

Derided *ekmukterizo* (1592), "to hold up the nose in derision at" (*ek*, "from," used intensively, *mukterizo*, "to mock"; from *mukter*, "the nose"), is translated "scoffed at" in **Luke 16:14**, RV (KJV, "derided"), of the Pharisees in their derision of Christ on account of His teaching; in **23:35** (ditto), of the mockery of Christ on the cross by the rulers of the people. In the Sept., Ps. 2:4; 22:7; 35:16.

16:15 And he said unto them, Ye are they which justify yourselves before men; but God knoweth your hearts: for that which is highly esteemed among men is abomination in the sight of God.

Justify *see* Justified at *Luke 7:29*.

Before *see* *Luke 1:17*.

Knoweth *see* Know at *Luke 1:34*.

Highly esteemed *hupselos* (5308), "high, lofty," is used (a) naturally, of mountains, Matt. 4:8; 17:1; Mark 9:2; Rev. 21:10; of a wall, Rev. 21:12; (b) figuratively, of the arm of God, Acts 13:17; of heaven, "on high," plural, lit., "in high (places)," Heb. 1:3; (c) metaphorically, **Luke 16:15**, RV, "exalted" (KJV, "highly esteemed"); Rom. 11:20, in the best texts, "high-minded" [lit., "mind (not) high things"]; 12:16.

Abomination *bdelugma* (946), denotes an "object of disgust, an abomination." This is said of the image to be set up by Antichrist, Matt. 24:15; Mark 13:14; of that which is highly esteemed amongst men, in contrast to its real character in the sight of God, **Luke 16:15**. The constant association with idolatry suggests that what is highly esteemed among men constitutes an idol in the human heart. In Rev. 21:27, entrance is forbidden into the Holy City on the part of the unclean, or one who "maketh an abomination and a lie." It is also used of the contents of the golden cup in the hand of the evil woman described in Rev. 17:4, and of the name ascribed to her in the following verse.

Sight *see* Before at *Luke 12:6*.

16:16 The law and the prophets *were* until John: since that time the kingdom of God is preached, and every man presseth into it.

Law *nomos* (3551), akin to *nemo*, "to divide out, distribute," primarily meant "that which is assigned"; hence, "usage, custom," and then, "law, law as prescribed by custom, or by statute"; the word *ethos*, "custom," was retained for unwritten "law," while *nomos* became the established name for "law" as decreed by a state and set up as the standard for the administration of justice. In the NT it is used,

(a) of "law" in general, e.g., Rom. 2:12, 13, "a law" (RV), expressing a general principle relating to "law"; v. 14, last part; 3:27, "By what manner of law?" i.e., "by what sort of principle (has the glorying been excluded)?"; 4:15 (last part); 5:13, referring to the period between Adam's trespass and the giving of the Law; 7:1 (1st part, RV marg., "law"); against those graces which constitute the fruit of the Spirit "there is no law," Gal. 5:23...

(b) of a force or influence impelling to action, Rom. 7:21, 23 (1st part), "a different law," RV;

(c) of the Mosaic Law, the "law" of Sinai, (1) with the definite article, e.g., Matt. 5:18; John 1:17; Rom. 2:15, 18, 20, 26, 27; 3:19; 4:15; 7:4, 7, 14, 16, 22; 8:3, 4, 7; Gal. 3:10, 12, 19, 21, 24; 5:3; Eph. 2:15; Phil. 3:6; 1 Tim. 1:8; Heb. 7:19; Jas. 2:9; (2) without the article, thus stressing the Mosaic Law in its quality as "law," e.g., Rom. 2:14 (1st part); 5:20; 7:9, where the stress in the quality lies in this, that "the commandment which was unto (i.e., which he thought would be a means of) life," he found to be "unto (i.e., to have the effect of revealing his actual state of) death"; 10:4; 1 Cor. 9:20; Gal. 2:16, 19, 21; 3:2, 5, 10 (1st part), 11, 18, 23; 4:4, 5, 21 (1st part); 5:4, 18; 6:13; Phil. 3:5, 9; Heb. 7:16; 9:19; Jas. 2:11; 4:11...

(d) by metonymy, of the books which contain the "law," (1) of the Pentateuch, e.g., Matt. 5:17; 12:5; **Luke 16:16; 24:44**; John 1:45; Rom. 3:21; Gal. 3:10; (2) of the Psalms, John 10:34; 15:25; of the Psalms, Isaiah, Ezekiel and Daniel, 12:34, the Psalms and Isaiah, Rom. 3:19 (with vv. 10-18); Isaiah, 1 Cor. 14:21; from all this it may be inferred that "the law" in the most comprehensive sense was an alternative title to "The Scriptures."

That time *see* Then at *Luke 11:26*.

Kingdom of God *see* Gospel at *Luke 7:22*.

Every *pas* (3956), signifies (1) with nouns without the article, (a) "every one" of the class denoted by the noun connected with *pas*, e.g., Matt. 3:10, "every tree"; Mark 9:49, "every sacrifice"; see also John 2:10; Acts 2:43; Rom. 2:9; Eph. 1:21; 3:15; 2 Thess. 2:4; 2 Tim. 3:16, RV; (b) "any and every, of every kind, all manner of," e.g., Matt. 4:23; "especially with nouns denoting virtues or vices, emotions, condition, indicating every mode in which a quality manifests itself; or any object to which the idea conveyed by the noun belongs" (GrimmThayer). This is often translated "all," e.g., Acts 27:20; Rom. 15:14; 2 Cor. 10:6; Eph. 4:19, 31; Col. 4:12, "all the will of God," i.e., everything God wills; (2) without a noun, "every one, everything, every man" (i.e., person), e.g., **Luke 16:16**; or with a negative, "not everyone," e.g., Mark 9:49; with a participle and the article, equivalent to a relative clause, everyone who, e.g., 1 Cor. 9:25; Gal. 3:10, 13; 1 John 2:29; 3:3-4, 6, 10, 15, rendered "whosoever." So in the neuter, 1 John 2:16; 5:4, often rendered "whatsoever"; governed by the preposition *en*, "in," without a noun following, it signifies "in every matter, or condition," Phil. 4:6; 1 Thess. 5:18; "in every way or particular," 2 Cor. 4:8, translated "on every side"; so 2 Cor. 7:5; "in everything," Eph. 5:24; Phil. 4:12, lit., "in everything and (perhaps "even") in all things."

Presseth *biazo* (971), in the middle voice, "to press violently" or "force one's way into," is translated "presseth" in **Luke 16:16**, KJV, RV, "entereth violently," a meaning confirmed by the papyri. Moulton and Milligan also quote a passage from D. S. Sharp's *Epictetus and the NT*, speaking of "those who (try to) force their way in"; the verb suggests forceful endeavor.

16:17 And it is easier for heaven and earth to pass, than one tittle of the law to fail.

Easier *see Luke 5:23*.

Pass *see Luke 11:42*.

Tittle *keraia* or *kerea* (2762), "a little horn" (*keras*, "a horn"), was used to denote the small stroke distinguishing one Hebrew letter from another. The rabbis attached great importance to these; hence the significance of the Lord's statements in Matt. 5:18 and **Luke 16:17**, charging the Pharisees with hypocrisy, because, while professing the most scrupulous reverence to the Law, they violated its spirit. Grammarians used the word to denote the accents in Greek words.

Fail *pipto* (4098), "to fall," is used of the law of God in its smallest detail, in the sense of losing its authority or ceasing to have force, **Luke 16:17**. In 1 Cor. 13:8 it is used of love (some mss. have *ekpipto*, "to fall off").

16:18 Whosoever putteth away his wife, and marrieth another, committeth adultery: and whosoever marrieth her that is put away from *her* husband committeth adultery.

Putteth away *apoluo* (630), "to let loose from, let go free" (*apo*, "from," *luo*, "to loose"), is translated "is divorced" in the KJV of Matt. 5:32 (RV, "is put away"); it is further used of "divorce" in Matt. 1:19; 19:3, 7-9; Mark 10:2, Mk 4:11; **Luke 16:18**. The Lord also used it of the case of a wife putting away her husband, Mark 10:12, a usage among Greeks and Romans, not among Jews.

Marrieth *see* Married at *Luke 14:20*.

Adultery *moicheuo* (3431), is used in Matt. 5:27-28, 32; 19:18; Mark 10:19; **Luke 16:18**; **18:20**; John 8:4; Rom. 2:22; 13:9; Jas. 2:11; in Rev. 2:22, metaphorically, of those who are by a Jezebel's solicitations drawn away to idolatry.

Husband *see Luke 2:36*.

16:19 There was a certain rich man, which was clothed in purple and fine linen, and fared sumptuously every day:

Rich *see Luke 6:24*.

Clothed *see* Ware at *Luke 8:27*.

Purple *porphura* (4209), originally denoted the "purple-fish," then, "purple dye" (extracted from certain shell fish): hence, "a purple garment," Mark 15:17, 20; **Luke 16:19**; Rev. 18:12.

Linen *bussos* (1040), "fine linen," made from a special species of flax, a word of Aramean origin, used especially for the Syrian *byssus* (Arab. *bus* is still used for native "linen"). Cf. Heb. *bus*, in all OT passages quoted here, except Ezek. 27:7; It is the material mentioned in 1 Chron. 4:21, wrought by the house of Ashbea; 15:27, *bussinos*, (David's robe); 2 Chron. 3:14, *bussos* (the veil of the Temple); 5:12, *bussinos* (the clothing of the Levite singers); Esth. 1:6 (the cords of the hangings in the king's garden); 8:15 (Mordecai's dress); Ezek. 27:7 (*bussos*, in Syrian trade with Tyre). In the NT, **Luke 16:19**, the clothing of the "rich man."

Fared *euphraino* (2165), in the active voice, signifies "to cheer, gladden," 2 Cor. 2:2; in the passive, "to rejoice, make merry"; translated "faring sumptuously" in **Luke 16:19**, especially of food (RV, marg., "living in mirth and splendor"). *See also* Merry at *Luke 12:19*.

Sumptuously *lampros* (2988), the corresponding adverb, is used in Luke 16:19, "sumptuously."

Every *see Luke 2:41*.

16:20 And there was a certain beggar named Lazarus, which was laid at his gate, full of sores,

Beggar *see* Poor at *Luke 14:13*.

Laid *ballo* (906), "to cast, throw, place, put," is used in the passive voice signifying "to be laid," e.g., Mark 7:30; **Luke 16:20**.

Gate *pulon* (4440), primarily signifies "a porch or vestibule," e.g., Matt. 26:71; **Luke 16:20**; Acts 10:17; 12:13, 14; then, the "gateway" or "gate tower" of a walled town, Acts 14:13; Rev. 21:12, 13, 15, 21, 25; 22:14.

Sores *helkoo* (1669), "to wound, to ulcerate," is used in the passive voice, signifying "to suffer from sores," to be "full of sores," **Luke 16:20** (perfect participle).

16:21 And desiring to be fed with the crumbs which fell from the rich man's table: moreover the dogs came and licked his sores.

Desiring *epithumeo* (1937), "to desire earnestly," stresses the inward impulse rather than the object desired. It is translated "to desire" in **Luke 16:21**; **17:22**; **22:15**; 1 Tim. 3:1; Heb. 6:11; 1 Pet. 1:12; Rev. 9:6. *See also* **Fain** at *Luke 15:16*.

Fed *chortazo* (5526), "to feed, to fatten," is used (a) primarily of animals, Rev. 19:21; (b) of persons, to fill or satisfy with food. It is usually translated by the verb "to fill," but is once rendered "to be fed," in **Luke 16:21**, of Lazarus, in his desire for the crumbs (he could be well supplied with them) that fell from the rich man's table, a fact which throws light upon the utter waste that went on at the table of the latter. The crumbs that fell would provide no small meal.

Crumbs *psichion* (5589), "a small morsel," a diminutive of *psix*, "a bit, or crumb", of bread or meat, it is used in Matt. 15:27 and Mark 7:28; some mss. have it in **Luke 16:21**.

Rich *see Luke 6:24*.

Table *trapeza* (5132), is used of (a) "a dining table," Matt. 15:27; Mark 7:28; **Luke 16:21**; **22:21**, **30**; (b) "the table of shewbread," Heb. 9:2; (c) by metonymy, of "what is provided on the table" (the word being used of that with which it is associated), Acts 16:34; Rom. 11:9 (figurative of the special privileges granted to Israel and centering in Christ); 1 Cor. 10:21 (twice), "the Lord's table," denoting all that is provided for believers in Christ on the ground of His death (and thus expressing something more comprehensive than the Lord's Supper); "the table of demons," denoting all that is partaken of by idolaters as the result of the influence of demons in connection with their sacrifices; (d) "a moneychanger's table," Matt. 21:12; Mark 11:15; John 2:15; (e) "a bank," **Luke 19:23** (cf. *trapezites*); (f) by metonymy for "the distribution of money," Acts 6:2.

Dogs *kuon* (2965), is used in two senses, (a) natural, Matt. 7:6; **Luke 16:21**; 2 Pet. 2:22; (b) metaphorical, Phil. 3:2; Rev. 22:15, of those whose moral impurity will exclude them from the New Jerusalem. The Jews used the term of Gentiles, under the idea of ceremonial impurity. Among the Greeks it was an epithet of impudence. Lat., *canis*, and Eng., "hound" are etymologically akin to it.

Licked *epileicho* (1952a), "to lick over" (*epi*, "over," *leicho*, "to lick"), is said of the dogs in **Luke 16:21**. Some mss. have *apoleicho*, "to lick off."

Sores *helkos* (1668), "a sore" or "ulcer" (primarily a wound), occurs in **Luke 16:21**; Rev. 16:2, 11.

16:22 And it came to pass, that the beggar died, and was carried by the angels into Abraham's bosom: the rich man also died, and was buried;

Beggar *see* **Poor** at *Luke 14:13*.

Bosom *see Luke 6:38*.

Rich *see Luke 6:24*.

Buried *thapto* (2290), occurs in Matt. 8:21-22, and parallels in Luke; Matt. 14:12; **Luke 16:22**; Acts 2:29; 5:6, 9-10; of Christ's "burial," 1 Cor. 15:4.

16:23 And in hell he lift up his eyes, being in torments, and seeth Abraham afar off, and Lazarus in his bosom.

Hell *see Luke 10:15*.

Lift *see* **Lifted** at *Luke 6:20*.

Torments *basanos* (931), primarily "a touchstone," employed in testing metals, hence, "torment," is used (a) of physical diseases, Matt. 4:24: (b) of a condition of retribution in Hades, **Luke 16:23**, **28**.

Bosom *see Luke 6:38*.

16:24 And he cried and said, Father Abraham, have mercy on me, and send Lazarus, that he may dip the tip of his finger in water, and cool my tongue; for I am tormented in this flame.

Cried *see Luke 8:8*.

Dip *bapto* (911), "to immerse, dip" (derived from a root signifying "deep"), also signified "to dye," which is suggested in Rev. 19:13, of the Lord's garment "dipped (i.e. dyed) in blood" (RV, "sprinkled" translates the verb *rhantizo*. It is elsewhere translated "to dip," **Luke 16:24**; John 13:26. Cf the longer form *baptizo* (primarily a frequentative form).

Tip *akron* (206), "the top, an extremity," is translated "tip" in **Luke 16:24**.

Finger *see Luke 11:20*.

Cool *katapsucho* (2711), **Luke 16:24**, denotes "to cool off, make cool" (*kata*, "down," *psucho*, "to cool"). In the Sept., Gen. 18:4.

Tormented *eodunao* (3600), in the passive voice is rendered "I am (thou art) tormented" in **Luke 16:24, 25**, KJV. *See also* **Sorrowing** at *Luke 2:48*.

Flame *phlox* (5395), akin to Lat. *fulgeo*, "to shine," is used apart from *pur*, "fire," in **Luke 16:24**; with *pur*, it signifies "a fiery flame," lit., "a flame of fire," Acts 7:30; 2 Thess. 1:8, where the fire is to be understood as the instrument of divine judgment; Heb. 1:7, where the meaning probably is that God makes His angels as active and powerful as a "flame" of fire; in Rev. 1:14; 2:18; 19:12, of the eyes of the Lord Jesus as emblematic of penetrating judgment, searching out evil.

16:25 But Abraham said, Son, remember that thou in thy lifetime receivedst thy good things, and likewise Lazarus evil things: but now he is comforted, and thou art tormented.

Lifetime *zoe* (2222), (Eng., "zoo," "zoology") is used in the NT "of life as a principle, life in the absolute sense, life as God has it, that which the Father has in Himself, and which He gave to the Incarnate Son to have in Himself, John 5:26, and which the Son manifested in the world, 1 John 1:2. From this life man has become alienated in consequence of the Fall, Eph. 4:18, and of this life men become partakers through faith in the Lord Jesus Christ, John 3:15, who becomes its Author to all such as trust in Him, Acts 3:15, and who is therefore said to be 'the life' of the believer, Col. 3:4, for the life that He gives He maintains, John 6:35, 63. Eternal life is the present actual possession of the believer because of his relationship with Christ, John 5:24; 1 John 3:14, and that it will one day extend its domain to the sphere of the body is assured by the Resurrection of Christ, 2 Cor. 5:4; 2 Tim. 1:10. This life is not merely a principle of power and mobility, however, for it has moral associations which are inseparable from it, as of holiness and righteousness. Death and sin, life and holiness, are frequently contrasted in the Scriptures.

"*Zoe* is also used of that which is the common possession of all animals and men by nature, Acts 17:25; 1 John 5:16, and of the present sojourn of man upon the earth with reference to its duration, **Luke 16:25**; 1 Cor. 15:19; 1 Tim. 4:8; 1 Pet. 3:10. 'This life' is a term equivalent to 'the gospel,' 'the faith,' 'Christianity,' Acts 5:20."

Receivedst *see* **Receive** at *Luke 6:34*.

Good *see Luke 1:53*.

Likewise *see Luke 5:33*. *See also Luke 10:32*.

Evil *kakos* (2556), stands for "whatever is evil in character, base," in distinction (wherever the distinction is observable) from *poneros*, which indicates "what is evil in influence and effect, malignant." *Kakos* is the wider term and often covers the meaning of *poneros*. *Kakos* is antithetic to *kalos*, "fair, advisable, good in character," and to *agathos*, "beneficial, useful, good in act"; hence it denotes what is useless, incapable, bad; *poneros* is essentially antithetic to *chrestos*, "kind, gracious, serviceable"; hence it denotes what is destructive, injurious, evil. As evidence that *poneros* and *kakos* have much in common, though still not interchangeable, each is used of thoughts, cf. Matt. 15:19 with Mark 7:21; of speech, Matt. 5:11 with 1 Pet. 3:10; of actions, 2 Tim. 4:18 with 1 Thess. 5:15; of man, Matt. 18:32 with 24:48. The use of *kakos* may be broadly divided as follows: (a) of what is morally or ethically "evil," whether of persons, e.g., Matt. 21:41; 24:48; Phil. 3:2; Rev. 2:2, or qualities, emotions, passions, deeds, e.g., Mark 7:21; John 18:23, 30; Rom. 1:30; 3:8; 7:19, 21; 13:4; 14:20; 16:19; 1 Cor. 13:5; 2 Cor. 13:7; 1 Thess. 5:15; 1 Tim. 6:10; 2 Tim. 4:14; 1 Pet. 3:9, 12; (b) of what is injurious, destructive, baneful, pernicious, e.g., **Luke 16:25**; Acts 16:28; 28:5; Titus 1:12; Jas. 3:8; Rev. 16:2, where *kakos* and *poneros* come in that order, "noisome and grievous."

Tormented *see Luke 16:24*.

16:26 And beside all this, between us and you there is a great gulf fixed: so that they which would pass from hence to you cannot; neither can they pass to us, that *would come* from thence.

Between *see Luke 11:51*.

Gulf *chasma* (5490), akin to *chasko*, "to yawn" (Eng., "chasm"), is found in **Luke 16:26**. In the Sept., 2 Sam. 18:17, two words are used with reference to Absalom's body, *bothunos* which signifies "a great pit," and *chasma*, "a yawning abyss, or precipice," with a deep pit at the bottom, into which the body was cast.

Fixed *sterizo* (4741), "to set forth, make fast, fix," is translated "fixed" in **Luke 16:26**, of the great gulf separating Hades or Sheol from the region called "Abraham's bosom." *See also* **Set** at *Luke 9:51*.

Pass *diabaino* (1224), "to step across, cross over," is translated "to pass" in **Luke 16:26** (of "passing" across the fixed gulf); in Heb. 11:29, "passed through."

Hence *enthen* (1782), is found in the best mss. in Matt. 17:20; **Luke 16:26**.

Pass *diaperao* (1276), "to pass over, cross over" (used in **Luke 16:26**, 2nd part).

16:27 Then he said, I pray thee therefore, father, that thou wouldest send him to my father's house:

Pray *see Luke 14:18.*

16:28 For I have five brethren; that he may testify unto them, lest they also come into this place of torment.

Testify *diamarturomai* (1263), "to testify or protest solemnly," an intensive form, is translated "to testify" in **Luke 16:28**; Acts 2:40; 8:25; 10:42; 18:5; 20:21, 23, 24; 23:11; 28:23; 1 Thess. 4:6; Heb. 2:6; "to charge" in 1 Tim. 5:21; 2 Tim. 2:14; 4:8.

Torment *see* Torments at *Luke 16:23.*

16:29-30 Abraham saith unto him, They have Moses and the prophets; let them hear them.
And he said, Nay, father Abraham: but if one went unto them from the dead, they will repent.

Nay *see Luke 12:51.*

Repent *see* Repented at *Luke 10:13.*

16:31 And he said unto him, If they hear not Moses and the prophets, neither will they be persuaded, though one rose from the dead.

Persuaded *peitho* (3982), in the active voice, signifies "to apply persuasion, to prevail upon or win over, to persuade," bringing about a change of mind by the influence of reason or moral considerations, e.g., in Matt. 27:20; 28:14; Acts 13:43; 19:8; in the passive voice, "to be persuaded, believe," e.g., **Luke 16:31; 20:6**; Acts 17:4, RV (KJV, "believed"); 21:14; 26:26; Rom. 8:38; 14:14; 15:14; 2 Tim. 1:5, 12; Heb. 6:9; 11:13, in some mss.; 13:18, RV (KJV, "trust").

Chapter 17

17:1 Then said he unto the disciples, It is impossible but that offences will come: but woe *unto him*, through whom they come!

Impossible *anendektos* (418), signifies "inadmissible" (*a*, negative, *n*, euphonic, and *endechomai*, "to admit, allow"), **Luke 17:1**, of occasions of stumbling, where the meaning is "it cannot be but that they will come."

Offences *skandalon* (4625), originally was "the name of the part of a trap to which the bait is attached, hence, the trap or snare itself, as in Rom. 11:9, RV, 'stumblingblock,' quoted from Psa. 69:22, and in Rev. 2:14, for Balaam's device was rather a trap for Israel than a stumblingblock to them, and in Matt. 16:23, for in Peter's words the Lord perceived a snare laid for Him by Satan.

Thus it is used (a) of Christ in Rom. 9:33, "(a rock) of offense"; so 1 Pet. 2:8; 1 Cor. 1:23 (KJV and RV, "stumblingblock"), and of His cross, Gal. 5:11 (RV, ditto); of the "table" provided by God for Israel, Rom. 11:9; (b) of that which is evil, e.g., Matt. 13:41, RV, "things that cause stumbling" (KJV, "things that offend"), lit., "all stumblingblocks"; 18:7, RV, "occasions of stumbling" and "occasion"; **Luke 17:1** (ditto); Rom. 14:13, RV, "an occasion of falling" (KJV, "an occasion to fall"), said of such a use of Christian liberty as proves a hindrance to another; 16:17, RV, "occasions of stumbling," said of the teaching of things contrary to sound doctrine; 1 John 2:10, "occasion of stumbling," of the absence of this in the case of one who loves his brother and thereby abides in the light. Love, then, is the best safeguard against the woes pronounced by the Lord upon those who cause others to stumble.

Woe *see Luke 6:24.*

17:2 It were better for him that a millstone were hanged about his neck, and he cast into the sea, than that he should offend one of these little ones.

Better *lusiteleo* (3081), signifies "to indemnify, pay expenses, pay taxes" (from *luo*, "to loose," *telos*, "toll, custom"); hence, "to be useful, advantageous, to be better" **Luke 17:2**. *See also* More at *Luke 15:7.*

Millstone *mulikos* (3457), "of a mill," occurs in **Luke 17:2**; *lithos* (3037), is used literally, of (a) the "stones" of the ground, e.g., Matt. 4:3, 6; 7:9; (b) "tombstones," e.g., Matt. 27:60, 66; (c) "building stones," e.g., Matt. 21:42; (d) "a millstone," **Luke 17:2**; cf. Rev. 18:21; (e) the "tables (or tablets)" of the Law, 2 Cor. 3:7; (f) "idol images," Acts 17:29; (g) the "treasures" of commercial Babylon, Rev. 18:12, 16.

Hanged *perikeimai* (4029), signifies "to lie round" (*peri*, "around," *keimai*, "to lie"); then, "to be hanged round," said of "a great millstone" (lit., "a millstone turned by an ass"), Mark 9:42, RV, and marg., to be "hung" round the neck of him who causes one of Christ's "little ones" to stumble; in **Luke 17:2**, "a millstone."

Neck *see Luke 15:20.*

Cast *see* Thrown at *Luke 4:35.*

Sea *thalassa* (2281), is used (a) chiefly literally, e.g., "the Red Sea," Acts 7:36; 1 Cor. 10:1; Heb. 11:29; the "sea" of Galilee or Tiberias, Matt. 4:18; 15:29; Mark 6:48, 49, where the acts of Christ testified to His deity; John 6:1; 21:1; in general, e.g., **Luke 17:2**; Acts 4:24; Rom. 9:27; Rev. 16:3; 18:17; 20:8, 13; 21:1; (b) metaphorically, of "the ungodly men" described in Jude 13 (cf. Isa. 57:20); (c) symbolically, in the apocalyptic vision of "a glassy sea like unto crystal," Rev. 4:6, emblematic of the fixed purity and holiness of all that appertains to the authority and judicial dealings of God; in 15:2, the same, "mingled with fire," and, standing by it (RV) or on it (KJV and RV marg.), those who had "come victorious from the beast" (ch. 13); of the wild and restless condition of nations, Rev. 13:1 (see 17:1, 15), where "he stood" (RV) refers to the dragon, not John (KJV); from the midst of this state arises the beast, symbolic of the final gentile power dominating the federated nations of the Roman world (see Dan., chs. 2, 7, etc.).

17:3 Take heed to yourselves: If thy brother trespass against thee, rebuke him; and if he repent, forgive him.

Heed *prosecho* (4337), lit., "to hold to," signifies "to turn to, turn one's attention to"; hence, "to give heed"; it is rendered "take heed" in Matt. 6:1; **Luke 17:3**; **21:34**; Acts 5:35; 20:28; 2 Pet. 1:19; to give heed to, in Acts 8:6, 10; in v. 11 (KJV, "had regard to"); 16:14 (KJV, "attended unto"); 1 Tim. 1:4; 4:1, 13 (KJV, "give attendance to"); Titus 1:14; Heb. 2:1, lit., "to give heed more earnestly."

Trespass *hamartano* (264), "to sin," is translated "to trespass," in the KJV of Matt. 18:15, and **Luke 17:3, 4** (RV, "to sin"). *See also* **Sinned** at *Luke 15:18.*

Rebuke *see* Rebuked at *Luke 4:35.*

Repent *see* Repented at *Luke 10:13.*

Forgive *see* Forgiven at *Luke 5:20.*

17:4 And if he trespass against thee seven times in a day, and seven times in a day turn again to thee, saying, I repent; thou shalt forgive him.

Trespass *see Luke 17:3. See also* Sinned at *Luke 15:18.*

Seven times *heptakis* (2034), occurs in Matt. 18:21, 22; **Luke 17:4** (twice).

Repent *see* Repented at *Luke 10:13.*

17:5 And the apostles said unto the Lord, Increase our faith.

Increase *prostithemi* (4369), "to put to" (*pros*, "to," *tithemi*, "to put"), "to add, or to place beside" (the primary meaning), in **Luke 17:5** is translated "increase," in the request "increase our faith"; in **Luke 20:11-12**, "he sent yet" (KJV, "again he sent"), lit., "he added and sent," as in **19:11**, "He added and spake." In Acts 12:3, RV, "proceeded," KJV, "proceeded further" (of repeating or continuing the action mentioned by the following verb); in Acts 13:36, "was laid unto"; in Heb. 12:19, "more ... be spoken," (lit., "that no word should be added"). In Gal. 3:19, "What then is the law?" It was "added" because of transgressions, there is no contradiction of what is said in v. 15, where the word is *epidiatasso*, for there the latter word conveys the idea of supplementing an agreement already made; here in v. 19 the meaning is not that something had been 'added' to the promise with a view to complete it, which the apostle denies, but that something had been given "in addition" to the promise, as in Rom. 5:20, "The law came in beside."

Our In **Luke 17:5**, "increase our faith" is, lit., "add faith to us."

17:6 And the Lord said, If ye had faith as a grain of mustard seed, ye might say unto this sycamine tree, Be thou plucked up by the root, and be thou planted in the sea; and it should obey you.

Grain *see Luke 13:19.*

Mustard *see Luke 13:19.*

Sycamine *sukaminos* (4507), occurs in **Luke 17:6**. It is generally recognized as the black mulberry, with fruit like blackberries. The leaves are too tough for silkworms and thus are unlike the white mulberry. Neither kind is the same as the mulberry of 2 Sam. 5:23, 24, etc. The town Haifa was called Sycaminopolis, from the name of the tree.

Plucked *ekrizoo* (1610), "to pluck up by the roots" (*ek*, "out," *rhiza*, "a root"), is so translated in Jude 12 (figuratively), and in the KJV in **Luke 17:6**, RV, "rooted up"; "root up," Matt. 13:29; "shall be rooted up," 15:13.

Planted *see Luke 13:6.*

Obey *see Luke 8:25.*

17:7 But which of you, having a servant plowing or feeding cattle, will say unto him by and by, when he is come from the field, Go and sit down to meat?

Plowing *arotriao* (722), a later form of *aroo*, "to plow," occurs in **Luke 17:7** and 1 Cor. 9:10.

Feeding *poimaino* (4165), "to act as a shepherd" (from *poimen*, "a shepherd"), is used (a) literally, **Luke 17:7**, RV, "keeping sheep," for KJV, "feeding cattle"; 1 Cor. 9:7, (b) metaphorically, "to tend, to shepherd"; said of Christ, Matt. 2:6, RV, "shall be Shepherd of" (for KJV, "shall rule"); of those who act as spiritual shepherds under Him, John 21:16, RV, "tend" (for KJV "feed"), so 1 Pet. 5:2; Acts 20:28, "to feed" ("to tend" would have been a consistent rendering; a shepherd does not only "feed" his flock); of base shepherds, Jude 12.

Cattle The verb *poimaino,* "to act as a shepherd" (*poimen*), "to keep sheep," is translated "keeping sheep" in **Luke 17:7**, RV, for KJV "feeding cattle."

By and by The phrase "by and by" in the KJV is in several places misleading. The three words *exautes,* Mark 6:25, *euthus,* Matt. 13:21, and *eutheos,* **Luke 17:7**; **21:9**, mean "straightway," "immediately." See under these words.

Go *eiserchomai* (1525), "to come into, or to go into" (*eis,* "into"), e.g., **Luke 17:7.**

See also Pass at *Luke 11:42.*

Sit *see* Sat at *Luke 11:37.*

17:8 And will not rather say unto him, Make ready wherewith I may sup, and gird thyself, and serve me, till I have eaten and drunken; and afterward thou shalt eat and drink?

Rather *alla* (235), "but, on the contrary," is translated "and rather" in **Luke 17:8.**

Sup *deipneo* (1172), "to sup" (said of taking the chief meal of the day), occurs in **Luke 17:8**; **22:20** (in the best texts), lit., "(the) supping"; so 1 Cor. 11:25; metaphorically in Rev. 3:20, of spiritual communion between Christ and the faithful believer.

Gird *see* Girded at *Luke 12:35.*

Serve *see Luke 10:40. See also* Ministered at *Luke 4:39.*

17:9 Doth he thank that servant because he did the things that were commanded him? I trow not.

Thank *see Luke 6:32. See also* Grace at *Luke 2:40.*

Commanded *see Luke 8:55.*

Trow Some mss. have *dokeo,* "to think," in **Luke 17:9**, KJV, "I trow (not)."

17:10 So likewise ye, when ye shall have done all those things which are commanded you, say, We are unprofitable servants: we have done that which was our duty to do.

Likewise *see Luke 3:14.*

Unprofitable *achreios* (888), "useless" (*chreia,* "use"), "unprofitable," occurs in Matt. 25:30 and **Luke 17:10.** In the Sept., 2 Sam. 6:22.

Duty *opheilo* (3784), "to owe, to be indebted," is translated "it was our duty," in **Luke 17:10**, lit., "we owe (ought) to do"; so in Rom. 15:27, KJV, "their duty is"; RV, "they owe it."

17:11 And it came to pass, as he went to Jerusalem, that he passed through the midst of Samaria and Galilee.

Midst *see Luke 4:30.*

17:12 And as he entered into a certain village, there met him ten men that were lepers, which stood afar off:

Met *see* Meet at *Luke 14:31.*

Lepers *see Luke 4:27.*

Afar *porrothen* (4207), "afar off," from *porro,* "at a distance, a great way off," is found in **Luke 17:12** and Heb. 11:13.

17:13 And they lifted up *their* voices, and said, Jesus, Master, have mercy on us.

Lifted *airo* (142), signifies (a) "to raise take up, lift, draw up," (b) "to bear, carry," (c) "to take or carry away." It is used of "lifting" up the voice, **Luke 17:13**; Acts 4:24; eyes, John 11:41; hand, Rev. 10:5.

Master *see Luke 5:5.*

17:14 And when he saw *them*, he said unto them, Go shew yourselves unto the priests. And it came to pass, that, as they went, they were cleansed.

Shew *epideiknumi* (1925), signifies (a) "to exhibit, display," Matt. 16:1; 22:19; 24:1; **Luke 17:14** (in some mss. **24:40**); in the middle voice, "to display," with a special interest in one's own action, Acts 9:39; (b) "to point out, prove, demonstrate," Acts 18:28; Heb. 6:17.

17:15 And one of them, when he saw that he was healed, turned back, and with a loud voice glorified God,

Turned *see Luke 2:45.*

17:16 And fell down on *his* face at his feet, giving him thanks: and he was a Samaritan.

Thanks *eucharisteo* (2168), "to give thanks," (a) is said of Christ, Matt. 15:36; 26:27; Mark 8:6; 14:23; **Luke 22:17, 19**; John 6:11, 23, 11:41; 1 Cor. 11:24; (b) of the Pharisee in **Luke 18:11** in his selfcomplacent prayer; (c) is used by Paul at the beginning of all his epistles, except 2 Cor. (see, however, *eulogetos* in 1:3), Gal., 1 Tim., 2 Tim. (see, however, *charin echo,* 1:3), and Titus, (1) for his readers, Rom. 1:8; Eph. 1:16; Col. 1:3; 1 Thess. 1:2; 2 Thess. 1:3 (cf. 2:13); virtually so in

"No duty is more urgent than that of returning thanks."

ST. AMBROSE

Philem. 4; (2) for fellowship shown, Phil. 1:3; (3) for God's gifts to them, 1 Cor. 1:4; (d) is recorded (1) of Paul elsewhere, Acts 27:35; 28:15; Rom. 7:25; 1 Cor. 1:14; 14:18; (2) of Paul and others, Rom. 16:4; 1 Thess. 2:13; of himself, representatively, as a practice, 1 Cor. 10:30; (3) of others, **Luke 17:16**; Rom. 14:6 (twice); 1 Cor. 14:17; Rev. 11:17; (e) is used in admonitions to the saints, the Name of the Lord Jesus suggesting His character and example, Eph. 5:20; Col. 1:12; 3:17; 1 Thess. 5:18; (f) as the expression of a purpose, 2 Cor. 1:11, RV; (g) negatively of the ungodly, Rom. 1:21. "Thanksgiving" is the expression of joy Godward, and is therefore the fruit of the Spirit (Gal. 5:22); believers are encouraged to abound in it (e.g., Col. 2:7).

17:17 And Jesus answering said, Were there not ten cleansed? but where *are* the nine?

Nine *ennea* (1767), is found in **Luke 17:17**, and in connection with "ninety."

17:18 There are not found that returned to give glory to God, save this stranger.

Returned *see Luke 1:56.*

Glory *see Luke 2:9.*

Stranger *allogenes* (241), (*allos*, "another," *genos*, "a race") occurs in **Luke 17:18**, of a Samaritan. Moulton and Milligan illustrate the use of the word by the inscription on the Temple barrier, "let no foreigner enter within the screen and enclosure surrounding the sanctuary"; according to Mommsen this inscription was cut by the Romans.

17:19 And he said unto him, Arise, go thy way: thy faith hath made thee whole.

Go *see Luke 7:22.*

17:20 And when he was demanded of the Pharisees, when the kingdom of God should come, he answered them and said, The kingdom of God cometh not with observation:

Demanded *see Luke 3:14. See also* Asking at *Luke 2:46.*

Kingdom *see* Kingdoms at *Luke 4:5.*

Observation *parateresis* (3907), "attentive watching" (akin to *paratereo*, "to observe"), is used in **Luke 17:20**, of the manner in which the kingdom of God (i.e., the operation of the spiritual kingdom in the hearts of men) does not come, "in such a manner that it can be watched with the eyes" (Grimm-Thayer), or, as KJV marg., "with outward show."

17:21 Neither shall they say, Lo here! or, lo there! for, behold, the kingdom of God is within you.

Kingdom *see* Kingdoms at *Luke 4:5.*

Within *entos* (1787), an adverb denoting "within," or "among," is once used with the article, as a noun, of "the inside (of the cup and of the platter)," Matt. 23:26, RV (KJV, "that which is within, etc."); elsewhere, **Luke 17:21**. *See also Luke 7:39.*

17:22 And he said unto the disciples, The days will come, when ye shall desire to see one of the days of the Son of man, and ye shall not see *it*.

Desire *see* Desiring at *Luke 16:21. See also* Fain at *Luke 15:16.*

17:23-24 And they shall say to you, See here; or, see there: go not after *them*, nor follow *them*.

For as the lightning, that lighteneth out of the one *part* under heaven, shineth unto the other *part* under heaven; so shall also the Son of man be in his day.

Lightning *see Luke 10:18.*

Lighteneth *astrapto* (797), "to flash forth lighten as lightning" (akin to *astrape*, "lightning"), occurs in **Luke 17:24; 24:4** (KJV "shining"; RV, "dazzling").

Shineth *lampo* (2989), "to shine as a torch," occurs in Matt. 5:15, 16, 17:2; **Luke 17:24**; Acts 12:7; 2 Cor. 4:6 (twice).

17:25 But first must he suffer many things, and be rejected of this generation.

Rejected *see Luke 9:22.*

17:26-27 And as it was in the days of Noe, so shall it be also in the days of the Son of man.

They did eat, they drank, they married wives, they were given in marriage, until the day that Noe entered into the ark, and the flood came, and destroyed them all.

Married *see Luke 14:20.*

Given in marriage *gamizo* (1061), "to give in marriage," is used in the passive voice in Matt. 22:30 (2nd clause); Mark 12:25 (*gamisko* in some mss.); **Luke 17:27** (*ekgamizo* in some mss.); **20:35** (last word), passive (*gamisko* and *ekgamizo* in some mss.); in the active voice Matt. 24:38 (*gamisko* and *ekgamizo* in some mss.); further, of giving a daughter in "marriage," 1 Cor. 7:38 (twice), RV (*ekgamizo* in some mss.), which, on the whole, may be taken as the meaning. In this part of the Epistle, the apostle was answering a number of questions on matters about which the church at Corinth had written to him, and in this particular matter the formal transition from "marriage" in general to the subject of giving a daughter in "marriage," is simple. Eastern customs naturally would involve the inclusion of the latter in the inquiry and the reply.

Ark *kibotos* (2787), "a wooden box, a chest," is used of (a) Noah's vessel, Matt. 24:38; **Luke 17:27**; Heb. 11:7; 1 Pet. 3:20; (b) the "ark" of the covenant in the tabernacle, Heb. 9:4; (c) the "ark" seen in vision in the heavenly temple, Rev. 11:19.

Flood *kataklusmos* (2627), "a deluge" (Eng., "cataclysm"), akin to *katakluzo*, "to inundate," 2 Pet. 3:6, is used of the "flood" in Noah's time, Matt. 24:38, 39; **Luke 17:27**; 2 Pet. 2:5.

17:28 Likewise also as it was in the days of Lot; they did eat, they drank, they bought, they sold, they planted, they builded;

Likewise *see Luke 5:33.*

Planted *see Luke 13:6.*

17:29 But the same day that Lot went out of Sodom it rained fire and brimstone from heaven, and destroyed *them* all.

Rained *see* Wash at *Luke 7:38.*

Brimstone *theion* (2303), originally denoted "fire from heaven." It is connected with sulphur. Places touched by lightning were called *theia*, and, as lightning leaves a sulphurous smell, and sulphur was used in pagan purifications, it received the name of *theion*, **Luke 17:29**; Rev. 9:17-18; 14:10; 19:20; 20:10; 21:8.

17:30 Even thus shall it be in the day when the Son of man is revealed.

Thus In **Luke 17:30**, KJV, *kata tauta*, lit., "according to these things," is rendered "thus" (RV, "after the same manner," follows the reading *kata ta auta*, lit., "according to the same things").

See also Manner at *Luke 6:23.*

Revealed *see Luke 2:35.*

17:31 In that day, he which shall be upon the housetop, and his stuff in the house, let him not come down to take it away: and he that is in the field, let him likewise not return back.

Housetop *see Luke 5:19.*

Stuff *skeuos* (4632), "a vessel," denotes "goods" in Matt. 12:29; Mark 3:27; **Luke 17:31**, RV (KJV, stuff). *See also* Vessel at *Luke 8:16.*

Likewise *see Luke 5:33.*

Return *see* Returned at *Luke 2:39.*

Back *see Luke 9:62.*

17:32 Remember Lot's wife.

Remember *mnemoneuo* (3421), signifies "to call to mind, remember"; it is used absolutely in Mark 8:18; everywhere else it has an object, (a) persons, **Luke 17:32**; Gal. 2:10; 2 Tim. 2:8, where the RV rightly has "remember Jesus Christ, risen from the dead"; Paul was not reminding Timothy (nor did he need to) that Christ was raised from the dead (KJV), what was needful for him was to "remember" (to keep in mind) the One who rose, the Source and Supplier of all his requirements; (b) things, e.g., Matt. 16:9; John 15:20; 16:21; Acts 20:35; Col. 4:18; 1 Thess. 1:3; 2:9; Heb. 11:15, "had been mindful of"; 13:7; Rev. 18:5; (c) a clause, representing a circumstance, etc., John 16:4; Acts 20:31; Eph. 2:11; 2 Thess. 2:5; Rev. 2:5; 3:3; in Heb. 11:22 it signifies "to make mention of."

17:33 Whosoever shall seek to save his life shall lose it; and whosoever shall lose his life shall preserve it.

Save *peripoieo* (4046), "to save for oneself, gain," is in the middle voice in the best mss. in **Luke 17:33**, RV, gain. *See also* Heal at *Luke 7:3.*

Preserve *zoogoneo* (2225), denotes "to preserve alive" (from *zoos*, "alive," and *ginomai*, "to come to be, become, be made"); in **Luke 17:33**, "shall preserve (it)," i.e., his life, RV marg., "save (it) alive"; cf. the parallels *sozo*, "to save," in Matt. 16:25, and *phulaso*, "to keep," in John 12:25; in Acts 7:19, "live," negatively of the efforts of Pharaoh to destroy the babes in Israel; in 1 Tim. 6:13, according to the best mss. (some have *zoopoieo*, "to cause to live"), "quickeneth" (RV, marg., "preserveth ... alive," the preferable rendering).

17:34 I tell you, in that night there shall be two *men* in one bed; the one shall be taken, and the other shall be left.

Two In **Luke 17:34** *duo* stands for "two men"; in v. **35** for "two women."

Taken *paralambano* (3880), besides its meaning "to receive," denotes "to take to (or with) oneself," of "taking" a wife, e.g., Matt. 1:20, 24;

of "taking" a person or persons with one, e.g., Matt. 2:13, 14, 20, 21; 4:5, 8; of demons, 12:45; of Christ and His disciples, 17:1; 20:17; Mark 9:2; 10:32; 14:33; of witnesses, Matt. 18:16; of the removal of persons from the earth in judgment, when "the Son of Man is revealed," Matt. 24:40, 41; **Luke 17:34, 35** (cf. the means of the removal of corruption, in v. **37**); of the "taking" of Christ by the soldiers for scourging, Matt. 27:27, RV, and to crucifixion, John 19:16; see also Acts 15:39; 16:33; 21:24, 26, 32; 23:18.

17:35 Two *women* shall be grinding together; the one shall be taken, and the other left.

Two *see Luke 17:34.*

Grinding *aletho* (229), signifies "to grind at the mill," Matt. 24:41; **Luke 17:35**. The Sept. has both the earlier form *aleo,* Isa. 47:2,, and the later one *aletho,* used in the *Koine* period, Num. 11:8; Judg. 16:21; Eccl. 12:3, 4.

Together In the following, "together" translates the phrase *epi to auto,* lit., "to (upon, or for) the same," Matt. 22:34; **Luke 17:35**; Acts 1:15; 2:44 (3:1, in some texts); 4:26; 1 Cor. 7:5; 14:23, RV.

Taken *see Luke 17:34.*

17:36 Two *men* shall be in the field; the one shall be taken, and the other left.

Taken *see Luke 17:34.*

17:37 And they answered and said unto him, Where, Lord? And he said unto them, Wheresoever the body *is*, thither will the eagles be gathered together.

Thither *ekei* (1563), signifies (a) "there," e.g., Matt. 2:13, frequently in the Gospels; (b) "thither," e.g., **Luke 17:37**; in Rom. 15:24, "thitherward."

Eagles *aetos* (105), "an eagle" (also a vulture), is perhaps connected with *aemi,* "to blow," as of the wind, on account of its windlike flight. In Matt. 24:28 and **Luke 17:37** the vultures are probably intended. The meaning seems to be that, as these birds of prey gather where the carcass is, so the judgments of God will descend upon the corrupt state of humanity. The figure of the "eagle" is used in Ezek. 17 to represent the great powers of Egypt and Babylon, as being employed to punish corrupt and faithless Israel. Cf. Job 39:30; Prov. 30:17. The "eagle" is mentioned elsewhere in the NT in Rev. 4:7; 8:13 (RV); 12:14. There are eight species in Palestine.

Chapter 18

18:1 And he spake a parable unto them *to this end*, that men ought always to pray, and not to faint;

End *eis,* "unto," followed by the article and the infinitive mood of a verb, signifies "to the end that ..." marking the aim of an action, Acts 7:19; Rom. 1:11; 4:16, 18; Eph. 1:12; 1 Thess. 3:13; 2 Thess. 1:5; 2:2, 6; 1 Pet. 3:7. In **Luke 18:1**, *pros,* "to," has the same construction and meaning.

Faint *enkakeo* or *ekkakeo* (1573), "to lack courage, lose heart, be fainthearted" (*en,* "in," *kakos,* "base"), is said of prayer, **Luke 18:1**; of gospel ministry, 2 Cor. 4:1, 16; of the effect of tribulation, Eph. 3:13; as to well doing, 2 Thess. 3:13, "be not weary" (KJV marg., "fain not"). Some mss. have this word in Gal. 6:9.

18:2 Saying, There was in a city a judge, which feared not God, neither regarded man:

Judge *see* Judges at *Luke 11:19.*

Regarded *entrepo* (1788), "to turn about" (*en,* "in," *trepo,* "to turn"), is metaphorically used of "putting to shame," e.g., 1 Cor. 4:14; in the middle voice, "to reverence, regard," translated "regard" in **Luke 18:2, 4**.

18:3 And there was a widow in that city; and she came unto him, saying, Avenge me of mine adversary.

Widow *see Luke 2:37.*

Avenge *ekdikeo* (1556), *ek,* "from," *dike,* "justice," i.e., that which proceeds from justice, means (a) "to vindicate a person's right," (b) "to avenge a thing." With the meaning (a), it is used in the parable of the unjust judge, **Luke 18:3, 5**, of the "vindication" of the rights of the widow; with the meaning (b) it is used in Rev. 6:10 and 19:2, of the act of God in "avenging" the blood of the saints; in 2 Cor. 10:6, of the apostle's readiness to use his apostolic authority in punishing disobedience on the part of his readers; here the RV substitutes "avenge" for the KJV, "revenge"; in Rom. 12:19 of "avenging" oneself, against which the believer is warned.

Adversary *see Luke 12:58.*

18:4 And he would not for a while: but afterward he said within himself, Though I fear not God, nor regard man;

While *see Luke 8:13.*

Regard *see* Regarded at *Luke 18:2.*

18:5 Yet because this widow troubleth me, I will avenge her, lest by her continual coming she weary me.

Widow *see Luke 2:37.*

Troubleth *see* Trouble at *Luke 11:7.*

Avenge *see Luke 18:3.*

Continual The following phrases contain *telos* (the word itself coming under one or other of the above): *eis telos,* "unto the end," e.g., Matt. 10:22; 24:13; **Luke 18:5**, "continual"; John 13:1; 2 Cor. 3:13, "on the end" (RV); *heos telous,* "unto the end," 1 Cor. 1:8; 2 Cor. 1:13; *achri telous,* "even to the end" (a stronger expression than the preceding); Heb. 6:11; Rev. 2:26 (where "even" might well have been added); *mechri telous,* with much the same meaning as *achri telous,* Heb. 3:6, 14.

Weary *hupopiazo* (5299), lit., "to strike under the eye" (from *hupopion,* "the part of the face below the eye"; *hupo,* "under," *ops,* "an eye"), hence, to beat the face black and blue (to give a black eye), is used metaphorically, and translated "buffet" in 1 Cor. 9:27 (KJV, "keep under"), of Paul's suppressive treatment of his body, in order to keep himself spiritually fit (RV marg., "bruise") and is translated "wear (me) out" in **Luke 18:5**, RV (KJV, "weary"). For this and the somewhat different application in 1 Cor. 9:27.

18:6 And the Lord said, Hear what the unjust judge saith.

Unjust *see Luke 16:8. See also* **Iniquity** at *Luke 13:27.*

Judge *see* **Judges** at *Luke 11:19.*

18:7 And shall not God avenge his own elect, which cry day and night unto him, though he bear long with them?

Avenge *ekdikesis* (1557), vengeance," is used with the verb *poieo,* "to make," i.e., to avenge, in **Luke 18:7-8**; Acts 7:24; twice it is used in statements that "vengeance" belongs to God, Rom. 12:19; Heb. 10:30. In 2 Thess. 1:8 it is said of the act of divine justice which will be meted out to those who know not God and obey not the gospel, when the Lord comes in flaming fire at His second advent. In the divine exercise of judgment there is no element of vindictiveness, nothing by way of taking revenge. In **Luke 21:22**, it is used of the "days of vengeance" upon the Jewish people; in 1 Pet. 2:14, of civil governors as those who are sent of God "for vengeance on evildoers" (KJV, "punishment"); in 2 Cor. 7:11, of the "self-avenging" of believers, in their godly sorrow for wrong doing, RV, "avenging," for KJV, "revenge."

Elect *eklektos* (1588), lit. signifies "picked out, chosen" (*ek,* "from," *lego,* "to gather, pick out"), and is used of (a) Christ, the "chosen" of God, as the Messiah, **Luke 23:35**, and metaphorically as a "living Stone," "a chief corner Stone," 1 Pet. 2:4, 6; some mss. have it in John 1:34, instead of *huios,* "Son"; (b) angels, 1 Tim. 5:21, as "chosen" to be of especially high rank in administrative association with God, or as His messengers to human beings, doubtless in contrast to fallen angels (see 2 Pet. 2:4 and Jude 6); (c) believers (Jews or Gentiles), Matt. 24:22, 24, 31; Mark 13:20, 22, 27; **Luke 18:7**; Rom. 8:33; Col. 3:12; 2 Tim. 2:10; Titus 1:1; 1 Pet. 1:1; 2:9 (as a spiritual race); Matt. 20:16; 22:14 and Rev. 17:14, "chosen"; individual believers are so mentioned in Rom. 16:13; 2 John 1, 13. Believers were "chosen" "before the foundation of the world" (cf. "before times eternal," 2 Tim. 1:9), in Christ, Eph. 1:4, to adoption, Eph. 1:5; good works, 2:10; conformity to Christ, Rom. 8:29; salvation from the delusions of the Antichrist and the doom of the deluded, 2 Thess. 2:13; eternal glory, Rom. 9:23. The source of their "election" is God's grace, not human will, Eph. 1:4, 5; Rom. 9:11; 11:5. They are given by God the Father to Christ as the fruit of His death, all being foreknown and foreseen by God, John 17:6 and Rom. 8:29. While Christ's death was sufficient for all men, and is effective in the case of the "elect," yet men are treated as responsible, being capable of the will and power to choose. For the rendering "being chosen as firstfruits," an alternative reading in 2 Thess. 2:13.

> *"Pray as you can, and do not try to pray as you can't."*
>
> JOHN CHAPMAN

Cry *see* **Crying** at *Luke 3:4.*

Though *kai* In some passages *kai* has the meaning "and yet," e.g., Matt. 3:14, "and yet comest Thou to me?"; 6:26, "and yet (RV 'and,' KJV, 'yet') your Heavenly Father feedeth them"; **Luke 18:7**, "and yet He is longsuffering"; John 3:19, "and yet men loved the darkness"; 4:20, "and yet we say"; 6:49, "and yet they died"; 1 Cor. 5:2, "and yet ye are puffed up"; 1 John 2:9, "and yet hateth his brother." The same is probably the case in John 7:30, "and yet no man laid hands on Him", some rule this and similar cases out because of the negative in the sentence following the *kai,* but that seems hardly tenable.

Bear long *makrothumeo* (3114), "to be long-tempered" (*makros,* "long," *thumos,* "temper"), is translated "is longsuffering over" in **Luke 18:7**, RV (KJV, "bear long with").

18:8 I tell you that he will avenge them speedily. Nevertheless when the Son of man cometh, shall he find faith on the earth?

Speedily For "speedily," *en tachei*, in Luke 18:8.

Earth *see* Land at *Luke 4:25*.

18:9 And he spake this parable unto certain which trusted in themselves that they were righteous, and despised others:

Trusted *see Luke 11:22*.

Despised *exoutheneo* (1848), "to make of no account" (*ex*, "out," *oudeis*, "nobody," alternatively written, *outheis*), "to regard as nothing, to despise utterly, to treat with contempt." This is usually translated to "set at nought," **Luke 18:9**, RV, KJV, "despised." So in Rom. 14:3. Both have "set at nought" in **Luke 23:11**; Acts 4:11; Rom. 14:10. Both have "despise" in 1 Cor. 16:11; Gal. 4:14, and 1 Thess. 5:20; in 2 Cor. 10:10, RV, "of no account," for KJV, "contemptible"; in 1 Cor. 1:28, KJV and RV, "despised."

Others *see Luke 8:10*.

18:10 Two men went up into the temple to pray; the one a Pharisee, and the other a publican.

Publican *see* Publicans at *Luke 3:12*.

18:11 The Pharisee stood and prayed thus with himself, God, I thank thee, that I am not as other men *are*, extortioners, unjust, adulterers, or even as this publican.

Thus *touto*, the neuter of *houtos*, "this," is translated "thus" in 2 Cor. 1:17; 5:14; Phil. 3:15; the neuter plural, *tauta*, "these things," e.g., in **Luke 18:11**; **19:28**; John 9:6; 11:43; 13:21; 20:14; Acts 19:41.

God *see Luke 1:35*.

Thank *see* Thanks at *Luke 1:3*.

Other *see* Others at *Luke 8:10*.

Extortioners *harpax* (727), "rapacious," is translated as a noun, "extortioners," in **Luke 18:11**; 1 Cor. 5:10-11; 6:10; in Matt. 7:15 "ravening" (of wolves). In the Sept., Gen. 49:27.

Unjust *adikos* (94), "not in conformity with *dike*, 'right,'" is rendered "unjust" in the KJV and RV in Matt. 5:45; **Luke 18:11**; Acts 24:15; elsewhere for the KJV "unjust" the RV has "unrighteous."

Adulterers *moichos* (3432), denotes one "who has unlawful intercourse with the spouse of another," **Luke 18:11**; 1 Cor. 6:9; Heb. 13:4.

Publican *see* **Publicans** at *Luke 3:12*.

18:12 I fast twice in the week, I give tithes of all that I possess.

Fast *see Luke 5:33*.

Twice *dis* (1364), occurs in Mark 14:30, 72; **Luke 18:12**; Jude 12; combined with *muriades*, "ten thousand," in Rev. 9:16; rendered "again" in Phil. 4:16 and 1 Thess. 2:18.

Week *sabbaton* (4521), is used (a) in the plural in the phrase "the first day of the week," Matt. 28:1; Mark 16:2, 9; **Luke 24:1**; John 20:1, 19; Acts 20:7; 1 Cor. 16:2; (b) in the singular, **Luke 18:12**, "twice in the week," lit., "twice of the sabbath," i.e., twice in the days after the sabbath.

Tithe *apodekateuo* (586), "to give tithes," in **Luke 18:12**. *See also Luke 11:42*.

Possess *ktaomai* (2932), "to procure for oneself, acquire, obtain," hence, "to possess," has this meaning in **Luke 18:12** and 1 Thess. 4:4; in **Luke 21:19**, RV, "ye shall win" (KJV, "possess ye"), where the probable meaning is "ye shall gain the mastery over your souls," i.e., instead of giving way to adverse circumstances.

18:13 And the publican, standing afar off, would not lift up so much as *his* eyes unto heaven, but smote upon his breast, saying, God be merciful to me a sinner.

Publican *see* Publicans at *Luke 3:12*.

Lift *see* Lifted at *Luke 6:20*.

Smote *see* Smiteth at *Luke 6:29*.

Breast *stethos* (4738), connected with *histemi*, "to stand," i.e., that which stands out, is used of mourners in smiting the "breast," **Luke 18:13**; **23:48**; of John in reclining on the "breast" of Christ, John 13:25; 21:20; of the "breasts" of the angels in Rev. 15:6.

God *see Luke 1:35*.

Merciful *hilaskomai* (2433), in profane Greek meant "to conciliate, appease, propitiate, cause the gods to be reconciled"; their goodwill was not regarded as their natural condition, but as something to be earned. The heathen believed their gods to be naturally alienated in feeling from man. In the NT the word never means to conciliate God; it signifies (a) "to be propitious, merciful," **Luke 18:13**, in the prayer of the publican; (b) "to expiate, make propitiation for," Heb. 2:17, "make propitiation."

18:14 I tell you, this man went down to his house justified *rather* than the other: for every one that exalteth himself shall be abased; and he that humbleth himself shall be exalted.

Other *see Luke 11:42*.

Exalteth, Exalted *see* Exalted at *Luke 1:52*.

Abased *see* Brought low at *Luke 3:5*.

18:15 And they brought unto him also infants, that he would touch them: but when *his* disciples saw *it*, they rebuked them.

Infants *see* Babe at *Luke 1:41*.

Rebuked *see Luke 4:35*.

18:16 But Jesus called them *unto him*, and said, Suffer little children to come unto me, and forbid them not: for of such is the kingdom of God.

Suffer *see* Suffered at Luke *8:51*.

18:17 Verily I say unto you, Whosoever shall not receive the kingdom of God as a little child shall in no wise enter therein.

Receive *see* Took at *Luke 2:28*.

18:18 And a certain ruler asked him, saying, Good Master, what shall I do to inherit eternal life?

Ruler *see Luke 8:41*.

Inherit *see Luke 10:25*.

18:19 And Jesus said unto him, Why callest thou me good? none *is* good, save one, *that is*, God.

Good *see Luke 1:53*.

One *see Luke 4:40*.

18:20 Thou knowest the commandments, Do not commit adultery, Do not kill, Do not steal, Do not bear false witness, Honour thy father and thy mother.

Adultery *see Luke 16:18*.

Kill *phoneuo* (5407), "to murder," akin to *phoneus*, "a murderer," is always rendered by the verb "to kill" (except in Matt. 19:18, KJV, "do ... murder," and in Matt. 23:35, KJV and RV, "ye slew"); Matt. 5:21 (twice); 23:31; Mark 10:19; **Luke 18:20**; Rom. 13:9; Jas. 2:11 (twice); 4:2; 5:6.

Steal *klepto* (2813), "to steal," akin to *kleptes*, "a thief" (cf. Eng., "kleptomania"), occurs in Matt. 6:19, 20; 19:18; 27:64; 28:13; Mark 10:19; **Luke 18:20**; John 10:10; Rom. 2:21 (twice); 13:9; Eph. 4:28 (twice).

Witness *pseudomartureo* (5576), "to bear false witness" (*pseudes*, "false"), occurs in Matt. 19:18; Mark 10:19; 14:56, 57; **Luke 18:20**; in some texts, Rom. 13:9.

Honour *timao* (5091), "to honor," is used of (a) valuing Christ at a price, Matt. 27:9; (b) "honoring" a person: (1) the "honor" done by Christ to the Father, John 8:49; (2) "honor" bestowed by the Father upon him who serves Christ, John 12:26; (3) the duty of all to "honor" the Son equally with the Father, 5:23; (4) the duty of children to "honor" their parents, Matt. 15:4; 19:19; Mark 7:10; 10:19; **Luke 18:20**; Eph. 6:2; (5) the duty of Christians to "honor" the king, and all men, 1 Pet. 2:17; (6) the respect and material assistance to be given to widows "that are widows indeed," 1 Tim. 5:3; (7) the "honor" done to Paul and his companions by the inhabitants of Melita, Acts 28:10; (8) mere lip profession of "honor" to God, Matt. 15:8; Mark 7:6.

18:21 And he said, All these have I kept from my youth up.

Kept *see* Keeping at *Luke 2:8*.

Youth *neotes* (3503), from *neos*, "new," occurs in Mark 10:20; **Luke 18:21**; Acts 26:4; 1 Tim. 4:12 (in some mss., Matt. 19:20).

18:22 Now when Jesus heard these things, he said unto him, Yet lackest thou one thing: sell all that thou hast, and distribute unto the poor, and thou shalt have treasure in heaven: and come, follow me.

Lackest *leipo* (3007), "to leave," denotes (a) transitively, in the passive voice, "to be left behind, to lack," Jas. 1:4, "ye may be lacking in (nothing)," RV (KJV, "wanting"); v. 5, "lacketh" (KJV, "lack"); 2:15, RV, "be ... in lack" (KJV, "be ... destitute"); (b) intransitively, active voice, **Luke 18:22**, "(one thing thou) lackest," is, lit., "(one thing) is lacking (to thee)"; Titus 1:5, "(the things) that were wanting"; 3:13, "(that nothing) be wanting."

Distribute *see* Divideth at *Luke 11:22*.

Poor *see Luke 6:20*.

Treasure *see Luke 6:45*.

Come *deuro*, "hither, here," is used (sometimes with verbs of motion) in the singular number, in calling a person to come, Matt. 19:21; Mark 10:21; **Luke 18:22**; John 11:43; Acts 7:3, 34; Rev. 17:1; 21:9.

18:23 And when he heard this, he was very sorrowful: for he was very rich.

Sorrowful *perilupos* (4036), "very sad, deeply grieved" (*peri*, intensive), is used in Matt. 26:38 and Mark 14:34, "exceeding sorrowful"; Mark 6:26; **Luke 18:23** (v. **24** in some mss.).

Very *sphodra* (4970), properly the neuter plural of *sphodros*, "excessive, violent" (from a root indicating restlessness), signifies "very, very much, exceedingly," Matt. 2:10; 17:6, "sore"; 17:23; 18:31, RV, "exceeding," for KJV, "very"; 19:25; 26:22; 27:54, RV, "exceedingly" for KJV, "greatly"; Mark 16:4, "very"; **Luke 18:23** (ditto); Acts 6:7, RV, "exceedingly," for KJV, greatly; Rev. 16:21.

Rich *see Luke 6:24*.

18:24 And when Jesus saw that he was very sorrowful, he said, How hardly shall they that have riches enter into the kingdom of God!

Sorrowful *see Luke 18:23.*

Hardly *duskolos* (1423), is used in Matt. 19:23; Mark 10:23; **Luke 18:24** of the danger of riches.

Riches *chrema* (5536), lit., "a thing that one uses" (akin to *chraomai* "to use"), hence, (a) "wealth, riches," Mark 10:23, 24; **Luke 18:24**; (b) "money," Acts 4:37, singular number, "a sum of money"; plural in 8:18, 20; 24:26.

Enter *see Luke 8:16.*

18:25 For it is easier for a camel to go through a needle's eye, than for a rich man to enter into the kingdom of God.

Easier *see Luke 5:23.*

Needle *belone* (956), akin to *belos*, "a dart," denotes a sharp point, hence, "a needle," **Luke 18:25.**

Eye *trumalia* (5168), is used of the "eye" of a needle, Mark 10:25 (from *trume*, "a hole," *truo*, "to wear away"). Cf. *trema*, "a hole, perforation," Matt. 19:24 (some texts have *trupema*, "a hole," from *trupao*, "to bore a hole") and **Luke 18:25**, as in the most authentic mss. (some texts have *trumalia* here).

Rich *see Luke 6:24.*

Enter *see* Go in at *Luke 8:51.*

18:26-27 And they that heard *it* said, Who then can be saved?
And he said, The things which are impossible with men are possible with God.

Impossible *adunatos* (102), from *a*, negative, and *dunatos*, "able, strong," is used (a) of persons, Acts 14:8, "impotent"; figuratively, Rom. 15:1, "weak"; (b) of things, "impossible," Matt. 19:26; Mark 10:27; **Luke 18:27**; Heb. 6:4, 18; 10:4; 11:6; in Rom. 8:3, "for what the Law could not do," is, more lit., "the inability of the law"; the meaning may be either "the weakness of the Law," or "that which was impossible for the Law"; the latter is perhaps preferable; literalism is ruled out here, but the sense is that the Law could neither justify nor impart life.

Possible *dunatos* (1415), "strong, mighty, powerful, able (to do)," in its neuter form signifies "possible," Matt. 19:26; 24:24; 26:39; Mark 9:23; 10:27; 13:22; 14:35, 36; **Luke 18:27**; Acts 2:24; 20:16 (27:39, in some mss; *dunamai*, "to be able," in the most authentic, RV, "they could"); Rom. 12:18; Gal. 4:15.

18:28-30 Then Peter said, Lo, we have left all, and followed thee.
And he said unto them, Verily I say unto you, There is no man that hath left house, or parents, or brethren, or wife, or children, for the kingdom of God's sake,
Who shall not receive manifold more in this present time, and in the world to come life everlasting.

Receive *lambano* (2983), denotes either "to take" or "to receive," (I) literally, (a) without an object, in contrast to asking, e.g., Matt. 7:8; Mark 11:24, RV, "have received" (the original has no object); (b) in contrast to giving, e.g., Matt. 10:8; Acts 20:35; (c) with objects, whether things, e.g., Mark 10:30; **Luke 18:30**, in the best mss. (some have *apolambano*); John 13:30; Acts 9:19, RV, "took" (KJV, "received"); 1 Cor. 9:25, RV, "receive" (KJV, "obtain"); or persons, e.g., John 6:21; 13:20; 16:14, RV, "take"; 2 John 10; in Mark 14:65, RV, "received (Him with blows of their hands)"; this has been styled a vulgarism; (II) metaphorically, of the word of God, Matt. 13:20; Mark 4:16; the sayings of Christ, John 12:48; the witness of Christ, John 3:11; a hundredfold in this life, and eternal life in the world to come, Mark 10:30; mercy, Heb. 4:16, RV, "may receive" (KJV, "may obtain"); a person (*prosopon*), **Luke 20:21**, "acceptest," and Gal. 2:6, "accepteth," an expression used in the OT either in the sense of being gracious or kind to a person, e.g., Gen. 19:21; 32:20, or (negatively) in the sense of being impartial, e.g., Lev. 19:15; Deut. 10:17; this latter is the meaning in the two NT passages just mentioned. *See also* ***Luke 6:34.***

Manifold *pollaplasion* (4179), "many times more" (from *polus*, "much"), occurs in **Luke 18:30**, "manifold more," and in many ancient authorities in Matt. 19:29 (RV, marg.; some editions in text); KJV and RV text "a hundredfold," translating *hekatontaplasiona*.

Time *kairos* (2540), primarily "due measure, due proportion," when used of "time," signified "a fixed or definite period, a season," sometimes an opportune or seasonable "time," e.g., Rom. 5:6, RV, "season"; Gal. 6:10, "opportunity." In Mark 10:30 and **Luke 18:30**, "this time" (*kairos*), i.e., "in this lifetime," is contrasted with "the coming age." In 1 Thess. 5:1, "the times and the seasons," "times" (*chronos*) refers to the duration of the interval previous to the Parousia of Christ and the length of "time" it will occupy, as well as other periods; "seasons" refers to the characteristics of these periods.

18:31-32 Then he took *unto him* the twelve, and said unto them, Behold, we go up to Jerusalem, and all things that are written by

the prophets concerning the Son of man shall be accomplished.

For he shall be delivered unto the Gentiles, and shall be mocked, and spitefully entreated, and spitted on:

Mocked *see* Mock at *Luke 14:29.*

Spitefully *see* Reproachest at *Luke 11:45.*

Spitted *emptuo* (1716), "to spit upon," occurs in Matt. 26:67; 27:30; Mark 10:34; 14:65; 15:19; **Luke 18:32**. In the Sept., Num. 12:14, in some texts; Deut. 25:9.

18:33 And they shall scourge *him*, and put him to death: and the third day he shall rise again.

Scourge In John 19:1 the "scourging" of Christ is described by *mastigoo*, as also in His prophecy of His sufferings, Matt. 20:19; Mark 10:34; **Luke 18:33**. In Acts 22:25 the similar punishment about to be administered to Paul is described by *mastizo* (the "scourging" of Roman citizens was prohibited by the Porcian law of 197 BC).

Death *apokteino* (615), to kill, is so translated in the RV, for the KJV, "put to death," in Mark 14:1; **Luke 18:33**; in John 11:53; 12:10 and 18:31, RV, "put to death."

Third *see Luke 9:22.*

Rise *see* Rose at *Luke 4:29.*

18:34 And they understood none of these things: and this saying was hid from them, neither knew they the things which were spoken.

Understood *see* Known at *Luke 7:39.*

Saying *see* Sayings at *Luke 1:65.*

Hid *krupto* (2928), "to cover, conceal, keep secret" (Eng., "crypt," "cryptic," etc.), is used (a) in its physical significance, e.g., Matt. 5:14; 13:44; 25:18; (b) metaphorically, e.g., Matt. 11:25; 13:35, RV, "(things) hidden"; KJV, "(things) which have been kept secret"; **Luke 18:34**; **19:42**; John 19:38, "secretly."

18:35 And it came to pass, that as he was come nigh unto Jericho, a certain blind man sat by the way side begging:

Come nigh *see* Came nigh at *Luke 7:12.*

Begging *prosaiteo* (4319), lit., "to ask besides" (*pros*, "towards," used intensively, and *aiteo*), "to ask earnestly, to importune, continue asking," is said of the blind beggar in John 9:8. In Mark 10:46 and **Luke 18:35** certain mss. have this verb; the most authentic have *prosaites*, "a beggar," a word used in John 9:8, as well as the verb (see the RV).

18:36 And hearing the multitude pass by, he asked what it meant.

Pass by *diaporeuo* (1279), "to carry over," used in the passive voice with the meaning "to pass by, to journey through," is translated "in my journey," in Rom. 15:24, lit., "journeying through"; in **Luke 18:36**, RV, "going by" (KJV "pass by"). *See also* Went at *Luke 6:1.*

Asked *see Luke 15:26.*

Meant *see Luke 15:26.*

18:37 And they told him, that Jesus of Nazareth passeth by.

Passeth *see* Pass at *Luke 11:42.*

18:38 And he cried, saying, Jesus, *thou* Son of David, have mercy on me.

Cried *see* Crying at *Luke 3:4.*

18:39 And they which went before rebuked him, that he should hold his peace: but he cried so much the more, *Thou* Son of David, have mercy on me.

Rebuked *see Luke 4:35.*

Peace *see* Close at *Luke 9:36.*

18:40 And Jesus stood, and commanded him to be brought unto him: and when he was come near, he asked him,

Commanded *keleuo* (2753), "to urge, incite, order," suggests a stronger injunction, Matt. 14:9, 19; 15:35; 18:25; 27:58, 64; **Luke 18:40**; Acts 4:15 (frequently in Acts, not subsequently in the NT).

Near *engizo* (1448), transitively, "to bring near" (not in NT; in the Sept., e.g., Gen. 48:10; Isa. 5:8); intransitively, "to draw near," e.g., Matt. 21:34; **Luke 18:40**; **19:41**, RV, "draw nigh."

18:41 Saying, What wilt thou that I shall do unto thee? And he said, Lord, that I may receive my sight.

Sight *anablepo* (308), "to look up," also denotes "to receive or recover sight," e.g., Matt. 11:5; 20:34; Mark 10:51, 52; **Luke 18:41-43**; John 9:11, 15, 18 (twice); Acts 9:12, 17, 18; 22:13.

18:42-43 And Jesus said unto him, Receive thy sight: thy faith hath saved thee.

And immediately he received his sight, and followed him, glorifying God: and all the people, when they saw *it*, gave praise unto God.

Immediately *see Luke 1:64.*

Praise *ainos* (136), primarily "a tale, narration," came to denote "praise"; in the NT only of praise to God, Matt. 21:16; **Luke 18:43**.

Chapter 19

19:1 And *Jesus* entered and passed through Jericho.

Passed *see* Pierce at *Luke 2:35.*

19:2 And, behold, *there was* a man named Zacchaeus, which was the chief among the publicans, and he was rich.

Named *see Luke 2:21.*

Chief *architelones* (754), denotes "a chief tax-collector, or publican," Luke 19:2.

Rich *see Luke 6:24.*

19:3 And he sought to see Jesus who he was; and could not for the press, because he was little of stature.

Press *see Luke 8:19.*

Little *see Luke 12:32.*

Stature *see Luke 2:52.*

19:4 And he ran before, and climbed up into a sycomore tree to see him: for he was to pass that *way*.

Ran before *protrecho* (4390), primarily, "to run forward" (*pro*, "forward" or "before," *trecho*, "to run"), is used with *tachion*, "more quickly," in John 20:4, "outran," RV (KJV, "did outrun"), lit., "ran forward more quickly"; in **Luke 19:4**, "he ran on before," RV (KJV, "ran before"). In the Sept., 1 Sam. 8:11; in some texts, Job 41:13, "destruction runneth before him," in the Eng. versions, v. 22.

Climbed up *anabaino* (305), "to ascend," is used of climbing up, in **Luke 19:4** and John 10:1.

Sycomore *sukomorea* (4509), occurs in **Luke 19:4**. This tree is of the fig species, with leaves like the mulberry and fruit like the fig. It is somewhat less in height than the sycamine and spreads to cover an area from 60 to 80 feet in diameter. It is often planted by the roadside, and was suitable for the purpose of Zacchaeus. Seated on the lowest branch he was easily within speaking distance of Christ.

Was *see Luke 7:6.*

Pass *see* Pierce at *Luke 2:35.*

Way *see Luke 5:19.*

19:5 And when Jesus came to the place, he looked up, and saw him, and said unto him, Zacchaeus, make haste, and come down; for to day I must abide at thy house.

Haste *see Luke 2:16.*

Must *see Luke 2:49.*

19:6 And he made haste, and came down, and received him joyfully.

Haste *see Luke 2:16.*

Received *see Luke 10:38.*

Joyfully *chairo* (5463), "to rejoice, be glad," is translated "joyfully" in **Luke 19:6**, lit., "rejoicing"; "we joyed," 2 Cor. 7:13; "I joy," Phil. 2:17; "do ye joy," 2:18; "joying," Col. 2:5; "we joy," 1 Thess. 3:9. It is contrasted with weeping and sorrow, e.g., in John 16:20, 22; Rom. 12:15; 1 Cor. 7:30 (cf. Ps. 30:5). *See also* Rejoice at *Luke 1:14.*

19:7 And when they saw *it*, they all murmured, saying, That he was gone to be guest with a man that is a sinner.

Murmured *see Luke 15:2.*

Guest For *kataluo*, "to unloose," rendered "to be a guest" in **Luke 19:7**, KJV, (RV, "to lodge", *see Luke 9:12*).

Sinner *see Luke 7:37. See also* Sinful at *Luke 5:8.*

19:8 And Zacchaeus stood, and said unto the Lord; Behold, Lord, the half of my goods I give to the poor; and if I have taken any thing from any man by false accusation, I restore *him* fourfold.

Stood *see* Stand, Stood at *Luke 6:8.*

Half *hemisus* (2255), an adjective, is used (a) as such in the neuter plural, in **Luke 19:8**, lit., "the halves (of my goods)"; (b) as a noun, in the neuter sing., "the half," Mark 6:23; "half (a time)," Rev. 12:14; "a half," 11:9, 11, RV.

Goods *see Luke 11:21.*

Taken ... by false accusation *see* Accuse at *Luke 3:14.*

Restore *apodidomi* (591), "to give back," is translated "I restore" in **Luke 19:8**.

Fourfold *tetraploos* (5073), an adjective, is found in **Luke 19:8**.

19:9 And Jesus said unto him, This day is salvation come to this house, forsomuch as he also is a son of Abraham.

This day *see Luke 4:21.*

Salvation *see Luke 1:69.*

Forsomuch *see* Because at *Luke 1:7.*

19:10 For the Son of man is come to seek and to save that which was lost.

Save *see* Made ... whole at *Luke 8:48.*

Lost *see* Lose at *Luke 9:25.*

19:11 And as they heard these things, he added and spake a parable, because he was nigh to Jerusalem, and because they

thought that the kingdom of God should immediately appear.

Added *see* Increase at *Luke 17:5.*

Nigh *engus* (1451), "near, nigh," is used (a) of place, e.g., **Luke 19:11**, "nigh"; John 3:23; 11:54, "near"; 6:19, 23, "nigh"; metaphorically in Rom. 10:8; Eph. 2:13, 17, "nigh"; (b) of time, e.g., Matt. 24:32-33, "nigh"; so **Luke 21:30-31**; as a preposition, Heb. 6:8, "nigh unto (a curse)," and 8:13, "nigh unto (vanishing away)."

Should *mello* (3195), "to be about to," e.g., Mark 10:32, RV, "were to"; **Luke 19:11**, RV, "was to"; "should" in **22:23**; **24:21**; John 6:71; 7:39, RV, "were to"; 11:51; 12:4, 33; 18:32; Acts 11:28; 23:27, RV, "was about (to be slain)"; 1 Thess. 3:4, RV, "are to"; Rev. 6:11.

Immediately *see Luke 1:64.*

Appear *anaphaino* (398), *ana*, "forth, or up," perhaps originally a nautical term, "to come up into view," hence, in general, "to appear suddenly," is used in the passive voice, in **Luke 19:11**, of the Kingdom of God; active voice, in Acts 21:3, "to come in sight of," RV; "having sighted" would be a suitable rendering (KJV, "having discovered").

19:12 He said therefore, A certain nobleman went into a far country to receive for himself a kingdom, and to return.

Nobleman *eugenes* (2104), an adjective, lit., "well born" (*eu*, "well," and *genos*, "a family, race"), (a) signifies "noble," 1 Cor. 1:26; (b) is used with *anthropos*, "a man," i.e., "a nobleman," in **Luke 19:12**. In the Sept., Job 1:3.

Far *see Luke 15:13.*

Country *see Luke 2:8.*

Return *see* Returned at *Luke 1:56.*

19:13 And he called his ten servants, and delivered them ten pounds, and said unto them, Occupy till I come.

Delivered *see Luke 7:15.*

Ten *deka* (1176), whence the Eng. prefix "deca-," is regarded by some as the measure of human responsibility, e.g., **Luke 19:13, 17**; Rev. 2:10; it is used in a figurative setting in Rev. 12:3; 13:1; 17:3, 7, 12, 16.

Pounds *mna* (3414), a Semitic word, both "a weight" and "a sum of money," 100 shekels (cf. 1 Kings 10:17, *maneh*; Dan. 5:25, 26, *mene*), in Attic Greek 100 *drachmai*, in weight about 15 oz., in value near about L/4 Is. 3d., occurs in **Luke 19:13, 16** (twice), **18** (twice), **20, 24** (twice), **25**.

Occupy *pragmateuomai* (4231), is rendered "trade ye" in **Luke 19:13**, RV, which adds "*herewith.*"

19:14 But his citizens hated him, and sent a message after him, saying, We will not have this *man* to reign over us.

Citizens *see* Citizen at *Luke 15:15.*

Hated *see* Hate at *Luke 6:22.*

Sent *see* Sendeth at *Luke 14:32.*

Message *see* Ambassage at *Luke 14:32.*

Reign *see Luke 1:33.*

19:15 And it came to pass, that when he was returned, having received the kingdom, then he commanded these servants to be called unto him, to whom he had given the money, that he might know how much every man had gained by trading.

Returned In **Luke 19:15**, KJV, *epanerchomai*, "to come back again" (RV) is translated "returned." *See also* Come at *Luke 10:35.*

Commanded *see* Command at *Luke 4:3.*

Called *see* Call at *Luke 14:12.*

Money *see Luke 9:3.*

Much In **Luke 19:15**, KJV, the pronoun *ti*, "what" (RV), is translated "how much."

Gained *diapragmateuomai* (1281), signifies "to gain by trading," **Luke 19:15** (from *dia*, "through," used intensively, and *pragmateuomai*, "to busy oneself, to be engaged in business").

Trading *diapragmateuomai* (1281), "to accomplish by traffic, to gain by trading," occurs in **Luke 19:15**.

19:16 Then came the first, saying, Lord, thy pound hath gained ten pounds.

Pound, Pounds *see* Pounds at *Luke 19:13.*

Gained In **Luke 19:16**, KJV, *prosergazomai*, "to work out in addition," or "to earn in addition," is translated "gained" (RV, "made"); in v. **18** the verb *poieo*, "to make," is translated in the same way, the English verb "make" standing both for "earning" and for "producing."

19:17 And he said unto him, Well, thou good servant: because thou hast been faithful in a very little, have thou authority over ten cities.

Well *eu* (2095), primarily the neuter of an old word, *eus*, "noble, good," is used (a) with verbs, e.g., Mark 14:7, "do (*poieo*) ... good"; Acts 15:29 (*prasso*); Eph. 6:3 (*ginomai*, "to be"); (b) in replies, "good," "well done," Matt. 25:21, 23; in **Luke 19:17**, *eu ge* (in the best texts). The word is the opposite of *kakos*, "evilly."

Good *see Luke 1:53.*

Little *elachistos* (1646), is translated "a very little" in Luke 19:17. *See also* Least at *Luke 12:26*.

Ten *see Luke 19:13*.

19:18 And the second came, saying, Lord, thy pound hath gained five pounds.

Pound, Pounds *see* Pounds at *Luke 19:13*.

Gained *see Luke 19:16*. *See also* Make at *Luke 5:34*.

19:19 And he said likewise to him, Be thou also over five cities.

Likewise *see Luke 3:14*.

19:20 And another came, saying, Lord, behold, *here is* thy pound, which I have kept laid up in a napkin:

Pound *see* Pounds at Luke *19:13*.

Have *see Luke 12:4*.

Kept *echo* (2192), "to have, to hold," is rendered "I kept" in **Luke 19:20**, RV (KJV, "I have kept"), of "keeping" a pound laid up in a napkin.

Laid *apokeimai* (606), "to be laid away, or up," is used of money in a napkin, **Luke 19:20**; metaphorically, of a hope, Col. 1:5; the crown of righteousness, 2 Tim. 4:8. In Heb. 9:27, said of physical death, it is translated "it is appointed" (RV marg., "laid up").

Napkin *soudarion* (4676), is translated "napkin" in **Luke 19:20**; John 11:44; 20:7. In **Luke 19:20** the reference may be to a towel or any kind of linen cloth or even a sort of headdress, any of which might be used for concealing money.

19:21 For I feared thee, because thou art an austere man: thou takest up that thou layedst not down, and reapest that thou didst not sow.

Austere *austeros* (840), akin to *auo*, "to dry up" (Eng., "austere"), primarily denotes "stringent to the taste," like new wine not matured by age, unripe fruit, etc., hence, "harsh, severe," **Luke 19:21-22**.

Layedst *see* Laid at *Luke 1:66*.

Reapest *see* Reap at *Luke 12:24*.

Sow *speiro* (4687), "to sow seed," is used (1) literally, especially in the Synoptic Gospels; elsewhere, 1 Cor. 15:36, 37; 2 Cor. 9:10, "the sower", (2) metaphorically, (a) in proverbial sayings, e.g., Matt. 13:3, 4; **Luke 19:21, 22**; John 4:37; 2 Cor. 9:6; (b) in the interpretation of parables, e.g., Matt. 13:19-23 (in these vv., RV, "was sown," for KJV, "received seed"); (c) otherwise as follows: of "sowing" spiritual things in preaching and teaching, 1 Cor. 9:11; of the interment of the bodies of deceased believers, 1 Cor. 15:42-44; of ministering to the necessities of others in things temporal (the harvest being proportionate to the "sowing"), 2 Cor. 9:6, 10; of "sowing" to the flesh, Gal. 6:7, 8 ("that" in v. 7 is emphatic, "that and that only," what was actually "sown"); in v. 8, *eis*, "unto," signifies "in the interests of"; of the "fruit of righteousness" by peacemakers, Jas. 3:18.

19:22 And he saith unto him, Out of thine own mouth will I judge thee, *thou* wicked servant. Thou knewest that I was an austere man, taking up that I laid not down, and reaping that I did not sow:

Mouth *see Luke 1:64*.

Wicked *see* Evil at *Luke 11:4*.

Laid *see Luke 1:66*.

Reaping *see* Reap at *Luke 12:24*.

Sow *see Luke 19:21*.

19:23 Wherefore then gavest not thou my money into the bank, that at my coming I might have required mine own with usury?

Wherefore Some phrases introduced by the preposition *dia*, "on account of," *dia touto*, "on account of this," e.g., Matt. 12:31; Rom. 5:12; Eph. 1:15; 3 John 10; *dia hen* (the accusative feminine of *hos*, "who"), "on account of which" (*aitia*, "a cause," being understood), e.g., Acts 10:21 (with *aitia*, expressed, Titus 1:13; Heb. 2:11); *dia ti* "on account of what?" (sometimes as one word, *diati*) e.g., **Luke 19:23**; Rom. 9:32; 2 Cor. 11:11; Rev. 17:7.

Money *see Luke 9:3*.

Bank *trapeza* (5132), primarily "a table," denotes (a) an eating-table, e.g., Matt. 15:27; (b) food, etc., placed on "a table," Acts 6:2; 16:34; (c) "a feast, a banquet," 1 Cor. 10:21; (d) "the table or stand" of a moneychanger, where he exchanged money for a fee, or dealt with loans and deposits, Matt. 21:12; Mark 11:15; **Luke 19:23**; John 2:15. *See also* Table at *Luke 16:21*.

Required *prasso* (4238), "to do, practice, perform," is used financially in the sense of "exacting" payment, in **Luke 19:23**. *See also* Exact at *Luke 3:13*.

Usury *tokos* (5110), primarily "a bringing forth, birth" (from *tikto*, "to beget"), then, "an offspring," is used metaphorically of the produce of money lent out, "interest," usury, Matt. 25:27; **Luke 19:23**The RV, "interest," Matt. 25:27; **Luke 19:23**, is the preferable rendering of *tokos* here.

19:24 And he said unto them that stood by, Take from him the pound, and give *it* to him that hath ten pounds.

Stood *see* Stand at *Luke 1:19*.

Pound, Pounds *see* Pounds at *Luke 19:13*.

19:25 (And they said unto him, Lord, he hath ten pounds.)

Pounds *see Luke 19:13*.

19:26-27 For I say unto you, That unto every one which hath shall be given; and from him that hath not, even that he hath shall be taken away from him.

But those mine enemies, which would not that I should reign over them, bring hither, and slay *them* before me.

Enemies *see Luke 1:71*.

Reign *see Luke 1:33*.

Slay *katasphazo* (2695V), "to kill off," is used in Luke 19:27. In the Sept., Ezek. 16:40; Zech. 11:5.

Before *see* Sight at *Luke 10:21*.

19:28 And when he had thus spoken, he went before, ascending up to Jerusalem.

Thus *see Luke 18:11*.

Went *see* Go at *Luke 17:7*.

Before *see* Sight at *Luke 10:21*.

19:29 And it came to pass, when he was come nigh to Bethphage and Bethany, at the mount called *the mount* of Olives, he sent two of his disciples,

Nigh *see Luke 7:12*.

Mount *see* Mountain at *Luke 3:5*.

Olives *elaion* (1638), "an olive grove" or "olive garden," the ending—*on*, as in this class of noun, here indicates "a place set with trees of the kind designated by the primitive" (Thayer); hence it is applied to the Mount of Olives, Luke 19:29; 21:37; Acts 1:12 ("Olivet"): in the first two of these and in Mark 11:1.

19:30 Saying, Go ye into the village over against *you*; in the which at your entering ye shall find a colt tied, whereon yet never man sat: loose him, and bring *him hither*.

Over against *katenanti* (2713), *kata*, "down," with *enanti*, lit., "down over against," is used (a) of locality, e.g., Mark 11:2; 13:3; Luke 19:30; (b) as "in the sight of," Rom. 4:17; in most mss. in 2 Cor. 2:17; 12:19.

Entering *see* Enter at *Luke 8:16*.

Tied *deo* (1210), "to bind," is rendered "to tie" in Matt. 21:2; Mark 11:2, 4; Luke 19:30.

Never *popote* follows *oudeis*, "no one," in the dative case ("to no man") in John 8:33, RV, "never yet" (KJV, "never"); so in Luke 19:30, where *oudeis* is in the nominative case, RV, "no man ever yet" (KJV, "yet never man").

19:31 And if any man ask you, Why do ye loose *him*? thus shall ye say unto him, Because the Lord hath need of him.

Thus *see Luke 1:25*.

Lord *see Luke 5:8*.

19:32 And they that were sent went their way, and found even as he had said unto them.

Way *aperchomai*, "to go away," is rendered "to go one's way," e.g., Matt. 13:25; 20:4; Mark 11:4; 12:12; Luke 19:32; John 11:46; Acts 9:17; Jas. 1:24.

19:33 And as they were loosing the colt, the owners thereof said unto them, Why loose ye the colt?

Owners *kurios* (2962), "one having power" (*kuros*) or "authority, a lord, master," signifies "an owner" in Luke 19:33. *See also* Lord at *Luke 5:8*.

19:34-35 And they said, The Lord hath need of him.

And they brought him to Jesus: and they cast their garments upon the colt, and they set Jesus thereon.

Cast *epiripto* (1977), "to cast upon," (a) lit., "of casting garments on a colt," Luke 19:35; (b) figuratively, "of casting care upon God," 1 Pet. 5:7.

Set *see Luke 10:34*.

19:36 And as he went, they spread their clothes in the way.

Spread *hupostronnuo* (5291), "to spread under" (*hupo*), of clothes, is used in Luke 19:36.

19:37 And when he was come nigh, even now at the descent of the mount of Olives, the whole multitude of the disciples began to rejoice and praise God with a loud voice for all the mighty works that they had seen;

Nigh *see Luke 7:12*.

Descent *katabasis* (2600), denotes "a going down," a way down," Luke 19:37.

Mount *see* Mountain at *Luke 3:5*.

Olives *elaia* (1636), denotes (a) "an olive tree," Rom. 11:17, 24; Rev. 11:4 (plural); the Mount of Olives was so called from the numerous olive trees there, and indicates the importance attached to such; the

Mount is mentioned in the NT in connection only with the Lord's life on earth, Matt. 21:1; 24:3; 26:30; Mark 11:1; 13:3; 14:26; **Luke 19:37**; **22:39**; John 8:1; (b) "an olive," Jas. 3:12, RV (KJV, "olive berries").

Whole *hapas* (537), is rendered "the whole," e.g., in **Luke 19:37**; **23:1**.

Multitude *see Luke 1:10*.

Praise *see Luke 2:13*.

19:38 Saying, Blessed *be* the King that cometh in the name of the Lord: peace in heaven, and glory in the highest.

Highest *see Luke 2:14*.

19:39 And some of the Pharisees from among the multitude said unto him, Master, rebuke thy disciples.

Rebuke *see* Rebuked at *Luke 4:35*.

19:40 And he answered and said unto them, I tell you that, if these should hold their peace, the stones would immediately cry out.

Peace *see* Dumb at *Luke 1:20*.

19:41 And when he was come near, he beheld the city, and wept over it,

Near *see Luke 18:40*.

19:42 Saying, If thou hadst known, even thou, at least in this thy day, the things *which belong* unto thy peace! but now they are hid from thine eyes.

Least In **Luke 19:42**, the adverbial phrase *kai ge*, "at least," is found in some mss.; the RV follows those in which it is absent.

Day *see* Years at *Luke 1:18*.

Belong This word represents (a) a phrase consisting of *eimi*, "to be," with or without a preposition and a noun, and usually best rendered, as in the RV, by the verb "to be," Mark 9:41, lit., "ye are of Christ"; **Luke 23:7** and Heb. 5:14; cf. Rom. 12:19, "belongeth unto Me," RV; (b) a phrase consisting of the neuter plural of the definite article, either with the preposition *pros*, "unto," as in **Luke 19:42**, where the phrase "the things which belong unto peace" (RV) is, lit., "the (things) unto peace," or with the genitive case of the noun, as in 1 Cor. 7:32, KJV, "the things that belong to the Lord," RV, suitably, "the things of the Lord"; (c) a distinct verb, e.g., *metecho*, "to partake of, share in," Heb. 7:13 RV, "belongeth to (another tribe)," KJV, "pertaineth to."

Peace *see Luke 1:79*.

Hid *see Luke 18:34*.

19:43 For the days shall come upon thee, that thine enemies shall cast a trench about thee, and compass thee round, and keep thee in on every side,

Come *heko* (2240), means (a) "to come, to be present"; (b) "to come upon, of time and events," Matt. 24:14; John 2:4; 2 Pet. 3:10; Rev. 18:8; (c) metaphorically, "to come upon one, of calamitous times, and evils," Matt. 23:36; **Luke 19:43**.

Enemies *see Luke 1:71*.

Cast *periballo* (4016), "to cast about, or around," is used in 23 of its 24 occurrences, of putting on garments, clothing, etc.; it is translated "cast about" in Mark 14:51; Acts 12:8, in **Luke 19:43**, used of "casting" up a bank or palisade against a city (see RV and marg.), KJV, "shall cast a trench about thee."

Trench *charax* (5482), primarily "a pointed stake," hence, "a palisade or rampart," is rendered "trench" in **Luke 19:43**, KJV (RV, "bank," marg., "palisade"). In AD 70, Titus, the Roman general, surrounded Jerusalem with a palisaded mound. The Jews in one of their sorties destroyed this *charax*, after which Titus surrounded the city with a wall of masonry.

Compass *perikukloo* (4033), is used in **Luke 19:43**, "shall compass ... round." *See also* **Taken** at *Luke 4:38*.

Keep *sunecho* (4912), "to hold together," is translated "shall ... keep (thee) in," in **Luke 19:43**.

Every side *pantothen* (3840), or *pantachothen*, "from all sides," is translated "from every quarter," Mark 1:45; in **Luke 19:43**, "on every side"; in Heb. 9:4, "round about."

19:44And shall lay thee even with the ground, and thy children within thee; and they shall not leave in thee one stone upon another; because thou knewest not the time of thy visitation.

Lay *edaphizo* (1474), "to beat level with the earth," e.g., as a threshing floor (cf. *edaphos*, "the ground"), **Luke 19:44**; RV, "shall dash (thee) to the ground"; (KJV, "shall lay (thee) even with the ground").

Even In **Luke 19:44** (KJV, "shall lay thee even with the ground"), there is no word representing "even"; the verb *edaphizo* signifies "to beat level" (like a threshing floor); hence, "to dash to the ground".

Within *see Luke 7:39*.

One ... another In Matt. 24:2; Mark 13:2; **Luke 19:44**, and **21:6**, "one (stone upon) another" is, lit., "stone upon stone."

Visitation *episkope* (1984), denotes "a visitation," whether in mercy, **Luke 19:44**, or in judgment, 1 Pet. 2:12.

19:45-46 And he went into the temple, and began to cast out them that sold therein, and them that bought;

Saying unto them, It is written, My house is the house of prayer: but ye have made it a den of thieves.

Den *spelaion* (4693), "a grotto, cavern, den" (Lat., *spelunca*), "cave," John 11:38, is said of the grave of Lazarus; in the RV in Heb. 11:38 and Rev. 6:15 (KJV, "dens"); in the Lord's rebuke concerning the defilement of the Temple, Matt. 21:13; Mark 11:17; **Luke 19:46**, "den" is used.

19:47 And he taught daily in the temple. But the chief priests and the scribes and the chief of the people sought to destroy him,

Chief *protos* (4413), denotes "the first," whether in time or place. It is translated "chief" in Mark 6:21, RV, of men of Galilee, in Acts 13:50, of men in a city; in 28:7, of the "chief" man in the island of Melita; in 17:4, of "chief" women in a city; in 28:17, of Jews; in 1 Tim. 1:15-16, of a sinner. In the following, where the KJV has "chief," or "chiefest," the RV renderings are different: Matt. 20:27 and Mark 10:44, "first"; **Luke 19:47** and Acts 25:2, "principal men"; Acts 16:12, said of Philippi, "the first (city) of the district," RV, for incorrect KJV, "the chief city of that part of Macedonia." Amphipolis was the "chief" city of that part. *Protos* here must mean the first in the direction in which the apostle came.

19:48 And could not find what they might do: for all the people were very attentive to hear him.

Find *see* Found at *Luke 1:30*.

Attentive *ekkremannumi* (1582), "to hang from, or upon," is used in the middle voice (*ekkremamai*) metaphorically in **Luke 19:48**, RV, "(the people all) "hung" upon (Him, listening)," KJV, "were very attentive." In the Sept, Gen. 44:30.

Chapter 20

20:1 And it came to pass, *that* on one of those days, as he taught the people in the temple, and preached the gospel, the chief priests and the scribes came upon *him* with the elders,

Came *see Luke 2:9*.

20:2 And spake unto him, saying, Tell us, by what authority doest thou these things? or who is he that gave thee this authority?

What *see Luke 5:19*.

20:3 And he answered and said unto them, I will also ask you one thing; and answer me:

Also *see Luke 11:49*.

Thing *logos* (3056), "a word," is translated "question" in Matt. 21:24 (KJV, "thing"); in Mark 11:29 (RV, marg., "word") and **Luke 20:3**, KJV, "one thing:" there is no word in the original for "one," hence the RV, "a question." *See also* Things at *Luke 1:4*.

20:4-5 The baptism of John, was it from heaven, or of men?

And they reasoned with themselves, saying, If we shall say, From heaven; he will say, Why then believed ye him not?

Reasoned *sullogizomai* (4817), "to compute" (*sun*, "with," and *logizomai*, cf. Eng., "syllogism"), also denotes "to reason," and is so rendered in **Luke 20:5**.

20:6 But and if we say, Of men; all the people will stone us: for they be persuaded that John was a prophet.

Stone *katalithazo* (2642), an intensive form "to cast stones at," occurs in **Luke 20:6**.

Persuaded *see Luke 16:31*.

20:7 And they answered, that they could not tell whence *it was*.

Could *oida* (1492), "to know by perception," is the word in Pilate's remark "make it as sure as ye can" (marg. "sure, as ye know"), Matt. 27:65. The phrases "cannot tell," "canst not tell," etc., are in the RV rendered "know not," etc., Matt. 21:27; Mark 11:33; **Luke 20:7**; John 3:8; 8:14; 16:18; 2 Cor. 12:2-3.

Tell In the following, *oida*, "to know," is translated "tell" in the KJV (RV, "know"), Matt. 21:27; Mark 11:33; **Luke 20:7**; John 3:8; 8:14; 16:18; 2 Cor. 12:2.

20:8 And Jesus said unto them, Neither tell I you by what authority I do these things.

What *see Luke 5:19*.

20:9 Then began he to speak to the people this parable; A certain man planted a vineyard, and let it forth to husbandmen, and went into a far country for a long time.

Planted *see Luke 13:6*.

Let ... forth *ekdidomi* (1554), primarily, "to give out, give up, surrender" (*ek*, "out, from," *didomi*, "to give"), denotes "to let out for hire"; in the

NT it is used, in the middle voice, with the meaning "to let out to one's advantage," in the parable of the husbandman and his vineyard, Matt. 21:33, 41; Mark 12:1; **Luke 20:9**, KJV, "let ... forth"; RV, "let out."

Husbandmen *georgos* (1092), from *ge*, "land, ground," and *ergo* (or *erdo*), "to do" (Eng., "George"), denotes (a) "a husbandman," a tiller of the ground, 2 Tim. 2:6; Jas. 5:7; (b) "a vinedresser," Matt. 21:33-35, 38, 40, 41; Mark 12:1, 2, 7, 9; **Luke 20:9, 10, 14, 16**; John 15:1, where Christ speaks of the Father as the "Husbandman," Himself as the Vine, His disciples as the branches, the object being to bear much fruit, life in Christ producing the fruit of the Spirit, i.e., character and ways in conformity to Christ.

Went *see* Journey at *Luke 15:13*.

Far *see Luke 15:13*.

Country *see Luke 15:13*.

Long *see Luke 8:27*.

Time *see Luke 4:5*.

20:10 And at the season he sent a servant to the husbandmen, that they should give him of the fruit of the vineyard: but the husbandmen beat him, and sent *him* away empty.

Sent *see Luke 1:19*.

Husbandmen *see Luke 20:9*.

Beat *see* Beaten at *Luke 12:47*.

Empty *see Luke 1:53*.

20:11 And again he sent another servant: and they beat him also, and entreated *him* shamefully, and sent *him* away empty.

Again *see* Increase at *Luke 17:5*.

Sent *see Luke 4:26*.

Entreated ... shamefully *atimazo* (818), signifies "to dishonour, treat shamefully, insult," whether in word, John 8:49, or deed, Mark 12:4; **Luke 20:11**, RV "handled (him) shamefully," (RV "entreated ... shamefully"); Rom. 1:24; 2:23, "dishonorest;" Jas. 2:6, RV, "ye have dishonored (the poor)," (KJV, "despised"); in the passive voice, to suffer dishonor, Acts 5:41 (KJV, "suffer shame").

20:12 And again he sent a third: and they wounded him also, and cast *him* out.

Sent *see Luke 4:26*.

Third *tritos* (5154), is used (a) as a noun, e.g., **Luke 20:12, 31**; in Rev. 8:7-12 and 9:15, 18, "the third part," lit., "the third"; (b) as an adverb, with the article, "the third time," e.g., Mark 14:41; John 21:17 (twice); without the article, lit., "a third time," e.g., John 21:14; 2 Cor. 12:14; 13:1; in enumerations, in Matt. 26:44, with *ek*, "from," lit., "from the third time" (the *ek* indicates the point of departure, especially in a succession of events, cf. John 9:24; 2 Pet. 2:8); absolutely, in the accusative neuter, in 1 Cor. 12:28, "thirdly"; (c) as an adjective (its primary use), e.g., in the phrase the third heaven, 2 Cor. 12:2; in the phrase "the third hour," Matt. 20:3; Mark 15:25; Acts 2:15 ("... of the day"); 23:23 ("... of the night"); in a phrase with *hemera*, "a day," "on the third day" (i.e., "the next day but one"), e.g., Matt. 16:21; **Luke 24:46**; Acts 10:40; in this connection the idiom "three days and three nights," Matt. 12:40, is explained by ref to 1 Sam. 30:12, 13, and Esth. 4:16 with 5:1; in Mark 9:31 and 10:34, the RV, "after three days," follows the texts which have this phrase, the KJV, "the third day," those which have the same phrase as in Matt. 16:21, etc.

Wounded *traumaizo* (5135), "to wound," occurs in **Luke 20:12** and Acts 19:16.

20:13 Then said the lord of the vineyard, What shall I do? I will send my beloved son: it may be they will reverence *him* when they see him.

Send *see* Sent at *Luke 4:26*.

May *isos* (2481), "equally" (from the adjective *isos*, "equal"), is translated "it may be" in **Luke 20:13** (i.e., "perhaps").

Reverence *entrepo* (1788), lit., "to turn in" (i.e., upon oneself), "to put to shame," denotes, when used in the passive voice, "to feel respect for, to show deference to, to reverence," Matt. 21:37; Mark 12:6; **Luke 20:13**; Heb. 12:9.

20:14 But when the husbandmen saw him, they reasoned among themselves, saying, This is the heir: come, let us kill him, that the inheritance may be ours.

Husbandmen *see Luke 20:9*.

Reasoned *see* Cast at *Luke 1:29*.

Heir *kleronomos* (2818), lit. denotes "one who obtains a lot or portion (*kleros*, "a lot," *nemomai*, "to possess"), especially of an inheritance. The NT usage may be analyzed as under: "(a) the person to whom property is to pass on the death of the owner, Matt. 21:38; Mark 12:7; **Luke 20:14**; Gal. 4:1; (b) one to whom something has been assigned by God, on possession of which, however, he has not yet entered, as Abraham, Rom. 4:13, 14; Heb. 6:17; Christ, Heb. 1:2; the poor saints, Jas. 2:5; (c) believers, inasmuch as they share in the new order of things to be ushered in at the return of Christ, Rom. 8:17; Gal. 3:29; 4:7; Titus 3:7; (d) one who receives something other than by merit, as Noah, Heb. 11:7." In the Sept., Judg. 18:7; 2 Sam. 14:7; Jer. 8:10; Mic. 1:15.

Inheritance *see Luke 12:13.*

Ours This usually translates *hemon*, the genitive of *hemeis*, "we," lit., "of us," e.g., Matt. 6:9, 11-12. It is translated "ours," e.g., in Mark 12:7; **Luke 20:14**; 1 Cor. 1:2; 2 Cor. 1:14.

20:15-16 So they cast him out of the vineyard, and killed *him*. What therefore shall the lord of the vineyard do unto them?
He shall come and destroy these husbandmen, and shall give the vineyard to others. And when they heard *it*, they said, God forbid.

Husbandmen *see Luke 20:9.*

Forbid The phrase *me genoito*, lit., "let it not be" (*me*, negative, and *ginomai*, "to become"), is idiomatically translated "God forbid" in **Luke 20:16**; Rom. 3:4, 6, 31; 6:2, 15; 7:7, 13; 9:14; 11:1, 11; 1 Cor. 6:15; Gal. 2:17; 3:21, and in the KJV of 6:14; here the RV has "far be it from me (to glory)," which the American RV uses in the OT. In Paul's Epistles it is almost entirely used to express the apostle's repudiation of an inference which he apprehends may be drawn from his argument.

20:17 And he beheld them, and said, What is this then that is written, The stone which the builders rejected, the same is become the head of the corner?

Beheld *emblepo* (1689), expresses "earnest looking," e.g., in the Lord's command to "behold" the birds of the heaven, with the object of learning lessons of faith from them, Matt. 6:26. See also 19:26; Mark 8:25; 10:21, 27; 14:67; **Luke 20:17**; **22:61**; John 1:36; of the Lord's looking upon Peter, John 1:42; Acts 1:11; 22:11.

Builders *oikodomeo* (3618), lit., "to build a house," (a) usually signifies "to build," whether literally, or figuratively; the present participle, lit., "the (ones) building," is used as a noun, "the builders," in Matt. 21:42; Mark 12:10; **Luke 20:17**; Acts 4:11 (in some mss.; the most authentic have the noun *oikodomos*;) 1 Pet. 2:7; (b) is used metaphorically, in the sense of "edifying," promoting the spiritual growth and development of character of believers, by teaching or by example, suggesting such spiritual progress as the result of patient labor. It is said (1) of the effect of this upon local churches, Acts 9:31; 1 Cor. 14:4; (2) of the individual action of believers towards each other, 1 Cor. 8:1; 10:23; 14:17; 1 Thess. 5:11; (3) of an individual in regard to himself, 1 Cor. 14:4. In 1 Cor. 8:10, where it is translated "emboldened," the apostle uses it with pathetic irony, of the action of a brother in "building up" his brother who had a weak conscience, causing him to compromise his scruples; "strengthened," or "confirmed," would be suitable renderings.

Rejected *see Luke 9:22.*

Corner *gonia* (1137), "an angle" (Eng., "coign"), signifies (a) "an external angle," as of the "corner" of a street, Matt. 6:5; or of a building, 21:42; Mark 12:10; **Luke 20:17**; Acts 4:11; 1 Pet. 2:7, "the corner stone or headstone of the corner"; or the four extreme limits of the earth, Rev. 7:1; 20:8; (b) "an internal corner," a secret place, Acts 26:26.

20:18 Whosoever shall fall upon that stone shall be broken; but on whomsoever it shall fall, it will grind him to powder.

Broken *sunthlao* (4917), *sun*, "together" (intensive), and *thlao*, "to break or crush, to break in pieces, to shatter," is used in Matt. 21:44 and **Luke 20:18** of the physical effect of falling on a stone.

Grind In Matt. 21:44 and **Luke 20:18**, *likmao*, "to winnow," as of grain, by throwing it up against the wind, to scatter the chaff and straw, hence has the meaning "to scatter," as chaff or dust, and is translated "will scatter ... as dust," RV (KJV, "will grind ... to powder"). In the Sept. it is used of being scattered by the wind or of sifting (cf. Amos 9:9). The use of the verb in the papyri writings suggests the meaning, "to ruin, destroy" (Deissmann).

Powder *likmao* (3039), primarily, "to winnow" (from *likmos*, "a winnowing-fan"), hence, "to scatter" as chaff or dust, is used in Matt. 21:44 and **Luke 20:18**, RV, "scatter as dust," KJV, "grind to powder." There are indications in the papyri writings that the word came to denote "to ruin, to destroy."

20:19 And the chief priests and the scribes the same hour sought to lay hands on him; and they feared the people: for they perceived that he had spoken this parable against them.

Same *see Luke 12:12.*

And *kai* Occasionally *kai* tends towards an *adversative* meaning, expressing a contrast, "yet," almost the equivalent of *alla*, "but"; see, e.g., Mark 12:12, "yet they feared"; **Luke 20:19**; John 18:28, "yet they themselves entered not." Some take it in this sense in Rom. 1:13, where, however, it may be simply parenthetic. Sometimes in the English versions the "yet" has been added in italics, as in 2 Cor. 6:8, 9, 10.

People *see Luke 1:21.*

Perceived *see* Known at *Luke 7:39.*

20:20 And they watched *him*, and sent forth spies, which should feign themselves just men, that they might take hold of his words, that so they might deliver him unto the power and authority of the governor.

Watched *see Luke 6:7.*

Sent forth *see* Departeth at *Luke 9:39.*

Spies *enkathetos* (1455), an adjective denoting "suborned to lie in wait" (*en*, "in," *kathiemi*, "to send down"), is used as a noun in **Luke 20:20**, "spies." In the Sept., Job. 19:12; 31:9.

Feign *hupokrinomai* (5271), primarily denotes "to answer"; then, "to answer on the stage, play a part," and so, metaphorically, "to feign, pretend," **Luke 20:20**. Cf. *hupokrites*, "a hypocrite," and *hupokrisis*, "hypocrisy."

Just *see Luke 2:25.*

Might "May," "might," sometimes translate the prepositional phrase *eis*, "unto," with the definite article, followed by the infinitive mood of some verb, expressing purpose, e.g., Acts 3:19, "may be blotted out," lit., "unto the blotting out of"; Rom. 3:26, "that he might be," lit., "unto his being"; so 8:29; 2 Cor. 1:4, "that we may be able," lit., "unto our being able"; Eph. 1:18, "that ye may know," lit., "unto your knowing"; Acts 7:19; Rom. 1:11; 4:16; 12:2; 15:13; Phil. 1:10; 1 Thess. 3:10, 13; 2 Thess. 1:5; 2:6, 10; Heb. 12:10. In **Luke 20:20** the best mss. have *hoste*, "so as to," RV, as, e.g., in 1 Pet. 1:21. Sometimes the article with the infinitive mood without a preceding preposition, expresses result, e.g., **Luke 21:22**; Acts 26:18 (twice), "that they may turn," RV; cf. Rom. 6:6; 11:10; 1 Cor. 10:13; Phil. 3:10, "that I may know"; Jas. 5:17.

Hold *epilambano* (1949), "to lay hold of, to take hold of" (*epi*, "upon," *lambano*, "to take"), with a special purpose, always in the middle voice, is so translated in **Luke 20:20**, **26**, of taking "hold" of Christ's words; in **23:26** and Acts 21:33, RV, of laying "hold" of persons; in 1 Tim. 6:12, 19, of laying "hold" on eternal life, i.e., practically appropriating all the benefits, privileges and responsibilities involved in the possession of it; in Heb. 2:16, RV "He taketh hold" (KJV "took on") perhaps to be viewed in connection with "deliver" (v. 15) and "succor" (v. 18).

Words *logos* (3056), akin to *lego*, most frequently rendered "word," signifies "speech," as follows: (a) "discourse," e.g., **Luke 20:20**, RV, "speech" (KJV, "words"); Acts 14:12; 20:7; 1 Cor. 2:1, 4; 4:19, KJV (RV, "word"); 2 Cor. 10:10; (b) "the faculty of speech," e.g., 2 Cor. 11:6; (c) "the manner of speech," e.g., Matt. 5:37, RV, "speech" (KJV, "communication"); Col. 4:6; (d) "manner of instruction," Titus 2:8; 1 Cor. 14:9, RV (KJV, "words"); Eph. 4:29, RV (KJV, "communication").

Power *arche* (746), "a beginning, rule," is translated "power" in **Luke 20:20**, KJV (RV, "rule").

Governor *hegemon* (2232), is a term used (a) for "rulers" generally, Mark 13:9; 1 Pet. 2:14; translated "princes" (i.e., leaders) in Matt. 2:6; (b) for the Roman procurators, referring, in the Gospels to Pontius Pilate, e.g., Matt. 27:2; **Luke 20:20** (so designated by Tacitus, *Annals*, xv. 44); to Felix, Acts 23:26. Technically the procurator was a financial official under a proconsul or propretor, for collecting the imperial revenues, but entrusted also with magisterial powers for decisions of questions relative to the revenues. In certain provinces, of which Judea was one (the procurator of which was dependent on the legate of Syria), he was the general administrator and supreme judge, with sole power of life and death. Such a governor was a person of high social standing. Felix, however, was an ex-slave, a freedman, and his appointment to Judea could not but be regarded by the Jews as an insult to the nation. The headquarters of the governor of Judea was Caesarea, which was made a garrison town.

20:21 And they asked him, saying, Master, we know that thou sayest and teachest rightly, neither acceptest thou the person *of any*, but teachest the way of God truly:

Asked *see* Asking at *Luke 2:46.*

Rightly *see Luke 7:43.*

Acceptest *see* Receive at *Luke 18:30.*

Person *prosopon* (4383), is translated "person" or "persons" in Matt. 22:16; Mark 12:14; **Luke 20:21**; 2 Cor. 1:11; 2 Cor. 2:10; Gal. 2:6; Jude 16, lit., "(admiring, or showing respect of, RV) persons."

Truly *aletheia* (225), "truth," is used (a) objectively, signifying "the reality lying at the basis of an appearance; the manifested, veritable essence of a matter" (Cremer), e.g., Rom. 9:1; 2 Cor. 11:10; especially of Christian doctrine, e.g., Gal. 2:5, where "the truth of the Gospel" denotes the "true" teaching of the gospel, in contrast to perversions of it; Rom. 1:25, where "the truth of God" may be "the truth concerning God" or "God whose existence is a verity"; but in Rom. 15:8 "the truth of God" is indicative of His faithfulness in the fulfillment of His promises as exhibited in Christ; the word has an absolute force in John 14:6; 17:17; 18:37, 38; in Eph. 4:21, where the RV, "even as truth is in Jesus," gives the correct rendering, the meaning is not merely ethical "truth," but "truth" in all its fullness and scope, as embodied in Him; He was the perfect expression of the truth; this is virtually equivalent to His statement in John 14:6; (b) subjectively, "truthfulness," "truth," not merely verbal, but sincerity and integrity of character, John 8:44; 3 John 3, RV; (c) in phrases, e.g., "in truth" (*epi*, "on the basis of"), Mark 12:14; **Luke 20:21**; with *en*, "in," 2 Cor. 6:7; Col. 1:6; 1 Tim. 2:7, RV (KJV, "in ... verity"), 1 John 3:18; 2 John 1, 3, 4.

20:22 Is it lawful for us to give tribute unto Caesar, or no?

Tribute *phoros* (5411), akin to *phero*, "to bring," denotes "tribute" paid by a subjugated nation, **Luke 20:22; 23:2**; Rom. 13:6, 7.

20:23 But he perceived their craftiness, and said unto them, Why tempt ye me?

Perceived *see* Known at *Luke 7:39. See also* Perceivest at *Luke 6:41*.

Craftiness *panourgia* (3834), lit., "all-working," i.e., doing everything (*pan*, "all," *ergon*, "work"), hence, "unscrupulous conduct, craftiness," is always used in a bad sense in the NT, **Luke 20:23**; 1 Cor. 3:19; 2 Cor. 4:2; 11:3; Eph. 4:14, KJV, "cunning craftiness." In the Sept. it is used in a good sense, Prov. 1:4; 8:5; indifferently in Num. 24:22 and Josh. 9:4.

20:24 Shew me a penny. Whose image and superscription hath it? They answered and said, Caesar's.

Image *eikon* (1504), denotes "an image"; the word involves the two ideas of representation and manifestation. "The idea of perfection does not lie in the word itself, but must be sought from the context" (Lightfoot); the following instances clearly show any distinction between the imperfect and the perfect likeness. The word is used ... of an "image" or a coin (not a mere likeness), Matt. 22:20; Mark 12:16; **Luke 20:24**; so of a statue or similar representation (more than a resemblance), Rom. 1:23; Rev. 13:14, 15 (thrice); 14:9, 11; 15:2; 16:2; 19:20; 20:4; of the descendants of Adam as bearing his image, 1 Cor. 15:49, each a representation derived from the prototype ...

Superscription *epigraphe* (1923), lit., "an overwriting" (*epi*, "over," *grapho*, "to write") (the meaning of the anglicized Latin word "superscription"), denotes "an inscription, a title." On Roman coins the emperor's name was inscribed, Matt. 22:20; Mark 12:16; **Luke 20:24**. In the Roman Empire, in the case of a criminal on his way to execution, a board on which was inscribed the cause of his condemnation, was carried before him or hung round his neck; the inscription was termed a "title" (*titlos*). The four Evangelists state that at the crucifixion of Christ the title was affixed to the cross, Mark (15:26), and Luke (**23:38**) call it a "superscription"; Mark says it was "written over" (*epigrapho*, the corresponding verb). Matthew calls it "His accusation"; John calls it "a title" (a technical term). The wording varies: the essential words are the same, and the variation serves to authenticate the narratives, showing that there was no consultation leading to an agreement as to the details.

20:25 And he said unto them, Render therefore unto Caesar the things which be Caesar's, and unto God the things which be God's.

Render *see* Give at *Luke 16:2*.

God *see Luke 1:35*.

20:26 And they could not take hold of his words before the people: and they marvelled at his answer, and held their peace.

Hold *see Luke 20:20*.

Before *enantion* (1726), from *en*, "in," and *anti*, "over against," the neuter of the adjective *enantios*, and virtually an adverb, is also used as a preposition signifying "in the presence of, in the sight of," **Luke 20:26**; Acts 7:10; 8:32.

Answer *see* Answers at *Luke 2:47*.

Peace *see* Close at *Luke 9:36*.

20:27 Then came to *him* certain of the Sadducees, which deny that there is any resurrection; and they asked him,

Deny *antilego* (483), means "to speak against, contradict." In **Luke 20:27**, the RV, "they which say that there is no resurrection," follows the texts which have the simple verb *lego*; for the KJV, which translates the verb *antilego*, "which deny that there is any resurrection."

Resurrection *see* Rising at *Luke 2:34*.

Asked *see* Asking at *Luke 2:46*.

20:28 Saying, Master, Moses wrote unto us, If any man's brother die, having a wife, and he die without children, that his brother should take his wife, and raise up seed unto his brother.

Children *ateknos* (815), from *a*, negative, and *teknon*, signifies "childless," **Luke 20:28-30**.

Raise *exanistemi* (1817), is used of "raising" up seed, Mark 12:19; **Luke 20:28**; elsewhere, Acts 15:5, "to rise up."

20:29-31 There were therefore seven brethren: and the first took a wife, and died without children.

And the second took her to wife, and he died childless.

And the third took her; and in like manner the seven also: and they left no children, and died.

Third *see* ***Luke 20:12***.

Manner *hosautos* (5615), a strengthened form of *hos*, "thus," signifies "just so, likewise, in like manner," e.g., 1 Tim. 2:9; in the following the RV has "in like manner," for KJV, "likewise"; Mark 14:31; **Luke 22:20**; Rom. 8:26; 1 Tim. 3:8; 5:25; in **Luke 20:31** the RV has "likewise," KJV, "in like manner."

20:32 Last of all the woman died also.

Last *see* **Afterward** at ***Luke 4:2***.

20:33 Therefore in the resurrection whose wife of them is she? for seven had her to wife.

Resurrection *see* **Rising** at ***Luke 2:34***.

20:34 And Jesus answering said unto them, The children of this world marry, and are given in marriage:

World *see* ***Luke 16:8***.

Marry *see* **Married** at ***Luke 14:20***.

Marriage *gamisko* (1061), **Luke 20:34**; in some mss. in Mark 12:25; **Luke 20:35**.

20:35 But they which shall be accounted worthy to obtain that world, and the resurrection from the dead, neither marry, nor are given in marriage:

Accounted *kataxioo* (2661), denotes "to account worthy" (*kata*, "intensive," *axios*, "worthy"), "to judge worthy," **Luke 20:35**; some mss. have it in **21:36** (so the KJV); the most authentic mss. have the verb *katischuo*, "to prevail"; Acts 5:41, "were counted worthy"; so 2 Thess. 1:5.

Worthy *kataxioo* (2661), occurs in **Luke 20:35**; **21:36**, in some texts; Acts 5:41; 2 Thess. 1:5.

Obtain *tunchano* (5177), "to reach, meet with," signifies "to attain to," in **Luke 20:35**, RV (for KJV, obtain).

Resurrection *see* **Rising** at ***Luke 2:34***.

Marry *see* **Married** at ***Luke 14:20***.

20:36 Neither can they die any more: for they are equal unto the angels; and are the children of God, being the children of the resurrection.

Angels *isangelos*, "equal to the angels," occurs in **Luke 20:36**.

Children *see* ***Luke 6:35***.

Resurrection *see* **Rising** at ***Luke 2:34***.

20:37 Now that the dead are raised, even Moses shewed at the bush, when he calleth the Lord the God of Abraham, and the God of Isaac, and the God of Jacob.

Raised *see* ***Luke 1:69***.

Shewed *menuo* (3377), "to disclose, make known" (what was secret), is rendered "to show" in **Luke 20:37**; 1 Cor. 10:28; in a forensic sense, John 11:57; Acts 23:30, RV (KJV, "it was told").

Bush *see* ***Luke 6:44***.

20:38 For he is not a God of the dead, but of the living: for all live unto him.

Live *see* **Living** at ***Luke 15:13***.

20:39-40 Then certain of the scribes answering said, Master, thou hast well said.

And after that they durst not ask him any *question at all*.

Durst *tolmao* (5111), signifies "to dare," (a) in the sense of not dreading or shunning through fear, Matt. 22:46; Mark 12:34; Mark 15:43, "boldly," lit., "having dared, went in"; **Luke 20:40**; John 21:12; Acts 5:13; 7:32; Rom. 15:18; 2 Cor. 10:2, RV, "show courage," (KJV, "be bold"); 10:12, RV, "are (not) bold", 11:21; Phil. 1:14, "are bold"; Jude 9; (b) in the sense of bearing, enduring, bringing oneself to do a thing, Rom. 5:7; 1 Cor. 6:1. Cf. *apotolmao*, "to be very bold," Rom. 10:20.

Ask *see* **Asking** at ***Luke 2:46***.

20:41-42 And he said unto them, How say they that Christ is David's son?

And David himself saith in the book of Psalms, The LORD said unto my Lord, Sit thou on my right hand,

Book *see* ***Luke 3:4***.

Psalms *psalmos* (5568), primarily denoted "a striking or twitching with the fingers (on musical strings)"; then, "a sacred song, sung to musical accompaniment, a psalm." It is used (a) of the OT book of "Psalms," **Luke 20:42**; **24:44**; Acts 1:20; (b) of a particular "psalm," Acts 13:33 (cf. v. 35); (c) of "psalms" in general, 1 Cor. 14:26; Eph. 5:19; Col. 3:16.

20:43 Till I make thine enemies thy footstool.

Make *tithemi* (5087), "to put," Matt. 22:44, Mark 12:36; **Luke 20:43**; Acts 2:35; 1 Cor. 9:18 (of making the gospel without charge); Heb. 1:13; 10:13; 2 Pet. 2:6; Rom. 4:17.

Enemies *see Luke 1:71.*

Footstool *hupopodion* (5286), from *hupo*, "under," and *pous*, "a foot," is used (a) literally in Jas. 2:3, (b) metaphorically, of the earth as God's "footstool," Matt. 5:35; of the foes of the Lord, Matt. 22:44 (in some mss.); Mark 12:36, "underneath" (in some mss.), **Luke 20:43**; Acts 2:35; 7:49; Heb. 1:13; 10:13. The RV, adhering to the literal rendering, translates the phrase "the footstool of My (Thy, His) feet," for the KJV, "My (etc.) footstool," but in Matt. 22:44, "(till I put Thine enemies) underneath thy feet."

20:44-46 David therefore calleth him Lord, how is he then his son?

Then in the audience of all the people he said unto his disciples,

Beware of the scribes, which desire to walk in long robes, and love greetings in the markets, and the highest seats in the synagogues, and the chief rooms at feasts;

Beware *see Luke 12:1.*

Robes *stole* (4749), is translated "robe" in Mark 16:5, RV (KJV, "garment"); "long robes" in **Luke 20:46**. *See also* Robe at *Luke 15:22.*

Greetings *see* Salutation at *Luke 1:29.*

Markets *see* Marketplace at *Luke 7:32.*

Seats *see Luke 11:43.*

Chief *see* Uppermost at *Luke 11:43.*

Feasts *see* Supper at *Luke 14:12.*

20:47 Which devour widows' houses, and for a shew make long prayers: the same shall receive greater damnation.

Widows *see* Widow at *Luke 2:37.*

Shew *prophasis* (4392), either from *pro*, "before," and *phaino*, "to cause to appear, shine," or, more probably, from *pro*, and *phemi*, "to say," is rendered "cloke" (of covetousness) in 1 Thess. 2:5; "excuse" in John 15:22 (KJV "cloke"); "pretense" in Matt. 23:14; Mark 12:40; **Luke 20:47** (KJV "show"); Phil. 1:18; "color" in Acts 27:30. It signifies the assuming of something so as to disguise one's real motives.

Long *see* Far at *Luke 15:13.*

Greater *perissoteros* (4055), the comparative of *perissos*, "over and above, abundant," signifies "more abundant, greater," e.g., of condemnation, Mark 12:40; **Luke 20:47**.

Chapter 21

21:1 And he looked up, and saw the rich men casting their gifts into the treasury.

Rich *see Luke 6:24.*

Gifts *doron* (1435), akin to *didomi*, "to give," is used (a) of "gifts" presented as an expression of honor, Matt. 2:11; (b) of "gifts" for the support of the temple and the needs of the poor, Matt. 15:5; Mark 7:11; **Luke 21:1, 4**; (c) of "gifts" offered to God, Matt. 5:23, 24; 8:4; 23:18, 19; Heb. 5:1; 8:3, 4; 9:9; 11:4; (d) of salvation by grace as the "gift" of God, Eph. 2:8; (e) of "presents" for mutual celebration of an occasion, Rev. 11:10.

Treasury *gazophulakion* (1049), from *gaza*, "a treasure," *phulake*, "a guard," is used by Josephus for a special room in the women's court in the Temple in which gold and silver bullion was kept. This seems to be referred to in John 8:20; in Mark 12:41 (twice), 43 and **Luke 21:1** it is used of the trumpet-shaped or ram's-horn-shaped chests, into which the temple offerings of the people were cast. There were 13 chests, six for such gifts in general, seven for distinct purposes.

21:2 And he saw also a certain poor widow casting in thither two mites.

Poor *penichros* (3998), "needy, poor," is used of the widow in **Luke 21:2**; it is used frequently in the papyri. In the Sept., Ex. 22:25; Prov. 28:15; 29:7.

Widow *see Luke 2:37.*

Mites *see* Mite at *Luke 12:59.*

21:3 And he said, Of a truth I say unto you, that this poor widow hath cast in more than they all:

Truth *see Luke 9:27.*

Poor *see Luke 6:20.*

Widow *see Luke 2:37.*

21:4 For all these have of their abundance cast in unto the offerings of God: but she of her penury hath cast in all the living that she had.

Abundance *see* Remained at *Luke 9:17.*

Offerings *see* Gifts at *Luke 21:1.*

Penury *husterema* (5303), denotes (a) "that which is lacking, deficiency, shortcoming" (akin to *husteroo*, "to be behind, in want"),

1 Cor. 16:17; Phil. 2:30; Col. 1:24, RV, "that which is lacking" [KJV, "that which is behind" (of the afflictions of Christ)], where the reference is not to the vicarious sufferings of Christ but to those which He endured previously, and those which must be endured by His faithful servants; 1 Thess. 3:10, where "that which is lacking" means that which Paul had not been able to impart to them, owing to the interruption of his spiritual instruction among them; (b) "need, want, poverty," **Luke 21:4**, RV, "want" (KJV, "penury"); 2 Cor. 8:14 (twice) "want;" 9:12, "wants" (KJV, "want"); 11:9, RV, "(the measure of my) want" [KJV, "that which was lacking (to me)"].

Living *see* Life at *Luke 8:14*.

21:5 And as some spake of the temple, how it was adorned with goodly stones and gifts, he said,

Adorned *see* Garnished at *Luke 11:25*.

Gifts *anathema* (334), denotes "a gift set up in a temple, a votive offering" (*ana*, "up," *tithemi*, "to place"), **Luke 21:5**, RV "offerings" (KJV, "gifts"), Cf. *anathema*.

21:6 *As for* these things which ye behold, the days will come, in the which there shall not be left one stone upon another, that shall not be thrown down.

One . . . another *see Luke 19:44*.

Thrown down *see* Lodge at *Luke 9:12*.

21:7 And they asked him, saying, Master, but when shall these things be? and what sign *will there be* when these things shall come to pass?

Shall *see Luke 9:44*.

Sign *see Luke 2:12*.

21:8 And he said, Take heed that ye be not deceived: for many shall come in my name, saying, I am *Christ*; and the time draweth near: go ye not therefore after them.

Heed *see Luke 8:18*.

Draweth near *see* Come nigh at *Luke 10:9*.

Go *see* Departed at *Luke 4:42*.

21:9 But when ye shall hear of wars and commotions, be not terrified: for these things must first come to pass; but the end *is* not by and by.

Commotions *akatastasia* (181), "instability," (*a*, negative, *kata*, "down," *stasis*, "a standing"), denotes "a state of disorder, disturbance, confusion, tumult," 1 Cor. 14:33; Jas. 3:16, "revolution or anarchy"; translated "tumults" in **Luke 21:9** (KJV, "commotions"); 2 Cor. 6:5; 12:20.

Terrified *ptoeo* (4422), "to terrify," is used in the passive voice, **Luke 21:9; 24:37**.

By and by *see Luke 17:7*.

21:10-11 Then said he unto them, Nation shall rise against nation, and kingdom against kingdom:

And great earthquakes shall be in divers places, and famines, and pestilences; and fearful sights and great signs shall there be from heaven.

Earthquakes *seismos* (4578), "a shaking, a shock," from *seio*, "to move to and fro, to shake," chiefly with the idea of concussion (Eng., "seismic," "seismology," "seismometry"), is used (a) of a "tempest" in the sea, Matt. 8:24; (b) of "earthquakes," Matt. 24:7; 27:54; 28:2; Mark 13:8; **Luke 21:11**; Acts 16:26; Rev. 6:12; 8:5; 11:13 (twice), 19; 16:18 (twice).

Divers The phrase *kata topous*, lit., "throughout places" (*kata*, "down, or throughout," in a distributive sense, *topos*, "a place"), is translated "in divers places," in Matt. 24:7; Mark 13:8 and **Luke 21:11**.

Famines *see* Famine at *Luke 4:25*.

Pestilences *loimos* (3061), "a pestilence, any deadly infectious malady," is used in the plural in **Luke 21:11** (in some mss., Matt. 24:7); in Acts 24:5, metaphorically, "a pestilent fellow."

Fearful In **Luke 21:11**, *phobetron* denotes a terror, RV, "terrors," for KJV, "fearful sights," i.e., objects or instruments of terror.

Sights *phobetron* (5400), "that which causes fright, a terror," is translated "terrors" in **Luke 21:11**, RV (KJV, "fearful sights"). *See also* **Sight** at *Luke 4:18*.

Signs *see* Sign at *Luke 2:12*.

21:12 But before all these, they shall lay their hands on you, and persecute *you*, delivering *you* up to the synagogues, and into prisons, being brought before kings and rulers for my name's sake.

Persecute *see Luke 11:49*.

Rulers In Mark 13:9 and **Luke 21:12**, KJV, *hegemon*, "a leader, a governor of a province," is translated "ruler" (RV, "governor").

21:13 And it shall turn to you for a testimony.

Turn *apobaino* (576), "to go from," is used metaphorically of events, "to issue, turn out," **Luke 21:13**; Phil. 1:19.

21:14 Settle *it* therefore in your hearts, not to meditate before what ye shall answer:

Settle *tithemi* (5087), "to put, place," is translated "settle (it therefore in your hearts)" in **Luke 21:14**, active voice in the best texts (some have the middle), the aorist tense signifying complete decision, i.e., "resolve" (not "consider"); cf. Acts 5:4, "to conceive in the heart," and contrast **Luke 1:66**, "to lay up" (both have aorist tense, middle voice).

Meditate *promeletao* (4304), "to premeditate," is used in **Luke 21:14** In the corresponding passage in Mark 13:11, the most authentic mss. have the verb *promerimnao*, "to be anxious beforehand" (RV).

Answer *see Luke 12:11.*

21:15 For I will give you a mouth and wisdom, which all your adversaries shall not be able to gainsay nor resist.

Mouth *see Luke 1:64.*

Wisdom *see Luke 2:40.*

Your *see Luke 16:11.*

Adversaries *see Luke 13:17.*

Gainsay *anteipon* (483), is rendered "gainsay" in **Luke 21:15**; "say against" in Acts 4:14.

21:16 And ye shall be betrayed both by parents, and brethren, and kinsfolks, and friends; and *some* of you shall they cause to be put to death.

Kinsfolks *see* Cousins at *Luke 1:58. See also* Cousin at *Luke 1:36.*

Friends *see Luke 7:6.*

Death *thanatoo* (2289), "to put to death," in Matt. 10:21; Mark 13:12; **Luke 21:16**, is translated "shall ... cause (them) to be put to death," lit., "shall put (them) to death" (RV marg.). It is used of the death of Christ in Matt. 26:59; 27:1; Mark 14:55 and 1 Pet. 3:18. In Rom. 7:4 (passive voice) it is translated "ye ... were made dead," RV (for KJV, "are become"), with reference to the change from bondage to the Law to union with Christ; in 8:13, "mortify" (marg., "make to die"), of the act of the believer in regard to the deeds of the body; in 8:36, "are killed"; so in 2 Cor. 6:9.

21:17 And ye shall be hated of all *men* for my name's sake.

Name *see Luke 1:49.*

21:18 But there shall not an hair of your head perish.

Hair *see* Hairs at *Luke 7:38.*

21:19 In your patience possess ye your souls.

Patience *see Luke 8:15.*

Possess *see Luke 18:12.*

Souls *see* Soul at *Luke 1:46.*

21:20 And when ye shall see Jerusalem compassed with armies, then know that the desolation thereof is nigh.

Compassed *kukloo* (2944), (cf. Eng., cycle"), signifies "to move in a circle, to compass about," as of a city "encompassed" by armies, **Luke 21:20**; Heb. 11:30; in Acts 14:20, "stood round about.

Armies *stratopedon* (4760), from *stratos*, "a military host," *pedon*, "a plain," strictly denotes "an army encamped, a camp"; in **Luke 21:20**, of the soldiers which were to be encamped about Jerusalem in fulfillment of the Lord's prophecy concerning the destruction of the city; the phrase might be translated "by camps" (or encampments).

Desolation *eremosis* (2050), denotes "desolation," (a) in the sense of "making desolate," e.g., in the phrase "the abomination of desolation," Matt. 24:15; Mark 13:14; the genitive is objective, "the abomination that makes desolate"; (b) with stress upon the effect of the process, **Luke 21:20**, with reference to the "desolation" of Jerusalem.

21:21 Then let them which are in Judaea flee to the mountains; and let them which are in the midst of it depart out; and let not them that are in the countries enter thereinto.

Mountains *see* Mountain at *Luke 3:5.*

Depart *ekchoreo* (1633), signifies "to depart out" (*ek*), "to leave a place," Luke 21:21.

Countries *see* Country at *Luke 2:8.*

21:22 For these be the days of vengeance, that all things which are written may be fulfilled.

Vengeance *see* Avenge at *Luke 18:7*

May *see* Might at *Luke 20:20.*

Fulfilled *see Luke 4:21.*

21:23 But woe unto them that are with child, and to them that give suck, in those days! for there shall be great distress in the land, and wrath upon this people.

Woe *see Luke 6:24.*

Suck *see* Sucked at *Luke 11:27.*

Distress *ananke* (318), denotes (a) "a necessity," imposed whether by external circumstances, e.g., **Luke 23:17**, or inward pressure, e.g., 1 Cor. 9:16; (b) "straits, distress,"

Luke **21:23** (in v. 25 "distress" translates *sunoche*); 1 Cor. 7:26; 1 Thess. 3:7; the last two refer to the lack of material things.

Wrath *see* *Luke 3:7*.

21:24 And they shall fall by the edge of the sword, and shall be led away captive into all nations: and Jerusalem shall be trodden down of the Gentiles, until the times of the Gentiles be fulfilled.

Edge *stoma* (4750), the mouth (cf. Eng., "stomach," from *stomachos*, 1 Tim. 5:23), has a secondary and figurative meaning in reference to the "edge of a sharp instrument, as of a sword," **Luke 21:24**; Heb. 11:34 (cf. the Sept., e.g., Gen. 34:26; Judg. 18:27). *See also* **Mouth** at *Luke 1:64*.

Sword *machaira* (3162), "a short sword or dagger," e.g., Matt. 26:47, 51, 52 and parallel passages; **Luke 21:24**; **22:38**, possibly "a knife" (Field, *Notes on the Translation of the NT*); Heb. 4:12; metaphorically and by metonymy, (a) for ordinary violence, or dissensions, that destroy peace, Matt. 10:34; (b) as the instrument of a magistrate or judge, e.g., Rom. 13:4; (c) of the Word of God, "the sword of the Spirit," probing the conscience, subduing the impulses to sin, Eph. 6:17.

Captive *aichmalotizo* (163), practically synonymous with *aichmaloteuo*, denotes either "to lead away captive," **Luke 21:24**, or "to subjugate, to bring under control," said of the effect of the Law in one's members in bringing the person into captivity under the law of sin, Rom. 7:23; or of subjugating the thoughts to the obedience of Christ, 2 Cor. 10:5; or of those who took captive "silly women laden with sins," 2 Tim. 3:6.

Trodden *see* **Tread** at *Luke 10:19*.

Fulfilled *see* *Luke 4:21*.

21:25 And there shall be signs in the sun, and in the moon, and in the stars; and upon the earth distress of nations, with perplexity; the sea and the waves roaring;

Signs *see* **Sign** at *Luke 2:12*.

Sun *helios* (2246), whence Eng. prefix "helio-," is used (a) as a means of the natural benefits of light and heat, e.g., Matt. 5:45, and power, Rev. 1:16; (b) of its qualities of brightness and glory, e.g., Matt. 13:43; 17:2; Acts 26:13; 1 Cor. 15:41; Rev. 10:1; 12:1; (c) as a means of destruction, e.g., Matt. 13:6; Jas. 1:11; of physical misery, Rev. 7:16; (d) as a means of judgment, e.g., Matt. 24:29; Mark 13:24; **Luke 21:25**; **23:45**; Acts 2:20; Rev. 6:12; 8:12; 9:2; 16:8.

Moon *selene* (4582), from *selas*, "brightness" (the Heb. words are *yareach*, "wandering," and *lebanah*, "white"), occurs in Matt. 24:29; Mark 13:24; **Luke 21:25**; Acts 2:20; 1 Cor. 15:41; Rev. 6:12; 8:12; 12:1; 21:23. In Rev. 12:1, "the moon under her feet" is suggestive of derived authority, just as her being clothed with the sun is suggestive of supreme authority, everything in the symbolism of the passage centers in Israel. In 6:12 the similar symbolism of the sun and "moon" is suggestive of the supreme authority over the world, and of derived authority, at the time of the execution of divine judgments upon nations at the close of the present age.

Stars *astron* (798), is used (a) in the sing. in Acts 7:43, "the star of the god Rephan," RV, the symbol or "figure," probably of Saturn, worshiped as a god, apparently the same as Chiun in Amos 5:26 (Rephan being the Egyptian deity corresponding to Saturn, Chiun the Assyrian); (b) in the plur., **Luke 21:25**; Acts 27:20; Heb. 11:12.

Distress *sunoche* (4928), lit., "a holding together, or compressing" (*sun*, "together," *echo*, "to hold"), was used of the narrowing of a way. It is found only in its metaphorical sense, of "straits, distress, anguish," **Luke 21:25**, "distress of nations," and 2 Cor. 2:4, "anguish of heart." *See also* ***Luke 21:23***.

Perplexity *aporia* (640), is translated "perplexity" in **Luke 21:25** (lit., "at a loss for a way," *a*, negative, *poros*, "a way, resource"), of the distress of nations, finding no solution to their embarrassments; papyri illustrations are in the sense of being at one's wit's end, at a loss how to proceed, without resources.

Waves *salos* (4535), denotes "a tossing," especially the rolling swell of the sea, **Luke 21:25**, KJV, "waves" (RV, "billows").

Roaring *echos* (2279), "a noise" or "sound" (Eng., "echo"), is used of the "roaring" of the sea in **Luke 21:25**, in the best mss., "for the roaring (of the sea and the billows)," RV; some mss. have the present participle of *echeo*, "to sound," KJV "(the sea and the waves) roaring.

21:26 Men's hearts failing them for fear, and for looking after those things which are coming on the earth: for the powers of heaven shall be shaken.

Hearts In **Luke 21:26**, where there is no word for "hearts" in the original, the RV has "men fainting (for fear)."

Failing In **Luke 21:26**, *apopsucho*, lit., "to breathe out life," hence, "to faint," is translated "hearts failing," in the KJV, RV, "fainting."

Looking *prosdokia* (4329), "a watching for, expectation," is used in the NT only of the "expectation" of evil, **Luke 21:26**, RV, "expectation," KJV, "looking for," regarding impending calamities; Acts 12:11, "the expectation" of the execution of Peter.

Coming *see* Come at *Luke 1:35*.

Earth *oikoumene* (3625), the present participle, passive voice, of *oikeo*, "to dwell, inhabit," denotes the "inhabited earth." It is translated "world" in every place where it has this significance, save in **Luke 21:26**, KJV, where it is translated "earth." *See also* World at *Luke 2:1*.

Shaken *see Luke 6:38*.

21:27-28 And then shall they see the Son of man coming in a cloud with power and great glory.

And when these things begin to come to pass, then look up, and lift up your heads; for your redemption draweth nigh.

Look *anakupto* (352), "to lift oneself up" (*ana*, "up"), is translated "look up" in **Luke 21:28**, of being elated in joyous expectation (followed by *epairo*, "to lift up").

Lift *epairo* (1869), "to lift up" (*epi*, "up," *airo*, "to raise"), is said (a) literally, of a sail, Acts 27:40; hands, **Luke 24:50**; 1 Tim. 2:8; heads, **Luke 21:28**; eyes, Matt. 17:8, etc.; (b) metaphorically, of "exalting" oneself, being "lifted up" with pride, 2 Cor. 10:5; 11:20. *See also* Lifted at *Luke 6:20*.

Redemption *apolutrosis* (629), lit., "a releasing, for (i.e., on payment of) a ransom." It is used of (a) "deliverance" from physical torture, Heb. 11:35; (b) the deliverance of the people of God at the coming of Christ with His glorified saints, "in a cloud with power and great glory," **Luke 21:28**, a "redemption" to be accomplished at the "outshining of His Parousia," 2 Thess. 2:8, i.e., at His second advent; (c) forgiveness and justification, "redemption" as the result of expiation, deliverance from the guilt of sins, Rom. 3:24, "through the redemption that is in Christ Jesus"; Eph. 1:7, defined as "the forgiveness of our trespasses," RV; so Col. 1:14, "the forgiveness of our sins," indicating both the liberation from the guilt and doom of sin and the introduction into a life of liberty, "newness of life" (Rom. 6:4); Heb. 9:15, "for the redemption of the transgressions that were under the first covenant," RV, here "redemption of" is equivalent to "redemption from," the genitive case being used of the object from which the "redemption" is effected, not from the consequence of the transgressions, but from the transgressions themselves; (d) the deliverance of the believer from the presence and power of sin, and of his body from bondage to corruption, at the coming (the Parousia in its inception) of the Lord Jesus, Rom. 8:23; 1 Cor. 1:30; Eph. 1:4; 4:30.

Draweth nigh *see* Come nigh at *Luke 10:9*.

21:29 And he spake to them a parable; Behold the fig tree, and all the trees;

Fig tree *see Luke 13:6*. *See also* Tree at *Luke 6:43*.

21:30 When they now shoot forth, ye see and know of your own selves that summer is now nigh at hand.

Shoot forth *proballo* (4261), lit., "to throw before," is used of "the putting forth of leaves, blossom, fruit," said of trees in general, **Luke 21:30**, "shoot forth."

Your own selves *see* Yourselves at *Luke 3:8*.

Summer *theros* (2330), akin to *thero*, "to heat," occurs in Matt. 24:32; Mark 13:28; **Luke 21:30**.

Nigh *see Luke 19:11*.

At hand *engus* (1451), "near, nigh," frequently rendered "at hand," is used (a) of place, e.g., of the Lord's sepulchre, John 19:42, "nigh at hand"; (b) of time, e.g., Matt. 26:18; **Luke 21:30**, **31**, RV, "nigh," KJV, "nigh at hand"; in Phil. 4:5, "the Lord is at hand," it is possible to regard the meaning as that either of (a) or (b); the following reasons may point to (b): (1) the subject of the preceding context has been the return of Christ, 3:20, 21; (2) the phrase is a translation of the Aramaic "Maranatha," 1 Cor. 16:22, a Christian watchword, and the use of the title "the Lord" is appropriate; (3) the similar use of the adverb in Rev. 1:3 and 22:10; (4) the similar use of the corresponding verb in Rom. 13:12; Heb. 10:25, "drawing nigh," RV; Jas. 5:8; cf. 1 Pet. 4:7.

21:31 So likewise ye, when ye see these things come to pass, know ye that the kingdom of God is nigh at hand.

Likewise *see Luke 3:14*.

At hand *see Luke 21:30*.

21:32 Verily I say unto you, This generation shall not pass away, till all be fulfilled.

Generation *see* Generations at *Luke 1:48*.

Pass *see Luke 11:42*.

Fulfilled *ginomai*, "to become, to take place," is rendered "fulfilled" in the KJV of Matt. 5:18; 24:34; **Luke 21:32**, RV, "accomplished," in each place.

"I hope that the day is near at hand when the advent of the great God will appear, for all things everywhere are boiling, burning, moving, falling, sinking, groaning."

MARTIN LUTHER

21:33 Heaven and earth shall pass away: but my words shall not pass away.

Pass *see Luke 11:42.*

21:34 And take heed to yourselves, lest at any time your hearts be overcharged with surfeiting, and drunkenness, and cares of this life, and *so* that day come upon you unawares.

Heed *see Luke 17:3.*

Yourselves *see Luke 3:8.*

Lest *see Luke 4:11.*

Overcharged *bareo* (916), or *baruno*, is rendered "overcharged" in **Luke 21:34**. *See also* **Heavy** at *Luke 9:32.*

Surfeiting *kraipale* (2897), signifies "the giddiness and headache resulting from excessive winebibbing, a drunken nausea," "surfeiting," **Luke 21:34**. Trench (*Syn.* Sec.lxi) distinguishes this and the synonymous words, *methe*, "drunkenness," *oinophlugia*, "wine-bibbing" (KJV, "excess of wine," 1 Pet. 4:3), *komos*, "revelling."

Drunkenness *methe* (3178), "strong drink" (akin to *methu*, "wine"), denotes "drunkenness, habitual intoxication," **Luke 21:34**; Rom. 13:13; Gal. 5:21.

Cares *see Luke 8:14.*

Life *biotikos* (982), "pertaining to life" (*bios*), is translated "of this life," in **Luke 21:34**, with reference to cares; in 1 Cor. 6:3 "(things) that pertain to this life," and v. 4, "(things) pertaining to this life," i.e., matters of this world, concerning which Christians at Corinth were engaged in public lawsuits one with another; such matters were to be regarded as relatively unimportant in view of the great tribunals to come under the jurisdiction of saints hereafter. Moulton and Milligan (*Vocab.*) illustrate the word from phrases in the papyri, e.g., "business (documents)"; "business concerning my livelihood"; "(stories) of ordinary life."

Unawares *aiphnidios* (160), "sudden," occurs in 1 Thess. 5:3, where it has the place of emphasis at the beginning of the sentence, as *olethros*, "destruction," which the adjective qualifies, has at the end; in **Luke 21:34**, it is used adverbially, RV, "suddenly" (KJV, "unawares").

21:35 For as a snare shall it come on all them that dwell on the face of the whole earth.

Snare *pagis* (3803), "a trap, a snare" (akin to *pegnumi*, "to fix," and *pagideuo*, "to ensnare," which see), is used metaphorically of (a) the allurements to evil by which the Devil "ensnares" one, 1 Tim. 3:7; 2 Tim. 2:26; (b) seductions to evil, which "ensnare" those who "desire to be rich," 1 Tim. 6:9; (c) the evil brought by Israel upon themselves by which the special privileges divinely granted them and centering in Christ, became a "snare" to them, their rejection of Christ and the gospel being the retributive effect of their apostasy, Rom. 11:9; (d) of the sudden judgments of God to come upon those whose hearts are "overcharged with surfeiting, and drunkenness, and cares of this life," **Luke 21:34** (v. **35** in KJV).

Dwell *kathemai* (2521), "to sit down," is translated "dwell," in **Luke 21:35**. *See also* **Sit** at *Luke 1:79.*

Face *see Luke 9:51.*

Earth *see* **Land** at *Luke 4:25.*

21:36 Watch ye therefore, and pray always, that ye may be accounted worthy to escape all these things that shall come to pass, and to stand before the Son of man.

Watch *agrupneo* (69), "to be sleepless" (from *agreuo*, "to chase," and *hupnos*, "sleep"), is used metaphorically, "to be watchful," in Mark 13:33; **Luke 21:36**; Eph. 6:18; Heb. 13:17. The word expresses not mere wakefulness, but the "watchfulness" of those who are intent upon a thing.

Pray *see* **Besought** at *Luke 5:12.*

Always Two phrases, rendered "always" or "alway" in the KJV, are *en panti kairo* (lit., "in every season"), **Luke 21:36**, RV, "at every season," Eph. 6:18, RV, "at all seasons," and *pasas tas hemeras,* (lit., "all the days"), Matt. 28:20, KJV and RV, "alway."

Accounted *see Luke 20:35.*

Worthy *see Luke 20:35.*

Escape *ekpheugo* (1628), "to flee out of a place," is said of the "escape" of prisoners, Acts 16:27; of Sceva's sons, "fleeing" from the demoniac, 19:16; of Paul's escape from Damascus, 2 Cor. 11:33; elsewhere with reference to the judgments of God, **Luke 21:36**; Rom. 2:3; Heb. 2:3; 12:25; 1 Thess. 5:3.

Shall *see Luke 9:44.*

21:37 And in the day time he was teaching in the temple; and at night he went out, and abode in the mount that is called *the mount* of Olives.

Day *see* Daily at *Luke 11:3.*

Abode *aulizomai* (835), "to lodge," originally "to lodge in the *aule*, or courtyard," is said of shepherds and flocks; hence, to pass the night in the open air, as did the Lord, **Luke 21:37**; "to lodge in a house," as of His visit to Bethany, Matt. 21:17.

Olives *see Luke 19:29.*

21:38 And all the people came early in the morning to him in the temple, for to hear him.

Morning *orthrizo* (3719), "to do anything early in the morning," is translated "came early in the morning," in **Luke 21:38**.

Chapter 22

22:1 Now the feast of unleavened bread drew nigh, which is called the Passover.

Bread *azumos* (106), denotes "unleavened bread," i.e., without any process of fermentation; hence, metaphorically, "of a holy, spiritual condition," 1 Cor. 5:7, and of "sincerity and truth" (v. 8). With the article it signifies the feast of unleavened bread, Matt. 26:17; Mark 14:1, 12; **Luke 22:1**, 7; Acts 12:3; 20:6.

22:2 And the chief priests and scribes sought how they might kill him; for they feared the people.

Kill *anaireo* (337), denotes (a) "to take up" (*ana*, "up," *haireo*, "to take"), said of Pharaoh's daughter, in "taking up" Moses, Acts 7:21; (b) "to take away" in the sense of removing, Heb. 10:9, of the legal appointment of sacrifices, to bring in the will of God in the sacrificial offering of the death of Christ; (c) "to kill," used physically only, e.g., **Luke 22:2**; in 2 Thess. 2:8, instead of the future tense of this verb, some texts (followed by RV marg.) read the future of *analisko*, "to consume."

22:3 Then entered Satan into Judas surnamed Iscariot, being of the number of the twelve.

Satan *see Luke 4:8.*

Surname *epikaleo* (1941), "to put a name upon" (*epi*, "upon," *kaleo*, "to call"), "to surname," is used in this sense in the passive voice, in some texts in Matt. 10:3 (it is absent in the best); in **Luke 22:3**, in some texts (the best have *kaleo*, "to call"); Acts 1:23; 4:36; 10:5, 18, 32; 11:13; 12:12, 25; in some texts, 15:22 (the best have *kaleo*).

Number *arithmos* (706), number, "a number" (Eng., "arithmetic," etc.), occurs in **Luke 22:3**; John 6:10; Rom. 9:27; elsewhere five times in Acts, ten times in Revelation.

22:4 And he went his way, and communed with the chief priests and captains, how he might betray him unto them.

Communed *sullaleo* (4814), "to talk together," is translated "communed" in **Luke 22:4**, of the conspiracy of Judas with the chief priests. *See also* Spake at *Luke 4:36.*

Captains *strategos* (4755), originally the commander of an army (from *stratos*, "an army," and *ago*, "to lead"), came to denote "a civil commander, a governor" (Latin, *duumvir*), the highest magistrate, or any civil officer in chief command, Acts 16:20, 22, 35-36, 38; also the "chief captain" of the Temple, himself Levite, having command of the Levites who kept guard in and around the Temple, **Luke 22:4**, **52**; Acts 4:1; 5:24, 26. Cf. Jer. 20:1.

22:5 And they were glad, and covenanted to give him money.

Glad *see Luke 15:32.*

Covenanted *suntithemi* (4934), lit., "to put together" (*sun*, "with," *tithemi*, "to put"), in the middle voice, means "to make an agreement, or to assent to"; translated "covenanted" in **Luke 22:5**; "agreed" in John 9:22, and Acts 23:20; "assented" in Acts 24:9.

Money *see Luke 9:3.*

22:6 And he promised, and sought opportunity to betray him unto them in the absence of the multitude.

Promised *exomologeo* (1843), "to agree openly, to acknowledge outwardly, or fully" (*ex*, "for," *ek*, "out," intensive), is translated "consented" in the RV of **Luke 22:6** (KJV, promised). *See also* Thank at *Luke 10:21.*

Opportunity *eukairia* (2120), "a fitting time, opportunity," occurs in Matt. 26:16 and **Luke 22:6**. Cf. *eukairos*, "seasonable".

Absence *ater* (817), means "without," **Luke 22:35**, "without purse"; in v. **6**, "in the absence (of the multitude)," marg., "without tumult." *See also* Without at *Luke 11:40.*

22:7 Then came the day of unleavened bread, when the passover must be killed.

Bread *see Luke 22:1.*

Passover *pascha* (3957), the Greek spelling of the Aramaic word for the

Passover, from the Hebrew *pasach*, "to pass over, to spare," a feast instituted by God in commemoration of the deliverance of Israel from Egypt, and anticipatory of the expiatory sacrifice of Christ. The word signifies (I) "the Passover Feast," e.g., Matt. 26:2; John 2:13, 23; 6:4; 11:55; 12:1; 13:1; 18:39; 19:14; Acts 12:4; Heb. 11:28; (II) by metonymy, (a) "the Paschal Supper," Matt. 26:18, 19; Mark 14:16; **Luke 22:8, 13**; (b) "the Paschal lamb," e.g., Mark 14:12 (cf. Exod. 12:21); **Luke 22:7**; (c) "Christ Himself," 1 Cor. 5:7.

Killed *thuo* (2380), is used of "sacrificing by slaying a victim," (a) of the "sacrifice" of Christ, 1 Cor. 5:7, RV, "hath been sacrificed" (KJV, "is sacrificed"); (b) of the Passover "sacrifice," Mark 14:12, RV, "they sacrificed" (KJV, "they killed"); **Luke 22:7**, RV, "(must) be sacrificed," KJV, "(must) be killed"; (c) of idolatrous "sacrifices," Acts 14:13, 18; 1 Cor. 10:20 (twice). *See also* Kill at *Luke 15:23*.

22:8 And he sent Peter and John, saying, Go and prepare us the passover, that we may eat.

Sent *see Luke 1:19*.

Passover *see Luke 22:7*.

22:9-10 And they said unto him, Where wilt thou that we prepare?

And he said unto them, Behold, when ye are entered into the city, there shall a man meet you, bearing a pitcher of water; follow him into the house where he entereth in.

Entered, Entereth *see* Enter at *Luke 8:16*.

Meet *see* Met at *Luke 9:37*.

Bearing *see* Bare at *Luke 7:14*.

Pitcher *keramion* (2765), "an earthen vessel" (*keramos*, "potter's clay"), "a jar" or "jug," occurs in Mark 14:13; **Luke 22:10**.

22:11 And ye shall say unto the goodman of the house, The Master saith unto thee, Where is the guestchamber, where I shall eat the passover with my disciples?

Goodman *see Luke 12:39*.

Master *see* Doctors at *Luke 2:46*.

Guestchamber *see* Room at *Luke 2:7*.

Disciples *see Luke 6:17*.

22:12 And he shall shew you a large upper room furnished: there make ready.

Large *megas* (3173), "great, large, of physical magnitude," is translated "large" in Mark 14:15 and **Luke 22:12**, of the upper room.

Room *anagaion* or *anogeon* (508), "an upper room" (*ana*, "above," *ge*, "ground"), occurs in Mark 14:15; **Luke 22:12**, "a chamber," often over a porch, or connected with the roof, where meals were taken and privacy obtained.

Furnished *stronnumi* (4766), or *stronnuo*, "to spread," is used of "furnishing a room," Mark 14:15; **Luke 22:12**; of "making a bed," Acts 9:34; in Matt. 21:8; Mark 11:8, "spread" (KJV, "strawed," twice).

22:13 And they went, and found as he had said unto them: and they made ready the passover.

Passover *see Luke 22:7*.

22:14 And when the hour was come, he sat down, and the twelve apostles with him.

Sat *see Luke 11:37*.

22:15 And he said unto them, With desire I have desired to eat this passover with you before I suffer:

Desire, Desired *epithumia* (1939), "a desire, craving, longing, mostly of evil desires," frequently translated "lust," is used in the following, of good "desires": of the Lord's "wish" concerning the last Passover, **Luke 22:15**, of Paul's "desire" to be with Christ, Phil. 1:23; of his "desire" to see the saints at Thessalonica again, 1 Thess. 2:17. With regard to evil "desires," in Col. 3:5 the RV has "desire," for the KJV, "concupiscence"; in 1 Thess. 4:5, RV, "lust," for KJV, "concupiscence"; there the preceding word *pathos* is translated "passion," RV, for KJV, "lust"; also in Col. 3:5 *pathos* and *epithumia* are associated, RV, "passion," for KJV, "inordinate affection." *Epithumia* is combined with *pathema*, in Gal. 5:24; for the KJV, "affections and lusts," the RV has "passions, and the lusts thereof." *Epithumia* is the more comprehensive term, including all manner of "lusts and desires"; *pathema* denotes suffering; in the passage in Gal. (l.c.) the sufferings are those produced by yielding to the flesh; *pathos* points more to the evil state from which "lusts" spring. Cf *orexis*, "lust," Rom. 1:27. *See also* Fain at *Luke 15:16;* Desiring at *Luke 16:21*.

Suffer *see* Suffered at *Luke 13:2*.

22:16 For I say unto you, I will not any more eat thereof, until it be fulfilled in the kingdom of God.

Fulfilled *see Luke 4:21*.

22:17 And he took the cup, and gave thanks, and said, Take this, and divide *it* among yourselves:

Took *see Luke 2:28*.

Thanks *see* ***Luke 17:16.***

Divide *see* Divided at *Luke 11:17.*

22:18 For I say unto you, I will not drink of the fruit of the vine, until the kingdom of God shall come.

Fruit *see* Fruits at *Luke 12:18.*

22:19 And he took bread, and gave thanks, and brake *it*, and gave unto them, saying, This is my body which is given for you: this do in remembrance of me.

Gave *see* Delivered at *Luke 4:17.*

Thanks *see* ***Luke 17:16.***

Brake *klao* or *klazo* (2806), "to break, to break off pieces," is used of "breaking bread," (a) of the Lord's act in providing for people, Matt. 14:19; 15:36; Mark 8:6, 19; (b) of the "breaking of bread" in the Lord's Supper, Matt. 26:26; Mark 14:22; **Luke 22:19**; Acts 20:7; 1 Cor. 10:16; 11:24; (c) of an ordinary meal, Acts 2:46; 20:11; 27:35; (d) of the Lord's act in giving evidence of His resurrection, **Luke 24:30.**

My *see* All that I have at *Luke 15:31.*

Remembrance *anamnesis* (364), "a remembrance" (*ana*, "up," or "again," and *mimnesko*), is used (a) in Christ's command in the institution of the Lord's Supper, **Luke 22:19**; 1 Cor. 11:24, 25, not "in memory of" but in an affectionate calling of the Person Himself to mind; (b) of the "remembrance" of sins, Heb. 10:3, RV, "a remembrance" (KJV, "a remembrance again"; but the prefix *ana* does not here signify "again"); what is indicated, in regard to the sacrifices under the Law, is not simply an external bringing to "remembrance," but an awakening of mind. In the Sept., Lev. 24:7; Num. 10:10; Pss. 38 and 70, Titles.

Me In **Luke 22:19** the possessive pronoun *emos*, "my," is rendered "of Me," lit., "(into) My (remembrance)."

22:20 Likewise also the cup after supper, saying, This cup *is* the new testament in my blood, which is shed for you.

Likewise *see* Manner at *Luke 20:31.*

Supper *see* Sup at *Luke 17:8.*

Testament *see* Covenant at *Luke 1:72.*

Shed *ekchuno* (1632), or *ekchunno*, a Hellenistic form, is used of the blood of Christ, **Luke 22:20**, RV "is poured out" (KJV, "is shed"); of the Holy Spirit, Acts 10:45. *See also* ***Luke 11:50.***

22:21 But, behold, the hand of him that betrayeth me *is* with me on the table.

Table *see* ***Luke 16:21.***

22:22 And truly the Son of man goeth, as it was determined: but woe unto that man by whom he is betrayed!

Determined *horizo* (3724), denotes "to bound, to set a boundary" (Eng., "horizon"); hence, "to mark out definitely, determine"; it is translated "to determine" in **Luke 22:22**, of the foreordained pathway of Christ; Acts 11:29, of a "determination" to send relief; 17:26, where it is used of fixing the bounds of seasons. In Acts 2:23 the verb is translated "determinate," with reference to counsel. Here the verbal form might have been adhered to by the translation "determined"; that is to say, in the sense of "settled."

Woe *see* ***Luke 6:24.***

22:23 And they began to enquire among themselves, which of them it was that should do this thing.

Enquire *suzeteo* (4802), or *sunzeteo*, "to search together," "to discuss, dispute," is translated "to question" (or "question with or together") in Mark 1:27; 8:11; 9:10, 14, 16; 12:28, RV (KJV, "reasoning together"); **Luke 22:23**, RV (KJV, "inquire"); **24:15**, RV (KJV, "reasoned").

Should *see* ***Luke 19:11.***

22:24 And there was also a strife among them, which of them should be accounted the greatest.

Strife *philoneikia* (5379), lit., "love of strife" (*phileo*, "to love," *neikos*, "strife"), signifies "eagerness to contend"; hence, a "contention," said of the disciples, **Luke 22:24.**

Accounted *dokeo* (1380), primarily, "to be of opinion, think, suppose," also signifies "to seem, be accounted, reputed," translated "accounted" in Mark 10:42; **Luke 22:24.** It is not used ironically here, nor in Gal. 2:2, 6, 9, "those who were of repute."

Greatest *see* ***Luke 9:46.***

22:25 And he said unto them, The kings of the Gentiles exercise lordship over them; and they that exercise authority upon them are called benefactors.

Exercise lordship *kurieuo* (2961), "to be lord over, rule over, have dominion over," is used of (a) divine authority over men, Rom. 14:9, "might be Lord"; (b) human authority over men, **Luke 22:25**, "lordship," 1 Tim. 6:15, "lords" (RV, marg., "them that rule as lords"); (c) the permanent immunity of Christ from the "dominion" of death, Rom. 6:9; (d) the deliverance of the believer from the "dominion" of sin, Rom. 6:14; (e) the "dominion" of law over men, Rom. 7:1; (f) the "dominion" of a person over the faith of other believers, 2 Cor. 1:24 (RV, "lordship").

Authority *exousiazo* (1850), signifies "to exercise power," **Luke 22:25**; 1 Cor. 6:12; 7:4 (twice).

Benefactors *euergetes* (2110), "a benefactor," expresses the agent, **Luke 22:25**.

22:26 But ye *shall* not *be* so: but he that is greatest among you, let him be as the younger; and he that is chief, as he that doth serve.

Greatest *meizon* (3187), is the comparative degree of *megas*, e.g., Matt. 11:11; in Matt. 13:32, the RV rightly has "greater than" (KJV, "the greatest among"); 23:17; in **Luke 22:26**, RV, "the greater (among you)" (KJV, "greatest"); in Jas. 3:1, RV, "the heavier (marg., greater) judgment" (KJV, "the greater condemnation"); it is used in the neuter plural in John 1:50, "greater things"; in 14:12, "greater works" (lit., "greater things"); in 1 Cor. 12:31, RV, "the greater," KJV, "the best". *See also Luke 9:46*.

Younger *see Luke 15:12*.

Chief *hegeomai* (2233), "to lead the way, to preside, rule, be the chief," is used of the ambition "to be chief" among the disciples of Christ, **Luke 22:26**; of Paul as the "chief" speaker in gospel testimony at Lystra, Acts 14:12; of Judas and Silas, as chief (or rather, "leading") men among the brethren at Jerusalem, Acts 15:22.

Serve *see Luke 10:40. See also* Ministered at *Luke 4:39*.

22:27 For whether *is* greater, he that sitteth at meat, or he that serveth? *is* not he that sitteth at meat? but I am among you as he that serveth.

Sitteth *see* Sat at *Luke 7:37*.

Serveth *see* Serve at *Luke 10:40. See also* Ministered at *Luke 4:39*.

Among *see* Midst at *Luke 4:30*.

22:28 Ye are they which have continued with me in my temptations.

Continued *see* Remained at *Luke 1:22*.

Temptations *see* Temptation at *Luke 4:13*.

22:29 And I appoint unto you a kingdom, as my Father hath appointed unto me;

Appoint, Appointed *diatithemi* (1303), is used in the middle voice only. The Lord used it of His disciples with reference to the kingdom which is to be theirs hereafter, and of Himself in the same respect, as that which has been "appointed" for Him by His Father, **Luke 22:29**.

22:30 That ye may eat and drink at my table in my kingdom, and sit on thrones judging the twelve tribes of Israel.

Table *see Luke 16:21*.

Kingdom *see* Kingdoms at *Luke 4:5*.

Thrones *see* Throne at *Luke 1:32*.

Twelve *dodeka* (1427), is used frequently in the Gospels for the twelve apostles, and in Acts 6:2; 1 Cor. 15:5; Rev. 21:14b; of the tribes of Israel, Matt. 19:28; **Luke 22:30**; Jas. 1:1; Rev. 21:12c (cf. 7:5-8; 12:1); in various details relating to the heavenly Jerusalem, Rev. 21:12-21; 22:2. The number in general is regarded as suggestive of divine administration.

Tribes *see* Tribe at *Luke 2:36*.

22:31 And the Lord said, Simon, Simon, behold, Satan hath desired *to have* you, that he may sift *you* as wheat:

Satan *see Luke 4:8*.

Desired In **Luke 22:31**, RV, *exaiteomai* is rendered "hath asked to have."

Sift *siniazo* (4617), "to winnow, sift" (*sinion*, "a sieve"), is used figuratively in **Luke 22:31**.

Wheat *see Luke 3:17*.

22:32 But I have prayed for thee, that thy faith fail not: and when thou art converted, strengthen thy brethren.

Prayed *see* Besought at *Luke 5:12*.

Fail *see Luke 16:9*.

Converted *epistrepho* (1994), "to turn about, turn towards," is used transitively, and so rendered "convert" (of causing a person to turn) in Jas. 5:19-20. Elsewhere, where the KJV translates this verb, either in the middle voice and intransitive use, or the passive, the RV adheres to the middle voice significance, and translates by "turn again," Matt. 13:15; Mark 4:12; **Luke 22:32**; Acts 3:19; 28:27.

Strengthen *see* Set at *Luke 9:51*.

22:33 And he said unto him, Lord, I am ready to go with thee, both into prison, and to death.

Ready *see Luke 12:40*.

22:34 And he said, I tell thee, Peter, the cock shall not crow this day, before that thou shalt thrice deny that thou knowest me.

Cock *alektor* (220), "a cock," perhaps connected with a Hebrew phrase for the oncoming of the light, is found in the passages concerning Peter's denial of the Lord, Matt. 26:34,

74-75; Mark 14:30, 68, 72; Luke **22:34, 60-61**; John 13:38; 18:27.

This day *see Luke 4:21*.

Deny *see Luke 9:23*.

22:35 And he said unto them, When I sent you without purse, and scrip, and shoes, lacked ye any thing? And they said, Nothing.

Without *see Luke 11:40. See also* Absence at *Luke 22:6*.

Purse *see Luke 10:4*.

Scrip *see Luke 9:3*.

Lacked *hustereo* (5302), "to come or be behind," is used in the sense of "lacking" certain things, Matt. 19:20; Mark 10:21; **Luke 22:35**; in the sense of being inferior, 1 Cor. 12:24 (middle voice). Elsewhere it is translated in various ways.

Nothing *ouden* (3762), the neuter of *oudeis*, "no one," occurs, e.g., in Matt. 5:13; 10:26; 23:16; adverbially, e.g., in Matt. 27:24; 2 Cor. 12:11 (1st part), "in nothing"; 1 Tim. 4:4; in the dative case, after *en*, "in," Phil. 1:20. Westcott and Hort adopt the spelling *outhen* in **Luke 22:35; 23:14**; Acts 15:9; 19:27; 26:26; 1 Cor. 13:2.

22:36 Then said he unto them, But now, he that hath a purse, let him take *it*, and likewise *his* scrip: and he that hath no sword, let him sell his garment, and buy one.

Likewise *see Luke 5:33*.

Scrip *see Luke 9:3*.

22:37 For I say unto you, that this that is written must yet be accomplished in me, And he was reckoned among the transgressors: for the things concerning me have an end.

"If I could hear Christ praying for me in the next room, I would not fear a million enemies. Yet the distance makes no difference; he is praying for me!"

ROBERT MURRAY MCCHEYNE

Reckoned *logizomai* (3049), is properly used (a) of "numerical calculation," e.g., **Luke 22:37**; (b) metaphorically, "by a reckoning of characteristics or reasons, to take into account," Rom. 2:26, "shall ... be reckoned," RV (KJV, "counted"), of "reckoning" uncircumcision for circumcision by God's estimate in contrast to that of the Jew regarding his own condition (v. 3); in 4:3, 5, 6, 9, 11, 22, 23, 24, of "reckoning" faith for righteousness, or "reckoning" righteousness to persons, in all of which the RV uses the verb "to reckon" instead of the KJV "to count or to impute ... (c) "to consider, calculate," translated "to reckon" in Rom. 6:11; 8:36; 2 Cor. 10:11, RV, "let (such a one) reckon (this)"; (d) "to suppose, judge, deem," translated "to reckon" in Rom. 2:3, "reckonest thou (this)," RV (KJV, "thinkest"); 3:28 (KJV, "we conclude"); 8:18; 2 Cor. 11:5 (KJV, "I suppose).

Transgressors *anomos* (459), "without law" (*a*-, negative), is translated "transgressors" in **Luke 22:37** (in some texts, Mark 15:28), in a quotation from Isa. 53:12.

End *see Luke 1:33*.

22:38 And they said, Lord, behold, here *are* two swords. And he said unto them, It is enough.

Swords *see* Sword at *Luke 21:24*.

Enough *hikanos* (2425), "sufficient, competent, fit" (akin to *hikano* and *hiko*, "to reach, attain" and *hikanoo*, "to make sufficient"), is translated "enough" in **Luke 22:38**, of the Lord's reply to Peter concerning the swords.

22:39 And he came out, and went, as he was wont, to the mount of Olives; and his disciples also followed him.

Wont In **Luke 22:39**, KJV, *ethos*, "a custom," preceded by *kata* and the article, lit., "according to the (i.e., His) custom," is translated "as He was wont" (RV, "as His custom was"). *See also* Custom at *Luke 2:42*.

Mount *see* Mountain at *Luke 3:5*.

Olives *see Luke 19:37*.

22:40 And when he was at the place, he said unto them, Pray that ye enter not into temptation.

Temptation *see Luke 4:13*.

22:41 And he was withdrawn from them about a stone's cast, and kneeled down, and prayed,

Withdrawn *apospao* (645), "to draw away," lit., "to wrench away from," is used of a sword, Matt. 26:51, of "drawing" away disciples into error, Acts 20:30; of Christ's "withdrawal" from the disciples, in Gethsemane, **Luke 22:41**, KJV, "was withdrawn," RV, "was parted" (or "was reft away from them"); of "parting" from a company, Acts 21:1 (KJV, "were gotten," RV, "were parted").

About *see Luke 3:23*.

Cast *belos* (956), akin to *ballo*, "to throw," denotes "a missile, an arrow, javelin, dart, etc.," Eph. 6:16. Cf. *bole*, "a stone's throw or cast," **Luke 22:41**; *bolizo*, "to sound" (to fathom the depth of water), Acts 27:28.

22:42 Saying, Father, if thou be willing, remove this cup from me: nevertheless not my will, but thine, be done.

Willing *boulomai* (1014), is rendered "(if) Thou be willing" in **Luke 22:42**; in 2 Pet. 3:9, KJV (RV, wishing).

Remove *paraphero* (3911), lit., "to bring to or before" (*para*, "beside," *phero*, "to carry"), "to take or carry away," is translated "remove" in the Lord's prayer in Gethsemane, Mark 14:36, RV (KJV, "take away"); **Luke 22:42**. In the Sept., 1 Sam. 21:13.

Cup *poterion* (4221), a diminutive of *poter*, denotes, primarily, a "drinking vessel"; hence, "a cup" (a) literal, as, e.g., in Matt. 10:42. The "cup" of blessing, 1 Cor. 10:16, is so named from the third (the fourth according to Edersheim) "cup" in the Jewish Passover feast, over which thanks and praise were given to God. This connection is not to be rejected on the ground that the church at Corinth was unfamiliar with Jewish customs. That the contrary was the case, see 5:7; (b) figurative, of one's lot or experience, joyous or sorrowful (frequent in the Psalms; cf. Ps. 116:18, "cup of salvation"); in the NT it is used most frequently of the sufferings of Christ, Matt. 20:22-23; 26:39; Mark 10:38-39; 14:36; **Luke 22:42**; John 18:11; also of the evil deeds of Babylon, Rev. 17:4; 18:6; of divine punishments to be inflicted, Rev. 14:10; 16:19. Cf. Ps. 11:6; 75:8; Isa. 51:17; Jer. 25:15; Ezek. 23:32-34; Zech. 12:2.

22:43 And there appeared an angel unto him from heaven, strengthening him.

Strengthening *enischuo* (1765), is used in **Luke 22:43** and Acts 9:19.

22:44 And being in an agony he prayed more earnestly: and his sweat was as it were great drops of blood falling down to the ground.

Agony *agonia* (74), Eng., "agony," was used among the Greeks as an alternative to *agon*, "a place of assembly"; then for the contests or games which took place there, and then to denote intense emotion. It was more frequently used eventually in this last respect, to denote severe emotional strain and anguish. So in **Luke 22:44**, of the Lord's "agony" in Gethsemane.

Prayed "Prayer is properly addressed to God the Father Matt. 6:6; John 16:23; Eph. 1:17; 3:14, and the Son, Acts 7:59; 2 Cor. 12:8; but in no instance in the NT is prayer addressed to the Holy Spirit distinctively, for whereas the Father is in Heaven, Matt. 6:9, and the Son is at His right hand, Rom. 8:34, the Holy Spirit is in and with the believers, John 14:16, 17. The Holy Spirit, being the sole interpreter of the needs of the human heart, makes His intercession therein; and inasmuch as prayer is impossible to man apart from His help, Rom. 8:26, believers are exhorted to pray at all seasons in the Spirit, Eph. 6:18; cf. Jude 20, and Jas. 5:16, the last clause of which should probably be read 'the inwrought [i.e., by the Holy Spirit] supplication of righteous man availeth much' (or 'greatly prevails' *ischuo*, as in Acts 19:16, 20). None the less on this account is the understanding to be engaged in prayer, 1 Cor. 14:15, and the will, Col. 4:12; Acts 12:5 (where 'earnestly' is, lit., 'stretched out') and so in **Luke 22:44**. Faith is essential to prayer, Matt. 21:22; Mark 11:24; Jas. 1:5-8, for faith is the recognition of, and the committal of ourselves and our matters to, the faithfulness of God. Where the Jews were numerous, as at Thessalonica, they had usually a Synagogue, Acts 17:1; where they were few, as at Philippi, they had merely a *proseuche*, or 'place of prayer,' of much smaller dimensions, and commonly built by a river for the sake of the water necessary to the preliminary ablutions prescribed by Rabbinic tradition, Acts 16:13, 16."

Earnestly *ektenesteron* (1617), used as an adverb in this neuter form, denotes "more earnestly, fervently," **Luke 22:44**.

Sweat *hidros* (2402), is used in **Luke 22:44**. In the Sept., Gen. 3:19.

Drops *thrombos* (2361), "a large, thick drop of clotted blood" (etymologically akin to *trepho*, "to curdle"), is used in **Luke 22:44**, in the plural, in the narrative of the Lord's agony in Gethsemane.

Falling *katabaino* (2597), denotes "to come (or fall) down," **Luke 22:44**; in Rev. 16:21, "cometh down," RV.

22:45 And when he rose up from prayer, and was come to his disciples, he found them sleeping for sorrow,

Rose *see Luke 4:29*.

Sleeping *koimaomai* (2837), is used of natural "sleep," Matt. 28:13; **Luke 22:45**; John 11:12; Acts 12:6; of the death of the body, but only of such as are Christ's; yet never of Christ Himself, though He is "the firstfruits of them that have fallen asleep," 1 Cor. 15:20, of saints who departed before Christ came, Matt. 27:52; Acts 13:36; of Lazarus, while Christ was yet upon the earth, John 11:11; of believers since the Ascension, 1 Thess. 4:13-15, and Acts 7:60; 1 Cor. 7:39; 11:30; 15:6, 18, 51; 2 Pet. 3:4.

Sorrow *lupe* (3077), "grief, sorrow," is translated "sorrow" in **Luke 22:45**; John 16:6, 20-22; Rom. 9:2, RV (KJV, "heaviness"); 2 Cor. 2:1, RV; 2:3, 7; 7:10 (twice); Phil. 2:27 (twice).

22:46 And said unto them, Why sleep ye? rise and pray, lest ye enter into temptation.

Temptation *see Luke 4:13.*

22:47 And while he yet spake, behold a multitude, and he that was called Judas, one of the twelve, went before them, and drew near unto Jesus to kiss him.

Kiss *phileo* (5368), "to love," signifies "to kiss," in Matt. 26:48; Mark 14:44; **Luke 22:47**.

22:48 But Jesus said unto him, Judas, betrayest thou the Son of man with a kiss?

Kiss *see Luke 7:45.*

22:49 When they which were about him saw what would follow, they said unto him, Lord, shall we smite with the sword?

Follow In **Luke 22:49**, the phrase *to esomenon*, lit. "the (thing) about to be" (from *eimi*, "to be"), is translated "what would follow."

Smite *patasso* (3960), "to strike, smite," is used (I) literally, of giving a blow with the hand, or fist or a weapon, Matt. 26:51, RV, "smote" (KJV, "struck"); **Luke 22:49, 50**; Acts 7:24; 12:7; (II) metaphorically, (a) of judgment meted out to Christ, Matt. 26:31; Mark 14:27; (b) of the infliction of disease, by an angel, Acts 12:23; of plagues to be inflicted upon men by two divinely appointed witnesses, Rev. 11:6; (c) of judgment to be executed by Christ upon the nations, Rev. 19:15, the instrument being His Word, described as a sword.

22:50 And one of them smote the servant of the high priest, and cut off his right ear.

One *see Luke 4:40.*

Smote *see* Smite at *Luke 22:49.*

Cut *aphaireo* (851), "to take away, remove," is translated "cut off" in Mark 14:47, KJV, and **Luke 22:50**, and "smote off" in Matt. 26:51; RV, "struck off" in each place.

22:51 And Jesus answered and said, Suffer ye thus far. And he touched his ear, and healed him.

Suffer *see* Suffered at *Luke 4:41.*

Far In **Luke 22:51**, "thus far" translates the phrase *heos toutou*, lit., "unto this."

Ear *otion* (5621), a diminutive, but without the diminutive force, it being a common tendency in everyday speech to apply a diminutive form to most parts of the body, is used in Matt. 26:51; Mark 14:47 (in some mss.); **Luke 22:51**; John 18:10 (in some mss.) and v. 26, all with reference to the "ear" of Malchus.

22:52 Then Jesus said unto the chief priests, and captains of the temple, and the elders, which were come to him, Be ye come out, as against a thief, with swords and staves?

Captains *see Luke 22:4.*

"Jesus was in a garden, not of delight as the first Adam, in which he destroyed himself and the whole human race, but in one of agony, in which he saved himself and the whole human race."

BLAISE PASCAL

22:53 When I was daily with you in the temple, ye stretched forth no hands against me: but this is your hour, and the power of darkness.

Darkness *see Luke 1:79.*

Stretched forth *see* Put forth at *Luke 5:13.*

22:54 Then took they him, and led *him*, and brought him into the high priest's house. And Peter followed afar off.

Took *sullambano* (4815), lit., "to take together" (*sun*, "with," *lambano*, "to take or lay hold of"), chiefly signifies "to seize as a prisoner"; in the following the RV substitutes the more suitable and forceful verb, "to seize," for KJV, "to take": Matt. 26:55; Mark 14:48; **Luke 22:54**; John 18:12; Acts 12:3; 23:27; 26:21; in Acts 1:16, RV and KJV, "took."

Led *see Luke 4:1.*

22:55 And when they had kindled a fire in the midst of the hall, and were set down together, Peter sat down among them.

Kindled *periapto* (4012 and 681), properly, "to tie about, attach," is used of "lighting" a fire in the midst of a court in **Luke 22:55**.

Set *sunkathizo* (4776), denotes (a) transitively, "to make to sit together," Eph. 2:6; (b) intransitively, **Luke 22:55**, RV, "had sat down together" (KJV, "were set down").

Midst *see Luke 4:30.*

Hall *aule* (833), "a court," most frequently the place where a governor dispensed justice, is rendered "hall" in Mark 15:16 and **Luke 22:55**, KJV (RV, "court"). *See also* **Palace** at *Luke 11:21.*

22:56 But a certain maid beheld him as he sat by the fire, and earnestly looked upon him, and said, This man was also with him.

Maid *see* **Maidens** at *Luke 12:45.*

Earnestly *atenizo*, "to fix the eyes upon, gaze upon," is translated "earnestly looked" in **Luke 22:56**, KJV (RV, "looking steadfastly"); in Acts 3:12, KJV, "look ye earnestly," RV, "fasten ye your eyes on"; in Acts 23:1, KJV, "earnestly beholding," RV, "looking steadfastly on."

Looked *see* **Fastened** at *Luke 4:20.*

**22:57-58 And he denied him, saying, Woman, I know him not.
And after a little while another saw him, and said, Thou art also of them. And Peter said, Man, I am not.**

Little *brachus* (1024), "short," is used to some extent adverbially of (a) time, with the preposition *meta*, "after," **Luke 22:58**, "(after) a little while"; in Acts 5:34, without a preposition, RV, "a little while" (KJV, "a little space"); in Heb. 2:7, 9, "a little" (KJV marg. in v. 7, and RV marg., in both, "a little while"), where the writer transfers to time what the Sept. in Ps. 8:5 says of rank; (b) of quantity, John 6:7; in Heb. 13:22, preceded by the preposition *dia*, "by means of," and with *logo.*, "words" (genitive plural) understood, "(in) few words"; (c) of distance, Acts 27:28, RV, "a little space" (KJV, "a little further").

22:59 And about the space of one hour after another confidently affirmed, saying, Of a truth this *fellow* also was with him: for he is a Galilaean.

Space *diistemi* (1339), "to set apart, separate" (*dia*, "apart," *histemi*, "to cause to stand"), is rendered "after the space of" in **Luke 22:59**; in Acts 27:28, with *brachu*, "a little," RV, "after a little space" (KJV, "when they had gone a little further").

Hour *see* **Time** at *Luke 1:10.*

Confidently The adverb "confidently" is combined with the verb "affirm" to represent the verbs *diischurzomai*, **Luke 22:59** and Acts 12:15, RV (KJV, "constantly affirmed"),, and *diabebaioomai*, 1 Tim. 1:7, KJV, "affirm," and Titus 3:8, KJV, "affirm constantly."

Affirmed *diischurizomai* (1340), "to corroborate" (*ischuros* "strong") primarily signifies "to lean upon," hence, "to affirm stoutly, assert vehemently," **Luke 22:59**; Acts 12:15.

22:60 And Peter said, Man, I know not what thou sayest. And immediately, while he yet spake, the cock crew.

Immediately *see Luke 1:64.*

Cock *see Luke 22:34.*

22:61 And the Lord turned, and looked upon Peter. And Peter remembered the word of the Lord, how he had said unto him, Before the cock crow, thou shalt deny me thrice.

Looked *emblepo* (1689), to look at, is translated "to look upon" in Mark 10:27; 14:67; **Luke 22:61**; John 1:36. This verb implies a close, penetrating "look." *See also* **Beheld** at *Luke 20:17.*

Remembered *hupomimnesko* (5279), signifies "to cause one to remember, put one in mind of" (*hupo*, "under," often implies suggestion), John 14:26, "shall ... bring ... to (your) remembrance"; 2 Tim. 2:14, "put ... in remembrance"; Titus 3:1, "put ... in mind"; 3 John 10, RV, "I will bring to remembrance" (KJV, "I will remember"); Jude 5, "to put ... in remembrance." In **Luke 22:61** it is used in the passive voice, "(Peter) remembered," lit., "was put in mind."

Deny *see Luke 9:23.*

22:62 And Peter went out, and wept bitterly.

Bitterly *pikros* (4090), "bitterly," is used of the poignant grief of Peter's weeping for his denial of Christ, Matt. 26:75; **Luke 22:62**.

22:63 And the men that held Jesus mocked him, and smote *him*.

Held *sunecho* (4912), is used of "holding" a prisoner, in **Luke 22:63**. *See also* **Taken** at *Luke 4:38.*

Mocked *see* **Mock** at *Luke 14:29.*

Smote *dero* (1194), "to flay, to beat," akin to *derma*, "skin," is translated "to smite" in **Luke 22:63**, KJV (RV, "beat"); John 18:23; 2 Cor. 11:20. *See also* **Beaten** at *Luke 12:47.*

22:64 And when they had blindfolded him, they struck him on the face, and asked him, saying, Prophesy, who is it that smote thee?

Blindfolded *perikalupto* (4028), signifies "to blindfold" (*peri*, "around," *kalupto*, "to hide"), **Luke 22:64**.

Struck *tupto* (5180), from a root *tup-*, meaning "a blow," (*tupos*, "a figure or print") (Eng., "type") denotes "to smite, strike, or beat," usually not with the idea of giving a thrashing as with *dero*. It frequently signifies a "blow" of violence, and, when used in a continuous tense, indicates a series of "blows." In Matt. 27:30 the imperfect tense signifies that the soldiers kept on striking Christ on the head. So Mark 15:19. The most authentic mss. omit it in **Luke 22:64**. In that verse the word *paio*, "to smite," is used of the treatment given to Christ (*dero* in the preceding verse). The imperfect tense of the verb is again used in Acts 18:17, of the beating given to Sosthenes. Cf. Acts 21:32, which has the present participle. It is used in the metaphorical sense of "wounding," in 1 Cor. 8:12.

Asked *see* Asking at *Luke 2:46*.

Smote *paio* (3817), signifies "to strike or smite" (a) with the hand or fist, Matt. 26:68; **Luke 22:64**; (b) with a sword, Mark 14:47; John 18:10, KJV (RV, "struck"); (c) with a sting, Rev. 9:5, "striketh." *See also* Smiteth at *Luke 6:29*.

22:65 And many other things blasphemously spake they against him.

Blasphemously *blasphemeo* (987), "to blaspheme, rail at or revile," is used (a) in a general way, of any contumelious speech, reviling, calumniating, railing at, etc., as of those who railed at Christ, e.g., Matt. 27:39; Mark 15:29; **Luke 22:65** (RV, "reviling"); **23:39**; (b) of those who speak contemptuously of God or of sacred things, e.g., Matt. 9:3; Mark 3:28; Rom. 2:24; 1 Tim. 1:20; 6:1; Rev. 13:6; 16:9, 11, 21; "hath spoken blasphemy," Matt. 26:65; "rail at," 2 Pet. 2:10; Jude 8, 10; "railing," 2 Pet. 2:12; "slanderously reported," Rom. 3:8; "be evil spoken of," Rom. 14:16; 1 Cor. 10:30; 2 Pet. 2:2; "speak evil of," Titus 3:2; 1 Pet. 4:4; "being defamed," 1 Cor. 4:13. The verb (in the present participial form) is translated "blasphemers" in Acts 19:37; in Mark 2:7, "blasphemeth," RV, for KJV, "speaketh blasphemies." There is no noun in the original representing the English "blasphemer." This is expressed either by the verb, or by the adjective *blasphemos*.

22:66 And as soon as it was day, the elders of the people and the chief priests and the scribes came together, and led him into their council, saying,

Elders *presbuterion* (4244), "an assembly of aged men," denotes (a) the Council or Senate among the Jews, **Luke 22:66**; Acts 22:5; (b) the "elders" or bishops in a local church, 1 Tim. 4:14, "the presbytery."

Came *sunago*, "to gather together," is always so rendered in RV, e.g., Matt. 27:62; Mark 7:1; **Luke 22:66**; Acts 13:44; 15:6; 20:7.

Led *see* Taking at *Luke 4:5*.

22:67-68 Art thou the Christ? tell us. And he said unto them, If I tell you, ye will not believe:

And if I also ask *you*, ye will not answer me, nor let *me* go.

Let *see* Forgive, Forgiven at *Luke 6:37*.

22:69 Hereafter shall the Son of man sit on the right hand of the power of God.

Hereafter *see* Henceforth at *Luke 1:48*.

Sit *kathemai* (2521), "to sit, be seated," is translated "shall ... be seated" in **Luke 22:69**, RV; "is seated," Col. 3:1, RV (KJV, "shall ... sit" and "sitteth").

22:70-71 Then said they all, Art thou then the Son of God? And he said unto them, Ye say that I am.

And they said, What need we any further witness? for we ourselves have heard of his own mouth.

Need *see Luke 5:31*.

Further *eti* (2089), "yet, still, further," is used (a) of time, most usually translated "yet," e.g., Matt. 12:46; or negatively, "any more," "no more," e.g., Heb. 8:12; (b) of degree, translated "further," or "any further," Matt. 26:65; Mark 5:35; 14:63; **Luke 22:71**; Heb. 7:11 in Acts 21:28, RV, "moreover" (KJV, "further").

Witness *marturia* (3141), "testimony, a bearing witness," is translated "witness" in Mark 14:55, 56, 59; **Luke 22:71**; John 1:7, 19 (RV); 3:11, 32 and 33 (RV); 5:31, 32, 34 (RV), 36; RV in 8:13, 14, 17; 19:35; 21:24; KJV in Titus 1:13; KJV and RV in 1 John 5:9 (thrice), 10a; RV in 10b, 11; 3 John 12.

Chapter 23

23:1 And the whole multitude of them arose, and led him unto Pilate.

Whole *see Luke 19:37*.

Multitude *plethos* (4128), lit., "a fullness," hence denotes "a multitude, a large or full company," **Luke 23:1**; "a multitude," v. 27 (KJV, "a great company").

Led *see Luke 4:1*.

23:2 And they began to accuse him, saying, We found this *fellow* perverting the nation, and forbidding to give tribute to Caesar, saying that he himself is Christ a King.

Fellow *houtos*, "this," is translated "this fellow" in the KJV of **Luke 23:2** (RV, "this man"). So in John 9:29. Both versions have "this man," e.g., in Mark 2:7; John 6:52, in the same contemptuous sense.

Perverting *see* Perverse at *Luke 9:41*.

Nation *see Luke 7:5*.

Forbidding *see* Forbid at *Luke 6:29*.

Tribute *see Luke 20:22*.

He himself *heauton* (1438), "oneself, himself," is rendered "he himself" in **Luke 23:2** and Acts 25:4.

Christ *see Luke 2:11*.

23:3 And Pilate asked him, saying, Art thou the King of the Jews? And he answered him and said, Thou sayest *it*.

Asked *see* Asking at *Luke 2:46*.

23:4 Then said Pilate to the chief priests and *to* the people, I find no fault in this man.

Fault *aition* (158), properly the neuter of *aitios*, causative of, responsible for, is used as a noun, "a crime, a legal ground for punishment," translated "fault" in **Luke 23:4, 14**; in v. 22, cause.

23:5 And they were the more fierce, saying, He stirreth up the people, teaching throughout all Jewry, beginning from Galilee to this place.

Fierce In **Luke 23:5**, the verb *epischuo*, "to make or grow stronger" (from *epi*, "over," intensive, and *ischus*, "strength"), is used metaphorically, "they were the more urgent," RV, for KJV, "the more fierce."

Stirreth *anaseio* (383) primarily denotes "to shake back or out, move to and fro"; then, "to stir up," used metaphorically in Mark 15:11, RV, "stirred ... up" (KJV, "moved"), and **Luke 23:5**.

Jewry *see* Judea at *Luke 1:5*.

Place *hode* (5602), "here, hither," is translated "to ('unto,' RV) this place" in **Luke 23:5**.

23:6 When Pilate heard of Galilee, he asked whether the man were a Galilaean.

Asked *see* Asking at *Luke 2:46*.

23:7 And as soon as he knew that he belonged unto Herod's jurisdiction, he sent him to Herod, who himself also was at Jerusalem at that time.

Knew *see Luke 7:37*.

Belonged *see* Belong at *Luke 19:42*.

Jurisdiction *exousia* (1849), "power, authority," is used, by metonymy, to denote "jurisdiction," in **Luke 23:7**. For the different meanings of the word and other instances of its use by metonymy.

Sent *anapempo* (375), denotes (a) "to send up," to a higher authority, **Luke 23:7, 15**; Acts 25:21 (in the best texts); this meaning is confirmed by examples from the papyri (Moulton and Milligan), by Deissmann (*Bible Studies*, p. 229); see also Field, *Notes on the Trans. of the NT;* (b) "to send back," **Luke 23:11**; Philem. 12.

Time *see Luke 9:51*.

23:8 And when Herod saw Jesus, he was exceeding glad: for he was desirous to see him of a long *season*, because he had heard many things of him; and he hoped to have seen some miracle done by him.

Exceeding *lian* (3029), "very, exceedingly," is translated "exceeding" in Matt. 2:16; 4:8; 8:28; Mark 9:3; **Luke 23:8**.

Glad *see Luke 15:32*.

Long *see Luke 8:27*.

Season *see* Time at *Luke 4:5*.

Many In **Luke 23:8** some mss. have *polla*, "many things," though it is absent from the most authentic; see the RV.

Miracle *semeion* (4592), "a sign, mark, token" (akin to *semaino*, "to give a sign"; *sema*, "a sign"), is used of "miracles" and wonders as signs of divine authority; it is translated "miracles" in the RV and KJV of **Luke 23:8**; Acts 4:16, 22; most usually it is given its more appropriate meaning "sign," "signs," e.g., Matt. 12:38, 39, and in every occurrence in the Synoptists, excep **Luke 23:8**; in the following passages in John's Gospel the RV substitutes "sign" or "signs" for the KJV "miracle or miracles"; 2:11, 23; 3:2; 4:54; 6:2, 14, 26; 7:31; 9:16; 10:41; 11:47; 12:18, 37; the KJV also has "signs" elsewhere in this Gospel; in Acts, RV, "signs," KJV, "miracles," in 6:8; 8:6; 15:12; elsewhere only in Rev. 13:14; 16:14; 19:20.

23:9 Then he questioned with him in many words; but he answered him nothing.

Questioned *see* Questions at *Luke 2:46*. *See also* Asking at *Luke 2:46*.

Many *see Luke 8:32*.

23:10 And the chief priests and scribes stood and vehemently accused him.

Vehemently *eutonos* (2159), "vigorously, vehemently" (*eu*, "well," *teino*, "to stretch"), is translated "mightily" in Acts 18:28, KJV, of the power of Apollos in "confuting" the Jews (RV, "powerfully"); in **Luke 23:10** it is rendered "vehemently." In the Sept., Josh. 6:7, "(let them sound) loudly."

23:11 And Herod with his men of war set him at nought, and mocked *him*, and arrayed him in a gorgeous robe, and sent him again to Pilate.

Men of war *strateuma* (4753), denotes (a) "an army" of any size, large or small, Matt. 22:7; Rev. 9:16; 19:14, 19 (twice); (b) "a company of soldiers," such as Herod's bodyguard, **Luke 23:11** (RV, "soldiers"), or the soldiers of a garrison, Acts 23:10, 27 (RV, "the soldiers," for KJV, "an army").

Nought *see* Despised at *Luke 18:9*.

Mocked *see* Mock at *Luke 14:29*.

Gorgeous *lampros* (2986), "bright, splendid," is rendered "gorgeous" in **Luke 23:11** of the apparel in which Herod and his soldiers arrayed Christ.

Robe *esthes* (2066), and *esthesis* (2067), connected with *hennumi*, "to clothe" means "clothing, raiment," usually suggesting the ornate, the goodly. The former is found in **Luke 23:11**, RV, "apparel" (KJV, "robe"); **24:4** (KJV, "garments"); Acts 10:30 (KJV, "clothing); 12:21; Jas. 2:2 (RV, "clothing," twice; KJV, "apparel" and "raiment"); 2:3 ("clothing"). *Esthesis* is used in Acts 1:10, "apparel."

Sent *see Luke 23:7*.

23:12 And the same day Pilate and Herod were made friends together: for before they were at enmity between themselves.

Friends *see Luke 7:6*.

Together *allelon* (240), a reciprocal pronoun, preceded by the preposition *meta*, "with," signifies "with each other," **Luke 23:12**, RV, for KJV, "together." Similarly in **24:14** *pros allelous*, where *pros* suggests greater intimacy.

Before *prouparcho* (4391), "to exist before, or be beforehand," is found in **Luke 23:12**, and Acts 8:9, "beforetime." In the Sept., Job 42:18.

Enmity *echthra* (2189), from the adjective *echthros* is rendered "enmity" in **Luke 23:12**; Rom. 8:7; Eph. 2:15-16; Jas. 4:4; "enmities," Gal. 5:20, RV, for KJV, "hatred." It is the opposite of *agape*, "love."

23:13 And Pilate, when he had called together the chief priests and the rulers and the people,

Called *see Luke 9:1*.

Rulers *see* Ruler at *Luke 8:41*.

23:14 Said unto them, Ye have brought this man unto me, as one that perverteth the people: and, behold, I, having examined *him* before you, have found no fault in this man touching those things whereof ye accuse him:

Perverteth *apostrepho* (654), "to turn away" (*apo*, "from," *strepho*, "to turn"), is used metaphorically in the sense of "perverting" in **Luke 23:14**.

Examined *anakrino* (350), "to examine, investigate," is used (a) of searching or enquiry, Acts 17:11; 1 Cor. 9:3; 10:25, 27; (b) of reaching a result of the enquiry, judging, 1 Cor. 2:14-15; 4:3-4; 14:24; (c) forensically, of examining by torture, **Luke 23:14**; Acts 4:9; 12:19; 24:8; 28:18.

Found *anakrino* (350), "to distinguish, or separate out so as to investigate (*krino*) by looking throughout (*ana*, intensive) objects or particulars," hence signifies "to examine, scrutinize, question, to hold a preliminary judicial examination preceding the trial proper" (this first examination, implying more to follow, is often present in the nonlegal uses of the word), e.g. **Luke 23:14**; figuratively, in 1 Cor. 4:3; it is said of searching the Scriptures in Acts 17:11; of "discerning" or determining the excellence or defects of a person or thing, e.g., 1 Cor. 2:14, KJV, "discerned"; RV, "judged"; in 1 Cor. 10:27, "asking (no) question" (i.e., not raising the question as to whether the meat is the residue from an idolatrous sacrifice). Except in **Luke 23:14**, this word is found only in Acts and 1 Cor.

No *see* Nothing at *Luke 22:35*.

Fault *see Luke 23:4*.

23:15 No, nor yet Herod: for I sent you to him; and, lo, nothing worthy of death is done unto him.

Sent *see Luke 23:7*.

Worthy *see Luke 7:4*.

23:16 I will therefore chastise him, and release *him*.

Chastise *paideuo* (3811), primarily denotes "to train children," suggesting the broad idea of education (*pais*, "a child"), Acts 7:22; 22:3; see also Titus 2:12, "instructing" (RV), here of a training gracious and firm; grace, which brings salvation, employs means to give us full possession of it, hence, "to chastise," this being part of the training, whether (a) by correcting with words, reproving, and admonishing, 1 Tim. 1:20 (RV, "be taught"); 2 Tim. 2:25, or (b) by "chastening" by the infliction of evils and calamities, 1 Cor. 11:32; 2 Cor. 6:9; Heb. 12:6-7, 10; Rev. 3:19. The verb also has the meaning "to chastise with blows, to scourge," said of the command of a judge, **Luke 23:16, 22.**

Release *see* **Forgive, Forgiven** at *Luke 6:37.*

23:17 (For of necessity he must release one unto them at the feast.)

Necessity *ananke* (318), signifies (a) "a necessity," what must needs be, translated "necessity" (in some mss. in **Luke 23:17**) in 1 Cor. 7:37; 9:16; 2 Cor. 9:7 (with *ek* "out of"); Philem. 14 (with *kata*, "according to"); Heb. 7:12; 9:16; (b) "distress, pain," translated "necessities" in 2 Cor. 6:4; 12:10. *See also* **Distress** at *Luke 21:23.*

Release *see* **Forgive, Forgiven** at *Luke 6:37.*

23:18 And they cried out all at once, saying, Away with this *man*, and release unto us Barabbas:

Cried *see Luke 4:33.*

Once In **Luke 23:18**, KJV, *pamplethei*, denoting "with the whole multitude" (*pas*, "all," *plethos*, "a multitude"), is rendered "all at once," RV, "all together").

Away This word is to be taken in connection with various verbs. The verb *airo*, "to seize, to lift up, take away," is translated "away with," in **Luke 23:18**; John 19:15; Acts 21:36; 22:22, implying a forcible removal for the purpose of putting to death.

Release *see* **Forgive, Forgiven** at *Luke 6:37.*

23:19 (Who for a certain sedition made in the city, and for murder, was cast into prison.)

Who These are usually the translations of forms of the relative pronoun *hos*, or of the interrogative pronoun *tis;* otherwise of *hostis*, "whoever," usually of a more general subject than *hos*, e.g., Mark 15:7; **Luke 23:19**; Gal. 2:4; *hosos*, "as many as," Heb. 2:15; in Acts 13:7, KJV, *houtos*, "this (man)," is translated "who," RV, "the same."

Sedition *stasis* (4714), akin to *histemi*, "to make to stand," denotes (a) primarily, "a standing or place," Heb. 9:8; (b) "an insurrection, sedition," translated "insurrection" in Mark 15:7; "insurrections" in Acts 24:5, RV (KJV, "sedition"); in **Luke 23:19, 25** (KJV "sedition"), "riot," Acts 19:40, RV (KJV, "uproar"); (c) "a dissension," Acts 15:2; in Acts 23:7, 10, "dissension."

Murder *phonos* (5408), is used (a) of a special act, Mark 15:7; **Luke 23:19, 25**; (b) in the plural, of "murders" in general, Matt. 15:19; Mark 7:21 (Gal. 5:21, in some inferior mss.); Rev. 9:21; in the singular, Rom. 1:29; (c) in the sense of "slaughter," Heb. 11:37, "they were slain with the sword," lit., "(they died by) slaughter (of the sword)"; in Acts 9:1, "slaughter."

23:20 Pilate therefore, willing to release Jesus, spake again to them.

Willing *see Luke 10:29.*

Release *see* **Forgive, Forgiven** at *Luke 6:37.*

Spake *see* **Called** at *Luke 6:13.*

23:21 But they cried, saying, Crucify *him*, crucify him.

Cried *epiphoneo* (2019), signifies "to shout," either against, **Luke 23:21**; Acts 21:34; 22:24, or in acclamation, Acts 12:22.

23:22 And he said unto them the third time, Why, what evil hath he done? I have found no cause of death in him: I will therefore chastise him, and let *him* go.

Cause *see* **Fault** at *Luke 23:4.*

Chastise *see Luke 23:16.*

Let … go *see* **Forgive, Forgiven** at *Luke 6:37. See also* **Went** at *Luke 8:22.*

23:23 And they were instant with loud voices, requiring that he might be crucified. And the voices of them and of the chief priests prevailed.

Instant *epikeimai* (1945), "to lie" or "press upon," is rendered "they were instant" in **Luke 23:23** (Amer. RV, "they were urgent"). *See also* **Pressed** at *Luke 5:1.*

Requiring *aiteo* (154), more frequently suggests the attitude of a suppliant, the petition of one who is lesser in position than he to whom the petition is made; e.g., in the case of men in asking something from God, Matt. 7:7; a child from a parent, Matt. 7:9-10; a subject from a king, Acts 12:20; priests and people from Pilate, **Luke 23:23** (RV, "asking" for KJV, "requiring"); a beggar from a passer by, Acts 3:2. With reference to petitioning God, this verb is found in Paul's epistles in Eph. 3:20 and Col. 1:9; in James four times, 1:5-6; 4:2-3; in 1 John, five times, 3:22; 5:14, 15 (twice), 16.

Might *see* **May** at *Luke 21:36.*

Prevailed *katischuo* (2729), "to be strong against," is used in Matt. 16:18, negatively of the gates of hades; in **Luke 21:36** (in the most authentic mss., some have *kataxioo*, "to count worthy"; see KJV), of "prevailing" to escape judgments at the close of this age; in **Luke 23:23**, of the voices of the chief priests, rulers and people against Pilate regarding the crucifixion of Christ.

23:24 And Pilate gave sentence that it should be as they required.

Sentence *epikrino* (1948), "to give sentence," is used in **Luke 23:24**.

Required *aitema* (155), denotes "that which has been asked for" (akin to *aiteo*, "to ask"); in **Luke 23:24**, RV, "what they asked for" (KJV, "as they required"), lit., "their request (should be done, *ginomai*)"; in Phil. 4:6, "requests"; in 1 John 5:15, "petitions."

23:25 And he released unto them him that for sedition and murder was cast into prison, whom they had desired; but he delivered Jesus to their will.

Released *see* Forgive, Forgiven at *Luke 6:37*.

Sedition *see Luke 23:19*.

Murder *see Luke 23:19*.

Desired *aiteo* (154), "to ask," is rendered "to desire" in KJV, e.g., in Matt. 20:20; **Luke 23:25** [RV, always "to ask (for)"].

23:26 And as they led him away, they laid hold upon one Simon, a Cyrenian, coming out of the country, and on him they laid the cross, that he might bear *it* after Jesus.

Led *see* Lead at *Luke 13:15*.

Laid *see Luke 4:40*.

Hold *see Luke 20:20*.

Country *see Luke 8:34*.

Bear *phero* (5342), "to bring or bear," is translated in the RV by the latter verb in **Luke 23:26**; John 2:8 (twice); 12:24; 15:2 (twice); Heb. 13:13.

After *see* Behind at *Luke 8:44*.

23:27 And there followed him a great company of people, and of women, which also bewailed and lamented him.

Company *see* Multitude at *Luke 23:1*.

Bewailed *see Luke 8:52*.

Lamented *kopto* (2875), to cut or beat, used in the middle voice of "beating the breast or head in mourning" (cf. **Luke 23:27**), is translated "shall mourn" in Matt. 24:30. *See also* Mourned at *Luke 7:32*.

23:28 But Jesus turning unto them said, Daughters of Jerusalem, weep not for me, but weep for yourselves, and for your children.

Daughters *see Luke 1:5*.

Weep *see Luke 7:13*.

23:29 For, behold, the days are coming, in the which they shall say, Blessed *are* the barren, and the wombs that never bare, and the paps which never gave suck.

Barren *see Luke 1:7*.

Wombs *see* Womb at *Luke 1:15*.

Bare *see* Bear at *Luke 1:13*.

Paps *see Luke 11:27*.

Suck *see* Sucked at *Luke 11:27*. *See also* Brought at *Luke 4:16*

23:30 Then shall they begin to say to the mountains, Fall on us; and to the hills, Cover us.

Hills *see* Hill at *Luke 3:5*.

Cover *see* Covereth at *Luke 8:16*.

23:31 For if they do these things in a green tree, what shall be done in the dry?

Green *hugros* (5200), denotes "wet, moist" (the opposite of *xeros*, "dry"); said of wood, sappy, "green," **Luke 23:31**, i.e., if they thus by the fire of their wrath treated Christ, the guiltless, holy, the fruitful, what would be the fate of the perpetrators, who were like the dry wood, exposed to the fire of divine wrath.

Tree *xulon* (3586), "wood, a piece of wood, anything made of wood", is used, with the rendering "tree," (a) in **Luke 23:31**, where "the green tree" refers either to Christ, figuratively of all His living power and excellencies, or to the life of the Jewish people while still inhabiting their land, in contrast to "the dry," a figure fulfilled in the horrors of the Roman massacre and devastation in AD 70 (cf. the Lord's parable in **Luke 13:6–9**; see Ezek. 20:47, and cf. 21:3); (b) of "the cross," the tree being the *stauros*, the upright pale or stake to which Romans nailed those who were thus to be executed, Acts 5:30; 10:39; 13:29; Gal. 3:13; 1 Pet. 2:24; (c) of "the tree of life," Rev. 2:7; 22:2 (twice), 14, 19, RV, KJV, "book."

Dry *see* Withered at *Luke 6:6*.

23:32 And there were also two other, malefactors, led with him to be put to death.

Other *see Luke 4:43*.

Malefactors *kakourgos* (2557), an adjective, lit., "evil-working" (*kakos*, "evil," *ergon*, "work"), is used as a noun, translated "malefactor(-s)" in **Luke 23:32, 33, 39**, and in the RV in 2 Tim. 2:9 (KJV, "evil doer").

Led *see Luke 4:1*.

Death *anaireo* (337), lit., "to take or lift up or away," hence, "to put to death," is usually translated "to kill or slay"; in two places "put to death," **Luke 23:32**; Acts 26:10. It is used 17 times, with this meaning, in Acts.

23:33 And when they were come to the place, which is called Calvary, there they crucified him, and the malefactors, one on the right hand, and the other on the left.

Calvary *kranion* (2898), *kara*, "a head" (Eng., "cranium"), a diminutive of *kranon*, denotes "a skull" (Latin *calvaria*), Matt. 27:33; Mark 15:22; **Luke 23:33**; John 19:17. The corresponding Aramaic word is *Golgotha* (Heb., *gulgoleth*, see Judg. 9:53; 2 Kings 9:35).

Malefactors *see* ***Luke 23:32***.

One ... the other *hos men ... hos de* (in various forms of the pronoun), lit., "this indeed ... but that," e.g., **Luke 23:33**; Rom. 9:21; 14:5; 1 Cor. 11:21; 2 Cor. 2:16; Phil. 1:16-17; (f) *heteros ... heteros*, "one ... another," 1 Cor. 15:40.

Left *aristeros* (710), is used (a) of the "left" hand, in Matt. 6:3, the word "hand" being understood; in connection with the armor of righteousness, in 2 Cor. 6:7, "(on the right hand and) on the left," lit., "(of the weapons ... the right and) the left"; (b) in the phrase "on the left," formed by *ex* (for *ek*), "from," and the genitive plural of this adjective, Mark 10:37; **Luke 23:33**.

23:34 Then said Jesus, Father, forgive them; for they know not what they do. And they parted his raiment, and cast lots.

Parted *diamerizo* (1266), "to part among, to distribute," is translated by the verb "to part" (a) in the middle voice, with reference to the Lord's garments, Matt. 27:35, 1st part (in some mss., 2nd part); Mark 15:24; **Luke 23:34**; John 19:24; (b) in the active voice, of "the proceeds of the sale of possessions and goods," Acts 2:45; (c) in the passive voice in Acts 2:3, of the "parting asunder" (RV) of tongues like fire (KJV, "cloven"). *See also* Divided at *Luke 11:17*.

Raiment For *himation*, rendered "raiment" in Matt. 17:2, KJV (RV, "garments"), so Matt. 27:31; Mark 9:3; **Luke 23:34**; John 19:24; Acts 22:20; Rev. 3:5, 18; 4:4; KJV and RV, Acts 18:6.

Lots *kleros* (2819), denotes (a) an object used in casting or drawing lots, which consisted of bits, or small tablets, of wood or stone (the probable derivation is from *klao*, "to break"); these were sometimes inscribed with the names of persons, and were put into a receptacle or a garment ("a lap," Prov. 16:33), from which they were cast, after being shaken together; he whose "lot" first fell out was the one chosen. The method was employed in a variety of circumstances, e.g., of dividing or assigning property, Matt. 27:35; Mark 15:24; **Luke 23:34**; John 19:24 (cf., e.g., Num. 26:55); of appointing to office, Acts 1:26 (cf., e.g., 1 Sam. 10:20); for other occurrences in the OT, see, e.g., Josh. 7:14 (the earliest instance in Scripture), Lev.16:7-10; Esth. 3:7; 9:24; (b) "what is obtained by lot, an allotted portion," e.g., of the ministry allotted to the apostles, Acts 1:17, RV, "portion," marg., "lot" (KJV, "part"); in some mss. v. 25, KJV, "part" (the RV follows those which have *topos*, "place"); Acts 8:21; it is also used like *kleronomia*, "an inheritance," in Acts 26:18, of what God has in grace assigned to the sanctified; so Col. 1:12; in 1 Pet. 5:3 it is used of those the spiritual care of, and charge over, whom is assigned to elders, RV, "the charge allotted to you" (plural, lit., "the charges"), KJV, "(God's) heritage." From *kleros* the word "clergy" is derived (a transposition in the application of the term).

23:35 And the people stood beholding. And the rulers also with them derided *him*, saying, He saved others; let him save himself, if he be Christ, the chosen of God.

Beholding *see* Beheld at ***Luke 10:18***.

Rulers *see* Ruler at *Luke 8:41*.

Derided *see* *Luke 16:14*.

Saved, Save *see* Made ... whole at *Luke 8:48*.

Chosen *eklektos* (1588), signifies "chosen out, select," e.g., Matt. 22:14; **Luke 23:35**; Rom. 16:13 (perhaps in the sense of "eminent"), Rev. 17:14. In 1 Pet. 2:4, 9, the RV translates it "elect." *See also* Elect at *Luke 18:7*.

23:36 And the soldiers also mocked him, coming to him, and offering him vinegar,

Soldiers *see* *Luke 7:8*.

Mocked *see* Mock at *Luke 14:29*.

Offering *prosphero* (4374), primarily, "to bring to" (*pros*, "to," *phero*, "to bring"), also denotes "to offer," (a) of the sacrifice of Christ Himself, Heb. 8:3; of Christ in virtue of his High Priesthood (RV, "this *high priest*"; KJV, "this man"); 9:14, 25 (negative), 28; 10:12; (b) of offerings under, or according to, the Law, e.g., Matt. 8:4; Mark 1:44; Acts 7:42; 21:26; Heb. 5:1, 3; 8:3; 9:7, 9; 10:1-2, 8, 11; (c) of "offerings" previous to the Law, Heb. 11:4, 17 (of Isaac by Abraham); (d) of gifts "offered" to Christ, Matt. 2:11, RV, "offered" (KJV, "presented unto"); (e) of prayers "offered" by Christ, Heb. 5:7; (f) of the vinegar "offered" to Him in mockery by the soldiers at the cross, **Luke 23:36**; (g) of the slaughter of disciples by persecutors, who think they are "offering" service to God, John 16:2, RV (KJV, "doeth");

(h) of money "offered" by Simon the sorcerer, Acts 8:18.

Vinegar *oxos* (3690), akin to *oxus*, "sharp," denotes "sour wine," the ordinary drink of laborers and common soldiers; it is used in the four Gospels of the "vinegar" offered to the Lord at His crucifixion. In Matt. 27:34 the best texts have *oinos*, "wine" (RV). Some have *oxos* (KJV, "vinegar"), but Mark 15:23 (KJV and RV) confirms the RV in the passage in Matthew. This, which the soldiers offered before crucifying, was refused by Him, as it was designed to alleviate His sufferings; the "vinegar" is mentioned in Mark 15:36; so **Luke 23:36**, and John 19:29, 30. In the Sept., Num. 6:3; Ruth 2:14; Ps. 69:21; Prov. 25:20.

23:37-38 And saying, If thou be the king of the Jews, save thyself.

And a superscription also was written over him in letters of Greek, and Latin, and Hebrew, THIS IS THE KING OF THE JEWS.

Superscription *see Luke 20:24.*

Latin In **Luke 23:38**, some mss. have the adjective *Rhomaikos*, "of Latin," agreeing with "letters."

23:39 And one of the malefactors which were hanged railed on him, saying, If thou be Christ, save thyself and us.

Malefactors *see Luke 23:32*

Hanged *kremannumi* (2910), is used (a) transitively in Acts 5:30; 10:39; in the passive voice, in Matt. 18:6, of a millstone about a neck, and in **Luke 23:39**, of the malefactors; (b) intransitively, in the middle voice, in Matt. 22:40, of the dependence of "the Law and the prophets" (i.e., that which they enjoin) upon the one great principle of love to God and one's neighbor (as a door "hangs" on a hinge, or as articles "hang" on a nail); in Acts 28:4, of the serpent "hanging" from Paul's hand; in Gal. 3:13 the word is used in a quotation from the Sept. of Deut. 21:23.

Railed *blasphemeo* (987), "to blaspheme, rail, revile" is translated "to rail at, or on," in Matt. 27:39, RV (KJV, "reviled"); Mark 15:29; **Luke 23:39**; 2 Pet. 2:10, RV (KJV, "to speak evil of"); 2:12, RV (KJV, "speak evil of"). *See also* **Blasphemously** at *Luke 22:65.*

23:40 But the other answering rebuked him, saying, Dost not thou fear God, seeing thou art in the same condemnation?

Rebuked *see Luke 4:35.*

Condemnation *krima* (2917), denotes (a) "the sentence pronounced, a verdict, a condemnation, the decision resulting from an investigation," e.g., Mark 12:40; **Luke 23:40**; 1 Tim. 3:6; Jude 4; (b) "the process of judgment leading to a decision," 1 Pet. 4:17 ("judgment"), where *krisis* might be expected. In **Luke 24:20**, "to be condemned" translates the phrase *eis krima*, "unto condemnation" (i.e., unto the pronouncement of the sentence of "condemnation"). For the rendering "judgment," see, e.g., Rom. 11:33; 1 Cor. 11:34; Gal. 5:10; Jas. 3:1. In these (a) the process leading to a decision and (b) the pronouncement of the decision, the verdict, are to be distinguished. In 1 Cor. 6:7 the word means a matter for judgment, a lawsuit.

23:41 And we indeed justly; for we receive the due reward of our deeds: but this man hath done nothing amiss.

Justly *dikaios* (1346), "justly, righteously, in accordance with what is right," is said (a) of God's judgment, 1 Pet. 2:23; (b) of men, **Luke 23:41**, "justly;" 1 Cor. 15:34, RV, "righteously" (KJV, "to righteousness"); 1 Thess. 2:10, RV, "righteously;" Titus 2:12.

Receive *see Luke 6:34.*

Reward In **Luke 23:41**, *axios*, "worthy, befitting," used in the plur., is rendered "the due reward," lit., "things worthy." *See also* **Worthy** at *Luke 3:8.*

Our In **Luke 23:41**, "of our deeds," is, lit., "of what things we practiced."

Deeds *praxis* (4234), denotes "a doing, transaction, a deed the action of which is looked upon as incomplete and in progress" (cf. *prasso*, "to practice"); in Matt. 16:27, RV, "deeds," for KJV, "works"; in **Luke 23:51**, "deed"; in v. **41**, the verb *prasso* is used with the neuter plural of the relative pronoun "of our deeds"; lit., "(the things) which we practiced"; Acts 19:18; Rom. 8:13; Col. 3:9. In Rom. 12:4 it denotes an "action," business, or function, translated "office."

Amiss *atopos* (824), lit., "out of place" (*a*, negative, *topos*, "a place"), denotes unbecoming, not befitting. It is used four times in the NT, and is rendered "amiss" three times in the RV; in the malefactor's testimony of Christ, **Luke 23:41**; in Festus' words concerning Paul, Acts 25:5, "if there is anything amiss in the man" (KJV, "wickedness"); in Acts 28:6, of the expected effect of the viper's attack upon Paul (KJV, "harm"); in 2 Thess. 3:2, of men capable of outrageous conduct, "unreasonable."

23:42-43 And he said unto Jesus, Lord, remember me when thou comest into thy kingdom.

And Jesus said unto him,

Verily I say unto thee, To day shalt thou be with me in paradise.

To day *see* This day at *Luke 4:21*.

Paradise *paradeisos* (3857), is an Oriental word, first used by the historian Xenophon, denoting "the parks of Persian kings and nobles." It is of Persian origin (Old Pers. *pairidaeza*, akin to Gk. *peri*, "around," and *teichos*, "a wall") whence it passed into Greek. See the Sept., e.g., in Neh. 2:8; Eccl. 2:5; Song of Sol. 4:13. The Sept. translators used it of the garden of Eden, Gen. 2:8, and in other respects, e.g., Num. 24:6; Isa. 1:30; Jer. 29:5; Ezek. 31:8-9. In **Luke 23:43**, the promise of the Lord to the repentant robber was fulfilled the same day; Christ, at His death, having committed His spirit to the Father, went in spirit immediately into Heaven itself, the dwelling place of God (the Lord's mention of the place as "paradise" must have been a great comfort to the malefactor; to the oriental mind it expressed the sum total of blessedness). Thither the apostle Paul was caught up, 2 Cor. 12:4, spoken of as "the third heaven" (v. 3 does not introduce a different vision), beyond the heavens of the natural creation (see Heb. 4:14, RV, with reference to the Ascension). The same region is mentioned in Rev. 2:7, where the "tree of life," the figurative antitype of that in Eden, held out to the overcomer, is spoken of as being in "the Paradise of God" (RV), marg., "garden," as in Gen. 2:8.

23:44 And it was about the sixth hour, and there was a darkness over all the earth until the ninth hour.

Ninth *enatos*, or *enn-* (1766), is found in reference (a) to "the ninth hour" (3 o'clock, p.m.) in Matt. 20:5; 27:45-46; Mark 15:33-34; **Luke 23:44**; Acts 3:1; 10:3, 30; (b) to "the topaz" as the "ninth" foundation of the city wall in the symbolic vision in Rev. 21 (v. 20).

Earth *see* Land at *Luke 4:25*.

23:45 And the sun was darkened, and the veil of the temple was rent in the midst.

Sun *see Luke 21:25*.

Darkened *skotizo* (4654), "to deprive of light, to make dark," is used in the NT in the passive voice only, (a) of the heavenly bodies Matt. 24:29; Mark 13:24; Rev. 8:12; (b) metaphorically, of the mind, Rom. 1:21; 11:10; (some mss. have it in **Luke 23:45**). *See also* Fail at *Luke 16:9*.

Veil *katapetasma* (2665), lit., "that which is spread out" (*petannumi*) "before" (*kata*), hence, "a veil," is used (a) of the inner "veil" of the tabernacle, Heb. 6:19; 9:3; (b) of the corresponding "veil" in the Temple, Matt. 27:51; Mark 15:38; **Luke 23:45**; (c) metaphorically of the "flesh" of Christ, Heb. 10:20, i.e., His body which He gave up to be crucified, thus by His expiatory death providing a means of the spiritual access of believers, the "new and living way," into the presence of God.

Rent *see Luke 5:36*.

Midst *see Luke 4:30*.

23:46 And when Jesus had cried with a loud voice, he said, Father, into thy hands I commend my spirit: and having said thus, he gave up the ghost.

Cried *see Luke 8:8*.

Hands *see* Hand at *Luke 1:66*.

Commend *paratithemi* (3908), lit., "to put near" (*para*, "near"), in the Middle Voice, denotes "to place with someone, entrust, commit." In the sense of commending, it is said (a) of the Lord Jesus in "commending" His spirit into the Father's hands, **Luke 23:46**; (b) of "commending" disciples to God, Acts 14:23; (c) of "commending" elders to God, Acts 20:32.

Ghost *ekpneo* (1606), lit., "to breathe out" (*ek*, "out," *pneo*, "to breathe"), "to expire," is used in the NT, without an object, "soul" or "life" being understood, Mark 15:37, 39, and **Luke 23:46**, of the death of Christ. In Matt. 27:50 and John 19:30, where different verbs are used, the act is expressed in a way which stresses it as of His own volition: in the former, "Jesus ... yielded up His spirit (*pneuma*); in the latter, "He gave up His spirit."

23:47 Now when the centurion saw what was done, he glorified God, saying, Certainly this was a righteous man.

Certainly *ontos* (3689), "really, actually, verily" (from *eimi*, "to be"), is translated "certainly" in **Luke 23:47**.

23:48 And all the people that came together to that sight, beholding the things which were done, smote their breasts, and returned.

Came *sumparaginomai* (4836), (*sun*, "with," *para*, "near"), "to come together," is used in **Luke 23:48**; 2 Tim. 4:16, lit., "stood at my side with me."

Beholding *see* Beheld at *Luke 10:18*.

Smote *see* Smiteth at *Luke 6:29*.

Breasts *see* Breast at *Luke 18:13*.

Returned *see Luke 1:56*.

23:49 And all his acquaintance, and the women that followed him from Galilee, stood afar off, beholding these things.

Acquaintance *see Luke 2:44.*

Followed *sunakoloutheo* (4870), "to follow along with, to accompany a leader," is given its true rendering in the RV of Mark 5:37, "He suffered no man to follow with Him"; in 14:51, of the young man who "followed with" Christ; **Luke 23:49**, of the women who "followed with" Christ from Galilee.

23:50 And, behold, *there was* a man named Joseph, a counsellor; *and he was* a good man, and a just:

Was *see* Were at *Luke 16:14.*

Counsellor *bouleutes* (1010), Joseph of Arimathaea is described as "a councillor of honorable estate," Mark 15:43, RV; cf. **Luke 23:50** (not as KJV, "counsellor").

Good *see Luke 1:53.*

Just *see Luke 2:25.*

23:51 (The same had not consented to the counsel and deed of them;) *he was* of Arimathaea, a city of the Jews: who also himself waited for the kingdom of God.

Consented *sunkatatithemi* (4784), lit., "to put or lay down together with" (*sun*, "with," *kata*, "down," *tithemi*, "to put"), was used of depositing one's vote in an urn; hence, "to vote for, agree with, consent to." It is said negatively of Joseph of Arimathaea, who had not "consented" to the counsel and deed of the Jews, **Luke 23:51** (middle voice).

Counsel *see Luke 7:30.*

Deeds *see Luke 23:41.*

Waited *see* waiting at *Luke 2:25. See also* Looked at *Luke 2:38.*

23:52 This *man* went unto Pilate, and begged the body of Jesus.

Begged "Begged" in Matt. 27:58 and **Luke 23:52**, RV, "asked for," translates the verb *aiteo*.

23:53 And he took it down, and wrapped it in linen, and laid it in a sepulchre that was hewn in stone, wherein never man before was laid.

Took *kathaireo* (2507), "to take down" (*kata*), besides its meaning of "putting down by force," was the technical term for the "removal" of the body afler crucifixion, Mark 15:36, 46; **Luke 23:53**; Acts 13:29.

Wrapped *entulisso* (1794), "to wrap up, roll round or about," is translated "rolled up" in John 20:7, RV, of the cloth or "napkin" that had been wrapped around the head of the Lord before burial. Both the RV and the KJV, "wrapped together," might suggest that this cloth had been "rolled" or wrapped up and put in a certain part of the tomb at the Lord's resurrection, whereas, as with the body wrappings, the head cloth was lying as it had been "rolled" round His head, an evidence, to those who looked into the tomb, of the fact of His resurrection without any disturbance of the wrappings either by friend or foe or when the change took place. It is followed by *en*, "in," and translated "wrapped" in Matt. 27:59, a meaning and construction which Moulton and Milligan illustrate from the papyri; in **Luke 23:53** it is followed by the dative of the noun *sindon*, "linen cloth," used instrumentally.

Linen *sindon* (4616), was "a fine linen cloth, an article of domestic manufacture" (Prov. 31:24) used (a) as a garment or wrap, the "linen cloth" of Mark 14:51, 52; (b) as shrouds or winding sheets, Matt. 27:59; Mark 15:46, RV, "linen cloth," for KJV, "linen"; **Luke 23:53** (ditto). In the Sept., Judg. 14:2, "(thirty) sheets"; Prov. 31:24. The Mishna (the great collection of legal decisions by the ancient Rabbis) records that the material was sometimes used for curtains.

Laid *see Luke 1:66.*

Hewn *laxeutos* (2991), denotes "hewn in stone" (*las*, "a stone," *xeo*, "to scrape"), is used of Christ's tomb, in **Luke 23:53**.

Never *oudepo* (3764), "not yet," is translated "never (man) yet" in John 19:41 ("man" representing the idiomatically used negative pronoun *oudeis*, "no one"); some mss. have it in **Luke 23:53**, instead of *oupo*, "not yet."

Laid In **Luke 23:53**, the RV has "had lain," for KJV, "was laid." See also Lying at *Luke 2:12.*

23:54 And that day was the preparation, and the sabbath drew on.

Preparation *paraskeue* (3904), denotes "preparation, equipment." The day on which Christ died is called "the Preparation" in Mark 15:42 and John 19:31; in John 19:42 "the Jews' Preparation," RV; in 19:14 it is described as "the Preparation of the Passover"; in **Luke 23:54**, RV, "the day of the Preparation (and the Sabbath drew on)." The same day is in view in Matt. 27:62, where the events recorded took place on "the day after the Preparation" (RV). The reference would be to the 6th day of the week. The title arose from the need of preparing food, etc., for the Sabbath. Apparently it was first applied only to the afternoon of the 6th day; later, to the whole day. In regard to the phraseology in John 19:14, many hold this to indicate the "preparation" for the paschal feast. It probably means "the Preparation day," and thus falls in line with the Synoptic Gospels. In modern Greek and ecclesiastical Latin, *Parasceve* = Friday.

Drew *epiphosko* (2020), "to dawn" (lit., "to make to shine upon"), is said of the approach of the Sabbath, **Luke 23:54** (marg., "began to dawn"); cf. Matt. 28:1.

23:55 And the women also, which came with him from Galilee, followed after, and beheld the sepulchre, and how his body was laid.

Came with *sunerchomai* (4905), chiefly used of "assembling together," signifies "to accompany," in **Luke 23:55**; John 11:33; Acts 9:39; 10:45; 11:12; 15:38; 21:16. In Acts 1:21 it is said of men who had "companied with" the apostles all the time the Lord Jesus was with them.

Followed *katakoloutheo* (2628), "to follow behind or intently after," is used of the women on their way to Christ's tomb, **Luke 23:55**; of the demon-possessed maid in Philippi in "following" the missionaries, Acts 16:17.

Beheld *theaomai* (2300), "to behold, view attentively, contemplate," had, in earlier Greek usage, the sense of a wondering regard. This idea was gradually lost. It signifies a more earnest contemplation than the ordinary verbs for "to see," "a careful and deliberate vision which interprets ... its object," and is more frequently rendered "behold" in the RV than the KJV. Both translate it by "behold" in **Luke 23:55** (of the sepulchre); "we beheld," in John 1:14, of the glory of the Son of God; "beheld," RV, in John 1:32; Acts 1:11; 1 John 1:1 (more than merely seeing); 4:12, 14.

Laid *see Luke 1:66.*

23:56 And they returned, and prepared spices and ointments; and rested the sabbath day according to the commandment.

Returned *see Luke 1:56.*

Prepared *see* **Make ready** at *Luke 1:17.*

Spices *aroma* (759), "spice," occurs in Mark 16:1, RV "spices" (KJV, "sweet spice"); **Luke 23:56**; **24:1**; John 19:40. A papyrus document has it in a list of articles for a sacrifice.

Ointments *see* **Ointment** at *Luke 7:37.*

Rested *hesuchazo* (2270), "to be still, to rest from labor," is translated "they rested" in **Luke 23:56**. *See also* **Peace** at *Luke 14:4.*

Chapter 24

24:1 Now upon the first *day* of the week, very early in the morning, they came unto the sepulchre, bringing the spices which they had prepared, and certain *others* with them.

First *mia* (3391), a grammatically feminine form of *heis*, "one," is translated "first" in certain occurrences of the phrase "on the first day of the week," e.g., **Luke 24:1**; 1 Cor. 16:2.

Week *see Luke 18:12.*

Early *orthros* (3722), denotes "daybreak, dawn" (cf. Lat. *orior*, "to rise"). Used with the adverb *batheos*, "deeply," in **Luke 24:1**, it means "at early dawn" (RV). In John 8:2 it is used in the genitive case, *orthrou*, "at dawn," i.e., "early in the morning." In Acts 5:21, it is used with the article and preceded by the preposition *hupo*, "under," or about, lit., "about the dawn," "about daybreak," RV (for KJV, "early in the morning"). In **Luke 24:1**, some mss. have *batheos*, the genitive case, with *orthros*, "dawn"; the most authentic mss. have *batheos*, "deeply," i.e., very early.

Spices *see Luke 23:56.*

Others In **Luke 24:1**, the plural of *tis*, "a certain one," is found in some mss., and translated "certain others" in the KJV.

24:2 And they found the stone rolled away from the sepulchre.

Rolled *apokulio or apokulizo* (617), "to roll away" (*apo*, "from," *kulio*, "to roll"; cf. Eng., "cylinder," etc.), is used of the sepulchre stone, Matt. 28:2; Mark 16:3 (v. 4 in some mss.); **Luke 24:2**. In the Sept., Gen. 29:3, 8, 10.

24:3-4 And they entered in, and found not the body of the Lord Jesus.

And it came to pass, as they were much perplexed thereabout, behold, two men stood by them in shining garments:

Perplexed *aporeo* (639), always used in the middle voice, lit. means "to be without a way" (*a*, negative, *poros*, "a way, transit"), "to be without resources, embarrassed, in doubt, perplexity, at a loss," as was Herod regarding John the Baptist, Mark 6:20 (RV, following the most authentic mss., "was much perplexed"); as the disciples were, regarding the Lord's betrayal, John 13:22, "doubting"; and regarding the absence of His body from the tomb, **Luke 24:4**, "were perplexed"; as was Festus, about the nature of the accusations brought against Paul, Acts 25:20, KJV "doubted," RV, "being perplexed"; as Paul was, in his experiences of trial 2 Cor. 4:8, "perplexed," and, as to the attitude of the believers of the churches in Galatia towards Judaistic errors, Gal. 4:20, KJV, "I stand in doubt," RV, "I am perplexed." *See also* **Perplexity** at ***Luke 21:25***.

Thereabout The phrase *peri toutou*, "concerning this," is rendered "thereabout" in **Luke 24:4**.

Men *see* **Angels** at ***Luke 12:8***.

Stood *see* **Came** at ***Luke 2:9***.

Shining *see* **Lighteneth** at ***Luke 17:24***.

Garments *see* **Robe** at ***Luke 23:11***.

24:5 And as they were afraid, and bowed down *their* faces to the earth, they said unto them, Why seek ye the living among the dead?

Afraid *emphobos* (1719), lit., "in fear" (*en*, "in," *phobos*, "fear"), means "affrighted," **Luke 24:5**, RV (KJV "afraid"); **24:37**; Acts 10:4, RV (KJV, "afraid"); Rev. 11:13. The RV omits it in Acts 22:9.

Bowed *see* **Wear** at ***Luke 9:12***.

Seek *see* **Desired** at ***Luke 9:9***.

24:6 He is not here, but is risen: remember how he spake unto you when he was yet in Galilee,

Spake A characteristic of *lego* is that it refers to the purport or sentiment of what is said as well as the connection of the words; this is illustrated in Heb. 8:1, RV, "(in the things which) we are saying," KJV, "(which) we have spoken." In comparison with *laleo*, *lego* refers especially to the substance of what is "said," *laleo*, to the words conveying the utterance; see, e.g., John 12:49, "what I should say (*lego*, in the 2nd aorist subjunctive form *eipo*), and what I should speak (laleo)"; v. 50, "even as the Father hath said (*lego*, in the perfect form *eireke*) unto Me, so I speak" (*laleo*); cf. 1 Cor. 14:34, "saith (*lego*) the law"; v. 35, "to speak" (*laleo*). Sometimes *laleo* signifies the utterance, as opposed to silence, *lego* declares what is "said"; e.g., Rom. 3:19, "what things soever the law saith (*lego*), it speaketh (*laleo*) to them that are under the law"; see also Mark 6:50; **Luke 24:6**. In the NT *laleo* never has the meaning "to chatter."

24:7 Saying, The Son of man must be delivered into the hands of sinful men, and be crucified, and the third day rise again.

Hands *see* **Hand** at ***Luke 1:66***.

Sinful *see* ***Luke 5:8***.

Third *see* ***Luke 9:22***.

Rise *see* **Rose** at ***Luke 4:29***.

24:8-9 And they remembered his words,

And returned from the sepulchre, and told all these things unto the eleven, and to all the rest.

Eleven *hendeka* (1733), lit., "one ten" (Lat., *undecim*), is used only of the eleven apostles remaining after the death of Judas Iscariot, Matt. 28:16; Mark 16:14; **Luke 24:9**, **33**; Acts 1:26; 2:14.

Rest *see* **Others** at ***Luke 8:10***.

24:10 It was Mary Magdalene, and Joanna, and Mary *the mother* of James, and other *women that were* with them, which told these things unto the apostles.

Other *see* **Others** at ***Luke 8:10***.

24:11 And their words seemed to them as idle tales, and they believed them not.

"Jesus' resurrection makes it impossible for man's story to end in chaos – it has to move inexorably toward light, toward life, toward love."

CARLO CARRETTO

Seemed *phaino* (5316), signifies, in the active voice, "to shine"; in the passive, "to be brought forth into light, to become evident, to appear." In Rom. 7:13, concerning sin, the RV has "might be shewn to be," for KJV, "appear." It is used of the "appearance" of Christ to the disciples, Mark 16:9; of His future "appearing" in glory as the Son of Man, spoken of as a sign to the world, Matt. 24:30; there the genitive is subjective, the sign being the "appearing" of Christ Himself; of Christ as the light, John 1:5; of John the Baptist, 5:35; of the "appearing" of an angel of the Lord, either visibly, Matt. 1:20, or in a dream, 2:13; of a star, 2:7; of men who make an outward show, Matt. 6:5; 6:18 (see the RV); 23:27-28; 2 Cor. 13:7; of tares, Matt. 13:26; of a vapor, Jas. 4:14; of things physical in general, Heb. 11:3; used impersonally in Matt. 9:33, "it was never so seen"; also of what appears to the mind, and so in the sense of to think, Mark 14:64, or to seem, **Luke 24:11** (RV, appeared).

To *see* **Before** at ***Luke 1:17***.

Idle tales *leros* (3026), denotes "foolish talk, nonsense," **Luke 24:11**, RV, "idle talk" (KJV, "idle tales").

Believed ... not *apisteo* (569), "to be unbelieving" (*a*, negative, *pistis*, "faith"; cf. *apistos*, "unbelieving"), is translated "believed not," etc., in the KJV (except in 1 Pet. 2:7, "be disobedient"); "disbelieve" (or "disbelieved") in the RV, in Mark 16:11, 16; **Luke 24:11, 41**; Acts 28:24; "disbelieve" is the best rendering, implying that the unbeliever has had a full opportunity of believing and has rejected it; some mss. have *apeitheo*, "to be disobedient," in 1 Pet. 2:7; Rom. 3:3, RV, "were without faith"; 2 Tim. 2:13, RV, "are faithless."

24:12 Then arose Peter, and ran unto the sepulchre; and stooping down, he beheld the linen clothes laid by themselves, and departed, wondering in himself at that which was come to pass.

Stooping *parakupto* (3879), is rendered "to stoop down" in **Luke 24:12**; John 20:5, 11, RV, "stooping and looking in".

Beheld *see* **Beholdest** at *Luke 6:41*.

Linen *othonion* (3608), "a piece of fine linen," is used in the plural, of the strips of cloth with which the body of the Lord was bound, after being wrapped in the *sindon*, **Luke 24:12**; John 19:40; 20:5, 6, 7. In the Sept., Judg. 14:13, "changes of raiment"; Hos. 2:5, 9. The word is a diminutive of *othone*, "a sheet".

Laid In **Luke 24:12**, some mss. have the verb, with reference to the linen cloths (the clause is absent in the best mss.); the translation should be "lying," not as KJV, "laid."

24:13 And, behold, two of them went that same day to a village called Emmaus, which was from Jerusalem *about* threescore furlongs.

Same *see Luke 12:12*.

Called For *onoma*, "a name," translated "called," KJV, in **Luke 24:13**; Acts 10:1, *onomazo*, "to name," translated "called," KJV, 1 Cor. 5:11, and *eponomazo*, "to surname," translated "art called," Rom. 2:17.

Was *see Luke 7:6*.

From *see* **Have received** at *Luke 6:24*.

Threescore *hexekonta* (1835), occurs in Matt. 13:8, RV (KJV, "sixty-fold"); 13:23; Mark 4:8, where the RV and KJV reverse the translation, as in Matt. 13:8, while in Mark 4:20 the RV has "sixtyfold," KJV, "sixty"; in Rev. 13:18, RV, "sixty" (KJV, "threescore"). It is rendered "threescore" in **Luke 24:13**; 1 Tim. 5:9; Rev. 11:3; 12:6.

Furlongs *stoion* (4712), denotes (a) "a stadium," i.e., a measure of length, 600 Greek feet, or one-eighth of a Roman mile, Matt. 14:24 (in the best mss.); **Luke 24:13**; John 6:19; 11:18; Rev. 14:20; 21:16; (b) "a race course," the length of the Olympic course, 1 Cor. 9:24.

24:14 And they talked together of all these things which had happened.

Talked *homileo* (3656), from *homos*, "together," signifies "to be in company, to associate with any one"; hence, "to have intercourse with," **Luke 24:14** (RV, "communed"; KJV, "talked"), **15**; Acts 24:26; in 20:11, "talked with.

Together In 1 Thess. 5:11, KJV, *allelous*, "one another" (RV), is rendered "yourselves together"; in **Luke 23:12**, KJV, *meta allelon*, lit., "with one another," is rendered "together" (RV, "with each other"); so in **Luke 24:14**, KJV, *pros allelous*, RV, "with each other." *See also Luke 23:12*.

Happened *sumbaino* (4819), lit., "to go or come together" (*sun*, "with," *baino*, "to go"), signifies "to happen together," of things or events, Mark 10:32; **Luke 24:14**; Acts 3:10; 1 Cor. 10:11; 1 Pet. 4:12; 2 Pet. 2:22; "befell" in Acts 20:19; in Acts 21:35, "so it was."

24:15 And it came to pass, that, while they communed *together* and reasoned, Jesus himself drew near, and went with them.

Communed *see* **Talked** at *Luke 24:14*.

Reasoned *see* **Enquire** at *Luke 22:23*.

Went *see Luke 7:11*.

24:16 But their eyes were holden that they should not know him.

Holden *krateo* (2902), "to be strong, mighty, to prevail," (1) is most frequently rendered "to lay or take hold on" (a) literally, e.g., Matt. 12:11; 14:3; 18:28 and 21:46, RV (KJV, "laid hands on"); 22:6, RV (KJV, "took"); 26:55, KJV (RV, "took"); 28:9, RV, "took hold of" (KJV, "held by"); Mark 3:21; 6:17; 12:12; 14:51; Acts 24:6, RV (KJV, "took"); Rev. 20:2; (b) metaphorically, of "laying hold of the hope of the Lord's return," Heb. 6:18; (2) also signifies "to hold" or "hold fast," i.e., firmly, (a), literally, Matt. 26:48, KJV (RV, "take"); Acts 3:11; Rev. 2:1; (b) metaphorically, of "holding fast a tradition or teaching," in an evil sense, Mark 7:3, 4, 8; Rev. 2:14, 15; in a good sense, 2 Thess. 2:15; Rev. 2:25; 3:11; of "holding" Christ, i.e., practically apprehending Him, as the head of His church, Col. 2:19; a confession, Heb. 4:14; the name of Christ, i.e., abiding by all that His name implies, Rev. 2:13; of restraint, **Luke 24:16**, "(their eyes) were holden"; of the winds, Rev. 7:1; of the impossibility of Christ's being "holden" of death, Acts 2:24.

24:17 And he said unto them, What manner of communications *are* these that ye have one to another, as ye walk, and are sad?

Manner *see Luke 8:25.*

Communications *logos* (3056), "a word, that which is spoken" (*lego*, "to speak"), is used in the plural with reference to a conversation; "communication," Luke 24:17. Elsewhere with this significance the RV renders it "speech," Matt. 5:37; Eph. 4:29. The verb *antiballo*, "to throw in turn, to exchange," is used of conversation, lit., "what words are these that ye exchange one with another."

Sad *skuthropos*, "of a sad countenance" (*skuthros*, "gloomy, sad," *ops*, "an eye"), is used in Matt. 6:16 and Luke 24:17, "sad."

24:18 And the one of them, whose name was Cleopas, answering said unto him, Art thou only a stranger in Jerusalem, and hast not known the things which are come to pass there in these days?

Stranger *paroikeo* (3939), denotes "to dwell beside, among or by" (*para*, "beside," *oikeo*, "to dwell"); then, "to dwell in a place as a *paroikos*, a stranger," Luke 24:18, RV, "Dost thou (alone) sojourn ...?" [marg., "Dost thou sojourn (alone)" is preferable], KJV, "art thou (only) a stranger?" (*monos*, "alone," is an adjective, not an adverb); in Heb. 11:9, RV, "he became a sojourner" (KJV, "he sojourned"), the RV gives the force of the aorist tense.

There In Luke 24:18 and Acts 9:38, "there" translates the phrase *en aute*, "in it."

24:19 And he said unto them, What things? And they said unto him, Concerning Jesus of Nazareth, which was a prophet mighty in deed and word before God and all the people:

What *see Luke 5:19.*

Prophet *see Luke 1:76. See also* Man at *Luke 5:8.*

Mighty *see Luke 1:49.*

24:20 And how the chief priests and our rulers delivered him to be condemned to death, and have crucified him.

Rulers *see* Ruler at *Luke 8:41.*

Condemned *krima* (2917), denotes the result of the action signified by the verb *krino*, "to judge"; it is used (a) of a decision passed on the faults of others, Matt. 7:2; (b) of "judgment" by man upon Christ, Luke 24:20; (c) of God's "judgment" upon men, e.g., Rom. 2:2, 3; 3:8; 5:16; 11:33; 13:2; 1 Cor. 11:29; Gal. 5:10; Heb. 6:2; Jas. 3:1; through Christ, e.g., John 9:39; (d) of the right of "judgment," Rev. 20:4; (e) of a lawsuit, 1 Cor. 6:7. In John 9:39, "For judgment (*krima*) came I into this world," the meaning would appear to be, "for being judged" (as a touchstone for proving men's thoughts and characters), in contrast to 5:22, "hath given all judging (*krisis*) to the Son"; in Luke 24:20, "delivered Him up to be condemned to death," the latter phrase is, lit., "to a verdict (*krima*) of death" (which they themselves could not carry out); in Mark 12:40, "these shall receive greater condemnation" (*krima*), the phrase signifies a heavier verdict (against themselves). *See* Condemnation at *Luke 23:40.*

24:21 But we trusted that it had been he which should have redeemed Israel: and beside all this, to day is the third day since these things were done.

Trusted *elpizo* (1679), "to hope," is not infrequently translated in the KJV, by the verb "to trust"; the RV adheres to some form of the verb "to hope," e.g., John 5:45, "Moses, on whom ye have set your hope"; 2 Cor. 1:10, "on whom we have set our hope"; so in 1 Tim. 4:10; 5:5; 6:17; see also, e.g., Matt. 12:21; Luke 24:21; Rom. 15:12, 24. The verb is followed by three prepositions: (1) *eis*, rendered "on" in John 5:45 (as above); the meaning is really "in" as in 1 Pet. 3:5, "who hoped in God"; the "hope" is thus said to be directed to, and to center in, a person; (2) *epi*, "on," Rom. 15:12, "On Him shall the Gentiles hope," RV; so 1 Tim. 4:10; 5:5 (in the best mss.); 6:17, RV; this expresses the ground upon which "hope" rests; (3) *en*, "in," 1 Cor. 15:19, "we have hoped in Christ," RV, more lit., "we are (men) that have hoped in Christ," the preposition expresses that Christ is not simply the ground upon whom, but the sphere and element in whom, the "hope" is placed. The form of the verb (the perfect participle with the verb to be, lit., "are having hoped") stresses the character of those who "hope," more than the action; "hope" characterizes them, showing what sort of persons they are.

Should *see Luke 19:11.*

Redeemed *lutroo* (3084), "to release on receipt of ransom" (akin to *lutron*, "a ransom"), is used in the middle voice, signifying "to release by paying a ransom price, to redeem" (a) in the natural sense of delivering, Luke 24:21, of setting Israel free from the Roman yoke; (b) in a spiritual sense, Titus 2:14, of the work of Christ in "redeeming" men "from all iniquity" (*anomia*, "lawlessness," the bondage of self-will which rejects the will of God); 1 Pet. 1:18 (passive voice), "ye were redeemed," from a vain manner of life, i.e., from bondage to tradition. In both instances the death of Christ is stated as the means of "redemption."

To day is the third day *see* Led at *Luke 4:1.*

24:22 Yea, and certain women also of our company made us astonished, which were early at the sepulchre;

Yea In **Luke 24:22** the RV translates *alla kai* "moreover" (KJV, "yea ... and").

Our *see* Your at *Luke 16:12*.

Company The preposition *ex* (i.e., *ek*), "of," with the first personal pronoun in the genitive plural (*hemon*, "us"); signifies "of our company," lit., "of us," in **Luke 24:22**; so *ex auton*, in Acts 15:22, "men out of their company," lit., "men out of them."

Astonished *existemi* (1839), primarily and lit. means "to put out of position, displace": hence, (a) "to amaze," **Luke 24:22** (for KJV, "make ... astonished"); Acts 8:9, 11 (KJV, "bewitched "); or "to be amazed, astounded," Matt. 12:23; Mark 6:51; (b) "to be out of one's mind, to be beside oneself," Mark 3:21; 2 Cor. 5:13, in the latter of which it is contrasted with *sophroneo*, "to be of a sound mind, sober."

Early *orthrinos* (3720), "early," is a later form of *orthrios*. It is found, in the most authentic mss., in **Luke 24:22**, of the women at the sepulchre, lit., "early ones" (some texts have the form *orthrios*, "at daybreak"). *See also* Morning at *Luke 21:38*.

24:23 And when they found not his body, they came, saying, that they had also seen a vision of angels, which said that he was alive.

Vision *see Luke 1:22*.

Angels *see Luke 12:8*.

24:24-25 And certain of them which were with us went to the sepulchre, and found *it* even so as the women had said: but him they saw not.

Then he said unto them, O fools, and slow of heart to believe all that the prophets have spoken:

Fools *anoetos* (453), signifies "not understanding" (*a*, negative, *noeo*, "to perceive, understand"), not applying *nous*, "the mind," **Luke 24:25**; in Rom. 1:14 and Gal. 3:1, 3 it signifies "senseless," an unworthy lack of understanding; sometimes it carries a moral reproach (in contrast with *sophron*, "sober-minded, selfcontrolled") and describes one who does not govern his lusts, Titus 3:3; in 1 Tim. 6:9 it is associated with evil desires, lusts.

Slow *bradus* (1021), is used twice in Jas. 1:19, in an exhortation to "be slow to speak" and "slow to wrath"; in **Luke 24:25**, metaphorically of the understanding.

24:26 Ought not Christ to have suffered these things, and to enter into his glory?

Ought *dei* (1163), denotes "it is necessary," "one must"; in **Luke 24:26**, KJV, "ought" (RV "behoved it"); the neuter of the present participle, used as a noun, is translated "things which they ought (not)" in 1 Tim. 5:13; in Acts 19:36, "ye ought".

Suffer *see* Suffered at *Luke 13:2*.

24:27 And beginning at Moses and all the prophets, he expounded unto them in all the scriptures the things concerning himself.

Prophets *see* Prophet at *Luke 1:76*.

Expounded *diermeneuo* (1329), "to interpret fully" (*dia* "through," intensive, *hermeneuo*, "to interpret"); (Eng., "hermeneutics"), is translated, "He expounded" in **Luke 24:27**, KJV, RV, "interpreted"; in Acts 9:36, "by interpretation," lit., "being interpreted"; see also 1 Cor. 12:30; 14:5, 13, 27.

24:28 And they drew nigh unto the village, whither they went: and he made as though he would have gone further.

Made *prospoieo* (4364), primarily "to claim," is used in the middle voice with the meaning "to make as if," in **Luke 24:28**, of the Lord's action regarding the two on the way to Emmaus. In the Sept., 1 Sam. 21:13; Job 19:14.

Further *porroteron* (4208), the comparative degree of *porro*, "far off," signifies "further," **Luke 24:28**. *See also* Way at *Luke 14:32*.

24:29 But they constrained him, saying, Abide with us: for it is toward evening, and the day is far spent. And he went in to tarry with them.

Constrained *parabiazomai* (3849), primarily denotes "to employ force contrary to nature and right, to compel by using force" (*para*, "alongside," intensive, *biazo*, "to force"), and is used only of "constraining" by intreaty, as the two going to Emmaus did to Christ, **Luke 24:29**; as Lydia did to Paul and his companions, Acts 16:15.

Abide, Tarry *meno* (3306), "to abide," is translated by the verb "to abide," in the RV, for KJV, "to tarry," in Matt. 26:38; Mark 14:34; **Luke 24:29**; John 4:40; Acts 9:43; 18:20; the RV retains the verb "to tarry" in John 21:22, 23; in Acts 20:5, KJV, "tarried" (RV, "were waiting"). Some mss. have it in Acts 20:15 (KJV, "tarried").

Evening *hespera* (2073), properly, the feminine of the adjective *hesperos*, "of, or at, evening, western" (Lat., *vesper*, Eng., "vespers"), is used as a noun in **Luke 24:29**; Acts 4:3, "eventide"; 28:23. Some mss. have the word in 20:15, "in the evening (we touched)," instead of *hetera*, "next (day)."

Spent *klino* (2827), "to lean, decline," is said of the decline of day in **Luke 24:29**, "is (now) far spent," lit., "has declined." *See also* **Wear** at *Luke 9:12*.

24:30 And it came to pass, as he sat at meat with them, he took bread, and blessed *it*, and brake, and gave to them.

Sat *see Luke 7:36*.

Brake *see Luke 22:19*.

Gave *see* **Delivered** at *Luke 4:17*.

24:31 And their eyes were opened, and they knew him; and he vanished out of their sight.

Opened *see* **Openeth** at *Luke 2:23*.

Vanished In **Luke 24:31**, the adjective *aphantos*, "invisible," used with *ginomai*, "to become," and followed by *apo*, "from," with the plural personal pronoun, is rendered "He vanished out of their sight" (KJV, marg., "He ceased to be seen of them"), lit., "He became invisible from them."

24:32 And they said one to another, Did not our heart burn within us, while he talked with us by the way, and while he opened to us the scriptures?

Hearts *see Luke 1:51*.

Burn *see* **Burning** at *Luke 12:35*.

While *hos*, as, "while" in **Luke 24:32** (twice); John 12:35, 36; Acts 1:10; 10:17.

Talked *laleo* (2980), "to speak, say," is always translated "to speak" in the RV, where the KJV renders it by "to talk," Matt. 12:46; Mark 6:50; **Luke 24:32**; John 4:27 (twice); 9:37; 14:30; Acts 26:31; Rev. 4:1; 17:1; 21:9, 15. The RV rendering is preferable; the idea of "chat" or "chatter" is entirely foreign to the NT, and should never be regarded as the meaning in 1 Cor. 14:34, 35.

Opened *see* **Openeth** at *Luke 2:23*.

24:33 And they rose up the same hour, and returned to Jerusalem, and found the eleven gathered together, and them that were with them,

Same *see Luke 12:12*.

Eleven *see Luke 24:9*.

Gathered *athroizo* (119a), denotes "to assemble, gather together," **Luke 24:33** (according to the best mss.); the word is akin to *athroos*, "assembled in crowds" (not found in the NT).

24:34 Saying, The Lord is risen indeed, and hath appeared to Simon.

Indeed *ontos* (3689), an adverb from *on*, the present participle of *eimi*, "to be," denotes "really, actually"; it is translated "indeed" in Mark 11:32 (RV, "verily"); **Luke 24:34**; John 8:36; 1 Cor. 14:25, RV (KJV "of a truth"); 1 Tim. 5:3, 5, 16; 6:15, RV, where some mss. have *aionios*, "eternal" (KJV); in Gal. 3:21, "verily."

24:35 And they told what things *were done* in the way, and how he was known of them in breaking of bread.

Told *exegeomai* (1834), lit., "to lead out," signifies "to make known, rehearse, declare," **Luke 24:35** (KJV, "told"; RV, "rehearsed"); Acts 10:8; 15:12, 14; 21:19. In John 1:18, in the sentence "He hath declared Him," the other meaning of the verb is in view, to unfold in teaching, "to declare" by making known.

Done In **Luke 24:35**, the phrase "the things *that happened* in the way," RV (KJV, "what things were done in the way"), is, lit., "the things in the way."

Breaking *klasis* (2800), "a breaking," is used in **Luke 24:35** and Acts 2:42, of the "breaking" of bread.

24:36-37 And as they thus spake, Jesus himself stood in the midst of them, and saith unto them, Peace *be* unto you.
But they were terrified and affrighted, and supposed that they had seen a spirit.

Terrified *see Luke 21:9*.

Affrighted *see* **Afraid** at *Luke 24:5*.

Supposed *see* **Suppose** at *Luke 12:51*.

Spirit *see Luke 1:17*.

24:38 And he said unto them, Why are ye troubled? and why do thoughts arise in your hearts?

Troubled *see Luke 1:12*.

Thoughts *see Luke 2:35. See also* **Luke** *5:22*.

Arise *anabaino* (305), "to go up, to ascend," is once rendered "arise" in the RV, **Luke 24:38**, of reasonings in the heart; in Rev. 13:1, RV, "coming up," for KJV, "rise up," with reference to the beast; in 17:8, KJV, "ascend," for RV, "to come up"; in 19:3, RV, "goeth up," for KJV, "rose up."

Hearts *see Luke 1:51*.

24:39 Behold my hands and my feet, that it is I myself: handle me, and see; for a spirit hath not flesh and bones, as ye see me have.

Myself *autos* (846), "self" (a) with *ego*, "I," "I myself," **Luke 24:39**; Acts 10:26; Rom. 7:25; 9:3; 2 Cor. 10:1; 12:13; (b) without the personal pronoun, Acts 24:16 (as the subject of a verb); in the nominative case, Acts 25:22; 1 Cor. 9:27; Phil. 2:24; in the genitive case, Rom. 16:2, RV, "of mine own self."

Handle *pselaphao* (5584), "to feel, touch, handle," is rendered by the latter verb in **Luke 24:39**, in the Lord's invitation to the disciples to accept the evidence of His resurrection in His being bodily in their midst; in 1 John 1:1, in the apostle's testimony (against the gnostic error that Christ had been merely a phantom) that he and his fellow apostles had handled Him.

Spirit *see Luke 1:17*.

Bones *osteon* (3747), probably from a word signifying strength, or firmness, sometimes denotes "hard substances other than bones," e.g., the stone or kernel of fruit. In the NT it always denotes "bones," Matt. 23:27; **Luke 24:39**; John 19:36; Heb. 11:22.

24:40 And when he had thus spoken, he shewed them *his* hands and *his* feet.

Shewed *deiknumi*, or *deiknuo* (1166), denotes (a) "to show, exhibit," e.g., Matt. 4:8; 8:4; John 5:20; 20:20; 1 Tim. 6:15; (b) "to show by making known," Matt. 16:21; **Luke 24:40**; John 14:8, 9; Acts 10:28; 1 Cor. 12:31; Rev. 1:1; 4:1; 22:6; (c) "to show by way of proving," Jas. 2:18; 3:13. *See also* Shew at *Luke 17:14*.

24:41 And while they yet believed not for joy, and wondered, he said unto them, Have ye here any meat?

Believed not *see* Believed ... not at *Luke 24:11*.

Here *enthade* (1759); "here" in **Luke 24:41**; Acts 16:28; 25:24.

Meat *brosimos* (1034), "eatable," **Luke 24:41**, KJV, "any meat" (RV, "anything to eat").

24:42 And they gave him a piece of a broiled fish, and of an honeycomb.

Piece *meros* (3313), "a part," is translated "a piece (of a broiled fish)" in **Luke 24:42**.

Broiled *optos* (3702), "broiled" (from *optao*, "to cook, roast"), is said of food prepared by fire, **Luke 24:42**.

Honeycomb *melissios* (3193), signifying "made by bees" from *melissa*, "a bee," is found, with *kerion*, "a comb," in some mss. in **Luke 24:42**.

24:43 And he took *it*, and did eat before them.

Before *see Luke 1:17*.

24:44 And he said unto them, These *are* the words which I spake unto you, while I was yet with you, that all things must be fulfilled, which were written in the law of Moses, and *in* the prophets, and *in* the psalms, concerning me.

Fulfilled *see Luke 4:21*.

Law *see Luke 16:16*.

Psalms *see Luke 20:42*.

24:45 Then opened he their understanding, that they might understand the scriptures,

Opened *see* Openeth at *Luke 2:23*.

Understanding *nous* (3563), "mind," denotes, speaking generally, the seat of reflective consciousness, comprising the faculties of perception and understanding, and those of feeling, judging and determining. Its use in the NT may be analyzed as follows: it denotes (a) the faculty of knowing, the seat of the understanding, **Luke 24:45**; Rom. 1:28; 14:5; 1 Cor. 14:15, 19; Eph. 4:17; Phil. 4:7; Col. 2:18; 1 Tim. 6:5; 2 Tim. 3:8; Titus 1:15; Rev. 13:18; 17:9; (b) counsels, purpose, Rom. 11:34 (of the "mind" of God); 12:2; 1 Cor. 1:10; 2:16, twice (1) of the thoughts and counsels of God, (2) of Christ, a testimony to His Godhood; Eph. 4:23; (c) the new nature, which belongs to the believer by reason of the new birth, Rom. 7:23, 25, where it is contrasted with "the flesh," the principle of evil which dominates fallen man. Under (b) may come 2 Thess. 2:2, where it stands for the determination to be steadfast amidst afflictions, through the confident expectation of the day of rest and recompense mentioned in the first chapter.

24:46 And said unto them, Thus it is written, and thus it behoved Christ to suffer, and to rise from the dead the third day:

Behoved *dei* (1163), "it is necessary," is rendered "behoved," in **Luke 24:46**; RV, (that the Christ) "should" (suffer). *Dei* expresses a logical necessity, *opheilo*, a moral obligation; cf. *chre*, Jas. 3:10, "ought," which expresses a need resulting from the fitness of things (Trench, Sec. cvii).

Suffer *see* Suffered at *Luke 13:2*.

Rise *see* Rose at *Luke 4:29*.

Third *see Luke 20:12*. *See also Luke 9:22*.

24:47 And that repentance and remission of sins should be preached in his name among all nations, beginning at Jerusalem.

Remission *see* ***Luke 1:77.***

Preached *see* Preach at ***Luke 4:18.***

24:48 And ye are witnesses of these things.

Witnesses *see* Witness at ***Luke 11:48.***

24:49 And, behold, I send the promise of my Father upon you: but tarry ye in the city of Jerusalem, until ye be endued with power from on high.

Send *see* Sent at ***Luke 1:19.***

Promise *epangelia* (1860), primarily a law term, denoting "a summons" (*epi*, "upon," *angello*, "to proclaim, announce"), also meant "an undertaking to do or give something, a promise." Except in Acts 23:21 it is used only of the "promises" of God. It frequently stands for the thing "promised," and so signifies a gift graciously bestowed, not a pledge secured by negotiation; thus, in Gal. 3:14, "the promise of the Spirit" denotes "the promised Spirit": cf. **Luke 24:49**; Acts 2:33 and Eph. 1:13; so in Heb. 9:15, "the promise of the eternal inheritance" is "the promised eternal inheritance."

Tarry *kathizo* (2523), "to make to sit down," or, intransitively, "to sit down," is translated "tarry ye" in **Luke 24:49**.

Endued *enduo* (1746), in the middle voice, "to put on oneself, be clothed with," is used metaphorically of power, **Luke 24:49**, RV, clothed. *See also* Ware at ***Luke 8:27.***

Power *dunamis* (1411), "power," (a) used relatively, denotes "inherent ability, capability, ability to perform anything," e.g., Matt. 25:15, "ability"; Acts 3:12, "power"; 2 Thess. 1:7, RV, "(angels) of His power" (KJV, "mighty"); Heb. 11:11, RV, "power" (KJV, "strength"); (b) used absolutely, denotes (1) "power to work, to carry something into effect," e.g., **Luke 24:49**; (2) "power in action," e.g., Rom. 1:16; 1 Cor. 1:18; it is translated "might" in the KJV of Eph. 1:21 (RV, "power"); so 3:16; Col. 1:11 (1st clause); 2 Pet. 2:11; in Rom. 15:19, KJV, this noun is rendered "mighty"; RV, "(in the) power of signs." The RV consistently avoids the rendering "might" for *dunamis;* the usual rendering is "power." Under this heading comes the rendering "mighty works," e.g., Matt. 7:22, RV (KJV, "wonderful works"); 11:20-23; singular number in Mark 6:5; in Matt. 14:2 and Mark 6:14 the RV has "powers"; in 2 Cor. 12:12, RV, "mighty works" (KJV, "mighty deeds").

On high *see* ***Luke 1:78.***

24:50 And he led them out as far as to Bethany, and he lifted up his hands, and blessed them.

Led *exago* (1806), "to lead out," is rendered by the verb "to lead, out or forth," in Mark 15:20 (in some mss. in 8:23, the best have *ekphero*, "to bring out)"; **Luke 24:50**; John 10:3; Acts 7:36, 40 (KJV "brought"), and 13:17, RV; Acts 21:38; Heb. 8:9.

Far In the following, *heos*, used as a preposition, is translated "as far as" in the RV, for different words in the KJV; Acts 17:14, in the best mss., instead of *hos*, which the KJV renders "as it were"; 17:15, "unto"; 23:23, "to." Both versions have "as far as" in 11:19, 22; in **Luke 24:50**, the RV has "until they were over against," for KJV, "as far as to."

Lifted *see* ***Luke 6:20.*** *See also* Lift at ***Luke 21:28.***

24:51 And it came to pass, while he blessed them, he was parted from them, and carried up into heaven.

"Seek Him! Seek Him! What can we do without Him? Seek Him! Seek Him always. But go beyond seeking Him; expect Him. Do you expect anything to happen to you when you get up to preach in a pulpit? ... Seek this power, expect this power, yearn for this power; and when this power comes, yield to Him. Do not resist. Forget all about your sermon if necessary. Let him loose you, let Him manifest His power in you and through you."

DAVID MARTYN LLOYD-JONES

Blessed *see* **Praised** at ***Luke 1:64***.

Parted *diistemi* (1339), "to set apart, separate" (*dia*, "apart," *histemi*, "to cause to stand"), is used in the active voice in **Luke 24:51**, RV, "He parted (from them)," KJV, "was parted."

Carried *anaphero* (399), is used of "leading persons up to a higher place," and, in this respect, of the Lord's ascension, **Luke 24:51**. It is used twice of the Lord's propitiatory sacrifice, in His bearing sins on the cross, Heb. 9:28 and 1 Pet. 2:24; the KJV margin, "to the tree," is to be rejected. The KJV text, "on," and the RV "upon" express the phrase rightly.

24:52-53 And they worshipped him, and returned to Jerusalem with great joy:

And were continually in the temple, praising and blessing God. Amen.

Continually *diapantos* (1275), is, lit., "through all," i.e., through all time, (*dia*, "through," *pas*, "all"). In the best texts the words are separated. The phrase, which is used of the time throughout which a thing is done, is sometimes rendered "continually," sometimes "always"; "always" or "alway" in Mark 5:5; Acts 10:2; 24:16; Rom. 11:10; "continually" in **Luke 24:53**; Heb. 9:6; 13:15, the idea being that of a continuous practice carried on without being abandoned.

Praising *see* ***Luke 2:13***.

Blessing *see* **Praised** at ***Luke 1:64***.

John

Chapter 1

1:1 In the beginning was the Word, and the Word was with God, and the Word was God.

Word *logos* (3056), denotes (I) "the expression of thought" – not the mere name of an object – (a) as embodying a conception or idea, e.g., Luke 7:7; 1 Cor. 14:9, 19; (b) a saying or statement, (1) by God, e.g., **John 15:25**; Rom. 9:9; 9:28, RV, "word" (KJV, "work"); Gal. 5:14; Heb. 4:12; (2) by Christ, e.g., Matt. 24:35 (plur.); **John 2:22**; **4:41**; **14:23** (plur.); **15:20**. In connection with (1) and (2) the phrase "the word of the Lord," i.e., the revealed will of God (very frequent in the OT), is used of a direct revelation given by Christ, 1 Thess. 4:15; of the gospel, Acts 8:25; 13:49; 15:35, 36; 16:32; 19:10; 1 Thess. 1:8; 2 Thess. 3:1; in this respect it is the message from the Lord, delivered with His authority and made effective by His power (cf. Acts 10:36); for other instances relating to the gospel see Acts 13:26; 14:3; 15:7; 1 Cor. 1:18, RV; 2 Cor. 2:17; 4:2; 5:19; 6:7; Gal. 6:6; Eph. 1:13; Phil. 2:16; Col. 1:5; Heb. 5:13; sometimes it is used as the sum of God's utterances, e.g., Mark 7:13; **John 10:35**; Rev. 1:2, 9; (c) discourse, speech, of instruction, etc., e.g., Acts 2:40; 1 Cor. 2:13; 12:8; 2 Cor. 1:18; 1 Thess. 1:5; 2 Thess. 2:15; Heb. 6:1, RV, marg.; doctrine, e.g., Matt. 13:20; Col. 3:16; 1 Tim. 4:6; 2 Tim. 1:13; Titus 1:9; 1 John 2:7;

(II) "The Personal Word," a title of the Son of God; this identification is substantiated by the statements of doctrine in **John 1:1-18**, declaring in verses 1 and 2 (1) His distinct and superfinite Personality, (2) His relation in the Godhead (*pros*, "with," not mere company, but the most intimate communion), (3) His deity; in v. **3** His creative power; in v. **14** His incarnation ("became flesh," expressing His voluntary act; not as KJV, "was made"), the reality and totality of His human nature, and His glory "as of the only begotten from the Father," RV (marg., "an only begotten from a father"), the absence of the article in each place lending stress to the nature and character of the relationship; His was the *shekinah* glory in open manifestation; v. **18** consummates the identification: "the only-begotten Son (RV marg., many ancient authorities read "God only begotten,"), which is in the bosom of the Father, He hath declared Him," thus fulfilling the significance of the title "*Logos*," the "Word," the personal manifestation, not of a part of the divine nature, but of the whole deity.

The title is used also in 1 John 1, "the Word of life" combining the two declarations in **John 1:1** and **4** and Rev. 19:13.

God *theos* (2316), (I) in the polytheism of the Greeks, denoted "a god or deity," e.g., Acts 14:11; 19:26; 28:6; 1 Cor. 8:5; Gal. 4:8.

(II) (a) Hence the word was appropriated by Jews and retained by Christians to denote "the one true God." In the Sept. *theos* translates (with few exceptions) the Hebrew words *Elohim* and *Jehovah*, the former indicating His power and preeminence, the latter His unoriginated, immutable, eternal and self-sustained existence. In the NT, these and all the other divine attributes are predicated of Him. To Him are ascribed, e.g., His unity, or monism, e.g., Mark 12:29; 1 Tim. 2:5; self-existence, **John 5:26**; immutability, Jas. 1:17; eternity, Rom. 1:20; universality, Matt. 10:29; Acts 17:26-28; almighty power, Matt. 19:26; infinite knowledge, Acts 2:23; 15:18; Rom. 11:33, creative power, Rom. 11:36; 1 Cor. 8:6; Eph. 3:9; Rev. 4:11; 10:6; absolute holiness, 1 Pet. 1:15; 1 John 1:5; righteousness, **John 17:25**; faithfulness, 1 Cor. 1:9; 10:13; 1 Thess. 5:24; 2 Thess. 3:3; 1 John 1:9; love, 1 John 4:8, 16; mercy, Rom. 9:15, 18; truthfulness, Titus 1:2; Heb. 6:18.

(b) The divine attributes are

"The Incarnation is the most stupendous event which ever can take place on earth, and after it henceforth, I do not see how we can scruple at any miracle on the mere ground of it being unlikely to happen."

JOHN HENRY NEWMAN

likewise indicated or definitely predicated of Christ, e.g., Matt. 20:18-19; **John 1:1-3**; **1:18**, RV, marg.; **5:22-29**; **8:58**; **14:6**; **17:22-24**; **20:28**; Rom. 1:4; 9:5; Phil. 3:21; Col. 1:15; 2:3; Titus 2:13, RV; Heb. 1:3; 13:8; 1 John 5:20; Rev. 22:12, 13.

(c) Also of the Holy Spirit, e.g., Matt. 28:19; Luke 1:35; **John 14:16**; **15:26**; **16:7-14**; Rom. 8:9, 26; 1 Cor. 12:11; 2 Cor. 13:14.

(d) *Theos* is used (1) with the definite article, (2) without (i.e., as an anarthrous noun). As to this latter it is usual to employ the article with a proper name, when mentioned a second time. There are, of course, exceptions to this, as when the absence of the article serves to lay stress upon, or give precision to, the character or nature of what is expressed in the noun. A notable instance of this is in **John 1:1**, "and the Word was God"; here a double stress is on *theos*, by the absence of the article and by the emphatic position. To translate it literally, "a god was the Word," is entirely misleading. Moreover, that "the Word" is the subject of the sentence, exemplifies the rule that the subject is to be determined by its having the article when the predicate is without the article.

(e) In the following the nominative case is used for the vocative, and always with the article; Mark 15:34; Luke 18:11, 13; **John 20:28**; (Acts 4:24 in some mss.); Heb. 1:8; 10:7.

(III) The word is used of divinely appointed judges in Israel, as representing God in His authority, **John 10:34**, quoted from Ps. 82:6, which indicates that God Himself sits in judgment on those whom He has appointed. The application of the term to the Devil, 2 Cor. 4:4, and the belly, Phil. 3:19, virtually places these instances under (I).

1:2-3 The same was in the beginning with God.
All things were made by him; and without him was not any thing made that was made.

All *pas* (3956), radically means "all." Used without the article it means "every," every kind or variety. So the RV marg. in Eph. 2:21, "every building," and the text in 3:15, "every family," and the RV marg. of Acts 2:36, "every house"; or it may signify "the highest degree," the maximum of what is referred to, as, "with all boldness" Acts 4:29. Before proper names of countries, cities and nations, and before collective terms, like "Israel," it signifies either "all" or "the whole," e.g., Matt. 2:3; Acts 2:36. Used with the article, it means the whole of one object. In the plural it signifies "the totality of the persons or things referred to." Used without a noun it virtually becomes a pronoun, meaning "everyone" or "anyone." In the plural with a noun it means "all." The neuter singular denotes "everything" or "anything whatsoever." One form of the neuter plural (*panta*) signifies "wholly, together, in all ways, in all things," Acts 20:35; 1 Cor. 9:25. The neuter plural without the article signifies "all things severally," e.g., **John 1:3**; 1 Cor. 2:10; preceded by the article it denotes "all things," as constituting a whole, e.g., Rom. 11:36; 1 Cor. 8:6; Eph. 3:9.

Made *ginomai* (1096), "to become," is sometimes translated by the passive voice of the verb to make, e.g., Matt. 9:16; **John 1:3** (three times), **10**; **8:33**; Rom. 11:9; 1 Cor. 1:30; 3:13; 4:9, 13; Eph. 2:13; 3:7; Phil. 2:7 (but RV marg., "becoming"); Col. 1:23, 25; Heb. 5:5; 6:4; 7:12, 16, 21, 26; 11:3; Jas. 3:9; 1 Pet. 2:7. In many places the RV translates otherwise, and chiefly by the verb to become, e.g., Matt. 25:6, "there is"; 27:24, "was arising"; **John 1:14**, "became"; **John 2:9**, "become"; Rom. 1:3, "born"; 2:25, "is become"; 10:20, "became"; Gal. 3:13, "having become"; 4:4, "born" (twice); Heb. 3:14, "are become", 7:22, "hath ... become."

1:4 In him was life; and the life was the light of men.

Light *phos* (5457), akin to *phao*, "to give light" (from roots *pha–* and *phan–*, expressing "light as seen by the eye," and, metaphorically, as "reaching the mind," whence *phaino*, "to make to appear," *phaneros*, "evident," etc.); cf. Eng., "phosphorus" (lit., "light-bearing").

"Apart from natural phenomena, light is used in Scripture of (a) the glory of God's dwellingplace, 1 Tim. 6:16; (b) the nature of God, 1 John 1:5; (c) the impartiality of God, Jas. 1:17; (d) the favor of God, Ps. 4:6; of the King, Prov. 16:15; of an influential man, Job 29:24; (e) God, as the illuminator of His people, Isa. 60:19, 20; (f) the Lord Jesus as the illuminator of men, **John 1:4, 5, 9; 3:19; 8:12; 9:5; 12:35, 36, 46**; Acts 13:47; (g) the illuminating power of the Scriptures, Ps. 119:105; and of the judgments and commandments of God, Isa. 51:4; Prov. 6:23, cf. Ps. 43:3; (h) the guidance of God Job 29:3; Ps. 112:4; Isa. 58:10; and, ironically, of the guidance of man, Rom. 2:19; (i) salvation, 1 Pet. 2:9; (j) righteousness, Rom. 13:12; 2 Cor. 11:14, 15; 1 John 2:9, 10; (k) witness for God, Matt. 5:14, 16; **John 5:35**; (l) prosperity and general well-being, Esth. 8:16; Job 18:18; Isa. 58:8-10."

1:5 And the light shineth in darkness; and the darkness comprehended it not.

Light *see John 1:4.*

Shineth *phaino* (5316), signifies, in the active voice, "to shine"; in the passive, "to be brought forth into light, to become evident, to appear." In Rom. 7:13, concerning sin, the RV has "might be shewn to be," for KJV, "appear."

It is used of the "appearance" of Christ to the disciples, Mark 16:9; of His future "appearing" in glory as the Son of Man, spoken of as a sign to the world, Matt. 24:30; there the genitive is subjective, the sign being the "appearing" of Christ Himself; of Christ as the light, **John 1:5**; of John the Baptist, **5:35**; of the "appearing" of an angel of the Lord, either visibly, Matt. 1:20, or in a dream, 2:13; of a star, 2:7; of men who make an outward show, Matt. 6:5; 6:18 (see the RV); 23:27-28; 2 Cor. 13:7; of tares, Matt. 13:26; of a vapor, Jas. 4:14; of things physical in general, Heb. 11:3; used impersonally in Matt. 9:33, "it was never so seen"; also of what appears to the mind, and so in the sense of to think, Mark 14:64, or to seem, Luke 24:11 (RV, appeared).

Darkness *skotia* (4653), is used (a) of physical darkness, "dark," **John 6:17**, lit., "darkness had come on," and 20:1, lit., "darkness still being"; (b) of secrecy, in general, whether what is done therein is good or evil, Matt. 10:27; Luke 12:3; (c) of spiritual or moral "darkness," emblematic of sin, as a condition of moral or spiritual depravity, Matt. 4:16; **John 1:5; 8:12; 12:35, 46**; 1 John 1:5; 2:8-9, 11.

Comprehended *katalambano* (2638), properly signifies "to lay hold of"; then, "to lay hold of so as to possess as one's own, to appropriate." Hence it has the same twofold meaning as the Eng. "to apprehend"; (a), "to seize upon, take possession of," (1) with a beneficial effect, as of "laying hold" of the righteousness which is of faith, Rom. 9:30 (not there a matter of attainment, as in the Eng. versions, but of appropriation); of the obtaining of a prize, 1 Cor. 9:24 (RV, "attain"); of the apostle's desire "to apprehend," or "lay hold of," that for which he was apprehended by Christ, Phil. 3:12-13; (2) with a detrimental effect, e.g., of demon power, Mark 9:18; of human action in seizing upon a person, **John 8:3-4**; metaphorically, with the added idea of overtaking, of spiritual darkness in coming upon people, **John 12:35**; of the Day of the Lord, in suddenly coming upon unbelievers as a thief, 1 Thess. 5:4; (b), "to lay hold of" with the mind, to understand, perceive, e.g., metaphorically, of darkness with regard to light, **John 1:5**, though possibly here the sense is that of (a) as in **12:35**; of mental perception, Acts 4:13; 10:34; 25:25; Eph. 3:18.

1:6 There was a man sent from God, whose name *was* John.

Sent *apostello* (649), lit., "to send forth" (*apo*, "from"), akin to *apostolos*, "an apostle," denotes (a) "to send on service, or with a commission," (1) of persons; Christ, sent by the Father, Matt. 10:40; 15:24; 21:37; Mark 9:37; 12:6; Luke 4:18, 43; 9:48; 10:16; **John 3:17; 5:36, 38; 6:29, 57; 7:29; 8:42; 10:36; 11:42; 17:3, 8, 18** (1st part), **21, 23, 25; 20:21**; Acts 3:20 (future); 3:26; 1 John 4:9, 10, 14; the Holy Spirit, Luke 24:49; 1 Pet. 1:12; Rev. 5:6; Moses, Acts 7:35; John the Baptist, **John 1:6; 3:28**; disciples and apostles, e.g., Matt. 10:16; Mark 11:1; Luke 22:8; **John 4:38; 17:18** (2nd part); Acts 26:17; servants, e.g., Matt. 21:34; Luke 20:10; officers and officials, Mark 6:27; **John 7:32**; Acts 16:35; messengers, e.g., Acts 10:8, 17, 20; 15:27; evangelists, Rom. 10:15; angels, e.g., Matt. 24:31; Mark 13:27; Luke 1:19, 26; Heb. 1:14; Rev. 1:1; 22:6; demons, Mark 5:10; (2) of things, e.g., Matt. 21:3; Mark 4:29, RV, marg., "sendeth forth," text, "putteth forth" (KJV, "... in"); Acts 10:36; 11:30; 28:28; (b) "to send away, dismiss," e.g., Mark 8:26; 12:3; Luke 4:18, "to set (at liberty)."

1:7 The same came for a witness, to bear witness of the Light, that all *men* through him might believe.

Witness *marturia* (3141), "testimony, a bearing witness," is translated "witness" in Mark 14:55, 56, 59; Luke 22:71; **John 1:7, 19** (RV); **3:11, 32** and **33** (RV); **5:31, 32, 34** (RV), **36**; RV in **8:13, 14, 17; 19:35; 21:24**; KJV in Titus 1:13; KJV and RV in 1 John 5:9 (thrice), 10a; RV in 10b, 11; 3 John 12.

Bear witness *martureo* (3140), denotes (I) "to be a *martus*," or "to bear witness to," sometimes rendered "to testify"; it is used of the witness (a) of God the Father to Christ, **John**

5:32, 37; 8:18 (2nd part); 1 John 5:9, 10; to others, Acts 13:22; 15:8; Heb. 11:2, 4 (twice), 5, 39; (b) of Christ, **John 3:11, 32; 4:44; 5:31; 7:7; 8:13, 14, 18** (1st part); **13:21; 18:37**; Acts 14:3; 1 Tim. 6:13; Rev. 22:18, 20; of the Holy Spirit, to Christ, **John 15:26**; Heb. 10:15; 1 John 5:7, 8, RV, which rightly omits the latter part of v. 7 (it was a marginal gloss which crept into the original text); it finds no support in Scripture; (c) of the Scriptures, to Christ, **John 5:39**; Heb. 7:8, 17; (d) of the works of Christ, to Himself, and of the circumstances connected with His death, **John 5:36; 10:25**; 1 John 5:8; (e) of prophets and apostles, to the righteousness of God, Rom. 3:21; to Christ, **John 1:7, 8, 15, 32, 34; 3:26; 5:33**, RV; **15:27; 19:35; 21:24**; Acts 10:43; 23:11; 1 Cor. 15:15; 1 John 1:2; 4:14; Rev. 1:2; to doctrine, Acts 26:22 (in some texts, so KJV); to the Word of God, Rev. 1:2; (f) of others, concerning Christ, Luke 4:22; **John 4:39; 12:17**; (g) of believers to one another, **John 3:28**; 2 Cor. 8:3; Gal. 4:15; Col. 4:13; 1 Thess. 2:11; 3 John 3, 6, 12 (2nd part); (h) of the apostle Paul concerning Israel, Rom. 10:2; (i) of an angel, to the churches, Rev. 22:16; (j) of unbelievers, concerning themselves, Matt. 23:31; concerning Christ, **John 18:23**; concerning others, **John 2:25**; Acts 22:5; 26:5; (II) "to give a good report, to approve of," Acts 6:3; 10:22; 16:2; 22:12; 1 Tim. 5:10; 3 John 12 (1st part); some would put Luke 4:22 here.

1:8 He was not that Light, but *was sent* to bear witness of that Light.

Bear witness *see John 1:7.*

1:9 *That* was the true Light, which lighteth every man that cometh into the world.

True *alethinos* (228), denotes "true" in the sense of real, ideal, genuine; it is used (a) of God, **John 7:28; 17:3**; 1 Thess. 1:9; Rev. 6:10; these declare that God fulfills the meaning of His Name; He is "very God," in distinction from all other gods, false gods (*alethes*, signifies that He is veracious, "true" to His utterances, He cannot lie); (b) of Christ, **John 1:9; 6:32; 15:1**; 1 John 2:8; 5:20 (thrice); Rev. 3:7, 14; 19:11; His judgment, **John 8:16**; (c) God's words, **John 4:37**; Rev. 19:9, 21:5; 22:6; (d) His ways, Rev. 15:3; (e) His judgments, Rev. 16:7; 19:2; (to His riches, Luke 16:11; (g) His worshipers, **John 4:23**; (h) their hearts, Heb. 10:22; (i) the witness of the apostle John, **John 19:35**; (j) the spiritual, antitypical tabernacle, Heb. 8:2; 9:24, not that the wilderness tabernacle was false, but that it was a weak and earthly copy of the heavenly.

Light *see John 1:4.*

Lighteth *photizo* (5461), used (a) intransitively, signifies "to shine, give light," Rev. 22:5; (b) transitively, (1) "to illumine, to light, enlighten, to be lightened," Luke 11:36; Rev. 21:23; in the passive voice, Rev. 18:1; metaphorically, of spiritual enlightenment, **John 1:9**; Eph. 1:18; 3:9, "to make … see;" Heb. 6:4; 10:32, "ye were enlightened," RV (KJV, "… illuminated"); (2) "to bring to light," 1 Cor. 4:5 (of God's act in the future); 2 Tim. 1:10 (of God's act in the past).

World *kosmos* (2889), primarily "order, arrangement, ornament, adornment" (1 Pet. 3:3), is used to denote (a) the "earth," e.g., Matt. 13:35; **John 21:25**; Acts 17:24; Rom. 1:20 (probably here the universe: it had this meaning among the Greeks, owing to the order observable in it); 1 Tim. 6:7; Heb. 4:3; 9:26; (b) the "earth" in contrast with Heaven, 1 John 3:17 (perhaps also Rom. 4:13); (c) by metonymy, the "human race, mankind," e.g., Matt. 5:14; **John 1:9** [here "that cometh (RV, 'coming') into the world" is said of Christ, not of "every man"; by His coming into the world He was the light for all men]; v. **10; 3:16, 17** (thrice), **19; 4:42**, and frequently in Rom., 1 Cor. and 1 John; (d) "Gentiles" as distinguished from Jews, e.g., Rom. 11:12, 15, where the meaning is that all who will may be reconciled (cf. 2 Cor. 5:19); (e) the "present condition of human affairs," in alienation from and opposition to God, e.g., **John 7:7; 8:23; 14:30**; 1 Cor. 2:12; Gal. 4:3; 6:14; Col. 2:8; Jas. 1:27; 1 John 4:5 (thrice); 5:19; (f) the "sum of temporal possessions," Matt. 16:26; 1 Cor. 7:31 (1st part); (g) metaphorically, of the "tongue" as "a world (of iniquity)," Jas. 3:6, expressive of magnitude and variety.

1:10 He was in the world, and the world was made by him, and the world knew him not.

World *see John 1:9.*

Made *see John 1:3.*

1:11 He came unto his own, and his own received him not.

His own *idios* (2398), expresses "what is one's own" (hence, Eng. "idiot," in a changed sense, lit., "a person with his own opinions"); the neuter plural with the article (*ta idia*) signifies "one's own things." In 1 Thess. 4:11, the noun is not expressed in the original but is supplied in the English versions by "business," "your own business." For the same phrase, otherwise expressed, see **John 1:11**, "His own (things)"; **16:32** and **19:27**, "his own (home)"; Acts 21:6, "home." In Luke 2:49, the phrase "in My Father's house" (RV), "about My Father's business" (KJV), is, lit., "in the (things, the neuter plural of the article) of My Father."

Received *paralambano* (3880), "to receive from another" (*para*, "from beside"), or "to take," signifies "to receive," e.g., in Mark 7:4; **John 1:11**; **14:3**; 1 Cor. 11:23; 15:1, 3; Gal. 1:9, 12; Phil. 4:9; Col. 2:6; 4:17; 1 Thess. 2:13 (1st part); 4:1; 2 Thess. 3:6; Heb. 12:28.

1:12 But as many as received him, to them gave he power to become the sons of God, *even* to them that believe on his name:

Power *exousia* (1849), "authority, power," is translated "right" in the RV, for KJV, "power," in **John 1:12**; Rom. 9:21; 1 Cor. 9:4, 5, 6, 12 (twice), 18; 2 Thess. 3:9, where the "right" is that of being maintained by those among whom the ministers of the gospel had labored, a "right" possessed in virtue of the "authority" given them by Christ, Heb. 13:10; Rev. 22:14.

Exousia first denotes "freedom to act" and then "authority for the action." This is first true of God, Acts 1:7. It was exercised by the Son of God, as from, and in conjunction with, the Father when the Lord was upon earth, in the days of His flesh, Matt. 9:6; **John 10:18**, as well as in resurrection, Matt. 28:18; **John 17:2**. All others hold their freedom to act from God (though some of them have abused it), whether angels, Eph. 1:21, or human potentates, Rom. 13:1. Satan offered to delegate his authority over earthly kingdoms to Christ, Luke 4:6, who, though conscious of His "right" to it, refused, awaiting the divinely appointed time. *See also* ***John 17:2***.

Sons *teknon* (5043), "a child" (akin to *tikto*, "to beget, bear"), is used in both the natural and the figurative senses. In contrast to *huios*, "son", it gives prominence to the fact of birth, whereas *huios* stresses the dignity and character of the relationship. Figuratively, *teknon* is used of "children" of (a) God, **John 1:12**; (b) light, Eph. 5:8; (c) obedience, 1 Pet. 1:14; (d) a promise, Rom. 9:8; Gal. 4:28; (e) the Devil, 1 John 3:10; (f) wrath, Eph. 2:3; (g) cursing, 2 Pet. 2:14; (h) spiritual relationship, 2 Tim. 2:1; Philem. 10.

Sons *huios* (5207), primarily signifies the relation of offspring to parent (see **John 9:18-20**; Gal. 4:30). It is often used metaphorically of prominent moral characteristics. "It is used in the NT of (a) male offspring, Gal. 4:30; (b) legitimate, as opposed to illegitimate offspring, Heb. 12:8; (c) descendants, without reference to sex, Rom. 9:27; (d) friends attending a wedding, Matt. 9:15; (e) those who enjoy certain privileges, Acts 3:25; (f) those who act in a certain way, whether evil, Matt. 23:31, or good, Gal. 3:7; (g) those who manifest a certain character, whether evil, Acts 13:10; Eph. 2:2, or good, Luke 6:35; Acts 4:36; Rom. 8:14; (h) the destiny that corresponds with the character, whether evil, Matt. 23:15; **John 17:12**; 2 Thess. 2:3, or good, Luke 20:36; (i) the dignity of the relationship with God whereinto men are brought by the Holy Spirit when they believe on the Lord Jesus Christ, Rom. 8:19; Gal. 3:26....

"The Apostle John does not use *huios*, 'son,' of the believer, he reserves that title for the Lord; but he does use *teknon*, 'child,' as in his Gospel, **1:12**; 1 John 3:1, 2; Rev. 21:7 (*huios*) is a quotation from 2 Sam. 7:14. The Lord Jesus used *huios* in a very significant way, as in Matt. 5:9, 'Blessed are the peacemakers, for they shall be called the sons of God,' and vv. 44, 45, 'Love your enemies, and pray for them that persecute you; that ye may be (become) sons of your Father which is in heaven.' The disciples were to do these things, not in order that they might become children of God, but that, being children (note 'your Father' throughout), they might make the fact manifest in their character, might 'become sons.' See also 2 Cor. 6:17, 18. As to moral characteristics, the following phrases are used: (a) sons of God, Matt. 5:9, 45; Luke 6:35; (b) sons of the light, Luke 16:8; **John 12:36**; (c) sons of the day, 1 Thess. 5:5; (d) sons of peace, Luke 10:6; (e) sons of this world, Luke 16:8; (f) sons of disobedience, Eph. 2:2; (g) sons of the evil one, Matt. 13:38, cf. 'of the Devil,' Acts 13:10; (h) son of perdition, **John 17:12**; 2 Thess. 2:3. It is also used to describe characteristics other than moral, as: (i) sons of the resurrection, Luke 20:36; (j) sons of the Kingdom, Matt. 8:12; 13:38; (k) sons of the bridechamber, Mark 2:19; (l) sons of exhortation, Acts 4:36; (m) sons of thunder, Boanerges, Mark 3:17."

Name *onoma* (3686), is used (I) in general of the "name" by which a person or thing is called, e.g., Mark 3:16, 17, "(He) surnamed," lit., "(He added) the name"; 14:32, lit., "(of which) the name (was)"; Luke 1:63; **John 18:10**, sometimes translated "named," e.g., Luke 8:5, "named (Zacharias)," lit., "by name"; in the same verse, "named (Elizabeth)," lit., "the name of her," an elliptical phrase, with "was" understood; Acts 8:9, RV, "by name," 10:1; the "name" is put for the reality in Rev. 3:1; in Phil. 2:9, the "Name" represents "the title and dignity" of the Lord, as in Eph. 1:21 and Heb. 1:4;

(II) for all that a "name" implies, of authority, character, rank, majesty, power, excellence, etc., of everything that the "name" covers: (a) of the "Name" of God as expressing His attributes, etc., e.g., Matt. 6:9; Luke 1:49; **John 12:28; 17:6, 26**; Rom. 15:9; 1 Tim. 6:1; Heb. 13:15; Rev. 13:6; (b) of the "Name" of Christ, e.g., Matt. 10:22; 19:29; **John 1:12; 2:23; 3:18**; Acts 26:9; Rom. 1:5; Jas. 2:7; 1 John 3:23; 3 John 7; Rev. 2:13; 3:8; also the phrases rendered "in the name"; these may be analyzed as follows: (1) representing the authority of Christ, e.g., Matt. 18:5 (with *epi*, "on the ground of My authority"); so Matt. 24:5 (falsely) and parallel passages; as substantiated by the Father, **John 14:26; 16:23** (last clause), RV; (2) in the power of (with *en*, "in"), e.g., Mark 16:17; Luke 10:17; Acts 3:6; 4:10; 16:18; Jas. 5:14; (3) in acknowledgement or confession of, e.g., Acts 4:12; 8:16; 9:27, 28; (4) in recognition of the authority of (sometimes combined with the thought of relying or resting on), Matt. 18:20; cf. 28:19; Acts 8:16; 9:2 (*eis*, "into"); **John 14:13; 15:16**; Eph. 5:20; Col. 3:17; (5) owing to the fact that one is called by Christ's "Name" or is identified with Him, e.g. 1 Pet. 4:14 (with *en*, "in"); with *heneken*, "for the sake of," e.g., Matt. 19:29; with *dia*, "on account of," Matt. 10:22; 24:9; Mark 13:13; Luke 21:17; **John 15:21**; 1 John 2:12; Rev. 2:3;

1:13 Which were born, not of blood, nor of the will of the flesh, nor of the will of man, but of God.

Blood *haima* (129), (hence Eng., prefix *haem–*), besides its natural meaning, stands, (a) in conjunction with *sarx*, "flesh," "flesh and blood," Matt. 16:17; 1 Cor. 15:50; Gal. 1:16; the original has the opposite order, blood and flesh, in Eph. 6:12 and Heb. 2:14; this phrase signifies, by *synecdoche*, "man, human beings." It stresses the limitations of humanity; the two are essential elements in man's physical being; "the life of the flesh is in the blood," Lev. 17:11; (b) for human generation, **John 1:13**; (c) for "blood" shed by violence, e.g., Matt. 23:35; Rev. 17:6; (d) for the "blood" of sacrificial victims, e.g., Heb. 9:7; of the "blood" of Christ, which betokens His death by the shedding of His "blood" in expiatory sacrifice; to drink His "blood" is to appropriate the saving effects of His expiatory death, **John 6:53**. As "the life of the flesh is in the blood," Lev. 17:11, and was forfeited by sin, life eternal can be imparted only by the expiation made, in the giving up of the life by the sinless Savior.

Will *thelema* (2307), signifies (a) objectively, "that which is willed, of the will of God," e.g., Matt. 18:14; Mark 3:35, the fulfilling being a sign of spiritual relationship to the Lord, **John 4:34; 5:30; 6:39, 40**; Acts 13:22, plural, "my desires"; Rom. 2:18; 12:2, lit., "the will of God, the good and perfect and acceptable"; here the repeated article is probably resumptive, the adjectives describing the will, as in the Eng. versions; Gal. 1:4; Eph. 1:9; 5:17, "of the Lord"; Col. 1:9; 4:12; 1 Thess. 4:3; 5:18, where it means "the gracious design," rather than "the determined resolve"; 2 Tim. 2:26, which should read "which have been taken captive by him" [(*autou*), i.e., by the Devil; the RV, "by the Lord's servant," is an interpretation; it does not correspond to the Greek] unto His (*ekeinou*) will" (i.e., "God's will"; the different pronoun refers back to the subject of the sentence, viz., God); Heb. 10:10; Rev. 4:11, RV, "because of Thy will"; of human will, e.g., 1 Cor. 7:37; (b) subjectively, the "will" being spoken of as the emotion of being desirous, rather than as the thing "willed"; of the "will" of God, e.g., Rom. 1:10; 1 Cor. 1:1; 2 Cor. 1:1; 8:5; Eph. 1:1, 5, 11; Col. 1:1; 2 Tim. 1:1; Heb. 10:7, 9, 36; 1 John 2:17; 5:14; of human "will," e.g., **John 1:13**; Eph. 2:3, "the desires of the flesh"; 1 Pet. 4:3 (in some texts); 2 Pet. 1:21.

Flesh *sarx* (4561), has a wider range of meaning in the NT than in the OT. Its uses in the NT may be analyzed as follows:

"(a) "the substance of the body," whether of beasts or of men, 1 Cor. 15:39; (b) "the human body," 2 Cor. 10:3a; Gal. 2:20; Phil. 1:22; (c) by synecdoche, of "mankind," in the totality of all that is essential to manhood, i.e., spirit, soul, and body, Matt. 24:22; **John 1:13**; Rom. 3:20; (d) by synecdoche, of "the holy humanity" of the Lord Jesus, in the totality of all that is essential to manhood, i.e., spirit, soul, and body, **John 1:14**; 1 Tim. 3:16; 1 John 4:2; 2 John 7, in Heb. 5:7, "the days of His flesh," i.e., His past life on earth in distinction from His present life in resurrection; (e) by synecdoche, for "the complete person," **John 6:51-57**; 2 Cor. 7:5; Jas. 5:3; (f) "the weaker element in human nature," Matt. 26:41; Rom. 6:19; 8:3a; (g) "the unregenerate state of men," Rom. 7:5; 8:8, 9; (h) "the seat of sin in man" (but this is not the same thing as in the body), 2 Pet. 2:18; 1 John 2:16; (i) "the lower and temporary element in the Christian," Gal. 3:3; 6:8, and in religious ordinances, Heb. 9:10; (j) "the natural attainments of men," 1 Cor. 1:26; 2 Cor. 10:2, 3b; (k) "circumstances," 1 Cor. 7:28; the externals of life, 2 Cor. 7:1; Eph. 6:5; Heb. 9:13; (l) by metonymy, "the outward and seeming," as contrasted with the spirit, the inward and real, **John 6:63**; 2 Cor. 5:16; (m) "natural relationship, consanguine," 1 Cor. 10:18; Gal. 4:23, or marital, Matt. 19:5."

In Matt. 26:41; Rom. 8:4, 13; 1 Cor. 5:5; Gal. 6:8 (not the Holy Spirit, here), "flesh" is contrasted with spirit, in Rom. 2:28, 29, with heart and spirit; in Rom. 7:25, with the mind; cf. Col. 2:1, 5. It is coupled with the mind in Eph. 2:3, and with the spirit in 2 Cor. 7:1.

1:14 And the Word was made flesh, and dwelt among us, (and we beheld his glory, the glory as of the only begotten of the Father,) full of grace and truth.

Word *see John 1:1.*

Made *see John 1:3.*

Flesh *see John 1:13.*

Dwelt *skenoo* (4637), "to pitch a tent" (*skene*), "to tabernacle," is translated "dwelt," in **John 1:14**, KJV, RV marg., "tabernacled"; in Rev. 7:15, KJV, "shall dwell," RV, "shall spread (His) tabernacle"; in Rev. 12:12; 13:6; 21:3, "dwell."

Beheld *theaomai* (2300), "to behold, view attentively, contemplate," had, in earlier Greek usage, the sense of a wondering regard. This idea was gradually lost. It signifies a more earnest contemplation than the ordinary verbs for "to see," "a careful and deliberate vision which interprets ... its object," and is more frequently rendered "behold" in the RV than the KJV. Both translate it by "behold" in Luke 23:55 (of the sepulchre); "we beheld," in **John 1:14**, of the glory of the Son of God; "beheld," RV, in **John 1:32**; Acts 1:11; 1 John 1:1 (more than merely seeing); 4:12, 14.

Glory *doxa* (1391), "glory" (from *dokeo*, "to seem"), primarily signifies an opinion, estimate, and hence, the honor resulting from a good opinion. It is used (I) of the nature and acts of God in self-manifestation, i.e., what He essentially is and does, as exhibited in whatever way he reveals Himself in these respects, and particularly in the person of Christ, in whom essentially His "glory" has ever shone forth and ever will do, **John 17:5, 24**; Heb. 1:3; it was exhibited in the character and acts of Christ in the days of His flesh, **John 1:14**; **John 2:11**; at Cana both His grace and His power were manifested, and these constituted His "glory", so also in the resurrection of Lazarus **11:4, 40**; the "glory" of God was exhibited in the resurrection of Christ, Rom. 6:4, and in His ascension and exaltation, 1 Pet. 1:21, likewise on the Mount of Transfiguration, 2 Pet. 1:17 ... (II) of good reputation, praise, honor, Luke 14:10 (RV, "glory," for KJV, "worship"); **John 5:41** (RV, "glory," for KJV, "honor"); **7:18**; **8:50**; **12:43** (RV, "glory," for KJV, "praise"); 2 Cor. 6:8 (RV, "glory," for KJV "honor"); Phil. 3:19; Heb. 3:3; in 1 Cor. 11:7, of man as representing the authority of God, and of woman as rendering conspicuous the authority of man; in 1 Thess. 2:6, "glory" probably stands, by metonymy, for material gifts, an honorarium, since in human estimation "glory" is usually expressed in things material. The word is used in ascriptions of praise to God, e.g., Luke 17:18; **John 9:24**, RV, "glory" (KJV, "praise"); Acts 12:23; as in doxologies (lit., "glory-words"), e.g., Luke 2:14; Rom. 11:36; 16:27; Gal. 1:5; Rev. 1:6.

Only begotten *monogenes* (3439), is used five times, all in the writings of the apostle John, of Christ as the Son of God; it is translated "only begotten" in Heb. 11:17 of the relationship of Isaac to Abraham. With reference to Christ, the phrase "the only begotten from the Father," **John 1:14**, RV (see also the marg.), indicates that as the Son of God He was the sole representative of the Being and character of the One who sent Him. In the original the definite article is omitted both before "only begotten" and before "Father," and its absence in each case serves to lay stress upon the characteristics referred to in the terms used. The apostle's object is to demonstrate what sort of glory it was that he and his fellow apostles had seen. That he is not merely making a comparison with earthly relationships is indicated by *para*, "from." The glory was that of a unique relationship and the word "begotten" does not imply a beginning of His Sonship. It suggests relationship indeed, but must be distinguished from generation as applied to man. We can only rightly understand the term "the only begotten" when used of the Son, in the sense of unoriginated relationship. "The begetting is not an event of time, however remote, but a fact irrespective of time. The Christ did not *become*, but necessarily and eternally *is* the Son. He, a Person, possesses every attribute of pure Godhood. This necessitates eternity, absolute being; in this respect He is not 'after' the Father" (Moule). The expression also suggests the thought of the deepest affection, as in the case of the OT word *yachid*, variously rendered, "only one," Gen. 22:2, 12; "only son," Jer. 6:26; Amos 8:10; Zech. 12:10; "only beloved," Prov. 4:3, and "darling," Ps. 22:20; 35:17.

In **John 1:18** the clause "the only begotten son, which is in the bosom of the Father," expresses both His eternal union with the Father in the Godhead and the ineffable intimacy and love between them, the Son sharing all the Father's counsels and enjoying all His affections. Another reading is *monogenes*

Theos, "God only-begotten." In **John 3:16** the statement, "God so loved the world that He gave His only begotten son," must not be taken to mean that Christ became the only begotten son by incarnation. The value and the greatness of the gift lay in the Sonship of Him who was given. His Sonship was not the effect of His being given. In **John 3:18** the phrase "the name of the only begotten son of God" lays stress upon the full revelation of God's character and will, His love and grace, as conveyed in the name of One who, being in a unique relationship to Him, was provided by Him as the object of faith. In 1 John 4:9 the statement "God hath sent His only begotten son into the world" does not mean that God sent out into the world one who at His birth in Bethlehem had become His Son. Cf. the parallel statement, "God sent forth the Spirit of His Son," Gal. 4:6, RV, which could not mean that God sent forth One who became His Spirit when He sent Him.

Full *pleres* (4134), denotes "full," (a) in the sense of "being filled," materially, Matt. 14:20; 15:37; Mark 8:19 (said of baskets "full" of bread crumbs); of leprosy, Luke 5:12; spiritually, of the Holy Spirit, Luke 4:1; Acts 6:3; 7:55; 11:24; grace and truth, **John 1:14**; faith, Acts 6:5; grace and power, 6:8; of the effects of spiritual life and qualities, seen in good works, Acts 9:36; in an evil sense, of guile and villany, Acts 13:10; wrath, 19:28; (b) in the sense of "being complete," "full corn in the ear," Mark 4:28; of a reward hereafter, 2 John 8.

1:15 John bare witness of him, and cried, saying, This was he of whom I spake, He that cometh after me is preferred before me: for he was before me.

Bare witness *see* **Bear witness** at *John 1:7*.

Preferred In **John 1:15**, **30**, KJV, *ginomai*, "to become," is translated "is preferred" (RV, "is become"); some mss. have it again in v. **27**.

Before *emprocthen* (1715), is used of place or position only; adverbially, signifying "in front," Luke 19:28; Phil. 3:13; Rev. 4:6; as a preposition, e.g., Matt. 5:24; **John 10:4**; with the meaning "in the sight of a person," e.g., Matt. 5:16; 6:1; 17:2; Luke 19:27; **John 12:37**; 1 Thess. 2:19, RV, "before"; KJV, "in the presence of"; Rev. 19:10, RV, "before," especially in phrases signifying in the sight of God, as God wills, Matt. 11:26; 18:14 (lit., "a thing willed before your Father," RV, marg.); Luke 10:21; in the sense of "priority of rank or position or dignity," **John 1:15**, **30** (in some texts, v. **27**); in an antagonistic sense, "against," Matt. 23:13 (RV, marg., "before").

Before *protos* (4413), the superlative degree of *pro*, "before," is used (I) "of time or place," (a) as a noun, e.g., Luke 14:18; Rev. 1:17; opposite to "the last," in the neuter plural, Matt. 12:45; Luke 11:26; 2 Pet. 2:20; in the neuter singular, opposite to "the second," Heb. 10:9; in 1 Cor. 15:3, *en protois*, lit., "in the first (things, or matters)" denotes "first of all"; (b) as an adjective, e.g., Mark 16:9, used with "day" understood, lit., "the first (day) of (i.e., after) the Sabbath," in which phrase the "of" is objective, not including the Sabbath, but following it; in **John 20:4**, **8**; Rom. 10:19, e.g., equivalent to an English adverb; in **John 1:15**, lit., "first of me," i.e., "before me" (of superiority); (II) "of rank or dignity."

1:16 And of his fulness have all we received, and grace for grace.

And *kai*: The *epexegetic* or *explanatory* use. This may be represented by the expressions "namely," "again," "and indeed," "that is to say"; it is usually translated by "and." In such cases not merely an addition is in view. In Matt. 21:5, "and upon a colt" means "that is to say, upon a colt." In **John 1:16** the clause "and grace for grace" is explanatory of the "fullness." In **John 12:48**, "and receiveth not My sayings," is not simply an addition to "that rejecteth Me," it explains what the rejection involves, as the preceding verse shows. In Mark 14:1, "and the unleavened bread" is perhaps an instance, since the Passover feast is so defined in Luke 22:1. In Acts 23:6 the meaning is "the hope, namely, the resurrection of the dead." In Rom. 1:5 "grace and apostleship" may signify "grace expressed in apostleship." In Eph. 1:1 "and the faithful" does not mark a distinct class of believers, it defines "the saints"; but in this case it goes a little further than what is merely epexegetical, it adds a more distinctive epithet than the preceding and may be taken as meaning "yes indeed." For the suggestion as to the epexegetic use of *kai* see **John 3:5**, "water, even the Spirit."

Fulness *pleroma* (4138), denotes "fullness," that of which a thing is "full"; it is thus used of the grace and truth manifested in Christ, **John 1:16**; of all His virtues and excellencies, Eph. 4:13; "the blessing of Christ," Rom. 15:29, RV (not as KJV); the conversion and restoration of Israel, Rom. 11:12; the completion of the number of Gentiles who receive blessing through the gospel, v. 25; the complete products of the earth, 1 Cor. 10:26; the end of an appointed period, Gal. 4:4; Eph. 1:10; God, in the completeness of His Being, Eph. 3:19; Col. 1:19; 2:9;

the church as the complement of Christ, Eph. 1:23. In Mark 6:43, "basketfuls," RV, is, lit., "fullnesses of baskets."

1:17 For the law was given by Moses, *but* grace and truth came by Jesus Christ.

Law *nomos* (3551), akin to *nemo*, "to divide out, distribute," primarily meant "that which is assigned"; hence, "usage, custom," and then, "law, law as prescribed by custom, or by statute"; the word *ethos*, "custom," was retained for unwritten "law," while *nomos* became the established name for "law" as decreed by a state and set up as the standard for the administration of justice.

In the NT it is used of the Mosaic Law, the "law" of Sinai, (1) with the definite article, e.g., Matt. 5:18; **John 1:17**; Rom. 2:15, 18, 20, 26, 27; 3:19; 4:15; 7:4, 7, 14, 16, 22; 8:3, 4, 7; Gal. 3:10, 12, 19, 21, 24; 5:3; Eph. 2:15; Phil. 3:6; 1 Tim. 1:8; Heb. 7:19; Jas. 2:9; (2) without the article, thus stressing the Mosaic Law in its quality as "law," e.g., Rom. 2:14 (1st part); 5:20; 7:9.

Also, by metonymy, of the books which contain the "law," (1) of the Pentateuch, e.g., Matt. 5:17; 12:5; Luke 16:16; 24:44; **John 1:45**; Rom. 3:21; Gal. 3:10; (2) of the Psalms, **John 10:34**; **15:25**; of the Psalms, Isaiah, Ezekiel and Daniel, **12:34**, the Psalms and Isaiah, Rom. 3:19 (with vv. 10-18); Isaiah, 1 Cor. 14:21; from all this it may be inferred that "the law" in the most comprehensive sense was an alternative title to "The Scriptures."

The following phrases specify "laws" of various kinds; (a) "the law of Christ," Gal. 6:2, i.e., either given by Him (as in the Sermon on the Mount and in **John 13:14, 15**; **15:4**), or the "law" or principle by which Christ Himself lived (Matt. 20:28; **John 13:1**); these are not actual alternatives, for the "law" imposed by Christ was always that by which He Himself lived in the "days of His flesh." ... (g) "the law of the Spirit of life," Rom. 8:2, i.e., the animating principle by which the Holy Spirit acts as the imparter of life (cf. **John 6:63**).

Grace *charis* (5485), has various uses, (a) objective, that which bestows or occasions pleasure, delight, or causes favorable regard; it is applied, e.g., to beauty, or gracefulness of person, Luke 2:40; act, 2 Cor. 8:6, or speech, Luke 4:22, RV, "words of grace" (KJV, "gracious words"); Col. 4:6; (b) subjective, (1) on the part of the bestower, the friendly disposition from which the kindly act proceeds, graciousness, loving-kindness, goodwill generally, e.g., Acts 7:10; especially with reference to the divine favor or "grace," e.g., Acts 14:26; in this respect there is stress on its freeness and universality, its spontaneous character, as in the case of God's redemptive mercy, and the pleasure or joy He designs for the recipient; thus it is set in contrast with debt, Rom. 4:4, 16, with works, 11:6, and with law, **John 1:17**; see also, e.g., Rom. 6:14, 15; Gal. 5:4; (2) on the part of the receiver, a sense of the favor bestowed, a feeling of gratitude, e.g., Rom. 6:17 ("thanks"); in this respect it sometimes signifies "to be thankful," e.g., Luke 17:9 ("doth he thank the servant?" lit., "hath he thanks to"); 1 Tim. 1:12; (c) in another objective sense, the effect of "grace," the spiritual state of those who have experienced its exercise, whether (1) a state of "grace," e.g., Rom. 5:2; 1 Pet. 5:12; 2 Pet. 3:18, or (2) a proof thereof in practical effects, deeds of "grace," e.g., 1 Cor. 16:3, RV, "bounty" (KJV, "liberality"); 2 Cor. 8:6, 19 (in 2 Cor. 9:8 it means the sum of earthly blessings); the power and equipment for ministry, e.g., Rom. 1:5; 12:6; 15:15; 1 Cor. 3:10; Gal. 2:9; Eph. 3:2, 7.

Jesus *iesous* (2424), is a transliteration of the Heb. "Joshua," meaning "Jehovah is salvation," i.e., "is the Savior," "a common name among the Jews, e.g., Ex. 17:9; Luke 3:29 (RV); Col. 4:11. It was given to the Son of God in Incarnation as His personal name, in obedience to the command of an angel to Joseph, the husband of His Mother, Mary, shortly before He was born, Matt 1:21. By it He is spoken of throughout the Gospel narratives generally, but not without exception, as in Mark 16:19, 20; Luke 7:13, and a dozen other places in that Gospel, and a few in John.

"'Jesus Christ' occurs only in Matt. 1:1, 18; 16:21, marg.; Mark 1:1; **John 1:17**; **17:3**. In Acts the name 'Jesus' is found frequently. 'Lord Jesus' is the normal usage, as in Acts 8:16; 19:5, 17; see also the reports of the words of Stephen, 7:59, of Ananias, 9:17, and of Paul, 16:31; though both Peter, 10:36, and Paul, 16:18, also used 'Jesus Christ.' In the Epistles of James, Peter, John and Jude, the personal name is not once found alone, but in Rev. eight times (RV), 1:9; 12:17; 14:12; 17:6; 19:10 (twice); 20:4; 22:16. In the Epistles of Paul 'Jesus' appears alone just thirteen times, and in the Hebrews eight times; in the latter the title 'Lord' is added once only, at 13:20. In the Epistles of James, Peter, John, and Jude, men who had companied with the Lord in the days of His flesh, 'Jesus Christ' is the invariable order (in the RV) of the Name and Title, for this was the order of their experience; as 'Jesus' they knew Him first,

"The law sends us to the gospel, that we may be justified, and the gospel sends us to the law again to inquire what is our duty, being justified."

SAMUEL BOLTON

that He was Messiah they learnt finally in His resurrection. But Paul came to know Him first in the glory of heaven, Acts 9:1-6, and his experience being thus the reverse of theirs, the reverse order, 'Christ Jesus,' is of frequent occurrence in his letters, but, with the exception of Acts 24:24, does not occur elsewhere in the RV. In Paul's letters the order is always in harmony with the context. Thus 'Christ Jesus' describes the Exalted One who emptied Himself, Phil. 2:5, and testifies to His pre-existence; 'Jesus Christ' describes the despised and rejected One Who was afterwards glorified, Phil. 2:11, and testifies to His resurrection. 'Christ Jesus' suggests His grace, 'Jesus Christ' suggests His glory."

1:18 No man hath seen God at any time; the only begotten Son, which is in the bosom of the Father, he hath declared *him*.

Seen *horao* (3708), with its aorist form *eidon*, "to see" (in a few places the KJV uses the verb "to behold"), is said (a) of bodily vision, e.g., Mark 6:38; **John 1:18**, **46**; (b) of mental perception, e.g., Rom. 15:21; Col. 2:18; (c) of taking heed, e.g., Matt. 8:4; 1 Thess. 5:15; (d) of experience, as of death, Luke 2:26; Heb. 11:5; life, **John 3:36**; corruption, Acts 2:27; (e) of caring for, Matt. 27:4; Acts 18:15 (here the form *opsomai* is used).

God *see John 1:1.*

Time *popote* (4455), "ever yet," is rendered "at any time" in **John 1:18**; **5:37**; 1 John 4:12.

Only begotten *see John 1:14.*

Son *The Son of God* In this title the word "Son" is used sometimes (a) of relationship, sometimes (b) of the expression of character. "Thus, e.g., when the disciples so addressed Him, Matt. 14:33; 16:16; **John 1:49**, when the centurion so spoke of Him, Matt. 27:54, they probably meant that (b) He was a manifestation of God in human form. But in such passages as Luke 1:32, 35; Acts 13:33, which refer to the humanity of the Lord Jesus, ... the word is used in sense (a).

"The Lord Jesus Himself used the full title on occasion, **John 5:25**; **9:35** [some mss. have 'the Son of Man'; see RV marg.]; **11:4**, and on the more frequent occasions on which He spoke of Himself as 'the Son,' the words are to be understood as an abbreviation of 'the Son of God,' not of 'The Son of Man'; this latter He always expressed in full; see Luke 10:22; **John 5:19**, etc. John uses both the longer and shorter forms of the title in his Gospel, see **3:16-18**; **20:31**, e.g., and in his Epistles; cf. Rev. 2:18. So does the writer of Hebrews, 1:2; 4:14; 6:6, etc. An eternal relation subsisting between the Son and the Father in the Godhead is to be understood. That is to say, the Son of God, in His eternal relationship with the Father, is not so entitled because He at any time began to derive His being from the Father (in which case He could not be co-eternal with the Father), but because He is and ever has been the expression of what the Father is; cf. **John 14:9**, 'he that hath seen Me hath seen the Father.' The words of Heb. 1:3, 'Who being the effulgence of His (God's) glory, and the very image of His (God's) substance' are a definition of what is meant by 'Son of God.' Thus absolute Godhead, not Godhead in a secondary or derived sense, is intended in the title."

Other titles of Christ as the "Son of God" are: "His Son," 1 Thess. 1:10 (in Acts 13:13, 26, RV, *pais* is rendered "servant"); "His own Son," Rom. 8:32; "My beloved Son," Matt. 3:17; "His Only Begotten Son," **John 3:16**; "the Son of His love," Col. 1:13.

"The Son is the eternal object of the Father's love, **John 17:24**, and the sole Revealer of the Father's character, **John 1:14**; Heb. 1:3. The words, 'Father' and 'Son,' are never in the NT so used as to suggest that the Father existed before the Son; the Prologue to the Gospel according to John distinctly asserts that the Word existed 'in the beginning,' and that this Word is the Son, Who 'became flesh and dwelt among us.'"

In addressing the Father in His prayer in **John 17** He says, "Thou lovedst Me before the foundation of the world." Accordingly in the timeless past the Father and the "Son" existed in that relationship, a relationship of love, as well as of absolute Deity. In this passage the "Son" gives evidence that there was no more powerful plea in the Father's estimation than that coeternal love existing between the Father and Himself. The declaration "Thou art My Son, this day have I begotten Thee," Ps. 2:7, quoted in Acts 13:33; Heb. 1:5; 5:5, refers to the birth of Christ, not to His resurrection. In Acts 13:33 the verb "raise up" is used of the raising up of a person to occupy a special position in the nation, as of David in verse 22 (so of Christ as a Prophet in 3:22 and 7:37). The word "again" in the KJV in v. 33 represents nothing in the original. The RV rightly omits it. In v. 34 the statement as to the resurrection of Christ receives the greater stress in this respect through the emphatic contrast to that in v. 33 as to His being raised up in the nation, a stress imparted by the added words "from the dead." Accordingly v. 33 speaks of His incarnation, v. 34 of His resurrection. In Heb. 1:5, that the declaration refers to the Birth is confirmed by the contrast in verse 6. Here the word "again" is rightly placed in the RV, "when He again bringeth in the Firstborn into the world." This points on to His second advent, which is set in contrast to His first advent, when God brought His Firstborn into the world the first time. So again in Heb. 5:5, where the High Priesthood of Christ is shown to fulfill all that was foreshadowed in the Levitical priesthood, the passage stresses the facts of His humanity, the days of His flesh, His perfect obedience and His sufferings.

Son of Man In the NT this is a designation of Christ, almost entirely confined to the Gospels. Elsewhere it is found in Acts 7:56, the only occasion where a disciple applied it to the Lord and in Rev. 1:13; 14:14.

"Son of Man" is the title Christ used of Himself; **John 12:34** is not an exception, for the quotation by the multitude was from His own statement. The title is found especially in the Synoptic Gospels. The occurrences in John's Gospel, **1:51**; **3:13**, **14**; **5:27**; **6:27**, **53**, **62**; **8:28** (**9:35** in some texts); **12:23**, **34** (twice); **13:31**, are not parallel to those in the Synoptic Gospels. In the latter the use of the title falls into two groups, (a) those in which it refers to Christ's humanity, His earthly work, sufferings and death, e.g., Matt. 8:20; 11:19; 12:40; 26:2, 24; (b) those which refer to His glory in resurrection and to that of His future advent, e.g., Matt. 10:23; 13:41; 16:27, 28; 17:9; 24:27, 30 (twice), 37, 39, 44. While it is a messianic title it is evident that the Lord applied it to Himself in a distinctive way, for it indicates more than Messiahship, even universal headship on the part of One who is Man. It therefore stresses His manhood, manhood of a unique order in comparison with all other men, for He is declared to be of heaven, 1 Cor. 15:47, and even while here below, was "the Son of Man, which is in Heaven," **John 3:13**. As the "Son of Man" He must be appropriated spiritually as a condition of possessing eternal life, **John 6:53**. In His death, as in His life, the glory of His Manhood was displayed in the absolute obedience and submission to the will of the Father (**12:23**; **13:31**), and, in view of this, all judgment has been committed to Him, who will judge in full understanding experimentally of human conditions, sin apart, and will exercise the judgment as sharing the nature of those judged, **John 5:22**, **27**. Not only is He man, but He is "Son of Man," not by human generation but, according to the Semitic usage of the expression, partaking of the characteristics (sin apart) of manhood belonging to the category of mankind. Twice in Revelation, **1:13** and **14:14**, He is described as "One like unto a Son of man," RV (KJV, "... the Son of Man"), cf. Dan. 7:13. He who was thus seen was indeed the "Son of Man," but the absence of the article in the original serves to stress what morally characterizes Him as such. Accordingly in these passages He is revealed, not as the Person known by the title, but as the One who is qualified to act as the Judge of all men. He is the same Person as in the days of His flesh, still continuing His humanity with His Deity. The phrase "like unto" serves to distinguish Him as there seen in His glory and majesty in contrast to the days of His humiliation.

Bosom *kolpos* (2859), signifies (a) "the front of the body between the arms"; hence, to recline in the "bosom" was said of one who so reclined at table that his head covered, as it were, the "bosom" of the one next to him, **John 13:23**. Hence, figuratively, it is used of a place of blessedness with another, as with Abraham in paradise, Luke 16:22-23 (plural in v. 23), from the custom of reclining at table in the "bosom," a place of honor; of the Lord's eternal and essential relation with the Father, in all its blessedness and affection as intimated in the phrase, "The Only-begotten Son, which is in the bosom of the Father" (**John 1:18**); (b) "of the bosom of a garment, the hollow formed by the upper forepart of a loose garment, bound by a girdle and used for carrying or keeping things"; thus figuratively of repaying one liberally, Luke 6:38; cf. Isa. 65:6; Jer. 39:18; (c) "of an inlet of the sea," because of its shape, like a bosom, Acts 27:39.

Declared *exegeomai* (1834), lit., "to lead out," signifies "to make known, rehearse declare," Luke 24:35 (KJV, "told"; RV, "rehearsed"); Acts 10:8; 15:12, 14; 21:19. In **John 1:18**, in the sentence "He hath declared Him," the other meaning of the verb is in view, to unfold in teaching, "to declare" by making known.

1:19 And this is the record of John, when the Jews sent priests and Levites from Jerusalem to ask him, Who art thou?

Priests *hiereus* (2409), "one who offers sacrifice and has the charge of things pertaining thereto," is used (a) of a "priest" of the pagan god Zeus, Acts 14:13; (b) of Jewish "priests," e.g., Matt. 8:4; 12:4, 5; Luke 1:5, where allusion is made to the 24 courses of "priests" appointed for service in the Temple (cf. 1 Chron. 24:4ff.); **John 1:19**; Heb. 8:4.

Thou Frequently this forms part of the translation of a verb in the 2nd person, singular. Otherwise it translates (a) the pronoun *su*, used for emphasis or contrast, e.g., **John 1:19**, **21** (twice), **25**, **42** (twice); **8:5**, **13**, **25**, **33**, **48**, **52**, **53**; Acts 9:5; in addressing a person or place, e.g., Matt. 2:6; Luke 1:76; **John 17:5**; perhaps also in the phrase *su eipas*, "thou hast said," e.g., Matt. 26:64 (sometimes without emphasis, e.g., Acts 13:33); (b) in the oblique cases, e.g., the dative *soi*, lit., "to thee," e.g., Matt. 17:25, "what thinkest thou?" (lit., "what does it seem to thee?"); (c) *autos*, "self," e.g., Luke 6:42; Acts 21:24, "thou thyself"; (d) the reflexive pronoun, *seauton*, Rom. 2:19, "thou thyself."

1:20 And he confessed, and denied not; but confessed, I am not the Christ.

Confessed *homologeo* (3670), lit., "to speak the same thing" (*homos*, "same," *lego*, "to speak"), "to assent, accord, agree with," denotes, (a) "to confess, declare, admit," **John 1:20**; e.g., Acts 24:14; Heb. 11:13; (b) "to confess by way of admitting oneself guilty of what one is accused of, the result of inward conviction," 1 John 1:9; (c) "to declare openly by way of speaking out freely, such confession being the effect of deep conviction of facts," Matt. 7:23; 10:32 (twice) and Luke 12:8 (see next par.); **John 9:22**; **12:42**; Acts 23:8; Rom. 10:9-10 ("confession is made"); 1 Tim. 6:12 (RV); Titus 1:16; 1 John 2:23; 4:2, 15; 2 John 7 (in John's epistle it is the necessary antithesis to Gnostic doceticism); Rev. 3:5, in the best mss.; (d) "to confess by way of celebrating with praise," Heb. 13:15; (e) "to promise," Matt. 14:7.

Denied *arneomai* (720), signifies (a) "to say ... not, to contradict," e.g., Mark 14:70; **John 1:20**; **18:25**, **27**; 1 John 2:22; (b) "to deny" by way of disowning a person, as, e.g., the Lord Jesus as master, e.g., Matt. 10:33; Luke 12:9; **John 13:38** (in the best mss.); 2 Tim. 2:12; or, on the other hand, of Christ Himself, "denying" that a person is His follower, Matt. 10:33; 2 Tim. 2:12; or to "deny" the Father and the Son, by apostatizing and by disseminating pernicious teachings, to "deny" Jesus Christ as master and Lord by immorality under a cloak of religion, 2 Pet. 2:1; Jude 4; (c) "to deny oneself," either in a good sense, by disregarding one's own interests, Luke 9:23, or in a bad sense, to prove false to oneself, to act quite unlike oneself, 2 Tim. 2:13; (d) to "abrogate, forsake, or renounce a thing," whether evil, Titus 2:12, or good, 1 Tim. 5:8; 2 Tim. 3:5; Rev. 2:13; 3:8; (e)"not to accept, to reject" something offered, Acts 3:14; 7:35, "refused"; Heb. 11:24 "refused."

1:21 And they asked him, What then? Art thou Elias? And he saith, I am not. Art thou that prophet? And he answered, No.

Thou *see John 1:19.*

Prophet *prophetes* (4396), "one who speaks forth or openly", "a proclaimer of a divine message," denoted among the Greeks an interpreter of the oracles of the gods.

In the NT the word is used (a) of "the OT prophets," e.g., Matt. 5:12; Mark 6:15; Luke 4:27; **John 8:52**; Rom. 11:3; (b) of "prophets in general," e.g., Matt. 10:41; 21:46; Mark 6:4; (c) of "John the Baptist," Matt. 21:26; Luke 1:76; (d) of "prophets in the churches," e.g., Acts 13:1; 15:32; 21:10; 1 Cor. 12:28, 29; 14:29, 32, 37; Eph. 2:20; 3:5; 4:11; (e) of "Christ, as the aforepromised Prophet," e.g., **John 1:21**; **6:14**; **7:40**; Acts 3:22; 7:37, or, without the article, and, without reference to the Old Testament, Mark 6:15; Luke 7:16; in Luke 24:19 it is used with *aner*, "a man"; **John 4:19**; **9:17**; (f) of "two witnesses" yet to be raised up for special purposes, Rev. 11:10, 18; (g) of "the Cretan poet Epimenides," Titus 1:12; (h) by metonymy, of "the writings of prophets," e.g., Luke 24:27; Acts 8:28.

1:22 Then said they unto him, Who art thou? that we may give an answer to them that sent us. What sayest thou of thyself?

Answer *apokrisis* (612), lit., "a separation or distinction," is the regular word for "answer," Luke 2:47; 20:26; **John 1:22** and **19:9**.

1:23 He said, I *am* the voice of one crying in the wilderness, Make straight the way of the Lord, as said the prophet Esaias.

Crying *boao* (994), signifies (a) "to raise a cry," whether of joy, Gal. 4:27, or vexation, Acts 8:7; (b) "to speak with a strong voice," Matt. 3:3; Mark 1:3; 15:34; Luke 3:4; 9:38; **John 1:23**; Acts 17:6; 25:24 (some mss. have *epiboao* here); (c) "to cry out for help," Luke 18:7, 38.

Straight *euthuno* (2116), is used of the directing of a ship by the steersman, Jas. 3:4; metaphorically, of making "straight" the way of the Lord, **John 1:23**.

1:24-25 And they which were sent were of the Pharisees.

And they asked him, and said unto him, Why baptizest thou then, if thou be not that Christ, nor Elias, neither that prophet?

Thou *see John 1:19*.

1:26 John answered them, saying, I baptize with water: but there standeth one among you, whom ye know not;

Standeth *steko* (4739), a late present tense from *hesteka*, the perfect of *histemi*, is used (a) literally, Mark 3:31; 11:25; **John 1:26**, in the best texts (in some texts Rev. 12:4); (b) figuratively, Rom. 14:4, where the context indicates the meaning "standeth upright" rather than that of acquittal; of "standing fast," 1 Cor. 16:13, "in the faith," i.e., by adherence to it; Gal. 5:1, in freedom from legal bondage; Phil. 1:27, "in one spirit"; Phil. 4:1 and 1 Thess. 3:8, "in the Lord," i.e., in the willing subjection to His authority; 2 Thess. 2:15, in the apostle's teaching; some mss. have it in **John 8:44**, the most authentic have *histemi*, RV, "stood" (KJV, "abode").

Among *mesos* (3319), an adjective denoting "middle, in the middle or midst," is used in the following, in which the English requires a phrase, and the adjectival rendering must be avoided: Luke 22:55, "Peter sat in the midst of them," lit., "a middle one of (them)"; Luke 23:45, of the rending of the veil "in the midst"; here the adjective idiomatically belongs to the verb "was rent," and is not to be taken literally, as if it meant "the middle veil"; **John 1:26**, "in the midst of you (standeth One)," RV (lit., "a middle One"); Acts 1:18, where the necessity of avoiding the lit. rendering is obvious.

1:27 He it is, who coming after me is preferred before me, whose shoe's latchet I am not worthy to unloose

Preferred *see John 1:15*.

Before *see John 1:15*.

Latchet *himas* (2438), denotes "a thong, strap," whether for binding prisoners, Acts 22:25, "(the) thongs," or for fastening sandals, Mark 1:7; Luke 3:16; **John 1:27**. "Among the Orientals everything connected with the feet and shoes is defiled and debasing, and the stooping to unfasten the dusty latchet is the most insignificant in such service" (Mackie, in *Hastings' Bib. Dic.*).

Worthy *axios* (514), "of weight, worth, worthy," is said of persons and their deeds: (a) in a good sense, e.g., Matt. 10:10, 11, 13 (twice), 37 (twice), 38; 22:8; Luke 7:4; 10:7; 15:19, 21; **John 1:27**; Acts 13:25; 1 Tim. 5:18; 6:1; Heb. 11:38; Rev. 3:4; 4:11; 5:2, 4, 9, 12; (b) in a bad sense, Luke 12:48; 23:15; Acts 23:29; 25:11, 25; 26:31; Rom. 1:32; Rev. 16:6.

Unloose *luo* (3089), "to loose," is rendered "to unloose" in Mark 1:7; Luke 3:16; **John 1:27**; in Acts 13:25, RV.

1:28 These things were done in Bethabara beyond Jordan, where John was baptizing.

Beyond *peran* (4008), "on the other side, across," is used with the definite article, signifying the regions "beyond," the opposite shore, Matt. 8:18, etc. With verbs of going it denotes direction towards and "beyond" a place, e.g., **John 10:40**. It frequently indicates "beyond," of locality, without a verb of direction, Matt. 16:5; Mark 10:1, RV; **John 1:28**; **3:26**.

1:29 The next day John seeth Jesus coming unto him, and saith, Behold the Lamb of God, which taketh away the sin of the world.

Next day *epaurion* (1887), *epi*, "upon," and *aurion*; the RV always translates it "on (the) morrow"; in the following the KJV has "(the) next day," Matt. 27:62; **John 1:29**, **35** ("the next day after"); **12:12**; Acts 14:20; 21:8; 25:6; "(the) day following," **John 1:43**; **6:22**; "the morrow after," Acts 10:24.

Behold *ide* (2396), an aorist or point tense, marking a definite point of time, of the imperative mood of *eidon*, "to see" (taken as part of *horao*, "to see"), is used as an interjection, addressed either to one or many persons, e.g., Matt. 25:20, 22, 25; **John 1:29**, **36**, **47**; Gal. 5:2, the only occurrence outside Matthew, Mark and John.

Lamb *amnos* (286), "a lamb," is used figuratively of Christ, in **John 1:29**, **36**, with the article, pointing Him out as the expected One, the One to be well known as the personal fulfillment and embodiment of all that had been indicated in the OT, the One by whose sacrifice deliverance from divine judgment was to be obtained; in Acts 8:32 (from the Sept. of Is. 53:7) and 1 Pet. 1:19, the absence of the article stresses the nature and character of His sacrifice as set forth in the symbolism. The reference in each case is to the lamb of God's providing, Gen. 22:8, and the Paschal lamb of God's appointment for sacrifice in Israel, e.g., Ex. 12:5, 14, 27 (cf. 1 Cor. 5:7).

Taketh *airo* (142), "to lift, carry, take up or away," occurs very frequently with its literal meanings. In **John 1:29** it is used of Christ as "the Lamb of God, which taketh away the sin of the world," not the sins, but sin, that which has existed from the time of the Fall, and in regard to which God has had judicial dealings with the world; through the expiatory sacrifice of Christ the sin of the world will be replaced by everlasting righteousness; cf. the plural, "sins", in 1 John 3:5. Righteous judgment was "taken away" from Christ at human tribunals, and His life, while voluntarily given by Himself (**John 10:17, 18**), was "taken (from the earth)," Acts 8:33 (quoted from the Sept. of Isa. 53:8). In **John 15:2** it is used in the Lord's statement, "Every branch in Me that beareth not fruit, He taketh it away." This does not contemplate members of the "body" of Christ, but those who (just as a graft which being inserted, does not "abide" or "strike") are merely professed followers, giving only the appearance of being joined to the parent stem.

Sin *hamartia* (266), is, lit., "a missing of the mark," but this etymological meaning is largely lost sight of in the NT. It is the most comprehensive term for moral obliquity. It is used of "sin" as (a) a principle or source of action, or an inward element producing acts, e.g., Rom. 3:9; 5:12, 13, 20; 6:1, 2; 7:7 (abstract for concrete); 7:8 (twice), 9, 11, 13, "sin, that it might be shown to be sin," i.e., "sin became death to me, that it might be exposed in its heinous character": in the last clause, "sin might become exceeding sinful," i.e., through the holiness of the Law, the true nature of sin was designed to be manifested to the conscience;

(b) a governing principle or power, e.g., Rom. 6:6, "(the body) of sin," here "sin" is spoken of as an organized power, acting through the members of the body, though the seat of "sin" is in the will (the body is the organic instrument); in the next clause, and in other passages, as follows, this governing principle is personified, e.g., Rom. 5:21; 6:12, 14, 17; 7:11, 14, 17, 20, 23, 25; 8:2; 1 Cor. 15:56; Heb. 3:13; 11:25; 12:4; Jas. 1:15 (2nd part);

(c) a generic term (distinct from specific terms yet sometimes inclusive of concrete wrong doing, e.g., **John 8:21, 34, 46; 9:41; 15:22, 24; 19:11**); in Rom. 8:3, "God, sending His own Son in the likeness of sinful flesh," lit., "flesh of sin," the flesh stands for the body, the instrument of indwelling "sin" [Christ, pre-existently the Son of God, assumed human flesh, "of the substance of the Virgin Mary"; the reality of incarnation was His, without taint of sin], and *as an offering* for sin," i.e., "a sin offering" (so the Sept., e.g., in Lev. 4:32; 5:6, 7, 8, 9), "condemned sin in the flesh," i.e., Christ, having taken human nature, "sin" apart (Heb. 4:15), and having lived a sinless life, died under the condemnation and judgment due to our "sin"; for the generic sense see further, e.g., Heb. 9:26; 10:6, 8, 18; 13:11; 1 John 1:7, 8; 3:4 (1st part; in the 2nd part, "sin" is defined as "lawlessness," RV), 8, 9; in these verses the KJV use of the verb to commit is misleading; not the committal of an act is in view, but a continuous course of "sin," as indicated by the RV, "doeth." The apostle's use of the present tense of *poieo*, "to do," virtually expresses the meaning of *prasso*, "to practice," which John does not use (it is not infrequent in this sense in Paul's Epp., e.g., Rom. 1:32, RV; 2:1; Gal. 5:21; Phil. 4:9); 1 Pet. 4:1 (singular in the best texts), lit., "has been made to cease from sin," i.e., as a result of suffering in the flesh, the mortifying of our members, and of obedience to a Savior who suffered in flesh. Such no longer lives in the flesh, "to the lusts of men, but to the will of God"; sometimes the word is used as virtually equivalent to a condition of "sin," e.g., **John 1:29**, "the sin (not sins) of the world"; 1 Cor. 15:17; or a course of "sin," characterized by continuous acts, e.g., 1 Thess. 2:16; in 1 John 5:16 (2nd part) the RV marg., is probably to be preferred, "there is sin unto death," not a special act of "sin," but the state or condition producing acts; in v. 17, "all unrighteousness is sin" is not a definition of "sin" (as in 3:4), it gives a specification of the term in its generic sense;

1:30 This is he of whom I said, After me cometh a man which is preferred before me: for he was before me.

Preferred *see John 1:15.*

Before *see John 1:15.*

1:31-32 And I knew him not: but that he should be made manifest to Israel, therefore am I come baptizing with water.

And John bare record, saying, I saw the Spirit descending from heaven like a dove, and it abode upon him.

Bare record *see* **Bear witness** at *John 1:7.*

Saw *see* **Beheld** at *John 1:14.*

Like In the following the most authentic mss. have *hos*, "as," for *hosei*, "like," in the KJV; Mark 1:10; Luke 3:22; **John 1:32**; Rev. 1:14.

Dove *peristera* (4058), denotes "a dove or pigeon," Matt. 3:16; 10:16 (indicating its proverbial harmlessness); 21:12; Mark 1:10; 11:15;

Luke 2:24 ("pigeons"); 3:22; **John 1:32; 2:14, 16.**

Abode *meno* (3306), used (a) of place, e.g., Matt. 10:11, metaphorically 1 John 2:19, is said of God, 1 John 4:15; Christ, **John 6:56; 15:4**, etc.; the Holy Spirit, **John 1:32-33; 14:17**; believers, **John 6:56; 15:4**; 1 John 4:15, etc.; the Word of God, 1 John 2:14; the truth, 2 John 2, etc.; (b) of time; it is said of believers, **John 21:22-23**; Phil. 1:25; 1 John 2:17; Christ, **John 12:34**; Heb. 7:24; the Word of God, 1 Pet. 1:23; sin, **John 9:41**; cities, Matt. 11:23; Heb. 13:14; bonds and afflictions, Acts 20:23; (c) of qualities; faith, hope, love, 1 Cor. 13:13; Christ's love, **John 15:10**; afflictions, Acts 20:23; brotherly love, Heb. 13:1; the love of God, 1 John 3:17; the truth, 2 John 2. The RV usually translates it by "abide," but "continue" in 1 Tim. 2:15; in the following, the RV substitutes "to abide" for the KJV, "to continue," **John 2:12; 8:31; 15:9**; 2 Tim. 3:14; Heb. 7:24; 13:14; 1 John 2:24. Cf. the noun *mone*, below.

1:33 And I knew him not: but he that sent me to baptize with water, the same said unto me, Upon whom thou shalt see the Spirit descending, and remaining on him, the same is he which baptizeth with the Holy Ghost.

Sent *pempo* (3992), "to send," is used (a) of persons: Christ, by the Father, Luke 20:13; **John 4:34; 5:23, 24, 30, 37; 6:38, 39, (40), 44; 7:16, 18, 28, 33; 8:16, 18, 26, 29; 9:4; 12:44, 45, 49; 13:20** (2nd part); **14:24; 15:21; 16:5**; Rom. 8:3; the Holy Spirit, **John 14:26; 15:26; 16:7**; Elijah, Luke 4:26; John the Baptist, **John 1:33**; disciples and apostles, e.g., Matt. 11:2; **John 20:21**; servants, e.g., Luke 20:11, 12; officials, Matt. 14:10; messengers, e.g., Acts 10:5, 32, 33; 15:22, 25; 2 Cor. 9:3, Eph. 6:22; Phil. 2:19, 23, 25; 1 Thess. 3:2, 5; Titus 3:12; a prisoner, Acts 25:25, 27; potentates, by God, 1 Pet. 2:14; an angel, Rev. 22:16, demons, Mark 5:12; (b) of things, Acts 11:29; Phil. 4:16; 2 Thess. 2:11; Rev. 1:11; 11:10; 14:15, 18, RV, "send forth" (KJV, "thrust in").

Remaining *meno* (3306), "to stay, abide," is frequently rendered "to remain," e.g., Matt. 11:23; Luke 10:7; **John 1:33**, KJV (RV, "abiding"); **9:41** (in **15:11**, the best texts have the verb to be, see RV); **15:16**, KJV (RV, "abide"); **19:31**; Acts 5:4 (twice), RV, "whiles it remained, did it (not) remain (thine own)?"; 27:41; 1 Cor. 7:11; 15:6; 2 Cor. 3:11, 14; 9:9, KJV (RV, "abideth"); Heb. 12:27; 1 John 3:9.

1:34 And I saw, and bare record that this is the Son of God.

Bare record *see* Bear witness at *John 1:7.*

Son *eklektos* (1588), lit. signifies "picked out, chosen" (*ek*, "from," *lego*, "to gather, pick out"), and is used of (a) Christ, the "chosen" of God, as the Messiah, Luke 23:35, and metaphorically as a "living Stone," "a chief corner Stone," 1 Pet. 2:4, 6; some mss. have it in **John 1:34**, instead of *huios*, "Son"; (b) angels, 1 Tim. 5:21, as "chosen" to be of especially high rank in administrative association with God, or as His messengers to human beings, doubtless in contrast to fallen angels (see 2 Pet. 2:4 and Jude 6); (c) believers (Jews or Gentiles), Matt. 24:22, 24, 31; Mark 13:20, 22, 27; Luke 18:7; Rom. 8:33; Col. 3:12; 2 Tim. 2:10; Titus 1:1; 1 Pet. 1:1; 2:9 (as a spiritual race); Matt. 20:16; 22:14 and Rev. 17:14, "chosen"; individual believers are so mentioned in Rom. 16:13; 2 John 1, 13.

1:35 Again the next day after John stood, and two of his disciples;

Next day *see John 1:29.*

1:36 And looking upon Jesus as he walked, he saith, Behold the Lamb of God!

Looking upon *emblepo* (1689), from *en*, "in" (intensive), and *blepo*, expresses "earnest looking," e.g., in the Lord's command to "behold" the birds of the heaven, with the object of learning lessons of faith from them, Matt. 6:26. See also 19:26; Mark 8:25; 10:21, 27; 14:67; Luke 20:17; 22:61; **John 1:36**; of the Lord's looking upon Peter, **John 1:42**; Acts 1:11; 22:11. *See also* Behold at *John 1:29.*

Lamb *see John 1:29.*

1:37-38 And the two disciples heard him speak, and they followed Jesus.

Then Jesus turned, and saw them following, and saith unto them, What seek ye? They said unto him, Rabbi, (which is to say, being interpreted, Master,) where dwellest thou?

Rabbi *rabbei* or *rabbi* (4461), from a word *rab*, primarily denoting "master" in contrast to a slave; this with the added pronominal suffix signified "my master" and was a title of respect by which teachers were addressed. The suffix soon lost its specific force, and in the NT the word is used as courteous title of address. It is applied to Christ in Matt. 26:25, 49; Mark 9:5; 11:21; 14:45; **John 1:38** (where it is interpreted as *didaskalos*, "master," marg., "teacher" (see also "Rabboni" in **John 20:16**); v. **49; 3:2; 4:31; 6:25; 9:2; 11:8**; to John the Baptist in **John 3:26**. In Matt. 23:7, 8 Christ forbids his disciples to covet or use it. In the latter verse it is again explained as *didaskalos*, "master" (some mss. have *kathegetes*, "a guide").

Say The phrase *tout' esti* (i.e., *touto esti*), "that is," is so translated in Matt. 27:46, RV (KJV, "that is to say"); so Acts 1:19; in Heb. 9:11 and 10:20, KJV and RV, "that is to say"; in Mark 7:11 the phrase is *ho esti*, lit., "which is"; the phrase *ho legetai*, lit., "which is said," **John 1:38** and **20:16**, is rendered "which is to say."

Interpreted *methermeneuo* (3177), "to change or translate from one language to another, to interpret," is always used in the passive voice in the NT, "being interpreted," of interpreting the names, Immanuel, Matt. 1:23; Golgotha, Mark 15:22; Barnabas, Acts 4:36; in Acts 13:8, of Elymas, the verb is rendered "is ... by interpretation," lit., "is interpreted"; it is used of interpreting or translating sentences in Mark 5:41; 15:34; in the best mss., **John 1:38** (Rabbi, interpreted as "Master"); v. **41** (Messiah, interpreted as "Christ").

Master *didaskalos* (1320), "a teacher" (from *didasko*, "to teach"), is frequently rendered "Master" in the four Gospels, as a title of address to Christ, e.g., Matt. 8:19; Mark 4:38 (there are more instances in Luke than in the other Gospels); **John 1:38**, where it interprets "Rabbi"; **20:16**, where it interprets "Rabboni." It is used by Christ of Himself in Matt. 23:8 and **John 13:13-14**; by others concerning Him, Matt. 17:24; 26:18; Mark 5:35; 14:14; Luke 8:49; 22:11; **John 11:28**. In **John 3:10**, the Lord uses it in addressing Nicodemus, RV, "the teacher" (KJV, "a master"), where the article does not specify a particular "teacher," but designates the member of a class; for the class see Luke 2:46, "the doctors" (RV, marg., "teachers"). It is used of the relation of a disciple to his "master," in Matt. 10:24, 25; Luke 6:40. It is not translated "masters" in the rest of the NT, save in the KJV of Jas. 3:1 "(be not many) masters," where obviously the RV "teachers" is the meaning.

Dwellest *meno* (3306), "to abide, remain," is translated "to dwell," in the KJV of **John 1:38-39**; **6:56**; **14:10**, **17**; Acts 28:16. The RV adheres throughout to the verb "to abide."

1:39 He saith unto them, Come and see. They came and saw where he dwelt, and abode with him that day: for it was about the tenth hour.

Tenth *dekatos* (1182), an adjective from *deka*, "ten," occurs in **John 1:39**; Rev. 11:13; 21:20.

1:40 One of the two which heard John *speak*, and followed him, was Andrew, Simon Peter's brother.

Heard *akouo* (191), the usual word denoting "to hear," is used (a) intransitively, e.g., Matt. 11:15; Mark 4:23; (b) transitively when the object is expressed, sometimes in the accusative case, sometimes in the genitive. Thus in Acts 9:7, "hearing the voice," the noun "voice" is in the partitive genitive case [i.e., hearing (something) of], whereas in 22:9, "they heard not the voice," the construction is with the accusative. This removes the idea of any contradiction. The former indicates a "hearing" of the sound, the latter indicates the meaning or message of the voice (this they did not hear). "The former denotes the sensational perception, the latter (the accusative case) the thing perceived" (Cremer). In **John 5:25**, **28**, the genitive case is used, indicating a "sensational perception" that the Lord's voice is sounding; in **3:8**, of "hearing" the wind, the accusative is used, stressing "the thing perceived."

That God "hears" prayer signifies that He answers prayer, e.g., **John 9:31**; 1 John 5:14, 15. Sometimes the verb is used with *para* ("from beside"), e.g., **John 1:40**, "one of the two which heard John speak," lit., "heard from beside John," suggesting that he stood beside him; in **John 8:26**, **40**, indicating the intimate fellowship of the Son with the Father; the same construction is used in Acts 10:22 and 2 Tim. 2:2, in the latter case, of the intimacy between Paul and Timothy.

1:41 He first findeth his own brother Simon, and saith unto him, We have found the Messias, which is, being interpreted, the Christ.

Interpreted *see John 1:38.*

Christ *christos* (5547), "anointed," translates, in the Sept., the word "Messiah," a term applied to the priests who were anointed with the holy oil, particularly the high priest, e.g., Lev. 4:3, 5, 16. The prophets are called *hoi christoi Theou*, "the anointed of God," Ps. 105:15. A king of Israel was described upon occasion as *christos tou Kuriou*, "the anointed of the Lord," 1 Sam. 2:10, 35; 2 Sam. 1:14; Ps. 2:2; 18:50; Hab. 3:13; the term is used even of Cyrus, Isa. 45:1.

The title *ho Christos*, "the Christ," is not used of Christ in the Sept. version of the inspired books of the OT. In the NT the word is frequently used with the article, of the Lord Jesus, as an appellative rather than a title, e.g., Matt. 2:4; Acts 2:31; without the article, Luke 2:11; 23:2; **John 1:41**. Three times the title was expressly accepted by the Lord Himself, Matt. 16:17; Mark 14:61-62; **John 4:26**. It is added as an appellative to the proper name "Jesus," e.g.,

John **17:3**, the only time when the Lord so spoke of Himself; Acts 9:34; 1 Cor. 3:11; 1 John 5:6. It is distinctly a proper name in many passages, whether with the article, e.g., Matt. 1:17; 11:2; Rom. 7:4, 9:5; 15:19; 1 Cor. 1:6, or without the article, Mark 9:41; Rom. 6:4; 8:9, 17; 1 Cor. 1:12; Gal. 2:16. The single title Christos is sometimes used without the article to signify the One who by His Holy Spirit and power indwells believers and molds their character in conformity to His likeness, Rom. 8:10; Gal. 2:20; 4:19; Eph. 3:17. As to the use or absence of the article, the title with the article specifies the Lord Jesus as "the Christ"; the title without the article stresses His character and His relationship with believers. Again, speaking generally, when the title is the subject of a sentence it has the article; when it forms part of the predicate the article is absent.

1:42 And he brought him to Jesus. And when Jesus beheld him, he said, Thou art Simon the son of Jona: thou shalt be called Cephas, which is by interpretation, A stone.

Beheld *see* Looking upon at *John 1:36*.

Thou *see John 1:19*.

Stone In **John 1:42** *petros* stands for the proper name, Peter, as the RV (KJV, "a stone"; marg., "Peter"); *petros* denotes: "a piece of a rock, a detached stone or boulder," in contrast to *petra*, "a mass of rock."

1:43 The day following Jesus would go forth into Galilee, and findeth Philip, and saith unto him, Follow me.

Day following *see* Next day at *John 1:29*.

1:44-45 Now Philip was of Bethsaida, the city of Andrew and Peter.

Philip findeth Nathanael, and saith unto him, We have found him, of whom Moses in the law, and the prophets, did write, Jesus of Nazareth, the son of Joseph.

Law *see 1:17*.

1:46 And Nathanael said unto him, Can there any good thing come out of Nazareth? Philip saith unto him, Come and see.

Come *eimi* (1510), "to be," is, in the infinitive mood, rendered "come," in **John 1:46** and in the future indicative "will come," in 2 Tim. 4:3.

See *see* Seen at *John 1:18*.

1:47 Jesus saw Nathanael coming to him, and saith of him, Behold an Israelite indeed, in whom is no guile!

Behold *see John 1:29*.

Indeed *alethos* (230), "truly," is translated "indeed" in **John 1:47**; **4:42**; **8:31**.

Guile *dolos* (1388), "a bait, snare, deceit," is rendered "guile" in **John 1:47**, negatively of Nathanael; Acts 13:10, RV, KJV, "subtlety" (of Bar-Jesus); 2 Cor. 12:16, in a charge made against Paul by his detractors, of catching the Corinthian converts by "guile" (the apostle is apparently quoting the language of his critics); 1 Thess. 2:3, negatively, of the teaching of the apostle and his fellow missionaries; 1 Pet. 2:1, of that from which Christians are to be free; 2:22, of the guileless speech of Christ; 3:10, of the necessity that the speech of Christians should be guileless. See also Matt. 26:4; Mark 7:22; 14:1.

1:48 Nathanael saith unto him, Whence knowest thou me? Jesus answered and said unto him, Before that Philip called thee, when thou wast under the fig tree, I saw thee.

Fig tree *suke or sukea* (4808), "a fig tree," is found in Matt. 21:19, 20, 21; 24:32; Mark 11:13, 20, 21; 13:28; Luke 13:6, 7; 21:29; **John 1:48**, **50**, Jas. 3:12; Rev. 6:13.

1:49 Nathanael answered and saith unto him, Rabbi, thou art the Son of God; thou art the King of Israel.

Rabbi *see John 1:38*.

Son *see John 1:18*.

King *basileus* (935), "a king" (cf. Eng., "Basil"), e.g., Matt. 1:6, is used of the Roman emperor in 1 Pet. 2:13, 17 (a command of general application); this reference to the emperor is illustrated frequently in the *Koine*; of Herod the Tetrarch (used by courtesy), Matt. 14:9; of Christ, as the "King" of the Jews, e.g., Matt, 2:2; 27:11, 29, 37; as the "King" of Israel, Mark 15:32; **John 1:49**; **12:13**; as "King of kings," Rev. 17:14; 19:16; as "the King" in judging nations and men at the establishment of the millennial kingdom, Matt. 25:34, 40; of God, "the great King," Matt. 5:35; "the King eternal, incorruptible, invisible," 1 Tim. 1:17; "King of kings," 1 Tim. 6:15; "King of the ages," Rev. 15:3, RV (KJV, "saints"). Christ's "kingship" was predicted in the OT, e.g., Ps. 2:6, and in the NT, e.g., Luke 1:32, 33; He came as such e.g., Matt. 2:2; **John 18:37**; was rejected and died as such, Luke 19:14; Matt. 27:37; is now a "King" Priest, after the order of Melchizedek, Heb. 5:6; 7:1, 17; and will reign for ever and ever, Rev. 11:15.

1:50 Jesus answered and said unto him, Because I said unto thee, I saw thee under the fig tree, believest thou? thou shalt see greater things than these.

Under *hupokato* (5270), an adverb signifying "under," is used as a preposition and rendered "under" in Mark 6:11; 7:28; Luke 8:16; Heb. 2:8; Rev. 5:3, 13; 6:9; 12:1; "underneath" in Matt. 22:44, RV (Mark 12:36 in some mss.); **John 1:50**, RV (KJV, "under").

Fig tree *see John 1:48*.

Believest *pisteuo* (4100), "to believe," also "to be persuaded of," and hence, "to place confidence in, to trust," signifies, in this sense of the word, reliance upon, not mere credence. It is most frequent in the writings of the apostle John, especially the Gospel. He does not use the noun. For the Lord's first use of the verb, see **1:50**. Of the writers of the Gospels, Matthew uses the verb ten times, Mark ten, Luke nine, John ninety-nine. In Acts 5:14 the present participle of the verb is translated "believers."

Greater *meizon* (3187), is the comparative degree of *megas*, e.g., Matt. 11:11; in Matt. 13:32, the RV rightly has "greater than" (KJV, "the greatest among"); 23:17; in Luke 22:26, RV, "the greater (among you)" (KJV, "greatest"); in Jas. 3:1, RV, "the heavier (marg., greater) judgment" (KJV, "the greater condemnation"); it is used in the neuter plural in **John 1:50**, "greater things"; in **14:12**, "greater works" (lit., "greater things"); in 1 Cor. 12:31, RV, "the greater," KJV, "the best".

1:51 And he saith unto him, Verily, verily, I say unto you, Hereafter ye shall see heaven open, and the angels of God ascending and descending upon the Son of man.

Open *anoigo* (455), is used (1) transitively, (a) literally, of "a door or gate," e.g., Acts 5:19; graves, Matt. 27:52; a sepulchre, Rom. 3:13; a book, e.g., Luke 4:17; Rev. 5:2-5; 10:8; the seals of a roll, e.g., Rev. 5:9; 6:1; the eyes, Acts 9:40; the mouth of a fish, Matt. 17:27; "the pit of the abyss," Rev. 9:2, RV; heaven and the heavens, Matt. 3:16; Luke 3:21; Acts 10:11; Rev. 19:11; "the temple of the tabernacle of the testimony in heaven," Rev. 15:5; by metonymy, for that which contained treasures, Matt. 2:11; (b) metaphorically, e.g., Matt. 7:7-8; 25:11; Rev. 3:7; Hebraistically, "to open the mouth," of beginning to speak, e.g., Matt. 5:2; 13:35; Acts 8:32, 35; 10:34; 18:14; Rev. 13:6 (cf., e.g., Num. 22:28; Job. 3:1; Isa. 50:5); and of recovering speech, Luke 1:64; of the earth "opening," Rev. 12:16; of the "opening" of the eyes, Acts 26:18; the ears, Mark 7:35; (2) intransitively (perfect tense, active, in the Greek), (a) literally, of "the heaven," **John 1:51**, RV, "opened;" (b) metaphorically, of "speaking freely," 2 Cor. 6:11.

Chapter 2

2:1 And the third day there was a marriage in Cana of Galilee; and the mother of Jesus was there:

Marriage *gamos* (1062), "a marriage, wedding," or "wedding feast," is used to denote (a) the ceremony and its proceedings, including the "marriage feast," **John 2:1, 2**; of the "marriage ceremony" only, figuratively, Rev. 19:7, as distinct from the "marriage feast" (v. 9); (b) "the marriage feast," RV in Matt. 22:2-4, 9; in v. 8, 10, "wedding;" in 25:10, RV "marriage feast;" so Luke 12:36; 14:8; in Matt. 22:11, 12, the "wedding garment" is, lit., "a garment of a wedding." In Rev. 19, where, under the figure of a "marriage," the union of Christ, as the Lamb of God, with His heavenly bride is so described, the marriage itself takes place in heaven during the Parousia, v. 7 (the aorist or point tense indicating an accomplished fact; the bride is called "His wife"); the "marriage feast" or supper is to take place on earth, after the Second Advent, v. 9.

2:2 And both Jesus was called, and his disciples, to the marriage.

Marriage *see John 2:1*.

2:3 And when they wanted wine, the mother of Jesus saith unto him, They have no wine.

Wanted *hustereo* (5302), signifies "to be in want," Luke 15:14; 2 Cor. 11:9 (1st occurrence); Phil. 4:12, RV (KJV "to suffer need"); in **John 2:3**, KJV, "wanted" (RV, "failed").

2:4 Jesus saith unto her, Woman, what have I to do with thee? mine hour is not yet come.

Woman *gune* (1135), is used of a "woman" unmarried or married, e.g., Matt. 11:11; 14:21; Luke 4:26, of a "widow"; Rom. 7:2; in the vocative case, used in addressing a "woman," it is a term not of reproof or severity, but of endearment or respect, Matt. 15:28; **John 2:4**, where the Lord's words to His mother at the wedding in Cana, are neither rebuff nor rebuke. The question is, lit., "What to Me and to thee?" and the word "woman," the term of endearment, follows this. The meaning is "There is no obligation on Me or you, but love will supply the need." She confides in Him, He responds to her faith.

There was lovingkindness in both hearts. His next words about "His hour" suit this; they were not unfamiliar to her. Cana is in the path to Calvary; Calvary was not yet, but it made the beginning of signs possible. See also **4:21**; **19:26**.

Have In Matt. 27:19, "Have thou nothing to do with that righteous man" translates what is lit. "nothing to thee and that righteous man," the verb being omitted. Similarly with the phrase, "What have I to do with thee?" lit., "what (is) to me and thee?" Mark 5:7; Luke 8:28; **John 2:4**, where Westcott translates it "What is there to Me and to thee?"; Ellicott, "What is that to Me and to thee," i.e., "What is My concern and thine in the matter?" There is certainly nothing disparaging in the question. On the contrary, it answers what must have been the thought in Mary's heart, and suggests that while there is no obligation either on Him or her, yet the need is a case for rendering help. For the construction with the plural pronoun see Matt. 8:29; Mark 1:24; Luke 4:34.

Come *heko* (2240), means (a) "to come, to be present"; (b) "to come upon, of time and events," Matt. 24:14; **John 2:4**; 2 Pet. 3:10; Rev. 18:8; (c) metaphorically, "to come upon one, of calamitous times, and evils," Matt. 23:36; Luke 19:43.

2:5 His mother saith unto the servants, Whatsoever he saith unto you, do *it*.

Servants *diakonos* (1249), (Eng., "deacon"), primarily denotes a "servant," whether as doing servile work, or as an attendant rendering free service, without particular reference to its character. The word is probably connected with the verb *dioko*, "to hasten after, pursue" (perhaps originally said of a runner). "It occurs in the NT of domestic servants, **John 2:5**, **9**; the civil ruler, Rom. 13:4; Christ, Rom. 15:8; Gal. 2:17; the followers of Christ in relation to their Lord, **John 12:26**; Eph. 6:21; Col. 1:7; 4:7; the followers of Christ in relation to one another, Matt. 20:26; 23:11, Mark 9:35; 10:43; the servants of Christ in the work of preaching and teaching, 1 Cor. 3:5; 2 Cor. 3:6; 6:4; 11:23; Eph. 3:7; Col. 1:23, 25; 1 Thess. 3:2; 1 Tim. 4:6; those who serve in the churches, Rom. 16:1 (used of a woman here only in NT); Phil. 1:1; 1 Tim. 3:8, 12; false apostles, servants of Satan, 2 Cor. 11:15. Once *diakonos* is used where, apparently, angels are intended, Matt. 22:13; in v. 3, where men are intended, *doulos* is used."

Diakonos is, generally speaking, to be distinguished from *doulos*, "a bondservant, slave"; *diakonos* views a servant in relationship to his work, *doulos* views him in relationship to his master. See, e.g., Matt. 22:2-14; those who bring in the guests (vv. 3-4, 6, 8, 10) are *douloi* those who carry out the king's sentence (v. 13) are *diakonoi*.

2:6 And there were set there six waterpots of stone, after the manner of the purifying of the Jews, containing two or three firkins apiece.

Set *keimai* (2749), "to lie, to be laid" (used as the passive voice of *tithemi*), is translated "to be set," e.g., in Matt. 5:14 (of a city); Luke 2:34 (of Christ); **John 2:6** (of waterpots); **19:29** (of a vessel of vinegar); Phil. 1:16, RV (v. 17, KJV) (of the apostle Paul); Rev. 4:2 (of the throne in heaven).

Six *hex* (1803), whence Eng. prefix, "hex"-, is used separately from other numerals in Matt. 17:1; Mark 9:2; Luke 4:25; 13:14; **John 2:6**; **12:1**; Acts 11:12; 18:11; Jas. 5:17; Rev. 4:8. It sometimes suggests incompleteness, in comparison with the perfect number seven.

Waterpots *hudria* (5201), occurs in **John 2:6**, **7**; **4:28**.

Stone *lithinos* (3035), "of stone," occurs in **John 2:6**; 2 Cor. 3:3; Rev. 9:20.

Manner *kata* (2596), "according to," is translated "after the manner" in **John 2:6**, i.e., "in accordance with"; in Rom. 3:5; 1 Cor. 3:3; 9:8, RV, "after the manner of" (KJV, "as").

Purifying *katharismos* (2512), denotes "cleansing," (a) both the action and its results, in the Levitical sense, Mark 1:44; Luke 2:22, "purification"; 5:14, "cleansing"; **John 2:6**; **3:25**, "purifying"; (b) in the moral sense, from sins, Heb. 1:3; 2 Pet. 1:9, RV, "cleansing.

Jews *ioudaios* (2453), is used (a) adjectivally, with the lit. meaning, "Jewish," sometimes with the addition of *aner*, "a man," Acts 10:28; 22:3; in 21:39 with *anthropos*, in some mss. (a man in the generic sense); the best mss. omit the phrase here; in 13:6, lit., "a Jewish false-prophet"; in **John 3:22**, with the word *chora*, "land" or "country," signifying "Judean," lit., "Judean country"; used by metonymy for the people of the country; (b) as a noun, "a Jew, Jews," e.g., Matt. 2:2; Mark 7:3. The name "Jew" is primarily tribal (from Judah). It is first found in 2 Kings 16:6, as distinct from Israel, of the northern kingdom. After the Captivity it was chiefly used to distinguish the race from Gentiles, e.g., **John 2:6**; Acts 14:1; Gal. 2:15, where it denotes Christians of "Jewish" race; it distinguishes Jews from Samaritans, in **John 4:9**; from proselytes, in Acts

2:10. The word is most frequent in John's Gospel and the Acts; in the former "it especially denotes the typical representatives of Jewish thought contrasted with believers in Christ ... or with other Jews of less pronounced opinions, e.g., **John 3:25; 5:10; 7:13; 9:22**" (Lukyn Williams, in *Hastings' Bib. Dic.*); such representatives were found, generally, in opposition to Christ; in the Acts they are chiefly those who opposed the apostles and the gospel. In Rom. 2:28, 29 the word is used of ideal "Jews," i.e., "Jews" in spiritual reality, believers, whether "Jews" or Gentiles by natural birth. The feminine, "Jewess," is found in Acts 16:1; 24:24. It also denotes Judea, e.g., Matt. 2:1; Luke 1:5; **John 4:3**, the word "country" being understood [cf. (a) above]. In Luke 23:5 and **John 7:1**, where the KJV has "Jewry," the RV translates it as usual, "Judea."

Containing *choreo* (5562), signifies (a), lit., "to give space, make room" (*chora*, "a place"); hence, transitively, "to have space or room for a thing, to contain," said of the waterpots as "containing" a certain quantity, **John 2:6**; of a space large enough to hold a number of people, Mark 2:2; of the world as not possible of "containing" certain books, **John 21:25**; (b) "to go," Matt. 15:17; "to have place," **John 8:37**; "to come," 2 Pet. 3:9; (c) metaphorically, "of receiving with the mind," Matt. 19:11, 12; or "into the heart," 2 Cor. 7:2.

Two In the following phrases the numeral is used distributively: (a) *ana duo*, "two apiece," **John 2:6** (in some mss., Luke 9:3); in Luke 10:1, "two and two" ("by twos"); (b) *kata duo*, "by two," 1 Cor. 14:27; (c) *duo duo*, "by two and two," lit., "two (and) two," Mark 6:7 (not a Hebraism; the form of expression is used in the papyri); (d) *eis duo*, "into two," "in twain," Matt. 27:51 and Mark 15:38.

Firkins *metretes* (3355), is a liquid measure (akin to *metreo*, "to measure"), equivalent to one and a half Roman *amphorae*, or about nine gallons, **John 2:6**.

Apiece *ana* (303), used with numerals or measures of quantity with a distributive force, is translated "apiece" in Luke 9:3, "two coats apiece," KJV; in **John 2:6**, "two or three firkins apiece." In Matt. 20:9-10, "every man a penny," is a free rendering for "a penny apiece"; in Luke 9:14, the RV adds "each" to translate the *ana*, in 10:1, *ana duo* is "two by two." See Rev. 4:8, "each."

2:7 Jesus saith unto them, Fill the waterpots with water. And they filled them up to the brim.

Waterpots *see John 2:6.*

Brim *ano* (507), denotes "above, in a higher place," Acts 2:19 (the opposite to *kato*, "below"). With the article it means "that which is above," Gal. 4:26; Phil. 3:14, "the high calling" (RV marg., "upward"); with the plural article, "the things above," **John 8:23**, lit., "from the things above"; Col. 3:1-2. With *heos*, "as far as," it is translated "up to the brim," in **John 2:7**. It has the meaning "upwards" in **John 11:41** and Heb. 12:15.

2:8 And he saith unto them, Draw out now, and bear unto the governor of the feast. And they bare *it*.

Draw *antleo* (501), signified, primarily, "to draw out a ship's bilgewater, to bale or pump out" (from *antlos*, "bilge-water"), hence, "to draw water" in any way (*ana*, "up" and a root, *tel–*, "to lift, bear"), **John 2:8-9; 4:7, 15**.

Bear, Bare *phero* (5342), "to bring or bear," is translated in the RV by the latter verb in Luke 23:26; **John 2:8** (twice); **12:24; 15:2** (twice); Heb. 13:13.

Governor *architriklinos* (755), from *arche*, "rule," and *triklinos*, "a room with three couches," denotes "the ruler of a feast," **John 2:8**, RV (KJV, "the governor of the feast"), a man appointed to see that the table and couches were duly placed and the courses arranged, and to taste the food and wine.

2:9 When the ruler of the feast had tasted the water that was made wine, and knew not whence it was: (but the servants which drew the water knew;) the governor of the feast called the bridegroom,

Ruler *see* Governor at *John 2:8.*

Tasted *geuo* (1089), "to make to taste," is used in the middle voice, signifying "to taste" (a) naturally, Matt. 27:34; Luke 14:24; **John 2:9**; Col. 2:21; (b) metaphorically, of Christ's "tasting" death, implying His personal experience in voluntarily undergoing death, Heb. 2:9; of believers (negatively) as to "tasting" of death, Matt. 16:28; Mark 9:1; Luke 9:27; **John 8:52**; of "tasting" the heavenly gift (different from receiving it), Heb. 6:4; "the good word of God, and the powers of the age to come," 6:5; "that the Lord is gracious," 1 Pet. 2:3.

Made *see John 1:3.*

Servants *see John 2:5.*

2:10 And saith unto him, Every man at the beginning doth set forth good wine; and when men have well drunk, then that which is worse: *but* thou hast kept the good wine until now.

Every *pas* (3956), signifies with nouns without the article, (a) "every one" of the class denoted by the noun connected with *pas*, e.g., Matt. 3:10, "every tree"; Mark 9:49, "every sacrifice"; see also **John 2:10**; Acts 2:43; Rom. 2:9; Eph. 1:21; 3:15; 2 Thess. 2:4; 2 Tim. 3:16, RV; (b) "any and every, of every kind, all manner of," e.g., Matt. 4:23; "especially with nouns denoting virtues or vices, emotions, condition, indicating every mode in which a quality manifests itself; or any object to which the idea conveyed by the noun belongs" (Grimm-Thayer). This is often translated "all," e.g., Acts 27:20; Rom. 15:14; 2 Cor. 10:6; Eph. 4:19, 31; Col. 4:12, "all the will of God," i.e., everything God wills.

Beginning *proton* (4412), the neuter of *protos* (the superlative degree of *proteros*), "first, at the first," is rendered "at the beginning" in **John 2:10**, KJV, RV, "setteth on first."

Set *tithemi* (5087), "to put, to place," is translated "to set" in Acts 1:7, of times and seasons (KJV, "put"); Acts 13:47; Rev. 10:2; "setteth on" (of wine) in **John 2:10**, RV (KJV, "doth set forth"); in the KJV of Mark 4:21 (2nd part) and in Luke 8:16 it is rendered "set" (RV, "put"), of a lamp. In Mark 4:30 it is used of "setting" forth by parable the teaching concerning the kingdom of God, RV, "shall we set (it) forth" (KJV, "compare").

Wine *oinos* (3631), is the general word for "wine." The mention of the bursting of the wineskins, Matt. 9:17; Mark 2:22; Luke 5:37, implies fermentation. See also Eph. 5:18 (cf. **John 2:10**; 1 Tim. 3:8; Titus 2:3). In Matt. 27:34, the RV has "wine" (KJV, "vinegar," translating the inferior reading *oxos*). The drinking of "wine" could be a stumbling block and the apostle enjoins abstinence in this respect, as in others, so as to avoid giving an occasion of stumbling to a brother, Rom. 14:21. Contrast 1 Tim. 5:23, which has an entirely different connection.

Well For **John 2:10**, "have well drunk" (RV, "freely").

Drunk *methuo* (3184), from *methu*, "wine, to be drunk," is used in **John 2:10** in the passive voice, and is translated in the RV, "have drunk freely"; KJV, "have well drunk."

Worse *elasson* or *elatton* (1640), serves as a comparative degree of *mikros*, "little", and denotes "less" in (a) quality, as of wine, **John 2:10**, "worse;" (b) age, Rom. 9:12, "younger"; 1 Tim. 5:9, "under" neuter, adverbially; (c) rank, Heb. 7:7.

Now *arti* (737), expressing "coincidence," and denoting "strictly present time," signifies "just now, this moment," in contrast (a) to the past, e.g., Matt. 11:12; **John 2:10; 9:19, 25; 13:33**; Gal. 1:9-10; (b) to the future, e.g., **John 13:37; 16:12, 31**; 1 Cor. 13:12; 2 Thess. 2:7; 1 Pet. 1:6, 8; (c) sometimes without necessary reference to either, e.g., Matt. 3:15; 9:18; 26:53; Gal. 4:20; Rev. 12:10.

2:11 This beginning of miracles did Jesus in Cana of Galilee, and manifested forth his glory; and his disciples believed on him.

This (a) as a noun, "this one." In Acts 17:32 the RV rightly omits "*matter*"; in Heb. 4:5 "*place*" is italicized; it is frequently rendered "this man," e.g., Matt. 9:3; **John 6:52**; "of this sort," 2 Tim. 3:6, KJV (RV, "of these"); (b) as an adjective with a noun, either with the article and before it, e.g., Matt. 12:32, or after the noun (which is preceded by the article), e.g., Matt. 3:9 and 4:3, "these stones"; or without the article often forming a predicate, e.g., **John 2:11**; 2 Cor. 13:1.

Miracles *semeion* (4592), "a sign, mark, token" (akin to *semaino*, "to give a sign"; *sema*, "a sign"), is used of "miracles" and wonders as signs of divine authority; it is translated "miracles" in the RV and KJV of Luke 23:8; Acts 4:16, 22; most usually it is given its more appropriate meaning "sign," "signs," e.g., Matt. 12:38, 39, and in every occurrence in the Synoptists, except Luke 23:8; in the following passages in John's Gospel the RV substitutes "sign" or "signs" for the KJV "miracle or miracles"; **2:11, 23; 3:2; 4:54; 6:2, 14, 26; 7:31; 9:16; 10:41; 11:47; 12:18, 37**; the KJV also has "signs" elsewhere in this Gospel; in Acts, RV, "signs," KJV, "miracles," in 6:8; 8:6; 15:12; elsewhere only in Rev. 13:14; 16:14; 19:20. "Signs" confirmatory of what God had accomplished in the atoning sacrifice of Christ, His resurrection and ascension, and of the sending of the Holy Spirit, were given to the Jews for their recognition, as at Pentecost, and supernatural acts by apostolic ministry, as well as by the supernatural operations in the churches, such as the gift of tongues and prophesyings; there is no record of the continuance of these latter after the circumstances recorded in Acts 19:1-20.

Glory *see John 1:14*.

Forth In **John 2:11** the RV rightly omits "forth."

2:12 After this he went down to Capernaum, he, and his mother, and his brethren, and his disciples: and they continued there not many days.

Continued *see* Abode at *John 1:32*.

2:13 And the Jews' passover was at hand, and Jesus went up to Jerusalem,

Passover *pascha* (3957), the Greek spelling of the Aramaic word for the Passover, from the Hebrew *pasach*, "to pass over, to spare," a feast instituted by God in commemoration of the deliverance of Israel from Egypt, and anticipatory of the expiatory sacrifice of Christ. The word signifies (I) "the Passover Feast," e.g., Matt. 26:2; **John 2:13, 23; 6:4; 11:55; 12:1; 13:1; 18:39; 19:14**; Acts 12:4; Heb. 11:28; (II) by metonymy, (a) "the Paschal Supper," Matt. 26:18, 19; Mark 14:16; Luke 22:8, 13; (b) "the Paschal lamb," e.g., Mark 14:12 (cf. Exod. 12:21); Luke 22:7; (c) "Christ Himself," 1 Cor. 5:7.

2:14 And found in the temple those that sold oxen and sheep and doves, and the changers of money sitting:

Sold *poleo* (4453), "to exchange or barter, to sell," is used in the latter sense in the NT, six times in Matthew, three in Mark, six in Luke; in John only in connection with the cleansing of the Temple by the Lord, **2:14, 16**; in Acts only in connection with the disposing of property for distribution among the community of believers, 4:34, 37; 5:1; elsewhere, 1 Cor. 10:25; Rev. 13:17.

Oxen *bous* (1016), denotes an "ox" or "a cow," Luke 13:15; 14:5, 19; **John 2:14-15**; 1 Cor. 9:9 (twice); 1 Tim. 5:18.

Doves *see* Dove at *John 1:32*.

Changers *kermatistes* (2773), from *kermatizo* (not found in the NT), "to cut into small pieces, to make small change" (*kerma* signifies "a small coin," **John 2:15**; akin to *keiro*, "to cut short"). In the court of the Gentiles, in the temple precincts, were the seats of those who sold selected and approved animals for sacrifice, and other things. The magnitude of this traffic had introduced the bankers' or brokers' business, **John 2:14**.

2:15 And when he had made a scourge of small cords, he drove them all out of the temple, and the sheep, and the oxen; and poured out the changers' money, and overthrew the tables;

Scourge *phragellion* (5416), "a whip" (from Latin, *flagellum*), is used of the "scourge" of small cords which the Lord made and employed before cleansing the Temple, **John 2:15**. However He actually used it, the whip was in itself a sign of authority and judgment.

Cords *schoinion* (4979), "a cord or rope," a diminutive of *schoinos*, "a rush, bulrush," meant a "cord" made of rushes; it denotes (a) "a small cord," **John 2:15** (plural), (b) "a rope," Acts 27:32.

Drove *ekballo* (1544), denotes, lit., "to cast forth," with the suggestion of force (*ek*, "out," *ballo*, "to cast"); hence "to drive out or forth." It is translated "driveth" in Mark 1:12, RV, "driveth forth." In **John 2:15** for the KJV, "drove," the RV has "cast," the more usual translation.

Pour *ekcheo* (1632), "to pour out" (*ek*, "out"), is used (a) of Christ's act as to the changers' money, **John 2:15**; (b) of the Holy Spirit, Acts 2:17, 18, 33, RV, "He hath poured forth" (KJV, "... shed forth"); Titus 3:6, RV, "poured out" (KJV, "shed"); (c) of the emptying of the contents of the bowls (KJV, "vials") of divine wrath, Rev. 16:1-4, 8, 10, 12, 17; (d) of the shedding of the blood of saints by the foes of God, Rev. 16:6, RV, "poured out" (KJV, "shed"); some mss. have it in Acts 22:20.

Changers *kollubistes* (2855), from *kollubos* (lit., "clipped"), "a small coin or rate of change" (*koloboo* signifies "to cut off, to clip, shorten," Matt. 24:22), denotes "a money-changer," lit., money-clipper, Matt. 21:12; Mark 11:15; **John 2:15**. *See also John 2:14*.

Money *kerma* (2772), primarily "a slice" (akin to *keiro*, "to cut short"), hence, "a small coin, change," is used in the plural in **John 2:15**, "the changers' money," probably considerable heaps of small Coins.

Overthrew *anatrepo* (396), lit., "to turn up or over" (*ana*, "up," *trepo*, "to turn"), "to upset," is used (a) literally, in the most authentic mss., in **John 2:15**; (b) metaphorically, in 2 Tim. 2:18, "overthrow (the faith of some);" in Titus 1:11, RV, "overthrow (whole homes)," KJV, "subvert ... ," i.e., households. Moulton and Milligan (*Vocab.*) give an apt illustration from a 2nd cent. papyrus, of the complete upsetting of a family by the riotous conduct of a member. *Anastrepho* (390), is found in some mss. in **John 2:15**.

Tables *trapeza* (5132), is used of (a) "a dining table," Matt. 15:27; Mark 7:28; Luke 16:21; 22:21, 30; (b) "the table of shewbread," Heb. 9:2; (c) by metonymy, of "what is provided on the table" (the word being used of that with which it is associated), Acts 16:34; Rom. 11:9 (figurative of the special privileges granted to Israel and centering in Christ); 1 Cor. 10:21 (twice), "the Lord's table," denoting all that is provided for believers in Christ on the ground of His death (and thus expressing something more comprehensive than the Lord's Supper); "the table of demons," denoting all that is partaken of by idolaters as the result of the influence of demons in connection with their sacrifices; (d) "a moneychanger's table," Matt. 21:12; Mark 11:15; **John 2:15**; (e) "a bank," Luke 19:23 (cf. *trapezites*); (f) by metonymy for "the distribution of money," Acts 6:2.

2:16 And said unto them that sold doves, Take these things hence; make not my Father's house an house of merchandise.

Sold *see John 2:14.*

Doves *see* Dove at *John 1:32.*

Hence *enteuthen* (1782), is used (a) of place, "hence," or "from hence," Luke 4:9; 13:31; **John 2:16**; **7:3**; **14:31**; **18:36**; in **John 19:18**, "on either side (one)," lit., "hence and hence"; in Rev. 22:2, it is contrasted with *ekeithen*, "thence," RV, "on this side ... on that" (KJV, "on either side"), lit. "hence ... thence"; (b) causal; Jas. 4:1, "(come they not) hence," i.e., "owing to."

Make *poieo* (4160), "to do, to make," is used ... (c) with nouns involving the idea of action (or of something accomplished by action), so as to express the idea of the verb more forcibly (the middle voice is commonly used in this respect, suggesting the action as being of special interest to the doer); for the active voice see, e.g., Mark 2:23, of "making" one's way, where the idea is not that the disciples "made" a path through the standing corn, but simply that they went, the phrase being equivalent to going, "(they began) as they went (to pluck the ears)"; other instances of the active are Rev. 13:13, 14; 16:14; 19:20; for the middle voice (the dynamic or subjective middle), see, e.g., **John 14:23**, "will make Our abode"; in Acts 20:24, "none of these things move me," lit., "I make account of none of these things"; 25:17, "I made no delay" RV, Rom. 15:26; Eph. 4:16; Heb. 1:2; 2 Pet. 1:10; (d) to "make" ready or prepare, e.g., a dinner, Luke 14:12; a supper, **John 12:2**; (e) to acquire, provide a thing for oneself, Matt. 25:16; Luke 19:18; (f) to render or "make" one or oneself anything, or cause a person or thing to become something, e.g., Matt. 4:19; 12:16, "make (Him known)"; **John 5:11**, **15**, to "make" whole; **16:2**, lit., "they shall make (you put out of the synagogue)"; Eph. 2:14; Heb. 1:7; to change one thing into another, Matt. 21:13; **John 2:16**; **4:46**; 1 Cor. 6:15; (g) to constitute one anything, e.g., Acts 2:36, (h) to declare one or oneself anything, **John 5:18**, "making (Himself equal with God)"; **8:53**; **10:33**; **19:7**, **12**; 1 John 1:10; 5:10; (i) to "make" one do a thing, e.g., Luke 5:34; **John 6:10**; Rev. 3:9.

House *oikos* (3624), denotes "a house, a dwelling," e.g., Matt. 9:6, 7; 11:8; it is used of the Tabernacle, as the House of God, Matt. 12:4, and the Temple similarly, e.g., Matt. 21:13; Luke 11:51, KJV, "temple," RV, "sanctuary"; **John 2:16**, **17**; called by the Lord "your house" in Matt. 23:38 and Luke 13:35 (some take this as the city of Jerusalem); metaphorically of Israel as God's house, Heb. 3:2, 5, where "his house" is not Moses', but God's; of believers, similarly, v. 6, where Christ is spoken of as "over God's House" (the word "own" is rightly omitted in the RV); Heb. 10:21; 1 Pet. 2:5; 4:17; of the body, Matt. 12:44; Luke 11:24.

Merchandise *emporion* (1712), denotes "a trading place, exchange" (Eng., "emporium"), **John 2:16**, "(a house) of merchandise."

2:17 And his disciples remembered that it was written, The zeal of thine house hath eaten me up.

Zeal *zelos* (2205), denotes "zeal" in the following passages: **John 2:17**, with objective genitive, i.e., "zeal for Thine house"; so in Rom. 10:2, "a zeal for God"; in 2 Cor. 7:7, RV, "(your) zeal (for me)," KJV, "(your) fervent mind (toward me)"; used absolutely in 7:11; 9:2; Phil. 3:6 (in Col. 4:13 in some texts; the best have *ponos*, labor, RV).

House *see John 2:16.*

Eaten *katesthio* and *kataphago* (2719), signifies (a) "to consume by eating, to devour," said of birds, Matt. 13:4; Mark 4:4; Luke 8:5; of the Dragon, Rev. 12:4; of a prophet, "eating" up a book, suggestive of spiritually "eating" and digesting its contents, Rev. 10:9 (cf. Ezek. 2:8; 3:1-3; Jer. 15:16); (b) metaphorically, "to squander, to waste," Luke 15:30; "to consume" one's physical powers by emotion, **John 2:17**; "to devour" by forcible appropriation, as of widows' property, Matt. 23:14 (KJV only); Mark 12:40; "to demand maintenance," as false apostles did to the church at Corinth, 2 Cor. 11:20; "to exploit or prey on one another," Gal. 5:15, where "bite ... devour ... consume" form a climax, the first two describing a process, the last the act of swallowing down; to "destroy" by fire, Rev. 11:5; 20:9.

2:18 Then answered the Jews and said unto him, What sign shewest thou unto us, seeing that thou doest these things?

Answered *apokrinomai* (611), signifies either "to give an answer to a question" (its more frequent use) or "to begin to speak," but always where something has preceded, either statement or act to which the remarks refer, e.g., Matt. 11:25; Luke 14:3; **John 2:18**. The RV translates by "answered," e.g., Matt. 28:5; Mark 12:35; Luke 3:16, where some have suggested "began to say" or "uttered solemnly," whereas the speaker is replying to the unuttered thought or feeling of those addressed by him.

2:19 Jesus answered and said unto them, Destroy this temple, and in three days I will raise it up.

Temple *naos* (3485), "a shrine or sanctuary," was used (a) among the heathen, to denote the shrine containing the idol, Acts 17:24; 19:24 (in the latter, miniatures); (b) among the Jews, the sanctuary in the "Temple," into which only the priests could lawfully enter, e.g., Luke 1:9, 21, 22; Christ, as being of the tribe of Judah, and thus not being a priest while upon the earth (Heb. 7:13, 14; 8:4), did not enter the *naos*; (c) by Christ metaphorically, of His own physical body, **John 2:19, 21**; (d) in apostolic teaching, metaphorically, (1) of the church, the mystical body of Christ, Eph. 2:21; (2) of a local church, 1 Cor. 3:16, 17; 2 Cor. 6:16; (3) of the present body of the individual believer, 1 Cor. 6:19; (4) of the "Temple" seen in visions in Revelation, 3:12; 7:15; 11:19; 14:15, 17; 15:5, 6, 8; 16:1, 17; (5) of the Lord God Almighty and the Lamb, as the "Temple" of the new and heavenly Jerusalem, Rev. 21:22.

Raise *egeiro* (1453), is used (a) of "raising" the dead, active and passive voices, e.g. of the resurrection of Christ, Matt. 16:21; 17:23; 20:19, RV; 26:32, RV, "(after) I am raised up" (KJV, "... risen again"); Luke 9:22; 20:37; **John 2:19**; Acts 3:15; 4:10 [not 5:30, see (c) below]; 10:40 [not 13:23 in the best texts, see (c) below]; 13:30, 37; Rom. 4:24, 25; 6:4, 9; 7:4; 8:11 (twice); 8:34, RV; 10:9; 1 Cor. 6:14 (1st part); 15:13, 14, RV; 15:15 (twice), 16, 17; 15:20, RV; 2 Cor. 4:14; Gal. 1:1; Eph. 1:20; Col. 2:12; 1 Thess. 1:10; 1 Pet. 1:21; in 2 Tim. 2:8, RV, "risen"; (b) of the resurrection of human beings, Matt. 10:8; 11:5; Matt. 27:52, RV (KJV, "arose"); Mark 12:26, RV; Luke 7:22; **John 5:21; 12:1, 9, 17**; Acts 26:8; 1 Cor. 15:29 and 32, RV; 15:35, 42, 43 (twice), 44, 52; 2 Cor. 1:9; 4:14; Heb. 11:19; (c) of "raising" up a person to occupy a place in the midst of a people, said of Christ, Acts 5:30; in 13:23, KJV only (the best texts have *ago*, to bring, RV, "hath ... brought"); of David, Acts 13:22; (d) metaphorically, of a horn of salvation, Luke 1:69; (e) of children, from stones, by creative power, Luke 3:8; (f) of the Temple, as the Jews thought, **John 2:20**, RV, "wilt Thou raise (it) Up" (KJV, "rear"); (g) of "lifting" up a person, from physical infirmity, Mark 1:31, RV, "raised ... up" (KJV, "lifted"); so 9:27; Acts 3:7; 10:26, RV (KJV, "took"); Jas. 5:15, "shall raise ... up"; (h) metaphorically, of "raising" up affliction, Phil. 1:17, RV (in the best texts; the KJV, v. 16, following those which have *epiphero*, has "to add").

2:20 Then said the Jews, Forty and six years was this temple in building, and wilt thou rear it up in three days?

Six In combination with *tessarakonta*, "forty," it occurs in **John 2:20**; with *hebdomekonta*, "seventy," Acts 27:37, "(two hundred) threescore and sixteen."

Years *etos* (2094), is used ... (b) to mark a space of time, e.g., Matt. 9:20; Luke 12:19; 13:11; **John 2:20**; Acts 7:6, where the 400 "years" mark not merely the time that Israel was in bondage in Egypt, but the time that they sojourned or were strangers there (the RV puts a comma after the word "evil"); the Genevan Version renders Gen. 15:13 "thy posterity shall inhabit a strange land for 400 years"; Heb. 3:17; Rev. 20:2-7; (c) to date an event from one's birth, e.g., Mark 5:42; Luke 2:42; 3:23; **John 8:57**; Acts 4:22; 1 Tim. 5:9; (d) to mark recurring events, Luke 2:41 (with *kata*, used distributively); 13:7; (e) of an unlimited number, Heb. 1:12.

Building *oikodomeo* (3618), lit., "to build a house" (*oikos*, "a house," *domeo*, "to build"), hence, to build anything, e.g., Matt. 7:24; Luke 4:29; 6:48, RV, "well builded" (last clause of verse); **John 2:20**; is frequently used figuratively, e.g., Acts 20:32; Gal. 2:18; especially of edifying, Acts 9:31; Rom. 15:20; 1 Cor. 10:23; 14:4; 1 Thess. 5:11 (RV). In 1 Cor. 8:10 it is translated "emboldened" (marg., "builded up"). The participle with the article (equivalent to a noun) is rendered "builder," Matt. 21:42; Acts 4:11; 1 Pet. 2:7.

Rear *see* **Raise** at *John 2:19*.

2:21 But he spake of the temple of his body.

He *ekeinos* (1565), denotes "that one, that person"; its use marks special distinction, favorable or unfavorable; this form of emphasis should always be noted; e.g., **John 2:21** "(But) He (spake)"; **5:19**, "(what things soever) He (doeth)"; **7:11**; 2 Cor. 10:18, lit., "for not he that commendeth himself, he (*ekeinos*) is approved"; 2 Tim. 2:13, "He (in contrast to "we") abideth faithful"; 1 John 3:3, "(even as) He (is pure)"; v. 5, "He (was manifested)"; v. 7, "He (is righteous)"; v. 16, "He laid down"; 4:17, "(as) He (is)."

Temple *see John 2:19*.

2:22 When therefore he was risen from the dead, his disciples remembered that he had said this unto them; and they believed the scripture, and the word which Jesus had said.

Scripture *graphe* (1124), akin to *grapho*, "to write" (Eng., "graph," "graphic," etc.), primarily denotes "a drawing, painting"; then "a writing," (a) of the OT Scriptures, (1) in the plural, the whole, e.g., Matt. 21:42; 22:29; **John 5:39**; Acts 17:11; 18:24; Rom. 1:2, where "the prophets" comprises the OT writers in general; 15:4; 16:26, lit., "prophetic writings," expressing the character of all the Scriptures; (2) in the singular in reference to a particular passage, e.g., Mark 12:10; Luke 4:21; **John 2:22; 10:35** (though applicable to all); **19:24, 28, 36, 37; 20:9**; Acts 1:16; 8:32, 35; Rom. 4:3; 9:17; 10:11; 11:2; Gal. 3:8, 22; 4:30; 1 Tim. 5:18, where the 2nd quotation is from Luke 10:7, from which it may be inferred that the apostle included Luke's Gospel as "Scripture" alike with Deuteronomy, from which the first quotation is taken; in reference to the whole, e.g. Jas. 4:5 (see RV, a separate rhetorical question from the one which follows); in 2 Pet. 1:20, "no prophecy of Scripture," a description of all, with special application to the OT in the next verse; (b) of the OT Scriptures (those accepted by the Jews as canonical) and all those of the NT which were to be accepted by Christians as authoritative, 2 Tim. 3:16; these latter were to be discriminated from the many forged epistles and other religious "writings" already produced and circulated in Timothy's time. Such discrimination would be directed by the fact that "every Scripture," characterized by inspiration of God, would be profitable for the purposes mentioned; so the RV. The KJV states truth concerning the completed canon of Scripture, but that was not complete when the apostle wrote to Timothy.

The Scriptures are frequently personified by the NT writers (as by the Jews, **John 7:42**), (a) as speaking with divine authority, e.g., **John 19:37**; Rom. 4:3; 9:17, where the Scripture is said to speak to Pharaoh, giving the message actually sent previously by God to him through Moses; Jas. 4:5; (b) as possessed of the sentient quality of foresight, and the active power of preaching, Gal. 3:8, where the Scripture mentioned was written more than four centuries after the words were spoken. The Scripture, in such a case, stands for its divine Author with an intimation that it remains perpetually characterized as the living voice of God. This divine agency is again illustrated in Gal. 3:22 (cf. v. 10 and Matt. 11:13).

Word *see John 1:1.*

2:23 Now when he was in Jerusalem at the passover, in the feast *day*, many believed in his name, when they saw the miracles which he did.

Passover *see John 2:13.*

Feast In Mark 14:2 and **John 2:23** the KJV translates *heorte* by "feast day" (RV, "feast").

Name *see John 1:12.*

Miracles *see John 2:11.*

2:24 But Jesus did not commit himself unto them, because he knew all *men*,

Commit *pisteuo* (4100), "to believe," also means "to entrust," and in the active voice is translated "to commit," in Luke 16:11; **John 2:24**; in the passive voice, "to be intrusted with," Rom. 3:2, RV, "they were intrusted with" (KJV, "unto them were committed"), of Israel and the oracles of God; 1 Cor. 9:17, RV, "I have ... intrusted to me" (KJV, "is committed unto me"), of Paul and the stewardship of the gospel; so Gal. 2:7; Titus 1:3; in 1 Thess. 2:4, where he associates with himself his fellow missionaries, RV, "to be intrusted with" (KJV, "to be put in trust with").

2:25 And needed not that any should testify of man: for he knew what was in man.

Needed *chreia* (5532), denotes "a need," in such expressions as "there is a need"; or "to have need of" something, e.g., Matt. 3:14; 6:8; 9:12, RV, "(have no) need," KJV, "need (not)," the RV adheres to the noun form; so in 14:16; Mark 14:63; Luke 5:31; 22:71; Eph. 4:28; 1 Thess. 4:9; in the following, however, both RV and KJV use the verb form, "to need" (whereas the original has the verb *echo*, "to have," with the noun *chreia* as the object, as in the instances just mentioned): Luke 15:7; **John 2:25; 13:10; 16:30**; 1 Thess. 1:8; 1 John 2:27; Rev. 22:5; in all these the verb "to have" could well have been expressed in the translation.

Testify *martureo* (3140), is frequently rendered "to bear witness, to witness," in the RV, where KJV renders it "to testify," **John 2:25; 3:11, 32; 5:39; 15:26; 21:24**; 1 Cor. 15:15; Heb. 7:17; 11:4; 1 John 4:14; 5:9; 3 John 3. In the following, however, the RV, like the KJV, has the rendering "to testify," **John 4:39, 44; 7:7; 13:21**; Acts 26:5; Rev. 22:16, 18, 20. *See also* **Witness** at *John 1:7.*

Man *anthropos* (444), is used (a) generally, of "a human being, male or female," without reference to sex or nationality, e.g., Matt. 4:4; 12:35; **John 2:25**; (b) in distinction from God, e.g., Matt. 19:6; **John 10:33**; Gal. 1:11; Col. 3:23.

Chapter 3

3:1 There was a man of the Pharisees, named Nicodemus, a ruler of the Jews:

Ruler *archon* (758), the present participle of the verb *archo*, "to rule"; denotes "a ruler, a prince." It is used as follows ("p" denoting "prince," or "princes"; "r," "ruler" or "rulers"): (a) of Christ, as "the Ruler (KJV, Prince) of the kings of the earth," Rev. 1:5; (b) of rulers of nations, Matt. 20:25, RV, "r," KJV, "p"; Acts 4:26, "r"; 7:27, "r"; 7:35, "r" (twice); (c) of judges and magistrates, Acts 16:19, "r"; Rom. 13:3, "r"; (d) of members of the Sanhedrin, Luke 14:1, RV, "r" (KJV, "chief"); 23:13, 35, "r"; so 24:20, **John 3:1**; **7:26**, **48**; **12:42**, RV, "r" (KJV, "chief r."); "r" in Acts 3:17; 4:5, 8; 13:27; 14:5; (e) of rulers of synagogues, Matt. 9:18, 23, "r"; so Luke 8:41; 18:18; (f) of the Devil, as "prince" of this world, **John 12:31**; **14:30**; **16:11**; of the power of the air, Eph. 2:2, "the air" being that sphere in which the inhabitants of the world live and which, through the rebellious and godless condition of humanity, constitutes the seat of his authority; (g) of Beelzebub, the "prince" of the demons, Matt. 9:24; 12:24; Mark 3:22; Luke 11:15.

3:2 The same came to Jesus by night, and said unto him, Rabbi, we know that thou art a teacher come from God: for no man can do these miracles that thou doest, except God be with him.

Same *houtos* (3778), "this" (person or thing), or "he" (and the feminine and neuter forms), is sometimes translated "the same," e.g., **John 3:2**, **26**; **7:18**; Jas. 3:2; sometimes the RV translates it by "this" or "these," e.g., **John 12:21**, "these" (KJV, "the same"); 2 Cor. 8:6, "this" (KJV, "the same").

Night *nux* (3571), is used (I) literally, (a) of "the alternating natural period to that of the day," e.g., Matt. 4:2; 12:40; 2 Tim. 1:3; Rev. 4:8; (b) of "the period of the absence of light," the time in which something takes place, e.g., Matt. 2:14 (27:64), in some mss.); Luke 2:8; **John 3:2** (**7:50**, in some mss.); Acts 5:19; 9:25; (c) of "point of time," e.g., Matt. 14:27 (in some mss.), 30; Luke 12:20; Acts 27:23; (d) of "duration of time," e.g., Luke 2:37; 5:5; Acts 20:31; 26:7 (note the difference in the phrase in Mark 4:27); (II) metaphorically, (a) of "the period of man's alienation from God," Rom. 13:12; 1 Thess. 5:5, lit., "not of night," where "of" means 'belonging to;' cf. "of the Way," Acts 9:2; "of shrinking back" and "of faith," Heb. 10:39, marg.; (b) of "death," as the time when work ceases, **John 9:4**.

Rabbi *see John 1:38*.

Teacher *didaskalos* (1320), is rendered "teacher" or "teachers" in Matt. 23:8, by Christ, of Himself; in **John 3:2** of Christ; of Nicodemus in Israel, **3:10**, RV; of "teachers" of the truth in the churches, Acts 13:1; 1 Cor. 12:28, 29; Eph. 4:11; Heb. 5:12; Jas. 3:1, RV; by Paul of his work among the churches, 1 Tim. 2:7; 2 Tim. 1:11; of "teachers," wrongfully chosen by those who have "itching ears," 2 Tim. 4:3.

Miracles *see John 2:11*.

3:3 Jesus answered and said unto him, Verily, verily, I say unto thee, Except a man be born again, he cannot see the kingdom of God.

Man *tis* (5100), "some one, a certain one," is rendered "a man," "a certain man," e.g., in Matt. 22:24; Mark 8:4, KJV (RV, "one"); 12:19; **John 3:3**, **5**; **6:50**; **14:23**; **15:6**, **13**; Acts 13:41, KJV (RV, "one"); 1 Cor. 4:2; 1 Tim. 1:8; 2 Tim. 2:5, 21; Jas. 2:14, 18; 1 Pet. 2:19; 1 John 4:20.

Born *gennao* (1080), "to beget," in the passive voice, "to be born," is chiefly used of men "begetting" children, Matt. 1:2-16; more rarely of women "begetting" children, Luke 1:13, 57, "brought forth"; 23:29; **John 16:21**, "is delivered of," and of the child, "is born". In Gal. 4:24, it is used allegorically, to contrast Jews under bondage to the Law, and spiritual Israel, KJV, "gendereth," RV, "bearing children," to contrast the natural birth of Ishmael and the supernatural birth of Isaac. In Matt. 1:20 it is used of conception, "that which is conceived in her." It is used of the act of God in the birth of Christ, Acts 13:33; Heb. 1:5; 5:5, quoted from Psalm 2:7, none of which indicate that Christ became the Son of God at His birth. It is used metaphorically (a) in the writings of the apostle John, of the gracious act of God in conferring upon those who believe the nature and disposition of "children," imparting to them spiritual life, **John 3:3**, **5**, **7**; 1 John 2:29; 3:9; 4:7; 5:1, 4, 18; (b) of one who by means of preaching the gospel becomes the human instrument in the impartation of spiritual life, 1 Cor. 4:15; Philem. 10; (c) in 2 Pet. 2:12, with reference to the evil men whom the apostle is describing, the RV rightly has "born mere animals" (KJV, "natural brute beasts"); (d) in the sense of gendering strife, 2 Tim. 2:23.

Again *anothen* (509), lit., "from above," in the phrase rendered "anew" in the RV (KJV, "again") of **John 3:3**, **7**. Other words are rendered "again" in the KJV, which the RV corrects, namely, *deuteros* and *anothen*. *Deuteros* signifies "a second time," **John**

9:24; Acts 11:9. *Anothen* signifies "from above, or anew." See the RV of **John 3:3**, **7**, and the KJV and RV of v. **31**. Nicodemus was not puzzled about birth from heaven; what perplexed him was that a person must be born a second time. This the context makes dear. This is really the meaning in Gal. 4:9, where it is associated with *palin*, "over again." The idea is "anew," for, though the bondage would be the same in essence and effect, it would be new in not being in bondage to idols but to the Law. See also Matt. 27:51; Mark 15:38; **John 19:23**, "from the top." *Anothen* may mean "from the first," in Luke 1:3 and Acts 26:5. For the meaning "from above," see Jas. 1:17; 3:15, 17.

Kingdom *basileia* (932), is primarily an abstract noun, denoting "sovereignty, royal power, dominion," e.g., Rev. 17:18, translated "(which) reigneth," lit., "hath a kingdom" (RV marg.); then, by metonymy, a concrete noun, denoting the territory or people over whom a king rules, e.g., Matt. 4:8; Mark 3:24. It is used especially of the "kingdom" of God and of Christ.

"The Kingdom of God is (a) the sphere of God's rule, Ps. 22:28; 145:13; Dan. 4:25; Luke 1:52; Rom. 13:1, 2. Since, however, this earth is the scene of universal rebellion against God, e.g., Luke 4:5, 6; 1 John 5:19; Rev. 11:15-18, the "kingdom" of God is (b) the sphere in which, at any given time, His rule is acknowledged. God has not relinquished His sovereignty in the face of rebellion, demoniac and human, but has declared His purpose to establish it, Dan. 2:44; 7:14; 1 Cor. 15:24, 25. Meantime, seeking willing obedience, He gave His law to a nation and appointed kings to administer His "kingdom" over it, 1 Chron. 28:5. Israel, however, though declaring still a nominal allegiance shared in the common rebellion, Isa. 1:2-4, and, after they had rejected the Son of God, **John 1:11** (cf. Matt. 21:33-43), were "cast away," Rom. 11:15, 20, 25. Henceforth God calls upon men everywhere, without distinction of race or nationality, to submit voluntarily to His rule. Thus the "kingdom" is said to be "in mystery" now, Mark 4:11, that is, it does not come within the range of the natural powers of observation, Luke 17:20, but is spiritually discerned, **John 3:3** (cf. 1 Cor. 2:14). When, hereafter, God asserts His rule universally, then the "kingdom" will be in glory, that is, it will be manifest to all; cf. Matt. 25:31-34; Phil. 2:9-11; 2 Tim. 4:1, 18. Thus, speaking generally, references to the Kingdom fall into two classes, the first, in which it is viewed as present and involving suffering for those who enter it, 2 Thess. 1:5; the second, in which it is viewed as future and is associated with reward, Matt. 25:34, and glory, 13:43. See also Acts 14:22. Entrance into the Kingdom of God is by the new birth, Matt. 18:3; **John 3:5**, for nothing that a man may be by nature, or can attain to by any form of self-culture, avails in the spiritual realm. And as the new nature, received in the new birth, is made evident by obedience, it is further said that only such as do the will of God shall enter into His Kingdom, Matt. 7:21, where, however, the context shows that the reference is to the future, as in 2 Pet. 1:10, 11. Cf. also 1 Cor. 6:9, 10; Gal. 5:21; Eph. 5:5. The expression 'Kingdom of God' occurs four times in Matthew, 'Kingdom of the Heavens' usually taking its place. The latter (cf. Dan. 4:26) does not occur elsewhere in NT, but see 2 Tim. 4:18, "His heavenly Kingdom." ... This Kingdom is identical with the Kingdom of the Father (cf. Matt. 26:29 with Mark 14:25), and with the Kingdom of the Son (cf. Luke 22:30). Thus there is but one Kingdom, variously described: of the Son of Man, Matt. 13:41; of Jesus, Rev. 1:9; of Christ Jesus, 2 Tim. 4:1; "of Christ and God," Eph. 5:5; "of our Lord, and of His Christ," Rev. 11:15; "of our God, and the authority of His Christ," 12:10; "of the Son of His love," Col. 1:13. The Kingdom of Heaven is always the Kingdom of God, but the Kingdom of God is not limited to the Kingdom of Heaven, until in their final form, they become identical, e.g., Rev. 11:15, RV; **John 3:5**; Rev. 12:10."

> *"If Jesus Christ is only a teacher, then all he can do is to tantalize us, to erect a standard we cannot attain to; but when we are born again of the Spirit of God, we know that he did not come only to teach us, he came to make us what he teaches we should be."*
>
> OSWALD CHAMBERS

3:4 Nicodemus saith unto him, How can a man be born when he is old? can he enter the second time into his mother's womb, and be born?

Old *geron* (1088), denotes "an old man" (from the same root comes Eng., "gray"), **John 3:4**.

Second *deuteros* (1208), denotes "second in order" with or without the idea of time, e.g., Matt. 22:26, 39; 2 Cor. 1:15; Rev. 2:11; in Rev. 14:8, RV only ("a second angel"); it is used in the neuter, *deuteron*, adverbially, signifying a "second" time, e.g., **John 3:4**; **21:16**; Acts 7:13; Rev. 19:3, RV (KJV, "again"); Jude 5, "afterward" (RV, marg., "the second time"); used with *ek* ("of") idiomatically, the preposition signifying "for (the second time)," Mark 14:72; **John 9:24** and Acts 11:9, RV (KJV, "again"); Heb. 9:28; in 1 Cor. 12:28, KJV, "secondarily," RV, "secondly."

Womb *koilia* (2836), denotes "the womb," Matt. 19:12; Luke 1:15, 41, 42, 44; 2:21; 11:27; 23:29; **John 3:4**; Acts 3:2; 14:8; Gal. 1:15.

3:5 Jesus answered, Verily, verily, I say unto thee, Except a man be born of water and *of* the Spirit, he cannot enter into the kingdom of God.

"You must be born again. This is not a command, it is a foundation fact. The characteristic of the new birth is that I yield myself so completely to God that Christ is formed in me."

OSWALD CHAMBERS

Man *see John 3:3.*

Born *see John 3:3.*

Water *hudor* (5204), whence Eng. prefix, "hydro-," is used of the natural element, frequently in the Gospels; in the plural especially in Revelation; elsewhere, e.g., Heb. 9:19; Jas. 3:12 ... The word "water" is used symbolically in **John 3:5**, either (1) of the Word of God, as in 1 Pet. 1:23 (cf. the symbolic use in Eph. 5:26), or, in view of the preposition *ek*, "out of," (2) of the truth conveyed by baptism, this being the expression, not the medium, the symbol, not the cause, of the believer's identification with Christ in His death, burial and resurrection. So the New Birth is, in one sense, the setting aside of all that the believer was according to the flesh, for it is evident that there must be an entirely new beginning. Some regard the *kai*, "and," in **John 3:5**, as epexegetic, = "even," in which case the "water" would be emblematic of the Spirit, as in **John 7:38** (cf. **4:10**, **14**), but not in 1 John 5:8, where the Spirit and the "water" are distinguished. "The water of life," Rev. 21:6 and 22:1, 17, is emblematic of the maintenance of spiritual life in perpetuity. In Rev. 17:1 "the waters" are symbolic of nations, peoples, etc.

And *kai* (2532), a conjunction, is usually a mere connective, meaning "and"; it frequently, however, has an ascensive or climactic use, signifying "even," the thing that is added being out of the ordinary, and producing a climax. The determination of this meaning depends on the context. Examples are Matt. 5:46-47; Mark 1:27; Luke 6:33 (RV); 10:17; **John 12:42**; Gal. 2:13, 17, where "also" should be "even"; Eph. 5:12. Examples where the RV corrects the KJV "and" or "also," by substituting "even," are Luke 7:49; Acts 17:28; Heb. 11:11; in 1 John 4:3 the RV rightly omits "even." When followed by "if" or "though," *kai* often signifies "even," e.g., Matt. 26:35; **John 8:14**. So sometimes when preceded by "if," e.g., 1 Cor. 7:11, where "but and if" should be "but even if." The epexegetic or explanatory use of *kai* followed by a noun in apposition, and meaning "namely," or "even" is comparatively rare. Some think it has this sense in **John 3:5**, "water, even the Spirit," and Gal. 6:16, "even the Israel of God."

Kingdom *see John 3:3.*

3:6-7 That which is born of the flesh is flesh; and that which is born of the Spirit is spirit.
Marvel not that I said unto thee, Ye must be born again.

Must *dei* (1163), an impersonal verb, signifying "it is necessary" or "one must," "one ought," is found most frequently in the Gospels, Acts and Revelation, and is used (a) of a necessity lying in the nature of the case e.g., **John 3:30**; 2 Tim. 2:6; (b) of necessity brought about by circumstances, e.g., Matt. 26:35, RV, "must," KJV, "should"; **John 4:4**; Acts 27:21, "should"; 2 Cor. 11:30; in the case of Christ, by reason of the Father's will, e.g., Luke 2:49; 19:5; (c) of necessity as to what is required that something may be brought about, e.g., Luke 12:12, "ought"; **John 3:7**; Acts 9:6; 1 Cor. 11:19; Heb. 9:26; (d) of a necessity of law, duty, equity, e.g., Matt. 18:33, "shouldest"; 23:23, "ought"; Luke 15:32, "it was meet"; Acts 15:5, "it is needful" (RV); Rom. 1:27, RV, "was due," KJV, "was meet" (of a recompense due by the law of God); frequently requiring the rendering "ought," e.g., Rom. 8:26; 12:3; 1 Cor. 8:2; (e) of necessity arising from the determinate will and counsel of God, e.g., Matt. 17:10; 24:6; 26:54; 1 Cor. 15:53, especially regarding the salvation of men through the death, resurrection and ascension of Christ, e.g., **John 3:14**; Acts 3:21; 4:12.

Born *see John 3:3.*

Again *see John 3:3.*

3:8 The wind bloweth where it listeth, and thou hearest the sound thereof, but canst not tell whence it cometh, and whither it goeth: so is every one that is born of the Spirit.

Bloweth *pneo* (4154), signifies (a) "to blow," e.g., Matt. 7:25; **John 3:8**; in Acts 27:40 the present participle is used as a noun, lit., "to the blowing" (i.e., to the wind); (b) "to breathe."

Listeth *thelo* (2309), "to will, wish," is translated by the verb "to list" in Matt. 17:12; Mark 9:13; **John 3:8**.

Hearest *see* Heard at *John 1:40.*

Sound *phone* (5456), "a sound," is used of the voice (a) of God, Matt. 3:17; **John 5:37; 12:28, 30**; Acts 7:31; 10:13, 15; 11:7, 9; Heb. 3:7, 15; 4:7; 12:19, 26; 2 Pet. 1:17, 18; Rev. 18:4; 21:3; (b) of Christ, (1) in the days of His flesh, Matt. 12:19 (negatively); **John 3:29; 5:25; 10:3, 4, 16, 27; 11:43; 18:37**; (2) on the cross Matt. 27:46, and parallel passages; (3) from heaven, Acts 9:4, 7; 22:7, 9, 14; 26:14; Rev. 1:10, 12 (here, by metonymy, of the speaker), 15; 3:20; (4) at the resurrection "to life," **John 5:28**; 1 Thess. 4:16, where "the voice of the archangel" is, lit., "a voice of an archangel," and probably refers to the Lord's voice as being of an archangelic character; (5) at the resurrection to judgment, **John 5:28** [not the same event as (4)]; (c) of human beings on earth, e.g., Matt. 2:18; 3:3; Luke 1:42, in some texts, KJV, "voice", and frequently in the Synoptists; (d) of angels, Rev. 5:11, and frequently in Revelation; (e) of the redeemed in heaven, e.g., Rev. 6:10; 18:22; 19:1, 5; (f) of a pagan god, Acts 12:22; (g) of things, e.g., wind, **John 3:8**, RV, "voice" (KJV, "sound").

Canst *oida* (1492), "to know by perception," is the word in Pilate's remark "make it as sure as ye can" (marg. "sure, as ye know"), Matt. 27:65. The phrases "cannot tell," "canst not tell," etc., are in the RV rendered "know not," etc., Matt. 21:27; Mark 11:33; Luke 20:7; **John 3:8; 8:14; 16:18**; 2 Cor. 12:2-3.

Tell In the following, *oida*, "to know," is translated "tell" in the KJV (RV, "know"), Matt. 21:27; Mark 11:33; Luke 20:7; **John 3:8; 8:14; 16:18**; 2 Cor. 12:2.

Spirit *pneuma* (4151), primarily denotes "the wind" (akin to *pneo*, "to breathe, blow"); also "breath"; then, especially "the spirit," which, like the wind, is invisible, immaterial and powerful. The NT uses of the word may be analyzed approximately as follows:

"(a) the wind, **John 3:8** (where marg. is, perhaps, to be preferred), Heb. 1:7; cf. Amos 4:13, Sept.; (b) the breath, 2 Thess. 2:8; Rev. 11:11; 13:15; cf. Job 12:10, Sept. ... (q) the significance, as contrasted with the form, of words, or of a rite, **John 6:63**; Rom. 2:29; 7:6; 2 Cor. 3:6; (r) a vision, Rev. 1:10; 4:2; 17:3; 21:10."

3:9-10 Nicodemus answered and said unto him, How can these things be?

Jesus answered and said unto him, Art thou a master of Israel, and knowest not these things?

Master *see John 1:38.*

3:11 Verily, verily, I say unto thee, We speak that we do know, and testify that we have seen; and ye receive not our witness.

Testify *see John 2:25.*

Receive *lambano* (2983), denotes either "to take" or "to receive," (I) literally, (a) without an object, in contrast to asking, e.g., Matt. 7:8; Mark 11:24, RV, "have received" (the original has no object); (b) in contrast to giving, e.g., Matt. 10:8; Acts 20:35; (c) with objects, whether things, e.g., Mark 10:30; Luke 18:30, in the best mss.; **John 13:30**; Acts 9:19, RV, "took" (KJV, "received"); 1 Cor. 9:25, RV, "receive" (KJV, "obtain"); or persons, e.g., **John 6:21; 13:20; 16:14**, RV, "take"; 2 John 10; in Mark 14:65, RV, "received (Him with blows of their hands)"; this has been styled a vulgarism; (II) metaphorically, of the word of God, Matt. 13:20; Mark 4:16; the sayings of Christ, **John 12:48**; the witness of Christ, **John 3:11**; a hundredfold in this life, and eternal life in the world to come, Mark 10:30.

Witness *see John 1:7.*

3:12 If I have told you earthly things, and ye believe not, how shall ye believe, if I tell you *of* heavenly things?

Earthly *epigeios* (1919), "on earth" (*epi*, "on," *ge*, "the earth"), is rendered "earthly" in **John 3:12**; 2 Cor. 5:1; Phil. 3:19; Jas. 3:15; in Phil. 2:10, "on earth," RV; "terrestrial" in 1 Cor. 15:40 (twice).

3:13 And no man hath ascended up to heaven, but he that came down from heaven, *even* the Son of man which is in heaven.

Heaven *ouranos* (3772), probably akin to *ornumi*, "to lift, to heave," is used in the NT (a) of "the aerial heavens," e.g., Matt. 6:26; 8:20; Acts 10:12; 11:6 (RV, "heaven," in each place, KJV, "air"); Jas. 5:18; (b) "the sidereal," e.g., Matt. 24:29, 35; Mark 13:25, 31; Heb. 11:12, RV, "heaven," KJV, "sky"; Rev. 6:14; 20:11; they, (a) and (b), were created by the Son of God, Heb. 1:10, as also by God the Father, Rev. 10:6; (c) "the eternal dwelling place of God," Matt. 5:16; 12:50; Rev. 3:12; 11:13; 16:11; 20:9. From thence the Son of God descended to become incarnate, **John 3:13, 31; 6:38, 42**. In His ascension Christ "passed through the heavens," Heb. 4:14, RV; He "ascended far above all the heavens," Eph. 4:10, and was "made higher than the heavens," Heb. 7:26; He "sat down on the right hand of the throne of the Majesty in the heavens," Heb. 8:1; He is "on the right hand of God," having gone into heaven, 1 Pet. 3:22. Since His ascension it is the scene of His present life and activity, e.g., Rom. 8:34; Heb. 9:24. From thence the Holy Spirit descended at Pentecost, 1 Pet. 1:12. It is the abode of the angels, e.g., Matt. 18:10; 22:30; cf. Rev. 3:5. Thither Paul was "caught up," whether in the body or out of the body, he knew not, 2 Cor. 12:2. It is to be the eternal dwelling place of the saints in resurrection glory, 2 Cor. 5:1. From thence Christ will descend to the air to receive His saints at the Rapture, 1 Thess. 4:16; Phil. 3:20, 21, and will subsequently come with His saints and with His holy angels at His second advent, Matt. 24:30; 2 Thess. 1:7. In the present life "heaven" is the region of the spiritual citizenship of believers, Phil. 3:20. The present "heavens," with the earth, are to pass away, 2 Pet. 3:10, "being on fire," v. 12 (see v. 7); Rev. 20:11, and new "heavens" and earth are to be created, 2 Pet. 3:13; Rev. 21:1, with Isa. 65:17, e.g.

Son *see John 1:18.*

3:14 And as Moses lifted up the serpent in the wilderness, even so must the Son of man be lifted up:

Lifted up *hupsoo* (5312), "to lift up" (akin to *hupsos*, "height"), is used (a) literally of the "lifting" up of Christ in His crucifixion, **John 3:14; 8:28; 12:32, 34**; illustratively, of the serpent of brass, **John 3:14**; (b) figuratively, of spiritual privileges bestowed on a city, Matt. 11:23; Luke 10:15; of "raising" to dignity and happiness, Luke 1:52; Acts 13:17; of haughty self-exaltation, and, contrastingly, of being "raised" to honor, as a result of self-humbling, Matt. 23:12; Luke 14:11; 18:14; of spiritual "uplifting" and revival, Jas. 4:10; 1 Pet. 5:6; of bringing into the blessings of salvation through the gospel, 2 Cor. 11:7; (c) with a combination of the literal and metaphorical, of the "exaltation" of Christ by God the Father, Acts 2:33; 5:31.

Serpent *ophis* (3789), the characteristics of the "serpent" as alluded to in Scripture are mostly evil (though Matt. 10:16 refers to its caution in avoiding danger); its treachery, Gen. 49:17; 2 Cor. 11:3; its venom, Ps. 58:4; 1 Cor. 10:9; Rev. 9:19; its skulking, Job 26:13; its murderous proclivities, e.g., Ps. 58:4; Prov. 23:32; Eccl. 10:8, 11; Amos 5:19; Mark 16:18; Luke 10:19; the Lord used the word metaphorically of the scribes and Pharisees, Matt. 23:33 (cf. *echidna*, "viper," in Matt. 3:7; 12:34). The general aspects of its evil character are intimated in the Lord's rhetorical question in Matt. 7:10 and Luke 11:11. Its characteristics are concentrated in the archadversary of God and man, the Devil, metaphorically described as the serpent, 2 Cor. 11:3; Rev. 12:9, 14, 15; 20:2. The brazen "serpent" lifted up by Moses was symbolical of the means of salvation provided by God, in Christ and His vicarious death under the divine judgment upon sin, **John 3:14**. While the living "serpent" symbolizes sin in its origin, hatefulness, and deadly effect, the brazen "serpent" symbolized the bearing away of the curse and the judgment of sin; the metal was itself figurative of the righteousness of God's judgment.

Must *see John 3:7.*

Son *see John 1:18.*

3:15 That whosoever believeth in him should not perish, but have eternal life.

Perish *apollumi* (622), a strengthened form of *ollumi*, signifies "to destroy utterly"; in middle voice, "to perish." The idea is not extinction but ruin, loss, not of being, but of wellbeing. This is clear from its use, as, e.g., of the marring of wine skins, Luke 5:37; of lost sheep, i.e., lost to the shepherd, metaphorical of spiritual destitution, Luke 15:4, 6, etc.; the lost son, 15:24; of the perishing of food, **John 6:27**; of gold, 1 Pet. 1:7. So of persons, Matt. 2:13, "destroy"; 8:25, "perish"; 22:7; 27:20; of the loss of well-being in the case of the unsaved hereafter, Matt. 10:28; Luke 13:3, 5; **John 3:16** (v. **15** in some mss.); **10:28; 17:12**; Rom. 2:12; 1 Cor. 15:18; 2 Cor. 2:15, "are perishing"; 4:3; 2 Thess. 2:10; Jas. 4:12; 2 Pet. 3:9.

Life *zoe* (2222), (Eng., "zoo," "zoology") is used in the NT "of life as a principle, life in the absolute sense, life as God has it, that which the Father has in Himself, and which He gave to the Incarnate Son to have in Himself, **John 5:26**, and which the Son manifested in the world, 1 John 1:2. From this life man has become alienated in consequence of the Fall, Eph. 4:18, and of this life men become partakers through faith in the Lord Jesus Christ, **John 3:15**, who becomes its Author to all such as trust in Him, Acts 3:15, and who is therefore said to be 'the life' of the believer, Col. 3:4, for the life that He gives He maintains, **John 6:35, 63**. Eternal life is the present actual possession of the believer because of his relationship with Christ, **John 5:24**; 1 John 3:14, and that it will one day extend its domain to the sphere of the body is assured by the Resurrection of Christ, 2 Cor. 5:4; 2 Tim. 1:10. This life is not merely a principle of power and mobility, however, for it has moral associations which are inseparable from it, as of holiness and righteousness. Death and sin, life and holiness, are frequently contrasted in the Scriptures.

Death came through sin, Rom. 5:12, which is rebellion against God. Sin thus involved the forfeiting of the "life." "The life of the flesh is in the blood," Lev. 17:11. Therefore the impartation of "life" to the sinner must be by a death caused by the shedding of that element which is the life of the flesh. "It is the blood that maketh atonement by reason of the life" (*id.*, RV). The separation from God caused by the forfeiting of the "life" could be removed only by a sacrifice in which the victim and the offerer became identified. This which was appointed in the typical offerings in Israel received its full accomplishment in the voluntary sacrifice of Christ. The shedding of the blood in the language of Scripture involves the taking or the giving of the "life." Since Christ had no sins of his own to die for, His death was voluntary and vicarious, **John 10:15** with Isa. 53:5, 10, 12; 2 Cor. 5:21. In His sacrifice He endured the divine judgment due to man's sin. By this means the believer becomes identified with Him in His deathless "life," through His resurrection, and enjoys conscious and eternal fellowship with God.

3:16 For God so loved the world, that he gave his only begotten Son, that whosoever believeth in him should not perish, but have everlasting life.

Loved *agapao* (25), and the corresponding noun *agape* present "the characteristic word of Christianity, and since the Spirit of revelation has used it to express ideas previously unknown, inquiry into its use, whether in Greek literature or in the Septuagint, throws but little light upon its distinctive meaning in the NT. Cf, however, Lev. 19:18; Deut. 6:5.

"*Agape* and *agapao* are used in the NT (a) to describe the attitude of God toward His Son, **John 17:26**; the human race, generally, **John 3:16**; Rom. 5:8, and to such as believe on the Lord Jesus Christ particularly **John 14:21**; (b) to convey His will to His children concerning their attitude one toward another, **John 13:34**, and toward all men, 1 Thess. 3:12; 1 Cor. 16:14; 2 Pet. 1:7; (c) to express the essential nature of God, 1 John 4:8. Love can be known only from the actions it prompts. God's love is seen in the gift of His Son, 1 John 4:9, 10. But obviously this is not the love of complacency, or affection, that is, it was not drawn out by any excellency in its objects, Rom. 5:8. It was an exercise of the divine will in deliberate choice, made without assignable cause save that which lies in the nature of God Himself, Cf. Deut. 7:7, 8. Love had its perfect expression among men in the Lord Jesus Christ, 2 Cor. 5:14; Eph. 2:4; 3:19; 5:2; Christian love is the fruit of His Spirit in the Christian, Gal. 5:22. Christian love has God for its primary object, and expresses itself first of all in implicit obedience to His commandments, **John 14:15, 21, 23; 15:10**; 1 John 2:5; 5:3; 2 John 6. Selfwill, that is, self-pleasing, is the negation of love to God."

World *see John 1:9.*

Only begotten *see John 1:14.*

Son *see John 1:18.*

Perish *apollumi* (622), signifies (I) In the active voice, (a) "to destroy, destroy utterly, kill," e.g., Matt. 10:28; Mark 1:24; 9:22; (b) "to lose utterly," e.g., Matt. 10:42, of "losing" a reward; Luke 15:4 (1st part), of "losing" a sheep; Luke 9:25, of "losing" oneself (of the "loss" of well-being hereafter); metaphorically, **John 6:39**, of failing to save; **18:9**, of Christ's not "losing" His own; (II) in the middle voice (a) "to perish," of things, e.g., **John 6:12** "(that nothing) be lost"; of persons, e.g., Matt. 8:25, "we perish;" of the "loss" of eternal life, usually (always in the RV) translated to perish, **John 3:16; 17:12**, KJV, "is lost," RV, "perished"; 2 Cor. 4:3, "are perishing," KJV, "are lost"; (b) "to be lost," e.g., Luke 15:4 (2nd part), "which is lost"; metaphorically, from the relation between shepherd and flock, of spiritual destitution and alienation from God, Matt. 10:6, "(the) lost (sheep)" of the house of Israel; Luke 19:10 (the perfect tense translated "lost" is here intransitive). *See also John 3:15.*

Eternal *aionios* (166), "describes duration, either undefined but not endless, as in Rom. 16:25; 2 Tim. 1:9; Titus 1:2; or undefined because endless as in Rom. 16:26, and the other sixty-six places in the NT. "The predominant meaning of *aionios*, that in which it is used everywhere in the NT, save the places noted above, may be seen in 2 Cor. 4:18, where it is set in contrast with *proskairos*, lit., 'for a season,' and in Philem. 15, where only in the NT it is used without a noun. Moreover it is used of persons and things which are in their nature endless, as, e.g., of God, Rom. 16:26; of His power, 1 Tim. 6:16, and of His glory, 1 Pet. 5:10; of the Holy Spirit, Heb. 9:14; of the redemption effected by Christ, Heb. 9:12, and of the consequent salvation of men, 5:9, as well as of His future rule, 2 Pet. 1:11, which is elsewhere declared to be without end, Luke 1:33; of the life received by those who believe in Christ, **John 3:16**, concerning whom He said, 'they shall never perish,' **10:28**, and of the resurrection body, 2 Cor. 5:1, elsewhere said to be 'immortal,' 1 Cor. 15:53, in which that life will be finally realized, Matt. 25:46; Titus 1:2. *Aionios* is also used of the sin that 'hath never forgiveness,' Mark 3:29, and of the judgment of God, from which there is no appeal, Heb. 6:2, and of the fire, which is one of its instruments, Matt. 18:8; 25:41; Jude 7, and which is elsewhere said to be 'unquenchable,' Mark 9:43. The use of *aionios* here shows that the punishment referred to in 2 Thess. 1:9, is not temporary, but final, and, accordingly, the phraseology shows that its purpose is not remedial but retributive."

3:17 For God sent not his Son into the world to condemn the world; but that the world through him might be saved.

Sent *see John 1:6.*

World *see John 1:9.*

Condemn *krino* (2919), primarily denotes "to separate, select, choose"; hence, "to determine," and so "to judge, pronounce judgment." "The uses of this verb in the NT may be analyzed as follows: (a) to assume the office of a judge, Matt. 7:1; **John 3:17**; (b) to undergo process of trial, **John 3:18**; **16:11**; **18:31**; Jas. 2:12; (c) to give sentence, Acts 15:19; 16:4; 21:25; (d) to condemn, **John 12:48**; Acts 13:27; Rom. 2:27; (e) to execute judgment upon, 2 Thess. 2:12; Acts 7:7; (f) to be involved in a lawsuit, whether as plaintiff, Matt. 5:40; 1 Cor. 6:1; or as defendant, Acts 23:6; (g) to administer affairs, to govern, Matt. 19:28; cf. Judg. 3:10; (h) to form an opinion, Luke 7:43; **John 7:24**; Acts 4:19; Rom. 14:5; (i) to make a resolve, Acts 3:13; 20:16; 1 Cor. 2:2."

3:18 He that believeth on him is not condemned: but he that believeth not is condemned already, because he hath not believed in the name of the only begotten Son of God.

Condemned *see* Condemn at *John 3:17.*

Name *see John 1:12.*

Only begotten *see John 1:14.*

3:19 And this is the condemnation, that light is come into the world, and men loved darkness rather than light, because their deeds were evil.

Condemnation *krisis* (2920), (a) denotes "the process of investigation, the act of distinguishing and separating" (as distinct from *krima*, above); hence "a judging, a passing of judgment upon a person or thing"; it has a variety of meanings, such as judicial authority, **John 5:22**, **27**; justice, Acts 8:33; Jas. 2:13; a tribunal, Matt. 5:21-22; a trial, **John 5:24**; 2 Pet. 2:4; a judgment, 2 Pet. 2:11; Jude 9; by metonymy, the standard of judgment, just dealing, Matt. 12:18, 20; 23:23; Luke 11:42; divine judgment executed, 2 Thess. 1:5; Rev. 16:7; (b) sometimes it has the meaning "condemnation," and is virtually equivalent to *krima* (a); see Matt. 23:33; **John 3:19**; Jas. 5:12, *hupo krisin*, "under judgment."

Light *see John 1:4.*

World *see John 1:9.*

And *kai*, in some passages *kai* has the meaning "and yet," e.g., Matt. 3:14, "and yet comest Thou to me?"; 6:26, "and yet (RV 'and,' KJV, 'yet') your Heavenly Father feedeth them"; Luke 18:7, "and yet He is longsuffering"; **John 3:19**, "and yet men loved the darkness"; **4:20**, "and yet we say"; **6:49**, "and yet they died"; 1 Cor. 5:2, "and yet ye are puffed up"; 1 John 2:9, "and yet hateth his brother." The same is probably the case in **John 7:30**, "and yet no man laid hands on Him", some rule this and similar cases out because of the negative in the sentence following the *kai*, but that seems hardly tenable.

Darkness *skotos* (4655), a neuter noun frequent in the Sept., is used (a) of "physical darkness," Matt. 27:45; 2 Cor. 4:6, (b) of "intellectual darkness," Rom. 2:19; (c) of "blindness," Acts 13:11; (d) by metonymy, of the "place of punishment," e.g., Matt. 8:12; 2 Pet. 2:17; Jude 13; (e) metaphorically, of "moral and spiritual darkness," e.g., Matt. 6:23; Luke 1:79; 11:35; **John 3:19**; Acts 26:18; 2 Cor. 6:14; Eph. 6:12; Col. 1:13; 1 Thess. 5:4-5; 1 Pet. 2:9; 1 John 1:6; (f) by metonymy, of "those who are in moral or spiritual darkness," Eph. 5:8; (g) of "evil works," Rom. 13:12; Eph. 5:11, (h) of the "evil powers that dominate the world," Luke 22:53; (i) "of secrecy." While *skotos* is used more than twice as many times as *skotia* in the NT, the apostle John uses *skotos* only once, 1 John 1:6, but *skotia* 15 times out of the 18.

"With the exception of the significance of secrecy, darkness is always used in a bad sense. Moreover the different forms of darkness are so closely allied, being either cause and effect, or else concurrent effects of the same cause, that they cannot always be distinguished; 1 John 1:5; 2:8, e.g., are passages in which both spiritual and moral darkness are intended."

Rather *mallon* (3123), the comparative degree of *mala*, "very, very much," is frequently translated "rather," e.g., Matt. 10:6, 28; 1 Cor. 14:1, 5; sometimes followed by "than," with a connecting particle, e.g., Matt. 18:13 ("more than"); or without, e.g., **John 3:19**; Acts 4:19, RV (KJV, "more"); in 1 Cor. 9:12, KJV, "rather" (RV, "yet more"); 12:22, RV, "rather" (KJV, "more"); 2 Cor. 3:9 (ditto); Philem. 16 (ditto); in 2 Pet. 1:10, KJV, "the rather" (RV, "the more").

Evil *poneros* (4190), akin to *ponos*, "labor, toil," denotes "evil that causes labor, pain, sorrow, malignant evil"; it is used (a) with the meaning bad, worthless, in the physical sense, Matt. 7:17-18; in the moral or ethical sense, "evil," wicked; of persons, e.g., Matt. 7:11; Luke 6:45; Acts 17:5; 2 Thess. 3:2; 2 Tim. 3:13; of "evil" spirits, e.g., Matt. 12:45; Luke 7:21; Acts 19:12-13, 15-16; of a generation, Matt. 12:39, 45; 16:4; Luke 11:29; of things, e.g., Matt. 5:11; 6:23; 20:15; Mark 7:22; Luke 11:34; **John 3:19**; **7:7**; Acts 18:14; Gal. 1:4; Col. 1:21; 1 Tim. 6:4; 2 Tim. 4:18; Heb. 3:12; 10:22; Jas. 2:4; 4:16; 1 John 3:12; 2 John 11; 3 John 10; (b) with the meaning toilsome, painful, Eph. 5:16; 6:13; Rev. 16:2. Cf. *poneria*, "iniquity, wickedness."

3:20 For every one that doeth evil hateth the light, neither cometh to the light, lest his deeds should be reproved.

Doeth *prasso* (4238), signifies "to practice," though this is not always to be pressed. The apostle John, in his epistles, uses the continuous tenses of *poieo*, to indicate a practice, the habit of doing something, e.g., 1 John 3:4 (the KJV, "committeth" and "commit" in 1 John 3:8 and 9, e.g., is wrong; "doeth," RV, in the sense of practicing, is the meaning). He uses *prasso* twice in the Gospel, **3:20** and **5:29**. The apostle Paul uses *prasso* in the sense of practicing, and the RV so renders the word in Rom. 1:32; 2:2, instead of KJV, "commit," though, strangely enough, the RV translates it "committed," instead of "practiced," in 2 Cor. 12:21. Generally speaking, in Paul's epistles *poieo* denotes "an action complete in itself," while *prasso* denotes "a habit." The difference is seen in Rom. 1:32, RV. Again, *poieo* stresses the accomplishment, e.g., "perform," in Rom. 4:21; *prasso* stresses the process leading to the accomplishment, e.g., "doer," in 2:25. In Rom. 2:3 he who does, *poieo*, the things mentioned, is warned against judging those who practice them, *prasso*. The distinction in **John 3:20-21** is noticeable: "Every one that doeth (*prasso*, practiceth) ill ... he that doeth (*poieo*) the truth." While we cannot draw the regular distinction, that *prasso* speaks of doing evil things, and *poieo* of doing good things, yet very often "where the words assume an ethical tinge, there is a tendency to use the verbs with this distinction" (Trench, *Syn.*, Sec.xcvi).

Evil *phaulos* (5337), primarily denotes "slight, trivial, blown about by every wind"; then, "mean, common, bad," in the sense of being worthless, paltry or contemptible, belonging to a low order of things; in **John 5:29**, those who have practiced "evil" things, RV, "ill" (*phaula*), are set in contrast to those who have done good things (*agatha*); the same contrast is presented in Rom. 9:11 and 2 Cor. 5:10, in each of which the most authentic mss. have *phaulos* for *kakos*; he who practices "evil" things (RV, "ill") hates the light, **John 3:20**; jealousy and strife are accompanied by "every vile deed," Jas. 3:16. It is used as a noun in Titus 2:8.

Hateth *miseo* (3404), "to hate," is used especially (a) of malicious and unjustifiable feelings towards others, whether towards the innocent or by mutual animosity, e.g., Matt. 10:22; 24:10; Luke 6:22, 27; 19:14; **John 3:20**, of "hating" the light (metaphorically); **7:7**; **15:18, 19, 23-25**; Titus 3:3; 1 John 2:9, 11; 3:13, 15; 4:20; Rev. 18:2, where "hateful" translates the perfect participle passive voice of the verb, lit., "hated," or "having been hated"; (b) of a right feeling of aversion from what is evil; said of wrongdoing, Rom. 7:15; iniquity, Heb. 1:9; "the garment (figurative) spotted by the flesh," Jude 23; "the works of the Nicolaitans," Rev. 2:6 (and v. 15, in some mss.; see the KJV); (c) of relative preference for one thing over another, by way of expressing either aversion from, or disregard for, the claims of one person or thing relatively to those of another, Matt. 6:24, and Luke 16:13, as to the impossibility of serving two masters; Luke 14:26, as to the claims of parents relatively to those of Christ; **John 12:25**, of disregard for one's life relatively to the claims of Christ; Eph. 5:29, negatively, of one's flesh, i.e. of one's own, and therefore a man's wife as one with him.

Deeds *ergon* (2041), denotes "a work" (Eng., "work" is etymologically akin), "deed, act." When used in the sense of a "deed or act," the idea of "working" is stressed, e.g., Rom. 15:18; it frequently occurs in an ethical sense of human actions, good or bad, e.g., Matt. 23:3; 26:10; **John 3:20-21**; Rom. 2:7, 15; 1 Thess. 1:3; 2 Thess. 1:11, etc.; sometimes in a less concrete sense, e.g., Titus 1:16; Jas. 1:25 (RV, "that worketh," lit., "of work").

Reproved *elencho* (1651), signifies (a) "to convict, confute, refute," usually with the suggestion of putting the convicted person to shame; see Matt. 18:15, where more than telling the offender his fault is in view; it is used of "convicting" of sin, **John 8:46**; **16:8**; gainsayers in regard to the faith, Titus 1:9; transgressors of the Law, Jas. 2:9; some texts have the verb in **John 8:9**; (b) "to reprove," 1 Cor. 14:24, RV (for KJV, "convince"), for the unbeliever is there viewed as being reproved for, or "convicted" of, his sinful state; so in Luke 3:19; it is used of reproving works, **John 3:20**; Eph. 5:11, 13; 1 Tim. 5:20; 2 Tim. 4:2; Titus 1:13; 2:15; all these speak of reproof by word of mouth. In Heb. 12:5 and Rev. 3:19, the word is used of reproving by action.

3:21 But he that doeth truth cometh to the light, that his deeds may be made manifest, that they are wrought in God.

Manifest *phaneroo* (5319), signifies, in the active voice, "to manifest"; in the passive voice, "to be manifested"; so, regularly, in the RV, instead of "to appear." See 2 Cor. 7:12; Col. 3:4; Heb. 9:26; 1 Pet. 5:4; 1 John 2:28; 3:2; Rev. 3:18. To be manifested, in the Scriptural sense of the word, is more than to "appear." A person may "appear" in a false guise or without a disclosure of what he truly is; to be manifested is to be revealed in one's true character; this is especially the meaning of *phaneroo*, see, e.g., **John 3:21**; 1 Cor. 4:5; 2 Cor. 5:10-11; Eph. 5:13.

3:22 After these things came Jesus and his disciples into the land of Judaea; and there he tarried with them, and baptized.

Land *ge* (1093), denotes (a) "earth as arable land," e.g., Matt. 13:5, 8, 23; in 1 Cor. 15:47 it is said of the "earthly" material of which "the first man" was made, suggestive of frailty; (b) "the earth as a whole, the world," in contrast, whether to the heavens, e.g., Matt. 5:18, 35, or to heaven, the abode of God, e.g., Matt. 6:19, where the context suggests the "earth" as a place characterized by mutability and weakness; in Col. 3:2 the same contrast is presented by the word "above"; in **John 3:31** (RV, "of the earth," for KJV, "earthly") it describes one whose origin and nature are "earthly" and whose speech is characterized thereby, in contrast with Christ as the One from heaven; in Col. 3:5 the physical members are said to be "upon the earth," as a sphere where, as potential instruments of moral evils, they are, by metonymy, spoken of as the evils themselves; (c) "the inhabited earth," e.g., Luke 21:35; Acts 1:8; 8:33; 10:12; 11:6; 17:26; 22:22; Heb. 11:13; Rev. 13:8. In the following the phrase "on the earth" signifies "among men," Luke 12:49; 18:8; **John 17:4**, (d) "a country, territory," e.g. Luke 4:25; **John 3:22**; (e) "the ground," e.g., Matt. 10:29; Mark 4:26, RV, "(upon the) earth," for KJV, "(into the) ground"; (f) "land," e.g., Mark 4:1; **John 21:8-9**, **11**. Cf. Eng. words beginning with *ge–*, e.g., "geodetic," "geodesy," "geology," "geometry," "geography."

Tarried *diatribo* (1304), lit., "to wear through by rubbing, to wear away" (*dia*, "through," *tribo*, "to rub"), when used of time, "to spend or pass time, to stay," is found twice in John's Gospel, **3:22** and **11:54**, RV, "tarried," instead of "continued"; elsewhere only in the Acts, eight times, 12:19; 14:3, 28; 15:35; 16:12; 20:6; 25:6, 14.

3:23 And John also was baptizing in Aenon near to Salim, because there was much water there: and they came, and were baptized.

Near *engus* (1451), "near, nigh," is used (a) of place, e.g., Luke 19:11, "nigh"; **John 3:23**; **11:54**, "near"; **6:19**, **23**, "nigh"; metaphorically in Rom. 10:8; Eph. 2:13, 17, "nigh"; (b) of time, e.g., Matt. 24:32-33, "nigh"; so Luke 21:30-31; as a preposition, Heb. 6:8, "nigh unto (a curse)," and 8:13, "nigh unto (vanishing away)."

3:24-25 For John was not yet cast into prison.

Then there arose a question between *some* of John's disciples and the Jews about purifying.

Arose *ginomai* (1096), "to become, to take place," is sometimes suitably translated "arise"; e.g., Matt. 8:24; Mark 4:37, "there arose a great tempest." So of the arising of persecution, Matt. 13:21; Mark 4:17; this might be translated "taketh place"; of a tumult, Matt. 27:24, RV, "arising," for KJV, "made"; of a flood, Luke 6:48; a famine, 15:14; a questioning, **John 3:25**; a murmuring, Acts 6:1; a tribulation, 11:19 (RV); a stir in the city, 19:23; a dissension, 23:7; a great clamor, v. 9.

Question *zetesis* (2214), denotes, firstly, "a seeking" (*zeteo*, "to seek"), then, "a debate, dispute, questioning," Acts 15:2, 7 (some texts have *suzetesis*, "reasoning," in both verses), RV, "questioning," for KJV, "disputation" and "disputing"; for **John 3:25**; Acts 25:20; 1 Tim. 1:4; 6:4; 2 Tim. 2:23; Titus 3:9.

Between The phrase *ek meta* (*ek*, "out of," *meta*, "with") is translated "between ... and" in the KJV of **John 3:25** (RV, "on the part of ... with").

Jews *see John 2:6*.

Purifying *see John 2:6*.

3:26 And they came unto John, and said unto him, Rabbi, he that was with thee beyond Jordan, to whom thou barest witness, behold, the same baptizeth, and all *men* come to him.

Rabbi *see John 1:38*.

Beyond *see John 1:28*.

Witness *see John 1:7*.

Same *see John 3:2*.

3:27-28 John answered and said, A man can receive nothing, except it be given him from heaven.

Ye yourselves bear me witness, that I said, I am not the Christ, but that I am sent before him.

Ye yourselves The addition of *autoi*, "yourselves," to the pronoun marks especial emphasis, e.g., Mark 6:31; **John 3:28**; 1 Cor. 11:13; 1 Thess. 4:9. Sometimes *autoi* is used without the pronoun, e.g., Luke 11:46, 52; Acts 2:22; 20:34; 1 Thess. 2:1; 3:3; 5:2; 2 Thess. 3:7; Heb. 13:3.

Witness *see John 1:7*.

Sent *see John 1:6*.

3:29 He that hath the bride is the bridegroom: but the friend of the bridegroom, which standeth and heareth him, rejoiceth greatly because of the bridegroom's voice: this my joy therefore is fulfilled.

Bride *numphe* (3565), (Eng. "nymph") "a bride, or young wife," **John 3:29**; Rev. 18:23; 21:2, 9; 22:17, is probably connected with the Latin *nubo*, "to veil"; the "bride" was often adorned with embroidery and jewels (see Rev. 21:2), and was led veiled from her home to the "bridegroom." Hence the secondary meaning of "daughter-in-law," Matt. 10:35; Luke 12:53. For the relationship between Christ and a local church, under this figure, see 2 Cor. 11:2; regarding the whole church, Eph. 5:23-32; Rev. 22:17.

Bridegroom *numphios* (3566), "a bridegroom," occurs fourteen times in the Gospels, and in Rev. 18:23. "The friend of the bridegroom," **John 3:29**, is distinct from "the sons of the bridechamber" who were numerous. When John the Baptist speaks of "the friend of the Bridegroom," he uses language according to the customs of the Jews.

Greatly *chara* (5479), "joy," is used in the dative case adverbially with the verb *chairo*, "to rejoice," in **John 3:29**, "rejoiceth greatly," lit., "rejoiceth with joy."

Voice *see* **Sound** at *John 3:8*.

Fulfilled *pleroo* (4137), signifies (1) "to fill"; (2) "to fulfill, complete," (a) of time, e.g., Mark 1:15; Luke 21:24; **John 7:8** (KJV, "full come"); Acts 7:23, RV, "he was wellnigh forty years old" (KJV, "was full," etc.), lit., "the time of forty years was fulfilled to him"; v. 30, KJV, "were expired"; 9:23; 24:27 (KJV, "after two years"; RV, "when two years were fulfilled"); (b) of number, Rev. 6:11; (c) of good pleasure, 2 Thess. 1:11; (d) of joy, Phil. 2:2; in the passive voice, "to be fulfilled," **John 3:29** and **17:13**; in the following the verb is rendered "fulfilled" in the RV, for the KJV, "full," **John 15:11**; **16:24**; 1 John 1:4; 2 John 12; (e) of obedience, 2 Cor. 10:6; (f) of works, Rev. 3:2; (g) of the future Passover, Luke 22:16; (h) of sayings, prophecies, etc., e.g., Matt. 1:22 (twelve times in Matt., two in Mark, four in Luke, eight in John, two in Acts); Jas. 2:23; in Col. 1:25 the word signifies to preach "fully," to complete the ministry of the Gospel appointed.

3:30 He must increase, but I *must* decrease.

Must *see John 3:7*.

Increase *auxano* (837), "to grow or increase," of the growth of that which lives, naturally or spiritually, is used (a) transitively, signifying to make to increase, said of giving the increase, 1 Cor. 3:6, 7; 2 Cor. 9:10, the effect of the work of God, according to the analogy of His operations in nature; "to grow, become greater," e.g., of plants and fruit, Matt. 6:28; used in the passive voice in 13:32 and Mark 4:8, "increase"; in the active in Luke 12:27; 13:19; of the body, Luke 1:80; 2:40; of Christ, **John 3:30**, "increase"; of the work of the gospel of God, Acts 6:7, "increased"; 12:24; 19:20; of people, Acts 7:17; of faith, 2 Cor. 10:15 (passive voice), RV, "growth" (KJV, "is increased"); of believers individually, Eph. 4:15; Col. 1:6, RV, 10 (passive voice), "increasing"; 1 Pet. 2:2; 2 Pet. 3:18; of the church, Col. 2:19; of churches, Eph. 2:21.

Decrease *elattoo* (1642), signifies "to make less or inferior, in quality, position or dignity"; "madest ... lower" and "hast made ... lower," in Heb. 2:7, 9. In **John 3:30**, it is used in the middle voice, in John the Baptist's "I must decrease," indicating the special interest he had in his own "decrease," i.e., in authority and popularity.

> *"What other people think of me is becoming less and less important; what they think of Jesus because of me is critical."*
>
> SIR CLIFF RICHARD

3:31 He that cometh from above is above all: he that is of the earth is earthly, and speaketh of the earth: he that cometh from heaven is above all.

Above *anothen* (509), "from above," is used of place, (a) with the meaning "from the top," Matt. 27:51; Mark 15:38, of the temple veil; in **John 19:23**, of the garment of Christ, lit., "from the upper parts" (plural); (b) of things which come from heaven, or from God in Heaven, **John 3:31**; **19:11**; Jas. 1:17; 3:15, 17. It is also used in the sense of "again."

Earth *see* Land at *John 3:22*.

Heaven *see John 3:13*.

3:32 And what he hath seen and heard, that he testifieth; and no man receiveth his testimony.

Testifieth *see* Testify at *John 2:25*.

Testimony *marturia* (3141), "witness, evidence, testimony," is almost always rendered "witness" in the RV (for KJV, "testimony" in **John 3:32**, **33**; **5:34**; **8:17**; **21:24**, and always for KJV, "record," e.g., 1 John 5:10, 11), except in Acts 22:18 and in Revelation, where both, with one exception, have "testimony," 1:2, 9; 6:9; 11:7; 12:11, 17; 19:10 (twice); 20:4 (KJV, "witness"). In 19:10, "the testimony of Jesus" is objective, the "testimony" or witness given to Him (cf. 1:2, 9; as to those who will bear it, see Rev. 12:17, RV). The statement "the testimony of Jesus is the spirit of prophecy," is to be understood in the light, e.g., of the "testimony" concerning Christ and Israel in the Psalms, which will be used by the godly Jewish remnant in the coming time of "Jacob's Trouble." All such "testimony" centers in and points to Christ.

3:33 He that hath received his testimony hath set to his seal that God is true.

Testimony *see John 3:32*.

Seal *sphragizo* (4972), "to seal," is used to indicate (a) security and permanency (attempted but impossible), Matt. 27:66; on the contrary, of the doom of Satan, fixed and certain, Rev. 20:3, RV, "sealed it over"; (b) in Rom. 15:28, "when ... I have sealed to them this fruit," the formal ratification of the ministry of the churches of the Gentiles in Greece and Galatia to needy saints in Judea, by Paul's faithful delivery of the gifts to them; this material help was the fruit of his spiritual ministry to the Gentiles, who on their part were bringing forth the fruit of their having shared with them in spiritual things; the metaphor stresses the sacred formalities of the transaction; (c) secrecy and security and the postponement of disclosure, Rev. 10:4; in a negative command 22:10; (d) ownership and security, together with destination, Rev. 7:3, 4, 5; the same three indications are conveyed in Eph. 1:13, in the metaphor of the "sealing" of believers by the gift of the Holy Spirit, upon believing (i.e., at the time of their regeneration, not after a lapse of time in their spiritual life, "having also believed" – not as KJV, "after that ye believed" – ; the aorist participle marks the definiteness and completeness of the act of faith); the idea of destination is stressed by the phrase "the Holy Spirit of promise" (see also v. 14); so 4:30, "ye were sealed unto the day of redemption"; so in 2 Cor. 1:22, where the middle voice intimates the special interest of the Sealer in His act; (e) authentication by the believer (by receiving the witness of the Son) of the fact that "God is true," **John 3:33**; authentication by God in sealing the Son as the Giver of eternal life (with perhaps a figurative allusion to the impress of a mark upon loaves), **6:27**.

True *alethes* (227), primarily, "unconcealed, manifest" (*a*, negative, *letho*, "to forget," = *lanthano*, "to escape notice"), hence, actual, "true to fact," is used (a) of persons, "truthful," Matt. 22:16; Mark 12:14; **John 3:33**; **7:18**; **8:26**; Rom. 3:4; 2 Cor. 6:8; (b) of things, "true," conforming to reality, **John 4:18**, "truly," lit., "true"; **5:31**, **32**; in the best texts, **6:55** (twice), "indeed"; **8:13**, **14** (v. **16** in some texts), 17; 10:41; 19:35; 21:24; Acts 12:9; Phil. 4:8; Titus 1:13; 1 Pet. 5:12; 2 Pet. 2:22; 1 John 2:8, 27; 3 John 12. *See also* ***John 1:9***.

3:34 For he whom God hath sent speaketh the words of God: for God giveth not the Spirit by measure *unto him*.

Words *rhema* (4487), denotes "that which is spoken, what is uttered in speech or writing"; in the singular, "a word," e.g., Matt. 12:36; 27:14; 2 Cor. 12:4; 13:1; Heb. 12:19; in the plural, speech, discourse, e.g., **John**

3:34; **8:20**; Acts 2:14; 6:11, 13; 11:14; 13:42; 26:25; Rom. 10:18; 2 Pet. 3:2; Jude 17; it is used of the gospel in Rom. 10:8 (twice), 17, RV, "the word of Christ" (i.e., the "word" which preaches Christ); 10:18; 1 Pet. 1:25 (twice); of a statement, command, instruction, e.g., Matt. 26:75; Luke 1:37, RV, "(no) word (from God shall be void of power)", v. 38; Acts 11:16; Heb. 11:3. The significance of *rhema* (as distinct from *logos*) is exemplified in the injunction to take "the sword of the Spirit, which is the word of God," Eph. 6:17; here the reference is not to the whole Bible as such, but to the individual scripture which the Spirit brings to our remembrance for use in time of need, a prerequisite being the regular storing of the mind with Scripture.

Measure *metron* (3358), denotes (I) "that which is used for measuring, a measure," (a) of "a vessel," figuratively, Matt. 23:32; Luke 6:38 (twice); in **John 3:34**, with the preposition *ek*, "(He giveth not the Spirit) by measure," RV (which is a necessary correction; the italicized words "*unto him*," KJV, detract from the meaning). Not only had Christ the Holy Spirit without "measure," but God so gives the Spirit through Him to others. It is the ascended Christ who gives the Spirit to those who receive His testimony and set their seal to this, that God is true. The Holy Spirit is imparted neither by degrees, nor in portions, as if He were merely an influence, He is bestowed personally upon each believer, at the time of the New Birth; (b) of "a graduated rod or rule for measuring," figuratively, Matt. 7:2; Mark 4:24; literally, Rev. 21:15 (in the best mss.; see the RV); v. 17; (II) "that which is measured, a determined extent, a portion measured off," Rom. 12:3; 2 Cor. 10:13 (twice); Eph. 4:7, "(according to the) measure (of the gift of Christ)"; the gift of grace is "measured" and given according to the will of Christ; whatever the endowment, His is the bestowment and the adjustment; v. 13, "the measure (of the stature of the fullness of Christ)," the standard of spiritual stature being the fullness which is essentially Christ's; v. 16, "(according to the working in due) measure (of each several part)," i.e., according to the effectual working of the ministration rendered in due "measure" by every part.

3:35 The Father loveth the Son, and hath given all things into his hand.

Loveth *phileo* (5368), is to be distinguished from *agapao* in this, that *phileo* more nearly represents "tender affection." The two words are used for the "love" of the Father for the Son, **John 3:35** (*agapao*), and **5:20** (*phileo*); for the believer, **14:21** (*agapao*) and **16:27** (*phileo*); both, of Christ's "love" for a certain disciple, **13:23** (*agapao*), and **20:2** (*phileo*). Yet the distinction between the two verbs remains, and they are never used indiscriminately in the same passage; if each is used with reference to the same objects, as just mentioned, each word retains its distinctive and essential character. *Phileo* is never used in a command to men to "love" God; it is, however, used as a warning in 1 Cor. 16:22; *agapao* is used instead, e.g., Matt. 22:37; Luke 10:27; Rom. 8:28; 1 Cor. 8:3; 1 Pet. 1:8; 1 John 4:21. The distinction between the two verbs finds a conspicuous instance in the narrative of **John 21:15-17**. The context itself indicates that *agapao* in the first two questions suggests the "love" that values and esteems (cf. Rev. 12:11). It is an unselfish "love," ready to serve. The use of *phileo* in Peter's answers and the Lord's third question, conveys the thought of cherishing the Object above all else, of manifesting an affection characterized by constancy, from the motive of the highest veneration. Again, to "love" (*phileo*) life, from an undue desire to preserve it, forgetful of the real object of living, meets with the Lord's reproof, **John 12:25**. On the contrary, to "love" life (*agapao*) as used in 1 Pet. 3:10, is to consult the true interests of living. Here the word *phileo* would be quite inappropriate.

3:36 He that believeth on the Son hath everlasting life: and he that believeth not the Son shall not see life; but the wrath of God abideth on him.

Believeth not *apeitheo* (544), "to refuse to be persuaded, to refuse belief, to be disobedient," is translated "disobedient," or by the verb "to be disobedient," in the RV of Acts 14:2 (KJV, "unbelieving"), and 19:9 (KJV, "believed not"); it is absent from the most authentic mss. in Acts 17:5; in **John 3:36** "obeyeth not," RV (KJV, "believeth not"); in Rom. 2:8 "obey not"; in 10:21, "disobedient"; in 11:30, 31, "were disobedient" (KJV, "have not believed"); so in 15:31; Heb. 3:18; 11:31; in 1 Pet. 2:8, "disobedient"; so in 3:20; in 3:1 and 4:17, "obey not." In 2:7 the best mss. have *apisteo*, "to disbelieve."

See *see* Seen at *John 1:18*.

Wrath *orge* (3709), originally any "natural impulse, or desire, or disposition," came to signify "anger," as the strongest of all passions. It is used of the wrath of man, Eph. 4:31; Col. 3:8; 1 Tim. 2:8; Jas. 1:19-20; the displeasure of human governments, Rom. 13:4-5; the sufferings of the Jews at the hands of the Gentiles, Luke 21:23; the terrors of the Law, Rom. 4:15; "the anger" of the Lord Jesus, Mark 3:5; God's "anger" with Israel in the wilderness, in a quotation from the OT, Heb. 3:11; 4:3; God's present "anger" with the Jews nationally, Rom. 9:22; 1 Thess. 2:16; His present "anger" with those who disobey the Lord Jesus in His gospel, **John 3:36**; God's purposes in judgment, Matt. 3:7; Luke 3:7; Rom. 1:18; 2:5, 8; 3:5; 5:9; 12:19; Eph. 2:3; 5:6; Col. 3:6; 1 Thess. 1:10; 5:9.

Chapter 4

4:1 When therefore the Lord knew how the Pharisees had heard that Jesus made and baptized more disciples than John,

Lord *kurios* (2962), properly an adjective, signifying "having power" (*kuros*) or "authority," is used as a noun, variously translated in the NT, "'Lord,' 'master,' 'Master,' 'owner,' 'Sir,' a title of wide significance, occurring in each book of the NT save Titus and the Epistles of John. It is used (a) of an owner, as in Luke 19:33, cf. Matt. 20:8; Acts 16:16; Gal. 4:1; or of one who has the disposal of anything, as the Sabbath, Matt. 12:8; (b) of a master, i.e., one to whom service is due on any ground, Matt. 6:24; 24:50; Eph. 6:5; (c) of an Emperor or King, Acts 25:26; Rev. 17:14; (d) of idols, ironically, 1 Cor. 8:5, cf. Isa. 26:13; (e) as a title of respect addressed to a father, Matt. 21:30, a husband, 1 Pet. 3:6, a master, Matt. 13:27; Luke 13:8, a ruler, Matt. 27:63, an angel, Acts 10:4; Rev. 7:14; (f) as a title of courtesy addressed to a stranger, **John 12:21**; **20:15**; Acts 16:30; from the outset of His ministry this was a common form of address to the Lord Jesus, alike by the people, Matt. 8:2; **John 4:11**, and by His disciples, Matt. 8:25; Luke 5:8; **John 6:68**; (g) *kurios* is the Sept. and NT representative of Heb. Jehovah ('LORD' in Eng. versions), see Matt. 4:7; Jas. 5:11, e.g., of *adon*, Lord, Matt. 22:44, and of *Adonay*, Lord, 1:22; it also occurs for *Elohim*, God, 1 Pet. 1:25.

"Thus the usage of the word in the NT follows two main lines: one, *a–f*, customary and general, the other, *g*, peculiar to the Jews, and drawn from the Greek translation of the OT. Christ Himself assumed the title, Matt. 7:21, 22; 9:38; 22:41-45; Mark 5:19 (cf. Ps. 66:16; the parallel passage, Luke 8:39, has 'God'); Luke 19:31; **John 13:13**, apparently intending it in the higher senses of its current use, and at the same time suggesting its OT associations. His purpose did not become clear to the disciples until after His resurrection, and the revelation of His Deity consequent thereon. Thomas, when he realized the significance of the presence of a mortal wound in the body of a living man, immediately joined with it the absolute title of Deity, saying, 'My Lord and my God,' **John 20:28**. Thereafter, except in Acts 10:4 and Rev. 7:14, there is no record that *kurios* was ever again used by believers in addressing any save God and the Lord Jesus; cf. Acts 2:47 with 4:29, 30. Though John does not use 'Lord' in his Epistles, and though, like the other Evangelists, he ordinarily uses the personal Name in his narrative, yet he occasionally speaks of Him as 'the Lord,' **John 4:1**; **6:23**; **11:2**; **20:20**; **21:12**. The full significance of this association of Jesus with God under the one appellation, 'Lord,' is seen when it is remembered that these men belonged to the only monotheistic race in the world. To associate with the Creator one known to be a creature, however exalted, though possible to Pagan philosophers, was quite impossible to a Jew. It is not recorded that in the days of His flesh any of His disciples either addressed the Lord, or spoke of Him, by His personal Name."

4:2-3 (Though Jesus himself baptized not, but his disciples,) He left Judaea, and departed again into Galilee.

Left *aphiemi* (863), *apo*, "from," and *hiemi*, "to send," has three chief meanings, (a) "to send forth, let go, forgive"; (b) "to let, suffer, permit"; (c) "to leave, leave alone, forsake, neglect." It is translated by the verb "to leave" (c), in Matt. 4:11; 4:20, 22, and parallel passages; 5:24; 8:15, and parallel passages; 8:22, RV, "leave (the dead)," KJV, "let," and the parallel passage; 13:36, RV, "left (the multitude)," KJV, "sent ... away"; 18:12; 19:27, and parallel passages, RV, "we have left" (KJV, "we have forsaken"), so v. 29; 22:22, 25; 23:23, RV, "have left undone" (KJV, "have omitted," in the 1st part, "leave undone" in the second); 23:38, and the parallel passage; 24:2, 40, 41, and parallel passages; 26:56, RV, "left"; Mark 1:18, "left"; 1:31; 7:8, RV, "ye leave"; 8:13; 10:28, 29; 12:12, 19-22; 13:34; Luke 10:30; 11:42 (in some mss.); Luke 12:39, RV "have left," KJV "have suffered"; **John 4:3, 28, 52; 8:29; 10:12; 14:18, 27; 16:28, 32**; Rom. 1:27; 1 Cor. 7:11, RV, "leave" (KJV "put away"); 7:13 (KJV and RV); Heb. 2:8; 6:1; Rev. 2:4.

4:4 And he must needs go through Samaria.

Must *see John 3:7*.

Needs *dei* (1163), an impersonal verb, signifying "it is necessary," is rendered "must needs" in Mark 13:7; **John 4:4**; Acts 1:16, KJV (RV, "it was needful"); 17:3, KJV (RV, "it behoved"); (in some mss. in Acts 21:22); 2 Cor. 11:30; 12:1; in Acts 15:5, "it was needful."

4:5 Then cometh he to a city of Samaria, which is called Sychar, near to the parcel of ground that Jacob gave to his son Joseph.

Called *lego* (3004), "to speak," is used of all kinds of oral communication, e.g. "to call, to call by name," to surname, Matt. 1:16; 26:36; **John 4:5**; **11:54**; **15:15**; Rev. 2:2, RV, "call themselves," etc.

Near *plesion* (4139), "near, close by, neighboring" (the neuter of the adjective *plesios*, used as an adverb), occurs in **John 4:5**.

Ground *chorion* (5564), "a piece of land, a place, estate," is translated "parcel of ground" in **John 4:5**.

4:6 Now Jacob's well was there. Jesus therefore, being wearied with *his* journey, sat thus on the well: *and* it was about the sixth hour.

Well *pege* (4077), "a spring or fountain," is used of (a) "an artificial well," fed by a spring, **John 4:6**; (b) metaphorically (in contrast to such a well), "the indwelling Spirit of God," **4:14**; (c) "springs," metaphorically in 2 Pet. 2:17, RV, for KJV, "wells"; (d) "natural fountains or springs," Jas. 3:11, 12; Rev. 8:10; 14:7; 16:4; (e) metaphorically, "eternal life and the future blessings accruing from it," Rev. 7:17; 21:6; (f) "a flow of blood," Mark 5:29.

Wearied *kopiao* (2872), (a) "to grow tired with toil," Matt. 11:28; **John 4:6**; Rev. 2:3, also means (b) "to bestow labor, work with toil," Rom. 16:6; Gal. 4:11; in **John 4:38**, KJV, "bestowed (no) labor," RV, "have (not) labored," and, in the same verse, KJV and RV, "labored."

Journey *hodoiporia* (3597), "a wayfaring, journeying," is used of the Lord's journey to Samaria, **John 4:6**, and of Paul's "journeyings," 2 Cor. 11:26.

Sat *kathezomai* (2516), "to sit (down)," is used in Matt. 26:55; Luke 2:46; **John 4:6**; **11:20**; **20:12**; Acts 6:15.

Sixth *hektos* (1623), is used (a) of a month, Luke 1:26, 36; (b) an hour, Matt. 20:5; 27:45 and parallel passages; **John 4:6**; (c) an angel, Rev. 9:13, 14; 16:12; (d) a seal of a roll, in vision, Rev. 6:12; (e) of the "sixth" precious stone, the sardius, in the foundations of the wall of the heavenly Jerusalem, Rev. 21:20.

4:7 There cometh a woman of Samaria to draw water: Jesus saith unto her, Give me to drink.

Draw *see John 2:8*.

4:8 (For his disciples were gone away unto the city to buy meat.)

Meat *trophe* (5160), denotes "nourishment, food" (akin to *trepho*, "to rear, nourish, feed"); it is used literally, in the Gospels, Acts and Jas. 2:15; metaphorically, in Heb. 5:12, 14, RV, "(solid) food," KJV, "(strong) meat," i.e., deeper subjects of the faith than that of elementary instruction. The word is always rendered "food" in the RV, where the KJV has "meat"; e.g., Matt. 3:4; 6:25; 10:10; 24:45; Luke 12:23; **John 4:8**; Acts 2:46, "did take their food," RV (KJV, "did eat their meat"); 9:19, "took food"; 27:33, 34, 36. The KJV also has "food" in Acts 14:17 and Jas. 2:15.

4:9 Then saith the woman of Samaria unto him, How is it that thou, being a Jew, askest drink of me, which am a woman of Samaria? for the Jews have no dealings with the Samaritans.

Jew *see* Jews at *John 2:6*.

Have ... dealings with *sunchraomai* (4798), lit., "to use with" (*sun*, "with," *chraomai*, "to use"), "to have in joint use, and hence to have dealings with," is said, in **John 4:9**, of Jews and Samaritans.

4:10 Jesus answered and said unto her, If thou knewest the gift of God, and who it is that saith to thee, Give me to drink; thou wouldest have asked of him, and he would have given thee living water.

Gift *dorea* (1431), denotes "a free gift," stressing its gratuitous character; it is always used in the NT of a spiritual or supernatural gift, **John 4:10**; Acts 8:20; 11:17; Rom. 5:15; 2 Cor. 9:15; Eph. 3:7; Heb. 6:4; in Eph. 4:7, "according to the measure of the gift of Christ," the "gift" is that given by Christ; in Acts 2:28, "the gift of the Holy Ghost," the clause is epexegetical, the "gift" being the Holy Ghost Himself; cf. 10:45; 11:17, and the phrase, "the gift of righteousness," Rom. 5:17.

Living *zao* (2198), "to live, be alive," is used in the NT of "(a) God, Matt. 16:16; **John 6:57**; Rom. 14:11; (b) the Son in Incarnation, **John 6:57**; (c) the Son in Resurrection, **John 14:19**; Acts 1:3; Rom. 6:10; 2 Cor. 13:4; Heb. 7:8; (d) spiritual life, **John 6:57**; Rom. 1:17; 8:13b; Gal. 2:19, 20; Heb. 12:9; (e) the present state of departed saints, Luke 20:38; 1 Pet. 4:6; (f) the hope of resurrection, 1 Pet. 1:3; (g) the resurrection of believers, 1 Thess. 5:10; **John**

5:25; Rev. 20:4, and of unbelievers, v. 5, cf. v. 13; (h) the way of access to God through the Lord Jesus Christ, Heb. 10:20; (i) the manifestation of divine power in support of divine authority, 2 Cor. 13:4b; cf. 12:10, and 1 Cor. 5:5; (j) bread, figurative of the Lord Jesus, **John 6:51**; (k) a stone, figurative of the Lord Jesus, 1 Pet. 2:4; (l) water, figurative of the Holy Spirit, **John 4:10**; **7:38**; (m) a sacrifice, figurative of the believer, Rom. 12:1; (n) stones, figurative of the believer, 1 Pet. 2:5; (o) the oracles, *logion*, Acts 7:38, and word, *logos*, Heb. 4:12; 1 Pet. 1:23, of God; (p) the physical life of men, 1 Thess. 4:15; Matt. 27:63; Acts 25:24; Rom. 14:9; Phil. 1:21 (in the infinitive mood used as a noun with the article, 'living'), 22; 1 Pet. 4:5; (q) the maintenance of physical life, Matt. 4:4; 1 Cor. 9:14; (r) the duration of physical life, Heb. 2:15; (s) the enjoyment of physical life, 1 Thess. 3:8; (t) the recovery of physical life from the power of disease, Mark 5:23; **John 4:50**; (u) the recovery of physical life from the power of death, Matt. 9:18; Acts 9:41; Rev. 20:5; (v) the course, conduct, and character of men, (1) good, Acts 26:5; 2 Tim. 3:12; Titus 2:12; (2) evil, Luke 15:13; Rom. 6:2; 8:13a; 2 Cor. 5:15b; Col. 3:7; (3) undefined, Rom. 7:9; 14:7; Gal. 2:14; (w) restoration after alienation, Luke 15:32."

Water *see* ***John 3:5***.

4:11 The woman saith unto him, Sir, thou hast nothing to draw with, and the well is deep: from whence then hast thou that living water?

Sir *see* Lord at ***John 4:1***.

Draw In **John 4:11**, "to draw with" translates the corresponding noun *antlema*, "a bucket for drawing water by a rope."

Deep *bathus* (901), "deep," is said in **John 4:11**, of a well; in Acts 20:9, of sleep; in Rev. 2:24 the plural is used, of the "deep things," the evil designs and workings, of Satan.

Well *phrear* (5421), "a well, dug for water" (distinct from *pege*, "a fountain"), denotes "a pit" in Rev. 9:1, 2, RV, "the pit (of the abyss)," "the pit," i.e., the shaft leading down to the abyss, KJV, "(bottomless) pit"; in Luke 14:5, RV, well (KJV, "pit"); in **John 4:11, 12**, "well."

4:12 Art thou greater than our father Jacob, which gave us the well, and drank thereof himself, and his children, and his cattle?

Well *see* ***John 4:11***.

Cattle *thremma* (2353), "whatever is fed or nourished" (from *trepho*, "to nourish, nurture, feed"), is found in **John 4:12**.

4:13 Jesus answered and said unto her, Whosoever drinketh of this water shall thirst again:

Thirst *dipsao* (1372), is used (a) in the natural sense, e.g., Matt. 25:35, 37, 42; in v. 44, "athirst" (lit., "thirsting"); **John 4:13, 15**; **19:28**; Rom. 12:20; 1 Cor. 4:11; Rev. 7:16; (b) figuratively, of spiritual "thirst," Matt. 5:6; **John 4:14**; **6:35**; **7:37**; in Rev. 21:6 and 22:17, "that is athirst."

4:14 But whosoever drinketh of the water that I shall give him shall never thirst; but the water that I shall give him shall be in him a well of water springing up into everlasting life.

Drinketh *pino* (4095), "to drink," is used chiefly in the Gospels and in 1 Cor., whether literally (most frequently), or figuratively, (a) of "drinking" of the blood of Christ, in the sense of receiving eternal life, through His death, **John 6:53-54, 56**; (b) of "receiving" spiritually that which refreshes, strengthens and nourishes the soul, **John 7:37**; (c) of "deriving" spiritual life from Christ, **John 4:14**, as Israel did typically, 1 Cor. 10:4; (d) of "sharing" in the sufferings of Christ humanly inflicted, Matt. 20:22-23; Mark 10:38-39; (e) of "participating" in the abominations imparted by the corrupt religious and commercial systems emanating from Babylon, Rev. 18:3; (f) of "receiving" divine judgment, through partaking unworthily of the Lord's Supper, 1 Cor. 11:29; (g) of "experiencing" the wrath of God, Rev. 14:10; 16:6; (h) of the earth's "receiving" the benefits of rain, Heb. 6:7.

Water *see* ***John 3:5***.

I *ego* (1473), is the nominative case of the first personal pronoun. The pronoun, "I," however, generally forms a part of the verb itself in Greek; thus *luo* itself means "I loose," the pronoun being incorporated in the verb form. Where the pronoun *ego* is added to the verb, it is almost invariably, if not entirely, emphatic. The emphasis may not be so apparent in some instances, as e.g., Matt. 10:16, but even here it may be taken that something more of stress is present than if the pronoun were omitted. By far the greater number of instances are found in the Gospel of John, and there in the utterances of the Lord concerning Himself, e.g., **4:14, 26, 32, 38**; **5:34, 36, 43, 45**; **6:35, 40, 41, 48, 51** (twice), **63**, 70 instances in the Epistles are Rom. 7:9, 14, 17, 20 (twice), 24, 25; there are more in that chapter than in any other outside the Gospel of John. In other cases of the pronoun than the nominative, the pronoun is usually more necessary to the meaning, apart from any stress.

Never The phrase *eis ton aiona*, "for ever" (not to be rendered literally, "unto the age"), preceded by the double negative *ou me*, denotes: "never," **John 4:14**; **8:51-52**; **10:28**; **11:26**; **13:8**; so, preceded by *ouk*, "not," in Mark 3:29.

Thirst *see John 4:13.*

Well *see John 4:6.*

Springing *hallomai* (242), "to leap, spring," is rendered "springing up," of well water, in **John 4:14**, figurative of the Holy Spirit in the believer.

4:15 The woman saith unto him, Sir, give me this water, that I thirst not, neither come hither to draw.

Thirst *see John 4:13.*

Hither *enthade* (1759), has the meaning "hither," **John 4:15**, **16**; Acts 17:6; 25:17.

Draw *see John 2:8.*

4:16 Jesus saith unto her, Go, call thy husband, and come hither.

Husband *aner* (435), denotes, in general, "a man, an adult male" (in contrast to *anthropos*, which generically denotes "a human being, male or female"); it is used of man in various relations, the context deciding the meaning; it signifies "a husband," e.g., Matt. 1:16, 19; Mark 10:12; Luke 2:36; 16:18; **John 4:16**, **17**, **18**; Rom. 7:23.

Hither *see John 4:15.*

4:17 The woman answered and said, I have no husband. Jesus said unto her, Thou hast well said, I have no husband:

Husband *see John 4:16.*

4:18 For thou hast had five husbands; and he whom thou now hast is not thy husband: in that saidst thou truly.

Husbands, Husband *see* Husband at *John 4:16.*

Now *nun* (3568), is used (a) of time, the immediate present, whether in contrast to the past, e.g., **John 4:18**; Acts 7:52, or to the future, e.g., **John 12:27**; Rom. 11:31; sometimes with the article, singular or plural, e.g., Acts 4:29; 5:38; (b) of logical sequence, often partaking also of the character of (a), "now therefore, now however," as it is, e.g., Luke 11:39; **John 8:40**; **9:41**; **15:22**, **24**; 1 Cor. 5:11, RV marg., "as it is."

Truly *see* True at *John 3:33.*

4:19 The woman saith unto him, Sir, I perceive that thou art a prophet.

Perceive *theoreo* (2334), "to be a spectator of, look at, discern," is translated "to perceive" in **John 4:19** (indicating the woman's earnest contemplation of the Lord); so Acts 17:22; in **John 12:19**, RV, "behold" (KJV, "perceive ye").

Prophet *see John 1:21.*

4:20 Our fathers worshipped in this mountain; and ye say, that in Jerusalem is the place where men ought to worship.

Mountain *oros* (3735), is used (a) without specification, e.g., Luke 3:5 (distinct from *bounos*, "a hill"); **John 4:20**; (b) of "the Mount of Transfiguration," Matt. 17:1, 9; Mark 9:2, 9; Luke 9:28, 37 (KJV, "hill"); 2 Pet. 1:18; (c) of "Zion," Heb. 12:22; Rev. 14:1; (d) of "Sinai," Acts 7:30, 38; Gal. 4:24, 25; Heb. 8:5; 12:20; (e) of "the Mount of Olives," Matt. 21:1; 24:3; Mark 11:1; 13:3; Luke 19:29, 37; 22:39; **John 8:1**; Acts 1:12; (f) of "the hill districts as distinct from the lowlands," especially of the hills above the Sea of Galilee, e.g., Matt. 5:1; 8:1; 18:12; Mark 5:5; (g) of "the mountains on the east of Jordan" and "those in the land of Ammon" and "the region of Petra," etc., Matt. 24:16; Mark 13:14; Luke 21:21; (h) proverbially, "of overcoming difficulties, or accomplishing great things," 1 Cor. 13:2; cf. Matt. 17:20; 21:21; Mark 11:23; (i) symbolically, of "a series of the imperial potentates of the Roman dominion, past and future," Rev. 17:9.

And *see John 3:19.*

4:21 Jesus saith unto her, Woman, believe me, the hour cometh, when ye shall neither in this mountain, nor yet at Jerusalem, worship the Father.

Woman *see John 2:4.*

Worship *proskuneo* (4352), "to make obeisance, do reverence to" (from *pros*, "towards," and *kuneo*, "to kiss"), is the most frequent word rendered "to worship." It is used of an act of homage or reverence (a) to God, e.g., Matt. 4:10; **John 4:21-24**; 1 Cor. 14:25; Rev. 4:10; 5:14; 7:11; 11:16; 19:10 (2nd part) and 22:9; (b) to Christ, e.g., Matt. 2:2, 8, 11; 8:2; 9:18; 14:33; 15:25; 20:20; 28:9, 17; **John 9:38**; Heb. 1:6, in a quotation from the Sept. of Deut. 32:43, referring to Christ's second advent; (c) to a man, Matt. 18:26; (d) to the Dragon, by men, Rev. 13:4; (e) to the Beast, his human instrument, Rev. 13:4, 8, 12; 14:9, 11; (f) the image of the Beast, 13:15; 14:11; 16:2; (g) to demons, Rev. 9:20; (h) to idols, Acts 7:43.

4:22 Ye worship ye know not what: we know what we worship: for salvation is of the Jews.

Salvation *soteria* (4991), denotes "deliverance, preservation, salvation." "Salvation" is used in the NT (a) of material and temporal

"I remember two things; that I am a great sinner and that Christ is a great Savior."

JOHN NEWTON

deliverance from danger and apprehension, (1) national, Luke 1:69, 71; Acts 7:25, RV marg., "salvation" (text, "deliverance"); (2) personal, as from the sea, Acts 27:34; RV, "safety" (KJV, "health"); prison, Phil. 1:19; the flood, Heb. 11:7; (b) of the spiritual and eternal deliverance granted immediately by God to those who accept His conditions of repentance and faith in the Lord Jesus, in whom alone it is to be obtained, Acts 4:12, and upon confession of Him as Lord, Rom. 10:10; for this purpose the gospel is the saving instrument, Rom. 1:16; Eph. 1:13; (c) of the present experience of God's power to deliver from the bondage of sin, e.g., Phil. 2:12, where the special, though not the entire, reference is to the maintenance of peace and harmony; 1 Pet. 1:9; this present experience on the part of believers is virtually equivalent to sanctification; for this purpose, God is able to make them wise, 2 Tim. 3:15; they are not to neglect it, Heb. 2:3; (d) of the future deliverance of believers at the Parousia of Christ for His saints, a salvation which is the object of their confident hope, e.g., Rom. 13:11; 1 Thess. 5:8, and v. 9, where "salvation" is assured to them, as being deliverance from the wrath of God destined to be executed upon the ungodly at the end of this age (see 1 Thess. 1:10); 2 Thess. 2:13; Heb. 1:14; 9:28; 1 Pet. 1:5; 2 Pet. 3:15; (e) of the deliverance of the nation of Israel at the second advent of Christ at the time of "the epiphany (or shining forth) of His Parousia" (2 Thess. 2:8); Luke 1:71; Rev. 12:10; (f) inclusively, to sum up all the blessings bestowed by God on men in Christ through the Holy Spirit, e.g., 2 Cor. 6:2; Heb. 5:9; 1 Pet. 1:9, 10; Jude 3; (g) occasionally, as standing virtually for the Savior, e.g., Luke 19:9; cf. **John 4:22**; (h) in ascriptions of praise to God, Rev. 7:10, and as that which it is His prerogative to bestow, 19:1 (RV).

4:23 But the hour cometh, and now is, when the true worshippers shall worship the Father in spirit and in truth: for the Father seeketh such to worship him.

True *see John 1:9*.

Worshippers *proskunetes* (4353), akin to *proskuneo*, occurs in **John 4:23**.

4:24-25 God *is* a Spirit: and they that worship *him* must worship him in spirit and in truth.

The woman saith unto him, I know that Messias cometh, which is called Christ: when he is come, he will tell us all things.

Christ *see John 1:41*.

Tell *anangello* (312), signifies "to announce, report, bring back tidings" (*ana*, "back," *angello*, "to announce"). Possibly the *ana* carries the significance of upward, i.e., heavenly, as characteristic of the nature of the tidings. In the following, either the KJV or the RV translates the word by the verb "to declare"; in **John 4:25**, RV, "declare," KJV, "tell"; in **16:13-15**, RV, "declare," KJV, "shew"; in Acts 15:4, RV, "rehearsed," KJV, "declared"; in 19:18, RV, "declaring," KJV, "shewed" (a reference, perhaps, to the destruction of their idols, in consequence of their new faith); in 20:20, RV, "declaring," KJV, "have shewed"; in 1 John 1:5, RV, "announce," KJV, "declare."

4:26 Jesus saith unto her, I that speak unto thee am *he*.

I *see John 4:14*.

4:27 And upon this came his disciples, and marvelled that he talked with the woman: yet no man said, What seekest thou? or, Why talkest thou with her?

Talked *laleo* (2980), "to speak, say," is always translated "to speak" in the RV, where the KJV renders it by "to talk," Matt. 12:46; Mark 6:50; Luke 24:32; **John 4:27** (twice); **9:37; 14:30**; Acts 26:31; Rev. 4:1; 17:1; 21:9, 15. The RV rendering is preferable; the idea of "chat" or "chatter" is entirely foreign to the NT, and should never be regarded as the meaning in 1 Cor. 14:34, 35.

Yet *mentoi*, "nevertheless," **John 4:27**; 20:5.

4:28 The woman then left her waterpot, and went her way into the city, and saith to the men,

Left *see John 4:3*.

Waterpot *see* Waterpots at *John 2:6*.

4:29-31 Come, see a man, which told me all things that ever I did: is not this the Christ?

Then they went out of the city, and came unto him.

In the mean while his disciples prayed him, saying, Master, eat.

Mean while *metaxu* (3342), "in the midst, or between" (from *meta*, and *xun*, i.e., *sun*, "with"), is used as a preposition, (a) of mutual relation, Matt. 18:15; Acts 15:9; Rom. 2:15, RV, "one with another," lit., "between one another," for KJV, "the meanwhile"; (b) of place, Matt. 23:35; Luke 11:51; 16:26; Acts 12:6; (c) of time, "meanwhile," **John 4:31**. In Acts 13:42, the KJV marg. has "in the week between," the literal rendering.

Prayed *erotao* (2065), "to ask," is translated by the verb to pray in Luke 14:18, 19; 16:27; **John 4:31**; **14:16**; **16:26**; **17:9**, **15**, **20**; in Acts 23:18, RV, "asked" (KJV "prayed"); in 1 John 5:16, RV, "should make request" (KJV "shall pray").

Master *see John 1:38.*

4:32 But he said unto them, I have meat to eat that ye know not of.

I *see John 4:14.*

Meat *brosis* (1035), denotes (a) "the act of eating," 1 Cor. 8:4; (b) "food," translated "meat" in **John 4:32**; **6:27** (twice, the second time metaphorically, of spiritual food); **6:55**, RV, marg., "(true) meat"; Rom. 14:17, KJV, "meat," RV, "eating"; Col. 2:16; in Heb. 12:16, RV, "mess of meat," KJV, "morsel of meat"; in 2 Cor. 9:10, "food"; in Matt. 6:19, 20, "rust."

Eat *brosis* (1035), denotes (a) "the act of eating," e.g., Rom. 14:17; said of rust, Matt. 6:19-20; or, more usually (b) "that which is eaten, food" (like *broma*, "food"), "meat," **John 4:32**; **6:27**, **55**; Col. 2:16; Heb. 12:16 ("morsel of meat"); "food," 2 Cor. 9:10; "eating," 1 Cor. 8:4.

4:33-34 Therefore said the disciples one to another, Hath any man brought him *ought* to eat?

Jesus saith unto them, My meat is to do the will of him that sent me, and to finish his work.

My *emos* (1699), a possessive adjective of the first person, often used as a possessive pronoun with greater emphasis than the oblique forms of *ego*, a measure of stress which should always be observed; it denotes (I) subjectively, (a) "what I possess," e.g., **John 4:34**; **7:16** (1st part); **13:35**; 1 Cor. 16:21; Gal. 6:11; Col. 4:18 (1st clause); as a pronoun, absolutely (i.e., not as an adjective), e.g., Matt. 20:15; 25:27; Luke 15:31, RV, "(all that is) mine," KJV, "(all that) I have"; **John 16:14**, **15**; **17:10**; (b) "proceeding from me," e.g. Mark 8:38; **John 7:16** (2nd part); **8:37** (here the repetition of the article with the pronoun, after the article with the noun, lends special stress to the pronoun; more lit., "the word, that which is mine"); so in **John 15:12**. Such instances are to be distinguished from the less emphatic order where the pronoun comes between the article and the noun, as in **John 7:16**, already mentioned; (c) in the phrase "it is mine" (i.e., "it rests with me"), e.g., Matt. 20:23; Mark 10:40; (II) objectively, "pertaining or relating to me": (a) "appointed for me," e.g., **John 7:6**, "My time" (with the repeated article and special stress just referred to); (b) equivalent to an objective genitive ("of me") e.g., Luke 22:19, "(in remembrance) of Me" (lit., "in My remembrance"); so 1 Cor. 11:24.

Meat *broma* (1033), "food" (akin to *bibrosko*, "to eat," **John 6:13**), solid food in contrast to milk, is translated "food" in Matt. 14:15, RV (KJV, "victuals"); "meats," Mark 7:19; 1 Cor. 6:13 (twice); 1 Tim. 4:3; Heb. 9:10; 13:9; "meat," **John 4:34**; Rom. 14:15 (twice), 20; 1 Cor. 3:2; 8:8, 13; 10:3; "food," RV, for KJV, "meat," Luke 3:11; 9:13. *See also John 4:32.*

Will *see John 1:13.*

Sent *see John 1:33.*

Finish *teleioo* (5048), though distinct grammatically from *teleo*, has much the same meaning. The main distinction is that *teleo* more frequently signifies "to fulfill," *teleioo*, more frequently, "to make perfect," one of the chief features of the Epistle to the Hebrews, where it occurs nine times. It is rendered "accomplish" in the RV of **John 4:34**; **5:36**; **17:4**, and Acts 20:24.

Work *ergon* (2041), denotes (I) "work, employment, task," e.g., Mark 13:34; **John 4:34**; **17:4**; Acts 13:2; Phil. 2:30; 1 Thess. 5:13; in Acts 5:38 with the idea of enterprise; (II) "a deed, act," (a) of God, e.g., **John 6:28**, **29**; **9:3**; **10:37**; **14:10**; Acts 13:41; Rom. 14:20; Heb. 1:10; 2:7; 3:9; 4:3, 4, 10; Rev. 15:3; (b) of Christ, e.g., Matt. 11:2; especially in John, 5:36; 7:3, 21; 10:25, 32, 33, 38; 14:11, 12; 15:24; Rev. 2:26; (c) of believers, e.g., Matt. 5:16; Mark 14:6; Acts 9:36; Rom. 13:3; Col. 1:10; 1 Thess. 1:3, "work of faith," here the initial act of faith at conversion (turning to God, v. 9); in 2 Thess. 1:11, "*every* work of faith," RV, denotes every activity undertaken for Christ's sake; 2:17; 1 Tim. 2:10; 5:10; 6:18; 2 Tim. 2:21; 3:17; Titus 2:7, 14; 3:1, 8, 14; Heb 10:24; 13:21; frequent in James, as the effect of faith [in 1:25, KJV, "(a doer) of the work," RV, "(a doer) that worketh"]; 1 Pet. 2:12; Rev. 2:2 and in several other places in chs. 2 and 3; 14:13; (d) of unbelievers, e.g., Matt. 23:3, 5; **John 7:7**; Acts 7:41 (for idols); Rom. 13:12; Eph. 5:11; Col. 1:21; Titus 1:16 (1st part); 1 John 3:12; Jude 15, RV; Rev. 2:6, RV; of those who seek justification by works, e.g., Rom. 9:32; Gal. 3:10; Eph. 2:9; described as the works of the law, e.g., Gal. 2:16; 3:2, 5; dead works, Heb. 6:1; 9:14; (e) of Babylon, Rev. 18:6; (f) of the Devil, **John 8:41**; 1 John 3:8.

4:35 Say not ye, There are yet four months, and *then* cometh harvest? behold, I say unto you, Lift up your eyes, and look on the fields; for they are white already to harvest.

Months *tetramenos* (5072), an adjective, denoting of four "months," is used as a noun in **John 4:35** (where *chronos*, "time," may be understood).

Harvest *therismos* (2326), akin to *therizo*, "to reap," is used (a) of "the act of harvesting," **John 4:35**; (b) "the time of harvest," figuratively, Matt. 13:30, 39; Mark 4:29; (c) "the crop," figuratively, Matt. 9:37, 38; Luke 10:2; Rev. 14:15. The beginning of "harvest" varied according to natural conditions, but took place on the average about the middle of April in the eastern lowlands of Palestine, in the latter part of the month in the coast plains and a little later in high districts. Barley "harvest" usually came first and then wheat. "Harvesting" lasted about seven weeks, and was the occasion of festivities.

Lift *epairo* (1869), "to lift up, raise," is used of "lifting" up the eyes, Matt. 17:8; Luke 6:20; 16:23, 18:13; **John 4:35**; **6:5**; **17:1**; the head, Luke 21:28; the hands, Luke 24:50; 1 Tim. 2:8; the voice, Luke 11:27; Acts 2:14; 14:11; 22:22; a foresail, Acts 27:40 ("hoisting," RV); metaphorically, of the heel, **John 13:18**, as of one "lifting" up the foot before kicking; the expression indicates contempt and violence; in the passive voice, Acts 1:9, of Christ's ascension, "was taken up"; 2 Cor. 10:5, "is exalted" (with pride); 11:20, "exalteth himself."

Look *theaomai* (2300), "to behold" (of careful contemplation), is translated "look" in **John 4:35**, of "looking" on the fields; in 1 John 1:1, KJV (RV, "we beheld"), of the apostles' personal experiences of Christ in the days of His flesh, and the facts of His Godhood and Manhood.

"Watch where Jesus went. The one dominant note in his life was to do his Father's will. His is not the way of wisdom or of success, but the way of faithfulness."

OSWALD CHAMBERS

Fields *chora* (5561), (a) "a space, place," then, (b) "land, country, region," is translated "fields" in **John 4:35**; Jas. 5:4.

White *leukos* (3022), is used of (a) clothing (sometimes in the sense of "bright"), Matt. 17:2; 28:3; Mark 9:3; 16:5; Luke 9:29; **John 20:12**; Acts 1:10; symbolically, Rev. 3:4, 5, 18; 4:4; 6:11; 7:9, 13; 19:14 (2nd part); (b) hair, Matt. 5:36; Christ's head and hair (in a vision; cf. Dan. 7:9), Rev. 1:14 (twice); ripened grain, **John 4:35**; a stone, Rev. 2:17, an expression of the Lord's special delight in the overcomer, the new name on it being indicative of a secret communication of love and joy; a horse (in a vision), 6:2; 19:11-14 (1st part); a cloud, 14:14; the throne of God, 20:11.

4:36 And he that reapeth receiveth wages, and gathereth fruit unto life eternal: that both he that soweth and he that reapeth may rejoice together.

Reapeth *therizo* (2325), "to reap" (akin to *theros*, "summer, harvest"), is used (a) literally, Matt. 6:26; 25:24, 26; Luke 12:24; 19:21, 22; Jas. 5:4 (2nd part), KJV, "have reaped"; (b) figuratively or in proverbial expressions, **John 4:36** (twice), **37**, **38**, with immediate reference to bringing Samaritans into the kingdom of God, in regard to which the disciples would enjoy the fruits of what Christ Himself had been doing in Samaria; the Lord's words are, however, of a general application in respect of such service.

Wages *misthos* (3408), "hire," is rendered "wages" in **John 4:36**; in 2 Pet. 2:15, KJV (RV, hire).

Fruit *karpos* (2590), "fruit," is used (I) of the fruit of trees, fields, the earth, that which is produced by the inherent energy of a living organism, e.g., Matt. 7:17; Jas. 5:7, 18; plural, e.g., in Luke 12:17 and 2 Tim. 2:6; of the human body, Luke 1:42; Acts 2:30; (II) metaphorically, (a) of works or deeds, "fruit" being the visible expression of power working inwardly and invisibly, the character of the "fruit" being evidence of the character of the power producing it, Matt. 7:16. As the visible expressions of hidden lusts are the works of the flesh, so the invisible power of the Holy Spirit in those who are brought into living union with Christ (**John 15:2-8**, **16**) produces "the fruit of the Spirit," Gal. 5:22, the singular form suggesting the unity of the character of the Lord as reproduced in them, namely, "love, joy, peace, longsuffering, kindness, goodness, faithfulness, meekness, temperance," all in contrast with the confused and often mutually antagonistic "works of the flesh." So in Phil. 1:11, marg., "fruit of righteousness." In Heb. 12:11, "the fruit of righteousness" is described as "peaceable fruit," the outward effect of divine chastening; "the fruit of righteousness is sown in peace," Jas. 3:18, i.e., the seed contains the fruit; those who make peace, produce a harvest of righteousness; in Eph. 5:9, "the fruit of the light" (RV, and see context) is seen in "goodness and righteousness and truth," as the expression of the union of the Christian with God (Father, Son and Holy Spirit); for God is good, Mark 10:18, the Son is "the righteous One," Acts 7:52, the Spirit is "the Spirit of truth," **John 16:13**; (b) of advantage, profit, consisting (1) of converts as the result of evangelistic ministry, **John 4:36**; Rom. 1:13; Phil. 1:22; (2) of sanctification, through deliverance from a life of sin and through service to God, Rom. 6:22, in contrast to (3) the absence of anything regarded as advantageous as the result of former sins, v. 21; (4) of the reward for ministration to servants of God, Phil. 4:17; (5) of the effect of making confession to God's Name by the sacrifice of praise, Heb. 13:15.

Rejoice *chairo* (5463), "to rejoice," is most frequently so translated. As to this verb, the following are grounds and occasions for "rejoicing," on the part of believers: in the Lord, Phil. 3:1; 4:4; His incarnation, Luke 1:14; His power, Luke 13:17; His presence with the Father, **John 14:28**; His presence with them, **John 16:22**; **20:20**; His ultimate triumph, **8:56**; hearing the gospel, Acts 13:48; their salvation, Acts 8:39; receiving the Lord, Luke 19:6; their enrollment in Heaven, Luke 10:20; their liberty in Christ, Acts 15:31; their hope, Rom. 12:12 (cf. Rom. 5:2; Rev. 19:7); their prospect of reward, Matt. 5:12; the obedience and godly conduct of fellow believers, Rom. 16:19, RV, "I rejoice" (KJV, "I am glad"); 2 Cor. 7:7, 9; 13:9; Col. 2:5; 1 Thess. 3:9; 2 John 4; 3 John 3; the proclamation of Christ, Phil. 1:18; the gospel harvest, **John 4:36**; suffering with Christ, Acts 5:41; 1 Pet. 4:13; suffering in the cause of the gospel, 2 Cor. 13:9 (1st part); Phil. 2:17 (1st part); Col. 1:24; in persecutions, trials and afflictions, Matt. 5:12; Luke 6:23; 2 Cor. 6:10; the manifestation of grace, Acts 11:23; meeting with fellow believers, 1 Cor. 16:17, RV, "I rejoice"; Phil. 2:28; receiving tokens of love and fellowship, Phil. 4:10; the "rejoicing" of others, Rom. 12:15; 2 Cor. 7:13; learning of the well-being of others, 2 Cor. 7:16.

Together *homou* (3674), used in connection with place, in **John 21:2**; Acts 2:1 (in the best texts), RV, "together" (KJV, "with one accord," translating the inferior reading *homothumadon*), is used without the idea of place in **John 4:36**; **20:4**.

4:37 And herein is that saying true, One soweth, and another reapeth.

Herein This translates the phrase *en touto*, "in this," in **John 4:37**; **9:30**; **15:8**; Acts 24:16; 2 Cor. 8:10; 1 John 4:9 (KJV, "in this"), 10, 17.

Saying *logos* (3056), "a word," as embodying a conception or idea, denotes among its various meanings, "a saying, statement or declaration," uttered (a) by God; RV, "word" or "words" (KJV, "saying"), e.g., in **John 8:55**; Rom. 3:4; Rev. 19:9; 22:6, 7, 9, 10; (b) by Christ, e.g., Mark 8:32; 9:10; 10:22; Luke 9:28; **John 6:60**; **21:23**; the RV appropriately substitutes "word" or "words" for KJV, "saying" or "sayings," especially in John's Gospel, e.g. **7:36, 40**; **8:51, 52**; **10:19**; **14:24**; **15:20**; **18:9, 32**; **19:13**; (c) by an angel, Luke 1:29; (d) by OT prophets, **John 12:38** (RV, "word") Rom. 13:9 (ditto); 1 Cor. 15:54; (e) by the apostle Paul in the Pastoral Epp., 1 Tim. 1:15; 3:1; 4:9; 2 Tim. 2:11; Titus 3:8; (f) by other men, Mark 7:29; Acts 7:29; **John 4:37** (in general).

True *see John 1:9.*

Soweth *speiro* (4687), "to sow seed," is used (1) literally, especially in the Synoptic Gospels; elsewhere, 1 Cor. 15:36, 37; 2 Cor. 9:10, "the sower", (2) metaphorically, (a) in proverbial sayings, e.g., Matt. 13:3, 4; Luke 19:21, 22; **John 4:37**; 2 Cor. 9:6; (b) in the interpretation of parables, e.g., Matt. 13:19-23 (in these vv., RV, "was sown," for KJV, "received seed"); (c) otherwise as follows: of "sowing" spiritual things in preaching and teaching, 1 Cor. 9:11; of the interment of the bodies of deceased believers, 1 Cor. 15:42-44; of ministering to the necessities of others in things temporal (the harvest being proportionate to the "sowing"), 2 Cor. 9:6, 10; of "sowing" to the flesh, Gal. 6:7, 8 ("that" in v. 7 is emphatic, "that and that only," what was actually "sown"); in v. 8, *eis*, "unto," signifies "in the interests of"; of the "fruit of righteousness" by peacemakers, Jas. 3:18.

Reapeth *see John 4:36.*

4:38 I sent you to reap that whereon ye bestowed no labour: other men laboured, and ye are entered into their labours.

I *see John 4:14.*

Sent *see John 1:6.*

Reap *see* Reapeth at *John 4:36.*

Bestowed *see* Wearied at *John 4:6.*

Labour *kopos* (2873), primarily denotes "a striking, beating" (akin to *kopto*, "to strike, cut"), then, "toil resulting in weariness, laborious toil, trouble"; it is translated "labor" or "labors" in **John 4:38**; 1 Cor. 3:8;

15:58; 2 Cor. 6:5; 10:15; 11:23, 27, RV, "labor" (KJV, "weariness"); 1 Thess. 1:3; 2:9; 3:5; 2 Thess. 3:8; (in some mss., Heb. 6:10); Rev. 2:2 (RV "toil"); 14:13. In the following the noun is used as the object of the verb *parecho*, "to afford, give, cause," the phrase being rendered "to trouble," lit., "to cause toil or trouble," to embarrass a person by giving occasion for anxiety, as some disciples did to the woman with the ointment, perturbing her spirit by their criticisms, Matt. 26:10; Mark 14:6; or by distracting attention or disturbing a person's rest, as the importunate friend did, Luke 11:7; 18:5; in Gal. 6:17, "let no man trouble me," the apostle refuses, in the form of a peremptory prohibition, to allow himself to be distracted further by the Judaizers, through their proclamation of a false gospel and by their malicious attacks upon himself.

4:39 And many of the Samaritans of that city believed on him for the saying of the woman, which testified, He told me all that ever I did.

Testified *see* Testify at *John 2:25*.

4:40 So when the Samaritans were come unto him, they besought him that he would tarry with them: and he abode there two days.

So It translates *homoios*, "likewise," e.g., in Luke 5:10; *oun*, "therefore," e.g., **John 4:40, 53**.

Tarry *meno* (3306), "to abide," is translated by the verb "to abide," in the RV, for KJV, "to tarry," in Matt. 26:38; Mark 14:34; Luke 24:29; **John 4:40**; Acts 9:43; 18:20; the RV retains the verb "to tarry" in **John 21:22, 23**; in Acts 20:5, KJV, "tarried" (RV, "were waiting"). Some mss. have it in Acts 20:15 (KJV, "tarried").

4:41 And many more believed because of his own word;

Word *see John 1:1*.

4:42 And said unto the woman, Now we believe, not because of thy saying: for we have heard *him* ourselves, and know that this is indeed the Christ, the Saviour of the world.

Now *ouketi* (3765), a negative adverb of time, signifies "no longer, no more" (*ou*, "not," *k*, euphonic, *eti* "longer"), denying absolutely and directly, e.g., Matt. 19:6; **John 4:42; 21:6**, "now ... not"; **6:66**; Acts 20:25, 38; 2 Cor. 1:23, KJV, "not as yet"; Eph. 2:19; with another negative, to strengthen the negation, e.g., Matt. 22:46; Mark 14:25; 15:5, RV, "no more (anything)," KJV, "yet ... no (thing)"; Acts 8:39; Rev. 18:11, 14.

Saying *lalia* (2981), akin to *laleo*, denotes "talk, speech," (a) of "a dialect," Matt. 26:73; Mark 14:70; (b) "utterances," **John 4:42**, RV, "speaking" (KJV, "saying"); **8:43**.

Ourselves This translates (a) *autoi*, the plural of *autos*, "self," used emphatically either alone, e.g., **John 4:42**; Rom. 8:23 (1st part); 2 Cor. 1:4 (last part); 1:9, RV, "we ourselves" (1st part); or joined with the plural pronouns, e.g., *hemeis*, "we," Rom. 8:23 (2nd part); (b) the plural *hemeis* alone, e.g., Titus 3:3; in 2 Cor. 4:7, RV, *ex hemon*, is translated "from ourselves" (KJV, "of us"); (c) *heauton*, governed by the preposition *apo*, "from," e.g., 2 Cor. 3:5 (1st part), lit., "from ourselves" ("of ourselves," in the text); (d) *heautis*, the dative case of (c), e.g., Rom. 15:1; governed by *en*, "in," 2 Cor. 1:9 (1st part); by *epi*, "on" (2nd part). (e) *heautous*, the accusative case, e.g., Acts 23:14; 2 Cor. 3:1; 4:2, 5.

Indeed *see John 1:47*.

Saviour *soter* (4990), "a savior, deliverer, preserver," is used (a) of God, Luke 1:47; 1 Tim. 1:1; 2:3; 4:10 (in the sense of "preserver," since He gives "to all life and breath and all things"); Titus 1:3; 2:10; 3:4; Jude 25; (b) of Christ, Luke 2:11; **John 4:42**; Acts 5:31; 13:23 (of Israel); Eph. 5:23 (the sustainer and preserver of the church, His "body"); Phil. 3:20 (at His return to receive the Church to Himself); 2 Tim. 1:10 (with reference to His incarnation, "the days of His flesh"); Titus 1:4 (a title shared, in the context, with God the Father); 2:13, RV, "our great God and Savior Jesus Christ," the pronoun "our," at the beginning of the whole clause, includes all the titles; Titus 3:6; 2 Pet. 1:1, "our God and Savior Jesus Christ; RV, where the pronoun "our," coming immediately in connection with "God," involves the inclusion of both titles as referring to Christ, just as in the parallel in v. 11, "our Lord and Savior Jesus Christ" (KJV and RV); these passages are therefore a testimony to His deity; 2 Pet. 2:20; 3:2, 18; 1 John 4:14.

World *see John 1:9*.

4:43-44 Now after two days he departed thence, and went into Galilee.

For Jesus himself testified, that a prophet hath no honour in his own country.

Testified *see* Testify at *John 2:25*.

Honour *time* (5092), primarily "a valuing," hence, objectively, (a) "a price paid or received," e.g., Matt. 27:6, 9; Acts 4:34; 5:2, 3; 7:16, RV, "price" (KJV, "sum"); 19:19; 1 Cor. 6:20; 7:23; (b) of "the preciousness of Christ" unto believers, 1 Pet. 2:7, RV, i.e., the honor and inestimable value of Christ as appropriated by believers, who are joined, as living stones, to Him the cornerstone; (c) in the sense of value, of human ordinances, valueless against the indulgence of the flesh, or, perhaps of no value in attempts at asceticism, Col. 2:23; (d) "honor, esteem," (1) used in ascriptions of worship to God, 1 Tim. 1:17; 6:16; Rev. 4:9, 11; 5:13; 7:12; to Christ, 5:12, 13; (2) bestowed upon Christ by the Father, Heb. 2:9; 2 Pet. 1:17; (3) bestowed upon man, Heb. 2:7; (4) bestowed upon Aaronic priests, Heb. 5:4; (5) to be the reward hereafter of "the proof of faith" on the part of tried saints, 1 Pet. 1:7, RV; (6) used of the believer who as a vessel is "meet for the Master's use," 2 Tim. 2:21; (7) to be the reward of patience in well-doing, Rom. 2:7, and of working good (a perfect life to which man cannot attain, so as to be justified before God thereby), 2:10; (8) to be given to all to whom it is due, Rom. 13:7 (see 1 Pet. 2:17); (9) as an advantage to be given by believers one to another instead of claiming it for self, Rom. 12:10; (10) to be given to elders that rule well ("double honor"), 1 Tim. 5:17 (here the meaning may be an honorarium); (11) to be given by servants to their master, 1 Tim. 6:1; (12) to be given to wives by husbands, 1 Pet. 3:7; (13) said of the husband's use of the wife, in contrast to the exercise of the passion of lust, 1 Thess. 4:4 (some regard the "vessel" here as the believer's body); (14) of that bestowed upon; parts of the body, 1 Cor. 12:23, 24; (15) of that which belongs to the builder of a house in contrast to the house itself, Heb. 3:3; (16) of that which is not enjoyed by a prophet in his own country, **John 4:44**; (17) of that bestowed by the inhabitants of Melita upon Paul and his fellow-passengers, in gratitude for his benefits of healing, Acts 28:10; (18) of the festive honor to be possessed by nations, and brought into the Holy City, the heavenly Jerusalem, Rev. 21:26 (in some mss., v. 24); (19) of honor bestowed upon things inanimate, a potters' vessel, Rom. 9:21; 2 Tim. 2:20.

Country *patris* (3968), primarily signifies "one's fatherland, native country, of one's own town," Matt. 13:54, 57; Mark 6:1, 4; Luke 4:23-24; **John 4:44**; Heb. 11:14.

4:45 Then when he was come into Galilee, the Galilaeans received him, having seen all the things that he did at Jerusalem at the feast: for they also went unto the feast.

Received *dechomai* (1209), "to receive by deliberate and ready reception of what is offered," is used of (a) taking with the hand, taking hold, taking hold of or up, e.g., Luke 2:28, RV, "he received (Him)," KJV, "took he (Him) up"; 16:6, 7; 22:17; Eph. 6:17; (b) "receiving," said of a place "receiving" a person, of Christ into the Heavens, Acts 3:21; or of persons in giving access to someone as a visitor, e.g., **John 4:45**; 2 Cor. 7:15; Gal. 4:14; Col. 4:10; by way of giving hospitality, etc., e.g., Matt. 10:14, 40 (four times), 41 (twice); 18:5; Mark 6:11; 9:37; Luke 9:5, 48, 53; 10:8, 10; 16:4; v. 9, of reception, "into the eternal tabernacles," said of followers of Christ who have used "the mammon of unrighteousness" to render assistance to ("make ... friends of") others; of Rahab's reception of the spies, Heb. 11:31; of the reception, by the Lord, of the spirit of a departing believer, Acts 7:59; of "receiving" a gift, 2 Cor. 8:4 (in some mss.; RV follows those which omit it); of the favorable reception of testimony and teaching, etc., Luke 8:13; Acts 8:14; 11:1; 17:11; 1 Cor. 2:14; 2 Cor. 8:17; 1 Thess. 1:6; 2:13.

4:46 So Jesus came again into Cana of Galilee, where he made the water wine. And there was a certain nobleman, whose son was sick at Capernaum.

Made *see* Make at *John 2:16*.

Nobleman *basilikos* (937), an adjective, "royal, belonging to a king" (*basileus*), is used of the command, "thou shalt love thy neighbor as thyself," "the royal law," Jas. 2:8; this may mean a law which covers or governs other laws and therefore has a specially regal character (as Hort suggests), or because it is made by a King (a meaning which Deissmann assigns) with whom there is no respect of persons; it is used with the pronoun *tis*, "a certain one," in **John 4:46**, **49**, of a courtier, one in the service of a king, "a nobleman" (some mss. have the noun *basiliskos*, "a petty king," in these two verses). It is used of a country in Acts 12:20, "the king's (country)," and of royal apparel in v. 21.

Sick *astheneo* (770), lit., "to be weak, feeble" (*a*, negative, *sthenos*, "strength"), is translated "to be sick," e.g., in Matt. 10:8, "(the) sick"; 25:36; v. 39 in the best texts; Mark 6:56; Luke 4:40; 7:10 (RV omits the word); 9:2; **John 4:46**; **5:3**, RV (KJV, "impotent folk"); v. 7; **6:2**, RV (KJV, "were diseased"); **11:1-3**, **6**; Acts 9:37; 19:12; Phil. 2:26, 27; 2 Tim. 4:20; Jas. 5:14.

4:47 When he heard that Jesus was come out of Judaea into Galilee, he went unto him, and besought him that he would come down, and heal his son: for he was at the point of death.

Point "To be at the point of death" is a translation (a) of the verb *mello*, "to be about," with *teleutao*, "to end one's life, die," Luke 7:2; (b) of *mello* with *apothnesko*, "to die," **John 4:47**.

4:48-49 Then said Jesus unto him, Except ye see signs and wonders, ye will not believe.

The nobleman saith unto him, Sir, come down ere my child die.

Nobleman *see John 4:46.*

Child *paidion* (3813), a diminutive of *pais*, signifies "a little or young child"; it is used of an infant just born, **John 16:21**, of a male child recently born, e.g., Matt. 2:8; Heb. 11:23; of a more advanced child, Mark 9:24; of a son, **John 4:49**; of a girl, Mark 5:39, 40, 41; in the plural, of "children," e.g., Matt. 14:21. It is used metaphorically of believers who are deficient in spiritual understanding, 1 Cor. 14:20, and in affectionate and familiar address by the Lord to His disciples, almost like the Eng., "lads," **John 21:5**; by the apostle John to the youngest believers in the family of God, 1 John 2:13, 18; there it is to be distinguished from *teknia*, which term he uses in addressing all his readers (vv. 1, 12, 28).

4:50 Jesus saith unto him, Go thy way; thy son liveth. And the man believed the word that Jesus had spoken unto him, and he went his way.

Go *poreuomai* (4198), "to go on one's way, to proceed from one place to another" (from *poros*, "a passage, a ford," Eng., "pore"), is always used in the middle voice in the NT and the Sept., and is the most frequent verb signifying "to go"; it is more distinctly used to indicate procedure or course than the verb *eimi*, "to go" (not found in the NT). It is often rendered "go thy (your) way," in Oriental usage the customary dismissal, marking the close of a case in court. Hence, in ordinary parlance, marking the end of a conversation, etc., e.g., Luke 7:22; 17:19; **John 4:50**; Acts 9:15; 24:25; cf. Dan. 12:9; in Rom. 15:24 (1st part), RV, "go" (KJV, "take my journey"); in Acts 9:3 and 26:13, journeyed (KJV and RV).

Liveth *see* **Living** at *John 4:10.*

4:51 And as he was now going down, his servants met him, and told *him*, saying, Thy son liveth.

Met *apantao* (528), "to go to meet, to meet" (*apo*, "from," *antao*, "to meet with, come face to face with"), is used in Mark 14:13 and Luke 17:12. Some mss. have this verb in Matt. 28:9; Mark 5:2; Luke 14:31; **John 4:51**; Acts 16:16.

Met *hupantao* (5221), "to go to meet, to meet," is used in Matt. 8:28; Luke 8:27; **John 11:20**, **30**, and, in the most authentic mss., in Matt. 28:9; Mark 5:2; Luke 14:31 (of meeting in battle); **John 4:51**; **12:18** and Acts 16:16.

Son *Pais* is rendered "son" in **John 4:51**.

4:52 Then enquired he of them the hour when he began to amend. And they said unto him, Yesterday at the seventh hour the fever left him.

Enquired *punthanomai* (4441), "to inquire," is translated "inquired" in Matt. 2:4, and Acts 21:33, RV (KJV, "demanded"); in Luke 15:26; 18:36 and Acts 4:7 (KJV, "asked"); "inquired" (KJV, "inquired") in **John 4:52**; "inquire" (KJV, "inquire") in Acts 23:20; in Acts 23:34 it denotes "to learn by inquiry," KJV, and RV, "when (he) understood"; elsewhere it is rendered by the verb "to ask," Acts 10:18, 29; 23:19.

Amend *echo* (2192), the usual verb for "to have," is used with the following meanings: (a) "to hold, in the hand," etc., e.g., Rev. 1:16; 5:8; (b) "to hold fast, keep," Luke 19:20; metaphorically, of the mind and conduct, e.g., Mark 16:8; **John 14:21**; Rom. 1:28; 1 Tim. 3:9; 2 Tim. 1:13; (c) "to hold on, cling to, be next to," e.g., of accompaniment, Heb. 6:9, "things that accompany (salvation)," lit., "the things holding themselves of salvation" (RV, marg., "are near to"); of place, Mark 1:38, "next (towns)," lit., "towns holding nigh"; of time, e.g., Luke 13:33, "(the day) following," lit., "the holding (day)"; Acts 13:44; 20:15; 21:26; (d) "to hold, to count, consider, regard," e.g., Matt. 14:5; 21:46; Mark 11:32; Luke 14:18; Philem. 17; (e) "to involve," Heb. 10:35; Jas. 1:4; 1 John 4:18; (f) "to wear," of clothing, arms, etc., e.g., Matt. 3:4; 22:12; **John 18:10**; (g) "to be with child," of a woman, Mark 13:17; Rom. 9:10 (lit., "having conception"); (h) "to possess," the most frequent use, e.g., Matt. 8:20; 19:22; Acts 9:14; 1 Thess. 3:6; (i) of complaints, disputes, Matt. 5:23; Mark 11:25; Acts 24:19; Rev. 2:4, 20; (j) of ability, power, e.g., Luke 12:4; Acts 4:14 (lit., "had nothing to say"); (k) of necessity, e.g., Luke 12:50; Acts 23:17-19; (l) "to be in a certain condition," as of readiness, Acts 21:12 (lit., "I have readily"); of illness, Matt. 4:24, "all that were sick" (lit., "that had themselves sickly"); Mark 5:23, "lieth (lit., "hath herself") at the point of death"; Mark 16:18, "they shall recover" (lit., "shall have themselves well"), **John 4:52**, "he began to amend" (lit., "he had himself better"); of evil works, 1 Tim. 5:25, "they that are otherwise," (lit., "the things having otherwise"); to be so, e.g., Acts 7:1, "are these things so?" (lit., "have these things thus?"), of time, Acts 24:25, "for this time" (lit., "the thing having now").

Yesterday *echthes* or *chthes* (5504), occurs in **John 4:52**; Acts 7:28; Heb. 13:8.

Seventh *hebdomos* (1442), occurs in **John 4:52**; Heb. 4:4 (twice); Jude 14; Rev. 8:1; 10:7; 11:15; 16:17; 21:20.

Fever *puretos* (4446), "feverish heat" (from *pur*, "fire"), hence, "a fever," occurs in Matt. 8:15; Mark 1:31; **John 4:52**; Acts 28:8; in Luke 4:38, with *megas*, "great, a high fever"; v. 39. Luke, as a physician, uses the medical distinction by which the ancients classified fevers into great and little. In the Sept., Deut. 28:22.

Left *see John 4:3.*

4:53 So the father knew that *it was* at the same hour, in the which Jesus said unto him, Thy son liveth: and himself believed, and his whole house.

So *see John 4:40.*

House *oikia* (3614); in Attic law *oikos* denoted the whole estate, *oikia* stood for the dwelling only; this distinction was largely lost in later Greek. In the NT it denotes (a) "a house, a dwelling," e.g., Matt. 2:11; 5:15; 7:24-27; 2 Tim. 2:20; 2 John 10; it is not used of the Tabernacle or the Temple; (b) metaphorically, the heavenly abode, spoken of by the Lord as "My Father's house," **John 14:2**, the eternal dwelling place of believers; the body as the dwelling place of the soul, 2 Cor. 5:1; similarly the resurrection body of believers (*id.*); property, e.g., Mark 12:40; by metonymy, the inhabitants of a house, a household, e.g., Matt. 12:25; **John 4:53**; 1 Cor. 16:15.

4:54 This *is* again the second miracle *that* Jesus did, when he was come out of Judaea into Galilee.

Miracle *see* Miracles at *John 2:11.*

Chapter 5

5:1-2 After this there was a feast of the Jews; and Jesus went up to Jerusalem.

Now there is at Jerusalem by the sheep *market* a pool, which is called in the Hebrew tongue Bethesda, having five porches.

Sheep market *probatikos* (4262), an adjective, used in the grammatically feminine form, in **John 5:2**, to agree with *pule*, "a gate," understood, RV, "sheep *gate*" (not with *agora*, "a market," KJV, "sheep *market*"). In the Sept., Neh. 3:1, 32; 12:39. This "sheep gate" was near the Temple; the sacrifices for the Temple probably entered by it.

Pool *kolumbethra* (2861), denotes "a swimming pool" (akin to *kolumbao*, "to swim," Acts 27:43), **John 5:2** (v. **4** in some mss.), 7; **9:7** (v. **11** in some mss.).

Called *epilego* (1951), *epi* "upon," and *lego*, signifies "to call in addition," i.e., by another name besides that already intimated **John 5:2**; for its other meaning in Acts 15:40.

Tongue *hebraisti* (or *ebraisti*) (1447), denotes (a) "in Hebrew," Rev. 9:11, RV (KJV, "in the Hebrew tongue"); so 16:16; (b) in the Aramaic vernacular of Palestine, **John 5:2**, KJV, "in the Hebrew tongue" (RV, "in Hebrew"); in **19:13**, **17**, KJV, "in the Hebrew" (RV, "in Hebrew"); in v. **20**, KJV and RV, "in Hebrew"; in **20:16**, RV only, "in Hebrew (Rabboni)."

Porches *stoa* (4745), "a portico," is used (a) of the "porches" at the pool of Bethesda, **John 5:2**; (b) of the covered colonnade in the Temple, called Solomon's "porch," **John 10:23**; Acts 3:11; 5:12, a portico on the eastern side of the temple; this and the other "porches" existent in the time of Christ were almost certainly due to Herod's restoration. Cf. *Stoics* (Acts 17:18), "philosophers of the porch."

5:3 In these lay a great multitude of impotent folk, of blind, halt, withered, waiting for the moving of the water.

Lay *katakeimai* (2621), "to lie down," is used of the sick, Mark 1:30; 2:4; Luke 5:25; **John 5:3**, **6**; Acts 28:8; in Acts 9:33 it is rendered "had kept (his bed)," lit., "lying (on a bed)."

Multitude *plethos* (4128), lit., "a fullness," hence, "a large company, a multitude," is used (a) of things: of fish, Luke 5:6; **John 21:6**; of sticks ("bundle"), Acts 28:3; of stars and of sand, Heb. 11:12; of sins, Jas. 5:20; 1 Pet. 4:8; (b) of persons, (1) a "multitude": of people, e.g., Mark 3:7, 8; Luke 6:17; **John 5:3**; Acts 14:1; of angels, Luke 2:13; (2) with the article, the whole number, the "multitude," the populace, e.g., Luke 1:10; 8:37; Acts 5:16; 19:9; 23:7; a particular company, e.g., of disciples, Luke 19:37; Acts 4:32; 6:2, 5; 15:30; of elders, priests, and scribes, 23:7; of the apostles and the elders of the Church in Jerusalem, Acts 15:12.

Impotent *astheneo* (770), "to be without strength," is translated "impotent folk" in **John 5:3**, KJV; cf. v. **7** (the present participle, lit., "being impotent").

Halt *cholos* (5560), "lame," is translated "halt" in Matt. 18:8; Mark 9:45; **John 5:3**, in Acts 14:8, "cripple"; in Luke 14:21, KJV, "halt," RV, "lame"; elsewhere, "lame," Matt. 11:5; 15:30, 31; 21:14: Luke 7:22; 14:13; Acts 3:2; 8:7; Heb. 12:13; some mss. have it in Acts 3:11 (KJV, "the lame man"), RV, "he," translating *autou*, as in the best texts.

Withered *xeros* (3584), is used (a) naturally, of "dry" land, Heb. 11:29; or of land in general, Matt. 23:15, "land"; or of physical infirmity, "withered," Matt. 12:10; Mark 3:3; Luke 6:6, 8; **John 5:3**; (b) figuratively, in Luke 23:31, with reference to the spiritual "barrenness" of the Jews, in contrast to the character of the Lord. Cf. Ps. 1:3; Isa. 56:3; Ezek. 17:24; 20:47.

Waiting *ekdechomai* (1551), lit. and primarily, "to take or receive from" (*ek*, "from," *dechomai*, "to receive"), hence denotes "to await, expect," the only sense of the word in the NT; it suggests a reaching out in readiness to receive something; "expecting," Heb. 10:13; "expect," 1 Cor. 16:11, RV (KJV, "look for"); to wait for, **John 5:3** (KJV, only); Acts 17:16; 1 Cor. 11:33, RV (KJV, "tarry for"); Jas. 5:7; to wait, 1 Pet. 3:20 in some mss.; "looked for," Heb. 11:10.

Moving *kinesis* (2796), "a moving," is found in **John 5:3** (in many ancient authorities, RV, marg.), of the "moving" of the water at the pool of Bethesda.

5:4 For an angel went down at a certain season into the pool, and troubled the water: whosoever then first after the troubling of the water stepped in was made whole of whatsoever disease he had.

Pool *see John 5:2*.

Troubled, Troubling *tarosso* (5015), akin to *tarache*, is used (1) in a physical sense, **John 5:7** (in some mss. v. **4**), (2) metaphorically, (a) of the soul and spirit of the Lord, **John 11:33**, where the true rendering is "He troubled Himself"; (b) of the hearts of disciples, **14:1**, **27**; (c) of the minds of those in fear or perplexity, Matt. 2:3; 14:26; Mark 6:50; Luke 1:12; 24:38; 1 Pet. 3:14; (d) of subverting the souls of believers, by evil doctrine, Acts 15:24; Gal. 1:7; 5:10; (e) of stirring up a crowd, Acts 17:8; v. 13 in the best texts, "troubling (the multitudes)," RV.

Stepped in *embaino* (1684), "to go in" (*en*, "in"), is used only in the Gospels, of "entering" a boat, Matt. 8:23; 9:1; 13:2; 14:22, 32; 15:39; Mark 4:1; 5:18; 6:45; 8:10, 13; Luke 5:3; 8:22, 37; **John 6:17** (in some mss., in v. **22**), **24**, RV, "got into the boats," for KJV, "took shipping"; **21:3**; Acts 21:6 (in the best mss.); of stepping into water, **John 5:4** (RV omits the verb).

Whole *hugies* (5199), (cf. Eng., "hygiene") is used especially in the Gospels of making sick folk "whole," Matt. 12:13; 15:31; Mark 3:5; 5:34; Luke 6:10; **John 5:4**, **6**, **9**, **11**, **14**, **15**; **7:23**; also Acts 4:10; of "sound (speech)," Titus 2:8.

Disease *nosema* (3553), is found in some mss. in **John 5:4**. Cf. noseo, "to dote about, have a diseased craving for," 1 Tim. 6:4.

Had In **John 5:4** (in those mss. which contain the passage), *katecho*, "to hold fast," is used in the passive voice, in the phrase "whatsoever disease he had," lit., "(by whatsoever disease) he was held."

5:5 And a certain man was there, which had an infirmity thirty and eight years.

Eight *okto* (3638), "eight" (Lat., *octo, octavus;* cf. Eng., "octagon," "octave," "octavo," "October," etc.), is used in Luke 2:21; 9:28; **John 20:26**; Acts 9:33; 25:6; 1 Pet. 3:20; in composition with other numerals, *okto kai deka*, lit., "eight and ten, eighteen," Luke 13:4, 11, 16; *triakonta kai okto*, "thirty and eight," **John 5:5**.

5:6 When Jesus saw him lie, and knew that he had been now a long time *in that case*, he saith unto him, Wilt thou be made whole?

Lie *see* Lay at *John 5:3*.

Long *polus* (4183), "much," is used with *chronos*, "time," in Matt. 25:19; **John 5:6**; in Acts 27:21, with *asitia*, KJV, "long abstinence," RV, "long without food."

Case *echo* (2192), "to have," is idiomatically used in the sense of being in a case or condition, as with the infirm man at the pool of Bethesda, **John 5:6**, lit., "that he had already much time (in that case)."

Whole *see John 5:4*.

5:7 The impotent man answered him, Sir, I have no man, when the water is troubled, to put me into the pool: but while I am coming, another steppeth down before me.

Impotent *see John 5:3*.

Troubled *see John 5:4*.

Put *ballo* (906), "to throw, cast, put," is translated "to put," in Matt. 9:17 (twice); 25:27; 27:6; Mark 2:22; 7:33; Luke 5:37; **John 5:7**; **12:6**; **13:2** (of "putting" into the heart by the Devil); **18:11** (of "putting" up a sword), **20:25** (RV twice, KJV, "put" and "thrust"); v. **27**, RV; Jas, 3:3; Rev. 2:24 (RV, "cast").

Pool *see John 5:2*.

While In Acts 27:33 and Heb. 3:13 *achri* (or *achris*) followed by *hou*, the genitive case of the relative pronoun *hos*, lit., "until which," is rendered "while"; cf. *en ho*, in Mark 2:19; Luke 5:34; **John 5:7**; *en to*, in Luke 1:21, RV, "while"; in Heb. 3:15, "while it is said," is, lit., "in the being said" (*en*, with the article and the pres. infin., passive of *lego*); so, e.g., in Matt. 13:25.

Steppeth *katabaino* (2597), "to go, or come, down," is translated "steppeth down" in **John 5:7**.

5:8 Jesus saith unto him, Rise, take up thy bed, and walk.

Bed *krabbatos* (2895), a Macedonian word (Lat. *grabatus*), is "a somewhat mean bed, pallet, or mattress for the poor," Mark 2:4, 9, 11-12; 6:55; **John 5:8-11**; Acts 5:15; 9:33.

5:9 And immediately the man was made whole, and took up his bed, and walked: and on the same day was the sabbath.

Whole *see John 5:4.*

Sabbath *sabbaton* (4521), or *sabbata:* the latter, the plural form, was transliterated from the Aramaic word, which was mistaken for a plural; hence the singular, *sabbaton,* was formed from it. The root means "to cease, desist" (Heb., *shabath*; cf. Arab., *sabata,* "to intercept, interrupt"); the doubled *b* has an intensive force, implying a complete cessation or a making to cease, probably the former. The idea is not that of relaxation or refreshment, but cessation from activity.

The observation of the seventh day of the week, enjoined upon Israel, was a sign between God and His earthly people, based upon the fact that after the six days of creative operations He rested, Exod. 31:16, 17, with 20:8-11. The OT regulations were developed and systematized to such an extent that they became a burden upon the people (who otherwise rejoiced in the rest provided) and a byword for absurd extravagance. Two treatises of the Mishna (the *Shabbath* and *Erubin*) are entirely occupied with regulations for the observance; so with the discussions in the Gemara, on rabbinical opinions. The effect upon current opinion explains the antagonism roused by the Lord's cures wrought on the "Sabbath," e.g., Matt. 12:9-13; **John 5:5-16**, and explains the fact that on a "Sabbath" the sick were brought to be healed after sunset, e.g., Mark 1:32. According to rabbinical ideas, the disciples, by plucking ears of corn (Matt. 12:1; Mark 2:23), and rubbing them (Luke 6:1), broke the "sabbath" in two respects; for to pluck was to reap, and to rub was to thresh. The Lord's attitude towards the "sabbath" was by way of freeing it from these vexatious traditional accretions by which it was made an end in itself, instead of a means to an end (Mark 2:27).

5:10 The Jews therefore said unto him that was cured, It is the sabbath day: it is not lawful for thee to carry *thy* bed.

Jews *see John 2:6.*

Cured *therapeuo* (2323), (Eng., "therapeutics," etc.), denotes (a) primarily, "to serve" (cf. *therapeia* and *therapon*), Acts 17:25 (KJV, "worshiped"); then, (b) "to heal, restore to health, to cure"; it is usually translated "to heal," but "cure" in Matt. 17:16, 18; Luke 7:21; 9:1; **John 5:10**; Acts 28:9, RV.

Lawful *exesti* (1832), an impersonal verb, signifying "it is permitted, it is lawful" (or interrogatively, "is it lawful?"), occurs most frequently in the Synoptic Gospels and the Acts; elsewhere in **John 5:10; 18:31**; 1 Cor. 6:12; 10:23; 2 Cor. 12:4; in Acts 2:29, it is rendered "let me (speak)," lit., "it being permitted"; in the KJV of 8:37, "thou mayest," lit., "it is permitted;" 16:21; in 21:37, "may I," lit., "is it permitted."

5:11 He answered them, He that made me whole, the same said unto me, Take up thy bed, and walk.

Made *see* Make at *John 2:16.*

Whole *see John 5:4.*

> *"Sometimes the Lord disturbs the waters before sending His healing angel."*
>
> FR. JOHN HARPER

5:12-13 Then asked they him, What man is that which said unto thee, Take up thy bed, and walk?

And he that was healed wist not who it was: for Jesus had conveyed himself away, a multitude being in *that* place.

Wist *oida* (1492), "to know," in the pluperfect tense (with imperfect meaning) is rendered "wist" (the past tense of the verb "to wit": cf. WOT) in Mark 9:6; 14:40; Luke 2:49; **John 5:13**; Acts 12:9; 23:5.

Conveyed *ekneuo* (1593), primarily, "to bend to one side, to turn aside"; then "to take oneself away, withdraw," is found in **John 5:13**, of Christ's "conveying" Himself away from one place to another. Some have regarded the verb as having the same meaning as *ekneo,* "to escape," as from peril, "slip away secretly"; but the Lord did not leave the place where He had healed the paralytic in order to escape danger, but to avoid the applause of the throng.

5:14 Afterward Jesus findeth him in the temple, and said unto him, Behold, thou art made whole: sin no more, lest a worse thing come unto thee.

Whole *see John 5:4.*

Sin *hamartano* (264), lit., "to miss the mark," is used in the NT (a) of "sinning" against God, (1) by angels, 2 Pet. 2:4; (2) by man, Matt. 27:4; Luke 15:18, 21 (heaven standing, by metonymy, for God); **John 5:14**; **8:11**; **9:2**, **3**; Rom. 2:12 (twice); 3:23; 5:12, 14, 16; 6:15; 1 Cor. 7:28 (twice), 36; 15:34; Eph. 4:26; 1 Tim. 5:20; Titus 3:11; Heb. 3:17; 10:26; 1 John 1:10; in 2:1 (twice), the aorist tense in each place, referring to an act of "sin"; on the contrary, in 3:6 (twice), 8, 9, the present tense indicates, not the committal of an act, but the continuous practice of "sin"; in 5:16 (twice) the present tense indicates the condition resulting from an act, "unto death" signifying "tending towards death"; (b) against Christ, 1 Cor. 8:12; (c) against man, (1) a brother, Matt. 18:15, RV, "sin" (KJV, "trespass"); v. 21; Luke 17:3, 4, RV, "sin" (KJV, "trespass"); 1 Cor. 8:12; (2) in Luke 15:18, 21, against the father by the Prodigal Son, "in thy sight" being suggestive of befitting reverence; (d) against Jewish law, the Temple, and Caesar, Acts 25:8, RV, "sinned" (KJV, "offended"); (e) against one's own body, by fornication, 1 Cor. 6:18; (f) against earthly masters by servants, 1 Pet. 2:20, RV, "(when) ye sin (and are buffeted for it)," KJV, "(when ye be buffeted) for your faults," lit., "having sinned."

No more *meketi* (3371), generally expressing a prohibition, e.g., Matt. 21:19; **John 5:14**; Rom. 14:13; Eph. 4:28; 1 Tim. 5:23; 1 Pet. 4:2; indicating some condition expressed or implied, e.g., 1 Thess. 3:5; or nonexistence, when the existence might have been possible under certain conditions, e.g., Mark 1:45; 2:2, RV, "no longer" (KJV, "no").

Worse *cheiron* (5501), used as the comparative degree of *kakos*, "evil," describes (a) the condition of certain men, Matt. 12:45; Luke 11:26; 2 Pet. 2:20; (b) evil men themselves and seducers, 2 Tim. 3:13; (c) indolent men who refuse to provide for their own households, and are worse than unbelievers, 1 Tim. 5:8, RV; (d) a rent in a garment, Matt. 9:16; Mark 2:21; (e) an error, Matt. 27:64; (f) a person suffering from a malady, Mark 5:26; (g) a possible physical affliction, **John 5:14**; (h) a punishment, Heb. 10:29, "sorer."

5:15 The man departed, and told the Jews that it was Jesus, which had made him whole.

Told *anangello* (312), "to bring back word, announce," is sometimes rendered "to tell," e.g., **John 5:15**; 2 Cor. 7:7.

Made *see* Make at *John 2:16*.

Whole *see John 5:4*.

5:16 And therefore did the Jews persecute Jesus, and sought to slay him, because he had done these things on the sabbath day.

Persecute *dioko* (1377), has the meanings (a) "to put to flight, drive away," (b) "to pursue," whence the meaning "to persecute," Matt. 5:10-12, 44; 10:23; 23:34; Luke 11:49; 21:12; **John 5:16**; **15:20** (twice); Acts 7:52; 9:4, 5, and similar passages; Rom. 12:14; 1 Cor. 4:12; 15:9; 2 Cor. 4:9, KJV (RV, "pursued"); Gal. 1:13, 23; 4:29; Gal. 5:11, RV, "am ... persecuted" (KJV, "suffer persecution"); so 6:12; Phil. 3:6; 2 Tim. 3:12, "shall suffer persecution"; Rev. 12:13.

Slay Some mss. have it in **John 5:16** (KJV, "to slay").

5:17 But Jesus answered them, My Father worketh hitherto, and I work.

Answered *lego* (3004), primarily to pick out, gather," chiefly denotes "to say, speak, affirm," whether of actual speech, e.g., Matt. 11:17, or of unspoken thought, e.g., Matt. 3:9, or of a message in writing, e.g., 2 Cor. 8:8. The 2nd aorist form *eipon* is used to supply that tense, which is lacking in *lego*. Concerning the phrase "he answered and said," it is a well known peculiarity of Hebrew narrative style that a speech is introduced, not simply by "and he said," but by prefixing "and he answered" (*apokrinomai*, with *eipon*). In Matt. 14:27, "saying," and Mark 6:50, "and saith," emphasis is perhaps laid on the fact that the Lord, hitherto silent as He moved over the lake, then addressed His disciples. That the phrase sometimes occurs where no explicit question has preceded (e.g., Matt. 11:25; 17:4; 28:5; Mark 11:14; 12:35; Luke 13:15; 14:3; **John 5:17**, **19**), illustrates the use of the Hebrew idiom.

Worketh, Work *ergazomai* (2038), is used (I) intransitively, e.g., Matt. 21:28; **John 5:17**; **9:4** (2nd part); Rom. 4:4, 5; 1 Cor. 4:12; 9:6; 1 Thess. 2:9; 4:11; 2 Thess. 3:8, 10-12; (II) transitively, (a) "to work something, produce, perform," e.g., Matt. 26:10, "she hath wrought"; **John 6:28**, **30**; **9:4** (1st part); Acts 10:35; 13:41; Rom. 2:10; 13:10; 1 Cor. 16:10; 2 Cor. 7:10a, in the best texts; Gal. 6:10, RV, "let us work"; Eph. 4:28; Heb. 11:33; 2 John 8; (b) "to earn by working, work for," **John 6:27**, RV, "work" (KJV, "labor").

Hitherto The phrase *heos arti*, "until now," is rendered "hitherto" in **John 16:24**, KJV, and RV; in **5:17**, RV, "even until now," which more definitely expresses the meaning than the KJV, "hitherto"; the rest of the Father and the Son having been broken by man's sin, they were engaged in the accomplishment of their counsels of grace with a view to redemption.

5:18 Therefore the Jews sought the more to kill him, because he not only had broken the sabbath, but said also that God was his Father, making himself equal with God.

More *mallon* (3123), the comparative degree of *mala*, "very, very much," is used (a) of increase, "more," with qualifying words, with *pollo*, "much," e.g., Mark 10:48, "the more (a great deal)"; Rom. 5:15, 17, "(much) more"; Phil. 2:12 (ditto); with *poso*, "how much," e.g., Luke 12:24; Rom. 11:12; with *tosouto*, "by so much," Heb. 10:25; (b) without a qualifying word, by way of comparison, "the more," e.g., Luke 5:15, "so much the more"; **John 5:18**, "the more"; Acts 5:14 (ditto); Phil. 1:9; 1 Thess. 4:1, 10, "more and more"; 2 Pet. 1:10, RV, "the more" (KJV, "the rather"); in Acts 20:35, by a periphrasis, it is translated "more (blessed)"; in Gal. 4:27, "more (than)," lit., "rather (than)"; (c) with qualifying words, similarly to (a), e.g., Mark 7:36.

Only *monon* (3441), "only, exclusively," is translated "only," e.g., in Matt. 5:47; 8:8; **John 5:18**; **11:52**; **12:9**; **13:9**; frequently in Acts, Romans and Galatians.

Broken *luo* (3089), "to loosen," especially by way of deliverance, sometimes has the meaning of "breaking, destructively," e.g., of "breaking" commandments, not only infringing them, but loosing the force of them, rendering them not binding, Matt. 5:19; **John 5:18**; of "breaking" the Law of Moses, **John 7:23**; Scripture, **John 10:35**; of the "breaking up" of a ship, Acts 27:41; of the "breaking down" of the middle wall of partition, Eph. 2:14; of the marriage tie, 1 Cor. 7:27.

His These translate (a) forms of pronouns (a frequent use: in 1 Pet. 2:24, "His own self"); the form *autou*, "his," becomes emphatic when placed between the article and the noun, e.g., 1 Thess. 2:19; Titus 3:5; Heb. 2:4; **John 5:47**; **9:28**; 1 Cor. 10:28; 2 Cor. 8:9; 2 Tim. 2:26; Titus 3:7; 2 Pet. 1:16; (b) *heautou*, "of himself, his own"; the RV rightly puts "his own," for the KJV, "his," in Luke 11:21; 14:26; Rom. 4:19; 5:8, "His own (love)"; 1 Cor. 7:37; Gal. 6:8; Eph. 5:28, 33; 1 Thess. 2:11, 12; 4:4; in Rev. 10:7 the change has not been made; it should read "his own servants"; (c) *idios*, "one's own," "his own," in the RV, in Matt. 22:5; **John 5:18**; 2 Pet. 2:16; in Matt. 25:15, it is rendered "his several"; in **John 19:27**, "his own home," lit., "his own things"; in 1 Tim. 6:15, RV, "its own (times)," referring to the future appearing of Christ; in Heb. 4:10 (end of verse), both KJV and RV have "his," where it should be "his own"; so in Acts 24:23, for KJV and RV, "his"; in 1 Cor. 7:7, RV, "his own," KJV, "his proper"; (d) in Acts 17:28, the genitive case of the definite article, "His (offspring)," lit., "of the" (i.e., the one referred to, namely, God).

Making *see* **Make** at *John 2:16*.

Equal *isos* (2470), "the same in size, number, quality," etc., is translated "equal" in **John 5:18**; Phil. 2:6; in the latter the word is in the neuter plural, lit., "equalities"; "in the RV the words are translated 'on an equality with God,' instead of 'equal with God,' as in the KJV. The change is of great importance to the right interpretation of the whole passage. The rendering 'equal with God,' is evidently derived from the Latin Version.... It was apparently due at first to the fact that the Latin language had no adequate mode of representing the exact form and meaning of the Greek. The neuter plural denotes the various modes or states in which it was possible for the nature of Deity to exist and manifest itself as Divine."

5:19 Then answered Jesus and said unto them, Verily, verily, I say unto you, The Son can do nothing of himself, but what he seeth the Father do: for what things soever he doeth, these also doeth the Son likewise.

Answered, Said *see* **Answered** at *John 5:17*.

Son *see John 1:18*.

What In **John 5:19** "but what" translates a phrase, lit., "if not anything."

He *see John 2:21*.

Seeth *blepo* (991), "to have sight," is used of bodily vision, e.g., Matt. 11:4; and mental, e.g. Matt. 13:13, 14; it is said of God the Father in Matt. 6:4, 6, 18; of Christ as "seeing" what the Father doeth, **John 5:19**. It especially stresses the thought of the person who "sees."

Likewise *homoios* (3668), "in like manner," is rendered "likewise" in the KJV of Matt. 22:26; 27:41, Luke 10:32; 16:25; **John 5:19**; Jas. 2:25; 1 Pet. 3:1, 7; Jude 8; Rev. 8:12 (in all these the RV has "in like manner"); in the following, KJV and RV have "likewise"; Matt. 26:35; Luke 5:33; 6:31; 10:37; 17:28, 31; 22:36; **John 6:11**; **21:13**; Rom. 1:27; 1 Pet. 5:5.

5:20 For the Father loveth the Son, and sheweth him all things that himself doeth: and he will shew him greater works than these, that ye may marvel.

Loveth *see John 3:35*.

Sheweth, Shew *deiknumi* or *deiknuo* (1166), denotes (a) "to show, exhibit," e.g., Matt. 4:8; 8:4; **John 5:20**; **20:20**; 1 Tim. 6:15; (b) "to show by making known," Matt.

16:21; Luke 24:40; **John 14:8, 9**; Acts 10:28; 1 Cor. 12:31; Rev. 1:1; 4:1; 22:6; (c) "to show by way of proving," Jas. 2:18; 3:13.

5:21 For as the Father raiseth up the dead, and quickeneth *them*; even so the Son quickeneth whom he will.

Raiseth *see* **Raise** at *John 2:19*.

Quickeneth *zoopoieo* (2227), "to make alive, cause to live, quicken" (from *zoe*, "life," and *poieo*, "to make"), is used as follows: "(a) of God as the bestower of every kind of life in the universe, 1 Tim. 6:13, and, particularly, of resurrection life, **John 5:21**; Rom. 4:17; (b) of Christ, who also is the bestower of resurrection life, **John 5:21** (2nd part); 1 Cor. 15:45; cf. v. 22; (c) of the resurrection of Christ in "the body of His glory," 1 Pet. 3:18; (d) of the power of reproduction inherent in seed, which presents a certain analogy with resurrection, 1 Cor. 15:36; (e) of the 'changing,' or 'fashioning anew,' of the bodies of the living, which corresponds with, and takes place at the same time as, the resurrection of the dead in Christ, Rom. 8:11; (f) of the impartation of spiritual life, and the communication of spiritual sustenance generally, **John 6:63**; 2 Cor. 3:6; Gal. 3:21."

5:22 For the Father judgeth no man, but hath committed all judgment unto the Son:

Committed *Didomi*, "to give," is rendered "committed" in the KJV of **John 5:22** (RV, "given").

Judgment In **John 9:39**, "For judgment (*krima*) came I into this world," the meaning would appear to be, "for being judged" (as a touchstone for proving men's thoughts and characters), in contrast to **5:22**, "hath given all judging (*krisis*) to the Son"; in Luke 24:20, "delivered Him up to be condemned to death," the latter phrase is, lit., "to a verdict (*krima*) of death" (which they themselves could not carry out); in Mark 12:40, "these shall receive greater condemnation" (*krima*), the phrase signifies a heavier verdict (against themselves). *See also* **Condemnation** at *John 3:19*.

Son *see John 1:18*.

5:23 That all *men* should honour the Son, even as they honour the Father. He that honoureth not the Son honoureth not the Father which hath sent him.

Honour, Honoureth *timao* (5091), "to honor," is used of (a) valuing Christ at a price, Matt. 27:9; (b) "honoring" a person: (1) the "honor" done by Christ to the Father, **John 8:49**; (2) "honor" bestowed by the Father upon him who serves Christ, **John 12:26**; (3) the duty of all to "honor" the Son equally with the Father, **5:23**; (4) the duty of children to "honor" their parents, Matt. 15:4; 19:19; Mark 7:10; 10:19; Luke 18:20; Eph. 6:2; (5) the duty of Christians to "honor" the king, and all men, 1 Pet. 2:17; (6) the respect and material assistance to be given to widows "that are widows indeed," 1 Tim. 5:3; (7) the "honor" done to Paul and his companions by the inhabitants of Melita, Acts 28:10; (8) mere lip profession of "honor" to God, Matt. 15:8; Mark 7:6.

Sent *Pempo* is a more general term than *apostello*; *apostello* usually "suggests official or authoritative sending" (Thayer). A comparison of the usages mentioned above shows how nearly (in some cases practically quite) interchangeably they are used, and yet on close consideration the distinction just mentioned is discernible; in the Gospel of John, cf. *pempo* in **5:23, 24, 30, 37**, *apostello* in **5:33, 36, 38**; *pempo* in **6:38, 39, 44**, *apostello* in **6:29, 57**; the two are not used simply for the sake of variety of expression. *Pempo* is not used in the Lord's prayer in ch. **17**, whereas *apostello* is used six times. *See also John 1:33*.

5:24 Verily, verily, I say unto you, He that heareth my word, and believeth on him that sent me, hath everlasting life, and shall not come into condemnation; but is passed from death unto life.

Sent *see John 1:33*.

Life *see John 3:15*.

Condemnation *see John 3:19*.

Death *thanatos* (2288), "death," is used in Scripture of: (a) the separation of the soul (the spiritual part of man) from the body (the material part), the latter ceasing to function and turning to dust, e.g., **John 11:13**; Heb. 2:15; 5:7; 7:23. In Heb. 9:15, the KJV, "by means of death" is inadequate; the RV, "a death having taken place" is in keeping with the subject. In Rev. 13:3, 12, the RV, "death-stroke" (KJV, "deadly wound") is, lit., "the stroke of death";

(b) the separation of man from God; Adam died on the day he disobeyed God, Gen. 2:17, and hence all mankind are born in the same spiritual condition, Rom. 5:12, 14, 17, 21, from which, however, those who believe in Christ are delivered, **John 5:24**; 1 John 3:14. "Death" is the opposite of life; it never denotes nonexistence. As spiritual life is "conscious existence in communion with God," so spiritual "death" is "conscious existence in separation from God."

"Death, in whichever of the above-mentioned senses it is used, is always, in Scripture, viewed as the penal consequence of sin, and since sinners alone are subject to death, Rom. 5:12, it was as the Bearer of sin that the Lord Jesus submitted thereto on the Cross, 1 Pet. 2:24. And while the physical death of the Lord Jesus was of the essence of His sacrifice, it was not the whole. The darkness symbolized, and His cry expressed, the fact that He was left alone in the Universe, He was 'forsaken;' cf. Matt. 27:45-46."

5:25 Verily, verily, I say unto you, The hour is coming, and now is, when the dead shall hear the voice of the Son of God: and they that hear shall live.

Dead *nekros* (3498), is used of (a) the death of the body, cf. Jas. 2:26, its most frequent sense: (b) the actual spiritual condition of unsaved men, Matt. 8:22; **John 5:25**; Eph. 2:1, 5; 5:14; Phil. 3:11; Col. 2:13; cf. Luke 15:24: (c) the ideal spiritual condition of believers in regard to sin, Rom. 6:11: (d) a church in declension, inasmuch as in that state it is inactive and barren, Rev. 3:1: (e) sin, which apart from law cannot produce a sense of guilt, Rom. 7:8: (f) the body of the believer in contrast to his spirit, Rom. 8:10: (g) the works of the Law, inasmuch as, however good in themselves, Rom. 7:13, they cannot produce life, Heb. 6:1; 9:14: (h) the faith that does not produce works, Jas. 2:17, 26; cf. v. 20.

Hear *see* Heard at *John 1:40.*

Voice *see* Sound at *John 3:8.*

Son *see John 1:18.*

Live *see* Living at *John 4:10.*

5:26 For as the Father hath life in himself; so hath he given to the Son to have life in himself;

Life *see John 3:15.*

5:27 And hath given him authority to execute judgment also, because he is the Son of man.

Execute *poieo* (4160), "to do, to make," is thrice rendered "execute," of the Lord's authority and acts in "executing" judgment, (a) of His authority as the One to whom judgment is committed, **John 5:27**; (b) of the judgment which He will mete out to all transgressors at His second advent, Jude 15; (c) of the carrying out of His Word (not "work," as in the KJV) in the earth, especially regarding the nation of Israel, the mass being rejected, the remnant saved, Rom. 9:28. That He will "execute His Word finishing and cutting it short," is expressive of the summary and decisive character of His action.

Judgment *see* **Condemnation** at *John 3:19.*

Son *see John 1:18.*

5:28 Marvel not at this: for the hour is coming, in the which all that are in the graves shall hear his voice,

Hear *see* Heard at *John 1:40.*

Voice *see* Sound at *John 3:8.*

5:29 And shall come forth; they that have done good, unto the resurrection of life; and they that have done evil, unto the resurrection of damnation.

Come *ekporeuo* (1607), in the middle voice, "to come forth" (*ek*, "out of"), Mark 7:15, 20; **John 5:29**.

Done *see* Doeth at *John 3:20.*

Good *agathos* (18), describes that which, being "good" in its character or constitution, is beneficial in its effect; it is used (a) of things physical, e.g., a tree, Matt. 7:17; ground, Luke 8:8; (b) in a moral sense, frequently of persons and things. God is essentially, absolutely and consummately "good," Matt. 19:17; Mark 10:18; Luke 18:19. To certain persons the word is applied in Matt. 20:15; 25:21, 23; Luke 19:17; 23:50; **John 7:12**; Acts 11:24; Titus 2:5; in a general application, Matt. 5:45; 12:35; Luke 6:45; Rom. 5:7; 1 Pet. 2:18. The neuter of the adjective with the definite article signifies that which is "good," lit., "the good," as being morally honorable, pleasing to God, and therefore beneficial. Christians are to prove it, Rom. 12:2; to cleave to it, 12:9; to do it, 13:3; Gal. 6:10; 1 Pet. 3:11 (here, and here only, the article is absent); **John 5:29** (here, the neuter plural is used, "the good things"); to work it, Rom. 2:10; Eph. 4:28; 6:8; to follow after it, 1 Thess. 5:15; to be zealous of it, 1 Pet. 3:13; to imitate it, 3 John 11; to overcome evil with it, Rom. 12:21. Governmental authorities are ministers of "good," i.e., that which is salutary, suited to the course of human affairs, Rom. 13:4. In Philem. 14, "thy goodness," RV (lit., "thy good"), means "thy benefit." As to Matt. 19:17, "why askest thou Me concerning that which is good?" the RV follows the most ancient mss.

Resurrection *anastasis* (386), denotes (I) "a raising up," or "rising" (*ana*, "up," and *histemi*, "to cause to stand"), Luke 2:34, "the rising up"; the KJV "again" obscures the meaning; the Child would be like a stone against which many in Israel would stumble while many others would find in its strength and firmness a means of their salvation and spiritual life;

(II) of "resurrection" from the dead, (a) of Christ, Acts 1:22; 2:31; 4:33; Rom. 1:4; 6:5; Phil. 3:10; 1 Pet. 1:3; 3:21; by metonymy, of Christ as the Author of "resurrection," **John 11:25**; (b) of those who are Christ's at His Parousia, Luke 14:14, "the resurrection of the just"; Luke 20:33, 35, 36; **John 5:29** (1st part), "the resurrection of life"; **11:24**; Acts 23:6; 24:15 (1st part); 1 Cor. 15:21, 42; 2 Tim. 2:18; Heb. 11:35 (2nd part); Rev. 20:5, "the first resurrection"; hence the insertion of "is" stands for the completion of this "resurrection," of which Christ was "the firstfruits"; 20:6; (c) of "the rest of the dead," after the Millennium (cf. Rev. 20:5); **John 5:29** (2nd part), "the resurrection of judgment"; Acts 24:15 (2nd part), "of the unjust"; (d) of those who were raised in more immediate connection with Christ's "resurrection," and thus had part already in the first "resurrection," Acts 26:23 and Rom. 1:4 (in each of which "dead" is plural; see Matt. 27:52); (e) of the "resurrection" spoken of in general terms, Matt. 22:23; Mark 12:18; Luke 20:27; Acts 4:2; 17:18; 23:8; 24:21; 1 Cor. 15:12, 13; Heb. 6:2; (f) of those who were raised in OT times, to die again, Heb. 11:35 (1st part), lit., "out of resurrection."

Evil *see John 3:20.*

5:30 I can of mine own self do nothing: as I hear, I judge: and my judgment is just; because I seek not mine own will, but the will of the Father which hath sent me.

Mine own self *emautou* (1683), a reflexive pronoun, of the first person, lit., "of myself," is used (a) frequently after various prepositions, e.g., *hupo*, "under," Matt. 8:9; Luke 7:8; RV, "under myself"; *peri*, "concerning," **John 5:31**; **8:14**, **18**; Acts 24:10; *apo*, "from," **John 5:30**; **7:17**, RV, "from" (KJV, "of," which is ambiguous); so v. **28**; **8:28**, **42**; **10:18**; **14:10** (RV, "from"); *pros*, "unto," **John 12:32**, RV, "unto Myself"; **14:3**; Philem. 13, "with me"; *eis*, "to," 1 Cor. 4:6; *huper*, "on behalf of," 2 Cor. 12:5; *ek* (*ex*), "out of," or "from," **John 12:49**, RV, "from Myself"; (b) as the direct object of a verb, Luke 7:7; **John 8:54**; **14:21**; **17:19**; Acts 26:2; 1 Cor. 4:3; 9:19; 2 Cor. 11:7, 9; Gal. 2:18; Phil. 3:13; (c) in other oblique cases of the pronoun, without a preposition, e.g., Acts 20:24, "unto" (or to); 26:9, "with" (or "to"); Rom. 11:4, RV, "for" (KJV, "to"); 1 Cor. 4:4, RV, "against myself" (KJV, inaccurately, "by"); in all these instances the pronoun is in the dative case; in 1 Cor. 10:33, "mine own" (the genitive case); in 1 Cor. 7:7, "I myself" (the accusative case).

Just *dikaios* (1342), was first used of persons observant of *dike*, "custom, rule, right," especially in the fulfillment of duties towards gods and men, and of things that were in accordance with right. The Eng. word "righteous" was formerly spelt "rightwise," i.e., (in a) straight way. In the NT it denotes "righteous," a state of being right, or right conduct, judged whether by the divine standard, or according to human standards, of what is right. Said of God, it designates the perfect agreement between His nature and His acts (in which He is the standard for all men). It is used (1) in the broad sense, of persons: (a) of God, e.g., **John 17:25**; Rom. 3:26; 1 John 1:9; 2:29; 3:7; (b) of Christ, e.g., Acts 3:14; 7:52; 22:14; 2 Tim. 4:8; 1 Pet. 3:18; 1 John 2:1; (c) of men, Matt. 1:19; Luke 1:6; Rom. 1:17; 2:13; 5:7; (2) of things; blood (metaphorical), Matt. 23:35; Christ's judgment, **John 5:30**; any circumstance, fact or deed, Matt. 20:4 (v. 7, in some mss.); Luke 12:57; Acts 4:19; Eph. 6:1; Phil. 1:7; 4:8; Col. 4:1; 2 Thess. 1:6; "the commandment" (the Law), Rom. 7:12; works, 1 John 3:12, the ways of God, Rev. 15:3.

Will *see John 1:13.*

Sent *see John 1:33.*

5:31 If I bear witness of myself, my witness is not true.

Witness *see John 1:7.*

Myself *see* **Mine own self** at *John 5:30.*

True *see John 3:33.*

5:32 There is another that beareth witness of me; and I know that the witness which he witnesseth of me is true.

Witness *see John 1:7.*

True *see John 3:33.*

5:33 Ye sent unto John, and he bare witness unto the truth.

Sent *see John 5:23.*

Witness *see John 1:7.*

5:34 But I receive not testimony from man: but these things I say, that ye might be saved.

I *see John 4:14.*

Testimony *see John 3:32.*

5:35 He was a burning and a shining light: and ye were willing for a season to rejoice in his light.

Burning *kaio* (2545), "to set fire to, to light"; in the passive voice, "to be lighted, to burn," Matt. 5:15; **John 15:6**; Heb. 12:18; Rev. 4:5; 8:8, 10; 19:20; 21:8; 1 Cor. 13:3, is used metaphorically of the heart, Luke 24:32; of spiritual light, Luke 12:35; **John 5:35**.

Shining *see* Shineth at *John 1:5*.

Light *see John 1:4*.

Willing *thelo* (2309), is rendered "ye were willing" in **John 5:35**.

Season *hora* (5610), whence Lat., *hora*, Eng., "hour," primarily denoted any time or period, especially a season. In the NT it is used to denote "a part of the day," especially a twelfth part of day or night, an "hour," e.g., Matt. 8:13; Acts 10:3, 9; 23:23; Rev. 9:15; in 1 Cor. 15:30, "every hour" stands for "all the time"; in some passages it expresses duration, e.g., Matt. 20:12; 26:40; Luke 22:59; inexactly, in such phrases as "for a season," **John 5:35**; 2 Cor. 7:8; "for an hour," Gal. 2:5; "for a short season," 1 Thess. 2:17, RV (KJV, "for a short time," lit., "for the time of an hour").

Rejoice *agalliao* (21), "to rejoice greatly, to exult," is used, (I) in the active voice, of "rejoicing" in God, Luke 1:47; in faith in Christ, 1 Pet. 1:8, RV (middle voice in some mss.), "ye rejoice greatly"; in the event of the marriage of the Lamb, Rev. 19:7, "be exceeding glad," RV; (II) in the middle voice, (a) of "rejoicing" in persecutions, Matt. 5:12 (2nd part); in the light of testimony for God, **John 5:35**; in salvation received through the gospel, Acts 16:34, "he rejoiced greatly," RV; in salvation ready to be revealed, 1 Pet. 1:6; at the revelation of His glory, 1 Pet. 4:13, "with exceeding joy," lit., "ye may rejoice exulting"; (b) of Christ's "rejoicing" (greatly) "in the Holy Spirit," Luke 10:21, RV; said of His praise, as foretold in Ps. 16:9, quoted in Acts 2:26 (which follows the Sept., "My tongue"); (c) of Abraham's "rejoicing," by faith, to see Christ's day, **John 8:56**.

Light *luchnos* (3088), frequently mistranslated "candle," is a portable "lamp" usually set on a stand; the word is used literally, Matt. 5:15; Mark 4:21; Luke 8:16; 11:33, 36; 15:8; Rev. 18:23; 22:5; metaphorically, of Christ as the Lamb, Rev. 21:23, RV, "lamp" (KJV, "light"); of John the Baptist, **John 5:35**, RV, "the lamp" (KJV, "a ... light"); of the eye, Matt. 6:22, and Luke 11:34, RV, "lamp"; of spiritual readiness, Luke 12:35, RV, "lamps"; of "the word of prophecy," 2 Pet. 1:19, RV, "lamp."

5:36 But I have greater witness than *that* of John: for the works which the Father hath given me to finish, the same works that I do, bear witness of me, that the Father hath sent me.

I *see John 4:14*.

Witness *see John 1:7*.

Finish *see John 4:34*.

Sent *see John 1:6*.

5:37 And the Father himself, which hath sent me, hath borne witness of me. Ye have neither heard his voice at any time, nor seen his shape.

Sent *see John 1:33*.

Witness *see John 1:7*.

Voice *see* Sound at *John 3:8*.

Time *see John 1:18*.

Shape *eidos* (1491), properly "that which strikes the eye, that which is exposed to view," signifies the "external appearance, form, or shape," and in this sense is used of the Holy Spirit in taking bodily form, as a dove, Luke 3:22; of Christ, 9:29, "the fashion of His countenance." Christ used it, negatively, of God the Father, when He said "Ye have neither heard His voice at any time, nor seen His form," **John 5:37**. Thus it is used with reference to each person of the Trinity. Probably the same meaning attaches to the word in the apostle's statement, "We walk by faith, not by sight (*eidos*)," 2 Cor. 5:7, where *eidos* can scarcely mean the act of beholding, but the visible "appearance" of things which are set in contrast to that which directs faith. The believer is guided, then, not only by what he beholds but by what he knows to be true though it is invisible. It has a somewhat different significance in 1 Thess. 5:22, in the exhortation, "Abstain from every form of evil," i.e., every sort or kind of evil (not "appearance," KJV).

> *"If you check out the life of Jesus you will discover what made him perfect. He did not attain a state of perfection by carrying around in his pocket a list of rules and regulations, or by seeking to conform to the cultural mores of his time. He was perfect because he never made a move without his Father."*
>
> THOMAS SKINNER

This meaning was common in the papyri, the Greek writings of the closing centuries, BC, and the New Testament era.

5:38 And ye have not his word abiding in you: for whom he hath sent, him ye believe not.

Sent *see John 1:6.*

5:39 Search the scriptures; for in them ye think ye have eternal life: and they are they which testify of me.

Search *eraunao* or *ereunao,* an earlier form, (2045), "to search, examine," is used (a) of God, as "searching" the heart, Rom. 8:27; (b) of Christ, similarly, Rev. 2:23; (c) of the Holy Spirit, as "searching" all things, 1 Cor. 2:10, acting in the spirit of the believer; (d) of the OT prophets, as "searching" their own writings concerning matters foretold of Christ, testified by the Spirit of Christ in them, 1 Pet. 1:11; (e) of the Jews, as commanded by the Lord to "search" the Scriptures, **John 5:39**, KJV, and RV marg., "search," RV text, "ye search," either is possible grammatically; (f) of Nicodemus as commanded similarly by the chief priests and Pharisees, **John 7:52**.

Scriptures *see* Scripture at *John 2:22.*

Testify *see John 2:25.*

5:40-41 And ye will not come to me, that ye might have life.
I receive not honour from men.

Honour *doxa* (1391), "glory," is translated "honor" in the KJV of **John 5:41, 44** (twice); **8:54**; 2 Cor. 6:8, and Rev. 19:7; the RV keeps to the word "glory," as the KJV everywhere else.

5:42-43 But I know you, that ye have not the love of God in you.
I am come in my Father's name, and ye receive me not: if another shall come in his own name, him ye will receive.

I *see John 4:14.*

5:44 How can ye believe, which receive honour one of another, and seek not the honour that *cometh* from God only?

Honour *see John 5:41.*

Only *monos* (3441), "alone, solitary," is translated "only," e.g., in Matt. 4:10; 12:4; 17:8; 1 Cor. 9:6; 14:36; Phil. 4:15; Col. 4:11; 2 John 1; it is used as an attribute of God in **John 5:44; 17:3**; Rom. 16:27; 1 Tim. 1:17; 1 Tim. 6:15-16; Jude 4, 25; Rev. 15:4.

5:45 Do not think that I will accuse you to the Father: there is *one* that accuseth you, *even* Moses, in whom ye trust.

I *see John 4:14.*

Trust *elpizo* (1679), "to hope," is not infrequently translated in the KJV, by the verb "to trust"; the RV adheres to some form of the verb "to hope," e.g., **John 5:45**, "Moses, on whom ye have set your hope"; 2 Cor. 1:10, "on whom we have set our hope"; so in 1 Tim. 4:10; 5:5; 6:17; see also, e.g., Matt. 12:21; Luke 24:21; Rom. 15:12, 24. The verb is followed by three prepositions: (1) *eis,* rendered "on" in **John 5:45** (as above); the meaning is really "in" as in 1 Pet. 3:5, "who hoped in God"; the "hope" is thus said to be directed to, and to center in, a person; (2) *epi,* "on," Rom. 15:12, "On Him shall the Gentiles hope," RV; so 1 Tim. 4:10; 5:5 (in the best mss.); 6:17, RV; this expresses the ground upon which "hope" rests; (3) *en,* "in," 1 Cor. 15:19, "we have hoped in Christ," RV, more lit., "we are (men) that have hoped in Christ," the preposition expresses that Christ is not simply the ground upon whom, but the sphere and element in whom, the "hope" is placed. The form of the verb (the perfect participle with the verb to be, lit., "are having hoped") stresses the character of those who "hope," more than the action; "hope" characterizes them, showing what sort of persons they are.

5:46-47 For had ye believed Moses, ye would have believed me: for he wrote of me.
But if ye believe not his writings, how shall ye believe my words?

His *see John 5:18.*

Writings *gramma* (1121), primarily denotes "that which is traced or drawn, a picture"; then, "that which is written," (a) "a character, letter of the alphabet," 2 Cor. 3:7; "written," lit., "(in) letters", Gal. 6:11; here the reference is not to the length of the epistle (Paul never uses *gramma,* either in the singular or the plural of his epistles; of these he uses *epistole*), but to the size of the characters written by his own hand (probably from this verse to the end, as the use of the past tense, "I have written," is, according to Greek idiom, the equivalent of our "I am writing"). Moreover, the word for "letters" is here in the dative case, *grammasin,* "with (how large) letters"; (b) "a writing, a written document, a bond" (KJV, "bill") Luke 16:6, 7; (c) "a letter, by way of correspondence," Acts 28:21; (d) the Scriptures of the OT, 2 Tim. 3:15; (e) "learning," **John 7:15**, "letters"; Acts 26:24, "(much) learning" (lit., "many letters"); in the papyri an illiterate person is often spoken of as one who does not know "letters," "which never means anything else than inability to write" (Moulton and Milligan); (f) "the letter," the written commandments of the Word of God, in contrast to the inward operation of the Holy Spirit under the New Covenant, Rom. 2:27, 29; 7:6; 2 Cor. 3:6; (g) "the books of Moses," **John 5:47**.

Chapter 6

6:1 After these things Jesus went over the sea of Galilee, which is *the sea* of Tiberias.

Sea *thalassa* (2281), is used (a) chiefly literally, e.g., "the Red Sea," Acts 7:36; 1 Cor. 10:1; Heb. 11:29; the "sea" of Galilee or Tiberias, Matt. 4:18; 15:29; Mark 6:48, 49, where the acts of Christ testified to His deity; **John 6:1**; **21:1**; in general, e.g., Luke 17:2; Acts 4:24; Rom. 9:27; Rev. 16:3; 18:17; 20:8, 13; 21:1; (b) metaphorically, of "the ungodly men" described in Jude 13 (cf. Isa. 57:20); (c) symbolically, in the apocalyptic vision of "a glassy sea like unto crystal," Rev. 4:6, emblematic of the fixed purity and holiness of all that appertains to the authority and judicial dealings of God; in 15:2, the same, "mingled with fire," and, standing by it (RV) or on it (KJV and RV marg.), those who had "come victorious from the beast" (ch. 13).

6:2 And a great multitude followed him, because they saw his miracles which he did on them that were diseased.

Miracles *see John 2:11.*

Diseased *astheneo* (770), "to lack strength, to be weak, sick," is translated "were diseased" in **John 6:2**, KJV (RV, "were sick").

6:3 And Jesus went up into a mountain, and there he sat with his disciples.

Went *anerchomai* (424), "to go up" (*ana*), occurs in **John 6:3**; Gal. 1:17, 18.

6:4 And the passover, a feast of the Jews, was nigh.

Passover *see John 2:13.*

6:5 When Jesus then lifted up *his* eyes, and saw a great company come unto him, he saith unto Philip, Whence shall we buy bread, that these may eat?

Lifted *see* Lift at *4:35.*

Saw *theaomai* (2300), "to view attentively, to see with admiration, desire, or regard," stresses more especially the action of the person beholding; it is used in Matt. 11:7 (RV, "to behold"), while *idein*, the infinitive of *eidon* is used in the questions in the next two verses; in verse 7 the interest in the onlooker is stressed, in vv. 8, 9, the attention is especially directed to the object "seen." The verb is translated "to see" in the KJV and RV of Matt. 6:1; Mark 16:11, 14; **John 6:5**; Acts 8:18 (in some mss.); 21:27; Rom. 15:24; elsewhere, for the KJV, "to see," the RV uses the verb "to behold," bringing out its force more suitably.

Eat *bibrosko* (977), "to eat," is derived from a root, *bor–*, "to devour" (likewise seen in the noun *broma*, "food, meat"; cf Eng., "carnivorous," "voracious," from Lat. *vorax*). This verb is found in **John 6:13**. The difference between this and *phago* may be seen perhaps in the fact that whereas in the Lord's question to Philip in v. **5**, *phago* intimates nothing about a full supply, the verb *bibrosko*, in v. **13**, indicates that the people had been provided with a big meal, of which they had partaken eagerly.

6:6 And this he said to prove him: for he himself knew what he would do.

Prove *peirazo* (3985), "to try," either in the sense of attempting, e.g., Acts 16:7, or of testing, is rendered "to prove" in **John 6:6**.

Knew *oida* (1492), from the same root as *eidon*, "to see," is a perfect tense with a present meaning, signifying, primarily, "to have seen or perceived"; hence, "to know, to have knowledge of," whether absolutely, as in divine knowledge, e.g., Matt. 6:8, 32; **John 6:6**, **64**; **8:14**; **11:42**; **13:11**; **18:4**; 2 Cor. 11:31; 2 Pet. 2:9; Rev. 2:2, 9, 13, 19; 3:1, 8, 15; or in the case of human "knowledge," to know from observation, e.g., 1 Thess. 1:4, 5; 2:1; 2 Thess. 3:7. The differences between *ginosko* and *oida* demand consideration: (a) *ginosko*, frequently suggests inception or progress in "knowledge," while *oida* suggests fullness of "knowledge," e.g., **John 8:55**, "ye have not known Him" (*ginosko*), i.e., begun to "know," "but I know Him" (*oida*), i.e., "know Him perfectly"; **13:7**, "What I do thou knowest not now," i.e. Peter did not yet perceive (*oida*) its significance, "but thou shalt understand," i.e., "get to know (*ginosko*), hereafter"; **14:7**, "If ye had known Me" (*ginosko*), i.e., "had definitely come to know Me," "ye would have known My Father also" (*oida*), i.e., "would have had perception of": "from henceforth ye know Him" (*ginosko*), i.e., having unconsciously been coming to the Father, as the One who was in Him, they would now consciously be in the constant and progressive experience of "knowing" Him; in Mark 4:13, "Know ye not (*oida*) this parable? and how shall ye know (*ginosko*) all the parables?" (RV), i.e., "Do ye not understand this parable? How shall ye come to perceive all ..." the intimation being that the first parable is a leading and testing one; (b) while *ginosko* frequently implies an active relation between the one who "knows" and the person or thing "known," *oida* expresses the fact that the object has simply come within the scope of the "knower's" perception; thus in Matt. 7:23 "I never knew you" (*ginosko*) suggests "I have never been in approving connection with you," whereas in 25:12, "I know you not" (*oida*) suggests "you stand in no relation to Me."

6:7 Philip answered him, Two hundred pennyworth of bread is not sufficient for them, that every one of them may take a little.

Two hundred *diakosioi* (1250), occurs in Mark 6:37; **John 6:7**; **21:8**; Acts 23:23 (twice); 27:37, "two hundred (threescore and sixteen)"; Rev. 11:3, "(a thousand) two hundred (and threescore)"; so 12:6.

Pennyworth *denarion* (1220), a Roman coin, a *denarius*, a little less than the value of the Greek *drachme*, now estimated as amounting to about 9 1/2d. in the time of our Lord, occurs in the singular, e.g., Matt. 20:2; 22:19; Mark 12:15; Rev. 6:6; in the plural, e.g., Matt. 18:28; Mark 14:5; Luke 7:41; 10:35; **John 12:5**; "pennyworth" in Mark 6:37 and **John 6:7**, lit., "(loaves of two hundred) pence." Considering the actual value, "shilling" would have been a more accurate translation, as proposed by the American translators, retaining "penny" for the *as*, and "farthing" for the *quadrans*.

Sufficient *arkeo* (714), "to suffice," is rendered "is sufficient" in **John 6:7**; 2 Cor. 12:9; "it sufficeth" in **John 14:8**.

Little *brachus* (1024), "short," is used to some extent adverbially (a) of time, with the preposition *meta*, "after," Luke 22:58, "(after) a little while"; in Acts 5:34, without a preposition, RV, "a little while" (KJV, "a little space"); in Heb. 2:7, 9, "a little" (KJV marg. in v. 7, and RV marg., in both, "a little while"), where the writer transfers to time what the Sept. in Ps. 8:5 says of rank; (b) of quantity, **John 6:7**; in Heb. 13:22, preceded by the preposition *dia*, "by means of," and with *logo*., "words" (genitive plural) understood, "(in) few words"; (c) of distance, Acts 27:28, RV, "a little space" (KJV, "a little further").

6:8-9 One of his disciples, Andrew, Simon Peter's brother, saith unto him,

There is a lad here, which hath five barley loaves, and two small fishes: but what are they among so many?

Lad *paidarion* (3808), another diminutive of *pais*, is used of "boys and girls," in Matt. 11:16 (the best texts have *paidiois* here), and a "lad," **John 6:9**; the tendency in colloquial Greek was to lose the diminutive character of the word.

Barley *krithinos* (2916), signifies "made of barley," **John 6:9, 13**.

Fishes *opsarion* (3795), is a diminutive of *opson*, "cooked meat," or "a relish, a dainty dish, especially of fish"; it denotes "a little fish," **John 6:9, 11; 21:9, 10, 13**.

Many *tosoutos* (5118), "so great, so much, so many," (a) qualifying a noun, is rendered "these many (years)" in Luke 15:29; "so many," **John 12:37**; 1 Cor. 14:10; (b) without a noun, **John 6:9**; **21:11**; Gal. 3:4, "so many things."

6:10 And Jesus said, Make the men sit down. Now there was much grass in the place. So the men sat down, in number about five thousand.

Make *see John 2:16.*

Men *anthropos* (444), "man," without distinction of sex (cf. *aner*, "a male"), is translated "people" in **John 6:10**, RV (KJV, "men").

Sit, Sat *anapipto* (377), "to fall back" (*ana*, "back," *pipto*, "to fall"), denotes, in the NT, "to recline for a repast," Matt. 15:35; Mark 6:40; 8:6; Luke 11:37; 14:10; 17:7; 22:14; **John 6:10** (twice); **13:12**; in **John 13:25** and **21:20** it is used of leaning on the bosom of Christ.

Grass *chortos* (5528), primarily denoted "a feeding enclosure" (whence Latin *hortus*, "a garden"; Eng.. "yard," and "garden"); then, "food," especially grass for feeding cattle; it is translated "grass" in Matt. 6:30; 14:19; Mark 6:39 (where "the green grass" is the first evidence of early spring); Luke 12:28; **John 6:10**; Jas. 1:10, 11; 1 Pet. 1:24; Rev. 8:7; 9:4; "blade" in Matt. 13:26; Mark 4:28; "hay" in 1 Cor. 3:12, used figuratively. In Palestine or Syria there are 90 genera and 243 species of grass.

Number *arithmos* (706), number, "a number" (Eng., "arithmetic," etc.), occurs in Luke 22:3; **John 6:10**; Rom. 9:27; elsewhere five times in Acts, ten times in Revelation.

Thousand The following compounds represent different multiples of a thousand: *dischilioi*, 2,000, Mark 5:13; *trischilioi*, 3,000, Acts 2:41; *tetrakischilioi*, 4,000, Matt. 15:38; 16:10; Mark 8:9, 20; Acts 21:35; *pentakischilioi*, 5,000, Matt. 14:21; 16:9; Mark 6:44; 8:9; Luke 9:14; **John 6:10**; *heplakischilioi*, 7,000, Rom. 11:4.

6:11 And Jesus took the loaves; and when he had given thanks, he distributed to the disciples, and the disciples to them that were set down; and likewise of the fishes as much as they would.

Thanks *eucharisteo* (2168), "to give thanks," (a) is said of Christ, Matt. 15:36; 26:27; Mark 8:6; 14:23; Luke 22:17, 19; **John 6:11, 23; 11:41;** 1 Cor. 11:24; (b) of the Pharisee in Luke 18:11 in his selfcomplacent prayer; (c) is used by Paul at the beginning of all his epistles, except 2 Cor. (see, however, *eulogetos* in 1:3), Gal., 1 Tim., 2 Tim. (see, however, *charin echo,* 1:3), and Titus, (1) for his readers, Rom. 1:8; Eph. 1:16; Col. 1:3; 1 Thess. 1:2; 2 Thess. 1:3 (cf. 2:13); virtually so in Philem. 4; (2) for fellowship shown, Phil. 1:3; (3) for God's gifts to them, 1 Cor. 1:4; (d) is recorded (1) of Paul elsewhere, Acts 27:35; 28:15; Rom. 7:25; 1 Cor. 1:14; 14:18; (2) of Paul and others, Rom. 16:4; 1 Thess. 2:13; of himself, representatively, as a practice, 1 Cor. 10:30; (3) of others, Luke 17:16; Rom. 14:6 (twice); 1 Cor. 14:17; Rev. 11:17; (e) is used in admonitions to the saints, the Name of the Lord Jesus suggesting His character and example, Eph. 5:20; Col. 1:12; 3:17; 1 Thess. 5:18; (f) as the expression of a purpose, 2 Cor. 1:11, RV; (g) negatively of the ungodly, Rom. 1:21. "Thanksgiving" is the expression of joy Godward, and is therefore the fruit of the Spirit (Gal. 5:22); believers are encouraged to abound in it (e.g., Col. 2:7).

Distributed *diadidomi* (1239), lit., "to give through," (*dia,* "through," *didomi,* "to give"), as from one to another, "to deal out," is said of "distributing" to the poor, Luke 18:22; Acts 4:35, "distribution was made," or to a company of people, **John 6:11**. It is translated "divideth" in Luke 11:22. In Rev. 17:13 the most authentic mss. have the verb *didomi,* to give, instead of the longer form.

Set *anakeimai* (345), "to recline at table" (*ana,* "up" *keimai,* "to lie"), is rendered "to sit at meat" in Matt. 9:10 (RV, marg., "reclined"); 26:7; 26:20, RV, "He was sitting at meat" (KJV, "He sat down"); Mark 16:14; in some mss. Luke 7:37; 22:27 (twice); in Mark 14:18, "sat"; in **John 6:11**, "were set down"; **John 12:2** in the best texts.

Likewise *see John 5:19.*

Fishes *see John 6:9.*

Much In **John 6:11** *hosos* denotes "as much as."

6:12 When they were filled, he said unto his disciples, Gather up the fragments that remain, that nothing be lost.

Filled *empiplemi* (1705), or *empletho,* "to fill full, to satisfy," is used (a) of "filling" the hungry, Luke 1:53; **John 6:12**; of the abundance of the rich, Luke 6:25; (b) metaphorically, of a company of friends, Rom. 15:24, RV, "satisfied," for KJV, "filled."

Gather *sunago* (4863), "to assemble" (*sun,* "together," *ago,* "to bring"), is used of the "gathering together" of people or things; in Luke 12:17-18, "bestow," with reference to the act of "gathering" one's goods; so in Luke 15:13, suggesting that the Prodigal, having "gathered" all his goods together, sold them off; in **John 6:12**, of "gathering" up fragments; in **John 18:2**, "resorted," with reference to the "assembling" of Christ with His disciples in the garden of Gethsemane, there in the passive voice (unsuitable, however, in an English translation). In Acts 11:26, the RV has "were gathered together (with the church)," for KJV, "assembled themselves" (possibly "they were hospitably entertained by"). The verb is not found in the most authentic mss. in Rev. 13:10.

Fragments *klasma* (2801), "a broken piece" (from *klao,* "to break") is used of the broken pieces from the feeding of the multitudes, RV, "broken pieces," KJV, "fragments," Matt. 14:20; Mark 6:43; 8:19, 20; Luke 9:17; **John 6:12, 13**; in Matt. 15:37 and Mark 8:8, RV, "broken pieces" (KJV, "broken meat").

Remain *perisseuo* (4052), "to abound, to be over and above, to remain over," is rendered "(that which) remained over" in Matt. 14:20, RV; and Luke 9:17, RV (KJV, "remained"); **John 6:12, 13** (KJV, "... over and above").

Lost *see* Perish at *John 3:16.*

6:13 Therefore they gathered *them* together, and filled twelve baskets with the fragments of the five barley loaves, which remained over and above unto them that had eaten.

Filled *see John 6:12.*

Baskets *kophinos* (2894), was "a wicker basket," originally containing a certain measure of capacity, Matt. 14:20; 16:9; Mark 6:43 (RV, "basketfuls"); 8:19; Luke 9:17; 13:8 in some mss.; **John 6:13**.

Fragments *see John 6:12.*

Barley *see John 6:9.*

Remained *see* Remain at *John 6:12.*

Eaten *see* Eat at *John 6:5.*

6:14 Then those men, when they had seen the miracle that Jesus did, said, This is of a truth that prophet that should come into the world.

Miracle *see* **Miracles** at *John 2:11*.

Truth *alethos* (230), "truly, surely," is rendered "of a truth" in Matt. 14:33; 26:73 and Mark 14:70, RV, (KJV, "surely"); Luke 9:27; 12:44; 21:3; **John 6:14; 7:40; 17:8**, RV, "of a truth" (KJV, "surely"); Acts 12:11, RV (KJV, "of a surety"); "in truth," 1 Thess. 2:13; "truly," Matt. 27:54; Mark 15:39.

Prophet *see John 1:21*.

6:15 When Jesus therefore perceived that they would come and take him by force, to make him a king, he departed again into a mountain himself alone.

Perceived *ginosko* (1097), "to know by experience and observation," is translated "to perceive" in Matt. 12:15, RV (KJV, "knew"); 16:8; 21:45; 22:18; 26:10, RV, (KJV, "understood"); Mark 8:17; 12:12 and 15:10, RV (KJV, "knew"); so Luke 9:11; 18:34; in Luke 7:39, RV (KJV, "known"); 20:19; **John 6:15**; **8:27**, RV (KJV, "understood"); **16:19**, RV (KJV, "knew"); Acts 23:6; Gal. 2:9; in 1 John 3:16, KJV, "perceive" (RV, "know," perfect tense, lit., "we have perceived," and therefore "know").

Take ... by force *harpazo* (726), "to snatch or catch away," is said of the act of the Spirit of the Lord in regard to Philip in Acts 8:39; of Paul in being "caught" up to paradise, 2 Cor. 12:2, 4; of the rapture of the saints at the return of the Lord, 1 Thess. 4:17; of the rapture of the man child in the vision of Rev. 12:5. This verb conveys the idea of force suddenly exercised, as in Matt. 11:12, "take (it) by force"; 12:29, "spoil" (some mss. have *diarpazo* here), in 13:19, RV, "snatcheth"; for forceful seizure, see also **John 6:15**; **10:12, 28-29**; Acts 23:10; in Jude 23, RV, "snatching."

Departed *anachoreo* (402), "to go back, recede, retire" (*ana*, "back or up," *choreo*, "to make room for, betake oneself," *choros*, "a place"), is translated "departed" in Matt. 2:12–14; 4:12 (RV, "withdrew"); so in 14:13 and 15:21, but "departed" in 27:5; "withdrew" in **John 6:15**. In Matt. 2:22 the RV has "withdrew," which is preferable to the KJV, "turned aside." The most suitable translation wherever possible, is by the verb "to withdraw."

6:16-17 And when even was *now* come, his disciples went down unto the sea,

And entered into a ship, and went over the sea toward Capernaum. And it was now dark, and Jesus was not come to them.

Entered *see* **Stepped in** at *John 5:4*.

Now *ede* (2235), denotes "already, now already," "the subjective present, with a suggested reference to some other time, or to some expectation" (Thayer), e.g., Matt. 3:10; 14:24; Luke 11:7; **John 6:17**; Rom. 1:10; 4:19; 13:11; Phil. 4:10.

Dark *see* **Darkness** at *John 1:5*.

6:18 And the sea arose by reason of a great wind that blew.

Arose *diegeiro* (1326), signifies "to rouse, to awaken from sleep." The active voice is not used intransitively. In Matt. 1:24, RV, "Joseph arose from his sleep," the passive participle is, lit., "being aroused." In Mark 4:39 (KJV, "he arose," RV, "he awoke"), the lit. rendering is "he being awakened." In **John 6:18** the imperfect tense of the passive voice is used, and the rendering should be, "the sea was being aroused.

Great *megas* (3173), is used (a) of external form, size, measure, e.g., of a stone, Matt. 27:60; fish, **John 21:11**; (b) of degree and intensity, e.g., of fear, Mark 4:41; wind, **John 6:18**; Rev. 6:13, RV, "great" (KJV, "mighty"); of a circumstance, 1 Cor. 9:11; 2 Cor. 11:15; in Rev. 5:2, 12, the RV has "great" (KJV, "loud"), of a voice; (c) of rank, whether of persons, e.g., God, Titus 2:13; Christ as a "great Priest," Heb. 10:21, RV; Diana, Acts 19:27, Simon Magus, Acts 8:9 "(some) great one"; in the plural "great ones," Matt. 20:25; Mark 10:42, those who hold positions of authority in gentile nations; or of things, e.g., a mystery, Eph. 5:32. Some mss. have it in Acts 8:8, of joy.

6:19 So when they had rowed about five and twenty or thirty furlongs, they see Jesus walking on the sea, and drawing nigh unto the ship: and they were afraid.

Rowed *elauno* (1643), "to drive," is used of "rowing" or sailing a boat, Mark 6:48; **John 6:19**.

About *hos* (5613), usually means "as." Used with numerals it signifies "about," e.g., Mark 5:13; 8:9; **John 1:40; 6:19; 11:18**; Acts 1:15; Rev. 8:1.

Twenty *eikosi* (1501), occurs in Luke 14:31; **John 6:19**; Acts 1:15; 27:28; 1 Cor. 10:8; of the "four and twenty" elders, in Rev. 4:4 (twice), 10; 5:8; 11:16; 19:4 (combined in one numeral with *tessares*, "four," in some mss.).

Furlongs *stoion* (4712), denotes (a) "a stadium," i.e., a measure of length, 600 Greek feet, or one-eighth of a Roman mile, Matt. 14:24 (in the best mss.); Luke 24:13; **John 6:19**; **11:18**; Rev. 14:20; 21:16; (b) "a race course," the length of the Olympic course, 1 Cor. 9:24.

Drawing *ginomai* (1096), "to become, begin to be," is translated "drawing nigh," in **John 6:19**.

Nigh *see* **Near** at *John 3:23*.

6:20-21 But he saith unto them, It is I; be not afraid.

Then they willingly received him into the ship: and immediately the ship was at the land whither they went.

Willingly *thelo* (2309), usually expresses "desire" or "design"; it is most frequently translated by "will" or "would"; see especially Rom. 7:15, 16, 18-21. In 1 Tim. 2:4, RV, "willeth" signifies the gracious "desire" of God for all men to be saved; not all are "willing" to accept His condition, depriving themselves either by the self-established criterion of their perverted reason, or because of their self-indulgent preference for sin. In **John 6:21**, the KJV renders the verb "willingly" (RV, "they were willing"); in 2 Pet. 3:5, KJV, the present participle is translated "willingly" (RV, "wilfully"). The following are RV renderings for the KJV, "will": Matt. 16:24, 25, "would"; "wouldest," 19:21 and 20:21; "would," 20:26, 27; Mark 8:34, 35; 10:43, 44; "would fain," Luke 13:31; "would," **John 6:67**; "willeth," **7:17**; in **8:44**, "it is your will (to do)"; "wouldest," Rom. 13:3; "would," 1 Cor. 14:35 and 1 Pet. 3:10.

Received *see* **Receive** at *John 3:11*.

Land *ge* (1093), in one of its usages, denotes (a) "land" as distinct from sea or other water, e.g., Mark 4:1; 6:47; Luke 5:3; **John 6:21**; (b) "land" as subject to cultivation, e.g., Luke 14:35; (c) "land" as describing a country or region, e.g., Matt. 2:20, 21; 4:15; Luke 4:25; in 23:44, RV, "(the whole) land," KJV, "(all the) earth"; Acts 7:29; Heb. 11:9, RV, "a land (not his own)," KJV "a (strange) country;" Jude 5. In Acts 7:11 the KJV follows a reading of the noun with the definite article which necessitates the insertion of "land."

6:22 The day following, when the people which stood on the other side of the sea saw that there was none other boat there, save that one whereinto his disciples were entered, and that Jesus went not with his disciples into the boat, but *that* his disciples were gone away alone;

Following *see John 1:43*.

Side *peran* (4008), an adverb, signifying "beyond, on the other side," is used (a) as a preposition and translated "on the other side of," e.g., in Mark 5:1; Luke 8:22; **John 6:1**, RV; **6:22, 25**; (b) as a noun with the article, e.g., Matt. 8:18, 28; 14:22; 16:5.

Boat *ploiarion* (4142), "a skiff or small boat," is a diminutive of *ploion*, Mark 3:9; 4:36; **John 6:22, 23, 24; 21:8**.

Entered *see* **Stepped in** at *John 5:4*.

Went In the following, the verbs mentioned, translated in the KJV by some form of the verb "to go," are rendered in the RV more precisely in accordance with their true meaning: (a) *zeteo*, "to seek," so the RV in **John 7:19, 20**; Acts 21:31; Rom. 10:3 (KJV, "to go about"); (b) *peirazo*, "to make an attempt," Acts 24:6, RV, "assayed" (KJV, "have gone about"); (c) *peirao*, "to attempt," Acts 26:21, RV, "assayed" KJV, "went about"); (d) *epistrepho*, "to return," Acts 15:16, RV, "let us return" (KJV, "let us go again"); (e) *huperbaino*, "to overstep," 1 Thess. 4:6, RV, "transgress" (KJV, "go beyond"); (f) *diistemi*, "to set apart, make an interval," Acts 27:28, RV, "(after) a space" (KJV, "had gone further"); (g) *suneiserchomai*, "to go in with," **John 6:22** and **18:15**, RV, "entered (in) with" (KJV, "went ... with"); (h) *phero*, in the middle voice, lit., "to bear oneself along," Heb. 6:1, RV, "let us press on" (KJV, "let us go on"); (i) *ekklino*, "to bend or turn away," Rom. 3:12, RV, "have turned aside" (KJV, "have gone out of the way"); (j) *diaperao*, "to pass through, or across," Matt. 14:34, RV, "had crossed over" (KJV, "were gone over"); (k) *strateuomai*, "to serve in war," 1 Cor. 9:7, RV, "(what) soldier ... serveth" (KJV, "goeth a warfare").

6:23 (Howbeit there came other boats from Tiberias nigh unto the place where they did eat bread, after that the Lord had given thanks:)

Boats *see* **Boat** at *John 6:22*.

Nigh *see* **Near** at *John 3:23*.

Lord *see John 4:1*.

Thanks *see John 6:11*.

6:24 When the people therefore saw that Jesus was not there, neither his disciples, they also took shipping, and came to Capernaum, seeking for Jesus.

Took In **John 6:24**, KJV, *embaino*, "to enter," is rendered "took (shipping)," RV, "got into (the boats)."

Shipping *ploiarion* (4142), is translated "ship" in the KJV of Mark 3:9; 4:36 and **John 21:8**; "(took) shipping" in **John 6:24**, KJV, RV "(got into the) boats.

Seeking *zeteo* (2212), signifies (a) "to seek, to seek for," e.g., Matt. 7:7, 8; 13:45; Luke 24:5; **John 6:24**; of plotting against a person's life, Matt. 2:20; Acts 21:31; Rom. 11:3; metaphorically, to "seek" by thinking, to "seek" how to do something, or what to obtain, e.g., Mark 11:18; Luke 12:29; to "seek" to ascertain a meaning, **John 16:19**, "do ye inquire"; to "seek" God, Acts 17:27, RV; Rom. 10:20; (b) "to seek or strive after, endeavor, to desire," e.g., Matt. 12:46, 47, RV, "seeking" (KJV, "desiring"); Luke 9:9, RV, "sought" (KJV, "desired"); **John 7:19**, RV, "seek ye" (KJV, "go ye about"); so v. **20**; Rom. 10:3, RV, "seeking" (KJV, "going about"); of "seeking" the kingdom of God and His righteousness, in the sense of coveting earnestly, striving after, Matt. 6:33; "the things that are above," Col. 3:1; peace, 1 Pet. 3:11; (c) "to require or demand," e.g., Mark 8:12; Luke 11:29; 1 Cor. 4:2, "it is required"; 2 Cor. 13:3, "ye seek."

6:25 And when they had found him on the other side of the sea, they said unto him, Rabbi, when camest thou hither?

Side *see John 6:22.*

Rabbi *see John 1:38.*

Hither *hode* (5602), primarily an adverb of manner then, of place, (a) of "motion" or "direction towards a place," e.g., Matt. 8:29; Mark 11:3; Luke 9:41; **John 6:25**; (b) of "position."

6:26 Jesus answered them and said, Verily, verily, I say unto you, Ye seek me, not because ye saw the miracles, but because ye did eat of the loaves, and were filled.

Miracles *see John 2:11.*

6:27 Labour not for the meat which perisheth, but for that meat which endureth unto everlasting life, which the Son of man shall give unto you: for him hath God the Father sealed.

Labour In **John 6:27** and 1 Thess. 2:9, KJV, *ergazomai*, "to work," is translated respectively "labor" and "laboring" (RV, "working"). It is used of manual work here and in 4:11 and Eph. 4:28; of work for Christ in general, in 1 Cor. 16:10. *See also* **Worketh, Work** at *John 5:17.*

Meat *see John 4:32.*

Perisheth *see* **Perish** at *John 3:15.*

Endureth *meno* (3306), "to abide," is rendered "to endure" in the KJV of **John 6:27** and 1 Pet. 1:25 (RV, "abideth"); Heb. 10:34, KJV, "enduring (substance)," RV, "abiding."

Son *see John 1:18.*

Sealed *see* **Seal** at *John 3:33.*

6:28 Then said they unto him, What shall we do, that we might work the works of God?

Shall Sometimes the subjunctive mood of a verb, used as a deliberative, is rendered "must," etc., **John 6:28**, "(what) must (we do)," RV (KJV, shall).

Work, Works *see John 4:34.*

6:29 Jesus answered and said unto them, This is the work of God, that ye believe on him whom he hath sent.

Work *see John 4:34.*

Sent *see John 1:6.*

6:30 They said therefore unto him, What sign shewest thou then, that we may see, and believe thee? what dost thou work?

Shewest *poieo* (4160), "to make, to do," is translated, "He hath showed" in Luke 1:51; "to show (mercy)," v. 72, RV (KJV, "perform"); "showed (mercy)," 10:37; **John 6:30**, KJV, "showest Thou," RV, "doest Thou (for a sign)"; Acts 7:36, KJV, "showed," RV, "wrought"; Jas. 2:13, "showed (no mercy)"; in Mark 13:22 in the best texts (some have *didomi*), "shall show (signs)."

Work *see* **Worketh, Work** at *John 5:17.*

6:31 Our fathers did eat manna in the desert; as it is written, He gave them bread from heaven to eat.

Manna *manna* (3131), the supernaturally provided food for Israel during their wilderness journey (for details see Exod. 16 and Num. 11). The Hebrew equivalent is given in Exod. 16:15, RV marg., "*man hu.*" The translations are, RV, "what is it?"; KJV and RV marg., "it is manna." It is described in Ps. 78:24, 25 as "the corn of heaven" and "the bread of the mighty," RV text and KJV marg. ("angels' food," KJV text), and in 1 Cor. 10:3, as "spiritual meat." The vessel appointed to contain it as a perpetual memorial, was of gold, Heb. 9:4, with Exod. 16:33. The Lord speaks of it as being typical of Himself, the true Bread from Heaven, imparting eternal life and sustenance to those who by faith partake spiritually of Him, **John 6:31-35**. The "hidden manna" is promised as one of the rewards of the overcomer, Rev. 2:17; it is thus suggestive of the moral excellence of Christ in His life on earth, hid from the eyes of men, by whom He was "despised and rejected"; the path of the overcomer is a reflex of His life. None of the natural substances called "manna" is to be identified with that which God provided for Israel.

Desert *eremos* (2048), used as a noun, has the same meaning as *eremia,* in Luke 5:16 and 8:29, RV, "deserts," for KJV, "wilderness"; in Matt. 24:26 and **John 6:31**, RV, "wilderness," for KJV, "desert." As an adjective, it denotes (a), with reference to persons, "deserted," desolate, deprived of the friends and kindred, e.g. of a woman deserted by a husband, Gal 4:21; (b) so of a city, as Jerusalem, Matt. 23:38; or uninhabited places, "desert," e.g., Matt. 14:13, 15; Acts 8:26; in Mark 1:35, RV, "desert," for KJV, solitary.

6:32 Then Jesus said unto them, Verily, verily, I say unto you, Moses gave you not that bread from heaven; but my Father giveth you the true bread from heaven.

True *see John 1:9.*

6:33 For the bread of God is he which cometh down from heaven, and giveth life unto the world.

Bread *artos* (740), "bread" (perhaps derived from *aro*, "to fit together," or from a root *ar*–, "the earth"), signifies (a) "a small loaf or cake," composed of flour and water, and baked, in shape either oblong or round, and about as thick as the thumb; these were not cut, but broken and were consecrated to the Lord every Sabbath and called the "shewbread" (loaves of presentation), Matt. 12:4; when the "shewbread" was reinstituted by Nehemiah (Neh. 10:32) a poll-tax of 1/3 shekel was laid on the Jews, Matt. 17:24; (b) "the loaf at the Lord's Supper," e.g., Matt. 26:26 ("Jesus took a loaf," RV, marg.); the breaking of "bread" became the name for this institution, Acts 2:42; 20:7; 1 Cor. 10:16; 11:23; (c) "bread of any kind," Matt. 16:11; (d) metaphorically, "of Christ as the Bread of God, and of Life," **John 6:33, 35**; (e) "food in general," the necessities for the sustenance of life, Matt. 6:11; 2 Cor. 9:10, etc.

6:34 Then said they unto him, Lord, evermore give us this bread.

Evermore *pantote* (3842), "at all times, always" (akin to *pas*, "all"), is translated "ever" in Luke 15:31; **John 18:20**; 1 Thess. 4:17; 5:15; 2 Tim. 3:7; Heb. 7:25; "evermore" in **John 6:34**; in 1 Thess. 5:16, RV, "alway," for KJV, "evermore." It there means "on all occasions," as, e.g., in 1 Thess. 1:2; 3:6; 5:15; 2 Thess. 1:3, 11; 2:13.

6:35 And Jesus said unto them, I am the bread of life: he that cometh to me shall never hunger; and he that believeth on me shall never thirst.

I *see John 4:14.*

Bread *see John 6:33.*

Life *see John 3:15.*

Never In 2 Pet. 1:10, "never" is the translation of *ou me pote*, i.e., "by no means ever"; so with the double negative followed by the extended word *popote*, i.e., "by no means not even at any time," **John 6:35** (2nd part).

Hunger *peinao* (3983), "to hunger, be hungry, hungered," is used (a) literally, e.g., Matt. 4:2; 12:1; 21:18; Rom. 12:20; 1 Cor. 11:21, 34; Phil. 4:12, Rev. 7:16; Christ identifies Himself with His saints in speaking of Himself as suffering in their sufferings in this and other respects, Matt. 25:35, 42; (b) metaphorically, Matt. 5:6; Luke 6:21, 25; **John 6:35**.

Thirst *see John 4:13.*

6:36 But I said unto you, That ye also have seen me, and believe not.

Seen *horao* (3708), with the form *eidon*, serving for its aorist tense, and *opsomai*, for its future tense (middle voice), denotes "to see," of bodily vision, e.g., **John 6:36**; and mental, e.g., Matt. 8:4; it is said of Christ as "seeing" the Father, **John 6:46**, and of what He had "seen" with the Father, **8:38**. It especially indicates the direction of the thought to the object "seen."

> *"When we are right with God, he gives us our desires and aspirations. Our Lord had only one desire, and that was to do the will of his Father, and to have this desire is characteristic of a disciple."*
>
> OSWALD CHAMBERS

6:37-38 All that the Father giveth me shall come to me; and him that cometh to me I will in no wise cast out.

For I came down from heaven, not to do mine own will, but the will of him that sent me.

Heaven *see John 3:13.*

Sent *see John 1:33.*

6:39 And this is the Father's will which hath sent me, that of all which he hath given me I should lose nothing, but should raise it up again at the last day.

Will *see John 1:13.*

Sent *see John 1:33.*

Lose *see* Perish at *John 3:16.*

Nothing *me* (3361), "not," is translated "nothing" in **John 6:39** in a clause expressing purpose; in the KJV of Luke 7:42 (RV, "not"), in a temporal clause.

Raise *anistemi* (450), "to stand up or to make to stand up," according as its use is intransitive or transitive (*ana*, "up," *histemi*, "to stand"), is used (a) of a physical change of position, e.g., of "rising" from sleep, Mark 1:35; from a meeting in a synagogue, Luke 4:29; of the illegal "rising" of the high priest in the tribunal in Matt. 26:62; of an invalid "rising" from his couch, Luke 5:25; the "rising" up of a disciple from his vocation to follow Christ, Luke 5:28; cf. **John 11:31**; "rising" up from prayer, Luke 22:45; of a whole company, Acts 26:30; 1 Cor. 10:7; (b) metaphorically, of "rising" up antagonistically against persons, e.g. of officials against people, Acts 5:17; of a seditious leader, 5:36, of the "rising" up of Satan, Mark 3:26; of false teachers, Acts 20:30; (c) of "rising" to a position of preeminence or power; e.g., of Christ as a prophet, Acts 3:22; 7:37; as God's servant in the midst of the nation of Israel, Acts 3:26; as the Son of God in the midst of the nation, 13:33 (not here of resurrection, but with reference to the Incarnation: the KJV "again" has nothing corresponding to it in the original, it was added as a misinterpretation: the mention of His resurrection is in the next verse, in which it is stressed by way of contrast and by the addition, "from the dead"); as a priest, Heb. 7:11, 15; as king over the nations, Rom. 15:12; (d) of a spiritual awakening from lethargy, Eph. 5:14; (e) of resurrection from the dead: (1) of the resurrection of Christ, Matt. 17:9; 20:19; Mark 8:31; 9:9-10, 31; 10:34; Luke 18:33; 24:7, 46; **John 20:9**; Acts 2:24, 32; 10:41; 13:34; 17:3, 31; 1 Thess. 4:14; (2) of believers, **John 6:39-40, 44, 54; 11:24**; 1 Thess. 4:16; of unbelievers, Matt. 12:41.

Last *eschatos* (2078), "last, utmost, extreme," is used (a) of place, e.g., Luke 14:9, 10, "lowest;" Acts 1:8 and 13:47, "uttermost part;" (b) of rank, e.g., Mark 9:35; (c) of time, relating either to persons or things, e.g., Matt. 5:26, "the last (farthing)," RV (KJV, "uttermost"); Matt. 20:8, 12, 14; Mark 12:6, 22; 1 Cor. 4:9, of apostles as "last" in the program of a spectacular display; 1 Cor. 15:45, "the last Adam"; Rev. 2:19; of the "last" state of persons, Matt. 12:45, neuter plural, lit., "the last (things)"; so Luke 11:26; 2 Pet. 2:20, RV, "the last state" (KJV, "the latter end"); of Christ as the Eternal One, Rev. 1:17 (in some mss. v. 11); 2:8; 22:13; in eschatological phrases as follows: (a) "the last day," a comprehensive term including both the time of the resurrection of the redeemed, **John 6:39, 40, 44, 54** and **11:24**, and the ulterior time of the judgment of the unregenerate, at the Great White Throne, **John 12:48**; (b) "the last days," Acts 2:17, a period relative to the supernatural manifestation of the Holy Spirit at Pentecost and the resumption of the divine interpositions in the affairs of the world at the end of the present age, before "the great and notable Day of the Lord," which will usher in the messianic kingdom; (c) in 2 Tim. 3:1, "the last days" refers to the close of the present age of world conditions; (d) in Jas. 5:3, the phrase "in the last days" (RV) refers both to the period preceding the Roman overthrow of the city and the land in AD 70, and to the closing part of the age in consummating acts of gentile persecution including "the time of Jacob's trouble" (cf. verses 7, 8); (e) in 1 Pet. 1:5, "the last time" refers to the time of the Lord's second advent; (f) in 1 John 2:18, "the last hour" (RV) and, in Jude 18, "the last time" signify the present age previous to the Second Advent.

6:40 And this is the will of him that sent me, that every one which seeth the Son, and believeth on him, may have everlasting life: and I will raise him up at the last day.

Will *see John 1:13.*

Sent *see John 1:33.*

I *see John 4:14.*

Raise *see John 6:39.*

Last *see John 6:39.*

6:41 The Jews then murmured at him, because he said, I am the bread which came down from heaven.

Murmured *gonguzo* (1111), "to mutter, murmur, grumble, say anything in a low tone" (Eng., "gong"), an onomatopoeic word, representing the significance by the sound of the word, as in the word "murmur" itself, is used of the laborers in the parable of the householder, Matt. 20:11; of the scribes and Pharisees, against Christ, Luke 5:30; of the Jews, **John 6:41, 43**, of the disciples, **6:61**; of the people, **7:32** (of debating secretly); of the Israelites, 1 Cor. 10:10 (twice), where it is also used in a warning to believers. In the papyri it is used of the "murmuring" of a gang of workmen, also in a remark interposed, while the Emperor (late 2nd cent. AD) was interviewing a rebel, that the Romans were then "murmuring" (Moulton and Milligan, *Vocab.*).

I *see John 4:14.*

6:42 And they said, Is not this Jesus, the son of Joseph, whose father and mother we know? how is it then that he saith, I came down from heaven?

Heaven *see John 3:13.*

6:43 Jesus therefore answered and said unto them, Murmur not among yourselves.

Murmur *see* **Murmured** at *John 6:41.*

6:44 No man can come to me, except the Father which hath sent me draw him: and I will raise him up at the last day.

Sent *see John 1:33.*

Draw *helkuo* (or *helko*) (1670), "to draw," differs from *suro*, as "drawing" does from violent "dragging." It is used of "drawing" a net, **John 21:6, 11**; Trench remarks, "At vv. **6** and **11** *helko* (or *helkuo*) is used; for there a *drawing* of the net to a certain point is intended; by the disciples to themselves in the ship, by Peter to himself upon the shore. But at v. **8** *helko* gives place to *suro*: for nothing is there intended but the *dragging* of the net, which had been fastened to the ship, after it through the water" (*Syn.*, Sec.xxi). This less violent significance, usually present in *helko*, but always absent from *suro*, is seen in the metaphorical use of *helko*, to signify "drawing" by inward power, by divine impulse, **John 6:44; 12:32**. So in the Sept., e.g., Song of Sol. 1:4, and Jer. 31:3, "with lovingkindness have I drawn thee." It is used of a more vigorous action, in **John 18:10**, of "drawing" a sword; in Acts 16:19; 21:30, of forcibly "drawing" men to or from a place; so in Jas. 2:6, KJV, "draw," RV, "drag." *See also* **Dragging** at *John 21:8.*

Raise *see John 6:39.*

Last *see John 6:39.*

6:45 It is written in the prophets, And they shall be all taught of God. Every man therefore that hath heard, and hath learned of the Father, cometh unto me.

Taught *didaktos* (1318), primarily "what can be taught," then, "taught," is used (a) of persons, **John 6:45**; (b) of things, 1 Cor. 2:13 (twice), "(not in words which man's wisdom) teacheth, (but which the Spirit) teacheth," lit., "(not in words) taught (of man's wisdom, but) taught (of the Spirit)."

6:46 Not that any man hath seen the Father, save he which is of God, he hath seen the Father.

Seen *see John 6:36.*

He *houtos* (3778), "this, this person here," is always emphatic; it is used with this meaning, sometimes to refer to what precedes, e.g., Matt. 5:19, "he (shall be called great)"; **John 6:46**, "he (hath seen)"; often rendered "this," e.g., Rom. 9:9, or "this man," e.g., Matt. 27:58, RV; Jas. 1:25; "the same," e.g., Luke 9:48.

Of In **John 6:46; 15:15; 17:7**; Acts 17:9, the RV, "from" is to be observed, as rightly translating *para* (KJV, "of").

6:47-48 Verily, verily, I say unto you, He that believeth on me hath everlasting life.
I am that bread of life.

I *see John 4:14.*

6:49 Your fathers did eat manna in the wilderness, and are dead.

Eat *trogo* (5176), primarily, "to gnaw, to chew," stresses the slow process; it is used metaphorically of the habit of spiritually feeding upon Christ, **John 6:54, 56-58** (the aorists here do not indicate a definite act, but view a series of acts seen in perspective); of the constant custom of "eating" in certain company, **John 13:18**; of a practice unduly engrossing the world, Matt. 24:38. In **John 6**, the change in the Lord's use from the verb *esthio (phago)* to the stronger verb *trogo*, is noticeable. The more persistent the unbelief of His hearers, the more difficult His language and statements became. In vv. **49** to **53** the verb *phago* is used; in **54, 58**, *trogo* (in v. **58** it is put into immediate contrast with *phago*). The use of *trogo* in Matt. 24:38 and **John 13:18** is a witness against pressing into the meaning of the word the sense of munching or gnawing; it had largely lost this sense in its common usage.

And *see John 3:19.*

6:50 This is the bread which cometh down from heaven, that a man may eat thereof, and not die.

Man *see John 3:3.*

Die *apothnesko* (599), lit., "to die off or out," is used (a) of the separation of the soul from the body, i.e., the natural "death" of human beings, e.g., Matt. 9:24; Rom. 7:2; by reason of descent from Adam, 1 Cor. 15:22; or of violent "death," whether of men or animals; with regard to the latter it is once translated "perished," Matt. 8:32; of vegetation, Jude 12; of seeds, **John 12:24**; 1 Cor. 15:36; it is used of "death" as a punishment in Israel under the Law, in Heb. 10:28; (b) of the separation of man from God, all who are descended from Adam not only "die" physically, owing to sin, see (a) above, but are naturally in the state of separation from God, 2 Cor. 5:14. From this believers are freed both now and eternally, **John**

6:50; **11:26**, through the "death" of Christ, Rom. 5:8, e.g.; unbelievers, who "die" physically as such, remain in eternal separation from God, **John 8:24**. Believers have spiritually "died" to the Law as a means of life, Gal. 2:19; Col. 2:20; to sin, Rom. 6:2, and in general to all spiritual association with the world and with that which pertained to their unregenerate state, Col. 3:3, because of their identification with the "death" of Christ, Rom. 6:8. As life never means mere existence, so "death," the opposite of life, never means nonexistence.

6:51 I am the living bread which came down from heaven: if any man eat of this bread, he shall live for ever: and the bread that I will give is my flesh, which I will give for the life of the world.

I *see John 4:14.*

Living *see John 4:10.*

Flesh *see John 1:13.*

6:52 The Jews therefore strove among themselves, saying, How can this man give us *his* flesh to eat?

Strove *machomai* (3164), "to fight, to quarrel, dispute," is rendered "to strive" in **John 6:52**; Acts 7:26; 2 Tim. 2:24.

Themselves Regarding *allelon*, "of one another," and its other forms, the RV substitutes "one another" for the KJV "themselves" in Mark 8:16; 9:34; Luke 4:36; **John 6:52; 11:56; 16:17; 19:24**; Acts 26:31; 28:4; Rom. 2:15, but adheres to the rendering "themselves" in Mark 15:31; Acts 4:15; 28:25.

This man *Houtos*, "this," is translated "this fellow" in the KJV of Luke 23:2 (RV, "this man"). So in **John 9:29**. Both versions have "this man," e.g., in Mark 2:7; **John 6:52**, in the same contemptuous sense. *See also* This at *John 2:11.*

6:53 Then Jesus said unto them, Verily, verily, I say unto you, Except ye eat the flesh of the Son of man, and drink his blood, ye have no life in you.

Eat *see John 6:49.*

Son *see John 1:18.*

Drink *see* Drinketh at *John 4:14.*

Blood *see John 1:13.*

6:54 Whoso eateth my flesh, and drinketh my blood, hath eternal life; and I will raise him up at the last day.

Eateth *see* Eat at *John 6:49.*

Raise *see John 6:39.*

Last *see John 6:39.*

6:55 For my flesh is meat indeed, and my blood is drink indeed.

Meat *see John 4:32.*

Indeed *alethes* (227), "true," is rendered "indeed" in **John 6:55** (twice), see RV marg.

Drink *posis* (4213), suggests "the act of drinking," **John 6:55**; Rom. 14:17, "drinking," RV; Col. 2:16.

6:56 He that eateth my flesh, and drinketh my blood, dwelleth in me, and I in him.

Eateth *see* Eat at *John 6:49.*

Drinketh *see John 4:14.*

Dwelleth *see* Dwellest at *John 1:38.*

6:57 As the living Father hath sent me, and I live by the Father: so he that eateth me, even he shall live by me.

Living *see John 4:10.*

Sent *see John 1:6.*

Even In **John 6:57** *kakeinos* (for *kai ekeinos*, "also he"), is translated "he also," RV, for KJV, "even he."

6:58 This is that bread which came down from heaven: not as your fathers did eat manna, and are dead: he that eateth of this bread shall live for ever.

Eateth *see* Eat at *John 6:49.*

6:59-60 These things said he in the synagogue, as he taught in Capernaum.

Many therefore of his disciples, when they had heard *this*, said, This is an hard saying; who can hear it?

Hard Synonymous with *austeros*, but to be distinguished from it, is *skleros* (4642) (from *skello*, "to be dry"). It was applied to that which lacks moisture, and so is rough and disageeable to the touch, and hence came to denotes: "harsh, stern, hard." It is used by Matthew to describe the unprofitable servant's remark concerning his master, in the parable corresponding to that in Luke 19 (see *austeros*, above). *Austeros* is derived from a word having to do with the taste, *skleros*, "with the touch." *Austeros* is not necessarily a term of reproach, whereas *skleros* is always so, and indicates a harsh, even inhuman character. *Austeros* is "rather the exaggeration of a virtue pushed too far, than an absolute vice" (Trench, *Syn.* Sec. xiv). *Skleros* is used of the character of a man, Matt. 25:24; of a saying, **John 6:60**; of the difficulty and pain of kicking against the ox-goads, Acts 9:5; 26:14; of rough winds, Jas. 3:4 and of harsh speeches, Jude 15. Cf. *sklerotes*, "hardness," *skleruno*, "to harden," *sklerokardia*, "hardness of heart," and *sklerotrachelos*, "stiff-necked."

Saying *see John 4:37.*

6:61 When Jesus knew in himself that his disciples murmured at it, he said unto them, Doth this offend you?

Murmured *see John 6:41.*

6:62 *What* and if ye shall see the Son of man ascend up where he was before?

Son *see John 1:18.*

Before *proteron* (4386), the neuter of *proteros*, the comparative degree of *pro*, is always used of time, and signifies "aforetime, before," e.g., **John 6:62**; **9:8**; 2 Cor. 1:15; Heb. 7:27; in Gal. 4:13, "the first time" (RV), lit., "the former time," i.e., the former of two previous visits; in Heb. 10:32 it is placed between the article and the noun, "the former days"; so in 1 Pet. 1:14, "the former lusts," i.e., the lusts formerly indulged.

6:63 It is the spirit that quickeneth; the flesh profiteth nothing: the words that I speak unto you, *they* are spirit, and *they* are life.

Spirit *see John 3:8.*

Quickeneth *see John 5:21.*

Flesh *see John 1:13.*

Profiteth *opheleo* (5623), is translated "to profit" in Matt. 15:5; 16:26; Mark 7:11; 8:36; Luke 9:25, RV; **John 6:63**; Rom. 2:25; 1 Cor. 13:3; 14:6; Gal. 5:2; Heb. 4:2; 13:9.

I *see John 4:14.*

6:64 But there are some of you that believe not. For Jesus knew from the beginning who they were that believed not, and who should betray him.

Knew *see John 6:6.*

Betray *paradidomi* (3860), "to betray" (*para*, "up," *didomi*, "to give"), lit., "to give over," is used either (a) in the sense of delivering a person or thing to be kept by another, to commend, e.g., Acts 28:16; (b) to deliver to prison or judgment, e.g., Matt. 4:12; 1 Tim. 1:20; (c) to deliver over treacherously by way of "betrayal," Matt. 17:22 (RV, "delivered"); 26:16; **John 6:64**, etc.; (d) to hand on, deliver, e.g., 1 Cor. 11:23; (e) to allow of something being done, said of the ripening of fruit, Mark 4:29, RV, "is ripe" (marg., "alloweth").

6:65-66 And he said, Therefore said I unto you, that no man can come unto me, except it were given unto him of my Father.

From that *time* many of his disciples went back, and walked no more with him.

Time In Matt., *apo tote*, "from that time," lit., "from then," occurs thrice, 4:17; 16:21; 26:16; in Luke 16:16, RV (KJV, "since that time"); in **John 6:66**, KJV, "from that time" translates *ek toutou*, lit., "from, or out of, this," RV, "upon this."

Disciples *mathetes* (3101), lit., "a learner" (from *manthano*, "to learn," from a root *math*–, indicating thought accompanied by endeavor), in contrast to *didaskalos*, "a teacher"; hence it denotes "one who follows one's teaching," as the "disciples" of John, Matt. 9:14; of the Pharisees, Matt. 22:16; of Moses, **John 9:28**; it is used of the "disciples" of Jesus (a) in a wide sense, of Jews who became His adherents, **John 6:66**; Luke 6:17, some being secretly so, **John 19:38**; (b) especially of the twelve apostles, Matt. 10:1; Luke 22:11, e.g.; (c) of all who manifest that they are His "disciples" by abiding in His Word, **John 8:31**, cf. **13:35**; **15:8**; (d) in the Acts, of those who believed upon Him and confessed Him, **6:1-2**, **7**; **14:20**, **22**, **28**; **15:10**; **19:1**, etc. A "disciple" was not only a pupil, but an adherent; hence they are spoken of as imitators of their teacher; cf. **John 8:31**; **15:8**.

Back *opiso* (3694), connected with *hepomai*, "to follow," is used adverbially, of place, with the meaning "back," "backward," in the phrase *eis ta opiso*, lit., "unto the things behind," in Mark 13:16; Luke 9:62; 17:31; **John 6:66**; **18:6**; **20:14**. Cf. Phil. 3:13, "the things which are behind.

6:67-68 Then said Jesus unto the twelve, Will ye also go away?

Then Simon Peter answered him, Lord, to whom shall we go? thou hast the words of eternal life.

Lord *see John 4:1.*

6:69 And we believe and are sure that thou art that Christ, the Son of the living God.

Sure In the KJV of **John 16:30**; Rom. 2:2 and 15:29, the verb *oida*, "to know," is translated "to be sure" (RV, in each place, "to know"). So with *ginosko*, "to know," in **John 6:69**.

6:70 Jesus answered them, Have not I chosen you twelve, and one of you is a devil?

Chosen *eklego* (1586), "to pick out, select," means, in the middle voice, "to choose for oneself," not necessarily implying the rejection of what is not chosen, but "choosing" with the subsidiary ideas of kindness or favor or love, Mark 13:20; Luke 6:13; 9:35 (RV); 10:42; 14:7; **John 6:70**; **13:18**; **15:16**, **19**; Acts 1:2, 24; 6:5; 13:17; 15:22, 25; in 15:7 it is rendered "made choice"; 1 Cor. 1:27-28; Eph. 1:4; Jas. 2:5.

Devil *diabolos* (1228), "an accuser, a slanderer" (from *diaballo*, "to accuse, to malign"), is one of the names of Satan. From it the English word "Devil" is derived, and should be applied only to Satan, as a proper name. *Daimon*, "a demon," is frequently, but wrongly, translated "devil"; it should always be translated "demon," as in the RV margin. There is one "Devil," there are many demons. Being the malignant enemy of God and man, he accuses man to God, Job 1:6-11; 2:1-5; Rev. 12:9, 10, and God to man, Gen. 3. He afflicts men with physical sufferings, Acts 10:38. Being himself sinful, 1 John 3:8, he instigated man to sin, Gen. 3, and tempts man to do evil, Eph. 4:27; 6:11, encouraging him thereto by deception, Eph. 2:2. Death having been brought into the world by sin, the "Devil" had the power of death, but Christ through His own death, has triumphed over him, and will bring him to nought, Heb. 2:14; his power over death is intimated in his struggle with Michael over the body of Moses, Jude 9. Judas, who gave himself over to the "Devil," was so identified with him, that the Lord described him as such, **John 6:70** (see **13:2**). As the "Devil" raised himself in pride against God and fell under condemnation, so believers are warned against similar sin, 1 Tim. 3:6; for them he lays snares, v. 7, seeking to devour them as a roaring lion, 1 Pet. 5:8; those who fall into his snare may be recovered therefrom unto the will of God, 2 Tim. 2:26, "having been taken captive by him (i.e., by the 'Devil')"; "by the Lord's servant" is an alternative, which some regard as confirmed by the use of *zogreo* ("to catch alive") in Luke 5:10; but the general use is that of taking captive in the usual way. If believers resist he will flee from them, Jas. 4:7. His fury and malignity will be especially exercised at the end of the present age, Rev. 12:12. His doom is the lake of fire, Matt. 25:41; Rev. 20:10. The noun is applied to slanderers, false accusers, 1 Tim. 3:11; 2 Tim. 3:3; Titus 2:3.

6:71 He spake of Judas Iscariot *the son* of Simon: for he it was that should betray him, being one of the twelve.

Should *mello* (3195), "to be about to," e.g., Mark 10:32, RV, "were to"; Luke 19:11, RV, "was to"; "should" in 22:23; 24:21; **John 6:71**; **7:39**, RV, "were to"; **11:51**; **12:4**, **33**; **18:32**; Acts 11:28; 23:27, RV, "was about (to be slain)"; 1 Thess. 3:4, RV, "are to"; Rev. 6:11.

Chapter 7

7:1 After these things Jesus walked in Galilee: for he would not walk in Jewry, because the Jews sought to kill him.

Jewry, Jews *see* Jews at *John 2:6*.

7:2 Now the Jews' feast of tabernacles was at hand.

Tabernacles *skenopegia* (4634), properly "the setting up of tents or dwellings", represents the word "tabernacles" in "the feast of tabernacles," **John 7:2**. This feast, one of the three Pilgrimage Feasts in Israel, is called "the feast of ingathering" in Exod. 23:16; 34:22; it took place at the end of the year, and all males were to attend at the "tabernacle" with their offerings. In Lev. 23:34; Deut. 16:13, 16; 31:10; 2 Chron. 8:13; Ezra 3:4 (cf. Neh. 8:14-18), it is called "the feast of tabernacles" (or "booths," *sukkoth*), and was appointed for seven days at Jerusalem from the 15th to the 22nd Tishri (approximately October), to remind the people that their fathers dwelt in these in the wilderness journeys. Cf. Num. 29:15-38, especially v. 35-38, for the regulations of the eighth or "last day, the great day of the feast" (**John 7:37**).

7:3 His brethren therefore said unto him, Depart hence, and go into Judaea, that thy disciples also may see the works that thou doest.

Depart *metabaino* (3327), is rendered "to depart" in Matt. 8:34; 11:1; 12:9; 15:29; **John 7:3**; **13:1**; Acts 18:7.

Hence *see John 2:16*.

Also *kai* The particle *kai*, "and," chiefly used for connecting words, clauses and sentences (the copulative or connective use), not infrequently signifies "also." This is the *adjunctive*, or *amplificatory*, use, and it is to be distinguished from the purely copulative significance "and." A good illustration is provided in Matt. 8:9, in the words of the centurion, "I also am a man under authority." Other instances are Matt. 5:39, 40; 8:9; 10:18; 18:33; 20:4; Luke 11:49; 12:41, 54, 57; 20:3; **John 5:26**, "the Son also," RV; **7:3**; **12:10**; **14:1**, **3**, **7**, **19**; **15:9**, **27**; **17:24**; Acts 11:17; Rom. 1:13; 6:11; 1 Cor. 7:3; 11:25; 15:30; Gal. 6:1; Phil. 4:12, "I know also," RV, 1 Thess. 3:12. In 1 Cor. 2:13 the *kai* phrase signifies "which are the very things we speak, with the like power of the Holy Spirit." This use includes the meanings "so," or "just so," by way of comparison, as in Matt. 6:10, and "so also," e.g., **John 13:33**; cf. Rom. 11:16. In Heb. 7:26 the most authentic mss. have *kai* in the first sentence, which may be rendered "for such a High Priest also became us." Here it virtually has the meaning "precisely."

7:4 For *there is* no man *that* doeth any thing in secret, and he himself seeketh to be known openly. If thou do these things, shew thyself to the world.

Secret *kruptos* (2927), "secret, hidden" (akin to *krupto*, "to hide"), Eng., "crypt," "cryptic," etc., is used as an adjective and rendered "secret" in Luke 8:17, KJV (RV, "hid"); in the neuter, with *en*, "in," as an adverbial phrase, "in secret," with the article, Matt. 6:4, 6 (twice in each v.), without the article, **John 7:4, 10; 18:20**; in the neuter plural, with the article, "the secrets (of men)," Rom. 2:16; of the heart, 1 Cor. 14:25; in Luke 11:33, KJV, "a secret place" (RV, "cellar").

Openly *parrhesia* (3954), from *pas*, "all," *rhesis*, "speech," denotes (a), primarily, "freedom of speech, unreservedness of utterance," Acts 4:29, 31; 2 Cor. 3:12; 7:4; Philem. 8; or "to speak without ambiguity, plainly," **John 10:24**; or "without figures of speech," **John 16:25**; (b) "the absence of fear in speaking boldly; hence, confidence, cheerful courage, boldness, without any connection necessarily with speech"; the RV has "boldness" in the following; Acts 4:13; Eph. 3:12; 1 Tim. 3:13; Heb. 3:6; 4:16; 10:19, 35; 1 John 2:28; 3:21; 4:17; 5:14. It is used adverbially in the dative case and translated "openly" in Mark 8:32, of a saying of Christ; in **John 7:13**, of a public statement; in **11:54**, of Christ's public appearance; in **7:26** and **18:20**, of His public testimony; preceded by the preposition *en*, "in," **John 7:4**, lit., "in boldness" (cf. v. **10**, RV, "publicly").

Shew *phaneroo*, **John 7:4; 21:1** (twice), **14**; Rom. 1:19, "to manifest."

7:5-6 For neither did his brethren believe in him.

Then Jesus said unto them, My time is not yet come: but your time is alway ready.

My *see John 4:34*.

Come *pareimi* (3918), signifies (a) "to be by, at hand or present," of persons, e.g., Luke 13:1; Acts 10:33; 24:19; 1 Cor. 5:3; 2 Cor. 10:2, 11; Gal. 4:18, 20; of things, **John 7:6**, of a particular season in the Lord's life on earth, "is (not yet) come," or "is not yet at hand"; Heb. 12:11, of chastening "(for the) present" (the neuter of the present participle, used as a noun); in 13:5 "such things as ye have" is, lit., "the things that are present"; 2 Pet. 1:12, of the truth "(which) is with (you)" (not as KJV, "the present truth," as if of special doctrines applicable to a particular time); in v. 9 "he that lacketh" is lit., "to whom are not present"; (b) "to have arrived or come," Matt. 26:50, "thou art come," RV; **John 11:28**; Acts 10:21; Col. 1:6.

Your The possessive pronoun, *humeteros*, "your," is used in Luke 6:20; **John 7:6; 8:17; 15:20**; Acts 27:34; Rom. 11:31; 1 Cor. 15:31; 16:17; 2 Cor. 8:8; Gal. 6:13; in Luke 16:12, "your own."

Ready *hetoimos* (2092), "prepared, ready" (akin to *hetoimasia*, "preparation"), is used (a) of persons, Matt. 24:44; 25:10; Luke 12:40; 22:33; Acts 23:15, 21 (for 2 Cor. 10:6); Titus 3:1; 1 Pet. 3:15; (b) of things, Matt. 22:4 (2nd part), 8; Mark 14:15, RV, "ready" (KJV, "prepared"); Luke 14:17; **John 7:6**; 2 Cor. 9:5; 10:16, RV, "things ready" (KJV, "things made ready"); 1 Pet. 1:5.

7:7 The world cannot hate you; but me it hateth, because I testify of it, that the works thereof are evil.

World *see John 1:9*.

Hate, Hateth *see* Hateth at *John 3:20*.

Testify *see John 2:25*.

Works *see* Work at *John 4:34*.

Evil *see John 3:19*.

7:8-10 Go ye up unto this feast: I go not up yet unto this feast; for my time is not yet full come.

When he had said these words unto them, he abode *still* in Galilee.

But when his brethren were gone up, then went he also up unto the feast, not openly, but as it were in secret.

Openly *phaneros* (5320), manifestly, is rendered "openly" in Mark 1:45; "publicly" in **John 7:10**, RV (opposite to "in secret"); in Acts 10:3, RV, "openly," for KJV, "evidently." *See also John 7:4*.

Secret *see John 7:4*.

7:11 Then the Jews sought him at the feast, and said, Where is he?

He *see John 2:21*.

7:12 And there was much murmuring among the people concerning him: for some said, He is a good man: others said, Nay; but he deceiveth the people.

Murmuring *gongusmos* (1112), "a murmuring, muttering," is used (a) in the sense of secret debate among people, **John 7:12** (as with the verb in v. **32**); (b) of displeasure or complaining (more privately than in public), said of Grecian Jewish converts against Hebrews, Acts 6:1; in general admonitions, Phil. 2:14; 1 Pet. 4:9, RV, "murmuring" (KJV "grudging").

Good *see John 5:29*.

Nay *ou* (3756), "no, not," expressing a negation absolutely, is rendered "nay," e.g., in Matt. 5:37; 13:29; **John 7:12**, KJV (RV, "not so"); Acts 16:37; 2 Cor. 1:17-19; Jas. 5:12.

Deceiveth *planao* (4105), (Eng., "planet"), in the passive form sometimes means "to go astray, wander," Matt. 18:12; 1 Pet. 2:25; Heb. 11:38; frequently active, "to deceive, by leading into error, to seduce," e.g., Matt. 24:4, 5, 11, 24; **John 7:12**, "leadeth astray," RV (cf. 1 John 3:7). In Rev. 12:9 the present participle is used with the definite article, as a title of the Devil, "the Deceiver," lit., "the deceiving one." Often it has the sense of "deceiving oneself," e.g., 1 Cor. 6:9; 15:33; Gal. 6:7; Jas. 1:16, "be not deceived," RV, "do not err," KJV.

People *ochlos* (3793), is used frequently in the four Gospels and the Acts; elsewhere only in Rev. 7:9; 17:15; 19:1, 6; it denotes (a) "a crowd or multitude of persons, a throng," e.g., Matt. 14:14, 15; 15:33; often in the plural, e.g., Matt. 4:25; 5:1; with *polus*, "much" or "great," it signifies "a great multitude," e.g., Matt. 20:29, or "the common people," Mark 12:37, perhaps preferably "the mass of the people." Field supports the meaning in the text, but either rendering is suitable. The mass of the people was attracted to Him (for the statement "heard Him gladly," cf. what is said in Mark 6:20 of Herod Antipas concerning John the Baptist); in **John 12:9**, "the common people," RV, stands in contrast with their leaders (v. **10**); Acts 24:12, RV, "crowd"; (b) "the populace, an unorganized multitude," in contrast to *demos*, "the people as a body politic," e.g., Matt. 14:5; 21:26; **John 7:12** (2nd part); (c) in a more general sense, "a multitude or company," e.g., Luke 6:17, RV, "a (great) multitude (of His disciples)," KJV, "the company"; Acts 1:15, "a multitude (of persons)," RV, KJV, "the number (of names)"; Acts 24:18, RV, "crowd" (KJV, "multitude").

7:13 Howbeit no man spake openly of him for fear of the Jews.

Openly *see John 7:4.*

Jews *see John 2:6.*

7:14 Now about the midst of the feast Jesus went up into the temple, and taught.

Midst *mesoo* (3322), "to be in the middle," is used of time in **John 7:14**, translated "when it was ... the midst (of the feast)," lit., "(the feast) being in the middle."

7:15 And the Jews marvelled, saying, How knoweth this man letters, having never learned?

Letters *gramma* (1121), "a letter," is used in the plural in Acts 26:24, with the meaning "learning": "(thy much) learning (doth turn thee to madness)," RV, possibly an allusion to the Jewish Scriptures, to which the apostle had been appealing; in **John 7:15**, "(How knoweth this Man) letters" (KJV marg., "learning"), the succeeding phrase "not having learned" is illustrated in the papyri, where it indicates inability to write.

Never In Mark 14:21, KJV, the negative particle *ouk*, "not," is translated "never" (RV, "not"); the negative particle *me*, "not" (which suggests nonexistence when the existence was after all possible, or even probable, in contrast to *ou*, which implies nonexistence absolutely), is translated "never" in **John 7:15**, KJV and RV.

Learned *manthano* (3129), denotes "to learn" (akin to *mathetes*, "a disciple"), "to increase one's knowledge," or "be increased in knowledge," frequently "to learn by inquiry, or observation," e.g., Matt. 9:13; 11:29; 24:32; Mark 13:28; **John 7:15**; Rom. 16:17; 1 Cor. 4:6; 14:35; Phil. 4:9; 2 Tim. 3:14; Rev. 14:3; said of "learning" Christ, Eph. 4:20, not simply the doctrine of Christ, but Christ Himself, a process not merely of getting to know the person but of so applying the knowledge as to walk differently from the rest of the Gentiles.

7:16 Jesus answered them, and said, My doctrine is not mine, but his that sent me.

My *see John 4:34.*

Sent *see John 1:33.*

7:17 If any man will do his will, he shall know of the doctrine, whether it be of God, or *whether* I speak of myself.

Will *see* Willingly at *John 6:21.*

Of In the KJV of **John 16:13**, "He shall not speak of Himself," the preposition is *apo*, "from," as in the RV; the Spirit of God often speaks of Himself in Scripture, the Lord's assurance was that the Holy Spirit would not be the source of His utterances. So with regard to Christ's utterances, **John 7:17**, RV, "I speak from (*apo*) Myself": and **14:10**.

Myself *see* Mine own self at *John 5:30.*

7:18 He that speaketh of himself seeketh his own glory: but he that seeketh his glory that sent him, the same is true, and no unrighteousness is in him.

Glory *see John 1:14.*

Sent *see John 1:33.*

Same *see John 3:2.*

True *see John 3:33.*

7:19 Did not Moses give you the law, and *yet* none of you keepeth the law? Why go ye about to kill me?

Keepeth *poieo* (4160), "to do, make," signifies "to keep," in Matt. 26:18, in the Lord's statement, "I will keep the passover;" so in Acts 18:21, in some mss.; in **John 7:19**, where the KJV has "keepeth (the law)," the RV adheres to the usual meaning "doeth."

Go *see* Went at *John 6:22*.

7:20 The people answered and said, Thou hast a devil: who goeth about to kill thee?

Goeth *see* Went at *John 6:22*.

7:21-23 Jesus answered and said unto them, I have done one work, and ye all marvel.

Moses therefore gave unto you circumcision; (not because it is of Moses, but of the fathers;) and ye on the sabbath day circumcise a man.

If a man on the sabbath day receive circumcision, that the law of Moses should not be broken; are ye angry at me, because I have made a man every whit whole on the sabbath day?

Broken *see John 5:18*.

Angry *cholao* (5520), connected with *chole*, "gall, bile," which became used metaphorically to signify bitter anger, means "to be enraged," **John 7:23**, "wroth," RV, in the Lord's remonstrance with the Jews on account of their indignation at His having made a man whole on the Sabbath Day.

Every whit *holos* (3650), "all, whole, complete," is rendered "every whit" in **John 7:23**; **13:10**.

Whole *see John 5:4*.

7:24 Judge not according to the appearance, but judge righteous judgment.

Judge *see* Condemn at *John 3:17*.

Appearance *opsis* (3799), from *ops*, "the eye," connected with *horao*, "to see," primarily denotes "seeing, sight"; hence, "the face, the countenance," **John 11:44** ("face"); Rev. 1:16 ("countenance"); the outward "appearance," the look, **John 7:24**, only here, of the outward aspect of a person.

7:25-26 Then said some of them of Jerusalem, Is not this he, whom they seek to kill?

But, lo, he speaketh boldly, and they say nothing unto him. Do the rulers know indeed that this is the very Christ?

Know *ginosko* (1097), signifies "to be taking in knowledge, to come to know, recognize, understand," or "to understand completely," e.g., Mark 13:28, 29; **John 13:12**; **15:18**; **21:17**; 2 Cor. 8:9; Heb. 10:34; 1 John 2:5; 4:2, 6 (twice), 7, 13; 5:2, 20; in its past tenses it frequently means "to know in the sense of realizing," the aorist or point tense usually indicating definiteness, Matt. 13:11; Mark 7:24; **John 7:26**; in **10:38** "that ye may know (aorist tense) and understand, (present tense)"; **19:4**; Acts 1:7; 17:19; Rom. 1:21; 1 Cor. 2:11 (2nd part), 14; 2 Cor. 2:4; Eph. 3:19; 6:22; Phil. 2:19; 3:10; 1 Thess. 3:5; 2 Tim. 2:19; Jas. 2:20; 1 John 2:13 (twice), 14; 3:6; 4:8; 2 John 1; Rev. 2:24; 3:3, 9. In the passive voice, it often signifies "to become known," e.g., Matt. 10:26; Phil. 4:5. In the sense of complete and absolute understanding on God's part, it is used, e.g., in Luke 16:15; **John 10:15** (of the Son as well as the Father); 1 Cor. 3:20. In Luke 12:46, KJV, it is rendered "he is ... aware." In the NT *ginosko* frequently indicates a relation between the person "knowing" and the object known; in this respect, what is "known" is of value or importance to the one who knows, and hence the establishment of the relationship, e.g., especially of God's "knowledge," 1 Cor. 8:3, "if any man love God, the same is known of Him"; Gal. 4:9, "to be known of God"; here the "knowing" suggests approval and bears the meaning "to be approved"; so in 2 Tim. 2:19; cf. **John 10:14**, **27**; Gen. 18:19; Nah. 1:7; the relationship implied may involve remedial chastisement, Amos 3:2. The same idea of appreciation as well as "knowledge" underlies several statements concerning the "knowledge" of God and His truth on the part of believers, e.g., **John 8:32**; **14:20**, **31**; **17:3**; Gal. 4:9 (1st part); 1 John 2:3-13, 14; 4:6, 8, 16; 5:20; such "knowledge" is obtained, not by mere intellectual activity, but by operation of the Holy Spirit consequent upon acceptance of Christ. Nor is such "knowledge" marked by finality; see e.g., 2 Pet. 3:18; Hos. 6:3, RV.

7:27-28 Howbeit we know this man whence he is: but when Christ cometh, no man knoweth whence he is.

Then cried Jesus in the temple as he taught, saying, Ye both know me, and ye know whence I am: and I am not come of myself, but he that sent me is true, whom ye know not.

Cried *krazo* (2896), "to cry out," an onomatopoeic word, used especially of the "cry" of the raven; then, of any inarticulate cries, from fear, pain, etc.; of the "cry" of a Canaanitish woman, Matt. 15:22 (so the best mss., instead of *kraugazo*); of the shouts of the children in the Temple, Matt. 21:15; of the people who shouted for Christ to be crucified, 27:23; Mark 15:13-14; of the "cry" of Christ on the Cross at the close of His sufferings, Matt. 27:50; Mark 15:39. In John's Gospel it is used three times, out of the six, of Christ's utterances, **7:28**, **37**; **12:44**. In the Acts it is not used of "cries" of distress, but chiefly of the shouts of opponents; in Revelation, chiefly of the utterances of heavenly beings concerning earthly matters; in Rom. 8:15 and Gal. 4:6, of the appeal of believers to God the Father; in Rom. 9:27, of a prophecy concerning Israel; in Jas. 5:4, metaphorically, of hire kept back by fraud.

Myself *see* **Mine own self** at *John 5:30*.

Sent *see John 1:33*.

True *see John 1:9*.

7:29 But I know him: for I am from him, and he hath sent me.

Sent *see John 1:6*.

7:30 Then they sought to take him: but no man laid hands on him, because his hour was not yet come.

But *see* And at *John 3:19*.

Take, Laid hands on *piazo* (4084), "to lay hold of," with the suggestion of firm pressure or force, is used in the Gospels only in John, six times of efforts to seize Christ and is always rendered "take" in the RV, **7:30**, **32**, **44**; **8:20**; **10:39**; **11:57**. The KJV has "laid hands on" in **8:20**. In Acts 12:4 and 2 Cor. 11:32 (KJV), it is translated respectively "apprehended" and "apprehend" (RV, "had taken," and "take"). In Rev. 19:20 it is used of the seizure of the Beast and the False Prophet. In **John 21:3**, **10** it is used of catching fish. Elsewhere in Acts 3:7.

7:31 And many of the people believed on him, and said, When Christ cometh, will he do more miracles than these which this *man* hath done?

Miracles *see John 2:11*.

7:32 The Pharisees heard that the people murmured such things concerning him; and the Pharisees and the chief priests sent officers to take him.

Murmured *see John 6:41*.

Officers *huperetes* (5257), is translated "officer," with the following applications, (a) to a magistrate's attendant, Matt. 5:25; (b) to officers of the synagogue, or officers or bailiffs of the Sanhedrin, Matt. 26:58; Mark 14:54, 65; **John 7:32**, **45-46**; **18:3**, **12**, **18**, **22**; **19:6**; Acts 5:22, 26.

Sent *see John 1:6*.

Take *see John 7:30*.

7:33 Then said Jesus unto them, Yet a little while am I with you, and *then* I go unto him that sent me.

Little *mikros* (3398), "little, small" (the opposite of *megos*, "great"), is used (a) of persons, with regard to (1) station, or age, in the singular, Mark 15:40, of James "the less" (RV marg., "little"), possibly referring to age; Luke 19:3; in the plural, "little" ones, Matt. 18:6, 10, 14; Mark 9:42; (2) rank or influence, e.g., Matt. 10:42 (see context); Acts 8:10; 26:22, "small," as in Rev. 11:18; 13:16; 19:5, 18; 20:12; (b) of things, with regard to (1) size, e.g., Jas. 3:5; (2) quantity, Luke 12:32; 1 Cor. 5:6; Gal. 5:9; Rev. 3:8; (3) time, **John 7:33**; **12:35**; Rev. 6:11; 20:3.

While *chronos*, "time," is rendered "while" in Luke 18:4; **John 7:33**; **12:35** (1st part); 1 Cor. 16:7; *kairos*, "a season," "a while," Luke 8:13; in Acts 19:22, RV, "while" (KJV, "season"); for the different meanings of these words

Sent *see John 1:33*.

7:34 Ye shall seek me, and shall not find *me*: and where I am, *thither* ye cannot come.

Thither In **John 7:34**, **36**, KJV, *hopou*, "where" (RV) is amplified by the italicized word "thither."

7:35 Then said the Jews among themselves, Whither will he go, that we shall not find him? will he go unto the dispersed among the Gentiles, and teach the Gentiles?

Will *mello* (3195), "to be about to," is translated "will" in Matt. 2:13 and **John 7:35** (twice); "wilt," **John 14:22**; "will," Acts 17:31; "wouldest," 23:20; "will," 27:10 and Rev. 3:16.

Dispersed *diaspora* (1290), "a scattering, a dispersion," was used of the Jews who from time to time had been scattered among the Gentiles, **John 7:35**; later with reference to Jews, so "scattered," who had professed, or actually embraced, the Christian faith, "the Dispersion," Jas. 1:1, RV; especially of believers who were converts from Judaism and "scattered" throughout certain districts, "sojourners of the Dispersion," 1 Pet. 1:1, RV. In the Sept., of Israelites, "scattered" and exiled, e.g., Deut. 28:25; 30:4; Neh. 1:9.

Gentiles *hellen* (1672), originally denoted the early descendants of Thessalian Hellas; then, Greeks as opposed to barbarians, Rom. 1:14. It became applied to such Gentiles as spoke the Greek language, e.g., Gal. 2:3; 3:28. Since that was the common medium of intercourse in the Roman Empire, Greek and

Gentile became more or less interchangeable terms. For this term the RV always adheres to the word "Greeks," e.g., **John 7:35**; Rom. 2:9, 10; 3:9; 1 Cor. 10:32, where the local church is distinguished from Jews and Gentiles; 12:13.

7:36 What *manner of* saying is this that he said, Ye shall seek me, and shall not find *me*: and where I am, *thither* ye cannot come?

Manner In Luke 24:17, KJV, the pronoun *tis*, "who, what," in the plural (RV, "what") is translated "what manner of"; similarly, in the singular in Mark 4:41; Luke 8:25 (RV, "who"), **John 7:36**.

Saying *see John 4:37*.

Thither *see John 7:34*.

7:37 In the last day, that great *day* of the feast, Jesus stood and cried, saying, If any man thirst, let him come unto me, and drink.

Cried *see John 7:28*.

Thirst *see John 4:13*.

Drink *see* Drinketh at *John 4:14*.

7:38 He that believeth on me, as the scripture hath said, out of his belly shall flow rivers of living water.

Belly *koilia* (2836), from *koilos*, "hollow" (Lat., *coelum*, "heaven," is connected), denotes the entire physical cavity, but most frequently was used to denote "the womb." In **John 7:38** it stands metaphorically for the innermost part of man, the soul, the heart.

Flow *rheo* (4482), "to flow," is used figuratively in **John 7:38** of the Holy Spirit, acting in and through the believer.

Rivers *potamos* (4215), denotes (a) "a stream," Luke 6:48, 49; (b) "a flood or floods," Matt. 7:25, 27; (c) "a river," natural, Matt. 3:6, RV; Mark 1:5; Acts 16:13; 2 Cor. 11:26, RV (KJV, "waters"); Rev. 8:10; 9:14; 16:4, 12; symbolical, Rev. 12:15 (1st part), RV, "river" (KJV, "flood"); so v. 16; 22:1, 2 (cf. Gen. 2:10; Ezek. 47); figuratively, **John 7:38**, "the effects of the operation of the Holy Spirit in and through the believer."

Living *see John 4:10*.

Water *see John 3:5*.

7:39 (But this spake he of the Spirit, which they that believe on him should receive: for the Holy Ghost was not yet *given*; because that Jesus was not yet glorified.)

Spirit, Holy Ghost The "Holy Spirit" is spoken of under various titles in the NT ("Spirit" and "Ghost" are renderings of the same word, *pneuma*; the advantage of the rendering "Spirit" is that it can always be used, whereas "Ghost" always requires the word "Holy" prefixed.) In the following list the omission of the definite article marks its omission in the original: "Spirit, Matt. 22:43; Eternal Spirit, Heb. 9:14; the Spirit, Matt. 4:1; Holy Spirit, Matt. 1:18; the Holy Spirit, Matt. 28:19; the Spirit, the Holy, Matt. 12:32; the Spirit of promise, the Holy, Eph. 1:13; Spirit of God, Rom. 8:9; Spirit of (the) living God, 2 Cor. 3:3; the Spirit of God, 1 Cor. 2:11; the Spirit of our God, 1 Cor. 6:11; the Spirit of God, the Holy, Eph. 4:30; the Spirit of glory and of God, 1 Pet. 4:14; the Spirit of Him that raised up Jesus from the dead (i.e., God), Rom. 8:11; the Spirit of your Father, Matt. 10:20; the Spirit of His Son, Gal. 4:6; Spirit of (the) Lord, Acts 8:39; the Spirit of (the) Lord, Acts 5:9; (the) Lord, (the) Spirit, 2 Cor. 3:18; the Spirit of Jesus, Acts 16:7; Spirit of Christ, Rom. 8:9; the Spirit of Jesus Christ, Phil. 1:19; Spirit of adoption, Rom. 8:15; the Spirit of truth, **John 14:17**; the Spirit of life, Rom. 8:2; the Spirit of grace, Heb. 10:29."

The use or absence of the article in the original where the "Holy Spirit" is spoken of cannot always be decided by grammatical rules, nor can the presence or absence of the article alone determine whether the reference is to the "Holy Spirit." Examples where the Person is meant when the article is absent are Matt. 22:43 (the article is used in Mark 12:36); Acts 4:25, RV (absent in some texts); 19:2, 6; Rom. 14:17; 1 Cor. 2:4; Gal. 5:25 (twice); 1 Pet. 1:2. Sometimes the absence is to be accounted for by the fact that *Pneuma* (like *Theos*) is substantially a proper name, e.g., in **John 7:39**. As a general rule the article is present where the subject of the teaching is the Personality of the Holy Spirit, e.g., **John 14:26**, where He is spoken of in distinction from the Father and the Son. See also **15:26** and cf. Luke 3:22. The full title with the article before both *pneuma* and *hagios* (the "resumptive" use of the article), lit., "the Spirit the Holy," stresses the character of the Person, e.g., Matt. 12:32; Mark 3:29; 12:36; 13:11; Luke 2:26; 10:21 (RV); **John 14:26**; Acts 1:16; 5:3; 7:51; 10:44, 47; 13:2; 15:28; 19:6; 20:23, 28; 21:11; 28:25; Eph. 4:30; Heb. 3:7; 9:8; 10:15. The Personality of the Spirit is emphasized at the expense of strict grammatical procedure in **John 14:26**; **15:26**; **16:8, 13, 14**, where the emphatic pronoun *ekeinos*, "He," is used of Him in the masculine, whereas the noun *pneuma* is neuter in Greek, while the corresponding word in Aramaic, the language in which our Lord probably spoke, is feminine (*rucha*, cf. Heb. *ruach*). The rendering "itself" in Rom. 8:16, 26, due to the Greek gender, is corrected to "Himself" in the RV. The subject of the "Holy Spirit" in the NT may be considered as to His divine attributes; His distinct Personality in the Godhead; His operation in connection with the Lord Jesus in His birth, His life, His baptism, His death; His operations in the world; in the church; His having been sent at Pentecost by the Father and by Christ; His operations in the individual believer; in local churches; His operations in the production of Holy Scripture; His work in the world, etc.

Should *see John 6:71*.

Yet *oupo*, "not yet," **John 7:39** and 1 Cor. 8:2 (*oudepo*, in some mss., KJV, "nothing yet"); *oudepo*, **John 19:41**, "never yet"; **20:9**, "as yet ... not".

Glorified *doxazo* (1392), primarily denotes "to suppose" (from *doxa*, "an opinion"); in the NT (a) "to magnify, extol, praise," especially of "glorifying"; God, i.e., ascribing honor to Him, acknowledging Him as to His being, attributes and acts, i.e., His glory, e.g., Matt. 5:16; 9:8; 15:31; Rom. 15:6, 9; Gal. 1:24; 1 Pet. 4:16; the Word of the Lord, Acts 13:48; the Name of the Lord, Rev. 15:4; also of "glorifying" oneself, **John 8:54**; Rev. 18:7; (b) "to do honor to, to make glorious," e.g., Rom. 8:30; 2 Cor. 3:10; 1 Pet. 1:8, "full of glory," passive voice (lit., "glorified"); said of Christ, e.g., **John 7:39**; **8:54**, RV, "glorifieth," for KJV, "honor" and "honoreth" (which would translate *timao*, "to honor"); of the Father, e.g., **John 13:31**, **32**; **21:19**; 1 Pet. 4:11; of "glorifying" one's ministry, Rom. 11:13, RV, "glorify" (KJV, "magnify"); of a member of the body, 1 Cor. 12:26, "be honored" (RV marg., "be glorified").

"As the glory of God is the revelation and manifestation of all that He has and is ... , it is said of a Self-revelation in which God manifests all the goodness that is His, **John 12:28**. So far as it is Christ through whom this is made manifest, He is said to glorify the Father, **John 17:1**, **4**; or the Father is glorified in Him, **13:31**; **14:13**; and Christ's meaning is analogous when He says to His disciples, 'Herein is My Father glorified, that ye bear much fruit; and so shall ye be My disciples,' **John 15:8**. When *doxazo* is predicated of Christ ... , it means simply that His innate glory is brought to light, is made manifest; cf. **11:4**. So **7:39**; **12:16**, **23**; **13:31**; **17:1**, **5**. It is an act of God the Father in Him.... As the revelation of the Holy Spirit is connected with the glorification of Christ, Christ says regarding Him, 'He shall glorify Me,' **16:14**" (Cremer).

7:40 Many of the people therefore, when they heard this saying, said, Of a truth this is the Prophet.

Many In **John 7:40** there is no word in the original representing "some" or "many."

Saying *see John 4:37*.

Truth *see John 6:14*.

Prophet *see John 1:21*.

7:41-42 Others said, This is the Christ. But some said, Shall Christ come out of Galilee?
Hath not the scripture said, That Christ cometh of the seed of David, and out of the town of Bethlehem, where David was?

Scripture *see John 2:22*.

Seed *sperma* (4690), akin to *speiro*, "to sow" (Eng., "sperm," "spermatic," etc.), has the following usages, (a) agricultural and botanical, e.g., Matt. 13:24, 27, 32; 1 Cor. 15:38; 2 Cor. 9:10; (b) physiological, Heb. 11:11; (c) metaphorical and by metonymy for "offspring, posterity," (1) of natural offspring, e.g., Matt. 22:24, 25, RV, "seed" (KJV, "issue"); **John 7:42**; **8:33**, **37**; Acts 3:25; Rom. 1:3; 4:13, 16, 18; 9:7 (twice), 8, 29; 11:1; 2 Cor. 11:22; Heb. 2:16; 11:18; Rev. 12:17; Gal. 3:16, 19, 29; in the 16th v., "He saith not, And to seeds, as of many; but as of one, And to thy seed, which is Christ," quoted from the Sept. of Gen. 13:15 and 17:7, 8, there is especial stress on the word "seed," as referring to an individual (here, Christ) in fulfillment of the promises to Abraham—a unique use of the singular. While the plural form "seeds," neither in Hebrew nor in Greek, would have been natural any more than in English (it is not so used in Scripture of human offspring; its plural occurrence is in 1 Sam. 8:15, of crops), yet if the divine intention had been to refer to Abraham's natural descendants, another word could have been chosen in the plural, such as "children"; all such words were, however, set aside, "seed" being selected as one that could be used in the singular, with the purpose of showing that the "seed" was Messiah. Some of the rabbis had even regarded "seed," e.g., in Gen. 4:25 and Isa. 53:10, as referring to the Coming One. Descendants were given to Abraham by other than natural means, so that through him Messiah might come, and the point of the apostle's argument is that since the fulfillment of the promises of God is secured alone by Christ, they only who are "in Christ" can receive them; (2) of spiritual offspring, Rom. 4:16, 18; 9:8; here "the children of the promise are reckoned for a seed" points, firstly, to Isaac's birth as being not according to the ordinary course of nature but by divine promise, and, secondly, by analogy, to the fact that all believers are children of God by spiritual birth; Gal. 3:29. As to 1 John 3:9, "his seed abideth in him," it is possible to understand this as meaning that children of God (His "seed") abide in Him, and do not go on doing (practicing) sin (the verb "to commit" does not represent the original in this passage). Alternatively, the "seed" signifies the principle of spiritual life as imparted to the believer, which abides in him without possibility of removal or extinction; the child of God remains eternally related to Christ, he who lives in sin has never become so related, he has not the principle of life in him. This meaning suits the context and the general tenor of the Epistle.

Town *kome* (2968), "a village," or "country town," primarily as distinct from a walled town, occurs in the Gospels; elsewhere only in Acts 8:25. The difference between *polis*, "a city," and *kome*, is maintained in the NT, as in Josephus. Among the Greeks the point of the distinction was not that of size or fortification, but of constitution and land. In the OT the city and the village are regularly distinguished. The Mishna makes the three distinctions, a large city, a city, and a village. The RV always substitutes "village(-s)" for KJV, "town(-s)," Matt. 10:11; Mark 8:23, 26, 27; Luke 5:17; 9:6, 12; **John 7:42; 11:1, 30.**

7:43 So there was a division among the people because of him.

Division *schisma* (4978), (Eng., "schism"), denotes "a cleft, a rent," Matt. 9:16; Mark 2:21, then, metaphorically, "a division dissension," **John 7:43; 9:16; 10:19;** 1 Cor. 1:10; 11:18; in 1 Cor. 12:25 it is translated "schism" (marg., "division"). The root is *skid*– seen in the corresponding verb *schizo*, "to cleave" (Lat. *scindo*). Cf. *hairesis*, a sect.

7:44 And some of them would have taken him; but no man laid hands on him.

Taken, Laid hands on *see John 7:30.*

7:45 Then came the officers to the chief priests and Pharisees; and they said unto them, Why have ye not brought him?

Officers *see John 7:32.*

7:46 The officers answered, Never man spake like this man.

Like In **John 7:46**, KJV, the combination of the adverb *houtos*, thus, with *hos*, "as," is translated "like," RV "(never man) so (spake)."

7:47-48 Then answered them the Pharisees, Are ye also deceived?
Have any of the rulers or of the Pharisees believed on him?

Rulers *see* Ruler at *John 3:1.*

7:49 But this people who knoweth not the law are cursed.

Cursed *eparatos* (1883a), "accursed," is found, in the best mss., in **John 7:49**, RV, "accursed."

7:50 Nicodemus saith unto them, (he that came to Jesus by night, being one of them,)

Night *see John 3:2.*

7:51 Doth our law judge *any* man, before it hear him, and know what he doeth?

Before *proton* (4412), the neuter of the adjective *protos*, is used as an adverb, signifying "first, firstly," e.g., of time, Matt. 8:21; of order, Rom. 3:2 (KJV, "chiefly"); in **John 7:51**, RV, "except it first hear from himself" (the KJV "before it hear him").

7:52 They answered and said unto him, Art thou also of Galilee? Search, and look: for out of Galilee ariseth no prophet.

Search *see John 5:39.*

Look *eidon* (3708), used as the aorist tense of *horao*, "to see," in various senses, is translated "to look," in the KJV of **John 7:52**, RV, "see;" Rev. 4:1 (RV, "I saw"); so in 6:8; 14:1, 14 (as in KJV of v. 6), and 15:5.

7:53 And every man went unto his own house.

Chapter 8

8:1 Jesus went unto the mount of Olives.

Mount *see* Mountain at *John 4:20.*

Olives *elaia* (1636), denotes (a) "an olive tree," Rom. 11:17, 24; Rev. 11:4 (plural); the Mount of Olives was so called from the numerous olive trees there, and indicates the importance attached to such; the Mount is mentioned in the NT in connection only with the Lord's life on earth, Matt. 21:1; 24:3; 26:30; Mark 11:1; 13:3; 14:26; Luke 19:37; 22:39; **John 8:1**; (b) "an olive," Jas. 3:12, RV (KJV, "olive berries").

8:2 And early in the morning he came again into the temple, and all the people came unto him; and he sat down, and taught them.

"Lead kindly light, amid th'encircling gloom; / lead thou me on. / The night is dark, and I am far from home; / lead thou me on. / Keep thou my fear; I do not ask to see / the distant scene – one step enough for me."

JOHN HENRY NEWMAN

Early *orthros* (3722), denotes "daybreak, dawn" (cf. Lat. *orior*, "to rise"). Used with the adverb *batheos*, "deeply," in Luke 24:1, it means "at early dawn" (RV). In **John 8:2** it is used in the genitive case, *orthrou*, "at dawn," i.e., "early in the morning." In Acts 5:21, it is used with the article and preceded by the preposition *hupo*, "under," or about, lit., "about the dawn," "about daybreak," RV (for KJV, "early in the morning.").

8:3 And the scribes and Pharisees brought unto him a woman taken in adultery; and when they had set her in the midst,

Scribes *grammateus* (1122), from *gramma*, "a writing," denotes "a scribe, a man of letters, a teacher of the law"; the "scribes" are mentioned frequently in the Synoptists, especially in connection with the Pharisees, with whom they virtually formed one party (see Luke 5:21), sometimes with the chief priests, e.g., Matt. 2:4; Mark 8:31; 10:33; 11:18, 27; Luke 9:22. They are mentioned only once in John's Gospel, **8:3**, three times in the Acts, 4:5; 6:12; 23:9; elsewhere only in 1 Cor. 1:20, in the singular. They were considered naturally qualified to teach in the synagogues, Mark 1:22. They were ambitious of honor, e.g., Matt. 23:5-11, which they demanded especially from their pupils, and which was readily granted them, as well as by the people generally. Like Ezra (Ezra 7:12), the "scribes" were found originally among the priests and Levites. The priests being the official interpreters of the Law, the "scribes" ere long became an independent company; though they never held political power, they became leaders of the people. Their functions regarding the Law were to teach it, develop it, and use it in connection with the Sanhedrin and various local courts. They also occupied themselves with the sacred writings both historical and didactic. They attached the utmost importance to ascetic elements, by which the nation was especially separated from the Gentiles. In their regime piety was reduced to external formalism. Only that was of value which was governed by external precept. Life under them became a burden; they themselves sought to evade certain of their own precepts, Matt. 23:16ff.; Luke 11:46; by their traditions the Law, instead of being a help in moral and spiritual life, became an instrument for preventing true access to God, Luke 11:52. Hence the Lord's stern denunciations of them and the Pharisees.

Taken *katalambano* (2638), "to lay hold of," is rendered "to take," in Mark 9:18; **John 8:3, 4**.

Adultery *moicheia* (3430), "adultery," is found in Matt. 15:19; Mark 7:21; **John 8:3** (KJV only).

Set *histemi* (2476), "to cause to stand," is translated "to set" in Matt. 4:5 (aorist tense in the best texts; some have the present, as in KJV); 18:2; 25:33; Mark 9:36; Luke 4:9; 9:47; **John 8:3**; Acts 4:7; 5:27; 6:6; v. 13, "set up"; 22:30; in Jude 24, RV, "to set" (KJV, "to present").

8:4 They say unto him, Master, this woman was taken in adultery, in the very act.

Taken *see John 8:3.*

Adultery *moicheuo* (3431), is used in Matt. 5:27-28, 32; 19:18; Mark 10:19; Luke 16:18; 18:20; **John 8:4**; Rom. 2:22; 13:9; Jas. 2:11; in Rev. 2:22, metaphorically, of those who are by a Jezebel's solicitations drawn away to idolatry.

Act *epautophoro* (1888), primarily signifies "caught in the act of theft" (*epi*, "upon," intensive, *autos*, "self," *phor*, "a thief"); then, "caught in the act" of any other crime, **John 8:4**. In some texts the preposition *epi* is detached from the remainder of the adjective, and appears as *ep' autophoro*.

8:5 Now Moses in the law commanded us, that such should be stoned: but what sayest thou?

Commanded *entello* (1781), signifies "to enjoin upon, to charge with"; it is used in the Middle Voice in the sense of commanding, Matt. 19:7; 28:20; Mark 10:3; 13:34; **John 8:5**; **15:14**, **17**; Acts 13:47; Heb. 9:20; 11:22, "gave commandment."

Stoned *lithoboleo* (3036), "to pelt with stones," "to stone to death," occurs in Matt. 21:35; 23:37; Luke 13:34 (**John 8:5** in some mss.); Acts 7:58, 59; 14:5; Heb. 12:20.

Thou *see John 1:19.*

8:6 This they said, tempting him, that they might have to accuse him. But Jesus stooped down, and with *his* finger wrote on the ground, *as though he heard them not*.

Tempting *peirazo* (3985), signifies (1) "to try, attempt, assay"; (2) "to test, try, prove," in a good sense, said of Christ and of believers, Heb. 2:18, where the context shows that the temptation was the cause of suffering to Him, and only suffering, not a drawing away to sin, so that believers have the sympathy of Christ as their High Priest in the suffering which sin occasions to those who are in the enjoyment of communion with God; so in the similar passage in 4:15; in all the temptations which Christ endured, there was nothing within Him that answered to sin. There was no sinful infirmity in Him. While He was truly man, and His divine nature was not in any way inconsistent with His Manhood, there was nothing in Him such as is produced in us by the sinful nature which belongs to us; in Heb. 11:37, of the testing of OT saints; in 1 Cor. 10:13, where the meaning has a wide scope, the verb is used of "testing" as permitted by God, and of the believer as one who should be in the realization of his own helplessness and his dependence upon God; in a bad sense, "to tempt" (a) of attempts to ensnare Christ in His speech, e.g., Matt. 16:1; 19:3; 22:18, 35, and parallel passages; **John 8:6**; (b) of temptations to sin, e.g., Gal. 6:1, where one who would restore an erring brother is not to act as his judge, but as being one with him in liability to sin, with the possibility of finding himself in similar circumstances, Jas. 1:13, 14; of temptations mentioned as coming from the Devil, Matt. 4:1; and parallel passages; 1 Cor. 7:5; 1 Thess. 3:5; (c) of trying or challenging God, Acts 15:10; 1 Cor. 10:9 (2nd part); Heb. 3:9; the Holy Spirit, Acts 5:9.

Stooped *kupto* (2955), "to bow the head, stoop down," occurs in Mark 1:7; **John 8:6, 8**.

Down *kato* (2736), signifies (a) "down, downwards," Matt. 4:6; Luke 4:9; **John 8:6, 8**; Acts 20:9; (b) "below, beneath," of place, Mark 14:66; the realms that lie below in contrast to heaven, **John 8:23**; the earth, as contrasted with the heavens, Acts 2:19; with *heos*, "unto," Matt. 27:51; Mark 15:38. The comparative degree, *katotero*, "under," is used in Matt. 2:16.

Finger *daktulos* (1147), Matt. 23:4; Mark 7:33; Luke 11:46; 16:24; **John 8:6; 20:25, 27**, is used metaphorically in Luke 11:20, for the power of God, the effects of which are made visible to men (cf. Matt. 12:28, "by the Spirit of God"; cf. also Exod. 8:19).

Wrote *grapho* (1125), is used (a) of "forming letters" on a surface or writing material, **John 8:6**; Gal. 6:11, where the apostle speaks of his having "written" with large letters in his own hand, which not improbably means that at this point he took the pen from his amanuensis and finished the epistle himself; this is not negatived by the fact that the verb is in the aorist or past definite tense, lit., "I wrote," for in Greek idiom the writer of a letter put himself beside the reader and spoke of it as having been "written" in the past; in Eng. we should say "I am writing," taking our point of view from the time at which we are doing it; cf. Philem. 19 (this Ep. is undoubtedly a holograph), where again the equivalent English translation is in the present tense (see also Acts 15:23; Rom. 15:15); possibly the apostle, in Galatians, was referring to his having "written" the body of the epistle but the former alternative seems the more likely; in 2 Thess. 3:17 he says that the closing salutation is written by his own hand and speaks of it as "the token in every epistle" which some understand as a purpose for the future rather than a custom; see, however, 1 Cor. 16:21 and Col. 4:18. The absence of the token from the other epistles of Paul can be explained differently, their authenticity not being dependent upon this; (b) "to commit to writing, to record," e.g., Luke 1:63; **John 19:21, 22**; it is used of Scripture as a standing authority, "it is written," e.g., Mark 1:2; Rom. 1:17 (cf. 2 Cor. 4:13); (c) of "writing directions or giving information," e.g., Rom. 10:5, "(Moses) writeth," RV (KJV, "describeth"); 15:15; 2 Cor. 7:12; (d) of "that which contained a record or message," e.g., Mark 10:4, 5; **John 19:19; 21:25**; Acts 23:25.

8:7 So when they continued asking him, he lifted up himself, and said unto them, He that is without sin among you, let him first cast a stone at her.

Continued *epimeno* (1961), lit., "to remain on," i.e., in addition to, "to continue long, still to abide," is used of "continuing" to ask, **John 8:7**; to knock, Acts 12:16; in the grace of God, 13:43; in sin, Rom. 6:1; in God's goodness, 11:22; in unbelief, 11:23 (KJV, "abide"); in the flesh, Phil. 1:24; in the faith, Col. 1:23; in doctrine, 1 Tim. 4:16; elsewhere of abiding in a place.

Lifted *anakupto* (352), "to lift oneself up," is used (a) of the body, Luke 13:11; **John 8:7, 10**; (b) metaphorically, of the mind, to look up, to be elated, Luke 21:28; an instance is found in the papyri in which a person speaks of the impossibility of ever looking up again in a certain place, for very shame (Moulton and Milligan, *Vocab.*). In the Sept., Job 10:15.

Sin *anamartetos* (361), "without sin," is found in **John 8:7**. In the Sept., Deut. 29:19.

8:8 And again he stooped down, and wrote on the ground.

Stooped *see John 8:6.*

Down *see John 8:6.*

8:9 And they which heard *it*, being convicted by *their own* conscience, went out one by one, beginning at the eldest, *even* unto the last: and Jesus was left alone, and the woman standing in the midst.

Eldest *presbuteros* (4245), an adjective, the comparative degree of *presbus,* "an old man, an elder," is used of age, whether of the "elder" of two persons, Luke 15:25, or more, **John 8:9**, "the eldest", or of a person advanced in life, a senior, Acts 2:17; in Heb. 11:2, the "elders" are the forefathers in Israel so in Matt. 15:2; Mark 7:3, 5 the feminine of the adjective is used of "elder" women in the churches, 1 Tim. 5:2, not in respect of position but in seniority of age.

8:10 When Jesus had lifted up himself, and saw none but the woman, he said unto her, Woman, where are those thine accusers? hath no man condemned thee?

Lifted *see John 8:7.*

But *plen* (4133), an adverb, most frequently signifying "yet, howbeit," or "only," sometimes has the meaning "except (that)," "save (that)," Acts 20:23; Phil. 1:18, RV, "only that," for KJV, "notwithstanding." It is also used as a preposition, signifying "except, save," Mark 12:32, "but"; **John 8:10**, "but" (KJV only); Acts 8:1, "except"; Acts 15:28, "than"; 27:22, "but (only)."

Accusers *kategoros* (2725), "an accuser," is used in **John 8:10**; Acts 23:30, 35; 24:8; 25:16, 18. In Rev. 12:10, it is used of Satan. In the Sept., Prov. 18:17.

8:11 She said, No man, Lord. And Jesus said unto her, Neither do I condemn thee: go, and sin no more.

Sin *see John 5:14.*

8:12 Then spake Jesus again unto them, saying, I am the light of the world: he that followeth me shall not walk in darkness, but shall have the light of life.

Light *see John 1:4.*

Darkness *see John 1:5.*

8:13 The Pharisees therefore said unto him, Thou bearest record of thyself; thy record is not true.

Thou *see John 1:19.*

Record *see* Witness at *John 1:7.*

True *see John 3:33.*

8:14 Jesus answered and said unto them, Though I bear record of myself, *yet* my record is true: for I know whence I came, and whither I go; but ye cannot tell whence I come, and whither I go.

Record *see* Witness at *John 1:7.*

Myself *see* Mine own self at *John 5:30.*

True *see John 3:33.*

Know *see* Knew at *John 6:6.*

Cannot *see* Canst at *John 3:8.*

Tell *see John 3:8.*

8:15-16 Ye judge after the flesh; I judge no man.

And yet if I judge, my judgment is true: for I am not alone, but I and the Father that sent me.

Yet The following, in which the RV gives the correct meaning for the KJV, "yet": *ede,* "now," Mark 13:28; *pote,* "ever," Eph. 5:29 (KJV, "ever yet"); *kai ... de,* **John 8:16**, "yea and" (KJV, "and yet"); *ou pleious,* Acts 24:11, "not more".

True *see John 3:33.*

Sent *see John 1:33.*

8:17 It is also written in your law, that the testimony of two men is true.

Your *see John 7:6.*

Testimony *see John 3:32.*

8:18 I am one that bear witness of myself, and the Father that sent me beareth witness of me.

Witness *see John 1:7.*

Myself *see* Mine own self at *John 5:30.*

Sent *see John 1:33.*

8:19-20 Then said they unto him, Where is thy Father? Jesus answered, Ye neither know me, nor my Father: if ye had known me, ye should have known my Father also.

These words spake Jesus in the treasury, as he taught in the temple: and no man laid hands on him; for his hour was not yet come.

Words *see John 3:34.*

Treasury *gazophulakion* (1049), from *gaza*, "a treasure," *phulake*, "a guard," is used by Josephus for a special room in the women's court in the Temple in which gold and silver bullion was kept. This seems to be referred to in **John 8:20**; in Mark 12:41 (twice), 43 and Luke 21:1 it is used of the trumpet-shaped or ram's-horn-shaped chests, into which the temple offerings of the people were cast. There were 13 chests, six for such gifts in general, seven for distinct purposes.

Laid hands on *see John 7:30.*

8:21 Then said Jesus again unto them, I go my way, and ye shall seek me, and shall die in your sins: whither I go, ye cannot come.

Sins *see* Sin at *John 1:29.*

8:22-23 Then said the Jews, Will he kill himself? because he saith, Whither I go, ye cannot come.

And he said unto them, Ye are from beneath; I am from above: ye are of this world; I am not of this world.

Beneath *see* Down at *John 8:6.*

Above *see* Brim at *John 2:7.*

World *see John 1:9.*

8:24 I said therefore unto you, that ye shall die in your sins: for if ye believe not that I am *he*, ye shall die in your sins.

Die *see John 6:50.*

8:25 Then said they unto him, Who art thou? And Jesus saith unto them, Even *the same* that I said unto you from the beginning.

Thou *see John 1:19.*

Said *laleo* (2980), "to speak," is sometimes translated "to say"; in the following where the KJV renders it thus, the RV alters it to the verb "to speak," e.g., **John 8:25** (3rd part), **26**; **16:6**; **18:20** (2nd part), **21** (1st part); Acts 3:22 (2nd part); 1 Cor. 9:8 (1st part); Heb. 5:5; in the following the RV uses the verb "to say," **John 16:18**; Acts 23:18 (2nd part); 26:22 (2nd part); Heb. 11:18.

Beginning *arche* (746), means "a beginning." The root *arch* primarily indicated what was of worth. Hence the verb *archo* meant "to be first," and *archon* denoted "a ruler." So also arose the idea of "a beginning," the origin, the active cause, whether a person or thing, e.g., Col. 1:18. In Heb. 2:3 the phrase "having at the first been spoken" is, lit., "having received a beginning to be spoken." In 2 Thess. 2:13 ("God chose you from the beginning"), there is a well supported alternative reading, "chose you as firstfruits" (i.e., *aparchen*, instead of *ap' arches*). In Heb. 6:1, where the word is rendered "first principles," the original has "let us leave the word of the beginning of Christ," i.e., the doctrine of the elementary principles relating to Christ. In **John 8:25**, Christ's reply to the question "Who art Thou?" "Even that which I have spoken unto you from the beginning," does not mean that He had told them before; He declares that He is consistently the unchanging expression of His own teaching and testimony from the first, the immutable embodiment of His doctrine.

8:26 I have many things to say and to judge of you: but he that sent me is true; and I speak to the world those things which I have heard of him.

Say *see* Said at *John 8:25.*

Sent *see John 1:33.*

True *see John 3:33.*

Heard *see John 1:40.*

8:27 They understood not that he spake to them of the Father.

Understood *ginosko* (1097), "to know, to come to know," is translated "to understand" in the KJV in Matt. 26:10 and **John 8:27** (RV, "to perceive"); KJV and RV in **John 8:43**; **10:6**; in **10:38**, RV (in some texts *pisteuo*, KJV, "believe"); KJV and RV in **12:16**; **13:7** RV, KJV, "know"; Acts 8:30; in Phil. 1:12, KJV, RV, "know" (in some texts, Acts 24:11, KJV).

8:28 Then said Jesus unto them, When ye have lifted up the Son of man, then shall ye know that I am *he*, and *that* I do nothing of myself; but as my Father hath taught me, I speak these things.

Lifted up *see John 3:14.*

Son *see John 1:18.*

Myself *see* Mine own self at *John 5:30.*

8:29 And he that sent me is with me: the Father hath not left me alone; for I do always those things that please him.

Sent *see John 1:33.*

Left *see John 4:3.*

Please *arestos* (701), denotes "pleasing, agreeable," **John 8:29**, RV, "(the things that are) pleasing," KJV, "(those things that) please", KJV and RV in 1 John 3:22; in Acts 6:2, "fit" (RV marg., "pleasing"); 12:3, "it pleased," lit., "it was pleasing."

8:30-31 As he spake these words, many believed on him.

Then said Jesus to those Jews which believed on him, If ye continue in my word, *then* are ye my disciples indeed;

"Christianity is not true because it works. It works because it is true."

OS GUINNESS

Disciples *see John 6:66.*

Indeed *see John 1:47.*

8:32 And ye shall know the truth, and the truth shall make you free.

Know *epiginosko* (1921), denotes (a) "to observe, fully perceive, notice attentively, discern, recognize"; it suggests generally a directive, a more special, recognition of the object "known" than does *ginosko*; it also may suggest advanced "knowledge" or special appreciation; thus, in Rom. 1:32, "knowing the ordinance of God" (*epiginosko*) means "knowing full well," whereas in verse 21 "knowing God" (*ginosko*) simply suggests that they could not avoid the perception. Sometimes *epiginosko* implies a special participation in the object "known," and gives greater weight to what is stated; thus in **John 8:32**, "ye shall know the truth," *ginosko* is used, whereas in 1 Tim. 4:3, "them that believe and know the truth," *epiginosko* lays stress on participation in the truth. Cf. the stronger statement in Col. 1:6 (*epiginosko*) with that in 2 Cor. 8:9 (*ginosko*), and the two verbs in 1 Cor. 13:12, "now I know in part (*ginosko*); but then shall I know (*piginosko*) even as also I have been known (*epiginosko*)," "a knowledge" which perfectly unites the subject with the object; (b) "to discover, ascertain, determine," e.g., Luke 7:37; 23:7; Acts 9:30; 19:34; 22:29; 28:1; in 24:11 the best mss. have this verb; hence the RV, "take knowledge." J. Armitage Robinson (on Ephesians) points out that *epignosis* is "knowledge directed towards a particular object, perceiving, discerning," whereas *gnosis* is knowledge in the abstract.

Free *eleutheroo* (1659), "to make free," is used of deliverance from (a) sin, **John 8:32, 36**; Rom. 6:18, 22; (b) the Law, Rom. 8:2; Gal. 5:1; (c) the bondage of corruption, Rom. 8:21.

8:33 They answered him, We be Abraham's seed, and were never in bondage to any man: how sayest thou, Ye shall be made free?

Seed *see John 7:42.*

Never *popote* follows *oudeis*, "no one," in the dative case ("to no man") in **John 8:33**, RV, "never yet" (KJV, "never"); so in Luke 19:30, where *oudeis* is in the nominative case, RV, "no man ever yet" (KJV, "yet never man").

Bondage *douleuo* (1398), "to serve as a *doulos*," is used (a) of serving God (and the impossibility of serving mammon also), Matt. 6:24 and Luke 16:13; Rom. 7:6; in the gospel, Phil. 2:22; (b) Christ, Acts 20:19; Rom. 12:11; 14:18; 16:18; Eph. 6:7; Col. 3:24; (c) the law of God, Rom. 7:25; (d) one another, Gal. 5:13, RV, "be servants to" (KJV, "serve"); (e) a father, Luke 15:29 (with a suggestion of acting as a slave); (f) earthly masters, Matt. 6:24; Luke 16:13; 1 Tim. 6:2, RV, "serve"; (g) the younger by the elder, Rom. 9:12; (h) of being in bondage to a nation, Acts 7:7; Gal. 4:25, to the Romans, actually, though also spiritually to Judaizers; (i) to idols, Gal. 4:8, RV, "were in bondage" (KJV, "did service"); (j) to "the weak and beggarly rudiments," v. 9 (RV), "to be in bondage" (aorist tense in the best texts, suggesting "to enter into bondage"), i.e., to the religion of the Gentiles ("rudiments" being used in v. 3 of the religion of the Jews); (k) sin, Rom. 6:6, RV, "be in bondage" (KJV, "serve"); (l) "divers lusts and pleasures," Titus 3:3; (m) negatively, to any man – a proud and thoughtless denial by the Jews, **John 8:33**.

Thou *see John 1:19.*

Made *see John 1:3.*

Free *eleutheros* (1658), primarily of "freedom to go wherever one likes," is used (a) of "freedom from restraint and obligation" in general, Matt. 17:26; Rom. 7:3; 1 Cor. 7:39, RV, "free," of the second marriage of a woman; 9:1, 19; 1 Pet. 2:16; from the Law, Gal. 4:26; from sin, **John 8:36**; with regard to righteousness, Rom. 6:20 (i.e., righteousness laid no sort of bond upon them, they had no relation to it); (b) in a civil sense, "free" from bondage or slavery, **John 8:33**; 1 Cor. 7:21, 22, 2nd part; 12:13; Gal. 3:28; Eph. 6:8; Rev. 13:16; 19:18; as a noun, "freeman," Col. 3:11, RV; Rev. 6:15; "freewoman," Gal. 4:22, 23, 30, and v. 31, RV.

8:34 Jesus answered them, Verily, verily, I say unto you, Whosoever committeth sin is the servant of sin.

Committeth *poieo* (4160), "to do, cause, etc.," sometimes signifies "to commit, of any act, as of murder," Mark 15:7; sin, **John 8:34**; 2 Cor. 11:7; Jas. 5:15.

Sin *see John 1:29.*

Servant *doulos* (1401), an adjective, signifying "in bondage," Rom. 6:19 (neuter plural, agreeing with *mele*, "members"), is used as a noun, and as the most common and general word for "servant," frequently indicating subjection without the idea of bondage; it is used (a) of natural conditions, e.g., Matt. 8:9; 1 Cor. 7:21, 22 (1st part); Eph. 6:5; Col. 4:1; 1 Tim. 6:1; frequently in the four Gospels; (b) metaphorically of spiritual, moral and ethical conditions: "servants" (1) of God, e.g., Acts 16:17; Titus 1:1; 1 Pet. 2:16; Rev. 7:3; 15:3; the perfect example being Christ Himself, Phil. 2:7; (2) of Christ, e.g., Rom. 1:1; 1 Cor. 7:22 (2nd part); Gal. 1:10; Eph. 6:6; Phil. 1:1; Col. 4:12; Jas. 1:1; 2 Pet. 1:1; Jude 1; (3) of sin, **John 8:34** (RV, "bondservants"); Rom. 6:17, 20; (4) of corruption, 2 Pet. 2:19 (RV, "bondservants"); cf. the verb *douloo*.

8:35-36 And the servant abideth not in the house for ever: *but* the Son abideth ever.

If the Son therefore shall make you free, ye shall be free indeed.

Free *see John 8:33.*

Indeed *ontos* (3689), an adverb from *on*, the present participle of *eimi*, "to be," denotes "really, actually"; it is translated "indeed" in Mark 11:32 (RV, "verily"); Luke 24:34; **John 8:36**; 1 Cor. 14:25, RV (KJV "of a truth"); 1 Tim. 5:3, 5, 16; 6:15, RV, where some mss. have *aionios*, "eternal" (KJV); in Gal. 3:21, "verily."

8:37 I know that ye are Abraham's seed; but ye seek to kill me, because my word hath no place in you.

Seed *see John 7:42.*

My *see John 4:34.*

Place For *choreo* in **John 8:37**, KJV, "hath ... place."

8:38 I speak that which I have seen with my Father: and ye do that which ye have seen with your father.

Seen *see John 6:36.*

Father *pater* (3962), from a root signifying "a nourisher, protector, upholder" (Lat., *pater*, Eng., "father," are akin), is used (a) of the nearest ancestor, e.g., Matt. 2:22; (b) of a more remote ancestor, the progenitor of the people, a "forefather," e.g., Matt. 3:9; 23:30; 1 Cor. 10:1; the patriarchs, 2 Pet. 3:4; (c) one advanced in the knowledge of Christ, 1 John 2:13; (d) metaphorically, of the originator of a family or company of persons animated by the same spirit as himself, as of Abraham, Rom. 4:11, 12, 16, 17, 18, or of Satan, **John 8:38, 41, 44**; (e) of one who, as a preacher of the gospel and a teacher, stands in a "father's" place, caring for his spiritual children, 1 Cor. 4:15 (not the same as a mere title of honor, which the Lord prohibited, Matt. 23:9); (f) of the members of the Sanhedrin, as of those who exercised religious authority over others, Acts 7:2; 22:1; (g) of God in relation to those who have been born anew (**John 1:12, 13**), and so are believers, Eph. 2:18; 4:6 (cf. 2 Cor. 6:18), and imitators of their "Father," Matt. 5:45, 48; 6:1, 4, 6, 8, 9, etc. Christ never associated Himself with them by using the personal pronoun "our"; He always used the singular, "My Father," His relationship being unoriginated and essential, whereas theirs is by grace and regeneration, e.g., Matt. 11:27; 25:34; **John 20:17**; Rev. 2:27; 3:5, 21; so the apostles spoke of God as the "Father" of the Lord Jesus Christ, e.g., Rom. 15:6; 2 Cor. 1:3; 11:31; Eph. 1:3; Heb. 1:5; 1 Pet. 1:3; Rev. 1:6; (h) of God, as the "Father" of lights, i.e., the Source or Giver of whatsoever provides illumination, physical and spiritual, Jas. 1:17; of mercies, 2 Cor. 1:3; of glory, Eph. 1:17; (i) of God, as Creator, Heb. 12:9 (cf. Zech. 12:1).

8:39-40 They answered and said unto him, Abraham is our father. Jesus saith unto them, If ye were Abraham's children, ye would do the works of Abraham.

But now ye seek to kill me, a man that hath told you the truth, which I have heard of God: this did not Abraham.

Now *see John 4:18.*

Told *laleo* (2980), is usually rendered "to speak," in the RV (for KJV, "to tell"), e.g., Matt. 26:13; Luke 1:45; 2:17, 18, 20; Acts 11:14; 27:25; but RV and KJV, "to tell" in **John 8:40**; Acts 9:6; 22:10.

Heard *see John 1:40.*

8:41 Ye do the deeds of your father. Then said they to him, We be not born of fornication; we have one Father, *even* God.

Deeds *see* Work at *John 4:34.*

Fornication *porneia* (4202), is used (a) of "illicit sexual intercourse," in **John 8:41**; Acts 15:20, 29; 21:25; 1 Cor. 5:1; 6:13, 18; 2 Cor. 12:21; Gal. 5:19; Eph. 5:3; Col. 3:5; 1 Thess. 4:3; Rev. 2:21; 9:21; in the plural in 1 Cor. 7:2; in Matt. 5:32 and 19:9 it stands for, or includes, adultery; it is distinguished from it in 15:19 and Mark 7:21; (b) metaphorically, of "the association of pagan idolatry with doctrines of, and professed adherence to, the Christian faith," Rev. 14:8; 17:2, 4; 18:3; 19:2; some suggest this as the sense in 2:21.

Father *see John 8:38.*

8:42 Jesus said unto them, If God were your Father, ye would love me: for I proceeded forth and came from God; neither came I of myself, but he sent me.

Father *see John 8:38.*

Proceeded *exerchomai* (1831), is translated "proceed" in Matt. 15:19, KJV (RV, "come forth"); **John 8:42**, RV, "came forth"; Jas. 3:10. The verb "to proceed" is not so suitable.

Came *erchomai* (2064), the most frequent verb, denoting either "to come, or to go," signifies the act, in contrast with *heko*, which stresses the arrival, as, e.g., "I am come and am here," **John 8:42** and Heb. 10:9.

Myself *see* **Mine own self** at *John 5:30.*

Sent *see John 1:6.*

8:43 Why do ye not understand my speech? *even* because ye cannot hear my word.

Understand *see* **Understood** at *John 8:27.*

Speech *see* **Saying** at *John 4:42.*

8:44 Ye are of *your* father the devil, and the lusts of your father ye will do. He was a murderer from the beginning, and abode not in the truth, because there is no truth in him. When he speaketh a lie, he speaketh of his own: for he is a liar, and the father of it.

Father *see John 8:38.*

Murderer *anthropoktonos* (443), an adjective, lit., "manslaying," used as a noun, "a manslayer, murderer" (*anthropos*, "a man," *kteino*, "to slay"), is used of Satan, **John 8:44**; of one who hates his brother, and who, being a "murderer," has not eternal life, 1 John 3:15 (twice).

Abode *histemi* (2476), "to stand, to make to stand," is rendered "abode" in **John 8:44**, KJV; "continue," in Acts 26:22. In these places the RV corrects to "stood" and "stand." This word is suggestive of fidelity and stability. It is rendered "lay ... to the charge" in Acts 7:60.

histemi (2476), (a) transitively, denotes "to cause to stand, to set"; in the passive voice, "to be made to stand," e.g., Matt. 2:9, lit., "was made to stand"; so Luke 11:18; 19:8 (Col. 4:12 in some mss.); in Rev. 13:1 the RV follows the best texts, "he stood" (not as KJV, "I stood"); the reference is to the Dragon. In the middle voice, "to take one's stand, place oneself," e.g., Rev. 18:15; (b) intransitively, in the 2nd aorist and perfect active, "to stand, stand by, stand still," e.g., Matt. 6:5; 20:32, "stood still"; in Luke 6:8, "stand forth" and "stood forth"; metaphorically, "to stand firm," **John 8:44** (negatively), in the truth; Rom. 5:2, in grace; 1 Cor. 15:1, in the gospel; Rom. 11:20, "by thy faith," RV; 2 Cor. 1:24, "by faith" (marg., "by your faith"); of steadfastness, 1 Cor. 7:37; Eph. 6:11, 13, 14; Col. 4:12.

Truth *aletheia* (225), "truth," is used (a) objectively, signifying "the reality lying at the basis of an appearance; the manifested, veritable essence of a matter" (Cremer), e.g., Rom. 9:1; 2 Cor. 11:10; especially of Christian doctrine, e.g., Gal. 2:5, where "the truth of the Gospel" denotes the "true" teaching of the Gospel, in contrast to perversions of it; Rom. 1:25, where "the truth of God" may be "the truth concerning God" or "God whose existence is a verity"; but in Rom. 15:8 "the truth of God" is indicative of His faithfulness in the fulfillment of His promises as exhibited in Christ; the word has an absolute force in **John 14:6**; **17:17**; **18:37**, **38**; in Eph. 4:21, where the RV, "even as truth is in Jesus," gives the correct rendering, the meaning is not merely ethical "truth," but "truth" in all its fullness and scope, as embodied in Him; He was the perfect expression of the truth; this is virtually equivalent to His statement in **John 14:6**; (b) subjectively, "truthfulness," "truth," not merely verbal, but sincerity and integrity of character, **John 8:44**; 3 John 3, RV; (c) in phrases, e.g., "in truth" (*epi*, "on the basis of"), Mark 12:14; Luke 20:21; with *en*, "in," 2 Cor. 6:7; Col. 1:6; 1 Tim. 2:7, RV (KJV, "in ... verity"), 1 John 3:18; 2 John 1, 3, 4.

Lie *pseudos* (5579), "a falsehood, lie", is translated "lie" in **John 8:44** (lit., "the lie"); Rom. 1:25, where it stands by metonymy for an idol, as, e.g., in Isa. 44:20; Jer. 10:14; 13:25; Amos 2:4 (plural); 2 Thess. 2:11, with special reference to the lie of v. 4, that man is God (cf. Gen. 3:5); 1 John 2:21, 27; Rev. 21:27; 22:15; in Eph. 4:25, KJV, "lying," RV, "falsehood," the practice; in Rev. 14:5, RV, "lie" (some mss. have *dolos*, "guile," KJV); 2 Thess. 2:9, where "lying wonders" is, lit., "wonders of falsehood," i.e., wonders calculated to deceive (cf. Rev. 13:13-15), the purpose being to deceive people into the acknowledgement of the spurious claim to deity on the part of the Man of Sin.

Liar *pseustes* (5583), "a liar," occurs in **John 8:44, 55**; Rom. 3:4; 1 Tim. 1:10; Titus 1:12; 1 John 1:10; 2:4, 22; 4:20; 5:10.

8:45-46 And because I tell *you* the truth, ye believe me not. Which of you convinceth me of sin? And if I say the truth, why do ye not believe me?

Which This is the translation of (a) the article with nouns, adjectives, numerals, participles, etc., e.g., "that which," etc.; (b) the relative pronoun *hos*, "who," in one of its forms (a frequent use); (c) *hostis*, "whoever," differing from *hos* by referring to a subject in general, as one of a class, e.g., Rom. 2:15; Gal. 4:24 (twice); 5:19; Rev. 2:24; 20:4; (d) the interrogative pronoun *tis*, "who? which?" e.g., Matt. 6:27; **John 8:46**; (e) *hoios*, "of what kind," e.g., Phil. 1:30; (f) *poios*, the interrogative of (e), e.g., **John 10:32**; (g) *hosos*, "whatsoever," etc.; plural, how many, translated "which" in Acts 9:39.

Convinceth *see* Reproved at *John 3:20.*

Sin *see 1:29.* Christ is predicated as having been without "sin" in every respect, e.g., (a), (b), (c) above, 2 Cor. 5:21 (1st part); 1 John 3:5; **John 14:30**; (d) **John 8:46**; Heb. 4:15; 1 Pet. 2:22.

8:47-48 He that is of God heareth God's words: ye therefore hear *them* not, because ye are not of God.

Then answered the Jews, and said unto him, Say we not well that thou art a Samaritan, and hast a devil?

Thou *see John 1:19.*

8:49 Jesus answered, I have not a devil; but I honour my Father, and ye do dishonour me.

Honour *see John 5:23.*

Dishonour *atimazo* (818), signifies "to dishonor, treat shamefully, insult," whether in word, **John 8:49**, or deed, Mark 12:4; Luke 20:11, RV, "handled (him) shamefully," (RV, "entreated ... shamefully"); Rom. 1:24; 2:23, "dishonorest;" Jas. 2:6, RV, "ye have dishonored (the poor)," (KJV, "despised"); in the passive voice, to suffer dishonor, Acts 5:41 (KJV, "suffer shame").

8:50 And I seek not mine own glory: there is one that seeketh and judgeth.

Glory *see John 1:14.*

8:51 Verily, verily, I say unto you, If a man keep my saying, he shall never see death.

Saying *see John 4:37.*

Never *see John 4:14.*

See *theoreo* (2334), from *theoros*, "a spectator," is used of one who looks at a thing with interest and for a purpose, usually indicating the careful observation of details; see, e.g., Mark 15:47; Luke 10:18; 23:35; **John 20:6** (RV, "beholdeth," for KJV, "seeth"); so in verses **12** and **14**; "consider," in Heb. 7:4. It is used of experience, in the sense of partaking of, in **John 8:51**; **17:24**. Cf. *theoria*, "sight," Luke 23:48, only.

8:52 Then said the Jews unto him, Now we know that thou hast a devil. Abraham is dead, and the prophets; and thou sayest, If a man keep my saying, he shall never taste of death.

Thou *see John 1:19.*

Prophets *see* Prophet at *John 1:21.*

Saying *see John 4:37.*

Taste *see* Tasted at *John 2:9.*

8:53 Art thou greater than our father Abraham, which is dead? and the prophets are dead: whom makest thou thyself?

Thou *see John 1:19.*

Makest *see* Make at *John 2:16.*

8:54 Jesus answered, If I honour myself, my honour is nothing: it is my Father that honoureth me; of whom ye say, that he is your God:

Honour *doxazo* (1392), "to glorify," is rendered "honor" and "honoureth" in the KJV of **John 8:54**; in 1 Cor. 12:26, however, in reference to the members of the body, both KJV and RV have "honored" (RV marg., "glorified"). Everywhere else it is translated by some form of the verb "to glorify," "have glory," or "be made glorious," except in Rom. 11:13, "magnify," KJV.

> *"Satan deals with confusion and lies. Put the truth in front of him and he is gone."*
>
> PAUL MATTOCK

Myself *see* Mine own self at *John 5:30.*

8:55 Yet ye have not known him; but I know him: and if I should say, I know him not, I shall be a liar like unto you: but I know him, and keep his saying.

Known, Know *see* Knew at *John 6:6.*

Liar *see John 8:44.*

Like *homoios* (3664), "like, resembling, such as, the same as," is used (a) of appearance or form **John 9:9**; Rev. 1:13, 15; 2:18; 4:3 (twice), 6, 7; 9:7 (twice), 10, 19; 11:1; 13:2, 11; 14:14; (b) of ability, condition, nature, Matt. 22:39; Acts 17:29; Gal. 5:21, "such like," lit., "and the (things) similar to these"; 1 John 3:2; Rev. 13:4; 18:18; 21:11, 18; (c) of comparison in parables, Matt. 13:31, 33, 44, 45, 47; 20:1; Luke 13:18, 19, 21; (d) of action, thought, etc., Matt. 11:16; 13:52; Luke 6:47, 48, 49; 7:31, 32; 12:36; **John 8:55**; Jude 7.

Saying *see John 4:37.*

8:56 Your father Abraham rejoiced to see my day: and he saw *it*, and was glad.

Rejoiced *see* Rejoice at *John 4:36.*

Day *hemera* (2250), "a day," is used of (a) the period of natural light, Gen. 1:5; Prov. 4:18; Mark 4:35; (b) the same, but figuratively, for a period of opportunity for service, **John 9:4**; Rom. 13:13; (c) one period of alternate light and darkness, Gen. 1:5; Mark 1:13; (d) a period of undefined length marked by certain characteristics, such as "the day of small things," Zech. 4:10; of perplexity and distress, Isa. 17:11; Obad. 12-14; of prosperity and of adversity, Ecc. 7:14; of trial or testing, Ps. 95:8; of salvation, Isa. 49:8; 2 Cor. 6:2; cf. Luke 19:42; of evil, Eph. 6:13; of wrath and revelation of the judgments of God, Rom. 2:5; (e) an appointed time, Ecc. 8:6; Eph. 4:30; (f) a notable defeat in battle, etc., Isa. 9:4; Psa. 137:7; Ezek. 30:9; Hos. 1:11; (g) by metonymy = "when," "at the time when"; (1), of the past, Gen. 2:4; Num. 3:13; Deut. 4:10, (2), of the future, Gen. 2:17; Ruth 4:5; Matt. 24:50; Luke 1:20; (h) a judgment or doom, Job 18:20. (i) of a time of life, Luke 1:17-18 ("years"). As the "day" throws light upon things that have been in darkness, the word is often associated with the passing of judgment upon circumstances. In 1 Cor. 4:3, "man's day," KJV, "man's judgement," RV, denotes mere human judgment upon matters ("man's" translates the adjective *anthropinos*, "human"), a judgment exercised in the present period of human rebellion against "God"; probably therefore "the Lord's Day," Rev. 1:10, or "the Day of the Lord" (where an adjective, *kuriakos*, is similarly used), is the day of His manifested judgment on the world. The phrases "the day of Christ," Phil. 1:10; 2:16; "the day of Jesus Christ," 1:6; "the day of the Lord Jesus," 1 Cor. 5:5; 2 Cor. 1:14; "the day of our Lord Jesus Christ," 1 Cor. 1:8, denote the time of the Parousia of Christ with His saints, subsequent to the Rapture, 1 Thess. 4:16-17. In 2 Pet. 1:19 this is spoken of simply as the day. From these the phrase "the day of the Lord" is to be distinguished; in the OT it had reference to a time of the victorious interposition by God for the overthrow of the foes of Israel, e.g., Isa. 2:12; Amos 5:18; if Israel transgressed in the pride of their hearts, the Day of the Lord would be a time of darkness and judgment. For their foes, however, there would come "a great and terrible day of the Lord," Joel 2:31; Mal. 4:5. That period, still future, will see the complete overthrow of gentile power and the establishment of Messiah's kingdom, Isa. 13:9-11; 34:8; Dan. 2:34, 44; Obad. 15; cf. Isa. 61:2; **John 8:56**. In the NT "the day of the Lord" is mentioned in 1 Thess. 5:2 and 2 Thess. 2:2, RV, where the apostle's warning is that the church at Thessalonica should not be deceived by thinking that "the Day of the Lord is now present." This period will not begin till the circumstances mentioned in verses 3 and 4 take place. For the eventual development of the divine purposes in relation to the human race see 2 Pet. 3:12, "the Day of God."

Glad *chairo* (5463), is the usual word for "rejoicing, being glad"; it is rendered by the verb "to be glad" in Mark 14:11; Luke 15:32; 22:5; 23:8; **John 8:56**; **11:15**; **20:20**; Acts 11:23; 13:48; in the following the RV has "to rejoice" for KJV, "to be glad," Rom. 16:19; 1 Cor. 16:17; 2 Cor. 13:9; 1 Pet. 4:13; Rev. 19:7.

8:57 Then said the Jews unto him, Thou art not yet fifty years old, and hast thou seen Abraham?

Fifty *pentekonta* (4004), is found in Luke 7:41; 16:6; **John 8:57**; **21:11**; Acts 13:20; in Mark 6:40 with *kata* (in the most authentic mss.), according to, "by fifties"; in Luke 9:14, with *ana*, "up," used distributively, "fifty each," RV (Luke adds *hosei*, "about").

Years *see John 2:20.*

Old In **John 8:57**, *echo*, "to have," is used with "fifty years" as the object, signifying, "Thou art (not yet fifty years) old," lit., "Thou hast not yet fifty years."

8:58-59 Jesus said unto them, Verily, verily, I say unto you, Before Abraham was, I am.

Then took they up stones to cast at him: but Jesus hid himself, and went out of the temple, going through the midst of them, and so passed by.

Chapter 9

9:1 And as *Jesus* passed by, he saw a man which was blind from *his* birth.

Birth *genete* (1079), "a being born, or the hour of birth" (related to *genea*, "race, generation"), is connected with *ginomai*, "to become, to be born," and is used in **John 9:1**.

9:2 And his disciples asked him, saying, Master, who did sin, this man, or his parents, that he was born blind?

Master *see John 1:38.*

Sin *see John 5:14.*

9:3 Jesus answered, Neither hath this man sinned, nor his parents: but that the works of God should be made manifest in him.

Sinned *see* Sin at *John 5:14*.

Works *see* Work at *John 4:34*.

9:4 I must work the works of him that sent me, while it is day: the night cometh, when no man can work.

Work, Works *see* Worketh, Work at *John 5:17*.

Sent *see John 1:33*.

While The conjunction *heos*, "until," etc., has the meaning "while" in Matt. 14:22; Mark 6:45; 14:32; in some texts, **John 9:4**; **12:35**, **36**; with *hotou*, "whatever" (an oblique case, neuter, of *hostis*, "whoever"), "whiles," Matt. 5:25.

Day *see John 8:56*.

Night *see John 3:2*.

9:5 As long as I am in the world, I am the light of the world.

Light *see John 1:4*. *See also* Dedication at *John 10:22*.

9:6 When he had thus spoken, he spat on the ground, and made clay of the spittle, and he anointed the eyes of the blind man with the clay,

Thus *touto*, the neuter of *houtos*, "this," is translated "thus" in 2 Cor. 1:17; 5:14; Phil. 3:15; the neuter plural, *tauta*, "these things," e.g., in Luke 18:11; 19:28; **John 9:6**; **11:43**; **13:21**; **20:14**; Acts 19:41.

Spat *ptuo* (4429), "to spit," occurs in Mark 7:33; 8:23; **John 9:6**. In the Sept., Num. 12:14.

Ground *chamai* (5476), (akin to Lat., *humi*, "on the ground," and *homo*, "man"), signifies "on the ground," **John 9:6**, of the act of Christ in spitting on the "ground" before anointing the eyes of a blind man; in **18:6**, "to the ground," of the fall of the rabble that had come to seize Christ in Gethsemane.

Clay *pelos* (4081), "clay," especially such as was used by a mason or potter, is used of moist "clay," in **John 9:6**, **11**, **14-15**, in connection with Christ's healing the blind man; in Rom. 9:21, of potter's "clay," as to the potter's right over it as an illustration of the prerogatives of God in His dealings with men.

Spittle *ptusma* (4427), akin to *ptuo*, "to spit," occurs in **John 9:6**.

Anointed *epichrio* (2025), primarily, "to rub on" (*epi*, "upon"), is used of the blind man whose eyes Christ "anointed," and indicates the manner in which the "anointing" was done, **John 9:6**, **11**.

9:7 And said unto him, Go, wash in the pool of Siloam, (which is by interpretation, Sent.) He went his way therefore, and washed, and came seeing.

Wash, Washed *nipto* (3538), is chiefly used of "washing part of the body," **John 13:5-6**, **8** (twice, figuratively in 2nd clause), **12**, **14** (twice); in 1 Tim. 5:10, including the figurative sense; in the middle voice, to wash oneself, Matt. 6:17; 15:2; Mark 7:3; **John 9:7**, **11**, **15**; **13:10**. For the corresponding noun

Pool *see John 5:2*.

Interpretation *see* Interpreted at *John 1:38*

9:8 The neighbours therefore, and they which before had seen him that he was blind, said, Is not this he that sat and begged?

Before *see John 6:62*.

Blind In **John 9:8**, the most authentic mss. have *prosaites*, "a beggar," RV, instead of *tuphlos*, "blind."

Begged *prosaiteo* (4319), lit., "to ask besides" (*pros*, "towards," used intensively, and *aiteo*), "to ask earnestly, to importune, continue asking," is said of the blind beggar in **John 9:8**. In Mark 10:46 and Luke 18:35 certain mss. have this verb; the most authentic have *prosaites*, "a beggar," a word used in **John 9:8**, as well as the verb (see the RV).

9:9 Some said, This is he: others *said*, He is like him: *but* he said, I am *he*.

Some In the following *alloi*, "others" ("some" in the KJV), is translated "others" in the RV, Matt. 13:5, 7; Mark 4:7 ("other"); 8:28; Luke 9:19; **John 9:9**. Followed by a correlative expression it denotes "some," e.g., Acts 19:32; 21:34.

Others *allos* (243), indicates numeral distinction of objects of similar character, and is used (a) absolutely, e.g., Matt. 20:3 (plural); (b) attached to a noun, e.g., Matt. 21:36; (c) with the article, e.g., Matt. 5:39; 1 Cor. 14:29 (plural, RV); in Matt. 13:5; Luke 9:19; **John 9:9**, e.g., RV, "others" (KJV, "some"); in Matt. 25:20, RV, "other" (KJV, "beside them ... more").

Like *see John 8:55*.

9:10-11 Therefore said they unto him, How were thine eyes opened?

He answered and said, A man that is called Jesus made clay, and anointed mine eyes, and said unto me, Go to the pool of Siloam, and wash: and I went and washed, and I received sight.

Clay *see John 9:6*.

Anointed *see John 9:6*.

Pool *see John 5:2*.

Wash, Washed *see John 9:7.*

Sight *anablepo* (308), "to look up," also denotes "to receive or recover sight," e.g., Matt. 11:5; 20:34; Mark 10:51, 52; Luke 18:41-43; **John 9:11, 15, 18** (twice); Acts 9:12, 17, 18; 22:13.

9:12-13 Then said they unto him, Where is he? He said, I know not. They brought to the Pharisees him that aforetime was blind.

Aforetime *pote* (4218), signifies "once, at some time," **John 9:13** (cf. *proteron*, in v. **8**); Eph. 2:2, 11; Col. 3:7; Titus 3:3; Philem. 11; 1 Pet. 3:5, 20. In all these the RV translates it "aforetime." The KJV varies it with "in time past," "some time," "sometimes," "in the old time."

9:14 And it was the sabbath day when Jesus made the clay, and opened his eyes.

Sabbath In Matt. 12:1 and 11, where the plural is used, the KJV (as the RV) rightly has the singular, "the sabbath day"; in v. 5 the KJV has the plural. Where the singular is used the RV omits the word "day," v. 2; 24:20; Mark 6:2; Luke 6:1 ("on a sabbath"); 14:3; **John 9:14** ("it was the sabbath on the day when ..."). As to the use or omission of the article the omission does not always require the rendering "a sabbath"; it is absent, e.g., in Matt. 12:2.

Clay *see John 9:6.*

9:15 Then again the Pharisees also asked him how he had received his sight. He said unto them, He put clay upon mine eyes, and I washed, and do see.

Asked *erotao* (2065), more frequently suggests that the petitioner is on a footing of equality or familiarity with the person whom he requests. It is used of a king in making request from another king, Luke 14:32; of the Pharisee who "desired" Christ that He would eat with him, an indication of the inferior conception he had of Christ, Luke 7:36; cf. 11:37; **John 9:15; 18:19.** In this respect it is significant that the Lord Jesus never used *aiteo* in the matter of making request to the Father. "The consciousness of His equal dignity, of His potent and prevailing intercession, speaks out in this, that as often as He asks, or declares that He will ask anything of the Father, it is always *erotao*, an asking, that is, upon equal terms, **John 14:16; 16:26; 17:9, 15, 20,** never *aiteo*, that He uses. Martha, on the contrary, plainly reveals her poor unworthy conception of His person, that ... she ascribes that *aiteo* to Him which He never ascribes to Himself, **John 11:22**" (Trench, *Syn.* Sec. xl). In passages where both words are used, the distinction should be noticed, even if it cannot be adequately represented in English. In **John 16:23**, "in that day ye shall ask Me nothing," the verb is *erotao*, whereas in the latter part of the verse, in the sentence, "If ye shall ask anything of the Father," the verb is *aiteo*. The distinction is brought out in the RV margin, which renders the former clause "Ye shall ask Me no question," and this meaning is confirmed by the fact that the disciples had been desirous of "asking" Him a question (*erotao*, v. **19**). If the Holy Spirit had been given, the time for "asking" questions from the Lord would have ceased. In **John 14:14**, where, not a question, but a request is made by the disciples, *aiteo*, is used. Both verbs are found in 1 John 5:16: in the sentence "he shall ask, and God will give him life for them that sin not unto death," the verb is *aiteo*, but with regard to the sin unto death, in the sentence "not concerning this do I say that he shall make request," the verb is *erotao*. Later, the tendency was for *erotao* to approximate to *aiteo*.

Sight *see John 9:11.*

Put *epitithemi* (2007), "to put on, upon," is so rendered in Matt. 19:13, KJV (RV, "lay"); so Mark 7:32; 8:25; Matt. 21:7; 27:29; **John 9:15; 19:2** (1st part); Acts 9:12 (RV, "laying ... on"); 15:10.

Washed *see* **Wash, Washed** at *John 9:7.*

9:16 Therefore said some of the Pharisees, This man is not of God, because he keepeth not the sabbath day. Others said, How can a man that is a sinner do such miracles? And there was a division among them.

Sinner *hamartolos* (268), an adjective, akin to *hamartano*, "to sin," is used as an adjective, "sinful" in Mark 8:38; Luke 5:8; 19:7 (lit., "a sinful man"); 24:7; **John 9:16,** and **24** (lit., "a man sinful"); Rom. 7:13. Elsewhere it is used as a noun, sinner. The noun is frequently found in a common phrase in sepulchral epitaphs in the S.W. of Asia Minor, with the threat against any desecrator of the tomb, "let him be as a sinner before the subterranean gods" (Moulton and Milligan).

Miracles *see John 2:11.*

Division *see John 7:43.*

9:17 They say unto the blind man again, What sayest thou of him, that he hath opened thine eyes? He said, He is a prophet.

Prophet *see John 1:21.*

9:18 But the Jews did not believe concerning him, that he had been blind, and received

his sight, until they called the parents of him that had received his sight.

Sight *see John 9:11.*

9:19 And they asked them, saying, Is this your son, who ye say was born blind? how then doth he now see?

Son *see* Sons at *John 1:12.*

Now *see John 2:10.*

9:20-21 His parents answered them and said, We know that this is our son, and that he was born blind:

But by what means he now seeth, we know not; or who hath opened his eyes, we know not: he is of age; ask him: he shall speak for himself.

Means *pos* (4459), an interrogative adverb, "how, in what way," Luke 8:36, KJV, "by what means," RV, "how"; so **John 9:21**.

Age *helikia* (2244), primarily "an age," as a certain length of life, came to mean (a) "a particular time of life," as when a person is said to be "of age," **John 9:21, 23**, or beyond a certain stage of life, Heb. 11:11; (b) elsewhere only "of stature," e.g., Matt. 6:27; Luke 2:52; 12:25; 19:3; Eph. 4:13. Some regard Matt. 6:27 and Luke 12:25 as coming under (a). It is to be distinguished from *aion* and *genea,* since it has to do simply with matters relating to an individual, either his time of life or his height.

9:22 These *words* spake his parents, because they feared the Jews: for the Jews had agreed already, that if any man did confess that he was Christ, he should be put out of the synagogue.

Jews *see John 2:6.*

Agreed *suntithemi* (4934), lit., "to put together" (*sun,* "with," *tithemi,* "to put"), in the middle voice, means "to make an agreement, or to assent to"; translated "covenanted" in Luke 22:5; "agreed" in **John 9:22**, and Acts 23:20; "assented" in Acts 24:9.

Confess *see* Confessed at *John 1:20.*

Synagogue *aposunagogos* (656), an adjective denoting "expelled from the congregation, excommunicated," is used (a) with *ginomai,* "to become, be made," **John 9:22; 12:42**; (b) with *poieo,* "to make," **John 16:2**. This excommunication involved prohibition not only from attendance at the "synagogue," but from all fellowship with Israelites.

9:23 Therefore said his parents, He is of age; ask him.

Age *see John 9:21.*

9:24 Then again called they the man that was blind, and said unto him, Give God the praise: we know that this man is a sinner.

Again *see John 3:3.*

Praise In the following the KJV translates *doxa,* "glory," by "praise" (RV, "glory"); **John 9:24**, where "give glory to God" signifies "confess thy sins" (cf. Josh. 7:19, indicating the genuine confession of facts in one's life which gives glory to God); **12:43** (twice); 1 Pet. 4:11.

Sinner *see John 9:16.*

9:25 He answered and said, Whether he be a sinner *or no,* I know not: one thing I know, that, whereas I was blind, now I see.

Now *see John 2:10.*

9:26-27 Then said they to him again, What did he to thee? how opened he thine eyes?

He answered them, I have told you already, and ye did not hear: wherefore would ye hear *it* again? will ye also be his disciples?

Already *ede* (2235), is always used of time in the NT and means "now, at (or by) this time," sometimes in the sense of "already," i.e., without mentioning or insisting upon anything further, e.g., 1 Tim. 5:15. In 1 Cor. 4:8 and 1 John 2:8, the RV corrects the KJV "now," and, in 2 Tim. 4.6, the KJV, "now ready to be," by the rendering "already." See also **John 9:27** (KJV, "already," RV, "even now") and 1 Cor. 6:7 (KJV, "now," RV, "already").

Wherefore *ti,* "what, why," **John 9:27**; Acts 22:30; Gal. 3:19, KJV (RV, "what").

9:28 Then they reviled him, and said, Thou art his disciple; but we are Moses' disciples.

Revile *loidoreo* (3058), denotes "to abuse, revile," **John 9:28**; Acts 23:4; 1 Cor. 4:12; 1 Pet. 2:23 (1st clause).

His *see John 5:18.*

Disciple, Disciples *see* Disciples at *John 6:66.*

9:29 We know that God spake unto Moses: *as for* this *fellow,* we know not from whence he is.

Fellow *see* Man at *John 6:52.*

9:30 The man answered and said unto them, Why herein is a marvellous thing, that ye know not from whence he is, and *yet* he hath opened mine eyes.

Herein *see John 4:37.*

Marvellous *thaumastos* (2298), "marvelous," is said (a) of the Lord's doing in making the rejected Stone the Head of the corner, Matt. 21:42; Mark 12:11; (b) of the erstwhile blind man's astonishment that the Pharisees knew not from whence Christ had come, and yet He had given him sight, **John 9:30**, RV, "the marvel," KJV, "a marvelous thing"; (c) of the spiritual light into which believers are brought, 1 Pet. 2:9; (d) of the vision of the seven angels having the seven last plagues, Rev. 15:1; (e) of the works of God, 15:3.

9:31 Now we know that God heareth not sinners: but if any man be a worshipper of God, and doeth his will, him he heareth.

Heareth *see* Heard at *John 1:40.*

9:32 Since the world began was it not heard that any man opened the eyes of one that was born blind.

Began In the following passages the KJV faulty translations, "since the world began," etc., are rightly rendered in the RV by "before times eternal" and similar phrases, Rom. 16:25; Eph. 3:9; 2 Tim. 1:9; Titus 1:2. The alteration has not been made, however, in Luke 1:70; **John 9:32**; Acts 3:21; 15:18.

9:33-34 If this man were not of God, he could do nothing.

They answered and said unto him, Thou wast altogether born in sins, and dost thou teach us? And they cast him out.

Altogether *holos* (3650), "whole," is rendered "altogether" in **John 9:34**. It is sometimes subjoined to an adjective or a verb, as in this case, to show that the idea conveyed by the adjective or verb belongs to the whole person or thing referred to. So here, lit., "thou wast altogether (i.e., completely) born in sins." Cf. Matt. 13:33, RV; Luke 11:36; 13:21; **John 13:10**, RV (rendered "every whit").

9:35 Jesus heard that they had cast him out; and when he had found him, he said unto him, Dost thou believe on the Son of God?

Son *see John 1:18.*

9:36-37 He answered and said, Who is he, Lord, that I might believe on him?

And Jesus said unto him, Thou hast both seen him, and it is he that talketh with thee.

Talketh *see* Talked at *John 4:27.*

9:38 And he said, Lord, I believe. And he worshipped him.

Worshipped *see* Worship at *John 4:21.*

9:39 And Jesus said, For judgment I am come into this world, that they which see not might see; and that they which see might be made blind.

Judgment *krima* (2917), denotes the result of the action signified by the verb *krino*, "to judge"; it is used (a) of a decision passed on the faults of others, Matt. 7:2; (b) of "judgment" by man upon Christ, Luke 24:20; (c) of God's "judgment" upon men, e.g., Rom. 2:2, 3; 3:8; 5:16; 11:33; 13:2; 1 Cor. 11:29; Gal. 5:10; Heb. 6:2; Jas. 3:1; through Christ, e.g., **John 9:39**; (d) of the right of "judgment," Rev. 20:4; (e) of a lawsuit, 1 Cor. 6:7.

9:40 And *some* of the Pharisees which were with him heard these words, and said unto him, Are we blind also?

Also *kai* (2532), has three chief meanings, "and," "also," "even." When *kai* means "also" it precedes the word which it stresses. In English the order should be reversed. In **John 9:40**, e.g., the RV rightly has "are we also blind?" instead of "are we blind also?" In Acts 2:26 the RV has "moreover My flesh also," instead of "moreover also ...."

9:41 Jesus said unto them, If ye were blind, ye should have no sin: but now ye say, We see; therefore your sin remaineth.

Sin *see John 1:29.*

Now *see John 4:18.*

Remaineth *see* Remaining at *John 1:33.*

Chapter 10

10:1 Verily, verily, I say unto you, He that entereth not by the door into the sheepfold, but climbeth up some other way, the same is a thief and a robber.

Sheepfold *aule* (833), first signifies "an open courtyard" before a house; then, "an enclosure" in the open, "a sheepfold," **John 10:1**, **16**. In the papyri "the word is extremely common, denoting the court attached to a house" (Moulton and Milligan, *Vocab.*). The "sheepfold" was usually surrounded by a stone wall, Numb. 32:16, preferably near a well, Exod. 2:16; Ps. 23:2, and often protected by a tower, 2 Chron. 26:10; Mic. 4:8.

Climbeth up *anabaino* (305), "to ascend," is used of climbing up, in Luke 19:4 and **John 10:1**.

Way In **John 10:1**, the adverb *allachothen*, "from some other place" (from *allos*, "another"), is translated "some other way."

Thief *kleptes* (2812), is used (a) literally, Matt. 6:19, 20; 24:43; Luke 12:33, 39; **John 10:1, 10; 12:6**; 1 Cor. 6:10; 1 Pet. 4:15; (b) metaphorically of "false teachers," **John 10:8**.

Robber *lestes* (3027), "a robber, brigand" (akin to *leia*, "booty"), "one who plunders openly and by violence" (in contrast to *kleptes*, "a thief"), is always translated "robber" or "robbers" in the RV, as the KJV in **John 10:1, 8, 18:40**; 2 Cor. 11:26; the KJV has "thief" or "thieves" in Matt. 21:13, and parallel passages; 26:55, and parallel passages; 27:38, 44 and Mark 15:27; Luke 10:30, 36; but "thief" is the meaning of *kleptes*.

10:2 But he that entereth in by the door is the shepherd of the sheep.

Shepherd *poimen* (4166), is used (a) in its natural significance, Matt. 9:36; 25:32; Mark 6:34; Luke 2:8, 15, 18, 20; **John 10:2, 12**; (b) metaphorically of Christ, Matt. 26:31; Mark 14:27; **John 10:11, 14, 16**; Heb. 13:20; 1 Pet. 2:25; (c) metaphorically of those who act as pastors in the churches, Eph. 4:11.

Sheep *probaton* (4263), from *probaino*, "to go forward," i.e., of the movement of quadrupeds, was used among the Greeks of small cattle, sheep and goats; in the NT, of "sheep" only (a) naturally, e.g., Matt. 12:11, 12; (b) metaphorically, of those who belong to the Lord, the lost ones of the house of Israel, Matt. 10:6; of those who are under the care of the Good Shepherd, e.g., Matt. 26:31; **John 10:1**, lit., "the fold of the sheep," and vv. **2-27; 21:16, 17** in some texts; Heb. 13:20; of those who in a future day, at the introduction of the millennial kingdom, have shown kindness to His persecuted earthly people in their great tribulation, Matt. 25:33; of the clothing of false shepherds, Matt. 7:15; (c) figuratively, by way of simile, of Christ, Acts 8:32; of the disciples, e.g., Matt. 10:16; of true followers of Christ in general, Rom. 8:36; of the former wayward condition of those who had come under His Shepherd care, 1 Pet. 2:25; of the multitudes who sought the help of Christ in the days of His flesh, Matt. 9:36; Mark 6:34.

10:3 To him the porter openeth; and the sheep hear his voice: and he calleth his own sheep by name, and leadeth them out.

Porter *thuroros* (2377), "a doorkeeper" (*thura*, "a door," *ouros*, "a guardian"), is translated "porter" in Mark 13:34; **John 10:3**; it is used of a female in **John 18:16, 17**, translated "(her) that kept the door." In the Sept., 2 Sam. 4:6; 2 Kings 7:11; Ezek. 44:11.

Voice *see* **Sound** at *John 3:8*.

Calleth *phoneo* (5455), "to sound" (Eng., "phone"), is used of the crowing of a cock, e.g., Matt. 26:34; **John 13:38**; of "calling" out with a clear or loud voice, to cry out, e.g. Mark 1:26 (some mss. have *krazo* here), Acts 16:28; of "calling" to come to oneself, e.g., Matt. 20:32; Luke 19:15; of "calling" forth, as of Christ's call to Lazarus to come forth from the tomb, **John 12:17**; of inviting, e.g., Luke 14:12; of "calling" by name, with the implication of the pleasure taken in the possession of those "called," e.g., **John 10:3; 13:13**.

Leadeth *exago* (1806), "to lead out," is rendered by the verb "to lead, out or forth," in Mark 15:20 (in some mss. in 8:23, the best have *ekphero*, "to bring out)"; Luke 24:50; **John 10:3**; Acts 7:36, 40 (KJV "brought"), and 13:17, RV; Acts 21:38; Heb. 8:9.

> *"If a sheep stray from his fellows, the shepherd sets his dog after it, not to devour it, but to bring it in again; even so our Heavenly Shepherd."*
>
> DANIEL CAWDRAY

10:4 And when he putteth forth his own sheep, he goeth before them, and the sheep follow him: for they know his voice.

Putteth *ekballo* (1544), "to cast out," is translated "to put forth or out" in Matt. 9:25; Mark 5:40 (Luke 8:54 in some mss.); **John 10:4**; Acts 9:40.

Before *see John 1:15.*

Voice *see* **Sound** at *John 3:8.*

10:5 And a stranger will they not follow, but will flee from him: for they know not the voice of strangers.

Stranger *allotrios* (245), "strangers," Matt. 17:25, 26; **John 10:5** (twice).

10:6 This parable spake Jesus unto them: but they understood not what things they were which he spake unto them.

Parable *paroimia* (3942), denotes "a wayside saying" (from *paroimos*, "by the way"), "a byword," "maxim," or "problem," 2 Pet. 2:22. The word is sometimes spoken of as a "parable,"

"When I met Christ, I felt that I had swallowed sunshine."

ELI STANLEY JONES

John 10:6, i.e., a figurative discourse (RV marg., "proverb"); see also **16:25**, **29**, where the word is rendered "proverbs" (marg. "parables") and "proverb."

Understood *see John 8:27.*

10:7 Then said Jesus unto them again, Verily, verily, I say unto you, I am the door of the sheep.

Door *thura* (2374), "a door, gate" (Eng., "door" is connected), is used (a) literally, e.g., Matt. 6:6; 27:60; (b) metaphorically, of Christ, **John 10:7**, **9**; of faith, by acceptance of the gospel, Acts 14:27; of "openings" for preaching and teaching the Word of God, 1 Cor. 16:9; 2 Cor. 2:12; Col. 4:3; Rev. 3:8; of "entrance" into the Kingdom of God, Matt. 25:10; Luke 13:24-25; of Christ's "entrance" into a repentant believer's heart, Rev. 3:20; of the nearness of Christ's second advent, Matt. 24:33; Mark 13:29; cf. Jas. 5:9; of "access" to behold visions relative to the purposes of God, Rev. 4:1.

10:8 All that ever came before me are thieves and robbers: but the sheep did not hear them.

Robbers *see* Robber at *John 10:1.*

Thieves *see* Thief at *John 10:1.*

10:9 I am the door: by me if any man enter in, he shall be saved, and shall go in and out, and find pasture.

Door *see John 10:7.*

Saved *sozo* (4982), "to save," is used (as with the noun *soteria*, "salvation") (a) of material and temporal deliverance from danger, suffering, etc., e.g., Matt. 8:25; Mark 13:20; Luke 23:35; **John 12:27**; 1 Tim. 2:15; 2 Tim. 4:18 (KJV, "preserve"); Jude 5; from sickness, Matt. 9:22, "made ... whole" (RV, marg., "saved"); so Mark 5:34; Luke 8:48; Jas. 5:15; (b) of the spiritual and eternal salvation granted immediately by God to those who believe on the Lord Jesus Christ, e.g., Acts 2:47, RV "(those that) were being saved"; 16:31; Rom. 8:24, RV, "were we saved"; Eph. 2:5, 8; 1 Tim. 2:4; 2 Tim. 1:9; Titus 3:5; of human agency in this, Rom. 11:14; 1 Cor. 7:16; 9:22; (c) of the present experiences of God's power to deliver from the bondage of sin, e.g., Matt. 1:21; Rom. 5:10; 1 Cor. 15:2; Heb. 7:25; Jas. 1:21; 1 Pet. 3:21; of human agency in this, 1 Tim. 4:16; (d) of the future deliverance of believers at the second coming of Christ for His saints, being deliverance from the wrath of God to be executed upon the ungodly at the close of this age and from eternal doom, e.g., Rom. 5:9; (e) of the deliverance of the nation of Israel at the second advent of Christ, e.g., Rom. 11:26; (f) inclusively for all the blessings bestowed by God on men in Christ, e.g., Luke 19:10; **John 10:9**; 1 Cor. 10:33; 1 Tim. 1:15; (g) of those who endure to the end of the time of the Great Tribulation, Matt. 10:22; Mark 13:13; (h) of the individual believer, who, though losing his reward at the judgment seat of Christ hereafter, will not lose his salvation, 1 Cor. 3:15; 5:5; (i) of the deliverance of the nations at the Millennium, Rev. 21:24 (in some mss.).

Pasture *nome* (3542), denotes (a) "pasture, pasturage," figuratively in **John 10:9**; (b) "grazing, feeding," figuratively in 2 Tim. 2:17, of the doctrines of false teachers, lit., "their word will have feeding as a gangrene."

10:10 The thief cometh not, but for to steal, and to kill, and to destroy: I am come that they might have life, and that they might have *it* more abundantly.

Thief *see John 10:1.*

Steal *klepto* (2813), "to steal," akin to *kleptes*, "a thief" (cf. Eng., "kleptomania"), occurs in Matt. 6:19, 20; 19:18; 27:64; 28:13; Mark 10:19; Luke 18:20; **John 10:10**; Rom. 2:21 (twice); 13:9; Eph. 4:28 (twice).

Kill *thuo* (2380), primarily denotes "to offer firstfruits to a god"; then (a) "to sacrifice by slaying a victim," Acts 14:13, 18, to do sacrifice; 1 Cor. 10:20, to sacrifice; 1 Cor. 5:7, "hath been sacrificed," of the death of Christ as our Passover; (b) "to slay, kill," Matt. 22:4; Mark 14:12; Luke 15:23, 27, 30; 22:7; **John 10:10**; Acts 10:13; 11:7.

Life "Speaking generally, *psuche*, is the individual life, the living being, whereas *zoe*, is the life of that being, cf. Ps. 66:9, 'God ... which holdeth our soul (*psuche* in life (*zoe*),' and **John 10:10**, 'I came that they may have life (*zoe*),' with v. **11**, 'The Good Shepherd layeth down His life (*psuche*) for the sheep.'"

More *perissos* (4053), "more than sufficient, over and above, abundant," is translated "more," e.g., in Matt. 5:37-47. In **John 10:10** the neuter form is rendered "more abundantly," KJV, RV, "abundantly" (marg., "abundance").

10:11 I am the good shepherd: the good shepherd giveth his life for the sheep.

Shepherd *see John 10:2.*

Giveth In **John 10:11**, RV, *tithemi,* "to put, lay down," is rendered "layeth down," for the KJV, "giveth."

Life *see John 10:10.*

10:12 But he that is an hireling, and not the shepherd, whose own the sheep are not, seeth the wolf coming, and leaveth the sheep, and fleeth: and the wolf catcheth them, and scattereth the sheep.

Hireling *misthotos* (3411), an adjective denoting "hired," is used as a noun, signifying "one who is hired," "hired servants," Mark 1:20; "hireling," **John 10:12, 13**; here, it expresses, not only one who has no real interest in his duty (that may or may not be present in its use in Mark 1:20), but one who is unfaithful in the discharge of it; that sense attaches always to the word rendered "hireling."

Shepherd *see John 10:2.*

Wolf *lukos* (3074), occurs in Matt. 10:16; Luke 10:3; **John 10:12** (twice); metaphorically, Matt. 7:15; Acts 20:29.

Leaveth *see* Left at *John 4:3.*

Catcheth *harpazo* (726), "to snatch," is translated "to snatch" in the RV only, in Matt. 13:19, KJV, "catcheth away"; **John 10:12**, KJV, "catcheth"; **10:28, 29**, KJV, "pluck"; Jude 23, KJV, "pulling." *See also* **Take ... by force** at *John 6:15.*

Scattereth *skorpizo* (4650), "to scatter" (probably from a root, *skarp-*, signifying "to cut asunder," akin to *skorpios,* "a scorpion"), is used in Matt. 12:30; Luke 11:23; **John 10:12; 16:32**; in the RV of 2 Cor. 9:9, "scattered abroad" (KJV, "he hath dispersed abroad"), of one who liberally dispenses benefits.

10:13 The hireling fleeth, because he is an hireling, and careth not for the sheep.

Hireling *see John 10:12.*

Careth *melei* (3199), the third person sing. of *melo,* used impersonally, signifies that "something is an object of care," especially the care of forethought and interest, rather than anxiety, Matt. 22:16; Mark 4:38; 12:14; Luke 10:40; **John 10:13; 12:6**; Acts 18:17; 1 Cor. 9:9 (RV, "Is it for the oxen that God careth?" The KJV seriously misses the point. God does "care" for oxen, but there was a divinely designed significance in the OT passage, relating to the service of preachers of the gospel); 7:21; 1 Pet. 5:7.

10:14 I am the good shepherd, and know my *sheep*, and am known of mine.

Shepherd *see John 10:2.*

Know *see John 7:26.*

10:15 As the Father knoweth me, even so know I the Father: and I lay down my life for the sheep.

Knoweth *see* Know at *John 7:26.*

Even so *kago,* for *kai ego,* means either "even I" or "even so I" or "I also." In **John 10:15**, the RV has "and I" for the KJV, "even so ... I"; in **17:18** and **20:21**, KJV and RV, "even so I"; in the following, *kago* is preceded by *hos,* or *kathos,* "even as I," 1 Cor. 7:8; 10:33; "even as I also," 11:1; "as I also," Rev. 2:27.

Life *see John 3:15.*

10:16 And other sheep I have, which are not of this fold: them also I must bring, and they shall hear my voice; and there shall be one fold, *and* one shepherd.

Fold *poimne* (4167), akin to *poimen,* "a shepherd," denotes "a flock" (properly, of sheep), Matt. 26:31; Luke 2:8; 1 Cor. 9:7; metaphorically, of Christ's followers, **John 10:16**, RV, for the erroneous KJV, "fold." What characterizes Christ's sheep is listening to His voice, and the "flock" must be one as He is one. *See also* **Sheepfold** at *John 10:1.*

Voice *see* Sound at *John 3:8.*

Shepherd *see John 10:2.*

10:17 Therefore doth my Father love me, because I lay down my life, that I might take it again.

Lay *tithemi* (5087), "to put, place, set," frequently signifies "to lay," and is used of (a) "laying" a corpse in a tomb, Matt. 27:60; Mark 6:29; 15:47; 16:6; Luke 23:53, 55; **John 11:34; 19:41, 42; 20:2, 13, 15**; Acts 7:16; 13:29; Rev. 11:9, RV, "to be laid" (KJV, "to be put"); in an upper chamber, Acts 9:37; (b) "laying" the sick in a place, Mark 6:56; Luke 5:18; Acts 3:2; 5:15; (c) "laying" money at the apostles' feet, Acts 4:35, 37; 5:2; (d) Christ's "laying" His hands upon children, Mark 10:16, RV, "laying" (KJV, "put"); upon John, Rev. 1:17 (in the best mss.); (e) "laying" down one's life, (1) of Christ, **John 10:11**, RV, "layeth down" (KJV, "giveth"); vv. **17, 18** (twice); 1 John 3:16; (2) of Peter for Christ's sake, **John 13:37, 38**; (3) of Christ's followers, on behalf of others, 1 John 3:16; (4) of anyone, for his friends, **John 15:13**; (f) "laying" up sayings in one's heart, Luke 1:66 (middle voice, in the sense of "for themselves"); in 9:44, of letting Christ's words "sink" (middle voice, in the sense of "for oneself"; KJV, "sink down") into the ears; (g) "laying" a foundation (1) literally, Luke 6:48; 14:29; (2) metaphorically, of Christ in relation to an assembly, 1 Cor. 3:10, 11;

(h) in "laying" Christ as a "stone of stumbling" for Israel, Rom. 9:33; (i) Christ's "laying" aside His garments, **John 13:4**; (j) Christians, in "laying" money in store for the help of the needy, 1 Cor. 16:2 (lit., "let him put"); (k) "depositing" money, Luke 19:21, 22.

Take *see* Taketh at *John 1:29*.

10:18 No man taketh it from me, but I lay it down of myself. I have power to lay it down, and I have power to take it again. This commandment have I received of my Father.

Taketh *see John 1:29*.

Lay *see John 10:17*.

Myself *see* Mine own self at *John 5:30*.

Power *see John 1:12*.

10:19 There was a division therefore again among the Jews for these sayings.

Division *see John 7:43*.

Sayings *see* Saying at *John 4:37*.

10:20 And many of them said, He hath a devil, and is mad; why hear ye him?

Mad *mainomai* (3105), "to be mad, to rave," is said of one who so speaks that he appears to be out of his mind, Acts 26:24, translated "thou art beside thyself," KJV; RV, "thou art mad." In v. 25; **John 10:20**; Acts 12:15; 1 Cor. 14:23, both versions use the verb to be mad.

10:21 Others said, These are not the words of him that hath a devil. Can a devil open the eyes of the blind?

Devil *daimonizomai* (1139), signifies "to be possessed of a demon, to act under the control of a demon." Those who were thus afflicted expressed the mind and consciousness of the "demon" or "demons" indwelling them, e.g., Luke 8:28. The verb is found chiefly in Matt. and Mark; Matt. 4:24; 8:16, 28, 33; 9:32; 12:22; 15:22; Mark 1:32; 5:15-16, 18; elsewhere in Luke 8:36 and **John 10:21**, "him that hath a devil (demon)."

10:22 And it was at Jerusalem the feast of the dedication, and it was winter.

Dedication *enkainia* (1456), frequent in the Sept., in the sense of "dedication," became used particularly for the annual eight days' feast beginning on the 25th of Chisleu (mid. of Dec.), instituted by Judas Maccabaeus, 164 BC, to commemorate the cleansing of the Temple from the pollutions of Antiochus Epiphanes; hence it was called the Feast of the Dedication, **John 10:22**. This feast could be celebrated anywhere. The lighting of lamps was a prominent feature; hence the description "Feast of Lights." Westcott suggests that **John 9:5** refers to this.

Winter *cheimon* (5494), denotes "winter," in Matt. 24:20; Mark 13:18; **John 10:22**; 2 Tim. 4:21.

10:23 And Jesus walked in the temple in Solomon's porch.

Porch *see* Porches at *John 5:2*.

10:24 Then came the Jews round about him, and said unto him, How long dost thou make us to doubt? If thou be the Christ, tell us plainly.

Came *kukloo* (2944), denotes "to encircle, surround," and is found in the best texts in **John 10:24**, "came round about," and Rev. 20:9, of a camp surrounded by foes.

Us *psuche* (5590), denotes "the breath, the breath of life," then "the soul," in its various meanings. The NT uses "may be analyzed approximately as follows:

(a) the natural life of the body, Matt. 2:20; Luke 12:22; Acts 20:10; Rev. 8:9; 12:11; cf. Lev. 17:11; 2 Sam. 14:7; Esth. 8:11; (b) the immaterial, invisible part of man, Matt. 10:28; Acts 2:27; cf. 1 Kings 17:21; (c) the disembodied (or "unclothed" or "naked," 2 Cor. 5:3, 4) man, Rev. 6:9; (d) the seat of personality, Luke 9:24, explained as = "own self," v. 25; Heb. 6:19; 10:39; cf. Isa. 53:10 with 1 Tim. 2:6; (e) the seat of the sentient element in man, that by which he perceives, reflects, feels, desires, Matt. 11:29; Luke 1:46; 2:35; Acts 14:2, 22; cf. Ps. 84:2; 139:14; Isa. 26:9; (f) the seat of will and purpose, Matt. 22:37; Acts 4:32; Eph. 6:6; Phil. 1:27; Heb. 12:3; cf. Num. 21:4; Deut. 11:13; (g) the seat of appetite, Rev. 18:14; cf. Ps. 107:9; Prov. 6:30; Isa. 5:14 ("desire"); 29:8; (h) persons, individuals, Acts 2:41, 43; Rom. 2:9; Jas. 5:20; 1 Pet. 3:20; 2 Pet. 2:14; cf. Gen. 12:5; 14:21 ("persons"); Lev. 4:2 ('any one');Ezek. 27:13; of dead bodies, Num. 6:6, lit., "dead soul"; and of animals, Lev. 24:18, lit., "soul for soul"; (i) the equivalent of the personal pronoun, used for emphasis and effect: 1st person, **John 10:24** ("us"); Heb. 10:38; cf. Gen. 12:13; Num. 23:10; Jud. 16:30; Ps. 120:2 ("me"); 2nd person, 2 Cor. 12:15; Heb. 13:17; Jas. 1:21; 1 Pet. 1:9; 2:25; cf. Lev. 17:11; 26:15; 1 Sam. 1:26; 3rd person, 1 Pet. 4:19; 2 Pet. 2:8; cf. Exod. 30:12; Job 32:2, Heb. "soul," Sept. "self"; (j) an animate creature, human or other, 1 Cor. 15:45; Rev. 16:3; cf. Gen. 1:24; 2:7, 19; (k) "the inward man," the seat of the new life, Luke 21:19 (cf. Matt. 10:39); 1 Pet. 2:11; 3 John 2.

"Body and soul are the constituents of the man according to Matt. 6:25; 10:28; Luke 12:20; Acts

20:10; body and spirit according to Luke 8:55; 1 Cor. 5:3; 7:34; Jas. 2:26. In Matt. 26:38 the emotions are associated with the soul, in **John 13:21** with the spirit; cf. also Ps. 42:11 with 1 Kings 21:5. In Ps. 35:9 the soul rejoices in God, in Luke 1:47 the spirit. Apparently, then, the relationships may be thus summed up '*Soma*, body, and *pneuma*, spirit, may be separated, *pneuma* and *psuche*, soul, can only be distinguished' (Cremer)."

Plainly *parrhesia* (3954), "boldness," is used adverbially in its dative case and rendered "plainly" in **John 10:24**; **11:14**; **16:25**; **16:29** (with *en*, lit., "in plainness").

10:25 Jesus answered them, I told you, and ye believed not: the works that I do in my Father's name, they bear witness of me.

Witness *see John 1:7.*

10:26-27 But ye believe not, because ye are not of my sheep, as I said unto you.
My sheep hear my voice, and I know them, and they follow me:

Voice *see* Sound at *John 3:8.*

Know *see John 7:26.*

10:28 And I give unto them eternal life; and they shall never perish, neither shall any *man* pluck them out of my hand.

Eternal *see John 3:16.*

Never *see John 4:14.*

Perish *see John 3:15.*

Pluck ... out *harpazo* (726), "to seize, snatch," is rendered "pluck" in **John 10:28**, **29**, KJV, RV, "snatch." For the meaning. *See also* Catcheth at *John 10:12. See also* Take ... by force at *John 6:15.*

Hand *cheir* (5495), "the hand" (cf. Eng., "chiropody"), is used, besides its ordinary significance, (a) in the idiomatic phrases, "by the hand of," "at the hand of," etc., to signify "by the agency of," Acts 5:12; 7:35; 17:25; 14:3; Gal. 3:19 (cf. Lev. 26:46); Rev. 19:2; (b) metaphorically, for the power of God, e.g., Luke 1:66; 23:46; **John 10:28**, **29**; Acts 11:21; 13:11; Heb. 1:10; 2:7; 10:31; (c) by metonymy, for power, e.g., Matt. 17:22; Luke 24:7; **John 10:39**; Acts 12:11.

10:29 My Father, which gave *them* me, is greater than all; and no *man* is able to pluck *them* out of my Father's hand.

Pluck ... out *see John 10:28.*

Hand *see John 10:28.*

10:30 I and *my* Father are one.

One *heis* (1520), the first cardinal numeral, masculine (feminine and neuter nominative forms are *mia* and *hen*, respectively), is used to signify (1) (a) "one" in contrast to many, e.g., Matt. 25:15; Rom. 5:18, RV, "(through) one (trespass)," i.e., Adam's transgression, in contrast to the "one act of righteousness," i.e., the death of Christ (not as KJV, "the offense of one," and "the righteousness of one"); (b) metaphorically, "union" and "concord," e.g., **John 10:30**; **11:52**; **17:11**, **21-22**; Rom. 12:4-5; Phil. 1:27; (2) emphatically, (a) a single ("one"), to the exclusion of others, e.g., Matt. 21:24; Rom. 3:10; 1 Cor. 9:24; 1 Tim. 2:5 (twice); (b) "one, alone," e.g., Mark 2:7, RV (KJV, "only"); 10:18; Luke 18:19; (c) "one and the same," e.g., Rom. 3:30, RV, "God is one," i.e., there is not "one" God for the Jew and one for the Gentile; cf. Gal. 3:20, which means that in a promise there is no other party; 1 Cor. 3:8; 11:5; 12:11; 1 John 5:8 (lit., "and the three are into one," i.e., united in "one" and the same witness); (3) a certain "one," in the same sense as the indefinite pronoun *tis*, e.g., Matt. 8:19, RV, "a (scribe)," marg., "one (scribe)," KJV, "a certain (scribe)"; 19:16, "one;" in Rev. 8:13, RV marg., "one (eagle)"; *heis tis* are used together in Luke 22:50; **John 11:49**; this occurs frequently in the papyri (Moulton, *Prol.*, p. 96); (4) distributively, with *hekastos*, "each," i.e., "every one," e.g., Luke 4:40; Acts 2:6, "every man" (lit., "every one"); in the sense of "one ... and one," e.g., **John 20:12**; or "one" ... followed by *allos* or *heteros*, "the other," e.g., Matt. 6:24; or by a second *heis*, e.g., Matt. 24:40, RV, "one"; **John 20:12**. In Gal. 3:28, the RV adds the italicized word "man" ("ye all are one *man* in Christ Jesus"), in accordance with Eph. 2:15, which speaks of Jew and Gentile as becoming "one new man" in Christ. The figure is closely analogous to that of "the body." In these two passages "one" is masculine, i.e., "one person"; in **John 10:30**; **11:52**; **17:21**, **22**, **23**, "one" is neuter, "one thing," as in 1 Cor. 3:8; 11:5. The first two, in Gal. 3 and Eph. 2, express vital union, present and eternal; in **John 17** the union is moral, a process in course of accomplishment.

10:31 Then the Jews took up stones again to stone him.

Stones *see* Stoned at *John 8:5.*

Took up *bastazo* (941), signifies "to support as a burden." It is used with the meaning (a) "to take up," as in picking up anything stones, **John 10:31**; (b) "to carry" something, Matt. 3:11; Mark 14:13; Luke 7:14; 22:10; Acts 3:2; 21:35; Rev. 17:7; "to carry" on one's person, Luke 10:4; Gal. 6:17; in one's body, Luke 11:27; "to bear" a name in testimony, Acts 9:15; metaphorically, of a root "bearing" branches, Rom. 11:18; (c) "to bear" a burden, whether physically, as of the cross, **John 19:17**, or metaphorically in respect of sufferings endured in the cause of Christ, Luke 14:27; Rev. 2:3; it is said of physical endurance, Matt. 20:12; of sufferings "borne" on behalf of others, Matt. 8:17; Rom. 15:1; Gal. 6:2; of spiritual truths not able to be "borne," **John 16:12**; of the refusal to endure evil men, Rev. 2:2; of religious regulations imposed on others, Acts 15:10; of the burden of the sentence of God to be executed in due time, Gal. 5:10; of the effect at the judgment seat of Christ, to be "borne" by the believer for failure in the matter of discharging the obligations of discipleship, Gal. 6:5; (d) to "bear" by way of carrying off, **John 12:6; 20:15**.

10:32 Jesus answered them, Many good works have I shewed you from my Father; for which of those works do ye stone me?

Which *see John 8:46.*

10:33 The Jews answered him, saying, For a good work we stone thee not; but for blasphemy; and because that thou, being a man, makest thyself God.

Makest *see* Make at *John 2:16.*

Man *see John 2:25.*

10:34 Jesus answered them, Is it not written in your law, I said, Ye are gods?

Gods *see* God at *John 1:1.*

Law *see John 1:17.*

10:35 If he called them gods, unto whom the word of God came, and the scripture cannot be broken;

Called *eipon* (3004), "to say, speak," means "to call by a certain appellation," **John 10:35**.

Word *see John 1:1.*

Scripture *see John 2:22.*

Broken *see John 5:18.*

10:36 Say ye of him, whom the Father hath sanctified, and sent into the world, Thou blasphemest; because I said, I am the Son of God?

Sanctified *hagiazo* (37), "to sanctify," "is used of (a) the gold adorning the Temple and of the gift laid on the altar, Matt. 23:17, 19; (b) food, 1 Tim. 4:5; (c) the unbelieving spouse of a believer, 1 Cor. 7:14; (d) the ceremonial cleansing of the Israelites, Heb. 9:13; (e) the Father's Name, Luke 11:2; (f) the consecration of the Son by the Father, **John 10:36**; (g) the Lord Jesus devoting Himself to the redemption of His people, **John 17:19**; (h) the setting apart of the believer for God, Acts 20:32; cf. Rom. 15:16; (i) the effect on the believer of the Death of Christ, Heb. 10:10, said of God, and 2:11; 13:12, said of the Lord Jesus; (j) the separation of the believer from the world in his behavior – by the Father through the Word, **John 17:17, 19**; (k) the believer who turns away from such things as dishonor God and His gospel, 2 Tim. 2:21; (l) the acknowledgment of the Lordship of Christ, 1 Pet. 3:15.

Sent *see John 1:6.*

10:37 If I do not the works of my Father, believe me not.

Works *see* Work at *John 4:34.*

10:38 But if I do, though ye believe not me, believe the works: that ye may know, and believe, that the Father *is* in me, and I in him.

Know *see John 7:26.*

10:39 Therefore they sought again to take him: but he escaped out of their hand,

Take *see* Take, Laid hands on at *John 7:30.*

Escaped *exerchomai*, "to come or go out of a place," is rendered, "He escaped," in **John 10:39**, KJV, an unsuitable translation, both in meaning and in regard to the circumstances of the Lord's departure from His would-be captors. The RV "went forth" is both accurate and appropriate to the dignity of the Lord's actions.

Hand *see John 10:28.*

10:40 And went away again beyond Jordan into the place where John at first baptized; and there he abode.

Beyond *see John 1:28.*

10:41 And many resorted unto him, and said, John did no miracle: but all things that John spake of this man were true.

Resorted *erchomai* (2064), "to come," is translated "resorted" in Mark 2:13; in **John 10:41** (RV, "came").

Miracle *see* Miracles at *John 2:11.*

10:42 And many believed on him there.

Chapter 11

11:1 Now a certain *man* was sick, *named* Lazarus, of Bethany, the town of Mary and her sister Martha.

Sick *see John 4:46.*

Town *see John 7:42.*

11:2 (It was *that* Mary which anointed the Lord with ointment, and wiped his feet with her hair, whose brother Lazarus was sick.)

Anointed *aleipho* (218), is a general term used for "an anointing" of any kind, whether of physical refreshment after washing, e.g., in the Sept. of Ruth 3:3; 2 Sam. 12:20; Dan. 10:3; Micah 6:15; in the NT, Matt. 6:17; Luke 7:38, 46; **John 11:2**; **12:3**; or of the sick, Mark 6:13; Jas. 5:14; or a dead body, Mark 16:1. The material used was either oil, or ointment, as in Luke 7:38, 46. In the Sept. it is also used of "anointing" a pillar, Gen. 31:13, or captives, 2 Chron. 28:15, or of daubing a wall with mortar, Ezek. 13:10-12, 14-15; and, in the sacred sense, of "anointing" priests, in Exod. 40:15 (twice), and Num. 3:3.

Lord *see John 4:1.*

Ointment *muron* (3464), a word derived by the ancients from *muro*, "to flow," or from *murra*, "myrrh-oil." The "ointment" is mentioned in the NT in connection with the anointing of the Lord on the occasions recorded in Matt. 26:7, 9, 12; Mark 14:3-4; Luke 7:37-38, 46; **John 11:2**; **12:3** (twice), **5**. The alabaster cruse mentioned in the passages in Matthew, Mark and Luke was the best of its kind, and the spikenard was one of the costliest of perfumes. "Ointments" were used in preparing a body for burial, Luke 23:56 ("ointments"). Of the act of the woman mentioned in Matt. 26:6-13, the Lord said, "she did it to prepare Me for burial"; her devotion led her to antedate the customary ritual after death, by showing both her affection and her understanding of what was impending. For the use of the various kinds of "ointments" as articles of commerce, see Rev. 18:13.

Wiped *ekmasso* (1591), "to wipe out" (*ek*), "wipe dry," is used of "wiping" tears from Christ's feet, Luke 7:38, 44; **John 11:2**; **12:3**; of Christ's "wiping" the disciples' feet, **John 13:5**.

Hair *thrix* (2359), denotes the "hair," whether of beast, as of the camel's "hair" which formed the raiment of John the Baptist, Matt. 3:4; Mark 1:6; or of man. Regarding the latter (a) it is used to signify the minutest detail, as that which illustrates the exceeding care and protection bestowed by God upon His children, Matt. 10:30; Luke 12:7; 21:18; Acts 27:34; (b) as the Jews swore by the "hair," the Lord used the natural inability to make one "hair" white or black, as one of the reasons for abstinence from oaths, Matt. 5:36; (c) while long "hair" is a glory to a woman, and to wear it loose or dishevelled is a dishonor, yet the woman who wiped Christ's feet with her "hair" (in place of the towel which Simon the Pharisee omitted to provide), despised the shame in her penitent devotion to the Lord (slaves were accustomed to wipe their masters' feet), Luke 7:38, 44 (RV, "hair"); see also **John 11:2**; **12:3**; (d) the dazzling whiteness of the head and "hair" of the Son of Man in the vision of Rev. 1 (v. 14) is suggestive of the holiness and wisdom of "the Ancient of Days"; (e) the long "hair" of the spirit-beings described as locusts in Rev. 9:8 is perhaps indicative of their subjection to their satanic master (cf. 1 Cor. 11:10, RV); (f) Christian women are exhorted to refrain from adorning their "hair" for outward show, 1 Pet. 3:3.

11:3-4 Therefore his sisters sent unto him, saying, Lord, behold, he whom thou lovest is sick.
When Jesus heard *that*, he said, This sickness is not unto death, but for the glory of God, that the Son of God might be glorified thereby.

Sickness *astheneia* (769), lit., "lacking strength" (*a*, negative, *sthenos*, "strength"), "weakness, infirmity," is translated "diseases" in Matt. 8:17, RV, for KJV, "sicknesses," and in Acts 28:9. Its usual rendering is "infirmity" or "infirmities"; "sickness," in **John 11:4**.

Glory *see John 1:14.*

Son *see John 1:18.*

Glorified *see John 7:39.*

Thereby *Di'autes* occurs in Matt. 7:13; **John 11:4**; Heb. 12:11.

11:5-6 Now Jesus loved Martha, and her sister, and Lazarus.
When he had heard therefore that he was sick, he abode two days still in the same place where he was.

Sick *see John 4:46.*

11:7 Then after that saith he to *his* disciples, Let us go into Judaea again.

Then *epeita* (1899), "thereupon, thereafter," then (in some texts, Mark 7:5; *kai*, "and," in the best); Luke 16:7; **John 11:7**; 1 Cor. 12:28, RV, "then" (KJV, "after that"); 15:6 and 7 (ditto); v. 23, RV, KJV, "afterward"; v. 46 (ditto); Gal. 1:18; v. 21, RV (KJV, "afterwards"), 2:1; 1 Thess. 4:17; Heb. 7:2, RV (KJV, "after that"); v. 27; Jas. 3:17; 4:14.

Go *ago* (71), "to bring, lead," is used intransitively, signifying "let us go" (as if to say, "let us be leading on," with the point of departure especially in view), Matt. 26:46; Mark 1:38; 14:42; **John 11:7, 15, 16; 14:31**.

11:8 *His* disciples say unto him, Master, the Jews of late sought to stone thee; and goest thou thither again?

Master *see John 1:38.*

Late In **John 11:8**, KJV, "*nun*, now," is translated "of late" (RV, "but now").

Stone *see* Stoned at *John 8:5.*

11:9 Jesus answered, Are there not twelve hours in the day? If any man walk in the day, he stumbleth not, because he seeth the light of this world.

Stumbleth *proskopto* (4350), "to strike against," is used of "stumbling," (a) physically, **John 11:9, 10**; (b) metaphorically, (1) of Israel in regard to Christ, whose Person, teaching, and atoning death, and the gospel relating thereto, were contrary to all their ideas as to the means of righteousness before God, Rom. 9:32; 1 Pet. 2:8; (2) of a brother in the Lord in acting against the dictates of his conscience, Rom. 14:21.

11:10 But if a man walk in the night, he stumbleth, because there is no light in him.

Stumbleth *see John 11:9.*

11:11 These things said he: and after that he saith unto them, Our friend Lazarus sleepeth; but I go, that I may awake him out of sleep.

Sleepeth *koimaomai* (2837), is used of natural "sleep," Matt. 28:13; Luke 22:45; **John 11:12**; Acts 12:6; of the death of the body, but only of such as are Christ's; yet never of Christ Himself, though He is "the firstfruits of them that have fallen asleep," 1 Cor. 15:20, of saints who departed before Christ came, Matt. 27:52; Acts 13:36; of Lazarus, while Christ was yet upon the earth, **John 11:11**; of believers since the Ascension, 1 Thess. 4:13-15, and Acts 7:60; 1 Cor. 7:39; 11:30; 15:6, 18, 51; 2 Pet. 3:4.

Awake *exupnizo* (1852), from *ek*, "out of," and *hupnos*, "sleep," "to rouse a person out of sleep," is used metaphorically, in **John 11:11**.

11:12 Then said his disciples, Lord, if he sleep, he shall do well.

Sleep *see* Sleepeth at *John 11:11.*

Well In **John 11:12**, KJV, *sozo* (passive voice, "to be saved"), is rendered "he shall do well" (RV, "he will recover").

11:13 Howbeit Jesus spake of his death: but they thought that he had spoken of taking of rest in sleep.

Death *see John 5:24.*

Rest *koimesis* (2838), "a resting, reclining" (akin to *keimai*, "to lie"), is used in **John 11:13**, of natural sleep, translated "taking rest," RV.

11:14 Then said Jesus unto them plainly, Lazarus is dead.

Then *tote* (5119), a demonstrative adverb of time, denoting "at that time," is used (a) of concurrent events, e.g., Matt. 2:17; Gal. 4:8, "at that time"; v. 29, "then"; 2 Pet. 3:6, "(the world) that then was," lit., "(the) then (world)"; (b) of consequent events, "then, thereupon," e.g., Matt. 2:7; Luke 11:26; 16:16, "[from (KJV, "since")] that time"; **John 11:14**; Acts 17:14; (c) of things future, e.g., Matt. 7:23; 24:30 (twice), 40; eight times in ch. 25; 1 Cor. 4:5; Gal. 6:4; 1 Thess. 5:3; 2 Thess. 2:8. It occurs 90 times in Matthew, more than in all the rest of the NT together.

Plainly *see John 10:24.*

11:15 And I am glad for your sakes that I was not there, to the intent ye may believe; nevertheless let us go unto him.

Glad *see John 8:56.*

Intent In **John 11:15** the conjunction *hina*, "to the end that," is translated "to the intent," and in Eph. 3:10, "to the intent that."

Go *see John 11:7.*

11:16 Then said Thomas, which is called Didymus, unto his fellowdisciples, Let us also go, that we may die with him.

Go *see John 11:7.*

Fellowdisciples *summathetes* (4827), means "a fellow disciple," **John 11:16**.

11:17 Then when Jesus came, he found that he had *lain* in the grave four days already.

Lain In **John 11:17**, KJV, the verb *echo*, "to have, to hold," used with *en*, "in," signifying "to be in a certain condition," is translated "had *lain*" (RV, "*had been*").

11:18 Now Bethany was nigh unto Jerusalem, about fifteen furlongs off:

About *see John 6:19.*

Fifteen *dekapente* (1178), lit., "ten-five," occurs in **John 11:18**; Acts 27:28; Gal. 1:18.

Furlongs *see John 6:19.*

11:19 And many of the Jews came to Martha and Mary, to comfort them concerning their brother.

Comfort *paramutheomai* (3888), "to soothe, console, encourage," is translated, in **John 11:31**, "comforted", in v. **19**, RV, "console." In 1 Thess. 2:11 and 5:14, RV, "encourage," as the sense there is that of stimulating to the earnest discharge of duties.

11:20 Then Martha, as soon as she heard that Jesus was coming, went and met him: but Mary sat *still* in the house.

Met *see John 4:51.*

Sat *see John 4:6.*

11:21-22 Then said Martha unto Jesus, Lord, if thou hadst been here, my brother had not died.
But I know, that even now, whatsoever thou wilt ask of God, God will give *it* thee.

Ask *see* Asked at *John 9:15.*

11:23-24 Jesus saith unto her, Thy brother shall rise again.
Martha saith unto him, I know that he shall rise again in the resurrection at the last day.

Rise *see* Raise at *John 6:39.*

Resurrection *see John 5:29.*

Last *see John 6:39.*

11:25 Jesus said unto her, I am the resurrection, and the life: he that believeth in me, though he were dead, yet shall he live:

Resurrection *see John 5:29.*

Live In 1 Thess. 5:10, to live means to experience that change, 1 Cor. 15:51, which is to be the portion of all in Christ who will be alive upon the earth at the Parousia of the Lord Jesus, cf. **John 11:25**, and which corresponds to the resurrection of those who had previously died in Christ, 1 Cor. 15:52-54.

11:26 And whosoever liveth and believeth in me shall never die. Believest thou this?

Never *see John 4:14.*

Die *see John 6:50.*

11:27 She saith unto him, Yea, Lord: I believe that thou art the Christ, the Son of God, which should come into the world.

Yea *nai* (3483), a particle of affirmation, is used (a) in answer to a question, Matt. 9:28; 11:9; 13:51; 17:25; 21:16; Luke 7:26; **John 11:27; 21:15, 16**; Acts 5:8; 22:27; Rom. 3:29; (b) in assent to an assertion, Matt. 15:27, RV (KJV, "truth"); Mark 7:28; Rev. 14:13; 16:7, RV (KJV, "even so"); (c) in confirmation of an assertion, Matt. 11:26 and Luke 10:21, RV (KJV, "even so"); Luke 11:51, RV (KJV, "verily"); 12:5; Phil. 4:3 (in the best texts); Philem. 20; (d) in solemn asseveration, Rev. 1:7 (KJV and RV, "even so"); 22:20, RV (KJV, "surely"); (e) in repetition for emphasis, Matt. 5:37; 2 Cor. 1:17; Jas. 5:12; (f) singly in contrast to *ou*, "nay," 2 Cor. 1:18, 19 (twice), 20, "(the) yea," RV.

11:28 And when she had so said, she went her way, and called Mary her sister secretly, saying, The Master is come, and calleth for thee.

Secretly *lathra* (2977), "secretly, covertly" (from a root *lath*– indicating "unnoticed, unknown," seen in *lanthano*, "to escape notice," *lethe*, "forgetfulness"), is translated "privily" in Matt. 1:19; 2:7; Acts 16:37; "secretly" in **John 11:28** (in some mss., Mark 5:33).

Master *see John 1:38.*

Come *see John 7:6.*

11:29 As soon as she heard *that*, she arose quickly, and came unto him.

Quickly *tachu* (5035), the neuter of *tachus*, "swift, quick," signifies "quickly," Matt. 5:25; 28:7, 8; Mark 9:39, RV (KJV, "lightly"); Luke 15:22; **John 11:29**; Rev. 2:16 (v. 5 in some mss.); 3:11; 11:14; 22:7, 12, 20.

11:30 Now Jesus was not yet come into the town, but was in that place where Martha met him.

Yet *eti* (2089), "yet, as yet, still," is translated "still" in the RV in 1 Cor. 12:31; 2 Cor. 1:10; Gal. 1:10 and 5:11; KJV and RV in Rev. 22:11 (four times), where the word indicates the permanent character, condition and destiny of the unrighteous and the filthy, the righteous and the holy (for the verbs see the RV); in **John 11:30**, the best mss. have the word; so RV (KJV omits).

Town *see John 7:42.*

Met *see John 4:51.*

11:31 The Jews then which were with her in the house, and comforted her, when they saw Mary, that she rose up hastily and went out, followed her, saying, She goeth unto the grave to weep there.

Comforted *see* Comfort at *John 11:19.*

Rose *see* Raise at *John 6:39.*

Hastily *tacheos* (5030), "quickly," is used in a warning to lay hands "hastily" on no man (with a suggestion of rashness), 1 Tim. 5:22, RV (KJV, "suddenly"); in **John 11:31**, RV, "(she rose up) quickly" (KJV, "hastily").

Saying *dokeo* (1380), "to be of opinion," is translated "to suppose" in Mark 6:49; Luke 24:37; **John 20:15**; Acts 27:13; in the following, KJV "suppose," RV, "think," Luke 12:51; 13:2; Heb. 10:29. It is most frequently rendered "to think," always in Matthew; always in John, except **11:31**, "supposing," RV [where the best texts have this verb (for *lego*, KJV, "saying")], and **20:15**.

Weep *klaio* (2799), is used of "any loud expression of grief," especially in mourning for the dead, Matt. 2:18; Mark 5:38, 39; 16:10; Luke 7:13; 8:52 (twice); **John 11:31**, **33** (twice); **20:11** (twice), 13, 15; Acts 9:39; otherwise, e.g., in exhortations, Luke 23:28; Rom. 12:15; Jas. 4:9; 5:1; negatively, "weep not," Luke 7:13; 8:52; 23:28; Rev. 5:5 (cf. Acts 21:13); in 18:9, RV, "shall weep" (KJV, "bewail").

11:32-33 Then when Mary was come where Jesus was, and saw him, she fell down at his feet, saying unto him, Lord, if thou hadst been here, my brother had not died.

When Jesus therefore saw her weeping, and the Jews also weeping which came with her, he groaned in the spirit, and was troubled,

Weeping *see* Weep at *John 11:31*.

Came with *sunerchomai* (4905), chiefly used of "assembling together," signifies "to accompany," in Luke 23:55; **John 11:33**; Acts 9:39; 10:45; 11:12; 15:38; 21:16. In Acts 1:21 it is said of men who had "companied with" the apostles all the time the Lord Jesus was with them.

Groaned *embrimaomai* (1690), from *en*, "in," and *brime*, "strength," is rendered "groaned" in **John 11:33** (preferable to the RV marg., "He had indignation"); so in v. **38**. The Lord was deeply moved doubtless with the combination of circumstances, present and in the immediate future. Indignation does not here seem to express His feelings.

Troubled *see John 5:4*.

11:34 And said, Where have ye laid him? They said unto him, Lord, come and see.

Laid *see* Lay at *John 10:11*.

11:35 Jesus wept.

Wept *dakruo* (1145), "to shed tears" (*dakruon*, "a tear"), is used only of the Lord Jesus, **John 11:35**. The associated noun is *klauthmos*, "weeping."

11:36-37 Then said the Jews, Behold how he loved him!

And some of them said, Could not this man, which opened the eyes of the blind, have caused that even this man should not have died?

Caused *poieo* (4160), "to do," is translated by the verb "to cause" in **John 11:37**; Acts 15:3; Rom. 16:17; Col. 4:16; Rev. 13:15-16.

11:38 Jesus therefore again groaning in himself cometh to the grave. It was a cave, and a stone lay upon it.

Groaning *see* Groaned at *John 11:33*.

Cave *spelaion* (4693), "a grotto, cavern, den" (Lat., *spelunca*), "cave," **John 11:38**, is said of the grave of Lazarus; in the RV in Heb. 11:38 and Rev. 6:15 (KJV, "dens"); in the Lord's rebuke concerning the defilement of the Temple, Matt. 21:13; Mark 11:17; Luke 19:46, "den" is used.

Lay upon *epikeimai* (1945), "to lie upon, be laid upon," is translated with this meaning, intransitively in **John 11:38** and Acts 27:20; transitively, in the passive voice, in **John 21:9** and 1 Cor. 9:16.

11:39 Jesus said, Take ye away the stone. Martha, the sister of him that was dead, saith unto him, Lord, by this time he stinketh: for he hath been *dead* four days.

Dead *teleutao* (5053), "to end" (from *telos*, "an end"), hence, "to end one's life," is used (a) of the "death" of the body, Matt. 2:19; 9:18; 15:4, where "die the death" means "surely die," RV, marg., lit., "let him end by death"; Mark 7:10; Matt. 22:25, "deceased"; Luke 7:2; **John 11:39**; Acts 2:29; 7:15; Heb. 11:22 (RV, "his end was nigh"); (b) of the gnawings of conscience in self reproach, under the symbol of a worm, Mark 9:48 (vv. 44 and 46, KJV).

Time *ede* (2235), "already, now," is translated "by this time" in **John 11:39**.

Stinketh *ozo* (3605), "to emit a smell" (cf. Eng., "ozone"), occurs in **John 11:39**.

Four *tessares* (5064), "four," is not found in the NT outside the Gospels, the Acts and Revelation; in the last it is very frequent. *Tetartos*, "fourth," is found in Matt. 14:25; Mark 6:48 and seven times in Revelation; also in Acts 10:30, "four days ago," lit., "from a fourth day." *Dekatessares*, "fourteen" (lit., "ten-four"), is found in Matt. 1:17; 2 Cor. 12:2; Gal. 2:1; *tessareskaidekatos*, "fourteenth" (lit., "four-and-tenth"), Acts 27:27, 33; *tetrakosia*, "four hundred," Acts 5:36; 7:6; 13:20; Gal. 3:17. In Acts 7:6 the 400 years refers to Abraham's descendants and to the sojourning and the bondage. This agrees with Gen. 15:13. In Exod. 12:40 the 430 years dates from the call of Abraham himself. Likewise the giving of the Law was

430 years from the promise in Gen. 12:3, which agrees with Gal. 3:17. In **John 11:39** *tetartaios*, lit., "a fourth day (one)," is rendered "four days."

11:40 Jesus saith unto her, Said I not unto thee, that, if thou wouldest believe, thou shouldest see the glory of God?

Glory *see John 1:14.*

11:41 Then they took away the stone *from the place* where the dead was laid. And Jesus lifted up *his* eyes, and said, Father, I thank thee that thou hast heard me.

Laid In **John 11:41**, the verb is not found in the best mss.

Lifted *airo* (142), signifies (a) "to raise take up, lift, draw up," (b) "to bear, carry," (c) "to take or carry away." It is used of "lifting" up the voice, Luke 17:13; Acts 4:24; eyes, **John 11:41**; hand, Rev. 10:5.

Up The adverb is used with numerous Eng. verbs to translate single Greek verbs. In **John 11:41** and Heb. 12:15, however, the adverb *ano*, "up," is used separately.

Thank *see* Thanks at John *6:11.*

11:42 And I knew that thou hearest me always: but because of the people which stand by I said *it*, that they may believe that thou hast sent me.

Knew *see John 6:6.*

Stand *periistemi* (4026), intransitively, "to stand around" (*peri*), is so used in **John 11:42**; Acts 25:7.

Sent *see John 1:6.*

11:43 And when he thus had spoken, he cried with a loud voice, Lazarus, come forth.

Thus *see John 9:6.*

Voice *see* Sound at *John 3:8.*

Cried *kraugazo* (2905), "to make a clamor or outcry," is used in Matt. 12:19, in a prophecy from Isaiah of Christ; in Luke 4:41 (in the best mss., instead of *krazo*); **John 11:43**; **12:13** (in the best mss.); **18:40**; **19:6, 12, 19:15**; Acts 22:23.

Come *Deuro*, "hither, here," is used (sometimes with verbs of motion) in the singular number, in calling a person to come, Matt. 19:21; Mark 10:21; Luke 18:22; **John 11:43**; Acts 7:3, 34; Rev. 17:1; 21:9. It has a plural, *deute*, frequent in the Gospels; elsewhere in Rev. 19:17. In the following the RV *has a different rendering:*

Forth *exo* (1854), "outside, without" (from, *ek*, "out of, from"), frequently signifies "forth," especially after verbs of motion, e.g., **John 11:43**; **19:4, 13**.

11:44 And he that was dead came forth, bound hand and foot with graveclothes: and his face was bound about with a napkin. Jesus saith unto them, Loose him, and let him go.

Graveclothes *keiria* (2750), denotes, firstly, "a band" either for a bed girth, or bed sheets themselves (Sept. of Prov. 7:16.); then, "the swathings wrapped round a corpse"; it is used in the plural in **John 11:44**.

Face *see* Appearance at *John 7:24.*

Bound *perideo* (4019), "to bind around," is used in **John 11:44** of the napkin around the face of Lazarus. Cf. Job 12:18, Sept.

Napkin *soudarion* (4676), is translated "napkin" in Luke 19:20; **John 11:44**; **20:7**. In Luke 19:20 the reference may be to a towel or any kind of linen cloth or even a sort of headdress, any of which might be used for concealing money.

Loose *luo* (3089), denotes (a) "to loose, unbind, release," (1) of things, e.g., in Acts 7:33, RV, "loose (the shoes)," KJV, "put off"; Mark 1:7; (2) of animals, e.g., Matt. 21:2; (3) of persons, e.g., **John 11:44**; Acts 22:30; (4) of Satan, Rev. 20:3, 7, and angels, Rev. 9:14, 15; (5) metaphorically, of one diseased, Luke 13:16; of the marriage tie, 1 Cor. 7:27; of release from sins, Rev. 1:5 (in the most authentic mss.); (b) "to loosen, break up, dismiss, dissolve, destroy"; in this sense it is translated "to loose" in Acts 2:24, of the pains of death; in Rev. 5:2, of the seals of a roll.

Let ... go *aphiemi* (863), frequently denotes "to let, suffer, permit," e.g., Matt. 5:40 (translated "let ... have"); 7:4; 13:30; 15:14; 27:49 and Mark 15:36, RV, "let be," probably short for "let us see" (Moulton and Milligan, *Vocab.*); Mark 7:27; 11:6 ("let ... go"); 14:6 ("let ... alone"); so Luke 13:8; **John 11:48**; in Acts 5:38 (where some mss. have *eao*, "to permit, let, suffer"); in **John 11:44** and **18:8** ("let"); 1 Cor. 7:11, 12, RV, "let ... leave," KJV, "let ... put away"; 7:13 ("let ... leave").

11:45-46 Then many of the Jews which came to Mary, and had seen the things which Jesus did, believed on him.

But some of them went their ways to the Pharisees, and told them what things Jesus had done.

Ways *aperchomai*, "to go away," is rendered "to go one's way," e.g., Matt. 13:25; 20:4; Mark 11:4; 12:12; Luke 19:32; **John 11:46**; Acts 9:17; Jas. 1:24.

11:47 Then gathered the chief priests and the Pharisees a council, and said, What do we? for this man doeth many miracles.

Council *sunedrion* (4892), properly, "a settling together" (*sun*, "together," *hedra*, "a seat"), hence, (a) "any assembly or session of persons deliberating or adjusting," as in the Sept. of Ps. 26:4 (lit., "with a council of vanity"); Prov. 22:10; Jer. 15:17, etc.; in the NT, e.g., Matt. 10:17; Mark 13:9; **John 11:47**, in particular, it denoted (b) "the Sanhedrin," the Great Council at Jerusalem, consisting of 71 members, namely, prominent members of the families of the high priest, elders and scribes. The Jews trace the origin of this to Num. 11:16. The more important causes came up before this tribunal. The Roman rulers of Judea permitted the Sanhedrin to try such cases, and even to pronounce sentence of death, with the condition that such a sentence should be valid only if confirmed by the Roman procurator. In **John 11:47**, it is used of a meeting of the Sanhedrin; in Acts 4:15, of the place of meeting.

Miracles *see John 2:11.*

11:48 If we let him thus alone, all *men* will believe on him: and the Romans shall come and take away both our place and nation.

Let ... alone *aphiemi* (863), signifies "to send away, set free"; also "to let alone," Matt. 15:14; Mark 14:6; Luke 13:8; **John 11:48; 12:7** (RV, "suffer her"); in Acts 5:38 some texts have *easate* from *eao*, "to permit." *See also* **Let ... go** at *John 11:44.*

Romans *rhomaios* (4514), occurs in **John 11:48**; Acts 2:10, RV, "from Rome" (KJV, "of Rome"); 16:21, 37, 38; 22:25, 26, 27, 29; 23:27; 25:16; 28:17.

Nation *ethnos* (1484), originally "a multitude," denotes (a) "a nation" or "people," e.g., Matt. 24:7; Acts 10:35; the Jewish people, e.g., Luke 7:5; 23:2; **John 11:48, 50-52**; Acts 10:22; 24:2, 10, 17; in Matt. 21:43, the reference is to Israel in its restored condition, (b) in the plural "the nations" as distinct from Israel.

11:49 And one of them, *named* Caiaphas, being the high priest that same year, said unto them, Ye know nothing at all,

One *see John 10:30.*

Year *eniautos* (1763), originally "a cycle of time," is used (a) of a particular time marked by an event, e.g., Luke 4:19; **John 11:49, 51; 18:13**; Gal. 4:10; Rev. 9:15; (b) to mark a space of time, Acts 11:26; 18:11; Jas. 4:13; 5:17; (c) of that which takes place every year, Heb. 9:7.

Nothing In **John 11:49** the double negative *ouk* ("not") ... *ouden* ("nothing") is translated "nothing at all."

11:50 Nor consider that it is expedient for us, that one man should die for the people, and that the whole nation perish not.

Consider *logizomai* (3049), primarily signifies "to reckon," whether by calculation or imputation, e.g., Gal. 3:6 (RV, "reckoned"); then, to deliberate, and so to suppose, "account," Rom. 8:36; 14:14 (KJV, "esteemeth"); **John 11:50**; 1 Cor. 4:1; Heb. 11:19; (KJV, "consider"); Acts 19:27 ("made of no account"; KJV, "despised"); 1 Pet. 5:12 (KJV, "suppose"). It is used of love in 1 Cor. 13:5, as not taking "account" of evil, RV (KJV, "thinketh"). In 2 Cor. 3:5 the apostle uses it in repudiation of the idea that he and fellow-servants of God are so self-sufficient as to "account anything" (RV) as from themselves (KJV, "think"), i.e., as to attribute anything to themselves. Cf. 12:6. In 2 Tim. 4:16 it is used of laying to a person's "account" (RV) as a charge against him (KJV, "charge").

Expedient *sumphero* (4851), signifies (a), transitively, lit., "to bring together," (*sun*, "with," *phero*, "to bring"), Acts 19:19; (b) intransitively, "to be an advantage, profitable, expedient" (not merely 'convenient'); it is used mostly impersonally, "it is (it was) expedient"; so in Matt. 19:10, RV (negatively), KJV, "it is (not) good"; **John 11:50; 16:7; 18:14**; 1 Cor. 6:12; 10:23; 2 Cor. 8:10; 12:1; "it is profitable," Matt. 5:29-30; 18:6, RV; "was profitable," Acts 20:20; "to profit withal," 1 Cor. 12:7; in Heb. 12:10, used in the neuter of the present participle with the article as a noun, "for (our) profit." Cf. the adjective *sumphoros* (or *sumpheron*), "profitable," used with the article as a noun, 1 Cor. 7:35; 10:33.

People *laos* (2992), is used of (a) "the people at large," especially of people assembled, e.g., Matt. 27:25; Luke 1:21; 3:15; Acts 4:27; (b) "a people of the same race and language," e.g., Rev. 5:9; in the plural, e.g., Luke 2:31; Rom. 15:11; Rev. 7:9; 11:9; especially of Israel, e.g., Matt. 2:6; 4:23; **John 11:50**; Acts 4:8; Heb. 2:17; in distinction from their rulers and priests, e.g., Matt. 26:5; Luke 20:19; Heb. 5:3; in distinction from Gentiles, e.g., Acts 26:17, 23; Rom. 15:10; (c) of Christians as the people of God, e.g., Acts 15:14; Titus 2:14; Heb. 4:9; 1 Pet. 2:9.

Whole *holos* (3650), signifies "whole," (a) with a noun, e.g., Matt. 5:29, 30; Mark 8:36; 15:1, 16, 33; Luke 11:36 (1st part), though *holon* may here be used adverbially with *photeinon*, "wholly light"; **John 11:50**; 1 Cor. 12:17 (1st part); 1 John 2:2; 5:19; (b) absolutely, as a noun, e.g., Matt. 13:33; 1 Cor. 12:17 (2nd part).

Nation *see John 11:48.*

11:51 And this spake he not of himself: but being high priest that year, he prophesied that Jesus should die for that nation;

Year *see John 11:49.*

Prophesied *propheteia* (4394), signifies "the speaking forth of the mind and counsel of God"; in the NT it is used (a) of the gift, e.g., Rom. 12:6; 1 Cor. 12:10; 13:2; (b) either of the exercise of the gift or of that which is "prophesied," e.g., Matt. 13:14; 1 Cor. 13:8; 14:6, 22 and 1 Thess. 5:20, "prophesying(s)"; 1 Tim. 1:18; 4:14; 2 Pet. 1:20, 21; Rev. 1:3; 11:6; 19:10; 22:7, 10, 18, 19. "Though much of OT prophecy was purely predictive, see Micah 5:2, e.g., and cf. **John 11:51**, prophecy is not necessarily, nor even primarily, fore-telling. It is the declaration of that which cannot be known by natural means, Matt. 26:68, it is the forth-telling of the will of God, whether with reference to the past, the present, or the future, see Gen. 20:7; Deut. 18:18; Rev. 10:11; 11:3."

Should *see John 6:71.*

11:52 And not for that nation only, but that also he should gather together in one the children of God that were scattered abroad.

Only *see John 5:18.*

One *see John 10:30.*

Children *see* Sons at *1:12.*

Scattered *diaskorpizo* (1287), signifies "to scatter abroad," in Matt. 26:31; Mark 14:27, metaphorically of sheep; in Luke 1:51, of the proud; in **John 11:52**, of the "scattering" of the children of God; in Acts 5:37, of the followers of Judas of Galilee (KJV, "were dispersed"); of "scattering" grain by winnowing, Matt. 25:24, 26; in Luke 15:13 and 16:1, it signifies "to waste."

11:53 Then from that day forth they took counsel together for to put him to death.

Forth In Matt. 26:16, the RV omits "forth," as the similar *apo tote*, "from then," simply means "from that time"; in the similar phrase "from that day forth," Matt. 22:46; **John 11:53**, there is no word in the original representing "forth."

Took counsel *bouleuo* (1011), "to take counsel, to resolve," is used in the middle voice in the NT, "took counsel" in Acts 5:33, KJV (RV translates *boulomai*); both in 27:39; in Luke 14:31, RV "take counsel" (KJV, "consulteth"); in **John 11:53**, KJV and RV (so the best mss.); **12:10**, RV, "took counsel," for KJV, "consulted"; in 2 Cor. 1:17 (twice), "purpose." Also, *sumbouleuo* (4823), in the active voice, "to advise, to counsel," **John 18:14**, "gave counsel"; in Rev. 3:18, "I counsel"; in the middle voice, "to take counsel, consult," Matt. 26:4, RV, "took counsel together," for KJV, "consulted"; Acts 9:23, "took counsel" (RV adds "together"); in some mss. **John 11:53**.

Death *apokteino* (615), to kill, is so translated in the RV, for the KJV, "put to death," in Mark 14:1; Luke 18:33; in **John 11:53**; **12:10** and **18:31**, RV, "put to death."

11:54 Jesus therefore walked no more openly among the Jews; but went thence unto a country near to the wilderness, into a city called Ephraim, and there continued with his disciples.

Openly *see John 7:4.*

Near *see John 3:23.*

Called *see John 4:5.*

Continued The following are translated by the verb "to continue," in the KJV, in the places mentioned: *diatribo*, "to tarry," (according to inferior mss.) **John 11:54**; Acts 15:35 (RV, "tarried"); *histemi*, "to stand," Acts 26:22 (RV, "stand"): *kathizo*, "to sit down," Acts 18:11 (RV, "dwelt"): *parateino*, "to extend, stretch," Acts 20:7 (RV, "prolonged"); *parameno*, "to abide together with," Phil. 1:25, RV, "abide with"; the KJV, "continue," translating *sumparameno* (in some mss.), marks the difference from the preceding *meno*.

11:55 And the Jews' passover was nigh at hand: and many went out of the country up to Jerusalem before the passover, to purify themselves.

Passover *see John 2:13.*

Purify *hagnizo* (48), akin to *hagnos*, "pure", "to purify, cleanse from defilement," is used of "purifying" (a) ceremonially, **John 11:55**; Acts 21:24, 26; 24:18; (b) morally, the heart, Jas. 4:8; the soul, 1 Pet. 1:22; oneself, 1 John 3:3.

11:56 Then sought they for Jesus, and spake among themselves, as they stood in the temple, What think ye, that he will not come to the feast?

Themselves *see John 6:52.*

11:57 Now both the chief priests and the Pharisees had given a commandment, that, if any man knew where he were, he should shew *it*, that they might take him.

Shew *menuo* (3377), "to disclose, make known" (what was secret), is rendered "to show" in Luke 20:37; 1 Cor. 10:28; in a forensic sense, **John 11:57**; Acts 23:30, RV (KJV, "it was told").

Take *see* Take, Laid hands on at *John 7:30.*

Chapter 12

12:1 Then Jesus six days before the passover came to Bethany, where Lazarus was which had been dead, whom he raised from the dead.

Six *see John 2:6.*

Passover *see John 2:13.*

Raised *see* raise at *John 2:19.*

12:2 There they made him a supper; and Martha served: but Lazarus was one of them that sat at the table with him.

Made *see* Make at *John 2:16.*

Supper *deipnon* (1173), denotes (a) "the chief meal of the day," dinner or supper, taken at or towards evening; in the plural "feasts," Matt. 23:6; Mark 6:21; 12:39; Luke 20:46; otherwise translated "supper," Luke 14:12, 16, 17, 24; **John 12:2**; **13:2**, **4**; **21:20**; 1 Cor. 11:21 (of a social meal); (b) "the Lord's Supper," 1 Cor. 11:20; (c) "the supper or feast" which will celebrate the marriage of Christ with His spiritual Bride, at the inauguration of His Kingdom, Rev. 19:9; (d) figuratively, of that to which the birds of prey will be summoned after the overthrow of the enemies of the Lord at the termination of the war of Armageddon, 19:17 (cf. Ezek. 39:4, 17-20).

Served *diakoneo* (1247), signifies "to be a servant, attendant, to serve, wait upon, minister." In the following it is translated "to minister," except where "to serve" is mentioned: it is used (a) with a general significance, e.g., Matt. 4:11; 20:28; Mark 1:13; 10:45; **John 12:26** ("serve," twice); Acts 19:22; Philem. 13; (b) of waiting at table, "ministering" to the guests, Matt. 8:15; Luke 4:39; 8:3; 12:37; 17:8, "serve"; 22:26, "serve," v. 27, "serveth," twice; the 2nd instance, concerning the Lord, may come under (a); so of women preparing food, etc., Mark 1:31; Luke 10:40, "serve"; **John 12:2**, "served."

Sat *sunanakeimai* (4873), "to recline at table with or together," "to sit at meat or at table with," occurs in Matt. 9:10, "sat down"; 14:9; Mark 2:15, RV, "sat down with" (KJV, "sat ... together with"); 6:22; Luke 7:49; 14:10, 15; **John 12:2** (in some texts).

Table *anakeimai* (345), "to recline at a meal table," is rendered "sat at the table" in **John 12:2**, KJV, RV, "sat at meat" (some texts have *sunanakeimai*); "sat," of course does not express the actual attitude; in **John 13:23**, RV, "at the table reclining"; KJV, "leaning"; in **13:28**, "at the table" (KJV and RV), lit., "of (those) reclining."

12:3 Then took Mary a pound of ointment of spikenard, very costly, and anointed the feet of Jesus, and wiped his feet with her hair: and the house was filled with the odour of the ointment.

Pound *litra* (3046), was a Sicilian coin, the equivalent of a Latin *libra* or as (whence the metric unit, "liter"); in the NT it is used as a measure of weight, a pound, **John 12:3**; **19:39**.

Ointment *see John 11:2.*

Spikenard *nardos* (3487), is derived, through the Semitic languages (Heb. *nerd*, Syriac *nardin*), from the Sanskrit *nalada*, "a fragrant oil," procured from the stem of an Indian plant. The Arabs call it the "Indian spike." The adjective *pistikos* is attached to it in the NT, Mark 14:3; **John 12:3**; *pistikos*, if taken as an ordinary Greek word, would signify "genuine." There is evidence, however, that it was regarded as a technical term. It has been suggested that the original reading was *pistakes*, i.e., the *Pistacia Terebinthus*, which grows in Cyprus, Syria, Palestine, etc., and yields a resin of very fragrant odor, and in such inconsiderable quantities as to be very costly. "Nard was frequently mixed with aromatic ingredients ... so when scented with the fragrant resin of the *pistake* it would quite well be called *nardos pistakes*" (E. N. Bennett, in the *Classical Review* for 1890, Vol. iv, p. 319). The oil used for the anointing of the Lord's head must have been of the most valuable kind. In the Sept., Song of Sol. 1:12; 4:13, 14.

Costly *polutimos* (4186), lit., "of great value," is used of a pearl, Matt. 13:46; of spikenard, **John 12:3** (RV, "very precious," KJV, "very costly"). The comparative *polutimo (v.l.io) teros*, "much more precious," is used in 1 Pet. 1:7.

Anointed *see John 11:2.*

Wiped *see John 11:2.*

Hair *see John 11:2.*

Filled *pleroo* (4137), denotes (I) "to make full, to fill to the full"; in the passive voice, "to be filled, made full"; it is used (1) of things: a net, Matt. 13:48; a building, **John 12:3**; Acts 2:2; a city, Acts 5:28; needs, Phil. 4:19, KJV, "supply," RV, "fulfill"; metaphorically, of valleys, Luke 3:5; figuratively, of a measure of iniquity, Matt. 23:32; (2) of persons: (a) of the members of the church, the body of Christ, as filled by Him, Eph. 1:23 ("all things in all the members"); 4:10; in 3:19, of their being filled "into" (*eis*), RV, "unto," KJV, "with" (all the fullness of God); of their being "made full" in Him,

Col. 2:10 (RV, for KJV, "complete"); (b) of Christ Himself: with wisdom, in the days of His flesh, Luke 2:40; with joy, in His return to the Father, Acts 2:28; (c) of believers: with the Spirit, Eph. 5:18; with joy, Acts 13:52; 2 Tim. 1:4; with joy and peace, Rom. 15:13; with knowledge, Rom. 15:14; with comfort, 2 Cor. 7:4; with the fruits of righteousness, Phil. 1:11 (Gk. "fruit"); with the knowledge of God's will, Col. 1:9; with abundance through material supplies by fellow believers, Phil. 4:18; (d) of the hearts of believers as the seat of emotion and volition, **John 16:6** (sorrow); Acts 5:3 (deceitfulness); (e) of the unregenerate who refuse recognition of God, Rom. 1:29; (II) "to accomplish, complete, fulfill.

Odour *osme* (3744), "a smell, an odor" (akin to *ozo*, "to smell"), is translated "odor" in **John 12:3**; it is used metaphorically in Eph. 5:2, RV, "an odor (of a sweet smell)," KJV, "(a sweet smelling) savor," of the effects Godward of the sacrifice of Christ; in Phil. 4:18 of the effect of sacrifice, on the part of those in the church at Philippi, who sent material assistance to the apostle in his imprisonment. The word is translated "savor" in 2 Cor. 2:14, 16 (twice).

12:4 Then saith one of his disciples, Judas Iscariot, Simon's *son*, which should betray him,

Should *see John 6:71.*

12:5 Why was not this ointment sold for three hundred pence, and given to the poor?

Ointment *see John 11:2.*

Sold *piprasko* (4097), from an earlier form, *perao*, "to carry across the sea for the purpose of selling or to export," is used (a) literally, Matt. 13:46; 18:25; 26:9; Mark 14:5; **John 12:5**; Acts 2:45; 4:34; 5:4; (b) metaphorically, Rom. 7:14, "sold under sin," i.e., as fully under the domination of sin as a slave is under his master; the statement evinces an utter dissatisfaction with such a condition; it expresses, not the condemnation of the unregenerate state, but the evil of bondage to a corrupt nature, involving the futility of making use of the Law as a means of deliverance.

Three hundred *triakosioi* (5145), occurs in Mark 14:5 and **John 12:5**.

Pence *see* Pennyworth at *John 6:7.*

Poor *ptochos* (4434), has the broad sense of "poor," (a) literally, e.g., Matt. 11:5; 26:9, 11; Luke 21:3 (with stress on the word, "a conspicuously poor widow"); **John 12:5, 6, 8; 13:29**; Jas. 2:2, 3, 6; the "poor" are constantly the subjects of injunctions to assist them, Matt. 19:21; Mark 10:21; Luke 14:13, 21; 18:22; Rom. 15:26; Gal. 2:10; (b) metaphorically, Matt. 5:3; Luke 6:20; Rev. 3:17.

12:6 This he said, not that he cared for the poor; but because he was a thief, and had the bag, and bare what was put therein.

Cared *see* Careth at *John 10:13.*

Poor *see John 12:5.*

Thief *see John 10:1.*

Bag *glossokomon* (1101), from *glossa*, "a tongue," and *komeo*, "to tend," was, firstly, "a case" in which to keep the mouthpiece of wind instruments; secondly, "a small box" for any purpose, but especially a "casket or purse," to keep money in. It is used of the "bag" which Judas carried, **John 12:6; 13:29**; in the Sept. of 2 Chron. 24:8, 10, used of the "box" appointed by King Joash for offerings for the repair of the Temple.

Bare *see* Took up at *John 10:31.*

Put *see John 5:7.*

12:7 Then said Jesus, Let her alone: against the day of my burying hath she kept this.

Let ... alone *aphiemi* (863), "to send away," signifies "to permit, suffer," in Matt. 3:15 (twice); Matt. 19:14; 23:13; Mark 1:34; 5:19, 37; 10:14; 11:16; Luke 8:51; 12:39, KJV (RV, "left"); 18:16; **John 12:7**, RV, KJV and RV marg., "let (her) alone"; Rev. 11:9. *See also John 11:48.*

Burying *entaphiasmos* (1780), lit. "an entombing" (from *en*, "in," *taphos*, "a tomb"), "burying," occurs in Mark 14:8; **John 12:7**.

This *autos*; "he," rendered "this" in Matt. 11:14, lit., "he"; in **John 12:7**, KJV (RV, "it"); in the feminine, Luke 13:16.

12:8 For the poor always ye have with you; but me ye have not always.

Poor *see John 12:5.*

12:9 Much people of the Jews therefore knew that he was there: and they came not for Jesus' sake only, but that they might see Lazarus also, whom he had raised from the dead.

Much In **John 12:9**, the RV has "the common people" for "much people."

People *see John 7:12.*

Knew *ginosko* (1097), "to know by observation and experience," is translated "to learn," in the RV of Mark 15:45; **John 12:9**.

Only *see John 5:18.*

Raised *see* Raise at *John 2:19.*

12:10 But the chief priests consulted that they might put Lazarus also to death;

Consulted *bouleuo* (1011), used in the middle voice, means (a) "to consult," Luke 14:31; (b) "to resolve," **John 12:10**, KJV, "consulted"; RV, took counsel."

Also *see John 7:3.*

Death *see John 11:53.*

12:11-12 Because that by reason of him many of the Jews went away, and believed on Jesus.

On the next day much people that were come to the feast, when they heard that Jesus was coming to Jerusalem,

Next day *see John 1:29.*

Much *polus* (4183), is used (a) as an adjective of degree, e.g., Matt. 13:5, "much (earth)"; Acts 26:24, "much (learning)"; in v. 29, in the answer to Agrippa's "with but little persuasion," some texts have *pollo* (some *megalo*, "with great"), RV, "(whether with little or) with much"; of number, e.g., Mark 5:24, RV, "a great (multitude)," KJV, "much (people)"; so Luke 7:11; **John 12:12**; Rev. 19:1, etc.; (b) in the neuter singular form (*polu*), as a noun, e.g., Luke 16:10 (twice); in the plural (*polla*), e.g., Rom. 16:6, 12, "(labored) much," lit., "many things"; (c) adverbially, in the neuter singular, e.g., Acts 18:27; James 5:16; Matt. 26:9 (a genitive of price); in the plural, e.g., Mark 5:43, RV, "much" (KJV, "straitly"); Mark 9:26, RV, "much" (KJV, "sore"); **John 14:30**; and with the article, Acts 26:24; Rom. 15:22; 1 Cor. 16:19; Rev. 5:4.

12:13 Took branches of palm trees, and went forth to meet him, and cried, Hosanna: Blessed *is* the King of Israel that cometh in the name of the Lord.

Branches *baion* (902), of Egyptian origin, frequent in the papyri writings, denotes "a branch of the palm tree," **John 12:13**.

Palm trees *phoinix* (5404), denotes "the date palm"; it is used of "palm" trees in **John 12:13**, from which branches were taken; of the branches themselves in Rev. 7:9. The "palm" gave its name to Phoenicia and to Phoenix in Crete, Acts 27:12, RV. Jericho was the city of "palm trees," Deut. 34:3; Judg. 1:16; 3:13; 2 Chron. 28:15. They were plentiful there in the time of Christ.

Meet *hupantesis* (5222), "a going to meet," preceded by the preposition *eis*, "unto," lit., "unto a meeting," translated "to meet," is found in **John 12:13**, and in the most authentic mss. in Matt. 8:34 and 25:1.

Cried *see John 11:43.*

Hosanna *hosanna* (5614), in the Hebrew, means "save, we pray." The word seems to have become an utterance of praise rather than of prayer, though originally, probably, a cry for help. The people's cry at the Lord's triumphal entry into Jerusalem (Matt. 21:9, 15; Mark 11:9, 10; **John 12:13**) was taken from Ps. 118, which was recited at the Feast of Tabernacles in the great Hallel (Psalms 113 to 118) in responses with the priest, accompanied by the waving of palm and willow branches. "The last day of the feast" was called "the great Hosanna"; the boughs also were called "hosannas."

Blessed *eulogeo* (2127), lit., "to speak well of" (*eu*, "well," *logos*, "a word"), signifies, (a) "to praise, to celebrate with praises," of that which is addressed to God, acknowledging His goodness, with desire for His glory, Luke 1:64; 2:28; 24:51, 53; Jas. 3:9; (b) "to invoke blessings upon a person," e.g., Luke 6:28; Rom. 12:14. The present participle passive, "blessed, praised," is especially used of Christ in Matt. 21:9; 23:39, and the parallel passages; also in **John 12:13**; (c) "to consecrate a thing with solemn prayers, to ask God's blessing on a thing," e.g., Luke 9:16; 1 Cor. 10:16; (d) "to cause to prosper, to make happy, to bestow blessings on," said of God, e.g., in Acts 3:26; Gal. 3:9; Eph. 1:3. Cf. the synonym *aineo*, "to praise."

King *see John 1:49.*

12:14 And Jesus, when he had found a young ass, sat thereon; as it is written,

Ass *onos* (3688), is the usual word. *Onarion*, the diminutive of *onos*, "a young ass, or ass's colt," is used in **John 12:14**, together with *onos*.

12:15 Fear not, daughter of Sion: behold, thy King cometh, sitting on an ass's colt.

Daughter *thugater* (2364), "a daughter," (etymologically, Eng., "daughter" is connected), is used of (a) the natural relationship (frequent in the Gospels); (b) spiritual relationship to God, 2 Cor. 6:18, in the sense of the practical realization of acceptance with, and the approval of, God (cf. Isa. 43:6), the only place in the NT where it applies to spiritual relationship; (c) the inhabitants of a city or region, Matt. 21:5; **John 12:15** ("of Zion"); cf. Isa. 37:22; Zeph. 3:14 (Sept.); (d) the women who followed Christ to Calvary, Luke 23:28; (e) women of Aaron's posterity, Luke 1:5; (f) a female descendant of Abraham, Luke 13:16.

12:16 These things understood not his disciples at the first: but when Jesus was glorified, then remembered they that these

things were written of him, and *that* they had done these things unto him.

Understood *see John 8:27.*

Glorified *see John 7:39.*

12:17 The people therefore that was with him when he called Lazarus out of his grave, and raised him from the dead, bare record.

Called *see* Calleth at *John 10:3.*

Raised *see* Raise at *John 2:19.*

Record *see* Witness at *John 1:7.*

12:18 For this cause the people also met him, for that they heard that he had done this miracle.

Met *see John 4:51.*

Miracle *see* Miracles at *John 2:11.*

12:19 The Pharisees therefore said among themselves, Perceive ye how ye prevail nothing? behold, the world is gone after him.

Perceive *see John 4:19.*

Prevail *opheleo* (5623), signifies "to be useful, do good, profit," Rom. 2:25; with a negative, "to be of no use, to effect nothing," Matt. 27:24; **John 6:63**, "profiteth"; **12:19**, "prevail"; in Luke 9:25, KJV, "(what is a man) advantaged?" RV, "profited."

12:20-21 And there were certain Greeks among them that came up to worship at the feast:

The same came therefore to Philip, which was of Bethsaida of Galilee, and desired him, saying, Sir, we would see Jesus.

Same *see John 3:2.*

Sir *see* Lord at *John 4:1.*

Desired *erotao* (2065), in Luke 7:36 is translated "desired"; in 14:32, RV, "asketh," for KJV, "desireth"; so in **John 12:21**; Acts 16:39; 18:20; 23:20; in v. 18 "asked," for KJV, "prayed."

12:22-23 Philip cometh and telleth Andrew: and again Andrew and Philip tell Jesus.

And Jesus answered them, saying, The hour is come, that the Son of man should be glorified.

Son *see John 1:18.*

Glorified *see John 7:39.*

12:24 Verily, verily, I say unto you, Except a corn of wheat fall into the ground and die, it abideth alone: but if it die, it bringeth forth much fruit.

Corn *kokkos (2848)*, "a grain" (its regular meaning), is translated "corn" in the KJV of **John 12:24** (RV, "grain").

Wheat *sitos* (4621), "wheat, corn"; in the plural, "grain," is translated "corn" in Mark 4:28; "wheat," Matt. 3:12; 13:25, 29-30; Luke 3:17; 12:18 (some mss. have *genemata*, "fruits," here): 16:7; 22:31; **John 12:24**; Acts 27:38; 1 Cor. 15:37; Rev. 6:6; 18:13.

Die *see John 6:50.*

Bringeth forth *see* Bear, Bare at *John 2:8.*

12:25 He that loveth his life shall lose it; and he that hateth his life in this world shall keep it unto life eternal.

Loveth *see John 3:35.*

Hateth *see John 3:20.*

Keep *phulasso* (5442), denotes (a) "to guard, watch, keep watch," e.g., Luke 2:8; in the passive voice, 8:29; (b) "to keep by way of protection," e.g., Luke 11:21; **John 12:25; 17:12** (2nd part; *tereo* in 1st part and in v. 11); (c) metaphorically, "to keep a law precept," etc., e.g., Matt. 19:20 and Luke 18:21, "have observed"; Luke 11:28; **John 12:47** (in the best mss.); Acts 7:53; 16:4; 21:24; Rom. 2:26; Gal. 6:13; 1 Tim. 5:21 ("observe"); in the middle voice, Mark 10:20 ("have observed"); (d) in the middle voice, "to keep oneself from," Acts 21:25; elsewhere translated by the verb "to beware."

> *"God will never plant the seed of his life upon the soil of a hard, unbroken spirit. He will only plant that seed where conviction of his Spirit has brought brokenness, where the soil has been watered with the tears of repentance as well as the tears of joy."*
>
> ALAN REDPATH

12:26 If any man serve me, let him follow me; and where I am, there shall also my servant be: if any man serve me, him will *my* Father honour.

Servant *see* Servants at *John 2:5.*

Honour *see John 5:23.*

12:27 Now is my soul troubled; and what shall I say? Father, save me from this hour: but for this cause came I unto this hour.

Now *see John 4:18.*

Save *see* Saved at John *10:9.*

12:28 Father, glorify thy name. Then came there a voice from heaven, *saying*, I have both glorified *it*, and will glorify *it* again.

Glorify, Glorified *see* Glorified at *John 7:39.*

Name *see John 1:12.*

Voice *see* Sound at *John 3:8.*

12:29 The people therefore, that stood by, and heard *it*, said that it thundered: others said, An angel spake to him.

Thundered *bronte* (1027), in Mark 3:17 "sons of thunder" is the interpretation of Boanerges, the name applied by the Lord to James and John; their fiery disposition is seen in 9:38 and Luke 9:54; perhaps in the case of James it led to his execution. The name and its interpretation have caused much difficulty; some suggest the meaning "the twins." It is however most probably the equivalent of the Aramaic *bene regesh*, "sons of tumult"; the latter of the two words was no doubt used of "thunder" in Palestinian Aramaic; hence the meaning "the sons of thunder"; the cognate Hebrew word *ragash*, "to rage," is used in Ps. 2:1 and there only. In **John 12:29** *bronte* is used with *ginomai*, "to take place," and rendered "it had thundered"; lit., "there was thunder"; elsewhere, Rev. 4:5; 6:1; 8:5; 10:3, 4; 11:19; 14:2; 16:18; 19:6.

12:30 Jesus answered and said, This voice came not because of me, but for your sakes.

Voice *see* Sound at John *3:8.*

12:31 Now is the judgment of this world: now shall the prince of this world be cast out.

Prince *kosmokrator* (2888), denotes "a ruler of this world" (contrast *pantokrator*, "almighty"). In Greek literature, in Orphic hymns, etc., and in rabbinic writings, it signifies a "ruler" of the whole world, a world lord. In the NT it is used in Eph. 6:12, "the world rulers (of this darkness)," RV, KJV, "the rulers (of the darkness) of this world." The context ("not against flesh and blood") shows that not earthly potentates are indicated, but spirit powers, who, under the permissive will of God, and in consequence of human sin, exercise satanic and therefore antagonistic authority over the world in its present condition of spiritual darkness and alienation from God. The suggested rendering "the rulers of this dark world" is ambiguous and not phraseologically requisite. Cf. **John 12:31**; **14:30**; **16:11**; 2 Cor. 4:4. *See also* **Ruler** at *John 3:1.*

12:32 And I, if I be lifted up from the earth, will draw all *men* unto me.

Lifted up *see John 3:14.*

Draw *see John 6:44.*

Me *see* Mine own self at *John 5:30.*

12:33 This he said, signifying what death he should die.

Signifying *semaino* (4591), "to give a sign, indicate," "to signify," is so translated in **John 12:33**; **18:32**; **21:19**; Acts 11:28; 25:27; Rev. 1:1, where perhaps the suggestion is that of expressing by signs.

What Other words are (a) *hoios*, "of what kind," e.g., 2 Cor. 10:11, RV (KJV, "such as"); 1 Thess. 1:5, "what manner of men"; 2 Tim. 3:11 (twice), lit., "what sorts of things," "what sorts of persecutions"; (b) *poios*, "what sort of," e.g., Matt. 21:23, 24, 27; 24:42, 43; Luke 5:19; 6:32-34; 20:2, 8; 24:19; **John 12:33**, "what manner of"; so in **18:32**; **21:19**; Rom. 3:27; 1 Cor. 15:35; in Jas. 4:14, "what"; 1 Pet. 2:20 and Rev. 3:3 (ditto); 1 Pet. 1:11, "what manner of"; (c) *hopoios*, "what sort of," 1 Cor. 3:13; "what manner of," 1 Thess. 1:9; (d) *hosos*, "how great," Mark 6:30 (twice), RV, "whatsoever"; Acts 15:12; Rom. 3:19, "what things soever"; Jude 10 (1st part), "what soever things," RV; (2nd part) "what"; (e) *posos*, "how great, how much," 2 Cor. 7:11, "what (earnest care)," RV (*posos* here stands for the repeated words in the Eng. versions, the adjective not being repeated in the original); (f) *hostis*, "what (things)," Phil. 3:7; (g) in Matt. 26:40, *houtos*, "thus, so," is used as an exclamatory expression, translated "What" (in a word immediately addressed by the Lord to Peter), lit., "So"; (h) for *potapos*, rendered "what" in Mark 13:1 (2nd part), KJV; (i) in 1 Cor. 6:16, 19, KJV, the particle *e*, "or" (RV), is rendered "What?"; in 1 Cor. 14:36, KJV and RV, "what?" (j) in 1 Cor. 11:22, *gar*, "in truth, indeed," has its exclamatory use "What."

Should *see John 6:71.*

12:34 The people answered him, We have heard out of the law that Christ abideth for ever: and how sayest thou, The Son of man must be lifted up? who is this Son of man?

Law *see John 1:17.*

Abideth *see* Abode at *John 1:32.*

Son *see John 1:18.*

Lifted up *see John 3:14.*

12:35 Then Jesus said unto them, Yet a little while is the light with you. Walk while ye have the light, lest darkness come upon you: for he that walketh in darkness knoweth not whither he goeth.

Little *see John 7:33.*

While *Hos,* as, "while" in Luke 24:32 (twice); **John 12:35, 36**; Acts 1:10; 10:17. *See also John 7:33.*

Light *see John 1:4.*

Darkness *see John 1:5.*

Come upon *katalambano* (2638), "to lay hold of," has the significance of "overtaking," metaphorically, in **John 12:35** (RV, "overtake," KJV, "come upon") and 1 Thess. 5:4.

Knoweth *see* Comprehended at *John 1:5.*

12:36 While ye have light, believe in the light, that ye may be the children of light. These things spake Jesus, and departed, and did hide himself from them.

While *see John 9:4.*

Light *see John 1:4.*

12:37 But though he had done so many miracles before them, yet they believed not on him:

Many *see John 6:9.*

Miracles *see John 2:11.*

Before *see John 1:15.*

12:38 That the saying of Esaias the prophet might be fulfilled, which he spake, Lord, who hath believed our report? and to whom hath the arm of the Lord been revealed?

Saying *see John 4:37.*

Report *akoe* (189), "a hearing," is translated "report" in **John 12:38** and Rom. 10:16, and in the RV of Matt. 4:24; 14:1; Mark 1:28.

Arm *brachion* (1023), "the shorter part of the arm, from the shoulder to the elbow," is used metaphorically to denote strength, power, and always in the NT of the power of God, Luke 1:51; **John 12:38**; Acts 13:17; frequently so in the OT, especially in Deuteronomy, the Psalms and Isaiah; see, e.g., Deut. 4:34; 5:15; Ps. 44:3; 71:18, where "strength" is, lit., "arm"; 77:15; Isa. 26:11, where "hand" is, lit., "arm"; 30:30; 40:10-11, etc.

Revealed *apokalupto* (601), signifies "to uncover, unveil" (*apo,* "from," *kalupto,* "to cover"); both verbs are used in Matt. 10:26; in Luke 12:2, *apokalupto* is set in contrast to *sunkalupto,* "to cover up, cover completely." "The NT occurrences of this word fall under two heads, subjective and objective. The subjective use is that in which something is presented to the mind directly, as, (a) the meaning of the acts of God, Matt. 11:25; Luke 10:21; (b) the secret of the Person of the Lord Jesus, Matt. 16:17; **John 12:38**; (c) the character of God as Father, Matt. 11:27; Luke 10:22; (d) the will of God for the conduct of His children, Phil. 3:15; (e) the mind of God to the prophets of Israel, 1 Pet. 1:12, and of the Church, 1 Cor. 14:30; Eph. 3:5.

12:39-40 Therefore they could not believe, because that Esaias said again,

He hath blinded their eyes, and hardened their heart; that they should not see with *their* eyes, nor understand with *their* heart, and be converted, and I should heal them.

Blinded *tuphloo* (5186), "to blind" (from a root *tuph–,* "to burn, smoke"; cf. *tuphos,* "smoke"), is used metaphorically, of the dulling of the intellect, **John 12:40**; 2 Cor. 4:4; 1 John 2:11.

Eyes *ophthalmos* (3788), akin to *opsis,* "sight," probably from a root signifying "penetration, sharpness" (Curtius, Gk. Etym.) (cf. Eng., "ophthalmia," etc.). is used (a) of the physical organ, e.g., Matt. 5:38; of restoring sight, e.g., Matt. 20:33; of God's power of vision, Heb. 4:13; 1 Pet. 3:12; of Christ in vision, Rev. 1:14; 2:18; 19:12; of the Holy Spirit in the unity of Godhood with Christ, Rev. 5:6; (b) metaphorically, of ethical qualities, evil, Matt. 6:23; Mark 7:22 (by metonymy, for envy); singleness of motive, Matt. 6:22; Luke 11:34; as the instrument of evil desire, "the principal avenue of temptation," 1 John 2:16; of adultery, 2 Pet. 2:14; (c) metaphorically, of mental vision, Matt. 13:15; **John 12:40**; Rom. 11:8; Gal. 3:1, where the metaphor of the "evil eye" is altered to a different sense from that of bewitching (the posting up or placarding of an "eye" was used as a charm, to prevent mischief); by gospel-preaching Christ had been, so to speak, placarded before their "eyes"; the question may be paraphrased, "What evil teachers have been malignly fascinating you?"; Eph. 1:18, of the "eyes of the heart," as a means of knowledge.

Hardened *poroo* (4456), "to make hard, callous, to petrify," is used metaphorically, of the heart, Mark 6:52; 8:17; **John 12:40**; of the mind (or thoughts), 2 Cor. 3:14, of those in Israel who refused the revealed will and ways of God in the gospel, as also in Rom. 11:7, RV, "hardened" (KJV, "blinded"), in both places.

Heart *kardia* (2588), "the heart" (Eng., "cardiac," etc.), the chief organ of physical life ("for the life of the flesh is in the blood," Lev. 17:11), occupies the most important place in the human system. By an easy transition the word came to stand for man's entire mental and moral activity, both the rational and the emotional elements. In other words, the heart is used figuratively for the hidden springs of the personal life. As to its usage in the NT it denotes (a) the seat of physical life, Acts 14:17; Jas. 5:5; (b) the seat of moral nature and spiritual life, the seat of grief, **John 14:1**; Rom. 9:2; 2 Cor. 2:4; joy, **John 16:22**; Eph. 5:19; the desires, Matt. 5:28; 2 Pet. 2:14; the affections, Luke 24:32; Acts 21:13; the perceptions, **John 12:40**; Eph. 4:18; the thoughts, Matt. 9:4; Heb. 4:12; the understanding, Matt. 13:15; Rom. 1:21; the reasoning powers, Mark 2:6; Luke 24:38; the imagination, Luke 1:51; conscience, Acts 2:37; 1 John 3:20; the intentions, Heb. 4:12, cf. 1 Pet. 4:1; purpose, Acts 11:23; 2 Cor. 9:7; the will, Rom. 6:17; Col. 3:15; faith, Mark 11:23; Rom. 10:10; Heb. 3:12. The heart, in its moral significance in the OT, includes the emotions, the reason and the will.

Understand *noeo* (3539), "to perceive with the mind," as distinct from perception by feeling, is so used in Matt. 15:17, KJV, "understand," RV, "perceive"; 16:9, 11; 24:15 (here rather perhaps in the sense of considering) and parallels in Mark (not in Luke); **John 12:40**; Rom. 1:20; 1 Tim. 1:7; Heb. 11:3; in Eph. 3:4, KJV, "may understand" (RV, "can perceive"); 3:20, "think"; 2 Tim. 2:7, "consider."

Converted *strepho* (4762), denotes (1) in the active voice, (a) "to turn" (something), Matt. 5:39; (b) "to bring back," Matt. 27:3; (c) reflexively, "to turn oneself, to turn the back to people," said of God, Acts 7:42; (d) "to turn one thing into another," Rev. 11:6 (the only place where this word occurs after the Acts); (2) in the passive voice, (a) used reflexively, "to turn oneself," e.g. Matt. 7:6; **John 20:14, 16**; (b) metaphorically, Matt. 18:3, RV, "(except) ye turn" (KJV, "... be converted"); **John 12:40**.

Heal *iaomai* (4390), "to heal," is used (a) of physical treatment 22 times; in Matt. 5:28, KJV, "made whole," RV, "healed"; so in Acts 9:34; (b) figuratively, of spiritual "healing," Matt. 13:15; **John 12:40**; Acts 28:27; Heb. 12:13; 1 Pet. 2:24; possibly, Jas. 5:16 includes both (a) and (b); some mss. have the word, with sense (b), in Luke 4:18. Apart from this last, Luke, the physician, uses the word fifteen times.

12:41-42 These things said Esaias, when he saw his glory, and spake of him.

Nevertheless among the chief rulers also many believed on him; but because of the Pharisees they did not confess *him*, lest they should be put out of the synagogue:

Nevertheless *homos* (3676), "yet, nevertheless," is translated "even" in 1 Cor. 14:7 (KJV, "and even"); elsewhere **John 12:42**, "nevertheless"; Gal. 3:15, "yet" (i.e., "nevertheless," an example of hyperbaton, by which a word is placed out of its true position).

Chief *archon* (758), "a ruler," is rendered "chief" in the KJV of Luke 14:1 (RV, "ruler"); "chief rulers," in **John 12:42**, RV, "rulers (of the people)," i.e., of members of the Sanhedrin; "chief," in Luke 11:15 (RV, "prince"), in reference to Beelzebub, the prince of demons.

Rulers *see* Ruler at *John 3:1*.

Confess *see* Confessed at *John 1:20*.

Synagogue *see John 9:22*.

12:43 For they loved the praise of men more than the praise of God.

Praise *see John 9:24*.

12:44 Jesus cried and said, He that believeth on me, believeth not on me, but on him that sent me.

Cried *see John 7:28*.

Sent *see John 1:33*.

12:45 And he that seeth me seeth him that sent me.

Sent *see John 1:33*.

12:46 I am come a light into the world, that whosoever believeth on me should not abide in darkness.

Light *see John 1:4*.

Darkness *see John 1:5*.

12:47-48 And if any man hear my words, and believe not, I judge him not: for I came not to judge the world, but to save the world.

He that rejecteth me, and receiveth not my words, hath one that judgeth him: the word that I have spoken, the same shall judge him in the last day.

Rejecteth *atheteo* (114), properly, "to do away" with what has been laid down, to make *atheton* (i.e., "without place," *a*, negative, *tithemi*, "to place"), hence, besides its meanings "to set aside, make void, nullify, disannul," signifies "to reject"; in Mark 6:26, regarding Herod's pledge to Salome, it almost certainly has the meaning "to break faith with" (cf.

the Sept. of Jer. 12:6, and Lam. 1:2, "dealt treacherously"). Moulton and Milligan illustrate this meaning from the papyri. Field suggests "disappoint." In Mark 7:9 "ye reject (the commandment)" means "ye set aside"; in Luke 7:30, "ye reject" may have the meaning of "nullifying or making void the counsel of God"; in Luke 10:16 (four times), "rejecteth," RV (KJV, "despiseth"); "rejecteth" in **John 12:48**; "reject" in 1 Cor. 1:19 (KJV, "bring to nothing"); 1 Thess. 4:8, "to despise," where the reference is to the charges in v. 2; in 1 Tim. 5:12 RV, "have rejected" (KJV, "have cast off").

And *see John 1:16.*

Receiveth *see* Receive at *John 3:11.*

Judgeth *see* Condemn at *John 3:17.*

Last *see John 6:39.*

12:49 For I have not spoken of myself; but the Father which sent me, he gave me a commandment, what I should say, and what I should speak.

Myself *see* Mine own self at *John 5:30.*

Sent *see John 1:33.*

Say A characteristic of *lego* is that it refers to the purport or sentiment of what is said as well as the connection of the words; this is illustrated in Heb. 8:1, RV, "(in the things which) we are saying," KJV, "(which) we have spoken." In comparison with *laleo, lego* refers especially to the substance of what is "said," *laleo,* to the words conveying the utterance; see, e.g., **John 12:49**, "what I should say (*lego*, in the 2nd aorist subjunctive form *eipo*), and what I should speak (laleo)"; v. **50**, "even as the Father hath said (*lego*, in the perfect form *eireke*) unto Me, so I speak" (*laleo*); cf. 1 Cor. 14:34, "saith (*lego*) the law"; v. 35, "to speak" (*laleo*). Sometimes *laleo* signifies the utterance, as opposed to silence, *lego* declares what is "said"; e.g., Rom. 3:19, "what things soever the law saith (*lego*), it speaketh (*laleo*) to them that are under the law"; see also Mark 6:50; Luke 24:6. In the NT *laleo* never has the meaning "to chatter."

12:50 And I know that his commandment is life everlasting: whatsoever I speak therefore, even as the Father said unto me, so I speak.

Said *eiro* (3004), an obsolete verb, has the future tense *ereo*, used, e.g., in Matt. 7:4; Luke 4:23 (2nd part); 13:25 (last part); Rom. 3:5; 4:1; 6:1; 7:7 (1st part); 8:31; 9:14, 19, 20, 30; 11:19; 1 Cor. 15:35; 2 Cor. 12:6; Jas. 2:18. The perfect is used, e.g., in **John 12:50**. *See also* Say at *John 12:49.*

Chapter 13

13:1 Now before the feast of the passover, when Jesus knew that his hour was come that he should depart out of this world unto the Father, having loved his own which were in the world, he loved them unto the end.

Passover *see John 2:13.*

Depart *see John 7:3.*

End *telos* (5056), signifies (a) "the limit," either at which a person or thing ceases to be what he or it was up to that point, or at which previous activities were ceased, 2 Cor. 3:13; 1 Pet. 4:7; (b) "the final issue or result" of a state or process, e.g., Luke 1:33; in Rom. 10:4, Christ is described as "the end of the Law unto righteousness to everyone that believeth"; this is best explained by Gal. 3:23-26; cf. Jas. 5:11; the following more especially point to the issue or fate of a thing, Matt. 26:58; Rom. 6:21; 2 Cor. 11:15; Phil. 3:19; Heb. 6:8; 1 Pet. 1:9; (c) "a fulfillment," Luke 22:37, KJV, "(have) an end"; (d) "the utmost degree" of an act, as of the love of Christ towards His disciples, **John 13:1**; (e) "the aim or purpose" of a thing, 1 Tim. 1:5; (f) "the last" in a succession or series Rev. 1:8 (KJV, only, "ending"); 21:6; 22:13.

13:2 And supper being ended, the devil having now put into the heart of Judas Iscariot, Simon's *son*, to betray him;

Supper *deipnon* (1173), denotes "a supper" or "feast." In **John 13:2** the RV, following certain texts, has "during supper" (KJV, "supper being ended").

Ended In **John 13:2**, the verb *ginomai*, there signifying "to be in progress," and used in the present participle, is translated "during supper" (RV). A less authentic reading, is *genomenou*, "being ended" (KJV).

Devil *see John 6:70.*

Put *see John 5:7.*

13:3-4 Jesus knowing that the Father had given all things into his hands, and that he was come from God, and went to God;
He riseth from supper, and laid aside his garments; and took a towel, and girded himself.

Supper *see John 12:2.*

Laid *see* Lay at *John 10:17.*

Towel *lention* (3012), denotes "a linen cloth or towel" (Lat., *linteum*), as used by the Lord, **John 13:4, 5**; it was commonly used by servants in a household.

Girded *diazonnumi* (1241), "to gird round," i.e., firmly (*dia*, "throughout," used intensively), is used of the Lord's act in "girding" Himself with a towel, **John 13:4**, **5**, and of Peter's girding himself with his coat, **21:7**.

13:5 After that he poureth water into a bason, and began to wash the disciples' feet, and to wipe *them* with the towel wherewith he was girded.

After that *eita* (1534), denotes sequence (a) "of time, then, next," Mark 4:17, RV, "then"; 4:28, in some texts; 8:25, RV, "then" (KJV, "after that"); Luke 8:12; **John 13:5**; **19:27**; **20:27**; in some texts in 1 Cor. 12:28; 1 Cor. 15:5, 7, 24; 1 Tim. 2:13; 3:10; Jas. 1:15; (b) in argument, Heb. 12:9, "furthermore."

Poureth *ballo* (906), "to throw," is used of "pouring" liquids, Matt. 26:12, RV, marg., "cast" (of ointment); **John 13:5** (of water).

Bason *nipter* (3537), the vessel into which the Lord poured water to wash the disciples' feet, was "a large ewer," **John 13:5**. The word is connected with the verb *nipto*, "to wash."

Wash *see* **Wash, Washed** at ***John 9:7***.

Feet *pous* (4228), besides its literal meaning, is used, by metonymy, of "a person in motion," Luke 1:79; Acts 5:9; Rom. 3:15; 10:15; Heb. 12:13. It is used in phrases expressing subjection, 1 Cor. 15:27, RV; of the humility and receptivity of discipleship, Luke 10:39; Acts 22:3; of obeisance and worship, e.g., Matt. 28:9; of scornful rejection, Matt. 10:14; Acts 13:51. Washing the "feet" of another betokened the humility of the service and the comfort of the guest, and was a feature of hospitality, Luke 7:38; **John 13:5**; 1 Tim. 5:10 (here figuratively).

Wipe *see* **Wiped** at ***John 11:2***.

Towel *see* ***John 13:4***.

Girded *see* ***John 13:4***.

13:6-7 Then cometh he to Simon Peter: and Peter saith unto him, Lord, dost thou wash my feet?

Jesus answered and said unto him, What I do thou knowest not now; but thou shalt know hereafter.

Knowest, Know *see* **Knew** at ***John 6:6***.

Hereafter This adverb translates the phrase *meta tauta*, lit., "after these things," **John 13:7**; Rev. 1:19, and frequently in Revelation, see 4:1 (twice); 7:9; 9:12; 15:5; 18:1; 19:1; 20:3.

13:8 Peter saith unto him, Thou shalt never wash my feet. Jesus answered him, If I wash thee not, thou hast no part with me.

Never *see* ***John 4:14***.

Wash *see* **Wash, Washed** at **John *9:7***.

Part *meros* (3313), denotes (a) "a part, portion," of the whole, e.g., **John 13:8**; Rev. 20:6; 22:19; hence, "a lot" or "destiny," e.g., Rev. 21:8; in Matt. 24:51 and Luke 12:46, "portion"; (b) "a part" as opposite to the whole, e.g., Luke 11:36; **John 19:23**; **21:6**, "side"; Acts 5:2; 23:6; Eph. 4:16; Rev. 16:19; a party, Acts 23:9; the divisions of a province, e.g., Matt. 2:22; Acts 2:10; the regions belonging to a city, e.g., Matt. 15:21, RV, "parts" (KJV, "coasts"); 16:13 (ditto); Mark 8:10, KJV and RV, "parts"; "the lower parts of the earth," Eph. 4:9; this phrase means the regions beneath the earth; (c) "a class," or "category" (with *en*, in, "in respect of"), Col. 2:16; "in this respect," 2 Cor. 3:10; 9:3, RV (KJV, "in this behalf").

13:9 Simon Peter saith unto him, Lord, not my feet only, but also *my* hands and *my* head.

Only *see* ***John 5:18***.

13:10 Jesus saith to him, He that is washed needeth not save to wash *his* feet, but is clean every whit: and ye are clean, but not all.

Washed, Wash *louo* (3068), signifies "to bathe, to wash the body," (a) active voice, Acts 9:37; 16:33; (b) passive voice, **John 13:10**, RV, "bathed" (KJV, "washed"); Heb. 10:22, lit., "having been washed as to the body," metaphorical of the effect of the Word of God upon the activities of the believer; (c) middle voice, 2 Pet. 2:22. Some inferior mss. have it instead of *luo*, "to loose," in Rev. 1:5 (see RV). *See also* **Wash, Washed** at ***John 9:7***.

Needeth *see* **Needed** at ***John 2:25***.

Clean *katharos* (2513), "free from impure admixture, without blemish, spotless," is used (a) physically, e.g., Matt. 23:26; 27:59; **John 13:10** (where the Lord, speaking figuratively, teaches that one who has been entirely "cleansed," needs not radical renewal, but only to be "cleansed" from every sin into which he may fall); **15:3**; Heb. 10:22; Rev. 15:6; 19:8, 14; 21:18, 21; (b) in a Levitical sense, Rom. 14:20; Titus 1:15, "pure"; (c) ethically, with the significance free from corrupt desire, from guilt, Matt. 5:8; **John 13:10-11**; Acts 20:26; 1 Tim. 1:5; 3:9; 2 Tim. 1:3; 2:22; Titus 1:15; Jas. 1:27; blameless, innocent (a rare meaning for this word), Acts 18:6; (d) in a combined Levitical and ethical sense ceremonially, Luke 11:41, "all things are clean unto you."

Every whit *see* ***John 7:23***.

13:11 For he knew who should betray him; therefore said he, Ye are not all clean.

Knew *see John 6:6.*

13:12 So after he had washed their feet, and had taken his garments, and was set down again, he said unto them, Know ye what I have done to you?

Washed *see* Wash, Washed at *John 9:7.*

Set In **John 13:12**, KJV, *anapipto*, "to recline at table," is translated "was set down" (RV, "sat down"; marg., "reclined"). *See also* Sit, Sat at *John 6:10.*

Know *see John 7:26.*

13:13 Ye call me Master and Lord: and ye say well; for *so* I am.

Call *see* Calleth at *John 10:3.*

Master *see John 1:38.*

Lord *see John 4:1.*

13:14 If I then, *your* Lord and Master, have washed your feet; ye also ought to wash one another's feet.

Washed, Wash *see* Wash, Washed at John *9:7.*

Ought *opheilo* (3784), "to owe," is translated "ought," with various personal pronouns, in **John 13:14; 19:7**; Acts 17:29; Rom. 15:1; Heb. 5:3, KJV (RV, "he is bound"); 5:12; 1 John 3:16; 4:11; 3 John 8; with other subjects in 1 Cor. 11:7, 10; 2 Cor. 12:14; Eph. 5:28; 1 John 2:6.

13:15 For I have given you an example, that ye should do as I have done to you.

Example *hupodeigma* (5262), lit., "that which is shown" (from *hupo*, "under," and *deiknumi*, "to show"), hence, (a) "a figure, copy," Heb. 8:5, RV, "copy," for KJV, "example"; 9:23; (b) "an example," whether for imitation, **John 13:15**; Jas. 5:10, or for warning, Heb. 4:11; 2 Pet. 2:6, RV, example. *See also* Sanctify at *John 17:17.*

13:16 Verily, verily, I say unto you, The servant is not greater than his lord; neither he that is sent greater than he that sent him.

Sent In **John 13:16** *apostolos* is rendered "one (KJV, he) that is sent," RV marg., "an apostle."

13:17 If ye know these things, happy are ye if ye do them.

Happy *makarios* (3107), "blessed, happy," is rendered "happy" in the RV, in two places only, as in the KJV, Acts 26:2 and Rom. 14:22 (where "blessed" would have done); also the comparative "happier" in 1 Cor. 7:40. Elsewhere the RV uses "blessed" for KJV "happy," e.g., **John 13:17**; 1 Pet. 3:14; 4:14.

13:18 I speak not of you all: I know whom I have chosen: but that the scripture may be fulfilled, He that eateth bread with me hath lifted up his heel against me.

Chosen *see John 6:70.*

Eateth *see* Eat at *John 6:49.*

Lifted *see* Lift at *John 4:35.*

Heel *pterna* (4418), is found in **John 13:18**, where the Lord quotes from Ps. 41:9; the metaphor is that of tripping up an antagonist in wrestling. Cf. the verb in Gen. 27:36; Jer. 9:4; Hos. 12:3.

13:19 Now I tell you before it come, that, when it is come to pass, ye may believe that I am *he*.

Now *aparti* (534), sometimes written separately, *ap'arti*, denotes "from now, henceforth," **John 13:19; 14:7**; Rev. 14:13.

Come to pass *ginomai*, "to become, take place," is often translated "to come to pass"; frequently in the Synoptic Gospels and Acts; elsewhere in **John 13:19; 14:22**, RV, "(what) is come to pass ...?" KJV, "(how) is it ...?"; **14:29** (twice); 1 Thess. 3:4; Rev. 1:1.

13:20 Verily, verily, I say unto you, He that receiveth whomsoever I send receiveth me; and he that receiveth me receiveth him that sent me.

Receiveth *see* Receive at *John 3:11.*

Sent *see John 1:33.*

13:21 When Jesus had thus said, he was troubled in spirit, and testified, and said, Verily, verily, I say unto you, that one of you shall betray me.

Thus *see John 9:6.*

Spirit *see* Us at *John 10:24.*

Testified *see* Testify at *John 2:25.*

13:22 Then the disciples looked one on another, doubting of whom he spake.

Looked *blepo* (991), primarily, "to have sight, to see," then, "observe, discern, perceive," frequently implying special contemplation, is rendered by the verb "to look" in Luke 9:62, "looking (back)"; **John 13:22** "(the disciples) looked (one on another)"; Acts 1:9, RV, "were looking" (KJV, "beheld"); 3:4, "look (on us)"; 27:12, RV, "looking," KJV, "that lieth (towards)," of the haven Phenix; Eph. 5:15, RV, "look (therefore carefully how ye walk)," KJV, "see (that ye walk circumspectly)"; Rev. 11:9 and 18:9, RV, "look upon" (KJV, "shall see").

One another This translates a number of words and phrases, (a) *allelon*, a reciprocal pronoun in the genitive plural, signifying "of, or from, one another" (akin to *allos*, "another"), e.g., Matt. 25:32; **John 13:22**; Acts 15:39; 19:38; 1 Cor. 7:5; Gal. 5:17; the accusative *allelous* denotes "one another," e.g., Acts 7:26, lit., "why do ye wrong one another?"; 2 Thess. 1:3, RV; in Eph. 4:32 and Col. 3:13, e.g., RV, "each other"; in 1 Thess. 5:15, "one (toward) another," RV; the dative *allelois* denotes "one to another," e.g., Luke 7:32; (b) different forms of the plural of *heautou*, "of himself," used as a reciprocal pronoun, e.g., Eph. 5:19, RV, "one to another" (KJV, and RV marg., "to yourselves").

Doubting *aporeo* (639), always used in the middle voice, lit. means "to be without a way" (*a*, negative, *poros*, "a way, transit"), "to be without resources, embarrassed, in doubt, perplexity, at a loss," as was Herod regarding John the Baptist, Mark 6:20 (RV, following the most authentic mss., "was much perplexed"); as the disciples were, regarding the Lord's betrayal, **John 13:22**, "doubting"; and regarding the absence of His body from the tomb, Luke 24:4, "were perplexed"; as was Festus, about the nature of the accusations brought against Paul, Acts 25:20, KJV "doubted," RV, "being perplexed"; as Paul was, in his experiences of trial, 2 Cor. 4:8, "perplexed," and, as to the attitude of the believers of the churches in Galatia towards Judaistic errors, Gal. 4:20, KJV, "I stand in doubt," RV, "I am perplexed." Perplexity is the main idea. Cf. the noun *aporia*, "distress," Luke 21:25.

13:23 Now there was leaning on Jesus' bosom one of his disciples, whom Jesus loved.

Leaning *anakeimai* (345), lit., and in classical usage, "to be laid up, to lie," is used of reclining at table, and translated "leaning (on Jesus' bosom)" in the KJV of **John 13:23**, RV, "reclining." In v. **28**, it is translated "at the table," lit., "of (those) reclining."

Bosom *see John 1:18*.

Loved *see* **Loveth** at *John 3:35*.

13:24 Simon Peter therefore beckoned to him, that he should ask who it should be of whom he spake.

Beckoned *neuo* (3506), lit., "to give a nod, to signify by a nod," is used in **John 13:24**, of Peter's beckoning to John to ask the Lord of whom He had been speaking; in Acts 24:10, of the intimation given by Felix to Paul to speak.

13:25 He then lying on Jesus' breast saith unto him, Lord, who is it?

Lying *anapipto* (377), lit., "to fall back" (*ana*, "back," *pipto*, "to fall"), is used of reclining at a repast and translated "leaning back, (as he was, on Jesus' breast)" in **John 13:25**, RV (the KJV follows the mss. which have *epipipto*, and renders it "lying"); in **21:20**, "leaned back," the apostle's reminder of the same event in his experience.

Breast *stethos* (4738), connected with *histemi*, "to stand," i.e., that which stands out, is used of mourners in smiting the "breast," Luke 18:13; 23:48; of John in reclining on the "breast" of Christ, **John 13:25**; **21:20**; of the "breasts" of the angels in Rev. 15:6.

13:26 Jesus answered, He it is, to whom I shall give a sop, when I have dipped *it*. And when he had dipped the sop, he gave *it* to Judas Iscariot, *the son* of Simon.

Sop *psomion* (5596), a diminutive of *psomos*, "a morsel," denotes "a fragment, a sop," **John 13:26** (twice), **27**, **30**. It had no connection with the modern meaning of "sop," something given to pacify (as in the classical expression "a sop to Cerberus").

Dipped *bapto* (911), "to immerse, dip" (derived from a root signifying "deep"), also signified "to dye," which is suggested in Rev. 19:13, of the Lord's garment "dipped (i.e. dyed) in blood" (RV, "sprinkled" translates the verb *rhantizo*. It is elsewhere translated "to dip," Luke 16:24; **John 13:26**. Cf the longer form *baptizo* (primarily a frequentative form).

13:27 And after the sop Satan entered into him. Then said Jesus unto him, That thou doest, do quickly.

Sop *see John 13:26*.

Satan *satanas* (4567), a Greek form derived from the Aramaic (Heb., *Satan*), "an adversary," is used (a) of an angel of Jehovah in Num. 22:22 (the first occurrence of the Word in the OT); (b) of men, e.g., 1 Sam. 29:4; Ps. 38:20; 71:13; four in Ps. 109; (c) of "Satan," the Devil, some seventeen or eighteen times in the OT; in Zech. 3:1, where the name receives its interpretation, "to be (his) adversary," RV (see marg.; KJV, "to resist him"). In the NT the word is always used of "Satan," the adversary (a) of God and Christ, e.g., Matt. 4:10; 12:26; Mark 1:13; 3:23, 26; 4:15; Luke 4:8 (in some mss.); 11:18; 22:3; **John 13:27**; (b) of His people, e.g., Luke 22:31; Acts 5:3; Rom. 16:20; 1 Cor. 5:5; 7:5; 2 Cor. 2:11; 11:14; 12:7; 1 Thess. 2:18; 1 Tim. 1:20; 5:15; Rev. 2:9, 13 (twice), 24; 3:9; (c) of mankind, Luke 13:16; Acts 26:18; 2 Thess. 2:9; Rev. 12:9; 20:7. His doom, sealed at the

Cross, is foretold in its stages in Luke 10:18; Rev. 20:2, 10. Believers are assured of victory over him, Rom. 16:20. The appellation was given by the Lord to Peter, as a "Satan-like" man, on the occasion when he endeavored to dissuade Him from death, Matt. 16:23; Mark 8:33.

"Satan" is not simply the personification of evil influences in the heart, for he tempted Christ, in whose heart no evil thought could ever have arisen (**John 14:30**; 2 Cor. 5:21; Heb. 4:15); moreover his personality is asserted in both the OT and the NT, and especially in the latter, whereas if the OT language was intended to be figurative, the NT would have made this evident.

Quickly *tacheion* (5032), is translated "quickly" in **John 13:27**; "out(ran)" in **20:4**, RV, lit., "(ran before) more quickly (than Peter)"; "shortly" in 1 Tim. 3:14 and Heb. 13:23; in 13:19, "(the) sooner."

13:28 Now no man at the table knew for what intent he spake this unto him.

At the table *see* Leaning at John *13:23*.

Intent The phrase *pros ti*, lit., "in reference to what," is rendered "for what intent" in **John 13:28**.

13:29 For some *of them* thought, because Judas had the bag, that Jesus had said unto him, Buy *those things* that we have need of against the feast; or, that he should give something to the poor.

Some The indefinite pronoun *tis* in its singular or plural forms, frequently means "some," "some one" (translated "some man," in the KJV, e.g., of Acts 8:31; 1 Cor. 15:35), or "somebody," Luke 8:46; the neuter plural denotes "some things" in 2 Pet. 3:16; the singular denotes "something," e.g., Luke 11:54; **John 13:29** (2nd part); Acts 3:5; 23:18; Gal. 6:3, where the meaning is "anything," as in 2:6, "somewhat." It is translated "somewhat," in the more indefinite sense, in Luke 7:40; Acts 23:20; 25:26; 2 Cor. 10:8; Heb. 8:3.

Bag *see John 12:6*.

Poor *see John 12:5*.

13:30 He then having received the sop went immediately out: and it was night.

Received *see* Receive at *John 3:11*.

Sop *see John 13:26*.

13:31 Therefore, when he was gone out, Jesus said, Now is the Son of man glorified, and God is glorified in him.

Son *see John 1:18*.

Glorified *see John 7:39*.

13:32 If God be glorified in him, God shall also glorify him in himself, and shall straightway glorify him.

Glorified, Glorify *see* Glorified at *John 7:39*.

13:33 Little children, yet a little while I am with you. Ye shall seek me: and as I said unto the Jews, Whither I go, ye cannot come; so now I say to you.

Children *teknion* (5040), "a little child," is used only figuratively in the NT, and always in the plural. It is found frequently in 1 John, see 2:1, 12, 28; 3:7, 18; 4:4; 5:21; elsewhere, once in John's Gospel, **13:33**, once in Paul's epistles, Gal. 4:19. It is a term of affection by a teacher to his disciples under circumstances requiring a tender appeal, e.g., of Christ to the Twelve just before His death; the apostle John used it in warning believers against spiritual dangers; Paul, because of the deadly errors of Judaism assailing the Galatian churches. Cf. his use of *teknon* in Gal. 4:28.

Little *mikron* (3397), is used adverbially (a) of distance, Matt. 26:39; Mark 14:35; (b) of quantity, 2 Cor. 11:1, 16; (c) of time, Matt. 26:73, "a while"; Mark 14:70; **John 13:33**, "a little while", **14:19**; **16:16-19**; Heb. 10:37, with the repeated *hoson*, "how very," lit., "a little while, how little, how little."

And *see* Also at *John 7:3*.

Now *see John 2:10*.

13:34 A new commandment I give unto you, That ye love one another; as I have loved you, that ye also love one another.

New *kainos* (2537), denotes "new," of that which is unaccustomed or unused, not "new" in time, recent, but "new" as to form or quality, of different nature from what is contrasted as old. "'The new tongues,' kainos, of Mark 16:17 are the 'other tongues,' heteros, of Acts 2:4. These languages, however, were 'new' and 'different,' not in the sense that they had never been heard before, or that they were new to the hearers, for it is plain from v. 8 that this is not the case; they were new languages to the speakers, different from those in which they were accustomed to speak. The new things that the Gospel brings for present obedience and realization are: a new covenant, Matt. 26:28 in some texts; a new commandment, **John 13:34**; a new creative act, Gal. 6:15; a new creation, 2 Cor. 5:17; a new man, i.e., a new character of manhood, spiritual and moral, after the pattern of Christ, Eph. 4:24; a new man, i.e., 'the Church which is His

(Christ's) body,' Eph. 2:15. The new things that are to be received and enjoyed hereafter are: a new name, the believer's, Rev. 2:17; a new name, the Lord's, Rev. 3:12; a new song, Rev. 5:9; a new Heaven and a new Earth, Rev. 21:1; the new Jerusalem, Rev. 3:12; 21:2; 'And He that sitteth on the Throne said, Behold, I make all things new,' Rev. 21:5."

Love, Loved *see* Loved at John *3:16*.

13:35 By this shall all *men* know that ye are my disciples, if ye have love one to another.

My *see John 4:34*.

Disciples *see John 6:66*.

13:36 Simon Peter said unto him, Lord, whither goest thou? Jesus answered him, Whither I go, thou canst not follow me now; but thou shalt follow me afterwards.

Afterwards *husteron* (5305), "afterwards," with the suggestion of at length, is found in Matt. 4:2; 21:29, 32, 37 (KJV, "last of all"); 22:27; 25:11; 26:60 (KJV, "at the last"), Mark 16:14; Luke 4:2; 20:32 (KJV, "last"), **John 13:36**; Heb. 12:11.

13:37 Peter said unto him, Lord, why cannot I follow thee now? I will lay down my life for thy sake.

Now *see John 2:10*.

Lay *see John 10:17*.

13:38 Jesus answered him, Wilt thou lay down thy life for my sake? Verily, verily, I say unto thee, The cock shall not crow, till thou hast denied me thrice.

Lay *see John 10:17*.

Cock *alektor* (220), "a cock," perhaps connected with a Hebrew phrase for the oncoming of the light, is found in the passages concerning Peter's denial of the Lord, Matt. 26:34, 74-75; Mark 14:30, 68, 72; Luke 22:34, 60-61; **John 13:38**; **18:27**.

Denied *aparneomai* (533), a strengthened form of *arneomai*, with *apo*, "from," prefixed (Lat., *abnego*), means (a) "to deny utterly," to abjure, to affirm that one has no connection with a person, as in Peter's denial of Christ, Matt. 26:34-35, 75; Mark 14:30-31, 72; Luke 22:34, 61 (some mss. have it in **John 13:38**). This stronger form is used in the Lord's statements foretelling Peter's "denial," and in Peter's assurance of fidelity; the simple verb (*arneomai*) is used in all the records of his actual denial. The strengthened form is the verb used in the Lord's warning as to being "denied" in the presence of the angels, Luke 12:9; in the preceding clause, "he that denieth Me," the simple verb *arneomai* is used; the rendering therefore should be "he that denieth Me in the presence of men, shall be utterly denied in the presence of the angels of God"; (b) "to deny oneself" as a follower of Christ, Matt. 16:24; Mark 8:34; Luke 9:23. *See also John 1:20*.

Chapter 14

14:1 Let not your heart be troubled: ye believe in God, believe also in me.

Heart *see John 12:40*.

Troubled *see* Troubled at *John 5:4*.

Also *see John 7:3*.

14:2 In my Father's house are many mansions: if *it were* not *so*, I would have told you. I go to prepare a place for you.

House *see John 4:53*.

Mansions *mone* (3438), primarily "a staying abiding" (akin to *meno*, "to abide"), denotes an "abode" (Eng., "manor," "manse," etc.), translated "mansions" in **John 14:2**; "abode" in v. **23**. There is nothing in the word to indicate separate compartments in heaven; neither does it suggest temporary resting places on the road.

Prepare *hetoimazo* (2090), "to prepare, make ready," is used (I) absolutely, e.g., Mark 14:15; Luke 9:52; (II) with an object, e.g., (a) of those things which are ordained (1) by God, such as future positions of authority, Matt. 20:23; the coming Kingdom, 25:34; salvation personified in Christ, Luke 2:31; future blessings, 1 Cor. 2:9; a city, Heb. 11:16; a place of refuge for the Jewish remnant, Rev. 12:6; Divine judgments on the world, Rev. 8:6; 9:7, 15; 16:12; eternal fire, for the Devil and his angels, Matt. 25:41; (2) by Christ: a place in Heaven for His followers, **John 14:2**, **3**; (b) of human "preparation" for the Lord, e.g., Matt. 3:3; 26:17, 19; Luke 1:17 ("make ready"), 76; 3:4, KJV (RV, "make ye ready"); 9:52 ("to make ready"); 23:56; Rev. 19:7; 21:2; in 2 Tim. 2:21, of "preparation" of oneself for "every good work"; (c) of human "preparations" for human objects, e.g., Luke 12:20, RV, "thou hast prepared" (KJV, "provided"); Acts 23:23; Philem. 22.

14:3 And if I go and prepare a place for you, I will come again, and receive you unto myself; that where I am, *there* ye may be also.

Prepare *see John 14:2*.

Receive *see* Received at *John 1:11*.

Myself *see* Mine own self at John *5:30*.

May The phrases "may be," "might be," are frequently the rendering of the verb "to be," in the subjunctive or optative moods, preceded by a conjunction introducing a condition, or expressing a wish or purpose, e.g., Matt. 6:4; **John 14:3; 17:11**. Sometimes the phrase translates simply the infinitive mood of the verb *eimi*, "to be," e.g., Luke 8:38, lit., "to be (with Him)"; so the RV in 2 Cor. 5:9; in 2 Cor. 9:5, "that (the same) might be," lit., "(the same) to be."

Also *see John 7:3.*

14:4-6 And whither I go ye know, and the way ye know.

Thomas saith unto him, Lord, we know not whither thou goest; and how can we know the way?

Jesus saith unto him, I am the way, the truth, and the life: no man cometh unto the Father, but by me.

Way *hodos* (3598), denotes (a) "a natural path, road, way," frequent in the Synoptic Gospels; elsewhere, e.g., Acts 8:26; 1 Thess. 3:11; Jas. 2:25; Rev. 16:12; (b) "a traveler's way"; (c) metaphorically, of "a course of conduct," or "way of thinking," e.g., of righteousness, Matt. 21:32; 2 Pet. 2:21; of God, Matt. 22:16, and parallels, i.e., the "way" instructed and approved by God; so Acts 18:26 and Heb. 3:10, "My ways" (cf. Rev. 15:3); of the Lord, Acts 18:25; "that leadeth to destruction," Matt. 7:13; "... unto life," 7:14; of peace, Luke 1:79; Rom. 3:17; of Paul's "ways" in Christ, 1 Cor. 4:17 (plural); "more excellent" (of love), 1 Cor. 12:31; of truth, 2 Pet. 2:2; of the right "way," 2:15; of Balaam (*id.*), of Cain, Jude 11; of a "way" consisting in what is from God, e.g., of life, Acts 2:28 (plural); of salvation, Acts 16:17; personified, of Christ as the means of access to the Father, **John 14:6**; of the course followed and characterized by the followers of Christ, Acts 9:2; 19:9, 23; 24:22.

Truth *see John 8:44.*

14:7 If ye had known me, ye should have known my Father also: and from henceforth ye know him, and have seen him.

Known *see* Knew at *John 6:6.*

Also *see John 7:3.*

Henceforth *see* Now at *John 13:19.*

14:8 Philip saith unto him, Lord, shew us the Father, and it sufficeth us.

Shew *see* Sheweth, Shew at *John 5:20.*

Sufficeth *see* Sufficient at *John 6:7.*

14:9 Jesus saith unto him, Have I been so long time with you, and yet hast thou not known me, Philip? he that hath seen me hath seen the Father; and how sayest thou *then*, Shew us the Father?

Long *tosoutos* (5118), "so long," is used with *chronos* in John 14:9 and Heb. 4:7.

Shew *see* Sheweth, Shew at *John 5:20.*

14:10 Believest thou not that I am in the Father, and the Father in me? the words that I speak unto you I speak not of myself: but the Father that dwelleth in me, he doeth the works.

Of *see John 7:17.*

Myself *see* Mine own self at *John 5:30.*

Dwelleth *see* Dwellest at *John 1:17.*

Works *see John 4:34* Work.

"Fear imprisons, faith liberates; fear paralyzes, faith empowers; fear disheartens, faith encourages; fear sickens, faith heals; fear makes useless, faith makes serviceable – and, most of all, fear puts hopelessness at the heart of life, while faith rejoices in its God."

HARRY EMERSON FOSDICK

14:11 Believe me that I *am* in the Father, and the Father in me: or else believe me for the very works' sake.

Very Occasionally one of the forms of the pronoun *autos*, "self, same," is translated "very"; the RV rendering is sometimes "himself," etc., e.g., 1 Thess. 5:23, "(The God of peace) Himself"; see, however, **John 14:11**, "(the) very (works)"; Rom. 13:6 and Phil. 1:6, "(this) very (thing)"; Heb. 10:1, "(the) very (image)"; and the RV, "very" (KJV, "same") in Luke 12:12; 20:19; 24:13, 33; Acts 16:18; Rom. 9:17; Eph. 6:22.

14:12 Verily, verily, I say unto you, He that believeth on me,

the works that I do shall he do also; and greater *works* than these shall he do; because I go unto my Father.

Greater *see John 1:50.*

14:13 And whatsoever ye shall ask in my name, that will I do, that the Father may be glorified in the Son.

Name *see John 1:12.*

Glorified *see John 7:39.*

14:14 If ye shall ask any thing in my name, I will do *it*.

Ask *see* Asked at *John 9:15.*

14:15 If ye love me, keep my commandments.

Love *see* Loved at *John 3:16.*

Keep *tereo* (5083), denotes (a) "to watch over, preserve, keep, watch," e.g., Acts 12:5, 6; 16:23; in 25:21, RV (1st part), "kept" (KJV, "reserved"); the present participle is translated "keepers" in Matt. 28:4, lit., "the keeping (ones)"; it is used of the "keeping" power of God the Father and Christ, exercised over His people, **John 17:11, 12, 15**; 1 Thess. 5:23, "preserved"; 1 John 5:18, where "He that was begotten of God," RV, is said of Christ as the Keeper ("keepeth him," RV, for KJV, "keepeth himself"); Jude 1, RV, "kept for Jesus Christ" (KJV, "preserved in Jesus Christ"), Rev. 3:10; of their inheritance, 1 Pet. 1:4 ("reserved"); of judicial reservation by God in view of future doom, 2 Pet. 2:4, 9, 17; 3:7; Jude 6, 13; of "keeping" the faith, 2 Tim. 4:7; the unity of the Spirit, Eph. 4:3; oneself, 2 Cor. 11:9; 1 Tim. 5:22; Jas. 1:27; figuratively, one's garments, Rev. 16:15; (b) "to observe, to give heed to," as of keeping commandments, etc., e.g., Matt. 19:17; **John 14:15; 15:10; 17:6**; Jas. 2:10; 1 John 2:3, 4, 5; 3:22, 24; 5:2 (in some mss.), 3; Rev. 1:3; 2:26; 3:8, 10; 12:17; 14:12; 22:7, 9.

14:16 And I will pray the Father, and he shall give you another Comforter, that he may abide with you for ever;

Pray "Prayer is properly addressed to God the Father Matt. 6:6; **John 16:23**; Eph. 1:17; 3:14, and the Son, Acts 7:59; 2 Cor. 12:8; but in no instance in the NT is prayer addressed to the Holy Spirit distinctively, for whereas the Father is in Heaven, Matt. 6:9, and the Son is at His right hand, Rom. 8:34, the Holy Spirit is in and with the believers, **John 14:16, 17**. Prayer is to be offered in the Name of the Lord Jesus, **John 14:13**, that is, the prayer must accord with His character, and must be presented in the same spirit of dependence and submission that marked Him, Matt. 11:26; Luke 22:42. The Holy Spirit, being the sole interpreter of the needs of the human heart, makes His intercession therein; and inasmuch as prayer is impossible to man apart from His help, Rom. 8:26, believers are exhorted to pray at all seasons in the Spirit, Eph. 6:18; cf. Jude 20, and Jas. 5:16, the last clause of which should probably be read 'the inwrought [i.e., by the Holy Spirit] supplication of righteous man availeth much' (or 'greatly prevails' *ischuo*, as in Acts 19:16, 20). None the less on this account is the understanding to be engaged in prayer, 1 Cor. 14:15, and the will, Col. 4:12; Acts 12:5 (where 'earnestly' is, lit., 'stretched out') and so in Luke 22:44. Faith is essential to prayer, Matt. 21:22; Mark 11:24; Jas. 1:5-8, for faith is the recognition of, and the committal of ourselves and our matters to, the faithfulness of God. Where the Jews were numerous, as at Thessalonica, they had usually a Synagogue, Acts 17:1; where they were few, as at Philippi, they had merely a *proseuche*, or 'place of prayer,' of much smaller dimensions, and commonly built by a river for the sake of the water necessary to the preliminary ablutions prescribed by Rabbinic tradition, Acts 16:13, 16." *See also* **Prayed** at ***John 4:31***.

> *"The surest evidence of our love to Christ is obedience to the laws of Christ. Love is the root, obedience is the fruit."*
>
> MATTHEW HENRY

Another *allos* (243), and *heteros* (2087) have a difference in meaning, which despite a tendency to be lost, is to be observed in numerous passages. *Allos* expresses a numerical difference and denotes "another of the same sort"; *heteros* expresses a qualitative difference and denotes "another of a different sort." Christ promised to send "another Comforter" (*allos*, "another like Himself," not *heteros*), **John 14:16**. Paul says "I see a different (KJV, "another") law," *heteros*, a law different from that of the spirit of life (not *allos*, "a law of the same sort"), Rom. 7:23. After Joseph's death "another king arose," *heteros*, one of quite a different character, Acts 7:18. Paul speaks of "a different gospel (*heteros*), which is not another" (*allos*, another like the one he preached), Gal. 1:6-7. See *heteros* (not *allos*) in Matt. 11:3, and Acts 27:1; in Luke 23:32*heteroi* is used of the two malefactors crucified with Christ. The two words are only apparently interchanged in 1 Cor. 1:16 and 6:1; 12:8-10; 14:17 and 19, e.g., the difference being present, though not so readily discernible. They are not interchangeable in 1 Cor. 15:39-41; here *heteros* is used to distinguish the heavenly glory from the earthly, for these differ in genus, and *allos* to distinguish the flesh of men, birds, and fishes, which in each case is flesh differing not in genus but in species. *Allos* is used again to distinguish between the glories of the heavenly bodies, for these also differ not in kind but in degree only.

Comforter *parakletos* (3875), lit., "called to one's side," i.e., to one's aid, is primarily a verbal adjective, and suggests the capability or adaptability for giving aid. It was used in a court of justice to denote a legal assistant, counsel for the defense, an advocate; then, generally, one who pleads another's cause, an intercessor, advocate, as in 1 John 2:1, of the Lord Jesus. In the widest sense, it signifies a "succorer, comforter." Christ was this to His disciples, by the implication of His word "another (*allos*, "another of the same sort," not *heteros*, "different") Comforter," when speaking of the Holy Spirit, **John 14:16**. In **14:26**; **15:26**; **16:7** He calls Him "the Comforter." "Comforter" or "Consoler" corresponds to the name "*Menahem*," given by the Hebrews to the Messiah.

14:17 *Even* the Spirit of truth; whom the world cannot receive, because it seeth him not, neither knoweth him: but ye know him; for he dwelleth with you, and shall be in you.

Spirit *see* Spirit, Holy Ghost at *John 7:39*.

Seeth *theoreo* (2334), denotes "to be a spectator of," indicating the careful perusal of details in the object; it points especially to the action of the person beholding, e.g., Matt. 28:1; the RV frequently renders it by "to behold," for the KJV, "to see," e.g., **John 14:17**, **19**; **16:10**, **16**, **17**, **19**. The difference between this verb and *blepo* and *horao* is brought out in **John 20:5**, **6**, **8**; in v. **5** *blepo* is used of John's sight of the linen cloths in the tomb, without his entering in; he "saw" at a glance the Lord was not there; in v. **6** the closer contemplation by Peter is expressed in the verb *theoreo*. But in v. **8** the grasping by John of the significance of the undisturbed cloths is denoted by *eidon*.

Dwelleth *see* Abode at *John 1:32*.

14:18 I will not leave you comfortless: I will come to you.

Leave *see* Left at *John 4:3*.

Comfortless *orphanos* (3737), (Eng., "orphan"; Lat., "*orbus*"), signifies "bereft of parents or of a father." In Jas. 1:27 it is translated "fatherless." It was also used in the general sense of being "friendless or desolate." In **John 14:18** the Lord uses it of the relationship between Himself and His disciples, He having been their guide, teacher and protector; RV, "desolate," KJV, "comfortless." Some mss. have the word in Mark 12:40.

14:19 Yet a little while, and the world seeth me no more; but ye see me: because I live, ye shall live also.

Little *see John 13:33*.

Seeth *see John 14:17*.

Live *see* Living at *John 4:10*.

Also *see John 7:3*.

14:20 At that day ye shall know that I *am* in my Father, and ye in me, and I in you.

Know *see John 7:26*.

14:21 He that hath my commandments, and keepeth them, he it is that loveth me: and he that loveth me shall be loved of my Father, and I will love him, and will manifest myself to him.

Hath *see* Amend at *John 4:52*.

Loveth *see* Loved at *John 3:16*.

Manifest *emphanizo* (1718), from *en*, "in," intensive, and *phaino*, "to shine," is used, either of "physical manifestation," Matt. 27:53; Heb. 9:24; cf. **John 14:22**, or, metaphorically, of "the manifestation of Christ" by the Holy Spirit in the spiritual experience of believers who abide in His love, **John 14:21**. It has another, secondary meaning, "to make known, signify, inform." This is confined to the Acts, where it is used five times, 23:15, 22; 24:1; 25:2, 15. There is perhaps a combination of the two meanings in Heb. 11:14, i.e., to declare by oral testimony and to "manifest" by the witness of the life.

Myself *see* Mine own self at *John 5:30*.

14:22 Judas saith unto him, not Iscariot, Lord, how is it that thou wilt manifest thyself unto us, and not unto the world?

Wilt *see* Will at *John 7:35*.

Manifest *see John 14:21*.

14:23 Jesus answered and said unto him, If a man love me, he will keep my words: and my Father will love him, and we will come unto him, and make our abode with him.

Man *see John 3:3.*

Love *see* Loved at *John 3:16.*

Words *see* Word at *John 1:1.*

Make *see John 2:16.*

Abode *see* Mansions at *John 14:2.*

14:24 He that loveth me not keepeth not my sayings: and the word which ye hear is not mine, but the Father's which sent me.

Sayings *see* Saying at *John 4:37.*

Sent *see John 1:33.*

14:25 These things have I spoken unto you, being *yet* present with you.

Present In **John 14:25**, KJV, *meno*, "to abide," is translated "being present" (RV, "abiding").

"Jesus differs from all other teachers; they reach the ear, but he instructs the heart; they deal with the outward letter, but he imparts an inward taste for the truth."

CHARLES HADDON SPURGEON

14:26 But the Comforter, *which is* the Holy Ghost, whom the Father will send in my name, he shall teach you all things, and bring all things to your remembrance, whatsoever I have said unto you.

Comforter *see John 14:16.*

Holy Ghost *see* Spirit, Holy Ghost at *John 7:39.*

Send *see* Sent at *John 1:33.*

Name *see John 1:12.*

Teach *didasko* (1321), is used (a) absolutely, "to give instruction," e.g., Matt. 4:23; 9:35; Rom. 12:7; 1 Cor. 4:17; 1 Tim. 2:12; 4:11; (b) transitively, with an object, whether persons, e.g., Matt. 5:2; 7:29, and frequently in the Gospels and Acts, or things "taught," e.g., Matt. 15:9; 22:16; Acts 15:35; 18:11; both persons and things, e.g., **John 14:26**; Rev. 2:14, 20.

Your "Your" is most frequently the translation of *humon*, lit., "of you," the genitive plural of *su*, "thou, you"; it is translated "yours" in 1 Cor. 3:21, 22; in 8:9, "of yours"; 16:18; 2 Cor. 12:14. In the following the dative plural, *humin*, lit., "to you," is translated "your"; Luke 16:11, lit., "(who will entrust) to you"; in 21:15 "your adversaries" is, lit., "(those opposed) to you"; in 1 Cor. 6:5 and 15:34, KJV, "(I speak to) your (shame)," RV, "(I say *this* to move) you (to shame)," is, lit., "(I speak unto a shame) to you." The accusative plural, *humas*, preceded by *kata*, "according to," is rendered in Acts 18:15 "your own (law)," RV, KJV, "your (law)," lit., "(of the law) according to you," with emphasis and scorn; in Eph. 1:15 the same construction is used of faith, but *kata* here means "among," as in the RV, "(the faith ... which is) among you," KJV, "your (faith)"; in **John 14:26** "He shall ... bring to your remembrance" is, lit., "He shall ... put you in mind of."

Remembrance *hupomimnesko* (5279), signifies "to cause one to remember, put one in mind of," **John 14:26**, "shall ... bring ... to (your) remembrance"; 2 Tim. 2:14, "put ... in remembrance"; Titus 3:1, "put ... in mind"; 3 John 10, RV, "I will bring to remembrance" (KJV, "I will remember"); Jude 5, "to put ... in remembrance." In Luke 22:61 it is used in the passive voice, "(Peter) remembered," lit., "was put in mind."

14:27 Peace I leave with you, my peace I give unto you: not as the world giveth, give I unto you. Let not your heart be troubled, neither let it be afraid.

Peace *eirene* (1515), "occurs in each of the books of the NT, save 1 John and save in Acts 7:26 ['(at) one again'] it is translated "peace" in the RV. It describes (a) harmonious relationships between men, Matt. 10:34; Rom. 14:19; (b) between nations, Luke 14:32; Acts 12:20; Rev. 6:4; (c) friendliness, Acts 15:33; 1 Cor. 16:11; Heb. 11:31; (d) freedom from molestation, Luke 11:21; 19:42; Acts 9:31 (RV, 'peace,' KJV, 'rest'); 16:36; (e) order, in the State, Acts 24:2 (RV, 'peace,' KJV, 'quietness'); in the churches, 1 Cor. 14:33; (f) the harmonized relationships between God and man, accomplished through the gospel, Acts 10:36; Eph. 2:17; (g) the sense of rest and contentment consequent thereon, Matt. 10:13; Mark 5:34; Luke 1:79; 2:29; **John 14:27**; Rom. 1:7; 3:17; 8:6; in certain passages this idea is not distinguishable from the last, Rom. 5:1."

"The God of peace" is a title used in Rom. 15:33; 16:20; Phil. 4:9; 1 Thess. 5:23; Heb. 13:20; cf. 1 Cor.

14:33; 2 Cor. 13:11. The corresponding Heb. word *shalom* primarily signifies "wholeness": see its use in Josh. 8:31, "unhewn"; Ruth 2:12, "full"; Neh. 6:15, "finished"; Isa. 42:19, marg., "made perfect." Hence there is a close connection between the title in 1 Thess. 5:23 and the word *holokleros*, "entire," in that verse. In the Sept. *shalom* is often rendered by *soteria*, "salvation, e.g., Gen. 26:31; 41:16; hence the "peace-offering" is called the "salvation offering."

Leave *see* Left at *John 4:3*.

Troubled *see John 5:4*.

Afraid *deilia* (1167), "fearfulness" (from *deos*, "fright"), is rightly rendered "fearfulness" in 2 Tim. 1:7, RV (for KJV, "fear"). That spirit is not given us of God. The word denotes "cowardice and timidity" and is never used in a good sense. Cf. *deilos*, and *deiliao*, to be fearful (KJV, "afraid"), **John 14:27**.

14:28 Ye have heard how I said unto you, I go away, and come *again* unto you. If ye loved me, ye would rejoice, because I said, I go unto the Father: for my Father is greater than I.

Rejoice *see John 4:36*.

14:29 And now I have told you before it come to pass, that, when it is come to pass, ye might believe.

Told *eiro* (3004), is rendered "to tell" in Matt. 21:24; Mark 11:29; **John 14:29**; Rev. 17:7.

Before *prin* (4250), "before, formerly" (etymologically akin to *pro*, "before"), has the force of a conjunction, e.g., Matt. 1:18; 26:34, 75; **John 14:29**; Acts 7:2.

Come to pass *see John 13:19*.

14:30 Hereafter I will not talk much with you: for the prince of this world cometh, and hath nothing in me.

Hereafter In **John 14:30**, *ouk eti* is rendered "no more" in the RV (KJV, "Hereafter ... not").

Talk *see* Talked at *John 4:27*.

Much *see John 12:12*.

Prince *see* Ruler at *John 3:1*.

World *see John 1:9*.

14:31 But that the world may know that I love the Father; and as the Father gave me commandment, even so I do. Arise, let us go hence.

Know *see John 7:26*.

Go *see John 11:7*.

Hence *see John 2:16*.

Chapter 15

15:1 I am the true vine, and my Father is the husbandman.

True *see John 1:9*.

Vine *ampelos* (288), is used (a) lit., e.g., Matt. 26:29 and parallel passages; Jas. 3:12; (b) figuratively, (1) of Christ, **John 15:1, 4, 5**; (2) of His enemies, Rev. 14:18, 19, "the vine of the earth" (RV, "vintage" in v. 19), probably figurative of the remaining mass of apostate Christendom.

Husbandman *georgos* (1092), from *ge*, "land, ground," and *ergo* (or *erdo*), "to do" (Eng., "George"), denotes (a) "a husbandman," a tiller of the ground, 2 Tim. 2:6; Jas. 5:7; (b) "a vinedresser," Matt. 21:33-35, 38, 40, 41; Mark 12:1, 2, 7, 9; Luke 20:9, 10, 14, 16; **John 15:1**, where Christ speaks of the Father as the "Husbandman," Himself as the Vine, His disciples as the branches, the object being to bear much fruit, life in Christ producing the fruit of the Spirit, i.e., character and ways in conformity to Christ.

15:2 Every branch in me that beareth not fruit he taketh away: and every *branch* that beareth fruit, he purgeth it, that it may bring forth more fruit.

Branch *klema* (2814), akin to *klao*, "to break," denotes "a tender, flexible branch, especially the shoot of a vine, a vine sprout," **John 15:2, 4-6**.

Beareth *see* Bear at *John 2:8*.

Fruit *see John 4:36*.

Taketh *see John 1:29*.

Purgeth *kathairo* (2508), akin to *katharos*, "to cleanse," is used of pruning, **John 15:2**, KJV, "purgeth" (RV, "cleanseth"). In the Sept., 2 Sam. 4:6; Isa. 28:27; Jer. 38:28.

More *pleion* (4119), the comparative degree of *polus*, "much," is used (a) as an adjective, e.g., **John 15:2**; Acts 24:11, RV, "(not) more (than)" (KJV, "yet but"); Heb. 3:3; (b) as a noun, or with a noun understood, e.g., Matt. 20:10; Mark 12:43; Acts 19:32 and 27:12, "the more part"; 1 Cor. 9:19; (c) as an adverb, Matt. 5:20, "shall exceed," lit., "(shall abound) more (than)"; 26:53; Luke 9:13.

15:3 Now ye are clean through the word which I have spoken unto you.

Clean *see John 13:10*.

15:4 Abide in me, and I in you. As the branch cannot bear fruit of itself, except it abide in the vine; no more can ye, except ye abide in me.

"The destiny of every human being depends on his relationship to Jesus Christ. It is not on his relationship to life, or on his service or his usefulness, but simply and solely on his relationship to Jesus Christ."

OSWALD CHAMBERS

Abide *see* Abode at *John 1:32.*

Branch *see John 15:2.*

Vine *see John 15:1.*

No more In **John 15:4**, KJV, *houtos*, "so," followed by *oude*, "neither," is translated "no more" (RV, "so neither").

15:5 I am the vine, ye *are* the branches: He that abideth in me, and I in him, the same bringeth forth much fruit: for without me ye can do nothing.

Vine *see John 15:1.*

Bringeth *phero* (5342), "to bear, or carry," is used also of "bearing or bringing forth fruit," Mark 4:8; **John 15:5**, etc. To bring is the most frequent meaning.

Without *choris* (5565), is used both as an adverb and as a preposition. As an adverb it signifies "separately, by itself," **John 20:7**, of the napkin which had been around the Lord's head in the tomb; as a preposition (its more frequent use), "apart from, without, separate from." It is rendered "apart from" in the RV of **John 15:5**; Rom. 3:21, 28; 4:6; 2 Cor. 12:3; Heb. 9:22, 28; 11:40; Jas. 2:18, 20, 26.

15:6 If a man abide not in me, he is cast forth as a branch, and is withered; and men gather them, and cast *them* into the fire, and they are burned.

Man *see John 3:3.*

Withered *xeraino* (3583), "to dry up, parch, wither," is translated "to wither," (a) of plants, Matt. 13:6; 21:19, 20; Mark 4:6; 11:20, RV (KJV, "dried up"), 21; Luke 8:6; **John 15:6**; Jas. 1:11; 1 Pet. 1:24; (b) of members of the body, Mark 3:1, and, in some texts, 3.

Burned *see* Burning at *John 5:35.*

15:7-8 If ye abide in me, and my words abide in you, ye shall ask what ye will, and it shall be done unto you.
Herein is my Father glorified, that ye bear much fruit; so shall ye be my disciples.

Herein *see John 4:37.*

Glorified *see John 7:39.*

Disciples *see John 6:66.*

15:9 As the Father hath loved me, so have I loved you: continue ye in my love.

Continue *see* Abode at *John 1:32.*

15:10 If ye keep my commandments, ye shall abide in my love; even as I have kept my Father's commandments, and abide in his love.

Keep *see John 14:15.*

Abide *see* Abode at *John 1:32.*

Love *see* Loved at *John 3:16.*

15:11 These things have I spoken unto you, that my joy might remain in you, and *that* your joy might be full.

Remain *see* Remaining at *John 1:33.*

Full *see* Fulfilled at *John 3:29.*

15:12 This is my commandment, That ye love one another, as I have loved you.

My *see John 4:34.*

15:13 Greater love hath no man than this, that a man lay down his life for his friends.

Man *see John 3:3.*

Lay *see John 10:17.*

15:14 Ye are my friends, if ye do whatsoever I command you.

Command *see* Commanded at *John 8:5.*

15:15 Henceforth I call you not servants; for the servant knoweth not what his lord doeth: but I have called you friends; for all things that I have heard of my Father I have made known unto you.

Henceforth *ouketi* (3765), "no more, no longer," is rendered "no longer" in the RV of Mark 7:12 (KJV, "no more"); **John 15:15**, RV (KJV, "henceforth not"), Rom. 14:15, RV (KJV, "now ... not"); Gal. 2:20, RV (KJV, "yet not"), Gal. 3:25; 4:7 (KJV, "no more"); Philem. 16 (KJV, "not now").

Call *see* Called at *John 4:5.*

Knoweth *gnorizo* (1107), signifies (a) "to come to know, discover, know,"

Phil. 1:22, "I wot (not)," i.e., "I know not," "I have not come to know" (the RV, marg. renders it, as under (b), "I do not make known"); (b) "to make known," whether (I) communicating things before "unknown," Luke 2:15, 17; in the latter some mss. have the verb *diagnorizo* (hence the KJV, "made known abroad)"; **John 15:15**, "I have made known"; **17:26**; Acts 2:28; 7:13 (1st part); Rom. 9:22, 23; 16:26 (passive voice); 2 Cor. 8:1, "we make known (to you)," RV, KJV, "we do (you) to wit"; Eph. 1:9; 3:3, 5, 10 (all three in the passive voice); 6:19, 21; Col. 1:27; 4:7, 9, "shall make known" (KJV, "shall declare"); 2 Pet. 1:16; or (II) reasserting things already "known," 1 Cor. 12:3, "I give (you) to understand" (the apostle reaffirms what they knew); 15:1, of the gospel; Gal. 1:11 (he reminds them of what they well knew, the ground of his claim to apostleship); Phil. 4:6 (passive voice), of requests to God.

Of *see John 6:46.*

15:16 Ye have not chosen me, but I have chosen you, and ordained you, that ye should go and bring forth fruit, and *that* your fruit should remain: that whatsoever ye shall ask of the Father in my name, he may give it you.

Chosen *see John 6:70.*

Ordained *tithemi* (5087), "to put," is used of "appointment" to any form of service. Christ used it of His followers, **John 15:16** (RV, "appointed" for KJV, "ordained"). "I set you" would be more in keeping with the metaphor of grafting. The verb is used by Paul of his service in the ministry of the gospel, 1 Tim. 1:12 (RV, "appointing" for "putting"); 2:7 (RV, "appointed" for "ordained"); and 2 Tim. 1:11 (RV, "appointing" for "putting"); of the overseers, or bishops, in the local church at Ephesus, as those "appointed" by the Holy Ghost, to tend the church of God, Acts 20:28 ("hath made"); of the Son of God, as appointed Heir of all things, Heb. 1:2. It is also used of "appointment" to punishment, as of the unfaithful servant, Matt. 24:51; Luke 12:46; of unbelieving Israel, 1 Pet. 2:8. Cf. 2 Pet. 2:6.

Fruit *see John 4:36.*

Remain *see* Remaining at *John 1:33.*

Name *see John 1:12.*

15:17 These things I command you, that ye love one another.

Command *see* Commanded at *John 8:5.*

15:18 If the world hate you, ye know that it hated me before *it hated* you.

Hate *see* Hateth at *John 3:20.*

Know *see John 7:26.*

Before *proton* (4412), the neuter of the adjective *protos* (the superlative degree of *pro*, "before"), signifies "first, or at the first," (a) in order of time, e.g., Luke 10:5; **John 18:13**; 1 Cor. 15:46; 1 Thess. 4:16; 1 Tim. 3:10; (b) in enumerating various particulars, e.g., Rom. 3:2; 1 Cor. 11:18; 12:28; Heb. 7:2; Jas. 3:17. It is translated "before" in **John 15:18**.

15:19 If ye were of the world, the world would love his own: but because ye are not of the world, but I have chosen you out of the world, therefore the world hateth you.

Chosen *see John 6:70.*

Hateth *see John 3:20.*

15:20 Remember the word that I said unto you, The servant is not greater than his lord. If they have persecuted me, they will also persecute you; if they have kept my saying, they will keep yours also.

Remember *mnemoneuo* (3421), signifies "to call to mind, remember"; it is used absolutely in Mark 8:18; everywhere else it has an object, (a) persons, Luke 17:32; Gal. 2:10; 2 Tim. 2:8, where the RV rightly has "remember Jesus Christ, risen from the dead"; Paul was not reminding Timothy (nor did he need to) that Christ was raised from the dead (KJV), what was needful for him was to "remember" (to keep in mind) the One who rose, the Source and Supplier of all his requirements; (b) things, e.g., Matt. 16:9; **John 15:20**; **16:21**; Acts 20:35; Col. 4:18; 1 Thess. 1:3; 2:9; Heb. 11:15, "had been mindful of"; 13:7; Rev. 18:5; (c) a clause, representing a circumstance, etc., **John 16:4**; Acts 20:31; Eph. 2:11; 2 Thess. 2:5; Rev. 2:5; 3:3; in Heb. 11:22 it signifies "to make mention of."

Word *see John 1:1.*

Persecuted, Persecute *see* Persecute at *John 5:16.*

Saying *see John 4:37.*

Yours *see* Your at *John 7:6.*

15:21 But all these things will they do unto you for my name's sake, because they know not him that sent me.

Name *see John 1:12.*

Sent *see John 1:33.*

15:22 If I had not come and spoken unto them, they had not had sin: but now they have no cloke for their sin.

Now *see John 4:18.*

Cloke *prophasis* (4392), either from *pro*, "before," and *phaino*, "to cause to appear, shine," or, more probably, from *pro*, and *phemi*, "to say," is rendered "cloke" (of covetousness) in 1 Thess. 2:5; "excuse" in **John 15:22** (KJV "cloke"); "pretense" in Matt. 23:14; Mark 12:40; Luke 20:47 (KJV "show"); Phil. 1:18; "color" in Acts 27:30. It signifies the assuming of something so as to disguise one's real motives.

Sin *see John 1:29.*

15:23 He that hateth me hateth my Father also.

Hateth *see John 3:20.*

15:24 If I had not done among them the works which none other man did, they had not had sin: but now have they both seen and hated both me and my Father.

Sin *see John 1:29.*

Now *see John 4:18.*

15:25 But *this cometh to pass*, that the word might be fulfilled that is written in their law, They hated me without a cause.

Word *see John 1:1.*

Law *see John 1:17.*

Cause *dorean* (1432), lit., "as a gift, gratis," (connected with *doron*, "a gift"), is rendered "without a cause," **John 15:25**; "for nought," 2 Cor. 11:7; Gal. 2:21; 2 Thess. 3:8; "freely," Matt. 10:8; Rom. 3:24; Rev. 21:6; 22:17.

15:26 But when the Comforter is come, whom I will send unto you from the Father, *even* the Spirit of truth, which proceedeth from the Father, he shall testify of me:

Comforter *see John 14:16.*

Send *see* Sent at *John 1:33.*

Spirit *see* Spirit, Holy Ghost at *John 7:39.*

Proceedeth *ekporeuomai* (1607), "to go forth," is translated "to proceed out of" in Matt. 4:4; 15:11, RV; 15:18; Mark 7:15, RV; 7:20, RV; 7:21; 7:23, RV; Luke 4:22; **John 15:26**; Eph. 4:29; Rev. 1:16, RV; 4:5; 9:17, 18, RV (KJV, "issued"); 11:5; 19:15, RV; 19:21, KJV (RV, "came forth"); 22:1.

Testify *see John 2:25.*

15:27 And ye also shall bear witness, because ye have been with me from the beginning.

Ye These are most frequently the translations of various inflections of a verb; sometimes of the article before a nominative used as a vocative, e.g., Rev. 18:20, "ye saints, and ye apostles, and ye prophets" (lit., "the saints, etc."). When the 2nd person plural pronouns are used separately from a verb, they are usually one or other of the forms of *humeis*, the plural of *su*, "thou," and are frequently emphatic, especially when they are subjects of the verb, an emphasis always to be noticed, e.g., Matt. 5:13, 14, 48; 6:9, 19, 20; Mark 6:31, 37; **John 15:27a**; Rom. 1:6; 1 Cor. 3:17, 23; Gal. 3:28, 29a; Eph. 1:13a; 2:8; 2:11, 13; Phil. 2:18; Col. 3:4, 7a; 4:1; 1 Thess. 1:6; 2:10, 19, 20; 3:8; 2 Thess. 3:13; Jas. 5:8; 1 Pet. 2:9a; 1 John 2:20, 24 (1st and 3rd occurrences), 27a; 4:4; Jude 17, 20.

Also *see John 7:3.*

Witness *see John 1:7.*

Chapter 16

16:1-2 These things have I spoken unto you, that ye should not be offended.

They shall put you out of the synagogues: yea, the time cometh, that whosoever killeth you will think that he doeth God service.

Synagogues *see* Synagogue at *John 9:22.*

Yea *alla* (235), "but," is translated "yea" in **John 16:2**; Rom. 3:31, KJV (RV, "nay"); 1 Cor. 4:3; 2 Cor. 7:11 (six times); Gal. 4:17, KJV (RV, "nay"); Phil. 1:18; 2:17; 3:8; Jas. 2:18.

Time *hora* (5610), primarily, "any time or period fixed by nature," is translated "time" in Matt. 14:15; Luke 14:17; Rom. 13:11, "high time"; in the following the RV renders it "hour," for KJV, "time," Matt. 18:1; Luke 1:10; **John 16:2, 4, 25**; 1 John 2:18 (twice); Rev. 14:15; in Mark 6:35, RV, "day"; in 1 Thess. 2:17, RV, "a short (season)," lit., "(the season, KJV, 'time') of an hour."

Doeth *prosphero* (4374), primarily, "to bring to" (*pros*, "to," *phero*, "to bring"), also denotes "to offer," (a) of the sacrifice of Christ Himself, Heb. 8:3; of Christ in virtue of his High Priesthood (RV, "this *high priest*"; KJV, "this man"); 9:14, 25 (negative), 28; 10:12; (b) of offerings under, or according to, the Law, e.g., Matt. 8:4; Mark 1:44; Acts 7:42; 21:26; Heb. 5:1, 3; 8:3; 9:7, 9; 10:1-2, 8, 11; (c) of "offerings" previous to the Law, Heb. 11:4, 17 (of Isaac by Abraham); (d) of gifts "offered" to Christ, Matt. 2:11, RV, "offered" (KJV, "presented unto"); (e) of prayers "offered" by Christ, Heb. 5:7; (f) of the vinegar "offered" to Him in mockery by the soldiers at the cross, Luke 23:36; (g) of the slaughter of disciples by persecutors, who think they are "offering" service to God, **John 16:2**, RV (KJV, "doeth"); (h) of money "offered" by Simon the sorcerer, Acts 8:18.

Service *latreia* (2999), akin to *latreuo*, primarily "hired service," is used (a) of the "service" *of God* in connection with the tabernacle, Rom. 9:4; Heb. 9:1, "divine service"; v. 6, plural, RV, "services" (KJV, "service", and, in italics, "of God"); (b) of the intelligent "service" of believers in presenting their bodies to God, a living sacrifice, Rom. 12:1, RV marg., "worship"; (c) of imagined "service" to God by persecutors of Christ's followers, **John 16:2**.

16:3-4 And these things will they do unto you, because they have not known the Father, nor me.

But these things have I told you, that when the time shall come, ye may remember that I told you of them. And these things I said not unto you at the beginning, because I was with you.

Time *see John 16:2.*

Remember *see John 15:20.*

16:5 But now I go my way to him that sent me; and none of you asketh me, Whither goest thou?

Sent *see John 1:33.*

16:6 But because I have said these things unto you, sorrow hath filled your heart.

Said *see* Saith at *John 8:25.*

Sorrow *lupe* (3077), "grief, sorrow," is translated "sorrow" in Luke 22:45; **John 16:6, 20-22**; Rom. 9:2, RV (KJV, "heaviness"); 2 Cor. 2:1, RV; 2:3, 7; 7:10 (twice); Phil. 2:27 (twice).

Filled *see* Fulfilled at *John 3:29.*

16:7 Nevertheless I tell you the truth; It is expedient for you that I go away: for if I go not away, the Comforter will not come unto you; but if I depart, I will send him unto you.

Expedient *see John 11:50.*

Comforter *see John 14:16.*

Depart *poreuo* (4198), akin to *poros*, "a passage," in the middle voice signifies "to go on one's way, to depart from one place to another." In some places, where the KJV has the verb "to depart," the RV translates by "to go one's way," e.g., Matt. 2:9, "went their way"; 11:7; 24.1, "was going on His way." In the following the RV has the verb "to go," for the KJV "depart," Luke 4:42 (latter part of verse); 13:31; **John 16:7**; 2 Tim. 4:10. In Luke 21:8, "go (after)," is said of disciples or partisans. In some places both KJV and RV translate by the verb "to depart," e.g., Matt. 19:15; 25:41; Acts 5:41; Acts 22:21. This verb is to be distinguished from others signifying "to go." It is best rendered, as often as possible, "to go on one's way."

Send *see* Sent at *John 1:33.*

16:8 And when he is come, he will reprove the world of sin, and of righteousness, and of judgment:

Reprove *see* Reproved at *John 3:20.*

Of In the following, *peri*, "concerning," is so translated in the RV (for KJV, "of"), e.g., Acts 5:24; 1 Cor. 1:11; 1 John 1:1 (the RV is important); cf. **John 16:8**.

Righteousness *dikaiosune* (1343), is "the character or quality of being right or just"; it was formerly spelled "rightwiseness," which clearly expresses the meaning. It is used to denote an attribute of God, e.g., Rom. 3:5, the context of which shows that "the righteousness of God" means essentially the same as His faithfulness, or truthfulness, that which is consistent with His own nature and promises; Rom. 3:25, 26 speaks of His "righteousness" as exhibited in the death of Christ, which is sufficient to show men that God is neither indifferent to sin nor regards it lightly. On the contrary, it demonstrates that quality of holiness in Him which must find expression in His condemnation of sin.

"*Dikaiosune* is found in the sayings of the Lord Jesus, (a) of whatever is right or just in itself, whatever conforms to the revealed will of God, Matt. 5:6, 10, 20; **John 16:8, 10**; (b) whatever has been appointed by God to be acknowledged and obeyed by man, Matt. 3:15; 21:32; (c) the sum total of the requirements of God, Matt. 6:33; (d) religious duties, Matt. 6:1 (distinguished as almsgiving, man's duty to his neighbor, vv. 2-4, prayer, his duty to God, vv. 5-15, fasting, the duty of self-control, vv. 16–18)."

Judgment The Holy Spirit, the Lord said, would convict the world of (*peri*, "in respect of"), i.e., of the actuality of, God's "judgment," **John 16:8, 11**. Cf. 2 Thess. 1:5.

16:9-10 Of sin, because they believe not on me;

Of righteousness, because I go to my Father, and ye see me no more;

Righteousness *see John 16:8.*

See *see* Seeth at *John 14:17.*

16:11 Of judgment, because the prince of this world is judged.

Judgment *see John 16:8.*

Prince *see John 12:31.*

Judged *see* Condemn at *John 3:17.*

16:12 I have yet many things to say unto you, but ye cannot bear them now.

Bear *see* Took up at *John 10:31*.

Now *see John 2:10*.

16:13 Howbeit when he, the Spirit of truth, is come, he will guide you into all truth: for he shall not speak of himself; but whatsoever he shall hear, *that* shall he speak: and he will shew you things to come.

Spirit *see* Spirit, Holy Ghost at *John 7:39*.

Of *see John 7:17*.

Guide *hodegeo* (3594), "to lead the way," is used (a) literally, RV, "guide" (KJV, "lead"), of "guiding" the blind, in Matt. 15:14; Luke 6:39; of "guiding" unto fountains of waters of life, Rev. 7:17; (b) figuratively, in **John 16:13**, of "guidance" into the truth by the Holy Spirit; in Acts 8:31, of the interpretation of Scripture.

Shew *anangello* ("to declare"), Matt. 11:4, "tell"; **John 16:13–15**, "declare"; **16:25**, "shall tell"; Acts 19:18 and 20:20, "declaring".

16:14 He shall glorify me: for he shall receive of mine, and shall shew *it* unto you.

Glorify *see* Glorified at *John 7:39*.

Receive *see John 3:11*.

Mine *see* My at *John 4:34*.

16:15 All things that the Father hath are mine: therefore said I, that he shall take of mine, and shall shew *it* unto you.

Mine *see* My at *John 4:34*.

16:16 A little while, and ye shall not see me: and again, a little while, and ye shall see me, because I go to the Father.

Little *see John 13:33*.

See *see* Seeth at *John 14:17*.

16:17 Then said *some* of his disciples among themselves, What is this that he saith unto us, A little while, and ye shall not see me: and again, a little while, and ye shall see me: and, Because I go to the Father?

Themselves *see John 6:52*.

See *see* Seeth at *John 14:17*.

16:18 They said therefore, What is this that he saith, A little while? we cannot tell what he saith.

Saith *see* Said at *John 8:25*.

Cannot *see* Canst at *John 3:8*.

Tell *see John 3:8*.

16:19 Now Jesus knew that they were desirous to ask him, and said unto them, Do ye enquire among yourselves of that I said, A little while, and ye shall not see me: and again, a little while, and ye shall see me?

Now *oun* (3767), "therefore, so then," is sometimes used in continuing a narrative, e.g., Acts 1:18; 1 Cor. 9:25; or resuming it after a digression, usually rendered "therefore," e.g., Acts 11:19; 25:1, RV (KJV, now). In the following it is absent from the best mss., Mark 12:20; Luke 10:36; **John 16:19**; **18:24**; **19:29**.

Ask *see* Asked at *John 9:15*.

Enquire *zeteo* (2212), "to seek," is rendered "inquire" in **John 16:19**; "inquire ... for" in Acts 9:11.

See *see* Seeth at *John 14:17*.

16:20 Verily, verily, I say unto you, That ye shall weep and lament, but the world shall rejoice: and ye shall be sorrowful, but your sorrow shall be turned into joy.

Weep *threneo* (2354), "to lament, wail" (akin to *threnos*, "a lamentation, a dirge"), is used (a) in a general sense, of the disciples during the absence of the Lord, **John 16:20**, "lament"; (b) of those who sorrowed for the sufferings and the impending crucifixion of the Lord, Luke 23:27, "lamented"; the preceding word is *kopto*; (c) of "mourning" as for the dead, Matt. 11:17, RV, "wailed" (KJV, "have mourned"); Luke 7:32 (ditto).

Turned *ginomai* (1096), "to become," is rendered "shall be turned" in **John 16:20** (of sorrow into joy).

Rejoice, Joy *chairo* (5463), "to rejoice, be glad," is translated "joyfully" in Luke 19:6, lit., "rejoicing"; "we joyed," 2 Cor. 7:13; "I joy," Phil. 2:17; "do ye joy," 2:18; "joying," Col. 2:5; "we joy," 1 Thess. 3:9. It is contrasted with weeping and sorrow, e.g., in **John 16:20**, **22**; Rom. 12:15; 1 Cor. 7:30 (cf. Ps. 30:5).

Sorrow *see John 16:6*.

16:21 A woman when she is in travail hath sorrow, because her hour is come: but as soon as she is delivered of the child, she remembereth no more the anguish, for joy that a man is born into the world.

Travail *tikto* (5088), "to beget," is rendered "travail" in **John 16:21**.

Child *see John 4:49*.

Remembereth *see* Remember at *John 15:20*.

Anguish *thlipsis* (2347), primarily means "a pressing, pressure," anything which burdens the spirit. In two passages in Paul's Epistles it is used of future retribution, in the way of "affliction," Rom. 2:9; 2 Thess. 1:6. In Matt. 24:9, the KJV renders it as a verb, "to be afflicted," (RV, "unto tribulation"). It is coupled with *stenochoria*, "anguish," in Rom. 2:9; 8:35; with *ananke*, "distress," 1 Thess. 3:7; with *diogmos*, "persecution," Matt. 13:21; Mark 4:17; 2 Thess. 1:4. It is used of the calamities of war, Matt. 24:21, 29; Mark 13:19, 24; of want, 2 Cor. 8:13, lit., "distress for you"; Phil. 4:14 (cf. 1:16); Jas. 1:27; of the distress of woman in childbirth, **John 16:21**; of persecution, Acts 11:19; 14:22; 20:23; 1 Thess. 3:3, 7; Heb. 10:33; Rev. 2:10; 7:14; of the "afflictions" of Christ, from which (His vicarious sufferings apart) his followers must not shrink, whether sufferings of body or mind, Col. 1:24; of sufferings in general, 1 Cor. 7:28; 1 Thess. 1:6, etc.

Born *see John 3:3.*

16:22 And ye now therefore have sorrow: but I will see you again, and your heart shall rejoice, and your joy no man taketh from you.

Heart *see John 12:40.*

Rejoice *see John 4:36.*

Joy *see John 16:20.*

16:23 And in that day ye shall ask me nothing. Verily, verily, I say unto you, Whatsoever ye shall ask the Father in my name, he will give *it* you.

Ask *see* Asked at *John 9:15.*

Whatsoever See the RV of Mark 15:5; **John 16:23**; 1 Tim. 6:7; in Luke 24:41, the RV suitably has "anything to eat," for, KJV, "any meat."

Name *see John 1:12.*

16:24 Hitherto have ye asked nothing in my name: ask, and ye shall receive, that your joy may be full.

Hitherto *see John 5:17.*

Full *see* Fulfilled at *John 3:29.*

16:25 These things have I spoken unto you in proverbs: but the time cometh, when I shall no more speak unto you in proverbs, but I shall shew you plainly of the Father.

Proverbs *see* Parable at *John 10:6.*

Time *see John 16:2.*

Shew *see John 16:13.*

Plainly *see John 10:24.*

16:26 At that day ye shall ask in my name: and I say not unto you, that I will pray the Father for you:

Ask *see* Asked at *John 9:15.*

Pray *see* Prayed at *John 4:31.*

16:27 For the Father himself loveth you, because ye have loved me, and have believed that I came out from God.

Himself In **John 16:27**, "the Father Himself (*autos*)," Field (on the Translation of the NT) remarks that *autos* stands for *automatos*.

Loveth *see John 3:35.*

16:28 I came forth from the Father, and am come into the world: again, I leave the world, and go to the Father.

Leave *see* Left at *John 4:3.*

16:29 His disciples said unto him, Lo, now speakest thou plainly, and speakest no proverb.

Plainly *see John 10:24.*

Proverb *see* Parable at *John 10:6.*

16:30 Now are we sure that thou knowest all things, and needest not that any man should ask thee: by this we believe that thou camest forth from God.

Sure *see John 6:69.*

Needest *see* Needed at *John 2:25.*

16:31 Jesus answered them, Do ye now believe?

Now *see John 2:10.*

16:32 Behold, the hour cometh, yea, is now come, that ye shall be scattered, every man to his own, and shall leave me alone: and yet I am not alone, because the Father is with me.

Yea *kai* (2532), "and, even," is rendered "yea," e.g., Luke 2:35; **John 16:32**; 1 Cor. 2:10; 2 Cor. 8:3; in Acts 7:43, KJV (RV, "and").

Scattered *see* Scattereth at *John 10:12.*

His own *see John 1:11.*

Leave *see* Left at *John 4:3.*

16:33 These things I have spoken unto you, that in me ye might have peace. In the world ye shall have tribulation: but be of good cheer; I have overcome the world.

Cheer *tharseo* (2293), "to be of good courage, of good cheer" (*tharsos*, "courage, confidence"), is used only in the imperative mood, in the NT; "be of good cheer," Matt. 9:2, 22; 14:27; Mark 6:50; 10:49; Luke 8:48; **John 16:33**; Acts 23:11.

Overcome *nikao* (3528), is used (a) of God, Rom. 3:4 (a law term), RV, "mightest prevail"; (b) of Christ, **John 16:33**; Rev. 3:21; 5:5; 17:14; (c) of His followers, Rom. 12:21 (2nd part); 1 John 2:13-14; 4:4; 5:4-5; Rev. 2:7, 11, 17, 26; 3:5, 12, 21; 12:11; 15:2; 21:7; (d) of faith, 1 John 5:4; (e) of evil (passive voice), Rom. 12:21; (f) of predicted human potentates, Rev. 6:2; 11:7; 13:7.

Chapter 17

17:1 These words spake Jesus, and lifted up his eyes to heaven, and said, Father, the hour is come; glorify thy Son, that thy Son also may glorify thee:

Lifted *see* Lift at *John 4:35*.

Glorify *see* Glorified at *John 7:39*.

Son *see John 1:18*.

17:2 As thou hast given him power over all flesh, that he should give eternal life to as many as thou hast given him.

Power *exousia* (1849), denotes "authority" (from the impersonal verb *exesti*, "it is lawful"). From the meaning of "leave or permission," or liberty of doing as one pleases, it passed to that of "the ability or strength with which one is endued," then to that of the "power of authority," the right to exercise power, e.g., Matt. 9:6; 21:23; 2 Cor. 10:8; or "the power of rule or government," the power of one whose will and commands must be obeyed by others, e.g., Matt. 28:18; **John 17:2**; Jude 25; Rev. 12:10; 17:13; more specifically of apostolic "authority," 2 Cor. 10:8; 13:10; the "power" of judicial decision, **John 19:10**; of "managing domestic affairs," Mark 13:34. By metonymy, or name-change (the substitution of a suggestive word for the name of the thing meant), it stands for "that which is subject to authority or rule," Luke 4:6 (RV, "authority," for the KJV, "power"); or, as with the English "authority," "one who possesses authority, a ruler, magistrate," Rom. 13:1-3; Luke 12:11; Titus 3:1; or "a spiritual potentate," e.g., Eph. 3:10; 6:12; Col. 1:16; 2:10, 15; 1 Pet. 3:22. The RV usually translates it "authority." In 1 Cor. 11:10 it is used of the veil with which a woman is required to cover herself in an assembly or church, as a sign of the Lord's "authority" over the church. *See also John 1:12*.

Many In **John 17:2**, KJV, the neuter of *pas*, "all," followed by the neuter of the relative pronoun "what," and then by the plural of the personal pronoun, is translated "to as many as" (RV, "whatsoever ... to them").

> *"What were we made for? To know God. What aim should we set ourselves in life? To know God. What is the 'eternal life' that Jesus gives? Knowledge of God."*
>
> J. I. PACKER

17:3 And this is life eternal, that they might know thee the only true God, and Jesus Christ, whom thou hast sent.

Life *aion* (165), "an age, era" (to be connected with *aei*, "ever," rather than with *ao*, "to breathe"), signifies a period of indefinite duration, or time viewed in relation to what takes place in the period. The force attaching to the word is not so much that of the actual length of a period, but that of a period marked by spiritual or moral characteristics. This is illustrated in the use of the adjective in the phrase "life eternal," in **John 17:3**, in respect of the increasing knowledge of God. The phrases containing this word should not be rendered literally, but consistently with its sense of indefinite duration. Thus *eis ton aiona* does not mean "unto the age" but "for ever" (see, e.g., Heb. 5:6). The Greeks contrasted that which came to an end with that which was expressed by this phrase, which shows that they conceived of it as expressing interminable duration. The word occurs most frequently in the Gospel of John, the Hebrews and Revelation. It is sometimes wrongly rendered "world." It is a characteristic word of John's Gospel.

Know *see John 7:26*.

Only *see John 5:44*.

True *see John 1:9*.

Jesus *see John 1:17*.

Christ *see John 1:41*.

Sent *see John 1:6*.

17:4 I have glorified thee on the earth: I have finished the work which thou gavest me to do.

Glorified *see John 7:39*.

Earth *see* Land at *John 3:22*.

Finished *see John 4:34*.

Work *see John 4:34*.

17:5 And now, O Father, glorify thou me with thine own self with the glory which I had with thee before the world was.

Glorify *see* Glorified at *John 7:39*.

Thou *see John 1:19*.

Glory *see John 1:14*.

17:6 I have manifested thy name unto the men which thou gavest me out of the world: thine they were, and thou gavest them me; and they have kept thy word.

Name *see John 1:12.*

Kept *see* Keep at *John 14:15.*

17:7 Now they have known that all things whatsoever thou hast given me are of thee.

Of *see John 6:46.*

17:8 For I have given unto them the words which thou gavest me; and they have received *them*, and have known surely that I came out from thee, and they have believed that thou didst send me.

Surely In the KJV of Matt. 26:73; Mark 14:70; **John 17:8**, *alethos*, "truly," is rendered "surely" (RV, "of a truth"); so *pantos*, "at all events, altogether," in Luke 4:23 (RV, "doubtless"), and *nai*, "yea," in Rev. 22:20 (RV, "yea"). *See also* Truth at *John 6:14.*

Send *see* Sent at *John 1:6.*

17:9 I pray for them: I pray not for the world, but for them which thou hast given me; for they are thine.

Pray *see* Prayed at *John 4:31.*

17:10 And all mine are thine, and thine are mine; and I am glorified in them.

Mine *see* My at *John 4:34.*

17:11 And now I am no more in the world, but these are in the world, and I come to thee. Holy Father, keep through thine own name those whom thou hast given me, that they may be one, as we *are*.

Holy *hagios* (40), from the same root as *hagnos* (found in *hazo*, "to venerate"), fundamentally signifies "separated" (among the Greeks, dedicated to the gods), and hence, in Scripture in its moral and spiritual significance, separated from sin and therefore consecrated to God, sacred. It is predicated of God (as the absolutely "Holy" One, in His purity, majesty and glory): of the Father, e.g., Luke 1:49; **John 17:11**; 1 Pet. 1:15, 16; Rev. 4:8; 6:10; of the Son, e.g., Luke 1:35; Acts 3:14; 4:27, 30; 1 John 2:20; of the Spirit, e.g., Matt. 1:18 and frequently in all the Gospels, Acts, Romans, 1 and 2 Cor., Eph., 1 Thess.; also in 2 Tim. 1:14; Titus 3:5; 1 Pet. 1:12; 2 Pet. 1:21; Jude 20.

Keep *see John 14:15.*

May *see John 14:3.*

One *see John 10:30.*

17:12 While I was with them in the world, I kept them in thy name: those that thou gavest me I have kept, and none of them is lost, but the son of perdition; that the scripture might be fulfilled.

While *hote*, "when," is rendered "while" in **John 17:12**; Heb. 9:17.

Kept *phulasso* (5442), "to guard, watch, keep," is rendered by the verb "to guard" in the RV (KJV, "to keep") of Luke 11:21; **John 17:12**; Acts 12:4; 28:16; 2 Thess. 3:3; 1 Tim. 6:20; 2 Tim. 1:12, 14; 1 John 5:21; Jude 24. In Luke 8:29, "was kept under guard, RV (KJV, "kept"). *See also* Keep at *John 14:15.*

Lost *see* Perish at *John 3:16.*

17:13 And now come I to thee; and these things I speak in the world, that they might have my joy fulfilled in themselves.

Fulfilled *see John 3:29.*

17:14-15 I have given them thy word; and the world hath hated them, because they are not of the world, even as I am not of the world.

I pray not that thou shouldest take them out of the world, but that thou shouldest keep them from the evil.

Pray *see* Prayed at *John 4:31.*

Keep *see John 14:15.*

Evil *poneros* (4190), the adjective is used as a noun, (a) of Satan as the "evil" one, Matt. 5:37; 6:13; 13:19, 38; Luke 11:4 (in some texts); **John 17:15**; Eph. 6:16; 2 Thess. 3:3; 1 John 2:13-14; 3:12; 5:18-19; (b) of human beings, Matt. 5:45; (probably v. 39); 13:49; 22:10; Luke 6:35; 1 Cor. 5:13; (c) neuter, "evil (things)," Matt. 9:4; 12:35; Mark 7:23; Luke 3:19; "that which is evil," Luke 6:45; Rom. 12:9; Acts 28:21, "harm."

17:16-17 They are not of the world, even as I am not of the world.

Sanctify them through thy truth: thy word is truth.

Sanctify *hagiasmos* (38), "sanctification," is used of (a) separation to God, 1 Cor. 1:30; 2 Thess. 2:13; 1 Pet. 1:2; (b) the course of life befitting those so separated, 1 Thess. 4:3, 4, 7; Rom. 6:19, 22; 1 Tim. 2:15; Heb. 12:14. "Sanctification is that relationship with God into which men enter by faith in Christ, Acts 26:18; 1 Cor. 6:11, and to which their sole title is the death of Christ, Eph. 5:25, 26; Col. 1:22; Heb. 10:10, 29; 13:12.

"Sanctification is also used in NT of the separation of the believer from evil things and ways. This sanctification is God's will for the believer, 1 Thess. 4:3, and His purpose in calling him by the gospel, v. 7; it must be learned from God, v. 4, as He teaches it by His

"Division has done more to hide Christ from the view of men than all the infidelity that has ever been spoken."

GEORGE MACDONALD

Word, **John 17:17**, **19**, cf. Ps. 17:4; 119:9, and it must be pursued by the believer, earnestly and undeviatingly, 1 Tim. 2:15; Heb. 12:14. For the holy character, *hagiosune*, 1 Thess. 3:13, is not vicarious, i.e., it cannot be transferred or imputed, it is an individual possession, built up, little by little, as the result of obedience to the Word of God, and of following the example of Christ, Matt. 11:29; **John 13:15**; Eph. 4:20; Phil. 2:5, in the power of the Holy Spirit, Rom. 8:13; Eph. 3:16. The Holy Spirit is the Agent in sanctification, Rom. 15:16; 2 Thess. 2:13; 1 Pet. 1:2; cf. 1 Cor. 6:11.... The sanctification of the Spirit is associated with the choice, or election, of God; it is a Divine act preceding the acceptance of the Gospel by the individual."

Truth *see John 8:44.*

17:18 As thou hast sent me into the world, even so have I also sent them into the world.

Sent *see John 1:6.*

Even so *see John 10:15.*

17:19 And for their sakes I sanctify myself, that they also might be sanctified through the truth.

Myself *see* Mine own self at *John 5:30.*

Sanctify, Sanctified *see* Sanctify at *John 17:17.*

17:20 Neither pray I for these alone, but for them also which shall believe on me through their word;

Pray *see* Prayed at *John 4:31.*

Alone *monon* (3441), meaning "only, exclusively," e.g., Rom. 4:23; Acts 19:26, is translated "alone" in the KJV of **John 17:20**; RV, "only."

17:21 That they all may be one; as thou, Father, *art* in me, and I in thee, that they also may be one in us: that the world may believe that thou hast sent me.

One *see John 10:30.*

Sent *see John 1:6.*

17:22-23 And the glory which thou gavest me I have given them; that they may be one, even as we are one:
I in them, and thou in me, that they may be made perfect in one; and that the world may know that thou hast sent me, and hast loved them, as thou hast loved me.

Perfect *teleioo* (5048), "to bring to an end by completing or perfecting," is used (I) of "accomplishing"; (II) of "bringing to completeness," of persons: of Christ's assured completion of His earthly course, in the accomplishment of the Father's will, the successive stages culminating in His death, Luke 13:32; Heb. 2:10, to make Him "perfect," legally and officially, for all that He would be to His people on the ground of His sacrifice; cf. 5:9; 7:28, RV, "perfected" (KJV, "consecrated"); of His saints, **John 17:23**, RV, "perfected" (KJV, "made perfect"); Phil. 3:12; Heb. 10:14; 11:40 (of resurrection glory); 12:23 (of the departed saints); 1 John 4:18, of former priests (negatively), Heb. 9:9; similarly of Israelites under the Aaronic priesthood, 10:1.

Sent *see John 1:6.*

17:24 Father, I will that they also, whom thou hast given me, be with me where I am; that they may behold my glory, which thou hast given me: for thou lovedst me before the foundation of the world.

Also *see John 7:3.*

Behold *see* See at *John 8:51.*

Glory *see John 1:14.*

Foundation *katabole* (2602), lit., "a casting down," is used (a) of "conceiving seed," Heb. 11:11; (b) of "a foundation," as that which is laid down, or in the sense of founding; metaphorically, of "the foundation of the world"; in this respect two phrases are used, (1) "from the foundation of the world," Matt. 25:34 (in the most authentic mss. in 13:35 there is no phrase representing "of the world"); Luke 11:50; Heb. 4:3; 9:26; Rev. 13:8; 17:8; (2) "before the foundation of the world," **John 17:24**; Eph. 1:4; 1 Pet. 1:20. The latter phrase looks back to the past eternity.

17:25 O righteous Father, the world hath not known thee: but I have known thee, and these have known that thou hast sent me.

Righteous *see* Just at *John 5:30.*

Father *see John 8:38.*

Sent *see John 1:6.*

17:26 And I have declared unto them thy name, and will declare *it*: that the love wherewith thou hast loved me may be in them, and I in them.

Declared, Declare *gnorizo*, "to make known," rendered "to declare" in **John 17:26**; 1 Cor. 15:1 and Col. 4:7.

Name *see John 1:12*.

Love *see* Loved at *John 3:16*.

Chapter 18

18:1 When Jesus had spoken these words, he went forth with his disciples over the brook Cedron, where was a garden, into the which he entered, and his disciples.

Brook *cheimarrhos* (5493), lit., "winter-flowing" (from *cheima*, "winter," and *rheo*, "to flow"), a stream which runs only in winter or when swollen with rains, a "brook" **John 18:1**.

Garden *kepos* (2779), "a garden," occurs in Luke 13:19, in one of the Lord's parables; in **John 18:1**, **26**, of the garden of Gethsemane; in **19:41**, of the garden near the place of the Lord's crucifixion.

18:2 And Judas also, which betrayed him, knew the place: for Jesus ofttimes resorted thither with his disciples.

Resorted *sunago* (4863), "to gather or bring together" (*sun*, "with," *ago*, "to bring"), in the passive voice, "to be gathered or come together," is translated "resorted" in **John 18:2** (the aorist tense expressing repeated action viewed cumulatively).

18:3 Judas then, having received a band *of men* and officers from the chief priests and Pharisees, cometh thither with lanterns and torches and weapons.

Officers *see John 7:32*.

Lanterns *phanos* (5322), denotes either "a torch" or "a lantern" (from *phaino*, "to cause to shine, to give light"), **John 18:3**, where it is distinguished from *lampas*; it was "a link or torch consisting of strips of resinous wood tied together" (Rutherford). "Torch" would seem to be the meaning.

Torches *lampas* (2985), denotes "a torch" (akin to *lampo*, "to shine"), frequently fed, like a "lamp," with oil from a little vessel used for the purpose (the *angeion* of Matt. 25:4); they held little oil and would frequently need replenishing. Rutherford (*The New Phrynichus*) points out that it became used as the equivalent of *luchnos*, as in the parable of the ten virgins, Matt. 25:1, 3, 4, 7, 8; **John 18:3**, "torches"; Acts 20:8, "lights"; Rev. 4:5; 8:10 (RV, "torch," KJV, "lamp"). Cf. *phanos*, "a torch," **John 18:3** (translated "lanterns").

Weapons *hoplon* (3696), originally any tool or implement for preparing a thing, became used in the plural for "weapons of warfare." Once in the NT it is used of actual weapons, **John 18:3**; elsewhere, metaphorically, of (a) the members of the body as instruments of unrighteousness and as instruments of righteousness, Rom. 6:13; (b) the "armor" of light, Rom. 13:12; the "armor" of righteousness, 2 Cor. 6:7; the weapons of the Christian's warfare, 2 Cor. 10:4.

18:4 Jesus therefore, knowing all things that should come upon him, went forth, and said unto them, Whom seek ye?

Knowing *see* Knew at *John 6:6*.

18:5-6 They answered him, Jesus of Nazareth. Jesus saith unto them, I am *he*. And Judas also, which betrayed him, stood with them.

As soon then as he had said unto them, I am *he*, they went backward, and fell to the ground.

Backward *see* Back at *John 6:66*.

Fell *pipto* (4098), "to fall," is used (a) of descent, to "fall" down from, e.g., Matt. 10:29; 13:4; (b) of a lot, Acts 1:26; (c) of "falling" under judgment, Jas. 5:12 (cf. Rev. 18:2, RV); (d) of persons in the act of prostration, to prostrate oneself, e.g., Matt. 17:6; **John 18:6**; Rev. 1:17; in homage and worship, e.g., Matt. 2:11; Mark 5:22; Rev. 5:14; 19:4; (e) of things, "falling" into ruin, or failing, e.g., Matt. 7:25; Luke 16:17, RV, "fall," for KJV, "fail"; Heb. 11:30; (f), of "falling" in judgment upon persons, as of the sun's heat, Rev. 7:16, RV, "strike," KJV, "light"; of a mist and darkness, Acts 13:11 (some mss. have *epipipto*); (g) of persons, in "falling" morally or spiritually, Rom. 14:4; 1 Cor. 10:8, 12; Rev. 2:5.

Ground *see John 9:6*.

18:7 Then asked he them again, Whom seek ye? And they said, Jesus of Nazareth.

Asked *eperotao* (1905), is frequently used in the Synoptic Gospels, but only twice in the Gospel of John, **18:7**, **21**. In Rom. 10:20 it is rendered "asked of" (KJV, "asked after"). The more intensive character of the "asking" may be observed in Luke 2:46; 3:14; 6:9; 17:20; 20:21, 27, 40; 22:64, 23:3, 6, 9. In Matt. 16:1, it virtually signifies to demand (its meaning in later Greek).

18:8 Jesus answered, I have told you that I am *he*: if therefore ye seek me, let these go their way:

Let ... go *see John 11:44.*

18:9 That the saying might be fulfilled, which he spake, Of them which thou gavest me have I lost none.

Saying *see John 4:37.*

Lost *see* Perish at *John 3:16.*

18:10 Then Simon Peter having a sword drew it, and smote the high priest's servant, and cut off his right ear. The servant's name was Malchus.

Having *see* Amend at *John 4:52.*

Drew *see* Draw at *John 6:44.*

Smote *paio* (3817), signifies "to strike or smite" (a) with the hand or fist, Matt. 26:68; Luke 22:64; (b) with a sword, Mark 14:47; **John 18:10**, KJV (RV, "struck"); (c) with a sting, Rev. 9:5, "striketh."

Name *see John 1:12* Name.

Cut *apokopto* (609), "to cut off, or cut away," is used (a) literally, of members of the body, Mark 9:43, 45; **John 18:10, 26**; of ropes, Acts 27:32; (b) metaphorically, in the middle voice, of "cutting off oneself," to excommunicate, Gal. 5:12, of the Judaizing teachers, with a reference, no doubt, to circumcision.

Ear *otion* (5621), is used in Matt. 26:51; Mark 14:47 (in some mss.); Luke 22:51; **John 18:10** (in some mss.) and v. **26**, all with reference to the "ear" of Malchus. The most authentic mss. have the alternative diminutive *otarion*, in Mark 14:47 and **John 18:10**.

18:11 Then said Jesus unto Peter, Put up thy sword into the sheath: the cup which my Father hath given me, shall I not drink it?

Put *see John 5:7.*

Sheath *theke* (2336), "a place to put something in" (akin to *tithemi*, "to put"), "a receptacle, chest, case," is used of the "sheath" of a sword, **John 18:11**.

Cup *poterion* (4221), a diminutive of *poter*, denotes, primarily, a "drinking vessel"; hence, "a cup" (a) literal, as, e.g., in Matt. 10:42. The "cup" of blessing, 1 Cor. 10:16, is so named from the third (the fourth according to Edersheim) "cup" in the Jewish Passover feast, over which thanks and praise were given to God. This connection is not to be rejected on the ground that the church at Corinth was unfamiliar with Jewish customs. That the contrary was the case, see 5:7; (b) figurative, of one's lot or experience, joyous or sorrowful (frequent in the Psalms; cf. Ps. 116:18, "cup of salvation"); in the NT it is used most frequently of the sufferings of Christ, Matt. 20:22-23; 26:39; Mark 10:38-39; 14:36; Luke 22:42; **John 18:11**; also of the evil deeds of Babylon, Rev. 17:4; 18:6; of divine punishments to be inflicted, Rev. 14:10; 16:19. Cf. Ps. 11:6; 75:8; Isa. 51:17; Jer. 25:15; Ezek. 23:32-34; Zech. 12:2.

18:12 Then the band and the captain and officers of the Jews took Jesus, and bound him,

Captain *chiliarchos* (5506), denoting "a commander of 1000 soldiers" (from *chilios*, "a thousand," and *archo*, "to rule"), was the Greek word for the Persian vizier, and for the Roman military tribune, the commander of a Roman cohort, e.g., **John 18:12**; Acts 21:31-33, 37. One such commander was constantly in charge of the Roman garrison in Jerusalem. The word became used also for any military commander, e.g., a "captain" or "chief captain," Mark 6:21; Rev. 6:15; 19:18.

Officers *see John 7:32.*

Took *sullambano* (4815), lit., "to take together" (*sun*, "with," *lambano*, "to take or lay hold of"), chiefly signifies "to seize as a prisoner"; in the following the RV substitutes the more suitable and forceful verb, "to seize," for KJV, "to take": Matt. 26:55; Mark 14:48; Luke 22:54; **John 18:12**; Acts 12:3; 23:27; 26:21; in Acts 1:16, RV and KJV, "took."

18:13 And led him away to Annas first; for he was father in law to Caiaphas, which was the high priest that same year.

Led *apago* (520), "to lead away" (*apo*, "away"), is used of a way "leading" to destruction, Matt. 7:13, to life, v. 14; of those who "led" Christ away from Gethsemane, Mark 14:44; in some mss., **John 18:13**, to Annas; to Caiaphas, Matt. 26:57; Mark 14:53; to Pilate, Matt. 27:2; to the Praetorium, Mark 15:16; to crucifixion, Matt. 27:31; Luke 23:26; in some mss. **John 19:16**; of "leading" an animal away to watering, Luke 13:15; of being "led" away to idolatry, 1 Cor. 12:2, RV, "led away" (KJV, "carried away"). Some mss. have it in Acts 24:7 (KJV, "took away"). It is translated "bring" in 23:17. In 12:19 it signifies "to put to death."

Father in law *pentheros* (3995), "a wife's father" (from a root signifying "a bond, union"), is found in **John 18:13**.

Year *see John 11:49.*

18:14 Now Caiaphas was he, which gave counsel to the Jews, that it was expedient that one man should die for the people.

Counsel *see John 11:53.*

Expedient *see John 11:50.*

Die *apollumi*, "to destroy," is found in the middle voice in some mss. in **John 18:14**, and translated "die." The most authentic mss. have *apothnesko*.

18:15 And Simon Peter followed Jesus, and *so did* another disciple: that disciple was known unto the high priest, and went in with Jesus into the palace of the high priest.

Known *gnostos* (1110), a later form of *gnotos*, most frequently denotes "known"; it is used ten times in the Acts, always with that meaning (save in 4:16, where it means "notable"); twice in the Gospel of John, **18:15**, **16**; in Luke 2:44 and 23:49 it denotes "acquaintance"; elsewhere only in Rom. 1:19, "(that which) may be known (of God)," lit., "the knowable of God," referring to the physical universe, in the creation of which God has made Himself "knowable," that is, by the exercise of man's natural faculties, without such supernatural revelations as those given to Israel.

Went *see John 6:22.*

18:16 But Peter stood at the door without. Then went out that other disciple, which was known unto the high priest, and spake unto her that kept the door, and brought in Peter.

Known *see John 18:15.*

Kept the door For the phrase "that kept the door," *thuroros*, **John 18:16-17** ("porter" in Mark 13:34; **John 10:3**).

18:17 Then saith the damsel that kept the door unto Peter, Art not thou also *one* of this man's disciples? He saith, I am not.

Damsel *paidiske* (3814), denotes "a young girl, or a female slave"; "damsel," KJV, in **John 18:17**; Acts 12:13; 16:16; RV "maid" in each case.

18:18 And the servants and officers stood there, who had made a fire of coals; for it was cold: and they warmed themselves: and Peter stood with them, and warmed himself.

Officers *see John 7:32.*

Coals *anthrakia* (439), is "a heap of burning coals, or a charcoal fire," **John 18:18**; **21:9**.

Cold *psuchos* (5592), "coldness, cold," appears in **John 18:18**; Acts 28:2; 2 Cor. 11:27.

Warmed *thermaino* (2328), "to warm, heat" (Eng. "thermal," etc.), when used in the middle voice, signifies "to warm oneself," Mark 14:54, 67; **John 18:18** (twice), 25; Jas. 2:16.

18:19 The high priest then asked Jesus of his disciples, and of his doctrine.

Asked *see John 9:15.*

18:20 Jesus answered him, I spake openly to the world; I ever taught in the synagogue, and in the temple, whither the Jews always resort; and in secret have I said nothing.

Openly *see John 7:4.*

Ever *see* Evermore at *John 6:34.*

Resort *sunerchomai* (4905), "to come together" (*sun* "with"), e.g., **John 18:20**, is often translated by the verb "to assemble"; see the RV of 1 Cor. 11:20; 14:23. In the KJV of **John 18:20** and Acts 16:13, it is translated "to resort."

Secret *see John 7:4.*

Said *see John 8:25.*

18:21 Why askest thou me? ask them which heard me, what I have said unto them: behold, they know what I said.

Askest, Ask *see* Asked at *John 18:7.*

Said *see John 8:25.*

18:22 And when he had thus spoken, one of the officers which stood by struck Jesus with the palm of his hand, saying, Answerest thou the high priest so?

Officers *see John 7:32.*

Stood *paristemi* (3936), intransitively, denotes "to stand by or beside," Mark 14:47, 69, 70; 15:35, 39 (RV, "stood by"); Luke 19:24; **John 18:22**; **19:26**; Acts 1:10; 9:39; 23:2, 4; 27:23; in 27:24, "stand before"; in 4:10, "doth ... stand here"; in Luke 1:19, "stand"; Rom. 14:10, "we shall ... stand before" (middle voice); 2 Tim. 4:17, RV, "stood by" (KJV, "... with").

Struck *rhapisma* (4475), "a blow," in the plural, as the object of *didomi*, "to give," in **John 19:3** is translated "smote (Him) with their hands" (RV, "struck, etc."), lit., "gave ... blows" (RV marg., "with rods"); in **18:22** (where the phrase is used with the singular of the noun) the RV renders it "struck ... with his hand" (KJV, "struck ... with the palm of his hand"), marg. of both, "with a rod." The same word is used in Mark 14:65, "(received Him) with blows (of their hands)", RV [KJV, "did strike Him with the palms (of their hands)," RV margin, "strokes of rods"].

18:23 Jesus answered him, If I have spoken evil, bear witness of the evil: but if well, why smitest thou me?

Evil *kakos* (2556), stands for "whatever is evil in character, base," in distinction (wherever the distinction is observable) from *poneros*, which indicates "what is evil in influence and effect, malignant." *Kakos* is the wider term and often covers the meaning of *poneros*. *Kakos* is antithetic to *kalos*, "fair, advisable, good in character," and to *agathos*, "beneficial, useful, good in act"; hence it denotes what is useless, incapable, bad; *poneros* is essentially antithetic to *chrestos*, "kind, gracious, serviceable"; hence it denotes what is destructive, injurious, evil. As evidence that *poneros* and *kakos* have much in common, though still not interchangeable, each is used of thoughts, cf. Matt. 15:19 with Mark 7:21; of speech, Matt. 5:11 with 1 Pet. 3:10; of actions, 2 Tim. 4:18 with 1 Thess. 5:15; of man, Matt. 18:32 with 24:48. The use of *kakos* may be broadly divided as follows: (a) of what is morally or ethically "evil," whether of persons, e.g., Matt. 21:41; 24:48; Phil. 3:2; Rev. 2:2, or qualities, emotions, passions, deeds, e.g., Mark 7:21; **John 18:23, 30**; Rom. 1:30; 3:8; 7:19, 21; 13:4; 14:20; 16:19; 1 Cor. 13:5; 2 Cor. 13:7; 1 Thess. 5:15; 1 Tim. 6:10; 2 Tim. 4:14; 1 Pet. 3:9, 12; (b) of what is injurious, destructive, baneful, pernicious, e.g., Luke 16:25; Acts 16:28; 28:5; Titus 1:12; Jas. 3:8; Rev. 16:2, where *kakos* and *poneros* come in that order, "noisome and grievous."

Witness *see John 1:7*.

Smitest *dero* (1194), from a root *der*–, "skin" (*derma*, "a skin," cf. Eng., "dermatology"), primarily "to flay," then "to beat, thrash or smite," is used of the treatment of the servants of the owner of the vineyard by the husbandmen, in the parable in Matt. 21:35; Mark 12:3, 5; Luke 20:10-11; of the treatment of Christ, Luke 22:63, RV, "beat," for KJV, "smote"; **John 18:23**; of the followers of Christ, in the synagogues, Mark 13:9; Acts 22:19; of the punishment of unfaithful servants, Luke 12:47-48; of the "beating" of apostles by the High Priest and the Council of the Sanhedrin, Acts 5:40; by magistrates, 16:37. The significance of flogging does not always attach to the word; it is used of the infliction of a single blow, **John 18:23**; 2 Cor. 11:20, and of "beating" the air, 1 Cor. 9:26. The usual meaning is that of "thrashing or cudgelling," and when used of a blow it indicates one of great violence.

18:24 Now Annas had sent him bound unto Caiaphas the high priest.

Now *see John 16:19*.

18:25 And Simon Peter stood and warmed himself. They said therefore unto him, Art not thou also *one* of his disciples? He denied *it*, and said, I am not.

Denied *see John 1:20*.

18:26 One of the servants of the high priest, being *his* kinsman whose ear Peter cut off, saith, Did not I see thee in the garden with him?

Kinsman *sungenes* (4773), primarily denoting "congenital, natural, innate" (*sun*, "with," *genos*, "a family, race, offspring"), then, "akin to," is used as a noun, denoting (a) of "family relationship, kin, a kinsman, kinsfolk(s)," Luke 1:58, RV, "kinsfolk" (KJV, "cousins"); 14:12; 21:16; **John 18:26**; Acts 10:24; (b) of "tribal or racial kinship, fellow nationals," Rom. 9:3; 16:7, 11, 21.

Ear *see John 18:10*.

Cut *see John 18:10*.

Garden *see John 18:1*.

18:27 Peter then denied again: and immediately the cock crew.

Denied *see John 1:20*.

Cock *see John 13:38*.

18:28 Then led they Jesus from Caiaphas unto the hall of judgment: and it was early; and they themselves went not into the judgment hall, lest they should be defiled; but that they might eat the passover.

Led *ago* (71), "to bear, bring, carry, lead," is translated by the verb "to lead," e.g., in Mark 13:11; Luke 4:1; 4:9, RV; 4:29; 22:54; 23:1, KJV only; 23:32; **John 18:28** (present tense, RV), Acts 8:32; metaphorically in Rom. 2:4, of the goodness of God; 8:14 and Gal. 5:18, of the Spirit of God; 1 Cor. 12:2, of the powers of darkness instigating to idolatry; 2 Tim. 3:6, of divers lusts (in some mss., *aichmaloteuo*). In Luke 24:21 *ago* is used of the passing (or spending) of a day, and translated "it is (now the third day)"; here the verb is probably to be taken impersonally, according to idiomatic usage, in the sense "there is passing the third day."

Hall of judgment, Judgment hall *praitorion* (4232), is translated "common hall" in Matt. 27:27, KJV (RV, "palace"); "Praetorium" in Mark 15:16; "hall of judgment" or "judgment hall" in **John 18:28, 33; 19:9**; Acts 23:35 (RV, "palace," in each place); "praetorian guard," Phil. 1:13 (KJV, "palace").

And *kai* Occasionally *kai* tends towards an *adversative* meaning, expressing a contrast, "yet," almost the equivalent of *alla*, "but"; see, e.g., Mark 12:12, "yet they feared";

Luke 20:19; **John 18:28**, "yet they themselves entered not." Some take it in this sense in Rom. 1:13, where, however, it may be simply parenthetic. Sometimes in the English versions the "yet" has been added in italics, as in 2 Cor. 6:8, 9, 10.

Early *proi* (4404) or *proios* (4405), "early, at early morn", "early in the day, at morn," derived from *pro*, "before." In Mark 16:2, KJV, it is translated "early in the morning"; in Mark 16:9 and **John 18:28; 20:1**, "early"; in Matt. 16:3; 20:1; 21:18; Mark 1:35; 11:20; 13:35; 15:1, "in the morning"; in Acts 28:23, "(from) morning." It is used as a noun in the feminine form *proia*, "morning" in Matt. 27:1 and **John 21:4** (in some mss. in Matt. 21:18 and **John 18:28**).

Themselves *autos* (846), "he," also means "self," in the reflexive pronouns "myself, thyself, himself," etc., expressing distinction, exclusion, etc.; it is usually emphatic in the nominative case, e.g., Luke 6:42; 11:4; **John 18:28**; Rom. 8:16, RV, "Himself."

Defiled *miaino* (3392), primarily, "to stain, to tinge or dye with another color," as in the staining of a glass, hence, "to pollute, contaminate, soil, defile," is used (a) of "ceremonial defilement," **John 18:28**; so in the Sept., in Lev. 22:5, 8; Num. 19:13, 20, etc.; (b) of "moral defilement," Titus 1:15 (twice); Heb. 12:15; "of moral and physical defilement," Jude 8.

18:29 Pilate then went out unto them, and said, What accusation bring ye against this man?

Accusation *kategoria* (2724), "an accusation," is found in **John 18:29**; 1 Tim. 5:19 and Titus 1:6, lit., "not under accusation." This and the verb *kategoreo*, "to accuse," and the noun *kategoros*, "an accuser," all have chiefly to do with judicial procedure, as distinct from *diaballo*, "to slander." It is derived from *agora*, "a place of public speaking," prefixed by *kata*, "against"; hence, it signifies a speaking against a person before a public tribunal. It is the opposite to *apologia*, "a defense."

18:30 They answered and said unto him, If he were not a malefactor, we would not have delivered him up unto thee.

Malefactor *kakopoios* (2555), properly the masculine gender of the adjective, denotes an "evil-doer" (*kakon*, "evil," *poieo*, "to do"), 1 Pet. 2:12, 14; 4:15; in some mss. in 3:16 and **John 18:30** (so the KJV). *See also* Evil at *John 18:23.*

18:31 Then said Pilate unto them, Take ye him, and judge him according to your law. The Jews therefore said unto him, It is not lawful for us to put any man to death:

Judge *see* Condemn at *John 3:17.*

Lawful *see John 5:10.*

Put ... to death *apokteino* (615), "to kill," is used (a) physically, e.g., Matt. 10:28; 14:5, "put ... to death," similarly rendered in **John 18:31**; often of Christ's death; in Rev. 2:13, RV "was killed" (KJV, "was slain"); 9:15, RV, "kill" (KJV, "slay"); 11:13, RV, "were killed" (KJV, "were slain"); so in 19:21; (b) metaphorically, Rom. 7:11, of the power of sin, which is personified, as "finding occasion, through the commandment," and inflicting deception and spiritual death, i.e., separation from God, realized through the presentation of the commandment to conscience, breaking in upon the fancied state of freedom; the argument shows the power of the Law, not to deliver from sin, but to enhance its sinfulness; in 2 Cor. 3:6, "the letter killeth," signifies not the literal meaning of Scripture as contrasted with the spiritual, but the power of the Law to bring home the knowledge of guilt and its punishment; in Eph. 2:16 "having slain the enmity" describes the work of Christ through His death in annulling the enmity, "the Law" (v. 15), between Jew and Gentile, reconciling regenerate Jew and Gentile to God in spiritual unity "in one body." *See also* Death at *John 11:53.*

18:32 That the saying of Jesus might be fulfilled, which he spake, signifying what death he should die.

Saying *see John 4:37.*

Signifying *see John 12:33.*

What *see John 12:33.*

Should *see John 6:71.*

18:33 Then Pilate entered into the judgment hall again, and called Jesus, and said unto him, Art thou the King of the Jews?

Judgment hall *see* Hall of judgment, Judgment hall at *John 18:28.*

18:34 Jesus answered him, Sayest thou this thing of thyself, or did others tell it thee of me?

Thyself *heautou* (with *apo*, "from"), John 18:34, "of thyself," lit., "from thyself".

18:35-36 Pilate answered, Am I a Jew? Thine own nation and the chief priests have delivered thee unto me: what hast thou done?

Jesus answered, My kingdom is not of this world: if my kingdom were of this world, then would my servants fight,

that I should not be delivered to the Jews: but now is my kingdom not from hence.

Servants *huperetes* (5257), is translated "servants" in the KJV of Matt. 26:58; Mark 14:65 (RV, "officers"); in **John 18:36**, KJV and RV (RV, marg., "officers").

Fight *agonizomai* (75), denotes (a) "to contend" in the public games, 1 Cor. 9:25 ("striveth in the games," RV); (b) "to fight, engage in conflict," **John 18:36**; (c) metaphorically, "to contend" perseveringly against opposition and temptation, 1 Tim. 6:12; 2 Tim. 4:7 (in regard to the meaning there, the evidence of *Koine* inscriptions is against the idea of games-contests); to strive as in a contest for a prize, straining every nerve to attain to the object Luke 13:24; to put forth every effort, involving toil, Col. 1:29; 1 Tim. 4:10 (some mss. have *oneidizomai* here, "to suffer reproach"); to wrestle earnestly in prayer, Col. 4:12 (cf. *sunagonizomai*, Rom. 15:30).

Hence *see John 2:16*.

18:37 Pilate therefore said unto him, Art thou a king then? Jesus answered, Thou sayest that I am a king. To this end was I born, and for this cause came I into the world, that I should bear witness unto the truth. Every one that is of the truth heareth my voice.

Therefore *oukoun* (3766), an adverb formed from *ouk*, "not," *oun*, "therefore," with the negative element dropped, meaning "so then," is used in **John 18:37**.

King *see John 1:49*.

End The phrase *eis touto*, lit., "unto this," signifies "to this end," **John 18:37**, RV (twice; KJV, "for this cause," in the second clause); so Mark 1:38; Acts 26:16; Rom. 14:9; 2 Cor. 2:9; 1 Tim. 4:10 (KJV, "therefore"); 1 Pet. 4:6; 1 John 3:8 (KJV, "for this purpose").

Cause In **John 18:37**, *eis touto*, "unto this," denotes "unto this end," RV (KJV, "for this cause").

Witness *see John 1:7*.

Truth *see John 8:44*.

Voice *see* **Sound** at *John 3:8*.

18:38 Pilate saith unto him, What is truth? And when he had said this, he went out again unto the Jews, and saith unto them, I find in him no fault *at all*.

Truth *see John 8:44*.

Find *heurisko* (2147), denotes (a) "to find," either with previous search, e.g., Matt. 7:7, 8, or without, e.g., Matt. 27:32; in the passive voice, of Enoch's disappearance, Heb. 11:5; of mountains, Rev. 16:20; of Babylon and its occupants, 18:21, 22; (b) metaphorically, "to find out by enquiry," or "to learn, discover," e.g., Luke 19:48; **John 18:38**; **19:4, 6**; Acts 4:21; 13:28; Rom. 7:10; Gal. 2:17, which indicates "the surprise of the Jew" who learned for the first time that before God he had no moral superiority over the Gentiles whom he superciliously dubbed "sinners," while he esteemed himself to be "righteous"; 1 Pet. 1:7; Rev. 5:4; (c) in the middle voice, "to find for oneself, gain, procure, obtain," e.g. Matt. 10:39; 11:29, "ye shall find (rest)"; Luke 1:30; Acts 7:46; 2 Tim. 1:18.

Fault *aition* (158), properly the neuter of *aitios*, causative of, responsible for, is used as a noun, "a crime, a legal ground for punishment," translated "fault" in Luke 23:4, 14; in v. 22, cause, *aitia* is rendered "fault" in **John 18:38**; **19:4**, **6**, KJV (like *aition*, denoting "a ground for punishment").

18:39 But ye have a custom, that I should release unto you one at the passover: will ye therefore that I release unto you the King of the Jews?

Custom *sunetheia* (4914), *sun*, "with," *ethos*, denotes (a) "an intercourse, intimacy," a meaning not found in the NT; (b) "a custom, customary usage," **John 18:39**; 1 Cor. 11:16; "or force of habit," 1 Cor. 8:7, RV, "being used to" (some mss. here have *suneidsis*, "conscience"; whence KJV, "with conscience of").

Release *apoluo* (630), "to loose from," is translated "to release" in Matt. 18:27, RV (KJV, "loosed"); 27:15, 17, 21, 26; Mark 15:6, 9, 11, 15; Luke 6:37 (twice), RV (KJV, "forgive" and "ye shall be forgiven"); 23:16 (v. 17, in some mss.), 18, 20, 25; 23:22, RV (KJV, "let ... go"); **John 18:39** (twice); **19:10**; in **19:12**, in the 1st part, KJV and RV; in the 2nd part, RV, "release" (KJV, "let ... go"); so in Acts 3:13.

Passover *see John 2:13*.

18:40 Then cried they all again, saying, Not this man, but Barabbas. Now Barabbas was a robber.

Cried *see John 11:43*.

Robber *see John 10:1*.

Chapter 19

19:1 Then Pilate therefore took Jesus, and scourged *him*.

Scourged *mastigoo* (3146), in **John 19:1** the "scourging" of Christ, as also in His prophecy of His sufferings, Matt. 20:19; Mark 10:34; Luke 18:33.

19:2 And the soldiers platted a crown of thorns, and put *it* on his head, and they put on him a purple robe,

Platted *pleko* (4120), "to weave, twist, plait," is used of the crown of thorns inflicted on Christ, Matt. 27:29; Mark 15:17; **John 19:2**.

Crown *stephanos* (4735), primarily, "that which surrounds, as a wall or crowd" (from *stepho*, "to encircle"), denotes (a) "the victor's crown," the symbol of triumph in the games or some such contest; hence, by metonymy, a reward or prize; (b) "a token of public honor" for distinguished service, military prowess, etc., or of nuptial joy, or festal gladness, especially at the parousia of kings. It was woven as a garland of oak, ivy, parsley, myrtle, or olive, or in imitation of these in gold. In some passages the reference to the games is clear, 1 Cor. 9:25; 2 Tim. 4:8 ("crown of righteousness"); it may be so in 1 Pet. 5:4, where the fadeless character of "the crown of glory" is set in contrast to the garlands of earth. In other passages it stands as an emblem of life, joy, reward and glory, Phil. 4:1; 1 Thess. 2:19; Jas. 1:12 ("crown of life"); Rev. 2:10 (ditto); 3:11; 4:4, 10; of triumph, 6:2; 9:7; 12:1; 14:14. It is used of "the crown of thorns" which the soldiers plaited and put on Christ's head, Matt. 27:29; Mark 15:17; **John 19:2, 5**. At first sight this might be taken as an alternative for *diadema*, "a kingly crown", but considering the blasphemous character of that masquerade, and the materials used, obviously *diadema* would be quite unfitting and the only alternative was *stephanos*.

Thorns *akantha* (173), "a brier, a thorn" (from *ake*, "a point"), is always used in the plural in the NT, Matt. 7:16 and parallel passage in Luke 6:44; Matt. 13:7 (twice), 22 and parallels in Mark and Luke; in Matt. 27:29 and **John 19:2**, of the crown of "thorns" placed on Christ's head in mock imitation of the garlands worn by emperors. They were the effects of the divine curse on the ground (Gen. 3.18, contrast Isa. 55:13). The "thorns" of the crown plaited by the soldiers, are usually identified with those of the *Zizyphus spina Christi*, some 20 feet high or more, fringing the Jordan and abundant in Palestine; its twigs are flexible. Another species, however, the Arabian *qundaul*, crowns of which are plaited and sold in Jerusalem as representatives of Christ's crown, seems likely to be the one referred to. The branches are easily woven and adapted to the torture intended. The word *akantha* occurs also in Heb. 6:8.

Put *periballo* (4016), "to put or throw around," is translated "put on" in **John 19:2**, KJV (RV, "arrayed ... in"). *See also* ***John 9:15***.

Purple *porphureos* (4210), "purple, a reddish purple," is used of the robe put in mockery on Christ, **John 19:2, 5**; in Rev. 17:4; 18:16, as a noun (with *himation*, "a garment," understood).

Robe *himation* (2440), is translated "robe" in the KJV of **John 19:2, 5** (RV, "garment).

19:3 And said, Hail, King of the Jews! and they smote him with their hands.

"Bearing shame and scoffing rude, / In my place condemned He stood; / Sealed my pardon with His blood: / Hallelujah, what a Savior!"

PHILIPP PAUL BLISS

Hail *chairo* (5463), "to rejoice," is used in the imperative mood, (a) as a salutation, only in the Gospels; in this respect it is rendered simply "hail," in mockery of Christ, Matt. 26:49; 27:29; Mark 15:18; **John 19:3**; (b) as a greeting, by the angel Gabriel to Mary, Luke 1:28, and, in the plural, by the Lord to the disciples after His resurrection, Matt. 28:9.

Smote *see* **Struck** at *John 18:22*.

19:4 Pilate therefore went forth again, and saith unto them, Behold, I bring him forth to you, that ye may know that I find no fault in him.

Forth *see John 11:43*.

Know *see John 7:26*.

Find *see John 18:38*.

19:5 Then came Jesus forth, wearing the crown of thorns, and the purple robe. And *Pilate* saith unto them, Behold the man!

Wearing *phoreo* (5409), a frequentative form of *phero*, "to bear," and denoting "repeated or habitual action," is chiefly used of clothing, weapons, etc., of soft raiment, Matt. 11:8; fine clothing, Jas. 2:3; the crown of thorns, **John 19:5**.

Crown *see John 19:2.*

Thorns *akanthinos* (174), "of thorns," is used in Mark 15:17 and **John 19:5**. In the Sept., Isa. 34:13.

Purple *see John 19:2.*

Robe *see John 19:2.*

19:6 When the chief priests therefore and officers saw him, they cried out, saying, Crucify *him*, crucify *him*. Pilate saith unto them, Take ye him, and crucify *him*: for I find no fault in him.

Officers *see John 7:32.*

Cried *see John 11:43.*

Find *see John 18:38.*

19:7 The Jews answered him, We have a law, and by our law he ought to die, because he made himself the Son of God.

Ought *see John 13:14.*

Made *see* Make at *John 2:16.*

19:8-9 When Pilate therefore heard that saying, he was the more afraid;

And went again into the judgment hall, and saith unto Jesus, Whence art thou? But Jesus gave him no answer.

Judgment hall *see* Hall of judgment, Judgment hall at *John 18:28.*

Answer *see John 1:22.*

19:10 Then saith Pilate unto him, Speakest thou not unto me? knowest thou not that I have power to crucify thee, and have power to release thee?

Power *see John 17:2.*

Release *apoluo* (630), signifies "to set free, release, loose" (*apo*, "from," *luo*, "to loose"), e.g., Luke 13:12; **John 19:10**; forgive, Luke 6:37; to release, dismiss, send away, translated "to let go," e.g., in Luke 14:4; in some mss. 22:68; in Luke 23:22; **John 19:12** and Acts 3:13, KJV, "let ... go" (RV, "release"); in Acts 4:21, "they let ... go"; in v. 23 (passive voice), "being let go"; 5:40; in 15:33, KJV, "let go" (RV, "dismissed"); 16:35, 36; 17:9; in 23:22, RV, "let ... go" (KJV, "let ... depart"); in 28:18, KJV, "let ... go" (RV, "set ... at liberty"). *See also John 18:39.*

19:11 Jesus answered, Thou couldest have no power *at all* against me, except it were given thee from above: therefore he that delivered me unto thee hath the greater sin.

Above *see John 3:31.*

Sin *see John 1:29.*

19:12 And from thenceforth Pilate sought to release him: but the Jews cried out, saying, If thou let this man go, thou art not Caesar's friend: whosoever maketh himself a king speaketh against Caesar.

Thenceforth In **John 19:12**, KJV, *ek toutou*, "from this," is translated "from thenceforth" (RV, "upon this").

Release *see John 18:39.*

Cried *see John 11:43.*

Let *see* Release at *John 19:10.*

Go *hodoiporeo* ... (l), "to be on a journey," Acts 10:9, RV, "as they were on their journey" (KJV, "as they went, etc."); (m) *embaino*, "to enter," Matt. 13:2 and Luke 8:22, RV, "entered" (KJV, "went into"); in v. 37 (KJV, "went up into"); (n) *apoluo*, "to set free," Luke 23:22 and **John 19:12**, RV, "release" (KJV, "let ... go"); Acts 15:33, RV, "dismissed" (KJV, ditto); Acts 28:18, RV, "set at liberty" (KJV, ditto); (o) *epibaino*, "to go upon," Acts 21:4, RV, "set foot" (KJV, "go"); some mss. have *anabaino*; (p) *apangello*, "to announce," Acts 12:17, RV, "tell" (KJV, "go shew"); (q) *aperchomai*, "to go away," Matt. 5:30, RV, "go" (KJV, "be cast"); some mss. have *ballo*, "to cast"; (r) *peripateo*, "to walk," Mark 12:38, RV, "walk" (KJV "go"); (s) for "gone by," Acts 14:16, RV.

Maketh *see* Make at *John 2:16.*

Speaketh *antilego* (483), "to speak against," is so rendered in Luke 2:34; **John 19:12**; Acts 13:45, KJV (RV, "contradicted"); 28:19, 22.

19:13 When Pilate therefore heard that saying, he brought Jesus forth, and sat down in the judgment seat in a place that is called the Pavement, but in the Hebrew, Gabbatha.

Saying *see John 4:37.*

Forth *see John 11:43.*

Judgment seat *bema* (968), primarily, "a step, a pace" (akin to *baino*, "to go"), as in Acts 7:5, translated "to set (his foot) on," lit., "footroom," was used to denote a raised place or platform, reached by steps, originally that at Athens in the Pnyx Hill, where was the place of assembly; from the platform orations were made. The word became used for a tribune, two of which were provided in the law courts of Greece, one for the accuser and one for the defendant; it was applied to the tribunal of a Roman magistrate or ruler, Matt. 27:19; **John 19:13**; Acts 12:21, translated "throne"; 18:12, 16, 17; 25:6, 10, 17. In two passages the word is used of the divine tribunal before which all believers are hereafter to stand. In Rom. 14:10 it is called "The judgement seat of God," RV (KJV, "of Christ"), according to the most authentic mss. The same tribunal is called "the judgment seat of Christ," 2 Cor. 5:10, to whom the Father has given all judgment, **John 5:22, 27.** At this *bema* believers are to be made manifest, that each may "receive the things done in (or through) the body," according to what he has done, "whether it be good or bad." There they will receive rewards for their faithfulness to the Lord. For all that has been contrary in their lives to His will they will suffer loss, 1 Cor. 3:15. This judgment seat is to be distinguished from the premillennial, earthly throne of Christ, Matt. 25:31, and the postmillennial "Great White Throne," Rev. 20:11, at which only "the dead" will appear. The judgment seat of Christ will be a tribunal held "in His Parousia," i.e., His presence with His saints after His return to receive them to Himself.

Sat *kathizo* (2523), is used (a) transitively, "to make sit down," Acts 2:30; (b) intransitively, "to sit down," e.g., Matt. 5:1, RV, "when (He) had sat down" (KJV, "was set"); 19:28; 20:21, 23; 23:2; 25:31; 26:36; Mark 11:2, 7; 12:41; Luke 14:28, 31; 16:6; **John 19:13**; Acts 2:3 (of the tongues of fire); 8:31; 1 Cor. 10:7; 2 Thess. 2:4, "he sitteth," aorist tense, i.e., "he takes his seat" (as, e.g., in Mark 16:19); Rev. 3:21 (twice), RV, "to sit down" and "sat down"; 20:4.

Pavement *lithostrotos* (3038), an adjective, denoting "paved with stones" (*lithos*, "a stone," and *stronnuo*, "to spread"), especially of tessellated work, is used as a noun in **John 19:13**, of a place near the Praetorium in Jerusalem, called Gabbatha, a Greek transliteration of an Aramaic word. In the Sept., 2 Chron. 7:3; Esth. 1:6; Song of Sol. 3:10.

19:14 And it was the preparation of the passover, and about the sixth hour: and he saith unto the Jews, Behold your King!

Preparation *paraskeue* (3904), denotes "preparation, equipment." The day on which Christ died is called "the Preparation" in Mark 15:42 and **John 19:31**; in **John 19:42** "the Jews' Preparation," RV; in **19:14** it is described as "the Preparation of the Passover"; in Luke 23:54, RV, "the day of the Preparation (and the Sabbath drew on)." The same day is in view in Matt. 27:62, where the events recorded took place on "the day after the Preparation" (RV). The reference would be to the 6th day of the week. The title arose from the need of preparing food, etc., for the Sabbath. Apparently it was first applied only to the afternoon of the 6th day; later, to the whole day. In regard to the phraseology in **John 19:14**, many hold this to indicate the "preparation" for the paschal feast. It probably means "the Preparation day," and thus falls in line with the Synoptic Gospels. In modern Greek and ecclesiastical Latin, *Parasceve* = Friday.

Passover *see John 2:13.*

19:15 But they cried out, Away with *him*, away with *him*, crucify him. Pilate saith unto them, Shall I crucify your King? The chief priests answered, We have no king but Caesar.

Cried *see John 11:43.*

Away This word is to be taken in connection with various verbs. The verb *airo*, "to seize, to lift up, take away," is translated "away with," in Luke 23:18; **John 19:15**; Acts 21:36; 22:22, implying a forcible removal for the purpose of putting to death.

19:16 Then delivered he him therefore unto them to be crucified. And they took Jesus, and led *him* away.

Took *paralambano* (3880), besides its meaning "to receive," denotes "to take to (or with) oneself," of "taking" a wife, e.g., Matt. 1:20, 24; of "taking" a person or persons with one, e.g., Matt. 2:13, 14, 20, 21; 4:5, 8; of demons, 12:45; of Christ and His disciples, 17:1; 20:17; Mark 9:2; 10:32; 14:33; of witnesses, Matt. 18:16; of the removal of persons from the earth in judgment, when "the Son of Man is revealed," Matt. 24:40, 41; Luke 17:34, 35 (cf. the means of the removal of corruption, in v. 37); of the "taking" of Christ by the soldiers for scourging, Matt. 27:27, RV, and to crucifixion, **John 19:16**; see also Acts 15:39; 16:33; 21:24, 26, 32; 23:18.

Led *see John 18:13.*

19:17 And he bearing his cross went forth into a place called *the place* of a skull, which is called in the Hebrew Golgotha:

Bearing *see* Took up at *John 10:31.*

Skull *kranion* (2898), Lat., *cranium* (akin to *kara*, "the head"), is used of the scene of the Crucifixion, Matt. 27:33; Mark 15:22; **John 19:17**; in Luke 23:33, RV, "(the place which is called) The skull," KJV, "Calvary" (from Latin *calvaria*, "a skull": marg., "the place of a skull"). The locality has been identified by the traces of the resemblance of the hill to a "skull". In the Sept., Judg. 9:53; 2 Kings 9:35.

19:18 Where they crucified him, and two other with him, on either side one, and Jesus in the midst.

Either The adverb *enteuthen*, denoting "hence," is repeated in the phrase rendered "on either side," (lit., "hence and hence") in **John 19:18**. The RV of Rev. 22:2 translates it "on this side," distinguishing it from *ekeithen*, "on that side"; the KJV, following another reading for the latter adverb, has "on either side."

19:19 And Pilate wrote a title, and put *it* on the cross. And the writing was, JESUS OF NAZARETH THE KING OF THE JEWS.

Wrote *see John 8:6*.

Title *titlos* (5102), from Latin *titulus*, is used of the inscription above the cross of Christ, **John 19:19, 20**.

Put *tithemi* (5087), "to place, lay, set, put," is translated "to put" in Matt. 5:15; 12:18; in Matt. 22:44, RV, "put (underneath Thy feet)"; Mark 4:21 (1st part), in the 2nd part, RV, "put" (in some texts, KJV, "set"); 10:16, KJV (RV, "laying"); Luke 8:16 (1st part); 2nd part, RV (KJV, "setteth"); 11:33; **John 19:19**; Acts 1:7, KJV (RV, "set"); 4:3; 5:18, 25; 12:4; Rom. 14:13; 1 Cor. 15:25; 2 Cor. 3:13; 1 Tim. 1:12, KJV (RV, "appointing"); Rev. 11:9, KJV (RV, "laid").

Writing In **John 19:19**, KJV, "the writing (was)" is a translation of the perfect participle, passive voice, of *grapho*, RV, "(there was) written."

19:20 This title then read many of the Jews: for the place where Jesus was crucified was nigh to the city: and it was written in Hebrew, *and* Greek, *and* Latin.

Title *see John 19:19*.

Greek *Hellenisti*, "in Greek," **John 19:20**, RV; Acts 21:37, "Greek."

Latin *rhomaisti* (4515), an adverb, "in Latin," occurs in **John 19:20**, lit., "in Roman."

19:21 Then said the chief priests of the Jews to Pilate, Write not, The King of the Jews; but that he said, I am King of the Jews.

Write *see* Wrote at *John 8:6*.

19:22 Pilate answered, What I have written I have written.

Written *see* Wrote at *John 8:6*.

19:23 Then the soldiers, when they had crucified Jesus, took his garments, and made four parts, to every soldier a part; and also *his* coat: now the coat was without seam, woven from the top throughout.

Garments *chiton* (5509), denotes "the inner vest or undergarment," and is to be distinguished, as such, from the *himation*. The distinction is made, for instance, in the Lord's command in Matt. 5:40: "If any man would go to law with thee, and take away thy coat (*chiton*), (*himation*) also." The order is reversed in Luke 6:29, and the difference lies in this, that in Matt. 5:40 the Lord is referring to a legal process, so the claimant is supposed to claim the inner garment, the less costly. The defendant is to be willing to let him have the more valuable one too. In the passage in Luke an act of violence is in view, and there is no mention of going to law. So the outer garment is the first one which would be seized. When the soldiers had crucified Jesus they took His garments (*himation*, in the plural), His outer garments, and the "coat," the *chiton*, the inner garment, which was without seam, woven from the top throughout, **John 19:23**. The outer garments were easily divisible among the four soldiers, but they could not divide the *chiton* without splitting it, so they cast lots for it. Dorcas was accustomed to make coats (*chiton*) and garments (*himation*), Acts 9:39, that is, the close fitting undergarments and the long, flowing outer robes. A person was said to be "naked" (*gumnos*), whether he was without clothing, or had thrown off his outer garment, e.g., his *ependutes*, and was clad in a light undergarment, as was the case with Peter, in **John 21:7**. The high priest, in rending his clothes after the reply the Lord gave him in answer to his challenge, rent his undergarments (*chiton*), the more forcibly to express his assumed horror and indignation, Mark 14:63. In Jude 23, "the garment spotted by the flesh" is the *chiton*, the metaphor of the undergarment being appropriate; for it would be that which was brought into touch with the pollution of the flesh.

Parts, Part *see* Part at *John 13:8*.

Every *hekastos* (1538), "each" or "every," is used of any number separately, either (a) as an adjective qualifying a noun, e.g., Luke 6:44; **John 19:23**; Heb. 3:13, where "day by day," is, lit., "according to each day"; or, more emphatically with *heis*, "one," in Matt. 26:22; Luke 4:40; 16:5; Acts 2:3, 6, 20:31; 1 Cor. 12:18; Eph. 4:7, 16, RV, "each (several)," for KJV, "every"; Col. 4:6; 1 Thess. 2:11; 2 Thess. 1:3; (b) as a distributive pronoun, e.g., Acts 4:35; Rom. 2:6; Gal. 6:4; in Phil. 2:4, it is used in the plural; some mss. have it thus in Rev. 6:11. The repetition in Heb. 8:11 is noticeable "every man" (i.e., everyone). Prefixed by the preposition *ana*, "apiece" (a colloquialism), it is used, with stress on the individuality, in Rev. 21:21, of the gates of the heavenly city, "each one of the several," RV; in Eph. 5:33, preceded by *kath' hena*, "by one," it signifies "each (one) his own."

Coat *himatismos* (2441), in form a collective word, denoting "vesture, garments," is used generally of "costly or stately raiment," the apparel of kings, of officials, etc. See Luke 7:25, where "gorgeously apparelled" is, lit., "in gorgeous vesture." See also

Acts 20:33 and 1 Tim. 2:9, "costly raiment." This is the word used of the Lord's white and dazzling raiment on the Mount of Transfiguration, Luke 9:29. It is also used of His *chiton*, His undergarment, for which the soldiers cast lots, **John 19:23-24**, "vesture"; in Matt. 27:35 it is also translated vesture.

Now *de* (1161), "but, and, now," often implying an antithesis, is rendered "now" in **John 19:23**; 1 Cor. 10:11; 15:50; Gal. 1:20; Eph. 4:9; in Acts 27:9 (1st part), RV, "and" (KJV, "now"); in Gal. 4:1, RV, "but" (KJV, "now").

Without seam *araphos or arrhaphos* (729), denotes "without seam" (*a*, negative, and *rhapto*, "to sew"), **John 19:23**.

Woven *huphantos* (5307), from *huphaino*, "to weave" (found in good mss. in Luke 12:27), is used of Christ's garment, **John 19:23**.

Top In Matt. 27:51 and Mark 15:38, *apo anothen*, "from the top" (lit., "from above"), is used of the upper part of the Temple veil. In **John 19:23**, the different phrase *ek ton anothen* is used of the weaving of the Lord's garment (the *chiton*), lit., "from the parts above."

19:24 They said therefore among themselves, Let us not rend it, but cast lots for it, whose it shall be: that the scripture might be fulfilled, which saith, They parted my raiment among them, and for my vesture they did cast lots. These things therefore the soldiers did.

Themselves *see John 6:52.*

Rend *schizo* (4977), "to split, rend open," translated "to rend" in Matt. 27:51 (twice); Mark 1:10, RV, "rent asunder" (KJV, "open"); 15:38; Luke 5:36, RV, "rendeth (from)"; the KJV follows the mss. which omit it in the 1st part of this verse; 23:45; **John 19:24**; **21:11**, RV, "rent" (KJV, "broken"), of a net.

Lots *lanchano* (2975), denotes (a) "to draw lots," **John 19:24**; (b) "to obtain by lot, to obtain," Luke 1:9, "his lot was," lit., "he received by lot," i.e., by divine appointment; Acts 1:17, of the portion "allotted" by the Lord to His apostles in their ministry; 2 Pet. 1:1, "that have obtained (a like precious faith)," i.e., by its being "allotted" to them, not by acquiring it for themselves, but by divine grace (an act independent of human control, as in the casting of "lots").

Scripture *see John 2:22.*

Parted *diamerizo* (1266), "to divide through," i.e., "completely, to divide up," is translated "to divide" in Luke 11:17-18; 12:52-53; 22:17; "parted" in Matt. 27:35; Mark 15:24; Luke 23:34; **John 19:24**; Acts 2:45; in Acts 2:3, KJV, "cloven," RV, "parting asunder."

Raiment For *himation*, rendered "raiment" in Matt. 17:2, KJV (RV, "garments"), so Matt. 27:31; Mark 9:3; Luke 23:34; **John 19:24**; Acts 22:20; Rev. 3:5, 18; 4:4; KJV and RV, Acts 18:6. *Himatismos* is rendered "raiment" in Luke 9:29; *enduma* in Matt. 3:4; 6:25, 28; 28:3 and Luke 12:23. For *esthes*, translated "raiment" in Jas. 2:2 (2nd part), KJV.

Vesture *himatismos* (2441), used of "clothing in general," is translated "vesture" in Matt. 27:35, KJV, in a quotation from Ps. 22:18 (RV, following the better texts, omits the quotation); in **John 19:24**, KJV and RV.

19:25 Now there stood by the cross of Jesus his mother, and his mother's sister, Mary the *wife* of Cleophas, and Mary Magdalene.

Wife In **John 19:25** the article stands idiomatically for "the *wife* (of)"; in Matt. 1:6, the article is rendered "her *that had been the wife* (of)."

19:26 When Jesus therefore saw his mother, and the disciple standing by, whom he loved, he saith unto his mother, Woman, behold thy son!

Standing *see* Stood at *John 18:22.*

Woman *see John 2:4.*

19:27 Then saith he to the disciple, Behold thy mother! And from that hour that disciple took her unto his own *home*.

Then *see* After that at *John 13:5.*

Mother *meter* (3384), is used (a) of the natural relationship, e.g., Matt. 1:18; 2 Tim. 1:5; (b) figuratively, (1) of "one who takes the place of a mother," Matt. 12:49, 50; Mark 3:34, 35; **John 19:27**; Rom. 16:13; 1 Tim. 5:2; (2) of "the heavenly and spiritual Jerusalem," Gal. 4:26, which is "free" (not bound by law imposed externally, as under the Law of Moses), "which is our mother" (RV), i.e., of Christians, the metropolis, mother-city, used allegorically, just as the capital of a country is "the seat of its government, the center of its activities, and the place where the national characteristics are most fully expressed"; (3) symbolically, of "Babylon," Rev. 17:5, as the source from which has proceeded the religious harlotry of mingling pagan rites and doctrines with the Christian faith.

His *see John 5:18.*

19:28 After this, Jesus knowing that all things were now accomplished, that the scripture might be fulfilled, saith, I thirst.

Accomplished *teleo* (5055), "to bring to an end" (*telos*, "an end"), in the passive voice, "to be finished," is translated by the verb "to finish" in Matt. 13:53; 19:1; 26:1; **John 19:28**, where the RV "are ... finished" brings out the force of the perfect tense (the same word as in v. **30**, "It is finished"), which is missed in the KJV; as Stier says, "the word was in His heart before He uttered it", 2 Tim. 4:7; Rev. 10:7; 11:7; 20:3, RV, "should be finished" (KJV, "fulfilled"), 5, 7, RV, "finished" (KJV, "expired").

Scripture *see John 2:22.*

Fulfilled *teleioo* (5048), "to bring to an end, fulfill," is rendered "to fulfill," of days. Luke 2:43; of the Scripture, **John 19:28**.

Thirst *see John 4:13.*

19:29 Now there was set a vessel full of vinegar: and they filled a spunge with vinegar, and put *it* upon hyssop, and put *it* to his mouth.

Now *see John 16:19.*

Set *see John 2:6.*

Vessel *skeuos* (4632), is used (a) of "a vessel or implement" of various kinds, Mark 11:16; Luke 8:16; **John 19:29**; Acts 10:11, 16; 11:5; 27:17 (a sail); Rom. 9:21; 2 Tim. 2:20; Heb. 9:21; Rev. 2:27; 18:12; (b) of "goods or household stuff," Matt. 12:29 and Mark 3:27, "goods"; Luke 17:31, RV, "goods" (KJV, "stuff"); (c) of "persons," (1) for the service of God, Acts 9:15, "a (chosen) vessel"; 2 Tim. 2:21, "a vessel (unto honor)"; (2) the "subjects" of divine wrath, Rom. 9:22; (3) the "subjects" of divine mercy, Rom. 9:23; (4) the human frame, 2 Cor. 4:7; perhaps 1 Thess. 4:4; (5) a husband and wife, 1 Pet. 3:7; of the wife, probably, 1 Thess. 4:4; while the exhortation to each one "to possess himself of his own vessel in sanctification and honor" is regarded by some as referring to the believer's body [cf. Rom. 6:13; 1 Cor. 9:27], the view that the "vessel" signifies the wife, and that the reference is to the sanctified maintenance of the married state, is supported by the facts that in 1 Pet. 3:7 the same word *time*, "honor," is used with regard to the wife, again in Heb. 13:4, *timios*, "honorable" (RV, "in honor") is used in regard to marriage; further, the preceding command in 1 Thess. 4 is against fornication, and the succeeding one (v. 6) is against adultery. In Ruth 4:10, Sept., *ktaomai*, "to possess," is used of a wife.

Full *mestos* (3324), probably akin to a root signifying "to measure," hence conveys the sense of "having full measure," (a) of material things, a vessel, **John 19:29**; a net, **21:11**; (b) metaphorically, of thoughts and feelings, exercised (1) in evil things, hypocrisy, Matt. 23:28; envy, murder, strife, deceit, malignity, Rom. 1:29; the utterances of the tongue, Jas. 3:8; adultery, 2 Pet. 2:14; (2) in virtues, goodness, Rom. 15:14; mercy, etc., Jas. 3:17.

Vinegar *oxos* (3690), akin to *oxus*, "sharp," denotes "sour wine," the ordinary drink of laborers and common soldiers; it is used in the four Gospels of the "vinegar" offered to the Lord at His crucifixion. In Matt. 27:34 the best texts have *oinos*, "wine" (RV). Some have *oxos* (KJV, "vinegar"), but Mark 15:23 (KJV and RV) confirms the RV in the passage in Matthew. This, which the soldiers offered before crucifying, was refused by Him, as it was designed to alleviate His sufferings; the "vinegar" is mentioned in Mark 15:36; so Luke 23:36, and **John 19:29, 30**. In the Sept., Num. 6:3; Ruth 2:14; Ps. 69:21; Prov. 25:20.

Filled *pimplemi* (4130), and *pletho* (4130), lengthened forms of *pleo*, "to fill" (*pletho* supplies certain tenses of *pimplemi*), is used (1) of things; boats, with fish, Luke 5:7; a sponge, with vinegar, Matt. 27:48 (some mss. have this verb in **John 19:29**); a city, with confusion, Acts 19:29; a wedding, with guests, Matt. 22:10; (2) of persons (only in Luke's writings): (a) with the Holy Spirit, Luke 1:15, 41, 67; Acts 2:4; 4:8, 31; 9:17; 13:9; (b) with emotions: wrath, Luke 4:28; fear, 5:26; madness, 6:11; wonder, amazement, Acts 3:10; jealousy, 5:17, RV, for KJV, "indignation," and 13:45 (KJV, "envy"). For its other significance, "to complete."

Spunge *spongos* (4699), was the medium by which vinegar was carried to the mouth of Christ on the cross, Matt. 27:48; Mark 15:36; **John 19:29**.

Put *peritithemi* (4060), "to put around or on," is so used in Matt. 27:28; Mark 15:17, RV, "put on" (KJV, "... about"); 15:36; **John 19:29**. In **John 19:29**, KJV, *prosphero*, "to bring to," is translated "they put it to (His mouth)," RV, "they brought it ...."

Hyssop *hussopos* (5301), a bunch of which was used in ritual sprinklings, is found in Heb. 9:19; in **John 19:29** the reference is apparently to a branch or rod of "hyssop," upon which a sponge was put and offered to the Lord on the cross. The suggestion has been made that the word in the original may have been *hussos*, "a javelin"; there seems to be no valid reason for the supposition.

19:30 When Jesus therefore had received the vinegar, he said, It is finished: and he bowed his head, and gave up the ghost.

Vinegar *see John 19:29.*

Finished *see* Accomplished at *John 19:28.*

Bowed *klino* (2827), "to incline, to bow down," is used of the women who in their fright "bowed" their faces to the earth at the Lord's empty tomb, Luke 24:5; of the act of the Lord on the cross immediately before giving up His Spirit. What is indicated in the statement "He bowed His head," is not the helpless dropping of the head after death, but the deliberate putting of His head into a position of rest, **John 19:30**. The verb is deeply significant here. The Lord reversed the natural order. The same verb is used in His statement in Matt. 8:20 and Luke 9:58, "the Son of Man hath not where to lay His head." It is used, too, of the decline of day, Luke 9:12; 24:29; of turning enemies to flight, Heb. 11:34.

Gave up *paradidomi* (3860), "to give or hand over," is said of "giving" up the ghost, **John 19:30**; of "giving" persons up to evil, Acts 7:42; Rom. 1:24, 26; of "giving" one's body to be burned, 1 Cor. 13:3; of Christ's "giving" Himself up to death, Gal. 2:20; Eph. 5:2, 25.

Ghost *ekpneo* (1606), lit., "to breathe out" (*ek*, "out," *pneo*, "to breathe"), "to expire," is used in the NT, without an object, "soul" or "life" being understood, Mark 15:37, 39, and Luke 23:46, of the death of Christ. In Matt. 27:50 and **John 19:30**, where different verbs are used, the act is expressed in a way which stresses it as of His own volition: in the former, "Jesus ... yielded up His spirit (*pneuma*); in the latter, "He gave up His spirit."

19:31 The Jews therefore, because it was the preparation, that the bodies should not remain upon the cross on the sabbath day, (for that sabbath day was an high day,) besought Pilate that their legs might be broken, and *that* they might be taken away.

Preparation *see John 19:14.*

Remain *see* Remaining at *John 1:33.*

High *megas* (3173), "great," is translated "high" in **John 19:31**, of the Sabbath day at the Passover season; here the meaning is virtually equivalent to "holy."

Legs *skelos* (4628), "the leg from the hip downwards," is used only of the breaking of the "legs" of the crucified malefactors, to hasten their death, **John 19:31-33** (a customary act, not carried out in the case of Christ, in fulfillment of Exod. 12:46; Num. 9:12). The practice was known as *skelokopia* (from *kopto*, "to strike"), or, in Latin, *crurifragium* (from *crus*, "a leg," and *frango*, "to break").

Broken *katagnumi* (2608), is used of the "breaking" of a bruised reed, Matt. 12:20, and of the "breaking" of the legs of those who were crucified, **John 19:31, 32, 33**.

19:32 Then came the soldiers, and brake the legs of the first, and of the other which was crucified with him.

Brake *see* Broken at *John 19:31.*

Crucifed *sustauroo* (4957), "to crucify with" (*su-*, "for," *sun*, "with"), is used (a) of actual "crucifixion" in company with another, Matt. 27:44; Mark 15:32; **John 19:32**; (b) metaphorically, of spiritual identification with Christ in His death, Rom. 6:6, and Gal. 2:20.

19:33 But when they came to Jesus, and saw that he was dead already, they brake not his legs:

Brake *see* Broken at *John 19:31.*

19:34 But one of the soldiers with a spear pierced his side, and forthwith came there out blood and water.

Spear *lonche* (3057), primarily "a spearhead," then, "a lance or spear," occurs in **John 19:34**; some texts have it in Matt. 27:49.

Pierced *nusso* (3572), "to pierce" or "pierce through," often of inflicting severe or deadly wounds, is used of the piercing of the side of Christ, **John 19:34** (in some mss., Matt. 27:49).

Side *pleura* (4125), "a side" (cf. Eng., "pleurisy"), is used of the "side" of Christ, into which the spear was thrust, **John 19:34**; **20:20**, **25**, **27** (some mss. have it in Matt. 27:49; see RV marg.); elsewhere, in Acts 12:7.

Forthwith *euthus* (2117), is translated "forthwith" in the KJV of Mark 1:29; 1:43 (in the best mss.), and **John 19:34** (RV, straightway).

19:35 And he that saw *it* bare record, and his record is true: and he knoweth that he saith true, that ye might believe.

Record *see* Witness at *John 1:7.*

True *see John 1:9.*

19:36 For these things were done, that the scripture should be fulfilled, A bone of him shall not be broken.

Scripture *see John 2:22.*

Bone *osteon* (3747), probably from a word signifying strength, or firmness, sometimes denotes "hard substances other than bones," e.g., the stone or kernel of fruit. In the NT it always denotes "bones," Matt. 23:27; Luke 24:39; **John 19:36**; Heb. 11:22.

Broken *suntribo* (4937), lit., "to rub together," and so "to shatter, shiver, break in pieces by crushing," is said of the bruising of a reed, Matt. 12:20; the "breaking" of fetters in pieces, Mark 5:4; the "breaking" of an alabaster cruse, Mark 14:3; an earthenware vessel, Rev. 2:27; of the physical bruising of a person possessed by a demon, Luke 9:39; concerning Christ, "a bone of Him shall not be broken," **John 19:36**; metaphorically of the crushed condition of a "broken-hearted" person, Luke 4:18 (KJV only); of the eventual crushing of Satan, Rom. 16:20. This verb is frequent in the Sept. in the passive voice, e.g., Ps. 51:17; Isa. 57:15, of a contrite heart, perhaps a figure of stones made smooth by being rubbed together in streams. Cf. *suntrimma*, "destruction."

19:37 And again another scripture saith, They shall look on him whom they pierced.

Scripture *see John 2:22.*

Pierced *ekkenteo* (1574), primarily, "to prick out" (*ek*, "out," *kenteo*, "to prick"), signifies "to pierce," **John 19:37**; Rev. 1:7.

19:38 And after this Joseph of Arimathaea, being a disciple of Jesus, but secretly for fear of the Jews, besought Pilate that he might take away the body of Jesus: and Pilate gave *him* leave. He came therefore, and took the body of Jesus.

Disciple *see* Disciples at *John 6:66.*

Secretly *krupto* (2928), "to hide," is translated "secretly" in **John 19:38** [perfect participle, passive voice, lit., "(but) having been hidden"], referring to Nicodemus as having been a "secret" disciple of Christ; in Matt. 13:35, KJV, it is translated "kept secret" (RV, "hidden").

Leave *epitrepo* (2010), lit. denotes "to turn to" (*epi*, "upon, to," *trepo*, "to turn"), and so (a) "to commit, entrust" (not in NT); (b) "to permit, give leave, send," of Christ's permission to the unclean spirits to enter the swine, Mark 5:13; in Luke 8:32, RV, "give ... leave," "gave ... leave" (KJV, "suffer" and "suffered"); in **John 19:38**, of Pilate's permission to Joseph to take away the body of the Lord; in Acts 21:39, of Paul's request to the chief captain to permit him to address the people, RV, "give ... leave" (for KJV, "suffer"); in 21:40, "he had given him leave" (KJV, "... licence").

19:39 And there came also Nicodemus, which at the first came to Jesus by night, and brought a mixture of myrrh and aloes, about an hundred pound *weight*.

Mixture *migma* (3395), "a mixture" (akin to *mignumi*, "to mix, mingle"), occurs in **John 19:39** (some mss. have *heligma*, "a roll").

Aloes *aloe* (250), "an aromatic tree," the soft, bitter wood of which was used by Orientals for the purposes of fumigation and embalming, **John 19:39** (see also Num. 24:6; Ps. 45:8; Prov. 7:17). In the Sept., Song of Sol. 4:14.

Myrrh *smurna* (4666), whence the name "Smyrna," a word of Semitic origin, Heb., *mor*, from a root meaning "bitter," is a gum resin from a shrubby tree, which grows in Yemen and neighboring regions of Africa; the fruit is smooth and somewhat larger than a pea. The color of myrrh varies from pale reddish-yellow to reddish-brown or red. The taste is bitter, and the substance astringent, acting as an antiseptic and a stimulant. It was used as a perfume, Ps. 45:8, where the language is symbolic of the graces of the Messiah; Prov. 7:17; Song of Sol. 1:13; 5:5; it was one of the ingredients of the "holy anointing oil" for the priests, Ex. 30:23 (RV, "flowing myrrh"); it was used also for the purification of women, Esth. 2:12; for embalming, **John 19:39**; as an anodyne, it was one of the gifts of the Magi, Matt. 2:11.

Pound *see John 12:3.*

19:40 Then took they the body of Jesus, and wound it in linen clothes with the spices, as the manner of the Jews is to bury.

Body *soma* (4983), is "the body as a whole, the instrument of life," whether of man living, e.g., Matt. 6:22, or dead, Matt. 27:52; or in resurrection, 1 Cor. 15:44; or of beasts, Heb. 13:11; of grain, 1 Cor. 15:37-38; of the heavenly hosts, 1 Cor. 15:40. In Rev. 18:13 it is translated "slaves." In its figurative uses the essential idea is preserved. Sometimes the word stands, by *synecdoche*, for "the complete man," Matt. 5:29; 6:22; Rom. 12:1; Jas. 3:6; Rev. 18:13. Sometimes the person is identified with his or her "body," Acts 9:37; 13:36, and this is so even of the Lord Jesus, **John 19:40** with **42**. The "body" is not the man, for he himself can exist apart from his "body," 2 Cor. 12:2-3. The "body" is an essential part of the man and therefore the redeemed are not perfected till the resurrection, Heb. 11:40. The word is also used for physical nature, as distinct from *pneuma*, "the spiritual nature," e.g., 1 Cor. 5:3, and from *psuche*, "the soul," e.g., 1 Thess. 5:23. "*Soma*, 'body,' and *pneuma*, 'spirit,' may be separated; *pneuma* and *psuche*, 'soul,' can only be distinguished" (Cremer). It is also used metaphorically, of the mystic body of Christ, with reference to the whole church, e.g., Eph. 1:23; Col. 1:18, 22, 24; also of a local church, 1 Cor. 12:27.

Wound *deo* (1210), "to bind," is translated "wound (it in linen clothes)," **John 19:40**, KJV, of the body of Christ (RV, "bound").

Linen clothes *othonion* (3608), "a piece of fine linen," is used in the plural, of the strips of cloth with which the body of the Lord was bound, after being wrapped in the *sindon*, Luke 24:12; **John 19:40; 20:5, 6, 7**. In the Sept., Judg. 14:13, "changes of raiment"; Hos. 2:5, 9. The word is a diminutive of *othone*, "a sheet".

Spices *aroma* (759), "spice," occurs in Mark 16:1, RV "spices" (KJV, "sweet spice"); Luke 23:56; 24:1; **John 19:40**. A papyrus document has it in a list of articles for a sacrifice.

Manner *ethos* (1485), "a habit, custom" (akin to the verb *etho*, "to be accustomed"), is always translated "custom" in the RV ("manner" in the KJV of **John 19:40**; Acts 15:1; 25:16; Heb. 10:25).

Bury *entaphiazo* (1779), "to prepare a body for burial," is used of any provision for this purpose, Matt. 26:12; **John 19:40**.

19:41 Now in the place where he was crucified there was a garden; and in the garden a new sepulchre, wherein was never man yet laid.

Garden *see John 18:1*.

Never *oudepo* (3764), "not yet," is translated "never (man) yet" in **John 19:41** ("man" representing the idiomatically used negative pronoun *oudeis*, "no one"); some mss. have it in Luke 23:53, instead of *oupo*, "not yet."

Yet *see John 7:39*.

Laid *see* Lay at *John 10:17*.

19:42 There laid they Jesus therefore because of the Jews' preparation *day*; for the sepulchre was nigh at hand.

Laid *see John 10:17*.

Preparation *see John 19:14*.

At hand *engus* (1451), "near, nigh," frequently rendered "at hand," is used (a) of place, e.g., of the Lord's sepulchre, **John 19:42**, "nigh at hand"; (b) of time, e.g., Matt. 26:18; Luke 21:30, 31, RV, "nigh," KJV, "nigh at hand"; in Phil. 4:5, "the Lord is at hand," it is possible to regard the meaning as that either of (a) or (b); the following reasons may point to (b): (1) the subject of the preceding context has been the return of Christ, 3:20, 21; (2) the phrase is a translation of the Aramaic "Maranatha," 1 Cor. 16:22, a Christian watchword, and the use of the title "the Lord" is appropriate; (3) the similar use of the adverb in Rev. 1:3 and 22:10; (4) the similar use of the corresponding verb in Rom. 13:12; Heb. 10:25, "drawing nigh," RV; Jas. 5:8; cf. 1 Pet. 4:7.

Chapter 20

20:1 The first *day* of the week cometh Mary Magdalene early, when it was yet dark, unto the sepulchre, and seeth the stone taken away from the sepulchre.

Week *sabbaton* (4521), is used (a) in the plural in the phrase "the first day of the week," Matt. 28:1; Mark 16:2, 9; Luke 24:1; **John 20:1, 19**; Acts 20:7; 1 Cor. 16:2; (b) in the singular, Luke 18:12, "twice in the week," lit., "twice of the sabbath," i.e., twice in the days after the sabbath.

Early *see John 18:28*.

20:2 Then she runneth, and cometh to Simon Peter, and to the other disciple, whom Jesus loved, and saith unto them, They have taken away the Lord out of the sepulchre, and we know not where they have laid him.

Loved *see* Loveth at *John 3:35*.

Laid *see* Lay *at John 10:17*.

20:3-4 Peter therefore went forth, and that other disciple, and came to the sepulchre.

So they ran both together: and the other disciple did outrun Peter, and came first to the sepulchre.

Together *see John 4:36*.

Outrun *protrecho* (4390), primarily, "to run forward" (*pro*, "forward" or "before," *trecho*, "to run"), is used with *tachion*, "more quickly," in **John 20:4**, "outran," RV (KJV, "did outrun"), lit., "ran forward more quickly"; in Luke 19:4, "he ran on before," RV (KJV, "ran before"). In the Sept., 1 Sam. 8:11; in some texts, Job 41:13, "destruction runneth before him," in the Eng. versions, v. 22.

First *see* Before at *John 1:15*.

20:5 And he stooping down, *and looking in*, saw the linen clothes lying; yet went he not in.

Stooping *parakupto* (3879), is rendered "to stoop down" in Luke 24:12; **John 20:5, 11**, RV, "stooping and looking in".

Looking *parakupto* (3879), lit. and primarily, "to stoop sideways" *para*, "aside," *kupto*, "to bend forward"), denotes "to stoop to look into," Luke 24:12, "stooping and looking in" (KJV, "stooping down"), **John 20:5, 11**; metaphorically in Jas. 1:25, of "looking" into the perfect law of liberty; in 1 Pet. 1:12 of things which the angels desire "to look into.

Saw *see* Seeth at *John 14:17*.

Linen clothes *see John 19:40.*

Lying *keimai* (2749), "to be laid, to lie," used as the passive voice of *tithemi*, "to lay", is said (a) of the Child Jesus, Luke 2:12, 16; (b) of the dead body of the Lord, Matt. 28:6; **John 20:12**; in Luke 23:53, "had ... lain," RV, KJV, "was laid," in the tomb as hitherto empty; (c) of the linen cloths, **John 20:5, 6, 7**; (d) figuratively of a veil as "lying" upon the hearts of the Jews, 2 Cor. 3:15, RV, "lieth" (KJV, "is"); (e) metaphorically, of the world as "lying" in the evil one, 1 John 5:19, RV; (f) of the heavenly city, Rev. 21:16.

Yet *see John 4:27.*

20:6 Then cometh Simon Peter following him, and went into the sepulchre, and seeth the linen clothes lie,

Seeth *see John 14:17.*

Linen clothes *see John 19:40.*

Lie *see* Lying at *John 20:5.*

20:7 And the napkin, that was about his head, not lying with the linen clothes, but wrapped together in a place by itself.

Napkin *see John 11:44.*

Lying *see John 20:5.*

Linen clothes *see John 19:40.*

Wrapped *entulisso* (1794), "to wrap up, roll round or about," is translated "rolled up" in **John 20:7**, RV, of the cloth or "napkin" that had been wrapped around the head of the Lord before burial. Both the RV and the KJV, "wrapped together," might suggest that this cloth had been "rolled" or wrapped up and put in a certain part of the tomb at the Lord's resurrection, whereas, as with the body wrappings, the head cloth was lying as it had been "rolled" round His head, an evidence, to those who looked into the tomb, of the fact of His resurrection without any disturbance of the wrappings either by friend or foe or when the change took place. It is followed by *en*, "in," and translated "wrapped" in Matt. 27:59, a meaning and construction which Moulton and Milligan illustrate from the papyri; in Luke 23:53 it is followed by the dative of the noun *sindon*, "linen cloth," used instrumentally.

20:8 Then went in also that other disciple, which came first to the sepulchre, and he saw, and believed.

First *see* Before at John *1:15.*

Saw *see* Seeth at *John 14:17.*

20:9 For as yet they knew not the scripture, that he must rise again from the dead.

Yet *see John 7:39.*

Scripture *see John 2:22.*

Rise *see* Raise at *John 6:39.*

20:10-11 Then the disciples went away again unto their own home.

But Mary stood without at the sepulchre weeping: and as she wept, she stooped down, *and looked* into the sepulchre,

Weeping *see* Weep at *John 11:31.*

Stooped *see* Stooping at *John 20:5.*

Looked *see* Looking at *John 20:5.*

20:12 And seeth two angels in white sitting, the one at the head, and the other at the feet, where the body of Jesus had lain.

White *see John 4:35.*

Sitting *see* Sat at *John 4:6.*

One *see John 10:30.*

Lain *see* Lying at *John 20:5.*

20:13 And they say unto her, Woman, why weepest thou? She saith unto them, Because they have taken away my Lord, and I know not where they have laid him.

Laid *see* Lay at *John 10:17.*

20:14 And when she had thus said, she turned herself back, and saw Jesus standing, and knew not that it was Jesus.

Thus *see John 9:6.*

Turned *see* Converted at *John 12:40.*

Back *see John 6:66.*

Saw *see* See at *John 8:51.*

20:15 Jesus saith unto her, Woman, why weepest thou? whom seekest thou? She, supposing him to be the gardener, saith unto him, Sir, if thou have borne him hence, tell me where thou hast laid him, and I will take him away.

Supposing *see* Saying at *John 11:31.*

Gardener *kepouros* (2780), lit., "a gardenkeeper" (from *kepos*, "garden" and *ouros*, "a watcher"), occurs in John 20:15.

Sir *see* Lord at *John 4:1.*

Borne *see* Took up at *John 10:31.*

Laid *see* Lay at *John 10:17.*

20:16 Jesus saith unto her, Mary. She turned herself, and saith unto him, Rabboni; which is to say, Master.

Saith *see John 1:38.*

Turned *see* Converted at *John 12:40.*

Rabboni *rabbounei* or *rabboni* (4462), formed in a similar way to the above, was an Aramaic form of a title almost entirely applied to the president of the Sanhedrin, if such was a descendant of Hillel. It was even more respectful than Rabbi, and signified "My great master"; in its use in the NT the pronominal force of the suffix is apparently retained (contrast Rabbi above); it is found in Mark 10:51 in the best texts, RV, "Rabboni" (KJV, "Lord"), addressed to Christ by blind Bartimaeus, and in **John 20:16** by Mary Magdalene, where it is interpreted by *didaskalos*, "Master" (marg., "Teacher").

Master The form *Rabbounei* (*Rabboni*), in Mark 10:51, is retained in the RV (for KJV, "Lord"); in **John 20:16**, in both KJV and RV. This title is said to be Galilean; hence it would be natural in the lips of a woman of Magdala. It does not differ materially from "Rabbi." *See also* **Rabbi** at *John 1:38*.

20:17 Jesus saith unto her, Touch me not; for I am not yet ascended to my Father: but go to my brethren, and say unto them, I ascend unto my Father, and your Father; and *to* my God, and your God.

Touch *hapto* (681), primarily, "to fasten to," hence, of fire, "to kindle," denotes, in the middle voice (a) "to touch," e.g., Matt. 8:3, 15; 9:20, 21, 29; (b) "to cling to, lay hold of," **John 20:17**; here the Lord's prohibition as to clinging to Him was indicative of the fact that communion with Him would, after His ascension, be by faith, through the Spirit.

Father *see John 8:38*.

Brethren The disciples, and so, by implication, all believers, Matt. 28:10; **John 20:17**.

20:18-19 Mary Magdalene came and told the disciples that she had seen the Lord, and *that* he had spoken these things unto her.

Then the same day at evening, being the first *day* of the week, when the doors were shut where the disciples were assembled for fear of the Jews, came Jesus and stood in the midst, and saith unto them, Peace *be* unto you.

Week *see John 20:1*.

Shut *kleio* (2808), is used (a) of things material, Matt. 6:6; 25:10; Luke 11:7; **John 20:19**, **26**; Acts 5:23; 21:30; Rev. 20:3; figuratively, 21:25; (b) metaphorically, of the kingdom of heaven, Matt. 23:13; of heaven, with consequences of famine, Luke 4:25; Rev. 11:6; of compassion, 1 John 3:17, RV (KJV, "bowels *of compassion*"); of the blessings accruing from the promises of God regarding David, Rev. 3:7; of a door for testimony, 3:8.

20:20 And when he had so said, he shewed unto them *his* hands and his side. Then were the disciples glad, when they saw the Lord.

Shewed *see* Sheweth at *John 5:20*.

Side *see John 19:34*.

Glad *see John 8:56*.

Lord *see John 4:1*.

20:21 Then said Jesus to them again, Peace *be* unto you: as *my* Father hath sent me, even so send I you.

Even so *see John 10:15*.

Sent *see John 1:6*.

20:22 And when he had said this, he breathed on *them*, and saith unto them, Receive ye the Holy Ghost:

"Christ, the Lord, is risen today, / Hallelujah! / Sons of men and angels say: / Raise your joys and triumphs high; / Sing, ye heavens, and earth reply. / Vain the stone, the watch, the seal; / Christ hath burst the gates of hell; / Death in vain forbids Him rise; / Christ hath opened paradise."

CHARLES WESLEY

Breathed *emphusao* (1720), "to breathe upon," is used of the symbolic act of the Lord Jesus in breathing upon His apostles the communication of the Holy Spirit, **John 20:22**.

20:23 Whose soever sins ye remit, they are remitted unto them; *and* whose soever *sins* ye retain, they are retained.

Remit, Remitted *aphiemi* (863), "to send away," is translated "to remit" in **John 20:23** (twice), KJV (RV, "to forgive"). Scripture makes clear that the Lord's words could not have been intended to bestow the exercise of absolution, which

Scripture declares is the prerogative of God alone. There is no instance in the NT of this act on the part of the apostles. The words are to be understood in a "declarative" sense; the statement has regard to the effects of their ministry of the gospel, with its twofold effects of "remission" or retention. They could not, nor could anyone subsequently, forgive sins, any more than that Joseph actually restored the butler to his office and hanged the baker (Gen. 41:13), or any more than that the prophets actually accomplished things when they declared that they were about to be done (Jer. 1:10; Ezek. 43:3).

Retain, Retained *krateo* (2902), "to be strong, obtain, hold, hold fast," is translated "to retain," of sins, **John 20:23** (twice).

20:24-25 But Thomas, one of the twelve, called Didymus, was not with them when Jesus came.

The other disciples therefore said unto him, We have seen the Lord. But he said unto them, Except I shall see in his hands the print of the nails, and put my finger into the print of the nails, and thrust my hand into his side, I will not believe.

Print *tupos* (5179), primarily denoted "a blow" (from a root *tup–*, seen also in *tupto*, "to strike"), hence, (a) an impression, the mark of a "blow," **John 20:25**; (b) the "impress" of a seal, the stamp made by a die, a figure, image, Acts 7:43; (c) a "form" or mold, Rom. 6:17 (see RV); (d) the sense or substance of a letter, Acts 23:25; (e) "an ensample," pattern, Acts 7:44; Heb. 8:5, "pattern"; in an ethical sense, 1 Cor. 10:6; Phil. 3:17; 1 Thess. 1:7; 2 Thess. 3:9; 1 Tim. 4:12, RV, "ensample"; Titus 2:7, RV, "ensample," for KJV, "pattern"; 1 Pet. 5:3; in a doctrinal sense, a type, Rom. 5:14.

Nails *helos* (2247), occurs in the remarks of Thomas regarding the print of the nails used in Christ's crucifixion, **John 20:25**.

Put *see John 5:7.*

Finger *see John 8:6.*

Thrust *ballo* (906), is rendered "to thrust" in **John 20:25, 27**, KJV (RV, put); Acts 16:24, KJV (RV, "cast"); so Rev. 14:16, 19.

Side *see John 19:34.*

20:26 And after eight days again his disciples were within, and Thomas with them: *then* came Jesus, the doors being shut, and stood in the midst, and said, Peace *be* unto you.

Eight *see John 5:5.*

Within This is a translation of (a) *entos*; in Luke 17:21 the RV marg., "in the midst of," is to be preferred; the kingdom of God was not in the hearts of the Pharisees; (b) *en*, "of thinking or saying within oneself," e.g., Luke 7:39, 49 (marg., "among"); locally, e.g., Luke 19:44; (c) *esothen*, 2 Cor. 7:5; Rev. 4:8; 5:1; "from within," Mark 7:21, 23; Luke 11:7; "within," Matt. 23:25; Luke 11:40, RV, "inside"; in Matt. 23:27, 28, RV, "inwardly"; (d) *eso*, **John 20:26**; Acts 5:23; 1 Cor. 5:12 (i.e., "within" the church); (e) *pros*, to, or with, in Mark 14:4, KJV, "within" (RV, "among"); (f) *dia*, "through," rendered "within (three days)" in Mark 14:58, KJV (RV, "in," looking through the time to the event, and in keeping with the metaphor of building); (g) *esoteros*, Heb. 6:19, the comparative degree of *eso*, used with the article translated "that within," lit., "the inner (part of the veil)," i.e., "inside"; (h) in Luke 11:41, RV, *eneimi*, "to be in," is rendered "are within" (KJV, "ye have").

Shut *see John 20:19.*

20:27 Then saith he to Thomas, Reach hither thy finger, and behold my hands; and reach hither thy hand, and thrust *it* into my side: and be not faithless, but believing.

Reach *phero* (5342), "to bear, carry," is used of "reaching" forth the hand in **John 20:27** (twice).

Finger *see John 8:6.*

Thrust *see John 20:25.*

Side *see John 19:34.*

Then *see* After that at *John 13:5.*

Faithless *apistos* (571), is used with meanings (a) "untrustworthy," not worthy of confidence or belief, is said of things "incredible," Acts 26:8; (b) "unbelieving, distrustful," used as a noun, "unbeliever," Luke 12:46; 1 Tim. 5:8 (RV, for KJV, "infidel"); in Titus 1:15 and Rev. 21:8, "unbelieving"; "faithless" in Matt. 17:17; Mark 9:19; Luke 9:41; **John 20:27**. The word is most frequent in 1 and 2 Corinthians. (In the Sept., Prov. 17:6; 28:25; Isa. 17:10.).

Believing *pistos* (4103), (a) in the active sense means "believing, trusting"; (b) in the passive sense, "trusty, faithful, trustworthy." It is translated "believer" in 2 Cor. 6:15; "them that believe" in 1 Tim. 4:12, RV (KJV, "believers"); in 1 Tim. 5:16, "if any woman that believeth," lit. "if any believing woman." So in 6:2, "believing masters." In 1 Pet. 1:21 the RV, following the most authentic mss., gives the noun form, "are believers in God" (KJV, "do believe in God"). In **John 20:27** it is translated "believing." It is best understood with significance (a), above, e.g., in Gal. 3:9; Acts 16:1; 2 Cor. 6:15; Titus 1:6; it has significance (b), e.g., in 1 Thess. 5:24; 2 Thess. 3:3.

20:28 And Thomas answered and said unto him, My Lord and my God.

Lord *see John 4:1.*

God *see John 1:1.*

20:29-30 Jesus saith unto him, Thomas, because thou hast seen me, thou hast believed: blessed *are* they that have not seen, and *yet* have believed.

And many other signs truly did Jesus in the presence of his disciples, which are not written in this book:

Signs *see* Miracles at *John 2:11.*

Truly In **John 20:30**, KJV, the particle *oun*, therefore (RV), is rendered "truly."

Presence *enopion* (1799), is translated "in the presence of" in Luke 1:19; 13:26; 14:10; 15:10; **John 20:30**; Rev. 14:10 (twice); in 1 Cor. 1:29 KJV, "in His presence" (RV, "before God").

Book *biblion* (975), had in Hellenistic Greek almost lost its diminutive force and was ousting *biblos* in ordinary use; it denotes "a scroll or a small book." It is used in Luke 4:17, 20, of the "book" of Isaiah; in **John 20:30**, of the Gospel of John; in Gal. 3:10 and Heb. 10:7, of the whole of the OT; in Heb. 9:19, of the "book" of Exodus; in Rev. 1:11; 22:7, 9-10, 18 (twice), 19, of Revelation; in **John 21:25** and 2 Tim. 4:13, of "books" in general; in Rev. 13:8; 17:8; 20:12; 21:27, of the "Book" of Life; in Rev. 20:12, of other "books" to be opened in the Day of Judgment, containing, it would seem, the record of human deeds. In Rev. 5:1-9 the "Book" represents the revelation of God's purposes and counsels concerning the world. So with the "little book" in Rev. 10:8. In 6:14 it is used of a scroll, the rolling up of which illustrates the removal of the heaven. In Matt. 19:7 and Mark 10:4 the word is used of a bill of divorcement.

20:31 But these are written, that ye might believe that Jesus is the Christ, the Son of God; and that believing ye might have life through his name.

Son *see John 1:18.*

Chapter 21

21:1 After these things Jesus shewed himself again to the disciples at the sea of Tiberias; and on this wise shewed he *himself*.

Shewed *phaneroo* (5319), "to make visible, clear, manifest," known, is used especially in the writings of the apostles John and Paul), occurring 9 times in the Gospel, 9 times in 1 John, 2 in Rev.; in the Pauline Epistles (including Heb.) 24 times; in the other Gospels, only in Mark, 3 times; elsewhere in 1 Pet. 1:20; 5:4. The true meaning is "to uncover, lay bare reveal." The following are variations in the rendering, which should be noted: Mark 16:12, 14 (RV, "was manifested," KJV, "appeared"); **John 21:1** (RV, "manifested," KJV, "shewed"; cf. v. 14). *See also* Shew at *John 7:4.*

Sea *see John 6:1.*

On this wise *houtos or houto* (3779), "in this way, so, thus," is used (a) with reference to what precedes, e.g., Luke 1:25; 2:48; (b) with reference to what follows, e.g., Luke 19:31, rendered "on this wise," in Matt. 1:18; **John 21:1**, and before quotations, Acts 7:6; 13:34; Rom. 10:6, KJV (RV, "thus"); Heb. 4:4; (c) marking intensity, rendered "so," e.g., Gal. 1:6; Heb. 12:21; Rev. 16:18; (d) in comparisons, rendered "so," e.g., Luke 11:30; Rom. 5:15.

"Jesus Christ will be Lord of all or he will not be Lord at all."

ST. AUGUSTINE OF HIPPO

21:2 There were together Simon Peter, and Thomas called Didymus, and Nathanael of Cana in Galilee, and the *sons* of Zebedee, and two other of his disciples.

Together *see John 4:36.*

21:3 Simon Peter saith unto them, I go a fishing. They say unto him, We also go with thee. They went forth, and entered into a ship immediately; and that night they caught nothing.

Entered *see* Went into at *John 5:4.*

Caught *see* Take at *John 7:30.*

21:4 But when the morning was now come, Jesus stood on the shore: but the disciples knew not that it was Jesus.

Morning *see John 18:28.*

Shore *aigialos* (123), translated "shore" in the KJV in each place where it is used, Matt. 13:2, 48; **John 21:4**; Acts 21:5; 27:39-40, is always in the RV translated "beach." It is derived from a root signifying "to press, drive"; *aigis* denotes "a wind-storm."

21:5 Then Jesus saith unto them, Children, have ye any meat? They answered him, No.

Children In **John 21:5** the KJV marg. has "sirs" for *paidia*, "children." *See also* Child at *John 4:49*.

Meat *prosphagion* (4371), primarily "a dainty or relish" (especially cooked fish), to be eaten with bread, then, "fish" in general, is used in **John 21:5**, "Have ye aught to eat?" (KJV, "have ye any meat?"). Moulton remarks that the evidences of the papyri are to the effect that *prosphagion*, "is not so broad a word as 'something to eat.' The apostles had left even loaves behind them once, Mark 8:14; they might well have left the 'relish' on this occasion. It would normally be fish; cf. Mark 6:38" (Gram. of NT Greek, Vol. 1, p. 170).

21:6 And he said unto them, Cast the net on the right side of the ship, and ye shall find. They cast therefore, and now they were not able to draw it for the multitude of fishes.

Net *diktuon* (1350), a general term for a "net" (from an old verb *diko*, "to cast": akin to *diskos*, "a quoit"), occurs in Matt. 4:20-21; Mark 1:18-19; Luke 5:2, 4-6; **John 21:6, 8, 11** (twice). In the Sept. it was used for a "net" for catching birds, Prov. 1:17, in other ways, e.g., figuratively of a snare, Job 18:8; Prov. 29:5.

Now *see John 4:42*.

Draw *see John 6:44*.

Multitude *see John 5:3*.

21:7 Therefore that disciple whom Jesus loved saith unto Peter, It is the Lord. Now when Simon Peter heard that it was the Lord, he girt *his* fisher's coat *unto him*, (for he was naked,) and did cast himself into the sea.

Girt *see* Girded at *John 13:4*.

Coat *ependutes* (1903), denotes "an upper garment" (*epi*, "upon," *enduo*, "to clothe"). The word is found in **John 21:7**, where it apparently denotes a kind of linen frock, which fishermen wore when at their work. *See also John 19:23*.

Naked *gumnos* (1131), signifies (a) "unclothed," Mark 14:52; in v. 51 it is used as a noun ("*his*" and "*body*" being italicized); (b) "scantily or poorly clad," Matt. 25:36, 38, 43, 44; Acts 19:16 (with torn garments); Jas. 2:15; (c) "clad in the undergarment only" (the outer being laid aside), **John 21:7**; (d) metaphorically, (1) of "a bare seed," 1 Cor. 15:37; (2) of "the soul without the body," 2 Cor. 5:3; (3) of "things exposed to the allseeing eye of God," Heb. 4:13; (4) of "the carnal condition of a local church," Rev. 3:17; (5) of "the similar state of an individual," 16:15; (6) of "the desolation of religious Babylon," 17:16.

21:8 And the other disciples came in a little ship; (for they were not far from land, but as it were two hundred cubits,) dragging the net with fishes.

Ship *see* Shipping at *John 6:24*.

Land *see John 3:22*.

Far *makran* (3112), properly a feminine form of the adjective above, denotes "a long way, far," (a) literally, Matt. 8:30, RV, "afar off." Luke 7:6; 15:20, RV, "afar off"; **John 21:8**; Acts 17:27; 22:21; (b) metaphorically, "far (from the kingdom of God)," Mark 12:34; in spiritual darkness, Acts 2:39; Eph. 2:13, 17.

Two hundred *see John 6:7*.

Cubits *pechus* (4083), denotes the forearm, i.e., the part between the hand and the elbow joint; hence, "a measure of length," not from the wrist to the elbow, but from the tip of the middle finger to the elbow joint, i.e., about a foot and a half, or a little less than two feet, Matt. 6:27; Luke 12:25; **John 21:8**; Rev. 21:17.

Dragging *suro* (4951), "to draw, drag, haul," is used of a net, **John 21:8**; of violently "dragging" persons along, Acts 8:3, "haling"; 14:19, RV, "dragged," KJV, "drew"; 17:6 (ditto); Rev. 12:4, KJV, "drew," RV, "draweth." *See also* Draw at *John 6:44*.

Net *see John 21:6*.

21:9 As soon then as they were come to land, they saw a fire of coals there, and fish laid thereon, and bread.

Were come to *apobaino*, "to go away," is rendered, in the KJV of **John 21:9**, "were come to"; RV, "got out upon."

Coals *see John 18:18*.

There In **John 21:9**, "there" is used to translate the verb *keimai*.

Fish *see John 6:9*.

Laid *keimai* (2749), "to be laid, to lie," is used as the passive voice of *tithemi*, "to put," and is translated by some part of the verb "to be laid" in Matt. 3:10 and Luke 3:9, of an axe; Luke 12:19, of goods; **John 21:9**, where the verb has been omitted from the translation, after the words "a fire of coals"; 1 Cor. 3:11, of Christ, as a foundation.

Laid *epikeimai* (1945), "to be placed, to lie on," is translated by the verb "to be laid upon," in **John 21:9**, of a fish; in 1 Cor. 9:16, of necessity. *See also* Lay upon at *John 11:38*.

21:10 Jesus saith unto them, Bring of the fish which ye have now caught.

Bring *see* Take at *John 7:30*.

Fish *see John 6:9*.

21:11 Simon Peter went up, and drew the net to land full of great fishes, an hundred and fifty and three: and for all there were so many, yet was not the net broken.

Drew *see* Draw at *John 6:44.*

Net *see John 21:6.*

Land *see John 3:22.*

Full *see John 19:29.*

Great *see John 6:18.*

Hundred *hekaton* (1540), an indeclinable numeral, denotes "a hundred," e.g., Matt. 18:12, 28; it also signifies "a hundredfold," Matt. 13:8, 23, and the RV in the corresponding passage, Mark 4:8, 20 (for KJV, "hundred"), signifying the complete productiveness of sown seed. In the passage in Mark the phrase is, lit., "in thirty and in sixty and in a hundred." In Mark 6:40 it is used with the preposition *kata*, in the phrase "by hundreds." It is followed by other numerals in **John 21:11**; Acts 1:15; Rev. 7:4; 14:1, 3; 21:17.

Fifty *see John 8:57.*

Many *see John 6:9.*

Broken *see* Rend at *John 19:24.*

21:12 Jesus saith unto them, Come *and* dine. And none of the disciples durst ask him, Who art thou? knowing that it was the Lord.

Dine *aristao* (709), primarily, "to breakfast", was later used also with the meaning "to dine," e.g., Luke 11:37; in **John 21:12, 15**, RV, "break your fast," and "had broken their fast," for KJV, "dine"; obviously there it was the first meal in the day. In the Sept., Gen. 43:25; 1 Sam. 14:24; 1 Chron. 13:7.

Durst *tolmao* (5111), signifies "to dare," (a) in the sense of not dreading or shunning through fear, Matt. 22:46; Mark 12:34; Mark 15:43, "boldly," lit., "having dared, went in"; Luke 20:40; **John 21:12**; Acts 5:13; 7:32; Rom. 15:18; 2 Cor. 10:2, RV, "show courage," (KJV, "be bold"); 10:12, RV, "are (not) bold", 11:21; Phil. 1:14, "are bold"; Jude 9; (b) in the sense of bearing, enduring, bringing oneself to do a thing, Rom. 5:7; 1 Cor. 6:1. Cf. *apotolmao*, "to be very bold," Rom. 10:20.

Ask *exetazo* (1833), "to search out" (*ek*, "out," intensive, *etazo*, "to examine"), is translated "ask," in **John 21:12**, KJV (RV, "inquire"); in Matt. 2:8, KJV, "search"; RV, "search out," expressing the intensive force of the verb, so Matt. 10:11 (KJV, "inquire").

Lord *see John 4:1.*

21:13 Jesus then cometh, and taketh bread, and giveth them, and fish likewise.

Fish *see John 6:9.*

Likewise *see John 5:19.*

21:14 This is now the third time that Jesus shewed himself to his disciples, after that he was risen from the dead.

Third *tritos* (5154), is used (a) as a noun, e.g., Luke 20:12, 31; in Rev. 8:7-12 and 9:15, 18, "the third part," lit., "the third"; (b) as an adverb, with the article, "the third time," e.g., Mark 14:41; **John 21:17** (twice); without the article, lit., "a third time," e.g., **John 21:14**; 2 Cor. 12:14; 13:1; in enumerations, in Matt. 26:44, with *ek*, "from," lit., "from the third time" (the *ek* indicates the point of departure, especially in a succession of events, cf. **John 9:24**; 2 Pet. 2:8); absolutely, in the accusative neuter, in 1 Cor. 12:28, "thirdly"; (c) as an adjective (its primary use), e.g., in the phrase the third heaven, 2 Cor. 12:2; in the phrase "the third hour," Matt. 20:3; Mark 15:25; Acts 2:15 ("... of the day"); 23:23 ("... of the night"); in a phrase with *hemera*, "a day," "on the third day" (i.e., "the next day but one"), e.g., Matt. 16:21; Luke 24:46; Acts 10:40; in this connection the idiom "three days and three nights," Matt. 12:40, is explained by ref to 1 Sam. 30:12, 13, and Esth. 4:16 with 5:1; in Mark 9:31 and 10:34, the RV, "after three days," follows the texts which have this phrase, the KJV, "the third day," those which have the same phrase as in Matt. 16:21, etc.

Shewed *see John 21:1. See also* Shew at *John 7:4.*

21:15 So when they had dined, Jesus saith to Simon Peter, Simon, *son* of Jonas, lovest thou me more than these? He saith unto him, Yea, Lord; thou knowest that I love thee. He saith unto him, Feed my lambs.

"Ghosts, apparitions, and various psychological hallucinations may do a lot of things, but they don't fire up the charcoal grill and cook fish for breakfast."

PHEME PERKINS

Dined *see* Dine at *John 21:12.*

Lovest, Love *see* Loveth at *John 3:35.*

Yea *see John 11:27.*

Feed *bosko* (1006), "to feed," is primarily used of a herdsman (from *boo*, "to nourish," the special function being to provide food; the root is *bo*, found in *boter*, "a herdsman or herd," and *botane*, "fodder, pasture"), its uses are (a) literal, Matt. 8:30; in v. 33, the RV corrects the KJV, "they that kept," to "they that fed," as in Mark. 5:14 (KJV and RV) and Luke 8:34; in Mark 5:11 and Luke 8:32, "feeding"; Luke 15:15; (b) metaphorical, of spiritual ministry, **John 21:15, 17**. In **John 21:15, 16, 17**, the Lord, addressing Peter, first uses *bosko* (v. **15**) then *poimaino* (v. **16**), and then returns to *bosko* (v. **17**). These are not simply interchangeable (nor are other variations in His remarks). Nor, again, is there a progression of ideas. The lesson to be learnt, as Trench points out (*Syn.* Sec. xxv), is that, in the spiritual care of God's children, the "feeding" of the flock from the Word of God is the constant and regular necessity; it is to have the foremost place. The tending (which includes this) consists of other acts, of discipline, authority, restoration, material assistance of individuals, but they are incidental in comparison with the "feeding."

Lambs *arnion* (721), is a diminutive in form, but the diminutive force is not to be pressed. The general tendency in the vernacular was to use nouns in *-ion* freely, apart from their diminutive significance. It is used only by the apostle John, (a) in the plural, in the Lord's command to Peter, **John 21:15**, with symbolic reference to young converts; (b) elsewhere, in the singular, in Revelation, some 28 times, of Christ as the "Lamb" of God, the symbolism having reference to His character and His vicarious Sacrifice, as the basis both of redemption and of divine vengeance. He is seen in the position of sovereign glory and honor, e.g., 7:17, which He shares equally with the Father, 22:1, 3, the center of angelic beings and of the redeemed and the object of their veneration, e.g. 5:6, 8, 12, 13; 15:3, the Leader and Shepherd of His saints, e.g., 7:17; 14:4, the Head of his spiritual bride, e.g., 21:9, the luminary of the heavenly and eternal city, 21:23, the One to whom all judgment is committed, e.g., 6:1, 16; 13:8, the Conqueror of the foes of God and His people, 17:14; the song that celebrates the triumph of those who "gain the victory over the Beast," is the song of Moses ... and the song of the Lamb 15:3. His sacrifice, the efficacy of which avails for those who accept the salvation thereby provided, forms the ground of the execution of divine wrath for the rejector, and the defier of God, 14:10; (c) in the description of the second "Beast," Rev. 13:11, seen in the vision "like a lamb," suggestive of his acting in the capacity of a false messiah, a travesty of the true.

21:16 He saith to him again the second time, Simon, *son* of Jonas, lovest thou me? He saith unto him, Yea, Lord; thou knowest that I love thee. He saith unto him, Feed my sheep.

Second *see John 3:4.*

Yea *see John 11:27.*

Feed *poimaino* (4165), "to act as a shepherd" (from *poimen*, "a shepherd"), is used (a) literally, Luke 17:7, RV, "keeping sheep," for KJV, "feeding cattle"; 1 Cor. 9:7, (b) metaphorically, "to tend, to shepherd"; said of Christ, Matt. 2:6, RV, "shall be Shepherd of" (for KJV, "shall rule"); of those who act as spiritual shepherds under Him, **John 21:16**, RV, "tend" (for KJV "feed"), so 1 Pet. 5:2; Acts 20:28, "to feed" ("to tend" would have been a consistent rendering; a shepherd does not only "feed" his flock); of base shepherds, Jude 12. *See also John 21:15.*

Sheep *probation* (4263), "a little sheep," is found in the best texts in **John 21:16, 17**; distinct from *arnia*, "lambs" (v. **15**), but used as a term of endearment. *See also John 10:2.*

21:17 He saith unto him the third time, Simon, *son* of Jonas, lovest thou me? Peter was grieved because he said unto him the third time, Lovest thou me? And he said unto him, Lord, thou knowest all things; thou knowest that I love thee. Jesus saith unto him, Feed my sheep.

Knowest *see* Know at *John 7:26.*

Grieved *lupeo* (3076), denotes (a), in the active voice, "to cause pain, or grief, to distress, grieve," e.g., 2 Cor. 2:2 (twice, active and passive voices); v. 5 (twice), RV, "hath caused sorrow" (KJV, "have caused grief," and "grieved"); 7:8, "made (you) sorry"; Eph. 4:30, of grieving the Holy Spirit of God (as indwelling the believer); (b) in the passive voice, "to be grieved, to be made sorry, to be sorry, sorrowful," e.g., Matt. 14:9, RV, "(the king) was grieved" (KJV, "was sorry"); Mark 10:22, RV, "(went away) sorrowful" (KJV, "grieved"); **John 21:17**, "(Peter) was grieved", Rom. 14:15, "(if ... thy brother) is grieved"; 2 Cor. 2:4, "(not that) ye should be made sorry," RV, KJV, "ye should be grieved."

Feed *see John 21:15.*

Sheep *see John 10:1.*

21:18 Verily, verily, I say unto thee, When thou wast young, thou girdedst thyself, and walkedst whither thou wouldest: but when thou shalt be old, thou shalt stretch forth thy hands, and another shall gird thee, and carry *thee* whither thou wouldest not.

Young *neoteros* (3501), the comparative degree of *neos*, "new, youthful," is translated "young" in **John 21:18**; in the plural, Acts 5:6, "young men" (marg., "younger"); Titus 2:6, KJV, RV, "younger men."

Girdedst *zonnumi* (2224), or *zonnuo*, "to gird" in the middle voice, "to gird oneself," is used of the long garments worn in the east, **John 21:18**; Acts 12:8 (*perizonnumi* in some mss.).

Old *gerasko* (1095), from *geras*, "old age," "to grow old," is translated "thou shalt be old," in **John 21:18**; "waxeth aged," Heb. 8:13, RV (KJV, "waxeth old").

Stretch *ekteino* (1614), "to stretch out or forth," is so rendered in Matt. 12:13 (twice), 49; 14:31; 26:51; Mark 3:5 (twice), Luke 6:10; in Matt. 8:3; Mark 1:41 and Luke 5:13, RV (KJV, "put forth"); Luke 22:53; **John 21:18**; Acts 4:30; 26:1. For Acts 27:30

Carry *phero* (5342), "to bear, to bring," is translated "carry" only in **John 21:18**.

21:19 This spake he, signifying by what death he should glorify God. And when he had spoken this, he saith unto him, Follow me.

Signifying *see John 12:33.*

What *poios* (4169), "of what sort," is translated "by what manner of (death)" in **John 21:19**, RV, (KJV, "by what"); in Acts 7:49, "what manner of (house)"; Rom. 3:27, "what manner of law"; 1 Cor. 15:35, "what manner of body." *See also John 12:33.*

Glorify *see* Glorified at *John 7:39.*

21:20 Then Peter, turning about, seeth the disciple whom Jesus loved following; which also leaned on his breast at supper, and said, Lord, which is he that betrayeth thee?

Leaned *see* Lying at *John 13:25.*

Breast *see John 13:25.*

Supper *see John 12:2.*

21:21-22 Peter seeing him saith to Jesus, Lord, and what *shall* this man *do*?

Jesus saith unto him, If I will that he tarry till I come, what *is that* to thee? follow thou me.

Tarry *see* Abode at *John 1:32. See also John 4:40.*

21:23 Then went this saying abroad among the brethren, that that disciple should not die: yet Jesus said not unto him, He shall not die; but, If I will that he tarry till I come, what *is that* to thee?

Saying *see John 4:37.*

Tarry *see John 4:40.*

21:24 This is the disciple which testifieth of these things, and wrote these things: and we know that his testimony is true.

Testifieth *see* Testify at *John 2:25.*

Testimony *see John 3:32.*

21:25 And there are also many other things which Jesus did, the which, if they should be written every one, I suppose that even the world itself could not contain the books that should be written. Amen.

Written *see* Wrote at *John 8:6.*

Suppose *oiomai or oimai* (3633), signifies "to expect, imagine, suppose"; it is rendered "to suppose" in **John 21:25**; Phil. 1:17, RV (KJV, v. 16, "thinking"); "think" in Jas. 1:7.

World *see John 1:9.*

Contain *see John 2:6.*

Books *see* Book at *John 20:30.*

Acts

Chapter 1

1:1 The former treatise have I made, O Theophilus, of all that Jesus began both to do and teach,

Former *protos* (4413), "first," is translated "former" in **Acts 1:1**, of Luke's first treatise; in Rev. 21:4, RV, "first" (KJV, "former").

Treatise *logos* (3056), a word, denotes "a treatise or written narrative" in **Acts 1:1**.

Began *archomai* (756), denotes "to begin." In Luke 3:23 the present participle is used in a condensed expression, lit., "And Jesus Himself was beginning about thirty years." Some verb is to be supplied in English. The RV has "when He began to teach, was about thirty years of age." The meaning seems to be that He was about thirty years when He "began" His public career (cf. **Acts 1:1**). The KJV has "began to be about thirty years of age." In **Acts 11:4** the RV suitably has "began, and expounded," instead of "from the beginning."

1:2 Until the day in which he was taken up, after that he through the Holy Ghost had given commandments unto the apostles whom he had chosen:

Taken *analambano* (353), signifies (a) "to take up" (*ana*), e.g., **Acts 1:2, 11, 22** (RV, "received"), "He was received up" (KJV, "taken"); **10:16**; 1 Tim. 3:16; (b) "to take to oneself," **Acts 7:43**; or "to one's company," **20:13, 14**; **23:31**; 2 Tim. 4:11; of "taking up spiritual armor," Eph. 6:13, 16.

Chosen *eklego* (1586), "to pick out, select," means, in the middle voice, "to choose for oneself," not necessarily implying the rejection of what is not chosen, but "choosing" with the subsidiary ideas of kindness or favor or love, Mark 13:20; Luke 6:13; 9:35 (RV); 10:42; 14:7; John 6:70; 13:18; 15:16, 19; **Acts 1:2, 24**; **6:5**; **13:17**; **15:22, 25**; in **15:7** it is rendered "made choice"; 1 Cor. 1:27-28; Eph. 1:4; Jas. 2:5.

1:3 To whom also he shewed himself alive after his passion by many infallible proofs, being seen of them forty days, and speaking of the things pertaining to the kingdom of God:

Shewed *paristemi* (3936), denotes, when used transitively, "to place beside" (*para*, "by," *histemi*, "to set"), "to present," e.g., Luke 2:22; **Acts 1:3**, "He shewed (Himself)"; **9:41**; **23:33**; Rom. 6:13 (2nd part), RV, "present," KJV, "yield"; so 6:19 (twice); 12:1; 2 Cor. 4:14; 11:2; Eph. 5:27; Col. 1:22, 28; 2 Tim. 2:15, RV (KJV, "shew").

Alive *zao* (2198), "to live, be alive," is used in the NT of "(a) God, Matt. 16:16; John 6:57; Rom. 14:11; (b) the Son in Incarnation, John 6:57; (c) the Son in Resurrection, John 14:19; **Acts 1:3**; Rom. 6:10; 2 Cor. 13:4; Heb. 7:8; (d) spiritual life, John 6:57; Rom. 1:17; 8:13b; Gal. 2:19, 20; Heb. 12:9; (e) the present state of departed saints, Luke 20:38; 1 Pet. 4:6; (f) the hope of resurrection, 1 Pet. 1:3; (g) the resurrection of believers, 1 Thess. 5:10; John 5:25; Rev. 20:4, and of unbelievers, v. 5, cf. v. 13; (h) the way of access to God through the Lord Jesus Christ, Heb. 10:20; (i) the manifestation of divine power in support of divine authority, 2 Cor. 13:4b; cf. 12:10, and 1 Cor. 5:5; (j) bread, figurative of the Lord Jesus, John 6:51; (k) a stone, figurative of the Lord Jesus, 1 Pet. 2:4; (l) water, figurative of the Holy Spirit, John 4:10; 7:38; (m) a sacrifice, figurative of the believer, Rom. 12:1; (n) stones, figurative of the believer, 1 Pet. 2:5; (o) the oracles, *logion*, **Acts 7:38**, and word, *logos*, Heb. 4:12; 1 Pet. 1:23, of God; (p) the physical life of men, 1 Thess. 4:15; Matt. 27:63; **Acts 25:24**; Rom. 14:9; Phil. 1:21 (in the infinitive mood used as a noun with the article, 'living'), 22; 1 Pet. 4:5; (q) the maintenance of physical life, Matt. 4:4; 1 Cor. 9:14; (r) the duration of physical life, Heb. 2:15; (s) the enjoyment of physical life, 1 Thess. 3:8; (t) the recovery of physical life from the power of disease, Mark 5:23; John 4:50; (u) the recovery of physical life from the power of death, Matt. 9:18; **Acts 9:41**; Rev. 20:5; (v) the course, conduct, and character of men, (1) good, **Acts 26:5**; 2 Tim. 3:12; Titus 2:12; (2) evil, Luke 15:13; Rom. 6:2; 8:13a; 2 Cor. 5:15b; Col. 3:7; (3) undefined, Rom. 7:9; 14:7; Gal. 2:14; (w) restoration after alienation, Luke 15:32."

Passion *pascho* (3958), "to suffer," is used (I) of the "sufferings" of Christ (a) at the hands of men, e.g., Matt. 16:21; 17:12; 1 Pet. 2:23; (b) in His expiatory and vicarious sacrifice for sin, Heb. 9:26; 13:12; 1 Pet. 2:21; 3:18; 4:1; (c) including both (a) and (b), Luke 22:15; 24:26, 46; **Acts 1:3**, "passion"; **3:18**; **17:3**; Heb. 5:8; (d) by the antagonism of the evil one, Heb. 2:18; (II) of human "suffering" (a) of followers of Christ, **Acts 9:16**; 2 Cor. 1:6; Gal. 3:4; Phil. 1:29; 1 Thess. 2:14; 2 Thess. 1:5; 2 Tim. 1:12; 1 Pet. 3:14, 17; 5:10; Rev. 2:10; in identification with Christ in His crucifixion, as the spiritual ideal to be realized, 1 Pet. 4:1; in a wrong way, 4:15; (b) of others, physically, as the result of demoniacal power, Matt. 17:15, RV, "suffereth (grievously)," KJV, "is (sore) vexed"; cf. Mark 5:26; in a dream, Matt. 27:19; through maltreatment, Luke 13:2; 1 Pet. 2:19, 20; by a serpent (negatively), **Acts 28:5**, RV, "took" (KJV, "felt:"); (c) of the effect upon the whole body through the "suffering" of one member, 1 Cor. 12:26, with application to a church.

Proofs *tekmerion* (5039), "a sure sign, a positive proof" (from *tekmar*, "a mark, sign"), occurs in **Acts 1:3**, RV, "proofs" (KJV, "infallible proofs"; a "proof" does not require to be described as infallible, the adjective is superfluous).

Being seen *optano* (3700), in the middle voice signifies "to allow oneself to be seen." It is rendered "appearing" in **Acts 1:3**, RV, for KJV, "being seen," of the Lord's "appearances" after His resurrection; the middle voice expresses the personal interest the Lord took in this.

Forty *tessarakonta* (5062), is used in circumstances in Scripture which indicate the number as suggesting probation, separation or judgment, e.g., Matt. 4:2; **Acts 1:3**; Heb. 3:9, 17.

Pertaining to In **Acts 1:3**, KJV, the phrase *ta peri*, "the (things) concerning" (RV), is translated "the things pertaining to."

1:4 And, being assembled together with *them*, commanded them that they should not depart from Jerusalem, but wait for the promise of the Father, which, *saith he*, ye have heard of me.

Assembled *sunalizo* (4871), "to gather together, to assemble," with the suggestion of a crowded meeting (*sun*, "with," *halizo*, "to crowd, or mass:" the corresponding adjective is *hales*, "thronged"), is used in **Acts 1:4**. The meaning "to eat with," suggested by some, as if the word were derived from *hals*, "salt," is not to be accepted.

Commanded *parangello* (3853), lit., "to announce beside" (*para*, "beside," *angello*, "to announce"), "to hand on an announcement from one to another," usually denotes "to command, to charge," Luke 5:14; 8:56; 1 Cor. 7:10 (KJV, "command"), "give charge," RV; 11:17, "in giving you this charge," RV; 1 Tim. 1:3; 6:13, RV, and 6:17. It is rendered by the verb "to charge" in the RV of **Acts 1:4**; **4:18**; **5:28**; **15:5**; 1 Thess. 4:11. *See also* **Command** at **Acts 5:28**.

Depart *chorizo* (5563), "to put apart, separate," means, in the middle voice, "to separate oneself, to depart from," **Acts 1:4**; **18:1–2**; in marital affairs, 1 Cor. 7:10-11, 15; "departed" (RV corrects to "was parted"), Philem. 15. The verb is also used in Matt. 19:6; Mark 10:9; Rom. 8:35, 39; Heb. 7:26.

Wait *perimeno* (4037), "to await an event," is used in **Acts 1:4**, of "waiting" for the Holy Spirit, "the promise of the Father." In the Sept., Gen. 49:18.

Promise *epangelia* (1860), primarily a law term, denoting "a summons" (*epi*, "upon," *angello*, "to proclaim, announce"), also meant "an undertaking to do or give something, a promise." Except in **Acts 23:21** it is used only of the "promises" of God. It frequently stands for the thing "promised," and so signifies a gift graciously bestowed, not a pledge secured by negotiation; thus, in Gal. 3:14, "the promise of the Spirit" denotes "the promised Spirit": cf. Luke 24:49; **Acts 2:33** and Eph. 1:13; so in Heb. 9:15, "the promise of the eternal inheritance" is "the promised eternal inheritance." On the other hand, in **Acts 1:4**, "the promise of the Father," is the "promise" made by the Father. In Gal. 3:16, the plural "promises" is used because the one "promise" to Abraham was variously repeated (Gen. 12:1-3; 13:14-17; 15:18; 17:1-14; 22:15-18), and because it contained the germ of all subsequent "promises"; cf. Rom. 9:4; Heb. 6:12; 7:6; 8:6; 11:17; Gal. 3 is occupied with showing that the "promise" was conditional upon faith and not upon the fulfillment of the Law. The Law was later than, and inferior to, the "promise," and did not annul it, v. 21; cf. 4:23, 28. Again, in Eph. 2:12, "the covenants of the promise" does not indicate different covenants, but a covenant often renewed, all centering in Christ as the "promised" Messiah-Redeemer, and comprising the blessings to be bestowed through Him. In 2 Cor. 1:20 the plural is used of every "promise" made by God: cf. Heb. 11:33; in 7:6, of special "promises" mentioned. For other applications of the word, see, e.g., Eph. 6:2; 1 Tim. 4:8; 2 Tim. 1:1; Heb. 4:1; 2 Pet. 3:4, 9; in 1 John 1:5 some mss. have this word, instead of *angelia*, "message." The occurrences of the word in relation to Christ and what centers in Him, may be arranged under the headings (1) the contents of the "promise," e.g., **Acts 26:6**; Rom. 4:20; 1 John 2:25; (2) the heirs, e.g., Rom. 9:8; 15:8; Gal. 3:29; Heb. 11:9; (3) the conditions, e.g., Rom. 4:13, 14; Gal. 3:14-22; Heb. 10:36.

1:5 For John truly baptized with water; but ye shall be baptized with the Holy Ghost not many days hence.

Baptized *baptizo* (907), "to baptize," primarily a frequentative form of *bapto*, "to dip," was used among the Greeks to signify the dyeing of a garment, or the drawing of water by dipping a vessel into another, etc. Plutarchus uses it of the drawing of wine by dipping the cup into the bowl (*Alexis*, 67) and Plato, metaphorically, of being overwhelmed with questions (*Euthydemus*, 277 D). It is used in the NT in Luke 11:38 of washing oneself (as in 2 Kings 5:14, "dipped himself," Sept.); see also Isa. 21:4, lit., "lawlessness overwhelms me." In the early chapters of the four Gospels and in **Acts 1:5**; **11:16**; **19:4**, it is used of the rite performed by John the Baptist who called upon the people to repent that they might receive remission of sins. Those who obeyed came "confessing their sins," thus acknowledging their unfitness to be in the Messiah's coming kingdom. Distinct from this is the "baptism" enjoined by Christ, Matt. 28:19, a "baptism" to be undergone by believers, thus witnessing to their identification with Him in death, burial and resurrection, e.g., **Acts 19:5**; Rom. 6:3-4; 1 Cor. 1:13-17; 12:13; Gal. 3:27; Col. 2:12. The phrase in Matt. 28:19, "baptizing them into the Name" (RV; cf. **Acts 8:16**, RV), would indicate that the "baptized" person was closely bound to, or became the property of, the one into whose name he was "baptized." In **Acts 22:16** it is used in the middle voice, in the command given to Saul of Tarsus, "arise and be baptized," the significance of the middle voice form being "get thyself baptized." The experience of those who were in the ark at the time of the Flood was a figure or type of the facts of spiritual death, burial, and resurrection, Christian "baptism" being an *antitupon*, "a corresponding type," a "like figure," 1 Pet. 3:21. Likewise the nation of Israel was figuratively baptized when made to pass through the Red Sea under the cloud, 1 Cor. 10:2. The verb is used metaphorically also in two distinct senses: firstly, of "baptism" by the Holy Spirit, which took place on the Day of Pentecost; secondly, of the calamity which would come upon the nation of the Jews, a "baptism" of the fire of divine judgment for rejection of the will and word of God, Matt. 3:11; Luke 3:16.

Hence In **Acts 1:5**, the phrase "not many days hence" is, lit., "not after (*meta*) many days."

1:6 When they therefore were come together, they asked of him, saying, Lord, wilt thou at this time restore again the kingdom to Israel?

Restore *apokathistemi* or the alternative form *apokathistano* (600), is used (a) of "restoration" to a former condition of health, Matt. 12:13; Mark 3:5; 8:25; Luke 6:10; (b) of the divine "restoration" of Israel and conditions affected by it, including the renewal of the covenant broken by them, Matt. 17:11; Mark 9:12; **Acts 1:6**; (c) of "giving" or "bringing" a person back, Heb. 13:19. In the papyri it is used of financial restitution, of making good the breaking of a stone by a workman by his substituting another, of the reclamation of land, etc. (Moulton and Milligan).

1:7 And he said unto them, It is not for you to know the times or the seasons, which the Father hath put in his own power.

Know *ginosko* (1097), signifies "to be taking in knowledge, to come to know, recognize, understand," or "to understand completely," e.g., Mark 13:28, 29; John 13:12; 15:18; 21:17; 2 Cor. 8:9; Heb. 10:34; 1 John 2:5; 4:2, 6 (twice), 7, 13; 5:2, 20; in its past tenses it frequently means "to know in the sense of realizing," the aorist or point tense usually indicating definiteness, Matt. 13:11; Mark 7:24; John 7:26; in 10:38 "that ye may know (aorist tense) and understand, (present tense)"; 19:4; **Acts 1:7**; **17:19**; Rom. 1:21; 1 Cor. 2:11 (2nd part), 14; 2 Cor. 2:4; Eph. 3:19; 6:22; Phil. 2:19; 3:10; 1 Thess. 3:5; 2 Tim. 2:19; Jas. 2:20; 1 John 2:13 (twice), 14; 3:6; 4:8; 2 John 1; Rev. 2:24; 3:3, 9. In the passive voice, it often signifies "to become known," e.g., Matt. 10:26; Phil. 4:5. In the sense of complete and absolute understanding on God's part, it is used, e.g., in Luke 16:15; John 10:15 (of the Son as well as the Father); 1 Cor. 3:20. In Luke 12:46, KJV, it is rendered "he is ... aware."

Seasons *chronos* (5550), whence Eng. words beginning with "chron"–, denotes "a space of time," whether long or short: (a) it implies duration, whether longer, e.g., **Acts 1:21**, "(all the) time"; **Acts 13:18**; **20:18**, RV, "(all the) time" (KJV, "at all seasons"); or shorter, e.g., Luke 4:5; (b) it sometimes refers to the date of an occurrence, whether past, e.g., Matt. 2:7, or future, e.g., **Acts 3:21**; **7:17**. Broadly speaking, *chronos* expresses the duration of a period, *kairos* stresses it as marked by certain features; thus in **Acts 1:7**, "the Father has set within His own authority" both the times (*chronos*), the lengths of the periods, and the "seasons" (*kairos*), epochs characterized by certain events; in 1 Thess. 5:1, "times" refers to the length of the interval before the Parousia takes place (the presence of Christ with the saints when He comes to receive them to Himself at the Rapture), and to the length of time the Parousia will occupy; "seasons" refers to the special features of the period before, during, and after the Parousia. *Chronos* marks quantity, *kairos*, quality. Sometimes the distinction between the two words is not sharply defined as, e.g., in 2 Tim. 4:6, though even here the apostle's "departure" signalizes the time (*kairos*). The words occur together in the Sept. only in Dan. 2:21 and Eccl. 3:1. *Chronos* is rendered "season" in **Acts 19:22**, KJV (RV, "a while); **20:18** (RV, "all the time"); Rev. 6:11, KJV (RV, "time"); so 20:3. In Luke 23:8 it is used with *hikanos* in the plural, RV, "(of a long) time," more lit., "(for a sufficient number) of times."

Put *tithemi* (5087), "to place, lay, set, put," is translated "to put" in Matt. 5:15; 12:18; in Matt. 22:44, RV, "put (underneath Thy feet)"; Mark 4:21 (1st part), in the 2nd part, RV, "put" (in some texts, KJV, "set"); 10:16, KJV (RV, "laying"); Luke 8:16 (1st part); 2nd part, RV (KJV, "setteth"); 11:33; John 19:19; **Acts 1:7**, KJV (RV, "set"); **4:3**; **5:18**, **25**; **12:4**; Rom. 14:13; 1 Cor. 15:25; 2 Cor. 3:13; 1 Tim. 1:12, KJV (RV, "appointing"); Rev. 11:9, KJV (RV, "laid"). It is translated "to set" in **Acts 1:7**, of times and seasons (KJV, "put"); **Acts 13:47**; Rev. 10:2;

Power *exousia* (1849), denotes "freedom of action, right to act"; used of God, it is absolute, unrestricted, e.g., Luke 12:5 (RV marg., "authority"); in **Acts 1:7** "right of disposal" is what is indicated; used of men, authority is delegated. Angelic beings are called "powers" in Eph. 3:10 (cf. 1:21); 6:12; Col. 1:16; 2:15 (cf. 2:10).

1:8 But ye shall receive power, after that the Holy Ghost is come upon you: and ye shall be witnesses unto me both in Jerusalem, and in all Judaea, and in Samaria, and unto the uttermost part of the earth.

Witnesses *martus* or *martur* (3144), (whence Eng., "martyr," one who bears "witness" by his death) denotes "one who can or does aver what he has seen or heard or knows"; it is used (a) of God, Rom. 1:9; 2 Cor. 1:23; Phil. 1:8; 1 Thess. 2:5, 10 (2nd part); (b) of Christ, Rev. 1:5; 3:14; (c) of those who "witness" for Christ by their death, **Acts 22:20**; Rev. 2:13; Rev. 17:6; (d) of the interpreters of God's counsels, yet to "witness" in Jerusalem in the times of the Antichrist, Rev. 11:3; (e) in a forensic sense, Matt. 18:16; 26:65; Mark 14:63; **Acts 6:13**; **7:58**; 2 Cor. 13:1; 1 Tim. 5:19; Heb. 10:28; (f) in a historical sense, Luke 11:48; 24:48; **Acts 1:8**, **22**; **2:32**; **3:15**; **5:32**; **10:39**, **41**; **13:31**; **22:15**; **26:16**; 1 Thess. 2:10 (1st part); 1 Tim. 6:12; 2 Tim. 2:2; Heb. 12:1, "(a cloud) of witnesses," here of those mentioned in ch. 11, those whose lives and actions testified to the worth and effect of faith, and whose faith received "witness" in Scripture; 1 Pet. 5:1.

Uttermost *eschatos* (2078), "last, utmost, extreme," is used (a) of place, e.g., Luke 14:9, 10, "lowest;" **Acts 1:8** and **13:47**, "uttermost part;" (b) of rank, e.g., Mark 9:35; (c) of time, relating either to persons or things, e.g., Matt. 5:26, "the last (farthing)," RV (KJV, "uttermost"); Matt. 20:8, 12, 14; Mark 12.6, 22; 1 Cor. 4:9, of apostles as "last" in the program of a spectacular display; 1 Cor. 15:45, "the last Adam"; Rev. 2:19; of the "last" state of persons, Matt. 12:45, neuter plural, lit., "the last (things)"; so Luke 11:26; 2 Pet. 2:20, RV, "the last state" (KJV, "the latter end"); of Christ as the Eternal One, Rev. 1:17 (in some mss. v. 11); 2:8; 22:13; in eschatological phrases as follows: (a) "the last day," a comprehensive term including both the time of the resurrection of the redeemed, John 6:39, 40, 44, 54 and 11:24, and the ulterior time of the judgment of the unregenerate, at the Great White Throne, John 12:48; (b) "the last days," **Acts 2:17**, a period relative to the supernatural manifestation of the Holy Spirit at Pentecost and the resumption of the divine interpositions in the affairs of the world at the end of the present age, before "the great and notable Day of the Lord," which will usher in the messianic kingdom.

Earth *ge* (1093), denotes ... "the inhabited earth," e.g., Luke 21:35; **Acts 1:8**; **8:33**; **10:12**; **11:6**; **17:26**; **22:22**; Heb. 11:13; Rev. 13:8. In the following the phrase "on the earth" signifies "among men," Luke 12:49; 18:8; John 17:4.

"Witnessing is not something we do; it is something we are."

ANON

1:9 And when he had spoken these things, while they beheld, he was taken up; and a cloud received him out of their sight.

Beheld *blepo* (991), primarily, "to have sight, to see," then, "observe, discern, perceive," frequently implying special contemplation, is rendered by the verb "to look" in Luke 9:62, "looking (back)"; John 13:22 "(the disciples) looked (one on another)"; **Acts 1:9**, RV, "were looking" (KJV, "beheld"); **3:4**, "look (on us)"; **27:12**, RV, "looking," KJV, "that lieth (towards)," of the haven Phenix; Eph. 5:15, RV, "look (therefore carefully how ye walk)," KJV, "see (that ye walk circumspectly)"; Rev. 11:9 and 18:9, RV, "look upon" (KJV, "shall see").

Taken up *epairo* (1869), "to lift up, raise," is used of "lifting" up the eyes, Matt. 17:8; Luke 6:20; 16:23, 18:13; John 4:35; 6:5; 17:1; the head, Luke 21:28; the hands, Luke 24:50; 1 Tim. 2:8; the voice, Luke 11:27; **Acts 2:14**; **14:11**; **22:22**; a foresail, **Acts 27:40** ("hoisting," RV); metaphorically, of the heel, John 13:18, as of one "lifting" up the foot before kicking; the expression indicates contempt and violence; in the passive voice, **Acts 1:9**, of Christ's ascension, "was taken up"; 2 Cor. 10:5, "is exalted" (with pride); 11:20, "exalteth himself."

Cloud *nephele* (3507), "a definitely shaped cloud, or masses of clouds possessing definite form," is used, besides the physical element, (a) of the "cloud" on the mount of transfiguration, Matt. 17:5; (b) of the "cloud" which covered Israel in the Red Sea, 1 Cor. 10:1-2; (c) of "clouds" seen in the Apocalyptic visions, Rev. 1:7; 10:1; 11:12; 14:14-16; (d) metaphorically in 2 Pet. 2:17, of the evil workers there mentioned; but RV, "and mists" (*homichle*), according to the most authentic mss. In 1 Thess. 4:17, the "clouds" referred to in connection with the rapture of the saints are probably the natural ones, as also in the case of those in connection with Christ's second advent to the earth. See Matt. 24:30; 26:64, and parallel passages. So at the Ascension, **Acts 1:9**.

Received *hupolambano* (5274), signifies (a) "to take or bear up from beneath," **Acts 1:9**; (b) "to receive," 3 John 8; (c) "to suppose," Luke 7:43; **Acts 2:15**; (d) "to catch up (in speech), to answer," Luke 10:30; in sense (d) it indicates that a person follows what another has said, either by controverting or supplementing it.

Sight *ophthalmos* (3788), "an eye" (Eng. "ophthalmic," etc.) in **Acts 1:9** is translated "sight" (plur. lit., "eyes").

1:10 And while they looked stedfastly toward heaven as he went up, behold, two men stood by them in white apparel;

While *hos*, as, "while" in Luke 24:32 (twice); John 12:35, 36; **Acts 1:10**; **10:17**.

Looked *atenizo* (816), "to look fixedly, gaze," is translated "looking steadfastly" in Luke 22:56, RV (KJV, "... earnestly"); in **Acts 1:10**, "looking steadfastly;" in **3:12**, KJV, "look ... earnestly" (RV, "fasten ye your eyes," as in **3:4** and **11:6**); so in the RV of **6:15**; **10:4**; **13:9**; **14:9**; in **7:55**, "looked up steadfastly," in **23:1**, "looking steadfastly on" (KJV, "earnestly beholding"); in 2 Cor, 3:7, RV, "look steadfastly" (KJV, "steadfastly behold"); in 3:13, RV, ditto (KJV, "steadfastly look"). In Luke 4:20, "were fastened" (*ophthalmoi*, "eyes," being used separately).

Stood *paristemi* (3936), intransitively, denotes "to stand by or beside," Mark 14:47, 69, 70; 15:35, 39 (RV, "stood by"); Luke 19:24; John 18:22; 19:26; **Acts 1:10**; **9:39**; **23:2**, **4**; **27:23**; in **27:24**, "stand before"; in **4:10**, "doth ... stand here"; in Luke 1:19, "stand"; Rom. 14:10, "we shall ... stand before" (middle voice); 2 Tim. 4:17, RV, "stood by" (KJV, "... with").

White *leukos* (3022), is used of (a) clothing (sometimes in the sense of "bright"), Matt. 17:2; 28:3; Mark 9:3; 16:5; Luke 9:29; John 20:12; **Acts 1:10**; symbolically, Rev. 3:4, 5, 18; 4:4; 6:11; 7:9, 13; 19:14 (2nd part); (b) hair, Matt. 5:36; Christ's head and hair (in a vision; cf. Dan. 7:9), Rev. 1:14 (twice); ripened grain, John 4:35; a stone, Rev. 2:17, an expression of the Lord's special delight in the overcomer, the new name on it being indicative of a secret communication of love and joy; a horse (in a vision), 6:2; 19:11-14 (1st part); a cloud, 14:14; the throne of God, 20:11.

Apparel *esthes* (2066), and *esthesis* (2067), connected with *hennumi*, "to clothe" means "clothing, raiment," usually suggesting the ornate, the goodly. The former is found in Luke 23:11, RV, "apparel" (KJV, "robe"); 24:4 (KJV, "garments"); **Acts 10:30** (KJV, "clothing"); **12:21**; Jas. 2:2 (RV, clothing," twice; KJV, "apparel" and "raiment"); 2:3 ("clothing"). *Esthesis* is used in **Acts 1:10**, "apparel."

1:11 Which also said, Ye men of Galilee, why stand ye gazing up into heaven? this same Jesus, which is taken up from you into heaven, shall so come in like manner as ye have seen him go into heaven.

Gazing *emblepo* (1689), expresses "earnest looking," e.g., in the Lord's command to "behold" the birds of the heaven, with the object of learning lessons of faith from them, Matt. 6:26. See also 19:26; Mark 8:25; 10:21, 27; 14:67; Luke 20:17; 22:61; John 1:36; of the Lord's looking upon Peter, John 1:42; **Acts 1:11**; **22:11**.

Taken *see Acts 1:2*.

Manner *tropos* (5158), "a turning, fashion, manner, character, way of life," is translated "manner" in **Acts 1:11**, with reference to the Lord's ascension and return, in Jude 7, of the similarity of the evil of those mentioned in vv. 6 and 7.

Seen *theaomai* (2300), "to behold, view attentively, contemplate," had, in earlier Greek usage, the sense of a wondering regard. This idea was gradually lost. It signifies a more earnest contemplation than the ordinary verbs for "to see," "a careful and deliberate vision which interprets ... its object," and is more frequently rendered "behold" in the RV than the KJV. Both translate it by "behold" in Luke 23:55 (of the sepulchre); "we beheld," in John 1:14, of the glory of the Son of God; "beheld," RV, in John 1:32; **Acts 1:11**; 1 John 1:1 (more than merely seeing); 4:12, 14.

1:12 Then returned they unto Jerusalem from the mount called Olivet, which is from Jerusalem a sabbath day's journey.

Returned *hupostrepho* (5290), "to turn behind," or "back" (*hupo*, "under"), is translated "to return" (in some texts in Mark 14:40) in Luke 1:56; 2:20, 43; v. 45, RV (KJV, "turned back again"), 4:1, 14; 7:10; 8:37; 10:17; 11:24, KJV (RV, "I will turn back"); 17:18; 19:12; 23:48, 56; **Acts 1:12**; **12:25**; **13:13**; **13:34**; **20:3**; **21:6**; **22:17**, RV (KJV, "was come again"); **23:32**; Gal. 1:17; Heb. 7:1.

Mount *oros* (3735), is used (a) without specification, e.g., Luke 3:5 (distinct from *bounos*, "a hill"); John 4:20; (b) of "the Mount of Transfiguration," Matt. 17:1, 9; Mark 9:2, 9; Luke 9:28, 37 (KJV, "hill"); 2 Pet. 1:18; (c) of "Zion," Heb. 12:22; Rev. 14:1; (d) of "Sinai," **Acts 7:30**, **38**; Gal. 4:24, 25; Heb. 8:5; 12:20; (e) of "the Mount of Olives," Matt. 21:1; 24:3; Mark 11:1; 13:3; Luke 19:29, 37; 22:39; John 8:1; **Acts 1:12**; (f) of "the hill districts as distinct from the lowlands," especially of the hills above the Sea of Galilee, e.g., Matt. 5:1; 8:1; 18:12; Mark 5:5; (g) of "the mountains on the east of Jordan" and "those in the land of Ammon" and "the region of Petra," etc., Matt. 24:16; Mark 13:14; Luke 21:21; (h) proverbially, "of overcoming difficulties, or accomplishing great things," 1 Cor. 13:2; cf. Matt. 17:20; 21:21; Mark 11:23; (i) symbolically, of "a series of the imperial potentates of the Roman dominion, past and future," Rev. 17:9.

Olivet *elaion* (1638), "an olive grove" or "olive garden," the ending—*on*, as in this class of noun, here indicates "a place set with trees of the kind designated by the primitive" (Thayer); hence it is applied to the Mount of Olives, Luke 19:29; 21:37; **Acts 1:12** ("Olivet"): in the first two of these and in Mark 11:1.

From *engus* (1451), "nigh" or "near," is translated in both ways in Matt. 24:32-33 and Mark 13:28-29, KJV (RV, "nigh" in both); in **Acts 1:12**, with *echon*, present participle neuter of *echo*, "to have," RV, "nigh unto ... off" (KJV, from).

Journey *hodos* (3598), "a way, path, road," used of a traveler's way, a "journey," is rendered "journey" in Matt. 10:13; Mark 6:8; Luke 2:44, "a day's journey" (probably to Beeroth, six miles north of Jerusalem); 9:3; 11:6; **Acts 1:12**, "a Sabbath day's journey," i.e., the journey which a Jew was allowed to take on the Sabbath, viz., about 2,000 yards or cubits (estimates vary). The regulation was not a Mosaic enactment, but a rabbinical tradition, based upon an exposition of Exod. 16:29, and a comparison of the width of the suburb of a Levitical city as enjoined in Num. 35:4, 5, and the distance between the ark and the people at the crossing of the Jordan, Josh. 3:4. In regard to **Acts 1:12**, there is no discrepancy between this and Luke 24:50, where the RV rightly translates by "over against Bethany," which does not fix the exact spot of the Ascension.

"The fact that Jesus Christ is to come again is not a reason for star-gazing, but for working in the power of the Holy Ghost."

CHARLES HADDON SPURGEON

1:13 And when they were come in, they went up into an upper room, where abode both Peter, and James, and John, and Andrew, Philip, and Thomas, Bartholomew, and Matthew, James *the son* of Alphaeus, and Simon Zelotes, and Judas *the brother* of James.

Upper room *huperoon* (5253), the neuter of the adjective *huperoos*, "upper" (from *huper*, "above"), used as a noun, denoted in classical Greek "an upper story" or "room" where the women resided; in the Sept. and the NT, "an upper chamber, a roof-chamber," built on the flat "roof" of the house, **Acts 1:13**, **9:37**, **39**; **20:8** RV, "upper chamber" (KJV "upper room").

Abode *katameno* (2650), *kata*, "down" (intensive), and *meno*, is used in **Acts 1:13**. The word may signify "constant residence," but more probably indicates "frequent resort." In 1 Cor. 16:6, it denotes "to wait."

Zelotes *zelotes* (2207), is used adjectivally, of "being zealous" (a) "of the Law," **Acts 21:20**; (b) "toward God," lit., "of God," **22:3**, RV, "for God"; (c) "of spiritual gifts," 1 Cor. 14:12, i.e., for exercise of spiritual gifts (lit., "of spirits," but not to be interpreted literally); (d) "for (KJV, 'of') the traditions of my fathers," Gal. 1:14, of Paul's loyalty to Judaism before his conversion; (e) "of good works," Titus 2:14. The word is, lit., "a zealot," i.e., "an uncompromising partisan." The "Zealots" was a name applied to an extreme section of the Pharisees, bitterly antagonistic to the Romans. Josephus (*Antiq.* xviii. 1. 1, 6; *B.J.* ii. 8. 1) refers to them as the "fourth sect of Jewish philosophy" (i.e., in addition to the Pharisees, Sadducees, and Essenes), founded by Judas of Galilee (cf. Acts 5:37). After his rebellion in AD 6, the Zealots nursed the fires of revolt, which, bursting out afresh in AD 66, led to the destruction of Jerusalem in 70. To this sect Simon, one of the apostles, had belonged, Luke 6:15; **Acts 1:13**. The equivalent Hebrew and Aramaic term was "Cananaean" (Matt. 10:4); this is not connected with Canaan, as the KJV "Canaanite" would suggest, but is derived from Heb. *qanna*, "jealous."

Brother In Luke 6:16 and **Acts 1:13**, the RV has "son," for KJV, "brother."

1:14 These all continued with one accord in prayer and supplication, with the women, and Mary the mother of Jesus, and with his brethren.

Continued *proskartereo* (4342), lit., "to be strong towards" (*pros*, "towards," used intensively, and *kartereo*, "to be strong"), "to endure in, or persevere in, to be continually steadfast with a person or thing," is used of "continuing" in prayer with others, **Acts 1:14**; Rom. 12:12; Col. 4:2; in the apostles' teaching, **Acts 2:42**; in the Temple, **2:46** ("continuing steadfastly," RV), the adverb representing the intensive preposition; in prayer and the ministry, **6:4** (RV, "will continue steadfastly"); of Simon Magus with Philip, **8:13**. In Mark 3:9 and **Acts 10:7**, it signifies "to wait on"; in Rom. 13:6, to attend "continually" upon.

Accord *homothumadon* (3661), "of one accord" (from *homos*, "same," *thumos*, "mind"), occurs eleven times, ten in the Acts, **1:14**; **2:46**; **4:24**; **5:12**; **7:57**; **8:6**; **12:20**; **15:25**; **18:12**, **19:29**, and the other in Rom. 15:6, where, for KJV, "with one mind," the RV has "with one accord," as throughout the Acts.

1:15 And in those days Peter stood up in the midst of the disciples, and said, (the number of names together were about an hundred and twenty,)

Stood *anistemi* (450), "to raise," intransitively, "to rise," is translated "to stand up" in Matt. 12:41, RV; Mark 14:60; Luke 4:16; 10:25; **Acts 1:15**; **5:34**; **10:26**; **11:28**; **13:16**; in **14:10**, "stand upright."

Disciples In **Acts 1:15**, the RV translates the mss. which have *adelphon*, "brethren"; in **20:7**, RV, "we," for KJV, "disciples."

Names *onoma* (3686), is used (I) in general of the "name" by which a person or thing is called, e.g., Mark 3:16, 17, "(He) surnamed," lit., "(He added) the name"; 14:32, lit., "(of which) the name (was)"; Luke 1:63; John 18:10, sometimes translated "named," e.g., Luke 8:5, "named (Zacharias)," lit., "by name"; in the same verse, "named (Elizabeth)," lit., "the name of her," an elliptical phrase, with "was" understood; **Acts 8:9**, RV, "by name," **10:1**; the "name" is put for the reality in Rev. 3:1; in Phil. 2:9, the "Name" represents "the title and dignity" of the Lord, as in Eph. 1:21 and Heb. 1:4.

(II) for all that a "name" implies, of authority, character, rank, majesty, power, excellence, etc., of everything that the "name" covers: (a) of the "Name" of God as expressing His attributes, etc., e.g., Matt. 6:9; Luke 1:49; John 12:28; 17:6, 26; Rom. 15:9; 1 Tim. 6:1; Heb. 13:15; Rev. 13:6; (b) of the "Name" of Christ, e.g., Matt. 10:22; 19:29; John 1:12; 2:23; 3:18; **Acts 26:9**; Rom. 1:5; Jas. 2:7; 1 John 3:23; 3 John 7; Rev. 2:13; 3:8; also the phrases rendered "in the name"; these may be analyzed as follows: (1) representing the authority of Christ, e.g., Matt. 18:5 (with *epi*, "on the ground of My authority"); so Matt. 24:5 (falsely) and parallel passages; as substantiated by the Father, John 14:26; 16:23 (last clause), RV; (2) in the power of (with *en*, "in"), e.g., Mark 16:17; Luke 10:17; **Acts 3:6**; **4:10**; **16:18**; Jas. 5:14; (3) in acknowledgement or confession of, e.g., **Acts 4:12**; **8:16**; **9:27**, **28**; (4) in recognition of the authority of (sometimes combined with the thought of relying or resting on), Matt. 18:20; cf. 28:19; **Acts 8:16**; **9:2** (*eis*, "into"); John 14:13; 15:16; Eph. 5:20; Col. 3:17; (5) owing to the fact that one is called by Christ's "Name" or is identified with Him, e.g. 1 Pet. 4:14 (with *en*, "in"); with *heneken*, "for the sake of," e.g., Matt. 19:29; with *dia*, "on account of," Matt. 10:22; 24:9; Mark 13:13; Luke 21:17; John 15:21; 1 John 2:12; Rev. 2:3.

(III) as standing, by metonymy, for "persons," **Acts 1:15**; Rev. 3:4; 11:13 (RV, "persons").

Together In the following, "together" translates the phrase *epi to auto*, lit., "to (upon, or for) the same," Matt. 22:34; Luke 17:35; **Acts 1:15**; **2:44** (**3:1**, in some texts); **4:26**; 1 Cor. 7:5; 14:23, RV.

About *hos* (5613), usually means "as." Used with numerals it signifies "about," e.g., Mark 5:13; 8:9; John 1:40; 6:19; 11:18; **Acts 1:15**; Rev. 8:1.

Hundred *hekaton* (1540), an indeclinable numeral, denotes "a hundred," e.g., Matt. 18:12, 28; it also signifies "a hundredfold," Matt. 13:8, 23, and the RV in the corresponding passage, Mark 4:8, 20 (for KJV, "hundred"), signifying the complete productiveness of sown seed. In the passage in Mark the phrase is, lit., "in thirty and in sixty and in a hundred." In Mark 6:40 it is used with the preposition *kata*, in the phrase "by hundreds." It is followed by other numerals in John 21:11; **Acts 1:15**; Rev. 7:4; 14:1, 3; 21:17.

Twenty *eikosi* (1501), occurs in Luke 14:31; John 6:19; **Acts 1:15**; **27:28**; 1 Cor. 10:8; of the "four and twenty" elders, in Rev. 4:4 (twice), 10; 5:8; 11:16; 19:4 (combined in one numeral with *tessares*, "four," in some mss.).

1:16 Men *and* brethren, this scripture must needs have been fulfilled, which the Holy Ghost by the mouth of David spake before concerning Judas, which was guide to them that took Jesus.

Men *aner* (435), is never used of the female sex; it stands (a) in distinction from a woman, **Acts 8:12**; 1 Tim. 2:12; as a husband, Matt. 1:16; John 4:16; Rom. 7:2; Titus 1:6; (b) as distinct from a boy or infant, 1 Cor. 13:11; metaphorically in Eph. 4:13; (c) in conjunction with an adjective or noun, e.g., Luke 5:8, lit., "a man, a sinner"; 24:19, lit., "a man, a prophet"; often in terms of address, e.g., **Acts 1:16**; **13:15**, **26**; **15:7**, **13**, lit., "men, brethren"; with gentilic or local names (virtually a title of honor), e.g., **Acts 2:14**; **22:3**, lit., "Judean men," "a Judean man"; **3:12**; **5:35**, lit., "Israelite men"; **17:22**, "Athenian men"; **19:35**, lit., "Ephesian men"; in **Acts 14:15** it is used in addressing a company of "men," without any descriptive term. In this verse, however, the distinction between *aner* and *anthropos* (2nd part) is noticeable; (d) in general, "a man, a male person," (i.e., a certain "man"), e.g., Luke 8:41; in the plural, **Acts 6:11**.

Brethren Believers, with *aner*, "male," prefixed, and with "or sister" added, 1 Cor. 7:14 (RV), 15; Jas. 2:15, male as distinct from female, **Acts 1:16**; **15:7**, **13**, but not **6:3**.

Scripture *graphe* (1124), akin to *grapho*, "to write" (Eng., "graph," "graphic," etc.), primarily denotes "a drawing, painting"; then "a writing," (a) of the OT Scriptures, (1) in the plural, the whole, e.g., Matt. 21:42; 22:29; John 5:39; **Acts 17:11**; **18:24**; Rom. 1:2, where "the prophets" comprises the OT writers in general; 15:4; 16:26, lit., "prophetic writings," expressing the character of all the Scriptures; (2) in the singular in reference to a particular passage, e.g., Mark 12:10; Luke 4:21; John 2:22; 10:35 (though applicable to all); 19:24, 28, 36, 37; 20:9; **Acts 1:16**; **8:32**, **35**; Rom. 4:3; 9:17; 10:11; 11:2; Gal. 3:8, 22; 4:30; 1 Tim. 5:18, where the 2nd quotation is from Luke 10:7, from which it may be inferred that the apostle included Luke's Gospel as "Scripture" alike with Deuteronomy, from which the first quotation is taken; in reference to the whole, e.g. Jas. 4:5 (see RV, a separate rhetorical question from the one which follows); in 2 Pet. 1:20, "no prophecy of Scripture," a description of all, with special application to the OT in the next verse; (b) of the OT Scriptures (those accepted by the Jews as canonical) and all those of the NT which were to be accepted by Christians as authoritative, 2 Tim. 3:16; these latter were to be discriminated from the many forged epistles and other religious "writings" already produced and circulated in Timothy's time. Such discrimination would be directed by the fact that "every Scripture," characterized by inspiration of God, would be profitable for the purposes mentioned; so the RV.

Needs *dei* (1163), an impersonal verb, signifying "it is necessary," is rendered "must needs" in Mark 13:7; John 4:4; **Acts 1:16**, KJV (RV, "it was needful"); **17:3**, KJV (RV, "it behoved"); (in some mss. in **Acts 21:22**); 2 Cor. 11:30; 12:1; in **Acts 15:5**, "it was needful."

Holy Ghost The "Holy Spirit" is spoken of under various titles in the NT ("Spirit" and "Ghost" are renderings of the same word, *pneuma;* the advantage of the rendering "Spirit" is that it can always be used, whereas "Ghost" always requires the word "Holy" prefixed.) In the following list the omission of the definite article marks its omission in the original: "Spirit, Matt. 22:43; Eternal Spirit, Heb. 9:14; the Spirit, Matt. 4:1; Holy Spirit, Matt. 1:18; the Holy Spirit, Matt. 28:19; the Spirit, the Holy, Matt. 12:32; the Spirit of promise, the Holy, Eph. 1:13; Spirit of God, Rom. 8:9; Spirit of (the) living God, 2 Cor. 3:3; the Spirit of God, 1 Cor. 2:11; the Spirit of our God, 1 Cor. 6:11; the Spirit of God, the Holy, Eph. 4:30; the Spirit of glory and of God, 1 Pet. 4:14; the Spirit of Him that raised up Jesus from the dead (i.e., God), Rom. 8:11; the Spirit of your Father, Matt. 10:20; the Spirit of His Son, Gal. 4:6; Spirit of (the) Lord, **Acts 8:39**; the Spirit of (the) Lord, **Acts 5:9**; (the) Lord, (the) Spirit, 2 Cor. 3:18; the Spirit of Jesus, **Acts 16:7**; Spirit of Christ, Rom. 8:9; the Spirit of Jesus Christ, Phil. 1:19; Spirit of adoption, Rom. 8:15; the Spirit of truth, John 14:17; the Spirit of life, Rom. 8:2; the Spirit of grace, Heb. 10:29."

The use or absence of the article in the original where the "Holy Spirit" is spoken of cannot always be decided by grammatical rules, nor can the presence or absence of the article alone determine whether the reference is to the "Holy Spirit." Examples where the Person is meant when the article is absent are Matt. 22:43 (the article is used in Mark 12:36); **Acts 4:25**, RV (absent in some texts); **19:2**, 6; Rom. 14:17; 1 Cor. 2:4; Gal. 5:25 (twice); 1 Pet. 1:2. Sometimes the absence is to be accounted for by the fact that *Pneuma* (like *Theos*) is substantially a proper name, e.g., in John 7:39. As a general rule the article is present where the subject of the teaching is the Personality of the Holy Spirit, e.g., John 14:26, where He is spoken of in distinction from the Father and the Son. See also 15:26 and cf. Luke 3:22. The full title with the article before both *pneuma* and *hagios* (the "resumptive" use of the article), lit., "the Spirit the Holy," stresses the character of the Person, e.g., Matt. 12:32; Mark 3:29; 12:36; 13:11; Luke 2:26; 10:21 (RV); John 14:26; **Acts 1:16; 5:3; 7:51; 10:44, 47; 13:2; 15:28; 19:6; 20:23, 28; 21:11; 28:25**; Eph. 4:30; Heb. 3:7; 9:8; 10:15. The Personality of the Spirit is emphasized at the expense of strict grammatical procedure in John 14:26; 15:26; 16:8, 13, 14, where the emphatic pronoun *ekeinos*, "He," is used of Him in the masculine, whereas the noun *pneuma* is neuter in Greek, while the corresponding word in Aramaic, the language in which our Lord probably spoke, is feminine (*rucha*, cf. Heb. *ruach*).

Mouth *stoma* (4750), akin to *stomachos* (which originally meant "a throat, gullet"), is used (a) of "the mouth" of man, e.g., Matt. 15:11; of animals, e.g., Matt. 17:27; 2 Tim. 4:17 (figurative); Heb. 11:33; Jas. 3:3; Rev. 13:2 (2nd occurrence); (b) figuratively of "inanimate things," of the "edge" of a sword, Luke 21:24; Heb. 11:34; of the earth, Rev. 12:16; (c) figuratively, of the "mouth," as the organ of speech, (1) of Christ's words, e.g., Matt. 13:35; Luke 11:54; **Acts 8:32; 22:14**; 1 Pet. 2:22; (2) of human, e.g., Matt. 18:16; 21:16; Luke 1:64; Rev. 14:5; as emanating from the heart, Matt. 12:34; Rom. 10:8, 9; of prophetic ministry through the Holy Spirit, Luke 1:70; **Acts 1:16; 3:18; 4:25**; of the destructive policy of two world potentates at the end of this age, Rev. 13:2, 5, 6; 16:13 (twice); of shameful speaking, Eph. 4:29 and Col. 3:8; (3) of the Devil speaking as a dragon or serpent, Rev. 12:15, 16; 16:13; (d) figuratively, in the phrase "face to face" (lit., "mouth to mouth"), 2 John 12; 3 John 14; (e) metaphorically, of "the utterances of the Lord, in judgment," 2 Thess. 2:8; Rev. 1:16; 2:16; 19:15, 21; of His judgment upon a local church for its lukewarmness, Rev. 3:16; (f) by metonymy, for "speech," Matt. 18:16; Luke 19:22; 21:15; 2 Cor. 13:1.

Spake *proeipon* (4302), "to speak or say before" (a 2nd aorist tense from an obsolete present), is rendered "to speak before" in **Acts 1:16**; 2 Pet. 3:2; Jude 17.

Spake before *prolego* (4302), with the aorist form *proeipon*, and a perfect form *proeireka* (from *proereo*), signifies (1) "to declare openly" or "plainly," or "to say" or "tell beforehand" (*pro*, "before," *lego*, "to say"), translated in 2 Cor. 13:2 (in the first sentence), RV, "I have said beforehand," KJV, "I told ... before", in the next sentence, KJV, "I foretell," RV, "I do say beforehand" (marg., "plainly"); not prophecy is here in view, but a warning given before and repeated; (2) "to speak before, of prophecy," as "foretelling" the future, Mark 13:23, KJV, "have foretold," RV, "have told ... beforehand"; **Acts 1:16** (of the prophecy concerning Judas); Rom. 9:29; 2 Pet. 3:2; Jude 17; some inferior mss. have it in Heb. 10:15.

Guide *hodegos* (3595), "a leader on the way" (*hodos*, "a way," *hegeomai*, "to lead"), "a guide," is used (a) literally, in **Acts 1:16**; (b) figuratively, Matt. 15:14, RV, "guides" (KJV, "leaders"); Matt. 23:16, 24, "guides"; Rom. 2:19, "a guide."

Took *sullambano* (4815), lit., "to take together" (*sun*, "with," *lambano*, "to take or lay hold of"), chiefly signifies "to seize as a prisoner"; in the following the RV substitutes the more suitable and forceful verb, "to seize," for KJV, "to take": Matt. 26:55; Mark 14:48; Luke 22:54; John 18:12; **Acts 12:3**; **23:27**; **26:21**; in **Acts 1:16**, RV and KJV, "took."

1:17 For he was numbered with us, and had obtained part of this ministry.

Numbered *katarithmeo* (2674), "to number" or "count among," is used in **Acts 1:17**.

Obtained *lanchano* (2975), "to obtain by lot," is translated "that have obtained" in 2 Pet. 1:1; in **Acts 1:17**, KJV, "had obtained" (RV, "received"), with *kleros*, "a lot" or "portion."

Part *kleros* (2819), denotes (a) an object used in casting or drawing lots, which consisted of bits, or small tablets, of wood or stone (the probable derivation is from *klao*, "to break"); these were sometimes inscribed with the names of persons, and were put into a receptacle or a garment ("a lap," Prov. 16:33), from which they were cast, after being shaken together; he whose "lot" first fell out was the one chosen. The method was employed in a variety of circumstances, e.g., of dividing or assigning property, Matt. 27:35; Mark 15:24; Luke 23:34; John 19:24 (cf., e.g., Num. 26:55); of appointing to office, **Acts 1:26** (cf, e.g., 1 Sam. 10:20); for other occurrences in the OT, see, e.g., Josh. 7:14 (the earliest instance in Scripture), Lev.16:7-10; Esth. 3:7; 9:24; (b) "what is obtained by lot, an allotted portion," e.g., of the ministry allotted to the apostles, **Acts 1:17**, RV, "portion," marg., "lot" (KJV, "part"); in some mss. v. **25**, KJV, "part" (the RV follows those which have *topos*, "place"); **Acts 8:21**; it is also used like *kleronomia*, "an inheritance," in **Acts 26:18**, of what God has in grace assigned to the sanctified; so Col. 1:12; in 1 Pet. 5:3 it is used of those the spiritual care of, and charge over, whom is assigned to elders, RV, "the charge allotted to you" (plural, lit., "the charges"), KJV, "(God's) heritage." From *kleros* the word "clergy" is derived (a transposition in the application of the term).

Ministry *diakonua* (1248), "the office and work of a *diakonos*", "service, ministry," is used (a) of domestic duties, Luke 10:40; (b) of religious and spiritual "ministration," (1) of apostolic "ministry," e.g., **Acts 1:17**, **25**; **6:4**; **12:25**; **21:19**; Rom. 11:13, RV (KJV, "office"); (2) of the service of believers, e.g., **Acts 6:1**; Rom. 12:7; 1 Cor. 12:5, RV, "ministrations" (KJV, "administrations"); 1 Cor. 16:15; 2 Cor. 8:4; 9:1, 12, RV, "ministration"; v. 13; Eph. 4:12, RV, "ministering" (KJV, "the ministry," not in the sense of an ecclesiastical function); 2 Tim. 4:11, RV, "(for) ministering"; collectively of a local church, **Acts 11:29**, "relief" (RV marg. "for ministry"); Rev. 2:19, RV, "ministry" (KJV, "service"); of Paul's service on behalf of poor saints, Rom. 15:31; (3) of the "ministry" of the Holy Spirit in the gospel, 2 Cor. 3:8; (4) of the "ministry" of angels, Heb. 1:14, RV, "to do service" (KJV, "to minister"); (5) of the work of the gospel, in general, e.g., 2 Cor. 3:9, "of righteousness;" 5:18, "of reconciliation"; (6) of the general "ministry" of a servant of the Lord in preaching and teaching, **Acts 20:24**; 2 Cor. 4:1; 6:3; 11:8; 1 Tim. 1:12, RV, "(to His) service"; 2 Tim. 4:5; undefined in Col. 4:17; (7) of the Law, as a "ministration" of death, 2 Cor. 3:7; of condemnation, 3:9.

1:18 Now this man purchased a field with the reward of iniquity; and falling headlong, he burst asunder in the midst, and all his bowels gushed out.

Now *oun* (3767), "therefore, so then," is sometimes used in continuing a narrative, e.g. **Acts 1:18**; 1 Cor. 9:25; or resuming it after a digression, usually rendered "therefore," e.g., **Acts 11:19**; **25:1**, RV (KJV, now). In the following it is absent from the best mss., Mark 12:20; Luke 10:36; John 16:19; 18:24; 19:29.

Purchased *ktaomai* (2932), "to procure for oneself, get, gain, acquire," is translated "obtained" in **Acts 1:18**, RV (KJV, "purchased"); **8:20**, RV (KJV, "may be purchased"); **22:28**.

Field *chorion* (5564), denotes (a) "a place, region," (b) "a piece of land, property," rendered "field" in **Acts 1:18**, **19**.

Reward *misthos* (3408), primarily "wages, hire," and then, generally, "reward," (a) received in this life, Matt. 5:46; 6:2, 5, 16; Rom. 4:4; 1 Cor. 9:17, 18; of evil "rewards," **Acts 1:18**; (b) to be received hereafter, Matt. 5:12; 10:41 (twice), 42; Mark 9:41; Luke 6:23, 35; 1 Cor. 3:8, 14; 2 John 8; Rev. 11:18; 22:12.

Iniquity *adikia* (93), denotes "unrighteousness," lit., "unrightness" (*a*, negative, *dike*, "right"), a condition of not being right, whether with God, according to the standard of His holiness and righteousness, or with man, according to the standard of what man knows to be right by his conscience. In Luke 16:8 and 18:6, the phrases lit. are, "the steward of unrighteousness" and "the judge of injustice," the subjective genitive describing their character; in 18:6 the meaning is "injustice" and so perhaps in Rom.

9:14. The word is usually translated "unrighteousness," but is rendered "iniquity" in Luke 13:27; **Acts 1:18; 8:23**; 1 Cor. 13:6, KJV (RV, "unrighteousness"); so in 2 Tim. 2:19; Jas. 3:6.

Falling *ginomai* (1096), "to become," is translated "falling" (headlong) in **Acts 1:18**.

Headlong *prenes* (4248), an adjective denoting "headlong, prone," is used with the verb *ginomai*, "to become," in **Acts 1:18**, of the death of Judas, "falling headlong"; various suggestions have been made as to the actual details; some ascribe to the word the meaning "swelling up."

Burst asunder *lakeo* or *lasko* (2997), primarily, "to crack, or crash," denotes "to burst asunder with a crack, crack open" (always of making a noise), is used in **Acts 1:18**.

Midst *mesos* (3319), an adjective denoting "middle, in the middle or midst," is used in the following, in which the English requires a phrase, and the adjectival rendering must be avoided: Luke 22:55, "Peter sat in the midst of them," lit., "a middle one of (them)"; Luke 23:45, of the rending of the veil "in the midst"; here the adjective idiomatically belongs to the verb "was rent," and is not to be taken literally, as if it meant "the middle veil"; John 1:26, "in the midst of you (standeth One)," RV (lit., "a middle One"); **Acts 1:18**, where the necessity of avoiding the lit. rendering is obvious. Cf. the phrases "at midday," "at midnight." *Mesos* is used adverbially, in prepositional phrases, (a) *ana m.*, e.g., 1 Cor. 6:5, "between"; Matt. 13:25, "among"; Rev. 7:17, "in the midst"; (b) *dia m.*, e.g., Luke 4:30; 17:11, "through the midst"; (c) *en m.*, Luke 10:3, RV, "in the midst," KJV, "among"; so 22:27; 1 Thess. 2:7; with the article after *en*, e.g., Matt. 14:6, RV, "in the midst," KJV, "before"; (d) *eis m.*, Mark 14:60, "in the midst"; with the article, e.g., Mark 3:3, "forth" (lit., "into the midst"); (e) *ek m.*, "out of the way," lit., "out of the midst," Col. 2:14; 2 Thess. 2:7, where, however, removal is not necessarily in view; there is no accompanying verb signifying removal, as in each of the other occurrences of the phrase; with the article, e.g., 1 Cor. 5:2; 2 Cor. 6:17; (f) *kata m.*, **Acts 27:27**, "about mid(night)."

Bowels *splanchnon* (4698), always in the plural, properly denotes "the physical organs of the intestines," and is once used in this respect, **Acts 1:18**. The RV substitutes the following for the word "bowels": "affections," 2 Cor. 6:12; "affection," 2 Cor. 7:15; "tender mercies," Phil. 1:8; 2:1; "a heart (of compassion)," Col. 3:12; "heart," Philem. 12, 20; "hearts," Philem. 7; "compassion," 1 John 3:17. The word is rendered "tender" in the KJV and RV of Luke 1:78, in connection with the word mercy.

Gushed out *ekchuno*, or *ekchunno* (1632), a Hellenistic form of *ekcheo*, "to pour forth," is translated "gushed out" in **Acts 1:18**, of the bowels of Judas Iscariot.

1:19 And it was known unto all the dwellers at Jerusalem; insomuch as that field is called in their proper tongue, Aceldama, that is to say, The field of blood.

Known *gnostos* (1110), an adjective, signifying "known" (from *ginosko*, "to know"), is used (a) as an adjective, most usually translated "known," whether of facts, e.g., **Acts 1:19; 2:14; 4:10**; or persons, John 18:15-16; it denotes "notable" in **Acts 4:16**, of a miracle; (b) as a noun, "acquaintance," Luke 2:44 and 23:49.

Dwellers *katoikeo* (2730), the most frequent verb with this meaning, properly signifies "to settle down in a dwelling, to dwell fixedly in a place." Besides its literal sense, it is used of (a) the "indwelling" of the totality of the attributes and powers of the Godhead in Christ, Col. 1:19; 2:9; (b) the "indwelling" of Christ in the hearts of believers ("may make a home in your hearts"), Eph. 3:17; (c) the "dwelling" of Satan in a locality, Rev. 2:13; (d) the future "indwelling" of righteousness in the new heavens and earth, 2 Pet. 3:13. It is translated "dwellers" in **Acts 1:19; 2:9**; "inhabitants" in Rev. 17:2, KJV (RV, "they that dwell"), "inhabiters" in Rev. 8:13 and 12:12, KJV (RV, "them that dwell"). Cf. the nouns *katoikesis* (below), *katoikia*, "habitation," **Acts 17:26**; *katoiketerion*, "a habitation," Eph. 2:22; Rev. 18:2. Contrast *paroikeo*, "to sojourn," the latter being temporary, the former permanent.

Insomuch as *hoste* (5620), a consecutive particle, is used with the meaning "insomuch that," or "so that," or "that," to express the effect or result of anything, e.g., Matt. 8:24; 13:54; 15:31; 27:14; **Acts 1:19** (KJV, "insomuch as"); **5:15; 19:12** (KJV, "so that"); 2 Cor. 1:8; Gal. 2:13.

Field *see Acts 1:18.*

Proper *idios* (2398), "one's own," is found in some mss. in **Acts 1:19**, KJV, "proper"; in 1 Cor. 7:7, RV, "own" (KJV, "proper"); in Jude 6, RV, "their proper (habitation)," KJV, "their own."

Tongue *dialektos* (1258), "language" (Eng., "dialect"), is rendered "tongue" in the KJV of **Acts 1:19; 2:6, 8; 21:40; 22:2; 26:14**.

Say *The* phrase *tout' esti* (i.e., *touto esti*), "that is," is so translated in Matt. 27:46, RV (KJV, "that is to say"); so

Acts 1:19; in Heb. 9:11 and 10:20, KJV and RV, "that is to say"; in Mark 7:11 the phrase is *ho esti*, lit., "which is"; the phrase *ho legetai*, lit., "which is said," John 1:38 and 20:16, is rendered "which is to say."

1:20 For it is written in the book of Psalms, Let his habitation be desolate, and let no man dwell therein: and his bishoprick let another take.

Book *biblos* (976), (Eng. "Bible") was the inner part, or rather the cellular substance, of the stem of the papyrus (Eng. "paper"). It came to denote the paper made from this bark in Egypt, and then a written "book," roll, or volume. It is used in referring to "books" of Scripture, the "book," or scroll, of Matthew's Gospel, Matt. 1:1; the Pentateuch, as the "book" of Moses, Mark 12:26; Isaiah, as "the book of the words of Isaiah," Luke 3:4; the Psalms, Luke 20:42 and **Acts 1:20**; "the prophets," **Acts 7:42**; to "the Book of Life," Phil. 4:3; Rev. 3:5; 20:15. Once only it is used of secular writings, **Acts 19:19**.

Psalms *psalmos* (5568), primarily denoted "a striking or twitching with the fingers (on musical strings)"; then, "a sacred song, sung to musical accompaniment, a psalm." It is used (a) of the OT book of "Psalms," Luke 20:42; 24:44; **Acts 1:20**; (b) of a particular "psalm," **Acts 13:33** (cf. v. **35**); (c) of "psalms" in general, 1 Cor. 14:26; Eph. 5:19; Col. 3:16.

Habitation *epaulis* (1886), "a farm, a dwelling" (*epi*, "upon," *aulis*, "a place in which to pass the night, a country house, cottage or cabin, a fold"), is used in **Acts 1:20** of the habitation of Judas.

Desolate (2048), is translated "desolate" in the Lord's words against Jerusalem, Matt. 23:38; some mss. have it in Luke 13:35; in reference to the habitation of Judas, **Acts 1:20**, and to Sarah, from whom, being barren, her husband had turned, Gal. 4:27.

Bishoprick *episkope* (1984), besides its meaning, "visitation," e.g., 1 Pet. 2:12 (cf. the Sept. of Exod. 3:16; Isa. 10:3; Jer. 10:15), is rendered "office," in **Acts 1:20**, RV (KJV, "bishoprick"); in 1 Tim. 3:1 "the office of a bishop," lit., "(if any one seeketh) overseership," there is no word representing office.

1:21 Wherefore of these men which have companied with us all the time that the Lord Jesus went in and out among us,

Companied *sunerchomai* (4905), chiefly used of "assembling together," signifies "to accompany," in Luke 23:55; John 11:33; **Acts 9:39**; **10:45**; **11:12**; **15:38**; **21:16**. In **Acts 1:21** it is said of men who had "companied with" the apostles all the time the Lord Jesus was with them.

1:22 Beginning from the baptism of John, unto that same day that he was taken up from us, must one be ordained to be a witness with us of his resurrection.

Taken *see Acts 1:2*.

Ordained In **Acts 1:22**, KJV, *ginomai* "to become," is translated "be ordained" (RV, "become").

Witness *see* **Witnesses** at *Acts 1:8*.

Resurrection *anastasis* (386), denotes (I) "a raising up," or "rising" (*ana*, "up," and *histemi*, "to cause to stand"), Luke 2:34, "the rising up"; the KJV "again" obscures the meaning; the Child would be like a stone against which many in Israel would stumble while many others would find in its strength and firmness a means of their salvation and spiritual life; (II) of "resurrection" from the dead, (a) of Christ, **Acts 1:22**; **2:31**; **4:33**; Rom. 1:4; 6:5; Phil. 3:10; 1 Pet. 1:3; 3:21; by metonymy, of Christ as the Author of "resurrection," John 11:25; (b) of those who are Christ's at His Parousia, Luke 14:14, "the resurrection of the just"; Luke 20:33, 35, 36; John 5:29 (1st part), "the resurrection of life"; 11:24; **Acts 23:6**; **24:15** (1st part); 1 Cor. 15:21, 42; 2 Tim. 2:18; Heb. 11:35 (2nd part); Rev. 20:5, "the first resurrection"; hence the insertion of "is" stands for the completion of this "resurrection," of which Christ was "the firstfruits"; 20:6; (c) of "the rest of the dead," after the Millennium (cf. Rev. 20:5); John 5:29 (2nd part), "the resurrection of judgment"; **Acts 24:15** (2nd part), "of the unjust"; (d) of those who were raised in more immediate connection with Christ's "resurrection," and thus had part already in the first "resurrection," **Acts 26:23** and Rom. 1:4 (in each of which "dead" is plural; see Matt. 27:52); (e) of the "resurrection" spoken of in general terms, Matt. 22:23; Mark 12:18; Luke 20:27; **Acts 4:2**; **17:18**; **23:8**; **24:21**; 1 Cor. 15:12, 13; Heb. 6:2; (f) of those who were raised in OT times, to die again, Heb. 11:35 (1st part), lit., "out of resurrection."

1:23 And they appointed two, Joseph called Barsabas, who was surnamed Justus, and Matthias.

Appointed *histemi* (2476), "to make to stand," means "to appoint," in **Acts 17:31**, of the day in which God will judge the world by Christ. In **Acts 1:23**, with reference to Joseph and Barnabas, the RV has "put forward"; for these were not both "appointed" in the accepted sense of the term, but simply singled out, in order that it might be made known which of them the Lord had chosen.

Surnamed *epikaleo* (1941), "to put a name upon" (*epi*, "upon," *kaleo*, "to call"), "to surname," is used in this sense in the passive voice, in some texts in Matt. 10:3 (it is absent in the best); in Luke 22:3, in some texts (the best have *kaleo*, "to call"); **Acts 1:23; 4:36; 10:5, 18, 32; 11:13; 12:12, 25**; in some texts, **15:22** (the best have *kaleo*).

1:24 And they prayed, and said, Thou, Lord, which knowest the hearts of all *men*, shew whether of these two thou hast chosen,

Hearts *kardiognostes* (2589), "a knower of hearts" (*kardia* and *ginosko*, "to know"), is used in **Acts 1:24; 15:8**.

Shew *anadeiknumi* (322), signifies (a) "to lift up and show, show forth, declare," **Acts 1:24**; (b) to "appoint," Luke 10:1.

Whether In **Acts 1:24**, KJV, "whether" is, lit., and as the RV, "the one whom."

Chosen *see Acts 1:2.*

1:25 That he may take part of this ministry and apostleship, from which Judas by transgression fell, that he might go to his own place.

Part In **Acts 1:25**, where the best mss. have topos, "a place," RV, "(to take) the place (in this ministry)," some texts have *kleros*, which the KJV translates "part."

Ministry *see Acts 1:17.*

Apostleship *apostole* (651), "a sending, a mission," signifies an apostleship, **Acts 1:25**; Rom. 1:5; 1 Cor. 9:2; Gal. 2:8.

Transgression *parabaino* (3845), lit., "to go aside" (*para*), hence "to go beyond," is chiefly used metaphorically of "transgressing" the tradition of the elders, Matt. 15:2; the commandment of God, 15:3; in **Acts 1:25**, of Judas, KJV, "by transgression fell" (RV, "fell away"); in 2 John 9 some texts have this verb (KJV, "transgresseth"), the best have *proago*.

Place *topos* (5117), (Eng., "topic," "topography," etc.) is used of "a region" or "locality," frequently in the Gospels and Acts, in Luke 2:7 and 14:22, "room"; of a place which a person or thing occupies, a couch at table, e.g., Luke 14:9, 10, RV, "place" (KJV, "room"); of the destiny of Judas Iscariot, **Acts 1:25**; of the condition of the "unlearned" or nongifted in a church gathering, 1 Cor. 14:16, RV, "place"; the sheath of a sword, Matt. 26:52; a place in a book, Luke 4:17; see also Rev. 2:5; 6:14; 12:8; metaphorically, of "condition, occasion, opportunity" **Acts 25:16**, RV, "opportunity" (KJV, "license"); Rom. 12:19; Eph. 4:27.

1:26 And they gave forth their lots; and the lot fell upon Matthias; and he was numbered with the eleven apostles.

Gave *didomi* (1325), "to give," is used with various meanings according to the context; it is said, e.g., of seed "yielding fruit," Mark 4:7, 8; of "giving" (i.e., exercising) diligence, Luke 12:58; of giving lots, **Acts 1:26**, RV (KJV, "gave forth"); of "rendering" vengeance, 2 Thess. 1:8; of "striking or smiting" Christ, John 18:22 (lit., "gave a blow") and 19:3 (lit., "they gave Him blows"); of "putting" a ring on the hand, Luke 15:22; of Paul's "adventuring" himself into a place, **Acts 19:31**. (In Rev. 17:13 some mss. have *diadidomi*, "to divide".)

Lots, Lot *see* **Part** at *Acts 1:17.*

Fell *pipto* (4098), "to fall," is used (a) of descent, to "fall" down from, e.g., Matt. 10:29; 13:4; (b) of a lot, **Acts 1:26**; (c) of "falling" under judgment, Jas. 5:12 (cf. Rev. 18:2, RV); (d) of persons in the act of prostration, to prostrate oneself, e.g., Matt. 17:6; John 18:6; Rev. 1:17; in homage and worship, e.g., Matt. 2:11; Mark 5:22; Rev. 5:14; 19:4; (e) of things, "falling" into ruin, or failing, e.g., Matt. 7:25; Luke 16:17, RV, "fall," for KJV, "fail"; Heb. 11:30; (f), of "falling" in judgment upon persons, as of the sun's heat, Rev. 7:16, RV, "strike," KJV, "light"; of a mist and darkness, **Acts 13:11** (some mss. have *epipipto*); (g) of persons, in "falling" morally or spiritually, Rom. 14:4; 1 Cor. 10:8, 12; Rev. 2:5.

Numbered *sunkatapsephizo* (4785), "to vote or reckon (one) a place among" (*sun*, "with" or "among," *kata*, "down," and *psephizo*, "to count or vote," originally with pebbles, *psephos*, "a pebble"), is used of the "numbering" of Matthias with the eleven apostles, **Acts 1:26**.

Eleven *hendeka* (1733), lit., "one ten" (Lat., *undecim*), is used only of the eleven apostles remaining after the death of Judas Iscariot, Matt. 28:16; Mark 16:14; Luke 24:9, 33; **Acts 1:26; 2:14**.

Chapter 2

2:1 And when the day of Pentecost was fully come, they were all with one accord in one place.

Pentecost *pentekostos* (4005), an adjective denoting "fiftieth," is used as a noun, with "day" understood, i.e., the "fiftieth" day after the Passover, counting from the second day of the Feast, **Acts 2:1; 20:16**; 1 Cor. 16:8. For the divine instructions to Israel see Exod. 23:16; 34:22; Lev. 23:15-21; Num. 28:26-31; Deut. 16:9-11.

Come *sumpleroo* (4845), "to fill completely" (*sun*, "with," intensive), is used, in the passive voice, of time to be fulfilled or completed, Luke 9:51, "the days were well-nigh come"; **Acts 2:1**, "the day ... was now come" (KJV "was fully come"). In Luke 8:23, it is used in the active voice, of the filling of a boat in a storm.

One In **Acts 2:1** "in one place" translates *epi to auto*, lit., "to the same," which may mean "for the same (purpose)"; in 1 Cor. 11:20 and 14:23, the RV translates it "together."

Accord *homou* (3674), used in connection with place, in John 21:2; **Acts 2:1** (in the best texts), RV, "together" (KJV, "with one accord," translating the inferior reading *homothumadon*), is used without the idea of place in John 4:36; 20:4.

2:2 And suddenly there came a sound from heaven as of a rushing mighty wind, and it filled all the house where they were sitting.

Suddenly *aphno* (869), "suddenly," occurs in **Acts 2:2**; **16:26**; **28:6**.

Sound *echos* (2279), "a noise, a sound of any sort" (Eng., "echo"), is translated "sound" in **Acts 2:2**; Heb. 12:19.

Rushing *phero* (5342), "to bear," is used in the present participle, passive voice, in **Acts 2:2**, and translated "rushing," RV, "the rushing (of a mighty wind)," KJV "a rushing (mighty wind)" lit., "a violent wind borne (along)."

Mighty *biaios* (972), "violent" (from *bia*, "force, violence, strength," found in **Acts 5:26**; **21:35**; **24:7**; **27:41**), occurs in **Acts 2:2**, of wind.

Wind *pnoe* (4157), akin to *pneo*, "to blow," lit., "a blowing," signifies (a) "breath, the breath of life," **Acts 17:25**; (b) "wind," **Acts 2:2**.

Filled *pleroo* (4137), denotes "to make full, to fill to the full"; in the passive voice, "to be filled, made full"; it is used (1) of things: a net, Matt. 13:48; a building, John 12:3; **Acts 2:2**; a city, **Acts 5:28**; needs, Phil. 4:19, KJV "supply," RV, "fulfill"; metaphorically, of valleys, Luke 3:5; figuratively, of a measure of iniquity, Matt. 23:32; (2) of persons: (a) of the members of the church, the body of Christ, as filled by Him, Eph. 1:23 ("all things in all the members"); 4:10; in 3:19, of their being filled "into" (*eis*), RV, "unto," KJV, "with" (all the fullness of God); of their being "made full" in Him, Col. 2:10 (RV, for KJV, "complete"); (b) of Christ Himself: with wisdom, in the days of His flesh, Luke 2:40; with joy, in His return to the Father, **Acts 2:28**; (c) of believers: with the Spirit, Eph. 5:18; with joy, **Acts 13:52**; 2 Tim. 1:4; with joy and peace, Rom. 15:13; with knowledge, Rom. 15:14; with comfort, 2 Cor. 7:4; with the fruits of righteousness, Phil. 1:11 (Gk. "fruit"); with the knowledge of God's will, Col. 1:9; with abundance through material supplies by fellow believers, Phil. 4:18; (d) of the hearts of believers as the seat of emotion and volition, John 16:6 (sorrow); **Acts 5:3** (deceitfulness); (e) of the unregenerate who refuse recognition of God, Rom. 1:29.

2:3 And there appeared unto them cloven tongues like as of fire, and it sat upon each of them.

Cloven *diamerizo* (1266), *dia*, "through," and *merizo*, "to divide through," i.e., "completely, to divide up," is translated "to divide" in Luke 11:17-18; 12:52-53; 22:17; "parted" in Matt. 27:35; Mark 15:24; Luke 23:34; John 19:24; **Acts 2:45**; in **Acts 2:3**, KJV, "cloven," RV, "parting asunder."

Fire *pur* (4442), (akin to which are *pura*, and *puretos*, "a fever," Eng., "fire," etc.) is used (besides its ordinary natural significance): (a) of the holiness of God, which consumes all that is inconsistent therewith, Heb. 10:27; 12:29; cf. Rev. 1:14; 2:18; 10:1; 15:2; 19:12; similarly of the holy angels as His ministers Heb. 1:7 in Rev. 3:18 it is symbolic of that which tries the faith of saints, producing what will glorify the Lord. (b) of the divine judgment, testing the deeds of believers, at the judgment seat of Christ 1 Cor. 3:13 and 15. (c) of the fire of divine judgment upon the rejectors of Christ, Matt. 3:11 (where a distinction is to be made between the baptism of the Holy Spirit at Pentecost and the "fire" of divine retribution; **Acts 2:3** could not refer to baptism): Luke 3:16. (d) of the judgments of God at the close of the present age previous to the establishment of the kingdom of Christ in the world, 2 Thess. 1:8; Rev. 18:8. (e) of the "fire" of Hell, to be endured by the ungodly hereafter, Matt. 5:22; 13:42, 50; 18:8, 9; 25:41; Mark 9:43, 48; Luke 3:17. (f) of human hostility both to the Jews and to Christ's followers, Luke 12:49. (g) as illustrative of retributive judgment upon the luxurious and tyrannical rich, Jas. 5:3. (h) of the future overthrow of the Babylonish religious system at the hands of the Beast and the nations under him, Rev. 17:16. (i) of turning the heart of an enemy to repentance by repaying his unkindness by kindness, Rom. 12:20. (j) of the tongue, as governed by a "fiery" disposition and as exercising a destructive influence over others, Jas. 3:6.(k) as symbolic of the danger of destruction, Jude 23.

Sat *kathizo* (2523), is used (a) transitively, "to make sit down," **Acts 2:30**; (b) intransitively, "to sit down," e.g., Matt. 5:1, RV, "when (He) had sat down" (KJV, "was set"); 19:28; 20:21, 23; 23:2; 25:31; 26:36; Mark 11:2, 7; 12:41; Luke 14:28, 31; 16:6; John 19:13; **Acts 2:3** (of the tongues of fire); **8:31**; 1 Cor. 10:7; 2 Thess. 2:4, "he sitteth," aorist tense, i.e., "he takes his seat" (as, e.g., in Mark 16:19); Rev. 3:21 (twice), RV, "to sit down" and "sat down"; 20:4.

Each *hekastos* (1538), "each" or "every," is used of any number separately, either (a) as an adjective qualifying a noun, e.g., Luke 6:44; John 19:23; Heb. 3:13, where "day by day," is, lit., "according to each day"; or, more emphatically with *heis*, "one," in Matt. 26:22; Luke 4:40; 16:5; **Acts 2:3, 6, 20:31**; 1 Cor. 12:18; Eph. 4:7, 16, RV, "each (several)," for KJV, "every"; Col. 4:6; 1 Thess. 2:11; 2 Thess. 1:3; (b) as a distributive pronoun, e.g., **Acts 4:35**; Rom. 2:6; Gal. 6:4; in Phil. 2:4, it is used in the plural; some mss. have it thus in Rev. 6:11. The repetition in Heb. 8:11 is noticeable "every man" (i.e., everyone). Prefixed by the preposition *ana*, "apiece" (a colloquialism), it is used, with stress on the individuality, in Rev. 21:21, of the gates of the heavenly city, "each one of the several," RV; in Eph. 5:33, preceded by *kath' hena*, "by one," it signifies "each (one) his own."

> *"O Breath of life, come sweeping through us, / Revive your church with life and power; / O Breath of life, come, cleanse, renew us / And fit your church to meet this hour."*
>
> ELIZABETH A. P. HEAD

2:4 And they were all filled with the Holy Ghost, and began to speak with other tongues, as the Spirit gave them utterance.

Filled *pimplemi* (4130), and *pletho* (4130), lengthened forms of *pleo*, "to fill" (*pletho* supplies certain tenses of *pimplemi*), is used (1) of things; boats, with fish, Luke 5:7; a sponge, with vinegar, Matt. 27:48 (some mss. have this verb in John 19:29); a city, with confusion, **Acts 19:29**; a wedding, with guests, Matt. 22:10; (2) of persons (only in Luke's writings): (a) with the Holy Spirit, Luke 1:15, 41, 67; **Acts 2:4; 4:8, 31; 9:17; 13:9**; (b) with emotions: wrath, Luke 4:28; fear, 5:26; madness, 6:11; wonder, amazement, **Acts 3:10**; jealousy, **5:17**, RV, for KJV, "indignation," and **13:45** (KJV, "envy"). For its other significance, "to complete."

Other *heteros* (2087), indicates either numerical distinction, e.g., Luke 4:43; 5:7; or generic distinction, different in character, etc., e.g., Luke 9:29, "(the fashion of His countenance) was altered," lit., "became other"; 23:32, "two others (malefactors)," RV, where the plural serves to make the necessary distinction between them and Christ; **Acts 2:4; 19:39** ("other matters"); 1 Cor. 14:21, KJV, "other" (RV, "strange"); 2 Cor. 11:4 (2nd and 3rd parts, RV, "different"; in the 1st clause, *allos*, "another").

Tongues *glossa* (1100), is used of (1) the "tongues ... like as of fire" which appeared at Pentecost; (2) "the tongue," as an organ of speech, e.g., Mark 7:33; Rom. 3:13; 14:11; 1 Cor. 14:9; Phil. 2:11; Jas. 1:26; 3:5, 6, 8; 1 Pet. 3:10; 1 John 3:18; Rev. 16:10; (3) (a) "a language," coupled with *phule*, "a tribe," *laos*, "a people," *ethnos*, "a nation," seven times in the Apocalypse, 5:9; 7:9; 10:11; 11:9; 13:7; 14:6; 17:15; (b) "the supernatural gift of speaking in another language without its having been learnt"; in **Acts 2:4-13** the circumstances are recorded from the viewpoint of the hearers; to those in whose language the utterances were made it appeared as a supernatural phenomenon; to others, the stammering of drunkards; what was uttered was not addressed primarily to the audience but consisted in recounting "the mighty works of God"; cf. **2:46**; in 1 Cor., chapters 12 and 14, the use of the gift of "tongues" is mentioned as exercised in the gatherings of local churches; 12:10 speaks of the gift in general terms, and couples with it that of "the interpretation of tongues"; chapt. 14 gives instruction concerning the use of the gift, the paramount object being the edification of the church; unless the "tongue" was interpreted the speaker would speak "not unto men, but unto God," v. 2; he would edify himself alone, v. 4, unless he interpreted, v. 5, in which case his interpretation would be of the same value as the superior gift of prophesying, as he would edify the church, vv. 4-6; he must pray that he may interpret, v. 13; if there were no interpreter, he must keep silence, v. 28, for all things were to be done "unto edifying," v. 26. "If I come ... speaking with tongues, what shall I profit you," says the apostle (expressing the great object in all oral ministry), "unless I speak to you either by way of revelation, or of knowledge, or of prophesying, or of teaching?" (v. 6). "Tongues" were for a sign, not to believers, but to unbelievers, v. 22, and especially to unbelieving Jews (see v. 21): cf. the passages in the Acts.

Utterance For *apophthengomai*, rendered "utterance" in **Acts 2:4**.

2:5 And there were dwelling at Jerusalem Jews, devout men, out of every nation under heaven.

Devout *eulabes* (2126), lit., "taking hold well" (*eu*, "well," *lambano*, "to take hold"), primarily, "cautious," signifies in the NT, "careful as to the realization of the presence and claims of God, reverencing God, pious, devout", in Luke 2:25 it is said of Simeon, in **Acts 2:5**, of certain Jews; in **8:2**, of those who bore Stephen's body to burial; of Ananias, **22:12**. "In that mingled fear and love which, combined, constitute the piety of man toward God, the Old Testament placed its emphasis on the fear, the New places it on the love (though there was love in the fear of God's saints then, as there must be fear in their love now)," Trench, *Syn.*, Sec.xlviii.

2:6 Now when this was noised abroad, the multitude came together, and were confounded, because that every man heard them speak in his own language.

Noised *phone* (5456), most frequently "a voice," is translated "sound" in Matt. 24:31 (KJV marg., "voice"); John 3:8, KJV (RV, "voice"); so 1 Cor. 14:7 (1st part), 8; Rev. 1:15; 18:22 (2nd part, RV, "voice"); KJV and RV in 9:9 (twice); it is used with *ginomai* in **Acts 2:6**, KJV, "(this) was noised abroad," RV, "(this) sound was heard."

Confounded *suncheo* (4797), or *sunchunno* or *sunchuno*, lit., "to pour together, commingle," hence (said of persons), means "to trouble or confuse, to stir up," **Acts 19:32** (said of the mind); "to be in confusion," **21:31**, RV (KJV, "was in an uproar"); **21:27**, "stirred up"; **Acts 2:6**; **9:22**, "confounded."

Every *see* Each at *Acts 2:3*.

Man *heis* (1520), the first cardinal numeral, masculine (feminine and neuter nominative forms are *mia* and *hen*, respectively), is used to signify (1) (a) "one" in contrast to many, e.g., Matt. 25:15; Rom. 5:18, RV, "(through) one (trespass)," i.e., Adam's transgression, in contrast to the "one act of righteousness," i.e., the death of Christ (not as KJV, "the offense of one," and "the righteousness of one"); (b) metaphorically, "union" and "concord," e.g., John 10:30; 11:52; 17:11, 21-22; Rom. 12:4-5; Phil. 1:27; (2) emphatically, (a) a single ("one"), to the exclusion of others, e.g., Matt. 21:24; Rom. 3:10; 1 Cor. 9:24; 1 Tim. 2:5 (twice); (b) "one, alone," e.g., Mark 2:7, RV (KJV, "only"); 10:18; Luke 18:19; (c) "one and the same," e.g., Rom. 3:30, RV, "God is one," i.e., there is not "one" God for the Jew and one for the Gentile; cf. Gal. 3:20, which means that in a promise there is no other party; 1 Cor. 3:8; 11:5; 12:11; 1 John 5:8 (lit., "and the three are into one," i.e., united in "one" and the same witness); (3) a certain "one," in the same sense as the indefinite pronoun *tis*, e.g., Matt. 8:19, RV, "a (scribe)," marg., "one (scribe)," KJV, "a certain (scribe)"; 19:16, "one;" in Rev. 8:13, RV marg., "one (eagle)"; *heis tis* are used together in Luke 22:50; John 11:49; this occurs frequently in the papyri (Moulton, *Prol.*, p. 96); (4) distributively, with *hekastos*, "each," i.e., "every one," e.g., Luke 4:40; **Acts 2:6**, "every man" (lit., "every one"); in the sense of "one ... and one," e.g., John 20:12; or "one" ... followed by *allos* or *heteros*, "the other," e.g., Matt. 6:24; or by a second *heis*, e.g., Matt. 24:40, RV, "one"; John 20:12; in Rom. 12:5 *heis* is preceded by *kata* (*kath'* in the sense of "severally (members) one (of another)," RV (KJV, "every one ... one"); cf. Mark 14:19; in 1 Thess. 5:11 the phrase in the 2nd part, "each other," RV (KJV, "one another"), is, lit., "one the one".

Language *see* Tongue at *Acts 1:19*.

2:7-8 And they were all amazed and marvelled, saying one to another, Behold, are not all these which speak Galilaeans?
And how hear we every man in our own tongue, wherein we were born?

Our own *idios* (2398), "one's own," signifies "our own" in **Acts 3:12**; 1 Cor. 4:12; in **Acts 2:8**, with *hemon*, forming a strong possessive, lit., "each in his own language of us."

Tongue *see Acts 1:19*.

2:9 Parthians, and Medes, and Elamites, and the dwellers in Mesopotamia, and in Judaea, and Cappadocia, in Pontus, and Asia,

Dwellers *see Acts 1:19*.

2:10 Phrygia, and Pamphylia, in Egypt, and in the parts of Libya about Cyrene, and strangers of Rome, Jews and proselytes,

Parts *meros* (3313), denotes (a) "a part, portion," of the whole, e.g., John 13:8; Rev. 20:6; 22:19; hence, "a lot" or "destiny," e.g., Rev. 21:8; in Matt. 24:51 and Luke 12:46, "portion"; (b) "a part" as opposite to the whole, e.g., Luke 11:36; John 19:23; 21:6, "side"; **Acts 5:2**; **23:6**; Eph. 4:16; Rev.

16:19; a party, **Acts 23:9**; the divisions of a province, e.g., Matt. 2:22; **Acts 2:10**; the regions belonging to a city, e.g., Matt. 15:21, RV, "parts" (KJV, "coasts"); 16:13 (ditto); Mark 8:10, KJV and RV, "parts"; "the lower parts of the earth," Eph. 4:9; this phrase means the regions beneath the earth; (c) "a class," or "category" (with *en*, in, "in respect of"), Col. 2:16; "in this respect," 2 Cor. 3:10; 9:3, RV (KJV, "in this behalf").

Rome *rhomaios* (4514), occurs in John 11:48; **Acts 2:10**, RV, "from Rome" (KJV, "of Rome"); **16:21, 37, 38; 22:25, 26, 27, 29; 23:27; 25:16; 28:17**.

Jews *ioudaios* (2453), is used (a) adjectivally, with the lit. meaning, "Jewish," sometimes with the addition of *aner*, "a man," **Acts 10:28; 22:3**; in **21:39** with *anthropos*, in some mss. (a man in the generic sense); the best mss. omit the phrase here; in **13:6**, lit., "a Jewish false-prophet"; in John 3:22, with the word *chora*, "land" or "country," signifying "Judean," lit., "Judean country"; used by metonymy for the people of the country; (b) as a noun, "a Jew, Jews," e.g., Matt. 2:2; Mark 7:3. The name "Jew" is primarily tribal (from Judah). It is first found in 2 Kings 16:6, as distinct from Israel, of the northern kingdom. After the Captivity it was chiefly used to distinguish the race from Gentiles, e.g., John 2:6; **Acts 14:1**; Gal. 2:15, where it denotes Christians of "Jewish" race; it distinguishes Jews from Samaritans, in John 4:9; from proselytes, in **Acts 2:10**. The word is most frequent in John's Gospel and the Acts; in the former "it especially denotes the typical representatives of Jewish thought contrasted with believers in Christ ... or with other Jews of less pronounced opinions, e.g., John 3:25; 5:10; 7:13; 9:22" (Lukyn Williams, in *Hastings' Bib. Dic.*); such representatives were found, generally, in opposition to Christ; in the Acts they are chiefly those who opposed the apostles and the gospel. In Rom. 2:28, 29 the word is used of ideal "Jews," i.e., "Jews" in spiritual reality, believers, whether "Jews" or Gentiles by natural birth. The feminine, "Jewess," is found in **Acts 16:1; 24:24**. It also denotes Judea, e.g., Matt. 2:1; Luke 1:5; John 4:3, the word "country" being understood [cf. (a) above]. In Luke 23:5 and John 7:1, where the KJV has "Jewry," the RV translates it as usual, "Judea."

Proselytes *proselutos* (4339), akin to *proserchomai*, "to come to," primarily signifies "one who has arrived, a stranger"; in the NT it is used of converts to Judaism, or foreign converts to the Jewish religion, Matt. 23:15; **Acts 2:10; 6:5; 13:43**. There seems to be no connection necessarily with Palestine, for in **Acts 2:10** and **13:43** it is used of those who lived abroad. Cf. the Sept., e.g., in Exod. 22:21; 23:9; Deut. 10:19, of the "stranger" living among the children of Israel.

2:11 Cretes and Arabians, we do hear them speak in our tongues the wonderful works of God.

Our In Luke 24:22, "of our company" is, lit., "from among us." (S) *Hemeteros*, a possessive pronoun, more emphatic than *hemeis*, is used in Luke 16:12, in the best mss. (some have *humeteros*, "your own"); **Acts 2:11; 24:6**, in some mss.; **26:5**; 2 Tim. 4:15; Titus 3:14, "ours"; 1 John 1:3; 2:2, "ours."

Wonderful *megaleiotes* (3168), denotes "splendor, magnificence" (from *megaleios*, "magnificent, mighty," **Acts 2:11**, *megas*, "great"), translated "magnificence" in **Acts 19:27**, of the splendor of the goddess Diana. In Luke 9:43, RV (KJV, "mighty power"); in 2 Pet. 1:16, "majesty." In the papyri writings it is frequent as a ceremonial title. In **Acts 2:11**, KJV, the adjective *megaleios*, "magnificent," in the neuter plural with the article, is rendered "the wonderful works."

2:12 And they were all amazed, and were in doubt, saying one to another, What meaneth this?

Doubt *diaporeo* (1280), signifies "to be thoroughly perplexed," with a perplexity amounting to despair, **Acts 2:12; 5:24** and **10:17**, KJV, "were in doubt," "doubted," RV, "were (was) perplexed."

One to another *allos pros allon*, "one to another," **Acts 2:12**; (d) *allos ... heteros*, 1 Cor. 12:8; (e) *hos men ... hos de* (in various forms of the pronoun), lit., "this indeed ... but that," e.g., Luke 23:33; Rom. 9:21; 14:5; 1 Cor. 11:21; 2 Cor. 2:16; Phil. 1:16-17; (f) *heteros ... heteros*, "one ... another," 1 Cor. 15:40.

Meaneth *eimi* (1510), "to be," in certain of its forms, has an explicative force, signifying "to denote, to import," e.g., Matt. 9:13; 12:7, "(what this) meaneth," lit., "(what this) is"; Luke 18:36, "meant" (lit., "might be"); **Acts 10:17**, "might mean," RV (lit., "might be"); in Luke 15:26 the RV keeps to the verb "to be," "(what these things) might be" (KJV, "meant"). In **Acts 2:12** the verb "to be" is preceded by *thelo*, "to will," and the phrase is translated "(what) meaneth (this)," lit., "(what) does (this) will to be?" in **17:20**, lit., "(what do these things) will to be."

2:13 Others mocking said, These men are full of new wine.

Full *mestoo* (3325), "to fill full," from *mestos*, "full," is used of being "filled" with wine, **Acts 2:13**, RV, "are filled with."

Wine *gleukos* (1098), denotes sweet "new wine," or must, **Acts 2:13**, where the accusation shows that it was intoxicant and must have been undergoing fermentation some time. In the Sept, Job 32:19.

2:14 But Peter, standing up with the eleven, lifted up his voice, and said unto them, Ye men of Judaea, and all *ye* that dwell at Jerusalem, be this known unto you, and hearken to my words:

Eleven *see Acts 1:26.*

Lifted *see* taken up at *Acts 1:9.*

Said *apophthengomai* (669), "to speak forth," is so rendered in **Acts 2:14**, RV (KJV, "said"), and **26:25**; in **2:2** it denotes to give utterance.

Men *see Acts 1:16.*

Hearken *enotizomai* (1801), "to give ear to, to hearken" (from *en*, "in," and *ous*, "an ear"), is used in **Acts 2:14**, in Peter's address to the men of Israel.

Words *rhema* (4487), denotes "that which is spoken, what is uttered in speech or writing"; in the singular, "a word," e.g., Matt. 12:36; 27:14; 2 Cor. 12:4; 13:1; Heb. 12:19; in the plural, speech, discourse, e.g., John 3:34; 8:20; **Acts 2:14**; **6:11**, **13**; **11:14**; **13:42**; **26:25**; Rom. 10:18; 2 Pet. 3:2; Jude 17; it is used of the gospel in Rom. 10:8 (twice), 17, RV, "the word of Christ" (i.e., the "word" which preaches Christ); 10:18; 1 Pet. 1:25 (twice); of a statement, command, instruction, e.g., Matt. 26:75; Luke 1:37, RV, "(no) word (from God shall be void of power)", v. 38; **Acts 11:16**; Heb. 11:3. The significance of *rhema* (as distinct from *logos*) is exemplified in the injunction to take "the sword of the Spirit, which is the word of God," Eph. 6:17; here the reference is not to the whole Bible as such, but to the individual scripture which the Spirit brings to our remembrance for use in time of need, a prerequisite being the regular storing of the mind with Scripture.

2:15 For these are not drunken, as ye suppose, seeing it is *but* the third hour of the day.

Drunken *methuo* (3184), signifies "to be drunk with wine" (from *methu*, "mulled wine"; hence Eng., "mead, honey-wine"); originally it denoted simply "a pleasant drink." The verb is used of "being intoxicated" in Matt. 24:49; **Acts 2:15**; 1 Cor. 11:21; 1 Thess. 5:7*b*; metaphorically, of the effect upon men of partaking of the abominations of the Babylonish system, Rev. 17:2; of being in a state of mental "intoxication," through the shedding of men's blood profusely, v. 6.

Suppose *hupolambano* (5274), when used of mental action, signifies "to suppose," Luke 7:43, and **Acts 2:15**.

Third *tritos* (5154), is used (a) as a noun, e.g., Luke 20:12, 31; in Rev. 8:7-12 and 9:15, 18, "the third part," lit., "the third"; (b) as an adverb, with the article, "the third time," e.g., Mark 14:41; John 21:17 (twice); without the article, lit., "a third time," e.g., John 21:14; 2 Cor. 12:14; 13:1; in enumerations, in Matt. 26:44, with *ek*, "from," lit., "from the third time" (the *ek* indicates the point of departure, especially in a succession of events, cf. John 9:24; 2 Pet. 2:8); absolutely, in the accusative neuter, in 1 Cor. 12:28, "thirdly"; (c) as an adjective (its primary use), e.g., in the phrase the third heaven, 2 Cor. 12:2; in the phrase "the third hour," Matt. 20:3; Mark 15:25; **Acts 2:15** ("... of the day"); **23:23** ("... of the night"); in a phrase with *hemera*, "a day," "on the third day" (i.e., "the next day but one"), e.g., Matt. 16:21; Luke 24:46; **Acts 10:40**; in this connection the idiom "three days and three nights," Matt. 12:40, is explained by ref to 1 Sam. 30:12, 13, and Esth. 4:16 with 5:1; in Mark 9:31 and 10:34, the RV, "after three days," follows the texts which have this phrase, the KJV, "the third day," those which have the same phrase as in Matt. 16:21, etc.

"The question on Pentecost is not whether God is blessing our own plans and programs but whether we are open to the great opportunities to which his Spirit calls us."

CORRIE TEN BOOM

**2:16-17 But this is that which was spoken by the prophet Joel;
And it shall come to pass in the last days, saith God, I will pour out of my Spirit upon all flesh: and your sons and your daughters shall prophesy,
and your young men shall see visions, and your old men shall dream dreams:**

Shall The phrase "it shall come to pass" is the rendering of the future tense of *eimi*, "to be," in **Acts 2:17**, **21**; **3:23**; Rom. 9:26.

Pass In **Acts 2:17**, **21**; **3:23** and Rom. 9:26, the KJV translates the future of *eimi*, "to be," "it shall come to pass" (RV, "it shall be").

"Holy Spirit, power divine, / Fill and nerve this will of mine; / By Thee may I strongly live, / Bravely bear, and nobly strive."

SAMUEL LONGFELLOW

Last *see* **Uttermost** at *Acts 1:8*.

Pour *ekcheo* (1632), "to pour out" (*ek*, "out"), is used (a) of Christ's act as to the changers' money, John 2:15; (b) of the Holy Spirit, **Acts 2:17**, **18**, **33**, RV, "He hath poured forth" (KJV, "... shed forth"); Titus 3:6, RV, "poured out" (KJV, "shed"); (c) of the emptying of the contents of the bowls (KJV, "vials") of divine wrath, Rev. 16:1-4, 8, 10, 12, 17; (d) of the shedding of the blood of saints by the foes of God, Rev. 16:6, RV, "poured out" (KJV, "shed"); some mss. have it in **Acts 22:20**.

Young men *neaniskos* (3495), "a youth, a young man," occurs in Matt. 19:20, 22; Mark 14:51 (1st part; RV omits in 2nd part); 16:5; Luke 7:14; **Acts 2:17**; **5:10** (i.e., attendants); **23:18** (in the best texts), **22**; 1 John 2:13, 14, of the second branch of the spiritual family.

Visions *horasis* (3706), denotes (a) a vision (so the associated noun *horama*, e.g., **Acts 7:31**; *horasis* signifies especially the act of seeing, *horama* that which is seen), **Acts 2:17**; Rev. 9:17; (b) an appearance, Rev. 4:3, translated "to look upon" (twice in the RV; in the second instance the KJV has "in sight").

Old men *presbuteros* (4245), an adjective, the comparative degree of *presbus*, "an old man, an elder," is used (a) of age, whether of the "elder" of two persons, Luke 15:25, or more, John 8:9, "the eldest", or of a person advanced in life, a senior, **Acts 2:17**; in Heb. 11:2, the "elders" are the forefathers in Israel so in Matt. 15:2; Mark 7:3, 5 the feminine of the adjective is used of "elder" women in the churches, 1 Tim. 5:2, not in respect of position but in seniority of age; (b) of rank or positions of responsibility, (1) among Gentiles, as in the Sept. of Gen. 50:7; Num. 22:7, (2) in the Jewish nation, firstly, those who were the heads or leaders of the tribes and families, as of the seventy who assisted Moses, Num. 11:16; Deut. 27:1, and those assembled by Solomon; secondly, members of the Sanhedrin, consisting of the chief priests, "elders" and scribes, learned in Jewish law, e.g., Matt. 16:21; 26:47; thirdly, those who managed public affairs in the various cities, Luke 7:3; (3) in the Christian churches those who, being raised up and qualified by the work of the Holy Spirit, were appointed to have the spiritual care of, and to exercise oversight over, the churches. To these the term "bishops," *episkopoi*, or "overseers," is applied (see **Acts 20**, v. **17** with v. **28**, and Titus 1:5 and 7), the latter term indicating the nature of their work *presbuteroi* their maturity of spiritual experience. The divine arrangement seen throughout the NT was for a plurality of these to be appointed in each church, **Acts 14:23**; **20:17**; Phil. 1:1; 1 Tim. 5:17; Titus 1:5. The duty of "elders" is described by the verb *episkopeo*. They were appointed according as they had given evidence of fulfilling the divine qualifications, Titus 1:6 to 9; cf. 1 Tim. 3:1-7 and 1 Pet. 5:2; (4) the twenty-four "elders" enthroned in heaven around the throne of God, Rev. 4:4, 10; 5:5-14; 7:11, 13; 11:16; 14:3; 19:4. The number twenty-four is representative of earthly conditions. The word "elder" is nowhere applied to angels.

Dream, Dreams *enupniazo* (1797), used in **Acts 2:17**, in the passive voice in a phrase (according to the most authentic mss.) which means "shall be given up to dream by dreams," translated "shall dream dreams" metaphorically in Jude 8, of being given over to sensuous "dreamings," RV, KJV, "dreamers," and so defiling the flesh.

2:18 And on my servants and on my handmaidens I will pour out in those days of my Spirit; and they shall prophesy:

Handmaidens *doulos* (1401), from *deo*, "to bind," "a slave," originally the lowest term in the scale of servitude, came also to mean "one who gives himself up to the will of another," e.g., 1 Cor. 7:23; Rom. 6:17, 20, and became the most common and general word for "servant," as in Matt. 8:9, without any idea of bondage. In calling himself, however, a "bondslave of Jesus Christ," e.g., Rom. 1:1, the apostle Paul intimates (1) that he had been formerly a "bondslave" of Satan, and (2) that, having been bought by Christ, he was now a willing slave, bound to his new Master. The feminine, *doule*, signifies "a handmaid," Luke 1:38, 48; **Acts 2:18**.

Pour *see* *Acts 2:17*.

2:19 And I will shew wonders in heaven above, and signs in the earth beneath; blood, and fire, and vapour of smoke:

Wonders *teras* (5059), "something strange," causing the beholder to marvel, is always used in the plural, always rendered "wonders," and generally follows *semeia*, "signs"; the opposite order occurs in **Acts 2:22, 43; 6:8**, RV; **7:36**; in **Acts 2:19** "wonders" occurs alone. A sign is intended to appeal to the understanding, a "wonder" appeals to the imagination, a power (*dunamis*) indicates its source as supernatural. "Wonders" are manifested as divine operations in thirteen occurrences (9 times in Acts); three times they are ascribed to the work of Satan through human agents, Matt. 24:24; Mark 13:22 and 2 Thess. 2:9.

Above *ano* (507), denotes "above, in a higher place," **Acts 2:19** (the opposite to *kato*, "below"). With the article it means "that which is above," Gal. 4:26; Phil. 3:14, "the high calling" (RV marg., "upward"); with the plural article, "the things above," John 8:23, lit., "from the things above"; Col. 3:1-2. With *heos*, "as far as," it is translated "up to the brim," in John 2:7. It has the meaning "upwards" in John 11:41 and Heb. 12:15.

Signs *semeion* (4592), "a sign, mark, indication, token," is used (a) of that which distinguished a person or thing from others, e.g., Matt. 26:48; Luke 2:12; Rom. 4:11; 2 Cor. 12:12 (1st part); 2 Thess. 3:17, "token," i.e., his autograph attesting the authenticity of his letters; (b) of a "sign" as a warning or admonition, e.g., Matt. 12:39, "the sign of (i.e., consisting of) the prophet Jonas"; 16:4; Luke 2:34; 11:29, 30; (c) of miraculous acts (1) as tokens of divine authority and power, e.g., Matt. 12:38, 39 (1st part); John 2:11, RV, "signs"; 3:2 (ditto); 4:54, "(the second) sign," RV; 10:41 (ditto); 20:30; in 1 Cor. 1:22, "the Jews ask for signs," RV, indicates that the Apostles were met with the same demand from Jews as Christ had been: "signs were vouchsafed in plenty, signs of God's power and love, but these were not the signs which they sought.... They wanted signs of an outward Messianic Kingdom, of temporal triumph, of material greatness for the chosen people.... With such cravings the Gospel of a 'crucified Messiah' was to them a stumblingblock indeed" (Lightfoot); 1 Cor. 14:22; (2) by demons, Rev. 16:14; (3) by false teachers or prophets, indications of assumed authority, e.g., Matt. 24:24; Mark 13:22; (4) by Satan through his special agents, 2 Thess. 2:9; Rev. 13:13, 14; 19:20; (d) of tokens portending future events, e.g., Matt. 24:3, where "the sign of the Son of Man" signifies, subjectively, that the Son of Man is Himself the "sign" of what He is about to do; Mark 13:4; Luke 21:7, 11, 25; **Acts 2:19**; Rev. 12:1, RV; 12:3, RV; 15:1. "Signs" confirmatory of what God had accomplished in the atoning sacrifice of Christ, His resurrection and ascension, and of the sending of the Holy Spirit, were given to the Jews for their recognition, as at Pentecost, and supernatural acts by apostolic ministry, as well as by the supernatural operations in the churches, such as the gift of tongues and prophesyings; there is no record of the continuance of these latter after the circumstances recorded in **Acts 19:1-20**.

Beneath *kato* (2736), signifies (a) "down, downwards," Matt. 4:6; Luke 4:9; John 8:6, 8; **Acts 20:9**; (b) "below, beneath," of place, Mark 14:66; the realms that lie below in contrast to heaven, John 8:23; the earth, as contrasted with the heavens, **Acts 2:19**; with *heos*, "unto," Matt. 27:51; Mark 15:38. The comparative degree, *katotero*, "under," is used in Matt. 2:16.

Vapour *atmis* (822), is used of "smoke," **Acts 2:19**; figuratively of human life, Jas. 4:14.

Smoke *kapnos* (2586), "smoke," occurs in **Acts 2:19** and 12 times in the Apocalypse.

2:20 The sun shall be turned into darkness, and the moon into blood, before that great and notable day of the Lord come:

Sun *helios* (2246), whence Eng. prefix "helio–," is used (a) as a means of the natural benefits of light and heat, e.g., Matt. 5:45, and power, Rev. 1:16; (b) of its qualities of brightness and glory, e.g., Matt. 13:43; 17:2; **Acts 26:13**; 1 Cor. 15:41; Rev. 10:1; 12:1; (c) as a means of destruction, e.g., Matt. 13:6; Jas. 1:11; of physical misery, Rev. 7:16; (d) as a means of judgment, e.g., Matt. 24:29; Mark 13:24; Luke 21:25; 23:45; **Acts 2:20**; Rev. 6:12; 8:12; 9:2; 16:8.

Turned *metastrepho* (3344), signifies, in the passive voice, "to be turned" (of a change into something different, *meta*) in **Acts 2:20** and Jas. 4:9.

Moon *selene* (4582), from *selas*, "brightness" (the Heb. words are *yareach*, "wandering," and *lebanah*, "white"), occurs in Matt. 24:29; Mark 13:24; Luke 21:25; **Acts 2:20**; 1 Cor. 15:41; Rev. 6:12; 8:12; 12:1; 21:23. In Rev. 12:1, "the moon under her feet" is suggestive of derived authority, just as her being clothed with the sun is suggestive of supreme authority, everything in the symbolism of the passage centers in Israel. In 6:12 the similar symbolism of the sun and "moon" is suggestive of the supreme authority over the world, and of derived authority, at the time of the execution of divine judgments upon nations at the close of the present age.

Notable *epiphanes* (2016), "illustrious, renowned, notable" (akin to *epiphaino*, "to show forth, appear"; Eng., "epiphany"), is translated "notable" in **Acts 2:20**, of the great Day of the Lord. The appropriateness of this word to that future occasion is obvious.

2:21 And it shall come to pass, *that* whosoever shall call on the name of the Lord shall be saved.

Shall *see Acts 2:17.*

Pass *see Acts 2:17.*

Call *epikaleo* (1941), denotes (a) "to surname"; (b) "to be called by a person's name"; hence it is used of being declared to be dedicated to a person, as to the Lord, **Acts 15:17** (from Amos 9:12); Jas. 2:7; (c) "to call a person by a name by charging him with an offense," as the Pharisees charged Christ with doing His works by the help of Beelzebub, Matt. 10:25 (the most authentic reading has *epikaleo*, for *kaleo*); (d) "to call upon, invoke"; in the middle voice, "to call upon for oneself" (i.e., on one's behalf), **Acts 7:59**, or "to call upon a person as a witness," 2 Cor. 1:23, or to appeal to an authority, **Acts 25:11**, etc.; (e) "to call upon by way of adoration, making use of the Name of the Lord," **Acts 2:21**; Rom. 10:12-14; 2 Tim. 2:22.

2:22 Ye men of Israel, hear these words; Jesus of Nazareth, a man approved of God among you by miracles and wonders and signs, which God did by him in the midst of you, as ye yourselves also know:

Ye The addition of *autoi*, "yourselves," to the pronoun marks especial emphasis, e.g., Mark 6:31; John 3:28; 1 Cor. 11:13; 1 Thess. 4:9. Sometimes *autoi* is used without the pronoun, e.g., Luke 11:46, 52; **Acts 2:22**; **20:34**; 1 Thess. 2:1; 3:3; 5:2; 2 Thess. 3:7; Heb. 13:3.

Approved *apodeiknumi* (584), lit., "to point out, to exhibit" (*apo*, "forth," *deiknumi*, "to show"), is used once in the sense of proving by demonstration, and so bringing about an "approval." The Lord Jesus was "a Man approved of God by mighty works and wonders and signs," **Acts 2:22**.

Miracles *dunamis* (1411), "power, inherent ability," is used of works of a supernatural origin and character, such as could not be produced by natural agents and means. It is translated "miracles" in the RV and KJV in **Acts 8:13** (where variant readings give the words in different order); **19:11**; 1 Cor. 12:10, 28, 29; Gal. 3:5; KJV only, in **Acts 2:22** (RV, "mighty works"); Heb. 2:4 (RV, "powers"). In Gal. 3:5, the word may be taken in its widest sense, to include "miracles" both physical and moral.

Wonders *see Acts 2:19.*

2:23 Him, being delivered by the determinate counsel and foreknowledge of God, ye have taken, and by wicked hands have crucified and slain:

Delivered *ekdotos* (1560), lit., "given up" (*ek*, "out of," *didomi*, "to give"), "delivered up" (to enemies, or to the power or will of someone), is used of Christ in **Acts 2:23**.

Determinate *horizo* (3724), denotes "to bound, to set a boundary" (Eng., "horizon"); hence, "to mark out definitely, determine"; it is translated "to determine" in Luke 22:22, of the foreordained pathway of Christ; **Acts 11:29**, of a "determination" to send relief; **17:26**, where it is used of fixing the bounds of seasons. In **Acts 2:23** the verb is translated "determinate," with reference to counsel. Here the verbal form might have been adhered to by the translation "determined"; that is to say, in the sense of "settled." In Rom. 1:4 it is translated "declared," where the meaning is that Christ was marked out as the Son of God by His resurrection and that of others. In **Acts 10:42** and **17:31** it has its other meaning of "ordain," that is, "to appoint by determined counsel." In Heb. 4.7, it is translated "limiteth," but preferably in the RV, "defineth," with reference to a certain period; here again it approaches its primary meaning of marking out the bounds of.

Counsel *boule* (1012), from a root meaning "a will," hence "a counsel, a piece of advice," is to be distinguished from *gnome; boule* is the result of determination, *gnome* is the result of knowledge. *Boule* is everywhere rendered by "counsel" in the RV except in **Acts 27:12**, "advised," lit., "gave counsel." In **Acts 13:36** the KJV wrongly has "by the will of God fell on sleep"; the RV, "after he had served the counsel of God, fell on sleep." The word is used of the counsel of God, in Luke 7:30; **Acts 2:23**; **4:28**; **13:36**; **20:27**; Eph. 1:11; Heb. 6:17; in other passages, of the counsel of men, Luke 23:51; **Acts 27:12, 42**; 1 Cor. 4:5.

Foreknowledge *prognosis* (4268), "a foreknowledge," is used only of divine "foreknowledge," **Acts 2:23**; 1 Pet. 1:2. "Foreknowledge" is one aspect of omniscience; it is implied in God's warnings, promises and predictions. See **Acts 15:18**. God's "foreknowledge" involves His electing grace, but this does not preclude human will. He "foreknows" the exercise of faith which brings salvation. The apostle Paul stresses especially the actual purposes of God rather than the ground of the purposes, see, e.g., Gal. 1:16; Eph. 1:5, 11. The divine counsels will ever be unthwartable.

God *theos* (2316), (I) in the polytheism of the Greeks, denoted "a god or deity," e.g., **Acts 14:11**; **19:26**; **28:6**; 1 Cor. 8:5; Gal. 4:8.

(II) (a) Hence the word was appropriated by Jews and retained by Christians to denote "the one true God." In the Sept. *theos* translates (with few exceptions) the Hebrew words *Elohim* and *Jehovah*, the former indicating His power and preeminence, the latter His unoriginated, immutable, eternal and self-sustained existence.

In the NT, these and all the other divine attributes are predicated of Him. To Him are ascribed, e.g., His unity, or monism, e.g., Mark 12:29; 1 Tim. 2:5; self-existence, John 5:26; immutability, Jas. 1:17; eternity, Rom. 1:20; universality, Matt. 10:29; **Acts 17:26-28**; almighty power, Matt. 19:26; infinite knowledge, **Acts 2:23**; **15:18**; Rom. 11:33, creative power, Rom. 11:36; 1 Cor. 8:6; Eph. 3:9; Rev. 4:11; 10:6; absolute holiness, 1 Pet. 1:15; 1 John 1:5; righteousness, John 17:25; faithfulness, 1 Cor. 1:9; 10:13; 1 Thess. 5:24; 2 Thess. 3:3; 1 John 1:9; love, 1 John 4:8, 16; mercy, Rom. 9:15, 18; truthfulness, Titus 1:2; Heb. 6:18.

(b) The divine attributes are likewise indicated or definitely predicated of Christ, e.g., Matt. 20:18-19; John 1:1-3; 1:18, RV, marg.; 5:22-29; 8:58; 14:6; 17:22-24; 20:28; Rom. 1:4; 9:5; Phil. 3:21; Col. 1:15; 2:3; Titus 2:13, RV; Heb. 1:3; 13:8; 1 John 5:20; Rev. 22:12, 13.

(c) Also of the Holy Spirit, e.g., Matt. 28:19; Luke 1:35; John 14:16; 15:26; 16:7-14; Rom. 8:9, 26; 1 Cor. 12:11; 2 Cor. 13:14.

(d) *Theos* is used (1) with the definite article, (2) without (i.e., as an anarthrous noun). "The English may or may not have need of the article in translation. But that point cuts no figure in the Greek idiom. Thus in **Acts 27:23** ('the God whose I am,' RV) the article points out the special God whose Paul is, and is to be preserved in English. In the very next verse (*ho theos*) we in English do not need the article" (A. T. Robertson, *Gram. of Greek, NT*, p. 758).

In the following titles God is described by certain of His attributes; the God of glory, **Acts 7:2**; of peace, Rom. 15:33; 16:20; Phil. 4:9; 1 Thess. 5:23; Heb. 13:20; of love and peace, 2 Cor. 13:11; of patience and comfort, Rom. 15:5; of all comfort, 2 Cor. 1:3; of hope, Rom. 15:13; of all grace, 1 Pet. 5:10. These describe Him, not as in distinction from other persons, but as the source of all these blessings; hence the employment of the definite article. In such phrases as "the God of a person," e.g., Matt. 22:32, the expression marks the relationship in which the person stands to God and God to him.

(e) In the following the nominative case is used for the vocative, and always with the article; Mark 15:34; Luke 18:11, 13; John 20:28; (**Acts 4:24** in some mss.); Heb. 1:8; 10:7.

(f) The phrase "the things of God" (translated literally or otherwise) stands for (1) His interests, Matt. 16:23; Mark 8:33; (2) His counsels, 1 Cor. 2:11; (3) things which are due to Him, Matt. 22:21; Mark 12:17; Luke 20:25. The phrase "things pertaining to God," Rom. 15:17; Heb. 2:17; 5:1, describes, in the Heb. passages, the sacrificial service of the priest; in the Rom. passage the gospel ministry as an offering to God.

Wicked *anomos* (459), "without law," also denotes "lawless," and is so rendered in the RV of **Acts 2:23**, "lawless (men)," marg., "(men) without the law," KJV, "wicked (hands);" 2 Thess. 2:8, "the lawless one" (KJV, "that wicked"), of the man of sin (2 Th 2:4); in 2 Pet. 2:8, of deeds (KJV, "unlawful"), where the thought is not simply that of doing what is unlawful, but of flagrant defiance of the known will of God.

Crucified *prospegnumi* (4362), "to fix or fasten to anything" (*pros*, "to," *pegnumi*, "to fix"), is used of the "crucifixion" of Christ, **Acts 2:23**.

Slain *anaireo* (337), "to take away, destroy, kill," is rendered "to slay" in Matt. 2:16; **Acts 2:23**; **5:33**, **36**; **9:29**, KJV (RV, "to kill"); **10:39**; **13:28**; **22:20**; **23:15**, RV; in 2 Thess. 2:8 the best texts have this verb (for *analisko*, "to consume," KJV and RV marg.); hence the RV, "shall slay," of the destruction of the man of sin.

2:24 Whom God hath raised up, having loosed the pains of death: because it was not possible that he should be holden of it.

Raised *anistemi* (450), "to stand up or to make to stand up," according as its use is intransitive or transitive (*ana*, "up," *histemi*, "to stand"), is used (a) of a physical change of position, e.g., of "rising" from sleep, Mark 1:35; from a meeting in a synagogue, Luke 4:29; of the illegal "rising" of the high priest in the tribunal in Matt. 26:62; of an invalid "rising" from his couch, Luke 5:25; the "rising" up of a disciple from his vocation to follow Christ, Luke 5:28; cf. John 11:31; "rising" up from prayer, Luke 22:45; of a whole company, **Acts 26:30**; 1 Cor. 10:7; (b) metaphorically, of "rising" up antagonistically against persons, e.g., of officials against people, **Acts 5:17**; of a seditious leader, **5:36**, of the "rising" up of Satan, Mark 3:26; of false teachers, **Acts 20:30**; (c) of "rising" to a position of preeminence or power; e.g., of Christ as a prophet, **Acts 3:22**; **7:37**; as God's servant in the midst of the nation of Israel, **Acts 3:26**; as the Son of God in the midst of the nation, **13:33** (not here of resurrection, but with reference to the Incarnation: the KJV "again" has nothing corresponding to it in the original; this is confirmed by the latter part of the verse, which explains the "raising" up as being by way of His incarnation, and by the contrast in v. **34**, where stress is laid upon His being "raised" from the dead, the same verb being used); as a priest, Heb. 7:11, 15; as king over the nations, Rom. 15:12; (d) of a spiritual awakening from lethargy, Eph. 5:14; (e) of resurrection from the dead: (1) of the resurrection of Christ, Matt. 17:9; 20:19; Mark 8:31; 9:9-10, 31; 10:34; Luke 18:33; 24:7, 46; John 20:9; **Acts 2:24, 32; 10:41; 13:34; 17:3, 31**; 1 Thess. 4:14; (2) of believers, John 6:39-40, 44, 54; 11:24; 1 Thess. 4:16; of unbelievers, Matt. 12:41.

Loosed *luo* (3089), denotes (a) "to loose, unbind, release," (1) of things, e.g., in **Acts 7:33**, RV, "loose (the shoes)," KJV, "put off"; Mark 1:7; (2) of animals, e.g., Matt. 21:2; (3) of persons, e.g., John 11:44; **Acts 22:30**; (4) of Satan, Rev. 20:3, 7, and angels, Rev. 9:14, 15; (5) metaphorically, of one diseased, Luke 13:16; of the marriage tie, 1 Cor. 7:27; of release from sins, Rev. 1:5 (in the most authentic mss.); (b) "to loosen, break up, dismiss, dissolve, destroy"; in this sense it is translated "to loose" in **Acts 2:24**, of the pains of death; in Rev. 5:2, of the seals of a roll.

Pains *odin* (5604), "a birth pang, travail pain," is rendered "travail," metaphorically, in Matt. 24:8 and Mark 13:8, RV (KJV, "sorrows"); by way of comparison, in 1 Thess. 5:3; translated "pains (of death)," **Acts 2:24** (RV, "pangs"). Cf. *odino*, "to travail in birth."

Because *kathoti* (2530), from *kata*, "according to," and *hoti*, "that," lit., "because that," Luke 1:7; 19:9; **Acts 2:24**, is translated "according as" in **Acts 2:45**, RV (KJV, "as") and in **4:35**; "inasmuch as," **17:31**.

Possible *dunatos* (1415), "strong, mighty, powerful, able (to do)," in its neuter form signifies "possible," Matt. 19:26; 24:24; 26:39; Mark 9:23; 10:27; 13:22; 14:35, 36; Luke 18:27; **Acts 2:24**; **20:16** (**27:39**, in some mss; *dunamai*, "to be able," in the most authentic, RV, "they could"); Rom. 12:18; Gal. 4:15.

Holden *krateo* (2902), "to be strong, mighty, to prevail," (1) is most frequently rendered "to lay or take hold on," (a) literally, e.g., Matt. 12:11; 14:3; 18:28 and 21:46, RV (KJV, "laid hands on"); 22:6, RV (KJV, "took"); 26:55, KJV (RV, "took"); 28:9, RV, "took hold of" (KJV, "held by"); Mark 3:21; 6:17; 12:12; 14:51; **Act 24:6**, RV (KJV, "took"); Rev. 20:2; (b) metaphorically, of "laying hold of the hope of the Lord's return," Heb. 6:18; (2) also signifies "to hold" or "hold fast," i.e., firmly, (a) literally, Matt. 26:48, KJV (RV, "take"); **Acts 3:11**; Rev. 2:1; (b) metaphorically, of "holding fast a tradition or teaching," in an evil sense, Mark 7:3, 4, 8; Rev. 2:14, 15; in a good sense, 2 Thess. 2:15; Rev. 2:25; 3:11; of "holding" Christ, i.e., practically apprehending Him, as the head of His church, Col. 2:19; a confession, Heb. 4:14; the name of Christ, i.e., abiding by all that His name implies, Rev. 2:13; of restraint, Luke 24:16, "(their eyes) were holden"; of the winds, Rev. 7:1; of the impossibility of Christ's being "holden" of death, **Acts 2:24**.

2:25 For David speaketh concerning him, I foresaw the Lord always before my face, for he is on my right hand, that I should not be moved:

Before *enopion* (1799), from *en*, "in," and *ops*, "the eye," is the neuter of the adjective *enopios*, and is used prepositionally, (a) of place, that which is before or opposite a person, "towards which he turns his eyes," e.g., Luke 1:19; **Acts 4:10; 6:6**; Rev. 1:4; 4-10; 7:15; (b) in metaphorical phrases after verbs of motion, Luke 1:17; 12:9; **Acts 9:15**, etc.; signifying "in the mind or soul of persons," Luke 12:6; **Acts 10:31**; Rev. 16:19; (c) "in one's sight or hearing," Luke 24:43; John 20:30; 1 Tim. 6:12; metaphorically, Rom. 14:22; especially in Gal. 1:20; 1 Tim. 5:21; 6:13; 2 Tim. 2:14; 4:1; before, as "having a person present to the mind," **Acts 2:25**; Jas. 4:10; "in the judgment of a person," Luke 16:15; 24:11, RV, "in their sight," for KJV, "to"; **Acts 4:19**; Rom. 3:20; 12:17; 2 Cor. 8:21; 1 Tim. 2:3; "in the approving sight of God," Luke 1:75; **Acts 7:46; 10:33**; 2 Cor. 4:2; 7:12.

Foresaw *proorao* (4308), with the aorist form *proeidon* (used to supply tenses lacking in *proorao*), "to see before" (*pro*, "before," *horao*, "to see"), is used with reference (a) to the past, of seeing a person before, **Acts 21:29**; (b) to the future, in the sense of "foreseeing" a person or thing, **Acts 2:25**, with reference to Christ and the Father, RV, "beheld" (here the middle voice is used).

Moved *saleuo* (4531), "to agitate, shake," primarily of the action of stormy winds, waves, etc., is used (a) literally, of a reed, Matt. 11:7; Luke 7:24; a vessel, "shaken" in filling, Luke 6:38; a building, Luke 6:48; **Acts 4:31; 16:26**; the natural forces of the heavens and heavenly bodies, Matt. 24:29; Mark 13:25; Luke 21:26; the earth, Heb. 12:26, "shook"; (b) metaphorically, (1) of "shaking" so as to make insecure, Heb. 12:27 (twice); (2) of casting down from a sense of security, **Acts**

2:25, "I should (not) be moved"; (3) to stir up (a crowd), **Acts 17:13**; (4) to unsettle, 2 Thess. 2:2, "(to the end that) ye be not (quickly) shaken (from your mind)," i.e., from their settled conviction and the purpose of heart begotten by it, as to the return of Christ before the Day of the Lord begins; the metaphor may be taken from the loosening of a ship from its moorings by a storm.

2:26 Therefore did my heart rejoice, and my tongue was glad; moreover also my flesh shall rest in hope:

Rejoice *euphraino* (2165), in the active voice, "to cheer, gladden" (*eu*, "well," *phren*, "the mind"), signifies in the passive voice "to rejoice, make merry"; it is translated "to rejoice" in **Acts 2:26**, RV, "was glad," KJV, "did ... rejoice," of the heart of Christ as foretold in Ps. 16:9; in **Acts 7:41**, of Israel's idolatry; in Rom. 15:10 (quoted from the Sept. of Deut. 32:43, where it is a command to the Gentiles to "rejoice" with the Jews in their future deliverance by Christ from all their foes, at the establishment of the messianic kingdom) the apostle applies it to the effects of the gospel.

Glad *agalliao* (21), "to exult, rejoice greatly," is chiefly used in the middle voice (active in Luke 1:47; some mss. have the passive in John 5:35, "to be made glad"). In the OT, it is found abundantly in the Psalms, from 2:11 onward to 149:2, 5 (Sept.). It conveys the idea of jubilant exultation, spiritual "gladness," Matt. 5:12, "be exceeding glad," the Lord's command to His disciples; Luke 1:47, in Mary's song; 10:21, of Christ's exultation ("rejoiced"); cf **Acts 2:26**, "(My tongue) was glad," KJV (RV, "rejoiced"); John 8:56, of Abraham; **Acts 16:34**, RV, "rejoiced greatly" (of the Philippian jailor); 1 Pet. 1:6, 8; 4:13 ("with exceeding joy"), of believers in general; in Rev. 19:7, RV, "be exceeding glad" (KJV, "rejoice").

Moreover *eti* (2089), "yet, as yet, still," is translated "moreover" in **Acts 2:26**; in **21:28**, RV (KJV, "further"); Heb. 11:36.

Also *kai* (2532), has three chief meanings, "and," "also," "even." When *kai* means "also" it precedes the word which it stresses. In English the order should be reversed. In John 9:40, e.g., the RV rightly has "are we also blind?" instead of "are we blind also?" In **Acts 2:26** the RV has "moreover My flesh also," instead of "moreover also ...."

Rest *kataskenoo* (2681), "to pitch one's tent" (*kata*, "down," *skene*, "a tent"), is translated "lodge" in Matt. 13:32; Mark 4:32; Luke 13:19; in **Acts 2:26**, RV, "dwell," KJV, "rest."

2:27 Because thou wilt not leave my soul in hell, neither wilt thou suffer thine Holy One to see corruption.

Leave *enkataleipo* (1459), lit., "to leave behind in," signifies (a) "to leave behind," Rom. 9:29, "a seed"; (b) "to abandon, forsake," translated by the verb "to leave" in **Acts 2:27, 31** of the soul of Christ; in the following, by the verb "to forsake," Matt. 27:46; Mark 15:34; 2 Cor. 4:9; 2 Tim. 4:10, 16; Heb. 10:25; 13:5.

Soul *psuche* (5590), denotes "the breath, the breath of life," then "the soul," in its various meanings. The NT uses "may be analyzed approximately as follows: (a) the natural life of the body, Matt. 2:20; Luke 12:22; **Acts 20:10**; Rev. 8:9; 12:11; cf. Lev. 17:11; 2 Sam. 14:7; Esth. 8:11; (b) the immaterial, invisible part of man, Matt. 10:28; **Acts 2:27**; cf. 1 Kings 17:21; (c) the disembodied (or "unclothed" or "naked," 2 Cor. 5:3, 4) man, Rev. 6:9; (d) the seat of personality, Luke 9:24, explained as = "own self," v. 25; Heb. 6:19; 10:39; cf. Isa. 53:10 with 1 Tim. 2:6; (e) the seat of the sentient element in man, that by which he perceives, reflects, feels, desires, Matt. 11:29; Luke 1:46; 2:35; **Acts 14:2, 22**; cf. Ps. 84:2; 139:14; Isa. 26:9; (f) the seat of will and purpose, Matt. 22:37; **Acts 4:32**; Eph. 6:6; Phil. 1:27; Heb. 12:3; cf. Num. 21:4; Deut. 11:13; (g) the seat of appetite, Rev. 18:14; cf. Ps. 107:9; Prov. 6:30; Isa. 5:14 ("desire"); 29:8; (h) persons, individuals, **Acts 2:41, 43**; Rom. 2:9; Jas. 5:20; 1 Pet. 3:20; 2 Pet. 2:14; cf. Gen. 12:5; 14:21 ("persons"); Lev. 4:2 ('any one'); Ezek. 27:13; of dead bodies, Num. 6:6, lit., "dead soul"; and of animals, Lev. 24:18, lit., "soul for soul"; (i) the equivalent of the personal pronoun, used for emphasis and effect:—1st person, John 10:24 ("us"); Heb. 10:38; cf. Gen. 12:13; Num. 23:10; Jud. 16:30; Ps. 120:2 ("me"); 2nd person, 2 Cor. 12:15; Heb. 13:17; Jas. 1:21; 1 Pet. 1:9; 2:25; cf. Lev. 17:11; 26:15; 1 Sam. 1:26; 3rd person, 1 Pet. 4:19; 2 Pet. 2:8; cf.

"This one event of the cross of Christ is a final revelation both of the character and consequence of human sin and of the wonder and sacrifice of divine love."

ALAN M. STIBBS

Exod. 30:12; Job 32:2, Heb. "soul," Sept. "self"; (j) an animate creature, human or other, 1 Cor. 15:45; Rev. 16:3; cf. Gen. 1:24; 2:7, 19; (k) "the inward man," the seat of the new life, Luke 21:19 (cf. Matt. 10:39); 1 Pet. 2:11; 3 John 2....

"Body and soul are the constituents of the man according to Matt. 6:25; 10:28; Luke 12:20; **Acts 20:10**; body and spirit according to Luke 8:55; 1 Cor. 5:3; 7:34; Jas. 2:26. In Matt. 26:38 the emotions are associated with the soul, in John 13:21 with the spirit; cf. also Ps. 42:11 with 1 Kings 21:5. In Ps. 35:9 the soul rejoices in God, in Luke 1:47 the spirit. Apparently, then, the relationships may be thus summed up '*Soma*, body, and *pneuma*, spirit, may be separated, *pneuma* and *psuche*, soul, can only be distinguished' (Cremer)."

Hell *hades* (86), "the region of departed spirits of the lost" (but including the blessed dead in periods preceding the ascension of Christ). It has been thought by some that the word etymologically meant "the unseen" (from *a*, negative, and *eido*, "to see"), but this derivation is questionable; a more probable derivation is from *hado*, signifying "all-receiving." It corresponds to "Sheol" in the OT. In the KJV of the OT and NT; it has been unhappily rendered "hell," e.g., Ps. 16:10; or "the grave," e.g., Gen. 37:35; or "the pit," Num. 16:30, 33; in the NT the revisers have always used the rendering "hades"; in the OT, they have not been uniform in the translation, e.g. in Isa. 14:15 "hell" (marg., "Sheol"); usually they have "Sheol" in the text and "the grave" in the margin. It never denotes the grave, nor is it the permanent region of the lost; in point of time it is, for such, intermediate between decease and the doom of Gehenna. For the condition, see Luke 16:23-31. The word is used four times in the Gospels, and always by the Lord, Matt. 11:23; 16:18; Luke 10:15; 16:23; it is used with reference to the soul of Christ, **Acts 2:27**, **31**; Christ declares that He has the keys of it, Rev. 1:18; in Rev. 6:8 it is personified, with the signification of the temporary destiny of the doomed; it is to give up those who are therein, 20:13, and is to be cast into the lake of fire, v. 14.

Suffer In **Acts 2:27** and **13:35**, KJV, *didomi*, "to give" (RV), is rendered "to suffer."

Holy *hosios* (3741), signifies "religiously right, holy," as opposed to what is unrighteous or polluted. It is commonly associated with righteousness. It is used "of God, Rev. 15:4; 16:5; and of the body of the Lord Jesus, **Acts 2:27**; **13:35**, citations from Ps. 16:10, Sept.; Heb. 7:26; and of certain promises made to David, which could be fulfilled only in the resurrection of the Lord Jesus, **Acts 13:34**. In 1 Tim. 2:8 and Titus 1:8, it is used of the character of Christians.... In the Sept., *hosios* frequently represents the Hebrew word *chasid*, which varies in meaning between 'holy' and 'gracious,' or 'merciful;' cf. Ps. 16:10 with 145:17."

See *horao* (3708), with its aorist form *eidon*, "to see" (in a few places the KJV uses the verb "to behold"), is said (a) of bodily vision, e.g., Mark 6:38; John 1:18, 46; (b) of mental perception, e.g., Rom. 15:21; Col. 2:18; (c) of taking heed, e.g., Matt. 8:4; 1 Thess. 5:15; (d) of experience, as of death, Luke 2:26; Heb. 11:5; life, John 3:36; corruption, **Acts 2:27**; (e) of caring for, Matt. 27:4; **Acts 18:15** (here the form *opsomai* is used).

Corruption *diaphthora* (1312), "utter or thorough corruption," referring in the NT to physical decomposition and decay, is used six times, five of which refer, negatively, to the body of God's "Holy One," after His death, which body, by reason of His absolute holiness, could not see "corruption," **Acts 2:27**, **31**; **13:34-35**, **37**; once it is used of a human body, that of David, which, by contrast, saw "corruption," **Acts 13:36**.

2:28 Thou hast made known to me the ways of life; thou shalt make me full of joy with thy countenance.

Known *gnorizo* (1107), signifies (a) "to come to know, discover, know," Phil. 1:22, "I wot (not)," i.e., "I know not," "I have not come to know" (the RV, marg. renders it, as under (b), "I do not make known"); (b) "to make known," whether (I) communicating things before "unknown," Luke 2:15, 17; in the latter some mss. have the verb *diagnorizo* (hence the KJV, "made known abroad)"; John 15:15, "I have made known"; 17:26; **Acts 2:28**; **7:13**; Rom. 9:22, 23; 16:26 (passive voice); 2 Cor. 8:1, "we make known (to you)," RV, KJV, "we do (you) to wit"; Eph. 1:9; 3:3, 5, 10 (all three in the passive voice); 6:19, 21; Col. 1:27; 4:7, 9, "shall make known" (KJV, "shall declare"); 2 Pet. 1:16; or (II) reasserting things already "known," 1 Cor. 12:3, "I give (you) to understand" (the apostle reaffirms what they knew); 15:1, of the gospel; Gal. 1:11 (he reminds them of what they well knew, the ground of his claim to apostleship); Phil. 4:6 (passive voice), of requests to God.

Ways *hodos* (3598), denotes (a) "a natural path, road, way," frequent in the Synoptic Gospels; elsewhere, e.g., **Acts 8:26**; 1 Thess. 3:11; Jas. 2:25; Rev. 16:12; (b) "a traveler's way"; (c) metaphorically, of "a course of conduct," or "way of thinking," e.g., of righteousness, Matt. 21:32; 2 Pet. 2:21; of God, Matt. 22:16, and parallels, i.e., the "way" instructed and approved by God; so **Acts 18:26** and Heb. 3:10, "My ways" (cf. Rev. 15:3); of the Lord, **Acts 18:25**; "that leadeth to destruction," Matt. 7:13; "... unto life," 7:14; of peace, Luke 1:79; Rom. 3:17; of Paul's "ways" in Christ, 1 Cor. 4:17 (plural); "more excellent" (of love), 1 Cor. 12:31; of truth, 2 Pet. 2:2; of the right "way," 2:15; of Balaam (*id.*), of Cain, Jude 11; of a "way" consisting in what is from God, e.g., of life, **Acts 2:28** (plural); of salvation, **Acts 16:17**; personified, of Christ as the means of access to the Father, John 14:6; of the course followed and characterized by the followers of Christ, **Acts 9:2; 19:9, 23; 24:22.**

Full *see* **Filled** at *Acts 2:2*.

Joy *euphrosune* (2167), is rendered "joy" in the KJV of **Acts 2:28**, RV, "gladness," as in **14:17**.

Countenance *prosopon* (4383), is translated "countenance" in Luke 9:29; **Acts 2:28**, and in the KJV of 2 Cor. 3:7 (RV, "face").

2:29 Men *and* brethren, let me freely speak unto you of the patriarch David, that he is both dead and buried, and his sepulchre is with us unto this day.

Brethren People of the same nationality, **Acts 3:17, 22**; Rom. 9:3. With "men" (*aner*, "male"), prefixed, it is used in addresses only, **Acts 2:29, 37**, etc.

Let *exesti* (1832), an impersonal verb, signifying "it is permitted, it is lawful" (or interrogatively, "is it lawful?"), occurs most frequently in the Synoptic Gospels and the Acts; elsewhere in John 5:10; 18:31; 1 Cor. 6:12; 10:23; 2 Cor. 12:4; in **Acts 2:29**, it is rendered "let me (speak)," lit., "it being permitted"; in the KJV of **8:37**, "thou mayest," lit., "it is permitted;" **16:21**; in **21:37**, "may I," lit., "is it permitted."

Freely In **Acts 2:29** the noun *parrhesia* with the preposition *meta*, "with," is rendered "freely," lit., "with free-spokenness."

Patriarch *patriarches* (3966), from *patria*, "a family," and *archo*, "to rule," is found in **Acts 2:29; 7:8, 9**; Heb. 7:4. In the Sept., 1 Chron. 24:31; 27:22; 2 Chron. 19:8; 23:20; 26:12.

Buried *thapto* (2290), occurs in Matt. 8:21-22, and parallels in Luke; Matt. 14:12; Luke 16:22; **Acts 2:29; 5:6, 9-10**; of Christ's "burial," 1 Cor. 15:4.

Dead *teleutao* (5053), "to end" (from *telos*, "an end"), hence, "to end one's life," is used (a) of the "death" of the body, Matt. 2:19; 9:18; 15:4, where "die the death" means "surely die," RV, marg., lit., "let him end by death"; Mark 7:10; Matt. 22:25, "deceased"; Luke 7:2; John 11:39; **Acts 2:29; 7:15**; Heb. 11:22 (RV, "his end was nigh"); (b) of the gnawings of conscience in self reproach, under the symbol of a worm, Mark 9:48 (vv. 44 and 46, KJV).

Sepulchre *mnema* (3418), like which it signified "a memorial" or "record of a thing or a dead person," then "a sepulchral monument," and hence "a tomb"; it is rendered "graves" in the KJV of Rev. 11:9 (RV, "a tomb"); "tomb" or "tombs," Mark 5:3, 5 and 16:2 (KJV, "sepulchre"); Luke 8:27; **Acts 2:29** and **7:16** (KJV, "sepulchre").

2:30 Therefore being a prophet, and knowing that God had sworn with an oath to him, that of the fruit of his loins, according to the flesh, he would raise up Christ to sit on his throne;

Fruit *karpos* (2590), "fruit," is used (I) of the fruit of trees, fields, the earth, that which is produced by the inherent energy of a living organism, e.g., Matt. 7:17; Jas. 5:7, 18; plural, e.g., in Luke 12:17 and 2 Tim. 2:6; of the human body, Luke 1:42; **Acts 2:30**; (II) metaphorically, (a) of works or deeds, "fruit" being the visible expression of power working inwardly and invisibly, the character of the "fruit" being evidence of the character of the power producing it, Matt. 7:16. As the visible expressions of hidden lusts are the works of the flesh, so the invisible power of the Holy Spirit in those who are brought into living union with Christ (John 15:2-8, 16) produces "the fruit of the Spirit," Gal. 5:22, the singular form suggesting the unity of the character of the Lord as reproduced in them, namely, "love, joy, peace, longsuffering, kindness, goodness, faithfulness, meekness, temperance," all in contrast with the confused and often mutually antagonistic "works of the flesh." So in Phil. 1:11, marg., "fruit of righteousness." In Heb. 12:11, "the fruit of righteousness" is described as "peaceable fruit," the outward effect of divine chastening; "the fruit of righteousness is sown in peace," Jas. 3:18, i.e., the seed contains the fruit; those who make peace, produce a harvest of righteousness; in Eph. 5:9, "the fruit of the light" (RV, and see context) is seen in "goodness and righteousness and truth," as the expression of the union of the Christian with God (Father, Son and Holy Spirit); for God is good, Mark 10:18, the Son is "the righteous One," **Acts 7:52**, the Spirit is "the Spirit of truth," John 16:13; (b) of advantage, profit, consisting (1) of converts as the result of evangelistic ministry, John 4:36; Rom. 1:13; Phil. 1:22;

(2) of sanctification, through deliverance from a life of sin and through service to God, Rom. 6:22, in contrast to (3) the absence of anything regarded as advantageous as the result of former sins, v. 21; (4) of the reward for ministration to servants of God, Phil. 4:17; (5) of the effect of making confession to God's Name by the sacrifice of praise, Heb. 13:15.

Oath *horkos* (3727), is primarily equivalent to *herkos*, "a fence, an enclosure, that which restrains a person"; hence, "an oath." The Lord's command in Matt. 5:33 was a condemnation of the minute and arbitrary restrictions imposed by the scribes and Pharisees in the matter of adjurations, by which God's Name was profaned. The language of the apostle Paul, e.g., in Gal. 1:20 and 1 Thess. 5:27 was not inconsistent with Christ's prohibition, read in the light of its context. Contrast the "oaths" mentioned in Matt. 14:7, 9; 26:72; Mark 6:26. Heb. 6:16 refers to the confirmation of a compact among men, guaranteeing the discharge of liabilities; in their disputes "the oath is final for confirmation." This is referred to in order to illustrate the greater subject of God's "oath" to Abraham, confirming His promise; cf. Luke 1:73; **Acts 2:30**. Cf. the verbs *horkizo*, and *exorkizo*.

Loins *osphus* (3751), is used (a) in the natural sense in Matt. 3:4; Mark 1:6; (b) as "the seat of generative power," Heb. 7:5, 10; metaphorically in **Acts 2:30**; (c) metaphorically, (1) of girding the "loins" in readiness for active service for the Lord, Luke 12:35; (2) the same, with truth, Eph. 6:14, i.e., bracing up oneself so as to maintain perfect sincerity and reality as the counteractive in Christian character against hypocrisy and falsehood; (3) of girding the "loins" of the mind, 1 Pet. 1:13, RV, "girding," suggestive of the alertness necessary for sobriety and for setting one's hope perfectly on "the grace to be brought ... at the revelation of Jesus Christ" (the present participle, "girding," is introductory to the rest of the verse).

Exist *huparcho* (5225), primarily, "to make a beginning" (*hupo*, "under," *arche*, "a beginning"), denotes "to be, to be in existence," involving an "existence" or condition both previous to the circumstances mentioned and continuing after it. This is important in Phil. 2:6, concerning the deity of Christ. The phrase "being (existing) in the form (*morphe*, the essential and specific form and character) of God," carries with it the two facts of the antecedent Godhood of Christ, previous to His incarnation, and the continuance of His Godhood at and after the event of His Birth. It is translated "exist" in 1 Cor. 11:18, RV, for KJV, "there be." Cf. Luke 16:14; 23:50; **Acts 2:30**; **3:2**; **17:24**; **22:3** etc.

Raise *see* **Raised** at *Acts 2:24*.

Sit *kathizo* (2523), used transitively, signifies "to cause to sit down, set, appoint," translated "to set" in **Acts 2:30**, RV (KJV, incorrectly, "to sit"); in 1 Cor. 6:4, of appointing, i.e., obtaining the services of, judges in lawcourts; in Eph. 1:20, RV, "made (Him) to sit" (KJV, "set"). *See also* **Sat** at *Acts 2:3*.

Throne *thronos* (2362), "a throne, a seat of authority," is used of the "throne" (a) of God, e.g., Heb. 4:16, "the throne of grace," i.e., from which grace proceeds; 8:1; 12:2; Rev. 1:4; 3:21 (2nd part); 4:2 (twice); 5:1; frequently in Rev.; in 20:12, in the best texts, "the throne" (some have *Theos*, "God," KJV); cf. 21:3; Matt. 5:34; 23:22; **Acts 7:49**; (b) of Christ, e.g. Heb. 1:8; Rev. 3:21 (1st part); 22:3; His seat of authority in the Millennium, Matt. 19:28 (1st part); (c) by metonymy for angelic powers, Col. 1:16; (d) of the Apostles in millennial authority, Matt. 19:28 (2nd part); Luke 22:30; (e) of the elders in the heavenly vision, Rev. 4:4 (2nd and 3rd parts), RV, "thrones" (KJV, "seats"); so 11:16; (f) of David, Luke 1:32; **Acts 2:30**; (g) of Satan, Rev. 2:13, RV, "throne" (KJV, "seat"); (h) of "the beast," the final and federal head of the revived Roman Empire, Rev. 13:2; 16:10.

2:31 He seeing this before spake of the resurrection of Christ, that his soul was not left in hell, neither his flesh did see corruption.

Seeing ... before *proeidon* (4275), an aorist tense form without a present, "to foresee," is used of David, as foreseeing Christ, in **Acts 2:31**, RV, "foreseeing" (KJV, "seeing before"); in Gal. 3:8 it is said of the Scripture, personified, personal activity being attributed to it by reason of its divine source (cf. v. 22). "What saith the Scripture?" was a common formula among the Rabbis. In the Sept., Gen. 37:18; Ps. 16:8 (*proorao*); 139:3.

Christ *christos* (5547), "anointed," translates, in the Sept., the word "Messiah," a term applied to the priests who were anointed with the holy oil, particularly the high priest, e.g., Lev. 4:3, 5, 16. The prophets are called *hoi christoi Theou*, "the anointed of God," Ps. 105:15. A king of Israel was described upon occasion as *christos tou Kuriou*, "the anointed of the Lord," 1 Sam. 2:10, 35; 2 Sam. 1:14; Ps. 2:2; 18:50; Hab. 3:13; the term is used even of Cyrus, Isa. 45:1. The title *ho Christos*, "the Christ," is not used of Christ in the Sept. version of the inspired books of the OT. In the NT the word is frequently used with the article, of the Lord Jesus, as an appellative rather than a title, e.g., Matt. 2:4; **Acts 2:31**; without the article, Luke 2:11; 23:2; John 1:41. Three times the title was expressly accepted by the Lord Himself, Matt. 16:17; Mark 14:61-62; John 4:26. It is added as an appellative to the proper name "Jesus," e.g., John 17:3, the only time when the Lord so spoke of Himself; **Acts 9:34**; 1 Cor. 3:11; 1 John 5:6. It is distinctly a proper name in many passages, whether with the article, e.g., Matt. 1:17; 11:2; Rom. 7:4, 9:5; 15:19; 1 Cor. 1:6, or without the article, Mark 9:41; Rom. 6:4; 8:9, 17; 1 Cor. 1:12; Gal. 2:16. The single title Christos is sometimes used without the article to signify the One who by His Holy Spirit and power indwells believers and molds their character in conformity to His likeness, Rom. 8:10; Gal. 2:20; 4:19; Eph. 3:17. As to the use or absence of the article, the title with the article specifies the Lord Jesus as "the Christ"; the title without the article stresses His character and His relationship with believers. Again, speaking generally, when the title is the subject of a sentence it has the article; when it forms part of the predicate the article is absent.

Resurrection *see Acts 1:22.*

Left *see* Leave at Acts *2:27.*

Hell *see Acts 2:27.*

Corruption *see Acts 2:27.*

2:32 This Jesus hath God raised up, whereof we all are witnesses.

Raised *see Acts 2:24.*

Witnesses *see Acts 1:8.*

2:33 Therefore being by the right hand of God exalted, and having received of the Father the promise of the Holy Ghost, he hath shed forth this, which ye now see and hear.

Right hand *dexios* (1188), an adjective, used (a) of "the right" as opposite to the left, e.g., Matt. 5:29, 30; Rev. 10:5, RV, "right hand"; in connection with armor (figuratively), 2 Cor. 6:7; with *en*, followed by the dative plural, Mark 16:5; with *ek*, and the genitive plural, e.g., Matt. 25:33, 34; Luke 1:11; (b) of giving the "right hand" of fellowship, Gal. 2:9, betokening the public expression of approval by leaders at Jerusalem of the course pursued by Paul and Barnabas among the Gentiles; the act was often the sign of a pledge, e.g., 2 Kings 10:15; 1 Chron. 29:24, marg.; Ezra 10:19; Ezek. 17:18; figuratively, Lam. 5:6; it is often so used in the papyri; (c) metaphorically of "power" or "authority," **Acts 2:33**; with *ek*, signifying "on," followed by the genitive plural, Matt. 26:64; Mark 14:62; Heb. 1:13; (d) similarly of "a place of honor in the messianic kingdom," Matt. 20:21; Mark 10.37.

Exalted *hupsoo* (5312), "to lift up" (akin to *hupsos*, "height"), is used (a) literally of the "lifting" up of Christ in His crucifixion, John 3:14; 8:28; 12:32, 34; illustratively, of the serpent of brass, John 3:14; (b) figuratively, of spiritual privileges bestowed on a city, Matt. 11:23; Luke 10:15; of "raising" to dignity and happiness, Luke 1:52; **Acts 13:17**; of haughty self-exaltation, and, contrastingly, of being "raised" to honor, as a result of self-humbling, Matt. 23:12; Luke 14:11; 18:14; of spiritual "uplifting" and revival, Jas. 4:10; 1 Pet. 5:6; of bringing into the blessings of salvation through the gospel, 2 Cor. 11:7; (c) with a combination of the literal and metaphorical, of the "exaltation" of Christ by God the Father, **Acts 2:33; 5:31**.

Promise *see Acts 1:4.*

Shed *ekcheo* (1632), "to pour out," is translated "to shed" or "to shed forth" in **Acts 2:33**; Titus 3:6, KJV; of "shedding" blood in murder, Rom. 3:15.

2:34 For David is not ascended into the heavens: but he saith himself, The Lord said unto my Lord, Sit thou on my right hand,

Sit *kathemai* (2521), is used (a) of the natural posture, e.g., Matt. 9:9, most frequently in the Apocalypse, some 32 times; frequently in the Gospels and Acts; elsewhere only in 1 Cor. 14:30; Jas. 2:3 (twice); and of Christ's position of authority on the throne of God, Col. 3:1, KJV, "sitteth" (RV, "is, seated"); Heb. 1:13 (cf. Matt. 22:44; 26:64 and parallel passages in Mark and Luke, and **Acts 2:34**); often as antecedent or successive to, or accompanying, another act (in no case a superfluous expression), e.g., Matt. 15:29; 27:36; Mark 2:14; 4:1; (b) metaphorically in Matt. 4:16 (twice); Luke 1:79; of inhabiting a place (translated "dwell"), Luke 21:35; Rev. 14:6, RV marg., "sit" (in the best texts: some have *katoikeo*, "to dwell").

2:35 Until I make thy foes thy footstool.

Make *tithemi* (5087), "to put," Matt. 22:44, Mark 12:36; Luke 20:43; **Acts 2:35**; 1 Cor. 9:18 (of making the gospel without charge); Heb. 1:13; 10:13; 2 Pet. 2:6; **Acts 20:28**; Rom. 4:17.

Foes *echthros* (2190), an adjective, primarily denoting "hated" or "hateful" (akin to *echthos*, "hate";

perhaps associated with *ekos*, "outside"), hence, in the active sense, denotes "hating, hostile"; it is used as a noun signifying an "enemy," adversary, and is said (a) of the Devil, Matt. 13:39; Luke 10:19; (b) of death, 1 Cor. 15:26; (c) of the professing believer who would be a friend of the world, thus making himself an enemy of God, Jas. 4:4; (d) of men who are opposed to Christ, Matt. 13:25, 28; 22:44; Mark 12:36; Luke 19:27; 20:43; **Acts 2:35**; Rom. 11:28; Phil. 3:18; Heb. 1:13; 10:13; or to His servants, Rev. 11:5, 12; to the nation of Israel, Luke 1:71, 74; 19:43; (e) of one who is opposed to righteousness, **Acts 13:10**; (f) of Israel in its alienation from God, Rom. 11:28; (g) of the unregenerate in their attitude toward God, Rom. 5:10; Col. 1:21; (h) of believers in their former state, 2 Thess. 3:15; (i) of foes, Matt. 5:43-44; 10:36; Luke 6:27, 35; Rom. 12:20; 1 Cor. 15:25; of the apostle Paul because he told converts "the truth," Gal. 4:16. Cf. *echthra*, "enmity".

Footstool *hupopodion* (5286), from *hupo*, "under," and *pous*, "a foot," is used (a) literally in Jas. 2:3, (b) metaphorically, of the earth as God's "footstool," Matt. 5:35; of the foes of the Lord, Matt. 22:44 (in some mss.); Mark 12:36, "underneath" (in some mss.), Luke 20:43; **Acts 2:35**; **7:49**; Heb. 1:13; 10:13. The RV, adhering to the literal rendering, translates the phrase "the footstool of My (Thy, His) feet," for the KJV, "My (etc.) footstool," but in Matt. 22:44, "(till I put Thine enemies) underneath thy feet."

2:36 Therefore let all the house of Israel know assuredly, that God hath made that same Jesus, whom ye have crucified, both Lord and Christ.

All *pas* (3956), radically means "all." Used without the article it means "every," every kind or variety. So the RV marg. in Eph. 2:21, "every building," and the text in 3:15, "every family," and the RV marg. of **Acts 2:36**, "every house"; or it may signify "the highest degree," the maximum of what is referred to, as, "with all boldness" **Acts 4:29**. Before proper names of countries, cities and nations, and before collective terms, like "Israel," it signifies either "all" or "the whole," e.g., Matt. 2:3; **Acts 2:36**. Used with the article, it means the whole of one object. In the plural it signifies "the totality of the persons or things referred to." Used without a noun it virtually becomes a pronoun, meaning "everyone" or "anyone." In the plural with a noun it means "all." The neuter singular denotes "everything" or "anything whatsoever." One form of the neuter plural (*panta*) signifies "wholly, together, in all ways, in all things," **Acts 20:35**; 1 Cor. 9:25. The neuter plural without the article signifies "all things severally," e.g., John 1:3; 1 Cor. 2:10; preceded by the article it denotes "all things," as constituting a whole, e.g., Rom. 11:36; 1 Cor. 8:6; Eph. 3:9.

House *oikos* (3624), denotes (a) "a house, a dwelling," e.g., Matt. 9:6, 7; 11:8; it is used of the Tabernacle, as the House of God, Matt. 12:4, and the Temple similarly, e.g., Matt. 21:13; Luke 11:51, KJV, "temple," RV, "sanctuary"; John 2:16, 17; called by the Lord "your house" in Matt. 23:38 and Luke 13:35 (some take this as the city of Jerusalem); metaphorically of Israel as God's house, Heb. 3:2, 5, where "his house" is not Moses', but God's; of believers, similarly, v. 6, where Christ is spoken of as "over God's House" (the word "own" is rightly omitted in the RV); Heb. 10:21; 1 Pet. 2:5; 4:17; of the body, Matt. 12:44; Luke 11:24; (b) by metonymy, of the members of a household or family, e.g., Luke 10:5; **Acts 7:10**; **11:14**; 1 Tim. 3:4, 5, 12; 2 Tim. 1:16; 4:19, RV (KJV, "household"); Titus 1:11 (plural); of a local church, 1 Tim. 3:15; of the descendants of Jacob (Israel) and David, e.g., Matt. 10:6; Luke 1:27, 33; **Acts 2:36**; **7:42**.

Assuredly *asphalos* (806), means (a) "safely," Mark 14:44; **Acts 16:23**; (b) "assuredly," **Acts 2:36**; the knowledge there enjoined involves freedom from fear of contradiction, with an intimation of the impossibility of escape from the effects.

Made *poieo* (4160), "to do, to make," is used in the latter sense (a) of constructing or producing anything, of the creative acts of God, e.g., Matt. 19:4 (2nd part); **Acts 17:24**; of the acts of human beings, e.g., Matt. 17:4; **Acts 9:39**; (b) with nouns denoting a state or condition, to be the author of, to cause, e.g., peace, Eph. 2:15; Jas. 3:18; stumbling blocks, Rom. 16:17; (c) with nouns involving the idea of action (or of something accomplished by action), so as to express the idea of the verb more forcibly (the middle voice is commonly used in this respect, suggesting the action as being of special interest to the doer); for the active voice see, e.g., Mark 2:23, of "making" one's way, where the idea is not that the disciples "made" a path through the standing corn, but simply that they went, the phrase being equivalent to going, "(they began) as they went (to pluck the ears)"; other instances of the active are Rev. 13:13, 14; 16:14; 19:20; for the middle voice (the dynamic or subjective middle), see, e.g., John 14:23, "will make Our abode"; in **Acts 20:24**, "none of these things move me," lit., "I make account of none of these things"; **25:17**, "I made no delay" RV, Rom. 15:26; Eph. 4:16; Heb. 1:2; 2 Pet. 1:10; (d) to "make" ready or prepare, e.g., a dinner, Luke 14:12; a supper, John 12:2; (e) to acquire, provide a thing for oneself, Matt. 25:16; Luke 19:18; (f) to render or "make" one or oneself anything, or cause a person or thing to become something, e.g., Matt. 4:19; 12:16, "make (Him known)"; John 5:11, 15, to "make" whole; 16:2, lit., "they shall make (you put out of the synagogue)"; Eph. 2:14; Heb. 1:7; to change one thing into another, Matt. 21:13; John 2:16; 4:46; 1 Cor. 6:15; (g) to constitute one anything, e.g., **Acts 2:36**, (h) to declare one or oneself anything, John 5:18, "making (Himself equal with God)"; 8:53; 10:33; 19:7, 12; 1 John 1:10; 5:10; (i) to "make" one do a thing, e.g., Luke 5:34; John 6:10; Rev. 3:9.

Lord *kurios* (2962), properly an adjective, signifying "having power" (*kuros*) or "authority," is used as a noun, variously translated in the NT, "'Lord,' 'master,' 'Master,' 'owner,' 'Sir,' a title of wide significance, occurring in each book of the NT save Titus and the Epistles of John. It is used (a) of an owner, as in Luke 19:33, cf. Matt. 20:8; **Acts 16:16**; Gal. 4:1; or of one who has the disposal of anything, as the Sabbath, Matt. 12:8; (b) of a master, i.e., one to whom service is due on any ground, Matt. 6:24; 24:50; Eph. 6:5; (c) of an Emperor or King, **Acts 25:26**; Rev. 17:14; (d) of idols, ironically, 1 Cor. 8:5, cf. Isa. 26:13; (e) as a title of respect addressed to a father, Matt. 21:30, a husband, 1 Pet. 3:6, a master, Matt. 13:27; Luke 13:8, a ruler, Matt. 27:63, an angel, **Acts 10:4**; Rev. 7:14; (f) as a title of courtesy addressed to a stranger, John 12:21; 20:15; **Acts 16:30**; from the outset of His ministry this was a common form of address to the Lord Jesus, alike by the people, Matt. 8:2; John 4:11, and by His disciples, Matt. 8:25; Luke 5:8; John 6:68; (g) *kurios* is the Sept. and NT representative of Heb. Jehovah ('LORD' in Eng. versions), see Matt. 4:7; Jas. 5:11, e.g., of *adon*, Lord, Matt. 22:44, and of *Adonay*, Lord, 1:22; it also occurs for *Elohim*, God, 1 Pet. 1:25.

"Thus the usage of the word in the NT follows two main lines: one, *a–f*, customary and general, the other, *g*, peculiar to the Jews, and drawn from the Greek translation of the OT. Christ Himself assumed the title, Matt. 7:21, 22; 9:38; 22:41-45; Mark 5:19 (cf. Ps. 66:16; the parallel passage, Luke 8:39, has 'God'); Luke 19:31; John 13:13, apparently intending it in the higher senses of its current use, and at the same time suggesting its OT associations. His purpose did not become clear to the disciples until after His resurrection, and the revelation of His Deity consequent thereon. Thomas, when he realized the significance of the presence of a mortal wound in the body of a living man, immediately joined with it the absolute title of Deity, saying, 'My Lord and my God,' John 20:28. Thereafter, except in **Acts 10:4** and Rev. 7:14, there is no record that *kurios* was ever again used by believers in addressing any save God and the Lord Jesus; cf **Acts 2:47** with **4:29, 30**. How soon and how completely the lower meaning had been superseded is seen in Peter's declaration in his first sermon after the resurrection, 'God hath made Him—Lord,' **Acts 2:36**, and that in the house of Cornelius, 'He is Lord of all,' **10:36**, cf. Deut. 10:14; Matt. 11:25; **Acts 17:24**. In his writings the implications of his early teaching are confirmed and developed. Thus Ps. 34:8, 'O taste and see that Jehovah is good,' is applied to the Lord Jesus, 1 Pet. 2:3, and 'Jehovah of Hosts, Him shall ye sanctify,' Isa. 8:13, becomes 'sanctify in your hearts Christ as Lord,' 3:15. So also James who uses *kurios* alike of God, 1:7 (cf. v. 5); 3:9; 4:15; 5:4, 10, 11, and of the Lord Jesus, 1:1 (where the possibility that *kai* is intended epexegetically, i.e. = even, cf. 1 Thess. 3:11, should not be overlooked); 2:1 (lit., 'our Lord Jesus Christ of glory,' cf. Ps. 24:7; 29:3; **Acts 7:2**; 1 Cor. 2:8); 5:7, 8, while the language of 4:10; 5:15, is equally applicable to either...

"It is not recorded that in the days of His flesh any of His disciples either addressed the Lord, or spoke of Him, by His personal Name. Where Paul has occasion to refer to the facts of the gospel history he speaks of what the Lord Jesus said, **Acts 20:35**, and did, 1 Cor. 11:23, and suffered, 1 Thess. 2:15; 5:9, 10. It is our Lord Jesus who is coming, 1 Thess. 2:19, etc. In prayer also the title is given, 3:11; Eph. 1:3; the sinner is invited to believe on the Lord Jesus, **Acts 16:31**; **20:21**, and the saint to look to the Lord Jesus for deliverance, Rom. 7:24, 25, and in the few exceptional cases in which the personal Name stands alone a reason is always discernible in the immediate context. The title 'Lord,' as given to the Savior, in its full significance rests upon the resurrection, **Acts 2:36**; Rom. 10:9; 14:9, and is realized only in the Holy Spirit, 1 Cor. 12:3."

2:37 Now when they heard *this*, they were pricked in their heart, and said unto Peter and to the rest of the apostles, Men *and* brethren, what shall we do?

Pricked *katanusso* (2660), primarily, "to strike or prick violently, to stun," is used of strong emotion, in **Acts 2:37** (passive voice), "they were pricked (in their heart)." Cf. *katanuxis*, "stupor, torpor of mind," Rom. 11:8.

Heart *kardia* (2588), "the heart" (Eng., "cardiac," etc.), the chief organ of physical life ("for the life of the flesh is in the blood," Lev. 17:11), occupies the most important place in the human system. By an easy transition the word came to stand for man's entire mental and moral activity, both the rational and the emotional elements. In other words, the heart is used figuratively for the hidden springs of the personal life. "The Bible describes human depravity as in the 'heart,' because sin is a principle which has its seat in the center of man's inward life, and then 'defiles' the whole circuit of his action, Matt. 15:19, 20. On the other hand, Scripture regards the heart as the sphere of Divine influence, Rom. 2:15; **Acts 15:9**.... The heart, as lying deep within, contains 'the hidden man,' 1 Pet. 3:4, the real man. It represents the true character but conceals it" (J. Laidlaw, in *Hastings' Bible Dic.*). As to its usage in the NT it denotes (a) the seat of physical life, **Acts 14:17**; Jas. 5:5; (b) the seat of moral nature and spiritual life, the seat of grief, John 14:1; Rom. 9:2; 2 Cor. 2:4; joy, John 16:22; Eph. 5:19; the desires, Matt. 5:28; 2 Pet. 2:14; the affections, Luke 24:32; **Acts 21:13**; the perceptions, John 12:40; Eph. 4:18; the thoughts, Matt. 9:4; Heb. 4:12; the understanding, Matt. 13:15; Rom. 1:21; the reasoning powers, Mark 2:6; Luke 24:38; the imagination, Luke 1:51; conscience, **Acts 2:37**; 1 John 3:20; the intentions, Heb. 4:12, cf. 1 Pet. 4:1; purpose, **Acts 11:23**; 2 Cor. 9:7; the will, Rom. 6:17; Col. 3:15; faith, Mark 11:23; Rom. 10:10; Heb. 3:12. The heart, in its moral significance in the OT, includes the emotions, the reason and the will.

Brethren *see Acts 2:29.*

2:38 Then Peter said unto them, Repent, and be baptized every one of you in the name of Jesus Christ for the remission of sins, and ye shall receive the gift of the Holy Ghost.

Repent *metanoeo* (3340), lit., "to perceive afterwards" (*meta,* "after," implying "change," *noeo,* "to perceive"; *nous,* "the mind, the seat of moral reflection"), in contrast to *pronoeo,* "to perceive beforehand," hence signifies "to change one's mind or purpose," always, in the NT, involving a change for the better, an amendment, and always, except in Luke 17:3, 4, of "repentance" from sin. The word is found in the Synoptic Gospels (in Luke, nine times), in Acts five times (2:38; 3:19; 8:22; 17:30: 26:20), in Revelation twelve times, eight in the messages to the churches, 2:5 (twice), 16, 21 (twice), RV, "she willeth not to repent" (2nd part); 3:3, 19 (the only churches in those chapters which contain no exhortation in this respect are those at Smyrna and Philadelphia); elsewhere only in 2 Cor. 12:21.

Remission *aphesis* (859), "a dismissal, release" (from *aphiemi*), is used of the forgiveness of sins and translated "remission" in Matt. 26:28; Mark 1:4; Luke 1:77; 3:3; 24:47; **Acts 2:38**; **5:31** (KJV, "forgiveness"); **10:43**; **13:38**, RV (KJV, "forgiveness"); **26:18** (ditto); Heb. 9:22; 10:18.

2:39 For the promise is unto you, and to your children, and to all that are afar off, *even* as many as the Lord our God shall call.

Afar *makran* (3112), properly a feminine form of the adjective above, denotes "a long way, far," (a) literally, Matt. 8:30, RV, "afar off." Luke 7:6; 15:20, RV, "afar off"; John 21:8; Acts 17:27; 22:21; (b) metaphorically, "far (from the kingdom of God)," Mark 12:34; in spiritual darkness, **Acts 2:39**; Eph. 2:13, 17.

Many *hosos* (3745), "how much, how many, how great, as much as, as many as," is translated "as many as," e.g., in Matt. 14:36; Mark 3:10; Luke 9:5, RV (KJV, "whosoever"); **Acts 2:39**; in **9:16**, RV, "how many things" (KJV, "how great things"); in Rom. 6:3 the RV renders it by "all we who" (KJV, "so many of us as"), a necessary alteration, not singling out some believers from others, as if some were not baptized, but implying what was recognized as true of all (see **Acts 18:8**); in 2 Cor. 1:20, RV, "how many soever be" (KJV, "all").

Call *proskaleo* (4341), signifies (a) "to call to oneself, to bid to come"; it is used only in the middle voice, e.g., Matt. 10:1; **Acts 5:40**; Jas. 5:14; (b) "God's call to Gentiles through the gospel," **Acts 2:39**; (c) the divine call in entrusting men with the preaching of the gospel," **Acts 13:2**; **16:10**.

2:40 And with many other words did he testify and exhort, saying, Save yourselves from this untoward generation.

Many *pleion* (4119), "more, greater," is translated "many" in **Acts 2:40**; **13:31**; **21:10**; **24:17**; **25:14**; **27:20**; **28:23** (KJV; RV, "in great number"); with the article, "most," RV (or rather, "the more part") **Acts 19:32**; 1 Cor. 10:5, and Phil. 1:14 (for KJV, "many," an important change); in 2 Cor. 2:6, RV, "the many" (marg., "the more"); so 4:15; in 9:2, "very many" (marg., "the more part"); in Heb. 7:23, RV, "many in number" (KJV "many").

Words *logos* (3056), denotes (I) "the expression of thought"—not the mere name of an object—(a) as embodying a conception or idea, e.g., Luke 7:7; 1 Cor. 14:9, 19; (b) a saying or statement, (1) by God, e.g., John 15:25; Rom. 9:9; 9:28, RV, "word" (KJV, "work"); Gal. 5:14; Heb. 4:12; (2) by Christ, e.g., Matt. 24:35 (plur.); John 2:22; 4:41; 14:23 (plur.); 15:20. In connection with (1) and (2) the phrase "the word of the Lord," i.e., the revealed will of God (very frequent in the OT), is used of a direct revelation given by Christ, 1 Thess. 4:15; of the gospel, **Acts 8:25**; **13:49**; **15:35**, **36**; **16:32**; **19:10**; 1 Thess. 1:8; 2 Thess. 3:1; in this respect it is the message from the Lord, delivered with His authority and made effective by His power (cf. **Acts 10:36**); for other instances relating to the gospel see **Acts 13:26**; **14:3**; **15:7**; 1 Cor. 1:18, RV; 2 Cor. 2:17; 4:2; 5:19; 6:7; Gal. 6:6; Eph. 1:13; Phil. 2:16; Col. 1:5; Heb. 5:13; sometimes it is used as the sum of God's utterances, e.g., Mark 7:13; John 10:35; Rev. 1:2, 9; (c) discourse, speech, of instruction, etc., e.g., **Acts 2:40**; 1 Cor. 2:13; 12:8; 2 Cor. 1:18; 1 Thess. 1:5; 2 Thess. 2:15; Heb. 6:1, RV, marg.; doctrine, e.g., Matt. 13:20; Col. 3:16; 1 Tim. 4:6; 2 Tim. 1:13; Titus 1:9; 1 John 2:7; (II) "The Personal Word," a title of the Son of God.

Testify *diamarturomai* (1263), "to testify or protest solemnly," is translated "to testify" in Luke 16:28; **Acts 2:40**; **8:25**; **10:42**; **18:5**; **20:21**, **23**, **24**; **23:11**; **28:23**; 1 Thess. 4:6; Heb. 2:6; "to charge" in 1 Tim. 5:21; 2 Tim. 2:14; 4:8.

Untoward *skolios* (4646), "curved, crooked," was especially used (a) of a way, Luke 3:5, with spiritual import (see Prov. 28:18, Sept.); it is set in contrast to *orthos* and *euthus*, "straight"; (b) metaphorically, of what is morally "crooked," perverse, froward, of people belonging to a particular generation, **Acts 2:40** (KJV, "untoward"); Phil. 2:15; of tyrannical or unjust masters, 1 Pet. 2:18, "froward"; in this sense it is set in contrast to *agathos*, "good."

Generation *genea* (1074), connected with *ginomai*, "to become," primarily signifies "a begetting, or birth"; hence, that which has been begotten, a family; or successive members of a genealogy, Matt. 1:17, or of a race of people, possessed of similar characteristics, pursuits, etc., (of a bad character) Matt. 17:17; Mark 9:19; Luke 9:41; 16:8; **Acts 2:40**; or of the whole multitude of men living at the same time, Matt. 24:34; Mark 13:30; Luke 1:48; 21:32; Phil. 2:15, and especially of those of the Jewish race living at the same period, Matt. 11:16, etc. Transferred from people to the time in which they lived, the word came to mean "an age," i.e., a period ordinarily occupied by each successive generation, say, of thirty or forty years, **Acts 14:16**; **15:21**; Eph. 3:5; Col. 1:26; see also, e.g., Gen. 15:16. In Eph. 3:21 *genea* is combined with *aion* in a remarkable phrase in a doxology: "Unto Him be the glory in the church and in Christ Jesus, unto all generations for ever and ever (wrongly in KJV 'all ages, world without end')." The word *genea* is to be distinguished from *aion*, as not denoting a period of unlimited duration.

2:41 Then they that gladly received his word were baptized: and the same day there were added *unto them* about three thousand souls.

Gladly *asmenos* (780), "with delight, delightedly, gladly," is found in **Acts 21:17**. It is absent from the best texts in **2:41** (see the RV).

Received *apodechomai* (588), "to welcome, to accept gladly" (*apo*, "from"), "to receive without reserve," is used (a) literally, Luke 8:40, RV, "welcomed"; 9:11; **Acts 18:27**; **21:17**; **28:30**; (b) metaphorically, **Acts 2:41**; **24:3**, "we accept," in the sense of acknowledging, the term being used in a tone of respect.

"Evangelism never seemed to be an 'issue' in the New Testament. That is to say, one does not find the apostles urging, exhorting, scolding, planning and organizing for evangelistic programmes ... evangelism happened! Issuing effortlessly from the community of believers as light from the sun, it was automatic, spontaneous, continuous, contagious."

RICHARD CHRISTIAN HALVERSON

"The birth and rapid rise of the Christian Church remain an unsolved enigma for any historian who refuses to take seriously the only explanation offered by the Church itself."

CHARLES F. D. MOULE

About *hosei* (5616), "as if," before numerals, denotes "about, nearly, something like," e.g., Matt. 14:21; Luke 3:23; 9:14, 28; **Acts 2:41**; with a measure of space, Luke 22:41, "about a stone's cast."

Thousand The following compounds represent different multiples of a thousand: *dischilioi*, 2,000, Mark 5:13; *trischilioi*, 3,000, **Acts 2:41**; *tetrakischilioi*, 4,000, Matt. 15:38; 16:10; Mark 8:9, 20; **Acts 21:38**; *pentakischilioi*, 5,000, Matt. 14:21; 16:9; Mark 6:44; 8:9; Luke 9:14; John 6:10; *heplakischilioi*, 7,000, Rom. 11:4.

Souls *see* Soul at *Acts 2:27*.

2:42 And they continued stedfastly in the apostles' doctrine and fellowship, and in breaking of bread, and in prayers.

Continued *see Acts 1:14*.

Fellowship *koinonia* (2842), "a having in common (*koinos*), partnership, fellowship", denotes (a) the share which one has in anything, a participation, fellowship recognized and enjoyed; thus it is used of the common experiences and interests of Christian men, **Acts 2:42**; Gal. 2:9; of participation in the knowledge of the Son of God, 1 Cor. 1:9; of sharing in the realization of the effects of the blood (i.e., the death) of Christ and the body of Christ, as set forth by the emblems in the Lord's Supper, 1 Cor. 10:16; of participation in what is derived from the Holy Spirit, 2 Cor. 13:14 (RV, "communion"); Phil. 2:1; of participation in the sufferings of Christ, Phil. 3:10; of sharing in the resurrection life possessed in Christ, and so of fellowship with the Father and the Son, 1 John 1:3, 6-7; negatively, of the impossibility of "communion" between light and darkness, 2 Cor. 6:14; (b) fellowship manifested in acts, the practical effects of fellowship with God, wrought by the Holy Spirit in the lives of believers as the outcome of faith, Philem. 6, and finding expression in joint ministration to the needy, Rom. 15:26; 2 Cor. 8:4; 9:13; Heb. 13:16, and in the furtherance of the Gospel by gifts, Phil. 1:5.

Breaking *klasis* (2800), "a breaking," is used in Luke 24:35 and **Acts 2:42**, of the "breaking" of bread.

Bread *artos* (740), "bread" (perhaps derived from *aro*, "to fit together," or from a root *ar*–, "the earth"), signifies (a) "a small loaf or cake," composed of flour and water, and baked, in shape either oblong or round, and about as thick as the thumb; these were not cut, but broken and were consecrated to the Lord every Sabbath and called the "shewbread" (loaves of presentation), Matt. 12:4; when the "shewbread" was reinstituted by Nehemiah (Neh. 10:32) a poll-tax of 1/3 shekel was laid on the Jews, Matt. 17:24; (b) "the loaf at the Lord's Supper," e.g., Matt. 26:26 ("Jesus took a loaf," RV, marg.); the breaking of "bread" became the name for this institution, **Acts 2:42**; **20:7**; 1 Cor. 10:16; 11:23; (c) "bread of any kind," Matt. 16:11; (d) metaphorically, "of Christ as the Bread of God, and of Life," John 6:33, 35; (e) "food in general," the necessities for the sustenance of life, Matt. 6:11; 2 Cor. 9:10, etc.

2:43 And fear came upon every soul: and many wonders and signs were done by the apostles.

Fear *phobos* (5401), first had the meaning of "flight," that which is caused by being scared; then, "that which may cause flight," (a) "fear, dread, terror," always with this significance in the four Gospels; also e.g., in **Acts 2:43**; **19:17**; 1 Cor. 2:3; 1 Tim. 5:20 (lit., "may have fear"); Heb. 2:15; 1 John 4:18; Rev. 11:11; 18:10, 15; by metonymy, that which causes "fear," Rom. 13:3; 1 Pet. 3:14, RV, "(their) fear," KJV "(their) terror," an adaptation of the Sept. of Isa. 8:12, "fear not their fear"; hence some take it to mean, as there, "what they fear," but in view of Matt. 10:28, e.g., it seems best to understand it as that which is caused by the intimidation of adversaries; (b) "reverential fear," (1) of God, as a controlling motive of the life, in matters spiritual and moral, not a mere "fear" of His power and righteous retribution, but a wholesome dread of displeasing Him, a "fear" which banishes the terror that shrinks from His presence, Rom. 8:15, and which influences the disposition and attitude of one whose circumstances are guided by trust in God, through the indwelling Spirit of God, **Acts 9:31**; Rom. 3:18; 2 Cor. 7:1; Eph. 5:21 (RV, "the fear of Christ"); Phil. 2:12; 1 Pet. 1:17 (a comprehensive phrase: the reverential "fear" of God will inspire a constant carefulness in dealing with others in His "fear"); 3:2, 15; the association of "fear and trembling," as, e.g., in Phil. 2:12, has in the Sept. a much sterner import, e.g., Gen. 9:2; Exod. 15:16; Deut. 2:25; 11:25; Ps. 55:5; Isa. 19:16; (2) of superiors, e.g., Rom. 13:7; 1 Pet. 2:18.

Every *pas* (3956), signifies (1) with nouns without the article, (a) "every one" of the class denoted by the noun connected with *pas*, e.g., Matt. 3:10, "every tree"; Mark 9:49, "every sacrifice"; see also John 2:10; **Acts 2:43**; Rom. 2:9; Eph. 1:21; 3:15; 2 Thess. 2:4; 2 Tim. 3:16, RV; (b) "any and every, of every kind, all manner of," e.g., Matt. 4:23; "especially with nouns denoting virtues or vices, emotions, condition, indicating every mode in which a quality manifests itself; or any object to which the idea conveyed by the noun belongs" (Grimm-Thayer). This is often translated "all," e.g., **Acts 27:20**; Rom. 15:14; 2 Cor. 10:6; Eph. 4:19, 31; Col. 4:12, "all the will of God," i.e., everything God wills; (2) without a noun, "every one, everything, every man" (i.e., person), e.g., Luke 16:16; or with a negative, "not everyone," e.g., Mark 9:49; with a participle and the article, equivalent to a relative clause, everyone who, e.g., 1 Cor. 9:25; Gal. 3:10, 13; 1 John 2:29; 3:3-4, 6, 10, 15, rendered "whosoever." So in the neuter, 1 John 2:16; 5:4, often rendered "whatsoever"; governed by the preposition *en*, "in," without a noun following, it signifies "in every matter, or condition," Phil. 4:6; 1 Thess. 5:18; "in every way or particular," 2 Cor. 4:8, translated "on every side"; so 2 Cor. 7:5; "in everything," Eph. 5:24; Phil. 4:12, lit., "in everything and (perhaps "even") in all things."

Soul *see Acts 2:27.*

Wonders *see Acts 2:19.*

2:44 And all that believed were together, and had all things common;

Together *see Acts 1:15.*

Common *koinos* (2834), denotes (a) "common, belonging to several" (Lat., *communis*), said of things had in common, **Acts 2:44**; **4:32**; of faith, Titus 1:4; of salvation, Jude 3; it stands in contrast to *idios*, "one's own"; (b) "ordinary, belonging to the generality, as distinct from what is peculiar to the few", hence the application to religious practices of Gentiles in contrast with those of Jews; or of the ordinary people in contrast with those of the Pharisees; hence the meaning "unhallowed, profane," Levitically unclean (Lat., *profanus*), said of hands, Mark 7:2 (KJV, "defiled,") RV marg., "common"; of animals, ceremonially unclean, **Acts 10:14**; **11:8**; of a man, **10:28**; of meats, Rom. 14:14, "unclean"; of the blood of the covenant, as viewed by an apostate, Heb. 10:29, "unholy" (RV, marg., "common"); of everything unfit for the holy city, Rev. 21:27, RV, "unclean" (marg., "common"). Some mss. have the verb here.

2:45 And sold their possessions and goods, and parted them to all *men*, as every man had need.

Sold *piprasko* (4097), from an earlier form, *perao*, "to carry across the sea for the purpose of selling or to export," is used literally, Matt. 13:46; 18:25; 26:9; Mark 14:5; John 12:5; **Acts 2:45**; **4:34**; **5:4**.

Possessions *ktema* (2933), denotes "a possession, property," Matt. 19:22; Mark 10:22; **Acts 2:45**; **5:1**.

Goods *huparxis* (5223), primarily, "subsistence," then, "substance, property, goods" (akin to *huparcho*, "to exist, be, belong to"), is translated "goods" in **Acts 2:45**; "possession," RV (KJV, "substance") in Heb. 10:34.

Parted *see* Cloven at *Acts 2:3.*

Every The pronoun *tis*, "anyone," is rendered "any" in **Acts 2:45**, RV, for the incorrect KJV, "every." In Mark 15:24, the interrogative form is rendered "what each (should take)" (KJV, "every man"), lit., "who (should take) what."

2:46 And they, continuing daily with one accord in the temple, and breaking bread from house to house, did eat their meat with gladness and singleness of heart,

Continuing *see* Continued at *Acts 1:14.*

Accord *see Acts 1:14.*

Breaking *klao or klazo* (2806), "to break, to break off pieces," is used of "breaking bread," (a) of the Lord's act in providing for people, Matt. 14:19; 15:36; Mark 8:6, 19; (b) of the "breaking of bread" in the Lord's Supper, Matt. 26:26; Mark 14:22; Luke 22:19; **Acts 20:7**; 1 Cor. 10:16; 11:24; (c) of an ordinary meal, **Acts 2:46**; **20:11**; **27:35**; (d) of the Lord's act in giving evidence of His resurrection, Luke 24:30.

From house to house *oikos* (3624), "a house, dwelling," is used (a) with the preposition *eis*, "unto," with the meaning "to home," lit., "to a house," in Mark 8:3, RV, "to (their) home," KJV, "to (their own) houses"; so 8:26, "to (his) home"; Luke 15:6, "home," lit., "into the house"; (b) with the preposition *en*, "in," 1 Cor. 11:34, "(let him eat) at home"; 14:35, "(let them ask ...) at home"; (c) with the preposition *kata*, "down," **Acts 2:46**, "(breaking bread) at home," RV (KJV, "from house to house"); so in **5:42** (KJV, "in every house").

"Ultimately, evangelism is not a technique. It is the Lord of the Church who reserves to Himself His sovereign right to add to His Church."

JOHN R. W. STOTT

Eat The verb *metalambano*, "to take a part or share of anything with others, to partake of, share," is translated "did eat," in **Acts 2:46**, corrected in the RV to "did take"; a still more suitable rendering would be "shared," the sharing of food being suggested; cf. *metadidomi*, "to share," e.g., Luke 3:11.

Meat *trophe* (5160), denotes "nourishment, food" (akin to *trepho*, "to rear, nourish, feed"); it is used literally, in the Gospels, Acts and Jas. 2:15; metaphorically, in Heb. 5:12, 14, RV, "(solid) food," KJV, "(strong) meat," i.e., deeper subjects of the faith than that of elementary instruction. The word is always rendered "food" in the RV, where the KJV has "meat"; e.g., Matt. 3:4; 6:25; 10:10; 24:45; Luke 12:23; John 4:8; **Acts 2:46**, "did take their food," RV (KJV, "did eat their meat"); **9:19**, "took food"; **27:33, 34, 36**. The KJV also has "food" in **Acts 14:17** and Jas. 2:15.

Singleness *aphelotes* (858), denotes "simplicity," **Acts 2:46**, "singleness," for which Moulton and Milligan, from papyri examples, suggest "unworldly simplicity"; the idea here is that of an unalloyed benevolence expressed in act.

2:47 Praising God, and having favour with all the people. And the Lord added to the church daily such as should be saved.

Praising *aineo* (134), "to speak in praise of, to praise," is always used of "praise" to God, (a) by angels, Luke 2:13; (b) by men, Luke 2:2; 19:37; 24:53; **Acts 2:20, 47; 3:8, 9**; Rom. 15:11; Rev. 19:5.

Favour *charis* (5485), denotes (a) objectively, "grace in a person, graciousness," (b) subjectively, (1) "grace on the part of a giver, favor, kindness," (2) "a sense of favor received, thanks." It is rendered "favor" in Luke 1:30; 2:52; **Acts 2:47; 7:10, 46; 24:27** and **25:9**, RV (for KJV, "pleasure"); **25:3**. It has various uses, (a) objective, that which bestows or occasions pleasure, delight, or causes favorable regard; it is applied, e.g., to beauty, or gracefulness of person, Luke 2:40; act, 2 Cor. 8:6, or speech, Luke 4:22, RV, "words of grace" (KJV, "gracious words"); Col. 4:6; (b) subjective, (1) on the part of the bestower, the friendly disposition from which the kindly act proceeds, graciousness, loving-kindness, goodwill generally, e.g., **Acts 7:10**; especially with reference to the divine favor or "grace," e.g., **Acts 14:26**; in this respect there is stress on its freeness and universality, its spontaneous character, as in the case of God's redemptive mercy, and the pleasure or joy He designs for the recipient; thus it is set in contrast with debt, Rom. 4:4, 16, with works, 11:6, and with law, John 1:17; see also, e.g., Rom. 6:14, 15; Gal. 5:4; (2) on the part of the receiver, a sense of the favor bestowed, a feeling of gratitude, e.g., Rom. 6:17 ("thanks"); in this respect it sometimes signifies "to be thankful," e.g., Luke 17:9 ("doth he thank the servant?" lit., "hath he thanks to"); 1 Tim. 1:12; (c) in another objective sense, the effect of "grace," the spiritual state of those who have experienced its exercise, whether (1) a state of "grace," e.g., Rom. 5:2; 1 Pet. 5:12; 2 Pet. 3:18, or (2) a proof thereof in practical effects, deeds of "grace," e.g., 1 Cor. 16:3, RV, "bounty" (KJV, "liberality"); 2 Cor. 8:6, 19 (in 2 Cor. 9:8 it means the sum of earthly blessings); the power and equipment for ministry, e.g., Rom. 1:5; 12:6; 15:15; 1 Cor. 3:10; Gal. 2:9; Eph. 3:2, 7. To be in favor with is to find "grace" with, e.g., **Acts 2:47**; hence it appears in this sense at the beginning and the end of several epistles, where the writer desires "grace" from God for the readers, e.g., Rom. 1:7; 1 Cor. 1:3; in this respect it is connected with the imperative mood of the word *chairo*, "to rejoice," a mode of greeting among Greeks, e.g., **Acts 15:23**; Jas. 1:1 (marg.); 2 John 10, 11, RV, "greeting" (KJV, "God speed").

Lord *see Acts 2:36.*

Such as In **Acts 2:47**, KJV, the article with the present participle, passive, of *sozo*, "to save," lit., "the (ones), i.e., those, being saved," is translated "such as (should be saved)"; the RV, "those that (were being saved)," gives the correct meaning, marking the kind of persons who were added to the company.

Saved *sozo* (4982), "to save," is used (as with the noun *soteria*, "salvation") (a) of material and temporal deliverance from danger, suffering, etc., e.g., Matt. 8:25; Mark 13:20; Luke 23:35; John 12:27; 1 Tim. 2:15; 2 Tim. 4:18 (KJV, "preserve"); Jude 5; from sickness, Matt. 9:22, "made ... whole" (RV, marg., "saved"); so Mark 5:34; Luke 8:48; Jas. 5:15; (b) of the spiritual and eternal salvation granted immediately by God to those who believe on the Lord Jesus Christ, e.g., **Acts 2:47**, RV "(those that) were being saved"; **16:31**; Rom. 8:24, RV, "were we saved"; Eph. 2:5, 8; 1 Tim. 2:4; 2 Tim. 1:9; Titus 3:5; of human agency in this, Rom. 11:14; 1 Cor. 7:16; 9:22; (c) of the present experiences of God's power to deliver from the bondage of sin, e.g., Matt. 1:21; Rom. 5:10; 1 Cor. 15:2; Heb. 7:25; Jas. 1:21; 1 Pet. 3:21; of human agency in this, 1 Tim. 4:16; (d) of the future deliverance of believers at the second coming of Christ for His saints, being deliverance from the wrath of God to be executed upon the ungodly at the close of this age and from eternal doom, e.g., Rom. 5:9; (e) of the deliverance of the nation of Israel at the second advent of Christ, e.g., Rom. 11:26; (f) inclusively for all the blessings bestowed by God on men in Christ, e.g., Luke 19:10; John 10:9; 1 Cor. 10:33; 1 Tim. 1:15; (g) of those who endure to the end of the time of the Great Tribulation, Matt. 10:22; Mark 13:13; (h) of the individual believer, who, though losing his reward at the judgment seat of Christ hereafter, will not lose his salvation, 1 Cor. 3:15; 5:5; (i) of the deliverance of the nations at the Millennium, Rev. 21:24 (in some mss.).

Chapter 3

3:1 Now Peter and John went up together into the temple at the hour of prayer, *being* the ninth *hour*.

Together *see Acts 1:15.*

Ninth *enatos*, or *ennatos* (1766), is found in reference (a) to "the ninth hour" (3 o'clock, p.m.) in Matt. 20:5; 27:45-46; Mark 15:33-34; Luke 23:44; **Acts 3:1**; **10:3**, **30**; (b) to "the topaz" as the "ninth" foundation of the city wall in the symbolic vision in Rev. 21 (v. 20).

3:2 And a certain man lame from his mother's womb was carried, whom they laid daily at the gate of the temple which is called Beautiful, to ask alms of them that entered into the temple;

Lame *cholos* (5560), "lame," is translated "halt" in Matt. 18:8; Mark 9:45; John 5:3, in **Acts 14:8**, "cripple"; in Luke 14:21, KJV, "halt," RV, "lame"; elsewhere, "lame," Matt. 11:5; 15:30, 31; 21:14: Luke 7:22; 14:13; **Acts 3:2**; **8:7**; Heb. 12:13; some mss. have it in **Acts 3:11** (KJV, "the lame man"), RV, "he," translating *autou*, as in the best texts.

Womb *koilia* (2836), denotes "the womb," Matt. 19:12; Luke 1:15, 41, 42, 44; 2:21; 11:27; 23:29; John 3:4; **Acts 3:2**; **14:8**; Gal. 1:15.

Carried *bastazo* (941), signifies "to support as a burden." It is used with the meaning (a) "to take up," as in picking up anything stones, John 10:31; (b) "to carry" something, Matt. 3:11; Mark 14:13; Luke 7:14; 22:10; **Acts 3:2**; **21:35**; Rev. 17:7; "to carry" on one's person, Luke 10:4; Gal. 6:17; in one's body, Luke 11:27; "to bear" a name in testimony, **Acts 9:15**; metaphorically, of a root "bearing" branches, Rom. 11:18; (c) "to bear" a burden, whether physically, as of the cross, John 19:17, or metaphorically in respect of sufferings endured in the cause of Christ, Luke 14:27; Rev. 2:3; it is said of physical endurance, Matt. 20:12; of sufferings "borne" on behalf of others, Matt. 8:17; Rom. 15:1; Gal. 6:2; of spiritual truths not able to be "borne," John 16:12; of the refusal to endure evil men, Rev. 2:2; of religious regulations imposed on others, **Acts 15:10**; of the burden of the sentence of God to be executed in due time, Gal. 5:10; of the effect at the judgment seat of Christ, to be "borne" by the believer for failure in the matter of discharging the obligations of discipleship, Gal. 6:5; (d) to "bear" by way of carrying off, John 12:6; 20:15.

Laid *tithemi* (5087), "to put, place, set," frequently signifies "to lay," and is used of (a) "laying" a corpse in a tomb, Matt. 27:60; Mark 6:29; 15:47; 16:6; Luke 23:53, 55; John 11:34; 19:41, 42; 20:2, 13, 15; **Acts 7:16**; **13:29**; Rev. 11:9, RV, "to be laid" (KJV, "to be put"); in an upper chamber, **Acts 9:37**; (b) "laying" the sick in a place, Mark 6:56; Luke 5:18; **Acts 3:2**; **5:15**; (c) "laying" money at the apostles' feet, **Acts 4:35**, **37**; **5:2**; (d) Christ's "laying" His hands upon children, Mark 10:16, RV, "laying" (KJV, "put"); upon John, Rev. 1:17 (in the best mss.); (e) "laying" down one's life, (1) of Christ, John 10:11, RV, "layeth down" (KJV, "giveth"); vv. 17, 18 (twice); 1 John 3:16; (2) of Peter for Christ's sake, John 13:37, 38; (3) of Christ's followers, on behalf of others, 1 John 3:16; (4) of anyone, for his friends, John 15:13; (f) "laying" up sayings in one's heart, Luke 1:66 (middle voice, in the sense of "for themselves"); in 9:44, of letting Christ's words "sink" (middle voice, in the sense of "for oneself"; KJV, "sink down") into the ears; (g) "laying" a foundation (1) literally, Luke 6:48; 14:29; (2) metaphorically, of Christ in relation to an assembly, 1 Cor. 3:10, 11; (h) in "laying" Christ as a "stone of stumbling" for Israel, Rom. 9:33; (i) Christ's "laying" aside His garments, John 13:4; (j) Christians, in "laying" money in store for the help of the needy, 1 Cor. 16:2 (lit., "let him put"); (k) "depositing" money, Luke 19:21, 22.

Daily The following phrases contain the word *hemera*, "day," and are translated "daily" or otherwise: (a) *kath' hemeran*, lit., "according to, or for, (the) day, or throughout the day," "day by day," e.g., Luke 11:3; **Acts 3:2**; **16:5**; 1 Cor. 15:31; Heb. 7:27; (b) *hemera kai hemera*, lit., "day and day," "day by day," 2 Cor. 4:16; (c) *hemeran ex hemeras*, lit., "day from day," "from day to day," 2 Pet. 2:8; (d) *semeron*, "this day," or "today," used outside the Synoptists and the Acts, in 2 Cor. 3:14-15, eight times in Hebrews, and in Jas. 4:13; (e) *tessemeron hemeras*, "(unto) this very day," Rom. 11:8 (RV); (f) *tas hemeras*, Luke 21:37, RV, "every day," for KJV, "in the daytime"; (g) *pasan hemeran*, **Acts 5:42**, RV, "every day"; preceded by *kata* in **Acts 17:17**, RV, "every day"; (h) *kath' hekasten hemeran*, lit., "according to each day," Heb. 3:13, "day by day," RV.

Gate In **Acts 3:2** *thura* denotes, not a "gate," but a "door," RV.

Beautiful *horaios* (5611), describes "that which is seasonable, produced at the right time," as of the prime of life, or the time when anything is at its loveliest and best (from *hora*, "a season," a period fixed by natural laws and revolutions, and so the best season of the year). It is used of the outward appearance of whited sepulchres in contrast to the corruption within Matt. 23:27; of the Jerusalem gate called "Beautiful," **Acts 3:2**, **10**; of the feet of those that bring glad tidings, Rom. 10:15. In the Sept. it is very frequent, and especially in Genesis and the Song of Solomon. In Genesis it is said of all the trees in the garden of Eden, 2:9, especially of the tree of the knowledge of good and evil, 3:6; of the countenances of Rebekah, 26:7, Rachel, 29:17 and Joseph, 39:6. It is used five times in the Song of Solomon, 1:16; 2:14; 4:3 and 6:3, 5.

Ask *aiteo* (154), "to ask," more frequently suggests the attitude of a suppliant, the petition of one who is lesser in position than he to whom the petition is made; e.g., in the case of men in asking something from God, Matt. 7:7; a child from a parent, Matt. 7:9-10; a subject from a king, **Acts 12:20**; priests and people from Pilate, Luke 23:23 (RV, "asking" for KJV, "requiring"); a beggar from a passer by, **Acts 3:2**. With reference to petitioning God, this verb is found in Paul's epistles in Eph. 3:20 and Col. 1:9; in James four times, 1:5-6; 4:2-3; in 1 John, five times, 3:22; 5:14, 15 (twice), 16.

Alms *eleemosune* (1654), connected with *eleemon*, "merciful," signifies (a) "mercy, pity, particularly in giving alms," Matt. 6:1, 2-4; **Acts 10:2**; **24:17**; (b) the benefaction itself, the "alms" (the effect for the cause), Luke 11:41; 12:33; **Acts 3:2-3**, **10**; **9:36**, "alms-deeds"; **10:2**, **4**, **31**.

Entered *eisporeuomai* (1531), "to go into," found only in the Synoptists and Acts, is translated "to enter," in the RV of Mark 1:21; 6:56; 11:2; Luke 8:16; 11:33 (KJV, "come in"); 19:30 (KJV, "at your entering"); 22:10; in the following the RV has the verb "to go," for the KJV, "to enter," Matt. 15:17; Mark 5:40; 7:15, 18-19; in **Acts 28:30**, "went," KJV, "came"; in **9:28**, RV, "going," KJV, "coming"; in the following both KJV and RV have the verb "to enter," Mark 4:19; Luke 18:24 (in the best mss.); **Acts 3:2**; **8:3**.

3:3 Who seeing Peter and John about to go into the temple asked an alms.

About *mello* (3195), signifies (a) "of intention, to be about to do something," e.g., **Acts 3:3**; **18:14**; **20:3**; Heb. 8:5; (b) "of certainty, compulsion or necessity, to be certain to act," e.g., John 6:71.

Go *eiseimi* (1524), "to go into, enter," is used in **Acts 3:3**; **21:18**, **26**; Heb. 9:6, RV, "go in" (KJV, "went ... into").

3:4 And Peter, fastening his eyes upon him with John, said, Look on us.

Fastening his eyes *see* **Looked** at *Acts 1:10*.

Look *see* **Beheld** at *Acts 1:9*.

3:5 And he gave heed unto them, expecting to receive something of them.

Heed *epecho* (1907), lit., "to hold upon," then, "to direct towards, to give attention to," is rendered "gave heed," in **Acts 3:5**; "take heed," in 1 Tim. 4:16.

Expecting *prosdokao* (4328), "to watch toward, to look for, expect" (*pros*, "toward," *dokeo*, "to think": *dokao* "does not exist"), is translated "expecting" in Matt. 24:50 and Luke 12:46, RV (KJV, "looketh for"); Luke 3:15, "were in expectation"; **Acts 3:5**, "expecting" (KJV and RV); **28:6** (twice), "expected that," RV (KJV, "looked when") and "when they were long in expectation" (KJV, "after they had looked a great while").

Something The indefinite pronoun *tis* in its singular or plural forms, frequently means "some," "some one" (translated "some man," in the KJV, e.g., of **Acts 8:31**; 1 Cor. 15:35), or "somebody," Luke 8:46; the neuter plural denotes "some things" in 2 Pet. 3:16; the singular denotes "something," e.g., Luke 11:54; John 13:29 (2nd part); **Acts 3:5**; **23:18**; Gal. 6:3, where the meaning is "anything," as in 2:6, "somewhat." It is translated "somewhat," in the more indefinite sense, in Luke 7:40; **Acts 23:20**; **25:26**; 2 Cor. 10:8; Heb. 8:3.

3:6 Then Peter said, Silver and gold have I none; but such as I have give I thee: In the name of Jesus Christ of Nazareth rise up and walk.

Silver *argurion* (694), is rendered "silver" in **Acts 3:6**; **8:20**, RV (KJV, "money"); **20:33**; 1 Cor. 3:12 (metaphorical); 1 Pet. 1:18.

Gold *chrusion* (5553), is used (a) of "coin," **Acts 3:6**; **20:33**; 1 Pet. 1:18; (b) of "ornaments," 1 Pet. 3:3, and the following, 1 Tim. 2:9; Rev. 17:4; 18:16; (c) of "the metal in general," Heb. 9:4; 1 Pet. 1:7; Rev. 21:18, 21; metaphorically, (d) of "sound doctrine and its effects," 1 Cor. 3:12; (e) of "righteousness of life and conduct," Rev. 3:18.

Have *huparcho* (5225), "to be in existence, to be ready, at hand," is translated by the verb "to have" in **Acts 3:6**, lit., "silver and gold is not to me" (in the next clause, "such as I have," *echo* is used); **4:37**, "having (land)," lit., "(land) being (to him)"; Matt. 19:21, "that (thou) hast," lit., "(things that) are (thine)," i.e., "thy belongings"; similarly Luke 12:33; 44; 14:33.

Name *see* Names at *Acts 1:15*.

3:7 And he took him by the right hand, and lifted *him* up: and immediately his feet and ankle bones received strength.

Took *piazo* (4084), "to lay hold of," with the suggestion of firm pressure or force, is used in the Gospels only in John, six times of efforts to seize Christ and is always rendered "take" in the RV, 7:30, 32, 44; 8:20; 10:39; 11:57. The KJV has "laid hands on" in 8:20. In **Acts 12:4** and 2 Cor. 11:32 (KJV), it is translated respectively "apprehended" and "apprehend" (RV, "had taken," and "take"). In Rev. 19:20 it is used of the seizure of the Beast and the False Prophet. In John 21:3, 10 it is used of catching fish. Elsewhere in **Acts 3:7**. In the Sept., Song of Sol. 2:15.

Lifted *egeiro* (1453), "to awaken, raise up," is used in Matt. 12:11, of "lifting" a sheep out of a pit. It is used (a) of "raising" the dead, active and passive voices, e.g. of the resurrection of Christ, Matt. 16:21; 17:23; 20:19, RV; 26:32, RV, "(after) I am raised up" (KJV, "... risen again"); Luke 9:22; 20:37; John 2:19; **Acts 3:15**; **4:10** [not **5:30**, see (c) below]; **10:40** [not **13:23** in the best texts, see (c) below]; **13:30**, **37**; Rom. 4:24, 25; 6:4, 9; 7:4; 8:11 (twice); 8:34, RV; 10:9; 1 Cor. 6.14 (1st part), 15.13, 14, RV; 15:15 (twice), 16, 17; 15:20, RV; 2 Cor. 4:14; Gal. 1:1; Eph. 1:20; Col. 2:12; 1 Thess. 1:10; 1 Pet. 1:21; in 2 Tim. 2:8, RV, "risen"; (b) of the resurrection of human beings, Matt. 10:8; 11:5; Matt. 27:52, RV (KJV, "arose"); Mark 12:26, RV; Luke 7:22; John 5:21; 12:1, 9, 17; **Acts 26:8**; 1 Cor. 15:29 and 32, RV; 15:35, 42, 43 (twice), 44, 52; 2 Cor. 1:9; 4:14; Heb. 11:19; (c) of "raising" up a person to occupy a place in the midst of a people, said of Christ, **Acts 5:30**; in **13:23**, KJV only (the best texts have *ago*, to bring, RV, "hath ... brought"); of David, **Acts 13:22**; (d) metaphorically, of a horn of salvation, Luke 1:69; (e) of children, from stones, by creative power, Luke 3:8; (f) of the Temple, as the Jews thought, John 2:20, RV, "wilt Thou raise (it) Up" (KJV, "rear"); (g) of "lifting" up a person, from physical infirmity, Mark 1:31, RV, "raised ... up" (KJV, "lifted"); so 9:27; **Acts 3:7**; **10:26**, RV (KJV, "took"); Jas. 5:15, "shall raise ... up"; (h) metaphorically, of "raising" up affliction, Phil. 1:17, RV (in the best texts; the KJV, v. 16, following those which have *epiphero*, has "to add").

Immediately *parachrema* (3916), lit., "with the matter (or business) itself" (*para*, "with," *chrema*, "a business," or "event"), and so, "immediately," Matt. 21:19 (KJV, "presently"), 20; Luke 1:64; 4:39; 5:25; 8:44, 47, 55; 13:13; 18:43; 19:11; 22:60; **Acts 3:7**; **5:10**; **12:23**; **13:11**; **16:26**, **33**; it is thus used by Luke only, save for the two instances in Matthew. It is also rendered "presently," "soon," "straightway."

Feet *basis* (939), lit., "a step" (akin to *baino*, "to go"), hence denotes that with which one steps, "a foot," and is used in the plural in **Acts 3:7**.

Ankle bones *sphuron* (4974), or *sphudron* (4974a), denotes the "ankle, or ankle-bone" (from *sphura*, "a hammer," owing to a resemblance in the shape), **Acts 3:7**.

Received strength *stereoo* (4732), "to make firm, or solid" (akin to *stereos*, "hard, firm, solid"; cf Eng., "stereotype"), is used only in Acts, (a) physically, **3:7**, "received strength"; **3:16**, "hath made strong"; (b) metaphorically, of establishment in the faith, **16:5**, RV, "strengthened," for KJV established.

3:8 And he leaping up stood, and walked, and entered with them into the temple, walking, and leaping, and praising God.

Leaping up *exallomai* (1814), "to leap up," is said in **Acts 3:8** (1st part) of the cripple healed by Peter.

Leaping *hallomai* (242), "to leap" (akin to *halma*, "a leap"), is used (a) metaphorically, of the "springing" up of water, John 4:14; (b) literally, of the "leaping" of healed cripples, **Acts 3:8** (2nd part); **14:10**.

Praising *see Acts 2:47*.

3:9 And all the people saw him walking and praising God:

Praising *see Acts 2:47*.

"Miracles are not contrary to nature but only contrary to what we know about nature."

ST. AUGUSTINE OF HIPPO

3:10 And they knew that it was he which sat for alms at the Beautiful gate of the temple: and they were filled with wonder and amazement at that which had happened unto him.

Alms *see Acts 3:2.*

Beautiful *see Acts 3:2.*

Gate *pule* (4439), is used (a) literally, for a larger sort of "gate," in the wall either of a city or palace or temple, Luke 7:12, of Nain (burying places were outside the "gates" of cities); **Acts 3:10**; **9:24**; **12:10**; Heb. 13:12; (b) metaphorically, of the "gates" at the entrances of the ways leading to life and to destruction, Matt. 7:13, 14; some mss. have *pule*, for *thura*, "a door," in Luke 13:24 (see the RV); of the "gates" of Hades, Matt. 16:18, than which nothing was regarded as stronger. The importance and strength of "gates" made them viewed as synonymous with power. By metonymy, the "gates" stood for those who held government and administered justice there.

Filled *see Acts 2:4.*

Wonder *thambos* (2285), "amazement, wonder," is probably connected with a root signifying "to render immovable"; it is frequently associated with terror as well as astonishment, as with the verb in **Acts 9:6**. It occurs in Luke 4:36; 5:9; **Acts 3:10**.

Amazement *ekstasis* (1611), is, lit., "a standing out" (*ek*, "out of," *stasis*, "a standing"). Eng. "ecstasy" is a transliteration. It is translated "amazement" in **Acts 3:10**. It was said of any displacement, and especially, with reference to the mind, of that alteration of the normal condition by which the person is thrown into a state of surprise or fear, or both; or again, in which a person is so transported out of his natural state that he falls into a trance, **Acts 10:10**; **11:5**; **22:17**. As to the other meaning, the RV has "amazement" in Mark 5:42 and Luke 5:26, but "astonishment" in Mark 16:8.

Happened *sumbaino* (4819), lit., "to go or come together" (*sun*, "with," *baino*, "to go"), signifies "to happen together," of things or events, Mark 10:32; Luke 24:14; **Acts 3:10**; 1 Cor. 10:11; 1 Pet. 4:12; 2 Pet. 2:22; "befell" in **Acts 20:19**; in **Acts 21:35**, "so it was."

3:11 And as the lame man which was healed held Peter and John, all the people ran together unto them in the porch that is called Solomon's, greatly wondering.

Lame *see Acts 3:2.*

Held *see* Holden at *Acts 2:24.*

Ran *suntrecho* (4936), "to run together with" (*sun*, "with"), is used (a) literally, Mark 6:33; **Acts 3:11**; (b) metaphorically, 1 Pet. 4:4, of "running" a course of evil with others. In the Sept., Ps. 50:18.

Porch *stoa* (4745), "a portico," is used (a) of the "porches" at the pool of Bethesda, John 5:2; (b) of the covered colonnade in the Temple, called Solomon's "porch," John 10:23; **Acts 3:11**; **5:12** a portico on the eastern side of the temple; this and the other "porches" existent in the time of Christ were almost certainly due to Herod's restoration. Cf. *Stoics* (**Acts 17:18**), "philosophers of the porch."

Greatly wondering *ekthambos* (1569), is found in **Acts 3:11**. The intensive force of the word is brought out by the rendering "greatly wondering.

3:12 And when Peter saw *it*, he answered unto the people, Ye men of Israel, why marvel ye at this? or why look ye so earnestly on us, as though by our own power or holiness we had made this man to walk?

Look *see Acts 1:10.*

Earnestly *atenizo*, "to fix the eyes upon, gaze upon," is translated "earnestly looked" in Luke 22:56, KJV (RV, "looking steadfastly"); in **Acts 3:12**, KJV, "look ye earnestly," RV, "fasten ye your eyes on"; in **Acts 23:1**, KJV, "earnestly beholding," RV, "looking steadfastly on."

Our own *see Acts 2:8.*

Power *dunamis* (1411), "power," (a) used relatively, denotes "inherent ability, capability, ability to perform anything," e.g., Matt. 25:15, "ability"; **Acts 3:12**, "power"; 2 Thess. 1:7, RV, "(angels) of His power" (KJV, "mighty"); Heb. 11:11, RV, "power" (KJV, "strength"); (b) used absolutely, denotes (1) "power to work, to carry something into effect," e.g., Luke 24:49; (2) "power in action," e.g., Rom. 1:16; 1 Cor. 1:18; it is translated "might" in the KJV of Eph. 1:21 (RV, "power"); so 3:16; Col. 1:11 (1st clause); 2 Pet. 2:11; in Rom. 15:19, KJV, this noun is rendered "mighty"; RV, "(in the) power of signs." The RV consistently avoids the rendering "might" for *dunamis;* the usual rendering is "power." Under this heading comes the rendering "mighty works," e.g., Matt. 7:22, RV (KJV, "wonderful works"); 11:20-23; singular number in Mark 6:5; in Matt. 14:2 and Mark 6:14 the RV has "powers"; in 2 Cor. 12:12, RV, "mighty works" (KJV, "mighty deeds").

Holiness *eusebeia* (2150), from *eu,* "well," and *sebomai,* "to be devout," denotes that piety which, characterized by a Godward attitude, does that which is well-pleasing to Him. This and the corresponding verb and adverb are frequent in the Pastoral Epistles, but do not occur in previous epistles of Paul. The apostle Peter has the noun four times in his 2nd Epistle, 1:3, 6, 7; 3:11. Elsewhere it occurs in **Acts 3:12**; 1 Tim. 2:2; 3:16; 4:7, 8; 6:3, 5, 6, 11; 2 Tim. 3:5; Titus 1:1. In 1 Tim. 6:3 "the doctrine which is according to godliness" signifies that which is consistent with "godliness," in contrast to false teachings; in Titus 1:1, "the truth which is according to godliness" is that which is productive of "godliness"; in 1 Tim. 3:16, "the mystery of godliness" is "godliness" as embodied in, and communicated through, the truths of the faith concerning Christ; in 2 Pet. 3:11, the word is in the plural, signifying acts of "godliness."

Man *see* Men at *Acts 1:16.*

3:13 The God of Abraham, and of Isaac, and of Jacob, the God of our fathers, hath glorified his Son Jesus; whom ye delivered up, and denied him in the presence of Pilate, when he was determined to let *him* go.

Presence *prosopon* (4383), denotes "the countenance," lit., "the part towards the eyes" (from *pros,* "towards," *ops,* "the eye"), and is used (a) of the "face," Matt. 6:16-17; 2 Cor. 3:7, 2nd part (KJV, "countenance"); in 2 Cor. 10:7, in the RV, "things that are before your face" (KJV, "outward appearance"), the phrase is figurative of superficial judgment; (b) of the look, i.e., the "face," which by its various movements affords an index of inward thoughts and feelings, eg., Luke 9:51, 53; 1 Pet. 3:12; (c) the presence of a person, the "face" being the noblest part, e.g., **Acts 3:13**, RV, "before the face of," KJV, "in the presence of"; **5:41**, "presence"; 2 Cor. 2:10, "person"; 1 Thess. 2:17 (first part), "presence"; 2 Thess. 1:9, RV, "face," KJV, "presence"; Rev. 12:14, "face"; (d) the person himself, e.g., Gal. 1:22; 1 Thess. 2:17 (second part); (e) the appearance one presents by his wealth or poverty, his position or state, Matt. 22:16; Mark 12:14; Gal. 2:6; Jude 16; (f) the outward appearance of inanimate things, Matt. 16:3; Luke 12:56; 21:35; **Acts 17:26**.

Determined *krino* (2919), primarily "to separate, select, choose"; hence, "to determine," and so "to judge, pronounce judgment," used in this sense in **Acts 3:13**; **20:16**; **25:25**; **27:1**; 1 Cor. 2:2; 2 Cor. 2:1; Titus 3:12. "The uses of this verb in the NT may be analyzed as follows: (a) to assume the office of a judge, Matt. 7:1; John 3:17; (b) to undergo process of trial, John 3:18; 16:11; 18:31; Jas. 2:12; (c) to give sentence, **Acts 15:19**; **16:4**; **21:25**; (d) to condemn, John 12:48; **Acts 13:27**; Rom. 2:27; (e) to execute judgment upon, 2 Thess. 2:12; **Acts 7:7**; (f) to be involved in a lawsuit, whether as plaintiff, Matt. 5:40; 1 Cor. 6:1; or as defendant, **Acts 23:6**; (g) to administer affairs, to govern, Matt. 19:28; cf. Judg. 3:10; (h) to form an opinion, Luke 7:43; John 7:24; **Acts 4:19**; Rom. 14:5; (i) to make a resolve, **Acts 3:13**; **20:16**; 1 Cor. 2:2."

Let ... go *apoluo* (630), signifies "to set free, release, loose" (*apo,* "from," *luo,* "to loose"), e.g., Luke 13:12; John 19:10; forgive, Luke 6:37; to release, dismiss, send away, translated "to let go," e.g., in Luke 14:4; in some mss. 22:68; in Luke 23:22; John 19:12 and **Acts 3:13**, KJV, "let ... go" (RV, "release"); in **Acts 4:21**, "they let ... go"; in v. **23** (passive voice), "being let go"; **5:40**; in **15:33**, KJV, "let go" (RV, "dismissed"); **16:35**, **36**; **17:9**; in **23:22**, RV, "let ... go" (KJV, "let ... depart"); in **28:18**, KJV, "let ... go" (RV, "set ... at liberty").

3:14 But ye denied the Holy One and the Just, and desired a murderer to be granted unto you;

Denied *arneomai* (720), signifies (a) "to say ... not, to contradict," e.g., Mark 14:70; John 1:20; 18:25, 27; 1 John 2:22; (b) "to deny" by way of disowning a person, as, e.g., the Lord Jesus as master, e.g., Matt. 10:33; Luke 12:9; John 13:38 (in the best mss.); 2 Tim. 2:12; or, on the other hand, of Christ Himself, "denying" that a person is His follower, Matt. 10:33; 2 Tim. 2:12; or to "deny" the Father and the Son, by apostatizing and by disseminating pernicious teachings, to "deny" Jesus Christ as master and Lord by immorality under a cloak of religion, 2 Pet. 2:1; Jude 4; (c) "to deny oneself," either in a good sense, by disregarding one's own interests, Luke 9:23, or in a bad sense, to prove false to oneself, to act quite unlike oneself, 2 Tim. 2:13; (d) to "abrogate, forsake, or renounce a thing," whether evil, Titus 2:12, or good, 1 Tim. 5:8; 2 Tim. 3:5; Rev. 2:13; 3:8; (e) "not to accept, to reject" something offered, **Acts 3:14**; **7:35**, "refused"; Heb. 11:24, "refused."

Holy *hagios* (40), which are from the same root as *hagnos* (found in *hazo*, "to venerate"), fundamentally signifies "separated" (among the Greeks, dedicated to the gods), and hence, in Scripture in its moral and spiritual significance, separated from sin and therefore consecrated to God, sacred.

(a) It is predicated of God (as the absolutely "Holy" One, in His purity, majesty and glory): of the Father, e.g., Luke 1:49; John 17:11; 1 Pet. 1:15, 16; Rev. 4:8; 6:10; of the Son, e.g., Luke 1:35; **Acts 3:14**; **4:27, 30**; 1 John 2:20; of the Spirit, e.g., Matt. 1:18 and frequently in all the Gospels, Acts, Romans, 1 and 2 Cor., Eph., 1 Thess.; also in 2 Tim. 1:14; Titus 3:5; 1 Pet. 1:12; 2 Pet. 1:21; Jude 20.

(b) It is used of men and things in so far as they are devoted to God. Indeed the quality, as attributed to God, is often presented in a way which involves divine demands upon the conduct of believers. These are called *hagioi*, "saints," i.e., "sanctified" or "holy" ones.

This sainthood is not an attainment, it is a state into which God in grace calls men; yet believers are called to sanctify themselves (consistently with their calling, 2 Tim. 1:9), cleansing themselves from all defilement, forsaking sin, living a "holy" manner of life, 1 Pet. 1:15; 2 Pet. 3:11, and experiencing fellowship with God in His holiness. The saints are thus figuratively spoken of as "a holy temple", 1 Cor. 3:17 (a local church); Eph. 2:21 (the whole Church), cp. 5:27; "a holy priesthood," 1 Pet. 2:5; "a holy nation," 2:9.

The adjective is also used of the outer part of the tabernacle, Heb. 9:2 (RV, "the holy place"); of the inner sanctuary, 9:3, RV, "the Holy of Holies"; 9:4, "a holy place," RV; v. 25 (plural), of the presence of God in heaven, where there are not two compartments as in the tabernacle, all being "the holy place"; 9:8, 12 (neuter plural); 10:19, "the holy place," RV (KJV, "the holiest," neut. plural); of the city of Jerusalem. Rev. 11:2; its temple, **Acts 6:13**; of the faith, Jude 20; of the greetings of saints, 1 Cor. 16:20; of angels, e.g., Mark 8:38; of apostles and prophets, Eph. 3:5; of the future heavenly Jerusalem, Rev. 21:2, 10; 22:19.

Just *dikaios* (1342), was first used of persons observant of *dike*, "custom, rule, right," especially in the fulfillment of duties towards gods and men, and of things that were in accordance with right. The Eng. word "righteous" was formerly spelt "rightwise," i.e., (in a) straight way. In the NT it denotes "righteous," a state of being right, or right conduct, judged whether by the divine standard, or according to human standards, of what is right. Said of God, it designates the perfect agreement between His nature and His acts (in which He is the standard for all men). It is used (1) in the broad sense, of persons: (a) of God, e.g., John 17:25; Rom. 3:26; 1 John 1:9; 2:29; 3:7; (b) of Christ, e.g., **Acts 3:14**; **7:52**; **22:14**; 2 Tim. 4:8; 1 Pet. 3:18; 1 John 2:1; (c) of men, Matt. 1:19; Luke 1:6; **Acts 10:22**; Rom. 1:17; 2:13; 5:7, (2) of things; blood (metaphorical), Matt. 23:35; Christ's judgment, John 5:30; any circumstance, fact or deed, Matt. 20:4 (v. 7, in some mss.); Luke 12:57; **Acts 4:19**; Eph. 6:1; Phil. 1:7; 4:8; Col. 4:1; 2 Thess. 1:6; "the commandment" (the Law), Rom. 7:12; works, 1 John 3:12, the ways of God, Rev. 15:3.

Murderer *phoneus* (5406), akin to *phoneuo* and *phonos*, is used (a) in a general sense, in the singular, 1 Pet. 4:15; in the plural, Rev. 21:8; 22:15; (b) of those guilty of particular acts, Matt. 22:7; **Acts 3:14**, lit. "a man (*aner*), a murderer"; **7:52**; **28:4**.

Granted *charizomai* (5483), primarily denotes "to show favor or kindness," as in Gal. 3:18, RV, "hath granted" (KJV, "gave"); then, to "give" freely, bestow graciously; in this sense it is used almost entirely of that which is "given" by God, **Acts 27:24**, "God hath granted thee all them that sail with thee" (RV); in Rom. 8:32, "shall ... freely give"; 1 Cor. 2:12, "are freely given"; Phil. 1:29, "it hath been granted" (said of believing on Christ and suffering for Him); 2:9, "hath given" (said of the name of Jesus as "given" by God); Philem. 22, "I shall be granted unto you" (RV). In Luke 7:21, it is said in regard to the blind, upon whom Christ "bestowed" sight (RV). The only exceptions, in this sense of the word, as to divinely imparted "gifts," are **Acts 3:14**, of the "granting" of Barabbas by Pilate to the Jews, and **Acts 25:11**, **16**, of the "giving" up of a prisoner to his accusers or to execution.

3:15 And killed the Prince of life, whom God hath raised from the dead; whereof we are witnesses.

Prince *archegos* (747), translated "Prince" in **Acts 3:15** (marg., "Author") and **5:31**, but "Author" in Heb. 2:10, RV, "Captain," RV marg., and KJV, and "Author" in 12:2, primarily signifies "one who takes a lead in, or provides the first occasion of, anything." In the Sept. it is used of the chief of a tribe or family, Num. 13:2 (RV, prince); of the "heads" of the children of Israel, v. 3; a captain of the whole people, 14:4; in Micah 1:13, of Lachish as the leader of the sin of the daughter of Sion: there, as in Heb. 2:10, the word suggests a combination of the meaning of leader with that of the source from whence a thing proceeds. That Christ is the Prince of life signifies, as Chrysostom says, that "the life

He had was not from another; the Prince or Author of life must be He who has life from Himself." But the word does not necessarily combine the idea of the source or originating cause with that of leader. In Heb. 12:2 where Christ is called the "Author and Perfecter of faith," He is represented as the one who takes precedence in faith and is thus the perfect exemplar of it. The pronoun "our" does not correspond to anything in the original, and may well be omitted. Christ in the days of His flesh trod undeviatingly the path of faith, and as the Perfecter has brought it to a perfect end in His own person. Thus He is the leader of all others who tread that path.

Life *zoe* (2222), (Eng., "zoo," "zoology") is used in the NT "of life as a principle, life in the absolute sense, life as God has it, that which the Father has in Himself, and which He gave to the Incarnate Son to have in Himself, John 5:26, and which the Son manifested in the world, 1 John 1:2. From this life man has become alienated in consequence of the Fall, Eph. 4:18, and of this life men become partakers through faith in the Lord Jesus Christ, John 3:15, who becomes its Author to all such as trust in Him, **Acts 3:15**, and who is therefore said to be 'the life' of the believer, Col. 3:4, for the life that He gives He maintains, John 6:35, 63. Eternal life is the present actual possession of the believer because of his relationship with Christ, John 5:24; 1 John 3:14, and that it will one day extend its domain to the sphere of the body is assured by the Resurrection of Christ, 2 Cor. 5:4; 2 Tim. 1:10. This life is not merely a principle of power and mobility, however, for it has moral associations which are inseparable from it, as of holiness and righteousness. Death and sin, life and holiness, are frequently contrasted in the Scriptures.

"*Zoe* is also used of that which is the common possession of all animals and men by nature, **Acts 17:25**; 1 John 5:16, and of the present sojourn of man upon the earth with reference to its duration, Luke 16:25; 1 Cor. 15:19; 1 Tim. 4:8; 1 Pet. 3:10. 'This life' is a term equivalent to 'the gospel,' 'the faith,' 'Christianity,' **Acts 5:20**."

Raised *see* Lifted at *Acts 3:7*.

Witnesses *see Acts 1:8*.

3:16 And his name through faith in his name hath made this man strong, whom ye see and know: yea, the faith which is by him hath given him this perfect soundness in the presence of you all.

Strong *see* Strength at *Acts 3:7*.

Soundness *holokleria* (3647), "completeness, soundness" (akin to *holokleros*), occurs in **Acts 3:16**. In the Sept., Isa. 1:6.

Presence *apenanti* (561), lit., "from over against, opposite to" (*apo*, "from," *enantios*, "against"), is translated "contrary to" in **Acts 17:7**; "before" in Matt. 27:24; Rom. 3:18; "over against"; in Matt. 27:61; "in the presence of," in **Acts 3:16**; "against," **Acts 17:7**.

3:17 And now, brethren, I wot that through ignorance ye did *it*, as *did* also your rulers.

Brethren *see Acts 2:29*.

Wot *oida*, "to know," in **Acts 3:17**; **7:40**; Rom. 11:2.

Ignorance *agnoia* (52), lit., "want of knowledge or perception" (akin to *agnoeo*, "to be ignorant"), denotes "ignorance" on the part of the Jews regarding Christ, **Acts 3:17**; of Gentiles in regard to God, **17:30**; Eph. 4:18 (here including the idea of willful blindness: see Rom. 1:28, not the "ignorance" which mitigates guilt); 1 Pet. 1:14, of the former unregenerate condition of those who became believers (RV, "in *the time of* your ignorance").

Rulers *archon* (758), the present participle of the verb *archo*, "to rule"; denotes "a ruler, a prince." It is used as follows ("p" denoting "prince," or "princes"; "r," "ruler" or "rulers"): (a) of Christ, as "the Ruler (KJV, Prince) of the kings of the earth," Rev. 1:5; (b) of rulers of nations, Matt. 20:25, RV, "r," KJV, "p"; **Acts 4:26**, "r"; **7:27**, "r"; **7:35**, "r" (twice); (c) of judges and magistrates, **Acts 16:19**, "r"; Rom. 13:3, "r"; (d) of members of the Sanhedrin, Luke 14:1, RV, "r" (KJV, "chief"); 23:13, 35, "r"; so 24:20, John 3:1; 7:26, 48; 12:42, RV, "r" (KJV, "chief r"); "r" in **Acts 3:17**; **4:5, 8**; **13:27**; **14:5**; (e) of rulers of synagogues, Matt. 9:18, 23, "r"; so Luke 8:41; 18:18; (f) of the Devil, as "prince" of this world, John 12:31; 14:30; 16:11; of the power of the air, Eph. 2:2, "the air" being that sphere in which the inhabitants of the world live and which, through the rebellious and godless condition of humanity, constitutes the seat of his authority; (g) of Beelzebub, the "prince" of the demons, Matt. 9:24; 12:24; Mark 3:22; Luke 11:15.

3:18 But those things, which God before had shewed by the mouth of all his prophets, that Christ should suffer, he hath so fulfilled.

Before ... shewed *prokatangello* (4293), "to announce beforehand" (*pro*, "before," *katangello*, "to proclaim"), is translated "foreshewed" in **Acts 3:18**, RV (KJV, "before had shewed"); in **7:52**, KJV and RV, "shewed before."

Mouth *see Acts 1:16.*

Suffer *see* Passion at *Acts 1:3.*

3:19 Repent ye therefore, and be converted, that your sins may be blotted out, when the times of refreshing shall come from the presence of the Lord;

Repent *see Acts 2:38.*

Converted *epistrepho* (1994), "to turn about, turn towards" (*epi*, "towards" and *strepho*), is used transitively, and so rendered "convert" (of causing a person to turn) in Jas. 5:19-20. Elsewhere, where the KJV translates this verb, either in the middle voice and intransitive use, or the passive, the RV adheres to the middle voice significance, and translates by "turn again," Matt. 13:15; Mark 4:12; Luke 22:32; **Acts 3:19**; **28:27**.

May "May," "might," sometimes translate the prepositional phrase *eis*, "unto," with the definite article, followed by the infinitive mood of some verb, expressing purpose, e.g., **Acts 3:19**, "may be blotted out," lit., "unto the blotting out of"; Rom. 3:26, "that he might be," lit., "unto his being"; so 8:29; 2 Cor. 1:4, "that we may be able," lit., "unto our being able"; Eph. 1:18, "that ye may know," lit., "unto your knowing"; **Acts 7:19**; Rom. 1:11; 4:16; 12:2; 15:13; Phil. 1:10; 1 Thess. 3:10, 13; 2 Thess. 1:5; 2:6, 10; Heb. 12:10. In Luke 20:20 the best mss. have *hoste*, "so as to," RV, as, e.g., in 1 Pet. 1:21. Sometimes the article with the infinitive mood without a preceding preposition, expresses result, e.g., Luke 21:22; **Acts 26:18** (twice), "that they may turn," RV; cf. Rom. 6:6; 11:10; 1 Cor. 10:13; Phil. 3:10, "that I may know"; Jas. 5:17.

Blotted out *exaleipho* (1813), from *ek*, "out," used intensively, and *aleipho*, "to wipe," signifies "to wash, or to smear completely." Hence, metaphorically, in the sense of removal, "to wipe away, wipe off, obliterate"; **Acts 3:19**, of sins; Col. 2:14, of writing; Rev. 3:5, of a name in a book; Rev. 7:17; 21:4, of tears.

Times *kairos* (2540), primarily, "due measure, fitness, proportion," is used in the NT to signify "a season, a time, a period" possessed of certain characteristics, frequently rendered "time" or "times"; in the following the RV substitutes "season" for the KJV "time," thus distinguishing the meaning from *chronos*: Matt. 11:25; 12:1; 14:1; 21:34; Mark 11:13; **Acts 3:19**; **7:20**; **17:26**; Rom. 3:26; 5:6; 9:9; 13:11; 1 Cor. 7:5; Gal. 4:10; 1 Thess. 2:17, lit., "for a season (of an hour)", 2 Thess. 2:6; in Eph. 6:18, "at all seasons" (KJV, "always"); in Titus 1:3, "His own seasons" (marg., "its"; KJV, "in due times"); in the preceding clause *chronos* is used. The characteristics of a period are exemplified in the use of the term with regard, e.g. to harvest, Matt. 13:30; reaping, Gal. 6:9; punishment, Matt. 8:29; discharging duties, Luke 12:42; opportunity for doing anything, whether good, e.g., Matt. 26:18; Gal. 6:10 ("opportunity"); Eph. 5:16; or evil, e.g., Rev. 12:12; the fulfillment of prophecy, Luke 1:20; **Acts 3:19**; 1 Pet. 1:11; a time suitable for a purpose, Luke 4:13, lit., "until a season"; 2 Cor. 6:2.

Refreshing *anapsuxis* (403), "a refreshing," occurs in **Acts 3:19**. In the Sept., Ex. 8:15. In the papyri it is used of "obtaining relief."

3:20 And he shall send Jesus Christ, which before was preached unto you:

Send *apostello* (649), lit., "to send forth" (*apo*, "from"), akin to *apostolos*, "an apostle," denotes (a) "to send on service, or with a commission." (1) of persons; Christ, sent by the Father, Matt. 10:40; 15:24; 21:37; Mark 9:37; 12:6; Luke 4:18, 43; 9:48; 10:16; John 3:17; 5:36, 38; 6:29, 57; 7:29; 8:42; 10:36; 11:42; 17:3, 8, 18 (1st part), 21, 23, 25; 20:21; **Acts 3:20** (future); 3:26; 1 John 4:9, 10, 14; the Holy Spirit, Luke 24:49; 1 Pet. 1:12; Rev. 5:6; Moses, **Acts 7:35**; John the Baptist, John 1:6; 3:28; disciples and apostles, e.g., Matt. 10:16; Mark 11:1; Luke 22:8; John 4:38; 17:18 (2nd part); **Acts 26:17**; servants, e.g., Matt. 21:34; Luke 20:10; officers and officials, Mark 6:27; John 7:32; **Acts 16:35**; messengers, e.g., **Acts 10:8**, **17**, **20**; **15:27**; evangelists, Rom. 10:15; angels, e.g., Matt. 24:31; Mark 13:27; Luke 1:19, 26; Heb. 1:14; Rev. 1:1; 22:6; demons, Mark 5:10; (2) of things, e.g., Matt. 21:3; Mark 4:29, RV, marg., "sendeth forth," text, "putteth forth" (KJV, "... in"); **Acts 10:36**; **11:30**; **28:28**; (b) "to send away, dismiss," e.g., Mark 8:26; 12:3; Luke 4:18, "to set (at liberty)."

Preached *prokerusso* (4296), lit., "to proclaim as a herald," is used in **Acts 13:24**, "had first preached." Some mss. have the verb in **Acts 3:20**. Also *procheirizo* (4400), from *procheiros*, "at hand," signifies (a) "to deliver up, appoint," **Acts 3:20** (RV, "appointed"); (b) in the middle voice, "to take into one's hand, to determine, appoint beforehand," translated "appointed" in **Acts 22:14**, RV (for KJV, "hath chosen"), and "to appoint" in **26:16** (for KJV, "to make").

3:21 Whom the heaven must receive until the times of restitution of all things, which God hath spoken by the mouth of all his holy prophets since the world began.

Must *dei* (1163), an impersonal verb, signifying "it is necessary" or "one must," "one ought," is found most frequently in the Gospels, Acts and the Apocalypse, and is used (a) of a necessity lying in the nature of the case e.g., John 3:30; 2 Tim. 2:6; (b) of necessity brought about by circumstances, e.g., Matt. 26:35, RV, "must," KJV, "should"; John 4:4; **Acts 27:21**, "should"; 2 Cor. 11:30; in the case of Christ, by reason of the Father's will, e.g., Luke 2:49; 19:5; (c) of necessity as to what is required that something may be brought about, e.g., Luke 12:12, "ought"; John 3:7; **Acts 9:6**; 1 Cor. 11:19; Heb. 9:26; (d) of a necessity of law, duty, equity, e.g., Matt. 18:33, "shouldest"; 23:23, "ought"; Luke 15:32, "it was meet"; **Acts 15:5**, "it is needful" (RV); Rom. 1:27, RV, "was due," KJV, "was meet" (of a recompense due by the law of God); frequently requiring the rendering "ought," e.g., Rom. 8:26; 12:3; 1 Cor. 8:2; (e) of necessity arising from the determinate will and counsel of God, e.g., Matt. 17:10; 24:6; 26:54; 1 Cor. 15:53, especially regarding the salvation of men through the death, resurrection and ascension of Christ, e.g., John 3:14; **Acts 3:21**; **4:12**.

Receive *dechomai* (1209), "to receive by deliberate and ready reception of what is offered," is used of (a) taking with the hand, taking hold, taking hold of or up, e.g., Luke 2:28, RV, "he received (Him)," KJV, "took he (Him) up"; 16:6, 7; 22:17; Eph. 6:17; (b) "receiving," said of a place "receiving" a person, of Christ into the Heavens, **Acts 3:21**; or of persons in giving access to someone as a visitor, e.g., John 4:45; 2 Cor. 7:15; Gal. 4:14; Col. 4:10; by way of giving hospitality, etc., e.g., Matt. 10:14, 40 (four times), 41 (twice); 18:5; Mark 6:11; 9:37; Luke 9:5, 48, 53; 10:8, 10; 16:4; v. 9, of reception, "into the eternal tabernacles," said of followers of Christ who have used "the mammon of unrighteousness" to render assistance to ("make ... friends of") others; of Rahab's reception of the spies, Heb. 11:31; of the reception, by the Lord, of the spirit of a departing believer, **Acts 7:59**; of "receiving" a gift, 2 Cor. 8:4 (in some mss.; RV follows those which omit it); of the favorable reception of testimony and teaching, etc., Luke 8:13; **Acts 8:14**; **11:1**; **17:11**; 1 Cor. 2:14; 2 Cor. 8:17; 1 Thess. 1:6; 2:13, where *paralambano* is used in the 1st part, "ye received," *dechomai* in the 2nd part, "ye accepted," RV (KJV, "received"), the former refers to the ear, the latter, adding the idea of appropriation, to the heart; Jas. 1:21; in 2 Thess. 2:10, "the love of the truth,:" i.e., love for the truth; cf. Matt. 11:14, "if ye are willing to receive it," an elliptical construction frequent in Greek writings; of "receiving," by way of bearing with, enduring, 2 Cor. 11:16; of "receiving" by way of getting, **Acts 22:5**; **28:21**, of becoming partaker of benefits, Mark 10:15; Luke 18:17; **Acts 7:38**; 2 Cor. 6:1; 11:4 (last clause "did accept": cf. *lambano* in previous clauses); Phil. 4:18.

Times *see* ***Acts 1:7***.

Restitution *apokatastasis* (605), from *apo*, "back, again," *kathistemi*, "to set in order," is used in **Acts 3:21**, RV, "restoration" (KJV, "restitution"). In the papyri it is used of a temple cell of a goddess, a "repair" of a public way, the "restoration" of estates to rightful owners, a "balancing" of accounts. Apart from papyri illustrations the word is found in an Egyptian reference to a consummating agreement of the world's cyclical periods, an idea somewhat similar to that in the Acts passage (Moulton and Milligan).

Began In the following passages the KJV faulty translations, "since the world began," etc., are rightly rendered in the RV by "before times eternal" and similar phrases, Rom. 16:25; Eph. 3:9; 2 Tim. 1:9; Titus 1:2. The alteration has not been made, however, in Luke 1:70; John 9:32; **Acts 3:21**; **15:18**.

3:22 For Moses truly said unto the fathers, A prophet shall the Lord your God raise up unto you of your brethren, like unto me; him shall ye hear in all things whatsoever he shall say unto you.

Prophet *prophetes* (4396), "one who speaks forth or openly", "a proclaimer of a divine message," denoted among the Greeks an interpreter of the oracles of the gods. In the NT the word is used (a) of "the OT prophets," e.g., Matt. 5:12; Mark 6:15; Luke 4:27; John 8:52; Rom. 11:3; (b) of "prophets in general," e.g., Matt. 10:41; 21:46; Mark 6:4; (c) of "John the Baptist," Matt. 21:26; Luke 1:76; (d) of "prophets in the churches," e.g., **Acts 13:1**; **15:32**; **21:10**; 1 Cor. 12:28, 29; 14:29, 32, 37; Eph. 2:20; 3:5; 4:11; (e) of "Christ, as the aforepromised Prophet," e.g., John 1:21; 6:14; 7:40; **Acts 3:22**; **7:37**, or, without the article, and, without reference to the Old Testament, Mark 6:15; Luke 7:16; in Luke 24:19 it is used with *aner*, "a man"; John 4:19; 9:17; (f) of "two witnesses" yet to be raised up for special purposes, Rev. 11:10, 18; (g) of "the Cretan poet Epimenides," Titus 1:12; (h) by metonymy, of "the writings of prophets," e.g., Luke 24:27; **Acts 8:28**.

Raise *see* **Raised** at ***Acts 2:24***.

Brethren *see* ***Acts 2:29***.

Like unto *hos* (5613), used as a relative adverb of manner, means "as, like as," etc., and is translated "like," e.g., in Matt. 6:29; Mark 4:31; Luke 12:27; in **Acts 3:22** and **7:37** (see RV, marg.); in **8:32** (2nd part), RV, "as" (KJV, "like"); Rev. 2:18, RV (the rendering should have been "as" here); 18:21, RV, "as it were" (KJV, "like"); 21:11, 2nd part (ditto).

Hear *akouo* (191), "to hear," is rendered "hearken" in the KJV and RV, in Mark 4:3; **Acts 4:19**; **7:2**; **15:13**; Jas. 2:5; in the RV only, in **Acts 3:22, 23**; **13:16** (KJV, "give audience"); **15:12**, "hearkened" (KJV "gave audience").

Say *laleo* (2980), "to speak," is sometimes translated "to say"; in the following where the KJV renders it thus, the RV alters it to the verb "to speak," e.g., John 8:25 (3rd part), 26; 16:6; 18:20 (2nd part), 21 (1st part); **Acts 3:22** (2nd part); 1 Cor. 9:8 (1st part); Heb. 5:5; in the following the RV uses the verb "to say," John 16:18; **Acts 23:18** (2nd part); **26:22** (2nd part); Heb. 11:18.

3:23 And it shall come to pass, *that* every soul, which will not hear that prophet, shall be destroyed from among the people.

Hear *see Acts 3:22*.

Shall *see Acts 2:17*.

Pass *see Acts 2:17*.

Destroyed *exolothreuo* (1842), "to destroy utterly to slay wholly," is found in **Acts 3:23**, RV, "utterly destroyed," referring to the "destruction" of one who would refuse to hearken to the voice of God through Christ.

3:24 Yea, and all the prophets from Samuel and those that follow after, as many as have spoken, have likewise foretold of these days.

Follow In **Acts 3:24**, the adverb *kathexes*, "successively, in order," is translated "(them) that followed after," i.e., those who succeeded (him), lit., "the (ones) successively (to him)."

After *kathexes* (2517), denotes "afterward," or "in order," Luke 1:3; 8:1; **Acts 3:24**; **11:4**; **18:23**.

Likewise *kai* (2532), "and, even," is translated "likewise" in the KJV and RV of Matt. 20:10 (last *kai* in the verse), more lit., "even they"; elsewhere the RV has "also," for the KJV, "likewise," Matt. 18:35; 24:33; Luke 3:14; 17:10; 19:19; 21:31; **Acts 3:24**; 1 Cor. 14:9; Col. 4:16; 1 Pet. 4:1; in Matt. 21:24, the KJV has "in like wise" (RV, "likewise").

Foretold In **Acts 3:24** some mss. have *prokatangello*; the most authentic have *katangello*, RV, "told."

3:25 Ye are the children of the prophets, and of the covenant which God made with our fathers, saying unto Abraham, And in thy seed shall all the kindreds of the earth be blessed.

Children *huios* (5207), primarily signifies the relation of offspring to parent (see John 9:18-20; Gal. 4:30). It is often used metaphorically of prominent moral characteristics. "It is used in the NT of (a) male offspring, Gal. 4:30; (b) legitimate, as opposed to illegitimate offspring, Heb. 12:8; (c) descendants, without reference to sex, Rom. 9:27; (d) friends attending a wedding, Matt. 9:15; (e) those who enjoy certain privileges, **Acts 3:25**; (f) those who act in a certain way, whether evil, Matt. 23:31, or good, Gal. 3:7; (g) those who manifest a certain character, whether evil, **Acts 13:10**; Eph. 2:2, or good, Luke 6:35; **Acts 4:36**; Rom. 8:14; (h) the destiny that corresponds with the character, whether evil, Matt. 23:15; John 17:12; 2 Thess. 2:3, or good, Luke 20:36; (i) the dignity of the relationship with God whereinto men are brought by the Holy Spirit when they believe on the Lord Jesus Christ, Rom. 8:19; Gal. 3:26....

"As to moral characteristics, the following phrases are used: (a) sons of God, Matt. 5:9, 45; Luke 6:35; (b) sons of the light, Luke 16:8; John 12:36; (c) sons of the day, 1 Thess. 5:5; (d) sons of peace, Luke 10:6; (e) sons of this world, Luke 16:8; (f) sons of disobedience, Eph. 2:2; (g) sons of the evil one, Matt. 13:38, cf. 'of the Devil,' **Acts 13:10**; (h) son of perdition, John 17:12; 2 Thess. 2:3. It is also used to describe characteristics other than moral, as: (i) sons of the resurrection, Luke 20:36; (j) sons of the Kingdom, Matt. 8:12; 13:38; (k) sons of the bridechamber, Mark 2:19; (l) sons of exhortation, **Acts 4:36**; (m) sons of thunder, Boanerges, Mark 3:17."

Covenant *diatheke* (1242), primarily signifies "a disposition of property by will or otherwise." In its use in the Sept., it is the rendering of a Hebrew word meaning a "covenant" or agreement (from a verb signifying "to cut or divide," in allusion to a sacrificial custom in connection with "covenant-making," e.g., Gen. 15:10, "divided" Jer. 34:18-19). In contradistinction to the English word "covenant" (lit., "a coming together"), which signifies a mutual undertaking between two parties or more, each binding himself to fulfill obligations, it does not in itself contain the idea of joint obligation, it mostly signifies an obligation undertaken by a single person. For instance, in Gal. 3:17 it is used as an alternative to a "promise" (vv. 16-18). God enjoined upon Abraham the rite of circumcision, but His promise to Abraham, here called a "covenant," was not conditional upon the observance of circumcision, though a penalty attached to its nonobservance.

"The NT uses of the word may be analyzed as follows: (a) a promise or undertaking, human or divine, Gal. 3:15; (b) a promise or undertaking on the part of God, Luke 1:72; **Acts 3:25**; Rom. 9:4; 11:27; Gal. 3:17Eph. 2:12; Heb. 7:22; 8:6, 8, 10; 10:16; (c) an agreement, a mutual undertaking, between God and Israel, see Deut. 29-30 (described as a 'commandment,' Heb. 7:18, cf. v. 22); Heb. 8:9; 9:20; (d) by metonymy, the token of the covenant, or promise, made to Abraham, **Acts 7:8**, (e) by metonymy, the record of the covenant, 2 Cor. 3:14; Heb. 9:4; cf. Rev. 11:19; (f) the basis, established by the death of Christ, on which the salvation of men is secured, Matt. 26:28; Mark 14:24; Luke 22:20; 1 Cor. 11:25; 2 Cor. 3:6; Heb. 10:29; 12:24; 13:20.

Made *diatithemi* (1303), "to arrange, dispose," is used only in the middle voice in the NT; in Heb. 9:16, 17, the present participle with the article, lit., "the (one) making a testament (or covenant)," virtually a noun, "the testator" (the covenanting one); it is used of "making a covenant" in 8:10 and 10:16 and **Acts 3:25**. In "covenant-making," the sacrifice of a victim was customary (Gen. 15:10; Jer. 34:18, 19). He who "made a covenant" did so at the cost of a life. While the terminology in Heb. 9:16, 17 has the appearance of being appropriate to the circumstances of making a will, there is excellent reason for adhering to the meaning "covenant-making." The rendering "the death of the testator" would make Christ a Testator, which He was not. He did not die simply that the terms of a testamentary disposition might be fulfilled for the heirs. Here He who is "the Mediator of a new covenant" (v. 15) is Himself the Victim whose death was necessary. The idea of "making a will" destroys the argument of v. 18. In spite of various advocacies of the idea of a will, the weight of evidence is confirmatory of what Hatch, in *Essays in Biblical Greek*, p. 48, says: "There can be little doubt that the word (*diatheke*) must be invariably taken in this sense of 'covenant' in the NT, and especially in a book ... so impregnated with the language of the Sept. as the Epistle to the Hebrews" (see also Westcott, and W. F. Moulton). We may render somewhat literally thus: 'For where a covenant (is), a death (is) necessary to be brought in of the one covenanting; for a covenant over dead ones (victims) is sure, since never has it force when the one covenanting lives' [Christ being especially in view]. The writer is speaking from a Jewish point of view, not from that of the Greeks. "To adduce the fact that in the case of wills the death of the testator is the condition of validity, is, of course, no proof at all that a death is necessary to make a covenant valid.... To support his argument, proving the necessity of Christ's death, the writer adduces the general law that he who makes a covenant does so at the expense of life" (Marcus Dods).

Seed *sperma* (4690), akin to *speiro*, "to sow" (Eng., "sperm," "spermatic," etc.), has the following usages, (a) agricultural and botanical, e.g., Matt. 13:24, 27, 32; 1 Cor. 15:38; 2 Cor. 9:10; (b) physiological, Heb. 11:11; (c) metaphorical and by metonymy for "offspring, posterity," (1) of natural offspring, e.g., Matt. 22:24, 25, RV, "seed" (KJV, "issue"); John 7:42; 8:33, 37; **Acts 3:25**; Rom. 1:3; 4:13, 16, 18; 9:7 (twice), 8, 29; 11:1; 2 Cor. 11:22; Heb. 2:16; 11:18; Rev. 12:17; Gal. 3:16, 19, 29; in the 16th v., "He saith not, And to seeds, as of many; but as of one, And to thy seed, which is Christ," quoted from the Sept. of Gen. 13:15 and 17:7, 8, there is especial stress on the word "seed," as referring to an individual (here, Christ) in fulfillment of the promises to Abraham—a unique use of the singular. While the plural form "seeds," neither in Hebrew nor in Greek, would have been natural any more than in English (it is not so used in Scripture of human offspring; its plural occurrence is in 1 Sam. 8:15, of crops), yet if the divine intention had been to refer to Abraham's natural descendants, another word could have been chosen in the plural, such as "children"; all such words were, however, set aside, "seed" being selected as one that could be used in the singular, with the purpose of showing that the "seed" was Messiah. Some of the rabbis had even regarded "seed," e.g., in Gen. 4:25 and Isa. 53:10, as referring to the Coming One. Descendants were given to Abraham by other than natural means, so that through him Messiah might come, and the point of the apostle's argument is that since the fulfillment of the promises of God is secured alone by Christ, they only who are "in Christ" can receive them; (2) of spiritual offspring, Rom. 4:16, 18; 9:8; here "the children of the promise are reckoned for a seed" points, firstly, to Isaac's birth as being not according to the ordinary course of nature but by divine promise, and, secondly, by analogy, to the fact that all believers are children of God by spiritual birth; Gal. 3:29.

Kindreds *patria* (3965), primarily "an ancestry, lineage," signifies in the NT "a family or tribe" (in the Sept. it is used of related people, but in a narrower sense than *phule*, "a tribe," e.g., Exod. 12:3; Num. 32:28); it is used of the "family" of David, Luke

2:4, RV, for KJV, "lineage"; in the wider sense of "nationalities, races," **Acts 3:25**, RV, "families," for KJV, "kindreds"; in Eph. 3:15, RV, "every family," for KJV, "the whole family," the reference being to all those who are spiritually related to God the Father, He being the Author of their spiritual relationship to Him as His children, they being united to one another in "family" fellowship (*patria* is akin to *pater*, "a father"); Luther's translation, "all who bear the name of children," is advocated by Cremer, p. 474. The phrase, however, is lit., "every family."

Blessed *eneulogeomai* (1757), "to bless," is used in the passive voice, **Acts 3:25**, and Gal. 3:8. The prefix *en* apparently indicates the person on whom the blessing is conferred.

3:26 Unto you first God, having raised up his Son Jesus, sent him to bless you, in turning away every one of you from his iniquities.

Raised *see Acts 2:24.*

Bless *eulogeo* (2127), lit., "to speak well of" (*eu*, "well," *logos*, "a word"), signifies, (a) "to praise, to celebrate with praises," of that which is addressed to God, acknowledging His goodness, with desire for His glory, Luke 1:64; 2:28; 24:51, 53; Jas. 3:9; (b) "to invoke blessings upon a person," e.g., Luke 6:28; Rom. 12:14. The present participle passive, "blessed, praised," is especially used of Christ in Matt. 21:9; 23:39, and the parallel passages; also in John 12:13; (c) "to consecrate a thing with solemn prayers, to ask God's blessing on a thing," e.g., Luke 9:16; 1 Cor. 10:16; (d) "to cause to prosper, to make happy, to bestow blessings on," said of God, e.g., in **Acts 3:26**; Gal. 3:9; Eph. 1:3. Cf. the synonym *aineo*, "to praise."

Turning *apostrepho* (654), denotes (a) "to cause to turn away (*apo*), to remove," Rom. 11:26; 2 Tim. 4:4 (1st clause); metaphorically, "to turn away from allegiance, pervert," Luke 23:14; (b) "to make to return, put back," Matt. 26:52, (c) in the passive voice, used reflexively, "to turn oneself away from," Matt. 5:42; 2 Tim. 1:15; Titus 1:14; Heb. 12:25; in the active voice, **Acts 3:26**.

Iniquities *poneria* (4189), akin to *poneo*, "to toil" (cf. *poneros*, "bad, worthless"), denotes "wickedness," and is so translated in Matt. 22:18; Mark 7:22 (plural); Luke 11:39; Rom. 1:29; 1 Cor. 5:8; Eph. 6:12; in **Acts 3:26**, "iniquities." Cf. *kakia*, "evil."

Chapter 4

4:1 And as they spake unto the people, the priests, and the captain of the temple, and the Sadducees, came upon them,

Captain *strategos* (4755), originally the commander of an army (from *stratos*, "an army," and *ago*, "to lead"), came to denote "a civil commander, a governor" (Latin, *duumvir*), the highest magistrate, or any civil officer in chief command, **Acts 16:20, 22, 35-36, 38**; also the "chief captain" of the Temple, himself Levite, having command of the Levites who kept guard in and around the Temple, Luke 22:4, 52; **Acts 4:1; 5:24, 26**. Cf. Jer. 20:1.

Came *ephistemi* (2186), signifies "to stand by or over" (*epi*, "upon"), Luke 2:9, RV; **Acts 12:7** "before," **Acts 11:11**; to come upon, Luke 20:1 (here with the idea of suddenness); **Acts 4:1; 6:12; 23:27**; 1 Thess. 5:3; "coming up," of the arrival of Anna at the Temple, Luke 2:38; "came up to (Him)," of Martha, Luke 10:40; "is come," 2 Tim. 4:6 (probably with the same idea as in Luke 20:1). The RV is significant in all these places.

4:2 Being grieved that they taught the people, and preached through Jesus the resurrection from the dead.

Grieved *diaponeo*, "to work out with labor," in the passive voice, "to be sore troubled," is rendered "being grieved" in **Acts 4:2** and **16:18**, KJV (RV, "sore troubled"). In some mss., Mark 14:4.

Preached *katangello*, "to proclaim," is always so translated in the RV; the KJV renders it by "to preach" in **Acts 4:2; 13:5, 38; 15:36; 17:3, 13**; 1 Cor. 9:14; Col. 1:28.

Resurrection *see Acts 1:22.*

4:3 And they laid hands on them, and put *them* in hold unto the next day: for it was now eventide.

Laid *epiballo* (1911), "to lay upon," is used of seizing men, to imprison them, **Acts 4:3**.

Put *see Acts 1:7.*

Hold *teresis* (5084), translated "hold" in **Acts 4:3**, KJV, "prison" in **5:18** (RV, "ward"), signifies (a) "a watching, guarding"; hence, "imprisonment, ward" (from *tereo*, "to watch, keep"); the RV, has "ward" in both places; (b) "a keeping," as of commandments, 1 Cor. 7:19.

Next day *aurion* (839), an adverb denoting "tomorrow," is used (a) with this meaning in Matt. 6:30; Luke 12:28; 13:32, 33; **Acts 23:15** (in some mss.), **20**; **25:22**; 1 Cor. 15:32; Jas. 4:13, (b) with the word *hemera*, "day," understood (occurring thus in the papyri), translated as a noun, "(the) morrow," Matt.

6:34 (twice); Luke 10:35; **Acts 4:3** (KJV, "next day"); **4:5**; Jas. 4:14. Also *epaurion*, "on the morrow," Matt. 27:62; John 1:29, 35; 12:12; **Acts 14:20**; **25:6**.

Eventide *hespera* (2073), properly, the feminine of the adjective *hesperos*, "of, or at, evening, western" (Lat., *vesper*, Eng., "vespers"), is used as a noun in Luke 24:29; **Acts 4:3**, "eventide"; **28:23**. Some mss. have the word in **20:15**, "in the evening (we touched)," instead of *hetera*, "next (day)."

4:4-5 Howbeit many of them which heard the word believed; and the number of the men was about five thousand.

And it came to pass on the morrow, that their rulers, and elders, and scribes,

Morrow *see* Next day at *Acts 4:3*.

Rulers *see Acts 3:17*.

Scribes *grammateus* (1122), from *gramma*, "a writing," denotes "a scribe, a man of letters, a teacher of the law"; the "scribes" are mentioned frequently in the Synoptists, especially in connection with the Pharisees, with whom they virtually formed one party (see Luke 5:21), sometimes with the chief priests, e.g., Matt. 2:4; Mark 8:31; 10:33; 11:18, 27; Luke 9:22. They are mentioned only once in John's Gospel, 8:3, three times in the Acts, **4:5**; **6:12**; **23:9**; elsewhere only in 1 Cor. 1:20, in the singular. They were considered naturally qualified to teach in the synagogues, Mark 1:22. They were ambitious of honor, e.g., Matt. 23:5–11, which they demanded especially from their pupils, and which was readily granted them, as well as by the people generally. Like Ezra (Ezra 7:12), the "scribes" were found originally among the priests and Levites. The priests being the official interpreters of the Law, the "scribes" ere long became an independent company; though they never held political power, they became leaders of the people. Their functions regarding the Law were to teach it, develop it, and use it in connection with the Sanhedrin and various local courts. They also occupied themselves with the sacred writings both historical and didactic. They attached the utmost importance to ascetic elements, by which the nation was especially separated from the Gentiles. In their regime piety was reduced to external formalism. Only that was of value which was governed by external precept. Life under them became a burden; they themselves sought to evade certain of their own precepts, Matt. 23:16ff.; Luke 11:46; by their traditions the Law, instead of being a help in moral and spiritual life, became an instrument for preventing true access to God, Luke 11:52. Hence the Lord's stern denunciations of them and the Pharisees.

4:6 And Annas the high priest, and Caiaphas, and John, and Alexander, and as many as were of the kindred of the high priest, were gathered together at Jerusalem.

Priest *archiereus* (749), designates "the high priests" of the Levitical order, frequently called "chief priests" in the NT, and including "ex-high priests" and members of "high priestly" families, e.g., Matt. 2:4; 16:21; 20:18; 21:15; in the singular, a "high priest," e.g., Abiathar, Mark 2:26; Annas and Caiaphas, Luke 3:2, where the RV rightly has "in the high priesthood of A. and C." (cf. **Acts 4:6**). As to the combination of the two in this respect, Annas was the "high priest" from AD 7-14, and, by the time referred

"If you were arrested for being a Christian, would there be enough evidence to convict you?"

DAVID OTIS FULLER

to, had been deposed for some years; his son-in-law, Caiaphas, the fourth "high priest" since his deposition, was appointed about AD 24. That Annas was still called the "high priest" is explained by the facts (1) that by the Mosaic law the high priesthood was held for life, Num. 35:25; his deposition was the capricious act of the Roman procurator, but he would still be regarded legally and religiously as "high priest" by the Jews; (2) that he probably still held the office of deputy-president of the Sanhedrin (cf. 2 Kings 25:18); (3) that he was a man whose age, wealth and family connections gave him a preponderant influence, by which he held the real sacerdotal power; indeed at this time the high priesthood was in the hands of a clique of some half dozen families; the language of the writers of the gospels is in accordance with this, in attributing the high priesthood rather to a caste than a person; (4) the "high priests" were at that period mere puppets of Roman authorities who deposed them at will, with the result that the title was used more loosely than in former days.

Kindred *genos* (1085), akin to *ginomai*, "to become," denotes (a) "a family," **Acts 4:6**, "kindred;" **7:13**, RV, "race" (KJV, "kindred"); **13:26**, "stock";

(b) "an offspring," **Acts 17:28**; Rev. 22:16; (c) "a nation, a race," Mark 7:26, RV, "race" (KJV, "nation"); **Acts 4:36**, RV "(a man of Cyprus) by race," KJV, "of the country (of Cyprus);" *genos* does not mean "a country;" the word here signifies "parentage" (Jews had settled in Cyprus from, or even before, the reign of Alexander the Great); **7:19**, RV, "race" (KJV, "kindred"); **18:2, 24**, RV, "by race" (KJV, "born"); 2 Cor. 11:26, "countrymen"; Gal. 1:14, RV, "countrymen" (KJV, "nation"); Phil. 3:5, "stock"; 1 Pet. 2:9, RV, "race" (KJV, "generation"); (d) "a kind, sort, class," Matt. 13:47, "kind"; in some mss. in 17:21, KJV, "kind;" Mark 9:29, "kind"; 1 Cor. 12:10, 28, "kinds" (KJV, "diversities"); 14:10 (ditto).

4:7 And when they had set them in the midst, they asked, By what power, or by what name, have ye done this?

Set *histemi* (2476), "to cause to stand," is translated "to set" in Matt. 4:5 (aorist tense in the best texts; some have the present, as in KJV); 18:2; 25:33; Mark 9:36; Luke 4:9; 9:47; John 8:3; **Acts 4:7**; **5:27**; **6:6**; v. **13**, "set up"; **22:30**; in Jude 24, RV, "to set" (KJV, "to present").

Asked *punthanomai* (4441), "to inquire," is translated "inquired" in Matt. 2:4, and **Acts 21:33**, RV (KJV, "demanded"); in Luke 15:26; 18:36 and **Acts 4:7** (KJV, "asked"); "inquired" (KJV, "inquired") in John 4:52; "inquire" (KJV, "inquire") in **Acts 23:20**; in **Acts 23:34** it denotes "to learn by inquiry," KJV, and RV, "when (he) understood"; elsewhere it is rendered by the verb "to ask," **Acts 10:18, 29**; **23:19**.

4:8 Then Peter, filled with the Holy Ghost, said unto them, Ye rulers of the people, and elders of Israel,

Filled *see Acts 2:4*.

Rulers *see Acts 3:17*.

People *laos* (2992), is used of (a) "the people at large," especially of people assembled, e.g., Matt. 27:25; Luke 1:21; 3:15; **Acts 4:27**; (b) "a people of the same race and language," e.g., Rev. 5:9; in the plural, e.g., Luke 2:31; Rom. 15:11; Rev. 7:9; 11:9; especially of Israel, e.g., Matt. 2:6; 4:23; John 11:50; **Acts 4:8**; Heb. 2:17; in distinction from their rulers and priests, e.g., Matt. 26:5; Luke 20:19; Heb. 5:3; in distinction from Gentiles, e.g., **Acts 26:17, 23**; Rom. 15:10; (c) of Christians as the people of God, e.g., **Acts 15:14**; Titus 2:14; Heb. 4:9; 1 Pet. 2:9.

4:9 If we this day be examined of the good deed done to the impotent man, by what means he is made whole;

Examined *anakrino* (350), "to examine, investigate," is used (a) of searching or enquiry, **Acts 17:11**; 1 Cor. 9:3; 10:25, 27; (b) of reaching a result of the enquiry, judging, 1 Cor. 2:14-15; 4:3-4; 14:24; (c) forensically, of examining by torture, Luke 23:14; **Acts 4:9**; **12:19**; **24:8**; **28:18**.

Of *epi*, "over," is so translated in Matt. 18:13, RV; "concerning" in **Acts 4:9**.

Good deed *euergesia* (2108), lit., "good work" (*eu*, "well," *ergon*, "work"), is found in **Acts 4:9**, "good deed," and 1 Tim. 6:2, "benefit."

Impotent *asthenes* (772), lit., "without strength," hence, "feeble, weak," is used of "bodily debility," Matt. 25:43, 44; some texts have it in Luke 9:2 (the best omit it, the meaning being "to heal" in general); 10:9; **Acts 5:15, 16**; in **4:9** it is rendered "impotent."

By what means In **Acts 4:9**, the phrase *en*, "in" or "by," with *tini* (from *tis*, "who"), lit., "in whom" (RV, marg.), is translated "by what means."

Whole *sozo* (4982), "to save," is sometimes rendered "to make whole," and, in the passive voice, "to be made whole," or "to be whole," e.g., Matt. 9:21, 22 (twice), and parallel passages; **Acts 4:9**.

4:10 Be it known unto you all, and to all the people of Israel, that by the name of Jesus Christ of Nazareth, whom ye crucified, whom God raised from the dead, *even* by him doth this man stand here before you whole.

Name *see* Names at *Acts 1:15*.

Raised *see* Lifted at *Acts 3:7*.

Stand *see* Stood at *Acts 1:10*.

Before *see Acts 2:25*.

Whole *hugies* (5199), (cf. Eng., "hygiene") is used especially in the Gospels of making sick folk "whole," Matt. 12:13; 15:31; Mark 3:5; 5:34; Luke 6:10; John 5:4, 6, 9, 11, 14, 15; 7:23; also **Acts 4:10**; of "sound (speech)," Titus 2:8.

4:11 This is the stone which was set at nought of you builders, which is become the head of the corner.

Set at nought *exoutheneo* (1848), "to make of no account" (*ex*, "out," *oudeis*, "nobody," alternatively written, *outheis*), "to regard as nothing, to despise utterly, to treat with contempt." This is usually translated to "set at nought," Luke 18:9, RV, KJV, "despised." So in Rom. 14:3. Both have "set at nought" in Luke 23:11; **Acts 4:11**; Rom. 14:10. Both have "despise" in 1 Cor. 16:11; Gal. 4:14, and 1 Thess. 5:20; in 2 Cor. 10:10, RV, "of no account," for KJV, "contemptible"; in 1 Cor. 1:28, KJV and RV, "despised." For the important rendering in 1 Cor. 6:4, RV.

Builders *oikodomeo* (3618), lit., "to build a house" (*oikos*, "a house," *domeo*, "to build"), hence, to build anything, e.g., Matt. 7:24; Luke 4:29; 6:48, RV, "well builded" (last clause of verse); John 2:20; is frequently used figuratively, e.g., **Acts 20:32** (some mss. have *epoikodomeo* here); Gal. 2:18; especially of edifying, **Acts 9:31**; Rom. 15:20; 1 Cor. 10:23; 14:4; 1 Thess. 5:11 (RV). In 1 Cor. 8:10 it is translated "emboldened" (marg., "builded up"). The participle with the article (equivalent to a noun) is rendered "builder," Matt. 21:42; **Acts 4:11**; 1 Pet. 2:7.

Corner *gonia* (1137), "an angle" (Eng., "coign"), signifies (a) "an external angle," as of the "corner" of a street, Matt. 6:5; or of a building, 21:42; Mark 12:10; Luke 20:17; **Acts 4:11**; 1 Pet. 2:7, "the corner stone or headstone of the corner"; or the four extreme limits of the earth, Rev. 7:1; 20:8; (b) "an internal corner," a secret place, **Acts 26:26**.

4:12 Neither is there salvation in any other: for there is none other name under heaven given among men, whereby we must be saved.

Salvation *soteria* (4991), denotes "deliverance, preservation, salvation." "Salvation" is used in the NT (a) of material and temporal deliverance from danger and apprehension, (1) national, Luke 1:69, 71; **Acts 7:25**, RV marg., "salvation" (text, "deliverance"); (2) personal, as from the sea, **Acts 27:34**; RV, "safety" (KJV, "health"); prison, Phil. 1:19; the flood, Heb. 11:7; (b) of the spiritual and eternal deliverance granted immediately by God to those who accept His conditions of repentance and faith in the Lord Jesus, in whom alone it is to be obtained, **Acts 4:12**, and upon confession of Him as Lord, Rom. 10:10; for this purpose the gospel is the saving instrument, Rom. 1:16; Eph. 1:13; (c) of the present experience of God's power to deliver from the bondage of sin, e.g., Phil. 2:12, where the special, though not the entire, reference is to the maintenance of peace and harmony; 1 Pet. 1:9; this present experience on the part of believers is virtually equivalent to sanctification; for this purpose, God is able to make them wise, 2 Tim. 3:15; they are not to neglect it, Heb. 2:3; (d) of the future deliverance of believers at the Parousia of Christ for His saints, a salvation which is the object of their confident hope, e.g., Rom. 13:11; 1 Thess. 5:8, and v. 9, where "salvation" is assured to them, as being deliverance from the wrath of God destined to be executed upon the ungodly at the end of this age (see 1 Thess. 1:10); 2 Thess. 2:13; Heb. 1:14; 9:28; 1 Pet. 1:5; 2 Pet. 3:15; (e) of the deliverance of the nation of Israel at the second advent of Christ at the time of "the epiphany (or shining forth) of His Parousia" (2 Thess. 2:8); Luke 1:71; Rev. 12:10; (f) inclusively, to sum up all the blessings bestowed by God on men in Christ through the Holy Spirit, e.g., 2 Cor. 6:2; Heb. 5:9; 1 Pet. 1:9, 10; Jude 3; (g) occasionally, as standing virtually for the Savior, e.g., Luke 19:9; cf. John 4:22; (h) in ascriptions of praise to God, Rev. 7:10, and as that which it is His prerogative to bestow, 19:1 (RV).

Name *see* **Names** at ***Acts 1:15***.

Must be *dei*, it is necessary, expresses, not the obligation (as does *opheilo*) but the certainty or inevitableness of what is bound to happen, e.g., John 3:15, "must be lifted up" (i.e., inevitably), and **Acts 4:12**, "wherein we must be saved" (i.e., there is a certainty of salvation). *See also* **Must** at ***Acts 3:21***.

4:13 Now when they saw the boldness of Peter and John, and perceived that they were unlearned and ignorant men, they marvelled; and they took knowledge of them, that they had been with Jesus.

Boldness *parrhesia* (3954), from *pas*, "all," *rhesis*, "speech," denotes (a), primarily, "freedom of speech, unreservedness of utterance," **Acts 4:29, 31**; 2 Cor. 3:12; 7:4; Philem. 8; or "to speak without ambiguity, plainly," John 10:24; or "without figures of speech," John 16:25; (b) "the absence of fear in speaking boldly, hence, confidence, cheerful courage, boldness, without any connection necessarily with speech"; the RV has "boldness" in the following; **Acts 4:13**; Eph. 3:12; 1 Tim. 3:13; Heb. 3:6; 4:16; 10:19, 35; 1 John 2:28; 3:21; 4:17; 5:14; (c) the deportment by which one becomes conspicuous, John 7:4; 11:54, acts openly, or secures publicity, Col. 2:15.

Perceived *katalambano* (2638), properly signifies "to lay hold of"; then, "to lay hold of so as to possess as one's own, to appropriate." Hence it has the same twofold meaning as the Eng. "to apprehend"; (a), "to seize upon, take possession of," (1) with a beneficial effect, as of "laying hold" of the righteousness which is of faith, Rom. 9:30 (not there a matter of attainment, as in the Eng. versions, but of appropriation); of the obtaining of a prize, 1 Cor. 9:24 (RV, "attain"); of the apostle's desire "to apprehend," or "lay hold of," that for which he was apprehended by Christ, Phil. 3:12-13; (2) with a detrimental effect, e.g., of demon power, Mark 9:18; of human action in seizing upon a person, John 8:3-4; metaphorically, with the added idea of overtaking, of spiritual darkness in coming upon people, John 12:35; of the Day of the Lord, in suddenly coming upon unbelievers as a thief, 1 Thess. 5:4; (b), "to lay hold of" with the mind, to understand, perceive, e.g., metaphorically, of darkness with regard to light, John 1:5, though possibly here the sense is that of (a) as in 12:35; of mental perception, **Acts 4:13**; **10:34**; **25:25**; Eph. 3:18.

Unlearned *agrammatos* (62), lit., "unlettered" (*grammata*, "letters": *grapho*, "to write") **Acts 4:13**, is explained by GrimmThayer as meaning "unversed in the learning of the Jewish schools"; in the papyri, however, it occurs very frequently in a formula used by one who signs for another who cannot write, which suggests that the rulers, elders and scribes regarded the apostles as "unlettered" (Moulton and Milligan).

Ignorant *idiotes* (2399), primarily "a private person" in contrast to a state official, hence, "a person without professional knowledge, unskilled, uneducated, unlearned," is translated "unlearned" in 1 Cor. 14:16, 23, 24, of those who have no knowledge of the facts relating to the testimony borne in and by a local church; "rude" in 2 Cor. 11:6, of the apostle's mode of speech in the estimation of the Corinthians; "ignorant men," in **Acts 4:13**, of the speech of the apostle Peter and John in the estimation of the rulers, elders and scribes in Jerusalem. While *agrammatoi* ("unlearned") may refer to their being unacquainted with rabbinical learning, *idiotai* would signify "laymen," in contrast with the religious officials.

4:14 And beholding the man which was healed standing with them, they could say nothing against it.

Could *echo* (2192), the usual verb for "to have," is used with the following meanings: (a) "to hold, in the hand," etc., e.g., Rev. 1:16; 5:8; (b) "to hold fast, keep," Luke 19:20; metaphorically, of the mind and conduct, e.g., Mark 16:8; John 14:21; Rom. 1:28; 1 Tim. 3:9; 2 Tim. 1:13; (c) "to hold on, cling to, be next to," e.g., of accompaniment, Heb. 6:9, "things that accompany (salvation)," lit., "the things holding themselves of salvation" (RV, marg., "are near to"); of place, Mark 1:38, "next (towns)," lit., "towns holding nigh"; of time, e.g., Luke 13:33, "(the day) following," lit., "the holding (day)"; **Acts 13:44**; **20:15**; **21:26**; (d) "to hold, to count, consider, regard," e.g., Matt. 14:5; 21:46; Mark 11:32; Luke 14:18; Philem. 17; (e) "to involve," Heb. 10:35; Jas. 1:4; 1 John 4:18; (t) "to wear," of clothing, arms, etc., e.g., Matt. 3:4; 22:12; John 18:10; (g) "to be with child," of a woman, Mark 13:17; Rom. 9:10 (lit., "having conception"); (h) "to possess," the most frequent use, e.g., Matt. 8:20; 19:22; **Acts 9:14**; 1 Thess. 3:6; (i) of complaints, disputes, Matt. 5:23; Mark 11:25; **Acts 24:19**; Rev. 2:4, 20; (j) of ability, power, e.g., Luke 12:4; **Acts 4:14** (lit., "had nothing to say"); (k) of necessity, e.g., Luke 12:50; **Acts 23:17-19**; (l) "to be in a certain condition," as of readiness, **Acts 21:12** (lit., "I have readily"); of illness, Matt. 4:24, "all that were sick" (lit., "that had themselves sickly"); Mark 5:23, "lieth (lit., "hath herself") at the point of death"; Mark 16:18 "they shall recover" (lit., "shall have themselves well"), John 4:52, "he began to amend" (lit., "he had himself better"); of evil works, 1 Tim. 5:25, "they that are otherwise," (lit., "the things having otherwise"); to be so, e.g., **Acts 7:1**, "are these things so?" (lit., "have these things thus?"), of time, **Acts 24:25**, "for this time" (lit., "the thing having now").

Say ... against *anteipon* (483), which serves as an aorist tense of *antilego*, is rendered "gainsay" in Luke 21:15; "say against" in **Acts 4:14**.

4:15 But when they had commanded them to go aside out of the council, they conferred among themselves,

Commanded *keleuo* (2753), "to urge, incite, order," Matt. 14:9, 19; 15:35; 18:25; 27:58, 64; Luke 18:40; **Acts 4:15** (frequently in Acts, not subsequently in the NT).

Them Regarding *allelon*, "of one another," and its other forms, the RV substitutes "one another" for the KJV "themselves" in Mark 8:16; 9:34; Luke 4:36; John 6:52; 11:56; 16:17; 19:24; **Acts 26:31**; **28:4**; Rom. 2:15, but adheres to the rendering "themselves" in Mark 15:31; **Acts 4:15**; **28:25**.

Go *aperchomai* (565), "to go away" (*apo*, "from"), is chiefly used in the gospels; it signifies "to go aside" in **Acts 4:15**.

Council *sunedrion* (4892), properly, "a settling together" (*sun*, "together," *hedra*, "a seat"), hence, (a) "any assembly or session of persons deliberating or adjusting," as in the Sept. of Ps. 26:4 (lit., "with a council of vanity"); Prov. 22:10; Jer. 15:17, etc.; in the NT, e.g., Matt. 10:17; Mark 13:9; John 11:47, in particular, it denoted (b) "the Sanhedrin," the Great Council at Jerusalem, consisting of 71 members, namely, prominent members of the families of the high priest, elders and scribes. The Jews trace the origin of this to Num. 11:16. The more important causes came up before this tribunal. The Roman rulers of Judea permitted the Sanhedrin to try such cases, and even to pronounce sentence of death, with the condition that such a sentence should be valid only if confirmed by the Roman procurator. In John 11:47, it is used of a meeting of the Sanhedrin; in **Acts 4:15**, of the place of meeting.

Conferred *sumballo* (4820), lit., "to throw together" (*sun*, "with," *ballo*, "to throw"), is used of "conversation, to discourse or consult together, confer," **Acts 4:15**.

4:16 Saying, What shall we do to these men? for that indeed a notable miracle hath been done by them *is* manifest to all them that dwell in Jerusalem; and we cannot deny *it*.

Notable *gnostos* (1110), a later form of *gnotos*, most frequently denotes "known"; it is used ten times in the Acts, always with that meaning (save in **4:16**, where it means "notable"); twice in the Gospel of John, 18:15, 16; in Luke 2:44 and 23:49 it denotes "acquaintance"; elsewhere only in Rom. 1:19, "(that which) may be known (of God)," lit., "the knowable of God," referring to the physical universe, in the creation of which God has made Himself "knowable," that is, by the exercise of man's natural faculties, without such supernatural revelations as those given to Israel. *See also* **Known** at *Acts 1:19*.

Miracle *semeion* (4592), "a sign, mark, token" (akin to *semaino*, "to give a sign"; *sema*, "a sign"), is used of "miracles" and wonders as signs of divine authority; it is translated "miracles" in the RV and KJV of Luke 23:8; **Acts 4:16, 22**; most usually it is given its more appropriate meaning "sign," "signs," e.g., Matt. 12:38, 39, and in every occurrence in the Synoptists, excep Luke 23:8; in the following passages in John's Gospel the RV substitutes "sign" or "signs" for the KJV "miracle or miracles"; 2:11, 23; 3:2; 4:54; 6:2, 14, 26; 7:31; 9:16; 10:41; 11:47; 12:18, 37; the KJV also has "signs" elsewhere in this Gospel; in Acts, RV, "signs," KJV, "miracles," in **6:8**; **8:6**; **15:12**; elsewhere only in Rev. 13:14; 16:14; 19:20.

Manifest *phaneros* (5318), "open to sight, visible, manifest," is translated "manifest" in Luke 8:17; **Acts 4:16**; **7:13**, RV (KJV, "known"); Rom. 1:19; 1 Cor. 3:13; 11:19; 14:25; Gal. 5:19; Phil. 1:13; 1 Tim. 4:15 (KJV "appear"); 1 John 3:10.

4:17 But that it spread no further among the people, let us straitly threaten them, that they speak henceforth to no man in this name.

Spread *dianemo* (1268), "to distribute," is used in the passive voice in **Acts 4:17**, "spread," lit., "be spread about" (*dia*). In the Sept., Deut. 29:26, "to assign" or "divide" (concerning the worship of other gods).

Straitly In **Acts 4:17** some mss. have *apeile*, "a threat," with *apeilo* (middle voice), lit., "let us threaten them with a threat," KJV, "let us straitly threaten"; the best texts omit the noun (so RV). Moulton and Milligan (*Vocab.*), arguing for the presence of the noun, consider that it "clearly reflects the literal rendering of a Semitic original reported to Luke from an eye-witness—was it Paul."

Threaten *apeileo* (546), is used of Christ, negatively, in 1 Pet. 2:23; in the middle voice, **Acts 4:17**, hence the KJV, "let us straitly threaten," lit., "let us threaten ... with threatening"; *apeile* (547), akin to *apeileo*, occurs in **Acts 4:29** (in some mss. v. **17**); **9:1**; Eph. 6:9.

Henceforth Negatively, "henceforth ... not" (or "no more") translates one or other of the negative adverbs *ouketi* and *meketi*, "no longer," e.g., **Acts 4:17**, KJV, and RV, "henceforth (to no man)"; in the following the RV has "no longer" for the KJV, "henceforth" (with a negative), John 15:15; Rom. 6:6; 2 Cor. 5:15; Eph. 4:17; in 2 Cor. 5:16 (last part), RV, "no more"; in Matt. 21:19 and Mark 11:14, "no (fruit ...) henceforward"; KJV in the latter, "hereafter."

4:18 And they called them, and commanded them not to speak at all nor teach in the name of Jesus.

Commanded *see Acts 1:4*.

Speak *phthengomai* (5350), "to utter a sound or voice," is translated "to speak" in **Acts 4:18**; 2 Pet. 2:16; in 2:18, KJV, "speak" (RV, "utter").

All The synonym *katholou*, a strengthened form of *holou* signifies "at all," **Acts 4:18**.

4:19 But Peter and John answered and said unto them, Whether it be right in the sight of God to hearken unto you more than unto God, judge ye.

Right *dikaios* (1342), "just, righteous, that which is in accordance with" *dike*, "rule, right, justice," is translated "right" in Matt. 20:4; v. 7, KJV only (RV omits, according to the most authentic mss., the clause having been inserted from v. 4, to the detriment of the narrative); Luke 12:57; **Acts 4:19**; Eph. 6:1; Phil. 1:7, RV (KJV, "meet"); 2 Pet. 1:13 (KJV, "meet").

Hearken *see* **Hear** at *Acts 3:22*.

More *mallon* (3123), the comparative degree of *mala*, "very, very much," is frequently translated "rather," e.g., Matt. 10:6, 28; 1 Cor. 14:1, 5; sometimes followed by "than," with a connecting particle, e.g., Matt. 18:13 ("more than"); or without, e.g., John 3:19; **Acts 4:19**, RV (KJV, "more"); in 1 Cor. 9:12, KJV, "rather" (RV, "yet more"); 12:22, RV, "rather" (KJV, "more"); 2 Cor. 3:9 (ditto); Philem. 16 (ditto); in 2 Pet. 1:10, KJV, "the rather" (RV, "the more").

Judge *see* Determined at *Acts 3:13*.

4:20-21 For we cannot but speak the things which we have seen and heard.

So when they had further threatened them, they let them go, finding nothing how they might punish them, because of the people: for all *men* glorified God for that which was done.

Threatened *prosapeileo* (4324), "to threaten further," occurs in the middle voice in **Acts 4:21**.

Let ... go *see Acts 3:13*.

Finding *heurisko* (2147), denotes (a) "to find," either with previous search, e.g., Matt. 7:7, 8, or without, e.g., Matt. 27:32; in the passive voice, of Enoch's disappearance, Heb. 11:5; of mountains, Rev. 16:20; of Babylon and its occupants, 18:21, 22; (b) metaphorically, "to find out by enquiry," or "to learn, discover," e.g., Luke 19:48; John 18:38; 19:4, 6; **Acts 4:21**; **13:28**; Rom. 7:10; Gal. 2:17, which indicates "the surprise of the Jew" who learned for the first time that before God he had no moral superiority over the Gentiles whom he superciliously dubbed "sinners," while he esteemed himself to be "righteous"; 1 Pet. 1:7; Rev. 5:4; (c) in the middle voice, "to find for oneself, gain, procure, obtain," e.g. Matt. 10:39; 11:29, "ye shall find (rest)"; Luke 1:30; **Acts 7:46**; 2 Tim. 1:18.

Nothing *meden* (3367), the neuter of *medeis*, "no one"; so with the negatives *ou* and *me*, "not," in all their usage and connections. Thus it is found, not in direct negative statements, but in warnings, prohibitions, etc., e.g., Matt. 27:19; **Acts 19:36**; in expressions conveying certain impossibilities, e.g., **Acts 4:21**; comparisons, e.g., 2 Cor. 6:10; intimating a supposition to the contrary, 1 Tim. 6:4; adverbially, e.g., 2 Cor. 11:5, "not a whit." Westcott and Hort adopt the spelling *methen* in **Acts 27:33**.

Punish *kolazo* (2849), primarily denotes "to curtail, prune, dock" (from *kolos*, "docked"); then, "to check, restrain, punish"; it is used in the middle voice in **Acts 4:21**; passive voice in 2 Pet. 2:9, KJV, "to be punished" (RV, "under punishment," lit., "being punished"), a futurative present tense.

4:22 For the man was above forty years old, on whom this miracle of healing was shewed.

Above In **Acts 4:22**, KJV, the adjective *pleion*, "more," is translated "above," the RV corrects to "more than (forty years)."

Years *etos* (2094), is used (a) to mark a point of time at or from which events take place, e.g., Luke 3:1 (dates were frequently reckoned from the time when a monarch began to reign); in Gal. 3:17 the time of the giving of the Law is stated as 430 "years" after the covenant of promise given to Abraham; there is no real discrepancy between this and Ex. 12:40; the apostle is not concerned with the exact duration of the interval, it certainly was not less than 430 "years"; the point of the argument is that the period was very considerable; Gal. 1:18 and 2:1 mark events in Paul's life; as to the former the point is that three "years" elapsed before he saw any of the apostles; in 2:1 the 14 "years" may date either from his conversion or from his visit to Peter mentioned in 1:18; the latter seems the more natural; (b) to mark a space of time, e.g., Matt. 9:20; Luke 12:19; 13:11; John 2:20; **Acts 7:6**, where the 400 "years" mark not merely the time that Israel was in bondage in Egypt, but the time that they sojourned or were strangers there (the RV puts a comma after the word "evil"); the Genevan Version renders Gen. 15:13 "thy posterity shall inhabit a strange land for 400 years"; Heb. 3:17; Rev. 20:2-7; (c) to date an event from one's birth, e.g., Mark 5:42; Luke 2:42; 3:23; John 8:57; **Acts 4:22**; 1 Tim. 5:9; (d) to mark recurring events, Luke 2:41 (with *kata*, used distributively); 13:7; (e) of an unlimited number, Heb. 1:12.

Miracle *see Acts 4:16*.

Healing *iasis* (2392), "a healing, a cure" (akin to *iaomai*, "to heal," and *iatros*, "a physician"), is used in the plural in Luke 13:32; in **Acts 4:22**, "healing", in **4:30** with the preposition *eis* "unto," lit., "unto healing," translated "heal."

Shewed *ginomai* ("to become"), **Acts 4:22**, "was wrought".

4:23 And being let go, they went to their own company, and reported all that the chief priests and elders had said unto them.

Let ... go *see Acts 3:13*.

Company *idios* (2398), "one's own," is used in the plural with the article in **Acts 4:23**, to signify "their own (company)."

Reported *apangello* (518), "to report" (*apo*, "from," *angello*, "to give a message"), "announce, declare" (by a messenger, speaker, or writer), is translated "reported" in **Acts 4:23**; **16:36**, RV (KJV, "told"); v. **38** (KJV, "told"); "report" in 1 Cor. 14:25,

KJV (RV, "declaring"); 1 Thess. 1:9, RV, "report" (KJV, "shew"); so **Acts 28:21**.

All *hosa* (3745), the neuter plural of *hosos*, "as much as," chiefly used in the plural, is sometimes rendered "all that," e.g., **Acts 4:23**; **14:27**. It really means "whatsoever things." See Luke 9:10, RV, "what things."

4:24 And when they heard that, they lifted up their voice to God with one accord, and said, Lord, thou *art* God, which hast made heaven, and earth, and the sea, and all that in them is:

Lifted *airo* (142), signifies (a) "to raise take up, lift, draw up," (b) "to bear, carry," (c) "to take or carry away." It is used of "lifting" up the voice, Luke 17:13; **Acts 4:24**; eyes, John 11:41; hand, Rev. 10:5.

God *see Acts 2:23.*

Accord *see Acts 1:14.*

Lord *despotes* (1203), "a master, lord, one who possesses supreme authority," is used in personal address to God in Luke 2:29; **Acts 4:24**; Rev. 6:10; with reference to Christ, 2 Pet. 2:1; Jude 4; elsewhere it is translated "master," "masters," 1 Tim. 6:1, 2; 2 Tim. 2:21 (of Christ); Titus 2:9; 1 Pet. 2:18.

Sea *thalassa* (2281), is used (a) chiefly literally, e.g., "the Red Sea," **Acts 7:36**; 1 Cor. 10:1; Heb. 11:29; the "sea" of Galilee or Tiberias, Matt. 4:18; 15:29; Mark 6:48, 49, where the acts of Christ testified to His deity; John 6:1; 21:1; in general, e.g., Luke 17:2; **Acts 4:24**; Rom. 9:27; Rev. 16:3; 18:17; 20:8, 13; 21:1; (b) metaphorically, of "the ungodly men" described in Jude 13 (cf. Isa. 57:20); (c) symbolically, in the apocalyptic vision of "a glassy sea like unto crystal," Rev. 4:6, emblematic of the fixed purity and holiness of all that appertains to the authority and judicial dealings of God; in 15:2, the same, "mingled with fire," and, standing by it (RV) or on it (KJV and RV marg.), those who had "come victorious from the beast" (ch. 13); of the wild and restless condition of nations, Rev. 13:1 (see 17:1, 15), where "he stood" (RV) refers to the dragon, not John (KJV); from the midst of this state arises the beast, symbolic of the final gentile power dominating the federated nations of the Roman world (see Dan., chs. 2, 7, etc.).

4:25 Who by the mouth of thy servant David hast said, Why did the heathen rage, and the people imagine vain things?

Mouth *see Acts 1:16.*

Servant *pais* (3816), also denotes "an attendant"; it is translated "servant" (a) of natural conditions, in Matt. 8:6, 8, 13; 14:2; Luke 7:7 ("menservants" in 12:45); 15:26; (b) of spiritual relation to God, (1) of Israel, Luke 1:54; (2) of David, Luke 1:69; **Acts 4:25**; (3) of Christ, so declared by God the Father, Matt. 12:18; spoken of in prayer, **Acts 4:27, 30**, RV (KJV, "child"); the argument advanced by Dalman for the rendering "Child" in these passages, is not sufficiently valid as against the RV, "Servant" in **Acts 4**, and the KJV and RV in Matt. 12 (cf, e.g., the use of *pais* in the Sept. of Gen. 41:38; Jer. 36:24). The Matt. 12 passage by direct quotation, and the **Acts 4** passages by implication, refer to the ideal "Servant of Jehovah" (Sept., *pais Kuriou*), of Isa. 42:1 and following passages, thus identifying the Servant with the Lord Jesus; for the same identification, cf. **Acts 8:35**.

Rage *phruasso* (5433), was primarily used of "the snorting, neighing and prancing of horses"; hence, metaphorically, of "the haughtiness and insolence of men," **Acts 4:25**. In the Sept., Ps. 2:1.

> *"Prayer meetings are the throbbing machinery of the Church."*
>
> CHARLES HADDON SPURGEON

Imagine *meletao* (3191), signifies "to care for" (*melete*, "care"); then, "to attend to," "be diligent in," 1 Tim. 4:15, RV, i.e., to practice as the result of devising or planning; thirdly, "to ponder," "imagine," **Acts 4:25**, RV, marg., "meditate." Some inferior mss. have it in Mark 13:11.

Vain *kenos* (2756), "empty," with special reference to quality, is translated "vain" (as an adjective) in **Acts 4:25**; 1 Cor. 15:10, 14 (twice); Eph. 5:6; Col. 2:8; Jas. 2:20; in the following the neuter, *kenon*, follows the preposition *eis*, "in," and denotes "in vain," 2 Cor. 6:1; Gal. 2:2; Phil. 2:16 (twice); 1 Thess. 3:5. The synonymous word *mataios*, "vain," signifies "void" of result, it marks the aimlessness of anything. The vain (*kenos*) man in Jas. 2:20 is one who is "empty" of divinely imparted wisdom; in 1:26 the vain (*mataios*) religion is one that produces nothing profitable. *Kenos* stresses the absence of quality, *mataios*, the absence of useful aim or effect. Cf. the corresponding adverb *kenos*, "in vain," in Jas. 4:5, the noun *kenodoxia*, "vainglory," Phil. 2:3, the adjective *kenodoxos*, "vainglorious," Gal. 5:26, and the noun *kenophonia*, "vain," or "empty," babblings, 1 Tim. 6:20; 2 Tim. 2:16.

"The only New Testament precedents for spreading the gospel are godly living, praying and bold speaking."

GEOFFREY THOMAS

4:26 The kings of the earth stood up, and the rulers were gathered together against the Lord, and against his Christ.

Rulers *see Acts 3:17.*

Together *see Acts 1:15.*

4:27 For of a truth against thy holy child Jesus, whom thou hast anointed, both Herod, and Pontius Pilate, with the Gentiles, and the people of Israel, were gathered together,

Holy *see Acts 3:14.*

Child *pais* (3816), denotes "a boy" (in contrast to *paidion*, a diminutive of *pais*, and to *teknon*, "a child"). With reference to Christ, instead of the KJV "child," the RV suitably translates otherwise as follows: Luke 2:43, "the boy Jesus"; **Acts 4:27, 30**, "Thy Holy Servant, Jesus." So in the case of others, Matt. 17:18 and Luke 9:42 ("boy").

Anointed *chrio* (5548), is confined to "sacred and symbolical anointings"; of Christ as the "Anointed" of God, Luke 4:18; **Acts 4:27; 10:38**, and Heb. 1:9, where it is used metaphorically in connection with "the oil of gladness." The title Christ signifies "The Anointed One," The word (*Christos*) is rendered "(His) Anointed" in **Acts 4:26**, RV. Once it is said of believers, 2 Cor. 1:21. *Chrio* is very frequent in the Sept., and is used of kings, 1 Sam. 10:1, and priests, Ex. 28:41, and prophets, 1 Kings 19:16. Among the Greeks it was used in other senses than the ceremonial, but in the Scriptures it is not found in connection with secular matters.

People *see Acts 4:8.*

4:28 For to do whatsoever thy hand and thy counsel determined before to be done.

Counsel *see Acts 2:23.*

Determined *proorizo* (4309), denotes "to mark out beforehand, to determine before, foreordain"; in **Acts 4:28**, KJV, "determined before," RV, "foreordained"; so the RV in 1 Cor. 2:7, KJV, "ordained", in Rom. 8:29-30 and Eph. 1:5, 11, KJV, "predestinate," RV, "foreordain."

4:29 And now, Lord, behold their threatenings: and grant unto thy servants, that with all boldness they may speak thy word,

Now *nun* (3568), is used (a) of time, the immediate present, whether in contrast to the past, e.g., John 4:18; **Acts 7:52**, or to the future, e.g., John 12:27; Rom. 11:31; sometimes with the article, singular or plural, e.g., **Acts 4:29; 5:38**; (b) of logical sequence, often partaking also of the character of (a), "now therefore, now however," as it is, e.g., Luke 11:39; John 8:40; 9:41; 15:22, 24; 1 Cor. 5:11, RV marg., "as it is."

Lord *see Acts 2:36.*

Behold *epide* (1896), is used in **Acts 4:29** of the entreaty made to the Lord to "behold" the threatenings of persecutors. *See also* **Foresaw** at *Acts 2:25.*

Threatenings *see* **Threaten** at *Acts 4:17.*

Grant *didomi* (1325), "to give," is rendered "grant" in Mark 10:37; Luke 1:74; **Acts 4:29; 11:18; 14:3.**

All *see Acts 2:36.*

Boldness *see Acts 4:13.*

4:30 By stretching forth thine hand to heal; and that signs and wonders may be done by the name of thy holy child Jesus.

Stretching *ekteino* (1614), "to stretch out or forth," is so rendered in Matt. 12:13 (twice), 49; 14:31; 26:51; Mark 3:5 (twice), Luke 6:10; in Matt. 8:3; Mark 1:41 and Luke 5:13, RV (KJV, "put forth"); Luke 22:53; John 21:18; **Acts 4:30; 26:1**. *See also* **Cast** at *Acts 27:30.*

Heal *see* **Healing** at *Acts 4:22.*

Holy *see Acts 3:14.*

Child *see Acts 4:27.*

4:31 And when they had prayed, the place was shaken where they were assembled together; and they were all filled with the Holy Ghost, and they spake the word of God with boldness.

Prayed *deomai* (1189), "to desire, to long for," usually representing the word "need," is sometimes translated "beseech," e.g., Luke 5:12; **Acts 21:39**; 2 Cor. 10:2; Gal. 4:12. It is used of prayer to God, in Matt. 9:38; Luke 10:2; 21:36; 22:32; **Acts 4:31; 8:22, 24; 10:2**; Rom. 1:10; 1 Thess. 3:10.

Shaken *see* **Moved** at *Acts 2:25.*

Filled *see Acts 2:4.*

Boldness *see Acts 4:13.*

4:32 And the multitude of them that believed were of one heart and of one soul: neither said any *of them* that ought of the things which he possessed was his own; but they had all things common.

Multitude *plethos* (4128), lit., "a fullness," hence, "a large company, a multitude," is used (a) of things: of fish, Luke 5:6; John 21:6; of sticks ("bundle"), **Acts 28:3**; of stars and of sand, Heb. 11:12; of sins, Jas. 5:20; 1 Pet. 4:8; (b) of persons, (1) a "multitude": of people, e.g., Mark 3:7, 8; Luke 6:17; John 5:3; **Acts 14:1**; of angels, Luke 2:13; (2) with the article, the whole number, the "multitude," the populace, e.g., Luke 1:10; 8:37; **Acts 5:16**; **19:9**; **23:7**; a particular company, e.g., of disciples, Luke 19:37; **Acts 4:32**; **6:2**, **5**; **15:30**; of elders, priests, and scribes, **23:7**; of the apostles and the elders of the Church in Jerusalem, **Acts 15:12**.

Soul *see Acts 2:27.*

Possessed *huparcho* (5225), "to be in existence," and, in a secondary sense, "to belong to," is used with this meaning in the neuter plural of the present participle with the article signifying one's "possessions," "the things which he possesseth," Luke 12:15; **Acts 4:32**; in Heb. 10:34, RV, "possessions" (KJV, "goods").

Common *see Acts 2:44.*

4:33 And with great power gave the apostles witness of the resurrection of the Lord Jesus: and great grace was upon them all.

Gave *apodidomi* (591), signifies "to give up or back, to restore, return, render what is due, to pay, give an account," e.g., of an account. Matt. 5:26; 12:36; Luke 16:2; **Acts 19:40**; Heb. 13:17; 1 Pet. 4:5; of wages, etc., e.g., Matt. 18:25-34; 20:8; of conjugal duty, 1 Cor. 7:3; of a witness, **Acts 4:33**; frequently of recompensing or rewarding, 1 Tim. 5:4; 2 Tim. 4:8, 14; 1 Pet. 3:9; Rev. 18:6; 22:12. In the middle voice it is used of "giving" up what is one's own; hence, "to sell," **Acts 5:8**; **7:9**; Heb. 12:16.

Witness *marturion* (3142), "testimony or witness as borne, a declaration of facts," is translated "witness" in Matt. 24:14, KJV; **Acts 4:33**; **7:44** (KJV); Jas. 5:3 (KJV).

Resurrection *see Acts 1:22.*

4:34 Neither was there any among them that lacked: for as many as were possessors of lands or houses sold them, and brought the prices of the things that were sold,

Lacked *endees* (1729), from *endeo*, "to lack," signifies "needy, in want," translated "that lacked" in **Acts 4:34**.

Possessors *ktetor* (2935), "a possessor, an owner," occurs in **Acts 4:34**.

Lands *chorion* (5564), is translated "land" in the sense of property, in **Acts 4:34**; **5:3**, **8**; **28:7**, RV, "lands" (KJV, "possessions").

Sold *poleo* (4453), "to exchange or barter, to sell," is used in the latter sense in the NT, six times in Matthew, three in Mark, six in Luke; in John only in connection with the cleansing of the Temple by the Lord, 2:14, 16; in Acts only in connection with the disposing of property for distribution among the community of believers, **4:34**, **37**; **5:1**; elsewhere, 1 Cor. 10:25; Rev. 13:17. *See also Acts 2:45.*

Prices *time* (5092), primarily "a valuing," hence, objectively, (a) "a price paid or received," e.g., Matt. 27:6, 9; **Acts 4:34**; **5:2**, **3**; **7:16**, RV, "price" (KJV, "sum"); **19:19**; 1 Cor. 6:20; 7:23; (b) of "the preciousness of Christ" unto believers, 1 Pet. 2:7, RV, i.e., the honor and inestimable value of Christ as appropriated by believers, who are joined, as living stones, to Him the cornerstone; (c) in the sense of value, of human ordinances, valueless against the indulgence of the flesh, or, perhaps of no value in attempts at asceticism, Col. 2:23; (d) "honor, esteem," ... of that bestowed by the inhabitants of Melita upon Paul and his fellow-passengers, in gratitude for his benefits of healing, **Acts 28:10**.

4:35 And laid *them* down at the apostles' feet: and distribution was made unto every man according as he had need.

Laid *see Acts 3:2.*

Distribution *diadidomi* (1239), lit., "to give through," (*dia*, "through," *didomi*, "to give"), as from one to another, "to deal out," is said of "distributing" to the poor, Luke 18:22; **Acts 4:35**, "distribution was made," or to a company of people, John 6:11. It is translated "divideth" in Luke 11:22. In Rev. 17:13 the most authentic mss. have the verb *didomi*, to give, instead of the longer form.

Every *see* Each at *Acts 2:3.*

According as *see* Because at *Acts 2:24.*

He The indefinite pronoun *tis*, "anyone, any man," is rendered "he" in **Acts 4:35**, KJV (RV, rightly, "any one"); in Heb. 10:28, RV, "a man."

4:36 And Joses, who by the apostles was surnamed Barnabas, (which is, being interpreted, The son of consolation,) a Levite, *and* of the country of Cyprus,

Surnamed *see Acts 1:23.*

Interpreted *methermeneuo* (3177), "to change or translate from one language to another, to interpret," is always used in the passive voice in the NT, "being interpreted," of interpreting the names, Immanuel, Matt. 1:23; Golgotha, Mark 15:22; Barnabas, **Acts 4:36**; in **Acts 13:8**, of Elymas, the verb is rendered "is ... by interpretation," lit., "is interpreted"; it is used of interpreting or translating sentences in Mark 5:41; 15:34; in the best mss., John 1:38 (Rabbi, interpreted as "Master"); v. 41 (Messiah, interpreted as "Christ").

Son *see* Children at *Acts 3:25.*

Consolation *paraklesis* (3874), is translated "consolation," in both KJV and RV, in Luke 2:25; 6:24; **Acts 15:31**; in 1 Cor. 14:3, KJV, "exhortation," RV, "comfort"; in the following the KJV has "consolation," the RV, "comfort," Rom. 15:5; 2 Cor. 1:6-7; 7:7; Phil. 2:1; 2 Thess. 2:16; Philem. 7; in **Acts 4:36**, RV, "exhortation"; in Heb. 6:18, RV, "encouragement."

Country *genos*, "a race," is mistranslated "country" in the KJV of **Acts 4:36** (RV, "by race").

4:37 Having land, sold *it*, and brought the money, and laid *it* at the apostles' feet.

Having *see* Have at *Acts 3:6.*

Land *agros* (68), "a field," or "piece of ground," or "the country" as distinct from the town, is translated "lands" in Matt. 19:29; Mark 10:29, 30; **Acts 4:37.**

Sold *see Acts 4:34.*

Money *chrema* (5536), lit., "a thing that one uses" (akin to *chraomai* "to use"), hence, (a) "wealth, riches," Mark 10:23, 24; Luke 18:24; (b) "money," **Acts 4:37**, singular number, "a sum of money"; plural in **8:18, 20; 24:26.**

Laid *see Acts 3:2.*

Chapter 5

5:1 But a certain man named Ananias, with Sapphira his wife, sold a possession,

Possession *see* Possessions at *Acts 2:45.*

Sold *see* Sell at *Acts 4:34.*

5:2 And kept back *part* of the price, his wife also being privy *to it*, and brought a certain part, and laid *it* at the apostles' feet.

Kept *nosphizo* (3557), "to set apart, remove," signifies, in the middle voice, "to set apart for oneself, to purloin," and is rendered "purloining" in Titus 2:10; "kept back" (and "keep") in **Acts 5:2, 3**, of the act of Ananias and his wife in "retaining" part of the price of the land.

Part *see* Parts at *Acts 2:10.*

Price *see* Prices at *Acts 4:34.*

Privy *sunoida* (4923), denotes (a) "to share the knowledge of, be privy to," **Acts 5:2**; (b) "to be conscious of," especially of guilty consciousness, 1 Cor. 4:4, "I know nothing against (KJV, by) myself." The verb is connected with *suneidon*, found in **Acts 12:12; 14:6** (in the best texts).

Laid *see Acts 3:2.*

5:3 But Peter said, Ananias, why hath Satan filled thine heart to lie to the Holy Ghost, and to keep back *part* of the price of the land?

Satan *satanas* (4567), a Greek form derived from the Aramaic (Heb., *Satan*), "an adversary," is used (a) of an angel of Jehovah in Num. 22:22 (the first occurrence of the Word in the OT); (b) of men, e.g., 1 Sam. 29:4; Ps. 38:20; 71:13; four in Ps. 109; (c) of "Satan," the Devil, some seventeen or eighteen times in the OT; in Zech. 3:1, where the name receives its interpretation, "to be (his) adversary," RV (see marg.; KJV, "to resist him"). In the NT the word is always used of "Satan," the adversary (a) of God and Christ, e.g., Matt. 4:10; 12:26; Mark 1:13; 3:23, 26; 4:15; Luke 4:8 (in some mss.); 11:18; 22:3; John 13:27; (b) of His people, e.g., Luke 22:31; **Acts 5:3**; Rom. 16:20; 1 Cor. 5:5; 7:5; 2 Cor. 2:11; 11:14; 12:7; 1 Thess. 2:18; 1 Tim. 1:20; 5:15; Rev. 2:9, 13 (twice), 24; 3:9; (c) of mankind, Luke 13:16; **Acts 26:18**; 2 Thess. 2:9; Rev. 12:9; 20:7.

Filled *see Acts 2:2.*

Lie *pseudo* (5574), "to deceive by lies" (always in the middle voice in the NT), is used (a) absolutely, in Matt. 5:11, "falsely," lit., "lying" (v, marg.); Rom. 9:1; 2 Cor. 11:31; Gal. 1:20; Col. 3:9 (where the verb is followed by the preposition *eis*, "to"); 1 Tim. 2:7; Heb. 6:18; Jas. 3:14 (where it is followed by the preposition *kata*, "against"); 1 John 1:6; Rev. 3:9; (b) transitively, with a direct object (without a preposition following), **Acts 5:3** (with the accusative case) "to lie to (the Holy Ghost)," RV marg., "deceive"; v. **4** (with the dative case) "thou hast (not) lied (unto men, but unto God)."

Holy Ghost *see Acts 1:16.*

Keep *see* Kept at *Acts 5:2.*

Price *see* Prices at *Acts 4:34.*

Land *see* Lands at *Acts 4:34.*

5:4 Whiles it remained, was it not thine own? and after it was sold, was it not in thine own power? why hast thou conceived this thing in thine heart? thou hast not lied unto men, but unto God.

Remained *meno* (3306), "to stay, abide," is frequently rendered "to remain," e.g., Matt. 11:23; Luke 10:7; John 1:33, KJV (RV, "abiding"); 9:41 (in 15:11, the best texts have the verb to be, see RV); 15:16, KJV (RV, "abide"); 19:31; **Acts 5:4** (twice), RV, "whiles it remained, did it (not) remain (thine own)?"; **27:41**; 1 Cor. 7:11; 15:6; 2 Cor. 3:11, 14; 9:9, KJV (RV, "abideth"); Heb. 12:27; 1 John 3:9.

Was When not part of another verb, or phrase, these translate *eimi*, "to be," e.g., Matt. 1:18, or the following: (a) *ginomai*, "to become," e.g., Matt. 8:26; (b) *huparcho*, "to exist," especially when referring to an already existing condition, e.g., Luke 8:41; **Acts 5:4** (2nd part); **16:3**; **27:12**; Rom. 4:19, KJV, "when he was" (RV, "he being"); (c) *echo*, "to have," e.g., **Acts 12:15**; (d) *apecho*, "to be away, to be distant," e.g., Luke 7:6; 24:13; (e) *mello*, "to be about to," e.g., Luke 19:4; **Acts 21:27**, **37**, KJV (RV, "was about to"); (f) *sumbaino*, "to come to pass, happen," e.g., **Acts 21:35**; (g) in Gal. 4:28, the preposition *kata*, "according to," is rendered "was," in the phrase "as Isaac was," lit., "like Isaac"; as Isaac's birth came by divine interposition, so does the spiritual birth of every believer.

Thine One of the oblique cases of *su*, "thou"; *sou*, "of thee," e.g., Matt. 1:20; 7:3 (2nd part), "thine own"; *soi*, "to thee," e.g., Mark 5:9; with *meno*, "to remain," **Acts 5:4** (1st part), "thine own," lit., "remain to thee"; in Matt. 26:18, *pros se*, "at thy house," lit., "with thee".

Own In **Acts 5:4**, "was it not thine own?" is, lit., "did it not remain (*meno*) to thee."

Sold *see* *Acts 2:45*.

Conceived *tithemi* (5087), to put, set, is used in **Acts 5:4**, of the sin of Ananias, in "conceiving" a lie in his heart.

Thing *pragma* (4229), is translated thing in Matt. 18:19, as part of the word "anything," lit., "every thing"; Luke 1:1, KJV only; **Acts 5:4**; in Heb. 6:18; 10:1, and 11:1, "things."

Lied *see* **Lie** at *Acts 5:3*.

5:5 And Ananias hearing these words fell down, and gave up the ghost: and great fear came on all them that heard these things.

Ghost *ekpsucho* (1634), "to expire," lit., "to breathe out the soul (or life), to give up the ghost" (*ek*, "out," *psuche*, "the soul"), is used in **Acts 5:5**, **10**; **12:23**.

5:6 And the young men arose, wound him up, and carried *him* out, and buried *him*.

Young *neoteros* (3501), the comparative degree of *neos*, "new, youthful," is translated "young" in John 21:18; in the plural, **Acts 5:6**, "young men" (marg., "younger"); Titus 2:6, KJV, RV, "younger men."

Wound *sustello* (4958), denotes (a) "to draw together" (*sun*, "together," *stello*, "to bring, gather"), "to contract, shorten," 1 Cor. 7:29, RV, "(the time) is shortened" (KJV, "... is short"); the coming of the Lord is always to be regarded as nigh for the believer, who is to be in constant expectation of His return, and thus is to keep himself from being the slave of earthly conditions and life's relationships; (b) "to wrap up," of enshrouding a body for burial, **Acts 5:6**, RV, "they wrapped (KJV, wound) ... up."

Carried *ekphero* (1627), is used, literally, "of carrying something forth, or out," e.g., a garment, Luke 15:22; sick folk, **Acts 5:15**; a corpse, **Acts 5:6**, **9-10**; of the impossibility of "carrying" anything out from this world at death, 1 Tim. 6:7. The most authentic mss. have this word in Mark 8:23, of the blind man, whom the Lord brought out of the village (RV). It is also used of the earth, in "bringing forth" produce, Heb. 6:8.

Buried *see* *Acts 2:29*.

5:7 And it was about the space of three hours after, when his wife, not knowing what was done, came in.

Space *diastema* (1292), "an interval, space," is used of time in **Acts 5:7**.

5:8 And Peter answered unto her, Tell me whether ye sold the land for so much? And she said, Yea, for so much.

Sold *apodidomi* (591), "to give up or back," also means, in the middle voice, "to give up of one's own will"; hence, "to sell"; it is so used in Peter's question to Sapphira as to "selling" the land, **Acts 5:8**; of the act of Joseph's brothers, **7:9**; of Esau's act in "selling" his birthright, Heb. 12:16. *See also* **Gave** at *Acts 4:33*.

Land *see* **Lands** at *Acts 4:34*.

Much The adjective *tosoutos*, "so great, so much," is translated "so much (bread)," in Matt. 15:33, plural, RV, "so many (loaves)"; in the genitive case, of price, in **Acts 5:8**, "for so much"; in the dative case, of degree, in Heb. 1:4, RV, "by so much" (KJV, "so much"); so in Heb. 10:25; in Heb. 7:22 "by so much" translates the phrase *kata tosouto;* in Rev. 18:7, "so much."

Yea *nai* (3483), a particle of affirmation, is used (a) in answer to a question, Matt. 9:28; 11:9; 13:51; 17:25; 21:16; Luke 7:26; John 11:27; 21:15, 16; **Acts 5:8**; **22:27**; Rom.

3:29; (b) in assent to an assertion, Matt. 15:27, RV (KJV, "truth"); Mark 7:28; Rev. 14:13; 16:7, RV (KJV, "even so"); (c) in confirmation of an assertion, Matt. 11:26 and Luke 10:21, RV (KJV, "even so"); Luke 11:51, RV (KJV, "verily"); 12:5; Phil. 4:3 (in the best texts); Philem. 20; (d) in solemn asseveration, Rev. 1:7 (KJV and RV, "even so"); 22:20, RV (KJV, "surely"); (e) in repetition for emphasis, Matt. 5:37; 2 Cor. 1:17; Jas. 5:12; (f) singly in contrast to *ou*, "nay," 2 Cor. 1:18, 19 (twice), 20, "(the) yea," RV.

5:9 Then Peter said unto her, How is it that ye have agreed together to tempt the Spirit of the Lord? behold, the feet of them which have buried thy husband *are* at the door, and shall carry thee out.

Agreed *sumphoneo* (4856), lit., "to sound together" (*sun*, "together," *phone*, "a sound"), i.e., "to be in accord, primarily of musical instruments," is used in the NT of the "agreement" (a) of persons concerning a matter, Matt. 18:19; 20:2, 13; **Acts 5:9**; (b) of the writers of Scripture, **Acts 15:15**; (c) of things that are said to be congruous in their nature, Luke 5:36.

Tempt *peirazo* (3985), signifies (1) "to try, attempt, assay"; (2) "to test, try, prove," in a good sense, said of Christ and of believers, Heb. 2:18, where the context shows that the temptation was the cause of suffering to Him, and only suffering, not a drawing away to sin, so that believers have the sympathy of Christ as their High Priest in the suffering which sin occasions to those who are in the enjoyment of communion with God; so in the similar passage in 4:15; in all the temptations which Christ endured, there was nothing within Him that answered to sin. There was no sinful infirmity in Him. While He was truly man, and His divine nature was not in any way inconsistent with His Manhood, there was nothing in Him such as is produced in us by the sinful nature which belongs to us; in Heb. 11:37, of the testing of OT saints; in 1 Cor. 10:13, where the meaning has a wide scope, the verb is used of "testing" as permitted by God, and of the believer as one who should be in the realization of his own helplessness and his dependence upon God; in a bad sense, "to tempt" (a) of attempts to ensnare Christ in His speech, e.g., Matt. 16:1; 19:3; 22:18, 35, and parallel passages; John 8:6; (b) of temptations to sin, e.g., Gal. 6:1, where one who would restore an erring brother is not to act as his judge, but as being one with him in liability to sin, with the possibility of finding himself in similar circumstances, Jas. 1:13, 14; of temptations mentioned as coming from the Devil, Matt. 4:1; and parallel passages; 1 Cor. 7:5; 1 Thess. 3:5; (c) of trying or challenging God, **Acts 15:10**; 1 Cor. 10:9 (2nd part); Heb. 3:9; the Holy Spirit, **Acts 5:9**.

Spirit *see* **Holy Ghost** at *Acts 1:16*.

Feet *pous* (4228), besides its literal meaning, is used, by metonymy, of "a person in motion," Luke 1:79; **Acts 5:9**; Rom. 3:15; 10:15; Heb. 12:13. It is used in phrases expressing subjection, 1 Cor. 15:27, RV; of the humility and receptivity of discipleship, Luke 10:39; **Acts 22:3**; of obeisance and worship, e.g., Matt. 28:9; of scornful rejection, Matt. 10:14; **Acts 13:51**. Washing the "feet" of another betokened the humility of the service and the comfort of the guest, and was a feature of hospitality, Luke 7:38; John 13:5; 1 Tim. 5:10 (here figuratively).

Buried *see Acts 2:29*.

5:10 Then fell she down straightway at his feet, and yielded up the ghost: and the young men came in, and found her dead, and, carrying *her* forth, buried *her* by her husband.

Straightway *see* **Immediately** at *Acts 3:7*.

Yielded In **Acts 5:10**, KJV, *ekpsucho*, "to breathe one's last, expire" (*ek*, "out," *psuche*, "the life"), is translated "yielded up (RV, "gave up") the ghost."

Ghost *see Acts 5:5*.

Young *see Acts 2:17*.

5:11-12 And great fear came upon all the church, and upon as many as heard these things.
And by the hands of the apostles were many signs and wonders wrought among the people; (and they were all with one accord in Solomon's porch.

Hands *cheir* (5495), "the hand" (cf. Eng., "chiropody"), is used, besides its ordinary significance, (a) in the idiomatic phrases, "by the hand of," "at the hand of," etc., to signify "by the agency of," **Acts 5:12**; **7:35**; **17:25**; **14:3**; Gal. 3:19 (cf. Lev. 26:46); Rev. 19:2; (b) metaphorically, for the power of God, e.g., Luke 1:66; 23:46; John 10:28, 29; **Acts 11:21**; **13:11**; Heb. 1:10; 2:7; 10:31; (c) by metonymy, for power, e.g., Matt. 17:22; Luke 24:7; John 10:39; **Acts 12:11**.

Wrought *ginomai* (1096), "to become, take place," is rendered "wrought" in Mark 6:2; **Acts 5:12**, "were ... wrought."

Accord *see Acts 1:14*.

Porch *see Acts 3:11*.

5:13 And of the rest durst no man join himself to them: but the people magnified them.

Durst *tolmao* (5111), signifies "to dare," (a) in the sense of not dreading or shunning through fear, Matt. 22:46; Mark 12:34; Mark 15:43, "boldly," lit., "having dared, went in"; Luke 20:40; John 21:12; **Acts 5:13**; **7:32**; Rom. 15:18; 2 Cor. 10:2, RV, "show courage," (KJV, "be bold"); 10:12, RV, "are (not) bold", 11:21; Phil. 1:14, "are bold"; Jude 9; (b) in the sense of bearing, enduring, bringing oneself to do a thing, Rom. 5:7; 1 Cor. 6:1. Cf. *apotolmao*, "to be very bold," Rom. 10:20.

Join *kollao* (2853), primarily, "to glue or cement together," then, generally, "to unite, to join firmly," is used in the passive voice signifying "to join oneself to, to be joined to," Luke 15:15; **Acts 5:13**; **8:29**; **9:26**; **10:28**, RV (KJV, "to keep company with"); 1 Cor. 6:16, 17; elsewhere, "to cleave to," Luke 10:11; **Acts 17:34**; Rom. 12:9.

Magnified *megaluno* (3170), "to make great" (*megas*), is translated "to magnify" in Luke 1:46; in v. 58, RV, "had magnified (His mercy)," KJV, "had shewed great (mercy)"; **Acts 5:13**; **10:46**; **19:17**; 2 Cor. 10:15, RV (KJV, "we shall be enlarged"), i.e., by their faith in its practical effect he will be so assisted as to enlarge the scope of his gospel ministry and carry its message to regions beyond them; in Phil. 1:20, of the "magnifying" of Christ by him in his body, i.e., in all his activities and ways. In Matt. 23:5, it signifies "to enlarge."

5:14 And believers were the more added to the Lord, multitudes both of men and women.)

Believers *pisteuo* (4100), "to believe," also "to be persuaded of," and hence, "to place confidence in, to trust," signifies, in this sense of the word, reliance upon, not mere credence. It is most frequent in the writings of the apostle John, especially the Gospel. He does not use the noun. For the Lord's first use of the verb, see 1:50. Of the writers of the Gospels, Matthew uses the verb ten times, Mark ten, Luke nine, John ninety-nine. In **Acts 5:14** the present participle of the verb is translated "believers."

More *mallon* (3123), the comparative degree of *mala*, "very, very much," is used (a) of increase, "more," with qualifying words, with *pollo*, "much," e.g., Mark 10:48, "the more (a great deal)"; Rom. 5:15, 17, "(much) more"; Phil. 2:12 (ditto); with *poso*, "how much," e.g., Luke 12:24; Rom. 11:12; with *tosouto*, "by so much," Heb. 10:25; (b) without a qualifying word, by way of comparison, "the more," e.g., Luke 5:15, "so much the more"; John 5:18, "the more"; **Acts 5:14** (ditto); Phil. 1:9; 1 Thess. 4:1, 10, "more and more"; 2 Pet. 1:10, RV, "the more" (KJV, "the rather"); in **Acts 20:35**, by a periphrasis, it is translated "more (blessed)"; in Gal. 4:27, "more (than)," lit., "rather (than)"; (c) with qualifying words, similarly to (a), e.g., Mark 7:36.

5:15 Insomuch that they brought forth the sick into the streets, and laid *them* on beds and couches, that at the least the shadow of Peter passing by might overshadow some of them.

Insomuch that *see* Insomuch as at *Acts 1:19*.

Brought *see* Carried at *Acts 5:6*.

Sick *see* Impotent at *Acts 4:9*.

Streets *plateia* (4113), grammatically the feminine of *platus*, "broad," is used as a noun (*hodos*, "a way," being understood, i.e., "a broad way"), "a street," Matt. 6:5; 12:19 (in some texts, Mark 6:56); Luke 10:10; 13:26; 14:21; **Acts 5:15**; Rev. 11:8; 21:21; 22:2.

Laid *see Acts 3:2*.

Beds *krabbatos* (2895), a Macedonian word (Lat. *grabatus*), is "a somewhat mean bed, pallet, or mattress for the poor," Mark 2:4, 9, 11-12; 6:55; John 5:8-11; **Acts 5:15**; **9:33**.

Least In **Acts 5:15**, the phrase *k'an* (for *kai ean*, "even if") denotes "at the least."

Shadow *skia* (4639), is used (a) of "a shadow," caused by the interception of light, Mark 4:32; **Acts 5:15**; metaphorically of the darkness and spiritual death of ignorance, Matt. 4:16; Luke 1:79; (b) of "the image" or "outline" cast by an object, Col. 2:17, of ceremonies under the Law; of the tabernacle and its appurtenances and offerings, Heb. 8:5; of these as appointed under the Law, Heb. 10:1.

Passing In **Acts 5:15**, KJV, *erchomai*, "to come," is translated "passing by" (RV, "came by").

Overshadow *episkiazo* (1982), "to throw a shadow upon" (*epi*, "over," *skia*, "a shadow"), "to overshadow," is used (a) of the bright cloud at the Transfiguration, Matt. 17:5; Mark 9:7; Luke 9:34; (b) metaphorically of the power of "the Most High" upon the Virgin Mary, Luke 1:35; (c) of the apostle Peter's shadow upon the sick, **Acts 5:15**.

5:16 There came also a multitude *out* of the cities round about unto Jerusalem, bringing sick folks, and them which were vexed with unclean spirits: and they were healed every one.

Multitude *see Acts 4:32.*

Round about *perix* (4038), from the preposition *peri*, "around," occurs in **Acts 5:16**, "round about" (of cities).

Sick *see* **Impotent** at **Acts** *4:9.*

Vexed *ochleo* (3791), "to disturb, trouble," is used in the passive voice, of being "troubled" by evil spirits, **Acts 5:16**.

Unclean *akathartos* (169), "unclean, impure" (*a*, negative, *kathairo*, "to purify"), is used (a) of "unclean" spirits, frequently in the Synoptists, not in John's Gospel; in **Acts 5:16**; **8:7**; Rev. 16:13; 18:2a (in the 2nd clause the birds are apparently figurative of destructive satanic agencies); (b) ceremonially, **Acts 10:14, 28**; **11:8**; 1 Cor. 7:14; (c) morally, 2 Cor. 6:17, including (b), RV; "no unclean thing"; Eph. 5:5; Rev. 17:4, RV, "the unclean things" (KJV follows the text which have the noun *akathartes*, "the filthiness").

They In **Acts 5:16**, *hoitines*, the plural of *hostis*, "anyone who," is translated "they"; so in **23:14**, translated "and they"; in 17:11, "in that they" (some texts have it in Matt. 25:3).

Every *hapas* (537), signifies "all, the whole, altogether"; it is translated "every one" in **Acts 5:16**, where it occurs in the plural. In Mark 8:25, the KJV, "every man" translates the text with the masculine plural; the best mss. have the neuter plural, RV, "all things."

One For "every one" in **Acts 5:16**.

5:17 Then the high priest rose up, and all they that were with him, (which is the sect of the Sadducees,) and were filled with indignation,

Rose *see* **Raised** at *Acts 2:24.*

Sect *hairesis* (139), denotes (a) "a choosing, choice" (from *haireomai*, "to choose"); then, "that which is chosen," and hence, "an opinion," especially a self-willed opinion, which is substituted for submission to the power of truth, and leads to division and the formation of sects, Gal. 5:20 (marg., "parties"); such erroneous opinions are frequently the outcome of personal preference or the prospect of advantage; see 2 Pet. 2:1, where "destructive" (RV) signifies leading to ruin; some assign even this to (b); in the papyri the prevalent meaning is "choice" (Moulton and Milligan, *Vocab.*); (b) "a sect"; this secondary meaning, resulting from (a), is the dominating significance in the NT, **Acts 5:17; 15:5; 24:5, 14; 26:5; 28:22**; "heresies" in 1 Cor. 11:19 (see marg.).

Filled *see Acts 2:4.*

Indignation *zelos* (2205), "zeal, jealousy," is rendered "jealousy" in the RV (KJV, "envying") in Rom. 13:13; 1 Cor. 3:3; Jas. 3:14, 16; in 2 Cor. 12:20 (KJV, "envyings"); in Gal. 5:20, RV "jealousies" (KJV, "emulations"); in **Acts 5:17** (KJV, "indignation"); in **13:45** (KJV, "envy"); in 2 Cor. 11:2 it is used in the phrase "with a godly jealousy," lit., "with a jealousy of God" (RV, marg.).

5:18 And laid their hands on the apostles, and put them in the common prison.

Laid *see Acts 4:3.*

Put *see Acts 1:7.*

Common *demosios* (1219), "belonging to the people" (*demos*, "the people"), is translated "public" in **Acts 5:18**, RV, "public (ward)", KJV, "common (prison)." In **Acts 16:37**, KJV, the dative case of the adjective *demosios*, "belonging to the people" (*demos*, "a people"), "public" (so RV), used adverbially, is translated "openly"; in **18:28** and **20:20**, "publicly."

Prison *teresis* (5084), "a watching, keeping," then "a place of keeping" is translated "prison" in **Acts 5:18** KJV (RV "ward"). The prison at Jerusalem (**Acts 5:18**) was controlled by the priests and probably attached to the high priest's palace, or the Temple. Paul was imprisoned at Jerusalem in the fort Antonia, **Acts 23:10**; at Caesarea, in Herod's Praetorium, **23:35**; probably his final imprisonment in Rome was in the Tullianum dungeon.

5:19 But the angel of the Lord by night opened the prison doors, and brought them forth, and said,

Night *nux* (3571), is used (I) literally, (a) of "the alternating natural period to that of the day," e.g., Matt. 4:2; 12:40; 2 Tim. 1:3; Rev. 4:8; (b) of "the period of the absence of light," the time in which something takes place, e.g., Matt. 2:14 (27:64), in some mss.); Luke 2:8; John 3:2 (7:50, in some mss.); **Acts 5:19; 9:25**; (c) of "point of time," e.g., Matt. 14:27 (in some mss.), 30; Luke 12:20; **Acts 27:23**; (d) of "duration of time," e.g., Luke 2:37; 5:5; **Acts 20:31**; **26:7** (note the difference in the phrase in Mark 4:27); (II) metaphorically, (a) of "the period of man's alienation from God," Rom. 13:12; 1 Thess. 5:5, lit., "not of night," where "of" means 'belonging to;' cf. "of the Way," **Acts 9:2**; "of shrinking back" and "of faith," Heb. 10:39, marg.; (b) of "death," as the time when work ceases, John 9:4.

Opened *anoigo* (455), is used (1) transitively, (a) literally, of "a door or gate," e.g., **Acts 5:19**; graves, Matt. 27:52; a sepulchre, Rom. 3:13; a book, e.g., Luke 4:17; Rev. 5:2-5; 10:8; the seals of a roll, e.g., Rev. 5:9; 6:1; the eyes, **Acts 9:40**; the mouth of a fish, Matt. 17:27; "the pit of the abyss," Rev. 9:2, RV; heaven and the heavens, Matt. 3:16; Luke 3:21; **Acts 10:11** (for **7:56**, see *dianoigo*); Rev. 19:11; "the temple of the tabernacle of the testimony in heaven," Rev. 15:5; by metonymy, for that which contained treasures, Matt. 2:11; (b) metaphorically, e.g., Matt. 7:7-8; 25:11; Rev. 3:7; Hebraistically, "to open the mouth," of beginning to speak, e.g., Matt. 5:2; 13:35; **Acts 8:32, 35; 10:34; 18:14**; Rev. 13:6 (cf., e.g., Num. 22:28; Job. 3:1; Isa. 50:5); and of recovering speech, Luke 1:64; of the earth "opening," Rev. 12:16; of the "opening" of the eyes, **Acts 26:18**; the ears, Mark 7:35; (2) intransitively (perfect tense, active, in the Greek), (a) literally, of "the heaven," John 1:51, RV, "opened;" (b) metaphorically, of "speaking freely," 2 Cor. 6:11.

Prison *phulake* (5438), denotes a "prison," e.g., Matt. 14:10; Mark 6:17; **Acts 5:19**; 2 Cor. 11:23; in 2 Cor. 6:5 and Heb. 11:36 it stands for the condition of imprisonment; in Rev. 2:10; 18:2, "hold" (twice, RV, marg., "prison"; in the 2nd case, KJV, "cage"); 20:7.

Brought *exago* (1806), "to lead out, bring forth," **Acts 5:19; 7:36, 40**, etc.

5:20 Go, stand and speak in the temple to the people all the words of this life.

Life *see Acts 3:15.*

5:21 And when they heard *that*, they entered into the temple early in the morning, and taught. But the high priest came, and they that were with him, and called the council together, and all the senate of the children of Israel, and sent to the prison to have them brought.

Early *orthros* (3722), denotes "daybreak, dawn" (cf. Lat. *orior*, "to rise"). Used with the adverb *batheos*, "deeply," in Luke 24:1, it means "at early dawn" (RV). In John 8:2 it is used in the genitive case, *orthrou*, "at dawn," i.e., "early in the morning." In **Acts 5:21**, it is used with the article and preceded by the preposition *hupo*, "under," or about, lit., "about the dawn," "about daybreak," RV (for KJV, "early in the morning").

Called *sunkaleo* (4779), signifies "to call together," Mark 15:16; Luke 9:1; 15:6, 9; 23:13; **Acts 5:21; 10:24; 28:17**.

Senate *gerousia* (1087), "a council of elders" (from *geron*, "an old man," a term which early assumed a political sense among the Greeks, the notion of age being merged in that of dignity), is used in **Acts 5:21**, apparently epexegetically of the preceding word *sunedrion*, "council," the Sanhedrin.

Prison *desmoterion* (1201), "a place of bonds" (from *desmos*, "a bond," *deo*, "to bind"), "a prison," occurs in Matt. 11:2, in **Acts 5:21, 23** and **16:26**, RV, "prison house" (KJV, "prison").

5:22 But when the officers came, and found them not in the prison, they returned, and told,

Officers *huperetes* (5257), is translated "officer," with the following applications, (a) to a magistrate's attendant, Matt. 5:25; (b) to officers of the synagogue, or officers or bailiffs of the Sanhedrin, Matt. 26:58; Mark 14:54, 65; John 7:32, 45-46; 18:3, 12, 18, 22; 19:6; **Acts 5:22, 26**.

Returned *anastrepho* (390), "to turn back," is translated "to return" in **Acts 5:22** and **15:16**.

5:23 Saying, The prison truly found we shut with all safety, and the keepers standing without before the doors: but when we had opened, we found no man within.

Prison *see Acts 5:21.*

Truly *asphaleia* (803), primarily, "not liable to fall, steadfast, firm," hence denoting "safety," **Acts 5:23**, and 1 Thess. 5:3, has the further meaning, "certainty," Luke 1:4.

Shut *kleio* (2808), is used (a) of things material, Matt. 6:6; 25:10; Luke 11:7; John 20:19, 26; **Acts 5:23; 21:30**; Rev. 20:3; figuratively, 21:25; (b) metaphorically, of the kingdom of heaven, Matt. 23:13; of heaven, with consequences of famine, Luke 4:25; Rev. 11:6; of compassion, 1 John 3:17, RV (KJV, "bowels *of compassion*"); of the blessings accruing from the promises of God regarding David, Rev. 3:7; of a door for testimony, 3:8.

Safety *asphaleia* (803), "certainty, safety," is translated "safety" in **Acts 5:23**; 1 Thess. 5:3.

Keepers *phulax* (5441), "a guard, keeper" (akin to *phulasso*, "to guard, keep"), is translated "keepers" in **Acts 5:23**; in **12:6, 19**, RV, "guards" (KJV, "keepers").

Within This is a translation of ... *eso*, John 20:26; **Acts 5:23**; 1 Cor. 5:12 (i.e., "within" the church).

5:24 Now when the high priest and the captain of the temple and the chief priests heard these things, they doubted of them whereunto this would grow.

Captain *see Acts 4:1.*

Things *logos* (3056), "a word, an account," etc., is translated "thing" in Matt. 21:24, KJV (1st part), and Luke 20:3, KJV, RV, "question" (in Matt. 21:24, 2nd part, "these things" translates *tauta*, the neut. plur. of *houtos*, "this"); Luke 1:4; **Acts 5:24**, KJV (RV, "words").

Doubted *see* **Doubt** at *Acts 2:12.*

Of In the following, *peri*, "concerning," is so translated in the RV (for KJV, "of"), e.g., **Acts 5:24**; 1 Cor. 1:11; 1 John 1:1 (the RV is important); cf. John 16:8.

Grow *ginomai* (1096), "to become or come to be," is translated "grow" in **Acts 5:24**, of the development of apostolic work.

5:25 Then came one and told them, saying, Behold, the men whom ye put in prison are standing in the temple, and teaching the people.

One *tis* (5100), an indefinite pronoun signifying "a certain one, some one, any one, one" (the neuter form *ti* denotes "a certain thing"), is used (a) like a noun, e.g., **Acts 5:25**; **19:32**; **21:34**; 1 Cor. 3:4; or with the meaning "someone," e.g., **Acts 8:31**, RV, "some one" (KJV, "some man"); Rom. 5:7; (b) as an adjective.

Put *see Acts 1:7*.

5:26 Then went the captain with the officers, and brought them without violence: for they feared the people, lest they should have been stoned.

Captain *see Acts 4:1*.

Officers *see Acts 5:22*.

Without In **Acts 5:26**, *ou*, "not," *meta*, "with," is rendered "without (violence)."

Violence *bia* (970), denotes "force, violence," said of men, **Acts 5:26**; **21:35**; **24:7**; of waves, **27:41**.

Stoned *lithazo* (3034), "to stone," occurs in John 8:5 (in the most authentic mss.); 10:31-33; 11:8; **Acts 5:26**; **14:19**; 2 Cor. 11:25; Heb. 11:37.

5:27 And when they had brought them, they set *them* before the council: and the high priest asked them,

Set *see Acts 4:7*.

5:28 Saying, Did not we straitly command you that ye should not teach in this name? and, behold, ye have filled Jerusalem with your doctrine, and intend to bring this man's blood upon us.

Straitly A similar construction, *parangello* with the noun *parangelia*, occurs in **Acts 5:28**, "we straitly charged you," lit., "we charged you with a charge."

Command *parangelia* (3852), "a proclamation, a command or commandment," is strictly used of commands received from a superior and transmitted to others. It is rendered "charge" in **Acts 16:24**; 1 Thess. 4:2, RV (where the word is in the plural); 1 Tim. 1:5 (RV) and v. 18. In **Acts 5:28** the lit. meaning is "Did we not charge you with a charge?" *See also* **Commanded** at *Acts 1:4*.

Filled *see Acts 2:2*.

Intend *boulomai* (1014), "to will, wish, desire, purpose" (expressing a fixed resolve, the deliberate exercise of volition), is translated "intend" in **Acts 5:28**, and "intending" in **12:4**.

Bring *epago* (1863), "to bring upon," **Acts 5:28**; 2 Pet. 2:1, 5.

5:29 Then Peter and the *other* apostles answered and said, We ought to obey God rather than men.

Obey *peitharcheo* (3980), "to obey one in authority," is translated "obey" in **Acts 5:29, 32**; "to be obedient," Titus 3:1, RV (KJV, "to obey magistrates"); in **Acts 27:21**, "hearkened."

5:30 The God of our fathers raised up Jesus, whom ye slew and hanged on a tree.

Raised *see* Lifted at *Acts 3:7*.

Slew *diacheirizo* (1315), primarily, "to have in hand, manage" (*cheir*, "the hand"), is used in the middle voice, in the sense of "laying hands on" with a view to "kill," or of actually "killing," **Acts 5:30**, "ye slew"; **26:21**, "to kill."

Hanged *kremannumi* (2910), is used (a) transitively in **Acts 5:30**; **10:39**; in the passive voice, in Matt. 18:6, of a millstone about a neck, and in Luke 23:39, of the malefactors; (b) intransitively, in the middle voice, in Matt. 22:40, of the dependence of "the Law and the prophets" (i.e., that which they enjoin) upon the one great principle of love to God and one's neighbor (as a door "hangs" on a hinge, or as articles "hang" on a nail); in **Acts 28:4**, of the serpent "hanging" from Paul's hand; in Gal. 3:13 the word is used in a quotation from the Sept. of Deut. 21:23.

Tree *xulon* (3586), "wood, a piece of wood, anything made of wood", is used, with the rendering "tree," (a) in Luke 23:31, where "the green tree" refers either to Christ, figuratively of all His living power and excellencies, or to the life of the Jewish people while still inhabiting their land, in contrast to "the dry," a figure fulfilled in the horrors of the Roman massacre and devastation in AD 70 (cf. the Lord's parable in Luke 13:6–9; see Ezek. 20:47, and cf. 21:3); (b) of "the cross," the tree being the *stauros*, the upright pale or stake to which Romans nailed those who were thus to be executed, **Acts 5:30**; **10:39**; **13:29**; Gal. 3:13; 1 Pet. 2:24; (c) of "the tree of life," Rev. 2:7; 22:2 (twice), 14, 19, RV, KJV, "book."

5:31 Him hath God exalted with his right hand *to be* a Prince and a Saviour, for to give repentance to Israel, and forgiveness of sins.

Exalted *see Acts 2:33.*

Prince *see Acts 3:15.*

Saviour *soter* (4990), "a savior, deliverer, preserver," is used (a) of God, Luke 1:47; 1 Tim. 1:1; 2:3; 4:10 (in the sense of "preserver," since He gives "to all life and breath and all things"); Titus 1:3; 2:10; 3:4; Jude 25; (b) of Christ, Luke 2:11; John 4:42; **Acts 5:31**; **13:23** (of Israel); Eph. 5:23 (the sustainer and preserver of the church, His "body"); Phil. 3:20 (at His return to receive the Church to Himself); 2 Tim. 1:10 (with reference to His incarnation, "the days of His flesh"); Titus 1:4 (a title shared, in the context, with God the Father); 2:13, RV, "our great God and Savior Jesus Christ," the pronoun "our," at the beginning of the whole clause, includes all the titles; Titus 3:6; 2 Pet. 1:1, "our God and Savior Jesus Christ"; RV, where the pronoun "our," coming immediately in connection with "God," involves the inclusion of both titles as referring to Christ, just as in the parallel in v. 11, "our Lord and Savior Jesus Christ" (KJV and RV); these passages are therefore a testimony to His deity; 2 Pet. 2:20; 3:2, 18; 1 John 4:14.

Repentance *metanoia* (3341), "afterthought, change of mind, repentance," is used of "repentance" from sin or evil, except in Heb. 12:17, where the word "repentance" seems to mean, not simply a change of Isaac's mind, but such a change as would reverse the effects of his own previous state of mind. Esau's birthright-bargain could not be recalled; it involved an irretrievable loss. As regards "repentance" from sin, (a) the requirement by God on man's part is set forth, e.g., in Matt. 3:8; Luke 3:8; **Acts 20:21**; **26:20**; (b) the mercy of God in giving "repentance" or leading men to it is set forth, e.g., in **Acts 5:31**; **11:18**; Rom. 2:4; 2 Tim. 2:25. The most authentic mss. omit the word in Matt. 9:13 and Mark 2:17, as in the RV.

Forgiveness *aphesis* (859), denotes "a dismissal, release"; it is used of the remission of sins, and translated "forgiveness" in Mark 3:29; Eph. 1:7; Col. 1:14, and in the KJV of **Acts 5:31**; **13:38**; **26:18**, in each of which the RV has "remission." Eleven times it is followed by "of sins," and once by "of trespasses." It is never used of the remission of sins in the Sept., but is especially connected with the Year of Jubilee (Lev. 25:10, etc.). Cf. the RV of Luke 4:18, "release" (KJV, "liberty"). For the significance in connection with remission of sins and the propitiatory sacrifice of Christ, see the different word *paresis*, "a passing over, a remission," of sins committed under the old covenant, Rom. 3:25. The RV should be used here. This passing over, or by, was neither forgetting nor "forgiving"; it was rather a suspension of the just penalty; cf. **Acts 17:30**, "the times of ignorance God overlooked," RV; see also, e.g., Ps. 78:38.

5:32 And we are his witnesses of these things; and *so is* also the Holy Ghost, whom God hath given to them that obey him.

Witnesses *see Acts 1:8.*

Things *rhema* (4487), "a saying, word," is translated "thing" in Luke 2:15; v. 19, KJV (RV, "saying"); in **Acts 5:32**, "things."

Obey *see Acts 5:29.*

5:33 When they heard *that*, they were cut *to the heart*, and took counsel to slay them.

Cut *diaprio* (1282), signifies "to saw asunder" (*dia*, "asunder," *prio*, "to saw"), "to divide by a saw" (as in 1 Chron. 20:3, Sept.), hence, metaphorically, "to be sawn through mentally, to be rent with vexation, to be cut to the heart," is used in **Acts 5:33**; **7:54**.

Counsel *bouleuo* (1011), "to take counsel, to resolve," is used in the middle voice in the NT, "took counsel" in **Acts 5:33**, KJV (RV translates *boulomai*); both in **27:39**; in Luke 14:31, RV "take counsel" (KJV, "consulteth"); in John 11:53, KJV and RV (so the best mss.); 12:10, RV, "took counsel," for KJV, "consulted"; in 2 Cor. 1:17 (twice), "purpose."

Slay *see* Slain at *Acts 2:23.*

5:34 Then stood there up one in the council, a Pharisee, named Gamaliel, a doctor of the law, had in reputation among all the people, and commanded to put the apostles forth a little space;

Stood *see Acts 1:15.*

Doctor *nomodidaskalos* (3547), "a teacher of the Law," with reference to the teachers of the Mosaic Law, Luke 5:17; **Acts 5:34**; also of those who went about among Christians, professing to be instructors of the Law, 1 Tim. 1:7.

Reputation *timios* (5093), from *time*, "honor, price," signifies (a) primarily, "accounted as of great price, precious, costly," 1 Cor. 3:12; Rev. 17:4; 18:12, 16; 21:19, and in the superlative degree, 18:12; 21:11; the comparative degree is found in 1 Pet. 1:7 (*polutimoteros*, in the most authentic mss., "much more precious"); (b) in the metaphorical sense, "held in honor, esteemed, very dear," **Acts 5:34**, "had in honor," RV (KJV, "had in reputation"); so in Heb. 13:4, RV, "let marriage be had in honor"; KJV, "is honorable"; **Acts 20:24**, "dear," negatively of Paul's estimate of his life; Jas. 5:7, "precious" (of fruit); 1 Pet. 1:19, "precious" (of the blood of Christ); 2 Pet. 1:4 (of God's promises). Cf. *timiotes*, preciousness, Rev. 18:19.

Put *poieo* (4160), "to do, make," is translated "to put" (with *exo*, "forth") in **Acts 5:34**, lit., "do (them) outside."

Little *brachus* (1024), "short," is used to some extent adverbially of (a) time, with the preposition *meta*, "after," Luke 22:58, "(after) a little while"; in **Acts 5:34**, without a preposition, RV, "a little while" (KJV, "a little space"); in Heb. 2:7, 9, "a little" (KJV marg. in v. 7, and RV marg., in both, "a little while"), where the writer transfers to time what the Sept. in Ps. 8:5 says of rank; (b) of quantity, John 6:7; in Heb. 13:22, preceded by the preposition *dia*, "by means of," and with *logo*., "words" (genitive plural) understood, "(in) few words"; (c) of distance, **Acts 27:28**, RV, "a little space" (KJV, "a little further").

Space In **Acts 5:34**, KJV, *brachu* (the neuter of *brachus*, "short"), used adverbially, is translated "a little space" (RV "... while").

5:35 And said unto them, Ye men of Israel, take heed to yourselves what ye intend to do as touching these men.

Men *see Acts 1:16*.

Heed *prosecho* (4337), lit., "to hold to," signifies "to turn to, turn one's attention to"; hence, "to give heed"; it is rendered "take heed" in Matt. 6:1; Luke 17:3; 21:34; **Acts 5:35**; **20:28**; 2 Pet. 1:19; to give heed to, in **Acts 8:6, 10**; in v. **11** (KJV, "had regard to"); **16:14** (KJV, "attended unto"); 1 Tim. 1:4; 4:1, 13 (KJV, "give attendance to"); Titus 1:14; Heb. 2:1, lit., "to give heed more earnestly."

Yourselves The reflexive pronoun "yourselves" represents the various plural forms of the reflexive pronoun *heautou* (frequently governed by some preposition), e.g., Matt. 3:9; 16:8; 23:31; 25:9; Mark 9:50; Luke 3:8; 12:33, 57; 16:9; 21:30, "of your own selves"; 21:34; **Acts 5:35**; in Rom. 11:25, "in your own (conceits)," lit., "in (*en;* some texts have *para*, 'among') yourselves"; so 12:16 (with *para*); 1 Pet. 4:8; Jude 20, 21; in Eph. 5:19, RV, "one to another" (KJV, and RV marg., "to yourselves"). In 1 Thess. 5:11, KJV, *allelous*, "one another" (RV), is rendered "yourselves together."

Intend *mello* (3195), "to be about to do a thing," indicating simply the formation of a design, is translated "intend" in **Acts 5:35**, KJV (RV, "are about"); "intending," in **Acts 20:7**, RV (KJV, "ready"); **20:13** (1st part); in the 2nd part of the v., RV, "intending" (KJV, "minding").

5:36 For before these days rose up Theudas, boasting himself to be somebody; to whom a number of men, about four hundred, joined themselves: who was slain; and all, as many as obeyed him, were scattered, and brought to nought.

Rose *see* **Raised** at *Acts 2:24*.

Boasting In **Acts 5:36**, the verb *lego*, "to say," is rendered "boasting" in the KJV; "giving out" (RV).

Four hundred *tessares* (5064), "four," is not found in the NT outside the Gospels, the Acts and Apocalypse; in the last it is very frequent. *Tetartos*, "fourth," is found in Matt. 14:25; Mark 6:48 and seven times in the Apocalypse; also in **Acts 10:30**, "four days ago," lit., "from a fourth day." *Dekatessares*, "fourteen" (lit., "ten-four"), is found in Matt. 1:17; 2 Cor. 12:2; Gal. 2:1; *tessareskaidekatos*, "fourteenth" (lit., "four-and-tenth"), **Acts 27:27, 33**; *tetrakosia*, "four hundred," **Acts 5:36**; **7:6**; **13:20**; Gal. 3:17. In **Acts 7:6** the 400 years refers to Abraham's descendants and to the sojourning and the bondage. This agrees with Gen. 15:13. In Exod. 12:40 the 430 years dates from the call of Abraham himself. Likewise the giving of the Law was 430 years from the promise in Gen. 12:3, which agrees with Gal. 3:17. In John 11:39 *tetartaios*, lit., "a fourth day (one)," is rendered "four days."

Joined *proskollao* (4347), "to stick to," a strengthened form of *kollao*, with *pros*, "to," intensive, is used in the passive voice, reflexively, in a metaphorical sense, with the meanings (a) "to join oneself to," in **Acts 5:36**; (b) "to cleave to," of the husband with regard to the wife, Matt. 19:5; Mark 10:7; in Eph. 5:31, KJV, "shall cleave to" (KJV, "shall be joined to").

Slain *see Acts 2:23*.

Obeyed *peitho* (3982), "to persuade, to win over," in the passive and middle voices, "to be persuaded, to listen to, to obey," is so used with this meaning, in the middle voice, e.g., in **Acts 5:36-37** (in v. **40**, passive voice, "they agreed"); Rom. 2:8; Gal. 5:7; Heb. 13:17; Jas. 3:3. The "obedience" suggested is not by submission to authority, but resulting from persuasion. "*Peitho* and *pisteuo*, 'to trust,' are closely related etymologically; the difference in meaning is that the former implies the obedience that is produced by the latter, cf. Heb. 3:18-19, where the disobedience of the Israelites is said to be the evidence of their unbelief Faith is of the heart, invisible to men; obedience is of the conduct and may be observed. When a man obeys God he gives the only possible evidence that in his heart he believes God. Of course it is persuasion of the truth that results in faith (we believe because we are persuaded that the thing is true, a thing does not become true because it is believed), but *peitho*, in NT suggests an actual and outward result of the inward persuasion and consequent faith."

Scattered *dialuo* (1262), "to dissolve," is translated "scattered" in **Acts 5:36**, KJV.

Brought In **Acts 5:36**, *ginomai*, "to become," is rendered "came (to nought)," RV, for KJV, "were brought." So in 1 Cor. 15:54, "come to pass," for "shall be brought to pass."

Nought *ouden* (3762), "nothing" (the neuter of *oudeis*, no one), is translated "nought" in **Acts 5:36**.

5:37 After this man rose up Judas of Galilee in the days of the taxing, and drew away much people after him: he also perished; and all, *even* as many as obeyed him, were dispersed.

Taxing *apographe* (582), primarily denotes "a written copy," or, as a law term, "a deposition"; then, "a register, census, enrollment," Luke 2:2; **Acts 5:37**, RV, for KJV, "taxing." Luke's accuracy has been vindicated, as against the supposed inconsistency that as Quirinius was governor of Syria in AD 6, ten years after the birth of Christ, the census, as "the first" (RV), could not have taken place. At the time mentioned by Luke, Cilicia, of which Quirinius was governor, was separated from Cyprus and joined to Syria. His later direct governorship of Syria itself accounts for the specific inclusion of, and reference to, his earlier connection with that province. Justin Martyr, a native of Palestine, writing in the middle of the 2nd century, asserts thrice that Quirinius was present in Syria at the time mentioned by Luke (see Apol., 1:34, 46; Trypho 78). Noticeable, too, are the care and accuracy taken by Luke in his historical details, 1:3, RV. As to charges made against Luke's accuracy, Moulton and Milligan say as follows:—"The deduction so long made ... about the census apparently survives the demonstration that the blunder lay only in our lack of information: the microbe is not yet completely expelled. Possibly the salutary process may be completed by our latest inscriptional evidence that Quirinius was a legate in Syria for census purposes in 8-6 BC."

Drew away *aphistemi* (868), in the active voice, used transitively, signifies "to cause to depart, to cause to revolt," **Acts 5:37**; used intransitively, "to stand off, or aloof, or to depart from anyone," Luke 4:13; 13:27; **Acts 5:38** ("refrain from"); **12:10**; **15:38**; **19:9**; **22:29**; 2 Cor. 12:8; metaphorically, "to fall away," 2 Tim. 2:19; in the middle voice, "to withdraw or absent oneself from," Luke 2:37; to "apostatize," Luke 8:13; 1 Tim. 4:1; Heb. 3:12, RV, "falling away."

Much *hikanos* (2425), "enough, much, many," is translated "much," e.g., in Luke 7:12 (in some mss. **Acts 5:37**; see the RV); **Acts 11:24**, **26**; **19:26**; **27:9**.

Dispersed *diaskorpizo* (1287), *dia*, "through," and *skorpizo*, signifies "to scatter abroad," in Matt. 26:31; Mark 14:27, metaphorically of sheep; in Luke 1:51, of the proud; in John 11:52, of the "scattering" of the children of God; in **Acts 5:37**, of the followers of Judas of Galilee (KJV, "were dispersed").

5:38 And now I say unto you, Refrain from these men, and let them alone: for if this counsel or this work be of men, it will come to nought:

Now *see Acts 4:29.*

Refrain *aphistemi* (868), "to cause to depart," is used intransitively, in the sense of "departing from, refraining from," **Acts 5:38**.

Let ... alone *aphiemi* (863), signifies "to send away, set free"; also "to let alone," Matt. 15:14; Mark 14:6; Luke 13:8; John 11:48; 12:7 (RV, "suffer her"); in **Acts 5:38** some texts have *easate* from *eao*, "to permit."

Work *ergon* (2041), denotes (I) "work, employment, task," e.g., Mark 13:34; John 4:34; 17:4; **Acts 13:2**; Phil. 2:30; 1 Thess. 5:13; in **Acts 5:38** with the idea of enterprise; (II) "a deed, act," (a) of God, e.g., John 6:28, 29; 9:3; 10:37; 14:10; **Acts 13:41**; Rom. 14:20; Heb. 1:10; 2:7; 3:9; 4:3, 4, 10; Rev. 15:3; (b) of Christ, e.g., Matt. 11:2; especially in John, 5:36; 7:3, 21; 10:25, 32, 33, 38; 14:11, 12; 15:24; Rev. 2:26; (c) of believers, e.g., Matt. 5:16; Mark 14:6; **Acts 9:36**; Rom. 13:3; Col. 1:10; 1 Thess. 1:3, "work of faith," here the initial act of faith at conversion (turning to God, v. 9); in 2 Thess. 1:11, "*every* work of faith," RV, denotes every activity undertaken for Christ's sake; 2:17; 1 Tim. 2:10; 5:10; 6:18; 2 Tim. 2:21; 3:17; Titus 2:7, 14; 3:1, 8, 14; Heb. 10:24; 13:21; frequent in James, as the effect of faith [in 1:25, KJV, "(a doer) of the work," RV, "(a doer) that worketh"]; 1 Pet. 2:12; Rev. 2:2 and in several other places in chs. 2 and 3; 14:13; (d) of unbelievers, e.g., Matt. 23:3, 5; John 7:7; **Acts 7:41** (for idols); Rom. 13:12; Eph. 5:11; Col. 1:21; Titus 1:16 (1st part); 1 John 3:12; Jude 15, RV; Rev. 2:6, RV; of those who seek justification by works, e.g., Rom. 9:32; Gal. 3:10; Eph. 2:9; described as the works of the law, e.g., Gal. 2:16; 3:2, 5; dead works, Heb. 6:1; 9:14; (e) of Babylon, Rev. 18:6; (f) of the Devil, John 8:41; 1 John 3:8.

Come to nought In **Acts 5:38**, *kataluo*, lit., "to loosen down," hence, "to overthrow," is translated "it will come to nought" (RV, "it will be overthrown").

5:39 But if it be of God, ye cannot overthrow it; lest haply ye be found even to fight against God.

Overthrow *kataluo* (2647), "to destroy utterly, to overthrow completely," is rendered "destroy," in Matt. 5:17, twice, of the Law; Matt. 24:2; 26:61; 27:40; Mark 13:2; 14:58; 15:29; Luke 21:6, of the Temple; in **Acts 6:14**, of Jerusalem; in Gal. 2:18, of the Law as a means of justification; in Rom. 14:20 (KJV, "destroy," RV, "overthrow"), of the marring of a person's spiritual well-being; in **Acts 5:38** and **39** (RV, "overthrow") of the failure of purposes; in 2 Cor. 5:1, of the death of the body ("dissolved"). For its other meaning, "to lodge," see Luke 9:12 and 19:7.

Haply *me pote* (3379), lit., "lest ever," "lest haply," e.g., Luke 14:29, of laying a foundation, with the possibility of being unable tofinish the building; **Acts 5:39**, of the possibility of being found fighting against God; Heb. 3:2, RV, "lest haply," of the possibility of having an evil heart of unbelief. The RV usually has "lest haply" (KJV "lest at any time"), e.g., Matt. 4:6; 5:25; 13:15; Mark 4:12; Luke 4:11; 21:34; Heb. 2:1; in Matt. 25:9, the RV has "peradventure"; in 2 Tim. 2:25, KJV and RV, have "if peradventure"; in John 7:26 the RV has "Can it be that," for the word "Do" in the KJV.

Fight *theomachos* (2314), "fighting against God" occurs in **Acts 5:39** (KJV, "to fight"), lit., "God-fighters."

5:40 And to him they agreed: and when they had called the apostles, and beaten *them*, they commanded that they should not speak in the name of Jesus, and let them go.

Agreed *peitho* (3982), "to persuade," is rendered "agreed" in **Acts 5:40**, where the meaning is "they yielded to him." *See also* **Obeyed** at *Acts 5:36*.

Called *see* **Call** at *Acts 2:39*.

Beaten *dero* (1194), from a root *der*—, "skin" (*derma*, "a skin," cf. Eng., "dermatology"), primarily "to flay," then "to beat, thrash or smite," is used of the treatment of the servants of the owner of the vineyard by the husbandmen, in the parable in Matt. 21:35; Mark 12:3, 5; Luke 20:10-11; of the treatment of Christ, Luke 22:63, RV, "beat," for KJV, "smote"; John 18:23; of the followers of Christ, in the synagogues, Mark 13:9; **Acts 22:19**; of the punishment of unfaithful servants, Luke 12:47-48; of the "beating" of apostles by the High Priest and the Council of the Sanhedrin, **Acts 5:40**; by magistrates, **16:37**. The significance of flogging does not always attach to the word; it is used of the infliction of a single blow, John 18:23; 2 Cor. 11:20, and of "beating" the air, 1 Cor. 9:26. The usual meaning is that of "thrashing or cudgelling," and when used of a blow it indicates one of great violence.

Let *see Acts 3:13*.

5:41 And they departed from the presence of the council, rejoicing that they were counted worthy to suffer shame for his name.

Departed *poreuo* (4198), akin to *poros*, "a passage," in the middle voice signifies "to go on one's way, to depart from one place to another." In some places, where the KJV has the verb "to depart," the RV translates by "to go one's way," e.g., Matt. 2:9, "went their way"; 11:7; 24:1, "was going on His way." In the following the RV has the verb "to go," for the KJV "depart," Luke 4:42 (latter part of verse); 13:31; John 16:7; 2 Tim. 4:10. In Luke 21:8, "go (after)," is said of disciples or partisans. In some places both KJV and RV translate by the verb "to depart," e.g., Matt. 19:15; 25:41; **Acts 5:41**; **Acts 22:21**. This verb is to be distinguished from others signifying "to go." It is best rendered, as often as possible, "to go on one's way."

Presence *see Acts 3:13*.

Rejoicing *chairo* (5463), "to rejoice," is most frequently so translated. As to this verb, the following are grounds and occasions for "rejoicing," on the part of believers: in the Lord, Phil. 3:1; 4:4; His incarnation, Luke 1:14; His power, Luke 13:17; His presence with the Father, John 14:28; His presence with them, John 16:22; 20:20; His ultimate triumph, 8:56; hearing the gospel, **Acts 13:48**; their salvation, **Acts 8:39**; receiving the Lord, Luke 19:6; their enrollment in Heaven, Luke 10:20; their liberty in Christ, **Acts 15:31**; their hope, Rom. 12:12 (cf. Rom. 5:2; Rev. 19:7); their prospect of reward, Matt. 5:12; the obedience and godly conduct of fellow believers, Rom. 16:19, RV, "I rejoice" (KJV, "I am glad"); 2 Cor. 7:7, 9; 13:9; Col. 2:5; 1 Thess. 3:9; 2 John 4; 3 John 3;

the proclamation of Christ, Phil. 1:18; the gospel harvest, John 4:36; suffering with Christ, **Acts 5:41**; 1 Pet. 4:13; suffering in the cause of the gospel, 2 Cor. 13:9 (1st part); Phil. 2:17 (1st part); Col. 1:24; in persecutions, trials and afflictions, Matt. 5:12; Luke 6:23; 2 Cor. 6:10; the manifestation of grace, **Acts 11:23**; meeting with fellow believers, 1 Cor. 16:17, RV, "I rejoice"; Phil. 2:28; receiving tokens of love and fellowship, Phil. 4:10; the "rejoicing" of others, Rom. 12:15; 2 Cor. 7:13; learning of the well-being of others, 2 Cor. 7:16.

Counted *kataxioo* (2661), denotes "to account worthy" (*kata*, "intensive," *axios*, "worthy"), "to judge worthy," Luke 20:35; some mss. have it in 21:36 (so the KJV); the most authentic mss. have the verb *katischuo*, "to prevail"; **Acts 5:41**, "were counted worthy"; so 2 Thess. 1:5.

Worthy *kataxioo* (2661), occurs in Luke 20:35; 21:36, in some texts; **Acts 5:41**; 2 Thess. 1:5.

Shame *atimazo* (818), signifies "to dishonour, treat shamefully, insult," whether in word, John 8:49, or deed, Mark 12:4; Luke 20:11, RV "handled (him) shamefully," (RV "entreated ... shamefully"); Rom. 1:24; 2:23, "dishonorest;" Jas. 2:6, RV, "ye have dishonored (the poor)," (KJV, "despised"); in the passive voice, to suffer dishonor, **Acts 5:41** (KJV, "suffer shame").

5:42 And daily in the temple, and in every house, they ceased not to teach and preach Jesus Christ.

Daily *see Acts 3:2.*

Every The preposition *kata*, "down," is sometimes found governing a noun, in the sense of "every," e.g., Luke 2:41, "every year"; 16:19, "every day"; Heb. 9:25, "every year" (RV, "year by year"); so 10:3. This construction sometimes signifies "in every ... ," e.g., **Acts 14:23**, "in every church"; **15:21**, "in every city"; so **20:23**; Titus 1:5; **Acts 22:19**, "in every synagogue" (plural); **Acts 8:3** "(into) every house." In Luke 8:1 the phrase means "throughout every city," as in the KJV; in v. 4 "of every city," RV. In **Acts 5:42** the RV renders *kat' oikon* "at home," for KJV, "in every house"; in **2:46**, for KJV, "from house to house" (marg., "at home"). In **Acts 15:21** (last part) the adjective *pas*, "all," is placed between the preposition and the noun for the sake of emphasis. In **Acts 26:11**, *kata*, followed by the plural of *pas* and the article before the noun, is rendered "in all the synagogues," RV, for KJV, "in every synagogue." The presence of the article confirms the RV.

House For "in every house," **Acts 5:42** (cf. **2:46**).

Ceased *pauo* (3973), "to stop, to make an end," is used chiefly in the middle voice in the NT, signifying "to come to an end, to take one's rest, a willing cessation" (in contrast to the passive voice which denotes a forced cessation), Luke 5:4, of a discourse; 8:24, of a storm, 11:1, of Christ's prayer; **Acts 5:42**, of teaching and preaching; **6:13**, of speaking against; **13:10**, of evil doing; **20:1**, of an uproar; **20:31**, of admonition; **21:32**, of a scourging; 1 Cor. 13:8, of tongues; Eph. 1:16, of giving thanks; Col. 1:9, of prayer; Heb. 10:2, of sacrifices; 1 Pet. 4:1, of "ceasing" from sin. It is used in the active voice in 1 Pet. 3:10, "let him cause his tongue to cease from evil."

Preach *euangelizo* (2097), "to bring or announce glad tidings" (Eng., "evangelize"), is used (a) in the active voice in Rev. 10:7 ("declared") and 14:6 ("to proclaim," RV, KJV, "to preach"); (b) in the passive voice, of matters to be proclaimed as "glad tidings," Luke 16:16; Gal. 1:11; 1 Pet. 1:25; of persons to whom the proclamation is made, Matt. 11:5; Luke 7:22; Heb. 4:2, 6; 1 Pet. 4:6; (c) in the middle voice, especially of the message of salvation, with a personal object, either of the person preached, e.g., **Acts 5:42**; **11:20**; Gal. 1:16, or, with a preposition, of the persons evangelized, e.g., **Acts 13:32**, "declare glad tidings"; Rom. 1:15; Gal. 1:8; with an impersonal object, e.g., "the word," **Acts 8:4**; "good tidings," **8:12**; "the word of the Lord," **15:35**; "the gospel," 1 Cor. 15:1; 2 Cor. 11:7; "the faith," Gal. 1:23; "peace," Eph. 2:17; "the unsearchable riches of Christ," 3:8.

Chapter 6

6:1 And in those days, when the number of the disciples was multiplied, there arose a murmuring of the Grecians against the Hebrews, because their widows were neglected in the daily ministration.

Multiplied *plethuno* (4129), used (a) transitively, denotes "to cause to increase, to multiply," 2 Cor. 9:10; Heb. 6:14 (twice); in the passive voice, "to be multiplied," Matt. 24:12, RV, "(iniquity) shall be multiplied" (KJV, "shall abound"); **Acts 6:7**; **7:17**; **9:31**; **12:24**; 1 Pet. 1:2; 2 Pet. 1:2; Jude 2; (b) intransitively it denotes "to be multiplying," **Acts 6:1**, RV, "was multiplying" (KJV, "was multiplied").

Arose *ginomai* (1096), "to become, to take place," is sometimes suitably translated "arise"; e.g., Matt. 8:24; Mark 4:37, "there arose a great tempest." So of the arising of persecution, Matt. 13:21; Mark 4:17; this might be translated "taketh place"; of a tumult, Matt. 27:24, RV, "arising," for KJV, "made"; of a flood, Luke 6:48; a famine, 15:14; a questioning, John 3:25; a murmuring, **Acts 6:1**; a tribulation, **11:19** (RV); a stir in the city, **19:23**; a dissension, **23:7**; a great clamor, v. **9**.

Murmuring *gongusmos* (1112), "a murmuring, muttering," is used (a) in the sense of secret debate among people, John 7:12 (as with the verb in v. 32); (b) of displeasure or complaining (more privately than in public), said of Grecian Jewish converts against Hebrews, **Acts 6:1**; in general admonitions, Phil. 2:14; 1 Pet. 4:9, RV, "murmuring" (KJV, "grudging").

Widows *chera* (5503), Matt. 28:13 (in some texts); Mark 12:40, 42, 43; Luke 2:37; 4:25, 26, lit., "a woman a widow"; 7:12; 18:3, 5; 20:47; 21:2, 3; **Acts 6:1**; **9:39, 41**; 1 Tim. 5:3 (twice), 4, 5, 11, 16 (twice); Jas. 1:27; 1 Tim. 5:9 refers to elderly "widows" (not an ecclesiastical "order"), recognized, for relief or maintenance by the church (cf. vv. 3, 16), as those who had fulfilled the conditions mentioned; where relief could be ministered by those who had relatives that were "widows" (a likely circumstance in large families), the church was not to be responsible; there is an intimation of the tendency to shelve individual responsibility at the expense of church funds. In Rev. 18:7, it is used figuratively of a city forsaken.

Neglected *paratheoreo* (3865), primarily, "to examine side by side, compare" (*para*, "beside," *theoreo*, "to look at"), hence, "to overlook, to neglect," is used in **Acts 6:1**, of the "neglect" of widows in the daily ministration in Jerusalem.

Daily *kathemerinos* (2522), means, lit., "according to" (*kata*) "the day" (*hemera*), "day by day, daily," **Acts 6:1**.

Ministration *see* **Ministry** at *Acts 1:17*.

6:2 Then the twelve called the multitude of the disciples *unto them*, and said, It is not reason that we should leave the word of God, and serve tables.

Twelve *dodeka* (1427), is used frequently in the Gospels for the twelve apostles, and in **Acts 6:2**; 1 Cor. 15:5; Rev. 21:14b; of the tribes of Israel, Matt. 19:28; Luke 22:30; Jas. 1:1; Rev. 21:12c (cf. 7:5-8; 12:1); in various details relating to the heavenly Jerusalem, Rev. 21:12-21; 22:2. The number in general is regarded as suggestive of divine administration.

Multitude *see Acts 4:32*.

Reason *arestos* (701), denotes "pleasing, agreeable," John 8:29, RV, "(the things that are) pleasing," KJV, "(those things that) please", KJV and RV in 1 John 3:22; in **Acts 6:2**, "fit" (RV marg., "pleasing"); **12:3**, "it pleased," lit., "it was pleasing."

Leave *kataleipo* (2641), a strengthened form of *leipo*, "to leave," signifies (a) "to leave, to leave behind," e.g., Matt. 4:13; (b) "to leave remaining, reserve," e.g., Luke 10:40; (c) "to forsake," in the sense of abandoning, translated "to forsake" in the RV of Luke 5:28 and **Acts 6:2**; in Heb. 11:27 and 2 Pet. 2:15, KJV and RV. In this sense it is translated "to leave," in Mark 10:7; 14:52; Luke 15:4; Eph. 5:31.

Serve *diakoneo* (1247), signifies "to be a servant, attendant, to serve, wait upon, minister." In the following it is translated "to minister," except where "to serve" is mentioned: it is used (a) with a general significance, e.g., Matt. 4:11; 20:28; Mark 1:13; 10:45; John 12:26 ("serve," twice); **Acts 19:22**; Philem. 13; (b) of waiting at table, "ministering" to the guests, Matt. 8:15; Luke 4:39; 8:3; 12:37; 17:8, "serve"; 22:26, "serve," v. 27, "serveth," twice; the 2nd instance, concerning the Lord, may come under (a); so of women preparing food, etc., Mark 1:31; Luke 10:40, "serve"; John 12:2, "served"; (c) of relieving one's necessities, supplying the necessaries of life, Matt. 25:44; 27:55; Mark 15:41; **Acts 6:2**, "serve"; Rom. 15:25; Heb. 6:10; more definitely in connection with such service in a local church, 1 Tim. 3:10, 13 [there is nothing in the original representing the word "office"; RV, "let them serve as deacons," "they that have served (well) as deacons"]; (d) of attending, in a more general way, to anything that may serve another's interests, as of the work of an amanuensis, 2 Cor. 3:3 (metaphorical): of the conveyance of material gifts for assisting the needy, 2 Cor. 8:19, 20, RV, "is ministered" (KJV, "is administered"); of a variety of forms of service, 2 Tim. 1:18; of the testimony of the OT prophets, 1 Pet. 1:12; of the ministry of believers one to another in various ways, 1 Pet. 4:10, 11 (not here of discharging ecclesiastical functions).

Tables *trapeza* (5132), is used of (a) "a dining table," Matt. 15:27; Mark 7:28; Luke 16:21; 22:21, 30; (b) "the table of shewbread," Heb. 9:2; (c) by metonymy, of "what is provided on the table" (the word being used of that with which it is associated), **Acts 16:34**; Rom. 11:9 (figurative of the special privileges granted to Israel and centering in Christ); 1 Cor. 10:21 (twice), "the Lord's table," denoting all that is provided for believers in Christ on the ground of His death (and thus expressing something more comprehensive than the Lord's Supper); "the table of demons," denoting all that is partaken of by idolaters as the result of the influence of demons in connection with their sacrifices; (d) "a moneychanger's table," Matt. 21:12; Mark 11:15; John 2:15; (e) "a bank," Luke 19:23 (cf. *trapezites*); (f) by metonymy for "the distribution of money," **Acts 6:2**.

6:3 Wherefore, brethren, look ye out among you seven men of honest report, full of the Holy Ghost and wisdom, whom we may appoint over this business.

Wherefore *oun*, a particle expressing sequence or consequence, e.g., Matt. 24:26; **Acts 6:3**.

Brethren *see* ***Acts 1:16***.

Look *episkeptomai* (1980), primarily, "to inspect" (a late form of *episkopeo*, "to look upon, care for, exercise oversight"), signifies (a) "to visit" with help, of the act of God, Luke 1:68, 78; 7:16; **Acts 15:14**; Heb. 2:6; (b) "to visit" the sick and afflicted, Matt. 25:36, 43; Jas. 1:27; (c) "to go and see," "pay a visit to," **Acts 7:23**; **15:36**; (d) "to look out" certain men for a purpose, **Acts 6:3**

Honest In **Acts 6:3**, "men of honest (RV, 'good') report" translates the passive voice of *martureo*, lit., "having had witness borne."

Report *martureo* (3140), denotes (I) "to be a *martus*," or "to bear witness to," sometimes rendered "to testify"; it is used of the witness (a) of God the Father to Christ, John 5:32, 37; 8:18 (2nd part); 1 John 5:9, 10; to others, **Acts 13:22**; **15:8**; Heb. 11:2, 4 (twice), 5, 39; (b) of Christ, John 3:11, 32; 4:44; 5:31; 7:7; 8:13, 14, 18 (1st part); 13:21; 18:37; **Acts 14:3**; 1 Tim. 6:13; Rev. 22:18, 20; of the Holy Spirit, to Christ, John 15:26; Heb. 10:15; 1 John 5:7, 8, RV, which rightly omits the latter part of v. 7 (it was a marginal gloss which crept into the original text); it finds no support in Scripture; (c) of the Scriptures, to Christ, John 5:39; Heb. 7:8, 17; (d) of the works of Christ, to Himself, and of the circumstances connected with His death, John 5:36; 10:25; 1 John 5:8; (e) of prophets and apostles, to the righteousness of God, Rom. 3:21; to Christ, John 1:7, 8, 15, 32, 34; 3:26; 5:33, RV; 15:27; 19:35; 21:24; **Acts 10:43**; **23:11**; 1 Cor. 15:15; 1 John 1:2; 4:14; Rev. 1:2; to doctrine, **Acts 26:22** (in some texts, so KJV; see *marturomai*); to the Word of God, Rev. 1:2; (f) of others, concerning Christ, Luke 4:22; John 4:39; 12:17; (g) of believers to one another, John 3:28; 2 Cor. 8:3; Gal. 4:15; Col. 4:13; 1 Thess. 2:11; 3 John 3, 6, 12 (2nd part); (h) of the apostle Paul concerning Israel, Rom. 10:2; (i) of an angel, to the churches, Rev. 22:16; (j) of unbelievers, concerning themselves, Matt. 23:31; concerning Christ, John 18:23; concerning others, John 2:25; **Acts 22:5**; **26:5**; (II) "to give a good report, to approve of," **Acts 6:3**; **10:22**; **16:2**; **22:12**; 1 Tim. 5:10; 3 John 12 (1st part); some would put Luke 4:22 here.

Full *pleres* (4134), denotes "full," (a) in the sense of "being filled," materially, Matt. 14:20; 15:37; Mark 8:19 (said of baskets "full" of bread crumbs); of leprosy, Luke 5:12; spiritually, of the Holy Spirit, Luke 4:1; **Acts 6:3**; **7:55**; **11:24**; grace and truth, John 1:14; faith, **Acts 6:5**; grace and power, **6:8**; of the effects of spiritual life and qualities, seen in good works, **Acts 9:36**; in an evil sense, of guile and villany, **Acts 13:10**; wrath, **19:28**; (b) in the sense of "being complete," "full corn in the ear," Mark 4:28; of a reward hereafter, 2 John 8.

Wisdom *sophia* (4678), is used with reference to (a) God, Rom. 11:33; 1 Cor. 1:21, 24; 2:7; Eph. 3:10; Rev. 7:12; (b) Christ, Matt. 13:54; Mark 6:2; Luke 2:40, 52; 1 Cor. 1:30; Col. 2:3; Rev. 5:12; (c) "wisdom" personified, Matt. 11:19; Luke 7:35; 11:49; (d) human "wisdom" (1) in spiritual things, Luke 21:15; **Acts 6:3**, **10**; **7:10**; 1 Cor. 2:6 (1st part); 12:8; Eph. 1:8, 17; Col. 1:9, RV, "(spiritual) wisdom," 28; 3:16; 4:5; Jas. 1:5; 3:13, 17; 2 Pet. 3:15; Rev. 13:18; 17:9; (2) in the natural sphere, Matt. 12:42; Luke 11:31; **Acts 7:22**; 1 Cor. 1:17, 19, 20, 21 (twice), 22; 2:1, 4, 5, 6 (2nd part), 13; 3:19; 2 Cor. 1:12; Col. 2:23; (3) in its most debased form, Jas. 3:15, "earthly, sensual, devilish" (marg., "demoniacal").

Appoint *kathistemi* (2525), usually signifies "to appoint a person to a position." In this sense the verb is often translated "to make" or "to set," in appointing a person to a place of authority, e.g., a servant over a household, Matt. 24:45, 47; 25:21, 23; Luke 12:42, 44; a judge, Luke 12:14; **Acts 7:27**, **35**; a governor, **Acts 7:10**; man by God over the work of His hands, Heb. 2:7. It is rendered "appoint," with reference to the so-called seven deacons in **Acts 6:3**. The RV translates it by "appoint" in Titus 1:5, instead of "ordain," of the elders whom Titus was to "appoint" in every city in Crete. Not a formal ecclesiastical ordination is in view, but the "appointment," for the recognition of the churches, of those who had already been raised up and qualified by the Holy Spirit, and had given evidence of this in their life and service. It is used of the priests of old, Heb. 5:1; 7:28; 8:3 (RV, "appointed").

Business *chreia* (5532), translated "business" in **Acts 6:3**, of the distribution of funds, signifies "a necessity, a need," and is used in this place concerning duty or business.

6:4 But we will give ourselves continually to prayer, and to the ministry of the word.

Give For *proskartereo*, "to give oneself continually," **Acts 6:4**.

Ourselves In **Acts 6:4**, KJV, *proskartereo*, "to continue steadfastly" (RV), is translated "give ourselves continually."

Continually *see* Continued at *Acts 1:14*.

Ministry *see Acts 1:17*.

6:5 And the saying pleased the whole multitude: and they chose Stephen, a man full of faith and of the Holy Ghost, and Philip, and Prochorus, and Nicanor, and Timon, and Parmenas, and Nicolas a proselyte of Antioch:

Pleased *aresko* (700), signifies (a) "to be pleasing to, be acceptable to," Matt. 14:6; Mark 6:22; **Acts 6:5**; Rom. 8:8; 15:2; 1 Cor. 7:32-34; Gal. 1:10; 1 Thess. 2:15; 4:1 (where the preceding *kai*, "and," is epexegetical, "even," explaining the "walking," i.e., Christian manner of life as "pleasing" God; in Gen. 5:22, where the Hebrew has "Enoch walked with God," the Sept. has "Enoch pleased God"; cf. Mic. 6:8; Heb. 11:5); 2 Tim. 2:4; (b) "to endeavor to please," and so, "to render service," doing so evilly in one's own interests, Rom. 15:1, which Christ did not, v. 3; or unselfishly, 1 Cor. 10:33; 1 Thess. 2:4. This sense of the word is illustrated by Moulton and Milligan (*Vocab.*) from numerous inscriptions, especially describing "those who have proved themselves of use to the commonwealth."

Multitude *see Acts 4:32*.

Chose *see* Chosen at *Acts 1:2*.

Full *see Acts 6:3*.

Proselyte *see* Proselytes at *Acts 2:10*.

6:6 Whom they set before the apostles: and when they had prayed, they laid *their* hands on them.

Set *see Acts 4:7*.

Before *see Acts 2:25*.

Laid ... on *epitithemi* (2007), "to add to, lay upon," etc., is used of "laying" hands on the sick, for healing, Matt. 9:18; 19:13, RV, "lay" (KJV, "put"); 19:15; Mark 5:23; 6:5; 7:32; 8:23, RV, "laid" (KJV, "put"); so in v. 25; 16:18; Luke 4:40; 13:13; **Acts 6:6**; **8:17**, **19**; **9:12** and **17**, RV, "laying" (KJV, "putting"); **13:3**; **19:6**; **28:8**; in some mss. in Rev. 1:17; of "laying" hands on a person by way of public recognition, 1 Tim. 5:22; of a shepherd's "laying" a sheep on his shoulders, Luke 15:5; "of laying" the cross on Christ's shoulders, Luke 23:26; of "laying" on stripes, **Acts 16:23**; wood on a fire, **28:3**; metaphorically, of "laying" burden's on men's shoulders, Matt. 23:4; similarly of "giving" injunctions, **Acts 15:28** (cf. "put ... upon" in v. **10**). *Epithesis* (1936), "a laying on" (*epi*, "on," *tithemi*, "to put"), is used in the NT (a) of the "laying" on of hands by the apostles accompanied by the impartation of the Holy Spirit in outward demonstration, in the cases of those in Samaria who had believed, **Acts 8:18**.

6:7 And the word of God increased; and the number of the disciples multiplied in Jerusalem greatly; and a great company of the priests were obedient to the faith.

Increased *auxano* (837), "to grow or increase," of the growth of that which lives, naturally or spiritually, is used transitively, signifying to make to increase, said of giving the increase, 1 Cor. 3:6, 7; 2 Cor. 9:10, the effect of the work of God, according to the analogy of His operations in nature; "to grow, become greater," e.g. of plants and fruit, Matt. 6:28; used in the passive voice in 13:32 and Mark 4:8, "increase"; in the active in Luke 12:27; 13:19; of the body, Luke 1:80; 2:40; of Christ, John 3:30, "increase"; of the work of the gospel of God, **Acts 6:7**, "increased"; **12:24**; **19:20**; of people, **Acts 7:17**; of faith, 2 Cor. 10:15 (passive voice), RV, "growth" (KJV, "is increased"); of believers individually, Eph. 4:15; Col. 1:6, RV, 10 (passive voice), "increasing"; 1 Pet. 2:2; 2 Pet. 3:18; of the church, Col. 2:19; of churches, Eph. 2:21.

Multiplied *see Acts 6:1*.

Greatly *sphodra* (4970), properly the neuter plural of *sphodros*, "excessive, violent" (from a root indicating restlessness), signifies "very, very much, exceedingly," Matt. 2:10; 17:6, "sore"; 17:23; 18:31, RV, "exceeding," for KJV, "very"; 19:25; 26:22; 27:54, RV, "exceedingly" for KJV, "greatly"; Mark 16:4, "very"; Luke 18:23 (ditto); **Acts 6:7**, RV, "exceedingly," for KJV, "greatly"; Rev. 16:21.

Company *ochlos* (3793), "a throng of people, an irregular crowd," most usually "a disorganized throng"; in **Acts 6:7**, however, it is said of a company of the priests who believed; the word here indicates that they had not combined to bring this about. The RV usually translates this word "company" or "multitude."

Obedient *hupakouo* (5219), "to listen, attend" (as in **Acts 12:13**), and so, "to submit, to obey," is used of "obedience" (a) to God, Heb. 5:9; 11:8; (b) to Christ, by natural elements,

Matt. 8:27; Mark 1:27; 4:41; Luke 8:25; (c) to disciples of Christ, Luke 17:6; (d) to the faith, **Acts 6:7**; the gospel, Rom. 10:16; 2 Thess. 1:8; Christian doctrine, Rom. 6:17 (as to a form or mold of teaching); (e) to apostolic injunctions, Phil. 2:12; 2 Thess. 3:14; (f) to Abraham by Sarah, 1 Pet. 3:6; (g) to parents by children, Eph. 6:1; Col. 3:20; (h) to masters by servants, Eph. 6:5; Col. 3:22; (i) to sin, Rom. 6:12; (j) in general, Rom. 6:16.

Faith *pistis* (4102), primarily, "firm persuasion," a conviction based upon hearing (akin to *peitho*, "to persuade"), is used in the NT always of "faith in God or Christ, or things spiritual." The word is used of (a) trust, e.g., Rom. 3:25; 1 Cor. 2:5; 15:14, 17; 2 Cor. 1:24; Gal. 3:23; Phil. 1:25; 2:17; 1 Thess. 3:2; 2 Thess. 1:3; 3:2; (b) trust-worthiness, e.g., Matt. 23:23; Rom. 3:3, RV, "the faithfulness of God"; Gal. 5:22 (RV, "faithfulness"); Titus 2:10, "fidelity"; (c) by metonymy, what is believed, the contents of belief, the "faith," **Acts 6:7**; **14:22**; Gal. 1:23; 3:25 [contrast 3:23, under (a)]; 6:10; Phil. 1:27; 1 Thess. 3:10; Jude 3, 20 (and perhaps 2 Thess. 3:2); (d) a ground for "faith," an assurance, **Acts 17:31** (not as in KJV, marg., "offered faith"); (e) a pledge of fidelity, plighted "faith," 1 Tim. 5:12.

6:8 And Stephen, full of faith and power, did great wonders and miracles among the people.

Full *see Acts 6:3.*

Faith In **Acts 6:8** the most authentic mss. have *charis*, "grace," RV, for *pistis*, "faith."

Wonders *see Acts 2:19.*

Miracles *see* Miracle at *Acts 4:16.*

6:9 Then there arose certain of the synagogue, which is called *the synagogue* of the Libertines, and Cyrenians, and Alexandrians, and of them of Cilicia and of Asia, disputing with Stephen.

Disputing *suzeteo* (4802), lit., "to seek or examine together," signifies "to discuss," but is translated "to dispute" in **Acts 6:9**, and **9:29**; elsewhere only in Mark and Luke.

6:10 And they were not able to resist the wisdom and the spirit by which he spake.

Resist *anthistemi* (436), "to set against" (*anti*, "against," *histemi*, "to cause to stand"), used in the middle (or passive) voice and in the intransitive 2nd aorist and perfect active, signifying "to withstand, oppose, resist," is translated "to resist" in Matt. 5:39; **Acts 6:10**, KJV (RV, withstand); Rom. 9:19, KJV (RV, "withstandeth"); 13:2 (2nd and 3rd parts), KJV (RV, "withstandeth" and "withstand"); Gal. 2:11, RV (KJV, "withstood"); 2 Tim. 3:8 (2nd part), KJV (RV, "withstand"); Jas. 4:7; 1 Pet. 5:9, KJV (RV, "withstand"); "to withstand" in **Acts 13:8**; Eph. 6:13; 2 Tim. 3:8 (1st part); 4:15.

Wisdom *see Acts 6:3.*

6:11 Then they suborned men, which said, We have heard him speak blasphemous words against Moses, and *against* God.

Suborned *hupoballo* (5260), "to throw or put under, to subject," denoted "to suggest, whisper, prompt"; hence, "to instigate," translated "suborned" in **Acts 6:11**. To "suborn" in the legal sense is to procure a person who will take a false oath. The idea of making suggestions is probably present in this use of the word.

Men *see Acts 1:16.*

Blasphemous *blasphemos* (989), "abusive, speaking evil," is translated "blasphemous," in **Acts 6:11, 13**; "a blasphemer," 1 Tim. 1:13; "railers," 2 Tim. 3:2, RV; "railing," 2 Pet. 2:11.

Words *see Acts 2:14.*

6:12 And they stirred up the people, and the elders, and the scribes, and came upon *him*, and caught him, and brought *him* to the council,

Stirred up *sunkineo* (4787), "to move together" (*sun*, "together," *kineo*, "to move"), "to stir up, excite," is used metaphorically in **Acts 6:12**.

Scribes *see Acts 4:5.*

Came *see Acts 4:1.*

Caught *sunarpazo* (4884), "to snatch, to seize, to keep a firm grip of," is used only by Luke, and translated "caught" in the KJV of Luke 8:29, of demon-possession; in **Acts 6:12**, of the act of the elders and scribes in seizing Stephen, RV, more suitably, "seized." So in **Acts 19:29**. In **27:15**, it is used of the effects of wind upon a ship.

6:13 And set up false witnesses, which said, This man ceaseth not to speak blasphemous words against this holy place, and the law:

Set *see Acts 4:7.*

False *pseudes* (5571), is used of "false witnesses," **Acts 6:13**; "false apostles," Rev. 2:2, RV, "false," KJV, "liars"; Rev. 21:8, "liars."

Witnesses *see Acts 1:8.*

Ceaseth *see* Ceased at *Acts 5:42.*

Blasphemous *see Acts 6:11.*

Words *see Acts 2:14.*

Holy *see Acts 3:14.*

6:14 For we have heard him say, that this Jesus of Nazareth shall destroy this place, and shall change the customs which Moses delivered us.

Destroy *see* Overthrow at *Acts 5:39.*

Change *allasso* (236), "to make other than it is" (from *allos*, "another"), "to transform, change," is used (a) of the effect of the gospel upon the precepts of the Law, **Acts 6:14**; (b) of the effect, on the body of a believer, of Christ's return, 1 Cor. 15:51-52; (c) of the final renewal of the material creation, Heb. 1:12; (d) of a change in the apostle's mode of speaking (or dealing), Gal. 4:20. In Rom. 1:23 it has its other meaning, "to exchange."

Customs *ethos* (1485), denotes (a) "a custom, usage, prescribed by law," **Acts 6:14**; **15:1**; **25:16**; "a rite or ceremony," Luke 2:42; (b) a "custom, habit, manner," Luke 22:39; John 19:40; Heb. 10:25 (KJV, "manner").

6:15 And all that sat in the council, looking stedfastly on him, saw his face as it had been the face of an angel.

Sat *kathezomai* (2516), "to sit (down)," is used in Matt. 26:55; Luke 2:46; John 4:6; 11:20; 20:12; **Acts 6:15**.

Looking stedfastly *see* **Looked** at *Acts 1:10.*

Chapter 7

7:1 Then said the high priest, Are these things so?

Are these things so *see* **Could** at *Acts 4:14.*

7:2 And he said, Men, brethren, and fathers, hearken; The God of glory appeared unto our father Abraham, when he was in Mesopotamia, before he dwelt in Charran,

Hearken *see* Hear at *Acts 3:22.*

God *see Acts 2:23.*

Father *pater* (3962), from a root signifying "a nourisher, protector, upholder" (Lat., *pater*, Eng., "father," are akin), is used (a) of the nearest ancestor, e.g., Matt. 2:22; (b) of a more remote ancestor, the progenitor of the people, a "forefather," e.g., Matt. 3:9; 23:30; 1 Cor. 10:1; the patriarchs, 2 Pet. 3:4; (c) one advanced in the knowledge of Christ, 1 John 2:13; (d) metaphorically, of the originator of a family or company of persons animated by the same spirit as himself, as of Abraham, Rom. 4:11, 12, 16, 17, 18, or of Satan, John 8:38, 41, 44; (e) of one who, as a preacher of the gospel and a teacher, stands in a "father's" place, caring for his spiritual children, 1 Cor. 4:15 (not the same as a mere title of honor, which the Lord prohibited, Matt. 23:9); (f) of the members of the Sanhedrin, as of those who exercised religious authority over others, **Acts 7:2**; **22:1**; (g) of God in relation to those who have been born anew (John 1:12, 13), and so are believers, Eph. 2:18; 4:6 (cf. 2 Cor. 6:18), and imitators of their "Father," Matt. 5:45, 48; 6:1, 4, 6, 8, 9, etc. Christ never associated Himself with them by using the personal pronoun "our"; He always used the singular, "My Father," His relationship being unoriginated and essential, whereas theirs is by grace and regeneration, e.g., Matt. 11:27; 25:34; John 20:17; Rev. 2:27; 3:5, 21; so the apostles spoke of God as the "Father" of the Lord Jesus Christ, e.g., Rom. 15:6; 2 Cor. 1:3; 11:31; Eph. 1:3; Heb. 1:5; 1 Pet. 1:3; Rev. 1:6; (h) of God, as the "Father" of lights, i.e., the Source or Giver of whatsoever provides illumination, physical and spiritual, Jas. 1:17; of mercies, 2 Cor. 1:3; of glory, Eph. 1:17; (i) of God, as Creator, Heb. 12:9 (cf. Zech. 12:1).

Before *prin* (4250), "before, formerly" (etymologically akin to *pro*, "before"), has the force of a conjunction, e.g., Matt. 1:18; 26:34 75; John 14:29; **Acts 7:2**.

7:3 And said unto him, Get thee out of thy country, and from thy kindred, and come into the land which I shall shew thee.

Get *exerchomai* (1831), "to come or go out," is translated "get ... out" in Luke 13:31; **Acts 7:3**; **22:18**.

Country *ge*, "earth, land," is translated "country" in the KJV of Matt. 9:31 and **Acts 7:3**; RV, land.

Kindred *sungeneia* (4772), primarily denotes "kinship"; then, "kinsfolk, kindred" (cf. *sungenes*, "a kinsman"), Luke 1:61; **Acts 7:3, 14**.

Come *deuro*, "hither, here," is used (sometimes with verbs of motion) in the singular number, in calling a person to come, Matt. 19:21; Mark 10:21; Luke 18:22; John 11:43; **Acts 7:3, 34**; Rev. 17:1; 21:9. For its other meaning, "hitherto," Rom. 1:13. It has a plural, *deute*, frequent in the Gospels; elsewhere in Rev. 19:17.

7:4 Then came he out of the land of the Chaldaeans, and dwelt in Charran: and from thence, when his father was

dead, he removed him into this land, wherein ye now dwell.

Thence *ekeithen* (1564), is used (a) of place, e.g., Matt. 4:21, "from thence"; 5:26; in **Acts 20:13**, "there"; often preceded by *kai*, written *kakeithen*, e.g., Mark 9:30 and Luke 11:53 (in the best texts); **Acts 7:4**; **14:26**; (b) of time, **Acts 13:21**, "and afterward."

Removed *metoikizo* (3351), "to remove to a new abode, cause to migrate" (*meta*, implying "change," *oikos*, "a dwelling place"), is translated "removed" in **Acts 7:4**; "I will carry ... away" (v. **43**).

7:5 And he gave him none inheritance in it, no, not *so much as* to set his foot on: yet he promised that he would give it to him for a possession, and to his seed after him, when *as yet* he had no child.

Inheritance *kleronomia* (2817), "a lot," properly "an inherited property, an inheritance." "It is always rendered inheritance in NT, but only in a few cases in the Gospels has it the meaning ordinarily attached to that word in English, i.e., that into possession of which the heir enters only on the death of an ancestor. The NT usage may be set out as follows: (a) that property in real estate which in ordinary course passes from father to son on the death of the former, Matt. 21:38; Mark 12:7; Luke 12:13; 20:14; (b) a portion of an estate made the substance of a gift, **Acts 7:5**; Gal. 3:18, which also is to be included under (c); (c) the prospective condition and possessions of the believer in the new order of things to be ushered in at the return of Christ, **Acts 20:32**; Eph. 1:14; 5:5; Col. 3:24; Heb. 9:15; 1 Pet. 1:4; (d) what the believer will be to God in that age, Eph. 1:18."

Set For **Acts 7:5**, "to set his foot on."

Foot In **Acts 7:5** *bema*, "a step," is used with podos, the genitive case of *pous*, lit., "the step of a foot," i.e., "a foot breadth," what the "foot" can stand on, "(not so much as) to set his foot on."

Promised *epangello* (1861), "to announce, proclaim," has in the NT the two meanings "to profess" and "to promise," each used in the middle voice; "to promise" (a) of "promises" of God, **Acts 7:5**; Rom. 4:21; in Gal. 3:19, passive voice; Titus 1:2; Heb. 6:13; 10:23; 11:11; 12:26; Jas. 1:12; 2:5; 1 John 2:25; (b) made by men, Mark 14:11; 2 Pet. 2:19.

Possession *kataschesis* (2697), primarily "a holding back," then, "a holding fast," denotes "a possession," **Acts 7:5**, or "taking possession," v. **45**, with the article, lit., "in the (i.e., their) taking possession."

7:6 And God spake on this wise, That his seed should sojourn in a strange land; and that they should bring them into bondage, and entreat *them* evil four hundred years.

On this wise *houtos or houto* (3779), "in this way, so, thus," is used (a) with reference to what precedes, e.g., Luke 1:25; 2:48; (b) with reference to what follows, e.g., Luke 19:31, rendered "on this wise," in Matt. 1:18; John 21:1, and before quotations, **Acts 7:6**; **13:34**; Rom. 10:6, KJV (RV, "thus"); Heb. 4:4; (c) marking intensity, rendered "so," e.g., Gal. 1:6; Heb. 12:21; Rev. 16:18; (d) in comparisons, rendered "so," e.g., Luke 11:30; Rom. 5:15.

Sojourn *paroikos* (3941), an adjective, lit., "dwelling near," then, "foreign, alien" (found with this meaning in inscriptions), hence, as a noun, "a sojourner," is used with *eimi*, "to be," in **Acts 7:6**, "should sojourn," lit., "should be a sojourner"; in **7:29**, RV, "sojourner" (KJV, "stranger"); in Eph. 2:19, RV, "sojourners" (KJV, "foreigners"), the preceding word rendered "strangers" is *xenos;* in 1 Pet. 2:11, RV, ditto (KJV, "strangers").

Strange *allotrios* (245), denotes (a) "belonging to another" (*allos*); (b) "alien, foreign, strange," **Acts 7:6**; Heb. 11:9, KJV, RV, "(a land) not his own." Cf. *allophulos*, **Acts 10:28**; *xenos*, Matt. 25:35, 38, 43; 27:7; **Acts 17:21**, etc.

Bondage *douloo* (1402), transitive, signifies "to make a slave of, to bring into bondage," **Acts 7:6**; 1 Cor. 9:19, RV; in the passive voice, "to be brought under bondage," 2 Pet. 2:19; "to be held in bondage," Gal. 4:3 (lit., "were reduced to bondage"); Titus 2:3, "of being enslaved to wine"; Rom. 6:18, "of service to righteousness" (lit., "were made bondservants"). As with the purchased slave there were no limitations either in the kind or the time of service, so the life of the believer is to be lived in continuous obedience to God.

Evil *kakoo* (2559), "to ill-treat," is rendered "to entreat evil" in **Acts 7:6**, **19**; "made (them) evil affected," **14:2**.

Four hundred *see Acts 5:36.*

Years *see Acts 4:22.*

7:7 And the nation to whom they shall be in bondage will I judge, said God: and after that shall they come forth, and serve me in this place.

Judge *see* Determined at *Acts 3:13*.

Be in bondage *douleuo* (1398), "to serve as a *doulos*," is used (a) of serving God (and the impossibility of serving mammon also),

Matt. 6:24 and Luke 16:13; Rom. 7:6; in the gospel, Phil. 2:22; (b) Christ, **Acts 20:19**; Rom. 12:11; 14:18; 16:18; Eph. 6:7; Col. 3:24; (c) the law of God, Rom. 7:25; (d) one another, Gal. 5:13, RV, "be servants to" (KJV, "serve"); (e) a father, Luke 15:29 (with a suggestion of acting as a slave); (f) earthly masters, Matt. 6:24; Luke 16:13; 1 Tim. 6:2, RV, "serve"; (g) the younger by the elder, Rom. 9:12; (h) of being in bondage to a nation, **Acts 7:7**; Gal. 4:25, to the Romans, actually, though also spiritually to Judaizers.

Serve *latreuo* (3000), primarily "to work for hire" (akin to *latris*, "a hired servant"), signifies (1) to worship, (2) to "serve"; in the latter sense it is used of service (a) to God, Matt. 4:10; Luke 1:74 ("without fear"); 4:8; **Acts 7:7**; **24:14**, RV, "serve" (KJV, "worship"); **26:7**; **27:23**; Rom. 1:9 ("with my spirit"); 2 Tim. 1:3; Heb. 9:14; 12:28, KJV, "we may serve," RV, "we may offer service"; Rev. 7:15; (b) to God and Christ ("the Lamb"), Rev. 22:3; (c) in the tabernacle, Heb. 8:5, RV; 13:10; (d) to "the host of heaven," **Acts 7:42**, RV, "to serve" (KJV, "to worship"); (e) to "the creature," instead of the Creator, Rom. 1:25, of idolatry.

7:8 And he gave him the covenant of circumcision: and so *Abraham* begat Isaac, and circumcised him the eighth day; and Isaac *begat* Jacob; and Jacob *begat* the twelve patriarchs.

Covenant *see Acts 3:25.*

Circumcision *peritome* (4061), lit., "a cutting round, circumcision" (the verb is *peritemno*), was a rite enjoined by God upon Abraham and his male descendants and dependents, as a sign of the covenant made with him, Gen. 17; **Acts 7:8**; Rom. 4:11. Hence Israelites termed Gentiles "the uncircumcised," Judg. 15:18; 2 Sam. 1:20. So in the NT, but without the suggestion of contempt, e.g., Rom. 2:26; Eph. 2:11. The rite had a moral significance, Ex. 6:12, 30, where it is metaphorically applied to the lips; so to the ear, Jer. 6:10, and the heart, Deut. 30:6; Jer. 4:4. Cf. Jer. 9:25-26. It refers to the state of "circumcision," in Rom. 2:25-28; 3:1; 4:10; 1 Cor. 7:19; Gal. 5:6; 6:15; Col. 3:11. Upon the preaching of the gospel to, and the conversion of, Gentiles, a sect of Jewish believers arose who argued that the gospel, without the fulfillment of "circumcision," would make void the Law and make salvation impossible, **Acts 15:1**. Hence this party was known as "the circumcision," **Acts 10:45**; **11:2**; Gal. 2:12; Col. 4:11; Titus 1:10 (the term being used by metonymy, the abstract being put for the concrete, as with the application of the word to Jews generally, Rom. 3:30; 4:9, 12; 15:8; Gal. 2:7-9; Eph. 2:11). It is used metaphorically and spiritually of believers with reference to the act, Col. 2:11 and Rom. 2:29; to the condition, Phil. 3:3. The apostle Paul's defense of the truth, and his contention against this propaganda, form the main subject of the Galatian epistle. Cf. *katatome*, "concision," Phil. 3:2.

Eighth *ogdoos* (3590), "eighth" (connected with the preceding), is used in Luke 1:59; **Acts 7:8**; 2 Pet. 2:5; Rev. 17:11; 21:20.

Patriarchs *see* **Patriarch** at *Acts 2:29.*

7:9 And the patriarchs, moved with envy, sold Joseph into Egypt: but God was with him,

Patriarchs *see* **Patriarch** at *Acts 2:29.*

Envy *zeloo* (2206), "to be jealous, to burn with jealousy" (otherwise, to seek or desire eagerly), is rendered "moved with jealousy," in **Acts 7:9** and **17:5**, RV (KJV, "moved with envy"); in 1 Cor. 13:4, "envieth (not)," KJV and RV; in Jas. 4:2, RV marg., "are jealous" (text "covet;" KJV, "desire to have").

Sold *see Acts 5:8. See also* **Gave** at *Acts 4:33.*

7:10 And delivered him out of all his afflictions, and gave him favour and wisdom in the sight of Pharaoh king of Egypt; and he made him governor over Egypt and all his house.

Delivered *exaireo* (1807), lit., "to take out," denotes, in the middle voice, "to take out for oneself," hence, "to deliver, to rescue," the person who does so having a special interest in the result of his act. Thus it is used, in Gal. 1:4, of the act of God in "delivering" believers "out of this present evil world," the middle voice indicating His pleasure in the issue of their "deliverance." It signifies to "deliver" by rescuing from danger, in **Acts 12:11**; **23:27**; **26:17**; from bondage, **Acts 7:10**, **34**. For its other meaning, "to pluck out of," Matt. 5:29; 18:9.

Favour *see Acts 2:47.*

Wisdom *see Acts 6:3.*

Sight *enantion* (1726), from *en*, "in," and *anti*, "over against," the neuter of the adjective *enantios*, and virtually an adverb, is also used as a preposition signifying "in the presence of, in the sight of," Luke 20:26; **Acts 7:10**; **8:32**; "in the judgment of," Luke 24:9. Translated "in the sight of" in **Acts 7:10**. *enanti* (1725), an adverb, used as a preposition, "before," Luke 1:8; "in the judgment of," **Acts 8:21**. Some texts have the word in **Acts 7:10**.

Made *kathistemi* (2525), "to set down, set in order, appoint," is used in **Acts 7:10**, **27**, **35**; Heb. 7:28, KJV (RV, "appointeth"). *See also* **Appoint** at *Acts 6:3.*

Governor *hegeomai* (2233), is used in the present participle to denote "a governor," lit., "(one) governing," Matt. 2:6; **Acts 7:10**.

House *see Acts 2:36.*

7:11 Now there came a dearth over all the land of Egypt and Chanaan, and great affliction: and our fathers found no sustenance.

Dearth *limos* (3042), is translated "hunger" in Luke 15:17; 2 Cor. 11:27; elsewhere it signifies "a famine," and is so translated in each place in the RV; the KJV has the word "dearth" in **Acts 7:11** and **11:28**, and "hunger" in Rev. 6:8; the RV "famine" is preferable there; see Matt. 24:7; Mark 13:8; Luke 4:25; 15:14; 21:11; Rom. 8:35; Rev. 18:8.

Land *ge* (1093), in one of its usages, denotes (a) "land" as distinct from sea or other water, e.g., Mark 4:1; 6:47; Luke 5:3; John 6:21; (b) "land" as subject to cultivation, e.g., Luke 14:35; (c) "land" as describing a country or region, e.g., Matt. 2:20, 21; 4:15; Luke 4:25; in 23:44, RV, "(the whole) land," KJV, "(all the) earth"; **Acts 7:29**; Heb. 11.9, RV, "a land (not his own)," KJV "a (strange) country;" Jude 5. In **Acts 7:11** the KJV follows a reading of the noun with the definite article which necessitates the insertion of "land."

Sustenance *chortasma* (5527), "fodder," is used in the plural in **Acts 7:11**, "sustenance." In the Sept., Gen. 24:25, 32; 42:27; 43:24; Deut. 11:15; Jud. 19:19.

7:12 But when Jacob heard that there was corn in Egypt, he sent out our fathers first.

Corn *sition* (4621), "corn, grain," is found in **Acts 7:12**.

Sent *exapostello* (1821), denotes (a) "to send forth": of the Son by God the Father, Gal. 4:4; of the Holy Spirit, 4:6; Luke 24:49 in the best texts; an angel, **Acts 12:11**; the ancestors of Israel, **Acts 7:12**; Paul to the Gentiles, **22:21**; of the word of salvation, **13:26**; (b) "to send away," Luke 1:53; 20:10, 11; **Acts 9:30**; **11:22**; **17:14**.

7:13 And at the second *time* Joseph was made known to his brethren; and Joseph's kindred was made known unto Pharaoh.

Second *deuteros* (1208), denotes "second in order" with or without the idea of time, e.g., Matt. 22:26, 39; 2 Cor. 1:15; Rev. 2:11; in Rev. 14:8, RV only ("a second angel"); it is used in the neuter, *deuteron*, adverbially, signifying a "second" time, e.g., John 3:4; 21:16; **Acts 7:13**; Rev. 19:3, RV (KJV, "again"); Jude 5, "afterward" (RV, marg., "the second time"); used with *ek* ("of") idiomatically, the preposition signifying "for (the second time)," Mark 14:72; John 9:24 and **Acts 11:9**, RV (KJV, "again"); Heb. 9:28; in 1 Cor. 12:28, KJV, "secondarily," RV, "secondly."

Known In **Acts 7:13**, some mss. have the verb *anagnorizo*, "to make oneself known," "was made known." The KJV, "was made known" translates the phrase *phaneros ginomai*, "to become manifest" (RV, "became manifest"). *See also Acts 2:28* and **Manifest** at *Acts 4:16*.

Kindred *see Acts 4:6.*

7:14 Then sent Joseph, and called his father Jacob to *him*, and all his kindred, threescore and fifteen souls.

Called *metakaleo* (3333), "to call from one place to another, to summon" (cf. the Sept. of Hos. 11:1), is used in the middle voice only, "to call for oneself, to send for, call hither," **Acts 7:14**; **10:32**; **20:17**; **24:25**.

Kindred *see Acts 7:3.*

Threescore and fifteen *hebdomekonta* (1440), occurs in Luke 10:1, 17; in **Acts 7:14** it precedes *pente*, "five," lit., "seventy-five," rendered "threescore and fifteen"; in **23:23** it is translated "threescore and ten"; in **27:37** it precedes *hex*, "six," lit., "seventy-six," rendered "threescore and sixteen."

7:15 So Jacob went down into Egypt, and died, he, and our fathers,

Died *see* **Dead** at *Acts 2:29.*

7:16 And were carried over into Sychem, and laid in the sepulchre that Abraham bought for a sum of money of the sons of Emmor *the father* of Sychem.

Carried *metatithemi* (3346), "to place among, put in another place" (*meta*, implying "change," and *tithemi*, "to put"), has this latter meaning in **Acts 7:16**, "carried over."

Laid *see Acts 3:2.*

Sepulchre *see Acts 2:29.*

Bought *oneomai* (5608), "to buy, in contradistinction to selling," is used in **Acts 7:16**, of the purchase by Abraham of a burying place.

Sum For *kephalaion*, **Acts 22:28**; Heb. 8:1. For time, **Acts 7:16**. *See also* **Prices** at *Acts 4:34.*

Money In **Acts 7:16**, for the KJV, "(a sum of) money," the RV has "(a price in) silver."

7:17 But when the time of the promise drew nigh, which God had sworn to Abraham, the people grew and multiplied in Egypt,

Time *see* Times at *Acts 1:7.*

Drew nigh *engizo* (1448), "to draw near, to approach," from *engus*, "near," is used (a) of place and position, literally and physically, Matt. 21:1; Mark 11:1; Luke 12:33; 15:25; figuratively, of drawing near to God, Matt. 15:8; Heb. 7:19; Jas. 4:8; (b) of time, with reference to things that are imminent, as the kingdom of heaven, Matt. 3:2; 4:17; 10:7; the kingdom of God, Mark 1:15; Luke 10:9, 11; the time of fruit, Matt. 21:34; the desolation of Jerusalem, Luke 21:8; redemption, 21:28; the fulfillment of a promise, **Acts 7:17**; the Day of Christ in contrast to the present night of the world's spiritual darkness, Rom. 13:12; Heb. 10:25; the coming of the Lord, Jas. 5:8; the end of all things, 1 Pet. 4:7. It is also said of one who was drawing near to death, Phil. 2:30.

Sworn *homologeo* (3670), "to agree," is found in the best texts in **Acts 7:17**, and rendered "vouchsafed," RV, with reference to God's promise to Abraham; some mss. have *omosen*, "swore" (*omnumi*, "to swear"), as in KJV.

Grew *see* Increased at *Acts 6:7.*

Multiplied *see Acts 6:1.*

7:18 Till another king arose, which knew not Joseph.

Another *allos* (243), and *heteros* (2087) have a difference in meaning, which despite a tendency to be lost, is to be observed in numerous passages. *Allos* expresses a numerical difference and denotes "another of the same sort"; *heteros* expresses a qualitative difference and denotes "another of a different sort." Christ promised to send "another Comforter" (*allos*, "another like Himself," not *heteros*), John 14:16. Paul says "I see a different (KJV, "another") law," *heteros*, a law different from that of the spirit of life (not *allos*, "a law of the same sort"), Rom. 7:23. After Joseph's death "another king arose," *heteros*, one of quite a different character, **Acts 7:18**. Paul speaks of "a different gospel (*heteros*), which is not another" (*allos*, another like the one he preached), Gal. 1:6-7. See *heteros* (not *allos*) in Matt. 11:3, and **Acts 27:1**; in Luke 23:32 *heteroi* is used of the two malefactors crucified with Christ. The two words are only apparently interchanged in 1 Cor. 1:16 and 6:1; 12:8-10; 14:17 and 19, e.g., the difference being present, though not so readily discernible. They are not interchangeable in 1 Cor. 15:39-41; here *heteros* is used to distinguish the heavenly glory from the earthly, for these differ in genus, and *allos* to distinguish the flesh of men, birds, and fishes, which in each case is flesh differing not in genus but in species. *Allos* is used again to distinguish between the glories of the heavenly bodies, for these also differ not in kind but in degree only.

7:19 The same dealt subtilly with our kindred, and evil entreated our fathers, so that they cast out their young children, to the end they might not live.

Dealt *Katasophizomai*, "to circumvent by fraud, conquer by subtle devices" (*kata*, "down," intensive, and *sophizo*, "to devise cleverly or cunningly"; cf. Eng., "sophist, sophistry"), is translated "dealt subtilly," in **Acts 7:19**, of Pharaoh's dealings with the Israelites. This is the word in the Sept. of Ex. 1:10.

Subtilly *katasophizomai* (2686), "to deal subtly" (from *kata*, "against, under," *sophos*, "wise, subtle," used in the Sept. in 2 Sam. 13:3, of Jonadab), occurs in **Acts 7:19**. In the Sept. Ex. 1:10.

Kindred *see Acts 4:6.*

Evil *see Acts 7:6.*

Cast *ektithemi* (1260), "to expose, cast out" (*ek*, "out," *tithemi*, "to put"), is said of a new-born child in **Acts 7:21**. In v. **19** "cast out" translates the phrase *poieo*, "to make," with *ekthetos*, "exposed," a verbal form of *ektithemi*.

Young In **Acts 7:19**, KJV, *brephos*, in the neuter plural, is rendered "young children," RV, "babes."

Children For *brephos*, "a new born babe," always rendered "babe" or "babes" in the RV (KJV, "young children," **Acts 7:19**; "child," 2 Tim. 3:15).

End *eis*, "unto," followed by the article and the infinitive mood of a verb, signifies "to the end that ..." marking the aim of an action, **Acts 7:19**; Rom. 1:11; 4:16, 18; Eph. 1:12; 1 Thess. 3:13; 2 Thess. 1:5; 2:2, 6; 1 Pet. 3:7. In Luke 18:1, *pros*, "to," has the same construction and meaning.

Might *see* May at *Acts 3:19.*

Live *zoogoneo* (2225), denotes "to preserve alive" (from *zoos*, "alive," and *ginomai*, "to come to be, become, be made"); in Luke 17:33, "shall preserve (it)," i.e., his life, RV marg., "save (it) alive"; cf. the parallels *sozo*, "to save," in Matt. 16:25, and *phulaso*, "to keep," in John 12:25; in **Acts 7:19**, "live," negatively of the efforts of Pharaoh to destroy the babes in Israel; in 1 Tim. 6:13, according to the best mss. (some have *zoopoieo*, "to cause to live"), "quickeneth" (RV, marg., "preserveth ... alive," the preferable rendering).

7:20 In which time Moses was born, and was exceeding fair, and nourished up in his father's house three months:

Time *see* Times at *Acts 3:19*.

·**Exceeding** In **Acts 7:20**, the phrase "exceeding fair" (*asteios*) is, lit., "fair to God" (see marg.).

Fair *asteios* (791), lit., "of the city" (from *astu*, "a city"; like Lat. *urbanus*, from *urbs*, "a city"; Eng., "urbane"; similarly, "polite," from *polis*, "a town"), hence, "fair, elegant" (used in the papyri writings of clothing), is said of the external form of a child, **Acts 7:20**, of Moses "(exceeding) fair," lit., "fair to God"; Heb. 11:23 (RV, "goodly," KJV, "proper").

Nourished *anatrepho* (397), "to nurse, bring up," is translated "nourished" in **Acts 7:20** (KJV, "nourished up"); in **21**, "nourished," KJV and RV.

Months *men* (3376), connected with *mene*, "the moon," akin to a Sanskrit root *ma*—, "to measure" (the Sanskrit *masa* denotes both moon and month, cf, e.g., Lat. *mensis*, Eng., "moon" and "month," the moon being in early times the measure of the "month"). The interval between the 17th day of the second "month" (Gen. 7:11) and the 17th day of the seventh "month," is said to be 150 days (8:3, 4), i.e., five months of 30 days each; hence the year would be 360 days (cf. Dan. 7:25; 9:27; 12:7 with Rev. 11:2-3; 12:6, 14; 13:5; whence we conclude that 3½ years or 42 months = 1260 days, i.e., one year = 60 days); this was the length of the old Egyptian year; later, five days were added to correspond to the solar year. The Hebrew year was as nearly solar as was compatible with its commencement, coinciding with the new moon, or first day of the "month." This was a regular feast day, Num. 10:10; 28:11-14; the Passover coincided with the full moon (the 14th of the month Abib). Except in Gal. 4:10; Jas. 5:17; Rev. 9:5, 10, 15; 11:2; 13:5; 22:2, the word is found only in Luke's writings, Luke 1:24, 26, 36, 56; 4:25; **Acts 7:20**; **18:11**; **19:8**; **20:3**; **28:11**, examples of Luke's care as to accuracy of detail.

7:21 And when he was cast out, Pharaoh's daughter took him up, and nourished him for her own son.

Cast *see Acts 7:19*.

Took *anaireo* (337), "to take up" (*ana*, "up," and *haireo*, "to take"), is used of Pharaoh's daughter in "taking up" the infant Moses, **Acts 7:21**; of God's act in "taking away" the typical animal sacrifices under the Law, Heb. 10:9.

Nourished *see Acts 7:20*.

7:22 And Moses was learned in all the wisdom of the Egyptians, and was mighty in words and in deeds.

Learned *paideuo* (3811), primarily denotes "to train children," suggesting the broad idea of education (*pais*, "a child"), **Acts 7:22**; **22:3**; see also Titus 2:12, "instructing" (RV), here of a training gracious and firm; grace, which brings salvation, employs means to give us full possession of it, hence, "to chastise," this being part of the training, whether (a) by correcting with words, reproving, and admonishing, 1 Tim. 1:20 (RV, "be taught"); 2 Tim. 2:25, or (b) by "chastening" by the infliction of evils and calamities, 1 Cor. 11:32; 2 Cor. 6:9; Heb. 12:6-7, 10; Rev. 3:19. The verb also has the meaning "to chastise with blows, to scourge," said of the command of a judge, Luke 23:16, 22.

Wisdom *see Acts 6:3*.

Mighty *dunatos* (1415), "powerful, mighty," is used, with that significance, (1) of God, Luke 1:49, "mighty"; Rom. 9:22, "power" (here the neuter of the adjective is used with the article, as a noun, equivalent to *dunamis*); frequently with the meaning "able"; (2) of Christ, regarded as a prophet, Luke 24:19 ("in deed and word"); (3) of men: Moses, **Acts 7:22** ("in his words and works"); Apollos, **18:24**, "in the Scriptures"; of those possessed of natural power, 1 Cor. 1:26; of those possessed of spiritual power, 2 Cor. 10:4. For the shades of meaning in the translation "strong," see Rom. 15:1; 2 Cor. 12:10; 13:9.

7:23 And when he was full forty years old, it came into his heart to visit his brethren the children of Israel.

Full *pleroo* (4137), signifies (1) "to fill"; (2) "to fulfill, complete," (a) of time, e.g., Mark 1:15; Luke 21:24; John 7:8 (KJV, "full come"); **Acts 7:23**, RV, "he was wellnigh forty years old" (KJV, "was full," etc.), lit., "the time of forty years was fulfilled to him"; v. **30**, KJV, "were expired"; **9:23**; **24:27** (KJV, "after two years"; RV, "when two years were fulfilled"); (b) of number, Rev. 6:11; (c) of good pleasure, 2 Thess. 1:11; (d) of joy, Phil. 2:2; in the passive voice, "to be fulfilled," John 3:29 and 17:13; in the following the verb is rendered "fulfilled" in the RV, for the KJV, "full," John 15:11; 16:24; 1 John 1:4; 2 John 12; (e) of obedience, 2 Cor. 10:6; (f) of works, Rev. 3:2; (g) of the future Passover, Luke 22:16; (h) of sayings, prophecies, etc., e.g., Matt. 1:22 (twelve times in Matt., two in Mark, four in Luke, eight in John, two in Acts); Jas. 2:23; in Col. 1:25 the word signifies to preach "fully," to complete the ministry of the Gospel appointed.

Forty *tessarakontaetes*, "forty years" (*etos*, "a year"), is found in **Acts 7:23**; **13:18**.

Visit *see* Look at *Acts 6:3*.

Brethren Male descendants of the same parents, **Acts 7:23**, **26**; Heb. 7:5.

7:24 And seeing one *of them* suffer wrong, he defended *him*, and avenged him that was oppressed, and smote the Egyptian:

Wrong *adikeo* (91), "to do wrong," is used (a) intransitively, to act unrighteously, **Acts 25:11**, RV, "I am a wrongdoer" (KJV, "... an offender"); 1 Cor. 6:8; 2 Cor. 7:12 (1st part); Col. 3:25 (1st part); cf. Rev. 22:11; (b) transitively, "to wrong," Matt. 20:13; **Acts 7:24** (passive voice), 26, 27; 25:10; 2 Cor. 7:2, v. 12 (2nd part; passive voice); Gal. 4:12, "ye did (me no) wrong," anticipating a possible suggestion that his vigorous language was due to some personal grievance; the occasion referred to was that of his first visit; Col. 3:25 (2nd part), lit., "what he did wrong," which brings consequences both in this life and at the judgment seat of Christ; Philem. 18; 2 Pet. 2:13 (1st part); in the middle or passive voice, "to take or suffer wrong, to suffer (oneself) to be wronged," 1 Cor. 6:7.

Defended *amuno* (292), "to ward off," is used in the middle voice in **Acts 7:24**, of the assistance given by Moses to his fellow Israelite against an Egyptian (translated, "defended"). The middle voice indicates the special personal interest Moses had in the act.

Avenged *ekdikesis* (1557), "vengeance," is used with the verb *poieo*, "to make," i.e., to avenge, in Luke 18:7-8; **Acts 7:24**; twice it is used in statements that "vengeance" belongs to God, Rom. 12:19; Heb. 10:30. In 2 Thess. 1:8 it is said of the act of divine justice which will be meted out to those who know not God and obey not the gospel, when the Lord comes in flaming fire at His second advent. In the divine exercise of judgment there is no element of vindictiveness, nothing by way of taking revenge. In Luke 21:22, it is used of the "days of vengeance" upon the Jewish people; in 1 Pet. 2:14, of civil governors as those who are sent of God "for vengeance on evildoers" (KJV, "punishment"); in 2 Cor. 7:11, of the "self-avenging" of believers, in their godly sorrow for wrong doing, RV, "avenging," for KJV, "revenge."

Oppressed *kataponeo* (2669), primarily, "to tire down with toil, exhaust with labor" (*kata*, "down," *ponos*, "labor"), hence signifies "to afflict, oppress"; in the passive voice, "to be oppressed, much distressed"; it is translated "oppressed" in **Acts 7:24**, and "sore distressed" in 2 Pet. 2:7, RV, (KJV, "vexed").

Smote *patasso* (3960), "to strike, smite," is used (I) literally, of giving a blow with the hand, or fist or a weapon, Matt. 26:51, RV, "smote" (KJV, "struck"); Luke 22:49, 50; **Acts 7:24**; **12:7**; (II) metaphorically, (a) of judgment meted out to Christ, Matt. 26:31; Mark 14:27; (b) of the infliction of disease, by an angel, **Acts 12:23**; of plagues to be inflicted upon men by two divinely appointed witnesses, Rev. 11:6; (c) of judgment to be executed by Christ upon the nations, Rev. 19:15, the instrument being His Word, described as a sword.

7:25 For he supposed his brethren would have understood how that God by his hand would deliver them: but they understood not.

Supposed *nomizo* (3543), "to consider, suppose, think," is rendered "to suppose" in Matt. 20:10; Luke 2:34; 3:23; **Acts 7:25**; **14:19**; **16:27**; **21:29**; 1 Tim. 6:5; in 1 Cor. 7:26, KJV (RV, "I think"); in **Acts 16:13**, the RV adheres to the meaning "to suppose," "(where) we supposed (there was a place of prayer)"; this word also signifies "to practice a custom" (*nomos*) and is commonly so used by Greek writers. Hence the KJV, "was wont (to be made)"; it is rendered "to think" in Matt. 5:17; 10:34; **Acts 8:20**; **17:29**; 1 Cor. 7:36.

Understood *suniemi* (4920), primarily, "to bring or set together," is used metaphorically of "perceiving, understanding, uniting" (*sun*), so to speak, the perception with what is perceived, e.g., Matt. 13:13-15, 19, 23, 51; 15:10; 16:12; 17:13, and similar passages in Mark and Luke; **Acts 7:25** (twice); **28:26**, **27**; in Rom. 3:11, the present participle, with the article, is used as a noun, lit., "there is not the understanding (one)," in a moral and spiritual sense; Rom. 15:21; 2 Cor. 10:12, RV, "are (without) understanding," KJV, "are (not) wise"; Eph. 5:17, RV, "understand."

Deliver In the following the RV gives the correct rendering: **Acts 7:25**, "was giving them deliverance" (KJV, "would deliver them"); **Acts 10:40**, "gave Him to be made manifest" (KJV, "shewed Him openly"); Rev. 13:14, 15, "it was given him" (KJV, "he had power"). *See also* **Salvation** at *Acts 4:12*.

7:26 And the next day he shewed himself unto them as they strove, and would have set them at one again, saying, Sirs, ye are brethren; why do ye wrong one to another?

Next *epeimi* (1909 and 1510), "to come upon," or, of time, "to come on or after" (*epi*, "upon," and *eimi*, "to go"), is used in the present participle as an adjective, in reference to a day, in **Acts 7:26**; **16:11**; **20:15**; **21:18**; a night, **23:11**, RV, "following," in each place (KJV, "next").

Day *epiousios* (1967), is found in Matt. 6:11 and Luke 11:3. Some would derive the word from *epi*, "upon," and *eimi*, "to be," as if to signify "(bread) present," i.e., sufficient bread, but this formation is questionable. The same objection applies to the conjecture, that it is derived from *epi*, and *ousia*, and signifies "(bread) for sustenance." The more probable derivation is from *epi*, and *eimi*, "to go," (bread) for going on, i.e., for the morrow and after, or (bread) coming (for us). See the RV marg. This suits the added *semeron*, "to-day," i.e., the prayer is to be for bread that suffices for this day and next, so that the mind may conform to Christ's warning against anxiety for the morrow. Confirmation of this derivation is also to be found in the word *epious*, in the phrase "the next day," **Acts 7:26**; **16:11**.

Shewed *ophthe* (lit., "was seen"), **Acts 7:26**, "He appeared".

Strove *machomai* (3164), "to fight, to quarrel, dispute," is rendered "to strive" in John 6:52; **Acts 7:26**; 2 Tim. 2:24.

Set *sunallasso* (4862, 236), "to reconcile" (*sun*, "together," *allasso*, "to change or exchange"), is translated "he ... would have set (them at one, lit., 'into peace') again" in **Acts 7:26** (the imperfect tense being conative, expressing an attempt); some mss. have *sunelauno*, "to drive together, force together."

One In **Acts 7:26**, "at one," is, lit., "unto peace".

Sirs *aner* (435), "a man," is translated "sirs" in **Acts 7:26**; **14:15**; **19:25**; **27:10, 21, 25**.

Brethren *see Acts 7:23*.

One to another This translates a number of words and phrases, (a) *allelon*, a reciprocal pronoun in the genitive plural, signifying "of, or from, one another" (akin to *allos*, "another"), e.g., Matt. 25:32; John 13:22; **Acts 15:39**; **19:38**; 1 Cor. 7:5; Gal. 5:17; the accusative *allelous* denotes "one another," e.g., **Acts 7:26**, lit., "why do ye wrong one another?"; 2 Thess. 1:3, RV; inEph. 4:32 and Col. 3:13, e.g., RV, "each other"; in 1 Thess. 5:15, "one (toward) another," RV; the dative *allelois* denotes "one to another," e.g., Luke 7:32; (b) different forms of the plural of *heautou*, "of himself," used as a reciprocal pronoun, e.g., Eph. 5:19, RV, "one to another" (KJV, and RV marg., "to yourselves").

7:27 But he that did his neighbour wrong thrust him away, saying, Who made thee a ruler and a judge over us?

Neighbour *plesion* (4139), the neuter of the adjective *plesios* (from *pelas*, "near"), is used as an adverb accompanied by the article, lit., "the (one) near"; hence, one's "neighbor"; **Acts 7:27**.

Thrust *apotheo* (638), "to thrust away," is used in the middle voice, "to thrust away from oneself," and translated "thrust away" in **Acts 7:27, 39**; "thrust ... from," **13:46**, RV (KJV, "put ... from"); "having thrust from them," 1 Tim. 1:19, RV (KJV, "having put away").

Made *see Acts 7:10*. *See also* Appoint at *Acts 6:3*.

Ruler *see* Rulers at *Acts 3:17*.

Judge *dikastes* (1348), denotes "a judge" (from *dike*, "right, a judicial hearing, justice"; akin to *dikazo*, "to judge"), **Acts 7:27, 35**; some mss. have it in Luke 12:14; while *dikastes* is a forensic term, *krites* "gives prominence to the mental process" (Thayer). At Athens the *dikastes* acted as a juryman, the *krites* being the presiding "judge."

7:28 Wilt thou kill me, as thou diddest the Egyptian yesterday?

Yesterday *echthes or chthes* (5504), occurs in John 4:52; **Acts 7:28**; Heb. 13:8.

7:29 Then fled Moses at this saying, and was a stranger in the land of Madian, where he begat two sons.

Saying *logos* (3056), "a word," as embodying a conception or idea, denotes among its various meanings, "a saying, statement or declaration," uttered (a) by God; RV, "word" or "words" (KJV, "saying"), e.g., in John 8:55; Rom. 3:4; Rev. 19:9; 22:6, 7, 9, 10; (b) by Christ, e.g., Mark 8:32; 9:10; 10:22; Luke 9:28; John 6:60; 21:23; the RV appropriately substitutes "word" or "words" for KJV, "saying" or "sayings," especially in John's Gospel e.g. 7:36, 40; 8:51, 52; 10:19; 14:24; 15:20; 18:9, 32; 19:13; (c) by an angel, Luke 1:29; (d) by OT prophets, John 12:38 (RV, "word") Rom. 13:9 (ditto); 1 Cor. 15:54; (e) by the apostle Paul in the Pastoral Epp., 1 Tim. 1:15; 3:1; 4:9; 2 Tim. 2:11; Titus 3:8; (f) by other men, Mark 7:29; **Acts 7:29**; John 4:37 (in general).

Stranger *see* Sojourn at *Acts 7:6*.

Land *see Acts 7:11*.

7:30 And when forty years were expired, there appeared to him in the wilderness of mount Sina an angel of the Lord in a flame of fire in a bush.

Expired In **Acts 7:30**, the KJV "were expired" translates the verb *pleroo*, "to fulfill" (RV). In Rev. 20:7, the KJV "are expired" translates the verb *teleo*, "to finish" (RV).

Mount *see Acts 1:12*.

Flame *phlox* (5395), akin to Lat. *fulgeo*, "to shine," is used apart from *pur*, "fire," in Luke 16:24; with *pur*, it signifies "a fiery flame," lit., "a flame of fire," **Acts 7:30**; 2 Thess. 1:8, where the fire is to be understood as the instrument of divine judgment; Heb. 1:7, where the meaning probably is that God makes His angels as active and powerful as a "flame" of fire; in Rev. 1:14; 2:18; 19:12, of the eyes of the Lord Jesus as emblematic of penetrating judgment, searching out evil.

Bush *batos* (942), denotes "a bramble bush," as in Luke 6:44. In Mark 12:26 and Luke 20:37 the phrase "in the place concerning the Bush" signifies in that part of the book of Exodus concerning it. See also **Acts 7:30, 35**.

7:31 When Moses saw *it*, he wondered at the sight: and as he drew near to behold *it*, the voice of the Lord came unto him,

Saw *see* Visions at *Acts 2:17*.

Sight *horama* (3705), "that which is seen" (*horao*), denotes (a) "a spectacle, sight," Matt. 17:9; **Acts 7:31** ("sight"); (b) "an appearance, vision," **Acts 9:10** (v. **12** in some mss.): **10:3, 17, 19; 11:5; 12:9; 16:9, 10; 18:9**.

Drew *proserchomai* (4334), is translated "draw near" in Heb. 4:16; 7:25, RV, and 10:22, KJV and RV; in **Acts 7:31**, "drew near."

Near *proserchomai* (4334), "to come to, go to," is translated "drew near" in **Acts 7:31** and Heb. 10:22.

Behold *katanoeo* (2657), "to perceive clearly," "to understand fully, consider closely," is used of not "considering" thoroughly the beam in one's own eye, Matt. 7:3 and Luke 6:41 (KJV, "perceivest"); of carefully "considering" the ravens, Luke 12:24; the lilies, v. 27; of Peter's full "consideration" of his vision, **Acts 11:6**; of Abraham's careful "consideration" of his own body, and Sarah's womb, as dead, and yet accepting by faith God's promise, Rom. 4:19 (RV); of "considering" fully the Apostle and High Priest of our confession, Heb. 3:1; of thoughtfully "considering" one another to provoke unto love and good works, Heb. 10:24. It is translated by the verbs "behold," **Acts 7:31-32**; Jas. 1:23-24; "perceive," Luke 20:23; "discover," **Acts 27:39**.

Voice *phone* (5456), "a sound," is used of the voice (a) of God, Matt. 3:17; John 5:37; 12:28, 30; **Acts 7:31; 10:13, 15; 11:7, 9**; Heb. 3:7, 15; 4:7; 12:19, 26; 2 Pet. 1:17, 18; Rev. 18:4; 21:3; (b) of Christ, (1) in the days of His flesh, Matt. 12:19 (negatively); John 3:29; 5:25; 10:3, 4, 16, 27; 11:43; 18:37; (2) on the cross Matt. 27:46, and parallel passages; (3) from heaven, **Acts 9:4**, 7; **22:7, 9, 14; 26:14**; Rev. 1:10, 12 (here, by metonymy, of the speaker), 15; 3:20; (4) at the resurrection "to life," John 5:28; 1 Thess. 4:16, where "the voice of the archangel" is, lit., "a voice of an archangel," and probably refers to the Lord's voice as being of an archangelic character; (5) at the resurrection to judgment, John 5:28 [not the same event as (4)]; (c) of human beings on earth, e.g., Matt. 2:18; 3:3; Luke 1:42, in some texts, KJV, "voice", and frequently in the Synoptists; (d) of angels, Rev. 5:11, and frequently in the Apocalypse; (e) of the redeemed in heaven, e.g., Rev. 6:10; 18:22; 19:1, 5; (f) of a pagan god, **Acts 12:22**; (g) of things, e.g., wind, John 3:8, RV, "voice" (KJV, "sound").

7:32 *Saying*, I *am* the God of thy fathers, the God of Abraham, and the God of Isaac, and the God of Jacob. Then Moses trembled, and durst not behold.

Trembled *entromos* (1790), an adjective signifying "trembling with fear" (*en*, "in," *tremo*, "to tremble"), is used with *eimi*, "to be," in Heb. 12:21 (some mss. have *ektromos*, with the same meaning), "I quake," lit., "I am trembling." It is used with *ginomai*, "to become," in **Acts 7:32**, "trembled," lit., "became trembling," and **16:29**, RV, "trembling for fear" (KJV, "came trembling).

Durst *see Acts 5:13*.

7:33 Then said the Lord to him, Put off thy shoes from thy feet: for the place where thou standest is holy ground.

Put In **Acts 7:33**, KJV, *luo*, "to loose" (RV), is translated "put off."

7:34 I have seen, I have seen the affliction of my people which is in Egypt, and I have heard their groaning, and am come down to deliver them. And now come, I will send thee into Egypt.

Affliction *kakosis* (2561), "affliction, ill treatment," is used in **Acts 7:34**.

Groaning *stenagmos* (4726), is used in **Acts 7:34**, in a quotation from Exod. 3:7, but not from the Sept., which there has *krauge*, "a cry"; the word is used, however, in Exod. 2:24; in Rom. 8:26, in the plural, of the intercessory groanings of the Holy Spirit.

Come *see Acts 7:3*.

Deliver *see* Delivered at *Acts 7:10*.

7:35 This Moses whom they refused, saying, Who made thee a ruler and a judge? the same

did God send *to be* a ruler and a deliverer by the hand of the angel which appeared to him in the bush.

Refused *arneomai* (720), "to deny, renounce, reject," in late Greek came to signify "to refuse to acknowledge, to disown," and is translated "to refuse" in **Acts 7:35**; Heb. 11:24. *See also* Denied at *Acts 3:14.*

Made *see Acts 7:10. See also* Appoint at *Acts 6:3.*

Ruler *see* Rulers at *Acts 3:17.*

Judge *see Acts 7:27.*

Send *see Acts 3:20.*

Deliverer *lutrotes* (3086), "a redeemer, one who releases", is translated "deliverer" in **Acts 7:35** (RV marg., "redeemer").

Hand *see* Hands at *Acts 5:12.*

Bush *see Acts 7:30.*

7:36 He brought them out, after that he had shewed wonders and signs in the land of Egypt, and in the Red sea, and in the wilderness forty years.

Brought *exago* (1806), "to lead out," is rendered by the verb "to lead, out or forth," in Mark 15:20 (in some mss. in 8:23, the best have *ekphero*, "to bring out)"; Luke 24:50; John 10:3; **Acts 7:36, 40** (KJV "brought"), and **13:17**, RV; **Acts 21:38**; Heb. 8:9. *See also Acts 5:19.*

Shewed *poieo* (4160), "to make, to do," is translated, "He hath showed" in Luke 1:51; "to show (mercy)," v. 72, RV (KJV, "perform"); "showed (mercy)," 10:37; John 6:30, KJV, "showest Thou," RV, "doest Thou (for a sign)"; **Acts 7:36**, KJV, "showed," RV, "wrought"; Jas. 2:13, "showed (no mercy)"; in Mark 13:22 in the best texts (some have *didomi*), "shall show (signs)."

Wonders *see Acts 2:19.*

Red *eruthros* (2063), denotes "red" (the ordinary color); the root *rudh*– is seen, e.g., in the Latin *rufus*, Eng., "ruby," "ruddy," "rust," etc. It is applied to the Red Sea, **Acts 7:36**; Heb. 11:29. The origin of the name is uncertain; it has been regarded as due, e.g., to the color of the corals which cover the Red Sea bed or line its shores, or to the tinge of the mountains which border it, or to the light of the sky upon its waters.

Sea *see Acts 4:24.*

7:37 This is that Moses, which said unto the children of Israel, A prophet shall the Lord your God raise up unto you of your brethren, like unto me; him shall ye hear.

Raise *see* Raised at *Acts 2:24.*

Prophet *see Acts 3:22.*

Like unto *see Acts 3:22.*

7:38 This is he, that was in the church in the wilderness with the angel which spake to him in the mount Sina, and *with* our fathers: who received the lively oracles to give unto us:

Church *ekklesia* (1577), from *ek*, "out of," and *klesis*, "a calling" (*kaleo*, "to call"), was used among the Greeks of a body of citizens "gathered" to discuss the affairs of state, **Acts 19:39**. In the Sept. it is used to designate the "gathering" of Israel, summoned for any definite purpose, or a "gathering" regarded as representative of the whole nation. In **Acts 7:38** it is used of Israel; in **19:32, 41**, of a riotous mob. It has two applications to companies of Christians, (a) to the whole company of the redeemed throughout the present era, the company of which Christ said, "I will build My Church," Matt. 16:18, and which is further described as "the Church which is His Body," Eph. 1:22; 5:23, (b) in the singular number (e.g., Matt. 18:17, RV marg., "congregation"), to a company consisting of professed believers, e.g., **Acts 20:28**; 1 Cor. 1:2; Gal. 1:13; 1 Thess. 1:1;2 Thess. 1:1; 1 Tim. 3:5, and in the plural, with reference to churches in a district. There is an apparent exception in the RV of **Acts 9:31**, where, while the KJV has "churches," the singular seems to point to a district; but the reference is clearly to the church as it was in Jerusalem, from which it had just been scattered, **8:1**. Again, in Rom. 16:23, that Gaius was the host of "the whole church," simply suggests that the "assembly" in Corinth had been accustomed to meet in his house, where also Paul was entertained.

Mount *see Acts 1:12.*

Received *see* Receive at *Acts 3:21.*

Lively This is the KJV translation of the present participle of the verb; *zao*, "to live," in three passages, in each of which the RV has "living," **Acts 7:38**; 1 Pet. 1:3; 2:5. *See also* Alive at *Acts 1:3.*

Oracles *logion* (3051), a diminutive of *logos*, "a word, narrative, statement," denotes "a divine response or utterance, an oracle"; it is used of (a) the contents of the Mosaic Law, **Acts 7:38**; (b) all the written utterances of God through OT writers, Rom. 3:2; (c) the substance of Christian doctrine, Heb. 5:12; (d) the utterances of God through Christian teachers, 1 Pet. 4:11.

7:39 To whom our fathers would not obey, but thrust *him* from them, and in their hearts turned back again into Egypt,

Obey *hupekoos* (5255), "obedient," "giving ear, subject," occurs in **Acts 7:39**, RV, "(would not be) obedient," KJV, "(would not) obey"; 2 Cor. 2:9; Phil. 2:8, where the RV "*even*" is useful as making clear that the "obedience" was not to death but to the Father.

Thrust *see Acts 7:27.*

7:40 Saying unto Aaron, Make us gods to go before us: for *as for* this Moses, which brought us out of the land of Egypt, we wot not what is become of him.

Go *proporeuomai* (4313), "to go before," is used in Luke 1:76 and **Acts 7:40**.

Brought *see Acts 5:19. See also Acts 7:36.*

Wot *see Acts 3:17.*

7:41 And they made a calf in those days, and offered sacrifice unto the idol, and rejoiced in the works of their own hands.

Calf *moschopoieo* (3447), signifies "to make a calf" (*moschos*, and *poieo*, "to make"), **Acts 7:41**.

Offered In **Acts 7:41**, KJV, *anago*, "to lead up" or "bring up," is rendered "offered" (RV, "brought").

Sacrifice *thusia* (2378), primarily denotes "the act of offering"; then, objectively, "that which is offered" (a) of idolatrous "sacrifice," **Acts 7:41**; (b) of animal or other "sacrifices," as offered under the Law, Matt. 9:13; 12:7; Mark 9:49; 12:33; Luke 2:24; 13:1; **Acts 7:42**; 1 Cor. 10:18; Heb. 5:1; 7:27 (RV, plural); 8:3; 9:9; 10:1, 5, 8 (RV, plural), 11; 11:4; (c) of Christ, in His "sacrifice" on the cross, Eph. 5:2; Heb. 9:23, where the plural antitypically comprehends the various forms of Levitical "sacrifices" in their typical character; 9:26; 10:12, 26; (d) metaphorically, (1) of the body of the believer, presented to God as a living "sacrifice," Rom. 12:1; (2) of faith, Phil. 2:17; (3) of material assistance rendered to servants of God, Phil. 4:18; (4) of praise, Heb, 13:15; (5) of doing good to others and communicating with their needs, Heb. 13:16; (6) of spiritual "sacrifices" in general, offered by believers as a holy priesthood, 1 Pet. 2:5.

Idol *eidolon* (1497), primarily "a phantom or likeness" (from *eidos*, "an appearance," lit., "that which is seen"), or "an idea, fancy," denotes in the NT (a) "an idol," an image to represent a false god, **Acts 7:41**; 1 Cor. 12:2; Rev. 9:20; (b) "the false god" worshipped in an image, **Acts 15:20**; Rom. 2:22; 1 Cor. 8:4, 7; 10:19; 2 Cor. 6:16; 1 Thess. 1:9; 1 John 5:21. "The corresponding Heb. word denotes 'vanity,' Jer. 14:22; 18:15; 'thing of nought,' Lev. 19:4, marg., cf. Eph. 4:17. Hence what represented a deity to the Gentiles, was to Paul a 'vain thing,' **Acts 14:15**; 'nothing in the world,' 1 Cor. 8:4; 10:19. Jeremiah calls the idol a 'scarecrow' ('pillar in a garden,' 10:5, marg.), and Isaiah, 44:9-20, etc., and Habakkuk, 2:18, 19 and the Psalmist, 115:4-8, etc., are all equally scathing. It is important to notice, however, that in each case the people of God are addressed. When he speaks to idolaters, Paul, knowing that no man is won by ridicule, adopts a different line, **Acts 14:15-18**; **17:16**, **21-31**." *See also* **Work** at *Acts 5:38.*

Rejoiced *see* **Rejoice** at *Acts 2:26.*

Works *see* **Work** at *Acts 5:38.*

7:42 Then God turned, and gave them up to worship the host of heaven; as it is written in the book of the prophets, O ye house of Israel, have ye offered to me slain beasts and sacrifices *by the space of* forty years in the wilderness?

Turned *strepho* (4762), denotes (1) in the active voice, (a) "to turn" (something), Matt. 5:39; (b) "to bring back," Matt. 27:3 (in the best texts); (c) reflexively, "to turn oneself, to turn the back to people," said of God, **Acts 7:42**; (d) "to turn one thing into another," Rev. 11:6 (the only place where this word occurs after the Acts); (2) in the passive voice, (a) used reflexively, "to turn oneself," e.g. Matt. 7:6; John 20:14, 16; (b) metaphorically, Matt. 18:3, RV, "(except) ye turn" (KJV, "... be converted"); John 12:40.

Gave *paradidomi* (3860), "to give or hand over," is said of "giving" up the ghost, John 19:30; of "giving" persons up to evil, **Acts 7:42**; Rom. 1:24, 26; of "giving" one's body to be burned, 1 Cor. 13:3; of Christ's "giving" Himself up to death, Gal. 2:20; Eph. 5:2, 25.

Worship *latreuo* (3000), "to serve, to render religious service or homage," is translated "to worship" in Phil. 3:3, "(who) worship (by the Spirit of God)," RV, KJV, "(which) worship (God in the spirit)"; the RV renders it "to serve" (for KJV, "to worship") in **Acts 7:42**; **24:14**; KJV and RV, "(the) worshipers" in Heb. 10:2, present participle, lit., "(the ones) worshiping." *See also* **Serve** at *Acts 7:7.*

Host *stratia* (4756), "an army," is used of angels, Luke 2:13; of stars, **Acts 7:42**; some mss. have it instead of *strateia*, in 2 Cor. 10:4 ("warfare"). Cf. *strateuma*, "an army."

Book *see Acts 1:20.*

House *see Acts 2:36.*

Offered *prosphero* (4374), primarily, "to bring to" (*pros*, "to," *phero*, "to bring"), also denotes "to offer," (a) of the sacrifice of Christ Himself, Heb. 8:3; of Christ in virtue of his High Priesthood (RV, "this *high priest*"; KJV, "this man"); 9:14, 25 (negative), 28; 10:12; (b) of offerings under, or according to, the Law, e.g., Matt. 8:4; Mark 1:44; **Acts 7:42; 21:26**; Heb. 5:1, 3; 8:3; 9:7, 9; 10:1-2, 8, 11; (c) of "offerings" previous to the Law, Heb. 11:4, 17 (of Isaac by Abraham); (d) of gifts "offered" to Christ, Matt. 2:11, RV, "offered" (KJV, "presented unto"); (e) of prayers "offered" by Christ, Heb. 5:7; (f) of the vinegar "offered" to Him in mockery by the soldiers at the cross, Luke 23:36; (g) of the slaughter of disciples by persecutors, who think they are "offering" service to God, John 16:2, RV (KJV, "doeth"); (h) of money "offered" by Simon the sorcerer, **Acts 8:18**.

Slain *sphazo*, or *sphatto* (4969), "to slay, to slaughter," especially victims for sacrifice, is most frequently translated by the verb "to slay"; so the RV in Rev. 6:4 (KJV, "should kill"), in 13:3, RV, "smitten unto death" (KJV, "wounded"). Cf. *katasphazo*, "to kill off," Luke 19:27; *sphage*, "slaughter," e.g., **Acts 8:32**, and *sphagion*, "a victim for slaughter," **Acts 7:42**.

Beasts *sphagion* (4968), from *sphazo*, "to slay," denotes "a victim slaughtered for sacrifice, a slain beast," **Acts 7:42**, in a quotation from Amos 5:25.

Sacrifices *see* Sacrifice at *Acts 7:41*.

7:43 Yea, ye took up the tabernacle of Moloch, and the star of your god Remphan, figures which ye made to worship them: and I will carry you away beyond Babylon.

Yea *kai* (2532), "and, even," is rendered "yea," e.g., Luke 2:35; John 16:32; 1 Cor. 2:10; 2 Cor. 8:3; in **Acts 7:43**, KJV (RV, "and").

Took *see* Taken at *Acts 1:2*.

Tabernacle *skene* (4633), "a tent, booth, tabernacle," is used of (a) tents as dwellings, Matt. 17:4; Mark 9:5; Luke 9:33; Heb. 11:9, KJV, "tabernacles" (RV, "tents"); (b) the Mosaic tabernacle, **Acts 7:44**; Heb. 8:5; 9:1 (in some mss.); 9:8, 21, termed "the tent of meeting," RV (i.e., where the people were called to meet God), a preferable description to "the tabernacle of the congregation," as in the KJV in the OT; the outer part 9:2, 6; the inner sanctuary, 9:3; (c) the heavenly prototype, Heb. 8:2; 9:11; Rev. 13:6; 15:5; 21:3 (of its future descent); (d) the eternal abodes of the saints, Luke 16:9, RV, "tabernacles" (KJV, "habitations"); (e) the Temple in Jerusalem, as continuing the service of the tabernacle, Heb. 13:10; (f) the house of David, i.e., metaphorically of his people, **Acts 15:16**; (g) the portable shrine of the god Moloch, **Acts 7:43**.

Star *astron* (798), is used (a) in the sing. in **Acts 7:43**, "the star of the god Rephan," RV, the symbol or "figure," probably of Saturn, worshiped as a god, apparently the same as Chiun in Amos 5:26 (Rephan being the Egyptian deity corresponding to Saturn, Chiun the Assyrian); (b) in the plur., Luke 21:25; **Acts 27:20**; Heb. 11:12.

Figures *tupos* (5179), primarily denoted "a blow" (from a root *tup–*, seen also in *tupto*, "to strike"), hence, (a) an impression, the mark of a "blow," John 20:25; (b) the "impress" of a seal, the stamp made by a die, a figure, image, **Acts 7:43**; (c) a "form" or mold, Rom. 6:17 (see RV); (d) the sense or substance of a letter, **Acts 23:25**; (e) "an ensample," pattern, **Acts 7:44**; Heb. 8:5, "pattern"; in an ethical sense, 1 Cor. 10:6; Phil. 3:17; 1 Thess. 1:7; 2 Thess. 3:9; 1 Tim. 4:12, RV, "ensample"; Titus 2:7, RV, "ensample," for KJV, "pattern"; 1 Pet. 5:3; in a doctrinal sense, a type, Rom. 5:14.

Worship *proskuneo* (4352), "to make obeisance, do reverence to" (from *pros*, "towards," and *kuneo*, "to kiss"), is the most frequent word rendered "to worship." It is used of an act of homage or reverence (a) to God, e.g., Matt. 4:10; John 4:21-24; 1 Cor. 14:25; Rev. 4:10; 5:14; 7:11; 11:16; 19:10 (2nd part) and 22:9; (b) to Christ, e.g., Matt. 2:2, 8, 11; 8:2; 9:18; 14:33; 15:25; 20:20; 28:9, 17; John 9:38; Heb. 1:6, in a quotation from the Sept. of Deut. 32:43, referring to Christ's second advent; (c) to a man, Matt. 18:26; (d) to the Dragon, by men, Rev. 13:4; (e) to the Beast, his human instrument, Rev. 13:4, 8, 12; 14:9, 11; (f) the image of the Beast, 13:15; 14:11; 16:2; (g) to demons, Rev. 9:20; (h) to idols, **Acts 7:43**.

Carry … away *see* Removed at *Acts 7:4*.

Beyond *epekeina* (19), *epi*, "upon," and *ekeina*, "those," the word "parts" being understood, is used in **Acts 7:43**.

7:44 Our fathers had the tabernacle of witness in the wilderness, as he had appointed, speaking unto Moses, that he should make it according to the fashion that he had seen.

Tabernacle *see Acts 7:43*.

Witness *see Acts 4:33*.

Appointed *diatasso* (1299), a strengthened form (*dia*, "through," intensive), frequently denotes "to arrange, appoint, prescribe," e.g., of what was "appointed" for tax collectors to collect, Luke 3:13; of the tabernacle, as "appointed" by God for Moses to make, **Acts 7:44**; of the arrangements "appointed" by Paul with regard to himself and his travelling companions, **Acts 20:13**; of what the apostle "ordained" in all the churches in regard to marital conditions, 1 Cor. 7:17; of what the Lord "ordained" in regard to the support of those who proclaimed the gospel, 1 Cor. 9:14; of the Law as divinely "ordained," or administered, through angels, by Moses, Gal. 3:19. In Titus 1:5, KJV, "had appointed thee," the sense is rather that of commanding, RV, "gave thee charge."

Fashion *tupos* (5179), "a type, figure, example," is translated "fashion" in the KJV of **Acts 7:44**, RV, "figure," said of the tabernacle. *See also* Figures at *Acts 7:43*.

7:45 Which also our fathers that came after brought in with Jesus into the possession of the Gentiles, whom God drave out before the face of our fathers, unto the days of David;

Came after *diadechomai* (1237), "to receive through another, to receive in turn" (*dia*, "through," *dechomai*, "to receive"), occurs in **Acts 7:45**, RV, "in their turn ... when they entered" (KJV, "that came after"); the meaning here is "having received (it) after," i.e., as from Moses under Joshua's leadership. In the papyri the word is used similarly of visiting as deputy.

Possession *see Acts 7:5*.

Drave *exotheo* (1856), "to thrust out" (*ek*, "out," *otheo*, "to push, thrust"), is translated "thrust" in **Acts 7:45**, RV (KJV, "drave"); in **27:39**, of "driving" a storm-tossed ship ashore (RV, "drive," KJV, "thrust").

7:46 Who found favour before God, and desired to find a tabernacle for the God of Jacob.

Found *see* Shewed at *Acts 4:21*.

Favour *see Acts 2:47*.

Before *enopion* (1799), is translated "in the sight of" in the RV (for KJV, "before") in Luke 12:6; 15:18; 16:15; **Acts 7:46**; **10:33**; **19:19**; 1 Tim. 5:4, 21; 2 Tim. 2:14; 4:1; Rev. 13:12. The RV is more appropriate in most passages, as giving the real significance of the word. *See also Acts 2:25*.

Tabernacle *skenoma* (4638), occurs in **Acts 7:46**; 2 Pet. 1:13, 14.

7:47-48 But Solomon built him an house.

Howbeit the most High dwelleth not in temples made with hands; as saith the prophet,

High *hupsistos* (5310), "most high," is a superlative degree, the positive not being in use; it is used of God in Luke 1:32, 35, 76; 6:35, in each of which the RV has "the most High," for KJV, "the highest", KJV and RV in Mark 5:7; Luke 8:28; **Acts 7:48**; **16:17**; Heb. 7:1.

Hands *cheiropoietos* (5499), "made by hand," of human handiwork (*cheir*, and *poieo*, "to make"), is said of the temple in Jerusalem, Mark 14:58; temples in general, **Acts 7:48** (RV, "houses"); **17:24**; negatively, of the heavenly and spiritual tabernacle, Heb. 9:11; of the holy place in the earthly tabernacle, v. 24; of circumcision, Eph. 2:11. In the Sept., of idols, Lev. 26:1, 30; Isa. 2:18; 10:11; 16:12; 19:1; 21:9; 31:7; 46:6.

7:49 Heaven *is* my throne, and earth *is* my footstool: what house will ye build me? saith the Lord: or what *is* the place of my rest?

Throne *see Acts 2:30*.

Footstool *see Acts 2:35*.

What *poios* (4169), "of what sort," is translated "by what manner of (death)" in John 21:19, RV, (KJV, "by what"); in **Acts 7:49**, "what manner of (house)"; Rom. 3:27, "what manner of law"; 1 Cor. 15:35, "what manner of body."

Rest *katapausis* (2663), in classical Greek, denotes "a causing to cease" or "putting to rest"; in the NT, "rest, repose"; it is used (a) of God's "rest," **Acts 7:49**; Heb. 3:11, 18; 4:1, 3 (twice), RV (1st part), "that rest" (the KJV, "rest," is ambiguous), 5, 11; (b) in a general statement, applicable to God and man, 4:10.

7:50-51 Hath not my hand made all these things?

Ye stiffnecked and uncircumcised in heart and ears, ye do always resist the Holy Ghost: as your fathers *did*, so *do* ye.

Stiffnecked *sklerotrachelos* (4644), from *skleros*, "harsh, hard," *trachelos*, "a neck," is used metaphorically in **Acts 7:51**.

Uncircumcised *aperitmetos* (564), "uncircumcised" (*a*, negative, *peri*, "around," *temno*, "to cut"), is used in **Acts 7:51**, metaphorically, of "heart and ears."

Ears *ous* (3775), Latin *auris*, is used (a) of the physical organ, e.g., Luke 4:21; **Acts 7:57**; in **Acts 11:22**, in the plural with *akouo*, "to hear," lit., "was heard into the ears of someone," i.e., came to the knowledge of, similarly, in the singular, Matt. 10:27, in familiar private conversation; in Jas. 5:4 the phrase is used with *eiserchomai*, "to enter into"; in Luke 1:44, with *ginomai*, "to become, to come"; in Luke 12:3, with *lalein*, "to speak" and *pros*, "to", (b) metaphorically, of the faculty of perceiving with the mind, understanding and knowing, Matt. 13:16; frequently with *akouo*, "to hear," e.g., Matt. 11:15; 13:9, 43; Rev. 2 and 3, at the close of each of the messages to the churches, in Matt. 13:15 and **Acts 28:27**, with *bareos*, "heavily," of being slow to understand and obey; with a negative in Mark 8:18; Rom. 11:8; in Luke 9:44 the lit. meaning is "put those words into your ears," i.e., take them into your mind and keep them there, in **Acts 7:51** it is used with *aperitmetos*, "uncircumcised." As seeing is metaphorically associated with conviction, so hearing is with obedience (*hupakoe*, lit., "hearing under"; the Eng., "obedience" is etymologically "hearing over against," i.e., with response in the hearer).

Always *aei* (104), has two meanings: (a) "perpetually, incessantly," **Acts 7:51**; 2 Cor. 4:11; 6:10; Titus 1:12; Heb. 3:10; (b) "invariably, at any and every time," of successive occurrences, when some thing is to be repeated, according to the circumstances, 1 Pet. 3:15; 2 Pet. 1:12.

Resist *antipipto* (496), lit., and primarily, "to fall against or upon" (*anti*, "against," *pipto*, "to fall"), then, "to strive against, resist," is used in **Acts 7:51** of "resisting" the Holy Spirit.

Holy Ghost *see Acts 1:16.*

7:52 Which of the prophets have not your fathers persecuted? and they have slain them which shewed before of the coming of the Just One; of whom ye have been now the betrayers and murderers:

Persecuted *dioko* (1377), has the meanings (a) "to put to flight, drive away," (b) "to pursue," whence the meaning "to persecute," Matt. 5:10-12, 44; 10:23; 23:34; Luke 11:49; 21:12; John 5:16; 15:20 (twice); **Acts 7:52**; **9:4**, **5**, and similar passages; Rom. 12:14; 1 Cor. 4:12; 15:9; 2 Cor. 4:9, KJV (RV, "pursued"); Gal. 1:13, 23; 4:29; Gal. 5:11, RV, "am ... persecuted" (KJV, "suffer persecution"); so 6:12; Phil. 3:6; 2 Tim. 3:12, "shall suffer persecution"; Rev. 12:13.

Slain *apokteino* (615), the usual word for "to kill," is so translated in the RV wherever possible (e.g., for KJV, "to slay," in Luke 11:49; **Acts 7:52**; Rev. 2:13; 9:15; 11:13; 19:21); in the following the verb "to kill" would not be appropriate, Rom. 7:11, "slew," metaphorically of sin, as using the commandment; Eph. 2:16, "having slain," said metaphorically of the enmity between Jew and Gentile.

Shewed *see Acts 3:18.*

Coming *eleusis* (1660), "a coming" (from *erchomai*, "to come"), is found in **Acts 7:52**.

Just *see Acts 3:14. See also* Fruit at *Acts 2:30.*

Now *see Acts 4:29.*

Betrayers *prodotes* (4273), "a betrayer," is translated "betrayers" in **Acts 7:52**; "traitor," "traitors," in Luke 6:16 and 2 Tim. 3:4.

Murderers *see* Murderer at *Acts 3:14.*

7:53 Who have received the law by the disposition of angels, and have not kept *it*.

Disposition *diatage* (1296), an ordinance, e.g., Rom. 13:2 (cf. *diatasso*, "to appoint, ordain"), is rendered "disposition" in **Acts 7:53**; RV, "as it (the law) was ordained by angels" (marg., "as the ordinance of angels"; lit., "unto ordinances of angels"). Angels are mentioned in connection with the giving of the Law of Moses in Deut. 33:2. In Gal. 3:19 and Heb. 2:2 the purpose of the reference to them is to show the superiority of the gospel to the Law. In **Acts 7:53** Stephen mentions the angels to stress the majesty of the Law.

Kept *phulasso* (5442), denotes (a) "to guard, watch, keep watch," e.g., Luke 2:8; in the passive voice, 8:29; (b) "to keep by way of protection," e.g., Luke 11:21; John 12:25; 17:12; (c) metaphorically, "to keep a law precept," etc., e.g., Matt. 19:20 and Luke 18:21, "have observed"; Luke 11:28; John 12:47 (in the best mss.); **Acts 7:53**; **16:4**; **21:24**; Rom. 2:26; Gal. 6:13; 1 Tim. 5:21 ("observe"); in the middle voice, Mark 10:20 ("have observed"); (d) in the middle voice, "to keep oneself from," **Acts 21:25**; elsewhere translated by the verb "to beware."

7:54 When they heard these things, they were cut to the heart, and they gnashed on him with *their* teeth.

Cut *see Acts 5:33.*

Gnashed *brucho* (1031), primarily, "to bite or eat greedily" (akin to *bruko*, "to chew"), denotes "to grind or gnash with the teeth," **Acts 7:54**.

Teeth *odous* (3599), is used in the sing. in Matt. 5:38 (twice); elsewhere in the plural, of "the gnashing of teeth," the gnashing being expressive of anguish and indignation, Matt. 8:12; 13:42, 50; 22:13; 24:51; 25:30; Mark 9:18; Luke 13:28; **Acts 7:54**; in Rev. 9:8, of the beings seen in a vision and described as locusts.

7:55 But he, being full of the Holy Ghost, looked up stedfastly into heaven, and saw the glory of God, and Jesus standing on the right hand of God,

Full *see Acts 6:3.*

Looked *see Acts 1:10.*

Stedfastly *see Acts 1:10.*

7:56 And said, Behold, I see the heavens opened, and the Son of man standing on the right hand of God.

Opened *dianoigo* (1272), "to open up completely" (*dia*, "through," intensive, and *anoigo*), is used (a) literally, Luke 2:23; **Acts 7:56**, in the best mss.; (b) metaphorically, of the eyes, Mark 7:34; Luke 24:31; of the Scriptures, v. 32 and **Acts 17:3**; of the mind, Luke 24:45, RV (KJV, "understanding"); of the heart, **Acts 16:14**. *See also* ***Acts 5:19***.

Son *Son of Man* In the NT this is a designation of Christ, almost entirely confined to the Gospels. Elsewhere it is found in **Acts 7:56**, the only occasion where a disciple applied it to the Lord and in Rev. 1:13; 14:14. "Son of Man" is the title Christ used of Himself; John 12:34 is not an exception, for the quotation by the multitude was from His own statement. The title is found especially in the Synoptic Gospels. The occurrences in John's Gospel, 1:51; 3:13, 14; 5:27; 6:27, 53, 62; 8:28 (9:35 in some texts); 12:23, 34 (twice); 13:31, are not parallel to those in the Synoptic Gospels. In the latter the use of the title falls into two groups, (a) those in which it refers to Christ's humanity, His earthly work, sufferings and death, e.g., Matt. 8:20; 11:19; 12:40; 26:2, 24; (b) those which refer to His glory in resurrection and to that of His future advent, e.g., Matt. 10:23; 13:41; 16:27, 28; 17:9; 24:27, 30 (twice), 37, 39, 44. While it is a messianic title it is evident that the Lord applied it to Himself in a distinctive way, for it indicates more than Messiahship, even universal headship on the part of One who is Man. It therefore stresses His manhood, manhood of a unique order in comparison with all other men, for He is declared to be of heaven, 1 Cor. 15:47, and even while here below, was "the Son of Man, which is in Heaven," John 3:13. As the "Son of Man" He must be appropriated spiritually as a condition of possessing eternal life, John 6:53. In His death, as in His life, the glory of His Manhood was displayed in the absolute obedience and submission to the will of the Father (12:23; 13:31), and, in view of this, all judgment has been committed to Him, who will judge in full understanding experimentally of human conditions, sin apart, and will exercise the judgment as sharing the nature of those judged, John 5:22, 27. Not only is He man, but He is "Son of Man," not by human generation but, according to the Semitic usage of the expression, partaking of the characteristics (sin apart) of manhood belonging to the category of mankind. Twice in the Apocalypse, 1:13 and 14:14, He is described as "One like unto a Son of man," RV (KJV, "... the Son of Man"), cf. Dan. 7:13. He who was thus seen was indeed the "Son of Man," but the absence of the article in the original serves to stress what morally characterizes Him as such. Accordingly in these passages He is revealed, not as the Person known by the title, but as the One who is qualified to act as the Judge of all men. He is the same Person as in the days of His flesh, still continuing His humanity with His Deity. The phrase "like unto" serves to distinguish Him as there seen in His glory and majesty in contrast to the days of His humiliation.

7:57 Then they cried out with a loud voice, and stopped their ears, and ran upon him with one accord,

Stopped *sunecho* (4912), "to hold together, confine, secure, to hold fast" (*echo*, "to have or hold"), "to constrain," is said (a) of the effect of the word of the Lord upon Paul, **Acts 18:5** (KJV, "was pressed in spirit," RV, "was constrained by the word"); of the effect of the love of Christ, 2 Cor. 5:14; (b) of being taken with a disease, Matt. 4:24; Luke 4:38; **Acts 28:8**; with fear, Luke 8:37; (c) of thronging or holding in a person, Luke 8:45; being straitened, Luke 12:50; being in a strait betwixt two, Phil. 1:23; keeping a city in on every side, Luke 19:43; keeping a tight hold on a person, as the men who seized the Lord Jesus did, after bringing Him into the High Priest's house, Luke 22:63; (d) of stopping the ears in refusal to listen, **Acts 7:57**. Luke uses the word nine times out of its twelve occurrences in the NT.

Ears *see* ***Acts 7:51***.

Ran *hormao*, "to set in motion, urge on," but intransitively, "to hasten on, rush," is always translated "to rush" in the RV; KJV, "ran violently," Matt. 8:32; Mark 5:13; Luke 8:33; "ran," **Acts 7:57**; "rushed", **19:29**.

Accord *see* ***Acts 1:14***.

7:58 And cast *him* out of the city, and stoned *him*: and the witnesses laid down their clothes at a young man's feet, whose name was Saul.

Stoned *lithoboleo* (3036), "to pelt with stones," "to stone to death," occurs in Matt. 21:35; 23:37; Luke 13:34 (John 8:5 in some mss.); **Acts 7:58, 59**; **14:5**; Heb. 12:20.

Witnesses *see* ***Acts 1:8***.

Laid *apotithemi* (659), "to put off from oneself," always in the middle voice in the NT, is used metaphorically in Heb. 12:1, "laying aside (every weight);" in Jas. 1:21, KJV, "lay apart," RV, "putting away"; in **Acts 7:58** of "laying" down garments, after taking them off, for the purpose of stoning Stephen.

Young *neanias* (3494), "a young man," occurs in **Acts 7:58**; **20:9**; **23:17, 18** (in some texts).

Name *kaleo* (2564), "to call," is translated "named" in **Acts 7:58**, RV (KJV, "whose name was").

7:59 And they stoned Stephen, calling upon *God*, and saying, Lord Jesus, receive my spirit.

Stoned *see Acts 7:58*.

Calling *epikaleo* (1941), "to call upon," has the meaning "appeal" in the middle voice, which carries with it the suggestion of a special interest on the part of the doer of an action in that in which he is engaged. Stephen died "calling upon the Lord," **Acts 7:59**. In the more strictly legal sense the word is used only of Paul's "appeal" to Caesar, **Acts 25:11-12**, **21**, **25**; **26:32**; **28:19**. *See also* **Call** at *Acts 2:21*.

Jesus *iesous* (2424), is a transliteration of the Heb. "Joshua," meaning "Jehovah is salvation," i.e., "is the Savior," "a common name among the Jews," e.g., Ex. 17:9; Luke 3:29 (RV); Col. 4:11. It was given to the Son of God in Incarnation as His personal name, in obedience to the command of an angel to Joseph, the husband of His Mother, Mary, shortly before He was born, Matt. 1:21. By it He is spoken of throughout the Gospel narratives generally, but not without exception, as in Mark 16:19, 20; Luke 7:13, and a dozen other places in that Gospel, and a few in John. "'Jesus Christ' occurs only in Matt. 1:1, 18; 16:21, marg.; Mark 1:1; John 1:17; 17:3. In Acts the name 'Jesus' is found frequently. 'Lord Jesus' is the normal usage, as in **Acts 8:16**; **19:5**, **17**; see also the reports of the words of Stephen, **7:59**, of Ananias, **9:17**, and of Paul, **16:31**; though both Peter, **10:36**, and Paul, **16:18**, also used 'Jesus Christ.' In the Epistles of James, Peter, John and Jude, the personal name is not once found alone, but in Rev. eight times (RV), 1:9; 12:17; 14:12; 17:6; 19:10 (twice); 20:4; 22:16. In the Epistles of Paul 'Jesus' appears alone just thirteen times, and in the Hebrews eight times; in the latter the title 'Lord' is added once only, at 13:20. In the Epistles of James, Peter, John, and Jude, men who had companied with the Lord in the days of His flesh, 'Jesus Christ' is the invariable order (in the RV) of the Name and Title, for this was the order of their experience; as 'Jesus' they knew Him first, that He was Messiah they learnt finally in His resurrection. But Paul came to know Him first in the glory of heaven, **Acts 9:1-6**, and his experience being thus the reverse of theirs, the reverse order, 'Christ Jesus,' is of frequent occurrence in his letters, but, with the exception of **Acts 24:24**, does not occur elsewhere in the RV. In Paul's letters the order is always in harmony with the context. Thus 'Christ Jesus' describes the Exalted One who emptied Himself, Phil. 2:5, and testifies to His preexistence; 'Jesus Christ' describes the despised and rejected One Who was afterwards glorified, Phil. 2:11, and testifies to His resurrection. 'Christ Jesus' suggests His grace, 'Jesus Christ' suggests His glory."

Receive *see Acts 3:21*.

Spirit *pneuma* (4151), primarily denotes "the wind" (akin to *pneo*, "to breathe, blow"); also "breath"; then, especially "the spirit," which, like the wind, is invisible, immaterial and powerful. The NT uses of the word may be analyzed approximately as follows:

"(a) the wind, John 3:8 (where marg. is, perhaps, to be preferred); Heb. 1:7; cf. Amos 4:13, Sept.; (b) the breath, 2 Thess. 2:8; Rev. 11:11; 13:15; cf. Job 12:10, Sept.; (c) the immaterial, invisible part of man, Luke 8:55; **Acts 7:59**; 1 Cor. 5:5; Jas. 2:26; cf. Eccl. 12:7, Sept.; (d) the disembodied (or 'unclothed,' or 'naked,' 2 Cor. 5:3, 4) man, Luke 24:37, 39; Heb. 12:23; 1 Pet. 4:6; (e) the resurrection body, 1 Cor. 15:45; 1 Tim. 3:16; 1 Pet. 3:18; (f) the sentient element in man, that by which he perceives, reflects, feels, desires, Matt. 5:3; 26:41; Mark 2:8; Luke 1:47, 80; **Acts 17:16**; **20:22**; 1 Cor. 2:11; 5:3, 4; 14:4, 15; 2 Cor. 7:1; cf. Gen. 26:35; Isa. 26:9; Ezek. 13:3; Dan. 7:15; (g) purpose, aim, 2 Cor. 12:18; Phil. 1:27; Eph. 4:23; Rev. 19:10; cf. Ezra 1:5; Ps. 78:8; Dan. 5:12; (h) the equivalent of the personal pronoun, used for emphasis and effect: 1st person, 1 Cor. 16:18; cf. Gen. 6:3; 2nd person, 2 Tim. 4:22; Philem. 25; cf. Ps. 139:7; 3rd person, 2 Cor. 7:13; cf. Isa. 40:13; (i) character, Luke 1:17; Rom. 1:4; cf. Num. 14:24; (j) moral qualities and activities: bad, as of bondage, as of a slave, Rom. 8:15; cf. Isa. 61:3; stupor, Rom. 11:8; cf. Isa. 29:10; timidity, 2 Tim. 1:7; cf. Josh. 5:1; good, as of adoption, i.e., liberty as of a son, Rom. 8:15; cf. Ps. 51:12; meekness, 1 Cor. 4:21; cf. Prov. 16:19; faith, 2 Cor. 4:13; quietness, 1 Pet. 3:4; cf. Prov. 14:29; (k) the Holy Spirit, e.g., Matt. 4:1; Luke 4:18; (l) 'the inward man' (an expression used only of the believer, Rom. 7:22; 2 Cor. 4:16; Eph. 3:16); the new life, Rom. 8:4-6, 10, 16; Heb. 12:9; cf. Ps. 51:10; (m) unclean spirits, demons, Matt. 8:16; Luke 4:33; 1 Pet. 3:19; cf. 1 Sam. 18:10; (n) angels, Heb. 1:14; cf. **Acts 12:15**; (o) divine gift for service, 1 Cor. 14:12, 32; (p) by metonymy, those who claim to be depositories of these gifts, 2 Thess. 2:2; 1 John 4:1-3; (q) the significance, as contrasted with the form, of words, or of a rite, John 6:63; Rom. 2:29; 7:6; 2 Cor. 3:6; (r) a vision, Rev. 1:10; 4:2; 17:3; 21:10."

7:60 And he kneeled down, and cried with a loud voice, Lord, lay not this sin to their charge. And when he had said this, he fell asleep.

Lay *histemi* (2476), "to stand, to make to stand," is rendered "abode" in John 8:44, KJV; "continue," in **Acts 26:22**. In these places the RV corrects to "stood" and "stand." This word is suggestive of fidelity and stability. It is rendered "lay ... to the charge" in **Acts 7:60**.

Sin *hamartia* (266), is, lit., "a missing of the mark," a sinful deed, an act of "sin," e.g., Matt. 12:31; **Acts 7:60**; Jas. 1:15 (1st part); 2:9; 4:17; 5:15, 20; 1 John 5:16 (1st part).

Charge In **Acts 7:60***histemi*, "to cause to stand," is rendered "lay ... to the charge."

Asleep *koimaomai* (2837), is used of natural "sleep," Matt. 28:13; Luke 22:45; John 11:12; **Acts 12:6**; of the death of the body, but only of such as are Christ's; yet never of Christ Himself, though He is "the firstfruits of them that have fallen asleep," 1 Cor. 15:20, of saints who departed before Christ came, Matt. 27:52; **Acts 13:36**; of Lazarus, while Christ was yet upon the earth, John 11:11; of believers since the Ascension, 1 Thess. 4:13-15, and **Acts 7:60**; 1 Cor. 7:39; 11:30; 15:6, 18, 51; 2 Pet. 3:4.

"Persecution is one of the surest signs of the genuineness of our Christianity."

BENJAMIN E. FERNANDO

Chapter 8

8:1 And Saul was consenting unto his death. And at that time there was a great persecution against the church which was at Jerusalem; and they were all scattered abroad throughout the regions of Judaea and Samaria, except the apostles.

Consenting *suneudokeo* (4909), lit., "to think well with" (*sun*, "with," *eu*, "well," *dokeo*, "to think"), to take pleasure with others in anything, to approve of, to assent, is used in Luke 11:48, of "consenting" to the evil deeds of predecessors (KJV, "allow"); in Rom. 1:32, of "consenting" in doing evil; in **Acts 8:1**; **22:20**, of "consenting" to the death of another. All these are cases of "consenting" to evil things. In 1 Cor. 7:12-13, it is used of an unbelieving wife's "consent" to dwell with her converted husband, and of an unbelieving husband's "consent" to dwell with a believing wife (KJV, "be pleased"; RV, "be content").

Death *anairesis* (336), another word for "death," lit. signifies "a taking up or off" (*ana*, "up," *airo*, "to take"), as of the taking of a life, or "putting to death"; it is found in **Acts 8:1**, of the murder of Stephen. Some mss. have it in **22:20**. In the Sept., Num. 11:15; Judg. 15:17, "the lifting of the jawbone."

Time In Luke 9:51 and **Acts 8:1**, KJV, *hemera*, "a day," is translated "time," in the former, plural, RV, "the days"; in Luke 23:7 (plural), RV "(in these) days," KJV, "(at that) time."

Persecution *diogmos* (1375), occurs in Matt. 13:21; Mark 4:17; 10:30; **Acts 8:1**; **13:50**; Rom. 8:35; 2 Cor. 12:10; 2 Thess. 1:4; 2 Tim. 3:11, twice. In the Sept., Prov. 11:19; Lam. 3:19.

Church *see Acts 7:38*.

Scattered *diaspeiro* (1289), "to scatter abroad" (*dia*, "throughout," *speiro*, "to sow seed"), is used in **Acts 8:1, 4**; **11:19**, all of the church in Jerusalem "scattered" through persecution; the word in general is suggestive of the effects of the "scattering" in the sowing of the spiritual seed of the Word of life.

Regions *chora* (5561), "a space lying between two limits, a country, land," is translated "region" in Matt. 4:16; Luke 3:1; **Acts 8:1**; **13:49**; **16:6**; **18:23**, RV. In the last three passages it has the technical sense of a subdivision of a Roman province, Lat. *regio*; as also *perichoros* in **Acts 14:6**.

Except *plen* (4133), an adverb, most frequently signifying "yet, howbeit," or "only," sometimes has the meaning "except (that)," "save (that)," **Acts 20:23**; Phil. 1:18, RV, "only that," for KJV, "notwithstanding." It is also used as a preposition, signifying "except, save," Mark 12:32, "but"; John 8:10, "but" (KJV only); **Acts 8:1**, "except"; **Acts 15:28**, "than"; **27:22**, "but (only)."

8:2 And devout men carried Stephen *to his burial*, and made great lamentation over him.

Devout *see Acts 2:5*.

Carried *sunkomizo* (4792), "to carry together, to help in carrying" (*sun*, "with," *komizo*, "to carry"), is used in **Acts 8:2**, RV, "buried," for KJV, "carried to his burial." The verb has also the meaning of "recovering or getting back a body."

Lamentation *kopto* (2875), primarily, "to beat, smite"; then, "to cut off," Matt. 21:8; Mark 11:8, is used in the middle voice, of beating oneself, beating the breast, as a token of grief; hence, "to bewail," Matt. 11:17 (RV, "mourn," for KJV, "lament");

24:30, "mourn"; Rev. 1:7 (RV, "mourn"; KJV, "wail"); in Luke 8:52; 23:27 "bewail"; in Rev. 18:9, "wail" (for KJV, "lament"). Cf. *kopetos*, "lamentation," **Acts 8:2**.

8:3 As for Saul, he made havock of the church, entering into every house, and haling men and women committed *them* to prison.

Made havock *lumainomai* (3075), "to maltreat, to outrage" (from *lume*, "a brutal outrage"), is translated "laid waste" (the church), in **Acts 8:3**, RV (KJV, "made havoc of").

Entering *see* Entered at *Acts 3:2*.

Every *see Acts 5:42*.

Haling *suro* (4951), "to draw, drag, haul," is used of a net, John 21:8; of violently "dragging" persons along, **Acts 8:3**, "haling"; **14:19**, RV, "dragged," KJV, "drew"; **17:6** (ditto); Rev. 12:4, KJV, "drew," RV, "draweth."

Committed *paradidomi* (3860), "to give over," is often rendered by the verb "to commit," e.g., to prison, **Acts 8:3**; to the grace of God, **Acts 14:26**; to God, 1 Pet. 2:23; by God to pits of darkness, 2 Pet. 2:4.

8:4 Therefore they that were scattered abroad went every where preaching the word.

Scattered *see Acts 8:1*.

Preaching *see* Preach at *Acts 5:42*.

8:5 Then Philip went down to the city of Samaria, and preached Christ unto them.

Preached *kerusso* (2784), signifies (a) "to be a herald," or, in general, "to proclaim," e.g., Matt. 3:1; Mark 1:45, "publish"; in Luke 4:18, RV, "to proclaim," KJV, "to preach"; so verse 19; Luke 12:3; **Acts 10:37**; Rom. 2:21; Rev. 5:2. In 1 Pet. 3:19 the probable reference is, not to glad tidings (which there is no real evidence that Noah preached, nor is there evidence that the spirits of antediluvian people are actually "in prison"), but to the act of Christ after His resurrection in proclaiming His victory to fallen angelic spirits; (b) "to preach the gospel as a herald," e.g., Matt. 24:14; Mark 13:10, RV, "be preached" (KJV, "be published"); 14:9; 16:15, 20; Luke 8:1; 9:2; 24:47; **Acts 8:5**; **19:13**; **28:31**; Rom. 10:14, present participle, lit., "(one) preaching," "a preacher"; 10:15 (1st part); 1 Cor. 1:23; 15:11, 12; 2 Cor. 1:19; 4:5; 11:4; Gal. 2:2; Phil. 1:15; Col. 1:23; 1 Thess. 2:9; 1 Tim. 3:16; (c) "to preach the word," 2 Tim. 4:2 (of the ministry of the Scriptures, with special reference to the gospel). Translated "to proclaim" in the RV, for KJV, "to preach," in Matt. 10:27; Luke 4:19; **Acts 8:5**; **9:20**.

8:6 And the people with one accord gave heed unto those things which Philip spake, hearing and seeing the miracles which he did.

Accord *see Acts 1:14*.

Gave *prosecho* (4337), "to turn one's mind to, attend to," is used of "giving" oneself up to, 1 Tim. 3:8 (to wine); of "giving" heed to, **Acts 8:6**, **10**, **11** (RV); **16:14** (RV); 1 Tim. 1:4; 4:1, 13 (RV); Titus 1:14; Heb. 2:1.

Heed *see Acts 5:35*.

Miracles *see* Miracle at *Acts 4:16*.

8:7 For unclean spirits, crying with loud voice, came out of many that were possessed *with them*: and many taken with palsies, and that were lame, were healed.

Unclean *see Acts 5:16*.

Crying *boao* (994), signifies (a) "to raise a cry," whether of joy, Gal. 4:27, or vexation, **Acts 8:7**; (b) "to speak with a strong voice," Matt. 3:3; Mark 1:3; 15:34; Luke 3:4; 9:38 (some mss. have *anaboao* here); John 1:23; **Acts 17:6**; **25:24** (some mss. have *epiboao* here); (c) "to cry out for help," Luke 18:7, 38. For **Acts 21:34**, see *epiphoneo*: *see* **Shout** at *Acts 12:22*.

Possessed In **Acts 8:7** and **16:16**, KJV, *echo*, "have," is translated "to be possessed of," RV, "had" and "having."

Palsies *paraluo* (3886), lit., "to loose from the side," hence, "to set free," is used in the passive voice of "being enfeebled by a paralytic stroke, palsied," Luke 5:18, RV, "palsied" (KJV, "taken with a palsy"); 5:24 (ditto), in the best mss.; **Acts 8:7** (ditto); **9:33**, RV, "he was palsied" (KJV, "was sick of the palsy"); Heb. 12:12, RV, "palsied (knees)," KJV, "feeble."

Lame *see Acts 3:2*.

8:8 And there was great joy in that city.

Great *megas* (3173), is used (a) of external form, size, measure, e.g., of a stone, Matt. 27:60; fish, John 21:11; (b) of degree and intensity, e.g., of fear, Mark 4:41; wind, John 6:18; Rev. 6:13, RV, "great" (KJV, "mighty"); of a circumstance, 1 Cor. 9:11; 2 Cor. 11:15; in Rev. 5:2, 12, the RV has "great" (KJV, "loud"), of a voice; (c) of rank, whether of persons, e.g., God, Titus 2:13; Christ as a "great Priest," Heb. 10:21, RV; Diana, **Acts 19:27**, Simon Magus, **Acts 8:9** "(some) great one"; in the plural "great ones," Matt. 20:25; Mark 10:42, those who hold positions of authority in gentile nations; or of things, e.g., a mystery, Eph. 5:32. Some mss. have it in **Acts 8:8**, of joy. Some manuscripts have *polus* (4183), "much, many, great," is used of number, e.g., Luke 5:6; **Acts 11:21**; degree, e.g., of harvest, Matt. 9:37; mercy, 1 Pet. 1:3, RV "great" (KJV, "abundant"); glory, Matt. 24:30; joy, Philem. 7, RV, "much" (KJV, "great"); peace, **Acts 24:2**. The best mss. have it in **Acts 8:8** (RV, "much"), of joy.

8:9 But there was a certain man, called Simon, which beforetime in the same city used sorcery, and bewitched the people of Samaria, giving out that himself was some great one:

Called *see* Names at *Acts 1:15*.

Beforetime *prouparcho* (4391), "to exist before, or be beforehand," is found in Luke 23:12, and **Acts 8:9**, "beforetime." In the Sept., Job 42:18.

Sorcery *mageuo* (3096), "to practice magic," **Acts 8:9**, "used sorcery," is used ... of Simon Magnus.

Bewitched *existemi* (1839), lit. means "to stand out from." Like the noun, this is used with two distinct meanings: (a) in the sense of amazement, the word should be invariably rendered "amazed," as in the RV, e.g., in the case of Simon Magus (for KJV, "bewitched"), **Acts 8:9** and **11**. It is used, in the passive voice, of Simon himself in the **13**th v., RV, "he was amazed," for KJV, "wondered." "Amaze" is preferable to "astonish" throughout; (b) in Mark 3:21 and 2 Cor. 5:13 it is used with its other meaning of being beside oneself.

People *ethnos* (1484), denotes (a) "a nation," e.g., Matt. 24:7; **Acts 10:35**; "the Jewish people," e.g., Luke 7:5; **Acts 10:22**; **28:19**; (b) in the plural, "the rest of mankind" in distinction from Israel or the Jews, e.g., Matt. 4:15; **Acts 28:28**; (c) "the people of a city," **Acts 8:9**; (d) gentile Christians, e.g., Rom. 10:19; 11:13; 15:27; Gal. 2:14.

Giving *lego* (3004), "to say," is rendered "giving out," of the self-advertisement of Simon Magus, **Acts 8:9**.

Great *see Acts 8:8*.

8:10 To whom they all gave heed, from the least to the greatest, saying, This man is the great power of God.

Gave *see Acts 8:6*.

Heed *see Acts 5:35*.

Least *mikros* (3398), "little, small" (the opposite of *megos*, "great"), is used (a) of persons, with regard to (1) station, or age, in the singular, Mark 15:40, of James "the less" (RV marg., "little"), possibly referring to age; Luke 19:3; in the plural, "little" ones, Matt. 18:6, 10, 14; Mark 9:42; (2) rank or influence, e.g., Matt. 10:42 (see context); **Acts 8:10**; **26:22**, "small," as in Rev. 11:18; 13:16; 19:5, 18; 20:12; (b) of things, with regard to (1) size, e.g., Jas. 3:5; (2) quantity, Luke 12:32; 1 Cor. 5:6; Gal. 5:9; Rev. 3:8; (3) time, John 7:33; 12:35; Rev. 6:11; 20:3.

Greatest *megas* (3173), is translated "the greatest," in **Acts 8:10** and Heb. 8:11. The whole phrase, lit., "from small to great," is equivalent to the Eng. idiom "one and all." It is used in the Sept., e.g., in 1 Sam. 5:9: "God smote the people of Gath from the least to the greatest," ("both small and great"). So 1 Sam. 30:19; 2 Chron. 34:30, etc.

8:11 And to him they had regard, because that of long time he had bewitched them with sorceries.

Had *see* Gave at *Acts 8:6*.

Regard *prosecho* (4337), "to take or give heed," is translated "they had regard" in **Acts 8:11**, KJV (RV, "they gave heed").

Long *hikanos* (2425), "sufficient, much, long," is used with *chronos*, "time," in Luke 8:27; in 20:9 and 23:8 (KJV, "season") the plural is used, lit., "long times"; **Acts 8:11**; **14:3**.

Bewitched *see Acts 8:9*.

Sorceries *magia* (or *-eia*) (3095), "the magic art," is used in the plural in **Acts 8:11**, "sorceries."

8:12 But when they believed Philip preaching the things concerning the kingdom of God, and the name of Jesus Christ, they were baptized, both men and women.

Preaching *see* Preach at *Acts 5:42*.

Things *euangelizo* (2097), is used of any message designed to cheer those who receive it; it is rendered "to bring, declare, preach," or "show good or glad tidings," e.g., Luke 1:19; 2:10; 3:18, RV; 4:43, RV; 7:22, RV; 8:1; **Acts 8:12** and **10:36**, RV; **14:15**, RV; in 1 Thess. 3:6, "brought us glad (KJV, good) tidings"; in Heb. 4:2, RV, "we have had good tidings preached"; similarly, 4:6; in 1 Pet. 1:25 *rhema*, "a word," is coupled with this verb, "the word of good tidings which was preached," RV (KJV, "the word which by the gospel is preached").

Men *see Acts 1:16*.

8:13 Then Simon himself believed also: and when he was baptized, he continued with Philip, and wondered, beholding the miracles and signs which were done.

Continued *see Acts 1:14*.

Wondered *see* Bewitched at *Acts 8:9*.

Miracles For *existemi*, **Acts 8:13**, KJV. *See also* *Acts 2:22*.

Signs *see Acts 2:22.*

8:14 Now when the apostles which were at Jerusalem heard that Samaria had received the word of God, they sent unto them Peter and John:

Received *see* Receive at *Acts 3:21.*

8:15-16 Who, when they were come down, prayed for them, that they might receive the Holy Ghost:

(For as yet he was fallen upon none of them: only they were baptized in the name of the Lord Jesus.)

Fallen *epipipto* (1968), "to fall upon," is used (a) literally, Mark 3:10, "pressed upon"; **Acts 20:10, 37**; (b) metaphorically, of fear, Luke 1:12; **Acts 19:17**; Rev. 11:11; reproaches, Rom. 15:3; of the Holy Spirit, **Acts 8:16; 10:44; 11:15.**

Baptized *see Acts 1:5.*

Name *see* Names at *Acts 1:15.*

Jesus *see Acts 7:59.*

8:17 Then laid they *their* hands on them, and they received the Holy Ghost.

Laid ... on *see Acts 6:6.*

8:18 And when Simon saw that through laying on of the apostles' hands the Holy Ghost was given, he offered them money,

Saw *theaomai* (2300), "to view attentively, to see with admiration, desire, or regard," stresses more especially the action of the person beholding; it is used in Matt. 11:7 (RV, "to behold"), while *idein*, the infinitive of *eidon*, is used in the questions in the next two verses; in verse 7 the interest in the onlooker is stressed, in vv. 8, 9, the attention is especially directed to the object "seen." The verb is translated "to see" in the KJV and RV of Matt. 6:1; Mark 16:11, 14; John 6:5; **Acts 8:18** (in some mss.); **21:27**; Rom. 15:24; elsewhere, for the KJV, "to see," the RV uses the verb "to behold," bringing out its force more suitably.

Laying on *see* Laid ... on at *Acts 6:6.*

Offered *see Acts 7:42.*

Money *see Acts 4:37.*

8:19 Saying, Give me also this power, that on whomsoever I lay hands, he may receive the Holy Ghost.

Lay *see* Laid ... on at *Acts 6:6.*

8:20 But Peter said unto him, Thy money perish with thee, because thou hast thought that the gift of God may be purchased with money.

Money *see* Silver at *Acts 3:6.*

Perish *apoleia* (684), indicating "loss of well-being, not of being," is used (a) of things, signifying their waste, or ruin; of ointment, Matt. 26:8; Mark 14:4; of money, **Acts 8:20** ("perish"); (b) of persons, signifying their spiritual and eternal perdition, Matt. 7:13; John 17:12; 2 Thess. 2:3, where "son of perdition" signifies the proper destiny of the person mentioned; metaphorically of men persistent in evil, Rom. 9:22, where "fitted" is in the middle voice, indicating that the vessels of wrath fitted themselves for "destruction", of the adversaries of the Lord's people, Phil. 1:28 ("perdition"); of professing Christians, really enemies of the cross of Christ, Phil. 3:19 (RV, "perdition"); of those who are subjects of foolish and hurtful lusts, 1 Tim. 6:9; of professing Hebrew adherents who shrink back into unbelief, Heb. 10:39; of false teachers, 2 Pet. 2:1, 3; of ungodly men, 3:7; of those who wrest the Scriptures, 3:16; of the Beast, the final head of the revived Roman Empire, Rev. 17.8, 11; (c) of impersonal subjects, as heresies, 2 Pet. 2:1, where "destructive heresies" (RV; KJV, "damnable") is, lit., "heresies of destruction" (marg., "sects of perdition"); in v. 2 the most authentic mss. have *aselgeiais*, "lascivious," instead of *apoleiais*.

> *"The experience of revival is nothing more than a new beginning of obedience to God."*
>
> CHARLES GRANDISON FINNEY

Thought *see* Supposed at *Acts 7:25.*

Gift *dorea* (1431), denotes "a free gift," stressing its gratuitous character; it is always used in the NT of a spiritual or supernatural gift, John 4:10; **Acts 8:20**; **11:17**; Rom. 5:15; 2 Cor. 9.15; Eph. 3:7; Heb. 6:4; in Eph. 4:7, "according to the measure of the gift of Christ," the "gift" is that given by Christ; in **Acts 2:28**, "the gift of the Holy Ghost," the clause is epexegetical, the "gift" being the Holy Ghost Himself; cf. **10:45**; **11:17**, and the phrase, "the gift of righteousness," Rom. 5:17.

Purchased *see Acts 1:18.*

8:21 Thou hast neither part nor lot in this matter: for thy heart is not right in the sight of God.

Part *meris* (3310), denotes (a) "a part" or "portion," Luke 10:42; **Acts 8:21**; 2 Cor. 6:15 (RV, "portion"); in Col. 1:12, "partakers," lit., "unto the part of"; (b) "a district" or "division," **Acts 16:12**, RV, "district" (KJV, "part").

Lot *see* **Part** at *Acts 1:17*.

Matter *logos* (3056), "a word, speech, discourse, account," hence also "that which is spoken of, a matter, affair, thing," is translated "matter" in Mark 1:45; **Acts 8:21**; **15:6**; **19:38**; RV of Phil. 4:15, "in the matter of" (KJV, "concerning").

Right *euthus* (2117), "straight," hence, metaphorically, "right," is so rendered in **Acts 8:21**, of the heart; **13:10**, of the ways of the Lord; 2 Pet. 2:15.

Sight of *enanti* (1725), is translated "in the sight of" in **Acts 8:21**, KJV.

8:22 Repent therefore of this thy wickedness, and pray God, if perhaps the thought of thine heart may be forgiven thee.

Repent *see Acts 2:38*.

Wickedness *kakia* (2549), "evil," is rendered "wickedness" in **Acts 8:22**; RV in Jas. 1:21, KJV, "naughtiness."

Pray *see* **Prayed** at *Acts 4:31*.

Perhaps *ara* (686), a particle, "then," sometimes marking a result about which some uncertainty is felt, is translated "perhaps" in **Acts 8:22**.

Thought *epinoia* (1963), "a thought by way of a design" (akin to *epinoeo*, "to contrive," *epi*, intensive, *noeo*, "to consider"), is used in **Acts 8:22**. In the Sept., Jer. 20:10.

Forgiven *aphiemi* (863), primarily, "to send forth, send away" (*apo*, "from," *hiemi*, "to send"), denotes, besides its other meanings, "to remit or forgive" (a) debts, Matt. 6:12; 18:27, 32, these being completely cancelled; (b) sins, e.g., Matt. 9:2, 5, 6; 12:31, 32; **Acts 8:22** ("the thought of thine heart"); Rom. 4:7; Jas. 5:15; 1 John 1:9; 2:12. In this latter respect the verb, like its corresponding noun (below), firstly signifies the remission of the punishment due to sinful conduct, the deliverance of the sinner from the penalty divinely, and therefore righteously, imposed; secondly, it involves the complete removal of the cause of offense; such remission is based upon the vicarious and propitiatory sacrifice of Christ. In the OT atoning sacrifice and "forgiveness" are often associated, e.g., Lev. 4:20, 26. The verb is used in the NT with reference to trespasses (*paraptoma*), e.g., Matt. 6:14, 15; sins (*hamartia*), e.g., Luke 5:20; debts (*opheilema*), Matt. 6:12; (*opheile*), 18:32; (*daneion*), 18:27; the thought (*dianoia*) of the heart, **Acts 8:22**. Cf. *kalupto*, "to cover," 1 Pet. 4:8; Jas. 5:20; and *epikalupto*, "to cover over," Rom. 4:7, representing the Hebrew words for "atonement." Human "forgiveness" is to be strictly analogous to divine "forgiveness," e.g., Matt. 6:12. If certain conditions are fulfilled, there is no limitation to Christ's law of "forgiveness," Matt. 18:21, 22. The conditions are repentance and confession, Matt. 18:15-17; Luke 17:3. As to limits to the possibility of divine "forgiveness," see Matt. 12:32, 2nd part and 1 John 5:16.

8:23 For I perceive that thou art in the gall of bitterness, and *in* the bond of iniquity.

Perceive In **Acts 8:23**, KJV, *horao*, "to see," is translated "I perceive" (RV, "I see").

Gall *chole* (5521), a word probably connected with *chloe*, "yellow," denotes "gall," (a) literal, Matt. 27:34 (cf. Ps. 69:21); some regard the word here as referring to myrrh, on account of Mark 15:23; (b) metaphorical, **Acts 8:23**, where "gall of bitterness" stands for extreme wickedness, productive of evil fruit. In the OT it is used (a) of a plant characterized by bitterness (probably wormwood), Deut. 29:18; Hos. 10:4; Amos 6:12; (b) as the translation of the word *mererah*, "bitterness," Job. 13:26, e.g.; (c) as the translation of *rosh*, "venom"; in Deut. 32:32 "(grapes) of gall." In Job 20:25, the gall bladder is referred to (the receptacle of bile). The ancients supposed that the poison of serpents lay in the gall (see Job 20:14).

Bitterness *pikria* (4088), denotes "bitterness." It is used in **Acts 8:23**, metaphorically, of a condition of extreme wickedness, "gall of bitterness" or "bitter gall"; in Rom. 3:14, of evil speaking; in Eph. 4:31, of "bitter" hatred; in Heb. 12:15, in the same sense, metaphorically, of a root of "bitterness," producing "bitter" fruit.

Bond *sundesmos* (4886), "that which binds together," is said of "the bond of iniquity," **Acts 8:23**; "the bond of peace," Eph. 4:3; "the bond of perfectness," Col. 3:14 (figurative of the ligaments of the body); elsewhere; Col. 2:19, "bands," figuratively of the bands which unite the church, the body of Christ.

Iniquity *see Acts 1:18*.

8:24 Then answered Simon, and said, Pray ye to the Lord for me, that none of these things which ye have spoken come upon me.

Pray *see* **Prayed** at *Acts 4:31*.

8:25 And they, when they had testified and preached the word of the Lord, returned to Jerusalem, and preached the gospel in many villages of the Samaritans.

Testified *see* **Testify** at *Acts 2:40*.

Preached *laleo*, "to speak," is translated "preached," Mark 2:2, KJV, "preached" (RV, "spake"); in **Acts 8:25**, 1st part, KJV (RV, "spoken"); so in **13:42** and **14:25**; "preaching" in **Acts 11:19**, KJV, but what is indicated here is not a formal "preaching" by the believers scattered from Jerusalem, but a general testimony to all with whom they came into contact; in **16:6**, RV, "to speak" (KJV, "to preach").

Word *see* Words at *Acts 2:40*.

Villages *kome* (2968), "a village," or "country town," primarily as distinct from a walled town, occurs in the Gospels; elsewhere only in **Acts 8:25**. The difference between *polis*, "a city," and *kome*, is maintained in the NT, as in Josephus. Among the Greeks the point of the distinction was not that of size or fortification, but of constitution and land. In the OT the city and the village are regularly distinguished. The Mishna makes the three distinctions, a large city, a city, and a village. The RV always substitutes "village(-s)" for KJV, "town(-s)," Matt. 10:11; Mark 8:23, 26, 27; Luke 5:17; 9:6, 12; John 7:42; 11:1, 30.

8:26 And the angel of the Lord spake unto Philip, saying, Arise, and go toward the south unto the way that goeth down from Jerusalem unto Gaza, which is desert.

South *mesembria* (3314), lit., "middle-day" (*mesos*, "middle," and *hemera*, "a day"), signifies (a) "noon," **Acts 22:6**; (b) "the south," **Acts 8:26**.

Way *see* Ways at *Acts 2:28*.

Which In **Acts 8:26**, KJV, *haute* (the feminine of *houtos*, "this"), "the same" (RV), is translated "which."

Desert *eremos* (2048), used as a noun, has the same meaning as *eremia*, in Luke 5:16 and 8:29, RV, "deserts," for KJV, "wilderness"; in Matt. 24:26 and John 6:31, RV, "wilderness," for KJV, "desert." As an adjective, it denotes (a), with reference to persons, "deserted," desolate, deprived of the friends and kindred, e.g. of a woman deserted by a husband, Gal 4:21; (b) so of a city, as Jerusalem, Matt. 23:38; or uninhabited places, "desert," e.g., Matt. 14:13, 15; **Acts 8:26**; in Mark 1:35, RV, "desert," for KJV, "solitary."

8:27 And he arose and went: and, behold, a man of Ethiopia, an eunuch of great authority under Candace queen of the Ethiopians, who had the charge of all her treasure, and had come to Jerusalem for to worship,

Eunuch *eunouchos* (2135), denotes (a) "an emasculated man, a eunuch," Matt. 19:12; (b) in the 3rd instance in that verse, "one naturally incapacitated for, or voluntarily abstaining from, wedlock"; (c) one such, in a position of high authority in a court, "a chamberlain," **Acts 8:27-39**.

Authority *dunastes* (1413), akin to *dunamis*, "power," (Eng., "dynasty,") signifies "a potentate, a high officer"; in **Acts 8:27**, of a high officer, it is rendered "of great authority"; in Luke 1:52, RV, "princes," (KJV, "the mighty"); in 1 Tim. 6:15 it is said of God ("Potentate").

Queen *basilissa* (938), the feminine of *basileus*, "a king," is used (a) of the "Queen of Sheba," Matt. 12:42; Luke 11:31; of "Candace," **Acts 8:27**; (b) metaphorically, of "Babylon," Rev. 18:7.

Charge In **Acts 8:27**, the RV translates the verb *eimi*, "to be," with *epi*, "over," "was over," KJV, "had the charge of."

Treasure *gaza* (1047), a Persian word, signifying "royal treasure," occurs in **Acts 8:27**.

8:28 Was returning, and sitting in his chariot read Esaias the prophet.

Chariot *harma* (716), akin to *ararisko*, "to join," denotes "a war chariot with two wheels," **Acts 8:28, 29, 38**; Rev. 9:9.

Read *anaginosko* (314), primarily, "to know certainly, to know again, recognize" (*ana*, "again," *ginosko*, "to know"), is used of "reading" written characters, e.g., Matt. 12:3, 5; 21:16; 24:15; of the private "reading" of Scripture, **Acts 8:28, 30, 32**; of the public "reading" of Scripture, Luke 4:16; **Acts 13:27**; **15:21**; 2 Cor. 3:15; Col. 4:16 (thrice); 1 Thess. 5:27; Rev. 1:3.

Prophet *see Acts 3:22*.

8:29 Then the Spirit said unto Philip, Go near, and join thyself to this chariot.

Go The following verbs signify both "to come" and "to go," with prefixed prepositions accordingly: *erchomai*; *eiserchomai*; *exerchomai*; *dierchomai*; *katerchomai*; Luke 17:7, *parerchomai*; *proserchomai*, "go near," **Acts 8:29**; *sunerchomai*, "went with," **Acts 9:39**; **15:38**; **21:16**; *anabaino*; *katabaino*; *paraginomai*, **Acts 23:16**, KJV, "went," RV, "entered"; *ekporeuo*; *choreo*, Matt. 15:17, KJV, "goeth," RV, "passeth"; *anabaino*, Luke 19:28, RV, "going up"; *ekbaino*.

Join *see Acts 5:13*.

Chariot *see Acts 8:28*.

8:30 And Philip ran thither to *him*, and heard him read the prophet Esaias, and said, Understandest thou what thou readest?

Ran *prostrecho* (4370), "to run to," is used in Mark 9:15; 10:17; **Acts 8:30**.

Read, Readest *see* **Read** at *Acts 8:28*.

Understandest *ginosko* (1097), "to know, to come to know," is translated "to understand" in the KJV in Matt. 26:10 and John 8:27 (RV, "to perceive"); KJV and RV in John 8:43; 10:6; in 10:38, RV (in some texts *pisteuo*, KJV, "believe"); KJV and RV in 12:16; 13:7 RV, KJV, "know"; **Acts 8:30**; in Phil. 1:12, KJV, RV, "know" (in some texts, **Acts 24:11**, KJV).

8:31 And he said, How can I, except some man should guide me? And he desired Philip that he would come up and sit with him.

Some *see* **One** at *Acts 5:25*.

Some man *see* **Something** at *Acts 3:5*.

Guide *hodegeo* (3594), "to lead the way," is used (a) literally, RV, "guide" (KJV, "lead"), of "guiding" the blind, in Matt. 15:14; Luke 6:39; of "guiding" unto fountains of waters of life, Rev. 7:17; (b) figuratively, in John 16:13, of "guidance" into the truth by the Holy Spirit; in **Acts 8:31**, of the interpretation of Scripture.

Desired *parakaleo* (3870), the most frequent word with this meaning, lit. denotes "to call to one's side," hence, "to call to one's aid." It is used for every kind of calling to a person which is meant to produce a particular effect, hence, with various meanings, such as "comfort, exhort, desire, call for," in addition to its significance "to beseech," which has a stronger force than *aiteo*. See, e.g., the RV "besought" in Mark 5:18; **Acts 8:31**; **19:31**; 1 Cor. 16:12.

Sit *see* **Sat** at *Acts 2:3*.

8:32 The place of the scripture which he read was this, He was led as a sheep to the slaughter; and like a lamb dumb before his shearer, so opened he not his mouth:

Place *perioche* (4042), primarily "a circumference, compass" *peri*, "around," *echo*, "to have"), hence denotes "a portion circumscribed," that which is contained, and in reference to a writing or book, "a portion or passage of its contents," **Acts 8:32**, "(the) place."

Scripture *see* *Acts 1:16*.

Read *see* *Acts 8:28*.

Led *ago* (71), "to bear, bring, carry, lead," is translated by the verb "to lead," e.g., in Mark 13:11; Luke 4:1; 4:9, RV; 4:29; 22:54; 23:1, KJV only; 23:32; John 18:28 (present tense, RV), **Acts 8:32**; metaphorically in Rom. 2:4, of the goodness of God; 8:14 and Gal. 5:18, of the Spirit of God; 1 Cor. 12:2, of the powers of darkness instigating to idolatry; 2 Tim. 3:6, of divers lusts (in some mss., *aichmaloteuo*). In Luke 24:21 *ago* is used of the passing (or spending) of a day, and translated "it is (now the third day)"; here the verb is probably to be taken impersonally, according to idiomatic usage, in the sense "there is passing the third day."

As *see* **Like unto** at *Acts 3:22*.

Sheep *probaton* (4263), from *probaino*, "to go forward," i.e., of the movement of quadrupeds, was used among the Greeks of small cattle, sheep and goats; in the NT, of "sheep" only (a) naturally, e.g., Matt. 12:11, 12; (b) metaphorically, of those who belong to the Lord, the lost ones of the house of Israel, Matt. 10:6; of those who are under the care of the Good Shepherd, e.g., Matt. 26:31; John 10:1, lit., "the fold of the sheep," and vv. 2-27; 21:16, 17 in some texts; Heb. 13:20; of those who in a future day, at the introduction of the millennial kingdom, have shown kindness to His persecuted earthly people in their great tribulation, Matt. 25:33; of the clothing of false shepherds, Matt. 7:15; (c) figuratively, by way of simile, of Christ, **Acts 8:32**; of the disciples, e.g., Matt. 10:16; of true followers of Christ in general, Rom. 8:36; of the former wayward condition of those who had come under His Shepherd care, 1 Pet. 2:25; of the multitudes who sought the help of Christ in the days of His flesh, Matt. 9:36; Mark 6:34.

Slaughter *sphage* (4967), is used in two quotations from the Sept., **Acts 8:32** from Isa. 53:7, and Rom. 8:36 from Ps. 44:22; in the latter the quotation is set in a strain of triumph, the passage quoted being an utterance of sorrow. In Jas. 5:5 there is an allusion to Jer. 12:3, the luxurious rich, getting wealth by injustice, spending it on their pleasures, are "fattening themselves like sheep unconscious of their doom." *See also* **Slain** at *Acts 7:42*.

Lamb *amnos* (286), "a lamb," is used figuratively of Christ, in John 1:29, 36, with the article, pointing Him out as the expected One, the One to be well known as the personal fulfillment and embodiment of all that had been indicated in the OT, the One by whose sacrifice deliverance from divine judgment was to be obtained; in **Acts 8:32** (from the Sept. of Is. 53:7) and 1 Pet. 1:19, the absence of the article stresses the nature and character of His sacrifice as set forth in the symbolism. The reference in each case is to the lamb of God's providing, Gen. 22:8, and the Paschal lamb of God's appointment for sacrifice in Israel, e.g., Ex. 12:5, 14, 27 (cf. 1 Cor. 5:7).

Dumb *aphonos* (880), lit., "voiceless, or soundless" (*a*, negative, and *phone*, "a sound"), has reference to voice, **Acts 8:32**; 1 Cor. 12:2; 2 Pet. 2:16, while *alalos* has reference to words. In 1 Cor. 14:10 it is used metaphorically of the significance of voices or sounds, "without signification." In the Sept. Isa. 53:7.

Before *see* **Sight** at *Acts 7:10*.

Shearer *keiro* (2751), is used (a) of "shearing sheep," **Acts 8:32**, "shearer," lit., "the (one) shearing": (b) in the middle voice, "to have one's hair cut off, be shorn," **Acts 18:18**; 1 Cor. 11:6.

Opened *see Acts 5:19*.

Mouth *see Acts 1:16*.

8:33 In his humiliation his judgment was taken away: and who shall declare his generation? for his life is taken from the earth.

Humiliation *tapeinosis* (5014), akin to *tapeinos*, is rendered "low estate" in Luke 1:48; "humiliation," **Acts 8:33**; Phil. 3:21, RV "(the body of our) humiliation," KJV, "(our) vile (body)"; Jas. 1:10, where "in that he is made low," is, lit., "in his humiliation."

Judgment *krisis* (2920), (a) denotes "the process of investigation, the act of distinguishing and separating"; hence "a judging, a passing of judgment upon a person or thing"; it has a variety of meanings, such as judicial authority, John 5:22, 27; justice, **Acts 8:33**; Jas. 2:13; a tribunal, Matt. 5:21-22; a trial, John 5:24; 2 Pet. 2:4; a judgment, 2 Pet. 2:11; Jude 9; by metonymy, the standard of judgment, just dealing, Matt. 12:18, 20; 23:23; Luke 11:42; divine judgment executed, 2 Thess. 1:5; Rev. 16:7; (b) sometimes it has the meaning "condemnation," and is virtually equivalent to *krima* (a); see Matt. 23:33; John 3:19; Jas. 5:12, *hupo krisin*, "under judgment."

Declare *diegeomai* (1334), "to conduct a narration through to the end" (*dia*, "through," intensive, *hegeomai*, "to lead"), hence denotes "to recount, to relate in full," Mark 5:16; Luke 8:39; 9:10; **Acts 8:33**; **9:27**; **12:17**; in Mark 9:9 and Heb. 11:32, "tell."

Taken *airo* (142), "to lift, carry, take up or away," occurs very frequently with its literal meanings. In John 1:29 it is used of Christ as "the Lamb of God, which taketh away the sin of the world," not the sins, but sin, that which has existed from the time of the Fall, and in regard to which God has had judicial dealings with the world; through the expiatory sacrifice of Christ the sin of the world will be replaced by everlasting righteousness; cf. the plural, "sins", in 1 John 3:5. Righteous judgment was "taken away" from Christ at human tribunals, and His life, while voluntarily given by Himself (John 10:17, 18), was "taken (from the earth)," **Acts 8:33** (quoted from the Sept. of Isa. 53:8). In John 15:2 it is used in the Lord's statement, "Every branch in Me that beareth not fruit, He taketh it away." This does not contemplate members of the "body" of Christ, but those who (just as a graft which being inserted, does not "abide" or "strike") are merely professed followers, giving only the appearance of being joined to the parent stem. The Law described in Col. 2:14 as "the bond written in ordinances that was against us," Christ "took" out of the way at His cross. In 1 Cor. 5:2, *airo* is used in the best texts, of the divine judgment which would have been exercised in "taking away" from the church the incestuous delinquent, had they mourned before God.

Earth *see Acts 1:8*.

8:34-35 And the eunuch answered Philip, and said, I pray thee, of whom speaketh the prophet this? of himself, or of some other man?

Then Philip opened his mouth, and began at the same scripture, and preached unto him Jesus.

Opened *see Acts 5:19*.

Scripture *see Acts 1:16*.

8:36 And as they went on *their* way, they came unto a certain water: and the eunuch said, See, *here is* water; what doth hinder me to be baptized?

Hinder *koluo* (2967), "to hinder, forbid, restrain," is translated "to hinder" in Luke 11:52; **Acts 8:36**; Rom. 1:13, RV (KJV, "was let"); Heb. 7:23, RV (KJV, "were not suffered").

8:37 And Philip said, If thou believest with all thine heart, thou mayest. And he answered and said, I believe that Jesus Christ is the Son of God.

Mayest *see* Let at *Acts 2:29*.

8:38 And he commanded the chariot to stand still: and they went down both into the water, both Philip and the eunuch; and he baptized him.

Chariot *see Acts 8:28*.

8:39-40 And when they were come up out of the water, the Spirit of the Lord caught away Philip, that the eunuch saw him no more: and he went on his way rejoicing.

But Philip was found at Azotus: and passing through he preached in all the cities, till he came to Caesarea.

Spirit *see* Holy Ghost at *Acts 1:16*.

Caught *harpazo* (726), "to snatch or catch away," is said of the act of the Spirit of the Lord in regard to Philip in **Acts 8:39**; of Paul in being "caught" up to paradise, 2 Cor. 12:2, 4; of the rapture of the saints at the return of the Lord, 1 Thess. 4:17; of the rapture of the man child in the vision of Rev. 12:5. This verb conveys the idea of force suddenly exercised, as in Matt. 11:12, "take (it) by force"; 12:29, "spoil" (some mss. have *diarpazo* here), in 13:19, RV, "snatcheth"; for forceful seizure, see also John 6:15; 10:12 28-29; **Acts 23:10**; in Jude 23, RV, "snatching."

No more *ouketi* (3765), a negative adverb of time, signifies "no longer, no more" (*ou*, "not," *k*, euphonic, *eti* "longer"), denying absolutely and directly, e.g., Matt. 19:6; John 4:42, "now ... not"; 6:66; **Acts 20:25**, **38**; 2 Cor. 1:23, KJV, "not as yet"; Eph. 2:19; with another negative, to strengthen the negation, e.g., Matt. 22:46; Mark 14:25; 15:5, RV, "no more (anything)," KJV, "yet ... no (thing)"; **Acts 8:39**; Rev. 18:11, 14.

Rejoicing *see Acts 5:41*.

Chapter 9

9:1 And Saul, yet breathing out threatenings and slaughter against the disciples of the Lord, went unto the high priest,

Breathing *empneo* (1709), lit., "to breathe in, or on," is used in **Acts 9:1**, indicating that threatening and slaughter were, so to speak, the elements from which Saul drew and expelled his breath.

Threatenings *see* Threaten at *Acts 4:17*.

Slaughter *phonos* (5408), is used (a) of a special act, Mark 15:7; Luke 23:19, 25; (b) in the plural, of "murders" in general, Matt. 15:19; Mark 7:21 (Gal. 5:21, in some inferior mss.); Rev. 9:21; in the singular, Rom. 1:29; (c) in the sense of "slaughter," Heb. 11:37, "they were slain with the sword," lit., "(they died by) slaughter (of the sword)"; in **Acts 9:1**, "slaughter."

9:2 And desired of him letters to Damascus to the synagogues, that if he found any of this way, whether they were men or women, he might bring them bound unto Jerusalem.

Letters *epistole* (1992), primarily "a message" (from *epistello*, "to send to"), hence, "a letter, an epistle," is used in the singular, e.g., **Acts 15:30**; in the plural, e.g., **Acts 9:2**; 2 Cor. 10:10. "Epistle is a less common word for a letter. A letter affords a writer more freedom, both in subject and expression, than does a formal treatise. A letter is usually occasional, that is, it is written in consequence of some circumstance which requires to be dealt with promptly. The style of a letter depends largely on the occasion that calls it forth." "A broad line is to be drawn between the letter and the epistle. The one is essentially a spontaneous product dominated throughout by the image of the reader, his sympathies and interests, instinct also with the writer's own soul: it is virtually one half of an imaginary dialogue, the suppressed responses of the other party shaping the course of what is actually written.... the other has a general aim, addressing all and sundry whom it may concern: it is like a public speech and looks towards publication" (J. V. Bartlet, in *Hastings' Bib. Dic.*). In 2 Pet. 3:16 the apostle includes the Epistles of Paul as part of the God-breathed Scriptures.

Synagogues *sunagoge* (4864), properly "a bringing together" (*sun*, "together," *ago*, "to bring"), denoted (a) "a gathering of things, a collection," then, of "persons, an assembling, of Jewish religious gatherings," e.g., **Acts 9:2**; an assembly of Christian Jews, Jas. 2:2, RV, "synagogue" (KJV, marg.; text, "assembly"); a company dominated by the power and activity of Satan, Rev. 2:9; 3:9; (b) by metonymy, "the building" in which the gathering is held, e.g. Matt. 6:2; Mark 1:21. The origin of the Jewish "synagogue" is probably to be assigned to the time of the Babylonian exile. Having no temple, the Jews assembled on the Sabbath to hear the Law read, and the practice continued in various buildings after the return. Cf. Ps. 74:8.

Way *see* Ways at *Acts 2:28*.

9:3 And as he journeyed, he came near Damascus: and suddenly there shined round about him a light from heaven:

Journeyed *poreuomai* (4198), "to go on one's way, to proceed from one place to another" (from *poros*, "a passage, a ford," Eng., "pore"), is always used in the middle voice in the NT and the Sept., and is the most frequent verb signifying "to go"; it is more distinctly used to indicate procedure or course than the verb *eimi*, "to go" (not found in the NT). It is often rendered "go thy (your) way," in Oriental usage the customary dismissal, marking the close of a case in court. Hence, in ordinary parlance, marking the end of a conversation, etc., e.g., Luke 7:22; 17:19; John 4:50; **Acts 9:15**; **24:25**; cf. Dan. 12:9; in Rom. 15:24 (1st part), RV, "go" (KJV, "take my journey"); in **Acts 9:3**; **22:6** and **26:13**, "journeyed" (KJV and RV).

Came near *engizo* (1448), "to come near draw nigh" (akin to *engus*, "near"), is translated by the verb "draw near or nigh," in the RV, Luke 12:33, KJV, "approacheth"; Heb. 10:25, KJV, "approaching"; Luke 18:35; 19:29, 37; **Acts 22:6**, KJV, "was come nigh"; Luke 7:12 "came nigh"; **Acts 9:3**, "came near."

Suddenly *exaiphnes* (1810), occurs in Mark 13:36; Luke 2:13; 9:39; **Acts 9:3**; **22:6**.

Shined *periastrapto* (4015), "to flash around, shine round about" (*peri*, and *astrape*, "shining brightness"), is used in **Acts 9:3** and **22:6** of the same circumstance as in **26:13**.

9:4 And he fell to the earth, and heard a voice saying unto him, Saul, Saul, why persecutest thou me?

Voice *see Acts 7:31.*

Persecutest *see* Persecuted at *Acts 7:52.*

9:5 And he said, Who art thou, Lord? And the Lord said, I am Jesus whom thou persecutest: *it is* hard for thee to kick against the pricks.

Thou Frequently this forms part of the translation of a verb in the 2nd person, singular. Otherwise it translates (a) the pronoun *su*, used for emphasis or contrast, e.g., John 1:19, 21 (twice), 25, 42 (twice); 8:5, 13, 25, 33, 48, 52, 53; **Acts 9:5**; in addressing a person or place, e.g., Matt. 2:6; Luke 1:76; John 17:5; perhaps also in the phrase *su eipas*, "thou hast said," e.g., Matt. 26:64 (sometimes without emphasis, e.g., **Acts 13:33**); (b) in the oblique cases, e.g., the dative *soi*, lit., "to thee," e.g., Matt. 17:25, "what thinkest thou?" (lit., "what does it seem to thee?"); (c) *autos*, "self," e.g., Luke 6:42; **Acts 21:24**, "thou thyself"; (d) the reflexive pronoun, *seauton*, Rom. 2:19, "thou thyself."

Persecutest *see* Persecuted at *Acts 7:52.*

Hard Synonymous with *austeros*, but to be distinguished from it, is *skleros* (from *skello*, "to be dry"). It was applied to that which lacks moisture, and so is rough and disageeable to the touch, and hence came to denotes "harsh, stern, hard." It is used by Matthew to describe the unprofitable servant's remark concerning his master, in the parable corresponding to that in Luke 19 (see *austeros*, above). *Austeros* is derived from a word having to do with the taste, *skleros*, "with the touch." *Austeros* is not necessarily a term of reproach, whereas *skleros* is always so, and indicates a harsh, even inhuman character. *Austeros* is "rather the exaggeration of a virtue pushed too far, than an absolute vice" (Trench, *Syn.* Sec. xiv). *Skleros* is used of the character of a man, Matt. 25:24; of a saying, John 6:60; of the difficulty and pain of kicking against the ox-goads, **Acts 9:5**; **26:14**; of rough winds, Jas. 3:4 and of harsh speeches, Jude 15. Cf. *sklerotes*, "hardness," *skleruno*, "to harden," *sklerokardia*, "hardness of heart," and *sklerotrachelos*, "stiff-necked."

Kick *laktizo* (2979), "to kick" (from *lax*, an adverb signifying "with the foot"), is used in **Acts 26:14** (some mss. have it in **9:5**).

Pricks *kentron* (2759), from *kenteo*, "to prick," denotes (a) "a sting," Rev. 9:10; metaphorically, of sin as the "sting" of death, 1 Cor. 15:55, 56; (b) "a goad," **Acts 26:14**, RV, "goad" (marg., "goads"), for KJV, "pricks" (in some mss. also in **9:5**), said of the promptings and misgivings which Saul of Tarsus had resisted before conversion.

9:6 And he trembling and astonished said, Lord, what wilt thou have me to do? And the Lord *said* unto him, Arise, and go into the city, and it shall be told thee what thou must do.

Trembling *tremo* (5141), "to tremble, especially with fear," is used in Mark 5:33; Luke 8:47 (**Acts 9:6**, in some mss.); 2 Pet. 2:10, RV, "they tremble (not)," KJV, "they are (not) afraid."

Astonished *thambeo* (2284), is used in Mark 1:27; 10:24, 32 (and **Acts 9:6**, KJV). The RV has "amazed" in each place; KJV "astonished," in Mark 110:24. *See also* Amazement at *Acts 3:10.*

Told *laleo* (2980), is usually rendered "to speak," in the RV (for KJV, "to tell"), e.g., Matt. 26:13; Luke 1:45; 2:17, 18, 20; **Acts 11:14**; **27:25**; but RV and KJV, "to tell" in John 8:40; **Acts 9:6**; **22:10**.

Must *see Acts 3:21.*

9:7 And the men which journeyed with him stood speechless, hearing a voice, but seeing no man.

Journeyed *sunodeuo* (4922), "to journey with," occurs in **Acts 9:7**. In the Sept., Zech. 8:21.

Speechless *eneos* (or *enneos*) (1769), "dumb, speechless," occurs in **Acts 9:7**. In the Sept., Prov. 17:28; Isa. 56:10.

Hearing *akouo* (191), the usual word denoting "to hear," is used (a) intransitively, e.g., Matt. 11:15; Mark 4:23; (b) transitively when the object is expressed, sometimes in the accusative case, sometimes in the genitive. Thus in **Acts 9:7**, "hearing the voice," the noun "voice" is in the partitive genitive case [i.e., hearing (something) of], whereas in **22:9**, "they heard not the voice," the construction is with the accusative. This removes the idea of any contradiction. The former indicates a "hearing" of the sound, the latter indicates the meaning or message of the voice (this they did not hear). "The former denotes the sensational perception, the latter (the accusative case) the thing perceived" (Cremer). In John 5:25, 28, the genitive case is used, indicating a "sensational perception" that the Lord's voice is sounding; in 3:8, of "hearing" the wind, the accusative is used, stressing "the thing perceived." That God "hears" prayer signifies that He answers prayer, e.g., John 9:31; 1 John 5:14, 15. Sometimes the verb is used with *para* ("from beside"), e.g., John 1:40, "one of the two which heard John speak," lit., "heard from beside John," suggesting that he stood beside him; in John 8:26, 40, indicating the intimate fellowship of the Son with the Father; the same construction is used in **Acts 10:22** and 2 Tim. 2:2, in the latter case, of the intimacy between Paul and Timothy.

Voice *see Acts 7:31*.

9:8 And Saul arose from the earth; and when his eyes were opened, he saw no man: but they led him by the hand, and brought *him* into Damascus.

Hand *cheiragogeo* (5496), "to lead by the hand," is used in **Acts 9:8; 22:11**.

9:9 And he was three days without sight, and neither did eat nor drink.

Sight *anablepsis* (309), denotes "recovering of sight" (*ana*, "again," *blepo*, "to see"), Luke 4:18. In the Sept, Isa. 61:1. In Luke 7:21, the infinitive mood of *blepo*, "to see," is used as a noun, "(He bestowed, KJV, 'gave') sight." In **Acts 9:9** it is used in the present participle with *me*, "not," "without sight" (lit., "not seeing").

9:10 And there was a certain disciple at Damascus, named Ananias; and to him said the Lord in a vision, Ananias. And he said, Behold, I *am here*, Lord.

Vision *see* **Sight** at *Acts 7:31*.

9:11 And the Lord *said* unto him, Arise, and go into the street which is called Straight, and enquire in the house of Judas for *one* called Saul, of Tarsus: for, behold, he prayeth,

Street *rhume* (4505), in earlier Greek meant "the force or rush or swing of a moving body" in later times, "a narrow road lane or street", it is translated "lanes" in Luke 14:21; "streets" in Matt. 6:2; "street" in **Acts 9:11; 12:10**. In the Sept., Isa. 15:3.

Straight *euthus* (2117), "direct, straight, right," is translated "straight," figuratively, of the paths of the Lord, Matt. 3:3; Mark 1:3; Luke 3:4; in v. 5 of the rectification of the crooked, with reference to moral transformation; in **Acts 9:11**, the name of a street in Damascus, still one of the principal thoroughfares.

Enquire *zeteo* (2212), "to seek," is rendered "inquire" in John 16:19; "inquire ... for" in **Acts 9:11**.

9:12 And hath seen in a vision a man named Ananias coming in, and putting *his* hand on him, that he might receive his sight.

Vision *see* **Sight** at *Acts 7:31*.

Putting *epitithemi* (2007), "to put on, upon," is so rendered in Matt. 19:13, KJV (RV, "lay"); so Mark 7:32; 8:25; Matt. 21:7; 27:29; John 9:15; 19:2 (1st part); **Acts 9:12** (RV, "laying ... on"); **15:10**. *See also* **Laid ... on** at *Acts 6:6*.

Sight *anablepo* (308), "to look up," also denotes "to receive or recover sight," e.g., Matt. 11:5; 20:34; Mark 10:51, 52; Luke 18:41-43; John 9:11, 15, 18 (twice); **Acts 9:12, 17, 18; 22:13**.

9:13-14 Then Ananias answered, Lord, I have heard by many of this man, how much evil he hath done to thy saints at Jerusalem:

And here he hath authority from the chief priests to bind all that call on thy name.

Hath *see* **Could** at *Acts 4:14*.

9:15 But the Lord said unto him, Go thy way: for he is a chosen vessel unto me, to bear my name before the Gentiles, and kings, and the children of Israel:

Go *see* **Journeyed** at *Acts 9:3*.

Chosen *ekloge* (1589), "a picking out, choosing" (Eng., "eclogue"), is translated "chosen" in **Acts 9:15**, lit., "he is a vessel of choice unto Me." In the six other places where this word is found it is translated "election."

Vessel *skeuos* (4632), is used (a) of "a vessel or implement" of various kinds, Mark 11:16; Luke 8:16; John 19:29; **Acts 10:11, 16; 11:5; 27:17** (a sail); Rom. 9:21; 2 Tim. 2:20; Heb. 9:21; Rev. 2:27; 18:12; (b) of "goods or household stuff," Matt. 12:29 and Mark 3:27, "goods"; Luke 17:31, RV, "goods" (KJV, "stuff"); (c) of "persons," (1) for the service of God, **Acts 9:15**, "a (chosen) vessel"; 2 Tim. 2:21, "a vessel (unto honor)"; (2) the "subjects" of divine wrath, Rom. 9:22; (3) the "subjects" of divine mercy, Rom. 9:23; (4) the human frame, 2 Cor. 4:7; perhaps 1 Thess. 4:4; (5) a husband and wife, 1 Pet. 3:7; of the wife, probably, 1 Thess. 4:4; while the exhortation to each one "to possess himself of his own vessel in sanctification and honor" is regarded by some as referring to the believer's body [cf. Rom. 6:13; 1 Cor. 9:27], the view that the "vessel" signifies the wife, and that the reference is to the sanctified maintenance of the married state, is supported by the facts that in 1 Pet. 3:7 the same word *time*, "honor," is used with regard to the wife, again in Heb. 13:4, *timios*, "honorable" (RV, "in honor") is used in regard to marriage; further, the preceding command in 1 Thess. 4 is against fornication, and the succeeding one (v. 6) is against adultery. In Ruth 4:10, Sept., *ktaomai*, "to possess," is used of a wife.

Bear *see* Carried at *Acts 3:2*.

Before *see Acts 2:25*.

9:16 For I will shew him how great things he must suffer for my name's sake.

Shew *hupodeiknumi* (5263), primarily, "to show secretly (*hupo*, 'under'), or by tracing out," hence, "to make known, warn," is translated "to show" in Luke 6:47; **Acts 9:16**; in **20:35**, KJV (RV, "I gave ... an example").

Great *hosos* (3745), "how much, how many," is used in the neuter plural to signify how great things, Mark 5:19, 20; Luke 8:39 (twice); **Acts 9:16**, KJV (RV, "how many things"); in Rev. 21:16 (in the best mss.), "as great as," RV (KJV, "as large as," said of length). *See also* Many at *Acts 2:39*.

Suffer *see* Passion at *Acts 1:3*.

9:17 And Ananias went his way, and entered into the house; and putting his hands on him said, Brother Saul, the Lord, *even* Jesus, that appeared unto thee in the way as thou camest, hath sent me, that thou mightest receive thy sight, and be filled with the Holy Ghost.

Way *aperchomai*, "to go away," is rendered "to go one's way," e.g., Matt. 13:25; 20:4; Mark 11:4; 12:12; Luke 19:32; John 11:46; **Acts 9:17**; Jas. 1:24.

Putting *see* Laid ... on at *Acts 6:6*.

Jesus *see Acts 7:59*.

Sight *see Acts 9:12*.

Filled *see Acts 2:4*.

9:18 And immediately there fell from his eyes as it had been scales: and he received sight forthwith, and arose, and was baptized.

Fell *apopipto* (634), "to fall from" (*apo*, "from"), is used in **Acts 9:18**, of the scales which "fell" from the eyes of Saul of Tarsus.

Scales *lepis* (3013), from *lepo*, "to peel," occurs in **Acts 9:18**.

Sight *see Acts 9:12*.

9:19 And when he had received meat, he was strengthened. Then was Saul certain days with the disciples which were at Damascus.

Received *lambano* (2983), denotes either "to take" or "to receive," literally, (a) without an object, in contrast to asking, e.g., Matt. 7:8; Mark 11:24, RV, "have received" (the original has no object); (b) in contrast to giving, e.g., Matt. 10:8; **Acts 20:35**; (c) with objects, whether things, e.g., Mark 10:30; Luke 18:30, in the best mss.; John 13:30; **Acts 9:19**, RV, "took" (KJV, "received"); 1 Cor. 9:25, RV, "receive" (KJV, "obtain"); or persons, e.g., John 6:21; 13:20; 16:14, RV, "take"; 2 John 10; in Mark 14:65, RV, "received (Him with blows of their hands)"; this has been styled a vulgarism.

Meat *see Acts 2:46*.

Strengthened *enischuo* (1765), is used in Luke 22:43 and **Acts 9:19**.

9:20 And straightway he preached Christ in the synagogues, that he is the Son of God.

Preached *see Acts 8:5*

9:21 But all that heard *him* were amazed, and said; Is not this he that destroyed them which called on this name in Jerusalem, and came hither for that intent, that he might bring them bound unto the chief priests?

Destroyed *portheo*, "to ruin by laying waste, to make havock of," is translated "destroyed" in **Acts 9:21**, of the attacks upon the church in Jerusalem by Saul of Tarsus; "wasted," in Gal. 1:13, with reference to the same; "destroyed" in Gal. 1:23, where "the faith" is put by metonymy (one thing being put for another associated with it), for those who held the faith. In each of these places the RV consistently translates by "made havock of."

Intent The phrase *eis touto*, lit., "unto this," i.e., "for this purpose," is rendered "for this (KJV, 'that') intent" in **Acts 9:21**, RV

9:22 But Saul increased the more in strength, and confounded the Jews which dwelt at Damascus, proving that this is very Christ.

Strength *endunamoo* (1743), "to make

strong," is rendered "increased ... in strength" in **Acts 9:22**; "to strengthen" in Phil. 4:13; 2 Tim. 2:1, RV, "be strengthened"; 4:17.

Confounded *see Acts 2:6*.

Proving *sumbibazo* (4822), "to join together," signifies "to prove" in **Acts 9:22**.

9:23 And after that many days were fulfilled, the Jews took counsel to kill him:

Many *hikanos* (2425), "sufficient," when used of number sometimes signifies "many," suggesting a sufficient number, (a) with nouns, Luke 8:32; 23:9; **Acts 9:23, 43; 20:8; 27:7**; (b) absolutely, some noun being understood, e.g., **Acts 12:12; 14:21; 19:19**; 1 Cor. 11:30.

Fulfilled *see* Full at *Acts 7:23*.

Counsel *sumbouleuo* (4823), in the active voice, "to advise, to counsel," John 18:14, "gave counsel"; in Rev. 3:18, "I counsel"; in the middle voice, "to take counsel, consult," Matt. 26:4, RV, "took counsel together," for KJV, "consulted"; **Acts 9:23**, "took counsel" (RV adds "together"); in some mss. John 11:53.

9:24 But their laying await was known of Saul. And they watched the gates day and night to kill him.

Laying await *epiboule* (1917), lit., "a plan against" (*epi*, "against," *boule*, "a counsel, plan"), is translated "plot" in the RV (KJV, "laying await" and "lying in wait") in **Acts 9:24; 20:3, 19; 23:30**.

Watched *paratereo* (3906), "to observe," especially with sinister intent, is rendered "to watch" in Mark 3:2; Luke 6:7; 14:1; 20:20; **Acts 9:24**.

Gates *see* Gate *at Acts 3:10*.

9:25 Then the disciples took him by night, and let *him* down by the wall in a basket.

Night *see Acts 5:19*.

Let ... down *kathiemi* (2524), "to send," or "let down" (*kata*, "down," *hiemi*, "to send"), is translated "to let down," with reference to (a) the paralytic in Luke 5:19; (b) Saul of Tarsus, **Acts 9:25**; (c) the great sheet in Peter's vision, **10:11** and **11:5**.

chalao (5465), "to slacken, loosen, let loose," denotes in the NT, "to let down, to lower"; it is used with reference to (a) the paralytic, in Mark 2:4; (b) Saul of Tarsus, **Acts 9:25**, "lowering"; 2 Cor. 11:33, "was I let down" (passive voice); (c) nets, Luke 5:4, 5 (in the latter, RV, "nets"; KJV, "net"); (d) the gear of a ship, **Acts 27:17**, RV, "they lowered (the gear)," KJV, "they strake (sail)"; (e) a ship's boat, v. **30**, RV, "lowered" (KJV, "let down").

Wall *teichos* (5038), "a wall," especially one around a town, is used (a) literally, **Acts 9:25**; 2 Cor. 11:33; Heb. 11:30; (b) figuratively, of the "wall" of the heavenly city, Rev. 21:12, 14, 15, 17, 18, 19.

Basket *spuris* (4711), or *sphuris*, signifies "something round, twisted or folded together" (connected with *speira*, "anything rolled into a circle"; Eng., "sphere"); hence a reed basket, plaited, a capacious kind of hamper, sometimes large enough to hold a man, Matt. 15:37; 16:10; Mark 8:8, 20 (RV, "basketfuls"); **Acts 9:25**.

9:26 And when Saul was come to Jerusalem, he assayed to join himself to the disciples: but they were all afraid of him, and believed not that he was a disciple.

Join *see Acts 5:13*.

9:27 But Barnabas took him, and brought *him* to the apostles, and declared unto them how he had seen the Lord in the way, and that he had spoken to him, and how he had preached boldly at Damascus in the name of Jesus.

Declared *see Acts 8:33* Declare.

Preached *parrhesiazomai* (3955), "to be bold in speech," is translated "to preach boldly" in **Acts 9:27** (2nd part); in v. **29**, RV (KJV, "he spake boldly").

Boldly *parrhesiazomai* (3955), "to speak boldly, or freely," primarily had reference to speech, but acquired the meaning of "being bold, or waxing bold," 1 Thess. 2:2; in **Acts 13:46**, RV, "spake out boldly" (the aorist participle here signifies "waxing bold"); **Acts 9:27, 29**, "preached boldly" (see also **18:26; 19:8**); in **26:26**, "speak freely."

Name *see* Names at *Acts 1:15*.

9:28 And he was with them coming in and going out at Jerusalem.

Coming in *eisporeuomai* (1531), "to go in, enter," is never rendered by the verb "to come in," in the RV. See, e.g., Luke 11:33, "enter"; **Acts 9:28**, going in; **28:30**, "went in." *See also* Entered at *Acts 3:2*.

9:29 And he spake boldly in the name of the Lord Jesus, and disputed against the Grecians: but they went about to slay him.

Boldly *see Acts 9:27*.

Disputed *see* Disputing at *Acts 6:9*.

Went *epicheireo* (2021), lit., "to put the hand to" (*epi*, "to," *cheir*, "the hand"), "to take in hand, undertake," occurs in Luke 1:1, "have taken in hand"; in **Acts 9:29**, "they went about"; in **19:13**, "took upon them."

Slay *see* Slain at *Acts 2:23*.

9:30 *Which* when the brethren knew, they brought him down to Caesarea, and sent him forth to Tarsus.

Knew *epiginosko* (1921), denotes (a) "to observe, fully perceive, notice attentively, discern, recognize"; it suggests generally a directive, a more special, recognition of the object "known"; it also may suggest advanced "knowledge" or special appreciation; thus, in Rom. 1:32, "knowing the ordinance of God" (*epiginosko*) means "knowing full well," whereas in verse 21 "knowing God" (*ginosko*) simply suggests that they could not avoid the perception. Sometimes *epiginosko* implies a special participation in the object "known," and gives greater weight to what is stated; thus in John 8:32, "ye shall know the truth," *ginosko* is used, whereas in 1 Tim. 4:3, "them that believe and know the truth," *epiginosko* lays stress on participation in the truth. Cf. the stronger statement in Col. 1:6 (*epiginosko*) with that in 2 Cor. 8:9 (*ginosko*), and the two verbs in 1 Cor. 13:12, "now I know in part (*ginosko*); but then shall I know (*piginosko*) even as also I have been known (*epiginosko*)," "a knowledge" which perfectly unites the subject with the object; (b) "to discover, ascertain, determine," e.g., Luke 7:37; 23:7; **Acts 9:30**; **19:34**; **22:29**; **28:1**; in **24:11** the best mss. have this verb; hence the RV, "take knowledge."

Brought *katago* (2609), "to bring down," **Acts 9:30**; **22:30**; **23:15**, **20**; Rom. 10:6; "to bring forth," **Acts 23:28**; of boats, "to bring to land," Luke 5:11.

Sent *see Acts 7:12*.

9:31 Then had the churches rest throughout all Judaea and Galilee and Samaria, and were edified; and walking in the fear of the Lord, and in the comfort of the Holy Ghost, were multiplied.

Churches *see* Church at *Acts 7:38*.

Rest *eirene* (1515), "occurs in each of the books of the NT, save 1 John and save in **Acts 7:26** ['(at) one again'] it is translated "peace" in the RV. It describes (a) harmonious relationships between men, Matt. 10:34; Rom. 14:19; (b) between nations, Luke 14:32; **Acts 12:20**; Rev. 6:4; (c) friendliness, **Acts 15:33**; 1 Cor. 16:11; Heb. 11:31; (d) freedom from molestation, Luke 11:21; 19:42; **Acts 9:31** (RV, 'peace,' KJV, 'rest'); **16:36**; (e) order, in the State, **Acts 24:2** (RV, 'peace,' KJV, 'quietness'); in the churches, 1 Cor. 14:33; (f) the harmonized relationships between God and man, accomplished through the gospel, **Acts 10:36**; Eph. 2:17; (g) the sense of rest and contentment consequent thereon, Matt. 10:13; Mark 5:34; Luke 1:79; 2:29; John 14:27; Rom. 1:7; 3:17; 8:6; in certain passages this idea is not distinguishable from the last, Rom. 5:1."

Edified *see* Builders at *Acts 4:11*.

Walking *poreuo* (4198), is used in the middle voice and rendered "to walk" in Luke 1:6, of the general activities of life; so in Luke 13:33, KJV, "walk" (RV, "go on My way"); **Acts 9:31**; **14:16**; 1 Pet. 4:3; 2 Pet. 2:10; Jude 16, 18.

Fear *see Acts 2:43*.

Comfort *see* Consolation at *Acts 4:36*.

Multiplied *see Acts 6:1*.

9:32 And it came to pass, as Peter passed throughout all *quarters*, he came down also to the saints which dwelt at Lydda.

Quarters In **Acts 9:32** the phrase *dia panton*, lit., "throughout all," is rendered "throughout all parts," RV (*meros*, "a part," being understood), KJV, "throughout all *quarters*."

9:33 And there he found a certain man named Aeneas, which had kept his bed eight years, and was sick of the palsy.

Kept *katakeimai* (2621), "to lie down," is used of the sick, Mark 1:30; 2:4; Luke 5:25; John 5:3, 6; **Acts 28:8**; in **Acts 9:33** it is rendered "had kept (his bed)," lit., "lying (on a bed)."

Bed *see* Beds at *Acts 5:15*.

Eight *okto* (3638), "eight" (Lat., *octo, octavus;* cf. Eng., "octagon," "octave," "octavo," "October," etc.), is used in Luke 2:21; 9:28; John 20:26; **Acts 9:33**; **25:6**; 1 Pet. 3:20; in composition with other numerals, *okto kai deka*, lit., "eight and ten, eighteen," Luke 13:4, 11, 16; *triakonta kai okto*, "thirty and eight," John 5:5.

Sick For "sick of the palsy," Luke 5:24; **Acts 9:33**.

Palsy *see* Palsies at *Acts 8:7*.

9:34 And Peter said unto him, Aeneas, Jesus Christ maketh thee whole: arise, and make thy bed. And he arose immediately.

Christ *see Acts 2:31*.

Whole *iaomai* (4390), "to heal," is used (a) of physical treatment 22 times; in Matt. 5:28, KJV, "made whole," RV, "healed"; so in **Acts 9:34**; (b) figuratively, of spiritual "healing," Matt. 13:15; John 12:40; **Acts 28:27**; Heb. 12:13; 1 Pet. 2:24; possibly, Jas. 5:16 includes both (a) and (b); some mss. have the word, with sense (b), in Luke 4:18. Apart from this last, Luke, the physician, uses the word fifteen times.

Make *stronnumi* (4766), or *stronnuo*, "to spread," is used of "furnishing a room," Mark 14:15; Luke 22:12; of "making a bed," **Acts 9:34**; in Matt. 21:8; Mark 11:8, "spread" (KJV, "strawed," twice).

Bed The verb *stronnuo* or *stronnumi*, "to spread," signifies, in **Acts 9:34**, "to make a bed"; elsewhere it has its usual meaning.

9:35-36 And all that dwelt at Lydda and Saron saw him, and turned to the Lord.

Now there was at Joppa a certain disciple named Tabitha, which by interpretation is called Dorcas: this woman was full of good works and almsdeeds which she did.

Disciple *mathetria* (3102), "a female disciple," is said of Tabitha, **Acts 9:36**.

Interpretation *diermeneuo* (1329), a strengthened form of *dia*, "through," used intensively, signifies "to interpret fully, to explain." In Luke 24:27, it is used of Christ in interpreting to the two on the way to Emmaus "in all the Scriptures the things concerning Himself," RV, "interpreted" (KJV, "expounded"); in **Acts 9:36**, it is rendered "is by interpretation," lit., "being interpreted" (of Tabitha, as meaning Dorcas); in 1 Cor. 12:30 and 14:5, 13, 27, it is used with reference to the temporary gift of tongues in the churches; this gift was inferior in character to that of prophesying unless he who spoke in a "tongue" interpreted his words, 14:5; he was, indeed, to pray that he might interpret, v. 13; only two, or at the most three, were to use the gift in a gathering, and that "in turn" (RV); one was to interpret; in the absence of an interpreter, the gift was not to be exercised, v. 27.

Full *see Acts 6:3*.

Works *see* Work at *Acts 5:38*.

Almsdeeds *see* Alms at *Acts 3:2*.

9:37 And it came to pass in those days, that she was sick, and died: whom when they had washed, they laid *her* in an upper chamber.

Sick *astheneo* (770), lit., "to be weak, feeble" (*a*, negative, *sthenos*, "strength"), is translated "to be sick," e.g., in Matt. 10:8, "(the) sick"; 25:36; v. 39 in the best texts; Mark 6:56; Luke 4:40; 7:10 (RV omits the word); 9:2; John 4:46; 5:3, RV (KJV, "impotent folk"); v. 7; 6:2, RV (KJV, "were diseased"); 11:1-3, 6; **Acts 9:37**; **19:12**; Phil. 2:26, 27; 2 Tim. 4:20; Jas. 5:14.

Washed *louo* (3068), signifies "to bathe, to wash the body," (a) active voice, **Acts 9:37**; **16:33**; (b) passive voice, John 13:10, RV, "bathed" (KJV, "washed"); Heb. 10:22, lit., "having been washed as to the body," metaphorical of the effect of the Word of God upon the activities of the believer; (c) middle voice, 2 Pet. 2:22. Some inferior mss. have it instead of *luo*, "to loose," in Rev. 1:5 (see RV).

Laid *see Acts 3:2*.

Chamber *see* Room at *Acts 1:13*.

9:38 And forasmuch as Lydda was nigh to Joppa, and the disciples had heard that Peter was there, they sent unto him two men, desiring *him* that he would not delay to come to them.

There In Luke 24:18 and **Acts 9:38**, "there" translates the phrase *en aute*, "in it."

Desiring *parakaleo* (3870), "to beseech, comfort, exhort," is rendered by the verb "to intreat" in Luke 8:31, RV, "intreated" (KJV, "besought"); 15:28; **Acts 9:38**, RV, "intreating" (KJV, "desiring"); **28:20**, RV (KJV, "called for"); 1 Cor. 4:13; 2 Cor. 9:5, RV (KJV, "exhort"); 10:1, RV (KJV, "beseech"); 1 Tim. 5:1, KJV (RV, "exhort").

Delay *okneo* (3635), akin to *oknos*, "a shrinking, to be loath or slow to do a thing, to hesitate, delay," is used in **Acts 9:38**. In the Sept. in Num. 22:16, "do not delay"; Judg. 18:9.

Come *dierchomai* (1330), "to come or go through" (*dia*, "through"), e.g., **Acts 9:38**.

9:39 Then Peter arose and went with them. When he was come, they brought him into the upper chamber: and all the widows stood by him weeping, and shewing the coats and garments which Dorcas made, while she was with them.

Went *see* Go at *Acts 8:29*.

Brought *anago* (321), "to lead or bring up to," Luke 2:22; **Acts 9:39**, etc.; "to bring forth," **Acts 12:4**; "to bring again," Heb. 13:20; "to bring up again," Rom. 10:7.

Chamber *see* Room at *Acts 1:13*.

Widows *see Acts 6:1*.

Stood *see Acts 1:10*.

Weeping *klaio* (2799), is used of "any loud expression of grief," especially in mourning for the dead, Matt. 2:18; Mark 5:38, 39; 16:10; Luke 7:13; 8:52 (twice); John 11:31, 33 (twice); 20:11 (twice), 13, 15; **Acts 9:39**; otherwise, e.g., in exhortations, Luke 23:28; Rom. 12:15; Jas. 4:9; 5:1; negatively, "weep not," Luke 7:13; 8:52; 23:28; Rev. 5:5 (cf. **Acts 21:13**); in **18:9**, RV, "shall weep" (KJV, "bewail").

Shewing *epideiknumi* (1925), signifies (a) "to exhibit, display," Matt. 16:1; 22:19; 24:1; Luke 17:14; in the middle voice, "to display," with a special interest in one's own action, **Acts 9:39**; (b) "to point out, prove, demonstrate," **Acts 18:28**; Heb. 6:17.

Coats *chiton* (5509), denotes "the inner vest or undergarment," and is to be distinguished, as such, from the *himation*. The distinction is made, for instance, in the Lord's command in Matt. 5:40: "If any man would go to law with thee, and take away thy coat (*chiton*), (*himation*) also." The order is reversed in Luke 6:29, and the difference lies in this, that in Matt. 5:40 the Lord is referring to a legal process, so the claimant is supposed to claim the inner garment, the less costly. The defendant is to be willing to let him have the more valuable one too. In the passage in Luke an act of violence is in view, and there is no mention of going to law. So the outer garment is the first one which would be seized. When the soldiers had crucified Jesus they took His garments (*himation*, in the plural), His outer garments, and the "coat," the *chiton*, the inner garment, which was without seam, woven from the top throughout, John 19:23. The outer garments were easily divisible among the four soldiers, but they could not divide the *chiton* without splitting it, so they cast lots for it. Dorcas was accustomed to make coats (*chiton*) and garments (*himation*), **Acts 9:39**, that is, the close fitting undergarments and the long, flowing outer robes.

Which This is the translation of (a) the article with nouns, adjectives, numerals, participles, etc., e.g., "that which," etc.; (b) the relative pronoun *hos*, "who," in one of its forms (a frequent use); (c) *hostis*, "whoever," differing from *hos* by referring to a subject in general, as one of a class, e.g., Rom. 2:15; Gal. 4:24 (twice); 5:19; Rev. 2:24; 20:4; (d) the interrogative pronoun *tis*, "who? which?," e.g., Matt. 6:27; John 8:46; (e) *hoios*, "of what kind," e.g., Phil. 1:30; (f) *poios*, the interrogative of (e), e.g., John 10:32; (g) *hosos*, "whatsoever," etc.; plural, how many, translated "which" in **Acts 9:39**.

Made *see Acts 2:36.*

9:40 But Peter put them all forth, and kneeled down, and prayed; and turning *him* to the body said, Tabitha, arise. And she opened her eyes: and when she saw Peter, she sat up.

Put *ekballo* (1544), "to cast out," is translated "to put forth or out" in Matt. 9:25; Mark 5:40 (Luke 8:54 in some mss.); John 10:4; **Acts 9:40**.

Opened *see Acts 5:19.*

Sat *anakathizo* (339), "to set up," is used intransitively, "to sit up," of two who were raised from the dead, Luke 7:15; **Acts 9:40**.

9:41 And he gave her *his* hand, and lifted her up, and when he had called the saints and widows, presented her alive.

Lifted *anistemi* (450), "to raise up" (*ana*, "up," *histemi*, "to cause to stand"), is translated "lifted (her) up," in **Acts 9:41**, KJV; RV, "raised (her) up."

Widows *see Acts 6:1.*

Presented *see* Shewed at *Acts 1:3.*

Alive *see Acts 1:3.*

9:42-43 And it came to pass, that he tarried many days in Joppa with one Simon a tanner.

Tarried *meno* (3306), "to abide," is translated by the verb "to abide," in the RV, for KJV, "to tarry," in Matt. 26:38; Mark 14:34; Luke 24:29; John 4:40; **Acts 9:43**; **18:20**; the RV retains the verb "to tarry" in John 21:22, 23; in **Acts 20:5**, KJV, "tarried" (RV, "were waiting"). Some mss. have it in **Acts 20:15** (KJV, "tarried").

Many *see Acts 9:23.*

Tanner *burseus* (1038), "a tanner" (from *bursa*, "a hide"), occurs in **Acts 9:43; 10:6, 32**.

Chapter 10

10:1 There was a certain man in Caesarea called Cornelius, a centurion of the band called the Italian *band*,

Called For *onoma*, "a name," translated "called," KJV, in Luke 24:13; **Acts 10:1**, *onomazo*, "to name," translated "called," KJV, 1 Cor. 5:11, and *eponomazo*, "to surname," translated "art called," Rom. 2:17. *See also* Names at *Acts 1:15.*

Centurion *hekatontarches* (1543), e.g., **Acts 10:1**, **22**. The Sept. has this word frequently, to denote "captains of hundreds."

10:2 A devout *man*, and one that feared God with all his house, which gave much alms to the people, and prayed to God alway.

Devout *eusebes* (2152), from *eu*, "well," *sebomai*, "to reverence," the root *seb-* signifying "sacred awe," describes "reverence" exhibited especially in actions, reverence or awe well directed. Among the Greeks it was used, e.g., of practical piety towards parents. In the NT it is used of a pious attitude towards God, **Acts 10:2**, **7**; (in some mss. in **22:12**); "godly," in 2 Pet. 2:9. In the Sept., Prov. 12:12; Isa. 24:16; 26:7; 32:8; Mic. 7:2.

Feared *phobeo* (5399), in earlier Greek, "to put to flight," in the NT is always in the passive voice, with the meanings either (a) "to fear, be afraid," its most frequent use, e.g., **Acts 23:10**, according to the best mss.; or (b) "to show reverential fear," (1) of men, Mark 6:20; Eph. 5:33, RV, "fear," for KJV, "reverence"; (2) of God, e.g., **Acts 10:2**, **22**; **13:16**, **26**; Col. 3:22 (RV, "the Lord"); 1 Pet. 2:17; Rev. 14:7; 15:4; 19:5; (a) and (b) are combined in Luke 12:4, 5, where Christ warns His followers not to be afraid of men, but to "fear" God.

Alms *see Acts 3:2*.

Prayed *see Acts 4:31*.

Alway *diapantos* (1275), is, lit., "through all," i.e., through all time, (*dia*, "through," *pas*, "all"). In the best texts the words are separated. The phrase, which is used of the time throughout which a thing is done, is sometimes rendered "continually," sometimes "always"; "always" or "alway" in Mark 5:5; **Acts 10:2**; **24:16**; Rom. 11:10; "continually" in Luke 24:53; Heb. 9:6; 13:15, the idea being that of a continuous practice carried on without being abandoned.

10:3 He saw in a vision evidently about the ninth hour of the day an angel of God coming in to him, and saying unto him, Cornelius.

Vision *see* Sight at *Acts 7:31*.

Evidently *phaneros* (5320), manifestly, is rendered "openly" in Mark 1:45; "publicly" in John 7:10, RV (opposite to "in secret"); in **Acts 10:3**, RV, "openly," for KJV, evidently.

Ninth *see Acts 3:1*.

Hour *hora* (5610), whence Lat., *hora*, Eng., "hour," primarily denoted any time or period, expecially a season. In the NT it is used to denote (a) "a part of the day," especially a twelfth part of day or night, an "hour," e.g., Matt. 8:13; **Acts 10:3**, **9**; **23:23**; Rev. 9:15; in 1 Cor. 15:30, "every hour" stands for "all the time"; in some passages it expresses duration, e.g., Matt. 20:12; 26:40; Luke 22:59; inexactly, in such phrases as "for a season," John 5:35; 2 Cor. 7:8; "for an hour," Gal. 2:5; "for a short season," 1 Thess. 2:17, RV (KJV, "for a short time," lit., "for the time of an hour"); (b) "a period more or less extended," e.g., 1 John 2:18, "it is the last hour," RV; (c) "a definite point of time," e.g., Matt. 26:45, "the hour is at hand"; Luke 1:10; 10:21; 14:17, lit., "at the hour of supper"; **Acts 16:18**; **22:13**; Rev. 3:3; 11:13; 14:7; a point of time when an appointed action is to begin, Rev. 14:15; in Rom. 13:11, "it is high time," lit., "it is already an hour," indicating that a point of time has come later than would have been the case had responsibility been realized. In 1 Cor. 4:11, it indicates a point of time previous to which certain circumstances have existed.

Angel *angelos* (32), "a messenger" (from *angello*, "to deliver a message"), sent whether by God or by man or by Satan, "is also used of a guardian or representative in Rev. 1:20, cf. Matt. 18:10; **Acts 12:15** (where it is better understood as 'ghost'), but most frequently of an order of created beings, superior to man, Heb. 2:7; Ps. 8:5, belonging to Heaven, Matt. 24:36; Mark 12:25, and to God, Luke 12:8, and engaged in His service, Ps. 103:20. "Angels" are spirits, Heb. 1:14, i.e., they have not material bodies as men have; they are either human in form, or can assume the human form when necessary, cf. Luke 24:4, with v. 23, **Acts 10:3** with v. **30**."

10:4 And when he looked on him, he was afraid, and said, What is it, Lord? And he said unto him, Thy prayers and thine alms are come up for a memorial before God.

Looked *see Acts 1:10*.

Afraid *emphobos* (1719), lit., "in fear" (*en*, "in," *phobos*, "fear"), means "affrighted," Luke 24:5, RV (KJV "afraid"); 24:37; **Acts 10:4**, RV (KJV, "afraid"); Rev. 11:13. The RV omits it in **Acts 22:9**.

Lord *see Acts 2:36*.

Alms *see Acts 3:2*.

Memorial *mnemosunon* (3422), denotes "a memorial," that which keeps alive the memory of someone or something (from *mnemon*, "mindful"), Matt. 26:13; Mark 14:9; **Acts 10:4**.

10:5 And now send men to Joppa, and call for *one* Simon, whose surname is Peter:

Send *pempo* (3992), "to send," is used (a) of persons: Christ, by the Father, Luke 20:13; John 4:34; 5:23, 24, 30, 37; 6:38, 39, (40), 44; 7:16, 18, 28, 33; 8:16, 18, 26, 29; 9:4; 12:44, 45, 49; 13:20 (2nd part); 14:24; 15:21; 16:5; Rom. 8:3; the Holy Spirit, John 14:26; 15:26; 16:7; Elijah, Luke 4:26; John the Baptist, John 1:33; disciples and apostles, e.g., Matt. 11:2; John 20:21; servants, e.g., Luke 20:11, 12; officials, Matt. 14:10; messengers, e.g., **Acts 10:5**, **32**, **33**; **15:22**, **25**; 2 Cor. 9:3, Eph. 6:22; Phil. 2:19, 23, 25; 1 Thess. 3:2, 5; Titus 3:12;

a prisoner, **Acts 25:25, 27**; potentates, by God, 1 Pet. 2:14; an angel, Rev. 22:16, demons, Mark 5:12; (b) of things, **Acts 11:29**; Phil. 4:16; 2 Thess. 2:11; Rev. 1:11; 11:10; 14:15, 18, RV, "send forth" (KJV, "thrust in").

Call for *metapempo* (3343), "to send after or for, fetch" (*meta*, "after"), is used only in the Acts; in the middle voice, translated "to send for" in **10:22, 29** (2nd part: passive voice in the 1st part); **20:1**, RV only (some texts have *proskaleo*); **24:24, 26**; **25:3**; in **10:5** and **11:13**, RV, fetch.

Surname *see* Surnamed at *Acts 1:23*.

10:6 He lodgeth with one Simon a tanner, whose house is by the sea side: he shall tell thee what thou oughtest to do.

Lodgeth *xenizo* (3579), "to receive as a guest" (*xenos*, "a guest, stranger"), "to entertain, lodge," is used in the active voice in **Acts 10:23**; **28:7**, RV, "entertained" (KJV, "lodged"); Heb. 13:2, "have entertained"; in the passive voice, **Acts 10:6** (lit., "he is entertained"), **18, 32**; **21:16**. Its other meaning, "to think strange," is found in 1 Pet. 4:4, 12.

Tanner *see Acts 9:43*.

10:7 And when the angel which spake unto Cornelius was departed, he called two of his household servants, and a devout soldier of them that waited on him continually;

Household servants *oiketes* (3610), "a house-servant," is translated "household-servants" in **Acts 10:7**; elsewhere, "servant" or "servants," Luke 16:13; Rom. 14:4; 1 Pet. 2:18.

Devout *see Acts 10:2*.

Waited on *proskartereo* (4342), to continue steadfastly, is rendered "to wait on," in Mark 3:9 and **Acts 10:7**.

Continually *see* Continued at *Acts 1:14*.

10:8 And when he had declared all *these* things unto them, he sent them to Joppa.

Declared *exegeomai* (1834), lit., "to lead out," signifies "to make known, rehearse declare," Luke 24:35 (KJV, "told"; RV, "rehearsed"); **Acts 10:8**; **15:12, 14**; **21:19**. In John 1:18, in the sentence "He hath declared Him," the other meaning of the verb is in view, to unfold in teaching, "to declare" by making known.

Sent *see* Send at *Acts 3:20*.

10:9 On the morrow, as they went on their journey, and drew nigh unto the city, Peter went up upon the housetop to pray about the sixth hour:

Went *hodoiporeo*, "to be on a journey," **Acts 10:9**, RV, "as they were on their journey" (KJV, "as they went, etc."); (m) *embaino*, "to enter," Matt. 13:2 and Luke 8:22, RV, "entered" (KJV, "went into"); in v. 37 (KJV, "went up into"); (n) *apoluo*, "to set free," Luke 23:22 and John 19:12, RV, "release" (KJV, "let ... go"); **Acts 15:33**, RV, "dismissed" (KJV, ditto); **Acts 28:18**, RV, "set at liberty" (KJV, ditto); (o) *epibaino*, "to go upon," **Acts 21:4**, RV, "set foot" (KJV, "go"); some mss. have *anabaino*; (p) *apangello*, "to announce," **Acts 12:17**, RV, "tell" (KJV, "go shew"); (q) *aperchomai*, "to go away," Matt. 5:30, RV, "go" (KJV, "be cast"); some mss. have *ballo*, "to cast"; (r) *peripateo*, "to walk," Mark 12:38, RV, "walk" (KJV "go"); (s) for "gone by," **Acts 14:16**, RV.

Journey *hodoiporeo* (3596), "to travel, journey," is found in **Acts 10:9**.

Housetop *doma* (1430), akin to *demo*, "to build," denotes a housetop. The housetop was flat, and guarded by a low parapet wall (see Deut. 22:8). It was much frequented and used for various purposes, e.g., for proclamations, Matt. 10:27; Luke 12:3; for prayer, **Acts 10:9**. The house was often built round a court, across the top of which cords were fixed from the parapet walls for supporting a covering from the heat. The housetop could be reached by stairs outside the building; the paralytic in Luke 5:19 could be let down into the court or area by rolling back the covering. External flight from the housetop in time or danger is enjoined in Matt. 24:17; Mark 13:15; Luke 17:31.

Hour *see Acts 10:3*.

10:10 And he became very hungry, and would have eaten: but while they made ready, he fell into a trance,

Hungry *prospeinos* (4361), signifies "hungry" (*pros*, "intensive," *peina*, "hunger"), **Acts 10:10**, KJV, "very hungry," RV, "hungry."

Eaten *geuo* (1089), primarily, "to cause to taste, to give one a taste of," is used in the middle voice and denotes (a) "to taste," its usual meaning; (b) "to take food, to eat," **Acts 10:10**; **20:11**; **23:14**; the meaning to taste must not be pressed in these passages, the verb having acquired the more general meaning. As to whether **Acts 20:11** refers to the Lord's Supper or to an ordinary meal, the addition of the words "and eaten" is perhaps a sufficient indication that the latter is referred to here, whereas v. **7**, where the single phrase "to break bread" is used, refers to the Lord's Supper. A parallel instance is found in **Acts 2:43, 46**. In the former verse the phrase "the breaking of bread," unaccompanied by any word about taking food, clearly stands for the Lord's Supper; whereas in v. **46** the phrase "breaking bread at home" is immediately explained by "they did take their food," indicating their ordinary meals.

Made ready *paraskeuazo* (3903), "to prepare, make ready" (*para*, "beside"), is used of making ready a meal, **Acts 10:10**: in the middle voice, of "preparing" oneself for war, 1 Cor. 14:8, RV; in the passive voice, of "preparing" an offering for the needy, 2 Cor. 9:2, "hath been prepared," RV (KJV, "was ready"); v. 3, "ye may be prepared," RV (KJV, "ye may be ready").

Fell Some mss. have this verb in John 13:25; **Acts 10:10**; **13:11**.

Trance *ekstasis* (1611), denotes "a trance" in **Acts 10:10**; **11:5**; **22:17**, a condition in which ordinary consciousness and the perception of natural circumstances were withheld, and the soul was susceptible only to the vision imparted by God. *See* also **Amazement** *at Acts 3:10.*

10:11 And saw heaven opened, and a certain vessel descending unto him, as it had been a great sheet knit at the four corners, and let down to the earth:

Opened *see Acts 5:19.*

Vessel *see Acts 9:15.*

Sheet *othone* (3607), primarily denoted "fine linen," later, "a sheet," **Acts 10:11**; **11:5**. Cf. *othonion*, "linen."

Knit In **Acts 10:11** some mss. have the verb *deo*, "to bind," translated "knit," of the four corners of the sheet in Peter's vision.

Corners *arche* (746), "a beginning" (its usual meaning), "first in time, order, or place," is used to denote the extremities or "corners" of a sheet, **Acts 10:11**; **11:5**.

Let down *see* **Let ... down** at *Acts 9:25.*

10:12 Wherein were all manner of fourfooted beasts of the earth, and wild beasts, and creeping things, and fowls of the air.

Fourfooted beasts *tetrapous* (5074), from *tetra*, "four" (used in compound words), and *pous*, "a foot," is used of "beasts," **Acts 10:12**; **11:6**; Rom. 1:23.

Earth *see Acts 1:8.*

Creeping *herpeton* (2062), signifies "a creeping thing" (*herpo*, "to creep"; Eng., "serpent," Jas. 3:7 (RV, "creeping things," for KJV, "serpents," which form only one of this genus); it is set in contrast to quadrupeds and birds, **Acts 10:12**; **11:6**; Rom. 1:23.

Fowls *peteinon* (4071), signifies "that which is able to fly, winged." It is connected with *ptenon* signifying "feathered, winged," which is used in 1 Cor. 15:39. Cf. *petomai* and *petaomai*, "to fly." In the Gospels the RV always translates it "birds," e.g., Matt. 6:26; but "fowls" in **Acts 10:12**; **11:6**. The KJV unsuitably has "fowls," in the Gospels, except Matt. 8:20; 13:32; Luke 9:58.

Air *ouranos* (3772), probably akin to *ornumi*, "to lift, to heave," is used in the NT of "the aerial heavens," e.g., Matt. 6:26; 8:20; **Acts 10:12**; **11:6** (RV, "heaven," in each place, KJV, "air"); Jas. 5:18.

10:13 And there came a voice to him, Rise, Peter; kill, and eat.

Voice *see Acts 7:31.*

Kill *thuo* (2380), primarily denotes "to offer firstfruits to a god"; then (a) "to sacrifice by slaying a victim," **Acts 14:13**, **18**, to do sacrifice; 1 Cor. 10:20, to sacrifice; 1 Cor. 5:7, "hath been sacrificed," of the death of Christ as our Passover; (b) "to slay, kill," Matt. 22:4; Mark 14:12; Luke 15:23, 27, 30; 22:7; John 10:10; **Acts 10:13**; **11:7**.

10:14 But Peter said, Not so, Lord; for I have never eaten any thing that is common or unclean.

Common *see Acts 2:44.*

Unclean *akathartos* (169), denotes "unclean, impure" (*a*, negative, and *kathairo*, "to purify"), (a) ceremonially, e g., **Acts 10:14**, **28**; (b) morally, always, in the Gospels, of unclean spirits; it is translated "foul" in the KJV of Mark 9:25 and Rev. 18:2, but always "unclean" in the RV. Since the word primarily had a ceremonial significance, the moral significance is less prominent as applied to a spirit, than when *poneros*, "wicked," is so applied. Cf. *akatharsia*, "uncleanness." *See also* ***Acts 5:16.***

10:15 And the voice *spake* unto him again the second time, What God hath cleansed, *that* call not thou common.

Voice *see Acts 7:31.*

Cleansed *katharizo* (2511), signifies (1) "to make clean, to cleanse" (a) from physical stains and dirt, as in the case of utensils, Matt. 23:25 (figuratively in verse 26); from disease, as of leprosy, Matt. 8:2; (b) in a moral sense, from the defilement of sin, **Acts 15:9**; 2 Cor. 7:1; Heb. 9:14; Jas. 4:8, "cleanse" from the guilt of sin, Eph. 5:26; 1 John 1:7; (2) "to pronounce clean in a Levitical sense," Mark 7:19, RV; **Acts 10:15**; **11:9**; "to consecrate by cleansings," Heb. 9:22, 23; 10:2.

Common *koinoo* (2840), denotes (a) "to make common"; hence, in a ceremonial sense, "to render unholy, unclean, to defile," Matt. 15:11, 18, 20; Mark 7:15, 18, 20, 23; **Acts 21:28**

(RV, "defiled"; KJV, "polluted"); Heb. 9:13 (RV, "them that have been defiled," KJV, "the unclean"); (b) "to count unclean," **Acts 10:15**; **11:9**. In Rev. 21:27, some mss. have this verb, "defileth"; the most authentic have the adjective, *koinos*, "unclean."

10:16 This was done thrice: and the vessel was received up again into heaven.

Thrice *tris* (5151), occurs in Matt. 26:34, 75 and parallel passages; in **Acts 10:16** and **11:10**, preceded by *epi*, "up to"; 2 Cor. 11:25 (twice); 12:8.

Vessel *see Acts 9:15*.

Received *see* Taken at *Acts 1:2*.

10:17 Now while Peter doubted in himself what this vision which he had seen should mean, behold, the men which were sent from Cornelius had made enquiry for Simon's house, and stood before the gate,

While *see Acts 1:10*.

Doubted *see* Doubt at *Acts 2:12*.

Vision *see* Sight at Acts *7:31*.

Mean *see* Meaneth at *Acts 2:12*.

Sent *see* Send at *Acts 3:20*.

Enquiry *dierotao* (1331), "to find by inquiry, to inquire through to the end" (*dia*, intensive, *erotao*, "to ask") is used in **Acts 10:17**.

Stood *ephistemi* (2186), used intransitively, denotes "to stand upon or by, be present," Luke 2:9 and **Acts 12:7**, "stood by," RV (KJV, "came upon"); Luke 4:39, "stood over"; 24:4 and **Acts 23:11**, "stood by"; **Acts 10:17**, "stood"; **22:13**, "standing by (me)," RV; so v. **20**, KJV and RV.

Gate *pulon* (4440), primarily signifies "a porch or vestibule," e.g., Matt. 26:71; Luke 16:20; **Acts 10:17**; **12:13**, **14**; then, the "gateway" or "gate tower" of a walled town, **Acts 14:13**; Rev. 21:12, 13, 15, 21, 25; 22:14.

10:18 And called, and asked whether Simon, which was surnamed Peter, were lodged there.

Asked *see Acts 4:7*.

Surnamed *see Acts 1:23*.

Lodged *see* Lodgeth at *Acts 10:6*.

There *enthade* (759), "here, hither," is rendered "there" in **Acts 10:18**.

10:19 While Peter thought on the vision, the Spirit said unto him, Behold, three men seek thee.

Thought *dienthumeomai* (1223), "to consider deeply," is used of Peter in **Acts 10:19**, in the best texts.

Vision *see* Sight at Acts *7:31*.

10:20 Arise therefore, and get thee down, and go with them, doubting nothing: for I have sent them.

Get *katabaino* (2597), "to descend," is translated "get … down," in **Acts 10:20**.

Doubting *diakrino* (1252), lit., "to separate throughout, to make a distinction," **Acts 15:9**, RV, is translated "to make to differ," in 1 Cor. 4:7. In Jude 22, where the middle voice is used, the KJV has "making a difference"; the RV, adopting the alternative reading, the accusative case, has "who are in doubt," a meaning found in Matt. 21:21; Mark 11:23; **Acts 10:20**; Rom. 14:23; Jas. 1:6; 2:4.

Sent *see* Send at *Acts 3:20*.

10:21 Then Peter went down to the men which were sent unto him from Cornelius; and said, Behold, I am he whom ye seek: what *is* the cause wherefore ye are come?

Wherefore Some phrases introduced by the preposition *dia*, "on account of," *dia touto*, "on account of this," e.g., Matt. 12:31; Rom. 5:12; Eph. 1:15; 3 John 10; *dia hen* (the accusative feminine of *hos*, "who"), "on account of which" (*aitia*, "a cause," being understood), e.g., **Acts 10:21** (with *aitia*, expressed, Titus 1:13; Heb. 2:11); *dia ti* "on account of what?" (sometimes as one word, *diati*), e.g., Luke 19:23; Rom. 9:32; 2 Cor. 11:11; Rev. 17:7.

Come *pareimi* (3918), signifies (a) "to be by, at hand or present," of persons, e.g., Luke 13:1; **Acts 10:33**; **24:19**; 1 Cor. 5:3; 2 Cor. 10:2, 11; Gal. 4:18, 20; of things, John 7:6, of a particular season in the Lord's life on earth, "is (not yet) come," or "is not yet at hand"; Heb. 12:11, of chastening "(for the) present" (the neuter of the present participle, used as a noun); in 13:5 "such things as ye have" is, lit., "the things that are present"; 2 Pet. 1:12, of the truth "(which) is with (you)" (not as KJV, "the present truth," as if of special doctrines applicable to a particular time); in v. 9 "he that lacketh" is lit., "to whom are not present"; (b) "to have arrived or come," Matt. 26:50, "thou art come," RV; John 11:28; **Acts 10:21**; Col. 1:6.

10:22 And they said, Cornelius the centurion, a just man, and one that feareth God, and of good report among all the nation of the Jews, was warned from God by an holy angel to send for thee into his house, and to hear words of thee.

Centurion *see Acts 10:1.*

Just *see Acts 3:14.*

Feareth *see* Feared at *Acts 10:2.*

Report *see Acts 6:3.*

Nation *ethnos* (1484), originally "a multitude," denotes (a) "a nation" or "people," e.g., Matt. 24:7; **Acts 10:35**; the Jewish people, e.g., Luke 7:5; 23:2; John 11:48, 50-52; **Acts 10:22**; **24:2**, **10**, **17**; in Matt. 21:43, the reference is to Israel in its restored condition, (b) in the plural "the nations" as distinct from Israel. *See also* People at *Acts 8:9.*

Warned *chrematizo* (5537), is translated "to warn" in Matt. 2:12, 22; **Acts 10:22**; Heb. 8:5, RV (KJV, "admonished"); 11:7; 12:25, RV (KJV, "spake").

Send *see Acts 10:5.*

Hear *see* Hearing at *Acts 9:7.*

10:23 Then called he them in, and lodged *them*. And on the morrow Peter went away with them, and certain brethren from Joppa accompanied him

Called *eiskaleo* (1528), lit., "to call in," hence, "to invite," is found in **Acts** 10:23.

Lodged *see* Lodgeth at *Acts 10:6.*

10:24 And the morrow after they entered into Caesarea. And Cornelius waited for them, and had called together his kinsmen and near friends.

Morrow *epaurion* (1887); the RV always translates it "on (the) morrow"; in the following the KJV has "(the) next day," Matt. 27:62; John 1:29, 35 ("the next day after"); 12:12; **Acts 14:20**; **21:8**; **25:6**; "(the) day following," John 1:43; 6:22; "the morrow after," **Acts 10:24**.

Waited *prosdokao* (4328), "to await," is rendered "to wait for" in Luke 1:21; 8:40; **Acts 10:24**; in **27:33**, RV, "ye wait" (KJV, "have tarried").

Called *see Acts 5:21.*

Kinsmen *sungenes* (4773), primarily denoting "congenital, natural, innate" (*sun*, "with," *genos*, "a family, race, offspring"), then, "akin to," is used as a noun, denoting (a) of "family relationship, kin, a kinsman, kinsfolk(s)," Luke 1:58, RV, "kinsfolk" (KJV, "cousins"); 14:12; 21:16; John 18:26; **Acts 10:24**; (b) of "tribal or racial kinship, fellow nationals," Rom. 9:3; 16:7, 11, 21.

Near *anankaios* (316), "necessary" (from *ananke*, "necessity"), is so rendered in **Acts 13:46**; 1 Cor. 12:22; 2 Cor. 9:5; Phil. 2:25; Titus 3:14; Heb. 8:3, RV (KJV, "of necessity"); for **Acts 10:24**, "near friends."

10:25 And as Peter was coming in, Cornelius met him, and fell down at his feet, and worshipped *him*.

Coming in *eiserchomai* (1525), "to come into" (*eis*, "in," *erchomai*, "to come"), is frequently rendered "entered" in the RV for KJV, "went into," e.g., Matt. 9:25; 21:12; or "go in," e.g., Matt. 7:13; Luke 8:51; "go," Luke 18:25; "was coming in," **Acts 10:25**.

Met *sunantao* (4876), "to meet with," lit., "to meet together with," is used in Luke 9:37 (in v. 18, in some mss.); 22:10; **Acts 10:25**; Heb. 7:1, 10; metaphorically in **Acts 20:22** ("shall befall").

10:26 But Peter took him up, saying, Stand up; I myself also am a man.

Took In **Acts 10:26**, KJV, *egeiro*, "to raise" (RV), is rendered "took ... up." *See also* Lifted at *Acts 3:7.*

Stand *see* Stood at *Acts 1:15.*

Myself *autos* (846), "self" (a) with *ego*, "I," "I myself," Luke 24:39; **Acts 10:26**; Rom. 7:25; 9:3; 2 Cor. 10:1; 12:13; (b) without the personal pronoun, **Acts 24:16** (as the subject of a verb); in the nominative case, **Acts 25:22**; 1 Cor. 9:27; Phil. 2:24; in the genitive case, Rom. 16:2, RV, "of mine own self."

10:27 And as he talked with him, he went in, and found many that were come together.

Talked *sunomileo* (4926), "to converse, talk with," occurs in **Acts 10:27**.

10:28 And he said unto them, Ye know how that it is an unlawful thing for a man that is a Jew to keep company, or come unto one of another nation; but God hath shewed me that I should not call any man common or unclean.

Know *epistamai* (1987), "to know, know of, understand" (probably an old middle voice form of *ephistemi*, "to set over"), is used in Mark 14:68, "understand," which follows *oida* "I (neither) know"; most frequently in the Acts, **10:28**; **15:7**; **18:25**; **19:15**, **25**; **20:18**; **22:19**; **24:10**; **26:26**; elsewhere, 1 Tim. 6:4; Heb. 11:8; Jas. 4:14; Jude 10.

Unlawful *athemitos* (111), a late form for *athemistos* (*themis*, "custom, right"; in classical Greek "divine law"), "contrary to what is right," is rendered "an unlawful thing" (neuter) in **Acts 10:28**; in 1 Pet. 4:3, "abominable."

Jew *see* Jews at *Acts 2:10.*

Keep company *kollao*, "to join," is rendered "keep company," in **Acts 10:28**, KJV; RV, "join himself." *See also* Join at *Acts 5:13.*

Nation *allophulos* (246), "foreign, of another race" (*allos*, "another," *phulon*, "a tribe"), is used in **Acts 10:28**, "one of another nation." *See also* Strange at *Acts 7:6*.

Shewed *deiknumi*, or *deiknuo* (1166), denotes (a) "to show, exhibit," e.g., Matt. 4:8; 8:4; John 5:20; 20:20; 1 Tim. 6:15; (b) "to show by making known," Matt. 16:21; Luke 24:40; John 14:8, 9; **Acts 10:28**; 1 Cor. 12:31; Rev. 1:1; 4:1; 22:6; (c) "to show by way of proving," Jas. 2:18; 3:13.

Common *see Acts 2:44*.

Unclean *see Acts 5:16. See also Acts 10:14.*

10:29 Therefore came I *unto you* without gainsaying, as soon as I was sent for: I ask therefore for what intent ye have sent for me?

Gainsaying *anantirrhetos* (369), is translated "without gainsaying" in **Acts 10:29**; it might be rendered "unquestioningly."

Sent *see* Send at *Acts 10:5*.

Ask *see* Asked at *Acts 4:7*.

Intent *logos* (3056), "a word, account, etc.," sometimes denotes "a reason, cause; intent," e.g., Matt. 5:32, "cause"; it is rendered "intent" in **Acts 10:29**.

10:30 And Cornelius said, Four days ago I was fasting until this hour; and at the ninth hour I prayed in my house, and, behold, a man stood before me in bright clothing,

Four *see* Four hundred at *Acts 5:36*.

Fasting *nesteuo* (3522), "to fast, to abstain from eating," is used of voluntary "fasting," Matt. 4:2; 6:16, 17, 18; 9:14, 15; Mark 2:18, 19, 20; Luke 5:33, 34, 35; 18:12; **Acts 13:2, 3**. Some of these passages show that teachers to whom scholars or disciples were attached gave them special instructions as to "fasting." Christ taught the need of purity and simplicity of motive. The answers of Christ to the questions of the disciples of John and of the Pharisees reveal His whole purpose and method. No doubt He and His followers observed such a fast as that on the Day of Atonement, but He imposed no frequent "fasts" in addition. What He taught was suitable to the change of character and purpose which He designed for His disciples. His claim to be the Bridegroom, Matt. 9:15, and the reference there to the absence of "fasting," virtually involved a claim to be the Messiah (cf. Zech. 8:19). Some mss. have the verb in **Acts 10:30**.

Ninth *see Acts 3:1*.

Bright *lampros* (2986), "shining, brilliant, bright," is used of the clothing of an angel, **Acts 10:30** and Rev. 15:6; symbolically, of the clothing of the saints in glory, Rev. 19:8, RV, in the best texts (KJV, "white"); of Christ as the Morning Star, 22:16; of the water of life, 22:1, KJV, "clear."

Clothing *esthes* (2066), "clothing," **Acts 10:30**. *See also* Apparel at *Acts 1:10*.

10:31 And said, Cornelius, thy prayer is heard, and thine alms are had in remembrance in the sight of God.

Heard *eisakouo* (1522), "to listen to," has two meanings, (a) "to hear and to obey," 1 Cor. 14:21, "they will not hear"; (b) "to hear so as to answer," of God's answer to prayer, Matt. 6:7; Luke 1:13; **Acts 10:31**; Heb. 5:7.

Alms *see Acts 3:2*.

Remembrance *mimnesko* (3403), from the older form *mnaomai*, in the active voice signifies "to remind"; in the middle voice, "to remind oneself of," hence, "to remember, to be mindful of"; the later form is found only in the present tense, in Heb. 2:6, "are mindful of," and 13:3, "remember"; the perfect tense in 1 Cor. 11:2 and in 2 Tim. 1:4 (RV, "remembering," KJV, "being mindful of"), is used with a present meaning. RV variations from the KJV are, in Luke 1:54, RV, "that He might remember" (KJV, "in remembrance of"); 2 Pet. 3:2, "remember" (KJV, "be mindful of"); Rev. 16:19 (passive voice), "was remembered" (KJV, "came in remembrance"). The passive voice is used also in **Acts 10:31**, KJV and RV, "are had in remembrance."

In the sight of *see* Before at *Acts 2:25*.

10:32 Send therefore to Joppa, and call hither Simon, whose surname is Peter; he is lodged in the house of *one* Simon a tanner by the sea side: who, when he cometh, shall speak unto thee.

Send *see Acts 10:5*.

Call *see* Called at *Acts 7:14*.

Surname *see* Surnamed at *Acts 1:23*.

Lodged *see* Lodgeth at *Acts 10:6*.

Tanner *see Acts 9:43*.

10:33 Immediately therefore I sent to thee; and thou hast well done that thou art come. Now therefore are we all here present before God, to hear all things that are commanded thee of God.

Immediately *exautes* (1824), "at once" (from, *ek*, "out of," and *autes*, the genitive case of *autos*, "self or very," agreeing with "hour" understood, i.e., "from that very hour"), is translated "forthwith" in the RV in Mark 6:25 (KJV, "by and by"); **Acts 10:33** (KJV, "immediately"); **11:11** (ditto); **21:32** (ditto); **23:30** (KJV, "straightway"); Phil. 2:23 (KJV, "presently"). The word is frequent in the period of the *koine* Greek (see Preface).

Sent *see* Send at *Acts 10:5.*

Present *see* Come at *Acts 10:21.*

Before *see Acts 2:25. See also Acts 7:46.*

Commanded *prostasso* (4367), denotes "to arrange or set in order towards" (*pros*, "towards," *tasso*, "to arrange"); hence "to prescribe, give command," Matt. 1:24; 8:4; Mark 1:44; Luke 5:14; **Acts 10:33, 48.**

10:34 Then Peter opened *his* mouth, and said, Of a truth I perceive that God is no respecter of persons:

Opened *see Acts 5:19.*

Perceive *see* Perceived at *Acts 4:13.*

Persons *prosopolemptes* (4381), denotes "a respecter of persons" (*prosopon*, "a face" or "person," *lambano*, "to lay hold of"), **Acts 10:34.**

10:35 But in every nation he that feareth him, and worketh righteousness, is accepted with him.

Nation *see Acts 10:22. See also* people at *Acts 8:9.*

Worketh *ergazomai* (2038), is used (I) intransitively, e.g., Matt. 21:28; John 5:17; 9:4 (2nd part); Rom. 4:4, 5; 1 Cor. 4:12; 9:6; 1 Thess. 2:9; 4:11; 2 Thess. 3:8, 10-12; (II) transitively, (a) "to work something, produce, perform," e.g., Matt. 26:10, "she hath wrought"; John 6:28, 30; 9:4 (1st part); **Acts 10:35; 13:41**; Rom. 2:10; 13:10; 1 Cor. 16:10; 2 Cor. 7:10a; Gal. 6:10, RV, "let us work"; Eph. 4:28; Heb. 11:33; 2 John 8; (b) "to earn by working, work for," John 6:27, RV, "work" (KJV, "labor").

Accepted *dektos* (1184), denotes "a person or thing who has been regarded favorably," Luke 4:19, 24; **Acts 10:35**; 2 Cor. 6:2; Phil. 4:18.

10:36 The word which *God* sent unto the children of Israel, preaching peace by Jesus Christ: (he is Lord of all:)

Word *see* Words at *Acts 2:40.*

Sent *see* Send *at Acts 3:20.*

Preach *see* Things at *Acts 8:12.*

Peace *see* Rest at *Acts 9:31.*

Jesus *see Acts 7:59* Jesus.

Lord *see Acts 2:36* Lord.

10:37 That word, *I say*, ye know, which was published throughout all Judaea, and began from Galilee, after the baptism which John preached;

Published *ginomai* (1096), "to become, come to be," is translated "was published" in **Acts 10:37**, lit., "came to be."

Preached *see Acts 8:5.*

10:38 How God anointed Jesus of Nazareth with the Holy Ghost and with power: who went about doing good, and healing all that were oppressed of the devil; for God was with him.

Anointed *see Acts 4:27.*

Good *euergeteo* (2109), "to bestow a benefit, to do good" (*eu*, "well," and a verbal form akin to *ergon*), is used in **Acts 10:38.**

Devil *diabolos* (1228), "an accuser, a slanderer" (from *diaballo*, "to accuse, to malign"), is one of the names of Satan. From it the English word "Devil" is derived, and should be applied only to Satan, as a proper name. *Daimon*, "a demon," is frequently, but wrongly, translated "devil"; it should always be translated "demon," as in the RV margin. There is one "Devil," there are many demons. Being the malignant enemy of God and man, he accuses man to God, Job 1:6-11; 2:1-5; Rev. 12:9, 10, and God to man, Gen. 3. He afflicts men with physical sufferings, **Acts 10:38.** Being himself sinful, 1 John 3:8, he instigated man to sin, Gen. 3, and tempts man to do evil, Eph. 4:27; 6:11, encouraging him thereto by deception, Eph. 2:2. Death having been brought into the world by sin, the "Devil" had the power of death, but Christ through His own death, has triumphed over him, and will bring him to nought, Heb. 2:14; his power over death is intimated in his struggle with Michael over the body of Moses, Jude 9. Judas, who gave himself over to the "Devil," was so identified with him, that the Lord described him as such, John 6:70 (see 13:2). As the "Devil" raised himself in pride against God and fell under condemnation, so believers are warned against similar sin, 1 Tim. 3:6; for them he lays snares, v. 7, seeking to devour them as a roaring lion, 1 Pet. 5:8; those who fall into his snare may be recovered therefrom unto the will of God, 2 Tim. 2:26, "having been taken captive by him (i.e., by the 'Devil')"; "by the Lord's servant" is an alternative, which some regard as confirmed by the use of *zogreo* ("to catch alive") in Luke 5:10; but the general use is that of taking captive in the usual way. If believers resist he will flee from them, Jas. 4:7. His fury and malignity will be especially exercised at the end of the present age, Rev. 12:12. His doom is the lake of fire,

Matt. 25:41; Rev. 20:10. The noun is applied to slanderers, false accusers, 1 Tim. 3:11; 2 Tim. 3:3; Titus 2:3.

Oppressed *katadunasteuo* (2616), "to exercise power over" (*kata*, "down," *dunastes*, "a potentate": *dunamai* "to have power"), "to oppress," is used, in the passive voice, in **Acts 10:38**; in the active, in Jas. 2:6.

10:39 And we are witnesses of all things which he did both in the land of the Jews, and in Jerusalem; whom they slew and hanged on a tree:

Witnesses *see Acts 1:8.*

Land *chora* (5561), properly denotes "the space lying between two limits or places"; accordingly it has a variety of meanings: "country," Matt. 2:12; 8:28; Mark 1:5, RV (KJV, "land"); 5:1, 10; Luke 2:8; 8:26; 15:13-14, RV (KJV, land), 15; 19:12; 21:21; **Acts 10:39**, RV (KJV, "land"); **12:20**; **26:20**, RV (KJV, "coasts"); **27:27**; in Mark 6:55 (in the best mss.) and **Acts 18:23**, RV, region.

Slew *see* Slain at *Acts 2:23.*

Hanged *see Acts 5:30.*

Tree *see Acts 5:30.*

10:40 Him God raised up the third day, and shewed him openly;

Raised *see* Lifted at *Acts 3:7.*

Third *see Acts 2:15.*

Shewed … openly In **Acts 10:40**, *emphanes*, "manifest," with *didomi*, "to give," and *ginomai*, "to become," gave … to be made manifest" (KJV "showed … openly"). *See also* Deliver at *Acts 7:25.*

10:41 Not to all the people, but unto witnesses chosen before of God, *even* to us, who did eat and drink with him after he rose from the dead.

Witnesses *see Acts 1:8.*

Chosen *procheirotoneo* (4401), signifies "to choose before," **Acts 10:41**, where it is used of a choice made before by God.

Eat *sunesthio* (4906), "to eat with," is found in Luke 15:2; **Acts 10:41**; **11:3**; 1 Cor. 5:11; Gal. 2:12.

Drink *sumpino* (4844), "to drink together," is found in **Acts 10:41**.

Rose *see* Raised at *Acts 2:24.*

10:42 And he commanded us to preach unto the people, and to testify that it is he which was ordained of God *to be* the Judge of quick and dead.

Testify *see Acts 2:40.*

Ordained *horizo* (3724), is twice used of Christ as divinely "ordained" to be the Judge of men, **Acts 10:42**; **17:31**. *See also* Determinate at *Acts 2:23.*

Judge *krites* (2923), "a judge," is used (a) of God, Heb. 12:23, where the order in the original is "to a Judge who is God of all"; this is really the significance; it suggests that He who is the Judge of His people is at the same time their God; that is the order in 10:30; the word is also used of God in Jas. 4:12, RV; (b) of Christ, **Acts 10:42**; 2 Tim. 4:8; Jas. 5:9; (c) of a ruler in Israel in the times of the Judges, **Acts 13:20**; (d) of a Roman procurator, **Acts 24:10**; (e) of those whose conduct provides a standard of "judging," Matt. 12:27; Luke 11:19; (f) in the forensic sense, of one who tries and decides a case, Matt. 5:25 (twice); Luke 12:14; 12:58 (twice); 18:2; 18:6 (lit., "the judge of unrighteousness," expressing subjectively his character); **Acts 18:15**; (g) of one who passes, or arrogates to himself, judgment on anything, Jas. 2:4 (see the RV); 4:11.

"'God does not show favouritism but accepts anyone from every nation who fears him and does what is right.' In these words Peter was 'sweeping away the racial prejudices of centuries.'"

F. F. BRUCE

Quick *zao* is translated "quick" (i.e., "living") in **Acts 10:42**; 2 Tim. 4:1; 1 Pet. 4:5; in Heb. 4:12, KJV (RV, "living").

10:43 To him give all the prophets witness, that through his name whosoever believeth in him shall receive remission of sins.

Witness *see* Report at *Acts 6:3.*

Remission *see Acts 2:38.*

10:44 While Peter yet spake these words, the Holy Ghost fell on all them which heard the word.

Fell *see* Fallen at *Acts 8:16.*

Holy Ghost *see Acts 1:16.*

10:45 And they of the circumcision which believed were astonished, as many as came with Peter, because that on the Gentiles also was poured out the gift of the Holy Ghost.

Circumcision *see Acts 7:8.*

Came with *see* Companied at *Acts 1:21*.

Also *kai*: The *ascensive* use. This is somewhat similar to the epexegetic significance. It represents, however, an advance in thought upon what precedes and has the meaning "even." The context alone can determine the occurrences of this use. The following are some instances ... In **Acts 10:45**, the *kai*, rendered "also," in the phrase "on the Gentiles also," seems necessary to be regarded in the same way, in view of the amazement manifested by those of the circumcision, and thus the rendering will be "even on the Gentiles was poured out the gift"; cf. **11:1**.

Poured *ekchuno*, or *ekchunno* (1632), is used of the voluntary giving up of His life by Christ through the "shedding" of His blood in crucifixion as an atoning sacrifice, Matt. 26:28; Mark 14:24; Luke 22:20, KJV, "is shed," RV, "is poured out"; these passages do not refer to the effect of the piercing of His side (which took place after His death); of the murder of servants of God, Matt. 23:35; Luke 11:50; **Acts 22:20**; of the love of God in the hearts of believers through the Holy Spirit, Rom. 5:5. For the "pouring out" of the Holy Spirit, **Acts 10:45**.

Gift *see Acts 8:20*.

10:46 For they heard them speak with tongues, and magnify God. Then answered Peter,

Magnify *see* Magnified at *Acts 5:13*.

10:47 Can any man forbid water, that these should not be baptized, which have received the Holy Ghost as well as we?

Forbid *koluo* (2967), "to hinder, restrain, withhold, forbid" (akin to *kolos*, "docked, lopped, clipped"), is most usually translated "to forbid," often an inferior rendering to that of hindering or restraining, e.g., 1 Thess. 2:16; Luke 23:2; 2 Pet. 2:16, where the RV has "stayed"; in **Acts 10:47** "forbid." In Luke 6:29, the RV has "withhold not (thy coat also)."

Holy Ghost *see Acts 1:16*.

Well *hos*, "as," with *kai*, "also (and)," is rendered "as well as" in **Acts 10:47** (*kathos* in some mss.) and 1 Cor. 9:5.

10:48 And he commanded them to be baptized in the name of the Lord. Then prayed they him to tarry certain days.

Commanded *see Acts 10:33*.

Tarry *epimeno* (1961), to abide, continue, is translated "to tarry" in **Acts 10:48**; **21:4**, **10**; **28:12**, **14**; 1 Cor. 16:7, 8; Gal. 1:18, RV (KJV, "abode").

Chapter 11

11:1 And the apostles and brethren that were in Judaea heard that the Gentiles had also received the word of God.

Also *see Acts 10:45*.

Received *see* Receive at Acts *3:21*.

11:2 And when Peter was come up to Jerusalem, they that were of the circumcision contended with him,

Circumcision *see Acts 7:8*.

Contended *diakrino* (1252), lit., "to separate throughout or wholly" (*dia*, "asunder," *krino*, "to judge," from a root *kri*, meaning "separation"), then, to distinguish, decide, signifies, in the middle voice, "to separate oneself from, or to contend with," as did the circumcisionists with Peter, **Acts 11:2**; as did Michael with Satan, Jude 9. See RV marg. of v. 22, where the thought may be that of differing in opinion.

11:3 Saying, Thou wentest in to men uncircumcised, and didst eat with them.

Uncircumcised *akrobustia* (203), "uncircumcision," is used (a) of the physical state, in contrast to the act of "circumcision," **Acts 11:3** (lit., "having uncircumcision"); Rom. 2:25-26; 4:10-11 ("though they be in uncircumcision," RV), 12; 1 Cor. 7:18-19; Gal. 5:6; 6:15; Col. 3:11; (b) by metonymy, for Gentiles, e.g., Rom. 2:26-27; 3:30; 4:9; Gal. 2:7; Eph. 2:11; (c) in a metaphorical or transferred sense, of the moral condition in which the corrupt desires of the flesh still operate, Col. 2:13.

Eat *see Acts 10:41*.

11:4 But Peter rehearsed *the matter* from the beginning, and expounded *it* by order unto them, saying,

Rehearsed In **Acts 11:4**, the KJV translates the middle voice of *archo*, "to begin," "rehearsed ... from the beginning," RV, "began, (and)."

Beginning *see* Began at *Acts 1:1*.

Expounded *ektithemi* (1620), "to set out expose" (*ek*, "out," *tithemi*, "to place"), is used (a) literally, **Acts 7:21**; (b) metaphorically, in the middle voice, to set forth, "expound," of circumstances, **Acts 11:4**; of the way of God, **18:26**; of the kingdom of God, **28:23**.

Order *kathexes* (2517), is translated "in order" in Luke 1:3; **Acts 11:4**, RV (KJV, "by order); **Acts 18:23**.

11:5 I was in the city of Joppa praying: and in a trance I saw a vision, A certain vessel descend, as it had been a great sheet,

let down from heaven by four corners; and it came even to me:

Trance *see Acts 10:10. See also* Amazement at *Acts 3:10.*

Vision *see* Sight at *Acts 7:31.*

Vessel *see Acts 9:15.*

Sheet *see Acts 10:11.*

Let down *see* Let ... down at *Acts 9:25.*

Corners *see Acts 10:11.*

11:6 Upon the which when I had fastened mine eyes, I considered, and saw fourfooted beasts of the earth, and wild beasts, and creeping things, and fowls of the air.

Fastened *see* Stedfastly at *Acts 1:10.*

Considered *see* Behold at *Acts 7:31.*

Fourfooted beasts *see Acts 10:12.*

Earth *see Acts 1:8.*

Creeping *see Acts 10:12.*

Fowls *see Acts 10:12.*

Air *see Acts 10:12.*

11:7 And I heard a voice saying unto me, Arise, Peter; slay and eat.

Voice *see Acts 7:31.*

Slay For *thuo,* Acts **11:7**, KJV, "slay" (RV, "kill"). *See also* Kill at *Acts 10:13.*

11:8 But I said, Not so, Lord: for nothing common or unclean hath at any time entered into my mouth.

Nothing In Acts **11:8** *pan,* "everything," with *oudepote,* "not even ever," is rendered "nothing ... ever," RV, KJV, "nothing ... at any time."

Common *see Acts 2:44.*

Unclean *see Acts 5:16.*

11:9 But the voice answered me again from heaven, What God hath cleansed, *that* call not thou common.

Voice *see Acts 7:31.*

Again Other words are rendered "again" in the KJV, which the RV corrects, namely, *deuteros* and *anothen. Deuteros* signifies "a second time," John 9:24; Acts **11:9**. *Anothen* signifies "from above, or anew." See the RV of John 3:3, 7, and the KJV and RV of v. 31. Nicodemus was not puzzled about birth from heaven; what perplexed him was that a person must be born a second time. This the context makes dear. This is really the meaning in Gal. 4:9, where it is associated with *palin,* "over again." The idea is "anew," for, though the bondage would be the same in essence and effect, it would be new in not being in bondage to idols but to the Law. See also Matt. 27:51; Mark 15:38; John 19:23, "from the top." *Anothen* may mean "from the first," in Luke 1:3 and **Acts 26:5**. For the meaning "from above," see Jas. 1:17; 3:15, 17. *See also* Second at *Acts 7:13.*

Cleansed *see Acts 10:15.*

Call *see Acts 10:15.*

Common *see Acts 10:15.*

11:10 And this was done three times: and all were drawn up again into heaven.

Three times *see* Thrice at *Acts 10:16.*

Drawn *anaspao* (385), "to draw up," is used of "drawing" up an animal out of a pit, Luke 14:5 (RV, "draw up"; KJV, "pull out"), and of the "drawing" up of the sheet into heaven, in the vision in **Acts 11:10**.

11:11 And, behold, immediately there were three men already come unto the house where I was, sent from Caesarea unto me.

Immediately *see Acts 10:33.*

Come *see* Came at *Acts 4:1.*

11:12 And the Spirit bade me go with them, nothing doubting. Moreover these six brethren accompanied me, and we entered into the man's house:

Bade *eipon* (3004), used as the aorist tense of *lego,* "to speak, to say," sometimes has the meaning of "commanding, or bidding," and is translated "bid," or "bade," e.g., in Matt. 16:12; 23:3; Luke 10:40; 9:54, KJV, "command," RV, "bid"; **Acts 11:12**; "bidding," **Acts 22:24**, RV.

Doubting *diakrino* (1252); in **Acts 11:12**, KJV, "nothing doubting," RV, "making no distinction"; in Jude 22, RV, "who are in doubt" (KJV, "making a difference," RV, marg., "while they dispute"); in Jas. 1:6, KJV, "wavereth," RV, "doubteth." This verb suggests, not so much weakness of faith, as lack of it.

Moreover *de* (1161), a particle signifying "and" or "but," is translated "moreover" in Matt. 18:15, KJV (RV, "and"); **Acts 11:12** (RV, "and"); Rom. 5:20, KJV (RV, "but"); 8:30 ("and"); 1 Cor. 15:1 (RV, "now"); 2 Cor. 1:23 (RV, "but"); 2 Pet. 1:15 (RV, "yea").

Six *hex* (1803), whence Eng. prefix, "hex"-, is used separately from other numerals in Matt. 17:1; Mark 9:2; Luke 4:25; 13:14; John 2:6; 12:1; **Acts 11:12**; **18:11**; Jas. 5:17; Rev. 4:8. It sometimes suggests incompleteness, in comparison with the perfect number seven.

Accompanied *see* Companied at *Acts 1:21.*

11:13 And he shewed us how he had seen an angel in his house, which stood and said unto him, Send men to Joppa, and call for Simon, whose surname is Peter;

Send *see Acts 10:5.*

Call *see Acts 10:5.*

Surname *see* Surnamed at *Acts 1:23.*

11:14 Who shall tell thee words, whereby thou and all thy house shall be saved.

Tell *see* Told at *Acts 9:6.*

Words *see Acts 2:14.*

House *see Acts 2:36.*

11:15 And as I began to speak, the Holy Ghost fell on them, as on us at the beginning.

Fell *see* Fallen at *Acts 8:16.*

11:16 Then remembered I the word of the Lord, how that he said, John indeed baptized with water; but ye shall be baptized with the Holy Ghost.

Word *see* Words at *Acts 2:14.*

Baptized *see Acts 1:5.*

11:17 Forasmuch then as God gave them the like gift as *he did* unto us, who believed on the Lord Jesus Christ; what was I, that I could withstand God?

Like *isos* (2470), "equal" (the same in size, quality, etc.), is translated "like," of the gift of the Spirit, **Acts 11:17.**

Gift *see Acts 8:20.*

Withstand *koluo* (2967), "to hinder," is rendered "withstand" in **Acts 11:17.**

11:18 When they heard these things, they held their peace, and glorified God, saying, Then hath God also to the Gentiles granted repentance unto life.

Peace *hesuchazo* (2270), signifies "to be still"; it is used of holding one's "peace," being silent, Luke 14:4; **Acts 11:18; 21:14,** "we ceased."

Granted *see* Grant at *Acts 4:29.*

Repentance *see Acts 5:31.*

11:19 Now they which were scattered abroad upon the persecution that arose about Stephen travelled as far as Phenice, and Cyprus, and Antioch, preaching the word to none but unto the Jews only.

Now *see Acts 1:18.*

Scattered *see Acts 8:1.*

Persecution *thlipsis* (2347), primarily means "a pressing, pressure," anything which burdens the spirit. In two passages in Paul's Epistles it is used of future retribution, in the way of "affliction," Rom. 2:9; 2 Thess. 1:6. In Matt. 24:9, the KJV renders it as a verb, "to be afflicted," (RV, "unto tribulation"). It is coupled with *stenochoria,* "anguish," in Rom. 2:9; 8:35; with *ananke,* "distress," 1 Thess. 3:7; with *diogmos,* "persecution," Matt. 13:21; Mark 4:17; 2 Thess. 1:4. It is used of the calamities of war, Matt. 24:21, 29; Mark 13:19, 24; of want, 2 Cor. 8:13, lit., "distress for you"; Phil. 4:14 (cf. 1:16); Jas. 1:27; of the distress of woman in childbirth, John 16:21; of persecution, **Acts 11:19; 14:22; 20:23;** 1 Thess. 3:3, 7; Heb. 10:33; Rev. 2:10; 7:14; of the "afflictions" of Christ, from which (His vicarious sufferings apart) his followers must not shrink, whether sufferings of body or mind, Col. 1:24; of sufferings in general, 1 Cor. 7:28; 1 Thess. 1:6, etc.

Arose *see Acts 6:1.*

Travelled *dierchomai* (1330), "to go or pass through," is translated "travelled" in **Acts 11:19.**

Far In the following, *heos,* used as a preposition, is translated "as far as" in the RV, for different words in the KJV; **Acts 17:14,** in the best mss., instead of *hos,* which the KJV renders "as it were"; **17:15,** "unto"; **23:23,** "to." Both versions have "as far as" in **11:19, 22;** in Luke 24:50, the RV has "until they were over against," for KJV, "as far as to."

Preaching *see* Preached at *Acts 8:25.*

11:20 And some of them were men of Cyprus and Cyrene, which, when they were come to Antioch, spake unto the Grecians, preaching the Lord Jesus.

Preaching *see* Preach at *Acts 5:42.*

11:21 And the hand of the Lord was with them: and a great number believed, and turned unto the Lord.

Hand *see* Hands at *Acts 5:12.*

Great *see Acts 8:8.*

Turned *epistrepho* (1994), is used (a) transitively, "to make to turn towards" (*epi*), Luke 1:16, 17; Jas. 5:19, 20 (to convert); (b) intransitively, "to turn oneself round," e.g., in the passive voice, Mark 5:30; in the active voice, Matt. 13:15, RV, "turn again" (KJV, "be converted"); **Acts 11:21; 14:15; 15:19;** 1 Thess. 1:9, "ye turned," the aorist tense indicating an immediate and decisive change, consequent upon a deliberate choice; conversion is a voluntary act in response to the presentation of truth.

11:22 Then tidings of these things came unto the ears of the church which was in Jerusalem: and they sent forth Barnabas, that he should go as far as Antioch.

Tidings In **Acts 11:22**, KJV, *logos*, "a word, a report" (RV), is rendered "tidings."

Ears *see Acts 7:51.*

Sent *see Acts 7:12.*

Far *see Acts 11:19.*

11:23 Who, when he came, and had seen the grace of God, was glad, and exhorted them all, that with purpose of heart they would cleave unto the Lord.

Glad *chairo* (5463), is the usual word for "rejoicing, being glad"; it is rendered by the verb "to be glad" in Mark 14:11; Luke 15:32; 22:5; 23:8; John 8:56; 11:15; 20:20; **Acts 11:23; 13:48**; in the following the RV has "to rejoice" for KJV, "to be glad," Rom. 16:19; 1 Cor. 16:17; 2 Cor. 13:9; 1 Pet. 4:13; Rev. 19:7. *See also* **Rejoicing** at *Acts 5:41.*

Purpose *prothesis* (4286), "a setting forth" (used of the "showbread"), "a purpose," is used (a) of the "purposes of God," Rom. 8:28; 9:11; Eph. 1:11; 3:11; 2 Tim. 1:9; (b) of "human purposes," as to things material, **Acts 27:13**; spiritual, **Acts 11:23**; 2 Tim. 3:10.

Heart *see Acts 2:37.*

Cleave *prosmeno* (4357), "to abide still longer, continue with" (*pros*, "with") is used (a) of place, Matt. 15:32; Mark 8:2; **Acts 18:18**; 1 Tim. 1:3; (b) metaphorically, "of cleaving unto a person," **Acts 11:23**, indicating persistent loyalty; of continuing in a thing, **Acts 13:43**; 1 Tim. 5:5. In the Sept., Judg. 3:25.

11:24 For he was a good man, and full of the Holy Ghost and of faith: and much people was added unto the Lord.

Good *agathos* (18), describes that which, being "good" in its character or constitution, is beneficial in its effect; it is used (a) of things physical, e.g., a tree, Matt. 7:17; ground, Luke 8:8; (b) in a moral sense, frequently of persons and things. God is essentially, absolutely and consummately "good," Matt. 19:17; Mark 10:18; Luke 18:19. To certain persons the word is applied in Matt. 20:15; 25:21, 23; Luke 19:17; 23:50; John 7:12; **Acts 11:24**; Titus 2:5; in a general application, Matt. 5:45; 12:35; Luke 6:45; Rom. 5:7; 1 Pet. 2:18.

Full *see Acts 6:3.*

Much *see Acts 5:37.*

11:25 Then departed Barnabas to Tarsus, for to seek Saul:

Seek *anazeteo* (327), "to seek carefully," is used of searching for human beings, difficulty in the effort being implied Luke 2:44, 45, **Acts 11:25**; numerous illustrations of this particular meaning in the papyri are given by Moulton and Milligan. In the Sept., Job 3:4; 10:6.

11:26 And when he had found him, he brought him unto Antioch. And it came to pass, that a whole year they assembled themselves with the church, and taught much people. And the disciples were called Christians first in Antioch.

Whole *holos* (3650), "the whole, all," is most frequently used with the article followed by a noun, e.g., Matt. 4:23. It is used with the article alone, in John 7:23, "every whit"; **Acts 11:26; 21:31; 28:30**; Titus 1:11; Luke 5:5, in the best texts.

Year *eniautos* (1763), originally "a cycle of time," is used (a) of a particular time marked by an event, e.g., Luke 4:19; John 11:49, 51; 18:13; Gal. 4:10; Rev. 9:15; (b) to mark a space of time, **Acts 11:26; 18:11**; Jas. 4:13; 5:17; (c) of that which takes place every year, Heb. 9:7; with *kata*, Heb. 9:25; 10:1, 3.

Assembled *sunago* (4863), "to assemble" (*sun*, "together," *ago*, "to bring"), is used of the "gathering together" of people or things; in Luke 12:17-18, "bestow," with reference to the act of "gathering" one's goods; so in Luke 15:13, suggesting that the Prodigal, having "gathered" all his goods together, sold them off; in John 6:12, of "gathering" up fragments; in John 18:2, "resorted," with reference to the "assembling" of Christ with His disciples in the garden of Gethsemane, there in the passive voice (unsuitable, however, in an English translation). In **Acts 11:26**, the RV has "were gathered together (with the church)," for KJV, "assembled themselves" (possibly "they were hospitably entertained by"). The verb is not found in the most authentic mss. in Rev. 13:10.

Taught *chrematizo* (5537), primarily, "to transact business," then, "to give advice to enquirers" (especially of official pronouncements of magistrates), or "a response to those consulting an oracle," came to signify the giving of a divine "admonition" or instruction or warning, in a general way; "admonished" in Heb. 8:5, KJV (RV, "warned"). Elsewhere it is translated by the verb "to warn." The word is derived from *chrema*, "an affair, business." Names were given to men from the nature of their business (see the same word in **Acts 11:26**; Rom. 7:3); hence, the idea of dealing with a person and receiving instruction.

In the case of oracular responses, the word is derived from *chresmos*, "an oracle."

Much *see Acts 5:37.*

Called *chrematizo* (5337), occasionally means "to be called or named," **Acts 11:26** (of the name "Christians") and Rom. 7:3, the only places where it has this meaning. Its primary significance, "to have business dealings with," led to this. They "were (publicly) called" Christians, because this was their chief business.

Christians *christianos* (5546), "Christian," a word formed after the Roman style, signifying an adherent of Jesus, was first applied to such by the Gentiles and is found in **Acts 11:26**; **26:28**; 1 Pet. 4:16. Though the word rendered "were called" in **Acts 11:26** might be used of a name adopted by oneself or given by others, the "Christians" do not seem to have adopted it for themselves in the times of the apostles. In 1 Pet. 4:16, the apostle is speaking from the point of view of the persecutor, cf. "as a thief," "as a murderer." Nor is it likely that the appellation was given by Jews. As applied by Gentiles there was no doubt an implication of scorn, as in Agrippa's statement in **Acts 26:28**. Tacitus, writing near the end of the first century, says, "The vulgar call them Christians. The author or origin of this denomination, Christus, had, in the reign of Tiberius, been executed by the procurator, Pontius Pilate" (Annals xv. 44). From the second century onward the term was accepted by believers as a title of honor.

First *protos* (4413), "firstly," is used in **Acts 11:26**, "first."

11:27-28 And in these days came prophets from Jerusalem unto Antioch.

And there stood up one of them named Agabus, and signified by the Spirit that there should be great dearth throughout all the world: which came to pass in the days of Claudius Caesar.

Stood *see Acts 1:15.*

Signified *semaino* (4591), "to give a sign, indicate," "to signify," is so translated in John 12:33; 18:32; 21:19; **Acts 11:28**; **25:27**; Rev. 1:1, where perhaps the suggestion is that of expressing by signs.

Should *mello* (3195), "to be about to," e.g., Mark 10:32, RV, "were to"; Luke 19:11, RV, "was to"; "should" in 22:23; 24:21; John 6:71; 7:39, RV, "were to"; 11:51; 12:4, 33; 18:32; **Acts 11:28**; **23:27**, RV, "was about (to be slain)"; 1 Thess. 3:4, RV, "are to"; Rev. 6:11. Also "it needs, it should," e.g., Matt. 18:33; **Acts 27:21**.

Dearth *see Acts 7:11.*

World *oikoumene* (3625), "the inhabited earth", is used (a) of the whole inhabited world, Matt. 24:14; Luke 4:5; 21:26; Rom. 10:18; Heb. 1:6; Rev. 3:10; 16:14; by metonymy, of its inhabitants, **Acts 17:31**; Rev. 12:9; (b) of the Roman Empire, the world as viewed by the writer or speaker, Luke 2:1; **Acts 11:28**; **24:5**; by metonymy, of its inhabitants, **Acts 17:6**; **19:27**; (c) the inhabited world in a coming age, Heb. 2:5.

Days In Mark 2:26, KJV, "in the days of," there is no word for "days" in the original; RV (from best mss.), "when" in **Acts 11:28**, "in the days of."

11:29 Then the disciples, every man according to his ability, determined to send relief unto the brethren which dwelt in Judaea:

Ability *euporeo* (2141), lit., "to journey well" (*eu*, "well," *poreo*, "to journey"), hence, "to prosper," is translated "according to (his) ability," in **Acts 11:29**.

Determined *see* Determinate at *Acts 2:23.*

Send *see Acts 10:5.*

Relief *diakonia* (1248), "ministry," is translated "relief" in **Acts 11:29** [RV, marg., "for (*eis*) ministry"]. *See also* Ministry at *Acts 1:17.*

11:30 Which also they did, and sent it to the elders by the hands of Barnabas and Saul.

Sent *see Acts 3:20.*

Chapter 12

12:1 Now about that time Herod the king stretched forth *his* hands to vex certain of the church.

Stretched *epiballo* (1911), "to put to or unto," is so translated in Matt. 9:16; Luke 5:36; 9:62; in **Acts 12:1**, RV, "put forth (his hands)," KJV, "stretched forth."

Vex *kakoo* (2559), is translated "afflict, in **Acts 12:1**, RV (KJV, "vex").

12:2-3 And he killed James the brother of John with the sword.

And because he saw it pleased the Jews, he proceeded further to take Peter also. (Then were the days of unleavened bread.)

Pleased *see* Reason at *Acts 6:2.*

Proceeded *prostithemi* (4369), "to put to" (*pros*, "to," *tithemi*, "to put"), "to add, or to place beside" (the primary meaning), in Luke 17:5 is translated "increase," in the request "increase our faith"; in Luke 20:11-12, "he sent yet" (KJV, "again he sent"), lit., "he added and sent," as in 19:11, "He added and spake." In **Acts 12:3**, RV, "proceeded," KJV, "proceeded further" (of repeating or continuing the action mentioned by the following verb); in **Acts 13:36**, "was laid unto"; in Heb. 12:19, "more ... be spoken," (lit., "that no word should be added"). In Gal. 3:19, "What then is the law?" It was "added" because of transgressions, there is no contradiction of what is said in v. 15, where the word is *epidiatasso*, for there the latter word conveys the idea of supplementing an agreement already made; here in v. 19 the meaning is not that something had been 'added' to the promise with a view to complete it, which the apostle denies, but that something had been given "in addition" to the promise, as in Rom. 5:20, "The law came in beside."

Take *see* Took at *Acts 1:16*.

Bread *azumos* (106), denotes "unleavened bread," i.e., without any process of fermentation; hence, metaphorically, "of a holy, spiritual condition," 1 Cor. 5:7, and of "sincerity and truth" (v. 8). With the article it signifies the feast of unleavened bread, Matt. 26:17; Mark 14:1, 12; Luke 22:1, 7; **Acts 12:3**; **20:6**.

12:4 And when he had apprehended him, he put *him* in prison, and delivered *him* to four quaternions of soldiers to keep him; intending after Easter to bring him forth to the people.

Apprehended *see* Took at *Acts 3:7*.

Put *see Acts 1:7*.

Quaternions *tetradion* (5069), "a group of four" (*tetra-*, "four"), occurs in **Acts 12:4**. A "quaternion" was a set of four men occupied in the work of a guard, two soldiers being chained to the prisoner and two keeping watch; alternatively one of the four watched while the other three slept. The night was divided into four watches of three hours each; there would be one "quaternion" for each watch by day and by night. Cf. the "guard" in Matt. 27:65 and 28:11.

Keep *phulasso* (5442), "to guard, watch, keep," is rendered by the verb "to guard" in the RV (KJV, "to keep") of Luke 11:21; John 17:12; **Acts 12:4**; **28:16**; 2 Thess. 3:3; 1 Tim. 6:20; 2 Tim. 1:12, 14; 1 John 5:21; Jude 24. In Luke 8:29, "was kept under guard," RV (KJV, "kept").

Intending *see* Intend at *Acts 5:28*.

Easter *pascha* (3957), mistranslated "Easter" in **Acts 12:4**, KJV, denotes the Passover (RV). The phrase "after the Passover" signifies after the whole festival was at an end. The term "Easter" is not of Christian origin. It is another form of *Astarte*, one of the titles of the Chaldean goddess, the queen of heaven. The festival of Pasch held by Christians in post-apostolic times was a continuation of the Jewish feast, but was not instituted by Christ, nor was it connected with Lent. From this Pasch the pagan festival of "Easter" was quite distinct and was introduced into the apostate Western religion, as part of the attempt to adapt pagan festivals to Christianity.

Bring *see* Brought at *Acts 9:39*.

12:5 Peter therefore was kept in prison: but prayer was made without ceasing of the church unto God for him.

Kept *tereo* (5083), denotes (a) "to watch over, preserve, keep, watch," e.g., **Acts 12:5**, **6**; **16:23**; in **25:21**, RV (1st part), "kept" (KJV, "reserved"); the present participle is translated "keepers" in Matt. 28:4, lit. "the keeping (ones)"; it is used of the "keeping" power of God the Father and Christ, exercised over His people, John 17:11, 12, 15; 1 Thess. 5:23, "preserved"; 1 John 5:18, where "He that was begotten of God," RV, is said of Christ as the Keeper ("keepeth him," RV, for KJV, "keepeth himself"); Jude 1, RV, "kept for Jesus Christ" (KJV, "preserved in Jesus Christ"), Rev. 3:10; of their inheritance, 1 Pet. 1:4 ("reserved"); of judicial reservation by God in view of future doom, 2 Pet. 2:4, 9, 17; 3:7; Jude 6, 13; of "keeping" the faith, 2 Tim. 4:7; the unity of the Spirit, Eph. 4:3; oneself, 2 Cor. 11:9; 1 Tim. 5:22; Jas. 1:27; figuratively, one's garments, Rev. 16:15; (b) "to observe, to give heed to," as of keeping commandments, etc., e.g., Matt. 19:17; John 14:15; 15:10; 17:6; Jas. 2:10; 1 John 2:3, 4, 5; 3:22, 24; 5:2 (in some mss.), 3; Rev. 1:3; 2:26; 3:8, 10; 12:17; 14:12; 22:7, 9.

Prayer "Prayer is properly addressed to God the Father Matt. 6:6; John 16:23; Eph. 1:17; 3:14, and the Son, **Acts 7:59**; 2 Cor. 12:8; but in no instance in the NT is prayer addressed to the Holy Spirit distinctively, for whereas the Father is in Heaven, Matt. 6:9, and the Son is at His right hand, Rom. 8:34, the Holy Spirit is in and with the believers, John 14:16, 17. Prayer is to be offered in the Name of the Lord Jesus, John 14:13, that is, the prayer must accord with His character, and must be presented in the same spirit of dependence and submission that marked Him, Matt. 11:26; Luke 22:42. The Holy Spirit, being the sole interpreter of the needs of the human heart, makes His intercession therein; and inasmuch as prayer is impossible to man apart from His help,

Rom. 8:26, believers are exhorted to pray at all seasons in the Spirit, Eph. 6:18; cf. Jude 20, and Jas. 5:16, the last clause of which should probably be read 'the inwrought [i.e., by the Holy Spirit] supplication of righteous man availeth much' (or 'greatly prevails' *ischuo*, as in **Acts 19:16, 20**). None the less on this account is the understanding to be engaged in prayer, 1 Cor. 14:15, and the will, Col. 4:12; **Acts 12:5** (where 'earnestly' is, lit., 'stretched out') and so in Luke 22:44. Faith is essential to prayer, Matt. 21:22; Mark 11:24; Jas. 1:5-8, for faith is the recognition of, and the committal of ourselves and our matters to, the faithfulness of God. Where the Jews were numerous, as at Thessalonica, they had usually a Synagogue, **Acts 17:1**; where they were few, as at Philippi, they had merely a *proseuche*, or 'place of prayer,' of much smaller dimensions, and commonly built by a river for the sake of the water necessary to the preliminary ablutions prescribed by Rabbinic tradition, **Acts 16:13, 16**."

Without ceasing *ektenes* (1618), denotes "strained, stretched" (*ek*, "out," *teino*, "to stretch"); hence, metaphorically, "fervent," 1 Pet. 4:8. Some mss. have it in **Acts 12:5**, for the adverb. Cf. *ekteneia* (with *en*), "intently, strenuously," in **Acts 26:7**, KJV, "instantly," RV, "earnestly."

12:6 And when Herod would have brought him forth, the same night Peter was sleeping between two soldiers, bound with two chains: and the keepers before the door kept the prison.

Brought *proago* (4254), "to bring or lead forth," e.g., **Acts 12:6; 16:30; 25:26**.

Sleeping *see* Asleep at *Acts 7:60*.

Between *metaxu* (3342), "in the midst, or between" (from *meta*, and *xun*, i.e., *sun*, "with"), is used as a preposition, (a) of mutual relation, Matt. 18:15; **Acts 15:9**; Rom. 2:15, RV, "one with another," lit., "between one another," for KJV, "the meanwhile"; (b) of place, Matt. 23:35; Luke 11:51; 16:26; **Acts 12:6**; (c) of time, "meanwhile," John 4:31. In **Acts 13:42**, the KJV marg. has "in the week between," the literal rendering.

Chains *halusis* (254), denotes "a chain or bond for binding the body, or any part of it (the hands or feet)." Some derive the word from *a*, negative, and *luo*, "to loose," i.e., "not to be loosed"; others from a root connected with a word signifying "to restrain." It is used in Mark 5:3-4; Luke 8:29; **Acts 12:6-7; 21:33; 28:20**; Eph. 6:20; 2 Tim. 1:16; Rev. 20:1.

Keepers *see Acts 5:23*.

Kept *see Acts 12:5*.

12:7 And, behold, the angel of the Lord came upon *him*, and a light shined in the prison: and he smote Peter on the side, and raised him up, saying, Arise up quickly. And his chains fell off from *his* hands.

Came *see Acts 4:1. See also* **Stood** at *Acts 10:17*.

Shined *lampo* (2989), "to shine as a torch," occurs in Matt. 5:15, 16, 17:2; Luke 17:24; **Acts 12:7**; 2 Cor. 4:6 (twice).

Prison *oikema* (3612), lit., "a habitation" (akin to *oikeo*, "to dwell"), is euphemistically put for "a prison," in **Acts 12:7**, RV, "cell."

Smote *see Acts 7:24*.

Side *pleura* (4125), "a side" (cf. Eng., "pleurisy"), is used of the "side" of Christ, into which the spear was thrust, John 19:34; 20:20, 25, 27 (some mss. have it in Matt. 27:49; see RV marg.); elsewhere, in **Acts 12:7**.

Arise *egeiro* (1453), is used, (a) in the active voice, of "arousing a person from sleep" in Matt. 8:25 of the act of the disciples in awaking the Lord; in **Acts 12:7**, of the awaking of Peter, RV, "awake him"; (b) in the passive voice, with a middle significance, of the virgins, in "arousing themselves" from their slumber, Matt. 25:7; in Rom. 13:11, and Eph. 5:14, metaphorically, "of awaking from a state of moral sloth."

Fell *ekpipto* (1601), "to fall out of," "is used in the NT, literally, of flowers that wither in the course of nature, Jas. 1:11; 1 Pet. 1:24; of a ship not under control, **Acts 27:17, 26, 29, 32**; of shackles loosed from a prisoner's wrist, **12:7**; figuratively, of the Word of God (the expression of His purpose), which cannot "fall" away from the end to which it is set, Rom. 9:6; of the believer who is warned lest he "fall" away from the course in which he has been confirmed by the Word of God, 2 Pet. 3:17." So of those who seek to be justified by law, Gal. 5:4, "ye are fallen away from grace." Some mss. have this verb in Mark 13:25; so in Rev. 2:5.

Off The preposition *ek* (or *ex*), which frequently signifies "out of" or "from the midst of," has a variety of meanings, among which is "from," as virtually equivalent to *apo*, "away from," e.g., 2 Cor. 1:10, "who delivered us out of so great a death, and will deliver"; since death was not actually experienced, but was impending, *ek* here does not signify "out of the midst of" In **Acts 12:7** it is used in the statement "his chains fell off from his hands." In Matt. 17:9 it is used of descending from a mountain, not "out of"; "we are not to suppose that they had been in a cave" (Dr. A. T. Robertson, *Gram. of the Greek NT*). In 1 Thess. 1:10, "even Jesus, which delivereth us from the wrath to come," RV, the question whether *ek* here means "out of the midst of" or "away from," is to be determined by some statement of Scripture where the subject is specifically mentioned; this is provided, e.g., in 5:9, the context of which makes clear that believers are to be delivered from (not "out of") the divine wrath to be executed on the nations at the end of the present age.

12:8 And the angel said unto him, Gird thyself, and bind on thy sandals. And so he did. And he saith unto him, Cast thy garment about thee, and follow me.

Gird *zonnumi* (2224), or *zonnuo*, "to gird" in the middle voice, "to gird oneself," is used of the long garments worn in the east, John 21:18; **Acts 12:8**. In some mss. *perizonnumi* (4024), "to gird around or about," is used (a) literally, of "girding" oneself for service, Luke 12:37; 17:8; for rapidity of movement, **Acts 12:8**.

Bind *hupodeo* (5265), *hupo*, "to bind underneath," is used of binding of sandals, **Acts 12:8**; rendered "shod" in Mark 6:9 and Eph. 6:15

Sandals *sandalion* (4547), a diminutive of *sandalon*, probably a Persian word, Mark 6:9; **Acts 12:8**. The "sandal" usually had a wooden sole bound on by straps round the instep and ankle.

Cast *periballo* (4016), "to cast about, or around," is used in 23 of its 24 occurrences, of putting on garments, clothing, etc.; it is translated "cast about" in Mark 14:51; **Acts 12:8**, in Luke 19:43, used of "casting" up a bank or palisade against a city (see RV and marg.), KJV, "shall cast a trench about thee."

12:9 And he went out, and followed him; and wist not that it was true which was done by the angel; but thought he saw a vision.

Wist *oida* (1492), "to know," in the pluperfect tense (with imperfect meaning) is rendered "wist" (the past tense of the verb "to wit") in Mark 9:6; 14:40; Luke 2:49; John 5:13; **Acts 12:9; 23:5**.

True *alethes* (227), primarily, "unconcealed, manifest" (*a*, negative, *letho*, "to forget," = *lanthano*, "to escape notice"), hence, actual, "true to fact," is used (a) of persons, "truthful," Matt. 22:16; Mark 12:14; John 3:33; 7:18; 8:26; Rom. 3:4; 2 Cor. 6:8; (b) of things, "true," conforming to reality, John 4:18, "truly," lit., "true"; 5:31, 32; in the best texts, 6:55 (twice), "indeed"; 8:13, 14, 17; 10:41; 19:35; 21:24; **Acts 12:9**; Phil. 4:8; Titus 1:13; 1 Pet. 5:12; 2 Pet. 2:22; 1 John 2:8, 27; 3 John 1:2.

Vision *see* **Sight** at *Acts 7:31*.

12:10 When they were past the first and the second ward, they came unto the iron gate that leadeth unto the city; which opened to them of his own accord: and they went out, and passed on through one street; and forthwith the angel departed from him.

Ward *phulake* (5438), "a guard," is used of the place where persons are kept under guard (akin to *phulax*, "a keeper"), and translated "ward" in **Acts 12:10**.

Iron *sidereos* (4603), "of iron," occurs in **Acts 12:10**, of an iron gate; "of iron," Rev. 2:27; 9:9; 12:5; 19:15.

Gate *see Acts 3:10*.

Leadeth *phero* (5342), "to bear, carry," is used metaphorically of a gate, as "leading" to a city, **Acts 12:10**.

Accord *automatos* (844), from *autos*, "self," and a root *ma–*, signifying "desire," denotes of oneself, moved by one's own impulse. It occurs in Mark 4:28, of the power of the earth to produce plants and fruits of itself; **Acts 12:10**, of the door which opened of its own accord. In the Sept., Lev. 25:5, "spontaneous produce"; v. 11, "produce that comes of itself"; Josh. 6:5; 2 Kings 19:29, "(that which groweth) of itself"; Job 24:24, of an ear of corn "(falling off) of itself (from the stalk)."

Passed *proerchomai* (4281), "to go before, precede, go forward or farther" (*pro*, "before"), is used of (a) place, e.g., Matt. 26:39; **Acts 12:10**, "passed on through"; (b) time, Luke 1:17; **Acts 20:5, 13**; 2 Cor. 9:5.

Street *see Acts 9:11*.

Forthwith *eutheos* (2112), "at once, straightway" (from the adjective, *euthus*, "straight"), is translated "forthwith," in the KJV of Matt. 13:5; 26:49; (it occurs in some mss. in Mark 5:13; the RV omits it); **Acts 12:10; 21:30** (RV, "straightway," in each place).

Departed *see* **Dispersed** at *Acts 5:37*.

12:11 And when Peter was come to himself, he said, Now I know of a surety, that the Lord hath sent his angel, and hath delivered me out of the hand of Herod, and *from* all the expectation of the people of the Jews.

Surety *alethos* (230), "truly, surely," is rendered "of a truth" in Matt. 14:33; 26:73 and Mark 14:70, RV, (KJV, "surely"); Luke 9:27; 12:44; 21:3; John 6:14; 7:40; 17:8, RV, "of a truth" (KJV, "surely"); **Acts 12:11**, RV (KJV, "of a surety"); "in truth," 1 Thess. 2:13; "truly," Matt. 27:54; Mark 15:39.

Sent *see Acts 7:12.*

Delivered *see Acts 7:10.*

Hand *see* Hands at *Acts 5:12.*

Expectation *prosdokia* (4329), "a watching for, expectation," is used in the NT only of the "expectation" of evil, Luke 21:26, RV, "expectation," KJV, "looking for," regarding impending calamities; **Acts 12:11**, "the expectation" of the execution of Peter.

12:12 And when he had considered *the thing*, he came to the house of Mary the mother of John, whose surname was Mark; where many were gathered together praying.

Considered *suneidon* (4894), used as the aorist tense of *sunorao*, to see with one view, to be aware, conscious, as the result of mental perception, is translated "considered" in **Acts 12:12**, of Peter's consideration of the circumstances of his deliverance from.

Surname *see* Surnamed at *Acts 1:23.*

Many *see Acts 9:23.*

Gathered *sunathroizo* (4867), signifies (a) "to gather together," **Acts 19:25**, RV (KJV, "called together"); in the passive voice, **12:12**.

12:13 And as Peter knocked at the door of the gate, a damsel came to hearken, named Rhoda.

Knocked *krouo* (2925), "to strike, knock," is used in the NT of "knocking" at a door, (a) literally, Luke 12:36; **Acts 12:13, 16**; (b) figuratively, Matt. 7:7, 8; Luke 11:9, 10 (of importunity in dealing with God); 13:25; Rev. 3:20.

Gate *see Acts 10:17.*

Damsel *paidiske* (3814), denotes "a young girl, or a female slave"; "damsel," KJV, in John 18:17; **Acts 12:13; 16:16**; RV "maid" in each case.

Hearken In **Acts 12:13**, *hupakouo*, lit., "to hearken," with the idea of stillness, or attention (*hupo*, "under," *akouo*, "to hear"), signifies "to answer a knock at a door," RV, "to answer" (KJV, "to hearken").

12:14 And when she knew Peter's voice, she opened not the gate for gladness, but ran in, and told how Peter stood before the gate.

Gate *see Acts 10:17.*

Gladness *chara* (5479), "joy, delight," is rendered "gladness" in the KJV of Mark 4:16; **Acts 12:14** and Phil. 2:29 (RV "joy", as elsewhere in both versions).

Ran *eistrecho* (1532), "to run in" (*eis*, "in"), occurs in **Acts 12:14**.

12:15 And they said unto her, Thou art mad. But she constantly affirmed that it was even so. Then said they, It is his angel.

Mad *mainomai* (3105), "to rage, be mad," is translated by the verb "to be mad" in John 10:20; **Acts 12:15; 26:24, 25**; 1 Cor. 14:23.

Affirmed *diischurizomai* (1340), and *ischurizosai*, "to corroborate" primarily signifies "to lean upon," hence, "to affirm stoutly, assert vehemently," Luke 22:59; **Acts 12:15**.

Was *see Acts 5:4.*

Angel *see Acts 10:3. See also* **Spirit** at *Acts 7:59.*

12:16 But Peter continued knocking: and when they had opened *the door*, and saw him, they were astonished.

Continued *epimeno* (1961), lit., "to remain on," i.e., in addition to, "to continue long, still to abide," is used of "continuing" to ask, John 8:7; to knock, **Acts 12:16**; in the grace of God, **13:43**; in sin, Rom. 6:1; in God's goodness, 11:22; in unbelief, 11:23 (KJV, "abide"); in the flesh, Phil. 1:24; in the faith, Col. 1:23; in doctrine, 1 Tim. 4:16; elsewhere of abiding in a place.

Knocking *see* Knocked at *Acts 12:13.*

12:17 But he, beckoning unto them with the hand to hold their peace, declared unto them how the Lord had brought him out of the prison. And he said, Go shew these things unto James, and to the brethren. And he departed, and went into another place.

Beckoning *kataseio* (2678), lit., "to shake down" (*kata*, "down," *seio*, "to shake"), of shaking the hand, of waving, expresses a little more vigorously the act of "beckoning," **Acts 12:17; 13:16; 19:33; 21:40**. *Neuo* and its compounds have primary reference to a movement of the head; *kataseio*, to that of the hand.

Peace *sigao* (4601), signifies (a), used intransitively, "to be silent" (from *sige*, "silence"), translated "to hold one's peace," in Luke 9:36; 18:39; 20:26; **Acts 12:17; 15:13** (in v. **12**, "kept silence"; similarly rendered in 1 Cor. 14:28, 30, KJV, "hold his peace," 34); (b) used transitively, "to keep secret"; in the passive voice, "to be kept secret," Rom. 16:25, RV, "hath been kept in silence."

Declared *see* Declare at *Acts 8:33.*

Went *see Acts 10:9.*

12:18 Now as soon as it was day, there was no small stir among the soldiers, what was become of Peter.

Small *oligos* (3641), "little, small" (of amount, number, time), is translated "small" in **Acts 12:18**; **15:2**; **19:23**; v. **24**; KJV (RV, "little"); **27:20**.

Stir *tarachos* (5017), akin to *tarache*, "trouble," and *tarasso*, "to trouble," is rendered "stir" in **Acts 12:18**; **19:23**.

12:19 And when Herod had sought for him, and found him not, he examined the keepers, and commanded that *they* should be put to death. And he went down from Judaea to Caesarea, and *there* abode.

Sought *epizeteo* (1934), "to seek after" (directive, *epi*, "towards") is always rendered in the RV, by some form of the verb "to seek," **Acts 13:7**, "sought" (KJV, "desired"); **19:39**, "seek" (KJV, "inquire"); Phil. 4:17, "seek for" (KJV, "desire"), twice; elsewhere, Matt. 6:32; 12:39; 16:4; Mark 8:12 (in some texts); Luke 12:30; **Acts 12:19**; Rom. 11:7; Heb. 11:14; 13:14.

Examined *see* ***Acts 4:9***.

Keepers *see* ***Acts 5:23***.

Put to death *apago* (520), "to lead away" (*apo*, "away"), is used of a way "leading" to destruction, Matt. 7:13, to life, v. 14; of those who "led" Christ away from Gethsemane, Mark 14:44; in some mss., John 18:13, to Annas; to Caiaphas, Matt. 26:57; Mark 14:53; to Pilate, Matt. 27:2; to the Praetorium, Mark 15:16; to crucifixion, Matt. 27:31; Luke 23:26; in some mss. John 19:16; of "leading" an animal away to watering, Luke 13:15; of being "led" away to idolatry, 1 Cor. 12:2, RV, "led away" (KJV, "carried away"). Some mss. have it in **Acts 24:7** (KJV, "took away"). It is translated "bring" in **23:17**. In **12:19** it signifies "to put to death."

Abode *diatribo* (1304), is invariably rendered "to tarry," in the RV; KJV, twice, John 3:22; **Acts 25:6**; "continued" in John 11:54; **Acts 15:35**; "abode," **Acts 12:19**; **14:3**, **28**; **20:6**; "abiding," **16:12**, "had been," **25:14**.

12:20 And Herod was highly displeased with them of Tyre and Sidon: but they came with one accord to him, and, having made Blastus the king's chamberlain their friend, desired peace; because their country was nourished by the king's *country*.

Displeased *thumomacheo* (2371), lit., "to fight with great animosity" (*thumos*, "passion," *machomai*, "to fight"), hence, "to be very angry, to be highly displeased," is said of Herod's "displeasure" with the Tyrians and Sidonians, **Acts 12:20**.

Accord *see* ***Acts 1:14***.

Friend *peitho* (3982), "to persuade, influence," is rendered "having made ... their friend" in **Acts 12:20**, of the folks of Tyre and Sidon in winning the good will of Blastus, Herod's chamberlain, possibly with bribes.

Desired *see* **Ask** at ***Acts 3:2***.

Country *see* **Land** at ***Acts 10:39***.

Nourished *trepho* (5142), "to rear, feed, nourish," is translated by the verb "to nourish" in Jas. 5:5 (of luxurious living); Rev. 12:14 (of God's care for Israel against its enemies); so v. 6, RV (KJV, "feed"); in **Acts 12:20**, RV, "was fed" (KJV, "was nourished").

King's country *basilikos* (937), an adjective, "royal, belonging to a king" (*basileus*), is used of the command, "thou shalt love thy neighbor as thyself," "the royal law," Jas. 2:8; this may mean a law which covers or governs other laws and therefore has a specially regal character (as Hort suggests), or because it is made by a King (a meaning which Deissmann assigns) with whom there is no respect of persons; it is used with the pronoun *tis*, "a certain one," in John 4:46, 49, of a courtier, one in the service of a king, "a nobleman" (some mss. have the noun *basiliskos*, "a petty king," in these two verses). It is used of a country in **Acts 12:20**, "the king's (country)," and of royal apparel in v. **21**.

12:21 And upon a set day Herod, arrayed in royal apparel, sat upon his throne, and made an oration unto them.

Set *taktos* (5002), an adjective, "ordered, fixed, set," is said of an appointed day, in **Acts 12:21**. In the Sept., Job 12:5.

Royal *basilikos* (937), "belonging to a king," is translated "royal" in **Acts 12:21**; Jas. 2:8. *See also* **King's country** at ***Acts 12:20***.

Apparel *see* ***Acts 1:10***.

Throne *bema* (968), is used of the throne or tribunal of Herod, **Acts 12:21**.

Oration *demegoreo* (1215), from *demos*, "the people" and *agoreuo*, "to speak in the public assembly, to deliver an oration," occurs in **Acts 12:21**.

12:22 And the people gave a shout, *saying, It is* the voice of a god, and not of a man.

People *demos* (1218), "the common people, the people generally" (Eng., "demagogue," "democracy," etc.), especially the mass of the "people" assembled in a public place, **Acts 12:22**; **17:5**; **19:30**, **33**.

Shout *epiphoneo* (2019), signifies "to shout," either against, Luke 23:21; **Acts 21:34**; **22:24**, or in acclamation, **Acts 12:22**.

Voice *see* ***Acts 7:31***.

12:23 And immediately the angel of the Lord smote him, because he gave not God the glory: and he was eaten of worms, and gave up the ghost.

Immediately *see Acts 3:7.*

Smote *see Acts 7:24.*

Glory *doxa* (1391), "glory" (from *dokeo*, "to seem"), primarily signifies an opinion, estimate, and hence, the honor resulting from a good opinion. It is used (I) (a) of the nature and acts of God in self-manifestation, i.e., what He essentially is and does, as exhibited in whatever way he reveals Himself in these respects, and particularly in the person of Christ, in whom essentially His "glory" has ever shone forth and ever will do, John 17:5, 24; Heb. 1:3; it was exhibited in the character and acts of Christ in the days of His flesh, John 1:14; John 2:11; at Cana both His grace and His power were manifested, and these constituted His "glory", so also in the resurrection of Lazarus 11:4, 40; the "glory" of God was exhibited in the resurrection of Christ, Rom. 6:4, and in His ascension and exaltation, 1 Pet. 1:21, likewise on the Mount of Transfiguration, 2 Pet. 1:17. In Rom. 1:23 His "everlasting power and Divinity" are spoken of as His "glory," i.e., His attributes and power as revealed through creation; in Rom. 3:23 the word denotes the manifested perfection of His character, especially His righteousness, of which all men fall short; in Col. 1:11 "the might of His glory" signifies the might which is characteristic of His "glory"; in Eph. 1:6, 12, 14, "the praise of the glory of His grace" and "the praise of His glory" signify the due acknowledgement of the exhibition of His attributes and ways; in Eph. 1:17, "the Father of glory" describes Him as the source from whom all divine splendor and perfection proceed in their manifestation, and to whom they belong; (b) of the character and ways of God as exhibited through Christ to and through believers, 2 Cor. 3:18 and 4:6; (c) of the state of blessedness into which believers are to enter hereafter through being brought into the likeness of Christ, e.g., Rom. 8:18, 21; Phil. 3:21 (RV, "the body of His glory"); 1 Pet. 5:1, 10; Rev. 21:11; (d) brightness or splendor, (1) supernatural, emanating from God (as in the *shekinah* "glory," in the pillar of cloud and in the Holy of Holies, e.g., Exod. 16:10; 25:22), Luke 2:9; **Acts 22:11**; Rom. 9:4; 2 Cor. 3:7; Jas. 2:1; in Titus 2:13 it is used of Christ's return, "the appearing of the glory of our great God and Savior Jesus Christ" (RV); cf. Phil. 3:21, above; (2) natural, as of the heavenly bodies, 1 Cor. 15:40, 41; (II) of good reputation, praise, honor, Luke 14:10 (RV, "glory," for KJV, "worship"); John 5:41 (RV, "glory," for KJV, "honor"); 7:18; 8:50; 12:43 (RV, "glory," for KJV, "praise"); 2 Cor. 6:8 (RV, "glory," for KJV "honor"); Phil. 3:19; Heb. 3:3; in 1 Cor. 11:7, of man as representing the authority of God, and of woman as rendering conspicuous the authority of man; in 1 Thess. 2:6, "glory" probably stands, by metonymy, for material gifts, an honorarium, since in human estimation "glory" is usually expressed in things material. The word is used in ascriptions of praise to God, e.g.. Luke 17:18; John 9:24, RV, "glory" (KJV, "praise"); **Acts 12:23**; as in doxologies (lit., "glory-words"), e.g., Luke 2:14; Rom. 11:36; 16:27; Gal. 1:5; Rev. 1:6.

Worms *skolekobrotos* (4662), denotes "devored by worms" (*skolex*, and *bibrosko*, "to eat"), **Acts 12:23**.

Ghost *see Acts 5:5.*

12:24 But the word of God grew and multiplied.

Grew *see* Increased at *Acts 6:7.*

Multiplied *see Acts 6:1.*

12:25 And Barnabas and Saul returned from Jerusalem, when they had fulfilled *their* ministry, and took with them John, whose surname was Mark.

Returned *see Acts 1:12.*

Ministry *see Acts 1:17.*

Took *sumparalambano* (4838), denotes "to take along with oneself," as a companion, **Acts 12:25**; **15:37, 38**; Gal. 2:1.

Surname *see* Surnamed at *Acts 1:23.*

Chapter 13

13:1 Now there were in the church that was at Antioch certain prophets and teachers; as Barnabas, and Simeon that was called Niger, and Lucius of Cyrene, and Manaen, which had been brought up with Herod the tetrarch, and Saul.

Prophets *see* Prophet at *Acts 3:22.*

Teachers *didaskalos* (1320), is rendered "teacher" or "teachers" in Matt. 23:8, by Christ, of Himself; in John 3:2 of Christ; of Nicodemus in Israel, 3:10, RV; of "teachers" of the truth in the churches, **Acts 13:1**; 1 Cor. 12:28, 29; Eph. 4:11; Heb. 5:12; Jas. 3:1, RV; by Paul of his work among the churches, 1 Tim. 2:7; 2 Tim. 1:11; of "teachers," wrongfully chosen by those who have "itching ears," 2 Tim. 4:3.

Brought In **Acts 13:1**, *suntrophos* denotes "a foster-brother," RV (KJV, marg.).

Tetrarch *tetraarches or tetrarches* (5076), denotes "one of four rulers" (*tetra*, "four," *arche*, "rule"), properly, "the governor of the fourth part of a region"; hence, "a dependent princeling," or "any petty ruler" subordinate to kings or ethnarchs; in the NT, Herod Antipas, Matt. 14:1; Luke 3:19; 9:7; **Acts 13:1**.

13:2 As they ministered to the Lord, and fasted, the Holy Ghost said, Separate me Barnabas and Saul for the work whereunto I have called them.

Ministered *leitourgeo* (3008), in classical Greek, signified at Athens "to supply public offices at one's own cost, to render public service to the State"; hence, generally, "to do service," said, e.g., of service to the gods. In the NT it is used (a) of the prophets and teachers in the church at Antioch, who "ministered to the Lord," **Acts 13:2**; (b) of the duty of churches of the Gentiles to "minister" in "carnal things" to the poor Jewish saints at Jerusalem, in view of the fact that the former had "been made partakers" of the "spiritual things" of the latter, Rom. 15:27; (c) of the official service of priests and Levites under the Law, Heb. 10:11 (in the Sept., e.g., Exod. 29:30; Num. 16:9).

Fasted *see* Fasting at *Acts 10:30*.

Holy Ghost *see Acts 1:16*.

Work *see Acts 5:38*.

Called *see* Call at *Acts 2:39*.

13:3 And when they had fasted and prayed, and laid *their* hands on them, they sent *them* away.

Fasted *see* Fasting at *Acts 10:30*.

Laid ... on *see Acts 6:6*.

Sent *apoluo* (630), "to set free, to let go," is translated "to send away" in Matt. 14:15, 22, 23; Mark 6:36, 45; 8:3, 9; Luke 8:38; **Acts 13:3**, where the "sending" is not that of commissioning, but of letting go, intimating that they would gladly have retained them (contrast *ekpempo*, the act of commissioning by the Holy Spirit in v. 4).

13:4 So they, being sent forth by the Holy Ghost, departed unto Seleucia; and from thence they sailed to Cyprus.

Sent *ekpempo* (1599), denotes "to send forth" (*ek*, "out of"), **Acts 13:4**, "being sent forth"; **17:10**, "sent away." *See also Acts 13:3*.

Departed *katerchomai* (2718), "to come down" (its usual meaning), is translated "departed" in **Acts 13:4**, KJV (RV, "went down").

Sailed *apopleo* (636), "to sail away," occurs in **Acts 13:4**; **14:26**; **20:15**; **27:1**.

13:5 And when they were at Salamis, they preached the word of God in the synagogues of the Jews: and they had also John to *their* minister.

Preached *see Acts 4:2*.

Minister *huperetes* (5257), properly "an under rower" (*hupo*, "under," *eretes*, "a rower"), as distinguished from *nautes*, "a seaman" (a meaning which lapsed from the word), hence came to denote "any subordinate acting under another's direction"; in Luke 4:20, RV, "attendant," KJV, "minister" it signifies the attendant at the synagogue service; in **Acts 13:5**, it is said of John Mark, RV, "attendant," KJV, "minister;" in **Acts 26:16**, "a minister," it is said of Paul as a servant of Christ in the gospel; so in 1 Cor. 4:1, where the apostle associates others with himself, as Apollos and Cephas, as "ministers of Christ."

"The Spirit was given not to make us comfortable but to make us missionaries."

MICHAEL GREEN

13:6 And when they had gone through the isle unto Paphos, they found a certain sorcerer, a false prophet, a Jew, whose name *was* Barjesus:

Isle *nesos* (3520), "an island," occurs in **Acts 13:6**; **27:26**; **28:1**, **7**, **9**, **11**; Rev. 1:9; 6:14; 16:20.

Sorcerer *magos* (3097), (a) "one of a Median caste, a magician"; (b) "a wizard, sorcerer, a pretender to magic powers, a professor of the arts of witchcraft," **Acts 13:6**, **8**, where Bar-Jesus was the Jewish name, Elymas, an Arabic word meaning "wise." Hence the name Magus, "the magician," originally applied to Persian priests. In the Sept., only in Dan. 2:2, 10, of the "enchanters," RV (KJV, "astrologers"), of Babylon. The superior Greek version of Daniel by Theodotion has it also at 1:20; 2:27; 4:7; 5:7, 11, 15.

Prophet *pseudoprophetes* (5578), "a false prophet," is used of such (a) in OT times, Luke 6:26; 2 Pet. 2:1; (b) in the present period since Pentecost, Matt. 7:15; 24:11, 24; Mark 13:22; **Acts 13:6**; 1 John 4:1; (c) with reference to a false "prophet" destined to arise as the supporter of the "Beast" at the close of this age, Rev. 16:13; 19:20; 20:10 (himself described as "another beast," 13:11).

Jew *see* Jews at *Acts 2:10*.

13:7 Which was with the deputy of the country, Sergius Paulus, a prudent man; who called for Barnabas and Saul, and desired to hear the word of God.

Deputy *anthupatos* (446), from *anti*, "instead of," and *hupatos*, "supreme," denotes "a consul, one acting in place of a consul, a proconsul, the governor of a senatorial province" (i.e., one which had no standing army). The "proconsuls" were of two classes, (a) exconsuls, the rulers of the provinces of Asia and Africa, who were therefore "proconsuls" (b) those who were ex-pretors or "proconsuls" of other senatorial provinces (a pretor being virtually the same as a consul). To the former belonged the "proconsuls" at Ephesus, **Acts 19:38** (KJV, "deputies"); to the latter, Sergius Paulus in Cyprus, **Acts 13:7, 8, 12**, and Gallio at Corinth, **18:12**. In the NT times Egypt was governed by a prefect. Provinces in which a standing army was kept were governed by an imperial legate (e.g., Quirinius in Syria, Luke 2:2).

Prudent *sunetos* (4908), signifies "intelligent, sagacious, understanding" (akin to *suniemi*, "to perceive"), translated "prudent" in Matt. 11:25, KJV (RV, "understanding"); Luke 10:21 (ditto); **Acts 13:7**, RV, "(a man) of understanding"; in 1 Cor. 1:19, "prudent," RV and KJV. Cf. *asunetos*, "without understanding."

Who These are usually the translations of forms of the relative pronoun *hos*, or of the interrogative pronoun *tis;* otherwise of *hostis*, "whoever," usually of a more general subject than *hos*, e.g., Mark 15:7; Luke 23:19; Gal. 2:4; *hosos*, "as many as," Heb. 2:15; in **Acts 13:7**, KJV, *houtos*, "this (man)," is translated "who," RV, "the same."

Desired *epizeteo*, "to seek earnestly," in **Acts 13:7**, RV, "sought"; in Phil. 4:17, RV, "seek for" (twice). *See also* **Sought** at *Acts 12:19*.

13:8 But Elymas the sorcerer (for so is his name by interpretation) withstood them, seeking to turn away the deputy from the faith.

Sorcerer *see Acts 13:6*.

Interpretation *see* **Interpreted** at *Acts 4:36*.

Withstood *anthistemi* (436), "to set against," is translated "to withstand" in **Acts 13:8** (middle voice); in the intransitive 2nd aorist, active voice, Eph. 6:13; 2 Tim. 3:8 (1st part; middle voice in 2nd part); 4:15. *See also* **Resist** at *Acts 6:10*.

Turn away *diastrepho* (1294), "to distort, twist" (*dia*, "through," and *strepho*), is translated "to pervert" in Luke 23:2; **Acts 13:10** [in v. 8, "to turn aside" (KJV, "away")]; in the perfect participle, passive voice, it is translated "perverse," lit., "turned aside, corrupted," in Matt. 17:17; Luke 9:41; **Acts 20:30**; Phil. 2:15.

Deputy *see Acts 13:7*.

13:9 Then Saul, (who also *is called* Paul,) filled with the Holy Ghost, set his eyes on him,

Filled *see Acts 2:4*.

Set In **Acts 13:9**, KJV, *atenizo*, "to look fixedly, gaze," is rendered "set his eyes on" (RV, "fastened his eyes on"). *See also* **Looked** at *Acts 1:10*.

13:10 And said, O full of all subtilty and all mischief, *thou* child of the devil, *thou* enemy of all righteousness, wilt thou not cease to pervert the right ways of the Lord?

Full *see Acts 6:3*.

Subtilty *dolos* (1388), "a bait, snare, deceit," is rendered "guile" in John 1:47, negatively of Nathanael; **Acts 13:10**, RV, KJV, "subtlety" (of Bar-Jesus); 2 Cor. 12:16, in a charge made against Paul by his detractors, of catching the Corinthian converts by "guile" (the apostle is apparently quoting the language of his critics); 1 Thess. 2:3, negatively, of the teaching of the apostle and his fellow missionaries; 1 Pet. 2:1, of that from which Christians are to be free; 2:22, of the guileless speech of Christ; 3:10, of the necessity that the speech of Christians should be guileless. See also Matt. 26:4; Mark 7:22; 14:1.

Mischief *rhadiourgia* (4468), lit. and primarily denotes "ease in working" (*rhadios*, "easy," *ergon*, "work"), "easiness, laziness"; hence "recklessness, wickedness," **Acts 13:10**, RV, "villany," KJV, "mischief." In the papyri it is used of "theft."

Child *see* **Children** at *Acts 3:25*.

Enemy *see* **Foes** at *Acts 2:35*.

Cease *see* **Ceased** at *Acts 5:42*.

Pervert *see* **Turn away** at *Acts 13:8*.

Right *see Acts 8:21*.

13:11 And now, behold, the hand of the Lord *is* upon thee, and thou shalt be blind, not seeing the sun for a season. And immediately there fell on him a mist and a darkness; and he went about seeking some to lead him by the hand.

Hand *see* **Hands** at *Acts 5:12*.

Blind *tuphlos* (5185), "blind," is used both physically and metaphorically, chiefly in the Gospels; elsewhere four times; physically, **Acts 13:11**; metaphorically, Rom. 2:19; 2 Pet. 1:9; Rev. 3:17. The word is frequently used as a noun, signifying "a blind man."

Immediately *see Acts 3:7.*

Fell *see Acts 1:26.*

Mist *achlus* (887), "a mist," especially a dimness of the eyes, is used in **Acts 13:11**. "In the single place of its NT use it attests the accuracy in the selection of words, and not least of medical words, which 'the beloved physician' so often displays. For him it expresses the mist of darkness ... which fell on the sorcerer Elymas, being the outward and visible sign of the inward spiritual darkness which would be his portion for a while in punishment for his resistance to the truth" (Trench, *Syn.*, Sec.c).

Darkness *skotos* (4655), a neuter noun frequent in the Sept., is used in the NT (a) of "physical darkness," Matt. 27:45; 2 Cor. 4:6; (b) of "intellectual darkness," Rom. 2:19; (c) of "blindness," **Acts 13:11**; (d) by metonymy, of the "place of punishment," e.g., Matt. 8:12; 2 Pet. 2:17; Jude 13; (e) metaphorically, of "moral and spiritual darkness," e.g., Matt. 6:23; Luke 1:79; 11:35; John 3:19; **Acts 26:18**; 2 Cor. 6:14; Eph. 6:12; Col. 1:13; 1 Thess. 5:4-5; 1 Pet. 2:9; 1 John 1:6; (f) by metonymy, of "those who are in moral or spiritual darkness," Eph. 5:8; (g) of "evil works," Rom. 13:12; Eph. 5:11, (h) of the "evil powers that dominate the world," Luke 22:53; (i) "of secrecy." While *skotos* is used more than twice as many times as *skotia* in the NT, the apostle John uses *skotos* only once, 1 John 1:6, but *skotia* 15 times out of the 18.

Went about *periago* (4013), "to lead about," as in 1 Cor. 9:5, is used intransitively with the meaning "to go about"; "went about," Matt. 4:23, 9:35; Mark 6:6; **Acts 13:11**; in Matt. 23:15, "ye compass."

Lead ... by the hand *cheiragogos* (5497), lit., "a hand-leader" (*cheir,* "the hand," *ago,* "to lead"), is used as a noun (plural) in **Acts 13:11**, "some to lead him by the hand."

13:12 Then the deputy, when he saw what was done, believed, being astonished at the doctrine of the Lord.

Deputy *see Acts 13:7.*

13:13 Now when Paul and his company loosed from Paphos, they came to Perga in Pamphylia: and John departing from them returned to Jerusalem.

Company The phrase in **Acts 13:13**, *hoi peri Paulon,* lit., "the (ones) about Paul," signifies "Paul and his company."

Loosed *anago* (321), "to bring up" (*ana,* "up," *ago,* "to lead"), is used in the middle voice as a nautical term signifying "to put to sea"; it is translated "launch forth" in Luke 8:22; "set sail" in **Acts 13:13**, RV (KJV, "loosed"); similarly in **16:11**; in **18:21**, for KJV, "sailed"; similarly in **20:3, 13**; in **21:1**, RV, "set sail," (KJV, "launched"), and in v. **2**, for KJV, "set forth"; in **27:2** and **4** the RV has the verb "to put to sea," for KJV "to launch"; in v. **12** for KJV, "depart"; in v. **21**, RV, "set sail" (KJV, "loosed"); in **28:10, 11**, "sailed" and "set sail" (KJV, "departed").

Departing *apochoreo* (672), "to depart from" (*apo*), is so translated in Matt. 7:23; Luke 9:39; **Acts 13:13** (both KJV and RV). Some mss. have it in Luke 20:20.

Returned *see Acts 1:12.*

13:14 But when they departed from Perga, they came to Antioch in Pisidia, and went into the synagogue on the sabbath day, and sat down.

Departed *dierchomai* (1330), "to come or go through, to pass through to a place," is translated "departed" in **Acts 13:14**, KJV; RV, "passing through"; elsewhere it is usually translated "pass through" or "go through."

13:15 And after the reading of the law and the prophets the rulers of the synagogue sent unto them, saying, *Ye* men *and* brethren, if ye have any word of exhortation for the people, say on.

Reading *anagnosis* (320), in nonbiblical Greek denoted "recognition" or "a survey" (the latter found in the papyri); then, "reading"; in the NT the public "reading" of Scripture, **Acts 13:15**; 2 Cor. 3:14; 1 Tim. 4:13, where the context makes clear that the reference is to the care required in reading the Scriptures to a company, a duty ever requiring the exhortation "take heed." Later, readers in churches were called *anagnostai.* In the Sept, Neh. 8:8.

Rulers of the synagogue *archisunagogos* (752), denotes "the administrative official," with the duty of preserving order and inviting persons to read or speak in the assembly, Mark 5:22, 35, 36, 38; Luke 8:49; 13:14; **Acts 13:15**; "chief ruler" (KJV) in **Acts 18:8, 17**.

Men *see Acts 1:16.*

Say on In Luke 7:40 and **Acts 13:15**, the imperative mood of *eipon* and *lego,* respectively, is rendered "say on."

13:16 Then Paul stood up, and beckoning with *his* hand said, Men of Israel, and ye that fear God, give audience.

Give audience *see* Hear at *Acts 3:22.*

Stood *see Acts 1:15.*

Beckoning *see Acts 12:17.*

Fear *see* Feared at *Acts 10:2.*

13:17 The God of this people of Israel chose our fathers, and exalted the people when they dwelt as strangers in the land of Egypt, and with an high arm brought he them out of it.

Chose *see* Chosen at *Acts 1:2.*

Exalted *see Acts 2:33.*

Dwelt *paroikia* (3940), denotes "a sojourning," **Acts 13:17**, lit., "in the sojourning," translated "when they sojourned," RV (KJV, "dwelt as strangers"); in 1 Pet. 1:17, "sojourning."

Strangers *paroikia* (3940), "a sojourning," occurs in **Acts 13:17**, rendered "they sojourned," RV, KJV, "dwelt as strangers," lit., "in the sojourning"; in 1 Pet. 1:17, "sojourning."

High *hupselos* (5308), "high, lofty," is used (a) naturally, of mountains, Matt. 4:8; 17:1; Mark 9:2; Rev. 21:10; of a wall, Rev. 21:12; (b) figuratively, of the arm of God, **Acts 13:17**; of heaven, "on high," plural, lit., "in high (places)," Heb. 1:3; (c) metaphorically, Luke 16:15, RV, "exalted" (KJV, "highly esteemed"); Rom. 11:20, in the best texts, "high-minded" [lit., "mind (not) high things"]; 12:16.

Arm *brachion* (1023), "the shorter part of the arm, from the shoulder to the elbow," is used metaphorically to denote strength, power, and always in the NT of the power of God, Luke 1:51; John 12:38; **Acts 13:17**; frequently so in the OT, especially in Deuteronomy, the Psalms and Isaiah; see, e.g., Deut. 4:34; 5:15; Ps. 44:3; 71:18, where "strength" is, lit., "arm"; 77:15; Isa. 26:11, where "hand" is, lit., "arm"; 30:30; 40:10-11, etc.

Brought *see Acts 7:36.*

13:18 And about the time of forty years suffered he their manners in the wilderness.

Time *see* Seasons at *Acts 1:7.*

Forty *see Acts 7:23.*

Suffered ... manners *tropophoreo* (5159), "to bear another's manners," is translated "suffered He (their) manners" in **Acts 13:18**.

13:19 And when he had destroyed seven nations in the land of Chanaan, he divided their land to them by lot.

Destroyed *kathaireo* (2507), "to cast down, pull down by force, etc.," is translated "to destroy" in **Acts 13:19**. In **Acts 19:27**, KJV, "should be destroyed," the RV suitably has "should be deposed."

Divided In **Acts 13:19**, the KJV, "He divided their land ... by lot," represents the verb *kataklerodoteo*, from *kata*, suggesting "distribution," *kleros*, "a lot," *didomi*, "to give." The most authentic mss. have *katakleronomeo*, "to distribute," as an inheritance, from *kleronomia*, "an inheritance"; hence RV, "He gave them their land for an inheritance." For *schizo*, **Acts 14:4; 23:7**.

13:20 And after that he gave *unto them* judges about the space of four hundred and fifty years, until Samuel the prophet.

Judges *see* Judge at *Acts 10:42.*

Four hundred *see Acts 5:36.*

Fifty *pentekonta* (4004), is found in Luke 7:41; 16:6; John 8:57; 21:11; **Acts 13:20**; in Mark 6:40 with *kata* (in the most authentic mss.), according to, "by fifties"; in Luke 9:14, with *ana*, "up," used distributively, "fifty each," RV (Luke adds *hosei*, "about").

13:21 And afterward they desired a king: and God gave unto them Saul the son of Cis, a man of the tribe of Benjamin, by the space of forty years.

Afterward *ekeithen* (1564), "thence," is once used to signify "afterwards," in the sense of "then, from that time," **Acts 13:21**. *See also* **Thence** at *Acts 7:4.*

Tribe *phule* (5443), "a company of people united by kinship or habitation, a clan, tribe," is used (a) of the peoples of the earth, Matt. 24:30; in the following the RV has "tribe(-s)" for KJV, "kindred(-s)," Rev. 1:7; 5:9; 7:9; 11:9; 13:7; 14:6; (b) of the "tribes" of Israel, Matt. 19:28; Luke 2:36; 22:30; **Acts 13:21**; Rom. 11:1; Phil. 3:5; Heb. 7:13, 14; Jas. 1:1; Rev. 5:5; 7:4-8; 21:12.

13:22 And when he had removed him, he raised up unto them David to be their king; to whom also he gave testimony, and said, I have found David the *son* of Jesse, a man after mine own heart, which shall fulfil all my will.

Removed *methistemi* (3179), is used transitively in the sense of causing "to remove," in **Acts 13:22**, of the "removing" of King Saul, by bringing about his death; in 1 Cor. 13:2, of "removing" mountains.

Raised *egeiro* (1453), is frequently used in the NT in the sense of "raising" (active voice), or "rising" (middle and passive voices): (a) from sitting, lying, sickness, e.g., Matt. 2:14; 9:5, 7, 19; Jas. 5:15; Rev. 11:1; (b) of causing to appear, or, in the passive, appearing, or raising up so as to occupy a place in the midst of people, Matt. 3:9; 11:11; Mark 13:22; **Acts 13:22**. It is thus said of Christ in **Acts 13:23**; (c) of rousing, stirring up, or "rising" against, Matt. 24:7; Mark 13:8; (d) of "raising buildings," John 2:19-20; (e) of "raising or rising" from the dead; (1) of Christ, Matt. 16:21; and frequently elsewhere (but not in Phil., 2 Thess., 1 Tim., Titus, Jas., 2 Pet., 1, 2, 3 John, and Jude); (2) of Christ's "raising" the dead, Matt. 11:5; Mark 5:41; Luke 7:14; John 12:1, 9, 17; (3) of the act of the disciples, Matt. 10:8; (4) of the resurrection of believers, Matt. 27:52; John 5:21; 1 Cor. 15:15-16, 29, 32, 35, 42-44 52; 2 Cor. 1:9; 4:14; of unbelievers, Matt. 12:42. *Egeiro* stands in contrast to *anistemi* (when used with reference to resurrection) in this respect, that *egeiro* is frequently used both in the transitive sense of "raising up" and the intransitive of "rising," whereas *anistemi* is comparatively infrequent in the transitive use. *See also* Lifted at *Acts 3:7*.

Testimony *see* Report at *Acts 6:3*.

Fulfill *poieo*, "to do," is so rendered in the RV, for KJV "fulfill," in **Acts 13:22**; Eph. 2:3; Rev. 17:17.

Will *thelema* (2307), signifies (a) objectively, "that which is willed, of the will of God," e.g., Matt. 18:14; Mark 3:35, the fulfilling being a sign of spiritual relationship to the Lord, John 4:34; 5:30; 6:39, 40; **Acts 13:22**, plural, "my desires"; Rom. 2:18; 12:2, lit., "the will of God, the good and perfect and acceptable"; here the repeated article is probably resumptive, the adjectives describing the will, as in the Eng. versions; Gal. 1:4; Eph. 1:9; 5:17, "of the Lord"; Col. 1:9; 4:12; 1 Thess. 4:3; 5:18, where it means "the gracious design," rather than "the determined resolve"; 2 Tim. 2:26, which should read "which have been taken captive by him" [(*autou*), i.e., by the Devil; the RV, "by the Lord's servant" is an interpretation; it does not correspond to the Greek] unto His (*ekeinou*) will" (i.e., "God's will"; the different pronoun refers back to the subject of the sentence, viz., God); Heb. 10:10; Rev. 4:11, RV, "because of Thy will"; of human will, e.g., 1 Cor. 7:37; (b) subjectively, the "will" being spoken of as the emotion of being desirous, rather than as the thing "willed"; of the "will" of God, e.g., Rom. 1:10; 1 Cor. 1:1; 2 Cor. 1:1; 8:5; Eph. 1:1, 5, 11; Col. 1:1; 2 Tim. 1:1; Heb. 10:7, 9, 36; 1 John 2:17; 5:14; of human "will," e.g., John 1:13; Eph. 2:3, "the desires of the flesh"; 1 Pet. 4:3 (in some texts); 2 Pet. 1:21.

13:23 Of this man's seed hath God according to *his* promise raised unto Israel a Saviour, Jesus:

Raised *see Acts 13:22*. *See also* Lifted at *Acts 3:7*.

Saviour *see Acts 5:31*.

13:24 When John had first preached before his coming the baptism of repentance to all the people of Israel.

Preached *see Acts 3:20*.

Before In **Acts 13:24** *prosopon* is translated "before" (lit., "before the presence of His coming").

Coming *eisodos* (1529), "an entrance" (*eis*, "in," *hodos*, "a way"), "an entering in," is once translated "coming," **Acts 13:24**, of the coming of Christ into the nation of Israel. For its meaning "entrance" see 1 Thess. 1:9; 2:1; Heb. 10:19; 2 Pet. 1:11.

13:25 And as John fulfilled his course, he said, Whom think ye that I am? I am not *he*. But, behold, there cometh one after me, whose shoes of *his* feet I am not worthy to loose.

Course *dromos* (1408), properly, "a running, a race" (from *edramon*, "to run"), hence, metaphorically, denotes "a career, course of occupation, or of life," viewed in a special aspect, **Acts 13:25**; **20:24**; 2 Tim. 4:7.

Think *huponoeo* (5282), "to suppose, conjecture, surmise," is translated "deemed" in **Acts 27:27**, KJV (RV, "surmised"); in **13:25**, "think ye" (KJV); RV, "suppose ye"; in **25:18**, supposed.

Worthy *axios* (514), "of weight, worth, worthy," is said of persons and their deeds: (a) in a good sense, e.g., Matt. 10:10, 11, 13 (twice), 37 (twice), 38; 22:8; Luke 7:4; 10:7; 15:19, 21; John 1:27; **Acts 13:25**; 1 Tim. 5:18; 6:1; Heb. 11:38; Rev. 3:4; 4:11; 5:2, 4, 9, 12; (b) in a bad sense, Luke 12:48; 23:15; **Acts 23:29**; **25:11**, **25**; **26:31**; Rom. 1:32; Rev. 16:6.

Loose *luo* (3089), "to loose," is rendered "to unloose" in Mark 1:7; Luke 3:16; John 1:27; in **Acts 13:25**, RV.

13:26 Men *and* brethren, children of the stock of Abraham, and whosoever among you feareth God, to you is the word of this salvation sent.

Men *see Acts 1:16*.

Stock *see* Kindred at *Acts 4:6*.

Feareth *see* Feared at *Acts 10:2*.

Word *see* Words at *Acts 2:40*.

Sent *see Acts 7:12*.

13:27 For they that dwell at Jerusalem, and their rulers, because they knew him not, nor yet the voices of the prophets which are read every sabbath day, they have fulfilled *them* in condemning *him*.

Rulers *see Acts 3:17*.

Knew … not *agnoeo* (50), signifies (a) "to be ignorant, not to know," either intransitively, 1 Cor. 14:38 (in the 2nd occurrence in this verse, the RV text translates the active voice, the margin the passive); 1 Tim. 1:13, lit., "being ignorant (I did it)"; Heb. 5:2, "ignorant"; or transitively, 2 Pet. 2:12, KJV, "understand not," RV, "are ignorant (of)"; **Acts 13:27**, "knew (Him) not"; **17:23**, RV, "(what ye worship) in ignorance," for KJV, "(whom ye) ignorantly (worship)," lit., "(what) not knowing (ye worship"; also rendered by the verb "to be ignorant that," or "to be ignorant of," Rom. 1:13; 10:3; 11:25; 1 Cor. 10:1; 12:1; 2 Cor. 1:8; 2:11; 1 Thess. 4:13; to know not, Rom. 2:4; 6:3; 7:1; to be unknown (passive voice), 2 Cor. 6:9; Gal. 1:22; (b) "not to understand," Mark 9:32; Luke 9:45.

Read *see Acts 8:28.*

Condemning *krino* (2919), "to distinguish, choose, give an opinion upon, judge," sometimes denotes "to condemn," e.g., **Acts 13:27**; Rom. 2:27; Jas. 5:9 (in the best mss.).

13:28 And though they found no cause of death *in him*, yet desired they Pilate that he should be slain.

Found *see* **Finding** at *Acts 4:21.*

Cause *aitia* (156), probably has the primary meaning of "a cause, especially an occasion of something evil, hence a charge, an accusation." It is used in a forensic sense, of (a) an accusation, **Acts 25:18** (RV, "charge"), **27**; (b) a crime, Matt. 27:37; Mark 15:26, John 18:38; 19:4, 6; **Acts 13:28**; **23:28**; **28:18**.

Slain *see Acts 2:23.*

13:29 And when they had fulfilled all that was written of him, they took *him* down from the tree, and laid *him* in a sepulchre.

Fulfilled *teleo* (5055), "to end" (akin to *telos*, "an end"), signifies, among its various meanings, "to give effect to," and is translated "fulfill," of the Law, intentionally, Jas. 2:8, or unconsciously, Rom. 2:27; of the prophetic Scriptures concerning the death of Christ, **Acts 13:29**; prohibitively, of the lust of the flesh, Gal. 5:16.

Took *kathaireo* (2507), "to take down" (*kata*), besides its meaning of "putting down by force," was the technical term for the "removal" of the body afler crucifixion, Mark 15:36, 46; Luke 23:53; **Acts 13:29**.

Tree *see Acts 5:30.*

Laid *see Acts 3:2.*

Sepulchre *mnemeion* (3419), primarily denotes "a memorial" (akin to *mnaomai*, "to remember"), then, "a monument" (the significance of the word rendered "tombs," KJV, "sepulchres," in Luke 11:47), anything done to preserve the memory of things and persons; it usually denotes a tomb, and is translated either "tomb" or "sepulchre" or "grave." Apart from the Gospels, it is found only in **Acts 13:29**. Among the Hebrews it was generally a cavern, closed by a door or stone, often decorated. Cf. Matt. 23:29.

13:30 But God raised him from the dead:

Raised *see* **Lifted** at *Acts 3:7.*

13:31 And he was seen many days of them which came up with him from Galilee to Jerusalem, who are his witnesses unto the people.

Many *see Acts 2:40.*

Came *sunanabaino* (4872), "to come up with" (*sun*, "with," *ana*, "up"), is used in Mark 15:41; **Acts 13:31**.

Witnesses *see Acts 1:8.*

13:32 And we declare unto you glad tidings, how that the promise which was made unto the fathers,

Declare … glad tidings *euangelizo* (2097), is almost always used of "the good news" concerning the Son of God as proclaimed in the gospel [exceptions are e.g., Luke 1:19; 1 Thess. 3:6, in which the phrase "to bring (or show) good (or glad) tidings" does not refer to the gospel]; Gal. 1:8 (2nd part). With reference to the gospel the phrase "to bring, or declare, good, or glad, tidings" is used in **Acts 13:32**; Rom. 10:15; Heb. 4:2. In Luke 4:18 the RV "to preach good tidings" gives the correct quotation from Isaiah, rather than the KJV "to preach the Gospel." In the Sept. the verb is used of any message intended to cheer the hearers, e.g. 1 Sam. 31:9; 2 Sam. 1:20. *See also* **Preach** at *Acts 5:42.*

13:33 God hath fulfilled the same unto us their children, in that he hath raised up Jesus again; as it is also written in the second psalm, Thou art my Son, this day have I begotten thee.

Fulfilled *ekpleroo* (1603), strengthened formof accomplish, "to fulfill," lit., "fill out," is used in **Acts 13:33**, of the fulfillment of a divine promise of the resurrection of Christ.

Raised *see Acts 2:24. See also* **Lifted** at *Acts 3:7.*

Second In **Acts 13:33** some mss. have *protos*, "(in the) first (psalm)"; the 1st and 2nd Psalms were originally one, forming a prologue to the whole book; hence the numbering in the Sept.

Psalm *see* **Psalms** at *Acts 1:20.*

Thou *see Acts 9:5.*

Son *The Son of God* In this title the word "Son" is used sometimes (a) of relationship, sometimes (b) of the expression of character. "Thus, e.g., when the disciples so addressed Him, Matt. 14:33; 16:16; John 1:49, when the centurion so spoke of Him, Matt. 27:54, they probably meant that (b) He was a manifestation of God in human form. But in such passages as Luke 1:32, 35; **Acts 13:33**, which refer to the humanity of the Lord Jesus, ... the word is used in sense (a).

"The Lord Jesus Himself used the full title on occasion, John 5:25; 9:35 [some mss. have 'the Son of Man'; see RV marg.]; 11:4, and on the more frequent occasions on which He spoke of Himself as 'the Son,' the words are to be understood as an abbreviation of 'the Son of God,' not of 'The Son of Man'; this latter He always expressed in full; see Luke 10:22; John 5:19, etc. John uses both the longer and shorter forms of the title in his Gospel, see 3:16-18; 20:31, e.g., and in his Epistles; cf. Rev. 2:18. So does the writer of Hebrews, 1:2; 4:14; 6:6, etc. An eternal relation subsisting between the Son and the Father in the Godhead is to be understood. That is to say, the Son of God, in His eternal relationship with the Father, is not so entitled because He at any time began to derive His being from the Father (in which case He could not be co-eternal with the Father), but because He is and ever has been the expression of what the Father is; cf. John 14:9, 'he that hath seen Me hath seen the Father.' The words of Heb. 1:3, 'Who being the effulgence of His (God's) glory, and the very image of His (God's) substance' are a definition of what is meant by 'Son of God.' Thus absolute Godhead, not Godhead in a secondary or derived sense, is intended in the title."

Other titles of Christ as the "Son of God" are: "His Son," 1 Thess. 1:10 (in **Acts 13:13, 26**, RV, *pais* is rendered "servant"); "His own Son," Rom. 8:32; "My beloved Son," Matt. 3:17; "His Only Begotten Son," John 3:16; "the Son of His love," Col. 1:13.

"The Son is the eternal object of the Father's love, John 17:24, and the sole Revealer of the Father's character, John 1:14; Heb. 1:3. The words, 'Father' and 'Son,' are never in the NT so used as to suggest that the Father existed before the Son; the Prologue to the Gospel according to John distinctly asserts that the Word existed 'in the beginning,' and that this Word is the Son, Who 'became flesh and dwelt among us.'"

In addressing the Father in His prayer in John 17 He says, "Thou lovedst Me before the foundation of the world." Accordingly in the timeless past the Father and the "Son" existed in that relationship, a relationship of love, as well as of absolute Deity. In this passage the "Son" gives evidence that there was no more powerful plea in the Father's estimation than that coeternal love existing between the Father and Himself. The declaration "Thou art My Son, this day have I begotten Thee," Ps. 2:7, quoted in **Acts 13:33**; Heb. 1:5; 5:5, refers to the birth of Christ, not to His resurrection. In **Acts 13:33** the verb "raise up" is used of the raising up of a person to occupy a special position in the nation, as of David in verse **22** (so of Christ as a Prophet in **3:22** and **7:37**). The word "again" in the KJV in v. **33** represents nothing in the original. The RV rightly omits it. In v. **34** the statement as to the resurrection of Christ receives the greater stress in this respect through the emphatic contrast to that in v. **33** as to His being raised up in the nation, a stress imparted by the added words "from the dead." Accordingly v. **33** speaks of His incarnation, v. **34** of His resurrection. In Heb. 1:5, that the declaration refers to the Birth is confirmed by the contrast in verse 6. Here the word "again" is rightly placed in the RV, "when He again bringeth in the Firstborn into the world." This points on to His second advent, which is set in contrast to His first advent, when God brought His Firstborn into the world the first time. So again in Heb. 5:5, where the High Priesthood of Christ is shown to fulfill all that was foreshadowed in the Levitical priesthood, the passage stresses the facts of His humanity, the days of His flesh, His perfect obedience and His sufferings. *See also* ***Acts 7:56.***

Begotten *gennao* (1080), "to beget," in the passive voice, "to be born," is chiefly used of men "begetting" children, Matt. 1:2-16; more rarely of women "begetting" children, Luke 1:13, 57, "brought forth"; 23:29; John 16:21, "is delivered of," and of the child, "is born." In Gal. 4:24, it is used allegorically, to contrast Jews under bondage to the Law, and spiritual Israel, KJV, "gendereth," RV, "bearing children," to contrast the natural birth of Ishmael and the supernatural birth of Isaac. In Matt. 1:20 it is used of conception, "that which is conceived in her." It is used of the act of God in the birth of Christ, **Acts 13:33**; Heb. 1:5; 5:5, quoted from Psalm 2:7, none of which indicate that Christ became the Son of God at His birth.

13:34 And as concerning that he raised him up from the dead, *now* no more to return to corruption, he said on this wise, I will give you the sure mercies of David.

Raised *see* ***Acts 2:24.***

Return *see* Returned at *Acts 1:12*.

Corruption *see Acts 2:27*.

On this wise *see Acts 7:6*.

Sure *pistos* (4103), a verbal adjective, akin to *peitho*, is used in two senses, (a) passive, "faithful, to be trusted, reliable," said of God, e.g., 1 Cor. 1:9; 10:13; 2 Cor. 1:18 (KJV, "true"); 2 Tim. 2:13; Heb. 10:23; 11:11; 1 Pet. 4:19; 1 John 1:9; of Christ, e.g., 2 Thess. 3:3; Heb. 2:17; 3:2; Rev. 1:5; 3:14; 19:11; of the words of God, e.g., **Acts 13:34**, "sure"; 1 Tim. 1:15; 3:1 (KJV, "true"); 4:9; 2 Tim. 2:11; Titus 1:9; 3:8; Rev. 21:5; 22:6; of servants of the Lord, Matt. 24:45; 25:21, 23; **Acts 16:15**; 1 Cor. 4:2, 17; 7:25; Eph. 6:21; Col. 1:7; 4:7, 9; 1 Tim. 1:12; 3:11; 2 Tim. 2:2; Heb. 3:5; 1 Pet. 5:12; 3 John 5; Rev. 2:13; 17:14; of believers, Eph. 1:1; Col. 1:2; (b) active, signifying "believing, trusting, relying," e.g., **Acts 16:1** (feminine); 2 Cor. 6:15; Gal. 3:9 seems best taken in this respect, as the context lays stress upon Abraham's "faith" in God, rather than upon his "faithfulness." In John 20:27 the context requires the active sense, as the Lord is reproaching Thomas for his want of "faith." With regard to believers, they are spoken of sometimes in the active sense, sometimes in the passive, i.e., sometimes as believers, sometimes as "faithful." See Lightfoot on Galatians, p. 155.

Mercies In **Acts 13:34**, *hosia*, lit., "holy things," is translated "the holy and sure blessings," RV; the KJV, following the mss. in which the words "holy and" are absent, has "the sure mercies," but notices the full phrase in the margin.

13:35 Wherefore he saith also in another *psalm*, Thou shalt not suffer thine Holy One to see corruption.

Psalm *see* Psalms at *Acts 1:20*.

Holy *see Acts 2:27*.

Suffer *see Acts 2:27*.

13:36 For David, after he had served his own generation by the will of God, fell on sleep, and was laid unto his fathers, and saw corruption:

Served *hupereteo* (5256), "to do the service of a *huperetes*," properly, "to serve as a rower on a ship," is used (a) of David, as serving the counsel of God in his own generation, **Acts 13:36**, RV, expressive of the lowly character of his service for God; (b) of Paul's toil in working with his hands, and his readiness to avoid any pose of ecclesiastical superiority, **Acts 20:34**; (c) of the service permitted to Paul's friends to render to him, **24:23**.

Will In **Acts 13:36**, KJV, *boule*, "counsel" (RV), is translated "will." *See also* Counsel at *Acts 2:23*.

Sleep *see* Asleep at *Acts 7:60*.

Laid *prostithemi* (4369), ."to put to, add," is used in the passive voice in **Acts 13:36**, "was laid" (unto his fathers), of the burial of David.

Corruption *see Acts 2:27*.

13:37 But he, whom God raised again, saw no corruption.

Raised *see* Lifted at *Acts 3:7*.

Corruption *see Acts 2:27*.

13:38 Be it known unto you therefore, men *and* brethren, that through this man is preached unto you the forgiveness of sins:

Preached *see Acts 4:2*.

Forgiveness *see Acts 5:31*. *See also* Remission at *Acts 2:38*.

13:39-40 And by him all that believe are justified from all things, from which ye could not be justified by the law of Moses. Beware therefore, lest that come upon you, which is spoken of in the prophets;

Beware *blepo* (991), "to see," is applied to mental vision, and is sometimes used by way of warning "to take heed" against an object, Mark 8:15; 12:38; **Acts 13:40**; Phil. 3:2 (three times); in Col. 2:8, RV, "take heed," marg., "see whether."

Lest *me* (3361), a negative particle, often used as a conjunction, is frequently translated "lest," e.g., Mark 13:36 (in v. 5, RV, "that no," for KJV, "lest"); **Acts 13:40**; **23:10**.

13:41 Behold, ye despisers, and wonder, and perish: for I work a work in your days, a work which ye shall in no wise believe, though a man declare it unto you.

Despisers *kataphronetes* (2707), lit., "one who thinks down against," hence, "a despiser," is found in **Acts 13:41**. In the Sept., Hab. 1:5; 2:5 and Zeph. 3:4.

Perish *aphanizo* (853), "to make unseen" (*a*, negative, *phaino*, "to cause to appear"), in the passive voice, is translated "perish" in **Acts 13:41** (RV, marg., "vanish away").

Work *see Acts 5:38*.

Man *tis* (5100), "some one, a certain one," is rendered "a man," "a certain man," e.g., in Matt. 22:24; Mark 8:4, KJV (RV, "one"); 12:19; John 3:3, 5; 6:50; 14:23; 15:6, 13; **Acts 13:41**, KJV (RV, "one"); 1 Cor. 4:2; 1 Tim. 1:8; 2 Tim. 2:5, 21; Jas. 2:14, 18; 1 Pet. 2:19; 1 John 4:20.

Declare *ekdiegeomai* (1555), properly, "to narrate in full," came to denote, "to tell, declare"; it is used in **Acts 13:41**; **15:3**.

13:42 And when the Jews were gone out of the synagogue, the Gentiles besought that these words might be preached to them the next sabbath.

Gone out of *exeimi* (1826), "to go out" (*ex*, "out," *eimi* "to go"), is rendered "went out" in **Acts 13:42**; in **27:43**, "got," of mariners getting to shore; in **17:15**, "departed"; in **20:7**, "to depart."

Words *see Acts 2:14*.

Preached *see Acts 8:25*.

Next *metaxu* (3342), signifies "between, next," in **Acts 13:42**. *See also* **Between** at *Acts 12:6*.

13:43 Now when the congregation was broken up, many of the Jews and religious proselytes followed Paul and Barnabas: who, speaking to them, persuaded them to continue in the grace of God.

Congregation *sunagoge* (4864), lit., "a place where people assemble." In **Acts 13:43** the RV suitably has "synagogue," for the KJV "congregation," the building standing by metonymy for the people therein (cf. Matt. 10:17, etc.). In Jas. 2:2 (KJV, "assembly") the word is "synagogue" (RV).

Religious *sebomai* (4576), "to feel awe," whether before God or man, "to worship," is translated "devout," in **Acts 13:43**, RV (KJV, "religious"); **13:50**; **17:4**, **17**.

Proselytes *see Acts 2:10*.

Speaking *proslaleo* (4354), "to speak to or with," is used in **Acts 13:43** and **28:20**.

Persuaded *peitho* (3982), in the active voice, signifies "to apply persuasion, to prevail upon or win over, to persuade," bringing about a change of mind by the influence of reason or moral considerations, e.g., in Matt. 27:20; 28:14; **Acts 13:43**; **19:8**; in the passive voice, "to be persuaded, believe," e.g., Luke 16:31; 20:6; **Acts 17:4**, RV (KJV, "believed"); **21:14**; **26:26**; Rom. 8:38; 14:14; 15:14; 2 Tim. 1:5, 12; Heb. 6:9; 11:13, in some mss.; 13:18, RV (KJV, "trust").

Continue *see* **Continued** at *Acts 12:16*. *See also* **Cleave** at *Acts 11:23*.

13:44 And the next sabbath day came almost the whole city together to hear the word of God.

Next *erchomai* (2064), "to come," is used in the present participle in **Acts 13:44**, "(the) next (sabbath)." *See also* **Could** at *Acts 4:14*.

Came *sunago*, "to gather together," is always so rendered in RV, e.g., Matt. 27:62; Mark 7:1; Luke 22:66; **Acts 13:44**; **15:6**; **20:7**.

Almost *schedon* (4975), is used either (a) of locality, **Acts 19:26**, or (b) of degree, **Acts 13:44**; Heb. 9:22.

City *polis* (4172), primarily "a town enclosed with a wall" (perhaps from a root *ple*–, signifying "fullness," whence also the Latin *pleo*, "to fill," Eng., "polite, polish, politic, etc."), is used also of the heavenly Jerusalem, the abode and community of the redeemed, Heb. 11:10, 16; 12:22; 13:14. In the Apocalypse it signifies the visible capital of the heavenly kingdom, as destined to descend to earth in a coming age e.g., Rev. 3:12; 21:2, 14, 19. By metonymy the word stands for the inhabitants, as in the English use, e.g., Matt. 8:34; 12:25; 21:10; Mark 1:33; **Acts 13:44**.

13:45 But when the Jews saw the multitudes, they were filled with envy, and spake against those things which were spoken by Paul, contradicting and blaspheming.

Filled *see Acts 2:4*.

Envy *zelos*, "zeal or jealousy," translated "envy" in the KJV, in **Acts 13:45**; Rom. 13:13; 1 Cor. 3:3; 2 Cor. 12:20; Jas. 3:14, 16, is to be distinguished from *phthonos*, and, apart from the meanings "zeal" and "indignation," is always translated "jealousy" in the RV. The distinction lies in this, that "envy" desires to deprive another of what he has, "jealousy" desires to have the same or the same sort of thing for itself. *See also* **Indignation** at *Acts 5:17*.

Spake against *antilego* (483), "to speak against," is so rendered in Luke 2:34; John 19:12; **Acts 13:45**, KJV (RV, "contradicted"); **28:19**, **22**.

Contradicting *antilego* (483), lit., "to speak against" (*anti*, "against," *lego*, "to speak"), is translated "contradict" in **Acts 13:45**.

13:46 Then Paul and Barnabas waxed bold, and said, It was necessary that the word of God should first have been spoken to you: but seeing ye put it from you, and judge yourselves unworthy of everlasting life, lo, we turn to the Gentiles.

Bold *see* **Boldly** at *Acts 9:27*.

Necessary *see* **Near** at *Acts 10:24*.

Put *see* **Thrust** at *Acts 7:27*.

Unworthy In **Acts 13:46**, "unworthy" represents the adjective *axios*, preceded by the negative *ouk*.

13:47 For so hath the Lord commanded us, *saying*, I have set thee to be a light of the Gentiles, that thou shouldest be for salvation unto the ends of the earth.

Commanded *entello* (1781), signifies "to enjoin upon, to charge with"; it is used in the Middle Voice in the sense of commanding, Matt. 19:7; 28:20; Mark 10:3; 13:34; John 8:5; 15:14, 17; **Acts 13:47**; Heb. 9:20; 11:22, "gave commandment."

Set *see* Put at *Acts 1:7.*

Light *phos* (5457), akin to *phao*, "to give light" (from roots *pha–* and *phan–*, expressing "light as seen by the eye," and, metaphorically, as "reaching the mind," whence *phaino*, "to make to appear," *phaneros*, "evident," etc.); cf. Eng., "phosphorus" (lit., "light-bearing"). "Primarily light is a luminous emanation, probably of force, from certain bodies, which enables the eye to discern form and color. Light requires an organ adapted for its reception (Matt. 6:22). Where the eye is absent, or where it has become impaired from any cause, light is useless. Man, naturally, is incapable of receiving spiritual light inasmuch as he lacks the capacity for spiritual things, 1 Cor. 2:14. Hence believers are called 'sons of light,' Luke 16:8, not merely because they have received a revelation from God, but because in the New Birth they have received the spiritual capacity for it. "Apart from natural phenomena, light is used in Scripture of (a) the glory of God's dwellingplace, 1 Tim. 6:16; (b) the nature of God, 1 John 1:5; (c) the impartiality of God, Jas. 1:17; (d) the favor of God, Ps. 4:6; of the King, Prov. 16:15; of an influential man, Job 29:24; (e) God, as the illuminator of His people, Isa. 60:19, 20; (f) the Lord Jesus as the illuminator of men, John 1:4, 5, 9; 3:19; 8:12; 9:5; 12:35, 36, 46; **Acts 13:47**; (g) the illuminating power of the Scriptures, Ps. 119:105; and of the judgments and commandments of God, Isa. 51:4; Prov. 6:23, cf. Ps. 43:3; (h) the guidance of God Job 29:3; Ps. 112:4; Isa. 58:10; and, ironically, of the guidance of man, Rom. 2:19; (i) salvation, 1 Pet. 2:9; (j) righteousness, Rom. 13:12; 2 Cor. 11:14, 15; 1 John 2:9, 10; (k) witness for God, Matt. 5:14, 16; John 5:35; (l) prosperity and general well-being, Esth. 8:16; Job 18:18; Isa. 58:8-10."

Ends *eschatos* (2078), "last, utmost, extreme," is used as a noun (a) of time, rendered "end" in Heb. 1:2, RV, "at the "end" of these days," i.e., at the "end" of the period under the Law, for KJV, "in these last days"; so in 1 Pet. 1:20, "at the end of the times." In 2 Pet. 2:20, the plural, *ta eschata*, lit., "the last things," is rendered "the latter end," KJV, (RV, "the last state"); the same phrase is used in Matt. 12:45; Luke 11:26; (b) of place, **Acts 13:47**, KJV, "ends (of the earth)," RV, "uttermost part." *See also* Uttermost at *Acts 1:8.*

13:48 And when the Gentiles heard this, they were glad, and glorified the word of the Lord: and as many as were ordained to eternal life believed.

Glad *see Acts 11:23.*

Glorified *doxazo* (1392), primarily denotes "to suppose" (from *doxa*, "an opinion"); in the NT (a) "to magnify, extol, praise" (see *doxa* below), especially of "glorifying"; God, i.e., ascribing honor to Him, acknowledging Him as to His being, attributes and acts, i.e., His glory, e.g., Matt. 5:16; 9:8; 15:31; Rom. 15:6, 9; Gal. 1:24; 1 Pet. 4:16; the Word of the Lord, **Acts 13:48**; the Name of the Lord, Rev. 15:4; also of "glorifying" oneself, John 8:54; Rev. 18:7; (b) "to do honor to, to make glorious," e.g., Rom. 8:30; 2 Cor. 3:10; 1 Pet. 1:8, "full of glory," passive voice (lit., "glorified"); said of Christ, e.g., John 7:39; 8:54, RV, "glorifieth," for KJV, "honor" and "honoreth" (which would translate *timao*, "to honor"); of the Father, e.g., John 13:31, 32; 21:19; 1 Pet. 4:11; of "glorifying" one's ministry, Rom. 11:13, RV, "glorify" (KJV, "magnify"); of a member of the body, 1 Cor. 12:26, "be honored" (RV marg., "be glorified"). *See also* Rejoicing at *Acts 5:41.*

Ordained *tasso* (5021), "to place in order, arrange," signifies "to appoint," e.g., of the place where Christ had "appointed" a meeting with His disciples after His resurrection, Matt. 28:16; of positions of military and civil authority over others, whether "appointed" by men, Luke 7:8, or by God, Rom. 13:1, "ordained." It is said of those who, having believed the gospel, "were ordained to eternal life," **Acts 13:48**. The house of Stephanas at Corinth had "set themselves" to the ministry of the saints (KJV, "addicted"), 1 Cor. 16:15. Other instances of the arranging of special details occur in Acts 15:2; 22:10; 28:23.

13:49 And the word of the Lord was published throughout all the region.

Word *see* Words at *Acts 2:40.*

Published *diaphero* (1308), used (a) transitively, means "to carry through" or "about" (*dia*, "through," *phero*, "to carry"), Mark 11:16 ("carry ... through"); **Acts 13:49; 27:27** ("driven to and fro"); (b) intransitively, (1) "to differ," Rom. 2:18; Gal. 2:6; Phil. 1:10; (2) "to excel, be better," e.g., Matt. 6:26; 10:31 ("of more value"); 12:12; Luke 12:7, 24; 1 Cor. 15:41; Gal. 4:1; some would put Rom. 2:18 and Phil. 1:10 here (see marg.).

Region *see* Regions at *Acts 8:1.*

13:50 But the Jews stirred up the devout and honourable women, and the chief men of the city,

and raised persecution against Paul and Barnabas, and expelled them out of their coasts.

Stirred up *parotruno* (3951), from *para*, used intensively, beyond measure, and *otruno*, "to urge on, rouse," occurs in **Acts 13:50**, "stirred up."

Devout *see* Religious at *Acts 13:43*.

Honourable *euschemon* (2158), signifies "elegant, comely, of honorable position," KJV, "honorable," RV, "of honorable estate," Mark 15:43; **Acts 13:50**; **17:12**; for other renderings in 1 Cor. 7:35 and 12:24

Chief *protos* (4413), denotes "the first," whether in time or place. It is translated "chief" in Mark 6:21, RV, of men of Galilee, in **Acts 13:50**, of men in a city; in **28:7**, of the "chief" man in the island of Melita; in **17:4**, of "chief" women in a city; in **28:17**, of Jews; in 1 Tim. 1:15-16, of a sinner. In the following, where the KJV has "chief," or "chiefest," the RV renderings are different: Matt. 20:27 and Mark 10:44, "first"; Luke 19:47 and **Acts 25:2**, "principal men"; **Acts 16:12**, said of Philippi, "the first (city) of the district," RV, for incorrect KJV, "the chief city of that part of Macedonia." Amphipolis was the "chief" city of that part. *Protos* here must mean the first in the direction in which the apostle came.

Raised In **Acts 13:50**, KJV, *epegeiro*, "to rouse up, excite," is translated "raised" (RV, "stirred up," as in KJV and RV in **14:2**).

Persecution *see Acts 8:1*.

Coasts *horion* (3725), "the border of a country or district" (cf. Eng., "horizon"), is always used in the plural. The KJV has "coasts," but "borders" in Matt. 4:13; the RV always "borders," Matt. 2:16; 4:13; 8:34; 15:22, 39; 19:1; Mark 5:17; 7:31 (twice); 10:1; **Acts 13:50**. In some of these it signifies territory.

13:51 But they shook off the dust of their feet against them, and came unto Iconium.

Shook *ektinasso* (1621), "to shake out," is used of "shaking off" the dust from the feet, Matt. 10:14; Mark 6:11; **Acts 13:51**; of "shaking out" one's raiment, **Acts 18:6**.

Dust *koniortos* (2868), "raised or flying dust" (*konia*, "dust," *ornumi*, "to stir up"), is found in Matt. 10:14; Luke 9:5; 10:11; **Acts 13:51**; **22:23**.

Feet *see Acts 5:9*.

13:52 And the disciples were filled with joy, and with the Holy Ghost.

Filled *see Acts 2:2*.

Chapter 14

14:1 And it came to pass in Iconium, that they went both together into the synagogue of the Jews, and so spake, that a great multitude both of the Jews and also of the Greeks believed.

Together In **Acts 14:1**, it translates *kata to auto*, "at the same"; it may mean "in the same way" (i.e., as they had entered the synagogue at Pisidian Antioch).

Jews *see Acts 2:10*.

Multitude *see Acts 4:32*.

14:2 But the unbelieving Jews stirred up the Gentiles, and made their minds evil affected against the brethren.

Unbelieving *apeitheo* (544), "to refuse to be persuaded, to refuse belief, to be disobedient," is translated "disobedient," or by the verb "to be disobedient," in the RV of **Acts 14:2** (KJV, "unbelieving"), and **19:9** (KJV, "believed not"); it is absent from the most authentic mss. in **Acts 17:5**; in John 3:36 "obeyeth not," RV (KJV, "believeth not"); in Rom. 2:8 "obey not"; in 10:21, "disobedient"; in 11:30, 31, "were disobedient" (KJV, "have not believed"); so in 15:31; Heb. 3:18; 11:31; in 1 Pet. 2:8, "disobedient"; so in 3:20; in 3:1 and 4:17, "obey not." In 2:7 the best mss. have *apisteo*, "to disbelieve."

Stirred up *epegeiro* (1892), "stirred up" in **Acts 14:2**. *See also Acts 13:50.*

Minds In three places, **Acts 14:2**; Phil. 1:27; Heb. 12:3, the KJV translates *psuche*, "the soul," by "mind" (RV, "soul"). *See also* Soul at *Acts 2:27*.

Evil *see Acts 7:6*.

Affected *kakoo* (2559), from *kakos*, "evil, to treat badly, to hurt," also means "to make evil affected, to embitter," **Acts 14:2**.

14:3 Long time therefore abode they speaking boldly in the Lord, which gave testimony unto the word of his grace, and granted signs and wonders to be done by their hands.

Long *see Acts 8:11*.

Abode *see Acts 12:19*.

Testimony *see* Report at *Acts 6:3*.

Word *see* Words at *Acts 2:40*.

Granted *see* Grant at *Acts 4:29*.

Hands *see Acts 5:12*.

14:4 But the multitude of the city was divided: and part held with the Jews, and part with the apostles.

Divided *schizo* (4977), "to split, to rend open," is said of the veil of the temple, Matt. 27:51; the rending of rocks, Matt. 27:51; the rending of the heavens, Mark 1:10; a garment,

Luke 5:36; John 19:24; a net, John 21:11; in the passive voice, metaphorically, of being divided into factions, **Acts 14:4**; **23:7**. *See also Acts 13:19.*

Held *eimi* (1510), "to be," is used in the imperfect tense, with the preposition, *sun*, "with," in the idiomatic phrase "held with," in **Acts 14:4**, lit., "were with."

Apostles *apostolos* (652), is, lit., "one sent forth" (*apo*, "from," *stello*, "to send"). "The word is used of the Lord Jesus to describe His relation to God, Heb. 3:1; see John 17:3. The twelve disciples chosen by the Lord for special training were so called, Luke 6:13; 9:10. Paul, though he had seen the Lord Jesus, 1 Cor. 9:1; 15:8, had not 'companied with' the Twelve 'all the time' of His earthly ministry, and hence was not eligible for a place among them, according to Peter's description of the necessary qualifications, **Acts 1:22**. Paul was commissioned directly, by the Lord Himself, after His Ascension, to carry the gospel to the Gentiles. "The word has also a wider reference. In **Acts 14:4**, **14**, it is used of Barnabas as well as of Paul; in Rom. 16:7 of Andronicus and Junias. In 2 Cor. 8:23 (RV, margin) two unnamed brethren are called 'apostles of the churches'; in Phil. 2:25 (RV, margin) Epaphroditus is referred to as 'your apostle.' It is used in 1 Thess. 2:6 of Paul, Silas and Timothy, to define their relation to Christ."

14:5 And when there was an assault made both of the Gentiles, and also of the Jews with their rulers, to use *them* despitefully, and to stone them,

Assault *horme* (3730), rendered "assault" in **Acts 14:5**, KJV; RV, "onset," corresponds to *hormao*, to rush.

Rulers *see Acts 3:17.*

Despitefully *hubrizo* (5195), used transitively, denotes "to outrage, treat insolently"; "to entreat shamefully" in Matt. 22:6, RV (KJV, "spitefully"); so in Luke 18:32, RV; in **Acts 14:5** (KJV, "use despitefully"); in 1 Thess. 2:2, KJV and RV; in Luke 11:45, "reproachest."

Stone *see* Stoned at *Acts 7:58.*

14:6 They were ware of *it*, and fled unto Lystra and Derbe, cities of Lycaonia, and unto the region that lieth round about:

Ware of For *sunoida*, translated "were ware" in **Acts 14:6**, KJV (RV, "became aware of it"). *See also* Privy at *Acts 5:2.*

Fled *katapheugo* (2703), "to flee for refuge," is used (a) literally in **Acts 14:6**; (b) metaphorically in Heb. 6:18, of "fleeing" for refuge to lay hold upon hope.

Region *perichoros* (4066), "a country or region round about" *peri*), is translated "region round about" in Matt. 3:5; 14:35, RV; Mark 1:28 (in some mss. Mark 6:55); Luke 3:3, RV; 4:14; 4:37, RV; 7:17; **Acts 14:6**. *See also* Regions at *Acts 8:1.*

14:7-8 And there they preached the gospel.

And there sat a certain man at Lystra, impotent in his feet, being a cripple from his mother's womb, who never had walked:

Impotent *adunatos* (102), from *a*, negative, and *dunatos*, "able, strong," is used (a) of persons, **Acts 14:8**, "impotent"; figuratively, Rom. 15:1, "weak"; (b) of things, "impossible," Matt. 19:26; Mark 10:27; Luke 18:27; Heb. 6:4, 18; 10:4; 11:6; in Rom. 8:3, "for what the Law could not do," is, more lit., "the inability of the law"; the meaning may be either "the weakness of the Law," or "that which was impossible for the Law"; the latter is perhaps preferable; literalism is ruled out here, but the sense is that the Law could neither justify nor impart life.

Cripple *see* Lame at *Acts 3:2.*

Womb *see Acts 3:2.*

14:9 The same heard Paul speak: who stedfastly beholding him, and perceiving that he had faith to be healed,

Stedfastly *see Acts 1:10.*

Beholding *atenizo* (816), from *atenes*, "strained, intent," denotes "to gaze upon," "beholding earnestly," or "steadfastly" in **Acts 14:9**; **23:1**.

Perceiving *eidon* (3708), (akin to *oida*, "to know"), an aorist form used to supply that tense of *horao*, "to see," is translated "to perceive" in Matt. 13:14; Mark 4:12; **Acts 28:26**; in Luke 9:47, KJV (RV, "saw"); in **Acts 14:9**, KJV, "perceiving" (RV, "seeing").

14:10 Said with a loud voice, Stand upright on thy feet. And he leaped and walked.

Stand *see* Stood at *Acts 1:15.*

Upright *orthos* (3717), used of height, denotes "upright," **Acts 14:10**; of line of direction, figuratively, said of paths of righteousness, Heb. 12:13.

Leaped *see* Leaping at *Acts 3:8.*

14:11 And when the people saw what Paul had done, they lifted up their voices, saying in the speech of Lycaonia, The gods are come down to us in the likeness of men.

Lifted *see* Taken up at *Acts 1:9.*

Speech In **Acts 14:11** "the speech of Lycaonia" translates the adverb *Lukaonisti.* Lycaonia was a large country in the center and south of the plateau of Asia Minor; the villages retained the native language, but cities like Lystra probably had a Seleucid tone in their laws and customs (Ramsay on Galatians).

Gods *see* **God** at *Acts 2:23.*

Likeness *homoioo* (3666), "to make like," is used (a) especially in the parables, with the significance of comparing, "likening," or, in the passive voice, "being likened," Matt. 7:24, 26; 11:16; 13:24; 18:23; 22:2 (RV, "likened"); 25:1; Mark 4:30; Luke 7:31; 13:18, RV, "liken" (KJV, "resemble"); v. 20; in several of these instances the point of resemblance is not a specific detail, but the whole circumstances of the parable; (b) of making "like," or, in the passive voice, of being made or becoming "like," Matt. 6:8; **Acts 14:11**, "in the likeness of (men)," lit., "being made like" (aorist participle, passive); Rom. 9:29; Heb. 2:17, of Christ in being "made like" unto His brethren, i.e., in partaking of human nature, apart from sin (cf. v. 14).

14:12 And they called Barnabas, Jupiter; and Paul, Mercurius, because he was the chief speaker.

Chief *hegeomai* (2233), "to lead the way, to preside, rule, be the chief," is used of the ambition "to be chief" among the disciples of Christ, Luke 22:26; of Paul as the "chief" speaker in gospel testimony at Lystra, **Acts 14:12**; of Judas and Silas, as chief (or rather, "leading") men among the brethren at Jerusalem, **Acts 15:22**. In **Acts 14:12** the verb *hegeomai,* "to lead the way, be the chief," is used in the present participle with the article (together equivalent to a noun), followed by the genitive case of *logos,* "speech," with the article, the phrase being rendered "the chief speaker," lit., "the leader of the discourse."

Speech *logos* (3056), akin to *lego,* most frequently rendered "word," signifies "speech," as follows: (a) "discourse," e.g., Luke 20:20, RV, "speech" (KJV, "words"); **Acts 14:12; 20:7**; 1 Cor. 2:1, 4; 4:19, KJV (RV, "word"); 2 Cor. 10:10; (b) "the faculty of speech," e.g., 2 Cor. 11:6; (c) "the manner of speech," e.g., Matt. 5:37, RV, "speech" (KJV, "communication"); Col. 4:6; (d) "manner of instruction," Titus 2:8; 1 Cor. 14:9, RV (KJV, "words"); Eph. 4:29, RV (KJV, "communication").

14:13 Then the priest of Jupiter, which was before their city, brought oxen and garlands unto the gates, and would have done sacrifice with the people.

Priest *hiereus* (2409), "one who offers sacrifice and has the charge of things pertaining thereto," is used (a) of a "priest" of the pagan god Zeus, **Acts 14:13**; (b) of Jewish "priests," e.g., Matt. 8:4; 12:4, 5; Luke 1:5, where allusion is made to the 24 courses of "priests" appointed for service in the Temple (cf. 1 Chron. 24:4ff.); John 1:19; Heb. 8:4; (c) of believers, Rev. 1:6; 5:10; 20:6. Israel was primarily designed as a nation to be a kingdom of "priests," offering service to God, e.g., Ex. 19:6, the Israelites having renounced their obligations, Ex. 20:19, the Aaronic priesthood was selected for the purpose, till Christ came to fulfil His ministry in offering up Himself; since then the Jewish priesthood has been abrogated, to be resumed nationally, on behalf of Gentiles, in the millennial kingdom, Is. 61:6; 66:21. Meanwhile all believers, from Jews and Gentiles, are constituted "a kingdom of priests," Rev. 1:6, "a holy priesthood," 1 Pet. 2:5, and "royal," v. 9. The NT knows nothing of a sacerdotal class in contrast to the laity; all believers are commanded to offer the sacrifices mentioned in Rom. 12:1; Phil. 2:17; 4:18; Heb. 13:15, 16; 1 Pet. 2:5; (d) of Christ, Heb. 5:6; 7:11, 15, 17, 21; 8:4 (negatively); (e) of Melchizedek, as the foreshadower of Christ, Heb. 7:1, 3.

Oxen *tauros* (5022), Latin *taurus,* is translated "oxen" in Matt. 22:4 and **Acts 14:13**; "bulls" in Heb. 9:13 and 10.4.

Garlands *stemma* (4725), denotes "a wreath" (from *stepho,* "to put around, enwreath"), as used in sacrifices, **Acts 14:13**.

Gates *see* **Gate** at *Acts 10:17.*

Sacrifice *thuo* (2380), is used of "sacrificing by slaying a victim," (a) of the "sacrifice" of Christ, 1 Cor. 5:7, RV, "hath been sacrificed" (KJV, "is sacrificed"); (b) of the Passover "sacrifice," Mark 14:12, RV, "they sacrificed" (KJV, "they killed"); Luke 22:7, RV, "(must) be sacrificed," KJV, "(must) be killed"; (c) of idolatrous "sacrifices," **Acts 14:13, 18**; 1 Cor. 10:20 (twice). *See also* **Kill** at *Acts 10:13.*

14:14 *Which* when the apostles, Barnabas and Paul, heard *of,* they rent their clothes, and ran in among the people, crying out,

Apostles *see Acts 14:4.*

Rent *diarrhesso,* or *diaresso* (1284), a late form of *diarrhegnumi,* "to break asunder, rend" (*dia,* "through," and *rhegnumi*), is used of "rending" one's garments, Matt. 26:65; Mark 14:63; **Acts 14:14**.

Ran In **Acts 14:14**, RV, *ekpedao*, "to spring forth," is translated "sprang forth" (this verb is found in the papyri); the KJV, "ran in" translates the mss. which have *eispedao*, "to spring in."

14:15 And saying, Sirs, why do ye these things? We also are men of like passions with you, and preach unto you that ye should turn from these vanities unto the living God, which made heaven, and earth, and the sea, and all things that are therein:

Sirs *see Acts 7:26.*

Things *see Acts 8:12.*

Men *anthropos* (444), is used (a) generally, of "a human being, male or female," without reference to sex or nationality, e.g., Matt. 4:4; 12:35; John 2:25; (b) in distinction from God, e.g., Matt. 19:6; John 10:33; Gal. 1:11; Col. 3:23; (c) in distinction from animals, etc., e.g., Luke 5:10; (d) sometimes, in the plural, of "men and women," people, e.g., Matt. 5:13, 16; in Mark 11:2 and 1 Tim. 6:16, lit., "no one of men"; (e) in some instances with a suggestion of human frailty and imperfection e.g., 1 Cor. 2:5; **Acts 14:15** (2nd part); (f) in the phrase translated "after man," "after the manner of men," "as a man" (KJV), lit. "according to (*kata*) man," is used only by the apostle Paul ... (j) as equivalent simply to "a person," or "one," whether "man" or woman, e.g., **Acts 19:16**; Rom. 3:28; Gal. 2:16; Jas. 1:19; 2:24; 3:8 (like the pronoun *tis*, "someone"; *tis* is rendered "man" in Matt. 8:28); or, again (as *tis* sometimes signifies), "a man," e.g., Matt. 17:14; Luke 13:19; (k) definitely, with the article, of some particular person, Matt. 12:13; Mark 3:3, 5; or with the demonstrative pronoun and the article, e.g., Matt. 12:45; Luke 14:30. For "the man of sin," 2 Thess. 2:3. *See also* ***Acts 1:16.***

Passions *homoiopathes* (3663), "of like feelings or affections" (Eng., "homeopathy"), is rendered "of like passions" in **Acts 14:15** (RV marg., "nature"); in Jas. 5:17, RV, ditto (KJV, "subject to like passions").

Turn *see* Turned at *Acts 11:21.*

Vanities *mataios* (3152), "void of result," is used of (a) idolatrous practices, **Acts 14:15**, RV, "vain things" (KJV, "vanities"); (b) the thoughts of the wise, 1 Cor. 3:20; (c) faith, if Christ is not risen, 1 Cor. 15:17; (d) questionings, strifes, etc., Titus 3:9; (e) religion, with an unbridled tongue, Jas. 1:26; (f) manner of life, 1 Pet. 1:18. *See also* Idol at *Acts 7:41.*

14:16 Who in times past suffered all nations to walk in their own ways.

Times For *genea*, rendered "times" in **Acts 14:16**, "time" in **15:21** (RV, "generations"). *See also* Generation at *Acts 2:40.*

Past *paroichomai* (3944), "to have passed by, to be gone by," is used in **Acts 14:16**, of past generations, KJV, "(in times) past," RV, "(in the generations) gone by."

Suffered *eao* (1439), "to let, permit," is translated "to suffer" in Matt. 24:43; Luke 4:41; 22:51; **Acts 14:16**; **16:7**; **19:30**; **28:4**; 1 Cor. 10:13.

Walk *see* Walking at *Acts 9:31*. *See also* Went at *Acts 10:9.*

14:17 Nevertheless he left not himself without witness, in that he did good, and gave us rain from heaven, and fruitful seasons, filling our hearts with food and gladness.

Witness *amarturos* (267), denotes "without witness" (*a*, negative, and *martus*), **Acts 14:17**.

Good *agathopoieo* (15), is used (a) in a general way, "to do well," 1 Pet. 2:15, 20; 3:6, 17; 3 John 11; (b) with pointed reference "to the benefit of another," Luke 6:9, 33, 35; in Mark 3:4 the parts of the word are separated in some mss. Some mss. have it in **Acts 14:17**. Cf. the noun *agathopoiia*, "well-doing," 1 Pet. 4:19, and the adjective *agathopoios*, "doing well," 1 Pet. 2:14. *agathourgeo* (14), for *agathoergeo*, "to do good," is used in **Acts 14:17** (in the best mss.), where it is said of God's beneficence towards man, and 1 Tim. 6:18, where it is enjoined upon the rich.

Rain *huetos* (5205), from *huo*, "to rain," is used especially, but not entirely, of "showers," and is found in **Acts 14:17**; **28:2**; Heb. 6:7; Jas. 5:7; 5:18; Rev. 11:6.

Heaven *ouranothen* (3771), denoting "from heaven," is used of (a) the aerial heaven, **Acts 14:17**; (b) heaven, as the uncreated sphere of God's abode, **26:13**.

Fruitful *karpophoros* (2593), denotes "fruitful," **Acts 14:17**.

Filling *empiplao* (1705), is found in **Acts 14:17**, "filling (your hearts)," of God's provision for mankind.

Hearts *see* Heart at *Acts 2:37.*

Food *see* Bread at *Acts 2:46.*

Gladness *see* Joy at *Acts 2:28.*

14:18 And with these sayings scarce restrained they the people, that they had not done sacrifice unto them.

Sayings In **Acts 14:18**, "with these sayings" is lit., "saying (*lego*) these things." For *lalia*, "saying," John 4:42, KJV.

Scarce *molis* (3433), signifies "with difficulty, hardly" (from *molos*, "toil"). In Luke 9:39, it is rendered "hardly," of the "difficulty" in the departure of a demon. In **Acts 27:7, 8, 16**, where the KJV has three different renderings, "scarce," "hardly," and "much work," respectively, the RV has "with difficulty" in each place. For its other meanings, "scarce, scarcely," see **Acts 14:18**; Rom. 5:7 1 Pet. 4:18.

Restrained *katapauo* (2664), used transitively, signifies "to cause to cease, restrain," **Acts 14:18**; "to cause to rest," Heb. 4:8; intransitively, "to rest," Heb. 4:4, 10.

Sacrifice *see Acts 14:13. See also* Kill at *Acts 10:13.*

14:19 And there came thither *certain* Jews from Antioch and Iconium, who persuaded the people, and, having stoned Paul, drew *him* out of the city, supposing he had been dead.

Came *eperchomai* (1904), "to come or go upon" (*epi*, "upon"), e.g., Luke 1:35; in Luke 21:26, used of "coming" events, suggesting their certainty; in Eph. 2:7, said of the "oncoming" of the ages; in **Acts 14:19**, of Jews coming to (lit., "upon") a place.

Stoned *see Acts 5:26.*

Drew *see* Haling at *Acts 8:3.*

Supposing *see* Supposed at *Acts 7:25.*

14:20 Howbeit, as the disciples stood round about him, he rose up, and came into the city: and the next day he departed with Barnabas to Derbe.

Stood round about *kukloo* (2944), (cf. Eng., cycle"), signifies "to move in a circle, to compass about," as of a city "encompassed" by armies, Luke 21:20; Heb. 11:30; in **Acts 14:20**, "stood round about."

"In our evangelism ... should we not remind our neighbours of the goodness of God in our lives? It is a simple and direct approach."

ROY JOSLIN

Next day *see Acts 4:3. See also* Morrow at *Acts 10:24.*

14:21 And when they had preached the gospel to that city, and had taught many, they returned again to Lystra, and *to* Iconium, and Antioch,

Taught *matheteuo* (3100), is used in the active voice, intransitively, in some mss., in Matt. 27:57, in the sense of being the "disciple" of a person; here, however, the best mss. have the passive voice, lit., "had been made a disciple," as in Matt. 13:52, RV, "who hath been made a disciple." It is used in this transitive sense in the active voice in 28:19 and **Acts 14:21**.

Many *see Acts 9:23.*

14:22 Confirming the souls of the disciples, *and* exhorting them to continue in the faith, and that we must through much tribulation enter into the kingdom of God.

Confirming *episterizo* (1991), "to make to lean upon, strengthen" (*epi*, "upon," *sterix*, "a prop, support"), is used of "confirming" souls **Acts 14:22**, brethren, **15:32**; churches, **15:41**; disciples, **18:23**, in some mss. ("stablishing," RV, "strengthening," KJV); the most authentic mss. have *sterizo* in **18:23**.

Souls *see* Soul at *Acts 2:27.*

Continue *emmeno* (1696), "to remain in" (*en*, "in"), is used of "abiding in a house," **Acts 28:30** (in the best mss.); of "continuing" in the faith, **Acts 14:22**; in the Law, Gal. 3:10; in God's covenant, Heb. 8:9.

Faith *see Acts 6:7.*

Tribulation *thlipsis* (2347), is translated "tribulation" in the RV (for KJV, "affliction") in Mark 4:17; 13:19; plural in 2 Thess. 1:4, KJV, "tribulations," RV, "afflictions"; in **Acts 14:22** "many tribulations" (KJV, "much tribulation"); in Matt. 24:9, "unto tribulation" (KJV, "to be afflicted"); in 2 Cor. 1:4; 7:4; 2 Thess. 1:6, KJV, "tribulation" for RV, "affliction"; RV and KJV, "tribulation(-s)," e.g., in Rom. 2:9; 5:3 (twice); 8:35; 12:12; Eph. 3:13; Rev. 1:9; 2:9, 10, 22. *See also* Persecution at *Acts 11:19.*

Kingdom *basileia* (932), is primarily an abstract noun, denoting "sovereignty, royal power, dominion," e.g., Rev. 17:18, translated "(which) reigneth," lit., "hath a kingdom" (RV marg.); then, by metonymy, a concrete noun, denoting the territory or people over whom a king rules, e.g., Matt. 4:8; Mark 3:24. It is used especially of the "kingdom" of God and of Christ.

"The Kingdom of God is (a) the sphere of God's rule, Ps. 22:28; 145:13; Dan. 4:25; Luke 1:52; Rom. 13:1, 2. Since, however, this earth is the scene of universal rebellion against God, e.g., Luke 4:5, 6; 1 John 5:19; Rev. 11:15-18, the "kingdom" of God is (b) the sphere in which, at any given time, His rule is acknowledged. God has not relinquished His sovereignty in the face of rebellion, demoniac and human, but has declared His purpose to establish it, Dan. 2:44; 7:14; 1 Cor. 15:24, 25. Meantime, seeking willing obedience, He gave His law to a nation and appointed kings to administer His "kingdom" over it, 1 Chron. 28:5. Israel, however, though declaring still a nominal allegiance shared in the common rebellion, Isa. 1:2-4, and, after they had rejected the Son of God, John 1:11 (cf. Matt. 21:33-43), were "cast away," Rom. 11:15, 20, 25. Henceforth God calls upon men everywhere, without distinction of race or nationality, to submit voluntarily to His rule. Thus the "kingdom" is said to be "in mystery" now, Mark 4:11, that is, it does not come within the range of the natural powers of observation, Luke 17:20, but is spiritually discerned, John 3:3 (cf. 1 Cor. 2:14). When, hereafter, God asserts His rule universally, then the "kingdom" will be in glory, that is, it will be manifest to all; cf. Matt. 25:31-34; Phil. 2:9-11; 2 Tim. 4:1, 18. Thus, speaking generally, references to the Kingdom fall into two classes, the first, in which it is viewed as present and involving suffering for those who enter it, 2 Thess. 1:5; the second, in which it is viewed as future and is associated with reward, Matt. 25:34, and glory, 13:43. See also **Acts 14:22.** The fundamental principle of the Kingdom is declared in the words of the Lord spoken in the midst of a company of Pharisees, "the Kingdom of God is in the midst of you," Luke 17:21, marg., that is, where the King is, there is the Kingdom. Thus at the present time and so far as this earth is concerned, where the King is and where His rule is acknowledged, is, first, in the heart of the individual believer, **Acts 4:19**; Eph. 3:17; 1 Pet. 3:15; and then in the churches of God, 1 Cor. 12:3, 5, 11; 14:37; cf. Col. 1:27, where for "in" read "among." Now, the King and His rule being refused, those who enter the Kingdom of God are brought into conflict with all who disown its allegiance, as well as with the desire for ease, and the dislike of suffering and unpopularity, natural to all. On the other hand, subjects of the Kingdom are the objects of the care of God, Matt. 6:33, and of the rejected King, Heb. 13:5."

14:23 And when they had ordained them elders in every church, and had prayed with fasting, they commended them to the Lord, on whom they believed.

Ordained *cheirotoneo* (5500), primarily used of voting in the Athenian legislative assembly and meaning "to stretch forth the hands" (*cheir*, "the hand," *teino*, "to stretch"), is not to be taken in its literal sense; it could not be so taken in its compound *procheirotoneo*, "to choose before," since it is said of God, **Acts 10:41**. *Cheirotoneo* is said of "the appointment" of elders by apostolic missionaries in the various churches which they revisited, **Acts 14:23**, RV, "had appointed," i.e., by the recognition of those who had been manifesting themselves as gifted of God to discharge the functions of elders. It is also said of those who were "appointed" (not by voting, but with general approbation) by the churches in Greece to accompany the apostle in conveying their gifts to the poor saints in Judea, 2 Cor. 8:19.

Elders *presbuteros*, "an elder," is another term for the same person as bishop or overseer. See **Acts 20:17** with verse **28**. The term "elder" indicates the mature spiritual experience and understanding of those so described; the term "bishop," or "overseer," indicates the character of the work undertaken. According to the divine will and appointment, as in the NT, there were to be "bishops" in every local church, **Acts 14:23**; **20:17**; Phil. 1:1; Titus 1:5; Jas. 5:14. Where the singular is used, the passage is describing what a "bishop" should be, 1 Tim. 3:2; Titus 1:7. Christ Himself is spoken of as "the ... Bishop of our souls," 1 Pet. 2:25. *See also* **Old men** at *Acts 2:17*.

Every *see Acts 5:42*.

Fasting *nesteia* (3521), "a fasting, fast" (from *ne*, a negative prefix, and *esthio*, "to eat"), is used (a) of voluntary abstinence from food, Luke 2:37; **Acts 14:23** (some mss. have it in Matt. 17:21 and Mark 9:29); "fasting" had become a common practice among Jews, and was continued among Christians; in **Acts 27:9**, "the Fast" refers to the Day of Atonement, Lev. 16:29; that time of the year would be one of dangerous sailing; (b) of involuntary abstinence (perhaps voluntary is included), consequent upon trying circumstances, 2 Cor. 6:5; 11:27.

Commended *paratithemi* (3908), lit., "to put near" (*para*, "near"), in the Middle Voice, denotes "to place with someone, entrust, commit." In the sense of commending, it is said (a) of the Lord Jesus in "commending" His spirit into the Father's hands, Luke 23:46; (b) of "commending" disciples to God, **Acts 14:23**; (c) of "commending" elders to God, **Acts 20:32**.

14:24-25 And after they had passed throughout Pisidia, they came to Pamphylia.

And when they had preached the word in Perga, they went down into Attalia:

Preached *see Acts 8:25.*

14:26 And thence sailed to Antioch, from whence they had been recommended to the grace of God for the work which they fulfilled.

Thence *see Acts 7:4.*

Sailed *see Acts 13:4.*

Recommended *paradidomi* (3860), lit., to give or deliver over" (*para*, "over" *didomi*, "to give"), is said of "commending," or "committing," servants of God to Him (KJV, "recommend), **Acts 14:26**; **15:40**. *See also* **Committed** at *Acts 8:3.*

Grace *see* **Favour** at *Acts 2:47.*

14:27 And when they were come, and had gathered the church together, they rehearsed all that God had done with them, and how he had opened the door of faith unto the Gentiles.

Rehearsed *anangello* (312), "to bring back word" (*ana*, "back," *angello*, "to announce"), is translated "to rehearse" in **Acts 14:27**; **15:4**, RV.

All *see Acts 4:23.*

Door *thura* (2374), "a door, gate" (Eng., "door" is connected), is used (a) literally, e.g., Matt. 6:6; 27:60; (b) metaphorically, of Christ, John 10:7, 9; of faith, by acceptance of the gospel, **Acts 14:27**; of "openings" for preaching and teaching the Word of God, 1 Cor. 16:9; 2 Cor. 2:12; Col. 4:3; Rev. 3:8; of "entrance" into the Kingdom of God, Matt. 25:10; Luke 13:24-25; of Christ's "entrance" into a repentant believer's heart, Rev. 3:20; of the nearness of Christ's second advent, Matt. 24:33; Mark 13:29; cf. Jas. 5:9; of "access" to behold visions relative to the purposes of God, Rev. 4:1.

14:28 And there they abode long time with the disciples.

Abode *see Acts 12:19.*

Long *In* **Acts 14:28**, KJV, the adjective *oligos*, "little," with the negative *ou*, "not," and qualifying *chronos*, is rendered "long time;" RV, "no little (time)."

Chapter 15

15:1 And certain men which came down from Judaea taught the brethren, *and said*, Except ye be circumcised after the manner of Moses, ye cannot be saved.

Circumcised *see* **Circumcision** at *Acts 7:8.*

Manner *ethos* (1485), "a habit, custom" (akin to the verb *etho*, "to be accustomed"), is always translated "custom" in the RV ("manner" in the KJV of John 19:40; **Acts 15:1**; **25:16**; Heb. 10:25). *See also* **Customs** at *Acts 6:14.*

15:2 When therefore Paul and Barnabas had no small dissension and disputation with them, they determined that Paul and Barnabas, and certain other of them, should go up to Jerusalem unto the apostles and elders about this question.

Had *ginomai* (1096), "to begin to be, come to pass, happen," is rendered "have" in Matt. 18:12; "had" in **Acts 15:2**; "shall have" in 1 Cor. 4:5, lit., "praise shall be," or come to pass.

Small *see Acts 12:18.*

Dissension *stasis* (4714), akin to *histemi*, "to stand," denotes (a) "a standing, stability," Heb. 9:8, "(while as the first tabernacle) is yet standing"; (b) "an insurrection, uproar," Mark 15:7; Luke 23:19, 25; **Acts 19:40**; **24:5**; (c) "a dissension, **Acts 15:2**; **23:7**, **10**.

Disputation *zetesis* (2214), denotes, firstly, "a seeking" (*zeteo*, "to seek"), then, "a debate, dispute, questioning," **Acts 15:2**, **7** (some texts have *suzetesis*, "reasoning," in both verses), RV, "questioning," for KJV, "disputation" and "disputing"; for John 3:25; **Acts 25:20**; 1 Tim. 1:4; 6:4; 2 Tim. 2:23; Titus 3:9.

Determined *see* **Ordained** at *Acts 13:48.*

Question *zetema* (2213), generally speaking, suggesting in a concrete form the subject of an inquiry, occurs in **Acts 15:2**; **18:15**; **23:29**; **25:19**; **26:3**.

15:3 And being brought on their way by the church, they passed through Phenice and Samaria, declaring the conversion of the Gentiles: and they caused great joy unto all the brethren.

Brought ... way *propempo* (4311), "to send forth, to bring on one's way," **Acts 15:3**; **20:38**, RV; **21:5**; Rom. 15:24; 1 Cor. 16:6, 11; 2 Cor. 1:16; Titus 3:13; 3 John 6.

Declaring *see* **Declare** at *Acts 13:41.*

Conversion *epistrophe* (1995), "a turning about, or round, conversion," is found in **Acts 15:3**. The word implies "a turning from and a turning to"; corresponding to these are repentance and faith; cf. "turned to God from idols" (1 Thess. 1:9). Divine grace is the efficient cause, human agency the responding effect.

Caused *poieo* (4160), "to do," is translated by the verb "to cause" in John 11:37; **Acts 15:3**; Rom. 16:17; Col. 4:16; Rev. 13:15-16.

15:4 And when they were come to Jerusalem, they were received of the church, and *of* the apostles and elders, and they declared all things that God had done with them.

Received *paradechomai* (3858), "to receive or admit with approval" (*para*, "beside"), is used (a) of persons, **Acts 15:4**; Heb. 12:6; (b) of things, Mark 4:20, KJV, "receive" (RV, "accept"); **Acts 16:21**; **22:18**; 1 Tim. 5:9. In the Sept., Ex. 23:1; Prov. 3:12.

Of For *hupo*, "by," see the RV of Matt. 1:22; 2:16; 11:27; Luke 9:7; **Acts 15:4**; 1 Cor. 14:24; 2 Cor. 8:19; Phil. 3:12.

Declared *anangello* (312), signifies "to announce, report, bring back tidings" (*ana*, "back," *angello*, "to announce"). Possibly the *ana* carries the significance of upward, i.e., heavenly, as characteristic of the nature of the tidings. In the following, either the KJV or the RV translates the word by the verb "to declare"; in John 4:25, RV, "declare," KJV, "tell"; in 16:13-15, RV, "declare," KJV, "shew"; in **Acts 15:4**, RV, "rehearsed," KJV, "declared"; in **19:18**, RV, "declaring," KJV, "shewed" (a reference, perhaps, to the destruction of their idols, in consequence of their new faith); in **20:20**, RV, "declaring," KJV, "have shewed"; in 1 John 1:5, RV, "announce," KJV, "declare." *See also* Rehearsed at *Acts 14:27.*

15:5 But there rose up certain of the sect of the Pharisees which believed, saying, That it was needful to circumcise them, and to command *them* to keep the law of Moses.

Rose up *exanistemi* (1817), is used of "raising" up seed, Mark 12:19; Luke 20:28; elsewhere, **Acts 15:5**, "to rise up."

Sect *see Acts 5:17.*

Needful *see* Needs at *Acts 1:16. See also* Must at *Acts 3:21.*

Command *see* Commanded at *Acts 1:4.*

15:6 And the apostles and elders came together for to consider of this matter.

Came *see Acts 13:44.*

Consider *eidon* (3708), used as the aorist tense of *horao*, "to see," is translated "to consider" in **Acts 15:6**, of the gathering of the apostles and elders regarding the question of circumcision in relation to the gospel.

Matter *see Acts 8:21.*

15:7 And when there had been much disputing, Peter rose up, and said unto them, Men *and* brethren, ye know how that a good while ago God made choice among us, that the Gentiles by my mouth should hear the word of the gospel, and believe.

Disputing *see* Disputation at *Acts 15:2.*

Men *see Acts 1:16.*

Brethren *see Acts 1:16.*

Know *see Acts 10:28.*

A good while ago *archaios* (744), "original, ancient" (from *arche*, "a beginning": Eng., "archaic," "archaeology," etc.), is used (a) of persons belonging to a former age, "(to) them of old time," Matt. 5:21, 33, RV; in some mss. v. 27; the RV rendering is right; not ancient teachers are in view; what was said to them of old time was "to be both recognized in its significance and estimated in its temporary limitations, Christ intending His words to be regarded not as an abrogation, but a deepening and fulfilling" (Cremer); of prophets, Luke 9:8, 19; (b) of time long gone by, **Acts 15:21**; (c) of days gone by in a person's experience, **Acts 15:7**, "a good while ago," lit., "from old (days)," i.e., from the first days onward in the sense of originality, not age; (d) of Mnason, "an early disciple," **Acts 21:16**, RV, not referring to age, but to his being one of the first who had accepted the gospel from the beginning of its proclamation; (e) of things which are "old" in relation to the new, earlier things in contrast to things present, 2 Cor. 5:17, i.e., of what characterized and conditioned the time previous to conversion in a believer's experience, RV, "they are become new," i.e., they have taken on a new complexion and are viewed in an entirely different way; (f) of the world (i.e., the inhabitants of the world) just previous to the Flood, 2 Pet. 2:5; (g) of the Devil, as "that old serpent," Rev. 12:9; 20:2, "old," not in age, but as characterized for a long period by the evils indicated.

Choice *see* Chosen at *Acts 1:2.*

Word *see* Words at *Acts 2:40.*

Gospel *euangelion* (2098), originally denoted a reward for good tidings; later, the idea of reward dropped, and the word stood for "the good news" itself. The Eng. word "gospel," i.e. "good message," is the equivalent of *euangelion* (Eng., "evangel"). In the NT it denotes the "good tidings" of the kingdom of God and of salvation through Christ, to be received by faith, on the basis of His expiatory death, His burial, resurrection, and ascension, e.g., **Acts 15:7**; **20:24**; 1 Pet. 4:17. Apart from those references and those in the Gospels of Matthew and Mark, and Rev. 14:6, the noun is confined to Paul's epistles. The apostle uses it of two associated yet distinct things, (a) of the basic facts of the death, burial and resurrection of Christ, e.g., 1 Cor. 15:1-3; (b) of the interpretation of these facts, e.g., Rom. 2:16; Gal. 1:7, 11; 2:2; in (a) the "gospel" is viewed historically, in (b) doctrinally, with reference to the interpretation of the facts, as is sometimes indicated by the context. The following phrases describe the subjects or nature or purport of the message; it is the "gospel" of God, Mark 1:14; Rom. 1:1; 15:16; 2 Cor. 11:7; 1 Thess. 2:2, 9; 1 Pet. 4:17; God, concerning His Son, Rom. 1:1-3; His Son, Rom. 1:9; Jesus Christ, the Son of God, Mark 1:1; our Lord Jesus, 2 Thess. 1:8; Christ, Rom. 15:19, etc.; the glory of Christ, 2 Cor. 4:4; the grace of God, **Acts 20:24**; the glory of the blessed God, 1 Tim. 1:11; your salvation, Eph. 1:13; peace, Eph. 6:15. Cf. also "the gospel of the Kingdom," Matt. 4:23; 9:35; 24:14; "an eternal gospel," Rev. 14:6. In Gal. 2:14, "the truth of the gospel" denotes, not the true "gospel," but the true teaching of it, in contrast to perversions of it. The following expressions are used in connection with the "gospel": (a) with regard to its testimony; (1) *kerusso*, "to preach it as a herald, e.g., Matt. 4:23; Gal. 2:2; (2) *laleo*, "to speak," 1 Thess. 2:2; (3) *diamarturomai*, "to testify (thoroughly)," **Acts 20:24**; (4) *euangelizo*, "to preach," e.g., 1 Cor. 15:1; 2 Cor. 11:7; Gal. 1:11; (5) *katangello*, "to proclaim," 1 Cor. 9:14; (6) *douleuo eis*, "to serve unto" ("in furtherance of"), Phil. 2:22; (7) *sunathleo en*, "to labor with in," Phil. 4:3; (8) *hierourgeo*, "to minister," Rom. 15:16; (9) *pleroo*, "to preach fully," Rom. 15:19; (10) *sunkakopatheo*, "to suffer hardship with," 2 Tim. 1:8; (b) with regard to its reception or otherwise: (1) *dechomai*, "to receive," 2 Cor. 11:4; *hupakouo*, "to hearken to, or obey," Rom. 10:16; 2 Thess. 1:8; *pisteuo en*, "to believe in," Mark 1:15; *metastrepho*, "to pervert," Gal. 1:7.

15:8 And God, which knoweth the hearts, bare them witness, giving them the Holy Ghost, even as *he did* unto us;

Hearts *see Acts 1:24.*

Witness *see* Report at *Acts 6:3.*

15:9 And put no difference between us and them, purifying their hearts by faith.

Put In **Acts 15:9**, KJV, *diakrino*, "to make a distinction" (RV), is translated "put (no) difference."

No *ouden* (3762), the neuter of *oudeis*, "no one," occurs, e.g., in Matt. 5:13; 10:26; 23:16; adverbially, e.g., in Matt. 27:24; 2 Cor. 12:11 (1st part), "in nothing"; 1 Tim. 4:4; in the dative case, after *en*, "in," Phil. 1:20. Westcott and Hort adopt the spelling *outhen* in Luke 22:35; 23:14; **Acts 15:9**; **19:27**; **26:26**; 1 Cor. 13:2.

Difference *see* Doubting at *Acts 10:20.*

Between *see Acts 12:6.*

Purifying *katharizo* (2511), "to cleanse, make free from admixture," is translated "to purify" in **Acts 15:9**, KJV (RV, "cleansing"); Titus 2:14; Heb. 9:23, KJV (RV, "cleansed"). *See also* Cleansed at *Acts 10:15.*

Hearts *see* Heart at *Acts 2:37.*

15:10 Now therefore why tempt ye God, to put a yoke upon the neck of the disciples, which neither our fathers nor we were able to bear?

Tempt *see Acts 5:9.*

Put *see* Putting at *Acts 9:12. See also* Laid ... on at *Acts 6:6.*

Yoke *zugos* (2218), "a yoke," serving to couple two things together, is used metaphorically, (a) of submission to authority, Matt. 11:29, 30, of Christ's "yoke," not simply imparted by Him but shared with Him; (b) of bondage, **Acts 15:10** and Gal. 5:1, of bondage to the Law as a supposed means of salvation; (c) of bond service to masters, 1 Tim. 6:1; (2) to denote "a balance," Rev. 6:5.

Neck *trachelos* (5137), is used (a) literally, Matt. 18:6; Mark 9:42; Luke 17:2; of "embracing," Luke 15:20; **Acts 20:37**; (b) metaphorically, in **Acts 15:10**, of "putting a yoke upon": Rom. 16:4, singular in the original, "(laid down their) neck," indicating the figurative use of the term rather than the literal. Prisca and Aquila in some way had risked their lives for the apostle (the phrase is found with this significance in the papyri).

Bear *see* Carried at *Acts 3:2.*

15:11 But we believe that through the grace of the Lord Jesus Christ we shall be saved, even as they.

Even as In **Acts 15:11**, the phrase *kath' hon tropon*, "according to what manner," is translated "in like manner as," RV (KJV, "even as").

15:12 Then all the multitude kept silence, and gave audience to Barnabas and Paul, declaring what miracles and wonders God had wrought among the Gentiles by them.

Multitude *see Acts 4:32.*

Silence *see* Peace at *Acts 12:17.*

Gave audience *see* Hear at *Acts 3:22.*

Declaring *see* Declared at *Acts 10:8.*

What Other words are (a) *hoios*, "of what kind," e.g., 2 Cor. 10:11,

RV (KJV, "such as"); 1 Thess. 1:5, "what manner of men"; 2 Tim. 3:11 (twice), lit., "what sorts of things," "what sorts of persecutions"; (b) *poios*, "what sort of," e.g., Matt. 21:23, 24, 27; 24:42, 43; Luke 5:19; 6:32-34; 20:2, 8; 24:19; John 12:33, "what manner of"; so in 18:32; 21:19; Rom. 3:27; 1 Cor. 15:35; in Jas. 4:14, "what"; 1 Pet. 2:20 and Rev. 3:3 (ditto); 1 Pet. 1:11, "what manner of"; (c) *hopoios*, "what sort of," 1 Cor. 3:13; "what manner of," 1 Thess. 1:9; (d) *hosos*, "how great," Mark 6:30 (twice), RV, "whatsoever"; **Acts 15:12**; Rom. 3:19, "what things soever"; Jude 10 (1st part), "what soever things," RV; (2nd part) "what"; (e) *posos*, "how great, how much," 2 Cor. 7:11, "what (earnest care)," RV (*posos* here stands for the repeated words in the Eng. versions, the adjective not being repeated in the original); (f) *hostis*, "what (things)," Phil. 3:7; (g) in Matt. 26:40, *houtos*, "thus, so," is used as an exclamatory expression, translated "What" (in a word immediately addressed by the Lord to Peter), lit., "So"; (h) for *potapos*, rendered "what" in Mark 13:1 (2nd part), KJV; (i) in 1 Cor. 6:16, 19, KJV, the particle *e*, "or" (RV), is rendered "What?"; in 1 Cor. 14:36, KJV and RV, "what?" (j) in 1 Cor. 11:22, *gar*, "in truth, indeed," has its exclamatory use "What."

Miracles *see* Miracle at *Acts 4:16*.

Wrought *poieo* (4160), "to do," is rendered "to work" in Matt. 20:12, KJV (RV, "spent"); **Acts 15:12**, "had wrought"; **19:11**; **21:19**; Heb. 13:21; Rev. 16:14; 19:20; 21:27, KJV (RV, "maketh"; marg., "doeth").

15:13 And after they had held their peace, James answered, saying, Men *and* brethren, hearken unto me:

Peace *see Acts 12:17*.

Men *see Acts 1:16*.

Brethren *see Acts 1:16*.

Hearken *see* Hear at *Acts 3:22*.

15:14 Simeon hath declared how God at the first did visit the Gentiles, to take out of them a people for his name.

Declared *see Acts 10:8*.

Visit *see* Look at *Acts 6:3*.

People *see Acts 4:8*.

15:15 And to this agree the words of the prophets; as it is written,

Agree *see* Agreed at *Acts 5:9*.

15:16 After this I will return, and will build again the tabernacle of David, which is fallen down; and I will build again the ruins thereof, and I will set it up:

Return In the following, the verbs mentioned, translated in the KJV by some form of the verb "to go," are rendered in the RV more precisely in accordance with their true meaning: (a) *zeteo*, "to seek," so the RV in John 7:19, 20; **Acts 21:31**; Rom. 10:3 (KJV, to go about); (b) *peirazo*, "to make an attempt," **Acts 24:6**, RV, "assayed" (KJV, "have gone about"); (c) *peirao*, "to attempt," **Acts 26:21**, RV, "assayed" KJV, "went about"); (d) *epistrepho*, "to return," **Acts 15:16**, RV, "let us return" (KJV, "let us go again"); (e) *huperbaino*, "to overstep," 1 Thess. 4:6, RV, "transgress" (KJV, "go beyond"); (f) *diistemi*, "to set apart, make an interval," **Acts 27:28**, RV, "(after) a space" (KJV, "had gone further"); (g) *suneiserchomai*, "to go in with," John 6:22 and 18:15, RV, "entered (in) with" (KJV, "went ... with"); (h) *phero*, in the middle voice, lit., "to bear oneself along," Heb. 6:1, RV, "let us press on" (KJV, "let us go on"); (i) *ekklino*, "to bend or turn away," Rom. 3:12, RV, "have turned aside" (KJV, "have gone out of the way"); (j) *diaperao*, "to pass through, or across," Matt. 14:34, RV, "had crossed over" (KJV, "were gone over"); (k) *strateuomai*, "to serve in war," 1 Cor. 9:7, RV, "(what) soldier ... serveth" (KJV, "goeth a warfare"). *See also* Returned at *Acts 5:22*.

Build *anoikodomeo* (456), signifies "to build again" (*ana*, "again"), **Acts 15:16**.

Tabernacle *see Acts 7:43*.

Ruins *katestrammena* (2690), the neuter plural, perfect participle, passive, of *katastrepho*, "to overturn," is translated "ruins" in **Acts 15:16** (some mss. have *kataskapto*, "to dig down").

Set *anorthoo* (461), "to set straight, set up" (*ana*, "up," *orthos*, "straight"), is used in **Acts 15:16** in God's promise to "set" up the fallen tabernacle (*skene*, "tent") of David. The word is used in the papyri of rearing buildings again.

15:17 That the residue of men might seek after the Lord, and all the Gentiles, upon whom my name is called, saith the Lord, who doeth all these things.

Residue *kataloipos* (2645), an adjective denoting "left remaining" (*kata*, "after, behind," *leipo*, "to leave"), is translated "residue" in **Acts 15:17**, from the Sept. of Amos 9:12.

Seek *ekzeteo* (1567), signifies (a) "to seek out (*ek*) or after, to search for"; e.g., God Rom. 3:11; the Lord, **Acts 15:17**; in Heb. 11:6, RV, "seek after" (KJV, "diligently seek"); 12:17, RV, "sought diligently" (KJV, "sought carefully"); 1 Pet. 1:10, RV, "sought" (KJV, "have inquired"), followed by *exeraunao*, "to search diligently", (b) "to require or demand," Luke 11:50, 51.

Called *see* Call at *Acts 2:21*.

15:18 Known unto God are all his works from the beginning of the world.

Known *see* Foreknowledge at *Acts 2:23*.

God *see Acts 2:23*.

Beginning *see* Began at *Acts 3:21*.

15:19 Wherefore my sentence is, that we trouble not them, which from among the Gentiles are turned to God:

Wherefore *dio* = *dia ho* (the neuter of the relative pronoun *hos*), "on account of which (thing)," e.g., Matt. 27:8; **Acts 15:19**; **20:31**; **24:26**; **25:26**; **27:25**, **34**; Rom. 1:24; 15:7; 1 Cor. 12:3; 2 Cor. 2:8; 5:9; 6:17; Eph. 2:11; 3:13; 4:8, 25; 5:14; Phil. 2:9; 1 Thess. 5:11; Philem. 8; Heb. 3:7, 10; 10:5; 11:16; 12:12, 28; 13:12; Jas. 1:21; 4:6; 1 Pet. 1:13; 2 Pet. 1:10, 12; 3:14.

Sentence *krino* (2919), "to judge, to adjudge," is translated "(my) sentence is" in **Acts 15:19**, KJV, RV, "(my) judgment is," lit., "I (*ego*, emphatic) judge," introducing the substance or draft of a resolution. *See also* Determined at *Acts 3:13*.

Trouble *parenochleo* (3926), "to annoy concerning anything," occurs in **Acts 15:19**, "we trouble (not them)."

Turned *see Acts 11:21*.

15:20 But that we write unto them, that they abstain from pollutions of idols, and *from* fornication, and *from* things strangled, and *from* blood.

Write *epistello* (1989), denotes "to send a message by letter, to write word" (*stello*, "to send"; Eng., "epistle"), **Acts 15:20**; **21:25** (some mss. have *apostello*, "to send"); Heb. 13:22.

Abstain *apecho* (568), "to hold oneself from" (*apo*, "from," *echomai*, the middle voice of *echo*, "to have," i.e., to keep oneself from), in the NT, invariably refers to evil practices, moral and ceremonial, **Acts 15:20**, **29**; 1 Thess. 4:3; 5:22; 1 Tim. 4:3; 1 Pet. 2:11; so in the Sept. in Job 1:1; 2:3.

Pollutions *alisgema* (234), akin to a late verb *alisgeo*, "to pollute," denotes "a pollution, contamination," **Acts 15:20**, "pollutions of idols," i.e., all the contaminating associations connected with idolatry including meats from sacrifices offered to idols.

Idols *see* Idol at *Acts 7:41*.

Fornication *porneia* (4202), is used (a) of "illicit sexual intercourse," in John 8:41; **Acts 15:20**, **29**; **21:25**; 1 Cor. 5:1; 6:13, 18; 2 Cor. 12:21; Gal. 5:19; Eph. 5:3; Col. 3:5; 1 Thess. 4:3; Rev. 2:21; 9:21; in the plural in 1 Cor. 7:2; in Matt. 5:32 and 19:9 it stands for, or includes, adultery; it is distinguished from it in 15:19 and Mark 7:21; (b) metaphorically, of "the association of pagan idolatry with doctrines of, and professed adherence to, the Christian faith," Rev. 14:8; 17:2, 4; 18:3; 19:2; some suggest this as the sense in 2:21.

Strangled *pniktos* (4156), from *pnigo*, "to choke," occurs in **Acts 15:20**, **29**; **21:25**, of the flesh of animals killed by strangling, without shedding their blood (see, e.g., Lev. 17:13, 14).

15:21 For Moses of old time hath in every city them that preach him, being read in the synagogues every sabbath day.

Of old time *see* A good while ago at *Acts 15:7*. *See also* Generation at *Acts 2:40*; Past at *Acts 14:16*.

Read *see Acts 8:28*.

15:22 Then pleased it the apostles and elders, with the whole church, to send chosen men of their own company to Antioch with Paul and Barnabas; *namely*, Judas surnamed Barsabas, and Silas, chief men among the brethren:

Pleased *dokeo* (1380), denotes (a) "to be of opinion" (akin to *doxa*, "opinion"), e.g., Luke 8:18, RV, "thinketh" (KJV, "seemeth"); so 1 Cor. 3:18; to think, suppose, Jas. 1:26, RV, "thinketh himself (KJV, "seem"); (b) "to seem, to be reputed," e.g., **Acts 17:18**; 1 Cor. 11:16; 12:22; 2 Cor. 10:9; Heb. 4:1; 12:11; for Gal. 2:2, 6, 9; (c) impersonally (1) to think, (2) to "seem" good, Luke 1:3; **Acts 15:22**, RV, "it seemed good" (KJV, "it pleased"); **15:25**, **28** (v. **34** in some mss.); in Heb. 12:10, the neuter of the present participle is used with the article, lit., "the (thing) seeming good," RV, "(as) seemed good," KJV, "after (their own) pleasure."

Send *see Acts 10:5*.

Chosen *see Acts 1:2*.

Company The preposition *ex* (i.e., *ek*), "of," with the first personal pronoun in the genitive plural (*hemon*, "us"); signifies "of our company," lit., "of us," in Luke 24:22; so *ex auton*, in **Acts 15:22**, "men out of their company," lit., "men out of them."

Surnamed *see Acts 1:23*.

Chief *see Acts 14:12*.

15:23 And they wrote *letters* by them after this manner; The apostles and elders and brethren *send* greeting unto

the brethren which are of the Gentiles in Antioch and Syria and Cilicia:

Manner In **Acts 15:23** some mss. have the demonstrative pronoun *tode* used adverbially and rendered "after this manner" (KJV). The RV, adhering to the mss. in which it is absent, inserts the word "*thus*" in italics.

Greeting *chairo* (5463), "to rejoice," is thrice used as a formula of salutation in **Acts 15:23**, KJV, "send greeting," RV, "greeting"; so **23:26**; Jas. 1:1. In 2 John 10, 11, the RV substitutes the phrase (to give) "greeting," for the KJV (to bid) "God speed." *See also* **Favour** at *Acts 2:47*.

15:24 Forasmuch as we have heard, that certain which went out from us have troubled you with words, subverting your souls, saying, *Ye must* be circumcised, and keep the law: to whom we gave no *such* commandment:

Troubled *tarosso* (5015), akin to *tarache*, is used (1) in a physical sense, John 5:7 (in some mss. v. 4), (2) metaphorically, (a) of the soul and spirit of the Lord, John 11:33, where the true rendering is "He troubled Himself"; (b) of the hearts of disciples, 14:1, 27; (c) of the minds of those in fear or perplexity, Matt. 2:3; 14:26; Mark 6:50; Luke 1:12; 24:38; 1 Pet. 3:14; (d) of subverting the souls of believers, by evil doctrine, **Acts 15:24**; Gal. 1:7; 5:10; (e) of stirring up a crowd, **Acts 17:8**; v. **13** in the best texts, "troubling (the multitudes)," RV.

Subverting *anaskeuazo* (384), primarily, "to pack up baggage" (*ana*, "up," *skeuos*, "a vessel"), hence, from a military point of view, "to dismantle a town, to plunder," is used metaphorically in **Acts 15:24**, of unsettling or "subverting" the souls of believers. In the papyri it is used of going bankrupt.

Commandment *diastellomai* (1291), lit., "to draw asunder" (*dia*, "asunder," *stello*, "to draw"), signifies "to admonish, order, charge," Matt. 16:20; Mark 5:43; 7:36 (twice); 8:15; 9:9. In **Acts 15:24** it is translated "gave commandment"; in Heb. 12:20, KJV, "commanded," RV, "enjoined."

15:25 It seemed good unto us, being assembled with one accord, to send chosen men unto you with our beloved Barnabas and Paul,

Seemed *see* **Pleased** at *Acts 15:22*.

Assembled In **Acts 15:25**, *ginomai*, "to become," is translated "having come to (one accord)," correcting the KJV, "being assembled with (one accord)."

Accord *see Acts 1:14*.

Send *see Acts 10:5*.

Chosen *see Acts 1:2*.

15:26 Men that have hazarded their lives for the name of our Lord Jesus Christ.

Hazarded *paradidomi* (3860), "to give over, deliver," signifies "to risk, to hazard," in **Acts 15:26**, of Barnabas and Paul, who "hazarded" their lives for the name of the Lord Jesus.

15:27 We have sent therefore Judas and Silas, who shall also tell *you* the same things by mouth.

Sent *see* **Send** at *Acts 3:20*.

Mouth In **Acts 15:27**, *logos*, "a word," is translated "word of mouth," RV (KJV, "mouth," marg., "word").

15:28 For it seemed good to the Holy Ghost, and to us, to lay upon you no greater burden than these necessary things;

Seemed *see* **Pleased** at *Acts 15:22*.

Holy Ghost *see Acts 1:16*.

Lay *see* **Laid ... on** at *Acts 6:6*.

Greater *pleion* (4119), the comparative of *polus*, is used (a) as an adjective, "greater, more," e.g., **Acts 15:28**; (b) as a noun, e.g., Matt. 12:41, "a greater (than Jonah)"; v. 42, "a greater (than Solomon)"; in these instances the neuter *pleion*, "something greater," is "a fixed or stereotyped form" of the word; in 1 Cor. 15:6, "the greater part" (masculine plural); (c) as an adverb, e.g., Matt. 5:20, lit., "(except your righteousness abound) more greatly (than of scribes and Pharisees)"; so 26:53, "more"; Luke 9:13.

Burden *baros* (922), denotes "a weight, anything pressing on one physically," Matt. 20:12, or "that makes a demand on one's resources," whether material, 1 Thess. 2:6 (to be burdensome), or spiritual, Gal. 6:2; Rev. 2:24, or religious, **Acts 15:28**. In one place it metaphorically describes the future state of believers as "an eternal weight of glory," 2 Cor. 4:17.

Than *see* **Except** at *Acts 8:1*.

Necessary *epanankes* (1876), an adjective akin to the preceding, with *epi* used intensively, found only in the neuter form, is used as an adverb signifying "of necessity" and translated as an adjective in **Acts 15:28**, "necessary," lit., "(things) of necessity."

15:29 That ye abstain from meats offered to idols, and from blood, and from things strangled, and from fornication:

from which if ye keep yourselves, ye shall do well. Fare ye well.

Abstain *see Acts 15:20.*

Meats In **Acts 15:29**, KJV, the neuter plural of *eidolothutos*, "sacrificed to idols," is translated "meats offered to idols" (RV, "things ... ," as elsewhere in the KJV).

Offered to idols *eidolothutos* (1494), is an adjective signifying "sacrificed to idols" (*eidolon*, as above, and *thuo*, "to sacrifice"), **Acts 15:29**; **21:25**; 1 Cor. 8:1, 4, 7, 10; 10:19 (in all these the RV substitutes "sacrificed" for the KJV); Rev. 2.14, 20 (in these the RV and KJV both have "sacrificed"). Some inferior mss. have this adjective in 1 Cor. 10:28. The flesh of the victims, after sacrifice, was eaten or sold.

Strangled *see Acts 15:20.*

Fornication *see Acts 15:20.*

Keep *diatereo* (1301), "to keep carefully," is said of "the mother of Jesus," in keeping His sayings in her heart, Luke 2:51, and of the command of the apostles and elders in Jerusalem to gentile converts in the churches to "keep" themselves from the evils mentioned in **Acts 15:29**.

Well *eu* (2095), primarily the neuter of an old word, *eus*, "noble, good," is used (a) with verbs, e.g., Mark 14:7, "do (*poieo*) ... good"; **Acts 15:29** (*prasso*); Eph. 6:3 (*ginomai*, "to be"); (b) in replies, "good," "well done," Matt. 25:21, 23; in Luke 19:17, *eu ge* (in the best texts). The word is the opposite of *kakos*, "evilly."

Fare *rhonnumi* (4517), "to strengthen, to be strong," is used in the imperative mood as a formula at the end of letters, signifying "Farewell," **Acts 15:29**; some mss. have it in **23:30** (the RV omits it, as do most Versions).

15:30 So when they were dismissed, they came to Antioch: and when they had gathered the multitude together, they delivered the epistle:

Dismissed *apoluo* (630), lit., "to loose from" (*apo*, "from," *luo*, "to loose"), is translated "dismiss" in **Acts 15:30**, **33**, RV (KJV, "let go") and **19:41**.

Multitude *see Acts 4:32.*

Delivered *epididomi* (1929), signifies (a) "to give by handing, to hand" (*epi*, "over"), e.g., Matt. 7:9, 10; Luke 4:17; 24:30, here of the Lord's act in "handing" the broken loaf to the two at Emmaus, an act which was the means of the revelation of Himself as the crucified and risen Lord; the simple verb, *didomi*, is used of His "handing" the bread at the institution of the Lord's Supper, Matt. 26:26; Mark 14:22; Luke 22:19; this meaning of the verb *epididomi* is found also in **Acts 15:30**, "they delivered"; (b) "to give in, give way," **Acts 27:15**, RV, "we gave way to it."

Epistle *see* Letters at *Acts 9:2.*

15:31 *Which* when they had read, they rejoiced for the consolation.

Rejoiced *see* Rejoicing at *Acts 5:41.*

Consolation *see Acts 4:36.*

15:32 And Judas and Silas, being prophets also themselves, exhorted the brethren with many words, and confirmed *them*.

Prophets *see* Prophet at *Acts 3:22.*

Confirmed *see* Confirming at *Acts 14:22.*

15:33 And after they had tarried *there* a space, they were let go in peace from the brethren unto the apostles.

Tarried *poieo* (4160), "to do, make," is used of spending a time or tarrying, in a place, **Acts 15:33**; **20:3**; in 2 Cor. 11:25 it is rendered "I have been (a night and a day)"; a preferable translation is "I have spent," as in Jas. 4:13, "spend a year" (RV). So in Matt. 20:12. Cf., the English idiom "did one hour"; in Rev. 13:5 "continue" is perhaps the best rendering.

Space In **Acts 15:33** and Rev. 2:21, KJV, *chronos*, "time" (RV), is translated "space."

Let *see Acts 3:13. See also* Went at *Acts 10:9;* Dismissed at *Acts 15:30.*

15:34 Notwithstanding it pleased Silas to abide there still.

Pleased *see Acts 15:22.*

There *autou* (847), the genitive case, neuter, of *autos*, he, lit., "of it," is used as an adverb, "there," in **Acts 18:19**; **21:4** (in some texts in **15:34**).

15:35 Paul also and Barnabas continued in Antioch, teaching and preaching the word of the Lord, with many others also.

Continued The following are translated by the verb "to continue," in the KJV, in the places mentioned: *diatribo*, "to tarry," (according to inferior mss.) John 11:54; **Acts 15:35** (RV, "tarried"); *histemi*, "to stand," **Acts 26:22** (RV, "stand"): *kathizo*, "to sit down," **Acts 18:11** (RV, "dwelt"): *parateino*, "to extend, stretch," **Acts 20:7** (RV, "prolonged"); *parameno*, "to abide together with," Phil. 1:25, RV, "abide with"; the KJV, "continue," translating *sumparameno* (in some mss.), marks the difference from the preceding *meno*. *See also* Abode at *Acts 12:19.*

Teaching *didasko* (1321), is used (a) absolutely, "to give instruction," e.g., Matt. 4:23; 9:35; Rom. 12:7; 1 Cor. 4:17; 1 Tim. 2:12; 4:11;

(b) transitively, with an object, whether persons, e.g., Matt. 5:2; 7:29, and frequently in the Gospels and Acts, or things "taught," e.g., Matt. 15:9; 22:16; **Acts 15:35**; **18:11**; both persons and things, e.g., John 14:26; Rev. 2:14, 20.

Preaching *see* Preach at *Acts 5:42*.

Word *see* Words at *Acts 2:40*.

15:36 And some days after Paul said unto Barnabas, Let us go again and visit our brethren in every city where we have preached the word of the Lord, *and see* how they do.

Go again *epistrepho* (1994), "to turn about," or "towards," is translated "to return" in Matt. 12:44; 24:18; Mark 13:16, RV (KJV, "turn back again"); Luke 2:39; 8:55, RV (KJV, "came again"); 17:31; **Acts 15:36**, RV (KJV, "go again").

And *de* (1211), a consecutive particle, giving stress to the word or words to which it is attached, sometimes with hardly any exact Eng. equivalent, is translated "now" in Luke 2:15, in the words of the shepherds; in **Acts 15:36**, RV (KJV, "and"). Some mss. have it in 2 Cor. 12:1; see RV marg.

Visit *see* Look at *Acts 6:3*.

Preached *see Acts 4:2*.

Word *see* Words at *Acts 2:40*.

Do *echo* (2192), "to have," is used idiomatically in **Acts 15:36**, RV, "(how) they fare," KJV, "how they do."

15:37 And Barnabas determined to take with them John, whose surname was Mark.

Determined *boulomai*, "to be minded, to purpose," from *bouleuo* (1011), "to take counsel, to resolve," is translated "determined" in **Acts 15:37**; RV, was minded.

Take *see* Took at *Acts 12:25*.

Surname *kaleo* (2564), derived from the root *kal–*, whence Eng. "call" and "clamor," is used (a) with a personal object, "to call anyone, invite, summon," e.g., Matt. 20:8; 25:14; it is used particularly of the divine call to partake of the blessings of redemption, e.g., Rom. 8:30; 1 Cor. 1:9; 1 Thess. 2:12; Heb. 9:15; (b) of nomenclature or vocation, "to call by a name, to name"; in the passive voice, "to be called by a name, to bear a name." Thus it suggests either vocation or destination; the context determines which, e.g., Rom. 9:25-26; "surname," in **Acts 15:37**, KJV, is incorrect (RV, "was called").

15:38 But Paul thought not good to take him with them, who departed from them from Pamphylia, and went not with them to the work.

Thought *axioo* (515), "to deem worthy," is translated "desire" in **Acts 28:22**, where a suitable rendering would be "We think it meet (or good) to hear of thee"; so in **15:38**.

Take *see* Took at *Acts 12:25*.

Departed *see* Dispersed at *Acts 5:37*.

Went *see* Go at *Acts 8:29*. *See also* Companied at *Acts 1:21*.

15:39 And the contention was so sharp between them, that they departed asunder one from the other: and so Barnabas took Mark, and sailed unto Cyprus;

Contention *paroxusmos* (3948), (Eng., "paroxysm"), lit., "a sharpening," hence "a sharpening of the feeling, or action" (*para*, "beside," intensive, *oxus*, "sharp"), denotes an incitement, a sharp contention, **Acts 15:39**, the effect of irritation; elsewhere in Heb. 10:24, "provoke," unto love.

Departed *apochorizo* (673), signifies "to separate off" (*apo*); in the middle voice, "to depart from," **Acts 15:39**, KJV, "departed asunder"; RV, "parted asunder"; Rev. 6:14, RV, "was removed."

One ... the other *see* One to another at *Acts 7:26*.

Took *paralambano* (3880), besides its meaning "to receive," denotes "to take to (or with) oneself," of "taking" a wife, e.g., Matt. 1:20, 24; of "taking" a person or persons with one, e.g., Matt. 2:13, 14, 20, 21; 4:5, 8; of demons, 12:45; of Christ and His disciples, 17:1; 20:17; Mark 9:2; 10:32; 14:33; of witnesses, Matt. 18:16; of the removal of persons from the earth in judgment, when "the Son of Man is revealed," Matt. 24:40, 41; Luke 17:34, 35 (cf. the means of the removal of corruption, in v. 37); of the "taking" of Christ by the soldiers for scourging, Matt. 27:27, RV, and to crucifixion, John 19:16; see also **Acts 15:39**; **16:33**; **21:24**, **26**, **32**; **23:18**.

15:40 And Paul chose Silas, and departed, being recommended by the brethren unto the grace of God.

Chose *epilego* (1951), in the middle voice, signifies "to choose," either in addition or in succession to another. It has this meaning in **Acts 15:40**, of Paul's choice of Silas. For its other meaning, "to call or name," John 5:2.

Recommended *see Acts 14:26*.

15:41 And he went through Syria and Cilicia, confirming the churches.

Confirming *see Acts 14:22*.

Chapter 16

16:1 Then came he to Derbe and Lystra: and, behold, a certain disciple was there, named Timotheus, the son of a certain woman, which was a Jewess, and believed; but his father *was* a Greek:

Came *katantao* (2658), denotes (a) "to come to, or over against, a place, arrive," **Acts 16:1**; **18:19**, **24**; **20:15** (in **21:7** and **25:13**, RV, "arrived"; in **27:12**, "reach," for KJV, "attain to"); **28:13**; (b) of things or events, "to arrive at a certain time, or come upon certain persons in the period of their lifetime," 1 Cor. 10:11; or "to come to persons" so that they partake of, as of the gospel, 1 Cor. 14:36. For the remaining instances, **Acts 26:7**; Eph. 4:13; Phil. 3:11.

Jewess *see* Jews at *Acts 2:10*.

Believed *pistos* (4103), (a) in the active sense means "believing, trusting"; (b) in the passive sense, "trusty, faithful, trustworthy." It is translated "believer" in 2 Cor. 6:15; "them that believe" in 1 Tim. 4:12, RV (KJV, "believers"); in 1 Tim. 5:16, "if any woman that believeth," lit., "if any believing woman." So in 6:2, "believing masters." In 1 Pet. 1:21 the RV, following the most authentic mss., gives the noun form, "are believers in God" (KJV, "do believe in God"). In John 20:27 it is translated "believing." It is best understood with significance (a), above, e.g., in Gal. 3:9; **Acts 16:1**; 2 Cor. 6:15; Titus 1:6; it has significance (b), e.g., in 1 Thess. 5:24; 2 Thess. 3:3. *See also* Sure at *Acts 13:34*.

16:2 Which was well reported of by the brethren that were at Lystra and Iconium.

Reported *see* Report at *Acts 6:3*.

16:3 Him would Paul have to go forth with him; and took and circumcised him because of the Jews which were in those quarters: for they knew all that his father was a Greek.

Quarters *topos* (5117), "a place," is translated "parts" in **Acts 16:3**, RV (KJV, "quarters").

Was *see Acts 5:4*.

16:4 And as they went through the cities, they delivered them the decrees for to keep, that were ordained of the apostles and elders which were at Jerusalem.

Went *diaporeuomai* (1279), "to go through," "to pass across," is translated "to go through," in Luke 6:1; 13:22, "went on His way through," RV; **Acts 16:4**; "going by" in Luke 18:36, RV (KJV, "pass by"); "in my journey" in Rom. 15:24 (2nd part).

Decrees *dogma* (1378), transliterated in English, primarily denoted "an opinion or judgment" (from *dokeo*, "to be of opinion"), hence, an "opinion expressed with authority, a doctrine, ordinance, decree"; "decree," Luke 2:1; **Acts 16:4**; **17:7**; in the sense of ordinances, Eph. 2:15; Col. 2:14.

Keep *see* Kept at *Acts 7:53*.

Ordained *krino* (2919), "to divide, separate, decide, judge," is translated "ordained" in **Acts 16:4**, of the decrees by the apostles and elders in Jerusalem. *See also* Determined at *Acts 3:13*.

16:5 And so were the churches established in the faith, and increased in number daily.

Established *see* Received strength at *Acts 3:7*.

Increased *perisseo* (4052), "to be over and above, to abound," is translated "increased" in **Acts 16:5**, of churches; "increase" in the KJV of 1 Thess. 4:10 (RV, abound).

Number *perisseuo* (4052), is used intransitively (a) "of exceeding a certain number, or measure, to be over, to remain," of the fragments after feeding the multitude (cf. *perisseuma*), Luke 9:17; John 6:12-13; "to exist in abundance"; as of wealth, Luke 12:15; 21:4; of food, 15:17. In this sense it is used also of consolation, 2 Cor. 1:5, of the effect of a gift sent to meet the need of saints, 2 Cor. 9:12; of rejoicing, Phil. 1:26; of what comes or falls to the lot of a person in large measure, as of the grace of God and the gift by the grace of Christ, Rom. 5:15, of the sufferings of Christ, 2 Cor. 1:5. In Mark 12:44 and Luke 21:4, the RV has "superfluity." (b) "to redound to, or to turn out abundantly for something," as of the liberal effects of poverty, 2 Cor. 8:2; in Rom. 3:7, argumentatively of the effects of the truth of God, as to whether God's truthfulness becomes more conspicuous and His glory is increased through man's untruthfulness; of numerical increase, **Acts 16:5**.

Daily *see Acts 3:2*.

16:6 Now when they had gone throughout Phrygia and the region of Galatia, and were forbidden of the Holy Ghost to preach the word in Asia,

Region *see* Regions at *Acts 8:1*.

Preach *see* Preached at *Acts 8:25*.

16:7 After they were come to Mysia, they assayed to go into Bithynia: but the Spirit suffered them not.

"The Spirit of Christ is the spirit of missions, and the nearer we get to him, the more intensely missionary we must become."

HENRY MARTYN

Assayed *peirazo* (3985), is rendered "to try" in Heb. 11:17; Rev. 2:2, 10; 3:10. In **Acts 16:7** it is rendered "assayed"; in **24:6**, RV, "assayed" (KJV, "hath gone about"). Cf. *peirao* in **Acts 26:21**, RV, "assayed" (KJV, "went about").

Spirit *see* Holy Ghost at *Acts 1:16*.

Suffered *see Acts 14:16*.

16:8 And they passing by Mysia came down to Troas.

Passing *parerchomai* (3928), from *para*, "by," *erchomai*, "to come" or "go," denotes (I) literally, "to pass, pass by," (a) of persons, Matt. 8:28; Mark 6:48; Luke 18:37; **Acts 16:8**; (b) of things, Matt. 26:39, 42; of time, Matt. 14:15; Mark 14:35; **Acts 27:9**, KJV, "past" (RV, "gone by"); 1 Pet. 4:3; (II) metaphorically, (a) "to pass away, to perish," Matt. 5:18; 24:34, 35; Mark 13:30, 31; Luke 16:17; 21:32, 33; 2 Cor. 5:17; Jas. 1:10; 2 Pet. 3:10; (b) "to pass by, disregard, neglect, pass over," Luke 11:42; 15:29, "transgressed." For the meaning "to come forth or come," see Luke 12:37; 17:7, RV (**Acts 24:7** in some mss.).

16:9 And a vision appeared to Paul in the night; There stood a man of Macedonia, and prayed him, saying, Come over into Macedonia, and help us.

Vision *see* Sight at *Acts 7:31*.

Prayed *parakaleo*, "to call to one's aid," is rendered by the verb "to pray" in the KJV in the following: Matt. 26:53 (RV, "beseech"); so Mark 5:17, 18; **Acts 16:9**; in **24:4**, RV, "intreat"; in **27:34**, RV, "beseech."

Come *diabaino* (1224), "to pass through," is translated "come over" in **Acts 16:9**; "pass" in Luke 16:26; "pass through" in Heb. 11:29.

Help *boetheo* (997), "to come to the aid of anyone, to succor," is used in Matt. 15:25; Mark 9:22, 24; **Acts 16:9**; **21:28**; 2 Cor. 6:2, "did I succour"; Heb. 2:18, "to succour"; Rev. 12:16.

16:10 And after he had seen the vision, immediately we endeavoured to go into Macedonia, assuredly gathering that the Lord had called us for to preach the gospel unto them.

Vision *see* Sight at *Acts 7:31*.

Endeavoured *zeteo* (2212), "to seek after," is translated "endeavor" in **Acts 16:10**, KJV, RV, "sought".

Assuredly In **Acts 16:10**, for the KJV (of *sumbibazomai*), "assuredly gathering."

Gathering *sumbibazo* (4822), lit., "to make to come together," is translated "concluding" in **Acts 16:10**, RV, for the KJV, "assuredly gathering."

Called *see* Call at *Acts 2:39*.

16:11 Therefore loosing from Troas, we came with a straight course to Samothracia, and the next *day* to Neapolis;

Loosing *see* Loosed at *Acts 13:13*.

Course Connected with *dromos*, is *euthudromeo*, "to make (or run) a straight course" (*euthus*, "straight"), **Acts 16:11** and **21:1**.

Next *see Acts 7:26*.

Day *see Acts 7:26*.

16:12 And from thence to Philippi, which is the chief city of that part of Macedonia, *and* a colony: and we were in that city abiding certain days.

Chief *see Acts 13:50*.

Part *see Acts 8:21*.

Colony *kolonia* (2862), transliterates the Latin *colonia*. Roman colonies belonged to three periods and classes, (a) those of the earlier republic before 100 BC, which were simply centers of Roman influence in conquered territory; (b) agrarian "colonies," planted as places for the overflowing population of Rome; (c) military "colonies" during the time of the Civil wars and the Empire, for the settlement of disbanded soldiers. This third class was established by the *imperator*, who appointed a legate to exercise his authority. To this class Philippi belonged as mentioned in **Acts 16:12**, RV, "a Roman colony." They were watch towers of the Roman state and formed on the model of Rome itself. The full organization of Philippi as such was the work of Augustus, who, after the battle of Actium, 31 BC, gave his soldiers lands in Italy and transferred most of the inhabitants there to other quarters including Philippi. These communities possessed the right of Roman freedom, and of holding the soil under Roman law, as well as exemption from poll-tax and tribute. Most Roman "colonies" were established on the coast.

Abiding *see* Abode at *Acts 12:19*.

16:13 And on the sabbath we went out of the city by a river side, where prayer was wont to be made; and we sat down, and spake unto the women which resorted *thither*.

Sabbath In **Acts 16:13**, "on the sabbath day," is, lit., "on the day of the sabbath" (plural).

City In **Acts 16:13**, the most authentic mss. have *pule*, "gate," RV, "without the gate."

River *potamos* (4215), denotes (a) "a stream," Luke 6:48, 49; (b) "a flood or floods," Matt. 7:25, 27; (c) "a river," natural, Matt. 3:6, RV; Mark 1:5; **Acts 16:13**; 2 Cor. 11:26, RV (KJV, "waters"); Rev. 8:10; 9:14; 16:4, 12; symbolical, Rev. 12:15 (1st part), RV, "river" (KJV, "flood"); so v. 16; 22:1, 2 (cf. Gen. 2:10; Ezek. 47); figuratively, John 7:38, "the effects of the operation of the Holy Spirit in and through the believer."

Prayer *proseuche* (4335), denotes (a) "prayer" (to God), the most frequent term, e.g., Matt. 21:22; Luke 6:12, where the phrase is not to be taken literally as if it meant, "the prayer of God" (subjective genitive), but objectively, "prayer to God." In Jas. 5:17, "He prayed fervently," RV, is, lit., "he prayed with prayer" (a Hebraistic form); in the following the word is used with *deesis*: Eph. 6:18; Phil. 4:6; 1 Tim. 2:1; 5:5; (b) "a place of prayer," **Acts 16:13, 16**, a place outside the city wall, RV.

Wont In **Acts 16:13** the KJV, "was wont," translates the texts which have the passive voice of *nomizo* with its meaning "to hold by custom"; the RV, "we supposed," translates the texts which have the imperfect tense, active, with the meaning "to consider, suppose." *See also* Supposed at *Acts 7:25*.

Made In **Acts 16:13**, KJV, the infinitive mood of *eimi*, "to be," is translated "to be made" (of prayer), RV, "there was (a place of prayer)."

Resorted *sunerchomai* (4905), "to come together" (*sun*, "together," *erchomai* "to come"), is once rendered "assemble," Mark 14:53, KJV. It is frequently used of "coming together," especially of the "gathering" of a local church, 1 Cor. 11:17-18, 20, 33-34; 14:23, 26; it is rendered "resorted" in **Acts 16:13**, KJV, where the RV adheres to the lit. rendering, "came together."

16:14 And a certain woman named Lydia, a seller of purple, of the city of Thyatira, which worshipped God, heard *us*: whose heart the Lord opened, that she attended unto the things which were spoken of Paul.

Seller of purple *porphuropolis* (4211), denotes "a seller of purple fabrics" (from *porphura*, and *poleo*, "to sell"), **Acts 16:14**.

Worshipped *sebomai* (4576), "to revere," stressing the feeling of awe or devotion, is used of "worship" (a) to God, Matt. 15:9; Mark 7:7; **Acts 16:14; 18:7, 13**; (b) to a goddess, **Acts 19:27**.

Opened *see Acts 7:56*.

Attended *prosecho* (4337), "to take heed, give heed," is said of the priests who "gave attendance at the altar," Heb. 7:13. It suggests devotion of thought and effort to a thing. In 1 Tim. 4:13 (in the exhortation regarding the public reading of the Scriptures), the RV translates it "give heed," for the KJV, "give attendance." In **Acts 16:14**, "to give heed" (for KJV, "attended"). *See also* Heed at *Acts 5:35*.

16:15 And when she was baptized, and her household, she besought *us*, saying, If ye have judged me to be faithful to the Lord, come into my house, and abide *there*. And she constrained us.

Household *oikos* (3624), is translated "household" in **Acts 16:15**; 1 Cor. 1:16; in the KJV of 2 Tim. 4:19 (RV, "house").

Faithful *see* Sure at *Acts 13:34*.

Constrained *parabiazomai* (3849), primarily denotes "to employ force contrary to nature and right, to compel by using force" (*para*, "alongside," intensive, *biazo*, "to force"), and is used only of "constraining" by intreaty, as the two going to Emmaus did to Christ, Luke 24:29; as Lydia did to Paul and his companions, **Acts 16:15**.

16:16 And it came to pass, as we went to prayer, a certain damsel possessed with a spirit of divination met us, which brought her masters much gain by soothsaying:

Prayer *see Acts 16:13*.

Damsel *see Acts 12:13*.

Possessed *see Acts 8:7*.

Divination *puthon* (4436), (Eng., "python"), in Greek mythology was the name of the Pythian serpent or dragon, dwelling in Pytho, at the foot of mount Parnassus, guarding the oracle of Delphi, and slain by Apollo. Thence the name was transferred to Apollo himself Later the word was applied to diviners or soothsayers, regarded as inspired by Apollo. Since demons are the agents inspiring idolatry, 1 Cor. 10:20, the young woman in **Acts 16:16** was possessed by a demon instigating the cult of Apollo, and thus had "a spirit of divination."

Met *hupantao* (5221), "to go to meet, to meet," is used in Matt. 8:28; Luke 8:27; John 11:20, 30, and, in the most authentic mss., in Matt. 28:9; Mark 5:2; Luke 14:31 (of meeting in battle); John 4:51; 12:18 and **Acts 16:16**. Some mss. have *apantao* (528) in Matt. 28:9; Mark 5:2; Luke 14:31; John 4:51; **Acts 16:16**.

Brought *parecho* (3930), usually, "to offer, furnish, supply" (lit., "to have near"), "to bring, in the sense of supplying," **Acts 16:16**; **19:24**.

Masters *kurios* (2962), "a lord, one who exercises power," is translated "masters" in Matt. 6:24; 15:27; Mark 13:35; Luke 16:13; **Acts 16:16**, **19**; Rom. 14:4, KJV (RV, "lord"); Eph. 6:5, 9 (twice), the 2nd time of Christ; so in Col. 3:22; 4:1. *See also* **Lord** at *Acts 2:36*.

Gain *ergasia* (2039), signifies (a) "work, working, performance" (from *ergon*, "work"), Eph. 4:19; in Luke 12:58, "diligence"; (b) "business or gain got by work," **Acts 16:16**, **19**; in **19:24**, **25**, the RV adheres to the meaning "business" (KJV, "gain" and "craft").

Soothsaying *manteuomai* (3132), "to divine, practice divination" (from *mantis*, "a seer, diviner"), occurs in **Acts 16:16**. The word is allied to *mainomai*, "to rave," and *mania*, "fury" displayed by those who were possessed by the evil spirit (represented by the pagan god or goddess) while delivering their oracular messages. Trench (*Syn.* Sec.vi) draws a distinction between this verb and *propheteuo*, not only as to their meanings, but as to the fact of the single occurrence of *manteuomai* in the NT, contrasted with the frequency of *propheteuo*, exemplifying the avoidance by NT writers of words the employment of which "would tend to break down the distinction between heathenism and revealed religion."

16:17 The same followed Paul and us, and cried, saying, These men are the servants of the most high God, which shew unto us the way of salvation.

Followed *katakoloutheo* (2628), "to follow behind or intently after," is used of the women on their way to Christ's tomb, Luke 23:55; of the demon-possessed maid in Philippi in "following" the missionaries, **Acts 16:17**.

Servants *doulos* (1401), an adjective, signifying "in bondage," Rom. 6:19 (neuter plural, agreeing with *mele*, "members"), is used as a noun, and as the most common and general word for "servant," frequently indicating subjection without the idea of bondage; it is used (a) of natural conditions, e.g., Matt. 8:9; 1 Cor. 7:21, 22 (1st part); Eph. 6:5; Col. 4:1; 1 Tim. 6:1; frequently in the four Gospels; (b) metaphorically of spiritual, moral and ethical conditions: "servants" (1) of God, e.g., **Acts 16:17**; Titus 1:1; 1 Pet. 2:16; Rev. 7:3; 15:3; the perfect example being Christ Himself, Phil. 2:7; (2) of Christ, e.g., Rom. 1:1; 1 Cor. 7:22 (2nd part); Gal. 1:10; Eph. 6:6; Phil. 1:1; Col. 4:12; Jas. 1:1; 2 Pet. 1:1; Jude 1; (3) of sin, John 8:34 (RV, "bondservants"); Rom. 6:17, 20; (4) of corruption, 2 Pet. 2:19 (RV, "bondservants").

High *see Acts 7:48*.

Shew *katangello* (2605), **Acts 16:17**; **26:23**; 1 Cor. 11:26, "proclaim"; in the last passage the partaking of the elements at the Lord's Supper is not a "showing forth" of His death, but a proclamation of it.

Way *see* **Ways** at *Acts 2:28*.

16:18 And this did she many days. But Paul, being grieved, turned and said to the spirit, I command thee in the name of Jesus Christ to come out of her. And he came out the same hour.

Grieved *see Acts 4:2*.

Name *see* **Names** at *Acts 1:15*.

Jesus *see Acts 7:59*.

Same Occasionally one of the forms of the pronoun *autos*, "self, same," is translated "very"; the RV rendering is sometimes "himself," etc., e.g., 1 Thess. 5:23, "(The God of peace) Himself"; see, however, John 14:11, "(the) very (works)"; Rom. 13:6 and Phil. 1:6, "(this) very (thing)"; Heb. 10:1, "(the) very (image)"; and the RV, "very" (KJV, "same") in Luke 12:12; 20:19; 24:13, 33; **Acts 16:18**; Rom. 9:17; Eph. 6:22.

Hour *see Acts 10:3*.

16:19 And when her masters saw that the hope of their gains was gone, they caught Paul and Silas, and drew *them* into the marketplace unto the rulers,

Masters *see Acts 16:16*.

Hope *elpis* (1680), in the NT, "favorable and confident expectation" (contrast the Sept. in Isa. 28:19, "an evil hope"). It has to do with the unseen and the future, Rom. 8:24, 25. "Hope" describes (a) the happy anticipation of good (the most frequent significance), e.g., Titus 1:2; 1 Pet. 1:21; (b) the ground upon which "hope" is based, **Acts 16:19**; Col. 1:27, "Christ in you the hope of glory"; (c) the object upon which the "hope" is fixed, e.g., 1 Tim. 1:1. Various phrases are used with the word "hope," in Paul's epistles and speeches: (1) **Acts 23:6**, "the hope and resurrection of the dead"; this has been regarded as a hendiadys (one by means of two), i.e., the "hope" of the resurrection; but the *kai*, "and," is epexegetic, defining the "hope," namely, the resurrection; (2) **Acts 26:6**, **7**, "the hope of the promise (i.e., the fulfillment of the promise) made unto the fathers"; (3) Gal. 5:5, "the hope of righteousness"; i.e., the believer's complete conformity to God's will, at the coming of Christ; (4) Col. 1:23, "the hope of the Gospel," i.e., the "hope" of the fulfillment of all the promises presented in the gospel; cf. 1:5; (5) Rom. 5:2, "(the) hope of the glory of God," i.e., as in Titus 2:13, "the blessed hope and appearing of the glory of our great God and Savior Jesus Christ"; cf. Col. 1:27; (6) 1 Thess. 5:8, "the hope of salvation," i.e., of the rapture of believers, to take place at the opening of the Parousia of Christ; (7) Eph. 1:18, "the hope of His (God's) calling," i.e., the prospect before those who respond to His call in the gospel; (8) Eph. 4:4, "the hope of your calling," the same as (7), but regarded from the point of view of the called; (9) Titus 1:2, and 3:7, "the hope of eternal life," i.e., the full manifestation and realization of that life which is already the believer's possession; (10) **Acts 28:20**, "the hope of Israel," i.e., the expectation of the coming of the Messiah. In Eph. 1:18; 2:12 and 4:4, the "hope" is objective. The objective and subjective use of the word need to be distinguished, in Rom. 15:4, e.g., the use is subjective. In the NT three adjectives are descriptive of "hope": "good," 2 Thess. 2:16; "blessed," Titus 2:13; "living," 1 Pet. 1:3. To these may be added Heb. 7:19, "a better hope," i.e., additional to the commandment, which became disannulled (v. 18), a hope centered in a new priesthood. In Rom. 15:13 God is spoken of as "the God of hope," i.e., He is the author, not the subject, of it. "Hope" is a factor in salvation, Rom. 8:24; it finds its expression in endurance under trial, which is the effect of waiting for the coming of Christ, 1 Thess. 1:3; it is "an anchor of the soul," staying it amidst the storms of this life, Heb. 6:18, 19; it is a purifying power, "every one that hath this hope set on Him (Christ) purifieth himself, even as He is pure," 1 John 3:3, RV (the apostle John's one mention of "hope"). The phrase "fullness of hope," Heb. 6:11, RV, expresses the completeness of its activity in the soul; cf. "fullness of faith," 10:22, and "of understanding," Col. 2:2 (RV, marg.).

Gains *see* Gain at *Acts 16:16*.

Caught *epilambano* (1949), "to lay hold," is translated "caught" in **Acts 16:19**, KJV; RV, "laid hold."

Drew *helkuo (or helko)* (1670), "to draw," differs from *suro*, as "drawing" does from violent "dragging." It is used of "drawing" a net, John 21:6, 11, Trench remarks, "At vv. 6 and 11 *helko* (or *helkuo*) is used; for there a *drawing* of the net to a certain point is intended; by the disciples to themselves in the ship, by Peter to himself upon the shore. But at v. 8 *helko* gives place to *suro*: for nothing is there intended but the *dragging* of the net, which had been fastened to the ship, after it through the water" (*Syn.*, Sec. xxi). This less violent significance, usually present in *helko*, but always absent from *suro*, is seen in the metaphorical use of *helko*, to signify "drawing" by inward power, by divine impulse, John 6:44; 12:32. So in the Sept., e.g., Song of Sol. 1:4, and Jer. 31:3, "with lovingkindness have I drawn thee." It is used of a more vigorous action, in John 18:10, of "drawing" a sword; in **Acts 16:19**; **21:30**, of forcibly "drawing" men to or from a place; so in Jas. 2:6, KJV, "draw," RV, "drag."

Marketplace *agora* (58), primarily "an assembly," or, in general, "an open space in a town" (akin to *ageiro*, "to bring together"), became applied, according to papyri evidences, to a variety of things, e.g., "a judicial assembly," "a market," or even "supplies, provisions" (Moulton and Milligan, *Vocab.*). In the NT it denotes "a place of assembly, a public place or forum, a marketplace." A variety of circumstances, connected with it as a public gathering place, is mentioned, e.g., business dealings such as the hiring of laborers, Matt. 20:3; the buying and selling of goods, Mark 7:4 (involving risk of pollution); the games of children, Matt. 11:16; Luke 7:32; exchange of greetings, Matt. 23:7; Mark 12:38; Luke 11:43; 20:46; the holding of trials, **Acts 16:19**; public discussions, **Acts 17:17**. Mark 6:56 records the bringing of the sick there. The word always carries with it the idea of publicity, in contrast to private circumstances. The RV always translates it "marketplace" or in the plural. The KJV sometimes changes the rendering to "markets" and translates it "streets" in Mark 6:56.

Rulers *see Acts 3:17*.

16:20 And brought them to the magistrates, saying, These men, being Jews, do exceedingly trouble our city,

Brought *prosago* (4317), "to bring to, or unto," **Acts 16:20**; 1 Pet. 3:18.

Magistrates *strategos* (4755), besides its application to "the captain of the Temple", denotes "a magistrate or governor," **Acts 16:20, 22, 35, 36, 38**. These were, in Latin terminology, the *duumviri* or *praetores*, so called in towns which were Roman colonies. They were attended by lictors or "sergeants," who executed their orders. In the circumstances of **Acts 16** they exceeded their powers, in giving orders for Roman citizens to be scourged; hence they became suppliants. *See also* **Captain** at *Acts 4:1*.

Trouble *ektarasso* (1613), "to throw into great trouble, agitate," is used in **Acts 16:20**, "do exceedingly trouble (our city)." In the Sept., Ps. 18:4; 88:16.

16:21 And teach customs, which are not lawful for us to receive, neither to observe, being Romans.

Teach *katangello* (2605), "to declare, proclaim," is translated "set forth" in **Acts 16:21**, RV (KJV, "teach"); "set I forth" in **Acts 17:23**, RV (KJV, "declare I").

Lawful *see* Let at *Acts 2:29*.

Receive *see* Received at *Acts 15:4*.

Observe *poieo* (4160), "to do," is translated "to observe" in **Acts 16:21**.

Romans *see* Rome at *Acts 2:10*.

16:22 And the multitude rose up together against them: and the magistrates rent off their clothes, and commanded to beat *them*.

Rose *sunephistemi* (4911), "to rise up together" (*sun*, together, *epi*, "up," *histemi*, "to stand"), is used in **Acts 16:22**, of the "rising up" of a multitude against Paul and Silas.

Magistrates *see* Captain at *Acts 4:1*.

Rent *perirrhegnumi*, or *periregnumi* (4048), "to tear off all round" (*peri*, "around"), is said of garments in **Acts 16:22**.

Beat *rhabdizo* (4463), "to beat with a rod, or stick, to cudgel," is the verbal form of *rhabdos*, "a rod, or staff," **Acts 16:22**; 2 Cor. 11:25.

16:23 And when they had laid many stripes upon them, they cast *them* into prison, charging the jailor to keep them safely:

Laid *see* Laid ...on at *Acts 6:6*.

Stripes *plege* (4127), "a blow, stripe, wound" (akin to *plesso*, "to strike," and *plektes*, "a striker"), is rendered "stripes" in Luke 12:48 (the noun is omitted in the original in v. 47 and the 2nd part of v. 48); **Acts 16:23, 33**; 2 Cor. 6:5; 11:23.

Jailor *desmophulax* (1200), "a prison keeper, jailer" (*desmos*, "a band," *phulax*, "a guard, keeper"), occurs in **Acts 16:23, 27, 36**.

Keep *see* Kept at *Acts 12:5*.

Safely *asphalos* (806), "safely," is so rendered in Mark 14:44 and **Acts 16:23**. In the Sept., Gen. 34:25. *See also* Assuredly at *Acts 2:36*.

16:24 Who, having received such a charge, thrust them into the inner prison, and made their feet fast in the stocks.

Charge *see* Command at *Acts 5:28*.

Thrust *ballo* (906), is rendered "to thrust" in John 20:25, 27, KJV (RV, put); **Acts 16:24**, KJV (RV, "cast"); so Rev. 14:16, 19.

Inner *esoteros* (2082), denotes "inner," **Acts 16:24** (of a prison); Heb. 6:19, with the article, and practically as a noun, "that which is within (the veil)," lit., "the inner (of the veil)." Cf. Eng., esoteric.

Fast *asphalizo* (805), "to make secure, safe, firm" (akin to *asphales*, "safe"), (*a*, negative, and *sphallo*, "to trip up"), is translated "make ... fast," in **Acts 16:24**, of prisoners' feet in the stocks. In Matt. 27:64, 65, 66, it is rendered "to make sure."

Stocks *xulon* (3586), "wood," is used of stocks in **Acts 16:24**.

16:25 And at midnight Paul and Silas prayed, and sang praises unto God: and the prisoners heard them.

Midnight *mesonuktion* (3317), an adjective denoting "at, or of, midnight," is used as a noun in Mark 13:35; Luke 11:5; **Acts 16:25; 20:7**.

Praises *humneo* (5214), denotes (a) transitively, "to sing, to laud, sing to the praise of" (Eng., "hymn"), **Acts 16:25**, KJV, "sang praises" (RV, "singing hymns"); Heb. 2:12, RV, "will I sing (Thy) praise," KJV, "will I sing praise (unto Thee)," lit., "I will hymn Thee"; (b) intransitively, "to sing," Matt. 26:30; Mark 14:26, in both places of the singing of the paschal hymns (Ps. 113-118, and 136), called by Jews the Great Hallel.

Prisoners *desmios* (1198), an adjective, primarily denotes "binding, bound," then, as a noun, "the person bound, a captive, prisoner" (akin to *deo*, "to bind"), Matt. 27:15, 16; Mark 15:6; **Acts 16:25, 27; 23:18; 25:14**, RV (KJV, "in bonds"), **27; 28:16, 17**; Eph. 3:1; 4:1; 2 Tim. 1:8; Philem. 1, 9; in Heb. 10:34 and 13:3, "in bonds."

Heard *epakroaomai* (1874), "to listen attentively to," is used in **Acts 16:25**, "(the prisoners) were listening to (them)," RV, expressive of rapt attention.

16:26 And suddenly there was a great earthquake, so that the foundations of the prison were shaken: and immediately all the doors were opened, and every one's bands were loosed.

Suddenly *see Acts 2:2*.

Earthquake *seismos* (4578), "a shaking, a shock," from *seio*, "to move to and fro, to shake," chiefly with the idea of concussion (Eng., "seismic," "seismology," "seismometry"), is used (a) of a "tempest" in the sea, Matt. 8:24; (b) of "earthquakes," Matt. 24:7; 27:54; 28:2; Mark 13:8; Luke 21:11; **Acts 16:26**; Rev. 6:12; 8:5; 11:13 (twice), 19; 16:18 (twice).

Foundations *themelios,* or *themelion* (2310), is properly an adjective denoting "belonging to a foundation" (connected with *tithemi,* "to place"). It is used (1) as a noun, with *lithos,* "a stone," understood, in Luke 6:48, 49; 14:29; Heb. 11:10; Rev. 21:14, 19; (2) as a neuter noun in **Acts 16:26**, and metaphorically, (a) of "the ministry of the gospel and the doctrines of the faith," Rom. 15:20; 1 Cor. 3:10, 11, 12; Eph. 2:20, where the "of" is not subjective (i.e., consisting of the apostles and prophets), but objective (i.e., laid by the apostles, etc.); so in 2 Tim. 2:19, where "the foundation of God" is "the foundation laid by God,"—not the Church (which is not a "foundation"), but Christ Himself, upon whom the saints are built; Heb. 6:1; (b) "of good works, 1 Tim. 6:19.

Prison *see Acts 5:21.*

Shaken *see* Moved at *Acts 2:25.*

Immediately *see Acts 3:7.*

Bands *desmos* (1199), from *deo,* "to bind", is usually found in the plural, either masculine or neuter; (a) it stands thus for the actual "bonds" which bind a prisoner, as in Luke 8:29; **Acts 16:26**; **20:23** (the only three places where the neuter plural is used); **22:30**; (b) the masculine plural stands frequently in a figurative sense for "a condition of imprisonment," Phil. 1:7, 13, i.e., "so that my captivity became manifest as appointed for the cause of Christ"; verses 14, 16; Col. 4:18; 2 Tim. 2:9; Philem. 10, 13; Heb. 10:34. In Mark 7:35 "the bond (KJV, string)" stands metaphorically for "the infirmity which caused an impediment in his speech." So in Luke 13:16, of the infirmity of the woman who was bowed together.

Loosed *aniemi* (447), "to send back" (*ana,* "back," *hiemi,* "to send"), "to leave, forbear," is translated "to loose," in **Acts 16:26**, of the "loosening" of bonds; **27:40**, rudder bands. Elsewhere, Eph. 6:9; Heb. 13:5.

16:27 And the keeper of the prison awaking out of his sleep, and seeing the prison doors open, he drew out his sword, and would have killed himself, supposing that the prisoners had been fled.

Keeper *see* Jailor at *Acts 16:23.*

Awaking *exupnos* (1853), "roused out of sleep" (*ek,* "out of," *hupnos,* "sleep"), occurs in **Acts 16:27**.

Out of … sleep *exupnos* (1853), **Acts 16:27**, signifies "out of sleep."

Drew *spao* (4685), "to draw or pull," is used, in the middle voice of "drawing" a sword from its sheath, Mark 14:47; **Acts 16:27**.

Supposing *see* Supposed at *Acts 7:25.*

Prisoners *see Acts 16:25.*

Fled *ekpheugo* (1628), "to flee away, escape," is translated "fled" in **Acts 16:27** (KJV only); **19:16**.

16:28 But Paul cried with a loud voice, saying, Do thyself no harm: for we are all here.

Cried *phoneo* (5455), "to utter a loud sound or cry," whether of animals, e.g., Matt. 26:34; or persons, Luke 8:8; 16:24; this is the word which Luke uses to describe the "cry" of the Lord at the close of His sufferings on the cross, Luke 23:46; also, e.g., **Acts 16:28**; Rev. 14:18.

Thyself *seauton,* "(as) thyself," Rom. 13:9; *seautou,* "of thyself," e.g., Matt. 4:6; *seauto,* "to thyself," **Acts 16:28**.

Harm *kakos* (2556), stands for "whatever is evil in character, base," in distinction (wherever the distinction is observable) from *poneros,* which indicates "what is evil in influence and effect, malignant." *Kakos* is the wider term and often covers the meaning of *poneros. Kakos* is antithetic to *kalos,* "fair, advisable, good in character," and to *agathos,* "beneficial, useful, good in act"; hence it denotes what is useless, incapable, bad; *poneros* is essentially antithetic to *chrestos,* "kind, gracious, serviceable"; hence it denotes what is destructive, injurious, evil. As evidence that *poneros* and *kakos* have much in common, though still not interchangeable, each is used of thoughts, cf. Matt. 15:19 with Mark 7:21; of speech, Matt. 5:11 with 1 Pet. 3:10; of actions, 2 Tim. 4:18 with 1 Thess. 5:15; of man, Matt. 18:32 with 24:48. The use of *kakos* may be broadly divided as follows: (a) of what is morally or ethically "evil," whether of persons, e.g., Matt. 21:41; 24:48; Phil. 3:2; Rev. 2:2, or qualities, emotions, passions, deeds, e.g., Mark 7:21; John 18:23, 30; Rom. 1:30; 3:8; 7:19, 21; 13:4; 14:20; 16:19; 1 Cor. 13:5; 2 Cor. 13:7; 1 Thess. 5:15; 1 Tim. 6:10; 2 Tim. 4:14; 1 Pet. 3:9, 12; (b) of what is injurious, destructive, baneful, pernicious, e.g., Luke 16:25; **Acts 16:28**; **28:5**; Titus 1:12; Jas. 3:8; Rev. 16:2, where *kakos* and *poneros* come in that order, "noisome and grievous."

Here *enthade* (1759), "here" in Luke 24:41; **Acts 16:28**; **25:24**.

16:29 Then he called for a light, and sprang in, and came trembling, and fell down before Paul and Silas,

Called *ait eo* (154), "to ask," is translated "called for" in **Acts 16:29** ("he called for lights").

Sprang *eispedao* (1530), "to spring" or "leap in," occurs in **Acts 16:29**, "sprang in." In the Sept., Amos 5:19.

Trembling *see* Trembled at *Acts 7:32*.

Fell *prospipto* (4363), "to fall towards anything" (*pros*, "towards"), "to strike against," is said of "wind," Matt. 7:25; it also signifies to "fall" down at one's feet, "fall" prostrate before, Mark 3:11; 5:33; 7:25; Luke 5:8; 8:28, 47; **Acts 16:29**.

16:30 And brought them out, and said, Sirs, what must I do to be saved?

Brought *see Acts 12:6*.

Sirs *see* Lord at *Acts 2:36*.

16:31 And they said, Believe on the Lord Jesus Christ, and thou shalt be saved, and thy house.

Lord *see Acts 2:36*.

Jesus *see Acts 7:59*.

Saved *see Acts 2:47*.

16:32 And they spake unto him the word of the Lord, and to all that were in his house.

Word *see* Words at *Acts 2:40*.

16:33 And he took them the same hour of the night, and washed *their* stripes; and was baptized, he and all his, straightway.

Took *see Acts 15:39*.

Washed *see Acts 9:37*.

Stripes *see Acts 16:23* e.

Straightway *see* Immediately at *Acts 3:7*.

16:34 And when he had brought them into his house, he set meat before them, and rejoiced, believing in God with all his house.

Set *paratithemi* (3908), "to place beside," "to set forth," of a parable, Matt. 13:24, RV (KJV, "put forth"); "to set before," of food, Mark 6:41; 8:6 (twice), 7; Luke 9:16; 10:8; 11:6; **Acts 16:34**; 1 Cor. 10:27.

Meat *trapeza* (5132), "a table" (Eng., "trapeze"), is used, by metonymy, of "the food on the table," in **Acts 16:34** (RV, marg., "a table") and translated "meat"; cf. "table" in Rom. 11:9; 1 Cor. 10:21. *See also* Tables at *Acts 6:2*.

Rejoiced *see* Glad at *Acts 2:26*.

House *panoikei* (3832), denotes "with all the house," **Acts 16:34**, i.e., "the household."

16:35 And when it was day, the magistrates sent the serjeants, saying, Let those men go.

Magistrates *see* Captain at *Acts 4:1*.

Sent *see* Send at *Acts 3:20*.

Serjeants *rhabdouchos* (4465), "a rod bearer" (*rhabdos*, "a rod," *echo*, "to hold"), one who carries a staff of office, was, firstly, an umpire or judge, later, a Roman lictor, **Acts 16:35, 38**. The duty of these officials was to attend Roman magistrates to execute their orders, especially administering punishment by scourging or beheading; they carried as their sign of office the *fasces* (whence "Fascist"), a bundle of rods with an axe inserted. At Philippi they acted under the *strategoi* or *pretors*.

16:36 And the keeper of the prison told this saying to Paul, The magistrates have sent to let you go: now therefore depart, and go in peace.

Keeper *see* Jailor at *Acts 16:23*.

Told *see* Reported at *Acts 4:23*.

Magistrates *see* Captain at *Acts 4:1*.

Let *see Acts 3:13*.

Peace *see* Set at *Acts 7:26*.

16:37 But Paul said unto them, They have beaten us openly uncondemned, being Romans, and have cast *us* into prison; and now do they thrust us out privily? nay verily; but let them come themselves and fetch us out.

Beaten *see Acts 5:40*.

Openly *see* Common at *Acts 5:18*.

Uncondemned *akatakritos* (178), rendered "uncondemned" in **Acts 16:37; 22:25** (*a*, negative, *katakrino*, "to condemn"), properly means "without trial, not yet tried." Sir W. M. Ramsay points out that the apostle, in claiming his rights, would probably use the Roman phrase *re incognita*, i.e., "without investigating our case" (*The Cities of St. Paul*, p. 225).

Romans *see* Rome at *Acts 2:10*.

Thrust *ekballo* (1544), "to cast out," is rendered "thrust ... out" in Luke 4:29, KJV (RV, "cast ... forth"); so 13:28 and **Acts 16:37**.

Privily *lathra* (2977), "secretly, covertly" (from a root *lath*– indicating "unnoticed, unknown," seen in *lanthano*, "to escape notice," *lethe*, "forgetfulness"), is translated "privily" in Matt. 1:19; 2:7; **Acts 16:37**; "secretly" in John 11:28 (in some mss., Mark 5:33).

Nay *ou* (3756), "no, not," expressing a negation absolutely, is rendered "nay," e.g., in Matt. 5:37; 13:29; John 7:12, KJV (RV, "not so"); **Acts 16:37**; 2 Cor. 1:17-19; Jas. 5:12.

Verily In **Acts 16:37**, *gar*, "for," is translated "verily."

Fetch In **Acts 16:37**, the RV gives to *exago*, "to bring out," the adequate meaning "let them ... bring us out," for the KJV, "let them fetch us out." "Fetch" is not sufficiently dignified for the just demand made.

16:38 And the serjeants told these words unto the magistrates: and they feared, when they heard that they were Romans.

Serjeants *see Acts 16:35.*

Told *see* Reported at *Acts 4:23.*

Magistrates *see* Captain at *Acts 4:1.*

Romans *see* Rome at *Acts 2:10.*

16:39-40 And they came and besought them, and brought *them* out, and desired *them* to depart out of the city.

And they went out of the prison, and entered into *the house of* Lydia: and when they had seen the brethren, they comforted them, and departed.

Desired *erotao* (2065), in Luke 7:36 is translated "desired"; in 14:32, RV, "asketh," for KJV, "desireth"; so in John 12:21; **Acts 16:39**; **18:20**; **23:20**; in v. **18** "asked," for KJV, "prayed."

Chapter 17

17:1 Now when they had passed through Amphipolis and Apollonia, they came to Thessalonica, where was a synagogue of the Jews:

Passed *diodeuo* (1353), "to travel through, or along" (*dia*, "through," hodos "a way"), is translated "they had passed through" in **Acts 17:1**, lit., "having passed through"; in Luke 8:1, "He went about," RV (KJV, "throughout").

17:2 And Paul, as his manner was, went in unto them, and three sabbath days reasoned with them out of the scriptures,

Manner *etho* (1486), "to be accustomed," is used in the passive participle as a noun, signifying "a custom," Luke 4:16; **Acts 17:2** (KJV, "manner"; RV, "custom"); in Matt. 17:15 and Mark 10:1, "was wont."

Reasoned *dialegomai* (1256), "to think different things with oneself, to ponder," then, "to dispute with others," is translated "to reason in **Acts 17:2**, KJV and RV; **17:17**, RV; **18:4**, **19**, KJV and RV; **19:8**, **9**, RV; **24:25**, KJV and RV; Heb. 12:5, RV, "reasoneth (with you)," KJV, "speaketh (unto you)."

17:3 Opening and alleging, that Christ must needs have suffered, and risen again from the dead; and that this Jesus, whom I preach unto you, is Christ.

Opening *see* Opened at *Acts 7:56.*

Alleging *paratithemi* (3908), "to place beside or to set before" (*para*, "beside," *tithemi*, "to put"), while often used in its literal sense of material things, as well as in its more common significance, "to commit, entrust," twice means "to set before one in teaching," as in putting forth a parable, Matt. 13:24, 31, RV. Once it is used of setting subjects before one's hearers by way of argument and proof, of Paul, in "opening and alleging" facts concerning Christ, **Acts 17:3**.

Needs *see Acts 1:16.*

Suffered *see* Passion at *Acts 1:3.*

Risen *see* Raised at *Acts 2:24.*

Preach *see* Preached at *Acts 4:2.*

17:4 And some of them believed, and consorted with Paul and Silas; and of the devout Greeks a great multitude, and of the chief women not a few.

Believed *peitho* (3982), "to persuade," in the middle and passive voices signifies "to suffer oneself to be persuaded," e.g., Luke 16:31; Heb. 13:18; it is sometimes translated "believe" in the RV, but not in **Acts 17:4**, RV, "were persuaded," and **27:11**, "gave (more) heed"; in **Acts 28:24**, "believed." *See also* **Persuaded** at *Acts 13:43.*

Consorted *proskleroo* (4345), lit., "to assign by lot" (*pros*, "to," *kleros*, "a lot"), "to allot," is found in **Acts 17:4**, "consorted with," imparting to the passive voice (the form of the verb there) a middle voice significance, i.e., "they joined themselves to," or "threw in their lot with." The passive voice significance can be retained by translating (in the stricter sense of the word), "they were allotted" (i.e., by God) to Paul and Silas, as followers or disciples.

Devout *see* Religious at *Acts 13:43.*

Chief *see Acts 13:50.*

17:5 But the Jews which believed not, moved with envy, took unto them certain lewd fellows of the baser sort, and gathered a company, and set all the city on an uproar, and assaulted the house of Jason, and sought to bring them out to the people.

Believed not *see* Unbelieving at *Acts 14:2.*

Moved with envy *see* Envy at *Acts 7:9.*

Took *proslambano* (4355), "to take to oneself" (*pros*), is used of food, **Acts 27:33-36**; of persons, of Peter's act toward Christ, Matt. 16:22; Mark 8:32; for evil purposes, **Acts 17:5**; for good purposes, **18:26**.

Lewd *poneros* (4190), akin to *ponos*, "labor, toil," denotes "evil that causes labor, pain, sorrow, malignant evil"; it is used (a) with the meaning bad, worthless, in the physical sense, Matt. 7:17-18; in the moral or ethical sense, "evil," wicked; of persons, e.g., Matt. 7:11; Luke 6:45; **Acts 17:5** (KJV, "lewd"); 2 Thess. 3:2; 2 Tim. 3:13; of "evil" spirits, e.g., Matt. 12:45; Luke 7:21; **Acts 19:12-13, 15-16**; of a generation, Matt. 12:39, 45; 16:4; Luke 11:29; of things, e.g., Matt. 5:11; 6:23; 20:15; Mark 7:22; Luke 11:34; John 3:19; 7:7; **Acts 18:14**; Gal. 1:4; Col. 1:21; 1 Tim. 6:4; 2 Tim. 4:18; Heb. 3:12; 10:22; Jas. 2:4; 4:16; 1 John 3:12; 2 John 11; 3 John 10; (b) with the meaning toilsome, painful, Eph. 5:16; 6:13; Rev. 16:2. Cf. *poneria*, "iniquity, wickedness."

Fellows *aner* (435), denotes "a man," in relation to his sex or age; in **Acts 17:5** (plural) it is rendered "fellows," as more appropriate to the accompanying description of them.

Baser *agoraios* (60), translated in the KJV of **Acts 17:5** "of the baser sort," RV, "of the rabble," signifies, lit., "relating to the market place"; hence, frequenting markets, and so sauntering about idly. It is also used of affairs usually transacted in the market-place, and hence of judicial assemblies, **Acts 19:38**, RV "courts" (KJV, "law"); the margin in both RV and KJV has "court days are kept."

Company *ochlopoieo*, lit., "to make a crowd" (*ochlos*, "a crowd," *poieo*, "to make"), is translated "gathered a company," in **Acts 17:5**, KJV; the RV corrects this to "gathering a crowd."

Uproar *thorubeo* (2350), "to make an uproar, to throw into confusion, or to wail tumultuously," is rendered "make ... ado," in Mark 5:39; elsewhere in Matt. 9:23; **Acts 17:5**; **20:10**.

Assaulted *ephistemi* (2186), lit., "to stand over" (*epi*, "over," *histemi*, "to stand"), signifies "to assault"; said in **Acts 17:5**, of those who attacked the house of Jason. For its usual meanings

People see *Acts 12:22*.

17:6 And when they found them not, they drew Jason and certain brethren unto the rulers of the city, crying, These that have turned the world upside down are come hither also;

Drew see Haling at *Acts 8:3*.

Rulers *politarches* (4173), "a ruler of a city" (*polis*, "a city," *archo*, "to rule"), "a politarch," is used in **Acts 17:6, 8**, of the magistrates in Thessalonica, before whom the Jews, with a mob of market idlers, dragged Jason and other converts, under the charge of showing hospitality to Paul and Silas, and of treasonable designs against the emperor. Thessalonica was a "free" city and the citizens could choose their own politarchs. The accuracy of Luke has been vindicated by the use of the term, for while classical authors use the terms *poliarchos* and *politarchos* of similar "rulers," the form used by Luke is supported by inscriptions discovered at Thessalonica, one of which mentions Sosipater, Secundus, and Gaius among the politarchs, names occurring as those of Paul's companions.

Crying see *Acts 8:7*.

Turned *anastatoo* (387), "to excite, unsettle," or "to stir up to sedition," is so translated in **Acts 21:38**, RV (KJV, "madest an uproar"); in **17:6**, "have turned (the world) upside down," i.e., "causing tumults"; in Gal. 5:12, RV, "unsettle" (KJV, "trouble"), i.e., by false teaching (here in the continuous present tense, lit., "those who are unsettling you"). The word was supposed not to have been used in profane authors. It has been found, however, in several of the papyri writings.

World see *Acts 11:28*.

Hither *enthade* (1759), "hither," John 4:15, 16; **Acts 17:6**; **25:17**.

17:7 Whom Jason hath received: and these all do contrary to the decrees of Caesar, saying that there is another king, *one* Jesus.

Received *hupodechomai* (5264), denotes "to receive under one's roof" (*hupo*, "under"), "receive as a guest, entertain hospitably," Luke 10:38; 19:6; **Acts 17:7**; Jas. 2:25.

Do *prasso* (4238), "to do, to practice," is translated "act" in the RV of **Acts 17:7** (KJV, "do").

Contrary see Presence at *Acts 3:16*.

Decrees see *Acts 16:4*.

17:8 And they troubled the people and the rulers of the city, when they heard these things.

Troubled see *Acts 15:24*.

Rulers see *Acts 17:6*.

17:9 And when they had taken security of Jason, and of the other, they let them go.

Security *hikanos* (2425), "sufficient," is used in its neuter form with the article, as a noun, in **Acts 17:9**, "(when they had taken) security," i.e., satisfaction, lit., "the sufficient." The use of *hikanos* in this construction is a Latinism in Greek. See Moulton, *Proleg.*, p. 20. Probably the bond given to the authorities by Jason and his friends included an undertaking that Paul would not return to Thessalonica. Any efforts to have the bond cancelled were unsuccessful; hence the reference to the hindrance by Satan (1 Thess. 2:18).

Of In John 6:46; 15:15; 17:7; **Acts 17:9**, the RV, "from" is to be observed, as rightly translating *para* (KJV, "of").

Other *loipos* (3062), "remaining," is frequently used to mean "the rest," and is generally so translated in the RV (KJV, "others" in Luke 8:10; **Acts 28:9**; Eph. 2:3; 1 Thess. 4:13; 5:6; 1 Tim. 5:20; KJV, "other" in Luke 18:11; **Acts 17:9**; Rom. 1:13; 2 Cor. 12:13; 13:2; Gal. 2:13; Phil. 1:13; 4:3); the neut. plur., lit., "remaining things," is used in Luke 12:26; 1 Cor. 11:34.

Let *see Acts 3:13.*

17:10 And the brethren immediately sent away Paul and Silas by night unto Berea: who coming *thither* went into the synagogue of the Jews.

Sent *see Acts 13:4.*

Went *apeimi* (549), "to go away," is found in **Acts 17:10**.

17:11 These were more noble than those in Thessalonica, in that they received the word with all readiness of mind, and searched the scriptures daily, whether those things were so.

Noble *eugenesteros* (2104), occurs in **Acts 17:11**, "more noble," i.e., "more nobleminded."

Received *see* Receive at *Acts 3:21.*

Readiness *prothumia* (4288), "eagerness, willingness, readiness" (*pro*, "forward," *thumos*, "mind, disposition," is translated "readiness of mind" in **Acts 17:11**, "readiness" in 2 Cor. 8:11; in v. 12, RV (KJV, "a willing mind"); in v. 19, RV "(our) readiness," KJV, "(your) ready mind"; in 9:2, RV, "readiness" (KJV, "forwardness of ... mind").

Searched *anakrino* (350), "to distinguish, or separate out so as to investigate (*krino*) by looking throughout (*ana*, intensive) objects or particulars," hence signifies "to examine, scrutinize, question, to hold a preliminary judicial examination preceding the trial proper" (this first examination, implying more to follow, is often present in the nonlegal uses of the word), e.g., Luke 23:14; figuratively, in 1 Cor. 4:3; it is said of searching the Scriptures in **Acts 17:11**; of "discerning" or determining the excellence or defects of a person or thing, e.g., 1 Cor. 2:14, KJV, "discerned"; RV, "judged"; in 1 Cor. 10:27, "asking (no) question" (i.e., not raising the question as to whether the meat is the residue from an idolatrous sacrifice). Except in Luke 23:14, this word is found only in Acts and 1 Cor. *See also* **Examined** at *Acts 4:9.*

Scriptures *see* **Scripture** at *Acts 1:16.*

17:12 Therefore many of them believed; also of honourable women which were Greeks, and of men, not a few.

Honourable *see Acts 13:50.*

17:13 But when the Jews of Thessalonica had knowledge that the word of God was preached of Paul at Berea, they came thither also, and stirred up the people.

Preached *see Acts 4:2.*

Stirred up *saleuo* (4531), "stirred up" in **Acts 17:13**. *See also* **Moved** at *Acts 2:25;* **Troubled** at *Acts 15:24.*

17:14 And then immediately the brethren sent away Paul to go as it were to the sea: but Silas and Timotheus abode there still.

"If I were the devil, one of my first aims would be to stop folk from digging into the Bible."

J. I. PACKER

Then *tote* (5119), a demonstrative adverb of time, denoting "at that time," is used (a) of concurrent events, e.g., Matt. 2:17; Gal. 4:8, "at that time"; v. 29, "then"; 2 Pet. 3:6, "(the world) that then was," lit., "(the) then (world)"; (b) of consequent events, "then, thereupon," e.g., Matt. 2:7; Luke 11:26; 16:16, "[from (KJV, "since")] that time"; John 11:14; **Acts 17:14**; (c) of things future, e.g., Matt. 7:23; 24:30 (twice), 40; eight times in ch. 25; 1 Cor. 4:5; Gal. 6:4; 1 Thess. 5:3; 2 Thess. 2:8. It occurs 90 times in Matthew, more than in all the rest of the NT together.

Sent *see Acts 7:12* Send.

As it were *see* **Far** at *Acts 11:19.*

Abode *hupomeno* (5278), lit., "to abide under" (*hupo*, "under"), signifies "to remain in a place instead of leaving it, to stay behind," e.g., Luke 2:43; **Acts 17:14**; or "to persevere," Matt. 10:22; 24:13; Mark 13:13; in each of which latter it is used with the phrase "unto the end"; or "to endure bravely and trustfully," e.g., Heb. 12:2-3, 7, suggesting endurance under what would be burdensome. See also Jas. 1:12; 5:11; 1 Pet. 2:20. Cf., *makrothumeo*, "to be longsuffering."

17:15 And they that conducted Paul brought him unto Athens:

and receiving a commandment unto Silas and Timotheus for to come to him with all speed, they departed.

Conducted *kathistemi* (2525), lit., "to stand down or set down" (*kata*, "down," *histemi*, "to stand"), has, among its various meanings, "the significance of bringing to a certain place, conducting," **Acts 17:15** (so the Sept. in Josh. 6:23; 1 Sam. 5:3; 2 Chron. 28:15).

Unto *see* **Far** at *Acts 11:19*.

Commandment *entole* (1785), denotes, in general, "an injunction, charge, precept, commandment." It is the most frequent term, and is used of moral and religious precepts, e.g., Matt. 5:19; it is frequent in the Gospels, especially that of John, and in his Epistles. See also, e.g., **Acts 17:15**; Rom. 7:8-13; 13:9; 1 Cor. 7:19; Eph. 2:15; Col. 4:10.

Speed In **Acts 17:15** "with all speed" is the rendering of the phrase *hos*, "as," *tachista*, "most speedily" (the superlative of *tachu*, "speedily"), i.e., "as speedily as possible."

Departed *see* **Gone out** at *Acts 13:42*.

17:16 Now while Paul waited for them at Athens, his spirit was stirred in him, when he saw the city wholly given to idolatry.

Waited *ekdechomai* (1551), lit. and primarily, "to take or receive from" (*ek*, "from," *dechomai*, "to receive"), hence denotes "to await, expect," the only sense of the word in the NT; it suggests a reaching out in readiness to receive something; "expecting," Heb. 10:13; "expect," 1 Cor. 16:11, RV (KJV, "look for"); to wait for, John 5:3 (KJV only); **Acts 17:16**; 1 Cor. 11:33, RV (KJV, "tarry for"); Jas. 5:7; to wait, 1 Pet. 3:20 in some mss.; "looked for," Heb. 11:10.

Spirit *see Acts 7:59*.

Stirred *paroxuno* (3947), primarily, "to sharpen," is used metaphorically, signifying "to rouse to anger, to provoke," in the passive voice, in **Acts 17:16**, RV, "was provoked" (KJV, "was stirred"); in 1 Cor. 13:5, RV, "is not provoked" (the word "easily" in KJV, represents no word in the original).

Wholly given to idolatry *kateidolos* (2712), an adjective denoting "full of idols" (*kata*, "throughout," and *eidolon*), is said of Athens in **Acts 17:16**, RV, and KJV, marg. (KJV, "wholly given to idolatry"). *See also* **Idol** at *Acts 7:41*.

17:17 Therefore disputed he in the synagogue with the Jews, and with the devout persons, and in the market daily with them that met with him.

Disputed *dialegomai* (1256), primarily signifies "to think different things with oneself, to ponder"; then, with other persons, "to converse, argue, dispute"; it is translated "to dispute" in Mark 9:34, the RV and KJV "had disputed" is somewhat unsuitable here, for the delinquency was not that they had wrangled, but that they had reasoned upon the subject at all; in **Acts 17:17**, KJV (RV, "reasoned," as in the KJV of **18:4**, **19**); in **19:8-9** (RV, "reasoning"); in **24:12**, "disputing"; in Jude 9, "disputed." *See also* **Reasoned** at *Acts 17:2*.

Devout *see* **Religious** at *Acts 13:43*.

Market *see* **Marketplace** at *Acts 16:19*.

Daily *see Acts 3:2*.

Met *paratunchano* (3909), "to happen to be near or present, to chance to be by" (*para*, "beside, near," *tunchano*, "to happen"), occurs in **Acts 17:17**, "met with (him)."

17:18 Then certain philosophers of the Epicureans, and of the Stoicks, encountered him. And some said, What will this babbler say? other some, He seemeth to be a setter forth of strange gods: because he preached unto them Jesus, and the resurrection.

Philosophers *philosophos* (5386), lit., "loving wisdom" (*philos*, "loving," *sophia*, "wisdom"), occurs in **Acts 17:18**.

Encountered *sumballo* (4820), lit., "to throw together" (*sun*, "with," *ballo*, "to throw"), is used of "encountering" in war, Luke 14:31, RV, "to encounter ... (in war)," for KJV, "to make war against"; of meeting in order to discuss, in **Acts 17:18**, "encountered," of the philosophers in Athens and the apostle.

Babbler *spemologos* (4691), "a babbler," is used in **Acts 17:18**. Primarily an adjective, it came to be used as a noun signifying a crow, or some other bird, picking up seeds (*sperma*, "a seed," *lego*, "to collect"). Then it seems to have been used of a man accustomed to hang about the streets and markets, picking up scraps which fall from loads; hence a parasite, who lives at the expense of others, a hanger on. Metaphorically it became used of a man who picks up scraps of information and retails them secondhand, a plagiarist, or of those who make a show, in unscientific style, of knowledge obtained from misunderstanding lectures. Prof. Ramsay points out that there does not seem to be any instance of the classical use of the word as a "babbler" or a mere talker. He finds in the word a piece of Athenian slang, applied to one who was outside any literary circle, an ignorant plagiarist. Other suggestions have been made, but without satisfactory evidence.

Seemeth *see* Pleased at *Acts 15:22.*

Setter forth *katangeleus* (2604), "a proclaimer, herald" (akin to *katangello*, "to proclaim"), is used in **Acts 17:18**, "a setter forth (of strange gods)." It is found in inscriptions in connection with proclamations made in public places.

Strange *xenos* (3581), denotes (a) "foreign, alien," **Acts 17:18**, of gods; Heb. 13:9, of doctrines; (b) "unusual," 1 Pet. 4:12, 2nd part, of the fiery trial of persecution.

Gods *daimonion* (1140), not a diminutive of *daimon*, but the neuter of the adjective *daimonios*, pertaining to a demon, is also mistranslated "devil," "devils." In **Acts 17:18**, it denotes an inferior pagan deity.

Resurrection *see Acts 1:22.*

17:19 And they took him, and brought him unto Areopagus, saying, May we know what this new doctrine, whereof thou speakest, *is*?

May *dunamai* (1410), "to be able, have power," whether by personal ability, permission, or opportunity, is sometimes rendered "may" or "might," e.g., Matt. 26:9; Mark 14:5; **Acts 17:19**; 1 Thess. 2:6. In the following the RV substitutes "can," "canst," "couldst," for the KJV, e.g., Matt. 26:42; Mark 4:32; 14:7; Luke 16:2; **Acts 24:11**; **25:11**; **27:12**; 1 Cor. 7:21; 14:31 (here the alteration is especially important, as not permission for all to prophesy, but ability to do so, is the meaning); Eph. 3:4. In the following the RV substitutes the verb "to be able," **Acts 19:40**; **24:8**; Rev. 13:17.

Know *see Acts 1:7.*

17:20 For thou bringest certain strange things to our ears: we would know therefore what these things mean.

Bringest *eisphero* (1533), denotes "to bring to," **Acts 17:20**; "to bring into," Luke 5:18, 19; 1 Tim. 6:7; Heb. 13:11.

Strange *xenizo* (3579), denotes "to think something strange," 1 Pet. 4:4, 12, passive voice, i.e., "they are surprised," and "be (not) surprised"; in **Acts 17:20**, the present participle, active, is rendered "strange," i.e., "surprising."

Ears *akoe* (189), "hearing," akin to *akouo*, "to hear," denotes (a) the sense of "hearing," e.g., 1 Cor. 12:17; 2 Pet. 2:8; (b) that which is "heard," a report, e.g., Matt. 4:24; (c) the physical organ, Mark 7:35, standing for the sense of "hearing"; so in Luke 7:1, RV, for KJV, "audience"; **Acts 17:20**; 2 Tim. 4:3-4 (in v. 3, lit., "being tickled as to the ears"); (d) a message or teaching, John 12:38; Rom. 10:16-17; Gal. 3:2, 5; 1 Thess. 2:13; Heb. 4:2, RV, "(the word) of hearing," for KJV, "(the word) preached."

Mean *see* Meaneth at *Acts 2:12.*

17:21 (For all the Athenians and strangers which were there spent their time in nothing else, but either to tell, or to hear some new thing.)

Strangers *xenos* (3581), "strange", denotes "a stranger, foreigner," Matt. 25:35, 38, 43, 44; 27:7; **Acts 17:21**; Eph. 2:12, 19; Heb. 11:13; 3 John 5. *See also* **Sojourn** at *Acts 7:6.*

There In **Acts 17:21**, "there" forms part of the translation of *epidemeo*, "to sojourn," "sojourning there," RV ("which were there," KJV).

Spent … time *eukaireo* (2119), "to have leisure or devote one's leisure to," is translated "spent their time," in **Acts 17:21**.

Either *e* (2228), is a disjunctive particle. One of its uses is to distinguish things which exclude each other, or one of which can take the place of another. It is translated "either" in Matt. 6:24; 12:33; Luke 16:13; **Acts 17:21**; 1 Cor. 14:6. The RV rightly omits it in Luke 6:42, and translates it by "or" in Luke 15:8; Phil. 3:12 and Jas. 3:12.

17:22 Then Paul stood in the midst of Mars' hill, and said, *Ye* men of Athens, I perceive that in all things ye are too superstitious.

Hill In **Acts 17:22**, KJV, *pagos* is translated "hill." "The Areopagus," RV, stands for the council (not hill) held near by.

Men *see Acts 1:16.*

Perceive *theoreo* (2334), "to be a spectator of, look at, discern," is translated "to perceive" in John 4:19 (indicating the woman's earnest contemplation of the Lord); so **Acts 17:22**; in John 12:19, RV, "behold" (KJV, "perceive ye").

Superstitious *deisidaimon* (1175), "reverent to the deity" (*deido*, "to fear"; *daimon*, "a demon," or "pagan god"), occurs in **Acts 17:22** in the comparative degree, rendered "somewhat superstitious," RV (KJV, "too superstitious"), a meaning which the word sometimes has; others, according to its comparative form, advocate the meaning "more religious (than others)," "quite religious" (cf. the noun in **25:19**). This is supported by Ramsay, who renders it "more than others respectful of what is divine"; so Deissmann in *Light from the Ancient East*, and others. It also agrees with the meaning found in Greek writers; the context too suggests that the adjective is used in a good sense; perhaps, after all with kindly ambiguity (Grimm-Thayer). An ancient epitaph has it in the sense of "reverent" (Moulton and Milligan).

17:23 For as I passed by, and beheld your devotions, I found an altar with this inscription, TO THE UNKNOWN GOD. Whom therefore ye ignorantly worship, him declare I unto you.

Beheld *anatheoreo* (333), is translated "beheld," in **Acts 17:23**, RV, "observed"; "considering" in Heb. 13:7.

Devotions *sebasma* (4574), denotes "an object of worship"; **Acts 17:23**; in 2 Thess. 2:4, "that is worshiped"; every object of "worship," whether the true God or pagan idols, will come under the ban of the Man of Sin.

Altar *bomos* (1041), properly, "an elevated place," always denotes either a pagan "altar" or an "altar" reared without divine appointment. In the NT the only place where this is found is **Acts 17:23**, as this is the only mention of such. Three times in the Sept., but only in the Apocrypha, *bomos* is used for the divine altar. In Josh. 22 the Sept. translators have carefully observed the distinction, using *bomos* for the altar which the two and a half tribes erected, vv. 10-11, 16, 19, 23, 26, 34, no divine injunction being given for this; in vv. 19, 28-29, where the altar ordained of God is mentioned, *thuciasterion* is used.

Inscription *epigrapho* (1924), "to write upon, inscribe" (*epi*, "upon," *grapho*, "to write"), is usually rendered by the verb "to write upon, over, or in," Mark 15:26; Heb. 8:10; 10:16; Rev. 21:12; it is translated by a noun phrase in **Acts 17:23**, "(with this) inscription," lit., "(on which) had been inscribed." Cf. the noun *epigraphe*, "a superscription."

Unknown *agnostos* (57), "unknown," is found in **Acts 17:23**.

Ignorantly *see* **Knew ... not** at *Acts 13:27*.

Worship *eusebeo* (2151), "to reverence, to show piety" towards any to whom dutiful regard is due (akin to *eusebes*, "pious, godly, devout"), is used in 1 Tim. 5:4 of the obligation on the part of children and grandchildren (RV) to express in a practical way their dutifulness "towards their own family"; in **Acts 17:23** of worshiping God.

Declare *katangello* (2605), lit., "to report down" (*kata*, intensive), is ordinarily translated "to preach"; "declare" in **Acts 17:23**, KJV (RV, "set forth"); in 1 Cor. 2:1, RV, "proclaiming," for KJV, "declaring." It is nowhere translated by "declare" in the RV.

17:24 God that made the world and all things therein, seeing that he is Lord of heaven and earth, dwelleth not in temples made with hands;

Made *see Acts 2:36*.

World *kosmos* (2889), primarily "order, arrangement, ornament, adornment" (1 Pet. 3:3), is used to denote (a) the "earth," e.g., Matt. 13:35; John 21:25; **Acts 17:24**; Rom. 1:20 (probably here the universe: it had this meaning among the Greeks, owing to the order observable in it); 1 Tim. 6:7; Heb. 4:3; 9:26; (b) the "earth" in contrast with Heaven, 1 John 3:17 (perhaps also Rom. 4:13); (c) by metonymy, the "human race, mankind," e.g., Matt. 5:14; John 1:9 [here "that cometh (RV, 'coming') into the world" is said of Christ, not of "every man"; by His coming into the world He was the light for all men]; v. 10; 3:16, 17 (thrice), 19; 4:42, and frequently in Rom., 1 Cor. and 1 John; (d) "Gentiles" as distinguished from Jews, e.g., Rom. 11:12, 15, where the meaning is that all who will may be reconciled (cf. 2 Cor. 5:19); (e) the "present condition of human affairs," in alienation from and opposition to God, e.g., John 7:7; 8:23; 14:30; 1 Cor. 2:12; Gal. 4:3; 6:14; Col. 2:8; Jas. 1:27; 1 John 4:5 (thrice); 5:19; (f) the "sum of temporal possessions," Matt. 16:26; 1 Cor. 7:31 (1st part); (g) metaphorically, of the "tongue" as "a world (of iniquity)," Jas. 3:6, expressive of magnitude and variety.

Lord *see Acts 2:36*.

Temples *naos* (3485), "a shrine or sanctuary," was used (a) among the heathen, to denote the shrine containing the idol, **Acts 17:24**; **19:24** (in the latter, miniatures); (b) among the Jews, the sanctuary in the "Temple," into which only the priests could lawfully enter, e.g., Luke 1:9, 21, 22; Christ, as being of the tribe of Judah, and thus not being a priest while upon the earth (Heb. 7:13, 14; 8:4), did not enter the *naos*; for 2 Thess. 2:4; (c) by Christ metaphorically, of His own physical body, John 2:19, 21; (d) in apostolic teaching, metaphorically, (1) of the church, the mystical body of Christ, Eph. 2:21; (2) of a local church, 1 Cor. 3:16, 17; 2 Cor. 6:16; (3) of the present body of the individual believer, 1 Cor. 6:19; (4) of the "Temple" seen in visions in the Apocalypse, 3:12; 7:15; 11:19; 14:15, 17; 15:5, 6, 8; 16:1, 17; (5) of the Lord God Almighty and the Lamb, as the "Temple" of the new and heavenly Jerusalem, Rev. 21:22.

Hands *see Acts 7:48*.

17:25 Neither is worshipped with men's hands, as though he needed any thing, seeing he giveth to all life, and breath, and all things;

Worshipped *therapeuo* (2323), (Eng., "therapeutics," etc.), denotes (a) primarily, "to serve" (cf. *therapeia* and *therapon*), **Acts 17:25** (KJV, "worshiped"); then, (b) "to heal, restore to health, to cure"; it is usually translated "to heal," but "cure" in Matt. 17:16, 18; Luke 7:21; 9:1; John 5:10; **Acts 28:9**, RV.

Men's *anthropinos* (442), "human, belonging to man," is used (a) of man's wisdom, in 1 Cor. 2:13 (some mss. have it in v. 4, where indeed it is implied; see, however, the RV); (b) of "man's judgement," 1 Cor. 4:3 (marg., "day"); (c) of "mankind," Jas. 3:7, lit., "the human nature," RV marg. (KJV marg., "nature of man"); (d) of human ordinance, 1 Pet. 2:13; Moulton and Milligan show from the papyri how strongly antithetic to the divine the use of the word is in this respect; (e) of temptation, 1 Cor. 10:13, RV, "such as man can bear" (KJV, "such as is common to man"), i.e., such as must and does come to "men"; of "men's" hands, **Acts 17:25**; (g) in the phrase "after the manner of men," Rom. 6:19.

Hands *see Acts 5:12.*

Needed *prosdeomai* (4326), "to want besides, to need in addition" (*pros*, "besides," *deomai*, "to want"), is used in **Acts 17:25**, "(as though) He needed (anything)"; the literal sense of *pros* is not to be stressed. In the Sept., Prov. 12:9, "lacking (bread)."

Life *see Acts 3:15.*

Breath *see* Wind at *Acts 2:2.*

17:26 And hath made of one blood all nations of men for to dwell on all the face of the earth, and hath determined the times before appointed, and the bounds of their habitation;

Blood In **Acts 17:26** (RV, "of one"; KJV, "of one blood"), the most authentic mss. do not contain the noun *haima*, "blood." So with the phrase "through His blood," in Col. 1:14.

Dwell *see* Dwellers at *Acts 1:19.*

Face *see* Presence at *Acts 3:13.*

Earth *see Acts 1:8.*

Determined *see* Determinate at *Acts 2:23.*

Times *see Acts 3:19.*

Appointed *horizo* (3724), (Eng., "horizon"), lit., "to mark by a limit," hence, "to determine, ordain," is used of Christ as ordained of God to be a judge of the living and the dead, **Acts 17:31**; of His being "marked out" as the Son of God, Rom. 1:4; of divinely appointed seasons, **Acts 17:26**, "having determined."

Bounds *horothesia* (3734), "the fixing of a boundary," rather than the boundary itself (from *horos*, "a boundary," and *tithemi*, "to place"), is used in **Acts 17:26**, "bounds."

Habitation *katoikia* (2733), "a settlement, colony, dwelling" (*kata*, and *oikos*), is used in **Acts 17:26**, of the localities divinely appointed as the dwelling places of the nations.

17:27 That they should seek the Lord, if haply they might feel after him, and find him, though he be not far from every one of us:

Seek *zeteo* (2212), signifies (a) "to seek, to seek for," e.g., Matt. 7:7, 8; 13:45; Luke 24:5; John 6:24; of plotting against a person's life, Matt. 2:20; **Acts 21:31**; Rom. 11:3; metaphorically, to "seek" by thinking, to "seek" how to do something, or what to obtain, e.g., Mark 11:18; Luke 12:29; to "seek" to ascertain a meaning, John 16:19, "do ye inquire"; to "seek" God, **Acts 17:27**, RV; Rom. 10:20; (b) "to seek or strive after, endeavor, to desire," e.g., Matt. 12:46, 47, RV, "seeking" (KJV, "desiring"); Luke 9:9, RV, "sought" (KJV, "desired"); John 7:19, RV, "seek ye" (KJV, "go ye about"); so v. 20; Rom. 10:3, RV, "seeking" (KJV, "going about"); of "seeking" the kingdom of God and His righteousness, in the sense of coveting earnestly, striving after, Matt. 6:33; "the things that are above," Col. 3:1; peace, 1 Pet. 3:11; (c) "to require or demand," e.g., Mark 8:12; Luke 11:29; 1 Cor. 4:2, "it is required"; 2 Cor. 13:3, "ye seek."

Feel *pselaphao* (5584), "to feel or grope about" (from *psao*, "to touch"), expressing the motion of the hands over a surface, so as to "feel" it, is used (a) metaphorically, of seeking aher God, **Acts 17:27**; (b) literally, of physical handling or touching, Luke 24:39 with 1 John 1:1; Heb. 12:18.

Far *see* Afar at *Acts 2:39.*

17:28 For in him we live, and move, and have our being; as certain also of your own poets have said, For we are also his offspring.

Move *kineo* (2795), "to set in motion, move" (hence, e.g., Eng. "kinematics," "kinetics," "cinema"), is used (a) of wagging the head, Matt. 27:39; Mark 15:29; (b) of the general activity of the human being, **Acts 17:28**; (c) of the "moving" of mountains, Rev. 6:14, in the sense of removing, as in Rev. 2:5, of removing a lampstand (there figuratively of causing a local church to be discontinued); (d) figuratively, of exciting, stirring up feelings and passions, **Acts 21:30** (passive voice); **24:5**, "a mover"; (e) of "moving burdens," Matt. 23:4. Cf. *sunkineo*, "to stir up," **Acts 6:12**.

And *kai* (2532), a conjunction, is usually a mere connective, meaning "and"; it frequently, however, has an ascensive or climactic use, signifying "even," the thing that is added being out of the ordinary, and producing a climax. The determination of this meaning depends on the context. Examples are Matt. 5:46-47; Mark 1:27; Luke 6:33 (RV); 10:17; John 12:42; Gal. 2:13, 17, where "also" should be "even"; Eph. 5:12. Examples where the RV corrects the KJV "and" or "also," by substituting "even," are Luke 7:49; **Acts 17:28**; Heb. 11:11; in 1 John 4:3 the RV rightly omits "even." When followed by "if" or "though," *kai* often signifies "even," e.g., Matt. 26:35; John 8:14. So sometimes when preceded by "if," e.g., 1 Cor. 7:11, where "but and if" should be "but even if." The epexegetic or explanatory use of *kai* followed by a noun in apposition, and meaning "namely," or "even" is comparatively rare. Winer's cautionary word needs heeding, that "this meaning has been introduced into too many passages" (Gram. of the NT, p. 546.). Some think it has this sense in John 3:5, "water, even the Spirit," and Gal. 6:16, "even the Israel of God."

Poets *poietes* (4163), primarily "a maker," later "a doer" (*poieo* "to make, to do"), was used, in classical Greek, of "an author," especially a "poet"; so **Acts 17:28**.

His These translate (a) forms of pronouns under he, (a frequent use: in 1 Pet. 2:24, "His own self"); the form *autou*, "his," becomes emphatic when placed between the article and the noun, e.g., 1 Thess. 2:19; Titus 3:5; Heb. 2:4; (in which "his" is emphasized), e.g., John 5:47; 9:28; 1 Cor. 10:28; 2 Cor. 8:9; 2 Tim. 2:26; Titus 3:7; 2 Pet. 1:16; (b) *heautou*, "of himself, his own"; the RV rightly puts "his own," for the KJV, "his," in Luke 11:21; 14:26; Rom. 4:19; 5:8, "His own (love)"; 1 Cor. 7:37; Gal. 6:8; Eph. 5:28, 33; 1 Thess. 2:11, 12; 4:4; in Rev. 10:7 the change has not been made; it should read "his own servants"; (c) *idios*, "one's own," "his own," in the RV, in Matt. 22:5; John 5:18; 2 Pet. 2:16; in Matt. 25:15, it is rendered "his several"; in John 19:27, "his own home," lit., "his own things"; in 1 Tim. 6:15, RV, "its own (times)," referring to the future appearing of Christ; in Heb. 4:10 (end of verse), both KJV and RV have "his," where it should be "his own"; so in **Acts 24:23**, for KJV and RV, "his"; in 1 Cor. 7:7, RV, "his own," KJV, "his proper"; (d) in **Acts 17:28**, the genitive case of the definite article, "His (offspring)," lit., "of the" (i.e., the one referred to, namely, God).

Offspring *genos* (1085), "a race, family" (akin to *ginomai*, "to become"), denotes "an offspring," **Acts 17:28, 29**; Rev. 22:16. *See also* **Kindred** at *Acts 4:6.*

17:29 Forasmuch then as we are the offspring of God, we ought not to think that the Godhead is like unto gold, or silver, or stone, graven by art and man's device.

Offspring *see Acts 17:28.*

Ought *opheilo* (3784), "to owe," is translated "ought," with various personal pronouns, in John 13:14; 19:7; **Acts 17:29**; Rom. 15:1; Heb. 5:3, KJV (RV, "he is bound"); 5:12; 1 John 3:16; 4:11; 3 John 8; with other subjects in 1 Cor. 11:7, 10; 2 Cor. 12:14; Eph. 5:28; 1 John 2:6.

Think *see* **Supposed** at *Acts 7:25.*

Godhead *theios* (2304), "divine" (from *theos*, "God"), is used of the power of God, 2 Pet. 1:3, and of His nature, v. 4, in each place, as that which proceeds from Himself. In **Acts 17:29** it is used as a noun with the definite article, to denote "the Godhead," the Deity (i.e., the one true God). This word, instead of *theos*, was purposely used by the apostle in speaking to Greeks on Mars Hill, as in accordance with Greek usage. In the Sept., Exod. 31:3; 35:31; Job 27:3; 33:4; Prov. 2:17.

Like unto *homoios* (3664), "like, resembling, such as, the same as," is used (a) of appearance or form John 9:9; Rev. 1:13, 15; 2:18; 4:3 (twice), 6, 7; 9:7 (twice), 10, 19; 11:1; 13:2, 11; 14:14; (b) of ability, condition, nature, Matt. 22:39; **Acts 17:29**; Gal. 5:21, "such like," lit., "and the (things) similar to these"; 1 John 3:2; Rev. 13:4; 18:18; 21:11, 18; (c) of comparison in parables, Matt. 13:31, 33, 44, 45, 47; 20:1; Luke 13:18, 19, 21; (d) of action, thought, etc. Matt. 11:16; 13:52; Luke 6:47, 48, 49; 7:31, 32; 12:36; John 8:55; Jude 7.

Gold *chrusos* (5557), is used (a) of "coin," Matt. 10:9; Jas. 5:3; (b) of "ornaments," Matt. 23:16, 17; Jas. 5:3 (perhaps both coin and ornaments); Rev. 18:12; some mss. have it in 1 Cor. 3:12; (c) of "images," **Acts 17:29**; (d) of "the metal in general," Matt. 2:11; Rev. 9:7 (some mss. have it in Rev. 18:16).

Silver *arguros* (696), akin to *argos*, "shining," denotes "silver." In each occurrence in the NT it follows the mention of gold, Matt. 10:9; **Acts 17:29**; Jas. 5:3; Rev. 18:12.

Stone *lithos* (3037), is used (I) literally, of (a) the "stones" of the ground, e.g., Matt. 4:3, 6; 7:9; (b) "tombstones," e.g., Matt. 27:60, 66; (c) "building stones," e.g., Matt. 21:42; (d) "a millstone," Luke 17:2; cf. Rev. 18:21; (e) the "tables (or tablets)" of the Law, 2 Cor. 3:7; (f) "idol images," **Acts 17:29**; (g) the "treasures" of commercial Babylon, Rev. 18:12, 16; (II) metaphorically, of (a) Christ, Rom. 9:33; 1 Pet. 2:4, 6, 8; (b) believers, 1 Pet. 2:5; (c) spiritual edification by scriptural teaching, 1 Cor. 3:12; (d) the adornment of the foundations of the wall of the spiritual and heavenly Jerusalem, Rev. 21:19; (e) the adornment of the seven angels in Rev. 15:6, RV (so the best texts; some have *linon*, "linen," KJV); (f) the adornment of religious Babylon, Rev. 17:4; (III) figuratively, of Christ, Rev. 4:3; 21:11, where "light" stands for "Light-giver" (*phoster*).

Graven *charagma* (5480), from *charasso*, "to engrave" (akin to *charakter*, "an impress," RV, marg., of Heb. 1:3), denotes (a) "a mark" or "stamp," e.g., Rev. 13:16, 17; 14:9, 11; 16:2; 19:20; 20:4; 15:2 in some mss.; (b) "a thing graven," **Acts 17:29**.

Art *techne* (5078), "an art, handicraft, trade," is used in **Acts 17:29**, of the plastic art; in **Acts 18:3**, of a trade or craft (KJV, "occupation," RV, "trade"); in Rev. 18:22, "craft" (cf. *technites*, "a craftsman," Eng., "technical").

Device *enthumesis* (1761), "a cogitation, an inward reasoning" (generally, evil surmising or supposition), is formed from *en*, "in," and *thumos*, "strong feeling, passion" (cf. *thumoo*, in the middle voice, "to be wroth, furious"); Eng., "fume" is akin; the root, *thu*, signifies "to rush, rage." The word is translated "device" in **Acts 17:29**, of man's production of images; elsewhere, "thoughts," Matt. 9:4; 12:25; Heb. 4:12, where the accompanying word *ennoia* denotes inward intentions.

17:30 And the times of this ignorance God winked at; but now commandeth all men every where to repent:

Ignorance *see Acts 3:17.*

Winked at *hupereidon* (5237), "to overlook" (an aorist form), is med in **Acts 17:30**, RV (KJV, "winked at"), i.e., God bore with them without interposing by way of punishment, though the debasing tendencies of idolatry necessarily developed themselves. *See also* **Forgiveness** at *Acts 5:31.*

Every where *pantachou* (3837), is translated "everywhere" in Mark 1:28, RV, of the report throughout Galilee concerning Christ; in Mark 16:20, of preaching; Luke 9:6, of healing; **Acts 17:30**, of a divine command for repentance; **28:22**, of disparagement of Christians; 1 Cor. 4:17, of apostolic teaching; in **Acts 24:3**, it is rendered "in all places." In the Sept., Isa. 42:22.

Repent *see Acts 2:38.*

17:31 Because he hath appointed a day, in the which he will judge the world in righteousness by *that* man whom he hath ordained; *whereof* he hath given assurance unto all *men*, in that he hath raised him from the dead.

Appointed *see Acts 1:23.*

World *see Acts 11:28.*

Will *mello* (3195), "to be about to," is translated "will" in Matt. 2:13 and John 7:35 (twice); "wilt," John 14:22; "will," **Acts 17:31**; "wouldest," **23:20**; "will," **27:10** and Rev. 3:16.

Ordained *see Acts 10:42. See also* **Determinate** at *Acts 2:23.*

Given *parecho* (3930), in the active voice, signifies "to afford, furnish, provide, supply" (lit., "to hold out or towards"; *para*, "near," *echo*, "to hold"); it is translated "hath given" in **Acts 17:31**; "giveth" in 1 Tim. 6:17 (in the sense of affording); in Col. 4:1, RV, "render" (KJV, "give").

Assurance *putis* (4102), "faith," has the secondary meaning of "an assurance or guarantee, e.g., **Acts 17:31**; by raising Christ from the dead, God has given "assurance" that the world will be judged by Him (the KJV margin, "offered faith" does not express the meaning). Cf. 1 Tim. 5:12, where "faith" means "pledge." *See also* **Faith** at *Acts 6:7.*

"The primitive church thought more about the Second Coming of Jesus Christ than about death or about heaven. The early Christians were looking not for a cleft in the ground called a grave but for a cleavage in the sky called Glory. They were watching not for the undertaker but for the uppertaker."

ALEXANDER MACLAREN

Raised *see Acts 2:24.*

17:32 And when they heard of the resurrection of the dead, some mocked: and others said, We will hear thee again of this *matter*.

Mocked *chleuazo* (5512), "to jest, mock, jeer at" (from *chleue*, "a jest"), is said of the ridicule of some of the Athenian philosophers at the apostle's testimony concerning the resurrection of the dead, **Acts 17:32**.

Others The plural of the definite article is translated "others" in **Acts 17:32**; in Jude 23, KJV, "others" (RV, "some").

This In **Acts 17:32** the RV rightly omits "*matter*"; in Heb. 4:5 "*place*" is italicized; it is frequently rendered "this man," e.g., Matt. 9:3; John 6:52; "of this sort," 2 Tim. 3:6, KJV (RV, "of these"); (b) as an adjective with a noun, either with the article and before it, e.g., Matt. 12:32, or after the noun (which is preceded by the article), e.g., Matt. 3:9 and 4:3, "these stones"; or without the article often forming a predicate, e.g., John 2:11; 2 Cor. 13:1.

Matter In **Acts 17:32**, the KJV adds "*matter*" to the pronoun "this," RV, "(concerning) this."

17:33-34 So Paul departed from among them.

Howbeit certain men clave unto him, and believed: among the which *was* Dionysius the Areopagite, and a woman named Damaris, and others with them.

Clave *see* **Join** at *Acts 5:13*.

Chapter 18

18:1 After these things Paul departed from Athens, and came to Corinth;

Departed *see* **Depart** at *Acts 1:4*.

18:2 And found a certain Jew named Aquila, born in Pontus, lately come from Italy, with his wife Priscilla; (because that Claudius had commanded all Jews to depart from Rome:) and came unto them.

Born *genos* (1085), "a generation, kind, stock," is used in the dative case, with the article, to signify "by race," in **Acts 18:2** and **24**, RV, for the KJV, "born." *See also* **Kindred** at *Acts 4:6*.

Lately *prosphatos* (4373), denotes "recently, lately," from the adjective *prosphatos*, "new, fresh, recent"; primarily, "newly slain," Heb. 10:20 (*phatos*, "slain"), is also found in **Acts 18:2**. In the Sept., Deut. 24:5; Ezek. 11:3.

Commanded *diatasso* (1299), signifies "to set in order, appoint, command," Matt. 11:1; Luke 8:55; 17:9-10; **Acts 18:2**; **23:31**; "gave order," 1 Cor. 16:1, RV. So in **Acts 24:23**, where it is in the middle voice.

18:3 And because he was of the same craft, he abode with them, and wrought: for by their occupation they were tentmakers.

Craft *homotechnos* (3673), "one of the same trade" (from *homos*, "same," and *techne*), is used in **Acts 18:3** (RV, "trade"). Cf. *architekton*, "master-builder," 1 Cor. 3:10. *See also* **Art** at *Acts 17:29*.

Occupation *techne* (5078), "an art" (Eng., "technique," "technical"), is used in **Acts 18:3** (2nd part) of a "trade," RV (KJV, "occupation").

Tentmakers *skenopoios* (4635), an adjective, "tentmaking" (*skene*, "a tent," *poieo*, "to make"), is used as a noun in **Acts 18:3**.

18:4 And he reasoned in the synagogue every sabbath, and persuaded the Jews and the Greeks.

Reasoned *see Acts 17:2*. *See also* **Disputed** at *Acts 17:17*.

18:5 And when Silas and Timotheus were come from Macedonia, Paul was pressed in the spirit, and testified to the Jews *that* Jesus *was* Christ.

Pressed *sunecho* (4912), "to hold together," is used physically of being held, or thronged, Luke 8:45; 19:43; 22:63; of being taken with a malady, Matt. 4:24; Luke 4:38; **Acts 28:8**; with fear, Luke 8:37; of being straitened or pressed in spirit with desire, Luke 12:50; **Acts 18:5**; Phil. 1:23; with the love of Christ, 2 Cor. 5:14. In one place it is used of the stopping of their ears by those who killed Stephen. *See also* **Stopped** at *Acts 7:57*.

Testified *see* **Testify** at *Acts 2:40*.

18:6 And when they opposed themselves, and blasphemed, he shook *his* raiment, and said unto them, Your blood *be* upon your own heads; I *am* clean: from henceforth I will go unto the Gentiles.

Opposed *antitasso* (498), is used in the middle voice in the sense of setting oneself against (*anti*, "against," *tasso*, "to order, set"), "opposing oneself to," **Acts 18:6**; elsewhere rendered by the verb "to resist," Rom. 13:2; Jas. 4:6; 5:6; 1 Pet. 5:5.

Shook *see Acts 13:51*.

Raiment For *himation*, rendered "raiment" in Matt. 17:2, KJV (RV, "garments"), so Matt. 27:31; Mark 9:3; Luke 23:34; John 19:24; **Acts 22:20**; Rev. 3:5, 18; 4:4; KJV and RV, **Acts 18:6**. *Himatismos* is rendered "raiment" in Luke 9:29; *enduma* in Matt. 3:4; 6:25, 28; 28:3 and Luke 12:23.

Heads *kephale* (2776), besides its natural significance, is used (a) figuratively in Rom. 12:20, of heaping coals of fire on a "head"; in **Acts 18:6**, "Your blood be upon your own heads," i.e., "your blood-guiltiness rest upon your own persons," a mode of expression frequent in the OT, and perhaps here directly connected with Ezek. 3:18, 20; 33:6, 8; see also Lev. 20:16; 2 Sam. 1:16; 1 Kings 2:37; (b) metaphorically, of the authority or direction of God in relation to Christ, of Christ in relation to believing men, of the husband in relation to the wife, 1 Cor. 11.3, of Christ in relation to the Church, Eph. 1:22; 4:15; 5:23; Col. 1:18; 2:19; of Christ in relation to principalities and powers, Col. 2:10. As to 1 Cor. 11:10, taken in connection with the context, the word "authority" probably stands, by metonymy, for a sign of authority (RV), the angels being witnesses of the preeminent relationship as established by God in the creation of man as just mentioned, with the spiritual significance regarding the position of Christ in relation to the Church; cf. Eph. 3:10; it is used of Christ as the foundation of the spiritual building set forth by the Temple, with its "corner stone," Matt. 21:42; symbolically also of the imperial rulers of the Roman power, as seen in the apocalyptic visions, Rev. 13:1, 3; 17:3, 7, 9.

Clean *katharos* (2513), "free from impure admixture, without blemish, spotless," is used (a) physically, e.g., Matt. 23:26; 27:59; John 13:10 (where the Lord, speaking figuratively, teaches that one who has been entirely "cleansed," needs not radical renewal, but only to be "cleansed" from every sin into which he may fall); 15:3; Heb. 10:22; Rev. 15:6; 19:8, 14; 21:18, 21; (b) in a Levitical sense, Rom. 14:20; Titus 1:15, "pure"; (c) ethically, with the significance free from corrupt desire, from guilt, Matt. 5:8; John 13:10-11; **Acts 20:26**; 1 Tim. 1:5; 3:9; 2 Tim. 1:3; 2:22; Titus 1:15; Jas. 1:27; blameless, innocent (a rare meaning for this word), **Acts 18:6**; (d) in a combined Levitical and ethical sense ceremonially, Luke 11:41, "all things are clean unto you."

Henceforth Positively, "henceforth" stands for the following: (a) *ap' arti* (i.e., *apo arti*), lit., "from now," e.g., Matt. 26:64; Luke 22:69; John 13:19, RV, and KJV marg., "from henceforth"; Rev. 14:13 (where *aparti* is found as one word in the best mss.); (b) *to loipon*, lit., "(for) the remaining (time)," Heb. 10:13; *tou loipou*, Gal. 6:17; (c) *apo tou nun*, lit., "from the now," e.g., Luke 1:48; 5:10; 12:52; **Acts 18:6**; 2 Cor. 5:16 (1st part).

18:7 And he departed thence, and entered into a certain *man's* house, named Justus, *one* that worshipped God, whose house joined hard to the synagogue.

Departed *metabaino* (3327), is rendered "to depart" in Matt. 8:34; 11:1; 12:9; 15:29; John 7:3; 13:1; **Acts 18:7**.

Entered *erchomai*, "to come," is never translated "to enter," in the RV; in the KJV, Mark 1:29; **Acts 18:7**.

Worshipped *see* ***Acts 16:14***.

Joined *sunomoreo* (4927), "to border on," is used of a house as being contiguous with a synagogue, in **Acts 18:7**, "joined hard to."

18:8 And Crispus, the chief ruler of the synagogue, believed on the Lord with all his house; and many of the Corinthians hearing believed, and were baptized.

Chief *archisunagogos* (752), "a ruler of a synagogue," translated "chief ruler of the synagogue," in **Acts 18:8, 17**, KJV, was the administrative officer supervising the worship.

Ruler of the synagogue *see* **Rulers of the synagogue** at ***Acts 13:15***.

Many *see* ***Acts 2:39***.

18:9 Then spake the Lord to Paul in the night by a vision, Be not afraid, but speak, and hold not thy peace:

Vision *see* **Sight** at ***Acts 7:31***.

Peace *siopao* (4623), "to be silent or still, to keep silence" (from *siope*, "silence"), is translated "to hold one's peace," in Matt. 20:31; 26:63; Mark 3:4; 9:34; 10:48; 14:61; Luke 19:40; **Acts 18:9**; in the Lord's command to the sea, in Mark 4:39, it is translated "peace"; in Luke 1:20, RV, "thou shalt be silent" (KJV, "dumb").

18:10 For I am with thee, and no man shall set on thee to hurt thee: for I have much people in this city.

Set *epitithemi* (2007), "to put, set or lay upon," is used of the placing over the head of Christ on the cross "His accusation," Matt. 27:37, "set up"; of attacking a person, **Acts 18:10**, "shall set on."

Hurt *kakoo* (2559), "to do evil to a person," is rendered "harm" in 1 Pet. 3:13, and in the RV of **Acts 18:10** (KJV, "hurt").

18:11 And he continued *there* a year and six months, teaching the word of God among them.

Continued *kathizo* (2523), "to sit down," denotes "to dwell," in **Acts 18:11** (RV, "dwelt," for KJV, "continued"). *See also* ***Acts 15:35***.

Year *see Acts 11:26.*

Six *see Acts 11:12.*

Months *see Acts 7:20.*

Teaching *see Acts 15:35.*

18:12 And when Gallio was the deputy of Achaia, the Jews made insurrection with one accord against Paul, and brought him to the judgment seat,

Deputy *see Acts 13:7. Anthupateo,* "to be proconsul," is in some texts in **Acts 18:12.**

Insurrection *katephistemi* (2721), signifies "to rise up against" (lit., "to cause to stand forth against," *kata,* "against," *epi,* "forth," *histemi,* "to cause to stand"), **Acts 18:12,** KJV, "made insurrection" (RV, "rose up against").

Accord *see Acts 1:14.*

Judgment seat *bema* (968), primarily, "a step, a pace" (akin to *baino,* "to go"), as in **Acts 7:5,** translated "to set (his foot) on," lit., "footroom," was used to denote a raised place or platform, reached by steps, originally that at Athens in the Pnyx Hill, where was the place of assembly; from the platform orations were made. The word became used for a tribune, two of which were provided in the law courts of Greece, one for the accuser and one for the defendant; it was applied to the tribunal of a Roman magistrate or ruler, Matt. 27:19; John 19:13; **Acts 12:21,** translated "throne"; **18:12, 16, 17; 25:6, 10, 17.** In two passages the word is used of the divine tribunal before which all believers are hereafter to stand. In Rom. 14:10 it is called "The judgement seat of God," RV (KJV, "of Christ"), according to the most authentic mss. The same tribunal is called "the judgment seat of Christ," 2 Cor. 5:10, to whom the Father has given all judgment, John 5:22, 27. At this *bema* believers are to be made manifest, that each may "receive the things done in (or through) the body," according to what he has done, "whether it be good or bad." There they will receive rewards for their faithfulness to the Lord. For all that has been contrary in their lives to His will they will suffer loss, 1 Cor. 3:15. This judgment seat is to be distinguished from the premillennial, earthly throne of Christ, Matt. 25:31, and the postmillennial "Great White Throne," Rev. 20:11, at which only "the dead" will appear. The judgment seat of Christ will be a tribunal held "in His Parousia," i.e., His presence with His saints after His return to receive them to Himself.

18:13 Saying, This *fellow* persuadeth men to worship God contrary to the law.

Persuadeth *anapeitho* (374), "to persuade, induce," in an evil sense, is used in **Acts 18:13.** In the Sept., Jer. 29:8.

Worship *see* **Worshipped** at *Acts 16:14.*

Contrary *para* (3844), "beside," has the meaning "contrary to" in **Acts 18:13**; Rom. 11:24; 16:17; "other than" in Gal. 1:8.

18:14 And when Paul was now about to open *his* mouth, Gallio said unto the Jews, If it were a matter of wrong or wicked lewdness, O *ye* Jews, reason would that I should bear with you:

About *see Acts 3:3.*

Open *see* **Opened** at *Acts 5:19.*

Wrong *adikema* (92), denotes "a misdeed, injury," in the concrete sense, **Acts 18:14,** "a matter of wrong"; **24:20,** RV, "wrongdoing" (KJV, "evil doing").

Wicked *poneros* (4190), is translated "wicked" in the KJV and RV in Matt. 13:49; 18:32; 25:26; Luke 19:22; **Acts 18:14**; 1 Cor. 5:13; in the following the RV substitutes "evil" for KJV, "wicked": Matt. 12:45 (twice); 13:19; 16:4; Luke 11:26; Col. 1:21; 2 Thess. 3:2; and in the following, where Satan is mentioned as "the (or that) evil one": Matt. 13:38; Eph. 6:16; 1 John 2:13, 14; 3:12 (1st part); 5:18; in v. 19 for KJV, "wickedness"; he is so called also in KJV and RV in John 17:15; 2 Thess. 3:3; KJV only in Luke 11:4; in 3 John 10, KJV, the word is translated "malicious," RV, "wicked."

Lewdness *rhadiourgema* (4467), "a reckless act," occurs in **Acts 18:14,** RV, "villany" (KJV, "lewdness"). *See also* **Lewd** at *Acts 17:5.*

Reason *logos* (3056), "a word," etc., has also the significance of "the inward thought itself, a reckoning, a regard, a reason," translated "reason" in **Acts 18:14,** in the phrase "reason would," *kata logon,* lit., "according to reason (I would bear with you)"; in 1 Pet. 3:15, "a reason (concerning the hope that is in you)."

18:15 But if it be a question of words and names, and *of* your law, look ye *to it*; for I will be no judge of such *matters*.

Question *see Acts 15:2.*

Your "Your" is most frequently the translation of *humon,* lit., "of you," the genitive plural of *su,* "thou, you"; it is translated "yours" in 1 Cor. 3:21, 22; in 8:9, "of yours"; 16:18; 2 Cor. 12:14. In the following the dative plural, *humin*, lit., "to you," is translated "your"; Luke 16:11, lit., "(who will entrust) to you"; in 21:15 "your adversaries" is, lit., "(those opposed) to you"; in 1 Cor. 6:5 and 15:34, KJV, "(I speak to) your (shame)," RV, "(I say *this* to move) you (to shame)," is, lit., "(I speak unto a shame) to you." The accusative plural, *humas*, preceded by *kata*, "according to," is rendered in **Acts 18:15** "your own (law)," RV, KJV, "your (law)," lit., "(of the law) according to you," with emphasis and scorn; in Eph. 1:15 the same construction is used of faith, but *kata* here means "among," as in the RV, "(the faith ... which is) among you," KJV, "your (faith)"; in John 14:26 "He shall ... bring to your remembrance" is, lit., "He shall ... put you in mind of."

Look *optomai* (3700), "to see" (from *ops*, "the eye"; cf. Eng. "optical," etc.), in the passive sense, "to be seen, to appear," is used (a) objectively, with reference to the person or thing seen, e.g., 1 Cor. 15:5-8, RV "appeared," for KJV, "was seen"; (b) subjectively, with reference to an inward impression or a spiritual experience, John 3:36, or a mental occupation, **Acts 18:15**, "look to it"; cf. Matt. 27:4, 24, "see (thou) to it," "see (ye) to it," throwing responsibility on others. *Optomai* is to be found in dictionaries under the word *horao*, "to see"; it supplies some forms that are lacking in that verb. *Horao* (3708), "to see", has the meaning of "seeing to" or "caring for a thing" in Matt. 27:4, "see (thou to it);" in **Acts 18:15**, "look to it (yourselves)"; the future (sing. *opsei*, plural, *opsesthe*), is used for the tense which is wanting in *horao*, and stands for the imperative. *See also* **See** at *Acts 2:27*.

Judge *see Acts 10:42*.

18:16 And he drave them from the judgment seat.

Drave *apelauno* (556), "to drive from" is used in **Acts 18:16**.

Judgment seat *see Acts 18:12*.

18:17 Then all the Greeks took Sosthenes, the chief ruler of the synagogue, and beat *him* before the judgment seat. And Gallio cared for none of those things.

Chief *see Acts 18:8*.

Judgment seat *see Acts 18:12*.

Ruler of the synagogue *see* **Rulers of the synagogue** at *Acts 13:15*.

Beat *tupto* (5180), from a root *tup*—, meaning "a blow," (*tupos*, "a figure or print") (Eng., "type") denotes "to smite, strike, or beat," usually not with the idea of giving a thrashing as with *dero*. It frequently signifies a "blow" of violence, and, when used in a continuous tense, indicates a series of "blows." In Matt. 27:30 the imperfect tense signifies that the soldiers kept on striking Christ on the head. So Mark 15:19. The most authentic mss. omit it in Luke 22:64. In that verse the word *paio*, "to smite," is used of the treatment given to Christ (*dero* in the preceding verse). The imperfect tense of the verb is again used in **Acts 18:17**, of the beating given to Sosthenes. Cf. **Acts 21:32**, which has the present participle. It is used in the metaphorical sense of "wounding," in 1 Cor. 8:12.

Cared *melei* (3199), the third person sing. of *melo*, used impersonally, signifies that "something is an object of care," especially the care of forethought and interest, rather than anxiety, Matt. 22:16; Mark 4:38; 12:14; Luke 10:40; John 10:13; 12:6; **Acts 18:17**; 1 Cor. 9:9 (RV, "Is it for the oxen that God careth?" The KJV seriously misses the point. God does "care" for oxen, but there was a divinely designed significance in the OT passage, relating to the service of preachers of the gospel); 7:21; 1 Pet. 5:7.

18:18 And Paul *after this* tarried *there* yet a good while, and then took his leave of the brethren, and sailed thence into Syria, and with him Priscilla and Aquila; having shorn *his* head in Cenchrea: for he had a vow.

Tarried *prosmeno* (4357), "to abide still, continue," is translated "tarried" in **Acts 18:18**, suggesting patience and steadfastness in remaining after the circumstances which preceded; in 1 Tim. 1:3, RV, "to tarry" (KJV, "to abide still"). *See also* **Cleave** at *Acts 11:23*.

While In **Acts 18:18**, RV, *hikanos* is rendered "many" (KJV, "good").

Took leave *apotasso* (657), used in the middle voice in the NT, lit. signifies "to arrange oneself off" (*apo*, "from," *tasso*, "to arrange"); hence, "to take leave of," Mark 6:46, RV, "had taken leave of" (KJV, "had sent ... away"); **Acts 18:18; 18:21**, RV, "taking his leave of" (KJV, "bade ... farewell"); 2 Cor. 2:13; in Luke 9:61 "to bid farewell"; in Luke 14:33 it has its other meaning "renouncing" (KJV, "forsaking").

Shorn *xurao* (3587), a late form of *xureo*, or *xuro*, from *xuron*, "a razor," occurs in **Acts 21:24** (middle voice), in connection with a vow (Num. 6:2-18; cf. **Acts 18:18**); 1 Cor. 11:5, 6 (2nd part in each). *See also* **Shearer** at *Acts 8:32*.

Vow *euche* (2171), denotes also "a vow," **Acts 18:18; 21:23**, with reference to the "vow" of the Nazirite (wrongly spelt Nazarite), see Num. 6, RV; in Jas. 5:15, "prayer."

18:19 And he came to Ephesus, and left them there: but he himself entered into the synagogue, and reasoned with the Jews.

Came *see Acts 16:1.*

There *see Acts 15:34.*

Reasoned *see Acts 17:2. See also* Disputed at *Acts 17:17.*

18:20 When they desired *him* to tarry longer time with them, he consented not;

Desired *see Acts 16:39.*

Tarry *see* Tarried at *Acts 9:43.*

Longer *pleion* (4119), "more," is used with *chronos*, "time," in Acts 18:20, "a longer time," RV (KJV, "longer").

Consented *epineuo* (1962), lit. "signifies to nod to" (*epi*, "upon or to," *neuo*, "to nod"); hence, "to nod assent, to express approval, consent," Acts 18:20.

18:21 But bade them farewell, saying, I must by all means keep this feast that cometh in Jerusalem: but I will return again unto you, if God will. And he sailed from Ephesus.

Bade ... farewell *see* Took leave at *Acts 18:18.*

All means *pantos* (3843), from *pas*, "all," is translated in various ways. The rendering "altogether" is found only in 1 Cor. 5:10 (where the RV margin gives the alternative meaning, "not at all" (meaning the fornicators of this world) and 9:10 (marg., "doubtless"). The other renderings are, in Luke 4:23, "doubtless" (KJV, "surely"); in Acts 18:21, "by all means," (KJV, "only"); so in1 Cor. 9:22, both RV and KJV; in Acts 21:22, "certainly" (KJV, "needs," which does not give an accurate meaning); in Acts 28:4, "no doubt"; in Rom. 3:9, "in no wise" (lit., "not at all"), so in 1 Cor. 16:12. In Acts 26:29 the KJV has given a misleading rendering in the phrase "both almost and altogether"; there is no Greek word here which means "altogether"; the RV corrects to "whether with little or with much."

Keep *poieo* (4160), "to do, make," signifies "to keep," in Matt. 26:18, in the Lord's statement, "I will keep the passover;" so in Acts 18:21, in some mss.; in John 7:19, where the KJV has "keepeth (the law)," the RV adheres to the usual meaning "doeth."

Feast *heorte* (1859), "a feast or festival," is used (a) especially of those of the Jews, and particularly of the Passover; the word is found mostly in John's Gospel (seventeen times); apart from the Gospels it is used in this way only in Acts 18:21; (b) in a more general way, in Col. 2:16, KJV, "holy day," RV, "a feast day."

Return *anakampto* (344), "to turn or bend back," occurs in Matt. 2:12; Luke 10:6 (i.e., as if it was unsaid); Acts 18:21; Heb. 11:15.

Sailed *see* Loosed at *Acts 13:13.*

18:22 And when he had landed at Caesarea, and gone up, and saluted the church, he went down to Antioch.

Landed *katerchomai* (2718), "to come down, or go down, descend," is used of coming to port by ship, in Acts 18:22, "landed"; 21:3 (ditto); 27:5, "came to."

18:23 And after he had spent some time *there*, he departed, and went over *all* the country of Galatia and Phrygia in order, strengthening all the disciples.

After *see Acts 3:24.*

Country *see* Land at *Acts 10:39. See also* Regions at *Acts 8:1.*

Order *see Acts 11:4.*

Strengthening *episterizo* is found in some texts in Acts 18:23, KJV, "strengthening." *See also* Confirming at *Acts 14:22.*

18:24 And a certain Jew named Apollos, born at Alexandria, an eloquent man, *and* mighty in the scriptures, came to Ephesus.

Born *see Acts 18:2. See also* Kindred at *Acts 4:6.*

Eloquent *logios* (3052), an adjective, from *logos*, "a word," primarily meant "learned, a man skilled in literature and the arts." In the KJV of Acts 18:24, it is translated "eloquent," said of Apollos; the RV is almost certainly right in translating it "learned." It was much more frequently used among the Greeks of one who was erudite than of one who was skilled in words. He had stores of "learning" and could use it convincingly.

Mighty *see Acts 7:22.*

Scriptures *see* Scripture at *Acts 1:16.*

Came *see Acts 16:1.*

18:25 This man was instructed in the way of the Lord; and being fervent in the spirit, he spake and taught diligently the things of the Lord, knowing only the baptism of John.

Instructed *katecheo* (2727), "to teach orally, inform, instruct," is translated by the verb "to instruct" in Luke 1:4; Acts 18:25 (RV marg., "taught by word of mouth"); Rom. 2:18; 1 Cor. 14:19, RV (KJV, "teach").

Way *see* Ways at *Acts 2:28.*

Fervent *zeo* (2204), "to be hot, to boil" (Eng. "zeal" is akin), is metaphorically used of "fervency" of spirit, **Acts 18:25**; Rom. 12:11.

Diligently *akribos* (199), means "accurately, exactly." The KJV translates it "diligently" in Matt. 2:8 and **Acts 18:25**; "perfectly" in 1 Thess. 5:2 (cf. Luke 1:3).

Knowing *see* Know at *Acts 10:28*.

18:26 And he began to speak boldly in the synagogue: whom when Aquila and Priscilla had heard, they took him unto *them*, and expounded unto him the way of God more perfectly.

Boldly *see Acts 9:27*.

Took *see Acts 17:5*.

Expounded *see Acts 11:4*.

Way *see* Ways at *Acts 2:28*.

Perfectly *akribesteron* (197), the comparative degree of *akribos*, "accurately, carefully," is used in **Acts 18:26**, KJV, "more perfectly," RV, "more carefully"; **23:15**, KJV, "more perfectly," RV, "more exactly"; so v. **20**; **24:22**, KJV, "more perfect," RV, "more exact" (lit., "knowing more exactly"). Cf. *akribeia*, "precision, exactness," **Acts 22:3**, and *akriboo*, "to learn carefully, to enquire with exactness," Matt. 2:7, 16.

18:27 And when he was disposed to pass into Achaia, the brethren wrote, exhorting the disciples to receive him: who, when he was come, helped them much which had believed through grace:

Disposed *boulomai* (1014), "to wish, to purpose, to will deliberately," indicating a predisposition acting through the deliberate will, is translated "was disposed" in **Acts 18:27**, KJV (RV, "was minded"). It expresses more strongly than *thelo*, the deliberate exercise of the will.

Exhorting *protrepo* (4389), lit., "to turn forward, propel" (*pro*, "before," *trepo*, "to turn"); hence, "to impel morally, to urge forward, encourage," is used in **Acts 18:27**, RV, "encouraged him" (Apollos), with reference to his going into Achaia; KJV, "exhorting the disciples"; while the encouragement was given to Apollos, a letter was written to the disciples in Achaia to receive him.

Receive *see* **Received** at *Acts 2:41*.

Helped *sumballo* (4820), lit., "to throw together" (*sun*, "with," *ballo*, "to throw"), is used in the middle voice in **Acts 18:27**, of helping or benefiting believers by discussion or ministry of the Word of God.

Much *polus* (4183), is used (a) as an adjective of degree, e.g., Matt. 13:5, "much (earth)"; **Acts 26:24**, "much (learning)"; in v. **29**, in the answer to Agrippa's "with but little persuasion," some texts have *pollo* (some *megalo*, "with great"), RV, "(whether with little or) with much"; of number, e.g., Mark 5:24, RV, "a great (multitude)," KJV, "much (people)"; so Luke 7:11; John 12:12; Rev. 19:1, etc.; (b) in the neuter singular form (*polu*), as a noun, e.g., Luke 16:10 (twice); in the plural (*polla*), e.g., Rom. 16:6, 12, "(labored) much," lit., "many things"; (c) adverbially, in the neuter singular, e.g., **Acts 18:27**; James 5:16; Matt. 26:9 (a genitive of price); in the plural, e.g., Mark 5:43, RV, "much" (KJV, "straitly"); Mark 9:26, RV, "much" (KJV, "sore"); John 14:30; and with the article, **Acts 26:24**; Rom. 15:22; 1 Cor. 16:19; Rev. 5:4.

18:28 For he mightily convinced the Jews, *and that* publickly, shewing by the scriptures that Jesus was Christ.

Mightily *eutonos* (2159), "vigorously, vehemently" (*eu*, "well," *teino*, "to stretch"), is translated "mightily" in **Acts 18:28**, KJV, of the power of Apollos in "confuting" the Jews (RV, "powerfully"); in Luke 23:10 it is rendered "vehemently." In the Sept., Josh. 6:7, "(let them sound) loudly."

Convinced *diakatelenchomai* (1246), "to confute powerfully," is an intensive form of *elencho*, "to convict" (*dia*, "through," *kata*, "down," both intensive), **Acts 18:28**, implying that "he met the opposing arguments in turn (*dia*), and brought them down to the ground (*kata*)." It carries also the thought that he brought home moral blame to them.

Publickly *see* **Common** at *Acts 5:18*.

Shewing *see Acts 9:39*.

Chapter 19

19:1 And it came to pass, that, while Apollos was at Corinth, Paul having passed through the upper coasts came to Ephesus: and finding certain disciples,

Upper *anoterikos* (510), "upper," is used in the plural in **Acts 19:1**, to denote "upper regions," with KJV, "coast," RV, "country," i.e., the high central plateau, in contrast to the roundabout way by the river through the valley.

Coasts *meros*, "a part," is translated "coasts" in Matt. 15:21; 16:13, KJV (RV, "parts,"); "country," RV, in **Acts 19:1**, KJV, "coasts"; this refers to the high land in the interior of Asia Minor.

19:2 He said unto them, Have ye received the Holy Ghost since ye believed? And they said unto him, We have not so much as heard whether there be any Holy Ghost.

Holy Ghost *see Acts 1:16.*

Much The negatives *oude* and *mede*, "not even" (RV) are translated "not so much as" in the KJV in Mark 2:2; Luke 6:3 and 1 Cor. 5:1; in the following the RV and KJV translate them "not so much as," Mark 3:20 (some mss. have *mete*, with the same meaning); **Acts 19:2**; in Mark 6:31 "no (leisure) so much as."

19:3-4 And he said unto them, Unto what then were ye baptized? And they said, Unto John's baptism.
Then said Paul, John verily baptized with the baptism of repentance, saying unto the people, that they should believe on him which should come after him, that is, on Christ Jesus.

Baptized, Baptism *see* Baptized at *Acts 1:5.*

19:5 When they heard *this*, they were baptized in the name of the Lord Jesus.

Baptized *see Acts 1:5.*

Jesus *see Acts 7:59.*

19:6 And when Paul had laid *his* hands upon them, the Holy Ghost came on them; and they spake with tongues, and prophesied.

Laid *see* Laid ... on at *Acts 6:6.*

Holy Ghost *see Acts 1:16.*

19:7-8 And all the men were about twelve.
And he went into the synagogue, and spake boldly for the space of three months, disputing and persuading the things concerning the kingdom of God.

Boldly *see Acts 9:27.*

Space In **Acts 19:8** and 10, *epi*, "for or during" (of time), is translated "for the space of"; in **19:34**, "about the space of."

Months *see Acts 7:20.*

Disputing *see* **Disputed** at *Acts 17:17. See also* **Reasoned** at *Acts 17:2.*

Persuading *see* **Persuaded** at *Acts 13:43.*

19:9 But when divers were hardened, and believed not, but spake evil of that way before the multitude, he departed from them, and separated the disciples, disputing daily in the school of one Tyrannus.

Divers The pronoun *tines*, "some" (the plural of *tis*, "someone"), is translated "divers" in the KJV of Mark 8:3 and **Acts 19:9**; RV, "some."

Hardened *skleruno* (4645), "to make dry or hard," is used in **Acts 19:9**; in Rom. 9:18, illustrated by the case of Pharaoh, who first persistently "hardened" his heart (see the RV marg. of Ex. 7:13, 22; 8:19; text of v. 32 and 9:7), all producing the retributive "hardening" by God, after His much long-suffering, 9:12, etc.; in Heb. 3:8, 13, 15; 4:7, warnings against the "hardening" of the heart.

Believed not *see* **Unbelieving** at *Acts 14:2.*

Spake evil *kakologeo* (2551), "to speak evil" (*kakos*, "evil," *lego*, "to speak"), is translated by the verb "to curse" in Matt. 15:4, and Mark 7:10, "to speak evil of father and mother," not necessarily "to curse," is what the Lord intended (RV). KJV and RV have the verb "to speak evil" in Mark 9:39 and **Acts 19:9**.

Way *see* **Ways** at *Acts 2:28.*

Multitude *see Acts 4:32.*

Departed *see* **Drew away** at *Acts 5:37.*

Separated *aphorizo* (873), "to mark off by bounds" (*apo*, "from," *horizo*, "to determine"; *horos*, "a limit"), "to separate," is used of "(a) the Divine action in setting men apart for the work of the gospel, Rom. 1:1; Gal. 1:15; (b) the Divine judgment upon men, Matt. 13:49; 25:32; (c) the separation of Christians from unbelievers, **Acts 19:9**; 2 Cor. 6:17; (d) the separation of believers by unbelievers, Luke 6:22; (e) the withdrawal of Christians from their brethren, Gal. 2:12. In (c) is described what the Christian must do, in (d) what he must be prepared to suffer, and in (e) what he must avoid."

Disputing *see* **Reasoned** at *Acts 17:2.*

School *schole* (4981), (whence Eng., "school") primarily denotes "leisure," then, "that for which leisure was employed, a disputation, lecture"; hence, by metonymy, "the place where lectures are delivered, a school," **Acts 19:9**.

19:10 And this continued by the space of two years; so that all they which dwelt in Asia heard the word of the Lord Jesus, both Jews and Greeks.

Continued *ginomai* (1096), signifies (a) "to begin to be" (suggesting origin); (b) "to become" (suggesting entrance on a new state); (c) "to come to pass" (suggesting effect); hence with the meaning (c) it is translated "continued" in **Acts 19:10**.

Word *see* **Words** at *Acts 2:40.*

19:11 And God wrought special miracles by the hands of Paul:

Wrought *see Acts 15:12.*

Miracles *see Acts 2:22.*

19:12 So that from his body were brought unto the sick handkerchiefs or aprons, and the diseases departed from them, and the evil spirits went out of them.

So that *see* Insomuch as at *Acts 1:19.*

Body *chros* (5559), signifies "the surface of a body," especially of the human body, **Acts 19:12**, with reference to the handkerchiefs carried from Paul's body to the sick.

Brought *apophero* (667), "to carry forth," is rendered "bring," in the KJV of 1 Cor. 16:3; **Acts 19:12** (RV, "carried away"); some mss. have *epiphero* here.

Sick *see Acts 9:37.*

Handkerchiefs *soudarion* (4676), a Latin word, *sudarium* (from *sudor*, "sweat"), denotes (a) "a cloth for wiping the face," etc., Luke 19:20; **Acts 19:12**; (b) "a headcovering for the dead," John 11:44; 20:7.

Aprons *simikinthion* (4612), "a thing girded round half the body" (Latin, *semicinctium*), was a narrow apron, or linen covering, worn by workmen and servants, **Acts 19:12**.

Diseases *nosos* (3554), akin to Lat., *nocere*, "to injure" (Eng., "nosology"), is the regular word for "disease, sickness," Matt. 4:23; 8:17; 9:35; 10:1, RV, "disease," KJV, "sickness"; in Matt. 4:24; Mark 1:34; Luke 4:40; 6:17; 9:1; **Acts 19:12**, KJV and RV render it "diseases." In Luke 7:21, KJV has "infirmities." The most authentic mss. omit the word in Mark 3:15.

Departed *apallasso* (525), lit., "to change from" (*apo*, "from," *allasso*, "to change"), is used once of "departing," said of the removal of diseases, **Acts 19:12**. In Heb. 2:15 it signifies "to deliver, release." In Luke 12:58, it is used in a legal sense, "to be quit of."

Evil *see* Lewd at *Acts 17:5.*

19:13 Then certain of the vagabond Jews, exorcists, took upon them to call over them which had evil spirits the name of the Lord Jesus, saying, We adjure you by Jesus whom Paul preacheth.

Vagabond *perierchomai* (4022), "to go about," as an itinerant (*peri*, "around," *erchomai*, "to go"), is used of certain Jews in **Acts 19:13**, RV, "strolling" (KJV, "vagabond").

Exorcists *exorkistes* (1845), denotes (a) "one who administers an oath"; (b) "an exorcist" (akin to *exorkizo*, "to adjure," from *orkos*, "an oath"), "one who employs a formula of conjuration for the expulsion of demons," **Acts 19:13**. The practice of "exorcism" was carried on by strolling Jews, who used their power in the recitation of particular names.

Took *epicheireo* (2021), "to take in hand" (*epi*, "upon," *cheir*, "the hand"), "to attempt, take upon oneself," is rendered "have taken in hand," Luke 1:1; "took upon (them)," **Acts 19:13**. *See also* **Went** at *Acts 9:29.*

Name *onomazo* (3687), denotes (a) "to name," "mention," or "address by name," **Acts 19:13**, RV, "to name" (KJV, "to call"); in the passive voice, Rom. 15:20; Eph. 1:21; 5:3; to make mention of the "Name" of the Lord in praise and worship, 2 Tim. 2:19; (b) "to name, call, give a name to," Luke 6:13, 14; passive voice, 1 Cor. 5:11, RV, "is named" (KJV, "is called"); Eph. 3:15 (some mss. have the verb in this sense in Mark 3:14 and 1 Cor. 5:1).

Adjure *horkizo* (3726), "to cause to swear, to lay under the obligation of an oath" (*horkos*, Mark 5:7; **Acts 19:13**), is connected with the Heb. word for a thigh, cf. Gen. 24:2, 9; 47:29. Some mss. have this word in 1 Thess. 5:27.

Preacheth *see* Preached at *Acts 8:5.*

19:14-15 And there were seven sons of *one* Sceva, a Jew, *and* chief of the priests, which did so.
And the evil spirit answered and said, Jesus I know, and Paul I know; but who are ye?

Evil *see* Lewd at *Acts 17:5.*

Know *see Acts 10:28.*

19:16 And the man in whom the evil spirit was leaped on them, and overcame them, and prevailed against them, so that they fled out of that house naked and wounded.

Man *see* Men at *Acts 14:15.*

Leaped *ephallomai* (2177), "to leap upon," is said of the demoniac in **Acts 19:16**.

Overcame *katakurieuo* (2634), is translated "overcome" in **Acts 19:16**.

Prevailed *ischuo* (2480), signifies (a) "to be strong in body, to be robust, in sound health," Matt. 9:12; Mark 2:17; (b) "to have power," as of the gospel, **Acts 19:20**; to prevail against, said of spiritual enemies, Rev. 12:8; of an evil spirit against exorcists, **Acts 19:16**; (c) "to be of force, to be effective, capable of producing results," Matt. 5:13 ("it is good for nothing"; lit., "it availeth nothing"); Gal. 5:6; in Heb. 9:17 it apparently has the meaning "to be valid" (RV, "for doth it ever avail ...?" for KJV, "it is of no strength"). It is translated "avail" with reference to prayer, in Jas. 5:16; cf. the strengthened form *exischuo* in Eph. 3:18.

Fled *see Acts 16:27.*

Naked *gumnos* (1131), signifies (a) "unclothed," Mark 14:52; in v. 51 it is used as a noun (*"his"* and *"body"* being italicized); (b) "scantily or poorly clad," Matt. 25:36, 38, 43, 44; **Acts 19:16** (with torn garments); Jas. 2:15; (c) "clad in the undergarment only" (the outer being laid aside), John 21:7; (d) metaphorically, (1) of "a bare seed," 1 Cor. 15:37; (2) of "the soul without the body," 2 Cor. 5:3; (3) of "things exposed to the allseeing eye of God," Heb. 4:13; (4) of "the carnal condition of a local church," Rev. 3:17; (5) of "the similar state of an individual," 16:15; (6) of "the desolation of religious Babylon," 17:16.

Wounded *traumaizo* (5135), "to wound," occurs in Luke 20:12 and **Acts 19:16.**

19:17 And this was known to all the Jews and Greeks also dwelling at Ephesus; and fear fell on them all, and the name of the Lord Jesus was magnified.

Fear *see Acts 2:43.*

Fell *see* **Fallen** at *Acts 8:16.*

Jesus *see Acts 7:59.*

Magnified *see Acts 5:13.*

19:18 And many that believed came, and confessed, and shewed their deeds.

Confessed *exomologeo* (1843), "to confess forth," i.e., "freely, openly," is used (a) "of a public acknowledgment or confession of sins," Matt. 3:6; Mark 1:5; **Acts 19:18**; Jas. 5:16; (b) "to profess or acknowledge openly," Matt. 11:25 (translated "thank," but indicating the fuller idea); Phil. 2:11; (c) "to confess by way of celebrating, giving praise," Rom. 14:11; 15:9. In Luke 10:21, it is translated "I thank," the true meaning being "I gladly acknowledge." In Luke 22:6 it signifies to consent (RV), for KJV, "promised." *See also* **Declared** at *Acts 15:4.*

Shewed *anangello* ("to declare"), Matt. 11:4, "tell"; John 16:13–15, "declare"; 16:25, "shall tell"; **Acts 19:18** and **20:20**, "declaring".

Deeds *praxis* (4234), denotes "a doing, transaction, a deed the action of which is looked upon as incomplete and in progress" (cf. *prasso*, "to practice"); in Matt. 16:27, RV, "deeds," for KJV, "works"; in Luke 23:51, "deed"; in v. 41, the verb is used; **Acts 19:18**; Rom. 8:13; Col. 3:9. In Rom. 12:4 it denotes an "action," business, or function, translated "office."

19:19 Many of them also which used curious arts brought their books together, and burned them before all *men*: and they counted the price of them, and found *it* fifty thousand *pieces* of silver.

Many *see Acts 9:23.*

Used *prasso* (4238), is translated by the verb "to practice" in the RV in the following passages (the KJV nowhere renders the verb thus): John 3:20 (marg.); 5:29 (marg.); **Acts 19:19**; Rom. 1:32 (twice); 2:1, 2, 3; 7:15, 19; Gal. 5:21. In **Acts 19:19**, KJV, *prasso*, "to practice" (RV), is rendered "used."

Curious arts *periergos* (4021), lit., "a work about" (*peri*, "about," *ergon*, "a work"), hence, "busy about trifles," is used, in the plural, of things superfluous, "curious (or magical) arts," **Acts 19:19**; in 1 Tim. 5:13, "busybodies."

Brought *sumphero* (4851), signifies (a), transitively, lit., "to bring together," (*sun*, "with," *phero*, "to bring"), **Acts 19:19**; (b) intransitively, "to be an advantage, profitable, expedient" (not merely 'convenient'); it is used mostly impersonally, "it is (it was) expedient"; so in Matt. 19:10, RV (negatively), KJV, "it is (not) good"; John 11:50; 16:7; 18:14; 1 Cor. 6:12; 10:23; 2 Cor. 8:10; 12:1; "it is profitable," Matt. 5:29-30; 18:6, RV; "was profitable," **Acts 20:20**; "to profit withal," 1 Cor. 12:7; in Heb. 12:10, used in the neuter of the present participle with the article as a noun, "for (our) profit." Cf. the adjective *sumphoros* (or *sumpheron*), "profitable," used with the article as a noun, 1 Cor. 7:35; 10:33.

Books *see* **Book** at *Acts 1:20.*

Burned *katakaio* (2618), signifies "to burn up, burn utterly," as of chaff, Matt. 3:12; Luke 3:17; tares, Matt. 13:30, 40; the earth and its works, 2 Pet. 3:10; trees and grass, Rev. 8:7. This form should be noted in **Acts 19:19**; 1 Cor. 3:15; Heb. 13:11, Rev. 17:16. In each piace the full rendering "burn utterly" might be used, as in Rev. 18:8.

Before *see Acts 7:46.*

Counted *sumpsephizo* (4860), "to count up," occurs in **Acts 19:19.**

Price *see* **Prices** at *Acts 4:34.*

Thousand *murias*, "a myriad, a vast number," "many thousands," Luke 12:1, RV; **Acts 21:20**; it also denotes 10,000, **Acts 19:19**, lit., "five ten-thousands"; Jude 14, "ten thousands"; in Rev. 5:11 "ten thousand times ten thousand" is, lit., "myriads of myriads"; in Rev. 9:16 in the best texts, *dismuriades muriadon*, "twice ten thousand times ten thousand" RV (KJV, "two hundred thousand thousand").

Pieces *argurion* (694), which frequently denotes "money," also represents "a silver coin," of the value of a shekel or *tetradrachmon* (four times the *drachme*); it is used in the plural in Matt. 26:15; 27:3-9. In **Acts 19:19**, "fifty thousand pieces of silver," is, lit., "fifty thousand of silver" (probably drachmas).

19:20 So mightily grew the word of God and prevailed.

Grew *see* Increased at *Acts 6:7*.

Prevailed *see Acts 19:16*.

19:21 After these things were ended, Paul purposed in the spirit, when he had passed through Macedonia and Achaia, to go to Jerusalem, saying, After I have been there, I must also see Rome.

Ended *pleroo* (4137), (a) "to fill," (b) "to fulfill, complete, end," is translated "had ended" in Luke 7:1; "were ended" (passive) in **Acts 19:21**

Purposed *tithemi* (5087), "to put, place," is used in the middle voice in **Acts 19:21**, "purposed," in the sense of resolving.

19:22 So he sent into Macedonia two of them that ministered unto him, Timotheus and Erastus; but he himself stayed in Asia for a season.

Ministered *see* Serve at *Acts 6:2*.

Stayed *epecho* (1907), has the meaning "to wait in a place, to stay," in **Acts 19:22**.

Season *chronos*, "time," is rendered "while" in Luke 18:4; John 7:33; 12:35 (1st part); 1 Cor. 16:7; *kairos*, "a season," "a while," Luke 8:13; in **Acts 19:22**, RV, "while" (KJV, "season"); for the different meanings of these words. *See also* Seasons at *Acts 1:7*.

19:23 And the same time there arose no small stir about that way.

Arose *see Acts 6:1*.

Small *see Acts 12:18*.

Stir *see Acts 12:18*.

Way *see* Ways at *Acts 2:28*.

19:24 For a certain *man* named Demetrius, a silversmith, which made silver shrines for Diana, brought no small gain unto the craftsmen;

Silversmith *argurokopos* (695), from *arguros* "silver" and *kopto*, "to beat," occurs in **Acts 19:24**. In the Sept., Judg. 17:4; Jer. 6:29.

Silver *argureos* (693), signifies "made of silver," **Acts 19:24**; 2 Tim. 2:20; Rev. 9:20.

Shrines *naos* (3485), "the inmost part of a temple, a shrine," is used in the plural in **Acts 19:24**, of the silver models of the pagan "shrine" in which the image of Diana (Greek Artemis) was preserved. The models were large or small, and were signs of wealth and devotion on the part of purchasers. The variety of forms connected with the embellishment of the image provided "no little business" for the silversmiths. *See also* **Temples** at *Acts 17:24*.

Brought *see Acts 16:16*.

Small *see Acts 12:18*.

Gain *ergasia* (2039), denotes "a business," **Acts 19:24, 25**, RV, KJV, "gain" and "craft" (from *ergon*, "work"). *See also Acts 16:16*.

Craftsmen *technites* (5079), "an artificer, artisan, craftsman," is translated "craftsman" in **Acts 19:24, 38** and Rev. 18:22. It is found elsewhere in Heb. 11:10 "builder"; but this is practically the same as "maker." Trench, *Syn.* Sec. qv., suggests that *technites* brings out the artistic side of creation, viewing God as "moulding and fashioning ... the materials which He called into existence." This agrees with the usage of the word in the Sept.

19:25 Whom he called together with the workmen of like occupation, and said, Sirs, ye know that by this craft we have our wealth.

Called together *sunathroizo*, "to assemble," is translated "he called together," in the KJV of **Acts 19:25**; RV, "he gathered together." *See also* Gathered at *Acts 12:12*.

Workmen *ergates* (2040), is translated "workers" in Luke 13:27 ("of iniquity"); 2 Cor. 11:13 ("deceitful"); Phil. 3:2 ("evil"); "workman," Matt. 10:10, KJV (RV, "laborer"); "workman," 2 Tim. 2:15; "workmen," **Acts 19:25**.

Occupation The phrase "of like occupation" in **Acts 19:25** translates the phrase *peri* ("about") *ta* ("the") *toiauta* ("such things"), i.e., lit., "(occupied) about such things." *See also* Gain at *Acts 16:16; 19:24*.

Sirs *see Acts 7:26*.

Know *see Acts 10:28*.

Wealth *euporia* (2142), primarily "facility" (*eu*, "well," *poros*, "a passage"), hence "plenty, wealth," occurs in **Acts 19:25**. Cf. *euporeo*, "to be well provided for, to prosper," Acts 11:29.

19:26 Moreover ye see and hear, that not alone at Ephesus, but almost throughout all Asia, this Paul hath persuaded and turned away much people, saying that they be no gods, which are made with hands:

Moreover *kai* (2532), and, is translated "moreover" in **Acts 24:6**; in the KJV, where the RV has "and," **Acts 19:26**.

Alone *monon* (3441), meaning "only, exclusively," e.g., Rom. 4:23; **Acts 19:26**, is translated "alone" in the KJV of John 17:20; RV, "only."

Almost *see* ***Acts 13:44***.

Turned *methistemi* (3179), is used metaphorically in **Acts 19:26**, "turned away (much people)."

Much *see* ***Acts 5:37***.

Gods *see* **God** at ***Acts 2:23***.

19:27 So that not only this our craft is in danger to be set at nought; but also that the temple of the great goddess Diana should be despised, and her magnificence should be destroyed, whom all Asia and the world worshippeth.

Craft *meros* (3313), "a part, portion," is translated "craft" in **Acts 19:27**, KJV; "trade," RV (cf. *ergasia* in v. 25).

Danger *kinduneuo* (2793), properly signifies "to run a risk, face danger," but is used in the NT in the sense of "being in danger, jeopardy," **Acts 19:27**, **40**. It is translated "were in jeopardy" in Luke 8:23, and "stand we in jeopardy," 1 Cor. 15:30.

Set at nought *apelegmos* (557), from *apo*, "from," and *elencho*, "to refute," denotes "censure, repudiation" (of something shown to be worthless), hence, "contempt," "disrepute," **Acts 19:27**, RV, "(come into) disrepute," for KJV, "(to be) set at nought." In **Acts 19:27**, KJV, the accusative case of *apelegmos*, "confutation, disrepute," preceded by the verb *erchomai*, "to come," and *eis*, "unto" or "into," is translated "be set at nought" (RV, "come into disrepute"). *See also* **No** at ***Acts 15:9***.

Temple *hieron* (2411), the neuter of the adjective *hieros*, "sacred," is used as a noun denoting "a sacred place, a temple," that of Artemis (Diana), **Acts 19:27**; that in Jerusalem, Mark 11:11, signifying the entire building with its precincts, or some part thereof, as distinct from the *naos*, "the inner sanctuary"; apart from the Gospels and Acts, it is mentioned only in 1 Cor. 9:13. Christ taught in one of the courts, to which all the people had access. *Hieron* is never used figuratively. The Temple mentioned in the Gospels and Acts was begun by Herod in 20 BC, and destroyed by the Romans in AD 70.

Great *see* ***Acts 8:8***.

Goddess *thea* (2299), is found in **Acts 19:27** (in some mss. in vv. **35**, **37**).

Despised *logizomai* (3049), primarily signifies "to reckon," whether by calculation or imputation, e.g., Gal. 3:6 (RV, "reckoned"); then, to deliberate, and so to suppose, "account," Rom. 8:36; 14:14 (KJV, "esteemeth"); John 11:50; 1 Cor. 4:1; Heb. 11:19; (KJV, "consider"); **Acts 19:27** ("made of no account"; KJV, "despised"); 1 Pet. 5:12 (KJV, "suppose"). It is used of love in 1 Cor. 13:5, as not taking "account" of evil, RV (KJV, "thinketh"). In 2 Cor. 3:5 the apostle uses it in repudiation of the idea that he and fellow-servants of God are so selfsufficient as to "account anything" (RV) as from themselves (KJV, "think"), i.e., as to attribute anything to themselves. Cf. 12:6. In 2 Tim. 4:16 it is used of laying to a person's "account" (RV) as a charge against him (KJV, "charge").

Magnificence *see* **Wonderful** at ***Acts 2:11***.

Destroyed *kathaireo* (2507), lit. signifies "to take down" (*kata*, "down," *haireo*, "to take"), the technical term for "removing a body after crucifixion," e.g., Mark 15:36; hence, "to pull down, demolish"; in **Acts 19:27**, according to the most authentic mss., the translation is (as the RV) "that she (Diana) should even be deposed from her magnificence" (possibly, in the partitive sense of the genitive, "destroyed from, or diminished in, somewhat of her magnificence"). *See also* ***Acts 13:19***.

World *see* ***Acts 11:28***.

Worshippeth *see* **Worshipped** at ***Acts 16:14***.

19:28 And when they heard *these sayings*, they were full of wrath, and cried out, saying, Great *is* Diana of the Ephesians.

Full *see* ***Acts 6:3***.

Wrath *thumos* (2372), "hot anger, passion," is translated "wrath" in Luke 4:28; **Acts 19:28**; Rom. 2:8, RV; Gal. 5:20; Eph. 4:31; Col. 3:8; Heb. 11:27; Rev. 12:12; 14:8, 10, 19; 15:1, 7; 16:1; 18:3; "wraths" in 2 Cor. 12:20; "fierceness" in Rev. 16:19; 19:15.

19:29 And the whole city was filled with confusion: and having caught Gaius and Aristarchus, men of Macedonia, Paul's companions in travel, they rushed with one accord into the theatre.

Filled *see* ***Acts 2:4***.

Confusion *sunchusis* (4799), "a pouring or mixing together" (*sun*, "with," *cheo*, "to pour"); hence "a disturbance, confusion, a tumultuous disorder, as of riotous persons," is found in **Acts 19:29**.

Caught *see* ***Acts 6:12***.

Companions *sunekdemos* (4898), "a fellow-traveler" (*sun*, "with," *ek*, "from," *demos*, "people"; i.e., "away from one's people"), is used in **Acts 19:29**, of

Paul's companions in travel, in 2 Cor. 8:19, "travel with"; a closer rendering would be "(as) our fellow-traveler."

Rushed *see* Ran at *Acts 7:57.*

Accord *see Acts 1:14.*

Theatre *theatron* (2302), "a theater," was used also as "a place of assembly," **Acts 19:29, 31**; in 1 Cor. 4:9 it is used of "a show" or "spectacle."

19:30 And when Paul would have entered in unto the people, the disciples suffered him not.

People *see Acts 12:22.*

Suffered *see Acts 14:16.*

19:31 And certain of the chief of Asia, which were his friends, sent unto him, desiring *him* that he would not adventure himself into the theatre.

Chief *asiarches* (775), "an Asiarch," was one of certain officers elected by various cities in the province of Asia, whose function consisted in celebrating, partly at their own expense, the public games and festivals; in **Acts 19:31**, RV, the word is translated "chief officers of Asia" (KJV, "chief of Asia"). It seems probable, according to Prof. Ramsay, that they were "the high priests of the temples of the Imperial worship in various cities of Asia"; further, that "the Council of the Asiarchs sat at stated periods in the great cities alternately ... and were probably assembled at Ephesus for such a purpose when they sent advice to St. Paul to consult his safety." A festival would have brought great crowds to the city.

Desiring *see* Desired at *Acts 8:31. See also* Gave at *Acts 1:26.*

Adventure *didomi* (1325), "to give," is once used of giving oneself to go into a place, "to adventure" into, **Acts 19:31**, of Paul's thought of going into the midst of the mob in the theater at Ephesus.

Theatre *see Acts 19:29.*

19:32 Some therefore cried one thing, and some another: for the assembly was confused; and the more part knew not wherefore they were come together.

Some In the following *alloi*, "others" ("some" in the KJV), is translated "others" in the RV, Matt. 13:5, 7; Mark 4:7 ("other"); 8:28; Luke 9:19; John 9:9. Followed by a correlative expression it denotes "some," e.g., **Acts 19:32; 21:34**.

One *see Acts 5:25.*

Assembly *see* Church at *Acts 7:38.*

Confused *see* Confounded at *Acts 2:6.*

More *pleion* (4119), the comparative degree of *polus*, "much," is used (a) as an adjective, e.g., John 15:2; **Acts 24:11**, RV, "(not) more (than)" (KJV, "yet but"); Heb. 3:3; (b) as a noun, or with a noun understood, e.g., Matt. 20:10; Mark 12:43; **Acts 19:32** and **27:12**, "the more part"; 1 Cor. 9:19; (c) as an adverb, Matt. 5:20, "shall exceed," lit., "(shall abound) more (than)"; 26:53; Luke 9:13. *See also* Many at *Acts 2:40.*

Wherefore *heneka* with *tinos* (the genitive case of *ti*), "because of what," **Acts 19:32**.

19:33 And they drew Alexander out of the multitude, the Jews putting him forward. And Alexander beckoned with the hand, and would have made his defence unto the people.

Drew ... out In **Acts 19:33**, where the most authentic mss. have *sumbibazo*, the RV translates it "brought" (marg., "instructed"), KJV, "draw out." Some mss. have *probibazo*, "to bring or drag forward."

Putting ... forward *proballo* (4261), "to put forward," is so used in **Acts 19:33**.

Beckoned *see* Beckoning at *Acts 12:17.*

Defence *apologeomai* (626), "to talk oneself off from" (*apo*, "from," *lego*, "to speak"), "to answer by way of making a defense for oneself" (besides its meaning "to excuse," Rom. 2:15; 2 Cor. 12:19), is translated "answer" in Luke 12:11; 21:14; in **Acts 19:33**, KJV and RV both have "made defense"; in **Acts 24:10; 25:8; 26:1-2**, the RV has the verb to make a defense, for the KJV, "to answer," and in **26:24** for the KJV, "spake for himself."

People *see Acts 12:22.*

19:34 But when they knew that he was a Jew, all with one voice about the space of two hours cried out, Great *is* Diana of the Ephesians.

Knew *epiginosko* (1921), "to gain a full knowledge of, to become fully acquainted with," is translated "to perceive" in Mark 5:30, RV (KJV, "knowing"); Luke 1:22; 5:22; **Acts 19:34**, RV (KJV, "knew"). *See also Acts 9:30.*

Space *see Acts 19:8.*

19:35 And when the townclerk had appeased the people, he said, *Ye* men of Ephesus, what man is there that knoweth not how that the city of the Ephesians is a worshipperof the great goddess Diana, and of the *image* which fell down from Jupiter?

Townclerk *grammateus* (1122), "a writer, scribe," is used in **Acts 19:35** of a state "clerk," an important official, variously designated, according to inscriptions found in Graeco-Asiatic cities. He was responsible for the form of decrees first approved by the Senate, then sent for approval in the popular assembly, in which he often presided. The decrees having been passed, he sealed them with the public seal in the presence of witnesses. Such an assembly frequently met in the theater. The Roman administration viewed any irregular or unruly assembly as a grave and even capital offense, as tending to strengthen among the people the consciousness of their power and the desire to exercise it. In the circumstances at Ephesus the town clerk feared that he might himself be held responsible for the irregular gathering.

Appeased *katastello* (2687), "to quiet" (lit., "to send down," *kata,* "down," *stello,* "to send"), in the passive voice, "to be quiet, or to be quieted," is used in **Acts 19:35** and **36**, in the former verse in the active voice, KJV, "appeased"; RV, "quieted"; in the latter, the passive, "to be quiet" (lit., 'to be quieted').

Men, Man *see* **Men** at *Acts 1:16.*

Worshipper *neokoros* (3511), **Acts 19:35**, RV, and KJV marg., "temple keeper" (KJV, "worshiper"), is used in profane Greek of "one who has charge of a temple." Coin inscriptions show that it was an honorary title given to certain cities, especially in Asia Minor, where the cult of some god or of a deified human potentate had been established, here to Ephesus in respect of the goddess Artemis. Apparently the imperial cult also existed at Ephesus.

Goddess *see Acts 19:27.*

Fell In **Acts 19:35** *diopetes,* from *dios,* "heaven," *pipto,* "to fall," i.e., "fallen" from the sky, is rendered "image which fell down from Jupiter" (RV marg., "heaven").

19:36 Seeing then that these things cannot be spoken against, ye ought to be quiet, and to do nothing rashly.

Spoken against *anantirrhetos* (368), lit., "not to be spoken against" (*a,* negative, *n,* euphonic, *anti,* "against," *rhetos,* "spoken"), is rendered "cannot be gainsaid" in **Acts 19:36**, RV.

Ought *dei* (1163), denotes "it is necessary," "one must"; in Luke 24:26, KJV, "ought" (RV "behoved it"); the neuter of the present participle, used as a noun, is translated "things which they ought (not)" in 1 Tim. 5:13; in **Acts 19:36**, "ye ought".

Quiet *see* **Appeased** at *Acts 19:35.*

Nothing *see Acts 4:21.*

Rashly *propetes* (4312), lit. means "falling forwards" (from *pro,* "forwards," and *pipto,* "to fall"); it is used metaphorically to signify "precipitate, rash, reckless," and is said (a) of persons, 2 Tim. 3:4; "headstrong" is the appropriate rendering; (b) of things, **Acts 19:36**, RV, "(nothing) rash" (KJV, "rashly").

19:37 For ye have brought hither these men, which are neither robbers of churches, nor yet blasphemers of your goddess.

Blasphemers *blasphemeo* (987), "to blaspheme, rail at or revile," is used (a) in a general way, of any contumelious speech, reviling, calumniating, railing at, etc., as of those who railed at Christ, e.g., Matt. 27:39; Mark 15:29; Luke 22:65 (RV, "reviling"); 23:39; (b) of those who speak contemptuously of God or of sacred things, e.g., Matt. 9:3; Mark 3:28; Rom. 2:24; 1 Tim. 1:20; 6:1; Rev. 13:6; 16:9, 11, 21; "hath spoken blasphemy," Matt. 26:65; "rail at," 2 Pet. 2:10; Jude 8, 10; "railing," 2 Pet. 2:12; "slanderously reported," Rom. 3:8; "be evil spoken of," Rom. 14:16; 1 Cor. 10:30; 2 Pet. 2:2; "speak evil of," Titus 3:2; 1 Pet. 4:4; "being defamed," 1 Cor. 4:13. The verb (in the present participial form) is translated "blasphemers" in **Acts 19:37**; in Mark 2:7, "blasphemeth," RV, for KJV, "speaketh blasphemies." There is no noun in the original representing the English "blasphemer." This is expressed either by the verb, or by the adjective *blasphemos.*

Robbers *hierosulos* (2417), an adjective signifying "robbing temples" (*hieron,* "a temple," and *sulao,* "to rob"), is found in **Acts 19:37**. Cf. *hierosuleo,* "to rob a temple," Rom. 2:22, KJV, "commit sacrilege."

Goddess *see Acts 19:27.*

19:38 Wherefore if Demetrius, and the craftsmen which are with him, have a matter against any man, the law is open, and there are deputies: let them implead one another.

Craftsmen *see Acts 19:24.*

Matter *see Acts 8:21.*

Law The verb *ago* is used in **Acts 19:38** of "keeping" certain occasions, as of the holding of law courts, RV "(the courts) are open," KJV marg., "court days are kept"; Moulton and Milligan illustrate from the papyri the use of the adjective *agoraios,* in the plural with *hemerai,* "days," understood, in regard to certain market days; certain court days are what are indicated here. The conjecture that the meaning is "courts are now being held" (*sunodoi* being understood as meetings of the court instead of "days") is scarcely so appropriate to the circumstances. *See also* Baser at *Acts 17:5*.

Open *ago* (71), "to lead," or "to keep or spend a day," is so used in **Acts 19:38**.

Deputies *see* Deputy at *Acts 13:7*.

Implead *enkaleo* (1458), "to bring a charge against, or to come forward as an accuser against," lit. denotes "to call in" (*en*, "in," *kaleo*, "to call"), i.e., "to call (something) in or against (someone)"; hence, "to call to account, to accuse," **Acts 19:38**, RV (KJV, "implead"); in v. **40**, "accused" (KJV, "call in question"). It is used in four other places in the Acts, **23:28-29**; **26:2**, 7, and elsewhere in Rom. 8:33, "shall lay to the charge."

One another *see* One to another at *Acts 7:26*.

19:39 But if ye enquire any thing concerning other matters, it shall be determined in a lawful assembly.

Enquire *epizeteo*, "to seek after or for" (*epi*, "after," *zeteo*, "to seek"), is rendered "inquire" in **Acts 19:39**, KJV (RV, "seek"). *See also* Sought at *Acts 12:19*.

Other *see Acts 2:4*.

Determined *epiluo* (1956), lit., "to loosen upon," denotes "to solve, expound," Mark 4:34; "to settle," as of a controversy, **Acts 19:39**, KJV, "it shall be determined," RV, "it shall be settled."

Lawful *ennomos* (1772), (a) "lawful, legal," lit., "in law" (*en*, "in," and *nomos*), or strictly, "what is within the range of law," is translated "lawful" in **Acts 19:39**, KJV (RV, "regular"), of the legal tribunals in Ephesus; (b) "under law" (RV), in relation to Christ, 1 Cor. 9:21, where it is contrasted with *anomos*; the word as used by the apostle suggests not merely the condition of being under "law," but the intimacy of a relation established in the loyalty of a will devoted to his Master.

Assembly *see* Church at *Acts 7:38*.

19:40 For we are in danger to be called in question for this day's uproar, there being no cause whereby we may give an account of this concourse.

Danger *see Acts 19:27*.

Called in question *enkaleo*, **Acts 19:40**, KJV, "called in question," signifies "to accuse," as always in the RV. *See also* Implead at *Acts 19:38*.

Uproar *stasis* (4714), primarily "a standing" (akin to *histemi*, "to cause to ("stand"), then "an insurrection," is translated "riot" in **Acts 19:40** RV (KJV, "uproar"). *See also* Dissension at *Acts 15:2*.

Cause *aition* (158), "a fault," is translated "cause (of death)" in Luke 23:22; "cause" in **Acts 19:40** (of a riot); "fault" in Luke 23:4, 14.

May *see Acts 17:19*.

Give *see* Gave at *Acts 4:33*.

Account *logos* (3056), "a word or saying," also means "an account which one gives by word of mouth," Matt. 12:36; Matt. 18:23, RV, "reckoning"; 16:2; **Acts 19:40**; **20:24** (KJV, "count"); Rom. 14:12; Phil. 4:17; Heb. 13:17; 1 Pet. 4:5.

Concourse *suntrophe* (4963), "a turning together" (*sun*, "with," *trepo*, "to turn"), signifies (a) that which is rolled together; hence (b) a dense mass of people, concourse, **Acts 19:40**.

19:41 And when he had thus spoken, he dismissed the assembly.

Thus *touto*, the neuter of *houtos*, "this," is translated "thus" in 2 Cor. 1:17; 5:14; Phil. 3:15; the neuter plural, *tauta*, "these things," e.g., in Luke 18:11; 19:28; John 9:6; 11:43; 13:21; 20:14; **Acts 19:41**.

Dismissed *see Acts 15:30*.

Assembly *see* Church at *Acts 7:38*.

Chapter 20

20:1 And after the uproar was ceased, Paul called unto *him* the disciples, and embraced *them*, and departed for to go into Macedonia.

Uproar *thorubos* (2351), "a noise, uproar, tumult," is rendered "tumult" in Matt. 27:24 and Mark 5:38; in Matt. 26:5, RV (KJV, "uproar"), so in Mark 14:2; in **Acts 20:1**, "uproar," KJV and RV; in **24:18**, "tumult"; in **21:34**, KJV, "tumult" (RV, "uproar").

Ceased *see Acts 5:42*.

Called *see* Called for at *Acts 10:5*.

Embraced *aspazomai* (782), lit. signifies "to draw to oneself"; hence, "to greet, salute, welcome," the ordinary meaning, e.g., in Rom. 16, where it is used 21 times. It also signifies "to bid farewell," e.g., **Acts 20:1**, RV, "took leave of" (KJV, "embraced"). A "salutation or farewell" was generally made by embracing and kissing (see Luke 10:4, which indicates the possibility of delay on the journey by frequent salutation). In Heb. 11:13 it is said of those who greeted the promises from afar, RV, "greeted," for KJV, "embraced." Cf. *aspasmos*, "a salutation."

20:2-3 And when he had gone over those parts, and had given them much exhortation, he came into Greece,

And *there* abode three months. And when the Jews laid wait for him, as he was about to sail into Syria, he purposed to return through Macedonia.

Abode *see* Tarried at *Acts 15:33.*

Months *see Acts 7:20.*

Laid wait *epiboule* (1917), lit., "a plan against," is translated "lying in wait," **Acts 20:19**, KJV, and "laid wait," **20:3**; **23:30**. *See also* **Laying await** at *Acts 9:24.*

About *see Acts 3:3.*

Sail *see* Loosed at *Acts 13:13.*

Purposed *gnome* (1106), "an opinion, purpose, judgment," is used in the genitive case with *ginomai*, "to come to be," in **Acts 20:3**, "he purposed," KJV (RV, "he determined"), lit., "he came to be of purpose."

Return *see* Returned at *Acts 1:12.*

20:4 And there accompanied him into Asia Sopater of Berea; and of the Thessalonians, Aristarchus and Secundus; and Gaius of Derbe, and Timotheus; and of Asia, Tychicus and Trophimus.

Accompanied *sunepomai* (4902), lit., "to follow with" (*sun*, "with," *hepomai*, "to follow"), came to mean simply "to accompany," **Acts 20:4**.

20:5 These going before tarried for us at Troas.

Going *see* Went at *Acts 12:10.*

Tarried *see Acts 9:43.*

20:6 And we sailed away from Philippi after the days of unleavened bread, and came unto them to Troas in five days; where we abode seven days.

Bread *see Acts 12:3.*

Abode *see Acts 12:19.*

20:7 And upon the first *day* of the week, when the disciples came together to break bread, Paul preached unto them, ready to depart on the morrow; and continued his speech until midnight.

First *see* Man at *Acts 2:6.*

Week *sabbaton* (4521), is used (a) in the plural in the phrase "the first day of the week," Matt. 28:1; Mark 16:2, 9; Luke 24:1; John 20:1, 19; **Acts 20:7**; 1 Cor. 16:2.

Disciples *see Acts 1:15.*

Came *see Acts 13:44.*

Break *see* Breaking at *Acts 2:46.*

Bread *see Acts 2:42.*

Preached For *dialegomai*, in KJV of **Acts 20:7, 9**.

Ready *mello* (3195), "to be about to," is translated "to be ready" in 2 Pet. 1:12, RV, where the future indicates that the apostle will be prepared, as in the past and the present, to remind his readers of the truths they know (some mss. have *ouk ameleso*, "I will not be negligent," KJV; cf., however, v. 15. Field, in *Notes on the Translation of the NT*, suggests that the true reading is *meleso*, the future of *melo*, "to be a care, or an object of care"); in Rev. 3:2, RV, "were ready" (some texts have the present tense, as in the KJV). Elsewhere, where the KJV has the rendering to be ready, the RV gives renderings in accordance with the usual significance as follows: Luke 7:2, "was ... at the point of"; **Acts 20:7**, "intending"; Rev. 12:4, "about (to)." *See also* Intend at *Acts 5:35.*

Depart *see* Gone out of at *Acts 13:42.*

Continued *parateino* (3905), "to stretch out along" (*para*, "along," *teino*, "to stretch"), is translated "prolonged" in **Acts 20:7**, RV, of Paul's discourse. *See also* **Acts 15:35.**

Speech *dialegomai* (1256), primarily denotes "to ponder, resolve in one's mind" (*dia*, "through," *lego*, "to say"); then, "to converse, dispute, discuss, discourse with"; most frequently, "to reason or dispute with." In Heb. 12:5 the RV, "reasoneth with" is to be preferred to the KJV, "speaketh unto." The KJV translates it "preached," in **Acts 20:7** and **9**; this the RV corrects to "discoursed," lit., "dialogued," i.e., not by way of a sermon, but by a "discourse" of a more conversational character. In the Sept., Exod. 6:27; Judg. 8:1; Isa. 63:1. *See also* **Acts 14:12.**

Midnight *see Acts 16:25.*

20:8 And there were many lights in the upper chamber, where they were gathered together.

Many *see Acts 9:23.*

Lights *lampas* (2985), denotes "a torch" (akin to *lampo*, "to shine"), frequently fed, like a "lamp," with oil from a little vessel used for the purpose (the *angeion* of Matt. 25:4); they held little oil and would frequently need replenishing. Rutherford (*The New Phrynichus*) points out that it became used as the equivalent of *luchnos*, as in the parable of the ten virgins, Matt. 25:1, 3, 4, 7, 8; John 18:3, "torches"; **Acts 20:8**, "lights"; Rev. 4:5; 8:10 (RV, "torch," KJV, "lamp").

Chamber *see* Room at *Acts 1:13.*

20:9 And there sat in a window

a certain young man named Eutychus, being fallen into a deep sleep: and as Paul was long preaching, he sunk down with sleep, and fell down from the third loft, and was taken up dead.

Window *thuris* (2376), a diminutive of *thura*, "a door," occurs in **Acts 20:9**; 2 Cor. 11:33.

Young *see Acts 7:58.*

Fallen, Sunk *kataphero* (2702), "to bring down or against" (*kata*, "down"), said of an accusation in **Acts 25:7** (in the best mss.), and of being "borne down" with sleep, **20:9**, RV, is used of casting a ballot or "giving" a vote in **26:10**.

Deep *bathus* (901), "deep," is said in John 4:11, of a well; in **Acts 20:9**, of sleep; in Rev. 2:24 the plural is used, of the "deep things," the evil designs and workings, of Satan.

Long *pleion* (4119), the neuter of *pleion*, "more," the comparative degree of *polu*, "much," is rendered "longer" in **Acts 20:9**, RV (KJV "long").

Preaching *see* Preached at *Acts 20:7.*

Down *see* Beneath at *Acts 2:19.*

Third loft *tristegos* (5152), an adjective denoting "of three stories" (*treis*, "three," *stege*, "a roof"), occurs in **Acts 20:9** (with *oikema*, "a dwelling," understood), RV, "the third story" (KJV, "the third loft").

20:10 And Paul went down, and fell on him, and embracing *him* said, Trouble not yourselves; for his life is in him.

Fell *see* Fallen at *Acts 8:16.*

Embracing *sumperilambano* (4843), lit., "to take around with," (*sun*, "with" *peri* "around," *lambano*, "to take"), "to embrace," is used in **Acts 20:10**, in connection with Paul's recovery of Eutychus. In the Sept., Ezra 5:3, "to enclose."

Trouble *thorubeo* (2350), akin to *thorubos*, "a tumult," in the middle voice, "to make an uproar," is rendered "trouble not yourselves" in **Acts 20:10**, KJV. *See also* **Uproar** at *Acts 17:5.*

Life *psuche* (5590), besides its meanings, "heart, mind, soul," denotes "life" in two chief respects, (a) "breath of life, the natural life," e.g., Matt. 2:20; 6:25; Mark 10:45; Luke 12:22; **Acts 20:10**; Rev. 8:9; 12:11 (cf. Lev. 17:11; Esth. 8:11); (b) "the seat of personality," e.g., Luke 9:24, explained in v. 25 as "own self." *See also* Soul at *Acts 2:27.*

20:11 When he therefore was come up again, and had broken bread, and eaten, and talked a long while, even till break of day, so he departed.

Broken *see* Breaking at *Acts 2:46.*

Eaten *see* Eat at *Acts 2:46.*

Talked *homileo* (3656), from *homos*, "together," signifies "to be in company, to associate with any one"; hence, "to have intercourse with," Luke 24:14 (RV, "communed"; KJV, "talked"), 15; **Acts 24:26**; in **20:11**, "talked with."

While In **Acts 20:11** *hikanos*, "sufficient," is rendered "a long while."

Day *auge* (827), "brightness, bright, shining, as of the sun"; hence, "the beginning of daylight," is translated "break of day" in **Acts 20:11**.

20:12 And they brought the young man alive, and were not a little comforted.

Young man *pais* (3816), signifies (a) "a child in relation to descent," (b) "a boy or girl in relation to age," (c) "a servant, attendant, maid, in relation to condition." As an instance of (a) see Matt. 21:15, "children," and **Acts 20:12** (RV, "lad"). In regard to (b) the RV has "boy" in Matt. 17:18 and Luke 9:42. In Luke 2:43 it is used of the Lord Jesus. In regard to (c), see Matt. 8:6, 8, 13, etc. As to (a) note Matt. 2:16, RV, male children.

Little *metrios* (3357), moderately, occurs in **Acts 20:12**, "a little."

20:13 And we went before to ship, and sailed unto Assos, there intending to take in Paul: for so had he appointed, minding himself to go afoot.

Went *see Acts 12:10.*

Sailed *see* Loosed at *Acts 13:13.*

There *ekeithen* (1564), "thence," is rendered "there" in **Acts 20:13**. *See also* Thence at *Acts 7:4.*

Intending *see* Intend at *Acts 5:35.*

Take *see* Taken at *Acts 1:2.*

Appointed *see Acts 7:44.*

Minding In **Acts 20:13**, KJV, *mello*, "to be about to, to intend," is translated "minding" (RV, "intending").

Afoot In **Acts 20:13**, *pezeuo*, "to travel by land" or "on foot" (*pezos*, "on foot"; *pous*, "a foot"), is translated "to go by land," RV, KJV, "to go afoot," and RV marg., "to go on foot."

20:14 And when he met with us at Assos, we took him in, and came to Mitylene.

Met *sumballo* (4820), "to confer, to fall in with, meet with," is translated "met" in **Acts 20:14**, RV (KJV, "met with"), of the apostle Paul's "meeting" his companions at Assos.

Took *see* Taken at *Acts 1:2.*

20:15 And we sailed thence, and came the next *day* over against Chios; and the next *day* we arrived at Samos, and tarried at Trogyllium; and the next *day* we came to Miletus.

Sailed *see Acts 13:4.*

Came *see Acts 16:1.*

Next *echo* (2192), "to have," in the middle voice, sometimes signifies "to be next to," said of towns, in Mark 1:38; of a day, **Acts 21:26**; in **20:15** (2nd part), *hemera*, "day," is unexpressed. In **Acts 20:15** (mid. of verse) *heteros*, "other," signifies "next," with *hemera*, understood. *See also Acts 7:26. See also* **Eventide** at *Acts 4:3;* **Could** at *Acts 4:14.*

Arrived *paraballo* (3846), *para*, "alongside," *ballo*, "to throw," signifies, nautically, "touched at"; so the RV of **Acts 20:15** (KJV, "arrived"); or, perhaps, to strike across, from one place to another. In Mark 4:30, some mss. have this verb (KJV, "compare"); the most authentic have *tithemi*, to set forth (with the word "parable"). *See also* **Came** at *Acts 16:1.*

Tarried *see Acts 9:43.*

20:16 For Paul had determined to sail by Ephesus, because he would not spend the time in Asia: for he hasted, if it were possible for him, to be at Jerusalem the day of Pentecost.

Determined *see Acts 3:13.*

Sail *parapleo* (3896), "to sail by" (*para*), occurs in **Acts 20:16**.

Spend *chronotribeo* (5551), "to spend time" (*chronos*, "time," *tribo*, "to rub, to wear out"), occurs in **Acts 20:16**.

Hasted *speudo* (4692), denotes (a) intransitively, "to hasten," Luke 2:16, "with haste," lit., "(they came) hastening"; Luke 19:5, 6; **Acts 20:16**; **22:18**; (b) transitively, "to desire earnestly," 2 Pet. 3:12, RV, "earnestly desiring" (marg., "hastening"), KJV, "hasting" (the day of God), i.e., in our practical fellowship with God as those who are appointed by Him as instruments through prayer and service for the accomplishment of His purposes, purposes which will be unthwartably fulfilled both in time and manner of accomplishment. In this way the earnest desire will find its fulfillment.

Possible *see Acts 2:24.*

Pentecost *see Acts 2:1.*

20:17 And from Miletus he sent to Ephesus, and called the elders of the church

Called *see Acts 7:14.*

Elders *see Acts 14:23. See also* **Old men** at *Acts 2:17.*

20:18 And when they were come to him, he said unto them, Ye know, from the first day that I came into Asia, after what manner I have been with you at all seasons,

Come *epibaino* (1910), "to come to or into, or go upon," is rendered, in **Acts 20:18**, RV, set foot in.

Know *see Acts 10:28.*

Manner *pos* (4459), how, is translated "after what manner" in **Acts 20:18**.

Seasons *chronos* (5550), denotes "a space of time," whether short, e.g., Matt. 2:7; Luke 4:5, or long, e.g., Luke 8:27; 20:9; or a succession of "times," shorter, e.g., **Acts 20:18**, or longer, e.g., Rom. 16:25, RV, "times eternal"; or duration of "time," e.g., Mark 2:19, 2nd part, RV, "while" (KJV, "as long as"), lit., "for whatever time." *See also Acts 1:7.*

20:19 Serving the Lord with all humility of mind, and with many tears, and temptations, which befell me by the lying in wait of the Jews:

Serving *douleuo* (1398), "to serve as a slave, to be a slave, to be in bondage," is frequently used without any association of slavery, e.g., **Acts 20:19**; Rom. 6:6; 7:6; 12:11; Gal. 5:13. *See also* **Serve** at *Acts 7:7.*

Humility *tapeinophrosune* (5012), "lowliness of mind" (*tapeinos* and *phren*, "the mind"), is rendered "humility of mind" in **Acts 20:19**, KJV (RV, "lowliness of mind"); in Eph. 4:2, "lowliness"; in Phil. 2:3, "lowliness of mind"; in Col. 2:18, 23, of a false "humility"; in Col. 3:12, KJV, "humbleness of mind," RV, "humility"; 1 Pet. 5:5, "humility."

Tears *dakruon* or *dakru* (1144), akin to *dakruo*, "to weep," is used in the plural, Mark 9:24; Luke 7:38, 44 (with the sense of washing therewith the Lord's feet); **Acts 20:19, 31**; 2 Cor. 2:4; 2 Tim. 1:4; Heb. 5:7; 12:17; Rev. 7:17; 21:4.

Temptations *peirasmos* (3986), is used of (1) "trials" with a beneficial purpose and effect, (a) of "trials" or "temptations," divinely permitted or sent, Luke 22:28; **Acts 20:19**; Jas. 1:2; 1 Pet. 1:6; 4:12, RV, "to prove," KJV, "to try"; 2 Pet. 2:9 (singular); Rev. 3:10, RV, "trial" (KJV, "temptation"); in Jas. 1:12, "temptation" apparently has meanings (1) and (2) combined and is used in the widest sense; (b) with a good or neutral significance, Gal. 4:14, of Paul's physical infirmity, "a temptation" to the Galatian converts, of such a kind as to arouse feelings of natural repugnance; (c) of "trials" of a varied character, Matt. 6:13 and Luke 11:4, where believers are commanded to pray not to be led into such by forces beyond their own control; Matt. 26:41; Mark 14:38; Luke 22:40, 46, where they are commanded to watch and pray against entering into "temptations" by their own carelessness or disobedience; in all such cases God provides "the way of escape," 1 Cor. 10:13 (where *peirasmos* occurs twice). (2) Of "trial" definitely designed to lead to wrong doing, "temptation," Luke 4:13; 8:13; 1 Tim. 6:9; (3) of "trying" or challenging God, by men, Heb. 3:8.

Befell *sumbaino* (4819), lit., "to walk, or go together" (*sun*, "with," *baino*, "to go"), is used of things which happen at the same time; hence, "to come to pass, befall," **Acts 20:19**. In **21:35**, it is translated "so it was." *See also* Happened at *Acts 3:10*.

Lying in wait *see* Laid wait at *Acts 20:3*. *See also* Laying await at *Acts 9:24*.

20:20 *And* how I kept back nothing that was profitable *unto you*, but have shewed you, and have taught you publickly, and from house to house,

Kept In **Acts 20:20**, *hupostello*, "to shrink, draw back from," is translated "I shrank (not)" (middle voice), RV, KJV, "I kept back (nothing)."

Profitable *sumphero* (4851), "to be profitable," Matt. 5:29, 30; **Acts 20:20**.

Shewed *see Acts 19:18*. *See also* Declared at *Acts 15:4*.

Publickly *see* Common at *Acts 5:18*.

20:21 Testifying both to the Jews, and also to the Greeks, repentance toward God, and faith toward our Lord Jesus Christ.

Testifying *see* Testify at *Acts 2:40*.

Repentance *see Acts 5:31*.

Lord *see Acts 2:36*.

20:22 And now, behold, I go bound in the spirit unto Jerusalem, not knowing the things that shall befall me there:

Bound *deo* (1210), "to bind," is used (a) literally, of any sort of "binding," e.g., **Acts 22:5; 24:27**, (b) figuratively, of the Word of God, as not being "bound," 2 Tim. 2:9, i.e., its ministry, course and efficacy were not hindered by the bonds and imprisonment suffered by the apostle. A woman who was bent together, had been "bound" by Satan through the work of a demon, Luke 13:16. Paul speaks of himself, in **Acts 20:22**, as being "bound in the spirit," i.e., compelled by his convictions, under the constraining power of the Spirit of God, to go to Jerusalem. A wife is said to be "bound" to her husband, Rom. 7:2; 1 Cor. 7:39; and the husband to the wife, 1 Cor. 7:27. The Lord's words to the apostle Peter in Matt. 16:19, as to "binding," and to all the disciples in 18:18, signify, in the former case, that the apostle, by his ministry of the Word of Life, would keep unbelievers outside the kingdom of God, and admit those who believed. So with regard to 18:18, including the exercise of disciplinary measures in the sphere of the local church; the application of the rabbinical sense of forbidding is questionable.

Spirit *see Acts 7:59*.

Befall *sunantao* (4876), "to meet with" (*sun*, "with," *antao*, "to meet"), is used much in the same way as *sumbaino*, of events which come to pass; "befall," **Acts 20:22**. *See also* Met at *Acts 10:25*.

20:23 Save that the Holy Ghost witnesseth in every city, saying that bonds and afflictions abide me.

Save *see* Except at *Acts 8:1*.

Holy Ghost *see Acts 1:16*.

Witnesseth *see* Testify at *Acts 2:40*.

Every *see Acts 5:42*.

Bonds *see* Bands at *Acts 16:26*.

Afflictions *see* Persecution at *Acts 11:19*.

Abide *meno* (3306), used (a) of place, e.g., Matt. 10:11, metaphorically 1 John 2:19, is said of God, 1 John 4:15; Christ, John 6:56; 15:4, etc.; the Holy Spirit, John 1:32-33; 14:17; believers, John 6:56; 15:4; 1 John 4:15, etc.; the Word of God, 1 John 2:14; the truth, 2 John 2, etc.; (b) of time, it is said of believers, John 21:22-23; Phil. 1:25; 1 John 2:17; Christ, John 12:34; Heb. 7:24; the Word of God, 1 Pet. 1:23; sin, John 9:41; cities, Matt. 11:23; Heb. 13:14; bonds and afflictions, **Acts 20:23**; (c) of qualities; faith, hope, love, 1 Cor. 13:13; Christ's love, John 15:10; afflictions, **Acts 20:23**; brotherly love, Heb. 13:1; the love of God, 1 John 3:17; the truth, 2 John 2.

20:24 But none of these things move me, neither count I my life dear unto myself, so that I might finish my course with joy, and the ministry, which I have received of the Lord Jesus, to testify the gospel of the grace of God.

Move In **Acts 20:24** some mss. have a phrase translated "none of these things move me." The text for which there is most support gives the rendering "but I hold not my life of any account, as dear unto myself." Field suggests a reading, the translation of which is, "neither make I account of anything, nor think my life dear unto myself." *See also* Made at *Acts 2:36*.

Count *echo* (2192), "to have, to hold"; then, "to hold in the mind, to regard, to count," has this significance in Matt. 14:5, "they counted Him as a prophet"; Philem. 17, "If then thou countest me a partner"; Mark 11:32, KJV, (RV, "hold"); **Acts 20:24**, KJV. *See also* Account at *Acts 19:40.*

Dear *see* Reputation at *Acts 5:34.*

Myself *emautou* (1683), a reflexive pronoun, of the first person, lit., "of myself," is used (a) frequently after various prepositions, e.g., *hupo*, "under," Matt. 8:9; Luke 7:8; RV, "under myself"; *peri*, "concerning," John 5:31; 8:14, 18; **Acts 24:10**; *apo*, "from," John 5:30; 7:17, RV, "from" (KJV, "of," which is ambiguous); so v. 28; 8:28, 42; 10:18; 14:10 (RV, "from"); *pros*, "unto," John 12:32, RV, "unto Myself"; 14:3; Philem. 13, "with me"; *eis*, "to," 1 Cor. 4:6; *huper*, "on behalf of," 2 Cor. 12:5; *ek* (*ex*), "out of," or "from," John 12:49, RV, "from Myself"; (b) as the direct object of a verb, Luke 7:7; John 8:54; 14:21; 17:19; **Acts 26:2**; 1 Cor. 4:3; 9:19; 2 Cor. 11:7, 9; Gal. 2:18; Phil. 3:13; (c) in other oblique cases of the pronoun, without a preposition, e.g., **Acts 20:24**, "unto" (or to); **26:9**, "with" (or "to"); Rom. 11:4, RV, "for" (KJV, "to"); 1 Cor. 4:4, RV, "against myself" (KJV, inaccurately, "by"); in all these instances the pronoun is in the dative case; in 1 Cor. 10:33, "mine own" (the genitive case); in 1 Cor. 7:7, "I myself" (the accusative case).

Finish *teleioo* (5048), akin to the adjective *teleios*, "complete, perfect," and to *teleo*, denotes "to bring to an end" in the sense of completing or perfecting, and is translated by the verb "to finish" in John 4:34; 5:36; 17:4; **Acts 20:24**.

Course *see Acts 13:25.*

Ministry *see Acts 1:17.*

Testify *see Acts 2:40.*

Gospel *see Acts 15:7.*

20:25 And now, behold, I know that ye all, among whom I have gone preaching the kingdom of God, shall see my face no more.

More *ouketi* (3765), is translated "no more," e.g., in Matt. 19:6; Luke 15:19, 21; **Acts 20:25, 38**; Eph. 2:19. *See also* No more at *Acts 8:39.*

20:26 Wherefore I take you to record this day, that I *am* pure from the blood of all *men*.

Take ... to record *marturomai* (3143), primarily, "to summon as witness," then, "to bear witness" (sometimes with the suggestion of solemn protestation), is rendered "to testify" in **Acts 20:26**, RV (KJV, "I take ... to record"); **26:22**, in the best texts, RV; Gal. 5:3; Eph. 4:17; 1 Thess. 2:11, in the best texts, RV, "testifying" (KJV, "charged").

Pure *see* Clean at *Acts 18:6.*

20:27 For I have not shunned to declare unto you all the counsel of God.

Counsel *see Acts 2:23.*

20:28 Take heed therefore unto yourselves, and to all the flock, over the which the Holy Ghost hath made you overseers, to feed the church of God, which he hath purchased with his own blood.

Heed *see Acts 5:35.*

Flock *poimnion* (4168), is used in the NT only metaphorically, of a group of Christ's disciples, Luke 12:32; of local churches cared for by elders, **Acts 20:28, 29**; 1 Pet. 5:2, 3.

Holy Ghost *see Acts 1:16.*

Made *tithemi* (5087), "to put," is used of "appointment" to any form of service. Christ used it of His followers, John 15:16 (RV, "appointed" for KJV, "ordained"). "I set you" would be more in keeping with the metaphor of grafting. The verb is used by Paul of his service in the ministry of the gospel, 1 Tim. 1:12 (RV, "appointing" for "putting"); 2:7 (RV, "appointed" for "ordained"); and 2 Tim. 1:11 (RV, "appointing" for "putting"); of the overseers, or bishops, in the local church at Ephesus, as those "appointed" by the Holy Ghost, to tend the church of God, **Acts 20:28** ("hath made"); of the Son of God, as appointed Heir of all things, Heb. 1:2. It is also used of "appointment" to punishment, as of the unfaithful servant, Matt. 24:51; Luke 12:46; of unbelieving Israel, 1 Pet. 2:8. Cf. 2 Pet. 2:6. *See also* Make at *Acts 2:35.*

Overseers *episkopos* (1985), lit., an overseer" (*epi*, "over," *skopeo*, "to look or watch"), whence Eng. "bishop," which has precisely the same meaning, is found in **Acts 20:28**; Phil. 1:1; 1 Tim. 3:2; Titus 1:7; 1 Pet. 2:25. *See also* Old men at *Acts 2:17;* Elders at *Acts 14:23.*.

Feed *poimaino* (4165), "to act as a shepherd" (from *poimen*, "a shepherd"), is used (a) literally, Luke 17:7, RV, "keeping sheep," for KJV, "feeding cattle"; 1 Cor. 9:7, (b) metaphorically, "to tend, to shepherd"; said of Christ Matt. 2:6, RV, "shall be Shepherd of" (for KJV, "shall rule"); of those who act as spiritual shepherds under Him, John 21:16, RV, "tend" (for KJV "feed"), so 1 Pet. 5:2; **Acts 20:28**, "to feed" ("to tend" would have been a consistent rendering; a shepherd does not only "feed" his flock); of base shepherds, Jude 12.

Church *see Acts 7:38.*

Purchased *peripoieo* (4046), signifies "to gain" or "get for oneself, purchase"; middle voice in **Acts 20:28** and 1 Tim. 3:13 (RV "gain").

20:29 For I know this, that after my departing shall grievous wolves enter in among you, not sparing the flock.

Departing *aphixis* (867), most frequently "an arrival" (akin to *aphikneomas*), also signifies a "departure" (*apo*, "from," *hikneomai*, "to come": etymologically, to come far enough, reach; cf. *hikanos*, "sufficient"), the "departure" being regarded in relation to the end in view. Thus Paul speaks of his "departing," **Acts 20:29**.

Grievous *barus* (926), denotes "heavy, burdensome"; it is always used metaphorically in the NT, and is translated "heavy" in Matt. 23:4, of Pharisaical ordinances; in the comparative degree "weightier," 23:23, of details of the law of God; "grievous," metaphorically of wolves, in **Acts 20:29**; of charges, **25:7**; negatively of God's commandments, 1 John 5:3 (causing a burden on him who fulfills them); in 2 Cor. 10:10, "weighty," of Paul's letters.

Wolves *lukos* (3074), occurs in Matt. 10:16; Luke 10:3; John 10:12 (twice); metaphorically, Matt. 7:15; **Acts 20:29**.

Sparing *pheidomai* (5339), "to spare," i.e., "to forego" the infliction of that evil or retribution which was designed, is used with a negative in **Acts 20:29**; Rom. 8:32; 11:21 (twice); 2 Cor. 13:2; 2 Pet. 2:4, 5; positively, in 1 Cor. 7:28; 2 Cor. 1:3; rendered "forbear" in 2 Cor. 12:6.

Flock *see Acts 20:28.*

20:30 Also of your own selves shall men arise, speaking perverse things, to draw away disciples after them.

Arise *see* Raised at *Acts 2:24.*

Perverse *see* Turn away at *Acts 13:8.*

Draw *apospao* (645), "to draw away," lit., "to wrench away from," is used of a sword, Matt. 26:51, of "drawing" away disciples into error, **Acts 20:30**; of Christ's "withdrawal" from the disciples, in Gethsemane, Luke 22:41, KJV, "was withdrawn," RV, "was parted" (or "was reft away from them"); of "parting" from a company, **Acts 21:1** (KJV, "were gotten," RV, "were parted").

20:31 Therefore watch, and remember, that by the space of three years I ceased not to warn every one night and day with tears.

Therefore *see* Wherefore at *Acts 15:19.*

Watch *gregoreo* (1127), "to watch," is used (a) of "keeping awake," e.g., Matt. 24:43; 26:38, 40, 41; (b) of "spiritual alertness," e.g., **Acts 20:31**; 1 Cor. 16:13; Col. 4:2; 1 Thess. 5:6, 10; 1 Pet. 5:8, RV, "be watchful" (KJV, "be vigilant"); Rev. 3:2, 3; 16:15.

Remember *mnemoneuo* (3421), signifies "to call to mind, remember"; it is used absolutely in Mark 8:18; everywhere else it has an object, (a) persons, Luke 17:32; Gal. 2:10; 2 Tim. 2:8, where the RV rightly has "remember Jesus Christ, risen from the dead"; Paul was not reminding Timothy (nor did he need to) that Christ was raised from the dead (KJV), what was needful for him was to "remember" (to keep in mind) the One who rose, the Source and Supplier of all his requirements; (b) things, e.g., Matt. 16:9; John 15:20; 16:21; **Acts 20:35**; Col. 4:18; 1 Thess. 1:3; 2:9; Heb. 11:15, "had been mindful of"; 13:7; Rev. 18:5; (c) a clause, representing a circumstance, etc., John 16:4; **Acts 20:31**; Eph. 2:11; 2 Thess. 2:5; Rev. 2:5; 3:3; in Heb. 11:22 it signifies "to make mention of."

"The spiritual leader influences others not by the power of his own personality alone but by that personality irradiated and interpenetrated and empowered in the Holy Spirit. Because he permits the Holy Spirit undisputed control of his life, the Spirit's power can flow through him to others unhindered."

J. OSWALD SANDERS

Years *trietia* (5148), denotes "a space of three years," **Acts 20:31**.

Ceased *see Acts 5:42.*

Warn *noutheteo* (3560), cf. the noun above, means "to put in mind, admonish," **Acts 20:31** (KJV, "warn"); Rom. 15:14; 1 Cor. 4:14 (KJV, "warn"); Col. 1:28 (KJV, "warning"); Col. 3:16; 1 Thess. 5:12, 14 (KJV, "warn"); 2 Thess. 3:15. It is used, (a) of instruction, (b) of warning. It is thus distinguished from *paideuo*, "to correct by discipline, to train by act," Heb. 12:6; cf. Eph. 6:4. "The difference between 'admonish' and 'teach' seems to be that, whereas the former has mainly in view the things that are wrong and call for warning, the latter has to do chiefly with the impartation of positive truth, cf. Col. 3:16; they were to let the Word of Christ dwell richly in them, so that they might be able (1) to teach and 'admonish' one another, and (2) to abound in the praises of God."

Every *see* Each at *Acts 2:3*.

Night *see Acts 5:19*.

Tears *see Acts 20:19*.

20:32 And now, brethren, I commend you to God, and to the word of his grace, which is able to build you up, and to give you an inheritance among all them which are sanctified.

Commend *see* Commended at *Acts 14:23*.

Build *epoikodomeo* (2026), signifies "to build upon" (*epi*, "upon"), 1 Cor. 3:10, 12, 14; Eph. 2:20; Jude 20; or up, **Acts 20:32**; Col. 2:7. *See also* Builders at *Acts 4:11*.

Inheritance *see Acts 7:5*.

Sanctified *hagiazo* (37), "to sanctify," "is used of (a) the gold adorning the Temple and of the gift laid on the altar, Matt. 23:17, 19; (b) food, 1 Tim. 4:5; (c) the unbelieving spouse of a believer, 1 Cor. 7:14; (d) the ceremonial cleansing of the Israelites, Heb. 9:13; (e) the Father's Name, Luke 11:2; (f) the consecration of the Son by the Father, John 10:36; (g) the Lord Jesus devoting Himself to the redemption of His people, John 17:19; (h) the setting apart of the believer for God, **Acts 20:32**; cf. Rom. 15:16; (i) the effect on the believer of the Death of Christ, Heb. 10:10, said of God, and 2:11; 13:12, said of the Lord Jesus; (j) the separation of the believer from the world in his behavior – by the Father through the Word, John 17:17, 19; (k) the believer who turns away from such things as dishonor God and His gospel, 2 Tim. 2:21; (l) the acknowledgment of the Lordship of Christ, 1 Pet. 3:15.

20:33 I have coveted no man's silver, or gold, or apparel.

Coveted *epithumeo* (1937), "to fix the desire upon" (*epi*, "upon," used intensively, *thumos*, "passion"), whether things good or bad; hence, "to long for, lust after, covet," is used with the meaning "to covet evilly" in **Acts 20:33**, of "coveting money and apparel"; so in Rom. 7:7; 13:9.

Silver *see Acts 3:6*.

Gold *see Acts 3:6*.

Apparel *himatismos* (2441), in form a collective word, denoting "vesture, garments," is used generally of "costly or stately raiment," the apparel of kings, of officials, etc. See Luke 7:25, where "gorgeously apparelled" is, lit., "in gorgeous vesture." See also **Acts 20:33** and 1 Tim. 2:9, "costly raiment." This is the word used of the Lord's white and dazzling raiment on the Mount of Transfiguration, Luke 9:29. It is also used of His *chiton*, His undergarment, for which the soldiers cast lots, John 19:23-24, "vesture"; in Matt. 27:35 it is also translated vesture.

20:34 Yea, ye yourselves know, that these hands have ministered unto my necessities, and to them that were with me.

Ye, Yourselves *see* Ye at *Acts 2:22*.

Ministered *see* Served at *Acts 13:36*.

Necessities *chreia* (5532), "a need," and almost always so translated, is used in the plural in **Acts 20:34**, "necessities"; Rom. 12:13, RV (KJV, "necessity"); in Phil. 4:16, KJV, "necessity," RV, "need."

20:35 I have shewed you all things, how that so labouring ye ought to support the weak, and to remember the words of the Lord Jesus, how he said, It is more blessed to give than to receive.

Shewed *see* Shew at *Acts 9:16*.

All *see Acts 2:36*.

Labouring *kopiao* (2872), has the two different meanings (a) "growing weary," (b) "toiling"; it is sometimes translated "to bestow labor". It is translated by the verb "to labor" in Matt. 11:28; John 4:38 (2nd part); **Acts 20:35**; Rom. 16:12 (twice); 1 Cor. 15:10; 16:16; Eph. 4:28; Phil. 2:16; Col. 1:29; 1 Thess. 5:12; 1 Tim. 4:10; 5:17; 2 Tim. 2:6; Rev. 2:3; 1 Cor. 4:12, RV, "toil" (KJV, "labor").

Support *antilambano* (482), lit., "to take instead of, or in turn," is used in the middle voice, and rendered "He hath holpen" in Luke 1:54; "to help," RV, "to support," KJV, in **Acts 20:35**; its other meaning, to partake of, is used of partaking of things, 1 Tim. 6:2, "that partake of," for KJV, "partakers of."

Remember *see Acts 20:31*.

Lord *see Acts 2:36*.

More *see Acts 5:14*.

Receive *see* Received at *Acts 9:19*.

20:36-37 And when he had thus spoken, he kneeled down, and prayed with them all.

And they all wept sore, and fell on Paul's neck, and kissed him,

Wept *klauthmos* (2805), denotes "weeping, crying," Matt. 2:18; 8:12;

13:42, 50, RV (KJV, "wailing"); 22:13; 24:51; 25:30; Luke 13:28; **Acts 20:37**.

Sore *hikanos* (2425), used of things, occasionally denotes "much," translated "sore" in **Acts 20:37**, lit., "there was much weeping of all."

Fell *see* Fallen at *Acts 8:16*.

Neck *see Acts 15:10*.

Kissed *kataphileo* (2705), denotes "to kiss fervently"; the stronger force of this verb has been called in question, but the change from *phileo* to *kataphileo* in Matt. 26:49 and Mark 14:45 can scarcely be without significance, and the act of the traitor was almost certainly more demonstrative than the simple kiss of salutation. So with the kiss of genuine devotion, Luke 7:38, 45; 15:20; **Acts 20:37**, in each of which this verb is used.

20:38 Sorrowing most of all for the words which he spake, that they should see his face no more. And they accompanied him unto the ship.

Sorrowing *odunao* (3600), "to cause pain," is used in the middle voice in Luke 2:48; **Acts 20:38**.

Most *malista* (3122), "most, most of all, above all," is the superlative of *mala*, "very much"; translated "especially" in **Acts 26:3**; Gal. 6:10; 1 Tim. 5:17; 2 Tim. 4:13; Phil. 4:22, RV (for KJV, "chiefly"); "specially," **Acts 25:26**; 1 Tim. 4:10; 5:8; Titus 1:10; Philem. 16; in **Acts 20:38**, "most of all."

No more *see Acts 8:39*. *See also* More at *Acts 20:25*.

Accompanied *see* Brought ... way at *Acts 15:3*.

Chapter 21

21:1 And it came to pass, that after we were gotten from them, and had launched, we came with a straight course unto Coos, and the *day* following unto Rhodes, and from thence unto Patara:

Gotten In **Acts 21:1**, KJV, *apospao*, "to withdraw or part from," is rendered "we had gotten (from)," RV, "had parted (from)." After the scene described at the end of ch. 20, it may well have the force of "being reft away" (or tearing themselves away) from them. Cf. the same verb in Luke 22:41 ("He was reft away from them"). *See also* Draw at *Acts 20:30*.

Launched *see* Loosed at *Acts 13:13*.

Course *see Acts 16:11*.

Following *hexes* (1836), an adverb (akin to *echo*, "to have") denoting "in order, successively, next," is used adjectivally, qualifying the noun "day" in Luke 9:37; **Acts 21:1**, RV, "next" (KJV, "following"); **25:17**, RV, "next" (KJV, "on the morrow"); in **27:18**, with *hemera*, "day," understood, in Luke 7.11, in the best mss., with the word *chronos*, "time," understood, "soon afterwards" (marg., "on the next day," according to some ancient authorities).

21:2 And finding a ship sailing over unto Phenicia, we went aboard, and set forth.

Finding *aneurisko* (429), "to find out" (by search), "discover," implying diligent searching, is used in Luke 2:16, of the shepherds in searching for and "finding" Mary and Joseph and the Child; in **Acts 21:4**, of Paul and his companions, in searching for and "finding" "the disciples" at Tyre [in **Acts 21:2**, *heurisko* (2147), is used].

Sailing *diaperao* (1276), "to pass over, to cross over" (*dia*, "through," *perao*, "to pass": akin to this are *peran*, "across," *peras*, "a boundary," Latin, *porta*, "a gate," Eng., "portal, port," etc.), is translated by the verb "to cross" in the RV, but differently in the KJV; in Matt. 9:1; Mark 5:21; 6:53 (KJV, "passed"); Matt. 14:34 (KJV, "were gone"); Luke 16:26 (KJV, "neither can they pass"); **Acts 21:2** (KJV, "sailing"). In the Sept., Deut. 30:13; Isa. 23:2.

Went aboard *epibaino* (1910), "to go upon" (*epi*, "upon," *baino*, "to go"), is once translated "we went aboard," **Acts 21:2**, the single verb being short for "going aboard ship." In v. **6** it is rendered "we went on board", in **27:2** "embarking"; in Matt. 21:5, "riding upon."

Set forth In **Acts 21:2**, KJV, *anago*, "to set sail" (RV), is translated "set forth". *See also* Loosed at *Acts 13:13*.

21:3 Now when we had discovered Cyprus, we left it on the left hand, and sailed into Syria, and landed at Tyre: for there the ship was to unlade her burden.

Discovered *anaphaino* (398), *ana*, "forth, or up," perhaps originally a nautical term, "to come up into view," hence, in general, "to appear suddenly," is used in the passive voice, in Luke 19:11, of the Kingdom of God; active voice, in **Acts 21:3**, "to come in sight of," RV; "having sighted" would be a suitable rendering (KJV, "having discovered"). In **Acts 21:3**, some mss. have the verb *katago*, with reference to Cyprus.

Left *euonumos* (2176), lit., "of good name," or "omen" (*eu*, "well," *onoma*, "a name"), a word adopted to avoid the ill-omen attaching to the "left" (omens from the "left" being unlucky, but a good name being desired for them, cf. *aristeros*, lit., "better of two," euphemistic for the ill-omened *laios* and *skaios*; cf, too, the Eng., "sinister," from the Latin word meaning "left"), is used euphemistically for *aristeros* (710), either (a) simply as an adjective in Rev. 10:2, of the "left" foot; in **Acts 21:3**, "on the left" (lit., "left"); or (b) with the preposition *ex* (for *ek*), signifying "on the left hand," Matt. 20:21, 23; 25:33, 41; 27:38; Mark 10:40; 15:27.

Sailed *pleo* (4126), "to sail," occurs in Luke 8:23; **Acts 21:3**; **27:2**, **6**, **24**; Rev. 18:17, RV, "saileth".

Landed *see Acts 18:22.*

There *ekeise* (1566), properly, "thither," signifies "there" in **Acts 21:3**; **22:5**. In the Sept., Job 39:29.

Unlade *apophortizo* (670), "to discharge a cargo" (*apo*, "from," *phortizo*, "to load"), is used in **Acts 21:3**.

Burden *gomos* (1117), from a root *gem-*, signifying "full, or heavy," seen in *gemo*, "to be full," *gemizo*, "to fill," Lat. *gemo*, "to groan," denotes "the lading of freight of a ship," **Acts 21:3**, or "merchandise conveyed in a ship," and so "merchandise in general," Rev. 18:11-12.

21:4 And finding disciples, we tarried there seven days: who said to Paul through the Spirit, that he should not go up to Jerusalem.

Finding *see Acts 21:2.*

Tarried *see* Tarry at *Acts 10:48.*

There *see Acts 15:34.*

Go *see* Went at *Acts 10:9.*

21:5 And when we had accomplished those days, we departed and went our way; and they all brought us on our way, with wives and children, till *we were* out of the city: and we kneeled down on the shore, and prayed.

Accomplished *exartizo* (1822), "to fit out," (from *ek*, "out," and a verb derived from *artos*, "a joint"), means "to furnish completely," 2 Tim. 3:17, or "to accomplish," **Acts 21:5**, there said of a number of days, as if to render the days complete by what was appointed for them. In the Sept., Exod. 28:7.

Brought *see Acts 15:3.*

Way *see Acts 15:3.*

Shore *aigialos* (123), translated "shore" in the KJV in each place where it is used, Matt. 13:2, 48; John 21:4; **Acts 21:5**; **27:39-40**, is always in the RV translated "beach." It is derived from a root signifying "to press, drive"; *aigis* denotes "a wind-storm."

21:6 And when we had taken our leave one of another, we took ship; and they returned home again.

Taken ... leave *apaspazomai* (575 and 782), "to bid farewell" (*apo*, "from," *aspazomai*, "to greet"), is used in **Acts 21:6**, KJV, "had taken our leave of"; RV, "bade ... farewell."

Took ship *embaino* (1684), "to go in" (*en*, "in"), is used only in the Gospels, of "entering" a boat, Matt. 8:23; 9:1; 13:2; 14:22, 32; 15:39; Mark 4:1; 5:18; 6:45; 8:10, 13; Luke 5:3; 8:22, 37; John 6:17, (in some mss., in v. 22), 24, RV, "got into the boats," for KJV, "took shipping"; 21:3; **Acts 21:6** (in the best mss.); of stepping into water, John 5:4 (RV omits the verb). *See also* Went aboard at *Acts 21:2.*

Returned *see Acts 1:12.*

Home *idios* (2398), expresses "what is one's own" (hence, Eng. "idiot," in a changed sense, lit., "a person with his own opinions"); the neuter plural with the artide (*ta idia*) signifies "one's own things." In 1 Thess. 4:11, the noun is not expressed in the original but is supplied in the English versions by "business," "your own business." For the same phrase, otherwise expressed, see John 1:11, "His own (things)"; 16:32 and 19:27, "his own (home)"; **Acts 21:6**, "home." In Luke 2:49, the phrase "in My Father's house" (RV), "about My Father's business" (KJV), is, lit., "in the (things, the neuter plural of the article) of My Father."

21:7 And when we had finished *our* course from Tyre, we came to Ptolemais, and saluted the brethren, and abode with them one day.

Came *see Acts 16:1.*

Course *ploos* or *plous* (4144), is rendered "a voyage" (*pleo*, "to sail") in **Acts 27:10** (KJV and RV); in **21:7**, RV (KJV, "course"); in **27:9**, RV (KJV, "sailing").

21:8 And the next *day* we that were of Paul's company departed, and came unto Caesarea: and we entered into the house of Philip the evangelist, which was *one* of the seven; and abode with him.

Next day *see* Morrow at *Acts 10:24.*

Company In **Acts 21:8**, the phrase translated "that were of Paul's company" is absent from the best texts.

Evangelist *euangelistes* (2099), lit., "a messenger of good" (*eu*, "well," *angelos*, "a messenger"), denotes a "preacher of the gospel," **Acts 21:8**; Eph. 4:11, which makes clear the distinctiveness of the function in the churches; 2 Tim. 4:5.

Cf. *euangelizo*, "to proclaim glad tidings," and *euangelion*, "good news, gospel." Missionaries are "evangelists," as being essentially preachers of the gospel.

21:9 And the same man had four daughters, virgins, which did prophesy.

Virgins *parthenos* (3933), is used (a) of "the Virgin Mary," Matt. 1:23; Luke 1:27; (b) of the ten "virgins" in the parable, Matt. 25:1, 7, 11; (c) of the "daughters" of Philip the evangelist, **Acts 21:9**; (d) those concerning whom the apostle Paul gives instructions regarding marriage, 1 Cor. 7:25, 28, 34; in vv. 36, 37, 38, the subject passes to that of "virgin *daughters*" (RV), which almost certainly formed one of the subjects upon which the church at Corinth sent for instructions from the apostle; one difficulty was relative to the discredit which might be brought upon a father (or guardian), if he allowed his daughter or ward to grow old unmarried. The interpretation that this passage refers to a man and woman already in some kind of relation by way of a spiritual marriage and living together in a vow of virginity and celibacy, is untenable if only in view of the phraseology of the passage; (e) figuratively, of "a local church" in its relation to Christ, 2 Cor. 11:2; (f) metaphorically of "chaste persons," Rev. 14:4.

21:10 And as we tarried *there* many days, there came down from Judaea a certain prophet, named Agabus.

Tarried *see* Tarry at *Acts 10:48.*

Many *see Acts 2:40.*

Prophet *see Acts 3:22.*

21:11 And when he was come unto us, he took Paul's girdle, and bound his own hands and feet, and said, Thus saith the Holy Ghost, So shall the Jews at Jerusalem bind the man that owneth this girdle, and shall deliver *him* into the hands of the Gentiles.

Girdle *zone* (2223), Eng., "zone," denotes "a belt or girdle," Matt. 3:4; Mark 1:6; **Acts 21:11**; Rev. 1:13; 15:6; it was often hollow, and hence served as a purse, Matt. 10:9; Mark 6:8.

Thus *tade*, these things (the neuter plural of *hode*, "this"), is translated "thus" in **Acts 21:11**.

Holy Ghost *see Acts 1:16.*

Owneth In **Acts 21:11**, "that owneth this girdle," is lit., "whose is (*esti*) this girdle."

21:12 And when we heard these things, both we, and they of that place, besought him not to go up to Jerusalem.

Place The adjective *entopios*, "of that place," occurs in **Acts 21:12**.

21:13 Then Paul answered, What mean ye to weep and to break mine heart? for I am ready not to be bound only, but also to die at Jerusalem for the name of the Lord Jesus.

Mean In **Acts 21:13**, KJV, *poieo*, "to do," is translated "(what) mean ye (to weep)"; RV, "(what) do ye, (weeping)."

Weep *see* Weeping at *Acts 9:39.*

Break *sunthrupto* (4919), *sun*, and *thrupto*, "to crush, to break small, weaken," is used metaphorically of "breaking" one's heart **Acts 21:13**.

Heart *see Acts 2:37.*

Ready *hetoimos* (2093), "readily," is used with *echo*, "to have," lit., "to have readily," i.e., "to be in readiness, to be ready," **Acts 21:13**; 2 Cor. 12:14; 1 Pet. 4:5.

21:14 And when he would not be persuaded, we ceased, saying, The will of the Lord be done.

Persuaded *see Acts 13:43.*

Ceased *see* Peace at *Acts 11:18.*

21:15 And after those days we took up our carriages, and went up to Jerusalem.

Took up our carriages *episkeuazo* (643), "to furnish with things necessary"; in the middle voice, "to furnish for oneself"; it was used of equipping baggage animals for a journey; in **Acts 21:15**, RV, it is translated "we took up our baggage" (KJV, "we took up our carriages"). The form is the 1st aorist participle, and lit. means "having made ready (the things that were necessary for the journey)."

21:16 There went with us also *certain* of the disciples of Caesarea, and brought with them one Mnason of Cyprus, an old disciple, with whom we should lodge.

Went *see* Go at *Acts 8:29. See also* Companied at *Acts 1:21.*

Old *see* A good while ago at *Acts 15:7.*

Lodge *see* Lodgeth at *Acts 10:6.*

21:17 And when we were come to Jerusalem, the brethren received us gladly.

Received *see Acts 2:41.*

Gladly *see Acts 2:41.*

21:18 And the *day* following Paul went in with us unto James; and all the elders were present.

Following *see* Next at *Acts 7:26.*

Went *see* Go at *Acts 3:3.*

Present *paraginomai* (3854), "to be beside" (*para*, "by," *ginomai*, "to become"), is translated "were present" in **Acts 21:18**.

21:19 And when he had saluted them, he declared particularly what things God had wrought among the Gentiles by his ministry.

Declared *see Acts 10:8.*

Particularly In **Acts 21:19**, for the KJV "particularly" the RV has "one by one," translating the phrase, lit., "according to each one."

Wrought *see Acts 15:12.*

Ministry *see Acts 1:17.*

21:20 And when they heard *it*, they glorified the Lord, and said unto him, Thou seest, brother, how many thousands of Jews there are which believe; and they are all zealous of the law:

Many *posos* (4214), "how much, how great, how many," has the last meaning in Matt. 15:34; 16:9, 10; 27:13 ("how many things"); Mark 6:38; 8:5, 19, 20; 15:4 ("how many things"); Luke 15:17; **Acts 21:20**.

Thousands *see* Thousand at *Acts 19:19.*

Zealous *see* Zelotes at *Acts 1:13.*

21:21 And they are informed of thee, that thou teachest all the Jews which are among the Gentiles to forsake Moses, saying that they ought not to circumcise *their* children, neither to walk after the customs.

Informed *katecheo* (2727), primarily denotes "to resound" (*kata*, "down," *echos* "a sound"); then, "to sound down the ears, to teach by word of mouth, instruct, inform" (Eng., "catechize, catechumen"); it is rendered, in the passive voice, by the verb "to inform," in **Acts 21:21, 24**. Here it is used of the large numbers of Jewish believers at Jerusalem whose zeal for the Law had been stirred by information of accusations made against the Apostle Paul, as to certain anti-Mosaic teaching he was supposed to have given the Jews.

Forsake *apostasia* (646), "a defection, revolt, apostasy," is used in the NT of religious apostasy; in **Acts 21:21**, it is translated "to forsake," lit., "thou teachest apostasy from Moses." In 2 Thess. 2:3 "the falling away" signifies apostasy from the faith. In papyri documents it is used politically of rebels.

Walk *peripateo* (4043), is used (a) physically, in the Synoptic Gospels (except Mark 7:5); always in the Acts except in **21:21**; never in the Pauline Epistles, nor in those of John; (b) figuratively, "signifying the whole round of the activities of the individual life, whether of the unregenerate, Eph. 4:17, or of the believer, 1 Cor. 7:17; Col. 2:6. It is applied to the observance of religious ordinances, **Acts 21:21**; Heb. 13:9, marg., as well as to moral conduct. The Christian is to walk in newness of life, Rom. 6:4, after the spirit, 8:4, in honesty, 13:13, by faith, 2 Cor. 5:7, in good works, Eph. 2:10, in love, 5:2, in wisdom, Col. 4:5, in truth, 2 John 4, after the commandments of the Lord, v. 6. And, negatively, not after the flesh, Rom. 8:4; not after the manner of men, 1 Cor. 3:3; not in craftiness, 2 Cor. 4:2; not by sight, 5:7; not in the vanity of the mind, Eph. 4:17; not disorderly, 2 Thess. 3:6."

21:22 What is it therefore? the multitude must needs come together: for they will hear that thou art come.

Needs *see Acts 1:16. See also* All means at *Acts 18:21.*

21:23 Do therefore this that we say to thee: We have four men which have a vow on them;

Have *eimi* (1510), "to be," is often used in its various forms with some case of the personal pronoun, to signify "to be to," or "of, a person," e.g., Matt. 19:27, "(what then) shall we have," lit., "what then shall be to us?"; **Acts 21:23**, "we have four men," lit., "there are to us, etc."

Vow *see Acts 18:18.*

21:24 Them take, and purify thyself with them, and be at charges with them, that they may shave *their* heads: and all may know that those things, whereof they were informed concerning thee, are nothing; but *that* thou thyself also walkest orderly, and keepest the law.

Take *see* Took at *Acts 15:39.*

Purify *hagnizo* (48), akin to *hagnos*, "pure", "to purify, cleanse from defilement," is used of "purifying" (a) ceremonially, John 11:55; **Acts 21:24, 26; 24:18**; (b) morally, the heart, Jas. 4:8; the soul, 1 Pet. 1:22; oneself, 1 John 3:3.

Charges *dapanao* (1159), "to be at the expense of anything," is translated "be at charges," in **Acts 21:24**.

Shave *see* Shorn at *Acts 18:18.*

Informed *see Acts 21:21.*

Thou *see Acts 9:5.*

Walkest *stoicheo* (4748), from *stoichos*, "a row," signifies "to walk in line," and is used metaphorically of "walking" in relation to others; in **Acts 21:24**, it is translated "walkest orderly"; in Rom. 4:12, "walk (in ... steps)"; in Gal. 5:25 it is used of walking "by the Spirit," RV, in an exhortation to keep step with one another in submission of heart to the Holy Spirit, and therefore of keeping step with Christ, the great means of unity and harmony in a church; in 6:16 it is used of walking by the rule expressed in vv. 14, 15; in Phil. 3:16 the reference is to the course pursued by the believer who makes "the prize of the high calling" the object of his ambition. In the Sept., Eccl. 1:16.

Orderly For *stoicheo*, in **Acts 21:24**, "thou walkest orderly."

Keepest *see* Kept at *Acts 7:53*.

21:25 As touching the Gentiles which believe, we have written *and* concluded that they observe no such thing, save only that they keep themselves from *things* offered to idols, and from blood, and from strangled, and from fornication.

Written *see* Write at *Acts 15:20*

Concluded *see* Determined at *Acts 3:13*.

Only The conjunction *ei*, "if," with the negative *me*, "not," is translated "but only" in Luke 4:26, RV (KJV, "save"); 4:27 (KJV, "saving"); "only" in 1 Cor. 7:17 (KJV, "but"); in some mss. in **Acts 21:25** (KJV "save only").

Keep *phulasso* (5442), "to guard, watch, keep," is used, in the middle voice, of being "on one's guard against" (the middle v. stressing personal interest in the action), Luke 12:15, "beware of," RV, "keep yourselves from," as in **Acts 21:25**; in 2 Tim. 4:15, "be thou ware"; in 2 Pet. 3:17, "beware." *See also* Kept at *Acts 7:53*.

Offered *see Acts 15:29*.

Idols *see Acts 15:29*.

Strangled *see Acts 15:20*.

Fornication *see Acts 15:20*.

21:26 Then Paul took the men, and the next day purifying himself with them entered into the temple, to signify the accomplishment of the days of purification, until that an offering should be offered for every one of them.

Took *see Acts 15:39*.

Next *see Acts 20:15*. *See also* Could at *Acts 4:14*.

Purifying *see* Purify at *Acts 21:24*.

Entered *see* Go at *Acts 3:3*.

Signify *diangello* (1229), lit., "to announce through," hence, "to declare fully, or far and wide" (*dia*, "through"), is translated "declaring" in **Acts 21:26**, RV (KJV, "to signify"); in Luke 9:60, RV, "publish abroad" (for KJV, "preach"), giving the verb its fuller significance; so in Rom. 9:17, for KJV, "declared."

Accomplishment *ekplerosis* (1604), means "an entire fulfillment" (*ek*, "out," *plerosis*, "a filling"), **Acts 21:26**, of the "fulfillment" of days of purification.

Purification *hagnismos* (49), denotes "a ceremonial purification," **Acts 21:26**, for the circumstances of which with reference to the vow of a Nazirite (RV), see Num. 6:9-13.

Offering *prosphora* (4376), lit., "a bringing to," hence an "offering," in the NT a sacrificial "offering," (a) of Christ's sacrifice, Eph. 5:2; Heb. 10:10 (of His body); 10:14; negatively, of there being no repetition, 10:18; (b) of "offerings" under, or according to, the Law, **Acts 21:26**; Heb. 10:5, 8; (c) of gifts in kind conveyed to needy Jews, **Acts 24:17**; (d) of the presentation of believers themselves (saved from among the Gentiles) to God, Rom. 15:16.

Offered *see Acts 7:42*.

21:27 And when the seven days were almost ended, the Jews which were of Asia, when they saw him in the temple, stirred up all the people, and laid hands on him,

Were *see* Was at *Acts 5:4*.

Almost *mello* (3195), "to be about to do anything, or to delay," is used in connection with a following verb in the sense of "almost," in **Acts 21:27**, lit., "And when the seven days were about to be completed." In **Acts 26:28** the KJV, "Almost thou persuadest me to be a Christian" obscures the sense; the RV rightly has "with but little persuasion"; lit., "in a little."

Ended *sunteleo* (4931), signifies (a) "to bring to an end, finish completely" (*sun*, "together," imparting a perfective significance to *teleo*), Matt. 7:28 (in some mss.); Luke 4:2, 13; **Acts 21:27**, RV, "completed"; (b) "to bring to fulfillment," Mark 13:4; Rom. 9:28; (c) "to effect, make," Heb. 8:8.

Saw *see Acts 8:18*.

Stirred up *suncheo* (4797), "to pour together," is used metaphorically in **Acts 21:27**, stirred up. *See also* Confounded at *Acts 2:6*.

21:28 Crying out, Men of Israel, help: This is the man, that teacheth all *men* every where against the people, and the law, and this place: and further brought Greeks also into the temple, and hath polluted this holy place.

Help *see Acts 16:9.*

Every where *pantache* (3837), "everywhere," is used in **Acts 21:28**.

Further *eti* (2089), "yet, still, further," is used (a) of time, most usually translated "yet," e.g., Matt. 12:46; or negatively, "any more," "no more," e.g., Heb. 8:12; (b) of degree, translated "further," or "any further," Matt. 26:65; Mark 5:35; 14:63; Luke 22:71; Heb. 7:11 in **Acts 21:28**, RV, "moreover" (KJV, "further"). *See also* **Moreover** at *Acts 2:26.*

Polluted *bebeloo* (953), primarily, "to cross the threshold," hence, "to profane, pollute," occurs in Matt. 12:5 and **Acts 24:6** (the latter as in **21:28, 29**). *See also* **Common** at *Acts 10:15.*

21:29 (For they had seen before with him in the city Trophimus an Ephesian, whom they supposed that Paul had brought into the temple.)

Seen before *see* **Foresaw** at *Acts 2:25.*

Supposed *see Acts 7:25.*

21:30 And all the city was moved, and the people ran together: and they took Paul, and drew him out of the temple: and forthwith the doors were shut.

Moved *see* **Stirred up** at *Acts 6:12.*

Ran In **Acts 21:30**, *sundrome*, "a running together," with *ginomai*, "to become, take place," is translated "ran together," lit. "a running together took place."

Drew *helko* (1670), is translated "to draw" in the KJV, of **Acts 21:30** and Jas. 2:6. *See also Acts 16:19.*

Forthwith *see Acts 12:10.*

Shut *see Acts 5:23.*

21:31 And as they went about to kill him, tidings came unto the chief captain of the band, that all Jerusalem was in an uproar.

Went about *see* **Return** at *Acts 15:16. See also* **Seek** at *Acts 17:27.*

Tidings *phasis* (5334), akin to *phemi*, "to speak," denotes "information," especially against fraud or other delinquency, and is rendered "tidings" in **Acts 21:31**.

Captain *chiliarchos* (5506), denoting "a commander of 1000 soldiers" (from *chilios*, "a thousand," and *archo*, "to rule"), was the Greek word for the Persian vizier, and for the Roman military tribune, the commander of a Roman cohort, e.g., John 18:12; **Acts 21:31-33, 37**. One such commander was constantly in charge of the Roman garrison in Jerusalem. The word became used also for any military commander, e.g., a "captain" or "chief captain," Mark 6:21; Rev. 6:15; 19:18.

All *see* **Whole** at *Acts 11:26.*

Uproar For *suncheo*, "to confuse," **Acts 21:31** (KJV, "was in an uproar"); for *anastatoo*, **Acts 21:38** (KJV, "madest an uproar"). *See also* **Counfounded** at *Acts 2:6.*

21:32 Who immediately took soldiers and centurions, and ran down unto them: and when they saw the chief captain and the soldiers, they left beating of Paul.

Immediately *see Acts 10:33.*

Took *see Acts 15:39.*

Ran *katatrecho*, "to run down" occurs in **Acts 21:32**.

Left *pauo* (3973), "to make to cease," is used in the middle voice, signifying "to cease, leave off," and is translated "had left" in Luke 5:4; "left" in **Acts 21:32**; elsewhere, "to cease." *See also* **Ceased** at *Acts 5:42.*

Beating *see* **Beat** at *Acts 18:17.*

21:33 Then the chief captain came near, and took him, and commanded *him* to be bound with two chains; and demanded who he was, and what he had done.

Took *epilambano* (1949), "to lay hold of, to take hold of" (*epi*, "upon," *lambano*, "to take"), with a special purpose, always in the middle voice, is so translated in Luke 20:20, 26, of taking "hold" of Christ's words; in 23:26 and **Acts 21:33**, RV, of laying "hold" of persons; in 1 Tim. 6:12, 19, of laying "hold" on eternal life, i.e., practically appropriating all the benefits, privileges and responsibilities involved in the possession of it; in Heb. 2:16, RV "He taketh hold" (KJV "took on") perhaps to be viewed in connection with "deliver" (v. 15) and "succor" (v. 18).

Chains *see Acts 12:6.*

Demanded *punthanomai* (4441), to ask by way of enquiry, not by way of making a request for something, is found in the Gospels and the Acts, five times in the former, seven in the latter; in Matt. 2:4, KJV, "demanded," RV, "enquired, so **Acts 21:33**. *See also* **Asked** at *Acts 4:7.*

21:34 And some cried one thing, some another, among the multitude: and when he could not know the certainty for the tumult, he commanded him to be carried into the castle.

Some *see Acts 19:32.*

Cried *see* **Crying** at *Acts 8:7.*

One *see Acts 5:25.*

Multitude *ochlos* (3793), "a confused throng," is usually translated "multitude." The RV translates it "crowd" (KJV, "press" in some) in Matt. 9:23, 25; Mark 2:4; 3:9; 5:27, 30; Luke 8:19; 19:3; **Acts 21:34-35; 24:12, 18.**

Certainty *asphales* (804), safe, is translated "certainty," **Acts 21:34; 22:30**; "certain," **Acts 25:26**; "safe," Phil. 3:1; "sure," Heb. 6:19.

Tumult *see* Uproar at *Acts 20:1.*

Castle *parembole* (3925), lit., "a casting in among, an insertion" (*para*, "among," *ballo*, "to throw"), in the Macedonian dialect, was a military term. In the NT it denotes the distribution of troops in army formation, "armies," Heb. 11:34; a camp, as of the Israelites, Exod. 19:17; 29:14; 32:17; hence, in Heb. 13:11, 13, of Jerusalem, since the city was to the Jews what the camp in the wilderness had been to the Israelites; in Rev. 20:9, the "armies" or camp of the saints, at the close of the Millennium. It also denoted a castle or barracks, **Acts 21:34, 37; 22:24; 23:10, 16, 32.**

21:35 And when he came upon the stairs, so it was, that he was borne of the soldiers for the violence of the people.

Stairs *anabathmos* (304), "an ascent" (akin to *anabaino*, "to go up"), denotes "a flight of stairs," **Acts 21:35, 40.** These were probably the steps leading down from the castle of Antonia to the Temple. (See Josephus, *B.J.*, v., 5, 8.) In the Sept., it is used, e.g., in the titles of the Songs of Ascents, Ps. 120-134.

So *sumbaino*, when used of events, signifies "to come to pass, happen"; in **Acts 21:35** it is rendered "so it was." *See also* Happened *at Acts 3:10;* Befell at *Acts 20:19.*

Was *see Acts 5:4.*

Borne *see* Carried at *Acts 3:2.*

Violence *see Acts 5:26. See also* Mighty at *Acts 2:2.*

21:36 For the multitude of the people followed after, crying, Away with him.

Away This word is to be taken in connection with various verbs. The verb *airo*, "to seize, to lift up, take away," is translated "away with," in Luke 23:18; John 19:15; **Acts 21:36; 22:22**, implying a forcible removal for the purpose of putting to death.

21:37 And as Paul was to be led into the castle, he said unto the chief captain, May I speak unto thee? Who said, Canst thou speak Greek?

Was *see Acts 5:4.*

Led *eisago* (1521), "to bring into," is translated "to be led into" in **Acts 21:37**, KJV (RV, "to be brought into").

Castle *see Acts 21:34.*

Captain *see Acts 21:31.*

May *see* Let at *Acts 2:29.*

Greek Cf. *Hellenisti*, "in Greek," John 19:20, RV; **Acts 21:37**, "Greek."

21:38 Art not thou that Egyptian, which before these days madest an uproar, and leddest out into the wilderness four thousand men that were murderers?

Uproar *see Acts 21:31. See also* Turned at *Acts 17:6.*

Leddest *see* Brought at *Acts 7:36.*

Thousand *see Acts 2:41.*

Murderers *sikarios* (4607), is a Latin word (*sicarius*, "from" *sica*, "a dagger") denoting "one who carries a dagger or short sword under his clothing, an assassin," **Acts 21:38**, RV. Here it is used as a proper name (see the RV) of the Sicarii, "assassins," the fanatical Jewish faction which arose in Judea after Felix had rid the country of the robbers referred to by Josephus (Ant., XX). They mingled with the crowds at festivals and stabbed their political opponents unobserved (KJV, "murderers").

21:39 But Paul said, I am a man *which am* a Jew of Tarsus, *a city* in Cilicia, a citizen of no mean city: and, I beseech thee, suffer me to speak unto the people.

Jew *see* Jews at *Acts 2:10.*

Citizen *polites* (4177), "a member of a city or state, or the inhabitant of a country or district," Luke 15:15, is used elsewhere in Luke 19:14; **Acts 21:39**, and, in the most authentic mss., in Heb. 8:11 (where some texts have *plesion*, "a neighbor"). Apart from Heb. 8:11, the word occurs only in the writings of Luke (himself a Greek).

Mean *asemos* (767), lit., "without mark" (*a*, negative, *sema*, "a mark"), i.e., "undistinguished, obscure," was applied by the apostle Paul negatively, to his native city, Tarsus, **Acts 21:39**. Moulton and Milligan (*Vocab.*) have a note as follows: "This word occurs perpetually in the papyri to denote a man who is 'not distinguished' from his neighbors by the convenient scars on eyebrow or arm or right shin, which identify so many individuals in formal documents." Deissmann suggests that the word may have been the technical term for "uncircumcised," among the Greek Egyptians. In another papyrus document a pair of silver bracelets are described as of "unstamped" (*asemos*) silver.

Beseech *see* Prayed at *Acts 4:31*.

Suffer *epitrepo* (2010), lit. denotes "to turn to" (*epi*, "upon, to," *trepo*, "to turn"), "to permit, give leave, send," of Christ's permission to the unclean spirits to enter the swine, Mark 5:13; in Luke 8:32, RV, "give ... leave," "gave ... leave" (KJV, "suffer" and "suffered"); in John 19:38, of Pilate's permission to Joseph to take away the body of the Lord; in **Acts 21:39**, of Paul's request to the chief captain to permit him to address the people, RV, "give ... leave" (for KJV, "suffer"); in **21:40**, "he had given him leave" (KJV, "... licence"). It is rendered "to suffer" in KJV and RV in Matt. 8:21; Mark 10:4; Luke 9:59; **Acts 28:16**; RV only, Luke 9:61 (KJV, "let"); KJV only, **Acts 21:39**; in some texts, Matt. 8:31, KJV only.

21:40 And when he had given him licence, Paul stood on the stairs, and beckoned with the hand unto the people. And when there was made a great silence, he spake unto *them* in the Hebrew tongue, saying,

Licence *see* Suffer at *Acts 21:39*.

Stairs *see Acts 21:35*.

Beckoned *see* **Beckoning** at *Acts 12:17*.

Silence *sige* (4602), occurs in **Acts 21:40**; Rev. 8:1, where the "silence" is introductory to the judgments following the opening of the seventh seal.

Spake *prosphoneo* (4377), "to address, call to," is rendered "spake unto" (or "to") in Luke 23:20; **Acts 21:40**; **22:2**; "to call unto" (or "to") in Matt. 11:16; Luke 6:13; 7:32; 13:12.

Tongue *see Acts 1:19*.

Chapter 22

22:1 Men, brethren, and fathers, hear ye my defence *which I make* now unto you.

Fathers *see Acts 7:2*.

Defence *apologia* (627), a "verbal defense, a speech in defense," is sometimes translated "answer," in the KJV, **Acts 25:16**; 1 Cor. 9:3; 2 Tim. 4:16, all which the RV corrects to "defense." See **Acts 22:1**; Phil. 1:7, 16; 2 Cor. 7:11, "clearing." Once it signifies an "answer," 1 Pet. 3:15.

Make In **Acts 22:1** the verb "I make" represents no word in the original, lit., "hear now my defense unto you."

Now *nuni* (3570), is used (a) of time, e.g., **Acts 22:1** (in the best mss.); **24:13**; Rom. 6:22; 15:23, 25; (b) with logical import, e.g., Rom. 7:17; 1 Cor. 13:13, which some regard as temporal.

22:2 (And when they heard that he spake in the Hebrew tongue to them, they kept the more silence: and he saith,)

Spake *see Acts 21:40*.

Tongue *see Acts 1:19*.

Kept In **Acts 22:2**, KJV, *parecho*, "to afford, give, cause," is rendered "kept (the more silence)," RV, "were (the more quiet)."

Silence *hesuchia* (2271), denotes "quietness," 2 Thess. 3:12; it is so translated in the RV of 1 Tim. 2:11, 12 (KJV, "silence"); in **Acts 22:2**, RV, "(they were the more) quiet," KJV, "(they kept the more) silence," lit., "they kept quietness the more."

22:3 I am verily a man *which am* a Jew, born in Tarsus, *a city* in Cilicia, yet brought up in this city at the feet of Gamaliel, *and* taught according to the perfect manner of the law of the fathers, and was zealous toward God, as ye all are this day.

Am, Are *see* Exist at *Acts 2:30*.

Man *see* Men at *Acts 1:16*.

Jew *see* Jews at *Acts 2:10*.

Feet *see Acts 5:9*.

Taught *see* Learned at *Acts 7:22*.

Perfect *see* Perfectly at *Acts 18:26*.

Manner *akribeia* (195), "exactness, precision" (akin to *akribes*, "exact, careful"; see *akriboo*, "to inquire carefully," and *akribos*, "carefully"), occurs in **Acts 22:3**, RV, "strict manner" (KJV, "perfect manner").

Fathers *patroos* (3971), signifies "of one's fathers," or "received from one's fathers," **Acts 22:3**; **24:14**; **28:17**. In the Sept., Prov. 27:10.

Zealous *see* Zelotes at *Acts 1:13*.

22:4 And I persecuted this way unto the death, binding and delivering into prisons both men and women.

Binding *desmeuo* or *desmeo* (1195), signifies "to put in fetters or any kind of bond," Luke 8:29; **Acts 22:4**, or "to bind a burden upon a person," Matt. 23:4.

22:5 As also the high priest doth bear me witness, and all the estate of the elders: from whom also I received letters unto the brethren, and went to Damascus, to bring them which were there bound unto Jerusalem, for to be punished.

Witness *see* Report at *Acts 6:3*.

Estate In **Acts 22:5**, *presbuterion*, "presbytery, a body of elders," is translated "estate of the elders," lit., "the presbytery," i.e., the Sanhedrin.

Elders *presbuterion* (4244), "an assembly of aged men," denotes (a) the Council or Senate among the Jews, Luke 22:66; Acts 22:5; (b) the "elders" or bishops in a local church, 1 Tim. 4:14, "the presbytery."

Received *see* Receive at *Acts 3:21.*

There *see Acts 21:3.*

Bound *see Acts 20:22.*

Punished *timoreo* (5097), primarily, "to help," then, "to avenge" (from *time*, "value, honor," and *ouros*, "a guardian"), i.e., "to help" by redressing injuries, is used in the active voice in Acts 26:11, RV, "punishing" (KJV, "I punished"); passive voice in 22:5, lit., "(that) they may be punished."

22:6 And it came to pass, that, as I made my journey, and was come nigh unto Damascus about noon, suddenly there shone from heaven a great light round about me.

Journey *see* Journeyed at *Acts 9:3.*

Come nigh *see* Came near at *Acts 9:3.*

Noon *see* South at *Acts 8:26.*

Suddenly *see Acts 9:3.*

Shone *see* Shined at *Acts 9:3.*

Great *hikanos* (2425), lit., "reaching to" (from *hikano*, "to reach"), denotes "sufficient, competent, fit," and is sometimes rendered "great," e.g., of number (of people), Mark 10:46; of degree (of light), Acts 22:6.

22:7 And I fell unto the ground, and heard a voice saying unto me, Saul, Saul, why persecutest thou me?

Ground *edaphos* (1475), "a bottom, base," is used of the "ground" in Acts 22:7, suggestive of that which is level and hard.

Voice *see Acts 7:31.*

22:8-9 And I answered, Who art thou, Lord? And he said unto me, I am Jesus of Nazareth, whom thou persecutest.

And they that were with me saw indeed the light, and were afraid; but they heard not the voice of him that spake to me.

Afraid *see Acts 10:4.*

Heard *see* Hearing at *Acts 9:7.*

Voice *see Acts 7:31.*

22:10 And I said, What shall I do, Lord? And the Lord said unto me, Arise, and go into Damascus; and there it shall be told thee of all things which are appointed for thee to do.

Told *see Acts 9:6.*

Appointed *see* Ordained at *Acts 13:48.*

22:11 And when I could not see for the glory of that light, being led by the hand of them that were with me, I came into Damascus.

Could *emblepo* in Acts 22:11, lit., "I was not seeing," is translated "I could not see."

See *emblepo* (1689), "to look at," used of earnestly looking, is translated "saw" in Mark 8:25 (last part); "could (not) see" in Acts 22:11. *See also* Gazing at *Acts 1:11.*

Glory *see Acts 12:23.*

Hand *see Acts 9:8.*

22:12 And one Ananias, a devout man according to the law, having a good report of all the Jews which dwelt *there*,

Devout *see Acts 2:5.*

Report *see Acts 6:3.*

22:13 Came unto me, and stood, and said unto me, Brother Saul, receive thy sight. And the same hour I looked up upon him.

Stood *see Acts 10:17.*

Sight *see Acts 9:12.*

Hour *see Acts 10:3.*

22:14 And he said, The God of our fathers hath chosen thee, that thou shouldest know his will, and see that Just One, and shouldest hear the voice of his mouth.

Chosen *see* Preached at *Acts 3:20.*

Just *see Acts 3:14.*

Voice *see Acts 7:31.*

Mouth *see Acts 1:16.*

22:15 For thou shalt be his witness unto all men of what thou hast seen and heard.

Witness *see* Witnesses at *Acts 1:8.*

22:16 And now why tarriest thou? arise, and be baptized, and wash away thy sins, calling on the name of the Lord.

Tarriest *mello* (3195), "to be about to," is rendered "(why) tarriest thou?" in Acts 22:16.

Baptized *see Acts 1:5.*

Wash *apolouo* (628), "to wash off or away," is used in the middle voice, metaphorically, "to wash oneself," in Acts 22:16, where the command to Saul of Tarsus to "wash away" his sins indicates that by his public confession, he would testify to the removal of his sins, and to the complete change from his past life; this "washing away" was not in itself the actual remission of his sins, which had taken place at his conversion; the middle voice implies his own particular interest in the act (as with the preceding verb "baptize," lit., "baptize thyself," i.e., "get thyself baptized"); the aorist tenses mark the decisiveness of the acts; in 1 Cor. 6:11, lit., "ye washed yourselves clean"; here the middle voice (rendered in the Passive in KJV and RV, which do not distinguish between this and the next two passives; see RV marg.) again indicates that the converts at Corinth, by their obedience to the faith, voluntarily gave testimony to the complete spiritual change divinely wrought in them. In the Sept., Job 9:30.

22:17 And it came to pass, that, when I was come again to Jerusalem, even while I prayed in the temple, I was in a trance;

Come For "was come again," **Acts 22:17**, KJV. *See also* **Returned** at *Acts 1:12*.

Trance *see Acts 10:10*. *See also* **Amazement** at *Acts 3:10*.

22:18 And saw him saying unto me, Make haste, and get thee quickly out of Jerusalem: for they will not receive thy testimony concerning me.

Haste *see* **Hasted** at *Acts 20:16*.

Get *see Acts 7:3*.

Receive *see* **Received** at *Acts 15:4*.

Testimony *marturia* (3141), "witness, evidence, testimony," is almost always rendered "witness" in the RV (for KJV, "testimony" in John 3:32, 33; 5:34; 8:17; 21:24, and always for KJV, "record," e.g., 1 John 5:10, 11), except in **Acts 22:18** and in Revelation, where both, with one exception, have "testimony," 1:2, 9; 6:9; 11:7; 12:11, 17; 19:10 (twice); 20:4 (KJV, "witness"). In 19:10, "the testimony of Jesus" is objective, the "testimony" or witness given to Him (cf. 1:2, 9; as to those who will bear it, see Rev. 12:17, RV). The statement "the testimony of Jesus is the spirit of prophecy," is to be understood in the light, e.g., of the "testimony" concerning Christ and Israel in the Psalms, which will be used by the godly Jewish remnant in the coming time of "Jacob's Trouble." All such "testimony" centers in and points to Christ.

22:19 And I said, Lord, they know that I imprisoned and beat in every synagogue them that believed on thee:

Know *see Acts 10:28*.

Imprisoned *phulakizo* (5439), "to imprison," akin to *phulax*, "a guard, a keeper," and *phulasso*, "to guard," is used in **Acts 22:19**.

Beat *see* **Beaten** at *Acts 5:40*.

Every *see Acts 5:42*.

22:20 And when the blood of thy martyr Stephen was shed, I also was standing by, and consenting unto his death, and kept the raiment of them that slew him.

Martyr *see* **Witnesses** at *Acts 1:8*.

Shed *see* **Pour** at *Acts 2:17*. *See also* **Poured** at *Acts 10:45*.

Standing *see* **Stood** at *Acts 10:17*.

Consenting *see Acts 8:1*.

Death *see Acts 8:1*.

Raiment *see Acts 18:6* t.

Slew *see* **Slain** at *Acts 2:23*.

22:21 And he said unto me, Depart: for I will send thee far hence unto the Gentiles.

Depart *see* **Departed** at *Acts 5:41*.

Send *see* **Sent** at *Acts 7:12*.

Far *see* **Afar** at *Acts 2:39*.

Hence For *makran*, "far hence," in **Acts 22:21**.

22:22 And they gave him audience unto this word, and *then* lifted up their voices, and said, Away with such a *fellow* from the earth: for it is not fit that he should live.

Lifted *see* **Taken up** at *Acts 1:9*.

Away *see Acts 21:36*.

Fellow *toioutos*, an adjective, "such a one," is often used as a noun, e.g., **Acts 22:22**, where it is translated "such a fellow."

Earth *see Acts 1:8*.

Fit *katheko* (2520), "to come or reach down to" (*kata*, "down"), hence, "to befit, be proper," is translated "is (not fit)" in **Acts 22:22**; in Rom. 1:28, RV, "fitting" (KJV, "convenient").

22:23 And as they cried out, and cast off *their* clothes, and threw dust into the air,

Cried *kraugazo* (2905), "to make a clamor or outcry," is used in Matt. 12:19, in a prophecy from Isaiah of Christ; in Luke 4:41 (in the best mss., instead of *krazo*); John 11:43; 12:13 (in the best mss.); 18:40; 19:6, 12, 19:15; **Acts 22:23**.

Cast *rhipto* (4496), denotes "to throw with a sudden motion, to jerk, cast forth"; "cast down," Matt. 15:30 and 27:5; "thrown down," Luke 4:35; "thrown," 17:2 (KJV, "cast"); [*rhipteo* in **Acts 22:23** (KJV, "cast off"), of the "casting" off of clothes (in the next sentence *ballo* is used of "casting" dust into the air)]; in **27:19** "cast out," of the tackling of a ship, in v. **29** "let go" (KJV, "cast"), of anchors; in Matt. 9:36, "scattered," said of sheep.

Threw *ballo* (906), "to cast, to throw," is rendered "to throw" in Mark 12:42, KJV (RV, "cast"); so **Acts 22:23** (2nd part); "to throw down," Rev. 18:21 (2nd part), KJV (RV, "cast down").

Dust *see Acts 13:51.*

Air *aer* (109), Eng., "air," signifies "the atmosphere," certainly in five of the seven occurrences **Acts 22:23**; 1 Cor. 9:26; 14:9; Rev. 9:2; 16:11, and almost certainly in the other two, Eph. 2:2 and 1 Thess. 4:17.

22:24 The chief captain commanded him to be brought into the castle, and bade that he should be examined by scourging; that he might know wherefore they cried so against him.

Castle *see Acts 21:34.*

Bade *see Acts 11:12.*

Examined *anetazo* (426), "to examine judicially" (*ana,* "up," *etazo,* "to test"), is used in **Acts 22:24, 29**. Cf. the synonymous verb *exetazo,* "to search" or "enquire carefully," Matt. 2:8; 10:11; John 21:12.

Scourging *mastix* (3148), "a whip, scourge," is used (a) with the meaning "scourging," in **Acts 22:24**, of the Roman method, (b) in Heb. 11:36, of the "sufferings" of saints in the OT times. Among the Hebrews the usual mode, legal and domestic, was that of beating with a rod (see 2 Cor. 11:25); (c) metaphorically, of "disease" or "suffering".

Cried *see* Shout at *Acts 12:22.*

22:25 And as they bound him with thongs, Paul said unto the centurion that stood by, Is it lawful for you to scourge a man that is a Roman, and uncondemned?

Bound *proteino* (4385), lit., "to stretch forth" (*pro,* "forth," *teino,* "to stretch"), is used in **Acts 22:25**, KJV, "they bound"; RV, "they had tied (him) up," in reference to the preparations made for scourging, probably, to stretch the body forward, to make it tense for severer punishment.

See also ***Acts 20:22.***

Thongs *himas* (2438), denotes "a thong, strap," whether for binding prisoners, **Acts 22:25**, "(the) thongs," or for fastening sandals, Mark 1:7; Luke 3:16; John 1:27. "Among the Orientals everything connected with the feet and shoes is defiled and debasing, and the stooping to unfasten the dusty latchet is the most insignificant in such service" (Mackie, in *Hastings' Bib. Dic.*).

Scourge *mastizo* (3147), occurs in **Acts 22:25**. In the Sept., Num. 22:25.

Roman *see* Rome at *Acts 2:10.*

Uncondemned *see Acts 16:37.*

22:26 When the centurion heard *that*, he went and told the chief captain, saying, Take heed what thou doest: for this man is a Roman.

Heed *horao* (3708), "to see," usually expressing the sense of vision, is rendered "take heed" in Matt. 16:6; 18:10, KJV (RV, "see"); Mark 8:15; Luke 12:15; **Acts 22:26** (KJV only).

Roman *see* Rome at *Acts 2:10.*

22:27 Then the chief captain came, and said unto him, Tell me, art thou a Roman? He said, Yea.

Roman *see* Rome at *Acts 2:10.*

Yea *see Acts 5:8.*

22:28 And the chief captain answered, With a great sum obtained I this freedom. And Paul said, But I was *free* born.

Great *kephalaion* (2774), akin to the adjective *kephalaios,* "belonging to the head," and *kephale,* "the head," denotes the chief point or principal thing in a subject, Heb. 8:1, "the chief point is this" (KJV, "the sum"); elsewhere in **Acts 22:28** (of principal, as to money), "(a great) sum." Certain compound nouns involving the significance of chief, are as follows.

Sum *see Acts 7:16.*

Obtained *see* Purchased at *Acts 1:18.*

Freedom *politeia* (4174), signifies (a) "the relation in which a citizen stands to the state, the condition of a citizen, citizenship," **Acts 22:28**, "with a great sum obtained I this citizenship" (KJV, "freedom"). While Paul's "citizenship" of Tarsus was not of advantagre outside that city, yet his Roman "citizenship" availed throughout the Roman Empire and, besides private rights, included (1) exemption from all degrading punishments; (2) a right of appeal to the emperor after a sentence; (3) a right to be sent to Rome for trial before the emperor if charged with a capital offense. Paul's father might have obtained "citizenship" (1) by manumission; (2) as a reward of merit; (3) by purchase; the contrast implied in **Acts 22:28** is perhaps against the last mentioned; (b) "a civil polity, the condition of a state, a commonwealth," said of Israel, Eph. 2:12.

22:29 Then straightway they departed from him which should have examined him: and the chief captain also was afraid, after he knew that he was a Roman, and because he had bound him.

Departed *see* Drew away at *Acts 5:37*.

Examined *see Acts 22:24*.

Knew *see Acts 9:30*.

Roman *see* Rome at *Acts 2:10*.

22:30 On the morrow, because he would have known the certainty wherefore he was accused of the Jews, he loosed him from *his* bands, and commanded the chief priests and all their council to appear, and brought Paul down, and set him before them.

Because *ti*, "what, why," John 9:27; **Acts 22:30**; Gal. 3:19, KJV (RV, "what").

Certainty *see Acts 21:34*.

Accused *kategoreo* (2723), "to speak against, accuse," is used (a) in a general way, "to accuse," e.g., Luke 6:7, RV, "how to accuse"; Rom. 2:15; Rev. 12:10; (b) before a judge, e.g., Matt. 12:10; Mark 15:4 (RV, "witness against"); **Acts 22:30**; **25:16**. In **Acts 24:19**, RV renders it "make accusation," for the KJV, "object."

Loosed *see Acts 2:24* e.

Bands *see Acts 16:26*.

Commanded *boulomai* (1014), "to wish, to will deliberately," expresses more strongly than *thelo* the deliberate exercise of the will; it is translated "to desire" in the RV of the following: **Acts 22:30**; **23:28**; **27:43**; **28:18**; 1 Tim. 2:8; 5:14; 6:9 and Jude 5.

Appear In **Acts 22:30** *sunerchomai* (in its aorist form), "to come together," is translated "appear," KJV; RV, "come together."

Brought *see Acts 9:30*.

Set *see Acts 4:7*.

Chapter 23

23:1 And Paul, earnestly beholding the council, said, Men *and* brethren, I have lived in all good conscience before God until this day.

Earnestly *see Acts 3:12*.

Beholding *see Acts 14:9. See also* Looked at Acts 1:10.

Lived *politeuo* (4176), "to be a citizen (*polites*), to live as a citizen," is used metaphorically of conduct as in accordance with the characteristics of the heavenly community; in **Acts 23:1**, "I have lived"; in Phil. 1:27, "let your manner of life (KJV, conversation) be."

Conscience *suneidesis* (4893), lit., "a knowing with" (*sun*, "with," *oida*, "to know"), i.e., "a co-knowledge (with oneself), the witness borne to one's conduct by conscience, that faculty by which we apprehend the will of God, as that which is designed to govern our lives"; hence (a) the sense of guiltiness before God; Heb. 10:2; (b) that process of thought which distinguishes what it considers morally good or bad, commending the good, condemning the bad, and so prompting to do the former, and avoid the latter; Rom. 2:15 (bearing witness with God's law); 9:1; 2 Cor. 1:12; acting in a certain way because "conscience" requires it, Rom. 13:5; so as not to cause scruples of "conscience" in another, 1 Cor. 10:28-29; not calling a thing in question unnecessarily, as if conscience demanded it, 1 Cor. 10:25, 27; "commending oneself to every man's conscience," 2 Cor. 4:2; cf. 5:11. There may be a "conscience" not strong enough to distinguish clearly between the lawful and the unlawful, 1 Cor. 8:7, 10, 12 (some regard consciousness as the meaning here). The phrase "conscience toward God," in 1 Pet. 2:19, signifies a "conscience" (or perhaps here, a consciousness) so controlled by the apprehension of God's presence, that the person realizes that griefs are to be borne in accordance with His will. Heb. 9:9 teaches that sacrifices under the Law could not so perfect a person that he could regard himself as free from guilt. For various descriptions of "conscience" see **Acts 23:1**; **24:16**; 1 Cor. 8:7; 1 Tim. 1:5, 19; 3:9; 4:2; 2 Tim. 1:3; Titus 1:15; Heb. 9:14; 10:22; 13:18; 1 Pet. 3:16, 2l.

23:2 And the high priest Ananias commanded them that stood by him to smite him on the mouth.

Commanded *epitasso* (2004), signifies to appoint over, put in charge (*epi*, "over," *tasso*, "to appoint"); then, "to put upon one as a duty, to enjoin," Mark 1:27; 6:27, 39; 9:25; Luke 4:36; 8:25, 31; 14:22; **Acts 23:2**; Philem. 8.

Stood *see Acts 1:10*.

Smite *tupto* (5180), "to strike, smite, beat," is rendered "to smite" in Matt. 24:49, KJV (RV, "beat"); 27:30; Mark 15:19; Luke 6:29; 18:13; in some texts in 22:64 (1st part: RV omits); 23:48; **Acts 23:2, 3** (twice).

23:3 Then said Paul unto him, God shall smite thee, *thou* whited wall: for sittest thou to judge me after the law, and commandest me to be smitten contrary to the law?

Shall *mello* (3195), "to be about (to be or do)," is used of purpose, certainty, compulsion or necessity. It is rendered simply by "shall" or "should" (which frequently represent elsewhere part of the future tense of the verb) in the following (the RV sometimes translates differently, as noted): Matt. 16:27 (1st part), lit., "is about to come"; 17:12, 22; 20:22, RV, "am about"; 24:6; Mark 13:4 (2nd part), RV, "are about"; Luke 9:44; 21:7 (2nd part), RV, "are about"; v. 36; **Acts 23:3; 24:15; 26:2**, RV, "I am (to)"; Rom. 4:24; 8:13 (1st part), RV, "must"; v. 18; 2 Tim. 4:1; Heb. 1:14; 10:27; Jas. 2:12, RV "are to"; 1 Pet. 5:1; Rev. 1:19; 2:10 (1st and 2nd parts), RV, "art about," "is about"; 3:10, RV, "is (to)"; 17:8 (1st part), RV, "is about."

Smite *see Acts 23:2.*

Whited *koniao* (2867), from *konia*, "dust, lime," denotes "to whiten, whitewash," of tombs, Matt. 23:27; figuratively of a hypocrite, **Acts 23:3**. In the Sept., Deut. 27:2, 4; Prov. 21:9.

Wall *toichos* (5109), "a wall," especially of a house, is used figuratively in **Acts 23:3**, "(thou whited) wall."

Law *paranomeo* (3891), "to transgress law" (*para*, "contrary to," and *nomos*), is used in the present participle in **Acts 23:3**, and translated "contrary to the law," lit., "transgressing the law."

23:4 And they that stood by said, Revilest thou God's high priest?

Stood *see Acts 1:10.*

Revilest *loidoreo* (3058), denotes "to abuse, revile," John 9:28; **Acts 23:4**; 1 Cor. 4:12; 1 Pet. 2:23 (1st clause).

23:5 Then said Paul, I wist not, brethren, that he was the high priest: for it is written, Thou shalt not speak evil of the ruler of thy people.

Wist *see Acts 12:9.*

Evil *kakos* (2560), "badly, evilly," is used in the physical sense, "to be sick," e.g., Matt. 4:24; Mark 1:32, 34; Luke 5:31. In Matt. 21:41 this adverb is used with the adjective, "He will miserably destroy those miserable men," more lit., "He will evilly destroy those men (evil as they are)," with stress on the adjective; (b) in the moral sense, "to speak evilly," John 18:23; **Acts 23:5**; to ask evilly, Jas. 4:3.

23:6 But when Paul perceived that the one part were Sadducees, and the other Pharisees, he cried out in the council, Men *and* brethren, I am a Pharisee, the son of a Pharisee: of the hope and resurrection of the dead I am called in question.

Perceived *ginosko* (1097), "to know by experience and observation," is translated "to perceive" in Matt. 12:15, RV (KJV, "knew"); 16:8; 21:45; 22:18; 26:10, RV, (KJV, "understood"); Mark 8:17; 12:12 and 15:10, RV (KJV, "knew"); so Luke 9:11; 18:34; in Luke 7:39, RV (KJV, "known"); 20:19; John 6:15; 8:27, RV (KJV, "understood"); 16:19, RV (KJV, "knew"); **Acts 23:6**; Gal. 2:9; in 1 John 3:16, KJV, "perceive" (RV, "know," perfect tense, lit., "we have perceived," and therefore "know").

Part *see* Parts at *Acts 2:10.*

Pharisees, Pharisee *pharisaios* (5330), from an Aramaic word *peras* (found in Dan. 5:28), signifying "to separate," owing to a different manner of life from that of the general public. The "Pharisees" and Sadducees appear as distinct parties in the latter half of the 2nd cent. BC, though they represent tendencies traceable much earlier in Jewish history, tendencies which became pronounced after the return from Babylon (537 BC). The immediate progenitors of the two parties were, respectively, the Hasidaeans and the Hellenizers; the latter, the antecedents of the Sadducees, aimed at removing Judaism from its narrowness and sharing in the advantages of Greek life and culture. The Hasidaeans, a transcription of the Hebrew *chasidim*, i.e., "pious ones," were a society of men zealous for religion, who acted under the guidance of the scribes, in opposition to the godless Hellenizing party; they scrupled to oppose the legitimate high priest even when he was on the Greek side. Thus the Hellenizers were a political sect, while the Hasidaeans, whose fundamental principle was complete separation from non-Jewish elements, were the strictly legal party among the Jews, and were ultimately the more popular and influential party. In their zeal for the Law they almost deified it and their attitude became merely external, formal, and mechanical. They laid stress, not upon the righteousness of an action, but upon its formal correctness. Consequently their opposition to Christ was inevitable; His manner of life and teaching was essentially a condemnation of theirs; hence His denunciation of them, e.g., Matt. 6:2, 5, 16; 15:7 and chapter 23. While the Jews continued to be divided into these two parties, the spread of the testimony of the gospel must have produced what in the public eye seemed to be a new sect, and in the extensive development which took place at Antioch, **Acts 11:19-26**, the name "Christians" seems to have become a popular term applied to the disciples as a sect, the primary cause, however, being their witness to Christ. The opposition of both "Pharisees" and Sadducees (still mutually antagonistic, **Acts 23:6-10**) against the new "sect" continued unabated during apostolic times.

Hope *see Acts 16:19.*

And *kai* The *epexegetic* or *explanatory* use. This may be represented by the expressions "namely," "again," "and indeed," "that is to say"; it is usually translated by "and." In such cases not merely an addition is in view. In Matt. 21:5, "and upon a colt" means "that is to say, upon a colt." In John 1:16 the clause "and grace for grace" is explanatory of the "fullness." In John 12:48, "and receiveth not My sayings," is not simply an addition to "that rejecteth Me," it explains what the rejection involves, as the preceding verse shows. In Mark 14:1, "and the unleavened bread" is perhaps an instance, since the Passover feast is so defined in Luke 22:1. In **Acts 23:6** the meaning is "the hope, namely, the resurrection of the dead." In Rom. 1:5 "grace and apostleship" may signify "grace expressed in apostleship." In Eph. 1:1 "and the faithful" does not mark a distinct class of believers, it defines "the saints"; but in this case it goes a little further than what is merely epexegetical, it adds a more distinctive epithet than the preceding and may be taken as meaning "yes indeed."

Resurrection *see Acts 1:22.*

Called *krino* (2919), "to judge," is translated "to call in question," in **Acts 23:6**; **24:21**. *See also* **Determined** at *Acts 3:13.*

23:7 And when he had so said, there arose a dissension between the Pharisees and the Sadducees: and the multitude was divided.

So Some form of *houtos*, "this," is sometimes rendered "so," e.g., **Acts 23:7**; Rom. 12:20.

Arose *see Acts 6:1.*

Dissension *see Acts 15:2.*

Multitude *plethos* (4128), "a multitude, the whole number," is translated "assembly" in **Acts 23:7**, RV. *See also Acts 4:32.*

Divided *see Acts 13:19. See also Acts 14:4.*

23:8 For the Sadducees say that there is no resurrection, neither angel, nor spirit: but the Pharisees confess both.

Resurrection *see Acts 1:22.*

Confess *homologeo* (3670), lit., "to speak the same thing" (*homos*, "same," *lego*, "to speak"), "to assent, accord, agree with," denotes, (a) "to confess, declare, admit," John 1:20; e.g., **Acts 24:14**; Heb. 11:13; (b) "to confess by way of admitting oneself guilty of what one is accused of, the result of inward conviction," 1 John 1:9; (c) "to declare openly by way of speaking out freely, such confession being the effect of deep conviction of facts," Matt. 7:23; 10:32 (twice) and Luke 12:8 (see next par.); John 9:22; 12:42; **Acts 23:8**; Rom. 10:9-10 ("confession is made"); 1 Tim. 6:12 (RV); Titus 1:16; 1 John 2:23; 4:2, 15; 2 John 7 (in John's epistle it is the necessary antithesis to Gnostic doceticism); Rev. 3:5, in the best mss.; (d) "to confess by way of celebrating with praise," Heb. 13:15; (e) "to promise," Matt. 14:7. In Matt. 10:32 and Luke 12:8 the construction of this verb with *en*, "in," followed by the dative case of the personal pronoun, has a special significance, namely, to "confess" in a person's name, the nature of the "confession" being determined by the context, the suggestion being to make a public "confession." Thus the statement, "every one ... who shall confess Me (lit. "in Me," i.e., in My case) before men, him (lit., "in him," i.e., in his case) will I also confess before My Father ... ," conveys the thought of "confessing" allegiance to Christ as one's Master and Lord, and, on the other hand, of acknowledgment, on His part, of the faithful one as being His worshipper and servant, His loyal follower; this is appropriate to the original idea in *homologeo* of being identified in thought or language.

23:9 And there arose a great cry: and the scribes *that were* of the Pharisees' part arose, and strove, saying, We find no evil in this man: but if a spirit or an angel hath spoken to him, let us not fight against God.

Arose *see Acts 6:1.*

Cry *krauge* (2906), an onomatopoeic word, is used in Matt. 25:6; Luke 1:42 (some mss. have *phone*); **Acts 23:9**, RV, "clamor"; Eph. 4:31, "clamor"; Heb. 5:7; Rev. 21:4, "crying." Some mss. have it in Rev. 14:18 (the most authentic have *phone*).

Scribes *see Acts 4:5.*

Part *see* Parts at *Acts 2:10.*

Strove *diamachomai* (1264), "to struggle against" (*dia*, intensive, and *machomai*), is used of "contending" in an argument, **Acts 23:9**, "strove."

Evil *kakon* (2556), is used with the article, as a noun, e.g., **Acts 23:9**; Rom. 7:21; Heb. 5:14; in the plural, "evil things," e.g., 1 Cor. 10:6; 1 Tim. 6:10, "all kinds of evil," RV.

Fight In **Acts 23:9** some mss. have the verb *theomacheo*, "to fight against God."

23:10 And when there arose a great dissension, the chief captain, fearing lest Paul should have been pulled in pieces of them, commanded the soldiers to go down, and to take him by force from among them, and to bring *him* into the castle.

Dissension *see Acts 15:2.*

Fearing *see* Feared at *Acts 10:2.*

Lest *see Acts 13:40.*

Pulled *diaspao* (1288), "to break or tear asunder," is translated "should be torn in pieces" in **Acts 23:10**, RV (KJV, "... pulled ...").

Soldiers *strateuma* (4753), denotes (a) "an army" of any size, large or small, Matt. 22:7; Rev. 9:16; 19:14, 19 (twice); (b) "a company of soldiers," such as Herod's bodyguard, Luke 23:11 (RV, "soldiers"), or the soldiers of a garrison, **Acts 23:10, 27** (RV, "the soldiers," for KJV, "an army").

Take In Matt. 11:12; John 6:15; **Acts 23:10** *harpazo* is rendered "take ... by force." *See also* Caught at *Acts 8:39.*

Force *harpazo* (726), "to snatch away, carry off by force," is used in the next sentence in Matt. 11:12, "men of violence (KJV 'the violent') take it by force," the meaning being, as determined by the preceding clause, that those who are possessed of eagerness and zeal, instead of yielding to the opposition of religious foes, such as the scribes and Pharisees, press their way into the kingdom, so as to possess themselves of it. It is elsewhere similarly rendered in John 6:15, of those who attempted to seize the Lord, and in **Acts 23:10**, of the chief captain's command to the soldiers to rescue Paul. Cf. *diarpazo*, "to plunder," e.g., Matt. 12:29, and *sunarpazo*, "to seize and carry away," e.g., **Acts 6:12**, and *harpax*, "rapacious, ravening," e.g., Matt. 7:15.

Castle *see Acts 21:34.*

23:11 And the night following the Lord stood by him, and said, Be of good cheer, Paul: for as thou hast testified of me in Jerusalem, so must thou bear witness also at Rome.

Following *see* Next at *Acts 7:26.*

Stood *see Acts 10:17.*

Cheer *tharseo* (2293), "to be of good courage, of good cheer" (*tharsos*, "courage, confidence"), is used only in the imperative mood, in the NT; "be of good cheer," Matt. 9:2, 22; 14:27; Mark 6:50; 10:49; Luke 8:48; John 16:33; **Acts 23:11**.

Testified *see* Testify at *Acts 2:40.*

Witness *see* Report at *Acts 6:3.*

23:12 And when it was day, certain of the Jews banded together, and bound themselves under a curse, saying that they would neither eat nor drink till they had killed Paul.

Banded *poieo sustrophen* (4160, 4963), **Acts 23:12**, of the Jews who "banded together" with the intention of killing Paul, consists of the verb *poieo*, "to make," and the noun *sustrophe*, primarily "a twisting up together, a binding together"; then, "a secret combination, a conspiracy." Accordingly it might be translated "made a conspiracy."

Curse *anathematizo* (332), signifies "to declare anathema," i.e., "devoted to destruction, accursed, to curse," Mark 14:71, or "to bind by a curse," **Acts 23:12, 14, 21**.

23:13 And they were more than forty which had made this conspiracy.

Conspiracy *sunomosia* (4945), denotes, lit., "a swearing together" (*sun*, "with," *omnumi*, "to swear"), a "being leagued by oath, and so a conspiracy," **Acts 23:13**.

23:14 And they came to the chief priests and elders, and said, We have bound ourselves under a great curse, that we will eat nothing until we have slain Paul.

They *see Acts 5:16.*

Ourselves This translates (a) *autoi*, the plural of *autos*, "self," used emphatically either alone, e.g., John 4:42; Rom. 8:23 (1st part); 2 Cor. 1:4 (last part); 1:9, RV, "we ourselves" (1st part); or joined with the plural pronouns, e.g., *hemeis*, "we," Rom. 8:23 (2nd part); (b) the plural *hemeis* alone, e.g., Titus 3:3; in 2 Cor. 4:7, RV, *ex hemon*, is translated "from ourselves" (KJV, "of us"); (c) *heauton*, governed by the preposition *apo*, "from," e.g., 2 Cor. 3:5 (1st part), lit., "from ourselves" ("of ourselves," in the text); (d) *heautis*, the dative case of (c), e.g., Rom. 15:1; governed by *en*, "in," 2 Cor. 1:9 (1st part); by *epi*, "on" (2nd part). (e) *heautous*, the accusative case, e.g., **Acts 23:14**; 2 Cor. 3:1; 4:2, 5.

Curse *anathema* (33), transliterated from the Greek, is frequently used in the Sept., where it translates the Heb. *cherem*, "a thing devoted to God," whether (a) for His service, as the sacrifices, Lev. 27:28 (cf. *anathema*, a votive offering, gift), or (b) for its destruction, as an idol, Deut. 7:26, or a city, Josh. 6:17. Later it acquired the more general meaning of "the disfavor of Jehovah," e.g., Zech. 14:11. This is the meaning in the NT. It is used of (a) the sentence pronounced, **Acts 23:14** (lit., "cursed themselves with a curse"; see *anathematizo* below); (b) of the object on which the "curse" is laid, "accursed"; in the following, the RV keeps to the word "anathema," Rom. 9:3; 1 Cor. 12:3; 16:22; Gal. 1:8-9, all of which the KJV renders by "accursed" except 1 Cor. 16:22, where it has "Anathema." In Gal. 1:8-9, the apostle declares in the strongest manner that the gospel he preached was the one and only way of salvation, and that to preach another was to nullify the death of Christ. *See also Acts 23:12.*

Eat *see Acts 2:46.*

23:15 Now therefore ye with the council signify to the chief captain that he bring him down unto you to morrow, as though ye would enquire something more perfectly concerning him: and we, or ever he come near, are ready to kill him.

Signify *emphanizo* (1718), from *en*, "in," intensive, and *phaino*, "to shine," is used, either of "physical manifestation," Matt. 27:53; Heb. 9:24; cf. John 14:22, or, metaphorically, of "the manifestation of Christ" by the Holy Spirit in the spiritual experience of believers who abide in His love, John 14:21. It has another, secondary meaning, "to make known, signify, inform." This is confined to the Acts, where it is used five times, **23:15**, **22**; **24:1**; **25:2**, **15**. There is perhaps a combination of the two meanings in Heb. 11:14, i.e., to declare by oral testimony and to "manifest" by the witness of the life.

Bring *see* Brought at *Acts 9:30.*

Morrow *see* Next day at *Acts 4:3.*

Enquire *diaginosko*, "to distinguish," Acts **23:15**, "to judge" (KJV, "enquire"), or "determine," **24:22**, RV (KJV, "know the uttermost of").

Perfectly *see Acts 18:26.*

Ready *hetoimos* (2092), "prepared, ready" (akin to *hetoimasia*, "preparation"), is used (a) of persons, Matt. 24:44; 25:10; Luke 12:40; 22:33; **Acts 23:15**, **21** (for 2 Cor. 10:6); Titus 3:1; 1 Pet. 3:15; (b) of things, Matt. 22:4 (2nd part), 8; Mark 14:15, RV, "ready" (KJV, "prepared"); Luke 14:17; John 7:6; 2 Cor. 9:5; 10:16, RV, "things ready" (KJV, "things made ready"); 1 Pet. 1:5.

Kill *see* Slain at *Acts 2:23.*

23:16 And when Paul's sister's son heard of their lying in wait, he went and entered into the castle, and told Paul.

Lying in wait *enedra* or *enedron* (1747, 1749), "a lying in wait, an ambush," occurs in **Acts 23:16** (where some mss. have the form *enedron*); **25:3**, "laying wait," lit., "making an ambush." In the Sept., Josh. 8:7, 9; Ps. 10:8.

Went *see* Go at *Acts 8:29.*

Castle *see Acts 21:34.*

23:17 Then Paul called one of the centurions unto *him*, and said, Bring this young man unto the chief captain: for he hath a certain thing to tell him.

Bring *apago* (520), "to lead away, bring forth, bring unto," **Acts 23:17**. *See also* Put to death at *Acts 12:19.*

Young *see Acts 7:58.*

Hath *see* Could at *Acts 4:14.*

Certain The rendering "certain," is frequently changed in the RV, or omitted, e.g., Luke 5:12; 8:22; **Acts 23:17**; Heb. 2:6; 4:4.

23:18 So he took him, and brought *him* to the chief captain, and said, Paul the prisoner called me unto *him*, and prayed me to bring this young man unto thee, who hath something to say unto thee.

Took *see Acts 15:39.*

Said *see Acts 3:22.*

Prisoner *see* Prisoners at *Acts 16:25.*

Prayed *erotao* (2065), "to ask," is translated by the verb to pray in Luke 14:18, 19; 16:27; John 4:31; 14:16; 16:26; 17:9, 15, 20; in **Acts 23:18**, RV, "asked" (KJV "prayed"); in 1 John 5:16, RV, "should make request" (KJV "shall pray"). *See also* Desired at *Acts 16:39.*

Young *see Acts 7:58.*

Something *see Acts 3:5.*

23:19 Then the chief captain took him by the hand, and went *with him* aside privately, and asked *him*, What is that thou hast to tell me?

Went *anachoreo* (402), signifies "to withdraw," often in the sense of avoiding danger, e.g., **Acts 23:19**, RV, "going aside" (KJV, "went ... aside").

Asked *see Acts 4:7.*

23:20 And he said, The Jews have agreed to desire thee that thou wouldest bring down Paul to morrow into the council, as though they would enquire somewhat of him more perfectly.

Agreed *suntithemi* (4934), lit., "to put together" (*sun*, "with," *tithemi*, "to put"), in the middle voice, means "to make an agreement, or to assent to"; translated "covenanted" in Luke 22:5; "agreed" in John 9:22, and **Acts 23:20**; "assented" in **Acts 24:9**.

Desire *see* Desired at *Acts 16:39.*

Bring *see* Brought at *Acts 9:30.*

Morrow *see* Next day at *Acts 4:3.*

Would *see* Will at *Acts 17:31.*

Enquire *see* Asked at *Acts 4:7.*

Somewhat *see* Something at *Acts 3:5.*

Perfectly *see Acts 18:26.*

23:21 But do not thou yield unto them: for there lie in wait for him of them more than forty men, which have bound themselves with an oath, that

they will neither eat nor drink till they have killed him: and now are they ready, looking for a promise from thee.

Yield *peitho* (3982), "to persuade," in the passive voice, "to be persuaded," is translated "do (not) thou yield," **Acts 23:21**.

Lie in wait *enedreuo* (1748), "to lie in wait for, to lay wait for" (from *en*, "in," and *hedra*, "a seat"), occurs in Luke 11:54, "laying wait for"; **Acts 23:21**, "there lie in wait for."

Oath For *anathematizo* in **Acts 23:21**, KJV, "have bound (themselves) with an oath." *See also* **Curse** at *Acts 23:12*.

Ready *see Acts 23:15*.

Promise *see Acts 1:4*.

23:22 So the chief captain *then* let the young man depart, and charged *him, See thou* tell no man that thou hast shewed these things to me.

Let *see Acts 3:13*.

Young *see Acts 2:17*.

Depart *apoluo* (630), "to loose from" (*apo*), in the middle voice, signifies "to depart," Luke 2:29; **Acts 23:22**, RV, "let go"; **28:25**.

Tell *eklaleo* (1583), "to speak out" (*ek*), is translated "tell" in **Acts 23:22**.

Shewed *emphanizo* ("to manifest"), **Acts 23:22**, "hast signified". See also **Signify** at *Acts 23:15*.

23:23 And he called unto *him* two centurions, saying, Make ready two hundred soldiers to go to Caesarea, and horsemen threescore and ten, and spearmen two hundred, at the third hour of the night;

Unto *see* **Far** at *Acts 11:19*.

Make ready *hetoimazo* (2090), "to prepare, make ready," is used (I) absolutely, e.g., Mark 14:15; Luke 9:52; (II) with an object, e.g., (a) of those things which are ordained (1) by God, such as future positions of authority, Matt. 20:23; the coming Kingdom, 25:34; salvation personified in Christ, Luke 2:31; future blessings, 1 Cor. 2:9; a city, Heb. 11:16; a place of refuge for the Jewish remnant, Rev. 12:6; Divine judgments on the world, Rev. 8:6; 9:7, 15; 16:12; eternal fire, for the Devil and his angels, Matt. 25:41; (2) by Christ: a place in Heaven for His followers, John 14:2, 3; (b) of human "preparation" for the Lord, e.g., Matt. 3:3; 26:17, 19; Luke 1:17 ("make ready"), 76; 3:4, KJV (RV, "make ye ready"); 9:52 ("to make ready"); 23:56; Rev. 19:7; 21:2; in 2 Tim. 2:21, of "preparation" of oneself for "every good work"; (c) of human "preparations" for human objects, e.g., Luke 12:20, RV, "thou hast prepared" (KJV, "provided"); **Acts 23:23**; Philem. 22.

Two hundred *diakosioi* (1250), occurs in Mark 6:37; John 6:7; 21:8; **Acts 23:23** (twice); **27:37**, "two hundred (threescore and sixteen)"; Rev. 11:3, "(a thousand) two hundred (and threescore)"; so 12:6.

Horsemen *hippeus* (2460), "a horseman," is used in the plural in **Acts 23:23, 32**.

Threescore and ten In **Acts 23:23**, *hebdomekonta*, "seventy," is translated "threescore and ten." *See also* **Threescore and fifteen** at *Acts 7:14*.

Spearman *dexiolabos* (1187), from *dexios*, "the right (hand)," and *lambano*, "to lay hold of," is used in the plural in **Acts 23:23**, "spearmen." Some texts have *dexiobolos*, "one who throws with his right hand" (*ballo*, "to throw"), "right-handed slingers."

Third *see Acts 2:15*.

Hour *see Acts 10:3*.

23:24 And provide *them* beasts, that they may set Paul on, and bring *him* safe unto Felix the governor.

Provide *paristemi* (3936), "to present," signifies "to provide" in **Acts 23:24**.

Beasts *ktenos* (2934), primarily denotes "property" (the connected verb *ktaomai* means "to possess"); then, "property in flocks and herds." In Scripture it signifies, (a) a "beast" of burden, Luke 10:34; **Acts 23:24**, (b) "beasts" of any sort, apart from those signified by *therion*, 1 Cor. 15:39; Rev. 18:13, (c) animals for slaughter; this meaning is not found in the NT, but is very frequent in the Sept.

Set *epibibazo* (1913), "to place upon," is used of causing persons to mount animals for riding, Luke 10:34; 19:35; **Acts 23:24**.

Safe *diasozo* (1295), "to bring safely through," is used (a) of the healing of the sick by the Lord, Matt. 14:36, RV, "were made whole" (KJV adds "perfectly"); Luke 7:3; (b) of bringing "safe" to a destination, **Acts 23:24**; (c) of keeping a person "safe," **27:43**; (d) of escaping through the perils of shipwreck, **27:44**; **28:1**, **4**, passive voice; (e) through the Flood, 1 Pet. 3:20. In 2 Pet. 2:5, KJV, *phulasso*, "to guard, keep, preserve," is translated "saved" (RV, "preserved").

23:25 And he wrote a letter after this manner:

Wrote *grapho* (1125), is used (a) of "forming letters" on a surface or writing material, John 8:6; Gal. 6:11, where the apostle speaks of his having "written" with large letters in his own hand, which not improbably means that at this point he took the pen from his amanuensis and finished the epistle himself; this is not negatived by the fact that the verb is in the aorist or past definite tense, lit., "I wrote," for in Greek idiom the writer of a letter put himself beside the reader and spoke of it as having been "written" in the past; in Eng. we should say "I am writing," taking our point of view from the time at which we are doing it; cf. Philem. 19 (this Ep. is undoubtedly a holograph), where again the equivalent English translation is in the present tense (see also Acts 15:23; Rom. 15:15); possibly the apostle, in Galatians, was referring to his having "written" the body of the epistle but the former alternative seems the more likely; in 2 Thess. 3:17 he says that the closing salutation is written by his own hand and speaks of it as "the token in every epistle" which some understand as a purpose for the future rather than a custom; see, however, 1 Cor. 16:21 and Col. 4:18. The absence of the token from the other epistles of Paul can be explained differently, their authenticity not being dependent upon this; (b) "to commit to writing, to record," e.g., Luke 1:63; John 19:21, 22; it is used of Scripture as a standing authority, "it is written," e.g., Mark 1:2; Rom. 1:17 (cf. 2 Cor. 4:13); (c) of "writing directions or giving information," e.g., Rom. 10:5, "(Moses) writeth," RV (KJV, "describeth"); 15:15; 2 Cor. 7:12; (d) of "that which contained a record or message," e.g., Mark 10:4, 5; John 19:19; 21:25; **Acts 23:25**.

After this manner *periecho* (4023), lit., "to have round" (*peri*, "around," *echo*, "to have"), means "to encompass, enclose, contain," as a writing contains details, 1 Pet. 2:6. Some mss. have it in **Acts 23:25**, lit., "having this form" (the most authentic have *echo*, "to have"). For the secondary meaning, "amazed" (KJV, "astonished"), Luke 5:9 (lit., "amazement encompassed," i.e., seized, him).

Manner *tupos* (5179), "the representation or pattern" of anything, is rendered "form" in Rom. 6:17, "that form (or mold) of teaching whereunto ye were delivered," RV. The metaphor is that of a cast or frame into which molten material is poured so as to take its shape. The Gospel is the mould; those who are obedient to its teachings become conformed to Christ, whom it presents. In **Acts 23:25**, it is used of a letter, RV, "form" (KJV, "manner"), with reference to the nature of the contents. *See also* Figures at *Acts 7:43*.

23:26 Claudius Lysias unto the most excellent governor Felix *sendeth* greeting.

Excellent *kratistos* (2903), "mightiest, noblest, best," the superlative degree of *kratus*, "strong" (cf. *kratos*, "strength"), is used as a title of honor and respect, "most excellent," Luke 1:3 (Theophilus was quite possibly a man of high rank); **Acts 23:26**; **24:3** and **26:25**, RV, for KJV, "most noble."

Governor *hegemon* (2232), is a term used (a) for "rulers" generally, Mark 13:9; 1 Pet. 2:14; translated "princes" (i.e., leaders) in Matt. 2:6; (b) for the Roman procurators, referring, in the Gospels to Pontius Pilate, e.g., Matt. 27:2; Luke 20:20 (so designated by Tacitus, *Annals*, xv. 44); to Felix, **Acts 23:26**. Technically the procurator was a financial official under a proconsul or propretor, for collecting the imperial revenues, but entrusted also with magisterial powers for decisions of questions relative to the revenues. In certain provinces, of which Judea was one (the procurator of which was dependent on the legate of Syria), he was the general administrator and supreme judge, with sole power of life and death. Such a governor was a person of high social standing. Felix, however, was an ex-slave, a freedman, and his appointment to Judea could not but be regarded by the Jews as an insult to the nation. The headquarters of the governor of Judea was Caesarea, which was made a garrison town.

Greeting *see Acts 15:23*.

23:27 This man was taken of the Jews, and should have been killed of them: then came I with an army, and rescued him, having understood that he was a Roman.

Taken *see* Took at *Acts 1:16*.

Should *see Acts 11:28*.

Came *see Acts 4:1*.

Army *see* Soldiers at *Acts 23:10*.

Rescued *exaireo* (1807), "to take out" (*ek*, "from," *haireo*, "to take"), is used of "delivering" from persons and circumstances, and translated "rescued" in **Acts 23:27**. *See also* Delivered at *Acts 7:10*.

Understood *manthano* (3129), denotes (a) "to learn" (akin to *mathetes*, "a disciple"), "to increase one's knowledge," or "be increased in knowledge," frequently "to learn by inquiry, or observation," e.g., Matt. 9:13; 11:29; 24:32; Mark 13:28; John 7:15; Rom. 16:17; 1 Cor. 4:6; 14:35; Phil. 4:9; 2 Tim. 3:14; Rev. 14:3; said of "learning" Christ, Eph. 4:20, not simply the doctrine of Christ, but Christ Himself, a process not merely of getting to know the person but of so applying the knowledge as to walk differently from the rest of the Gentiles; (b) "to ascertain," **Acts 23:27**,

RV, "learned" (KJV, "understood"); Gal. 3:2, "This only would I learn from you," perhaps with a tinge of irony in the enquiry, the answer to which would settle the question of the validity of the new Judaistic gospel they were receiving; (c) "to learn by use and practice, to acquire the habit of, be accustomed to," e.g., Phil. 4:11; 1 Tim. 5:4, 13; Titus 3:14; Heb. 5:8.

Roman *see* Rome at *Acts 2:10.*

23:28 And when I would have known the cause wherefore they accused him, I brought him forth into their council:

Would *see Acts 22:30.*

Cause *see Acts 13:28.*

Brought *see Acts 9:30.*

23:29 Whom I perceived to be accused of questions of their law, but to have nothing laid to his charge worthy of death or of bonds.

Perceived In **Acts 23:29**, KJV, *heurisko*, "to find," is translated "perceived" (RV, "found").

Accused, Laid to his charge *enklema* (1462), is "an accusation made in public," but not necessarily before a tribunal. That is the case in **Acts 23:29**, "laid to his charge." In **25:16** it signifies a matter of complaint; hence, the RV has "the matter laid against him" (KJV, "crime").

Questions *see* Question at *Acts 15:2.*

Worthy *see Acts 13:25.*

23:30 And when it was told me how that the Jews laid wait for the man, I sent straightway to thee, and gave commandment to his accusers also to say before thee what *they had* against him. Farewell.

Told *menuo* (3377), "to disclose, make known" (what was secret), is rendered "to show" in Luke 20:37; 1 Cor. 10:28; in a forensic sense, John 11:57; **Acts 23:30**, RV (KJV, "it was told").

Laid wait *see Acts 20:3. See also* Laying await at *Acts 9:24.* In **Acts 23:30**, the word *epiboule*, "a plot," necessitates the RV "(that there would be) a plot."

Straightway *see* Immediately at *Acts 10:33.*

Accusers *kategoros* (2725), "an accuser," is used in John 8:10; **Acts 23:30, 35; 24:8; 25:16, 18.** In Rev. 12:10, it is used of Satan. In the Sept., Prov. 18:17.

Farewell *see* Fare at *Acts 15:29.*

23:31 Then the soldiers, as it was commanded them, took Paul, and brought *him* by night to Antipatris.

Commanded *see Acts 18:2.*

Took *see* Taken at *Acts 1:2.*

23:32 On the morrow they left the horsemen to go with him, and returned to the castle:

Left *eao* (1439), signifies (a) "to let, permit, suffer," e.g., Matt. 24:43; (b) "to leave," **Acts 23:32**, of "leaving" horsemen; **27:40**, of "leaving" anchors in the sea, RV [KJV, "committed (themselves)"].

Horsemen *see Acts 23:23.*

Returned *see Acts 1:12.*

Castle *see Acts 21:34.*

23:33 Who, when they came to Caesarea, and delivered the epistle to the governor, presented Paul also before him.

Delivered *anadidomi* (325), "to deliver over, give up," is used of "delivering" the letter mentioned in **Acts 23:33.**

Presented *see* Shewed at *Acts 1:3.*

23:34 And when the governor had read *the letter,* he asked of what province he was. And when he understood that *he was* of Cilicia;

Asked *see Acts 4:7.*

Province *eparcheia*, or *-ia* (1885), was a technical term for the administrative divisions of the Roman Empire. The original meaning was the district within which a magistrate, whether consul or pretor, exercised supreme authority. The word *provincia* acquired its later meaning when Sardinia and Sicily were added to the Roman territories, 227 BC. On the establishment of the empire the proconsular power over all "provinces" was vested in the emperor. Two "provinces," Asia and Africa, were consular, i.e., held by ex-consuls; the rest were praetorian. Certain small "provinces," e.g. Judea and Cappadocia, were governed by procurators. They were usually districts recently added to the empire and not thoroughly Romanized. Judea was so governed in the intervals between the rule of native kings; ultimately it was incorporated in the "province" of Syria. The "province" mentioned in **Acts 23:34** and **25:1** was assigned to the jurisdiction of an *eparchos*, "a prefect or governor." In the Sept., Esth. 4:11.

Understood *punthanomai* (4441), "to inquire," is rendered "to understand" in **Acts 23:34.**

23:35 I will hear thee, said he, when thine accusers are also come. And he commanded him to be kept in Herod's judgment hall.

Hear *diakouo* (1251), "to hear through, hear fully," is used technically, of "hearing" judicially, in **Acts 23:35**, of Felix in regard to the charges against Paul. In the Sept., Deut. 1:16; Job 9:33.

Said *phemi* (5346), "to declare, say," (a) is frequently used in quoting the words of another, e.g., Matt. 13:29; 26:61; (b) is interjected into the recorded words, e.g., **Acts 23:35**; (c) is used impersonally, 2 Cor. 10:10.

Accusers *see Acts 23:30.*

Judgment hall *praitorion* (4232), signified originally "a general's (praetor's) tent." Then it was applied to "the council of army officers"; then to "the official residence of the governor of a province"; finally, to "the imperial bodyguard." In the KJV the word appears only once, Mark 15:16, "the hall, called Praetorium" (RV, "within the court which is the Praetorium," marg., "palace"); in the Greek of the NT it also occurs in Matt. 27:27, KJV, "the common hall," marg., "the governor's house"; RV, "palace," see marg.; John 18:28 (twice), KJV, "the hall of judgment"; and "judgment hall," marg., "Pilate's house," RV, "palace"; 18:33 and 19:9, KJV, "judgment hall," RV, "palace," see marg.; so in **Acts 23:35**; in Phil. 1:13, KJV, "in all the palace," marg., "Caesar's court," RV, "throughout the whole praetorian guard," marg., "in the whole Praetorium."

"In the Gospels the term denotes the official residence in Jerusalem of the Roman governor, and the various translations of it in our versions arose from a desire either to indicate the special purpose for which that residence was used on the occasion in question, or to explain what particular building was intended. But whatever building the governor occupied was the Praetorium. It is most probable that in Jerusalem he resided in the well-known palace of Herod.... Pilate's residence has been identified with the castle of Antonia, which was occupied by the regular garrison. The probability is that it was the same as Herod's palace. Herod's palace in Caesarea was used as the Praetorium there, and the expression in **Acts 23:35**, marg., 'Herod's praetorium,' is abbreviated from 'the praetorium of Herod's palace.'" (*Hastings' Bib. Dic.*).

Chapter 24

24:1 And after five days Ananias the high priest descended with the elders, and *with* a certain orator *named* Tertullus, who informed the governor against Paul.

Descended *katabaino* (2597), "to go down" (*kata*, "down," *baino*, "to go"), used for various kinds of motion on the ground (e.g., going, walking, stepping), is usually translated "to descend." The RV uses the verb "to come down," for KJV, "descend," in Mark 15:32; **Acts 24:1**; Rev. 21:10.

Orator *rhetor* (4489), from an obsolete present tense, *rheo*, "to say" (cf. Eng., "rhetoric"), denotes "a public speaker, an orator," **Acts 24:1**, of Tertullus. Such a person, distinct from the professional lawyer, was hired, as a professional speaker, to make a skillful presentation of a case in court. His training was not legal but rhetorical.

Informed *emphanizo* (1718), "to manifest, exhibit," in the middle and passive voices, "to appear, also signifies to declare, make known," and is translated "informed" in **Acts 24:1; 25:2, 15.** *See also* **Signify** at *Acts 23:15.*

24:2 And when he was called forth, Tertullus began to accuse *him*, saying, Seeing that by thee we enjoy great quietness, and that very worthy deeds are done unto this nation by thy providence,

Enjoy *tunchano* (5177), used transitively, denotes "to hit upon, meet with"; then, "to reach, get, obtain"; it is translated "enjoy" (i.e., obtain to our satisfaction) in **Acts 24:2**.

Great *see Acts 8:8.*

Quietness *eirene* (1515), "peace," is translated "quietness" in **Acts 24:2**, KJV (RV, "peace").

Worthy *diorthoma* (1357), signifies "a reform, amendment, correction," lit., "a making straight" (*dia*, "through," *orthoo*, "to make straight"). In **Acts 24:2**, lit., "reformations come about (or take place, lit., 'become')," the RV has "evils are corrected," KJV, "worthy deeds are done"; there is no word for "worthy" or for "deeds" in the original. Some texts have *katorthoma*, which has the same meaning. See *diorthosis*, "reformation," Heb. 9:10.

Deeds In **Acts 24:2**, *diorthoma*, "a straightening," with *ginomai*, "to become," is translated in the KJV, "very worthy deeds are done," RV, "evils are corrected"; more lit., "reforms take place."

Nation *see Acts 10:22.*

Providence *pronoia* (4307), "forethought" (*pro*, "before," *noeo*, "to think"), is translated "providence" in **Acts 24:2**; "provision" in Rom. 13:14.

24:3 We accept *it* always, and in all places, most noble Felix, with all thankfulness.

Accept *see* **Received** at *Acts 2:41.*

Always *pante* (3839), and *pantote* (3842) are derived from *pas*, "all." The former is found in **Acts 24:3**. The latter is the usual word for "always."

Places *pantachou* (3837), "everywhere," is translated "in all places" in **Acts 24:3**. *See also* **Every where** at *Acts 17:30*.

Noble *kratistos* (2903), is translated "most noble" in the KJV of **Acts 24:3** and **26:25** (RV, most excellent). *See also* **Excellent** at *Acts 23:26*.

Thankfulness *eucharistia* (2169), *eu*, "well," *charizomai*, "to give freely" (Eng., "eucharist"), denotes (a) "gratitude," "thankfulness," **Acts 24:3**; (b) "giving of thanks, thanksgiving," 1 Cor. 14:16; 2 Cor. 4:15; 9:11, 12 (plur.); Eph. 5:4; Phil. 4:6; Col. 2:7; 4:2; 1 Thess. 3:9 ("thanks"); 1 Tim. 2:1 (plur.); 4:3, 4; Rev. 4:9, "thanks"; 7:12.

24:4 Notwithstanding, that I be not further tedious unto thee, I pray thee that thou wouldest hear us of thy clemency a few words.

Tedious *enkopto* (1465), "to hinder," is rendered "to be tedious" in **Acts 24:4**, of detaining a person unnecessarily.

Pray *see* **Prayed** at *Acts 16:9*.

Clemency *epieikeia* (1932), "mildness, gentleness, kindness" (what Matthew Arnold has called "sweet reasonableness"), is translated "clemency" in **Acts 24:4**; elsewhere, in 2 Cor. 10:1, of the gentleness of Christ.

Few *suntomos* (4935), "concisely, briefly, cut short" (from *suntemno*, "to cut in pieces," *sun*, used intensively, *temno*, "to cut"), occurs in the speech of Tertullus, **Acts 24:4**.

Words For *suntomos*, **Acts 24:4**, "a few words."

24:5 For we have found this man *a* pestilent *fellow*, and a mover of sedition among all the Jews throughout the world, and a ringleader of the sect of the Nazarenes:

Pestilent *loimos* (3061), "a pestilence, any deadly infectious malady," is used in the plural in Luke 21:11 (in some mss., Matt. 24:7); in **Acts 24:5**, metaphorically, "a pestilent fellow."

Fellow In **Acts 24:5** *loimos*, "a plague, a pest," is rendered "a pestilent fellow." This is a sample of the strongest use of the epithet "fellow."

Mover *see* **Stirred** at *Acts 6:12*.

Sedition *stasis* (4714), "a dissension, an insurrection," is translated "sedition" in **Acts 24:5**, KJV (RV, "insurrections"). *See also* **Sect** at *Acts 5:17*; **Dissension** at *Acts 15:2*.

World *see Acts 11:28*.

Ringleader *protostates* (4414), "one who stands first" (*protos*, "first," *histemi*, "to cause to stand"), was used of soldiers, one who stands in the front rank; hence, metaphorically, "a leader," **Acts 24:5**.

24:6 Who also hath gone about to profane the temple: whom we took, and would have judged according to our law.

Also *see* **Moreover** at *Acts 19:26*.

Gone about *see* **Return** at *Acts 15:16*. *See also* **Assayed** at *Acts 16:7*.

Profane *see* **Polluted** at *Acts 21:28*.

Took *krateo* (2902), "to take hold of, get possession of," is translated "to take" in Matt. 9:25; 22:6; 26:4; Mark 1:31; 5:41; 9:27; 14:1, 44, 46, 49; Luke 8:54; **Acts 24:6**. *See also* **Holden** at *Acts 2:24*.

Our *see Acts 2:11*.

24:7 But the chief captain Lysias came *upon us*, and with great violence took *him* away out of our hands,

Came *parerchomai* (3928), signifies (a) "to come or go forth, or arrive," e.g., Luke 12:37; 17:7 (last part); **Acts 24:7**; (b) "to pass by," e.g., Luke 18:37; (c) "to neglect," e.g., Luke 11:42. *See also* **Passing** at *Acts 16:8*.

Violence *see Acts 5:26*. *See also* **Mighty** at *Acts 2:2*.

Took *see* **Put to death** at *Acts 12:19*. Some texts have *apago*, "to take away," in **Acts 24:7**.

24:8 Commanding his accusers to come unto thee: by examining of whom thyself mayest take knowledge of all these things, whereof we accuse him.

Accusers *see Acts 23:30*.

Examining *see* **Examined** at *Acts 4:9*.

Mayest *dunamai* (1410), "to be able, to have power," whether by virtue of one's own ability and resources, e.g., Rom. 15:14; or through a state of mind, or through favorable circumstances, e.g., 1 Thess. 2:6; or by permission of law or custom, e.g., **Acts 24:8, 11**; or simply "to be able, powerful," Matt. 3:9; 2 Tim. 3:15, etc. *See also* **May** at *Acts 17:19*.

24:9 And the Jews also assented, saying that these things were so.

Assented *see* **Agreed** at *Acts 23:20*.

Saying *phasko* (5335), a frequentative form of the verb *phemi*, denotes "to allege, to affirm by way of alleging or professing," **Acts 24:9** (RV, "affirming," KJV, "saying"); **25:19**; Rom. 1:22, "professing." Some mss. have it in Rev. 2:2, instead of the verb *lego*, "to say."

24:10 Then Paul, after that the governor had beckoned unto him to speak, answered, Forasmuch as I know that thou hast been of many years a judge unto this nation, I do the more cheerfully answer for myself:

Beckoned *neuo* (3506), lit., "to give a nod, to signify by a nod," is used in John 13:24, of Peter's beckoning to John to ask the Lord of whom He had been speaking; in **Acts 24:10**, of the intimation given by Felix to Paul to speak.

Answered, Answer *see* Defence at *Acts 19:33*.

Know *see Acts 10:28*.

Judge *see Acts 10:42*.

Nation *see Acts 10:22*.

Cheerfully *euthumos* (2115), cheerfully, is found in the most authentic mss. in **Acts 24:10**, instead of the comparative degree, *euthumoteron*.

Myself *see Acts 20:24*.

24:11 Because that thou mayest understand, that there are yet but twelve days since I went up to Jerusalem for to worship.

Mayest *see Acts 24:8*. *See also* May at *Acts 17:19*.

Understand *see* Understandest at *Acts 8:30*; Knew at *Acts 9:30*.

Yet The following, in which the RV gives the correct meaning for the KJV, "yet": *ede*, "now," Mark 13:28; *pote*, "ever," Eph. 5:29 (KJV, "ever yet"); *kai ... de*, John 8:16, "yea and" (KJV, "and yet"); *ou pleious*, **Acts 24:11**, "not more". *See also* More at *Acts 19:32*.

24:12 And they neither found me in the temple disputing with any man, neither raising up the people, neither in the synagogues, nor in the city:

Disputing *see* Disputed at *Acts 17:17*.

Raising *epistasis* (1999), primarily "a stopping, halting" (as of soldiers), then, "an incursion, onset, rush, pressure" (akin to *ephistemi*, "to set upon"), is so used in 2 Cor. 11:28, "(that which) presseth upon (me)," KJV, "cometh upon," lit., "(the daily) pressure (upon me)"; some have taken the word in its other meaning "attention," which perhaps is accounted for by the variant reading of the pronoun (*mou*, "my", instead of *moi*, "to me, upon me"), but that does not adequately describe the "pressure" or onset due to the constant call upon the apostle for all kinds of help, advice, counsel, exhortation, decisions as to difficulties, disputes, etc. Cf. the other occurrence of the word in **Acts 24:12**, "stirring up," RV (KJV, "raising"), lit. "making a stir" (in some mss., *episustasis*). In **Acts 24:12**, *poieo*, to make, is used with *epistasis*, a collection of people, and translated "stirring up (a crowd)," RV, lit., 'making a collection (of a crowd)'; some mss. have *episustasis*, a riotous throng, KJV, "raising up (the people)."

People *ochlos* (3793), is used frequently in the four Gospels and the Acts; elsewhere only in Rev. 7:9; 17:15; 19:1, 6; it denotes (a) "a crowd or multitude of persons, a throng," e.g., Matt. 14:14, 15; 15:33; often in the plural, e.g., Matt. 4:25; 5:1; with *polus*, "much" or "great," it signifies "a great multitude," e.g., Matt. 20:29, or "the common people," Mark 12:37, perhaps preferably "the mass of the people." Field supports the meaning in the text, but either rendering is suitable. The mass of the people was attracted to Him (for the statement "heard Him gladly" cf. what is said in Mark 6:20 of Herod Antipas concerning John the Baptist); in John 12:9, "the common people," RV, stands in contrast with their leaders (v. 10); **Acts 24:12**, RV, "crowd"; (b) "the populace, an unorganized multitude," in contrast to *demos*, "the people as a body politic," e.g., Matt. 14:5; 21:26; John 7:12 (2nd part); (c) in a more general sense, "a multitude or company," e.g., Luke 6:17, RV, "a (great) multitude (of His disciples)," KJV, "the company"; **Acts 1:15**, "a multitude (of persons)," RV, KJV, "the number (of names)"; **Acts 24:18**, RV, "crowd" (KJV, "multitude"). *See also* **Multitude** at *Acts 21:34*.

24:13 Neither can they prove the things whereof they now accuse me.

Prove *paristemi* (3936), "to present," signifies "to prove" in **Acts 24:13**.

Now *see Acts 22:1*.

24:14 But this I confess unto thee, that after the way which they call heresy, so worship I the God of my fathers, believing all things which are written in the law and in the prophets:

Confess *see Acts 23:8*.

Heresy *see* Sect at *Acts 5:17*.

Worship *see Acts 7:42*. *See also* Serve at *Acts 7:7*.

Fathers *see Acts 22:3*.

24:15 And have hope toward God, which they themselves also allow, that there shall be a resurrection of the dead, both of the just and unjust.

Allow *prosdechomai* (4327), mistranslated "allow" in **Acts 24:15**, KJV, means "to wait for," in contrast to rejection, there said of entertaining a hope; hence the RV, "look for."

Shall *see Acts 23:3.*

Resurrection *see Acts 1:22.*

Unjust *adikos* (94), "not in conformity with *dike*, 'right,'" is rendered "unjust" in the KJV and RV in Matt. 5:45; Luke 18:11; **Acts 24:15**; elsewhere for the KJV "unjust" the RV has "unrighteous."

24:16 And herein do I exercise myself, to have always a conscience void of offence toward God, and *toward* men.

Herein This translates the phrase *en touto*, "in this," in John 4:37; 9:30; 15:8; **Acts 24:16**; 2 Cor. 8:10; 1 John 4:9 (KJV, "in this"), 10, 17.

Exercise *askeo* (778), signifies "to form by art, to adorn, to work up raw material with skill"; hence, in general, "to take pains, endeavor, exercise by training or discipline," with a view to a conscience void of offense, **Acts 24:16**.

Myself *see Acts 10:26.*

Always *see* Alway at *Acts 10:2.*

Conscience *see Acts 23:1.*

Offence *aproskopos* (677), with *a*, negative, prefixed, is used (a) in the active sense, "not causing to stumble," in 1 Cor. 10:32, metaphorically of "refraining from doing anything to lead astray" either Jews or Greeks or the church of God (i.e., the local church), RV, "no occasion of stumbling" (KJV, "none offense"); (b) in the passive sense, "blameless, without stumbling," **Acts 24:16**, "(a conscience) void of offense;" Phil. 1:10, "void of (KJV, 'without') offense." The adjective is found occasionally in the papyri writings.

24:17 Now after many years I came to bring alms to my nation, and offerings.

Many *see Acts 2:40.*

Alms *see Acts 3:2.*

Nation *see Acts 10:22.*

Offerings *see* Offering at *Acts 21:26.*

24:18 Whereupon certain Jews from Asia found me purified in the temple, neither with multitude, nor with tumult.

Purified *see* Purify at *Acts 21:24.*

Multitude *see* People *at Acts 24:12. See also Acts 21:34.*

Tumult *see* Uproar at *Acts 20:1.*

24:19 Who ought to have been here before thee, and object, if they had ought against me.

Here *pareimi* (3918), "to be by or beside or here" (*para*, "by," and *eimi*, "to be"), is rendered "to have been here" in **Acts 24:19**. *See also* Come at *Acts 10:21.*

Object *see* Accused at *Acts 22:30.*

Had *see* Could at *Acts 4:14.*

24:20 Or else let these same *here* say, if they have found any evil doing in me, while I stood before the council,

Evil *adikema*, "an injustice" (*a*, negative, *dikaios*, "just"), is translated "evil-doing," in **Acts 24:20**, KJV, RV, "wrong-doing." *See also* Wrong at *Acts 18:14.*

24:21 Except it be for this one voice, that I cried standing among them, Touching the resurrection of the dead I am called in question by you this day.

Resurrection *see Acts 1:22.*

Called *see Acts 23:6.*

24:22 And when Felix heard these things, having more perfect knowledge of *that* way, he deferred them, and said, When Lysias the chief captain shall come down, I will know the uttermost of your matter.

Perfect *see* Perfectly at *Acts 18:26.*

Way *see* Ways at *Acts 2:28.*

Deferred *anaballo* (306), lit., "to throw up" (*ana*, "up," *ballo*, "to throw"), hence "to postpone," is used in the middle voice in **Acts 24:22**, in the forensic sense of "deferring" the hearing of a case.

Know For *diaginosko*, in **Acts 24:22**, "I will know the uttermost of."

Uttermost *see* Enquire at *Acts 23:15.*

24:23 And he commanded a centurion to keep Paul, and to let *him* have liberty, and that he should forbid none of his acquaintance to minister or come unto him.

Commanded *see Acts 18:2.*

Keep *tereo* (5083), "to keep, to guard," is translated "to be kept in charge," in **Acts 24:23**; **25:4**, RV (KJV, kept).

Liberty *anesis* (425), "a loosening, relaxation of strain" (akin to *aniemi*, "to relax, loosen"), is translated "indulgence" in **Acts 24:23**, RV (KJV, "liberty"), in the command of Felix to the centurion, to moderate restrictions upon Paul. The papyri and inscriptions illustrate the use of the word as denoting relief (Moulton and Milligan, *Vocab.*) In the NT it always carries the thought of relief from tribulation or persecution; so 2 Thess. 1:7, "rest"; in 2 Cor. 2:13 and 7:5 it is rendered "relief," RV (KJV, "rest"); in 8:13, "eased." Josephus speaks of the rest or relief (*anesis*) from plowing and tillage, given to the land in the Year of Jubilee.

His *see* *Acts 17:28.*

Acquaintance *idios* (2398), "one's own," is translated "acquaintance" in the KJV of **Acts 24:23**, "friends" (RV).

Minister *see* **Served** at *Acts 13:36.*

24:24 And after certain days, when Felix came with his wife Drusilla, which was a Jewess, he sent for Paul, and heard him concerning the faith in Christ.

Jewess *see* **Jews** at *Acts 2:10.*

Sent *see* **Send** at *Acts 10:5.*

Christ *see* **Jesus** at *Acts 7:59.*

24:25 And as he reasoned of righteousness, temperance, and judgment to come, Felix trembled, and answered, Go thy way for this time; when I have a convenient season, I will call for thee.

Reasoned *see* *Acts 17:2.*

Temperance *enkrateia* (1466), from *kratos*, "strength," occurs in **Acts 24:25**; Gal. 5:23; 2 Pet. 1:6 (twice), in all of which it is rendered "temperance"; the RV marg., "self-control" is the preferable rendering, as "temperance" is now limited to one form of self-control; the various powers bestowed by God upon man are capable of abuse; the right use demands the controlling power of the will under the operation of the Spirit of God; in **Acts 24:25** the word follows "righteousness," which represents God's claims, self-control being man's response thereto; in 2 Pet. 1:6, it follows "knowledge," suggesting that what is learned requires to be put into practice.

Trembled The adjective *emphobos*, used with *ginomai*, "to become," is rendered "trembled" in **Acts 24:25** (RV, "was terrified"); in Luke 24:5, RV, "they were affrighted," KJV, "they were afraid."

Go *see* **Journeyed** at *Acts 9:3.*

Time In 1 Cor. 16:12, KJV, nun, "now" (RV), is rendered "at this time"; in **Acts 24:25**, the phrase *to nun echon*, lit., "the now having," is rendered "at this time" (the verb is adjectival); the phrase is more expressive than the simple "now." Cf. *heos tou nun*, "until now," Matt. 24:21 and Mark 13:19, RV, KJV, "unto (this time)."

Have *metalambano* (3335), "to have," or "get a share of," is rendered "I have (a convenient season)," in **Acts 24:25**. *See also* **Could** at *Acts 4:14.*

Call *see* **Called** at *Acts 7:14.*

24:26 He hoped also that money should have been given him of Paul, that he might loose him: wherefore he sent for him the oftener, and communed with him.

Withal *hama* (260), at the same time, is rendered "withal" in **Acts 24:26**, RV (KJV, "also"); 1 Tim. 5:13 (with *kai*, "also"); Philem. 22.

Money *see* *Acts 4:37.*

Wherefore *see* *Acts 15:19.*

Sent *see* **Send** at *Acts 10:5.*

Oftener *puknoteron* (4437), the neuter singular of the comparative degree of *puknos*, "very often," or "so much the oftener," **Acts 24:26**, "the oftener."

Communed *see* **Talked** at *Acts 20:11.*

24:27 But after two years Porcius Festus came into Felix' room: and Felix, willing to shew the Jews a pleasure, left Paul bound.

After *see* **Full** at *Acts 7:23.*

Years *dietia* (1333), denotes "a space of two years," **Acts 24:27; 28:30.**

Came In **Acts 24:27**, *lambano*, with *diadochos*, "a successor," KJV, "came into the room of," RV, "was succeeded by."

Room In **Acts 24:27**, KJV, *diadochos*, "a successor," with *lambano*, "to receive," is translated "came into (Felix') room," RV, "(Felix) was succeeded by." *Diadochos* often meant "a deputy, a temporary successor."

Willing *thelo* (2309), "to will, to wish," implying volition and purpose, frequently a determination, is most usually rendered "to will." It is translated "to desire" in the RV of the following: Matt. 9:13; 12:7; Mark 6:19; Luke 10:29; 14:28; 23:20; **Acts 24:27; 25:9**; Gal. 4:17; 1 Tim. 5:11; Heb. 12:17; 13:18.

Shew *katatithemi* ("to lay up"), **Acts 24:27**, "to gain".

Pleasure For *charis*, translated "pleasure" in the KJV of **Acts 24:27** and **25:9**. *See also* **Favour** at *Acts 2:47.*

Bound *see* *Acts 20:22.*

Chapter 25

25:1 Now when Festus was come into the province, after three days he ascended from Caesarea to Jerusalem.

Now *see* *Acts 1:18.*

Come *anabaino* (305), "to come upon, to arrive in a place" (*ana*, "up or upon"), is translated "come into" in **Acts 25:1.**

Province *see* *Acts 23:34.*

25:2 Then the high priest and the chief of the Jews informed him against Paul, and besought him,

Chief *protos* (4413), "first," is translated "principal men" in the RV of Luke 19:47 and **Acts 25:2**. *See also Acts 13:50.*

Informed *see Acts 24:1. See also* Signify at *Acts 23:15.*

25:3 And desired favour against him, that he would send for him to Jerusalem, laying wait in the way to kill him.

Favour *see Acts 2:47.*

Send *see Acts 10:5.*

Laying wait *see* Lying in wait at *Acts 23:16.*

25:4 But Festus answered, that Paul should be kept at Caesarea, and that he himself would depart shortly *thither*.

Kept *see* Keep at *Acts 24:23.*

He himself *heauton* (1438), "oneself, himself," is rendered "he himself" in Luke 23:2 and **Acts 25:4**.

Depart *ekporeuo* (1607), *ek*, "from," in the middle and passive, "to proceed from or forth," more expressive of a definite course than simply "to go forth," is translated "go forth," in Mark 6:11; "went out" in Matt. 20:29, RV (KJV, "departed"); both have "depart" in **Acts 25:4**. It is frequently translated by the verb "to proceed," and is often best so rendered, e.g., in Rev. 9:17-18, RV, for KJV, "issued."

25:5 Let them therefore, said he, which among you are able, go down with *me*, and accuse this man, if there be any wickedness in him.

Go *sunkatabaino* (4782), "to go down with," is used in **Acts 25:5**. In the Sept., Ps. 49:17.

Wickedness *atopos* (824), lit., "out of place" (*a*, negative, *topos*, "a place"), denotes unbecoming, not befitting. It is used four times in the NT, and is rendered "amiss" three times in the RV; in the malefactor's testimony of Christ, Luke 23:41; in Festus' words concerning Paul, **Acts 25:5**, "if there is anything amiss in the man" (KJV, "wickedness"); in **Acts 28:6**, of the expected effect of the viper's attack upon Paul (KJV, "harm"); in 2 Thess. 3:2, of men capable of outrageous conduct, "unreasonable."

25:6 And when he had tarried among them more than ten days, he went down unto Caesarea; and the next day sitting on the judgment seat commanded Paul to be brought.

Tarried *see* Abode at *Acts 12:19.*

Ten *see* Eight at *Acts 9:33.*

Next day *see Acts 4:3. See also* Morrow at *Acts 10:24.*

Judgment seat *see Acts 18:12.*

25:7 And when he was come, the Jews which came down from Jerusalem stood round about, and laid many and grievous complaints against Paul, which they could not prove.

Stood *periistemi* (4026), in the active voice, means "to stand around" (*peri*, "around," *histemi*, "to stand"), John 11:42; **Acts 25:7**; in the middle voice, "to turn oneself about," for the purpose of avoiding something, "to avoid, shun," said of profane babblings, 2 Tim. 2:16; of foolish questions, genealogies, strife, etc., Titus 3:9 (KJV, "avoid").

Laid In **Acts 25:7**, KJV, *phero*, "to bear, bring," is rendered "laid ... (complaints)," RV, "bringing ... (charges)." *See* **Fallen, Sunk** at *Acts 20:9.*

Grievous *see Acts 20:29.*

Complaints *aitioma* (157), "a charge," is translated "complaints" in **Acts 25:7**, KJV.

Prove *apodeiknumi* (584), "to show forth," signifies "to prove" in **Acts 25:7**.

25:8 While he answered for himself, Neither against the law of the Jews, neither against the temple, nor yet against Caesar, have I offended any thing at all.

Answered *see* Defence at *Acts 19:33.*

Offended *hamartano* (264), lit., "to miss the mark," is used in the NT (a) of "sinning" against God, (1) by angels, 2 Pet. 2:4; (2) by man, Matt. 27:4; Luke 15:18, 21 (heaven standing, by metonymy, for God); John 5:14; 8:11; 9:2, 3; Rom. 2:12 (twice); 3:23; 5:12, 14, 16; 6:15; 1 Cor. 7:28 (twice), 36; 15:34; Eph. 4:26; 1 Tim. 5:20; Titus 3:11; Heb. 3:17; 10:26; 1 John 1:10; in 2:1 (twice), the aorist tense in each place, referring to an act of "sin"; on the contrary, in 3:6 (twice), 8, 9, the present tense indicates, not the committal of an act, but the continuous practice of "sin"; in 5:16 (twice) the present tense indicates the condition resulting from an act, "unto death" signifying "tending towards death"; (b) against Christ, 1 Cor. 8:12; (c) against man, (1) a brother, Matt. 18:15, RV, "sin" (KJV, "trespass"); v. 21; Luke 17:3, 4, RV, "sin" (KJV, "trespass"); 1 Cor. 8:12; (2) in Luke 15:18, 21, against the father by the Prodigal Son, "in thy sight" being suggestive of befitting reverence; (d) against Jewish law, the Temple, and Caesar, **Acts 25:8**, RV, "sinned" (KJV, "offended"); (e) against one's own body, by fornication, 1 Cor. 6:18; (f) against earthly masters by servants, 1 Pet. 2:20, RV, "(when) ye sin (and are buffeted for it)," KJV, "(when ye be buffeted) for your faults," lit., "having sinned."

25:9 But Festus, willing to do the Jews a pleasure, answered Paul, and said, Wilt thou go up to Jerusalem, and there be judged of these things before me?

Willing *see Acts 24:27.*

Do In **Acts 25:9** *katatithemi*, "to deposit, or lay up, for future use, to lay up favor for oneself with a person," is translated "to do (the Jews a pleasure)," KJV; RV, "to gain (favor with the Jews)."

Pleasure *see Acts 24:27. See also* Favour at *Acts 2:47.*

25:10 Then said Paul, I stand at Caesar's judgment seat, where I ought to be judged: to the Jews have I done no wrong, as thou very well knowest.

Judgment seat *see Acts 18:12.*

Well *kalos* (2573), "finely" (akin to *kalos*, "good, fair"), is usually translated "well," indicating what is done rightly, in the Epistles it is most frequent in 1 Tim. (3:4, 12, 13; 5:17); twice it is used as an exclamation of approval, Mark 12:32; Rom. 11:20; the comparative degree *kallion*, "very well," occurs in Acts 25:10.

25:11 For if I be an offender, or have committed any thing worthy of death, I refuse not to die: but if there be none of these things whereof these accuse me, no man may deliver me unto them. I appeal unto Caesar.

Offender In **Acts 25:11**, KJV, *adikeo*, "to do wrong," is translated "be an offender" (RV, "am a wrong-doer"). *See also* Wrong at *Acts 7:24.*

Committed *prasso* (4238), "to do, work, practice," is said of continuous action, or action not yet completed, **Acts 25:11, 25**; it is rendered "practice" in the RV, for the incorrect KJV "commit," in Rom. 1:32; 2:2.

Worthy *see Acts 13:25.*

Refuse *paraiteo mai* (3868), denotes "to refuse" in **Acts 25:11**; 1 Tim. 4:7; 5:11; 2 Tim. 2:23, RV (KJV, "avoid"); Titus 3:10, RV (marg., "avoid"; KJV, "reject"); Heb. 12:25 (twice), perhaps in the sense of "begging off."

May *see Acts 17:19.*

Deliver *charizomai* (5483), "to gratify, to do what is pleasing to anyone," is translated "deliver" in the KJV of **Acts 25:11, 16**; RV, "give up" (marg., "grant by favor," i.e., to give over to the Jews so as to gratify their wishes). *See also* Granted at *Acts 3:14.*

Appeal *see* Calling at *Acts 7:59. See also* Call at *Acts 2:21.*

25:12 Then Festus, when he had conferred with the council, answered, Hast thou appealed unto Caesar? unto Caesar shalt thou go.

Conferred *sullaleo* (4814), "to speak together with" (*sun*, "with," *laleo*, "to speak"), is translated "conferred" in **Acts 25:12**; elsewhere of talking with Matt. 17:3; Mark 9:4; Luke 4:36; 9:30; "communed" in Luke 22:4.

Council *sumboulion* (4824), "a uniting in counsel" (*sun*, "together," *boule*, "counsel, advice"), denotes (a) "counsel" which is given, taken and acted upon, e.g., Matt. 12:14, RV, "took counsel," for KJV, "held a council"; 22:15; hence (b) "a council," an assembly of counsellors or persons in consultation, **Acts 25:12**, of the "council" with which Festus conferred concerning Paul. The governors and procurators of provinces had a board of advisers or assessors, with whom they took "counsel," before pronouncing judgment.

25:13 And after certain days king Agrippa and Bernice came unto Caesarea to salute Festus.

After *diaginomai* (1230), used of time, denotes "to intervene, elapse, pass," Mark 16:1, "was past"; **Acts 25:13**, RV, "were passed"; **27:9**, "was spent."

Came *see Acts 16:1.*

Salute *aspazomai* (782), signifies "to greet welcome," or "salute." In the KJV it is chiefly rendered by either of the verbs "to greet" or "to salute." "There is little doubt that the revisers have done wisely in giving 'salute' ... in the passages where KJV has 'greet.' For the cursory reader is sure to imagine a difference of Greek and of meaning when he finds, e.g., in Phil. 4:21, 'Salute every saint in Christ Jesus. The brethren which are with me greet you,' or in 3 John 14, 'Our friends salute thee. Greet the friends by name'" (Hastings, *Bible Dic.*). In **Acts 25:13** the meaning virtually is "to pay his respects to."

25:14 And when they had been there many days, Festus declared Paul's cause unto the king, saying, There is a certain man left in bonds by Felix:

Had been there *see* Abode at *Acts 12:19.*

Many *see Acts 2:40.*

Declared *anatithemi* (394), "to put up or before" (*ana*), is used in the middle voice of "laying" a case before an authority, **Acts 25:14**, RV, "laid before," for KJV, "declared unto"; of "setting forth" a matter for consideration, Gal. 2:2, RV, "laid before (them the gospel)," for KJV, "communicated unto."

Cause In **Acts 25:14** the phrase in the original is "the things concerning Paul," KJV, "cause" (as if translating *aitia*); RV, "Festus laid Paul's case before the king."

Bonds *desmios* (1198), "a binding," denotes "a prisoner," e.g., **Acts 25:14**, RV, for the KJV, "in bonds"; Heb. 13:3, "them that are in bonds." Paul speaks of himself as a prisoner of Christ, Eph. 3:1; 2 Tim. 1:8; Philem. 1, 9; "in the Lord," Eph. 4:1. *See also* Prisoners at *Acts 16:25.*

25:15 About whom, when I was at Jerusalem, the chief priests and the elders of the Jews informed *me*, desiring *to have* judgment against him.

Informed *see Acts 24:1. See also* Signify at *Acts 23:15.*

Judgment *katadike* (2613), "a judicial sentence, condemnation," is translated "sentence" in **Acts 25:15**, RV (KJV, "judgment"); some mss. have *dike.*

25:16 To whom I answered, It is not the manner of the Romans to deliver any man to die, before that he which is accused have the accusers face to face, and have licence to answer for himself concerning the crime laid against him.

Answered, Answer *see* Defence at *Acts 22:1.*

Manner *see Acts 15:1. See also* Customs at *Acts 6:14.*

Romans *see* Rome at *Acts 2:10.*

Deliver *see Acts 25:11. See also* Granted at *Acts 3:14.*

Have In Mark 12:22, in some mss., *lambano*, "to take" or "receive," is translated "had," in the statement "the seven had her"; in **Acts 25:16**, RV, "have had" (KJV, "have"); in Heb. 11:36, "had."

Accusers *see Acts 23:30.*

Face *kata prosopon* (*kata*, "over against," and *prosopon*, "face"), **Acts 25:16.**

Licence *topos* (5117), "a place," is translated "opportunity" in **Acts 25:16**, RV (KJV, "licence"). *See also* Place at *Acts 1:25.*

Crime *see* Accused, Laid to his charge at *Acts 23:29.*

25:17 Therefore, when they were come hither, without any delay on the morrow I sat on the judgment seat, and commanded the man to be brought forth.

Hither *see Acts 17:6. See also* Here at *Acts 16:28.*

Without In **Acts 25:17**, KJV, "without (any delay)" represents *poieo*, "to make," and *medemian*, "no," RV, "I made no (delay)." *See also* Made at *Acts 2:36.*

Delay *anabole* (311), lit. signifies "that which is thrown up" (*ana*, "up," *ballo*, "to throw"); hence "a delay," Acts 25:17.

Morrow In **Acts 25:17**, KJV, the adverb *hexes*, "next, successively, in order," is translated "on (the) morrow." *See also* Following at *Acts 21:1.*

Judgment seat *see Acts 18:12.*

25:18 Against whom when the accusers stood up, they brought none accusation of such things as I supposed:

Accusers *see Acts 23:30.*

Brought *epiphero* (2018), signifies (a) "to bring upon, or to bring against," Jude 9; (b) "to impose, inflict, visit upon," Rom. 3:5. Some mss. have it in **Acts 25:18**; some in Phil. 1:16 (RV, v. 17, "raise up," translating *egeiro*).

Accusation *see* Cause at *Acts 13:28.*

Supposed *see* Think at *Acts 13:25.*

25:19 But had certain questions against him of their own superstition, and of one Jesus, which was dead, whom Paul affirmed to be alive.

Certain In **Acts 25:20** a phrase lit. rendered "(as to) the inquiry concerning these things" (or according to some mss. "this person," whether "Jesus" or "Paul," v. **19**), is translated "of such manner of questions," KJV (RV, "how to inquire concerning these things").

Questions *see* Question at *Acts 15:2.*

Superstition *deisidaimonia* (1175), primarily denotes "fear of the gods" (from *deido*, "to fear," *daimon*, "a pagan deity," Eng., "demon"), regarded whether as a religious attitude, or, in its usual meaning, with a condemnatory or contemptuous significance, "superstition." That is how Festus regarded the Jews' "religion," **Acts 25:19**, KJV and RV marg., "superstition" (RV, "religion"). *See also* Superstitious at *Acts 17:22.*

Affirmed *see* Assented at *Acts 24:9.*

25:20 And because I doubted of such manner of questions, I asked *him* whether he would go to Jerusalem, and there be judged of these matters.

Doubted *aporeo* (639), always used in the middle voice, lit. means "to be without a way" (*a*, negative, *poros*, "a way, transit"), "to be without resources, embarrassed, in doubt, perplexity, at a loss," as was Herod regarding John the Baptist, Mark 6:20 (RV, following the most authentic mss., "was much perplexed"); as the disciples were, regarding the Lord's betrayal, John 13:22, "doubting"; and regarding the absence of His body from the tomb, Luke 24:4, "were perplexed"; as was Festus, about the nature of the accusations brought against Paul, **Acts 25:20**, KJV "doubted," RV, "being perplexed"; as Paul was, in his experiences of trial 2 Cor. 4:8, "perplexed," and, as to the attitude of the believers of the churches in Galatia towards Judaistic errors, Gal. 4:20, KJV, "I stand in doubt," RV, "I am perplexed." Perplexity is the main idea. Cf. the noun *aporia*, "distress," Luke 21:25.

Manner *see* **Certain** at *Acts 25:19*.

Questions *zetesis* (2214), primarily "a seeking, search" (*zeteo*, "to seek"), is used in John 3:25; **Acts 25:20**, RV, "(being perplexed) how to inquire (concerning these things)," KJV "(because I doubted of such manner) of questions," lit., "being perplexed as to the inquiry (or discussion) concerning these things"; in 1 Tim. 1:4 (in some mss.); 6:4; 2 Tim. 2:23; Titus 3:9. *See also* **Disputation** at *Acts 15:2*.

Asked *lego* (3004), "to say," occasionally signifies "to ask," as of an inquiry, the reason being that *lego* is used for every variety of speaking, e.g., **Acts 25:20**, "I asked whether he would come to Jerusalem."

25:21 But when Paul had appealed to be reserved unto the hearing of Augustus, I commanded him to be kept till I might send him to Caesar.

Appealed *see* **Calling** at *Acts 7:59*.

Reserved *tereo* (5083), "to guard, keep, preserve, give heed to," is translated "to reserve," (a) with a happy issue, 1 Pet. 1:4; (b) with a retributive issue, 2 Pet. 2:4; v. 9, KJV (RV, "keep"); 2:17; 3:7; Jude 6, KJV (RV, "hath kept"); v. 13; and referenced (c) the possibility either of deliverance or execution, **Acts 25:21**, KJV (RV, kept). *See also* **Kept** at *Acts 12:5*.

Hearing *diagnosis* (1233), transliterated in English, primarily denotes "a discrimination" (*dia*, "apart," *ginosko*, "to know"), hence, "a judicial decision," which is its meaning in **Acts 25:21**, RV, "for the decision of the Emperor" (KJV, "hearing").

Send *anapempo* (375), denotes (a) "to send up," to a higher authority, Luke 23:7, 15; **Acts 25:21** (in the best texts; some have *pempo*); this meaning is confirmed by examples from the papyri (Moulton and Milligan), by Deissmann (*Bible Studies*, p. 229); see also Field, *Notes on the Trans. of the NT;* (b) "to send back," Luke 23:11; Philem. 12.

Caesar *sebastos* (4575), "august, reverent," the masculine gender of an adjective (from *sebas*, "reverential awe"), became used as the title of the Roman emperor, **Acts 25:21, 25**, RV, for KJV, "Augustus"; then, taking its name from the emperor, it became a title of honor applied to certain legions or cohorts or battalions, marked for their valor, **Acts 27:1**.

25:22 Then Agrippa said unto Festus, I would also hear the man myself. To morrow, said he, thou shalt hear him.

Would *boulomai* (1014), in Mark 15:15, RV, is translated "wishing" (KJV, "willing"); so 2 Pet. 3:9; in **Acts 25:22**, RV, "could wish" (KJV, "would).

Myself *see* *Acts 10:26*.

Morrow *see* **Next day** at *Acts 4:3*.

25:23 And on the morrow, when Agrippa was come, and Bernice, with great pomp, and was entered into the place of hearing, with the chief captains, and principal men of the city, at Festus' commandment Paul was brought forth.

Pomp *phantasia* (5325), as a philosophic term, denoted "an imagination"; then, "an appearance," like *phantasma*, "an apparition"; later, "a show, display, pomp" (Eng., "phantasy"), **Acts 25:23**. In the Sept., Hab. 2:18; 3:10; Zech. 10:1.

Place of hearing *akroaterion* (201), denotes "a place of audience" (*akroaomai*, "to listen"), **Acts 25:23**, "place of hearing."

Principal In **Acts 25:23** the phrase *kat' exochen*, lit., "according to eminence," is translated "principal (men)"; *exoche*, primarily a projection (akin to *execho*, "to stand out"), is used here metaphorically of eminence. In the Sept., Job 39:28.

25:24 And Festus said, King Agrippa, and all men which are here present with us, ye see this man, about whom all the multitude of the Jews have dealt with me, both at Jerusalem, and *also* here, crying that he ought not to live any longer.

Here *see* *Acts 16:28*.

Present *sumpareimi* (4840), "to be present with," is used in **Acts 25:24**.

Dealt with In **Acts 25:24**, *entunchano*, "to fall in with, meet and talk with," and hence "to make suit to a person" by way of pleading with him, is translated "have dealt with" in the KJV; correctly in the RV, "have made suit to," of the Jews in appealing to Festus against Paul.

Crying *epiboao* (1916), "to cry out, exclaim vehemently," is used in some mss. in **Acts 25:24**. *See also Acts 8:7.*

Live *see* Alive at *Acts 1:3.*

Longer *meketi* (3371), means "no more, no longer," but generally suggests what is a matter of thought or supposition. It is rendered "any longer" in **Acts 25:24**; "no longer," in Mark 2:2, RV, "no longer (room)," KJV, "no (room);" 2 Cor. 5:15, RV (KJV, "not henceforth"); Eph. 4:14, RV (KJV, "no more"); 4:17, RV (KJV, "henceforth ... not"); 1 Thess. 3:1, 5; 1 Tim. 5:23; 1 Pet. 4:2.

25:25 But when I found that he had committed nothing worthy of death, and that he himself hath appealed to Augustus, I have determined to send him.

Found *katalambano* (2638), "to lay hold of," said of mental action, "to comprehend" by laying hold of or "finding" facts, is translated "I found," of Festus regarding charges made against Paul, **Acts 25:25**. *See also* Perceived at *Acts 4:13.*

Committed *see Acts 25:11.*

Worthy *see Acts 13:25.*

Appealed *see* Calling at *Acts 7:59.*

Determined *see Acts 3:13.*

Send *see Acts 10:5.*

25:26 Of whom I have no certain thing to write unto my lord. Wherefore I have brought him forth before you, and specially before thee, O king Agrippa, that, after examination had, I might have somewhat to write.

Certain *see* Certainty at *Acts 21:34.*

Wherefore *see Acts 15:19.*

Brought *see Acts 12:6.*

Specially *see* Most at *Acts 20:38.*

King *see* Lord at *Acts 2:36.*

Examination *anakrisis* (351), from *ana*, "up or through," and *krino*, "to distinguish," was a legal term among the Greeks, denoting the preliminary investigation for gathering evidence for the information of the judges, **Acts 25:26**.

Somewhat *see* Something at *Acts 3:5.*

25:27 For it seemeth to me unreasonable to send a prisoner, and not withal to signify the crimes *laid* against him.

Unreasonable *alogos* (249), "without reason, irrational," is rendered "unreasonable" in **Acts 25:27**. It is translated "brute" in the KJV of 2 Pet. 2:12 and Jude 10, and signifies "without reason," RV, though, as J. Hastings points out, "brute beasts" is not at all unsuitable, as "brute" is from Latin *brutus*, which means "dull, irrational."

Send *see Acts 10:5.*

Prisoner *see* Prisoners at *Acts 16:25.*

Withal In **Acts 25:27**, *kai*, "also," is rendered "withal."

Signify *see* Signified at *Acts 11:28.*

Crimes *aitia* (156), "a cause, accusation," is rendered "charges" in **Acts 25:27** (KJV, crimes); cf. v. 18. *See also* Cause at *Acts 13:28.*

Chapter 26

26:1 Then Agrippa said unto Paul, Thou art permitted to speak for thyself. Then Paul stretched forth the hand, and answered for himself:

Permitted *epitrepo* (2010), lit., "to turn to" (*epi*, "to," *trepo*, "to turn"), "to entrust," signifies "to permit," **Acts 26:1**; 1 Cor. 14:34; 1 Cor. 16:7; 1 Tim. 2:12, RV "permit" (KJV, "suffer"); Heb. 6:3.

Stretched *see* Stretching at *Acts 4:30.*

Answered *see* Defence at *Acts 19:33.*

26:2 I think myself happy, king Agrippa, because I shall answer for myself this day before thee touching all the things whereof I am accused of the Jews:

Think *hegeomai* (2233), is rendered "to think" in **Acts 26:2**; 2 Cor. 9:5, "I thought"; Phil. 2:6, KJV (RV, "counted"); 2 Pet. 1:13.

Myself *see Acts 20:24.*

Happy *makarios* (3107), "blessed, happy," is rendered "happy" in the RV, in two places only, as in the KJV, **Acts 26:2** and Rom. 14:22 (where "blessed" would have done); also the comparative "happier" in 1 Cor. 7:40. Elsewhere the RV uses "blessed" for KJV "happy," e.g., John 13:17; 1 Pet. 3:14; 4:14.

Shall *see Acts 23:3.*

Accused *see* Implead at *Acts 19:38.*

26:3 Especially *because I know* thee to be expert in all customs and questions which are among the Jews: wherefore I beseech thee to hear me patiently.

Especially *see* Most at *Acts 20:38.*

Expert *gnostes* (1109), "one who knows" (akin to *ginosko*, "to know"), denotes "an expert, a connoisseur," Acts **26:3**. Cf. *gnostos*, "known."

Questions *see* Question at *Acts 15:2*.

Patiently *makrothumos* (3116), denotes "patiently," Acts **26:3**.

26:4 My manner of life from my youth, which was at the first among mine own nation at Jerusalem, know all the Jews;

Life *biosis* (981), from *bioo*, "to spend one's life, to live," denotes "a manner of life," **Acts 26:4**.

Youth *neotes* (3503), from *neos*, "new," occurs in Mark 10:20; Luke 18:21; **Acts 26:4**; 1 Tim. 4:12 (in some mss., Matt. 19:20).

First *arche* (746), "a beginning," is translated "first" in Heb. 5:12, "of the first (principles of the oracles of God)," lit. "(the principles) of the beginning (of the oracles of God)"; in 6:1 "the first (principles) of Christ," lit., "(the account) of the beginning of Christ," i.e., the elementary teaching concerning Christ. In **Acts 26:4**, where the word is preceded by *apo*, "from," the KJV has "at the first," the RV, "from the beginning."

26:5 Which knew me from the beginning, if they would testify, that after the most straitest sect of our religion I lived a Pharisee.

Knew *proginosko* (4267), "to know beforehand," is used (a) of the divine "foreknowledge" concerning believers, Rom. 8:29; Israel, 11:2; Christ as the Lamb of God, 1 Pet. 1:20, RV, "foreknown" (KJV, "foreordained"); (b) of human previous "knowledge," of a person, **Acts 26:5**, RV, "having knowledge of" (KJV, "which knew"); of facts, 2 Pet. 3:17.

Beginning *see* Again at *Acts 11:9*.

Testify *martureo* (3140), is frequently rendered "to bear witness, to witness," in the RV, where KJV renders it "to testify," John 2:25; 3:11, 32; 5:39; 15:26; 21:24; 1 Cor. 15:15; Heb. 7:17; 11:4; 1 John 4:14; 5:9; 3 John 3. In the following, however, the RV, like the KJV, has the rendering "to testify," John 4:39, 44; 7:7; 13:21; **Acts 26:5**; Rev. 22:16, 18, 20. *See also* Report at *Acts 6:3*.

Straitest *akribestatos* (196), the superlative degree of *akribes*, "accurate, exact" (cf. *akribos*), occurs in **Acts 26:5**, "the straitest (sect)," RV (KJV, "most straitest").

Sect *see Acts 5:17*.

Our *see Acts 2:11*.

Religion *threskeia* (2356), signifies "religion" in its external aspect (akin to *threskos*), "religious worship," especially the ceremonial service of "religion"; it is used of the "religion" of the Jews, **Acts 26:5**; of the "worshiping" of angels, Col. 2:18, which they themselves repudiate (Rev. 22:8, 9); "there was an officious parade of humility in selecting these lower beings as intercessors rather than appealing directly to the Throne of Grace" (Lightfoot); in Jas. 1:26, 27 the writer purposely uses the word to set in contrast that which is unreal and deceptive, and the "pure religion" which consists in visiting "the fatherless and widows in their affliction," and in keeping oneself "unspotted from the world." He is "not herein affirming ... these offices to be the sum total, nor yet the great essentials, of true religion, but declares them to be the body, the *threskeia*, of which godliness, or the love of God, is the informing soul" (Trench).

Lived *see* Alive at *Acts 1:3*.

26:6 And now I stand and am judged for the hope of the promise made of God unto our fathers:

Hope *see Acts 16:19*.

Promise *see Acts 1:4*.

26:7 Unto which *promise* our twelve tribes, instantly serving *God* day and night, hope to come. For which hope's sake, king Agrippa, I am accused of the Jews.

Twelve tribes *dodekaphulos* (1429), an adjective signifying "of twelve tribes," used as a noun in the neuter, occurs in **Acts 26:7**.

Instantly For the phrase *en ekteneia*, rendered "instantly" in **Acts 26:7**, KJV. *See also* **Without ceasing** at *Acts 12:5*.

Serving *see* Serve at *Acts 7:7*.

Night *see Acts 5:19*.

Hope *see Acts 16:19*.

Come *katantao* (2658), a strengthened form of *antao*, "to come opposite to," signifies "to reach, to arrive at." It is used in its local significance several times in the Acts, e.g. **27:12**, RV, "could reach." In its metaphorical sense of "attaining" to something it is used in three places: **Acts 26:7**, of the fulfillment of the promise of God made to the ancestors of Israel, to which promise the twelve tribes "hope to attain" (RV); in Eph. 4:13, of "attaining" to the unity of the faith and of the knowledge of the Son of God; in Phil. 3:11, of the paramount aims of the apostle's life, "if by any means," he says, "I might attain unto the resurrection from the dead," not the physical resurrection, which is assured to all believers hereafter, but to the present life of identification with Christ in His resurrection. For the metaphorical sense in 1 Cor. 10:11 and 14:36. *See also* **Came** at *Acts 16:1*.

Accused *see* **Implead** at *Acts 19:38*.

26:8 Why should it be thought a thing incredible with you, that God should raise the dead?

Thought In **Acts 26:8**, KJV, *krino*, "to judge, reckon," is translated "should it be thought" (RV, "is it judged").

Incredible *apistos* (571), is once rendered "incredible," **Acts 26:8**, of the doctrine of resurrection; elsewhere it is used of persons, with the meaning "unbelieving."

Raise *see* **Lifted** at *Acts 3:7*.

26:9 I verily thought with myself, that I ought to do many things contrary to the name of Jesus of Nazareth.

Verily The particle *men* is rendered "verily," e.g., in 1 Cor. 5:3; 14:17; Heb. 12:10; in the KJV, Heb. 3:5; 7:5, 18; 1 Pet. 1:20; in **Acts 26:9** it is combined with *oun* ("therefore").

Myself *see Acts 20:24*.

Contrary *enantios* (1727), "over against" (*en*, "in," *antios*, "against"), is used primarily of place, Mark 15:39; of an opposing wind, Matt. 14:24; Mark 6:48; **Acts 27:4**; metaphorically, opposed as an adversary, antagonistic, **Acts 26:9**; 1 Thess. 2:15; Titus 2:8; **Acts 28:17**, "against."

Name *see* **Names** at *Acts 1:15*.

26:10 Which thing I also did in Jerusalem: and many of the saints did I shut up in prison, having received authority from the chief priests; and when they were put to death, I gave my voice against *them*.

Shut up *katakleio* (2623), lit., "to shut down" (the *kata* has, however, an intensive use), signifies "to shut up in confinement," Luke 3:20; **Acts 26:10**. In the Sept., Jer. 32:3.

Death *anaireo* (337), lit., "to take or lift up or away," hence, "to put to death," is usually translated "to kill or slay"; in two places "put to death," Luke 23:32; **Acts 26:10**. It is used 17 times, with this meaning, in Acts.

Gave *see* **Fallen, Sunk** at *Acts 20:9*.

Voice *psephos* (5586), "a smooth stone, a pebble," worn smooth as by water, or polished (akin to *psao*, "to rub"), denotes (a) by metonymy, a vote (from the use of "pebbles" for this purpose; cf. *psephizo*, "to count"), **Acts 26:10**, RV (KJV, "voice"); (b) a (white) "stone" to be given to the overcomer in the church at Pergamum, Rev. 2:17 (twice); a white "stone" was often used in the social life and judicial customs of the ancients; festal days were noted by a white "stone," days of calamity by a black; in the courts a white "stone" indicated acquittal, a black condemnation. A host's appreciation of a special guest was indicated by a white "stone" with the name or a message written on it; this is probably the allusion here.

26:11 And I punished them oft in every synagogue, and compelled *them* to blaspheme; and being exceedingly mad against them, I persecuted *them* even unto strange cities.

Punished *see Acts 22:5*.

Every *see Acts 5:42*.

Compelled *anankazo* (315), denotes "to put constraint upon (from *ananke*, 'necessity'), to constrain, whether by threat, entreaty, force or persuasion"; Christ "constrained" the disciples to get into a boat, Matt. 14:22; Mark 6:45; the servants of the man who made a great supper were to constrain people to come in, Luke 14:23 (RV, "constrain"); Saul of Tarsus "strove" to make saints blaspheme, **Acts 26:11**, RV (KJV, "compelled"); Titus, though a Greek, was not "compelled" to be circumcised, Gal. 2:3, as Galatian converts were, 6:12, RV; Peter was "compelling" Gentiles to live as Jews, Gal. 2:14; Paul was "constrained" to appeal to Caesar, **Acts 28:19**, and was "compelled" by the church at Corinth to become foolish in speaking of himself, 2 Cor. 12:11.

Exceedingly *perissos* (4057), is used in Matt. 27:23, RV, "exceedingly," for KJV, "the more"; Mark 10:26, RV, "exceedingly," for KJV, "out of measure"; in **Acts 26:11**, "exceedingly." In Mark 15:14, the most authentic mss. have this word (RV, "exceedingly") (KJV, "the more exceedingly").

Mad *emmainomai* (1693), implying "fierce rage, to be furious against"; it is rendered "being exceedingly mad" in **Acts 26:11** (cf. **9:1**).

Strange *exo* (1845), outside, is rendered "strange" in **Acts 26:11**, KJV.

26:12 Whereupon as I went to Damascus with authority and commission from the chief priests,

Commission *epitrope* (2011), denotes "a turning over (to another), a referring of a thing to another" (*epi* "over," *trepo*, "to turn"), and so a committal of full powers, "a commission," **Acts 26:12**.

26:13 At midday, O king, I saw in the way a light from heaven, above the brightness of the sun, shining round about me and them which journeyed with me.

Midday In **Acts 26:13**, "at midday" translates the adjective *mesos*, "middle," and the noun *hemera*, "a day," in a combined adverbial phrase.

Heaven *see Acts 14:17.*

Brightness *lamprotes* (2987), "brightness," is found in **Acts 26:13**.

Sun *see Acts 2:20.*

Shining *perilampo* (4034), "to shine around," is used in Luke 2:9, "shone round about," of the glory of the Lord; so in **Acts 26:13**, of the light from Heaven upon Saul of Tarsus. *See also* Shined at *Acts 9:3.*

Journeyed *see Acts 9:3.*

26:14 And when we were all fallen to the earth, I heard a voice speaking unto me, and saying in the Hebrew tongue, Saul, Saul, why persecutest thou me? *it is* hard for thee to kick against the pricks.

Fallen *katapipto* (2667), "to fall down," is used in Luke 8:6 (in the best mss.); **Acts 26:14**; 28:6.

Voice *see Acts 7:31.*

Tongue *see Acts 1:19.*

Hard *see Acts 9:5.*

Kick *see Acts 9:5.*

Pricks *see Acts 9:5.*

26:15-16 And I said, Who art thou, Lord? And he said, I am Jesus whom thou persecutest.

But rise, and stand upon thy feet: for I have appeared unto thee for this purpose, to make thee a minister and a witness both of these things which thou hast seen, and of those things in the which I will appear unto thee;

Purpose The following phrases are translated with the word "purpose": (a) *eis auto touto*, "for this same (or very) purpose," lit., "unto this same (thing)," Rom. 9:17; Eph. 6:22; Col. 4:8; (b) *eis touto*, "for this purpose," **Acts 26:16**, KJV (RV, "to this end"), lit., "unto this"; so 1 John 3:8; (c) *eis ti*, "to what purpose," Matt. 26:8, lit., "unto what"; Mark 14:4, RV, "to what purpose" (KJV, "why").

Make In **Acts 26:16**, KJV, *procheirizo*, "to determine, choose," is translated "make" (RV, "appoint"). *See also* Preached at *Acts 3:20.*

Minister *see Acts 13:5.*

Witness *see* Witnesses at *Acts 1:8.*

26:17 Delivering thee from the people, and *from* the Gentiles, unto whom now I send thee,

Delivering *see* Delivered at *Acts 7:10.*

People *see Acts 4:8.*

Send *see Acts 3:20.*

26:18 To open their eyes, *and* to turn *them* from darkness to light, and *from* the power of Satan unto God, that they may receive forgiveness of sins, and inheritance among them which are sanctified by faith that is in me.

Open *see* Opened at *Acts 5:19.*

Darkness *see Acts 13:11.*

Satan *see Acts 5:3.*

May *see Acts 3:19.*

Forgiveness *see Acts 5:31. See also* Remission at *Acts 2:38.*

Inheritance *see* Part at *Acts 1:17.*

Sanctified *hagiasmos* (38), "sanctification," is used of (a) separation to God, 1 Cor. 1:30; 2 Thess. 2:13; 1 Pet. 1:2; (b) the course of life befitting those so separated, 1 Thess. 4:3, 4, 7; Rom. 6:19, 22; 1 Tim. 2:15; Heb. 12:14. "Sanctification is that relationship with God into which men enter by faith in Christ, **Acts 26:18**; 1 Cor. 6:11, and to which their sole title is the death of Christ, Eph. 5:25, 26; Col. 1:22; Heb. 10:10, 29; 13:12."

26:19 Whereupon, O king Agrippa, I was not disobedient unto the heavenly vision:

Disobedient *apeithes* (545), signifies "unwilling to be persuaded, spurning belief, disobedient," Luke 1:17; **Acts 26:19**; Rom. 1:30; 2 Tim. 3:2; Titus 1:16; 3:3.

Heavenly *ouranios* (3770), signifying "of heaven, heavenly," is used (a) as an appellation of God the Father, Matt. 6:14, 26, 32, "your heavenly Father"; 15:13, "My heavenly Father"; (b) as descriptive of the holy angels, Luke 2:13; (c) of the vision seen by Paul, **Acts 26:19**.

Vision *optasia* (3701), (a late form of *opsis*, "the act of seeing"), from *optano*, "to see, a coming into view," denotes a "vision" in Luke 1:22; 24:23; **Acts 26:19**; 2 Cor. 12:1.

26:20 But shewed first unto them of Damascus, and at Jerusalem, and throughout all the coasts of Judaea, and *then* to the Gentiles, that they should repent and turn to God, and do works meet for repentance.

Shewed *apangello* ("to announce"), Matt. 11:4, "tell"; 12:18, "declare"; 28:11, "told"; Luke 14:21, "told"; **Acts 26:20**, "declared"; **28:21**, "report"; 1 Thess. 1:9, "report"; 1 John 1:2, "declare".

Coasts *chora*, "a country," rendered "coasts" in **Acts 26:20**, KJV, is corrected in the RV to "country." *See also* Land at *Acts 10:39.*

Repent *see Acts 2:38.*

Repentance *see Acts 5:31.*

Meet *axios* (514), has the meaning of being of "weight, value, worth"; also "befitting, becoming, right on the ground of fitness," e.g., Matt. 3:8, KJV, "meet" (RV, "worthy"); so **Acts 26:20**; Luke 3:8 ("worthy"); 23:41 ("due reward").

26:21 For these causes the Jews caught me in the temple, and went about to kill *me*.

Caught *sullambano* (4815), "to seize," is used, in **Acts 26:21**, of the act of the Jews in seizing Paul in the temple. *See also* Took at *Acts 1:16.*

Went about *see* Return at *Acts 15:16. See also* Assayed at *Acts 16:7.*

Kill *see* Slew at *Acts 5:30.*

26:22 Having therefore obtained help of God, I continue unto this day, witnessing both to small and great, saying none other things than those which the prophets and Moses did say should come:

Obtained *tunchano* (5177), "to meet with, light upon," also signifies "to obtain, attain to, reach, get" (with regard to things), translated "to obtain" in **Acts 26:22**, of "the help that is from God"; 2 Tim. 2:10, of "the salvation which is in Christ Jesus with eternal glory"; Heb. 8:6, of the ministry obtained by Christ; 11:35, of "a better resurrection."

Help *epikouria* (1947), strictly denotes such aid as is rendered by an *epikouros*, "an ally, an auxiliary"; Paul uses it in his testimony to Agrippa, "having therefore obtained the help that is from God," Acts 26:22, RV.

Continue *see* Continued at *Acts 15:35. See also* Lay at *Acts 7:60.*

Witnessing *see* Report at *Acts 6:3. See also* Take ... to record at *Acts 20:26.*

Small *mikros* (3398), "little, small" (of age, quantity, size, space), is translated "small" in **Acts 26:22**; Rev. 11:18; 13:16; 19:5, 18; 20:12. *See also* Least at *Acts 8:10.*

Saying *see* Say at *Acts 3:22.*

Other In **Acts 26:22**, KJV, *ouden ektos*, lit., "nothing besides" is translated "none other things" (RV, "nothing but").

Than *ektos* (1622), an adverb, lit., "outside," is used with *ei me*, as an extended conjunction signifying "except"; so in 1 Cor. 14:5; in 15:2, RV, for KJV, "unless"; in 1 Tim. 5:19, RV, for KJV, "but." It has the force of a preposition in the sense of (a) "outside of," in 1 Cor. 6:18, "without; in 2 Cor. 12:2, "out of"; (b) "besides," except, in **Acts 26:22**, RV, "but," for KJV, "other than"; in 1 Cor. 15:27 "excepted." For its use as a noun see Matt. 23:26, "(the) outside."

26:23 That Christ should suffer, *and* that he should be the first that should rise from the dead, and should shew light unto the people, and to the Gentiles.

Suffer *pathetos* (3805), akin to *pascho*, denotes "one who has suffered," or "subject to suffering," or "destined to suffer"; it is used in the last sense of the "suffering" of Christ, **Acts 26:23**.

Rise For the KJV, "should rise" in **Acts 26:23**. *See also* Resurrection at *Acts 1:22.*

Shew *see Acts 16:17.*

People *see Acts 4:8.*

26:24 And as he thus spake for himself, Festus said with a loud voice, Paul, thou art beside thyself; much learning doth make thee mad.

Spake In **Acts 26:24**, KJV, *apologeomai*, "to make a defense" (RV), is rendered "spake for himself." *See also* Defence at *Acts 19:33.*

Beside thyself *See* Mad at *Acts 12:15.*

Much *see Acts 18:27.*

Learning *gramma* (1121), primarily denotes "that which is traced or drawn, a picture"; then, "that which is written," (a) "a character, letter of the alphabet," 2 Cor. 3:7; "written," lit., "(in) letters", Gal. 6:11; here the reference is not to the length of the epistle (Paul never uses *gramma*, either in the singular or the plural of his epistles; of these he uses *epistole*), but to the size of the characters written by his own hand (probably from this verse to the end, as the use of the past tense, "I have written," is, according to Greek idiom, the equivalent of our "I am writing"). Moreover, the word for "letters" is here in the dative case, *grammasin*, "with (how large) letters"; (b) "a writing, a written document, a bond" (KJV, "bill") Luke 16:6, 7; (c) "a letter, by way of correspondence," **Acts 28:21**; (d) the Scriptures of the OT, 2 Tim. 3:15; (e) "learning," John 7:15, "letters"; **Acts 26:24**, "(much) learning" (lit., "many letters"); in the papyri an illiterate person is often spoken of as one who does not know "letters," "which never means anything else than inability to write" (Moulton and Milligan); (f) "the letter," the written commandments of the Word of God, in contrast to the inward operation of the Holy Spirit under the New Covenant, Rom. 2:27, 29; 7:6; 2 Cor. 3:6; (g) "the books of Moses," John 5:47.

Make *peritrepo* (4062), "to turn about" (*peri*), is rendered "doth turn (thee to madness)" in **Acts 26:24**, RV, KJV, "doth make (thee mad)."

Mad *mania* (3130), transliterated into English, denotes "frenzy, madness," **Acts 26:24** "(thy much learning doth turn thee to) madness," RV; KJV, "(doth make thee) mad."

26:25 But he said, I am not mad, most noble Festus; but speak forth the words of truth and soberness.

Mad *see Acts 12:15.*

Noble *see Acts 24:3. See also* Excellent at *Acts 23:26.*

Speak *see Acts 2:14.*

Words *see Acts 2:14.*

Soberness *sophrosune* (4997), denotes "soundness of mind", **Acts 26:25**, "soberness"; 1 Tim. 2:9, 15, "sobriety"; "sound judgment" practically expresses the meaning; "it is that habitual inner self-government, with its constant rein on all the passions and desires, which would hinder the temptation to these from arising, or at all events from arising in such strength as would overbear the checks and barriers which *aidos* (shamefastness) opposed to it" (Trench *Syn.* Sec.xx, end).

26:26 For the king knoweth of these things, before whom also I speak freely: for I am persuaded that none of these things are hidden from him; for this thing was not done in a corner.

Knoweth *see* Know at *Acts 10:28.*

Freely In **Acts 26:26** *parrhesiazomai*, "to be bold in speech," is translated, "to speak freely." *See also* **Boldly** at *Acts 9:27.*

Persuaded *see Acts 13:43.*

None *see* No at *Acts 15:9.*

Hidden *lanthano* (2990), "to escape notice, to be hidden from," is rendered "(could not) be hid" in Mark 7:24, of Christ; "was (not) hid," Luke 8:47, of the woman with the issue of blood; "is hidden," **Acts 26:26**, of the facts concerning Christ; the sentence might be rendered "none of these things has escaped the king's notice."

Corner *see Acts 4:11.*

26:27-28 King Agrippa, believest thou the prophets? I know that thou believest.

Then Agrippa said unto Paul, Almost thou persuadest me to be a Christian.

Almost *see Acts 21:27.*

Persuadest For **Acts 26:28**, KJV, "thou persuadest."

Christian *see* Christians at *Acts 11:26.*

26:29 And Paul said, I would to God, that not only thou, but also all that hear me this day, were both almost, and altogether such as I am, except these bonds.

Would *euchomai* (2172), "to pray (to God)," is used with this meaning in 2 Cor. 13:7; v. 9, RV, "pray" (KJV, "wish"); Jas. 5:16; 3 John 2, RV, "pray" (KJV, "wish"). Even when the RV and KJV translate by "I would," **Acts 26:29**, or "wished for," **Acts 27:29** (RV, marg., "prayed"), or "could wish," Rom. 9:3 (RV, marg., "could pray"), the indication is that "prayer" is involved.

Altogether *see* All means at *Acts 18:21.*

Such as "Such as" is a rendering of certain relative pronouns: *hoios*, "what sort of," e.g., Matt. 24:21; 2 Cor. 12:20 (twice); Rev. 16:18; *hostis*, "whoever," e.g., Mark 4:20; *hopoios*, "of what sort," preceded by *toioutos*, "of such a sort," **Acts 26:29**.

Except *parektos* (3924), a strengthened form of *para*, "beside," is used (a) as an adverb, signifying "without," 2 Cor. 11:28; lit., "the things without," i.e., the things happening without; (b) as a preposition signifying "except"; in Matt. 5:32, "saving"; in **Acts 26:29**, except.

26:30 And when he had thus spoken, the king rose up, and the governor, and Bernice, and they that sat with them:

Rose *see* Raised at *Acts 2:24.*

Sat *sunkathemai* (4775), "to sit with," occurs in Mark 14:54; **Acts 26:30**. In the Sept., Ps. 101:6, "dwell."

26:31 And when they were gone aside, they talked between themselves, saying, This man doeth nothing worthy of death or of bonds.

Talked *laleo* (2980), "to speak, say," is always translated "to speak" in the RV, where the KJV renders it by "to talk," Matt. 12:46; Mark 6:50; Luke 24:32; John 4:27 (twice); 9:37; 14:30; **Acts 26:31**; Rev. 4:1; 17:1; 21:9, 15. The RV rendering is preferable; the idea of "chat" or "chatter" is entirely foreign to the NT, and should never be regarded as the meaning in 1 Cor. 14:34, 35.

Themselves *see Acts 4:15.*

Worthy *see Acts 13:25.*

26:32 Then said Agrippa unto Festus, This man might have been set at liberty, if he had not appealed unto Caesar.

Liberty *apoluo* (630), is translated "to set at liberty" in **Acts 26:32** and Heb. 13:23.

Appealed *see* Calling at *Acts 7:59.*

Chapter 27

27:1 And when it was determined that we should sail into Italy, they delivered Paul and certain other prisoners unto *one* named Julius, a centurion of Augustus' band.

Determined *see Acts 3:13.*

Sail *see* Sailed at *Acts 13:4.*

Other *see* Another at *Acts 7:18.*

Prisoners *desmotes* (1202), occurs in Acts 27:1, 42.

27:2 And entering into a ship of Adramyttium, we launched, meaning to sail by the coasts of Asia; *one* Aristarchus, a Macedonian of Thessalonica, being with us.

Entering *see* Went aboard at *Acts 21:2.*

Launched *anago* (321), "to lead or bring up," is used nautically of "putting" out to sea, **Acts 27:2, 4**, RV. *See also* Loosed at *Acts 13:13.*

Meaning In **Acts 27:2**, KJV, *mello*, "to be about to," is translated "meaning" (RV, "was about to"), with reference to the ship (according to the best mss.).

Sail *see* Sailed at *Acts 21:3.*

Coasts In **Acts 27:2** the phrase in the RV, "on the coast of," translates the preposition *kata*, "along," and the complete clause, "unto the places on the coast of Asia," RV, is curiously condensed in the KJV to "by the coasts of Asia."

27:3 And the next *day* we touched at Sidon. And Julius courteously entreated Paul, and gave *him* liberty to go unto his friends to refresh himself.

Touched *katago* (2609), to bring down, is used of bringing a ship to land in **Acts 27:3**.

Courteously *philanthropos* (5364), is translated "courteously" in **Acts 27:3**, KJV; RV, "kindly" (Eng., "philanthropically").

Entreated *chraomai* (5531), denotes (a) "to use" (of things); (b) "to use well or ill, to treat, deal with" (of persons); "treated (kindly)," **Acts 27:3**, RV, KJV, "(courteously) entreated." The remaining ten instances come under (a).

Liberty In **Acts 27:3**, KJV, *epitrepo* is rendered "gave ... liberty" (RV "gave ... leave").

Refresh In **Acts 27:3**, the verb *tunchano*, "to obtain or receive," with the object *epimeleia*, "care," is translated "to refresh himself" (RV, marg., "to receive attention," i.e., to enjoy the kind attention of his friends).

27:4 And when we had launched from thence, we sailed under Cyprus, because the winds were contrary.

Launched *see Acts 27:2. See also* Loosed at *Acts 13:13.*

Sailed under *hupopleo* (5284), "to sail under" (*hupo*), i.e., "under the lee of," occurs in **Acts 27:4, 7**.

Contrary *see Acts 26:9.*

27:5 And when we had sailed over the sea of Cilicia and Pamphylia, we came to Myra, *a city* of Lycia.

Sailed *diapleo* (1277), "to sail across" (*dia*, "through"), occurs in **Acts 27:5**.

Sea *pelagos* (989), "the deep sea, the deep," is translated "the depth" in Matt. 18:6, and is used of the "Sea of Cilicia" in **Acts 27:5**. *Pelagos* signifies "the vast expanse of open water," *thalassa*, "the sea as contrasted with the land" (Trench, *Syn.*, Sec.xiii).

Came to *see* Landed at *Acts 18:22.*

27:6 And there the centurion found a ship of Alexandria sailing into Italy; and he put us therein.

Sailing *see* Sailed at *Acts 21:3.*

Put *embibazo* (1688), "to put in" (*en*, "in," *bibazo*, not found in the NT), is used of "putting" persons on board ship, **Acts 27:6**. In the Sept., 2 Kings 9:28; Prov. 4:11.

27:7 And when we had sailed slowly many days, and scarce were come over against Cnidus, the wind not suffering us, we sailed under Crete, over against Salmone;

Sailed *braduploeo* (1020), "to sail slowly" (*bradus*, "slow," *plous*, "a voyage"), occurs in **Acts 27:7**. *See also Acts 27:4.*

Many *see Acts 9:23.*

Scarce *see Acts 14:18.*

Suffering *proseao* (4330), "to permit further," occurs in **Acts 27:7**.

27:8 And, hardly passing it, came unto a place which is called The fair havens; nigh whereunto was the city *of* Lasea.

Hardly *molis* (3433), "with difficulty, scarcely, hardly" (akin to *molos*, "toil"), occurs in the most authentic mss. in Luke 9:39; it is rendered "hardly" in **Acts 27:8**, KJV. *See also* Scarce at *Acts 14:18.*

Passing *paralego* (3881), "to lay beside" (*para*), is used in the middle voice, of "sailing past" in **Acts 27:8**, RV, "coasting along" (KJV, "passing"); v. **13**, RV, "sailed along" (KJV, "sailed").

Fair *kalos* (2570), "beautiful, fair, in appearance," is used as part of the proper name, Fair Havens, **Acts 27:8**.

Havens *limen* (3040), is mentioned in **Acts 27:8**, "Fair Havens," and v. **12**. The first mention in the Bible is in Gen. 49:13 (see RV marg.).

27:9 Now when much time was spent, and when sailing was now dangerous, because the fast was now already past, Paul admonished *them*,

Now *de* (1161), "but, and, now," often implying an antithesis, is rendered "now" in John 19:23; 1 Cor. 10:11; 15:50; Gal. 1:20; Eph. 4:9; in **Acts 27:9** (1st part), RV, "and" (KJV, "now"); in Gal. 4:1, RV, "but" (KJV, "now").

Much *see Acts 5:37.*

Spent *diaginomai* (1230), used of time, "to intervene, elapse," is rendered "was spent" in **Acts 27:9**. *See also* After at *Acts 25:13.*

Sailing *see* Course at *Acts 21:7.*

Dangerous *episphales* (2000), lit., "prone to fall" (*epi*, "upon," i.e., near upon, *sphallo*, "to fall"), hence, "insecure, dangerous," is used in **Acts 27:9**.

Fast *see* Fasting at *Acts 14:23.*

Past *see* Passing at *Acts 16:8.*

Admonished *paraineo* (3867), "to admonish by way of exhorting or advising," is found in **Acts 27:9** ("Paul admonished them") and v. 22 ("and now I exhort you").

27:10 And said unto them, Sirs, I perceive that this voyage will be with hurt and much damage, not only of the lading and ship, but also of our lives.

Sirs *see Acts 7:26.*

Voyage *see* Course at *Acts 21:7.*

Will *see Acts 17:31.*

Hurt *hubris* (5196), is rendered "hurt" in **Acts 27:10**, KJV only.

Damage *zemia* (2209), is used in **Acts 27:10**, RV, "loss" (KJV, "damage"); v. **21**, KJV and RV, "loss," of ship and cargo; in Phil. 3:7, 8 of the apostle's estimate of the things which he formerly valued, and of all things on account of "the excellency of the knowledge of Christ Jesus."

Lading *phortion* (5413), "a burden, load" (a diminutive of *phortos*, "a load," from *phero*, "to bear"), is used of the cargo of a ship, **Acts 27:10**, "lading" (some mss. have *phortos*).

27:11 Nevertheless the centurion believed the master and the owner of the ship, more than those things which were spoken by Paul.

Believed *see Acts 17:4.*

Master *kubernetes* (2942), "the pilot or steersman of a ship," or, metaphorically, "a guide or governor" (akin to *kubernao*, "to guide": Eng., "govern" is connected; cf. *kubernesis*, "a steering, pilotage," 1 Cor. 12:28, "governments"), is translated "master" in **Acts 27:11**; "shipmaster" in Rev. 18:17. In the Sept., Prov. 23:34; Ezek. 27:8, 27-28.

Owner *naukleros* (3490), "a ship owner" (*naus*, "a ship," *kleros*, "a lot"), "a shipmaster," occurs in **Acts 27:11**, "(the) owner of the ship."

27:12 And because the haven was not commodious to winter in, the more part advised to depart thence also, if by any means they might attain to Phenice, *and there* to winter; *which is* an haven of Crete, and lieth toward the south west and north west.

Haven *see* Havens at Acts *27:8.*

Was *see Acts 5:4.*

Commodious *aneuthetos* (428), "not commodious," lit., "not-well-placed" (from *a*, "not," *n*, euphonic, *eu*, "well," *thetos*, "from" *tithemi* "to put, place"), is found in **Acts 27:12**, where it is said of the haven at the place called Fair Havens.

Winter In **Acts 27:12** (1st part) *paracheimasia*, "a wintering," is rendered "(to) winter in."

More *see Acts 19:32.*

Advised *see* Counsel at *Acts 2:23.*

Depart *anago* (321), lit., "to lead up" (*ana*, "up," *ago*, "to lead"), is used, in the middle voice, as a nautical term, signifying "to set sail, put to sea"; "to depart," **Acts 27:12**, KJV (RV, "put to sea"); **28:10** (RV, "sailed"); v. **11** (RV, "set sail"). Cf. *epanago*, in Luke 5:3, to put out. *See also* Loosed at *Acts 13:13.*

By any means *pos* (4458), "at all, somehow, in any way," is used after the conjunction (a) *ei*, "if," meaning "if by any means," e.g., **Acts 27:12**; Rom. 1:10; 11:14; Phil. 3:11; (b) *me*, "lest, lest by any means," e.g., 1 Cor. 8:9; 9:27; 2 Cor. 2:7, RV (KJV, "perhaps"); 9:4, RV (KJV, "haply"); 11:3; 12:20, RV; Gal. 2:2; 4:11, RV (KJV, "lest"); 1 Thess. 3:5 (KJV, "lest by some means").

Might *see* May at *Acts 17:19.*

Attain *katantao* (2628), "to come to a place," is translated "reach" in **Acts 27:12**, RV (KJV, "attain to"). *See also* Came at *Acts 16:1;* Come at *Acts 26:7.*

Phenice *phoinix* (5404), denotes "the date palm"; it is used of "palm" trees in John 12:13, from which branches were taken; of the branches themselves in Rev. 7:9. The "palm" gave its name to Phoenicia and to

Phoenix in Crete, **Acts 27:12**, RV. Jericho was the city of "palm trees," Deut. 34:3; Judg. 1:16; 3:13; 2 Chron. 28:15. They were plentiful there in the time of Christ.

Winter *paracheimazo* (3914), denotes "to winter at a place," **Acts 27:12** (2nd part); **28:11**; 1 Cor. 16:6; Titus 3:12.

Lieth In **Acts 27:12**, KJV, *blepo*, "to look," is rendered "lieth," of the situation of the haven Phoenix (KJV, Phenice); RV, "looketh." *See also* **Beheld** at *Acts 1:9*.

South west *lips* (3047), lit., "Libyan," denotes "the S.W. wind," **Acts 27:12**, "(looking) northeast (and southeast)," RV, lit., "(looking down) the southwest wind (and down the northwest wind)"; to look down a wind was to look in the direction in which it blows. A S.W. wind blows towards the N.E.; the aspect of the haven answers to this.

North west *choros* (5566), Lat., *corus*, the Latin name for "the north-west wind," hence, "the north-west," occurs in **Acts 27:12**, KJV, RV, "(north-east and) south-east," as the N.W. wind blows towards the S.E.

27:13 And when the south wind blew softly, supposing that they had obtained *their* purpose, loosing *thence*, they sailed close by Crete.

South wind *notos* (3558), denotes (a) "the south wind," Luke 12:55; **Acts 27:13**; **28:13**; (b) "south," as a direction, Luke 13:29; Rev. 21:13; (c) "the South," as a region, Matt. 12:42; Luke 11:31.

Blew *hupopneo* (5285), denotes "to blow softly," **Acts 27:13**.

Supposing *dokeo* (1380), "to be of opinion," is translated "to suppose" in Mark 6:49; Luke 24:37; John 20:15; **Acts 27:13**; in the following, KJV "suppose," RV, "think," Luke 12:51; 13:2; Heb. 10:29. It is most frequently rendered "to think," always in Matthew; always in John, except 11:31, "supposing," RV [where the best texts have this verb (for *lego*, KJV, "saying")], and 20:15.

Obtained *krateo* (2902), "to be strong," also means "to get possession of, obtain," e.g., in **Acts 27:13**, "they had obtained (their purpose)."

Purpose *see Acts 11:23*.

Loosing *ankura* (45), (Eng., "anchor"), was so called because of its curved form (*ankos*, "a curve"), **Acts 27:29-30, 40**; Heb. 6:19. In **Acts 27:13** the verb *airo*, "to lift," signifies "to lift anchor" (the noun being understood), RV, "they weighed anchor" (KJV, "loosing thence").

Sailed *see* **Passing** at *Acts 27:8*.

Close *asson* (788), the comparative degree of *anchi*, "near," is found in **Acts 27:13**, of sailing "close" by a place.

27:14 But not long after there arose against it a tempestuous wind, called Euroclydon.

Long *polus* (4183), in one or other of its neuter forms, singular or plural, is used (a) of degree, "greatly, much, many," e.g., Mark 1:45; (b) of time, e.g., **Acts 27:14**.

Arose *ballo* (906), "to throw or cast," is once rendered "beat," **Acts 27:14** RV, of the tempestuous wind that "beat" down upon the ship, "arose" in the KJV.

Tempestuous *tuphonikos* (5189), from *tuphon*, "a hurricane, typhoon," is translated "tempestuous" in **Acts 27:14**.

27:15 And when the ship was caught, and could not bear up into the wind, we let *her* drive.

Caught *see Acts 6:12*.

Bear *phero* (5342), "to bear," is translated "driven" in **Acts 27:15**, **17**, of "being borne" in a storm-tossed ship.

Drive *anemizo* (416), "to drive by the wind" (*anemos*, "wind"), is used in Jas. 1:6. For "let ... drive," **Acts 27:15**.

27:16 And running under a certain island which is called Clauda, we had much work to come by the boat:

Running *hupotrecho* (5295), "to run under" (*hupo*, "under"), is used nautically in **Acts 27:16**.

Certain For "a certain island," **Acts 27:16**, see the RV, "small island."

Island *nesion* (3519), "a small island," occurs in **Acts 27:16**, Cauda, RV.

Much work In **Acts 27:16**, KJV, *ischuo*, "to be able," with *molis*, "scarcely," is translated "had much work" (RV, "were able, with difficulty"). *See also* **Scarce** at *Acts 14:18*.

Come by *perikrates* (4031), an adjective, signifies "having full command of" (*peri*, "around, about," *krateo*, "to be strong, to rule"), it is used with *ginomai*, "to become," in **Acts 27:16**, RV, "to secure (the boat)," KJV, "to come by."

Boat *skaphe* (4627), is, lit., "anything dug or scooped out" (from *skapto*, "to dig"), "as a trough, a tub, and hence a light boat, or skiff, a boat belonging to a larger vessel," **Acts 27:16, 30, 32**.

27:17 Which when they had taken up, they used helps, undergirding the ship; and, fearing lest they should fall into the quicksands, strake sail, and so were driven.

Taken up *airo* (142), "to raise," is used of "hoisting up" a skiff, or little boat, before undergirding the ship, **Acts 27:17**, RV, "had hoisted up," for KJV, "had taken up."

Used *chraomai* (5531), from *chre*, "it is necessary," denotes "to use," **Acts 27:17**; 1 Cor. 7:21, where "use it rather" means "use your bondservice rather"; 7:31, where "they that use (this world)" is followed by the strengthened form *katachraomai*, rendered "abusing," or "using to the full" (RV, marg.); 9:12, 15; 2 Cor. 1:17; 3:12; 13:10; 1 Tim. 1:8, of "using" the Law lawfully, i.e., agreeably to its designs; 1 Tim. 5:23.

Helps *boetheia* (996), from *boe*, "a shout," and *theo*, "to run," denotes "help, succour," Heb. 4:16, lit., "(grace) unto (timely) help"; in **Acts 27:17**, where the plural is used, the term is nautical, "frapping."

Undergirding *hupozonnumi* (5269), *hupo*, "under," *zonnumi*, "to gird," is used of frapping a ship, **Acts 27:17**, bracing the timbers of a vessel by means of strong ropes.

Ship *see* **Vessel** at *Acts 9:15.*

Fall *see* **Fell** at *Acts 12:7.*

Quicksands This is the KJV rendering in **Acts 27:17** of *Surtis*, "Syrtis" (RV). The Syrtes, Major and Minor, lie on the north coast of Africa, between the headlands of Tunis and Barca. They have been regarded as dangerous to mariners from very early times, both from the character of the sands and from the crosscurrents of the adjoining waters. In the voyage described in this chapter the vessel had left the shelter of the island of Cauda and was drifting before the N.E. wind Euraquilo. The mariners might well fear that they would be driven on the Syrtes on the leeward of their course. The changing character of the tempest, however, drove them into the sea of Adria.

Strake For *chalao*, "to let go," **Acts 27:17**, KJV, "strake." *See also* **Let ... down** at *Acts 9:25.*

Sail *skeuos* (4632), "an implement, vessel, utensil," is used of the tackling or "gear" of a ship, **Acts 27:17**, RV (KJV, "sail").

Driven *see* **Drive** at *Acts 27:15.*

27:18 And we being exceedingly tossed with a tempest, the next *day* they lightened the ship;

Exceedingly *sphodros* (4971), "exceedingly", is used in **Acts 27:18**.

Tossed *cheimazo* (5492), from *cheima*, "winter cold," primarily, "to expose to winter cold," signifies "to drive with a storm"; in the passive voice, "to be driven with storm, to be tempest-tossed," **Acts 27:18**, RV, "as (we) labored with the storm" (KJV, "being ... tossed with a tempest").

Tempest *cheimazo* (5492), from *cheima*, "winter cold," primarily "to expose to winter cold," signifies "to drive with a storm"; in the passive voice, "to be driven with storm, to be tempest-tossed," **Acts 27:18**, RV, "as (we) labored with the storm" (KJV, "being ... tossed with a tempest").

Next *see* **Following** at *Acts 21:1.*

Lightened *ekbole* (1546), lit., "a throwing out" (from *ekballo*, "to throw out"), denotes "a jettison, a throwing out of cargo," **Acts 27:18**, lit., "they made a throwing out," RV, "they began to throw the freight overboard," KJV, "they lightened the ship." In the Sept., Exod. 11:1; Jonah 1:5.

27:19 And the third *day* we cast out with our own hands the tackling of the ship.

Cast *see* *Acts 22:23.*

Hands *autocheir* (849), a noun (*autos*, "self," *cheir*, "the hand"), is used in the plural in **Acts 27:19**, "with their own hands."

Tackling *skeue* (4631), denotes "gear, equipment, tackling" (of a ship), **Acts 27:19**.

27:20 And when neither sun nor stars in many days appeared, and no small tempest lay on *us*, all hope that we should be saved was then taken away.

Stars *see* **Star** at *Acts 7:43.*

Many *see* *Acts 2:40.*

Appeared *epiphaino* (2014), *epi* signifying "upon," is used in the active voice with the meaning "to give light," Luke 1:79; in the passive voice, "to appear, become visible." It is said of heavenly bodies, e.g., the stars, **Acts 27:20** (RV, "shone"); metaphorically, of things spiritual, the grace of God, Titus 2:11; the kindness and the love of God, 3:4.

Small *see* *Acts 12:18.*

Tempest *cheimon* (5494), "winter, a winter storm," hence, in general, "a tempest," is so rendered in **Acts 27:20**.

Lay *epikeimai* (1945), "to lie upon, be laid upon," is translated with this meaning, intransitively in John 11:38 and **Acts 27:20**; transitively, in the passive voice, in John 21:9 and 1 Cor. 9:16.

All *see* **Every** at *Acts 2:43.*

Then *loipon* (3063), "finally, for the rest," the neuter of *loipos*, "(the) rest," used adverbially, is rendered "then" in **Acts 27:20**, KJV (RV, "now").

Taken *periaireo* (4014), "to take away that which surrounds" (*peri*, "around"), is used (a) literally, of "casting off" anchors, **Acts 27:40**,

RV (KJV, "having taken up"); 28:13 in some texts, for *periercomai*, "to make a circuit"; (b) metaphorically, of "taking away" the veil off the hearts of Israel, 2 Cor. 3:16; of hope of rescue, **Acts 27:20**; of sins (negatively), Heb. 10:11.

27:21 But after long abstinence Paul stood forth in the midst of them, and said, Sirs, ye should have hearkened unto me, and not have loosed from Crete, and to have gained this harm and loss.

Long *polus* (4183), "much," is used with *chronos*, "time," in Matt. 25:19; John 5:6; in **Acts 27:21**, with *asitia*, KJV, "long abstinence," RV, "long without food."

Abstinence The noun "abstinence" in **Acts 27:21**, KJV, translates *asitia*, "without food," RV (*a*, negative, *sitos*, "food"). Cf. *asitos*, "fasting," v. 33.

Sirs *see Acts 7:26.*

Should *see Acts 11:28. See also* **Must** at *Acts 3:21.*

Hearkened *peitharcheo* (3980), "to obey one in authority, be obedient" (*peithomai*, "to be persuaded," *arche*, "rule"), is translated "to hearken unto" in **Acts 27:21**, in Paul's reminder to the shipwrecked mariners that they should have given heed to his counsel. *See also* **Obey** at *Acts 5:29.*

Loosed *see Acts 13:13.*

Gained *kerdaino* (2770), "to gain," is rendered "have gotten" in **Acts 27:21**, RV (of injury and loss); the word is there used metaphorically, however, of avoiding, or saving oneself from. For the meaning, "to get gain," Jas. 4:13.

Loss *see* **Damage** at *Acts 27:10.*

27:22 And now I exhort you to be of good cheer: for there shall be no loss of *any man's* life among you, but of the ship.

Exhort *see* **Admonished** at *Acts 27:9.*

Cheer *euthumeo* (2114), signifies, in the active voice, "to put in good spirits, to make cheerful" (*eu*, "well," *thumos*, "mind or passion"); or, intransitively, "to be cheerful," **Acts 27:22, 25**; Jas. 5:13 (RV, "cheerful," for KJV, "merry").

Loss *apobole* (580), lit., "casting away" (*apo*, "away," *ballo*, "to cast"), is translated "loss" in **Acts 27:22**; in Rom. 11:15, "casting away," of the temporary exclusion of the nation of Israel from its position of divine favor involving the reconciling of the world (i.e., the provision made through the gospel, which brings the world within the scope of reconciliation).

Man's In **Acts 27:22** there is no word representing "man's"; the RV has "of life."

But *see* **Except** at *Acts 8:1.*

27:23 For there stood by me this night the angel of God, whose I am, and whom I serve,

Stood *see Acts 1:10.*

Night *see Acts 5:19.*

God *see Acts 2:23.*

Serve *see Acts 7:7.*

27:24 Saying, Fear not, Paul; thou must be brought before Caesar: and, lo, God hath given thee all them that sail with thee.

Brought In Mark 13:9, the verb translated "be brought," KJV, is *histemi*, "to stand" (RV); in **Acts 27:24**, *paristemi*, "to stand before" (KJV, "be brought before"). *See also* **Stood** at *Acts 1:10.*

Given *see* **Granted** at *Acts 3:14.*

Sail *see* **Sailed** at *Acts 21:3.*

27:25 Wherefore, sirs, be of good cheer: for I believe God, that it shall be even as it was told me.

Wherefore *see Acts 15:19.*

Sirs *see Acts 7:26.*

Cheer *see Acts 27:22.*

Told *see Acts 9:6.*

27:26 Howbeit we must be cast upon a certain island.

Cast *see* **Fell** at *Acts 12:7.*

Island *see* **Isle** at *Acts 13:6.*

27:27 But when the fourteenth night was come, as we were driven up and down in Adria, about midnight the shipmen deemed that they drew near to some country;

Fourteenth *see* **Four hundred** at *Acts 5:36.*

Driven *diaphero* (1308), lit., "to bear through," in **Acts 27:27** signifies "to be borne hither and thither" (RV, "were driven to and fro"; KJV, "up and down"). *See also* **Published** at *Acts 13:49.*

Midnight In Matt. 25:6 "at midnight" translates the adjective *mesos*, and noun *nux*, "night," in the combined adverbial phrase. In **Acts 27:27** "about midnight" translates an adverbial phrase consisting of *kata*, "towards," followed by *mesos*, "middle" and *nux*, "night," with the article, lit., "towards (the) middle of the night." *See also* **Midst** at *Acts 1:18.*

Shipmen *nautes* (3492), "a seaman, mariner, sailor" (from *naus*, "a ship," Eng., "nautical"), is translated "sailors" in **Acts 27:27**, **30**, RV (KJV, "shipmen"); in Rev. 18:17, RV, "mariners" (KJV, "sailors").

Deemed *see* **Think** at *Acts 13:25.*

Drew *prosago* (4317), used transitively, "to bring to"; intransitively, "to draw near," is so rendered in **Acts 27:27**.

Near *prosago* (4317), is used (a) transitively, "to bring," **Acts 16:20**; 1 Pet. 3:18; (b) intransitively, "to draw near," in the latter sense in **Acts 27:27**.

Country *see* **Land** at *Acts 10:39.*

27:28 And sounded, and found *it* twenty fathoms: and when they had gone a little further, they sounded again, and found *it* fifteen fathoms.

Sounded *bolizo* (1001), "to heave the lead" (*bolis*, "that which is thrown or hurled," akin to *ballo*, "to throw"; sounding-lead), to take soundings, occurs in **Acts 27:28** (twice).

Twenty *see Acts 1:15.*

Fathoms *orguia* (3712), akin to *orego*, "to stretch," is the length of the outstretched arms, about six feet, **Acts 27:28** (twice).

Gone *see* **Return** at *Acts 15:16.*

Little *brachus* (1024), denotes (a) "short," in regard to time, e.g., Heb. 2:7; or distance, **Acts 27:28**; (b) "few," in regard to quantity, Heb. 13:22, in the phrase *dia bracheon*, lit., "by means of few," i.e., "in few words." *See also Acts 5:34.*

Further In **Acts 27:28**, *brachu*, "a little," is rendered "a little further," KJV (RV, "after a little space").

Fifteen *dekapente* (1178), lit., "ten-five," occurs in John 11:18; **Acts 27:28**; Gal. 1:18.

27:29 Then fearing lest we should have fallen upon rocks, they cast four anchors out of the stern, and wished for the day.

Lest *mepou*, or *me pou* (3361), and (4225), "lest perhaps," is used in **Acts 27:29**, RV, "lest haply" (KJV, "lest").

Fallen *see* **Fell** at *Acts 12:7.*

Rocks *trachus* (5138), "rough, uneven," is used of paths, Luke 3:5; of rocky places, **Acts 27:29**. In **Acts 27:29**, KJV, the phrase *tracheis topoi*, lit., "rough places," is translated "rocks" (RV, "rocky ground").

Cast *ekpipto* (1601), lit., "to fall out," is translated "be cast ashore," in **Acts 27:29**, RV, KJV, have fallen upon. A number of compound verbs consisting of *ballo* or *rhipto*, with prepositions prefixed, denote to cast, with a corresponding English preposition. *See also Acts 22:23.*

Anchors *see* **Loosing** at *Acts 27:13.*

Stern *prumna* (4403), the feminine form of the adjective *prumnos*, "hindmost," is rendered "stern" in **Acts 27:29**; and in the RV in v. **41** and Mark 4:38.

Wished *euchomai* (2172), is rendered "to wish" in **Acts 27:29** (RV marg., "prayed"); so Rom. 9:3; in 2 Cor. 13:9 and 3 John 2, RV, "pray". *See also* **Would** at *Acts 26:29.*

27:30 And as the shipmen were about to flee out of the ship, when they had let down the boat into the sea, under colour as though they would have cast anchors out of the foreship,

Shipmen *see Acts 27:27.*

About *zeteo*, "to seek," is translated "were about" in the KJV of **Acts 27:30**; RV, correctly, "were seeking to."

Let down *see* Let ... down at *Acts 9:25.*

Boat *see Acts 27:16.*

Colour *prophasis* (4392), either from *pro*, "before," and *phaino*, "to cause to appear, shine," or, more probably, from *pro*, and *phemi*, "to say," is rendered "cloke" (of covetousness) in 1 Thess. 2:5; "excuse" in John 15:22 (KJV "cloke"); "pretense" in Matt. 23:14; Mark 12:40; Luke 20:47 (KJV "show"); Phil. 1:18; "color" in **Acts 27:30**. It signifies the assuming of something so as to disguise one's real motives.

Cast *ekteino* (1614), "to stretch out or forth," especially of the hand, is used of "laying" out anchors from a vessel, in **Acts 27:30**, RV, "lay out" (KJV, "cast ... out"). *See also* **Stretching** at *Acts 4:30.*

Foreship *prora* (4408), denotes the forward part of a ship, "the prow," **Acts 27:30**; in v. **41** (KJV, "forepart") in contrast to *prumna*, "the stern."

27:31-32 Paul said to the centurion and to the soldiers, Except these abide in the ship, ye cannot be saved.

Then the soldiers cut off the ropes of the boat, and let her fall off.

Cut *apokopto* (609), "to cut off, or cut away," is used (a) literally, of members of the body, Mark 9:43, 45; John 18:10, 26; of ropes, **Acts 27:32**; (b) metaphorically, in the middle voice, of "cutting off oneself," to excommunicate, Gal. 5:12, of the Judaizing teachers, with a reference, no doubt, to circumcision.

Ropes *schoinion* (4979), a diminutive of *schoinos*, "a rush," is used of the small cords of which Christ made a scourge, John 2:15; of the "ropes" of a boat, **Acts 27:32**.

Boat *see Acts 27:16.*

Let *eao* (1439), "to let," occurs in **Acts 27:32.**

Fall *see* **Fell** at *Acts 12:7.*

27:33 And while the day was coming on, Paul besought *them* all to take meat, saying, This day is the fourteenth day that ye have tarried and continued fasting, having taken nothing.

While In **Acts 27:33** and Heb. 3:13 *achri* (or *achris*) followed by *hou*, the genitive case of the relative pronoun *hos*, lit., "until which," is rendered "while"; cf. *en ho*, in Mark 2:19; Luke 5:34; John 5:7; *en to*, in Luke 1:21, RV, "while"; in Heb. 3:15, "while it is said," is, lit., "in the being said" (*en*, with the article and the pres. infin., passive of *lego*); so, e.g., in Matt. 13:25

Coming *ginomai* (1096), "to become," signifies a change of condition, state or place, e.g., Mark 4:35. In **Acts 27:33**, the verb is used with *mello*, "to be about to," to signify the coming on of day.

Take *metalambano* (3335), "to get, or have, a share of," is rendered "to take (food)" in **Acts 2:46**, RV (KJV, "did eat"); **27:33**, i.e., "to share it together."

Meat *see Acts 2:46.*

Fourteenth *see* **Four hundred** at **Acts** *5:36.*

Tarried In **Acts 27:33**, KJV, *prosdokao*, "to wait, look for," is translated "have tarried" (RV, "wait"). *See also* **Waited** at *Acts 10:24.*

Continued *diateleo* (1300), "to bring through to an end" (*dia*, "through," *telos*, "an end"), "to finish fully" or, when used of time, "continue right through," is said of "continuing" fasting up to the time mentioned, **Acts 27:33.**

Fasting *asitos* (777), "without food" (*a*, negative, *sitos*, "corn, food"), is used in **Acts 27:33**, "fasting." *See also* **Abstinence** at *Acts 27:21.*

Nothing *see Acts 4:21.*

27:34 Wherefore I pray you to take *some* meat: for this is for your health: for there shall not an hair fall from the head of any of you.

Wherefore *see Acts 15:19.*

Pray *see* **Prayed** at *Acts 16:9.*

Meat *see Acts 2:46.*

Your The possessive pronoun, *humeteros*, "your," is used in Luke 6:20; John 7:6; 8:17; 15:20; **Acts 27:34**; Rom. 11:31; 1 Cor. 15:31; 16:17; 2 Cor. 8:8; Gal. 6:13; in Luke 16:12, "your own."

Health In **Acts 27:34**, *soteria*, "salvation, safety," is translated "health" in the KJV; the RV, gives the right meaning, "safety." *See also* **Salvation** at *Acts 4:12.*

Hair *thrix* (2359), denotes the "hair," whether of beast, as of the camel's "hair" which formed the raiment of John the Baptist, Matt. 3:4; Mark 1:6; or of man. Regarding the latter (a) it is used to signify the minutest detail, as that which illustrates the exceeding care and protection bestowed by God upon His children, Matt. 10:30; Luke 12:7; 21:18; **Acts 27:34**; (b) as the Jews swore by the "hair," the Lord used the natural inability to make one "hair" white or black, as one of the reasons for abstinence from oaths, Matt. 5:36; (c) while long "hair" is a glory to a woman, and to wear it loose or dishevelled is a dishonor, yet the woman who wiped Christ's feet with her "hair" (in place of the towel which Simon the Pharisee omitted to provide), despised the shame in her penitent devotion to the Lord (slaves were accustomed to wipe their masters' feet), Luke 7:38, 44 (RV, "hair"); see also John 11:2; 12:3; (d) the dazzling whiteness of the head and "hair" of the Son of Man in the vision of Rev. 1 (v. 14) is suggestive of the holiness and wisdom of "the Ancient of Days"; (e) the long "hair" of the spirit-beings described as locusts in Rev. 9:8 is perhaps indicative of their subjection to their satanic master (cf. 1 Cor. 11:10, RV); (f) Christian women are exhorted to refrain from adorning their "hair" for outward show, 1 Pet. 3:3.

Fall *apollumi* (622), "to destroy," signifies, in the middle voice, "to perish," and is thus used (a) of things, e.g., Matt. 5:29, 30; Luke 5:37; **Acts 27:34**, RV, "perish" (in some texts *pipto*, "to fall," as KJV); Heb. 1:11; 2 Pet. 3:6; Rev. 18:14 (2nd part), RV, "perished" (in some texts *aperchomai*, "to depart," as KJV); (b) of persons, e.g., Matt. 8:25; John 3:15), 16; 10:28; 17:12, RV, "perished" (KJV, "is lost"); Rom. 2:12; 1 Cor. 1:18, lit., "the perishing," where the perfective force of the verb implies the completion of the process of destruction (Moulton, *Proleg.*, p. 114); 8:11; 15:18; 2 Pet. 3:9; Jude 11.

27:35 And when he had thus spoken, he took bread, and gave thanks to God in presence of them all: and when he had broken *it*, he began to eat.

Thanks *eucharisteo* (2168), "to give thanks," (a) is said of Christ, Matt. 15:36; 26:27; Mark 8:6; 14:23; Luke 22:17, 19; John 6:11, 23; 11:41; 1 Cor. 11:24; (b) of the Pharisee in Luke 18:11 in his selfcomplacent prayer; (c) is used by Paul at the beginning of all his epistles, except 2 Cor. (see, however, *eulogetos* in 1:3), Gal., 1 Tim., 2 Tim. (see, however, *charin* *echo,* 1:3), and Titus, (1) for his readers, Rom. 1:8; Eph. 1:16; Col. 1:3; 1 Thess. 1:2; 2 Thess. 1:3 (cf. 2:13); virtually so in Philem. 4; (2) for fellowship shown, Phil. 1:3; (3) for God's gifts to them, 1 Cor. 1:4; (d) is recorded (1) of Paul elsewhere, **Acts 27:35; 28:15**; Rom. 7:25; 1 Cor. 1:14; 14:18; (2) of Paul and others, Rom. 16:4; 1 Thess. 2:13; of himself, representatively, as a practice, 1 Cor. 10:30; (3) of others, Luke 17:16; Rom. 14:6 (twice); 1 Cor. 14:17; Rev. 11:17; (e) is used in admonitions to the saints, the Name of the Lord Jesus suggesting His character and example, Eph. 5:20; Col. 1:12; 3:17; 1 Thess. 5:18; (f) as the expression of a purpose, 2 Cor. 1:11, RV; (g) negatively of the ungodly, Rom. 1:21. "Thanksgiving" is the expression of joy Godward, and is therefore the fruit of the Spirit (Gal. 5:22); believers are encouraged to abound in it (e.g., Col. 2:7).

Broken *see* Breaking at *Acts 2:46.*

27:36 Then were they all of good cheer, and they also took *some* meat.

Cheer *euthumos* (2115), means "of good cheer," **Acts 27:36**.

Meat *see Acts 2:46.*

27:37 And we were in all in the ship two hundred threescore and sixteen souls.

Two hundred In **Acts 27:37**, some ancient authorities read "about threescore and sixteen souls" (RV, margin). The confusion was quite natural when the word *diakosioi* was not written in full but represented by one Greek letter. The larger number is by no means improbable: Josephus sailed for Rome in AD 63 in a ship which had 600 on board (*Life,* ch. 3). *See also Acts 23:23.*

Threescore and sixteen *see* Threescore and fifteen at *Acts 7:14.*

27:38 And when they had eaten enough, they lightened the ship, and cast out the wheat into the sea.

Eaten *korennumi* (2880), "to satiate, to satisfy," as with food, is used in the middle voice in **Acts 27:38**, "had eaten enough"; in 1 Cor. 4:8, "ye are filled."

Enough *korennumi* (2880), "to satisfy" (akin to *koros,* "a surfeit"), is used metaphorically of spiritual things, in 1 Cor. 4:8, RV, "ye are filled"; in **Acts 27:38**, "had eaten enough," lit., "having being satisfied with food."

Lightened *kouphizo* (2893), "to make light, lighten" (the adjective *kouphos,* not in NT, denotes "slight, light, empty"), is used of "lightening" the ship, in **Acts 27:38**.

Wheat *sitos* (4621), "wheat, corn"; in the plural, "grain," is translated "corn" in Mark 4:28; "wheat," Matt. 3:12; 13:25, 29-30; Luke 3:17; 12:18 (some mss. have *genemata,* "fruits," here); 16:7; 22:31; John 12:24; **Acts 27:38**; 1 Cor. 15:37; Rev. 6:6; 18:13.

27:39 And when it was day, they knew not the land: but they discovered a certain creek with a shore, into the which they were minded, if it were possible, to thrust in the ship.

Land *see* Shore at *Acts 21:5.*

Discovered *katanoeo* (2657), "to perceive distinctly, discern clearly, descry," is translated "discovered" in **Acts 27:39**, KJV, of finding a bay with a creek (RV, "perceived"). *See also* Behold at *Acts 7:31.*

Creek *kolpos* (2859), signifies (a) "the front of the body between the arms"; hence, to recline in the "bosom" was said of one who so reclined at table that his head covered, as it were, the "bosom" of the one next to him, John 13:23. Hence, figuratively, it is used of a place of blessedness with another, as with Abraham in paradise, Luke 16:22-23 (plural in v. 23), from the custom of reclining at table in the "bosom," a place of honor; of the Lord's eternal and essential relation with the Father, in all its blessedness and affection as intimated in the phrase, "The Only-begotten Son, which is in the bosom of the Father" (John 1:18); (b) "of the bosom of a garment, the hollow formed by the upper forepart of a loose garment, bound by a girdle and used for carrying or keeping things"; thus figuratively of repaying one liberally, Luke 6:38; cf. Isa. 65:6; Jer. 39:18; (c) "of an inlet of the sea," because of its shape, like a bosom, **Acts 27:39**.

Minded *bouleuo* (1011), "to take counsel," is translated "to be minded" in **Acts 27:39**; 2 Cor. 1:17, middle voice in each case. *See also* Counsel at *Acts 5:33.*

Possible *see Acts 2:24.*

Thrust In **Acts 27:39**, KJV, *exotheo,* "to drive out," is rendered "to thrust in," RV, "drive (the ship) upon (it [i.e., the beach])." *See also* Drave at *Acts 7:45.*

27:40 And when they had taken up the anchors, they committed *themselves* unto the sea, and loosed the rudder bands, and hoised up the mainsail to the wind, and made toward shore.

Taken *periaireo* (4014), "to take away," is used in **Acts 27:40**, as a nautical term, RV, casting off, KJV, taken up. *See also Acts 27:20.*

Anchors *see* Loosing at *Acts 27:13.*

Committed In **Acts 27:40**, *eao*, "to let, leave," is rendered in the RV, "left (the anchors) in," for KJV, "committed themselves to." *See also* **Left** at *Acts 23:32*.

Loosed *see Acts 16:26*.

Rudder *pedalion* (4079), "a rudder" (akin to *pedos*, "the blade of an oar"), occurs in Jas. 3:4, RV, "rudder" (KJV, "helm"), and **Acts 27:40**, plural, RV, "(the bands of) the rudders," KJV, "the rudder (bands)." The *pedalia* were actually steering paddles, two of which were used as "rudders" in ancient ships.

Bands *zeukteria* (2202), "a bond" (connected with *zugos*, "a yoke"), is found once, of the rudder band of a ship, **Acts 27:40**.

Hoised up *epairo* (1869), "to raise up," is used of "hoisting up" the foresail of a vessel, **Acts 27:40**, RV, "hoisting up." *See* also **Taken up** at *Acts 1:9*.

Mainsail *artemon* (736), from *artao*, "to fasten to," is rendered "mainsail" in **Acts 27:40**, KJV; RV, "foresail." As to the particular kind of sail there mentioned, Sir William Ramsay, quoting from Juvenal concerning the entrance of a disabled ship into harbor by means of a prow-sail, indicates that the *artemon* would be a sail set on the bow.

Wind *pneo* (4154), signifies (a) "to blow," e.g., Matt. 7:25; John 3:8; in **Acts 27:40** the present participle is used as a noun, lit., "to the blowing" (i.e., to the wind); (b) "to breathe."

Made *katecho* (2722), "to hold fast" (*kata*, "down," intensive, *echo*, "to hold"), is used of "making" for a place, in **Acts 27:40**, RV, "they made for" (KJV, "they made toward").

27:41 And falling into a place where two seas met, they ran the ship aground; and the forepart stuck fast, and remained unmoveable, but the hinder part was broken with the violence of the waves.

Falling *peripipto* (4045), "to fall around" (*peri*, "around"), hence signifies to "fall" in with, or among, to light upon, come across, Luke 10:30, "among (robbers)"; **Acts 27:41**, KJV, "falling into," RV, "lighting upon," a part of a shore; Jas. 1:2, into temptation (i.e., trials). In the Sept., Ruth 2:3; 2 Sam. 1:6; Prov. 11:5.

Seas *dithalassos* (1337), primarily signifies "divided into two seas" (*dis*, "twice," and *thalassa*), then, "dividing the sea," as of a reef or rocky projection running out into the "sea," **Acts 27:41**.

Ran *epikello* or *epokello* (2207), "to drive upon," is used in **Acts 27:41** of "running" a ship ashore.

Ship *naus* (3491), denotes "a ship" (Lat. *navis*, Eng. "nautical," "naval," etc.), **Acts 27:41**. *Naus*, in classical Greek the ordinary word for a "ship," survived in Hellenistic Greek only as a literary word, but disappeared from popular speech (Moulton, *Proleg.*, p. 25). Blass (*Philology of the Gospels*, p. 186) thinks the solitary Lucan use of *naus* was due to a reminiscence of the Homeric phrase for beaching a "ship."

Forepart *see* **Foreship** at *Acts 27:30*.

Stuck fast *ereido* (2043), primarily "to prop, fix firmly," is used intransitively in **Acts 27:41** of a ship driving ashore, RV, "struck."

Remained *see Acts 5:4*.

Immoveable *asaleutos* (761), "unmoved, immoveable," is translated "unmoveable" in **Acts 27:41**; "which cannot be moved" in Heb. 12:28, KJV (RV, "that cannot be shaken"). In the Sept., Exod. 13:16; Deut. 6:8; 11:18.

Hinder *see* **Stern** at *Acts 27:29*.

Part In Mark 4:38 and **Acts 27:41**, KJV, *prumna*, "a stern", is translated "hinder part" (RV, "stern").

Broken *luo* (3089), "to loosen," especially by way of deliverance, sometimes has the meaning of "breaking, destructively," e.g., of "breaking" commandments, not only infringing them, but loosing the force of them, rendering them not binding, Matt. 5:19; John 5:18; of "breaking" the Law of Moses, John 7:23; Scripture, John 10:35; of the "breaking up" of a ship, **Acts 27:41**; of the "breaking down" of the middle wall of partition, Eph. 2:14; of the marriage tie, 1 Cor. 7:27.

Violence *see Acts 5:26*. *See also* **Mighty** at *Acts 2:2*.

Waves *kuma* (2949), from *kuo*, "to be pregnant, to swell," is used (a) literally in the plural, Matt. 8:24; 14:24; Mark 4:37 (**Acts 27:41**, in some mss.); (b) figuratively, Jude 13.

27:42 And the soldiers' counsel was to kill the prisoners, lest any of them should swim out, and escape.

Counsel *see Acts 2:23*.

Prisoners *see Acts 27:1*.

Swim *ekkolumbao* (1579), "to swim out of" (*ek*), occurs in **Acts 27:42**.

Escape *diapheugo* (1309), lit., "to flee through," is used of the "escaping" of prisoners from a ship, **Acts 27:42**.

"They travel lightly whom God's grace carries."

THOMAS À KEMPIS

27:43 But the centurion, willing to save Paul, kept them from *their* purpose; and commanded that they which could swim should cast *themselves* first *into the sea*, and get to land:

Save *see* Safe at *Acts 23:24*.

Kept *koluo* (2967), "to hinder," is rendered "stayed" in **Acts 27:43**, RV (KJV, "kept"); so in 2 Pet. 2:16, RV (KJV, "forbad").

Purpose *boulema* (1013), "a purpose or will" (akin to *boulomai*, "to will, wish, purpose"), "a deliberate intention," occurs in **Acts 27:43**, "purpose"; Rom. 9:19, "will"; 1 Pet. 4:3, in the best mss. (some have *thelema*), KJV, "will," RV, "desire."

Commanded *see Acts 22:30*.

Swim *kolumbao* (2860), "to dive, plunge, into the sea," hence, "to swim," occurs in **Acts 27:43**.

Cast *aporipto* (641), "to cast off," **Acts 27:43**, of shipwrecked people in throwing themselves into the water.

Get *exeimi* (1826), "to go or come out," is used in **Acts 27:43** of "getting" to land. *See also* **Gone out of** at *Acts 13:42*.

27:44 And the rest, some on boards, and some on *broken pieces* of the ship. And so it came to pass, that they escaped all safe to land.

Boards *sanis* (4548), denotes "a plank, or board," **Acts 27:44**.

Pieces In **Acts 27:44**, for KJV, "*broken pieces*," the RV translates *epi* ("on") *tinon* ("certain things") *ton* ("the," i.e., "those namely") by "on *other* things"; there is no word in the original representing "pieces."

Escaped ... safe *see* **Safe** at *Acts 23:24*.

Chapter 28

28:1 And when they were escaped, then they knew that the island was called Melita.

Escaped *see* Safe at *Acts 23:24*.

Knew *see Acts 9:30*.

Island *see* Isle at *Acts 13:6*.

28:2 And the barbarous people shewed us no little kindness: for they kindled a fire, and received us every one, because of the present rain, and because of the cold.

Barbarous *barbaros* (915), properly meant "one whose speech is rude, or harsh"; the word is onomatopoeic, indicating in the sound the uncouth character represented by the repeated syllable "bar-bar." Hence it signified one who speaks a strange or foreign language. See 1 Cor. 14:11. It then came to denote any foreigner ignorant of the Greek language and culture. After the Persian war it acquired the sense of rudeness and brutality. In **Acts 28:2, 4**, it is used unreproachfully of the inhabitants of Malta, who were of Phoenician origin. So in Rom. 1:14, where it stands in distinction from Greeks, and in implied contrast to both Greeks and Jews. Cf. the contrasts in Col. 3:11, where all such distinctions are shown to be null and void in Christ. "Berber" stood similarly in the language of the Egyptians for all non-Egyptian peoples.

Shewed *parecho* (3930), "to afford, give, show," etc., in the active voice, is translated "showed" in **Acts 28:2**; in the middle voice, "showing" in Titus 2:7 (1st part).

No little *tunchano*, "to happen," is used as an adjective in **Acts 28:2**, of the kindness shown by the people of Melita to the shipwrecked company; KJV, "(no) little"; RV, "(no) common"; the idea suggested by the verb is that which might happen anywhere or at all times; hence, "little, ordinary, or casual."

Kindness *philanthropia* (5363), from *philos*, "loving," *anthropos*, "man" (Eng., "philanthropy"), denotes "kindness," and is so translated in **Acts 28:2**, of that which was shown by the inhabitants of Melita to the shipwrecked voyagers; in Titus 3:4, of the "kindness" of God, translated "(His) love toward man."

Kindled *hapto* (681), properly, "to fasten to," is used in **Acts 28:2** (in the most authentic mss.), of "kindling a fire."

Fire *pura* (4443), denotes "a heap of fuel" collected to be set on fire (hence Eng., "pyre"), **Acts 28:2, 3**.

Received *proslambano* (4355), denotes "to take to oneself" (*pros*, "to") or "to receive," always in the middle voice, signifying a special interest on the part of the receiver, suggesting a welcome, **Acts 28:2**; Rom. 14:1, 3; 15:7; Philem. 12 (in some mss.; the best omit it); v. 17.

Present *ephistemi* (2186), "to set over, stand over," is translated "present" in **Acts 28:2**.

Rain *see Acts 14:17*.

Cold *psuchos* (5592), "coldness, cold," appears in John 18:18; **Acts 28:2**; 2 Cor. 11:27.

28:3 And when Paul had gathered a bundle of sticks, and laid *them* on the fire, there came a viper out of the heat, and fastened on his hand.

Gathered *sustrepho* (4962), signifies (a) "to twist together or roll into a mass" (*sun*, "together," *strepho*, "to turn"), said of the bundle of sticks "gathered" by Paul, **Acts 28:3**; (b) "to assemble or gather together" (possibly, to journey about together), of persons, Matt. 17:22 (in the best mss.), RV, marg.

Bundle *plethos* (4128), "a great number" (akin to *pleo*, "to fill"), is the word for the "bundle of sticks" which Paul put on the fire, **Acts 28:3**. *See also* **Multitude** at *Acts 4:32.*

Sticks *phruganon* (5434), denotes "a dry stick" (from *phrugo*, "to parch"); in the plural, "brushwood," **Acts 28:3**.

Laid ... on *see Acts 6:6.*

Fire *see Acts 28:2.*

Viper *echidna* (2191), is probably a generic term for "poisonous snakes." It is rendered "viper" in the NT, (a) of the actual creature, **Acts 28:3**; (b) metaphorically in Matt. 3:7; 12:34; 23:33; Luke 3:7.

Heat *therme* (2329), denotes "warmth, heat," **Acts 28:3** (Eng., "thermal," etc.).

Fastened *kathapto* (2510), "to fasten on, lay hold of, attack," is used of the serpent which fastened on Paul's hand, **Acts 28:3**.

28:4 And when the barbarians saw the *venomous* beast hang on his hand, they said among themselves, No doubt this man is a murderer, whom, though he hath escaped the sea, yet vengeance suffereth not to live.

Barbarians *see* **Barbarous** at *Acts 28:2.*

Beast *therion* (2342), to be distinguished from *zoon*, almost invariably denotes "a wild beast." In **Acts 28:4**, "venomous beast" is used of the viper which fastened on Paul's hand. *Zoon* stresses the vital element, *therion* the bestial. The idea of a "beast" of prey is not always present. Once, in Heb. 12:20, it is used of the animals in the camp of Israel, such, e.g., as were appointed for sacrifice: But in the Sept. *therion* is never used of sacrificial animals; the word *ktenos* is reserved for these.

Hang *see* **Hanged** at *Acts 5:30.*

Themselves *see Acts 4:15.*

No doubt *see* **All means** at *Acts 18:21.*

Murderer *see Acts 3:14.*

Escaped *see* **Safe** at *Acts 23:24.*

Vengeance *dike* (1349), primarily "custom, usage," came to denote "what is right"; then, "a judicial hearing"; hence, "the execution of a sentence," "punishment," 2 Thess. 1:9, RV; Jude 7, "punishment," RV (KJV, "vengeance"). In **Acts 28:4** (KJV, "vengeance") it is personified and denotes the goddess Justice or Nemesis (Lat., *Justitia*), who the Melita folk supposed was about to inflict the punishment of death upon Paul by means of the viper.

Suffereth *see* **Suffered** at *Acts 14:16.*

28:5 And he shook off the beast into the fire, and felt no harm.

Shook *apotinasso* (660), "to shake off" (*apo*, "from," *tinasso*, "to shake"), is used in Luke 9:5, of dust from the feet; **Acts 28:5**, of a viper from the hand. In the Sept., Judg. 16:20; 1 Sam. 10:2; Lam. 2:7.

Felt In **Acts 28:5** *pascho*, "to suffer," is rendered "felt (no harm)," RV, "took," lit., "suffered no ill (effect)." *See also* **Passion** at *Acts 1:3.*

Harm *see Acts 16:28.*

28:6 Howbeit they looked when he should have swollen, or fallen down dead suddenly: but after they had looked a great while, and saw no harm come to him, they changed their minds, and said that he was a god.

Looked In **Acts 28:6**, KJV, *prosdokao*, "to expect," is translated "they looked" (RV, "they expected"), and "they had looked" (RV, "they were long in expectation"). *See also* **Expecting** at *Acts 3:5.*

Swollen *pimpremi* (4092), primarily, "to blow, to burn," later came to denote "to cause to swell," and, in the middle voice, "to become swollen," **Acts 28:6**. In the Sept., Num. 5:21, 22, 27.

Fallen *see Acts 26:14.*

Suddenly *see Acts 2:2.*

While In **Acts 28:6**, KJV, *epi polu*, lit., "upon much," is rendered "a great while" (RV, "long").

Harm *see* **Wickedness** at *Acts 25:5.*

Changed *metaballo* (3328), *meta*, and *ballo*, "to throw," signifies "to turn quickly," or, in the middle voice, "to change one's mind," and is found in **Acts 28:6**.

God *see Acts 2:23.*

28:7 In the same quarters were possessions of the chief man of the island, whose name was Publius; who received us, and lodged us three days courteously.

Possessions In **Acts 28:7**, KJV, *choria*, "lands" (RV), is translated "possessions." *See also* **Lands** at *Acts 4:34.*

Chief *see Acts 13:50.*

Island *see* **Isle** at *Acts 13:6.*

Received *anadechomai* (324), "to receive gladly," is used in **Acts 28:7**, of the reception by Publius of the shipwrecked company in Melita; in Heb. 11:17, of Abraham's reception of God's promises, RV, "gladly (*ana*, "up," regarded as intensive) received." Moulton and Milligan point out the frequency of this verb in the papyri in the legal sense of taking the responsibility of something, becoming security for, undertaking, and say "The predominance of this meaning suggests its application in Heb. 11:17. The statement that Abraham had 'undertaken,' 'assumed the responsibility of,' the promises, would not perhaps be alien to the thought." The responsibility would surely be that of his faith in "receiving" the promises. In Classical Greek it had the meaning of "receiving," and it is a little difficult to attach any other sense to the circumstances, save perhaps that Abraham's faith undertook to exercise the assurance of the fulfillment of the promises.

Lodged *xenizo* (3579), signifies (a) "to receive as a guest" (*xenos*, "a guest") rendered "entertained" in **Acts 28:7**, RV, for KJV, "lodged"; in Heb. 13:2, "have entertained." *See also* **Lodgeth** at *Acts 10:6*.

Courteously *philophronos* (5390), lit., "friendly," or, more fully, "with friendly thoughtfulness" (*philos*, "friend," *phren*, "the mind"), is found in **Acts 28:7**, of the hospitality showed by Publius to Paul and his fellow-shipwrecked travelers.

28:8 And it came to pass, that the father of Publius lay sick of a fever and of a bloody flux: to whom Paul entered in, and prayed, and laid his hands on him, and healed him.

Lay *see* **Kept** at *Acts 9:33. See also* **Stopped** at *Acts 7:57;* **Pressed** at *Acts 18:5.*

Sick *sunecho* (4912), "to hold in, hold fast," is used, in the passive voice, of "being seized or afflicted by ills," **Acts 28:8**, "sick" (of the father of Publius, cf. Matt. 4:24; Luke 4:38, taken with).

Fever *puretos* (4446), "feverish heat" (from *pur*, "fire"), hence, "a fever," occurs in Matt. 8:15; Mark 1:31; John 4:52; **Acts 28:8**; in Luke 4:38, with *megas*, "great, a high fever"; v. 39. Luke, as a physician, uses the medical distinction by which the ancients classified fevers into great and little. In the Sept., Deut. 28:22.

Bloody flux *dusenterion* (1420), whence Eng., "dysentery," is so translated in **Acts 28:8**, RV, for KJV "bloody flux" (*enteron* denotes an "intestine").

Laid ... on *see Acts 6:6*.

28:9 So when this was done, others also, which had diseases in the island, came, and were healed:

Others *loipos* (3062), signifies "remaining, the rest." It is translated "other," or "others," e.g., in Matt. 25:11: Mark 4:19; Luke 18:9; 24:10 (in v. 9, "the rest"); but in Luke 8:10; **Acts 28:9**; Rom. 1:13; 1 Cor. 9:5; Eph. 2:3; 1 Thess. 4:13; 5:6; 1 Tim. 5:20, e.g., the RV renders this word "the rest" (KJV, "other" or "others"); in Eph. 4:17, some mss. have *loipa*, neuter plural, KJV, "other (Gentiles)." *See also* **Other** at *Acts 17:9*.

Diseases *astheneia* (769), lit., "lacking strength" (*a*, negative, *sthenos*, "strength"), "weakness, infirmity," is translated "diseases" in Matt. 8:17, RV, for KJV, "sicknesses," and in **Acts 28:9**. Its usual rendering is "infirmity" or "infirmities"; "sickness," in John 11:4.

Island *see* **Isle** at *Acts 13:6*.

Healed *see* **Worshipped** at *Acts 17:25*.

28:10 Who also honoured us with many honours; and when we departed, they laded *us* with such things as were necessary.

Honoured *timao* (5091), "to honor," is used of (a) valuing Christ at a price, Matt. 27:9; (b) "honoring" a person: (1) the "honor" done by Christ to the Father, John 8:49; (2) "honor" bestowed by the Father upon him who serves Christ, John 12:26; (3) the duty of all to "honor" the Son equally with the Father, 5:23; (4) the duty of children to "honor" their parents, Matt. 15:4; 19:19; Mark 7:10; 10:19; Luke 18:20; Eph. 6:2; (5) the duty of Christians to "honor" the king, and all men, 1 Pet. 2:17; (6) the respect and material assistance to be given to widows "that are widows indeed," 1 Tim. 5:3; (7) the "honor" done to Paul and his companions by the inhabitants of Melita, **Acts 28:10**; (8) mere lip profession of "honor" to God, Matt. 15:8: Mark 7:6.

Honours *see* **Prices** at *Acts 4:34*.

Departed *see* **Depart** at *Acts 27:12. See also* **Loosed** at *Acts 13:13*.

Laded In **Acts 28:10**, KJV, *epitithemi*, "to put on" (*epi*, "on," *tithemi*, "to put"), is translated "they laded (us) with," RV, "they put on (board)."

Necessary *chreia* (5532), denotes "a need," in such expressions as "there is a need"; or "to have need of" something, e.g., Matt. 3:14; 6:8; 9:12, RV, "(have no) need," KJV, "need (not)," the RV adheres to the noun form; so in 14:16; Mark 14:63; Luke 5:31; 22:71; Eph. 4:28; 1 Thess. 4:9; in the following, however, both RV and KJV use the verb form, "to need" (whereas the original has the verb *echo*, "to have," with the noun *chreia* as the object, as in the instances just mentioned):

Luke 15:7; John 2:25; 13:10; 16:30; 1 Thess. 1:8; 1 John 2:27; Rev. 22:5; in all these the verb "to have" could well have been expressed in the translation. In Luke 10:42 it is translated "needful," where the "one thing" is surely not one dish, or one person, but is to be explained according to Matt. 6:33 and 16:26. In Eph. 4:29, for the KJV, "(to) the use (of edifying)," the RV more accurately has "(for edifying) as the need may be," marg., "the building up of the need," i.e., "to supply that which needed in each case"; so Westcott, who adds "The need represents a gap in the life which the wise word 'builds up,' fills up solidly and surely." In Phil. 4:19 the RV has "every need of yours" (KJV, "all your need"); in 1 Thess. 4:12, RV, "need" (KJV, "lack"); in **Acts 28:10**, RV, "(such things) as we needed" (KJV, "as were necessary"), lit., "the things for the needs (plural)."

28:11 And after three months we departed in a ship of Alexandria, which had wintered in the isle, whose sign was Castor and Pollux.

Months *see Acts 7:20.*

Departed *see* Depart at *Acts 27:12. See also* Loosed at *Acts 13:13.*

Wintered *see* Winter at *Acts 27:12.*

Isle *see Acts 13:6.*

Sign *parasemos* (3902), an adjective meaning "marked at the side" (*para*, "beside," *sema*, "a mark"), is used in **Acts 28:11** as a noun denoting the figurehead of a vessel.

28:12 And landing at Syracuse, we tarried *there* three days.

Landing In **Acts 28:12**, RV, *katago*, "to bring down," used as a nautical term in the passive voice, is translated "touching" (KJV, "landing").

Tarried *see* Tarry at *Acts 10:48.*

28:13 And from thence we fetched a compass, and came to Rhegium: and after one day the south wind blew, and we came the next day to Puteoli:

From thence In **Acts 28:13**, *hothen*, "from whence," is translated "from thence."

Fetched a compass *perierchomai* (4022), lit., "to go, or come, about" (*peri*, "about," *erchomai*, "to come"), is translated in **Acts 28:13**, KJV, "fetched a compass." *See also* Taken at *Acts 27:20.*

Came *see Acts 16:1.*

South wind *see Acts 27:13.*

Blew In **Acts 28:13**, *epiginomai*, "to come on," is used of the springing up of a wind, KJV, "blew"; RV, "sprang up."

Next day *deuteraios* (1206), an adjective with an adverbial sense, is used in **Acts 28:13**, RV, "on the second day" (KJV, "the next day"), lit., "second day (persons we came)."

28:14 Where we found brethren, and were desired to tarry with them seven days: and so we went toward Rome.

Tarry *see Acts 10:48.*

28:15 And from thence, when the brethren heard of us, they came to meet us as far as Appii forum, and The three taverns: whom when Paul saw, he thanked God, and took courage.

Meet *apantesis* (529), "a meeting," occurs in Matt. 25:6 (in some mss. in v. 1, and in 27:32, in some mss.); **Acts 28:15**; 1 Thess. 4:17. It is used in the papyri of a newly arriving magistrate. "It seems that the special idea of the word was the official welcome of a newly arrived dignitary" (Moulton, *Greek Test. Gram.* Vol. 1, p. 14).

Thanked *see* Thanks at *Acts 27:35.*

Courage *tharsos* (2294), akin to *tharseo*, "to be of good cheer," is found in **Acts 28:15**.

28:16 And when we came to Rome, the centurion delivered the prisoners to the captain of the guard: but Paul was suffered to dwell by himself with a soldier that kept him.

Delivered *paradidomi* (3860), "to betray" (*para*, "up," *didomi*, "to give"), lit., "to give over," is used either (a) in the sense of delivering a person or thing to be kept by another, to commend, e.g., **Acts 28:16**; (b) to deliver to prison or judgment, e.g., Matt. 4:12; 1 Tim. 1:20; (c) to deliver over treacherously by way of "betrayal," Matt. 17:22 (RV, "delivered"); 26:16; John 6:64 etc.; (d) to hand on, deliver, e.g., 1 Cor. 11:23; (e) to allow of something being done, said of the ripening of fruit, Mark 4:29, RV, "is ripe" (marg., "alloweth").

Prisoners *see Acts 16:25.*

Captain In **Acts 28:16** some mss. have the word *stratopedarches* (lit., "camp-commander"), which some take to denotes a praetorian prefect, or commander of the praetorian cohorts, the Emperor's bodyguard, "the captain of the praetorian guard." There were two praetorian prefects, to whose custody prisoners sent bound to the Emperor were consigned. But the word probably means the commander of a detached corps connected with the commissariat and the general custody of prisoners.

Guard *see* Keep at *Acts 12:4.*

Suffered *see* Suffer at *Acts 21:39.*

Dwell *meno* (3306), "to abide, remain," is translated "to dwell," in the KJV of John 1:38-39; 6:56; 14:10, 17; **Acts 28:16**. The RV adheres throughout to the verb "to abide."

28:17 And it came to pass, that after three days Paul called the chief of the Jews together: and when they were come together, he said unto them, Men *and* brethren, though I have committed nothing against the people, or customs of our fathers, yet was I delivered prisoner from Jerusalem into the hands of the Romans.

Called *see Acts 5:21.*

Chief *see Acts 13:50.*

Against *see* Contrary at *Acts 26:9.*

Fathers *see Acts 22:3.*

Prisoner *see* Prisoners at *Acts 16:25.*

Romans *see* Rome at *Acts 2:10.*

28:18 Who, when they had examined me, would have let *me* go, because there was no cause of death in me.

Examined *see Acts 4:9.*

Would *see Acts 22:30.*

Let ... go *see Acts 3:13. See also* Went at *Acts 10:9.*

Cause *see Acts 13:28.*

28:19 But when the Jews spake against *it*, I was constrained to appeal unto Caesar; not that I had ought to accuse my nation of.

People *see Acts 8:9.*

Spake *see Acts 13:45.*

Constrained *see* Compelled at *Acts 26:11.*

Appeal *see* Calling at *Acts 7:59.*

28:20 For this cause therefore have I called for you, to see *you*, and to speak with *you*: because that for the hope of Israel I am bound with this chain.

Called *parakaleo*, "to beseech, intreat," is rendered "have called for" in **Acts 28:20**, KJV; RV, "did intreat" (marg., "call for"). It is used only here with this meaning. *See also* Desiring at *Acts 9:38.*

Speak *see* Speaking at *Acts 13:43.*

Hope *see Acts 16:19.*

Bound *perikeimai* (4029), lit., "to lie around" (*peri*, "around," *keimai*, "to lie"), "to be compassed," is used of binding fetters around a person, **Acts 28:20**; in Mark 9:42, and Luke 17:2, to hang about a person's neck; in Heb. 5:2, to compass about, metaphorically of infirmities; in 12:1, of those who have witness borne to their faith.

Chain *see* Chains at *Acts 12:6.*

28:21 And they said unto him, We neither received letters out of Judaea concerning thee, neither any of the brethren that came shewed or spake any harm of thee.

Received *see* Receive at *Acts 3:21.*

Letters *see* Learning at *Acts 26:24.*

Shewed *see Acts 26:20. See also* Reported at *Acts 4:23.*

Harm *poneros* (4190), the adjective, is used as a noun, (a) of Satan as the "evil" one, Matt. 5:37; 6:13; 13:19, 38; Luke 11:4 (in some texts); John 17:15; Eph. 6:16; 2 Thess. 3:3; 1 John 2:13-14; 3:12; 5:18-19; (b) of human beings, Matt. 5:45; (probably v. 39); 13:49; 22:10; Luke 6:35; 1 Cor. 5:13; (c) neuter, "evil (things)," Matt. 9:4; 12:35; Mark 7:23; Luke 3:19; "that which is evil," Luke 6:45; Rom. 12:9; **Acts 28:21**, "harm."

28:22 But we desire to hear of thee what thou thinkest: for as concerning this sect, we know that every where it is spoken against.

Desire *see* Thought at *Acts 15:38.*

Every where *see Acts 17:30.*

Sect *see Acts 5:17.*

Spoken *see* Spake at *Acts 13:45.*

28:23 And when they had appointed him a day, there came many to him into *his* lodging; to whom he expounded and testified the kingdom of God, persuading them concerning Jesus, both out of the law of Moses, and *out of* the prophets, from morning till evening.

Appointed *see* Ordained at *Acts 13:48.*

Many *see Acts 2:40.*

Lodging *xenia* (3578), denotes (a) "hospitality, entertainment," Philem. 22; (b) by metonymy, "a place of entertainment, a lodging-place," **Acts 28:23** (some put Philem. 22 under this section).

Expounded *see Acts 11:4.*

Testified *see* Testify at *Acts 2:40.*

Morning *proi* (4404), "early in the day, at morn," is derived from *pro*, "before." In Mark 16:2, KJV, it is translated "early in the morning"; in Mark 16:9 and John 18:28; 20:1, "early"; in Matt. 16:3; 20:1; 21:18; Mark 1:35; 11:20; 13:35; 15:1, "in the morning"; in **Acts 28:23**, "(from) morning."

Evening *see* Eventide at *Acts 4:3.*

28:24 And some believed the things which were spoken, and some believed not.

Believed *see Acts 17:4.*

Believed not *apisteo* (569), "to be unbelieving" (*a,* negative, *pistis,* "faith"; cf. *apistos,* "unbelieving"), is translated "believed not," etc., in the KJV (except in 1 Pet. 2:7, "be disobedient"); "disbelieve" (or "disbelieved") in the RV, in Mark 16:11, 16; Luke 24:11, 41; **Acts 28:24**; "disbelieve" is the best rendering, implying that the unbeliever has had a full opportunity of believing and has rejected it; some mss. have *apeitheo,* "to be disobedient," in 1 Pet. 2:7; Rom. 3:3, RV, "were without faith"; 2 Tim. 2:13, RV, "are faithless."

28:25 And when they agreed not among themselves, they departed, after that Paul had spoken one word, Well spake the Holy Ghost by Esaias the prophet unto our fathers,

Agreed not *asumphonos* (800), "inharmonious" (*a* negative, *sumphonos,* "harmonious"), is used in **Acts 28:25**, "they agreed not."

Themselves *see Acts 4:15.*

Departed *see* Depart at *Acts 23:22.*

Holy Ghost *see Acts 1:16.*

28:26 Saying, Go unto this people, and say, Hearing ye shall hear, and shall not understand; and seeing ye shall see, and not perceive:

Hearing *akoe* (189), denotes (a) "the sense of hearing," 1 Cor. 12:17; 2 Pet. 2:8; a combination of verb and noun is used in phrases which have been termed Hebraic as they express somewhat literally an OT phraseology, e.g., "By hearing ye shall hear," Matt. 13:14; **Acts 28:26**, RV, a mode of expression conveying emphasis. *See also* Ears at *Acts 17:20.*

Understand *see* Understood at *Acts 7:25.*

Perceive *see* Perceiving at *Acts 14:9.*

28:27 For the heart of this people is waxed gross, and their ears are dull of hearing, and their eyes have they closed; lest they should see with *their* eyes, and hear with *their* ears, and understand with *their* heart, and should be converted, and I should heal them.

Waxed gross *pachuno* (3975), from *pachus,* "thick," signifies "to thicken, fatten"; in the passive voice, "to grow fat"; metaphorically said of the heart, to wax gross or dull, Matt. 13:15; **Acts 28:27**.

Ears *see Acts 7:51.*

Dull *bareos* (917), "heavily, with difficulty" (*barus,* "heavy"), is used with *akouo,* "to hear," in Man. 13:15, and **Acts 28:27** (from Isa. 6:10), lit., "to hear heavily, to be dull of hearing." In the Sept., Gen. 31:35 (lit., "bear it not heavily"); Isa. 6:10.

Hearing For the phrase to be dull of hearing, lit., "to hear heavily," Matt. 13:15; **Acts 28:27**.

Closed *kammuo* (2576), derived by syncope (i.e., shortening and assimilation of *t* to *m*) from *katamuo,* i.e., *kata,* "down," and *muo,* from a root *mu*–, pronounced by closing the lips, denotes "to close down"; hence, "to shut the eyes," Matt. 13:15 and **Acts 28:27**, in each place of the obstinacy of Jews in their opposition to the gospel.

Understand *see* Understood at *Acts 7:25.*

Converted *see Acts 3:19.*

Heal *see* Whole at *Acts 9:34.*

28:28 Be it known therefore unto you, that the salvation of God is sent unto the Gentiles, and *that* they will hear it.

Salvation *soterion* (4992), the neuter of the adjective, is used as a noun in Luke 2:30; 3:6, in each of which it virtually stands for the Savior; in **Acts 28:28**; in Eph. 6:17, where the hope of "salvation" is metaphorically described as "a helmet."

Sent *see* Send at *Acts 3:20.*

Gentiles *see* People at *Acts 8:9.*

28:29 And when he had said these words, the Jews departed, and had great reasoning among themselves.

Reasoning In those mss. which contain **Acts 28:29**, occurs *suzetesis,* "a disputation," which is translated "reasoning" (KJV).

28:30 And Paul dwelt two whole years in his own hired house, and received all that came in unto him,

Dwelt *misthoma* (3410), primarily, "a price, a hire" (akin to *misthos,* "wages, hire" and *misthoo,* "to let out for hire") is used in **Acts 28:30** to denote "a hired dwelling." *See also* Continue at *Acts 14:22.*

Years *see Acts 24:27.*

Hired house *misthoma* (3410), primarily denotes "a hire," as in the Sept. of Deut. 23:18; Prov. 19:13; Ezek. 16:31, 34, 41, etc.; in the NT, it is used of "a hired dwelling," **Acts 28:30**.

Received *see Acts 2:41.*

All *see* Whole at *Acts 11:26.*

Came *see* Entered at *Acts 3:2*. *See also* Coming in at *Acts 9:28*.

28:31 Preaching the kingdom of God, and teaching those things which concern the Lord Jesus Christ, with all confidence, no man forbidding him.

Preaching *see* Preached at *Acts 8:5*.

Confidence *parrhesia* (3954), often rendered "confidence" in the KJV, is in all such instances rendered "boldness" in the RV, **Acts 28:31**; Heb. 3:6; 1 John 2:28; 3:21; 5:14.

Forbidding *akolutos* (209), "without hindrance" (translated "none forbidding him," in **Acts 28:31**. From the 2nd century AD onwards the word is found constantly in legal documents (Moulton and Milligan, Vocab., who draw attention to the triumphant note on which the word brings the Acts to a close).

www.ingramcontent.com/pod-product-compliance
Lightning Source LLC
LaVergne TN
LVHW090428230725
816804LV00022B/757
* 9 7 8 0 7 1 8 0 3 6 8 9 8 *